The New Interpreter's Bible
Commentary

In Ten Volumes

Volume I	Introduction to the Pentateuch; Genesis; Exodus; Leviticus; Numbers; Deuteronomy
Volume II	Introduction to Narrative Literature; Joshua; Judges; Ruth; 1 & 2 Samuel; 1 & 2 Kings; 1 & 2 Chronicles
Volume III	Introduction to Hebrew Poetry; Job; Psalms; Introduction to Wisdom Literature; Proverbs; Ecclesiastes; Song of Songs
Volume IV	Ezra; Nehemiah; Introduction to Prophetic Literature; Isaiah; Jeremiah; Baruch; Letter of Jeremiah; Lamentations
Volume V	Ezekiel; Hosea; Joel; Amos; Obadiah; Jonah; Micah; Nahum; Habakkuk; Zephaniah; Haggai; Zechariah; Malachi
Volume VI	Esther; Additions to Esther; Tobit; Judith; 1 & 2 Maccabees; Book of Wisdom; Sirach; Introduction to Apocalyptic Literature; Daniel; Additions to Daniel
Volume VII	The Gospels and Narrative Literature; Jesus and the Gospels; Matthew; Mark
Volume VII	Luke; John
Volume IX	Acts; Introduction to Epistolary Literature; Romans; 1 & 2 Corinthians; Galatians
Volume X	Ephesians; Philippians; Colossians; 1 & 2 Thessalonians; 1 & 2 Timothy; Titus; Philemon; Hebrews; James; 1 & 2 Peter; 1, 2 & 3 John; Jude; Revelation

Editorial Board

Leander E. Keck
    Convener and Senior New Testament Editor
    Winkley Professor of Biblical Theology, Emeritus
    Yale University Divinity School

Thomas G. Long
    Senior Homiletics Editor
    Bandy Professor of Preaching
    Candler School of Theology
    Emory University

David L. Petersen
    Senior Old Testament Editor
    Professor of Old Testament
    Candler School of Theology
    Emory University

Bruce C. Birch
    Old Testament Editor
    Dean and Woodrow W. and Mildred B. Miller
      Professor of Biblical Theology
    Wesley Theological Seminary

John J. Collins
    Old Testament Editor
    Holmes Professor of Old Testament Criticism
      and Interpretation
    Yale University Divinity School

Katheryn Pfisterer Darr
    Old Testament Editor
    Associate Professor of Hebrew Bible
    The School of Theology
    Boston University

James Earl Massey
    Homiletics Editor
    Dean Emeritus and Distinguished
      Professor-at-Large
    The School of Theology
    Anderson University

William L. Lane
    New Testament Editor
    Paul T. Walls Professor of Wesleyan and
      Biblical Studies, Emeritus
    Department of Religion
    Seattle Pacific University

Marion L. Soards
    New Testament Editor
    Professor of New Testament
    Louisville Presbyterian Theological Seminary

Gail R. O'Day
    Homiletics Editor
    Almar H. Shatford Professor of Homiletics
    Candler School of Theology
    Emory University

* The credentials listed here reflect the positions held at the time of the original publication.

The New Interpreter's™ Bible Commentary

Volume Ten

Ephesians
Philippians
Colossians
1 & 2 Thessalonians
1 & 2 Timothy
Titus
Philemon
Hebrews
James
1 & 2 Peter
1, 2 & 3 John
Jude
Revelation

ABINGDON PRESS
Nashville

THE NEW INTERPRETER'S BIBLE COMMMENTARY
VOLUME X

Copyright © 2015 by Abingdon Press

This volume is a compilation of the following previously published material:
The New Interpreter's® Bible in Twelve Volumes, Volume XI (Ephesians, Philippians, Colossians, 1 & 2 Thessalonians, 1 & 2 Timothy, Titus), Copyright © 2000 by Abingdon Press.
The New Interpreter's® Bible in Twelve Volumes, Volume XII (Hebrews; James; 1 & 2 Peter; 1, 2, & 3 John; Jude; Revelation), Copyright © 1998 by Abingdon Press.

All rights reserved.
No part of this work may be reproduced or transmitted in any form or by any means, electronic or mechanical, including photocopying and recording, or by any information storage or retrieval system, except as may be expressly permitted by the 1976 Copyright Act or in writing from the publisher. Requests for permission should be addressed to Permissions, Abingdon Press, 2222 Rosa L. Parks Boulevard, PO Box 280988, Nashville, TN 37228, or permissions@abingdonpress.org.

This book is printed on acid-free paper.

Library of Congress Cataloging-in-Publication Data has been requested.

ISBN 978-1-4267-3586-8

Quotations from the HOLY BIBLE, NEW INTERNATIONAL VERSION. NIV. Copyright © 1973, 1978, 1984 by International Bible Society. Used by permission of Zondervan Publishing House. All rights reserved.

Quotations from the NEW REVISED STANDARD VERSION OF THE BIBLE. Copyright © 1989, Division of Christian Education of the National Council of the Churches of Christ in the United States of America. Used by permission. All rights reserved.

Quotations from the following are used by permission: *The Good News Bible*-Old Testament, copyright © American Bible Society 1976; New Testament, copyright © American Bible Society 1966, 1971, 1976. THE JERUSALEM BIBLE, copyright © 1966 by Darton, Longman & Todd, Ltd. and Doubleday, a division of Bantam Doubleday Dell Publishing Group, Inc. The New American Standard Bible, copyright © The Lockman Foundation 1960, 1962, 1968, 1971, 1972, 1973, 1975, 1977. *The New English Bible*, copyright © The Delegates of the Oxford University press and the Syndics of the Cambridge University Press 1961, 1970. *The Revised English Bible*, copyright © 1989 Oxford University Press and Cambridge University Press. *The Revised Standard Version of the Bible*, copyright © 1946, 1952, 1971 by the Division of Christian Education of the National Council of Churches in the USA. *The TANAKH: The New JPS Translation According to the Traditional Hebrew Text*, copyright © 1985 by Jewish Publication Society.

17 18 19 20 21 22 23 24—10 9 8 7 6 5 4

MANUFACTURED IN THE UNITED STATES OF AMERICA

Contributors

Pheme Perkins
  Professor of New Testament
  Boston College
  Chestnut Hill, Massachusetts
  (The Roman Catholic Church)
  Ephesians

Morna D. Hooker
  Lady Margaret's Professor of Divinity, Emeritus
  The Divinity School
  University of Cambridge
  Cambridge, England
  (The Methodist Church [Great Britain])
  Philippians

Andrew T. Lincoln
  Professor of New Testament
  Wycliffe College
  University of Toronto
  Toronto, Ontario
  Canada
  (The Church of England)
  Colossians

Abraham Smith
  Associate Professor of New Testament
  Andover Newton Theological School
  Newton Centre, Massachusetts
  (The National Baptist Convention, USA, Inc.)
  1 & 2 Thessalonians

James D. G. Dunn
  Lightfoot Professor of Divinity
  Department of Theology
  University of Durham
  Durham, England
  (The Methodist Church [Great Britain])
  1 & 2 Timothy, Titus

Cain Hope Felder
  Professor of New Testament Language
    and Literature
  The School of Divinity
  Howard University
  Washington, D.C.
  (The United Methodist Church)
  Philemon

Fred B. Craddock
  Bandy Distinguished Professor of Preaching
    and New Testament, Emeritus
  Candler School of Theology
  Emory University
  Atlanta, Georgia
  (Christian Church [Disciples of Christ])
  Hebrews

Luke Timothy Johnson
  Robert W. Woodruff Professor of New
    Testament and Christian Origins
  Candler School of Theology
  Emory University
  Atlanta, Georgia
  (The Roman Catholic Church)
  James

* The credentials listed here reflect the positions held at the time of the original publication.

CONTRIBUTORS

DAVID L. BARTLETT
  Lantz Professor of Preaching and
    Communication
  Yale University Divinity School
  New Haven, Connecticut
  (American Baptist Churches in the U.S.A.)
    1 Peter

DUANE F. WATSON
  Associate Professor of New Testament Studies
  Department of Religion and Philosophy
  Malone College
  Canton, Ohio
  (The United Methodist Church)
    2 Peter, Jude

C. CLIFTON BLACK
  Otto A. Piper Professor of Biblical Theology
  Princeton Theological Seminary
  Princeton, New Jersey
  (The United Methodist Church)
    1, 2 & 3 John

CHRISTOPHER C. ROWLAND
  Dean Ireland's Professor of the Exegesis of
    Holy Scripture
  The Queen's College
  Oxford, England
  (The Church of England)
    Revelation

Contents

VOLUME X

Ephesians
Pheme Perkins 1

Philippians
Morna D. Hooker 105

Colossians
Andrew T. Lincoln 179

1 Thessalonians
Abraham Smith 281

2 Thessalonians
Abraham Smith 341

1 & 2 Timothy and Titus
James D. G. Dunn 371

Philemon
Cain Hope Felder 461

Hebrews
Fred B. Craddock 481

James
Luke Timothy Johnson 629

1 Peter
David L. Bartlett 675

Contents

2 Peter
Duane F. Watson — 759

1, 2 & 3 John
C. Clifton Black — 793

Jude
Duane F. Watson — 887

Revelation
Christopher C. Rowland — 915

Abbreviations — 1107

THE LETTER TO THE EPHESIANS
INTRODUCTION, COMMENTARY, AND REFLECTIONS
BY
PHEME PERKINS

THE LETTER TO THE EPHESIANS

INTRODUCTION

REMEMBERING THE APOSTLE: GENRE, CHARACTER, AND SOURCES

Although some still argue that Paul was the author of Ephesians,[1] most scholars agree that the letter is pseudonymous. For an audience accustomed to appropriating all written texts orally—that is, through hearing their contents read and perhaps even explicated by the person who actually conveyed the letter to its recipients—multiple voices in a text were a common experience. Consequently, when scholars speak of Paul as the "implied" or "fictive" author of Ephesians, they do not mean that the writer is making a fraudulent use of Pauline authority. The gap between this letter and Paul's personal correspondence is not hard to detect.[2] Ephesians lacks the personal greetings characteristic of Paul. No associates or fellow Christians are mentioned as co-senders. Those to whom Ephesians speaks do not know the apostle (1:15; 3:2). Yet, as Gentiles who have now been brought into the people of God (2:11-13), they owe a great debt to him. Paul's insight into the mystery (μυστήριον *mystērion*) of God's saving plan forms the basis of the gospel message (3:1-13). Their familiarity with the apostle has been mediated through writing rather than through his personal presence (3:2-4).

Paul's own letters contain specific details of the relationship between the apostle and those to whom he writes. Figuring out the prior history of the apostle's ministry in a particular church plays a crucial part in understanding those letters. Ephesians has no such clues. Sometimes interpreters supply reasons for a particular theme in Ephesians that have been taken from the context of another of Paul's letters. For example, the assumption that the growing numbers of

---

1. Markus Barth, *Ephesians*, 2 vols., AB 34-34A (Garden City, N.Y.: Doubleday, 1974); Peter T. O'Brien, *Letter to the Ephesians* (Grand Rapids: Eerdmans, 1999).
2. Ernest Best, "Recipients and Title of the Letter to the Ephesians: Why and When the Designation 'Ephesians'?" in *Aufstieg und Niedergang der römischen Welt* II 25/4, ed. Wolfgang Haase (Berlin: DeGruyter, 1987).

Gentiles in the church have begun to denigrate the Jewish heritage of Christian faith (a concern of Romans 9:1–11) is proposed as the reason for writing Ephesians.[3]

Attempts to construct a setting for Ephesians run up against the literary genre of the work.[4] The author has adopted ancient rhetorical forms of celebratory and hortatory discourse.[5] The first half of the epistle (1:3–3:21) invites the audience to join in praising and thanking God for the plan of salvation that has united them with Christ. It concludes with a brief doxology (3:20-21). The second half encourages readers to persevere in the social and personal dimensions of their lives as new creations in Christ (4:1–6:20). It concludes in a dramatic peroration (6:10-20). Believers stand armed and ready to vanquish evil powers (6:10-17). They will also assist the imprisoned apostle in continuing his bold witness by remembering him in prayer (6:18-20).

Despite this clear understanding of the genre of the work, Andrew T. Lincoln cannot resist assuming that the rhetorical appeals to the audience built into the genres in question provide information about the epistle's readers. This methodological difficulty is masked by assuming that such mirror reading gives access to what literary critics mean by "implied readers." Not so, if the addressees recognize the rhetorical *topoi* involved. Lincoln comments, "It can be inferred from the implied author's prayers for them (3.14-19) and from his appeals which introduce and conclude the parenesis (cf. 4.1-16; 6.10-20) that their main problems are powerlessness, instability and a lack of resolve, and these are related to an insufficient sense of identity."[6] In fact, these passages tell us nothing about the problems of particular readers, actual or implied.[7] They do establish powerful images of Christian identity. The consolidation of communal identity can be understood as the basic function of celebratory rhetoric. A community that hears praises of its imperial—or, in this case, divine—benefactor, of the peace and well-being that a benefactor's gracious use of power has bestowed on it, that community also comes to know itself in relationship to the benefactor.

The lack of detail even appears in the opening greeting (1:1-2). The phrase "in Ephesus" (ἐν Ἐφέσῳ *en Ephesō*) does not occur in many of the earliest manuscripts. Nor would that locale be appropriate for an audience that does not know the apostle. Paul had worked extensively in Ephesus. He may even have been imprisoned there (1 Cor 15:32). Unlike either Colossians (Col 4:14; 5:6-7) or the Pastorals (1 Tim 1:18-20; 4:1-7), Ephesians never refers to false teachers whose doctrines must be avoided. Therefore, the epistle appears to be addressed to Christian churches in general, not to a particular situation. Some interpreters suggest that the author was concerned with the impact of the pagan religious environment in the Lycus Valley and wrote the epistle as a circular letter to churches in the environs of Laodicea and Hierapolis.[8] Nevertheless, the author does not appear to have any personal knowledge of the addressees. The discourse alternates between the second-person plural "you" and the first-person plural "we." Sometimes "we" designates Jewish Christians associated with the author, in contrast to "you" Gentile converts. Sometimes "we" refers to all Christians as a group. Ephesians never uses the common Christian designation "brothers" (ἀδελφοί *adelphoi*) in addressing the audience. The only use of the term occurs in the conclusion, where it is a third-person plural reference (*adelphoi*).

Ephesians encourages the audience to "imitate God" (Γίνεσθε οὖν μιμηταὶ τοῦ θεοῦ *Ginesthe oun mimētai tou Theou*, 5:1) rather than the apostle, unlike the usual practice in Paul's letters. Even the Pastoral Epistles retain the motif of imitating Paul (2 Tim 1:8; 3:10-14). Since imitation of those who possess virtues is key to ancient paraenesis, the absence of the theme in Ephesians highlights the distance between its audience and the apostle.[9] With the exception of *topoi* in the

---

3. Ralph P. Martin, *Ephesians, Colossians and Philemon* (Atlanta: John Knox, 1991).
4. David G. Meade, *Pseudonymity and Canon: An Investigation into the Relationship of Authorship and Authority in the Jewish and Earliest Christian Tradition*, WUNT 39 (Tübingen: Mohr-Siebeck, 1986) 140-42.
5. See Andrew T. Lincoln, *Ephesians*, WBC 42 (Dallas: Word, 1990) xl-xlii; and "'Stand, therefore . . .': Ephesians 6:10-20 as *Peroratio*," *Biblical Interpretation* 3 (1995) 99-114.
6. Andrew T. Lincoln and A. J. M. Wedderburn, *The Theology of the Later Pauline Letters* (Cambridge: Cambridge University Press, 1993) 82-83.
7. For a cautious treatment of the assumptions that Ephesians makes concerning its readers, see Ernest Best, *A Critical and Exegetical Commentary on Ephesians*, ICC (Edinburgh: T. & T. Clark, 1998) 1-6.
8. Larry J. Kreitzer, "'Crude Language' and 'Shameful Things Done in Secret' (Eph 5:1, 4, 12): Allusions to the Cult of Demeter/Cybele in Hierapolis?" *JSNT* 71 (1988) 51-77; and "The Plutonium of Hierapolis and the Descent of Christ into the 'Lowermost Parts of the Earth' (Ephesians 4:1, 9)," *Biblica* 79 (1998) 381-93.
9. Meade, *Pseudonymity and Canon*, 153.

household code, Ephesians has no significant parallels with the Pastoral Epistles.[10] Although the author has made extensive use of Colossians, he drops Timothy as co-sender from the opening greeting (1:1; cf. Col 1:1), even though this omission lives on in an odd first-person plural at the end (6:22; cf. Col 4:8). Perhaps this detail is more significant than it appears at first. The author and recipients of Ephesians do not belong to the circle of churches in which Timothy's or Paul's other closest associates had been active.

Does Ephesians represent the first introduction these Christians have had to the apostle? Attempts to treat Ephesians as a summary designed to introduce an early collection of Pauline letters (assumed as the referent of 3:3-4) founder on the genre of the work. Ephesians does not read as an epitome of the apostle's teaching either in its formal rhetorical structure or its content. Further, the passage said to refer to other writings (3:3-4) does not indicate an established canon of Pauline letters. It could refer to the reading of Ephesians as a further explanation of what was said about the mystery (*mystērion*) in a previous letter. Ephesians may have taken its cue from Col 2:1-6. The apostle's trials are to benefit not only Christians known to him, but also others who have never seen him. Ephesians is claiming to express the mystery (*mystērion*) about which Paul was speaking.[11]

Verbal comparisons of Ephesians and Colossians are found in the tables that accompany the relevant sections of the Commentary. The sum total of such evidence makes a strong case for the view that the author of Ephesians knew and used much of Colossians in his own epistle. But Ephesians has also recontextualized and changed the order of images and phrases taken from Colossians.[12] Even those sections that are substantially new contain some echoes of Colossians (1:3-14; 2:5-21; 4:8-16; 5:8-14, 22-33; 6:11-17).[13] Echoes of other Pauline letters are noted in the Commentary.[14] Romans is more frequently evident in parallels to Ephesians than any other Pauline letter. Consequently, it does not seem likely that Ephesians relies simply on oral traditions circulating in Pauline churches. Knowledge of some Pauline letters themselves must be presupposed. But one can only make this argument with regard to the author of Ephesians. It is impossible to tell from the epistle whether the recipients were familiar with the passages that are cited here as parallels. The Commentary will argue that the rhetorical strategies used in the letter presuppose that the audience recognizes what it hears as tradition, not new instruction. Lincoln has suggested using the phrase "actualization of an authoritative tradition" for the reuse of Pauline material in Ephesians.[15]

David Trobisch's study of letter collections has shed new light on the place of Ephesians in the Pauline corpus. Often the first collection of an author's letters was prepared by the author himself. Trobisch argues that Paul is responsible for creating a collection composed of Romans, 1–2 Corinthians, and Galatians. After an author's death other letters would be added at the end of the original group. Finally, someone might prepare a comprehensive collection from all available versions. Trobisch suggests that the first letter to break the principle that orders a collection indicates the point at which such expansion of an existing collection takes place. For the Pauline letters, the ordering principle appears to be length. However, on that criterion, Ephesians should come before Galatians. Therefore, it represents the first epistle added to the primitive collection produced by the apostle.[16] This research tells us nothing about the original addressees or how the Pauline letter canon came to be formed. It only indicates that Ephesians represented the first letter to be added to the originating collection of four major Pauline epistles.

---

10. Lincoln, *Ephesians*, lvi.
11. Meade, *Pseudonymity and Canon*, 150-51.
12. Best highlights the shifts in language between Colossians and Ephesians to argue for a more complex relationship between the two. Rather than conclude that Ephesians is directly dependent upon Colossians, Best concludes that Colossians and Ephesians are independent representatives of a Pauline school tradition. See Best, *A Critical and Exegetical Commentary on Ephesians*, 20-25. Such a hypothesis has as many difficulties as the assumption that Ephesians is reworking Col. For a detailed analysis that argues that Ephesians is dependent upon Colossians and other written Pauline letters, see Michael Gese, *Das Vermächtnis des Apostels, Die Rezeption der paulinischen Theologie im Epheserbrief*, WUNT 2 Reihe, 99 (Tübingen: J.C.B. Mohn [Paul Siebeck], 1997) 39-54.
13. So Rudolf Schnackenburg, *The Epistle to the Ephesians*, trans. H. Heron (Edinburgh: T. & T. Clark, 1991) 30-31.
14. Also see the chart of these relationships in Gese, *Das Vermächtnis des Apostels*, 76-78.
15. Lincoln, *Ephesians*, lviii.
16. David Trobisch, *Paul's Letter Collection: Tracing the Origins* (Minneapolis: Fortress, 1994) 50-52.

If the more speculative side of Trobisch's argument holds—namely, that the apostle himself was responsible for Romans through Galatians—then the question of which letters other churches may have possessed looks slightly different. An early collection by the apostle himself may have been designed to be circulated. If Ephesians assumes that its audience has heard actual letters from the apostle, then this group of letters is most likely the group that was circulated. Ephesians may not presume that Colossians was read in the churches to which the apostle writes. Instead, Colossians provided the impetus for Ephesians to formulate Paul's own account of the mystery of salvation.

The basic picture of the apostle that Ephesians leaves with its readers contains few details. He is presented as the great apostle to the Gentiles whose Spirit-endowed insight (1:17; 3:2-3) has made the hidden plan of salvation accessible to all. This "mystery" (*mystērion*) made known through the apostle is also the tradition of the apostles and prophets who are the foundation of the church (2:20-22). Finally, the apostle's imprisonment is "for the sake of you Gentiles" (3:1 NRSV) and calls for courage to continue boldly proclaiming the gospel (6:19-20). Even these Christians who have no direct connection to the apostle's own churches are assured that the apostle suffers on their behalf. One cannot be sure whether the letter's audience knows that Paul has suffered martyrdom. Unlike the letters that Paul wrote from prison earlier, Ephesians never anticipates the possibility of his release. Unlike 2 Tim 4:6-18, Ephesians never hints that his death is near. But the conclusion of Acts indicates that an author and readers who know full well that the apostle has died may celebrate his heroic witness to the gospel without recounting his death.

WHERE EPHESIANS DIFFERS: THEOLOGY, LANGUAGE, AND STYLE

Ephesians was not composed as an epitome of Paul's teaching or as the celebration of an apostle hero. It focuses on God's foreordained plan of salvation, uniting Jew and Gentile in the body of the risen Christ. This theological insight develops a number of themes found in Paul's letters in a new direction. One no longer finds the event of salvation focused on the cross, though the traditional formulae concerning the redemptive effects of Christ's death do appear. Instead of speaking of the power of sin to hold humans in bondage, Ephesians refers to sins in the plural (ἁμαρτίαι *hamartiai*). Bondage is associated with evil powers whose effectiveness is linked to the earthly regions. Consequently, the dominant metaphor for redemption from their influence is exaltation "in the heavenly regions" with the risen Christ.[17]

1. Shifting Language. The language of Ephesians also departs markedly from Paul's style. The author constructs extensive, periodic sentences out of dependent clauses introduced by participles and infinitive phrases. In order to provide a readable text, translations break up these long sentences. However, the tables that compare the language of Ephesians with other Pauline letters will provide as literal a rendering as possible in order to indicate similarities of wording. Readers should consult commentaries based on the Greek text for detailed information about the elaborate Greek style in Ephesians. Such commentaries also provide lists of the unusual vocabulary used in Ephesians. Many words are either unique in the New Testament or appear in Ephesians and another New Testament writing, but not elsewhere in the Pauline letters. Some expressions appear to replace Pauline equivalents; for example, Ephesians uses "in the heavenly places" (ἐν τοῖς ἐπουρανίοις *en tois epouraniois*; 1:3, 20; 2:6; 3:10; 6:12) where Paul would speak of "in the heavens" (ἐν οὐρανοῖς *en ouranois*; 2 Cor 5:1; Phil 3:20; Col 1:5, 16, 20).[18] Instead of Paul's "Satan" (Σατανᾶς *Satanas*), one finds "devil" (διάβολος *diabolos*) in Ephesians. The formula used to introduce citations from Scripture, "therefore it says" (διὸ λέγει *dio legei*), is also not found in Pauline letters, and the expression "good works" (ἔργοις ἀγαθοῖς *ergois agathois*) in the plural (2:10) does not appear there, though it does occur in the Pastorals.[19]

---

17. Arland J. Hultgren, *Christ and His Benefits: Christology and Redemption in the New Testament* (Philadelphia: Fortress, 1987) 92-93.
18. See the discussion of the phrase "in the heavenlies" in Best, *A Critical and Exegetical Commentary on Ephesians*, 115-18.
19. Schnackenburg, *The Epistle to the Ephesians*, 25-27.

Other features of Pauline letter form are missing, such as expressions of confidence, the formal opening to the body of a letter with a request or disclosure formula. The apostle typically uses a χάρις (*charis*, translated "thanks") formula as a contrast to a previously described negative situation (e.g., 2 Cor 2:12-15).[20] Ephesians does not use such contrastive formulae. Instead, *charis* (translated "grace") appears as the foundation of salvation and appears in expressions where one would expect "faith" if Paul had composed the letter (e.g., "by grace [*charis*] you have been saved through faith," 2:8). Or one would anticipate a discussion of righteousness in connection with the salvation of the Gentiles in 2:8-10. Instead, Ephesians refers to grace as the gift of God in opposition to works. The term "works" (ἔργα *erga*) also appears without Paul's normal qualifier "of the law" (νόμου *nomou*). In 2:10, the non-Pauline plural "good works" (*ergois agathois*) appears to refer to the moral conduct of those who are in Christ. The term "law" (νόμος *nomos*) only appears in 2:15, where the "law with its commandments and ordinances" has been canceled by the cross. There is no more distinction between Jew and Gentile. The whole complex of linguistic formulae that the apostle created to describe the inclusion of Gentiles in the promise of salvation has vanished with hardly a trace.[21]

This shift may be grounded in rhetoric as well as theology. Marc Schoeni's study of the "how much the more" formulae in Romans 5:1 discovered an important semantic distinction between using the topic "justification" and using "reconciliation." The language of justification is structured in such a way that it discriminates and divides. It acknowledges the singular differences between Jew and Gentile. Reconciliation "sublates and unites." By incorporating the differentiated singularities into a greater whole, reconciliation denies their significance.[22] Though Paul works with both reconciliation and justification, Ephesians has taken the reconciliation imagery of Rom 5:1-11 to be the Pauline understanding of salvation. Consequently, distinctions in Paul's terminology will be overridden by unity.

2. "Mystery" of Salvation. Several linguistic shifts are associated with the term "mystery" (μυστήριον *mystērion*). Ephesians often uses expressions that have their closest parallels in the Essene writings from Qumran, in which we find the "mystery" of the divine plan of salvation hidden in the prophets until the end time. Paul also uses "mystery" (*mystērion*) for God's preordained eschatological plan of salvation.[23] "Mystery" designates different aspects of the overall plan of salvation: (a) 1 Cor 2:1, 7, the crucifixion; (b) 1 Cor 15:51, the end-time transformation of the righteous into resurrected bodies; and (c) Rom 11:25, the present hardening of Israel as a condition for salvation of the Gentiles, to be followed by salvation for "all Israel." In 1 Cor 4:1, Paul refers to the apostles, specifically himself and Apollos, as "stewards of God's mysteries" and uses the term in a general way for revealed knowledge in 1 Cor 13:2 (also 14:2, ironically?). Its use for the salvation of the Gentiles as hidden in the prophets until the present at Rom 16:25-27 may be an addition to the letter, but it maintains the overtones of apocalyptic revelation characteristic of Paul's usage.

When Paul applies the term "mystery" to his gospel in Rom 11:25, he is not only thinking of God's plan to summon all humanity to salvation, but he is also thinking of the story of Israel. God's promises to the covenant people and their apparent inability to recognize Christ as the fulfillment of the law issue in Paul's conviction that God must still bring salvation to Israel.[24] For Ephesians, only the first side of Paul's thought remains: God intends to bring all to salvation in Christ (3:8-9). This mystery is grounded in the will of God from the beginning (1:9) and has been made known through the preaching of the apostle (6:19). It is also embodied in his writing (3:3-4). These examples are easily viewed as developments of Paul's own usage. After the apostle's death it would be natural to consider the written expression of his gospel as the way in which the mystery becomes known to others. However, a more significant shift becomes evident when Ephesians is compared with the immediate source for these expressions, Colossians

---

20. Linda L. Belleville, *Reflections of Glory: Paul's Polemical Use of the Moses-Doxa Tradition in 2 Corinthians 3:1.1-18*, JSNTSup 52 (Sheffield: JSOT, 1991) 92-93.
21. Schnackenburg, *The Epistle to the Ephesians*, 26-27; Lincoln and Wedderburn, *The Theology of the Later Pauline Letters* 130-37.
22. Marc Schoeni, "The Hyperbolic Sublime as a Master Trope in Romans," in *Rhetoric and the New Testament: Essays from the 1992 Heidelberg Conference*, ed. Stanley E. Porter and Thomas H. Olbricht, JSNTSup 90 (Sheffield: JSOT, 1993) 181.
23. See the study of Markus Bockmuehl, *Revelation and Mystery in Ancient Judaism and Pauline Christianity* (Grand Rapids: Eerdmans, 1977).
24. See James D. G. Dunn, *The Theology of Paul the Apostle* (Grand Rapids: Eerdmans, 1998) 526-29.

(Col 1:27; 2:2; 4:3). In every one of the Colossians examples the shorthand that clarifies the term "mystery" (*mystērion*) is "Christ." For Colossians, the mystery is the fact that salvation comes to all people through faith in Christ.

Ephesians shifts the playing field. The focus of the mystery is not the cosmic Christ of Colossians but the body of Christ, the church. The problem is not how Gentiles can participate in God's salvation while remaining free from the law. Instead, Ephesians conceives the problem as one of unity. The series of "with . . ." or "co-" terms in Eph 3:6 makes this point about the church: The Gentiles are "heirs with" (συγκληρονόμαι *sygklēronomai*), "body with" (σύσσωμα *syssōma*), and "sharers [συμμέτοχα *symmetocha*] of the promise in Christ through the gospel." This perspective makes it quite natural for Ephesians to speak of the union of Christ, the head, with his body, the church, as a "mystery" (Eph 5:32).

3. Church as Body of Christ. This use of "body of Christ" (σῶμα τοῦ Χριστοῦ *sōma tou Christou*) goes beyond Paul's own use of the expression. Paul employed a common image from the political philosophy of his day to appeal for order and harmony in the Corinthian church. Christians should understand that the Spirit has provided diverse gifts within the community so that the whole body can function together. Strife over gifts among Christians is as absurd as parts of the body claiming that they do not belong because they are not some other part (1 Cor 12:12-31). The image is repeated in the same sense in Rom 12:3-8. He can also extend the metaphor of Christians as members of the "body of Christ" to argue for appropriate separation from the two forms of immorality that Jews commonly associated with paganism—sexual immorality (1 Cor 6:15) and idolatrous cultic practices (1 Cor 10:17). Thus for the apostle the expression "body of Christ" (*sōma tou Christou*) involves a metaphor for how to order the concrete details of everyday Christian life. Like the term "church" (ἐκκλησία *ekklēsia*) in Paul's letters, the term "body of Christ" designates local communities of Christians.[25]

Ephesians does not address a local community. Its vision of the church is set in the largest possible framework, the cosmic body of all the faithful united with its head, the risen Christ (1:22-23; 2:6). When the image of the church as the "body of Christ" comes into the ethical exhortation, the picture is one of a "new human being" growing into the body of Christ, which serves under its head (4:13-16). Paul's reference to concrete gifts of ministry in the body are incorporated into this larger vision of the church as the agent through whom its growth takes place (4:11-12). The development toward a more cosmic image of "body of Christ" is anticipated in the hymnic tradition. Colossians 1:15-20 depicts Christ first as divine wisdom active in creation, then as redeemer. Christ the redeemer is head of the body that is the church by virtue of being "firstborn from the dead" (Col 1:18). Colossians 1:19 introduces another term that will figure in the cosmic vision of church found in Ephesians, "fullness" (πλήρωμα *plērōma*). For Colossians, "fullness" refers to divinity dwelling in Christ. For Ephesians, it will refer to the way in which Christ dwells in the cosmic body, the church (1:23; 3:19; 4:13).

Other metaphors used for the church are drawn into this picture of the church as "body of Christ." It can be described as a building or temple being built up into Christ (2:20-21). Christians are members of God's household as children of God, not as strangers or resident aliens (2:19). Because the "body of Christ" is depicted as a heavenly reality, some of the attributes that describe the church follow as natural consequences. The church must be a unity (2:14-16; 4:1-3, 10-13), holy (1:3-8; 4:17-22; 5:3-5, 25-27), universal (2:16; 3:1-6). It cannot be considered part of this world as though it were a sociopolitical institution (5:18-20).[26] If it were, the church would be subject to the powers and authorities that govern the lower regions. Because the body of Christ is the preordained vehicle by which God has chosen to unite all things with God and to subjugate the lower powers (3:10), the church has always belonged to the divine plan of salvation. The doxology of 3:21 insists that God is praised "in the church and in Christ Jesus."

---

25. L. O. R. Yorke, *The Church as the Body of Christ in the Pauline Corpus: A Re-examination* (Lanham: University Press of America, 1991); Dunn, *The Theology of Paul the Apostle*, 548-64.
26. Yorke, *The Church as the Body of Christ in the Pauline Corpus*, 101-3.

Those who consider such a vision of the church as a dangerous precedent should attend to the metaphors used. None of them attach the reality of the cosmic body of Christ to a particular group of human authorities. No single community could embody the church. Rudolf Schnackenburg remarks:

> For the author all the congregations which lie within his field of vision do not yet, even taken together, constitute "the *ekklēsia*." This is rather an entity which has precedence over all, in which they participate and in accordance with which they should orient their lives.[27]

Similarly the "mystery" (*mystērion*) of the church united to Christ as bride thus transforms a common Jewish metaphor for Israel as the "bride of Yahweh" (Isa 65:5; Jer 2:2; Ezek 16:1; Hosea 1:1–3) by highlighting the realism of the unity between Christ and the church. Christ's self-offering on the cross is the foundation of its holiness (Eph 5:2, 25). Christ's loving concern for the welfare of the church extends to the realities of Christian life in this world. It is not merely a reference to the heavenly unity of the saints with their head (2:5-6). If Ephesians can use this concern to describe the conduct of husbands toward their wives in marriage, then it should also be reflected in the ways that Christian leaders go about their various ministries.

4. Ministries in the Church. The references to such ministries in Ephesians also create some difficulties. When Paul refers to himself as apostle (ἀπόστολος *apostolos*, 1:1) or servant (διάκονος *diakonos*) of the gospel chosen by God to make God's salvation known to the Gentiles (3:7-9), we are on familiar ground. The self-deprecating comment "although I am the very least of all the saints, this grace was given to me" (3:8 NRSV) sounds close to Paul's own account of his apostleship (1 Cor 15:8-10). But Ephesians appears to have slipped out of the apostolic perspective in Eph 3:5. The mystery unknown to previous generations has now been revealed to God's "holy apostles and prophets by the Spirit." Since "prophets" follows the reference to apostles, the speaker does not appear to mean the Old Testament prophets. The author appears to be looking back on a revelation transmitted by Christian apostles and prophets. When Paul refers to Christian prophets, they are not associated with the apostolic witness to the gospel. Their function involves speaking, prayer, and exhortation within the local assembly (1 Cor 11:2-16; 14:29, 32, 37). When he refers to other apostles positively, Paul highlights the unity of his message with theirs (see 1 Cor 15:11).[28]

Ephesians 2:20 puts "apostles and prophets" in the past. They are the foundation of the building, the church, which is growing into Christ. By contrast, Paul describes himself as the master builder (ἀρχιτέκτων *architektōn*) who builds on the foundation, Jesus Christ (1 Cor 3:10-14). The paraenetic section of the letter treats the term "apostles" (ἀπόστολοι *apostoloi*) as first in a list of gifts to the church: apostles, prophets, evangelists, pastors, and teachers (4:11). They are to equip Christians for service in building up the body of Christ until all attain maturity, the fullness of Christ (τοῦ πληρώματος τοῦ Χριστοῦ *tou plērōmatos tou Christou*, 4:12-13). Once again the relationship between such persons and local church communities remains undefined.[29] Only the last two, pastors (ποιμέναι *poimenai*) and teachers (διδάσκαλοι *didaskaloi*), clearly designate resident leaders of the local church. The terms may not describe any particular church order. Ephesians merely wishes to indicate in a general way that God has charged certain persons with nurturing the church by aiding others to grow in unity and knowledge of God. This concern for harmony, internal unity, and growth might represent the concerns of a church facing the death of the apostolic generation.

5. Eschatological Shift. The cosmic picture of the church already united with the risen Christ shifts attention away from the end-time coming of the Lord (as in 1 Thess 4:13–5:11).

---

27. Schnackenburg, *The Epistle to the Ephesians*, 295. Others see the universalism in Ephesians as a loss for the theology of local church communities. Dunn remarks, "It is also true that Paul's own transforming vision was itself soon transformed, with many of its distinctive features lost to sight. His vision of the church of God as fully manifested in the local church was displaced by the thought of the Church universal (already in Ephesians)." Dunn, *The Theology of Paul the Apostle*, 563.

28. See Dunn, *The Theology of Paul the Apostle*, 579-82.

29. Lack of concern with the local community forms a striking contrast to Paul's understanding of the local character of all church ministry, including his own office as an apostle. See Dunn, *The Theology of Paul the Apostle*, 578-79.

For Paul, all things are not yet subjected to Christ. When they are, when every authority and power is destroyed, then Christ will bring all under God's rule (1 Cor 15:24-28). Ephesians refers to the subjection of all authorities and powers as a present reality. The risen and exalted Christ is far above all powers, whether in this age or in the age to come (Eph 1:19-23). Similarly, believers have been freed from the powers of darkness and raised up with Christ in the heavens. This exaltation also demonstrates God's extraordinary graciousness toward the faithful in the coming ages (Eph 2:5-7). Elements of future eschatology remain part of the author's conceptual world, but they do not serve as criteria to determine one's present position in the world. Nor is a culminating event in God's saving plan anticipated in the near future. Ephesians never uses the term "mystery" (*mystērion*) to designate a future act of redemption. The mystery of bringing all things together in Christ may not be completed, but it has already become a reality in the church (1:10).

This eschatological shift is evident in another formal difference between Ephesians and other Pauline letters. The apostle typically concludes major sections with references to elements of future judgment or salvation (e.g., Rom 11:31-36; 1 Cor 1:9-10; 15:54-58; Phil 1:10-11; 3:20–4:1; 1 Thess 1:9-10; 2:19-20; 3:11-13). Such references carry a hortatory message to the audience: Take care to persevere so that God may "strengthen your hearts in holiness that you may be blameless before our God and Father at the coming of our Lord Jesus with all his saints" (1 Thess 3:13 NRSV). Ephesians retains the liturgical character of Pauline transitions by using formulaic expressions (as in 1:20-23) or doxologies (as in 3:20-21). It uses "saints" (ἅγιοι *hagioi*) as its designation for believers (e.g., 1:1, 15; 2:19; 3:18; 5:3; 6:18). Concerns that the church be "holy and blameless" (ἅγιος καὶ ἄμωμος *hagios kai amōmos*) are reflected in the opening prayer (1:4) and the paraenesis (4:24; 5:27) but never appear with the reference to the Lord's coming in judgment. The conclusion to the whole letter (6:10-20) takes up the motif of divine armor, which occurs as part of the eschatological conclusion to 1 Thessalonians (1 Thess 5:8). Even here, where one would expect standing fast to be accompanied by an explicit indication that these are the "last days," there is no reference to a judgment day. All that remains are the linguistic tags "withstand on that evil day" (6:13) and "keep alert" (6:18). Ephesians never speaks of Christ's coming in judgment. Its ecclesiology short-circuits such language, since the church already exists in the unity of the saints with their exalted head.

SEARCHING FOR A SOCIORELIGIOUS CONTEXT

Scholars have mined various features of the letter to construct a background for its author or audience. Since the destination "Ephesus" was not original, those theories built on archaeological and religious descriptions of ancient Ephesus and its Artemis cult have no foundation in the text. Some advocates of an Ephesus argument claim that the pluralism of religious cults and magic practices evident there is representative of the environment of cities in Asia Minor. Since the emphasis on Christ's exaltation above the powers of the cosmos and the identification of believers with their exalted head forms the center of Ephesians, this imagery might be read as a response to pagan religion. The Artemis cult in Ephesus demonstrates the superiority of the goddess to all forces; she is queen of the cosmos, as the signs of the zodiac around her neck and the magic letters on her scepter demonstrate. Associated with her, one finds Hecate, goddess of the underworld.[30] Similar zodiac imagery is connected with other goddess figures, like Diana and Isis. Funerary reliefs at Philippi depict the deified male or female child being conducted into heavenly places.[31] Other authors compare the "seated in the heavenly places" of Ephesians with the heavenly ascent of Mithraism.[32] These parallels say little about the details of Ephesians, but they suggest religious images and prior convictions that its audience would bring with them to the letter.

---

30. Clinton E. Arnold, *Ephesians: Power and Magic: The Concept of Power in Ephesians in the Light of Its Historical Setting*, SNTSMS 63 (Cambridge: Cambridge University Press, 1989).

31. Valerie A. Abrahamsen, *Women and Worship at Philippi: Diana, Artemis, and Other Cults in the Early Christian Era* (Portland, Me.: Astarte Shell, 1995).

32. Timothy B. Cargal, "'Seated in the Heavenlies': Cosmic Mediators in the Mysteries of Mithras and the Letter to the Ephesians," SBLSP, ed. Eugene H. Lovering (Atlanta: Scholars Press, 1994) 804-21.

Other interpreters follow the lead of classic commentaries[33] and look to ancient gnostic mythologies. The separation between the heavenly regions in which those with knowledge of God are linked with the redeemer and the lower world of darkness governed by hostile forces forms a central element in their speculation. The second- and third-century CE gnostic texts provide suggestive parallels to some of the images in Ephesians. Gnostic writers claim Ephesians as evidence that the apostle taught a gnostic doctrine of the soul fallen from heaven and trapped by hostile powers. Once awakened and enlighted by the heavenly revealer from heaven, the soul is superior to the powers. However, peculiarly gnostic terminology or theologoumena do not appear in Ephesians, so emerging gnostic sectarianism does not provide an explanation for the theological innovations found in the epistles.

Some interpreters have tried to combine all of these motifs. A gnostic dualism between the heavenly and earthly regions is said to cause the turn toward astrology and magic in order to gain security in a dangerous, hostile universe.[34] Or they assume that since Ephesians speaks of access to God through the knowledge that comes in Christ, it must be opposed to visionaries who claim to have ascended into heaven and to have been seated in God's presence.[35] Such visionary practices linked to Jewish speculation about heavenly realities have been more easily linked the false teaching rejected in Col 2:8–3:4.[36] Though Ephesians adopts the image of believers seeking what belongs to the risen Christ (Col 3:1-4), none of the polemic details of the Colossians text are found in Ephesians. Further, as noted above, Ephesians erases the eschatological reservation found in earlier Pauline letters. Colossians does not. It limits the believers' identification with the exalted Christ to the future coming of Christ. For Ephesians, the saints are already one with their Lord. Once again, Ephesians shows no evidence of engaging a particular religious situation.

Since Ephesians highlights the incorporation of Gentiles with Israel in the new creation that God had planned from the beginning (2:11-18; 3:6), a natural context would appear to have been relationships between Jewish and Gentile Christians. Some interpreters lift the problematic of Gentile conversion from Pauline Epistles to explain the need for ethical instruction in Ephesians. But though the center of the apostle's gospel did require that both Jew and Gentile be made righteous on the same basis, through faith (Gal 2:15-21), Ephesians never deals with those concrete details of the law that distinguish Jew and Gentile and make Paul's emphasis on righteousness through faith, not works of the law, essential. Ephesians can refer to "circumcision" and "uncircumcision" as markers of the two communities (2:11) without any indication that the distinction created a problem for relationships between Jewish and Gentile Christians in their unity. Contrast Colossians, where circumcision is spiritualized (Col 2:11) and Jewish sabbaths, holy days, and food laws are rejected (Col 2:16-17). Ephesians 2:15 refers without difficulty to the "law with its commandments and ordinances" abolished by the cross. Consequently, many scholars agree that the churches to which Ephesians was written cannot include an active Jewish Christian group.[37]

If the community envisaged by the letter consists solely of Gentiles being encouraged to remember themselves as brought into a common inheritance with Jewish believers, does the reminder provide any hints about the setting of the letter? Many of our best parallels to its religious language can be found among the Essene texts from Qumran. Such comparisons, along with the exegetical forms used by the author, suggest a person with a background in first-century CE Jewish sectarianism. At the same time, the ornate Greek rhetorical style suggests a Jew with a Hellenistic education. This combination is similar to that of Paul himself. In Paul's case, the sectarian piety through which he assimilated Judaism was Pharisaism. In this case, it was some form of sectarian piety closer to that of the Essenes. The author of Ephesians not only looks to the apostle Paul as the recipient of special understanding of God's plan, but he is also a student

---

33. Esp. Heinrich Schlier, *Der Brief an die Epheser* (Dusseldorf: Patmos, 1957).
34. Martin, *Ephesians, Colossians and Philemon*.
35. Michael Gouldner, "Vision and Knowledge," *JSNT* 56 (1994) 53-71.
36. James D. G. Dunn, "The Colossian Philosophy: A Confident Jewish Apologetic," *Bib* 76 (1995) 153-81.
37. A. Lindemann, "Bemerkungen zu den Adressaten und zum Anlass des Epheserbriefes," *ZNW* 67 (1976) 235-51, insists not only that there were no Jewish Christians in the audience of Ephesians, but also that the author was not a Jewish Christian either. He has adopted Paul's persona to bolster faith in a church threatened by persecution.

of Paul's letters. Given the Essene interest in texts, including preserving and continuing an exegetical tradition linked to its founder, one might infer that such a person had made an effort to obtain copies of Paul's letters.

Other interpreters suggest that Ephesians attempts to ward off a crisis similar to that addressed by Paul in Rom 11:17-36. Its repeated use of "with..." formulae, as well as the priority given "us" into which "you," Gentiles, have been incorporated, indicates a desire to hang on to the Jewish roots of Christianity.[38] But Ephesians has surrendered the careful distinction between the church and Israel so important to Paul. Its exhortations have nothing to do with Judaism. Rather, the Gentile audience must remain committed to the new Christian way of life, to worship, to mutual love and assistance among believers, and to the moral reform that marks them as "children of God."

On the one hand, it seems more accurate to think of the early Christian movement as an "internal migration" of a sectarian group within Judaism than as a "new religion."[39] On the other hand, Ephesians clearly perceives the Jew and Gentile believers who constitute the body of the risen Christ as a "new creation," not merely the righteous remnant of Israel with some Gentiles thrown in. For its readers, the existence of any actual relationships with the Jewish communities of Asia Minor remains in doubt.[40]

Ephesians presumes that preaching the gospel involves persuading others to turn away from paganism as cultic practice and from moral laxity in conduct to become part of the Christian community. But does this orientation reflect an attitude that the Gentile Christian mission assimilated from the Hellenistic synagogue? Martin Goodman has recently assembled considerable evidence against the view that either Jews or pagans thought it would be preferable if all humans worshiped the same God.[41] Scholars find the social boundaries of those Gentile sympathizers often referred to as "god-fearers" increasingly difficult to fix clearly. Without doubt, some outsiders found their way into Judaism as proselytes (see Tob 1:8).[42] When women of the Herodian family married, they required that their husbands be converted to Judaism.[43] In some areas, though by no means everywhere, one finds Jewish communities with a range of Gentile sympathizers or benefactors. Why would outsiders act as benefactors to the Jewish community? They must have been encouraged that such acts would have a reward (cf. Rom 2:12-16). Persons within the Jewish community may have encouraged such benefactors, whose assistance they required in order to maintain the political independence of their community.[44]

Would such Gentiles have been drawn to the early Christian movement as Acts suggests (see Acts 16:11-14; 17:1-5)? Some synagogue benefactors clearly retained their pagan ties and even priesthoods within pagan cult associations.[45] If that was a normal pattern of benefaction, then the language of Ephesians that highlights the radical break of conversion might be directed toward those who thought they could retain earlier associations while belonging to the Christian group (as in 1 Cor 10:1-22). What else these Gentiles from Asia Minor might have known about Jews can only be suggested by supplementing the few hints in the letter with general evidence for the region. Ephesians itself assumes that readers are familiar with "circumcision" as the decisive criterion for belonging to Israel, with Jewish monotheism and its critique of pagan gods, with Scripture, and in a general way with Jews as separated from non-Jews by "commandments and ordinances." None of these observations go beyond what ordinary Gentiles might know about Jews. Indeed, Ephesians does not refer to the other common items of information, sabbath

---

38. Meade, *Pseudonymity and Canon,* 146.
39. So Dieter Georgi, "The Early Church: Internal Jewish Migration or New Religion?" *HTR* 88 (1995) 35-68, who does not deal with Ephesians.
40. On the paucity of evidence for Jewish life in Asia Minor during the first century CE, see John M. G. Barclay, *Jews in the Mediterranean Diaspora from Alexander to Trajan (323 BCE–117 CE)* (Berkeley: University of California Press, 1996) 259-81. Lack of involvement in the Jewish revolts of the period suggests that Jews in Asia Minor maintained friendly relations with non-Jewish neighbors.
41. Martin Goodman, *Mission and Conversion: Proselytizing in the Religious History of the Roman Empire* (Oxford: Clarendon, 1994).
42. Josephus *Against Apion* 2.210. However, Roman authors are aware of the difference between persons who are Jewish sympathizers and actual proselytes. See Peter Schäfer, *Judeophobia: Attitudes Toward the Jews in the Ancient World* (Cambridge, Mass.: Harvard University Press, 1997) 80-115. Schäfer concludes that the pressure on collecting the *discus Judaicus* under Domitian was a response to increasing proselytism in Roman society (Schäfer, *Judeophobia,* 115).
43. Josephus *Antiquities of the Jews* 20.139, 145; Goodman, *Mission and Conversion,* 63-65.
44. Goodman, *Mission and Conversion,* 87-88.
45. Paul R. Trebilco, *Jewish Communities in Asia Minor,* SNTSMS 69 (Cambridge: Cambridge University Press, 1991) 58-59.

observance and food laws, even though they appear in Colossians. This omission may indicate that Jewish or Jewish Christian practice was not an issue for the author or his audience.

Early Christian churches appear in those cities of Asia Minor that also had Jewish communities. Louis Feldman suggests that the lack of Pharisaic influence in the inland cities of Asia Minor indicates that Judaism there was less bound to the land of Israel. Jewish inscriptions lack the pious Jewish sentiments of longing for the Temple or artistic representations of the ark or the menorah so common elsewhere. Sardis appears to have been the exception to the rule of a lower degree of Jewish identity in inland Asia Minor. Its large, wealthy, and prosperous community evoked sharp anti-Jewish polemic from Melito, Bishop of Sardis in the second century. Even in the fourth century, the remodeled Jewish synagogue was a larger and more impressive building than the Christian church.[46] If the relative strength and social prestige of the two communities were as Feldman suggests, such that the Jewish community far outweighed that of the Christian offshoot, then the emphasis on Jewish origins evident in Ephesians might serve to intensify communal identity among the Christian minority.

After all, Ephesians makes the extraordinary claim that God's plan for humanity is represented by this community. Some have even compared that language to claims for the peace created by the Roman Empire.[47] Though there is no clear evidence that Ephesians is concerned with imperial ideology, the suggestion points to the spiritual importance of its message. The case for creating unity through imperial expansion was evident in the architecture of the great cities of Asia Minor. The Jewish community in many Asia Minor cities owed Roman power an important debt; appeals to Roman authorities secured Jewish rights to sabbath observance, protection of money collected for the Jerusalem Temple, and the like. Ephesians envisages a different basis for human unity, a religious one. As far as one can tell, this realization was unique to the Christian mission. Not even the Romans thought that all the citizens of their empire would worship Roman gods. Jews never undertook a systematic policy of proselytism to bring pagans to the worship of God. Ephesians has set Paul's own concern for a mission that would reach the ends of the Roman Empire (Rom 15:18-23) in a global perspective. God planned to unite all things in Christ even before creation.[48]

46. Louis H. Feldman, *Jew and Gentile in the Ancient World* (Princeton, N.J.: Princeton University Press, 1993) 73.
47. Franz Mussner, *Der Brief an die Epheser* (Gütersloh: Gerd Mohn, 1982).
48. Portions of this commentary appeared originally in Pheme Perkins, *Ephesians*, ANTC (Nashville: Abingdon, 1997).

BIBLIOGRAPHY

Commentaries:

Barth, Markus. *Ephesians*. 2 vols. AB 34; 34A. New York: Doubleday, 1974. Argues that Paul wrote Ephesians during his Roman imprisonment. Use of liturgical material accounts for the differences between Ephesians and early Pauline letters. Extensive comparisons between Ephesians and the earlier epistles.

Best, Ernest. *A Critical and Exegetical Commentary on Ephesians*. ICC. Edinburgh: T. & T. Clark, 1998. The most thorough commentary on the Greek text. Sees the author of Ephesians as a member of the Pauline school, which accounts for the similarity to Colossians, whose author was writing to show Gentile Christians what their new faith requires.

Kitchen, Martin. *Ephesians*. London: Routledge, 1994. A series of essays that sees Ephesians as a summing up of the Pauline tradition after the destruction of Jerusalem in 70 CE. Includes a helpful discussion of the use of pseudepigraphy in preserving religious traditions.

Lincoln, Andrew. *Ephesians*. WBC 42. Dallas: Word, 1990. A detailed study of the Greek text that is informed by knowledge of ancient rhetorical traditions. Argues that Ephesians has made a free adaptation of material from Colossians and other Pauline letters to encourage lagging faith among Christians in the Lycus Valley.

Martin, Ralph P. *Ephesians, Colossians, and Philemon.* Atlanta: John Knox, 1991. Comments on sections of the letter for the general reader. Treats Ephesians as an encyclical letter written by a disciple of Paul to the churches in Asia Minor against gnosticizing tendencies in the area. Includes suggestions for pastors and preachers.

Mitton, C. L. *The Epistle to the Ephesians.* Oxford: Clarendon, 1951. Detailed statistics on words shared between Ephesians and Colossians that played a significant role in establishing the view that Ephesians used the latter as a source.

O'Brien, Peter T. *The Letter to the Ephesians.* Pillar NT Commentary. Grand Rapids: Eerdmans, 1999. Continues to argue for the view that Paul wrote Ephesians from his Roman imprisonment in the 60s CE, against most contemporary scholars. Seeks to show the continuity between Ephesians and Paul's earlier letters. The commentary quotes the NIV translation but analyzes the Greek text.

Schnackenburg, Rudolf. *The Epistle to the Ephesians.* Translated by H. Heron. Edinburgh: T. & T. Clark, 1991 [Ger. 1982]. Particularly helpful analysis of the logical flow of the letter. Concludes with extended discussion of the theological impact of Ephesians in classical Roman Catholic and Protestant theology of predestination, Christ and redemption, church, and Christian life.

Specialized Studies:

Adams, Edward. *Constructing the World: A Study of Paul's Cosmological Language.* Edinburgh: T. & T. Clark, 2000. Studies the use of "world," "creation," and "new creation" in the major Pauline letters (Romans; 1–2 Corinthians; Galatians).

Arnold, Clinton E. *Ephesians: Power and Magic. The Concept of Power in Ephesians in Light of Its Historical Setting.* SNTSMS 63. Cambridge: Cambridge University Press, 1989. Argues from a study of ancient religious cults and magical practices that Ephesians seeks to show the superiority of Christ's power to Christians who remained fearful of attacks by evil cosmic powers.

Best, Ernest. *Essays on Ephesians.* Edinburgh: T. & T. Clark, 1997. Reprints the author's articles on important topics in Ephesians.

Caragounis, Chrys C. *The Ephesian Mysterion: Meaning and Context.* ConB 8. Lund: Gleerup, 1977. A study of the use of the term "mystery" in Ephesians that emphasizes its use to designate God's plan of salvation history.

Dawes, Gregory W. *The Body in Question: Metaphor and Meaning in the Interpretation of Ephesians 5:21-33.* Biblical Interpretation Series 30. Leiden: Brill, 1998. Studies the comparison of marriage to the relationship between the church and Christ from the perspective of modern studies of metaphor. Emphasizes the links between this passage and the rest of the letter.

Harris, W. Hall, III. *The Descent of Christ: Ephesians 4:7-11 and Traditional Hebrew Imagery.* AGAJU 32. Leiden: Brill, 1996. Concludes that a tradition of Moses' ascending Mt. Sinai to receive Torah has been transferred to Christ in the quotation of Ps 68:19.

Klauck, Hans-Josef. *The Religious Context of Early Christianity: A Guide to Graeco-Roman Religions.* Translated by Brian McNeil. Edinburgh: T. & T. Clark, 2000. A survey of religious and philosophical movements in the non-Jewish world of early Christianity. Concludes with a discussion of Gnosticism.

Lincoln, Andrew T., and A. J. M. Wedderburn. *The Theology of the Later Pauline Letters.* Cambridge: Cambridge University Press, 1993. Contains a synthesis of the theology of Ephesians for general readers by A. T. Lincoln; concludes with an essay on the critical appropriation of the theology of Ephesians.

Meade, David G. *Pseudonymity and Canon: An Investigation into the Relationship of Authorship and Authority in the Jewish and Earliest Christian Tradition.* WUNT 39. Tübingen: J. C. B. Mohr (Paul Siebeck), 1986. A study of the role played by pseudonymous authorship in Jewish and early Christian authors; argues that the death of Paul, and hence the loss of his presence as an authority, motivated the composition of Ephesians.

Neufeld, T. Y. *Put On the Armour of God: The Divine Warrior from Isaiah to Ephesians*. Sheffield: Sheffield Academic, 1997. Studies the background to the image of divine armor in Eph 6:10-17.

Usami, Kōshi. *Somatic Comprehension of Unity: The Church in Ephesus*. AnBib 101. Rome: Pontifical Biblical Institute, 1983. Detailed analysis of the use of bodily imagery to understand the church in Ephesians.

Wiles, G. P. *Paul's Intercessory Prayers: The Significance of the Intercessory Prayer Passages in the Letters of St. Paul*. SNTSMS 24. Cambridge: Cambridge University Press, 1974. Studies Paul's use of prayer formulae in the epistles.

OUTLINE OF EPHESIANS

I. Ephesians 1:1-2, Greeting

II. Ephesians 1:3-14, Eulogy on Salvation

III. Ephesians 1:15-23, Thanksgiving Prayer Report

IV. Ephesians 2:1–6:20, Body of the Letter

    A. 2:1–3:21, Theological Reflection on Salvation in the Body of the Exalted Christ
        2:1-10, Conversion from Death to New Life
        2:11-22, Unity in Christ
        3:1-13, Paul as Prisoner for the Gospel
        3:14-21, The Apostle's Prayer
    B. 4:1–6:9, Ethical Exhortations on Living as Christians
        4:1-16, Building the Body of Christ
        4:17-32, Two Ways of Life
        5:1-14, Live as Children of Light
        5:15-21, Wisdom as Thanksgiving
        5:22–6:9, Household Code
    C. 6:10-20, Peroration: Be Armed with the Power of God

V. Ephesians 6:21-24, Final Greeting

EPHESIANS 1:1-2

GREETING

COMMENTARY

Ancient letters begin with a greeting that identifies the sender and the recipients. Pauline letters expand the traditional formula with expressions of Christian faith or references to the divine origin of Paul's apostolic authority (1 Cor 1:1-3; Col 1:1-2). Some ancient manuscripts lack the words "in Ephesus" (ἐν Ἐφέσῳ *en Ephesō*). Without a concrete place reference, the greeting is grammatically awkward, since the designation "to the saints" is followed by the words "who are and faithful." The translation in the NRSV note, "to the saints who are also faithful," treats the "and" (καί *kai*) as "also" rather than as a conjunction.[49] Though there are no ancient examples, some commentators suggest that Ephesians was originally a circular letter into which the name of a particular church could be inserted. Since Ephesians reformulates sections from Colossians, one would expect the addressees to be designated "to the saints in Ephesus" (cf. Col 1:2). The "grace and peace" formula (v. 2) adds "and the Lord Jesus Christ" (see Rom 1:7) to Col 1:2. Conflation of Col 1:1-2 with Rom 1:7 may explain the dangling "who are" (τοῖς οὖσιν *tois ousin*), since Rom 1:7 has "to all those *who are* in Rome" (the NRSV changes the sentence structure).

Assuming that the author was a disciple of Paul who used Colossians and other Pauline letters to compose a letter of instruction explains the lack of precision about the addressees. Ephesians indicates that Paul was unknown to its audience (so 1:15; 3:2), but such personal distance would not be true of Ephesus, where the apostle spent considerable time (Acts 19:1-22) and from which he wrote to the Corinthians. Ephesus was probably the locus of the "mortal threat" mentioned in 2 Cor 1:8-11 (also 1 Cor 15:32), possibly the imprisonment of Philippians 1:1 and 2. The ties between Paul and Ephesus explain how an ancient scribe attached "in Ephesus" to this text. The mention of Tychicus as the letter carrier in Eph 6:21, combined with the assertion that he was sent to Ephesus in 2 Tim 4:12, could also generate the address.

Expressions found in the greeting are central to the letter's depiction of the author and his audience. Surprisingly, the author never again speaks of himself as "apostle" (ἀπόστολος *apostolos*). Instead, the word "apostle" appears in lists of those whose past activities provide the foundation for the church (2:20; 3:5; 4:11). The letter's "Paul" speaks of himself as the imprisoned ambassador for a gospel that revealed God's saving plan for the Gentiles (3:1-13; 4:1; 6:19-20). The reference to the "will of God" (θέλημα Θεοῦ *thelēma Theou*) introduces a theme that is echoed in the rest of the letter. The "will of God" lies behind the plan that the Gentiles would be included in salvation (1:5, 9, 11). The phrase appears in the hortatory material to highlight the orientation of Christian life (5:17; 6:6).

Of the two terms used to describe the addressees, "faithful" (πιστοί *pistoi*) and "saints" (ἅγιοι *hagioi*; lit., "holy ones"), the former never returns except in reference to Tychicus (6:21, from Col 4:7), but "saints" echoes throughout the letter. It is a standard designation for members of the Christian community (1:15, 18; 2:19; 3:8, 18; 4:12; 5:3; 6:18), but it also designates the moral purity to which Christians are called (1:4; 5:3, 27). A common self-designation among early Christians (see Acts 9:13; Rom 1:7; 1 Cor 1:2; 2 Cor 1:1), the expression was taken from OT references to Israel as a people set apart for the Lord (Lev 11:44; 19:2; 20:26). Its primary emphasis in the OT is not moral

---

49. On the grammatical problems of this translation, see Lincoln, *Ephesians*, 2.

perfection but the dedication of persons, places, or objects to the service of God (Exod 28:2; Pss 2:6; 24:3). These cultic connotations emerge in Ephesians when Christians are described as "a holy temple" (Eph 2:21).

Paul regularly replaced the secular epistolary "greeting" with "grace and peace" (see Rom 1:7; 1 Cor 1:3; Gal 1:3; Phil 1:2). God is "father" (πατήρ *patēr*) both of the "Lord Jesus Christ" (Eph 1:3; see Rom 15:6; 2 Cor 1:3) and of believers, who are God's adopted children in Christ (Eph 1:5; see Rom 8:14-17; Gal 4:4-7). Their access to God as Father is possible through the Spirit (Eph 2:18; see Rom 8:16, 27; Gal 4:6). God as our common "Father" (*patēr*) is the focus of both prayer (Eph 3:14; 5:20) and the unity of the church that God's activity has brought into being (Eph 4:6). However, there is a change in how Ephesians uses the language of God as "Father." Ephesians does not correlate it with references to either Jesus as "son" ("Son of God" appears only in 4:13) or believers as "sons." Instead, Christians attain their special relationship to God because they belong to the exalted, heavenly Christ who is head of the body, a new creation of the perfect human. References to God as "Father" occur either in set formulae of blessing, prayer, or confession (1:2-3, 17; 4:5; 6:23) or in references to prayer (2:18; 3:14; 5:20).

Another shift in imagery attaches to the theological use of the terms "grace" and "peace." "Grace" (χάρις *charis*) appears as a well-understood agent of salvation (2:5, 8); as an attribute of God that merits human praise (1:6-7; 2:7); as God's gift to Paul for the ministry he carries out (3:2-8); or as a gift to individual believers (4:7). "Peace" (εἰρήνη *eirēnē*) appears in a central image for the "mystery" (μυστήριον *mystērion*) of God's saving activity: the reconciliation of Jew and Gentile in one new human being (Eph 2:15-17). That image reshapes the exhortation to peace within the community (Eph 4:3).

Whether directed to an individual, a particular community, or—as appears to have been the case with Ephesians—to several churches, the Pauline letter was always a public event. Colossians 4:16 speaks of the reading and exchange of letters between churches in neighboring cities. The power of a whole letter, read out to an expectant community, is an important part of the event of communication. Ephesians uses the conventional greeting formulae to ready the audience for the reading that follows. Hearing the letter will remind them of how God and the Lord Jesus Christ have reshaped their lives. The ornate rhetorical style sweeps the audience up into the author's vision of membership in a cosmic church united with its exalted head.

EPHESIANS 1:3-14
EULOGY ON SALVATION

COMMENTARY

Greek letters usually followed the greeting with a brief thanksgiving or wish for the health of recipients. Pauline letters have transformed that feature into a longer thanksgiving for their faith, which also telegraphs themes found in the body of the letter (see Rom 1:8-9, 10-15; Phil 1:3-11; Col 1:3-8). In 2 Cor 1:3-11 the opening takes the form of a blessing (2 Cor 1:3a). Ephesians employs both the blessing (1:3-14) and the thanksgiving prayer report (1:15-23). Each consists of a single sentence, elaborately crafted from a sequence of subordinate participial and prepositional clauses. English translations break up these sentences into shorter sentences.

Unlike the undisputed Pauline letters, Ephesians does not refer in this section to the situation of its audience. Instead, the blessing period evokes the liturgical origin of the blessing formula as found in the psalms (LXX Pss 66:20; 68:35). The liturgical sense of blessing (εὐλογέω *eulogeō*) God for deeds of salvation has been combined with the rhetorical understanding of "eulogy" as eloquence or fine speaking in praise of someone. Thus Ephesians telegraphs its intention to the audience. We are about to hear a fine speech in praise of "God [the] Father of our Lord Jesus Christ." True to the rhetorical conventions of such speech, Ephesians indicates that such praise is the appropriate response to benefits conferred. In the secular sphere, speech in praise of a benefactor might elicit future benefactions by cementing the relationship between a powerful individual and those who participate in his praise.

Ephesians takes up this tradition by repeatedly underlining the fact that the blessings its audience has received come from a beneficent God who consistently intended to confer salvation. The passage is punctuated by references to election and divine will (vv. 4-5, 9, 11). Another set of phrases refers to the praise that the recipients of salvation owe their divine benefactor (vv. 6, 12, 14). The conclusion treats the present experience of salvation as the guarantee of a future inheritance and ongoing praise of God's glory. Ephesians weaves the function of Christ as heavenly mediator into the praise of God as benefactor. A series of clauses beginning with "in whom" (ἐν ᾧ *en hō*) spell out the Christian promise of salvation (vv. 7-10, 11-12, 13-14). The NRSV has created sentences that focus our attention on the benefits of salvation received in Christ: God blessed us in Christ (vv. 3-4) and destined us for adoption in Christ (vv. 5-6); redemption is through the blood of Christ (vv. 7-8a); knowledge of God's will unites all things in Christ (vv. 8b-10); we are destined to praise God in Christ (vv. 11-12), and Gentiles ("you") are included in this inheritance through preaching the gospel (vv. 13-14). Verses 9-10 have a central place in the theological understanding of Ephesians. The exaltation of Christ in the heavens provides the foundation for bringing the entire creation into unity under Christ as head. Appropriately, the final words of v. 14 pick up the intent of the whole section, "to the praise of his [God's] glory."

The biblical tradition insists that praise is the appropriate human response to God's acts of salvation (Pss 96:1-4; 118:1). Without the appearance of Jesus, God's full plan for salvation would have remained hidden (vv. 9-10). The expression "with every spiritual blessing" (ἐν πάσῃ εὐλογίᾳ πνευματικῇ *en pasē eulogia pneumatikē*) highlights the completeness of divine salvation. Unlike human benefactors, God has not conferred a partial blessing. Jewish roots for this expression lie in the blessing of Joseph by Jacob (Gen 49:25) and in the liturgical language of the Essenes, "May [my Lord] bless you [from his holy residence]. . . . May he bestow upon you all the blessings [. . .] in the congregation of the holy ones."[50] The reference to "the holy ones" assimilates the Essene congregation to the angels who are in the heavens with God.

Ephesians has modified this Jewish form by substituting the exalted Christ for the angelic hosts and using a peculiar plural form, "the heavenlies" (ἐπουράνιοι *epouranioi*; NRSV, "the heavenly places"), to refer to heaven. That expression appears only in Ephesians, where it is used both for God's dwelling (1:3, 20; 2:6) and for a sphere in which hostile powers are active (3:10; 6:12). Descriptions of the universe in the first century CE assumed that the earth was in the center of a cosmos that stretched out to the sphere of the stars. The moon, the sun, and the planets (through Saturn) circled the earth. The region from the earth to the moon was one in which decay and death occurred. Earthy, heavy, watery, and dark substances tended toward the earth. Fire and air tended toward the heavens. In order to reach the realm of the divine, the soul would have had to ascend through all of these heavenly regions. Spiritual beings, sometimes depicted as demonic, could be associated with the planetary spheres and their power to dictate the fate of humans and nations.

This picture of the cosmos was replicated in Jewish apocalypses that described the ascent of a seer to a vision of the divine throne. By the first century CE most apocalypses assumed that the journey would require passing through multiple heavens.[51] Ordinarily the fear or awe felt by the visionary is mitigated by the protection of his angelic guide. Ephesians does not develop the details of multiple heavenly regions.[52]

The explanation in v. 4 picks up the agency of Christ as the mediator of salvation and expands the description of God's plan of salvation in a temporal direction. God's plan to redeem humanity preexists the foundation of the world. The image of God's election of the righteous and condemnation of the wicked prior to creation appears in Essene texts.[53]

According to these texts God ordained the course of all the cosmic powers as well as those of humankind in the act of creation.[54] Ephesians agrees with the Essene view that the elect follow the paths of holiness that God established for creatures. The formulation in v. 4 does not imply the preexistence of the individual souls of the righteous.[55] Nor does Ephesians spell out the connection between the Christ in whom the righteous are elect and God's creative activity. Its emphasis is on the experience of salvation. Those who come to believe in Christ find themselves participating in God's eternal plan.

The phrase "in love" (ἐν ἀγάπῃ *en agapē*) at the conclusion of v. 4 appears so awkward that some have treated it as the motive for the divine "destined" (i.e., "predestined," προορίσας *proorisas*) in v. 5.[56] However, it matches the phrase "in the Beloved" (ἐν τῷ ἠγαπημένῳ *en tō ēgapēmenō*), which concludes v. 6. Therefore, the expression appears to be a stylistic marker. It may be intended to refer to divine election in Christ rather than to human behavior.

Verses 5-6 develop the previous reference to divine election in Christ by introducing the Pauline motif of adoption (Rom 8:15-23; Gal 4:4-7). A striking difference between the use of predestination language in Ephesians and similar expressions found at Qumran is the lack of any reference to the wicked. Ephesians knows such language, as later references to "those who are disobedient" (τῆς ἀπειθείας *tēs apeitheias*; 2:2-3; 5:6) indicate. But in keeping with the author's vision of unity, God's gracious election could not be expressed as the sharp division of humankind into a righteous remnant, the holy elect, over against a majority who will never experience God's grace. Predestination also has this positive tenor in Paul's usage (see Rom 8:29-30; 1 Cor 2:7).

The description of election in Ephesians is consistently theocentric. God calls a people "for himself." Consequently, the Greek of v. 5*a* follows "adoption through Jesus Christ" with the prepositional phrase "in him" (εἰς αὐτόν *eis auton*), which refers to God rather

---

50. 1QSb 1:3-5
51. Martha Himmelfarb, *Ascents into Heaven in Jewish and Christian Apocalypses* (Oxford: Oxford University Press, 1993), 32. See also *T. Levi* 2–3; 8; *2 Enoch* 3–21; *Apoc. Mos.* 35:2; 2 Cor 12:1-3.
52. For a survey of ancient traditions concerning the structure and inhabitants of the heavens, see J. Edward Wright, *The Early History of Heaven* (New York: Oxford University Press, 2000).
53. CD 2:7; 1QS 3:15-17.
54. 1QH 9[1]:10-20; 1QS 3:15-17.
55. Best observes that for Ephesians predestination is not primarily a doctrine about individual salvation but about God's purpose. See Best, *A Critical and Exegetical Commentary on Ephesians*, 119-20.
56. Best, *A Critical and Exegetical Commentary on Ephesians*, 123.

than to the Son. This focus diverges from the Pauline formula in Rom 8:29, which treats the calling of the elect as necessary to provide brothers and sisters for Christ the firstborn. Verse 6 spells out the reason for the existence of the elect community: worship and praise of the one whose gracious benefits they have received through the Beloved (Jesus Christ).

Traditional Christian formulae underlie the description in vv. 7-8 of how believers receive grace through Christ: His death brings forgiveness of sins. Verse 7 adds "through his blood" and the conclusion "according to the riches of his [God's] grace" to a formula from Col 1:14. The term "redemption" (ἀπολύτρωσις *apolytrōsis*; also see Rom 3:24) can be used for freeing a slave (LXX Exod 21:8; Dan 4:34). God obtained Israel as a people by liberating them from Egypt (Exod 15:16; Ps 74:2) or from captivity (Isa 51:11). Since it also came to refer to God's end-time action on Israel's behalf (Ps 130:7-8; Isa 59:29), early Christian usage points to Christ's death as effecting this salvation. The formula quoted in Rom 3:24-26 indicates that Christ's death was understood as the expiation for sin that makes redemption—God's free gift to believers—a reality.

The present tense of the verb "we have" (ἔχομεν *echomen*, v. 7) suggests that Christ continues to be the source of deliverance from sin for believers. Verse 8 specifies the expression of God's graciousness as "wisdom and insight" (σοφία καὶ φρόνησις *sophia kai phronēsis*) bestowed on believers. In the OT, insight and wisdom are characteristic of the pious who attend to God's revelation by living according to the law (Prov 1:2-7; 2:2-10; Ps 37:30-31). The Dead Sea Scrolls speak of wisdom or understanding of God's way as a special gift to the teacher(s) of the sect.[57] This revelation separates the sectaries from the rest of humanity, who lack wisdom and understanding).[58] Thus understanding forms part of the imagery of election. Characteristic of its modification of such metaphors, Ephesians bypasses the dualistic framework in the Qumran texts, which restricts knowledge to an elite minority.

The Essene examples include other virtues along with understanding: deeds of truth instead of sin, justice, loving what God loves, hatred of evil, love of God, wholehearted devotion to the quest for wisdom. The ethical section of Ephesians (4:1–6:20) takes up the concrete expression of such understanding in Christian life. Verse 9, with its reference to "mystery" (μυστήριον *mystērion*), continues to parallel the language of election found in the Essene writings. The Aramaic equivalent to "mystery" (רז *rāz,*; Dan 2:18) appears in Essene interpretation of prophetic texts to refer to the secret plan of God's salvation that has been revealed to the sectaries.[59] Paul uses "mystery" (*mystērion*) in this sense to refer to God's plan for the salvation of humanity in Christ. It has a future reference, that Jews who reject Christ will be included in salvation (Rom 11:25-32). Paul designates the presence of salvation unknown to the rulers of the cosmos when they crucified the Lord of glory as "God's wisdom" (1 Cor 2:7). Like the teacher(s) of the Essene sect,[60] Paul can describe the apostles as persons who dispense these mysteries to others (1 Cor 4:1). Colossians 2:1-3 presents knowledge of the hidden mystery of God as part of the wisdom Christians attain through Paul's teaching. This mystery of salvation was hidden from prior ages but has been made manifest to the saints in Paul's preaching Christ among the Gentiles (Col 1:26-27).

The connection between revelation of the mystery and a preordained divine plan is firmly embedded in Essene writings.[61] However, Ephesians lacks the interest in the succession of times characteristic of apocalyptic speculation that anticipates the end of the present evil age by divine judgment.[62] As v. 10 suggests, the times have reached their fulfillment. The term "plan" (οἰκονομία *oikonomia*) has a range of meanings. The primary secular meanings have to do with the management of a household or city. An individual designated as οἰκονόμος (*oikonomos*) may be the treasurer of a city (Rom 16:23), the estate administrator, or the manager of a household. Often such persons were slaves with considerable power over others, but other examples indicate that freemen may have been

---

57. 1QH 5[13]:7-9] 6[14]:8-9, 25-27.
58. 1QS 11:5-6.
59. 1QpHab 7:1-4, 13-14; 8:1-3.
60. 1QH 12[4]:27.
61. See 1QS 4:18-19, with reference to the future destruction of all evil.
62. 4 Ezra 4:37; *2 Apoc. Bar.* 40:3; 81:4.

administrators for extensive enterprises.[63] When "plan" (*oikonomia*) is associated with God, it refers to God's providential direction of all things in the cosmos.

The connection between the term "plan" (*oikonomia*) and "the fullness of time" (πλήρωμα τῶν καιρῶν *plērōma tōn kairōn*, v. 10) suggests a temporal plan rather than a providential ordering of the world. Paul used the expression "fullness of time" for the coming of Jesus as redeemer from the law and source of Christian adoption as children of God (Gal 4:4-5).[64] That expression designates a moment in the past that marked the transition from divine promise to its fulfillment. But, as we have seen when Paul uses the term "mystery" (*mystērion*) in Rom 11:25, he assumes that God's plan of salvation has not been completed. First Corinthians 15:51-57 also uses "mystery" (*mystērion*) for future stages in the unfolding story of salvation: subjection of all things to the Son, the bodily resurrection of those who belong to Christ, and finally, the return of everything to the Father. Does Ephesians assume that the exaltation of Christ in the heavenly regions marks the end of all significant times of salvation? Some argue that all the divine promises have been realized and are present now in the experience of believers who participate in the heavenly exaltation of Christ.[65]

Ephesians appears to come down somewhere between anticipating a future stage of salvation and assuming that all salvation is present in Christ. On the one hand, its eschatology departs from common apocalyptic patterns in not anticipating any future critical acts of salvation from God's side. The formulaic statement in v. 10*b* of what the fullness of time entails suggests more a static reality than a dynamic process. On the other hand, one cannot ignore the ongoing appropriation of the gospel by human beings, which implies further unfolding of salvation.

Ephesians describes the "all things" (τὰ πάντα *ta panta*) gathered up in Christ in cosmic terms, all things in heaven and on earth. *How* all things are united in Christ is not specified at this point. Ephesians will develop that motif with the image of Christ as head of the cosmic body, the church.[66] The confession of Christ's present power over the cosmos can be found in the ancient Christian hymn cited in Phil 2:9-11. Colossians 1:15-20 grounds its depiction of Christ's rule over all things in the role of the preexistent son of God in creation.

Ephesians continues in vv. 11-12 with the benefits received by the elect. The expression "obtain an inheritance" (κληρονομέω *klēronomeō*) evokes echoes of Israel's destiny to be God's "lot" or heritage (Deut 9:29). The Essenes frequently used this expression to describe their community.[67] Ephesians makes the risen Christ the basis for Christians to obtain their inheritance. It agrees with the Essenes that the elect have been called to praise God. Compare the Essene hymn, "I shall bless him for (his) great marvels and shall meditate on his power and shall rely on his compassion."[68] The concluding phrase in this section, "we, who were the first to set our hope on Christ," has led some scholars to suggest that the author has shifted to the perspective of the Jewish Christian "we" found in 2:11–3:6.[69] In that case, the phrase would employ the ambiguity of the Greek word Χριστός (*Christos*); it can mean both "Christ" (a specific reference to Jesus) and "Messiah" (the object of Jewish hopes). The next verse appears to contrast the "we" of this verse with the "you" of the Gentile readers. However, Ephesians has not yet introduced the Jew and Gentile distinction. Nor is such a division appropriate to the genre that draws speaker and audience together in praise of its subject.

One might treat the switch to "you" in v. 13 as a rhetorical way of drawing the audience into the act of praising God.[70] Since the audience's tacit participation is, however, presumed by the genre, another explanation

---

63. See Arion's administration of Hyrcannus's wealth in Josephus *Antiquities of the Jews* 12.199-200. See also Ceslas Spicq, *Theological Lexicon of the New Testament*, 3 vols., trans. James Ernest (Peabody, Mass.: Hendrickson, 1994).

64. Best observes that unlike Gal 4:4-5, Ephesians has no reference to the incarnation. See Best, *A Critical and Exegetical Commentary on Ephesians*, 139.

65. Andreas Lindemann, *Die Aufhebung der Zeit: Geschichtsverständnis und Eschatologie im Epheserbrief* (Gütersloh: Gerd Mohn, 1975) 49-66, 95.

66. "Somatic unity." See Kōshi Usami, *Somatic Comprehension of Unity: The Church in Ephesus*, AnBib 101 (Rome: Pontifical Biblical Institute, 1983) 112-24.

67. 1QS 4:26; 11:7.

68. 1QS 10:16.

69. Gordon Fee notes a typical Pauline telegraphing of a theme in the body of the letter. See Gordon D. Fee, *God's Empowering Presence: The Holy Spirit in the Letters of Paul* (Peabody, Mass.: Hendrickson, 1994) 669.

70. So Lincoln, *Ephesians* 38.

would seem to be required. The verse alludes to the audience's conversion upon hearing the preaching of the gospel. This mission terminology, drawn from the earlier Pauline writings (Rom 10:14-17; Col 1:5), distinguishes the speaker from the audience.[71] Paul is the agent through whom the gospel comes to be known. The "we" of v. 12 would refer to Paul. The Essenes also combine the language of truth revealed through their teacher(s) with an initiation that includes knowledge of the mysteries of God, forgiveness of sin, and cleansing by God's Spirit.[72]

The combination of "sealing" and "down payment" (NRSV, "pledge") with reference to the Spirit appears in 2 Cor 1:21-22. Though sealing would later become part of the baptismal rite,[73] there is no evidence for those associations in 2 Cor 1:21-22 or Eph 1:13. However, the Essene example mentioned above does tie purification by "lustral waters" with the cleansing power of God's Spirit. The phrase "Holy Spirit of the promise" (NRSV, "the promised Holy Spirit") has inverted Gal 3:14, "promise of the Spirit." There the promise to Abraham has been received through faith in Christ. If the Spirit itself is understood to be the content of the promise, then OT passages that refer to the presence of God's Spirit in the last days serve as the basis for the expression (see Ezek 36:26-27; 37:14; Joel 2:28-30). Commentators who see the "you" of v. 13 as Gentiles who have been incorporated into the faith of the Jewish believers treat the Spirit as evidence that the promise of Jew and Gentile joined together is being fulfilled.[74] This reading reflects the theological use of Spirit and promise in Gal 3:14. If the "we"/"you" contrast between v. 12 and v. 13 is not read as referring to Jewish and then Gentile believers respectively,[75] then there is little reason to explicate this expression as a theological account for the election of the Gentiles. The language suits poetic celebrations of divine election similar to that in Essene sources.

Although Ephesians depicts the gifts of salvation as fully present in the lives of believers, the designation "pledge" suggests a future perfection to this experience. A Semitic loan word, "pledge" (ἀρραβών *arrabōn*) is used in commercial texts for "security," "guarantee," or "deposit." The translation "pledge" would be misleading if it suggested a legal promise to fulfill a commitment that establishes a human right against God. Rather, the deposit indicates that one has already received part of what has been promised to secure future delivery. Throughout the eulogy, Ephesians emphasizes the abundance of divine graciousness (vv. 3, 6, 8). The congruence between present and future salvation is reinforced by the phrase that specifies inheritance, "toward redemption as God's own people" (lit., "toward redemption of his possession"). Verse 7 indicated that believers have "redemption" (ἀπολύτρωσις *apolytrōsis*) from sin through the death of Christ. The meaning of "possession" (περιποίησις *peripoiēsis*; NRSV, "God's own people") in v. 14 is contested. If taken as a nominal form that designates an action, it would mean "the possessing." The expression might then be a shorthand reference to believers' taking possession of their inheritance. However, the word can also be used to refer to a possession, in this case the people as God's possession (so NRSV; see LXX Mic 3:17; 1 Pet 2:9; Acts 20:28).

In keeping with the genre of praising a benefactor, the expression might refer to God's redeeming God's own (or Christ's) possession. The benefits experienced by the speakers in the present will continue to characterize their lives. Their experience of the Spirit guarantees this relationship. God is, and will continue to be, the redeemer of the people. Finally, the eulogy concludes with the human response to divine graciousness, praise of God's glory (v. 14c).

The compressed poetic style of the opening eulogy suggests a number of theological themes without providing a conceptual development for any of them. The linguistic and metaphoric parallels from the OT, from Jewish and non-Jewish writings of the Greco-Roman period, and from the earlier Pauline letters provide hints as to what first-century Christian audiences may have brought to their understanding of each phrase. It is easy to apprehend the dynamic involvement of God with human destiny that runs through this section.

---

71. See Best, *A Critical and Exegetical Commentary on Ephesians*, 148, on the mission terminology in this section.
72. 1QS 4:18-22.
73. *2 Clem.* 7:6; 8:6; *Herm. Sim.* viii 6.3; ix 16.3-6.
74. Fee, *God's Empowering Presence*, 670.
75. Schnackenburg, *The Epistle to the Ephesians*, 64-65.

Its language of election embraces all things in a divine plan that existed before anything came into being. Despite their minority status in the world of first-century CE Asia Minor, Christians found themselves the center of God's cosmic design because they belonged to the risen Lord, who is exalted over all of the heavenly powers. Benefits that humans might expect to receive from "the heavens" have been conferred by God in Christ.

We have seen that Ephesians adopted images that were suited to the cosmic picture of its age. The simpler OT imagery of a heavenly dome over the earth was replaced by a multiplicity of heavenly regions. God's power operates through all of them. The "mystery" (*mystērion*) of God's plan invites believers to recognize that all things in the cosmos are brought together in the risen Christ. Ancient readers would readily think of a divine force behind the observed motions of the cosmos. Ancient audiences could imagine the arduous journey of the soul beyond the regions of the earth and moon through the spheres to the divine heavens.[76]

Ephesians is making a claim about the universe as Paul's readers know it. The imagery of heavenly regions is not merely decoration for asserting the powerful sovereignty of God. Anyone who could journey like an apocalyptic visionary to the most distant regions of the universe would find God's creative and saving power at work to gather all things into Christ. Ephesians is not interested in a divine plan that was simply programmed into the creation of the universe as some Stoic cosmologies envisaged the multiple formations of a divine, rational spirit generating the universe. For Ephesians, the providential action of divine power is oriented forward, toward a redemption that brings all things in the cosmos together in Christ.

The dilemma of God's presence to believers in a vast universe was eloquently framed by Augustine. The God who is inside us, closer than we are to ourselves, is also "outside," quite beyond our comprehension. We cannot reach God without God's having come toward us. Citing Joel 2:28, Augustine comments on the conceptual dilemma of divine presence:

> When you are "poured out" (see Joel 2:28) upon us, you are not wasted on the ground. You raise us upright. You are not scattered but reassemble us. In filling all things, you fill them all with the whole of yourself.[77]

Augustine also recognized that the distinction between God as creator and human creatures is essential to the dynamic of praise. Ephesians indicates that the purpose of our election is to praise God's glory. We cannot engage in that praise without the ability to perceive God's redeeming power at work.

Ephesians uses the language of divine election to describe the experience of God's grace touching the lives of believers. In this context, it is important to note the difference between Ephesians and the linguistic background provided by the Essene writings. Unlike the Qumran texts, Ephesians does not depict election as the division between a few righteous and the majority of human beings who are alienated from God. Instead, Ephesians sees redemption as the purpose that God has embedded in creation as a whole. Though Ephesians recognizes the human need for redemption from sin, its imagery suggests that God would have brought all things together in Christ even if Adam had not sinned. Forgiveness enables the elect to live before God in the holiness to which they are called (1:4).

---

76. See M. R. Wright, *Cosmology in Antiquity* (New York: Routledge, 1995). J. E. Wright argues that poorly understood Hellenistic cosmology led 1st-cent. Jewish and Christian authors to shift from the traditional single heaven to multiple heavenly regions. See J. Edward Wright, *The Early History of Heaven*, 139-84.

77. Augustine, *Confessions*, 1.4 (3), in Augustine, *Confessions*, trans. Henry Chadwick (Oxford: Oxford University Press, 1992) 4.

REFLECTIONS

The opening words of Ephesians, after the epistolary greeting, are, "Blessed be the God and Father of our Lord Jesus Christ" (1:3). These words are a variation of "Blessed be God" or "Blessed are you, Lord God," which are standard formulae that ring through Jewish prayers. In the Passover seder, the prayer that accompanies the lighting of the candles is, "Blessed are you, Lord, our God, who makes us holy with your commandments and commands us to light the festival lights." Every prayer for the rest of the meal will begin with the same Hebrew phrase, "Blessed are you, O Lord, our God." Even visitors have it down by the end.

This opening prayer introduces several motifs that echo through Ephesians: God's rule over the universe, the holiness of God's people, a religious life as light shining in darkness, the joy that we take in salvation. The writer Anne Lamott, apologizing for her simple religion, has said that she had only two basic prayers: "Help, help, help" and "Thank you, thank you, thank you."[78] "Blessed be God"—these words remind us that the first movements of prayer should be thanksgiving and praise directed to God. The moments of asking, lament, or reaching out in the emptiness of despair, equally necessary to the life of prayer, make no sense without this framework. God is Lord of the universe, but not a distant force unconcerned about human beings. Instead, God is our greatest benefactor. Inhabitants of Greco-Roman cities were familiar with elaborate orations in praise of wealthy benefactors. Augustine complained that as holder of the chair of rhetoric in Milan he would be expected to eulogize the emperor on state occasions. Lies were the price of the honor that he was seeking: "I was preparing to recite praises of the emperor, most of which were lies, and by so lying win favor from those who knew [that they were lies]."[79] Ephesians has combined the traditional Jewish prayer with the familiar civic rhetoric of eulogy to drive home the point that God is the true source of goodness. Praise of God is the whole truth, not a pack of lies.

We also see the sense of a powerful new expression of God's person and love reshaping traditional forms of articulation. God is not simply "ruler of the universe." God is "Father of our Lord Jesus Christ." The Gospels tell the story of the life and ministry of Jesus, but Ephesians does not reflect in the same way on the human life of Jesus. Rather, it begins with the ongoing, present life of Christ, the risen Christ exalted in heavenly glory. In traditional Jewish formulae, the commandments are seen as the sign of God's blessing; but in Ephesians, because of Jesus' death on the cross and his heavenly exaltation, the signs of God's favor are spiritual blessing, forgiveness of sin, and, most important, election or adoption as God's people. We see the importance of this shift later in the letter (2:11-22). The commandments separated Jews from non-Jews. The spiritual blessings that have been won on the cross are for all people. Even today it is easy to forget that claim.

There is more to the tale. Ephesians sees the plan of salvation as a hidden order that existed even before the universe was created. This vision takes an even more dramatic turn when we translate it into the twenty-first-century cosmos. We have stunning visual photos as well as color renderings of radiation from other spectra that map the universe further and further back in time. Rather than check our astronomy at the church door, we need to bring these pictures in. There is no reason for today's believers to keep their faith locked up in the smaller universe of the first century. Add to that vision the mathematical speculations of physicists who imagine that there are other universes.[80] Ephesians suggests that we stretch our imaginations. Before any of this even existed, God's plan encompassed the human story of faith. Various astronomical theories, equations, and observations speculate about the probable fate of the material universe, but Ephesians assures us that God's plan of salvation does not depend on these calculations and that somehow the universe is ordered so that all things return to God in Christ.

---

78. Anne Lamott, *Traveling Mercies: Some Thoughts on Faith* (New York: Pantheon, 1999).
79. Augustine *Confessions* VI.6 (author's trans.).
80. See, e.g., Brian Greene, *The Elegant Universe: Superstrings, Hidden Dimensions, and the Quest for the Ultimate Theory* (New York: Norton, 1999).

The structure for the spiritual return of all things to God is already unrolled from its hiding place in God's eternal wisdom. That is the mystery Ephesians invites us to contemplate. What is the structure? The cosmic body of Christ (1:10). Remember that this section of Ephesians is poetic rhetoric, not the theological language of dogmatic textbooks. The nuts and bolts of a theological explanation for this vision are not provided. But put its affirmation of faith into the dramatic sweep of twenty-first-century science, and the consequences are breathtaking. Cosmology will not prove the truth about the hidden faith structure of the universe, whether it is dressed up in first-century or twenty-first-century garb; but it will instruct us about imagining God. We are summoned to a vision of a God who encompasses the whole cosmos and who is active in all of creation.

There is another question that Ephesians puts to the modern imagination that concerns the path of holiness. It is a fundamental tenet of biblical theology that creation is a witness to God (see Pss 19:1-4; 104:14-23; Isa 40:25-26; Rom 1:19-22).[81] That witness calls for human response of praise and piety, walking in holiness. We are familiar with poets and artists who find God through the beauty of creation. The nineteenth-century Jesuit poet Gerard Manley Hopkins ends his poem "Pied Beauty" with, "All things . . . he fathers-forth whose beauty is past change: Praise him."[82] Ephesians points to a further movement beyond awe and praise, that of discipleship. Holiness is a way of life that corresponds to the God revealed in creation. Creation has not lost its power to inspire awe in the twenty-first century. Praise of the Creator, who is greater than the beauty that "he fathers-forth," should follow. But that is the step we often find missing in the modern imagination. For example, Christians might well ask what happened to faith in the science fiction movies. Perhaps you have noticed. In most "sci-fi" movies (not to mention computer games) religion has been written out of most, if not all, of "the universe"—whether we take it in spacial, galactic terms or in temporal ones. The implicit prediction is that God will not be around in 3030. Think about it. People would have said the same about the long-term chances of the emerging Christian faith in 60 CE. They would have thought that empires, gods, perhaps even Rome, would remain to 1000 CE. But this group of believers?

---

81. See the discussion of this motif in Walter Brueggemann, *Theology of the Old Testament: Testimony, Dispute, Advocacy* (Minneapolis: Fortress, 1997) 528-51.

82. The poem can be found in Christopher Ricks, ed., *The Oxford Book of English Verse* (Oxford: Oxford University Press, 1999) no. 584.

EPHESIANS 1:15-23

THANKSGIVING PRAYER REPORT

COMMENTARY

The thanksgiving of Pauline letters often signals themes taken up in what follows. The second, long periodic sentence in Ephesians serves that function. Ephesians combines phrases from Colossians (Col 1:3-4, 9, 18) with its own emphasis on knowledge of God's saving power in Christ to create its thanksgiving. Rhetorically, the thanksgiving can be a way of gaining the goodwill of one's audience. The eulogy joined author and audience in the praise of their common benefactor, God (v. 13). Now the thanksgiving assures Christians who had not known the apostle Paul that their reputation for faith and love has won them a place in his prayers. Paul used a similar strategy in addressing Christians in Rome, whom he had not yet visited (Rom 1:8-15).

The thanksgiving falls into three sections: (a) the formal thanksgiving and prayer report (vv. 15-16); (b) the content of Paul's intercession (vv. 17-19); and (c) a christological expansion on God's energizing power in the exalted Christ (vv. 20-23). The intercessory report asks for insight and wisdom (vv. 17-19). The content of that knowledge returns to phrases from the eulogy: (a) Spirit, wisdom, revelation, and one's ability to "come to know" (ἐν ἐπιγνώσει *en epignōsei*) in v. 17 echo the wisdom, insight, and making "known to us the mystery" (μυστήριον *mystērion*) of vv. 8-9; (b) hope, riches, and inheritance in v. 18 pick up the earlier "first to set our hope" (v. 12), wealth (v. 7), and inheritance (v. 14).

Many commentators detect a hymnic formula describing the exaltation of Christ in vv. 20-21, which has been expanded by a scriptural proof text (Ps 110:1) and its application to Christ and the church. Emphasis on the role of the church in God's plan (v. 22) is an addition peculiar to Ephesians.[83] The combination of Ps 110:1 and Ps 8:6 describes the eschatological triumph of the Lord independently of ecclesial imagery elsewhere in the NT (see 1 Cor 15:25-27; Heb 2:8-9).[84] The image of the risen Christ as head of the church derives from Col 1:18. The puzzling concluding clause (v. 23c), "the fullness of him who fills all in all" (τὸ πλήρωμα τοῦ τὰ πάντα ἐν πᾶσιν πληρουμένου *to plērōma tou ta panta en pasin plēroumenou*), reformulates the mystery of God's plan from v. 10.

1:15-16. The prayer report combines Col 1:3-4 and Phlm 4-5. Pauline thanksgivings make it clear that the appropriate response to evangelization is a reputation for Christian faith. The apostle's preaching would not be successful if his churches did not become known to others as places of faith and mutual love (see 1 Thess 1:3-12).

1:17-19. The thanksgiving modulates into the prayer wish for the readers in these verses. The theocentric focus of the eulogy continues. A key element in the praise of God was "glory" (δόξα *doxa*, vv. 12, 14). This emphasis leads to a reformulation of the title for God. The earlier "Father of our Lord Jesus Christ" (v. 3) becomes "God of our Lord Jesus Christ" and "Father of glory" (v. 17a). The phrase "Father of glory" (ὁ πατήρ τῆς δόξης *ho patēr tēs doxēs*) is not a common expression for God. Paul refers to Jesus as "the Lord of glory" in 1 Cor 2:8. The phrase "God of glory" occurs in Ps 28:3 (LXX), where "glory" (*doxa*) is associated with the storm-god theophany tradition. James 1:17 refers to the "Father of lights" as the source of every good gift, a sentiment similar to that in Eph 1:3.

The initial content of the petition also reminds readers of the earlier emphasis on wisdom and knowledge of God's plan (vv. 8-9,

---

83. Lincoln concludes that these verses cite traditional material but are not taken from a hymn. See Lincoln, *Ephesians*, 51.

84. James D. G. Dunn, *Christology in the Making: A New Testament Inquiry into the Origins of the Doctrine of the Incarnation* (Philadelphia: Westminster, 1980) 108-9.

17b). Given the earlier reference to believers as being "marked with the seal of the promised Holy Spirit" (v. 13), the expression "spirit of wisdom" (πνεῦμα σοφίας *pneuma sophias*) probably intends more than human perception of divine wisdom. God's Spirit is the source of all wisdom and knowledge among the elect. The author is not thinking of particular charismatic gifts that are possessed only by some members of the community, such as the special insight possessed by the apostle (3:3, 5).

Verse 18 describes the result of wisdom as "the eyes of your heart enlightened" (πεφωτισμένους τοὺς ὀφθαλμοὺς τῆς καρδίας *pephōtismenous tous ophthalmous tēs kardias*). This expression resembles the Essene language of election as in the blessing pronounced over those who enter the covenant: "May he illuminate your heart with the discernment of life and grace you with eternal knowledge."[85] By the second century, baptism was commonly described as enlightenment.[86] Ephesians 4:18 speaks of Gentiles who do not know God as "darkened in their understanding." The addressees are warned not to return to that state. Ephesians treats the darkness-to-light image as a reference to the moral conversion associated with turning to God. The fact that individuals might revert to darkness shows that illumination of the heart is not a transformation that becomes permanent as soon as someone becomes a Christian.

Although the OT regularly uses "heart" (לֵב *lēb*) for the seat of human understanding (Ps 10:11; Prov 2:2), the phrase "eyes of your heart" (*tous opthalmous tēs kardias*) has no biblical antecedents. However, Prov 20:27 (LXX) speaks of the breath of humans as the light of the Lord searching out hidden storerooms of the belly. Other Jewish texts refer to the darkened or clouded eye as equivalent to a depraved will.[87] These examples suggest that the expression "eyes of your heart" is associated with change in conduct. Greek moralists may have contributed to such expressions. Matthew 6:22-23 also refers to an "eye" (ὀφθαλμός *ophthalmos*) that is healthy and one that is evil or diseased. This saying refers to the inner light required for ethical discernment. Platonic and Stoic philosophers commonly link that light with reason. Matthew challenges the philosophic assumption that humans can rely on such inner light, since the eye can be darkened.[88]

The content of enlightenment reiterates earlier statements about Christian hope (vv. 18b, c, 14a). Since the passage speaks of "his [God's] glorious inheritance," some commentators presume that the meaning of "saints" (ἅγιοι *hagioi*) has shifted from saints as God's elect to saints as "the holy ones"—that is, angels (so Deut 33:2-3; Ps 89:6, 8; Dan 8:13). On this reading, Ephesians would be similar to the Essene writings in claiming that the heritage of the elect lies with the angelic hosts.[89] Against this interpretation of v. 18, v. 15 has used "saints" (*hagioi*) for those who are fellow Christians within the audience.

Verse 19 shifts from knowledge of one's place among God's elect to recognition of the power of God at work in those who believe. An echo of Col 1:11, the phrase is replete with words for power. The author does not focus on the cosmological manifestations of divine power.[90] Just as the eulogy's account of God's activity in creation (vv. 3-5) was not cosmological but soteriological, so also v. 19 describes the power of God as "for us who believe" (εἰς ἡμᾶς τοὺς πιστεύοντας *eis hēmas tous pisteuontas*). Verse 19b shifts from "you" (plural) to the inclusive "we" in order to set up the parallelism between God's work in the believer and what God has done in raising Christ (v. 20).[91]

The expression "working of his great power" connects v. 19b with v. 20a. Some interpreters treat it as the introduction to the next section.[92] Colossians 1:29b speaks of God's powerful energy at work in the struggles of Paul's ministry. Colossians 2:12 speaks of God's power ("energy") to raise the dead. Since Ephesians uses expressions associated with divine energy and power to connect God's activity within believers and

---

85. 1QS 2:3.
86. So Justin Martyr *1 Apol.* 61.12; 65.1; *Dialogue with Trypho* 39.2; 122.1, 2, 6.
87. *T. Iss.* 4:6; *T. Benj.* 4:2. See Spicq, *Theological Lexicon of the New Testament*.
88. Hans Dieter Betz, *Galatians* (Philadelphia: Fortress, 1979) 84-87.
89. Schnackenburg, *The Epistle to the Ephesians*, 75. See 1QS 11:7-8.
90. As in, e.g., 1QS 11:18-19.
91. Joachim Gnilka, *Der Epheserbrief*, HTKNT (Freiburg: Herder & Herder, 1980) 91; Best, *A Critical and Exegetical Commentary on Ephesians*, 169.
92. Lincoln, *Ephesians*, 60.

the resurrection of Christ, the phrase may be derived from earlier Christian formulae.

1:20-23. The concluding section of this chapter is widely recognized as the development of a creedal formula. Attempts to isolate the specific words of a hymn have not been persuasive.[93] Verse 20 alludes to the ancient tradition of resurrection as heavenly exaltation at God's right hand (Dan 12:2-3; Acts 2:32-33; Phil 2:9-11). The audience already knows that Christ serves to mediate God's gracious blessings from the heavens (v. 3). Ephesians treats the exaltation of Jesus rather than the cross as the focus of God's saving power.[94] Paul links the resurrection of Jesus and divine power in contexts that contrast resurrection with the cross (Rom 1:4; 1 Cor 6:14; 2 Cor 13:4; Phil 3:10). Ephesians may have shifted the traditional emphasis in order to highlight the permanent victory of God's power.

Hellenistic Jewish court tales celebrated exaltation as the victory of a righteous sage over the enemy (see Daniel 1:1–7). Daniel 7:13-27 depicts a human figure ascending to God's throne. With his ascent comes vindication for the righteous and eternal dominion for the "holy ones of the Most High" (Dan 7:27). With the corporate interpretation of the heavenly figure as representative of the righteous, Dan 7:13-27 provides a key to the connection between heavenly exaltation of a figure to God's throne and the eventual triumph of God's elect. This apocalyptic scenario also includes two other elements that are represented in Ephesians: (a) use of the "holy ones" (Dan 7:18, 21, 25, 27) in a way that could refer to the righteous or the angelic hosts[95] and (b) exaltation as victory over powers that threaten human and divine order (Dan 7:23-25).

The exaltation christology of Ephesians requires that Christ be superior to all the heavenly powers (v. 21). The text does not indicate whether the reader should consider this catalog of powers as hostile (so Daniel) or angelic (so Heb 1:3-4). Colossians 1:16 associates a list of powers with the affirmation that the cosmos was created in Christ, "whether thrones or dominions or rulers or powers" (ἐξουσία *exousia*). Ephesians 1:21*a* omits "thrones" and includes δύναμις (*dynamis*; NRSV, "power"; for *exousia* the NRSV shifts to "authority"). Similar lists in apocalyptic texts can be associated with angels[96] or with Satan's cohorts.[97] Ephesians concludes the list of powers with the statement that Christ has the name above every name. This topos appears elsewhere in early christological formulae (see Phil 2:9-11, "Lord"; Heb 1:4-5, "Son"). The concluding phrase (v. 21*c*) evokes the apocalyptic picture of present and future ages. Just as the Son of Man and the holy ones in Dan 7:13-27 receive an eternal dominion, so also the exalted Christ enjoys eternal rule. This affirmation raises a theological question when this passage is compared with Paul's account in 1 Cor 15:23-28. There the Second Coming will be needed to complete the Son's domination of all the powers. At that point, Christ will hand dominion over to the Father. Though Ephesians focuses on the Father in its depiction of divine power, the author does not anticipate a "handing over" of the kingdom to God.

The scenario in Ephesians cannot be squared with the historical perspective of apocalypses like Daniel, which correlate heavenly or symbolic figures with political powers. In such historical apocalypses no claim to dethrone hostile powers could be sustained without the corresponding defeat of evil in its sociopolitical manifestations. The significance of language about Christ's exaltation over the powers in Colossians and Ephesians remains contested. Ephesians refers to an angelic leader of the hostile powers (2:2; 6:11). If the powers of this list are hostile, then Christ is a victorious conqueror.[98] Others have highlighted the reference to Christ's superior name. They suggest that Ephesians is concerned with the use of angelic names in magical texts. The Christ whose name is superior to those of any such powers has rendered the powers of magic impotent.[99] When Ephesians is read over against the ideology of the Roman emperor cult, its encomium to the exalted Christ (esp. 2:11-22) appears

---

93. Lincoln, *Ephesians*, 51.
94. Markus Barth and Helmut Blanke, *Colossians*, AB 34B (New York: Doubleday, 1994) 169.
95. John Collins, *Daniel* (Minneapolis: Fortress, 1993).
96. See *1 Enoch* 61:10; *2 Enoch* [J] 20:1; *T. Levi* 3:8.
97. *Ascen. Isa.* 2:2.
98. Schnackenburg, *The Epistle to the Ephesians*, 77.
99. Arnold, *Ephesians*, 55ff.

to copy the style of speeches in praise of the emperor.[100]

Identification of the list of powers with causes of sociopolitical or individual evil presumes that the powers in this list are the demonic powers referred to later in Ephesians. Since the eulogy and the thanksgiving both depend upon traditional formulaic phrases for divine blessing, the positive use of angelic powers and name formulae in christological acclamations and hymns seems to be more appropriate in this section. God has made all things subject to the risen and exalted Lord (1 Cor 15:25). That same power will be effective in the resurrection of the faithful (Phil 3:21).

In the earlier Pauline letters, references to the future completion of salvation indicate that the present subjection of all things remains a stage in an ongoing process: (a) Christ turns all things over to the Father (1 Cor 15:28); (b) believers are transformed into the image of the risen one (Phil 3:21). Unlike these examples, Ephesians remains focused on the present evidence of salvation. Verse 22b takes from Ps 110:1 the image of Christ as head over the universal church: "He has put all things under his feet." This motif picks up the earlier statement that God's preordained plan was to bring all things together in Christ (v. 10). Ephesians consistently uses "church" (ἐκκλησία *ekklēsia*) in the universal sense found in Colossians (e.g., Col 1:18, 24).

In 1 Cor 12:12-27 (and Rom 12:4-5) Paul adopts a common philosophical image for the political community as a body in which each has an assigned role. Differences in status, activity, and power are necessary for the well-being of the whole. Paul's appropriation of this image to promote concord in the Corinthian community also fits common philosophical usage.[101] Colossians 1:18 has universalized the image by alluding to philosophical traditions that transferred the communal sense of "body" (σῶμα *sōma*) to the harmonious coordination of the cosmos. The universe was considered to be a living being. Hence the move to describing it as a body was not as great as it would be for today's readers.[102] For Colossians, the image of Christ as head of the body makes a natural transition between the creation of all things in Christ and the church that comes into being through the death and resurrection of Jesus.

Ephesians has adopted the imagery of Colossians for a different purpose: to express the completeness of salvation. Christ's superiority to the powers of the cosmos makes the existence of the church possible. However, Ephesians distinguishes the subjection of the powers from the function of Christ as head of the church. Christ is not a distant potentate ruling the church.[103] The concluding description of the "body" (*sōma*) as "fullness" (πλήρωμα *plērōma*) involves several exegetical difficulties. Is "fullness" in apposition to "body" or to Christ (as in Col 1:19; 2:9)? In Ephesians, "fullness" (*plērōma*) makes better grammatical sense as a reference to the body.

The meaning of the term "fullness" (*plērōma*) is more problematic. Elaborate discussions of a divine "fullness" as the goal of salvation appear in gnostic writings from the second and third centuries CE. There "fullness" refers to the realm of divine light that is permanently separated from the darkness, chaos, and evil of this world. A primordial fall led to elements of that light being held captive in this world by the rulers of the planetary spheres (often equated with the OT God). Christ, or some other redeemer figure, must break into this world in order to provide the souls that possess light with the means to return to the "fullness."[104] Gnostic texts often suggest that when all the light has been restored the "deficiency"—that is, the lower world—vanishes.[105] However, Ephesians shows no evidence of the gnostic dualism.[106] Therefore, it is more probable that Ephesians has taken the term from a hymnic tradition like Col 1:19.[107]

---

100. Eberhard Faust, *Pax Christi et Pax Caesaris. Religionsgeschichtliche, traditionsgeschichtliche und sozial geschichtliche Studien zum Epheserbrief*, NTOA 24 (Freiburg: Universitätsverlag; Göttingen: Vandenhoeck & Ruprecht, 1993) 324-80.
101. Tacitus *Annals* 1.12, 13; Plutarch *Life of Galba* 4.3; Philo *On the Special Laws* 1.210; Cicero *On Duties* 1.25.85.
102. E.g., Plato *Timaeus* 30B-34B; 47C-48B; Cicero *On the Nature of the Gods* 1.35; 3.9; Seneca *On Anger* 2.31.7, 8.
103. Usami, *Somatic Comprehension of Unity*, 154-66.
104. E.g., *Gos. Truth* 41, 1-16; *Ap. John* 30, 16.
105. Craig A. Evans, "The Meaning of *plērōma* in Nag Hammadi," *Bib* 65 (1984) 259-65.
106. Karl Martin Fischer, *Tendenz und Absicht des Epheserbriefes*, FRLANT 111 (Göttingen: Vandenhoeck & Ruprecht, 1973) 173-200.
107. Schackenburg, *The Epistle to the Ephesians*, 74.

The noun "fullness" (*plērōma*) can have an active sense ("that which fills") or a passive sense ("that which is filled"); it can also refer to the activity of filling. In the OT the noun is used in the active sense (Pss 95:11; 23:1; 49:12; Jer 8:6; Ezek 12:19; 19:7; 30:12). Ephesians 1:23 echoes OT descriptions of God or a divine attribute filling all things (Isa 6:3; Jer 23:23-24 LXX; Isa 6:3; Wis 1:7; 7:24). Later in the epistle, both Christ (4:10) and the Spirit (5:18) are agents of filling. Since Eph 4:10 refers to the ascent of Christ above the heavens in order to fill (πληρόω *plēroō*) the universe, the phrase "fullness of him who fills all in all" probably belongs to the same tradition. Nothing remains outside the Christ who fills all.[108] Ephesians does not indicate how the church as Christ's fullness is related to his presence to all things.

The ecclesial conclusion of the thanksgiving sounds a motif that will reappear in the letter. Christ's body, the church, experiences the divine life and power of God that fills all things. Readers sometimes assume that the equation between the church and "fullness" (*plērōma*) is a call to action, that the Christian mission is responsible for filling the world with Christ. Ephesians does not identify the church with the "all things" (πάντα *panta*) of the cosmos. Instead, without explaining how the two activities of "filling" are related, this section of Ephesians suggests a special relationship between the church and Christ by using the image of head and body.

The opening of the thanksgiving period gave a more conventional picture of the addressees as the community of the elect. They have become known to others as a community that has faith in the Lord Jesus and demonstrates that faith in love. They believe that the risen Lord has been exalted at God's right hand and have experienced God's power in their lives. When the prayer report turns to imagery of the cosmic power of Christ, Ephesians moves beyond the world as structured by human powers and communities to a world that includes the heavens and ranks of angelic (or demonic) powers. Verse 21 insists that Christ has the name greater than any other, not only in the present age but also in the future. Whether involved in magical practices or not, many persons in the first century CE would have agreed that proper knowledge of angelic or magical names was critical to one's life. Magicians could use the knowledge of such names to enlist the aid of cosmic powers. Angelic powers might be named to facilitate the soul's journey into the heavens either at death or as part of a mystical vision. For the apocalyptic visions of the rise and fall of earthly rulers, the angelic or demonic figures behind the human community were also perceived as a real threat. Consequently, the vision of Christ's exaltation found in Ephesians removes believers from the influence of all other powers.

The lists of powers in Colossians and Ephesians aim to embrace all forces that are thought to control humans and events in the cosmos. Since neither angelic nor magical names are used, the claims made for God's effective power in the risen Christ are not wedded to a particular mythological scenario. A modern list of cosmic powers could be substituted for the ancient examples.[109] Perhaps the ambiguity over whether the powers are demonic or angelic was also deliberate. Ephesians intends to fold all "powers" in the cosmos into the power of God expressed through the exalted Christ. Christians should not assume that other powers in the cosmos, or in the political order, stand between them and salvation. Nor do other powers contribute positive benefits to human life.

The "filling" (*plēroō*) already exists as a divine reality (v. 23). Christians are not subject to powers that must be overcome, as was the case for those who thought that heavenly powers stood between the soul and salvation in the heavens. If Christians recognize the presence and power of God in all things, they have a secure basis for the hope for the "riches of [God's] glorious inheritance" (v. 18). The theology of election in Ephesians reminds Christians that God is the source of their hope and faith. Hope (ἐλπίς *elpis*) as a Christian virtue is not a psychological trait but a response to what God is.[110]

Finally, Ephesians challenges the tendency to define the church from the perspective of its existence as a sociopolitical institution. It

---

108. Lincoln, *Ephesians*, 77.
109. Barth and Blanke, *Colossians*, 202.
110. Hans Conzelmann, "Der Brief an die Epheser," in *Die Briefe an die Galater, Epheser, Philipper, Kolosser, Thessalonicher und Philemon*, ed. Jürgen Becker, Hans Conzelmann, and Gerhard Friedrich (Göttingen/Zürich: Vandenhoeck & Ruprecht, 1985).

stands the earlier Pauline usage of church on its head. The local assemblies to which the earlier letters refer have given place to the cosmic vision of church as a divine reality. The "body" image was used for both sociopolitical entities and for the universe as a whole. Consequently, Ephesians builds on the earlier tradition in order to expand the vision of church from local to cosmic community.

Since Ephesians shows no signs of the gnostic dualism between the divine realm and the material world, the "fullness" (*plērōma*) of the body is not limited to the heavenly realm where Christ is exalted. Ancient thinkers who depicted the divine spirit or wisdom pervading the universe[111] presumed that this spirit had a natural affinity with human intellectual and spiritual capacities. Ephesians rejects the view that human knowledge of God is part of creation as such. It is received as divine gift. The shift from cosmological to soteriological imagery highlights another central conviction of this letter: Redemption belonged to the divine plan prior to creation. Unlike gnostic myth, creation is not a hostile trap for light that belongs to the divine world. It is oriented toward salvation that comes in Christ. Knowledge of God comes with the conversion of human understanding through revelation (vv. 17-18).

111. As in Philo *Allegorical Interpretation of the Laws* 3.4.

REFLECTIONS

Reputation or publicity? How do our churches become known for their faith in Jesus and loving service to others? In the ancient secular letter form, the ones sending the letters often indicated that they had heard some good news from or about the recipients and expressed pleasure about learning it. In an age before instant global communication, people could go for weeks or months without news of family, friends, or business associates, and such news was always treasured. Likewise, in the thanksgiving sections of Paul's letters, he also often expresses pleasure about some news he has heard about the recipients, but the news he mentions is always more than routine events. The news for which Paul gives thanks has to do with the fundamental Christian virtues: faith, love, and hope (1:15, 18).

All churches, it could be argued, have some measure of these virtues, but what impresses the author of Ephesians is that this congregation has a word-of-mouth reputation for them. "I have *heard* of your faith in the Lord Jesus and your love toward all the saints," Ephesians says in the thanksgiving prayer section. What is the difference between a reputation based on word of mouth and one generated through a publicity blitz? One big difference is the source. We know who is making a recommendation or telling us a bit of news when we hear something by word of mouth. Paul names sources of information about particular churches in some of his letters (e.g., 1 Cor 1:11; 1 Thess 3:6-10). Since Ephesians is a general essay in the Pauline tradition, we do not find specific details, but the opening formula suggests the intimacy of a word-of-mouth report.

We are familiar with the fact that "word of mouth" can take what filmmakers consider a small movie to big-time status. Some record companies started paying teens in tickets, posters, and CDs to talk up their favorite stars on the Internet. But for all the marketing research, focus groups, and big-budget advertising, no one has found a way to turn publicity into reputation. How does "the buzz" get going around a particular church? Not by advertising. When people come to our worship, our Bible study, our church school, our church suppers, and all the other things we do, they have to feel that special spirit. And Ephesians reminds us that the source of the energy, power, and spirit at work in the church is ultimately God (1:19-20).

Ephesians' thanksgiving prayer tells us something else about the genuinely successful church. The people in such a church have a goal, a destination. And because they know where they are going, they are people of hope.

Sometimes people find it difficult to distinguish hope from faith, but Ephesians makes the distinction very easily. Faith is "in the Lord Jesus" (1:15); that is to say, faith is entrusting our lives to Jesus today, in the present tense. Hope is about the future, about where it is that our present trust in Jesus eventually leads. Hope, therefore, requires wisdom, knowledge, or insight into the glorious heavenly inheritance that awaits believers (1:17-18).

What is it that we need to know about that destiny? Some Christians think that the way to find out is to study reports about near-death experiences. Scholars have compared these modern reports on brushes with death to medieval accounts of mystical journeys into the heavens.[112]

Ephesians shows no evidence of "traveling to the other side," of advocating a spiritual asceticism aimed at gaining visions of the enthroned Christ and his angels.[113] Instead, Ephesians relies upon a theological insight grounded in early Christian exegesis of Pss 8:6 and 110:1. The risen Christ is exalted above all the powers in the universe (Eph 1:20-22a). Combining that insight with the Pauline metaphor of the church as the "body of Christ," originally an image of local churches, produces the striking new image of Eph 1:22b-23: Christ is head of a body that fills the entire cosmos. The main purpose of this image is not to give us a secret peek into the heavenly places but to give us confidence in the power of God, "who fills all in all."

What has that to do with the Christian need to know? Many Christians still think of heaven in spatial terms as a house or a castle or a park area filled with people. They fail to adjust their imagination of heaven (or, to use the odd term favored by the writer of Ephesians, "the heavenlies") to suit this cosmic picture of God's power and glory. The danger in thinking of heaven in spatial terms rather than in terms of God's power was brought home to me one day when a woman timidly knocked on my office door. It was several months after her mother's funeral, and the woman, in obvious distress, said that she had to have an answer to a question because one of her siblings was in real despair over it. The problem? Given the billions and billions of people who had died since humans first emerged on earth and were likely to die before the end of the world, she feared that her mother had to be lost in so vast a crowd. Given the enormous number of people jammed into heaven, she could not see how God could restore the bond of love, the relationship between the mother and her children.

"No problem," I assured her. As far back as the Middle Ages this question has been argued. People have wondered how God could get the bits of bodies shattered by martyrdom or accident back together again. It must be by God's creative power, they concluded. Today we have an even easier way to imagine it. Think of that DNA code or the capacity of computers to store, sort, find patterns, and match data. If puny little human brains can figure out ways to do that, God can restore bodies and families. Remember, God is not an object generated by the laws of physics and biology. Neither is the reality of being transformed into God, being with the holy ones in heaven. It is that creative power of God to touch, be embedded in, or linked to every single part of the universe. A few weeks later, I ran into her in the market. "That was so helpful," she said, "but how did you know it?" "Just theology," I replied.

So even though the metaphors in this section of Ephesians seem strange, both the working of God's power (1:19-20) and the exaltation christology that has the body of Christ "filling all in all" (1:23) have an important message about Christian hope.

---

112. Carol Zaleski, *Otherworld Journeys: Accounts of Near Death Experiences in Medieval and Modern Times* (New York: Oxford, 1987).

113. That some form of this spirituality was being promulgated among the churches of the Lycus Valley seems the best understanding of the false teaching opposed in Col 2:6-23. See James D. G. Dunn, *The Epistles to the Colossians and to Philemon*, NIGTC (Grand Rapids: Eerdmans, 1996) 145-87.

EPHESIANS 2:1–6:20

BODY OF THE LETTER

EPHESIANS 2:1–3:21, THEOLOGICAL REFLECTION ON SALVATION IN THE BODY OF THE EXALTED CHRIST

Ephesians 2:1-10, Conversion from Death to New Life

COMMENTARY

The body of the letter picks up the "you" and "us" of 1:18-19 in a long Greek sentence (vv. 1-7) that the NRSV and the NIV have divided into several sentences. The section shifts from the Gentile past of the letter's audience, "you," to the experience of salvation shared by all Christians, "we." The expression "by grace you have been saved" (v. 5c) returns in the conclusion of this section, which also moves from "you" (vv. 8-9) to "we" (v. 10).

The Greek sentence in vv. 1-7 divides into two halves, each beginning with a plural pronoun and a variation of the phrase "being dead in trespasses" (vv. 1, 5). The first half begins with "you" and contains a lengthy expansion on sins that then incorporate "us" (v. 3) in the story of sin and grace (v. 4). The second half continues with the "us" from vv. 3-4 and depicts salvation as being raised to the heavens (v. 6). The "you" of the first half of the sentence reappears in a parenthetical phrase in v. 5b, "by grace you have been saved." This phrase returns in the next sentence (vv. 8-9) to anchor a Pauline "faith not works" contrast. Verse 10 returns to the "we" who are predestined to good works.

Grammatically, the "you" and "we" of vv. 1 and 3 are objects of God's action. The subject of the Greek sentence (vv. 1-7) is not mentioned until v. 4. "God, who is rich in mercy" is the agent of new life and exaltation. The adjective "rich" (πλούσιος *plousios*) in v. 4 and the "riches of his grace" (πλοῦτος τῆς χάριτος *ploutos tēs charitos*) in v. 7 provide a link to the previous sections: "riches of his grace" (1:7) and "riches of his glorious inheritance" (1:18). Thus the opening section stresses the graciousness of God's life-giving power, not the sinfulness of life without God.

Three negative statements are reversed in the event of salvation:[114] (a) dead through trespasses (vv. 1, 5), made alive in Christ (v. 5); (b) living according to passions (v. 3), risen with Christ (v. 6); (c) subject to a demonic power (v. 2; v. 3b, treating "children of wrath" as equivalent to "those who are disobedient"), seated in the heavenly regions with Christ (v. 6). Romans 6:1-14 uses a number of "with" compounds to insist that Christians no longer live under sin or the passions of the body (vv. 12-14): crucified with, died with, buried with, live with. There "raised" lacks the "with" prefix when applied to believers. For Romans, being in the risen Christ remains for the future (Rom 6:8). Colossians 2:10-13 attaches similar verbs to a concrete issue: that Christians are free from physical circumcision through baptism—by being buried with, raised with, and made alive with Christ (Col 2:12-13). Ephesians may have derived its language of conversion from these two passages. Although Colossians combines Christ's victory over the powers with the Christian's present participation in resurrection, there is

---

114. Michel Bouttier, *L'Épître de Saint Paul aux Ephésiens*, Commentaire du Nouveau Testament, 2nd série Ixb (Geneva: Labor et Fides, 1991) 93.

no parallel to the co-enthronement language of Eph 2:6. The exhortation to set the mind on "things that are above, where Christ is" in Col 3:1-2 avoids placing Christians "in the heavens." Ephesians removes all spatial and temporal separation between believers and the exalted Christ by including "seated us with him in the heavenly places" (v. 6) as a consequence of conversion.

2:1-3. The author turns to address his audience. The connection between sin and death (v. 1) is characteristic of the Pauline tradition (Rom 5:12-21; 1 Cor 15:56; Col 2:13). The Essenes also describe persons who join the sect as being raised from the "worms of the dead" to the "lot of your holy ones."[115]

Verse 2 introduces a familiar apocalyptic topos: All who are not among the elect belong to a sinful humanity inspired by a demonic angelic power. The designation "sons of disobedience" (τοῖς υἱοῖς τῆς ἀπειθείας *tois huiois tēs apeitheias*; NRSV and NIV, "those who are disobedient") exhibits a pattern familiar from the Essene writings: "sons of darkness," "sons of deceit," "sons of guilt."[116] An angelic power inspires the evil deeds that human beings do: "in the hand of the Angel of Darkness is total dominion over the sons of deceit; they walk on paths of darkness."[117]

The two "following the course of" clauses attached to "you once lived" are unclear. The expression "course of this world" combines a temporal word, αἰών (*aiōn*, "course"; translated "age" in 1:21; 2:7), and a spatial one, "world" (1:4; 2:12). Since gnostic sources often used the term *aiōn* for the spiritual beings associated with levels of the heavenly "fullness," interpreters who see gnostic influence in Ephesians treat *aiōn* as a spiritual being. This reading makes the two clauses variants of each other.[118] However, to fit the gnostic examples, *aiōn* could not be used to describe this world. For example, the hostile Jewish God is described as "god, the *archōn* (ἄρχων) of the aeons and powers" or as "the *archōn* of the powers."[119] The Johannine expression "*archōn* of this world" (John 12:31; 16:11; NRSV, "ruler"; NIV, "prince") is the expression one would expect of a spiritual power responsible for evil (also see 1 Cor 2:6, 8; 2 Cor 4:4, "god of this *aiōn*"; NRSV, "god of this world"; NIV, "god of this age").

Since *aiōn* is consistently used as a temporal term in Pauline writings and elsewhere in Ephesians, it should have that meaning here.[120] The NRSV obscures the difficulties in the text by translating the phrase "course of this world." That expression is too neutral. When either an apocalyptic or a Pauline text refers to "this age," the assumption is that the evil powers that dominate the present age are under divine judgment. For the Essenes, the present time involves conflict between those who follow paths of truth and those who do deeds of injustice. God's plan will bring that situation to an end: "There exists a violent conflict in respect of all his decrees since they do not walk together. God, in the mysteries of his knowledge and the wisdom of his glory, has determined an end to injustice and on the occasion of his visitation he will obliterate it forever."[121]

Ephesians has not developed the dualism found in such apocalyptic writings, but the imagery in this section echoes apocalyptic language. Therefore *aiōn* must refer to the temporal span of this world as limited by God's judgment. The second "following" clause clearly refers to a demonic figure responsible for evil. Unlike the Essene writings that depict a dualistic struggle in the hearts of humans between the Angel of Darkness and the Prince of Lights,[122] Ephesians highlights the overwhelming power of God. Since Christ is above every "authority" (ἐξουσία *exousia*, 1:21), the ruler of such powers has no authority over believers.

Gnostic mythology embedded the triumph over the powers in a mythological reading of the Genesis story. The evil *archōn* whose power is shattered by the coming of the revealer is the God of Genesis. When awakened to their divine nature, the gnostic descendants of the spiritual Adam and Eve can laugh at the vain attempts of the *archōn* and his powers to govern the elect. For example, *Hypostasis of the Archons* has the gnostic ancestress Norea confront the chief

---

115. 1QH 19[11]:10-14.
116. See respectively, 1QS 1:10; 1QM 1:7, 16; 1QS 3:21; 1QH 13[5]:7.
117. 1QS 3:20-21.
118. Gnilka, *Der Epheserbrief,* 66.
119. *Apoc. Adam* 64, 20-26; *Hypostasis of the Archons* 92, 8-10.

120. Lincoln, *Ephesians,* 95.
121. 1QS 4:17-19.
122. 1QS 3:20-21.

archōn with the defiant words: "It is you who are the rulers of darkness who are accursed. . . . For I am not your descendant; rather it is from the world above that I am come."[123] The introduction to this tractate in the fourth-century codex tells the recipient that it has been copied because of an inquiry about the reality of the powers described by the apostle in phrases taken from Col 1:13 and Eph 6:12. Even in antiquity, gnostic myths were used to provide clues to the cosmological soteriology of Ephesians.

However, this same text shows what is not gnosticizing about Ephesians. The key lies in the description of the ruler as governing the "power of the air" (ἐξουσία τοῦ ἀέρος *exousia tou aeros*). The region of the "air" continues the engagement with popular Hellenistic cosmology evident in the expression "heavenly regions."[124] "Air" is the murky, polluted region between the planet earth and the moon in which the four elements (earth, water, air, and fire) are mixed.[125] In some accounts, the visible universe is divided into three regions connected to each of the four elements: (a) the stars and the sun are linked with fire; (b) the moon with air; and (c) the earth with water.[126] Ancient writers regularly argued that "demons," in the neutral sense of spiritual beings, must occupy the air. Philo treats the δαιμόνια (*daimonia*) as both beneficent agents of God and as evil angels.[127] Plutarch's teacher Ammonius, whose views also appear in Philo, developed Plato's demiurge into a lower power that rules the sublunary world. This power was also designated Hades or Pluto.[128]

To a first-century reader familiar with such cosmology, Eph 2:2 attributes human sinfulness to the rulers of the sublunary region. Read in astrological terms, the connection between phases of the moon and the passions would provide an explanation for the action of the lower powers. Firmicus says that horoscopes that have the waning moon in relation to mercury indicate a particularly malicious character: "They willingly associate themselves with all kind of wickedness, defend evil men and evil deeds, and their depravity increases from day to day; they are even hostile to men of their own kind."[129] The parallel formulation in Eph 2:3 refers to those trapped in sin as following "the desires or urgings of flesh and thoughts" (τὰ θελήματα τῆς σαρκὸς καὶ τῶν διανοιῶν *ta thelēmata tēs sarkos kai tōn dianoiōn*; NRSV, "senses"). As the astrological example demonstrates, planetary forces work on both the physical body and the ideas in an individual's mind. The term "spirit" (πνεῦμα *pneuma*) in v. 2 has no connection with references to God's "spirit" elsewhere in Ephesians. Popular Stoic defenses of astrology used the all-pervading "spirit" as an explanation of how astrological influences are transmitted.[130]

Some interpreters see the combination of Hellenistic cosmology and Jewish apocalyptic imagery of vv. 1-3 as a demonizing of the "neutral" (though not always beneficent) powers that would imply that a personal power of evil is at work in leading people into sin.[131] Ephesians assumes that disobedience means not walking in the paths established by God but does not require a cosmic being opposed to God in order to make that point. The letter derives its language about the universality of sin from Paul. The "we" links the sender with the audience in a past of alienation from God. God's wrath (Eph 5:6; Col 3:5, 6) belongs to the demonstration of divine righteousness in Paul (Rom 1:18, 25; 3:5; 4:15; 5:9; 9:22; 12:19; 13:4-5). The comments on grace and works in vv. 8-9 recall Paul's discussion of the law, but unlike Paul, Ephesians uses "righteousness" (δικαιοσύνη *dikaiosynē*) only in a conventional, moral sense as the opposite of "sin." This letter sees no need to defend the possibility of righteousness apart from the law, a central problem of Paul's theology.[132]

Verse 3c asserts that "we . . . like everyone else" are subject to God's wrath "by nature" (φύσει *physei*). Sometimes Paul uses "nature" (φύσις *physis*) for the natural or created order (Rom 1:26; 1 Cor 11:14). In Gal 2:15, those who are Jewish "by nature" (*physei*)—that is, by birth—are not sinners like Gentiles (and in a similar sense of

---

123. *Hypostasis of the Archons* 92, 22-26.
124. Bouttier, *L'Épître de Saint Paul aux Éphésiens*, 99.
125. Tamsyn Barton, *Ancient Astrology* (London: Routledge, 1994).
126. Plutarch *On the Face in the Moon* 943F, citing Xenocrates.
127. Philo *The Giants* 8-18.
128. See Philo *Questions and Solutions on Genesis* 4.8. See also John Dillon, *The Middle Platonists* (London: Duckworth, 1977) 169-70.
129. Firmicus *Mathēsis* 5.6.10.
130. Barton, *Ancient Astrology*, 104.
131. Lincoln, *Ephesians*, 95.
132. On Paul's argument, see Dunn, *The Theology of Paul the Apostle*, 354-85.

Gentiles, Rom 2:27). Thus, though Paul can speak of all humans as being implicated in sin from the beginning (Rom 5:12-21), he would hardly describe the Jew as "child of wrath" by nature (*physei*). Wisdom 13:1 exhibits the Jewish patterns of speech employed by the apostle. Without the law, human beings are by nature idolaters. The expression "by nature, children of wrath" fits the depiction of Gentile ignorance of God in Rom 1:18-32.

Romans 2:14-16 indicates that Gentiles who do not have the law but perform its requirements "by nature" (*physei*) will be appropriately rewarded by God. Consequently, Paul does not use "nature" (*physis*) to describe a principle that separates humans from God. Use of Eph 2:3 as evidence for the doctrine of original sin belongs to later theological development. The formula in this passage must be based on the general Jewish tradition of Gentile sinfulness, even though the "we" includes Paul as a Jewish Christian.[133]

2:4-7. The subject of this section finally emerges in v. 4: God's graciousness toward those lost in sin. "Rich in mercy" (πλούσιος ἐν ἐλέει *plousios en eleei*) and "love" (ἀγάπη *agapē*) were introduced as characteristics of God's actions toward us in the eulogy (1:5, 7-8) and thanksgiving (1:18). Elsewhere the expression "make alive with Christ" is embedded in Pauline descriptions of baptism (Rom 6:1-14; Col 2:11-13). Some interpreters think that readers would naturally understand a reference to baptism here.[134] However, Ephesians moves in a different direction. Its emphasis lies on the power of God evident in heavenly exaltation. The gift of life in vv. 5-6 develops the christological vision of 1:19-23. The earlier passage described God's power; here it depicts God's love. In both instances, exaltation above the heavens with the risen Christ is the key to the Ephesians' understanding of salvation.

The three "with" expressions—"made alive with" (συζωοποιέω *syzōopoieō*), "raised up with" (συνεγείρω *synegeirō*), and "seated with" (συγκαθίζω *sygkathizō*)—are interrupted by a parenthetical comment, "by grace you have been saved" (v. 5c). The same expression opens the next sentence (v. 8). Ephesians 1:7 attached the grace of God to a formulaic description of the cross as sin offering. Since vv. 1-3 described the past life of sin as "being dead," the parenthetical comment in v. 5 may be intended to remind readers of the fact that forgiveness of sin is central to "being made alive." It also suggests that the traditional Pauline juxtaposition of cross (dying with Christ) and resurrection (Rom 6:1-4) has not been completely erased by the emphasis on heavenly exaltation.

An Essene parallel to the exaltation of the righteous has been found in a scroll fragment that links exaltation and suffering.[135] The text speaks of God's saving activity toward the righteous: "and upon the poor he will place his spirit, and the faithful he will renew with strength. For he will honor *the devout upon the throne of eternal royalty* . . . and the Lord will perform marvellous acts such as have not existed, just as he sa[id] for he will heal the badly wounded and will *make the dead live.*"[136] Ephesians makes the exaltation of the faithful a function of their identification with the exalted Christ (1:20-22). This relationship erases the temporal gap between the present in which the righteous live and their future glory.

Verse 7 provides an apparent reason for the heavenly exaltation of the righteous: to prove a point and show "the immeasurable riches of his grace." The Greek expression ἐν τοῖς αἰῶσιν τοῖς ἐπερχομένοις (*en tois aiōsin tois eperchomenois*), translated "in the ages to come" by the NRSV, could have a very different reading. Should the word αἰών (*aiōn*, "age") be taken as a temporal term or as a reference to the powers that dominate human life? Ephesians 3:10 speaks of the manifestation of God's wisdom to the rulers and authorities in the heavenly places. If *aiōn* referred to powers, then this phrase would be a variant of 3:9-10.[137]

This understanding requires the participle (*eperchomenois*) to mean "attack" rather than the more usual meaning of "coming on" or "approaching." But several grammatical problems make this reading difficult.

---

133. Schnackenburg, *The Epistle to the Ephesians*, 92.
134. Fischer, *Tendenz und Absicht des Epheserbriefes*, 121-22.
135. 4Q521.
136. 4Q521 frag. 2 col. 2:6-7, 12, italics added.
137. See Schlier, *Der Brief an die Epheser*, 112-14; Martin Dibelius and D. Heinrich Greeven, *An die Kolosser, Epheser, an Philemon*, HNT 12 (Tübingen: Mohr-Siebeck, 1953); Conzelmann, "Der Brief an die Epheser"; Lindemann, *Die Aufhebung der Zeit*, 129-30.

The Greek verb ἐνδείκνυμαι (*endeiknymai*; NRSV and NIV, "show") uses the preposition εἰς (*eis*) or the dative case for those to whom something is shown. However, this phrase begins with ἐν (*en*, "in").[138] A temporal sense of *aiōn*, combined with the usual meaning of "approaching" for the participle (*eperchomenois*), provides a grammatically acceptable reading, "in coming ages" (as in the NIV). Verse 7 extends the manifestation of salvation that has taken place in the exaltation of Christ (1:6-10), in the inheritance given the faithful (1:18-20), and in their exaltation with Christ (2:6) into the indefinite future.

2:8-10. The parenthetical reference from v. 5 to salvation by grace returns in vv. 8-9 with a number of familiar Pauline expressions: grace (Rom 3:24; 11:6), faith (Gal 2:16), gift (Rom 3:24), boasting excluded by faith (Rom 3:27). The speaker shifts from "you" to addressing the audience as "we." Verse 8*b* underlines the fact that salvation is entirely God's gift, not the result of human effort. Verse 9 highlights that point by rejecting works. Though these expressions are easily expanded in the light of Paul's theological controversies over the role of the law, it is less clear why they are introduced at this point in Ephesians. Certainly, the Essene parallels to the language of election in the epistle would have assumed that obedience to the law is required for salvation. The shorthand "works" (ἔργα *erga*) in v. 9 alludes to the Pauline "works of the law" (Rom 3:27-28; 4:2-5; 9:32; Gal 2:16; 3:2-5, 9-10; Rom 11:6 contrasts works and grace). However, the parallel phrase in v. 8, "your own doing" (ἐξ ὑμῶν *ex hymōn*), allows a more general reading. An audience familiar with the conversion language of popular philosophical teachers might conclude that turning away from sin, the powers of the cosmos, can be accomplished by human efforts or human teaching.

This passage also departs from its Pauline antecedents in substituting "being saved" for Paul's term "justification." Grace prohibits boasting rather than the cross or justification through faith (as in Rom 3:27; 1 Cor 1:28-31). The "for" (γάρ *gar*) that attaches v. 10 to the preceding indicates a further explanation of why boasting is excluded. This sentence shifts back to the generalized "we" of vv. 4-7. It also qualifies the apparent rejection of works in v. 9 by suggesting that the righteous have been elected to perform certain good works. The last phrase, "be our way of life," provides an inclusion with the "you once lived" in v. 2.

Essene writings would agree that divine election is expressed in the "good works" of the righteous, walking according to God's decrees. But this view generally takes the form of predestination. The good works of the sons of light are contrasted with the works of those dominated by the spirit of injustice, "in agreement with man's birthright in justice and in truth, so he abhors injustice; and according to his share in the lot of injustice he acts irreverently in it and so abhors the truth."[139] Though Paul rejects the idea that good works create the righteousness that will stand up in God's judgment, he can describe the moral conduct that God expects as "good work" (Rom 2:7; 13:3; 2 Cor 9:8; Col 1:9-10). The ethical exhortation that concludes Ephesians requires holy and blameless conduct. The thanksgiving opened with a reminder that the faith for which the Ephesians were known included love of one another. With its emphasis on the present reality of salvation, some readers might infer that ritual identification with the risen Christ and particular convictions about the powers of the cosmos form the core of Christian experience. Verse 10*b* points to the purpose of divine election, the good works that have also been preordained by God.

Verse 10*a* introduces the image of Christians as God's special creation. The Greek word for "what he has made us" (ποίημα *poiēma*) is used in the LXX for creation as God's work (Pss 9:14; 14:25). It has the same sense in Rom 1:20. By itself the affirmation that "we are [God's] creation" could refer to God's original creation. Ephesians 1:4 described election to "holy and blameless" conduct as established before the creation. The next clause contains the phrase "created in Christ" (κτισθέντες ἐν Χριστῷ *ktisthentes en Christō*), though most interpreters assume that Ephesians is not referring to the divine plan in creation, but to the Pauline "new creation" (Gal 6:15; 2 Cor 5:17).

---

138. Lincoln, *Ephesians*, 109-10.

139. 1QS 4:24.

Galatians 6:15 uses "new creation" as the replacement for the divisive categories of Jew or Gentile. Ephesians may have introduced this expression as a link to the theme of the next section.

The opening of the body of the letter continues the tone set by the eulogy and thanksgiving concerning God's salvation. The initial description of sin raises a question: What does it mean to speak of humans as trapped in sin or subject to a malevolent power? Traditional Christian theology understands all humans as subject to original sin. Taking "by nature" (*physei*, v. 3) in the common sense of "by birth," humans are alienated from God and implicated in the sinfulness that began with Adam. A variant understanding appears in the Essene accounts of predestination. Though God is not directly responsible for the deeds of the wicked, God does permit the existence of the two conflicting powers and foreknows the existence of two "lots" of human beings. This predestination does not vitiate the need for God's grace among the righteous. They recognize that God's spirit enlightens, cleanses from sin, and sustains the life of holiness.

We have seen that Ephesians' use of "ruler of the power of air" to describe the force that governs the lives of sinners enabled its author to connect with first-century cosmological speculation. Augustine refers to Rom 7:7-25 as evidence that the irrational divisions of human willing are punishment for the sinful condition of humans in Adam. He rejects the dualistic view of the Manichees that attributes such divisions to the conflict between good and evil powers.[140] This caveat indicates the dangers of personifying the dualistic powers of apocalyptic. Individuals may conclude that they are not implicated in the works to which they have been predestined. Does Ephesians imply that human psychic and intellectual life is inherently distorted? Ephesians 2:3 treats the entire human person, bodily desires and mental life, as alienated from God. The dark side of this perspective hints that humans are not able to devise the needed "good works" on their own. Yet the dualism implied by such a reading conflicts with another motif in Ephesians: the close connection between the world that God created and salvation. As we have seen, v. 10 speaks of "us" as God's creation in a way that encompasses both God's initial creation and redemption.[141]

Ephesians has placed its description of sin in subordinate clauses. The focus of the opening period is God's grace and love experienced by the redeemed. That experience of God is not inherently known to human beings. Conversion implies turning away from a life in which God was absent. Ephesians uses the religious metaphors of its age in speaking of the past as "dead in sins" or as following the powers that govern the age and the lower world. By depicting believers alive, risen, and exalted in the heavens with Christ, Ephesians breaks the sense that humans are constrained by a complex web of powers that are not under their control. When the question of evil arises, no Christian can claim that he or she had no choice but to participate. God did not predestine God's creatures to works of injustice but to good works.

---

140. Augustine *Confessions* viii 9.21–10.22, 24.

141. Gnilka suggests reference sto the combination of the two in Col 1:15-20. See Gnilka, *Der Epheserbrief*, 112-22.

REFLECTIONS

There is a puzzle about evil that often escapes our attention. People can be trapped, or as Ephesians calls it "dead in your sins" (2:1), and not know it. Part of the reason why such effects of sin are not obvious can be found in the mythological-sounding phrases in the next verse: People are "following the course of this world, following the ruler of the power of the air, that spirit that is now at work among those who are disobedient" (2:2). In first-century mythology, an audience would have no trouble imagining a demonic ruler. The practices of magic were directed at harnessing or warding off the influences of such powers. Some scholars think that Ephesians drew up its picture of the body of Christ filling the cosmos to prove to believers that such forces had no way to enter their lives. In the industrialized world of the twenty-first century, we do not typically describe the force that drives people to destructive behavior as independent powers. But we do know that people are subject to many formative influences that mask the reality of "being dead in sins." Our most obvious examples come from persons in programs to aid in their recovery from addictions to drugs, alcohol, or gambling. They know the experience of being ruled by "powers."

On the one hand, in addressing sin Ephesians seems to fit the addiction-recovery model very well. First, according to Ephesians, before we can see our former lives as darkness, we must first experience self-recognition and conversion. Second, no one can make the journey from a way of life that is marked by death to a new life single-handedly. Not only does it take the shared power of other persons, but it also takes the power of God to break the deadly patterns of the old life. It takes the power of God to sustain the new life. Ephesians speaks of this process using the familiar language of grace, "for by grace you have been saved through faith, and this is not your own doing; it is the gift of God" (2:8a).

On the other hand, however, Ephesians looks at conversion from a point of view unlike the personal, psychological focus of modern recovery movements. Just as Paul understood that his conversion from persecuting the church to Christian apostle had been God's preordained plan (Gal 1:11-17), so also the writer of Ephesians sees every Christian life as preordained by God. Each life has a purpose, "good works, which God prepared beforehand to be our way of life" (2:10).

We often assume that speaking of a divine plan for a person's life only makes sense when we are speaking about the great heroes of faith, such as Martin Luther King, Jr., Nelson Mandela, Gandhi, Billy Graham, and Pope John Paul II. They are the modern successors to the apostles, since their lives changed the world. Ephesians makes the transition from heroes of the faith, like Paul, to every Christian. Every Christian has some "good works" that are his or her divine calling. These works are not burdensome commandments but an appropriate response to the extraordinary salvation already extended to us by God. How do we decide what good works are God's plan for us? They cannot be simple variants of the passions that motivate the actions of all human beings. Ignatius of Loyola (d. 1556) composed a process of spiritual discernment for Christians who are seeking to find out what God intends for them. The most important rule is, "The love which moves me and makes me choose something has to descend from above, from the love of God."[142]

The quotation from Ignatius indicates the significance of spatial imagery, which plays an important role in Ephesians as well. Christians need to order their way of life around God first. The passions and concerns of daily life remain part of Christian experience, but they now belong to something greater. Ephesians goes so far as to instruct Christians that they are "seated in the heavenly places" (2:6). Of course, that image cannot describe the actual experience of Christians in this life. However, it establishes a perspective. Suppose we could look down on our lives from above, from God's presence. What would the script for that life be? Surprisingly, perhaps, there is more freedom in that world than in the old life controlled by sin and death.

142. Ignatius of Loyola *Spiritual Exercises* 184. See Ignatius of Loyola, *Personal Writings*, trans. Joseph A. Munitiz and Philip Endean (London: Penguin, 1996) 319.

Ephesians 2:11-22, Unity in Christ

COMMENTARY

The "you" are now identified specifically as Gentiles, while the "we" belong to the "commonwealth of Israel." The "once but now" pattern applies to the prior division of the two groups, now brought together as one. Since the next section (3:1-21) depicts the apostle as the one who proclaimed this mystery, some interpreters treat 2:11–3:21 as a single section. However, 3:1 marks a strong rhetorical transition by introducing the apostle's character. Therefore, it introduces a new section in the epistle.

Alterations between "you," "us both," and "you" divide this section into three parts: vv. 11-13; vv. 14-18; and vv. 19-22. The middle section contains a number of formulaic phrases that have been described as fragments of an early Christian hymn (vv. 14-16).[143] This liturgical-sounding piece has been combined with an echo of Isa 57:19 and applied to the argument (vv. 17-18). The catchword "peace" (εἰρήνη *eirēnē*) ties the two parts of this section together. A reference to the cross in v. 16*b* ties the midsection to the conclusion of the first "you" section (v. 13).

The final "you" section (vv. 19-22) introduces a new image for the community: the household of God. It highlights the results of becoming part of Christ by describing the dwelling of God as being built up. Antithetical parallels with the first "you" section make the second "you" section a response to the first.[144] Verse 11 speaks of the Jew/Gentile distinction as "in the flesh by human hands." The new dwelling is "in the Spirit" (ἐν πνεύματι *en pneumati*, v. 22; NRSV, "spiritually"), a temple that has not been made by humans (v. 21). Verse 12 reminds the audience that they were once "without Christ." Now they are built on the cornerstone that is Jesus Christ (v. 20). Finally, v. 12 speaks of Gentiles as being alienated from the polity of Israel, as strangers and "without God in the world." Now they can count themselves as fellow citizens and members of God's household (v. 19).

Phrases from Col 1:19-22 inform Eph 2:14-16. Colossians describes "peace" (*eirēnē*) as the reconciliation with God brought about through Christ's death on the cross. However, Colossians does not provide the image of a dividing wall of hostility that is central to Ephesians (vv. 14, 16*c*). Ephesians departs from the cosmological perspective of Colossians, which referred to reconciling heaven and earth, to focus on the human dimension. Salvation has brought Jew and Gentile together in a single body.

2:11-13. "Remember" (vv. 11-12) calls the audience's attention back to their former state just as "you were dead" did at the beginning of v. 1. They were once called "the uncircumcision" by the "circumcision." What is the significance of such an observation? The description of circumcision as "in the flesh by human hands" plays down its crucial significance as a sign of the covenant with God (Gen 17:11-14). Echoes of earlier Pauline conflicts seem to be at work (Gal 2:1-14; Phil 3:2-3; Col 2:11). The fact that Jews required circumcision was well known.[145]

Colossians 2:11 speaks of believers receiving a circumcision "not of human hands" (see 2:13). Within first-century Judaism, references to "spiritual circumcision" or circumcision of the heart distinguish members of sects that claim true devotion to God from other Jews (Deut 10:16; Jer 4:4).[146] By speaking of the "circumcision made in the flesh by human hands" (also Rom 2:25-29), the speaker in Ephesians dissociates himself from those Jews who used the derogatory term "uncircumcised" for the Gentiles. The expression "in the flesh" (ἐν σαρκί *en sarki*) was used for those born Gentiles in v. 11*a* (NRSV, "by birth") and then for the external circumcision of Jews in v. 11*b*. Whatever exists merely "in the flesh" cannot express God's new creation (v. 10).

Lest the audience shrug off this bit of ethnic backbiting, v. 12 details the privileges enjoyed by those who belong to Israel. The formulation echoes Rom 9:4-5, but has converted positive statements in Romans to negative expressions describing what the Gentiles lack. The list begins where Rom 9:4-5 ends, with Christ. Romans 9:5 treats the fact that the Christ (Messiah) was Jewish as the culmination of Israel's privileges. The opening "without Christ" in Eph 2:12 forms a counterpart to the beginning of v. 13, "but now

---

143. Gerhard Wilhelmi, "Der Versöhner-Hymnus in Eph 2:1,14ff," *ZNW* 78 (1987) 145-52.
144. Bouttier, *L'Épître de Saint Paul aux Éphésiens*.
145. Josephus *Antiquities of the Jews* 1.192; Tacitus *Histories* 5.5, 2. Given the practice of circumcision by other peoples, its use as the sole identifying criterion to class a person as "Jew" can be debated. Shaye J. D. Cohen, *The Beginnings of Jewishness: Boundaries, Varieties, Uncertainties* (Berkeley: University of California Press, 1999) 39-49, finds no evidence that first-century Jews used circumcision as a mark to identify fellow Jews.
146. *Jub.* 1.23; Philo *On the Special Laws* 1.205; 1QpHab 11:13; 1QS 5:5.

in Christ Jesus," and stands in parallel to the concluding phrase "without God in the world."

The middle two phrases of v. 12 situate the deficiencies—being without the Christ, hope, and God—in the fact that the audience did not belong to the Jewish people. Ordinarily the term "alienated" (ἀπηλλοτριωμένοι *appēllotriōmenoi*; NRSV, "being aliens") refers to separation from someone or something to which one was formerly attached. This meaning hardly fits the case of Gentiles and Israel, since the Gentiles were excluded from the prior covenant (Exod 19:6; Pss 80:8-9; 105). The term "commonwealth" (or "body politic," πολιτεία *politeia*) can be used of those who possess citizenship rights.[147] Ephesians may be referring to the OT depiction of Israel as God's people (Deut 5:1-3; Isa 65:9) rather than the particular ethnic or citizenship status of Jews and Gentiles. The phrase "covenants of promise" serves as a generalizing reference to the OT covenants.

The emphasis on uniting Jew and Gentile suggests a context that includes actual experiences of Jew and Gentile separation in the first century CE. Jewish exclusiveness frequently led to charges of misanthropy.[148] There is considerable debate over the extent to which first-century Jews encouraged sympathetic Gentiles to join the commonwealth of Israel.[149] When the initiative came from the Gentile convert, Jews did accept proselytes.[150] Relationships between Jews and Gentiles in the cities of Asia Minor seem to have been more complex than a simple division suggests. For example, inscriptions and other documents show that Jews and Gentiles exchanged benefactions.[151]

Evidence for relationships between followers of Jesus and the Jewish communities of Asia Minor remains scant.[152] Paul's sufferings there (2 Cor 1:8-9) appear to have been at the hands of civil authorities. Matthew's polemic against the Pharisees reflects the situation in Syria (Matt 23:34-36). Expulsion of Johannine believers from the synagogue cannot be securely located (John 9:22). The "synagogue of Satan" sayings in Revelation do refer to cities in Asia Minor (Rev 2:9; 3:9). Josephus preserves evidence from the first century BCE that Jews in Asia Minor asked Roman authorities or local city councils to confirm their rights to follow ancestral customs.[153] By the beginning of the second century CE, there were fledgling Christian churches in all the cities of Asia Minor where we know of Jewish communities. This convergence suggests that these Christian groups began among the Jews of the synagogues.[154]

The description of what Gentiles lack may have been common in Jewish communities. The related expression in Col 1:21 lacks the details about belonging to the community of Israel and sharing its covenant promises. The expression "without God" (ἄθεοι *atheoi*) in Eph 2:12 refers to a frequent motif in the Bible—that is, the Gentiles are ignorant of God (LXX Jer 10:25; 1 Thess 1:9; 4:5; Gal 4:8). The expression can be used for someone considered to be godless in the sense of impious. That usage makes it parallel to the expression "those who are disobedient" in v. 2.[155] In that case, the meaning of Eph 2:12 would be close to Gal 4:8, "not know[ing] God . . . enslaved to beings that by nature are not gods." However, the expression "without God" might reflect local polemics. Josephus reports the slander against Jews that they were "atheists [*atheoi*, "without God"] and haters of humankind."[156]

Despite the Jewish cast to its depiction of Gentiles, the "now" (νυνί *nyni*) does not speak of Gentiles joining the commonwealth of Israel. Instead, Ephesians uses the expression "brought near by the blood of Christ" (v. 13). Ephesians 1:7 spoke of redemption in Christ's blood as forgiveness. More immediately, readers have been reminded that they are exalted in the heavenly places with Christ (2:6). This set of spatial terms would lead the

---

147. In his apologetic reply to calumnies against the Jewish people, Josephus speaks of their ancient constitution (*politeia*; Against Apion 2.188, 222, 226, 287) derived from the virtuous lawgiver and prophet, Moses (*Against Apion* 2.154-63). See the discussion in Paul Spilsbury, *The Image of the Jew in Flavius Josephus' Paraphrase of the Bible*, TSAJ 69 (Tübingen: J. C. B. Mohr [Paul Siebeck], 1988) 100-102. The peculiarity of using *politeia* in Ephesians arises because the characteristic of a constitution, its laws and ordinances, has been abolished.
148. Josephus *Against Apion* 2.258; Tacitus *Histories* 5.5.1.
149. See Goodman, *Mission and Conversion*.
150. Josephus *Against Apion* 2.210.
151. Trebilco, *Jewish Communities in Asia Minor*.
152. Jack T. Sanders, *Schismatics, Sectarians, Dissidents, Deviants: The First One Hundred Years of Jewish-Christian Relations* (Valley Forge: Trinity Press International, 1993).
153. Josephus *Antiquities of the Jews* 14.259-61; 16.163. See Feldman, *Jew and Gentile in the Ancient World*.
154. Feldman, *Jew and Gentile in the Ancient World*, 73.
155. So Gnilka, *Der Epheserbrief*.
156. Josephus *Against Apion* 2.148.

audience to conclude that they have been brought near to God rather than to the commonwealth of Israel as such.

The OT refers to Gentiles as "far off" (see Deut 28:49; 29:22; 1 Kgs 8:41; Isa 5:26; Jer 5:15). The term "come near" or "approach" (ἐγενήθητε ἐγγύς *egenēthēte engys*) also appears in Essene writings for joining the sect[157] or for the knowledge of the law, which comes through God's Spirit. Persons who "approach" in this sense are separated from others who disregard the law: "To the degree that I approach my fervour against all those who act wickedly . . . increases; for everyone who approaches you, does not defy your orders."[158] Thus for the Essenes, to "come near" could mean increasing distance from other Jews whose observance of the law did not meet the standards of the sect.[159]

2:14-18. Attempts to isolate a continuous hymnic piece in vv. 14-16 have resulted in very different solutions, though most agree that the phrases "dividing wall" and "in his flesh" (v. 14), "the law with its commandments and ordinances" and "in himself" (v. 15), and "through the cross" (v. 16) are likely to be expansions by the author of Ephesians. Rudolf Schnackenburg prefers to read vv. 14-16 as an elaborate periodic sentence similar to those found earlier in Ephesians. Its phrases alternate between references to the negative things that must be destroyed and to the positive result of Christ's coming, making peace. References to Christ are threaded throughout: (a) "himself . . . in his own flesh" (v. 14); (b) "in himself" (v. 15); (c) "in one body . . . in himself" (v. 16).

The negative phrases all refer to what must be destroyed: (a) a barrier (v. 14*b*); (b) law of commandments and decrees (v. 15*a*); (c) enmity (vv. 14*c*, 16*b*). Unity is not merely the end of human enmity. It also involves reconciliation with God through the cross. Verse 16 is the only explicit reference to "the cross" in Ephesians. This reference is connected with images in this section taken from Col 1:20-22: "making peace," God's willingness to "reconcile," the "blood of his cross," and being "estranged." Ephesians has used the hymnic phrases from Colossians to depict the new unity of Jew and Gentile.[160]

Verse 14 shifts from the "you" form of the previous verse to "we." "Christ is our . . ." formulae appear elsewhere in the Pauline Epistles, with Christ being called wisdom, righteousness, sanctification, redemption (1 Cor 1:30), life (Col 3:4), and hope (1 Tim 1:2). Making peace between estranged parties does not always imply that they become "one." The body metaphor requires harmonious concord, but such peace could embrace differentiated parts. However, readers know that God planned to bring all things together in Christ (1:10). If the Gentile deficiencies result from being separated from Israel, one might have thought Ephesians would argue that "brought near" (*egenēthēte engys*) meant incorporation into Israel. Since that is not what occurs, some interpreters assume that Ephesians has the reconciliation of Gentile and Jewish believers in mind (as Rom 15:7-13).[161]

Spacial and sociopolitical estrangement become enmity in v. 14*c*. Evidence for severe or sustained hostility between Jews and Gentiles in Asia Minor is weak. If we look to the Essene usage of "come near" for joining the sect, enmity would imply intrasectarian polemic. The pious Essene becomes the enemy of all Jews who are not observant. Ephesians appears to view the law as a source of enmity, since Christ has made peace by abolishing its various precepts (v. 14*b*).

Jews often faced the accusation that their law made them "haters of humanity." Josephus replies that any fair observer would find that the law has quite a different result. His account of the Jewish constitution should show any reader of goodwill that "we possess laws best designed to produce piety, fellowship with one another and sympathy toward humanity at large, as well as justice, strength in hardships and contempt for death."[162]

The law as a "dividing wall" that protects the holiness of the people appears in an

---

157. 1QS 9:15-16.
158. 1QH 14[6]:13-15.
159. Ephesians uses "come near" for Gentile converts in a way that masks the break with family and associates required of proselytes. See Philo, *Virt.* 20.102-21.108; *Spec. Law* 1,9.51-55). Cohen, *The Beginnings of Jewishness*, 156-62, finds that classification of proselytes was asymmetrical. Non-Jews considered proselytes to have become Jews. However, treatment of proselytes within the Jewish community indicates that they were not considered to be Jews. Ephesians can only be speaking as an outsider to the Jewish community in formulating this account of the unity of Jew and Gentile.
160. Schnackenburg, *The Epistle to the Ephesians*, 107.
161. Bouttier, *L'Épître de Saint Paul aux Éphésiens*, 115-20.
162. Josephus *Against Apion* 2.146.

apologetic context in the *Letter of Aristeas*: "The legislator . . . being endowed by God for the knowledge of universal truths, surrounded us with unbroken palisades and iron walls to prevent our mixing with any of the other peoples . . . thus being kept pure in body and soul . . . and worshipping the only God omnipotent over creation."[163] The overloaded Greek phrase in Eph 2:14*b*, τὸ μεσότοιχον τοῦ φραγμοῦ (*to mesotoichon tou phragmou*, "the dividing wall of the hedge," or "fence," encircling a vineyard) may be a reflection of a phrase like the "palisades and walls" of *Aristeas*. By itself, *to mesotoichon* might suggest the dividing wall in the temple area that prohibited Gentiles from entering on pain of death (Acts 21:27-31). The parallel phrase in v. 15*a* makes it clear that what the author has in mind as the barrier between Jew and Gentile is the law with its various ordinances.[164]

The sectarian polemic in Essene legal texts connects building a "wall"—that is, sectarian legal interpretation—and separation. Echoing Mic 7:1, the *Damascus Document* has "the wall is built, the boundary far removed."[165] The same text also speaks of those who have removed the boundary, "builders of the wall" who go astray after false teaching, "in the age of devastation of the land there arose those who shifted the boundary and made Israel stray."[166] Such apostate "builders of the wall," and those who follow their interpretations of the law, will be subject to God's wrath.[167] Concluding a letter that contains a number of halakhic rules concerning temple offerings and purity regulations, the Essene author comments, "We have segregated ourselves from the rest of the people and we avoid . . . associating with them in these things." Since the letter is addressed to an outsider whose group its author encourages to adopt similar halakhic rulings,[168] one must assume that such action would lead to reconciliation between the two groups. From a sectarian point of view, destroying the "dividing wall" could only mean destroying the separation created by divergent legal rulings.

The expression τὸν νόμον τῶν ἐντολῶν ἐν δόγμασιν (*ton nomon tōn entolōn en dogmasin*, "the law of commands in decrees"; NRSV, "the law with its commandments and ordinances"; NIV, "commandments and regulations") has sometimes been understood to imply that only part of the law is abolished: the ceremonial or other statutes that divide Jews from Gentiles, or those elements that are "in decrees" made by those who interpret the law, what the NT elsewhere refers to as "traditions of the elders" (Matt 23:1-4, 15-24; Mark 7:5-8).[169] The assumption that the law is divisible has little support in Jewish texts. Both apologetic writers like Josephus and the writer of *Letter of Aristeas* and intrasectarian texts like the CD and 4QMMT assume that Moses' legislation, including the peculiarly Jewish rites and customs and proper halakhic interpretation, belong together. As the Essenes would say, interpretation enables individuals to "turn away from the path of the people on account of God's love."[170] Therefore, Ephesians refers to the whole law. The additional nouns, "commandments and ordinances," exclude understanding what is abolished as a sectarian reading of the law. Though Paul carefully avoids speaking of the law as "abolished" (Rom 3:31), Ephesians has no concern to affirm the divine character of the law (cf. Rom 7:12).

Verse 15*b* fills out the positive hints in v. 14, completing the rhetorical structure of the section by matching the final "making peace" with the earlier "he is our peace." The expression "made both groups into one" is elaborated as "he might create in himself one new humanity in place of the two." Creation of the new humanity is the result of abolishing the law. Galatians 3:26-28 links being "in Christ" with abolition of the fundamental categories that divide persons. Paul used the formula to support his contention that righteousness that comes through faith has no place for inheriting God's promises by being under the law (Gal 3:23-25, 29). Since the expression "no male and female" in the Galatians formula alludes to Gen 1:27, the connection between baptism and "new creation," or restoration of the state of humankind prior to its alienation

---

163. *Letter of Aristeas* 139.
164. Best, *A Critical and Exegetical Commentary on Ephesians*, 259-61.
165. CD 4:12.
166. CD 4:19; CD 5:20.
167. CD-B 19:21-32.
168. 4QMMTa 92-93. 4QMMTa 113-14.
169. Barth, *Ephesians*, 287-91.
170. CD-A 19:29.

from God, probably belonged to the original formula.[171]

A gnostic reading of Eph 2:14-15 would draw upon speculation about the division of Adam and Eve from their original unity. In this myth the creator god gained control over beings who were spiritually superior to him. For example, Adam tells his son Seth:

> And we resembled the great eternal angels, for we were higher than the god who had created us and the powers with him. . . . The god, the ruler of the aeons and the powers, divided us in wrath. Then we became two aeons. And the glory in our hearts left us, along with the first knowledge that breathed within us.[172]

Though some gnostic texts treat baptism as renewing the androgynous, divine image, *The Apocalypse of Adam* concludes with what appears to be polemic against the angelic guardians of baptism for permitting its waters to be defiled.[173] Any who would receive those rites become subject to the rule of the powers.

Unlike either Galatians or later gnostic readers, Ephesians does not connect its new humanity with baptism. Some commentators spontaneously assume that all conversion language in Ephesians has a baptismal *Sitz im Leben*.[174] The expression "new creation" or "new creature" rather than "new humanity" appears in Paul's writings (2 Cor 5:17; Gal 6:15). Ephesians is probably dependent upon Col 3:10 for the idea. However, Ephesians departs from both Colossians and the later Gnostics by not speaking of the image of God when referring to new creation.

The connection between "new creation" and a humanity reconciled with God through the death of Christ appears in 2 Cor 5:17-21. The connection between v. 15 and reconciliation in v. 16 suggests that Ephesians has that imagery in view.[175] Verse 16 employs traditional formulae about the effectiveness of the death of Christ (see v. 13; Rom 5:10; 2 Cor 5:18). The traditional formulation might have used "body" as a reference to Christ's body. Since Ephesians uses "one body" (ἐνὶ σώματι *eni sōmati*) for the unity created in Christ, described earlier as exalted head of the body (1:23), the expression here must refer to the new entity of Jew and Gentile, the church. "Through the cross" indicates that the death of Christ is understood as the sacrifice that brings reconciliation (also 5:2).

Although Ephesians does not use a citation formula, v. 17 alludes to Isa 57:19 (and possibly Isa 52:7), in which the peace is preached (εὐαγγελίζω *euangelizō*) to both those near and far off.[176] Verse 18 employs a Pauline theme: All Christians have access to God in the Spirit (Rom 5:1-2; Gal 3:18). The following points of v. 18 parallel v. 16: (a) reconcile to God; access to the Father; (b) both groups; (c) in one body; in one Spirit; (d) through the cross; through him. It is impossible to tell whether ἐν (*en*, "in") designates the spirit as locus of access to God or as its instrument.[177] The phrase "in one Spirit" (ἐν ἑνὶ πνεύματι *en heni pneumati*) is framed by "access to the Father" (τὴν προσαγὴν . . . πρὸς τὸν πατέρα *tēn prosagēn . . . pros ton patera*). It recalls the earlier description of the Gentiles as "without God in the world" (v. 12). The term "access" (προσαγωγή *prosagōgē*) also brings the audience back to the eulogy in which God was depicted as a powerful benefactor. In a secular context the expression "we gain access" (ἔχομεν τὴν προσαγωγήν *echomen tēn prosagōgēn*) might be used of persons who are fortunate enough to be admitted to the presence of the emperor. Whether ambassadors or individuals, the purpose of such an audience was to press a request for benefits. Readers in the cities of Asia Minor would be familiar with efforts to gain access to the governor as he made his rounds of the province. Verse 18 makes a striking point about abolishing hostility in Christ: Access for one group does not mean exclusion for others.

2:19-22. The next shift in imagery can be linked to the imperial example in v. 18. Access to a powerful person often implied entry into an impressive building. Slaves who served powerful men could assert authority over freedmen of higher status by granting or

---

171. So Betz, *Galatians*, 181-85; Dennis R. MacDonald, *There Is No Male and Female: The Fate of a Dominical Saying in Paul and Gnosticism*, HDR 20 (Philadelpha: Fortress, 1987).
172. *Apoc. Adam* V 64, 14-28.
173. *Apoc. Adam* 84, 5-22.
174. Schnackenburg, *The Epistle to the Ephesians*, 94, 121.
175. Lincoln, *Ephesians*, 193-94.
176. Best, *A Critical and Exegetical Commentary on Ephesians*, 270.
177. Fee opts for the locative sense. See Fee, *God's Empowering Presence*, 683.

denying physical access to their master and his household. Cities in Asia Minor vied with one another to secure imperial favor by building a temple to Augustus.[178] In religious contexts the issue becomes access to God associated with a temple.[179] Ephesians combines both images by calling Christians "members of the household of God" and "holy temple in the Lord." Referring to concrete examples of temple construction, Ephesians depicts the temple as in the process of being built up (vv. 21-22).

Verse 19a returns to the description of the Gentiles as strangers. The term "aliens" (ξένοι *xenoi*) refers to persons who dwell in a place that is not their homeland. Since the LXX does not make a sharp distinction between the Greek words translated "strangers" (*xenoi*) and "aliens" (πάροικοι *paroikoi*), the second may be a rhetorical variant of "stranger." It corresponds to "aliens from the commonwealth of Israel" (v. 12) since aliens do not enjoy citizenship rights. First Peter 2:11 uses "aliens" (*paroikoi*) when speaking of Christians in an exhortation to watch their conduct among "Gentiles" (non-Christians). The designation "citizens with" (συμπολῖται *sympolitai*) reverses their previous exclusion from citizenship. However, the phrase "with the saints" is ambiguous. If v. 19 were strictly parallel with v. 12, "the saints" (οἱ ἅγιοι *hoi hagioi*) should be used as in Jewish texts to refer to the righteous of Israel. Since Ephesians has announced the destruction of the law, it would make little sense to declare that Christ has made the Gentiles "fellow citizens" (*sympolitai*) with Israel. Without its founding legislation, Israel could not claim to be a "commonwealth." Therefore "saints" (*hoi hagioi*) must designate those who are Christian believers regardless of their origins. The shift from the civic metaphor to the familial, "members of the household" (οἰκεῖοι *oikeioi*; cf. Gal 6:10), has been prepared by the earlier indication that Christians were preordained to be God's children (1:5).

Verse 20 shifts from household members to the building itself. Paul used a building image in 1 Cor 3:9-11, where the foundation is the Lord, the apostle is the master builder, and others build upon his work. Ephesians has shifted the imagery. Christ is portrayed as either a capstone or a cornerstone (see below). Apostles and prophets are the foundation. This comment places "apostles" (ἀπόστολοι *apostoloi*) in the past relative to the epistle and its audience. Ephesians 3:5 explains how the apostles serve as foundation, and how they are the ones to whom the mystery of God's plan has been revealed. The Essene writings show a similar regard for their founder: God's revelation to him provided the insight necessary to found the new community. Since Ephesians uses "prophets" (προφῆται *prophētai*) after the term "apostles," it appears to have Christian prophets in mind (e.g., Matt 7:15; 1 Cor 12:10, 28).

Old Testament texts about the cornerstone in Zion were applied to Jesus (Isa 8:14; see also Luke 2:34; Rom 9:32; 1 Pet 2:8). However, the capstone held the building together. Its location at the top of an arch also fits Ephesians' consistent references to the exaltation of Christ (4:16). The unity of the initially separate "you" and "us" gains the organic form of a building whose diverse materials must be properly fitted together and held in place by the capstone.

Designation of the building as "temple" retrieves the access to God image from v. 18, along with its reference to the Spirit. Though the term "grow" (αὔξω *auxō*) has been seen as discordant with Christ as capstone of a building, it anticipates the later description of the body growing together in the unity of the Spirit (4:3, 11-16). The presence of God's Spirit in the community described as temple was well-established in Paul's writings (1 Cor 3:16; 6:19-20). By shifting to the temple in which the Spirit dwells, Ephesians suggests that the community will be the locus of God's presence in the world.[180]

Every comment about Jew and Gentile in this section belongs to well-established motifs in Jewish apologetic or sectarian writings except the extraordinary claim that God abolished the law in order to unify the two. This concern extends Paul's own polemic against those who thought Christians ought to be incorporated into Israel by adopting peculiarly Jewish observances. However,

---

178. Faust, *Pax Christi et Pax Caesaris*.
179. Access to the throne room of the powerful, whether monarch or deity, required passing through gates, pillared antechambers, and the like. The architecture of palace and temple was seen to reflect that of the heavenly throne room. See J. Edward Wright, *The Early History of Heaven*, 75-78.

180. Fee, *God's Empowering Presence*, 684-85.

attempts to find a particular Jewish or Jewish Christian problem behind this section of Ephesians have failed. Although v. 12 might suggest that the Gentiles are to be brought into Israel, Ephesians avoids claiming that the church has replaced Israel. In the present reality of the church as a single community built up together in Christ, there is no distinction between Christian and Jew. Even the concern for harmony between Jewish and Gentile believers evident in Rom 15:1-13 is moderated. Nothing in Ephesians suggests that tensions between the two groups were creating difficulties (cf. Rom 14:1-23).

It is also impossible to use Ephesians to support theories of an ongoing covenant with Israel that will bring it to salvation outside of Christ. Ephesians consistently insists that God's plan from the beginning has been a "new creation" that requires abandoning the barriers that distinguished Jew from Gentile.[181] At the same time, Ephesians does not presume that all of the covenants, images, and promises of Israel belong to Gentile Christians by virtue of their Jewish heritage. The church is not separated from the God revealed in the story of Israel, but only exists through God's new act of creation. To recognize Christ's exaltation as head of the body of Christian believers requires an insight into the mystery of God's plan that is not available to nonbelievers.

Indeed, Ephesians leaves no opening for the continuing observance of the law by Jewish Christians.[182] Despite the differences in their origins, both Jewish and Gentile believers are reconciled to God through Christ. Both are brought into the body of Christ and have the same Spirit. They have a common foundation and belong to a building designed to be held together by one capstone. While diversity of origins is no barrier to coming into the church, it is not an excuse for a building of clashing architectural styles! Thus the emphasis on unity in Ephesians rejects the possibility of God's people being divided into multiple sects.

Since all legal ordinances are abolished, the church cannot be a sect within Judaism like the Essenes—a group grounded on claims not only to the Spirit, but also to a founder with inspired insight into God's will and to identification as "the holy ones" of God's promise. Though Ephesians shares many religious images with Essene writings, it does not understand the church as a religious group centered on interpreting the teachings and halakhic ordinances of a human founder. Instead, Ephesians insists that the reality of the church is in its head, the exalted Christ made present through the Spirit. Whatever the particular arrangements in local communities, they should reflect the symbolic truth about the church. Its unity is based in incorporation of different groups into a new humanity that no longer preserves the socioreligious boundaries established by the law.

181. See the extended argument in Andrew T. Lincoln, "The Church and Israel in Ephesians 2:1," *CBQ* 49 (1987) 605-24.

182. Sanders, *Schismatics, Sectarians, Dissidents, Deviants,* 196-98.

REFLECTIONS

1. *Baptismal Unity.* After describing conversion as the transition from death to new life, a jarring shift introduces a gap between the Jewish Christian speaker and his Gentile audience, "So remember that you were once gentiles in the flesh" (2:11; the NRSV has "by birth," which weakens the metaphor). It goes on to list everything that those who are not part of God's covenant people lack, ending with the dramatic *atheoi tou kosmou,* "without God in the world." When the Greek term *atheos* was applied to someone, it did not simply mean that this person did not believe in the God of the Jews (as the NRSV suggests by capitalizing the word). Instead, it was a term of cultural insult, a form of what we might call "hate speech," since it was often used derisively of someone who disdained or denied the gods and their laws—in short the structure and glue of civil society. In essence, to call someone *atheos* was to say that he or she was "uncivilized." Pagans could sling the term back at Jews (and later at Christians) because they would not participate in the religious practices of everyone else. The most wonderful example of this expression as a "fight song" occurs in the martyrdom of Polycarp (d. 167). The Roman proconsul, not wishing to execute the aged bishop, tried to persuade Polycarp to renounce his faith by swearing an oath by the "good fortune" of Caesar and shouting, "Away with the atheists." Polycarp refused, but in a dramatic tour de force looked at the multitude gathered in the arena, waved his hand toward them, and looking up to heaven said, "Away with the atheists!"[183]

Given this background, it is a shocking turn for Ephesians to refer to the readers, even in passing, as *atheoi*, surprising for the preacher to suddenly stir up the ethnic and religious tensions that separated Jews from the larger society of the Greco-Roman cities in which they lived. Ephesians hangs a lot of weight on the past tense, "you once were," but now in Christ that gulf has been bridged (2:13-14). Of course, this passage recalls one of Paul's most important theological insights. As he argued that his Gentile converts should not be required to adopt Jewish customs, Paul formulated the insight that God had a different plan. God intended to bring all humanity together in a single people. Paul reached back behind the idea of covenants with Moses and David, which emphasized the separateness of Israel, to the covenants with Abraham (Rom 4:1-25; Gal 3:15-20).[184] Paul used the baptismal formula to insist that God did not intend for the church to be split along socioeconomic, ethnic, or gender lines (Gal 3:26-28). When the Corinthians were divided over various spiritual gifts, Paul referred to that formula again in combination with the metaphor of the church as the body of Christ (1 Cor 12:13). Baptism confers one Spirit, which works toward unity in building up the body of Christ.

Ephesians 2:11-22 incorporates these familiar Pauline themes. Yet the author's voice sounds the note of Israel, privileged to be the original recipient of God's promises, speaking to the "other," the Gentiles who have now been incorporated into God's people (2:18-19). The closest Paul comes to addressing Gentile Christians from the perspective of Jewish Christians is the famous metaphor of Gentile Christians as wild olive branches grafted onto God's carefully cultivated tree in Rom 11:11-36. However, the tone is quite different. Paul struggles to explain the weak Jewish response to the gospel in contrast to that of non-Jews. He warns Gentile Christians against overbearing pride. Reading Ephesians, we would never infer that such difficulties existed. One would infer, rather, that the entire heritage of Israel had passed into the church, which then extended God's summons to the rest of the world. Christians learned from the horrors of the Holocaust and its legacy that a religious vision that can no longer affirm a positive ongoing relationship between God and the Jewish people in the end fails the gospel.

How does Ephesians 2:1 contribute to Christian/Jewish relations today? We need to remember Paul's anguish over the fate of fellow Jews who did not accept Jesus as Messiah in Romans 9:1–11. Paul concluded that Jewish disbelief had opened the way for non-Jews. God's plan of salvation had to include a place for Israel (Rom 11:11-32). God's love for Israel did not end when the church came into being. Ephesians provides a sharp reminder to the Gentile converts that they owe their knowledge of God to the Jewish people. There is a special bond between Christians and Jews because of this inheritance. The other religions from which non-Jewish converts come to faith in Jesus cannot replace Judaism. Only the Scriptures written and preserved by the Jewish people provide authentic revelation about God. Jesus was not the incarnation of a global divine force, a Hindu avatar, or a Bodhisattva. He is the Son of the God who called Abraham, who appeared to Moses on Sinai, who made a covenant with David, and who inspired the prophets. So Christians recognize that we owe the Jewish

---

183. *Martyrdom of Polycarp* chap. 9. See *ANF* 1:41.
184. For a description of the theological significance of the three types of covenant, see Bernard Anderson, *Contours of Old Testament Theology* (Minneapolis: Fortress, 1999) 32-35.

community an enormous debt for our faith in God. We should come to dialogue with our Jewish friends as grateful learners, not as people who have all the answers.

Ephesians also posits a challenge to both Jews and Christians by insisting that cultural and religious divisions are contrary to God's vision of human salvation. Circumcision or lack of circumcision is "in the flesh," ethnic divisions (2:11) that divide people into opposing camps. So Christians and Jews should not just talk about shared beliefs and then go their separate ways. They should find ways to witness to faith in the God who unites us. Social projects that embody a shared concern for justice are one way of recognizing common values grounded in Scripture. Christian and Jewish leaders also have to speak out against anti-Semitic and racist incidents. When swastikas are spray painted on the local high school or a synagogue and its Torah scrolls are defaced, Christians have to show that they are as outraged as their Jewish neighbors. After all, God did not bring us non-Jews into the household of faith to trash the place. God brought us in to build a glorious new creation: the body of the Messiah.

2. *Architecture, Empire, and Peace.* The architectural images in this passage further develop the theme of reconciling traditional enemies. In 2:14-15 the law and the commandments are pictured as a wall that kept Jew and Gentile apart. That wall is now destroyed because the cross marked the end of the law. Was a physical wall intended? Some interpreters have seen behind this image the actual barrier in the Temple that prohibited Gentiles from going further on pain of death. By the time Ephesians was written, the Temple had been destroyed when Titus looted and burned the city to end the Jewish revolt in 70 CE. The late twentieth century witnessed the power of tearing down a wall when the wall that had separated communist East Berlin from West Berlin was destroyed. But the "wall" can also be spiritual, the separation between Jew and non-Jew that is built into the commandments that govern Jewish life. In that case, the wall only came down within the Christian community. That, too, can be a familiar experience. We may form close, personal relationships with people of very different racial, ethnic, socioeconomic, or educational backgrounds in the church community. But do such experiences translate into what happens at work, on the street, in school? Not always. When it does not, can we honestly say that Christ bridges the gap of our hostilities and differences?

The section concludes with another architectural image already familiar from Paul's letters: the church as a building or a temple (2:21). Combined with the claim that Christ has brought hostile factions together, this image poses a challenge to the erection of temples and other buildings dedicated to the glory of Rome and its emperor. Safety from pirates on the seas, growing prosperity and trade passing along the roads and through the harbors of the Roman East were all claimed as benefits bestowed by the emperor. New buildings told the story. Ephesians hints that Christians have a different story to tell. Empires may spread a dominant culture or language that forces former enemies to live together in peace. But that is not the new creation in which people are genuinely sisters and brothers in Christ. Take the power away, and the old tribal hatreds flare up with horrible costs in suffering for civilian populations. The former Soviet Union, the Balkans, Africa, the Philippines, Sri Lanka—all stories in a single day's paper. How to create peace? Unfortunately, the only quick solutions have been to put up various walls, a U.N. peace-keeping force, or a massive separation of the warring populations, creating hundreds of refugees. The peace of empires is not true peace. Religious voices that call for conversion, justice, mutual hospitality, and community as foundations for peace are often the first to die when hostility breaks out.

3. *Sign of the Cross.* Since Ephesians highlights the triumph of the risen Christ, readers might be tempted to minimize the cross. That would undercut a central conviction of Pauline theology. The cross has achieved what no human ever could: reconciliation of a sinful humanity with God. Does that mean that God is a stern, capricious ruler who needs to be appeased or "bought off"? Not for the writer of Ephesians. God is a loving benefactor, offering all people a stake in salvation. By dying on the cross, God breaks down a wall that separated humanity from God. Humans are too trapped in the deadly effects of sin to return to God on their own—or to even notice the wall that is keeping God out. Why is the cross important to Christians today? People still need to be convinced of God's unconditional love for them. "Lift high the cross, the love of Christ proclaim," the hymn announces. It is always a favorite. A very wise spiritual director once remarked, "People have to be loved into forgiveness." He liked to ask students to make two lists: (1) people you need to forgive and (2) people you would like to thank. The first list is the hard one to deal with, but if you start with the second list, forgiving starts to become a possibility, too.

Ephesians 3:1-13, Paul as Prisoner for the Gospel

COMMENTARY

Paul now becomes "prisoner for Christ," a phrase used in Philemon 1:1.[185] Verses 2-13 read as a long digression until the prayer report introduced in v. 14. The pattern of alternating pronouns continues: "you" (vv. 2-6); "I" to "we" (vv. 7-12); and "you" (v. 13).

Verse 1 is an anacoluthon (an abrupt mid-sentence shift to a different grammatical construction), which identifies the subject but lacks a verb. Verse 2 begins with a "for surely" that assumes that the audience has heard of the mission entrusted to Paul. Verses 3-7 spell out the origins and content of Paul's service. Verse 13 finally states the consequence that is to follow from recognizing what Paul's ministry is: Do not be discouraged by his imprisonment (cf. Phil 1:12-13; 2:17-18). The intervening sentences (vv. 8-12) expand the account of Paul's ministry by describing the content of the mystery being revealed. Reference to his boldness (v. 12) anticipates the exhortation to the audience in v. 13, so that they do not "lose heart over my sufferings."

This section forms a key piece of evidence for the hypothesis that Ephesians has drawn on the text of Colossians. It combines the sequence of topics in Col 1:23-28 with echoes of earlier parts of Ephesians, especially the previous section (2:11-22). Figure 1 sets out the parallels between the two letters; a more literal translation has been provided to make the verbal parallels clearer.

Ephesians has taken the basic structure of Paul's self-presentation from Colossians. In v. 3, "as I wrote" suggests that the audience would be familiar with the existence of other Pauline epistles. References to Eph 2:11-22 demonstrate how carefully this section has been integrated into the epistle: (a) you Gentiles (v. 1; 2:11); (b) "holy apostles and prophets" (v. 5; 2:20); (c) "with" expressions to designate incorporation of Gentiles (v. 6; 2:19); (d) share a promise (v. 6; excluded from promise, 2:12); (e) in the body of Christ (v. 6; 2:16); (f) access to God (v. 12; 2:18). Other expressions point to earlier sections of Ephesians: (a) "commission" (οἰκονομία *oikonomia*, "administration," vv. 2, 9; 1:10); (b) grace of God (vv. 2, 7-8; 1:6-7; 2:5, 7-8); (c) mystery revealed (vv. 3-4, 9; 1:9); (d) rulers and powers (v. 10; 1:21); (e) heavenly places (v. 10; 1:3, 20; 2:6).

Rhetorically, the account of Paul's ministry serves to establish the character of the speaker. Such descriptions often appear as digressions in ancient rhetoric. A key requirement is establishing the reliability of the speaker. Since the audience has no personal knowledge of Paul on which to judge his character, Ephesians asserts that they can discern the truth of his claim to special insight from what he has written (vv. 3-4). Ephesians also establishes a relationship between the apostle

---

185. The phrase *desmios tou Christou* ("prisoner of Christ") should not be spiritualized as though it indicated Paul's attachment to Christ. It implies that preaching the gospel is the reason for his imprisonment. See the discussion of the conditions of ancient imprisonment and the rhetoric of imprisonment in Paul's own letters by Craig S. Wansink, *Chained in Christ: The Experience and Rhetoric of Paul's Imprisonments*, JSNTSup 130 (Sheffield: Sheffield Academic, 1996).

Figure 1: Eph 3:1-13 and Col 1:23-28

Theme	Ephesians	Colossians
Introduce Apostle	**[3:1]** I, Paul, the prisoner for you	**[1:23c]** I, Paul, a servant (Eph 3:7)
Sufferings of the Apostle	**[3:1]** prisoner **[3:13]** in my trials for you	**[1:24a]** . . . for you **[1:24b]** the deficiency of the trials of Christ in my flesh for his body
Office of the Apostle	**[3:7]** of which I have become a servant	**[1:25]** of which I have become a servant
Revelation of the Mystery	**[3:2]** the administration of the grace of God given to me for you **[3:4-5a]** the mystery of Christ that was not known to other generations **[3:9]** the mystery hidden from the aeons **[3:5]** has now been revealed to his holy apostles and prophets	**[1:25]** according to the administration of God given to me for you **[1:26]** the mystery that was hidden from the aeons and the generations **[1:26]** but now has been manifested to his holy ones
Content of the Mystery	**[3:6]** that the Gentiles would be an inheritance with, body with, and sharers with the promise in Christ Jesus through the gospel	**[1:27]** the wealth of the glory . . . in the Gentiles, which is Christ in you, the hope of glory
Mystery Preached	**[3:8]** to preach to the Gentiles the incomprehensible wealth of Christ	**[1:27-28a]** to make known what the wealth of the glory of this mystery in the Gentiles, which is Christ in you . . . whom we announce
God's Power in the Apostle	**[3:7c]** according to the activity of his power	**[1:29b]** according to the activity that is working in me in power

and his audience by reminding them that the apostle's suffering benefits the Gentiles (from Col 1:24-25; also see Phil 1:5-7). The exhortation not to lose heart over his sufferings (v. 13) adds an element of pathos to the relationship between Paul and the audience.

3:1. "This is the reason" connects this section with the previous reference to the

Gentiles' being incorporated into the temple of God (2:22-23). The addition of "for the sake of you Gentiles" integrates the biographical notice into the theme of bringing Gentiles into the body of Christ. Verse 13 does not spell out how suffering is integral to the apostle's mission. Readers may be familiar with Paul's view that suffering confirms the connection between the apostle and the crucified (1 Cor 4:1-13; 2 Cor 6:3-11). Just as the cross is not a major theme in Ephesians, so also apostolic hardships are not a topic of discussion. The letter contains only two other references to the sufferings of the apostle (v. 13; 6:20). Both connect his imprisonment with bold speech. Neither passage uses the reference as evidence for the heroism of the apostle (cf. 2 Tim 2:8-10;[186] which equates Ephesians and 2 Timothy). Nor does Ephesians develop the soteriological picture of apostolic suffering in Col 1:24.[187]

3:2-7. The first half (vv. 2-4) of the lengthy digression in vv. 2-7 recalls what the audience may already know about Paul. Description of Paul's mission as "commission" (*oikonomia*) is taken from Col 1:25. Ephesians also uses *oikonomia* as God's plan of salvation (1:10; 3:9; NRSV, "plan"; NIV, "administration"). In those cases, "plan" connects the saving activity of God with the order established in creation. Consequently, the "commission" entrusted to Paul is part of the process by which God's plan to unite all things in Christ is effected. The experience of God's grace involves understanding the divine purpose in Christ (1:9-10).

Paul used the phrase "stewards [οἰκονόμοι *oikonomoi*] of God's mysteries" in 1 Cor 4:1. There the term "mystery" (μυστήριον *mystērion*) reminds readers of the cross as the mystery unknown to the powers (1 Cor 2:7). For Ephesians, "mystery" (*mystērion*) refers to bringing together all things in the exalted Christ. Verse 3 attributes the apostle's knowledge of the mystery to revelation.

The Essenes also attributed the insight of their founder to divine revelation. Revelation to the elect is essential to their salvation.[188] We have seen that Ephesians does not treat its revelation as the key to a sectarian version of inherited Jewish tradition. Nor does Ephesians argue that Paul's preaching represents what was already revealed in Scripture (cf. Rom 4:1-25; Gal 3:6-22; 4:21-31).

The phrase "as I wrote before briefly" (καθὼς προέγραψα *kathōs proegrapsa*) is enigmatic. In ordinary correspondence, it would imply previous communication between the author and the recipients. Or in some instances it would refer to attached correspondence.[189] However, Ephesians is not a letter between parties who have business or friendship with each other. Although its author is familiar with Paul's letters, and particularly Colossians, a reference to "wrote briefly" hardly suggests a collection of Paul's epistles. The NRSV translation ("as I wrote above in a few words") follows exegetes who conclude that the expression refers to an earlier passage in Ephesians (1:9-10; 2:11-22). But Ephesians could be assuming prior reading of individual Pauline letters or extracts from them in the churches.[190] Verse 4 makes the reading of the letter itself evidence of the apostle's insight.

In describing that mystery (vv. 5-7), the epistle returns to motifs already presented, especially in 2:11-22. The "with" verbs in v. 6 pick up use of such expressions in 2:19-22. The foundation stone of the building to which the Gentiles are joined in 2:20, the "apostles and prophets" are now the privileged recipients of insight into the mystery of Christ.

By insisting that the mystery was unknown in past ages, Ephesians appears to assert that not even the righteous persons or prophets of the OT had knowledge of the blessings to come to the Gentiles.[191] However, the phrase should not be pressed to yield a theology of prior revelation. In apocalyptic writings such revelation formulae indicate that readers now have insight into divine mysteries that have been concealed from the rest of humanity (e.g., Matt 13:17). In a historical apocalypse, the seer receives both a vision and its interpretation. Since the vision refers to future events, only divine inspiration could provide the required understanding (Dan 10:1). Or the apocalypse may reveal hidden wisdom given to an ancient seer but sealed

---

186. Contra Martin, *Ephesians, Colossians and Philemon*, 41; O'Brien, *The Letter to the Ephesians*, 252.
187. Contra Bouttier, *L'Épître de Saint Paul aux Éphésiens*, 138.
188. 1QS 11.6-7, 15-19.
189. See John L. White, *Light from Ancient Letters* (Philadelphia: Fortress, 1986) nos. 4 and 7.
190. Meade, *Pseudonymity and Canon*, 149.
191. Lincoln, "The Church and Israel in Ephesians 2:1," 619-22.

until the time of fulfillment (Dan 12:9; 2 Esdr 14:5-10). Thus "not made known . . . now revealed" is a way of indicating that the time of fulfillment has come. The reference to "apostles and prophets" (v. 5; 2:20) indicates that the author of Ephesians does not consider Paul the sole recipient of insight into God's plan of salvation.

The expression "*his* holy apostles and prophets" supports the claim that Ephesians was not composed by Paul. He would have used the expression "us apostles" (as in 1 Cor 4:9). Verse 7 uses the self-designation "servant of the gospel" from Col 1:23. Paul uses the Greek term διάκονος (*diakonos*, "servant") in a variety of senses: (a) political rulers, who need not be aware of a place in God's order (Rom 13:4); (b) individuals in local churches (Rom 16:1; Phil 1:1); and (c) himself (and Apollos) as missionaries who established churches (1 Cor 3:5-7; 2 Cor 3:6; 6:4). Since the false teachers who had come to Corinth take on a false appearance as "servants [NRSV, "ministers"] of righteousness" (2 Cor 11:15), "servant" plus a genitive expression was probably a common term for traveling missionaries.

Ephesians takes over the depiction of God's power (δύναμις *dynamis*) from Col 1:29. However, it drops the reference to apostleship as weakness and struggle found in Col 1:29a. Stylistically Ephesians needs a shorter phrase. Thematically, the sufferings of the apostle are not the topic of discussion. Ephesians repeatedly stresses the extraordinary manifestation of God's gracious power in the salvation of the Gentiles. See the use of "power" (*dynamis*) in 1:19. The power of God demonstrated in the resurrection and exaltation of Christ may have been taken from Col 2:12.[192]

3:8-13. Ephesians breaks off the previous sentence only to begin describing the apostle's mission again (v. 8; contrary to the NRSV and the NIV, v. 7 belongs to the digression that began in v. 2). The passage opens with a striking description of the apostle as "least [ἐλαχιστοτέρῳ *elachistoterō*] of all the saints." Readers familiar with Paul's letters immediately think of his self-designation "least of the apostles" (1 Cor 15:9). The apostle uses his late call and efforts in founding churches as evidence for the power of God's grace working in his mission (1 Cor 15:10). Since Ephesians has consistently used "saints" (ἅγιοι *hagioi*) for believers, referring to Paul as "least of all the saints" is somewhat puzzling. Earlier Ephesians described the Gentiles as being added to the "saints" ("us"), fellow "citizens with the saints" (2:19). The apostle whose knowledge of the mystery of God makes this incorporation possible can hardly be described as "least" among Christians. The expression may be dictated by the rhetorical requirements of self-praise. By having Paul deprecate his own achievement, Ephesians has him magnify the graciousness of the divine benefactor who has given him the task of preaching the gospel.[193]

The summary of his message intensifies earlier formulations of the mystery embedded in God's creative plan. The Greek text of v. 9a is uncertain. The twenty-seventh edition of the Nestle-Aland Greek text brackets the "all" (πάντας *pantas*; NRSV and NIV, "everyone") following the infinitive "to enlighten" (NRSV, "to make see"; NIV, "to make plain"). The problem is finding the referent of "all" (*pantas*). It does not agree grammatically with "Gentiles" in v. 8. "Saints" is too far away from the adjective, and such an assertion would in any case contradict the expression "least of the saints." Therefore some interpreters prefer to follow the manuscript tradition that lacks *pantas* (NRSV note, "to bring to light"). On that reading, the apostle illuminates the mystery itself, not individuals about the mystery.[194]

However, Eph 1:18 asks God to enlighten (φωτίζω *phōtizō*) the addressees. To "enlighten the heart" occurs in apocalyptic language as God's activity. Paul claims such enlightenment for his preaching in 2 Cor 4:6 with reference to God's creation of light in Gen 1:3. The "I" of the Essene teacher is described as mediating the divine illumination he received from God to the community through his teaching, "like perfect dawn you have revealed yourself to me with your light";[195] "you exhibit your power in me and reveal yourself in me with your strength to enlighten them";[196] "through me you have

---

192. So Barth and Blanke, *Colossians*, 270.
193. Schnackenburg, *The Epistle to the Ephesians*, 136.
194. See Schnackenburg, *The Epistle to the Ephesians*, 138n28.
195. 1QH 12[4]:6.
196. 1QH 12:23.

enlightened the face of the Many . . . for you have shown me your wondrous mysteries."[197] Comparison with Essene language indicates that "all" stands in place of its designation for those illuminated through the Teacher, "the many." Despite the grammatical difficulties, it would have to refer back to "the saints." The NRSV translation "make everyone see" does not capture the appropriate nuances of transmitting what is essentially God's illumination of the hearts of the elect. It suggests that the apostle fulfills a routine teaching task to provide cognitive information about God's design.

As the Essene example indicates, divine illumination operates within the community of those chosen by God. Readers of Ephesians know that community is the church. The cosmic images that Ephesians uses for the church also have some roots in this type of apocalyptic terminology. The church identifies with the exalted Christ, just as the Essenes spoke of their sect as joining the heavenly community of the "holy ones" (angels), "He [God] unites their assembly to the sons of the heavens."[198] From that perspective, it is not difficult to see how Ephesians can conclude that the church, which belongs in the heavenly regions with Christ, would make God's hidden plan of salvation apparent to the various powers of the universe (vv. 10-11). As we have already seen, the terminology of divine predestination "in accordance with the eternal purpose" belongs to this revelation pattern (v. 11; 1:11). Therefore, there is no reason to treat the "aeons" and "powers" in v. 10 (NRSV and NIV, "rulers and authorities") as mythological, hostile powers actively seeking to prevent souls from reaching heavenly regions as in gnostic accounts of salvation.[199] Ephesians does recognize the existence of evil forces in the cosmos that are defeated by God (2:2; 6:12). The existence of the church serves as evidence of God's power over evil. The teaching of individuals in the church is not a contest against mythological powers.[200]

Nevertheless, scholars continue to link the cosmological terms in Ephesians with religious cults that personified the soul's ascent into the heavens as a defeat for planetary powers. The claim that its author was opposed to the cosmic speculation in the Mithras cult depends upon reading αἰώνων (*aiōnōn*) as a reference to the god Aion rather than as a temporal term designating "ages."[201] Readers familiar with the zodiacal grades and astronomical speculation attached to the Mithras initiation rites could understand Ephesians to mean that such mystery cults have no power to liberate the soul. However, the apocalyptic terminology used throughout the letter suggests that the temporal reading of αἰών (*aiōn*) is intended in Eph 3:9-11.

Verse 12 returns to the apostle's character. Boldness (παρρησία *parrēsia*) in speech was widely regarded as an attribute of the wise or of those, like Moses, favored with special access to God. Both meanings are evident in Ephesians. Paul's boldness is demonstrated in apostolic preaching despite imprisonment (6:19-20). He does not teach for human rewards, or he would speak in a way that flatters the audience (1 Thess 2:2; 2 Cor 3:12; Phil 1:20; Philo *On the Special Laws* 1.321). In the religious context, "boldness" belongs with access to God in prayer, a motif already mentioned in 2:18 (Job 27:10; Philo *Who Is the Heir of Divine Things?* 5-7; Josephus *Antiquities of the Jews* 2.4.4; 5.1.3). Both uses connect with what follows. Bold speech in defense of the gospel belongs to the image of the imprisoned apostle (v. 13); direct access to God in prayer, to the prayer formula of vv. 14-21.

The final sentence in this section returns to the personal relationship between the author and the addressees that opened the long digression (vv. 1-2). Although their only connection with the apostle is through reading, the audience should have such appreciation for Paul's role in bringing salvation to the Gentiles that they despair at his suffering. Ephesians leaves the connection between Paul's suffering and the "glory" (δόξα *doxa*) that accrues to the Gentiles undefined. "Glory" is always associated with praising God or God's gift of salvation in Ephesians (1:6, 12, 14, 17-18; 3:16, 21).

Accustomed to the catalogs of apostolic suffering in other Pauline letters, the dramatic

---

197. 1QH 12:27.
198. 1QS 11:8.
199. Contra Schlier, *Der Brief an die Epheser*.
200. Contra Conzelmann, "Der Brief an die Epheser." See Lincoln, *Ephesians*, 186.
201. Cargal, "'Seated in the Heavenlies,'" 814-16.

pictures of Paul in prison and on trial in Acts, and later martyrdom stories, readers might expect to hear about the imprisoned apostle in Ephesians. Commentators often bring in details from 2 Timothy in referring to this section of Ephesians as the portrayal of a heroic martyr. Yet Ephesians has less to say about the apostle's sufferings than any other Pauline letter. The reference to bold speech and the willingness to suffer for such speech serve as proof of character. They indicate that the message has not been crafted to flatter or suit the prejudices of an audience and that the speaker does not seek some personal gain or advantage. This section of Ephesians concerns the message that God entrusted to the apostle, not the personal details of his life.

The description of the mystery of God in vv. 5-11 follows the same pattern of rhetorical celebration evident in the earlier sections of Ephesians. Its claims are repeated using established patterns of language for divine revelation, election, and salvation. Throughout this section of Ephesians the activity of God's gracious power forms the basis for many statements about human activity. Neither the apostle as one who brings enlightenment about the divine mystery nor the church as manifestation of the many-sided divine wisdom (v. 10) possesses what they convey. Depiction of the church as heavenly reality, not as a human institution, should not be taken as triumphalism, since its truth is a mystery of God's plan known to the elect, not an expansionist sociopolitical program.

From that perspective, Ephesians considers the church as the culmination of God's plan for the entire universe. Therefore, anyone who does not respond to the gospel and become one with Christ has no hope of salvation. Ephesians does mean to say that God intends all peoples to become one in Christ. It presents the church as the new humanity that results. But it is also important to note the perspective from which Ephesians makes such claims—a position of sociopolitical powerlessness. Christian communities emerged at the margins of Jewish communities, which were themselves minorities in the urban centers of Asia Minor.

The dramatic opening, "I Paul am a prisoner for Christ," evokes the fragile character of the early Christian movement. Its Jewish heritage, especially the apocalyptic images of divine election, provided an extraordinary self-understanding as the church was being transformed from a sect of Jewish believers into a Gentile church of Jewish heritage. Ephesians reminds readers of two essential factors in this surprising development: the sure grasp of God's mysterious plan by particular individuals (especially Paul) and the power of God working to extend salvation to all.

REFLECTIONS

Even though the first readers of Ephesians did not know Paul personally, they benefited from his missionary activity. Paul understood his own conversion as a calling to make Christ known among the Gentiles (Gal 1:15-16). He also understood that the considerable sufferings he endured in service to the gospel were a necessary part of the process. The apostle must show in his own life the "life out of death" pattern of the crucified and risen Jesus: "Always carrying in the body the death of Jesus, so that the life of Jesus may be made visible in our mortal flesh. So death is at work in us but life in you" (2 Cor 4:11-12 NRSV).

The writer of Ephesians uses the dramatic opening "I Paul am a prisoner of Christ Jesus for the sake of you Gentiles" (3:1 NRSV) to shock the audience into attention. The author then inserts a summary of the message that Gentiles are to be God's people (3:2-6). He reminds them that God gave Paul the mission to make this plan of salvation known (3:7-12). With a characteristic twist, the author of Ephesians finds a cosmic significance in the gospel. As the message of salvation is made known among human beings, it becomes known to the powers that control the world as well (3:10). We have such ready access to all forms of media that we *expect* religious leaders to attract the attention of world leaders. When one of the television networks recently ran a mini-series called "Jesus," it managed to bump the most popular show on television out of the top spot. It is hard to remember a time when the church was made up of small groups of people meeting in houses. It had no buildings at all. In an age without media, having no buildings, statues, or inscriptions means very little presence in the public sphere. How could Christians ever think that their existence was God's plan for the world? How could they go even further and imagine that it was revealing God's wisdom to the forces that control the universe?

Yet, that is exactly the kind of vision, courage, and faith that changes the world. Once a movement has succeeded in changing how we live or eradicating some injustice, it is easy to forget what it took to get there. It is easy to forget that some of our greatest human benefactors, people like Gandhi and Martin Luther King, Jr., went to jail for their efforts. Like Paul, they eventually paid with their lives for insisting that God intended us all to be merciful, just, equal. In short, it is to come closer to the vision of all humanity united as God's new creation that Ephesians emphasizes. These leaders had talents and education that would have enabled them to live comfortable and productive lives without getting involved in transforming humanity.

Letters from jail also play a significant role in encouraging the movement. We have several from Paul himself and from close associates writing in Paul's name. Martin Luther King, Jr.'s famous "Letter from a Birmingham Jail" explains that he could not stay comfortably in Atlanta. He had to go where injustice was, even though fellow ministers criticized his decision as foolish. Dr. King could appeal to precedent, of course, and he was not shy about reminding his readers of Paul's missionary journeys and of the great Hebrew prophets who left home to take God's Word elsewhere. He also insisted that ultimately all communities are related:

> Injustice anywhere is a threat to justice everywhere. We are caught in an inescapable network of mutuality, tied in a single garment of destiny. Whatever affects one directly, affects all indirectly. . . . Anyone who lives inside the United States can never be considered an outsider anywhere within its bounds.[202]

This quotation captures for a particular situation the significance of Paul's insight that in the end human beings cannot be considered separately. We need to see ourselves as interconnected members of the one body of Christ just as much as we need to see ourselves as united in a single political body. "No one can ever be considered an outsider"—that is what we hear Paul announcing to the Gentiles. And we might agree with him that his is, indeed, a revelation of God's plan, the full truth of which is still being revealed to the world.

---

202. Martin Luther King, Jr., "Letter from a Birmingham Jail," in *Norton Anthology of African American Literature*, ed. H. L. Gates, Jr., and N. Y. McKay (New York: Norton, 1997) 1854.

Ephesians 3:14-21, The Apostle's Prayer

COMMENTARY

"For this reason" picks up 3:1. The section continues with a prayer report (vv. 14-19) and a concluding doxology (vv. 20-21). The petitions (vv. 16-19) ask that the process of salvation be completed in the hearts and minds of the letter's recipients. The doxology returns to the theme of God's power at work within the community of faith.

This prayer report exemplifies boldness and access to God (v. 12). Since the apostle entrusted with the "commission of God's grace" (v. 2) prays for them, readers can be certain that God will grant his request. There is no reason to treat the petitions as evidence of difficulties in the churches.[203] Because the prayer asks for the love of Christ and fullness of God (v. 19), it forms an appropriate rhetorical conclusion to the speech in praise of God's powerful grace.[204] The letter next turns to a different type of speech: ethical exhortation (4:1–6:20). That section of the letter is framed by references to Paul's imprisonment (4:1; 6:20). The prayer report facilitates the transition between the two halves of the epistle by disposing the audience to a Christian way of life. The prayer report reintroduces the theme of love. The addressees are known for their love (1:15). God's love for us (2:4) has been demonstrated in the election to holiness, "to be holy and blameless before him in love" (1:4). The prayer report speaks of the community with its *roots* and *foundation* in love (3:17), an echo of the earlier image of the church in which Gentiles *grow together* with Jews into the temple *founded on* apostles and prophets (2:20-21).

3:14-15. The apostle's kneeling position departs from the usual custom of standing to pray (as in Mark 11:25; Luke 18:11, 13). Luke has Jesus kneel in Gethsemane (Luke 22:41) rather than lie prostrate on the ground, as in Mark (Mark 14:35). Luke also refers to kneeling at prayer in Acts (Acts 7:60; 9:40; 20:36; 21:5). With the exception of Acts 9:40, all of these scenes are associated with death. Jesus and Stephen are about to die. Paul is departing on the journey to Jerusalem that will lead to his imprisonment and death. Kneeling is often the gesture of suppliants begging for a favor from a powerful or important person (as in Matt 17:14; Mark 1:40; 10:17). In these scenes, kneeling expresses the deep emotions of those involved; here it adds pathos to the image of the imprisoned apostle.

The prayer includes a play on words that cannot be easily reproduced in English. He prays to the Father (πατήρ *patēr*) from whom every πατριά (*patria*; "clan," "group derived from a single ancestor," "race") is named (the NRSV's "family" must be understood as a reference to the extended family). Ephesians follows the common Christian tradition of referring to God as "father" ("and the Lord Jesus," 5:20, also 6:23; "our Father," 1:3, also 2:18; 4:6; "of Jesus," 1:4; "Father of glory," 1:17). But what is meant by the assertion that every clan "in heaven and on earth" is named from the Father? Some interpreters suggest that the phrase implies that God is superior to all the powers because God created them. Persons tempted to use the names of heavenly powers for magical purposes fail to recognize the origin of all those names in God.[205] Others suggest some form of Hellenistic cosmological speculation.[206] Stoic cosmology proposed a biological image of the origins of all things out of the divine spiritual substance, "God, mind, fate and Zeus are all one, and many other names are applied to him. In the beginning all by himself he turned the entire substance through air into water."[207] God appears as father in Platonist cosmologies as well.[208] In gnostic cosmologies, the "first" Father generates all of the subsequent aeons of the heavenly pleroma.[209]

Though Ephesians uses images characteristic of the cosmology of its time, the letter shows no evidence of debate on the subject. Its emphasis on God as creator (also 4:6) provides the general context for this play on words. Everything belongs to the one clan because everything has been created by the one Father-creator.

3:16-19. The first petition (vv. 16-17) returns to God's power (1:17-23). It also contains variations of phrases from Colossians ("riches of glory," Col 1:27; "hearts held together in love," Col 2:2; and "rooted and built up in him," Col 2:7). Two parallel expressions ask for inner strengthening of the faithful. The first depicts God as the agent of inner strengthening (v. 16). The power through which God raised Christ operates through believers (1:19; 3:6). Unlike Rom 7:22, Ephesians does not use the expression "inner being" (εἰς τὸν ἔσω ἄνθρωπον *eis ton esō anthrōpon*) as the antithesis to outer, bodily passions that overwhelm reason.

---

203. Contra Lincoln, *Ephesians*, 197-98.
204. Fee, *God's Empowering Presence*, 695ff.
205. Arnold, *Ephesians*, 58-59; Cargal, "'Seated in the Heavenlies,'" 155.
206. Bouttier, *L'Épître de Saint Paul aux Éphésiens*.
207. A. A. Long and D. N. Sedley, *The Hellenistic Philosophers*, vol. 1, *Translations* (Cambridge: Cambridge University Press, 1987) 46B.
208. Plato *Timaeus* 28C; 37C; 41A; Philo *On the Special Laws* 2.165; 3.189.
209. E.g., *Ap. John* II 2,27-5,11.

Nor does the expression refer to the "new humanity" (τὸν καικὸν ἄνθρωπον *ton kainon anthrōpon*; NRSV and NIV, "new self") of 4:24.[210] The parallel phrase in v. 17, "in your hearts" (ἐν ταῖς καρδίαις ὑμῶν *en tais kardiais hymōn*), indicates that "inner being" refers to the basic intelligence and will of human persons.

The second formulation of the petition (v. 17) specifies what is meant by the first. Strengthening by God's Spirit is not a prior condition for the indwelling of Christ. The phrase "rooted and grounded is a variation on the "rooted and built up" of Col 2:7. Since it also designates God's mercy and goodness toward the elect (v. 19; 2:4), "love" (ἀγάπη *agapē*) means both God's love in the faithful and their love for others (1:15).

The second petition (vv. 18-19*a*) indicates the other fruits of the Spirit. It also consists of two parallel expressions: Understanding and knowing are the objects of strengthening (1:9, 17; 3:4-5). The first object of understanding is not clearly specified. "Breadth and length and height and depth" (v. 18) are not dimensions of a particular object. The cosmological images in Ephesians might lead one to anticipate that they refer to God's presence to all parts of the cosmos (as in Ps 139:7-12). Only God's wisdom can comprehend the cosmos (Job 11:7-9). Sirach 1:1-10 personifies God's incomprehensible wisdom. At the same time, Wisdom is a gift that the Lord bestows on the righteous: "It is he who created her; he saw her and took her measure; he poured her out upon all his works, upon all the living according to his gift; he lavished her upon those who love him" (Sir 1:9-10 NRSV). Ephesians 3:10 presented God's multisided wisdom (σοφία *sophia*) as manifest to the powers through the church. These petitions ask that God endow believers with the wisdom needed to hold fast to the gift of salvation.

Others suggest that the expression indicates expansion of the human mind or spirit. An apocalyptic reading would treat "the saints" (οἱ ἅγιοι *hoi hagioi*) as a reference to the angelic hosts. The object whose dimensions are comprehended would be a heavenly object, such as the new Jerusalem (Ezek 48:16-17; Rev 3:18; 21:6) or the temple of God (Ezek 40:1–43:12). An extremely fragmentary wisdom text from Qumran that is introduced as instructions from a sage to the righteous contained a section involving something with roots from the heavens to the abyss being measured by God.[211] In another fragment, astronomical measurements had special significance as the hidden wisdom conveyed in a vision of the heavens ordered from God's throne by the movements of the sun and the moon.[212] Members of the sect needed this knowledge in order to follow a liturgical calendar that is in accord with the divine order. Participation in divine wisdom is also a presupposition of these texts. Although the apocalyptic timetable is foreign to Ephesians, Essene language is not. Exaltation to the heavens, where Christ is seated on the divine throne, would certainly endow the saints with such knowledge. It also sets them among the angels. Since Ephesians is using figurative language, not discursive description, a Jewish liturgical fragment may have been the basis for this prayer formula.

More distant possibilities include philosophical reflection on the ability of the human mind to encompass the vast expanses of the cosmos. In interpreting Exod 33:23, Philo distinguishes the mind's ability to know all things that exist below God from its inability to grasp the divine: "It is an ample gift for the best sort of mortals, knowledge of things bodily and immaterial below the Existent."[213] He also repeats an argument for natural knowledge of God as creator based on a survey of the order and harmony of the universe from the region of fixed stars down to the earth. Such knowledge is contrasted with direct apprehension of God apart from created things given to Moses.[214] Though Ephesians might concur with these views, nothing in the letter suggests a philosophical interest in the modes of knowing God.

Since "fullness" (πλήρωμα *plērōma*) occurs in the final petition (v. 19*b*), the dimensions of the heavenly pleroma in gnostic speculation have also been seen as the referent of this phrase in v. 18*b*. Only those whose origins lie in the heavenly church can conceive the dimensions and properties of the aeons that have come forth from the

---

210. Contra Schlier, *Der Brief an die Epheser*, 168.
211. 4Q298.
212. 4Q286 frag. 1.
213. Philo *On the Change of Names* 8-9.
214. Philo *Allegorical Interpretation of the Laws* 3.99, 100-1.

Father.²¹⁵ Reading Ephesians as a response to magical practices leads to comparison with prayers and spells designed to gain divine power for individuals.²¹⁶ The four dimensions are named in a prayer that the magician is to say in order to draw down and retain divine light.²¹⁷

The parallel expression in v. 19*a* indicates that Ephesians is not concerned with knowledge in terms of human minds stretched to their limits in apprehending the creator or with cosmological speculation but with the experience of the love of Christ (cf. Rom 8:38-39). Ephesians characteristically uses "the exceeding" (τὸ ὑπερβάλλον *to hyperballon*) with expressions for salvation ("immeasurable greatness of his power," 1:19; "immeasurable riches of his grace," 2:7). The shift from knowledge to "faith and love" in v. 17 indicates that Ephesians is not a speculative tract. There is no polemic in Ephesians against knowledge (unlike Col 2:2-3). The strengthening to which the prayer refers points to earlier images of the community, not to individual knowledge of God or the cosmos.

The final petition (v. 19*b*) reinforces this orientation. The community must become what the church in its heavenly reality already is, "filled with all the fullness [*plērōma*] of God." The phrase echoes Colossians, which speaks of the "fullness of deity in Christ" (see Col 1:19; 2:9) and of believers "filled in him" (see Col 2:10). Ephesians 1:23 has already established the immediate context for this phrase. The church is the "fullness of Christ," who in turn fills the entire cosmos. The expression "fullness of God" (πλήρωμα τοῦ Θεοῦ *plērōma tou Theou*) in this petition highlights the theocentric element in the epistle. God's preordained plan, which culminates in Christ, is the object of praise. The shift to divine fullness also indicates that no future revelations or acts in the drama of salvation remain to be achieved.²¹⁸

3:20-21. The concluding doxology cannot be entirely divided from the earlier prayer, since this is the only doxology in the NT to mention Christ and the church as the locus of praise. The reference to both "all the saints" and Christ in vv. 18-19 makes this focus appropriate. The doxology also fits the pattern of alternating pronouns so evident in the epistle. The "you" of the earlier prayer formula is once again joined to the author's "we." In addition, the reflection on God's power working within the believing community picks up the references to being strengthened in power (v. 16) and to being filled with God (v. 19). Therefore, the doxology should be seen to flow from the intercessory prayer formula.²¹⁹

Doxologies refer to the person being praised, contain a praise formula—usually with the word "glory" (δόξα *doxa*), an eternity formula—and often a concluding amen. The doxology typically occurs at or near the end of a letter ("to our God and Father be glory forever and ever. Amen" [Phil 4:20]; see also Rom 16:25-27; 2 Tim 4:18; Heb 13:21; 1 Pet 5:11). The doxology in Rom 11:36 concludes the theological section of that letter, as is the case here. Though doxologies are not ordinarily attached to a previous intercession, Phil 4:19 belongs to an expression of thanks that comes close to a prayer formula. The gifts that the Philippians have sent Paul in prison are to be repaid by Paul's "master God." Paul assures readers that their gift is a pleasing sacrifice (Phil 4:18) and that "God will repay every need of yours according to his riches in glory in Christ." Many of the terms in this sentence ("fill," "wealth," "glory," "in Christ") appear in Eph 3:14-19.

Ephesians begins by celebrating the power of God to deliver even more than humans might ask or think. It retrieves the description of the great power of God that raised Jesus and is at work in believers from 1:19-20. The doxology also models the praise of God's glory for which the elect were predestined (1:6, 12).

This ringing affirmation of God's extraordinary power picks up a note that is already evident in the intercessory prayer report: Believers have received the grace and Spirit of God long before they come to ask God for them. Such confidence is part of the access to God that Christians enjoy. The extraordinary character of such expressions becomes

---

215. So *Tripartite Tractate* 58, 29-60.1
216. Arnold, *Ephesians*, 89-96.
217. PGM IV 970-85. See Hans Dieter Betz, ed., *The Greek Magical Papyri in Translation*, vol. 1, *Texts* (Chicago: University of Chicago Press, 1986) 57
218. Lincoln, *Ephesians*, 215.

219. Fee, *God's Empowering Presence*, 696.

evident when one considers the usual mode of making a request of a powerful person or benefactor. Not only should the request be enveloped in extensive praise of the patron's goodness, but it should also be hedged with "if it would not be too much trouble . . . ," "if you could . . . ," and other similar expressions. If the person from whom one seeks a favor is considerably more powerful, intermediaries or a prior note of introduction will be produced. It is possible to see all of Ephesians 1:1–3 as an exposition of God's saving power.

The intercessory prayer report and doxology merely confirm what the letter has already stated. God has gathered the elect into the heavenly regions with Christ. In Ephesians, the apostle does not intercede with God to do things. Instead, the prayer asks God to bring to perfection the work of salvation that has already begun among the elect. What that will mean in the concrete terms of Christian life remains to be spelled out in the second half of the epistle.

REFLECTIONS

The previous section ended with Paul's concern that his sufferings might cause his audience to lose heart. Since Ephesians was written after Paul's martyrdom, its author could not express confidence that God could return the apostle to the mission field, which Paul himself used in earlier letters (see Phil 1:21-26; Phlm 22). Instead, Ephesians returns to two themes already sounded loud and clear in the opening chapter: glory (3:13) and prayer (3:14). This prayer concludes with a doxology praising God's power to go beyond anything we can imagine (3:20-21). Rhetorically, this prayer makes a dramatic statement of faith. Indirectly it answers the question that must have tugged at the hearts of second-generation Christians. As they saw the apostles arrested and martyred, they must have wondered whether the church could survive. Notice the slight twist that appears in the doxology, "to him be all glory *in the church* and in Jesus Christ" (3:21 NRSV, italics added). For us, "glory in the church" does not turn up in doxologies, but it certainly does in our imagination. We have TV shots of the worship at general conventions, at St. Peter's in Rome, at the Church of the Nativity in Bethlehem, and even at great stadium crusades. Those of us who regularly participate in such worship services may forget the extraordinary impact such experiences make on Christians from small churches who experience it for the first time. All those phrases about "glory in the heavenly realms" take on physical reality as the music of the choir echoes off the stone vaulting of Westminster Abbey or Chartres Cathedral.

Step back for a moment into the house-church world of the first century. The Temple in Jerusalem, which had been a marvel, lies in ruins. Even Jews have no physical site in which they could experience such dramatic worship of God. So who had the buildings, the sacred processions and sacrifices, the dramatic public events that could take your breath away? Neither Jews nor Christians. Those *atheoi* ("godless people") did. And the Roman imperial administration did. When Christians imagined Christ returning in glory or Christ enthroned in glory, they undoubtedly had such images in mind. They only had to look at their coins to see the imperial version: temples dedicated to Roman glory and deified emperors. We should not take the phrases about strengthening the hearts and inner being of Christians lightly. It must have required extraordinary inner confidence to remain a faithful Christian with no external signs of the truth of our faith. "That Christ may dwell in your hearts through faith, as you are being rooted and grounded in love" (3:17 NRSV) is an extraordinary prayer. Accomplish that, and you have the whole Christian life.

The Lutheran theologian Dietrich Bonhoeffer, who was jailed and executed for joining a plot to assassinate Hitler, left a prison correspondence that is one of the classics of twentieth-century theology. In one letter, he advises his friend to take in the Holy Week services in St. Peter's and St. John Lateran at Rome, mentions a service of some twenty years earlier in a Greek Orthodox church, and then mentions a small convent church outside Rome where the nuns' singing made an impression.[220] This letter shows what a powerful support such memories of the larger church at prayer can be in the life of faith. Like Paul, Bonhoeffer had put his life at risk for his suffering sisters and brothers. He had returned to Germany despite the urging of colleagues to remain in the United States, where he had been lecturing. He felt compelled to take the risk of direct attack against an evil that he could see was destroying his own country.

Yet prison does strange things to the mind. In the same letter, he muses on the lives of his generation in contrast to the great theologians and artists of the previous centuries. People no longer seemed to want to achieve what is great. "Where is there today the combination of fine *abandon* and large-scale planning that goes with such a life?" he remarked. That could issue in a bit of cynicism. There is nothing great to accomplish, so devote your life to chasing personal wealth. But Bonhoeffer has a different answer: Perhaps our lives can be fragments that God can sort out, consigning some to the dustbin and completing others: "The important thing today is that we should be able to discern from the fragment of our life who the whole was arranged . . . their completion can only be a matter for God and so they are fragments that must be fragments." Set this observation alongside the prayer report in Eph 3:14-21. Paul is not proclaiming a triumphalist Christianity that has conquered the world, as many people imagine when they read this prayer. He is providing prayers for the witnesses, prisoners, martyrs for the gospel and their friends—everyone whose life is somehow fragments in need of sorting. The Christian virtues of faith, hope, and love can latch on to the fullness of God and find completion in that experience.

---

220. Dietrich Bonhoeffer, "3 February 1944," in *Letters and Papers from Prison,* ed. Eberhard Bethge (New York: Macmillan, 1972) 218.

EPHESIANS 4:1–6:9, ETHICAL EXHORTATIONS ON LIVING AS CHRISTIANS

Ephesians 4:1-16, Building the Body of Christ

COMMENTARY

Ephesians presumes that conversion leads to moral renewal. The new moral life is indicated by the self-designation "saints" ("holy ones," ἅγιοι *hagioi*), praise for mutual love (1:15), and indications that the elect are "holy and blameless" (1:4) before God and are created for good works (2:10). Paul's letters frequently include sections of paraenesis (moral advice or admonition). Pauline paraenesis has stronger ties to the forms and content of Hellenistic philosophers than other sections of his epistles.[221] Ancient moralists held that people should be reminded of what they know so that they will act accordingly.[222] Therefore, the epistle's paraenesis need not reflect actual vices among the addressees. These moralists also held that a teacher's life was to provide a visible example of his teaching.

This section returns to the image of the imprisoned apostle (4:1) and establishes friendship between author and audience that was also considered fundamental to hortatory discourse. Paul's paraenesis often opens with the verb παρακαλέω (*parakaleō*, "I beg" or

---

221. Abraham J. Malherbe, "Hellenistic Moralists and the New Testament," in Haase, *Aufstieg und Niedergang der römischen Welt* II.

222. Dio Chrysostom *Orations* 17,2.

"I appeal"; Rom 12:1; 2 Cor 10:1; 1 Thess 4:1) and a brief list of virtues (v. 2). The beginning then shifts from convention to a theme of the letter: unity in the body of Christ (vv. 3-6). Verses 2-4 draw on Col 3:12-15. Verse 7 makes the transition from exhortation to the heavenly exaltation of Christ (vv. 8-10). His status is the basis for the gifts of salvation. The conclusion (vv. 11-16) describes unity as working together in the body of Christ. This concern refers back to the growth image (2:21).

4:1-6. The exhortation to "lead a life worthy of [your] calling" echoes Jewish understanding of divine election. God's calling is to create a people who are devoted to God's law. God works:

> to enlighten the heart of man, straighten out in front of him all the paths of justice and truth, establish in his heart respect for the precepts of God; it is a spirit of meekness, of patience, generous compassion, eternal goodness ... potent wisdom which trusts in all the deeds of God and depends upon his abundant mercy ... of generous compassion with all the sons of truth.[223]

Though Pauline churches no longer follow the law, the conviction that election leads to a new life remains (1 Thess 2:12).

An exhortation to holiness could be expanded by a list of virtues (vv. 2-3). For the Essenes, the virtues distinguish the community of the "sons of light" from the "sons of darkness," whose vices that text goes on to describe.[224] The list in v. 2—humility (ταπεινοφροσύνη *tapeinophrosynē*), gentleness (πραΰτη *prautē*), patience (μακαροθυμία *makrothymia*)—adopts the final three of the list in Col 3:12. These virtues are found in the Essene example also. "Humility" (*tapeinophrosynē*) does not appear outside Jewish and Christian lists. To the non-Jew, "humility" suggests demeaning lowliness.[225] "Gentleness" (*prautē*), on the other hand, does have positive connotations in Hellenistic ethics. It is opposed to wrath, disposed to forgiveness and to moderate punishment, and lives without jealousy or spite.[226] Those who have this trait can bear hardship or loss with tranquility. "Patience" (*makrothymia*) also belongs to both traditions. In Jewish and Christian sources, it appears as an attribute of God (Jer 15:15; Rom 2:4; 9:22; 1 Tim 1:16; 1 Pet 3:20) or of human beings (Prov 25:15; 2 Cor 6:6; Gal 5:22).

The exhortation "bearing with one another in love" appears in Col 3:13 and in the Essene description of the "sons of light." "Love" (ἀγάπη *agapē*) can be the foundation of all Christian virtues (1 Cor 13:1; Gal 5:14). Galatians 5:15 uses negative examples to highlight the communal implications of the love command. It dictates how persons relate to, and speak about, one another.

Verse 3 shifts to the specific focus of this section: unity. Two clauses, "unity of the Spirit" and "in the bond of peace," indicate that the fruit of the Spirit is peace (Rom 8:6; 14:17; 15:13; Gal 5:22). "Peace" (εἰρήνη *eirēnē*) as gift of the Spirit goes beyond social interest in communal concord. It refers to the fullness of salvation that comes from God (Rom 14:17; 15:13). The term "bond" (σύνδεσμος *syndesmos*) derives from Col 3:14-15, in which love is described as the "bond of perfection" (NRSV, "love, which binds everything together in perfect harmony"). It also creates a verbal echo with the apostle's self-designation "prisoner" (δέσμος *desmos*).

The reference to election from Col 3:15 introduces a list of "one" (ἕν *hen*) expressions (vv. 4-6). It ends with the one God who governs and fills the entire cosmos (v. 6). Some interpreters treat vv. 4-6 as an independent liturgical fragment.[227] However, the section appears to be an ad hoc creation from standard Pauline expressions. First Corinthians 12:12-13 (one body, Christ, one Spirit, baptized into one body) provides an initial framework for vv. 4-5, while 1 Cor 8:6 provides a formula for God's creative activity. Gordon Fee proposes an essentially trinitarian structure in the series that he calls "one of the more certain and specific Trinitarian passages in the corpus."[228] The first term in each verse provides its key image: one body (v. 4), one Lord (v. 5), and one God (v. 6). The first two verses indicate how persons have become

---

223. 1QS 4:2-5.
224. 1QS 4:9-11.
225. Spicq, *Theological Lexicon of the New Testament*.
226. Aristotle *Nichomachean Ethics* 4.11, 1125b; Plato *Republic* 3.387.
227. Barth, *Ephesians*, 429.
228. Fee, *God's Empowering Presence*, 702.

part of the body that is God's elect. Verse 6 has taken over a philosophical formulation for the creative activity of God.[229]

Conversion included coming to know the one God, creator of all (2:12b, 18). The creation formula that indicates the transcendence of God, God's activity, and God's omnipresence undergirds the letter's insistence that other forces in the cosmos have no effective power.

4:7-10. Verse 7 incorporates exhortation by referring to "grace" (χάρις *charis*). The expression "each of us was given grace" resembles Rom 12:6, where diversity of gifts is associated with the particular grace given to each person in the community. Ephesians substitutes "according to the measure of Christ's gift" for "grace given." This usage conflates Rom 12:6 with the reference to "measure" in Rom 12:3. There Paul warns against false estimation of one's own gifts. If Ephesians has this section of Romans in view, then one would anticipate what follows in vv. 11-13, a discussion of gifts that require proper understanding of one's place in the community.

A digression interrupts the development that v. 7 anticipates. Ephesians has depicted the creative activity of God as equivalent to the plan that culminates in the body of Christ (1:9-10, 20-23; 2:5-7; 3:9-11). Verses 8-10 contain another description of the soteriological activity of Christ. It uses a form of biblical exegesis familiar from the Qumran scrolls, the *pesher*.[230] Citation of a section of biblical text is followed by its application, often introduced by the formula, "its interpretation is that. . . ."[231] Interpretation involves demonstrating that the biblical text refers to events connected with the past, the present, or the future (end of all things) history of the sect. The Qumran text 1QpHab 7:4-5 treats the pesherim as revelations of divine mysteries: "Its interpretation (Hab 2:2) concerns the Teacher of Righteousness, to whom God has disclosed all the mysteries of the words of his servants, the prophets."

Ephesians 4:8-10 is a pesher on Ps 68:19 [67:19]. Fragments of a pesher on this psalm have been found at Qumran. That commentary connects with Ps 68:12-13, 26-27, 30-31, but the remains are too slight to permit any reconstruction of the sect's understanding. Ephesians may have taken its citation from a comparable text.

This type of interpretation begins with the theme and continues with as many details as fit the subject. Subunits of a text may be picked up, cited with an introduction ("as for when it says"), and followed by additional identifications. Applied to Eph 4:8-10, it is clear that the only phrase from the psalm citation on which the pesher comments is "he ascended." Nothing is said about either the "captivity taken captive" or the gifts bestowed on humankind. It is easy to link both of these themes to the overall imagery of Ephesians by understanding "captivity" (αἰχμαλωσία *aichmalōsia*) as the powers to whom Christ's ascent reveals God's plan. The author has "he gave," found in the psalm, in both v. 7 and v. 11. But the connection is not made in the exegetical style of a pesher. Therefore, the psalm interpretation was not originally formulated to fit the paraenesis in vv. 7 and 11-16.

Taken as a fragment of early Christian exegesis, the opening argument of the pesher is strikingly similar to John 3:13: "No one has ascended into heaven except the one who descended from heaven, the Son of Man" (NRSV).[232] A related piece of exegesis is connected with the use of Ps 110:1 in Acts 2:32-35 as David's prediction that the risen Jesus would be exalted to God's right hand. That psalm was incorporated into Eph 1:20-23. The argument in Acts 2:34 seeks to show that David was speaking prophetically of the Christ and not of himself. All of these examples use the ascent and descent imagery to advance Christian claims for Jesus as the one who has been exalted to God's right hand.

Both the form and the content of the pesher suggest that the regions to which Christ descends refers to the earth, not to some region below the earth (unlike Rom 10:7; 1 Pet 3:18-21; Rev 1:18). The objection that "lower regions of the earth" (τὰ κατώτερα μέρα τῆς γῆς *ta katōtera mera tēs gēs*) cannot mean simply earth and must mean hades ignores the fact that the regions of the air are

---

229. See Pseudo-Aristotle *On the Origin of the World* 6.397b, 11.14-15; Philo *The Cherubim* 125-126.
230. See Devorah Dimant, "Pesharim, Qumran," *ABD* 5:244-51.
231. E.g., Isa 40:3 in 1QS 8:13-16; Isa 24:17 in CD 4:13-15.

232. See Bouttier, *L'Épître de Saint Paul aux Éphésiens,* 183-85, who makes too much of the Moses typology.

also connected with earth in ancient cosmology.[233] Since Ephesians does not interpret the phrase about captives, one cannot treat it as the key to the passage as Arnold does in proposing that Eph 4:9 refers to initiation rites that involved descent to hades.[234] "The lower parts of the earth" (NRSV) and "the lower, earthly regions" (NIV) are suitably ambiguous translations. Though Eph 2:2 distinguishes the heavenly regions from the "air" (the area below the moon that has malevolent powers responsible for evil), it never refers to regions below the earth (cf. Phil 2:11).[235]

The final clause, "that he might fill [πληρόω *pleroō*] all things" (v. 10), fits the cosmological perspective of Ephesians. The phrase "filling the universe" was used earlier in connection with God's power and with the exalted Christ in his body (1:23; 3:19). Ephesians 4:13 speaks of the Christian community maturing in the "full stature of Christ." Cosmological images always serve the soteriological framework of the epistle. Here, the omnipresence of God (Eph 4:6; as in Philo *Allegorical Interpretation of the Laws* 3.4; *Life of Moses* 2.238) grounds the image of Christ as universal savior. God's preordained plan becomes known only when Christ is exalted in the heavens.

4:11-16. Verse 11 picks up the gifts mentioned in v. 7. A single Greek sentence (vv. 11-16) links a list of teaching functions in the community (vv. 11-12) with the need for the church to grow to perfection (vv. 13-16). Romans 12:3-8 orders those gifts that might cause division in the community: prophecy, ministry, teaching, exhorting, contributing to charity (ὁ μεταδιδούς *ho metadidous*; NRSV, "the giver"; for this meaning of the verb, see Job 31:17; Prov 11:26; Luke 3:11), serving as a leader (προιστάμενος *proistamenos*, "standing at the head"; with this meaning, cf. 1 Thess 5:12; 1 Tim 5:17),[236] and performing acts of mercy (ὁ ἐλεῶν *ho eleōn*; NRSV, "the compassionate"). Romans associates each task with a requisite virtue. These virtues provide the "measure" by which the performance of members of the community can be evaluated.

Ephesians 4:11-12 begins with a list of such functions, but unlike Rom 12:7-8, the list extends beyond the local church. "Apostle, prophet, evangelist" are clearly external to local churches. Ephesians has twice used "apostles and prophets" in a way that suggests an activity that has already been completed (2:20; 3:5). The term "evangelist" (εὐαγγελιστής *euangelistēs*) appears in only two other places in the NT (Acts 21:8, Philip; 2 Tim 4:5, Timothy). In both cases, the evangelist has been commissioned by the apostles to preach the gospel. Though the term "pastor" (ποιμήν *poimēn*) appears to be a particular designation for Peter (John 21:15-17), 1 Pet 5:1-5 indicates that the term applied to those who served as elders in the local communities of Asia Minor (also Acts 20:28). A pre-Christian example that uses the term "shepherd" for the community's supervisor also appears in an Essene text.[237] Teachers (διδάσκαλοι *didaskaloi*) appear in all the Pauline lists of church offices (Rom 12:7; 1 Cor 12:28). Teaching may refer to basic instruction or to ongoing exhortation (Gal 6:6). Paul can refer to himself as "teacher" (1 Cor 4:17; Col 1:28; 3:16), though "teacher" comes third after apostles and prophets in 1 Cor 12:28. Thus Ephesians begins with those functions connected with the founding of the community and moves on to those of local leaders.[238]

Ephesians treats these activities as service to the body of Christ (as in Rom 12:4-8; 1 Cor 12:12, 27-30). Diverse manifestations of the Spirit in the community are forms of service (so 1 Cor 12:5). Verses 12*b*-16 describe the purpose of service as equipping and building up the body. Paul used the verb "build up" in arguing that love should govern relationships among members of the church (1 Cor 8:1; 10:23; 14:3-5). Ephesians 2:21 used the noun "structure" (οἰκοδομή *oikodomē*) for the church as a temple being built for the Lord. That building is also spoken of as "growing" (αὔξω *auxō*), an image that this section will connect with both "body" (σῶμα *sōma*) and "love" (ἀγάπη *agapē*) in v. 16.

---

233. Cargal, "'Seated in the Heavenlies,'" 819.
234. Arnold, *Ephesians*, 57; Kreitzer, "The Plutonium of Hierapolis and the Descent of Christ into the 'Lowermost Parts of the Earth' (Ephesians 4:1, 9)," 381-93.
235. Schnackenburg, *The Epistle to the Ephesians*.
236. Josephus *Antiquities of the Jews* 8.123, sec. 300; Joseph A. Fitzmyer, *Romans*, AB 33 (Garden City, NY: Doubleday, 1993).
237. CD 13:7-11.
238. Schnackenburg, *The Epistle to the Ephesians*, 182.

Although the particular offices refer to those who are in charge of guiding churches after the apostle's death, Ephesians assumes that all Christians are part of the building process (cf. Gal 6:1-6). Maturity involves the community as a whole, and not merely particular individuals. A series of short phrases describes the goal of ministry: unity of faith, knowledge of the Son of God, "perfect man" (εἰς ἄνδρα τέλιον *eis andra telion*; NIV, "mature"; NRSV, "maturity"), measure of the full stature of Christ (v. 13). All of these phrases appear to be equivalent to the "new humanity" created in Christ (Eph 2:15). That expression described unity in concrete terms, Jews and Gentiles joined in a single community. But if the Jewish believer gives up those elements of the law that make him or her Jewish, then the "Jewish" side of the equation loses its significance.[239] Ephesians 4:4-5 included with "one Spirit, one Lord, one God" the terms "one body, one faith" and "one baptism." Presumably the "unity of faith" and "knowledge" depicted as future goals in v. 13 represent the same faith and knowledge that Christians already experience.

If the "unity of knowledge" is both present experience and future goal, then Ephesians is not dependent upon gnostic images of the church as a heavenly aeon. For Gnostics, the gathering of the scattered light from the world of darkness into the heavenly pleroma could be said to complete the deficiency in the heavenly church.[240]

The contrast between maturity and childishness (vv. 14-16) is commonplace in ethical exhortation. Paul uses it to castigate the Corinthians for their divisions (1 Cor 3:1-4). Philo uses "tossed around on the sea" for idolaters whose souls lack the necessary anchor in knowledge of the true God.[241] The problem of "trickery" and "deceitful scheming" that can lead the elect astray adds elements from Jewish apocalyptic to the philosophical picture of those who are morally immature. Essenes had to be on guard against the spirit of deceit.[242] Early Christians also anticipated the emergence of false prophets within their communities. The expression "deceit" for false teachers appears in later writings of the NT (2 Pet 2:18; 3:17; 1 John 4:6; Jude 11; also Acts 20:29-30; 1 Tim 4:1; 2 Tim 3:13). Since the author of Ephesians has read Colossians, he knows that Paul had warned against specific forms of false teaching (Col 2:2-4, 8). Since the word "scheming" (μεθοδεία *methodeia*; NIV, "schemes"; NRSV, "wiles") appears in 6:11 for the devil, the phrase "deceitful scheming" may suggest a demonic source for false teaching.

The concluding phrases in this long sentence shift back to the positive conditions for building up the body of Christ, speech as "the truth in love." Paul used "love" (*agapē*) as the key to communal solidarity (Rom 12:9-10). Love for fellow members was characteristic of the Essene sect.[243] Since Ephesians refers to "speaking truth in love" in contrast to deceit, its concern appears to be speech rather than solidarity. Jealousy and divisive speech show that the Corinthians remain "people of the flesh, as infants in Christ" (1 Cor 3:1 NRSV). Paul's open presentation of the gospel contrasts with the cunning of false teachers (2 Cor 4:2; 6:7). Truth opposes the error of false teaching, and love opposes its deceit.[244]

Verse 16 echoes the exhortation in Col 2:19 to resist false teaching. Ephesians shifts its focus from the head's holding parts of the body together to the body's growth into Christ (as in Eph 1:22-23). All of the parts need to work properly for the body to grow. The verb "knit together" (συμβιβάζω *symbibazō*) appeared in the architectural image of Eph 2:21. The phrase "every ligament . . . as each part is working properly" draws on terms used earlier in the letter: "according to the power [ἐνέργεια *energeia*, 1:19-20; 3:7] in measure [μέτρον *metron*, 4:7, 13] of each part." Though Ephesians has specified the functions of other parts of the body, the term "measure" implies God's gift to each one. Ephesians also uses *energeia* ("power") for God's active power present in the exalted Christ and working through the apostle. Though Ephesians does not make such associations, some interpreters assume that the ligaments are the teachers and "each part" the other members. Consequently, Rudolf Schnackenburg concludes that Ephesians

---

239. Sanders, *Schismatics, Sectarians, Dissidents, Deviants*, 200-1.
240. E.g., *Tripartite Tractate* 23, 3-23.
241. Philo *On the Decalogue* 67.
242. 1QS 3:21-22.
243. 1QS 1:9.
244. Lincoln, *Ephesians*, 276.

seeks to strengthen the power of the teachers in the community. Their office binds others to Christ.

Paraenesis played an important role in early Christian churches. Both teachers and individuals were expected to engage in such hortatory speech. Concern for the unity of religious and civic communities was also a common topic of deliberative rhetoric. Unlike the use of the "body" metaphor in 1 Corinthians and Romans, Ephesians does not point to a crisis of disunity. Exhortation serves the function of reminding the audience of what has already been true of its experience. Election requires that Christians live a style of life appropriate to that calling. Most of the concrete virtues listed (vv. 2, 14-15) support social cohesion, since they moderate competitive, divisive behavior.

The formula "one faith, one Lord, one baptism, one God" underscores the dilemma of religious pluralism. The phrases indicate that for Ephesians there can be only one true people of God. Those who are not part of the "body of Christ," whether Jews or Gentiles, are not included in salvation. The generalities of such formulae make a surface unity possible. The problems arise when people ask what the practical consequences ought to be. Ephesians does not grapple with situations of communal discord as Paul does in 1 Corinthians or Rom 14:1–15:13. The comments in vv. 11-16 suggest general emphasis on building up the church so that all grow to maturity in faith through sound teaching, speech that reflects love, mutual concern, and support of others. Ephesians does not explain how such activities are parceled out. Who are the shepherds and teachers? How do they relate to those founding figures in the common tradition, the apostles, the prophets, and the evangelists? How do the gifts that each member of the community receives serve the common task of building up the body of Christ?

The catalogs of charismata in Rom 12:6-8 and 1 Cor 12:8-11 that have influenced this section of Ephesians provide one possibility for filling out the picture of individual activities within the body of Christ. Other interpreters reach back to the earlier section on the unity of Jew and Gentile (2:14-22). The "one" formula refers to bringing together in a single community, body, and temple building those who were formerly divided. Following medical discussions of the time in which the operation of the body was explained by its being articulated and joined together with the head through nerves, Ephesians can attribute all of the growth in the body to Christ. The special feature of this body for Ephesians is bringing into one the foreign peoples to whom the gospel has been preached.[245]

245. Usami, *Somatic Comprehension of Unity*.

REFLECTIONS

Ephesians 4:1 adds to what is otherwise a standard opening for a section of moral exhortation the note that Paul is imprisoned. This reminder directs our attention back to a similar phrase in 3:1 and the reference to Paul's afflictions in 3:13. Perhaps we are even to think that he continues in the unusual kneeling posture of 3:14, as the NRSV's translation "beg" for the Greek *parakal* suggests. However, the verb can have a more positive meaning of encouraging someone; hence the NIV's "urge." We all know the difference between begging or pleading with someone whom we doubt will follow our advice and encouraging someone to continue an effort already well begun. The tone we imagine Paul using makes all the difference to our interpretation of this advice. Since Ephesians shows no evidence of seeking to correct the failures to live out the gospel of a particular community—unlike 1 Corinthians, for instance—let us assume that the author is encouraging Christians in a way of life already well begun. Even the list of basic Christian virtues in 4:2 could reflect habits that the audience is seeking to cultivate.

These virtues have a communal orientation, since they enhance the unity that is the defining characteristic of the Christian community. Ephesians 4:3 makes the transition from the general, other-centered virtues of humility, gentleness, generosity of spirit, and love to unity with a metaphorical prison image. What holds them all in place? Not the bands that hold a bundle together or the fetters that bind Paul, the prisoner. What holds them all together is a bond or fetter of peace.

It is easy to see chains as a reminder of slavery and prison cruelty. But we also live in a society in which any kind of permanent tie to others is treated as optional. Coaches tell kids that they cannot be on teams unless they will show up for practice and games on Sunday morning. People think nothing of ditching a community or church meeting or even a social event if something they would rather do comes along. Hardly evidence of persons who are "making every effort to maintain the unity of the Spirit" (4:3). Ephesians 4:4-6 picks up Paul's image of the church as a single body with one Spirit and adds a string of "one" clauses, concluding with the most important unity of all, that of God operating through all things. Our bond of unity with the church community and its presence to the larger human community should be more important than any of those alternatives that drag us away.

Ephesians 4:7 begins to specify how we are obligated to the church community by speaking of God as benefactor once again. God has distributed gifts to all members of the church so that it can be built up. At our college, the most popular spring break activity is not getting drunk on Florida beaches. It is the volunteer option, spending the week in some poor area of the East Coast, from Maine to North Carolina, building housing, cleaning out old houses, painting houses for the poor, fixing parks for children, and the like. Even students faced with twenty-hour bus rides, rusty cold showers, rats, bats, and garbage come back encouraging their friends to sign up. What did they discover that made such an impact? A spirit binding people together in a common effort to build up the human and church community. Those who have never used tools before discover some gifts they never knew they had. Ephesians 4:11 lists the experts charged with spreading the gospel and caring for the church. The danger is thinking that professionals create the church. Paul originally used the image in 1 Cor 12:14-31 to undercut those who thought their spiritual gifts of speaking in tongues made them superior to others. He insisted on the diversity of gifts required for the one body to function well. Ephesians 4:11-16 is less concrete, but it also moves from church leaders to the body composed of all believers, which has to grow up in love (4:16).

Ephesians adds another note to this practical training in love, concord, humility, generosity, and the like: a concern for the truth. Children are easily tricked, since they lack the knowledge or experience necessary to protect themselves against deceitful persons or false information. Even respected journalists have been conned by what appeared to be reliable information from knowledgeable sources. Scientists say that at least 50 percent of such public information is wrong. People who make some effort to avoid being taken in by false or misleading information seem to lose all critical sense where religion is concerned. They presume that anything someone asserts about his or her religious tradition with sincerity and conviction is religious truth. In that respect, we may be worse off than the post-apostolic generation of Christians whom Ephesians urges toward maturity in understanding of their faith (4:14).[246]

246. P. Berthoud, "Vérité et foi," *La revue réformée* 48 (1997) 49-54.

Ephesians 4:17-32, Two Ways of Life

COMMENTARY

The call to turn aside from a past way of life occurs in Hellenistic moralists as well as in Christian catechesis. Those who were addressed as "you Gentiles" (2:11) are now encouraged to separate themselves from the immorality of the Gentiles (4:17; cf. 1 Pet 2:12). Rhetorically, this introduction creates a boundary between the readers and the larger world.[247] The section divides into two parts: (a) the vices typical of the outsiders (vv. 17-24) and (b) a catalog of virtues (vv. 25-32) that characterize the "new self" (v. 24). This division reflects a common theme in paraenesis: description of the "two ways," virtue and vice. In Essene writings, the ways of the sons of light (members of the sect) are contrasted with those of the sons of darkness.[248]

Ephesians continues to use "we" for the author and the audience. Address to the audience as "you" returns when the list of injunctions is expanded in vv. 29-32. The genre of hortatory discourse (instruction by someone who exemplifies the teaching given) makes the "you" address more appropriate than the inclusive "we." Verses 17-24 establish the two groups, "alienated from the life of God" and "renewed in . . . your minds." Verses 25-32 contain a series of imperatives, or moral *sententiae.* Verse 25 is the topic sentence that refers to one negative action, "putting away," and one positive one, "speak truth." Verses 26-31 describe what is to be put away, while v. 32 turns to positive relationships among Christians. This section has close relationships to Rom 1:21, 24 and Col 3:5-10 as Figs. 2 and 3 indicate.

247. Lincoln, *Ephesians.*
248. 1QS 4:2-17.

Figure 2: Eph 4:17-19 and Rom 1:21, 24

Item	Ephesians	Romans
non-Jews lack effective knowledge of God: mind	**4:17c** in emptiness (ματαιότης *mataiotēs*) of their minds	**1:21** they have been given over to worthlessness (ἐματαιώθησαν *emataiōthēsan*) in their thoughts
non-Jews lack effective knowledge of God: darkened intelligence	**4:18a** being darkened in understanding	**1:21** their foolish heart was darkened
consequences of idolatry: impurity	**4:19** they handed themselves over to the practice of every impurity	**1:24** God handed them over to impurity

Ephesians uses a graphic description of the Gentile way of life to encourage readers to remain separated from their former conduct. Colossians provides images for both the old way of life and the new human beings that Christians have become:

Figure 3: Eph 4:17-24 and Col 3:5-10

Item	Ephesians	Colossians
not like the Gentiles	**4:17** you no longer walk as the Gentiles walk	**3:7** in which you also once walked
vices: impurity, greediness	**4:19** in practice of every impurity in greediness	**3:5** sexual immorality, purity, passion, evil desire, and greediness (which is idolatry)

put off old human being	**4:22a** put off from yourselves the old human being according to the former way of life	**3:8** now you put off . . . **3:9** having taken off the old human being with the deeds . . .
reject passions of old human being	**4:22b** corrupted according to the passions of error	See vices in **3:5**
renew the intellect	**4:23** be renewed in the spirit of your mind	**3:10** renewed in knowledge
put on the new human being	**4:24** and put on the new human being	**3:10** and having put on the new
the new creation	**4:24** created according to God	**3:10** according to the image of the one who created him

Ephesians has not followed the order in Colossians and has introduced stylistic variants in phrasing. Verses 20-21 are a rhetorical appeal to the audience. They follow an established practice in paraenesis, invoking prior instruction. The variations in describing the new creation may have a theological motivation. Since v. 24 ends with a reference to the moral categories of righteousness and holiness, Ephesians is not thinking of the elect as created in God's image but as predestined to a way of life.

The second section (vv. 25-32) continues to echo Col 3:8-12. Both are employing a standard form of ethical teaching—lists of vices to be avoided and virtues to be practiced. This form of teaching is so common in antiquity that the vices in such a list should not be culled for evidence about the community. A number of the items in this section will reappear in what follows: (a) not conducting oneself like the Gentiles (4:25–5:2; 5:3-14, 15-20); (b) darkness (v. 18; 5:8, 11; 6:12); (c) error (v. 18; 5:6); (d) impurity and greed (v. 19; 5:3, 5); and (e) righteousness (v. 24; 5:9; 6:14).

4:17-24. Ephesians reminds the audience to reject the Gentile way of life. The word "Gentiles" (τὰ ἔθνη *ta ethnē*) was previously used for Christians of Gentile origins in contrast to Jewish Christians (2:11; 3:1). Now it designates "pagans," non-Christian Gentiles. Other phrases suggest baptismal conversion: "testify in the Lord" (v. 17a), being "unclothed" and "clothed" (vv. 22, 24).[249] The rest of the sentence uses characteristic terms for Gentile ignorance of God (e.g., Wis 12:1-15; 18:10-19).[250] Romans 1:19-21 employs similar language. Having abandoned knowledge of the creator, the Gentiles are locked in immorality and worship of false gods. Ephesians uses two expressions that refer to the mind: "futility of mind" and "darkened understanding." The LXX uses "understanding" interchangeably with "heart." In the OT the "heart" (לֵב *lēb*) is the seat of understanding. Ephesians has drawn its terminology from Rom 1:21, "they became futile in their thinking" and "their senseless minds [καρδία *kardia* "hearts"] were darkened." Ephesians has expanded the series to involve two forms of mental darkness followed by "hardness of heart" (v. 18). The OT frequently refers to disobedient Israel as hard hearted (Ps 95:8; Isa 6:10; 63:17; Jer 7:26; 17:23).

These phrases fill out the earlier reference to non-Christians as "those who are disobedient" (2:2). Such language seeks to gain an emotional response, not to provide information. All three descriptions are consequences of being separated from the "life of God"

---
249. Bouttier, *L'Épître de Saint Paul aux Éphésiens*; Schnackenburg, *The Epistle to the Ephesians*.
250. *Letter of Aristeas* 140; 277; *Sib. Or.* 3.220-35.

(4:18). This expression does not answer the question of whether any trace of God's life remains with those who do not know the creator. Rather, being alienated from the "life of God" describes those who are not participants in the covenant (Eph 2:12). Unfaithful Israelites can also be described with such language as Essene examples indicate, "for futile are all those who do not know the covenant. And all those who scorn his [God's] word he shall cause to vanish from the world."[251]

The concluding clause presents typical examples of pagan vice (v. 19; cf. Rom 1:24). The cover term "impurity" (ἀκαθαρσία *akatharsia*) appears in Essene material as the contrary to the holiness that comes from joining the new covenant community.[252] Unlike Rom 1:24, in which God hands the Gentiles over to immorality, Ephesians makes the Gentiles responsible for handing themselves over to vice. The Greek word that describes their having become callous (ἀπηλγηκότες *apēlgēkotes*) occurs only here in the New Testament and is not widely used elsewhere. Ephesians employs a few standard vices as illustrations—disordered sexual passions, greed, and uncleanness. Their only purpose is to awaken revulsion for the life that believers have left behind.

Verses 20-21 repeat the appeal to follow prior instruction with the unusual phrase "you learned Christ" (ἐμάθετε τὸν Χριστόν *emathete ton Christon*). For some interpreters, the continuation "as truth is in Jesus" suggests an audience familiar with traditions about the teaching of Jesus.[253] Others think Ephesians is combating speculation that separated the heavenly revealer from the earthly Jesus.[254] The text does not explain what is meant by the cryptic expression, though prior catechesis must be implied.[255]

Verses 22-24 are based on Col 3:8-10. They combine two motifs used for conversion: changing clothing (putting off vice, putting on Christ, Rom 13:12, 14; 1 Thess 5:8) and transformation from the old human being (Rom 6:6) into the new (Gal 3:27; Col 3:10). Putting off vices and putting on virtues are commonplace in ethical exhortation.[256] The difficulty with reading the old and the new "man" as Adam and Christ (Rom 5:12-21)[257] is that Paul always defers the believer's conformity to the image of Christ as spiritual Adam to the future resurrection (1 Cor 15:22-23, 53-54; Phil 3:21).

The general exhortation to "be renewed in the spirit of your minds" (v. 23) indicates the end of the intellectual deficiencies of pagan reasoning. The paraenesis in Romans begins with a similar expression: "Be transformed by the renewing of your minds" (Rom 12:2 NRSV). Ephesians has radicalized the inherited images by describing the believer as completely re-created "according to God" (see v. 24).[258] Ephesians omits the term "image" (εἰκών *eikōn*) from Col 3:10. Most interpreters assume that the Greek "according to God" (κατὰ θεόν *kata Theon*) means "according to the likeness of God" (so NRSV). However, Ephesians has shown little interest in the creation speculation of Colossians. The phrase "according to God" is complemented by the virtues that describe God's elect, "righteousness and holiness."[259] It anticipates the phrase in 5:1, "be imitators of God," and is oriented toward the present behavior of believers.[260] The Essene writings also employ the contrast between "deceit" and "truth" to distinguish those who belong to the community from outsiders.[261]

4:25-32. Ephesians shifts to a series of short exhortations, *sententiae*, that describe vices to be avoided and virtues to be cultivated. Colossians 3:8-9, 12-13 provides the core for these verses. Each exhortation describes what is to be done and provides a reason for such conduct. Truthful speech is to replace lying because of the corporate character of Christian life, since all are "members of one another" (v. 25; 4:12, 16; Rom 12:4-5). Verse 15 treated "speaking the truth in love" as key to building up the body of Christ. The connection between anger and work of

---

251. 1QS 5:19-20.
252. 1QS 5:20-21.
253. So Schnackenburg, *The Epistle to the Ephesians* 199.
254. So Schlier, *Der Brief an die Epheser*, 213.
255. Gnilka, *Der Epheserbrief*, 228.
256. On putting off vices, see *Letter of Aristeas* 122; Lucian *Dialogues on Death* 10.8.9. On putting on virtues, see Philo *On the Confusion of Tongues* 31.
257. So Barth, *Ephesians*.
258. Bouttier, *L'Épître de Saint Paul aux Éphésiens*, 211; Gnilka, *Der Epheserbrief*, 229.
259. Schnackenburg, *The Epistle to the Ephesians*, 201.
260. Lincoln, *Ephesians*, 287.
261. 1QS 4:2–5:10.

the devil (v. 27) echoes Gen 4:7 (and 6:11).²⁶² The topic of anger occurs in Greco-Roman moralists, in the Sermon on the Mount (Matt 5:21-22), and in Essene writings.²⁶³ *Testament of Dan* 5:1-2 provides the virtue of truth-telling with a motive clause that includes God's presence to the community and driving Beliar away.

The reference to the reformed thief (v. 28) has no parallel in Colossians but is also traditional (see 1 Cor 6:10; 1 Pet 4:15). The alternative in the second clause, laboring with one's hands, was established by Paul's own example (1 Thess 4:11; 2:9; as part of the apostolic hardship list, see 1 Cor 4:12; against the disorderly who take advantage of communal charity, see 2 Thess 3:6-11). Ephesians has generalized the advice. The motive clause points toward a communal concern, sharing what is gained by such labor with those in need. Exhortations to share appear elsewhere without the reference to earning one's own living (see Rom 12:13; 2 Cor 9:6-12). Such examples might suggest that the apostle merely requires those Christians who are wealthy enough to include fellow Christians among those who receive their benefactions (see 1 Tim 6:17-19).

The need to engage in manual work (v. 28), indicated in the catalogs of Paul's hardships by the phrases "in toil and hardship" (2 Cor 11:27) or "the work of our own hands" (1 Cor 4:12); "working for a living" (1 Cor 9:6); and "worked night and day" (1 Thess 2:9), describes the situation of the majority of believers (1 Cor 1:26). They are to provide for themselves and others rather than seek to live off the largess of wealthy patrons (1 Thess 4:11-12; 2 Thess 3:6-13). Some interpreters suggest that the original warning against stealing also spoke to particular social issues.²⁶⁴ Slaves or other servants were commonly accused of theft (e.g., Titus 2:10; Phlm 18). Thus this advice ensures the respectable behavior of Christians who are not among the elite and whose affiliation with the new religious movement might render them suspect. Verse 29 returns to the opening theme. Concern for what one says, here expressed by the semitism "come out of your mouths,"

is commonplace in Wisdom literature (see Prov 10:31-32; 12:17-19; Sir 5:10-14; 18:15-19). The Essenes required their members to control speech. After warnings against angry speech and lying, the *Rule of the Community* turns to misuse of communal property, retaliation, and then negligent speech.²⁶⁵ Penalties are attached to trivial speech and interrupting one's fellows. The context for this speech among the Essenes is a communal assembly for instruction. Ephesians will refer to assemblies for worship later (5:19). The concern for speech aimed at the religious edification of the hearer suggests conversation among fellow believers, not interaction with outsiders.

The reference to the Holy Spirit (v. 30) interrupts the series of concrete examples. Some commentators treat "and do not grieve the Holy Spirit of God" as a motive clause parallel to "do not make room for the devil" (v. 27) and "as God in Christ has forgiven you" (v. 32).²⁶⁶ As such, it reinforces the exhortation in v. 29. The phrase "grieve the Holy Spirit" is unusual, though 1 Thess 5:18 speaks of quenching the Holy Spirit in the context of communal prophecy. Essene texts refer to "defiling" the Holy Spirit that one has received from God.²⁶⁷ Neglecting the legal and moral precepts of the sect would be the occasion for such defilement. The phrase itself resembles the prophetic word in Isa 63:10, "They rebelled and grieved his holy spirit" (NRSV).

Ephesians indicates that the Spirit was conveyed in a ritual of "sealing." Since Eph 4:5 referred to "one baptism," the rite in question was probably baptism. The final phrase of v. 30, "for the day of redemption," may also be traditional. It introduces a rare note of future salvation into the letter. This passage highlights the effect of the Spirit in the community. Believers are to feel a particular concern for their behavior because it affects the holiness of the community.²⁶⁸

Another effect of incorporation into the Christian community, forgiveness (χαρίζομαι *charizomai*, v. 32), serves as the final motivating clause in this section. Verse 31 opens with a list of vices that Christians will avoid (bitterness, wrath, anger, wrangling, slander;

---

262. Bouttier, *L'Épître de Saint Paul aux Éphésiens*.
263. Plutarch *On Controlling Anger* 452E-464D. See CD 7:2-3
264. Gnilka, *Der Epheserbrief*, 271.
265. 1QS 7:2-11.
266. Fee, *God's Empowering Presence*, 713ff.
267. CD 5:11-12.
268. Schnackenburg, *The Epistle to the Ephesians*, 209.

see Col 3:5, 8). These vices all refer back to anger (ὀργίζομαι *orgizomai*, v. 26) and the behavior it causes. Concern to rise above anger and its manifestations forms a common element in both Greco-Roman and Jewish exhortation. The section concludes with communal love and harmony, virtues that are the opposite of the divisions caused by anger (v. 32; cf. Gal 5:22; Col 3:12-13). God's forgiveness as the motive for Christian forgiveness appears in Col 3:13 (as well as the Lord's prayer; see Matt 6:14).

Though composed of shorter exhortations, this section can be seen as the continuation of the last section. That section concluded with the metaphor of the body of Christ joined together and growing to maturity through love (vv. 15-16). The primary focus of both the virtues and the vices developed in this section can be said to be communal harmony. The audience must remain committed to a way of life that is unlike their previous life as "pagans," a life that accepted greed, sexual immorality, and other evils. Of course, the writer of Ephesians and its readers know that there were philosopher-preachers who sought to turn people away from their irrational accommodation to passions that swamp rational human behavior. True to its Jewish heritage, however, Ephesians assumes that those who are ignorant of the true God will not be capable of any consistent moral insight or activity.

Ephesians expresses an understanding of Christian life that runs throughout the Pauline tradition. Christians have been transformed in Christ. The Spirit of God works in the community of believers to effect a new way of life. At the same time, Christians must be actively engaged in strengthening what they already are. Conversion, baptism, putting off the old and putting on the new human being, and being sealed with the Spirit and freed from sin are not past events whose effects remain, as though the temple of God were a monumental piece of architecture. Rather, they have introduced believers into a new reality, the body of Christ, which is still in the process of growing into its head. Like the body, the development of the whole depends upon, and contributes to, the well-being of individual members.

The reference to the "day of redemption" reminds the audience that human conduct will be subject to divine judgment. However, the primary emphasis of the epistle remains the present life of the community. Relations with others are central to the concrete examples of the new Christian way of life. False speech, anger, theft, bitterness, slander, and the like destroy relationships among human beings. The many faces of anger indicate that ethical maturity is fairly rare. Believers would insist that only God's Spirit can transform us from the old way of life to the new.

Ephesians also recognizes that believers must constantly turn away from sinful behavior. They do not claim to be completely free of passions like the Stoic sage. When anger occurs, it must be put away and not harbored (v. 26). Hanging on to anger or other resentments provides opportunity for the devil. As we have seen from the Essene writings, "the devil" actively leads believers away from God. Though it is easy to think that many of the virtues listed in this section of Ephesians are "for saints only," this section does not support such an approach. All Christians are striving toward the holiness and perfection that are given by the Spirit.

The communal emphasis in Ephesians distinguishes its Jewish heritage from treatment of the same themes by pagan moralists. Virtues are not the result of individual reason and its ability to order human life. Rather, God calls together a community of persons to live in holiness and justice. The earlier section of the letter spoke of the Christian community in which Christians—both Jews and Gentiles—become one as the new human being (2:15). This creation was also predestined to walk in good works (2:10). The ethical section of the letter depicts those works. Their focus on the needs of others, as well as on harmonious relationships, indicates how the communal body grows into Christ. Christian community requires face-to-face involvement with others. The forms of speech being recommended are essential to the maturing of the body of Christ, words to support faith, expressions of love, and forgiveness.

REFLECTIONS

Most of the ethical exhortation in this section is standard fare, as the exegesis demonstrates. The author opens with a characteristically Jewish view of Gentile immorality. Earlier in the letter the Gentile otherness of the addressees formed a central element in the rhetorical affirmations of unity in Christ (2:11). Now those baptized into Christ are encouraged to separate themselves from the immorality of that Gentile past. What does the dualism of ethical conversion mean to contemporary Christians? For some, getting rid of a deluded way of thinking and a life-style marred by lust and greed describes their experience of coming to Christ. We all know that whenever we decide to make a major life change, perhaps to adopt new habits of diet and exercise or emotional and spiritual health, the transition takes time and discipline. Reminders or partners in improvement do not hurt either. Some people become so panicked about their exercise routine that they do not dare take a day or two off even when they need to rest a minor injury. Such compulsion usually spells trouble. Other people make changes that are not enough to make a difference and then announce, "It isn't working." Nutritionists find that many people consume more calories in low fat foods than they did before.

A pre-school teacher tells the story of the four-year-old who was sent to apologize to a child he had hit on the playground. Several minutes later, he struck again. When the teacher called him over, the boy explained, "That's okay. I'll apologize to him later." A major misunderstanding! It took the teacher quite a while to persuade him that hitting another child was never okay. That was not the point of apologizing.

When a pre-school child comes up with a skewed view of the moral universe, teachers and caretakers wonder what the child sees going on at home. We have all overheard the pre-school set solemnly imitating something we say or do, or recognized that the presence of the car-seat witness means a major change in driving habits. The difficulty with the dualism of old and new self is not that we lack old-self vices, bad habits, or lack of charity to get rid of. It is the separation between ourselves and others that the author seems to call for. We have friends and even family members who belong to different religious traditions or who reject all religion. We consider some of them good persons and others "bad apples," but the list does not fall along neat religious lines.

How do we deal with persons whose moral views and conduct we consider wrong? Ephesians 4:20-23 reminds us that we have not been taught to approve everything in the name of charity. When the kids start school, after-school debriefing about who said and did what becomes a major necessity—how to handle another child's misbehavior; when to run to the teacher and when to handle it themselves. In some inner-city classrooms where children go home to violent or disordered situations, debriefing in a morning circle helps the kids clear the emotional air so they can learn. Ephesians does not solve all the dilemmas that arise even on the school playground, but the collection of moral precepts focuses our attention on a key element: truthful speech.

Most of the items in the collection deal with aspects of speech and its impact on human relationships. We struggle constantly over definitions of "free speech," "hate speech" and the like. What is Christian speech? This passage gives us a list of things that it is not. No anger, quarreling, bitterness, ruining the reputation of another, lying, deceit. Christian speech is truthful, helpful, positive, builds up, is kind, has words of forgiveness—a much bigger order than avoiding language about other drivers that one does not wish to hear echoed from the car seat. We have begun to gain public agreement that women and minorities are not required to put up with verbal attacks or harassment in the workplace. Perhaps Christians could contribute to cleaning the verbal air. Christian speech does not mean verbally assaulting others with our religion at every turn. It does mean a higher standard of verbal interaction with others than many of us practice. And perhaps along with that focus on speech should go listening. A wise pastor with a reputation as a great listener once shared his secret. "After the initial greeting," he said, "I never make any statement until I have asked at least three questions and heard the answers."

Tucked into the sayings on anger and speech, we find an exhortation concerning work (4:28). Paul frequently encouraged congregations to follow his example of working at a trade. The alternatives for people who did not belong to the wealthy aristocracy were either criminal activity or living off wealthy patrons. The disdain for the worker in antiquity was such that those philosophers and intellectuals who were not aristocrats generally lived off such benefactors. Paul himself had to defend his way of life against criticism from wealthy Corinthian Christians who thought manual labor degrading to the apostle (1 Cor 9:3-27; 2 Cor 11:7-11). We live in a society where work has been undergoing global changes, not all of them beneficial to us as individuals or as a human community. We live in a culture in which what we do is more likely to define what people think of us as persons than what our family roots are.

Christian theology needs to catch up in the area of work. Ephesians provides two bits of advice that remain significant because they are so general: (a) Do not steal, and (b) the paycheck is not all yours; some has to be given away. Those who say, "I never steal," need to look around their workplace. We may not engage in it, but all sorts of theft goes on. Public officials steal from all of us by abusing privileges meant to help them serve others; workers, both blue and white collar, make off with materials that belong to the company; others—including teachers and ministers—steal by not giving the time and attention to their jobs that they should. We all know the demoralizing effect that working in such an environment has on us. The metaphor of our being connected to one another as though we were all parts of one body applies to that community as well.

Pope John Paul II's encyclical *Laborem exercens* (1981) called upon Roman Catholics to engage in serious Christian reflection about the nature of work. On the one hand, work is a spiritual necessity. Our identity as persons is bound up with what we create in working. On the other hand, social and economic systems can generate structures of injustice and inhuman working conditions that destroy human persons.[269] As Christians we need to continually examine the intersection between work and our ethical values.

269. For a discussion of the encyclical and its impact, see Gregory Baum, "Laborem Exercens," in *New Dictionary of Catholic Social Thought*, ed. Judith A. Dwyer (Collegeville, Minn.: Liturgical Press, 1994) 527-35.

Ephesians 5:1-14, Live as Children of Light

COMMENTARY

References to God and Christ link 5:1-2 with 4:32. A list of vices follows (vv. 3-5). The warning against being deceived contrasts "those who are disobedient" (v. 6) with "children of light" (v. 8). The section ends with a liturgical fragment celebrating Christ as light (v. 14). Some interpreters treat vv. 1-2 as the conclusion of the previous section. Others treat all of vv. 1-5 as part of the previous section, beginning a major section with "let no one deceive you" (v. 6) and continuing through v. 21. Lists of vices, however, do not typically open sections of paraenesis. Therefore, 5:1-2 must introduce the list.[270] The *UBSGNT* avoids that difficulty by treating 5:1-5 as the conclusion to a section that begins at 4:25. Their second division picks up the parallelism between v. 6, "let no one

270. Gnilka, *Der Epheserbrief*, 242.

deceive you," and v. 15, "be careful then how you live." Since vv. 15-21 introduce a new image, the wise and the foolish, it is preferable to treat them separately as the transition between the general exhortation and the household code of 5:22–6:9.

Ephesians 5:3-8 draws on Col 3:5-8, as the following chart indicates:

Figure 4: Eph 5:3-8 and Col 3:5-8

Item	Ephesians	Colossians
vices not even named among Christians	**5:3** sexual immorality and all impurity or greed	**3:5** sexual immorality, impurity . . . and greed
vices of speech to be replaced with thanksgiving	**5:4** indecency and foolish talk or vulgar talk	**3:8** indecent speech
those who have no inheritance in the kingdom	**5:5** every evil or impure or greedy person who is an idolater	**3:5** and the greed (which is idolatry)
God's judgment falls on the wicked	**5:6** for because of these things the wrath of God comes	**3:6** through which the wrath of God comes
contrast past with present	**5:8** once . . . but now	**3:7-8** once . . . and now

---

The vices are arranged in groups of three. They pick up themes from the previous section: impurity and greed (4:19); immorality as a consequence of idolatry (4:18); unguarded, degenerate speech (4:29); and divine judgment (4:30).

Verses 6-14 urge separation from the ways of darkness. These verses echo some of the dualistic language found in the Essene texts and conclude with a liturgical fragment (v. 14) that provides a christological basis for the light imagery.[271]

5:1-5. The graciousness of God (4:32) serves as the motivation for an appeal to be "imitators of God" (μιμηταί τοῦ θεοῦ *mimētai tou Theou*). Encouragement to find and imitate a model was a prominent feature of ancient paraenesis, "Nay, if you will but recall also your father's principles, you will have from your own house a noble illustration of what I am telling you . . . after whom you should pattern your life . . . regarding his conduct as your law, and striving to imitate and emulate your father's virtue."[272] Since the model indicates both what sort of person the young should aspire to be and what they should avoid, advice is typically given in an antithetical form, "not . . . but. . . ."

Paul uses this imitation pattern regularly. Christians may be encouraged to imitate other churches (1 Thess 2:14) or Christ (1 Thess 1:6). However, his most common usage follows the philosophic example of the child imitating a parent. Thus Paul underlines the "father in Christ"/"child" relationship between himself and those churches he founded (1 Cor 4:14; 11:1; Phil 3:17; 1 Thess 1:6). The phrase "as beloved children" in v. 1*b* recalls this pattern. Christians routinely refer to themselves as children of God (Rom 5:5; Gal 4:5-6; 8:15; Phil 2:15; "destined for adoption," Eph 1:5). However, the injunction to imitate God does not appear elsewhere in the NT. Philo does, however, speak of imitating God in the context of those who have power to rule others. They ought to copy God's beneficence: "The best is to use all their energies to assist people and not to injure them; for this is to act in imitation of God, since he also has the power to do either good or evil, but his inclination causes him only to

---

271. So Lincoln, *Ephesians*.
272. See Malherbe, "Hellenistic Moralists and the New Testament," 282-83. For Jewish examples, see *T.Benj.* 3.1; 4.1.

do good. And the creation and arrangement of the world shows this."[273]

Ephesians is not concerned with exercising power over others. Ephesians 4:24 referred to the new human being as "created according to the likeness of God in true righteousness and holiness." This expression develops the motif of the Christian as a new creation in God's image. Therefore, one would expect some account of the virtues that characterize God to follow. The expression "live in love" (περιπατεῖτε ἐν ἀγάπῃ *peripateite en agapē*, v. 2a) meets that requirement. God's love was introduced in the opening eulogy as the cause of election to holiness (1:4). "Love toward all the saints" described the audience in the epistolary thanksgiving (1:15; 4:2, 15-16). God's love is expressed in extending salvation to those separated from God by sin (2:4). The Christian's grounding in love is formed by knowledge of the love of Christ (3:17-19). The general exhortation to love in 5:2 continues with an illustrative clause, "as Christ loved us" (v. 2b). Christ's death as an acceptable self-offering to God provides the concrete example of that love (v. 2c). Ephesians 1:7 uses Christ's death as sin-offering to illustrate the extraordinary graciousness of God in bringing about salvation. The blood of the cross abolished the wall of separation between Jew and Gentile (2:13). This passage uses established formulae to highlight the self-offering in Christ's death (Gal 1:4; 2:20). A more concrete application of the exemplary love of Christ for the community of the faithful occurs when Ephesians applies the image to the traditional motif of the relationship between husbands and wives in 5:25-27.

There is a difference in orientation between the Ephesians vice list (vv. 3-5) and that in Col 3:5-8. Colossians describes the vices as being put to death by conversion. In Ephesians, the vice list describes pagan outsiders (4:17). This passage calls Christians to separate themselves from others in their environment. The term "fornication" (πορνεία *porneia*) includes a variety of illicit activities, including adultery and prostitution (Sir 23:16, 27; Philo *On Joseph* 43-44; *T. Reub.* 1.6; 2.1; 3.3; *T. Iss.* 7.2; 1 Thess 4:3; 1 Cor 6:12-20). Fornication and impurity (ἀκαθαρσία *akatharsia*) often appear together in vice lists (Gal 5:19; 2 Cor 12:21; Col 3:5; 1QS 4:10). Since the other two sins in the list refer to sexual activities, some scholars suggest that "greed" should be understood as unrestrained sexual greed, such as the violation of the command against coveting the neighbor's wife.[274] Ephesians is not merely warning against such behavior (cf. 1 Thess 4:3-8). Rather, Christians are not even to speak of such vices. The conclusion, "as is proper among saints," might be trading on the semantic ambiguity of the term "saints" (ἅγιοι *hagioi*). If translated "holy ones," the expression can refer to "the angels." This dual meaning provides the logical force behind the phrase. Such vices would not belong to speech among the angels.

The second triad includes two clear examples of censured speech: foolish talk and vulgar talk.[275] The Greek word εὐτραπελία (*eutrapelia*, "vulgar talk") has a more positive meaning in common usage than it does in this triad. Usually it refers to "witty" or clever speech.[276] The context in Ephesians indicates that the author has one of the Aristotelian excesses in mind: vulgar or obscene speech. This use of the word may reflect a cultural sense that the proper bearing of a wise person requires seriousness in speech. Persons who are facile with words are less appropriate models than those whose lives exemplify the words they utter: "Let us choose . . . not men who pour forth their words with the greatest glibness, turning out commonplaces . . . but men who teach us by their lives, men who tell us what we ought to do and then prove it by their practice."[277] Or the term may reflect the sectarian emphasis on disciplined speech that one observes in the Essene documents, "and whoever giggles inanely causing his voice to be heard shall be sentenced."[278] The speech of the Essene sectary avoids all vices, "From my mouth no vulgarity shall be heard or wicked deceptions. . . . I shall remove from my lips worthless words."[279]

---

273. Philo *On the Special Laws* 4.34, 186-87.
274. *T. Levi* 14.5-6; *T. Jud.* 18.2; 1QS 4:9-10.
275. Some scholars assume that "vulgar talk" does not refer to speech in general but to ritualized vulgarity that is connected with celebration of mystery cults in antiquity. See Schlier, *Der Brief an die Epheser*, 239; Kreitzer, "'Crude Language' and 'Shameful Things Done in Secret' (Ephesians 5:4, 12)," 51-77. Against such proposals see Lincoln, *Ephesians*, 330).
276. See Aristotle *Nichomachean Ethics* 4.8, 1128a.
277. Seneca *Epistles* 52,8. See Malherbe, "Hellenistic Moralists and the New Testament," 285.
278. 1QS 7:16.
279. 1QS 10:21-24.

Prohibited forms of speech are to be replaced by exhortation or thanksgiving. The philosopher exhorts others to virtue. The Essene turns speech to piety and the saving deeds of God: "With hymns shall I open my mouth and my tongue will ever number the just acts of God."[280] The thanksgiving proposed in Eph 5:4b fits this pattern. Ephesians 1:3-14 provided a concrete example of the type of speech the author has in mind. Ephesians 5:18-20 returns to the topic of communal speech in prayer and praise of God. Thanksgiving is central to the Christian life and prayer elsewhere in Paul's writings (2 Cor 4:15; Phil 4:6; 1 Thess 5:18).

The conclusion also has parallels in the Essene writings. Though the phrase "kingdom of God" is peculiarly Christian (on exclusion from the kingdom, see 1 Cor 6:9-10; 15:50; Gal 5:21), the "inheritance" terminology belongs to the language of Jewish piety. The wicked do not belong to God's covenant, "all those not numbered in his covenant will be segregated, they and all that belongs to them . . . all those who scorn his word, he shall cause to vanish from the world."[281] The righteous receive an inheritance that unites them with the angelic hosts ("sons of the heavens"), "to those whom God has selected he has given them [= righteousness, knowledge of God, and so forth] as an everlasting possession; until they inherit them in the lot of the holy ones. He unites their assembly to the sons of the heavens."[282]

The vices listed are typical examples of wickedness, sexual immorality, impurity, greed, and idolatry (see Wis 14:12; *T. Jud.* 19.1; 23.1; Philo *On the Special Laws* 1.23.25). Paul uses these vices in a longer list of those who *will not inherit* the kingdom (1 Cor 6:9-10). Ephesians employs the present tense "has any inheritance in" instead of the future. The Essene examples show that Jews could speak of both present and future participation in the inheritance of the elect.

The vice triad in v. 5 parallels the list in v. 3.[283] The unusual dual genitive in "kingdom of Christ and of God" recalls the references to God and then Christ in vv. 1-2. Verse 5 opens with a peculiar phrase, the second-person plural of the verb "to know" (ἴστε *iste*), followed by the participle γινώσκοντες (*ginōskontes*). The form *iste* may be either indicative or imperative. Most translations opt for the imperative and suggest that the additional participle reflects a semiticizing Hebrew infinitive absolute, hence the translation "be sure of this" (NRSV). However, some scholars treat the finite verb as an indicative that refers back to vv. 3-4, "for this you know." In this case, the participle would refer to what follows in v. 5, and could be translated "recognizing that." This reading makes the general orientation of the paraenesis in this section clearer. The author is not correcting believers who lack holiness that they ought to have but is reinforcing an established Christian way of life.

5:6-14. Ephesians insists on separation between "children of light" and "those who are disobedient." This dualism is characteristic of the Essene writings that have provided parallels for much of the imagery in Ephesians. The Essene texts also show a concern to avoid being deceived. They describe the agent of deceit in mythological terms as the "angel of darkness." The Prince of Lights guides the sectaries: "In the hand of the Prince of Lights is dominion over all the sons of justice; they walk on paths of light. And in the hand of the Angel of Darkness is total dominion over the sons of deceit."[284] Ephesians has not mythologized those who may lead its audience astray. There is no evidence that particular false teachers are in view. The unbelieving Gentile world is a sufficient source of "deception" (2:2-3; 4:17-18). Outsiders may seek to counter a Christian's new life by justifying their vices[285] or by the sort of ridicule and abuse described in 1 Pet 4:3-5.

The image of the wicked as persons who justify their actions by claiming that God does not judge was common in Jewish writing (see Exod 5:9 LXX; Deut 32:47; Wisdom 2; *T. Naph.* 3.1). In Eph 3:6 the author spoke of salvation as making the Gentile converts "sharers [συμμέτοχοι *symmetochoi*] in the promise." Here the same word is translated "be associated with" (v. 7) and warns against

---

280. 1QS 10:23.
281. 1QS 5:18-19.
282. 1QS 10:7-8.
283. On the chiastic structure of Eph 5:3-5, see Stanley E. Porter, "*Iste Ginōskontes* in Ephesians 5:1,5: Does Chiasm Solve a Problem?" *ZNW* 81 (1990) 270-76.
284. 1QS 3:20-22.
285. Schnackenburg, *The Epistle to the Ephesians*, 222.

sharing in the deeds of those who remain outside Christ (cf. 2 Cor 6:14–7:1). In the Essene case, the call for separation from the "sons of darkness" has a clear sociological meaning. Persons become members of a new community, with its own interpretation of the Mosaic law, ritual calendar, worship, and detailed instructions governing the lives of members. Contacts with outsiders are limited. It would be natural to read Ephesians as requiring a similar withdrawal, except that the letter nowhere hints at the kind of social structures required to sustain such a move. Therefore the dissociation required in this passage seems to apply primarily to the activities that characterized the life-style of non-Christians. The emphasis on "fruit of the light" and "pleasing to the Lord" in vv. 9-10 suggests that a Christian's general conduct is in view.

Ephesians may also anticipate that Christians will be active moral agents in their world. They are to "try to find out" (δοκιμάζω *dokimazō*, "discern" or "test") what is pleasing to the Lord (v. 10). This expression implies that believers must determine what is suitable behavior in concrete circumstances. For the philosopher, such moral discernment is the activity of reason.[286] Earlier, Ephesians spoke of the renewal of mind that comes with conversion (4:23). Romans 12:2 treats that renewal as the basis of the ability to discern God's will. Elsewhere Paul also uses the verb *dokimazō* in the sense of taking responsibility before the Lord, who is to come in judgment (Phil 1:10-11). Failure to "discern" what is required will lead to divine punishment (1 Cor 11:28-32).

Christian responsibility is not limited to one's own conduct. Verse 11 moves beyond refusal to participate in evil. Christians should also "expose" (ἐλέγχω *elegchō*) evil deeds. The verb can refer to divine condemnation (Wis 4:20; 2 Esdr 12:32-33). Or sinners can be "convicted" by persons who hold up their sin before their eyes (Lev 19:17 LXX; Sir 19:13-17; 1 Cor 14:24-25). The philosopher moralist also sought to upbraid hearers for their vices in order to effect reform. The philosopher as a good physician of the soul will vary his speech from stinging rebuke to gentle encouragement as suits the condition of his audience.[287]

Who is the audience of the rebuke envisaged by Ephesians? Some say it is fellow Christians in danger of falling back into their former life-style (as in Matt 18:15-17; Gal 6:1).[288] This policy can be found among the Essenes, who have nothing to do with outsiders, "He should not reproach or argue with the men of the pit but instead hide the counsel of the law in the midst of the men of sin. He should reproach with truthful knowledge and with just judgment those who choose the path, each one according to his spirit."[289] Or does Ephesians intend believers to confront outsiders with the evil of their actions? The description that follows in vv. 12-13 suggests that the latter interpretation should be preferred. Although the evils that such people do are not to be spoken of among believers (vv. 3, 12), they can be exposed. (See John 3:19-21 for a similar image.) Ephesians does not indicate what form such a confrontation might take. The epistle presumes that its readers are familiar with the process of conversion in their own experience of moving from darkness to light, from death to life (2:1-2; 4:17-18).[290]

The liturgical fragment that concludes this section (v. 14) clearly marks the transition back to the experience of conversion. The connection between the cryptic phrase "everything that becomes visible is light" and the citation said to illustrate the point is unclear. Ephesians spoke of "eyes of your heart enlightened" to recognize God's offer of salvation (1:18). Essene hymns speak of God "brightening the face" of the righteous or of their teacher: "I give you thanks Lord because you have brightened my face with your covenant. . . . Like perfect dawn you have revealed yourself to me with your light."[291] This passage contrasts the teacher illuminated by God with deceivers who would lead people astray. The hymnic fragment in Eph 5:14*b* identifies Christ as the source of illumination for the righteous.

---

286. Epictetus *Discourses* 1.20,7; 2.23,6.
287. Dio Chrysostom *Orations* 77/78, 38, 42. See Malherbe, "Hellenistic Moralists and the New Testament."
288. So Gnilka, *Der Epheserbrief*, 255ff.
289. 1QS 9:16-18a. See also 1QS 5:24-25.
290. Lincoln, *Ephesians*, 335.
291. 1QH 12[4]:5-6.

The origin of the citation is unclear. Within the epistle, "death" consistently refers to the preconversion situation. Consequently, the fragment seems to be associated with the baptismal imagery of arising from death (Rom 6:4, 13). The Christian remains awake and vigilant in anticipation of the day of the Lord, while others are in darkness or drunken sleep (Rom 13:11-14). Its form is similar to the short fragment in 1 Tim 3:16. Some commentators agree with those patristic authors who saw here images of Jerusalem from Isa 60:1 (also Isa 51:9; 52:1).[292] The Lord has summoned the captive city to awake, be clothed in festal garments, arisen and shine because the light of the Lord's glory has dawned. This imagery recurs in descriptions of the coming messiah.[293] Clement of Alexandria, in his exhortation to the pagans, treats this passage as a word of the Lord.[294]

Other commentators have turned to gnostic texts that picture humanity lost in drunken sleep until the revealer comes from the divine world of light to awaken them.[295] Ephesians was popular among second- and third-century Gnostics. This passage may have inspired the final section of a gnostic hymn that describes the descents of the revealer:

> And I filled my face with the light of the completion of their aeon. And I entered the midst of their prison which is the prison of the body. . . . And I said, "I am the Pronoia of pure light; . . . Arise and remember that it is you who hearkened, and follow your root, which is I, the merciful one, and guard yourself against the angels of poverty . . . and beware of the deep sleep and the enclosure of the inside of Hades." And I raised him up and sealed him in the light of the water with the five seals in order that death may not have power over him.[296]

This gnostic example also suggests a ritual context that included baptism and sealing against the powers of the lower world. It shares the cosmology of Ephesians in treating salvation as exaltation to a realm above the powers of this world. However, Ephesians does not exhibit the sharp dualism of the gnostic author. It does not equate the body with the imprisonment of the soul by passions. Nor does Ephesians show characteristic gnostic tendencies to either ascetic denial of bodily reality or its libertine overcoming. Therefore, gnostic parallels should be treated as dependent upon Ephesians rather than as its source.

This passage illustrates a feature that characterizes much of the ethical exhortation in the New Testament. On the one hand, lists of fairly specific vices indicate conduct that is unacceptable. On the other hand, the virtues to be cultivated are phrased in a more general way, such as love or imitation of Christ or discernment of what is pleasing to God. Unlike groups within Judaism—Pharisees or Essenes, for example—Christians did not attempt to specify the positive obligations of Christian life by interpreting the Law. Consequently, they had constantly to ask what conduct pleases God in every particular situation. Hans Dieter Betz has suggested that uneasiness about Christian freedom in the face of human sinfulness led the Judaizers in Galatia to advocate adopting Jewish customs.[297] Ephesians has learned from the apostle Paul that the law created a separation among people, that Christ has abolished.

Because Ephesians is not addressed to a particular crisis, its exhortation only expresses the guiding images of the Christian life. However, this section indicates that Christians take moral renewal seriously. They strive for a perfection that does not even need to speak of the evils that typify life without Christ. This injunction does not imply withdrawing from the world. The exhortation to name evils that are being hidden by others shows that Christians must act as a form of moral conscience for fellow believers. Though the two positions—not speaking of evils and exposing them—might appear contradictory at first glance, the philosophical moralists indicate how the two can work together. Vices do not have to be named or spoken of in a community where they do not occur. Anyone who has mastered a subject no longer thinks of the lessons that were required in order to do so. For the ancient moralists the ethical life is best learned by imitation rather than verbal

---

292. Bouttier, *L'Épître de Saint Paul aux Éphésiens*, 230.
293. *T.Levi* 18.3-4; *T.Jud.* 4.1.
294. Clement of Alexandria *Exhortation to the Greeks* 9.84.
295. Schlier, *Der Brief an die Epheser*, 239-40.
296. *Ap. John* II 31, 2-25.

297. Betz, *Galatians*, 5-8.

instruction. Nonetheless, verbal exhortation is needed. Such exhortation may take the mild form of reminder and encouragement as in Ephesians. Or it may take the harsh form of reprimand (as in 1 Cor 5:1-13, for example). The "wise" who serve as models for imitation do not need either type of parenesis. But they do have an obligation to instruct others. Ephesians has applied this model to the Christian life.

REFLECTIONS

The last section of Ephesians ended with a call to forgive "one another as God in Christ has forgiven you"—in other words, to imitate Christ in the act of forgiveness. This theme is continued in this section of the letter by the command to be "imitators of God" (5:1).

How do we "imitate" God? Most Christians look to the Gospels, to the actions and teachings of Jesus for a pattern. The command to love enemies (Matt 5:43-48), the petition "to forgive us . . . as we have been forgiven" in the Lord's prayer (Matt 6:12), and the parable of the unforgiving servant (Matt 18:21-35) are examples of how to shape the Christian life of love and forgiveness in imitation of the divine example. Moreover, Jesus' death appears as a motive for Christian love in the Johannine tradition (John 13:34; 15:11-17; 1 John 4:7-11).

So when Ephesians calls on Christians to imitate the sacrificial love of Christ, we are on familiar ground (even though Paul's letters ordinarily speak of God's love on the cross independently of the command to love others; see Gal 2:20; 5:14). How do we put life into such familiar Christian slogans? Mere repetition induces amnesia. The gospels turn to narrative to make their point. First John takes another tack. It asks readers to reflect on the love that is the very nature of God. The parable of the unforgiving servant contains a pointed lesson. Not all forgiveness transforms a person's behavior. It should do so, but it does not.

So we need to feed the imagination with powerful stories of the transforming effects of forgiveness and love. June Sprigg tells a delightful tale of three months spent living with the remaining elderly Shaker ladies at Canterbury Shaker Village in New Hampshire between her sophomore and junior years of college. She had been permitted to play their piano and small organ. When she was refused permission to play the grand organ, she went to her room and threw a toddler-sized fit—with a few added curse words that toddlers do not know. To her horror she realized that the elderly Sister Bertha in the office was on her way over: "The glint stayed in her eye, and I thought, God help anyone who really does hurt someone she loves. . . . I didn't know then . . . what she heard in my blubbering explanations that sometimes I just lost it. . . . The main point was, everything was all right. The thing I had dreaded most had happened, and it was still all right. Bertha had seen the worst side of me, and she loved me just the same. . . . God was in Heaven, all was right with the world."[298] The world is all right when people like sister Bertha imitate God by seeing the worst side and loving all the same. Those who have never been on the receiving end of such love will have a difficult time extending it to others.

This human example is an analogy for what Ephesians invites us to meditate on: God's love exhibited in the death of Jesus. Many people today will admit that they would prefer not to meditate on the cross. They are not alone. Paul knew some Christians in Corinth with a similar mental block (1 Cor 1:18-31). For twenty-first-century Americans the culture of pleasure has made the language of sacrifice dysfunctional. Yet it is impossible to speak about Jesus as God's love for us without it. God's Son gave up being God to die on a cross, to paraphrase the famous hymn in Phil 2:6-11. Ignatius of

---

298. June Sprigg, *Simple Gifts: Lessons from Living in a Shaker Village* (New York: Random House, 1998) 208-10.

Loyola concludes the *Spiritual Exercises* with directions for meditation to gain a sense of God's love. He suggests beginning much as this letter did, by recalling all the benefits received from God. He also points out that love only works when it is expressed in deeds more than in words. So contemplating benefits received should lead to consideration of what we can give back to the source of the general blessings of creation and salvation as well as the source of our individual talents.[299]

Ephesians moves to this second dimension, that love returns to God, by drawing upon the traditional patterns of moral exhortation. For an ancient reader, the language of sacrifice in 5:2 would evoke the idea of a sphere of sacred holiness that had to be kept pure because it belonged to God. Animals who were to be sacrificed had to be without blemish (Lev 1:3; 4:32). Persons entering the sanctuary might be required to wash or to wear special garments. Sometimes those seeking to consult a god or goddess at one of the oracle shrines also had to refrain from sex or food or other activities for several days beforehand. Moses had to warn the people of Israel away from Mount Sinai. He also told them to engage in purifying themselves by putting on clean clothing and abstaining from sex (Exod 19:12-15). People thought of God's holiness as a powerful force that had to be respected. An unholy offering would provoke God to destroy the person who made it (Lev 10:1-3). Both Jews and non-Jews would recognize that only special words could be spoken or sung in the context of a sacred offering. Ephesians combines that image with the idea that, as children of God, Christians belong to the heavenly regions, to light and not darkness. Once again the moral universe is described in dualistic categories that many modern Christians consider unrealistic. Communities, like that of the Shakers, that attempt to create zones of light independent of the world and its ways, are dead or dying. Of course, there is no evidence that Ephesians expected Christian "children of light" to move out of the world to separate community groups as the Jewish Essene sect had done. But Sprigg discovered a spirit among the Shakers that was not unrealistic at all: "They were human beings, not impossibly perfect saints. . . . Doing unto others as I would have them do unto me didn't mean that I had to be perfect or a Goody Two-shoes, or a Holy Roller, thank God. I could be my own real self. In fact God wanted me to be my own real self. All I needed was to keep in mind that kindness is never a mistake, that we all make mistakes, and that forgiveness is the key."[300] This summary may serve as a key for modern Christians wondering what it means to live in the light of Christ.

299. Ignatius of Loyola, *Spiritual Exercises*, secs. 230-37, in *Personal Writings*, 329-30.
300. Sprigg, *Simple Gifts*, 11.

Ephesians 5:15-21, Wisdom as Thanksgiving

COMMENTARY

This section opens as though it would conclude the paraenesis. It combines a summons to conduct oneself wisely (vv. 15-18a) with a quasi-doxology (vv. 18b-20). An additional hortatory phrase (v. 21) permits the author to insert the household code (5:22–6:9) before the peroration (6:10-20). Ephesians 5:15-20 consists of a series of "not . . . but" clauses derived from material found in Colossians, as the following table indicates:

> Figure 5: Eph 5:15-20 and Col 3:16-17; 4:5
>
> | Item | Ephesians | Colossians |
> |---|---|---|
> | not like the unwise | 5:15 how you walk, not like the unwise but the wise | 4:5 walk in wisdom toward those outside |
> | the times are evil | 5:16 employing the opportunity because the days are evil | 4:5 employing the opportunity |
> | forms of worship | 5:19a speaking to one another in psalms and hymns and spiritual songs | 3:16b instructing one another in all wisdom, singing psalms, hymns, spiritual songs |
> | sing to God from the heart | 5:19b singing and praising the Lord with your hearts | 3:16c singing with thanks in your hearts to God |
> | giving thanks to God | 5:20 giving thanks always for all things in the name of our Lord Jesus Christ to God the Father | 3:17 and everything whatever you do . . . all things in the name of the Lord Jesus, giving thanks to God the Father through him |

Ephesians draws on other traditional material in verses 17b-18a (see Prov 23:31; T. Jud. 14.1; Rom 12:2). The two sections highlight the purposes for which the new community exists: praise of God's graciousness (1:6, 11) and walking in good works (2:10). "Filled with the Spirit" forms a transition between the sapiential "not . . . but" clauses and the worship section. On the one hand, "filled with the Spirit" serves as the antithesis to being drunken. On the other hand, the Spirit inspires worship and thanksgiving. Groups of three structure the material: (a) three "not . . . but" phrases (vv. 15b, 17-18); (b) three types of music (v. 19a); and (c) three participial phrases in the worship section: speaking to one another (v. 19a), singing and praising (v. 19b), and giving thanks (v. 20).

The contrast between the wise and the foolish person (vv. 15-16) is common in wisdom material (see Prov 4:10-14). The Essenes internalized the feud between the spirits of light and darkness as the contest between Wisdom and Folly: "Until now the spirits of truth and injustice feud in the heart of man and they walk in wisdom or in folly."[301] Though Ephesians does not speak of a contest between spiritual beings, it does reflect elements in the apocalyptic scheme. The warning "be careful how you live" highlights the constant danger that the righteous might be deceived in the present evil age. Essenes separate from "men of sin" by careful observance of the law, "to convert from all evil and to keep themselves steadfast in all he prescribes in compliance with his will . . . those who persevere steadfastly in the covenant."[302]

The Essene covenant community protects its members in an age ruled by Belial, "all those who enter in the Rule of the Community shall establish a covenant before God in order to carry out all that he commands and in order not to stray from following him for any fear, dread or grief that might occur during the dominion of Belial."[303] Ephesians makes

301. 1QS 4:23-24.
302. 1QS 5:1, 4.
303. 1QS 1:16-18.

a similar point in 5:16. The verb ἐξαγοράζω (*exagorazō*; NRSV and NIV, "make the most of") means to purchase or to "buy back"—that is, "redeem"—something (as in Gal 3:13; 4:5). The meaning of the verb with the noun "time" is not clear. The Greek καιρός (*kairos*, "time") can refer to a particular time, a favorable time, or even the time of crisis in an eschatological sense (as in Rom 13:11). Ephesians picks up the eschatological overtones of *kairos* by adding the clause "because the days are evil" (v. 16*b*). The expression suggests that the times themselves require one to be cautious.[304]

The need for wisdom is intensified by the end-time perspective (vv. 17-18). While "being drunk" (μεθύσκομαι *methyskomai*) and its resulting folly is a common item in vice lists (see Prov 23:29-35), the blindness or unconsciousness of a drunken humanity also appears as a metaphor in eschatological contexts (see Rom 13:11-13; 1 Thess 5:1-10). The antithesis, "being drunk" or "being filled with the Spirit," has antecedents in the story of Hannah (1 Sam 1:12-18). Similarly, the crowd suspects the apostles of drunkenness on Pentecost (Acts 2:13).[305] There is no reason to assume that Ephesians speaks of abuses in the church (as was the case in 1 Cor 11:21-22)[306] or attraction to cultic orgies attached to a pagan god like Dionysus.[307] The positive injunction "be filled with the Spirit" (πληροῦσθε ἐν πνεύματι *plērousthe en pneumati*) supports a chain of participles used as examples of Spirit-filled behavior.

Entry into the Essene covenant involved being cleansed of sin by the Spirit: "He will sprinkle over him the Spirit of Truth like lustral water (in order to cleanse him) from all the abhorrences of deceit and from the defilement of the unclean spirit."[308] Humans were divided according to which spirit ruled their hearts: "For God has sorted them into equal parts until the appointed end and the new creation . . . so they decide the lot of every living being in compliance with the spirit there is in him [at the time of] the visitation."[309] Likewise, Christians received the Holy Spirit upon joining the church as the guarantee of their inheritance (1:12-14). The Spirit provides believers access to God (2:18) and dwells within them (3:16; 4:4).

Praise and thanksgiving (vv. 19-20) are the proper responses to what God has done in the believer (1:14; 3:20). Essene writers would agree that praising God is essential to the life of the righteous: "He shall bless his Creator in all that transpires . . . [and with the offering] of his lips he shall bless him."[310] It is not possible to distinguish the various types of song referred to. Hymns and liturgical fragments are often cited in didactic contexts by NT authors (e.g., Phil 2:5-11; 1 Tim 3:16).

Since v. 21 introduces the household code material, some commentators treat it as the beginning of that section. However, the participle belongs in the chain begun earlier. The phrase "reverence for Christ" reflects the OT "fear of God" (Ps 36:2 in Rom 3:18). Paul uses the verb ὑποτάσσω (*hypotassō*, "be subject") for obedience to rulers in Rom 13:5 (also 1 Pet 2:13; Titus 3:1). Some interpreters assume that Ephesians created v. 21 from the opening of the household code in Col 3:18. Others suggest that it represents a variant of NT exhortations to humility within the community (e.g., Rom 12:3, 10; Gal 6:2-3; Eph 4:2; Phil 2:3-4).

Essene writings provide another context in which the expression "submit" or "be subordinate" applies. Unity is a function of the ranks that members occupy: "No one shall move down . . . nor move up from the place of his lot. For all shall be in a single Community of truth, of proper meekness, of compassionate love and upright purpose, towards each other."[311] Order determined by the individual's insight and holiness governs relationships between members of the community, "each one obeys his fellow, junior under senior. And their spirit and their deeds must be tested year after year in order to upgrade one according to the extent of his insight and the perfection of his path. . . . Each should reproach his fellow in truth, in meekness and in compassionate love."[312] There is no such ranking in Ephesians. However, the Essene example also shows that "be subject to one

---

304. So Schnackenburg, *The Epistle to the Ephesians*, 233.
305. Against this connection, see Lincoln, *Ephesians*, 343
306. Contra Schlier, *Der Brief an die Epheser*, 246; Gnilka, *Der Epheserbrief*, 269.
307. Contra Mussner, *Der Brief an die Epheser*, 148.
308. 1QS 4:21-22.
309. 1QS 4:25-26.
310. 1QS 9:26.
311. 1QS 2:24-25.
312. 1QS 5:23-25.

another" is connected with virtues of humility and mutual correction as well as rank. Therefore, the expression in Ephesians indicates how exhortation is to be conducted within the church.

Both praise of God and conduct pleasing to the Lord require the assistance and participation of others. "Be subject to one another" as shorthand for the practice of mutual instruction and encouragement requires lives open to the observation and participation of others. Ephesians never forgets that believers are a single body in Christ. Its growth depends upon the well-being of all members. Mutual responsibility is particularly striking in churches like those addressed by Ephesians. The death of the apostles left others to carry on without the strong presence of an apostle-founder.

Believers must attend to their own conduct. Ephesians never suggests that such attention requires detailed moralism and legal observance. It does require consistent turning away from the old way of life. At the same time, this community exists as a worshiping community. Members must gather to offer praise and thanksgiving to God through Jesus Christ. Like their Jewish contemporaries, these Christians recognize that worshiping God and the blessing of God's presence in the Spirit are the keys to wisdom.

REFLECTIONS

The conclusion to chapter 5 injects an eschatological note. Evils were thought to increase as the world came to an end (e.g., Mark 13:3-23). But like the conclusion to the Lord's prayer, "do not bring us to the time of trial, and rescue us from the evil one" (Matt 6:13 NRSV), the reference to "evil days" (5:16) could be generalized to apply to any time or culture in which Christians find faith under pressure. Ephesians speaks of "wise" and "foolish" instead of the more apocalyptic "children of light" and "children of darkness," thus drawing upon the wisdom tradition. In this tradition, fools are ignorant of God (Psalm 14), and wisdom is life's greatest asset: "For the protection of wisdom is like the protection of money, and the advantage of knowledge is that wisdom gives life to the one who possesses it" (Eccl 7:12 NRSV). For the Jewish tradition, the wisdom that orders the world and calls the wise to banquet at her table (Prov 8:1–9:12) is embodied not only in the collections of general maxims, but also in the Torah. Sirach reflects the convergence of these two traditions in the second century BCE: "If you desire wisdom, keep the commandments and the Lord will lavish her upon you" (Sir 1:26 NRSV).[313] When Eph 5:17 exhorts the audience to avoid folly by seeking the will of the Lord, does the writer assume that they will go to Scripture, even though Christ has ended the binding force of the commandments (2:15)? Does he include, as the earlier wisdom writings do, the broad sweep of human experience and maxims from the general wisdom of the ancient Near East? Appeals to Scripture in the moral exhortation of both the Pauline and deutero-Pauline letters are so rare that one cannot be certain of the first. Use of maxims and ethical arguments that are common currency in the Greco-Roman studies suggests a positive reply to the second question.

So Christians today must incorporate the wisdom about human nature, society, and moral imperatives of their time into ethical deliberation. Modern medicine has revolutionized much of our understanding of life and death. We no longer think that women who find themselves unable to conceive a child are cursed by God. Instead, we face the question of how to choose appropriate medical intervention. We are on the threshold of a revolution in genetic testing that will require Christians to think long and hard about what knowledge is worth having. In other cases, medicine has given us clearer answers. We know that addicts need specialized help to break the physiological and psychological chains of addiction. They are not able to completely control

---

313. Brueggemann, *Theology of the Old Testament*, 689-90.

their actions. We know that persons with depression or bipolar disorder may commit suicide. But their families are no longer run out of the church. Nor do we conclude that the suicide is in rebellion against God. We understand that human actions have an impact on the environment, so we recognize that God's command to "fill the earth and subdue it" (Gen 1:28) cannot be a license to wipe out the diversity of God's creation. Our faith tells us to seek "all that is good and right and true" (Eph 5:5). Even when we disagree about the right thing to do in a particular situation, we should be trying to promote what is good.

The section concludes with public Christian speech, the language of worship. Psalms are included in the mix. What other hymns and songs are envisaged, we do not know. Though we are accustomed to think of music in the context of liturgical prayer, we do not always think singing necessary to forming a Christian character. Music was central to the Shaker experience. The famous dancing that brought believers closest to angels ended so long ago that in 1972 Sprigg met only one sister who had witnessed that tradition. "She said that dancing Believers looked like 'angels,' and she spoke with respect and awe of the effect of the dance on the faithful Believers, who found blessed unity in their efforts to move as one."[314] Shaker hymns remain. Some, like "Simple Gifts," have become secular hits, causing some consternation to Believers. Worldly fame does not regard the religious message of the hymn that the "right place" is living out Mother Ann's gospel.[315] These Shaker examples remind us that the songs of Christian worship are not individuals singing to themselves or performances by the choir. They are another way of drawing the community together in its common faith.

---

314. Sprigg, *Simple Gifts*, 85.
315. See the liner notes to the hymn in Joel Cohen with the Shakers of Sabbathday Lake, the Schola Cantorum, and The Boston Camerata, *Simple Gifts: Shaker Chants and Spirituals,* Erato Disques, 1995. No. 4509-98491-2.

Ephesians 5:22–6:9, Household Code

COMMENTARY

This section adopts a pattern of instruction on duties of household members from Col 3:18–4:1 (also see 1 Pet 2:18–3:7; Titus 2:1-10). The Stoic philosopher Hierocles detailed duties to gods, city, and household.[316] Other such descriptions occur in both Greco-Roman and Hellenistic Jewish writers.[317] Seneca wrote: "How a husband should conduct himself towards his wife, or how a father should bring up his children, or how a master should rule his slaves, this department of philosophy is accepted by some as the only significant part."[318] Comparative material extends back to Greek authors on household management and forward to neo-Pythagorean schools as well.[319]

Most scholars agree that the household code came to NT writers from Hellenistic Jewish sources. Some exegetes detect an apologetic accommodation to larger social mores in the household codes. Conversion by inferior members of a household could be viewed as dangerous insubordination. The attention paid to women and slaves in 1 Peter suggests that such exemplary behavior is being recommended in order to ameliorate tensions that adherence to the new sect is causing.[320]

---

316. See Abraham J. Malherbe, *Moral Exhortation: A Greco-Roman Sourcebook* (Philadelphia: Westminster, 1986) 85-104.
317. E.g., Greco-Roman writers: Cicero *On Duties* 1.17, 58; Dio Chrysostom *Orations* 4.91. Hellenistic Jewish writers: Pseudo-Phochylides 175-230; Philo *On the Posterity and Exile of Cain* 181.
318. Seneca *Epistles* 94.1; see Malherbe, *Moral Exhortation,* 127.
319. See Aristotle *Politics* 1235b 1-14; Xenophon *Household Management.* See also Dibelius and Greeven, *An die Kolosser, Epheser, an Philemon,* 48-50; Malherbe, "Hellenistic Moralists and the New Testament," 204-13; David L. Balch, "Neopythagorean Moralists and the New Testament Household Codes," in Haase, *Aufstieg und Niedergang der römischen Welt* II 26/1, 380-411.
320. So David L. Balch, *Let Wives Be Submissive: The Domestic Code in 1 Peter,* SBLMS 26 (Atlanta: Scholars Press, 1981) 63-80.

A wisdom text from Qumran includes instruction for husbands and wives after comments on the appropriate honor due one's parents.[321] The addressee is a poor person who might think that true piety is beyond his grasp. Unfortunately, the text is too fragmentary to determine what the sociological dynamics behind this reference to the addressee as poor might have been. The NT examples are atypical in addressing subordinate parties in the household first. In 1 Peter, a subsequent word to slave masters is lacking. That omission may reflect the socioeconomic situation of its community.

Colossians 3:18–4:1 provides single sentence instructions for each group except slaves, where the advice is expanded to include obedience to the heavenly Lord. In taking over the material from Colossians, Ephesians reformulates it to indicate that all parties are Christian. The most striking interruption of the parallel clause form comes in the address to husbands (vv. 25-32). That digression concludes with a statement that addresses both husbands and wives (v. 33).

Since the other Christian household codes invoke Christ either as the Lord to whom obedience is paid (Col 3:23) or as the model in suffering unjust treatment (1 Pet 2:18-25), the Christ and church application here probably originated as an example of subordination (Eph 5:23-24). Most conventional discourse on the topic of household management was addressed to males, for whom harmonious governing of the household and ability to rule were closely related.[322]

Though attached to the exhortation of slaves, Col 3:25 constitutes an independent judgment saying, which may have been intended to refer to the unjust masters.[323] Ephesians 6:9 read Col 3:25 in that sense and relocated the warning about divine impartiality to the end of the saying addressed to the masters. Two levels of development are evident in the rest of the household code: first, OT citations and comments to husbands (5:30-31) and children (6:2-3); second, the ecclesial imagery of Christ as head of the body (5:28-32; see also 1:22-23; 2:16; 3:6; 4:15-16, 25). The addition of OT citations is independent of the "body of Christ" ecclesiology. First Peter uses OT examples in its address to slaves and women. In the former case, OT allusions are associated with Christ as suffering servant. In the latter, Sarah is the exemplary holy woman. Such developments suggest that the household code material was used in catechesis. The audience of Ephesians would recognize this section of paraenesis as part of its own tradition.

5:22-24. Verse 22 lacks a verb. The participle "being subject" (ὑποτασσόμενοι *hypotassomenoi*) can be supplied from v. 21. The same verb can be used for subjection to authorities and masters or for voluntary subordination on the part of those who might otherwise command respect (1 Pet 5:5).[324] The household codes presuppose that Christians will subordinate themselves to others, as do the exhortations to obey civil authorities (Rom 13:1; Titus 3:1; 1 Pet 2:13). Of course, Christian women, slaves, or children cannot be subject to the religious opinions of husbands, masters, or parents if the latter oppose Christian faith.

Two parallel statements about the wife's subordination to her husband (vv. 23*a*, 24*b*) frame the two statements about the church (vv. 23*b*, 24*a*). The opening metaphor, "husband is the head of the wife," echoes Paul's use of "head" for an order of hierarchical subordination in 1 Cor 11:3. Ephesians 5:23*b* refers Christ's position as "head" (κεφαλή *kephalē*) to his role as savior. The depiction of Christ's exaltation as head (*kephalē*) of the church in 1:20-23 highlighted the cosmic dimensions of salvation. The question of how far to push the metaphor is raised by the juxtaposition of husband as head (*kephalē*) of his wife with Christ as head (*kephalē*) of the church. Some interpreters point to 1:20-23 as evidence that the image should be referred to the power that Christ exercises on behalf of those who are members of his body. Others attempt to push the effect of the metaphor further. Insofar as the husband's authority is compared to that of Christ, the phrase "in everything" (ἐν παντί *en panti*) does not require wives to accept degrading or unworthy (i.e., unchristlike) forms of subjection.

---

321. 4Q416 3:15-19, parents; 4:2, wife
322. See Balch, *Let Wives Be Submissive*, 36-40.
323. So Barth and Blanke, *Colossians*, 445-47.
324. See *Letter of Aristeas* 257; Barth and Blanke, *Colossians*, 433.

Figure 6: Eph 5:22–6:9 as Household Code

Item	Ephesians	Colossians and other parallels
to wives	**5:22** wives [be subject, from v. 21] to your own husbands as to the Lord	**Col 3:18** wives, be subject to your husbands as is proper in the Lord
	5:33*b* let the wife respect her husband	**1 Pet 3:1** likewise, wives be subject to your own husbands
		Titus 2:4-5 train young women to be loving of their husbands, loving of children . . . subject to their own husbands
reason for conduct	**5:23-24** husband head of wife as Christ is head of church [his body, Christ its savior]; church subject to Christ, wife subject to husband in everything	[**1 Cor 11:3** head of every man is Christ; head of a woman, her husband; head of Christ, God]
		Titus 2:5 that the word of God might not be slandered
		1 Pet 3:1*b*-2 unbelieving husbands may be won over without a word by reverent and chaste behavior
		[**1 Pet 3:3-6** expansion: inner virtue to replace outward adornment; follow example of holy women such as Sarah; do right and have nothing to fear]
to husbands	**5:25-27** husbands, love your wives, as Christ loved the church and gave himself up for her	**Col 3:19** husbands, love your wives and do not be harsh with them
		1 Pet 3:7*a* likewise, husbands live considerately (with your wives) as the weaker vessel, bestowing honor on the woman

Figure 6: Eph 5:22–6:9 as Household Code, *cont.*

	[**vv. 26-27** expansion: Christ cleanses church, presents her holy and unstained]	[cf. **1 Pet 3:2-6**, holiness of the virtuous wife]
	5:33a let each one love his wife as himself	
reason for conduct	**5:28-32** therefore husbands ought to love their wives as their own bodies; the one who loves his wife loves himself, no one hates his own flesh, but nourishes and cherishes it as Christ does the church, because we are members of his body [cites Gen 2:24 exegical comment, vv. 31-32]	**1 Pet 3:7b** because you are fellow heirs of the grace of life, so that your prayers may not be hindered
to children	**6:1** children, obey your parents in the Lord, for it is just	**Col 3:20** children, obey your parents in everything for this is pleasing to the Lord
reason for conduct	**6:2-3** cites Exod 20:12 + comment, "this is the first commandment with a promise"	
to fathers	**6:4** fathers, do not provoke your children to rage but nourish them with education and knowledge of the Lord	**Col 3:21** fathers, do not provoke your children
reason for conduct		lest they become discouraged
to slaves	**6:5-7** slaves obey your lords according to the flesh with fear and trembling, in your single heartedness, as to Christ, not with eye-	**Col 3:22-23** slaves, obey in all things your lords according to the flesh, not with eye-service as pleasing people but in single-heartedness,

Figure 6: Eph 5:22–6:9 as Household Code, *cont.*

	service as pleasing people, but as slaves of Christ, doing the will of God from the heart, serving with zeal, as to the Lord and not human beings	fearing the Lord. Whatever you do, work from the heart as for the Lord and not for human beings
		1 Pet 2:18 household slaves, be subject in all fear to your masters, not only to the good and gentle but also to the harsh
		Titus 2:9-10*a* slaves to be subject (ὑποτάσσεσθαι *hypotassesthai*) to their own masters in all things, to be pleasing, not to be obstinate, not thieving, but showing complete, good faithfulness
reason for conduct	**6:8** knowing that each, whatever good he does, this he will get back from the Lord, whether slave or freeman	**Col 3:24-25** knowing that from the Lord, you will receive back the reward of the inheritance; you serve the Lord Christ. For the wicked will get back the wrong he has done, and there is no partiality
		1 Pet 2:19 for this is as reason for gracious favor if in consciousness of God someone bears pains, suffering unjustly
		[**2:20** explanation: no merit in enduring deserved punishment; God bestows favor on (χάρις παρὰ θεῷ *charis para Theō*) those who do good and endure suffering]
		[**2:21-25** example for imitation: Christ as suffering servant brought salvation from sin and healing]

Figure 6: Eph 5:22–6:9 as Household Code, *cont.*

		Titus 2:10b so that in everything they may adorn the teaching of God our savior
to masters	**6:9a** and lords, do the same things toward them, giving up the threat	**Col 4:1** lords, treat your slaves justly and equitably
reason for conduct	**6:9b** knowing that their Lord and yours is in the heavens and there is no partiality with him	**Col 4:1b** knowing that you also have a Lord in heaven
		[see **Col 3:25b**]

Some commentators have seen this passage as evidence that gnostic images of the spiritual marriage between the soul and the savior influenced Ephesians.[325] Valentinian Gnostics enacted this mythological motif in a rite referred to as the "bridal chamber." That rite reversed the loss of humanity's original androgyny that occurred when Adam was divided from Eve. "His separation became the beginning of death. Because of this Christ came to repair the separation which was from the beginning and again unite the two, and to give life to those who died as a result. . . . But the woman is united to her husband in the bridal chamber."[326]

Another gnostic text refers to this section of Ephesians: "For they were originally joined to one another when they were with the father before the woman led astray the man, who is her brother. This marriage has brought them back together again and the soul has been joined to her true love, her real master, as it is written, 'For the master of the woman is her husband.'"[327] Other gnostic texts speak of the church as a preexistent entity in the divine world (πλήρωμα *plērōma*). "Those which exist have come forth from the Son and the Father like kisses . . . the kiss being a unity, although it involves many kisses. That is to say, it is the church consisting of many men that existed before the aeons, which is called in the proper sense "the aeon of aeons."[328] The Savior's function is to restore the preexistent church to its original unity. Though it is easy to understand why these later gnostic writers would read Ephesians as evidence for their views, the epistle itself never suggests that the church as body of Christ preexists except in God's foreordained plan of salvation. Nor does Ephesians use the gnostic imagery of the soul's reunion with its true spouse, returning instead to the traditional theology of the cross. Christ's death on the cross is the source of both the unity (2:14) and holiness (2:1-10; 5:2) of the church.

5:25-33. Ephesians begins the exhortation to husbands with "love your wives," but omits the conventional "never treat them harshly" found in Col 3:19. Instead, Ephesians develops the body of Christ motif. Christ's self-sacrifice is a model to be imitated (Eph 5:2). Paul spoke of the local church as the pure bride of Christ (2 Cor 11:2). Ephesians assumes that Christ's death brought into being a church that is holy and unblemished. Some interpreters also find references to

---
325. Schlier, *Der Brief an die Epheser*, 264-76; Fischer, *Tendenz und Absicht des Epheserbriefes*, 181-200.
326. *Gos. Phil.* 70,10-19.
327. *Exegesis on the Soul* 133,4-10.
328. *Tripartite Tractate* 58, 22-33.

the bride of the Song of Songs (Cant 5:1).[329] "Washing of water by the word" refers to baptism (1 Cor 6:11; Titus 2:14; 3:5). The "word" was probably the name of Christ used during the ritual. Old Testament images might also be involved. Ezekiel 16:8-14 describes God's bathing the battered nation, anointing and clothing her so that she can enter into a covenant with God, whose glory she now shares. For Ephesians, the church now exists in holiness and glory. The church as "bride" does not depict the eschatological future as a wedding in the manner of Rev 19:5-10.[330]

This extended description of the church as a bride prepared for the wedding highlights what has been accomplished by Christ's self-giving love. Husbands should love their wives with similar devotion. Ephesians does not imply that husbands are agents of holiness for their wives. Holiness comes to individual Christians through their incorporation into the body of Christ.[331] However, the audience might assume that husbands are responsible for instructing their wives in holiness (cf. 1 Cor 14:34-35).[332]

Ephesians resumes with another development of the metaphor (vv. 28-30). The wife is like her husband's own body. A similar sentiment appears in Plutarch, who insists that the husband should not rule his wife in the way in which a master rules property but in the same way that the soul directs the body.[333] When Ephesians speaks of "nourishing" (ἐκτρέφω *ektrephō*) one's own flesh, the letter uses terms that would have been familiar to its audience. Ancient marriage contracts often included the husband's obligation to provide his wife with clothing and nourishment.[334] The conclusion returns to the activity of Christ. Conventional images continue to be transposed into the larger picture of the church's relationship to Christ. The author interrupts his presentation with another insertion of the "we" perspective (v. 30) so that the entire community is designated "body of Christ."

Ephesians uses the term "mystery" (μυστήριον *mystērion*) here, as elsewhere, for the hidden purposes of God (v. 32; cf. 1:9; 3:3; 4:9; 6:19). The Essenes also speak of patient study of the law as learning to perceive the mysteries.[335] The quotation from Gen 2:24 appears in other contexts to bolster the prohibition of divorce (e.g., Mark 10:7-8). Essene legal codes use the related passage from Gen 1:27 in formulating their prohibition against divorce.[336] Ephesians may be familiar with the use of Gen 2:24 in such legal material. However, its exhortation to husbands gives no indication of addressing such issues.

Gnostic speculation regarded the division of Adam and Eve in Gen 2:23-24 as the source of death and human subjugation to the powers of the lower world. The savior comes to reveal that their true home lies above this world. The lost unity is restored when the soul is reunited with a heavenly counterpart. Consequently, gnostic exegetes interpreted Gen 2:24 as Adam's recognition of the heavenly wisdom figure:

> And Adam saw the woman beside him. In that moment the luminous Epinoia appeared, and she lifted the veil which lay over his mind. And he became sober from the drunkenness of darkness. And he recognized his counter-image, and he said, "This is indeed bone of my bones and flesh of my flesh." Therefore a man will leave his father and mother and cleave to his wife and they will both be one flesh. For they will send him his consort.[337]

For the gnostic interpreter the "mystery" (*mystērion*) involves liberation from the domination of the lower powers, including the god of the Genesis story. For some, this freedom implied ascetic renunciation of all passions and desires, since passions were widely regarded as the means by which the demonic powers controlled human behavior. Other Gnostics of the Valentinian school assimilated human marriage to the "bridal chamber" reunification of the soul with its counterpart. This section of Ephesians appears in references to that ritual.[338] The term

---

329. Bouttier, *L'Épître de Saint Paul aux Éphésiens*, 245; J. Paul Sampley, *"And the Two Shall Become One Flesh": A Study of Traditions in Eph 5:21-33*, SNTSMS 16 (Cambridge: Cambridge University Press, 1971) 45-51.
330. Contra Barth, *Ephesians*, 669.
331. Contra Mussner, *Der Brief an die Epheser*, 158.
332. 4Q416 frag. 2 1:6-9.
333. Plutarch *Advice to the Bride and Groom* 142E.
334. Gnilka, *Der Epheserbrief*, 285.
335. 4Q416 frag. 2 4:1.
336. CD 4:21.
337. *Ap. John* II 23, 4-15.
338. See *Gos. Phil.* 64, 31-32.

"mystery" (*mystērion*) refers to the gnostic sacrament, "Indeed marriage in the world is a mystery for those who have taken a wife. If there is a hidden quality to the marriage of defilement, how much more is the undefiled marriage a true mystery!"[339]

These gnostic texts exhibit a widespread concern over the passions that are involved in marriage. Paul's exchange with those in Corinth who viewed all sexuality as an obstacle to perfection provides an earlier example (1 Cor 7:1-31) of concern over these passions. When faced with Christians who resorted to prostitutes, Paul used the dual images of belonging to the body of Christ and becoming "one flesh" with a sexual partner to argue the immorality of that behavior (1 Cor 6:12-20). He argued that marriage is an appropriate vehicle to "glorify God in your body" (6:20) against the radical ascetic view. Ephesians may have taken the "one flesh" language from earlier Pauline instruction, but it shows no concern with the practical issues that Paul was addressing in that earlier context. Nor does Ephesians move in the Valentinian direction of explaining Christian marriage as an image of the heavenly union that restores the soul to freedom from passions and death. Translation of the term "mystery" *mystērion* by the Latin *sacramentum* in some versions of the Old Latin and Vulgate traditions gave rise to use of this text in support of marriage as a Christian sacrament.[340]

Ephesians does not mythologize human marriage. Instead the text limits application of the "mystery" (*mystērion*) to the relationship between Christ and the church (v. 32). The earlier description of the growth of the body into its head through the activity of nerves, tendons, and joints (4:15-16) had established an organic relationship between Christ and the church. This "mystery" (*mystērion*) is another aspect of that saving reality.

The final verse brings the long digression back to the essential point of the exhortation: the relationship between husband and wife. It reaffirms the hierarchical view of marriage and the household in ancient times. Modern translations prefer the more neutral term "respect" for the "fear" or "reverence" (φοβέομαι *phobeomai*) required of the wife.

The ancient author and his readers would presume that she, like all other members of the household, is subject to the authority of its male head. The term "fear" (*phobeomai*) can be used of all social relationships in which subordination is involved. On the other hand, the relationship between husband and wife is different from that between the husband/master and his slaves. The relationship between husband and wife modeled upon Christ's self-sacrificing love indicates a constant concern on the husband's part for her well-being that is not part of other hierarchical relationships in the household.

6:1-4. Ephesians returns in these verses to the traditional shorter exhortation. The Essene example indicates that "children" (τέκνα *tekna*) refers to adults obligated to care for and respect aging parents, "Honour your father in your poverty and your mother in your steps, for like grass for a man, so is his father, and like a pedestal for a man, so is his mother. For they are the oven of your origin, and just as they have dominion over you and form the spirit, so you must serve them."[341] Paul used the obligations of adult children toward their parents to describe relationships between himself and his converts. Paul refuses material support despite his needs. Rather, he insists that the Corinthians show him the love due a father (2 Cor 11:9).[342] As a solicitous father, Paul seeks to present the community to Christ as a pure bride (2 Cor 11:2).

The OT citation (vv. 2*a*, 3) is closer to LXX Exod 20:12 than to Deut 5:16. The conviction that the law teaches its followers "what is right" appears in Jewish apologetic. Attacks on paganism described the evil of disobedient children as the result of idolatry (Rom 1:29-31). This section affirms a conventional understanding of the appropriate relationship between children and parents. Some philosophers admit that children should disobey a father who tries to prohibit the study of philosophy.[343]

Ephesians focuses on the requirement that parents educate their children (v. 4). The

---

339. *Gos. Phil.* 82, 2-6.
340. Schnackenburg, *The Epistle to the Ephesians*, 256.
341. 4Q416 frag. 2, col. 3:16-17.
342. O. Larry Yarbrough, "Parents and Children in the Letters of Paul," in *The Social World of the First Christians: Essays in Honor of Wayne A. Meeks*, ed. L. Michael White and Larry Yarbough (Minneapolis: Fortress, 1995).
343. Barth and Blanke, *Colossians*, 441.

Essene example used the education received from parents as the basis for the obligation of adult children toward their parents. A treatise attributed to Plutarch argues that training one's children in philosophy will guarantee the social conformity that is the object of the household code paraenesis. The author writes: "Through philosophy . . . it is possible to attain knowledge of what is just and unjust . . . that one ought to reverence the gods, to honor one's parents . . . to be obedient to the laws, to yield to those in authority, to love one's friends, to be chaste with women, to be affectionate with children, and not to be overbearing with slaves."[344] Parental affection toward, and education of, children appears in Paul's use of parent/child imagery to describe his relationship to the churches he founded (1 Cor 4:14-21; 1 Thess 2:7-12).[345]

Sirach 30:1-13 recommends strict discipline, constant correction, and beating so that the son will become like his father. However, warnings against excessive harshness can also be found. The Pseudo-Plutarch treatise, for example, contrasts the education of freeborn children to that of slaves. Beating is for slaves. Exhortation, reasoning, and encouragement should be used for children.[346]

Ephesians is less interested in the negative aspects of discipline than in the positive responsibility for instruction. The term "discipline" (παιδεία *paideia*) spans the range between appropriate discipline for young children to the philosophical instruction of the older adolescent (Sir 1:27 connects "fear of the Lord," *paideia*, and wisdom"). The second term, "instruction" (νουθεσία *nouthesia*), refers to verbal correction or education. Thus Ephesians indicates that Christian fathers will be devoted to training their children in virtuous behavior.

6:5-9. The instruction to slaves (vv. 5-8) is more lengthy than that given the other subordinate groups. As Fig. 6 indicates, this material is an adaptation of Col 3:22-25. The conventional Christian modification (slaves serve the Lord, not just human masters) remains. Discussion of how slaves are to be treated appears in all ancient codes.[347] The NT codes are distinctive in addressing slaves directly rather than merely providing rules to the master. Slaves were members of early Christian communities (1 Cor 7:20-24; Gal 3:28; Philemon). Ancient authors often depicted slaves as unreliable, groveling and fawning on masters whom they secretly despise. If the master relaxes his stern discipline or turns his back, slaves become disobedient, steal from the household, and deserve punishment (cf. Luke 12:41-48). The virtuous slave depicted in the Christian household code is not to be lumped with such cultural stereotypes. His or her dignity lies in service to the Lord.[348] An owner might free, in his will, those slaves whom he considered zealous and affectionate.[349] Ephesians shifts that possibility of human reward for devoted service to the Lord, who governs the behavior of all Christians regardless of their status (v. 8).

Judgment brings the slave and the master under the same Lord. The warning that Col 3:25 addressed to wicked slaves has been reformulated in v. 8, which speaks of the Lord's rewarding each person, slave or free, for any good he or she does. The reminder that God is an impartial judge appears at the end, reinforcing this admonition to masters. The partiality that power and position gave individuals in human courts does not apply in front of the heavenly judge (cf. Rom 2:10-11; 2 Cor 5:10). Though the warning addressed to masters appears stronger than that in Col 4:1, the imperatives are weaker. Instead of the positive characteristics—just and equitable treatment—required of masters in Colossians, v. 9a has an unclear admonition to "do the same" (τὰ αὐτὰ ποιεῖτε *ta auta poieite*) and avoid threatening behavior. The latter reflects a common theme in master/slave relationships: the injuries that result from a master's rage. Consequently, philosophers exhort masters to avoid anger in dealing with slaves.[350] A female Pythagorean philosopher, Theano, directs similar advice on treatment of

---

344. Pseudo-Plutarch *Education of Children* 7DE; see Malherbe, *Moral Exhortation*, 30-31.
345. Yarbrough, "Parents and Children in the Letters of Paul."
346. Pseudo-Plutarch *Education of Children* 8F; see also Pseudo-Phocylides 207.
347. Balch, "Neopythagorean Moralists and the New Testament Household Codes," 380-411.
348. Barth and Blanke, *Colossians*, 446
349. *POxy* 494.6; see Lincoln, *Ephesians*, 419. Ancient slave names preserve the paternalism of this ideology with commonplaces such as *philodespotos* ("master loving") and *philokyrios* ("lord loving"). See Dale C. Martin, *Slavery as Salvation: The Metaphor of Slavery in Pauline Christianity* (New Haven: Yale University Press, 1990) 28-29.
350. Seneca *On Anger* 3.24.2; 32.1.

household slaves to young wives. They must avoid mistreating slaves through excessive toil and must restrain the cruel temper that some people exhibit in punishing slaves.[351] Thus the behavior required of Christian slaveowners does not differ appreciably from that enjoined by Hellenistic moralists. The difference appears in the motive clauses. The eschatological understanding that the Lord in the heavens treats all alike undermines a fundamental assumption in the hierarchy of power, that those in power enjoy their position through divine favor.[352]

Christians today often find the household code ethic an awkward accommodation to cultural patterns that would be considered unjust or, in the case of slavery, immoral. First-century readers of Ephesians would find its concern for proper roles and subordination quite natural. Women were expected to defer to their husbands. Adult children continued to be subject to the authority of their parents. In that context, Ephesians directs those in authority to moderate common forms of abusive power. The father's authority over wife and children requires self-sacrifice for their welfare. It does not permit subjecting them to dehumanizing labor or harsh punishments. Ephesians 5:22-33 contains a unique development of the traditional ethic in the extended description of the husband's love and concern for his wife.

[351]. Balch, "Neopythagorean Moralists and the New Testament Household Codes," 405.
[352]. Bouttier, *L'Épître de Saint Paul aux Éphésiens*, 255.

Ephesians presumes households in which both dominant and subordinate parties share a common faith, unlike the situation in 1 Peter where wives and slaves are subject to non-Christians. Since the household was considered the fundamental unit of the larger society, the relationship of Christians to the larger social structures is also at stake. Both Rom 13:1-7 and 1 Pet 2:13-17 incorporate the piece on civic hierarchy and concord that pertains to Greco-Roman treatments of household management.

Most exegetical attempts to detect some radical modification of the ethical injunctions based on special Christian insight or compassion fail to prove their case. Guiding images and motivational statements have been shaped by Christian language and views of the world. But the content and social implications of this paraenesis are not peculiar to the Christian variants. What is the significance of the early Christian appropriation of such ethical commonplaces? Does it lend the authority of Scripture to a particular sociocultural understanding of order or of family? Does the fact that the initial impetus for use of such material may have been apologetic or used to lessen the tensions between converts and those on whom they depended make the material irrelevant in another setting? Ephesians, which gives no evidence of the problems addressed in 1 Peter, would seem to counter that view. For Ephesians, this ethic describes a well-ordered Christian household independent of the views or actions of outsiders.

REFLECTIONS

1. When Eph 5:21 advises Christians to "be subject" to one another, no one bats an eye, but when the same verb is addressed to wives with regard to husbands in 5:22, protest erupts. Someone inevitably asks whether the verb has a different meaning. Popular substitutions, such as "defer to" or "respect," fail to capture the point of the verb. It does imply a hierarchy of command, though the obedience offered may be the voluntary submission of mutual Christian love, as in 5:21 (or 1 Cor 16:16), rather than military-style obedience to the command of a superior officer or government authorities (Rom 13:1). Of course, we do use "respect" to mean "do what they say" when we have police officers involved in schools and youth recreational programs to teach kids to respect law enforcement officers. We also intend that they come away from such experiences with the disposition to obey a command from the police immediately. Why? Because the orders are given in a context where the child's safety or that of a whole group of people is at stake. In an emergency, such as a building fire, the ability to follow orders quietly and quickly can mean the difference between life and death.

There is no inherent problem about the meaning of the verb in Scripture. Nor is it difficult to find social situations in which we expect the same sort of obedience. Without it, lives would be at risk. Couple the verb with the metaphor of the body, which dominates the development of the image in 5:23-24, and the command/response element of the verb becomes evident in another way. What happens when disease or accident cuts the link between the brain and the rest of the nervous system? We all know the answer: paralysis, various bodily movements or words and sounds unintended by the person. We can see the frustration of victims with a body out of control. What generates the hue and cry is not that the metaphor is dead, but that it no longer reflects either the experience or the ideal of respect in marriage for many Christians.[353] Conservatives reply that there would be less divorce and social disorder if the view of husband as head of the family were more widely accepted. Liberals retort that this text has been used to exonerate abuse against women and children. Moderates try to thread the needle by agreeing that families need respect for authority and that it is an abuse of Scripture to require wives and children to suffer violence. They propose a more contemporary view of headship in which husbands and wives share the responsibility according to their particular gifts and expertise. Even children have a role to play when it comes to computers or other modern electronics. The person who understands what needs to be done and has the expertise can direct and help the others. Such arrangements seem an obvious application of Eph 5:21, "be subject to one another."

Insofar as Ephesians employs the conventional wisdom of its time in adapting the household code to Christian use, Christians certainly must consider the social structures and wisdom of their own time in formulating an ethic for marriage. At the same time, we should be conscious of the fairly recent cultural origins of modern family relationships.[354] Merely replacing a patriarchal hierarchy determined by gender with an economic one determined by the size of one's paycheck is no improvement. If authority and responsibility are shared, then consensus and communication are critical virtues. Listening to others is an essential habit. The atomized American family is not a school for such virtues. Early in his freshman year, a Chinese American student commented on a visit to his roommate's house, "I couldn't get used to it. Everyone had their own TV, music system, computer, phone line. They thought I was poor because in our family we share these things." Equating individual liberty with the isolation of personal pleasures hardly represents an advance in ethical insight.

Ephesians has expanded the traditional household code with an elaborate metaphorical argument addressed to husbands (5:25-32). The terms "head" and "body" link the author's vision of Christ as head of a body, the church, with another tradition that applied Gen 2:24 in legal debates over divorce. This passage spawned elaborate mythological developments in later gnostic circles, but seems more rhetorical decoration to today's readers. The basic point that husbands should love and care for their wives with the same concern they show for their own bodies (5:28-29) is the take-home message for most congregations. The sacrificial and sanctifying actions of Christ in regard to the church (5:25-27) make sense as ecclesiology but translated usually emerge in commonplaces about marriage as a path of holiness. Lots of rhetoric to support moral commonplaces. Lincoln addresses this issue by pointing out that the readers of Ephesians were intensely involved in their new relationship with Christ, as is indicated in these verses. They experience themselves as being cleansed, beautified, made holy, and as obligated to respond with an appropriate life-style and thanksgiving. This involvement gives the metaphor its power. He comments, "Since they were

---

353. For a detailed survey of the theological and exegetical debate with concern for modern theories of metaphor, see Gregory W. Dawes, *The Body in Question: Metaphor and Meaning in Ephesians 5:21-33* (Leiden: Brill, 1998).
354. See E. J. Graff, *What Is Marriage For? The Strange Social History of Our Most Intimate Institution* (Boston: Beacon, 1999).

participating in the reality of this relationship, the writer's appeal to them to model their marriages on it, so that those marriages would be an equally real reflection of its dynamic, would have had a powerful effect."[355] In short, if the metaphor limps, it may say as much about our experience of the realities of salvation as it does about our view of marriage.

2. Ephesians 6:1-3 takes the generalized command to obey parents (Col 3:20) as an introduction to the specific commandment from the Decalogue (Exod 20:12; Deut 5:16). This citation indicates that the freedom from rules and regulations, which separated Israel as God's covenant people from Gentiles (2:15), did not apply to the Decalogue. Verse 2b attaches a particular significance to this commandment, the promise of a prosperous life in the land. Both Jews and Gentiles were accustomed to the legal conventions that gave the father of a family authority over the lives of all offspring regardless of their age, even though married children lived in separate households.[356] Such advice could be addressed to adult children in their relationships with parents as well as to those still in the household. Ephesians 6:4 indicates that the author has the latter in view. Anyone who deals with a group of school-aged children quickly finds a wide divergence in their willingness to obey parents or other adults.

Fear of punishment only compels short-term obedience. Parents and other adults sometimes try to discipline children with fear, but as soon as the adults are not looking, such kids are often out of control again. To name how a child's behavior might make parents or others feel is a much more reliable way to discipline. Older adolescents who avoid being drawn into serious trouble by their friends sometimes say that what kept them from going astray was their awareness of what it would have meant to a parent or some other family member if they had been injured or arrested. So Ephesians may have a point in shifting attention from the idea of a covenant curse, found in the earlier commandments, to the idea of promise, appended to this one. However, push the observable benefits of the promise too far into the future, and most young people lose motivation. The best coaches know that even a small taste of success does more to motivate compliance with a tough practice routine than threats or general promises.

Ephesians also modifies the instruction to fathers by dropping the motive clause from Col 3:21b and adding an injunction to provide children with an upbringing that includes knowledge of the Lord. What would such an education entail? If Deut 6:4-7 is the model envisaged, it makes concrete demands on Christian parents. Children have to see that their parents love God with their whole heart, that they know God's Word, and that they are anxious to share it with their children. "Keep these words that I am commanding you today in your heart. Recite them to your children and talk about them when you are at home and when you are away, when you lie down and when you rise" (Deut 6:6-7 NRSV).[357] Many churches, when an infant or an older child is baptized, ask parents to participate in some kind of faith-reflection experience, even if a parent is not a church member. Sometimes, as a result, an unbaptized parent comes to be baptized along with his or her son or daughter. The baptismal rituals in the various churches ask both the parents and the church community if they are willing to assume the responsibility for helping this child to grow up knowing the Lord. A Christian education is not information to be taught. It is a way of life to be lived. What is taught are the Scriptures, the songs, the prayers, and the faith stories that help us do that. But even more important, the parents and the larger community teach by example.

---

355. Lincoln, *Ephesians*, 390.
356. Yarbrough, "Parents and Children in the Letters of Paul," 128n9.
357. Also see Deut 6:20-25; Prov 22:6. For a general discussion of education in ancient Israel, see James L. Crenshaw, *Education in Ancient Israel: Across the Deadening Silence* (New York: Doubleday, 1998).

3. Despite acknowledging slaves as fellow members of the body of Christ, early Christians only condemn the more unpleasant aspects of the slave/master relationship: fawning, deceitful, and lazy behavior on the slave's part and harsh, threatening behavior on the master's. Christ is master of both slave and free Christian. Like the benevolent master, he will reward each according to the good service rendered. Scholars have pointed out that household and managerial slaves could anticipate advancement in the local pecking order; could benefit from an owner's patronage, and even possess names or epithets such as "master-loving" that support the patronal ideology of master/slave relations.[358] Introducing Christ as the master who owns both slave and master reinforces the institution as it was being lived. It does not pose a challenge to it. By affirming Christians on the wrong side of the abolition debate in the nineteenth-century United States, the exhortations to slaves in the New Testament have come to enjoy a prominence in twentieth- and twenty-first-century arguments over the authority of Scripture. Its support for other sociocultural institutions comes into question by analogy with the debate over slavery.

That an expansion of equal rights had to progress to challenge all barriers of race, class, gender, and ethnic group was evident to those involved in the women's movement after the Civil War. The country could not get over that division without a new vision of humanity. Frances Ellen Watkins Harper sounded the call at the 11th National Women's Rights Convention in 1866: "We are all bound up together in one great bundle of humanity, and society cannot trample on the weakest and feeblest of its members without receiving the curse in its own soul."[359] Injustice is fostered if the weakest and feeblest buy into the ideology of the power elite. W. E. B. Du Bois noted the fracture in the souls of black churches between those seeking assimilation to a white-dominated culture of power, education, and business success and those with the recognition that freedom does not yet exist: "Back of this still broods silently the deep religious feeling of the real Negro heart, the stirring, unguided might of powerful human souls who have lost the guiding star of the past and are seeking in the great night a new religious ideal."[360] Ephesians 6:5-9 poses a troubling question for the Christian conscience: Do we stifle the new movements of the Spirit by clothing assimilation to a cultural ideology as service to Christ?

---

358. Martin, *Slavery as Salvation*, 28-34.
359. Quoted in Henry Louis Gates Jr. and Nellie Y. McKay, *The Norton Anthology of African American Literature* (New York: W. W. Norton, 1966).
360. W. E. B. Du Bois, "The Souls of Black Folk," in Gates and McKay, *The Norton Anthology of African American Literature*, 711.

EPHESIANS 6:10-20, PERORATION: BE ARMED WITH THE POWER OF GOD

COMMENTARY

The final section of the letter returns to the theme of divine power, introduced in its opening section (1:19-21). Christ has triumphed over powers at work in the present age (1:21; 2:2; 3:10). His exaltation provides the energy at work in believers and in the ministry of the imprisoned apostle (3:7). Ephesians 6:10-20 is the peroration that brings the letter to a rhetorical conclusion.[361]

The unit falls into three sections. Verses 10-13 contain an opening statement and the command to take up God's weaponry against the hostile spiritual powers (see 2:2; 4:27). Verses 14-17 link items of divine armor with virtues or gifts of salvation. Finally, vv. 18-20 return to the theme of prayer. This prayer asks that the imprisoned apostle continue his bold witness to the mystery of salvation (vv. 19-20; cf. 3:1-13). Readers know the content

---

361. So Lincoln, "'Stand, therefore . . . ,'" 99-114.

of the "mystery of the gospel" (μυστήριον τοῦ εὐαγγελίου *mystērion tou euangeliou*, v. 19; from 1:9; 3:3-4, 9; 5:32). By enlisting their prayers on behalf of the apostle, Eph 6:18-20 indicates that the discourse has brought its audience to maturity as members of the body of Christ.

The call to battle marks a striking departure from the realized eschatology of exaltation above the heavenly powers, which suggested that the victory was already won. Lincoln detects an emotional appeal similar to those calls to battle that were composed for famous generals in the histories of the time.[362] If vv. 10-17 are the general's call to battle, what is the rhetorical impact of the shift in vv. 18-20? The general-orator is already in chains (v. 20)! Suddenly the image has shifted from armed soldier to the bold martyr able to disregard the threats of soldiers arrayed against him (cf. 2 Maccabees 7:1).

Both the image of the conquering general and that of the bold prisoner have antecedents in the Pauline letters. As prisoner, Paul testifies to imperial guards (Phil 1:12-14) and even fights with the beasts (1 Cor 15:32; a metaphorical expression for the hardships endured while preaching in Ephesus). As general, the apostle lays siege to those who resist knowledge of Christ with powers provided by God (2 Cor 10:3-6).[363] One may compare how first-century Cynic and Stoic philosophers spoke of the invulnerability of a wise man's soul when fortified by reason and secure virtue: "full of virtues human and divine, [the wise man] can lose nothing. . . . The walls which guard the wise man are safe from both flame and assault, they provide no means of entrance, are lofty, impregnable, godlike."[364] Cynics referred to their rough garb as armor in the war against the temptations of a soft life, lovers, false opinions, or other forms of cultural imprisonment.[365]

Dio argued that the philosopher's true weapons are words, not beggarly forms of dress.[366] Paul, however, does not give any description of the weapons that he uses, saying only that his weapons "have divine power to destroy" (2 Cor 10:4). The weapons appear to be the lowly form of life that his opponents have used as evidence against him (2 Cor 10:7-10).[367]

Second Corinthians 10:1-10 provides an indication that the general's call to arms and the bold prisoner image could be combined in describing the apostle. The apparent humiliation of imprisonment may even form part of the attack. The combination speaks eloquently to the rhetorical situation of the audience. Ephesians hints that imprisonment (and perhaps already death) has removed the apostle from the field. However, its readers are ready to take up the arms provided by God.

Details of divine armor do not occur in the earlier letters. First Thessalonians 5:8 picks two pieces of armor as metaphors: for the virtues of faith and love, the breastplate; and for hope of salvation, the helmet. Ephesians 6:14-17 must have created its picture of the armor from other sources. The closest parallels appear in descriptions from Isaiah, as Fig. 7 indicates.

A blessing of the "prince of the congregation" at Qumran also uses battle imagery to establish the new covenant: "He will renew the covenant . . . to establish the kingdom of his people forever [to judge the poor with justice]." This individual will be a fortress: "May the Lord raise you to an everlasting height, like a fortified tower upon the raised rampart." The word of his mouth is a sharp weapon: "May [you strike the peoples] with the power of your mouth. . . . With the breath of your lips may you kill the wicked." And he will be clad in armor: "May your justice be the belt [of your loins, and loyalty] the belt of your hips. May he place upon you horns of iron and horseshoes of bronze."[368]

---

362. E.g., Cyrus in Xenophon *The Education of Cyrus* 1.4; Hannibal and Scipio in Polybius 3.63; Anthony and Augustus in Dio Cassius *History* 1.16-30. See Lincoln, "'Stand, therefore . . .'"
363. Abraham J. Malherbe, "Antisthenes and Odysseus, and Paul at War," *HTR* 76 (1983) 143-73.
364. Seneca *On the Constancy of the Wise Man* 6.8. See Malherbe, *Moral Exhortation*, 160.
365. Pseudo-Diogenes *Epistles* 34.
366. Dio Chrysostom *Orations* 19.10-12.
367. Malherbe, "Antisthenes and Odysseus, and Paul at War."
368. 1Q28b 5:21-26.

Figure 7: Eph 6:14-17 and the Armor of the Lord

Item	Ephesians	Isaiah and other parallels
belt ("having girded your loins")	6:14 truth	Isa 11:5 (LXX) righteousness
breastplate	6:14 righteousness	Isa 59:17 (LXX) righteousness (also Wis 5:18)
military sandals ("having shod your feet")	6:15 equipment of the gospel of peace	[Isa 52:7 (LXX) "the feet of those who preach the tidings of peace"]
shield	6:16 faith	Wis 5:19 holiness
helmet	6:17 salvation	Isa 59:17 (LXX) salvation
		Wis 5:18 impartial judgment
sword	6:17 the Spirit, which is the word of God	[Isa 49:2 (LXX) placed in the mouth of the servant "a sharp sword"]
		Wis 5:20 "wrath as a large sword"

Use of the Isaiah material in the book of Wisdom and in 1Q28b shows that the metaphor did not include a fixed set of correlations between armor and virtues. The blessing of the Prince of the Congregation from Qumran also indicates that the armor of the Lord can be transferred from God to human agents. Both Qumran and Ephesians refer to this armor without any citation formulae. Both assume that the audience will recognize the biblical cast of the imagery. Such recognition plays an important part in the linguistic code of each document. In the Essene text, God's blessing on the leader of the renewed covenant people equips him to be the agent of divine justice and judgment among the peoples. In Ephesians, the enemies to be resisted are no longer human but spiritual, quasi-demonic powers that govern the lower world. God's armor expresses the superior power of the creator already evident in the exaltation of Christ into the heavens. The philosophical tradition of the sage armed against the passions and false reasonings of humankind would not be sufficient in either context.

6:10-13. The introduction in verse 10 echoes Col 1:11. A call to be vigilant frequently appears in apocalyptic conclusions. Readers know God's power in the salvation that they have already experienced (1:19; 3:16, 30). Wearing the soldier's armor (v. 11; from Wis 5:17) presents a more striking metaphor for divine protection than do the earlier references to divine power. Though the concrete details of the armor are biblical, not Roman, the audience probably envisaged the fully armed Roman soldier when they heard these words (Jdt 14:3).[369]

The idea that Satan has designs on the righteous is familiar (2:2). The paraenesis warned against permitting anger to provide opportunities for the devil (4:27), but the catalog of powers in v. 12 has been a source of controversy since antiquity. Gnostic authors

---
369. Polybius 6.23. See Lincoln, *Ephesians*, 435; Best, *A Critical and Exegetical Commentary on Ephesians*, 591.

used this verse as evidence that the soul is trapped in a world created by the evil creator and his subordinate powers. One account of this mythology is introduced as the revelation of the meaning of the apostle's words: "On account of the reality of the authorities inspired by the spirit of the father of truth, the great apostle referring to the 'authorities of darkness' [Col 1:13] told us that 'our contest is not against flesh and [blood]; rather, the authorities of the universe and the spirits of wickedness [Eph 6:12]."[370] Gnostic mythology gave more explicit expression to the hints in Ephesians that God has already given victory to the elect.[371]

Other exegetes have taken the peculiar term "cosmic powers" (κοσμοκράτορες *kosmokratores*) as evidence that Ephesians refers to the powers behind astrology and magic.[372] In inscriptions "cosmic power" implies that the deity invoked is omnipotent and universal. Use of the term in the plural is unusual, and Clinton Arnold contends that Ephesians wishes to demote Artemis and other deities in doing so. They are not universal rulers but members of the lower class of powers referred to as demons. Paul agrees that the pagan gods can be described as demons (1 Cor 10:20).

While the terms "ruler" (ἀρχή *archē*) and "authority" (ἐξουσία *exousia*) are frequently found in the New Testament (Eph 1:21; 3:10), the expressions "cosmic powers" and "spiritual forces of evil in the heavenly places" seem to have been coined by the author of Ephesians. They are equivalent to other descriptions of evil powers in Jewish apocalyptic (*Jub.* 10:3-13; *1 Enoch* 15:8-12; *T. Sim.* 4:9). By expanding the double expression "rulers and authorities" with these new terms, Ephesians has conveyed a sense that powers of evil pervade the cosmos. However, God's power is superior to any such forces. The expression found in v. 10 ("in the strength of his power") could be an allusion to Isa 40:26 LXX, "in the strength of might." Isaiah refers to the creative power of God in bringing forth the universe and its heavenly bodies.[373]

Verse 13 picks up the exhortation of v. 11. Given the strength of the forces arrayed against them, Christians must be well armed to withstand the day of battle. What does Ephesians mean by the expression "that evil day" ἐν τῇ ἡμέρα τῇ πονηρᾷ *en tē hēmera tē ponēra*)? Possibilities range from the evils of the time just before the end, particular instances of temptation, or simply everyday life in the present age. The apocalyptic background of much of the imagery makes a reference to end-time evil seem the most natural (cf. 1 Cor 7:26; 1 Thess 5:2-4). Elsewhere in Ephesians, however, apocalyptic expressions are usually converted to descriptions of present reality (see 1:21; 2:3, 7; 1:14, 18; 4:30; 5:5).[374] The vagueness of the concluding clause, "having done everything, to stand firm," suggests that the author has an indefinite future in mind. The structures of the present age will continue for an unknown period. The phrase does not specify what is meant by "having done everything." It could refer to having put on the armor or to having resisted the enemy when under attack.

6:14-17. Verse 14 picks up the verb "stand" (ἵστημι *histēmi*) from the end of the previous sentence. A series of participles describes being those standing as properly equipped with each piece of armor (vv. 14-17). As Fig. 7 indicates, the equipment and characteristics associated with the various items of armor have been taken from traditions concerning the armor of the Lord. Although the previous verses suggested that the combat was primarily defensive, most of the virtues in this section speak of positive actions. Such offensive acts bring the image closer to that of the Lord arming to come in judgment or to the Essene Prince of the Congregation ready to establish the new people of God. When Eph 4:24 uses the verb "clothe" (ἐνδύω *endyō*) for the new human being created in God's image, that new being is created in righteousness and holiness of truth. Righteousness, goodness, and truth are fruits of light (5:9). Thus virtues that Christians have "put on" when they were converted provide the desired armor. Military-style hobnailed sandals or short boots used as equipment for the gospel of peace suggest readiness for a long march, if readers associate

---

370. *Hypostasis of the Archons* 86,20-25.
371. Lindemann, *Die Aufhebung der Zeit*, 655.
372. Clinton E. Arnold, "The 'Exorcism' of Ephesians 6:1.12 in Recent Research: A Critique of Wesley Carr's View of the Rule of Evil Powers in First-Century AD Belief," *JSNT* (1987) 113-21.
373. Robert A. Wild, "The Warrior and the Prisoner: Some Reflections on Ephesians 6:10-20," *CBQ* 46 (1984) 287.

374. So Schnackenburg, *The Epistle to the Ephesians*, 275.

the image with Isa 52:7. Romans 10:15 uses the same passage from Isaiah for messengers of the gospel. For Ephesians, the peace that comes through preaching the gospel is constituted by the unity of Jew and Gentile in the body of Christ (2:14, 17).

Since v. 16 refers to withstanding an attack, some commentators reject the possibility that preaching the gospel is being referred to in v. 15.[375] Others suggest that the expression "whatever will make you ready to proclaim the gospel of peace" refers to the soldier as being armed to do battle in order to preserve a peace that has already been established, not to create that peace.[376] Ephesians speaks of peace as given by God's plan of salvation, harmoniously uniting all things in heaven and on earth in Christ (1:10). This plan has already been made known to the "rulers and authorities" in the heavens (3:10).

Unlike the small round shield (ἀσπίς *aspis*), the θυρεός (*thyreos*) was a full-length shield of leather-covered wood that protected the whole body.[377] Burning arrows have been used in attacks on besieged cities since Assyrian times. A soldier who became terrified by flaming arrows caught in his shield might throw it down and become vulnerable to enemy spears.[378] For the audience, these familiar images must also be linked to the use of "shield" for God (Gen 15:1; Pss 5:12; 18:30; 28:7) and to the arrows and sword God has readied for the wicked (Ps 7:12-13; Isa 50:11).

Arrows appear as metaphors for sins of speech (Prov 26:18). The blasphemous words that the wicked speak against God are fiery arrows that eventually ignite divine wrath.[379] The closest parallel to the image in Ephesians can be found in one of the Essene hymns. The righteous person, the speaker in this hymn, trusts in the Lord despite the attacks being mounted against him: "They—they attack my life on your account, so that you will be honored by the judgment of the wicked . . . heroes have set up camp against me surrounded by all their weapons of war; they loose off arrows without any cure; the tip of the spear, like fire which consumes trees."[380]

It is the speaker's testimony to the truth about God that excites the attack of the wicked: "You have set me as a reproach and a mockery of traitors, foundation of truth and of knowledge for those on the straight path."[381] Ephesians has already indicated that "the ruler of the power of the air" is the spirit working in "those who are disobedient" (2:2). Therefore the fiery arrows of the evil one might represent the speech of the wicked. If Ephesians makes the same associations with fiery darts that the Essene hymnist does, then the earlier reference to the "gospel of peace" should be taken in an active sense. The message conveyed by the faithful about God's salvation provokes the assaults that they suffer.

The active imagery returns in v. 17, which highlights offensive weapons. Along with the helmet, the faithful are encouraged to take up the sword that is the word of God. "Sword" refers to the short sword used in close combat. Ordinarily, the metaphor refers to the sword that comes from God's mouth to strike down God's enemies (Rev 1:16; 2:12, 16; 19:13, 15). In this context, "word" (ῥῆμα *rhēma*) must refer to the Christian message, the gospel (as in Rom 10:8; 1 Pet 1:25).

6:18-20. Ephesians concludes the peroration by returning to the theme of prayer that opened the letter. The formula has been appropriated from Col 4:2-4. By turning the reader's attention back to the imprisoned apostle, the writer softens the dramatic emotional impact of the call to arms. The author now appeals to the audience's emotions. They should be eager to follow the example of the heroic apostle that has been set before them. Ephesians has already indicated that prayer is necessary for those who would receive divine power (1:15-23; 3:14-21). Exhortations and references to continual prayer are a regular feature of Pauline letters (Rom 1:9-10; Col 1:3; 4:12; Phil 1:4; 4:6; 1 Thess 5:17). The phrase "for all the saints" reminds the audience of its ties to all believers (1:15; 3:18). Prayer is regularly described as the activity of the Spirit in the believer (Rom 8:15-16, 26-27; Gal 4:6).

Philippians speaks of the effects of Paul's imprisonment. It has made others confident in preaching the gospel (Phil 1:14-16). The prayers offered on his behalf by the Philippians

---

375. So Lincoln, *Ephesians*, 449.
376. Schnackenburg, *The Epistle to the Ephesians*, 278.
377. Polybius 6.23. See Lincoln, *Ephesians*.
378. Thucydides *The Peloponnesian War* 2.75,5.
379. CD 5:12-16; 1QH 11[3]:16; 27.
380. 1QH 10:23-26.

381. 1QH 10[2]:10.

can be credited with delivering the apostle from prison—along with the agency of the Spirit (Phil 1:19-20).

The prayer formula at the conclusion to Ephesians has generalized this pattern. One can no longer anticipate that the apostle will be freed from prison.[382] Ephesians even omits the reference to an "open door" for proclaiming the gospel from Col 4:3. However, the addressees can share Paul's courageous testimony to the gospel through praying for him.

The self-description of the apostle as "ambassador in chains" (v. 20) has taken the term "serve as ambassador" from 2 Cor 5:20. Philemon 9 combines the terms "ambassador" and "prisoner." The reference to chains appears elsewhere in Acts 28:20 and 2 Tim 1:16. Both the weight and the manner of chaining prisoners made chains extremely painful. Coupled with lack of nourishment, such imprisonment could result in permanent damage to the prisoner's limbs. Because of the physical torture involved in being chained, later legislation referred to slavery and low social rank as "the punishment of bonds."[383] When the realities of prison are grasped clearly, the suggestion that the apostle would continue to boldly proclaim the gospel is more evidently heroic than is the case for readers who think only of modern prisons. The prison context also indicates that to speak of an ambassador in chains would be considered an oxymoron.[384] A wretched, dirty creature in chains could hardly make the rhetorical show necessary to accomplish the task of ambassador. Nevertheless, both Philippians and Philemon indicate that Paul did manage to use imprisonment as an opportunity to spread the gospel. This section indicates that he will continue to do so.

Much of the drama of this peroration depends upon the range of emotional associations that an audience attaches to the rich imagery that makes up the passage. Life as a combat with astral powers located in the lower regions of the air has been coupled with believers, putting on the armor of the divine warrior. Swords and arrows will not be effective against such weapons. But the tone of victory may be swept away when Ephesians shifts to the imprisoned apostle. Though the harsh conditions of imprisonment would seem to make witness to the gospel impossible, Philemon demonstrates that Paul might even convert fellow prisoners.

Ephesians does not suggest that its readers are about to be imprisoned as Paul is. But the world in which they live is not going to be transformed. Hostile powers still govern the present age. They may attack the saints through the fiery arrows of verbal polemic. At one level, the armor appears to be equivalent to the new clothing that Christians put on when they are converted. At another, as the parenetic section of the letter indicates, preparation to withstand attack must be continuous. Believers must hear sermons, read scripture, talk with other Christians, engage in regular prayer, sing the praises of God, and so on.

Ancient philosophers highlight the connection between open or bold speech and freedom. Someone who has a secure grasp on his or her identity as a believer cannot be forced to surrender that truth. The armed soldier of this section provides an image of the secure believer. Such persons cannot be found shifting from one opinion to another, "tossed to and fro and blown about by every wind . . . by their craftiness in deceitful scheming" (4:14); their position should instead be "speaking the truth in love" (4:15).

---

382. On the uncertain fate of anyone sent to prison, the resulting depression and suicide, and the importance of that language for Paul's choice of life in Phil 1:19-26, see Wansink, *Chained in Christ*, 41-60; 96-125.

383. Brian Rapske, *The Book of Acts in Its First Century Setting*, vol. 3, *The Book of Acts and Paul in Roman Custody* (Grand Rapids: Eerdmans, 1994).

384. Lincoln, *Ephesians*, 454

REFLECTIONS

This section creates a striking visual image: the Christian standing as a fully armed Roman infantry soldier against assault, flaming arrows thrown down from above. By reminding us of armed guards at the beginning, the author also heightens the pathos of Paul, a chained prisoner speaking boldly as an ambassador for the gospel. No ambassador presented in chains has much of a chance for the success of his embassy. The initial depiction of humans armed against forces that are more than human, against spiritual powers, fits an established pattern in apocalyptic texts. Ordinarily, the conflicts of the evil times at the end of the world are described as demonic in inspiration. Angelic figures like Michael do battle against the spiritual forces that the faithful righteous ones struggle against on earth. This scenario understands the sufferings of the righteous as part of the testing that belongs to the last days.[385] Though its images suggest such a scenario, Ephesians departs from the apocalyptic vision in two ways: timetable and victory. There is no reference to the impending divine judgment that closes the time of struggle (cf. 1 Thess 5:1-11). Nor does Ephesians foresee a future victory over the powers, as in 1 Cor 15:24-28. The heavenly exaltation of Christ has already defeated them (Eph 1:20-23).

Consequently, the image of Christian life as a struggle between the soul, which belongs to the heavenly kingdom of Christ, and evil powers, which operate in this world from the heavens, provided a prime text for Gnostic and Manichaean salvation myths.[386] The spiritual practice of monks in the Egyptian desert saw the ascetic engaged in a direct struggle with the demons. Their appearance revealed the impurity of the monk's own heart. Recitation of phrases from Scripture had the power to drive demons away, even if the monk did not understand the meaning of those words.[387] Contemporary readers are less likely to see the demons as external beings than internal forces that infect the psyche. The quest for holiness forces a confrontation with the tangled web of confusion, sin, and ignorance in the human heart. Nor should the injunction to take up the armor of God and stand firm be limited to individuals. Groups are also subject to a dynamic that works for evil that no one individual would engage in separately. Psychologists note that group discussion can lead persons to extreme statements they would never make on their own. Combine that dynamic with religious ritual, and people who are ordinarily tolerant of others become capable of violence toward deviant members of the group or outsiders.[388] The concern Ephesians shows for the way Christians speak, pray, and sing indicates that the ethical consequences of language were already well known.

Remember the emphasis on bold preaching of the gospel in 6:19. That may be the key to the whole drama in this section. By the time Ephesians was written, the apostle Paul had died. Christ may have defeated the powers in the heavens, but the gospel still must be proclaimed on earth (6:15). Anyone who does so can expect to enter the arena against all the personal and social forces that resist transformation by the Word of God.[389] Father Wild suggests that we see this passage as an ideal image to encourage Christians in all the tasks required of them: "The cosmic and demonic powers still seek to exercise a tyranny over the Christian, and in that sense the Christian appears to be 'in bonds.' In actuality, however, the bonds are broken and the powers are defeated 'in Christ.' They have God's armor, and it is God who guarantees their freedom."[390]

---

385. For discussion of this scenario as it appears in the Dead Sea Scrolls, see John J. Collins, *Apocalypticism in the Dead Sea Scrolls* (London: Routledge, 1997) 57, 93-104.
386. Wild, "The Warrior and the Prisoner," 294-95.
387. Douglas Burton-Christie, *The Word in the Desert: Scripture and the Quest for Holiness in Early Christian Monasticism* (New York: Oxford, 1993) 123-24.
388. Robin Dunbar, *Grooming, Gossip, and the Evolution of Language* (Cambridge, Mass.: Harvard University Press, 1996) 143.
389. Arnold, *Ephesians*, 120-21.
390. Wild, "Warrior and the Prisoner," 294.

EPHESIANS 6:21-24

FINAL GREETING

COMMENTARY

Ancient letters ended with information about the sender's immediate plans, additional instructions, or words to particular individuals. Since Ephesians is not addressed to an audience that knew Paul personally, such concrete details are lacking. By contrast, Colossians ends with an extended list of greetings and instructions to named individuals (Col 4:10-17). Ephesians has taken wording for the final greeting from Colossians, as Fig. 8 indicates.

The final words diverge from Colossians. Ephesians does not conclude in the apostle's own hand (as do Gal 6:11; Phlm 19), and the reference to Paul's imprisonment has been relocated to the peroration (v. 20).

In Colossians the double reference to how Paul is doing (4:7) and how "we are" doing (4:8) makes sense because Col 1:1 identified Timothy as co-sender of the letter. There is no co-sender in Eph 1:1, but its author has retained the second plural reference anyway. Tychicus appears in Acts 20:4 as one of Paul's companions from Asia Minor. His name reappears in the pastorals as emissary to Ephesus and Crete (2 Tim 4:12; Titus 3:12). The notice that connected Tychicus and Ephesus provides a basis for the speculation—appearing in those manuscripts that add the phrase "in Ephesus" to the opening (1:1)—that this general letter was addressed to Christians in Ephesus.

The final greeting (vv. 23-24) expands the short form found in Colossians somewhat awkwardly. Its structure reflects the "grace to you and peace from God our Father and the Lord Jesus Christ" of the opening greeting (1:2). The expression "love with faith" (ἀγάπη μετὰ πίστεως *agapē meta pisteōs*) is unusual, as is the lack of a vocative or a second-person plural for those who are the object of the concluding blessing. Instead of personal greetings, Ephesians employs generalized expressions: "peace to the brothers" (NRSV, "the whole community") and "grace be with all who have an undying love for our Lord Jesus Christ." Consequently, any Christians who happen upon the letter may feel themselves included as its addressees. This form of address may indicate that Ephesians was composed as a circular letter.

Figure 8: Eph 6:21-24 and Col 4:7-9, 18

Item	Ephesians	Colossians
information about the sender	**6:21** and that you may know how I am and what I am doing,	**4:7** how I am doing,
person who brings the letter	**6:21b** Tychicus, the beloved brother, faithful minister in the Lord will make everything known to you	**4:7b** Tychicus, the beloved brother, faithful minister, and fellow servant in the Lord will make everything known to you

recommendation for the bearer	**6:22** whom I have sent to you for this purpose, that you may know how we are doing, and to be encouraged in your hearts	**4:8** whom I have sent to you for this purpose, that you may know how we are doing and be encouraged in your hearts
final blessing	**6:23-24** Peace to the brothers, and love with faith, from God the Father and the Lord Jesus Christ. Grace with all who love our Lord Jesus Christ in incorruptibility.	**4:18** I, Paul, write the greeting with my own hand. Remember my bonds. Grace be with you.

The letter's final prepositional phrase, "in incorruptibility" (ἐν ἀφθαρσίᾳ *en aptharsia*, translated as the adjectival "undying" in the NRSV and NIV), is awkward. One might expect the term "incorruptibility" to describe a divine attribute (Rom 1:23; 1 Tim 1:17). If so, the phrase refers to the Lord exalted in incorruptibility. But one would expect a verbal form to connect "the Lord" with the prepositional phrase or the adjective modifying that word. Therefore, the phrase probably modifies the verb "love" (ἀγαπάω *agapaō*) as in the NRSV and the NIV. It asserts that love of Christ is not subject to decay. This reading is grammatically clearer, though it still yields an awkward expression. First Corinthians 15:42 uses the prepositional phrase to describe the risen body. A formulaic passage in 2 Tim 1:10 speaks of Christ abolishing death and bringing to light life and incorruptibility through the gospel. These examples show that if "in incorruptibility" refers to believers, "incorruptibility" should refer to their eschatological situation, not the quality of their love of the Lord. Perhaps Ephesians is referring to those who love the Lord as the church that exists with him "in the heavenly places" (2:6-7). Its existence is the result and evidence of the richness of God's grace toward those who believe. Thus the author indirectly returns to one of the great themes of the letter. The existence of the church, united in love with its head, is the sign of God's loving providence. God wills to unite all people in the new creation. Like all divine attributes, the response to God's grace—love for the Lord Jesus—is also incorruptible.

THE LETTER TO THE PHILIPPIANS
INTRODUCTION, COMMENTARY, AND REFLECTIONS
BY
MORNA D. HOOKER

THE LETTER TO THE
PHILIPPIANS

INTRODUCTION

The characteristic note of Paul's letter to the Philippians is above all that of joy—a remarkable feature, in view of the fact that this letter was written in prison, where its author was held under a capital charge! Paul's faith triumphs over adversity and causes him to rejoice, whatever happens. The letter is written to a Christian community with whom Paul has had a long and happy relationship; though they are not yet perfect, they are nevertheless his joy and his crown, in whom he hopes to boast on the day of judgment (2:16; 4:1).

The founding of the Christian community at Philippi (probably in about 50 CE) had marked a significant development in Paul's ministry, opening up a new area for missionary work. According to Acts 16, Paul was prevented by the Holy Spirit from preaching in Asia or Bithynia, so he made his way to Troas, where he received a summons, in a dream, to go to Macedonia. This was considerably farther west than Paul had so far ventured. The Acts account is of particular interest, since it is at this precise point (Acts 16:10) that the "we" passages begin, suggesting that either Luke or his source had accompanied Paul on this mission.

Philippi was a fairly small city in the first century CE (approx. 10,000 inhabitants), situated on the Via Egnatia, which ran from east to west, taking travelers to the Adriatic coast and hence, by boat, to Italy. The port of Neapolis lay ten miles to the south and Thessalonica 100 miles to the southwest. Philippi had originally flourished because of gold mines nearby, but these had been worked out long before the first century CE, and the city was important mainly as an agricultural center, being situated on the edge of a fertile plain where grain and wine were produced. The original inhabitants of the area had been Thracians, but in the fourth century BCE it had been taken by Philip II of Macedon, who founded a Greek city on the site of an earlier village and gave it his own name. The city had come under Roman rule in the second century BCE, and after Antony and Octavian defeated Brutus and Cassius at the battles of Philippi in 42 BCE it had been refounded as a Roman colony, and many Italians had been brought in and settled. It was not (contra Acts 16:12) "the leading city of the district of Macedonia." Macedonia was in fact divided into four districts, and Philippi was in the first of these. (Luke may have been confused, or it is possible that he wrote "a city of the first district of Macedonia," as the NRSV margin suggests.) The fact that the city was a Roman colony gave its citizens great privileges, for they enjoyed considerable property and legal rights and were exempt from the taxes imposed on those without this status. Citizens of the colony were also citizens of Rome, and the city's administration was modeled on that of Rome.

When Paul came to Philippi, therefore, he would have found a sizable nucleus of Roman citizens, many of whom were Italian by birth and who constituted the aristocracy of the city. He would have found Roman administration and discipline as well as Roman culture. The official language was Latin (public inscriptions in the city were written in Latin), and the city was loyal to Rome, which meant, among other things, that the cult of the emperor would have been much in evidence. The men who are described in Acts 16:16-21 as dragging Paul and Silas before the magistrates are clearly understood by Luke to have been Roman citizens, but the majority of the inhabitants of the city would have been Greeks who had flocked in after the earlier conquest by Philip of Macedon. In the rural areas around Philippi in particular Paul would have found some of the original inhabitants of the land, the Thracians. No archaeological evidence has been found for a Jewish presence in the city; perhaps it was not sufficiently important commercially to attract them. It is notable that Luke makes no reference to a synagogue in Philippi; to be sure, Paul discovers "a place of prayer," but apparently the only people gathered there are women, and the one with whom Paul speaks is not herself Jewish, but a God-fearing Gentile. This account supports the belief that any Jewish presence in Philippi was minimal. Paul's converts would have been entirely, or almost entirely, Gentile. As for their previous religious beliefs, the mixed population of the city meant that various religious cults would have been practiced in the city, alongside the official cult of the emperor.

In the letter itself, there are possible reflections of these circumstances. The term Paul uses to address the Philippians in 4:15 is a Latin form of their name, rather than Greek. The name "Clement" in 4:3 is also Latin, but the names "Syntyche" and "Euodia" (4:2) are Greek. The reference to bishops and deacons in 1:1 may indicate a more developed organization (under Roman influence) than elsewhere, while the references to "citizenship" (see the Commentaries on 1:27 and 3:20) would have had a special nuance for the inhabitants of Philippi. Finally, the declaration of Jesus Christ as Lord in 2:11 may well have been intended as a deliberate challenge to the loyalty they were expected to give to the Roman emperor as Lord.

AUTHORSHIP AND INTEGRITY

The authenticity of the epistle is not seriously in dispute, though doubts have been expressed from time to time. F. C. Baur's objections were entirely subjective—the letter did not conform to what he expected from a Pauline epistle—and more recent attempts to apply objective literary tests to the letter (with a negative result) have been treated with considerable skepticism.[1]

More serious questions, however, have been raised concerning the epistle's integrity. Many commentators believe that it consists of two—or even three—letters that have been joined together. The arguments in favor of this hypothesis are as follows:

(1) There are abrupt jumps in Paul's argument, most notably at 3:1. It is suggested that these are easier to understand if they are due to an editor's piecing various letters together. In fact, however, this "solution" merely creates another problem: Why did an *editor* make such unsuitable joins? The more it is argued that it is difficult to understand why Paul should move abruptly from one topic to another, the more difficult it becomes to comprehend an editor's motives in doing so. Indeed, it is easier to attribute sudden changes in subject to Paul than to an editor!

(2) Paul had recently received a gift from the Philippian church, brought to him by Epaphroditus. Thus it is frequently assumed that one of the chief reasons why he had written to them was to thank them for that gift. This he does in 4:10-20, almost at the end of the letter, whereas courtesy and literary convention alike would surely have demanded that he begin his letter by

---

1. See A. Q. Morton and James McLeman, *Paul, the Man and the Myth* (London: Hodder & Stoughton, 1966); their method was based on too many questionable assumptions to carry conviction.

expressing his thanks. It is suggested, therefore, that 4:10-20 is part of an earlier "thank-you" letter. Since the earlier part of the letter was clearly written some time after the receipt of the gift (news about Epaphroditus's illness having reached the Philippians and information about their reaction having come to Paul, 2:26), it is possible that Paul has indeed already expressed his thanks, either by letter or by a message of some kind. If that is the case, then his apparently belated and comparatively muted reference to the Philippians' gift in 4:10-20 is understandable. This would, of course, mean that any such earlier letter has been lost. If, on the other hand, we assume that this letter has been incorporated into the existing letter, then part of it (its opening paragraph at the very least) has been lost; it would seem, moreover, that the editor who placed it here did not feel that this (to us) strange position was inappropriate.

It has been pointed out, however, that there are in 4:10-20 "echoes" of the vocabulary used in 1:3-11 and that the two passages thus form an inclusio. If this is deliberate, then not only does it suggest that one of Paul's main purposes in writing to the Philippians was to express his thanks for their gift, but it means also that the letter must have been composed as a unity.[2]

(3) In a letter written to the Philippian church by Polycarp, a second-century bishop and martyr, there is a reference to letters written by Paul to the Philippian church.[3] Unfortunately there is great debate as to whether the plural should be taken seriously and whether Polycarp was perhaps confused about the destination of some of Paul's epistles. Even if we take Polycarp's words as evidence that more than one letter to the Philippians was in existence in his time, however, this does not prove that these letters were later amalgamated. There is no textual evidence to support the view that letters that were still separate in Polycarp's day were subsequently brought together. If there was, in fact, more than one letter, the others appear to have been lost.

In spite of the various problems this theory involves, the view that what we know as the letter to the Philippians represents an amalgamation of two or three letters is popular among many commentators. Although there is considerable disagreement about precisely how to distribute the material, 1:1–3:1 is usually allocated to one letter and 4:10-20 to another; there is much debate, however, as to where the fragment of letter beginning in 3:2 might end, and this uncertainty is an indication of the fragility of the arguments. Moreover, attempts to produce a coherent series of letters leave us with a huge problem: *Why* should an editor piece Paul's letters together in this way? Had the originals been damaged, so that one or two letters existed as fragments only? If so, why did the editor make such a bad job of joining them together? The problems arising from this theory are such that it seems much easier to accept the letter as a unity. The features in Philippians that puzzle us (such as the sudden change of subject in 3:2 and the position of 4:10-20) are probably due to factors in Paul's situation that we do not fully understand.[4]

PLACE AND DATE

The place and date of writing the letter have proved equally contentious. It is clear that Paul was writing from prison (1:7, 12-18); therefore, the question at issue is where this prison was situated. The traditional answer (dating from at least the second century) was Rome, and there are strong arguments to back this up. The chief of these is that the situation reflected in the letter suits the conditions of Paul's imprisonment in Rome, insofar as these can be reconstructed from Acts. Paul had appealed to Caesar and had been taken as a prisoner to Rome. There he waited for a long time in custody (at least two years, according to Acts 28:30). Acts tells us that Paul was under house arrest during this time, but Luke does not complete the story. The tradition that Paul was martyred in Rome means that we must allow that at some stage he found himself in prison under a capital charge, which is the situation reflected in Philippians 1. Support for Rome as the place where the letter was written is found in two incidental references in

---

2. G. W. Peterman, *Paul's Gift from Philippi*, SNTS monograph 92 (Cambridge: Cambridge University Press, 1997) 90-120.
3. Polycarp *Epistle to the Philippians* 3.
4. Loveday Alexander has analyzed Philippians in the light of the structures of contemporary Hellenistic letters and argued that the latter are by no means inconsistent with the unity of the letter. See Alexander, "Hellenistic Letter-Forms and the Structure of Philippians," *JSNT* 37 (1989) 87-101.

Philippians. The first is the mention of the praetorium in 1:13; unfortunately the meaning of the word is uncertain, since it can refer to a building as well as to the praetorian guard, and both building and guard could be situated in cities other than Rome. However, the context of 1:13 seems to indicate that Paul had the guard in mind, and they would have been more likely to have been stationed in Rome than elsewhere. The second is the reference to Caesar's household in 4:22, a term that included a large number of officials. Again, they could be found throughout the empire, but there would certainly have been a far greater number of them in Rome than elsewhere.

Three arguments have been brought against Rome as the place of origin. The first is that Philippians is much more "like" earlier letters, such as Romans, than it is like the other letter Paul may have written from Rome—Colossians (though the authorship, as well as the place, of that letter is strongly disputed). This, however, is a subjective judgment. Philippians is "like" Romans in some ways, and unlike it in others; similarly, it has interesting parallels as well as differences with Colossians. These similarities and differences are hardly surprising, since letters reflect the particular circumstances in which and the situations for which they were written. Moreover, Romans was probably the last of Paul's letters to have been written before his Roman imprisonment.

A second argument has been given far more weight and relates to the distance between Rome and Philippi (approx. 800 miles), which would have made any journey between the two cities very long and tedious (approx. two months). Philippians implies several such journeys—news of Paul's imprisonment sent to Philippi, Epaphroditus sent by the Philippian church to Paul, news of Epaphroditus's illness sent to Philippi and news of their concern sent back to Paul, and now the letter itself sent to Philippi—far too many, it is suggested, to be possible if the distance was so great. The strength of this objection, too, seems to have been exaggerated. Communications in the ancient world were reasonably good, and Rome and Philippi were both strategically placed for such journeys. Travel was, of course, arduous and slow by modern standards—but this is reflected in the letter itself, in the reference to the anxiety of the Philippians as they await news of Epaphroditus. Moreover, since Paul spent at least two years in custody in Rome, there was plenty of time for numerous journeys.

The third objection to Rome as the place where this letter was written is that Paul says in 2:24 that he is hoping to visit the Philippians on his release, whereas in Rom 15:22-29 he had said that he planned to go on from Rome to Spain. If Paul is imprisoned east of Philippi, he could visit the city en route to Rome and Spain, but to visit it after Rome would be to head in the wrong direction. Romans 15:22-29 was written before his imprisonment, however, and several years in prison (both at Caesarea and at Rome) could well have caused Paul to change his mind. It would not have been the first time that Paul had altered his plans (see 2 Cor 1:15-23).

Two other suggestions as to the place of writing have been made. One is Caesarea, where Paul is said to have been imprisoned for two years (Acts 24:27) and where he was kept in a building called a praetorium (Acts 23:35). Caesarea was even farther from Philippi than was Rome, however, and the journey just as tedious. The serious objection to placing the letter's composition in Caesarea is that Paul was at no time in danger of execution while he was there, and it is difficult to relate his situation at Caesarea to what he says in Phil 1:19-26.

The other suggestion, which has gained wide support, is Ephesus, which is situated much closer to Macedonia so that the journey between the two cities would have been much shorter. There is, to be sure, nothing in Acts to indicate that Paul had been imprisoned there, but Paul says that he has been in prison many times (2 Cor 11:23). He also refers to an occasion when his life was in danger in Asia (2 Cor 1:8-10): Was this the occasion when he fought with wild beasts at Ephesus (1 Cor 15:32)? Unfortunately, we do not know what Paul was alluding to in that passage, but it can hardly have been meant literally, since he survived the experience. While it is possible that Paul was imprisoned in Ephesus, there is no evidence at all that he was incarcerated there for a considerable length of time under a capital charge. Moreover, Paul had many friends in Ephesus, whereas he appears to have been feeling extremely isolated when writing to Philippi.

If Paul wrote Philippians from Ephesus, then we would need to date it about 52–54 CE; if from Caesarea, then it would have been written about 60 CE. If, as seems most probable, we place it in Rome, then the date of composition would have been the early 60s.

PURPOSE FOR THE LETTER

Opinions differ widely as to the reason why Paul wrote the letter. Many commentators assume that his main purpose was to deal with some major problem in the Philippian church, which they deduce must have been that of disunity. Paul does not rebuke the church, however—apart from the implied mild rebuke directed to two leaders in 4:2. The gentleness with which Paul deals with that situation suggests that the problem is a minor one; when there were serious problems in a community Paul did not hesitate to deal with them vigorously.

Paul seems to have had two main reasons for writing. The first is to reassure his readers about his own situation. This he does—unusually—at the beginning of his letter (1:12-26), in order to allay their natural concern for him. The other reason is to commend Epaphroditus and to explain why he is returning to Philippi. Paul is probably anxious lest Epaphroditus be criticized for not staying with Paul.

A subsidiary reason for writing seems to have been to express his thanks (probably for a second time) for their gift to him. Although the section where he does so comes at the end of the letter (4:10-20), there are possible references earlier (1:5; 2:17, 25) that hint at his gratitude for what he regards as a response to the gospel rather than simply as a personal gift. The generosity of the church is witnessed to elsewhere (see 2 Cor 8:1-6).

It was probably Epaphroditus's return to Philippi that gave Paul the opportunity to send a letter. Paul took advantage of this journey to offer the Philippians encouragement and advice. How much of this was particularly related to the situation in Philippi we do not know, for what Paul wrote was appropriate to any Christian community. The references to suffering are particularly apt in the Philippian situation, however, since we know that the members of the church were being persecuted (1:28-29), and the stress on mutual forbearance was apposite in view of 4:2. The warning against Judaizers in 3:2 is fleeting, perhaps because Paul realized that there was no great danger from Judaizers in a city where there were almost no Jews.

These Judaizers are only one group among several who are often labeled "opponents." It is, perhaps, helpful to distinguish between them, since there appear to have been four distinct groups who are referred to in this letter: (1) Those who are personally opposed to Paul and whose motives in preaching the gospel are questionable (1:15-18). These people are nevertheless regarded as Christians, since they are acknowledged to preach the gospel. (2) The people who are described as opponents of the Philippians and who are persecuting them (1:28-29). This group consists of pagan outsiders. (3) Those attacked in 3:2 who are almost certainly Judaizers, whether Jewish or Gentile by birth. (4) The people described as "enemies of the cross of Christ" (3:18-19), who appear to be a group of libertines claiming to be Christians, but whom Paul clearly considers to be living in a manner totally at variance with the gospel.

IMPORTANCE OF PHILIPPIANS

Philippians has had a great influence on the thought of later theologians, largely because of the significant ideas expressed in the so-called hymn in 2:6-11. To a large extent, the passage was interpreted in a way never intended by Paul. Poetic langage was analyzed as though it were the language of dogma, and the passage was taken as an authoritative statement about the divine and human natures of Christ. In the nineteenth century, the "kenotic" theory of the incarnation was based upon it. If we wish to attempt to understand the passage in its historical context, we need to remember that Paul wrote what he did here, not in order to deal with the issues of Christ's divinity and humanity that so exercised the Church Fathers in the fourth and fifth centuries, but to spell out the way in which those who are in Christ ought to live. The passage is, indeed, an important christological statement—but its importance lies not only in what it says about Christ, but also in its implications for the lives of those who acknowledge Christ as Lord. It is Paul's insight into the relevance of divinity (who and what God is and does) to true humanity (who and what men and women should be and do)—of what we term "theology" to "ethics"—that makes this letter of great and lasting theological significance.

BIBLIOGRAPHY

Commentaries:

Bockmuehl, Markus. *The Epistle to the Philippians.* Black's NT Commentary. Peabody, Mass.: Hendrickson, 1998. Orig. pub. London: A & C Black, 1997. A balanced commentary, based on the author's own translation. Scholarly but readable, this is likely to appeal to a broad range of readers.

Caird, G. B. *Paul's Letters from Prison.* NCB. Oxford: Oxford University Press, 1976. A short commentary based on the RSV text. A useful guide in spite of its brevity.

Fee, Gordon D. *Paul's Letter to the Philippians.* NICNT. Grand Rapids: Eerdmans, 1995. A very thorough, but nevertheless readable, commentary, since detailed discussion is confined to the footnotes. Based on the NIV translation, though with frequent disagreements.

Lightfoot, J. B. *Saint Paul's Epistle to the Philippians.* 7th ed. London: Macmillan, 1883. A classic commentary on the Greek text. Dated, but still valuable. Contains a famous essay, "The Christian Ministry."

O'Brien, Peter T. *The Epistle to the Philippians.* NIGTC. Grand Rapids: Eerdmans, 1991. A useful modern commentary for those who wish to grapple with the Greek text.

Specialized Studies:

Bloomquist, L. Gregory. *The Function of Suffering in Philippians.* JSNTSup 78. Sheffield: Sheffield Academic Press, 1993. A technical study that applies the insights of rhetorical and epistolary analysis to Philippians to see what light they throw on the theme of suffering.

Martin, R. P. *Carmen Christi: Philippians 2:5-11 in Recent Interpretation and in the Setting of Christian Worship.* SNTSMS 4. Grand Rapids: Eerdmans, 1983. A classic survey of the history of interpretation of Phil 2:5-11, together with the author's own exegesis. Now inevitably somewhat dated.

Martin, Ralph P., and Brian J. Dodd, eds. *Where Christology Began: Essays on Philippians 2.* Lousiville: Westminster John Knox, 1998. A useful collection of essays assessing recent interpretation of Phil 2:5-11.

Peterman, G. W. *Paul's Gift from Philippi: Conventions of Gift Exchange and Christian Giving.* SNTSMS 92. Cambridge: Cambridge University Press, 1997. A technical study of Paul's response to the financial help he received from the church in Philippi, in the light of contemporary conventions regarding the exchange of gifts.

Wright, N. T. *The Climax of the Covenant: Christ and the Law in Pauline Theology.* Edinburgh: T. & T. Clark, 1991. Contains, among much else, a revised version of an essay orginally published in *JTS,* NS 37 (1986) on the meaning of ἁρπαγμός (*harpagmos*) in Phil 2:6.

Outline of Philippians

I. Philippians 1:1-11, Letter Introduction

    A. 1:1-2, Address
    B. 1:3-8, Thanksgiving
    C. 1:9-11, Intercession

II. Philippians 1:12-26, Paul's News About Himself

    A. 1:12-18*a*, Paul's Imprisonment
    B. 1:18*b*-26, The Approaching Crisis

III. Philippians 1:27–2:18, The Christian Life, Part 1

    A. 1:27-30, Stand Fast!
    B. 2:1-4, Our Life in Christ
    C. 2:5-11, The Mind of Christ
    D. 2:12-18, Our Necessary Response

IV. Philippians 2:19-30, Future Plans

    A. 2:19-24, Timothy
    B. 2:25-30, Epaphroditus

V. Philippians 3:1–4:1, The Christian Life, Part 2

    A. 3:1-11, The True Basis for Confidence
    B. 3:12–4:1, Keep Going!

VI. Philippians 4:2-23, Letter Conclusion

    A. 4:2-9, Various Exhortations
    B. 4:10-20, A Personal Note of Thanks
    C. 4:21-23, Closing Words

PHILIPPIANS 1:1-11
LETTER INTRODUCTION

OVERVIEW

This opening section follows the typical pattern of Paul's letters: The greeting or address (vv. 1-2) is followed by a thanksgiving (vv. 3-8), which here merges into a prayer of intercession (vv. 9-11). Paul's thanksgivings frequently introduce the themes that are going to be taken up in the body of the letter.[5] We find Paul touching here on three topics to which he is going to return: (1) the Philippians' participation in the gospel, (2) the way in which God is going to continue the work begun in them until it is brought to completion on the day of Jesus Christ, and (3) Paul's own imprisonment and defense of the gospel.

It is interesting to note that there is no specific reference in these verses to the need for unity in the Philippian community, unless the frequent use of the word "all/every" (πᾶς *pas*), found seven times in the first nine verses, is a hint of this. The fact that Paul does not here refer directly to the theme of unity throws doubt on the assumption of many commentators that disunity and personal ambition were serious problems in the Philippian community.

---

5. See Paul Schubert, *The Form and Function of the Pauline Thanksgivings*, BZNTW 20 (Berlin: A. Töpelmann, 1939) 180.

PHILIPPIANS 1:1-2, ADDRESS

COMMENTARY

Ancient letters usually began with the opening formula, "X to Y, Greetings." Paul adopts the formula but transforms it at every point: The writers, recipients, and greetings are all defined in Christian terms. The letter is from Paul and Timothy. The reference to Timothy does not mean that he helped to dictate the letter, which is very much Paul's own (see also 2:19-24); he is included as a matter of courtesy, since he was known well to the Philippians (see Acts 16:1-12; subsequent visits are probably implied in Acts 19:22; 20:3-4). He is nevertheless listed with Paul as an equal, unlike 2 Corinthians, Colossians, and Philemon, where Paul describes himself as "an apostle [or prisoner] of Christ Jesus" and refers to Timothy as "our brother."

In such opening greetings, Paul typically describes himself as an "apostle" (e.g., 1 and 2 Corinthians; Galatians), but here he refers to both Timothy and himself as "servants of Christ Jesus" (see also Romans). Is this, perhaps, because he does not feel the need to emphasize his own authority as an apostle when writing to the Philippians? Or is there some particular reason for choosing the word "servants"? The Greek term is δοῦλοι (*douloi*), a word that in the ancient world was used of slaves (see the NRSV note). Has it perhaps been chosen because Paul already has in mind the theme elaborated on in chap. 2, where he speaks of Christ's taking the form of a slave (2:7)? Certainly in chap. 3 Paul describes his Christian calling in terms of being conformed to the pattern of Christ, and he urges the Philippians to imitate his example. Is Paul using the term *douloi* here, then, because he wishes to remind the Philippians that they must not think too highly of themselves (see 2:1-4)?

The parallel with Philippians 2 is not a good one, however, since δοῦλος (*doulos*) there suggests a lack of status and subjection to the powers that hold humanity enslaved. The phrase "*douloi* of Christ" on the other hand is, paradoxically, a term of honor. To be a "*doulos* of God" was an honorable calling in the OT. The psalms contain frequent references to God's people as *douloi* (e.g., Ps 19:11, 13 [18:12, 14]), and David, in particular, is described as God's *doulos* (Ps 89:3[88:4]). If the word does have a forward look here, then it must also be to 2:11, where Christ is proclaimed as κύριος (*kurios*), "Lord." Paul and Timothy proudly declare their allegiance to Christ and then send greetings in his name (v. 2).

The letter is addressed to "all the saints in Christ Jesus at Philippi." "The saints" (οἱ ἅγιοι *hoi hagioi*) is a term used of the people of God (e.g., Ps 34:9[33:10]), called to be holy because they belonged to a holy God (cf. Lev 19:2; Deut 7:6; 14:2). But these "saints" owe their status to the fact that they are "in Christ Jesus." Already in the opening verse of the epistle we find this crucial phrase "in Christ," which is so important for Paul. Those who are in Christ are those who have been baptized into him, who have metaphorically shared his death and resurrection, dying to their old lives of sin in order to live with him a new life of righteousness. In chap. 2, Paul will remind the Philippians of what it means to be in Christ Jesus, including the fact that the community should be united. Some have argued that it is in order to stress this essential unity that the letter is addressed to *all* the saints.

Somewhat surprisingly, Paul adds the phrase "with the bishops and deacons," as though they were not included among "the saints." This is the only Pauline letter in which they are specifically addressed. For some reason he appears to wish to single them out for special mention. But why? And who were they? The use of the two words ἐπίσκοποι (*episkopoi*, "bishops") and διάκονοι (*diakonoi*, "deacons") together in v. 1 suggests that particular office bearers are in mind. Nevertheless, the words are not yet technical terms; the fact that they follow the reference to Paul and Timothy as *douloi* is a clear indication that we are not yet dealing with any kind of hierarchy. (The variant reading *"fellow* bishops," properly ignored by the translators, is clearly due to a scribe who was worried on this point.) For this reason, the NIV's "overseers" is preferable to the NRSV's "bishops" (see also the NRSV note), although the more general term "superintendents" might be better. The word *episkopoi* is used in the plural, and there is no suggestion as yet of a monarchical bishop. Rather, it refers to those who have pastoral oversight of the congregation (cf. 1 Thess 5:12). Elsewhere in the NT the term appears to be used synonymously with the word πρεσβύτεροι (*presbyteroi*, "elders"; Acts 20:17, 28; Titus 1:5-7; 1 Pet 5:1-2), a word that in the Pauline corpus is found only in the Pastoral Epistles (1 Tim 5:1-2, 17, 19; Titus 1:5). Commentators writing in the early centuries of the common era agreed that the two terms were used interchangeably in the NT. Apart from the Pastorals (1 Tim 3:2; Titus 1:7), this is the only occurrence of *episkopos* in the Pauline corpus. The term διάκονος (*diakonos*) is used more frequently, usually in a way that emphasizes the service being rendered (e.g., Rom 15:8, of Christ; 1 Cor 3:5; 2 Cor 6:4). The reference to Phoebe as a *diakonos* of the church in Cenchrae (Rom 16:1) shows how the word was beginning to be used of someone called to a specific ministry, but "deacon" is an anachronistic translation, while the NRSV's "helpers" is too vague. The more general "ministers" is preferable.

Is Paul referring to two groups of people or one? *Diakonos* cannot be regarded (like πρεσβύτερος *presbyteros*) as a synonym of ἐπίσκοπος (*episkopos*), since it denotes service, not seniority; but it is possible that we should translate the whole phrase as "superintendents who are also ministers"—that is, "leaders of the community who also serve." It seems more likely, however, that Paul is referring to two groups, and this suggests that some kind of structural organization is beginning to emerge in the Philippian Christian community. It will not be long before the words he uses here have become technical terms.

Although none of Paul's other letters begin in this way, there are plenty of examples of contemporary official letters that began by greeting both the community and its leaders. As in Philippians, these leaders are not usually mentioned again in the text of the letters, but they would presumably have had a particular responsibility for dealing with the matters raised in them. Why does Paul follow this custom of naming specific leaders here? Three explanations have been suggested. The first is that the *episkopoi* and the *diakonoi* had organized the gift that had been sent to Paul from the church (4:10-19), and he therefore thought it appropriate to acknowledge this fact by sending them a special greeting. The second is that he considered them to need a special word of encouragement (or reprimand) and was indicating that he hoped they would take note of what he was about to write. Were the leaders of the Philippian community tending to regard themselves as better than others? Were they therefore in need of the warning given in 2:3? Were the two women mentioned in 4:2, Euodia and Syntyche, among these leaders? Or did Paul perhaps follow the term "overseers" with the term "ministers" in order to remind the leaders gently that they should be serving the community? The third explanation is that the Christian community in Philippi was influenced by the structures of the society in which it existed, thus reflecting the Roman genius for organization. Written late in Paul's life, the letter indicates the beginnings of a need for structural organization that would later develop throughout the church. Of these three explanations, the first seems the most probable, but they are by no means exclusive.

Paul greets his readers in his usual manner (v. 2), wishing them grace and peace. The usual secular opening, "Greetings," is replaced by the reference to divine grace; "peace" is the customary Jewish greeting. Both gifts derive from "God our Father," whose people the readers are, and from "the Lord Jesus Christ," in whom they have their existence and whose servants Paul and Timothy are (v. 1).

REFLECTIONS

1. From its very first line, Philippians reflects the transformation brought by the gospel to every part of human life. The traditional epistolary opening formula is subtly changed. Writers and recipients alike are defined by their relationship to God and to Christ, and what the writers wish for their readers consists of gifts from God the Father and the Lord Jesus Christ. More than two thousand years later, it is easy to miss this significant emphasis; phrases that would have impressed the Philippians by their innovative approach now seem to us merely part of the conventional letter opening. To their first readers, however, these opening verses would have been a reminder that the whole of life had been transformed by the proclamation of the gospel.

2. Whatever the reason for the special reference to those who held office in the Philippian church, the letter is addressed to the whole community. All are "in Christ Jesus" and so belong to the fellowship of God's people. Once again, the terms have become so familiar that we no longer appreciate their real significance. We think of "saints" as very special people and forget that we are *all* called to be saints—to be members of God's people and, therefore holy, like God. This new status belongs to those who are "in Christ," who claim their new relationship with God because of their relationship with Christ. It is because Christ is God's holy one that those who belong to him are "saints" (the Greek word ἅγιοι [*hagioi*] means "holy ones"). Our proper emphasis on individual responsibility has tended to make us think of sanctity as something personal and private, but Christianity is primarily a calling to belong to a community. The church is not simply a group of individuals who happen to have responded to the gospel; it is the community of God's people, whose corporate life is an essential expression of their divine calling. Paul would certainly have endorsed John Wesley's maxim that "Christianity is essentially a social religion; and that to turn it into a solitary religion, is indeed to destroy it."[6] Paul's emphatic "all" (1:4, 7-8) will remind us how important this idea is.

---

6. John Wesley, *Forty-four Sermons*, XIX.1.1.

3. The terms "bishop" and "deacon" signify to us offices within the church. However, we need to remember that for Paul and his first readers, the words referred primarily to functions rather than to status. The bishops had pastoral oversight, and the deacons were those who served the community. Status was undoubtedly as important in first-century Philippi as it is in our modern world; yet, for himself and for Timothy, Paul claims the title "slaves [NRSV and NIV, "servants"] of Christ." The gospel throws all our human values on their heads: The truly great are servants, and those who are really first are those who are slaves of all (Mark 10:44). It is notable that although Paul uses the terms "slave/servant" and "servant/minister" of both Jesus and himself, he never uses the term "bishop" of either. The essence of the gospel is seen in service, not in the exercise of authority.

PHILIPPIANS 1:3-8, THANKSGIVING

COMMENTARY

Paul's thanksgiving for the Philippian community is unqualified and intensely personal. Timothy has been forgotten, and Paul has lapsed into the first-person singular. He expresses joy (v. 4), gratitude (v. 5), confidence (v. 6), affection (v. 7), and longing for them all (v. 8). His opening words, stressing his constant prayer for them, are typical of his letters (see esp. 1 Thess 1:2-3): He thanks God every time he remembers them (v. 3). It is possible, however, that we should translate the last phrase of this sentence (lit., "at your every remembrance") somewhat differently and read it as "for your every remembrance [of me]," rather than "at [my] every remembrance of you." This suggestion is attractive because it would mean that Paul begins his letter by thanking the Philippians (or rather God!) for their gift, instead of apparently somewhat ungraciously ignoring it until the last page of his letter. This translation, however, is grammatically difficult; we would ordinarily expect the object of the remembrance (in this case "me") to be expressed. Theologically, it is even more difficult: Would the Philippians' gift have been the first thing Paul mentioned? Was he not far more grateful to God for their progress in the gospel than for any financial gift?

The reference to joy (v. 4) is typical of this epistle, in which joy is a constant theme. The noun χαρά (*chara*) and the cognate verbs "to rejoice" (χαίρω *chairō*) and "to rejoice with" (συγχαίρω *sygchairō*) are used fourteen times. The four occurrences of "all" (πᾶς *pas*) in two lines of Greek text ("every," "constantly/ always," "every/all," "all") are surely indications of the measure of Paul's gratitude, rather than hints of the need for unity, as some suggest. The first particular cause of Paul's joy is the Philippians' participation ("sharing/ partnership") in the gospel (v. 5). This could be a reference to the way in which the Philippians have supported Paul by their prayers, but it seems to suggest rather more. In 4:3 he describes Euodia and Syntyche as having struggled beside him in the cause of the gospel, and he speaks of others at Philippi who have been his "co-workers." It is possible, however, that what Paul has in mind particularly in v. 5 is the financial help they have given him. The word κοινωνία (*koinōnia*, "sharing," "partnership") is, in fact, used elsewhere in Paul's letters with reference to financial contributions (Rom 15:26; 2 Cor 8:4; 9:13), as is the cognate verb κοινωνέω (*koinōneō*, Rom 12:13; Gal 6:6; Phil 4:15). If Paul is thinking of their gift, then it is interesting to note the way in which he refers to it: By their giving the Philippians have become partners *in the gospel*. What they have given is not a personal gift to Paul (though it has brought him material comfort), but rather a means whereby they share in the task of spreading the good news.

If this is the meaning, then we do have a reference to the Philippians' recent gift in the opening lines of the letter. Their generosity toward him is one of the reasons why Paul remembers them constantly with joy. They have shared in the promotion of the gospel "from the first day until now" (v. 5), and we know from 4:15-16 that they had given financial aid in the early days of Paul's ministry in Macedonia. Their readiness to share in the work of the gospel is seen in v. 6 as "a good work"—not, however, a good work for which they are responsible, but one begun in them by God and one that Paul is "confident" will be brought to completion by the day of Christ Jesus. (A similar contrast and connection between beginning and completing is found in Gal 3:3.) As always, Paul's confidence about the future is grounded in what God has already done in the past (cf. Rom 5:9-10). However, we should, perhaps, see the "good work" as referring to more than the Philippians' partnership in the gospel. Paul probably has in mind God's work in saving the community, of which their eagerness to assist in spreading the gospel is evidence.

The OT expectation of the day of the Lord is here interpreted as "the day of Christ Jesus." Paul sometimes refers to this event as "the day" (Rom 13:12; 1 Cor 3:13; 1 Thess 5:4) or "that day" (2 Thess 1:10), sometimes uses the OT expression "the day of the Lord" (1 Thess 5:2; 2 Thess 2:2; probably 1 Cor 5:5), and occasionally specifies that it is "our Lord Jesus Christ" (1 Cor 1:8) or "our Lord Jesus" (2 Cor 1:14). In Philippians, however, he prefers the phrase "the day of Christ" (1:10; 2:16) or, as here, "the day of Christ Jesus." The reference to Christ would certainly remind the Philippians once again that what will happen in the future is the completion of what has already been begun: It is the Christ in whom they believe, and whose story is told in 2:5-11, whose coming is now expected. Paul gives no hint as to when he expects this day to arrive. It will be a day of judgment, bringing both salvation and condemnation; judgment will be made "through Jesus Christ" (Rom 2:16), and Christ will save his own from wrath (1 Thess 1:10). This is why Paul is confident (v. 6).

"It is right" (i.e., "only natural," REB), says Paul, for him to think/feel this way about the Philippians (v. 7). Here we have the first occurrence of the key verb φρονέω (*phroneō*, "to think/feel"), used ten times in Philippians. Its meaning is less cerebral than "think" but more deliberate than "feel"; we lack an appropriate English verb that combines the activity of heart and head. It refers to an attitude or mind-set; it will be used in 2:5 of the attitude of Christ himself, an attitude that should be shared by those who are "in him." Perhaps there is already something of this sense in the use of the word in v. 8, for Paul goes on to say that he longs for the Philippians "with the compassion/affection [lit., bowels] of Christ." In Hebrew thought the bowels were regarded as the seat of human emotion, but Paul claims to love the Philippians with the bowels of Christ. That is, his affection for them is no mere human affection but is rooted in the love and compassion of Christ—a love and compassion that will be spelled out in 2:6-11.

The reason why he should feel this way toward them is stated in v. 7, but the first phrase is ambiguous, as the different translations of the NRSV ("you hold me in your heart") and the NIV ("I have you in my heart"; cf. the NRSV note) indicate. The Greek construction can be understood either way, but the order of the words slightly supports the NIV. Either interpretation makes sense, since the basis of this special regard is the fact that the Philippians are all participants with Paul in the grace experienced both during his imprisonment and in the defense and confirmation of the gospel. The Greek word meaning "fellow participants" (συγκοινωνοί *sygkoinōnoi*, "share") echoes the word used in v. 5. In what sense do the Philippians "share [with Paul] in God's grace"? Is this another reference to the financial assistance they have given him in prison? Or is Paul linking their experience to his because they are involved in the same struggle as he, a struggle that inevitably brings suffering (vv. 19-30)? Whichever it is, it is notable that Paul describes it as a sharing in grace, rather than as a sharing in labor or in suffering. Equally notable is his reference to the defense and confirmation of "the gospel." We might have expected him to refer to his *own* defense, but clearly he sees his own imminent trial as part of a much greater event in which the gospel itself is on trial. In this trial, the faith and behavior of the Philippians play a significant part. It is, perhaps, the legal imagery of v. 7 that leads Paul to call on God as his "witness" to "testify" how he longs for the Philippians (v. 8). He is clearly eager to assure them of the strength of his warm feelings for them.

REFLECTIONS

Because Christians are members of a community, their commitment is expressed in Christian fellowship. Paul refers twice in these verses to the fact that the Philippians have "shared" in the gospel and in grace; clearly they have shared not only in what they have received, but also in what they have given. The Christian community is called to partnership in the gospel (1:5) by helping the work of evangelism and in mutual support of other Christians by prayer and giving.

Many of our own letters begin with a "thank you," and in view of the fact that he has received money from the Philippians, we might well expect Paul to do the same. As in all his letters (with the exception of Galatians) Paul does, indeed, begin with thanksgiving, but his thanks are directed not to the Philippians but to God. Whether or not there is a subtle allusion to the Philippians' gift in these opening verses, it is God who is thanked for the Philippians' response to the gospel, since God is the source of that gospel (1:5) and the one who not only began the good work in them but can be depended upon to complete it as well. Paul praises God rather than the Philippians for their faithfulness and support, since whatever they do is a sharing in the gospel they have received and a sharing in God's grace as well (1:7). At the same time, Paul's thankfulness for the Philippians' progress in the gospel would certainly have encouraged them.

Our own prayers turn very quickly to petition and intercession, and we frequently take for granted the gift of the gospel and God's grace. Paul, on the contrary, pours out his heart in gratitude to God for all God has done and is continuing to do. When we remember Paul's situation in prison, with a capital sentence hanging over him, we are surely rebuked by his approach. This attitude pervades the whole epistle; even when Paul refers in 1:7 to his own imprisonment, he describes the Philippians as those who "share in God's grace." We might have expected him to say that they shared in his suffering! But he regards every circumstance as an experience of grace; therefore, his first response is thanksgiving, not petition. He remembers the Philippians constantly—with joy (1:4), with confidence (1:6), and with a love that is more than human affection, because it derives from Christ himself (1:8).

Paul's constant prayers of thanksgiving for the Philippian church would undoubtedly have strengthened his own bonds with that community. In our prayers for other Christians, do we spend enough time remembering them with joy, with confidence, and with love, or do we rush straight into intercession for them? We sometimes worry about how intercession works, as though prayer is empty unless it brings about certain results. Perhaps we ought to consider this problem in relation to the whole question of Christian prayer. We would do well to remember the saying of Meister Eckehart: "If the only prayer you ever say in your life is 'thank you,' that would be sufficient." Certainly we can see how Paul's outpouring of thanks would strengthen the Philippians' own faith as well as cement the relationship between them and Paul.

PHILIPPIANS 1:9-11, INTERCESSION

COMMENTARY

The introduction concludes with Paul's prayer for the Philippians, a prayer that their love may increase "more and more" in "knowledge" and "insight" (v. 9). The object of this love is not specified, but it is clear from the rest of the letter that it includes the people of Philippi as well as God. Paul's emphasis elsewhere on love as the fulfillment of the law (Rom 13:8-10; Gal 5:14) is open to the charge that it is too vague. Here he specifies that the Philippians need knowledge of God and insight so that they can distinguish the things that matter (v. 10), and thus make the right moral decision. The aim is that they should be "pure and blameless" on the day of Christ—something about which Paul has just expressed confidence (v. 6). "The harvest/fruit of righteousness" (v. 11) is ambiguous. It can mean either the fruit that *is* righteousness or the fruit that *comes from* righteousness. In the first case, "righteousness" (δικαιοσύνη *dikaiosynē*) is a synonym for the moral purity and blamelessness just described; in the second, it refers to the relationship with God that comes through being in Christ and that bears fruit in the form of purity and blamelessness. The second interpretation seems more likely, since the metaphor suggests that the "fruit" is produced by something else; it is supported by Paul's reference to the righteousness from God that comes through faith (3:9). Because their purity derives from the righteousness that is theirs through Jesus Christ, it will, of course, be to the glory and praise of God. There are some remakable variants in the Greek text, and one early manuscript (P[46]) reads "for the glory of God and my praise." This reading seems at first highly unlikely, but one wonders how it arose if it was not original. Moreover, the word ἔπαινος (*epainos*), meaning "approval," "commendation," or "praise," is ordinarily used in classical Greek and by Paul of a recognition directed to humans. Later in the epistle Paul speaks of boasting about the Philippians on the day of Christ (2:16) and describes them as his "joy and crown" (4:1), while in 1 Cor 4:5, when describing his ministry, he refers to the *epainos* everyone will receive from God when the Lord comes. It is just possible, then, that Paul was expressing this idea here; if so, then we have to remember that it is God who will do the commending/approving and that what Paul has been able to do among the Philippians has been done through the grace of God. But Jewish prayers commonly end in a doxology, and we expect this one to do the same. The text followed by both the NIV and the NRSV is almost certainly the correct one.

REFLECTIONS

1. When Paul finally turns to making requests, they are for the Philippians, and not for himself. What he asks for is a growth in Christian love—that it may overflow and that it may be enriched by knowledge and insight. Head and heart are not opposed: Our love for God grows as we learn more about God and about God's love for us. Augustine's dictum "Love and do as you like"[7] is far more profound than it might seem at first sight, for if our love is informed by knowledge and insight we will understand something of God's nature and will; therefore, what we want to do will be in accordance with God's purpose. Similarly, true Christian love for others is not a sentimental affection but a sincere desire for what is best for them. Love is often said to be blind, but such blindness can stop us from discerning the deepest needs of those we love. True love, on the other hand, requires knowledge and insight in order to help others reach their full potential.

2. The source of our love for God and for other people is God. The goal that we be "pure and blameless on the day of Christ" (1:10) will also be achieved by God, who "began a good work" in us (1:6). And what we offer to God is the "harvest/fruit of righteousness"—a righteousness, or right relationship with God, that we possess only because we are "in Christ." No wonder Paul concludes this section with the declaration that this is all to the glory of God! For Paul, this is the motive and goal for the whole of life. Is it, we may ask ourselves, also ours?

---

7. Augustine *Homilies on First Epistle of John* viii.8.

3. The introductory section of the epistle is permeated by Paul's confidence in God. He is confident that God will complete what God has begun (1:6); confident that God's grace is with him, even in prison (1:7); confident that his prayers for the Philippians will be answered and that by their lives God will be glorified. Paul's confidence is not just a vague hope; it is based firmly on what God has done in the past and on his conviction that God is consistent. God has begun a good work and will not give up; it will be completed on the day of Jesus Christ—the same Jesus who was crucified and exalted (2:6-11). Do we today base our hopes for the future on what God has done in the past? Or do we think of the future in terms of an escape from this life, rather than as a completion of what has been started here?

PHILIPPIANS 1:12-26
PAUL'S NEWS ABOUT HIMSELF

OVERVIEW

It is unusual for Paul to begin the main body of his letter by reporting his own news; 2 Corinthians is the only other exception. He probably does so here because he has heard that the Philippians are anxious about him. Even here, however, he tells them little about what is happening to him. His main concern is that, in spite of his imprisonment, his work as an apostle is continuing.

PHILIPPIANS 1:12-18a, PAUL'S IMPRISONMENT

COMMENTARY

Paul addresses the community as "brothers" (NIV; paraphrased as "beloved" in the NRSV; see also 4:8). The Greek term used here (ἀδελφοί *adelphoi*), though masculine in form, was understood to include women as well as men. He assures them that the setbacks he has endured have, in fact, helped the progress of the gospel (v. 12). This paradox is demonstrated, first, in the fact that the cause of his imprisonment has become widely known (v. 13) and, second, in the fact that other Christians have been emboldened by his imprisonment to preach the gospel (v. 14).

What has been made known is that Paul's imprisonment (lit., "chains") is "in Christ." The NIV and the NRSV both describe this as being "for Christ"; the phrase we might have expected Paul to use. In fact, however, he prefers his favorite expression, "in Christ" (ἐν Χριστῷ *en Christō*), which he has already used in v. 1 and which serves here to remind us that he interprets the suffering he experiences as a sharing in the suffering of Christ. Paul's imprisonment is thus not simply the *result* of his proclamation of the gospel, but a *means* of proclaiming it, since the fact that his imprisonment is "in Christ" has "become known/clear": φανερὸς γίνομαι (*phaneros ginomai*, "to make manifest/known/clear") is a phrase often used of revelation.

The cause of Paul's imprisonment has been made known "throughout the whole imperial/palace guard." The Greek word πραιτώριον (*praitōrion*) was used both of the imperial guard, whose headquarters were in Rome, and of the building that housed them there (see the alternative translations in the NRSV and the NIV margins); it was also used of the residency of a Roman governor in the provinces. Here, followed by "to everyone else," it probably refers to the guard itself, rather than to a building; since the guard could serve outside Rome, this does not settle the question of the place of Paul's imprisonment, though Rome seems the most likely option. For Paul, what is significant is that knowledge of the gospel has penetrated the Roman establishment.

Paradoxically, "most of the brothers" have been encouraged by Paul's imprisonment to speak the word with greater boldness (v. 14). Presumably, Paul's own courage and confidence in the Lord have inspired other Christians. The reference to boldness/courage and fear indicates that there is danger for them, too. The phrase "in the Lord" can be taken with the word that precedes it in Greek (NIV, "brothers in the Lord"), to which, however, it adds nothing. It should, therefore, probably be linked with the word that follows (NRSV, "confident in the Lord"), indicating the source of their encouragement. They speak "the word," a common expression for the gospel in the NT; its meaning is clear, whether or not we follow those MSS that read "of God" (as in the NIV; cf. NRSV).

We now discover that some of those who are fearlessly proclaiming the word have been emboldened to do so because Paul is out of the way! They preach Christ "from envy and rivalry . . . out of selfish ambition, not sincerely" (vv. 15a, 17). Their intention is to cause Paul distress in prison. Others, however, have precisely the opposite motives. They preach Christ from "goodwill" and out of "love," since they know that Paul has been put in prison "for the defense of the gospel" (vv. 15b-16). Whereas their actions arise from what they *know* (v. 16), the members of the other group are motivated by what they wrongly *suppose* (v. 17 NIV). The contrast between the two groups is emphasized by the chiastic structure of vv. 15-17. Astonishingly, Paul declares in v. 18 that their motives do not matter, since both groups are preaching Christ, and he, therefore, rejoices.

Both the NIV and the NRSV describe the second group as preaching from "goodwill" (v. 15). In fact, the Greek word εὐδοκία (*eudokia*) is more often used in the sense of "divine will/good pleasure," as it is in 2:13. Possibly Paul is not referring here to the preachers' attitude toward him but to the fact that they are preaching in obedience to the divine will and out of love—a love that is not for Paul alone, though it certainly includes him. They understand that Paul has been "put here [i.e., in prison] for the defense of the gospel" (v. 16; cf. v. 7). The "here" is missing in Greek, and the verb κεῖμαι (*keimai*) means "to stand," "to lie," "to be placed," or "to be appointed." There is probably something of this last sense here: Paul's imprisonment is not an accident of fortune, but part of the commission he has received from God.

Who were the people whom Paul describes as preaching Christ out of "false motives"? They certainly cannot be the "dogs" of 3:2, who glory in circumcision and not in Christ, for there is no suggestion in chap. 1 that those whom he had in mind were preaching the wrong gospel (cf. Gal 1:6-9, where the "different gospel" preached by the Judaizers is dismissed as a false gospel, and Gal 5:4, where those who accept this "other" gospel are said to cut themselves off from Christ). The people Paul had in mind in chap. 1 were apparently preaching the right gospel from the wrong motives, so they could not have been either Judaizers or Gnostics. Why were they envious of Paul? Was it because before his imprisonment he was winning more converts than they were? Was their rivalry the kind of rivalry reflected in 1 Cor 1:12, which gave undue honor to Christian leaders? Were these people like those whom Paul attacked in 2 Corinthians, who criticized him because they expected their leaders to be respected members of society, whereas Paul frequently experienced physical distress and humiliation—even imprisonment—for the sake of the gospel? Yet in 1 and 2 Corinthians, Paul appears to consider such attitudes to be a misunderstanding of the gospel, and it is difficult to understand how he thought Christ was being truly preached by these people if their motives were such a denial of love and Christian fellowship.

If the letter was written from Rome, there could well have been Christians living there who were suspicious of Paul and who felt that his approach was bringing the Christian community into conflict with the Roman authorities, and therefore into physical danger. They might have been relieved that Paul was out of the way, in prison, unable to cause trouble by disputing with his fellow Jews, which could so easily lead the state to intervene. Rumors of their activities would have reached Paul in prison, and he might have misunderstood their motives. He was clearly hurt, but his language here was perhaps exaggerated. Whatever the explanation, it seems that Paul did not criticize these people on the grounds of their doctrine or conduct—save only in their attitude to him. They proclaimed Christ (vv. 15, 17); therefore, he presumably regarded them as "brothers" (v. 14). In spite of their attitude, then, and in spite of his imprisonment, he rejoices! (See Reflections at 1:18b-26.)

PHILIPPIANS 1:18b-26, THE APPROACHING CRISIS

COMMENTARY

In v. 18b, Paul introduces another reason for rejoicing: the fact that he confidently expects "deliverance" (v. 19). What kind of deliverance does he have in mind? Could it be that he expects to be spared the need to stand trial? This seems unlikely, since in v. 20 he eagerly expects to speak boldly and not be put to shame—presumably at the trial. Does he expect to be vindicated at that trial and set free? This is possible, but if so, then his confidence in v. 19 would seem to be at odds with his doubts regarding the outcome in vv. 20-24, though it is certainly echoed in v. 25. The third possibility is that Paul has a heavenly vindication in mind. What he is confidently hoping for is a favorable verdict from God; the judgment of the earthly court, whether life or death, v. 20, is immaterial. This solution is supported by the fact that the words translated "this/what has happened to me will result in/turn out for my deliverance" are an exact quotation of the LXX version of Job 13:16, where Job expresses confidence about his vindication in a heavenly court. Moreover, although both the NRSV and the NIV have translated σωτηρία (sōtēria) as "deliverance," this word is used on every other occasion of its occurrence in the Pauline corpus in the sense of "salvation," God's final saving action (see the NIV marginal note). Paul's hope for a heavenly judgment in his favor is based on expectation regarding his behavior at the forthcoming earthly trial (v. 20). It is for this that he needs the Philippians' prayers and the support of "the Spirit of Jesus Christ." This is an unusual description of the Spirit, but it is highly appropriate, since Jesus was also put on trial before an earthly court and was vindicated by a heavenly judge, as we shall be reminded in 2:6-11. Paul is thus following in Jesus' footsteps. Perhaps Paul is also thinking of the Spirit as a paraclete or legal advocate, as does John (see John 14:16, 26; 15:26; 16:7-11; cf. 1 John 2:1).

It is Paul's eager expectation and firm hope (since it is founded upon God) that he will not be put to shame at the trial but will behave in such a way that now, as always, Christ will be exalted in him (v. 20). The possible shame stands in contrast to exaltation, but whereas it is Paul who might be ashamed, it is Christ who will be exalted by Paul's bold witness to him. The idea that God will come to the defense of the people, so that they are not put to shame and so that God is exalted, is common in the psalms, and the two verbs used here, meaning "to be ashamed" (αἰσχύνω aischynō) and "to exalt" (μεγαλύνω megalynō) are found together in the LXX (see Pss 34:3-5 [33:4-6]; 35:26-27[34:26]; 40:15-17[39:16-17]; cf. 1QH 4:23-24). The "now as always" indicates that Paul has had this experience before.

Christ will be exalted in Paul, "whether by life or death." The phrase "in my body" is a literal translation of the Greek but is somewhat misleading, for the word σῶμα (sōma) means more than a body of flesh. Paul does, to be sure, sometimes use the word in this sense, but the fact that Christ will be glorified in Paul's sōma whether he lives or dies indicates that Paul is not thinking here simply of his fleshly body. Rather, he is using sōma in the sense he often gives it, of the whole person. Thus whether Paul continues to live in the flesh or not, Christ will be exalted in him.

As far as Paul is concerned, however, "living/to live is Christ" (v. 21). These words are reminiscent of Gal 2:20, but they are balanced here by the parallel statement "dying/to die is gain." The verse is a neat rhetorical summary, especially effective when read aloud in Greek because of the similarity in sound of the words Χριστός (Christos) and κέρδος (kerdos, "gain"). There are parallels in ancient Greek writers to the idea that death can be a gain, in the sense that it is a release from troubles.[8] Paul, however, is far more positive. This verse suggests a very intimate relationship with Christ, but Paul is surely

---

8. E.g., Socrates. See Plato *Apology* 40c-d; Josephus *Antiquities of the Jews* 15:158 of death in battle.

thinking here of more than his own personal religious experience. The theme of the whole passage is the way in which the gospel is proclaimed, whatever Paul's own circumstances, and this verse links what is said in v. 20 with what follows in v. 22. For Paul, "to live is Christ" means not only that to live is to experience Christ, but also that to live is to magnify him; death will be gain because it will mean not only to "be with Christ," but also to find new ways to magnify him, perhaps through death itself.

Paul does not, in fact, spell out here the nature of the gain brought by death, though in v. 23 we learn that it means "to depart and be with Christ." Elsewhere he describes Christians who die as dying "in Christ" (1 Cor 15:18); they are "with Christ" (1 Thess 4:14); death cannot separate them from the love of God in Christ Jesus (Rom 8:38). In v. 22, however, he elaborates on what "living/to live" will mean. This, too, will involve a form of gain, since it will mean "fruitful labor," literally, "the fruit of labor." The phrase is ambiguous and could mean future fruit from past labor, but Paul is clearly thinking of the advantage of future work that will bear yet more fruit. The contrast between the gain brought by death (v. 21) and the fruit produced by life (v. 22) is once again underlined by the similarity of the words κέρδος (*kerdos*, "gain") and καρπός (*karpos*, "fruit"). The life that he is talking about is life "in the flesh" (NRSV). The NIV translates the expression as "in the body," but the Greek word used here is σάρξ (*sarx*, "flesh"). We see here the difference between *sarx*, which refers to the limitations of the life ended by death, and *sōma*, which embraces much more.

Paul does not know whether to hope for life or for death. "Choose" (NIV) and "prefer" (NRSV) are both proper translations of the Greek αἱρέω (*aireō*), but "prefer" is more appropriate here, since Paul is in no position to choose. He is "torn/hard pressed between the two"; the NRSV's "hard pressed" is closer to the literal meaning of the Greek, but the NIV's "torn" perhaps expresses the tension better. On the one hand, he wishes "to depart and be with Christ" (v. 23), and he piles up superlatives to express his conviction that this would be "better by far." The conviction that death would be gain has sometimes been interpreted as implying a belief in an intermediate afterlife between death and resurrection—a kind of "waiting room" where Christians await the next stage. There has been considerable debate as to whether this idea is consistent with Paul's teaching about the parousia and the resurrection in his earlier epistles. There, however, he uses verbs of sleeping to express the idea of dying, a common Jewish metaphor for death (see, e.g., 1 Cor 15:18; 1 Thess 4:14; 5:10). Since the image of sleep implies a lack of consciousness, the idea behind chap. 1 is perhaps that if Paul falls asleep in death, his next moment of awareness will be at the resurrection; hence, dying is seen as "gain." It is important to remember, however, that all these ideas are metaphors—attempts to explain something beyond our understanding. Since God is outside both time and space, questions about when and where are meaningless. Paul's conviction is simply that death will mean being with Christ and sharing his resurrection life.

To remain in the flesh (*sarx*), on the other hand, "is more necessary for you." Whatever his personal indecision, therefore, Paul is confident that for their sake he will "remain and continue" with them. There is a play on words in the Greek, which uses three different words for "remain" in vv. 24-25, all formed from the same root: ἐπιμένω (*epimenō*), μένω (*menō*), and παραμένω (*paramenō*). The last of these words can also have the meaning "to stay alive." What has persuaded Paul is not a sudden divine revelation, but his conviction that God will act for the benefit of the Philippians. The decisive factors here—as everywhere else in this epistle—are the needs of others and the progress of the gospel, and not one's personal preferences. The new lease on life he hopes for is not seen as a personal reward, but as an opportunity to be useful to his churches. It will thus serve their progress in the gospel.

The Greek word προκοπή (*prokopē*, "progress"), picks up a word used in v. 12, though this fact is disguised by both the NIV and the NRSV translations of that verse. The two occurrences form an inclusio, underlining the theme of the whole paragraph: Whatever happens to Paul is used by God to advance the gospel. Here the word should be linked with "the faith," which, unusually in Paul, is used with the definite article "only" (correctly translated in the NIV) and no further definition; it seems to have a meaning here similar to "the gospel." Paul's continuing ministry will also bring the Philippians joy (the keynote of the gospel). The result (v. 26) will be that the Philippians' boasting in Christ Jesus will overflow. The Greek word καύχημα (*kauchēma*) is properly translated "boasting" in the NRSV, in contrast to the NIV's "joy." The cause of boasting is Christ Jesus, but it is "on account of me" (the NIV translation is here preferable to that of the NRSV)—that is, "because of my coming to you again." The word for "coming" is παρουσία (*parousia*), the word used elsewhere of the coming of Christ at the end time, and in secular Greek of the triumphant entry of kings and governors into cities. It might perhaps have something of this sense of triumph here, but it is also the ordinary word for "coming" or "presence" (see, e.g., 2:12) and was probably simply the natural word for Paul to use.

REFLECTIONS

1. Once again, we find that a conventional feature of a letter has been transformed. Although Paul's opening words lead us to expect a report regarding his own situation, what he, in fact, gives us is a description of how the gospel is progressing, rather than simply how things are with him. As an apostle, this is his chief concern. He begins on a positive note ("what has happened to me has helped to advance the gospel"), and ends with a triumphant reference to future boasting in Christ. Throughout the whole section, we see how Paul confidently expects the message of the gospel (life through death) to be worked out in his own experience and in the experience of the church. He proclaims the gospel of crucifixion and resurrection not only with his lips, but also with his whole life.

Paul's own afflictions, therefore, are seen as an opportunity for the gospel: People talk about his case; therefore, they learn about the Christian faith, and other Christians are encouraged to make a similar stand. Christian churches that endure harassment and persecution today may draw comfort from Paul's words. Throughout history, persecution has often strengthened the church. In our own time, we have seen vigorous Christian communities emerge after years of oppression by state authorities. In spite of all its failures, the church bears witness to the power of the gospel, because the pattern of the gospel (life through death) is being worked out in the life of the church. The amazing fact that oppression leads to growth reflects the paradox that lies at the heart of the gospel—namely, that God's power is revealed through the weakness of the cross and that victory comes through apparent defeat (1 Cor 1:23-27).

Paul cheerfully accepts whatever circumstances he finds himself in, even imprisonment, acknowledging that he has been "put here for the defense of the gospel." Instead of chafing at the restrictions imposed upon him and pining for the time when he might preach freely again, he regards his imprisonment as an opportunity. His attitude is reflected in the searching words of the Methodist Covenant Service:

> Put me to what you will, rank me with whom you will; put me to doing, put me to suffering; let me be employed for you or laid aside for you, exalted for you or brought low for you; let me be full, let me be empty; let me have all things, let me have nothing.

Paul has been "laid aside" for God, but he sees even this as an opportunity for God to be glorified.

2. The fact that Paul elsewhere condemns those who preach false gospels (see, e.g., 3:2, 18-19) often leads us to suppose that he was totally intolerant of others' views. In this section, however, we see a remarkable tolerance of those whose motives are

dubious. This is because their jealousy of him and their ill will toward him are unimportant, so long as Christ is proclaimed. When Paul believes that the gospel is under attack, he is implacable; here he thinks the opposition is merely directed to him, and he can therefore be generous. This passage reminds us that the gospel is far greater than the worthiness of its ministers: God can work through men and women in spite of their faults and failings. Clearly there comes a point, however, at which our own selfish attitudes can contradict and swamp the message of the gospel. In the next section, Paul will urge his readers to live "in a manner worthy of the gospel" (1:27), which means having the message of the gospel stamped on their lives and attitudes. "Proclaiming Christ" is a matter of living out the gospel, not just of declaring its message.

Paul's words remind us, too, of how easy it is to delude ourselves about our motives in undertaking Christian service. Truly disinterested service is rare, indeed! The preacher is perhaps particularly in danger of succumbing to selfish ambition, enjoying the plaudits of those who are impressed by fluent oratory and good storytelling. Paul rightly contrasts true and false motives, but in practice most Christians probably belong to both camps. The battle against envy, rivalry, selfish ambition, and insincerity is a constant one.

3. Paul was clearly the kind of person who easily caused controversy and provoked opposition, not just from enemies, but from fellow Christians also. Those who are passionately committed to a cause frequently embarrass others who share the same aims, but who do so more quietly. Civil rights supporters, animal rights protestors, and environmentalists are all examples of groups who have been divided as to the best method by which to campaign for their cause. German church leaders who protested about what the Nazi Party was doing in the 1930s, campaigners for racial justice in the United States and South Africa; men and women who have protested against the exploitation of native peoples in South America, Indonesia, Nigeria, and Iran have all embarrassed others who believed in the same cause but who supported it in less aggressive ways. In the same way, Paul, who was so often imprisoned, must have been a great source of embarrassment to those Christians who preferred a softer approach. Sometimes these subtler ways work better, but the church certainly needs men and women with Paul's courage, who are not afraid to suffer for that in which they believe. There is a place for both approaches, and we must aim to live out God's particular calling for us.

4. Although in this passage Paul is discussing the possibility of his execution, the dominant notes are joy and hope; even imprisonment and the threat of death cannot extinguish them. Rabbi Hugo Gryn used to tell of his experiences in Auschwitz as a boy. Food supplies were meager, and the inmates took care to preserve every scrap that came their way. When the Festival of Hanukkah arrived, Hugo's father took a lump of margarine and, to the horror of young Hugo, used it as fuel for the light to be lit at the festival. When he was asked why, his father replied, "We know that it is possible to live for three weeks without food, but without hope it is impossible to live properly for three minutes."

Paul confidently expects "deliverance," but this deliverance, as we have seen, is not from death. What he hopes for is that he will be given the courage to stand firm at his trial and so be vindicated by the heavenly court. By contrast, we are, perhaps, inclined to pray too much for deliverance from illness and sorrow, pain and death, rather than for courage to endure these things. The real danger is to succumb to their power, instead of trusting in God (as Christ did) to bring us through them. Paul is convinced that God can be glorified not only by the way the Christian lives, but also by the way he or she dies. Living (and dying) "properly" means for Paul that Christ is exalted in his "body," or person. His thought is echoed centuries later in the line from George Herbert's hymn "King of Glory": "In my heart, though not in heaven, I can raise thee."

As for the outcome of his trial, Paul is uncertain what to hope for. As always, however, the needs of his congregations take priority over his own personal desires. Paul's spirituality, though intensely personal, is never an individual matter. He is a member of a community, the body of Christ, and the well-being of that community and the progress of the gospel are all-important. Our own piety tends to be far more individualistic. Many Christians regard religion as a private concern and think of the Christian gospel as primarily an offer of personal salvation. Without minimizing the necessity for the individual to respond to the gospel, we ought perhaps to remember the gospel's wider implications.

5. Underlying Paul's prayers for himself and for his churches is his conviction that God is in control of human destiny. Clearly he believes that the verdict at the trial lies ultimately in God's hands. But if God "looks after his own," it is definitely *not* in the sense that God will see to it that Paul is released! Rather, God can be relied on for the assurance that, whatever happens, there will be an opportunity to turn the situation to good effect. One of the temptations into which Christians frequently fall is to suppose that God "looks after his own" by saving them from disasters of all kinds and by blessing them with prosperity, health, and good fortune. The constant cry, "Why should this happen to me?" implies that God has let us down. We expect God to reward us for our allegiance and to save us from all trials and tribulations. The Christian gospel offers no such hope. What it does offer is the assurance that, whatever happens, the Christian who trusts in God will not be let down by God or be put to shame. Whatever experiences we undergo, we may confidently expect to find Christ sharing them with us, and so we discover that disaster leads to new opportunity, sorrow to joy, and death to resurrection life.

Perhaps our problem is our own limited horizon, which leads us to approach the gospel with the everyday attitudes that govern our behavior elsewhere. We might ask, "What's in it for me? What does the gospel offer me?" The answer to these questions is, of course, "A great deal!" But the questions ignore the fact that the gospel is primarily about God's self-revelation in Christ and about the things that God has done. The gospel invites us to forget, as Christ did, our own concerns and desires, and to find joy and salvation in offering praise and glory to God.

PHILIPPIANS 1:27–2:18
THE CHRISTIAN LIFE, PART 1

OVERVIEW

Paul now turns to pastoral advice, offered to a community facing opposition and persecution. This advice may well have been shaped in response to information that had reached him regarding the Philippian church, but it will also certainly reflect his own experiences and deliberations in prison. It is difficult to know which of these influences was the more important. There is, for example, a strong emphasis on unity in these verses, and many commentators believe that this emphasis reflects a situation of division and conflict in the Philippian church. The instruction in 4:2 to Euodia and Syntyche "to be of the same mind/agree with each other in the Lord" lends some support to this view; but Paul does not rebuke the community for a lack of unity, and the absence of such rebuke suggests that division was not a serious problem there. Nevertheless, the attitude he urges the Philippians to adopt is clearly the one he later presses on the women, and he may well have their disagreement in mind here. If Paul emphasizes the need for unity, however, this may well be in part because of the divisions referred to in 1:15-18 that he has himself encountered during his imprisonment. Preachers who exhort their congregations to particular courses of action are not necessarily rebuking them for their failures. These preachers may, of course, be emphasizing something because they know of certain problems within the communities they are addressing, but they are just as likely to be sharing insights into the gospel that have been shaped by their own experiences and meditations. Paul was well aware of the dangers and temptations facing a young Christian community subject to persecution and pressure.

This section gives advice on how the Philippians should behave. Apart from the emphasis on unity, the instructions are general rather than particular. The readers are to live "in a manner worthy of the gospel" (1:27); to "look to the interests of others" (2:4); to be "blameless" (2:15). What Paul is anxious to do is to instill an attitude—the attitude of Christ himself, set out in 2:5-11. Although Paul begins a new theme here, it is firmly linked to the preceding paragraphs, since the behavior he appeals for is that appropriate to the gospel, about which he has been speaking.

PHILIPPIANS 1:27-30, STAND FAST!

COMMENTARY

The opening word, μόνον (*monon*, "only," as in the NRSV), indicates the move to exhortation: "There is just one thing!" Although this one thing is then extensively discussed, it is in fact well summed up in the opening command, "Live your life/conduct yourselves in a manner worthy of the gospel of Christ." The verb πολιτεύομαι (*politeuomai*) is not the one Paul ordinarily employs in commands regarding behavior (indeed, he uses it nowhere else). It is derived from the noun used in 3:20, meaning "commonwealth" or "citizenship" (see the Commentary on 3:20). Its basic meaning is "to exercise the rights and duties of citizens," though it came to be used with the more general meaning of "to behave." The translations of the NRSV and the NIV: "live your life/

conduct yourselves" are, therefore, accurate, but they fail to convey the idea Paul was probably trying to express in using this particular word here—namely, that the behavior required of the Philippians is a reflection of the "citizenship" they now enjoy as members of the Christian community. Those members of the church in Philippi who were citizens of that city would also have been Roman citizens; thus they would have been well aware of the privileges and obligations of citizenship. Paul has probably chosen this particular verb because he thinks of Christian behavior not simply as something undertaken by individuals, but as the expression of the life of the whole community. His meaning is, "Let your life as a community be worthy of the gospel of Christ."[9]

If they do this, then the question of whether Paul is able to come and see them will be irrelevant. The life worthy of the gospel involves "standing firm in one spirit, striving side by side with one mind" (NRSV). Paul here uses the Greek terms for "spirit" (πνεῦμα *pneuma*) and "soul" (ψυχή *psychē*), but the NRSV aptly translates the latter word as "mind"; the community should act "as one person" (hence the NIV's "one man"). The words signify here that which unites the Philippians, not separate parts of the individual. "In one spirit" has no parallel in Greek literature and probably refers to the Holy Spirit (see 2:1). It is the Spirit that unites them and enables them to stand firmly and resist opposition. The "one mind" they share comes from the fact that they are all in Christ. Paul elaborates on what it means to be in one spirit and to have one mind in chap. 2. The verb "striving side by side" seems to be an athletic metaphor and points forward to the imagery of 3:14 (cf. 4:3); the NRSV translation here captures well the implication of "togetherness" in the Greek. "The faith," which was used in v. 25 in a sense parallel to "the gospel," appears here to be almost tautologous: "the faith which is the gospel."

We do not know who the opponents mentioned in v. 28 were. The fact that Paul speaks in vv. 29-30 of the Philippians' enduring suffering and being engaged in a struggle suggests that they were real opponents and not just potential ones. It is sometimes suggested that these opponents were Judaizers, the group of conservative Jewish Christians who gave Paul such problems in Galatia, but it seems more likely that the opposition came from outside the church. The community's enemies could be either Jews or pagans, but once again the reference to suffering and to the Philippians' sharing in "the same struggle" as Paul himself is enduring suggests that their problems may be with the civil authorities. According to Luke, Paul had met opposition in Philippi from businessmen in the city (Acts 16) who were annoyed because his mission was undermining their financial interests. The opposition faced by the Philippian community could well have arisen from similar grievances, leading to unrest and charges before the civil authorities, rather than from organized persecution.

The Greek underlying "This is evidence/a sign" (v. 28) is not nearly as clear as the English translations suggest. Paul uses the relative pronoun "which," and this probably refers to the behavior he is hoping the Philippians will show, though it might refer to "the faith of the gospel." One can certainly see how "the faith of the gospel" could be said to demonstrate both salvation and destruction, but the order of the Greek does not support this interpretation. It is difficult, however, to understand how the fact that the Philippians are standing firm and are not in any way intimidated can be a "sign" or "evidence" to their opponents of their own destruction and of the Philippians' salvation. They were surely very unlikely either to observe it or to heed it! It is not surprising, then, that there are variant readings in some MSS, which have either "but to you of salvation" or "but to us of salvation" instead of "but of your salvation." These, of course, solve only part of the difficulty and are clearly attempts to do so. In fact, it is easier to understand how the Philippians' steadfastness could be a sign to their opponents of the Christians' coming salvation than it is to see how the opponents could interpret it as a sign of their own coming destruction. The Greek word ἔνδειξις (*endeixis*) means "indication" or "demonstration." Paul perhaps means that when the gospel is lived out in an appropriate way, that is a proclamation of its message, a living demonstration of the salvation from

---

9. See Raymond R. Brewer, "The Meaning of *Politeuesthe* in Philippians 1:27," *JBL* 73 (1954) 76-83.

destruction that it offers. The Philippians' behavior is thus at one and the same time evidence of the truth of the gospel and a warning to those who oppose it.

The last clause of v. 28 is ambiguous. The NIV has taken it as a comment on what has just been said: The Philippians will be saved (and their opponents destroyed?) by God. But the preposition (ἀπό *apo*; lit., "from") denotes origin rather than agency, and Paul has used nouns, "destruction" and "salvation," not verbs. The ambiguity is better expressed by the NRSV's "And this is God's doing." But to what does "this" refer? Does it refer to the salvation and destruction, as the NIV supposes? Does it refer to the omen (the "sign" or "evidence") of that salvation or destruction? Or does it refer to that which was described as the "sign" or "evidence" of that salvation and destruction—namely, the Philippians' steadfastness in the face of suffering? These last two possibilities are not exclusive; if the "sign" is from God, so is the steadfastness of which it consists. Certainly the next verse seems to support the last possibility, since Paul speaks next of the Philippians' having been "granted" (the verb χαρίζομαι [*charizomai*] is a cognate of χάρις [*charis*], "grace") the privilege of suffering on Christ's behalf. Not only is their ability to resist evil a gift from God, but so also is the suffering itself, because it is ὑπὲρ Χριστοῦ (*hyper Christou*), "for/on behalf of Christ." This remarkable phrase, which is repeated at the end of the verse, is exactly parallel to the phrase used frequently in the NT, especially by Paul, to describe Christ's suffering and death for others.[10] Here, however, it is *Christians* who suffer *for Christ*. This reciprocal relationship is extraordinary. In what sense can the Philippians' sufferings be "for Christ"? Does Paul simply mean that they are suffering because they are Christians? The parallel between "believing in" and "suffering for" supports this, but the repetition of the phrase and the use of the verb *charizomai* suggest that there is more to it than this. We need to remember that although Paul speaks of Christ's dying *for* us, he also insists that the Christian needs to die *with* Christ (e.g., Rom 6:3-10) and is expected to suffer with him (e.g., Rom 8:17).

In 3:10, Paul speaks of his desire to know the fellowship of Christ's sufferings by being conformed to his death and so to his resurrection, but it is clear from 1:29-30 that both he and the Philippians are already experiencing that "sharing/fellowship" of suffering. Through baptism into Christ, we make his death our own, but this means that those who share Christ's sufferings and death are united to the power of his resurrection and life. This power is not something that stops short with them, however, since they become its channels, through whom grace and joy and comfort are brought to others. Suffering "for Christ" means, therefore, that the Philippians—because they are "in Christ"—are granted the privilege of sharing in the redemptive work of Christ. Their sufferings are in reality his and can, therefore, be used by him. Paul and the Philippians are, indeed, as he expressed in v. 7, "partners in grace."[11] The clearest expressions of this idea are to be found in 2 Cor 1:3-7; 4:7-12; and 6:4-10, where Paul describes his own experience, and in Col 1:24. We now understand why the Philippians are a sign of both salvation and destruction: In their believing and their suffering they are an embodiment of the gospel.

It is for good reason, then, that Paul returns to the theme of his own sufferings in v. 30. The Philippians are now sharing in the same "struggle" (ἀγών *agōn*), another athletic image, as they know Paul to have been and still be enduring. The reference to what the Philippians have witnessed in the past is presumably to the incident mentioned in 1 Thess 2:2, where Paul again uses the word *agōn* for the opposition he encountered in Philippi. He speaks there of being shamefully treated in Philippi, and this is likely to be a reference to the incident described by Luke in Acts 16:19-40. The struggle is the same, not because the Philippians are also suffering imprisonment (there is no hint of this), but because they, like Paul, are under attack from those who oppose the gospel and are engaged in a battle with the forces of evil. If the Philippians can take comfort from this, it

---

10. See, e.g., 1 Thess 5:10, "our Lord Jesus Christ died for us" (cf. Rom 5:8); 1 Cor 15:3, "Christ died for our sins" (cf. Gal 1:4); Rom 8:32, "[God] gave him up for all of us" (cf. Gal 2:20). See also John 10:15, "I lay down my life for the sheep," and Heb 2:9, where Christ is said to "taste death for everyone."

11. See M. D. Hooker, "A Partner in the Gospel: Paul's Understanding of His Ministry," in *Theology and Ethics in Paul and His Interpreters: Festschrift for V. P. Furnish*, ed. Eugene H. Lovering and Jerry L. Sumney (Nashville: Abingdon, 1996) 83-100.

is not simply because they are all, as it were, in the same boat, but because they have seen in Paul's case how suffering can be used "for Christ."

Many of the ideas in this paragraph are picked up by Paul in a later section of the epistle, 3:17–4:1, which suggests that the two passages mark the beginning and the end of a larger section of the epistle. The ideas taken up later include those of following Paul's example, sharing the sufferings of Christ, the future destinies of those opposed to the gospel (destruction) and of believers (salvation), the citizenship of Christians, and the exhortation to stand firm. (See Reflections at 2:12-18.)

PHILIPPIANS 2:1-4, OUR LIFE IN CHRIST

COMMENTARY

2:1-2. This section begins with a question headed by "If," but there is no doubt about the answer: "If—as is, of course, the case!" The assurance is conveyed in Greek by the word οὖν (*oun*), "therefore" (NRSV, "then"; unfortunately omitted by the NIV). The verb is missing and thus has to be supplied; the NRSV has chosen "there is," the NIV "you have." Paul's appeal is based on the "encouragement" the Philippians possess "in Christ." The word παράκλησις (*paraklēsis*), here translated "encouragement," can mean both "comfort" and "exhortation"; commentators are divided as to which meaning it has here, but it is perhaps unnecessary to choose. In fact, the English word "encouragement" conveys both senses, and the noun is probably used here to denote the power that enables the Philippians to do the things listed in vv. 2-4. In Christ, believers find both comfort and strength.

As in 1:27, union with Christ forms the basis of the appeal to an appropriate way of life. It is because Christians are "in Christ" that they are united to him and to one another and are able to share his mind and strength. It is this union that is the source of the "encouragement" that provides, in turn, the "consolation/comfort" of love, "sharing in/fellowship with the Spirit," "compassion/tenderness and sympathy/compassion." Paul (unlike the NIV) does not specify whose love he has in mind; no doubt Christ's love for us comes first, but he may well be thinking also of Christians' love for Christ and for one another. Similarly, although the Spirit is the origin of fellowship (the term is κοινωνία [*koinōnia*] once again; see 1:5; 3:10), Paul's phrase probably refers also to our participation in the life and work of the Spirit and the fellowship with other Christians that the Spirit creates. The word translated "compassion" in the NRSV and "tenderness" in the NIV is σπλάγχνα (*splagchna*; lit., "bowels"), which was used in 1:8 with the genitive "of Christ Jesus." It is clear from the context that Christ is the source of compassion here also.

On the basis of what they have in Christ, Paul now appeals to the Philippians to behave in such a way as will "make [his] joy complete" (v. 2). The Philippians have already brought him joy (1:4; cf. 4:1), and if their behavior reflects their common life in Christ, they will fulfill Paul's joy. The underlying exhortation is to "be what you are," to live "in a manner worthy of the gospel of Christ" (1:27). They are to "be of the same mind" (NRSV), literally, to "think the same." Here we have again the key verb φρονέω (*phroneō*), which Paul has already used in 1:7 (see the Commentary on 1:3-8). It occurs again in the last phrase of 2:2 ("being . . . of one mind," NRSV; this is obscured in the NIV's "one in . . . purpose") and in the opening words of v. 5. As has already been noted, the verb refers to attitude, rather than to intellectual thought. The members of the Christian community must share a common attitude, and what that attitude is will be spelled out in vv. 5-11. For the moment, the command to "be of the same mind" is amplified by the next three phrases: They are to "have the same love"—which is in effect the same love as Christ, since he is the source of love (v. 1)—to be "in full accord," and to think or feel one thing.

2:3-4. The same theme is continued in these verses, expressed in a couple of contrasts. Once again, the first verb is missing. The NRSV and the NIV supply "do," but perhaps we should understand *phronein*, since actions are based on attitudes. On the one side stand selfish ambition (cf. 1:17) and empty conceit. This latter term is κενοδοξία (*kenodoxia*); the *keno* part of the stem means "empty," and the *doxia* is related to δόξα (*doxa*), meaning "glory." Those who have illusions about themselves are also "vainglorious"; there is a contrast not only with the second part of the verse, but also with the true glory that comes at the climax of v. 11. On the other side we have the attitude that in humility considers others to be better than oneself. We are accustomed to thinking of humility as a virtue, but it was not considered to be such in the Greek world, where it was regarded as servility. Paul's converts might well have been surprised to find him urging them to behave with humility, but the reason will be made clear in v. 8. The noun ταπεινοφροσύνη (*tapeinophrosynē*) is akin to the verb ταπεινόω (*tapeinoō*) used in v. 8 and also to the verb φρονέω (*phroneō*); it refers to the attitude of being humble. The background to its use here is to be found in the OT. To be sure, men and women are often humbled by others, or by God (Ps 119:67, 71, 75), but those who are brought low may hope for God to save them (Job 5:11; Ps 142:6). Humility is the proper attitude toward God (Ps 138:6; Prov 3:34; 11:2). At Qumran, humility is recognized as the appropriate attitude both toward God and toward other members of the community (1QS 2:24; 4:3; 5:23, 25). Here, Paul urges the members of the Christian community in Philippi to regard others as better than themselves; this is not meant to foster false modesty or a lack of self-esteem, but to encourage a recognition of the rights and achievements of others. His choice of the word ἡγούμενοι (*hēgoumenoi*, "considering/ regarding") is significant, for the same verb will be used again in v. 6 of the attitude of Christ.

Verse 4 provides a parallel contrast between concern for one's own interests and concern for the interests of others. The NIV translation includes two words that are not in the NRSV: "only," which is not in the Greek, and "also," which represents the Greek word καί (*kai*) and is found in some Greek MSS but not in all. The addition weakens the contrast, and the passage seems to make better sense without it; others may have thought so, too, and so omitted it, which means that the word may well have been part of the original text. If that is the case, then Paul was perhaps more realistic than his later "corrector," and his instruction to be concerned with the interests of others *as well as* one's own is in line with the commandment to love one's neighbor *as oneself.* The shorter text, on the other hand, seems to agree with 1 Cor 10:24. But we should, perhaps, understand the *kai* as having the meaning "rather." That is, they should be looking to the interests of others *rather* than their own. What are the "interests" with which Christians are concerned? Paul does not specify. Indeed, there is no noun in the Greek, merely the definite article, followed by the words "your own" and "of others." Perhaps he is being intentionally vague; the phrases could refer to possessions, to rights, to spiritual gifts, or to points of view.

The themes of these four verses all lead into the "hymn" that follows. Christ's actions provide not simply an example for believers to copy but also the foundation of their Christian existence. (See Reflections at 2:12-18.)

PHILIPPIANS 2:5-11, THE MIND OF CHRIST

COMMENTARY

Origins of the Christological "Hymn." Philippians 2:5 introduces one of the best known and most influential passages in the Pauline corpus. It is commonly referred to as a hymn (and for the sake of convenience it will be referred to as such here). Whether or not it was composed as a hymn is uncertain. Its style is solemn and rhythmical, and thus it has a certain poetic quality, reflected in the fact that both the NIV and the NRSV set the passage as poetry. However, its structure does not conform to the rules of Greek poetry. Its pattern of regular stresses and the use of parallelism remind us of Hebrew poetry (as in the psalms); thus it has been suggested that it was originally composed in Aramaic. Its lines can be arranged in many different ways, and the very fact that this is possible should warn us to beware of imposing our own ideas of poetic structure onto the material. In particular, it is dangerous to do what some commentators do, and excise one or more lines as "Pauline additions" to an original passage, on the grounds that they do not fit the expected pattern.

It is, nevertheless, possible that Paul is quoting an earlier composition at this point. Certainly the introductory ὅς (*hos*, "who") in v. 6 suggests that what follows is a creedal statement of some kind—though we must beware of thinking that it is any kind of formal creed. Who, then, composed the passage? One possibility is Paul himself. We know from his other letters that he was capable of using colorful language as well as the rhetorical devices of parallelism and chiasm that are employed here. With his Jewish background, he was obviously capable of writing in a "Semitic" style. Another possibility is that it was a pre-Pauline composition that he took over and used. In support of this theory, we should note that the hymn contains many unusual words, some of which are not found in Paul's other writings or even elsewhere in the NT. This, of course, may be due to its poetic style, but many commentators believe that this passage, in fact, reflects the beliefs of the Christian community before Paul. But in that case, why should Paul quote it here? Was it something that was known to the Philippians? Or was it simply particularly appropriate to his purpose here? Certainly it was the latter, for, as we shall see, whatever its origin, Paul has used the passage in a very Pauline way, and its theology is much more Pauline than a superficial reading might suggest. A third possibility is that the "hymn" was originally not a Christian composition at all, but was "gnostic," celebrating the descent and exaltation of a redeemer figure, and that Paul took it over and adapted it. This view, at one time very popular, has almost nothing to be said for it. There is no evidence that the myth of the heavenly redeemer existed in pre-Christian times or that Paul was confronted by gnostic ideas at Philippi. Even if such a gnostic composition existed, it seems unlikely that it would be Semitic in form or that Paul would have made use of it. A final suggestion is that the "hymn" might have been composed by a member of one of Paul's churches (possibly even at Philippi), which would explain why the ideas are so similar to his, even though the language is somewhat different. Whether Paul actually composed these lines, however, he has used them, and by using them has made them his own.

Ideas. More important than the origins of the passage are the ideas it contains and their relevance to Paul's argument. But what are these ideas? And what is their background? Here again, we find widely diverging views.

The first thing to strike us is the fact that the passage falls into two main sections, the first dealing with Christ's voluntary humiliation, the second with his exaltation. This pattern is familiar from other passages in Paul's letters, though there are interesting differences. To begin with, the treatment of the theme is much more extended than usual. Second, the emphasis throughout the first section is on Christ's self-giving. Elsewhere, Paul usually speaks of God as the one who sends or gives his Son, though it is not unknown for him to refer to Christ's giving himself (cf. Gal 2:20 with Rom 8:32), and there is an interesting parallel with his reference to Christ's obedience in Rom 5:18-19. In Phil 2:6-8, the focus is on Christ's action. His exaltation in 2:9-11 is, however, the work of God, and here we have the third interesting difference from parallel Pauline expressions, for the language is of exaltation, rather than of resurrection. Where Paul speaks of exaltation elsewhere, it is something that *follows* resurrection (Rom 8:34; 1 Cor 15:27); that is, his usual contrast is between death and resurrection. Elsewhere, too, the confession of Jesus as Lord is linked with the belief in his resurrection (Rom 10:9-10; cf. Rom 1:3-4, where he is declared to be Son of God by resurrection from the dead).

Philippians 2 is the earliest passage in the Pauline literature to raise in our minds serious questions about the pre-existence of Christ. Already Paul has made statements implying a change in status on Christ's part, notably in 2 Cor 8:9, where Christ, who was rich, became poor for our sake—this is the language of incarnation. Now we find Christ, who was in the form of God, emptying himself, taking the form of a slave, and *becoming man*; his subsequent obedience to death is apparently the second stage in the process of self-emptying.

It is not surprising to find Christ being thought of here as pre-existent. In Jewish thought, to speak of something or someone in this way was to affirm that they were part of God's plan. Thus in Eph 1:4, Christians are said to have been chosen in Christ before the foundation of the world. Earlier Jewish writers, moreover, building on Genesis 1, where God speaks and the world is created, had described the role of God's Word (identified with wisdom and with the law) in creation (e.g., Prov 8:22-31; Wis 7:22-26; Sirach 24). For Paul, Christ is wisdom (1 Cor 1:24, 30) and the fulfillment of the law (Rom 8:3; 10:4); he represented God's nature and purpose from the beginning (2 Cor 4:4, 6). In 1 Cor 8:6 we find hints that Christ was being seen as the agent of creation, an idea elaborated later in Col 1:15-20. In Philippians 2, however, Paul is not concerned with Christ's activity in his pre-existent state, but with the idea, found already in 2 Cor 8:9, of his change in status. In Philippians 2 Paul spells this out more fully and goes on to describe Christ's subsequent exaltation. For the first time, therefore, we have a pattern that may be depicted in Fig. 1:

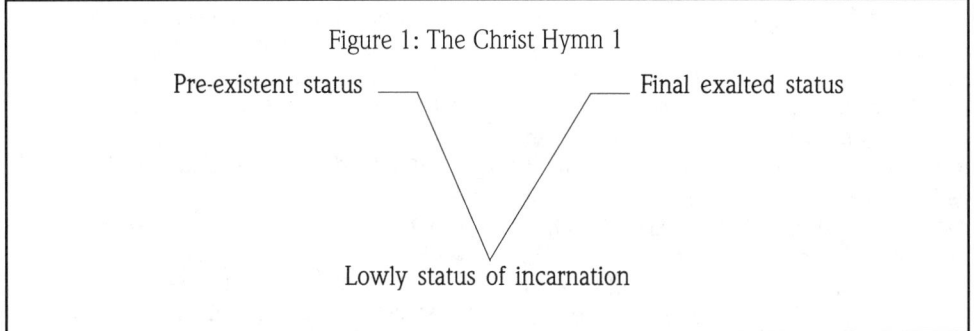

Figure 1: The Christ Hymn 1

We should note that Philippians 2 does not attempt to deal with questions about what the pre-incarnate Christ was *doing*; it is not until we come to Col 1:15-20 that this kind of problem is tackled. Nevertheless, we have moved a step beyond statements that "God sent his Son" to an emphatic declaration that Christ's incarnation was a deliberate act of self-emptying.

The turning point in the pattern is marked by the emphatic διό *dio*, "therefore") in 2:9. Because Christ acted in this way, God has highly exalted him. What is meant by the expression "highly exalted" (ὑπερύψωσεν *hyperypsōsen*)? Does the ὑπέρ (*hyper*) element indicate something more exalted than the status Christ enjoyed before? If it is only now that Christ is given "the name that is above every name," does this mean that the one who "was in the form of God" did not enjoy "equality with God" in his pre-existent state? If so, we must amend the diagram as follows:

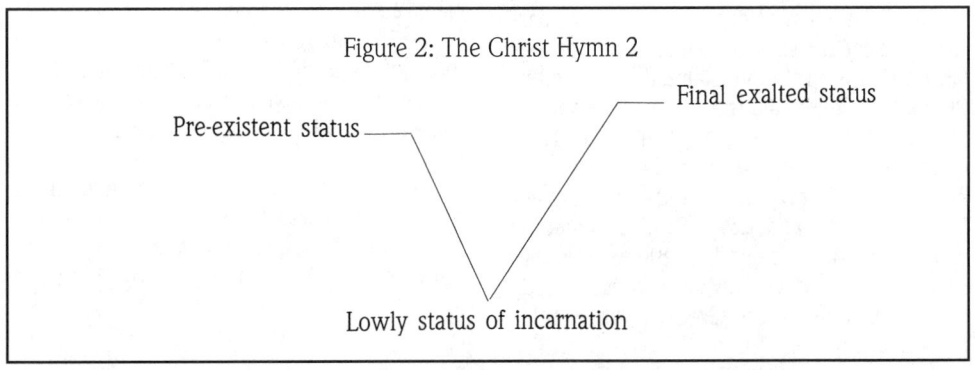

Figure 2: The Christ Hymn 2

To answer these questions, we must look closely at the text, but before we do so we must consider the question of background.

Background. If the roots of Paul's ideas in this passage are to be sought in Judaism (and not in Gnosticism), then where should we look to find them? Two main suggestions have been made, the first of which finds the background to Philippians 2 in the so-called Servant Song of Isaiah 53. The terminology is somewhat misleading. Isaiah 52:13–53:12 is the last of four passages that have been labeled "songs" by modern scholarship. In fact, there is nothing to isolate these passages from their context. Nor is there a distinct individual who is known as "my Servant." Rather, the phrase is used from time to time to refer to Israel or to a group within Israel, sometimes (possibly) to one individual. The parallels between Isaiah 53 and Philippians 2 have been found in the term "servant," in the idea of voluntary submission to suffering, and in the reference to death. On further investigation, however, these links prove to be illusory. The word used in the LXX of Isaiah 53 for "servant" is παῖς (*pais*), not δοῦλος (*doulos*), as in Phil 2:7. Moreover, the phrase "my servant" in Isa 52:13 is a title of honor—the very opposite of the degradation implied in the reference to a slave in Phil 2:7. It is true that the person described in Isaiah 52–53 dies a shameful death, but that is *in spite of*, and not *because of*, his status as God's servant. Moreover, it is by no means certain that the figure described in Isaiah 53 was understood to have suffered voluntarily. He suffered without protest (Isa 53:7); but that is not to say that he did so willingly, any more than a slaughtered lamb can be considered to be a willing victim. The assumption that Isaiah 53 describes voluntary sacrifice is the result of Christian interpretation of that passage, and the question at issue is whether that Christian interpretation is already reflected in Philippians 2. Finally, the phrase "he poured out himself/his life to death" in Isa 53:12 is often said to be reflected in the words ἑαυτὸν ἐκένωσεν (*heauton ekenōsen*), "he emptied himself" (v. 7), and μέχρι θανάτου (*mechri thanatou*), "unto death" (v. 8). As we shall see, however, not only are these words widely separated in the Greek, but they refer to two distinct actions on Christ's part: the action of the pre-existent Christ in emptying himself and becoming man and the action of the human Jesus in being obedient even to death. There is no justification for piecing them together and seeing them as an echo of Isa 53:12 (where the LXX verb is in any case quite different).

The alternative suggestion regarding the background of the passage is that it is based on the story of the fall of Adam in Genesis 3. Links have been found in the phrase "in the form of God," which is reminiscent of Gen 1:26, and in the contrast between Adam, who grasped at equality with God, and Christ, who did not grasp at/cling to/exploit that equality. Whereas Adam was stripped of his privileges, Christ deliberately emptied himself, becoming what Adam had become—a slave, subject to death. Adam's rebellion (though Adam himself is not named in Philippians 2) is thus contrasted with Christ's obedience. In favor of this interpretation we may point to Paul's use of Adam elsewhere (most clearly in Rom 5:12-21 and 1 Cor 15:21-22, 42-50) and to the language Paul uses at the end of Philippians 3 (where the implications of the "hymn" for Christians are, as we shall see, worked out), language that echoes that which he uses elsewhere to describe our restoration to the glory Adam lost (Rom 8:18-30, 39; 1 Cor 15:35-57; cf. 2 Cor 3:12–4:6). This interpretation has been objected to not only because the phrase ἐν μορφῇ θεοῦ (*en morphē theou*), "in the form of God," in v. 6 is not used in the LXX of Gen 1:26, but also because the word μορφή (*morphē*) is not synonymous with the word εἰκών (*eikōn*), "image," which *is* used there and which is used by Paul elsewhere (see in particular Rom 8:29; 2 Cor 3:18; 4:4; Col 1:15; 3:10). Moreover, although some have tried to exclude the idea of pre-existence from Philippians 2 and have argued that it is the actions of the human Jesus that are contrasted with those of Adam,[12] it is difficult to make sense of v. 7 without acknowledging that it was the *pre-existent* Christ who became man. How, then, can we have a figure who is described in Adamic terms, who then *becomes* man and takes on Adam's likeness?

The idea that Christ became man is found elsewhere in Paul, and it is perhaps wise to

---

12. Notably J. D. G. Dunn, *Christology in the Making* (London: SCM 1980) 113-21.

begin looking for an answer to this conundrum there. Particularly interesting is Rom 8:3, since the background of this verse is the idea of the renewal of creation and the restoration of the glory lost by Adam. God, we are told, sent his Son in the likeness of sinful flesh; the result is that men and women are delivered from slavery and themselves become children (lit., "sons") of God (Rom 8:14-17). The same ideas are expressed in Gal 4:4-7. In both these passages, however, unlike Philippians 2, the initative is taken by God, who sends the one described as God's Son. A parallel to Christ's self-emptying in Phil 2:7 is found in 2 Cor 8:9, where he is said to have become poor for the Corinthians' sake, with the result that they have been made rich. All three passages describe what we may term "incarnation," and in all three, the result of Christ's becoming man is that human beings are made what he eternally is.

Elsewhere, we find this same idea that men and women are conformed to what Christ is, and so become what they were meant to be. In 2 Cor 3:18, Christians see the glory of the Lord reflected in the face of Christ and are transformed into the same image; in 2 Cor 4:4 we learn that Christ is himself "the image." Similar ideas are developed in Colossians, where Christ is described as "the image of the invisible God" (Col 1:15) and where Christians are said to have taken off "the old man" and to have put on the new, which is being renewed after the image of its creator (Col 3:9-10). All these passages make use of Adamic language, since Adam was created after the image of God and was understood to have reflected the glory of God before the fall. Similar ideas seem to lie behind the passage at the end of Philippians 3, where we are told that the Lord Jesus Christ will transform our bodies of humiliation and conform them to his own body of glory.

There are two passages in which the comparisons between Adam and Christ are made explicit. In Rom 5:12-21, the comparison is the climax of the argument in the preceding chapters, where we are told that what happened in Christ was in many ways *not* the equivalent of what happened in Adam (Rom 5:15-17) because in Christ the grace of God was at work. The nature of this grace was spelled out in the opening verses of the chapter, where we were told that Christ died "for us" (Rom 5:8) and that we have been reconciled to God through the death of the Son (Rom 5:10). In 1 Cor 15:21-24, Christ stands over against Adam as the one who brings life instead of death and who is then identified as the Son who reigns until he hands everything over to his Father. Later in the chapter, Adam is described as the first man, who became a living soul (1 Cor 15:45, quoting Gen 2:7), whereas Christ is the second Adam, who is a life-giving Spirit. The first man is from the dust, the second man from heaven. Just as human beings have borne the image of the first man, so also they may bear the image of the second. The point of Paul's argument here is the nature of the future resurrection, when Christians will share the glorious body of Christ. In both these passages, Christ is understood to have reversed the effects of Adam's fall, and the reason why he is able to do so is because he is both man and Son of God. The relationship between Adam and Christ is not that of two successive competitors in a task, the first of whom fails while the second succeeds. Rather, Christ has to *undo* the failure of Adam, reverse his disobedience, and bring life where Adam brought death. Christ is thus greater than Adam.

The use of Adamic imagery elsewhere encourages us to suppose that it underlies Philippians 2–3, where we have similar ideas of Christ's becoming human, with the result that men and women become what he is. How, then, are we to deal with the objection that Phil 2:6 cannot be intended as a contrast between Adam and Christ, since the *result* of Christ's action is that he became man and took on human form? It is precisely in this anomaly that we find the solution to the problem. As has already been noted, Paul does not regard Adam and Christ as equals, since for him Christ is always greater than Adam. Christ is the true "image of God," after whom Christians are now being re-created, while Adam is the distorted copy, whose disobedience resulted in humanity's becoming enslaved to sin and death. If we were to set out the two actions of Adam and Christ diagrammatically, the pattern would not be that found in equating Adam with Christ but in seeing Christ as greater than Adam.

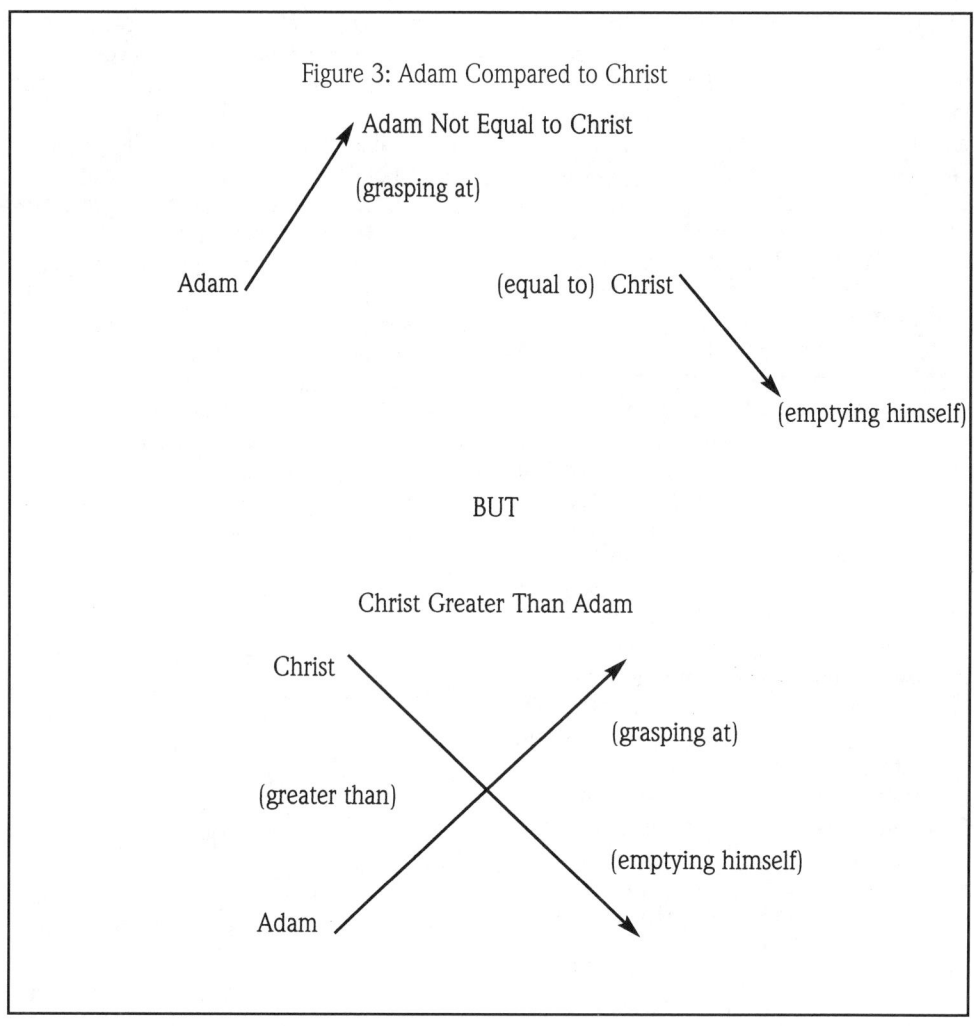

Figure 3: Adam Compared to Christ

To make sense of the parallel with Adam, therefore, we have to understand Christ to be the pattern of what humanity was meant to be: the perfect image of God and the reflection of God's glory. If Paul uses the phrase *en morphē Theou* rather than the one used of Adam in Genesis, that is with good reason, for it would make no sense at all to say that one who was created "after the image of God" (i.e., a man) became man! Christ is himself that image after whom Adam was created.

The fact that Paul does not use the word "image" here is thus no reason to reject the reference to Adam. The logic of the passage demands a contrast—between "the form of a slave," which expresses the condition into which Adam fell, and "the form of God," which expresses the condition of the one who is greater than Adam. Why, then, in Philippians 2 does Paul use the particular term *morphē*, whereas similar statements in Romans 8 and Galatians 4 refer to God's Son? The basic meaning of the word seems to be "visible form," and since children are often like their parents, it has been suggested that the phrase is comparable to the title "Son of God."[13] This visible form is perhaps to be identified with God's glory, which features in OT theophanies (e.g., Exodus 32). Or perhaps it is the expression of the inner reality that is at one and the same time concealed

---

13. C. A. Wanamaker, "Philippians 2.6-11: Son of God or Adamic Christology?" *NTS* 33 (1987) 179-93.

by and revealed by the glory. This presumably lies behind the NIV's "in very nature God," a translation that is nevertheless misleading (see below). The idea that God has a "form" that cannot be seen by humans is found in various Jewish writings.[14] Particularly interesting is the passage in the Talmud that interprets Gen 1:27 as meaning that God created Adam "in the image of the likeness of his form."[15] We do not know how early this particular interpretation came to be, but the fact that it distinguishes "the image" from "the form" is significant. A parallel idea is found in Philo (a contemporary of Paul) who uses the term "image" to describe what is closest to God. So God is the pattern of the image (who is also God's Word) and this image is in turn the pattern for humanity, since "God made the Man after the image of God."[16] In later Judaism, we find the hope of future restoration, when men and women will again be like God. Thus *Gen. Rab.* 21:7 interprets Gen 3:22 as referring to the world to come, when God will say, "Behold, the man *has become as one of us.*"

Ideas such as these may well lie behind Paul's use of Adamic language. For him, Christ is the *true* "image of God" (2 Cor 4:4; Col 1:15), the one who is "in his form," whereas Adam, who was created "after" God's image, became subject to sin and death because of his disobedience (Rom 5:12-21) and is now only a distorted copy of what he was meant to be. Those who have borne the image of the first Adam may, in turn, bear the image of the last Adam (1 Cor 15:42-49)—last, not in the sense that he came into existence last, but because he represents the eschatological goal of humanity, God's original purpose for creation.[17] He is the one through whom all things exist (1 Cor 8:6; Col 1:15-16), the embodiment of God's glory, according to whose image men and women are being restored (Rom 8:28-30; Col 3:9). If Phil 2:6 uses the phrase *en morphē Theou* rather than "the Son of God," this may well be precisely because the contrast of Christ with Adam is fundamental to the theme of the passage.[18]

2:5. The key to understanding how and why Paul uses this passage is found in v. 5, which reads literally: "Think this among you which also in Christ Jesus." Once again, we find that a missing verb has to be supplied after "which." What should that verb be? In v. 1, it made little difference whether we supplied "to be" or "to have," but here these two verbs can be interpreted in very different ways. The traditional interpretation was to understand the verb as "to be," as in the King James translation: "Let this mind be in you, which was also in Christ Jesus"; this interpretation is reflected in both the NRSV and the NIV. The Philippians are urged to have in themselves the disposition that Christ showed. It has been argued, however, that Paul's appeal in these verses (like his ethical appeals elsewhere) is not to the example of the earthly Jesus, but to the events of the saving kerygma.[19] In other words, Paul is not urging the Philippians to imitate Christ, but to be what they already are, "in him," to think among themselves what they think "in Christ." In this interpretation, the missing verb is once again φρονέω (*phroneō*), which is used at the beginning of the verse and which occurred twice in v. 2; we should understand Paul's command to mean "show among yourselves the attitude that arises from the fact that you are in Christ." In support of this view, we may note the use of Paul's customary phrase "in Christ" and the fact that if Paul is referring simply to the behavior of Christ as a model, then vv. 9-11 are strictly irrelevant. Syntactically, it is also much more natural to supply *phroneō* from the first part of the verse than the verb "to be" and to translate ἐν ὑμῖν (*en humin*) as "among yourselves" rather than "in yourselves."

The choice, then, is between a command to have the attitude that was in Christ Jesus and a command to have an attitude that belongs to those who are in him. This antithesis between imitation and kerygma, however, is too stark. It is true that ethical

---

14. See M. Bockmuehl, "'The Form of God' (Phil. 2:6): Variations on a Theme of Jewish Mysticism," *JTS* NS48 (1997) 1-23.
15. *b. Ket.* 8a.
16. Philo *Allegorical Interpretation of the Law* III.96.
17. If 1 Cor 15:47 describes Christ as "the second man," that is surely because, as man, Adam preceded Christ; in terms of our own experience, also, we share in the physical body of Adam before we are transformed into the spiritual body of Christ.

18. See further Morna D. Hooker, "Adam *Redivivus:* Philippians 2 Once More," in *The Old Testament in the New Testament: Essays in Honour of J. L. North Worth*, ed. Steve Mayise, JSNTSup 189 (Sheffield: Sheffield Academic, 2000) 220-34.
19. Notably by E. Käsemann, "Kritische Analyse von Phil 2:5-11," *ZThK* 47 (1950) 313-60; English trans., "A Critical Analysis of Phil 2:5-11," *JThC* 5 (1968) 45-88.

behavior is never simply a question of imitating Jesus, but it is not true that Paul does not appeal to the example of Jesus Christ when giving ethical exhortations (cf. Rom 15:1-3, 7; 2 Cor 8:9). Of course, the Philippians' behavior depends on the fact that they are in Christ, and the fact that they are "in Christ" depends on the saving events of the gospel. But the attitude that is appropriate to those who are in Christ is that shown by the historical person whom they know as "Jesus," and the very fact that they are in Christ is the result of that attitude. It is, perhaps, no accident that the phrase Paul uses in v. 5 is not "in Christ" but "in Christ *Jesus*," as though to remind the Philippians of what the one they now call Lord was like. The best translation of this verse, therefore, is one that conveys the whole extent of Paul's appeal, which is *both* to the attitude shown by Christ Jesus *and* to the attitude that is therefore appropriate to those who are "in him."[20] The NRSV's marginal note, which suggests the translation "Let the same mind be in you that you have in Christ Jesus," though probably intended to represent the kerygmatic interpretation, in fact best represents this ambiguity.

2:6. If the basic meaning of the word μορφή (*morphē*) is "visible form," then the NRSV's "in the form of God" is preferable to the NIV's "in very nature God." There is a certain (and necessary) anomaly in the expression, since the form of God cannot be seen. Similar ideas are expressed in Col 1:15, where Christ is described as "the image of the invisible God," and in John 1:18: "No one has ever seen God: the only Son [or the only God], who is in the Father's bosom, he has made him known."

The meaning of the word ἁρπαγμός (*harpagmos*), "something to be exploited/grasped" (v. 6), has proved even more contentious than that of the word *morphē*. From the time of the church fathers, there have been many different interpretations of it. The main dispute has been about whether the word referred to something Christ already possessed, but did not cling to, or whether it referred to something he did not yet possess, but might have clutched at. These two interpretations are represented in the two diagrams in Fig. 2 (p. 135).[21] If "equality with God" is regarded here as something the preexistent Christ already possessed, then how are we to explain the language of the second part of the "hymn," which suggests that God has now bestowed on Christ a status that he did not enjoy before? If, on the other hand, he did not yet possess equality with God, could he truly be said to be "in the form of God"?

It now seems, however, that the most likely interpretation of *harpagmos* is that it refers to "something to be exploited."[22] In this view, equality with God was something that Christ already possessed, but which he chose not to use for his own advantage. The implication of this passage is that God bestowed on him the status and honor he had not claimed for himself. (Christ's voluntary humiliation and the bestowal of this status of honor upon him are best represented by Fig. 2, p. 135.) There is another interesting parallel with the Fourth Gospel in the phrase "equality with God," since a very similar phrase is used in John 5:18, where Jesus is accused of making himself equal to God. His opponents regard his claim to be God's Son as a usurpation of a role that does not belong to him.

Verses 6-11 are unique in the Pauline literature in telling us what Christ did *not* do, before spelling out what he did. Why do they include this negative emphasis? One suggestion is that there is a reference here to Lucifer, who is said to have rebelled against God and to have attempted to make himself like God (Isa 14:12-14). Lucifer, however, was never "in the form of God," nor was he created "in the image of God," and all the objections to a contrast with Adam (and none of the arguments in favor) apply to him. The most likely explanation of the negative is that it is intended as a deliberate contrast with Adam, who desired to be like God (cf. Gen 3:5, 22). Logically Genesis presents us with a contradiction by affirming both that Adam was created "in the image and likeness of God"

---

20. See M. D. Hooker, "Philippians 2:6-11," in *Jesus und Paulus, Festschrift für Werner Georg Kümmel zum 70. Geburtstag,* ed. E. Earle Ellis and Erich Grässer (Göttingen: Vandenhoeck & Ruprecht, 1975) 151-64; reprinted in M. D. Hooker, *From Adam to Christ* (Cambridge: Cambridge University Press, 1990) 88-100.

21. For a full discussion of the various possibilities, see N. T. Wright, "ἁρπαγμός and the Meaning of Philippians 2:5-11," *JTS* NS 37 (1980) 321-52; reprinted in revised form in *The Climax of the Covenant* (Edinburgh: T. & T. Clark, 1991) 62-90.

22. See R. W. Hoover, "The *Harpagmos* Enigma: A Philological Solution," *HTR* 64 (1971) 95-119.

(Gen 1:26) and that he was tempted to become like God (Gen 3:5). This tension between *being* like God and *desiring* to be like God is due to the fact that different sources have been combined there, but can nevertheless be seen as expressing two aspects of the truth, since men and women are both *like* God, yet distant *from* God as well. Verse 6 perhaps reflects this tension and provides a christological solution: Christ, who was "in the form of God," might well have claimed the privileges of equality with God as his right, but did not do so. What Adam desired, Christ was content to forgo.

2:7-8. Whatever precise meaning we give to the first statement concerning what Christ did *not* do, the next verb, χενόω (*kenoō*), is clearly intended to describe the very opposite: "he emptied himself/made himself nothing" (v. 7). The NIV translation avoids raising the awkward question, Of what did he empty himself? This question led, in the nineteenth century, to the so-called kenotic theory of the incarnation, which held that in becoming man, Christ emptied himself of the attributes of divinity, such as omnipotence and omniscience. Paul shows no interest in such matters, and the verb (which he uses elsewhere in the sense of "to nullify"; Rom 4:14; 1 Cor 1:17; 9:15; 2 Cor 9:3) was probably chosen to stress the contrast between the possibility Christ rejected, of claiming what was rightfully his, and his abandonment of his privileges. Once again, there may also be an intended contrast with Adam, who, as a result of the fall, was stripped of his power.

The contrast between what Christ did and did not do is seen much more clearly in Greek than in either of the English translations, for (in spite of earlier warnings about imposing a pattern on the material!) there does seem to be a shape to vv. 6-7a. Literally, the passage reads as follows:

Who, being in the form of God,
   Did not consider as something-to-
   be-exploited
Equality with God,
   But made himself nothing,
Taking the form of a slave!

Here we see yet another clear contrast: between being in the form of God and taking the form of a slave. The OT name for God is "Lord"—the name that Christ himself is given in vv. 9-11. Had Christ exploited his equality with God, he might have been acknowledged as such from the beginning. Instead, he took the form—and status—of a slave. These final words shock us because of their incongruity: This is not what we expect of one who is in the form of God and who could, if he had wished, have claimed equality with God. There could be no greater contrast than this. Yet we should not think of this process as some kind of exchange. Christ did not cease to be "in the form of God" when he took the form of a slave, any more than he ceased to be the "Son of God" when he was sent into the world. On the contrary, it is *in his self-emptying and his humiliation that he reveals what God is like,* and it is through his taking the form of a slave that we see "the form of God." The NRSV's "though" in v. 6 is misleading. There is no conjunction in the Greek, but if we supply one, then it should perhaps be "because." There is an interesting parallel once again in the Fourth Gospel, where the glory of Jesus—and therefore of God—is revealed in the cross.

The condition of being a slave is now identified with that of being human, which suggests that the contrast between Adam and Christ is continuing. According to Gen 1:26, 28, Adam was intended to have dominion, as God's representative, over the earth, a dominion that he lost at the fall, when he was condemned to a life of servitude (Gen 3:17-19). Elsewhere, Paul describes the condition of men and women as that of slavery to cosmic forces, from which the Son of God rescues them (Gal 4:3-7; cf. Rom 8:15). In Romans 5–7, these forces are named as sin, the law, and death, and in various passages Paul speaks of Christ as coming under the power of all three (sin, insofar as he was "in the likeness of sinful flesh," Rom 8:3; law, Gal 4:4; and death, Phil 2:8). Christ deliberately identified himself with humanity, in bondage to evil forces (a similar idea is found in Heb 2:14-15). Whether Paul is thinking of these powers here we do not know; what is clear is that to adopt the form of a slave (with all the dishonor and lack of privileges that implies) is the complete opposite of claiming the status and privileges of equality with God.

Adam was created after the image and likeness of God, but now Christ is born "in human likeness" (ἐν ὁμοιώματι ἀνθρώπων *en homoiōmati anthrōpōn*) and is found in human form. The word translated "form" or "appearance" here is not *morphē* but σχῆμα (*schēma*). None of the three terms, *morphē*, *en homoiōmati anthrōpōn*, or *schēma*, is meant to suggest that Jesus was not truly human; they indicate, rather, that he shared fully in our human existence. If we are correct in understanding Paul to be thinking of Christ as the true image of God, according to whose image and likeness Adam was created, then there is a deep irony here. The true man now identifies himself with the condition of fallen humanity, and in place of the stark contrast in the first few clauses of the "hymn" we have two clauses in parallel. And the next line, "he humbled himself" (which corresponds to Christ's action of emptying himself in v. 7), introduces, not a contrast with his humanity, but its logical outcome: death (v. 8). Christ, however, was "obedient to the point of/to death"—and with that one word, "obedient" (ὑπήκοος *hypēkoos*), contrasts with Adam leap once again to mind. Adam was disobedient to God's command, and it was his disobedience that led to death for all (Rom 5:12-19). But to whom is Christ obedient? Paul does not say. The word "to" (μέχρι *mechri*) means "as far as." He was presumably obedient to the laws to which he was now enslaved, which decreed the universal rule of death; but ultimately he was obedient to God. Whereas for Adam death was the result of his disobedience, for Christ it was the result of his obedience in identifying himself totally with the human condition. Moreover, in his case this death was by crucifixion, the punishment reserved in the Roman world for rebels and disobedient slaves, thus marking the reality of Christ's self-identification with those who are slaves.

The last phrase in v. 8 is often excised as a Pauline addition to the original "hymn," because it is said to spoil the structure, but we should not amend the structures to suit our expectations. Moreover, the logic of the passage seems to demand this nadir of humiliation that, paradoxically, was for Paul the climax to the first half of the passage. More than two thousand years of Christian piety have obscured from us the shock and horror with which these final words would have been heard by their original audience. Crucifixion was the cruelest and most shameful of deaths, and there could be no greater contrast with the opening lines of the "hymn," or with the exaltation that follows.

There is, in fact, an interesting similarity between the first five lines (see above) and the five lines just examined. It is true that the structure is different (AABBC instead of ABABC), but that is because the content is different; these later lines explore what it meant for Christ to be human, rather than what it meant for one who was in the form of God to take on the form of a slave. For that reason, they use parallelism rather than contrast. But in this second group of lines, as in the first, the punch line comes at the end, with the shock of the reference to crucifixion:

> having become in human likeness,
> and being found in human appearance,
> *he humbled himself,*
> *becoming obedient to death,*
> even death on a cross!
> (author's trans.)

2:9-11. In the rest of the passage, we move into a totally different mood—and into a different structure again. The triumphant "Therefore" in v. 9 introduces the action of God, who now responds to Christ's self-emptying and humiliation. This final section appears to fall naturally into three shorter sections, each of three lines, coming to a climax in v. 11c:

> Therefore God has highly exalted him,
> and given to him the name
> *that is above all names,*
> that at the name of Jesus
> every knee should bow,
> *in heaven and on earth and under*
> *the earth,*
> and every tongue confess
> that Jesus Christ is Lord
> *to the glory of God the Father!*
> (author's trans.)

Throughout these final lines of the passage, the emphasis is on the superlative. The name given to Jesus is "the name that is above every name." The statement that "every knee" should bow or bend is further spelled out with the description of those to whom the knees belong and who are "in heaven and on earth and under the earth." Every living creature, including spiritual and demonic powers, will acknowledge Jesus as Lord; the adjective translated "under the earth" may well include the dead as well.

The verb ὑπερύψωσεν (*hyperypsōsen*), "highly exalted/exalted to the highest place," emphasizes the magnitude of the honor bestowed on Christ. The *hyper* element does not necessarily imply "higher than before," but since Christ made no claims for himself and is now exalted to the highest position possible, it does, in effect, mean that. He is now universally acknowledged to be "equal with God." The idea that the risen Jesus is given a status that he did not have before is implied in Rom 1:3-4 and 10:9 as well as in non-Pauline texts such as Matt 28:18 and Acts 2:36.

To give someone a name is to give him or her status and power. The name bestowed on Jesus here is "the name that is above every name," which is clearly the name of God (v. 9). Perhaps the fact that this name is not clearly specified is deliberate. By tradition, the name of God could not be spoken or written. Challenged by Moses to give a name in Exod 3:14, God replies, "I am who I am." But since the LXX commonly uses "the Lord" as a substitute for the divine name, we are not surprised to find in v. 11 the universal proclamation that "Jesus Christ is Lord." It is puzzling, then, to find the passage continuing with "that at the name of Jesus" (v. 10). In spite of what some commentators have occasionally argued,[23] the name that is given to Christ at his exaltation cannot be the name "Jesus," for that is the name he has already borne throughout his human life. Why, then, is it mentioned here? Presumably to emphasize that it is the one who came in the likeness of men (Jesus) who is now proclaimed as Lord. When the name of Jesus is mentioned, then all creation should acknowledge that "Jesus Christ is Lord" (cf. Rom 10:9; 1 Cor 12:3). In the Roman city of Philippi, where the cult of the emperor was so important, the proclamation of *Jesus* as Lord would be seen as a challenge to political loyalties. But the pattern of behavior that Paul had placed before the Philippians would have been just as much of a challenge to the whole Roman social ethos.

There is an obvious contrast between Christ's proclamation as Lord and the earlier references to his taking the form of a slave and dying a slave's death. There are possible contrasts with Adam also: in the declaration that Christ will be acknowledged "in heaven and on earth and under the earth," since Adam was given dominion over the earth alone, and in the final line, which declares that what is now done is "to the glory of God the Father." At the fall, Adam failed to honor God and ceased to reflect God's glory—an idea that may well have influenced Rom 1:23 and 3:23. What Adam failed to do, the one who became man and is now proclaimed as Lord is able to do. The exaltation of Jesus, far from diminishing God's own position and honor, actually resounds to God's glory. The words "every knee shall bow/bend . . . and every tongue confess" are taken from Isa 45:23, where they refer to the worship of God. Here, knees are bent at the name of Jesus, and the confession made in v. 11 is of the universal lordship of Jesus Christ—but the end result of offering praise to him is the glory of God. Once again, the final phrase takes us by surprise and forms the punch line of the stanza—and of the hymn. Yet we should not be surprised, for whoever honors Jesus must also glorify God, because in Jesus we see the one who is "in the form of God" and who mirrors God's glory. (See Reflections at 2:12-18.)

---

23. Notably C. F. D. Moule, "Further Reflexions on Philippians 2:5-11," in *Apostolic History and the Gospel: Festschrift for F. F. Bruce,* ed. W. Ward Gasque and Ralph P. Martin (Exeter: Paternoster, 1970).

PHILIPPIANS 2:12-18, OUR NECESSARY RESPONSE

COMMENTARY

2:12-13. Paul now continues with his appeal concerning the way in which the Philippians should behave, picking up many of the themes discussed in 1:27–2:4. As in 1:27, he urges the Philippians to live in a way that is appropriate to the gospel, whether he is present or absent. The introductory "therefore" shows us that this appeal is based firmly on what he has just said about Christ. He addresses his readers as "beloved" or "dear friends," another indication of the cordial relationship between them. There is no hint that the Philippians are not doing well. They have always been obedient, he says; so now, let them work out their own salvation with fear and trembling—not simply when he is with them, but even more when he is absent. Paul does not say to whom the Philippians were obedient; the NRSV assumes that it was to Paul himself, and there is some support for this in the references to his presence and absence. Ultimately, however, it is God to whom they owe obedience, and Paul is simply the one through whom God's commands are channeled.

The word used for "presence" (παρουσία *parousia*) also has the sense of "coming" and was used by Paul of his own hoped-for return to Philippi in 1:26. It is not clear whether Paul is referring to his presence with them in the past or to a possible future visit (cf. 2:24). Another possibility is that he is thinking of "presence" and "absence" in the more radical sense, discussed in 1:23-25, of remaining in this life or departing from it. If his intent is the latter, then his quotation in v. 15 from Moses' "farewell discourse" to the Israelites in Deuteronomy 32 is given added poignancy. It will certainly have occurred to Paul that this letter may well be his own farewell discourse to the Philippians. There may, indeed, already be an allusion (though not a linguistic one) to Deut 31:27, where Moses says that if the Israelites have been rebellious during his lifetime, they will surely be even more rebellious after his death.

The Philippians are to be obedient; the verb ὑπακούω (*hypakouō*) echoes the "obedient" used of Christ in v. 8. And they are to work out their own salvation "with fear and trembling." Such fear and trembling are not caused by any uncertainty regarding their salvation, but are the appropriate attitude in the presence of God, an attitude that might better be described in English as "awe." The "your" (better "your own," as in the NRSV) is slightly emphatic, and it may be intended to strengthen the point that Paul's presence or absence should be immaterial. The fact that the Philippians are urged to "work out" their own salvation does not conflict with the Pauline insistence that salvation is the work of God alone. Verses 6-11 have described the gracious action of God in Christ, but that gracious action demands a response—what Paul elsewhere describes as "the obedience of faith" (Rom 1:5). The Philippians are to complete what God has done by living it out in their own lives. But this is not simply an individual matter. Paul has already urged the Philippians to avoid selfish concern for their own interests (v. 4). The "your" is plural in Greek, and the life that is to be lived is that lived in the community of believers. Paul's words, like those of Moses, are addressed to the people of God, not to a collection of individuals.

Verse 13 reminds us of the other side of the equation. Although Paul has urged the Philippians to work out (κατεργάζομαι *katergazomai*) their own salvation, it is in fact God who is at work (ἐνεργέω *energeō*) in them. The two verbs are based on the same root, ἔργον (*ergon*), meaning "work" or "action," and the relation between the two activities is spelled out in the rest of the verse, since the purpose of God working in them is that they should will and work (the same verb, *energeō*) to God's good pleasure. What the Philippians now will and work is, in fact, the work of God within them. The NIV is ambiguous and perhaps understands

144

all the verbs to refer to the activity of God; the NRSV, which understands the willing and the working to be done by the Philippians—as a result of God's own work in them—is preferable. The fact that God is at work is the basis for Paul's confidence that his own presence or absence makes no difference to the Philippians' obedience. Once again, we may have an echo of Moses' farewell to Israel, when he assured the people that, though he was about to die, the Lord would still be with them (Deut 31:7-8).

2:14-16. What does this mean in practical terms? They are to do everything without murmuring/complaining or arguing (v. 14). Is this a hint that the Philippians are at present bickering among themselves? Many commentators think so, but there has been little evidence so far to support this view (but see the Commentary on 4:2). Why, then, should the Philippians be warned not to complain or argue? The answer is perhaps to be found in v. 15, where Paul says that the Philippians are "children of God without blemish/fault (ἄμωμα *amōma*, "without blame") in a crooked and perverse/depraved generation." These words are a clear echo of Deut 32:5, a verse that is confused in both Hebrew and Greek, but whose main sense is clear. The Israelites are accused of being blameworthy (μωμητά *mōmēta*), and described as no children of God, a crooked and perverse generation. Paul now turns this idea inside out: Christians have *become* God's children, and they must therefore live *without* blame in *the midst of* a crooked and perverse generation.

This contrast with the Israelites, who were denounced in the wilderness as unworthy to be called the children of God, gives us the explanation for the command to avoid complaining/murmuring and arguing, since the Israelites were frequently accused of complaining about God's provision for them. The first noun, γογγυσμός (*gongysmos*, "complaint"), and its cognate verb are used frequently in the OT of Israel's attitude toward God in the wilderness (e.g., Exod 16:1-12; Num 14:27-29). This complaining is referred to by Paul in 1 Cor 10:1-13, where he describes the behavior of the Israelites and what happened to them as a result as an "example" of what Christians must not do; in v. 10 he refers to the story in Numbers 16, where the people complained and many were destroyed. The second noun, διαλογισμός (*dialogismos*), which can mean simply "discussion," seems to be used here with the meaning "argument." Unlike *gongysmos*, it is not used in the Greek versions of the Pentateuch. Nevertheless, in view of the other echoes of the wilderness story, it is possible that Paul may have in mind the disputes between Moses and the people such as are recorded in Exod 17:1-7 and Num 16:1-11. Because of Christ's attitude and action, those who are in him are enabled to live as Israel was called (but failed) to live, as God's "blameless and innocent/pure children."

But who are the members of this new "crooked and perverse/depraved generation"? Does this phrase refer to those to whom it was once applied—namely, the Jews? If so, is that because, like Israel of old, they are rejecting what God offered them by opposing the gospel (cf. Matt 17:17)? Or does it refer to those people referred to in 1:28, whether Jews or Gentiles, whose refusal to accept the gospel was being expressed in opposition to the Philippian church? The phrase should probably be understood as a general one, referring to everyone who is not included among the children of God.

In contrast, the Philippian Christians "shine like stars." The verb could be understood as a command, but the NIV and the NRSV are probably correct in taking it to be a statement of fact. The word translated "stars" is φωστῆρες (*phōstēres*), which can refer to anything that gives light. There may be an echo of Dan 12:3 in this phrase, since there it is said that the wise will shine like the lights of the heaven and the implication is that they will illuminate others. But is that idea present in Philippians? Or is the emphasis in Philippians on the contrast between light and darkness? The answer to that question lies in v. 16 in the verb ἐπέχω (*epechō*): Does it mean "hold fast" (as in NRSV; cf. the NIV margin) or "hold out" (as in NIV)? If we follow the NIV, then the verb picks up the idea of light as showing the way, and the Christian community is seen as offering the gospel ("the word of life") to those among whom they live. If we accept the NRSV's translation, then Paul is continuing to think of the struggle in which the Philippian community is engaged (see

1:27-30). On the whole, this latter interpretation suits the context better. In contrast to those who met God's gifts with complaints and arguments, they *hold fast* to the word of life—but that means, inevitably, that they will also be an example to those around them (1:28).

Once again we find the expression "the day of Christ," which Paul has already used in 1:6 and 10. It is the Christ whose story Paul has just told who is now expected to come. Since every tongue has not yet confessed Jesus Christ to be Lord (vv. 10-11), Paul presumably assumes that this will take place then. Paul expects to boast on that day that his work has not been in vain. For Paul, boasting in his own achievements is excluded (e.g., Rom 3:27; 1 Cor 1:29), and the only proper ground for boasting is in what God has done in Christ (e.g., Rom 5:11; 1 Cor 1:31; Phil 3:3). But he frequently speaks of boasting about his congregations (see 1 Cor 15:31; 2 Cor 1:14; 7:4, 14; 9:2-3; 1 Thess 2:19). The reason for this is spelled out in Rom 15:17: "In Christ Jesus, then, I have reason to boast of my work for God." What he boasts of is not his own achievement, but what God has done in him and what God has enabled him to will and to do (v. 13) because he is in Christ. There is thus an interesting parallel between the idea that Paul will boast on the day of Christ and the statement in vv. 9-11 that the honor accorded to Jesus Christ as Lord is "to the glory of God the Father."

The image of "running in vain" (v. 16) is used again by Paul in Gal 2:2 (cf. 1 Cor 9:27). Here he links it with the idea of toiling in vain, a phrase that echoes words in Isa 49:4. In their original context, these words refer to the attempts of someone who was called to be God's servant to bring Israel back to the Lord, attempts that have apparently met with failure but that are followed by the summons to be a light to the Gentiles. The ideas are clearly relevant to Paul's own situation, but whether the echo is a conscious one we cannot be sure.

2:17-18. The idea that his efforts are in vain seems to bring Paul back in v. 17 to his own situation and the possibility of martyrdom that looms over him. Some commentators have doubted whether Paul is, in fact, contemplating martyrdom here, because a few verses later he expresses the hope that he will be released (v. 24). That hope depends, however, on "how things go with" him (v. 23), and there is no inconsistency between his attitude in v. 24 and his recognition in v. 17 that things may not go well; "but even if" the outcome is death, he will nevertheless rejoice. The metaphor he uses is that of "being poured out as a libation/like a drink offering." Libations of wine were the regular accompaniment to both Jewish burnt offerings (e.g., Exod 29:38-41; Num 28:1-15) and pagan sacrifices. But if it is Paul's own life that may be poured out in this way, who is it that offers "the sacrifice and the offering/service" that his libation accompanies? Is it Paul himself, who offers to God the faith of those Gentiles who have responded to the gospel (cf. Rom 15:16 where a different Greek word for "offering" is used)? Or is it the Philippians who make the sacrifice? The latter would seem more appropriate at the end of a paragraph urging them to respond to the gospel. Is it then their *faith* that they offer—or what grows out of their faith? Once again, the context suggests that Paul has in mind a sacrifice that is the *result* of their faith (NIV, "coming from your faith"); compare again the phrase "obedience of faith" in Rom 1:15, which refers to the obedience that issues from faith.

But why the sacrificial imagery, if Paul is thinking simply of conduct? Is it, perhaps, because their lives are to be seen as mirroring the self-sacrificial actions of Christ? Or (the suggestions are not exclusive) is Paul alluding once again to the gifts the Philippians have sent to him and that are, in effect, an offering to God? In favor of this interpretation we may point to the fact that the word for "sacrifice" (θυσία *thysia*) is used again in 4:18 of the gifts the Philippians sent to Paul, which are "an acceptable sacrifice, pleasing to God," while the noun translated "offering" or "service" (λειτουργία *leitourgia*) is used in 2:30 of the service that they wished to render Paul but were unable to offer. And over this sacrifice, Paul is ready, if necessary, to pour out his own life, thus making their partnership in the gospel (1:5) complete.

"Even if" this happens, Paul declares that he is glad and will rejoice with the Philippians, and he urges them to be glad and to rejoice with him in turn. As in 1:18*b*, the possibility of martyrdom cannot diminish his joy, a joy in which they should share. The emphatic use of the verbs χαίρω (*chairō*) and συγχαίρω (*sygchairō*; twice each) picks up the note of joy first sounded in 1:4, where it was caused by the fact that the Philippians had shared with him in the gospel "from the first day until now." If Paul is about to lose his life, then that "now" may mark the end and the climax of that partnership in the gospel.

REFLECTIONS

1. This section of Philippians (1:27–2:18) demonstrates clearly the way in which theology and ethics are inseparably joined together. As in Judaism, so in Christianity, theological affirmation leads to ethical demand; neither can exist without the other. The link is made clear in Paul's opening words, commanding the Philippians to live "in a manner worthy of the gospel of Christ" (1:27). Nor is this link a tenuous one. The account of Christ's gracious actions and subsequent exaltation in 2:6-11 forms the core of this passage, and everything before and after it depends on it. The demand to live in a certain way is a necessary obligation laid upon all Christians, arising from the fact that they are "in Christ" only as the result of what Christ has done. Those who claim Christ as Lord cannot refuse this demand without denying that truth—the truth of the gospel itself. If we are really "in Christ," then we must share the attitude that was his and that now belongs to all who are in him.

2. The theological statement in 2:6-11 concentrates on the actions of Christ and God. Later theologians were concerned to define the "nature" of God and of Christ, and we, like them, tend to assume that if we want to know about the "nature" of Christ, we must concentrate on the opening and closing lines of this passage, on the statement that he is "in the form of God," and on the declaration that he is Lord. But it is typical of the biblical material that God is revealed through what God does, and here we find that God is revealed through what Christ does. Having been told that Christ is "in the form of God," we find our attention immediately focused on what he did. Christ reveals himself in his gracious actions—in his refusal to exploit his rights, in his self-emptying, in his self-humiliation, and in his obedience, even to the point of death. And because he is "in the form of God," his actions reveal not simply his own character or nature, but what God is like as well. The birth, ministry, and death of Jesus are a consistent whole, and in them all, we see the divine character revealed. Christ's exaltation by God is the vindication of Christ's actions, and not their undoing; it is precisely because he is humble and obedient that he also is Lord. His exaltation is God's triumphant affirmation that in Christ's actions we have the perfect revelation of the love and compassion of God. To acknowledge this Jesus as universal Lord is to accept as Lord the humble, obedient figure on the cross. And since divine "being" is revealed in divine "action," we begin to understand why theology and ethics are inseparable. The basic ethical exhortation is to "be like God" (cf. Lev 19:2), which means, in effect, to *behave* like God. These few verses thus form one of the most profound statements in the Pauline corpus about the nature of God.

Asked to describe the nature of God, most people would probably appeal to ideas regarding omnipotence and omniscience, to God's immeasurable distance from us and God's unutterable holiness. Paul, by contrast, describes what he refers to elsewhere as "grace." What resounds to God's glory (in other words, what reveals God's nature) is the proclamation of the crucified Jesus as Lord. Paul's understanding of "glory" here is remarkably similar to that of the Fourth Evangelist, although the Evangelist takes the further step of identifying crucifixion and exaltation, and so speaks of the moment of Jesus' death as his glorification (John 12:16, 23; 13:31-32; 17:1). But Paul, too, apparently sees Christ's self-emptying and death as the revelation of God's glory, and he uses similar ideas elsewhere, notably in 1 Cor 1:25, where he speaks of God's "folly" and "weakness" as demonstrations of true wisdom and strength. This revelation of God's nature confounds all our expectations and turns our preconceptions upside down.

3. The nature of God is revealed in what *we* call "the incarnation," and if we want to know what it means to be "in the form of God," then we must look at one who took "the form of a slave." Paul, of course, does not use our technical term; nor does he concern himself with the problems of how it could take place. Yet he expresses, in his own way, what later came to be referred to as the divinity and the humanity of Christ. Christ is divine because, as we have seen, he did not cease to be "in the form of God" when he adopted "the form of a slave." He is human because, as Paul stresses, Christ completely identifies with our situation. And yet there is a difference between him and us! In contrast to men and women, Christ humbled himself and was obedient. And because the one who took the form of a slave was also "in the form of God," we know that his humility and his obedience are rooted in the will of God. It is by Christ's obedience to the will of God that the relationship between God and humanity, broken by Adam, is restored, and reconciliation takes place.

Paul, the theologian, expresses here in his own way the truth that Matthew and Luke spell out in very different ways in their nativity stories. Paul shows no knowledge of those traditions, choosing instead to sum up in theological language what the evangelists prefer to express in narrative. We may well feel that the nativity stories are easier to understand! But do we *really* comprehend them? It is easy to concentrate on the details in the stories—on the angels and the star, the shepherds and the wise men—and miss the point they are trying to make: God with us! The Son of God born in weakness and humility, accepting poverty and vulnerability. The familiarity of the stories obscures their meaning. Paul's statement reminds us of their significance—that God revealed his self-giving love for men and women in the birth of his Son.

4. What are the implications of these verses for Christian living? What does it mean for Christians to acknowledge *this* Jesus as their Lord? Because this passage upsets our normal assumptions about what God is like, it has a radical effect on our understanding of what God expects from us. Instinctive human attitudes are turned on their heads. Those who confess Jesus as Lord should not be looking for status or power; nor should they be acting from "selfish ambition or conceit" (2:3). Rather, they should be humbly considering others better than themselves. And because they are concerned with the interests of others (2:4), they will be of one mind and one purpose, "having the same love" and of one accord (2:2). In stark contrast to the modern spirit of encouraging competition and giving rewards to individuals who get to the top, Paul insists on mutual concern and service.

Paul's words are a terrible indictment of the lives and attitudes of many who have called themselves "Christian." How many of us have really taken the self-giving of Christ as a model for Christian behavior? How many have been more concerned with airing our own opinions than with coming to a common mind with others? How many church leaders have seen their own role in terms of position and power, and have forgotten that true honor comes to those who "make themselves nothing"? How many have been prepared to take on the role of a slave? We can all point to notable examples of Christians who have endeavored to show the same attitude as Christ. Mother Teresa may spring at once to mind. Unfortunately, the very fact that such examples are notable proves how exceptional they are. It has to be confessed that the church as a whole has never taken to heart the true significance of this passage. We have gloried in the sublime statement in 2:5-11, and have ignored its implications for our lives—attempting to detach theology from ethics, God's gracious act from the divine demand that follows, ignoring the "therefore" that insists we "work out" salvation in our lives. Some Christians have emphasized the idea that Christ suffers *for* us to such an extent that they have assumed that Christian life consists simply of enjoying the benefits of his passion, and have conveniently ignored the persistent emphasis in the New Testament on the need to share Christ's self-giving and poverty and sufferings. We have found it all too easy to forget, in the words of Kenneth Grayston, that those who acknowledge Jesus as Lord claim for themselves "not only the exaltation, but also the renunciation, and the service, and the willing obedience."[24] Is this, perhaps, why, in Philippians, the day of judgment is referred to as the day of Christ or the day of Christ Jesus (see the Commentary on 1:6), reminding us that it is by *his* actions and example that we shall be judged?

But if, as Christians, we feel indicted for our frequent failure to follow in the footsteps of Christ, we can also take courage from the description of his final triumph. Those who confess that "Jesus is Lord"—and who live in his service—can be assured that his way is God's way and that the final victory will be his. At a time when Christians formed a tiny minority in the ancient world, Paul confidently declared that ultimately every tongue would confess Jesus to be Lord and that every knee would one day bow before him. Christians today, who in certain parts of the world feel outnumbered and isolated, may take courage from these words.

5. As so often in Paul's letters, his instructions about how we should live and show our obedience are general and imprecise. We are told to live "in a manner worthy of the gospel of Christ," but most of his hints about what that might mean refer to the attitudes that are appropriate to the Christian community. We are sometimes tempted to wish that Paul had given more precise advice on just how Christians should behave in particular circumstances. But Christian obedience does not mean living in accordance with a set of rules; rather, it means responding in the appropriate way to the self-giving love of God. The vision that Paul provides us with is, in fact, far more valuable than any set of rules. Christians in the modern world are faced with innumerable ethical dilemmas, which multiply each year with advances in science and medicine. We cannot expect to find ready-made answers to these modern-day questions in the Bible! We may be grateful that Paul, in his ethical teaching, always went back to first principles. In effect, he is saying, "This is the gospel. This is what God is like. This is what God has done for you, and this is what God expects *you* to be like. Work out what that means for yourselves!" If we are to do that, then we, too, need to go back to first principles, to ask, What is the Christlike thing for us as a Christian community, for us as individual Christians, to be doing? How do we respond, in obedience, to what God has done?

The answers to these questions are not necessarily easy! In any particular ethical dilemma, we may well find Christians sincerely supporting opposite viewpoints. If someone is apparently in an irreversible coma, is it more "worthy of the gospel" to preserve life by continuing treatment or to allow the patient to die? When a tyrant like Hitler arises, is it right to resort to war in order to put a stop to his atrocities? What is the Christlike approach to using fetal tissue in medical research, in order to prevent disease? How does one balance the advantages and disadvantages to societies and environment when "development" seems to clash with "conservation"? In seeking to answer these questions, we may not always make the right choice. What is important is that we should approach all such problems in humility (not thinking we know the answers) and in love, looking to the interests of others, and not seeking to exploit what we consider to be our rights.

We see, then, that although Paul may not have given us precise guidelines about what to do in particular situations, he has, throughout this section, given us very significant hints. The basis for all our actions is our life in Christ. Unity is a "must" for those who are "one" in Christ. The humility (2:3) and obedience (2:12) expected of

---

24. Kenneth Grayston, *The Epistles to the Galatians and to the Philippians,* Epworth Preacher's Commentary (London: Epworth, 1957) 99.

Christians are rooted in the humility and obedience of Christ himself. The source of all these qualities is Christ, in whom Christians also find encouragement, love, fellowship, and compassion (2:1). In both 1:27–2:4 and 2:12-18, Paul appeals not only for unity and humility, but also for courage. The courage to stand firm (1:27-28; 2:16) is a way of witnessing to opponents, and it is especially necessary in view of the possibility of sharing Christ's own experience of suffering (1:29-30; 2:17). And because our suffering, like everything else, is "in Christ," we find that this, too, becomes, in a sense, *his* suffering. So it is "for others"; in 1:29, remarkably, it is "for Christ," and in 2:17 Paul speaks of his being poured out as a libation. Like everything else, suffering is transformed "in Christ"; whereas we usually think of suffering in negative terms, Paul views it positively, since it is used by God to witness to the truth of the gospel and to bring comfort to fellow Christians.

6. Throughout this section we see plainly (1) that Christian obedience must be understood as the response to God's grace, rather than to a set of rules; (2) that the response we are called on to make is the response made by Christ himself; (3) that we are enabled to make that response because we are in him; (4) that because in him we are one community, relationships within that community—rooted in love, selflessness, and concern for others—are especially important; and (5) that the result of our obedient response will be a powerful witness to others. When a Christian community really takes this teaching seriously, then they are like light in a dark world (2:15; cf. Matt 5:14-16). Christians can never see their response to the gospel merely as a matter between themselves and God. Once again we see the truth of Wesley's description of Christianity as "a social religion." What we believe is revealed in the way we behave, and whatever we do is inevitably a proclamation to others of the gospel we believe. The basic rule, therefore, is to make sure that we believe the right gospel with heart and mind and soul and strength. Our behavior should be the expression of that belief.

PHILIPPIANS 2:19-30
FUTURE PLANS

OVERVIEW

Paul turns from exhortation to practical matters. Although he is separated from the Philippians (2:12), he plans to keep in touch with them by sending Timothy and Epaphroditus to Philippi. These two paragraphs (vv. 19-24 and vv. 25-30) both read like letters of commendation, of the kind usually sent with letter bearers. Neither of these commendations is strictly necessary, since Timothy was well known to the Philippians and since Epaphroditus came from Philippi; but Paul takes the opportunity to speak warmly of them both. It is sometimes argued that "travel plans" of this kind are more appropriate at the end of a letter (cf. Rom 15:22-29; 1 Cor 16:1-12) and that this supports the idea that 3:2 is the beginning of a second letter. But Paul was not bound by structures in this way.

PHILIPPIANS 2:19-24, TIMOTHY

COMMENTARY

What Paul hopes to do is, like all his activities and plans, "in the Lord" (v. 19). Timothy seems to have been one of Paul's most constant companions, mentioned frequently in his letters as well as in Acts 16–20. In 1:1 he was named as co-author of the letter, but it is now clear that this was a matter of courtesy and that the real author is Paul alone. Paul plans to send Timothy to them soon, not immediately and not, therefore, as the bearer of the letter. Paul looks forward to receiving news of the Philippians via Timothy, and he is confident that this news will be good, since he expects to be cheered by it. The "also" (picked up in the NIV but missing from the NRSV) indicates his assumption that they will, of course, be cheered by Timothy's visit. Paul has no one else like Timothy, who is genuinely concerned for the welfare of the Philippians (v. 20). The contrast with everyone else who is pursuing his or her own interests (v. 21) reminds us of Paul's exhortation in 2:1-4. Clearly his concern there for the Philippian community reflected his own experience of the attitudes shown by those Christians with whom he is in touch in prison. These people are failing to do what Paul has urged the Philippians to do—namely, to put the interests of other people first.

If Paul is in prison in Rome, some 800 milies from Philippi, it is, perhaps, not surprising that he cannot find anyone else who is prepared to undertake the long journey to Philippi. Even from Ephesus, such a journey might be difficult. Timothy is already well known to the Philippians (according to Acts 16 he had accompanied Paul on his first visit to the city). Like a son learning a trade from his father, Timothy has served with Paul in the work of the gospel (v. 22). The verb "serve" (δουλεύω *douleuō*) picks up the δοῦλοι (*douloi*) of 1:1 as well as echoing the δοῦλος (*doulos*) of 2:7. Paul speaks of Timothy in similar terms in 1 Cor 4:17 and 16:10. And now we learn the reason for the delay in Timothy's visit: Paul plans to send him as soon as he sees "how things go" with him (v. 23)—presumably in order to bring news of the outcome of his trial to the Philippians. But since Paul has expressed confidence regarding his release, he trusts "in the Lord" that he will be able to visit them soon (v. 24). (See Reflections at 2:25-30.)

PHILIPPIANS 2:25-30, EPAPHRODITUS COMMENTARY

Paul considers it necessary to send Epaphroditus to Philippi as well—no doubt as the bearer of the letter (v. 25). Epaphroditus had been sent by the Philippian church to bring Paul their gift and to assist him in prison. Why is it now "necessary" for Paul to send him back? Apparently because the Philippians have heard that Epaphroditus has been seriously ill and are anxious as to whether he has made a full recovery (vv. 26, 28). This has made Epaphroditus long for the Philippians; the same verb (ἐπιποθέω *epipotheō*) was used of Paul's own longing for them in 1:8 (the reading in the NRSV margin, "to see," is almost certainly a later addition). Epaphroditus is described as Paul's "brother, co-worker/fellow worker and fellow soldier"; since he is mentioned only here and at 4:18, we do not know whether he and Paul had worked together in Philippi or whether this is a recognition of what Epaphroditus has done since—possibly in the fulfillment of his recent mission. He is also the Philippians' "messenger"; the word used is ἀπόστολος (*apostolos*), meaning "someone who is sent" to act on behalf of another. The NRSV note offers the transliteration "apostle," but the term is not being used here in the quasi-technical sense it has when Paul describes himself as "an apostle of Christ" (e.g., in 1 Cor 1:1). The task carried out by Epaphroditus is defined as being "minister to my need." Neither the NRSV nor the NIV's paraphrase, "to take care of my needs," conveys adequately the sense of the Greek. The noun is λειτουργός (*leitourgos*), a word that is usually used of someone who offers priestly service and is akin to the noun λειτουργία (*leitourgia*), used in 2:17 and 30. The word suggests that Paul regards Epaphroditus's ministry to his needs as a priestly offering to God, in whose service Paul is in prison. This ministry was a necessary one: As a prisoner, Paul would have been dependent on friends and relatives for the necessities of life, including food.

Epaphroditus's distress (v. 26) was caused by the difficulties of communication in the ancient world. News had reached the Philippians of his illness, and they needed to be reassured that he had fully recovered. His illness had clearly been severe—hardly an unusual event at that time. Commentators speculate about what it was and when it struck him, but we do not know these details. Paul attributes his recovery to divine mercy (v. 27): Epaphroditus had not died, and Paul had thus been spared additional sorrow. The phrase "sorrow upon sorrow/one sorrow after another" is a common one, and there is no need to ask what particular sorrow he had in mind. He had plenty! But since Epaphroditus is now better, Paul is "eager to send him" to Philippi, so that they may rejoice and so that Paul may be the more free from sorrow. Both the NRSV and the NIV understand the Greek ἀλυπότερος (*alypoteros*) to mean "less anxious," but the word is formed from the noun λύπη (*lypē*), "sorrow," used in v. 27. The English paraphrase probably arose from the difficulty of understanding how Paul could be saved sorrow by Epaphroditus's return: Would his departure not *add* to Paul's sorrow? The answer is probably to be found in the mutuality of experience that belongs to those who are "in Christ." In vv. 17-18 Paul spoke of the Philippians and himself rejoicing together. In 2 Cor 1:3-7, he describes the way in which God consoles those who are afflicted and how this consolation is then shared by others who are in Christ. Here, the fact that the Philippians will rejoice at Epaphroditus's return perhaps means that Paul expects to share their joy and so be relieved of his sorrow.

The Philippians are urged to welcome Epaphroditus (v. 29); some commentators have supposed that this means that they have been criticizing him for failing to complete his commission. There is no justification whatever for this notion in the text; we are told only that the Philippians have heard of his illness, and he could scarcely have been blamed for that! Perhaps, though, Paul wishes to assure them that Epaphroditus has accomplished the task entrusted to him, even though he is returning early. He is to be welcomed "in the Lord" with joy and to be held in honor because of what he has done for "the work of Christ." In this context, these words refer to his ministry to Paul, described in these terms because Paul is imprisoned for the sake of the gospel. In undertaking the work of Christ, Epaphroditus came close to death (v. 30). In this last phrase we have a fascinating echo of the words used in 2:8 of Christ's obedience "to death" μέχρι θανάτου (*mechri thanatou*). Like Timothy, who considered what would benefit others, and not himself, Epaphroditus has risked his life in order to make up for the help the Philippians could not give Paul. Paul's words at the end of v. 30 are not meant as criticism of the Philippians, for they had sent generous contributions to assist him. But they were not with him in prison and, therefore, could not minister to him personally. A similar expression is used in 1 Cor 16:17, where the arrival of some members of the church makes up for the absence of the rest. Paul urges the Philippians to honor their representative, who has not only carried out the task entrusted to him but also has done it at considerable personal cost.

REFLECTIONS

Paul's practical arrangements concerning the delivery of the letter, the return of Epaphroditus, and the visit of Timothy provide us with an insight into his theology. At a down-to-earth level, we now see what it means for men and women to live "in the Lord" (2:19, 24, 29) and, therefore, to work out in their daily lives how to share the attitude of Christ, being concerned for others rather than themselves. Paul's plans to send Timothy and Epaphroditus to Philippi arise out of his concern for the Philippian community, while Timothy, Epaphroditus, and the Philippians themselves have all demonstrated a Christlike attitude by their behavior. The community of believers "in the Lord" is bonded together by love. Such a society provides mutual support, of the kind provided by the Philippians through Epaphroditus. As with all loving relationships, however, its members are inevitably vulnerable, because they share the sorrows and cares of others, as well as their joys. Hence the mutual experience of joy and sorrow is shared by Paul, Epaphroditus, and the Philippians. Paul and Epaphroditus have shared the Philippians' concern at the news of Epaphroditus's illness. Now the joy the Philippians experience at his safe return is shared by Paul and overcomes his own sorrow at being left alone.

Paul's words remind us of the support and comfort that can be experienced by Christians, even when they are on their own. The mutual concern and prayers of those who belong to Christ mean that they need never be out of touch. Even with a capital charge hanging over his head and deliberately sending home the man who had come to suppport him in prison, Paul shares the joy of Epaphroditus's friends at his recovery. He does not need Epaphroditus's physical presence and material assistance to know the comfort of belonging to a community that is as concerned for him as he is for them. The fact that Christianity is not a solitary religion means that we are able to share with one another its rewards and joys as well as its demands and sorrows!

PHILIPPIANS 3:1–4:1
THE CHRISTIAN LIFE, PART 2

OVERVIEW

The very first word of this section in both the NRSV and the NIV, "Finally," is a surprise. We are just halfway through the letter. So why should Paul be drawing to a close? In fact, as we shall discover, he has a great deal still that he wishes to say! And the first issue that he discusses, in 3:2-11, appears to be a totally new one, introduced very abruptly in v. 2. When we note, in addition, that the Greek word χαίρετε (*chairete*) is translated as "farewell" instead of as "rejoice" in the NRSV note, we can understand why many commentators argue that 3:1*a* marks the end of one letter and the beginning of another, even though they have to assume that the concluding words of one and the opening words of the other are missing (the division is made either after v. 1*a* [see the break in the NRSV text] or at the end of v. 1). Others argue that the letter breaks off at 3:1*a* and resumes again at 4:4 and that 3:1*b*–4:3 is thus an insertion from another letter. This explanation leaves us with an even more puzzling problem, however, for the more vigorously modern interpreters argue that 3:1 leads naturally into 4:4, the more one is left wondering why an ancient editor should have inserted a fragment from another letter at such an unsuitable point! If either of these explanations is right, then we have to assume that a later editor joined two letters together, either because those letters (or the copies that he had) were incomplete or because (for reasons we can only guess at) he decided to omit parts of what Paul had written. Although there is no textual evidence to suggest that two letters have been joined at 3:2, those who support this theory point to the fact that Polycarp, when himself writing to the Philippians at the beginning of the second century, referred to the letters that Paul had written to them.[25] Since he may be referring to a letter or letters that have not survived at all, however, this proves nothing. The interpreter's decision on this matter, therefore, will depend on three things: (1) the translation of the opening words of 3:1, (2) whether or not the abrupt change of topic is probable within a single letter, and (3) whether the links between chaps. 1–2 and chaps. 3–4 are such as to suggest that they were written as a unity.

First, we should note that the Greek phrase τὸ λοιπόν (*to loipon*), translated here as "finally," is usually used with a much more general meaning. Here, it may mean "and so," in which case it is perhaps used to pick up and reiterate the command to rejoice in 2:18. Whichever way we translate the phrase, however, its use certainly does *not* indicate that the letter is near its end (cf., e.g., 1 Thess 4:1, where the word *loipon* is used to introduce what is in effect the main body of the epistle's teaching).

As in 1:12, Paul addresses the recipients of the letter as "brothers" (here, as often, paraphrased by the NRSV as "brothers and sisters"; see also 1:14; 3:17; 4:1). His command to rejoice is expressed in the same word (χαίρετε *chairete*) that he used in 2:18. In some contexts, however, the word could be employed as a term of greeting, although ordinarily on meeting rather than on parting. The infinitive χαίρειν (*chairein*) was commonly used at the beginning of a letter, as in Jas 1:1. Only in 2 Cor 13:11 is the verb used at the end of a letter, and there, as here, it is much more likely that it means "rejoice!"

Second, we have to examine whether the change of topic in 3:2 is too abrupt to be conceivable within a single letter. In a formal composition, we would not expect a writer to switch from one theme to another in this way; in a letter to people for whom Paul has pastoral responsibility, and whom he also

---
25. Polycarp *Epistle to the Philippians* 3.

regards as friends, it is less surprising that he jumps from one topic to another, as his active mind remembers other issues he felt it necessary to write about.

In fact, although Paul's outburst in 3:2 may seem an abrupt change of topic, the theme of the chapter as a whole picks up what he has said in chap. 2. Paul's warning in 3:2 quickly leads into a description of his own experience, which is clearly modeled on the example of Christ. Moreover, as we shall see, there are many echoes of the vocabulary of chap. 2. In particular, the commentary will argue that what Paul has to say in 3:20-21 not only looks back to 2:6-11, but also is the logical conclusion to that passage.

PHILIPPIANS 3:1-11, THE TRUE BASIS FOR CONFIDENCE

COMMENTARY

3:1. Paul half apologizes for writing "the same things" to the Philippians, while assuring them that he does not find it troublesome to do so. Is he referring to what he has just written: "rejoice in the Lord"? That seems unlikely, since such a command appears to be an improbable "safeguard" for the Philippians. Markus Bockmuehl argues in his commentary that joy was frequently regarded as the source of strength (so Neh 8:10); in the other passages he cites, however, strength appears to be the source of joy, which is hardly relevant.[26] The other possibility is that Paul is referring to what he is *about* to write—namely, his warning in v. 2. But since those he warns about have not been mentioned earlier in the letter, we must conclude that Paul is referring to warnings he has given in earlier letters or possibly by word of mouth (unless, of course, we decide that v. 1*b* introduces part of another letter that had already discussed these people). The fact that Paul's warnings are a safeguard suggests that he does not believe the Philippians to be in imminent danger but that he considers it wise to be issuing the warning in case the danger becomes a real one.

3:2. Since the term "safeguard" suggests that what follows is a warning, the first word of this verse, βλέπετε (*blepete*), which would ordinarily mean "pay attention to" when used, as here, with the accusative, has been translated "watch out for/beware of." The triple "beware" in the NRSV is perhaps too peremptory; but the tone is certainly emphatic, for the command is introduced abruptly and is given three times. The effect is heightened in Greek by the use of alliteration, with each warning being directed against something beginning with the letter *K*: τοὺς κύνας ... τοὺς κακοὺς ἐργάτας ... τὴν κατατομήν (*tous kynas ... tous kakous ergatas ... tēn katatomēn*). Those against whom Paul issues his warning are clearly Jews of some kind, though the terms he uses to describe them are totally unexpected. The epithet "dogs" was sometimes used by the Jews as a term of derision for Gentiles; dogs were scavengers and so were naturally associated with uncleanness.

Paul now applies the term to these people, thus indicating that the ones he has in mind are not, in fact, the people of God. "Evil workers/those who do evil" is equally unexpected. In the book of Psalms, it is those who do not obey the Torah who are repeatedly described as "evildoers" (e.g., Ps 5:5), while those who are faithful to the Torah are righteous (e.g., Pss 1:6; 5:12). Once again, the description is one that Jews would naturally apply to Gentiles and to non-observant Jews. The final warning, against "those who mutilate/mutilators of the flesh" is bizarre. The Greek word used here is κατατομή (*katatomē*), meaning "mutilation," and Paul has deliberately substituted it for the word περιτομή (*peritomē*), meaning "circumcision." The irony of his words reaches its climax here, as the Jews' proudest claim is turned on its head. Whereas circumcision was understood to be the sign of the covenant between God and Abraham,

---

26. See Markus Bockmuehl, *The Epistle to the Philippians*, Black's NT Commentary (Peabody, Mass.: Hendrickson, 1998).

mutilation—making gashes in the flesh—was something done by pagan priests. Mutilation was specifically forbidden to the priests of Israel (Lev 21:5), for any kind of physical defect debarred men from being priests, since they must be holy to their God (Lev 21:18-23).[27] For Paul, circumcision is worth nothing unless it is "circumcision of the heart" (Rom 2:28-29).

Three times over, Paul has applied to a group of Jews terms that they would have thought appropriate only for outsiders: "dogs," "evildoers," "mutilation." Taken together, his threefold description amounts to a denial of the claim of the people he has in mind to be true Jews. The people who pride themselves on being insiders are, in fact, in the position of those whom they despise. The irony of Paul's description lies in the fact that those whom he is describing are the very people who cared desperately about keeping themselves pure, about obeying the commandments of the Torah, and about preserving circumcision as the essential mark of those who belonged to Israel. But all this is the righteousness of the law (v. 6), which Paul now regards as worthless compared with the righteousness that comes to him in Christ (v. 9). If Paul urges the Philippians to "beware of" these people, then perhaps it is lest they, too, make the mistake of supposing that it is "the righteousness of the law" that is important.

Who *were* the people Paul is attacking here? Clearly it was some group who claimed to be Jewish. But were they Jewish by birth, or were they Gentile converts? And were they also Christians? It is sometimes suggested that Paul was referring to Jews who had rejected the gospel and were opposing the claims of Gentile Christians to belong to the people of God. Why, then, should he think it necessary to warn the Philippians against them? The answer could be that the Jewish community was persecuting the Christians in Philippi; Paul's own imprisonment had almost certainly come about because of the opposition of Jews in Jerusalem. His warning here, then, might echo the injunction in 1:27 to stand firm in the the face of opposition. But as we have already seen, there seem to have been very few Jews in Philippi! The argument in this chapter seems to suppose a more subtle danger, that of putting confidence "in the flesh." Moreover, Paul himself had once opposed the gospel and persecuted the Christian community (v. 6); yet, in describing his own life as a Jew in vv. 4-6 he does not refer to himself as a dog, as a worker of evil, or as belonging to the mutilation! On the contrary, he includes his devotion to the Torah among his former assets.

It is important to note that Paul's bitter attack here is not on Judaism per se. His argument in vv. 4-11 suggests that he probably had in mind a group of *Christian* Jews who disagreed with him about the terms on which one could belong to the people of God and were insisting that Gentile Christians become Jewish proselytes. This is supported by the reference to this group as "the mutilation," which suggests that Paul has in mind those who were actively pursuing a policy of circumcising converts.

These Judaizers might, of course, be *Gentile* Christians who, with all the enthusiasm of converts, assumed that it was necessary to accept all the practices of Judaism. It is sometimes argued that Paul's description of his own inherited privileges rules this interpretation out, since he is comparing his own credentials with those of fellow Jews. Since he is insisting that he had many of these privileges by birth and race, however, his argument would have added poignancy if it were directed against Gentile Judaizers who regard as essential the very things Paul has abandoned.

The meaning of the passage is not greatly affected by our decision on this point, since the focus of Paul's argument quickly shifts to his own experience. Nothing more is said about these people (unless vv. 18-19 are a reference to the same group), which suggests that Paul's words are indeed intended as a safeguard against possible danger rather than as a warning against an imminent threat to the Philippian community such as that which confronted the Galatians.

---

27. Deut 23:1 goes further, excluding from the assembly of the Lord those men whose sexual organs have been damaged. In some circles, 2 Sam 5:8 seems to have been understood as a perpetual prohibition of those who are blind or disabled in taking any part in worship. See 1QSa 2:5-7; *m. Hag.* 1:1. Mutilation is thus understood to put one outside the company of God's people. Sacrifices offered to God had to be "without blemish," so it was natural to think that those who worshiped God must meet the same requirement.

PHILIPPIANS 3:1-11 COMMENTARY

3:3-4. In contrast to those whose claims he has ridiculed, Paul declares: "For it is *we* who are the circumcision, who worship in/by the Spirit of God" (v. 3). The belief that true circumcision is not a literal one (Rom 2:28-29) is found in Jer 4:4 and 9:26 (cf. 1QS 5:5); for Paul it is faith, not circumcision, that is essential (Rom 4:9-12). The verb "to serve" (λατρεύω *latreuō*) is usually used of priestly service in the Temple; here that service is no longer offered by the priests but by *all* God's people. There are variant readings here, one of which is given in the NRSV note, but the text is almost certainly correct. The idea of a new spiritual worship is set out in John 4:23-24. The fact that the Spirit had been poured out on those who were *not* circumcised is a key element in Paul's argument with the "Judaizers" (Gal 3:1-5, 14; cf. Acts 10:44-8; 11:15-18).

The "we" are now identified further as those who "boast/glory" in Christ Jesus, a description that encompasses all Christians, whether Jews or Gentiles. By contrast, others "put/have . . . confidence in the flesh." The two verbs used here are almost synonymous in meaning, though "boasting" (καυχάομαι *kauchaomai*) perhaps goes a little beyond "having confidence" (πείθω *peithō*). It is *because* they have confidence in Christ that believers may justly boast of what God has done for them. Jews would certainly not have regarded boasting in the law as putting confidence in the flesh. For Paul, however, the law operates in the sphere of flesh and is ineffectual because of the weakness of the flesh (see Romans 7). There is added irony, of course, in the fact that the rite of circumcision is literally carried out in the flesh.

Those who mock earthly privileges are usually people who do not themselves have any. This is not true in Paul's case, however, since he has every reason to boast in the privileges that have come to him by birth and upbringing—except his overwhelming conviction that such privileges are worthless by comparison with those that have come to him "in Christ." What he now thinks about his former boast that he was a Jew is expressed in the phrase "to have confidence in the flesh," which he uses three times in vv. 3-4. The Greek word σάρξ (*sarx*), here translated "flesh," is used of humanity in its weakness. It denotes what is physical, external, visible, and temporal, in contrast to the spiritual, internal, invisible, and eternal. Flesh is not in itself sinful, though it can easily fall prey to sin. It represents everything that we would call "human" or "worldly." The contrast Paul makes here between having confidence "in the flesh" and boasting "in Christ" is similar to that expressed in Isa 31:3: "The Egyptians are human, and not God; their horses are flesh, and not spirit." The significant point to notice is that as a Christian, Paul regards all the privileges given by God to Israel as belonging to this sphere of "flesh"; those who belong to Christ, on the other hand, worship in/by *the Spirit* of God."

In human terms, then, Paul had every reason to be confident—more so than others. By "I have more," Paul perhaps meant simply that he had the best possible credentials that any Jew could have; but it is possible that the "anyone else" refers in particular to those Gentiles who had succumbed to the teaching of Judaizers and become proselytes. Paul himself had been circumcised on the eighth day, as the law required (Lev 12:3), because he was an Israelite by race (v. 5), and not a proselyte. The translation "of the people of Israel" in the NRSV and the NIV is misleading. The Greek word γένος (*genos*) implies racial descent, and Paul means that he was Jewish *by birth*. Paul had taken pride in the fact that he belonged to the tribe of Benjamin—perhaps because Benjamin was one of Jacob's favorite sons and because the tribe had later remained faithful to the house of David. His claims are summed up in the phrase "a Hebrew of Hebrews": He is a Hebrew, born of pure Hebrew stock. It is possible that the phrase implies a knowledge of the Hebrew language, which few Jews any longer spoke.

3:5-6. In addition to these inherited privileges, Paul had excelled in everything Jewish. He had been a member of the small sect of the Pharisees, who were faithful and sincere upholders of the law. Pharisees were renowned for their strict adherence to the law, and spelled out the implications of every regulation in the law in an attempt to avoid any accidental infringement. They also believed that the levitical rules of purity for the priests should be applied to all Jews, since the whole nation should be holy to God.

Paul's summary of his own credentials adds further irony to his description in v. 2 of a group of Jews as "dogs," "workers of evil," and "the mutilation": To Pharisees above all others, such people had no claim to belong to Israel. Paul's zeal for the law had been evidenced by his persecution of the church (v. 6; cf. Gal 1:13). And because he had lived in accordance with Pharisaic standards, he had been blameless in terms of what the law demanded. The NIV's "legalistic righteousness" is unfortunate. Paul is not caricaturing his previous life as a religion of legalism; on the contrary, he is listing it among the privileges he once possessed. But this was the righteousness specified in the law, not the righteousness of God (Rom 10:3), and being blameless according to its precepts was not sufficient (cf. Mark 10:20-21 and par.). The NRSV's triple "as to" in vv. 5-6 reflects well the rhythm of the Greek.

3:7-9. Paul now uses the image of a profit-and-loss account to compare the advantages he enjoyed as a Jew with those that have come to him as a result of his being in Christ. The things that he had once regarded as assets he now writes off as a loss for the sake of Christ (v. 7). After this initial contrast between the two sides of the ledger, the next few lines reiterate and amplify this idea of his overwhelming gain in Christ (the amplifications are in italics):

> He regards *everything* as loss for the *surpassing value/greatness* of *knowing* Christ Jesus *his Lord;* for the sake of Jesus Christ, indeed, he *has* lost all things and regards them *as rubbish,* in order that he might gain Christ *and be found in him.*

The core statement is repeated, with slight variations, three times over: "These/all things I consider loss/I have lost for the sake of Christ [Jesus my Lord]." A similar comparison between what was once regarded as valuable and the overwhelming value of what is now on offer is found in the parable of the pearl of great price (Matt 13:45-46).

Paul's skillful use of repetition and expansion emphasizes the point he is making. The noun "gain" (κέρδος *kerdos*, v. 7) is echoed by the verb "to gain" (κερδαίνω *kerdainō*, v. 8), the verb "regard/consider" (ἡγέομαι *hēgeomai*) is used three times, as is the name "Christ"; the noun "loss" (ζημία *zēmia*) occurs twice, followed by the verb "to lose" (ζημιόω *zēmioō*); the adjective πάντα (*panta*) is used twice, a fact that is obscured by English translations that switch from "everything" to "all things." The triple statement of the same theme (clearer in the NRSV than in the NIV) builds up to a climax that leaves us in no doubt that the gain of being "in Christ" far outweighs the value of everything Paul once possessed. The fact that on the third occasion he uses a passive verb (ἐζημιώθην *ezēmiōthēn*), "I have lost/suffered the loss," may indicate that he has been forcibly stripped of his privileges by his fellow Jews, who now disown him. Nevertheless, Paul's point is that he has willingly abandoned things that he no longer values. The word he now uses to describe them, σκύβαλα (*skybala*), is in fact more contemptuous than the translation "rubbish" suggests, for it means literally "excrement" or "refuse." That Paul now regards his former privileges in this way has already been demonstrated by his language in v. 2.

The things that Paul now prizes are "knowing Christ Jesus" (v. 8), being "found in him" (v. 9), and having the righteousness that comes "from God." What does Paul understand by "knowing Christ"? Some commentators have suggested that Paul is here influenced by the language of Gnosticism, but it seems more likely that the influence (if there was any) was in the other direction. It is far more probable that his words are rooted in the OT understanding of religion as the knowledge of God. The knowledge of God is based on God's self-revelation to the people and is, therefore, both an acknowledgment of what God has done and a recognition of God's claims upon the people. To know God is thus to honor God and to obey God's will; it is not simply to have knowledge of "facts" about God but to enter into a personal relationship. Here, however, Paul speaks about knowing *Christ Jesus his Lord.* This phrase immediately reminds us of the passage in the previous chapter in which Paul described how Christ Jesus acted in such a way that he was acknowledged as universal Lord. We have seen that this passage was an account of the unfolding of Christ's character, and hence also a revelation of the nature of God, and that it led into the demand for an appropriate response, in obedience, from the Philippians (2:12-13). The Christ whom Paul desires to know is the Christ who emptied himself and was obedient to death: To know him is to be like him. Precisely what it means to know Christ Jesus as Lord was spelled out in 2:1-15, and pointing us back to that passage is Paul's threefold use of the verb he used in 2:6 of Christ, "consider/regard" (*hēgeomai*), which he now uses of himself. Just as Christ considered the privileges that belonged to equality with God as something he should not exploit, and therefore abandoned them, so also Paul has now abandoned all the privileges that belonged to him as a Jew, because he does not consider them of value in comparison with knowing Christ. For Paul, therefore, to know Christ *as Lord* means to acknowledge his actions as the self-revelation *of God* and to recognize Christ's claims by adopting the same pattern for his own life.

These ideas are spelled out even more clearly in the third statement of Paul's theme in vv. 8-9. He has abandoned his old privileges in order to gain Christ and to be found in him. It is probably no accident that the word εὑρεθῶ (*heuretho*, "be found") echoes the participle used of Christ in 2:7: Christ was found in human form, and Paul is now found in Christ. This is an experience Paul already enjoys; there is, therefore, no need to assume, as some commentators have done, that Paul must be thinking of being found in Christ on the last day.

Paul now expresses the contrast in a new way: He has abandoned his own righteousness, a righteousness he described in vv. 5-6 as being "from the law," for that which comes "through faith in Christ" (v. 9). This new righteousness, which denotes a right relationship with Christ, is "from God" and is "based on/by faith." Paul has more to say about the righteousness he shares as a result of being in Christ than about the old righteousness he has abandoned, but it is worth noting which phrases here are balanced against each other. The obvious example is the contrast between the righteousness that is "from the law" and that which is "from God." The contrast is a familiar one in Pauline literature. In Rom 8:3, for example, he sums up his argument (set out in the preceding chapters) that the law could not bring true righteousness, by declaring that what the law could not do God has now done: God has sent the Son in the likeness of sinful flesh, with the result that men and women are declared righteous in him. The contrast in that passage between the law and God is not meant to suggest that the law is evil. Paul has spent the whole of Romans 7 arguing that the law (given by God!) is good, but that it is ineffectual because of the weakness of the flesh. We see echoes of this argument in Philippians in the description of Christ's incarnation (2:7), in the reference to the flesh (3:3-4), and in the contrast between the righteousness that comes from the law and that which comes from God.

In contrast to the righteousness Paul calls his own (cf. also Rom 10:3), based on his own endeavors, he sets that which is "through faith in Christ." The precise meaning of the phrase πίστις Χριστοῦ (*pistis Christou*), here translated "faith in Christ," is much disputed. The noun *pistis* is broader in meaning than our English word "faith," and it can also mean the faithfulness that is the basis of faith. However, the chief problem is that in Greek we have a genitive that may be either subjective or objective; it could mean, therefore, either the faith (or faithfulness) that was Christ's or our faith in Christ. The traditional English translation is the one given in the NRSV and the NIV, but the alternative is given in the NRSV note. Which is the correct interpretation here? Opinion is sharply divided, and for an informed judgment one needs to consider all the passages where Paul uses the phrase (the other examples are found at Rom 3:22, 26; Gal 2:16 [twice], 20; 3:22; and, in some MSS, 3:26). In Philippians, we should note that at the end of the verse Paul spells out the fact that the righteousness he has in Christ comes to him through faith: Is he simply repeating himself? This final phrase—"based on/by faith"—is not balanced by any comparable phrase about the righteousness that comes from the law, and it is difficult to explain why Paul should think it necessary to repeat the reference to faith if he has already said that the righteousness from God comes to us through *our* faith in Christ. Moreover, we expect the righteousness that is opposed to what he terms his own righteousness to be that which belongs to Christ himself—the righteousness pronounced by God on one who has faith or is faithful (cf. Paul's comment about the faith of Abraham in Rom 4:3) and now shared by those who are "found in him." This righteousness would then be understood as being *"from* God" but *through* the faithfulness of Christ (the preposition διά [*dia,* "through"], used with the genitive, has an instrumental sense). Finally, we should note that it is appropriate if Paul has Christ's own faith or faithfulness in mind here, in view of what was said in 2:6-11 about Christ's self-emptying and obedience (the result of faith!) and consequent vindication. For all these reasons, it seems likely that the genitive is subjective and that Paul is thinking here of the righteousness that is shared by those in Christ because of the faithfulness of Christ himself.[28]

3:10-11. Verse 10 introduces another purpose clause, though its precise relationship to what Paul has been saying is not clear. However we explain the grammar, this verse picks up and expands the idea of "knowing Christ," which was mentioned in v. 8. Paul's aim is "to know Christ and the power of his resurrection." We are surprised to find Paul mentioning Christ's resurrection before his sufferings and death, but he links our righteousness (v. 9) with Christ's resurrection elsewhere (Rom 4:25). The term used in Romans is δικαίωσις (*dikaiōsis*), meaning "vindication," rather than δικαιοσύνη (*dikaiosynē*), "righteousness" (as in v. 9), which suggests that there is a sense in which believers share in the vindication of Christ at his resurrection; see also Rom 5:18, where Christ's obedience (cf. Phil 2:8) leads to acquittal and to life for all. Belief in the resurrection of the body was a distinctively Jewish idea. It was taken over into Christianity, but was now understood to be dependent on the resurrection of Christ.

Christ's resurrection is described elsewhere as the result of an act of divine power (Rom 1:4). Here, it is seen as itself the source of power in the lives of believers. Those who are in Christ share his faith, his righteousness, and his resurrection—but only if they are prepared to share also in "his sufferings." Paul uses once again the word κοινωνία (*koinōnia*), meaning "sharing/fellowship," which he used in 1:5 (cf. 2:1 and 4:15, and in particular 1:7 and 4:14, where compounds of the word are used with reference to suffering). This is an experience that has already begun for Paul and the Philippians! Christians must be ready to become "like [Christ] in his death" (cf. Rom 8:17). The verb meaning "becoming like" (συμμορφόω *symmorphoō*), provides another echo of 2:6-7 (μορφή *morphē*), as does θάνατος (*thanatos*), "death," as though to remind us once again that being in Christ means following his example. Being conformed to Christ's death is an ongoing process in the life of the believer (cf. 2 Cor 4:10-12), but attaining "the resurrection from the dead" clearly lies in the future—even though Christians already know the power of Christ's resurrection (worked by God) in their lives! Now we realize that Paul mentions Christ's resurrection before his death because he is describing Christian experience. It is the power of Christ's resurrection that is at work in Paul's life, even in the midst of suffering, and that provides the assurance of his own future resurrection.

The introductory "if somehow" in v. 11 seems to introduce an element of doubt, but Paul can hardly be dubious about whether those who are in Christ will share his resurrection. The phrase is intended, rather, to remind the Philippians that Christians have not yet arrived at their final destination. Christ's resurrection has already occurred, but their own lies in the future, and it is necessary to go on "being conformed" to Christ's obedience and death if they are to attain the resurrection. The fact that their righteousness is "from God" does not absolve them from moral endeavor, for the goal still lies ahead—a theme Paul elaborates on in vv. 12-16.

---

28. For a discussion of "the faith of Christ," see Richard B. Hays, *The Faith of Jesus Christ: An Investigation of the Narrative Substructure of Galatians 3:1–4:11,* SBLDS 56 (Chico, Calif.: Scholars Press, 1983); M. D. Hooker, "ΠΙΣΤΙΣ ΧΡΙΣΤΟΥ," *NTS* 35 (1989) 321-42, reprinted in Hooker, *From Adam to Christ,* 165-86; I. G. Wallis, *The Faith of Jesus Christ in Early Christian Tradition* (Cambridge: Cambridge University Press, 1995) 118-24.

REFLECTIONS

1. At first sight, Paul's bitter attack on those whom he characterizes as "dogs" (3:2) does not seem very promising material for Christian exposition. We need to remember, however, that behind the sarcasm, what he is denouncing is the attitude that claims exclusive rights to divine favor and bars the great majority of men and women from fellowship with God. The language Paul uses is a parody of the terms that were used by devout Jews to distinguish between themselves and outsiders, and the terms he hurls at this group echo those that *they* would have used of those people who in their view were excluded from God's people. To them, Gentile "dogs" and those who did not observe the law—doers of evil—were outside God's covenant, the essential mark of which was circumcision. In contrast to their claim that they alone were God's holy people, Paul maintains that the true people of God consist of all who worship by the Spirit of God (3:3). It is the presence of God's Spirit, therefore, that is now the essential mark of God's people—the Spirit who was at work in Jesus and who was poured out on Jews and Gentiles alike when they believed the gospel—and through that Spirit they are now able to worship God sincerely. What Paul is offering us, therefore, is an *inclusive* model of the people of God rather than an exclusive one. No one need be kept out, for this community is open to all.

Unfortunately, the early Christians quickly succumbed to the temptation to adopt the exclusive model for themselves. They soon came to regard Jews as dogs.[29] All too quickly the conviction of a few that they alone were the elect of God infected, in turn, various sections of the Christian community, each of which claimed that *their* particular beliefs and practices were the essential hallmarks of the church, and that others, therefore, were not true believers. Far too often, religious people imagine that they "know" the mind of the Lord and suppose that God shares their prejudices and beliefs! The result is that they try to keep God to themselves and imagine that the privilege of belonging to God (a privilege meant for the entire human race) makes them superior to other people. In relationships with people from other denominations and of other faiths, it is very easy for Christians to suppose that their own prejudices and preferences represent God's will and that those of other people are inferior. If Paul were alive today, might he not condemn many of us for claiming exclusive understanding of the divine will and for forgetting that *all* who worship God by the Spirit belong to God's people? While the presence of the Spirit should mean unity, it does not mean uniformity, for the Spirit's gifts are many and varied (Romans 12; 1 Corinthians 12), and members of the Christian community are very different. But through the same Spirit, all may worship God.

As time passed and the Letter to the Philippians, along with Paul's other letters, was accepted as Scripture and became part of what we now know as the New Testament, the original circumstances in which Paul was writing were forgotten. Readers forgot that his purpose in this passage was to defend the rights of Gentiles to be Christians against a majority in the church who assumed that it was necessary to first become a Jew in order to be a Christian. The result was that Paul's words took on a very different meaning; taken out of their original context, they appeared to be a condemnation of all Jews. Tragically, this misunderstanding encouraged the growth of anti-Semitism in the church, and Paul's words were interpreted as anti-Jewish polemic. We need to be very careful when reading Scripture! It is so easy to misunderstand it and to assume that we can simply read it without considering what it meant to its original readers and why its authors were writing as they did. Precisely because it is so difficult to recover the original situation, many people today concentrate simply on the text as we have it.

---

29. See Shylock's famous complaint, many years later, in Shakespeare's *The Merchant of Venice* I.iii.

In this passage, we see clearly how, by doing that, one might assume that Paul was endorsing bigotry and exclusion, when, in fact, these were the attitudes he was attacking.

2. Privileges of birth and circumstance can easily lead to pride and boasting, and that is just as true in the modern world as it was for the first-century Jew. Perhaps it is surprising that Paul claims that Christians also boast—but this is a very different kind of boasting! Those who now belong to God's people are described as boasting/glorying *in Christ Jesus,* in contrast to those who have confidence in the flesh (3:3). Once again, Paul offers us an inclusive understanding of God's people instead of an exclusive one. Whereas the things about which Paul had once boasted (3:4-6) *separated* him from others, being in Christ *unites* all who boast in him, for they worship in the Spirit of God, relying on God alone. Thus no one can claim to be better than any other person. In the realm of what Paul calls "the flesh," some are inevitably superior to others; but in the realm of the Spirit, in which those who are "in Christ" live, these distinctions are abolished (Gal 3:28), and the different gifts given to individuals are signs of their *unity,* not of division. No one group of Christians can claim that the particular gift given to them is superior to those given to others, nor can they claim that they are superior to others (1 Corinthians 12–14). Those who are in Christ boast in him alone, and the fact that he was born in human likeness and lived a human life as it was meant to be lived has opened up to all humans the possibility of sharing that life.

3. In this passage, Paul is spelling out some of the implications of what it means to believe. To believe in the gospel is to put one's trust in God. We need at least four terms in English—"faith," "belief," "trust," "faithfulness"—to convey all the meanings of one Greek noun, πίστις (*pistis*). To trust in something or someone means to rely on them, and complete trust suggests that there is no need to rely on anything else. So if men and women come to put their trust in God, they must abandon all other props. It is easy to think of faith in very positive terms, as acceptance—acceptance of the grace of God at work in Christ—and to forget this other, more negative aspect of faith—the need for renunciation. Before Paul could accept Christ, he had to renounce those things on which, as a Jew, he had relied (3:7-11). Just as the rich young ruler had to renounce his wealth in order to become a disciple (Matt 19:16-26; Mark 10:17-27; Luke 18:18-26), so also Paul had to renounce the privileges that kept him from accepting the gifts that were now offered him in Christ. He does renounce them, not because they were wrong in themselves (both the law and circumcision had been given by God), but because they belong to the old era of the flesh and have been replaced by something far better: a new relationship with God, freely offered to all, and not confined to those who were able to claim to be righteous according to the law.

In spite of Paul's contrast between the righteousness of his own that he has abandoned and the righteousness that comes in Christ, it is all too easy for Christians to cling to what they regard as their own righteousness. We assume that our faithful attendance at church, our Christian conduct and adherence to moral principles, *deserve* some special consideration from God and constitute some special claim on God. Again and again, when disaster falls, people ask, "Why did this happen to me?" as though living an upright life ought to give them some kind of immunity from suffering. There are even some television evangelists who preach a perversion of the gospel, suggesting that God rewards believers with material goods. How seriously, then, do we take Paul's declaration that he regards his own righteousness as worthless, compared with that offered to him in Christ?

4. At his conversion, Paul renounced reliance on the law. The problem was not that the law was evil, but rather that the good could be the enemy of the best. Paul, in his zeal to keep the law of God, had persecuted Christians, a clear indication that righteousness according to the law could be opposed to the righteousness of God. Now he discovered that loving other people was more important than living according to a set of rules. Was this a lesson that had not been learned by one earnest Christian who caused his brother great pain because he thought it more important to worship in his own church on Sunday morning than to join a family lunch to celebrate his brother's eightieth birthday? It is easy to be so caught up in church activities and good works that we forget that God is worshiped and served in the ways we relate to others and in the way we live our everyday lives. It is possible to be so busy striving after what we are sure is right that we can miss more important needs. Yet we must be careful not to fall into the opposite temptation! Abandoning one's own righteousness for that of God can easily lead to the temptation to suppose that there is no need for moral endeavor or personal discipline. Paul insists that the Christian must become what he or she already is. Luther expressed the same idea somewhat differently when he said that the nature of a Christian does not lie in what he or she has become, but in what that person is becoming.

PHILIPPIANS 3:12–4:1, KEEP GOING!

COMMENTARY

3:12. What Paul has just said might perhaps be understood as complacency, so he hastens to remind the Philippians that he has not yet "obtained" what he is aiming for. The "this" (not expressed in the Greek) that he has not yet obtained is probably specifically "the resurrection from the dead," which he has just described as something he must still attain. However, it may refer to other aspects of that great gain for which he has abandoned "everything" (vv. 7-11); this understanding is reflected in the NIV's "all." Certainly Paul knows that he has not yet "been made perfect/reached the goal." The verb τελειόω (*teleioō*) means "to complete," "to bring to perfection," "to reach a goal." It was also used in the mystery religions in the sense of "to initiate," "to consecrate," and some commentators suggest that Paul is using it with that meaning here, and thus is possibly attacking a group of "gnostic Christians" who claimed to be perfect already.[30] Similar language is used in Judaism, however; for example, by the Qumran community, who regarded themselves as perfect because of their obedience to the law (see the Commentary on 3:15). Paul probably has in mind his previous way of life, in which he claimed to be "blameless/faultless" according to the law (v. 6). Now he realizes that he has not yet achieved his new—much greater—goal, which will be reached only at the resurrection. The NRSV translation already suggests the athletic imagery that dominates the rest of the paragraph: Paul presses forward to grasp what he has not yet obtained, which once again can mean either the resurrection in particular or the completion of the experience described in vv. 7-11. Both the NIV and the NRSV have understood the Greek phrase ἐφ' ᾧ (*eph hō*) in different ways—the NRSV as indicating result ("because"), the NIV as purpose ("for which"). The latter seems more appropriate in the context, since it emphasizes the fact that Paul's endeavors now are not simply the response to what Christ has done, but the completion of God's purpose for him.

3:13-14. For a third time Paul emphasizes that he has not yet reached his goal (v. 13), this time repeating the verb "to lay hold of/make my own" (καταλαμβάνω *katalambanō*), which he has already used twice in v. 12. The NIV has followed the text that is noted in the NRSV, reading οὔπω (*oupō*, "not yet") instead of οὐ (*ou*, "not"), even though the latter is better attested. The sense seems to require the "yet," which probably explains why the change was made. The "one thing" Paul does (v. 13) is to aim for the prize (v. 14), and like an athlete running a race, he ignores what is behind him and

---

30. This suggestion was made by Walter Schmithals in an article originally published in 1957, translated and republished in W. Schmithals, *Paul and the Gnostics* (Nashville: Abingdon, 1972) 95-104.

concentrates on the goal ahead (cf. Jesus' saying about the plowman, Luke 9:62). What is it that Paul does not look back at? Possibly it is the progress he has made thus far, but more probably he is thinking of the privileges he once prized but has now discarded (vv. 7-8). "The goal" on which Paul has set his eyes (the Greek σκοπός [*skopos*] is linked to the verb σκοπέω [*skopeō*], "to look at," used in v. 17) is "the prize," which is defined by the phrase (translated literally in the NRSV note) "of the upward calling of God in Christ Jesus." The precise meaning of this phrase is uncertain. Does it mean that the prize will be the divine summons to heaven? Or does it mean that the prize will be given to those who have obeyed the call of God, which is the way the NIV has understood it? Yet a third suggestion is that Paul is thinking of the ceremony at the end of a race, when the winner was called forward to receive a prize. Perhaps we should not attempt to choose between these various interpretations. Certainly the NIV is correct to remind us that the call of God came to Paul at the beginning of the race; thus he is pressing forward in order "to take hold of that for which Christ Jesus took hold of" him (v. 12). Nevertheless, the prize for which he is aiming will be the realization of that call.

3:15-16. Verse 15 is one of the passages in the letter that often has been seen as offering support to those who argue that Paul is writing to a divided community, since there are apparently people in Philippi who "think differently" from Paul on some matters. Moreover, the reference to those described as "mature" in the English translations has sometimes been taken as an ironic reference to a group who are claiming to be "perfect," since the Greek word τέλειος (*teleios*) can have both meanings. But the word can scarcely be ironic, since Paul includes himself among those who are "mature"! Paul's injunction in v. 15, "Let us be of the same mind/all of us should take such a view of things," picks up once again the verb φρονέω (*phroneō*), used in 2:5 of the attitude that belonged to Christ and to those who are in him, and in 2:2 (twice), where Paul urged the Philippians to "think the same." Here, it is not so much a question of having the *same* mind (as in the NRSV) as of thinking in a particular way; the lengthy English paraphrases represent a mere two words in Greek, meaning "this let us think." Paul's injunction is linked to what has just been said with the word οὖν (*oun*, "therefore"; NRSV, "then"; ignored in the NIV) and so refers to the attitude Paul has been describing, an attitude that has its origins in the attitude of Christ himself.

It is puzzling, however, to find Paul speaking of himself now as *teleios*, after using the cognate verb *teleioō* in v. 12 to deny that he had reached his goal. Nevertheless, he is certainly capable of using cognate words (or even the same word) in close proximity with slightly different meanings, and both the NIV and the NRSV are probably correct in understanding *teleios* here to mean "mature" rather than "perfect" (cf. 1 Cor 14:20, where it has this meaning). In the present context, however, *teleios* probably has a more specific meaning than is conveyed by the English word "mature." The word is sometimes used in the LXX of those who are wholeheartedly devoted to God and so blameless before God (e.g., Gen 6:9; Deut 18:13). A similar idea occurs in the Qumran literature (expressed in the Hebrew word תמים [*tamîm*]), where the members of the community were required to live "perfectly," in accordance with the law (1 QS 1:8; 2:2; 8:20). Paul has exchanged a life that was without fault according to the law (v. 6) for the purity and blamelessness that belong to Christ and to those who live in him; the new community consists of those who are *teleios* in Christ. Even though Christians will not finally be made perfect until the last day, the typical Pauline injunction to "be what you are" is reflected in the fact that they can be described already as "mature."

Those who are truly mature think about the Christian life in the way Paul has just described it, fully aware that they have *not* yet arrived at their final destination. "And if" on any point the Philippians "think differently," or otherwise than they should, God will reveal this to them also—how, Paul does not say, but this is presumably part of their growth in knowledge and insight, for which he prayed in 1:9. Paul's introductory "and" rather than "but" suggests that any different opinion that may exist in the Philippian community is not a major affair. Those whom Paul addresses are included, with himself, among the "mature," even though he recognizes that there is a possibility that some aspect of their thinking and behavior is not in line with the attitude he has been advocating. Paul's words are basically words of encouragement rather than of reprimand: Those who are truly mature are ready to recognize when they are wrong and to accept guidance. So Paul concludes this paragraph with an exhortation (again including himself) to "live up to/hold fast to" what has already been attained (v. 16). The verb στοιχέω (*stoicheō*, "to be in line with") suggests already the idea of imitation, which will be taken up in the next verse.

3:17. Paul now calls on the Philippians to "join" in imitating him. Out of context, this might sound extraordinarily conceited, but Paul is, of course, referring to the endeavors he has been describing in vv. 7-16, which are rooted in Christ's hold on him (v. 12). The apostle's task is to be a role model whose example can be imitated (cf. 1 Cor 4:16; 11:1; 1 Thess 1:6; 2 Thess 3:7, 9). But with whom are they to join? Is it with one another? This is how the NRSV has understood the command; the "others" in the NIV translation are not mentioned in the text. However, it is possible that Paul's words should be understood as meaning "be imitators *with* me" rather than "be imitators *of* me."[31] In this case, Paul would be appealing to the Philippians to join *him* in imitating Christ. The objection to this interpretation is that there is no specific reference to Christ, and the vast majority of commentators, therefore, understand Paul to be calling on the Philippians to imitate him. It is important to remember, however, that 2:6-11 is central to all of Paul's argument. As we have seen, 3:7-16 is, in effect, a description of how Paul has followed the example of Christ set out in 2:6-11, and that passage was itself introduced as a pattern for the life of the Philippian community. Moreover, we are about to have further echoes from 2:6-11 in the final verses of this chapter. Whichever way we translate these introductory words, therefore, there is an *implicit* command to imitate Christ. Paul's logic is very similar to 1 Cor 11:1, where he urges the Corinthians: "Be imitators of me, as I am of Christ!"

Although Paul himself is no longer among the Philippians, they can still observe the pattern they should be following in "those who live according to the example/pattern" given to the Philippians by Paul.

3:18-19. In these verses Paul refers once again to a very different group, whose way of life is opposed to the gospel. Whom does he have in mind now? Is it the same group described in v. 2? They seemed to be "Judaizers," Christian converts who placed great emphasis on keeping the law. The group now under attack regard their "belly/stomach" as their god and find their glory "in their shame." These words have, indeed, been interpreted by some commentators as a sarcastic attack on Jewish practices, with "belly" and "shame" understood as mocking references to the strict observance of food laws and the insistence on the rite of circumcision. Such language would be far more abusive than the irony used in v. 2, however, where Paul's words were carefully chosen to show how those who were *claiming* to be the people of God were in fact *not* members of God's people.

What Paul says in these verses seems far more appropriate if it is intended as an attack on those who really were living lives of indulgence. The existence of Christians who indulged in gluttony and shameful sexual practices is known to us from 1 Corinthians 5–6, where we find the Corinthians boasting (1 Cor 5:6) in spite of their immorality and toleration of people within their community who are "sexually immoral or greedy" (1 Cor 5:11). Some of these people seem to have been claiming that "all things are lawful" for Christians (1 Cor 6:12). Paul's teaching that Christians were not "under the law" was apparently being misunderstood as permitting self-indulgence (cf. 3 Macc 7:11, where Jews who abandoned the law are said to have transgressed the commandments for the sake of their bellies). In 1 Cor 6:13, Paul quotes what is apparently a slogan among these Christians: "Food is meant for the stomach [or belly] and the stomach [or belly] for food" (see also Paul's warning in Gal 5:13, 16-21). It would appear to be these people about whom Paul has "often told" the Philippians and now tells them again "with tears"— which suggests that, although Paul implicitly

---

31. In support of this interpretation, it has been pointed out that nowhere else in the NT is a compound formed with σύν (*syn-*, "with") such as we have here (συμμιμηταί *symmimētai*, "fellow imitators") used with an objective genitive denoting a person.

warns the Philippians against them, there is no one from this group in Philippi. In direct contrast to those who live in accordance with the pattern Paul has given them, these people "live as enemies of the cross of Christ" (v. 18); they are "enemies of the cross," because their whole manner of living is a denial of the revelation of God in Christ, whose self-emptying led to death on the cross. Paul's quarrel with these people concerns their behavior, not their teaching. They claim to be Christians, but fail completely to see the relevance of 2:6-11 for their own lives. Clearly they have not thought it necessary to "think like Christ," for (once again we have the familiar verb φρονέω [*phroneō*]) "their mind[s] is/are on earthly things" instead of on their heavenly call (v. 14). The "end/destiny" that awaits these people is not salvation but destruction, the fate that also lies in store for the opponents of the Philippian Christians, mentioned in 1:28.

3:20-21. In contrast to the "enemies of the cross," *our* citizenship is "in heaven" (v. 20; the word order emphasizes the "our"). The introductory "but" of the English translations stresses the contrast, but in Greek the link word is γάρ (*gar*), meaning "for." Paul has now returned to the theme he was pursuing in v. 17: Those who share the mind of Christ may confidently expect to share his victory, for they are already citizens of heaven. The word translated "citizenship" (πολίτευμα *politeuma*) echoes the verb πολιτεύομαι (*politeuomai*), which occurred in 3:20; it is used both of the commonwealth or state to which people belong and the citizenship (the privileges and duties) given to them. The idea that one belonged to a distant commonwealth could well have been familiar to Jews of the diaspora, but the term would have been particularly significant to the citizens of Philippi, who, because the city was a Roman colony, held citizenship in the distant city of Rome also. They may have been especially proud of their Roman citizenship. If Acts 16:12, 37-38 is to be believed, it was in Philippi that Paul declared himself to be a Roman citizen; perhaps, then, he is reminding the Philippians that they are all citizens of an even greater country. In fact, many of the Philippian Christians may well have been slaves and, therefore, without status of any kind; how much *more* meaningful it was to assure *them* that they were citizens of heaven! The idea that human beings have their citizenship in heaven is found also in Philo, a near contemporary of Paul.[32]

And from heaven, says Paul, "we are expecting/eagerly await a Savior," who is identified as the Lord Jesus Christ. The term "Savior" (σωτήρ *sōtēr*) is an unusual one for Paul (used nowhere else in the undisputed Pauline letters, though occurring once in Ephesians and no fewer than ten times in the Pastorals). Perhaps, again, it may have a particular nuance in this letter, since the Roman emperor was commonly given the title "Savior" in the imperial cult, where he was venerated as a god. The Philippians would have been well aware of this practice, as was Paul, who had appealed to Caesar, but who expected salvation from another source.

The idea that Christians can expect future salvation has already occurred in 1:19, 28 and 2:12. Now Paul links this specifically with the appearance of "the Lord Jesus Christ" from heaven (cf. 1 Thess 1:10; 5:2-10). Although Paul has described our citizenship as something that exists (already) "in heaven," his picture is of heaven brought to earth, rather than of our being translated to heaven. As in Rom 8:18-30 and 1 Cor 15:42-57, Paul speaks of the transformation of humanity. His expectation is part of the hoped-for restoration of a world that was plunged into chaos when Adam sinned. The imagery is thoroughly Jewish, envisaging the transformation of the body rather than the release of a soul from the body. Paul's language here echoes Rom 8:29, where Christians are destined to be conformed to the image of God's Son, and 1 Cor 15:42-44 and 52-54, where they are raised (if dead) or changed (if alive) from a mortal, perishable, physical body, characterized by weakness and dishonor, to an immortal, imperishable, spiritual body of power and glory. Here, however, Paul prefers to contrast "the body of our humiliation [ταπείνωσις *tapeinōsis*]" with "the body of his glory [δόξα *doxa*]." The NRSV's literal translation of these phrases (in contrast to the paraphrase of the NIV and the NRSV note) reminds us that Christ shared "the body of our humiliation" and that we hope to share in "the body of his glory." The language is a deliberate echo

32. See Philo *On the Confusion of Tongues.* 77-88.

of 2:6-11, where Christ humbled himself (ἐταπείνωσεν *etapeinōsen*) and where his consequent exaltation redounded to the glory (*doxa*) of God.

Paul's vocabulary here is, in fact, full of echoes of that earlier passage. The verb "is" (ὑπάρχει *hyparchei*) in v. 20 in the phrase "is in heaven" was used of Christ ("was") in 2:6; the phrase "Lord Jesus Christ" echoes the proclamation in 2:11; the verbs "transform" and "conformed/be like" (v. 27) are both compound verbs, the first based on the word μορφή (*morphē*, "form/very nature," vv. 6-7), the second on the word σχῆμα (*schēma*, "form/appearance," v. 8); the reference to "all things/everything" echoes the triple "every" of 2:9-11. The transformation of the body of our humiliation will be the work of Christ, through "the power that enables him [also] to make all things subject to himself/bring everything under his control"—the same power that was given him when every knee bowed to him and every tongue confessed him Lord (2:10-11). This power is ultimately the power of God, who has put everything under Christ's feet (1 Cor 15:28; cf. Ps 8:6).

The echoes of the vocabulary of 2:6-11 are not accidental. There is a sense in which 3:7-11 and 20-21 are the necessary completion of that passage, which told us of Christ's incarnation, death, and exaltation but said nothing about how these affect the believer. Now we realize that he was born in human likeness and shared our human death in order that Christians might be transformed into his likeness and share his vindication. This is a familiar theme in Paul, which is usually expressed in formulaic sayings that make clear the connection between what Christ became and what Christians become by means of a linking word (ἵνα *hina*, "in order that/so that"; see, e.g., 2 Cor 5:21; 8:9; Gal 3:13-14; 4:4-5). Sometimes these sayings refer to Christ's incarnation, sometimes to his death; in Phil 2:6-11 we find that both these aspects of Christ's sharing in our humanity are expressed. The interchange that allows Christians to become what Christ is occurs only when believers are "in Christ," however;[33] when they, in turn, are willing to share in Christ's death, then they experience his resurrection and become like him (3:9-10, 21).

4:1. The command (so rightly the NRSV) to "stand firm" provides another echo of 1:27, where the same verb was used; it thus brings this long section on the Christian life (which was interrupted by 2:19-30) to an end. Therefore, because of everything Paul has been saying, they must stand firm in the manner he has described ("in this way/that is how you should"). Paul heaps up laudatory descriptions of the Philippians: They are beloved and longed-for, his joy and his crown. The word "joy" (χαρά *chara*) repeats a theme that runs through Philippians; the term "crown" (στέφανος *stephanos*) is perhaps suggested by the image of the successful athlete in 3:12-14 (cf. 1 Cor 9:25). On the day of Christ, Paul expects to "boast" about the Philippians (2:16; cf. 1:3-11) and to be rewarded. Needless to say, they are to stand firm "in the Lord."

---

33. For further discussion, see Hooker, *From Adam to Christ*, 1-100.

REFLECTIONS

1. Paul's image of the Christian life as a race reminds us that we can never rest on our laurels. But this particular race is not a competition in which only one person can succeed: Like the so-called Caucus-race that is organized by the Dodo in Lewis Carroll's book *Alice's Adventures in Wonderland,* it is possible for everyone who takes part to win and for everyone to receive a prize. The end is assured, not because of what we are able to do (though we must do our best!), but by virtue of the fact that it rests ultimately on the hold Christ has on us: He has made us his own, and we belong to him (v. 13). The tension between what Christians already are and what they are called to be is neatly expressed in Paul's use of two words with the same root, first, to declare that he is not yet "perfect" (v. 12), and second, to appeal to those who, like himself, are "mature" (v. 15). John Wesley was only one person among many who have believed that Christian perfection is not only a proper aim but a real possibility—but Wesley was nevertheless skeptical about those who actually *claimed* to be perfect! It has been well said that the mark of true maturity is to know that one is *not* yet perfect. In this life, the goal always remains beyond us, demanding our continual endeavor, beckoning us forward.

2. Paul describes the goal of the Christian as "knowing Christ" or sharing his mind (3:8, 10). The pattern of the gospel must be stamped upon all who call Christ "Lord." Christ himself is the blueprint for Christian behavior, but the apostle, modeling himself on Christ, becomes in turn the pattern for the Philippians, because they know him (3:17). Now that Paul is no longer among them, there are other models to follow—those who live according to the pattern Paul gave them—and so the process continues. Individual Christians and Christian communities that embody the gospel serve to demonstrate the love of God to the world. The gospel is proclaimed in deed as much as in word. When Paul declares that "Christ Jesus has made me his own," he describes a task that is both a privilege and a responsibility. Teresa of Avila expressed this task well when she said: "Christ has no body on earth but yours. Yours are the eyes through which Christ's compassion is to look out to the world. Yours are the feet with which he is to go about doing good. Yours are the hands with which he is to bless us now." It is a privilege, indeed, to belong to him, and so to the people of God. But it is also a responsibility. And what a responsibility! Do others look at us and think, "In that person I can see something of what it means to be like Christ"? Would *we* dare to claim to be examples to others of what it means to live like Christ? Something of what can happen when that privilege and responsibility are taken seriously can be seen in the life of Lord Macleod of Iona, who worked first in the Glasgow slums and then built up the Christian community on Iona. Asked on one occasion "What makes you tick?" he promptly answered, "The fact that Christ Jesus made me his own."

3. To reject Paul's call to share Christ's mind and be like him is to live as an enemy of the cross (3:18). Two millennia later, we have forgotten the excruciating pain, the shame, and the horror that crucifixion involved; society has turned the cross into a hallowed symbol, and it is worn as a piece of jewelry or a charm. The result is that we are no longer appalled at the nature of Christ's death, and we no longer grasp the significance of what it means to share his sufferings and to become like him in death. Those who live as enemies of the cross see religion only in terms of benefit and advantage and are not prepared to share the humiliations and depravations that commitment to Christ can involve. In our modern world there are, however, men and women who have *not* been ashamed of the cross—men and women, for example, of the caliber of Dietrich Bonhoeffer, who was prepared to withstand the evil of Nazism and to accept the consequences.

4. At baptism, believers are marked with the sign of the cross, a reminder of what is involved in the confession of faith that is made, either by the person being baptized or by someone else on his or her behalf. To be marked with the sign of the cross implies an obligation to be conformed to the likeness of the crucified Lord—to love as he loved, to obey as he obeyed, and to be prepared to accept the consequences. Those who are not ashamed of the cross will not only be ready to share in Christ's sufferings and death, but they will also share in his exaltation (3:21). The Christian hope cannot be spelled out in detail, for we do not know—any more than did Paul—what lies beyond death. But Paul's conviction is that those who are like Christ in their lives and in their deaths will be like him in the life beyond. Because Christ was content to share our human life, he enables us to share his resurrection life, and he will one day make us truly like him.

PHILIPPIANS 4:2-23

LETTER CONCLUSION

PHILIPPIANS 4:2-9, VARIOUS EXHORTATIONS

COMMENTARY

4:2-3. In this appeal to Euodia and Syntyche we find at last clear evidence of dissension in the Philippian church. Many commentators believe this to have been a serious problem in the community and thus interpret these verses as an indication of Paul's real purpose in writing.[34] He deals with the women briefly and gently, however, speaking warmly of their work for the gospel, which suggests that, although they certainly needed to see the relevance of his teaching for their conduct, the matter was not out of hand. The fact that he addresses them by name supports this notion, since Paul frequently names his friends and fellow workers but very rarely those with whom he disagrees.

Paul addresses each woman in turn, using the same verb (the NRSV's "urge" is perhaps preferable to the NIV's "plead with" as a translation of παρακαλῶ *parakalō*), and so avoiding the taking of sides. He urges them "to be of the same mind/to agree with each other in the Lord"; the phrase is identical with that used in 2:2, although the NIV's translation disguises this fact. Paul also appeals to someone whom he addresses as "loyal companion/yokefellow" to help these two women, who have worked side by side with Paul in the cause of the gospel. In Philippi as elsewhere in the Pauline mission, women played an important role in the Christian community (for Philippi, see Acts 16:11-15; see also Rom 16:1-15). Euodia and Syntyche are described as having "struggled/contended" alongside Paul, and this verb (συναθλέω *synathleō*, used already in 1:27) continues the athletic imagery of 3:12-14. The punctuation used by the NIV and the NRSV could be thought to suggest that Paul is appealing for help to "Clement and other fellow workers," together with this loyal companion, but it is better to understand these words as belonging to the immediately preceding phrase and to assume that these people, too, have been working alongside Paul and the two women.

But who is the unnamed "loyal companion/yokefellow"? And why does Paul not name him? Many suggestions as to his identity have been made, some of which (such as that Paul is referring to his wife) can be ruled out (since the adjective is masculine in form). Some commentators have argued that the word translated "companion/yokefellow" is, in fact, a proper name, "Syzygus" (see the NIV and NRSV margins); unlike the names "Euodia" and "Syntyche," however, which are both found in Greek inscriptions of the period, there is no evidence that "Syzygus" was ever used as a name. Other suggestions have included Silas, Luke, and Timothy, but Timothy is both with Paul and remaining with him (2:19-24; unless, of course, we regard that passage as part of another letter). The best suggestion is, perhaps, the one favored by Lightfoot, that Paul is referring to Epaphroditus.[35] It is true that Epaphroditus was still with Paul when he wrote this letter (2:25-30), but he is about to set off for Philippi, presumably carrying the letter, and will be present when the letter is read. Had Paul been addressing anyone else, it is strange that this person is referred to in this way,

---

34. This view is argued at length by Davorin Peterlin, in *Paul's Letter to the Philippians in the Light of Disunity in the Church*, NovTSup (Leiden: Brill, 1995).

35. J. B. Lightfoot, *Saint Paul's Epistle to the Philippians*, 7th ed. (London: Macmillan, 1883).

rather than being named; but after the long reference to Epaphroditus earlier in the letter, it was, perhaps, not necessary to name him again. It is true that Paul could have given him the message in person—perhaps he did, which would make it even more unnecesary to name him here! The commission to him here would, however, give him extra authority to deal with what may have been a delicate situation.

Paul's reprimand of the two women is muted. He merely reminds them of the relevance of the teaching he has given earlier in the letter. He urges them to be of the same mind "in the Lord," a phrase that reminds us that the appeal for unity is based on the fact that those who are in Christ should share the attitude of Christ. Like Clement and the other leaders who are not named, these women have labored side by side with Paul for the sake of the gospel, and their "names are in the book of life." The image is a familiar one in both the OT (e.g., Exod 32:32; Ps 69:28; Dan 12:1) and the NT, especially in the book of Revelation (e.g., Rev 20:12-15). Citizens of Philippi, whose names would be recorded in the civic register, would certainly understand an image calling to mind its heavenly counterpart.

4:4-7. Paul repeats his command to rejoice, and this, too, is "in the Lord." (The alternative translation suggested in the NRSV note, "Farewell in the Lord always," makes no sense!) Christians should be known for a quality that is rendered in both the NIV and the NRSV as "gentleness." The Greek term ἐπιεικής (*epieikēs*) is more positive than that. It denotes generosity toward others and is a characteristic of Christ himself (cf. 2 Cor 10:1); the NEB's "magnanimity" and the REB's "consideration of others" catch its meaning.

This paragraph consists of a series of commands that appear to have little connection with each other. The abrupt statement that the Lord is near seems equally detached from what immediately precedes it. In what sense is he near? Is this a reference to space or to time? The words are reminiscent of Ps 145:18, "The LORD is near all who call upon him," but they could also have a sense similar to the prayer for the Lord's coming in 1 Cor 16:22. The former meaning leads naturally into the injunction not to be anxious, but the latter is also appropriate, since the statement would then echo the expectation of Phil 3:20. Perhaps Paul would have said that such questions are meaningless, for the Lord who is expected from heaven is also the Lord who is present with his people. Whether this nearness is primarily spatial or temporal, his people should rejoice.

The affirmation that the Lord is near leads naturally into the injunction not to be anxious in v. 6, a saying that is reminiscent of Jesus' teaching in Matt 6:25-34. All prayer and supplication are to be accompanied by thanksgiving, something that has characterized the whole of this letter. The result will be that the peace of God will guard their hearts and minds "in Christ Jesus." The peace promised here is far more than an absence of conflict. Rather, it is total well-being, and it comes from God—once again, to those who are in Christ Jesus and who share his attitude, so that his "heart and mind" become theirs.

4:8-9. Paul's final appeal is to "think about" various admirable qualities, all of which are appropriate to those whose minds are guarded by Christ. This time, the introductory "Finally" seems a more appropriate translation of the Greek phrase τὸ λοιπόν (*to loipon*) than it did in 3:1. Paul has reached the end of his injunctions, if not the end of his letter. The verb he employs here is not the familiar φρονέω (*phroneō*), which he has used repeatedly in this letter, but λογίζομαι (*logizomai*), "to consider," "to take into account," which he used in 3:13. The virtues listed here are often described as typical of the qualities that were admired in the pagan world, and certainly there is nothing particularly Christian about them (contrast the list at the beginning of chap. 2). The terms "true," "just/right," and "pure" echo familiar Pauline themes, but the vocabulary as a whole is unusual in the NT, and several of the words are not used elsewhere by Paul. Has he adopted a list of virtues from popular moral philosophy? If so, why? Is he making a deliberate attempt to show that Christianity is not incompatible with pagan culture at its best? Almost all the terms he uses here can be found in Jewish literature, however, so we cannot be certain about his source. What we can be sure of is that he is claiming that anything and everything that is "excellent or praiseworthy" is divine in origin.

Although the appeal in v. 8 is not specifically Christian, that in v. 9 is. Since Christ is himself the embodiment of all the virtues listed in v. 8, there is a logical link between Paul's appeal to "think about" these things and to "put into practice/keep on doing" what they have "learned and received" from Paul; the verbs are semitechnical, and refer to the learning and receiving of tradition—in this case, of the gospel. The Philippians have also heard and seen these things in Paul. Once again, therefore, they are urged to imitate Paul, who embodies for them the gospel message. The verse reminds us yet again of the close link between the proclamation of the gospel and the moral demand to be like Christ, which rests on those who respond.

Once again, Paul assures the Philippians that they will have peace, but this time the promise refers to the God of peace, rather than to the peace of God. The phrase is a familiar one in Pauline greetings. Here it reminds us that God (and not just the blessings that come from God) is with his people. (See Reflections at 4:21-23.)

PHILIPPIANS 4:10-20, A PERSONAL NOTE OF THANKS

COMMENTARY

The fact that this "thank-you note" comes almost at the end of the letter is something of a puzzle. Some commentators believe that Paul's main purpose in writing to the Philippians was to express his thanks for their gift to him. If that is the case, he has left it until very late in the letter to do so! There are, to be sure, possible references to their gift in 1:3, 5 and 2:25, 30, but these are scarcely expressions of thanks. Even now, Paul thanks the Lord, rather than the Philippians, for their concern for him! Why is Paul seemingly so tardy, and so reticent, to express his thanks?

One possible explanation is that Paul wrote to the Philippians when Epaphroditus first arrived. Some commentators suggest that the past tense in v. 10, "I rejoiced" (see the NRSV note) rather than "I rejoice," is an indication that the gift had arrived sometime earlier. Certainly there has been some communication between Paul (or those with him) and the Philippians, since the latter have heard of Epaphroditus's illness (2:26). If Paul wrote such a letter, then either we must conclude that it has not survived, or we must suppose that this is it and that an editor has combined two or more letters into one. An alternative suggestion is that Paul was embarrassed by the Philippians' gift, since it contravened his principle of not accepting financial assistance (see 1 Cor 9:15-18; 2 Cor 11:7-10; 1 Thess 2:9); hence his delay in mentioning it. For Paul to receive support from the Philippians when he was in prison, however, was a very different matter from receiving it from those among whom he was working. To accept money from Christians in Thessalonica and Corinth when he was working there might have seemed like profiting from the gospel, but the Philippians had long supported his missionary endeavors outside Philippi, and could, therefore, be seen as partners in his work—something about which Paul had indeed boasted to the Corinthians (2 Cor 11:7-10). There was no need for him, then, to feel embarrassed by their gift—except, perhaps, by the generosity of an impoverished church (2 Cor 11:7-10).

Recent study of social and rhetorical conventions in the Greco-Roman world has indicated that effusive thanks might have suggested a dependency on the donor or an obligation to reciprocate.[36] If Paul did not immediately express his thanks to the Philippians with the enthusiasm that seems appropriate to our modern ways, then this was because he regarded them as his partners in the gospel, and not as his paymasters. Moreover, although 1:3-8 is certainly not

---

36. See, e.g., G. W. Peterman, *Paul's Gift from Philippi*, SNTSMS 92 (Cambridge: Cambridge University Press, 1997).

a formal expression of thanks, the links in language ("joy/rejoice," 1:4; 4:10; "share," 1:5, 7; 4:14-15) and in theme (in the early days and now, 1:5; 4:10, 15) suggest that Paul had their gift very much in mind in those opening verses.

We wonder, however, whether commentators may not have exaggerated the problem. It is true that the Philippians sent Paul gifts of some kind (4:18). But their main contribution to his welfare may well have been to send Epaphroditus to look after his needs (2:25)—something that, under the circumstances, Epaphroditus was unable to do. Nevertheless, the Philippians have been partners with Paul in the gospel from the very beginning (1:5). In the early days, they shared in "giving and receiving" (4:15). Now they have again shown their concern for Paul (4:10) and shared in his troubles (4:14), not simply by their gifts but by sending Epaphroditus to him. It is clear from 2:30 how greatly Paul valued Epaphroditus's ministry, which mirrored the self-giving of Christ. Seen in this light, the fact that this section comes at the end of the letter is perhaps understandable. If there is any embarrassment on Paul's part, it is due to the fact that he has been forced by circumstance to send Epaphroditus back to Philippi, which might appear ungrateful. But it may well have been the Philippians, rather than Paul, who were in danger of feeling embarrassed, since their well-intentioned plan had foundered. Paul, therefore, emphasizes what he owes to the Philippians and how they have been his partners from the beginning (1:15; 2:25; 4:10-19). This partnership has been demonstrated not only in their gifts (4:15-16, 18) but also in their concern (2:25; 4;10, 14). The Philippians need not feel that Epaphroditus's return means that they have failed to give Paul what was due to him, since he has "been paid in full" (4:18).

4:10. This section is introduced as a thanksgiving with the familiar verb χαίρω (*chairō*, "to rejoice"). This is no hollow emotion; the adverb "greatly" (μεγάλως *megalōs*) is an indication of the strength of Paul's joy, which, like the joy he urges on the Philippians (3:1; 4:4), is "in the Lord." Equally familiar is the verb φρονέω (*phroneō*, "to think"), used here twice in the sense of "to be concerned." By their concern for Paul, the Philippians are showing precisely the Christlike attitude he has been urging them to share. The "[now] at last" sounds a bit grudging, as though their concern for him was belated. Some commentators suggest that the words are a quotation from a note to Paul from the Philippians: "At long last we are able to send you a gift." There was no way of indicating such a quotation in an ancient letter, but the recipients would, of course, have recognized it; there is almost certainly an example of such a quotation in 1 Cor 7:1. But even if the words are Paul's own, there is no need to suppose that they are meant as a rebuke. The sense is not "at long last you have thought about me," but "after all this time you have once again shown your concern for me, long after I might have expected you to do so." (The verb ἀναθάλλω [*anathallō*] means "to cause to bloom again.") In other words, the statement should be read positively, not negatively. In case his words should be misunderstood, however, Paul hastens to explain that the interval has been due to the lack of opportunity, and not to a lack of concern.

4:11-13. Paul's gratitude is not due to any real need on his part (v. 11), since he has learned to be content, whatever he has. Rather, as v. 14 will make clear, it arises from this tangible evidence of the special relationship between the Philippians and himself. The adjective translated "content" (αὐτάρκης *autarkēs*) means also "self-sufficient"; the noun is used at 2 Cor 9:8. The virtue of "self-sufficiency" or "contentment" was a favorite one among Cynics and Stoics, but Paul's self-sufficiency is of a very different kind, for—paradoxically—it comes from God. It arises from Paul's decision, described in 3:7-11, to give up everything in order to gain Christ. As a result, Paul can cope with every circumstance; he knows both how "to have plenty" and how "to have little/be in need." The verb here is ταπεινόω (*tapeinoō*) and means literally "to be humbled"; it echoes 2:8, where the verb was used of the action of Christ in humbling himself and reminds us once again that Paul's experience derives from his union with Christ. The verb translated "learned" here is μανθάνω (*manthanō*), commonly used of disciples or pupils learning from a rabbi or teacher. In the next verse, however, Paul uses a different verb, μυέω (*mueō*), in a similar sense; this word was often used of being initiated into the mystery religions, which is why the NIV and the NRSV render it, "I have learned the secret." It is possible that Paul is thinking of his achievement of "self-sufficiency" as a metaphorical initiation, but the verb could also be used in a more general sense. What he has learned is to be both well fed and hungry, to have plenty and to be in need—or, rather, how to cope with these situations; the NIV repeats the word "content" to make the meaning clear. Verse 13 reveals the secret of Paul's ability to do "everything"; it is through the one who gives him the strength he needs.

4:14-16. The paragraph division of the NRSV seems more logical than that of the NIV. In spite of what he has just said, it was nevertheless good of the Philippians to share in his distress. The verb συγκοινωνέω (*sygkoinōneō*, "to share") is a compound of the verb also translated "shared" in v. 15; equivalent nouns are used in 1:5 and 7 ("partnership" [κοινωνία *koinōnia*] and, lit., "fellow participants" [συγκοινωνοί *sygkoinōnoi*]). The fellowship of those in Christ involves sharing with one another at all levels: The Philippians have shared Paul's distress, just as they shared with him "in the matter of giving and receiving" (v. 15). This does not mean that the Philippians gave and Paul received. On the contrary, the giving and receiving were mutual, since he goes on to say that he has been paid in full (i.e., for what he has given them; v. 18). It has been shown recently that the commercial language Paul employs here echoes imagery commonly used in contemporary literature to describe the social reciprocity that should characterize relationships between equals.[37] The Philippians alone had shared with Paul in this particular way, and they alone had been true partners with him in the gospel (1:5). Paul refers to their support also in 2 Cor 11:8-9. The fact that the Philippians were the only Christians who supported Paul is significant, since it suggests that the bond between him and them was particularly strong. At least a part of the explanation as to why other churches did not contribute to his expenses seems to lie in Paul's own fierce independence and his refusal to depend on others for support (see 1 Cor 9:1-18; 1 Thess 2:9).

This financial support had been given to Paul "in the early days of the gospel" (v. 15). At first sight, this statement makes little sense. It was only *after* the early days (lit., "the beginning") of the gospel that Paul arrived in Philippi. The NIV has understood the statement from the Philippians' point of view—the early days of the gospel as far as they were concerned—and has paraphrased accordingly. Probably, however, Paul was thinking of the great expansion of missionary work following his departure from Philippi and, therefore, means the beginning of the spread of the gospel, which took place after he left Macedonia. Since Thessalonica is in Macedonia, v. 16 appears to be a bit of an afterthought: Even before he had left Macedonia, they had begun to help him.

4:17-19. Verse 17 picks up the theme of vv. 11-12. Paul does not need gifts, and he is certainly not "seeking/looking for" any. The fact that he insists that he is not asking for a gift so quickly after reminding the Philippians of their earlier assistance would seem to confirm that the Philippians may be feeling that they have not done as much for him as they would have liked. What he is looking for is not another gift, but the amount that stands to their credit, and this is more than enough. Paul has returned once again to the metaphor of the financial ledger, which he used in 3:7-8, and he hastens to assure them that the books have been balanced. "I have been paid in full," he declares; the Greek word ἀπέχω (*apechō*), which he uses here, is the word that would have been used on a receipt. Thus Paul has been paid more than enough. The implication seems to be that the Philippians had once been in his debt; what they owed him, of course, was the fact that he had brought them the gospel. Now Paul changes the metaphor again. The gifts brought by Epaphroditus were "a fragrant offering, an acceptable sacrifice, pleasing to God." Though the gifts were offered to Paul, they have in effect been offered to God, since they are being used for "the defense and confirmation of the gospel" (1:7). It seems, then, that the account is being held with God and that the Philippians are storing up treasure in heaven (cf. Matt 6:20; 19:21).

---

37. P. Marshall, *Enmity in Corinth*, WUNT 2:23 (Tübingen: J. C. B. Mohr [Siebeck], 1987) 157-64; Peterman, *Paul's Gift from Philippi*, 51-89.

It will be God, therefore, who recompenses them (v. 19). The unusual phrase "my God" (see also 1:3) is not intended to imply that Paul's God is not the God of the Philippians also; indeed, in the very next verse he refers to "our God." If he speaks of "my God" here, it is because he wishes to stress that he is relying on God to do for him what he is unable to do for himself. His God will "fully satisfy/supply" all their needs, just as Paul has been "fully satisfied/supplied" by the Philippians. Not only does the verb in v. 19 echo that used in v. 18, but also the word "need/needs" (χρεία *chreia*) is the same as that used in v. 16. Moreover, God will do this "according to his riches in glory in Christ Jesus"; since God's riches are immeasurable, God is able to meet every conceivable need. The NRSV follows the Greek more accurately than does the NIV here: These riches are "in glory," rather than "glorious." We are reminded of 3:21 and the promise that we will share Christ's body of glory. Paul is, perhaps, thinking now of what we would call "spiritual" needs rather than material ones. If the Philippians have not yet "been made perfect" (3:12), God will supply what they lack, and they will share the riches of God's glory "in Christ Jesus," whose self-emptying, death, and exaltation as Lord brought glory to God the Father (2:11).

4:20. It is hardly surprising that this section is rounded off with a doxology. The only possible response of the Christian church to this revelation of God's glory is to *give* God glory, and now, of course, this God is "*our* God and Father." The greatness and goodness of God are reflected and proclaimed by the worshiping community, and this process will continue "for ever and ever"—literally, "to the ages of ages," a thoroughly Jewish expression. The final "Amen" is the affirmation that this will be so. (See Reflections at 4:21-23.)

PHILIPPIANS 4:21-23, CLOSING WORDS

COMMENTARY

Paul's closing words follow the pattern of conventional letter-endings of his time, although this ending has, of course, been thoroughly Christianized. It may seem strange that after the doxology of v. 20 he should add greetings (vv. 21-22) and then the grace (v. 23). However, many NT letters (including, among Paul's, 1 and 2 Thessalonians and Galatians) conclude with a fourfold pattern consisting of:

(a) personal information or instruction
(b) formal benediction or doxology
(c) brief personal counsel or greetings
(d) simple benediction.

This pattern is followed here.

The greetings are general: to "every saint/all the saints in Christ Jesus" (the last phrase is probably a reminder, once again, of their fundamental relationship with Christ [echoing 1:1], though it is possible to take it with the word "Greet") from "the brothers/friends" who are with Paul and "all the saints." The distinction between "brothers [and sisters]" and "saints" is slightly puzzling, but Paul probably means by the former those who are fellow workers in the cause of the gospel. "Those who belong to Caesar's household" would have included officials and servants of all kinds who were employed in the service of the emperor, in particular, what we would term "civil servants." Although the majority of these persons would have resided in Rome, others would have been found throughout the empire (including Philippi); so once again this reference cannot settle the issue of the place of Paul's imprisonment, though it certainly points to Rome.

The grace in v. 23 is Paul's typical ending, though certainly no formality. We can scarcely read it without remembering his account of "the grace of the Lord Jesus Christ," which he has given us in chap. 2. Paul uses here the phrase "with your spirit" (see also Gal 6:18; Phlm 25) rather than his more typical "with you," but there is no real difference in meaning. Interestingly, he uses the plural "your" but the singular "spirit," perhaps because he thinks of the Christian community as a unity in Christ.

Many mss conclude the letter with a final "Amen" (see the NRSV note). It is difficult to decide whether the word was added at some stage or was accidentally omitted. Certainly it provides a fitting end to the epistle—but that may be precisely the reason why an ancient scribe added it! Both the NIV and the NRSV translators appear to have agreed that this was what happened, and they were probably correct.

REFLECTIONS

1. The note of joy continues to echo throughout this chapter. Paul urges the Philippians to rejoice (4:4), and he does so himself (4:10). What he refers to is not a superficial cheerfulness but a deep joy in what God has done in Christ and is continuing to do through the saints. The fact that this joy is "in the Lord" reminds us not only that it derives from the Lord, but also that it is shared by those who live in him. Paul is not thinking of something that is merely an emotional experience or that is in any sense transient but of the deep and lasting joy that comes through a deepening relationship with Christ; this joy is thus expressed in sharing his love and concern for others. If many Christians today lack such joy, is this perhaps because they see their faith to a great extent as an individual matter, and so do not see Christian life in terms of mutual respect and concern or experience the love and support of fellow Christians? Can we experience the *joy* of the gospel without *living* it?

2. Christians today can learn from the way in which Paul handled the problem of the dispute between Euodia and Syntyche. We do not know precisely what the trouble was, but it sounds all too familiar! Clearly there were rivalry and tension between them. By appealing to them "to be of the same mind," Paul reminds them of his teaching in 2:2 and his elaboration of what that meant in 2:3-4. But even more important, the appeal "to be of the same mind *in the Lord*" would remind them that this "mind" was the mind of Christ, who had emptied himself, had humbled himself, and had been obedient to death. As so often in his ethical appeals, Paul takes us back to the gospel and works things out from first principles: If Christ behaved like that, how must those who are "in Christ" behave? Put like that, it is clear what Euodia and Syntyche should do! If they do not do it, then they are in effect denying that they are "in Christ," denying that the way of Christ has been affirmed by God as God's way. Could we, perhaps, try more often to go back to first principles in attempting to sort out the problems that inevitably arise between members of the Christian community? Should we, perhaps, worry less about who is right and who is wrong and ask instead, "What does it mean for us, as a community, to have the mind of Christ?"

3. In 4:2-3, Paul is concerned with relations within the Christian community, but in 4:5 he turns to the church's dealings with those outside. Consideration of others is to be shown to *everyone,* not just to fellow Christians. Since this attitude, too, is a reflection of that seen in Christ, Paul is in effect urging the Philippians to let their lives be a proclamation of the gospel.

4. Like the concluding page of many a letter, this final chapter of the epistle is something of a hodgepodge—a collection of different ideas—as Paul mentions the various things he still wants to say, though there are unifying themes. In a series of commands, Paul has already urged the Philippians to live "in the Lord." They have been told to stand firm in the Lord (4:1), to be of the same mind in the Lord (4:2), to rejoice in the Lord (4:4), and to behave appropriately toward others (4:5). In 4:5-7, the command not to worry but to pray is sandwiched between a promise that the Lord is near and the assurance that the Philippians will be guarded by the peace of God.

Paul's declaration that "the Lord is near" in 4:5 may well cause us problems today. Two thousand years later, we wonder what this "nearness" means. For Paul, it certainly included a belief in a future coming. Ought Christians today expect an imminent parousia? Some, of course, do. But all too often this expectation leads them to opt out of everyday life and to do nothing except speculate about the date of the Second Coming and await its arrival. In contrast to this, Paul's words are intended to encourage the Philippians to behave with consideration toward others and to think positively about their present lives (4:6). Should we, then, interpret Paul's words in solely spatial terms? The Lord is certainly near in that sense, though too few of us are sufficiently aware of his presence. To know that Christ is with us in our everyday lives ought to be a great comfort to us. But we need also to remember that Paul's statement looked back to the promise in 3:21 that the Lord will come *to transform us and make us like himself.* In terms of human history, the final coming of the Lord may seem no nearer than when Paul wrote these words. But for those in Christ, the promise of 3:21 is sure. Paul's declaration that the Lord is near reminds us—paradoxically!—of a destiny that will be fulfilled *beyond* space and time.

5. Few of us find it easy to follow the advice of 4:6. We tend to worry about *everything*! Our attitude is the very opposite of the trust in God that Paul commends. It is sobering to remember that Paul was in prison, facing a capital charge, when he wrote this letter. And that was not his only problem, for his responsibility for the churches was a constant concern (2 Cor 11:28). Moreover, the people to whom he was writing were unlikely to be living comfortable lives. Most of them were poor, many were slaves, and few of them would have known the meaning of security. In marked contrast, those of us who live in comparative wealth and luxury today are frequently those who are most worried and anxious. The secret of Paul's composure is that he is relying on God, and not on material goods, as he goes on to spell out in 4:10-14. This freedom from worry and anxiety does not, of course, imply an irresponsible attitude toward life and one's obligations. It is interesting to note that the verb used in 4:6 was also used in 2:20 of the genuine concern Timothy felt for the Philippians' welfare. It is a mark of the Christian maturity spoken of in 3:15 to be able to distinguish between the anxiety that cripples and destroys the individual and the concern for others that builds up the whole community.

6. Paul directs the Philippians to pray (4:6)—with thanksgiving. Once again, we find that Paul's prayers are suffused with thanksgiving. And once again we should remember that Paul had a capital charge hanging over his head and was writing to people who had very little in material terms. All too often our own prayers are nothing but a "shopping list," *without* thanksgiving; our anxiety about the future obscures the benefits that have been showered upon us. Gratitude to God for all that we have been given will allow the peace of God to guard our hearts and minds, protecting us against all that might destroy us (4:7).

7. The virtues mentioned in 4:8 were among those that were honored in the pagan world, a fact that reminds us that we should not be afraid to take over the best in our secular world and claim it for Christ. In a sense, of course, this is but a recognition that everything that is true and pure comes from God. Christians, however, have often been afraid to acknowledge the good and true in the secular world—in art, for example, in music and drama, or in indigenous customs. We are appalled today to remember the way in which nineteenth-century missionaries refused to allow Africans to use drums and dancing in their worship, believing them to be "pagan." General William Booth, founder of the Salvation Army, was much sounder when he took over secular tunes for hymns, demanding, "Why should the devil have all the best tunes?" If God is the origin of all that is good and true and honorable, then Christians should certainly acknowledge these qualities, wherever they are found.

8. If Paul has taken over the principle of self-sufficiency (4:11) from the pagan world, then he has certainly turned it on its head. For the Stoics, the principle indicated a certain detachment from the world. This principle is still much admired today, for example, among those attracted by Buddhism. Although Paul could cope with plenty and with need, he does not cut himself loose from the concerns of the world. His gospel certainly cannot be interpreted as a message to the poor to put up with poverty. For the Stoics, again, self-sufficiency meant relying on one's inner resources. For Paul, it meant relying on God in Christ to provide the necessary resources. He has, he says, learned to be content, whatever his circumstances (4:11). Paul's language suggests that being content was not something that came easily, and this is hardly surprising, in view of the hardships and dangers in which his missionary work involved him. His contentment is no spineless resignation, but a joyful acceptance of what God provides.

And in Paul's case, God used the Philippians to provide what he needed. Their action in giving and receiving is described in sacrificial language, reminding us once again of the central theme of the gospel: Christ's gift of himself. They share in the divine giving, and the result, once again, is that God is given glory (4:20).

Paul reminds us here of something that we too often forget: The riches of God are sufficient to deal with all our needs. But unlike some propounders of popular "prosperity" gospels, he does not promise us earthly wealth. Far more valuable than that is the attitude Paul has acquired through being in Christ, an attitude that accepts riches and poverty with equal joy and thanksgiving.

9. In 4:11-20, Paul expresses his gratitude to God—and to the Philippians—for their gift. But far more important than the gift itself were the love and concern the Philippians showed toward Paul—a love and concern that led them to help him. As so often, it is the thought that counts! The most significant gifts often cost us very little—sometimes nothing, except a few moments to say a friendly word or to make a telephone call, the stamp to post a letter or a card. What matters is that someone has been remembered with affection and concern. Do we always remember to show appreciation for what others do for us in these simple ways? Do we remember to help those who, like Paul, are going through a rough patch and need our prayers and concern?

10. We can easily overlook the significance of the phrase "those of Caesar's household" in 4:22. These people are acknowledged by Paul to be "saints," members of God's people. It cannot have been easy in the ancient world for those who were in Caesar's employ to acknowledge Jesus as Lord. Not many years later, with the outbreak of persecution against Christians, it became impossible; those who continued to hold the faith lost their employment and usually their lives as well. The tension between various responsibilities and allegiances is one with which Christians have had to cope from the very earliest days. There are Christians in some countries today who still experience these tensions and whose witness to the gospel puts many of us to shame. We should remember them in our prayers. For those of us who are not in danger of active persecution, the temptations are more subtle. Are we willing to stand up for the gospel in a society that scorns its principles? If our faith comes into conflict with our career or our standard of living or our standing in society, which do we sacrifice? No doubt, Paul's answer would have been to point us back once more to Christ's own self-emptying and urge us yet again to share his mind.

THE LETTER TO THE COLOSSIANS
INTRODUCTION, COMMENTARY, AND REFLECTIONS
BY
ANDREW T. LINCOLN

THE LETTER TO THE COLOSSIANS

INTRODUCTION

Colossians is a rich and yet enigmatic Pauline letter. It contains a magnificent hymnic passage about the cosmic scope of Christ's role, develops the notion of believers' union with Christ, and has extensive exhortations about the ethical implications of this relationship. There are also fascinating treatments of the theme of reconciliation, of the heavenly world with its cosmic powers and its relation to the earthly realm, and of the notions of growth, maturity, and fullness; and there is the first occurrence in early Christian literature of the use of the "household code," the set of instructions for various groups within the household. While claiming to have been written by Paul (and Timothy), however, Colossians has a style quite distinct from earlier Pauline letters and theological and conceptual emphases that differ somewhat from these letters. In addition, its thought is developed in opposition to a teaching or philosophy about which the letter itself gives only a few scattered clues.

Much is to be gained simply by focusing on the text, following its argument closely, and thereby appreciating the impact of its message. But other questions—about the force of particular terms in their first-century context, about the situation of the writer and the first readers, about the teaching that is being opposed—arise naturally from a close reading. Clearly, the more that can be discovered about the historical setting, the better our appreciation of the message and the writer's pastoral strategy in conveying it. This Introduction looks at four key areas for the interpretation of Colossians: its form, structure, and persuasive strategy; the "philosophy" it opposes; the main themes that characterize its presentation of the Pauline gospel; and the identity of its author and those to whom it was addressed. The results of the discussion of these issues will inform the Commentary and Reflections that follow.

FORM, STRUCTURE, AND PERSUASIVE STRATEGY

The form of Colossians follows the Pauline letter's modification of the ancient letter form. The letter opening identifies the senders and the recipients and contains an initial greeting

(1:1-2). There follows a statement of thanksgiving, with its opening formula found in 1:3 ("we thank God") and its intercessory prayer report.[1]

The thanksgiving section of Colossians introduces major themes of the letter, but there has been much debate about whether it ends at 1:12, 1:14, 1:20, or 1:23. The note of thanksgiving clearly continues through 1:12-14 with the participle, "giving thanks" (εὐχαριστοῦντες *eucharistountes*) and its relative clauses that take up traditional liturgical formulations. These in turn lead into the Christ hymn of 1:15-20, which is no longer a discrete independent composition. It now serves the function of the thanksgiving section to signal significant themes, this time specifically christological ones. The closing part of the Pauline thanksgiving typically consists of liturgical material that reflects or substitutes for the Jewish *bĕrākâ*, or "blessing," and has at its conclusion an "eschatological climax" in which the present time of thanksgiving is linked with the final days of the supreme rule of God.[2] Here both its introduction and the hymnic passage itself provide the liturgical material, and an eschatological climax may be seen in the brief application of the hymn in 1:21-23, where the readers' own reconciliation with God is with a view to their being presented as "holy and blameless and irreproachable before" God (1:22*b*). The appropriation of the hymn's language of reconciliation for the change that has taken place in the readers indicates that 1:21-23 retains a close connection with what precedes it. The talk of not "shifting from the hope of the gospel that you heard, which has been proclaimed to every creature under heaven" both makes explicit the paraenetical implications of the earlier material in the thanksgiving and provides an inclusio (a literary bracketing device) with 1:5, which had mentioned the hope the readers had heard of in the gospel that was growing in the whole world. In this way 1:3-23 can be seen as a coherent unit that forms an extended thanksgiving.

The letter body then begins with 1:24. The last clause of 1:23*c* had provided a transition in which the language of the writer shifts from first-person plural to singular and focuses on Paul: "of which I, Paul, became a servant." Paul's relation to the readers becomes the subject of the next section up to 2:5, which can be seen as the body-opening. Again an inclusio confirms this as a distinct unit, since it begins and ends with an expression of rejoicing: "I am now rejoicing in my suffering for your sake" (1:24*a* NRSV) and "rejoicing to see your good order and the firmness of your faith in Christ" (2:5*b*). A disclosure formula frequently serves as evidence of the body-opening;[3] this is found in 2:1, "For I want you to know . . ." (NRSV), alerting the readers to the importance of what follows—namely, Paul's desire for their unity in love and their assured understanding of Christ.

The phrase "as therefore" in 2:6 serves as a transition, introducing the major concern of the letter in the body-middle. Scholars disagree about whether the paraenesis, or ethical exhortation, should be treated as part of the body of the Pauline letter or as a separate section following it. In the case of Colossians, this issue is made more complicated by the fact that from 2:6 through 4:6 all the material is structured by imperatives and is hortatory. A division is apparent, however, within this material. The warning of 2:8 is about being taken captive by philosophy and empty deceit and has a particular teaching in view. It is followed by an extensive warrant in 2:9-15 based on the writer's view of Christ and of believers' relationship to Christ. The exhortations of 2:16–3:4 are all directly related to elements in the teaching being opposed. What is more, if an eschatological climax indicates an occurrence of transition in thought,[4] then such a transition can be seen in the assertion of 3:4, "When Christ who is our life is revealed, then you also will be revealed with him in glory."

Although there is still some relation to the alternative teaching in what follows from 3:5, the exhortations become more general from this point and employ traditional paraenetical forms, such as the listing of vices (3:5-11) and virtues (3:12-17) and the household code (3:18–4:1). The exhortations also become more frequent in this section. Although there are six imperatives in 2:6–3:4, there are eighteen instances of a verb in the imperative mood in 3:5–4:6. If it is the

---

1. See P. T. O'Brien, *Introductory Thanksgivings in the Letters of Paul*, NovTSup 49 (Leiden: Brill, 1977) 100-104.
2. Cf. J. T. Sanders, "The Transition from Opening Epistolary Thanksgiving to Body in the Letters of the Pauline Corpus" *JBL* 81 (1962) 348-62.
3. Sanders, "The Transition from Opening Epistolary Thanksgiving to Body in the Letters of the Pauline Corpus," 354; J. L. White, "The Introductory Formulae in the Body of the Pauline Letter" *JBL* 90 (1971) 91-97.
4. J. L. White, *The Form and Function of the Body of the Greek Letter* (Missoula, Mont.: Scholars Press, 1972) 112-13n. 13.

case that the body of the Pauline letter has as a generally distinctive characteristic two parts to its argumentation—a more tightly organized theological part and a less tightly constructed appeal for the concrete working out of the view of Christian existence advocated earlier—then the central part of Colossians can still be seen to approximate these two parts. The exhortations of 2:6–3:4, with their focus on the alternative teaching and their more extended theological warrants, correspond to the first part, and the more general exhortations of 3:5–4:6 correspond to the usual paraenesis of the second part. In this way, 2:6–4:6 as a whole can be seen to constitute the body-middle.

The twenty-four imperatives of this section clearly make its tone one of warning, admonition, and exhortation. Issues raised in the thanksgiving section and the body-opening are elaborated here. The writer's concern about the recipients' knowledge and understanding (1:9; 2:2) and his related interest in their continued faithfulness to the gospel (1:23) are amplified in the exhortations of 2:6–3:4. The implicit paraenesis about "every good work," patient endurance, and thankfulness in 1:9-12 becomes explicit in the exhortations of 3:5–4:6. Assertions from the Christ hymn of 1:15-20 are employed in the christological warrant for the warning against the philosophy in 2:9-10, 15, 19, and what is involved in the reconciliation accomplished by Christ's death (1:22) is developed in 2:10-15.

The following section, 4:7-9, relates the intention to send Tychicus and Onesimus as emissaries. The sending of emissaries was one means, along with a visit of the apostle or the sending of a letter, of bringing about the benefit of Paul's presence. This mention of what has been called "the apostolic parousia" indicates the body-closing.[5]

There then comes the closing of the letter as a whole. Among the concluding elements found in the Pauline letters are hortatory remarks, requests for prayer, a wish of peace, greetings, a command to the recipients to greet one another with a holy kiss, an autographic subscription (i.e., a reference to the writer's own handwriting), and a grace benediction. With the exception of the request for prayer, made earlier in the paraenesis in 4:3-4, the wish of peace, and the mention of the greeting with the holy kiss, all these elements are found in the closing section of Colossians. Personal greetings from his companions and from Paul himself are listed in 4:10-15. The hortatory remarks are contained in 4:16-17, which urge the recipients to exchange letters with the church at Laodicea and to pass on a message to Archippus. The placing of these remarks is slightly unusual, since the only other letter closing that has an exhortation after the final greeting is 1 Thessalonians (see 1 Thess 5:27). Paul's autograph is appended in 4:18. Its call to the readers to remember his "chains" is unique to a letter-closing. The final item is the brief grace benediction in 4:18c ("grace be with you"); and, as in other Pauline letters, the parallel with the opening greeting in terms of grace can be seen to provide an epistolary inclusio.

Epistolary analysis, therefore, yields the following outline:

I. Letter Opening—Address and Greeting (1:1-2)
II. Extended Thanksgiving Section (1:3-23)
III. Letter Body (1:24–4:9)
    A. Body-Opening (1:24–2:5)
    B. Body-Middle (2:6–4:6)
        1. Exhortation Related to the Philosophy (2:6–3:4)
        2. More General Exhortation (3:5–4:6)
    C. Body-Closing (4:7-9)
IV. Letter Closing—Greetings, Hortatory Remarks, Autographic Subscription, and Grace Benediction (4:10-18)

Since the letter was a substitute for speech and since Paul's letters were meant to be read aloud to their recipients, it is also appropriate to view their contents in the light of the conventions of ancient rhetoric. Although the categories from the ancient rhetorical handbooks should

---

5. See R. W. Funk, "The Apostolic Parousia: Form and Function," in *Christian History and Interpretation,* ed. W. R. Farmer et al. (Cambridge: Cambridge University Press, 1966) 249-68.

not be applied rigidly or mechanically, they may be employed, where they fit, to illuminate the letter writer's persuasive strategy.

The rhetorical situation or exigency of Colossians is produced by the writer's awareness of what he considers to be a false teaching that will have harmful consequences for the readers if they are taken in by it. To dissuade them from being enticed by the proponents of this teaching, he first encourages the letter's recipients by reminding them of the gospel and its hope, which he and they have in common, of the change of status it has effected, and of the fruits of Christian behavior it has produced among them. Assuring them of his special relationship to this gospel and of his desire for their increased knowledge and understanding of it, he underlines that they must remain committed to it. He spells out what this continuing commitment will mean by exhorting them both to resist the baneful influence of the teachers of the philosophy and to exemplify distinctively Christian patterns of behavior.

Of the three main rhetorical genres—forensic, deliberative, and epideictic—the first, with its aim of persuading an audience to make a judgment about events in the past, can be dismissed in regard to Colossians. If the deliberative genre involves the author's seeking to bring about some action in the future by persuading or dissuading the audience, and if the epideictic involves the author's seeking to persuade the audience to hold or to reaffirm some present point of view by assigning praise or blame, then it is not immediately obvious which more appropriately describes Colossians. Exhortation can function in both deliberative and epideictic genres, depending on whether it is calling for a change of behavior or reiterating common values.[6] Colossians could, in fact, be viewed as a case in which the genres of epideictic and deliberative rhetoric are mixed and overlap. After all, the actions that the recipients are being persuaded to take in the future are precisely to hold on to the values of the gospel that the writer believes they at present share with him. Only 2:20-21 suggests that some of the recipients may have succumbed to the philosophy. In the main the letter simply contains warnings against the teaching and against allowing its proponents to condemn or disqualify the Colossian believers. Nevertheless, the fact that the central section of the letter has as its focus the call for the specific future action of resisting the philosophy does suggest that the deliberative genre of rhetoric predominates. To be sure, such an action is a consequence of the reaffirmation of present values, but it goes beyond mere reaffirmation.

In an analysis of Colossians as a persuasive speech, 1:3-23 constitutes the *exordium*. The *exordium* functioned as the introduction, indicating the aim of the speech and attempting to secure the hearer's goodwill.[7] Since in Colossians the author claims to have no personal acquaintance with the people being addressed, it is necessary for him to establish an initial positive relationship with them if they are to be receptive to his message. So expressing his thankfulness for their faith and love, declaring his knowledge of the fruitfulness of the gospel in their lives, seeing them as part of the worldwide growth of the Christian movement, mentioning Epaphras as the go-between, assuring them of his constant prayers, citing the Christ hymn, and reminding them of their change of status and relationship in respect to God are all part of establishing a positive relationship that will make them conducive to accept what follows. In particular, the Christ hymn draws readers into its praise, and its application explicitly appeals to their own experience of Christ's reconciling work. The two elements combine effectively to create an initial sympathy for the writer's thoughts and concerns.

The rest of the analysis takes up and modifies the suggestions of the French commentator J.-N. Aletti. He points out that if the *propositio,* or thesis, of a discourse is not a simple one, then its component elements are set out in a *partitio,* a division of the thesis into separate headings. He sees the *exordium* as concluding with such a *partitio* in 1:21-23. It has three headings: the work of Christ to achieve the holiness of believers (1:21-22); the need for the recipients to continue in the faith of the gospel (1:23*a*); and the recognition of the role of Paul in proclaiming this gospel (1:23*c*).[8] As has been noted, the exordium anticipates either directly or indirectly the

---

6. See D. E. Aune, *The New Testament in Its Literary Environment* (Philadelphia: Westminster, 1987) 191, 208.
7. See Aristotle *Rhetoric* 3.13-14.
8. J. N. Aletti, *St. Paul Épître aux Colossiens,* ÉB (Paris: Gabalda, 1993) 39.

themes to be dealt with in the discourse. Here at the end of the *exordium* there is a clear move to apply the preceding material to the letter's recipients. It would be natural, therefore, for this initial application to contain the main points to be made in this primarily deliberative discourse.

The *propositio* is usually followed by a section of proof, or *probatio*. This confirmation of the thesis can be seen to run from 1:24 to 4:1 and takes up both the language and the conceptuality of each of the elements of the *partitio,* but in reverse order. It functions not so much as the proof of propositions but more as the confirmation and elaboration of themes. Paul's role in the proclamation of the gospel is treated in 1:24–2:5, the need for faithfulness to this gospel in 2:6–3:4, and the holiness of believers' lives in 3:5–4:1.

This leaves 4:2-6 as the *peroratio*. According to Aristotle, the *peroratio* aimed to recapitulate leading themes, to make the audience well disposed toward the speaker, and to produce the required kind of emotion in the hearers.[9] Here the summing up is carried out in a generalizing fashion. It picks up particularly the key motifs of thanksgiving and prayer (4:2), recalling for readers not only the mention of thanksgiving in 1:12; 2:7; and 3:15-17 but also the writer's own extended introductory thanksgiving and its intercessory prayer report in 1:3-23. Talk of declaring the mystery of Christ (4:3), and doing so in the requisite manner (4:4), takes up the earlier references to the mystery and may well have in view what the author has attempted in his own rehearsal of the gospel in the face of opposing teaching in this discourse in 2:6–3:4.

The writer had also expressed his concern for the readers' spiritual wisdom (1:9) and made clear that such wisdom is to be found in Christ (2:3). Now he calls on the Colossians to live wisely in relation to outsiders (4:5). This requirement of wise living sums up well the exhortations of 3:5–4:1; the interest in outsiders points appropriately to the motivation behind the use of the household code of 3:18–4:1 in particular. Knowing how to answer everyone (4:6) can be seen as a summary of what the writer wishes his communication to achieve for his readers and would include, therefore, their being in a position to respond adequately to the proponents of the philosophy. The *peroratio*'s function of making the audience well disposed to the speaker and arousing emotion would be achieved by its request for prayer (4:3*a*), by the reminder of Paul's imprisonment for Christ (4:3*b*), and by the sense of urgency conveyed through the exhortations to be watchful (4:2*b*) and to make the most of the time (4:5*b*).

Aristotle delineated three modes of persuasion: "The first kind depends on the personal character of the speaker (*ethos*); the second on putting the audience into a certain frame of mind (*pathos*); the third on the proof, or apparent proof, provided by the words of the speech itself (*logos*)."[10] Ethos presents the speaker as having wisdom, excellent character, and goodwill. In Colossians the author's wisdom is displayed not only through the quality of the advice and instruction offered but also through the depiction of Paul's special role in his commission to make known God's Word, the previously hidden mystery (1:25-26; 4:3). Paul's character is conveyed through the unique role he has in respect to the sufferings of Christ (1:24) and by the references to Paul's imprisonment for the gospel (4:3, 18). His goodwill is manifested in his prayers for the Colossians (1:3-4, 9-12); in his relation to Epaphras as the link between him and the Colossians (1:7-8; 4:12-13); in conveying news and extending greetings (4:10-18); in the effort he expends to ensure that all believers, and especially the readers, will be mature, united in love, have assured understanding, and therefore not be deceived (1:28–2:4); and in assuring them of his spiritual presence with them and his rejoicing on their account (2:5).

A number of these features also function in the letter's pathos, putting the audience into a suitable frame of mind to receive the message by evoking their empathy and sympathy. The writer's rejoicing in the readers' faith, the mention of his prayers for them, and the references to his sufferings and imprisonment and to his struggles and efforts on their behalf are all intended to produce a positive emotional effect that will make them responsive to his exhortations. The use of the Christ hymn early in the letter evokes common feelings of praise and worship that also prepare the recipients for the message to follow.

---

9. Aristotle *Rhetoric* 3.19.
10. Aristotle *Rhetoric* 1.2.

If *logos* is the use of argument and appeal to reason to support the speaker's viewpoint and to convince the audience, then the assertions about Christ in the hymnic material can be seen as laying the groundwork for the arguments that follow and that take up its terminology in 2:9-15. The writer employs a form of deductive argument that involves a statement and a supporting reason. A number of his exhortations have warrants, and in these cases the exhortation constitutes the conclusion, and the supporting warrant constitutes the premise. Colossians, then, has all three modes of argumentation—*ethos, pathos,* and *logos*—in its rhetorical arsenal.

This rhetorical analysis has produced the following outline:

I. Exordium (1:3-23)
   concluding with Partitio (1:21-23)
II. Probatio (1:24–4:1)
   A. Paul's Role in the Proclamation of the Gospel (1:24–2:5)
   B. Exhortation to Faithfulness to the Gospel (2:6–3:4)
   C. Exhortation to Holiness of Life (3:5–4:1)
III. Peroratio (4:2-6)

The Outline that precedes the commentary combines structural elements from both epistolary and rhetorical analyses with more topical headings.

Colossians is a letter that attempts to persuade its recipients to take certain actions in the future. Ancient letters could be classified on the basis of the purpose they were meant to achieve or the circumstances they were designed to meet. In terms of the listings found in Pseudo-Demetrius and Pseudo-Libanius, Colossians would in all probability be called by the former an "advisory type" in which "we exhort (someone to) something or dissuade (him) from something" and by the latter a "paraenetic style" in which "we exhort someone by urging him to pursue something or to avoid something."[11] As a paraenetic letter, Colossians shares numerous features with other letters of moral guidance produced in the Greco-Roman philosophical schools. Teachers in these schools would also frequently combine the three major functions of affirmation, correction of rival views, and exhortation in the attempt to shape their students' lives. Sometimes their letters would be composed in the name of a past philosopher and addressed to figures from the past while clearly having a contemporary audience in view.[12]

THE "PHILOSOPHY" OPPOSED IN THE LETTER

A Variety of Proposals. Despite, and probably because of, the somewhat meager evidence provided by the letter, the academic industry of publishing books and articles on the teaching that provoked the writer's response shows no signs of abating. This commentary is not the place for interaction with the mass of secondary literature that also shows little sign of reaching a consensus. All that can be done here is to mention some of the more recent proposals, to caution the reader about the difficulties involved in any reconstruction, and then to provide a brief and tentative sketch of what appears to be the most plausible view.

In the past, scholars looked to a Jewish form of Gnosticism or to Jewish mysticism or to Hellenistic mystery cults or to neo-Pythagoreanism or to a syncretistic mix of some of these as the background that provides the identity of the philosophy. Recent monographs and commentaries have offered further variations. Sappington develops the view that some form of Jewish mysticism is the distinctive ingredient of the teaching, providing a full examination of the similar pattern of ascetic and mystical piety to be found in a number of Jewish apocalypses.[13] The distinctive contribution of DeMaris is to introduce Middle Platonism into the discussion as the context in which the letter's debate about achieving knowledge was conducted. He sees

---

11. See A. J. Malherbe, *Ancient Epistolary Theorists* (Atlanta: Scholars Press, 1988) 37, 69.
12. For an illuminating discussion of the similarities between Colossians and the moral exhortations of the Greco-Roman philosophical schools, see W. T. Wilson, *The Hope of Glory: Education and Exhortation in the Epistle to the Colossians* (Leiden: E. J. Brill, 1997) esp. 10-131, 219-29.
13. T. J. Sappington, *Revelation and Redemption at Colossae,* JSNTSup 53 (Sheffield: JSOT, 1991).

the teaching being opposed, therefore, as a mix of "popular Middle Platonic, Jewish and Christian elements that cohere around the pursuit of wisdom."[14] As the title of his monograph suggests, Arnold also finds a mix.[15] He provides the fullest investigation of local inscriptional and literary evidence, particularly that which deals with the practice of magic. For him the syncretistic teaching contained Jewish (cultic observances) and pagan (mystery cult initiation) elements that cohered within the general framework of magic and folk religion. Two further contributors to the debate refrain from a syncretistic solution. Dunn, in his commentary and in an article that preceded it, holds that the teaching was purely Jewish, a diaspora "synagogue apologetic promoting itself as a credible philosophy more than capable of dealing with whatever heavenly powers might be thought to control or threaten human existence."[16] Martin, on the other hand, views it as purely Hellenistic, claiming that Cynic teachers entered the Christian assembly to observe and then delivered a critical invective against Christian practices, to which the author of Colossians responds.[17]

The very number and variety of proposed solutions to the identity of the philosophy should caution against any overly confident claims to reconstruct it. Although the writer's prescription for curing the ailment he believed to be a threat to the well-being of his readers comes across reasonably clearly, the ailment itself defies any really accurate diagnosis. The writer had no reason for defining more exactly the teaching involved. He expects his readers to know perfectly well what he was talking about, and so he merely touches on some of its features, using some of its catchwords and slogans. Since the evidence the letter provides is piecemeal, it pushes the interpreter beyond the text to find an explanatory framework for the fragmented reflection of the teaching and its practices, found in the writer's response. Determining which does greatest justice to all the elements in the letter's polemic remains the criterion for evaluating the various proposals. Some of them fail to explain parts of the letter adequately, but in itself this criterion still allows for a number of competing hypotheses.

There are at least two further difficulties in any attempt to employ the letter to reconstruct the alternative teaching. How many of the writer's direct references to the philosophy in this polemical letter can be taken as straightforward description rather than negatively slanted caricature? And if reconstruction is based on the part of the letter that is in direct interaction with the opposing teaching, is it legitimate to see other parts of the letter as having the teaching more indirectly in view and to use their discussion to complete the reconstruction?

Despite the difficulties, and provided that one remains both self-conscious about how to proceed and tentative about one's conclusions, it is still worth the effort to take up the letter's clues, to point to similar concepts in the thought of that time, and thereby to endeavor to sketch the best picture available of the teaching in view. After all, this teaching caused the writer enough concern to provoke a response to it, and some historical reconstruction is necessary if we are to appreciate that response as fully as possible. This sketch will proceed in three stages. It will begin with the explicit terminology mentioned in 2:18, move to a more disputed issue involving 2:8, 20, and then suggest a general characterization of the teaching. Other aspects will be discussed in the course of the commentary.

Visionary Experience and Asceticism. Two major features of the philosophy, as the writer depicts it, appear to be the claim to visions (and "the worship of angels" associated with such visions) and ascetic practices (including fasting as a preparation for visionary experiences). Even this feature involves questions of interpretation, however, since 2:18, in which it is mentioned, has a number of difficulties. In it the readers are urged not to let anyone who (literally) "takes pleasure in or insists on self-abasement and the worship of angels, which he has seen when entering" disqualify them. The term ταπεινοφροσύνη (*tapeinophrosynē*), rendered here, as in the NRSV, as "self-abasement," as opposed to the NIV's "false humility," occurs three times in Colossians (2:18; 2:23; 3:12). In its third occurrence, it denotes the positive virtue of humility,

---

14. R. E. DeMaris, *The Colossian Controversy: Wisdom in Dispute at Colossae*, JSNTSup 96 (Sheffield: JSOT, 1994) 17.
15. C. Arnold, *The Colossian Syncretism*, WUNT 2/77 (Tübingen: J. C. B. Mohr, 1995).
16. J. D. G. Dunn, "The Colossian Philosophy: A Confident Jewish Apologia," *Biblica* 76 (1995) 153-81; *The Epistles to the Colossians and to Philemon*, NIGTC (Grand Rapids: Eerdmans, 1996) 35.
17. T. W. Martin, *By Philosophy and Empty Deceit. Colossians as Response to a Cynic Critique*, JSNTSup 118 (Sheffield: Sheffield Academic, 1996).

but that does not appear to be in view in the first two instances where it is connected with the philosophy. Because of its close association with worship in both cases, it is likely that it stands for some cultic practice rather than a disposition of lowliness and was a quasi-technical term in the philosophy for fasting. This makes sense in a context in which practices connected with food and drink (2:16); regulations about not handling, not tasting, not touching (2:20-21); and an emphasis on severe treatment of the body (2:23) are mentioned.[18]

This interpretation gains further strong support from the use of *tapeinophrosyne* as a technical term for fasting in Tertullian[19] and in *The Shepherd of Hermas*.[20] Cognate terms are also employed in the LXX for "fasting" in contexts where the practice is an expression of abasement before God (e.g., Lev 16:29, 31; 23:27, 29, 32; Isa 58:3, 5; Ps 34:13-14). Fasting was also frequently a preparation for visionary experience and the reception of divine revelations (Dan 10:2-9; 4 Ezra 5:13, 20; 9:23-25; 2 Bar 5:7-9; 12:5-7; 43:3). Sometimes it is the preparation specifically for entrance into the heavenly realm.[21] All this is highly relevant to Col 2:18, where the two elements associated with fasting are "the worship of angels" and visionary experience.

But what was this "worship of angels"? It was often assumed that the phrase referred straightforwardly to humans worshiping angels, either in place of or alongside Christ or God. But if that were the case, it is very strange that the writer is not more forthright in his condemnation of such a practice instead of simply mentioning it in passing. An attractive case has been made by F. O. Francis,[22] however, that the phrase should be taken as involving a subjective rather than an objective genitive construction and thus refers to the angels' worship—that is, the worship in which the angels are engaged. What has this to do with humans? Fasting would be the preparation that enabled human beings to share in heavenly worship with angels. The notion of participation in angelic worship was a common one in Second Temple Judaism. It is found in apocalypses[23] and in the Qumran literature where the community on earth is described as having liturgical fellowship with the inhabitants of heaven.[24] It is by no means foreign to the NT (cf. 1 Cor 11:10; Heb 12:22-23; Revelation 4; 5).

On the other hand, C. E. Arnold has mounted a strong case for taking the objective genitive not as actual worship of angels by humans but as the writer's way of describing the philosophy's practice of invoking angels in order to deal with the threat of hostile powers. He relies heavily on the evidence of the Greek magical papyri, believing that, although most date to the third and fourth centuries CE, they reflect ideas and practices that go back to the first century CE and earlier and that are corroborated by the lead curse tablets and magical amulets in use in this earlier period.[25] He shows convincingly that in both Jewish and pagan sources angels were invoked for protection, for revelations, for cursing other humans, for warding off evil, and for dealing with evil spirit powers. They were intermediaries who were also associated with the planets and stars and were viewed as being active in influencing the fate of humans. Moreover, the evidence for a syncretistic mixing of Jewish angelic and pagan divine names in magical practice is clear. Elements of Jewish belief about angels and actual Jewish names for angels could be combined with pagan deity cults. Frequently the setting for invoking angels is a visionary experience and the invocation is connected with stringent purity regulations.

Arnold bolsters his argument by isolating the evidence of this type of veneration of angels in popular Judaism and in paganism in Asia Minor, claiming that the invocation of angels in the context of magical practices was a major feature of Phrygian-Lydian folk belief.[26] Add to this his demonstration that the term θρησκεία (*thrēskeia*) in the sense of worship rather than religion was overwhelmingly employed with the genitive for the object of worship, and his case for treating the phrase "the worship of angels" as the writer's polemical depiction of the practice

---

18. See F. O. Francis's influential essay "Humility and Angelic Worship in Colossae," in *Conflict at Colossae*, ed. F. O. Francis and W. A. Meeks (Missoula, Mont.: Scholars Press, 1973) 163-95.
19. Tertullian *On Fasting* 12.
20. *The Shepherd of Hermas* Vision 3.10.6; Similitude 5.3.7.
21. See *Apoc. Abr.* 9, 12; Philo *On the Life of Moses* 1:67-70; *On Dreams* 1:33-37.
22. Francis, "Humility and Angelic Worship in Col 2:18," 163-95. Francis has been followed by numerous recent scholars.
23. E.g., *2 Enoch* 20:3-4; *T. Job* 48-50; *Apoc. Abr.* 17; *Asc. Isa.* 7:37; 9:28, 31, 33.
24. Cf. 1QH 3:20-22; 11:10-12; 1QSb 4:25-26.
25. Arnold, *The Colossian Syncretism*, esp. 8-102.
26. See Arnold, *The Colossian Syncretism*, 61-89.

of invoking angelic help becomes a very strong one indeed.[27] He rightly distinguishes between calling on, invoking, and praying to angels and an "angel cult" in which these intermediaries were the objects of adoration and worship. Although there is evidence of the latter in some of the pagan material, he finds none in Jewish or Christian texts and inscriptions. He shows easily, however, that the author of Colossians was not the only one to dub the veneration entailed by invocation as "worship of angels."[28]

In deciding between these two interpretations, we should recall that the evidence for taking the key phrase as a subjective genitive is very weak. In the two examples of *thrēskeia* in a subjective genitive construction that are usually cited (4 Macc 5:7 and Josephus *Antiquities of the Jews* 12.253), the reference is to the religion of the Jews, not to their act of worship; and there appear to be no texts where this term is employed for angelic activity. For this reason, and in the light of the case made by Arnold, it is more likely that "worship of angels" refers to the practice of invoking angels, a practice that the writer of Colossians, in line with his unfavorable evaluation of the philosophy as a whole, deems no better than worshiping angels. The practice may well have fulfilled the same functions that it did in popular magic—namely, coping with the threat of evil powers and providing special knowledge—but there is no need to follow the rest of Arnold's analysis and connect all of the philosophy's features with the magical tradition. It is one thing to see magic as being part of the religious milieu that helps to explain the appeal of the philosophy, but it is another to make magic the key that unlocks the door to the whole philosophy.

The next part of 2:18 fills out the reconstruction of the philosophy. What is insisted on by its proponents are fasting and veneration of angels "which he has seen when entering." The syntax could be construed as "entering into what he has seen," but it is more natural to take the neuter plural relative pronoun as modifying the whole of the preceding phrase, as in the previous verse, 2:17, and later in 3:6. The mention of "seeing" is a reference to what has been observed in visions. It may appear strange that fasting was part of what was seen in visions, but again such a feature was not uncommon in apocalyptic writings where instruction in fasting for the purpose of obtaining visions could itself be the subject of visions. The most likely reference of the participle translated "when entering" (ἐμβατεύων *embateuōn*) is to the visionary entering the heavenly realm. This, after all, is where a visionary is most likely to see and invoke angels; in apocalyptic writings, visionary experience was frequently conceived of in terms of the translation of the spirit and its entry into heavenly places (see, e.g., Rev 4:1-2).[29] The evidence of Col 2:18, then, indicates an insistence on fasting as preparation for visionary experience and invocation of angels in the heavenly realm.

The "Elemental Spirits of the Universe" and Dualistic Cosmology. Fasting, purity regulations, obtaining wisdom, visions, and even invocation of angels can all be found in various traditions within Judaism. Why not then simply conclude that the teaching being opposed was a particular strand of Judaism? This does not explain enough of the writer's emphases that appear to be directed against a strong dualistic strain in the philosophy. The stress in the hymnic material on Christ's agency in both creation and redemption and his reconciliation of heaven and earth, the insistence that God's presence and saving activity were in the physical body of Christ (1:22; 2:9), the discussion of "the body of flesh" in 2:11, and the treatment of the heavenly and earthly realms in 3:1-5 all suggest that the Jewish elements in the teaching had been assimilated into a framework that treated the earthly realm and the body as inferior and evil in contrast to the heavenly realm. In other words, the strands typical of Jewish apocalyptic writings and of popular Judaism now appear to be functioning within a Hellenistic dualistic cosmology. In addition, it is a reasonable inference from the letter's language about the principalities and powers (1:16, 20; 2:10, 15) that the philosophy held such heavenly powers to be threatening and hostile and in need of appeasement.[30] While belief in evil powers in heaven is, of course, found

---

27. Arnold, *The Colossian Syncretism*, 91-95.
28. Arnold, *The Colossian Syncretism*, 57-59.
29. See also *1 Enoch* 14:8; 71:1; *2 Enoch* 3:1; 36:1-2; *T. Abr.* 7-10; *Apoc. Abr.* 12, 15-16, 30; *T. Levi* 2:5-7, 10 ; 5:1, 3; *2 Bar* 6:4.
30. J. D. G. Dunn, *The Epistles to the Colossians and to Philemon*, NIGTC (Grand Rapids: Eerdmans, 1996) 184n. 35, admits that the weakest point of his hypothesis that the philosophy came from the Jewish synagogue is its failure to correlate such material satisfactorily and that this evidence provides the best support for the view that the philosophy was syncretistic.

in Jewish apocalypses, their role as intermediaries who had to be placated is much more difficult to discover and far more closely akin to the function of similar powers in Hellenistic cosmology.

A key question in this regard is how to interpret the phrase τὰ στοιχεῖα τοῦ κόσμου (*ta stoicheia tou kosmou*) in 2:8, 20. A minority of scholars take the phrase to refer to elementary principles or rudimentary teachings of the world (NIV, "the basic principles of this world"). But since the genitive is "of the world" and not "of this world," "world" in this context is most naturally taken to denote the cosmos.

The term *stoicheia* itself means first of all the component parts of a series and came to be applied to the physical components of the cosmos—earth, fire, water, and air (see 2 Pet 3:10, 12).[31] In Hellenistic thought these parts were believed to be under the control of spirit powers. Together with the stars and heavenly bodies they could be conceived of as personal forces who controlled the fate of humans. For this reason the majority of interpreters opt for a translation such as "the elemental spirits of the universe" (NRSV). This also fits well the context of thought in the letter, for elsewhere the writer emphasizes Christ's supremacy and victory over just such spiritual agencies. It is significant also that, when the same phrase was employed by Paul in Gal 4:3, 9, it was to warn Gentile Christians that to turn to the law would be equivalent to returning to their previous enslavement to the *stoicheia*, who are linked with their pagan deities, designated by Paul as "beings that by nature are not gods" (Gal 4:8).

One difficulty for this interpretation is that explicit use of *stoicheia* to refer to personified cosmic forces outside the NT is first found later in the *Testament of Solomon* 8:1-4; 18:1-5, where they are described as the cosmic rulers of darkness (see also Col 1:13). Moreover, the date of Pseudo-Callisthenes, in which King Nectabenos of Egypt is said to control the cosmic elemental spirits by his magical arts, is uncertain.[32] Given other pointers in the direction of such a reference, there is no reason why the NT might not be the first extant source for this explicit usage. Arnold, however, claims that these references and those in the magical papyri[33] belong to traditions that predate the actual writing and originate in the first century CE or earlier.[34] In any case, the book of Wisdom could earlier speak of the elements, referring to earth, air, fire, and water (Wis 7:15), and then condemn Gentiles for treating these elements as gods: "They supposed that either fire or wind or swift air, or the circle of the stars, or turbulent water, or the luminaries of heaven were the gods that rule the world" (Wis 13:2 NRSV). Philo also speaks of the *stoicheia* as "powers"[35] and reports worship of them as named deities.[36] Jewish apocalyptic literature had also already paved the way for this development by associating angels closely with the elements and heavenly bodies.[37]

In all probability, in the philosophy against which the letter is directed these elemental spirits were classed with the angels and were seen as controlling the heavenly realm and as posing a threat both to human well-being and to access to the divine presence. It was thought that an effective means of placating such powers was the rigorous subduing of the body in order to gain visionary experience of the heavenly dimension and to invoke the assistance of good angels in dealing with the hostile spirits. Through such visions also special knowledge and access to the divine presence could be obtained. This program as a whole, claiming to be wisdom (see 2:8, 23) and incorporating elements of Jewish calendrical and dietary law observances (2:16), appears to have been offered to the readers to supplement the apostolic gospel they had heard, so that in the view of the writer it undermined the sufficiency of what God had done in Christ. It reduced Christ to just another intermediary between humans and God, to one among a number of links to the heavenly dimension, one among a number of means of dealing with the hostile powers.

One of the chief concerns of Hellenistic religious thought was how a person could escape from the lower earthly realm and reach the heavenly world and the divine. Usually the purified

---

31. See also Diogenes Laertius 7, 136-37; Philo *Who Is the Heir of Divine Things?* 134.
32. Pseudo-Callisthenes I.12.1.
33. See PGM IV.475-829; XXXIX.18-21.
34. Arnold, *The Colossian Syncretism*, 170-73.
35. Philo *On the Eternity of the World* 107-9.
36. Philo *On the Contemplative Life* 3-4.
37. See 4 Ezra 6:3; *Jub.* 2:2; *1 Enoch* 60:11-12; *2 Enoch* 4:1; *T. Abr.* 13:11.

soul was believed to ascend after death and to remain above. It was possible, however, to experience this ascent of the soul during one's lifetime and to enter the heavenly sphere through various ecstatic experiences.[38] It was, of course, primarily the mystery cults that fostered this way of ascent. Often such cults demanded strict discipline, but their attraction was that by such means and through initiation into secret rites they promised freedom from the evil body, enlightenment, privileged knowledge, access to the heavenly realm, and union with the god or goddess. As people came to the view that, despite the apparent order of the heavenly regions, there were powers in them opposed to humanity, not only mystery religions but also magic flourished in order to influence the cosmic powers favorably. The philosophy being advocated in the Lycus Valley area, in which Colossae was located, would have spoken to these same needs, and, with certain features analogous to concerns of the mystery cults and magic traditions, would have seemed attractive for the same reason.

The "Philosophy" as Syncretistic. Despite the attempts of some scholars to avoid this conclusion, it seems clear from 2:18-19 that the one insisting on fasting and invocation of angels through visionary experience is viewed by the writer as a believer who is in some spiritual danger. This person is "puffed up without cause through a fleshly mind" (2:18) and is "not holding fast to the head, from whom the whole body . . . grows with a growth that is from God" (2:19 NRSV). The participle "holding" (κρατῶν *kratōn*) is singular in its Greek form and so does not refer to the readers but to the same person who was in view with the earlier singular form of the participle "insisting" (θέλων *thelōn*). It would make no sense for the writer to depict someone who made no claim to a relationship to Christ in the first place as not holding fast to Christ. This factor alone would appear to rule out viewing the philosophy simply as Judaism. Nor is there any evidence for use of the verb "to hold" meaning "to have an initial intellectual grasp," which would be required on the hypothesis that a Cynic critic of Christian worship is being described. Instead the proponent(s) of the teaching have taken a number of elements from Judaism and the Christian gospel and linked these with typical cosmological concerns from the Hellenistic world. It is quite plausible that a Hellenistic Jew who had left the synagogue to join a Pauline congregation or a Gentile convert who had had some previous contact with the synagogue would advocate such a philosophy, and the writer evidently was concerned that it might appeal to others among his preponderantly Gentile Christian readers. To label such teaching Hellenistic Jewish syncretism is not, therefore, simply an "easy both-and solution"[39] but an eminently plausible and fitting description of its components.

Obviously the Pauline gospel had a base in particular congregations in the Phrygian area, which included the Lycus Valley. It is equally clear that there was a strong Jewish presence in the area, because in 200 BCE Antiochus III had settled two thousand Jewish families in Lydia and Phrygia. It is not at all surprising, then, to find knowledge of specific features of Judaism in the syncretism that could have been picked up from the teaching of local synagogues. Jewish cultic regulations and calendrical observances have a role, but it remains significant that there is no mention of the law as such, as would surely be expected if the teaching were a straightforward variety of Judaism. It is also significant in this regard that the writer dismisses such elements as simply human tradition. This does not sound like the Paul of Galatians or Romans dealing with the law and having to account in his arguments for the claim that such observances were commanded by God, nor is it like the use of the charge of human tradition in Mark 7:1-13, where it is directed against the oral tradition. In addition, circumcision is mentioned in 2:11, but it functions in the writer's argument primarily as a metaphor for dealing with the physical body as a whole. The cultic and calendrical items and the interest in visionary experience also found in Judaism appear, then, to have been put to markedly different use in the philosophy.

The concepts of heaven and earth played an important part in Jewish thought, the apocalyptic writings included an increasing emphasis on the transcendent realm, and Hellenistic Judaism evidenced some similar cosmological concerns to those suggested for the philosophy. Yet in none of these strands was there the strong cosmological dualism that Colossians appears to combat.

---

38. See especially Plutarch *The Obsolescence of Oracles* 39-40; *Corpus Hermeticum* XI.20.
39. Dunn, *The Epistles to the Colossians and to Philemon*, 31.

Such spatial concepts, however, readily lent themselves to a dualistic framework, which, as we have seen, was current in Greco-Roman cosmological speculation. Still, cosmological dualism and an emphasis on special knowledge do not mean that there should be an identification of the philosophy with Gnosticism. At most what is suggested are certain "gnosticizing" tendencies. It is not until the Gnosticism attested in the Nag Hammadi documents that some of the letter's terminology is found in a clearly identifiable gnostic schema.

THE LETTER'S MAIN THEOLOGICAL THEMES

The writer does his theological reflection in response to the specific dangers he sees in the rival teaching and employs traditional materials in the process. Due attention will be given in the commentary to the way these elements shape the writer's thought, but it would be a mistake to reduce the letter's theology simply to the writer's mode of theologizing. This mode has produced the letter as we now have it, and it is the assertions of that final form that have made their impact on the development of Pauline thought and on the thinking of later Christians, however much or little we think we can know about the details of the preceding interaction with the philosophy or the writer's modifications of the traditional materials he employs to make his points. The following brief depiction of some of the letter's dominant theological emphases will concentrate primarily on the product of the writer's theologizing in the conviction that it is with these claims that contemporary readers of the letter need to engage. Although, for the sake of convenience, the depiction is divided into separate topics, it should be clear that in the theology of the letter these are inextricably interwoven and that what connects them is the assessment of the person and work of Christ. In the theology of Colossians, christology is central and everything else flows from the belief that Christ is the key to the understanding of reality.

The Apostolic Gospel. The writer addresses the situation faced by his readers with a combination of confidence in the sufficiency of the Pauline gospel and a pastoral concern that the readers should not weaken in their allegiance to this gospel. The theology of the letter consists in reflections on the implications of this apostolic gospel. It does so because the writer is convinced that the gospel is the word of truth (1:5), conveying reliable insight into God's purposes for humanity and the world through what has taken place in Christ. As such, it is also the conveyor of hope and of God's grace (1:5-6) and can be spoken of in a personified and dynamic fashion as bearing fruit and growing both among the readers and in the whole world (1:6). It is depicted as universal in its scope and spread ("proclaimed to every creature under heaven," 1:23), and its dynamic quality is again in view when the readers are exhorted to petition God to open a door for "the word" (4:3), to provide opportunities for the gospel to continue its progress. As the "word of God" (1:25), the gospel has its source in God, and, as "the word of Christ" (3:16), it has Christ as its content.

Another synonym for "gospel" is the term "mystery," with its connotation of a previously hidden purpose of God that has now been disclosed. The content of the mystery is Christ among you—that is, among the Gentiles (1:26-27)—or simply Christ (2:2; 4:3). This exclusive focus on Christ as being at the heart of the gospel message is reinforced when the notion of proclaiming the gospel can be expressed simply as proclaiming him (1:28). The gospel not only has at its center a person but it also entails received teaching about this person. In two places this is the force of the phrase "the faith" (1:23; 2:7), and in the latter context the formulation "Christ Jesus the Lord" encapsulates the tradition that has been received by the readers (2:6).

The gospel is the apostolic or, to be more precise, the Pauline gospel. The letter makes clear the intimate connection between the apostle and the gospel. The opening words provide the credentials for Paul's exposition of the gospel in response to the rival teaching. As apostle, he is the authorized representative of the one at the center of the message (1:1). But it is 1:23c–2:5 that underlines that, as Paul played his unique role in its missionary proclamation, he became the suffering servant of the gospel who participated in the same pattern of suffering experienced by Christ. Service of the gospel was also stewardship of the mystery on the part of Paul; just as the gospel has a teaching content and is universal in its scope, so also Paul's stewardship of it involves a teaching role that is universal in its reach, "teaching every human being" (1:28). His commitment to this gospel ministry entailed the strenuous effort of the athlete in a contest (1:29) and is symbolized by the chains of his imprisonment for the mystery of Christ (4:3, 18). Paul's service of the gospel is carried on by the team of his associates and coworkers. Epaphras was the initial link between the gospel the readers received and Paul (1:7), and he continues this role (4:12-13), while Tychicus and Onesimus have a similar function as further links with the apostle (4:7-9).

Christology. In responding to the rival teaching, the writer did not limit himself to criticisms of it; his positive recommendation of the Pauline gospel sets out some of the most profound reflections on the person of Christ to be found in the NT. The focus on Christ is such that there is almost no mention of the Spirit (but see 1:8-9; 3:16). Christ as the center of God's purposes and, therefore, the key to reality is what, according to the hymn, holds the cosmos together; but this notion of Christ is also, appropriately, what holds the thought of the letter together.

The most distinctive feature of the christology of Colossians is its sustained treatment of Christ in relation to both the creation and the reconciliation of the cosmos. Christ is not simply to be seen as the firstborn of all creation (1:15); rather, all things were created in, through, and for him (1:16). God is the Creator, but Christ is both an agent of creation and, more than that, its goal. The climactic "for him" in 1:16 adds to the assertions of 1 Cor 8:6 about Christ's agency that he is also the one to whom all creation is directed, the very purpose of its existence. Not only so, but all things hold together in him (1:17); their integrity and coherence depend on his role. The claim is not that it is some rational principle or even personified Wisdom that holds the key to the created universe but that it is the person believers confess as Christ who does so. The hymnic material does not explain why, although Christ has always been the agent and sustainer of creation, it is in need of reconciliation. Presupposing that need, it underlines that the one who was firstborn, agent, and goal in creation is also appropriately firstborn, agent, and goal of reconciliation in the new creation.

One major implication of this belief in the cosmic Christ is that he is sovereign over the powers of evil seen as threatening human life. In 1:15-20 such cosmic powers are depicted as being created in and for Christ, as having fallen out of harmony, and as being reconciled through Christ's death. Christ is, therefore, head over every ruler and authority (2:10). Whereas the hymnic material speaks of the powers' reintegration through Christ's death as a way of making peace and a reconciliation, in 2:15 what took place through the cross is described as stripping them of their power and triumphing over them. It looks very much, then, as if the making of peace is to be interpreted in terms of pacification. In the language of worship of 1:20 the hostile powers are depicted as already reconciled, but 1:13 has also made clear that the power of darkness is still operative and opposed to Christ's rule. The letter's thought about Christ's relation to the cosmic powers appears, then, to share the Pauline eschatological perspective with its "already" and "not yet." Through Christ the powers have already been pacified and reintegrated into God's purposes, and believers can already appropriate this achievement, but the full recognition of their new situation by the powers themselves awaits the eschaton.

A formulation about Christ in cosmic terms, echoing the thought of 1:15-20, is employed in an ecclesiological context in 3:11: "Christ is all and in all." In the first part of the verse, there is an adaptation of the baptismal formulation, found also in Gal 3:28 and 1 Cor 12:13, which states that in the new humanity there are no longer ethnic, cultural, and social distinctions. Rather, adds the second part, Christ is all and in all. If he has this status in the cosmos, then he most certainly has it in the church that is the focus for and the medium of his pervasive presence in the cosmos. Since Christ is now absolutely everything, all that matters, the old human categories of evaluation are rendered insignificant.

Colossians also characteristically describes Christ's status in terms of lordship. In line with assertions in the undisputed Pauline letters, it assumes that, by virtue of his exaltation to the right hand of God (3:1), Christ is Lord. He is now the one to whom believers are accountable (1:10) and owe absolute allegiance (2:6; 3:17). Even everyday life in the household is to reflect this relationship (3:18–4:1). Indeed, in the motivation slaves are to have, "fearing the Lord," Christ substitutes for Yahweh in Jewish scriptural terminology (3:22).

There are also other formulations used of God that are functionally equivalent to those employed of Christ. Being nourished by Christ the head is the same as receiving growth from God (2:19), and the "kingdom of his beloved Son" (1:13) is equivalent to the "kingdom of God" (4:11). Whereas the undisputed Pauline letters talk of creation as "for him" with reference to God (Rom 11:36; 1 Cor 8:6), Colossians uses this phrase of Christ (1:16); and while the undisputed letters of Paul speak of God as all in all (1 Cor 15:28), Colossians employs the same language of Christ (3:11).

Colossians depicts Christ's relationship to God in terms of oneness yet distinction. The Lord Jesus Christ still has a Father (1:3) and is the beloved Son (1:13). He is not the Creator but the agent and goal of creation. At the same time, in 1:15-20, his agency is portrayed in terms of Wisdom with the implication that all the qualities of Wisdom as God immanent in creation are now to be found in Christ (see also 2:3). The expression "image of the invisible God" (1:15) sums up the relationship well. Christ is the one who uniquely makes God's presence visible and God's purposes effective. Colossians does not call Christ "God," but the striking formulations of 1:19 and 2:9 put the two in the closest possible relationship and provide an equivalent to the Johannine notion of incarnation: All the fullness of God dwells in Christ bodily.

The letter's combination of universalism and particularism is related to its christology. On the one hand, it sets out the universal horizons of Christ's work and claims as Lord. Yet, on the other hand, it presses the necessity of faith in this particular person in whom God is uniquely revealed for entry into the new humanity.

Soteriology. The actual terminology of "salvation" is not employed in Colossians, but the language of rescue and transference is found in 1:13. Here the divine rescue act is from one dominion to another, from the power of darkness to the kingdom of the beloved Son. Both deliverance and redemption (1:14) stand for God's act of liberating humanity. Through Christ, believers are freed from the hold of the cosmic powers and their regulations (2:15-16, 20). Their liberation is experienced at present in terms of the forgiveness of sins (1:14; 2:13; 3:13), an emphasis needed because the opposing philosophy engendered a sense of guilt about life in the body that served to reinforce the hold of the powers.

The "once . . . now" contrast underlines the transference from plight to solution that God effects (1:21-22; 3:6-8). The depiction of the plight from which rescue is needed includes alienation and hostility (1:21), the old humanity and its vices (3:5-9), the wrath of God on this disobedient way of life (3:6), the flesh in its negative ethical sense (2:18, 23), and the death caused by sin (2:13). The depiction of the new situation and its benefits brought about through Christ includes reconciliation (1:22); the new humanity, both individual and corporate (3:10-11); and its virtues (3:12-14); the inheritance of God's people (1:12; 3:24); access to the heavenly realm (3:1-2); and being made alive (2:13). Among this variety of ways of portraying what God has achieved for humanity, reconciliation stands out. It appears in the hymnic material as the salvific image for God's accomplishment in Christ on a cosmic scale, where it is reinforced with the language of peacemaking (1:20), and it is this image that is then specifically applied to the readers (1:21-22). Later, too, they will be exhorted to appropriate the peace achieved by Christ in their corporate living (3:15).

The other major benefit highlighted in the letter can be termed wisdom (1:9, 28; 2:3, 23; 3:16; 4:5), knowledge (1:6, 9-10, 27; 2:2-3; 3:10), or understanding (1:9; 2:2). So God's rescue act in Christ also entails a revelation, a disclosure of God's previously hidden purposes in Christ, into which one can be given increasing insight. The mystery that was hidden has now been revealed to God's people (1:26-27), and the writer wants them to obtain "all the riches of assured understanding, the knowledge of God's mystery" (2:2).

Both the death and the resurrection of Christ play their part in the divine deliverance that produces the new humanity and the benefits it enjoys. Christ's death is spoken of as "the blood of his cross" (1:20), is seen as occurring in his body of flesh through death (1:22), and is described through the image of circumcision (2:11). Three further images describe how in Christ's death God overcame humanity's sense of condemnation: erasing the accusing record, setting it aside, and nailing it to the cross (2:14). It is not surprising that, when it comes to the reversal of death and the experience of new life, Christ's resurrection is at the fore as the means by which these are achieved for humanity. His resurrection makes him the firstborn from the dead, the first among brothers and sisters who will follow in his footsteps as they, too, are raised (1:18). Indeed, through union with Christ in his resurrection, they can already experience what it is to be made alive by God (2:12-13). Being raised with Christ also entails sharing his exaltation—thereby being given access to the heavenly realm—and participating in the future revelation in glory of Christ's life (3:1-4).

Eschatology. The letter's perspective on God's purposes for history and the cosmos provides the framework and presupposition for what it says about Christ and his agency in the rescuing of humanity. Colossians shares this basic eschatological framework with the undisputed Pauline letters in which Paul had in turn modified the Jewish eschatology he had inherited in the light of what he now believed to have taken place in Christ. Both these letters and Colossians see what God has done in Christ as having affected the whole cosmos with its two parts: heaven (in which there are also evil powers) and earth (the primary setting for humanity). They also see the time between Christ's death and resurrection and the eschaton as a period of tension between aspects of the blessings of the end times that can be experienced in the present and those that remain future. In Colossians, the stress is clearly on the present aspects. The decisive act that brings about the reintegration of the cosmos has already taken place, and believers can already appropriate its consequences so that they are no longer under the domination of the powers. Yet the powers continue to exist in their hostility to God's purposes and to pose a threat, so clearly the full realization of Christ's victory over them is not yet and is reserved for the eschaton.

Similarly, in response to the alternative teaching, Colossians emphasizes what has already taken place in believers' relationship of union with Christ. Romans 6 may well contain the notion of participation in Christ's resurrection, but it does not talk of this participation as having already taken place. Colossians does speak of believers as having been raised with Christ (2:12-13; 3:1). Indeed, it can go so far as to depict believers' lives as being linked with the life of the exalted Christ in heaven (3:2-3). Although the writer can appeal to a sense of urgency about the use of time (4:5), there is no imminent expectation of the end in this letter. Yet, as the writer moves away from thanksgiving and polemic to paraenesis or ethical exhortation, future references appear: negatively, to the coming wrath of God (3:6), and positively, to the reward of the inheritance (3:24).

Yet if Colossians can state that cosmic reconciliation has already been achieved and believers have already been raised with Christ, one might still want to ask whether anything substantial is left for the future. Crucial here is the assertion of 3:4 that Christ, who is believers' life, will be revealed, and believers will be revealed with him in glory. But will this be only the revelation of a present state of affairs, or will it involve some future change? Three considerations suggest that the latter option is in view. First, in 1:18 Christ has been described as the "firstborn from the dead" (πρωτότοκος ἐκ τῶν νεκρῶν *prōtotokos ek tōn nekrōn*). The clear implication is that, just as his resurrection was in bodily form, so also those who participate in the restored creation will experience a bodily resurrection from the dead. Second, the writer of Colossians stands in the Pauline school, and in Paul where life is found in an eschatological context it is equivalent to the resurrection or transformation of the body (Rom 8:11; 1 Cor 15:45; 2 Cor 5:4). Third, and similarly, if Colossians is interpreted as being in basic continuity with Paul, then, although it does not explicitly mention the resurrection of the body and the transformation of the cosmos, it is hard not to see these clear connotations of "glory" carrying over from Paul (Rom 8:17-23; 1 Cor 15:40-43; Phil 3:20-21).

The present and future aspects and the emphasis on eschatology in Colossians are summed up in its use of the term "hope" (ἐλπίς *elpis*). By definition hope entails some expectation about the future, and that temporal connotation is retained despite this letter's primary stress on its present content and heavenly dimension. Believers' hope is at present secured in heaven and so can be seen as foundational for their faith and love (1:4-5). Because Christ is the hope of glory (1:27), it is not surprising that this hope can be said to be located in heaven, where Christ now is until his revelation (3:1-4). Hope is closely identified with both Christ and the gospel (1:23). This is presumably because hope stands for confident assurance on the basis of what has already been achieved and is precisely what, in the writer's view, would be undermined by the philosophy.

Christian Existence in the Church and in the World. Believers' identity is dependent on their relationship with Christ. The primary way of viewing that relationship in Colossians is in terms of union with Christ, which is also the significance of the initiation rite of baptism (2:12). Believers can be said to be "in Christ" or "in the Lord" (1:2, 4, 28; 2:6-7), and the motif of incorporation into Christ is the thread running through 2:9-15. In union with Christ, readers have fullness (2:10). In him they were spiritually circumcised (2:11), and "with him" they died (2:20), were buried (2:12), were raised (2:12; 3:1), and were made alive (2:13). Since Christ is viewed as at present above, at the right hand of God, believers' union with him gives them a heavenly orientation that then is to be worked out on earth (3:1-2, 5). The relationship is such that believers' lives can be described as hidden with Christ in God (3:3); indeed, their life is Christ (3:4). Christian identity is inextricably bound up with the Christ who has died, been raised, is exalted in heaven, and is to be revealed.

Union with Christ is not a static relationship. It is seen in terms of growth (1:10; 2:19), leading to perfection or maturity (1:28; 3:14; 4:12). Those who are united to Christ have been filled (2:10), but the writer can also pray that they may be filled with the knowledge of God's will (1:9). Again there is an "already" and a "not yet" pattern to Christian existence. Believers have been given what is needed, but they must also appropriate this if they are to move toward their fullest potential. They have received Christ Jesus the Lord, but are exhorted to continue to live their lives in him (2:6-7) and are warned about the consequences of not continuing and holding fast (1:23; 2:19).

To live one's life in Christ the Lord (2:6) is to acknowledge his cosmic lordship as laying claim on all of life (3:17). The philosophy focused on specific rituals and on special days and abstinence from certain foods, but the sphere of Christ's lordship and, therefore, of obedient Christian response to that lordship is as broad as life itself. Everyday relationships in the most significant social and economic unit, the household, are singled out to illustrate what it means for the rule of the Christ who is Lord of the cosmos to be brought to bear within the structures of this world in which believers find themselves (3:18–4:1).

Believers have become new persons (3:10). This new humanity is not simply an individual but a corporate entity that transcends the divisions of the old humanity (3:11) and is an anticipation of the new creation as a whole. Reflecting its significant place in the writer's thought, in the Christ hymn the church is in fact mentioned before the reconciliation of the cosmos (1:18). Although Christ is the head over every ruler and authority, only the church, and not these powers or the cosmos as such, is designated his body (1:18, 24; 2:19; 3:15). Because of this special relationship to Christ, the church is the precursor of the reconciled cosmos. As Christ's body, it is distinctively related to its head, deriving its life and growth from him (2:19). Set in a cosmic context, Christ's body in Colossians is seen as a universal phenomenon. Similarly, Colossians employs the term ἐκκλησία (*ekklēsia*), for the assembly of the church with both a universal (1:18, 24) and a local (4:15-16) reference.

This church is a worshiping community. In implicit contrast to the veneration of angels and the ascetic regulations practiced by the philosophy, prominent in its worship are the word of Christ, the teaching of which inculcates wisdom, and thankful singing to God (3:16). The virtues that are to characterize the lives of its members are those that promote harmony and unity in the community (3:12-13). Peace, the reconciling activity of Christ that has been celebrated as affecting the cosmos (1:20), is to be appropriated particularly in the new community and allowed to rule (3:15). And what is necessary above all, if this community is to be what it is meant to be, is love (3:14; see also 1:4, 7).

A Theology of Wisdom and Grace. If setting out some of the themes of the letter reminds us that its theology transcends the setting that produced it, such a procedure may have its own dangers in obscuring this theology's essential characteristics. Perhaps what makes Colossians distinctive is its combination of a wisdom theology with a polemical theology of grace. Both elements are a result of the confrontation with the rival philosophy.

The philosophy's claims to wisdom (see 2:23) have provided the catalyst for a development of the Pauline gospel in terms of wisdom. This theme is explicit in each of the major sections of the letter's persuasive argument, occurring in the *exordium,* in each of the three sections of the *probatio,* and in the *peroratio.* In the first part of the letter, the intercessory prayer report reveals the concern that the recipients be "filled with the knowledge of God's will in all spiritual wisdom and understanding" (1:9), and the hymnic material in 1:15-20 is dominated by the application to Christ of the language and concepts associated with wisdom in the Hellenistic Jewish tradition.

In the body of the letter there is first a depiction of Paul and his gospel in terms of wisdom. Paul himself is humanity's great Christian wisdom teacher, "warning and teaching everyone in all wisdom" (1:28). The content of his gospel is "Christ himself, in whom are hidden all the treasures of wisdom and knowledge" (2:2-3). Next, in more direct interaction with the philosophy, the writer claims that its teachings may have a reputation for wisdom in its "worship of angels," fasting, and severity to the body. In fact, however, these are of no value in what he deems to be the real issue: dealing with the flesh in the negative sense of the sphere of humanity's opposition to God (2:23). Over against this otherworldly and ascetic wisdom, he then provides his own teaching on practical wisdom that is designed to deal with the sins of the old humanity. In the course of this, he makes clear that, because of their relationship to Christ, believers are to play their own role in such wise teaching of the community: "teach and admonish one another in all wisdom" (3:16). Finally, in the concluding exhortations, he can summarize the practical advice he has given, particularly in the household code, in terms of living wisely in regard to outsiders (4:5).

So wisdom features at all levels in the letter's theology. Christ embodies wisdom; Paul, supremely, but also all other believers are recipients and then teachers of wisdom; and Christian living is walking in wisdom. The wisdom christology of the hymn leads to the cosmic and univeral dimensions of the letter's theology. These in turn color the depiction of believers' relation to the exalted Christ. United to this Christ, they have a genuine heavenly orientation that works itself out in their lives on earth. James 3:13-18 contrasts two sorts of wisdom: a wisdom that is from above, displaying itself in a life of goodness and gentleness on earth, and a wisdom that is earthly, unspiritual, and devilish, characterized by envy and selfish ambition. Colossians can be seen as presenting, in contrast to what it regards as earthly wisdom, a wisdom that has its source where Christ is—above—but that then becomes firmly earthed in the everyday. The letter constitutes its writer's own wise teaching. What is more, he provides this in the typical wisdom mode of paraenesis, as he affirms, corrects, and exhorts in the attempt to produce other mature practitioners of wisdom.

This wisdom theology is universal in scope; however, its conviction that God's activity in Christ is the wisdom that provides the key to the understanding of reality is an exclusive one. At this point the polemical setting leaves a lasting mark on the theology. This version of the Pauline gospel sees itself as antithetical to other types of claims. Those espoused by the philosophy, according to the theological perspective of Colossians, should not be set alongside its own in a "both/and" relationship.

Colossians is polemical, because, like the Paul of Galatians in a different set of circumstances, it will not allow God's gracious activity in Christ to be undermined. To add new practices and regulations to the gospel is to suggest not only that believers are disqualified unless they adhere to them but also, more fundamentally, that what God has already done in Christ is deficient. Colossians is essentially Pauline in having none of this. In its defense of the apostolic gospel, Colossians does not make grace a separate theme so much as an underlying presupposition that it reinforces through both the content and the mode of its theologizing. This presupposition is made explicit in the very first mention of the gospel, where to hear the gospel and to comprehend the grace of God are equated (1:5-6). From then on, the insistence on what God has already achieved in Christ for the cosmos and for the church and the "realized eschatology," with its stress on the present experience of the benefits of end-time salvation, are in the service of this gospel of grace. This is also the force of the repetition of the motif of thanksgiving at key places throughout the letter (1:3, 11-12; 2:7; 3:15-17; 4:2). Christian thanksgiving is nothing other than the grateful recognition of the grace of God in Christ at the center of life. The mode of argumentation of Colossians is also in line with this element of its theology. Only after an extended thanksgiving section do the exhortations follow, and these are punctuated by the reminders to give thanks. For Colossians the gospel is grace, and no response to it can depart from that foundation by adding human achievements as a requirement. Instead, authentic Christian living is motivated by a response to and empowered by an appropriation of the undeserved favor of God in Christ.

Colossians is frequently referred to as having a bridging role between the undisputed and the disputed letters in the Pauline corpus. If its wisdom content and mode signal a significant development in the articulation of the Pauline gospel, its polemical theology of grace makes clear its essential continuity with that same gospel.

AUTHOR AND ADDRESSEES

Whereas there is widespread scholarly agreement that Ephesians and the Pastoral Epistles are pseudonymous, more dispute surrounds Colossians and 2 Thessalonians. Colossians is closely related to Ephesians. Although a tiny minority of scholars hold that Colossians is in some way dependent on Ephesians, for the majority it is clear that the dependency is the other way and that the author of Ephesians has used Colossians as the model on which he builds.[40] On this view, the relationship between Colossians and Ephesians plays no role in the debate about the authorship of the former.

In this debate the argument revolves around judgments on style, vocabulary, indications of what looks like a later setting than Paul's lifetime, and changes in theological perspective. In the case of Colossians, as with the other disputed letters, no one argument is decisive, although many consider that the issue of style comes very close to being so. Instead, it is a matter of a cumulative argument involving all these factors; of course, judgment will differ about the weight of any individual factor.

Colossians, however, allows a possible mediating position. Since it names both Paul and Timothy as it authors, some have suggested that the actual author could have been Timothy, writing either just before or just after Paul's death.[41] Nonetheless, the very fact that scholars opt for this solution indicates that they have accepted that the style differs so much from the undisputed Pauline letters that it cannot be attributed directly to Paul.

The introduction of the question of Paul's use of amanuenses, or secretaries, whom he may also in some instances have named as co-authors, complicates the issue of authorship still further. If secretaries are given the maximum possible role in the writing of the letters, this could mean that the only writings we actually have from Paul himself are the few brief passages he claims to have written in his own hand. If it is simply urged that we take the naming of co-authors with full seriousness, then Timothy is the co-author of 2 Corinthians, Philippians, and Philemon and, along with Silvanus, of 1 and 2 Thessalonians. Yet, with the exception of 2 Thessalonians, these are all among the undisputed letters, the comparison with which has caused the authorship of Colossians to be questioned in the first place. Clearly modern notions of authorship should not simply be assumed in regard to Paul's letters; on the other hand, we have no evidence of how Paul actually used any secretaries or co-authors. It appears best, then, to proceed cautiously with the criteria listed above in order to build a cumulative case that would indicate whether or not it is likely that Colossians was written in Paul's lifetime and that he put his name to it.

---

40. For a detailed discussion of the relation between Colossians and Ephesians and its role in the debate about the authorship of Ephesians, see A. T. Lincoln, *Ephesians* WBC (Dallas: Word, 1990) xlvii-lxxiii.

41. See, e.g., E. Schweizer, *The Letter to the Colossians* (Minneapolis: Augsburg, 1982); Dunn, *The Epistles to the Colossians and to Philemon*.

In regard to style, W. Bujard has provided the most thorough analysis of the letter, concluding that its style is not Paul's.[42] What is most telling here is that the grammar and syntax of Colossians differ so much from the undisputed Pauline letters. Colossians lacks the adversative, causal, consecutive, recitative, copulative, and disjunctive conjunctions that are characteristic of Paul's style. Instead it is characterized by long sentences with relative clauses, nouns linked in genitive constructions, and the piling up of synonyms. There are some thirty cases of amassed synonyms in Colossians. It also lacks completely the articular infinitive, a construction frequently employed by Paul to represent a dependent clause. Whereas Paul uses repetition to develop his argument in a logical direction, the repetitions in Colossians mostly function to build rhetorical effect. Colossians employs "which is" (ὅ ἐστιν *ho estin*) as a special idiom five times (1:24, 27; 2:10, 17; 3:14), a feature absent in the undisputed letters. Such differences bear on a writer's personal style. It is one thing to say that in order to address a new situation writers are likely to adapt their ideas or take on new vocabulary, but it is quite another thing to assert that they would abandon their characteristic style of writing for some other. There is nothing about the setting of the Colossian letter that would demand such a major shift in style.

The argument about vocabulary is less decisive. There are thirty-four words that do not occur elsewhere in the NT (*hapax legomena*) and a further ten that would be found only in Colossians were it not for the fact that they occur in Ephesians, which is dependent on Colossians. Also significant is the absence of so many key Pauline terms, such as "sin" (in the singular), "to believe," "promise," "law," "freedom," "boasting," the "justification" and "salvation" word groups, and, despite the actual address, the absence of the vocative "brothers and sisters" that is employed liberally in the body of the undisputed letters. Quite striking is the uncharacteristic combination of characteristic Pauline terms, so that, whereas "blood" and "cross" and "body" and "flesh" appear separately in the undisputed letters, here we have the phrases "blood of the cross" (1:20) and "body of flesh" (1:22; 2:11).

The changes of theological emphasis in the letter do not appear to be as decisive for authorship as some scholars claim. A number of these different emphases could be reasonably attributed to Paul's addressing his message to a different pastoral setting. So, for instance, the notion of realized eschatology using spatial categories is far more to the fore than in the undisputed Pauline letters, with this letter spelling out explicitly that believers have already been raised with Christ (2:12; 3:1) and stressing that hope is already present in heaven (1:5). Yet, it can be argued that these notions are in basic continuity with Paul's eschatology and are developed here because of the concern of the philosophy with cosmological questions and the need to assure believers of the security of their salvation. Similarly, the focus on a cosmic christology and the depiction of Christ's work of salvation in relation to the cosmic powers and the cosmos as a whole can be explained as the apostle's development of earlier strands in his teaching in the face of the philosophy's particular interests.

On the other hand, while Colossians does mention the future revelation of Christ in glory, there is no mention of the imminence of the parousia or the eschaton at all, and the Spirit is mentioned explicitly only once (1:8). There is no reason why the interaction with the philosophy should have caused these characteristic emphases to disappear to this extent. Their almost complete absence gives a quite different dynamic to the relation between eschatology and ethics than that found in the undisputed letters of Paul. In those letters, end-time events frequently shape ethical appeals and the Spirit and the fruit and gifts of the Spirit are seen as the present manifestation of the salvation of the end times among believers. In addition, while Paul could use the term "mystery" in a number of different ways, there is no such variety in Colossians, where its personal content in reference to the one at the heart of the gospel message, Christ, is constant (see 1:26-27; 2:2; 4:3). The notions of Christ's body and of the church now become universal entities (1:18, 24), in contrast to Paul's characteristic employment of them with reference to local groups of believers (although Colossians can also retain the reference of "church" to a local group in 4:15-16); and for the first time in the Pauline corpus the idea of Christ as the

---

42. W. Bujard, *Stilanalystische Untersuchungen zum Kolosserbrief als Beitrag zur Methodik von Sprachverglechen* (Göttingen: Vandenhoeck & Ruprecht, 1973). This work is summarized briefly in English in M. Kiley, *Colossians as Pseudepigraphy* (Sheffield: JSOT, 1986) 51-59.

head is brought into relation with that of the church as the body (1:18; 2:19). Despite this area of theological differences not being decisive in itself, since a number of the variations may well be explicable in terms of the circumstances of the letter, the question remains whether, when the differences are taken all together, Paul would have changed his perspective on so many significant matters.

Both the stress on "the faith" as a body of teaching (1:23; 2:7) and the inclusion of the household code (3:18–4:1) may well reflect a setting after the death of the apostle. In such a setting it would be necessary to maintain continuity with his teachings and to provide more help to churches of the Pauline mission on how to live in society over a longer period than Paul had anticipated. In particular, 1:24–2:5 reads very much like an admiring portrait of Paul from a follower. What stands out here in comparison with Paul's own reflections on his apostolic office are the exclusive focus on Paul and the stress on the universality of his mission. In Colossians, Paul alone is the apostle, while the undisputed letters mention other apostles, even if sometimes somewhat disparagingly. And here his ministry is for everyone without exception (1:28). There is no recognition that James, Peter, and John had a mission to Jews, while Paul and Barnabas were to go to Gentiles (see Gal 2:9). Indeed, Paul's gospel can be said to have been preached to every creature under heaven (1:23). Furthermore, while Paul can speak of his sufferings for the benefit of others (2 Cor 1:3-7), nowhere does he speak of these tribulations as making up a deficiency in Christ's sufferings or for the sake of the universal church (1:24).

The strongest arguments for the letter's authenticity are its close links with Philemon, whose Pauline authorship is undisputed, and the less than straightforward reading of 4:7-16, with its greetings to and mention of specific people, that is required if the letter is not authentic. Those who are persuaded on grounds of style and other factors that it is improbable that Paul wrote the bulk of the letter point out that there is a reasonable alternative explanation for the last section. Its features are typical of ancient pseudepigraphical letters that strive for verisimilitude as part of the device of pseudonymity.[43] Biographical reminiscences, personalia, and details of pseudo-recipients and their setting all further the appearance of genuineness. In Colossians not only does the author speak in Paul's name but, to add verisimilitude to his taking on the persona of Paul, he has also built on the list of greetings in Philemon and added one or two names known to the recipients from the Pauline mission. In the Pastoral Epistles, held by most scholars to be pseudepigraphical, the typical devices of verisimilitude are distributed throughout the letters, but also, as in Colossians, such details are grouped together at the end of 2 Timothy (see 2 Tim 4:9-22).

In the nature of the case, there can be no overwhelming proof for one's position on authorship; on balance, however, the cumulative argument that Paul was not the author and that Colossians was written by a follower after the apostle's death appears to have the greater probability. If this is indeed so, then there are implications for the identification of the addressees, since there are grave doubts about the existence of Colossae, let alone any church there, after 61 CE. Colossae was a small town in the Lycus Valley in the region of Phrygia. By the first century it was very much in the shadow of the neighboring cities of Laodicea and Hierapolis. But there are two ancient reports of an earthquake in the Lycus Valley. Tacitus says that Laodicea was destroyed by an earthquake in 60–61 CE,[44] and Eusebius talks of Laodicea, Hierapolis, and Colossae as all being destroyed by an earthquake in 63–64 CE.[45] It is usually suggested that these are references to the same earthquake and that the more important Hierapolis and Laodicea were rebuilt more quickly, while Colossae remained uninhabited for a considerable period. There are coins from the late second and the third century referring to Colossae but no mention of it in ancient evidence for the earlier period after 61 CE. So it is likely that it was not an inhabited site for quite a long time after Paul's death. Some have suggested, therefore, that the church at Colossae was chosen as the addressee as part of the letter's attempt at verisimilitude, precisely because there was a Pauline church there during the apostle's lifetime but not afterward. This

---

43. See L. R. Donelson, *Pseudepigraphy and Ethical Argument in the Pastoral Epistles* (Tübingen: Mohr, 1986) 7-66.
44. Tacitus *Annals* 14.27.
45. Eusebius *Chronicle* 1.21-22.

also meant that the writer was able to make use of the greetings in Philemon, a letter that was sent to Colossae. If all this is true, then an address to the Colossians is a convenient one in a pseudepigraphical letter actually intended for the former neighboring church of Laodicea and perhaps also that of Hierapolis, as the letter itself hints despite its address to pseudo-recipients (see 2:1; 4:13, 15-16).[46]

To conclude that Colossians is pseudonymous is, of course, not to detract in any way from the validity of its message or from its authority as part of the New Testament canon. What was canonized by the church were not the complete thoughts of Paul but those texts in which it recognized apostolic tradition. Pseudonymity was, in fact, a literary device for passing on authoritative tradition. In the Jewish Scriptures writings are attributed to great personages like Moses, David, Solomon, and Isaiah, and apocalypses, testaments, prayers, and collections of sayings were written in the name of ideal or authoritative figures from the past.[47] The earliest Christian writers of pseudepigrapha remained under the influence of such Jewish notions of authorship and revelation, whereby pseudonymity involved the assertion of authoritative tradition. The Epistle of Jeremiah, the Epistle of Enoch (*1 Enoch* 92–105), the Epistle of Baruch (*2 Apoc. Bar.* 78-87), the letters contained in 1 and 2 Maccabees, and the correspondence between Solomon, Hiram, and Pharaoh in Eupolemos and Josephus[48] provide examples from Jewish literature. However, the pseudepigraphical letter form employed by early Christians was particularly a Greco-Roman literary device. The pseudonymous didactic letters of the philosophical schools, such as the Pythagorean, Cynic, and Neo-Platonist school productions, attempted to convey the presence of the sender to the readers and in doing so would invent personal references and extraneous mundane details for the sake of verisimilitude. The purpose was to provide the occasion for passing on philosophical teaching and portraying a particular philosopher as a model.[49]

In evaluating this phenomenon, it should be remembered that the notion of "intellectual property," so essential to discussion of legitimate claims to authorship and to plagiarism in a modern context, played little or no role in ancient literary production. We know little about the circumstances of the composition of Colossians. Given its direct address to a particular problem, it does not seem likely that it was slipped into a letter collection in the hope that some later general readers would take it for one of Paul's originals and find it edifying. If, instead, it was intended for a specific group of readers in Asia Minor after Paul's death and came from one of Paul's close followers, it is reasonable to believe that its readers would have known of such a significant event as the death of the apostle and, therefore, would have taken the letter as a product of a trusted Pauline teacher who was presenting his teaching not simply as his own but as in the Pauline apostolic tradition. Whether written by Paul or by a disciple of his, the letter was treated as faithfully conveying the apostolic message and has a foundational status in the canon as part of the Pauline corpus. If written by a disciple of Paul, then Colossians, in its attempt to be both faithful and creative in its interpretation of the Pauline tradition in a later situation, provides a canonical model for those engaged in the same task of reflecting on the apostolic gospel and reformulating it in the face of changed circumstances and new challenges.

Although the following commentary is written from the perspective that the letter is to be dated sometime after Paul's death and that the interpretation of 1:24–2:5 and 4:7-16 in particular is to be linked to the device of pseudonymity, this is a matter still under dispute. For those who disagree with such a stance on authorship, all that is necessary in most of what follows is, of course, to make the mental substitution of "Paul" or "Timothy" or both for "the writer."[50]

---

46. So A. Lindemann, "Die Gemeinde von 'Kolossä.' Erwägungen zum 'Sitz im Leben' eines deuteropaulinischen Briefes," *WD* 16 (1981) 111-34; P. Pokorny, *Colossians: A Commentary*, trans. S. S. Schatzmann (Peabody, Mass.: Hendrickson, 1991) 21.
47. See D. G. Meade, *Pseudonymity and Canon* (Tübingen: Mohr, 1986).
48. Eupolemos, as preserved in Eusebius *Preparation for the Gospel* 9.31.1-34.5; Josephus *Antiquities of the Jews* 8.2.6-7.
49. See Donelson, *Pseudepigraphy and Ethical Argument in the Pastoral Epistles*, 7-66; Wilson, *The Hope of Glory*, esp. 49-50.
50. For a major commentary defending authorship of Colossians by Paul, see P. T. O'Brien, *Colossians, Philemon*, WBC 44 (Waco, Tex.: Word, 1982) esp. xli-xlix.

BIBLIOGRAPHY

Commentaries:

Barth, M., and H. Blanke. *Colossians.* Translated by A. B. Beck. AB 34B. New York: Doubleday, 1994. The original German draft of this full and detailed commentary was completed in 1991. Despite its publication date, its extensive bibliographical references are to works no later than 1986.

Dunn, J. D. G. *The Epistles to the Colossians and to Philemon.* NIGTC. Grand Rapids: Eerdmans, 1996. A recent full-scale commentary on the Greek text that interacts with a wide range of secondary literature but is readable and sensitive to the theological nuances of the letter.

Harris, M. J. *Colossians and Philemon.* Grand Rapids: Eerdmans, 1991. Provides detailed analysis of the Greek syntax and brief outlines for suggested homiletical expositions.

Lohse, E. *Colossians and Philemon.* Translated by W. R. Poehlmann and R. J. Karris. Hermeneia. Philadelphia: Fortress, 1971. For many years this has served as the standard detailed critical commentary on Colossians. Contains useful excursuses on key issues, including a comparison between the thought of Colossians and Pauline theology.

Martin, R. P. *Colossians and Philemon.* NCB. Greenwood, S.C.: Attic, 1974. A concise commentary, based on the RSV, with stimulating exegetical observations.

———. *Ephesians, Colossians, and Philemon.* Interpretation. Atlanta: John Knox, 1991. A short commentary geared to the needs of teachers and preachers.

O'Brien, P. T. *Colossians, Philemon.* WBC 44. Waco, Tex.: Word, 1982. A detailed commentary on the Greek text. The format of the series in which it appears allows its author to focus on each pericope's form, structure, and setting and to provide a brief summary of its thrust.

Pokorny, P. *Colossians: A Commentary.* Translated by S. S. Schatzmann. Peabody, Mass.: Hendrickson, 1991. A worthwhile resource with suggestive discussion of the structure of the letter and its argument. The original German commentary was published in 1987.

Schweizer, E. *The Letter to the Colossians.* Translated by A. Chester. Minneapolis: Augsburg, 1982. The German edition was published in 1976, but this remains a helpful critical commentary for preachers and teachers. Its writer says that no section was written without having first been preached, and the commentary contains a forty-five-page essay on the history of interpretation of Colossians.

Specialized Studies:

Arnold, C. E. *The Colossian Syncretism.* WUNT 2/77. Tübingen: J. C. B. Mohr, 1995. A worthwhile attempt to characterize the teaching the letter opposes and the author's response, utilizing more fully than others local inscriptional and textual evidence, including the magical papyri.

Barclay, J. M. G. *Colossians and Philemon.* Sheffield: Sheffield Academic, 1997. An excellent introductory guide to the issues of the letter's authorship, purpose, and theology.

D'Angelo, M. R. "Colossians." In *Searching the Scriptures.* Volume 2: *A Feminist Commentary.* Edited by E. Schüssler Fiorenza. New York: Crossroad, 1994. A concise commentary focusing on the issues most acute for feminist interpretation and endeavoring to uncover the collaboration of its theology of submission in the history of enslavement.

DeMaris, R. E. *The Colossian Controversy.* JSNTSS 96. Sheffield: JSOT, 1994. Argues that the teaching combated in the letter combined Jewish and Christian elements with popular Middle Platonism.

Francis, F. O., and W. A. Meeks, eds. *Conflict at Colossae.* Missoula, Mont.: Scholars Press, 1973. A collection of important essays in the debate about the nature of the Colossian "philosophy."

Kiley, M. *Colossians As Pseudepigraphy.* Sheffield: JSOT, 1986. A study of some of the issues surrounding the authorship of the letter, claiming that it is pseudonymous and in the process providing a useful summary of the thoroughgoing analysis of the style of Colossians by the German scholar W. Bujard.

Lincoln, A. T., and A. J. M. Wedderburn. *The Theology of the Later Pauline Letters.* New York: Cambridge University Press, 1993. Wedderburn writes on Colossians, focusing especially on theological and hermeneutical questions raised by the christological hymn of 1:15-20 and on the themes of baptism and eschatology.

Martin, T. W. *By Philosophy and Empty Deceit: Colossians as Response to a Cynic Critique.* JSNTSS 118. Sheffield: Sheffield Academic, 1996. A recent innovative study, claiming that the opposing teaching is straightforward Cynic philosophy and that the author is responding to Cynic criticisms of the Christian gospel.

Sappington, T. J. *Revelation and Redemption at Colossae.* JSNTSS 53. Sheffield: JSOT, 1991. Argues that the ascetic-mystical piety of Jewish apocalyptic literature provides the most appropriate background for interpreting Colossians and its polemic.

Wilson, W. T. *The Hope of Glory: Education and Exhortation in the Epistle to the Colossians.* Leiden: E. J. Brill, 1997. A fine study that is particularly helpful in setting Colossians in the context of the moral exhortations of the philosophical schools and in its analysis of the worldview of Colossians.

OUTLINE OF COLOSSIANS

I. Colossians 1:1-2, The Letter Opening

II. Colossians 1:3-23, An Extended Thanksgiving

    A. 1:3-12, Opening Thanksgiving and Intercessory Prayer Report
        1:3-8, Opening Thanksgiving
        1:9-12, Intercessory Prayer Report
    B. 1:13-23, Thanksgiving Through Introduction, Citation, and Application of Praise of Christ
        1:13-14, Transitional Introduction to the Praise of Christ
        1:15-20, Citation of Hymnic Material in Praise of Christ
        1:21-23, Application of Praise of Christ

III. Colossians 1:24–4:9, The Letter Body

    A. 1:24–2:5, Body-Opening: Paul's Proclamation of the Gospel and Its Relation to the Readers
    B. 2:6–4:6, Body-Middle: Exhortations
        2:6–3:4, Exhortation to Faithfulness to the Gospel
        2:6-7, Live in Accordance with the Tradition About Christ
        2:8-15, Do Not Be Captured by Human Tradition
        2:16-23, Do Not Be Judged by the Codes of a Different Teaching
        3:1-4, Seek the Things That Are Above
        3:5–4:1, Exhortation to Holiness of Life
        3:5-11, Put to Death What Is Earthly
        3:12-17, Put on Love, Appropriate the Peace of Christ, and Be Thankful
        3:18–4:1, Let Christ's Lordship Shape Household Relationships
        4:2-6, Concluding Exhortation: Pray, Live Wisely, and Speak Graciously
    C. 4:7-9, Body-Closing: Passing on News

IV. Colossians 4:10-18, The Letter Closing

COLOSSIANS 1:1-2

THE LETTER OPENING

COMMENTARY

The letter begins with the usual epistolary format of an introductory address and greetings. The senders are identified as Paul and Timothy. If the letter is Pauline, the placing of Timothy alongside Paul raises the issue of the former's role in the composition of the letter. Is he meant to be considered simply as a co-sender or also as a co-author? The naming of others in an address of a letter actually written by an individual was not the ordinary occurrence in antiquity.[51] This would suggest that Timothy is named because he had a significant role in collaborating as a co-author. It is easy to see why those who wish to give Timothy the dominant role in writing this letter as a way of accounting for the differences, especially stylistic ones, from the undisputed Pauline letters might favor this view. But it is a slim basis for such an explanation, since among the undisputed letters with which the style of Colossians has to be compared, 2 Corinthians, Philippians, and Philemon include Timothy in the address with Paul, and 1 Thessalonians includes not only Timothy but also Silvanus. Those who hold the letter to be pseudonymous would simply argue that at this point its author has used 2 Corinthians, Philippians, and Philemon as models.

In any case, as the letter stands, the primary authority for its message is Paul. Timothy's name comes second with the simple description "our brother" (cf. 2 Cor 1:1; Phlm 1); but Paul is named first, and only he is said to be "an apostle of Christ Jesus by the will of God" (cf. 2 Cor 1:1). Whether by Paul himself or by a follower writing in his name, an appeal is made to Paul's apostleship as the source of the letter's authority. Paul is seen, on account of his encounter with and commissioning by the risen Christ, as this Christ's authorized representative. Behind this apostolic role, it is claimed, lies the will of God; the letter will later expand on Paul's place in God's purposes in history (1:23c-29).

Whereas the Corinthian and Thessalonian correspondence and even Philemon contain an address "to the church," and Galatians is addressed "to the churches," Colossians designates its recipients as "the saints and faithful brothers and sisters in Christ." The former term signals that the readers are viewed as being set apart as God's elect people. None of the undisputed letters describes its recipients as "faithful brothers and sisters." The family metaphor for believers, found in various places in the Pauline letters, now becomes part of the address. Despite a relationship in which the writer claims not to have actually met the recipients (1:4, 9; 2:1), this gives the salutation a more intimate and personal note. Although the adjective translated as "faithful" (πιστοῖς *pistois*), could mean simply "believing," it is more likely that in view of its later usage in 1:7 and 4:7, 9 it refers to the readers' fidelity and steadfastness. The writer will later call on them to continue to exercise these qualities (1:23; 2:6-7).

The family metaphor continues into the greeting with its reference to "God our Father." The greeting begins as the usual Pauline one of grace and peace with its adaptation of Hebrew and Greek forms of greetings. But, unlike the greetings of the undisputed Pauline letters, there is no mention of "our Lord Jesus Christ" alongside "God the Father" as the source of grace and peace. The expression "grace to you and peace" is used in 1 Thess 1:1, but immediately preceding this the church is said to be "in God the Father and the Lord Jesus Christ." The omission of this phrase in Colossians might be explained by the fact that the writer has just previously designated the recipients as those "in Christ in Colossae," but a similar relating of the

---

51. See E. R. Richards, *The Secretary in the Letters of Paul*, WUNT 2/42 (Tübingen: J. C. B. Mohr, 1991) 47n. 138.

recipients to Christ in 1 Cor 1:2; Eph 1:1; and 2 Thess 1:1 does not prevent the writers of those letters from going on to mention Christ in the grace and peace greeting. The absence in Colossians of the usual reference to Christ in the actual greeting remains striking, particularly in a letter whose focus on Christ will be so strong.

What had become the typical Christian greeting in the Pauline letter in this case aptly sets the tone for what is to follow. What has been done for believers through God's undeserved favor in Christ will be the linchpin of the writer's argument; indeed, grace will stand as a synonym for the gospel in 1:6. In addition, peace will be highlighted as one of the major elements of that grace (1:20; 3:15), not simply as an inner contentment but as the experience of relationships on the cosmic and human levels being brought into conformity with the Creator's purposes for harmony.

REFLECTIONS

The double identification of the addressees as those who are "in Colossae" and "in Christ" (following the order in the Greek syntax) is suggestive both for the issues to be dealt with in Colossians and for broader questions about Christian identity. The readers are located both in their particular geographical environment, shaped by its religious, social, and political realities, and in the sphere of Christ's lordship. One of the key questions with which the letter grapples is how the latter bears on the former. The phrase "in Christ" refers to the relationship of believers' incorporation into and union with Christ. Again and again in various forms the writer will appeal to the implications of this relationship in his attempt to persuade the readers to remain true to the Pauline gospel in the way they view alternative teaching and live out their calling in the social structures of their day. Interpreters of Colossians will want to take advantage of their study of this letter's particular proposals to reflect on the same issue as it confronts contemporary Christians. The double identification of Christians can provide the lens for our self-understanding as we consider some of the dominant religious and social aspects of the culture that shapes us and what it means, in the midst of these, to be decisively reshaped by our relationship to Christ.

COLOSSIANS 1:3-23
AN EXTENDED THANKSGIVING

OVERVIEW

Colossians 1:3-23 is an extended thanksgiving section that, rhetorically speaking, can also be seen as an exordium (see Introduction). It functions to make the readers positively inclined to receive the letter's later exhortations and also introduces the main themes and concerns that inform those exhortations. The initial prayer of thanksgiving in 1:3-8 forms one sentence in the Greek text. It is followed by an even longer Greek sentence that extends to 1:17 and is further evidence of the distinctive style of Colossians in comparison to the undisputed Pauline letters. The first part of this sentence constitutes the usual intercessory prayer report of a Pauline letter in 1:9-12, which concludes on a note of thanksgiving. The thanksgiving is then extended by formulations about the salvation God has accomplished in Christ in 1:13-14, which lead into the citation of material in praise of Christ in 1:15-20. What is said in these verses about Christ's work of reconciliation is then applied to the readers in 1:21-23, where in particular the three main themes of the rest of the letter are set out before they are taken up in reverse order.

COLOSSIANS 1:3-12, OPENING THANKSGIVING AND INTERCESSORY PRAYER REPORT

Colossians 1:3-8, Opening Thanksgiving

COMMENTARY

The thanksgiving section is just as much a report on the writer's prayers for his readers, rather than a direct transcript of a prayer, as is the so-called intercessory prayer report. As such, it is now addressed to the readers rather than to God. While it reflects something of the writer's prayer life, its primary function is to assure the readers of the writer's goodwill toward them and his appreciation of the qualities of their Christian faith. Such opening thanksgivings in the Pauline letters frequently set the scene for the concerns of the letter, and this one is no exception. The writer does not hesitate to signal ahead of time some of the matters on which he will elaborate. For example, he mentions in the context of thanksgiving the readers' hope, laid up for them in heaven (v. 5), but he will remind them of this hope and its significance later. He mentions that the gospel they received was the word of truth from an apostolic representative (vv. 5, 7-8), but again this is a matter that will need reinforcing. In the light of the later message, his reference to their knowledge of the grace of God (v. 6) is also significant, for an understanding of the sufficiency of that grace is essential if the teaching that threatens the community is to be resisted.

1:3-5a. Despite these verses' being a report of a thanksgiving that now has an epistolary function of assuring the readers of the writer's goodwill toward them, the readers are not directly congratulated on their Christian virtues. This would clearly be inappropriate, since such virtues derive ultimately from God. Instead, the report speaks of the writer's constantly being thankful to God, who is described in the formula characteristic of the Pauline letters as "the Father of our Lord Jesus Christ" (cf. Rom 15:6; 2 Cor 1:3; 11:31). Paul and his churches held Jesus Christ to be Lord with all the connotations of κύριος (*kyrios*) from the Greek Scriptures where it was used of Yahweh (cf. Rom 10:13; Phil 2:10). At the same time, within a Jewish monotheistic framework, they still held that this Lord had a God but that this one God was now to be characterized by the intimate relationship with Christ of Father to Son.

The writer speaks only of having heard of the readers' faith and love, since Paul did not personally found the church at Colossae. The founder was Epaphras, who has provided this good report (vv. 7-8). Their faith is described as "in Christ Jesus." English translations disguise the fact that this phrase could refer either to the object of faith or to the sphere in which that faith is operative. Paul and the writer of Colossians elsewhere (cf. 2:5) do not use the preposition ἐν (*en*) for the object of faith, and so here it is likely that the reference is to Christ as the sphere in which believers live and exercise their faith. The notion of believers' status or standing "in Christ" is important for the writer (see his designation of the addressees as "faithful brothers and sisters in Christ" in v. 2), and he will later draw out some of the implications of this incorporation into and solidarity with Christ for the readers' lives (2:6-7, 10-12). The readers' love, which is also grounds for the writer's thanksgiving, is said to be "for all the saints," suggesting that they have given evidence of a practical concern for other believers that extends beyond the confines of their local group.

With the mention of "hope" in v. 5*a*, the familiar triad of Christian virtues—faith, hope, and love—is recalled (see Rom 5:1-5; 1 Cor 13:13; Gal 5:5-6; 1 Thess 1:3; 5:8). But what is distinctive about their association here is that faith and love are made dependent on hope and, as in Gal 5:5, hope is not so much a subjective Christian virtue as the content of salvation, that which is hoped for. By definition, hope, even as the content of salvation or the object of expectation, has a future dimension; but now the addition of the spatial description ("laid up for you in heaven") underlines that it exists not as a vague wish for the future but as an assured reality in the present. The language recalls other images for salvation in the NT, such as "treasures in heaven" (Matt 6:20) and "an inheritance . . . kept in heaven for you" (1 Pet 1:4). It reflects the concept found in Jewish apocalyptic literature that what will be manifested in history at the eschaton, at the consummation of salvation, is already present in heaven, a concept employed to stress the certainty of future salvation. This is also the force of such language in Colossians: The hope of believers' salvation is secured in heaven and nothing can alter that. The content of this hope is ultimately Christ, who will be called "the hope of glory" (v. 27); it is in heaven because the writer believes the exalted Christ is at present above (3:1). Later the writer will talk with equal seriousness about the possibility of the readers' shifting away from this hope (v. 23), but for now it is the security of the salvation God has provided through Christ that is underscored.

Some commentators have suggested that the stress on hope is because the rival teachers were robbing believers of this prospect by denying the future element in salvation and claiming that the resurrection was past already. But this is to misread the opposing teaching and to miss the force of the language. The threat of the rival teachers places the assured hope of salvation in jeopardy through its insistence on further means (rigorous ascetic observances, esoteric knowledge, and visionary experiences) in addition to the message about Christ as being necessary if full salvation is to be attained. Those readers exposed to such teaching need to know that there is nothing inadequate about the apostolic message they have received and to be assured, in the face of any insecurities induced by the teachers, that the gospel centered in Christ is well able to provide a certain hope.

1:5b-8. A further relative clause in the Greek text now makes explicit the link between the hope of which the writer has been speaking and the gospel that the readers have received. They have previously heard of that hope "in the word of truth, the gospel." By talking of the gospel in these terms the writer already is implicitly setting it over against the rival teaching, which he will label as "empty deceit" (2:8). Just as the psalmist could refer to God's commandments in the Torah as "the word of truth" (Ps 119:43; see also Ps 119:142, 160), so also the writer of Colossians can speak of the gospel as the word of truth and as "the word of God" (v. 25). Just as in the Jewish Scriptures God's Word can be personified, so also here the gospel takes on an almost personal quality as the writer speaks of its dynamic activity. The gospel has come to the readers and has taken a firm place in their lives. Indeed, it is "bearing fruit" (καρποφορέω *karpophoreō*), producing a crop of good deeds as a result of its reception, and is "growing" (αὐξάνω *auxanō*), attracting an increasing number of adherents in the whole world. This note of prophetic optimism about the universal proclamation of the gospel will be sounded again in v. 23. Here it is mentioned to remind the readers that in their adherence to the gospel they are part of a larger whole, a movement that is encompassing the Roman Empire. The universal appeal of the gospel may also be intended to counter the elitism of the rival teaching, which catered to initiates who were prepared to undergo certain rituals and observances. What the gospel was achieving on a broader scale, it was also effecting in the lives of the readers, bearing fruit among them from the time they first received its message.

Their initial hearing with faith is also characterized as a coming to know "the grace of God in truth." The phrase "in truth" (ἐν ἀληθείᾳ *en alētheia*) could be taken adverbially to refer to the readers' genuine comprehension, but more likely it links the grace of God with the truth of the gospel (v. 5). The reminder that the truth they first believed focused on the gracious activity of God is significant in the light of the place of human effort in the writer's sketch of the rival teaching. The realization that the readers owe their salvation to God's grace should serve to undermine those who would make ascetic and visionary achievements requirements for a full relationship with God.

The link between the apostolic gospel of Paul and Timothy and the readers is provided by Epaphras (vv. 7-8; see also 4:12-13; Phlm 23). In relation to the readers, Epaphras was the evangelist and teacher in the Lycus Valley from whom they had learned the gospel. If hearing the gospel (v. 6) draws attention to the initial reception, learning highlights the consequent catechesis (see also "just as you were taught," 2:7). As a result of his activity among the readers, Epaphras is depicted as being able to report to Paul and Timothy about their love in the Spirit. Again love is singled out (cf. v. 4) as a major fruit produced by the gospel, and this time it is associated, in one of the few references in this letter to the Spirit (see also 1:9; 3:16), with this power of the new age, whose first and all-encompassing fruit is love (cf. Gal 5:22).

In relation to Paul and Timothy, Epaphras is "our beloved fellow servant" and "a faithful minister of Christ on our behalf" (where the reading "on our behalf," rather than "on your behalf," has the much stronger external attestation). "Servant" or "slave of Christ" (δοῦλος χριστοῦ *doulos Christou*) was a self-designation of Paul as an apostle (cf. Rom 1:1; Gal 1:10; Phil 1:1—including Timothy), as was "minister" (διάκονος *diakonos*; see 1 Cor 3:5; 2 Cor 11:23), which could also be used of close co-workers such as Apollos, Timothy, or Tychicus (see 1 Cor 3:5; Col 4:7; 1 Thess 3:2). Together with the indications of affection ("beloved") and commendation ("faithful"), these terms place Epaphras in the closest possible relationship to Paul and his immediate co-workers and confirm for the readers that what has been presented to them by Epaphras has the seal of approval as the apostolic gospel. (See Reflections at 1:9-12.)

Colossians 1:9-12, Intercessory Prayer Report

COMMENTARY

The link with v. 8 through "for this reason" suggests that "since the day we heard" has in view the reception of the news about the readers from Epaphras. Certainly the report of the intercessions made on their behalf appears to be in the light of the full situation that Epaphras is depicted as having communicated. The stress in the first part of the report is on their growth in knowledge both of God's will and of God, a knowledge that involves spiritual wisdom and understanding (vv. 9-10). Again and again the letter will emphasize the true source of wisdom and knowledge (e.g., 1:27-28; 2:2-3; 3:10, 16). Together with the labeling of the rival teaching as a "philosophy" in 2:8 and the assertion in 2:23 that for all its claims it only has the appearance of wisdom, these emphases suggest that the prayer report has an eye on the alternative teaching being offered. The same may well be true of the language of growth and fullness it contains (see 2:9-10, 19). The writer's prayer for the readers, then, is for more, not less, than what others are offering; but he believes this will be found in an ever-increasing appropriation of what they already have in the gospel. In the OT, wisdom frequently involves practical knowledge—that is, the ability to choose right conduct—and here in Colossians the wisdom and insight produced by the Spirit have an explicitly ethical dimension. They are meant to enable the readers to "walk" (a Hebraism common in the LXX and taken up in the Pauline letters to refer to ethical conduct or a way of living) in a manner consistent with their confession of Christ as Lord and fully pleasing to him.

The writer elaborates on such a way of life in the four participial clauses that follow in vv. 10*b*-12. The first two participles were previously employed in v. 6 to speak of the activity of the gospel itself both in the world and among the readers. Now the fruitbearing and growth that were marks of the gospel are the characteristics to be desired for the readers. The fruit produced is to be good works, and the growth is to be in their knowledge of God. The good works contrast with and replace the "evil works" (v. 21) of the readers' previous way of life, a juxtaposition elaborated in the vices and virtues contained in the paraenesis in 3:5-17. For the undisputed Pauline letters, too, it should be remembered, authentic faith showed itself in doing good (see Rom 13:3; 2 Cor 5:10; Gal 6:10; 1 Thess 5:15); and the expression "every good work" is found in 2 Cor 9:8 (see also 2 Thess 2:17).

The third participial clause (v. 11) focuses on the power the readers will require to enable them to live lives that are fully pleasing to their Lord. It combines two nouns and a verb referring to power or strength and adds "all" before the first noun and "of glory" after the second in order to convey an impression of something of the divine might available to the readers and to make its point as forcefully as possible. Nothing less than God's glorious power at work within them will be necessary to live worthily of their Lord. But it is worth noting that this power is not for its own sake or for displays of wonder-working; it is "for all endurance and patience." The ability to face trials, distractions, and opposition in faithfulness requires more than a survivor instinct or stoic fortitude. Divine resources are needed; it is no accident that patience or long-suffering, which will be mentioned again in the paraenesis in 3:12, is depicted as a fruit of the divine Spirit in Gal 5:22.

The fourth and final participial clause indicates that the life worthy of the Lord, which the writer has requested in his prayer for the readers, will be marked by thankfulness and joy. Joy, of course, is yet another fruit of the Spirit (Gal 5:22; see also Rom 14:17; 1 Thess 1:6). It is a natural accompaniment to the activity of giving thanks to God, who is designated as Father (cf. v. 3), preparing the way for Christ to be called "his beloved Son" in the following verse. Thankfulness to God for all that God has done for believers in Christ is clearly one of the most essential Christian qualities for this writer; he will call for it again and again in his exhortations (see 2:7; 3:15, 17; 4:2). It is possible that this emphasis is made because thankfulness and joy were in short supply in the philosophy, with its severe ascetic regulations (see 2:20-23). The writer's own extended thanksgiving, within which this explicit mention of thankfulness occurs, can be seen as his modeling of the virtue he wishes to see in others.

Three activities of the Father that provide cause for believers' thanksgiving will be specified. The most immediate, in the relative clause that completes v. 12, is that God has qualified them "to share in the inheritance of the saints in light." In the Jewish Scriptures the inheritance of God's holy people was primarily the promised land. In fact, the two terms used together here in Colossians, μερίς (*meris*, "share" or "portion") and κλῆρος (*klēros*, "inheritance"), are frequently used together in the LXX with reference to the land (e.g., Deut 10:9; 32:9; Josh 19:9). But Yahweh as the source of salvation could also be seen as the portion of the people's inheritance (Ps 15:5 LXX). Here in Colossians, too, the inheritance of God's people moves beyond the terrestrial and is rather the transcendent realm of light. Light has connotations both of transcendent splendor, the environment of the heavenly world, and of holiness, ethical purity.

In the Qumran literature, with its dualism between light and darkness, the concept of inheritance had already been developed in this direction, so that the portion of God is that of light[52] and God's people inherit or share the portion of the Holy Ones,[53] the angels in heaven. Some have suggested that ἅγιοι (*hagioi*, "holy ones") in v. 12 should also be taken as "angels." With an eye on the rival teaching's veneration of angels (see 2:18), the writer would then be claiming that God had already provided for communion with the angels. Elsewhere in the Pauline writings "holy ones" can include angels in its range of meanings when the context requires (see 1 Thess 3:13; 2 Thess 1:7, 10), but ordinarily it is employed to refer to the saints—that is, to Christian believers. Since the writer uses the term "angels" in 2:18, if he had wanted the readers to find a reference to angels here, he would more likely have used the same term, particularly when he has just previously employed "holy ones" to designate believers as God's holy people in 1:2, 4 and will take up the same term in a similar way in 1:26 (see also 3:12). The thought here, then, is that God has enabled the readers to share with all God's chosen people an inheritance in the realm of light. It is a functional equivalent to the notion that their hope is already secure in heaven (1:5). Later in the paraenesis a future aspect to the inheritance will emerge, as in 3:24 it is viewed as still to be conferred; but here in the context of the thanksgiving the emphasis is that God has already enabled believers to share in the present in this inheritance in the realm of light.

Even if this reading does not present quite as striking and direct a counterpart to the philosophy, the latter may still be in view in two ways. First, if the realm of light has a transcendent heavenly dimension, then again the readers are being reminded that they already have the access to heaven that was of such concern for the rival teachers. Second, the reminder is underlined by the emphasis that God has already qualified them for access to heaven, in which case there can be no reason at all for allowing anyone to disqualify them by insisting on fasting, "the worship of angels," and visionary experience (2:18) as necessary for such access.

52. 1QM 13.5.
53. 1QS 11.7-8; 1QH 11.7.

REFLECTIONS

The thanksgiving (1:3-8) and intercessory prayer (1:9-12) are not actual prayers but *reports* that now serve conventional epistolary functions. They do not, therefore, provide a warrant for using public prayer to preach or to direct subtle messages to the congregation. It is, however, essential to the effectiveness of teaching and preaching that the congregation sense that the exhortations addressed to them come from someone who has identified with their needs, who is genuinely appreciative of their faith and commitment, who prays thankfully and faithfully for them, and whose prayers are directed toward growth and enrichment in their journey with God.

1. The prominence of hope in the thanksgiving is a reminder of the security of a salvation that is centered in Christ in the transcendent realm; it is not dependent on the feelings or efforts of humanity, not confined to the perspectives of this world. Later it will also be stressed that it is possible to shift away from this hope (1:23) and that what is distinctive about such salvation, as compared to the rival teaching, is that it is worked out within the structures of everyday life in this world (3:1–4:1). The tensions between assurance and the necessity of continuing in the faith and between transcendent and immanent aspects of salvation are vital parts of the preacher's theological framework. The discernment of knowing when to emphasize which pole, when to reassure or when to challenge, is an essential skill in the preacher's pastoral repertoire. Here, in the context of thanksgiving and as an antidote to any suggestion that the gospel message is inadequate, the emphasis on assurance and on the transcendent security of believers' hope in the exalted Christ is the writer's initial and appropriate pastoral stress.

2. There is a host of different ways in which contemporary believers can be tempted to feel that the basic gospel message is inadequate and that it needs to be supplemented by additional religious rites or disciplines, more sophisticated knowledge, or some compelling experience, if they are to be accepted by God or to reach their full potential as human beings. They need to hear that, although the gospel has riches that are yet to be fathomed and implications for all areas of life that are yet to be explored, there is no inadequacy about its basic message. They need to know that the hope that is at the heart of it and inseparable from the person of Christ is secure and that such hope is the potent incentive to a life of faith and love.

3. In a worthy desire to avoid abstraction and to do justice to the concreteness of their lives, perhaps too often Christians' prayers for one another remain at the level of immediate physical needs or specific direction in life or problems of relationships. Sometimes this may be because we wait to pray for others until they have a problem that requires attention or because we have a view of God in which God's primary role is to "fix" things for us. Sometimes such praying also unconsciously reveals our preoccupation with empirical reality and masks doubts about the reality of such dimensions to life as growth in the knowledge of God, spiritual wisdom, or divine empowering for patient and joyful endurance. These reports of prayers of thanksgiving and intercession teach us about holding individuals and communities before God in the whole of their relationship with God and, therefore, not being afraid to pray, both in thankfulness and in petition, in this large and more general way about their equally real spiritual well-being and progress.

4. What is striking in this initial section, even allowing for the hyperbole it contains, is the writer's confidence about the dynamic force and the progress of the gospel. Without such a perspective there can be, on the one hand, a lack of expectancy about any lives being transformed as a result of one's witness to the gospel. On the other hand, there may be an overreliance on one's own persuasive powers or on the latest communication techniques to produce results. The gospel that preachers are privileged to proclaim has its own inherent power. As Paul put it in Rom 1:16: "I am not ashamed of the gospel; it is the power of God for salvation for everyone who has faith" (NRSV). And the writer of Colossians is confident in his praying that the very dynamic of the gospel is also able to reproduce itself in and shape the lives of believers, as it bears fruit and grows (cf. 1:6 with 1:10).

5. Colossians 1:1-14 appears in Year C of the lectionary cycle paired with Old Testament readings emphasizing justice and Luke's parable of the Samaritan who acts as neighbor to the victim in the ditch. The broader theme can aid reflection on the significance of the discussion in Colossians of the spiritual wisdom and understanding that entail bearing fruit in every good work (1:9-10) and serve as a reminder that such good work will later be elaborated in terms of justice and fairness (4:1). In turn, the distinctive contribution of Colossians to the overall theme might well be seen in its stress on the hope of the gospel as the motivation for the faith and love that find their expression in the pursuit of justice.

COLOSSIANS 1:13-23, THANKSGIVING THROUGH INTRODUCTION, CITATION, AND APPLICATION OF PRAISE OF CHRIST

Colossians 1:13-14, Transitional Introduction to the Praise of Christ

COMMENTARY

These verses continue the reasons for giving thanks to God that the writer had begun to spell out in v. 12. The grounds for connecting them with what follows are (1) that the terminology for those who experience salvation switches from the second-person plural of v. 12, a reference to the readers, to the first-person plural, a reference to believers in general, and (2) that in the last part of v. 13 the focus shifts to Christ, who will be the subject of the hymnic material in vv. 15-20. In their formulations these two verses may already employ traditional confessional statements to lead into the praise of Christ.

Again both scriptural and Qumran references help to illuminate the language of v. 13. "Deliverance" (ῥύεσθαι *hryesthai*) is the LXX terminology (see, e.g., Exod 6:6; 14:30) for Israel's salvation from the Egyptians prior to the possession of the land as an inheritance (see v. 12). The Qumran literature extols God as the deliverer of the faithful from their enemies[54] and talks of the dominion of Belial over the sons of darkness.[55] Now the writer emphasizes as a cause for thanksgiving that God in a new rescue act has delivered believers from the dominion of darkness (and any tyranny of its hostile cosmic powers) and has transferred them into a new sphere of rule—namely, "the kingdom of his beloved Son." The undisputed Pauline letters usually speak of the kingdom of God (e.g., Rom 14:17; 1 Cor 6:9-10; 15:50; Gal 5:21), but in one place they see the kingdom of Christ as representing the present stage of God's rule (1 Cor 15:24-28). Given the mention of light in v. 12 and the contrast here between the dominion of darkness and the kingdom of Christ, the sphere over which the Son rules is to be seen as being bathed in the splendor and holiness of the divine radiance.

It is through their relationship to God's Son that believers experience redemption. This is simply another way of talking about God's rescue act. The term ἀπολύτρωσις (*apolytrōsis*, "redemption") was rare in nonbiblical Greek and is used only once in the LXX, but cognate verbs are employed of the divine act of deliverance or liberation from Egypt (Deut 7:8; 9:26; 13:5; 15:15; 24:18). Connotations of a ransom payment for release should be read into this term only if the context warrants it, and there are no explicit indications of such a force here. Since "the forgiveness of sins" is in apposition to redemption, this phrase depicts the primary way in which believers experience their liberation at present. They can be assured of a restored relationship with God in which they are freed from guilt and their offenses against God are no longer held against them.

Forgiveness will be mentioned again in 2:13, this time in connection with the term "trespasses" (παραπτώματα *paraptōmata*) instead of "sins" (ἁμαρτίαι *hamartiai*), in the context of the writer's interaction with the philosophy. The stress on what God has already done in releasing believers from the dominion of darkness and on their already having forgiveness may well be meant to reinforce for the readers that nothing more needs to be done to appease hostile powers of darkness, who can have no hold over them through their sinful deeds. The traditional formulations may also have baptismal associations. "Beloved Son" was the designation given Christ at his baptism (see Mark 1:11 par.), the forgiveness of sins was closely associated with baptism (e.g., Acts 2:38), and the

---

54. 1QH 2.35.
55. 1QS 1.18, 23-24; 1QM 14.9.

notion of a decisive transfer from one realm to another is also a baptismal theme (see Rom 6:1-11). Baptismal motivation is clearly at work later in chaps. 2–3 with the explicit mention of baptism in 2:12 and the employment of the language of dying and rising with Christ and putting off the old person and putting on the new. An allusion to baptism is a further effective means of recalling the significant change of status that the readers continually need to appropriate. (See Reflections at 1:21-23.)

Colossians 1:15-20, Citation of Hymnic Material in Praise of Christ

COMMENTARY

In its present form in the thanksgiving, the citation of the original hymn with its modifications falls into two parts: 1:15-17, dealing with Christ's role in the sphere of creation, and 1:18-20, dealing with his role in the sphere of redemption.

1:15-17. Christ is the one who supremely makes the invisible God visible. As "the image of the invisible God," he is the manifestation of the divine in the world of humans. This very first assertion about Christ draws our attention to the dynamic nature of the relation between the spheres of redemption and creation that produced the formulation of the hymn as a whole. Although the first part of the hymn speaks of Christ's agency in creation, it is what was first believed about his role in redemption that enabled early believers to make claims about his role in creation. In 1 Cor 15:49 and 2 Cor 4:4 Paul had used the term "image" (εἰκών *eikōn*) for the resurrected and exalted Christ, who as the last Adam now represented humanity as God had always intended it to be. This notion was then pushed back as far as it could go. If the resurrected Christ was the supreme expression of the image of God, then he must always have been so. This creates the paradox that the one who can be described in Adamic language (cf. Gen 1:27) can also be held to have existed before Adam and to have been on the side of the Creator as well as on the side of the creation. The sort of language that had been employed of Wisdom in Wis 7:26 ("she is a reflection of eternal light, a spotless mirror of the working of God, and an image of his goodness," NRSV) becomes a resource for expressing this belief about the status of Christ in God's purposes.

Wisdom could be spoken of in Proverbs as the beginning of God's work—the first of God's acts—and in Philo as firstborn.[56] Here in v. 15*b* Christ is similarly seen as "the firstborn of all creation." The term πρωτότοκος (*prōtotokos*) was employed frequently in the LXX, mostly in genealogical and historical contexts, to indicate not simply temporal priority but sovereignty of rank (e.g., Ps 89:27). Of course, if the term were taken simply in its strict temporal sense, it would make Christ the first of God's creatures, as in later christological debates the Arians held. In reply, Athanasius was quick to point out that the next lines of the passage in v. 16, with their assertion that all things were created in and through Christ, contradict such an interpretation: "But if all the creatures were created in him, he is other than the creatures, and he is not a creature, but the creator of the creatures."[57] At this early stage of christological reflection, such issues were not in view; no problem would have been contemplated in holding that, like Wisdom as God immanent in creation, Christ was both sovereign and first within creation and the divine agent of creation.

The comprehensive scope of Christ's agency in creation is stressed in v. 16. Twice it is asserted that "all things" were created in or through him. Both parts of the cosmos, the heavenly and invisible sphere as well as the earthly and visible realm, are included in this scope. To underline the significance of such an assertion made in worship, the writer spells out that the invisible things created in Christ include the cosmic powers, to

---

56. Prov 8:22; Philo *Questions and Answers on Genesis* 4.97.
57. Athanasius *Orations Against the Arians* II.62.

which some would give too much deference (see 2:10, 15).[58] This language about the cosmic powers can be traced to Jewish belief in angelic beings. Each of the four representative names here—thrones, dominions, rulers, powers—is mentioned in *2 Enoch* 20–22, where in the seventh heaven angels are set in rank (see also 2 Macc 3:24; *1 Enoch* 61:10; *T. Levi* 3). In the context of creation the powers are to be thought of as benign, but in v. 20 they are seen as part of the "all things" in need of reconciliation, and in the later references in the letter, as hostile and threatening to God's purposes in Christ and the well-being of believers. In v. 16 the thought is that if such powers were originally created in Christ and for him, then they are certainly in principle subject to him and should have no threatening hold over his people.

Whereas 1 Cor 8:6 could depict Christ as the medium and agent of all things and God as the goal, Col 1:16 goes further in its christological reflection so that here Christ can be said to be the goal of creation also. This addition of "to him" or "for him" also goes beyond what is said of Wisdom; thus it may reflect the hymn's understanding of Christ's role in redemption that it adds to the conceptuality of the wisdom tradition. It asserts that the creation of all things was for Christ and to enhance his glory. Something of what is intended by portraying Christ as the goal of creation will be developed in v. 20 in terms of reconciliation. Verse 17 is itself a summing-up of the two previous verses. Because of his agency in creating all things, Christ, again like Wisdom (cf. Sir 1:4), can be said to be before all things and, like the Logos (cf. Sir 43:26), the one in whom all things cohere. The one who, because of his preexistence, helped to bring all things into being is also the one who continues to sustain the whole creation and prevent its disintegration into chaos.

1:18-20. The hymnic material moves more explicitly to the realm of redemption by the addition of the term "the church" to what may originally have been simply a statement about the relationship of Christ to the cosmos as his body. In the original, Christ, like the Logos, would have been thought of as pervading with his presence and as ruling the cosmos. Now, in its present form in the thanksgiving, the praise of Christ's supremacy over the church as his body matches the earlier praise of his supremacy over the realm of creation.

It is easy, but probably mistaken, to see head and body as two parts of one anatomical image in which the head contains the brain that directs the body's nervous system. The two terms "head" and "body" had previously been employed separately by Paul, "head" for authoritative origin and "body" for the organic interdependence of believers in the church. They now come together for the first time in the Pauline corpus, and it is probably Hellenistic views about the cosmos that have provided the catalyst for the combination. As the excursus explains, the body was used as an image for the cosmos, and in that context "head" sometimes occurred with it (see Excursus: "The Existence, Structure, and Background of a Possible Hymn," 601-5). In an Orphic fragment, Zeus is seen as head of the cosmos, pervading it with his rule as it lies in his mighty body.[59] Philo used "head" for the Logos as the ruling principle of the cosmos as the body.[60] So this background of cosmic speculation and Paul's use of "body" for the church made it natural for the two separate images to be brought together for Christ's relation to believers. The term "head" (κεφαλή *kephalē*) denotes Christ's rule or authority over the church as his body. The LXX often employs this term to translate the Hebrew ראש (*rōš*) in the sense of "ruler" or "leader" (e.g., Deut 28:13; Judg 11:11; 2 Sam 22:44), and in the use of the term connotations of authority were often connected with those of origin or beginning, since the origin was held to be determinative for what followed from it.[61] Paul had employed *kephalē* in this sense in 1 Cor 11:3, and it will be used with this force again by the writer of Colossians in 2:10.

The transfer of "body" imagery from the cosmos to the church to indicate that the church is Christ's true body was natural enough, since Paul had already used this

---

58. Contra W. Wink, *Naming the Powers* (Philadelphia: Fortress, 1984) 11, 64-67, the powers are best understood not as including both things visible and things invisible but as an elaboration of the latter.

59. Fragment 168.
60. Philo *On Dreams* 1.128; See also Philo *Questions and Answers on Exodus* 2.117.
61. S. Bedale, "The Meaning of κεφαλή in the Pauline Epistles," *JTS* 5 (1954) 211-15.

imagery in connection with local groups of believers in Rom 12:4-5 and 1 Cor 10:16-17; 12:12-27. In this context, in v. 18, as later in v. 24, the reference is, however, to the universal church. In both passages, "body" (σῶμα *sōma*) is explained by the addition of the term "church" (ἐκκλησία *ekklēsia*). Paul had used the latter term most frequently for the actual gathering of a group of local Christians or for the local group itself, and Colossians retains that usage in 4:15-16. But in a number of places Paul appeared to indicate an entity broader than the merely local congregation (see 1 Cor 10:32; 12:28; 15:9; Gal 1:13; Phil 3:6), and here in vv. 18 and 24 it is certainly the universal church that is in view.

In v. 18*b* Christ is called "the beginning." Although this term had been used in Prov 8:22 LXX for Wisdom's position in the creation, here the following phrase "firstborn from the dead" makes clear that it is Christ's position in the new creation that is signified. Like both "head" and "firstborn," "beginning" (ἀρχή *archē*) had two linked connotations: primacy in the temporal sense and primacy with reference to authority or sovereignty. The clarifying phrase "firstborn from the dead," while providing a parallel with the earlier section through the designation "firstborn," indicates that Christ is to be ranked supreme in the new creation on account of his temporal primacy in the resurrection from the dead. As in the undisputed Pauline letters, Christ's resurrection makes him the firstborn among many brothers and sisters (Rom 8:29), the firstfruits of those who have died (1 Cor 15:20, 23). His resurrection is determinative for all those who will follow. If Christ has supremacy in the realm of new creation through his resurrection, then, the writer adds in v. 18*c* in an effort to ensure that his reason for citing this material will not be missed, God's undisputed purpose must be that Christ should have preeminence in everything.

Christ's preeminence is not simply because he happened to be one individual whom God raised ahead of time but because he is a particular individual with a unique relation to God and a unique role in God's work of reconciliation. This is made clear in the following two verses, introduced by "because." In Christ "all the fullness was pleased to dwell." Although the Greek text does not mention God in v. 19, both the NIV and the NRSV in their different ways relate the fullness to God in an interpretative gloss. Such an interpretation of the writer's meaning is surely justified by 2:9, since there he asserts that in Christ "the whole fullness of deity dwells bodily." It is also significant that the verb "was pleased" (εὐδόκησεν *eudokēsen*) would ordinarily be expected to have a personal subject. This, too, suggests that "all the fullness" stands for God in all the divine fullness. In the Jewish Scriptures God can be depicted as actively filling all things (e.g., Jer 23:24), so that outside of God nothing has existence. To say that this fullness of God dwells in Christ, then, is most likely to mean that just as there is nothing in heaven or earth that is outside the divine presence and power, so also there is nothing outside the scope of Christ's presence and power, because Christ now sums up all that God is in interaction with the cosmos.

Again speculation about Wisdom may have contributed to the language of the hymn. The writer of Wis 1:6-7 speaks of Wisdom as a kindly spirit and asserts that this spirit of the Lord has filled the world, using the verb "to fill" rather than the noun "fullness." The noun does occur in later syncretistic literature with a gnosticizing tendency, such as in *Corpus Hermeticum* 6.4; 16.3 and the *Odes of Solomon* 7.11, 13; 16.3; 17.7; 36.1-2. It also plays an important role in second-century Gnostic writings, where it denotes the totality of the emanations that come from God and represents the sphere of perfection and salvation in closest proximity to God and opposed to the lower material realm (e.g., *The Gospel of Truth*) 16.34-36, 41; *Tripartite Tractate* 70, 75, 77, 78, 80). It is possible that the writer of Colossians picks up on the term again in 2:9-10, because it played a part in the philosophy against which he warns, where it had a significance somewhere within the development between Hellenistic Jewish cosmic speculation and gnostic usage. It is not enough to dismiss this possibility by asserting that the use of the term here would have encouraged the very syncretism to which the writer is opposed.[62] The writer is quite capable of taking up the language and patterns of thought of opposing teaching and employing

---

62. Contra Dunn, *The Epistles to the Colossians and to Philemon*, 100-101.

them in line with his own understanding of the gospel. If the philosophy was advocating ascetic techniques and special knowledge gained through visions to placate the powers and to participate in the divine fullness, then this first reference in the hymnic material would reinforce that such fullness is not to be found outside of Christ. Since the divine fullness has taken up residence in him, it is not to be conceived as inherently inimical to the physical realm.

If we ask when the divine fullness was pleased to dwell in Christ, then the context presents us with two main options. Given the use of the same verb, "to be pleased," in the account of Jesus' baptism with its descent of the Spirit (cf. Mark 1:9-11), the designation "beloved Son" in v. 13 and the background of Wis 1:6-7, with its focus on the spirit of the Lord, it could be argued that baptism is the point at which the divine fullness indwelt Christ.[63] On the other hand, this verse is most immediately a supporting statement for a previous assertion that began with a reference to Christ's status by virtue of the resurrection, and so the resurrection might well have been intended as the point at which the divine fullness became resident in Christ (see Rom 1:4).[64] But to ask the question about a particular point in time may be pushing the text for information it was not intended to give. The claim may simply be a more general one: In Christ's existence as a whole, culminating, of course, in his death and resurrection, the divine fullness can be seen to have been displayed.

The second half of the supporting statement begun in v. 19 lends credence to this more general interpretation, since it brings into view, in connection with the indwelling of the divine fullness, the death of Christ. The subject and main verb of v. 20a carry over from the previous verse. It is God in the divine fullness who was pleased, at the same time as taking up residence in Christ, to reconcile all things through Christ. The implication of such a statement is, of course, that at some stage the cosmos with its original harmony, as God had created it in Christ, was put out of joint, so that it became in need of being restored to harmony through Christ. The compound form of the verb ἀποκαταλλάσσω (*apokatallassō*, "to reconcile") is employed here and in v. 22; it is used elsewhere in the NT only in Eph 2:16 in dependence on this passage. The simpler καταλλάσσω (*katallassō*) is found in Rom 5:10 and 2 Cor 5:18 for the reconciliation of humanity to God. It is preferable to take "to/for him" in v. 20a as a reference to Christ rather than to God (in contrast to both the NIV and the NRSV). In this way, the parallel with v. 16 is maintained, so that, there as here in vv. 19-20, the activity described is "in him," "through him," and "for him." And just as Christ is the means and the goal of creation, so also he is the means and the goal of reconciliation.

The verb "to be reconciled" (*apokatallassō*) is usually followed by the dative of the person to whom one is reconciled. The use here of εἰς (*eis*, "to" or "for") with the accusative reinforces the view that there has been a deliberate attempt to parallel the syntax of the earlier part of the hymnic material and that Christ is the goal of the reconciliation of all things rather than Christ or God being the one to whom all things are reconciled. The parallel clause in v. 20b explains that the reconciliation through Christ was a "making of peace" (εἰρηνοποιέω *eirēnopoieō*) through him. This is the only instance in the NT of the compound verb, and the masculine form of the participle confirms that the writer intended "all the fullness" to be taken in a personal sense. The enmity that had invaded the creation, reflected in the activity of hostile cosmic powers, is seen as having been overcome through Christ and in particular through the historical event of his death. The combination of images for that death in the phrase "through the blood of his cross" is not found in the undisputed Pauline letters. Paul employed the two images separately: "blood," to denote Christ's violently taken life in contexts where the sacrificial nature of his death was to the fore, and "cross," the more general image, to convey the ignominy of this death by Roman execution. The bringing together of the two in this context certainly roots Christ's cosmic reconciliation in a Pauline view of his death, but it may well indicate the work of a later disciple drawing on Paul's thought.

---

63. Pokorny, *Colossians*, 84-86.
64. A. J. M. Wedderburn, *The Theology of the Later Pauline Letters* (New York: Cambridge University Press, 1993) 32-33.

Just as the first part of the hymnic material underscored that the "all things" created through Christ were "in heaven and on earth, things visible and things invisible," so also the final part (v. 20c) stresses that the "all things" reconciled through him are to be understood equally comprehensively, "whether things on earth or things in heaven." Appropriately, because of its final position, the emphasis falls on the heavenly things, the cosmic powers added in explanation in v. 16c, since it is these powers in particular that the readers need to know have already been taken care of in God's purposes in Christ. Such powers do not require appeasing or reconciling by any special practices the readers may be urged to undertake themselves.

The immediate application of this passage in praise of Christ will be examined in the Commentary on 1:21-23, but it is worth noting at this point that there will be further application in the letter as a whole. It is a commonplace that the thanksgiving sections of Pauline letters frequently indicate concerns that will be dealt with later in the letter, but the distinctive hymnic material within the thanksgiving of Colossians has its own particular role in accomplishing this. Paul's ministry is treated in relation to Christ's body, the church, in v. 24 (see also v. 18). The notion that in Christ are all the treasures of wisdom (2:3) builds on the hymn's portrayal of Christ as embodying all the attributes of Wisdom. Christ's relation to the cosmic powers, his being indwelt by the fullness of deity, and his headship, all introduced in the hymn, are elaborated in 2:9-10, while 2:15 is a further interpretation of what took place between Christ and the powers on the cross (cf. 1:20). The head/body imagery of 1:18 is developed in 2:19, and the assertion that Christ is all and in all in 3:11 correlates with the cosmic conceptuality of the hymn and draws out its significance for the new creation.

In this way Col 1:15-20 functions as an effective part of the writer's rhetorical strategy in the exordium, constituted by the thanksgiving section. It establishes a positive relationship with the readers through the citation of material that they may well have in common with the writer; it encourages them to assent to its praise as they are carried along by its rhythms and flow; and it makes them conducive to accepting the subsequent message that has made the perspective of the hymn its foundation. (See Reflections at 1:21-23.)

❖ ❖ ❖ ❖

EXCURSUS: THE EXISTENCE, STRUCTURE, AND BACKGROUND OF A POSSIBLE HYMN

THE EXISTENCE OF A POSSIBLE HYMN

There is a major scholarly debate regarding these verses, and voluminous secondary literature has been written about their hymnic nature. Some of the questions raised are these: Is there a hymn to be found here at all? If so, did the writer compose it? Or was it a preformed hymn that he has used? In either case, what would be its background; from what sphere of thought does it come? What was its structure? If it was preformed, has the writer made some additions? If so, are these additions simply modifications, or are they corrections of the original? It is easy to become impatient with the intricacies and sometimes speculative nature of these discussions. Many of the questions admit of no definite solution. Yet, since most of them do arise from the text and even tentative conclusions about them affect one's exegesis, a brief summary of the issues is in order.

Colossians 1:15-20 forms a discrete unit within the thanksgiving. In contrast to both the preceding and the following contexts, which are marked by the number of personal pronouns, it contains no references to believers or to the readers in particular.

EXCURSUS: THE EXISTENCE, STRUCTURE, AND BACKGROUND OF A POSSIBLE HYMN

The relative pronoun ὅς (*hos*, "who"), which begins vv. 15, 18*b*, is not a natural part of the context. It has all the indications, as in 1 Tim 3:16, of being part of preformed material that may have been preceded by some such words as "We praise our Lord Jesus Christ. . . ." There is the repetition both of propositions with ἐστιν (*estin*, "is"), which provide a series of affirmations about Christ, and of various forms of πᾶς (*pas*, "all"), which emphasize the universal scope of Christ's activities. The designation "firstborn" occurs in vv. 15*b* and 18*b*. The notion of the creation of all things in relation to Christ's agency is found in both v. 16*a* and v. 16*d*. Verse 16 also contains the chiastically arranged phrases "in heaven and on earth, things visible and things invisible," while v. 20*c* speaks of "things on earth or things in heaven" (NIV). In vv. 17-18*a* there occur side by side two clauses that begin "and he is. . . ." The focused and elaborate description of Christ, the carefully constructed nature of the passage, the parallel correspondences in its parts, the recurrence of words and phrases in the same sequence, and the use of terms not found elsewhere in the Pauline corpus are all more natural in a liturgical formulation or hymn than in the free-flowing style of a letter, whose writer waxes poetical at this point. It is not a matter of conformity to an obvious Greek hymnic form. "The rhythm and pattern come, as in the Psalms which were also no doubt in the liturgical stock of Pauline churches, from verbal repetition and the reiteration of ideas in regular order."[65] Colossians 3:16 will speak about the singing of psalms, hymns, and spiritual songs, so it would not be at all strange if in the course of the letter the writer had recourse to quoting, either exactly or with some additional words of application, one such hymn that might also be known in the worship life of the addressees.

THE STRUCTURE OF AN ORIGINAL HYMN

How was the hymn structured? Were there one, two, or three strophes? Has the letter's writer made his own additions to the hymn? Scholars have developed no clear consensus about the number or content of the strophes in an original hymn, and so I shall set out here what appears to be the most plausible reconstruction, followed by some justifications for particular aspects.

Strophe I
who is the image of the invisible God
    the firstborn of all creation,
for in him were created all things
    in heaven and on earth
    things visible and invisible
[whether thrones or dominions or rulers or powers]—addition (i)

Transitional Strophe II
    all things were created through him and for him
and he himself is before all things
    and all things hold together in him
and he himself is the head of the body [the church]—addition (ii)

Strophe III
who is the beginning
    the firstborn from the dead
[so that he himself might have preeminence in all things]—addition (iii)
    for in him all the fullness was pleased to dwell

---

65. J. L. Houlden, *Paul's Letters from Prison* (Harmondsworth: Penguin, 1970) 157.

EXCURSUS: THE EXISTENCE, STRUCTURE, AND BACKGROUND OF A POSSIBLE HYMN

and through him to reconcile all things for him,
   making peace through him
   [through the blood of his cross]—addition (iv) after "making peace"
whether things on earth or things in heaven

As can be seen, this reconstruction proposes that some additions have been made to an original hymn. Some have argued that if additions were made to an original, then omissions could also have been made.[66] This is possible, but it does not entail the abandonment of any reconstruction. It only serves as a reminder that all such reconstruction is hypothetical and that we are working with probabilities, not certainties.

The lines beginning "who is . . ." followed by a second line designating Christ as firstborn, first in the realm of creation and then in the realm of redemption, mark the start of two separate strophes. Some scholars are satisfied with two strophes of quite different lengths. But it appears more likely that vv. 16d-18a, with the repetition of the creation theme, the two sets of parallelisms, and the description of Christ in the last line as the head of the body, form a transitional strophe that prepares for the move to the realm of redemption in the final section of the hymnic material. Unlike Martin's proposal,[67] this reconstruction includes "things visible and things invisible" as the last line of the original first strophe because of the chiasm with the preceding line and the repetition at the end of the last line of the term "invisible" (ἀόρατος *aoratos*) from the end of the first line. Again, unlike Martin's reconstruction,[68] here the clause "making peace through him" is included in the hymn, since the verb is a *hapax legomenon* in the Pauline corpus and has a fitting parallel in the previous line. The phrase "whether things on earth or things in heaven" is retained rather than being treated as an interpretive gloss, since it has a parallel in the first strophe, where the order is reversed.

The writer's first addition, "whether thrones or dominions or rulers or powers," spells out that the reference to Christ's agency in the creation of all created things includes the very cosmic powers some of the readers are being induced to see as a threat to their well-being (cf. 2:10, 15). The term σῶμα (*sōma*, "body") in v. 18a could have originally been, or could have been understood as, a reference to the cosmos, which was common in Philo[69] and Hellenistic Judaism; and so in the second addition the writer specifies that he understands Christ's headship as being over the church as the body. Paul had already used body imagery for the local congregation in 1 Corinthians and in Romans, and so in this context it is deemed appropriate to extend its scope to the universal church. Verse 18c, with its final or purpose clause ("so that he himself might have preeminence in all things"), fits awkwardly in terms of style; one would have expected a simple assertion or a participial clause in conformity with the rest of the material. It appears, therefore, to be a third addition, in which the writer wishes to elaborate on the significance of Christ's resurrection for the situation of the addressees. Its force is that, since Christ has preeminence in the realm of the resurrection as well as in the realm of creation, he was meant to have preeminence in everything, including by necessary implication their own perspective on the cosmos and its powers. The fourth addition ("through the blood of his cross," v. 20b) is meant to ensure that the reconciling work of Christ, though cosmic in scope, is not thought of in a speculative way but is anchored in the historical event of the crucifixion. The somewhat awkward insertion of this phrase before "through him" would also account for the uncertainty about the originality of the latter in the textual tradition.[70]

---

66. E.g., N. T. Wright, "Poetry and Theology in Colossians 1.15-20," *NTS* 36 (1990) 444-68.
67. R. P. Martin, *Colossians and Philemon*, NCB (Greenwood, S.C.: Attic, 1974) 56.
68. Martin, *Colossians and Philemon*, 60-61.
69. E.g., Philo *On Dreams* 1.128.
70. It is found, e.g., in P[46] ℵ A C Dc Ψ 048 33 181 326 syr[p, h] cop[bo] goth Chrysostom Theodoret and omitted in e.g., B D* G I 81 104 436 it[ar, c, d] vg cop[sa] arm eth Origen Ambrosiaster. The inclusion of the phrase constitutes the more difficult reading and, therefore, favors its originality.

EXCURSUS: THE EXISTENCE, STRUCTURE, AND BACKGROUND OF A POSSIBLE HYMN

THE HYMN'S BACKGROUND

Gnosticism

Käsemann held that, once the additions "of the church" and "through the blood of his cross" were removed, the original hymn no longer displayed any specifically Christian characteristics.[71] It could, in fact, be seen as a pre-Christian gnostic hymn that dealt with the metaphysical and supra-historical drama involving the gnostic redeemer. This hymn had been taken over into Christian usage in a baptismal liturgical reinterpretation and finally was cited by the writer in a refutation of what Käsemann considered to be the gnostic countermovement that provoked the letter. There is irony to this reconstruction, since the hymn had originally come from Gnosticism and was now being employed to refute it. But there is very little to be said in favor of the proposal. Apart from its being extremely doubtful whether one can speak of any clear gnostic redeemer myth in the first century CE, the hymn contains a perspective inimical to Gnosticism—namely, that creation and redemption are both related to the same source or agency. The Christian character of the phrase "the firstborn from the dead" cannot be doubted and appears to wreck any idea of a pre-Christian hymn. In addition, the repeated references to the creation of all things and the use of the verb "to be pleased," which was employed in the LXX for God's electing decree, recall the thought and language of the Jewish Scriptures.

Rabbinic Exegesis of Genesis 1:1

The influence of Jewish Scriptures is emphasized by Burney, followed by Davies and Caird, and more recently modified by Wright.[72] Burney attempts to demonstrate that the origin of the hymnic material lay in a typically Jewish interpretive exegesis of Gen 1:1 and its first Hebrew word, בראשית (*bĕrē'šît*, "in the beginning"), which was made possible by the use of ראשית (*rē'šît*, "beginning") in connection with Wisdom in Prov 8:22. The Hebrew of the latter text could be read as "the LORD created me at the beginning of his work" or "the LORD created me as the beginning of his work." Burney sees Col 1:15*b* ("the firstborn of all creation") as an allusion to Prov 8:22 and then claims that everything that might be said about Wisdom on the basis of Gen 1:1 is here applied to Christ. He asserts that this sort of connection would be obvious to a rabbinic scholar and that in Colossians 1 "we have an elaborate exposition of Bereshith in Gen 1:1 in the Rabbinic manner."[73] His proposal plays on the range of connotations of both the Hebrew preposition ב (*bĕ*) and the noun *rē'šît* and can be set out in summary form as follows:[74]

> *Bereshith* = in *reshith*—"in him all things were created" (1:16*a*)
> *Bereshith* = by *reshith*—"all things were created by or through him" (1:16*d*)
> *Bereshith* = into *reshith*—"all things were created to or for him" (1:16*d*)
> *Reshith* = beginning—"he himself is before all things" (1:17*a*)
> *Reshith* = sum total—"all things hold together in him" (1:17*b*)
> *Reshith* = head—"he is the head of the body" (1:18*a*)
> *Reshith* = firstfruits—"he is the beginning, the firstborn from the dead" (1:18*b*)
> Conclusion—Christ fulfills every meaning that may be extracted from reshith—
> "so that he himself might have preeminence in everything" (1:18*c*).

---

71. E. Käsemann, "A Primitive Christian Baptismal Liturgy," in *Essays on New Testament Themes* (London: SCM, 1964) 149-68.
72. C. F. Burney, "Christ as the ΑΡΧΗ of Creation," *JTS* 27 (1926) 160-77; W. D. Davies, *Paul and Rabbinic Judaism*, 3rd ed. (Philadelphia: Fortress, 1980) 150-52; G. B. Caird, *Paul's Letters from Prison* (Oxford: Clarendon, 1976) 175; Wright, "Poetry and Theology in Colossians 1.15-20," 444-68.
73. Burney, "Christ as the ΑΡΧΗ of Creation," 174-75.
74. Burney, "Christ as the ΑΡΧΗ of Creation," 176.

Excursus: The Existence, Structure, and Background of a Possible Hymn

Burney's proposal is ingenious, and although some have dismissed it as too ingenious, it might account for some of the process of thought that led up to the composition of part of the original hymn. It is strange that, despite its title, Burney's article actually underplays the significance of ἀρχή (*archē*, "beginning"), which would be the most natural correspondence to *rē'šît* as "beginning" in 1:15-20 and is in fact the term used to translate it in the LXX of Prov 8:22. This is a failure that Wright's modification of the proposal attempts to remedy.[75] The proposal provides, however, no explanation for the last part of the hymn, 1:19-20. And whether any of the Gentile Christians who made up the majority of the letter's addressees (3:5-7) would have caught or were meant to have caught any of these subtleties of Hebrew exegesis in a hymn composed in Greek must be extremely doubtful.

The Wisdom Tradition in Hellenistic Judaism

What cannot be doubted is that Burney was right to see the figure of Wisdom lying behind the hymn's depiction of Christ. Its language and thought resemble Jewish Hellenistic speculation not only about Wisdom but also about the Logos. Both Wisdom (Wis 7:26)[76] and the Logos[77] are spoken of as the image of God. Through Wisdom, God created all things (Prov 8:27-31; Sir 24:5-6).[78] Wisdom is depicted as firstborn,[79] as is the Logos.[80] The Logos (Sir 43:26) holds all things together,[81] and Wisdom is the beginning of God's ways (Prov 8:22). In Philo, the Logos is also head of the body, the world of souls,[82] announces God's peace,[83] and mediates between the disparate elements of the universe.[84] It looks very much, then, as if the Hellenistic Jewish composer of the hymn has taken the various attributes of Wisdom or the Logos and applied them to Christ in his relation to the cosmos. The hymn in its original form presupposes some major disruption in cosmic harmony and, therefore, sees Christ not only, like Wisdom or the Logos, as the divine agent in creation but also now as the divine agent in reconciliation, restoring harmony to the cosmos.

---

75. Wright, "Poetry and Theology in Colossians 1.15-20," 444-68.
76. See also Philo *Allegorical Interpretation* 1.43.
77. See Philo *On the Confusion of Tongues* 147; *The Special Laws* 1.81.
78. See also Philo *On Flight and Finding* 109.
79. Philo *Questions and Answers on Genesis* 4.97.
80. Philo *On the Confusion of Tongues* 146; *On Husbandry* 151; *On Dreams* 1.215.
81. Philo *On Flight and Finding* 112; *Who Is the Heir of Divine Things?* 23.
82. Philo *On Dreams* 1.128.
83. Philo *Who Is the Heir of Divine Things?* 206.
84. Philo *Concerning Noah's Work as a Planter* 10.

Colossians 1:21-23, Application of Praise of Christ

COMMENTARY

In one lengthy sentence the writer begins relating and applying the content of the hymn in praise of Christ to the situation of his readers and in so doing sets out the agenda for the rest of the letter. Addressing the readers directly, the writer employs the schema "once . . . now" to draw a contrast between their pre-Christian past and their Christian present (vv. 21-22a). This was not uncommon in the NT letters and probably originated in early Christian preaching. The people being addressed, too, have experienced the pattern of redemption depicted in the hymn, because at one time they were in a state of alienation, characterized by a hostile attitude accompanied by evil deeds, but now have been reconciled by God.[85] Such a description most appropriately fits a predominantly Gentile readership. Their reconciliation, as part of the cosmic reconciliation achieved by Christ, also took place through his death. As in the previous description of that death in v. 20, the writer again brings together two terms that appear separately in the undisputed Pauline letters, this time "body" (σῶμα *sōma*) and "flesh" (σάρξ *sarx*). While distinguishing this mention of the body from the earlier one with reference to the church, the combination stresses the physicality of Christ's death and, by making clear that the physical body of Christ was the means of reconciliation, may well have been meant to contrast this view of redemption with that of the philosophy and its denigration of the physical body (2:23).

The purpose of the reconciliation was to make those formerly alienated from God acceptable to God and to provide those previously characterized by evil actions with a new quality of life before God. "Before him" could be a reference to Christ in line with the earlier "his flesh" in this verse, but if "to be reconciled" is understood as a "divine passive" with God as the implied agent, then it makes sense to view the ultimate arbiter of believers' lives as God also. The verb "to present" (παρίστημι *paristēmi*) could be used in a cultic or legal context, and both images may be in view here, since, of the three accompanying adjectives, the first two have cultic and the third legal connotations. "Holy" (ἅγιος *hagios*) and "without blemish" (ἄμωμος *amōmos*) were employed of sacrificial animals that were consecrated to God and, therefore, had to be without defect (see Exod 29:37-38; Num 6:14; 19:2 LXX); they came to denote also ethical purity (see Pss 14:2; 17:24 LXX). Similarly the third term, ἀνέγκλητος (*anegklētos*), drawn from a judicial setting in which it meant "free from accusation," came also to have the force of "morally blameless" or "irreproachable."

For all the emphasis on the sufficiency and effectiveness of Christ's work of reconciliation, there is now an equal emphasis, no doubt provoked by the letter's occasion, on the readers' responsibility to continue in the faith. The conditional construction translated as "providing that . . ." need not express doubt that they will do so. But it does make clear that cosmic reconciliation is not some automatic process; it works itself out in history in relation to the response of faith, and that response entails not abandoning the content of faith. The definite article before "faith" suggests that it is not simply the attitude of faith that is meant but the teaching about the apostolic gospel, which is mentioned in the next part of the verse (see also 2:7).

The implied exhortation is reiterated through three terms that all make the same point. The readers are to be established or firmly founded; they are to be securely based or steadfast, and they are not to shift away from the content of their faith, whose base or foundation is now described as "the hope promised by the gospel that you heard." This recalls the language of v. 5, where, significantly, hope as the assured reality of salvation was the foundation for faith and love. Again this certain promise of hope is emphasized as the component of the gospel the readers had first heard and to which they must hold fast in the face of any teaching that might attempt to rob them of it. Finally, in v. 23c, in an attempt to underline the validity of this original gospel message, they are reminded of its universality and apostolicity. Echoing v. 6 and its mention of "the whole world," the writer talks of the gospel's being preached to every creature under heaven, again seeing the present Gentile mission as anticipating the completion of the worldwide proclamation and perhaps contrasting this with a teaching that was more local and specialized in its appeal. There then follows the assertion, lending the authority of Paul to the message and to be developed in the following section, that it is this gospel "of which I, Paul, became a servant."

As noted in the Introduction, the three parts of the application of the praise of Christ set the agenda for the rest of the letter—but in reverse order. The role of Paul in proclaiming the gospel (v. 23c) that is announced here

---

85. The NIV and the NRSV translate the aorist active third-person singular form of the verb, which is most widely attested in the manuscript traditions. The aorist passive second-person plural form, however, is the more difficult reading because it does not agree with the second-person plural accusative form of "you" in 1:21a. The latter form also has strong external attestation (P[46] and B) and provides the best explanation for the other variants that arose as an attempt to correct the syntax.

will be taken up in 1:24–2:5, the need to continue in the faith of the gospel the readers have heard (1:23a) will be treated in 2:6–3:4, and the holiness of believers achieved through the work of Christ (1:21-22) will be the subject of the exhortations in 3:5–4:1.

REFLECTIONS

Because this passage is so rich christologically, and yet its way of envisioning Christ may not be immediately comprehensible to contemporary Christians, these reflections will center around the cosmic role of Christ and the reconciliation accomplished in him.

1. Taking for granted the church's long tradition of worshiping Christ as God or becoming preoccupied with questions about the background of the Christ hymn can both, in their different ways, lead to overlooking the staggering claims of its content. For the writer, talk about the cosmic Christ is not about some abstract idea, not about the personified figure of Wisdom. Rather, as he has underscored through the terminology of "blood" and "cross," it is about a crucified person: Jesus. It must have taken a subsequent event of some magnitude to bring about the identification of a near contemporary, who had been ignominiously executed, with the assertions of this hymn. Early Christians held, of course, that this event was not just an inner experience of forgiveness or reconciliation on the part of Jesus' followers, which, as in 1:21-23, was seen as a consequence of what had happened to Christ, but was the raising of Christ from the dead, which led to the designation of him as "firstborn from the dead."

Today there are many, both Christians and others, who have a renewed interest in the historical Jesus of Nazareth but who are at a loss about how this is to be related to the church's confession of Christ as the second person of the Trinity. A sympathetic attempt to enter into the thought world of the Christ hymn may not only be enlightening about this early stage in the development of belief about Jesus, but it may also help in our own endeavors to understand both the humanity and the divinity of Christ. Without a belief that God raised Jesus from the dead or some experience of Christ's aliveness, there is little incentive to think of Jesus as any more than a Jewish prophet, sage, social revolutionary, or healer. But once we share that same essential starting point with early Christians, we face similar questions about the status of the resurrected Jesus.

Study of the hymn shows that early Christian thought moved from what was believed about Christ on the basis of his resurrection and of believers' experience of salvation through him to what he must have been from all time. This is reflected in the designations "image" and "firstborn" for his role in creation. A similar thought process is found in the Jewish Scriptures, where reflection on the activity of Yahweh in rescuing Israel in the exodus led back to the depiction of Yahweh's role in creation. In the Christian belief expressed in the hymn in Colossians, the movement back from Christ's role in redemption to his role in creation is aided by the transference to Christ of what Judaism held about Wisdom as the one God active in creation and in the world and revealed to Israel in the form of Torah. Now, as the embodiment of Wisdom, Christ is held to be the agent of the one God in creation, the one through whom creation is kept going, and, through his death and resurrection, the revealer and accomplisher of God's purposes for humanity and the cosmos. Just as in Judaism Wisdom was the figure that brought together transcendence and immanence, the universal and the particular, so also in Christian belief Jesus of Nazareth is seen as the point at which the particular and the universal, the human and the divine, uniquely intersect.

2. Recognition that the language of the Christ hymn of Colossians is that of poetry and praise should lead to a hesitancy to fill in its theological gaps in the light of later doctrinal formulations, but not to an unwillingness to stop and ask what we mean when, as contemporary Christians, we repeat its assertions. It is one thing to note that the notion of the preexistence of Wisdom as a personification of God's interaction with the created world is transferred to Christ. But what is going on when we claim that Christ was pre-existent? When this notion was applied in Jewish thought to Torah, its force was not so much to make a statement about the actual existence of the law before the world was created as to see the law as the climactic manifestation of the wise purposes of God in creation and thereby to ascribe ultimacy to its revelation of those purposes. Similarly, when we apply this notion to Christ, we are ascribing ultimacy to him in God's revelatory plan. The one whom we have come to know from the gospel tradition as the crucified and risen Jesus is to be thought of as, prior to his human existence, already at one with God in summing up God's purposes for creation. In terms of the Christ hymn, the divine Wisdom has now been fully embodied as God's human image, so that to speak of Christ is also to speak of God. Because of what we believe to be the perfect fit between God's purpose and the life, death, and resurrection of Jesus, Christians speak of Jesus Christ as pre-existent, although in his role in creation he had not yet become the human being Jesus of Nazareth. By way of loose analogy, although her coronation did not take place until 1953, British subjects can still talk of the *queen's* having been born in 1925.

Christians need to be clear that their ascription of ultimacy to Jesus Christ that leads to trinitarian formulations is not an abandonment of belief in one God. Again the Christ hymn helps here. Through the use of the traditions about Wisdom, it remains within the conceptuality of Jewish monotheism but, by applying such terminology to a human being, constitutes a new departure within that monotheism:

> Christ is *both* to be identified as the divine Wisdom, i.e., none other than the one creator God active in creation and now in redemption, *and* to be distinguished from the Father, not as in a dualism whereby two gods are opposed, nor as in a paganism where two gods are distinguished and given different (and in principle parallel) tasks, but within the framework of Jewish creational monotheism itself.[86]

Some will have a more urgent and existential question about the assertions of the hymnic passage. What does it mean in a world of fragmentation, suffering, and confusion to repeat its claim that all things cohere in Christ or that they have been reconciled in him? It reflects an absolutely basic conviction that, despite the vastness of the cosmos, its determinative principle is not impersonal. The God who is the ground of existence bears a human face—that of Jesus Christ. This means, too, that, despite fragmenting and chaotic forces at work, we humans can trust that the pattern of Christ's death and resurrection is more fundamental and gives the power that sustains the world its distinctive character. So, although it defies present empirical verification, we confess that what holds the world together is not the survival of the fittest or an unending cycle of violence but the reconciliation and peace of Christ. To look at the underside of a tapestry reveals no intelligent pattern. The alternative vision of the hymn holds that, when the upper side is seen, design and beauty will be apparent. The pattern with Christ at the center will be there for all to see when the reconciliation that has taken place through his death and resurrection is fully realized.

At present, as Colossians itself suggests, there remains a hiddenness to the particular pattern of believers' lives (3:3). There is much that remains ambiguous, unexplained, and painful. But this is also where the writer's emphasis on hope comes into play. The hope of cosmic harmony is an assured one, even though it is not yet visible. As believers, we have been given essential pieces of the overall pattern. Christ's resurrection is

---

86. Wright, "Poetry and Theology in Colossians 1.15-20," 463.

determinative for what is to follow—he is the firstborn from the dead. Thus, like the first readers of this letter, we need to see our own fragmentary experiences of reconciliation in the present as the pledge and guarantee of the fuller reconciliation to come.

3. The hymnic material in Colossians tells a story of Christ's role in the cosmos from creation to consummation. In our postmodern context, we frequently encounter an aversion to overarching stories or grand metanarratives. Such narratives are seen as making absolute claims that are inevitably oppressive and violent. We need to acknowledge that various formulations of the Christian story have had such lamentable consequences. But the key question is whether the overarching christological narrative implied by the hymn in Colossians necessarily perpetuates violence toward others.

Colossians 1:11-20 features in the lectionary cycle as one of the readings for the celebration of Christ the King Sunday in Year C, and this could provide an appropriate context for reflecting on this issue. The other readings all focus on the nature of kingly power, with Luke's crucifixion story underlining how different Jesus' kingship is from usual human expectations of royal rule. This is a reminder that in Colossians, too, the cosmic reign of Christ, meant to effect not uniformity but a harmonious unity, is described as being accomplished through violent means—"through the blood of his cross." But this violence is not perpetrated *by* Christ but rather the violence is perpetrated *on* him. This cosmic narrative has at its heart not a pantocrator's tyranny or benevolent dictatorship but the brutal death of a victim. There can be no universal statements without at the same time focusing on someone bleeding and suffocating on a cross. Paradoxically, this victim is the cosmic ruler; his rule is achieved through the experience of suffering, and his peacemaking is accomplished through the absorption of violence.

The hymnic material's story is oriented toward God's purposes of *shalôm* for the whole creation, including reconciliation for the alienated and marginalized and justice for the oppressed, purposes brought about through the solidarity of Christ in his death with suffering victims. The reference to his death is now set in the context of Christ's role in creation and his cosmic rule means that it was not just one more act in a cycle of unending violence. Rather, there are grounds, through the vindication of his resurrection, for the hope that alienation and suffering throughout the creation will cease. This christological narrative actually subverts violence. It is always open to misuse, but those who profess allegiance to it can have no excuse for employing it in a narrow partisan fashion that encourages the marginalization or exclusion of those who do not share the particular christological formulations of their own tradition. After all, the hymn tells of the Christ of the cosmos, not of one who is the exclusive possession of one particular group. Attempts to impose on others this hymn's particular beliefs about Christ should have been ruled out, because there can be no rehearsing or living out the hymn in any way other than the way of peace and reconciliation demonstrated in the death of its protagonist.

4. If what happened in Christ's death and resurrection happened to the one who is God's unique and supreme agent in the cosmos, then the implication is that the readers have given their allegiance not to one intermediary among others, not to one cultic god among others, but to one who has a rightful, unparalleled claim on their lives. They simply cannot afford, therefore, to neglect their relationship with him through the gospel and the apostolic teaching of that gospel (see 1:23). "Continuing steadfast in the faith" is not a defensive attitude of clinging to old formulations come what may but an essential aspect of all creative attempts to interpret the gospel in the midst of the competing ideologies of our own times, if such attempts are to retain continuity with the apostolic gospel.

Contemplating the significance of the person and work of the Christ who is celebrated in worship will also remain an indispensable means of developing roots in the faith. If the first readers of Colossians were familiar with the hymn lying behind the passage, then the writer is in effect asking whether they understand the significance of what they sing. For us, too, the proper perspective on any confusion being sown by the variety of versions of the Christian gospel will derive from a recognition of the supremacy and sufficiency of Christ in both creation and new creation that we acknowledge in our own praise. If this status of Christ is truly appreciated, then both the dualistic tendencies and the world-denying spirituality that are always in danger of creeping into the life of the Christian church are undercut. Since Christ is the one at work in creation as well as in redemption, then the created world is immeasurably enhanced, not relegated to some inferior status by the work of reconciliation. Salvation is not rescue from a totally evil world but the claiming of the rightful possession of this world by the one who was an agent in its creation. The scope of salvation is as broad as life and as vast as the cosmos.

The effect of such a belief should be to make redeemed humans more fully human. It should enable them to appreciate the creation and to work to transform the structures of this world rather than to produce a private piety or spirituality that attempts to cut itself off from the body, ignores the natural environment, and disdains culture. If reconciliation of all things in Christ is at the center of God's purposes, then the pursuit of peace and acts of reconciliation by Christians serve those purposes. Working for a fair distribution of the world's resources, being concerned for animal welfare, and struggling to prevent the collapse of the ecosystem through the pollution of air, soil, and water have everything to do with this passage's celebration of cosmic reconciliation.

5. It has always been a pressing question for Christians whether a loving God would consign the majority of humans, who do not believe in Christ, to perdition. The hymn of Colossians has often been thought to provide a resource for responding to this concern, and some have claimed that Col 1:20 teaches a universal reconciliation in which every human being will be saved.[87] Whatever the merits of such an interpretation of the triumph of God's grace, it appears to be putting a question to Colossians that it was not designed to answer. Certainly the purpose of God's reconciliation through the work of Christ is depicted as cosmic in scope, and this gives grounds for hope. Yet when reconciliation is related to human beings in the application to the readers, it is made abundantly clear that any experience of reconciliation cannot be separated from the response of faith. Indeed, there is no guarantee even here, unless there is a continuance in faith, and later in the letter the writer can assert that the future for those who are disobedient holds an experience of the wrath of God (3:6). Contemporary discussions about whether a Christian approach to salvation should be pluralist, exclusivist, or inclusivist, which of necessity have a different agenda from that of the writer of this letter, may well need not only to develop the implications of cosmic reconciliation but also to ensure that in doing so they take seriously the present necessity of faith and the future judgment of God, if they are to claim continuity with Colossians. We should certainly, therefore, hope that all will be saved, but whether and how this becomes reality has to be left in the hands of God, where, of course, it belongs.

Rather than a provocation to speculation about whether every individual will be included in salvation, perhaps the real challenge of this hymnic material lies in its depiction of the church as the forerunner of a reconciliation that will be cosmic and universal in scope. This is surely a major implication of the image of the church as Christ's body. The worldwide community of believers is meant to be a microcosm in which the divine purpose in reclaiming the entire creation is anticipated and through which, as a reconciled and reconciling community, that purpose is furthered. If this is the case, then the most urgent task of Christians is to play their part in making the church a place of healing for broken relationships, where divisions caused by class,

---

87. For a history of interpretation of this issue, see Schweizer, *The Letter to the Colossians,* 260-77.

race, wealth, education, age, gender, nationality, or religious tradition are overcome, and an agent of peace and justice in situations of conflict, whether in the home or the workplace, at the national or the international level. Whatever the details of the future prepared by a loving and just God, our present focus is to say and do all we can as agitators for the values of the coming new world.

6. All the talk about the use of a hymn and its possible structure should remind us that the writer of Colossians has chosen to use the language of praise of Christ at a vital point in his message in order to reinforce the perspective he and his readers shared and to draw out its implications. It is an effective means of communication because it builds on religious experience—that of worship—and taps the religious emotions so frequently associated with songs of praise. From the perspective of Old Testament studies, Brueggemann has called attention to the power of doxology in the encounter with contemporary idolatries and ideologies. In its response to God, he claims, praise is also an assertion of an alternative world. The liturgy sings and proclaims that God reigns, disestablishing worldly powers and exposing their claims to ultimacy and control.[88]

Much the same can be said of the hymn in praise of Christ in Colossians. Its doxological language reinforces for its readers the alternative vision of the Pauline gospel in which Christ is supreme in the cosmos over all powers and has dealt with their disintegrating threat through his work of reconciliation. The language of worship still has both an educative and affective force. Theological reflection and preaching would do well, therefore, to learn to employ the resources of traditional and contemporary hymns and poetry and to include a rhetoric of devotion in its repertoire in the attempt to instruct, to move, and to motivate congregations to live out of the alternative world of gospel values, where the crucified and risen Christ is cosmic Lord.

---

88. See W. Brueggemann, *Israel's Praise: Doxology Against Idolatry and Ideology* (Philadelphia: Fortress, 1988).

COLOSSIANS 1:24–4:9

THE LETTER BODY

COLOSSIANS 1:24–2:5, BODY-OPENING: PAUL'S PROCLAMATION OF THE GOSPEL AND ITS RELATION TO THE READERS

COMMENTARY

A major function of this body opening is to establish not only Paul's unique relation to the gospel and, therefore, his special apostolic authority but also his apostolic presence with the recipients (2:5a). The picture of Paul that emerges, while just possible as an actual self-portrait, is probably better interpreted as that of a follower looking back in admiration over the apostle's career. As part of the literary device of pseudonymity, the writer, by taking on the persona of the imprisoned apostle, establishes his credentials in the Pauline tradition and strengthens his bond with the readers so that they will be ready to accept the extensive exhortations that follow. At the same time the passage is rhetorically effective. The emphasis on Paul's sufferings on behalf of the church, on the energy he expends in proclaiming Christ, and on the intensity of his pastoral concern demonstrates the excellence of his character as an apostle (ethos) and at the same time arouses in the readers admiration and sympathy (pathos).

In addition, this section continues to stress the knowledge and wisdom available to the readers through the revelation provided by Paul's gospel, and it does so as it leads up to the first explicit mention of the opposing teaching or philosophy in 2:4. The apostolic gospel involves the fulfilling or completing of the word of God (1:25), the revealing or making known of the mystery of Christ (1:26-27), and the teaching in all wisdom (1:28) so that believers might have understanding and knowledge of the mystery—that is, of Christ, in whom are hidden all the treasures of wisdom and knowledge (2:2-3).

1:24. Paul is said to be rejoicing in his sufferings for the sake of readers he has neither evangelized nor visited. Even such readers are to see themselves as intimately linked with Paul, because his sufferings have all been part of the Gentile mission that has enabled them to hear and believe the gospel. The meaning of the elaboration of this thought in the second part of the verse has been highly disputed. It is strange to move from the hymnic material (1:15-20), stressing the all-sufficiency of Christ's reconciling work on the cross, to a statement that appears to suggest that there is something lacking in Christ's afflictions.

The claim is that in his physical body (presumably "flesh" [σάρξ *sarx*] is used because "body" [σῶμα *sōma*] will have an ecclesiological force in the last part of the clause) Paul is filling up what is lacking in Christ's afflictions and that he is doing this for the sake of Christ's body, the church. The term ὑστέρημα (*hysterēma*) occurs nine times in the NT in the sense of "need"/"want"/"deficiency," but this is the only place where it is associated with Christ. Similarly, this is the only place in which the noun θλῖψις (*thlipsis*), used elsewhere of the tribulations of the last days and of the afflictions experienced by various humans, is employed for the sufferings of Christ. The verb ἀνταναπληρόω (*antanaplēroō*, "to fill up/complete for someone else") is found nowhere else in the NT or the LXX. The combination of unusual usages may be confirmation that the formulation comes from someone other than Paul.

But what is to be made of this formulation? The interpretation that the sufferings endured by Christ for the redemption of believers were insufficient and needed to be supplemented by those of the church is highly unlikely. It is in conflict with the earlier emphasis on the sufficiency of Christ's reconciling work that the writer needs to make in the face of the implications of the Colossian philosophy. Another view looks to Paul's notion of the mystical union between Christ and believers and appeals to Phil 3:10, where Paul talks of sharing Christ's sufferings. But this provides no explanation for either how the sufferings are at the same time for other believers or how they complete what is lacking.

A more recent interpretation that has persuaded many suggests that the Jewish concept of the messianic woes makes sense of the formulation.[89] It is claimed that the idea was current in some Jewish apocalypses that there would be a period of worldwide tribulation, occasioned by the rising tide of human sin, a time that was to be both the death throes of this age and the birth pangs of the age to come. During this period a quota of suffering would have to be borne by the people of God before the age to come could be ushered in. Early Christians reinterpreted this concept, focusing attention on the messianic community, which, in the light of the Messiah's death and resurrection, must first share his suffering if it would share his glory (Rom 8:17). Certainly in Paul's thought and in other parts of the NT suffering is one of the major characteristics of the period of the overlap of the ages, and one of the others is the proclamation of the gospel (see also Mark 13:7-13; 2 Thess 2:3, 10-12). Within this pattern of thinking, it is claimed, the quota of suffering is no longer some arbitrary amount that has been assigned deterministically but that which the task of witness to the gospel demands (Rev 6:9-11).

Colossians 1:24 would fit such a pattern because the context here is also the worldwide proclamation of the gospel and Paul's unique vocation within it. Paul's sufferings are "for your sake" and "for the sake of his body, that is, the church" because they are part of his ministry to the Gentiles. That ministry is in turn hastening the day of glory, since, according to 1:27, Christ among the Gentiles is the hope of glory. Although *thlipsis* is used elsewhere in the NT of the final tribulation, it need not be held as part of this interpretation that "the afflictions of Christ" is a technical term meaning "the woes of the Messiah." The phrase could, in fact, be taken as an objective genitive meaning not the tribulations suffered by Christ but the tribulations suffered for Christ.

Despite its attractions, there are, however, problems with this view. The Jewish concept of the woes in fact had no place for a suffering Messiah and did not hold that the Messiah would come before the suffering of God's people took place. In addition, the assumption that there was at the time of the writing of this letter a clear-cut teaching about the "messianic woes" is dubious. There is considerable variation in the depiction of the nature, subject, and time of the woes in the writings from which the notion is said to come (e.g., 2 Bar 20; 25; *1 Enoch* 47; 4 Ezra 4:12, 33-37; 7; 13:16-19). And the thought of taking on a quota of suffering to hasten the inauguration of the new age does not fit particularly well in a letter that elsewhere contains no mention of the imminence of the eschaton. Perhaps the most that can be said is that the writer is taking up a greatly modified version of a still-developing tradition about the woes.

In any case, it seems safe to assert that the sufferings are not the redemptive sufferings of Christ (for which, as noted, *thlipsis* is never used) but the subsequent afflictions of Paul for the church in connection with his witness to the gospel. They can be called the afflictions of Christ in the sense that Paul actively participates in the same pattern of suffering that Christ experienced by continuing his role as servant (see the Commentary on 1:25-27). They are lacking so long as the work of proclamation is incomplete—that is, until the parousia. Paul, as the suffering apostle to the Gentiles, is depicted, then, as playing a major part in making up the deficiency through his unique missionary role. In this way his share in the afflictions of Christ is not redemptive but missionary in character. He is portrayed as rejoicing in such suffering because it is for the

---

89. See especially R. J. Bauckham, "Colossians 1:24 Again: The Apocalyptic Motif," *EvQ* 47 (1975) 168-70.

sake of his Gentile converts and, therefore, by no means meaningless. Instead, his suffering is part of the fulfillment of God's plan in bringing in the consummation through the worldwide proclamation of the gospel.

1:25-27. In 1:23 Paul is said to have become a servant of the gospel, and now in 1:25 he is called a servant of the church. Paul's vocation thus binds him together with the readers. It is part of the same divine initiative through which the readers have experienced the benefits of reconciliation. The combination of the twofold designation as servant with the stress on Paul's sufferings in 1:24 recalls the Suffering Servant figure from Isaiah 40–55. Paul himself appears to have defined his vocation in the light of this background. His description of his call in Gal 1:15-16 echoes the language of Isa 49:1, 5-6; and he can apply Isa 49:8 to his own preaching to the Corinthians in 2 Cor 6:1-2 and Isa 49:4 to his own mission in Phil 2:16. When he says in Rom 15:8-9 that Christ became a servant of the circumcised to confirm the promises to the patriarchs and in order that the Gentiles might glorify God for God's mercy, the second part of that statement is less appropriate to the mission of the earthly Jesus and more applicable to Paul's continuation of Jesus' servant ministry in his Gentile mission. That Paul sees himself completing that role is confirmed in Rom 15:20-21, where he cites Isa 52:15 to describe his own mission strategy. It is likely, then, that this depiction of Paul's role builds on the earlier strand of thought and takes his suffering to be a distinctive part of the extension and completion of Christ's mission as suffering servant.

All this is in line with the stewardship[90] Paul received from God for the benefit of the readers. In 1 Cor 4:1-2, Paul refers to Apollos and himself as stewards of the mysteries of God, and in 1 Cor 9:17 he speaks of his ministry as a stewardship with which he has been entrusted. Here also the stewardship is of a mystery. It involves fulfilling or completing the word of God (1:25c), a synonym for the apostolic gospel, which as the word of the truth (1:4) can now also be said to convey the very Word of God.

The word of God in the gospel is further described, taking up a "revelation schema" probably used in early Christian preaching,[91] as the mystery hidden throughout the ages and generations but now revealed. The term "mystery" was common in Jewish apocalypses (e.g., Dan 2:18-19, 27-30; 4 Ezra 14:5; *1 Enoch* 51:3; 103:2) and in the Qumran writings (e.g., 1QM 3.8; 16:9; 1QS 3.21-23; 1QH 7.27; 10.4), where it denoted a secret aspect of God's purposes that needed to be disclosed. It could, however, also carry connotations of the mysterious, that which is beyond ordinary human comprehension. In the apocalypses it usually referred to an event that would only be revealed at the end of history, although, since it was already prepared in heaven, the seer could have knowledge of it at present (e.g., 4 Ezra 14:5; *1 Enoch* 9:6). In the Qumran literature, however, "mystery" could also refer to an event that has already taken place, such as the community's participation in the angelic assembly (e.g., 1QS 11.5-8).

While Paul can employ both the singular and the plural of the term "mystery" (μυστήριον *mystērion*) with a variety of references, it is in Colossians that its use with reference to the heart of the gospel message, God's activity in Christ (1 Cor 2:7), becomes constant. Colossians 1:26-27; 2:2; and 4:3 all focus on the eschatological fulfillment of God's purposes of salvation in Christ. Whereas this mystery was hidden from previous ages and generations, it has "now" (the time of eschatological fulfillment) been revealed, and the privileged recipients of the revelation, via Paul's ministry, are God's "saints." All Christian believers as God's holy people (1:2), not a select few who have received special visions and knowledge (2:18), have access to the central mystery: God's plan for history and the cosmos.

The phrase "the riches of the glory" (1:27a) stresses the surpassing worth of this mystery that is now, in fact, an "open secret"; as a result of Paul's mission, it is "among the Gentiles," the means of incorporating the Gentiles into God's plan of salvation. The further summary of the mystery in 1:27b

---

90. By translating it as "commission," the NIV and the NRSV flatten out the force of οἰκονομία (*oikonomia*), which has in view the administration carried out by a steward.

91. See N. A. Dahl, "Form-Critical Observations on Early Christian Preaching," in *Jesus in the Memory of the Early Church* (Minneapolis: Augsburg, 1976) 32-33.

("which is Christ among you, the hope of glory") makes the same point in a different formulation. At the center of the mystery are the person and work of Christ; the glory of the mystery derives from the Christ who embodies the gospel's assured hope of the future glory to be restored to humanity and the cosmos (see 3:4; see also Rom 8:17-25). This Christ is not just among the Gentiles but now more specifically "among you," the Gentile Christian readers. The preposition ἐν (*en*) can be translated "in" (so NIV, NRSV), but in line with the first part of the verse, of which this second part is a further explanation, it more probably has the force of "among."[92]

1:28-29. The stress on the universal scope of the proclamation of the open secret constituted by Christ is continued through the threefold repetition of "every person." It is hard to avoid the conclusion that this is in opposition to the notion of mysteries and esoteric knowledge for a select group of initiates. In Paul's vocation, proclamation is not divorced from teaching, and instructing also involves admonishing. The activity of admonishing can take place through encouragement or reproof, but it usually implies that there is some difficulty or problem in the attitude or behavior of its recipients that needs to be overcome. The apostolic preaching and teaching about Christ "in all wisdom" can be seen, therefore, as an essential part of the answer to the writer's prayer for the readers in 1:9 that they might be filled with knowledge "in all wisdom." Paul is portrayed as a wisdom teacher whose teaching is not just for a select few but for everyone. Whatever other claims to wisdom there might be, his teaching provides the means to true wisdom, and the goal of his mission is to present every person perfect or mature in Christ (see 1:22). In this perspective, whether the language employed is that of perfection or of fullness (2:9-10), completion is available in believers' relationship to Christ and nowhere else. Because of such a conviction, Paul is depicted as pouring all his efforts into attaining this objective. The human effort and the toll it takes are immense ("I toil and struggle"), but they are matched by the equally immense divine resources for the task—literally, "in accordance with his energy that he energizes in me in power." The term "energy" (ἐνέργεια *energeia*) will be employed in connection with God's raising Christ from the dead (2:12); for the writer of Colossians, it was this power that was also operative in Paul's accomplishment of his missionary task. In this way, the proclamation of the mystery among the Gentiles can be traced back through Paul's apostleship to the power of God.

2:1-3. The readers of the letter are now drawn more specifically into the scope of Paul's mission as those on whose behalf his struggles have been carried out. The imagery of the athletic contest (ἀγών *agōn*) is continued from the preceding verse to underline the strenuous exertion demanded by Paul's missionary vocation (cf. 1 Cor 9:25-27). Yet no sooner have the recipients of Paul's task been narrowed from "every human being" (1:28) to "you" than they are broadened again to include "those in Laodicea" and "all who have not seen me face to face." This raises questions about who the intended recipients of the letter really are. If deutero-Pauline, was Colossians meant to be a general letter to all the churches of the Gentile mission in Asia Minor, with Laodicea as the immediate destination (cf. 4:13-16; see also the section "Author and Addressees," 577-83, in the Introduction)?

In 2:2 the goal of Paul's struggles for the recipients is expressed in terms of their hearts being encouraged (a formulation found only in the disputed Pauline letters; see 4:8; Eph 6:22; 2 Thess 2:17), and this encouragement will entail and foster the readers' unity as they are held together in love (see 3:14, where love is described as "the bond of perfection"). In the style typical of this writer, alliteration and the heaping up of synonyms are combined to underscore that the goal is "all the riches of the full assurance of understanding" and is "the knowledge of God's mystery, Christ." Here the content of the mystery is simply Christ rather than "Christ among you," as in 1:27. The understanding of Christ desired by the writer for his readers goes beyond merely an intellectual grasp and entails the full assurance or deep conviction

---

92. See E. Lohse, *Colossians and Philemon* Hermeneia (Philadelphia: Fortress, 1971) 76; Pokorný, *Colossians*, 103; M. Barth and H. Blanke, *Colossians* AB 34B (New York: Doubleday, 1994) 265. It is no objection to this interpretation to say, as does Dunn, *The Epistles to the Colossians and to Philemon*, 123, that it makes the phrase add hardly anything to the preceding "among the nations," since the style of Colossians contains many redundancies for effect with synonymous parallels and repetitions of thought.

that will enable them to appropriate and live out of the richness it provides (see also 2:6-7). They will be able to do this, because in Christ are all the resources they need—"all the treasures of wisdom and knowledge." All that Wisdom stood for (1:15-20), including instruction on living wisely (2 Bar 44:14 and 54:13 use the language of "treasures of wisdom" with reference to the teaching of the law), can now be found in Christ. Anyone who is interested in secret or hidden knowledge is to be assured that true wisdom and knowledge are "hidden" in Christ and, therefore, are also paradoxically no longer hidden but revealed to all those who believe in the apostolic gospel.

2:4-5. If all this talk of understanding, knowledge, wisdom, and mystery in 1:25–2:3 (and 1:9-10) has suggested that the writer has had an eye on the opposing teaching, then 2:4 explicitly confirms this. "I am saying this . . ." is retrospective, referring to what has just been said. And the reason for having said it is to prevent anyone from deceiving the readers by persuasive speech. The writer is naturally attempting to employ persuasive speech, and so the context with its mention of deceiving means that here the term should be taken negatively as connoting plausible, but in the end specious, arguments. Such claims about special wisdom and knowledge have the effect of undermining the sufficiency of the essential mystery of what God has done in Christ.

Yet, before launching into a more detailed interaction with the offending teaching and as part of his own persuasive strategy, the writer lets the addressees know that he is not issuing his warning because only he has assured understanding and they are all gullible and easily led astray. Instead, he assures them of his solidarity with them, even though he is not physically present, and of his joy at the reports he has received that the community is basically in good shape. It is frequently observed that the two terms used to describe their condition, "morale" (τάξις *taxis*) and "firmness" (στερέωμα *stereōma*), were also used in military contexts, where they denoted military formation or order and the solid front presented by an army. But the terms could be employed more generally in other contexts, and here they should be taken to indicate the good order that the community maintains and the firmness or solidity of its faith in Christ. "I rejoice" in 2:5*b* forms an inclusio with "I rejoice" in 1:24*a*, setting the tone of this section and its attempt to cement the links between the readers and the gospel originating in Paul's unique mission. Paul's vocation has been depicted as having been designed to meet precisely the need of the readers for growth in understanding and maturity in Christ. Thus both his sufferings for them and the effectiveness of his agonizing toil in producing well-grounded congregations like theirs are a cause for joy.

REFLECTIONS

1. What is the relationship between this depiction of Paul's ministry and present-day proclamation of the gospel? It is often assumed that, for this passage to have any bearing on the present, Paul should be taken as a model for Christian ministry and existence. Yet, as we have seen, the primary thrust of the passage does not move in this direction at all. Paul is portrayed, rather, as having a unique mission, as providing the foundational apostolic link with the gospel of Christ. Even his suffering, which in 2 Cor 1:6-7, for example, is seen as an experience shared by other believers, is in Colossians uniquely his own and has the special role of "completing what is lacking in Christ's afflictions for the sake of his body." Paul's suffering is described in the first-person singular, and there is no mention of the readers or the whole church joining him in his missionary role of suffering service. Here a suffering church is not the point; rather, it is the apostle suffering for the church.

Since the passage focuses so intensely on Paul and his ministry, it would certainly be in line with its purpose to preach a sermon celebrating the person and achievement of the apostle Paul and all that Christians, and in particular Gentile Christians, owe him in inheriting a law-free gospel together with his reflections on the implications of that gospel. Such a celebration could, of course, be critically appreciative. But, given the denigrating characterization of Paul as the distorter of the simple message of Jesus that is still all too frequently heard even in churches, it would be entirely appropriate to stress the immense debt of gratitude owed to the apostle. An interpretation in this vein need not remain simply at the level of a historical sketch or eulogy of a heroic human being. Taking its lead from the portrait of Paul in Colossians, a homily or lesson on Paul's impact and our links with him can draw out and reflect on (1) the theological dimensions of Paul's significant role as suffering servant, steward of the mystery, and wisdom teacher in the working out of God's reconciling purposes for the cosmos; (2) the centrality of Christ in his proclamation; (3) Paul's pastoral objectives for his Gentile converts; and (4) his sense of being energized for his struggles through the divine power at work in the resurrection of Christ.

Reflection on Paul's ministry of the Word would be appropriate when 1:15-28 appears in the lectionary in Year C (Proper 11) alongside Amos 8:1-12 and Luke 10:38-42. Amos pronounces God's judgment on Israel, which will entail a famine of hearing the words of the Lord, so that even those seeking the Lord's Word will not find it. The Gospel reading celebrates the salvation Jesus brings to Israel as Mary takes the "better part," the role of the disciple in attentively listening to the words of Jesus in defiance of the social codes. In this context, the Colossians passage underlines the privileges of the new era of salvation in which the Word of God is made fully known (1:25). Paul's preaching and teaching make it possible for ethnic barriers to be overcome and for Gentiles now to have access to Christ's wisdom, since what is proclaimed among them is the content of the Word of God or the revealed mystery is precisely Christ. And here there is no scarcity or famine but "the riches of the glory of this mystery" (1:27); as 1:15-20 has shown, everything that could be predicated of God's Wisdom and more is now made available in Christ.

2. Some of the items listed in the discussion of the portrait of Paul raise the persistent question of whether they are totally unique to Paul's ministry or whether they should also characterize any proclamation of the gospel. One might well point to the fact that the depiction of Paul's ministry of preaching and teaching in 1:28 shifts temporarily from the use of "I" to "we," indicating perhaps that not only Timothy (1:1) but also other apostolic coworkers may be in view. Certainly some of the language of 1:28-29 is employed of Epaphras in 4:12.

The rhetorical function of the passage may also help us here. The Commentary stresses its elements of ethos and pathos. Ethos points to the character of the speaker in such a way as to lend credence to the message. The characterization of Paul can then serve as a reminder of the intimate link between the message and the messenger. Audiences do judge the message by the character of the messenger as perceived through his or her attitudes and actions. The way Christian preachers and Christians in general live their lives, therefore, affects the way their message is received. The pathos of this passage may lie in its evoking from the readers both sympathy and admiration for the apostle. The latter aspect of admiration easily shades into emulation. Admiration for Paul's sense of vocation, for his keeping Christ central in his preaching, for his goal of presenting all believers as mature in Christ, and for his labors to achieve this goal can properly lead to these aspects of his ministry being considered models.

Despite Paul's sufferings having a special role, there may well also be justification for taking them as exemplary. Paul's sufferings have a unique place in the worldwide proclamation of the gospel. The extended delay of the parousia, however, means that the task of universal proclamation is not nearly as complete as Colossians supposes. It would be difficult to maintain either from an exegesis of the text or the history of the church that an implication of the passage is that Paul has absorbed such a disproportionate amount of the afflictions of Christ that the readers or other later believers can expect a life free from suffering or need only bear some minimal amount. Instead, while the missionary task remains, the afflictions of Christ continue regardless of the amount of them borne by Paul. Paul, then, can be seen as modeling the pain and cost of missionary proclamation and the ability to rejoice in the midst of such suffering. Indeed, in the undisputed letters he envisages that suffering, including suffering that is for the benefit of others, is the lot of other ministers of the new covenant and of all believers until the eschaton (see Rom 8:17-18; 2 Cor 1:3-11; 4:7-12).

3. The dominance of the theme of wisdom and its acompanying terminology of mystery and knowledge is also worth pondering. In our day, just as much as at the time of the Letter to the Colossians, there is no lack of those offering wisdom whether in the form of a return to ancient mysteries or of new scientific cosmologies. Gurus abound to offer their wit and wisdom about how to lead our lives, to cope with life's vicissitudes, and to find fulfillment. What does it mean for us if, with Colossians, we take Paul as our wisdom teacher, pointing us to and explicating the source of wisdom in God's revelation in Christ?

Since the wisdom found in Christ is cosmic in scope, Christians will claim to have already discovered the essential clues about meaning and life; but they will also know that they can never exhaust such wisdom and that their own grasp of it remains partial and provisional. They will, therefore, always be ready to explore new perspectives from their own foundation and to learn from the best of human knowledge and wisdom. Their own particular starting point in Christ and the rich tradition of Christian theology and wisdom will provide a basic means of discrimination in the face of other claims.

At the same time, if the church believes that all the treasures of wisdom and knowledge are hidden in Christ (2:3) and that its task is to teach wisdom (1:28; 3:16), a major but too often neglected implication is that it will do everything to encourage its members, whatever their particular field of vocation or interest, consciously to relate these to their faith in Christ. Without risking such a Christian perspective on all aspects of life and a corresponding acting out of its implications, the impression will be produced that the church has reduced the cosmic dimensions of wisdom, and indeed of Christ's lordship, to private religious convictions and corporate religious rites. Nor should we forget that Colossians will measure the wisdom of any teaching not simply by its claims but by its results (2:23)—what quality of living it produces—and that it will summarize much of its own ethical teaching about living all of life under the lordship of Christ as "walking in wisdom" (cf. 4:5).

COLOSSIANS 2:6–4:6, BODY-MIDDLE: EXHORTATIONS

OVERVIEW

It has been argued that on an epistolary analysis the heart of the letter is to be found in its body-middle, extending from 2:6 to 4:6. The present section would then constitute the opening half of the body-middle. On a rhetorical analysis, it has been suggested that this section is the middle of the three divisions of the *probatio,* the proof of the main propositions of the argument. Both analyses thus confirm the central significance for Colossians of this section, in which the writer interacts with the opposing teaching or philosophy. Certainly the letter is more than a polemical confrontation with the philosophy, but the positioning of this section reminds the interpreter that the danger from the opposing teaching is at the center of the letter's rhetorical situation. The teaching has provoked the writing of the letter, but the writer then uses the opportunity provided by the perceived danger to fashion a more general message of exhortation, in which the concerns and the language of the philosophy are taken up into a new framework and thereby given new content. In line with such a view of the role of the philosophy, the section begins (2:6-15) and ends (3:1-4) with passages that appear a little more general in orientation but still remain intimately connected to the writer's concern about misleading teaching.

Colossians 2:6–3:4, Exhortation to Faithfulness to the Gospel

Colossians 2:6-7, Live in Accordance with the Tradition About Christ

COMMENTARY

In many ways these two verses sum up everything the writer has to say. They make the general point that he will spell out in more detail in interaction with the philosophy. The "therefore" points back to the assurance he has expressed about the well-groundedness of the readers' faith (2:5*b*). Given this, his basic exhortation is that they are to carry on in the fashion in which they have begun and to become even more steadfast in the faith. Christ has been the beginning point for their faith, and the cultivation of their relationship with him will be the means by which they are enabled to continue effectively. The exhortation takes the form of a variation on the indicative/imperative construction. In the indicative part ("as you received Christ Jesus the Lord") the focus is not on the readers' initial experience of receiving Christ into their lives by exercising faith. Instead, the verb employed (παραλαμβάνω *paralambanō*) denotes the receiving of tradition that has been passed on (cf. 1 Cor 15:1, 3; Gal 1:9; 1 Thess 4:1; 2 Thess 3:6). Since the gospel centers in Christ and his lordship, the title "Christ Jesus the Lord" can serve as an effective encapsulation of this tradition. As 2:8 will make clear, the writer sets the Pauline gospel and the philosophy over against each other in terms of tradition. It is not that one is seen as gospel and the other as tradition, but rather that both take the form of tradition. The difference is that whereas the gospel is regarded as the apostolic tradition about Christ, the philosophy is depicted pejoratively as merely human tradition. But the personal aspect of this formulation about the gospel tradition remains significant. The writer believes that Christ as a living person and the reality of his lordship are mediated by the traditions about him, so that receiving those traditions entails not only learning about but also being shaped by Christ Jesus the Lord as the powerful source of a new way of life.

The imperative clause "walk in him" makes precisely this point. (On the force of "walk" [περιπατέω *peripateō*] see the Commentary on 1:10, where in the intercessory prayer report a similar relationship between believers' conduct and their confession of Christ's lordship is set out.) Given the earlier stress on the cosmic scope of Christ's lordship (1:15-20), it should occasion no surprise that the writer expects his readers' behavior to reflect this reality. Yet the motivation stressed here is not so much obedience to this Lord as it is living out of the resources of a relationship of incorporation into him, which is the force of the phrase "in him."

Four participles in v. 7 indicate aspects of living in relation to the Lord. The imagery of the first two conveys that Christ the Lord is the soil in which the readers are to continue to put down their roots and to grow, the foundation on which they are to continue to be built. The notion of solidity is also conveyed through the third participle. They are to be made firm or established in the faith, just as they were taught. This echoes the language of 1:23 and reinforces the importance of the tradition they have received (cf.

2:6) as that which must be appropriated for their living. The fourth participle introduces a different topic, but one that is typical of the letter: thanksgiving (cf. 1:12; 3:16-17; 4:2). The lives of those who appropriate the tradition are to have a surplus of thankfulness. This should not be a surprising emphasis in the context, for it is precisely in drawing on the tradition that believers are reminded of all that God has done in Christ on their behalf and thereby filled to overflowing with gratitude.

REFLECTIONS

1. These two verses make absolutely clear that in Christian existence orthodoxy and orthopraxis go hand in hand; "talking the talk" cannot be separated from "walking the walk." But what is said in Colossians takes us beyond such basic assertions. The pattern of this exhortation to Christian living that involves an indicative statement followed by an imperative is sometimes referred to by the slogan "Become what you are." This is helpful in pointing out that the indicative of the new life in Christ, to which the apostolic teaching points and which it attempts to safeguard, is more than simply a possibility; it is real. At the same time, the fact that an imperative is still needed makes clear that the new situation is still in progress and that the relationship between who one is in Christ and how one lives is not an automatic one. The pattern shares, therefore, in the eschatological tension typical of Pauline thought. The indicative reflects what God has already done in Christ in inaugurating the new order, while the imperative is the exhortation to appropriate and live this out in the midst of the powers of this present age that are still at work. Here the formulation about having "received Christ Jesus the Lord" (2:6) highlights that it is the implications of that lordship for all of believers' lives that need to be lived out.

In a letter that from this point will consist of a whole series of imperatives, it is crucial for the writer to establish what he sees as the proper perspective on Christian ethical exhortations. They do not represent an impossible ideal or a crushing burden. It is not uncommon to hear people complaining that their employers are increasing their workload or expanding their jobs but not providing them with the necessary resources. Colossians underscores that the necessary resources have already been made available for the task of Christian living and that there is no need to be numbed by the sense of powerlessness that makes us spectators in life. What is more, the motivation for living the good life is not a fear of punishment or a sense of duty or a need to be needed or a hope of reward (whether in the afterlife or in this life in terms of self-fulfillment). For those of us who are prone to be driven by such motivations, the relationship symbolized by the indicative and the imperative can provide a healthy reminder that the primary dynamic that should govern Christian behavior is rather a living out of our relationship to Christ, an appropriating of what God has already accomplished in Christ. This also puts the emphasis where it belongs in Christian living—not on human willpower or effort but on God's grace—and enables such living to be characterized by thankfulness (2:7).

2. In reflecting on how the church can best resist succumbing to today's alternative lordships that compete for adherence, we would do well to consider again the way in which these verses assign particular importance to the role of tradition and catechesis in the process of appropriating the reality of Christ's lordship. Colossians assumes that, if there is to be an effective demonstration of that lordship, believers will continually avail themselves of the resources of Christian teaching about their roots and foundation in order to nourish and support their active allegiance to Christ as Lord. Only those churches that are providing consistent Christian education will be in a position to make the same assumption.

Colossians 2:8-15, Do Not Be Captured by Human Tradition

COMMENTARY

This section consists of the issuing of a general warning against the opposing teaching, followed by a series of assertions about what God has done in Christ for the readers. In this context, the latter are clearly meant to function as antidotes to some basic features of the alternative teaching. It is not, however, until the next section (2:16-23), with its mention of practical aspects of the philosophy, that the philosophy's specifics come a little more clearly into view. For the present-day reader this necessitates that inferences drawn from these later, more explicit details are employed to fill out some of the positions against which the assertions of this earlier section appear to be aimed. (See the section "The 'Philosophy' Opposed in the Letter" in the Introduction for a general treatment of this issue.)

2:8. The strong warning to "beware" or "be on your guard against" indicates that the writer sees a real danger being posed by the views circulating in his readers' location. They are to beware lest anyone capture their allegiance and thereby lead them away from the Christ of the apostolic gospel. The Greek pronoun τίς (*tis*) is indefinite but singular, leaving open the possibility that writer and readers may be aware of a particular individual who is a key proponent of the teaching.

Three negative evaluations of the alternative teaching are given to dissuade the readers from being taken in by it. A variety of teachings and religions in the ancient world could be designated philosophies. "Philosophy" here has negative connotations simply because of the context, particularly the phrases that follow. This philosophy is seen as being in opposition to the faith, in which the readers are to be established (cf. 1:23; 2:7); the description "empty deceit" writes it off as being devoid of truth in comparison to the gospel, earlier described as "the word of truth" (1:5). It is seen as being in accordance with human tradition rather than the tradition that has Christ Jesus the Lord as its content and source (cf. 2:6). Whereas these antitheses have been implicit, the final depiction has an explicit antithesis: The alternative philosophy is according to "the elemental spirits of the universe" (NRSV) or "the basic principles of this world" (NIV) and not according to Christ. The contrasting translations represent the two main competing interpretations of a highly disputed phrase, though the NIV has inserted an extra interpretive gloss by translating τοῦ κόσμου (*tou kosmou*) as "this world" instead of "the world." (Reasons have already been given for opting for the interpretation represented by the NRSV. See the section "The 'Elemental Spirits of the Universe' and Dualistic Cosmology," in the Introduction.) So the writer bluntly asserts that the philosophy should not be seen as presenting the readers with a both . . . and situation, in which the gospel sits comfortably with elements from other traditions. Instead, the gospel about Christ is incompatible with the teaching into which it has been amalgamated. Two different authorities lie behind the philosophy and the Pauline gospel—in the one case the cosmic spirits or powers and in the other case Christ.

2:9-15. To reinforce the point about different authorities (see the "for" at the beginning of 2:9), the writer's strategy in these verses is to remind the readers of all that they already have "in Christ." The English translations often obscure this, but the phrase "in him" occurs at the beginning of v. 9 and at the end of v. 15, and "in him" or "in whom" is found five times in these verses. It is not surprising that, where incorporation into Christ is so dominant a note, a reminder of the readers' baptism, the event that represents their union with Christ, is an important part of this argument (vv. 11-12).

2:9-10. The earlier hymnic material had asserted of Christ, "in him all the fullness was pleased to dwell" (1:19). Now this language is taken up again. It is made clear that "all the fullness" refers to the fullness of the deity, and the present tense "dwells" replaces "was pleased to dwell." But the main change is the addition of the adverb "bodily" (σωματικῶς *sōmatikōs*). The assertion of v. 9 as a whole makes two points over against the philosophy. Since the totality of deity is embodied in Christ, there can be no grounds for a person who confesses Christ to seek God or fullness elsewhere or to think that the way to this divine fullness is through cosmic intermediaries. What is more, there is no dualism between the God of the higher world and the body viewed as some prisonhouse of the soul in the lower world. The apostolic gospel holds together the two concepts the philosophy deemed incompatible, because all the fullness of the deity not only dwells in Christ but dwells in him bodily—that is, it dwells in one who became incarnate in a body of flesh (cf. 1:22).

Through their incorporation into Christ, the readers have themselves been filled. This could be taken to mean that believers have all the fullness of deity within them, just as Christ does. But such an interpretation clearly runs counter to the unique status and role the writer has been anxious to claim for Christ. Its force is probably, therefore, more general. Because of their link with the fullness of deity through Christ, by definition there can be nothing lacking about their relation with God, no deficiency that needs to be filled by further teachings and practices offered by the philosophy.

This is also the case because the one through whom they have been filled is the head over every principality and power. Principalities and powers had already been shown to have been created and reconciled through Christ in 1:16, 20, and Christ had already been designated as head over the church in 1:18; now Christ's headship is said to be over these powers. Believers need not see themselves as subject to the powers. Instead, the cosmic powers are subject to the Christ through whom believers have been filled. To acknowledge the truth of this assertion would be to make the ascetic and cultic observances of the philosophy that were designed to appease the principalities and powers completely redundant. Everything depends, then, on the readers' appropriation by faith of God's saving actions in Christ, and it is this very thing that their baptism proclaimed.

2:11-12. Instead of talking about their union with Christ in his death, burial, and resurrection as proclaimed in baptism, as does Paul in Romans 6 and as might have been expected here, the writer speaks of their union with Christ in his circumcision, burial, and resurrection. This change in formulation produces a more complex argument, but it is highly significant. The use of the metaphor of circumcision for Christ's death is another means of taking on and undermining the viewpoint of the philosophy.

It is not that the philosophy is to be thought of as advocating physical circumcision and, therefore, as Jewish. After all, there is no clear polemic against circumcision, and it is not listed as among the philosophy's observances in vv. 16-23.[93] Nor is there any clear evidence that the philosophy employed the term "circumcision" for its own initiation rites, as some have held.[94] Rather, the use of the metaphor of circumcision enables the writer to deal once more with the philosophy's view of what has to be done with humans' body of flesh. The observance of detailed ascetic regulations was meant to enable people to divest themselves of the encumbrance of the physical body and rise above it in visionary experience of the upper realm. "The stripping off of the body of flesh" is the terminology the writer picks up in v. 11, as he claims that the stripping off of the body of flesh that really matters has already taken place for the readers in their union with Christ in his circumcision.

This is to take the phrase "the circumcision of Christ" as an objective rather than subjective genitive construction. In other words, it refers to the circumcision Christ underwent rather than to the circumcision that belongs to him or is effected by him (as opposed to the NIV).[95] The circumcision he underwent is his death. It was not merely the stripping off of a token part of the flesh, the foreskin, but a cutting off of his whole body of flesh through death. When taken in this

---

93. Dunn, *The Epistles to the Colossians and to Philemon*, 155-56, concedes the lightness of any polemic and holds that debate with Jews about the significance of spiritual circumcision should be envisaged.
94. E.g., Lohse, *Colossians and Philemon*, 102.
95. Cf. Martin, *Colossians and Philemon*, 82-83; O'Brien, *Colossians, Philemon*, 117; Dunn, *The Epistles to the Colossians and to Philemon*, 158. Contrary opinions can be found in Schweizer, *The Letter to the Colossians*, 143; M. J. Harris, *Colossians and Philemon* (Grand Rapids: Eerdmans, 1991) 103; Pokorny, *Colossians*, 124-25.

way, the phrase allows the argument to have the parallel already mentioned—that is, with the notion of union with Christ in his death, burial, and resurrection found in Romans 6.

Just as believers' dying with Christ is not a physical death but a spiritual dying to sin with clear ethical consequences, so also their being circumcised with Christ is not the cutting off of their physical existence in death but a spiritual circumcision that also has particular ethical consequences. Theirs is "a circumcision made without hands"; and "made without hands" always stands in implicit contrast to "made with hands," an expression typically employed in the LXX for idols as human constructs. The former refers to that which is the work of God and belongs to the new order inaugurated by the divine activity in Christ (see Mark 14:58; 2 Cor 5:1). What union with Christ in the stripping off of his body of flesh means ethically for believers will be spelled out later in 3:9, where the cognate verbal form "having stripped off" (ἀπεκδύομαι *apekdyomai*) is employed with reference to having put off the old humanity and its practices. This, together with the use of the same participle in 2:15, confirms that the notion of divesting oneself of the physical body is the key issue the writer is tackling at this point.

Union with Christ in his circumcision corresponds to union with Christ in his death, but the writer holds off actual mention of baptism until reminding the readers of their burial with Christ. The return to the more traditional formulation, taking up the language of Rom 6:4, indicates that the writer is moving away from direct engagement with the philosophy and is underscoring more generally the decisive significance of his readers' incorporation into Christ. The vivid imagery of burial, with its counterpart in immersion in the baptismal waters, stresses the reality of the death to and break with the life of the past. Neither the NRSV nor the NIV reflects the fact that the Greek syntax does not explicitly connect union with Christ in his resurrection with baptism. The Greek term ἐν ᾧ (*en hō*), which follows the mention of baptism in 2:12*b,* is best taken, with the majority of commentators, as "in him" rather than "in it" and as paralleling the same phrase at the beginning of 2:11.

The formulation about union with Christ in his resurrection does, however, differ from that of Romans 6. In Colossians believers are said to have already been raised with Christ, while in Rom 6:5, 8 the future tense is used of the relationship. The difference in formulation is real but should not be exaggerated. A closer examination of Romans 6 indicates that Paul could also speak there of a present as well as a future aspect of sharing Christ's resurrection life. In Rom 6:4 Paul talks of a present walk in newness of life; in Rom 6:10-11, he argues that in identification with Christ believers are to consider themselves alive to God; and in Rom 6:13 he urges them to live as those who have been brought from death to life. These expressions presuppose that in Paul's thinking about believers' union with Christ in his resurrection there was an "already" as well as a "not yet" aspect. The shift in emphasis to the "already" aspect in Colossians makes sense in this context, where the writer wants to underscore all that believers have in Christ and to minimize the uncertainty about salvation induced by the philosophy. Since this is a shift in emphasis rather than a major change of thought, it should not be made a decisive factor in the issue of authorship.

If baptism is still implicitly in view in the mention of having been raised with Christ, then it is significant that, while baptism as the external event is one aspect, faith as the internal response is the accompanying aspect of the one complex of "conversion/initiation." The faith that links believers to Christ's resurrection is "faith in the power of God who raised him from the dead."

2:13-15. The same power of God operative in Christ's resurrection has been effective for the readers. With a slight variation on the imagery of resurrection with Christ, the writer reminds them that God has made them alive together with Christ. And if this is the case, then their pre-Christian past must, comparatively speaking, be viewed as a condition of spiritual and moral death. Already in Judaism a life in disease, sin, alienation, or captivity could be seen as a life in Sheol, or the realm of death (see Pss 13:1-3; 30:3; 31:12; 88:3-6; 1QH 3.19; 11.10-14); and Paul depicts death as a power of the old age, connecting it closely with sin (see Rom 5:12-21; 6:23; 1 Cor 15:56). In Colossians this previous state of death was brought about and characterized by the readers' "trespasses," their deliberate acts of disobedience, and by what, from the writer's Jewish Christian perspective, is described as the "uncircumcision of your flesh." This phrase indicates both that the readers are Gentiles and that previously their uncircumcised physical state also represented a state of spiritual uncircumcision, an alienation from Israel's living God that entails death. But the power of God that was effective in Christ's being brought to life and that the readers have also experienced through their faith has reversed all this. The writer asserted in v. 11 that believers have undergone a circumcision made without hands in their union with Christ; v. 13c now goes on to make clear that their trespasses have also been dealt with, since God has granted full and free forgiveness.

The problem for the interpretation of v. 14 is to identify what has been dealt with by being erased and nailed to the cross. Both the NIV's "the written code with its regulations" and the NRSV's "the record . . . with its legal demands" could suggest that the Mosaic law is in view. But the term χειρόγραφον (*cheirographon*) denotes a handwritten document or a bond of indebtedness, while δόγματα (*dogmata*) refers to regulations or stipulations. The use of the latter term in Eph 2:15 clearly, because of the context, refers to the Mosaic law; but that cannot be determinative for this earlier usage in Colossians. The clue here is provided by the use of the cognate verb in v. 20 in connection with submitting to the ascetic regulations of the philosophy. The NIV correctly translates the twofold condemnatory function of the document. It is described as "against us" and as that which "was opposed to us." This language is just possible as a very harsh dismissal of the law, but so it is much more unguarded than even Paul in Galatians and very unlikely in a letter that nowhere else polemicizes against the law. And to argue that what is in view is not the law per se but only the law in its condemnatory function[96] is to have to read far too fine a distinction into the verse. The document itself is said to be opposed to humanity and, when one brings into play the ascetic regulations mentioned later, the clear implication is that it is condemnatory of humans because of their body of flesh.

The chirograph or document may well be best interpreted in the light of the use of this term in apocalyptic writings.[97] The motif of books in which good and evil deeds are written down with a view to the judgment is common (cf. *1 Enoch* 89:61-64, 70, 71; 108:7; *Apoc. Zeph.* 7:1-8; *T. Abr.* 12:7-18; 13:9-14; *2 Enoch* 53:2-3; Rev 20:12) and the actual term *cheirographon* is employed for such books in *Apoc. Zeph.* 3:6-9; 7:1-8 (where it is transliterated in the extant Coptic version) and *Apoc. Paul* 17 (where the Latin equivalent is found). A book of indictment held by an accusing heavenly power with regulations designed to deal with the body of flesh would fit well as the reference in this context. The writer is then claiming that God has erased[98] this indictment and has, literally, "taken it out of the middle," which was the position occupied by an accusing witness at a trial. The accusatory book has in effect been ruled out of court. It was canceled and set aside by being nailed to the cross.

The language of being nailed to the cross recalls either the *titulus*, which contained a person's indictment (see Mark 15:26), or Christ himself. Nailing the indictment to the cross would not in itself cancel it, and so it is likely that what is in view is that the indictment was nailed to the cross when the body of Christ was nailed to the cross, particularly when we remember that in both 1:22 and 2:11 the writer emphasized that it was Christ's body of flesh that underwent death on the cross. The thought may well be, then, that through the death of Christ's fleshly body any indictment of the body of flesh by the heavenly powers has already been dealt with by God. Such an interpretation is supported by the later reading of this text in *The Gospel of Truth* 20:24-25: "He put on that book; he was nailed to a tree." It need not be seen as the writer's endorsement of the philosophy's point of view about the body. Instead, he assumes its proponents' position for the sake of the argument and in order to undermine

---

96. Contra Dunn, *The Epistles to the Colossians and to Philemon*, 165-66.

97. See Sappington, *Revelation and Redemption at Colossae*, 214-20; also Martin, *Colossians and Philemon*, 84-85; Barth and Blanke, *Colossians*, 369-72; Dunn, *Colossians and Philemon*, 164-66.

98. The same notion is used in *1 Enoch* 108:3 and *Apoc. Zeph.* 7:8.

it. It is simply another way of making clear that there are no grounds for believers to feel guilty.

A quite different image for what was accomplished on the cross is employed in v. 15. It involves a further play on the "stripping off" terminology and thereby on the philosophy's view of the body of flesh. Now the writer's claim is that, instead of the readers' having to strip off the flesh to appease the powers, through Christ's death God has stripped off the principalities and powers. There is debate about whether the participle is to be taken as strictly middle in force, "having divested himself of," or as middle with an active sense, "having stripped or disarmed" the cosmic powers. Because of the difficulty of the notion of God divesting Godself of the powers and because of questions about how early the second meaning can be attested elsewhere, some have suggested that the subject of the clause has shifted to Christ. Thus Christ is pictured in his death as divesting himself of the powers like rags and thereby nullifying any influence they might have over humanity.[99] The later *Gospel of Truth* 20:30-31 interprets the passage in this way with Christ as subject: "having stripped himself of the perishable rags." But there are no grounds syntactically for arguing for a change of subject, particularly since the final "in him" is almost certainly to be taken as a reference to Christ.

Despite queries about the dating of the usage of the verb with an active force, taking the clause to mean that God has stripped the powers in the sense of divesting them of their accusing power is by far the best solution.[100] This is also supported by the context. After all, the previous image has made the point that the condemnatory record held by the powers has been dealt with, and the next clause speaks of their being exposed to public shame, which fits well with the notion of their having been stripped. What all this amounts to is that in Christ, particularly in his death, God has triumphed over the cosmic powers. The image of the triumphal procession that followed a military victory is evoked (cf. 2 Cor 2:14). Here the hostile powers are the defeated enemies who are paraded in God's train. Those who held the powers in such awe that they thought it necessary to appease them by whatever means possible are given a totally different perspective. The true attitude for Christian believers is to hold the powers in contempt as having been totally disgraced by God's redemptive activity on behalf of humanity and to celebrate and appropriate the victory and liberation God has achieved in Christ.

99. So Dunn, *Colossians and Philemon*, 167-68.

100. Cf. Harris, *Colossians and Philemon*, 110; O'Brien, *Colossians, Philemon*, 126-28; Pokorny, *Colossians*, 141; Schweizer, *The Letter to the Colossians*, 151.

REFLECTIONS

1. With a rich variety of imagery this section has made the point that the resources to be found in what God has already done in Christ and in believers' relationship of incorporation into Christ are more than sufficient to deal with whatever plight the opposing philosophy alleges the readers to be in. Faced with the strangeness of some of the imagery, the interpreter has a delicate task. On the one hand, there is a need to resist the impulse to translate these images immediately into more straightforward theological language. They had their original impact precisely as images or metaphors, and so first we need to do our best to enter the first-century world and attempt to appreciate their likely force. They are not mere ornaments to be discarded for more literal language that gives a greater purchase on the real world. These metaphors have their own unique function in bringing to expression insights into aspects of reality that would not be appreciated without them.

The central metaphors about Jesus' death's effecting forgiveness and constituting a victory have achieved classic status in the Christian tradition. They need to be explored as continuing ways of articulating God's action in the world and of shaping the life of the Christian community. However, some of the images attached to them, such as erasing a record book of angelic indictment, do not have the same status; it is probably futile to pretend that they can or that they should retain their original force in our own culture. What may be needed in such cases is to determine the analogies that underlie the metaphors and then in an act of imagination to explore whether there might be striking contemporary images to make graphic how Christ's death deals with whatever has a hold over people's lives in our world. For those under the thrall of consumerism, to visualize it as a symbol of the credit card being cut up when Christ was cut off from life might have the desired effect. The point is helping people to grasp that when Christ died to the old order and thereby took away its power, present-day gods and principalities were included in that event.

2. That last point reveals a stance on a major issue that has exercised writers on Paul and on Colossians: How to interpret the references to the cosmic powers and elemental spirits.[101] As the Commentary has made clear, the writer holds that Colossians, in its original context, was referring to supernatural spiritual agencies. He also holds that contemporary Christians are not bound by the specific cosmologies of the New Testament writers, including the cosmic demonology of Colossians. In our time, therefore, when for a variety of good reasons, including theological ones, the majority of Christians in the West do not operate with a belief in a host of evil spirits in the heavens called thrones or dominions, the most helpful appropriation of these texts is most likely to be by way of analogy. This entails seeing an equivalent to such cosmic powers in the systems, institutions, and ideologies of our day. In relation to human life they play a similar role to that of the elemental spirits of Colossians, because they have, within and beyond them, a driving force for good or evil that is more than the sum of the effects of any individuals who may represent them or of any of their tangible manifestations.

When faced with undesirable conditions in our world, such as the status of refugees, homelessness, or renewed tribal conflicts, we and our politicians are no strangers to talk of being the victims of economic or political forces beyond our control. Forces of evil larger than individual acts of sin can include some that have a counterpart in the first-century world, such as the lure of astrology or of the occult; but they will also include unjust social, political, and economic structures. They include ideologies that hold people in bondage, frequently without their being conscious of it, such as the ideology of redemptive violence in which peace and security are thought to be obtainable only through the violent use of power.[102] Among other such ideologies are materialism, consumerism, sexism, nationalism, and the type of postmodernism that denies any reality to truth and justice and asserts that the only realities are preference and desire. And forces of evil can include nuclear and chemical armaments, ecological disaster, and other consequences of human sin that have become destructive and threatening. The writer of Colossians brings the gospel of Christ's death and resurrection to bear on his readers' perception of evil in a first-century context. Contemporary interpreters need to take the same gospel and bring it to bear on the powers of evil and perceptions of them that pose a threat to faith in our time and location.

3. In this section, the good news of God's having dealt with the cosmic powers in Christ is expressed in terms of both Christ's headship over the powers (2:10) and Christ's death, which removes their indictment in a public triumph (2:14-15). Clearly this latter view of the salvation accomplished through Christ's death is part of the basis of what has become known as the Christus Victor model for the atonement.[103] From

---

101. For an extensive justification of the stance taken here, see A. T. Lincoln, "Liberation from the Powers: Supernatural Spirits or Societal Structures?" in *The Bible in Human Society*, ed. M. D. Carroll, D. J. A. Clines, and P. R. Davies (Sheffield: Sheffield Academic, 1995) 335-54. For a somewhat different approach, see the brilliant trilogy of W. Wink, *Naming the Powers* (Philadelphia: Fortress, 1984); *Unmasking the Powers* (Philadelphia: Fortress, 1986); and *Engaging the Powers* (Minneapolis: Fortress, 1992).
102. See Wink, *Engaging the Powers*, 13-31.
103. This model received particular emphasis and elaboration in the patristic period. See G. Aulén, *Christus Victor: An Historical Study of the Three Main Types of the Idea of the Atonement* (New York: Macmillan, 1969).

its perspective, the human need to which this solution corresponds is for liberation from both the consequences of sin and the powers of evil. The imagery for Christ's victory over the powers involves disarmament and triumphant procession, but any triumphalistic use of such a model ignores the paradox at its heart. The powers of evil are defeated not by some overwhelming display of divine power but by the weakness of Christ's death. By all ordinary standards of judgment, Christ's crucifixion looks like a victory for the violence of evil powers over God's purposes in this one who was the divine image. Christ was indicted, stripped, and nailed to the cross in the public humiliation of his death. Yet, Colossians can reverse this language because, seen in the light of his resurrection, the death of the victim, who has absorbed the destructive forces of the powers, becomes precisely the point at which their domination is decisively brought to an end. Their claims, their accusations, and their oppressive and divisive influence have all been subverted by a very different power: the power of the victim on the cross.

The challenge issued to the readers of Colossians is one that remains for Christians: Is this proclamation about Christ's death a metaphor by which we are prepared to live? Do we believe that this answer to the power of evil is really sufficient? The gospel proclaims that Christ has conquered evil; yet, evil still threatens and flourishes. So are additional means needed to cope with the reality of evil in our world? Presumably some of the original readers were tempted to turn to angelic powers for help for this very reason and thought this was compatible with their Christian faith. They reasoned that their confession of Jesus' lordship needed to be supplemented by other means of coping and bargaining with the forces of evil as they affected their daily lives. How far do contemporary Christians still make their own deals with other powers, whether materialism, rationalism, pragmatism, or violence, in order to live with the impact of evil on their lives and in society? For all readers of Colossians, a major test of authentic adherence to the gospel and to the confession of Christ as Lord is whether they are convinced enough of the sufficiency of God's action in the crucified Jesus to gamble their lives on the paradoxical power of the way of the cross rather than making compromises with other powers.

4. This passage has an obvious role to play in thinking about the significance of baptism. Colossians 2:12-13 focuses on the movement from the dominion of death and sin to the sphere of new life that is expressed through baptism, with its participation in Christ's burial and resurrection. This underlines that baptism is not simply an inititation rite but has to do with issues of life and death and with appropriation of the release from the domination of the powers of this age (cf. 2:20).

Baptism reminds believers that their pre-Christian past is to be regarded as a state of spiritual death, because their sins had cut them off from a living relationship with God. We need to be convinced, with the writer of Colossians, that to live life in pursuit of our own selfish ends is to be in the cul-de-sac that leads to death. Idolatry can be related to particular vices (see 3:5). The inevitable result of making something contingent and created the center of power rather than the Creator is not only a distortion of reality but also enslavement within the system of sin whose wages is death.

Bringing God into the analysis of the human plight gives it seriousness as a state of death, but it also provides the only hope. The conviction that the world is in the hands of a God who is the first and ultimate power, an actor in the drama who is more important than us, is what provides the opening to freedom. In Colossians this is formulated in terms of "faith in the power of God, who raised him from the dead" (2:12). If the plight is death, then the solution must involve a raising to life. Baptism proclaims that this is in fact what God has accomplished not only for Christ but also for believers. "God made you alive together with Christ" (2:13).

The claim involved is that the resurrection of Christ was an event through which God changed the power structures within history. Although there are many past events in which one feels no sense of personal involvement, there are others that are quite different. Most British people can still hardly think about the events of the Second World War without a sense of involvement, because they are members of a community that owes its continuity and some of its national characteristics to what happened then. Similarly, Colossians views Christ's resurrection as supremely an event that brings into being and defines a whole new situation and a new community. Baptism seals believers' involvement in that event. What God accomplished for Christ is to be seen as having been accomplished for him as representative of a new humanity that is included in him. Through faith and baptism, believers are linked with the life of this new resurrection power within history. It decisively shapes and identifies them, aligning them with a new center of power and breaking the system of sin and the hold of death over their lives.

5. Immediately after this passage has talked of believers' experience of the new order of life inaugurated through the resurrection, it moves on to assert God's forgiveness of all trespasses. To experience the forgiveness of sins is a sign that the hold of the past has been broken and that a new and liberated life has begun. Forgiveness remains really good news because it restores our relationship with the God who made us and with other human beings. It brings release from greed, from the need to exploit, from shortsighted self-interest, from the trap of believing that violence can be overcome only with violence, from all those attitudes that stand in the way of the achievement of God's purposes of love and justice for this world.

But a further issue arises from our interpretation of the philosophy and of 2:14 (see Commentary on 2:13-15). If our interpretation is correct, then from the perspective of the writer of Colossians, some of his readers are suffering from a sense of false guilt. The indictment against them is not based on God's law but on the philosophy's view that life in the body is sinful. It is out of a sense of guilt on this account that some are undergoing rigorous ascetic requirements. The writer's emphasis is that, whatever its origin, people need assurance that the sense of guilt that has a hold over them has been dealt with in Christ and that in God's eyes they are now forgiven and guilt-free people.

There is a pastoral point worth pondering here. Whether we consider people's guilt to be real or imagined, their *sense* of it is real to them. There may well be an analogy to be drawn between the sense of guilt of some of the first readers of Colossians and the condition we would diagnose today as shame. This is the unhealthy type of shame that is not attached to anything a person has done wrong but is the person's sense of being inferior, unworthy, or unacceptable as a person. When with Colossians we point to God's forgiveness in Christ, we may also need to make explicit that the grace that supplies such forgiveness is the grace that accepts us as we are. It is this dimension of forgiveness as producing acceptance in the eyes of the most significant Other that can begin to heal the sense of unhealthy shame. And the gospel of Colossians is the gospel of just such grace (see 1:6). The letter again and again stresses that, though they are undeserving, humans are considered worthy to receive all that God gives in Christ and, in the words of this passage, to receive fullness in Christ (2:10), to be made alive together with him (2:13), and to be liberated from any accusing forces that would tell them otherwise (2:14-15).

From a broader theological perspective, we may also need to see shame, whether about the body or about the self, as indeed part of the sin that needs forgiveness. Feminist theologians, among others, have pointed out that sin is not always to be thought of in terms of acts of proud self-assertion; it can also involve shameful self-diminution.[104] Both types of sin can be seen as culpable and requiring forgiveness, because they hinder the authentic relationship with God for which human beings were intended.[105]

---

104. See S. N. Dunfee, "The Sin of Hiding: A Feminist Critique of Reinhold Niebuhr's Account of the Sin of Pride," *Soundings* 65 (1982) 316-27.
105. See L. G. Jones, *Embodying Forgiveness* (Grand Rapids: Eerdmans, 1995) esp. 35-69.

Forgiveness is needed for complicity with shame. From this perspective, the writer of Colossians, in proclaiming God's forgiveness and depicting the effects of Christ's death in erasing and removing the specific requirements of the philosophy, can be seen as not only dealing with those requirements, but also, in so doing, offering the antidote to the complicity in shame about the body that has made them plausible.

This whole topic of forgiveness invites a more general biblical and theological treatment when Col 2:6-15 appears in the lectionary (Year C, Proper 12) alongside Old Testament readings (see Psalm 85; Hos 1:2-10), in which the theme of forgiveness is prominent, and Luke 11:1-13, with its petition, "Forgive us our sins, for we ourselves forgive everyone indebted to us" (NRSV).

Colossians 2:16-23, Do Not Be Judged by the Codes of a Different Teaching

COMMENTARY

2:16-17. As a consequence (again "therefore" provides the link) of his perspective on how God in Christ has dealt with the issue of the supposed hold of cosmic powers over humanity because of humanity's existence in physical bodies, the writer can now exhort the readers not to allow anyone to judge them negatively for failing to comply with the philosophy's regulations. The regulations singled out are requirements about food and drink and calendar observance. These are clearly parts of the philosophy taken over from Judaism, but now apparently they are put to use in its proponents' program for dealing with the cosmic powers. The issue of food and drink, however, is likely to be not so much one of purity laws as of abstinence as part of a strict asceticism. In the OT there are prohibitions against certain foods, but stipulations about drink are found only in regard to the particular cases of priests ministering in the tabernacle (see Lev 10:9) and those under Nazirite vows (see Num 6:3), though Jews in the diaspora were also cautious about wine in case it had been offered to idols. But there is no indication here that the motivation for abstinence from food and drink was due to observance of Torah. Rather, the requirement of abstinence should be linked with the mention of fasting in preparation for visions in v. 18, of ascetic regulations in vv. 21-22, and of severity to the body in v. 23.

The writer describes the calendar observances required by the philosophy in terms of feasts or festivals, new moons, and sabbaths.

These three calendrical features are listed together in the OT (see LXX 1 Chr 23:31; 2 Chr 2:3; 31:3; Ezek 45:17; Hos 2:13), where they were days on which special sacrifices were to be made to God.[106] Again there is no hint here that such special days are being observed because of the desire to obey Torah as such or because keeping them was a special mark of Jewish identity. Instead, it is probable that in the philosophy they were linked to a desire to please the cosmic powers, the "elemental spirits of the universe" (vv. 8, 20), held to be associated with the heavenly bodies and, therefore, in control of the calendar. Sabbath observance would have been no exception to this. Elchasai would later teach his followers that the sabbath was to be observed because it was one of the days controlled by the course of the stars.[107] It was precisely because of such links with cosmic beings that Paul had earlier found it so easy to make the point to the Gentile Christians in Galatia that to observe "days, months, seasons and years" under the law would be just like going back to enslavement under the elemental spirits of the universe (see Gal 4:9-10).

In addition to the earlier undermining of the need for such practices in vv. 9-15, the writer adds in v. 17 a further warrant for his exhortation. The observances are dismissed as mere "shadow" in comparison with the

---

106. See the chart "Agricultural and Civil Calendar," in *The New Interpreter's Bible*, vol. 1 (Nashville: Abingdon, 1994) 275.
107. See Hippolytus *Refutation of All Heresies* 9.16.2-3.

"body," the true reality that belongs to Christ. Such a comparison, deriving from Platonic thought, was common in Hellenistic writings, including Hellenistic Jewish texts.[108] "Shadow" represented the lower world of the senses, the world of appearances, in contrast most frequently to "image" but also to "body," representing the invisible realm of true ideas or true being. It may well be, as some have suggested,[109] that the writer is using the language of the philosophy to his own ends. In the perspective of the philosophy, the practices advocated for those in the lower earthly realm would have been the shadow that reflected and provided access to the true reality of the divine presence in the upper realm.

By introducing an eschatological element—the practices are the shadow of what is to come—the writer treats the regulations not as a present reflection of a heavenly reality but as belonging decisively to the past; for him, as for Paul, the age to come has already been inaugurated in Christ. The other element introduced into the comparison is the connection of the true reality with Christ. By asserting that the "body" belongs to Christ, the writer claims that with the presence of the true reality in Christ, who has already been designated the "image" of the invisible God in 1:15 and the one in whom all the fullness of the deity dwells in 1:19 and 2:10, the shadow no longer has any grounds for continued existence; the practices of the philosophy are superfluous.

2:18-19. A discussion of a number of aspects of v. 18, which is a key text for analysis of the teaching the writer is opposing, has been provided in the Introduction (see the section "Visionary Experience and Asceticism," in the Introduction), and so its results will be assumed here. Not only are the readers not to allow anyone to judge or condemn them (v. 16), but they are also not to let anyone disqualify them. The verb employed for "disqualify" (καταβραβεύω *katabrabeuō*) evokes the image of an umpire ruling against a contestant in a game and thereby depriving that person of any prize. The writer recognizes the potential of the philosophy for making the readers sense that they are missing out on the experience of the heavenly realm it offers through participation in its practices. In 3:1-3, he will claim that they can already experience this realm in Christ, but here he concentrates on providing a negative assessment of this major feature of the philosophy. It has already been argued that the phrase "the worship of angels" is to be taken as a derogatory description of the practice of invoking angelic aid and that the best translation of the most debated part of the verse (v. 18*b*) is that the proponent of the philosophy is depicted as "insisting on fasting and worship of angels, which he has seen, when entering." The "seeing" refers to visionary experience and the "entering" to entrance into the heavenly realm through such an experience. Fasting was required as the preparation for visions and for the visionary's ability to invoke the angels in the heavenly realm.

The writer characterizes the person who would insist on these experiences in a way that disqualifies those who have not had them as "puffed up without cause by his fleshly mind" (v. 18*c*). This characterization is doubly ironic or sarcastic. In the first place, the insistence on self-abasement in the form of fasting is said to have led to a pride or conceit that has no basis in reality. Second, to attribute this conceit to a mind of flesh would again be to combine two concepts that the philosophy would have held to be incompatible. In Hellenistic thought, it was the mind or the soul (the terms could be used interchangeably) that was deemed capable of escaping the realm of the physical to achieve in this life the experience of the upper realm and the divine (see the section "The 'Elemental Spirits of the Universe' and Dualistic Cosmology," in the Introduction). The writer denies that any such thing has happened and claims that instead the attitude of the philosophy's advocate is evidence that the mind has remained firmly bound to the whole realm of flesh; for a follower of Paul, there would remain connotations of the sinful sphere of the flesh in such an indictment (see Rom 8:5-6 for the closest correspondence to this language in the undisputed letters of Paul).

Such a person is also charged with "not holding fast to the head" (v. 19*a*). The clear implication is that the proponent of the

---

108. See Philo *On the Confusion of Tongues* 190; *On the Migration of Abraham* 12; Josephus *The Jewish War* 2.28.
109. See Lohse, *Colossians and Philemon*, 116-17; Martin, *Colossians and Philemon*, 91; Pokorny, *Colossians*, 144.

philosophy who is in view is someone who could be expected to adhere to Christ—namely, a Christian believer. One of the reasons why this person's hold on Christ is put in question is that the attitude of superiority and condemnation he or she shows toward other believers who do not share the philosophy's views amounts to ignoring the rest of the body (v. 19*b*) and is thereby detrimental to the well-being and growth of the body of all believers, over whom Christ is head. For the writer, one's attitude to the body, the church, is indicative of one's relation to its head, since the two are intimately connected. Christ, the head, is the source of the church's growth. His headship, therefore, is understood in the sense of both rule and origin. It is significant, however, that at the end of v. 19 this growth can also be said to come from God and so reflects the emphasis throughout the letter on Christ as the agent of God's activity.

There are, however, other agents in the church's growth: the members of the body. Paul had used "body" imagery for the church in Romans 12 and 1 Corinthians 12, which describe the mutual contributions of the body's members. Here the writer's stress is on corporate growth rather than simply interdependence. Believers are depicted as the ligaments and sinews that supply and connect the body and without whose proper functioning any growth would be severely impeded. By not holding firmly to the head, the philosophy's advocate is in danger of being deprived of the essential connection with the true source of fullness (see v. 10). By implication, such a person is a loose ligament out of alignment with the rest of the body, and the philosophy fails to pass the key test of contribution to the growth of the whole body.

2:20-23. The writer now approaches the task of distancing the readers from the philosophy from yet another angle. He reminds them of their union with Christ in his death, previously discussed using the imagery of circumcision (v. 11), and points out that through union with Christ they have died with Christ to the elemental spirits of the universe. Paul could talk of believers' having died to sin and the law as personified powers of the old age. Now the writer extends the thought to dying to the cosmic powers. In fact, the preposition employed in the formulation here is not "to" but "from," so that the force is that in their death with Christ the readers have come out from under the control of these powers. Since in Christ's death any hold of the powers over humanity on account of the body of flesh has been dealt with and the powers themselves have been disarmed and vanquished (cf. vv. 11, 14-15), participation in that death in union with Christ means that believers, too, enjoy liberation from the powers.

On this basis, the writer presses home the question: "Why, as living in the world, do you submit to regulations?" The clause "as living in the world" has proved difficult for interpreters. Does the participle "living" (ζῶντες *zōntes*) stand in contrast to having died with Christ, or is it a more general reference to existing? Since the writer does not appeal to resurrection with Christ until 3:1, the latter is probably to be preferred. Does "in the world" have a neutral force or the more negative sense of "this world" or worldly existence? Connected with this, how is ὡς (*hōs*, "as") to be taken? Many take it with the not very frequently attested meaning of "as if" and understand the expression as a whole to be saying that those being addressed are living as if they are still in the world in its negative sense. It appears simpler to take *hōs* in its more frequent sense of "while" and "world" (κόσμος *kosmos*) as alluding to the use of the term in the previously mentioned "elemental spirits of the universe or world." Thus the force of the question is, If you have come out from under the control of the elemental spirits of the world, why, while living in the world over which they can no longer lay claim, are you submitting to regulations that have as their presupposition that the elemental spirits are still in control? The natural implication of the present tense in this question is that some of the readers are, indeed, beginning to succumb to the rival teaching.

Three examples of the regulations are provided in v. 21. All are ascetic prohibitions. The first and third, "do not touch" and "do not handle," appear to be saying much the same thing. Some have attempted to find a distinction, claiming that the first refers to sexual abstinence, since the verb translated as "touch" (θιγγάνω *thinganō*) can refer to sexual relations (see 1 Cor 7:1). But elsewhere the context and the object of the verb make this connotation clear. The writer does not supply an object for any of the verbs, and it is fairly clear that the issue of food and drink that was dealt with in v. 16 is again in view. The verb *thinganō* could also be used with food as the object, meaning "to eat." It may well be that the attempt to pin down the exact reference of each prohibition is misguided. The examples function more as a caricature of the negative nature of the philosophy than as descriptions of actual regulations.[110] If any distinction is to be made, the force of the three prohibitions is most likely best captured by "Do not eat"; "Do not taste"; and "Do not even handle." The absolute nature of these formulations is part of the writer's ironic exageration of the philosophy's stance, which would not, of course, have treated all food and drink as taboo, but would have treated certain foods and drink as taboo at particular times for the purpose of subduing the physical body and being in a state of purity in readiness for visionary experience and access to heaven.

The writer can caricature the regulations because from his perspective they deal only with foodstuffs that are destined to perish with use anyway. This perspective is similar to that from which the Jesus of Mark 7:19 and Paul in 1 Cor 6:13 dealt with those who gave issues about food too high a priority. In the case of Colossians, regulations about food and drink are being given far too high a priority because they are simply human commands and teachings (v. 22*b;* see also 2:8), a phrase that recalls the Jesus tradition in Mark 7:7, which in turn had cited Isa 29:13. In Mark 7:7, the Isaiah passage had been employed with reference to the tradition of the elders, not of the Torah itself; and again this makes improbable the view that the Jewish purity laws as such are the content of the regulations in Colossians.[111] A Pauline disciple would scarcely have dismissed what, in fact, had been commanded by God in the Torah as merely human commandments.

The writer's third attack on the regulations to which some of the readers appear to be submitting is to suggest that their claims are a facade, masking a very different reality.

The details of the syntax of v. 23, however, are notoriously difficult to unravel. In all likelihood, the "and" between the term for "self-abasement" or "fasting" and the phrase "severity to the body" was not in the original text (contra the NRSV and the NIV)[112] but was added by scribes to provide a smoother reading. Without the "and" there is a clear reference back to the two practices mentioned in v. 18—worship and fasting—followed by a phrase in apposition that represents the writer's assessment of either the latter or both of these practices. The verse may well, then, be best translated: "which things [the regulations] have a reputation for wisdom in self-chosen worship and fasting, severity to the body but of no value to anyone for dealing with the gratification of the flesh" (author's trans.).

What is clear is that the writer's earlier stress on wisdom and knowledge (1:9-10, 28; 2:2-3) has been in response to the claims of the philosophy to provide these. He regards those claims as suspect; the reputation for wisdom is undeserved. The prefix "self-chosen," added to "worship," simply underscores that the invocation and veneration of angels is an activity undertaken freely and deliberately. The reason for questioning the reputation for wisdom comes in the evaluation at the end of the verse, and the key is the comparison between "body" and "flesh." For all the philosophy's strenuous ascetic requirements, designed to deal with the problem of the body, they turn out, according to the writer, to be of no value whatsoever in dealing with the problem of gratification of the flesh.

The question remains whether "flesh" (σάρξ *sarx*) here has the physical sense accorded it in the philosophy and in many of the writer's own earlier references or whether he is giving it a moral twist in line with both the predominant Pauline usage of the term and what is likely to be the case in 2:18. We have seen no reason to believe that the advocates of the philosophy are taking satisfaction in the flesh in the sense of their ethnic identity. It seems best, then, to see here an indictment parallel to that of 2:18, with the notion of a hollow reputation that matches being puffed up without cause and a gratification of the flesh that matches having a mind

---

110. See Lohse, *Colossians and Philemon*, 123.
111. Contra Dunn, *The Epistles to the Colossians and to Philemon*, 191-92.

112. See P[46], B. See also Dunn, *Colossians and Philemon*, 188.

of flesh. Later in 3:5, the writer also will give the terminology of the philosophy his own ethical connotations. Here the charge is that for all the effort taken to deal with the supposed problem of the body, the philosophy's regulations, as the attitudes of its advocates indicate, are of no value in dealing with the real problem: that of the flesh in the sense of the sphere of humanity in its sinfulness and opposition to God. In fact, the regulations pander to this dimension of human existence (cf. Paul's formulations about not gratifying the desires of the flesh in Rom 13:14; Gal 5:16).

REFLECTIONS

1. The polemical nature of the pastoral warnings in this passage raises questions about when it becomes necessary to issue a "health warning" against certain forms of spirituality or to expose a particular teaching's tenets as hollow wisdom and about how this is to be done. On the one hand, we need to be aware of the conventions of first-century polemics and resist imitating what may be elements of caricature in this writer's approach.[113] But, on the other hand, this should not prevent us from having the courage to be forthright, but fair, about what we deem to be the dangers of succumbing to misguided views and practices that have the potential for undermining adherence to the Christian gospel.

It is unlikely that we shall find any precise modern equivalent to the philosophy and its practices that are attacked in Colossians. Nevertheless, some of its features do tend to recur in a variety of forms and should put us on our guard when we encounter them. A list might include (1) emphasizing criteria in addition to the gospel message, whether they be visions and other special experiences or abstaining from wine or meat, as necessary for a "higher spirituality" by which other Christians are then judged defective; (2) a concern with other spiritual agencies or powers that detracts from the centrality and sufficiency of Christ; (3) teaching and practices that produce elite groups within the church to the detriment of the whole body of believers working and growing together; (4) claiming that a prime human need is to discover or rediscover some special esoteric knowledge in addition to what is found in the gospel and Christian teaching; and (5) dualistic views that treat the bodily and the material as inferior or evil and obscure the fact that humanity's plight is ethical—and by extension, views that treat any part of our humanity as inferior, asserting that the intellect or the personality needs to be transcended.

Obviously, discernment is needed in warning against suspect spiritualities. It would be foolish, for example, to discount asceticism and visions and dreams as part of spirituality and to ignore the contribution to the church's tradition from individuals and groups who value such practices and experiences. What is at issue is not these emphases themselves, which can be part of a healthy response to greed, lust, and materialism and to a reduction of human experience to the rational and empirical, but rather the motivation behind them and the attitude with which they are promoted. Fasting and other ascetic disciplines done during the season of Lent, for example, can be seen not as treating food and pleasures as evil but as a temporary suspension of the proper use of God's good gifts in order to gain perspective and to learn not to abuse them. A problem arises when particular practices or experiences are set up as requirements for others to fulfill if they are to be complete Christians, when they reflect a disparagement of ordinary physical existence, when they are accompanied by a spiritual pride that judges others, or when they are placed at the same level of importance in Christian living as the need for love and justice.

---

113. See L. T. Johnson, "The New Testament's Anti-Jewish Slander and the Conventions of Ancient Polemic," *JBL* 108 (1989) 419-41.

Taking our lead from Colossians, we also need to warn against the dualistic view that too frequently passes for Christianity, in which culture and sexuality are deeply suspect and in which the gospel is about being rescued from the world before it is finally destroyed and we are transported to some spiritual hereafter. This is a distortion of this letter's depiction of the Christ who has created and reconciled the cosmos and whose lordship of this world claims every area of human life, including culture and society. In line with Colossians, authentic spirituality will diagnose the real problem not as the body or the earth or any aspect of created reality but as the flesh (see 2:18, 23)—that is, the sphere of sin. True spirituality will see the solution as an appropriation of the reconciliation offered in Christ with its restoration of a proper relationship to the Creator and participation in the divine purposes of harmony for the whole creation.

2. The loose network of attitudes and beliefs that is often labeled "new age" spirituality provides some analogies to the philosophy opposed by Colossians. A wide variety of interests flows into it, including an emphasis on human potential, a fascination with extraterrestrial beings and UFOs, astrology, magic, witchcraft, ecological concerns, and channeling of spirits from the beyond. However, a major aspect of the phenomenon is a syncretistic spirituality that stresses experiences of transcendence in the attempt to go beyond the limitations of everyday life in the visible world. "New age" thinking is not a coherent system of beliefs, but its dominant attitude toward the world is holistic, with the self, the earth, and the spirit world all being linked within the one universe. Yet within this perspective there are dualistic features, and the questions "new age" thinking addresses are similar to those the philosophy raised: What powers are in control of life? What forces are available to be tapped into to help us control our own destinies?

Just as the writer of Colossians attempts to address the philosophy's concerns from his own perspective, rooted in the Pauline gospel, and to critique what he viewed as erroneous in the rival teaching, so also we need to develop our own twofold response to similar movements in our time. What do the concerns of their adherents say to the churches about what the latter have neglected in the resources of their own tradition? What elements have to be seen as antithetical to or undermining of that tradition?

In its concern to view human, animal, natural, and cosmic life as part of an undivided unity and in its reaction to the dualisms of Western thinking and the perceived dualisms of Christianity, "new age" thinking assumes a pantheistic monism. In this monism, Christ, when he is given attention, is seen as one of many manifestations of the all-pervasive divine consciousness. Certainly cosmic harmony is also a concern of Colossians. It may well be time, therefore, that we paid far greater attention to Christ as Wisdom, as the one who sustains and brings to harmony the ambiguities and complexities of the cosmos and who provides integration in our lives. Yet, for Colossians, this Christ is the unique manifestation of the divine Wisdom. As cosmic Lord, he is present and active within the natural order, but, rather than being identified with it or reduced to it, he remains transcendent and sovereign over it.

In contrast to "new age" philosophy, which views our problem as an ignorance that keeps us from discovering our true selves, the god within us, Christ's death and resurrection reveal our plight to be an alienation caused by our sin. In terms of the concepts of this passage (esp. 2:18, 23), what is needed is not the pseudo-wisdom of the search for mystical experiences that will open us to an awareness of cosmic consciousness or the cultivation of techniques that will unlock the treasures of wisdom that are hidden within us. What is needed, rather, is the wisdom of the crucified and risen Christ that releases us from the destructive and binding consequences of our selfish disruption of and resistance to God's purposes for cosmic harmony. In particular, it is our identification by faith with Christ's death (2:20) that has released us from the dominion of this alienated system of the old order and from the hold of any of its powers that would take advantage of our estrangement from the Creator. We are freed to live in alignment with the divine purposes of harmony for the cosmos as we maintain allegiance to the one in whom those purposes have been embodied and through whom they are being fulfilled.

3. Colossians reminds us that holding fast to Christ the head means that believers are not on a journey of individualistic spirituality but have become members of a community in which they need to live together in love and be accountable to one another in public worship (see 2:19). In this community, spiritual growth is not a private preoccupation but a corporate matter. Amid all the talk and activity associated with "church growth," and while by no means incompatible with a desire for and strategies to achieve greater numbers, the passage also reminds us that these are not the ultimate measures of growth. Genuine growth that comes from God and that is a result of authentic adherence to Christ as head is recognized by the way in which the whole body functions healthily as its members work together to provide nourishment and support for one another.

Colossians 3:1-4, Seek the Things That Are Above

COMMENTARY

This unit does not mark a new section of the letter but is closely connected with what precedes. Its exhortations are still in close interaction with the philosophy. But, whereas 2:16-23 had been a primarily negative critique, 3:1-4 contains the writer's positive counterpart to the philosophy's concerns. The following section also begins in direct interaction with the rival teaching in 3:5, but from then on its exhortations become more general and less immediately controlled by such interaction.

3:1. For his more positive exhortations, the writer returns to the theme of union with Christ. The opening clause, "if then you have been raised with Christ . . . ," picks up on the assertion of 2:12*b* and parallels the opening clause of 2:20, "if you died with Christ. . . ." Both dying with Christ and being raised with Christ have a close association with baptism, and so once more it is likely that the readers are being reminded of the significance of their baptism. Not only did it entail their death with Christ to the elemental spirits of the universe but also it signified that they now participate in the new life and order of the age to come. In Paul's thought, believers' present experience of the life of the age to come could be expressed in terms of their links with the heavenly realm (1 Cor 15:47-49; Gal 4:26; Phil 3:20). Here, too, the writer can phrase the imperative that follows from present possession of resurrection life in spatial terms: "Seek the things that are above."

"Above" (ἄνω *anō*) is synonymous with "heaven"; the writer indicates that there is, in his view, a valid and legitimate concern with the heavenly dimension in contrast to the misguided concern of the philosophy. In the face of the insistence on ascetic observances in order to participate in heavenly life, he asserts that through God's gracious initiative the readers have already been brought into such life. It is on the basis of their union with Christ in his resurrection that they are the ones—all of them, not a special group of initiates—who can be exhorted to further their relationship to the heavenly realm. Resurrection life is heavenly life, and by being united with Christ in his resurrection, the readers have access to the realm above.

The imperative here, then, is again based on an indicative. Since the readers already have access to the life of heaven, they are to pursue this access. There may no longer be any need for the rigorous activity entailed in the philosophy's achieving of visionary experiences, but there is to be the eager determination to take advantage of what has been achieved for them, to "seek" the genuine realm above. This is not an activity in addition to the salvation achieved by God's actions in Christ but a part of it, since "above," as the writer immediately points out, is where Christ is. In line with the rest of early

Christian thought, he holds that by virtue of the resurrection Christ had been exalted to heaven. This stress on where Christ is helps to make explicit the presupposition of the earlier indicative clause—namely, that their union with Christ's resurrection means that the readers participate in the heavenly realm where the resurrected Christ is at present.

It is clear, then, that the writer is not recommending seeking this realm above for its own sake. The motivation for the upward direction and the heavenly orientation to which he exhorts his readers is christological. "The things above" cannot be separated from the Christ who is there, and the centrality and supremacy of Christ in this realm are conveyed by the expression "seated at the right hand of God." Here, as earlier in Paul (cf. Rom 8:34; 1 Cor 15:25), the christological interpretation of Ps 110:1 common to the early church is taken up. Its function in this context is to underscore once more the rule of Christ over any cosmic powers the readers may associate with the heavenly realm. There need no longer be any sense of threat from above. Since the upper world centers around the one with whom they have been raised, and since he is in a position of authority at God's right hand, there is nothing to prevent believers from having permanent access to this heavenly world and to God's presence.

3:2. The writer issues a similar imperative in this verse, but this time the verb is varied and the exhortation is strengthened by the contrast between "things that are above" and "things that are on earth." The imperative amounts to an injunction to be heavenly minded rather than earthly minded. To set one's mind on some object implies concentration and firm purpose and indicates that more than isolated visionary experiences are in view. But what is to be made of the contrast between the heavenly and the earthly? For the philosophy, this entailed a cosmological dualism in which the upper realm was good because it was spiritual and immaterial, while the lower realm was evil because it was physical and material. The writer, however, is not telling the readers to avoid concern with the earthly creation as such. His contrast is controlled by his eschatological perspective and has an ethical dimension. Because of Christ's exaltation, heaven highlights the superiority of the life of the new age and is the source of the rule of Christ (v. 1) and of life (v. 3). The earth, on the other hand, takes on the connotations of the arena of this present evil age. "Things on earth" refers, then, to life in bondage to the cosmic powers (2:8, 20), the sphere of the flesh (2:18, 23), and the practices of the old humanity (3:5-9).

The writer's pastoral strategy can now be seen clearly. It might appear precarious to tell his readers to concentrate on the things above, when it was the excessive concern of the proponents of the philosophy with such matters that prompted the letter in the first place. He by no means completely disparages his readers' concern with the heavenly realm. Instead, he attempts to redirect it. In the process it emerges that two antithetical positions about participation in the heavenly realm are in confrontation. The philosophy's advocates take the earthly situation as their starting point, from which by their own efforts and techniques they will move beyond the body, gain visionary experience, and ascend into the heavenly spheres. The writer moves in the reverse direction, seeing the starting point and source of the believer's life in the resurrected Christ in heaven, from where it works itself out in earthly life (see 3:5-17) and from where it will eventually be publicly revealed (v. 4). Most important, he turns the tables on the philosophy by employing spatial and cosmic concepts to point to the sufficiency of Christ. The advocates of the philosophy appear to have wanted to add to belief in Christ the notion of appeasing other intermediaries in order to gain further knowledge and experience. For the writer of Colossians, there was no going beyond the one in the supreme position at God's right hand.

3:3-4. Believers' relationship with Christ is now elaborated in terms of its present hiddenness and future glory. The clear implication of "you have died" is that this is a reference to their having died with Christ (cf. 2:20), a dying both to the elemental spirits and to what have just been designated "earthly things." Because of their union with Christ in his death and resurrection, the readers' having died to the sphere of sin is inseparably connected to their new life. "Your life," then, is not simply a reference to their biological existence but to the existence that results from incorporation into Christ. This has a hidden aspect, however. Union with Christ is a hidden reality accessible to faith, not sight—not even visionary sight—but nevertheless a reality that provides the resources for believers living out their Christian existence in the world. The choice of the term "hidden" (κρύπτω *kryptō*) may have been prompted by the philosophy's interest in the notion of hidden or secret knowledge (cf. 2:3).

It is striking that believers' lives are said to be hidden "with Christ in God." They are "in God" because they are bound up with Christ, who is himself in God. In contrast to any ascent of the soul in order to appease the powers and achieve union with God, believers already have such a relationship on the basis of their link with Christ; and, by its very nature, being in God provides a security that needs no completion.

But for this writer, as for Jewish apocalyptic writings, hiddenness is not simply a mystical concept but is linked to God's purposes for history. That which is at present hidden in heaven is yet to be revealed in history. The mystery of God's plan for salvation has been revealed in Christ (1:26-27), but part of it remains hidden, including the true nature of believers' relationship with Christ, and awaits full revelation at the consummation.

The depiction of believers' relationship with Christ in v. 4 is also distinctive. Their lives are so bound up with Christ that the one who will be revealed at the end can be called "our life."[114] This identification between Christ and believers is reminiscent of Paul's formulations in Gal 2:20 and Phil 1:21 and sums up the way in which for believers Christ embodies what is of greatest value in life. Believers' relationship with Christ will be revealed in its full glory when Christ is manifested or revealed. Although some have disputed it, this is a reference to the parousia. It is true that being made manifest, or revealed, is not necessarily the same thing as "coming," but elsewhere in the Pauline corpus Christ's being revealed from heaven is synonymous with his coming (see 2 Thess 1:7, 10). The language of being revealed rather than coming is shaped by the hidden/revealed contrast of vv. 3-4, but nevertheless constitutes the letter's only reference to the parousia. At the parousia's unveiling of Christ's glory, the readers will also experience the unveiling of the consummation of their salvation as they share the glory of Christ that God had intended for humanity.

This formulation brings together a number of Pauline themes: the glory to be revealed, which includes the revelation of the sons and daughters of God and involves the redemption of their bodies (Rom 8:18-19, 23); the transformation of believers' bodies of humiliation into conformity with Christ's glorious body (Phil 3:21); and the resurrection of believers as entailing a body of glory in the image of the heavenly Christ (1 Cor 15:43, 49). The "then" in v. 4*b* makes the writer's assertion emphatic. Such experience of heavenly glory will only become available to sight at the consummation. This shows the normal Pauline eschatological reserve emerging forcefully despite the writer's earlier emphasis for the sake of his readers on "realized" eschatology. Colossians 3:1-4 can now be seen to demonstrate that believers' relationship "with Christ" receives its dynamic from the history of salvation. Believers have died and been raised with Christ, their lives are at present hidden in heaven with Christ, and they will be revealed in glory with Christ.

---

114. The choice between two textual variants here makes little difference to the meaning. The reading "your life" has the strongest external attestation, but, despite the NRSV and the NIV, it seems more likely that at an early stage a scribe changed an original "our" to "your" to conform to the surrounding syntax than that an awkward change was made in the other direction, because the identification of Christ with the readers' life appeared too exclusive.

REFLECTIONS

1. Appropriately, Col 3:1-4 serves as an alternative reading for Easter Day in Year A of the lectionary cycle. In that context, it underscores that Christ's resurrection is not to be viewed as some extraordinary, isolated event but one that inaugurated a new order in which believers have become participants.

The passage can serve, therefore, as a reminder that the real new age began with the resurrection of Jesus—not with a planetary shift from the Age of Pisces to the Age of Aquarius. In some aspects of the latter "new age" spirituality, with its concern for transcendence of the everyday material world, the claim is made that the universe is inhabited by spiritual beings who have to be placated by means of ceremonies and incantations and that ordinary people need the help of shamans, sorcerers, and mediums who, through long training, have learned to penetrate this spirit world and are equipped to show others the unity and fullness of cosmic life. Encounters with spirit guardians and "out of the body" experiences are offered through a variety of techniques, including use of drugs, meditation, and ritualized dance. Such claims do not appear too far removed from those of the philosophy. The letter writer's attempt to redirect his readers' concern with the heavenly realm and to advocate a genuine heavenly mindedness rooted in the Pauline gospel is suggestive for the contemporary church in the midst of those who are groping for transcendence. Christian proclamation will need to redirect contemporary interest in "the transcendent" to a relationship with a transcendent person, the risen and exalted Christ. The message of Colossians updated for such a situation might well be, "Since there is so much concern for experience of the transcendent, seek that transcendence in which the risen and exalted Christ is central." Contemporary readers of Colossians might do well to reflect on whether their worship, both public and private, is simply a routine exercise or an experience of transcendence shaped by encounter with the heavenly Christ and whether their lives are characterized by the sort of heavenly mindedness that transforms every part of life by seeing it in relation to the lordship of the exalted Christ.

2. Consideration of this section of Colossians in connection with what follows inevitably raises questions about the relationship of otherworldliness and this-worldliness in Christian existence. On the one hand, the extreme of this-worldliness might ask, "What can talk about spirituality and heavenly existence possibly mean to someone living on the poverty line and in squalid conditions?" On the other hand, the extreme of otherworldliness might ask, "What can the poverty line and squalid conditions matter to someone who has the hope of heaven?" For the writer of Colossians, being heavenly minded rather than earthly minded is not some compensation for life's ills but is motivated by attending to one's relation to the church's Lord, who from his position with God controls the course of human history and who will at its culmination bring the life of heaven to transform the earth. As becomes clear in the next section, heavenly mindedness is not to be understood as a form of absentmindedness about ordinary life or social and economic conditions. Having a heavenly reference point is, instead, the very thing that should drive believers on within their social situation to pursue justice and fairness (cf. 4:1).

This passage's exhortation to "seek the things above," when taken in context, provides no justification for the popular reduction of the Christian hope to the individualistic one of "going to heaven when I die." Both the notions of Christ's resurrection, participation in which opens up access to the heavenly, and of his future revelation in glory with believers at the parousia are part of the broader Pauline eschatological hope that is retained here. That hope is for believers to share Christ's resurrection life in transformed bodily form. We should not forget that the vision of the hymnic material in 1:15-20 is for a reconciled cosmos, explicitly including heaven and earth. In the meantime, believers' roles in the working out of this cosmic drama are sustained by their relationship to their Lord in heaven. This relationship is such that Christ is said to be the life of believers and their lives are depicted as being hidden with Christ in God, so that not even their physical death before the parousia will be able to affect their participation in the final act of the drama.

3. In the meantime, however, there does remain a "hiddenness" to believers' lives in Christ. Amid all the letter's emphasis on the wisdom and knowledge believers have in Christ, it is salutary to remember this. By no means everything about Christian living is apparent, not only to outsiders, for whom much of it appears foolish, but also to Christians themselves, for whom there remain mystery and much questioning until the final revelation. We will not see all that is entailed in our new identity until the eschaton, and there will be times when everything seems to tell against its reality. So while the relationship with Christ speaks of assurance, our present experience of it is partial and provisional. Its hiddenness necessitates that Christians live by faith and not by sight and, therefore, without all the answers to the meaning of many events in their lives.

Colossians 3:5–4:1, Exhortation to Holiness of Life

OVERVIEW

After the exhortations to genuine heavenly mindedness there now follows a series of ethical exhortations. The preceding exhortations and the first of the ethical exhortations are linked to the conceptuality of the philosophy and ensure that the ensuing more general paraenesis is not viewed as completely independent of the situation being addressed by the letter as a whole. Given the infrequency of exhortations about worship in paraenesis and the place of particular worship practices in the philosophy, it is probably more than a coincidence that 3:16 provides instruction about Christian worship. The paraenesis includes a collection of *sententiae*, ethical sentences, common among Hellenistic philosophers and adopted by Hellenistic Judaism, that were frequently in the form of imperatives and gave rules of conduct for daily life. From the same sources are derived the catalogs of vices and virtues in 3:5, 8, 12 and the household code taken up in 3:18–4:1. The contrast between two patterns of conduct reflected in the vices and virtues, the "Two Ways," is found both in Jewish Scriptures and in other writings (see Deut 30:15-20; Psalm 1; *T. Ash.* 1:3, 5; 1QS 3.13–4.26); it is also used frequently in Greco-Roman ethical thought, which had in turn influenced Hellenistic Judaism (see Wis 14:25-26).[115]

115. See also Philo *On the Sacrifices of Abel and Cain* 20-45.

Colossians 3:5-11, Put to Death What Is Earthly

COMMENTARY

3:5-8. The ascetic regulations insisted upon by the advocates of the philosophy were designed to deal with people's "members on the earth"—that is, their physical bodies, which are dependent on the lower, material realm. In v. 5, the writer takes up this notion but gives it his own ethical twist. Both the NRSV and the NIV miss the force of this with their paraphrases of v. 5a. The language at first sounds as if the writer is contradicting his previous polemic against asceticism and severity to the body: "Put to death the members on the earth." But then comes the list, not of physical parts of the body, as the reader might expect, but of vices. His point is that a genuine concern for the heavenly realm arising out of believers' union with Christ will not lead to the gratification of the flesh, for which he has criticized the philosophy (cf. 2:23). In the thought of Paul there is an "already" and a "not yet" to dying with Christ, whereby those who have died to sin (Rom 6:2-4) still need to be exhorted to put to death the deeds of the body (Rom 8:13). Similarly here, those who have died with Christ

(2:20; 3:3) still have to be told to put to death sinful practices.

The writer is fond of lists of five. In v. 5 he lists five vices, as also in v. 8, while in v. 12 he will catalog five virtues. The first five vices start off as explicitly sexual ones and gradually become more general. Heading the vices is "fornication" (πορνεία *porneia*), a broad term denoting general sexual immorality that is also used more particularly of adultery and intercourse with prostitutes. "Impurity" (ἀκαθαρσία *akatharsia*) is usually associated with sexual sin and is also found in combination with *porneia* in 2 Cor 12:21; Gal 5:19; and 1 Thess 4:3, 7. Because of its context here, the third vice, "passion" or "lust" (πάθος *pathos*), also has a primary connotation of uncontrolled sexual appetite. "Evil desire" (ἐπιθυμία κακή *epithymia kakē*) takes the list in a more general direction, referring to all forms of sinful desire, to what Paul might call "the desires of the flesh" (Rom 13:14; Gal 5:16, 24). The fifth vice, "covetousness" (πλεονεξία *pleonexia*), is the insatiable greed whereby people assume that things or other people exist simply for their own gratification. Interestingly, and in line with Jewish tradition, covetousness is equated with idolatry.[116] The thought is that all idolatry involves some form of covetousness. When humanity refuses to acknowledge the various aspects of life as the gifts of the Creator, it attempts to seize these things for itself and thereby elevates some desired object to the center of life. In the language of Rom 1:25, humanity ends up worshiping and serving created things rather than the Creator. This is the opposite attitude to the thanksgiving that recognizes God at the center of life (cf. 3:17).

An eschatological motivation is provided for putting to death these practices. The vices are so serious that on account of them the wrath of God is coming, and the implication is that those who are found indulging in them will experience that holy anger of God and the judgment that results from it. The implication is clear, although the original text in all likelihood did not contain the phrase "on the children of disobedience" (so NIV).[117] The "once . . . but now" contrast of vv. 7-8 (cf. 1:21-22) recalls the decisive change that has taken place for the readers, so that, whereas their lives were once characterized by such vices and deserved the coming wrath, this is no longer the case. Instead, the present is to be characterized by a total transformation in which the readers are responsible for putting aside or discarding like old clothes all vices.

A further list of five is provided to ensure that the readers understand the extent of their responsibility to abandon the old way of life. Anger, which heads this new list of sins, is given an overwhelmingly negative evaluation in the OT (see Prov 15:1, 18; 22:24; Eccl 7:9), in Hellenistic Judaism (see Sir 1:22; 27:30; *T. Dan* 2.1–5.1), and in the NT (see Matt 5:22; Gal 5:20; Jas 1:19-20), presumably because of the estrangement from others that nearly always accompanies its expression. "Rage" or "wrath" (θυμός *thymos*) is synonymous with "anger" (ὀργή *orgē*), though Stoic writers sometimes distinguished them, with rage denoting the initial explosion of anger.[118] "Malice" (κακία *kakia*) includes any attitude or action that intends harm to another. Malice can express itself through "slander" (βλασφημία *blasphēmia*), the abuse and vilifying of others; shameful, foul, or obscene language (αἰσχρολογία *aischrologia*) can be the form such abuse often takes. The vices listed here, then, would all be destructive of harmonious relationships, and there can be no place for them in the new way of life, in which believers are related to one another in the body of Christ.

3:9-11. The emphasis on sins of speech, which comes to the fore at the end of the catalog of vices, is continued in the prohibition of lying. There can be no room for lies in the new community, because they poison communication and breed suspicion instead of mutual trust. The warrant used for the exhortation is formulated in terms of the transformation believers have undergone. The imperative is based on the indicative of having stripped off the old person and its practices and having put on the new. The language of "stripping off," instead of simply "putting off," again picks up the ascetic terminology of the philosophy (cf. 2:11, 15) and this time gives it an ethical twist. This is

---

116. See *T. Jud.* 19:1 and Philo *The Special Laws* 1.23, 25 for the link between covetousness and idolatry. See also Wis 14:12; *T. Reub.* 4.6; and *T. Jud.* 23.1 for the link between fornication or sexual lust and idolatry.

117. See P[46], B. The later addition appears to have been made under the influence of the parallel in Eph 5:6.

118. E.g., Diogenes Laertius 7.114; Seneca *On Anger* 2.36.

not the stripping off of the physical body in acts of severity and self-abasement (cf. 2:16, 23) but a stripping off of the old sinful way of life. Paul talks of the old person's having been crucified with Christ in Rom 6:6 and about putting on Christ in Gal 3:27, where this is equivalent to being baptized into Christ; but he does not use the language of putting off the old person or putting on the new person. Some claim that this language derives from an early Christian baptismal practice of removing clothing before being baptized nude and then putting on a new garment.[119] This is possible, but the evidence for such a practice is actually from after the middle of the second century with *The Gospel of Philip* 101 and Hippolytus's *Apostolic Tradition*. The meaning of the imagery in *The Gospel of Thomas* 37, which contains no reference to baptism, is too doubtful for it to count as an allusion to the practice. In any case, the clothing imagery of putting off vices and putting on virtues was widespread among Greek and Hellenistic Jewish writers. It is far more certain that the imagery in Colossians is connected with the significance of baptism than with baptismal practice.

The translation of τὸν παλαιὸν ἄνθρωπον (*ton palaion anthrōpon*) as "old self" and τὸν νέον (*ton neon*) as "new self" (NRSV and NIV) though better than "old nature" and "new nature," tends to narrow the reference of its literal meaning, "person." The old person is the person as identified with the old humanity, living under the present evil age and its powers. The new person is the believer as identified with the new humanity, the new order of existence inaugurated by Christ's death and resurrection. Verse 10 makes clear that this new person is not yet totally new but is in process of renewal. The underlying thought is the familiar "already" and "not yet" of the new age.

The present focus of renewal is on knowledge. This is significant in the light of the letter's setting. Any search for further esoteric knowledge is to be seen as unnecessary for those who, as part of the new humanity, are continually being renewed in and growing in knowledge (cf. 1:10). The readers should expect to experience a constant development of perception that will result in their ability to live lives appropriate to the new order, a thought equivalent to Paul's formulation in Rom 12:2 about being "transformed by the renewing of your minds." That the renewal in knowledge of the new person is in conformity with the image of the one who created it underscores, through the allusion to Gen 1:27, that the believer is part of a new creation, a new humanity in whom the image of God is restored.

If v. 10 has focused primarily on the individual aspect of the new humanity, v. 11 highlights the corporate aspect, as it asserts that within the new humanity the barriers of the old order are abolished. This is an adaptation of the baptismal formula found in Gal 3:28. It is noticeable that here, however, as in 1 Cor 12:13, there is no mention of male and female. Given the problems Paul perceived about the conduct of women in the Corinthian church, the omission of this aspect in 1 Cor 12:13 is understandable. The omission may also be significant in Colossians, which will go on to introduce the household code, which demarcates more firmly different roles for husbands and wives. This should not, however, be overemphasized, since the code also discusses the roles of masters and slaves, and yet slave and free are mentioned in the Colossians version of the formula (v. 11). Nevertheless, women's asserting their freedom in Christ was a factor in the Pauline churches, while slaves' demanding their freedom apparently was not.

In the adaptation of the formula "Greek" is mentioned before "Jew" in the first pairing, possibly on account of the Gentile readership, although the dividing of humanity into Greek and Jew in the first place reflects the writer's Jewish perspective. The second pairing, "circumcision and uncircumcision," repeats the contrast, but this time puts greater emphasis on the religious aspects of the ethnic and cultural division. The thought of the new creation in v. 10 may have influenced this addition, since in Gal 6:15 Paul had written, "For neither circumcision nor uncircumcision is anything, but a new creation is everything!" Here the proclamation of Christ among the Gentiles (cf. 1:27) entails that the old humanity's categorization of people into these two classes is no longer meaningful in the new

---

119. E.g., W. A. Meeks, *The First Urban Christians: The Social World of the Apostle Paul* (New Haven: Yale University Press, 1983) 155.

humanity. If Jews divided humanity into Jews and Greeks, Greeks divided it into Greeks and barbarians, with the latter category denoting non-Greek speakers and conveying the additional overtones that such people were uncultured and uncivilized. The term "Scythian" intensifies the note of cultural contempt. The Scythian tribes around the Black Sea were considered the lowest kind of barbarian. Josephus considered them "little better than wild beasts" (see also 2 Macc 4:47 for an ironic statement indicating the low regard in which Scythians were held).[120] The terms "slave" and "free" will be discussed further under the household code. They are found in the earlier formulations in 1 Cor 12:13 and Gal 3:28; here the claim of the Pauline churches that this basic social division makes no difference in terms of believers' standing in Christ and in the new community is continued.

While the philosophy, with its condemnation of those who did not follow its rules and were still bound to the realm of the physical, introduced divisive distinctions into the body of Christ, this formulation stresses inclusiveness and does away with all distinctions based on ethnic, religious, cultural, or social criteria within the new humanity. The relation to Christ is all that matters and transcends these other categorizations. This is the force of "Christ is all and in all." He permeates and pervades the new humanity. This emphasis on Christ's centrality recalls the focus on his supremacy in both creation and redemption (1:15-20) and his paramount place in the realm above (3:1). If Christ is all in all in relation to the cosmos, then nothing less can be the case within the community of the new humanity.

120. Josephus *Against Apion* 2.269.

REFLECTIONS

1. The thrust of this passage provides another reminder that for the writer of Colossians the real issue is not learning special techniques to deal with the powerful forces at work for evil in our lives and in our society but is instead learning how to live the Christian life individually and corporately. He holds that there is no need for a diminished view of the self in which the body is deemed inferior and people are put in thrall to hostile powers that have a divisive influence. What is wrong is not an inherent flaw in the material world; it is sin, a flawed relationship with the Creator, that has produced alienation. Being restored in the image of the Creator through Christ, therefore, is what makes possible life as it was intended to be lived.

The lists of vices and virtues reflect the writer's assumption that the behavior of believers should at least match that enjoined by the conventional ethical wisdom of the day. In fact, the expectation that these standards will receive general consent adds to the persuasiveness of the appeal. In their new context, as part of the characterization of the old and new humanities, the vices and virtues selected are those that will either disrupt or enhance the life of the Christian community.

The vices, for which there is no longer any room in Christian existence, are of two main types: (1) sexual immorality and greed and (2) anger and hateful speech. That the exhortations are still needed today is indicated by the existence of some Christian groups and churches that are strongly judgmental of any failure to maintain the strictest standards of sexual conduct but are rife with malicious intrigue and spiteful gossip and of others that are so tolerant and keen to avoid any dissension that they are loath to rebuke or discipline even flagrant breaches of sexual morality.

It is easy to pass over these lists simply as conventional examples of early Christian moralism. Yet it may be worth pausing to reflect on some of the vices in a broader context. For example, it is because Christians want to celebrate the goodness of the sexual expression of human love in committed, lifelong relationships and to affirm the option of a healthy celibacy that they will be concerned, with the writer of Colossians, that the distorted practices of an uncontrolled and exploitative sexuality be rooted out or "put to death." The mention of "covetousness" invites us to broaden our reflections. It is, of course, colored by its context in a list that begins with sexual immorality, but it takes the issues in a more general direction. Greedy desire not only produces sexual exploitation but also fuels the materialism that controls the lives of individuals and societies, leading so frequently to a despising of the poor whose worship of this particular god of mammon is alleged not to be devoted enough. Anger, hatred, and malicious speech are at the roots of violence, whether that violence is domestic, leaving battered wives and children in its wake; national, producing civil wars and ethnic cleansings; or international, leading to the stockpiling of weapons through the arms trade and both the threat of their use and their actual use to wipe out human lives.

A broader perspective also compels us to ask whether anger is always a bad thing. What about the victims of violence and oppression? Should not they be allowed righteous anger? Have we not also learned that suppression of anger leads to repression and depression? A more qualified theological evaluation might well want and need to discuss how to express anger and resentment without being overcome by it, while still taking with full seriousness the destructive effects with which it is linked in Colossians. After all, anger can be evidence of the fact that evil is being taken seriously. The inability to be angry about injustice is surely a character deficiency. At the same time, anger and hatred can be a means of reestablishing a sense of self in the face of violation. Perhaps what needs to be stressed is that these appropriate human reactions are never meant to be the permanent characteristics of a life lived in the new order but a part of the costly process of moving to a love of one's enemies, not from a position of weakness but from one of appropriate strength. The listing of anger as a major vice reminds us, however, how easy it is even for victims of violence to perpetuate its cycle if they allow anger to fester and smolder into vengeance. Repressed bitterness and prolonged hatred, even as the result of acts that have wrecked our lives, have their own destructive effects.

The seriousness with which these lists of vices are to be treated emerges from the way they are evaluated theologically. In particular, the greed or covetousness that also underlies the sexual impurity the writer indicts is to be seen as idolatry. When we treat any part of the created order as ultimate, as a god, it then in fact functions like a god for us. But its control has destructive, rather than beneficial, ends. In terms of these lists of vices, sexual immorality, greed, and anger, seen as worship of the gods of Eros, Mammon, and Mars, can take over a person in a destructive way. The same is true of other objects of covetousness, such as power and prestige. But also the conduct of both lists is seen as characteristic of the old way of living, which incurs the righteous wrath of God (3:6). Two implications can be drawn from this assertion in its context. On the one hand, God's wrath, the divine judgment, is not on account of the body but on account of sin. On the other hand, the ultimate problem with sinful actions is not the harm they cause us or others, real though it is, but their affront to a holy God, with the consequence of that God's judgment.

2. Again there is benefit to be gained from seeing particularly 3:5-6 in the broader lectionary context (Year C, Proper 13). While Col 3:1-11 is the epistle reading, Hos 11:1-11 is the Old Testament reading and Luke 12:13-21 the Gospel. The parable of the rich man who fails to see his life and possessions as being on loan from God follows the warning, "Be on your guard against all kinds of greed." Hosea 11 depicts God's anguish in the face of people's propensity to idolatry. In the end, the divine anger and wrath, though merited by humans, will not be executed. They are real, but they do not have the last word, because they are in the service of God's kindness and love, which prevail. Here, too, in Colossians, despite the seriousness of the warning, it has become clear that the God of judgment is also a gracious giver, who has not only provided reconciliation instead of alienation (1:21-23) but has also made available new resources of life and power through Christ's resurrection (3:1-4) and has created the new person that is to be appropriated (3:10). Humans are required neither to save themselves from their plight nor to search for additional means to supplement the solution provided in the gospel. They are to realize that the one who knows the depth and seriousness of their plight has already provided at great cost a solution fully sufficient to match it and that all that is needed is to appropriate fully and thankfully what has been offered.

3. What are the contemporary equivalents of the categories listed in 3:11 that ought not to be obstacles to unity and reconciled relationships within the church? Certainly male and female still need to be added, and, in the light of contemporary understanding of sexual orientation, gay/lesbian and straight should be included. In a global context, the disparity between "First World" and "Two-thirds World" Christians scarcely reflects a universal community displaying the overcoming of differences in a loving and just reconciliation in Christ. Depending on our particular social location, we will also know how far there is to go in the church's being any different from our society's marginalization of particular ethnic groups, whether they be African American, Hispanic American, or Native American. The categories of "slave" and "free" in Colossians also remind us of the economic and class differences that are meant to be overcome in the church today.

As if such categories do not present enough of a challenge, since the time of Colossians the church has also experienced the barriers to unity produced by denominational and theological labeling. Is it more important to be known as evangelical or to promote a common gospel? Is it more important to be known as catholic or to focus on the one church and its sacraments? Is it more important to be thought liberal than to be concerned for a reasoned and critical articulation of the gospel in interaction with our culture? Is it more important to promote the charismatic movement than to be open to the variety of workings of the one Spirit?

Colossians 3:12-17, Put on Love, Appropriate the Peace of Christ, and Be Thankful

COMMENTARY

3:12. The writer now issues further exhortations about the qualities necessary for living in the new community. Just as believers have already stripped off the old person, but still need to discard specific vices, so now, although they have already put on the new person, they still need to clothe themselves with specific virtues. The readers are described as God's elect, holy and beloved. All three designations were used for Israel in the LXX (esp. Deut 7:6-8), and the cluster here provides a forceful reminder to the Gentile readers that through God's initiative in Christ they have now been chosen and set apart for God, who has bestowed upon them the divine love. So it is as the new people of God that they are to put on the qualities of the new humanity.

The five virtues listed in 3:12 are those required for harmonious living as a community. The new people of God need a deep and heartfelt sympathy for the situations of others and active consideration (compassion and kindness) for others' interests and needs. The term for humility (ταπεινοφροσύνη *tapeinophrosynē*) is the same word used in 2:18, 23 to refer to the self-abasement and fasting that were part of the philosophy's ascetic program. More generally in the Greco-Roman world, the term was associated with contemptible servility. Here, among the virtues, it is viewed positively as the ability to count others better than oneself (cf. Phil 2:3), which is based on a proper sense of self-worth and not simply weakness of character. Closely associated with this quality is gentleness (NIV), entailing courtesy, considerateness, and a willingness to waive one's rights rather than to be concerned for personal gain in one's relations with others. Also intimately related to these virtues is patience, the ability not to become frustrated and enraged but to make allowances for others' shortcomings and to tolerate their exasperating behavior.

3:13. The two participial clauses in this verse may well have imperative force; they function to underline the qualities required in the previous clause by highlighting the kinds of relationships in which they will need to be displayed. They reflect a realism about problems of relationships in any community and the inevitability of complaints, clashes, and grievances. The solution offered is bearing with one another and forgiving one another. Bearing with others involves fully accepting them for who they are, with their weaknesses and faults, and allowing them worth and space. The motivation and grounds for the all-important ability to forgive others lie in the readers' own experience of forgiveness (cf. 1:14). Knowing oneself to have been forgiven by Christ should release the generosity required to forgive others.

3:14-16. A verb needs to be supplied for the beginning of v. 14, which simply reads "above all these love . . ." That verb is the main verb from v. 12, "put on" (ἐνδύω *endyō*). However, it is not entirely clear how far the imagery of clothing is to be extended and whether it is being suggested that love is the item to be put on over the the other virtues (NIV) or whether the stress on the supreme importance of love is more general (NRSV). Either way, love is described as the "bond of perfection." The thought is reminiscent of 1 Corinthians 13, where love is the greatest of the virtues (1 Cor 13:13) and its depiction (1 Cor 13:4-7) encompasses the virtues listed here in v. 12 (see also Gal 5:22-23). Love functions in this way perfectly or in a way that leads to perfection or maturity; either construction is possible. In the latter case, the perfection in view is that of the community as a whole. The broader context of relationships within the new people of God (vv. 11-12) and the one body (v. 15) reinforces the implication that love acts as a bond not only for the other virtues but also for the community in which they are to be displayed. Perfection, then, is not some individually gained state but a corporate one achieved in a relationship of love.

In 1 Corinthians 13 love is a personified power of the new age; here it is like a garment to be put on or appropriated by believers. In Colossians, it is more explicitly the peace of Christ that is personified and seen as ruling in the new order. Through Christ, God has made peace and brought about reconciliation (1:20-22), and believers have been called by God into that peace. The notion of calling points to the actualization of God's electing purposes and recalls the designation "God's chosen" in v. 12. God has brought believers into this new order of peace. Now they are to let this peace have its sway and take control both at the center of their individual lives and in the one body that their calling had in view. God's gracious initiative and believers' responsibility to respond to that initiative go hand in hand. In being called into the one unified body of the corporate new humanity, the readers have been called to live out its transcending of divisions (v. 11); they have been called to appropriate Christ's peace. So far in the letter, the term "body" (σῶμα *sōma*) has been used of the universal body of Christ (1:18, 24; 2:19). The terminology of "one body" in v. 15 has reference to the unity of that same body, though drawing on the Pauline use of body imagery for the unity of the local church in Romans 12 and 1 Corinthians 12 and with the expectation that the primary sphere of realizing that unity for the readers will be in their local house churches.

The short exhortation of v. 15*c* ("And be thankful") sets the tone for the last part of this section and introduces a threefold emphasis on thanksgiving (cf. v. 16*c*, "with gratitude," and *v.* 17*b*, "giving thanks"). Thankfulness is a key response to the gospel in this letter (see the earlier references in 1:11-12; 2:7 and the writer's own extended thanksgiving in 1:3-23). Its grounds are all that has been accomplished in God's gracious initiative in Christ. The readers' thanksgiving will come to natural expression in their communal worship.

One of the features of the philosophy was what the writer calls its "worship of angels." This may well be one reason why the writer reminds his readers of the kind of worship in which they should be participating. In that worship, the word of Christ, the message of the gospel that centers in Christ, is to provide the focus. They are to give space to the word of Christ and allow it to dwell richly among them (cf. 1:27). This will entail listening to, meditating on, and responding in praise and thanksgiving to that word as it is preached and taught. Then it will be an abundant resource as it permeates their lives.

As the readers teach and admonish one another, the word of Christ will have a firm place in the community and will be the source for all the wisdom they need. In contrast to the philosophy's concern for wisdom, which results only in the appearance but not the reality (2:23), in attending to the word of Christ the readers will be taken up with the one "in whom are hidden all the treasures of wisdom" (2:3). And they will not travel the route to this wisdom alone but together, as they learn from one another. The task of teaching and admonishing in all wisdom, therefore, is seen to be not only that which Paul exercised (cf. 1:28) but also that of all believers.

In the Greek syntax the mention of "psalms, hymns and spiritual songs" is in the dative case and is linked more closely to the preceding participles "teaching and admonishing" (διδάσκοντες καὶ νουθετοῦντες *didaskontes kai nouthetountes*) than to the following one, "singing" (ἄδοντες *adontes*). The use of psalms, hymns, and songs, therefore, is a primary means by which mutual teaching and admonition take place. It is significant that when the writer of Ephesians takes up this language from Colossians in Eph 5:19, he clearly gives it this force. Hymns were meant to function as vehicles not only for worship but also for instruction. Much of what is hymnic in the Pauline corpus has a didactic and paraenetic function, and this writer has employed the hymnic material in 1:15-20 in this fashion (cf. Phil 2:6-11; 1 Tim 3:16).[121]

It is difficult to draw any hard and fast distinctions among the three categories of song mentioned here. They are the three most common terms for religious songs in the LXX, where they are used interchangeably. In all probability, the adjective "spiritual" (πνευματικός *pneumatikos*), signifying "inspired or prompted by the Spirit," applies to all three words and not just the last. Inspiration by the Spirit need not necessarily be equated with spontaneity, however. And all forms of hymnody found in the early church are likely to be in view, from liturgical pieces that had already become established in worship, such as 1:15-20, to chants and songs freshly created in the assembly. But of more importance than the type of songs sung was the attitude with which they were sung. The songs should flow out of gratitude and thanksgiving, come from the heart, and be directed in praise to God.

3:17. The language of this verse makes unmistakably clear that the scope of the paraenesis is being extended from community life and worship to encompass all of life. To do everything "in the name of the Lord Jesus" is to recognize that his lordship claims every part of a believer's life. But it also becomes clear that the obedience involved is not some burdensome duty but the accompaniment and natural expression of the thanksgiving believers offer to God through Christ, as the writer returns at the end of the section to one of his dominant motifs. By stressing that there can be no discontinuity between the readers' worship and everyday life, this verse provides an appropriate transition to the household code, whose duties now give more specificity to "whatever you do."

---

121. See S. E. Fowl, *The Story of Jesus in the Ethics of Paul: The Function of the Hymnic Material in the Pauline Corpus* (Sheffield: JSOT, 1990).

REFLECTIONS

Colossians 3:12-17 is the lection appointed for the First Sunday After Christmas (Year C). Its theme of the life of the new humanity is appropriate to the start of a new year, and its specific exhortations can give perspective and direction to the seasonal activity of making resolutions. What better resolve than to put on and grow in the virtues that will always remain incumbent for Christians and to find specific ways of expressing these.

COLOSSIANS 3:12-17 REFLECTIONS

1. It is important to realize that the forgiveness that is in view is in the context of relationships among believers and presupposes mutuality: "Forgive each other." Forgiveness is not the overlooking or absorbing of hurt that comes from a weak sense of our own selves. Those who are exhorted are first reminded of the identity they have been given as a result of God's calling. Their election as a holy people, consecrated to God's purposes, means that they are also loved by God (3:12). Knowing oneself to be loved by God in Christ provides the proper sense of self and the source for relating in forgiving love to others (3:13). In the context of a relationship to God in Christ and to others in the new community of the church, forgiveness has as its goal not merely the healing of one's emotions from an offense or a hurt but the reconciliation with others that will display God's purposes of harmony, being realized in Christ. The realistic recognition that believers as new persons are still in the process of renewal means that forgiveness is essential for the functioning of the new humanity. Any community in which forgiveness is not an integral part will be a superficial one. And what is required for sustaining community is likely to be more than a single act of forgiveness; rather, the lives of the people in that community will be characterized by the continuing practices of forgiveness that draw their resources from the forgiveness already enacted by Christ.[122]

Of course, the requirement of practicing forgiveness is not limited to settings of mutuality; sometimes these can be lacking even within the church. But when it comes to exhorting people to forgiveness in settings beyond those in which both parties can be assumed to desire reconciliation, care is needed. For some who are victims in relationships, this could result in the perpetuation of abuse and violence and a further diminution of any sense of self-worth. Forgiveness is not a remedy for healing all relationships. Sometimes those relationships simply have to be escaped or ended. But the issue of forgiving those who have made one's life hell on earth will remain.

2. Closely related to forgiveness is love. The sacrifice of one's own interests out of concern for the welfare of others is the quality above all that is necessary in the new humanity. Most of the evils that have marred the history of the church have been due to the absence of this virtue, which is meant to be the binding agent, the superglue in church unity. Hope always remains, because in Pauline thought just as sin is a power of the old age, so also love is a power of the new age. Here, too, it is available as the supreme virtue to be put on, the power to be appropriated, the resource that enables one to allow the concerns of another to weigh more heavily than one's own desire for self-fulfillment and to reach out toward another with no expectation of reward.

3. The goal of the costly activities of both forgiveness and love comes into view with the mention of the rule of Christ's peace both within believers' hearts and in the one body. This notion of the rule of peace would no doubt have called to mind the *Pax Romana,* the militarily imposed peace that brought the absence of war through Rome's adjudication or umpiring of disputes in the empire. The rule of Christ's peace is of a quite different kind, however, entailing a reconciliation with God, cosmic in its scope, that was brought about through Christ's becoming the victim of Roman crucifixion. Believers are now called to appropriate and live out the peace of Christ that has been achieved, to let it rule in their own lives and in the church. It involves not a removal from all conflict but a centeredness that comes from knowing that in the new humanity Christ is in control and all in all. Such peace removes the need for manipulation of others or fear about others' opinions and enables reconciliation to continue to be the hallmark of the body of Christ as it shapes and controls Christian vision and actions.

---

122. For a helpful discussion of forgiveness as "a habit that must be practised over time within the disciplines of Christian community," see Jones, *Embodying Forgiveness,* esp. 163-204.

4. The life of the Christian community living in the world as the bridgehead of the new humanity is to be distinguished not only by the quality of its interpersonal relationships but also by the quality of its worship. For Colossians, what is central is the word of Christ, the gospel, to which worship is the response. The focus is on its spoken proclamation, as attested by the mention of teaching and admonition that follows. By extension, we can see the centrality of the word of Christ maintained through Scripture, of which Colossians itself is now a part, and through the sacraments, which are at least visible words.

What is particularly telling is the relationship set out between the gospel and the community, as the readers are told to "let the word of Christ dwell in you richly." This suggests that the purpose of the focus on gospel proclamation is the formation and shaping of the community to embody the word of Christ in its witness in the world. The responsibility for the gospel's being allowed its continuing, settled, and distinctive function as an inexhaustible source for formation is not simply that of preachers and teachers but of the whole assembly as it engages in mutual wise admonition and teaching (3:16). How far do we ensure that our services, or at least house groups, give the opportunity for all believers to play a role as wisdom teachers?

For those who do have specific responsibilities for preaching and teaching the word of Christ, this emphasis in Colossians provides a reminder that such responsibilities are to be exercised on behalf of the community and will have as their goal the community's formation. This may sound like a statement of the obvious, but our experience of sermons may tell us that, if this insight were really absorbed, it would have much more impact on the way preaching is carried out. Rather than aiming simply to inform or persuade, the sermon would aim to shape the identity and life of the Christian community. Rather than simply being a distillation of the preacher's own experience of or insight into the gospel, the sermon would aim to allow the listeners to enter into their own encounter with the word of Christ, which addresses us through the Scriptures.

In the community's worship, psalms, hymns, and spiritual songs have a twofold function. On the one hand, they play a part in the community's being formed by the word of Christ. If Col 1:15-20 was originally part of such hymnody, then the letter itself is the writer's attempt to allow that particular word about Christ to do its job. On the other hand, such songs are an offering of praise to God. Praise is the appropriate response to the good news of God's actions in Christ; it is an indication that grace has had its liberating effect, moving us from preoccupation with ourselves to the worship of God that constitutes what it is to be truly human. Far from leading simply to a passive acceptance of the status quo, the thankfulness that underlies such praise is also the motivation that ensures that the worshiping community brings to bear the lordship of Christ in every aspect of its life in the world (3:17).

Colossians 3:18–4:1, Let Christ's Lordship Shape Household Relationships

COMMENTARY

In this section, the three basic relationships within the ancient household become the focus of the paraenesis, as the writer indicates that the heavenly mindedness to which he has exhorted his readers needs to be worked out in every aspect of daily life. In each of the three relationships, those expected to have the subordinate role in the relationship—wives, children, and slaves—are addressed first and then those who have the authoritative role—husbands, fathers, masters. In practice, of course, the address to the latter would frequently be to the same person, the male head of the household, in three different relationships. After the address of each group comes an imperative that, except in the case of husbands and fathers, is followed by a warrant giving the reason or motivation for the required conduct. The exhortation to slaves is the longest in the section, and in it the pattern of imperative followed by a warrant is repeated. The section constitutes the writer's adaptation of what has become known as "the household code" and appears to be the first instance of the use of such a schema in the NT.

❖   ❖   ❖   ❖

EXCURSUS: "THE HOUSEHOLD CODE": ITS ORIGIN AND ADAPTATION

Although some scholars had maintained that the household code was a Christian creation and others that it had been adapted from Stoic moral philosophy, the view that predominated for a considerable time was that the household code derived from the attempts of Philo and Josephus to show the links between the social duties of Judaism and Hellenistic moral philosophy. It was presumed that this type of Hellenistic Jewish ethical teaching was mediated to early Christianity via the Hellenistic synagogues.[123] More recently, however, it has been shown convincingly that such a hypothesis does not do sufficient justice to the more general discussion of household management in the ancient world and that the thought of Philo and Josephus needs to be situated within this broader stream of tradition.[124] This broader tradition, which also treats husband/wife, parent/child, and master/slave relationships and focuses on authority and subordination within these relationships, connects the topic of the household to the larger topic of the state and derives from the classical Greek philosophers.[125] All the elements of their discussion are continued down into the later Roman period. Philo and Josephus also adapted Aristotle's outline of household subordination in their interpretation and recommendation of Mosaic law.[126] Typical of the content of all such discussions is the notion that the man is intended by nature to rule as husband, father, and master and that failure to adhere to this proper hierarchy is detrimental not only to the household but also to the life of the state.

Setting the household code within this tradition becomes significant for assessing its use within early Christianity. The tradition reveals that proper household management was regarded as a matter of crucial social and political concern. Any upsetting of the household's traditional hierarchical order could be considered a potential threat to the order of society. In Greco-Roman culture, wives, children, and slaves were expected to accept the religion of the *paterfamilias,* the male head of the household, and so religious groups that attracted women and slaves were particularly seen as likely to be subversive of societal stability. Stereotyped criticism about breeding immorality and sedition was leveled by Greco-Roman writers against the cults of Dionysus and Isis, which attracted female devotees, and also against Judaism, because Jewish slaves rejected the worship of their Roman masters' gods. Dionysius of Halicarnassus criticized foreign mystery cults and praised the virtues of Roman households with their insistence on the

---

123. See J. E. Crouch, *The Origin and Intention of the Colossian Haustafel* (Göttingen: Vandenhoeck & Ruprecht, 1972) esp. 95-101, who provides the most detailed exposition of this view.
124. See D. L. Balch, *Let Wives Be Submissive: The Domestic Code in 1 Peter* (Chico, Calif.: Scholars Press, 1981), and also his review of the issues in "Household Codes," in *Greco-Roman Literature and the New Testament,* ed. D. E. Aune (Atlanta: Scholars Press, 1988) 25-50.
125. See Plato *Laws* 3.690A-D; 6.771E-7.824C; Aristotle *Politics* 1.1253b, 1259a.
126. See Philo *Hypothetica* 7.1-14; *On the Decalogue* 165-67; Josephus *Against Apion* 2.22-28.

EXCURSUS: "THE HOUSEHOLD CODE": ITS ORIGIN AND ADAPTATION

obedience of wives, children, and slaves.[127] And significantly, Josephus's stress on subordination within the three household relationships is a response to slander against the Jews in an attempt to show that Judaism was not subversive of the ethic demanded by Greco-Roman society.[128]

As women and slaves joined the new Christian movement in large numbers, it, too, became the object of suspicion and criticism. It may well, therefore, have been the need to respond to accusations from outsiders and to set standards in line with common notions of propriety as much as the need to respond to enthusiastic demands for freedom on the part of believers that led Christians to produce their own version of the household code. This was certainly a major factor by the time of the code's use in 1 Peter (see 1 Pet 2:12; 3:15-16).

In the first extant Christian household code here in Colossians, the reasons for its introduction are not made explicit. The primary reason for its adaptation appears to be that the writer found it appropriate in re-calling those who might have been attracted by the philosophy, with its stress on asceticism and visionary experiences, to the significance of earthly life with its domestic duties. It may well be, however, that his re-call takes this particular form precisely because of the social factors that have been noted. The philosophy had taken over some elements of Judaism in its observances, and they had become part of a package of teachings and practices that resembled those of mystery cults. What is more, by the second century CE, in popular thought asceticism, philosophy, and magic were all associated with signs of deviancy from social norms.[129] If "worship of angels" is the writer's description of the practice, frequently attested in magical traditions, of invoking angels in order to placate and ward off evil spirit powers, then the teaching being opposed in Colossians would bear all the marks of social deviance. It could be characterized as philosophy, was clearly ascetic, and advocated practices associated with popular magic. It would not be at all surprising that the writer would want to distance Pauline churches from outsiders' perception of this explosive combination. His instructions signal that, far from attempting to destabilize society, life in Christian households had its distinctive motivations but provided a model that those concerned with virtue in Greco-Roman society ought to be able to recognize not as subversive but as falling within the bounds of received wisdom about the household. The summarizing exhortation in 4:5 about living wisely in regard to outsiders lends support to this suggestion.

This first use of the code in Christian literature reflects a stage in which Christians were conscious of criticisms of subverting the social order and of the need to adjust to living as Christians in the Greco-Roman world without unnecessarily disrupting the status quo. The death of the apostle Paul and the delay of the parousia are also likely to have been secondary factors contributing to this need to take a more long-term perspective on assimilating to life in society while preserving a Christian identity. This use of the code can also be seen as part of the process of stabilizing communal relations in the Pauline churches while retaining continuity with their earlier ethos. As M. Y. MacDonald observes of the code, "On the one hand, the rule-like statements reflect a more conservative attitude toward the role of subordinate members of the household; they leave much less room for ambiguity and, consequently, for exceptional activity on the part of certain members. On the other hand, the instructions are not incompatible with Paul's own teaching about women and slaves (cf. 1 Cor 11:2-16; 1 Cor 14:34-36; 1 Cor 7:20-24; Philem 10-20)."[130]

What is distinctive about Colossians' and subsequent Christian adaptation of the code is the series of exhortations to different groups within the household, all of which are treated as moral agents in their own right. What is distinctive about the content of the

---

127. Dionysius of Halicarnassus *Roman Antiquities* 2.24.3–2.27.4.
128. Josephus *Against Apion* 2.24, 27, 30.
129. See J. A. Francis, *Subversive Virtue: Asceticism and Authority in the Second Century Pagan World* (University Park: University of Pennsylvania Press, 1995) esp. 47, 49, 53.
130. M. Y. MacDonald, *The Pauline Churches: A Socio-historical Study of Institutionalization in the Pauline and Deutero-Pauline Writings* (Cambridge: Cambridge University Press, 1988) 102-3.

Excursus: "The Household Code": Its Origin and Adaptation

code in Colossians is the way in which the warrants, with their motivation, link the exhortations to believers' relationship to Christ as Lord, so that each group, including by implication husbands and fathers, is seen as equally accountable to the church's one Lord.

In its context in Colossians, the household code now forms part of the paraenesis in the writer's version of apostolic wisdom. His prayer for his readers was that they be "filled with the knowledge of God's will in all spiritual wisdom and understanding, so that you may lead lives worthy of the Lord" (1:9-10). With their roots in the wisdom found in Christ (2:2-3), the recipients are to be wisdom teachers themselves (3:16) and to live wisely in regard to outsiders (4:5). The code is situated between these last two references to wisdom and represents the writer's perspective on wise living in the household. It is not surprising that household duties would have been seen as part of wise conduct, because the Jewish wisdom tradition contained practical advice for all three household groups. All three relationships are discussed in Sir 7:19-28. Elsewhere there are frequent mentions of what is considered wise behavior for husbands and wives (see, e.g., Prov 5:18-19; 12:4; 18:22; 19:13*b*; 31:10-31; Sir 9:1; 26:1-4, 13-18), for parents and children (see, e.g., Prov 1:8; 6:20; 10:1; 13:24; 15:20; 19:13*a*, 18, 26; 23:13-14; Sir 3:1-16; 30:1-13), and for masters and slaves (see, e.g., Prov 14:35; 17:2; 19:10; 27:27; 29:19, 21; Sir 33:25-33). Not only so, but the justice and equity demanded of masters in the code is explicitly said to be the product of wisdom in Prov 2:9, and, of course, the fear of the Lord, to which slaves are exhorted, is in this tradition deemed to be either the beginning of wisdom (Prov 9:9; Sir 1:14) or wisdom itself (Sir 1:27; 19:20). The wisdom tradition offered moral guidance based on the sages' experience of and observations on human affairs and life in the world and attempted to discern in this a divine pattern and purpose. Now the wisdom teaching of Colossians takes up an early Christian version of accumulated reflection on household management from the Aristotelian and Hellenistic Jewish traditions and by this means attempts to determine the shape of believers' conduct in the light of Christ's lordship.

3:18-19. Within the marriage relationship wives are addressed first and are exhorted to subordinate themselves voluntarily to their husbands. The verb ὑποτάσσεσθαι (*hypotassesthai*) refers to taking a subordinate role in relation to another person. What it involves more specifically depends on the social expectations attached to the relationship to which it is applied. Elsewhere in the NT it is employed of the relationship of wives to husbands in Eph 5:22 (where this verb is implied from the previous verse); Titus 2:5; and 1 Pet 3:1. Outside the NT there are only two examples of the use of this verb for the relationship,[131] while the more usual term is "to obey."[132]

In the light of the fact that this latter verb is employed here in the case of children (v. 20) and slaves (v. 22), some have argued that a distinction is to be made between "to submit/be subordinate" and "to obey." Although there is clearly a difference between willing submission and imposed obedience, there is really no meaningful difference between voluntary subordination and voluntary obedience. "To submit" is the broader term, but in the expectation of the ancient world a wife's submitting to her husband would have entailed her being willing to obey him. Submission and obedience of wives to husbands are explicitly paralleled in 1 Pet 3:5-6. The motivation for such submission ("as is fitting in the Lord") means that subordination is being required not simply because it is the role society has allotted the wife but also because, in the writer's view, it is appropriate for members of the community that confesses Christ as Lord (cf. 2:6-7). Thereby the

---

131. See Plutarch *Advice on Marriage* 33; Ps-Callisthenes *History of Alexander the Great* 1.22.4.
132. See Philo *Hypothetica* 7.3: "Wives must be in servitude to their husbands, a servitude not imposed by violent ill-treatment but promoting obedience in all things." See also Josephus *Against Apion* 2.24: "The woman, it [the law] says, is in all things inferior to the man. Let her accordingly be obedient, not for her humiliation, but that she may be directed; for God has given authority to the man."

patriarchal marriage pattern is reinforced and given a christological warrant.

The exhortation to husbands has both positive and negative formulations, both of which would make easier their wives' willingness to be subordinate. After the exhortation to wives to submit, the readers might well have expected that husbands would then be told to rule their wives. Instead, the exhortation is for them to love their wives. Such an exhortation is found in other ancient writings but is fairly infrequent, and the verb "love" (ἀγαπάω *agapaō*) never occurs in Greco-Roman discussions of household management that set out the husband's duties. So in terms of contemporary instructions on marriage, this writer's requirement of husbands is by no means merely conventional.

Earlier in the chapter (v. 14), love has been seen as the culmination of the virtues listed in vv. 12-13. The exhortation to sacrifice one's own interests for the welfare of others, which was so necessary for the harmony of the community, now finds a more specific application in the husband's role in contributing to marital harmony. Husbands are asked to exercise the self-giving love that has as its goal only their wives' good and that will care for their wives without expectation of reward.

Although both the NRSV and the NIV translate the negative formulation of the exhortation to husbands as a prohibition against them acting harshly, the passive form of the verb indicates that bitterness or harshness is being experienced by its subject. A better translation would be "do not be embittered with them." The opposite of compassionate love is a hard-heartedness that harbors resentment and bitterness toward others. It is against such an attitude and the conduct it engenders that the writer warns husbands.

3:20-21. The advice to children and parents is included, because it is one of the three basic household relationships treated in the discussion of household management in the Aristotelian tradition. But the general apologetic factors that had become linked with the code also applied to this relationship. When Tacitus attacked the Jews, he could charge, "Those who converted to their ways follow the same practice, and the earliest lesson they receive is to despise the gods, to disown their country, and to regard their parents, children, and brothers as of little account."[133] Attacks on the Christian movement also spoke of their subversion of children (cf. the variant readings of Luke 23:2 where Jesus is indicted for "leading astray both women and children").

The writer exhorts children to obey their parents in everything. This endorses the unanimous view in both Greco-Roman and Hellenistic Jewish writings. In Greco-Roman society in the first century CE, the father had almost absolute legal power over his children, and Hellenistic Judaism stressed the status and authority of parents. In both cultures parents were viewed as deserving of honor and obedience in all things. Colossians upholds this authority structure, but again relates it to Christ's lordship by adding, "this is pleasing in the Lord." The tradition of Judaism expressed by Philo as "If you honor parents . . . you will be pleasing before God"[134] has here been Christianized. The warrant now recalls the goal the writer has for all his readers in 1:10—that is, leading lives worthy of the Lord, fully pleasing to him. It treats children as persons who in their own right have a relationship with this Lord that both transcends and includes their duty to their parents. The term τέκνον (*teknon*, "child") denotes primarily a relationship rather than age and could be used of adults as well as small children. From the context, the children in view here are old enough to be conscious of a relationship to their Lord, to which appeal could be made, but young enough still to be living with their parents.

Fathers have obligations, as do their children as well. The plural "fathers" (πατέρες *pateres*) could be employed for both parents. However, the change of wording from "parents" in the previous verse and the fact that in Greco-Roman society the authority was vested in the father and that in Judaism the father was responsible for discipline make it almost certain that it is again the male heads of households who are being addressed, this time in their role as fathers. They are urged not to provoke or irritate their children lest the children become discouraged. This is in line with other advocates of moderation who advised gentle persuasion rather than harsh

---

133. Tacitus *Histories* 5.5.
134. Philo *On the Change of Names* 40.

threats.[135] Nevertheless, it is noticeable that the writer does not exhort fathers to exercise their authority. Instead, he presupposes that authority and then sets the bounds for its use. He also presupposes that children are not simply their fathers' legal property but are owed dignity as human beings in their own right. Fathers should not, therefore, drive their children to exasperation or resentment. This would rule out excessive discipline, unreasonably harsh demands, arbitrariness, constant nagging and condemnation, and any gross insensitivity to children's sensibilities that would break their spirit and make them listless and unresponsive.

3:22–4:1. In the longest section of the code (vv. 22-25) slaves are exhorted to obey their masters in everything, underlining the complete allegiance owed by slaves to the head of the household. In the traditional discussions of household management in both Greco-Roman and Hellenistic Jewish treatments, the ownership of slaves as property was simply axiomatic. The focus was on how a master should rule his slaves. In the first century CE a third of the population of Greece and Italy was enslaved, but the main supply of slaves was no longer through war or piracy but through birth in the house of a slave-owner. This produced a social climate in which houseborn slaves were given training for a wide variety of tasks and in which Roman legal practice had to keep pace by guaranteeing such slaves more humane treatment.[136] For this reason it should not be assumed that there was always a wide separation between the status of slave and freed person, that all slaves were badly treated, or that all who were enslaved were trying to free themselves. Clearly Pauline churches contained as equal members masters and slaves from the same household (see 3:11).

It could be that the greater proportion of paraenesis being addressed to slaves rather than masters reflects the social composition of the church or churches addressed, which would have contained more slaves than slave-owners, or that the code reflects the perspective of the leaders of the churches, which would have been more that of the masters than the slaves. Certainly the paraenesis reflects typical views of the behavior of slaves: attempting to ingratiate themselves (3:22-23), defrauding their masters and exploiting their good favor (3:25).[137]

On the other hand, it may well be that this section of the code is more extended because the writer sees the slave/master relationship as paradigmatic for the motivation of all the members of the household. Its warrants and motivations contain five references to Christ as Lord. The exhortations to slaves and masters place both in the same relation to Christ as Lord. The reference to "fearing the Lord," which recalls wisdom teaching, is found in the first exhortation to slaves (3:22c). But the last line of the code is also now highly significant for its reference to Christ's lordship. "Knowing that you also have a master or lord in heaven" now subjects the householder to the same binding obligation to Christ as that required of wives, children, and slaves; and since in the ancient household the masters were the same persons as the husbands and fathers, the force extends back to the earlier exhortations to those in the superior social position and places the whole household under the lordship of Christ. This notion that the masters of the household have a master over themselves is quite different from other discussions of the household in antiquity.[138] In line with this, the center of gravity in the Colossian code can now be seen to be the exhortations to slaves, "because it is precisely this group that is able to represent most adequately the relation of all Christians to Christ."[139] The writer does not say that in the slave/master relationship the master represents Christ, but the relationship within the ancient household that demonstrates both the possession of all believers by their Lord and their obligation to this Lord is that of slaves to their master. For this reason, it is the one that receives most attention as a paradigm for the motivation that should inform all members of the household and that is summed up in the command of 3:24b: "Serve the Lord

---

135. See, e. g., Menander in Stobaeus, *Anthology* 4.26.7, 13; Ps. Phocylides 207.

136. On the conditions for slaves, see especially S. S. Bartchy, ΜΑΛΛΟΝΧΠΗΣΑΙ: First Century Slavery and the Interpretation of 1 Corinthians 7:21 (Missoula, Mont.: Scholars Press, 1973) and ABD 6.58-73.

137. See K. R. Bradley, *Slaves and Masters in the Roman Empire* (New York: Oxford University Press, 1987) 26-31, 35, 343.

138. See M. Gielen, *Tradition und Theologie neustestamentlicher Haustafelsethik* (Frankfurt: Anton Hein, 1990) 118.

139. Gielen, *Tradition und Theologie neustestamentlicher Haustafelsethik*, 119.

Christ." The basic insight lying behind such a paradigm is, of course, indebted to Paul, since he had held that all humans are under some power and had used slavery as a metaphor for this perspective. Humans are either slaves to sin or slaves to God (Rom 6:15-23), and even if Christian believers are free persons in social terms they are still slaves of Christ (1 Cor 7:22).

In any case, the exhortations should not be interpreted as a reaction against unrest among Christian slaves caused by talk of Christian freedom or the baptismal formulations of Gal 3:28 and Col 3:11. There is simply no evidence that Christian slaves posed a social threat by calling for emancipation. The writer's own perspective evidently sees a distinction between the equal status of slaves and masters in the church and their roles in the Christian household, where the hierarchical social structures still pertain. Nevertheless, what remains striking and unprecedented about his use of the code in comparison with traditional discussions of household management is that slaves are addressed directly and not simply as members of the household but as full members of the church.

The appeal to slaves is to obey in everything their masters "according to the flesh." This designation already introduces a Christian perspective and points to a play on the term "lord/master" (κύριος *kyrios*), which runs through the passage. In obeying their fleshly masters, slaves are to see obedience as part of their responsibility to their true Master or Lord. After the initial literal use in 3:22a, all the other uses of the term in 3:22b-24 refer to Christ, and then in 4:1 fleshly or earthly masters are reminded that they have a heavenly Master or Lord.

Despite this relativizing of the relationship, slaves' obedience to their masters is to be thoroughgoing and exhibit integrity. This is described first negatively and then positively. It will exclude the dissimulation and fawning of trying to catch their masters' eye or of currying favor (3:22b). Rather, obedience will be carried out "in singleness of heart" (3:22c), a phrase underlining purity of motivation and singleness of purpose. This sort of inner commitment is made possible by "fearing the Lord" (3:22d). Just as the motivation and guiding principle for conduct in the Jewish Scriptures was the fear of Yahweh, so also now slaves are to carry out their duties motivated by awe of Christ and his sovereign claim as Lord. Those who fear the Lord will, in whatever they do, work, literally, "from the soul" (3:23a)—that is, wholeheartedy and unreservedly, because they are doing it for the Lord and not for other human beings (3:23b). This last point simply underscores that obedience to the heavenly Master is ultimately determinative and provides a specific application of the earlier exhortation of 3:17, "Whatever you do, in word or deed, do everything in the name of the Lord Jesus."

The exhortation of 3:23 is grounded in the reminder in 3:24 that the reward that really counts will come from this Master. Some discussions of household management recommended motivating slaves by holding out various rewards, such as praise, more food, or better clothes and shoes.[140] The writer of Colossians attempts to motivate Christian slaves by holding before them the prospect of eschatological reward: the inheritance previously described in 1:12. A contrast with Roman law, in which a slave could not inherit anything, may also be intended. Through their relationship with Christ, slaves are treated as sons and daughters with full rights to the inheritance of the saints in light.

Both the NRSV and the NIV take the verb in 3:24b (δουλεύετε *douleuete*, "serve") as indicative. In the light of the preceding and following assertions about rewards and the conjunction "for" in the following clause, which acts as a warrant, it may well best be taken as an imperative: "Be slaves of the Lord Christ." This provides a forceful underlining of the whole perspective of these exhortations to slaves and, though addressed to slaves, of the motivation in the code as a whole. Slaves are to see themselves, particularly in the light of future judgment and reward, as slaves first and foremost not of their fleshly masters, but of their true Master, Christ.

Unlike even the best of earthly masters, with this Lord there will be no hint of partiality, and this means that there will not only be reward for genuine service but retribution for wrongdoing. In the OT and other Jewish writings, impartiality in judgment is attributed to God (e.g., Deut 10:17; Sir 35:14-16;

---

140. See Xenophon *The Economist* 13.9-12.

Jub. 5:15-19), but here by implication this quality is transferred to Christ as Lord, who has been named as the one who recompenses (3:24*a*). Situated at the end of the exhortation to slaves and immediately before that to masters, the mention of retribution to wrongdoers and of impartiality may well function both as a warning to slaves and as a reassurance to them. Not only if they do wrong, but also if they are treated wrongly, they can know that there will be an impartial judgment by the one who is Master of both slaves and masters.

Indeed, in 4:1, when masters are addressed they are reminded of this very point that they, too, have a Master in heaven (cf. 3:1), to whom they are accountable. So, in the sphere of Christ's lordship, masters are on the same footing as slaves; they are slaves of a heavenly Master (see 3:26*b*). Again, for Colossians, a heavenly orientation is no escape from issues of social concern. Here it provides the motivation for the exhortation for slaveowners to treat their slaves in accordance with the fundamental principles of justice and fairness. What is required of masters, of course, is a complete reversal of the earlier view of Aristotle that the relationship between master and slave in the household was one in which it was inappropriate to talk about justice, since there can be no injustice in relating to things that are one's own, and a slave is a man's chattel.[141] More humane views of the treatment of slaves are found in the later traditions about household management. But the justice and equity required of Christian masters set a high standard. Indeed, they are to emulate the judgment of the heavenly Lord, who, according to Isa 11:3-4, "with righteousness [or justice] shall judge the poor, and decide with equity [or fairness] for the meek of the earth" (NRSV). Again this early Christian adaptation of the household code assumes the hierarchical structure of the master/slave relationship and has a view of justice that does not attempt to change the social structures (this was simply not an option for a powerless minority) but to ameliorate and transform conditions within them.

141. See Aristotle *Nicomachean Ethics* 5.1134b.

REFLECTIONS

To the question, "How would you preach on the household code?" one answer would be, "Follow the lectionary readings, and you will not have to do so!" *The Revised Common Lectionary* omits Col 3:18–4:1; Eph 5:21–6:9; Titus 2:1-10; and 1 Pet 2:13-18; 3:1-7. Whether this is the best way to handle these passages might be debated. Certainly at some point in the teaching ministry of the church their existence as part of Scripture needs to be faced, and questions need to be asked about how they are to be interpreted by contemporary Christians.

1. It is easy to dismiss Colossians' introduction of the household code as marking a greater emphasis on hierarchical than egalitarian aspects in the Pauline churches and as a retrograde step for the position of women and slaves in its accommodation to patriarchy and slavery. Certainly its painful heritage is still with us and cannot be ignored.

It is hard to know, however, whether the intention of the writer was in any way to restrict leadership in the church on the part of exceptional women and of slaves and to put power more firmly in the hands of male heads of households. Pauline churches still seem to have been able to make a distinction at this stage between what went on in the community's gatherings for worship and what went on in the everyday life of the household in closer contact with the surrounding society. It is significant that in Col 4:15 a house church in Laodicea can still be mentioned under the name of a woman, Nympha. Nevertheless, it has to be faced that there were negative implications for women and slaves as a probably unforeseen consequence of the household code's being taken over into Christian paraenesis. Later, by the time of the Pastoral Epistles, the distinction between church and household is ignored as the church itself is understood on the model of the patriarchal household. The author of those letters writes from the perspective of the male householder, forbidding women any roles that would give them authority over men and, in contrast to the reciprocity of Colossians, addresses only slaves and not masters about their duties.

2. Despite these negative consequences, the intent of the writer of Colossians in introducing the household code may still have something positive to say to us. In response to the philosophy's emphasis on visionary experiences and ascetic practices that detracted from the significance of the structures of everyday life, the introduction of the household code at this point in the letter enabled the writer to underline the value of such structures. It is part of his claim that any spirituality that does not enable believers to cope with ordinary life and live distinctively within its structures is bogus.

One concern of many contemporary Christians is the overcoming of the division between the sacred and the profane, of the separation between religion and culture. For those who agree with the assertion of Linda Sexson, "Religion is not a discrete category within human experience; it is rather a quality that pervades all experience,"[142] the code's construal of the mundane as sacred—ordinarily sacred—can be deemed an important contribution. Charles Taylor, too, has argued that central to contemporary notions of identity and crucial for any sense of the dignity of the self is the affirmation of ordinary life, the conviction that everyday living is not merely of infrastructural importance but can be "the very center of the good life."[143]

3. If it is the case that the Colossians code is part of the writer's wisdom teaching, then there is an important corollary. Everyday life is to be valued, but it is of the essence of the practical aspects of wisdom teaching that the form of such a claim needs continual reexamination. Brueggemann asserts that the sages:

> Are constantly facing new experience that must not only be integrated into the deposit of learning, but must be permitted to revise the deposit of learning in the light of new data. This means that their word of nurture and instruction is very much "on the run." . . . Wisdom teachers may encounter Yahweh with a tone of finality. It is known among such interpreters, however, that the work must all be done again, tomorrow.[144]

This knowledge, however, has often eluded interpreters of Colossians. The history of the code's interpretation shows all too clearly a reluctance to recognize that the evaluation of what wise living in the household and in society entails must by its very nature change with changing times and circumstances.

A critical appropriation of this passage, therefore, would entail present-day Christians' attempting to do something similar in their own settings to what the writer did in his. They need to bring to bear what they hold to be the heart of the Christian message and of their relationship to Christ as Lord on contemporary conventional values in regard to the family and to social structures. Those who consider love and justice to be the central thrust of the Bible's ethical teaching will, for example, in the area of marriage want to work out a view of marriage in which both partners are held in equal regard, in which justice will require that male domination not be tolerated, and in which love will ensure that the relationship does not degenerate into a sterile battle over each partner's rights to fulfillment. Instead of assigning love to the husband and submission to the wife, a contemporary appropriation of Colossians will be aware that the letter earlier required humility, forgiveness, and love from all. It will urge mutual expression of such qualities that challenge both assumptions about love as a romantic

---

142. Linda Sexson, *Ordinarily Sacred* (New York: Crossroad, 1982) 6.
143. Charles Taylor, *Sources of the Self: The Making of the Modern Identity* (Cambridge: Cambridge University Press, 1989) 13. For Taylor's tracing of the development of this conviction, see 211-302.
144. W. Brueggemann, *Theology of the Old Testament* (Minneapolis: Fortress, 1997) 685, 691.

feeling or ecstatic experience and assumptions about freedom and rights that result in self-centered competition for control.

In the case of children and parents, respect for parents and the honoring of children's dignity and worth can still be seen as expressions of Christian love and justice that speak to a society in which, on the one hand, parental power can frequently be abused, including even sexual abuse, and, on the other hand, attempts to exercise parental responsibility can be denounced in the name of children's rights or autonomy. In the case of slaves and masters, there is no really analogous pairing in most households in Western society. There is a significant difference between their situation in the ancient world and that of employees and employers, labor and management, in more democratic societies. Exceptions remain. Some Western businesses employ foreign workers for cheap labor under conditions that amount to slavery; and some families take on immigrants, often illegally, as little more than household slaves. This part of the code can still serve as a reminder that Christians will always have the responsibility of bringing the lordship of Christ to bear on their everyday work and its conditions of employment, even though specific applications of this lordship will become obsolete and new forms of social and economic obedience will need to be found to meet changing structures. Certainly two tasks will remain encumbent on believers whose concern is not human approval but serving the Lord Christ: ensuring that relationships within the church embody Christ's ultimate disregard for any distinctions based on social status and pursuing justice and fairness in their spheres of employment.

Colossians 4:2-6, Concluding Exhortation: Pray, Live Wisely, and Speak Graciously

COMMENTARY

On an epistolary analysis, this section constitutes the closing part of the body-middle, which runs from 2:6 to 4:6, rounding off the letter's main exhortations, while a rhetorical analysis has suggested that it can be read as the peroratio, the summing up of the letter's message. Either way, to treat its contents only as further general exhortations would be to miss the way in which they provide an important summarizing conclusion and recall earlier parts of the letter, not least its programmatic statement in 1:22-23. The stress on prayer and thanksgiving (4:2) not only reminds readers of the writer's own extended thanksgiving with its intercessory prayer report in 1:3-23, but also rounds off the motif of thanksgiving that has featured throughout (cf. 1:12; 2:7; 3:15-17). The reminder of Paul's imprisonment (4:3c) points back to the depiction of Paul and his suffering for the gospel in 1:24–2:5, which had been announced in 1:23c. The notion of declaring the mystery of Christ in the requisite manner summarizes what the writer has attempted to do in the face of the philosophy in 2:6–3:4 and which had been announced in 1:23ab. The need to walk wisely (4:5a) sums up the paraenesis of 3:5–4:1, and the need to have outsiders in view when doing so is an appropriate description of the motivation for the last part of such paraenesis in the household code of 3:18–4:1. Again the need for holiness of living had been announced ahead of time in 1:21-22. Finally, 4:6 can be seen as expressing what the writer hopes his message will achieve for the readers, putting them in a position to have the appropriate answer for people.

The peroratio was also expected to make an appeal to the readers in the process of its summing up. Features that would make the readers well disposed to the speaker (pathos) include the request for prayer for his ministry (4:3a) and the mention of Paul's chains (4:3c). The latter, together with the stress again on Paul's commission to declare the mystery of Christ (4:3b), would also strengthen the focus on the speaker's character (ethos). In addition, the section appeals to the readers'

4:2. The readers are urged to pursue a life characterized by prayer. The writer's own earlier prayer report indicates the importance he attaches to prayer (cf. esp. 1:3, 9). Prayer will reflect the readers' dependence on God, and for prayer they will need the perseverance that overcomes fatigue and discouragement (see Rom 12:12). They will also need the alertness that keeps at bay spiritual complacency. Staying alert and awake involves renouncing the sleep associated with absorption in the old way of life and its "dominion of darkness" (cf. 1:13). Such alertness will be motivated and accompanied not by anxiety but by thanksgiving, one of the letter's dominant themes. Thanksgiving is the proper response of those who are awake to all the blessings of God mediated in Christ. It was demonstrated earlier by the writer in his own prayer, in which he not only asked that the readers might give joyful thanks (1:12) but also offered such thanks to God (1:3-8, 15-20).

4:3-4. In their prayers the readers are to include intercession for the writer, who has taken on the persona of Paul (and Timothy) as part of the device of pseudonymity. In particular, prayer is asked for the apostolic ministry of proclaiming the mystery of Christ. In the earlier depiction of Paul's role in declaring it, the mystery was equated first with Christ among you (1:27) and then simply with Christ himself (2:2). In proclaiming this mystery, the apostle was dependent not only on his own strenuous efforts but on God's work within him as well (1:29). It is not surprising, then, that prayer for the apostolic ministry should take the form of asking that God open a door for the Word (cf. 1 Cor 16:9; 2 Cor 2:12)—that is, prepare the way by providing "windows of opportunity" for the gospel. This gospel is not only identified with Christ as its content but is also associated with Paul and his imprisonment (4:3c). Being bound was the mark of the suffering apostle (cf. 1:24), the appropriate insignia of the proclamation of the gospel among the Gentiles.

The prayer to be offered is not just for opportunities for proclamation but also that the proclamation be made in the requisite way: "that I may reveal it, in the way that it is necessary for me to speak" (v. 4). Both the NRSV and the NIV add the notion of clarity, but the verb φανερόω (*phaneroō*) is simply part of the terminology of disclosing or unveiling the mystery (cf. 1:26). The last clause could refer to the divine necessity or compulsion upon the apostle (cf. 1 Cor 9:16) to disclose the mystery or, more probably, to the necessity of expressing the disclosure in the appropriate way. Significantly, the writer of Ephesians takes this clause to be about the manner of proclamation and makes this clear by adding the idea of boldness (see Eph 6:20). Here, since the writer considers himself a representative of Paul, the exhortation can be understood as a request for prayer that he might proclaim the Pauline gospel in the appropriate manner. Presumably that is a manner that does justice to its truth, hope, dynamic, and scope (cf. 1:5-6).

4:5-6. The writer had earlier declared that all wisdom is to be found in Christ (2:3), and the hymn he had cited, in which Christ takes on the attributes of Wisdom, had given eloquent expression to this notion (1:15-20). Now he appeals to his readers to walk in wisdom, to live wisely. In the Jewish tradition, wisdom involved not simply right knowledge but skill in living—ethical insight into God's will as revealed in the Torah. For this writer, spiritual wisdom also involves living rightly, but now in displaying conduct worthy of or pleasing to Christ as Lord (cf. 1:9-10). This has been the burden of the ethical exhortations in 3:5–4:1 and particularly of 3:17 and the household code that follows in 3:18–4:1. This is particularly significant, since it is wise living in regard to outsiders that the writer has in view here. As we have seen, a prime reason for the introduction of the code was that it enabled the writer to address issues in the community's life that were of vital importance in outsiders' perception of whether Pauline churches were a threat to the stability of society.

Wise behavior entails having the right attitude to time. The imagery used is the commercial language of the marketplace and indicates that the readers are to buy up time eagerly, capitalizing on the opportunities it offers for living out what is pleasing to their Lord. Those who are awake and alert (4:2) as they wait for the revelation of Christ in glory (3:4) will not allow present opportunities for obedience to Christ as Lord to slip past unseized. Instead, they will be ready with the right word spoken in the right way. Only now does the focus change from the earlier proclamation of the word of the gospel in the apostolic ministry to the readers' regular conversation with others, in which answers to anyone's queries about their distinctive beliefs and conduct can be given (v. 6). The writer adapts a current idiom about attractive speech. Plutarch, for example, could talk of conveying "a certain grace by means of words as with salt."[145] So the readers' speech should always be gracious—that is, attractive, persuasive, and beneficial. It is not to be insipid or bland but salted with wit and wisdom.

By cultivating such speech Christians will know how to give appropriate and persuasive responses—they will, as 1 Pet 3:15 has it, always be prepared to give an answer to everyone who asks them to give the reason for the hope that they have. In many ways this has been precisely the model of the writer's own exposition of the gospel in answer to the claims of the philosophy: striving not only to be persuasive and attractive to those who might succumb to the rival claims but also to be forceful and ironic in attempting to expose those claims. What the writer has tried to accomplish in the letter is indeed to put his readers on a firmer footing in their understanding and appropriation of the Pauline gospel. From this basis they will be able to give an answer to advocates of the philosophy and to any other questioners of the validity and sufficiency of the gospel in which they believe.

145. Plutarch *On Talkativeness* 654F. See also Plutarch *Table-Talk* 685A.

REFLECTIONS

If these short concluding exhortations can be seen to serve a summarizing function, then any reflections on their content will appropriately draw on the overall message of the letter and its impact.

1. A life characterized by prayer is a recognition of our creaturely dependence on the Creator God and a sign that this relationship has been restored through reconciliation. Three elements of prayer are featured in this section: the necessity of alertness, its characterization by thanksgiving, and its participation in the mission of the proclamation of the gospel.

Alert prayer enables us to shake off and see through the deceptive values and shadows of the old order. It heightens our perception of and keeps us in touch with reality. And, since for Colossians at the heart of reality is the grace of God in Christ, such prayer will also entail a watchfulness that this grace is not jeopardized.

Prayer is to be accompanied by the thankfulness that is also an indispensable characteristic of the new community (see 1:12; 2:6-7; 3:15-17). Its presence or absence functions as a test of whether a person has truly understood that the gospel is one of grace, of undeserved gift. It is the mark not of striving to attain the fullness of knowledge and experience of God's presence, as in the philosophy, but of having received these freely in Christ. It is also the opposite of self-centered acquisitiveness and unproductive envy with their accompanying angry resentfulness or bitterness (see 3:5, 8). Thankfulness, then, is an essential aspect of the faith that acknowledges God as the Creator, Sustainer, and Redeemer of life, that recognizes, despite everything, that God's grace in Christ is at the center of life. Prayer characterized by such thankfulness is not a technique for ignoring life's problems and pain, but its practice enables these to be faced by placing them in their true context.

Prayer is also a major means of participating in the cosmic drama of reconciliation. For the writer of Colossians, Paul and his apostolic team, including his successors, have the primary responsibility for the proclamation of the gospel throughout the world. The role of members of the Pauline churches is to be in solidarity with that wider mission through prayer. Not surprisingly, at the heart of the mission is the gospel, designated as "the mystery of Christ," and the suffering, imprisoned apostle remains the model for missionary proclamation (see 1:24–2:5). Prayer, then, will focus on both the missionaries and their message. As in the depiction of the church's mission in the book of Acts, where prayer precedes major breakthroughs in the spread of the gospel, here it is expected that the provision of opportunities for proclamation will be in response to the church's praying.

2. The final exhortations to wise living in the world and appropriate verbal witness to the source for such living can be seen as major goals of the letter. What its message has aimed to produce is not withdrawal from the world but a reclaiming of that world for the one who is its Lord. The earlier grounding of the readers in the rich resources of wisdom in Christ has been meant to enable them to be not only wise teachers of one another, not only discriminating evaluators of counterfeit claims, but also practitioners of wisdom before a watching world and wise witnesses in the face of inquiries from outsiders. So in addition to their prayerful support for global mission, local communities of believers have the responsibility for working out and implementing the implications of Christ's lordship for family life, for the work sphere, for social structures, for economic matters—for all the areas of life in which onlookers will be able to catch a glimpse of the practical wisdom of gospel values. In the biblical tradition, the wise person discerns the times and seasons (see Eccl 3:1-8). Here the discerning use of time by believers entails buying up the opportunities to display Christ's lordship. Their lives are no longer determined by the times and seasons of the astral powers (see 2:16); rather, they have been released from their burdensome past through God's forgiveness (2:13-14), and so they are now free to make time serve the ends of the one who is Lord not only of space but also of time and to seize the moment for service.

3. Again it is worth noting that Colossians does not put a heavy burden on believers in regard to evangelism. The emphasis is not on marches for Jesus, preaching on street corners, or handing out tracts. There are those with special responsibilities for missionary proclamation and evangelism, but most of us are expected to use our time in wise living in the world. It is in that context, as outsiders observe transformed lives and different values, that questions will be asked and that we then have a responsibility for witness that provides answers. This will not be the sort of witness that provokes the taunt, "Christ is the answer, but what is the question?" because it will be a response to actual questions raised by the way we live. The answers this letter expects believers to cultivate will not trample on the sensibilities of their conversation partners or subject them to a harangue in the name of the gospel but will aim to be appropriate to each questioner and his or her specific queries, and, with the use of good humor and intelligence, to be a persuasive witness.

COLOSSIANS 4:7-9, BODY-CLOSING: PASSING ON NEWS

COMMENTARY

Some of the issues surrounding how both this and the following section of the letter are to be read, if one has come to the conclusion that what precedes was not written by Paul, have been raised in the Introduction (see the section "Author and Addressees"). One of the attractions of the mediating view that Timothy composed the letter in the names of both Paul and himself is that it enables these sections to be taken in a relatively straightforward way. It is not, however, as will become clear in the next section, without its own difficulties if, as nearly all who hold that Colossians was by Paul and/or Timothy argue, the letter was written at the same time as Philemon. Other letters in which Timothy is named as co-author have a quite different style. If Timothy was able to get Paul to write the closing greeting himself (4:18), it requires considerable speculation to explain why Paul would not have been able to dictate the rest of the letter and why he was able to write the companion letter to Philemon.

As has been noted, if the letter is pseudonymous, then 4:7-18 is its attempt at verisimilitude. Similar features can be found in other ancient pseudepigraphical letters, not least the Pastoral Epistles within the NT (see, e.g., the details about individuals and the greetings in 2 Tim 4:9-22). Since the author describes Onesimus as "one of you" (4:9), it is not surprising that all the names found in this section, with the exception of Tychicus and Nympha (and probably Jesus Justus), would be drawn by the writer from the letter of Paul that had been sent to Onesimus's owner—namely, Philemon.

In the final section of paraenesis the readers had been asked to pray for Paul's proclamation of the mystery of Christ and had been reminded of his imprisonment. It forms a natural progression for the writer to mention now that Tychicus is being sent to provide his readers with further information about Paul's welfare and circumstances. The commendation of an emissary is also found toward the end of some of Paul's letters (see Rom 16:1; 1 Cor 16:10). Its use here enables the writer to avoid having to say anything more specific about Paul's situation. He can instead simply point the readers to Tychicus. Tychicus features elsewhere in the NT as one of Paul's coworkers and is particularly associated with Asia Minor (see Acts 20:4; 2 Tim 4:12). He is likely to have been known to the letter's recipients as one of the leading representatives of the Pauline mission. The threefold description of him as "a beloved brother and faithful servant and fellow slave in the Lord" reinforces his close relationship with Paul and his proven record of reliable ministry and allegiance to Christ.

Two reasons are given for Tychicus's being sent (v. 8). The first repeats the explanation already supplied in v. 7: It is so that the readers "may know how we are." The second reason is so that Tychicus might encourage the hearts of the recipients, a task presumably to be accomplished not only by conveying the news about Paul but also by providing his own ministry to the readers in line with the concerns of the letter. The writer then adds that Tychicus will be accompanied in his mission by Onesimus, recommended as a Pauline coworker through the designation "the faithful and beloved brother." His links with Colossae are underlined by the additional clause, "who is one of you."

At the end of the recommendation (v. 9c), the readers are surprisingly told for the third time that the visit of the two is to let them know about "everything here." Clearly the writer wants to emphasize their role as links between Paul and the churches of the Lycus Valley, as links in the chain of Pauline tradition. Tychicus and Onesimus may well be seen, then, as representing the apostolic heritage in this region in succession to Epaphras, who had originally brought the gospel there (see 1:7; 4:12-13).

COLOSSIANS 4:10-18

THE LETTER CLOSING

COMMENTARY

The letter closing consists of a series of greetings from those said to be with Paul and from Paul himself (4:10-15), instructions about an exchange of letters with the church at Laodicea (4:16), a message to Archippus (4:17), Paul's autograph (4:18*a*), a final exhortation to remember his imprisonment (4:18*b*), and a very brief grace benediction (4:18*c*).

4:10-11. Greetings come first from the trio of those who are said to be the only Jewish Christian coworkers of Paul and who are commended as having been a comfort to him. Whereas in 1:12 he talked of "the kingdom of his beloved Son," the writer here employs the more traditional terminology in depicting these men as coworkers for "the kingdom of God." Aristarchus, who had been described in Philemon 24 as a fellow worker of Paul, is now said to be a fellow prisoner. It is unlikely that this designation is simply figurative, referring to a relationship to Christ. The readers are meant to assume that Aristarchus shared Paul's physical imprisonment. This is a difficulty for the view that Colossians was written by Paul or Timothy at about the same time as Philemon, since in that letter Aristarchus is not a prisoner and Epaphras is (Phlm 23), while in Colossians the status of the two is reversed.[146]

Next to be named in v. 10*b* is Mark (cf. Phlm 24), whose mention is elaborated. It is made clear that he is the cousin of Barnabas so that the readers are able to associate him with the tradition of the early missionary activity of Paul and Barnabas. The Acts account gives Paul's negative assessment of John Mark's earlier desertion as the cause of the split with Barnabas (Acts 15:38), but if Phlm 24 is set alongside the Acts tradition, the Mark's rift with Paul was temporary and he later rejoined Paul's mission. There is a further cryptic addition to the mention of Mark. The readers are told that they have already received instructions about him and that if he comes to them, they are to welcome him (v. 10*c*). This may play on the Acts tradition, suggesting that Pauline churches may have had reservations about Mark but that these are now to be put aside. Alternatively, it has been suggested that this may have been a way of referring to Mark's being known to have had a role in the region after Tychicus and Onesimus, so that at the time of the letter's composition, of all those listed as sending greetings, Mark may have been the only one still in contact with the letter's recipients.[147]

The third Jewish companion of Paul to send greetings is "Jesus, who is called Justus" (v. 11*a*). He has two names, since "Jesus" is the Greek form of his Hebrew name and "Justus" would have been the name he used in the Greco-Roman environment. Nothing further is known of him, although a number of scholars have supported the conjecture first made by Theodor Zahn that at the end of Phlm 23 the name "Jesus" in Greek should have a final sigma and, therefore, be associated not with the preceding Christ, but be seen as a separate name that leads off the list of those then mentioned in Phlm 24 as sending greetings.[148] It is possible that an early scribe was confused by the mention of another Jesus immediately after a reference to Christ, but there is no manuscript evidence to support this interesting conjecture.

4:12-13. Epaphras, also described, like Onesimus, as "one of you," is next listed as sending greetings. Having named Epaphras earlier as the initial link between the Pauline mission and Colossae (1:7-8), it would be

---

146. Dunn appeals to the hypothesis "that Paul's imprisonment was such as to permit certain of his associates to take turns sharing his confinement." See Dunn, *The Epistles to the Colossians and to Philemon*, 275-76.

147. See Pokorny, *Colossians*, 192.
148. See, e.g., Lohse, *Colossians and Philemon*, 172n. 26, 207n. 16.

natural for the writer to mention him again here. Earlier he was called a fellow slave and a servant of Christ; now he is simply a slave of Christ Jesus. A twofold commendation follows. First, Epaphras is depicted as being in constant prayer for the readers. This matches what has been said about Paul in 1:9; the rest of 4:11 also corresponds to the earlier depiction of the apostle. In his prayers, Epaphras struggles (cf. 1:29; 2:1), and the goal of those prayers is that the readers might stand as "perfect" or "mature" (cf. 1:28) and that they might be fully assured in all the will of God (cf. 1:9; 2:2). This first part of the commendation serves, then, to recall the purpose of the letter as a whole. The second part is the writer's witness to how much hard toil Epaphras is expending (the NIV, in contrast to the NRSV, rightly translates ἔχει πολὺν πόνον [echei polyn ponon] in the present tense) on behalf of the readers and of those in Laodicea, situated some ten miles from Colossae, and in Hierapolis, some fifteen miles away. Epaphras, then, is presented as the original representative of the Pauline mission in the whole Lycus Valley area, which has already been seen to be the object of the writer's concern (2:1).

4:14-15. The final pair of Paul's companions to extend greetings are Luke and Demas, also listed in Phlm 24. Later in the Pastoral Epistles, Demas will be mentioned negatively (2 Tim 4:10). Here only Luke has a further description added, the mention of his medical profession. That he is called "the beloved doctor" may suggest that the readers are expected to know of a tradition of his having been of help to Paul and his coworkers in times of sickness. Later traditions associate this same Luke with the author of Luke–Acts.

In v. 15 the readers are instructed to convey greetings from the writer to the brothers and sisters in Laodicea and to Nympha and the church in her house. If the letter were really from Paul to the church in Colossae, there are two difficulties at this point: There is no greeting to the church in Philemon's house, and the recipients are not told to greet one another, which was Paul's usual custom (cf. Rom 16:16; 1 Cor 16:20b; 2 Cor 13:12a; Phil 4:21a; 1 Thess 5:26), but instead are told to greet believers elsewhere, an instruction found nowhere else in the Pauline letters. And why would Paul want greetings extended to Laodicea via the Colossians when he says in the next verse that he has written a separate letter to the Laodiceans and that this letter to Colossae is in any case to be read to them? On the supposition of pseudonymity this feature is seen as providing a clue to the real recipients—namely, the Laodiceans (see 2:1). It could also be that Nympha, whose name is not drawn from elsewhere and who at least gave hospitality to a house church as a patroness to the Pauline movement and may possibly have been its leader, lived among the Laodicean recipients at the time the letter was written and was known by name to its writer.

4:16. The instruction that this letter be read to the church at Laodicea and that the addressees read the letter from Laodicea adds further support to the view that the device of pseudonymity allows the real recipients to become transparent at this point. If that is the case, the attempt to identify the Laodicean letter (whether as written from Laodicea by Epaphras or as Philemon or Ephesians or simply as a lost letter) was futile from the start. However, that the writer can draw on the practice of exchanging letters as part of the attempt to attain verisimilitude suggests that this was occurring in Pauline churches at the time of writing. The process of recognizing the more than occasional significance of the apostle's letters that later led to their achieving canonical status was apparently under way.

4:17. Though there are no greetings to any individuals associated with Colossae, the letter's recipients are told to pass on a message to Archippus. Again the formulation is slightly strange, because in Philippians, the only Pauline letter in which individuals are singled out for instruction, Euodia and Syntyche are addressed directly (Phil 4:2). Archippus had been mentioned in Phlm 2 as a member of Philemon's household and called a "fellow soldier." Here the message to be communicated to him is that he should pay attention to the service or ministry he has received in the Lord in order to complete it. Perhaps the best guess at the significance of this enigmatic message is that Archippus, who had been one of Paul's co-workers, is the only one of the addressees of Philemon still living in the Lycus Valley among the recipients of Colossians at the time of its writing. It may be that he needs to be re-called by them to the fulfilling of a role in keeping the Pauline tradition distinct from the views of the rival philosophy.[149]

4:18. The introduction of a greeting from Paul in his own hand takes up a feature of the closing sections of the undisputed letters (see 1 Cor 16:21; Gal 6:11; Phlm 19). The wording is, in fact, exactly the same as that of 1 Cor 16:21. On the supposition of pseudonymity, the writer of Colossians employs this feature to authenticate his letter as being in the Pauline tradition. It can also be seen as functioning to underscore the instruction to Archippus that has immediately preceded it and to evoke reminiscences of the apostle, as does the following exhortation.

The call to remember Paul's chains in v. 18*b* is unique for the closing section of a Pauline letter. It is a dramatic and rhetorical flourish. Paul himself used a similar technique effectively in Gal 6:17 with the more general mention of carrying the marks of Jesus branded on his body. Elsewhere in the undisputed letters Paul can call himself a "prisoner of Christ Jesus" (see Phlm 1, 9), but other references to his imprisonment arise naturally from the context and are not used for self-conscious effect (see Phil 1:7, 13-14, 17; Phlm 13). The appeal to others to remember "my chains" may be part of this writer's use of the device of pseudonymity designed to evoke sympathy and admiration for the persona of the imprisoned apostle whose identity he has taken on.

The final grace-benediction of v. 18*c* is shorter than that of any of the undisputed letters. The brief "grace be with you," however, not only recalls the opening greeting in 1:2*b* but also can be seen as an effective evocation of the central message of the letter with its stress on the sufficiency of all that God has provided for the readers in Christ. These benefits of salvation, which are already theirs, have come from the same grace of God that the writer now calls on to remain with them.

---

149. See Pokorny, *Colossians*, 195.

REFLECTIONS

In a letter that has treated the church as the body of Christ and has dealt with the cosmic scope of Christ's work and its implications for the lives of believers, the ending provides a further appropriate reminder that this same church is made up of particular individuals and local groups on earth and is dependent on social networks. The body of Christ fulfills its cosmic role in the midst of concrete, everyday relationships. Even if some of the features of the ending arise from the verisimilitude of a pseudepigraphical letter, they still reflect the need for the human structures of church life to be given constant attention. Team work, loyalty, praying for one another, and sheer hard work are indispensable. People need the reassurance of being greeted and made welcome. They need words of approval and recommendation for what they have done and reminders about tasks that still need to be done. Links between local groups need to be strengthened as introductions are made and communications are exchanged. In this way the apparently mundane contents of the letter's closure reinforce one of the main themes of its message: A right relationship to the exalted Christ manifests itself not in a spurious otherworldliness but in and through the real human relationships and structures of life in this world. It is here that believers are most in need of experiencing the reality of the letter's final benediction: grace in the ordinary.

THE FIRST LETTER TO THE THESSALONIANS

INTRODUCTION, COMMENTARY, AND REFLECTIONS
BY
ABRAHAM SMITH

THE FIRST LETTER TO THE
THESSALONIANS

INTRODUCTION

Both 1 and 2 Thessalonians are powerful witnesses to the early church's struggles with the suffering of its members. The Thessalonian letters make it clear that separation from leaders, alienation from former friends, and perennial threats of persecution and even death were not solely the concerns of the fledgling communities behind the Synoptic Gospels (Matthew, Mark, and Luke), the virtually introverted Johannine believers, and the persecuted minority group addressed by John's apocalypse.

These struggles and the constraints through which the early churches were pressed to view them resound on every page of 1 and 2 Thessalonians. In consequence, the two letters offer remarkable challenges to contemporary churches. Understanding these challenges, however, does not come easily. Since all letters (past or present) are occasional documents, they imply more than they state explicitly. The circumstances that the first-century letter writers and their audiences took for granted must be reconstructed before we can even begin to interpret their letters as responses to those circumstances. Moreover, certain thought patterns shared by Paul and the church at Thessalonica (but not directly obvious to us) also must be reconstructed because the letters assume these patterns without directly drawing attention to them.

Reconstruction of the letters' circumstances and some of the writer's thought patterns is enhanced by examining the general nature and functions of most ancient letters—that is, the various formulae expected in a typical first-century letter and the basic strategies letter writers used to make their letters effective. Over the years of biblical scholarship, proven methods of careful analysis have developed that highlight these aspects of first-century letters. These methods will be used in this commentary to place 1 and 2 Thessalonians in the historical and literary milieu of the first century CE. It is important as well to place them more directly in the environs of early Christianity, particularly Pauline Christianity, to the extent that we can reconstruct it from the surviving literary and historical evidence. Accordingly, this introduction will begin with an examination of several general historical contexts related to Paul and the city of Thessalonica, and then move to a more specific reconstruction of the specific occasions and purposes of each letter. Next, the Introduction will focus on the literary character of the letters. With these matters in place, it will then be possible for readers to move on to the in-depth analysis in the commentary with sufficient grounding for understanding each letter's challenges and reflecting on their meaning for today.

THE GENERAL HISTORICAL CONTEXTS OF 1 AND 2 THESSALONIANS

Three general historical contexts are essential for understanding 1 and 2 Thessalonians. Obviously, one critical historical context is Paul's work among the Gentiles. Equally important is the context of the city of Thessalonica itself, especially the city's ongoing dependence upon Roman patronage and the role that dependence likely played in the relations between Paul's church and the larger Thessalonian society. Yet another critical context is Paul's apocalyptic gospel—both the distinctive features of its thought pattern and its appeal to the church Paul founded in Thessalonica.

The Context of Paul's Work Among the Gentiles. Through the revelation of the risen Jesus to him (1 Cor 9:1; 15:8; 2 Cor 12:1-3; Acts 9:22, 26; Gal 1:12), Paul was called to preach the gospel among the Gentiles (Gal 1:16). He carried that gospel over considerable territory in the cities of the eastern Mediterranean. According to Wayne Meeks, the Pauline house-church movement took root in at least four provinces of the Roman Empire: Galatia (modern-day Turkey, e.g., the churches of Galatia), Asia (e.g., Colossae and Ephesus; see 1 Cor 16:19), Macedonia (e.g., the churches at Philippi and Thessalonica), and Achaia (the church at Corinth).[1]

In his Letter to the Romans (among whom he did not establish a church), Paul noted that his plan was to preach the gospel from Jerusalem to Illyricum (modern-day Dalmatia just to the east of the Adriatic Sea), to go on from there to Rome, and from there to Spain (Rom 15:19, 24). His goal, then, was a westward mission that would take him about ten thousand miles during the course of his career.[2] While it is possible to see Paul's travel to Thessalonica only as a reaction to difficulties he met at Philippi (1 Thess 2:1-2), the move was likely a strategic one, a part of the effort to move westward with his gospel to the Gentiles. Paul's letters and the book of Acts attest to his travel and to that of his coworkers, including Timothy, Titus, and Epaphroditus.

Just how Paul supported his house-church movement and extensive travel among the Gentiles is not altogether certain. On the basis of 1 Cor 4:12 (where Paul indicates that he "worked with his own hands") and Acts 18:3 (which identifies a trade for Paul), some scholars suggest that Paul's vocation involved some kind of leatherworking, whether that of making tents or other leather products.[3] If leatherworking was indeed Paul's vocation, we can imagine him traveling, like other artisans, with tools in hand, setting up a workshop wherever the local leatherworkers' guild of a city met. Even if we cannot identify Paul's exact occupation, however, we can still imagine him plying some trade to support himself (1 Thess 2:9), though he certainly received help from others, and from some of them repeatedly (e.g., the Macedonians, who included at least the Philippians; 2 Cor 11:8-9; Phil 4:15-16). For his intended work in Spain, moreover, Paul even desired help from the Roman churches, though he had not established those churches (Rom 1:13; 15:28–16:2).

More certain than his vocation is the pastoral care Paul extended to his churches in the course of his career.[4] Not only did he establish churches, but also his letters witness to his profound love for and anxiety about these assemblies as he shaped them and nurtured their growth (2 Cor 11:28). His letters also testify to his use of the hortatory tradition—that is, the well-known tradition of exhortation. Examination of the letters of Plato, Epicurus, and Seneca, among others, reveals the evolution of a tradition in which philosophers placed "exhortations to the philosophical life into the form of letters."[5] Such letters were designed to help the recipients

---

1. Wayne Meeks, *The First Urban Christians: The Social World of the Apostle Paul* (New Haven: Yale University Press, 1983) 41.
2. Ronald F. Hock, *The Social Context of Paul's Ministry: Tentmaking and Apostleship* (Philadelphia: Fortress, 1980) 27.
3. Hock, *The Social Context of Paul's Ministry*, 21.
4. Abraham J. Malherbe, *Paul and the Thessalonians: The Philosophic Tradition of Pastoral Care* (Philadelphia: Fortress, 1987).
5. Stanley Stowers, *Letter Writing in Greco-Roman Antiquity* (Philadelphia: Westminster, 1986) 37.

1 THESSALONIANS—INTRODUCTION

internalize the values of a particular philosophy, to help them "avoid feelings of isolation and the demoralizing effects they might have," and to affect their "habits and disposition."[6] Thus, in line with his call to take the gospel to the Gentiles, Paul seems to have planted house churches in strategic locations and to have sent them letters and emissaries in his absence in order to strengthen the solidarity of the assemblies and to correct any problems occurring in the wake of his departure. The church at Thessalonica was one of these assemblies that Paul established, molded, and nurtured.

The Context of the City of Thessalonica. In Paul's time Thessalonica was a part of the vast Roman Empire. When the city, named for Alexander's half-sister Thessaloniki, was founded in 316 BCE, one of Alexander's generals (Cassander) was its first benefactor. Due to the squabbles of Alexander's successors, however, Thessalonica eventually received Rome as its new patron in 167 BCE.[7]

The city was a commercial and cultic center. It did not stand toe to toe with Athens, the great intellectual capital. Nor did its size match that of Alexandria, the great international city of the day. Yet it was no mean place. With the construction of the Via Egnatia (Rome's gateway to its eastern colonies) in 130 BCE, Thessalonica benefited from the traffic of travelers and became a key trading center in the region.[8] Archaeological evidence suggests that the city enjoyed a rich cultic life—one that included indigenous Macedonian cults like those of Cabirus and Dionysus, foreign cults like those of Isis and Serapis, and the Roman imperial cult.[9]

The inhabitants of Thessalonica actively cultivated the beneficence of the Romans. The city's loyalty to the emperor Augustus (Octavian) and his successors favored it with the status of a free city (having an independent government) and with beneficence from both local and foreign Roman patrons. By the time Paul visited Thessalonica, sometime during the imperial reign of Claudius (41–54 CE), the Thessalonians had already erected a statue of Augustus as one of several honors to the Romans. Moreover, all of the Macedonians (in Thessalonica and beyond) had honored Augustus "by inaugurating an 'Augustan era.'"[10]

These data about the city in Paul's day are crucial to the interpretation of the Thessalonian epistles because the letters presuppose conflict between those in the church and other Thessalonians. It is likely that the Christians' glorification of Christ precipitated the conflict with the communities favorably disposed to the Roman government. If so, terms found in 1 Thessalonians, such as παρουσία (*parousia*, "coming" or "presence," 1 Thess 2:19; 3:13; 4:15; 5:23); ἀπάντησις (*apantēsis*, "meeting," 1 Thess 4:17) and ἀσφάλεια (*asphaleia*, "security," 1 Thess 5:3) are not politically innocuous. Rather, as Helmut Koester asserts, these terms present Paul's view of Jesus' "coming" or "return" as that of a king being greeted by a delegation that has come out to meet him.[11] Koester notes, moreover, that Paul's view of "peace and security" "points to the coming of the Lord as an event that will shatter the false peace and security of the Roman establishment."[12] Other terms in 1 and 2 Thessalonians could also be reread in the light of this possible political conflict. The attribution of the appellation "Father" to God may have been used in opposition to the imperial establishment, for the term figured in the ideology of Augustus Caesar as he sought to construe his empire as one large family.[13] Even such terms as "gospel" (εὐαγγέλιον *euangelion*) and "savior" (σωτήρ *sōtēr*) in 1 and 2 Thessalonians or any of the other letters attributed to Paul could well have suggested "opposition to the imperial religion of the *pax Romana* [Roman peace]."[14]

If these terms carried the political weight that has been suggested, it is not difficult to understand why some Thessalonians (those not accepting Paul's teachings) would castigate Paul's

---

6. Walter T. Wilson, *The Hope of Glory: Education and Exhortation in the Epistle to the Colossians* (Leiden: Brill, 1997) 47, 48.
7. R. Malcolm Errington, *A History of Macedonia*, trans. Catherine Errington (Berkeley: University of California Press, 1990) 133.
8. Meeks, *The First Urban Christians*, 17-18.
9. Craig Steven de Vos, *Church and Community Conflicts: The Relationships of the Thessalonian, Corinthian, and Philippian Churches with Their Wider Civic Communities*, (Atlanta: Scholars Press, 1997).
10. M. B. Sakellariou, *Macedonia: 4000 Years of Greek History and Civilization* (Athens: Ekdotike Athenon S.A., 1983) 196.
11. Helmut Koester, "From Paul's Eschatology to the Apocalyptic Schemata of 2 Thessalonians," in *The Thessalonian Correspondence*, ed. Raymond F. Collins (Leuven: University of Leuven Press, 1990) 446.
12. Koester, "From Paul's Eschatology to the Apocalyptic Schemata of 2 Thessalonians," 447.
13. Mary Rose D'Angelo, "'Abba' and 'Father': Imperial Theology and the Jesus Traditions," *JBL* 111 (1992) 623.
14. Richard Horsley, "Innovation in Search of Reorientation: New Testament Studies Rediscovering Its Subject Matter," *JAAR* 62 (1994) 1157.

salvific assembly, which viewed Jesus (not Augustus) as the benefactor and inaugurator of a new age.[15] In the eyes of these Thessalonians, support for Jesus weakened support for the Romans, who had brought tangible benefits to the city.

It is important to note, moreover, that criticism of the Pauline believers would have been severely hostile because most Gentiles vehemently opposed Christianity's exclusivistic claims on its adherents' lives. According to Segal, "Like the Jews and unlike the many clubs and associations that were a part of the civic life of the Hellenistic world, the Christians were exclusive in the sense that no *truly committed* gentile Christian could maintain cult membership. Thus, Christianity was subversive to the basic religious institutions of gentile society."[16] This shift in loyalty from various cult memberships to exclusive ties with the Christian assembly also meant that Christian believers lost the prestige they could have assumed through the commitments to their former networks.

Given this potential for conflict, why did any of the Thessalonians join this assembly? Why did they remain? What would they find valuable in Paul's gospel that could shape and nurture their lives? Answers to these questions are found in an exploration of Paul's apocalyptic gospel.

The Context of Paul's Apocalyptic Gospel. When Paul preached to the people of Thessalonica, some believed his gospel, even in the face of the hostile response of other Thessalonians (1 Thess 1:6; 2:13-16). But what exactly was Paul's gospel?

Beyond the hortatory tradition that seems to have shaped all of Paul's letters, both 1 and 2 Thessalonians are shaped by apocalyptic thought.[17] Proponents of this type of worldview hold that there is a fundamental distinction between the forces of good and the forces of evil. They envision an old age ruled by the forces of evil and a new one ruled by God, and they believe in an imminent judgment, at which time God will bring an end to the evil forces. Studies of Paul's letters reveal that all of Paul's churches and letter recipients struggled (healthily or unhealthily) with the delicate tension between the "already" and the "not-yet" aspects of his apocalyptic thought. The "already" refers to the things God accomplished through Jesus' death and resurrection; the "not yet" refers to those things yet to be accomplished at the parousia. Hence a reckoning of this tension—its distinctiveness and consequences—may give some insight into what Paul's hearers (and the followers of his tradition) took for granted about Paul's thought.

The *distinctiveness* of the delicate tension between the already and the not-yet lies in Paul's modification of Jewish apocalyptic thought. For many Jews, there were two sequential ages (or aeons)—one old and one new. For Paul, however, the power of the old age was already dealt a severe blow with the death and resurrection of Jesus (Gal 6:14-15), an event that also marked the dawning of the new age (Gal 1:4).[18] Moreover, for Paul, the manifestations of the old age—while doomed (1 Cor 2:6; 7:31)—are not yet at an end. They still affect believers, who await Jesus' parousia as the climactic event that will mark the consummation of the new age already begun (1 Cor 15:51-57). Therefore, believers live "between the times"—that is, between the already of what God has done through Jesus' death and resurrection and the not yet that awaits as the object of hope: resurrection (Phil 3:11), full adoption (and its consequence, heirship; Rom 8:15-17; Gal 4:4-7), and full conformity to Christ (Phil 3:21).[19]

Given the delicate tension of these aspects, what are the *consequences* of Paul's apocalyptic thought pattern? One consequence is that God's redemption or salvation of believers from sin's enslaving powers and death's corruption is a process that begins with God's free offering of grace (Rom 5:15), the creation of a new sphere of existence (2 Cor 5:17; Gal 6:15) not dependent on any previous entitlement (such as one's class status) or human performance (such as the keeping

---

15. On Roman imperial propaganda and its celebration of Augustus as the inaugurator of the new age, see Helmut Koester, "Jesus the Victim," *JBL* 111 (1992) 13.

16. Alan Segal, *Paul the Convert: The Apostolate and the Apostasy of Saul the Pharisee* (New Haven: Yale University Press, 1990) 164. Wayne Meeks, "Social Function of Apocalyptic Language in Pauline Christianity," in *Apocalypticism in the Mediterranean World and the Near East: Proceedings of the International Colloquium on Apocalypticism*, ed. David Hellholm (Tübingen: Mohr, 1983) 691. Charles Wanamaker, *The Epistles to the Thessalonians*, NIGTC (Grand Rapids: Eerdmans, 1990) 276.

17. According to Wilson, *The Hope of Glory*, 49, "The history of the early church evidences a tradition, established, it seems, primarily by the apostle Paul, of letter-writing as an instrument of moral instruction."

18. J. Paul Sampley, *Walking Between the Times: Paul's Moral Reasoning* (Minneapolis: Fortress, 1991) 10.

19. On Paul's thought world and the lives of believers between the death and resurrection of Jesus and his parousia, see Sampley, *Walking Between the Times*. See also W. Trilling, *Conversations with Paul* (New York: Crossroad, 1987).

of the law), and the declaration of justification by God through the believer's faith (or reorientation, Rom 5:1). That process—lived between the times—is one of sanctification, in which the Spirit both dwells in believers as God's pledge (or down payment, 2 Cor 1:22; 5:5) of the final consummation and acts as God's agency of transformation, conforming their lives to the image of God found in Jesus Christ (2 Cor 3:18). A second consequence is that believers struggle to live according to the spirit of the new age even while they still are plagued by manifestations of the old age—sin, trials, and death.

A third consequence of this tension is that believers—who have already conformed to Christ's death—presently conform to Christ's suffering and live expectantly in the hope that they will conform to his resurrection and glorification (Rom 5:2; Phil 3:10-11). Thus throughout the tenure of their lives "in Christ," from baptism to the other side of the parousia, the life of Jesus is the theme of their existence.

Finally, a fourth consequence of this tension is that the new sphere of existence entails products of transformation. These fruits show God at work in the edification of God's people, in the strengthening of the individual believer against the old age's manifestations, and in the persuasion of others through the proclamation of the gospel and the believer's conformity to Christ. The fruits of the Spirit (Gal 5:22) stand in opposition to the works of the flesh (or of the natural [and self-seeking] person; Gal 5:16,17).

While we cannot be sure of the full content of Paul's preaching in Thessalonica, it is known that he spoke strongly about the relationship that believers have with God. Paul's repeated references to God as "Father" only make sense if he shared with the community their incorporation into the family of God, a family in which Jesus is God's special son (1 Thess 1:10), but one in which all believers can be the children of God as well (1 Thess 1:1, 3; 3:11). It is also known that he preached about the death and resurrection of Jesus and how these events were the basis for rescue from the coming wrath of God (1 Thess 1:10). Accordingly, he likely spoke to the assembly about one of the ultimate benefits of the new age: God's deliverance of believers from death.

Paul's repeated emphasis on the role of the Holy Spirit and sanctification suggests that his message also covered the more immediate and ongoing benefits of the new age. In the course of his description of the foundational events, Paul repeatedly mentions the Holy Spirit as proof of God's choosing of believers for salvation (1 Thess 1:4-5) and as a source of inspiration in the face of opposition (1:6). Even his later comments on the Holy Spirit as a gift from God (4:8) that helps believers to do God's bidding (4:3-8) and as a presence that should not be quenched (5:19) are offered in the context of what the Thessalonians are already doing and what they should continue doing (4:11; 5:11). It is in the course of reiterating some of his previous instructions that Paul describes sanctification, or the ongoing maturation of believers, as the will of God (4:3).

Because Paul writes of continuing opposition as something that he warned them of when he was with the church (1 Thess 3:3-5; cf. 2:1-2), he likely spoke to the Thessalonian believers about the continuing manifestations of the old age as well. The hostilities they were suffering, in fact, were a sign of the old age; and Paul could assume that they would understand him when he spoke of his inability to get back to the church as due to opposition from Satan (2:18).

It appears, then, that the Thessalonian church would have known at least the rudimentary form of Paul's mature gospel: the initiative of God in incorporating believers into God's family, the overlapping of the two ages, and some of the benefits and costs accruing to believers because of the tensions between these two ages. Exactly what had appealed to the Thessalonian believers about this gospel is not clear, and we should resist unfounded assumptions. In earlier studies of this church, some scholars too quickly suggested that the appeal was based on the relative deprivation of the Thessalonians in general (the belief that the Thessalonian Christians before their conversion were among the lower classes, even though they lived at a time when the economic life of Thessalonica in general was on the upswing). Other scholars presumed that the appeal was based on status inconsistency, the belief that the achieved status of the Thessalonian Christians before conversion was radically different from their inherited status and thus a source of tension for which they found some ease in early Christianity. However, we simply do not have enough material evidence to determine the status levels of the Thessalonian believers. And in the judgment of the most recent careful assessment of the little evidence we have available, these descriptions are examples of "ethnocentric anachronisms."[20]

If we look to Paul, a possible appeal may be that his gospel came with "power" (1 Thess 1:5). Indeed, much of 1 Thessalonians seems to be directed toward reminding the church of the power of this gospel both over the Thessalonians who believed it (1:6-10; 2:13-16) and over the apostles who proclaimed it (2:1-12). It is also likely that the gospel's power brought a level of prestige to this community for which they were even willing to accept hostility of and alienation from their former networks of support and honor. As we shall see, the issue of the gospel's power and prestige will be crucial to both letters. Furthermore, we must not forget that both 1 and 2 Thessalonians, to the extent that they expose Paul's gospel, demonstrate the extraordinary hope of that gospel. Little wonder then that Jürgen Moltmann has advocated so forcefully that modern persons shun resignation and despair and embrace the hopefulness of Paul and other early Christians.[21] While many today might find difficulty in seeing the value of Paul's apocalyptic gospel, it was both an all-embracing statement about God's plan for the world and a "critique of this age and its values."[22] Many of those who heard Paul's preaching (including the Thessalonians) would have found in it a powerful challenge to the existing order. As we shall see as well, both Thessalonian letters also imply this challenge.

SPECIFIC OCCASIONS AND PURPOSES OF 1 AND 2 THESSALONIANS

Paul's gospel not only brought the church at Thessalonica into being, but also became the basis upon which Paul molded its character and sustained its growth. Thus one could expect his apocalyptic gospel to be tightly woven into the hortatory tradition that he adopted—a tradition noted for shaping the distinctiveness of communities and for providing them with nurturing resources.[23] Because history has afforded us with two exhortative letters addressed to the Thessalonians, we have the opportunity to explore the distinctive appropriations of Paul's gospel in two related, but different, hortatory documents.[24] It is necessary, therefore, to clarify as much as possible the circumstances that gave rise to each letter. An appreciation of the similar yet distinct occasions and purposes of each letter will help us to see their respective appropriations of Paul's gospel in stark relief.

Specific Occasion and Purposes of 1 Thessalonians. Drawing exclusively on Paul's writings, we can say little with certainty about the specific occasion of his earliest extant letter. Paul formed the church that received this letter shortly after he left Philippi, where he and others were "shamefully mistreated" (1 Thess 2:2). His stay at Thessalonica must have been long enough for him to receive support from the church at Philippi on more than one occasion (Phil 4:16). Still, the tenure in Thessalonica also met with difficulty (2:2) and, most unfortunately for both parties, with a painful separation (2:17). When efforts to return to the Thessalonian church proved futile (2:18), Paul dispatched Timothy from Athens (3:1-2) with instructions to strengthen the community. As a set of follow-up instructions, in line with his desire to form, mold, and nurture communities, Paul wrote the letter we now know as 1 Thessalonians.

If we rely somewhat on the material from Acts, a few more details about the circumstances are evident. From Athens, Paul moved on presumably to Corinth (Acts 18:11-17), the place from which he likely wrote the first Thessalonian letter. Acts also suggests that Paul arrived in Corinth before Gallio became proconsul (Acts 18:11-17). If, indeed, Paul wrote to the Thessalonians

---

20. De Vos, *Church and Community Conflicts*, 169.
21. Jürgen Moltmann, *Theology of Hope: On the Grounds and Implications of a Christian Eschatology* (New York: Harper & Row, 1967).
22. Sampley, *Walking Between the Times*, 108.
23. For more on the connections between apocalyptic language and the hortatory tradition, see Malherbe, *Paul and the Thessalonians*, 80.
24. This is the case even if Paul did not write both of the letters and even if we have no way of determining whether the same community actually received both letters. This commentary assumes that Paul wrote only 1 Thessalonians and that the dating of 2 Thessalonians and concrete details about its audience are difficult to determine. Still, it is justifiable to assume that the audience of 2 Thessalonians knew and respected 1 Thessalonians because 2 Thessalonians often adopts and adapts the language and style of 1 Thessalonians.

from Corinth, we may deduce that the letter was likely written around 50 or 51 CE because the famous Delphi inscription dates Gallio's arrival in Corinth to sometime between January and August of 51 CE.

Some details about the specific historical circumstances, however, differ between Paul's letter and the Acts account. While both suggest that the trip to Philippi preceded the trip to Thessalonica (Acts 17:1; cf. 16:11-40; 1 Thess 2:2), which was about 90 miles southwest of Philippi on the Via Egnatia, Acts gives the impression that the Thessalonian converts included both Jews and Gentiles (Acts 17:4), while Paul implies that there were Gentile converts only (as can be inferred from 1 Thess 1:9, 10). If one accepts 1 Thess 2:14-16 to be from Paul's hand and not an interpolation (see the Commentary), these verses also support an ethnic constituency of Gentiles.

Acts 17 also mentions Paul's going to a Jewish synagogue, which is not mentioned in 1 Thessalonians. To the extent of our archaeological data today, there is no evidence for a synagogue in Thessalonica at this early period. What must be remembered, however, is that Acts has a stereotyped pattern similar to ancient novelistic literature of the period. For example, in Chariton's *Chaereas and Callirhoe,* one of the ancient Greek novels, virtually everywhere the two protagonists, Chaereas and Callirhoe, go they find a shrine to Aphrodite, the goddess of love, where they offer her worship and thanks. Likewise, virtually everywhere Paul travels in Acts 13–28, he finds Jews and a Jewish synagogue. The function of the stereotyped narration of shrines in both cases is that the universal significance and power of an adherent's deity is highlighted if the writer can demonstrate that that the deity is worshiped all over the Mediterranean world.

If the Thessalonian Christians were a Gentile congregation, it is possible to posit some basic factors about the occasion of 1 Thessalonians. First, as has been noted, opposition from Gentile neighbors was likely a critical ingredient in the occasion of 1 Thessalonians. Their hostility was likely aroused by the Christian believers' countercultural glorification of Christ. A second factor in the letter's occasion was a concern for stability. Given the hostility from unbelievers, the congregation is encouraged to remain steady on its course. In 1 Thessalonians, Paul speaks of his leadership team (Paul, Silvanus, and Timothy) "living" if the community "stands firm" (3:8), and he implores God to "strengthen" the hearts of his congregation against external social alienation (3:13). Therefore, 1 Thessalonians seems written to encourage a beleaguered church to persist in its new way of life, in accordance with the apocalyptic gospel it has received, despite the fact that it might have been difficult for the members to see the power of God—and the prestige pertaining to that power—at work in their lives.

Specific Occasion and Purposes of 2 Thessalonians. Since some scholars are reticent to assign 2 Thessalonians to Pauline authorship, the determination of the specific occasion and purposes of the letter can only follow after a brief discussion of the evidence. Both 1 and 2 Thessalonians have simple letter openings (1 Thess 1:1; 2 Thess 1:2) and more than one thanksgiving notice (1 Thess 1:2; 2:13; 3:9; 2 Thess 1:3; 2:13). In addition, in both letters one of the thanksgiving notices (1 Thess 3:9; 2 Thess 2:13) is followed by a wish-prayer (1 Thess 3:11; 2 Thess 2:16) that itself is subsequently followed by the transitional marker "finally" (λοιπόν *loipon,* 1 Thess 4:1; 2 Thess 3:1).

These similarities could suggest that Paul wrote both letters. However, many scholars think the similarities simply indicate that the author of 2 Thessalonians (not Paul) mimicked a copy of 1 Thessalonians to give his work authority at a time when other followers of Paul were also composing works in the apostle's name (2:1-2; cf. 3:17). Furthermore, because scholars respect Paul's creative abilities, they suggest that the similarities are signs pointing to the pseudonymous character of 2 Thessalonians. Bonnie Thurston's lament is typical: "The question this evidence [of literary similarity] raises is why Paul would so slavishly follow his own precedent. Why would Paul use his own work so unimaginatively?"[25]

Arguments for or against Pauline authorship of 2 Thessalonians usually have to reckon with stylistic differences (e.g., the relatively limited diction of 2 Thessalonians), the different

---

25. Bonnie Thurston, *Reading Colossians, Ephesians, and 2 Thessalonians: A Literary and Theological Commentary* (New York: Crossroad, 1995) 160.

tones of the letters (e.g., the apparently "cooler" tone of 2 Thessalonians), and different uses of eschatology (e.g., the use of futuristic eschatology to create a distinction between believers and outsiders in 1 Thessalonians and its use to critique an overrealized eschatology within the Christian community in 2 Thessalonians).

While judgments can vary on each of these points, perhaps the most salient argument against Paul's authorship is that the letter seeks to authenticate itself from other apparently spurious letters (cf. 3:17). But it is difficult to understand how anyone could write a forgery while an author was still alive.

Any individual piece of evidence against Pauline authorship of 2 Thessalonians is not sufficient; however, the cumulative effect of these pieces of evidence leans more against it. Whatever one's conclusions about the debate, the force of this commentary's examination suggests that the more crucial matters are the difference in what occasioned the two letters and their common testament to the continuing influence of Paul's apocalyptic gospel.

As for the occasion of 2 Thessalonians, two issues appear to be prominent. On the one hand, the writer (as with Paul in 1 Thessalonians) has a general concern for stability in the face of continuing hostility from the congregation's neighbors. The writer of 2 Thessalonians assumes that the earlier opposition and loss of prestige faced by the Thessalonians at its foundation and shortly thereafter (see the section "Specific Occasion and Purposes of 1 Thessalonians") have not abated. In 2 Thessalonians the congregation is enjoined to "stand firm and hold fast to the traditions" (2:15), and the writer implores God to strengthen "the hearts" of the congregation (2:17) because of the mounting afflictions they are suffering from unbelievers. In this respect 2 Thessalonians is generally similar to 1 Thessalonians, and it is not surprising that the second letter mimics the first in form and diction.

On the other hand, a new issue emerges in 2 Thessalonians—namely, the introduction of an enthusiastic brand of apocalypticism, a view that compensates for the letter recipients' loss of power through an overrealized eschatology. Koester persuasively argues that the origin of the enthusiastic message—even if its proponents justified it on the basis of 1 Thessalonians—actually lies in "the apocalyptic fervor of the second half of the firstcentury."[26] It is not surprising that the writer uses several examples of apocalyptic material (assuming that the material will be convincing to his hearers) not to *support* the enthusiasm, but to *counter* it. Moreover, the writer's use of 1 Thessalonians is both plentiful (to show adequate acquaintance with it) and non-enthusiastic (to highlight the importance of not abandoning the everyday world as the enthusiasts would likely advocate).[27]

It is not necessary, then, to see 2 Thessalonians as Paul's correction of his own earlier writing, as some scholars purport. Nor need one postulate 2 Thessalonians as an argument advanced to dispute the claims of Colossians and Ephesians (though 2 Thessalonians does critique a realized eschatology on the order of the ones found in those letters). Rather, Earl Richard's hypothesis about 2 Thessalonians seems to be on target. The work was composed "to discredit the claims, made in Paul's name, of apocalyptic preachers which were causing alarm within the community (2:2) and social unrest within its ranks (3:6-12)."[28] It is critical to note, moreover, that Paul's apocalyptic thought (whether or not he wrote 2 Thessalonians) influenced the church that read 2 Thessalonians. Thus both 1 and 2 Thessalonians are apocalyptic documents, but the latter works against an enthusiastic brand of apocalypticism.

With these brief remarks about the letters' occasions and purposes, we are closer to understanding the circumstances and thought patterns of 1 and 2 Thessalonians. Another necessary step, however, is to consider some of the literary conventions of the day, to see how letters were read and heard in Paul's time in terms both of the various parts of ancient letters and of the special acoustical features that shaped the flow and argument of ancient letters.

---

26. Koester, "From Paul's Eschatology to the Apocalyptic Schemata of 2 Thessalonians," 455.
27. Koester, "From Paul's Eschatology to the Apocalyptic Schemata of 2 Thessalonians," 456.
28. Earl J. Richard, *First and Second Thessalonians* (Collegeville, Minn.: Liturgical, 1995) 299.

LITERARY CHARACTER OF 1 AND 2 THESSALONIANS

In determining the basic literary character of the two letters, Pauline scholarship profits from a variety of widely acknowledged perspectives and methods. This commentary assumes an audience-oriented perspective in which contemporary readers seek to understand the audience that each author had in mind when composing the respective letters. Generally, the audience-oriented approach used here draws on two methods, epistolary analysis and rhetorical criticism, not to restrict Paul and other early Christians to the handbooks of their age, but to make contemporary readers aware of the basic textual markers by which the audiences for the two letters would have read or heard them. It is generally accepted that early Christian letters offered nuanced variations on Hellenistic epistolary formulae as well as on the rhetorical practices of that age. Thus early Christian letters exploited the typical Hellenistic letter opening (prescript) and closing (postscript) formulae, variations of a typical health wish/thank you notice (to the gods or to the addressees) and prayer reports, and perhaps one or more parts of the conventional epistolary body (i.e., the main part of a letter).

As well, it is generally accepted that early Christian letters reflect rhetorical (or persuasive speech) conventions, as if the letters were all influenced by the rules that ancient Greeks and Romans applied to speeches. Accordingly, some scholars find in the letters the basic speech design indexed in handbooks on speech preparation—namely, an exordium (or opening of an argument), a *pistis* (or proof section, i.e., the central part of an argument) and the peroration (or closing of an argument). Others even characterize particular Christian letters in one of the three broad modal forms of argumentation: the deliberative mode (with the goal of persuading or dissuading), the epideictic mode (with the goal of praising and blaming), or the defensive mode (with the goal of accusing or defending).

Whether Paul learned the epistolary and rhetorical conventions in school or assimilated them from the larger culture is not known. What is generally believed, however, is that Paul (like anyone else of his time) was not straitjacketed by the rules and need not be held to exaction on the basis of either the set of practices in the handbooks of the period or those in the scholarly reckonings of our own age.

THEOLOGICAL CHALLENGES

Anticipating the results of the epistolary and rhetorical analyses of the two letters, the outlines that follow the bibliography are plausible reconstructions of the audience's apprehension of the textual markers for the two letters. Before turning to the bibliography and the outlines, however, contemporary readers can immediately appreciate some of the everyday theological challenges that these two texts present to modern audiences in the light of the historical and literary environments previously mentioned. In the course of the Commentary, the following challenges will be explored more fully.

Appreciating the signs of God's power already evident in a community lies at the heart of 1 Thessalonians (1:5; 2:13). Discovering that the effectiveness of the gospel extends beyond the limited parameters of one's own environs is a critical lesson as well (1 Thess 1:8; 2:14-16). Drawing on the past to discover models of perseverance in the face of present suffering is also a repeated challenge (1 Thess 1:6-7; 2:1-11; 3:1-11). Remaining firm in one's convictions without being beguiled by enticing words or false hopes is paramount for 2 Thessalonians (2:1-3). Knowing both how to wait on God and yet move toward practical pursuits is equally important (2 Thess 3:6-13). And discerning how to reach out in love to disorderly persons in the church without demonizing them is key to the spirit of 2 Thessalonians (3:14-15). These insights from 1 and 2 Thessalonians offer remarkable challenges for contemporary churches. But when fathomed sufficiently, 1 and 2 Thessalonians offer much deeper reservoirs of assistance to our world.

BIBLIOGRAPHY

Best, E. *A Commentary on the First and Second Epistles to the Thessalonians.* London: Black, 1972. A monumental work that critiques earlier German scholarship on interpolation and authenticity theories.

Collins, Raymond. *The Birth of the New Testament: The Origin and Development of the First Generation.* New York: Crossroad, 1993. An in-depth study with a variety of perspectives to show the value of 1 Thessalonians as the first work of the NT.

Gaventa, Beverly. *First and Second Thessalonians.* Interpretation. Louisville: John Knox, 1998. An exegetical work on 1 and 2 Thessalonians with interpretive insights for liturgy, Bible study, and preaching.

Hughes, F. W. *Early Christian Rhetoric and 2 Thessalonians.* Sheffield: JSOT, 1989. A rhetorical analysis of 2 Thessalonians that assumes it to be a pseudonymous work written against the realized eschatology found in Colossians and Ephesians.

Jewett, Robert. *The Thessalonian Correspondence: Pauline Rhetoric and Millenarian Piety.* Foundations and Facets. Philadelphia: Fortress, 1986. An audience-oriented rhetorical analysis that reads the two letters against the background of a radical form of millenarianism.

Malherbe, Abraham J. *Paul and the Thessalonians: The Philosophic Tradition of Pastoral Care.* Philadelphia: Fortress, 1987. An often-cited monograph on Paul's nurturing techniques of pastoral care.

Marshall, I. H. *1 and 2 Thessalonians.* Grand Rapids: Eerdmans, 1983. Traditional study with a careful and sustained critique of interpolation theories, letter-sequence hypotheses, and arguments on the pseudonymous character of 2 Thessalonians.

Menken, Maarten J. *2 Thessalonians.* London: Routledge, 1994. A literary analysis that situates 2 Thessalonians in several settings: its literary environment, Jewish apocalypticism, and the world of pseudonymity.

Richard, Earl J. *First and Second Thessalonians.* Sacra Pagina. Collegeville, Minn.: Liturgical, 1995. Assumes 1 Thess 2:14-16 to be an interpolation and 2 Thessalonians to be pseudonymous.

Smith, Abraham. *Comfort One Another: Reconstructing the Rhetoric and Audience of 1 Thessalonians.* Louisville: Westminster, 1995. An exploration of the ancient consolatory conventions in 1 Thessalonians.

Thurston, Bonnie. *Reading Colossians, Ephesians and 2 Thessalonians: A Literary and Theological Commentary.* New York: Crossroad, 1995. A commentary on 2 Thessalonians, Colossians, and Ephesians that reads 2 Thessalonians against the distinctive religious culture at Thessalonica.

Wanamaker, Charles. *The Epistles to the Thessalonians: A Commentary on the Greek Text.* NIGTC. Grand Rapids: Eerdmans, 1990. Combines rhetorical and social critical scholarship in an argument for both Pauline authorship of the two letters and a reverse sequence in the letters' composition.

OUTLINE OF 1 THESSALONIANS

I. 1 Thessalonians 1:1-5, The Exordium

II. 1 Thessalonians 1:6–5:22, Maintaining an Apocalyptic Way of Life

    A. 1:6–2:16, A Gospel of Consistent Power
        1:6-10, An Unstoppable Word
        2:1-12, Continuing with the Gospel
        2:13-16, The Word's Relentless Power
    B. 2:17–3:13, Concern for the Church's Survival and Moral Training
        2:17-20, Aborted Trips and the Parousia
        3:1-8, A Visit of Consolation in Hostile Times
        3:9-13, An Expected Trip and the Parousia
    C. 4:1–5:22, Commending Persistence in the Distinctive Life
        4:1-12, Walking a Distinctive Life
        4:13–5:11, Maintaining the Apocalyptic Hope
        5:12-22, Nurturing Resources for the Distinctive Life

III. 1 Thessalonians 5:23-28, The Peroration

1 THESSALONIANS 1:1-5

THE EXORDIUM

COMMENTARY

In epistolary analysis terms, 1 Thess 1:1-5 includes a prescript (1:1) and the first of three thanksgiving reports (1:2-5; see also 2:13; 3:9-10). In the epistolary patterns of his day, Paul opens the letter with a typical tripartite prescript (letter writer, letter recipient, and salutation; 1:1). Following the prescript, a thanksgiving report (1:2-5) presents three participial phrases that stress Paul and his coworkers (or his "pastoral care" team) praying for the community (1:2), remembering the Thessalonians' laudable resourcefulness (1:3), and acknowledging the community's election (1:4-5), respectively.[29] However, some scholars think the initial thanksgiving, as an introduction to the letter, continues—after an interruption at 2:1-12—from 2:13 to 2:16. Others even suggest that the thanksgiving extends to 3:13, with yet another interlude at 2:17–3:8.

In rhetorical terms, however, it seems best to limit the letter's initial introduction to 1:1-5 for two reasons. First, in Greek the first thanksgiving proceeds with a gradual increase in length for each of its three participial phrases as if to reach a resolution only in the last one (1:4-5). Second, with an initial prescript and a thanksgiving report ending in 1:5, the opening would conclude symmetrically with an acknowledgment both of what Paul's leadership team "knows" (εἰδότες *eidotes*) about the church (1:4-5) and what the church "knows" (οἴδατε *oidate*) about his leadership team (1:5).

One can argue that the first five verses of 1 Thessalonians alone sufficiently execute the twin goals of an ancient exordium—namely, to gain an audience's goodwill and to intimate a work's basic issues.[30] To gain the audience's goodwill, Paul presents an unadorned yet emotionally evocative prescript; a typical, yet important, thanksgiving report; and an acknowledgment of the powerful forces already and continuously unleashed in the church's life. The opening or prescript here (1:1), unlike those in the other undisputed Pauline letters (cf. 1 Cor 1:1-3; Phil 1:1-3), appears in an unelaborated form. No extended self-descriptions characterize the letter senders ("Paul, Silvanus, and Timothy"). Nothing but the basics are given in the depiction of the recipients ("To the church of the Thessalonians in God the Father and the Lord Jesus Christ"). Even the salutation ("Grace to you and peace"), likely Paul's variation of the Jewish "mercy and peace" greetings, is stated without embellishment. What the opening lacks in elaboration, however, it captures in its list of *dramatis personae* and in the powerful Jewish images it evokes.

Besides the recipients, other critical players include God, Jesus, and the founding figures: Paul, Silvanus (cf. Acts 17:9; 18:5), and Timothy (2 Cor 1:1; Phil 1:1; 2:19-34; Phlm 1). Timothy is a vivid part of the community's memory, moreover, because of the recent consolation and strength (3:2) he brought to the church. (Perhaps, though we cannot be sure, he also transported the letter to the church.)

The prescript also evokes at least two powerful Jewish images. Although the word ἐκκλησία (*ekklēsia*, "church," 1:1) could denote simply an "assembly" in profane Greek, it possibly evokes here a holy community called into being by God, as with the Hebrew expression קהל יהוה (*qĕhal YHWH*)

---

29. Paul's coworkers in his ministry among the Thessalonians include Silvanus and Timothy. Of course, Paul's plural verbal and nominal forms are not epistolary. That is, Paul bears sole authorship, as three later passages (2:18; 3:5; 5:27) using the first-person singular attest.

30. Robert Jewett, *The Thessalonian Correspondence: Pauline Rhetoric and Millenarian Piety*, Foundations and Facets (Philadelphia: Fortress, 1986) 76. On the *captatio benevolentiae* ("captivation of goodwill") in an exordium, see Quintilian 3.8.6; Cicero *De Inventione* 1.15.20; and Aristotle *Rhetoric* 3.14.7. On the exordium's forecasting function, see Cicero *De Part. Or.* 27.97; Quintilian 3.8.10; cf. Aristotle *Rhetoric* 3.13-14.

from the Old Testament. Hearing the expression Χριστός (*Christos*), the Greek term for the English expression "Christ," moreover, auditors would likely register the concept of the Jews' long-expected deliverer—only now, Paul's Gentile auditors can claim this deliverance as well. The critical players in place and some poignant Jewish images noted, Paul's prescript already provides a moving and comforting context for a church assaulted by the painful ordeal of alienation.

Like the prescript, the thanksgiving report captures the audience's goodwill. Its inclusion alone could have effected a *captatio benevolentiae* ("captivation of goodwill"), for the praise of the gods in any form was standard fare for securing the favorable disposition of ancient Greco-Roman audiences.[31] The specifics of the thanksgiving report could have had an endearing effect as well, for the three participial clauses depict the persistence of the foundational leaders' concern, the visible demonstration of the church's apocalyptic life, and the verities of the church members' status as believers. With a rhythmic and comforting diction, then, Paul announces the persistence with which his team makes their prayers (1:2; cf. Rom 1:9; Phlm 4; *Phaedrus* 254a; *Protagoras* 317e), continues with a recollection of discrete stages in the church's active life (i.e., the church's "work of faith," "labor of love" and "steadfastness of hope," 1:3; cf. Rom 5:2-5; 1 Cor 13:12; Gal 5:5), and finally indicates the church's hearty guarantees, including God's initiative and the gospel's powerful effect (1:4-5).

The thanksgiving's rhythmic flair is matched in rhetorical force only by its choice of diction, as if Paul brushed his epistolary canvas in colors drawn from the rich palette of the Septuagint or from other Jewish literature. Often deemed a signal of "group identity or a close sense of group kinship" (e.g., Deut 15:3),[32] the expression ἀδελφοί (*adelphoi*, "brothers and sisters") here connotes a fictive kinship group, all of whose members can claim God as their Father (cf. 1:1). Similarly, the expressions "beloved by God" (Deut 33:12) and "chosen" (Deut 4:37; 7:6-8; 10:14-15; 14:2) are election terms drawn from the OT, leading one scholar to aver: "It is clear by this early stage in his thinking Paul has already developed the concept of the church as the Israel of God."[33]

In sum, Paul's opening remarks touched the heart of the church because of the inclusion of an encomium to God, the persistence of his team's prayerful actions, the noting of the church's active life as believers, the consoling depiction of the church as secure in God's initiating work, and the characterization of the gospel as a powerful force.

The first five verses of the letter also announce three of the basic themes treated in Paul's missive. First, the verses announce the effectiveness of his leadership team's initial word (or gospel) and its subsequent practices. Besides its function in foreshadowing the letter's "knowledge" diction, the repetition of knowledge terms ("knowing" and "you know") also stresses *what* Paul and his coworkers know and *what* the church knows (1:4-5). Paul and his coworkers know the status of the church because of the effectiveness of the powerful gospel (1:4-5*a*). The church knows the effectiveness of Paul and his coworkers, whose subsequent actions and practices were effected for the sake of the church (1:5*b*). Accordingly, Paul will note repeatedly the knowledge (2:1-2, 5, 11; 3:3-4; 4:2; 5:2) or, with the related diction of remembrance (2:9-10; 3:6), the memory of the church. Furthermore, the rest of the letter will echo the effectiveness of the team's gospel (or word) and its pastoral care practices in providing a sufficient basis for the church's survival. For a young church beset by local hostility, reminders of these certainties were absolutely necessary.

Second, Paul's opening verses announce the theme of persistence—both that of Paul's leadership team and that of the church. Paul's emphasis on continually giving thanks to God (conveyed with the temporal adverb "always" [πάντοτε *pantote*], 1:2) and on the team's constant memory of the church (conveyed with the temporal adverb "constantly" [ἀδιαλείπτως *adialeiptōs*], 1:2) is complemented by the church's continuous signs of success, with the expression "steadfastness of hope" (1:3) vividly attesting to

---

31. See Quintillian 3.7.7.
32. Wanamaker, *The Epistles to the Thessalonians*, 77. See also Philo *On the Special Laws* 2.79; Josephus *Antiquities of the Jews* 10.20.

33. I. H. Marshall, "Election and Calling to Salvation in 1 and 2 Thessalonians." in Collins, *The Thessalonian Correspondence*, 262.

the church's endurance despite continuing alienation from the larger society. Moreover, because Paul prefaces his remarks about the church's continuing activity with the comprehensive category "all" [πάντων *pantōn*] of you" (1:2), Paul not only thanks God for all of the church, but he also speaks laudably about the continuing activity of all in the church. For a church plagued by the hostile actions of unbelievers, the persistence demanded (and for which Paul gives thanks) needs to be the goal of everyone in the assembly.

The focus on persistence—illustrated in the lives of Paul's leadership team and of all the church—is not surprising in a letter peppered with thanksgivings (2:13; 3:9-10), wish-prayers (3:11-13; 5:23), and a benediction (5:28). Nor is this focus surprising in a letter that commends the perennial life of joy, prayer, and thanksgiving (5:16-18) and exhorts the church to continue to do what it was taught to do (4:1-2), whether by God (4:9) or by Paul's leadership team (4:11). It is also not surprising that the persistence demanded has specific force for all of the church in a letter that charges individual members to be constant in their responsible behavior to each other (4:4-6; 5:11).

The emphasis on persistence was likely a needed message for Paul's church, for the fierceness of the hostility (read in the light of 2:14-16) suggests circumstances that could have precipitated a falling away. Paul apparently had that fear, as 3:5 makes clear. The letter, then, is certainly a paraenetic letter (one that encourages persistence in a certain way of life), as Malherbe has frequently noted, even if there are other factors at work as well.[34]

A third theme of the letter is the distinctiveness of the church from the rest of the Thessalonians. Perhaps Paul reveals this theme with the expression "in [ἐν *en*] God the Father and the Lord Jesus Christ" (1:1) in the salutation. Whether the term characterizes the present existence of the church or, more instrumentally, implies that the church of the Thessalonians "lies in what God accomplished by Christ's life, death and resurrection,"[35] the expression distinguishes Paul's *ekklēsia*, or church, from any other. The acknowledgment of the gospel's coming with the Holy Spirit (1:5), moreover, sets the church apart, especially if the auditors here understood the Holy Spirit—as some of Paul's later auditors and interpreters would discern—to be a pledge (or first installment) of the new age's final consummation (2 Cor 1:22; cf. Eph 1:14).

It is little wonder, then, that in the rest of the letter Paul makes distinctions between this community of believers and the larger society. As a part of a new and radically distinctive φιλία (*philia*), or friendship network, Paul's alternative community faces the temptation to return to its former networks for financial, social, and emotional support (3:5). Paul's highly dualistic diction, however, virtually places a wedge between the community and its fictive kin (Jesus, Paul, the churches of Judea and of Macedonia and Achaia), on the one hand, and the non-Christian Thessalonians, on the other hand (2:14). The church, while composed of Gentiles, is told not to act as the Gentiles do (4:5) and is commended to "behave properly toward outsiders" (4:12), as if the church's members are insiders (4:12). Indeed, the first instance of the "insiders/outsiders" typology beyond the first five verses occurs as early as 1:10 when Paul breaks into solemn—if not formulaic—diction with a declaration of Jesus' deliverance of "us" (ἡμᾶς *hēmas*), as if to separate all the believers from all the unbelievers.[36] "Others" or "outsiders" may grieve without hope, but for Paul's church, the coming of Jesus, or the parousia, neutralizes death and all other forms of separation (4:13-18). While others speak about "peace and security" as children of the darkness, Paul describes the Thessalonian believers as "children of the day" (5:1-11).

Even the support mechanisms the church once had in its *philia*, or friendship networks, in Thessalonica are now replaced within the circle of the new fellowship. For comfort and support in the wake of its leaders' absence, the members of the community are urged to look to one another (4:18; 5:11) and to demonstrate love toward each other and to all (3:12), especially through individuated aid to those requiring special attention (5:14). For

---

34. See, e.g., Malherbe, *Paul and the Thessalonians*, 70.
35. Ernest Best, *A Commentary on the First and Second Epistles to the Thessalonians* (London: Black, 1972) 62.

36. On the arguments for and against the formulaic character of 1:9-10, see Wanamaker, *The Epistles to the Thessalonians*, 84-89.

its sense of prestige, usually gained through traditional kin and clan networks, the community is exhorted to share in the kingdom and glory of God (2:12), a glory marked by the moral excellence of one's walk before God (cf. 2:12; 4:1). The church's life now is distinguished by its holiness (4:1-8).

So, with a powerful *captatio benevolentiae* achieved in the first five verses, Paul begins to write his letter. And given the themes of effectiveness, persistence, and distinctiveness announced in these verses, the specific goal of Paul's proposition for the entire letter seems clear. Paul writes to encourage a beleaguered church to use the words and practices of their foundational leaders as resources for persisting in the church's distinctive, apocalyptic life.

REFLECTIONS

Paul's thanksgiving notices often reveal his thanks to God for evidences of faith and fruitfulness in the lives of believers. What counts as a reason for thanksgiving in our churches? Is it numerical growth? Is it property lists? Is it the size of the office staff or figures in the annual budget? Or are these matters that only scratch the surface of church life?

The measuring stick by which we assess church life is too often influenced by our consumer-oriented and profit-driven culture. So profit driven is the larger culture that Jeffrey Goldfarb has commented that we now believe that "if something is profitable it is true, real, and good; if it is not, it is without true meaning."[37] Tragically, the identity of all too many churches is formed on the wheelbase of economics.

Paul's powerful thanksgiving (1:1-5), however, speaks appreciatively to God about a richness and a productiveness in the lives of the Thessalonian believers. To borrow the descriptive comparison of Peter Gomes, Paul's goal for those believers was not the "good life" (if that means getting all the material goods one can get) but the "life that is good" (i.e., the life that truly provides meaning).[38] Paul's thanksgiving highlights three indications of productivity in the life of the Thessalonian believers, three evidences of "the life that is good."

First, those believers had responded positively to the loving initiative of God. Although Paul dearly loved this community of believers, his words about his own love for them (2:8; 3:12) come only after he has spoken about God's effective love for the church (1:4). Paul was not content to describe the church's laudable attributes (1:3) without peering further back to call attention to God's active role in their history (1:4). To paraphrase the words of Abraham Heschel, "Long before we searched for God, God was already searching for us."[39]

Second, the believers at Thessalonica had welcomed and accepted caring leaders, leaders who not only brought to them the good news of the gospel, but who also cared enough to persistently monitor their growth as believers. Paul's constant prayers for and memories of that church reflect his consistent concern about the group's spiritual growth. The revolving door syndrome that plagues many churches today is often a woeful testament to ministries that spend too much time monitoring church building projects and not enough time building the lives of members. The quality of our witness to the larger world, however, depends not so much on our numbers as on our nurturing, not on our statistics but on our stability as people of God. As with Paul and his leadership team, our greatest concern ought to be that of inculcating convictions, aiding spiritual growth, and helping people to develop endurance to deal with life under pressure.

---

37. Jeffrey C. Goldfarb, *The Cynical Society: The Culture of Politics and the Politics of Culture in American Life* (Chicago: University of Chicago Press, 1991) 16.
38. Peter Gomes, *The Good Book: Reading the Bible with Mind and Heart* (New York: Morrow, 1996) 180.
39. Cf. Abraham J. Heschel, *God in Search of Man: A Philosophy of Judaism* (New York: Farrar, Straus & Cudahy, 1955) 136.

Third, Paul was thankful to God for the qualitative distinction in the lives of these believers. Paul's commendation is not just about their work, but their work of faith; not just their labor, but their labor of love; not just their steadfastness, but their steadfastness of hope in the Lord Jesus Christ (1:3). Their routines of life were now all transformed, supported by the decisive event of the coming of Jesus into the world and governed by a purposefulness that transcended yet included them.

A God who initiates salvation, caring leaders who nurture believers, and believers who eagerly follow a new orientation marked out by the gospel—these are the three realities that make for truly productive lives as believers. Without these, church members may merely have "the good life," but not "the life that is good."

1 THESSALONIANS 1:6–5:22

MAINTAINING AN APOCALYPTIC WAY OF LIFE

OVERVIEW

With its concerns for persistence in an apocalyptic way of life and self-sufficient survival apart from former networks of support, the letter shifts from its exordium to its proof (i.e., the larger portion of a document conveying its main argument). Here, Paul labors first to prepare a way (1:6–3:13) for his later challenge to the Thessalonians to continue walking in the ways of his apocalyptic gospel and its ethical imperatives (4:1–5:22). A sequential analysis of 1:6–5:22 supports this understanding, but two preliminary steps are in order. Given the audience-oriented nature of this commentary, first, it is important to observe the benefits of epistolary analysis in illuminating possible aural textual markers of the letter's epistolary structure in 1:6–5:22. Second, it is necessary to use any other critical tools to justify in broad strokes the larger rhetorical units of 1:6–5:22. Then the commentary can move forward with its sequential rhetorical analysis and examine more carefully the means Paul uses in persuading the church to maintain its distinctive life.

For our purposes, the benefits of epistolary analysis lie not with scholarly discussions about the ending of the epistolary thanksgiving or the beginning of its epistolary body. In fact, the repeated instances of thanksgiving notices in 1 Thessalonians, as we have seen, render hopeless a consensus on the beginning of the body of the letter. Furthermore (as noted in the Introduction), we need not think that Paul was straitjacketed by the theoretical epistolary patterns of his day. In fact, the presence of several thanksgiving notices should signal the greater importance for Paul of continuously giving thanks, just as he later directly exhorts the church to do (5:18).

Two important conclusions made by epistolary analysis, however, are fruitful for our discussion. First, although the largely autobiographical nature of the first three chapters and the abundance of imperatives in the last two could lead some interpreters to see a radical divide between these two sets of chapters, epistolary analysis suggests that the end of chapter 3 (3:9-13) functions like a hinge. That is, the final thanksgiving (3:9) and prayer formula (a petition, 3:10; and a concluding wish-prayer, 3:11-13)[40] together echo not only the earlier issues of Paul's desired visit (3:10; cf. 2:17-18) or the church's need for strength (3:13; cf. 3:2-3), but also the later issues about the life of holiness (3:13; cf. 4:3-8) and love (3:12; cf. 4:9-12) and about the parousia (3:13; cf. 4:13–5:11).[41] So it is not the case that only chapters 4 and 5 are exhortative. As with other letters of exhortation, additional features of exhortation—not just the inclusion of imperatives—are also prominent. First Thessalonians' focus on the imitation of models (1:6; 2:14), its use of prayer forms (1:2-5; 2:13; 3:9-13; 5:23), and the recalling of a teacher's previous instructions and deeds (2:1-12; 3:4; 4:2, 6) also bespeak its exhortative interest. Thus the entire letter is exhortative.

Second, if Jeffrey Weima is correct in his assertion that the Pauline letter closings, or postscripts, usually begin with a peace formula, that found in 5:23 ("May the God of peace . . .") marks a separate, final section in the letter (5:23-28).[42]

---

40. E.g., Peter T. O'Brien, *Introductory Thanksgivings in the Letters of Paul* (Leiden: Brill, 1977) 156.
41. O'Brien, *Introductory Thanksgivings in the Letters of Paul*, 160.
42. Jeffrey Weima, *Neglected Endings: The Significance of the Pauline Letter Closing* (Sheffield: JSOT, 1994) 187.

If we accept these results of epistolary analysis along with other distinctive markers, it is possible to support the division of the proof section into three discrete, yet interrelated, parts (1:6–2:16; 2:17–3:13; 4:1–5:22). Two additional pieces of evidence justify this partition. First, an obvious transitional marker between the material in the first three chapters and the last two is the adverb "finally" (λοιπόν *loipon*) in 4:1. In the undisputed Pauline letters, this same transitional expression marks a letter's final unit (cf. 2 Cor 13:11) or the last subsection of a unit (cf. Phil 3:1). Therefore, the presence of "finally" (*loipon*) suggests that 1 Thess 4:1 begins a new and final unit of the proof, though not one totally distinct from the previous material. Second, relative changes in the temporal perspectives of discrete units of 1 Thessalonians separate some parts of the letter from others. Accordingly, from 1:6 to 2:16, Paul remarks for the most part on events occurring in the more distant past. In 2:17–3:13, he turns to the more recent past to accentuate the struggles and joys of his leadership team and the church up to the time of the letter's composition. In 4:1–5:22, Paul shifts to a mostly imperative form to signal the behavior he desires in the believers' future, though to some extent he acknowledges that they are already doing what he wants them to continue to do. Thus the transitional nature of 3:9-13, the delineation of 5:23-28 as a separate part of the letter, the transitional marker "finally" in 4:1, and the letter's relative temporal changes all render the document into three separate units for the proof section.

1 THESSALONIANS 1:6–2:16, A GOSPEL OF CONSISTENT POWER

OVERVIEW

It is possible to demonstrate on rhetorical grounds that Paul's audience would have heard all of 1:6–2:16 as a string of three subunits (1:6-10; 2:1-12; 2:13-16). In accordance with one of the themes of the exordium (1:1-5), these three subunits together depict the effectiveness of the word of God (or gospel) and the pastoral care of Paul's leadership team.

Two of the subunits (1:6-10; 2:13-16) are parallel in their sequential development and in their effect. In their sequential development, these subunits practically begin with an emphasis on the church's commendable "reception" (δεξάμενοι *dexamenoi*, 1:6; ἐδέξασθε *edexasthe*, 2:13) of the word of God. Each subunit then continues its commendation of the church with illustrations of the believers' moral growth beyond their reception of the word even in the face of local opposition. So, in 1:6-10, Paul notes not only the church's initial reception of the word in affliction (1:6), but he also notes the church's continuing exemplary status as evinced by other believers (whose reports validated the Thessalonian believers' fundamental break with an old way of life and their continuing movement along the trajectory of their new lives, 1:9-10). And in 2:13-16, again Paul notes both the initial reception of the word (2:13*a*) and its ongoing work among the believers (2:13*b*) as revealed in their survival despite separation from their leaders (in a manner similar to the survival of the churches of Judea, 2:14-15). Finally, each subunit concludes with a note about God's wrath (1:10; 2:16; cf. Rom 1:2-8, 32; 2:8-9).

In their effect, both 1:6-10 and 2:13-16 have three goals. For one, they signal the importance of the word of God to the church in the foundational moments. "Word" here does not refer to the OT or the LXX but to an inspired word about God's actions in Christ that the foundational leaders preached to the church at Thessalonica. Second, these subunits widen the angle of Paul's scope to remind the church of other believers with whom they have solidarity, either because the church has become a model of endurance itself (1:7) or because the church has imitated the endurance of others (1:6; 2:14).

Third, these subunits encourage constancy or forbearance, another theme of the exordium (1:1-5), simply by amplifying that theme. In 1:6-10, the two infinitives "to serve" (δουλεύειν *douleuein*, 1:9) and "to wait" (ἀναμένειν *anamenein*, 1:10) signal both the community's constant devotion to a new way of life and their ongoing confidence in the return of Jesus. And in 2:13-16, the church's ability to survive beyond the initial foundational visit attests to its continuing forbearance. Thus the two subunits are parallel and direct their focus to the effectiveness of the word of God and of the leaders in shaping the Thessalonian believers into emulators and models of endurance.

With the second subunit (2:1-12), a virtual explanation of 1:6-10, Paul shifts to an emphasis on his leadership team. Yet the emphasis is not on the team's defense, as if it must exonerate itself against claims of financial exploitation or alterations in its theology, as some scholars have argued. Rather, it is on the team's ability to continue in its goals of the proclamation of the gospel and of the shaping and nurturing of the Thessalonian church despite the repeated instances of hostility the believers faced.

1 Thessalonians 1:6-10, An Unstoppable Word

COMMENTARY

As Paul begins to describe events in the more distant past, he commences in 1:6-10 with the foundational moments as he recalls them and as others have reported them to him. A critical element in the church's foundation is the role of the word of God. It is the "word" (of God) that the Thessalonians received in spite of "persecution" (1:6).[43] The result of that reception in the midst of persecution was not a weakening of his team's efforts. Rather, as indicated in a result clause (1:7), the Thessalonians became an "example" (τύπος *typos*) to other believers. Furthermore, the continuing power of the gospel has been demonstrated beyond the confines of Thessalonica, for Paul describes the "echoing" (ἐξηχέομαι *exēcheomai*) of the word of God in other parts of Macedonia and also in Achaia (1:8).

Thus Paul's earlier declaration of the gospel's power on the church (cf. 1:5) now receives elaboration with a striking description of the gospel's continuing power (1:6-10). With hyperbole, an apocalyptic orientation, and stirring images drawn from the currencies of his day, moreover, Paul lauds the Thessalonian believers for their imitation of their foundational leaders and the Lord, their own model behavior, and the persistence of their faith as acknowledged by others. Surely, his description of the church's exemplary behavior is exaggerated (1:8). In contrast to persons dwelling in the two Roman provinces of Macedonia and Achaia, could persons in every place (1:8) have known about the church's "faith in God"? Or does Paul here speak as one who wants to demonstrate his church's vitality by speaking about its renown in increasingly wider regions?

Notwithstanding Paul's exaggeration, the apocalyptic time in which the church's formation occurs is depicted in a straightforward manner. Two expressions, "persecution" (θλῖψις *thlipsis*, 1:6) and "wrath" (ὀργή *orgē*, 1:10), frame 1:6-10 and capture Paul's apocalyptic orientation. The first is a general category for affliction (cf. 3:3-4, 7) and probably refers to the Jewish apocalyptic belief that certain woes would precede the consummation of the new age (Dan 12:1; Matt 24:9-14; Mark 13:19, 24). The second is an expression connoting God's coming vengeance, from which the Thessalonians, in Paul's apocalyptic framework, are rescued. The church is praised, then, not only because it faced apocalyptic persecution from the very beginning of its existence, but also because its zeal, as given in the reports of others, has not flagged. Thus the power of the gospel is not a singular, one-time force on the church at the moment of the church's incorporation into the family of God. Even now its power

---

43. "Persecution" here and elsewhere in the commentary does not imply a widescale assault on Christianity. Rather, it refers to the experience of some kind of undefined and localized harassment by Paul and those who would have read 1 or 2 Thessalonians.

continues to make an impact on the church as the believers await Jesus' return.

To describe the extraordinary change in the lives of believers, Paul depends on three well-known images from his day: imitation, "turning," and slavery. The language of imitation was prevalent in Paul's time. Teachers often noted exemplary figures for their students.[44] Philosophers held up models from the past or present for emulation. Paul himself frequently uses the diction of imitation to talk about his relationship with the members of his churches (1 Cor 4:6; 11:1; Phil 3:17; 1 Thess 1:16; cf. 1 Cor 4:6; Gal 4:12). Notable in this case, however, is the church's impressive move from imitation (1:6) to example (1:7). That is, the church has so well grasped the conviction of those it imitated that it is now itself a model for other believers.

"Turning" language was equally prevalent in Paul's time. The word "to turn" (ἐπιστρέφω *epistrephō*, 1:9) was used in philosophical circles as one of the key words describing conversion to a philosophy.[45] Elsewhere, Paul uses the expression to speak about entrance into a new way of life (2 Cor 3:16; Gal 4:9). Others in Macedonia and Achaia were reporting the fundamental break, or turning, of the Thessalonian believers from their former cultic memberships to a new way of life (1:9).

The parlance of slavery was also commonplace in Paul's time, to describe both physical slavery and the powers over one's life in a metaphorical way. In his other letters Paul uses the diction of slavery repeatedly to depict the status of Jesus or of believers. In Philippians Paul calls himself and Timothy "slaves [δοῦλοι *douloi*] of Christ Jesus" (1:1) and later speaks of Jesus as one who took on the form of a "slave" (δοῦλος *doulos*, 2:7). Beyond its opening, where Paul both calls himself a "slave of Jesus Christ" (Rom 1:1) and speaks of the Romans as a part of the nations brought to "obedience" (ὑπακοή *hypakoē*, 1:5), the letter to the Romans redounds with the language of slavery. On the one hand, Paul writes about slavery to sin (6:6, 17, 20) and to decay (8:19-21), about a spirit of slavery (8:15), of obedient slaves to sin (6:16), and of "obedience to passions" (ὑπακούειν ταῖς ἐπιθυμίαις αὐτοῦ *hypakouein tais epithymiais autou*, 6:12). On the other hand, he writes about a slavery to righteousness (6:17) and to God (6:22), about service (i.e., slavery) to God (12:11) and to the law of God (7:25), and about the "obedience" (*hypakoē*) that leads to righteousness (6:16).[46] In Galatians Paul combines the language of turning with that of slavery:

> Formerly, when you did not know God, you were enslaved [ἐδουλεύσατε *edouleusate*] to beings that by nature are not gods. Now, however, that you have come to know God, or rather to be known by God, how can you turn [ἐπιστρέφετε *epistrephete*] back again to the weak and beggarly elemental spirits? How can you want to be enslaved [δουλεῦσαι *douleusai*] to them again? (Gal 4:8-9 NRSV)

Paul evidently found little problem employing the category of slavery in his arguments. Thus in the case of 1 Thessalonians, Paul uses the infinitive "to serve" (δουλεύειν *douleuein*, 1:9) to characterize the church's new allegiance.

Although some scholars think the phrases and themes of 1:9-10 are so unlike the rest of Paul that this material is temporally pre-Pauline, others suggest that the unusual wording is to be expected because Paul indicates that he is only reporting what others have said. Thus the verses, they assume, are contemporary to Paul's time, and they likely reflect a view of Christian beliefs espoused by other Jewish Christian preachers—a view that Paul edited for his purposes.[47]

In the case of the former opinion, some scholars hold that the expression "turned to God from idols," along with the description of God as "living and true," was a typical message preached to Gentiles before Paul's time. Some even locate the setting of the messages in the diaspora synagogue, where it is assumed that Gentiles would have first heard the Christian gospel.

In the case of the latter opinion, some scholars argue that 1:9-10 seems to combine

---

44. Boykin Sanders, "Imitating Paul: I Cor. 4:16," *HTR* 74 (1981) 358.

45. Malherbe, *Paul and the Thessalonians*, 26n. 89. On *epistrephō*, see (from Malherbe's list) Epictetus *Discourses* 3:16-15; 22:39; 23:16, 37; 4:4, 7.

46. For a careful look at Paul's slave terminology in Romans 8, see Wayne Rollins, "Greco-Roman Slave Terminology," *1987 SBL Papers*, ed. Kent H. Richards (Atlanta: Scholars Press, 1987).

47. Richard, *First and Second Thessalonians*, 75.

a message about the role of Jesus as an eschatological deliverer (in line with the Son of Man christology one finds in Q, the common source found in Matthew and Luke) to Paul's own interest in Jesus as the Son of God and as a resurrected figure.[48] Thus they insist that Paul simply revised a message that was probably preached elsewhere by others during the tenure of his ministry.

While either position may well be true, the debate need not consume us because we have no evidence that Paul's readers (or auditors) would have been able to make the distinctions assumed about Paul's redaction and the kinds of sources he used. More critical to Paul's young church was that these verses were written to inspire the believers to see that they were no longer subject to the presumed powers of the false gods (cf. 1 Cor 8:5) in whom they had originally believed. And against the possible temptation to return to the cult memberships of their non-Christian neighbors, the members of the church would now hear reminders of their new, distinctive, and ongoing life as believers.

Thus in the opening subunit of the proof, Paul's laudation describes the extraordinary change wrought on the lives of the Thessalonians. This laudation, however, actually commends the unstoppable character of the word of God. Neither difficulties nor distance can overcome it.

---

48. Richard, *First and Second Thessalonians,* 56, 75.

REFLECTIONS

In the aftermath of WWI, the English poet W. B. Yeats penned "The Second Coming," a prophetic poem of approaching anarchy. He wrote "things fall apart; the centre cannot hold," and he spoke of the crumbling of certainties on which people had grounded their lives. In like manner, Chinua Achebe's novel *Things Fall Apart* tells the story of an Igbo (Nigerian) farmer who commits suicide rather than face another day of his culture's disintegration. The center did not hold.

A meaningful life requires reliable resources—not a round of fads and fashions or words that fail to hold up under the heat of struggle. It is unfortunate that many people rest their fortunes and their lives on things that cannot hold: on beauty that fades, on perishable pharaohs who know Joseph, on antiquated perceptions, on supposed truths that last for but a season. When our lives are built on things that fall apart, consistency is difficult to maintain, and the end result may be disillusionment and the death of the spirit.

What helped the believers in Paul's young church at Thessalonica to remain stable? What helped them move from being imitators to being examples? What buoyed their lives so that despite affliction they served God and waited on their deliverance through Christ? It was their full reception of God's unstoppable word to them, the word that remained a reliable resource in their lives.

For us today, the unfailing truth of God's promises still provides us with a center that holds. When wells dry up, when famine comes, when disaster ruins all that is around us, the word of God remains a ready and reliable resource. It is both a ballast and a buffer—a ballast bringing security to otherwise insecure lives—and a buffer to shield us from self-destruction. R. Kelso Carter was right to sing:

Standing on the promises that cannot fail,
When the howling winds of doubt and fear assail,
By the living Word of God I shall prevail,
Standing on the promises of God.

1 Thessalonians 2:1-12, Continuing with the Gospel

COMMENTARY

Paul's introduction of the word "welcome" or "entrance" (εἴσοδος *eisodos*, 1:9) was likely a preparation for his use of the same word later when he describes the foundational "visit" (*eisodos*, 2:1) of his leadership team. In Greek, 2:1-12 is divisible into four discrete sections (vv. 1-2; vv. 3-4; vv. 5-8; vv. 9-12) by the repetition of a single transitional marker: "for" (γάρ *gar*). Still, the repetition of the word "gospel" (vv. 2, 4, 8, 9) in all four sections suggests that the common theme of the sections is the foundational leaders' continuous use of the gospel. Thus with a shift in focus from the church to the foundational leaders, Paul now continues his elaboration of the gospel's power (cf. 1:5) as it was used by his leadership team. As we shall see, the team never parted from the use of the gospel and maintained impeccable character despite repeated difficulties.

2:1-2. The first section, cast in the vocabulary of an athletic metaphor, presents the basic theme of the entire subunit—commitment to the noblest declaration and inculcation of the gospel's teaching despite continuing insults. With the expression "great opposition" (πολλῷ ἀγῶνι *pollō agōni*, v. 2), literally a "great contest," Paul speaks of the foundational leaders' difficulties in athletic terms, a commonplace among the Cynic and Stoic philosophers of his day.[49] Moreover, Paul's description of the difficulties in Philippi ("we had already suffered and been shamefully mistreated [προπαθόντες καὶ ὑβρισθέντες *propathontes kai hybristhentes*]") and of the foundational team's "courage" (ἐπαρρησιασάμεθα *eparrēsiasametha*) draws on the coinage of the Cynic philosophers' tradition of suffering.[50] Unlike the Cynics and the Stoics, however, the source of Paul's courage lies in God (v. 2), not in the individual. As readers would recall, although Paul mentions the foundational leaders' experience of "great opposition" (πολλῷ ἀγῶνι *pollō agōni*, v. 2) and he notes his church's reception of the word "in spite of persecution" (or better, "in great persecution" [ἐν θλίψει πολλῇ *en thlypsei pollē*], 1:6), he also notes in his exordium that the gospel came to the church not only in word, but also "with full conviction" (ἐν πληροφορίᾳ πολλῇ *en plērophoria pollē*, 1:5). Thus, unlike the Cynics and Stoics of Paul's day, the sufficiency of the foundational leaders and of the church was not in themselves, but in God—in the one who had brought about a conviction that was sufficient to meet every opposition that the believers would face. Furthermore, the struggle in which Paul is engaged is also different from that of the Cynics and the Stoics. For Paul, the contest is in the arena of proclaiming the gospel, not in all of life.[51]

The rich texture of antitheses in the second and third sections has suggested to many scholars that Paul seeks here to distinguish the foundational leaders from the hucksters who abused the otherwise noble philosophical practices of Paul's day. The distinction here from sham philosophers, however, should be viewed more as self-description than self-defense. Paul never says that he has been accused of improper motives, goals, methods, or actions. Furthermore, Abraham Malherbe has shown that some ancient philosophers[52] within the hortatory tradition used the antithetical style and even some of the same diction as 2:1-12 not in response to an actual accusation, but as a way of distinguishing what they did from other philosophers.[53]

2:3-4. In the second section Paul highlights his team's endurance and the distinctiveness of their motives and goals vis-à-vis the sham philosophers of the day. The vices listed in v. 3 (deceit, impure motives, trickery) were typical of charlatans.[54] By contrast, Paul's team has "been approved," literally tested through trial. And with language reminiscent of Jer 11:20 and 12:3, Paul speaks of God's continuous, ongoing testing of the

---

49. See Epictetus *Diss.* 1.24.1-2.
50. Abraham J. Malherbe, "Exhortation in First Thessalonians," *NovT* 25 (1983) 249.
51. Richard, *First and Second Thessalonians*, 93.
52. E.g., the Stoic Dio Chrysostom in *Discourses* 32.
53. Malherbe, *Paul and the Thessalonians*, 3-4.
54. Abraham J. Malherbe, "Gentle as a Nurse: The Cynic Background to 1 Thess 2:1," *NovT* 12 (1970) 203-17.

foundational team's hearts (cf. Gal 1:10; Prov 17:3).

2:5-8. In the third section Paul shifts from a focus on the source of the foundational leaders' courage and the nature of their motivations to their pedagogical style. With an appeal to the auditors' knowledge and to God as a witness (whether read simply as an oath or also as an allusion to Job 16:19 or Ps 89:37),[55] Paul lauds the foundational team for neither demanding glory (as did charlatans) nor treating their novices harshly (as did some austere philosophers). Thus, on the one hand, Paul and his coworkers avoided using flattery to gain goodwill[56] and even refused to exercise their rights or "demands" (βάρος *baros*; lit., using their "weight"). On the other hand, these leaders (like some of the Cynics) also avoided the method of severe criticism, seeking rather to exercise compassionate persuasion.

It should be noted that interpretations of v. 7 vary because the manuscript evidence is divided. A single Greek letter, ν (*n*), is added to the Greek word ἤπιοι (*ēpioi*, "gentle") in some manuscripts of 1 Thessalonians but not in others. So scholars wonder if Paul actually wrote "we were gentle" or "we were infants [νήπιοι *nēpioi*]" (see the NRSV note to v. 7). In the latter case, Paul would be saying that "the apostles were not 'heavies,' making much of themselves through various demands (v. 7a), but were as unassuming among the Thessalonians as infants."[57]

This commentary, however, agrees with those scholars who consider "gentle" (ἤπιοι *ēpioi*) to be the original formulation because Paul does not usually use νήπιοι (*nēpioi*, "infants") positively (cf. Rom 2:20; 1 Cor 3:1; 13:11; Gal 4:1, 3). Furthermore, if Paul draws on language found within the philosophical hortatory tradition throughout 2:1-12, it would not be uncommon for him to combine "gentleness" and nurse imagery. In his work *How to Tell a Flatterer from a Friend* (69 BCE), for example, Plutarch, in an attempt to critique the severe type of philosopher, writes:

The very circumstances in which the unfortunate find themselves leave them no room for frank speaking and sententious saws, but they do require gentle usage and help. When children fall down, the nurses do not rush up to them to berate them, but they take them, wash them up, and straighten their clothes, and, after all this is done, they then rebuke and punish them.[58]

Perhaps anticipating his use of the father/children metaphor to describe the foundational leaders' relationship to this church (v. 11; cf. 1 Cor 4:14-17; 2 Cor 6:11-13; Phlm 10), Paul initially writes about the nurse/children relationship. Nurses in that society were cherished for the affection they showed to children, and the idea of a nurse caring for her own children intensifies that affection.[59] Given the context of Paul's self-description of the foundational leaders' pedagogical style, moreover, Paul's use of the metaphor focuses on the role of nurses in the maturation of children or, in this case, the maturation of the Thessalonian believers (cf. Gal 4:19). In accordance with his mission of forming, shaping, and nurturing communities, Paul and his coworkers reached out to their own children during the foundational moments to shape them without severe chastisement. Ever noting the consistency of the foundational team's effort in those moments, Paul shifts metaphors from nurse to father as an oblique suggestion that the maturation process did not stop. From the earliest foundational moments to later ones, Paul and his coworkers continued to shape the development of the Thessalonian church.

2:9-12. Continuing the basic self-description of the foundational leaders' commitment, a fourth section commends the leadership team's self-sufficiency, evinces the effectiveness of the team's continuing pedagogical style, and orients the auditors toward God's rule and glory (not that of others). Paul's foundational team worked "night and day" (v. 9)—that is, constantly—to sustain themselves as they preached the gospel and not "to burden" (ἐπιβαρέω *epibareō*) financially or literally "to weigh in on" (cf. "demands," βάρος *baros*, in v. 7) anyone in the church (cf. 2 Cor 11:9b). Exactly what type of work they

---

55. On the witness diction, see Wanamaker, *The Epistles to the Thessalonians*, 97.
56. As did philosophers like Dio Chrysostom (*Discourses* 32) and Plutarch (*Ad Apollonium* 117F) as well.
57. Beverly R. Gaventa, *First and Second Thessalonians*, Interpretation (Louisville: John Knox, 1998) 27.
58. Malherbe, *Paul and the Thessalonians*, 55.
59. Richard, *First and Second Thessalonians*, 100.

did in Thessalonica is unknown, although some scholars infer manual labor through a reading of 1 Cor 4:12. What is clearer, however, is that Paul continued a pattern that he used elsewhere of never receiving funds from a church while he worked among the believers to establish and shape that church (2 Cor 11:7-9; Phil 4:15-16), even though Paul acknowledged that he had a right to be sustained financially for his work in proclaiming the gospel (1 Cor 9:14-18). What is also clear is that Paul's reference to the foundational team's self-sufficiency not only shows the great affection the team had for the Thessalonian believers, but it also serves as a model for them. Later Paul will charge the Thessalonians to "work with your hands" with the goal of not being dependent on outsiders (4:11).

Indeed, Paul's reference to the character and care of the foundational team's pedagogical activity throughout these verses is intended to be paradigmatic. Paul's description of the team as "holy," "righteous," and "blameless" (ἀμέμπτως *amemptos*, v. 10) at the foundational moments describes the type of character he desires among the Thessalonians, as revealed in his later wish-prayers (3:13 and 5:23). These wish-prayers show Paul's concern for the believers' sanctification or ongoing maturation, for he prays that their hearts might be established "unblamable in holiness" (ἀμέμπτους ἐν ἁγιωσύνῃ *amemptous en hagiōsynē*, 3:13) and that God will "sanctify" (ἁγιάζω *hagiazō*) them and make them "blameless" (ἀμέμπτως *amemptōs*, 5:23).

Likewise, the individuated care of Paul and his coworkers for members of the church is paradigmatic. That is, the foundational team was like fathers with their children, exhorting "each one of you" (v. 11). Like many philosophers in his day, Paul offered individuated pastoral care, and he seems to commend the same in his later advice when he urges the church to offer aid for different types of needs among the believers (5:14).

All of Paul's hortatory expressions in vv. 11-12 ("urging," παρακαλοῦντες *parakalountes*; "encouraging," παραμυθούμενοι *paramythoumenoi*; and "pleading," μαρτυρόμενοι *martyromenoi*) are paradigmatic as well. Paul uses παρακαλέω (*parakaleō*)—a word for which he displayed a considerable fondness throughout his writings (cf. Rom 12:8; 1 Cor 1:10; 14:3; 2 Cor 8:17; 9:5; Phlm 9-10)—repeatedly in this letter to indicate general exhortation or consolation (a specific type of exhortation, 3:2, 7; 4:1, 10, 18; 5:11, 14; cf. 2:3). The second of these hortatory terms, while not as common in Paul's letters as the first one (cf. Phil 2:1), appears again in 5:14 when Paul commends care for the fainthearted: "encourage the fainthearted." While the third term is rare in Paul (cf. Gal 5:3) and appears later in 1 Thessalonians in a different form ("solemnly warned," διαμαρτύρομαι *diamartyromai*, 4:6), Paul's exhortation with all three expressions had the goal of helping the church "to conduct [περιπατέω *peripateō*] . . . a life [or "to walk" or "live"] worthy of God" (v. 12). Thus all three terms, like those that described the special character of the foundational leaders among the believers (v. 10), were related to the development of the community's distinctive ethos.

As readers will recall, the church's distinctiveness was a key theme noted in the exordium. Its importance here for Paul, however, is made clearer when one notes this letter's repeated use of language related to walking. Paul's foundational concern that the church "walk" or (so NRSV) "lead" (περιπατεῖν *peripatein*, v. 12) a life worthy of God is the first instance of a refrain sounded again in the latter part of the letter (*peripatein*, "to walk" or "to live," 4:1; περιπατῆτε *peripatēte*, "to live," "to walk," or "to behave," 4:12).

Paul's imagery of "walking" could have emanated from Greco-Roman moral philosophy. Epictetus speaks of life as a walk or way.[60] Perhaps, however, the "walking" metaphor actually had its roots in the LXX (e.g., 1 Kgs 2:4; 36:6; Isa 38:3; Jer 3:17; 9:14; 11:8; Ezek 36:26-27). As a translation of the Hebrew word הלך (*hālak*), *peripateō*, or "walk," in the LXX usually connoted one's actions as "an expression of one's commitments and devotion."[61] According to James D. G. Dunn, "the characteristic Jewish use [of *hālak*] was

---

60. Wilson includes the following ancient witnesses to the idea of "walking" as a way of life: Epictetus *Diatribae* 2.12.3; Plutarch *De Profectibus in Virtute* 76C; Maximus of Tyre Orations 16.2. See Wilson, *The Hope of Glory*, 41.
61. For the previous list and the citation, see Joseph O. Holloway, "*Peripateo* as a Thematic Marker for Pauline Ethics" (Ph.D. diss., Southwestern Baptist Theological Seminary, 1990) 7.

in commendation of a 'walk in the law/statutes/ordinances/ways of God' (hence 'halakah')."[62] Also since Paul had been a Pharisee (Phil 3:5), he would have been familiar with halakah, the oral laws that were transmitted in the Pharisaic schools.

In a letter concerned with the consistency and the commitment of the church's life before God, *peripateō* was an apt expression. The "walk" toward which Paul charged the church was one grounded in God's continuous call, as suggested by the present-tense participle "is calling" (καλοῦντος *kalountos*, v. 12). Moreover, in the light of the present opposition and Paul's assertion that the worthy walk is that of a God who "calls you into his kingdom" (i.e., a sphere of eschatological inheritance in which some of the benefits of the end time were already available; 1 Cor 6:9,10; cf. Rom 14:17; 1 Cor 4:20; 15:24; Gal 5:21), that walk was also apocalyptic. It was an ethical imperative that demanded of believers an unbroken commitment to holiness (cf. 4:1) or the life of the new age despite the fact that they lived among people who believed in neither the dawn of the new age nor its imminent consummation (see the Introduction).[63] Thus the ethos Paul commends is one in which the members of his church would seek to live worthy lives—lives that would reflect their persistence or sanctification and God's continuous call.

Altogether, then, the individual sections of vv. 1-12 laud the foundational leaders' persistence in their roles of proclaiming the gospel and nurturing the Thessalonian believers despite the hostility they encountered and in the light of the worthy walk to which their lives and that of the church were oriented. Just as the foundational leaders established the church with the gospel of God (v. 2), their shaping of the community throughout their tenure after the initial foundational preaching also was grounded in that gospel (v. 9). At no point did the severity and persistence of their opposition or the tests of God change their character, weaken their resolve to shape the distinctiveness of the Thessalonian church, or lessen their commitment to the gospel. This was a gospel worth starting with and staying with.

62. James D. G. Dunn, "Echoes of Intra-Jewish Polemic in Paul's Letter to the Galatians," *JBL* 112 (1993) 462.

63. Holloway, "*Peripateō* as a Thematic Marker for Pauline Ethics," 223-24.

REFLECTIONS

1. Among the images Paul uses in this section of the Thessalonian letter, that of the teacher/student relationship, deserves special attention. On a popular level, the value of teachers has been captured indelibly in such films as *To Sir, with Love, Mr. Holland's Opus,* and *Stand and Deliver.*

Long before Paul wrote 1 Thessalonians, the Greek world also knew the value of teachers. Homer introduced Mentor in the *Odyssey.* Aeschylus, the Athenian playwright, portrayed the legendary teacher Prometheus chained to a rock in *Prometheus Bound.* And Plato's *Apology* depicts Socrates as one who shared knowledge, not for pay, but out of a passionate commitment to teaching the truth.[64] Teachers in the Greek world and in the later Roman culture exercised a variety of roles, including that of psychagogy, the leading of the soul. Paul's ruminations on the teacher/student relationship reflect one of the standard rules for that relationship—namely, the practice of commending advice and aid suited to the particular disposition of each student. Central to this practice is a sense of the differing needs of each student. Thus Paul writes that the foundational leaders treated "each one of you like a father with his children" (2:11). Perhaps his later advice commending aid for different types of persons in the church (5:14) also indicates this pedagogical posture. Care for God's people today requires what Daniel O. Aleshire calls "the ministry of attending," the ministry

64. See Dona Gower, "Hero, Healer, and Martyr," *Parabola* 14 (1989) 46-49.

of noticing carefully the development of individual believers so that "the Christian community of faith can help them learn a Christian way in the world and grow toward maturity in faith."[65] Not all believers are at the same place; not all grow at the same pace. But all deserve nurture and patience.

2. Another promising image in this section is that of walking. "Walking" is a response to the calling of God, a walk defined neither by the individual nor by the society. The "walk worthy of God" is a walk that pleases God, a walk "in which God's own will rules, rather than selfish passions or greed."[66] It is a way of life not governed by our own sets of desires.

Nor is the walk governed by a set of desires routinized by polite societies and accepted by individuals to gain social prestige. Paul speaks about pleasing God, not people (2:4). He seeks not a transient "glory" from mortals, but the eternal "glory" into which God calls believers (2:12). The walk is a way of life in which one's prestige or worth comes not from one's kin and clan, but from one's alliance with God. What a measure of liberation is found in this walk. Here true prestige is not governed by the fads and fashions of society, not determined by the size of one's portfolio, and not hindered by the color of one's skin, the region of one's origins, or the pedigree of one's birth. Rather, the prestige of the walk is the kind we can assert simply from knowing that God has placed a claim on our lives.

---

65. Daniel O. Aleshire, *Faithcare: Ministering to All God's People Through the Ages of Life* (Philadelphia: Westminster, 1988) 15.
66. Holloway, "*Peripateō* as a Thematic Marker for Pauline Ethics," 51.

1 Thessalonians 2:13-16, The Word's Relentless Power

COMMENTARY

Given the focus on the word of the Lord or the gospel that characterized the two previous subunits, it is not surprising that Paul continues that theme in 2:13-16. Elaborating on the events of the foundational moments, Paul recalls the church's acceptance of the word of God for what it really was—not the words of humans, though it was communicated through human beings, but the word of God (v. 13*a*). Paul declares further that the same word is at work even now among the believers (v. 13*b*). Thus the word of God that could not be stopped and to which the foundational leaders remained committed is actively at work among the Thessalonians.

But how is this so? Paul's brief notice about the present work of the word is quickly followed by a longer, explanatory clause (vv. 14-16) that has been the subject of much controversy. Indeed, because of the apparently anti-Jewish tone of these verses, some interpreters have deemed vv. 14-16 to be an interpolation. The apparent theological difficulties of vv. 14-16 and the fact that v. 13 represents a second thanksgiving notice in this letter also has caused some scholars to see all of 2:13-16 as an interpolation, thus confusing, if not missing altogether, the real value of 2:13-16 in the letter.

A few words are in order, then, about the second thanksgiving notice in v. 13 and about the apparently anti-Jewish tone of vv. 14-16 before we can see the positive value of 2:13-16. In a letter in which one of the key themes is persistence, the appearance of a second thanksgiving notice is not unusual. Paul's repeated notices about thanksgiving throughout the letter (1:2-3; 2:13; 3:9-10) simply prepare the way for his request of the church to be thankful constantly (5:18). Furthermore, just as Paul earlier acknowledged his constant thanks to God ("We always give thanks to God," 1:2) for the church's steadfastness because of the power of the foundational leaders' word (1:5; cf. 2:1-12), so also he reminds his audience now of his continuous thanks ("We also constantly give thanks to God for this," 1:13) because of the church's acceptance of that same word as the word of God (2:13). There is not, then, an abrupt rupture between v. 12 and v. 13, as some commentators suggest. Just as vv. 1-12 imply that the inhospitable treatment meted out to Paul's leadership team in one city (Philippi) did not terminate their work among the Gentiles, so also vv. 13-16 imply, by analogy, the same effectiveness of the word in the church of the Thessalonians despite the inhospitable treatment of the foundational leaders by the church's neighbors.

As for the suggestion that 1 Thess 2:14-16 is a non-Pauline anti-Jewish interpolation, there is no manuscript support for this claim. Of course, some scholars think the expression "oppose everyone" (v. 15) reflects a typical slur made against Jewish people in the first century. Yet, whether Paul and the Thessalonians knew the negative ancient stereotype of the Jews as haters of non-Jewish people, a stereotype noted in Tacitus and in Josephus,[67] hardly matters because 1 Thess 2:14-16 is not directed toward all Jews—just some. Obviously, Paul does not include himself in the lot. The prophets to whom he refers would themselves have been Jewish, but they, too, are not a part of the group against which Paul directs his polemic. According to Frank Gilliard the inclusion of a comma after "the Jews" in most English Bibles fails to indicate the way the rest of the Greek sentence restricts what is said about them. Paul's use of a participial phrase after "the Jews" reflects his customary use of a restrictive participial expression to qualify the meaning of the noun that precedes it. Thus Paul is not talking about *all* the Jews, just *some* Jews—those who opposed Jesus and his movement.[68]

If the passage is not directed against all the Jews, then any attempt to pinpoint "God's wrath" (v. 16) as being directed against all the Jews seems both speculative and misguided (although some interpreters still link God's wrath to the later destruction of the Temple or to the expulsion of the Jews from Rome in 49 CE or to the massacre of Jews in the temple court in 49 CE or to something else). And, if the passage is not directed against all the Jews, then it is also not in conflict with Romans 11, "where far from suggesting the final judgment of the Jews, [Paul] speaks concerning the continuing validity of God's covenant with them and indeed of their eventual salvation."[69]

Moreover, "in-house" Jewish debate was both active and vigorous in ancient times.[70] And Paul's expression "filling up the measure of their sins" is a typical lament "with which [some] Jews express[ed] their outrage at the faithlessness of other Jews."[71] It is not unreasonable to note, moreover, that members of certain minority groups within the Roman Empire would quickly quell the actions of other members of their own group at the slightest suggestion of subversive activity or if the actions outrightly could be deemed as treasonous by the imperial powers.

Yet what is often missed in readings of 2:14-16 is Paul's characterization of the relentlessness of those Jews who opposed the Judean churches. The litany of the opposition seems to go on and on until finally Paul concludes the list with the statement "they have constantly [πάντοτε *pantote*] been filling up the measure of their sins" (v. 16). The picture Paul draws is one of a group that appears to be unswerving in its efforts and obsessive in its pursuits.

With that description, three concerns seem critical for Paul. First, the description he gives is actually an analogy that depicts the character of the opposition in Thessalonica. Already Paul has mentioned the "persecution" (actually, the "great persecution") in which his Thessalonian church received the word (1:6) as well as the "great opposition" the foundational leaders faced in Thessalonica when they sought to declare the gospel (2:2). By analogy with the case of the Judean churches, what Paul now reveals is the constancy and relentlessness of that opposition in Thessalonica. That, of course, means that throughout the duration of the foundational visit, a time long enough for Paul to have received gifts "more than once" from the Philippians (Phil 4:16), his young church faced

---

67. Tacitus *Histories* 5.5.2. Josephus *Against Apion* 2.121.
68. Frank Gilliard, "The Problem of the Anti-Semitic Comma between 1 Thessalonians 2:14 and 15," *NTS* 35 (1989) 481-502. Cf. W. D. Davies, "Paul and the People of Israel," *NTS* 24 (1977) 6-9; Willi Marxsen, *Der erste Brief an die Thessalonicher* (Zuerich: Theologischer Verlag, 1979) 149.
69. Donald Hagner, "Paul's Quarrel with Judaism," in *Anti-Semitism and Christianity: Issues of Polemic and Faith*, ed. Craig A. Evans and Donald A. Hagner (Minneapolis: Fortress, 1993) 131.
70. See, e.g., Josephus *Antiquities of the Jews* 1.15.91; Philo *Cherubim* 17. See Luke Timothy Johnson, "The New Testament's Anti-Jewish Slander and the Conventions of Ancient Polemic," *JBL* 108 (1989) 419-41; Hagner, "Paul's Quarrel with Judaism," 130-36.
71. Gaventa, *First and Second Thessalonians*, 37. As examples, Gaventa cites Dan 8:23; 2 Macc 6:14; Wis 19:3-5.

constant opposition. In fact, the end result of this opposition was the separation of the foundational leaders from the church, a topic Paul will take up explicitly in vv. 17-18.[72]

Second, the description also breathes with apocalyptic hope, as readers can see in v. 16*b,* the translation of which is also debated. Because 2:14-16 has often been read as a polemic against all Jews, some scholars have shied away from a translation of εἰς τέλος (*eis telos*) as "at last" or "forever" or "completely" (see the NRSV textual note to 2:16). Instead, preference is given to "until the end," which would correspond better with Rom 11:26. However, if readers interpret the constancy of the aforementioned opposition as an indication of the apocalyptic worldview according to which the greater part of the old age's afflictions occur shortly before the end time (cf. Dan 12:1; Matt 24:9-14; Mark 13:19, 24), then "at last" or "finally" actually captures the apocalyptic urgency of the church's situation and conveys a word of assurance. In other words, Paul's reading of the times is that the greater volume of persecution that believers are now facing is an indicator of the imminence of the end. This interpretation, of course, requires that the verb that describes God's wrath be translated in a different way. Instead of rendering the expression as "God's wrath has overtaken [ἔφθασεν *ephthasen*] them at last," as in the NRSV, the text would read "God's wrath has drawn near [*ephthasen*] at last" (cf. Luke 11:20).[73]

Third, the description also speaks about the survival of the Thessalonian church despite constant opposition. What is often missed when considering this passage is that "the churches of God in Judea" (v. 14) evidently have survived. Even with the loss of their leaders—whether through death, as in the case of Christian prophets (e.g., Stephen and James the brother of John), or through separation, as with other Christian leaders like Paul, these churches did not disintegrate. Similarly, the church of Thessalonica, despite the absence of its leaders (as Paul will soon explicitly note, 3:6), still survives, a sign that God's word "is at work [right now] in you believers" (v. 13).

Thus after Paul gives a second thanksgiving report (v. 13*a*) and an acknowledgment of the auditors' acceptance of the foundational leaders' word (v. 13*b*), he then uses the diction of imitation to explain the ongoing effectiveness of the word on the church (vv. 14-16) and to amplify his earlier encomium about the church's endurance (1:1-10). In this case, however, Paul declares that the church became an imitator of the churches of God in Judea. What ties the church at Thessalonica to the churches of Judea, moreover, is the loss of its leaders, either through death or physical separation. So in 2:13-16, Paul describes what his church suffered throughout the duration of the foundational visit, especially the forced separation of its leaders from the believers (on the analogy of the Judean churches).

With 2:13-16, then, the first large unit of the letter (1:6–2:16) comes to a close. All three subunits highlight the effectiveness of the word of God on those who received it or on those who delivered it. All of 2:1-12 speaks of the word or gospel that Paul and his coworkers brought to the church (2:2-3, 5, 8-9). Both 1:6-10 and 2:13-16 speak of the word or gospel that the church heard. That word motivated its carriers and its receivers repeatedly to endure local hostility.

Thus Paul's first large unit does more than laud the church for its persistence. Implicitly, it indicates the resources for the church's persistence: the word or gospel and the leadership team's shaping and nurturing practices—its own persistence (vv. 1-2); its concern to please God, not others (vv. 3-8); its self-sufficiency (v. 9); its patience, evinced in Paul's metaphorical shift from "wet nurse" (v. 7) imagery to "father" imagery (vv. 11-12); its tailor-made psychagogy (v. 11); and its orientation toward a walk or way of life worthy of God (v. 12). In the next two large units, as we shall see, Paul will continue to give notice to these same resources for persistence.

---

72. While the order of the litany suggests opposition first to Jesus, then to the prophets (presumably Christian prophets because of the order), then to a group in which Paul includes himself, we are not given a specific timetable for the opposition of some Jews to Paul while he was with the Judean churches. From Acts, of course, some find opposition by Jewish persons to the Judean churches in Acts 8:1bff. and 11:19. If Paul indeed refers to this opposition, the irony is that he was driven out of Judea by an opposition of which he was originally a part. What seems clearer, however, is that Paul's language of being driven out from the churches of Judea is analogous to the same experience in Thessalonica and thus preparatory for 2:17. Even if the prophets are understood to be OT prophets on the order of Luke 13:31, the churches of Judea would still have lost those who were driven out with Paul.

73. I. H. Marshall, *1 and 2 Thessalonians* (Grand Rapids: Eerdmans, 1983) 80-81.

REFLECTIONS

In his play *As You Like It,* Shakespeare wrote:

All the world's a stage,
And all the men and women merely players.
They have their exits and their entrances,
And one man in his time plays many parts.
(2.7.139)

On occasion, however, some characters or character groups play hidden roles off the observable stage of life. They never speak or move in the drama, but the audience knows that the story is not complete without them.

Because Christian anti-Semitism has repeatedly and regrettably clouded so much of the good that can be found in Christianity, many who read 1 Thess 2:13-16 fail to appreciate all of the characters implied in this brief drama of tensions. When fully appreciated, this section does not lend itself to the demonization of the Jews or of any other group. Paul's denunciation here of "some" Jews and "some" Gentiles, however, speaks about the ways in which strategies of containment work when people have to deal with the larger unspoken, but very real, forces of imperialism. Both Jews and the largely Greek population of Thessalonica lived under the shadow of Roman imperialism. And here and there some Jews and some Greeks exercised strategies of containment or control on those members of their own people who might be reckoned as subversive in the face of the Roman government.

Simplistic analyses of the imperial context of Paul's time thus lead many of us to overlook the other major character group in this drama: the Romans with their forces of imperialism. What this text should alert us to is the need to look for the hidden characters and forces that govern our culture and profoundly influence the way we think. The text suggests the need for us to "unmask the powers," Walter Wink's expression for exposing "the invisible, intangible interiority of collective enterprises, the invariant, determining forces of nature and society, or the archetypal images of the unconscious, all of which shape, nurture, and all too often cripple human existence."[74]

It is imperative that we ask ourselves: Do our responses to each other reflect greater fears and deeper anxieties that deserve scrutiny? Are we influenced by anxieties concerning our own survival? Our church's survival? All the world may be a stage, but many of the systems, ideas, and perspectives that influence us are standing in the wings.

74. Walter Wink, *Unmasking the Powers: The Invisible Forces That Determine Human Existence* (Philadelphia: Fortress, 1986) 173.

1 THESSALONIANS 2:17–3:13, CONCERN FOR THE CHURCH'S SURVIVAL AND MORAL TRAINING

OVERVIEW

After presenting a first large unit virtually on the earliest moments of the church's apocalyptic life (1:6–2:16), Paul now offers a second large unit that basically depicts a more recent period, from the departure of Paul's leadership team to the time of the letter's composition (2:17–3:13). Repetitive features suggest the configuration of this second large unit to be a series of three subunits. Two of the subunits are similar in that they treat the foundational leaders' desire to revisit the church (2:17-20; 3:9-13), while a central subunit indicates Timothy's role as an envoy between Paul and Silvanus, on the one hand, and the church of the Thessalonians, on the other hand (3:1-8).

The two outer subunits are similar to each other in form and diction. In form, both use rhetorical questions to echo the leadership team's joy about the community's expected (2:19) or present survival (2:20; 3:9). In diction, both subunits cite desired visits (2:17; 3:10), unsuccessful ones in the past (2:17), and a desired one in the future (3:10-11). Both mention as well a glorious apocalyptic visit or arrival: the parousia (2:19; 3:13), the present thought of which provides consolation for Paul's failed attempts to return to his church. The middle subunit (3:1-8) continues the theme of visits, but does so with two flashback sections on Timothy: one on his visit to the church (3:1-5) and another on his subsequent return to Paul (3:6-8). Altogether, the three subunits resound with the language of visits and the arrival of Jesus, the tenderest depictions of the foundational leaders' affection and their continuing concern about the church's ability to survive, and a vibrant example of Timothy's nurturing practices.

1 Thessalonians 2:17-20, Aborted Trips and the Parousia

COMMENTARY

With the first subunit (2:17-20), Paul explicitly notes the last local opposition that occurred during the foundational visit—namely, the abrupt forced separation of the leaders from the church. With language that expresses the depths of sorrow, Paul now describes the distress of this separation (v. 17) and laments the futility of his efforts to return (v. 18). He also neutralizes any possible discouragement about the aborted visits with a declaration of benefits accruing to another visit or arrival: the parousia, a future grand visit or arrival similar to that of Hellenistic kings and rulers (vv. 19-20).[75]

The account in the book of Acts seems to suggest that the departure of the leaders from the Thessalonian church was caused by Jewish agitation (Acts 17:5-9). However, Acts' reckoning of the events of Paul's work in Thessalonica is difficult to reconcile with Paul's own account in several ways. For one, as has already been noted (see the Introduction), Paul's Thessalonian converts included Jews and Gentiles according to Acts 17:1-4, but only Gentiles according to 1 Thess 1:9-10; 2:14-16. Second, although 1 Thessalonians seems to involve Timothy explicitly in the foundational work at Thessalonica (1:1; 3:1-2, 6), Acts directly mentions the difficulties Paul and Silas encountered in Philippi and Thessalonica but only directly notes Timothy when the three leaders are together in Beroea (Acts 17:14). Third, because the form of the word "alone" (μόνοι *monoi*, 3:1) is plural in Greek, Paul gives the impression that he and presumably Silvanus were in Athens when Timothy was sent to the Thessalonians. Acts gives the impression, however, that (after Beroea) Silvanus and Timothy did not join up with Paul until they arrived in Corinth (Acts 18:5).

However one seeks to reconcile these accounts, Paul seems less interested in naming the exact cause of the separation than in indicating the heavy toll it exacted on the entire leadership team and on his personal life. Having already noted the great anguish of the separation for the church (v. 14), Paul uses vv. 17-20 to show the effect of the separation from the vantage point of the foundational leaders. The expression "we were made orphans" sufficiently translates the Greek word that lies behind it (ἀπορφανισθέντες *aporphanisthentes*, v. 17); however, the NRSV adds "by being separated from you" (v. 17), although these words are not actually a part of the Greek text. Still, Paul's lament that

---

75. Raymond Collins, *The Birth of the New Testament: The Origin and Development of the First Generation* (New York: Crossroad, 1993) 112.

his leadership team became orphans aptly catches the sense of deep grief caused by the separation.[76]

An indication of the depths of their grief is also shown in the way Paul heaps passionate phrases on top of one another to describe the attempts to return to Thessalonica. A literal translation of v. 17 would read: "As for us, brethren, when we were made orphans from you for a short time, in person [προσώπω *prosōpō*] not in heart, we even much more and with great longing made every effort to see your face [πρόσωπον *prosōpon*]."

As if the intensity of the leadership team's resolve is still not dramatized enough, however, Paul shifts from a description of the collective effects of the separation and recent endeavors to visit to his own personal strivings: "I, Paul . . ." (v. 18*b*). Shortly, as he continues to deal with the effects of the separation, Paul will similarly shift from the foundational leaders' inability to "bear" the separation to his own personal inability to do so (3:1, 5). For now, however, he seeks to expose the constancy of his effort to get back to the church. And constancy or persistence, as we have seen, is a recurring theme throughout the entire letter.

Exactly how often Paul tried to return is not known, for the expression "again and again" (lit., "once and twice [καὶ ἅπαξ καὶ δίς *kai hapax kai dis*]," v. 18*b*) connotes an "indefinite number of occasions"[77] (cf. Phil 4:16). Exactly what blocked his way is also not known, though some scholars speculate about a possible embargo or a physical malady.[78] What we do know, however, is that Paul's categorizing the obstruction as an effort of Satan is strategic on at least two levels.

On the one hand, this categorization reiterates Paul's apocalyptic ideas already noted in the letter. In his "already/not yet" apocalyptic understanding of reality, Satan is a deceiver who can take on the form of an angel of light, as can his envoys (2 Cor 2:11; 11:14). He is also a tempter (1 Cor 7:5; cf. 1 Thess 3:5) and one whom "God will shortly crush" (Rom 16:20). Thus, having already mentioned the "persecution" or "eschatological woes" (θλῖψις *thlipsis*, 1:6) in which the church received the word of God, Paul now highlights again the manifestations of the old age with a reference to the continuing hindrances of Satan. Once more, however, if the church recognizes that the intensity of the opposition described in vv. 14-16 is actually an indication of the imminence of God's wrath, the believers would likely recognize as well that Satan's repeated hindrances also signal the approaching end.

On the other hand, the categorization also anticipates Paul's next subunit, in which he will speak again in an oblique way about an evil force. In 3:5, Paul notes his former fear that the "tempter had tempted" his young church in the wake of his departure. Given that Satan was known as a tempter in Paul's apocalyptic worldview, it is likely that Paul is still speaking about the reality of the old age's pressure on believers (now with respect to the church). Indeed, Paul's use of the term "persecution" (θλίψεσιν *thlipsesin*, 3:3-4) also reinforces the apocalyptic context out of which Paul speaks. If he, indeed, is making the connection, he is also linking himself (and the other members of the leadership team) more solidly to his church. Both faced the pressures of the old age in the foundational moments of the work at Thessalonica; and the pressures continue.

Paul's reflections in vv. 17-20, however, do not end with his lament about the separation or his musings on Satan's hindrance. Because Satan's repeated hindrances would have signaled the imminence of the end to the Thessalonian addressees, Paul could not dwell on the hindrances alone. It is understandable why he would then launch out of the deep pathos of lamentation about the separation and aborted visits and shift the audience's thoughts to another visit or arrival, the parousia.

The word *parousia* has two essential meanings: "presence" (2 Macc 15:21; 3 Macc 3:17; 2 Cor 10:10; Phil 2:12) and "arrival" (Jdt 10:18; 2 Macc 8:12; 1 Cor 16:17; 2 Cor 7:6-7). Howard notes that the word "came to have particular associations with the arrival of a central figure." The word indicated both "the physical act of arrival" and "the attendant circumstances in which the ruler was honored."[79] It is generally

---

76. Other writers in Paul's time (Seneca, e.g., in *Ad Helviam* 18.7) used the image of an orphan to describe feelings associated with exile.
77. Marshall, *1 and 2 Thessalonians*, 86.
78. Marshall, *1 and 2 Thessalonians*, 86.
79. Tracy Howard, "The Literary Unity of 1 Thessalonians 4:13-5:11," *Grace Theological Journal* 9 (1988) 176.

believed that the early Christians adopted these "particular associations" to speak about Christ's coming. It is likely, moreover, that the term "would have evoked the image of the return of a triumphant conqueror in the Hellenistic world and the idea of a coronation on that occasion."[80]

For Paul, mentioning the parousia potentially had two results. First, with the imagery of a crown (v. 19), i.e., the laurel wreath won by an athletic victor, Paul could obliquely imply the success of his mission (cf. 1 Cor 9:25; Phil 4:1; 1 Thess 2:19). Presupposing the parousia as a time of mission assessment (cf. 1 Cor 4:10-15; 2 Cor 1:14), Paul makes the claim that the church will be his "crown of boasting" (cf. 1 Cor 9:25; Phil 4:1). That is, it will not disintegrate. The word of God that is still working in the believers will continue to do so (v. 13b), and the church will be the evidence of Paul's faithfulness to God in the call God assigned to him. Second, and related, because Paul and the Thessalonian believers will be together at the parousia, Paul is now neutralizing the present inability to get to them because of Satan's hindrances. Ultimately, he is suggesting that a reunion will occur between the foundational leaders and the church in spite of Satan's plots, even if that reunion must wait until his Lord's glorious parousia, the final blow to the manifestations of the old age. Indeed, he has joy (3:9) now as he thinks about the church in the light of that reunion. The church's joy was inspired by the Holy Spirit (1:6), God's pledge of all that is to come in the new age's consummation. Paul has joy as well as he thinks of that consummation. Satan has blocked his way, but not his joy.

---

80. Collins, *The Birth of the New Testament*, 112.

REFLECTIONS

Joy comes in a number of forms. Some works of visual art evoke joy: the marvelous landscapes of Edward M. Bannister or the magnificent *Water Lilies* of Claude Monet. Some sights evoke joy: a view of the Mediterranean Sea from atop the Notre Dame de la Garde in Marseilles or the snow-capped peak of Mt. Rainier above Seattle's foggy mists. Some musical compositions or performances evoke sheer joy: Bach's Flute Concerto, Kathleen Battle's sweeping rendition of "Were You There When They Crucified My Lord?" or the voices of the three tenors, José Carreras, Placido Domingo, and Luciano Pavarotti.

Thefts, nature's path of destruction, and death, however, can deprive us of the beauty of these joys. Yet the joy of which Paul speaks has no favorite season beyond which it can be felt no more. It neither originates from nor depends on transient forces. It can be experienced by women and men who can claim it personally in their lives, but it is not an isolated, private joy. It is both a hope for concrete benefits in the future and a present reality.

This is the joy that breaks through the gloomiest of days to buoy the otherwise disheartened. This is the joy that comes not from changing circumstances, but from a constant presence in the believer's life, the Holy Spirit. This is the joy that arises out of sights that are sure but not yet fully seen or realized. This is the joy that can stir the heart of a man to write "It Is Well with My Soul" even after the loss of family members at sea, as if to transform incomprehensible sorrow through a tireless declaration of the believer's peace in God. This is the joy of bruised and berated black bards who defied their circumstances with the simplest, yet weightiest, of words: "This joy that I have, the world did not give it to me." This is the joy of Archbishop Romero, whose last letter before his assassination spoke of the "spirit of joy at being accorded the privilege of running the same risks as [the poor], as Jesus did by identifying with the causes of the dispossessed."[81] This is Paul's view of joy.

---

81. Oscar A. Romero, "Letter to Bishop Pedro Casaldaliga, March 24, 1980," in Jon Sobrino, *Archbishop Romero: Memories and Reflections*, trans. Robert R. Barr (Maryknoll, N.Y.: Orbis, 1990) 40.

1 Thessalonians 3:1-8, A Visit of Consolation in Hostile Times

COMMENTARY

Studies of the Thessalonian correspondence argue that the foundational leaders not only established the Thessalonian church and then gave it shape through the inculcation of a distinctive ethos, but also sought to nurture it. That is, the team sought to provide the church with sustenance for its ongoing growth. Examinations of the hortatory tradition reveal three of the basic strategies through which teachers nurtured their students: (1) the commissioning of an emissary, (2) the use of letters of exhortation, and (3) the commendation of mutual nurturing.[82]

Paul used all three of these strategies. The whole of 1 Thessalonians is a letter of exhortation. And within the letter Paul repeatedly instructs the Thessalonian believers to exhort (console, encourage, or admonish) one another (4:18; 5:11-14). Here, in 3:1-8, in the form of two flashbacks (vv. 1-5 and vv. 6-8), Paul reminds them of the work of his emissary Timothy.

With an initial flashback (vv. 1-5), Paul offers repeated remarks about Timothy's role as a proclaimer of the word and as one of the foundational leaders (vv. 1-3a, 5) and a parenthetical statement of the foundational team's forewarning about suffering (vv. 3b-4). Both the remarks and the statement are critical.

The remarks (vv. 1-3a, 5) have at least two functions. First, Paul's description of Timothy's visit reveals the nurturing role the latter played in his visit to the Thessalonians. That is, Timothy was sent to "strengthen and to 'encourage'" (παρακαλέω *parakaleō*, v. 2), a role played by all the members of Paul's leadership team at their foundational visit in their "urging" (*parakaleō*; cf. 2:11) of the church. In that role, Timothy is described in the NRSV as "our brother and co-worker for God in . . . the gospel of Christ" (v. 2; cf. 2 Cor 6:2). While some manuscripts support the description of Timothy as "God's servant" or "our fellow-worker" or some combination of the two, most scholars accept the manuscript tradition that describes Timothy as God's coworker. The other manuscript traditions perhaps had problems conceiving of God as a coworker, but Paul has no problem perceiving the word that his team presents as the word of God (2:13). Thus, whatever role Timothy plays, God also was at work in it. Ultimately, God is the source of the church's nurturing.

Second, Paul's description of Timothy reveals the grave concern that the foundational leaders had for the stability of the church in the light of their acute separation. While Paul consistently praises the believers for their faith (1:3, 8; cf. 2:13), he also sends Timothy to find out about their faith (3:3, 5). Given the separation of the foundational leaders from the believers, he is concerned to know whether the church would be able to sustain itself without the nurturing presence of one or more members of his leadership team.

Paul's concern, however, is not narcissistic. It does not come from any self-aggrandizement on the part of the church's foundational leaders. Nor can it be chalked up simply to Paul's desire to visit all the churches that he established, although, in fact, he did have that desire. What is different about this church and what precipitates the grave concern here is the limited time the foundational leaders had with the believers. As Malherbe notes, "in no other letter does he write to people who had been Christians for so short a time and who were therefore especially in need of encouragement, preferably through personal contact."[83]

Because of the limited time he spent with the Thessalonian believers, Paul's fear was that the church might be "shaken" (σαίνομαι *sainomai*), or "unsettled emotionally" because of persecution,[84] with the result that his labor would be "in vain" (εἰς κενόν *eis kenon*), an expression he uses elsewhere to indicate his concern for the stability of his churches (Gal 2:2; Phil 2:16; cf. 1 Cor 15:58;

---

82. Malherbe, *Paul and the Thessalonians*, 61.
83. Malherbe, *Paul and the Thessalonians*, 63.
84. Malherbe, *Paul and the Thessalonians*, 65.

Gal 4:11). Thus Timothy's role was to provide additional nurturing or moral training for the young church in the light of the team's grave concerns about its stability.

While Paul does not elaborate on the nature of the "persecutions" (θλίψεσιν *thlipsesin*, v. 3; cf. v. 4), here or elsewhere when he uses the expression it has been noted that he likely has in mind the eschatological woes that were thought to precede the approaching end. Although Paul has talked at length about the effect of the separation and aborted visits on all of the foundational leaders or on himself alone, it is not a foregone conclusion that he understood the persecutions to be those of the foundational leaders exclusively. The similarities previously noted about Satan's hindrances and the tempter's pressure on the church suggest, in fact, that the persecutions include whatever troubles the Thessalonians were experiencing as well.

Furthermore, with respect to the Thessalonians, Paul's use of the language of temptation ("the tempter had tempted," v. 5) leads some scholars to suggest that the persecutions or afflictions also included social alienation or pressures from the former networks out of which the church members came. That is, the basic Greek word πειράζω (*peirazō*) connotes both the idea of testing through suffering, as in the case of persecutions, and the idea of temptation through seduction. Thus the Thessalonian believers may have been seduced to return to their former families and friends, especially in the light of the fact that the foundational leaders had only a brief time to inculcate the values of the Christian life in them. Until the time of Timothy's visit no one had returned to help solidify them against the hostilities from which their church, since the very beginning, had seen no respite or escape.

The parenthetical statement on what the church knows and what the team has already shared with them (vv. 3*b*-4) implicitly reiterates the foundational leaders' consistency in their hortatory practices. A typical strategy in the hortatory tradition was a forewarning of coming troubles so that exhorted persons might ready themselves to meet them. Paul employs this strategy, but his discussion of the forewarning is strategically placed as a parenthesis between comments about Timothy's visit to the Thessalonians. As well, the parenthesis repeatedly acknowledges what the church already knows: "Indeed, you yourselves know . . . ; so it turned out, as you know." What Paul tells the Thessalonians in vv. 1-5, therefore, is a reminder of what he has already said. Because the imperfect form of a Greek verb conveys ongoing, continuous action in the past, Paul's use of the imperfect verbal form "told you beforehand" (προελέγομεν *proelegomen*, v. 4) in his comments on the forewarning suggests that the team had shared the apocalyptic commentary on persecutions continuously while they were with the church.[85] Thus the parenthesis dramatizes the foundational leaders' consistency. Of course, the emphasis on the leaders' consistency is probably just another way in which Paul invites his church to be consistent. Given the constancy of Satan's hindrances and the repeated instances of hostility since its birth, how could Paul's church do less?

With a second flashback (vv. 6-8), Paul relates the survival of the church (v. 6*a*), the believers' constant remembrance of their foundational leaders (v. 6*b*), and even the value of Timothy's "good news" to the other members of the foundational team (v. 7). Ever the exhorter in this letter, Paul again obliquely nudges the church toward persistence by linking the foundational team's very life to the believers' firm stand in the face of local opposition (v. 8).[86]

As Timothy had gone to the Thessalonians, he now returns to Paul and Silvanus. As he was sent to "encourage" the believers (v. 2), he now returns to Paul and Silvanus, bringing words that "encouraged" them (v. 7). Evidently all is fine because the news reveals the church's consistency and the mutuality of affection and support between the foundational team and the believers. Timothy's report indicates that the church "always" (πάντοτε *pantote*) remembers the foundational team (v. 6). Paul used the same word earlier to speak about the constancy of the foundational team's thanksgiving (1:2). Given the context of the hortatory tradition, the church's constant remembrance of the foundational team could also indicate

---

85. See Marshall, *1 and 2 Thessalonians*, 92.
86. See Wanamaker, *The Epistles to the Thessalonians*, 136.

the believers' commitment to the values that the foundational leaders had shared with them.

Timothy's report also indicates the deep mutuality between the church and the foundational leaders. Paul's earlier description of the foundational team included their longing for the Thessalonian believers and their desire to see them (2:17). Likewise, the church longed to see the foundational team (v. 6). Thus the separation appears to have been a mutually heartbreaking experience, and each group desired to be reunited fully with the other.

The mutuality, however, was not only one of affection, but one of support as well. Obviously, the foundational leaders' efforts to get to the church reveal their desire to support the Thessalonians through their difficulties, to provide nourishment for their maintenance. Yet Paul indicates that the report about the church helped the foundational team as well: "During all our distress and persecution [or endtime woes] we have been encouraged [or consoled] about you through your faith" (v. 7; cf. 2 Cor 7:3-7).

What is remarkable about this mutuality of support is that Paul implies that this same church that became a type for other believers (1:7)—a community whose faith was known everywhere (1:8)—actually had within it the ability to bring consolation or encouragement to others. It is little wonder, then, that he later commands the believers to encourage one another (4:18; 5:11). They had already been a source of encouragement to the foundational team, and, according to Paul, their encouragement of one another was not a new practice (5:11). If they could be a source of encouragement, that should be a sign that they had really committed themselves to the foundational team's teachings.

To encourage the believers even further (if not also to challenge them), Paul adds: "For now we live, if you continue to stand firm in the Lord" (v. 8). Paul often used the language of "standing firm" in his exhortations to his other churches (1 Cor 16:13; Gal 5:1; Phil 1:27; 4:1). But what did Paul mean by the expression "we live"? In part, Paul speaks here about the "quality of life, i.e., that Timothy's message allows the missionaries a fuller, less anxious life."[87] As well, the linking of the quality of the mission team's life to the steadfastness of the church is Paul's way of exhorting them to stand fast, to persist in the ways of the gospel he has shared with them.

87. Richard, *First and Second Thessalonians*, 161.

REFLECTIONS

1. Readers will find much in this passage about the stresses of leadership, the importance of trustworthy people, the strategic value of teamwork, and the trials that can beset chuches. As for trust and teamwork, Timothy, Paul's trusted coworker, is pictured as a valued ally and an unselfish minister. Out of view of Paul and Silvanus, his elders, and working among the church members at Thessalonica, Timothy did not use the absence of his colleagues as an occasion for career advancement. He showed an acute perception of both the needs of those older, absent, anxious leaders and the needs of their solicitous church. Obviously, churches need comfort from time to time, but so do leaders. Leaders go through periods when they need to be on the receiving end, times when their leadership is particularly stressful, and they require rest, reassurance, and renewal. Timothy's work in Thessalonica helped the church and also helped to relieve Paul and Silvanus of anxiety about the Thessalonian Christians.

Timothy's unselfish spirit as a leader and team member is a worthy model of ministry in a time beset by the concerns of career building. He demonstrates the spirit of teamwork, showing how we can work trustingly with and for each other in fulfilling God's claim upon our lives.

2. It may be difficult for Christians who have never had to suffer for their beliefs to relate to the constant tests or afflictions that affected Paul and his church. If Paul's mention of "tests" is seen as an indication of a threat of apostasy, however, we may recognize his concern more clearly. Although we are not all tested directly by suffering for our faith, we are all familiar with being tempted because of our faith: tempted to ease up in our commitment, tempted to lose our convictions, tempted to relax our morality.

Dietrich Bonhoeffer, the German pastor and theologian who suffered imprisonment and made the ultimate sacrifice for his opposition to Nazism, argued in one of his writings that there is a relationship between these two types of tests. Bonhoeffer wrote: "Temptation to desire always includes the renunciation of the desire, that is to say, suffering. Temptation to suffering always includes the longing of freedom from suffering, that is to say, the desire. Thus the temptation of the flesh through desire and through suffering is at bottom one and the same."[88] Can it be that some of us face so few tests of suffering because we have given in too easily to so many tests of seduction?

---

88. Dietrich Bonhoeffer, *Creation and Fall, and Temptation: Two Biblical Studies* (New York: Macmillan, 1959) 118.

1 Thessalonians 3:9-13, An Expected Trip and the Parousia

COMMENTARY

A number of scholars suggest that the third subunit (3:9-13) of the second large unit (2:17–3:13) provides a brief summary of the argument's previous issues.[89] This is not an unreasonable assumption because Paul includes a wish-prayer (3:11-13), and wish-prayers generally summarize foregoing material (cf. 1 Thess 5:23; Rom 15:5-6). Thus, as previously mentioned, 3:9-13 parallels 2:17-20. In addition, Paul's reference to the foundational team's love (3:12), particularly a love that focused on each person (as one could infer from Paul's description of the believers' love "for one another"), could remind the audience of their leaders' great care at the foundational visit (cf. 2:8). The foundational team's care was expressed for "each person," for Paul affirms that "we dealt with each one of you like a father with his children" (2:11).

Still, 1 Thess 3:9-13 is also a foreshadowing of the material that follows. As noted by form critics, its thanksgiving and prayer formulas point ahead to the life of love and holiness and to the letter's later interest in the parousia. So, since the subunit focuses on a complete or comprehensive love, the audience will not be surprised when eventually Paul commends a love for one another and to all (4:9-12). Also, since Paul prays that the believers' hearts will be strengthened in "holiness" (3:13), the auditors can expect Paul later to charge the church to exemplify "holiness" (4:4), a distinctive characteristic of God (cf. Isa 1:4; Jer 50:9; Ezek 39:7). And since Paul speaks of the parousia and the greatness with which it is associated (3:13), his readers will not find it striking for him to speak about the parousia and for him to comment on those who will be a part of Jesus' prestigious entourage (4:13–5:11).

This subsection, however, is critical for three other reasons. First, it reveals yet again the constancy of the foundational team. The team continues to give thanks even if here (3:9) they recognize that their thanksgiving to God is never enough compared to the joy they feel because of the church. As before, moreover, their constancy implicitly encourages the constancy of the church.

Second, this subsection also exposes the realism of the foundational team. Despite all the good they can say about the church, the foundational team's apocalyptic understanding of the realities of evil—of persecution, of Satan's blocking techniques, of the temptation (or seduction) for the believers to return to their former networks of support—leads them to pray for an opportunity to "restore what is lacking" in the church's faith (3:10).

---

89. In agreement, see Jewett, *The Thessalonian Correspondence*, 140. Cf. Joseph O. Halloway, "*Peripateō* as a Thematic Marker for Pauline Ethics" (Ph.D. diss., Southwestern Baptist Theological Seminary, 1990) 37.

Paul does not state specifically what needs to be restored, and perhaps that would only be known when the foundational team's future visit was realized. What he does indicate, however, is that something is lacking. And given his apocalyptic understanding of reality, would not that always be the case until the parousia?

Third, Paul's brief comments on the parousia in conjunction with a wish-prayer for a reunion with the church emphasize the incredible strength the Thessalonian church could receive in thinking about the parousia. Paul is not sure whether he will get back to the church, although he prays for a chance to do so. He is certain, however, about the parousia's power to unite the people of God. So whether "all his saints" (NRSV) or "all his holy ones" (NIV) is the best translation of the Greek word that describes Jesus' entourage (ἅγιοι *hagioi*, 3:13), what Paul takes for granted is that the parousia will occur and that it will be a grand event of reunion. For an isolated church faced with continuous persecution, just knowing that they would be a part of that grand event would surely have brought them great encouragement. Satan would not have the last word.

Given the three subunits of the second large unit, how does the entire unit encourage the audience to maintain its apocalyptic way of life? Perhaps the believers are encouraged through Paul's emphasis on the persistence of both the foundational team and the church throughout hostilities and hindrances. The team's persistence was manifested through its embrace of the parousia as an event that neutralizes separation and through its persistent efforts to provide moral training for the church through Paul's acolyte, Timothy. Furthermore, the foundational leaders' persistence is evident in their continuous prayer to God (3:9-13). As for the church, its members evidently remain just as influenced by the apocalyptic word because Paul still hears something good about them. They continue to exhibit faith and love (3:6), and their remembrance of the foundational team is constant.

But what are the resources of persistence noted in the second large unit? They are, in fact, the very ones mentioned in the first large unit: the foundational team's earlier apocalyptic words and the consolatory or exhortatory practices of a specific leader, in this case Timothy. Paul continues to view the church's afflictions in the light of an apocalyptic prism. Yet, Timothy's presence is important as well. It is likely the case that Timothy secured the church with that apocalyptic word as he sought to strengthen and console the Thessalonian believers. With the word of God and the practices of moral training noted in two of the large units of Paul's letter, it is little wonder that the last large unit will feature the value of both the apocalyptic word and the practices of moral training. Paul's implicit emphasis on these resources anticipates the kinds of resources he will commend in 4:1–5:22 as he exhorts his church to persist in their distinctive way of life.

REFLECTIONS

Paul's love for the church spills over in this passage. Of course, the dearness of the church to Paul is found everywhere in the letter. Paul's metaphorical shift from wet nurse (2:7) to father (2:11-12) projects a friendly message, for the shift conveys the foundational leaders' continuous care for the converts from infancy onward. Paul praises the Thessalonians for their steadfastness (or their active and heroic constancy in the face of trials, 1:3) and for their continuous expressions of mutual support and comfort (4:1, 9; 5:11). A note of remembrance (1:3) registers Paul's admiration, and echoes of joy reverberate throughout the letter. Yet, only in 3:9-13—perhaps because Paul only now explicitly mentions the separation—do his deep affection and longing for the Thessalonian believers break through the surface to become a dominant theme as he confesses his intense desire to be present with them. Repeated hindrances follow repeated efforts to get to the church (2:17-18), and desperate agonizing over the church's survival leads to the dispatch of Timothy (3:1-5). Moreover, the separation is a mutually heartrending matter, for both Paul and the church long to see each other (2:17; 3:6, 10). And yet with all of the deep fondness and the relief that Timothy's report brings about the church's success, Paul, ever the pastor, speaks of his desire to "restore" or "supply" whatever is lacking in their faith (3:10).

These believers in Thessalonica are not like those in Corinth, with whom Paul would have a long and stormy relationship. Nor were they listening to outside agitators quibble about entrance requirements, as would be the case later among the Galatians. To the contrary, the church at Thessalonica was meritorious in many ways, moving from the rank of imitators to the rank of examples. Yet—for all the church's success—Paul's thanksgiving refrain is broken by a reminder that he wants not only to see the church, but also to supply whatever is still lacking in their faith (3:10).

Of the three thanksgiving reports, the other two simply laud the church for its success—for its active deployment of the triad of graces ("faith . . . love . . . hope," 1:3) or for its reception of the team's word as the word of God (2:13). But in the third one, Paul moves beyond an accounting of his joy before God for the church to a realism enriched by his apocalyptic vision. Again, Paul does not note exactly what is lacking. He just knows that something is.

This apocalyptic realism suggests that all is not yet complete. For Paul, as has been noted, manifestations of the old age still affect the believers who await Jesus' coming as the climactic event that will consummate the new age already begun with the death and resurrection of Jesus. Therefore, believers live between the "already" of what God has done through Jesus' death and resurrection and the "not yet" that awaits them.

This is hard realism for any church. As successful as a church may seem, something is still lacking because of the intrusions of the old age. As much light as the church may bring to others and as much good as it may do for the world, something is still lacking. Something inevitably needs the attention of those who lead the church, and God can be trusted to honor supplications on behalf of that need (cf. 3:11-13).

This realism bears witness to Paul's distinctive brand of apocalypticism—to the tension between the already and the not-yet of Paul's thought, as distilled from all of the undisputed letters. That same tension should rescue churches today from a one-sided view of salvation and its benefits. The value of the already dimension of God's work is that no one can make a claim to superiority based on previous entitlements outside of their lives in Christ. Whatever we are, we are by the grace of God already and always active in our lives. The value of the not-yet dimension of God's work, however, is that no one can claim perfection, as if the sanctification process is complete. Vestiges of the past still intrude, even if only in our memories, as if they are not dead, but only wounded and still seeking a toe-hold.[90] The goal for us, then, is to draw on the strength of the Holy Spirit, the seal or guarantee of the new age's consummation, and to wait with trust and diligence for the full transformation of our lives.

---

90. Sampley, *Walking Between the Times*, 10, 13.

1 THESSALONIANS 4:1–5:22, COMMENDING PERSISTENCE IN THE DISTINCTIVE LIFE

OVERVIEW

Having recalled the persistence of the church and the pastoral team at the foundational visit (1:6–2:16) and having recounted the recent events that occurred from the team's forced separation until the composition of the letter (2:17–3:13), Paul makes yet another temporal shift to urge the church to persist in its apocalyptic life in the face of local hostilities (4:1–5:22). Repetitive features in 4:1–5:22 suggest a large unit made up of three subunits: two units of explicit moral exhortation (4:1-12; 5:12-22) and a middle subunit with a direct focus on end-time events (4:13–5:11). Still, all of the material is exhortative, linking a number of imperatives to apocalyptic descriptions of the end time and describing for the church the distinctive life of love and holiness they must live before others as they wait with assurance for the parousia.

1 Thessalonians 4:1-12, Walking a Distinctive Life

COMMENTARY

All of 4:1-12 is held together by the repetition of the word "walk" (περιπατέω *peripateō*; see the Commentary on 2:12) at the beginning and end of this subunit. The Greek term is translated by the NRSV as "live" (v. 1) and "behave" (v. 12). Within these verses, three integrated sections clarify the believer's distinctive walk. One section (vv. 1-2), introductory in nature, acknowledges the believers' apprehension of a distinctive walk that pleases God. Two other sections (vv. 3-8 and vv. 9-12) render specific details about that walk. In 4:3-8, three specific injunctions (vv. 3*b*-6*a*) and three specific motivations (vv. 6*b*-8) follow a maxim about the holiness of the community (v. 3*a*). In 4:9-12, Paul presents specific challenges about love (whether for each other or for other believers in Macedonia) and specific directives on behavior toward outsiders.[91]

4:1-2. Four features of these verses give them an introductory character. First, they begin with "finally" (λοιπόν *loipon*), a familiar transitional expression in Paul's writings (2 Cor 13:11; Phil 3:1). In the case of 1 Thessalonians, "finally" marks the last of three large units of Paul's overall proof section.

Second, these initial verses are couched as general statements of exhortation, leaving the specifics for later (in vv. 3-8 and vv. 9-12). It is doubtful that the specifics indicate a lack in the moral character of the church. Paul's previous affirmation of the church's model behavior (1:7) suggests the contrary. Furthermore, Paul repeatedly acknowledges the appropriate comportment that he already sees in the church (vv. 1, 9).

Third, these verses set the tone for all of the material in 4:1–5:22—namely, an emphasis on persistence, with echoes of earlier themes treated in the two previous large units. According to Paul's description of his leadership team at its foundational visit in Thessalonica, the team's aim was to please God, not human beings (2:4). The exhortations "to live [walk] and to please God" (4:1) are synonymous infinitive expressions for the same activity (in technical jargon, an example of a hendiadys). They express what should also be the goal of the church.

Paul's declaration that his urging was something the church "learned" (παρελάβετε *parelabete*, v. 1*b*) from the foundational team

---

91. Some scholars think Περὶ δέ (*Peri de*, "and concerning") refers to a previous letter from the apostle. It is possible, however, simply to see *peri de* here and in 5:1 as a transitional marker. See the Commentary on 5:1.

also resonates with Paul's earlier statement that the church "received" (παραλαβόντες *paralabontes*) the word they heard as the word of God, not of humans (2:13). Though not clearly indicated in the NRSV's rendering of v. 1, Paul's request for a persistence in the "walking" activity ("as in fact you are doing, you should do so more and more," v. 1d) echoes the language of his earlier wish-prayer when he prays for the church's love to abound (3:12). It is with little wonder, then, that Paul will highlight love in 4:9-10 and also request that the love of the church abound more and more (4:11).

Fourth, these initial verses also highlight the distinctiveness of the practices and perspectives Paul will recommend in the rest of this large unit. Like other teachers of the first century, Paul offered his assemblies a reformatory ethics—that is, an ethics of moral instruction. Paul notes the distinctiveness of his reformatory ethics, however, by repeatedly indicating the sphere in which he offers his moral instruction: "in the Lord Jesus" (v. 1) and "through the Lord Jesus" (v. 2). Thus, even if, as we shall see, Paul will draw on other traditions to shape and nurture the church, he will do so with the intention of building up a community whose origins and destiny lie in the relationship they have with the Lord Jesus. Indeed, throughout 4:1–5:22, Paul seeks to define the boundaries of his church apart from the larger culture.

4:3-8. The theme of "sanctification" (ἁγιασμός *hagiasmos*, v. 3) or "holiness" (*hagiasmos* vv. 4, 7) is the common thread that Paul weaves throughout these verses. Accordingly, Paul begins with a general maxim on sanctification (v. 3) before offering three specific injunctions about the holy life (vv. 4-6a) and three motivations for living the holy life as enjoined (vv. 6b-8).

Before clarifying the meaning of the three injunctions, it is important to note that they pertain to activity that stands in contrast to "the will of God," an expression that Paul (and other Jews) often used to speak about proper conduct (Rom 2:18; 12:2; 1 Esdr 9:9; 4 Macc 18:16). In general, Paul often noted certain improprieties as a way of defining the boundary lines of his communities.[92] Some actions were simply not permissible because they reflected the former practices of Gentile converts (1 Cor 5:1) or because they indicated the desires of the flesh—that is, selfishness (Gal 5:19)—as opposed to the fruit of the Spirit (5:22). Paul even argues that certain actions—immorality usually leading the list—are the behaviors of persons who will not inherit God's kingdom (Gal 5:19-21; cf. 1 Cor 5:11).

Only the first of the three injunctions is readily clear: that the church abstain from "fornication" or immorality (v. 3b). The meaning of the other two, however, is mired in debate because some of Paul's expressions are ambiguous.

In the second injunction, the NRSV translates "body" (v. 4) for the Greek noun σκεῦος (*skeuos*), but the textual note suggests that the word can also mean "a wife" (the translation favored by the RSV). This noun literally means a vessel like an earthen jar or pot (cf. Luke 8:16). Yet, it could also have metaphorical meanings. A clear illustration of its metaphorical potential is seen elsewhere in Paul when he describes the physical life on earth as "treasure in clay jars" (2 Cor 4:7). Some scholars think that in 1 Thessalonians the noun is a metaphorical euphemism for genitalia, hence the term "body." Others, however, prefer the term "wife" because 1 Pet 3:7, in the patriarchal spirit of the times, uses the noun *skeuos* to refer to the wife as the "weaker vessel" or "weaker sex" (NRSV).

How one translates the noun is also related to the verb that accompanies it. Some scholars render "to control" for the Greek infinitive κτᾶσθαι (*ktasthai*), while others favor "to take" or "to acquire" (the verb itself being capable of both translations). So is Paul referring to the control of the body (genitalia) or to the acquisition or possession of a wife? On the one hand, those who support the former may be influenced by political correctness—not wanting Paul to speak exclusively here to men who could take a wife or for Paul to speak of a wife as a possession. On the other hand, those who favor "to take a wife" actually weaken their translation by resorting to 1 Peter because that text implies that both the husband and the wife are vessels.

Despite these competing positions on the ambiguous terms, Paul's challenge for his church is clear: that the church operate in

---

92. Sampley, *Walking Between the Times*, 57.

holiness (v. 4). Paul qualifies his directive by resorting to two well-known Jewish polemics against Gentiles: that they are sexually promiscuous (Wis 14:12-31; Philo *Allegorical Laws* 3:8) and that they are ignorant of God (Ps 79:6; Jer 10:25; Gal 4:8; Rom 1:28). Thus, both the first and the second injunctions are intended to accentuate the boundary lines of distinction between Paul and his church, on the one hand, and the larger society, on the other hand.

The ambiguity of the third injunction (v. 5) lies in the expression "matter" (πρᾶγμα *pragma*). Some scholars hold that all three injunctions speak about sexual behavior: against fornication (v. 3*b*); against sexual activity outside an act of marriage, as if *skeuos* refers to a wife (vv. 4-5); and against any kind of sexual activity that would wrong the husband or father of the woman involved, as if *pragma* refers to one of the two previous injunctions (v. 6*a*).[93] Still others read *pragma* as a command about proper business practices.[94]

Whatever the meanings of the enigmatic expressions, the motivations are clear: (1) a previous warning about God's vengeance (v. 6*b*); (2) God's call to holiness, not impurity (v. 7); and (3) God's gift of the Holy Spirit (v. 8). The first motivation is one Paul must have mentioned before with some insistency. The word he uses to describe his previous challenge (διεμαρτυράμεθα *diemartyrametha*, "solemnly warned," v. 6) echoes what he says earlier in his reflections on foundational efforts to shape the church, for "pleading" (μαρτυρόμενοι *martyromenoi*, 2:12) was a critical part of the foundational leaders' tutelage of the church to lead (or to walk) the life worthy of God.

Obviously, to speak of the Lord as an avenger (v. 6) removes any notion of self-vindication among those wronged—a point well worth saying in a context in which Paul wanted his church to display comportment that could influence outsiders (v. 12). Paul here also likely has all three injunctions in mind, for he claims that the Lord is an avenger in "all these things" (v. 6). Furthermore, Paul here likely refers to "Lord" as "God," not Jesus, because the subsequent motivations refer to God. The idea of the Lord as an avenger, moreover, also indicates the possibility for believers to come under judgment despite their status as being saved.

The second motivation, God's call to holiness, not to impurity (v. 7), resounds the theme of holiness but likewise echoes the former talk of a God who "calls" persons into the church (2:12). Paul's observation about God's calling the church actually suggests an ongoing call for the sake of sanctification. Earlier, at the foundational moments and even now, Paul's goal was consistent. In fact, just as the foundational team did not operate from "impure motives" (2:3) as it sought to declare the gospel to this church, so also the church cannot operate in "impurity" (4:7), for the life of holiness is one in which the chief aim is to "please" (2:4; 4:1) the God who entrusts special assignments (2:4) and calls believers (2:12).

The third motivation, God's gift of the Holy Spirit (v. 8), also focuses on God. God (as Lord) not only is responsible for judgment at the end of time (a time in which Paul thinks even believers will be assessed) but for the original call of believers into God's kingdom. God's continuous calling of the believers also equips them with what they need for the sanctified life, for growth and maturity—namely, the Holy Spirit. Rejection of the life of holiness, then, is not a rejection of human authority but of the very God who could help believers in the course of life, from their beginnings in the Lord until the moment of their full transformation at the parousia.

Altogether, then, vv. 3-8 are not a new commendation for this church. Paul had spoken earlier about the implication of God's call upon the believers' lives, and he continues to do so. The commendation, moreover, challenges the church to maintain a distinctive pattern of living—not as they once lived, but a life of holiness. As God's holy people and people whom God elected (1:4), the church has the responsibility of reflecting God's holiness as well.

4:9-12. These verses suggest the same emphasis on distinctive living—that is, on living a life distinct from that before conversion.

---

93. Jeffrey Weima, "How You Must Walk to Please God," in Collins, *The Thessalonian Correspondence*, 109.
94. Walter Bauer, William F. Arndt, F. Wilbur Gingrich, and Frederick W. Danker, *A Greek-English Lexicon of the New Testament and Other Early Christian Literature*, 2nd ed. (Chicago: University of Chicago Press, 1979) 203-4.

The section begins with a *paralipsis* (a feigned statement) as Paul avers that he will not mention anything about the church's love for one another when, in fact, he does just that (v. 9a). Next, Paul indicates both the source (v. 9b) and the extent (v. 10a) of the church's love for the brothers and sisters. Then, Paul exhorts the church "to do so more and more" (i.e., to love) and to strive to perform three concrete practices (v. 11) with the goals of modeling and achieving self-sufficiency (v. 12).

Paul's remarks about "the love of brothers and sisters" use a term (φιλαδελφία *philadelphia*, v. 9) that initially focused on the love among siblings but that by Paul's day had widened in Christian assemblies to indicate the love among believers. When Paul turns to the source of this expanded form of love, his coinage "taught by God" (θεοδίδακτοί *theodidaktoi*, v. 9) is distinctive, for it is not found in Greek literature before it appears in his letters. In the estimation of some scholars, Paul's "taught by God" is also intended as a contrast to the Epicureans, who considered themselves "self-taught"; but there is no evidence that Paul had a reason (given what we know about the Thessalonian Christians) to distinguish his church specifically from the Epicureans. What does seem clear is that Paul is continuing to place the life of this church in the hands of God—noting God's vengeance, calling, giving of the Holy Spirit, and now God's teaching.

The source of the love clearly depicted, Paul then highlights the extent of the church's love and "urges" them to do so "more and more" (v. 10). It is little wonder that their love is extended to believers throughout Macedonia, for, given Paul's earlier hyperbole, their faith has gone out everywhere (1:8) and Paul hears about them from others (1:9). Elsewhere, Paul speaks of one thing counting: faith working through love (Gal 5:6). Timothy's report seems to support the young church's ability to work forth its faith in concrete practices of love, for he notes both their "faith and love" (3:6).

Yet, Paul challenges his young church to love even more (v. 10). He shows himself to be the consummate pastor here because he sees the good and praises it but recognizes room for improvement as well. It should be noted that the improvement he seeks is something the foundational team models (given the constancy of their care for the church) and the very thing for which they have prayed (3:11).

The usual recourse of interpretation for assessing the three concrete practices to which Paul next turns (vv. 11-12) is to appeal (explicitly or implicitly) to 2 Thess 3:6-12 as a framework for interpreting 1 Thess 4:11-12, as if the practices were commended to calm "apocalyptic fervor."[95] As long as the authorship of 2 Thessalonians remains a matter of debate, however, a more convincing argument that arises from 1 Thessalonians is that the practices resound to Paul's theme about the church's distinctive love or care for others.

Two pieces of evidence support this claim. First, if ancient auditors followed the progression of the love theme in vv. 9-12, from love for the members of the church (v. 9) to love for the believers throughout Macedonia (v. 10), it is not difficult to suppose that they would then expect a further extension of the love theme directed to others—that is, to unbelievers in vv. 11-12. Second, if 3:9-13 is a prefiguring of the rest of the letter, one could expect Paul, at some point in 4:1–5:28, to treat his desired wish that the community's love "increase" (περισσεύω *perisseuō*) "for one another and for all" (εἰς ἀλλήλους καὶ εἰς πάντας *eis allēlous kai eis pantas*, 3:12). With the reference to the "outsiders" (πρὸς τοὺς ἔξω *pros tous exō*) in 4:12, it appears that Paul has, in fact, specified in concrete ways how the church's love could "increase" (*perisseuō*, v. 10) to others beyond the believers.

With the guiding context of the love theme, then, the concrete practices are all ways of solidifying the church into an ideal community with the purpose of providing a model or good form for the outsiders.[96] Readers familiar with the imperatival infinitive "to aspire" (φιλοτιμεῖσθαι *philotimeisthai*, v. 11a) as a term to "describe a person ambitious for [political] fame through the offer of beneficence to a community" would recognize an ironic twist in Paul's logic because

---

95. For a sterling critique of this position, see Richard, *First and Second Thessalonians*, 219ff.
96. Richard, *First and Second Thessalonians*, 220.

he actually recommends for the first concrete practice "a quiet life."[97] How is one to be ambitious but at the same time to seek a quiet life? Fame itself is not to be sought, but the community all together should seek to be distinctive—strikingly enough—by not aspiring to conventional forms of prestige.

Regarding Paul's admonition to "mind your own affairs," on the one hand, auditors familiar with the Platonic tradition could read the second (and related) concrete practice as a call away from public life to a smaller community or as a call to individuate one's contributions to the community to one's "own" natural gifts. On the other hand, this concrete practice could be more directly tied to the circumstances of the church. If the church faced local hostilities and alienation, the last thing they needed was to meddle in the affairs of the larger society. Indeed, given the imminence of the new age, such concerns would not be regarded as significant at all.

Given a context of local hostilities and alienation, moreover, auditors likely heard the expression "work with your hands" (v. 12) as a reference to the church's need to be self-sufficient. The pastoral team itself modeled self-sufficiency (2:9) in its foundational visit. Paul, in fact, notes that he is not saying anything new (4:11). Here, then, as elsewhere, Paul has already provided a model for the church in the concrete practices noted in the initial visit.

The aim of self-sufficiency, of course, is to "behave properly toward outsiders" (v. 12) or to provide a "good form" (εὐσχημόνως *euschēmonōs*). The early Christians, even if they drew boundaries around themselves, did not advocate "a need to go [completely] out of the world" before the parousia's consummation of the new age (cf. 1 Cor 5:10). Rather, they hoped to persuade outsiders to join them or to appreciate their conviction or to glorify the deity they represented through the model lives they lived before others. In 1 Peter, for example, believers are enjoined to allow their exemplary lives to influence others who may presently be the very cause of their suffering. In doing so, the believers both "silence the ignorance of the foolish" (1 Pet 2:15) and cause others eventually to "glorify God" (2:12). Perhaps, something similar lies behind Paul's reasoning in 1 Thessalonians as well (cf. 1 Cor 10:31-33).

Thus, in both 4:3-8 and 4:9-12, the theme is a distinctive walk, whether as a walk of holiness or as one of love for believers and outsiders. The distinctive life, moreover, is a life of consistency. The foundational leaders lived consistently before the Thessalonian church, and now Paul charges that church to continue the practices of their founding leaders with a similar consistency. If the church remained committed to its practices, perhaps the outsiders would be persuaded by their consistent quality of moral excellence and join them as believers in Paul's deity.

---

97. Abraham Smith, *Comfort One Another: Reconstructing the Rhetoric and Audience of 1 Thessalonians* (Louisville: Westminster, 1995) 40.

REFLECTIONS

1. We must be careful not to misunderstand Paul's emphasis on boundaries. If Christians are to be different from the larger society—and we are called to be different—our quest must not emanate from a will to retreat to remote corners of life. Our calling is not to isolate ourselves but to conduct ourselves as children of God. To be sure, there are those who become different—even unconventional—to make a personal statement. This may be symptomatic of something else, perhaps of poor self-esteem or of undue fear of losing one's individuality. In contrast, God's call to a life of holiness marks believers as different in healthy, unselfish, and strategic ways—and always for redemptive purposes.

Certainly, Paul does not define boundaries in 1 Thess 4:1-12 to commend parochialism of any sort. Rather, he challenges the Thessalonians to extend the limits of their love to all (1 Thess 4:9-12). We, too, are challenged to extend love to all, to transcend selfishness and short-sightedness. Insularity cripples spiritual growth and church outreach, and it may even give the impression that what we have is either too good for others or not worthy of their consideration.

2. A careful reading of 1 Thess 4:1-12 helps us to understand the comprehensive nature of Christian morality: its consideration for the individual, for others, and for God. Whatever the exact meaning of the passage, it is clear that Paul is addressing individuals, or "each of you" (4:4). At the same time, Paul goes further, addressing individuals in relation to others. The Christian life is not lived in personal isolation; unfortunately, too much Christian preaching has focused on individuals as if Christianity's goal was psychological fitness. Even the early Christian desert hermits withdrew to pray for the world. Yet, in the words of David Buttrick, "Most of our pulpits, Protestant and Catholic alike, have read scripture but then preached a psychological personalism for . . . decades, with sin as psychological dysfunction and salvation as inward good feeling. No wonder that American religion can be described as both 'gnosticism' and 'habits of the heart.'"[98]

Paul's consideration for the individual and for others is ultimately connected to consideration for God, the one who gives the Holy Spirit and the one who will issue vengeance upon those who exploit or violate others. Morality devoid of a consideration for God often leads to a static form of social relations, one that is ultimately not concerned with the wholeness of the entire universe. No wonder C. S. Lewis wrote, "Morality . . . seems to be concerned with three things. Firstly, with fair play and harmony between individuals. Secondly, with what might be called tidying up or harmonising the things inside each individual. Thirdly, with the general purpose of human life as a whole . . . what tune the conductor of the band [God] wants it to play."[99] If we miss the importance of these three elements, our lives will never rise above the din of society.

98. David Buttrick, *A Captive Voice: The Liberation of Preaching* (Louisville: Westminster/John Knox, 1994) 13-14.
99. C. S. Lewis, *Mere Christianity* (New York: Macmillan, 1943) 71.

1 Thessalonians 4:13–5:11, Maintaining the Apocalyptic Hope

COMMENTARY

The second subunit (4:13–5:11) of the last large unit (4:1–5:22) has two discrete parts: an explicit consolatory section about the hope of believers in Jesus' parousia (4:13-18), and a section on the requisite vigilance of the believers as they await the day of the Lord (5:1-11). Both of these sections depict end-time events. Both also conclude with a call for mutual consolation within the church (4:18; 5:11). The letter's recurring theme of persistence in the apocalyptic hope and the ethical life that flows from it, moreover, seems to guide the interpretation of both sets of verses even in those places where Paul's descriptive diction is hard to decipher.

4:13-18. A careful reading of these verses would include the following division: (1) an opening statement on the distinction between the believers and others who have no hope (v. 13); (2) descriptions of the basis for the believers' hope (vv. 14-17a); (3) an acknowledgment of the permanent union of the believers with the Lord (v. 17b); and (4) a commendation toward mutual consolation (v. 18).[100]

Though some scholars think the expression "we do not want you to be uninformed" (v. 13) indicates that Paul here introduces new information (a supposition based on other examples of the expression in Rom 1:13; 11:25; 1 Cor 10:1; 12:1; 2 Cor 1:8), the general exhortative character of 1 Thessalonians

100. Other issues not demanding our full attention are as follows: (1) The word διά (*dia*, "through") in 4:14 likely goes with Jesus and not with the dead ones, and (2) modern interpreters—not Paul—seem to have generated interest on the place where the dead will be brought in 4:14.

suggests that one need not infer the introduction of entirely new material,[101] as if the audience were totally unfamiliar with the subject of the resurrection itself.[102] Indeed, it is hard to imagine that Paul had talked about the resurrection of Jesus without talking about the resurrection of believers because Christ's resurrection, for Paul, was the very basis for his belief that the new age had dawned. And in Jewish thinking of the time, the new age was associated with the resurrection of believers.[103]

Instead, the expression could simply be a response to a grave need for consolation. Paul likely spoke to the church about the possibility of death even as he shared other afflictions that were manifestations of the old age (3:4). Death, albeit a traumatic manifestation, was still another instance of the old age's work. Yet, it is likely that the Thessalonians, despite hearing about the resurrection of the dead, honestly thought the parousia would come before any of their fellow believers died. Death having now visited them, Paul writes to console them about those who "sleep" (κοιμάομαι *koimaomai*, v. 13), Paul's euphemism for believers "who have died" (NRSV; cf. John 11:11-13; 1 Cor 7:39; 11:30).

As he consoles them, however, he also notes how different they are from those without the believers' hope. It is not accurate to say that others in Paul's world did not believe in the afterlife.[104] The hope that Paul has lies in the extraordinary power of the parousia as the consummation of the new age and the climactic conclusion to the old. That is, it has the power to raise the believers from the dead and to transform both the living and the risen into a lasting union with Christ (v. 17).

Paul's consolation includes two bases for the believers' hope, and both are related to Paul's apocalyptic understanding of the old and new ages. The first basis is expressed in a belief statement ("we believe that Jesus died and rose again," v. 14a) that is deemed to be a creedal formula. The belief statement is so considered because of its brevity and its description of the event as "Jesus rising" rather than Paul's customary language of "God raising Jesus" from the dead (Rom 4:24; 1 Cor 15:15; 2 Cor 4:14; Gal 1:1; 1 Thess 1:10).[105] From the creedal statement, Paul argues that God will secure the lives of believers who have died (v. 14b; cf. Rom 8:11). For Paul, as we have seen, Jesus' death and resurrection inaugurate the new age and sound a death knell to the old age.

A second basis for the believer's hope is the parousia, to which Paul turns after noting the death and resurrection of Jesus. Paul's description of the parousia here is introduced by the expression "by the word of the Lord" (v. 15). This expression need not indicate an actual word from Jesus (such as one would find in the later Synoptic and Johannine documents, which themselves depend on earlier traditions of Jesus' sayings).[106] Indeed, "Paul rarely explicitly identifies a saying as one of Jesus' (1 Cor 7:10)."[107] Relatedly, there is no way to know the origin of this "word of the Lord"—that is, to know whether Paul received it from an unknown medium (whether a post-Easter prophet or the church) or if "the word" is in fact an *agraphon*, an unwritten and thus unknown saying of Jesus—in the light of the fact that we may not have written testimony to all of Jesus' sayings. While scholars are able to see links between some of the written testimonies to the teachings of Jesus and Paul's own letters (cf. Matt 24:43; Luke 12:39-40; 1 Thess 5:2), Sampley has noted that "Paul's moral reflection did not follow a regular pattern of applying some teaching of Jesus to a problem at hand."[108] Gaventa has noted, moreover, that in the instance of 1 Thess 4:15, "nothing in the Gospels closely parallels the statements that follow [the expression "word of the Lord"] (although frequently Matt. 24:29-44 is invoked)."[109]

It seems more convincing, then, to suggest that Paul simply uses the expression "the word of the Lord" to give prophetic authority to words that he has already spoken in 4:14.[110] It is likely the case that Paul,

---

101. See Wanamaker, *The Epistles to the Thessalonians*, 165.
102. So Richard, *First and Second Thessalonians*, 232-33.
103. Bart D. Ehrman, *The New Testament: An Historical Introduction to the Early Christian Writings*, 2nd ed. (New York; Oxford, 2000) 270.
104. See Plato *Gorgias* 52D.
105. Gaventa, *First and Second Thessalonians*, 64; F. F. Bruce, *1 & 2 Thessalonians*, WBC (Waco, Tex.: Word, 1982) 97.
106. For a critique of this position, see J. Delobel, "The Fate of the Dead According to 1 Thess 4:1 and 1 Cor 15:1," in Collins, *The Thessalonian Correspondence*, 341.
107. Sampley, *Walking Between the Times*, 98.
108. Sampley, *Walking Between the Times*, 98.
109. Gaventa, *First and Second Thessalonians*, 65.
110. Richard, *First and Second Thessalonians*, 240.

like other hortatory guides in his age, gave his words authority by pointing to a higher authority deemed trustworthy by the readers.

Paul's description of the parousia (vv. 16-18), more richly symbolic than in the two previous allusions (2:19; 3:13), is a vivid yet terse apocalyptic drama that amplifies the value of Jesus' parousia. Against the backdrop of apocalyptic images like that of an "angel" (2 Esdr 4:36-37), the "trumpet of God" (*Pss Sol* 11:1; 2 Esdr 6:17-24), "[those] who are left" (Syriac Baruch 13:3; 76:2), and "clouds" (Dan 7:13), Paul portrays a group of brothers and sisters who will be united with each other and with the Lord imminently, powerfully, gloriously, and permanently.

The union will be imminent because Paul holds out the possibility that he will be one of those "who are left" (v. 17; but cf. 2 Cor 4:14). The union will be powerful because it will begin with "a cry of command" (v. 16), an image associated with a call to arms in a military battle. It will also be powerful because the dead believers (about whom the church now grieves) will live again (thus no longer subject to the powers of the old age). And it will likewise be powerful because those left "will be caught up" (lit., "will be snatched up," ἁρπαγησόμεθα *arpagēsometha*, v. 17), ironically a term often used to describe the action of death itself.[111] The union will be glorious not only because Paul uses the expression *parousia* (v. 15), which connoted (as previously shown) a grand affair, but it will be glorious as well because Paul uses the expression "meeting" (ἀπάντησις *apantēsis*), which at least connoted an entourage of citizens going out to meet a dignitary.[112]

The union, moreover, will be permanent as attested by the repetition of the preposition "with" (σύν *syn*, v. 17) and the result clause of v. 17b: "and so shall we be with the Lord forever." Paul envisions a reunion that can no longer be affected by the old age because, in fact, the parousia brings to an end all of the manifestations of the old age.

Paul closes his description of the parousia with a commendation to mutual consolation (v. 18). Thus here he speaks directly about some of the resources his church has for nurturing their lives together. Whether or not he can get to them, they have the power to console one another with the apocalyptic truths he has shared with them.

Before concluding this section, it is important to note that 1 Thess 4:13-18 should not be read in the light of 1 Corinthians 15. In part, given the audience-oriented perspective of this commentary, we should not read the Thessalonians passage in the light of the Corinthian passage because the church at Thessalonica would not have had 1 Corinthians 15 as a part of its repertoire for processing 1 Thess 4:13-18. In part, as well, 1 Corinthians 15 seems to have a different rhetorical interest from the one described for 1 Thess 4:13-18. While both texts note the death and resurrection of Jesus and appear to do so using pre-Pauline formulaic expressions, at least one of the rhetorical goals of 1 Corinthians 15 appears to be to challenge Corinthian enthusiasm or the overrealized eschatology within the Corinthian church through an insistence on the *future* resurrection of believers. Enthusiasm is not a problem in 1 Thessalonians. Furthermore, while the word "then" (ἔπειτα *epeita*) in 1 Cor 15:23 indicates the sequence of resurrection from "Christ the first fruits" to "those who belong to Christ," or all believers, the same word in 1 Thess 4:17 suggests a sequence from the dead in Christ to the living faithful.[113]

Altogether then, 1 Thess 4:13-18 encourages the church in the midst of its grief to recognize the hope they have and how that hope distinguishes them from others. Their hope lies in an apocalyptic drama that speaks of the great power both of the death and resurrection of Jesus and of his parousia with respect to one of the fiercest manifestations of the old age: death. Whether the audience had the apocalyptic background to understand all of the particulars Paul mentioned about the parousia is uncertain.[114] What they did know, however, was that Jesus' death and resurrection and his parousia were instruments of God's power. With hope in these instruments, not only could they expect to see their loved ones again but also they could expect a grand and permanent reunion for all the believers. This hope—this distinctive hope—is a

---

111. Plutarch uses the term "snatched up" several times in *Letter to Apollonius* 111C-D, 117B. See Abraham J. Malherbe, "Exhortation in First Thessalonians," *NovT* 25 (1983) 255-56.

112. Wanamaker, *The Epistles to the Thessalonians*, 175.

113. Bruce, *1 & 2 Thessalonians*, 101-2.

114. Gaventa, *First and Second Thessalonians*, 66.

resource they can use even now to console each other.

5:1-11. Some interpreters see tensions between 5:1-11 and 4:13-18. That is, they presuppose that Paul's "Now concerning" (Περὶ δέ *Peri de*, 5:1; lit., "and/but concerning") transition implies a strong adversative contrast between the ideas of 4:13-18 and 5:1-11. Some think, therefore, that there is a contrast between a presumed timetable in 5:1-11 and a presumed timetable in 4:13-18, as if the day of the Lord occurs at a different time from the parousia. Yet, 1 Thess 5:1-11 does not support the contention that the day of the Lord follows *after* living believers are "caught up" at the Lord's coming, as noted in 4:13-18.[115] As Tracy Howard has argued, neither section gives a systematic chronological timetable, and both sections are exhortative in purpose and parallel in content.[116] Both commend a certain type of behavior in the light of eschatological matters. Both discuss the same event, the parousia (or the day of the Lord), and draw on various apocalyptic images to clarify the importance of that day for believers in the present.

Alternatively, again implying a strong contrast, some read 5:1-11 as if the church failed to understand Paul or as if the passage—though Pauline—postdates the other parts of the letter and reflects Paul's effort to quiet gnostic agitation.[117] To the contrary, the repetition of the expression "with" (*syn*) the Lord (4:17; 5:10) in both passages and the similar endings of both sections (4:18; 5:11) argue that the two are not radically distinct. Rather, they differ only in perspective. Each section uses a distinctive diction to characterize the consummation of the new age (either the parousia or the day of the Lord). The distinctive perspective of 1 Thess 5:1-11, however, is that here Paul reveals more of his thought about the *present* impact of vindication or judgment in the new age on believers. Paul's reference to the parousia now as the Day of the Lord simply highlights his shift to a focus on judgment. That is, the Day of the Lord (understood as YHWH's day) originally was the day of YHWH's vindication of the righteous and judgment of the unrighteous (cf. Joel 2:31; Amos 5:18; Mal 4:5). Thus, in this subunit, Paul will distinguish the believers from the unbelievers with respect to how believers can already celebrate their vindication.

In 5:1-11, Paul extends his previous discussion of the parousia and its distinguishing effects. Transitional markers divide the subunit into six small subsections: (1) vv. 1-2, the auditors' knowledge of the coming of the day of the Lord; (2) v. 3, the unbelievers' ignorance about the day of the Lord; (3) vv. 4-5, eschatological contrasts between believers and unbelievers; (4) vv. 6-8, requisite sobriety of believers; (5) vv. 9-10, justification for sobriety; and (6) v. 11, commendation toward mutual consolation and edification.

Paul's first move in this subunit is to use a well-known hendiadys, or a set of synonymous expressions ("times and seasons," 5:1; cf. Dan 2:21; 7:12; Wis 8:8) that by the first century CE (cf. Acts 1:7; 3:20-21) simply meant "a time of judgment" (not two separate kinds of times) in a *paralipsis* (a feigned statement).[118] That is, feigning not to write about the time of judgment, he does just that. And while doing so, he notes the motivation for his reticence: The church already "know[s] very well" (5:2) the manner in which that time of judgment will come. The time of judgment will come in the surprising manner of a "thief at night," a well-known motif in apocalyptic traditions (5:2; cf. Luke 12:38-39; Rev 3:3).

Then, with a shift to a third-person style of writing and the use of the familiar apocalyptic diction of "labor pains" (5:3; cf. Ps 48:6; *1 Enoch* 62:4; Mark 13:8), Paul declares the destruction the day of the Lord will bring to the unbelievers whose lives were tethered exclusively to the present life. Given the auditors' familiarity with "peace and security" (5:3) as a propaganda slogan of the Roman imperial government (see the Introduction) moreover, the auditors likely recognized a pointed attack directed at the Roman Empire with which the Thessalonian outsiders had cast their lot of allegiance.

---

115. On this view, see John F. Walvoord, *The Blessed Hope and the Tribulation: A Biblical and Historical Study of Posttribulation* (Grand Rapids: Zondervan, 1976) 115.
116. Howard, "The Literary Unity of 1 Thessalonians 4:13–5:11," 163-90.
117. Walter Schmithals, *The Apocalyptic Movement*, trans. John E. Steely (Nashville: Abingdon, 1975) 16-167.

118. See Wanamaker, *The Epistles to the Thessalonians*, 178.

Shifting now again to the auditors (5:4), Paul next contrasts believers with unbelievers (5:4-5). Having already described unbelievers as persons capable of being surprised as if by a thief at night, Paul now presupposes that the "night" really represents a condition of unawareness or insensitivity. Thus he contrasts darkness and light imagery (or night and day imagery) as contrasting "spheres of existence."[119] Believers are not in a state of darkness (5:4) and do not have darkness as the source of their existence (5:5). Thus believers will not be surprised because they are "children of the day" (5:5), a Semitic expression that means that they belong to the realm of the day. By contrast, unbelievers are in darkness and have darkness as the source of their existence.

The imagery Paul uses here is that of eschatological battle, a familiar one in Jewish thought in Paul's time. Indeed, it is the imagery that the Qumran covenanters seized to portray the final eschatological battle.[120] With this imagery, Paul places the foundational team, along with the church, in an eschatological conflict, for he shifts from a second-person plural description of the church (all of you) to a first-person plural description ("we are not of the night or of darkness," 5:5).

With another transitional marker, "so then" (ἄρα οὖν *ara oun*, 5:6), Paul's declaration of the distinction between believers and unbelievers now shifts to the behavior required of believers, who are children of the light and children of the day (5:6-8). Paul's distinction between children of the day and those of the night is not just about contrasting spheres of awareness or existence but also of contrasting spheres of action. The requisite behavior for believers, who are in a battle, is one of vigilance, an idea Paul conveys through a call for the foundational team and the church to be "awake" and "sober" (5:6). Both terms figure in eschatological thought as examples of vigilance (cf. Rom 13:11-13; 1 Cor 16:13), but Paul strengthens his request for requisite behavior with allusions to the direct opposites of "awake" and "sober," respectively, "asleep" and "drunk" (5:7). To do so, moreover, he returns to the imagery of the night but now cast as the time in which the inappropriate behaviors take place.

Seizing more battle imagery (5:8), Paul continues his call for sober behavior commensurate with those who belong to the day. In this case he reconfigures the earlier triad of faith, love, and hope (cf. 1:3) as the church's "weaponry for the eschatological battle."[121] It is important to realize, however, that the aorist, or past tense participle, translated in the NRSV as "[let us] put on" (ἐνδυσάμενοι *endysamenoi*, 5:8), as if it were present, should actually be translated as "already having put on." Thus the action of sobriety is an action that flows out of the fact that the believers are already clothed in battle gear.

Paul's shift to a justification for sobriety (5:9-10), then, is really an ultimate explanation for why the foundational leaders and the church are already garbed and thus should act in a manner befitting who they are in the eschatological battle. The ultimate explanation, of course, is based on God's initiative or election (5:9). Paul's discussion of the consequences of God's initiative rhetorically signals connections between 5:1-11 and 4:13-18. That is, although Paul initially used the word "sleep" (καθεύδω *katheudō*) to connote insensibility ("let us not fall asleep," 5:6), he now uses it to imply death (5:10), perhaps alluding to Dan 12:2 LXX and the subject of death in 1 Thess 4:13-18. As well, 5:10*b* (attached as it is to what some scholars call a pre-Pauline formula: "who died for us," 5:10*a*; cf. 4:14; Gal 1:4) seems to hark back to 1 Thess 4:17 because both speak of believers being "with the Lord."[122]

If that is the case, Paul's expression "whether we are awake or asleep" shifts now from the concern with vigilance and the contrast between being awake and being asleep to the contrast between being alive and being dead. For Paul, because of God's initiative and Jesus' death, a reunion with the Lord is possible for all believers, whether they are awake (alive) or asleep (dead).

Finally, as 5:1-11 draws to a close, Paul connects 4:13–5:11 to 5:12-22. On the one hand, he repeats 4:18 with its emphasis on mutual consolation. On the other hand, he

---

119. Howard, "The Literary Unity of 1 Thessalonians 4:13–5:11," 172.
120. Helmut Koester, "From Paul's Eschatology to the Apocalyptic Schemata of 2 Thessalonians," 451. See also 1QS 3:13–4:26; 1 QM 1:1, 3.
121. Koester, "From Paul's Eschatology to the Apocalyptic Schemata of 2 Thessalonians," 451.
122. Bruce, *1 & 2 Thessalonians*, 113.

anticipates the edification section of 5:12-22 with the expression "build up each other."[123]

Thus 5:1-11 seeks to continue the theme of the parousia with judgment as the perspective from which Paul now distinguishes the believers from the unbelievers.[124] The believers, moreover, are already "children of the day" because of the death of their Lord Jesus Christ on their behalf. Still, the full consummation of the new age has not yet occurred. So the church must be vigilant in its vision of a life influsenced by that consummation and it must seek to offer consolation and individuated help to build one another up.

Throughout both sections (4:11-18; 5:1-11), Paul evinces the distinctiveness of the church—the distinctiveness of its hope or of its ethical life in the present as regulated by the events of the past (Jesus' death and resurrection) and the future (the parousia or day of the Lord). Like 4:1-12, then, the second subunit (4:13–5:11) of the last large unit (4:1–5:22) reinforces the idea of the church's distinctive apocalyptic life. For a church facing the painful ordeals of alienation, these words about a distinctive life likely provided a source of comfort. With little wonder it is, then, that Paul gives direct attention to his words at the closing of one of the sections: "Comfort one another with these words" (4:18).

---

123. On the relationship between 5:11 and 5:12-22, see Abraham J. Malherbe, "'Pastoral Care' in the Thessalonian Church," *NTS* 36 (1990) 388-89. Cf. Wanamaker, *The Epistles to the Thessalonians*, 191.
124. See Wanamaker, *The Epistles to the Thessalonians*, 177.

REFLECTIONS

When we read 1 Thess 4:13–5:11, we are prompted to think about end times, last things, and the ultimate destruction of the world as we know it. The proverbial "thief in the night" description of the day of the Lord of 1 Thessalonians (which is also mentioned in the Synoptics) appeared in medieval literature and continues to work its way in the thought of great texts today.[125] Julia Ward Howe's "Battle Hymn of the Republic" (1862) lyrically captures the 1 Thessalonians' end-time rhetoric about the Lord's coming with trumpets sounding forth (1 Thess 4:15-16). Paul's brief comments about believers being "caught up in the clouds" has become the basis for many books and for a degree of anxiety about a "rapture" of believers.

To be sure, these verses are saturated with apocalyptic imagery, that suggests an imminent end and final days. Yet Paul's apocalypticism inspired hope, gave comfort, and provided challenge to the socially alienated persons of his day. Reminders of God's provision for the absent (deceased) brothers and sisters in the future are powerful testaments to God's care for all believers in the present. Notices of permanent union with the Lord in the future are challenging statements about God's desire for believers to come together on earth right now, even though Martin Luther King, Jr.'s words are as true today as they were years ago: "At eleven o'clock on Sunday morning when we stand to sing 'In Christ there is no East or West,'" we stand in the most segregated hour of America."[126] Talk of eschatological battle is a serious invitation for us not to settle for easy "peace and security slogans" or other superficial changes that leave many people still confined to the margins of existence.

Thus, Paul's apocalyptic diction is not innocuous. It is radical and impinges on the quality of life lived in the present. In many ways, it is reminiscent of the apocalyptic spirit found in the Negro spirituals. Although the spirituals were noted for their otherworldly orientation, they also had this-worldly functions.[127]

---

125. Dwight H. Purdy, "Thief in the Night," in *A Dictionary of Biblical Tradition in English Literature,* ed. David Lyle Jeffrey (Grand Rapids: Eerdmans, 1992) 763.
126. Martin Luther King, Jr., "Remaining Awake Through a Great Revolution," in *A Knock at Midnight: Inspiration from the Great Sermons of Reverend Martin Luther King, Jr,* ed. Clayborne Carson and Peter Holloran (New York: Warner, 2000) 209.
127. Frazier regards them as "essentially religious in sentiment and . . . otherworldly in outlook." See E. Franklin Frazier, *The Negro Church in America* (New York: Schocken, 1974) 19. On the spirituals as aids in transcending circumstances, see Lawrence Levine, *Black Culture and Black Consciousness: Afro-American Folk Thought from Slavery to Freedom* (Oxford: Oxford University Press, 1977) 19, 23.

The slave's world was full of trouble, storms, and hard times, as the songs "Soon I Will Be Done," "Been in the Storm So Long," and "I Been Rebuked and I Been Scorned" attest. These songs expressed longing and hope for another world. Among the this-worldly functions, however, were the building up of community solidarity and the practice of a veiled form of critique and communication.[128] With an eye toward the future and yet with a challenge for community solidarity in the present circumstances, the slaves sang "Walk Together Children." In "Swing Low, Sweet Chariot" and "Steal Away to Jesus," the slave likely engaged in covert communication, cryptically requesting or signaling the help of the "underground railroad" (sweet chariot) to get "home" (the northern states or Canada).

Thus, the spirituals included both "apocalyptic visions and heroic exploits of the Scripture," despite the tensions between the two.[129] On the one hand, the slaves spoke of a future day of judgment, as in "That Great Gittin' Up Morning," "Roll, Jordan, Roll," and "My Lord, What a Morning." On the other hand, they spoke of biblical heroes (e.g., David, Joshua, Moses, and Noah) whom God had delivered in this world.[130]

Both the future and the present were important for them. In sum, the spirituals confronted the slaves' sordid experiences, remythologized the biblical concepts to speak cryptically but encouragingly, and provided a source of comfort and challenge. Their apocalyptic strain, like Paul's apocalyptic vision, read the present reality in the light of the future expectation.

---

128. On the spirituals as sources of communal bonding, especially through their antiphonal structure, see Levine, *Black Culture and Black Consciousnes*, 33. On the spirituals as veiled communication, see Levine, *Black Culture and Black Consciousness*, 51.
129. Levine, *Black Culture and Black Consciousnes*, 41.
130. Levine, *Black Culture and Black Consciousnes*, 50.

1 Thessalonians 5:12-22, Nurturing Resources for the Distinctive Life

COMMENTARY

The first (4:1-12) and second (4:13–5:11) subunits given, Paul now concludes his last large section with 5:12-22. A variety of markers aid the division of this material into three sections. First, the repetition of first-person plural verbs of exhortation, "we appeal" (ἐρωτῶμεν *erōtōmen*, v. 12) and "we urge" (παρακαλοῦμεν *parakaloumen*, v. 14), easily link the material in vv. 12 and 14 together. Likewise both vv. 12 and 14 include an address to the church ("Brothers and sisters"). Second, vv. 16-22 read like a series of terse imperatives all constructed with final verb formulations and interrupted in form only by the declarative sentence, "for this is the will of God in Christ Jesus for you" (v. 18a), as Fig. 1 suggests. Third, v. 15 seems to stand apart both from vv. 12-14 and vv. 16-22 because it is the only part of the section that uses the strong adversative transitional conjunction "but" (ἀλλά *alla*) and the only part imploring the church to direct its attention *inwardly* and *outwardly*. Fourth, if v. 15 constitutes a separate discrete part between vv. 12-14 and vv. 16-22, each of the three discrete parts now formed would virtually end with an emphasis on "all" (or with a cognate form of the word πᾶς *pas*). That is, each discrete part would stress "all" persons in a particular group (vv. 12-14) or "all" outsiders (v. 15) or "all" or "every" form of evil (v. 22).

The markers shown, readers should be able to divide 5:12-22 into three discrete sections: (1) exhortations on the recognition of ongoing models of moral training within the church and on the practices of moral training within the church (vv. 12-14); (2) a caveat against seeking retribution with an admonition consistently to seek the good toward all believers and toward outsiders (v. 15); and (3) a series of terse imperatives on the proper dispositions toward circumstances or the

> Figure 1: A Diagram of 1 Thess 5:16-22
>
> Always rejoice
> Constantly pray
> In all circumstances give thanks
>
> For this is the will of God in Christ Jesus for you
> The Spirit, do not quench.
> Prophecy (or words of prophets), do not despise
> Everything, test.
> The good, hold fast
> From every form of evil, abstain

nurturing resources accruing to the new age (vv. 16-22).

5:12-14. The first section describes moral training in the church from two perspectives. First, Paul addresses the church ("Brothers and sisters") on that which could build up the church (cf. 5:11). Using three participial expressions ("those who labor," "[those who] have charge," and "[those who] admonish"), Paul describes the ideal activities for aiding the community. Furthermore, the participle forms occur in the plural, as if Paul here speaks not about a single individual responsible for the activities or about single offices (which came later in the history of early Christianity) but about activities potentially practiced by several persons.[131] In addition, his final exhortation in vv. 12-14 commends the believers to have peace with one another.

Paul's injunction "to recognize" (εἰδέναι *eidenai*, v. 12a; the infinitive εἰδέναι [*eidenai*] should not be translated as "to respect") and "to esteem" (ἡγεῖσθαι *hēgeisthai*, v. 13) persons enaged in these edifying practices for their "work" (ἔργον *ergon*, v. 13) suggests that he favors those activities that are similar to the moral training practices mentioned earlier in the letter. Thus Paul's reference to "those who labor" (v. 12) recalls his use of "labor" (κόπος *kopos*) to describe the "labor" of the entire community (1:3), the "efforts" (or labor) of his foundational team (2:9),

and his foundational "labor" as it was under attack by the tempter (3:5). Relatedly, Paul also used cognate forms of "work" (*ergon*) to describe the "work" of the entire community (1:3, 4:11), the "efforts" (ἐργαζόμενοι *ergazomenoi*) of the foundational team (2:9), the "working" (ἐνεργεῖται *energeitai*) of God's word in the community (2:13), and the role of Timothy, God's "co-worker" (συνεργός *synergos*, 3:2; cf. 2 Cor 5:15–6:2).

Whatever the precise meanings of the words "labor" and "work," Paul's emphasis is on aid for the church—whether that aid comes from God, from the foundational leaders, or from the church itself. Thus "labor/work" is any form of aid that helps to make the church productive in its distinctive life. Because "work" and "labor" connote self-sufficiency in 2:9-12 and 4:11, moreover, it is possible that in 1 Thessalonians these expressions connote any efforts that could help the church maintain its self-sufficiency so as not to retreat to its former networks of support.

Second, Paul exhorts all of the church ("brothers and sisters") on the kinds of special needs that have to be addressed to build up one another in the church (cf. 5:11). As with the specific activities, the specific needs are relevant to the church's audience situation, especially as exposed by 2:1-12. Whatever the meaning of the terms ἀτάκτους (*ataktous*; NRSV, "idlers"), ὀλιγοψύχους (*oligopsychous*, "fainthearted"), and ἀσθενῶν (*asthenōn*, "weak"), the two commands to "admonish" (νουθετεῖτε *noutheteite*) and to "encourage" (παραμυθεῖσθε *paramytheisthe*), directed to the whole church, are used elsewhere in the letter. A cognate form of "admonish" is

---

[131]. While many interpreters quickly turn to Paul's list of exhortations in Romans 12 as a context for analyzing the exhortations in 1 Thess 5:12-22, a key difference needs to be noted. When Paul uses προϊστάμενος (*proistamenos*, "the leader") in Rom 12:8, the participle appears in a singular form, not the plural form as in 1 Thess 5:12. Following Malherbe, this commentary maintains that Paul refers not to a specific group of people in 5:12 as much as he refers to a specific group of activities that most of the church potentially could perform. See Malherbe, *Paul and the Thessalonians*, 88.

used in v. 12 to indicate the kind of activity the church should recognize and esteem. It can be inferred, then, that Paul continues to discuss moral training of some sort in v. 14 with a focus on how the church should look out for certain traits in the community. A cognate form of "encourage" was used earlier in 2:12 to indicate how the foundational leaders aided the church in its worthy walk. Both terms, then, are a part of Paul's moral training diction—that is, his language for efforts to make the church live out the new life to which God continuously calls them in the face of ongoing, difficult experiences.

We do not have any precise information about the specific needs of the church. Scholarly insistence that "idlers" is an appropriate translation of ἄτακτοι (*ataktoi*, v. 14) is misleading and likely based on construals of the audience situation in 2 Thessalonians (see the Introduction and the Commentary on 2 Thessalonians) where forms of the word appear again (3:6-7, 11). The term usually refers to those who "engage in anti-social conduct."[132] In the light of Paul's concern for the persistent worthy walk in the church, the expression *ataktoi* could simply refer to any type of person (of which there may be several) not in harmony with the mutual nurturing of the worthy walk.

Since "fainthearted" (ὀλιγοψύχους *oligopsychous*, v. 14; lit., "little-soul persons") never occurs again in Paul or elsewhere in the New Testament, it is difficult to know much about such people. The specific type of exhortation Paul recommends for them, however, is one of encouraging (or consoling), a type of exhortation that he has recommended for the entire congregation to offer each other (4:18; 5:11).

The identity of the "weak" (ἀσθενῶν *asthenōn*, v. 14) is also unclear though Paul elsewhere uses this word to describe persons with a deficiency of knowledge that renders them a limited measure of faith when compared to others (cf. 1 Cor 8:7-14). Whether this deficiency of knowledge is the issue for the "weak" in 1 Thessalonians is unclear, but Paul's term for the assistance they require ("help" or "support") is a need that anyone in the church could have had at one time or another.

Perhaps, then, all of these types—the "antisocial," the "fainthearted," and the "weak"— are persons who have to be exhorted by the church because they find it difficult at times either to engage in self-scrutiny or to take on the otherwise communal role of nurturing.[133] It must be noted, however, that the three traits are not the same. In fact, Paul likely mentions all three to show the church how its nurturing must be individuated to the differing needs that may arise in the church.[134] Regardless of the differences, Paul commends patience toward all of them (v. 14).

In focus here in 5:12-14, then, is a comprehensive form of mutual nurturing, a form of edification in which the church looks to itself both for expressions of nurture and for the recognition of the needs that require nurture. That kind of mutual nurturing—itself a part of other alternative communities (like the Epicureans)—was vitally necessary if the church was to maintain its distinctive holy life with a strong commitment to its apocalyptic hope in the face of local hostilities.

5:15. The second section warns the church against retribution (cf. Prov 20:22; Matt 5:38-39, 43; Rom 12:17) but enjoins the persistent seeking of the good. Lest the previous exhortations appear simply as directions to an introverted group, Paul uses the exhortation in this verse to cover both inner and outer relations. Auditors here would likely remember 4:9-12, which also included a shift from the church to others, including outsiders. Furthermore, Paul exploits here the same expression ("to one another and to all" [εἰς ἀλλήλους καὶ εἰς πάντας [*eis allēlous kai eis pantas*]) used earlier (3:12) to describe the church's need to extend its love or care outward. The edification process, then, is not one of distinctiveness for its own sake. Rather, Paul is ever the mission-directed pastor, even in his comments to a beleaguered church (cf. 4:12). He not only seeks edification within them, but also seeks to model appropriate behavior before outsiders who, in turn, will be influenced by the church's distinctive holy life.

5:16-22. The final section is sometimes labeled "Paul's shotgun paraenesis" because

---

132. Collins, *The Birth of the New Testament*, 94.

133. On the unreadiness of some novices for self-scrutiny, see Seneca *Letters to Lucilius* 2.1.
134. Cf. Seneca *On Tranquility of Mind* 6.1-2.

Paul quickly fires off one round of imperatives after another.[135] Scholars have noticed, moreover, that the first three imperatives (vv. 16-18) seem separated stylistically from the others because of constructions with initial adverbial expressions and because the adverbs are virtually synonymous (see Fig. 1).[136] In addition, the first three imperatives would likely remind the auditors of other instances in which Paul modeled the very commands he now advances.

Earlier Paul spoke of the church's reception of the word with joy (1:6) in affliction as an imitation of the foundational team and of the Lord. Joy in the midst of affliction, then, is something Paul's team has modeled. A clearer example of this kind of joy emerges in the two parallel subunits of the second large unit, 2:17-20 and 3:9-13. In those instances, Paul's joy is based not on his present circumstance—separation from the church—but on present or future manifestations of the new age (cf. Phil 4:4-5). To tell the church to "rejoice always" (5:16) is to tell the church to exult in the new age's manifestations, whether the manifestations are already apparent or can be expected at the glorious parousia.

Similarly, Paul's command "to pray without ceasing" (v. 17) is modeled earlier in the letter. Paul speaks of "making prayers" constantly" (1:2), and his thanksgiving reports and wish-prayers are abundant. Paul has also used the expression "always" (ἀδιαλείπτως *adialeiptōs*) twice (1:2; 2:13) before 5:17. As with "joy," Paul's prayers or thanks for the church's success are gratitude to God for manifestations of the new age—either its effectiveness in the present because of the death of Jesus or its manifestations in the future consummation (e.g., in the community's blamelessness at the parousia, 3:13). What Paul commends in both instances in vv. 16-17, then, is a disposition of constant joy or prayer because of the present and imminent manifestations of the new age. Yet, because the consummation of the new age is not yet in effect, the church has to face local hostilities. But it does not have to face them without some resources—that is, without joy and prayer.

Obviously, the same is true for the third imperative of this set (v. 18a). To "give thanks in all circumstances" is both modeled by Paul (see the repeated thanksgiving notices) and a response to what God has done in Paul's apocalyptic schema. What Paul has already modeled, then, becomes a command for the church as well.

It is little wonder that these three imperatives, all of which make an appeal for constancy, are followed by the declarative phrase "for this is the will of God in Christ Jesus for you" (v. 18b). Paul used the expression "will of God" earlier when he spoke about the sanctified life or the life of growing maturity (4:3). Furthermore, as noted before, "will of God" was often used in Jewish contexts as a descriptive term for proper activities.

In Greek, the last set of imperatives (vv. 19-22) all have a final verbal construction, as with the imperatives in vv. 16-18a (see Fig. 1). The last ones, however, do not begin with adverbial constructions. According to several scholars, what holds the last set together is an emphasis on the Spirit. Perhaps! Another interpretation is to see the last set as more resources accruing to those who are a part of the new age, as the following paragraphs suggest.

Certainly the Holy Spirit functions as evidence of the new age. Earlier, when Paul shared with the community evidence of the new age in their lives (1:1-5), he spoke of the Holy Spirit, which elsewhere he designates as a pledge (or a first installment, 2 Cor 1:22). Whether one can prove that the church already knew about the Spirit's role as a pledge is not important for this argument. What is critical is that the Holy Spirit is mentioned early in the letter as evidence of the new age's presence in the church. Later, Paul speaks about the Holy Spirit as an agent of inspiration (1:6) and of the Holy Spirit as God's gift to the believers, who have been called not to live as they once lived but in the distinctive life of holiness (4:7-8). The exhortation "not to quench the Spirit" (v. 19), then, makes absolute sense for this audience's situation. In order to face the local hostilities and gain inspiration and guidance, the church needs to avail itself of the resource of the Holy Spirit.

---

135. Calvin Roetzel, "1 Thess 5:12-28: A Case Study," in *Society of Biblical Literature Annual Papers*, ed. Lane McGaughy (Chico, Calif.: Scholars Press, 1972), 375.

136. Wanamaker, *The Epistles to the Thessalonians*, 199-200.

Whether the next resource should be translated as "words of prophets" (as in NRSV, v. 20) or as the "gift of prophecy" is uncertain. For a church subject to local hostilities, however, what seems incontrovertible is the need for this resource (in either form) for the survival of the church. Likewise, the last resource, testing or discernment (v. 2; cf. 1 Cor 14:29), is also crucial. The church is exhorted to test everything and to seize (that which is determined by the church to be) the good. Should the test apply to the prophetic utterances? Many scholars think so. The range of the tests, however, is comprehensive. They are to test "everything." Furthermore, just as they seek the good, they are to avoid "every" form of evil. The import of this exhortation and the others, then, is to show the church that they have what they need for every decision and every deliberation. They need not go beyond their alternative community for the resources they need to survive. Indeed, with the forces of moral training, the appropriate dispositions and the basic resources, the church has a sufficient base for its survival even if Paul, Silvanus, and Timothy can never return.

Before moving on to the last unit of the letter (5:23-28), a few words are in order about all of the subunits of the last large unit. First, all of the subunits reinforce the distinctiveness of the church—in its life of holiness and love, in its hope and ethical behavior because of that hope, and in the nurturing force of its resources for moral training. Second, the emphasis of these subunits on the church's distinctiveness does not distract from Paul's abiding concern for outsiders who could be influenced by the distinctiveness of the church. Third, the subunits reiterate the value of the resources for persistence noted in the two previous large units—namely, the words and practices of leaders who inculcate moral training. The words of these leaders—whether in past teachings (4:1, 9; 5:1-2), in authorized words of comfort (cf. 4:13-18, esp. 4:14), or in maxims (5:16-22)—are available to help the church through its present crisis of alienation. In addition, the practices of the foundational leaders are held up as a model already at work in the church (5:12-15), whether in the form of admonition, encouragement, patience, or doing and seeking good rather than retribution. For a church facing local hostilities, these resources could help them continue in their new apocalyptic life, even if the foundational team could never get back to them again. Thus these resources are given to strengthen a church against the possibility of returning to their former way or walk of living.

REFLECTIONS

"Give thanks in all circumstances" (5:16 NRSV). In *every* circumstance? In *all* things? Most of us would want to adjust Paul's words, to qualify his exhortation. Perhaps we wish Paul to say "in *some* circumstances" or "in *some* things." That would be more acceptable for our own practical tastes, more suitable for our own set of realities. But in *every* circumstance? That has to be one of the most adventurous voyages of thought ever embarked on the rough waters of reason. And logically, it seems destined for shipwreck.

Paul certainly does not qualify the circumstances. He means "all." The two previous imperatives also have a comprehensive, unqualified character: "Rejoice always, praying without ceasing" (5:16-17 NRSV). Has Paul asked his church to do the impossible? Can a person face a fresh set of abuses every day and give thanks? Can a person rise above the psychic doubts left by years of abuse at the hands of a parent and give thanks? "Give thanks in everything"!?

Paul's words may lack qualification, but they do presuppose at least two basic truths. Because of these two truths, it is possible and necessary to give thanks in everything. The first truth is that worship of God is the context for *all* of life, not just the part we devote to God during our time in a sanctuary. In Karl Rahner's words, "Everyday life must become itself our prayer."[137] If all of life is worship for those who seek to do God's will, then thanks is a necessary and inevitable product. But we should note that Paul does not say thanks should be governed by circumstances. The thanks is governed by the life of worship. Whether good or bad be the lot, a life of worship (of seeking to please and honor God and of doing God's will) means perpetual thanksgiving.

The second truth Paul presupposes is that life's depths, not solely its surfaces, must arrest our attention. Paul Tillich speaks of the "depth of existence" as the "ground of our historical life . . . the ultimate depth of history."[138] Tillich's words are not a call for residency near shallow waters, where thoughts are restricted to appearances near the shore. Yet, most of us live near such shallow waters. And we judge our lives by visible, surface, and indeed superficial determinants—that is, the occasional good things or bad things that happen to us.

Paul's (and Tillich's) challenge for us, however, is to move to a depth in which there are weightier truths that make it possible for us to give perpetual thanks. Paul's weightier truths are a part of his apocalyptic view of existence—his view of two ages (a new age and an old one), with Christ's death and resurrection securing us for salvation. From the depths of history, from which we get a comprehensive frame for life, we can defy circumstances (without ever glibly dismissing them). From the depths of life we can take the onetime cross of shame and declare it to be God's choice over that which conventionally accrues honor (cf. 1 Cor 26-31). From the depths of life, one can join the poet James Russell Lowell and say:

Truth forever on the scaffold
Wrong forever on the throne
But that scaffold sways the future
and beyond the dim unknown
Standeth God within the shadows
Keeping watch above God's own.

---

137. Karl Rahner, *The Content of Faith: The Best of Karl Rahner's Theological Writings,* ed. Karl Lehmann and Albert Raffelt, trans. Harvey D. Egan, S.J. (New York: Crossroad, 1992) 511.
138. Paul Tillich, *The Shaking of the Foundations* (New York: Scribner's, 1948) 58-59.

1 THESSALONIANS 5:23-28

THE PERORATION

COMMENTARY

Given the letter's goal of encouraging a beleaguered community, Paul writes the final lines (5:23-28) of his document. In epistolary analysis terms, all of these verses constitute the letter's closing. They include a peace benediction (v. 23), a concluding notice of encouragement, a brief series of exhortations (to pray a prayer of intercession, to greet one another with a kiss, and to read the letter to everyone), and a benediction.[139]

In terms of rhetorical analysis, the final section of a document is its peroration. Because the last large unit (4:1–5:22) ends at v. 22, v. 23 marks the beginning of 1 Thessalonians' peroration. Furthermore, with v. 23 as the beginning of the peroration, the entire letter is bound by a grace, peace (1:1), peace (v. 23), grace (v. 28) inclusio. The two intercessory prayers in 5:23 and 5:28 provide a nice final inclusio with both a notice of encouragement (v. 24) and exhortative material (vv. 25-27) occupying a central section. Assuming that the peroration includes all of 5:23-28, these final verses function in two ways. On the one hand, they stir the emotions; on the other hand, they summarize the contents of the letter.

Paul's use of an invocation at the beginning of the peroration gives his letter a closing emotional charge.[140] In addition, friendly terms and phrases in vv. 25-28 (e.g., "brothers and sisters," "greet with a holy kiss") bespeak an affectionate—even if exhortative—tone. The term "brothers" connotes the fictive kinship that Paul's team shared with the church of the Thessalonians and others as well. Furthermore, the "kiss" (cf. Rom 16:16; 1 Cor 16:20; 2 Cor 13:12), a symbol of "social union," also expressed the idea of a family.[141]

Just as the exordium (1:1-5) announced the letter's themes, so also the final verses (5:23-28) summarize some of those same themes. With final allusions to God's continuous calling (v. 24; cf. 1:4; 2:12; 4:7) and the parousia (v. 23; 2:19; 3:13; 4:15), Paul highlights the apocalyptic hope in which the church is exhorted to persist.[142] As well, Paul's wish-prayer (v. 23) signals that the church must persevere not only in its hope but in the requisite actions of that hope as well. Indeed, Paul intimates one of those requisite actions: continuous prayer, with the inclusion of prayer forms (vv. 23, 28) and the request for prayer (v. 25; Rom 15:30; Phlm 22).

Because Paul spells out some of those requisite actions, the church hears a final time about the distinctive life to which it has been charged. Repetitive diction about sanctification or holiness in the wish-prayer and in one of the exhortations describes the distinctive life (vv. 23, 26). That diction and the hope for the church's blamelessness vividly remind the church of its distinctiveness as signaled earlier in 3:9-13. Moreover, with the repeated emphasis on concern for "all," Paul reminds the church that the distinctive life must be the goal of "all" of its members (v. 26). Thus, even if some are not present for the reading of the letter, the letter must be read to them as well.

Even the earlier emphasis on the effectiveness (or importance) of the writer's word or presence receives its due in the peroration. Given the role of Hellenistic letters as substitutes for a writer's presence, Paul's command

---

139. Cf. Jeffrey Weima, *Neglected Endings: The Significance of the Pauline Letter Closing* (Sheffield: JSOT, 1994) 176.

140. It is to be noted that Quintilian, a 1st century CE rhetor, regarded invocations as appropriate for the peroration of a speech. He asserts that the "invocation of the gods usually gives the impression that our speaker is conscious of the justice of his cause." Quintilian, *Institutio Oratoria*, trans. H. E. Butler and N. Heinemann, LCL (New York: Putnam, 1920–22).

141. Collins, *The Birth of the New Testament*, 87.

142. It must be noted, however, that Paul's trichotomous anthropology ("spirit and soul and body," 5:23) indicates not Paul's personal acceptance of the anthropology but the recognition (from the church's perspective) that "it is the whole human being who is to be found blameless at the parousia." See Collins, *The Birth of the New Testament*, 158.

that the letter be read aloud evokes his presence as often as the letter must be so read to reach all of the members of the church.[143]

It should be stated finally that the peroration reminds the church again of its resources for persistence—the words and moral training practices of its foundational leaders. Given its terse, striking character, 1 Thess 5:24 ("The one who calls you is faithful, and he will do this"; cf. 1 Cor 1:8-9) assumes the force of a maxim, as if to provide a basic truth through which the church can maintain its apocalyptic hopes. Also, the injunction to have the letter read conveys the authority of the words of the foundational leaders for all the members of the church. Paul's wish-prayer, moreover, exemplifies his persistence in prayer and reminds the church of the constant concern he has exhibited for them. If the church continues to emulate this concern for its members, they will continue to embody one of Paul's key moral training practices.

143. f. Seneca *Letters to Lucilius* 40.1.

REFLECTIONS

One of the recurring images of 1 Thessalonians, that of brothers and sisters, finds its way into the letter's peroration as well. As noted earlier, the term "brothers" occurs in Jewish literature (Deut 15:3).[144] In 1 Thessalonians, Paul uses the term repeatedly with a compensatory function. Given the local hostilities faced by the church, language of brotherhood compensates for the loss of former family networks. In addition, the term is one of solidarity, gathering together all believers who could claim Paul's God as their father (cf. 1:1). In Paul's final words, he writes to ensure that the believers embrace the solidarity they share. No one is to be left out: *All* the brothers and sisters are to be greeted with a holy kiss, and the letter is to be read to *all* the brothers and sisters.

Some aspects of ancient family life could prove beneficial for the church today if we better understood and appreciated the solidarity expressed in such families. All collateral relations in ancient families were important for the family's stability, but the most important was that between brothers. Brothers were considered to be "the main supports of the house and . . . the family's continuity and solidarity."[145] For the sake of the family's public image and as an indication of family solidarity, brothers were expected to exhibit mutual trust, "emotional identification," self-sacrifice in the pursuit of common interests, and cooperation in the management and continuity of the family's property.[146] In addition, the ideal relations between brothers became the model for many of the relations that developed among the fictive kin of ancient clubs and associations. Thus, the ideal relations of blood brothers took on a metaphorical casting for the fictive kin, whether male or female, and whether near (in a particular city) or far (in another town).

Thinking of the church as a family with vital collateral relations of solidarity on the order of the ancient clubs and associations could prove helpful for the church today in several ways. First, the openness of the family is a breath of fresh air for our churches. The idea of family here, of course, is not that of a nuclear group with its issues of privacy and separation. Rather, the idea is more similar to the Latin American experience of the extended family that, according to Justo González, is "a much wider group of people, of uncertain and ever-expandable limits."[147] Second, in a world of wariness and suspicion, the practice of mutual trust is a lost art that needs to be found again. Third, the demonstration of solidarity through emotional identification is a welcomed ideal that should replace mere toleration. Fourth, the ability to measure one's life by pursuits shared by a larger group is a wholesome counterforce to the pervasive dominance of rank individualism.

144. See Philo *On the Special Laws* 2.79-80; Josephus *Antiquities of the Jews* 10.20. See also Wanamaker, *The Epistles to the Thessalonians*, 77.
145. Cynthia Jordan Bannon, "Consors Mecum Temporum Illorum: Brothers in Republican Rome" (Ph.D. diss., University of Michigan, 1991) 75.
146. See Bannon, "Consors Mecum Temporum Illorum: Brothers in Republican Rome," 37, 52-53, 86, 98, 101.
147. Justo L. González, "In Quest of a Protestant Hispanic Ecclesiology," in *Teología en Conjunto: A Collaborative Hispanic Protestant Theology,* ed. Jose David Rodriguez and Loida I. Martell-Otero (Louisville: Westminster John Knox, 1997) 92.

THE SECOND LETTER TO THE THESSALONIANS

INTRODUCTION, COMMENTARY, AND REFLECTIONS
BY
ABRAHAM SMITH

THE SECOND LETTER TO THE
THESSALONIANS

INTRODUCTION

Reflecting Paul's general concern for the church's stability in the face of mounting hostility from its neighbors and a more specific concern about an enthusiastic brand of apocalypticism, the writer of 2 Thessalonians crafts a letter to encourage the believers not to veer from his truth or traditions (2:15). That truth focuses on both the present and the future. Indeed, the present experiences of opposition are read in the light of traditions about the future, including the coming judgment at the parousia (1:5-10) and the apocalyptic events preceding the day of the Lord (2:1-12). Furthermore, the present works of the church are authorized when they stand in accordance with traditions that demand support for the image, care, and continuity of the whole church while it awaits its Lord's future revelation.

Like 1 Thessalonians, the letter falls within the hortatory tradition. It is a letter of exhortation not simply because it uses explicit hortatory appeals through imperatives, as in its requests for stability (2:15), prayer (3:1-2), and correct discipline (3:6-15). Like 1 Thessalonians and other letters of exhortation from the period, 2 Thessalonians uses other forms of exhortation: calls for imitation (3:7a, 9; cf. 1 Thess 1:6), reminders of a teacher's previous instruction (2:5, 15; 3:7b-10), and reminders of what recipients already know (2:6; 3:7; cf. 1 Thess 4:2; 5:2). Like 1 Thessalonians and unlike other letters of exhortation, however, 2 Thessalonians uses prayer forms with a hortatory intent as well (1:3-4; 2:13-14, 16-17; 3:5, 16; 1 Thess 1:2-5; 2:13; 3:9-13; 5:23).[1]

---

1. On the hortatory function of prayer forms, see Abraham J. Malherbe, *Paul and the Thessalonians* (Philadelphia: Fortress, 1987) 77.

For more discussion of the historical, theological, and literary background of 2 Thessalonians, see the Introduction to 1 Thessalonians. See also the annotated bibliography located there.

OUTLINE OF 2 THESSALONIANS

I. 2 Thessalonians 1:1-12, The Exordium

II. 2 Thessalonians 2:1–3:15, Maintaining the Traditions

    A. 2:1-17, Hortatory Appeals Against Apocalyptic Enthusiasm
        2:1-2, Do Not Be Shaken Up
        2:3-12, Do Not Be Deceived
        2:13-17, Reasons to Stand Firm and Hold On
    B. 3:1-15, Hortatory Appeals Against Irresponsible Behavior
        3:1-5, Doing What Is Commanded
        3:6-15, Doing What Is Responsible

III. 2 Thessalonians 3:16-18, The Peroration

2 THESSALONIANS 1:1-12

THE EXORDIUM

COMMENTARY

In epistolary terms, 2 Thessalonians 1:1-12 includes both a prescript (vv. 1-2) and a prayer formula (vv. 3-12) of two parts—namely, a thanksgiving notice (vv. 3-10) and an intercessory prayer report (vv. 11-12). With its tripartite structure (sender, recipient, and superscription formulae), the prescript (vv. 1-2) is similar to the prescripts of the undisputed Pauline letters, although both 1 and 2 Thessalonians lack an elaborate superscription.[2] Even with respect to 1 Thessalonians, however, 2 Thessalonians' prescript has two noticeable additions: (1) the inclusion of the pronoun "our" to describe the Father and (2) the addition of the longer greetings ("from God our Father and the Lord Jesus Christ," v. 2). Indeed, the greeting's repetition of "God our Father and Lord Jesus Christ," already given in the writer's description of the recipients (v. 1b), appears awkward—except for the fact that this kind of greeting elaboration can be found in all of the undisputed Pauline letters aside from 1 Thessalonians (cf. Rom 1:7b; 1 Cor 1:3; 2 Cor 1:2; Gal 1:3; Phil 1:2; Phlm 3).[3]

Typical of other thanksgiving notices, the initial one in 2 Thessalonians renders an assessment of the church's progress (vv. 3-4). In addition, the thanksgiving notice presents a commentary on God's justice (vv. 5-10) to contextualize the church's suffering. A closing intercessory prayer report (vv. 11-12) follows to commend appropriate thinking and acting throughout the church's life, from inception to glorification.

In rhetorical terms, the audience could have actualized the first twelve verses in at least two ways. On the one hand, perhaps the auditors could hear the two sentences that immediately follow the prescript. One sentence is long and loose (vv. 3-10), reporting the writer's thanks to God for both the church's success despite suffering and for the justice of God that will bring relief to the persecuted on the day of their Lord's revelation and glorification. The other sentence is short (vv. 11-12), reporting the content (v. 11) and purpose (v. 12) of Paul's intercessory prayer report. On the other hand, perhaps the auditors detected a framing pattern in the thanksgiving notice. That is, the explicit thanks in vv. 3-4 and the explicit intercessory prayer report in vv. 11-12 framed for the hearers a central section (vv. 5-10) on "apocalyptic retribution."[4]

In either case, the sonorous character of the intercessory prayer report (vv. 11-12), the use of the transitional expression "to this end" (v. 11), and the result clause with which the intercessory prayer report ends ("so that the name . . . ," v. 12) clearly mark v. 12 as the end of a unit of material. Furthermore, the repetition of the alliterative phrase "always . . . for you" (πάντοτε περὶ ὑμῶν *pantote peri hymōn*, vv. 3, 11) suggests that vv. 11-12 continue a unit that began at least with the thanksgiving notice of v. 3. Finally, the similar endings of v. 2 and v. 12 suggest that *all* of vv. 1-12 should be held together, not simply vv. 3-12. For our purposes, then, all of vv. 1-12 constitute a single unit with discrete sections: a prescript (vv. 1-2); a thanksgiving notice with its commentary (vv. 3-10), and an intercessory prayer report (vv. 11-12).

Many in the audience possibly heard all of the first twelve verses as an exordium. That is certainly the judgment of a number of scholars influenced by rhetorical criticism. Indeed, the prescript and the two sentences of vv. 1-12 together execute the twin goals of

---

2. On "grace and peace" as a variation of a Jewish formula, see the commentary on 1 Thessalonians.
3. As the textual note for this verse attests, another manuscript tradition omits the pronoun "our."

4. Gerhard Krodel, *The Deutero-Pauline Letters: Ephesians, Colossians, 2 Thessalonians, 1–2 Timothy, Titus*, Proclamation Commentaries (Minneapolis: Fortress, 1993) 43.

an exordium—namely, gaining goodwill and announcing the key issues of the document.⁵

However, some interpreters find it difficult to say that the initial thanksgiving of 2 Thessalonians was written to gain the audience's goodwill. For example, they point to the more effusive tone of friendship found in 1 Thessalonians or to the so-called obligatory thanks ("we must always give thanks") of the thanksgivings in vv. 3 and 13 as indications of the letter's coolness. Some interpreters even suspect that the obligatory thanks was a response to protests from a church that deemed itself far too unworthy to fit the claims of success intimated in the thanksgiving in 1 Thess 1:2-5. It seems more convincing, however, to state that the writer uses the language of obligatory thanks—a vernacular that was not unusual for his day—to express truthfully his thanks to God because of the abundance and constancy of successes in the church.⁶

The writer speaks of the church's faith not simply as "growing," for which he could have simply used the Greek word αὐξάνω (*auxanō*), but as "growing abundantly" (ὑπεραυξάνω *hyperauxanō*) to indicate an intensified type of growth (v. 3). Because the writer uses a present tense verbal form both to describe the growth of the church's faith and to indicate how the believers' love is "increasing" (πλεονάζει *pleonazei*, v. 3), he also indicates the endurance of the church's success: It is constant or ongoing. It should be noted as well that the writer qualifies the believers' love as the "love of everyone of you for one another." To note mutual love in the church, he could simply have written "love for one another" (as Paul did in 1 Thess 3:12; cf. 1 Thess 4:9). The expression here, one not found anywhere else in the NT, however, is emphatic. Thus the writer "must always give thanks" because he sees so many signs of success and at such a comprehensive level, all of which evoke feelings of thanks to God.

The argument about the writer's "coolness" set aside, the first twelve verses of the letter gain the goodwill of the audience in three salient ways: (1) by noting shared struggles and shared benefits, (2) by praising the church's model character, and (3) by expressing a passionate concern for the audience's suffering.⁷

As for the notices of shared struggles and shared benefits, the prescript, thanksgiving notice, and its attached commentary all accentuate important links between the Thessalonian church and the wider group of believers. In the epistolary prescript (vv. 1-2), the unifying pronoun "our" (ἡμῶν *hēmōn*) suggests that the writers and the letter's recipients share God as "our" Father.⁸ It is a small step to move from the claim of God as "our" Father to the related one of the believers as fictive "brothers" (and sisters), as expressed in the thanksgiving (v. 3). This section also implies shared bonds through the writer's assertion of boasting about the church to other churches of God (although they are not identified). The attached commentary (vv. 5-10) implies these bonds as well through the writer's insistence that the afflicted and the (implied) writer(s) ("us") will receive "relief" (or a cessation from suffering, v. 7). Likewise, the commentary section both places the church and the writer within the company of "all who have believed" (v. 10) and links them to all the believers who will marvel at the coming of the Lord. All of these connections would have had an endearing effect because ancient audiences were favorably disposed whenever they heard similarities shared between them and a speaker or writer.⁹

In remarking on the church's model character, the writer praises the believers for their progress in faith and steadfastness. Members of the audience would likely recognize this praise as the typical gesture of a teacher displaying deep concern for his students. Members of the audience who were familiar with 1 Thessalonians would likely discern as well the similar and yet nuanced laudatory remarks given in the initial thanksgiving of that letter. For example, the recipients of 1 Thessalonians received the word in spite of "persecution" (θλῖψις *thlipsis*, 1 Thess 1:6). Here, in 2 Thessalonians, the church is praised for its endurance of both "persecution" (διωγμός

---

5. Again, the exordium is the beginning part of a speech or argument. See Quintilian 3.8.59. Cf. Aristotle *Rhetoric* 3.13.12.
6. See Philo *On Special Laws* 1.224.
7. On the *captatio benevolentiae* (captivation of goodwill) in an exordium, see Quintilian 3.8.6; Cicero *De Inventione* 1.15. 20; and Aristotle *Rhetoric* 3.14.7.
8. On Silvanus and Timothy, see 1 Thess 1:1.
9. Aristotle *Rhetoric* 2.13.16.

diōgmos, v. 4) and "affliction" (*thlipsis*, v. 4), with the latter word for "suffering" being the more general of the two.[10] Also, a trace of the triad of graces—faith, love, and hope—of 1 Thessalonians lingers in 2 Thessalonians (cf. 1 Thess 1:3), for the writer commends the continuing increase of the church's faith and love. Although hope is not directly mentioned in the thanksgiving of 2 Thessalonians, in contrast to the earlier letter, the writer still praises the steadfastness of the church despite the quantity and constancy of its suffering. The recognition of the believers' endurance and faith is enhanced by the writer's insistence that he boasts about them to the churches of God (v. 4; cf. 1 Cor 11:16). Some in the audience would likely remember Paul's similar praise of the Thessalonian church as a model for "all the believers in Macedonia and in Achaia" in 1 Thess 1:7. Obviously, the church—in the estimation of the writer—has continued as a model.

Expressing passionate concern for the church's suffering, the writer presents not (in his estimation) an inaccurate timetable (cf. 2:3-12), but an explicit apocalyptic schema that insists on retribution for the afflicters (1:6), "relief" for the church (1:7), and a dazzling display of power that will cause the church and other believers to marvel (1:10). This concern is also displayed in the intercessory prayer report (1:11-12) when the writer restates his constancy in praying for the Thessalonian believers (1:11) and clarifies the past and the present that guarantee the future relief from suffering that they can expect. The church's past lies in the "call" of God (1:11), a call that indicates God's election of the church even as it is connected to the glory of the Lord Jesus (1:12; 2:14). The writer's prayer for God to make the church worthy of God's call defines the earlier expression "make you worthy of the kingdom of God" (1:5). Both expressions are likely drawn from 1 Thess 2:12 ("that you lead a life worthy of God, who calls you into his own kingdom and glory"); and both, like 1 Thess 2:12, focus on the ongoing commitment that believers must have because of God's initiative. In the case of 2 Thess 1:11, however, the writer clarifies "worthy" by adding "fulfill by his power every good resolve and work of faith, so that the name of the Lord may be glorified in you, and you in him, according to the grace of our God and the Lord Jesus" (1:11*b*-12).

The first expression (v. 11*b*) indicates the role God will continue to play in the church members' lives as they await the future relief. Whether "every good resolve" is God's resolve or (as is more likely in the light of Rom 15:14; Gal 5:22) the church's resolve or desire or pleasure (εὐδοκία *eudokia;* cf. 2:12), the concern is for the completion of that resolve and of the "work of faith" (or the work that comes out of faith; cf. 1 Thess 1:3) that God will bring about. And whether "by his power" is an indication of the Holy Spirit, which for Paul brings about the products of transformation (see the Introduction to 1 Thessalonians; cf. 2 Thess 2:13), or simply an indication of the manner in which the completion will be accomplished (i.e., "powerfully"), the accomplishment is the same: The called of God are sustained in their commitment to God in every respect because of God.

The second expression (v. 12), cast as a result clause, indicates why the God who called this church will sustain its commitment: It is for a mutual glorification process that is also made possible by the grace of God. On the one hand, because of God's grace the name (or authority) of Jesus is glorified on the order of the glorification of the name of YHWH (in Isa 66:5 LXX) through the present lives of the church members (cf. 1:10). On the other hand, the church can expect a glorification as well (cf. 2:14) because of that same grace.

Both expressions, cast in this sonorous prayer report, would likely encourage the beleaguered church because the report places the believers solidly in the hands of God—from their inception through their ongoing commitment to God even to their glorification. They are not alone or on their own in the midst of their suffering. What God has done, is doing, and will do all assure them of the future relief they will receive.

Thus, despite what others detect as the "cooler" tone of this letter, its opening verses still function as a *captatio benevolentiae* (captivation of goodwill). With an accentuation of

---

10. The NRSV is not consistent in its translation of this word. It is translated as "persecution" in 1 Thessalonians, but as "affliction" in 2 Thessalonians. Perhaps this is so in anticipation of 1:6, in which it would appear odd to say "it is indeed just of God to repay with 'persecution' [θλῖψιν *thlipsin*] those who 'persecute' [θλίβουσιν *thlibousin*] you."

common bonds, with a commendation of the church's praiseworthy progress, and with an apocalyptic framework for interpreting the meaning of the afflictions, the writer captures the attention and the goodwill of the audience.

The first twelve verses also announce three significant issues in the letter.[11] First, the initial verses prepare the auditors to see the critical importance of belief in the writer's gospel or testimony. These verses repeatedly mention the church's faith: It is "growing abundantly" (v. 3); the writer boasts about it (v. 4); the church is a part of a larger group, all of whom "have believed" (v. 10); the church "believed" the writer's testimony (v. 10); and the writer prays that God will complete in the church "every . . . work of faith" (v. 11). Faith (or its absence) remains a crucial concern elsewhere in the letter. Some persons believed "what is false" and "have not believed the truth" (2:11-12). The church, the writer maintains, was chosen "for salvation through sanctification by the Spirit and through belief in the truth" (2:13). The writer recognizes, moreover, that "not all [presumably outsiders] have faith" (3:2) and that the church must "keep away from believers who are living in idleness [or better, disorder] and not according to the tradition that they received from us" (3:6). Even still, the errant ones are to be warned as "believers" (3:15).

The repetition of language about faith in the initial verses suggests a basis upon which the writer can exhort his church. On the one hand, because the church believed his testimony and on that basis acquired a fate distinct from the unbelievers (1:10), he can consider presumably dissident thought (2:3-12) and behavior (3:6-15)—whether within or outside the church—as falsehood that should not be believed or supported. As Menken notes, "Belief in the gospel is what distinguishes in the present the oppressed from the oppressors, and in the future the elect from the damned."[12] On the other hand, the writer can deem the truth as that which he already shared with the church (2:5, 15; 3:10).

Relatedly, a second issue signaled by the writer is that of standing firm. In several places throughout the letter the writer accentuates the need for the church to remain firm (2:15) and to be strengthened (2:17; 3:3). Toward that end, the "steadfastness of Christ" (whether read as the "steadfastness that Christ possessed" or as "steadfastness toward Christ") is held up as an example (3:5). Furthermore, repeated remarks about "traditions" (2:15; 3:6) or about the things told (2:5) or commanded (3:7-10) to the church at a previous visit have the effect here, as in the case of 1 Thessalonians, of emphasizing stability (see the Commentary on 1 Thess 4:1-12). Because 2:15 appears as a counterweight to 2:1-2, moreover, some scholars suggests that "standing firm" is accentuated as well through the antonymous expression "to be quickly shaken in mind" (2:2).[13]

It is little wonder, then, that in the exordium the writer also commends the believers' steadfastness, which is the basis for his boasts to other churches of God (v. 4). Even the expression "enduring" (ἀνέχομαι *anechomai*), cast in the present tense (v. 4), implies the church's firm stance in the face of external difficulties up to the very moment of the letter's composition. With the intercessory prayer report (vv. 11-12), moreover, the scope of the church's commitment is clarified. The prayer report, as we have seen, implores God in the light of the initial call of the church and in the context of God's completion of "every resolve and work of faith" (v. 11). The scope of the believers' commitment extends beyond external difficulties to cover every aspect of their commitment to God. That is, the initial verses also prepare the audience for a commitment with respect to the specific internal issue raised in 3:6-15.

Third, these verses also signal God's continuing justice. Having commended the church for its endurance of persecutions and afflictions (v. 4), the writer next places its suffering in a more comprehensive apocalyptic context (vv. 5-10)—one that both defines or interprets the meaning of their suffering and contrasts the different fates of believers and unbelievers.

The interpretation of the suffering of the church is critical because a part of the audience's situation appears to be a potential

---

11. On the exordium's forecasting function, see Cicero *De Part. Or.* 27.97; Quintilian 3.8.10; cf. Aristotle *Rhetoric* 3.13.14.
12. Maarten J. J. Menken, *2 Thessalonians* (New York: Routledge, 1994) 92.
13. Jouette Bassler, "Peace in All Ways," in *Pauline Theology*, ed. Jouette Bassler (Minneapolis: Fortress, 1991) 1:78.

unsettling from their foundational apocalyptic moorings due to an "enthusiastic" interpretation of their affliction. That is, some understood their suffering to mean that the "day of the Lord has already come" (2:1-2), presumably thinking that this had taken place in short order in the wake of their experience of suffering. This kind of thinking was quite possible in an apocalyptic mindset, for many an apocalyptic thinker viewed suffering as a part of the eschatological woes that were expected to take place shortly before the end time. Paul himself thought this way (see the Commentary on 1 Thess 3:1), although he never inferred that the day of the Lord had already arrived because of suffering.

As we shall shortly see, the writer's focus on the Lord as one yet to be revealed (v. 7) and to come (v. 10) works against an enthusiastic interpretation of present suffering. In fact, in the later discussion of the events to occur, the writer painstakingly renders a timetable that frustrates efforts to pinpoint the exact time of Jesus' revealing or coming (2:8).

Likewise, the contrast between the fates of believers and unbelievers is critical because the writer seeks to drive a wedge between believers who follow the writer's traditions (2:15) and unbelievers who "believe what is false" (2:11). Ultimately, of course, the distinction is critical also because there are requisite actions that follow right belief and adherence to the writer's traditions (3:6-15).

This comprehensive apocalyptic context as given in vv. 5-10, however, requires sustained reflection. Its value in demonstrating God's continuing justice is not fully appreciated without some specific comments about the rhetorical force of v. 5 and of vv. 6-10.

The Rhetorical Force of 2 Thessalonians 1:5. To help modern readers, translations of 1:3-10 divide this long and loose sentence into discrete sections. In doing so, however, a problem of ambiguity may escape readers who only have access to an English translation. In Greek, 2 Thess 1:5 actually begins with the word "evidence" (ἔνδειγμα *endeigma*), in front of which the NRSV has placed "This is" and the NIV has affixed "All this is." Even with the help given by these translations, however, the antecedent of "[the] evidence of the righteous judgment of God" is ambiguous. Presumably, the antecedent can be found in one or all of the clauses of 1:3-4, but which one (or which ones) remains uncertain.

Some interpreters think the antecedent of "evidence" is the church's suffering. The immediate response to this assertion, however, is, "How is the innocent suffering of Christians evidence of the righteousness of God?"[14] The proponents of this view respond that the justice of God in 2 Thessalonians is similar to the view of God's justice found in 2 Bar 13:8-10 and the *Pss Sol* 13:10-12. In those texts, the justice of God is seen in the afflictions of the righteous, who are punished for their sins in the present so that they will not be punished for them at the end of time.[15] But this theology of suffering perspective seems unhelpful because it overlooks the fact that the writer does not speak here about the recipients' sins.[16] And would a writer who has spoken so wonderfully about a group so quickly explain their misery as a function of their sins anyway? Probably not!

An alternative position would be to see the antecedent of "evidence" as the ongoing endurance of the believers. That is, the evidence of God's righteous judgment is not their suffering, but that believers have been able successfully and constantly to withstand it. Thus, presupposing that some in the church think their continuous suffering is an indication of the end time, the writer initially focuses on how their endurance is evidence of the continuing righteous judgment of God. Then, drawing on the apocalyptic imagery of 1 Thess 2:12 ("that you lead a life worthy of God, who calls you into his own kingdom and glory"), the writer notes that their endurance (something actually granted rather than attained; see 1:11) in effect means that the believers are "counted worthy" or "made worthy" of the kingdom of God or of God's reign in the new age (1:5*b*). The church suffers for God's new order, but not in order to get into it. And the church's endurance is an indication of God's claim on their lives—that is, of God's previous call or election of

---

14. Bonnie Thurston, *Reading Colossians, Ephesians & 2 Thessalonians: A Literary and Theological Commentary* (New York: Crossroad, 1995) 171.
15. Jouette M. Bassler, "The Enigmatic Sign: 2 Thessalonians 1:5," *CBQ* 46 (1984) 501-6.
16. Beverly R. Gaventa, *First and Second Thessalonians*, Interpretation (Louisville: Westminster John Knox, 1998) 103.

them for salvation in that new order (cf. 1:10; 2:13).

The rhetorical force of 1:5, then, is to present an indication of God's righteous judgment in the ongoing present shortly before the long sentence of 1:3-10 continues with a more explicit apocalyptic scenario about God's justice in the future (1:6-10). Both parts reflect an apocalyptic view of reality, and both could prove encouraging, with 1:5 providing a shift from the present into the future.

The Rhetorical Force of 2 Thessalonians 1:6-10. Having described the present evidence of God's righteous judgment, the writer resumes the thought about God's justice, now looking toward the future, with a loose conditional ("If [or in this case, as shown below, Since] . . . then") statement (the statement is a loose construction because the expected transition "then" in the second clause has to be supplied). The statement has two parts: an initial clause that states what readers can take for granted (vv. 6-8) and a subsequent clause that applies more specifically the general principle of the initial clause (vv. 9-10).[17]

The initial clause (1:6-8) begins with the word "for" (εἴπερ *eiper*) or "since" because the type of Greek conditional statement used does not imply doubt but assumes with certainty that what follows is true. What is true and can be taken for granted by the recipients is that God is just in how God treats those who cause suffering and those who suffer (cf. Ps 7:10-13). With a play on words and an allusion to Isa 66:6, the writer notes God's retributive justice: God will "repay with affliction those who afflict you" (1:6). For the church and the writer ("us," 1:7), however, the promise is relief.

Yet it is clear from this initial clause that these things will happen "when the Lord Jesus is revealed," with "revealed" (ἀποκάλυψις *apokalypsis*) literally meaning "unveiled" (1:7). Thus the writer anticipates the issue of 2:1-8, for the Lord who will come (2:8) has not yet come. It is also clear from this clause that the justice of God will be meted out through Jesus with extraordinary force, consistency, and comprehensiveness.

The force is extraordinary because Jesus' unveiling from heaven will be accompanied by angels (1:7; cf. Zech 14:5; *1 Enoch* 1:9) and flaming fire (1:8; cf. Exod 3:2; Isa 66:15-16), both of which were identified with God in the OT but are now associated with Jesus. With respect to the angels, it is also clear in other NT texts that the early Christians expected Jesus to return with angels (Matt 13:49; 25:31).

The consistency is also extraordinary because precisely as a "just" (δίκαιος *dikaios*, 1:6) God "gives back" or "repays" (ἀνταποδίδωμι *antapodidōmi*, 1:6) with affliction those who afflict, the writer envisions Jesus "giving" (διδόντος *didontos*) "vengeance" or "recompense" (ἐκδίκησις *ekdikēsis*) to those not aligned with the people of God (1:8). While God exacted vengeance in the OT (Deut 32:35; Ps 94:1), Jesus does so now, according to 2 Thessalonians; but the idea of this vengeance is that the recipients get back no more than what they deserve (cf. Rom 12:19). In either case, vengeance is removed from the hands of "human beings who might act out of a spirit of retribution or vindictiveness rather than from motives of divine justice."[18]

The comprehensiveness is also extraordinary because the vengeance falls on all persons who have not aligned themselves with the people of God. Some scholars assume two groups as the recipients of the vengeance. One group, "those who do not know God" (1:8), is conventionally associated with the Gentiles (Ps 78:6; Jer 10:25). The expression "who do not know God" is found in 1 Thess 4:5, but the absence of the word for "Gentiles" (ἔθνη *ethnē*) in 2 Thessalonians suggests that this group is not necessarily limited to Gentiles alone. A second group, "those who do not obey the gospel of our Lord Jesus" (1:8), is conventionally limited exclusively to those Jews who did not accept the Christian gospel or, in Paul's words, "those who have not obeyed the gospel" (Rom 10:16 NRSV). If the two expressions are understood as synonymous, however, the latter group is also comprehensive.[19] This reckoning seems persuasive because a characteristic of

---

17. For explicit details of the construction, see Earl J. Richard, *First and Second Thessalonians*, Sacra Pagina (Collegeville, Minn.: Liturgical, 1995) 305-10.

18. Thurston, *Reading Colossians, Ephesians and 2 Thessalonians*, 172.

19. F. F. Bruce, *1 and 2 Thessalonians*, WBC (Waco, Tex.: Word, 1982) 151-52.

2 Thess 1:5-10 is the writer's transference of images related to God onto Jesus. In this case "those who do not know God" are the same as "those who have not obeyed the gospel of our Lord Jesus." Of course, within this comprehensive collection of persons receiving vengeance, the audience could place those who are afflicting the church (1:6) and, as we shall see, those who oppose the writer's attempt to spread the word of the Lord as well (3:1).

Having indicated what is taken for granted (that it is just for God to repay the afflicters and to grant rest to the afflicted), the writer's second clause (1:9-10) describes what that repayment entails and the benefits accruing to the believers. The repayment to be meted out includes suffering and separation. With an allusion to the aforementioned word "vengeance" (*ekdikēsis*, 1:8), the writer speaks of the afflicters as persons "who will suffer the punishment [δίκη *dikē*] of eternal destruction" (1:9). While some scholars think "destruction" (ὄλεθρος *olethros*, 1:9), a word Paul used in 1 Thess 5:3, is simply an instant annihilation that is eternal (1:9) and thus irreversible, others argue that the description of the separation that follows only makes sense if an eternal (constant) ruination is intended.

Supporting the latter claim is the backdrop of 1 Thess 4:17, in which the believers are "with the Lord forever," in contrast to the afflicters, who, according to this perspective, are banished from the presence of the Lord forever. Of course, the translations "separated" (NRSV) and "shut out" (NIV) do not actually occur in the Greek, but the expression "from the presence of the Lord" (in both the NRSV and the NIV) implies spatial exclusion.

The separation is described with an allusion to the LXX form of Isa 2:10, which speaks of a coming judgment when persons will hide "away from the face of the terror of the Lord, and from the glory of his power." While Isaiah 2:1 speaks about God's judgment against idolaters and the arrogant, the writer of 2 Thessalonians sees Jesus as the agent of justice, as the one from whose presence and glory the afflicters will be excluded. Thus the writer, in this clause, continues the transference of images associated with God in the OT to Jesus.

The appearance of Jesus also brings benefits to the believers (1:10). While the afflicters act in this age, they take on a passive role at the judgment as they are afflicted, inflicted, or shuttled away. For believers, however, those who witness the Lord's coming will have the opportunity to play an active role at the end. The believers (of whom the writer's church is a part) will be able to respond to the coming of Jesus in association with "his holy ones" (τοῖς ἁγίοις αὐτοῦ *tois hagiois autou;* translated as "saints" in the NRSV).

Because the likely background for 1:10 (Ps 88:8 LXX) views "his holy ones" as angels, there is uncertainty about whether the church is understood to be a part of "his holy ones." This problem is related to the translation of a similar expression in 1 Thess 3:13. For at least three reasons, however, some scholars (myself included) think the "holy ones" here include the believers. First, the glorification of the Lord by the "holy ones" in 1:10 possibly anticipates 1:12, where the writer speaks of the name of the Lord being "glorified in you." Second, the parallel nature of the two expressions in 1:10 (both are infinitive clauses: "to be glorified by his saints" and "to be marveled at . . . among all who have believed") could mean that the two expressions are synonymous. Third, the characteristic transference of images once attributed to God but now to Jesus may also imply a transference of "the image of God with his angels . . . to Christ with his church."[20] However one resolves the ambiguity, the church is assuredly a part of the group characterized as "all who have believed" (1:10*b*) and, accordingly, will play an active role in marveling at Jesus.

The timing for the marveling at Jesus' appearance is set in the future, another anticipation of the problem of 2:2. Earlier, Jesus' appearance (1:7*b*) was described as the time when Jesus would be "revealed" (*apokalypsis*). Here it is depicted as the time when he "comes [ἔλθῃ *elthē*] . . . on that day." "That day," appearing in Greek at the end of this clause, alludes to the day of YHWH in Isa 2:11. Here, with the characteristic transference we have come to expect, however, "that day" is not the day of God, but the day of Jesus, and thus the expression anticipates

---

20. Menken, *2 Thessalonians*, 91.

the discussion of the day of the Lord in 2 Thess 2:2.

The rhetorical force of the two clauses of this conditional statement presuppose the justice of God in the future. The initial clause assumes that the justice of God is performed through the agency of Jesus, whose future revelation brings forth relief to believers, but vengeance to unbelievers. The second clause, building on the first one, elucidates the specific consequences of God's future justice—eternal separation for unbelievers and an opportunity to marvel at the powerful coming of Jesus for believers. This explicit apocalyptic framework is a word of encouragement both because the timing of the drama refutes the misinformation noted in 2:2 and because the dazzling display of Jesus' godlike power assures this church that the avenging Jesus is able to bring the relief promised.

With the rhetorical force of 2 Thess 1:5 and of 1:6-10 having been noted, a final word is necessary about the role of 1:5-10 as a whole in its contribution to the exordium's emphasis on the continuing justice of God. In connection with 1:11-12, vv. 5-10 comment not exclusively on the issue of God's present and future "justice," but as well on the church's "worthiness." Verses 11-12 resume the theme first mentioned in 1:5: that of the worthiness of the church. The correct interpretation of suffering, then, is a comprehensive apocalyptic one that acknowledges the present endurance, the future retribution, and the ultimate glorification that God has set into operation. The problem with the enthusiastic apocalyptic message is not just that the timetable is inaccurate, but that it does not sufficiently adumbrate the continuing justice of God (in its present and future dimensions). Further, it does not place the suffering of believers within the larger discourse of God's program of glorification, thereby leaving out the church's route to prestige or worth through association with its powerful Lord. The enthusiastic apocalyptic message is both pallid and narrow.

The comprehensive apocalyptic framework of 1:5-10 thus helps the church to see the great power of Jesus. For a church that no longer has its former networks of power and honor, the honor it brings to its Lord is one part of the glorification process, for the church (and all the saints) will "obtain the glory of our Lord Jesus" (2:14; cf. 1:12).

Altogether, then, the initial verses of 2 Thessalonians function as an exordium not only because they capture the goodwill of the auditors, but as well because they announce the critical issues that will be addressed in chapters 2 and 3. Thus the auditors would already know the letter's emphasis on the importance of belief in the writer's word, on standing firm or remaining committed, and on the vindication of the afflicted.

REFLECTIONS

The words of 2 Thess 1:11 about "good resolve and work of faith" call to mind two persons from our own time whose lives reflected these in vivid detail: Martin Luther King, Jr., and Mother Teresa. Few have found points of comparison between them. Mohandas Gandhi usually comes to mind when one casts about for a counterpart for King. For the fundamental philosophy of his movement, King adopted Gandhi's principles of nonviolent direct action, principles that Gandhi had used in overcoming the colonial power of British rule in India. Both were motivated by love as a powerful agent of social change. And, alas, both men met death at the hands of an assassin.

But King and the diminutive saint from Calcutta? Few would connect them. The exordium in 2 Thessalonians, however, provides a unique link that forces us to think about the paradigmatic lives of King and Mother Teresa at the same time. The link is the measure of worth or prestige.

How does one measure prestige? What counts as an index of honor? Is it keeping up with the latest fashions and fads of the day? Is it having limitless financial resources at our disposal? How do we measure worth? This is the backdrop of the exordium in 2 Thess 1:1-12. The Greeks and the Romans, at all levels of society, had an undying interest in social prestige. No wonder that we read in one of the ancient documents: "Glory drags along the obscure no less than the nobly-bound to her shining chariot."[21] But the writer of 2 Thessalonians speaks about glory or prestige as if it is something that God grants to those who seek to do good to others (1:11).

This is the measure of worth that was basic to the lives of Martin Luther King, Jr., and Mother Teresa. One died young; the other old. One was assassinated; the other lived a relatively long life. Both gave the world incredible examples of "good resolve and work[s] of faith" (1:11). King captured true worth in his sermon "The Drum Major Instinct," in which he asked not to be remembered for his Nobel Peace Prize, his numerous awards, or where he went to school. He asked, rather, to be remembered as someone who "tried to love and serve humanity."[22] Mother Teresa may have been influenced by 2 Thessalonians when she prepared the following prayer:

Make us worthy, Lord,
to serve others throughout the world
who live and die
in poverty or hunger,
Give them, through our hands, this day their daily
bread, and by our understanding love,
give peace and joy.[23]

21. Horace *Satires* 1.6.23-24.
22. Martin Luther King, Jr., "The Drum Major Instinct," in *I Have a Dream: Writings and Speeches That Changed the World*, ed. James M. Washington (New York: HarperCollins, 1992) 191.
23. Mother Teresa of Calcutta, "Make Us Worthy, Lord," in *A Gift for God: Prayers and Meditations* (New York: Harper & Row, 1975) 71.

2 THESSALONIANS 2:1–3:15
MAINTAINING THE TRADITIONS

OVERVIEW

With its general concern for stability and its more specific concern about a misleading, enthusiastic brand of apocalypticism, the letter shifts from its exordium to a longer unit in which the writer encourages the church not to veer from the traditions they have received (2:15; 3:6). The unit (2:1–3:15) includes two sets of hortatory appeals: appeals to traditions against an apocalyptic enthusiasm (2:1-17) and appeals to traditions commending appropriate practical pursuits (3:1-15). A sequential analysis of 2:1–3:15 supports this contention, but two preliminary steps are in order. First, as in the case of the Commentary on 1 Thessalonians, it is important to note the various acoustic markers that clarify the broad strokes of the unit as discerned by epistolary analysis. Second, it is necessary to offer any other plausible arguments for the rhetorical delineation of 2:1–3:15. Those items in place, it will be possible to look sequentially and carefully at the discrete sections of verses that both constitute the two sets of hortatory appeals and advance the writer's argument about stability and the maintenance of traditions.

Epistolary analysis suggests the writer's inclusion of a thanksgiving report in 2:13-14 and wish-prayers in 2:16-17 and 3:5.[24] These prayer forms conventionally have the effect of summarizing previous material (as we have seen in the case of 1:11-12; cf. 1 Thess 3:11-13) or of anticipating subsequent material (again, note 1:11-12; cf. 1 Thess 1:3-5; 3:11-13). Thus, for example, 2:16-17 could be a conclusion to the material in 2:1-12.

Of course, determining the exact conclusion to 2:1-12 could appear confusing, for there are reasons to see 2:13-14, 2:15, or 2:16-17 as its conclusion. Like other prayer units, the thanksgiving in 2:13-14 is a fitting conclusion. We have already noticed how it is similar to the previous wish-prayer in 1:11-12, and its focus on constant thanks makes it obviously similar to the initial thanksgiving (1:3-4). Furthermore, it is directly related to 2:1-12 because it indicates that the fate of believers is different from that of the persons influenced by the delusion noted there since God chose (2:13) and called them (2:14). Yet 2:13-14 is quickly followed by "So then" (2:15), which also has the tone of a summation. Furthermore, in 2:15, the writer appears to contrast the traditions he had taught the church by word of mouth and letter with the enthusiastic agitation mentioned in 2:2. In addition, 2:16-17 is also a conclusion because it likewise indicates why the fate of believers is different from that of those under the delusion—namely, because God both loved them and gave them eternal consolation. It appears, therefore, that all three sections conclude 2:1-12 with 2:16-17 as its final conclusion because of its similarities with 1 Thess 3:11-13. That is, both 2 Thess 2:16-17 and 1 Thess 3:11-13 are wish-prayers, and both precede a transitional marker ("Finally," 2 Thess 3:1; 1 Thess 4:1).

Epistolary analysis also reveals the letter closing to begin at 3:16. According to Jeffrey Weima, the Pauline postscripts usually begin with a peace formula. Hence the peace formula of 3:16 (on the model of 1 Thess 5:23) marks the beginning of the closing unit (3:16-18) of 2 Thessalonians—that is, the peroration.[25]

If one accepts these benefits of the epistolary analysis along with some other specific rhetorical markers, it is possible to justify the delineation of 2:1–3:15 into two sets of appeals. Two pieces of evidence are crucial.

---

24. See, e.g., Peter T. O'Brien, *Introductory Thanksgivings in the Letters of Paul* (Leiden: Brill, 1977) 184-93. Cf. Gordon P. Wiles, *Paul's Intercessory Prayers: The Significance of the Intercessory Prayer in the Letters of Paul* (Cambridge: Cambridge University Press, 1974) 32n. 2.

25. Jeffrey Weima, *Neglected Endings: The Significance of the Pauline Letter Closing* (Sheffield: JSOT, 1994) 187.

First, the most obvious marker between the material in chaps. 2 and 3 is the transitional marker "finally" (λοιπόν *loipon*). In some of the undisputed Pauline letters, as has been noted, "finally" suggests either the last section of a letter (cf. 2 Cor 13:11; 1 Thess 4:1) or the last subsection of a unit (cf. Phil 3:1). In 2 Thess 3:1, "finally" probably marks the last large unit of the letter, although the repetition of cognate forms of "strengthen" (στηρίζω *stērizō*, 2:17; cf. 3:3) and "hearts" (καρδίας *kardias*, 2:17; 3:5) suggests a transitional role for 3:1-5.

Second, assuming the hortatory function of the writer's prayer reports and "finally" as a transitional marker, the rhetorical movement of the material in 2:1-17 appears to mirror that found in 3:1-15. On the one hand, consolatory exhortation couched in the solemn tones of prayer (2:13-17) appears to follow more explicit exhortations on the church's maintenance of its founding traditions (2:1-12) in 2:1-17. On the other hand, consolatory exhortation couched in solemn tones of prayer (3:1-5) appears to precede the more explicit exhortations on the church's maintenance of its founding traditions (3:6-15) in 3:1-15. Thus the transitional nature of 2:16-17, the delineation of 3:16-18 as a separate part of the letter, the transitional marker "finally" in 3:1, and the letter's reverse movements in 2:1-15 and 3:1-15 all suggest two separate large units for the proof section.

2 THESSALONIANS 2:1-17, HORTATORY APPEALS AGAINST APOCALYPTIC ENTHUSIASM

OVERVIEW

The first set of hortatory appeals easily divides into three parts: a brief initial section on the question of the parousia and the gathering of the believers (2:1-2); a longer section designed to refute the inaccurate information (2:3-12); and a set of concluding exhortations cast in the consolatory context of prayer (2:13-17). Of the three sections, both the initial and last ones are relatively straightforward. As we shall see, however, the middle section has been a source of puzzlement for centuries.

2 Thessalonians 2:1-2, Do Not Be Shaken Up

COMMENTARY

These verses, though brief, are judged by some scholars to be a terse introduction to the material following it. That is, these verses help readers to anticipate the context, the scope, and the aim of the subsequent verses. The context of 2:1-2 and (by implication) the rest of 2:1-17 is apocalyptic, for messages about the day of the Lord (or about his coming) were prevalent in the apocalyptic material of the writer's age (cf. Mark 13:1).[26]

The scope of vv. 1-2 is not limited to Jesus' parousia alone. Given the earlier claims made about the glorification of Jesus and believers (1:11-12), it is little wonder that the initial verses of this set of hortatory appeals focus both on Jesus and the believers—that is, on the believers' "eschatological gathering."[27] Of course, this kind of gathering was once used to describe God's gathering of exiles (Isa 52:12; 2 Macc 2:18), but in NT times

---

26. For arguments against reading the context as a gnostic one, see Menken, *2 Thessalonians*, 98. That Paul and the writer here viewed the day of the Lord and the parousia as the same event, see pp., 99-100.

27. Charles Wanamaker, *The Epistles to the Thessalonians*, NIGTC (Grand Rapids: Eerdmans, 1990) 238. On the gathering schema in apocalyptic literature, see *Pss Sol* 17:26-28.

the idea was transferred to Jesus, who was expected by Christians to gather God's people together (cf. Matt 23:37; Mark 13:27; Luke 13:34).

With this double interest in Jesus and the believers, these initial verses reveal that the entire first set of exhortations say as much about the believers as they do about Jesus. Indeed, as we shall soon see, the force of all the material in 2:1-17 is really an argument about the founding traditions that show a radical difference between believers and unbelievers, on the one hand, and Jesus and a figure called the "lawless one" (2:3, 8) on the other hand.

The aim of vv. 1-2 and its subsequent material is to refute an unfounded claim that the day of the Lord had already "appeared" (v. 2). Since the word "appeared" (ἐνέστηκεν *enestēken*) can only mean "the day of the Lord has already occurred," and not "the day of the Lord is imminent," the refutation is aimed against a misleading notion that events associated with that day had already happened.[28]

While it may seem obvious to us that the day of the Lord had not come, it must be remembered that the readers and auditors of 2 Thessalonians would have lived during what Koester calls "the apocalyptic fervor of the second half of the first century."[29] Furthermore, it would not be difficult for them to assume the arrival of the events of the day because of the expectation that those events would follow in close proximity the believers' experience of great suffering.

With vv. 1-2, the refutation can only begin by casting about for possible sources of the confusion: (1) a spirit or perhaps someone claiming to speak a word of prophecy inspired by the Spirit (cf. 1 Thess 5:20); (2) a word, possibly a teaching of some sort, but in any case a word determined apart from the Spirit; or (3) a letter purporting to be from the writer. The subsequent verses will show, however, that the claim did not emanate from the writer, even if it seems "as though from us" (v. 2; cf. v. 15). No wonder that the writer begins, not with the unfounded claim itself, but with strong words of insistence ("we beg you," v. 1), a word order that is reversed in the NRSV and the NIV. No wonder as well that the writer will go on to pile up prayerful words of encouragement on top of each other in 2:13-17 to remind the church of its secure and continuous salvation because of God's claim on and benefactions for their lives.

With 2:1-2, moreover, the writer introduces his refutation, not with an explicit argument against the unfounded claim, but with a concern that the claim not cause the church (in the NRSV) "to be quickly shaken in mind or alarmed" (v. 2). A better translation that captures the nuancing of the Greek words of v. 2 is that the claim should not "shock the church suddenly" or "repeatedly agitate" them (v. 2).[30] Indeed, one translation for the first expression could be that the church not "be quickly shaken out of . . . [its] wits."[31] Envisioned here is the idea that the church had been shaken at the very foundation and that the shaking—although it occurred only once, as is indicated by the kind of Greek verb the writer chose to describe the shock—had occurred easily. Furthermore, even if the shaking occurred once, the fallout of the shock had an enduring power. That is, the agitation it caused was ongoing. It appears that the agitation was similar to the kind that the Synoptic Gospels mention, for the writer and some of the synoptic gospel writers use forms of θροέω (*throeō*, "to agitate," 1 Thess 2:2; cf. Matt 24:6; Mark 13:7) to indicate a frenzied response to false claims on how the end-time events should be read. Finally, it must be noted that the precision with which the writer has spoken about the sudden shock and its enduring fallout reveals him to be a loving pastor. Here and elsewhere 2 Thessalonians is not a document by someone writing with a "cool" tone. Instead, it is the work of a loving pastor carefully warning his students against accepting false assumptions about reality.

---

28. Cf. Gaventa, *First and Second Thessalonians*, 109.
29. Helmut Koester, "From Paul's Eschatology to the Apocalyptic Schemata of 2 Thessalonians," in *The Thessalonian Correspondence*, ed. Raymond F. Collins (Leuven: University of Leuven Press, 1990) 455.
30. On this reading, see Thurston, *Reading Colossians, Ephesians and 2 Thessalonians*, 176.
31. Bruce, *1 and 2 Thessalonians*, 163.

REFLECTIONS

False claims exert a powerful force over the lives of people—precipitating needless panic, driving some to apostasy, and leading others to the precipice of despondency, if not over the cliff of despair. The writer of 2 Thess 2:1-2 also had to contend against false claims that had the potential to upset his church. One important lesson we can learn from him is that falsehood often comes wrapped in the same garb as truth. It seldom comes in the easily discernible guises of the fantastic, the iconoclastic, or the sophomoric. Rather, it moves with refined force. It comes in the name of science, declaring the depravity of some people and the superiority of those who would oppress and colonize them. It comes in the guise of a pastor's care, seeking personal gain and political grandstanding. It comes with the tone and touch of friendship, but it reveals private anguishes and intimate confidences spoken in closed chambers.

How, then, can we guard against falling prey to false claims that often appear as the truth—as a word, spirit, or letter "as though from us"? The answer is not to cave in to loveless logic or hateful science. Nor should we acquiesce to the fleecing of the faithful whether it emanates from the pulpit or the pew. And certainly we should not concede to a facile friendship with others who have not earned our trust through the tests of time. In all of these cases, rather, what is needed is an attitude of discernment, careful study, and relentless sifting of thought.

Christianity does not call us to be timid or gullible. It calls us, rather, to weigh every word, spirit, or letter carefully. Second Thessalonians shows us the great need for trained clergy and laity, for churches to make learning an everyday quest and a lifetime goal, and for all believers to take on that perennial pursuit first penned with precision in the Middle Ages by the great Anselm of Canterbury: "faith seeking understanding."

2 Thessalonians 2:3-12, Do Not Be Deceived

COMMENTARY

With 2:3-12, the writer treats the cosmic power dynamics of the realities of vengeance and vindication highlighted in 1:5-10 and assumed in 1:11-12. These verses do not skirt over the matter of the hostilities that the church faces or the consequences that its opponents must face. Rather, the verses describe in stark detail what will happen before and upon the coming of the Lord in accordance with what the writer has already said and on the basis of familiar apocalyptic traditions.

The stark detail, however, is not necessarily clear to modern interpreters. Descriptions of the material in vv. 3-12 range from "veiled and obscure" to "unconsciously vague."[32] One scholar suggests that the writer appears to "ransack the resources of apocalyptic thought to underscore his theme."[33] Perhaps, as we shall see, even veiled, vague, and unclear ransacking can have its purposes. For now, three concerns are relevant: (1) a division of the material in vv. 3-12; (2) some explanations of ambiguous clauses in vv. 3-5 and 6-7; and (3) an argument about the sequential logic of the verses.

Regarding the division, the material breaks nicely into two sections. An initial section focuses on the coming of a mysterious figure called "the lawless one" (vv. 3-7). A subsequent section renders the source(s) and consequences of the lawless one's arrival (vv. 8-12).

As for the ambiguous clauses in vv. 3-5 and 6-7, the one in vv. 3-5 is an ellipsis. The words "that day will not come" (v. 3a) in the

---

32. Respectively, see Thurston, *Reading Colossians, Ephesians and 2 Thessalonians*, 175; Koester, "From Paul's Eschatology to the Apocalyptic Schemata of 2 Thessalonians," 457.

33. Edgar Krentz, "Through a Lens," in Collins, *The Thessalonian Correspondence*, 61-62.

phrase "for that day will not come unless the rebellion comes first and the lawless one is revealed" (vv. 3a-b) are not found in the Greek, but are supplied by the NRSV to clarify what will not happen unless the rebellion comes first. Because the Greek sentence (vv. 3c-4) does not stop with its introduction of the lawless one, but winds on and on with more descriptions of this figure, the NRSV starts a new sentence at v. 4. Then the sentence is interrupted by a parenthetical clause about the writer's earlier words while he was with the church (v. 5), only to start again in v. 6. To note the interruption, the NRSV again begins a new sentence in v. 5.

In the case of vv. 6-7, there is ambiguity about the logic of using two different participial forms of the Greek verb "to restrain" (κατέχω *katechō*) to describe the restraint that is placed on the man of lawlessness. For one form, the NRSV gives the translation "what is now restraining" because that participle implies a thing rather than a person (v. 6). For the second, it gives the translation "the one who now restrains" because that participle implies the activity of a person (v. 7).[34] So scholars are not sure just what or who restrains the man of lawlessness. Is he restrained by a thing? By a person? And if only by one, why does the writer give both participles?

What we can know, however, is that because the restraint holds the man of lawlessness back, the day of the Lord has not occurred. In the reckoning of the writer, even though the "mystery of lawlessness" (perhaps a synonym for the activity of "those who do not know God," 1:8, or perhaps a cipher for the present persecutions) is already at work, the revelation or unveiling of the lawless one has not occurred (2:6). And until the restraint is removed, that revelation cannot occur. Furthermore, before the revelation, a rebellion (ἀποστασία *apostasia*, the word from which we get the English word "apostasy") must first occur (v. 3; cf. Matt 24:6-14; 1 Tim 4:1-14; 2 Tim 3:1-5; Jude 17:1-19). Then, with the revelation of the lawless one, the day of the Lord will come (v. 8).

With respect to the sequential logic, one must join the letter's first auditors, who would have heard vv. 3-12 as a refutation of the claim that the day of the Lord had appeared. To join them, however, requires that one note the force of the refutation, the intratextual context of the previous material, and the extratextual context that the auditors could have recalled in understanding the refutation.

Read apart from the preceding material, the force of much of the refutation is patently disturbing. That is, the writer's comprehensive schema suggests that the opposition will become more intense. As Krentz aptly notes: "The removal of that restraining person [or thing] will be the καιρός *kairos* [time] (2:6) for the ultimate revelation of ὁ ἄνθρωπός τῆς ἀνομίας (*ho anthrōpos tēs anomias* [lawless one]; 2:3), the nadir of apocalyptic misfortune."[35] How could the writer tell a group already facing external hostilities that the worst is yet to come? Would not his own words, at least until v. 8, cause the auditors to become "quickly shaken in mind or alarmed"? Precisely this is the reason why the preceding material of 1:5-12 had to be given first—to give the fuller drama of power in which the past and ongoing persecution should be set.

One must join the auditors, then, for an understanding of 2:3-12 that resonates with the preceding intratextual context given in 1:5-12. Given Jesus' own revelation as described in 1:7, the audience can expect the lawless one to have a revelation (2:3, 7). Indeed, the figure has a παρουσία (*parousia*, 2:9), as does Jesus (2:8). At least, therefore, as other scholars have noted, the audience could view the lawless one as a parody of Christ. Furthermore, the impression one gets of Jesus in 1:5-12 is that he comes as an agent of God who will inflict "vengeance on those who do not know God" (1:8). He does not seek glory, but both he (1:10) and his name (1:12) will be glorified. The picture of the lawless one, however, is that of a usurper: "He opposes and exalts himself above every so-called god or object of worship, so that he takes his seat in the temple of God, declaring himself to be God" (2:4). Unlike Jesus (1:8), the lawless one does not have a gospel, but

---

34. For the most part, the commentary agrees with arguments given by Wanamaker on these verses. See Wanamaker, *The Epistles to the Thessalonians*, 249-57.

35. Krentz, "Through a Lens," 53.

seeks to deceive people who "refused to love the truth" (2:10). If the authority of God lies behind Jesus' action of vengeance (1:8), Satan lies behind the activity of the lawless one (2:9; cf. 1 Thess 2:18). If Jesus' coming will be marveled at by "all who have believed" (1:10), the coming of the lawless one (1:9) sets into play God's delusion of persons who will "believe what is false" (2:11). Even given the great might of the lawless one, a might expressed through all kinds of "power [a general word connoting miraculous ability], signs, lying wonders" (cf. Exod 7:3; Deut 6:22; Acts 2:22, 43), he is no match for Jesus.

On the one hand, the mouth of Jesus will put an end to the lawless one. The image here reflects Isa 11:4 and other texts (cf. 4 Ezra 13:10; *1 Enoch* 62:2) in which the breath of God alone reduces enemies to nothing. On the other hand, the "manifestation" or epiphany (ἐπιφάνεια *epiphaneia*, 2:8) of Jesus' coming will reduce the effective work of the lawless one. The epiphany image here is Hellenistic. It is an image of the visit of a god to bring salvation or benefactions (cf. 1 Tim 6:14; 2 Tim 4:1, 8; Titus 2:13). Here, however, the visit brings both salvation and destruction.

In following the intratextual context and its contrasts between the lawless one and Jesus, readers probably will find it difficult to understand how God could be a deceiver. Robert Jewett offers a helpful explanation: "The phrases "having faith in" or "loving the truth" (vv. 2, 10) evoke the horizon of accepting or rejecting the gospel as the key to the judgment scheme in this apocalyptic theology."[36] Thus the delusion God brings is not the cause of the rejection of the gospel, but its result. The idea of God's sending a delusion, moreover, is not a unique expression. Elsewhere in biblical literature God grants the possibility for persons to be seduced or subjected to evil because of their failure to believe the truth about God (cf. Rom 1:18-32).

Another context important for joining the auditors is the extratextual context from which they could have understood their own plight in the light of the refutation given in 2:3-12. The commentary so far has deliberately not defined in explicit terms some of the key elements of the refutation—namely, the "lawless one" (vv. 3, 8), "what is now restraining" (v. 6), or the "the one who now restrains" (2:7). To gain even a provisional insight into these terms, one must be apprised of extratextual matters, both from the history of the subjugation of the Jewish subculture to which Paul and other early Christians belonged and from the larger political culture of the first century CE.

The "lawless man" or "man of lawlessness" is a Semitic expression that does not so much identify the figure as it describes his activity. This expression is qualified by the writer with yet a second Semitic expression, the "son of destruction" (v. 3).[37] Since this type of expression indicated the nature of a person or the realm to which a person belonged (cf. 1 Thess 5:4), the "son of destruction" also does not identify the figure, but aligns him with the cosmic forces of evil. He belongs to the realm of "destruction" (ἀπώλεια *apōleia*), and, indeed, his coming will be accompanied by deception "for those who are perishing" (ἀπόλλυμι *apollymi*, v. 10) or, as Richard has suggested, those "on the road to ruin."[38]

Beyond his aforementioned characterization as being against God and against Christ (though he is not called anti-Christ as in 1 John 2:18, 22; 4:3; 2 John 7), the figure could have connoted images of pseudo-prophets equipped with deceptive signs, as one finds in the synoptic apocalypses of the 70s and 80s CE.[39] Because the figure is associated with the Temple (presumably the Second Temple in Jerusalem) or is described as an "endtime tyrant," some scholars link him to the "king" in Dan 11:36-38 (i.e., Antiochus IV)[40] or to Roman figures, usually Pompey, who captured Jerusalem in 63 BCE,[41] or (better) Gaius Caligula, whose threat to set

---

36. Robert Jewett, "A Matrix of Grace: The Theology of 2 Thessalonians," in Bassler, *Pauline Theology*, 1:67. Cf. Thurston, *Reading Colossians, Ephesians and 2 Thessalonians*, 180.

37. The identification of the "man of lawlessness" actually assumes an earlier text-critical problem—namely, whether one supports the textual variant "man of sin" or the variant "man of lawlessness." The former variant is widely attested, but not usually preferred because the figure of 2:6 is later identified specifically as the "lawless one" in 2:8. See Leon Morris, *The First and Second Epistles to the Thessalonians: The English Text with Introduction, Exposition and Notes* (Grand Rapids: Eerdmans, 1959) 21-22.

38. Richard, *First and Second Thessalonians*, 327.

39. L. Hartman, "Eschatology of 2 Thessalonians" in Collins, *The Thessalonian Correspondence*, 480; C. H. Giblin, "2 Thessalonians 2:1 Re-read," in *The Thessalonian Correspondence*, 462.

40. Hartman, "Eschatology of 2 Thessalonians", 462.

41. See *Pss Sol* 17:11-15.

up statues of himself in Jerusalem in 40 CE almost succeeded.[42]

As noted earlier, both participles from the verb "to restrain" ("what is now restraining," v. 6; "the one who now restrains," v. 7) are interpretive hurdles. Some scholars wish to regard the first one in a positive way, as God[43] or as God's plan,[44] perhaps anticipating 2:8-12 where the writer will describe God as the ultimate source of the delusion promulgated by the lawless one and energized by Satan (cf. Rom 1:21-28). Notwithstanding God as the key designer of apocalyptic hopes in vv. 8-12, others read the initial participle in a negative way, as tantamount to the "mystery (μυστήριον *mystērion*) of lawlessness."[45] Some scholars also read the second participle in a positive way, suggesting that it refers to an angel of God or even to God, though one wonders how God could be removed (v. 7). The problem with the positive formulations is that they do not explain the necessity of two different participles to express the idea that God's plan or someone representing God was restraining the appearance of the lawless one.[46]

If the second participle ("the one who now restrains") has a negative referent (v. 7), it could be a contemporary emperor. As Wanamaker notes, "Paul and his contemporaries intuitively recognized that the type of evil that defies God and seeks to usurp his position derives from corrupt and unjust social and political institutions such as imperial rule under Gaius Caesar."[47] Yet one need not specifically identify the referent. Perhaps the writer gives "veiled, deliberately mysterious reference to the restrainer, be it magistrate, governor, or emperor."[48] In the light of the author's use of 1 Thessalonians, which highlights local hostility (v. 14) and the continuing hostilities in 2 Thessalonians, perhaps the author does not wish to limit the restrainer (whose removal will open up wide-scale rebellion and the revelation and deception of the lawless one) to a single figure. The problem is not a single instance of persecution. The problem is that the persecution that is already underway issues from many fronts.

The cryptic language, then, at least has the function of showing the varied character of the persecutions. In addition, as refutation, it makes it difficult for anyone to pinpoint the exact time of the future day of the Lord. With vv. 8-12 and their descriptions of the destruction of the lawless one and God's ultimate control, moreover, all of 2:3-12 functions as a source of encouragement for a beleaguered church. Indeed, the lawless one does not stand a chance. When he is revealed, he will exercise power and bring forth a deception. Yet, he will be destroyed or made inoperative by Jesus through "the breath of his mouth" (cf. Exod 15:8; 2 Sam 22:16). What the audience sees is that the power of the lawless one is no match for God's avenging agent.

42. See Josephus *The Jewish War* 2.184-185. See also Menken, *2 Thessalonians*, 104-6.
43. Thurston, *Reading Colossians, Ephesians and 2 Thessalonians*, 179; Hartman, "Eschatology of 2 Thessalonians," 481.
44. Menken, *2 Thessalonians*, 112.
45. Wanamaker, *The Epistles to the Thessalonians*, 253.
46. Wanamaker, *The Epistles to the Thessalonians*, 251.
47. Wanamaker, *The Epistles to the Thessalonians*, 248.
48. Krodel, *The Deutero-Pauline Letters*, 48.

REFLECTIONS

Despite the enigmatic character of 2:3-12 for us, the text likely breathed confidence into the lives of its original audience because it wove the plight of the church into a larger drama. Indeed, the text speaks even now to its readers and hearers with the challenge for us to respond to moments when life seems meaningless with a perspective that places life in a larger drama. There are persons who respond to moments of meaninglessness with a defeatist perspective. They look on the apparently hopeless individual scenes of life and wish to cry out with Macbeth: "Out, out, brief candle! Life is but a walking shadow, a poor player that struts and frets his hour upon the stage, and then is heard no more; it is a tale told by an idiot, full of sound and fury, signifying nothing." Others respond to these moments through denial. They resort to hedonistic solutions—numbing shattered dreams with mood-altering chemicals, holding madness at bay through countless hours of computerized or televised virtual reality, delaying the arrival of despair through relentless and promiscuous sexual pursuits, or nursing the deep wounds of emptiness with the swabs of self-centered acquisition.

The writer of 2 Thessalonians recommends neither a perspective of defeatism nor one of denial. Rather, the writer takes on a defiant position. He places the sordid experiences of the church's suffering within the larger drama of what God is doing and will do in the world. The momentary scenes of meaninglessness may represent an act in the drama, but the drama is not a one-act play. There is a larger picture, a grand movement in which every scene fits. The full horizon has not been sketched in. There is more to come. This perspective allowed Martin Luther King, Jr., to peer down the telescope of time to find a moment in history—albeit dreamlike—unsullied by oppression and unsoiled by discrimination. It helped Gandhi to advocate *Satyagraha* (or a devotion to truth) against the Transvaal government in South Africa and later against British rule in India. It convinced Archbishop Romero to minister to the poor in El Salvador. And it inspired Nelson Mandela's stability and hope as he struggled against South Africa's entrenched system of apartheid. This perspective has given courage to untold numbers of those who fight against injustice with its remarkable message: Evil will be defeated!

2 Thessalonians 2:13-17, Reasons to Stand Firm and Hold On

COMMENTARY

As noted earlier, 2:13-17 is cast as a conclusion to 2:1-12. This exhortative material easily divides into two sets of prayers around a more central set of exhortations. Thus 2:13-17 includes a thanksgiving notice (vv. 13-14), a request to stand firm (v. 15), and a wish-prayer (vv. 16-17).

The material here also anticipates the next large unit (3:1-15), particularly, the initial verses (3:1-5), which are also set in a context of prayers. Both speak about God's love (2:16; 3:5). Both speak of hearts (2:17; 3:5) and of the strengthening of the church (2:17; 3:3). Both give attention to the issue of belief, either the belief of the church (2:13) or others' lack of belief (3:2). Both also mention the writer's gospel (2:14) or the word of the Lord (3:1) and glory, either that obtained by the church (2:14) or by the word (3:1).

2:13-14. Like the thanksgiving in 1:3-4, the thanksgiving in these verses reflects the writer's obligation. Again, however, the obligation is not a challenge to a protest from the audience, but a genuine response to what God has done. The thanksgiving here also links God's call of the church to the writer's proclamation (v. 14). This is a critical link because the writer will later ask the church to stand firm and hold fast to traditions that he taught them (v. 15). It is also critical because a part of the audience's problem is its potential dissuasion from the writer's truth, even though the church came to belief through the writer. Little wonder it is, then, that the apocalyptic scenario given in vv. 3-12 is interrupted by a parenthesis in v. 5, in which the writer reminds the group that he had already told them the argument he was putting forth to refute the enthusiastic agitation. The inclusion of the initial words "But we" in this thanksgiving, moreover, sets up a contrast between the persons of doom noted in vv. 11-12 and the church. Those who are deceived will not be saved (v. 10), but the church was chosen for salvation (v. 13). The deceived ones are those who "refused to love the truth" (v. 10) and those who "have not believed the truth" (v. 12), but the church was chosen "through belief in the truth" (v. 13; cf. Deut 26:17-18 LXX).

It is also the case that this thanksgiving places the church's fate directly in God's hands—in what God has done, is doing, and will do. God's election of the church indicates

God's past actions, and the election is evinced both through the words "God chose you" and through the description of the church as "beloved" (see 1 Thess 1:4). God's concern for the believers is also found in their present, ongoing life, for the expression "the Spirit" mentioned in v. 13 is not a human spirit, but the source by which the church gains its sanctification or maturity (cf. 1 Thess 4:3-8).

God's activity in the lives of the believers can be seen if further attention is given to the text-critical problem in v. 13. Although some scholars accept the variant "first fruits" (as in the NRSV) as closer to the original,[49] it should be noted that the Thessalonians were not the "first fruits" in the Macedonian ministry (the Philippians were). Other scholars, then, opt for the expression "from the beginning" as closer to the original.[50] Read this way, the passage continues to show God's control over events, now peering back into the unfathomable moments of creation (v. 13) and eventually fastforwarding through time to speak about God's purpose in calling the church (to "obtain the glory of our Lord Jesus Christ," v. 14).

Thus, as noted earlier, the thanksgiving is one of the conclusions to the first set of hortatory appeals. After introducing the problem of the agitation and indicating the foundational traditions that refuted the enthusiastic message, the writer issues a word of prayer that reveals both the identity of the church (in contrast to those deceived by Satan) and the basis for that identity—namely, God's activity in their lives.

2:15. In the light of vv. 13-14, the writer asks the church in a positive form to do what he initially asked them to do in a negative form (v. 2). That is, if they stand fast and hold fast to the traditions that they already know (v. 6), they will not be shaken up. The writer's use of the word "traditions," however, is not simply to give a summation to the first set of hortatory appeals on maintaining the church's foundational traditions. It also prepares the audience for a similar discussion in the next set of hortatory appeals (cf. 3:6). In this case, the writer is refuting enthusiastic agitation. In the next large unit, the issue will be irresponsible behavior.

2:16-17. Even with the summation given in v. 15, the writer has not ended his hortatory appeals to return to the foundational traditions. And indeed, as already noted, this appeal will continue. In vv. 16-17, the writer gives a wish-prayer that both indicates the roles that the Lord Jesus and God have played in the church's lives and makes two appeals to God on the basis of those roles: a request for comfort and a request for strength or firming up of the hearts or inner beings of the church. Because this wish-prayer resembles the one in 1 Thess 3:11-13, the writer implicitly continues to make his point about maintaining the foundational traditions.

Thus in vv. 13-17 the writer offers comfort to the believers even as he exhorts them not to veer away from the apostolic traditions. Reminders that God chose them set the church apart from those deluded by Satan (v. 9). At the same time, the writer notes that salvation and glorification are related to the ongoing process of sanctification and a belief in the truth (vv. 13-14). With these reminders in place, he can emphatically admonish the church "to stand firm and hold fast to the traditions" (v. 15) and close out the first set of exhortations with a word about the eternal comfort God gives (v. 16).

Altogether, the first set of exhortative appeals (vv. 1-17) includes three parts: (1) a statement of the problem (vv. 1-2); (2) a refutation of the delusion (vv. 3-12); and (3) a prayer collection that concludes the refutation and contrasts the fates of believers and unbelievers (vv. 13-17). The exhortations encourage the auditors to remain firm in the traditions already taught to them (a typical course in the hortatory tradition) and to avoid being shaken by traditions that do not accurately and comprehensively treat the reward of the righteous or the fate of those who refuse to believe.

---

49. E.g., F. W. Hughes, *Early Christian Rhetoric and 2 Thessalonians* (Sheffield: JSOT, 1989) 61.

50. Wanamaker, *The Epistles to the Thessalonians*, 266; Thurston, *Reading Colossians, Ephesians and 2 Thessalonians*, 183.

REFLECTIONS

The writer of 2 Thessalonians speaks not only of God's comforting hearts, but (by implication) of God's strengthening them as well (2:17) The heart in ancient times referred to the inner convictions of a person. This is the strength for which the writer prayed and one that is sorely needed in our times. Our world is constantly bombarded by an emphasis on the outward, external appearance often to the exclusion of the internals. Nannie Helen Burroughs once said that maybe we have failed our children because we (as parents) have "been too bothered about the externals—clothes or money," but our young people need the internals and the eternals.[51] Indeed, when we read of inner-city youth willing to kill each other for the status that accrues to a designer jacket or fancy gym shoes, we must wonder if we have failed our children. And when sports figures are produced, packaged, and paraded as role models for the young by Madison Avenue with little regard for the violent behavior they promote in private or public spheres, we again must wonder if we have failed our children.

The focus on externals, however, extends beyond fashion trends. Consider the drug crisis in the world. So often countries focus on the outside in a quest to end drug use. Sure, something must be done to prohibit the traffic of drugs into or within a country. And those who deal this death rightly deserve prosecution and punishment. But it is also true that detox and rehabilitation centers must be available for those who are ready to resist these enslavers of the spirit. Yet even if drugs were eliminated totally from the planet, unless we grapple with the deeper cultural fixation on instant gratification, another evil will rise to take the place of drugs.

Or look at the almost exclusive attention that we place on the external physical self. Whole industries have developed to strengthen the physical body, to give us powerful physiques, carved and chiseled to aesthetic (or perhaps simply sensual) perfection. To be sure, proper care should be given to that which has been placed in our trust as God's stewards. But is a good physique everything? No, the life within must also be nourished. It must be fed and sustained to give us direction and stability. Lucie Campbell's great hymn of the church, "Something Within" (1919), is still appropriate:

Something within that holds the reins.
Something within that banishes pain.
Something within I cannot explain.
All that I know—there's something within.

51. Nannie Helen Burroughs, "Unload Your Uncle Toms," in *Black Women in White America: A Documentary History*, ed. Gerda Lerner (New York: Pantheon, 1972) 552.

2 THESSALONIANS 3:1-15, HORTATORY APPEALS AGAINST IRRESPONSIBLE BEHAVIOR

OVERVIEW

The second set of exhortations easily divides into two parts: (1) an initial section cast in the language of prayer (3:1-5) and (2) a longer section commending behavior requisite to the writer's tradition (3:6-15). Both sections reveal a concern for the church's stability. Both also encourage the church to turn to practical pursuits in accordance with the writer's commands.

2 Thessalonians 3:1-5, Doing What Is Commanded

COMMENTARY

The use of the word "finally" signals here the beginning of the last large unit (cf. 1 Thess 4:1). The five verses may be divided into three sections: a command for prayer, vv. 1-2; statements of confidence and assurance about the church's constancy, vv. 3-4; and a wish-prayer, v. 5. In part, the verses prepare the audience for 3:6-15.[52] In part, they also continue the consolatory "prayer mode begun at 2:13."[53] And in part, they reiterate the theme of maintaining the foundational traditions through their allusions to 1 Thessalonians in form and diction.

3:1-2. The writer's prayer request is reminiscent of 1 Thess 5:25 ("Beloved, pray for us"), but details are given here of what the prayer should include. For a writer who has repeatedly written with parallels and doublets, a prayer request with two concerns is not unusual. One concern focuses on the word of the Lord, that it might "spread rapidly" or "run swiftly." While Paul often used athletic language to speak about his ministry (Rom 9:16; 1 Cor 9:24-27; Gal 2:2; 5:7; Phil 2:16), the emphasis here is on the running of the word. Thus most scholars see Ps 147:15 (LXX, "his word runs swiftly") as the background for this request, with the writer, in characteristic form, attributing the word to the Lord (Jesus) rather than to God.

The additional focus of the initial concern is that the word of the Lord might "be glorified everywhere" (v. 1). To demonstrate this additional focus the writer speaks of the glorification of the word among his church's members. Whether the writer here indicates the past or present glorification is debated, but the word's glorification likely means its acceptance. Thus, given the context of opposition, the writer seeks to change others through their acceptance of the word of the Lord.

The second concern of the prayer request is more directly related to the writer. He may be a towering figure in the eyes of the church, but continuing use of first-person plural pronouns ("we" and "us") and the prayer request for deliverance from opposition suggest that he is not a lone hero. Furthermore, he *and* his church stand in opposition to others ("for not all have faith," v. 2), a somber, but realistic, recognition of the old age's presence and of the division of sides squared off against each other in the writer's apocalyptic perspective.[54]

3:3-4. In this passage the writer's consolatory statements of assurance about the Lord and the audience are reminiscent of 1 Thessalonians. God's faithfulness (1 Thess 5:24) now becomes the faithfulness of the Lord (Jesus, v. 3). And a wish-prayer for "strength" (1 Thess 3:13), already mentioned in the wish-prayer of 2 Thess 2:17, now becomes a statement of assurance (v. 3).

These verses, moreover, anticipate the content and tone of vv. 6-15. The writer's assurance that the church is "doing" (ποιεῖτε *poieite*) and will "do" (ποιήσετε *poiēsete*) the things he commands (v. 4) anticipates v. 13, a reminder to the church not to "be weary in doing [καλοποιοῦντες *kalopoiountes*] what is right." Also, the writer's tone of thoughtful concern for the larger church's battles with "the evil one" (τοῦ πονηροῦ *tou ponērou*; perhaps Satan, see Matt 13:19, 39; 1 John 2:13-14) or simply with "evil"—along with the earlier acknowledgment of the writer's own battles with πονηροὶ ἄνθρωποι (*ponēroi anthrōpoi*, "evil persons")—likely tips off the audience to the same kind of concern for thoughtfulness as noted in the example of useful work (vv. 7-9) given in the subsequent section. If so, at least one of the problems of those who live in "idleness" (as translated in the NRSV, v. 6) or "disorderliness" (ἀτάκτως *ataktōs*) is that their work does not give aid or consideration to the larger church as it faces external difficulties. With the expression "in the Lord" (v. 4), moreover, the writer's tone of thoughtful consideration of others is no less one of authority. Later, when the writer issues commands (vv. 6, 12), he uses a similar

---

52. Menken, *2 Thessalonians*, 125, reads 3:1-5 as preparation for the injunctions of 3:6-12.
53. Thurston, *Reading Colossians, Ephesians and 2 Thessalonians*, 185.
54. Cf. Menken, *2 Thessalonians*, 127.

expression to show the force or authority of his command.

3:5. In form, the wish-prayer in this verse is similar to 1 Thess 3:11-13. And it should not go unnoticed that the plenitude of prayer forms in 1 Thessalonians and the request for the church to pray without ceasing (1 Thess 5:17) and to give thanks in everything (1 Thess 5:18) probably influenced the writer's scattering of multiple prayers throughout 2 Thessalonians, including the ones in 3:1-5. In all of these ways, then, the writer continues to emphasize to the church the need to hold on to the foundational traditions.

More specifically, the wish-prayer here reiterates a concern for the "hearts" or inner convictions of the church (v. 5; cf. 2:17). Anticipating the thoughtfulness requested in the next section, however, the focus of the concern for the church's "hearts" here is on the "love of God" and the "steadfastness of Christ." While the Greek behind "love of God" could mean either God's kind of love or a love for God, the former is preferred because the writer does not elsewhere speak of a love for God. If hearts are directed to the love of God or God's kind of love, the church will have to show the constant concern for each other that God has demonstrated in loving (2:13) and sharing good gifts with this church (2:16). Likewise, while the Greek behind "steadfastness of Christ" could mean either Christ's own steadfastness or a steadfastness toward Christ, the former is preferred both because modeling is a key concern for the writer in anticipation of 3:6-15, and the writer has just stated his confidence that the church will "go on doing the things" he commands (v. 4).

Altogether, 3:1-5 provides a summary of the prayer mode begun earlier and a foreshadowing of the concern with proper conduct of the subsequent section. Its verses, while brief, give the second set of exhortations both a tone of proper regard for others and one of authority.

REFLECTIONS

While the Greek words behind the "love of God" (3:5) are ambiguous, the writer's theme of mutuality is not. Even before he lifts himself up as a model of thoughtful concern for others in 3:6-15, he models mutuality through his request of prayer from others and his prayer for others. This mutuality rescues people from either a lone hero syndrome or a selfish pursuit syndrome, both of which wreak havoc on the world.

According to Bernard Brandon Scott, in the American context this "lone hero" type likely owes its origin to the early "settler" individuals who found themselves faced with the vastness of a supposedly open frontier and the freedom to shape it and mold it into submission.[55] Perhaps the myth is supported by Hollywood through its string of "Duke" (John Wayne) westerns and its urban "Dirty Harry" (Clint Eastwood) action films, which offer a variation on this theme.[56] Robert N. Bellah notes that this "mythic individualism" also can be traced to stories of flight from society, as in James Fennimore Cooper's *The Deerslayer* and Herman Melville's *Moby Dick,* and to detective stories about Sam Spade or Serpico.[57] Whatever its origin and force, it has camped in on the American psyche—among extremists who have given up on prevailing ideas of justice and who want to take matters into their own hands, for example.

The selfish pursuit type, however, is just as harmful and often more cunning. This type has not listened to Abraham Heschel's warnings against "arrogating to the self what is not its due."[58] Nor has this type heard Samuel Proctor's lament about preachers who take the selfish route in the name of good: "What a temptation it is for some preachers . . . to use . . . ameliorative, and even revolutionary, causes to promote

---

55. Bernard Brandon Scott, "Toward a Hermeneutics of the Solo Savior: Dirty Harry and Romans 5:1–8," in *Intersections: Post-Critical Studies in Preaching,* ed. Richard L. Eslinger (Grand Rapids: Eerdmans, 1994) 123-24.
56. Scott, "Toward a Hermeneutics of the Solo Savior," 124-56.
57. Robert N. Bellah et al., *Habits of the Heart: Individualism and Commitment in American Life* (Berkeley: University of California Press, 1985) 144-47.
58. Abraham J. Heschel, *God in Search of Man: A Philosophy of Judaism* (New York: Harper and Bros., 1966) 400.

themselves, to seize every photo opportunity, to manipulate the press, to elbow to the front of and center of every rostrum, to maneuver themselves into the focus of every television camera, and to leap to the front of every parade."[59]

For the writer of 2 Thessalonians, only mutuality and solidarity can provide the real sustenance for which these types unwittingly cry out. For the first type, the writer answers not with his own vengeance, but with the promotion of the truth as found in the word of the Lord. And for the second type, he responds with the challenge that our hearts, our inner convictions, need to be directed by a force that rises above our individual pursuits.

59. Samuel D. Proctor, *The Certain Sound of the Trumpet: Crafting a Sermon of Authority* (Valley Forge: Judson, 1994) 135.

2 Thessalonians 3:6-15, Doing What Is Responsible

COMMENTARY

With the content and tone set by 3:1-5, the writer now directs his words both to the entire church (or to a group untouched by the disorderly behavior, vv. 6-10, 13-15) and to the erring ones (vv. 11-12).[60] As well, members of the audience recalling 1 Thessalonians would perhaps recognize with A. Van Aarde that vv. 6-12 are "the portion [of 2 Thessalonians] that has been most evidently taken over from 1 Thessalonians."[61] The language of exhortation "in the Lord" (v. 6; 1 Thess 4:1); imitation (vv. 7, 9; 1 Thess 1:6); disorderliness (vv. 6-7, 11; 1 Thess 5:14); useful work to avoid being a burden (vv. 8-9; 1 Thess 2:7-9); and quiet living (3:12; 1 Thess 4:11) clearly has its counterpart in 1 Thessalonians. Thus this section reinforces the theme of the maintenance of tradition.

3:6-10. This initial set of verses gives a specific command (v. 6) and a specific example drawn from the writer's previous visit and ongoing life while he was with the church (3:7-10).[62] On the one hand, the writer does not wish the church to be influenced by the conduct of those who depart from the writer's tradition (v. 6). Identification of the conduct is debated, with the NRSV describing the irresponsible behavior as "living in idleness"

(ἀτάκτως *ataktōs*, v. 11). The basic idea of the behavior, however, is that of disorder.[63]

In using the word "tradition," moreover, the writer does not now mean something passed on to him from another, as Paul had used this word with respect to the transmitted truths about the resurrection (1 Cor 15:3) or the worship life (1 Cor 11:23). Rather, the tradition is "a specific practice of the apostles themselves."[64]

On the other hand, the writer lifts up his own visit as a model for the church (vv. 7-10). In the course of doing so, he also draws on a Semitic idiom and a proverb. To "eat someone's bread" was an idiom meaning "to earn a living" (cf. Gen 3:19; 2 Kgs 9:7).[65] The expression "anyone unwilling to work should not eat" is not found in any of Paul's undisputed letters, but it resonates with a proverb found in Gen 3:19.[66] It is likely that the Semitic idiom and proverb, like the writer's example, would have reinforced the idea that the writer wished to emphasize traditions, either his own past example or the traditional wisdom of his heritage.

3:11-12. With the play on words in the exhortation directed to the erring ones, the writer clarifies the contrast between "the disorderly ones" (*ataktoi*) and his own "model" behavior. The erring ones are not "[really] working" (ἐργαζομένους *ergazomenous*) but "working around" (περιεργαζομένους *peri-*

---

60. On the view that the addressees of the positive exhortations are not the entire church, see Jouette Bassler, "Peace in All Ways," 1:79. It is clear, moreover, from v. 11 that the erring ones are an undefined quantity ("some") within the larger church.
61. A. Van Aarde, "The Struggle Against Heresy in the Thessalonian Correspondence and the Origin of the Apostolic Tradition," in Collins, *The Thessalonian Correspondence*, 423.
62. As Wanamaker noted, the imperfect form of παρηγγέλλομεν (*parēngellomen*) should be translated as "we used to command" (3:10). See Wanamaker, *The Epistles to the Thessalonians*, 285.

63. Xenophon *Cyropaedia* 7.26; Thucydides *Histories* 3.108.
64. Gaventa, *First and Second Thessalonians*, 129.
65. Richard, *First and Second Thessalonians*, 380.
66. Richard, *First and Second Thessalonians*, 381.

ergazomenous, v. 11).⁶⁷ Furthermore, their activity stands in contrast to the action requested in 1 Thessalonians, a part of their traditions—namely, that of working quietly (1 Thess 4:11). What they do, in contrast to the model of the writer, does not aid the larger church, and thus they must be admonished "in the Lord Jesus Christ" (v. 12). The use of an antithesis between the model and anti-models typically aids the moral guide (and in this case, the writer) in clarifying approved behavior.

3:13-15. The contrast in place and clarified, the writer next turns again to the larger church to stress its maintenance of good behavior and discipline. With the request that they not become "weary in doing what is right" (v. 13), he draws to a close with language reminiscent of the way he began this set of exhortations (cf. v. 4). The closing verses of the exhortation (vv. 14-15), moreover, invest the larger church with both the authority and the parameters for reforming the erring ones. On the one hand, the larger church has the authority to shame the erring ones because of the latter's deviation from the writer's word as given in the letter (v. 14). On the other hand, the parameters of the reform are clearly prescribed: The larger church must not regard the erring ones as enemies, but (as in 1 Thess 5:14) they must "warn" or "admonish" (νουθετέω *noutheteō*) them as believers (v. 15; cf. v. 6).⁶⁸

The entire second set of exhortations, therefore, has the force of responding to the specific problem of irresponsible behavior based on deviation from the writer's traditions. The analyses of both sets of exhortations in 2:1–3:15 suggest, moreover, that the aim is to get the entire church not to turn back to its former family networks, but to trust that God will both vindicate their suffering and send God's avenging agent, Jesus, on their behalf.

---

67. Cf. Demosthenes *Orations* 26.15; 32.28.

68. On 3:14-15 as a "clarification of v. 6," see Wanamaker, *The Epistles to the Thessalonians*, 288.

REFLECTIONS

In his famous "I Have a Dream" speech (1963), Martin Luther King, Jr., asked his government to live up to its economic promises, which had by then defaulted for many of its citizens.⁶⁹ He challenged the United States to act on its commitments to all of its people, to allow its deeds to match its ideals.

The same concern to match one's words with one's deeds was a serious consideration in the first century CE. In that age charlatans—not sages—acted in ways that did not match their words or thoughts.⁷⁰ Accordingly, the writer of 2 Thessalonians addresses not only the correct convictions or words that his church should espouse, but the correct actions as well. Indeed, a thread that runs throughout the textual fabric of the second set of exhortations is an emphasis on doing the right thing.

Beyond the challenge for the church to match its deeds to its words, the writer challenges his readers not to "be weary in doing what is right" (3:13). Under the weight of opposition or because of the influence of false claims, even those who otherwise desire to do right could face fatigue if not disillusionment in their struggle. Even today susceptibility to burnout is a real possibility. Yet the writer's challenge for the people of God to continue doing what is right is clarion and clear. So when we see the homeless sleeping on the streets, let us not be weary in doing what is right. When persons who are HIV positive or living with AIDS or other diseases cry out for assistance and for a cure, let us not be weary in doing what is right. When our children need us to rescue them from the throes of drug addiction or drug dealing, let us not be weary in doing what is right.

---

69. Martha Solomon, "Covenanted Rights: The Metaphoric Matrix of 'I Have a Dream,'" in *Martin Luther King, Jr., and the Sermonic Power of Public Discourse*, ed. Carolyn Calloway-Thomas and John Louis Lucaites (Tuscaloosa: University of Alabama Press, 1993) 77.

70. On the philosophical topos of the consistency of words and deeds, see Seneca *Epistle* 52.8-9; Philo *Life of Moses* 2.209-16; Epictetus *Discourses* 1:29-56; Dio Chrysostom *Oration* 4.28-39; 72.1; Maximus of Tyre *Discourse* 1.

2 THESSALONIANS 3:16-18

THE PERORATION

COMMENTARY

Given the letter's objective of encouraging a harassed church, how does the final section (3:16-18) contribute to the goals of a peroration—namely, to summarize the content of a document and to stir the emotions?

Its summarizing nature is clear to both epistolary and rhetorical analysts. Epistolary analysts not only see the peace wish in 3:16 as the beginning of the letter's closing, but they also suggest thematic functions for the letter's closing.[71] That is, they note how the letter's closing thematically reiterates two of the letter's earlier themes: (1) "conflict with the idlers" (or what this commentary has called persons acting disorderly or irresponsibly) and (2) "concern over Christ's return." For Weima, the writer addresses the "tensions and divisions caused by the idlers" in the double reference to peace in the benediction (v. 16), in the letter's repeated use of the word "all" (cf. vv. 16, 18), and in the letter's "autograph greeting and explanatory comment," which highlights the letter's authority for the "idlers." In addition, Weima suggests that the letter addresses the "concern over Christ's return" through its repeated references to the "Lord" (i.e., Jesus) in the "peace benediction" and "word of encouragement."[72]

Rhetorical criticism reveals other important links between the closing and the rest of the letter. Thurston notes how the letter closes as it opened "with a wish for peace (1:2)."[73] Similarly, Menken notes the letter's overall inclusio formed by the grace and peace formulae in the prescript and in the postscript.[74] Both Thurston and Menken also point out the similarities between the letter closings of 1 and 2 Thessalonians, particularly the similar peace wishes in 2 Thess 3:16 and 1 Thess 5:23 and the similar grace benedictions in 2 Thess 3:18 and 1 Thess 5:28.[75]

It should be stated as well that these last verses reiterate the themes noted in the exordium in at least three ways. First, the peroration's use of 1 Thessalonians reinforces both the theme about belief in the writer's gospel or testimony and the theme of standing firm. Second, the letter's pastoral insistence on restoration or reformation of the erring believers through an emphasis on "all" of the church implies the church's stability. That is, Paul's bare "The grace of our Lord Jesus Christ be with you" (1 Thess 5:28) is reinforced in 2 Thessalonians. In 2 Thessalonians, the writer has both "The Lord be with all of you" (3:16) and "The grace of our Lord Jesus Christ be with all of you" (3:18). He does not want anyone to be left out, and thus he envisions that all will remain stable. Third, the insistence that the Lord of peace would give peace "at all times and in all ways" (v. 16) represents the defiance with which the letter has characterized the continuous justice of God. We must be careful here, however, not to miss the import of the peace the writer emphasizes through redundancy. As Jouette Bassler has noted, "The fundamental meaning of peace in the Greek tradition is precisely this notion of a state of rest following war, strife, or tribulation [θλῖψις *thlipsis*]."[76] Accordingly, this is the kind of peace brought by Augustus to the Roman government when he ended its civil wars. The writer here, however, does not speak of the peace of someone whose rule would pass on to another by death or other vicissitudes of life. This Lord has already been dramatized as a powerful avenging agent for God (throughout

---

71. Weima, *Neglected Endings*, 187-201.
72. Weima, *Neglected Endings*, 189-90.
73. Thurston, *Reading Colossians, Ephesians and 2 Thessalonians*, 194.
74. Menken, *2 Thessalonians*, 54.
75. Menken, *2 Thessalonians*, 143. Thurston, *Reading Colossians, Ephesians and 2 Thessalonians*, 196.
76. Jouette Bassler, "Peace in All Ways," 1:77. Cf. Plutarch *Advice on Public Life* 824D.

chaps. 1 and 2). Thus this Lord of peace can bring peace in all ways and at all times (cf. Rom 16:20; 2 Cor 13:11; Phil 4:9; 1 Thess 5:23).

Beyond its summarizing character, this peroration also would likely stir the emotions of the church. Certainly, as in the case of 1 Thessalonians, the prayer form that opens the peroration (v. 16; cf. 1 Thess 5:23) would give the letter closing an emotional charge. The repetition of peace in v. 16 also would stir the emotions of a church for whom hostilities had been a constant threat. Given that Jesus as Lord has been placed in the role of an avenger, the writer is likely suggesting that the peace that the believers have, and which they have always, comes from one who is actually able to give permanent peace because of the great power associated with his role as God's agent of vindication for believers. Furthermore, because the wish-prayer speaks of peace in all times and "in every way" (v. 16), the church could find assurance that they would not have to face the multiple and mounting threats alone.[77]

Given the summarizing and stirring character of this peroration, what should we make of the authentication remarks in v. 17? Some scholars suggest that these formulae are simply used to respond to an epistolary situation in which "the disorderly ones" need to be corrected with authority. Others see the letter's remarks on its authentication as an indication that Paul actually did not write this letter. Paul's letters often included his closing words in his own handwriting (as opposed to that of an amanuensis, 1 Cor 16:21; Gal 6:11) "but never in order to authenticate his letter and distinguish it from forgeries."[78] Some scholars have noted that the wording "every letter" is odd and presupposes the presence of a collection that one would not have if 2 Thessalonians is *Paul's* own imitation of 1 Thessalonians, his *first* letter. Some scholars have also noted the closing's lack of a typical Pauline personal tone, and instead, the closing's greater concern "to authenticate its message rather than to produce the style and content of Paul's greetings."[79] In my estimation, however, even the authentication remarks could help a beleaguered church needing to make sure that the beliefs and behavior it has endorsed are appropriate as it awaits its Lord's revelation.

---

77. For the arguments supporting the variant "in every way" rather than "in every place," see Thurston, *Reading Colossians, Ephesians and 2 Thessalonians*, 194.

78. Krodel, *The Deutero-Pauline Letters*, 56.
79. Thurston, *Reading Colossians, Ephesians and 2 Thessalonians*, 196.

REFLECTIONS

Peace in all ways and at all times! This is a daring thought, an almost audacious assumption about hitherto unexperienced dimensions of life. It is a frontal assault on nihilism, a movement of optimism made with a cosmic consciousness, as if one could summarize all of life in one sweeping statement for all of time and eternity.

Yet this is a statement the writer needed to make for a church that was a part of the Roman Empire. The Romans prided themselves on their "peace," the end of Rome's own civil strife and protection from all of its enemies. The writer's description of Jesus as the Lord of peace is an attempt to indicate his great power. Like the Romans, Jesus has incredible power—the power to vindicate believers and destroy evil. The difference between the Lord of peace and the great figures of the Roman Empire, however, is that the writer's Lord brings thorough or absolute peace: "Peace in all ways and at all times."

What a defiant logic! Yet it is the kind of profound thought that echoes throughout the writings of the early Christians. In his Lyman Beecher Lectures, Gardner Taylor gives an almost poetic description of this defiance:

> They [the early Christian preachers] had nothing but a word-of-mouth report, and what an incredibly wild word it was. The bearers were not too impressive in their own persons....

What is more astonishing these men and women bore the most amazing tale ever spread.... How dare they to face the Empire! What foolishness and madness!" But Taylor adds, "And then, incredibly enough, the Empire bent its knee and called the name of Jesus as Lord and Saviour."[80]

Thank God even today for this kind of peace! No condition escapes its compass, and no period evades its parameters. The peace is always available. This is an inviolate, irrevocable peace, not a partial or removable peace, strained by tensions with others or dismissed by new rulers who take over kingdoms. It knows no end. It furnishes freedom from anxiety eternally. Steady are its benefits, and confident are its claims. It is the great confidence of the church. And it says to us that there is not a millennium into which we can march or a new era into which we can advance when God is absent and the promises of God null and void. It was a word of hope for all those who despaired in this writer's day. And it can rekindle that hope in hearts today as well.

80. Gardner Taylor, *How Shall They Preach* (Elgin, Ill.: Progressive Baptist Publishing House, 1977) 47-50.

THE FIRST AND SECOND LETTERS TO TIMOTHY AND THE LETTER TO TITUS

INTRODUCTION, COMMENTARY, AND REFLECTIONS
BY
JAMES D. G. DUNN

THE FIRST AND SECOND LETTERS TO TIMOTHY AND THE LETTER TO TITUS

INTRODUCTION

The Pastoral Epistles—1 and 2 Timothy and Titus—are among the most valued of New Testament writings. Yet the Pastorals are among the most discredited of NT writings. Why this paradox?

On the one hand, the Pastorals have been valued for a number of important reasons. They helped to establish the classic pattern of ministry and church structure (bishop, presybter, deacon), which was crucial in the triumph of the early Catholic Church over severe challenges from Marcionites and Gnosticism, and which has enabled the church to endure for nearly two millennia.[1] They helped to establish a pattern of "the truth," "the faith," and "sound teaching" as the yardstick and bulwark by which to judge and ward off false teaching and heresy.[2] And, less immediately obvious, they helped to secure the place of Paul within the NT canon; the more controversial aspects of his theology (e.g., seeming criticism of Peter in Galatians and a church order without bishops and elders in 1 Corinthians) were made more acceptable by the portrayal of Paul as founder of the tradition, ecclesiastical and dogmatic, by which the church lived and ordered its life. Recognition of this character of the letters lies behind their designation as "the Pastoral Epistles," common since the eighteenth century.[3]

On the other hand, the Pastorals have been widely disparaged for more than a century and a half. This is primarily because a majority consensus of scholarship has been convinced since then that the Pastorals were not written by Paul but by a later hand. Despite the same consensus that pseudonymity (false claim to authorship) was quite acceptable in those days, it has been difficult to escape the more negative modern judgment on pseudonymous writings: Can writings be so fully valued that misrepresent their hero so seriously? Bound up with this has been the particularly Protestant suspicion that the radicalism of the authentic Paul (the Paul of the

---

1. According to the Muratorian Fragment (traditionally dated to about 200 CE), the letters were held "in honor in the catholic church for the ordering of ecclesiastical discipline" (18-20).
2. As its preface indicates, with its explicit reference to 1 Tim 1:4, Irenaeus wrote his great work, *Against Heresies* (late 2nd cent. CE), in the spirit of the Pastorals.
3. See P. N. Harrison, *The Problem of the Pastoral Epistles* (London: Oxford University Press, 1921) 13-16.

undisputed Pauline letters)[4] has been compromised and blunted by the ecclesiastical orthodoxy of the Pastoral Epistles.

In the face of such a polarization of respected opinion, what is the modern reader of these letters to make of them? Before turning to the letters themselves, a number of issues need some clarification.

A SINGLE GROUP OR SEPARATE LETTERS?

The fashion has been to treat the three letters together, to talk of the theology or ecclesiology of the Pastorals, rather than of each letter separately. This can be misleading, since 2 Timothy has a significantly different scope. Most notably, the concerns for good order in church, household, and state that are such a feature of the other two letters are quite absent in 2 Timothy. Indeed, were it not for the other two, the personal character of 2 Timothy might have been sufficient within scholarly discussion to secure the authenticity of 2 Timothy on its own.[5] Tied in to this is the question of the order of the letters. In recent discussion, for example, Luke Johnson has placed 2 Timothy first.[6] On the other hand, Jerome Quinn tackled Titus first, its longer preface being treated as a preface to the whole three-letter corpus.[7] And both Gordon Fee and George Knight follow the order 1 Timothy, Titus, 2 Timothy.[8] The traditional order (1 Timothy, 2 Timothy, Titus), it should be remembered, was determined largely by length; the corpus of Pauline letters in the NT canon was laid out in decreasing length, and of the three 1 Timothy was the longest and Titus the shortest.

Overall, however, it does seem sensible to treat the three letters together. They are certainly closer to one another than they are to any other NT writings, including the undisputed letters of Paul. They share the same broad characteristic: Paul's counsel to two of his most important aides and coworkers. Indeed, 1 Timothy and Titus stand closely together. We need only compare 1 Tim 3:1-13 with Titus 1:5-9 (church officers), 1 Tim 5:1–6:2 with Titus 2:1-15 (good household management), and 1 Tim 2:1-2 with Titus 3:1-2 (civic authorities). But if 1 and 2 Timothy were written to the same person or situation we would not expect them to cover the same ground. More to the point is the similarity between the two letters to Timothy in terms of personal recollection (cf. 1 Tim 1:12-16 with 2 Tim 1:8-15; 1 Tim 1:20 with 2 Tim 2:17-18), personal commission (cf. 1 Tim 1:18 and 6:13 with 2 Tim 4:1; 1 Tim 4:14 with 2 Tim 1:6), and warnings against false teaching (cf. 1 Tim 1:3-7 and 4:1-3 with 2 Tim 3:1-5 and 4:1-4; 1 Tim 6:4, 20 with 2 Tim 2:14, 16, 23). And overall we find in all three letters the same high regard, as indicated by vocabulary and attitude, for "the faith"[9] and for piety/godliness,[10] and the same dismissive disparagement of alternatives.[11]

In view of the degree of cohesion between the letters, it does continue to make sense to treat them as a loose unit, sufficiently distinct as such within the NT canon. To attempt a closer analysis of their inter-relationship is unnecessary for this commentary. It is simplest, therefore, to treat them in their historic and canonical order. By analyzing each one in turn, however, we should be able to gain a clear enough sense of the emphases of each as well as of the whole.

---

4. The undisputed Pauline letters are generally reckoned to be Romans, 1–2 Corinthians, Galatians, Philippians, 1 Thessalonians, and Philemon. Many would also include 2 Thessalonians and Colossians. Not many would add Ephesians.

5. See particularly M. Prior, *Paul the Letter-Writer and the Second Letter to Timothy,* JSNTSup 23 (Sheffield: JSOT, 1989). J. Murphy-O'Connor, "2 Timothy Contrasted with 1 Timothy and Titus," *Revue Biblique* 98 (1991) 403-18, discusses over thirty points on which 1 Timothy and Titus agree against 2 Timothy and vice versa, but overstates the disagreements.

6. L. T. Johnson, *Letters to Paul's Delegates: 1 Timothy, 2 Timothy, Titus,* The New Testament in Context (Valley Forge: Trinity Press International, 1996).

7. J. D. Quinn, *The Letter to Titus,* AB 35 (New York: Doubleday, 1990) 190-200. Titus seems to have been placed first of the three in the Muratonian Fragment—"To Titus one and to Timothy two" (17).

8. G. D. Fee, *1 and 2 Timothy, Titus,* New International Bible Commentary (Peabody, Mass.: Hendrickson, 1984; rev. ed. 1988); G. W. Knight, *The Pastoral Epistles: A Commentary on the Greek Text,* NIGTC (Grand Rapids: Eerdmans, 1992).

9. "The faith"—1 Tim 1:19; 3:9, 13; 4:1, 6; 5:8; 6:10-12, 21; 2 Tim 1:13; 3:8; 4:7; Titus 1:1, 4, 13; 3:15. "Sound teaching/words"—1 Tim 1:10; 6:3; 2 Tim 1:13; 4:3; Titus 1:9; 2:1-2, 8. "Faithful saying"—1 Tim 1:15; 3:1; 4:9; 2 Tim 2:11; Titus 3:8. "The truth"—1 Tim 3:15; 4:3; 2 Tim 2:15, 18; 3:8; 4:4; Titus 1:14. "Knowledge of truth"—1 Tim 2:4; 2 Tim 3:7; Titus 1:1.

10. "Piety/godliness"—1 Tim 2:2; 3:16; 4:7-8; 5:4 (verb); 6:3, 5-6, 11; 2 Tim 3:5, 12 (adverb); Titus 1:1; 2:12 (adverb). "Good works/deeds"—1 Tim 2:10; 3:1; 5:10 (twice), 25; 6:18; 2 Tim 2:21; 3:17; Titus 1:16; 2:7, 14; 3:1, 8, 14.

11. 1 Tim 1:3-6; 4:1-3, 7; 6:3-5, 20; 2 Tim 2:16-17, 23; 3:15; 4:3-4; Titus 1:10, 15-16; 3:3, 9. "Myths"—1 Tim 1:4; 4:7; 2 Tim 4:4; Titus 1:14. "Empty/vain talk"—1 Tim 1:6; 6:20; 2 Tim 2:16; Titus 1:10.

Since few people will read the complete corpus of three letters at a sitting, it is more important that we focus attention on the internal coherence and thrust of each section within the letters.

AUTHORSHIP

Given, then, that the Pastoral Epistles form a relatively closely knit group, we may assume that they were written by the same person. But who? The obvious answer, of course, is Paul the apostle, the author of the other ten letters that bear his name. After all, each of the three letters explicitly claims to be from Paul. But for most of the last 150 years the majority of NT specialists have been more impressed by the differences between the Pastorals and the undisputed letters. So what is the answer?

For the last 150 years or so the debate on authorship of the Pastorals has been rehearsed over and over again. Those who want to pursue it in detail can easily do so by consulting any of the commentaries listed in the Bibliography (see especially the introductory paragraph there for the split in opinion between current commentaries). Here it will be sufficient to indicate the scope of the debate in broad terms, if only to alert readers to the features and factors that give the debate continued vitality. This seems to be the wiser course, since it is all too easy for this question to become the dominant one and for the value of the letters to be obscured by what in the end are questions of secondary importance.

The main features of the letters that continue to persuade the majority of specialists that they were not written by Paul are as follows:

(1) First is the distinctive vocabulary and style of the Pastorals. The most striking feature is the much higher proportion of *hapax legomena* (words occuring only once or only in the Pastorals) than in the other Paulines (between twice and four times as many as any other Pauline letter).[12] Style, of course, has an intangible quality, but it also leaves fingerprints in, for example, the choice of words, the use of conjunctions, and the structure of sentences; and in contrast to the typical liveliness of the earlier Pauline letters, the Pastorals seem consistently more prosaic.[13] These differences cannot be adequately explained by different subjects or different moods. The writer seems to be drawing from a different vocabulary pool, the writing to be of a different character. The perspective, in other words, seems to be at one remove from Paul, or one generation after Paul.

(2) The degree to which "faith" has been formalized into "the faith" (see footnote 9). The mood of the Pastorals is much less that of preaching faith than of preserving the faith, not so much of evangelism as of containment. In particular, it is notable that the most characteristic notes of Paul's gospel and theology appear in "faithful sayings" and formulae to be preserved (1 Tim 1:15; 2 Tim 1:9; 2:11-13; Titus 3:4-7). Clearly evident is the sense of a faith that was initially formulated by Paul and that has now to be passed on to future generations (esp. 2 Tim 1:12-14; 2:1-2).

(3) The threats to the gospel seem likewise to be different. Whereas the challenge from Christian Jews (usually designated "Judaizers") runs through the earlier Pauline correspondence (Romans 2–4; 2 Cor 2:14–4:6; 10–13; Galatians; Phil 3:2-11), all we hear in the Pastorals are at best echoes of that earlier dispute (1 Tim 1:7; Titus 1:10, 14). Notable again is the fact that the "faithful sayings" and formulae just mentioned lack the polemical thrust against Jewish Christians so characteristic of the earlier Paul. So, too, the degree of precision with which Paul aimed his counterthrusts, whether in matters of theology or those of praxis, enables the reader to gain a quite clear picture of the positions to which Paul objected. But in the Pastorals there is no such precision, and the dismissive fulminations generate much more heat than light.

(4) The degree of church structure seems more developed than anything in the earlier Paul. A distinctive office of "overseer (bishop)" has emerged (1 Tim 3:1; Titus 1:7), as also that of

---

12. See Harrison, *The Problem of the Pastoral Epistles*, 20-38. Despite qualifications, the basic contrast stands; see, e.g., J. N. D. Kelly, *The Pastoral Epistles*, Black's New Testament Commentaries (London: A. & C. Black, 1963), 22-24.

13. Quinn, *The Letter to Titus*, 6, states that the "PE read in a calm, slow, colorless, monotonous fashion. Their tone is sententious, stern, didactic, sober, stiff, domesticated." Quinn is in danger of overstatement, but not by much.

"deacon (minister)" (1 Tim 3:8). These titles were already in use in Phil 1:1, but the concept of a formal office is more in evidence. Likewise, the office of "elder" appears in the Pauline corpus for the first time (1 Tim 5:17; Titus 1:5). It looks as though on this point the Pastorals share the hindsight perspective evident also in Luke's account of Paul's mission (Acts 14:23; 20:17), of which there is no trace in the earlier Pauline letters.[14] It may also be significant, then, that the only use of the term "charism," so central to Paul's concept of the body of Christ (Rom 12:6-8; 1 Corinthians 12), is limited to talk of Timothy's charism given through the laying on of hands in the past (1 Tim 4:14; 2 Tim 1:6).

(5) Finally, what might be described as a greater accommodation with the norms and structures of contemporary society should be mentioned. It is not simply the readiness to accept the political structures of the day (1 Tim 2:1-2; Titus 3:1); that was already true in Rom 13:1-7. It is, rather, the degree to which the contemporary ideal of good household order has become also a norm for the writer of 1 Timothy and Titus (1 Timothy 5; Titus 2) and, indeed, a norm for the good order of the church (1 Tim 2:11-15; 3:4-5, 12, 15; 5:14). This accommodation is evident also in the fact that virtues like "dignity, seriousness, respectfulness"[15] and "prudence, moderation"[16] are so strongly commended, not least because of the respect they commanded within the wider society.

These features have to be weighed alongside (or against) two others in particular. One has already been mentioned: the fact that all three letters explicitly claim to have been written by Paul (1 Tim 1:1; 2 Tim 1:1; Titus 1:1). Against the view that they were pseudonymous, and known to be so, is the universal acceptance of them from the earliest attributions as written by Paul himself (from at least 200 CE). The other is the strikingly personal character of several passages within the letters, particularly 2 Tim 4:6-21 and Titus 3:12-13. It is difficult to conceive of a later writer's having composed such passages except as an attempt to deceive his readers.

The issue of pseudonymity is a difficult one for us to grasp at this distance, especially when the importance of copyright and the wrongs of plagiarism have become such fundamental features of modern literary culture. Suffice it to say that the principles were not at all so clearly grasped or the conventions so firmly drawn in those days. Of particular importance here is the fact that, particularly within the Jewish literary tradition, there seem to have been other conventions that rather cut across the issue. One was the attribution of writings to heroes from the past; most readers will have at least heard of the cycle of writings attributed to Enoch (Gen 5:24).[17]

More to the point here is what we might call the concept of "living tradition." That is, within Israel's history we can readily discern several different streams of tradition, each originating with an authoritative earlier figure, but elaborated and extended within the immediate circle of that figure's disciples and retained under the name of the originator of the tradition. The Pentateuch is generally recognized to have reached its final form in this way, and the present book of Isaiah to be the work of two or three generations. Just as David was remembered as the originator of a still-growing collection of psalms,[18] so also to Solomon was attributed a sequence of wisdom writings (most notably Proverbs and Ecclesiastes). A close comparison of the Gospels, even of the Synoptic Gospels alone, indicates that there was a basically similar elaboration and extension of the Jesus tradition within the Gospel format. John 21:24 attests to the activity of a circle around the Fourth Evangelist, who had at least some hand in the final form of John's Gospel. The Pastorals can be readily seen in similar terms. The point is that this practice was familiar and that attribution of the extended literary form to the originator of the form would not have been regarded as unacceptable or deceptive.[19]

---

14. 1 Cor 16:15-18 and 1 Thess 5:12-13 seem to be calls to respect for those who have displayed leadership initiative rather than for those already appointed to recognized posts ("elders").
15. Six of the seven occurrences of σεμνός, σεμνότης (*semnos, semnotēs*) are in the Pastorals (1 Tim 2:2; 3:4, 8, 11; Titus 2:2, 7; otherwise only Phil 4:8).
16. Four of the six forms of the word σώφρων (*sōphron*) are found only in the Pastorals—1 Tim 2:9, 15; 3:2; 2 Tim 1:7; Titus 1:8; 2:2, 4-6, 12.
17. The document usually known as *1 Enoch* is itself a compilation of five books.
18. Several more psalms attributed to David are found in the Qumran Psalms Scroll.
19. A fuller discussion can be found in J. D. G. Dunn, "Pseudepigraphy," in *Dictionary of the Later New Testament and Its Developments*, ed. R. P. Martin and P. H. Davids (Downers Grove, Ill.: InterVarsity, 1997) 997-1084, which draws particularly on D. Meade, *Pseudonymity and Canon* (Tübingen: Mohr, 1986). For an alternative view see E. E. Ellis, "Pseudonymity and Canonicity of New Testament Documents," in M. J. Wilkins and T. Paige, eds., *Worship, Theology and Ministry in the Early Church*, ed. M. J. Wilkins and T. Paige, JSNTSup 87 (Sheffield: JSOT, 1992) 212-24.

There is a corollary to this that is often neglected but should certainly be given some attention. If pseudonymous practice of this or some similar sort was accepted at the time of the writing of the Pastorals (so that the issue of pseudonymity loses its ethical dimension), then it follows that the pseudonymous writing would be attributed to the originator only if it was deemed to be an appropriate elaboration or extension of the original.[20] That is to say, the very factors of style and content that have moved modern scholars to deny Pauline authorship to the Pastorals would *not* have been deemed sufficient by the first readers to deny the letters to Paul. The Pastorals would have been deemed authentically Pauline; therefore, their attribution to Paul would have caused no problem. Already, in this early judgment, the canonical definition of what was and what was not "Pauline" was being determined.

If the problem of pseudonymity may thus be defused, what about the other feature that counts so strongly for Pauline authorship: the personal notes? There are probably only two choices here. Either they carry with them the whole sweep of the Pastorals, despite their differences from the earlier Paulines, in which case we have to envision Paul writing later in his career, his style changed by experiences later in a ministry extended beyond the limit suggested by Acts.[21] Or these personal notes were, in fact, brief notes, most of them dispatched or even smuggled from Paul's last imprisonment, treasured by the churches that received them, and used as a basis for the Pauline elaborations that are the Pastorals.[22]

Whatever the current answer, it is important not to let the issue of authorship weigh too heavily in one's appreciation of and response to the Pastorals.[23] On the one hand, if they were written by Paul himself, then we have to speak of a "late Paul" and of the earlier undisputed letters as bearing witness to the "early Paul." Recognition of Pauline authorship must not allow us either to blur the different and distinctive perspective we find in the Pastorals or to homogenize a thirteen-letter Paul. On the other hand, if they were written during some period subsequent to Paul's death, that should not allow us to justify their being devalued and treated as sub-Pauline.[24] They are *also* Pauline and show how the Pauline churches perceived and evaluated their great founding apostle and the heritage he left with them. Either way, they are invaluable evidence of how Christianity and Christian theology faced the challenges of the second generation and/or post-Pauline period.

DATE AND RECIPIENTS

These considerations permit a much briefer resolution of other introductory questions. If the Pastorals were written late in Paul's life (cf. 2 Tim 4:16-18), then we have to envisage that Paul had been freed from his (first) imprisonment in Rome (Acts 28), and that he had deemed it more important to return to the Aegean than to pursue his earlier plans to go to Spain (Rom 15:23-24, 28).[25] This would explain such references as 1 Tim 1:3 and Titus 1:5 and allow us to date the letters in the mid-60s. If, however, the letters are pseudonymous, then a date sometime between the deaths of Paul (early 60s) and of Ignatius (c. 110s) seems appropriate. This is principally because the more developed ecclesiology of the Pastorals seems to be in the process of formation (see Commentary on 1 Tim 5:17 and Titus 1:7) and still some way from the monoepiscopacy that Ignatius promotes but also was able to assume.[26] Nor has the false teaching attacked in the Pastorals such clear shape as that attacked in the 110s by Ignatius (see below). Some have

---

20. Tertullian *Concerning Baptism* 17 reports that the reason why the *Acts of Paul* were not accepted as Pauline is that they attributed to the woman Thecla an authority (in teaching and baptizing) that ran counter to 1 Cor 14:34-35.

21. The differences cannot adequately be explained by the use of different secretaries; the differences of emphasis and ethos are so integral to the letters that they have to be attributed to the author of the letters.

22. See Harrison, *The Problem of the Pastoral Epistles*, 115-35. The newest variation is that of J. D. Miller, *The Pastoral Letters as Composite Documents*, SNTSMS 93 (Cambridge: Cambridge University Press, 1997). In contrast, L. R. Donelson, *Pseudepigraphy and Ethical Argument in the Pastoral Epistles* (Tübingen: J. C. B. Mohr [Siebeck], 1986) 54-65, sees the personal notes as evidence of current pseudepigraphical practice.

23. As is the case, e.g., with Kelly, *Pastoral Epistles*, and Johnson, *Letters to Paul's Delegates*.

24. Quinn, *The Letter to Titus*, 6, states that the "PE read in a calm, slow, colorless, monotonous fashion. Their tone is sententious, stern, didactic, sober, stiff, domesticated." Quinn is in danger of overstatement, but not by much.

25. According to Eusebius *Church History* 2.22, "Tradition has it that after defending himself the apostle [Paul] was again sent on the ministry of preaching, and coming a second time to the same city, suffered martyrdom under Nero."

26. Particularly Ignatius *Smyrneans* 8.

argued for a still later date, but the later the exercise the less likely that a pseudonymous writing would have been accepted as still genuinely Pauline. Most elect for a date in the late 80s or 90s of the first century. The possible points of contact with Acts, which have suggested to some that Luke was the author,[27] also point to the latter years of the first century.

If the letters were written by Paul, then the recipients were those specified—Timothy and Titus (see Commentary on 1 Tim 1:2 and Titus 1:4)—each serving as an apostolic delegate, Timothy in Ephesus (1 Tim 1:3) and Titus in Crete (Titus 1:5). If, on the other hand, the letters are post-Pauline, the naming of the recipients as Timothy and Titus may indicate either that they were indeed the recipients or that they were the inspiration behind the letters (What would Paul want to say to us were he still alive?),[28] or simply that the letters were from the close circle of Paul's coworkers or immediate successors. Either way, Timothy and Titus are clearly envisaged as Paul's representatives, functioning in a unique role between church founder and local leadership. At the same time, we should not confuse the letters' personal address with their function. Whatever their origin, they were not intended for the eyes and ears of Timothy and Titus alone. The plural form of the final "you" in each case indicates that these letters were intended to be read to the church as a whole and, therefore, to function as manuals of discipline for the benefit of whole congregations. As such, their value in effect bypasses the question of the historical status of Timothy and Titus, just as it outlasts the death of Paul.

WHO WERE THE FALSE TEACHERS?

The other great debate concerns the opponents regularly castigated in the letters. It is difficult, however, to gain a firm handle on them, and the general assumption that they formed a single front should certainly be put under question. Most of the attack on false teaching is, as already indicated, vague and imprecise, often using conventional vilification of opponents, real or imagined.[29] There are only a few clear indications of concrete issues: 1 Tim 4:3, they forbid marriage and advocate abstinence from certain foods; 2 Tim 2:18, they claim that "the resurrection has already happened." These references, taken with the allusion to "knowledge [γνῶσις *gnōsis*] falsely so called" (1 Tim 6:20), could certainly be taken to imply an early form of Gnosticism, since all three features are present in the Gnostic systems of the later second century.

On the other hand, the references to those "desiring to be teachers of the law" (1 Tim 1:7) and to "those of the circumcision" (Titus 1:10) point to a Jewish dimension—that is, not just to Jewish elements in some syncretistic mix, but to people who prized a Jewish identity (see Commentary on Titus 1:10) and valued the principal Jewish identity marker (the law). The repeated references to "myths" (1 Tim 1:4; 4:7; 2 Tim 4:4; Titus 1:14) and to "genealogies" (1 Tim 1:4; Titus 3:9) in themselves could point in several directions, but the reference to "Jewish myths" (Titus 1:14) and the association of "genealogies" with "fights over the law" (Titus 3:9) again indicate an opposition more likely to be rooted in the local synagogues than anywhere else. The attempt to combine both sets of features into something like "Judaizing Gnosticism" (as many suggest)[30] is not very helpful, since "Judaizing" means "living as a Jew," and no gnostic system that we know of taught the need to Judaize.

As with other letters (notably 1 Corinthians), the older assumption that the threats addressed could be categorized simply in terms of religious or theological systems has been heavily qualified in more recent discussions. Social and financial pressures were obviously also a factor, particularly in 1 Timothy (1 Tim 2:9; 3:3, 8; 5:8, 17-19; 6:5-10, 17-19),[31] and the role of women in certain aspects of community life obviously worried the writer (1 Tim 2:9-15; 5:3-16).[32] In reading such passages we should recall how little we know of the situations envisaged and how

---

27. See particularly S. G. Wilson, *Luke and the Pastoral Epistles* (London: SPCK, 1979).
28. See particularly R. Bauckham, "Pseudo-Apostolic Letters," *JBL* 107 (1988) 469-94.
29. Documentation is provided by R. J. Karris, "The Background and Significance of the Polemic in the Pastoral Epistles," *JBL* 92 (1973) 549-64; A. J. Malherbe, "Medical Imagery in the Pastoral Epistles," *Paul and the Popular Philosophers* (Minneapolis: Fortress, 1989) 121-36.
30. The most recent variation is M. Goulder, "The Pastor's Wolves: Jewish Christian Visionaries Behind the Pastoral Epistles," *NovT* 38 (1996) 242-56.
31. See R. M. Kidd, *Wealth and Beneficence in the Pastoral Epistles: A "Bourgeois" Form of Early Christianity?* SBLDS 122 (Atlanta: Scholars Press, 1990).
32. See, e.g., A. Padgett, "Wealthy Women at Ephesus: 1 Timothy 2:8-15 in Social Context," *Int.* 41 (1987) 19-31.

much more complex they no doubt were than we can now appreciate. Straightforward transposition to contemporary situations of advice given in the Pastorals will rarely be wise.

THE THEOLOGY OF THE PASTORALS

The value of the Pastorals is reflected on at each stage throughout the following pages. Here we need simply to draw attention to the principal features.

(1) One is the strongly re-emphasized Jewish heritage. It is particularly clear in the insistence on affirming one of Israel's principal foundation pillars: the oneness of God (1 Tim 1:17; 2:5; 6:15-16). Other important features include the use of Israel's own self-identity: "the household of God, which is the church of the living God" (1 Tim 3:15 NRSV); "a people of his own" (Titus 2:14).[33] This is all the more important given that some opposition seems to have come from the synagogue. Here, in other words, we see not only early Christianity continuing to affirm its continuity and identity with its Jewish heritage, but also the importance to Pauline Christianity of that continuity and identity as integral to Christianity's own self-definition. It will be no accident that part of the same theology is the affirmation that God desires to save everyone (1 Tim 2:4, 6).

(2) The centrality of the christology and of "salvation" as the preeminent goal[34] is also clear, as the faithful sayings and creedal or hymnic formulae confirm (1 Tim 1:15; 2:4-6, 15; 3:16; 2 Tim 1:9-10; 2:11-13; Titus 3:4-7). The fact that God and Christ can equally be described as "Savior" (see Commentary on 1 Tim 1:1) is not an indication of confusion but of a recognition that Christ functions for God and that God has acted through Christ. The most careful formulations of the relationship between God and Christ are given in 1 Tim 2:4-6 and Titus 2:13-14, which should hardly be played off against each other. That salvation is a process working out between the two appearings of Christ[35] is a strong reaffirmation of a characteristically Pauline emphasis. Even if expressed primarily in traditional formulae, this gospel is still a matter of living faith[36] and may, indeed, have been freshly reformulated to present Christ as a more effective claimant to the title "Savior" than any emperor or other god.[37]

(3) The importance of faith clearly formulated and of the church well ordered has already been noted. Notable here is the affirmation of good household order as the model or criterion for good church order[38] and the concern for a proper respectability, or better, respect-worthiness as a measure of Christian conduct. One need not speculate about any influence of delay of parousia (of which there is no overt indication) to see in the Pastorals more helpful guidelines for churches confronted by a suspicious and dominant non-Christian society than in some of the earlier Paulines.

(4) Notable in this connection is the way in which theology and ethics are thoroughly integrated in the Pastorals—evident, not least, in the flow of argument in several passages (e.g., 1 Tim 2:1-6; 4:3-5; Titus 2:1-15; 3:1-7). Theology was not a mere clinging to old formulae; it issued directly in practical corollaries for daily living. Nor were ethics simply a nervous conformity to bourgeois ideals; their rationale was deeply rooted in the gospel.[39] The importance of this observation for churches of all time can hardly be overemphasized.

(5) Not least of value is the enriching of the church's memory of Paul. Whether the portrait is Paul's own or the beginning of a modest hagiography, the fuller portrayal of Paul is certainly to be cherished—from his conversion (1 Tim 1:12-16), through his ministry (2 Tim 1:11-12; 3:10), to his final testimony of trust (2 Tim 4:6-8). This portrayal serves not least to establish and keep open the line of continuity and tradition begun with Paul and so helps to ensure that

---

33. The degree to which the Pastorals draw on the OT is not usually appreciated, but see M. Davies, *The Pastoral Epistles*, Epworth Commentaries (London: Epworth, 1996) 15-16.
34. "Save"—1 Tim 1:15; 2:4, 15; 4:16; 2 Tim 1:9; 4:18; Titus 3:5; "salvation"—2 Tim 2:10; 3:15; "Savior"—1 Tim 1:1; 2:3; 4:10; 2 Tim 1:10; Titus 1:3-4; 2:10, 13; 3:4, 6; "saving"—Titus 2:11.
35. First "appearing"—2 Tim 1:10; Titus 2:11; 3:4. Second "appearing"—1 Tim 6:14; 2 Tim 4:1, 8; Titus 2:13.
36. Often missed is the fact that the Pastorals speak more of "faith" (1 Tim 1:2, 4-5, 14, 19; 2:7, 15; 3:13; 4:12; 6:11; 2 Tim 1:5, 13; 2:22; 3:15; Titus 1:1, 4; 2:10; 3:15) than of "the faith."
37. For more detail see M. Dibelius and H. Conzelmann, *The Pastoral Epistles*, Hermeneia (Philadelphia: Fortress, 1972) 100-103; F. Young, *The Theology of the Pastoral Letters*, New Testament Theology (Cambridge: Cambridge University Press, 1994) 63-65.
38. So particularly D. C. Verner, *The Household of God: The Social World of the Pastoral Epistles*, SBLDS 71 (Chico, Calif.: Scholars Press, 1983).
39. See particularly P. H. Towner, *The Goal of Our Instruction: The Structure of Theology and Ethics*, JSNTSup 34 (Sheffield: Sheffield Academic, 1989).

the Christianity that Paul did so much to shape and to spread remains in living communication with Paul, apostle to the Gentiles, model for the gospel preacher, and teacher of the church.[40]

40. See further M. C. de Boer, "Images of Paul in the Post-Apostolic Period," *CBQ* 42 (1980) 359-80.

BIBLIOGRAPHY

Two volumes stand as watersheds in the recent study of the Pastorals. P. N. Harrison's detailed analysis of the language of the letters, *The Problem of the Pastoral Epistles* (London: Oxford University Press, 1921), provides a definitive statement of the case for non-Pauline authorship. The still lively debate on the subject takes its starting point with Harrison, either in rebuttal (Guthrie, Kelly, Fee, Knight, Johnson) or as still more or less determinative (Barrett, Houlden, Hanson, Quinn, Bassler, Davies). Dibelius's commentary (2nd ed., 1931; revised by Conzelmann in 1955), with its presentation of a Christianity influenced by Hellenistic writings and emphasizing good citizenship, became equally a heritage both valued and disputed, but rarely ignored.

Commentaries:

Barrett, C. K. *The Pastoral Epistles.* New Clarendon Bible. Oxford: Clarendon, 1963. An excellent example of a brief treatment by one of the best NT commentators of the second half of the twentieth century.

Bassler, J. M. *1 Timothy, 2 Timothy, Titus.* ANTC. Nashville: Abingdon, 1996. A well-judged analysis, spiced with judicious use of background material and plenty of detail for further study and reflection.

Davies, M. *The Pastoral Epistles.* Epworth Commentaries. London: Epworth, 1996. Brief, but well informed.

Dibelius, M., and H. Conzelmann. *The Pastoral Epistles.* Hermeneia. Philadelphia: Fortress, 1972. The principal German commentary from the first three-quarters of the twentieth century.

Fee, G. D. *1 and 2 Timothy, Titus.* New International Biblical Commentary. Peabody, Mass.: Hendrickson, 1984; rev. ed. 1988. Useful treatment of the NIV text.

Guthrie, D. *The Pastoral Epistles: An Introduction and Commentary.* Tyndale New Testament Commentary. Leicester: InterVarsity Press, 1957. The first effective response to Harrison and a still-valuable exposition.

Hanson, A. T. *The Pastoral Epistles.* NCB. London: Marshall, Morgan & Scott, 1982. Insights variable, but Hanson was always his own man.

Houlden, J. L. *The Pastoral Epistles.* Pelican New Testament Commentaries. Harmondsworth: Penguin, 1976. Houlden has a good eye for questions of contemporary relevance and usefulness.

Johnson, L. T. *Letters to Paul's Delegates: 1 Timothy, 2 Timothy, Titus.* The New Testament in Context. Valley Forge: Trinity Press International, 1996. Johnson is one of today's most competent commentators, though the division of each passage into three sections (Notes on Translation, Literary Observations, Comment) makes it difficult to track down particular verses and leaves the Comment light on some important features of the text.

Kelly, J. N. D. *The Pastoral Epistles.* Black's New Testament Commentaries. London: A. & C. Black, 1963. The richness of Kelly's Patristic scholarship makes this a still very satisfying commentary to use.

Knight, G. W. *The Pastoral Epistles: A Commentary on the Greek Text.* NIGTC. Grand Rapids: Eerdmans, 1992. Heavy on detailed word and grammar study, though easy to lose sight of the woods for the trees.

Marshall, I. H. *The Pastoral Epistles.* ICC. Edinburgh: T. & T. Clark, 1999. The most recent detailed commentary; published too late to be used in what follows.

Quinn, J. D. *The Letter to Titus.* AB 35. New York: Doubleday, 1990. The fruit of nearly twenty-five years of study; full of rich detail.

Specialized Studies:

Davies, M. *The Pastoral Epistles.* New Testament Guides. Sheffield: Sheffield Academic, 1996. A valuable and up-to-date treatment of background, themes, and authorship.

Donelson, L. R. *Pseudepigraphy and Ethical Argument in the Pastoral Epistles.* Tübingen: J. C. B. Mohr (Siebeck), 1986. Argues for the deliberate use of pseudepigraphy to provide apostolic warrant for an orthodox ecclesiology and ethic.

Harrison, P. N. *The Problem of the Pastoral Epistles.* London: Oxford University Press, 1921. The most compelling statement of the case for post-Pauline authorship based on the language of the Pastorals.

Kidd, R. M. *Wealth and Beneficence in the Pastoral Epistles: A "Bourgeois" Form of Early Christianity?* SBLDS 122. Atlanta: Scholars Press, 1990. A study of the important social and cultural factors involved in the Pastorals.

MacDonald, D. T. *The Legend and the Apostle: The Battle for Paul in Story and Canon.* Philadelphia: Westminster, 1983. Argues that the Pastoral Epistles were written to contradict the image of Paul in popular legends.

Miller, J. D. *The Pastoral Letters as Composite Documents.* SNTSMS 93. Cambridge: Cambridge University Press, 1997. Argues that the Pastorals are composite documents based on brief, but genuine, Pauline notes written to Timothy and Titus.

Prior, M. *Paul the Letter-Writer and the Second Letter to Timothy.* JSNTSup 23. Sheffield: JSOT, 1989. The most thoroughgoing attempt to study 2 Timothy on its own as an authentic letter of Paul to Timothy.

Towner, P. H. *The Goal of Our Instruction: The Structure of Theology and Ethics.* JSNTSup 34. Sheffield: Sheffield Academic, 1989. Sees the overarching theological concern of the author as especially his emphasis on salvation as a present reality and the consequent task of the church.

Verner, D. C. *The Household of God: The Social World of the Pastoral Epistles.* SBLDS 71. Chico, Calif.: Scholars Press, 1983. Argues effectively that the hierarchical structure of the household provided the model for the structure of church authority.

Wilson, S. G. *Luke and the Pastoral Epistles.* London: SPCK, 1979. The most thoroughgoing attempt to argue that the real author of the Pastorals was Luke.

Young, F. *The Theology of the Pastoral Letters.* New Testament Theology. Cambridge: Cambridge University Press, 1994. Young's expertise in Patristic theology gives her a most insightful perspective.

OUTLINE OF THE PASTORALS

I. 1 Timothy 1:1–6:21

    A. 1:1-11, Address and Warning Against False Teachers
    B. 1:12-20, Paul's Example and Charge to Timothy
    C. 2:1-7, God's Concern Is for Everyone
    D. 2:8-15, The Role of Women Within This Strategy
    E. 3:1-16, Good Order in the Church
    F. 4:1-16, The Two Ways
    G. 5:1–6:2, On the Elderly, Widows, Elders, and Slaves
    H. 6:3-21, Putting Wealth in Its Place

II. 2 Timothy 1:1–4:22

    A. 1:1-7, Greetings and Personal Commendation
    B. 1:8-18, Paul's Own Testimony
    C. 2:1-26, Paul's Charge to Timothy
    D. 3:1-17, Lessons from Tradition
    E. 4:1-22, Paul's Final Charge and Requests to Timothy

III. Titus 1:1–3:15

    A. 1:1-4, Greetings and Reminder of Paul's Commission
    B. 1:5-16, The Church—Its Leadership and Enemies
    C. 2:1-15, Good Household Management and Its Theological Rationale
    D. 3:1-15, Of Grace and Works

1 TIMOTHY 1:1–6:21

1 TIMOTHY 1:1-11, ADDRESS AND WARNING AGAINST FALSE TEACHERS

COMMENTARY

The opening greeting (1:1-2) is quite typical of Paul's style. But unlike most of the earlier Pauline letters (and 2 Tim 1:3-5), there is no introductory thanksgiving or prayer for the readers. The letter begins, instead, with a forthright warning against other teachings regarded as false and dangerous (1:3-7). The writer evidently felt or intended his readers to feel that their faith was under threat. Most dangerous of all, some of their own number had already been caught up in this teaching and were being distracted from the faith. The theme continues into the next paragraph (1:8-11). Here the appeal is to the firm standard of the law as ruling out familiar categories of wrongdoing. But the thrust is in 1:10, where it becomes clear that the determinative standard of right and wrong is "the sound teaching."

1:1-2, The Greeting. The letter begins much as Paul would. He introduces himself and stresses his status as an apostle (v. 1). Fundamental to Paul's identity was the conviction, rooted already in his conversion (Gal 1:15-16), that he had been commissioned as an emissary ("apostle") of Messiah (Christ) Jesus, and in full accordance with God's intention (cf. 2 Tim 1:1). Typically Pauline is the association of Christ Jesus with God as equally the source of Paul's legitimacy as apostle (so also v. 2). The talk of Christ Jesus as "our hope" is reminiscent of Col 1:27 and recalls that Christian hope takes its character from the one hoped in rather than from any feelings of hopefulness (see also Commentary on Titus 1:2).

More distinctive, but also characteristic of the Pastorals, is the fuller description of God as Savior (also 2:3; 4:10; Titus 1:3; 2:10; 3:4), as characteristic, in fact, as the description of Christ Jesus as "Savior" (2 Tim 1:10; Titus 1:4; 2:13; 3:6), already touching on one of the central themes of the gospel according to the Pastorals (see Commentary on 1:15). A tension is thus set up: Are two salvations envisaged, or just one effected by both together or by one as the agent of the other? The point becomes steadily clearer through the subsequent references, but it is never fully clarified. The idea of God as "Savior" was, of course, familiar in the OT (e.g., Deut 32:15; Ps 27:1, 9; Isa 45:15, 21), and there were several "Savior" gods in Greco-Roman religion.[41] But the fact that "Savior" is used earlier in Paul only occasionally and only of Christ (Eph 5:23; Phil 3:20) suggests a distinctive development in the theology of the Pastorals.

The recipient, Timothy, was well known as Paul's chief lieutenant (v. 2). He had evidently been converted through Paul's ministry (Paul's child, cf. Acts 16:1-3; Phil 2:22), had been co-writer (or co-sender) of several of Paul's letters, and had acted as one of Paul's chief spokesmen in Thessalonica (1 Thess 3:2, 6) and Corinth (1 Cor 4:17; 16:10), as well as (by implication) here in Ephesus. The adjective describes literally a child born in wedlock, "legitimate," but its use here is probably figurative of the genuineness and mutual warmth of their relationship (Phil 2:20).

The typical Pauline greeting (v. 2) adapts the typical Greek "Greeting" (χαίρειν *chairein*) to the distinctive Christian "grace" (χάρις *charis*) and adds the typical Jewish "peace" (שלום *šālôm*, here translated as εἰρήνη *eirēnē*), rich in the sense of social well-being as well as individual tranquility.

---

41. "Savior" was also used of human benefactors. See F. W. Danker, *Benefactor: Epigraphic Study of a Greco-Roman and New Testament Semantic Field* (St. Louis: Clayton, 1982).

Here the Jewish character of the greeting is strengthened by adding "mercy" (ἔλεός *eleos*) the usual Greek translation of the strong Jewish term חסד (*ḥesed*), denoting God's "covenant love, loving kindness" (Exod 34:6-7), which had not been much used by Paul earlier (but note Rom 11:30-32; Gal 6:16).

1:3-11, Warning Against False Teachers. The indication that his mission in Ephesus was at Paul's explicit command (v. 3)[42] strengthens the line of command and the authority being asserted through Timothy. Characteristic of the initial polemic is the vagueness of the charge (vv. 3-7). It is "certain people" who are teaching otherwise (v. 3); the accusation is of preoccupation with "myths and endless genealogies," which simply promote "speculations" (v. 4); "some of them" have "turned away into fruitless talk" (v. 6).[43] "Myths" are a regular target (4:7; 2 Tim 4:4; Titus 1:14; otherwise only in 2 Pet 1:16), the term already familiar in the sense of "untrue story, fiction," as opposed to historical truth, and always used negatively in the NT. The basic meaning of "genealogy" (elsewhere only in Titus 3:9) is also clear enough. But more precise definition is not possible, the imprecision of the language having encouraged its own share of "speculation" and "fruitless talk." Later gnostic speculation about series of emanations from the divine have often been cited, but talk of the law (v. 7) suggests a speculation fed by the Pentateuch's patriarchal narratives (see Titus 1:14, "Jewish myths"). Of course, the original readers might well have known who was in mind (some of Paul's earlier polemic is equally vague; see Rom 3:8; 2 Cor 3:1; Gal 1:7; 2:12). But such imprecision can be intentional, to include as many targets as necessary, on the principle "if the shoe fits. . . ."

The most specific detail is the desire of some to be teachers of the law, but their talk and confident pronouncements are dismissed for their lack of understanding (v. 7). The impression is thus given of people anxious to know the pedigree of their new faith, fascinated by the possible connections with great figures of the past (or divine beings) and searching the Torah for clues (the whole sequence of writings about Enoch were stimulated by the single verse Gen 5:24). To be noted is the fact that these were not opponents of the church in Ephesus but were involved with it, and evidently eager to learn more. The writer's fear (v. 6) is that through such speculation they will "miss the mark" (similarly 6:21; 2 Tim 2:18) and "turn away" (also 5:15; 6:20; 2 Tim 4:4) to false teaching.

Over against all this the writer sets "faith" (already in v. 2). Here the word evokes the characteristic Pauline sense of trust (in God or Christ), though subsequently it is "the faith" as an already well-established pattern of teaching to be believed that is in view (see footnote 9). It is this faith that gives a clearer understanding of God's "ordering" (οἰκονομία *oikonomia*) of salvation (v. 4); the word is often taken in the sense of "training" (NRSV), but the echo of Eph 3:9 suggests a carryover of Paul's earlier confidence that he had been given to know the mystery of God's purpose for Jew and Gentile (Rom 11:25-26; Col 1:26-27). It is this faith "unfeigned, without hypocrisy," together with a "clean heart" and a "good conscience," that will achieve the goal of "love" (v. 5).[44] Here the central emphasis of Paul is sustained: On the human side, it is faith alone that is decisive for salvation; undue elaboration of that faith into speculative systems will usually mean a departure from that faith. At the same time, "clean heart" (v. 5; 2 Tim 2:22) and "good conscience" (vv. 5, 19) look like a single concept ("clean conscience," 3:9; 2 Tim 1:3), denoting a conscience instructed in a faith whose outline is already clearly drawn.

In an attempt to counter what he regards as abuse of the law, the writer reminds Timothy of its proper purpose. Where those warned against in v. 7 seem to have used also the narrative and other parts of the Torah (Pentateuch), the writer focuses exclusively on its function as law and implies that other use is unlawful (v. 8).[45] Echoing Rom 7:12, 16,

---

42. The awkwardness of the opening of v. 3 ("As I urged you . . ." the sentence being then left technically incomplete) may arise from the attempt to suggest that Timothy's commission derived from some time earlier, from Paul himself (cf. Acts 18:5; 19:22; 1 Cor 16:10-11; 1 Thess 3:2). Acts 20:25 implies that Paul never visited Ephesus again.

43. "Futile verbiage" (Kelly) "a wilderness of words" (NEB/REB).

44. As in the earlier Paul (Rom 13:8-10; 1 Cor 13; Gal 5:22), "love" is the most highly prized of the Christian graces. See 1 Tim 1:14; 2:15; 4:12; 6:11; 2 Tim 1:7, 13; 2:22; 3:10; Titus 2:2-10.

45. The wordplay ("law," "lawfully") perhaps pulls the latter term away from its normal use. So it can possibly be translated as "correctly" (Barrett) or "appropriately" (Johnson). The NRSV's "legitimately" is probably best. See C. K. Barrett, *The Pastoral Epistles*, New Clarendon Bible (Oxford: Clarendon, 1963); Johnson, *Letters to Paul's Delegates*.

he insists that the law is good and that its function is to define and warn off from lawless and undisciplined behavior (v. 9). There follows a list of those whom the law condemns for their behavior, initially in pairs, artistically contrived (the first five words all begin with "a"; cf. Rom 1:31), and using broad-brush terms ("lawless and undisciplined, godless and sinners, unholy and profane"). But then comes what seems to be a sequence of elaborations of the second table of the Ten Commandments: dishonoring parents, murder, adultery, theft, perjury. Today the most controversial of these is the putting of homosexual practice (v. 10; the term almost certainly comes from Lev 18:22; 20:13) under the prohibition of adultery; the teaching is consistent with Paul's views expressed earlier in Rom 1:26-27; 1 Cor 6:9-10.

With vv. 10-11 the criterion of "faith" is replaced by one of the most frequently recurring motifs in the Pastorals: "sound teaching" (v. 10; 2 Tim 4:3; Titus 1:9; 2:1), "sound words" (6:3; 2 Tim 1:13), "sound in faith" (Titus 1:13; 2:2). The image is of physical health, of being healthy, "sound in wind and limb."[46] This is linked, in turn, in a liturgically ringing phrase, with "the gospel of the glory of the blessed God" (see also 6:15). Over against the other teaching, marked by its speculations and fruitless talk, its misuse of the law and lack of discipline, is set the gospel, the faith that it promotes, the "sound teaching" that is its content, and the love that is its goal. Already there is a sense of a gospel and faith that is clearly defined (at least for the writer), and that provides a norm of "sound teaching." What is feared and attacked dismissively is teaching that fails to accord with this norm or goes beyond it needlessly.

46. See further Dibelius and Conzelmann, *The Pastoral Epistles*, 24-25. See also footnote 22.

REFLECTIONS

The situation addressed in these opening verses of 1 Timothy is one that can be well imagined early in the life of a new religious movement. The faith preached by Paul was not already well established or able to appeal to centuries of tradition behind it (as can be done by Christians today). Entirely to the contrary, it was one of those newcomer religious movements of which the more established religions will always be suspicious and speak dismissively. Acts 19:21-41 presents a vivid picture of the threat experienced in Ephesus by the ancient cult of Artemis, the city's established and famous religion.

This new faith in Jesus Christ was one of a number of new "sects" or "cults" (but finding the right word even to describe them is always difficult) that generally came from Egypt (particularly the cult of Isis) or from the East (particularly newly emerging Mithraism) and that were seeking to establish themselves in the major centers of the Roman Empire. For those moved by religious concerns or simply curious, there was a very active marketplace of possibilities. The more ancient a religion or its teaching could present itself to be, the more attractive it was to a culture that venerated the wisdom of age and of the ancients. The more divine its pedigree, or the pedigree it offered to inquirers, the more attractive it was to those anxious about their destiny or troubled by mortality.

The upshot is that many would be attracted to Christianity, without necessarily being committed to it; it was one option among many. Baptism could be regarded simply as the appropriate initiation into just one more cult. Attachment to Christianity would not necessarily dampen the religious questing and curiosity that had attracted them to it. Rather, Christianity's first statements of faith and its sacred book (Torah) could easily provide fresh matter (genealogies?) for fresh speculation. If the leaders of the Christian movement were to counter and contain such tendencies, it was necessary for them to develop clearer statements of faith and firmer patterns of acceptable behavior.

The situation has often been paralleled since then in the history of Christianity, in which more established patterns have been challenged both by movements of renewal within and by new teaching from without. The question church leaders have to face is how they can be open to renewal and fresh insight without losing hold on what continues to be fundamental. How can they attract the genuine seekers, the open-minded enquirers, without also encouraging an openness that might subvert their own foundations? How can they identify and affirm the fundamentals without turning their backs on the seekers after truth?

The strategy chosen by the writer of 1 Timothy is clear from this opening section. The gospel was already firmly drawn in outline, faith in Christ defined as "the sound teaching." What this faith consisted of will become clearer as he proceeds, but it is clear enough already that the "faith" gave him and his readers a firm foundation from which to engage with those other seekers, to warn them against more fanciful ideas. Here the dilemma is already clearly indicated, of a faith too little defined as to encourage fruitless discussion, or a faith too fully defined as to discourage growth in faith. Today one of the categories of conduct about whose lawlessness the writer was most confident (homosexual practice) has itself become a focus of debate. Today's Christian leaders have to determine whether its unacceptability is still part of the "sound teaching"—in particular whether current conduct should be guided more by the consistent emphasis in Pauline (and biblical) teaching, or by changing appreciation of the complexity of human sexuality. It is a test case in getting the balance right between the openness of "faith" and the more closed definition of "the faith."

1 TIMOTHY 1:12-20, PAUL'S EXAMPLE AND CHARGE TO TIMOTHY

COMMENTARY

In effect the whole of the opening section (1:3-20) is Paul's charge to Timothy. The linking term is "charge/command/commission" (vv. 3, 5, 18); the theme is the wrong teaching (vv. 3-7, 10-11), which can shipwreck faith (vv. 19-20), but from which people can be delivered, as Paul himself had been delivered (vv. 13-16). Paul is thus set forward as the great paradigm: the one with whom the gospel had been entrusted (v. 11), which was the measure of the sound teaching (v. 10), and the one who displayed the effects of grace in fullest measure to serve as the paradigm for other believers (vv. 13-16). Whether this is Paul himself speaking or a somewhat idealized Paul, the effect is the same: to root the gospel firmly in the commission of Paul and in the one who commissioned him. Timothy can thus be still more clearly presented as the one who stands in that line of authentic gospel tradition (Christ→Paul→Timothy; v. 18), set over against the antithetical paradigms of Hymenaeus and Alexander (vv. 19-20).

1:12. The typical thanksgiving of Paul's letters (for those to whom he writes) is replaced by a thanksgiving for Paul himself. The thought is similar to what we often find in the earlier Paulines: Paul's consciousness of divine commissioning and enabling (cf., e.g., 1 Cor 15:8-10; Phil 4:13). But the talk of God's appointing him because of his (future?) faithfulness introduces a different note (cf. 1 Cor 4:2; 7:25), underlining the need felt by the writer to draw a firm equation between Paul's "faith alone" and faithfulness measured by loyalty to the more elaborated faith of his own generation.

1:13. The memory of Paul as persecutor is deeply rooted in all texts related to Paul (e.g., Acts 9:4-5; 1 Cor 15:9; Gal 1:3, 24). New is the thought of him as "blasphemer" (an ironic echo of Acts 26:11) and "violent, insolent" (an echo of Rom 1:30?). "Blaspheme" does not necessarily denote insult of Christ; the term can connote simply slanderous speech (cf. 6:4), though it is probably stronger here (v. 20; 6:1); even so, what is in view is probably the insult to God implicit in such a rejection of Christ (cf. v. 20). Notable here is both the emphasis on Paul's guilt and the excuse that he acted ignorantly. In this, too, Paul can serve as an example; the seriousness of such sin is sufficient proof that the person committing it was unaware of its full nature.

1:14. Equally strongly stressed is the mercy and overflowing grace of the Lord (presumably Jesus). The language here is archtypically Pauline: It was Paul who established the term "grace" (χάρις *charis*) in the Christian vocabulary (used 100 times in the Pauline corpus); the imagery of grace "multiplying" is Paul's (Rom 5:20; 6:1); and there is little that is more typical of Paul's thought than talk of "faith and love in Christ Jesus" (Col 1:4; 1 Thess 1:3; 2 Thess 1:3; Phlm 5), though this form of "faith in Christ" only occurs in the later Paulines (cf. Col 1:4). In this not least Paul embodies what is most important about the gospel for which he was commissioned.

1:15-16. The point is made explicit in two ways here. First, the writer cites a "faithful saying and worthy of all acceptance" (v. 15). This is a formula he uses several times. In each case it seems to indicate an element of teaching that had become, or that the writer was trying to establish as, a more or less set formulation, encapsulating some gospel statement or principle regarding salvation or future life. In some cases, the identifying label comes before the saying (v. 15; 2 Tim 2:11), in others after it (3:1; 4:9; Titus 3:8). Here we can begin to see more clearly the content of the "sound teaching," by appeal to which the writer hoped to head off false teaching. In this case, the statement is as simple as it could be: the divine initiative embodied in Christ Jesus;[47] his mission to "save" (the key gospel term in the letters, v. 15; 2:4, 15; 4:16; 2 Tim 1:9; 4:18; Titus 3:5; "salvation," 2 Tim 2:10; 3:15); and the object "sinners," recalling a key term in Christian tradition, that summed up both the mission of Jesus (Mark 2:17; Luke 19:7-10) and the gospel for Paul (Gal 2:15-21).

Second, the point already made (vv. 13-14) is repeated for effect (vv. 15-16). Paul had been the worst of these "sinners," so that the mercy he received could serve as a model of the full sweep of God's patience toward those who were to believe subsequently. The overtone of the earlier talk of "sinner" as a term of condemnation used by those who judged the conduct of others to be unacceptable to God is not present here; as in Rom 5:19, the term simply means those who break or ignore God's law and are thus subject to God's judgment. This is the mercy of God that takes the initiative of grace not least to those who disdain God's directions for life (cf. 1 Cor 15:9-11).

1:17. As elsewhere (notably Rom 11:33-36), the thought of such undeserved mercy moves the writer to a paean of praise to such a God. It is the first of three passages in 1 Timothy that, very strikingly, affirm a strongly monotheistic faith (see also 2:5; 6:15-16). The language is characteristically Jewish: "king of the ages"—time conceived as a sequence of ages (cf., e.g., Gal 1:5; Col 1:26). That God was "incorruptible" was generally assumed, but "invisible" was a more distinctively Jewish claim (John 1:18; Rom 1:20; Col 1:15; Heb 11:27; common in the Jewish philosopher Philo), the one who alone is God (John 5:44; Rom 3:30; 16:27; Jude 25; Rev 15:4; cf. 2 Kgs 19:15, 19; Ps 86:10; Isa 37:20; 2 Macc 1:24-25). As in the earlier Paul, the strong christological claims are held within a monotheistic framework.

1:18-20. Rounding off the section, the initial charge to Timothy (vv. 3, 5) is repeated in v. 18. It is reinforced by a fresh appeal to the personal relationship between Paul and Timothy (v. 2). The reader has been reminded of just who this Paul was and how weighty, therefore, is the authority embodied in the charge to his "son" Timothy. The point is reinforced still further by pointing out that the charge was in accordance with prophecies that had earlier referred to him; the precise meaning is unclear, but the same episode may be referred to in 4:14. In other words, Timothy's authority was based not only in his personal link with the great apostle, but also in a direct indication from God through prophecy.

Notable is the fact that the commission is described as "fighting the good warfare" (v. 18). The imagery was familiar in those days (cf. 1 Cor 9:7; 2 Cor 10:3-4; Eph 6:10-17),

---

47. A rabbinic phrase describes human beings as "those who come into the world" and is probably reflected in John 1:9. So talk of Christ's coming into the world can be read as a description of his human existence (cf. 3:16), as in Rom 15:8 and Gal 4:4 (cf. Matt 1:21).

but here the context indicates that the reference was primarily to the need to fight to maintain the faith free from disabling distractions. To be noted is the fact that the metaphor envisages spiritual forces as the "enemies," not human beings; Paul does not encourage the idea of fighting against other people. The position from and for which the fighting is to be fought is once again given as "faith and a good conscience" (v. 19; see Commentary on 1:5).

Just as Paul had served as an example of "the faithful saying," so also others can serve as examples of what is being warned against. By rejecting conscience—that is, presumably, conscience instructed by those who had a clearer grasp of the faith—their faith had suffered shipwreck, a very vivid metaphor (v. 19) that Paul would certainly have appreciated (cf. 2 Cor 11:25). This third association of faith and conscience within a few verses (vv. 5, 19) drives home the point: Where faith and conscience are not in harmony, then shipwreck is likely.

Two cases in point are cited. Hymenaeus is mentioned only once elsewhere, in 2 Tim 2:17-18, where his (presumably the same) error is made explicit. He claimed that the resurrection had already taken place (see Commentary on 2 Tim 2:18). An Alexander is also mentioned in 2 Tim 4:14, but there is no hint that that Alexander ever came to faith (see Commentary on 2 Tim 4:14). If we generalize from Hymenaeus, however, the point of failure is clear: failure to hold to the understanding of resurrection on which Christian faith was based. Here we may have an example of how the faith was firming up, for whereas Paul simply argued against a denial of the resurrection of the dead (1 Cor 15:12), the writer here regards failure to hold to the belief expounded in 1 Corinthians 15:1 as tantamount to the shipwreck of faith in the resurrection.

The rather fearful-sounding final clause (v. 20) is almost certainly modeled on 1 Cor 5:5. In both cases some sort of excommunication (disfellowshipping) is probably intended; they would lose the protection of the "household of God" (cf. 1 Cor 5:9-13). In both cases, it is also important to recognize that the definite article is used—"the satan." In other words, the thought seems to be still of one who was ultimately God's agent and whose activities allowed by God were intended to test and prove those subjected to the satan's authority (Job 1–2; Zech 3:1-2). In both cases, then, handing over the individual to the power of the satan had in view that person's salvation (1 Cor 5:5) as well as discipline ("that they may learn"). The writer would certainly intend the reader to recall that Paul was the model of one who had learned not to "blaspheme" (v. 13).

REFLECTIONS

The use of examples from real life, the telling of how it worked out in someone else's experience, always makes a point far stronger than mere restatement. Here the writer follows in the train of psalmist and sage to cite the acts of God of time past. Just as the words and deeds of Jesus' own ministry were no doubt already being told and retold, so also the event of Paul's conversion was already gaining exemplary significance; in Acts it is recounted no less than three times. Similarly the sad tales of Balaam or Esau embody lessons for future generations, just as here do those of Hymenaeus and Alexander, both of whom and their fates were presumably known to the first readers.

In such circumstances there is always a temptation to add a flourish to the tale, to bring out the point being made more forcefully. Has that happened here? Where Paul described himself as "the least of the apostles, unfit to be called an apostle" (1 Cor 15:9), the writer here describes Paul as "first among sinners" (1:15). The motivation, presumably, is the same as when a Christian testimony describes pre-conversion life as plumbing the deepest depths of sin—that is, the more despairing the condition, the greater the grace that achieves redemption. There need be nothing dishonest or dishonorable in such hyperbole. A true mark of grace received is often a consciousness of the unworthiness of such grace, and without a degree of dramatic license there would be no art in storytelling. On the other hand, overstatement can easily slide into parody, and an element of unreality can enter that helps nobody.

Embedded within this testimony of Paul is the first "faithful saying," in which the gospel is summed up in eight words (in the Greek): "Christ Jesus came into the world to save sinners" (1:15). Evidently it was equally as important as the portrayal of Paul to be able to sum up the gospel in such simple terms. For those wanting greater precision, the formulation is overly simple and would hardly suffice for a theological analysis. But faith requires such slogan-like forms (like "Jesus is Lord") that can act as a unifying core, precisely by virtue of their degree of simplification or lack of sophistication; as such it can serve to anchor a wider range of faith seeking fuller definition (but not to be confused with "bumper sticker theology"). When even these do not provide that unifying core and anchor, then faith has, indeed, lost its identity.

Here, too, we may recall that the new Christian movement was still young. Its center was firmly fixed in the gospel of Jesus Christ, but its circumference was far from clear. The process of definition and boundary drawing required a firm hand; otherwise the identity of the new movement would be dissipated, and the movement itself might become just another scattering of elements in a wider syncretistic religiosity. Later generations may question some of these initial firm lines, but without them there would probably have been no lasting lines of definition from within which these questions could be posed.

At the same time, it should be again appreciated that the drawing of firm boundary lines cuts both ways in terms of evangelism and apostasy. Firmly drawn boundaries will exclude as well as retain. Permeable boundaries will leak as well as draw in. An open door allows people to exit as well as to enter. Is the former (exit) an inevitable corollary if the latter (enter) is to be successful? Arguably the most successful means of sustained local evangelism are groups that genuinely overlap the margins of a church. Perhaps, then, the loss of a Hymenaeus and an Alexander may be signs of a church's vitality!

1 TIMOTHY 2:1-7, GOD'S CONCERN IS FOR EVERYONE

COMMENTARY

After the initial charge to Timothy, the primary emphasis seems to be to stress the breadth of concern that Christians could express (vv. 1-2), and precisely (v. 3) as a reflection of the breadth of God's concern (vv. 4-6). The key word here is "all"; prayers should be made for all (v. 1), particularly all in authority (v. 2), for God wants all to be saved (v. 4), and Christ Jesus gave himself as a ransom for all (v. 6). This, too, is the gospel that Paul had been appointed to preach (v. 7).

There could be several reasons why this emphasis was given such high prominence ("first of all," v. 1). (1) It set the gospel in still sharper contrast with the other teachings already attacked (1:3-7, 10-11, 19); by implication, their concern was more introverted and self-centered. (2) It developed an emphasis that had been integral to the gospel from the beginning: good news for all, sinner and not just righteous, Jew first but also Gentile ("all" is equally prominent in Romans). The emphasis, then, is not necessarily directed against a Gnostic elitism; the older Jewish "exclusivism" (Jews only) could equally be a target. (3) It made clear that the young Christian movement was not an anarchistic revolution, but was concerned rather to be a positive force in and for society. This last concern provides the link of continuity into the next section; good order in the state leads naturally to thought of good order in the household (vv. 8-15; see also Titus 3:1-2).

2:1-2. Typical of the author is the heaping up of near synonyms—"supplications, prayers, intercessions and thanksgivings" (v. 1).[48] The whole range of prayer forms should be used to express Christian concern. And this concern should be for everyone (the Greek denotes all human beings, not just all "men"). The language, presumably, is not literally prescriptive, as though such prayer was practically possible (beyond the mere mouthing of "all"). Rather, it is indicative that Christian concern should exclude no one.

To be noted is the fact that the next requested prayer (for those in authority) is presented as a special case of this broader concern; the assumption is that good government is for the benefit of all, and that is why those in authority are to be prayed for (cf. Rom 13:1-7; 1 Pet 2:13-17). This, in fact, is spelled out in v. 2: The intention of such prayers is that we (Christians as part of society) might (be able to) lead a tranquil and quiet (again two near synonyms) life, in "all piety and dignity." These last terms are two of the key words in the Pastoral Epistles. The first, εὐσεβεία (*eusebeia*), occurs ten times (see footnote 10) and denotes religious obligation due to God—"piety," "godliness," even "religion."[49] The second, σεμνότης (*semnotēs*), which with its related adjective occurs six times (see footnote 16), has a range of meaning—"reverence," "dignity," "seriousness," "respectfulness," "holiness," "probity"—denoting the gravitas that a well-ordered religious life carries with it and that commands respect within the wider society.[50] Here is the other side of the universal concern being commended: that they themselves might be able to live in a way that wins the respect of all (cf. particularly 1 Thess 4:11-12).

Notable also are the echoes of older wisdom learned by those living under the yoke of foreign power: that prayers and offerings should be made for these rulers (Ezra 6:10; Jer 29:7; Bar 1:11-12; 1 Macc 7:33). In the often unfavorable realities of life, concern for others and self-interest need involve neither contradiction nor compromise.

2:3-4. Such concern for others and for rulers is not merely pragmatic policy but a theological necessity. It is fine and acceptable to God (the primary criterion), because "God our Savior" is not only "our Savior." There follows a statement that is as clear as any assertion of "Christian universalism": God wills the salvation of everyone. The God who wished to save Paul, "chief of sinners" (1:15), could hardly want anything less for everyone else (v. 4); the earlier Paul had spoken with equal boldness (Rom 11:32).

The traditional way of squaring this affirmation with the awareness of how few actually accept the gospel has been to distinguish between God's general will or desire and God's active determination of outcomes or permissive will in the face of human intransigence. But whatever the theological complications involved, it is important to recognize that the bottom line for the writer is God's concern for the salvation of everyone. The wholeness of the salvation in mind is indicated also in the complementary phrase "to come to knowledge of the truth" (v. 4), a phrase that appears regularly in the Pastorals (e.g., v. 4; 4:3; 2 Tim 2:25; Titus 1:1). Salvation includes a knowing, both intellectual and existential, an awareness and acknowledgment of the reality of oneself and of the world.

2:5-6. The ground for this theological claim is given in another creedal fragment, one of the most striking in these or any Pauline letter (see also 1:15; 2:15; 3:16; 2 Tim 1:9-10; 2:11-13; Titus 3:4-7). The fact that God is one (the primary Jewish confession, *Shema;* Deut 6:4) leads inevitably to the conclusion that God is God of all (as in Rom 3:29-30) and, therefore, is concerned for all. But the point of the creed is to integrate the oneness of God with the singular role of Christ Jesus (as in 1 Cor 8:6). This is the second affirmation of traditional Jewish monotheism (1:17); however lofty the claims to be made for Christ, they are to be held within that frame of reference. In a formulation pushing toward universalism ("gave himself a ransom for all"), the limitation of effective mediation

---

48. It is unlikely that the last term, εὐχαριστία (*eucharistia*), has the Lord's supper (eucharist) particularly in mind (as Kelly, *The Pastoral Epistles*, 60). The typical usage is much broader. See 1 Cor 14:16; 2 Cor 4:15; 9:11-12; Eph 5:4; Phil 4:6; Col 2:7; 4:2; 1 Thess 3:9.

49. Towner, *The Goal of Our Instruction*, 147-52, suggests that it functions as equivalent to the biblical phrase "the fear of the Lord," the knowledge of God that ensures reverence.

50. It is this passage that prompted Dibelius-Conzelmann's influential reflection on the Pastorals' advocacy of "the ideal of good Christian citizenship." See Dibelius and Conzelmann, *The Pastoral Epistles*, 39-41.

to Christ Jesus is not to exclude from salvation those who have not heard of Christ, but to affirm that effective salvation, wherever it is experienced, will be found to have been mediated through Christ. We may compare John 1:9 (the Word enlightens everyone) with John 14:6 (Jesus said, "No one comes to the Father except through me"). Particularly striking is the repeated antithesis between God and humankind: Christ comes from the side of human beings to act as mediator on their behalf with God (cf. 1:15). The thought is of a piece with Paul's earlier Adam christology: Christ is the second or last "man" who more than rectifies the damage done by the first (Rom 5:12-19; 1 Cor 15:21-22, 45-49).[51]

The second half of the creedal form echoes several earlier versions (Mark 10:45; Gal 1:4; 2:20; Eph 5:2, 25). The imagery is of something or someone given in place of others to secure their liberty (though 2 Tim 2:11 indicates that the imagery should not be overpressed). But the key linking word is again "all." The importance of the text is obvious for the old dispute about the scope of the atonement between Calvinists (atonement limited to the elect) and Arminians (atonement for all who will). Precisely what the final phrase means ("the testimony for its own times") is unclear, but the following verse and similar language elsewhere (Rom 3:26; 2 Cor 6:2; Gal 4:4-5; Col 1:25-26) suggest a sense of the climactic character within the purpose of God, both of Christ's death and of Paul's commission to proclaim it.

2:7. For the third time the writer stresses Paul's sense of commission (see also 1:11-12). The verse has some curious features. It reinforces Paul's claim to apostleship (1:1) and the particular scope of his mission as to "the Gentiles" (cf. Rom 11:13). But nowhere else outside the Pastorals does Paul describe himself as a "herald" or "teacher" (the language is closely repeated in 2 Tim 1:11). And the double vow of sincerity (cf. Rom 9:1; Gal 1:20) is a little surprising here; it sounds rather as though a known Pauline affirmation is being used to strengthen the potentially more controversial formulation of the universalism of the preceding verses.

---

51. For Adam christology, see J. D. G. Dunn, *The Theology of Paul the Apostle* (Grand Rapids: Eerdmans, 1998) 9.1, 10.2, 11.4-5.

REFLECTIONS

Do we begin to see in this passage the lust for social acceptance that can so easily blunt the cutting edge of the gospel, at both the individual and the social level? To be seen as loyal to the state, as motivated by concern for the well-being of everyone can be politically astute and possibly even open the way to political and social influence. But the same process can also mean a blurring of principles and an accommodation with practices that previously would have been wholeheartedly condemned. So here the desire for a "quiet life" can easily be disparaged by those eager to turn the world upside down, and the prizing of "piety and dignity" can be denigrated as desire for a "respectability" that stifles necessary criticism and unavoidable controversy.

But such a line of reflection would be unjust to the writer of these letters. The situation envisaged was nothing like the modern Western democracy, where nongovernmental organizations can exercise influence by freedom of speech and access to the media. It was, rather, the situation familiar to diaspora (and Palestinian) Jews for most of their history—the struggle to secure and maintain a foothold within a hostile environment, where political authorities would always tend to be suspicious of the little house groups whose legal status was at best ambiguous and be ready to act against them at short notice with little excuse (cf., e.g., Acts 18:2 with Rom 13:1-7). It was not yet a case of winning respectability, but of gaining basic respect. And only those whose "quiet and tranquility" have been little disturbed could begin to despise a desire for them as essential to any kind of security and prosperity in daily living. Here again, then, a sense of historical realism is necessary if such a passage is to be appreciated—not to mention a sense of empathy with little church groups struggling to survive in situations not so very different today.

Within this context a natural reaction is to become more secretive (like the ancient cults that celebrated secret mysteries) or to withdraw from the world to practice beliefs and principles as purely as possible (like the Qumran community, which withdrew to the Dead Sea). The first Christians chose the opposite alternative: to live within the world and for all their neighbors, high and low. That alternative inevitably involves some compromise with the principles and values governing the wider society, for where purity is possible only outside society, then "outside" has become an introverted self-concern cut off from wider community. But the theological imperative of "one God . . . and one mediator . . . who gave himself as a ransom for all" (2:5-6) left them no choice. The uncomfortable fact is that such universalism inevitably involves a fair degree of openness to the other and acceptance of the other in terms broader than one's own.

The problem with any theological system that turns its back on universalism, for no doubt good reasons of logic and self-reassurance, is that the resulting system postulates either a less generous God or a less omnipotent God than 1 Timothy envisions (cf. Rom 11:32). Here as elsewhere theological assertions need always to be qualified by the note of eschatological reserve. God's ultimate purpose is ultimate and, therefore, still unknown, as well as the divine means of achieving that purpose. All human judgment is subject to eschatological verification. At this point, theology must simply give way to wondering worship (as in Rom 11:33-36).

1 TIMOTHY 2:8-15, THE ROLE OF WOMEN WITHIN THIS STRATEGY

COMMENTARY

The train of thought is clear enough, with v. 8 signaling the continuity. It is of a piece with this wider concern for the common good that the believing women should dress and act in ways that commended their religion (vv. 9-10). This evidently included also the way wives should comport themselves in the church's gatherings for worship, where the key word is ἡσυχία (*hēsychia*, vv. 11-12), the same word used in v. 2 to connote a quiet life; for wives to be given a teaching or authority role in respect of their husbands would also mean upsetting the social tranquility so prized earlier. The point is reinforced by a theological deduction drawn from the original creation story of Adam and Eve (vv. 13-15) and is given added weight by being designated a "faithful saying" (3:1).[52]

2:8. The encouragement to pray is repeated, so that this verse forms a bracket with v. 1 and carries forward the logic behind the call to prayer into this paragraph also.[53] The verse confirms that a traditional manner of praying was with upraised hands (Ps 141:2), although talk of "holy hands" will be a carryover from the Jewish tradition of ritual purification prior to prayer. If the final phrase is more than conventional, it is a reminder that motives for prayer can often be mixed and that prayer itself can often be used as a factional weapon—praying at or against another or praying for a party point (cf. Rom 14:1).

The limitation of the advice to "men" (v. 8) prefaces a sequence directed to "women" (vv. 9-15). Since the two words ἀνήρ (*anēr*) and γυνή (*gynē*) also mean "husband" and "wife," it is more than likely that the advice has in view the good functioning of what was generally recognized to be society's basic household unit, formed around husband and wife; the point is much clearer in

---

52. Placing the label "Faithful is the saying" at the end of the saying is the practice also in 4:9 and Titus 3:8. The NIV and the NRSV, however, think that the label refers to what follows.

53. Barrett, *The Pastoral Epistles*, 54, thinks that "in every place" means every "meeting-place" (cf. Mal 1:10-11; 1 Cor 1:2; 1 Thess 1:8). But since Christians met for fellowship and worship in members' homes, it is less likely that "place" had such a specific meaning.

the parallel instructions of 1 Pet 3:1-6. As in more detailed "household codes" (rules for household management) elsewhere (e.g., Eph 5:21–6:9; Col 3:18–4:1), the advice is part of an attempt to gain wider respect for the church by ensuring that the then conventional subjection of wife to husband is not disturbed by the greater freedoms brought by the gospel (cf. Gal 3:28). The context, it should be recalled, is that of worship (vv. 8, 11-12; cf. 1 Cor 11:2-16), but v. 10 suggests that the thought reaches beyond the subject of dress appropriate for prayer meetings.

2:9. The first concern is for women's/wives' dress and appearance. The writer calls on them to adorn themselves in orderly or respectable apparel with modesty or reverence and reasonableness or moderation, or in reference to women, decently or chastely (the last word denotes a classic Greek "virtue," often alluded to in the Pastorals; see 2:9, 15; 3:2; 2 Tim 1:7; Titus 1:8; 2:2, 4-6, 12). The piling up of near synonyms is noticeable. Warning is given against braided hair, gold (ornaments), pearls, and expensive clothing. The warning presupposes the presence of some wealth in the congregations being addressed and a tendency on the part of well-to-do women (often severely limited in their freedom of action, not least since legally they were always dependent on a male relative) to find satisfaction in costly attire (the tendency is illustrated in poems, paintings, and sculptures of the time). A religion that saw its end result in such terms would be no more than a club for social advancement.

2:10. In place of adornment should be "good deeds," such as befits women/wives who profess worship of God. The commendation of "good deeds" is frequent in the Pastorals (fourteen times; see footnote 10); the category is broad, but most societies would have a reasonable idea of what constituted "good deeds." As in the earlier Paulines (particularly Rom 14:6), the criterion of acceptable conduct is whether the one who so acts can worship God in doing so.

2:11-12. With these verses the instruction becomes more specific and focuses on the gatherings for worship. The thought is clearly determined by the attitude behind the household codes. In the ancient household the male head of the family, the *paterfamilias*, had all authority and power, and this was deemed to be essential for the good order of the household, itself the basic unit of city and state. In consequence, the proper relation of the wife to her husband was one of "submission" (ὑποταγή *hypotagē*); the same key word appears in non-Christian household codes,[54] as well as Christian (Eph 5:22; Col 3:18; 1 Pet 3:1, 5).

The possibility of confusion arose because the first churches all met in private homes. Consequently there was uncertainty as to whether the norms of behavior were those of household or of church. Probably in the early days of Christianity there were wives who, in exercise of prophetic or other gifts, had been seen to be teaching or exhorting their husbands (cf. 1 Cor 14:29-35). Conceivably, this may have been acceptable in church, but since church was also household, the practice was too easily understood to be subversive of the good order of the household and of the authority of the *paterfamilias*.[55] For a church concerned to be seen as supportive of what was good for society, the only solution was to conform church order to that of the well-ordered household (hence 3:4-5, 12) and to forbid wives to teach (διδάσκω *didaskō*) or to have authority (αὐθεντέω *authenteō*; the meaning could be stronger: "domineer") over their husbands.

2:13-14. However, as with vv. 5-6 (and Titus 2), the author wanted to root his counsel theologically. At this point there enters a disturbing tendentiousness, pushing a line. He not only argues from the prior creation of Adam (Gen 2:7, 21-23), as in the more open 1 Cor 11:3, and he not only follows the Genesis account of Eve's initial deception (Gen 3:1-6), as in 2 Cor 11:3, but he also denies that Adam was deceived and puts the blame solely on the woman (Gen 3:13), in direct contrast to Paul's own earlier account of Adam's transgression (Rom 5:15-19; cf. Rom 7:11). Here the theology seems to be bending before social convention in spite of the biblical text referred to and the earlier Pauline use of it. (Would the "I" of Rom 7:11 be debarred from teaching authority by the same logic?) At the same time, however, the implication,

---

54. E.g., Plutarch *Moralia* 142E.
55. The wife had authority within the household, principally over domestic arrangements (5:14; cf. Titus 2:4-5). But that did not affect the husband's supreme authority.

supported by Gen 2:24, is that the relationship in view is still that of husband and wife, and not man and woman.

2:15. This verse confirms that notion, prompted no doubt by the punishment of the primal sin—for the woman/wife, labor pains in childbirth (Gen 3:16), which in those days could often be fatal. The implication is that childbearing is the means by which woman atones for her part in the primal sin, or, less negatively expressed, that labor pains are a sign of the out-of-jointedness of creation as a whole. In those days, childbearing was seen as woman's primary function, so that barrenness would be regarded typically as a cause of shame and rebuke (still reflected in the male tendency to blame failure to conceive on the wife). There have been attempts to refer "the childbearing" to the incarnation, but that thought seems to be far away at this point, and the qualification of the final clause implies that women endured the trauma of giving birth by their faith, love, and consecration, with moderation (the same word as in 2:9).[56] In designating the whole (or v. 15 alone) as a "faithful saying" (3:1), the author is appealing to and reinforcing a social tradition to which the early churches found it wiser to conform.

56. Alternatively, the plural "they" ("if they continue in . . .") could refer to the children thus born, and the reference would then include childrearing as well as giving birth. But that would seem to make the mother's salvation depend on her success in nurturing her children—that is, on the behavior of others, which is less likely. For a helpful discussion of 2:15, see S. E. Porter, "What Does It Mean to Be 'Saved by Childbirth' (1 Timothy 2:15)?" *JSNT* 49 (1993) 87-102.

REFLECTIONS

Few if any texts are more painful to modern sensitivities. The portrayal of women as effectively gagged in church, forbidden to exercise authority over men, and restricted to the role of childbearers, modest dressers, and doers of good deeds is about as remote from most twenty-first-century evaluations of women's roles in Western society, as one could imagine. What does one do with a text like this?

The tensions it sets up are partly relieved by the recognition that the focus of concern is not man and woman so much as husband and wife. It is not woman as woman who is to be subordinated to man as man, but woman as wife who is to be subordinated to man as husband. The freedom of the well-to-do unmarried woman or widow in business and in church would hardly be limitless, but would certainly be greater than that envisaged here (cf. Acts 18:26, Priscilla as instructor of Apollos; Rom 16:1-2, Phoebe as deacon and patron; Col 4:15, Nympha as host of the church in her house).

Still more to the point is the social context in which such instructions are given, including the norms and conventions of the time, and the consequently limited horizons and expectations of men and women of the time. Modern societies that only gave the vote to women within the last hundred years and that still connive at unequal opportunities for men and women should not be surprised that the earliest churches should be so conformist. The best minds of the day and the wisdom of the ancients all confirmed that the husband should have all legal authority and the wife should be subject to him. To challenge this then (nineteen centuries ahead of time!) would have been tantamount to calling marriage itself into question and would have been regarded as undermining the very foundations of society and state.

At the same time, recognition of the degree to which the counsel here was conditioned by the conventions of the time should caution against any attempt to transfer such directives directly into the different conditions of today's household—far less of church! To acknowledge the context-conditioned character of scripture teaching on relationships within marriage is not to deny authority to that teaching. Rather, it is to affirm the relevance of the teaching to the particular historical circumstances for which it was written. And it is to affirm that contemporary social teaching that does not take account of the (different) circumstances of today is that much less authoritative!

What emerges of lasting importance from this passage, therefore, is the concern to affirm the relationships that maintain the strength of marriage and the stability of the household. The perception of what these relationships are, and particularly of a wife's responsibility to and relation to her husband, have changed, though only in a radical way within the last hundred years. But arguably the principle of strong marriage and stable household remains fundamental to a Christianity that, like Jesus (Mark 10:7-8), looks back to Gen 2:24 as the most fundamental model for intimate human relationships. In this way, the force of the text can be recognized, while at the same time noting the time-conditioned character of its specific detail.

1 TIMOTHY 3:1-16, GOOD ORDER IN THE CHURCH

COMMENTARY

The concern for good order continues to direct the train of thought. Just as good order in the state (2:1-2) led into thoughts of good order in the household (2:9-15), so also that leads into thoughts of good order in the church (3:1-13). The transition would be all the more understandable for the author and his first readers, since, as already noted (see the Commentary on 2:11-12), the first churches all met in members' homes. Almost inevitably, therefore, the norms of good order within the home became the model for good order within the church and for the good order of their regular gatherings. This was already implicit in the restricted role allowed for wives (2:11-12), but the pattern now becomes explicit in the criteria for identifying those fit to take up the roles of overseer (3:4-5) and deacon (3:12).

The other criteria are an instructive mixture. Grosser acts or habits of intemperance (3:3, 8) would obviously rule someone out. Ability to teach (3:2) and clarity as to what "the mystery of the faith" consisted of (3:9) would also be expected, though at this point they are given little prominence. Hospitality (3:2) was widely recognized as a desirable and commendable social tradition. More striking is the indication that remarriage was frowned on (3:2, 12) and the indication that commensurate standards of behavior were expected of the candidate's wife (3:11). Most striking of all is the other string of words that begin the curriculum vitae expected of the would-be overseer (3:2) and the criterion that brings the paragraph to a close (3:7). Here again prominence is given to the impression made on others, the public face of the church: "without reproach, temperate, moderate, respectable" (3:2; the last two words echoing those in 2:9); "having a good testimony from those outside" (3:7). We are already in a church for which the good opinion of the wider community was important (see also 5:14; 6:1; Titus 2:5, 8, 10).

The final paragraph (3:14-16) confirms both the concern for good order ("how to behave in . . . the church," 3:15) and the household as the model for that good order ("the household of God, which is the church," 3:15). Somewhat late in the day (cf. 2:4-6 and 2:13-14; but note 3:9), the author recalls that the most fundamental issue is that of truth (3:15) and that the whole depends on and is intended to serve the mystery of piety and its confession (3:16).

3:1-7, Overseers. The traditional verse division attached the "faithful saying" to the following instructions regarding overseers (v. 1), and this remains the majority opinion among commentators. But a reference back to a statement regarding salvation (2:15) makes better sense (see Commentary on 1:15), whereas use of the formula to boost the emerging ecclesiastical structure (v. 1) would be without parallel.[57] At the same time the aspiration (lit., stretching oneself

---

57. However, the weakly attested variant—"This is a human/popular saying"—may have originated as a marginal note by a sarcastic scribe less enamored of the office of bishop.

or stretching out one's hand) for the role of overseer is commended as being one of the "fine/good works" to which believers should aspire. The singular need not imply that a single overseer in each place was meant.

The term ἐπισκοπή (*episkopē*; NRSV, "bishop"; NIV, "overseer") itself derives from the idea of a "visitation" to bring about good (e.g., Gen 50:24-25; Job 10:12; Wis 3:13; Luke 1:68, 78; 1 Pet 2:12), but already it had been extended to denote the regular function or office that had such oversight as its function (Num 4:16; Acts 1:20).[58] Ministries designated as "overseers" had already been in operation in Philippi (Phil 1:1); no hint is given regarding their function in that letter, though it is often assumed that they would have been financial officers (cf. Phil 4:10-18). Acts 20:28 envisages "overseers" as a function of "elders" appointed by Paul from the beginning (Acts 14:23), but most think Luke is at least giving greater formality to what had been much less clearly defined or designated ministries (cf. Titus 1:5-7). At any rate, whatever the precedents, vv. 2-7 are certainly the first clear attempt to define such ministry as an "office," with clearly identified conditions of candidature and some outline of responsibilities expected (hospitable, a good teacher and manager of the church as one would manage a household; cf Titus 1:7). Since the *paterfamilias* had such great authority, the model of the household implies an analogous weight of authority being granted to the overseer.

With v. 2 a rule begins to be formulated: "it is necessary that . . ." (as in Titus 1:7 NRSV, "Now a bishop must be . . ."). The first criterion is that the overseer must be "blameless, without reproach"; the word ἀνεπίλημπτος (*anepilēmptos*) is used only in 1 Timothy, of widows (5:7) and of Timothy himself (6:14). More curious is the second: "the husband of but one wife," which can hardly be taken to imply that polygamy was otherwise acceptable (cf. 5:9; presumably there was no thought that a woman could be polygamous), presumably means that widowers who aspired to oversee could not marry again. The logic here is unclear (Marriage should be for life? see 5:11-12), but still today the rule is maintained within the Orthodox Church. The third criterion, "temperate" (νηφάλιος *nēphalios*, v. 11; Titus 2:2), may reflect the more particular sense of temperance in drinking (cf. v. 3), so "sober," "clear-headed," "self-controlled." The next two words echo those used of wives in 2:9, "moderate," "respectable" (σώφρων *sōphrōn*, κόσμιος *kosmios*), with the same implication of making a good impression on outsiders looking to criticize. "Hospitality" (φιλόξενος *philoxenos*; again in adjectival form in Titus 1:8 and as a verb in 1 Tim 5:10) was a much-approved social grace (Rom 12:13; Heb 13:2; 1 Pet 4:9); travelers abroad would regularly look to countrymen or fellow believers for bed and board, especially since the available inns were frequently dangerous and usually full of bedbugs. Almost surprising in a list of such social talents comes "skillfull in teaching" (elsewhere only in 2 Tim 2:24); the role of the overseer as the acceptable public face of the church was evidently of greater importance than his role as instructor in faith!

With v. 3 the checklist takes an almost surreal turn: not a "drunkard, addicted to wine," not a "bully, pugnacious" (both elsewhere only in Titus 1:7), but "gentle, yielding" and "peaceable," literally "without fighting" (both again in Titus 3:2), "not a lover of money, greedy" (otherwise only Heb 13:5). But we recall that these were still frontier days for many of these new churches; pugnacious and combative characters could commend themselves to positions of leadership; positions of relative power and responsibility could quickly be undermined by drink or financial irregularity (cf. 1 Cor 11:20-21). Paul himself was evidently suspected of financial irregularities (2 Cor 8:20-21; 12:14-18), and it would certainly not be the last time that a bishop acted as a bully.

With vv. 4-5 it becomes evident that the meeting of the church in households was becoming the church as a household. In a so far not very effective or clear job description (vv. 2-3), the role of *paterfamilias* in a properly ordered household was the most obvious role model for an overseer. The key term προΐστημι (*proistēmi*), used twice in the two verses (also in v. 12; 5:17; Titus 3:8,

---

58. There is no reason why the office should be derived from the Qumran *mebaqqer* as such, a popular suggestion in the early days following the discovery of the Dead Sea Scrolls. The comparable responsibilities (so far as they are indicated) are quite different. The emergence of such leadership is more or less a sociological inevitability, whatever the theological rationalization.

14), means literally "place or stand before," with the double overtone of "give leadership to" and "take initiative on behalf of," so "be concerned about, care for." Either or both senses may be present in Rom 12:8 and 1 Thess 5:12; in v. 4 the initial thought is of firm leadership (linked to "keeping children in submission"), but in v. 5 "giving leadership to his own household" is set in parallel to "caring for God's church" (using a verb used elsewhere only in Luke 10:34-35). Again the idea of "keeping a child in submission" is jarring to modern ears but was in accordance with accepted parental wisdom well into the twentieth century ("Spare the rod and spoil the child"). Again, as with deacons in v. 8, their wives in v. 11, and earlier the wish for all (2:2), the desirable characteristic of such leadership is "dignity, respectfulness" (this last phrase probably continues the description of the overseer's attitude and conduct, not that of his children, as the NIV and the NRSV take it).

The leader must not be "a recent convert" (v. 6). The danger is that someone thus inexperienced would become conceited or be blinded by authority and act foolishly (the word νεόφυτος [*neophytos*] can have both meanings; it is used only in the Pastorals, here and in 6:4; 2 Tim 3:4), or that an untried convert could blind believers by his brilliant but superficial potential.[59] The counsel could be conventional wisdom, but suggests a young movement that had learned some harsh lessons; it would have been an attractive option in several circumstances to look to new converts of social standing and wealth to provide necessary leadership. To "fall into the condemnation of the devil," perhaps, implies a reference to the pride that had brought down the kings of Babylon and Tyre (Isa 14:12-15; Ezekiel 28:1), and already applied to the fall of Satan.

Verse 7 is the most explicit appeal to the impression made on others by a church leader, with a repeated "it is necessary that" (as in v. 2). The criteria were not simply what pleased the church; the overseer had to be the sort of person who would command respect among nonbelievers, and who would match up to the criteria of what was generally acknowledged to be "good" standards and conduct (cf. 6:2). Otherwise he would be vulnerable to the reproach and the traps of the slanderer (διάβολος *diabolos*; lit., "devil," but here probably playing on the alternative sense of "slanderer," as more often in the Pastorals; see v. 11; 2 Tim 3:3; Titus 2:3). Where a leader does not measure up to the highest standards of public esteem, he is vulnerable to malicious gossip and attack.

3:8-13, Deacons. The term used in this case, διάκονος (*diakonos*), often retains overtones of its original sense, "waiter at table" (as in John 2:5, 9) and so "servant." Jesus could be so described (Rom 15:8), an echo presumably of such traditions as Mark 9:35; 10:43-45. It was initially used to identify the character of ministry, rather than the ministry as such (e.g., 1 Cor 3:5; 2 Cor 6:4; Col 1:7, 23, 25; 1 Tim 4:6). The sense of "waiting at tables" invites a reference to Acts 6:1-6, but the term is not actually used there. It had, however, already been used more as a title in Rom 16:1 and Phil 1:1. Here the process is taken a step further, and an office of deacon emerges, with similar criteria for candidature and again little indication of responsibilities expected to be borne.

The specific instruction again begins with the ruling (implied): "It is necessary that . . ." (v. 8). As with the overseers, the first criterion is "respectable, dignified, serious" (the adjective related to the noun first used in 2:2), but again we should recall that it was of major importance for these new little churches to gain wider respect within the cities where they lived and met. "Not double-tongued" is clear enough, though it is discouraging that such had to be among the first requirements. Even more so are the next two—"not addicted to much wine, not fond of dishonest gain/greedy for money." The instruction is much the same as that in v. 3 and Titus 1:7. What a range of possible candidates for these roles that such instruction had to be given!

The most distinctively theological criterion in the whole chapter appears in v. 9: "holding the mystery of the faith with a clean conscience." The term "mystery" (μυστήριον *mystērion*) had been Paul's way of speaking about the great revelation (given to him in particular) that Gentiles were to be included

---

59. Lucian (2nd century) mocks Christians for being thus duped by the impressive sham Peregrinus, who, having started as a Cynic philosopher, was attracted for a time to Christianity, in which he quickly became a highly esteemed figure. See Lucian *Passing of Peregrinus* 11-13, 16.

with Jews in the saving purposes of God (Rom 11:25; Eph 3:3-9; Col 1:26-27). Here it is linked with "the faith," now evidently understood as a fuller statement of what Christians were to believe (see footnote 9). So presumably the thought is either still of the gospel as a hidden mystery revealed in Christ (cf. v. 16), or it is becoming more like the later sense of "the faith" as ultimately mysterious and, therefore, requiring someone skilled in understanding and exposition to unveil it to initiates. Not that the deacons are necessarily to fill that role (but see v. 13); here it is sufficient that they hold to that mystery—that is, affirm their commitment to the faith despite its mysterious quality and do so wholeheartedly, without undue qualms of conscience (see Commentary on 1:5). Confidence of faith was thus established as a crucial characteristic of leadership from very early on.

Equally striking is the counsel that deacons should "first be tested," and only if proved "blameless" should they serve (v. 10). The need for such testing was from early on (1 Thess 5:21) required by Paul as a way of preventing abuse of charismatic ministry (cf. 1 Cor 12:10; 14:29). Here the principle is extended to more established ministries. What the testing consisted of is not indicated (Are vv. 8-12 such a checklist?), nor is it clear whether a sort of probationary period for would-be deacons is intended.

Another puzzle is whether we should translate v. 11 as "likewise women" or "likewise their wives." The former is certainly possible, in view of Rom 16:1, and need not clash with 2:12 if "deacon" was a post of administrative responsibility (as in a well-ordered household) but not teaching responsibility.[60] The latter would indicate an early case of husbands' prospects for advancement being dependent on the behavior of their wives! Again the first word, σεμνός (*semnos*), is "respectable," "dignified," "serious" (as in v. 8). "Devils" (διαβόλους *diabolous*) should obviously be taken in its alternative sense of "slanderous." That they should be "temperate" was also required of overseers (v. 2). After such a list, "faithful in all things" comes closer to what might be found in an equivalent list today.

With v. 12 the criteria of "once married" and "experienced in good household management" again come to the fore (as in vv. 2, 4-5). Marriage and the household were seen as good testing grounds of leadership or ministry potential, and the degree to which administration of the church was being modeled on good household management is again evident.

Verse 13 gives the reason why the church had to be so choosy about its deacons—not least for their own sake: To serve well was to gain for oneself a "good step"—that is, presumably a step forward. The term βαθμόν καλόν (*bathmon kalon*, "good or excellent standing") may indicate a step of advancement within "the mystery of the faith" (vv. 9, 16) or even a "stage or rank." The imagery, somewhat unnervingly, may be akin to a stage in further initiation into the deeper mysteries of a cult. But a further factor was that those who served well could have "much boldness or confidence in faith" (cf. 2 Cor 3:12; Eph 3:12), again described as "faith in Christ Jesus" (as in 1:14). Or perhaps we should translate it as "much openness [in speaking], frankness or plainness of speech" (cf. Eph 6:19). In that case, somewhat surprisingly (cf. Acts 6:2), deacons were thought to have an important teaching ministry, into the deeper mysteries of the faith (though it is worth noting that in Acts 6–8 the ministries of Stephen and Philip soon became much more focused on teaching and evangelism than on administration).

3:14-16, The Reason for These Instructions. The instructions were intended as a substitute for Paul's personal presence (vv. 14-15). Paul's record of delay and disappointment in his planned visits would have been well known (e.g., Rom 1:13; 2 Cor 1:15-18), so that the letter became his principal means of giving advice and guidance. His frustrations over sailing schedules, bad weather, and repeated unexpected demands on his time have thus brought unexpected benefit to subsequent generations and successors to the churches he founded. It was natural, then, that a letter should still function as the voice of the great, but absent, apostle.

---

60. The syntax favors the identification. See J. H. Stiefel, "Women Deacons in 1 Timothy: A Linguistic and Literary Look at 'Women Likewise . . .' (1 Tim 3:1.11)," *NTS* 41 (1995) 442-57. Writing in 112 CE, Pliny, governor of Bithynia, refers to two Christians as "maids who were called ministers/deacons." See Pliny *Letters* 10.96.

The concern is that the recipients might know how it was "necessary" (δεῖ *dei*; the same term as in v. 2 and implied in v. 8) for believers to conduct themselves within "the household of God" (v. 15). The phrase partly echoes the idea of the Temple as "the house of God" (reflected in 1 Pet 2:5). But in this case, the thought is almost certainly more of "house" as "household" = family (as the preceding usages in vv. 4-5, 12 surely indicate). The ambiguity of "church" meeting in a "house" (not dissimilar to the ambiguity of "house/Temple") reinforces the point, emerging throughout the chapter, that structures of good household management should provide the model for the ordering of the church.[61] In this case, it is "the household of God" that is in view" in this household, the real *paterfamilias* is God, from whom all authority ultimately derives and with whom all authority ultimately rests.

The ambiguity is carried forward into the next phrase (v. 15), where the echo of OT usage continues. "The church of Yahweh" was a familiar description of the assembly of Israel (e.g., Num 16:3; Deut 23:1-3, 8; Mic 2:5),[62] and "the living God" characterized the Jewish conviction that all other gods were dead idols (cf. 2 Cor 6:16; 1 Thess 1:9). "Pillar and foundation" sustains the image of a building and in the sequence of imagery would again probably evoke thought of the Temple (cf. Rev 3:12). It was a high claim for themselves that these little churches around the edge of the Mediterranean made for themselves: They were God's family, in direct continuity with the Israel of the one Lord God. It was this conviction that bolstered their claim to have "the truth" (see footnote 9), to have been given such a firm insight into and grasp of the true state of affairs.

This truth is then summed up in what appears to be a hymnic form, which encapsulates "the mystery" of God's purpose as it has been revealed to them in Christ (v. 16; see Commentary on 3:9). Here it is described as "the mystery of the piety," where εὐσέβεια (*eusebeia*; see Commentary on 2:2) seems to epitomize the new Christian religion as a whole. The parallel with the populist acclamation in Ephesus, "Great is Artemis of the Ephesians" (Acts 19:28, 34), raises the intriguing possibility that this was intended as a Christian parallel and as a response to the dominant piety of Ephesus.

The six lines cited are one of the clearest examples of an early Christian hymn:[63] Christ is not even mentioned—the referent of the familiar lines needs no fuller identification (there is no antecedent to the opening "who");[64] the lines are set out in parallel passive phrases with "in" and the dative (only the third line omits the "in"); and they are structured in antithetical couplets in which the nouns ("flesh/spirit," "angels/nations" [the term can be translated "Gentiles" (NRSV), but the NIV's "nations" is preferable], "world/glory") are more determinative than the verbs, only the first of which ("revealed") links into the theology elsewhere in the Pastorals (cf. 2 Tim 1:10; Titus 1:3). The epigrammatic form makes for some awkward sense, particularly the second line (lit., "justified in spirit"), but the antithesis is clearly between Christ's pre-Easter earthly existence and his post-Easter exaltation (cf. 1 Pet 3:18). To look for greater precision of meaning in such a tight epigrammatic structure would be most unwise. The other lines probably do not form a chronological account but simply juxtapose Christ's increasing missionary impact on earth with his triumphal reception in heaven. Here is the faith to be preached and believed, the truth on whose foundation the household of God was being built: It is Christ.

---

61. This is the key thematic text for D. C. Verner, *The Household of God: The Social World of the Pastoral Epistles*, SBLDS 71 (Chico, Calif.: Scholars Press, 1983) 107-11.

62. The Greek term ἐκκλησία (*ekklēsia*), in the NT usually translated "church," is used about 100 times in the LXX.

63. A fuller treatment may be found in R. H. Gundry, "The Form, Meaning, and Background of the Hymn Quoted in 1 Timothy 3:16," in *Apostolic History and the Gospel*, F. F. Bruce Festschrift, ed. W. W. Gasque and R. P. Martin (Grand Rapids: Eerdmans, 1970) 203-22.

64. The lack of identification prompted some scribes to tidy up the Greek, including the reading of "God" (θεός *theos*) instead of "who" (ὅς *hos*).

REFLECTIONS

The linking word in this chapter is *household*. Its effect is to set the church in a double relation—on the one hand to the well-ordered family, and on the other hand to the Israel of old. Both are fundamental to the church's identity, and awareness of that double identity is fundamental to the church's well-being.

On the one hand, it is important to note here how natural it is that family and church are not set in opposition to each other, or that one is not posed as a threat to the other. Such opposition seems to be implied in some of Jesus' statements (e.g., Mark 3:31-35; Luke 14:26), and the challenge to discipleship and the missionary call will often mean hard choices between priorities. But the hyperbole of Jesus' teaching should not be made a rule; not all people were to leave home and literally follow him. His commendation of the fifth command is unreserved (Mark 7:9-13), and the prodigal son's leaving home is an antitype of discipleship (Luke 15:11-32). Despite some misunderstanding, Paul's commendation of marriage and the priority he gives to children's welfare should be clear enough in 1 Cor 7:3-5, 12-14, 36-38 (so also 1 Tim 4:3).

Here, however, the point is still clearer: The well-ordered family is the pattern for the well-ordered church (see also 5:1-2, 4, 8); those who are not good and effective husbands and fathers (3:4-5, 12) should not be expected to provide good and effective leadership in the church. As with the issue of husbands and wives (2:11-15), we should not confuse the form of that good management, as it was then conceived, with the principle here expressed. The language of "submission" (2:11; 3:4) reflects the conventional wisdom of the day, not a divinely instituted order. The principle remains that the family structure (here only husbands and wives, parents and children, are in view) provides a positive analogy to the structure of the church (see also Reflections at 2:8-15). It should be added, however, that the traditional family structure is only an analogy and that this analogy does not give grounds, for example, for debarring single persons from positions of church leadership. Other analogies (e.g., shepherd, servant, gardener) that indicate otherwise can easily be called upon.

It also follows that models for discipleship that set church and family in antithesis should be regarded as suspect. It would be odd, indeed, if the basic unit of society (the family) were seen, as a structural unit, to be hostile to the church, as though the church were a revolutionary structure that overturned and replaced any other; individual cases of conflict do not overturn the more fundamental principle. If 1 Timothy 3:1 has continuing relevance, then, the family itself is to be seen as the primary force for nurturing of discipleship and the primary arena for discipleship, and as such it should be the proving ground for the church in discipline and order.[65]

What could be taken for granted, then, when the church met in a house and the relationships and ordering of the one blended into the other, needs to be restated in terms more meaningful to the mobile society and transient groupings of today. It would be a pity if all that resulted was negative criticism of one-parent families, divorces, families in which both parents pursued professional careers, as compared with an older ideal of family (as though that ideal had ever been fully realized); or if church fellowship was presented as a replacement for family (on the ground that some families are dysfunctional); or if the teaching was set aside because it did not apply equally to all church members. Discussion time would be better spent asking how far the positive principles implicit in this section can be safeguarded and promoted, given and within the changing circumstances of today.

The link implied by church—*ekklēsia*—the assembly of Israel, also needs fuller rethinking. For centuries the church has seen itself as replacing historic Israel, much as some have seen the church replacing the historic family unit. The long-term result has

---

65. I am indebted here to my wife's thesis. See M. Dunn, "The Place of Family in Discipleship" (Ph.D. diss., Durham University, 1988).

been centuries of anti-Semitism, culminating in the Holocaust. But now in the revulsion against that tragic history, Paul's attempt to hold together church and Israel (Gal 6:16), Gentile and Jewish believers as together constituting the called people of God (Rom 9:24-29; 11:17-24) is being heard afresh. That is what lies behind the merging of household into house of God, into pillar and foundation of God's Temple (3:15). It is only as the church understands itself in terms of Israel and in direct continuity with Israel (cf. Romans 9–11; Gal 6:16; see also Titus 2:14) that it can begin to understand itself, its Lord (Messiah Jesus), and three-quarters of its Bible (the OT)!

Within this alternate imagery it is striking that the functionaries named are not "priest" or "high priest," but "overseer" and "deacon." Continuity there may be, but not in the central office-bearers and functionaries of Israel's Temple. The functions, so far as they can be determined, are contained in the names themselves—to keep an eye out for good, to serve. To that extent, we may say that these functions are every bit as charismatic (engraced and enabled by God's Spirit) as those more explicitly so in Paul's earlier conception of church ministry (Rom 12:6-8; 1 Cor 12:4-11, 28). That is to say, they are ill-defined as to specific function, since their specific function was determined by the motivation expressed in their names.

Coordinate with that is the weight of the writer's concern in describing the criteria for candidates for such office—little or no anxiety about what we would call theological training or administrative expertise, but concern for character and for a life that would justifiably be respected by others. One may wonder at several items in these lists of criteria, but the priorities, particularly in recently formed groups, probably strange in character to their neighbors, are worth noting. Here again the church, and not least the much more established churches of the early twenty-first century, is bidden to pause and take fresh thought about such matters. Have character and motivation, for example, as criteria of function, become too lost to sight behind procedural rules and political considerations, as determinants for office?

1 TIMOTHY 4:1-16, THE TWO WAYS

COMMENTARY

Chapter 4 broadly follows a pattern of exhortation with ancient precedents, in Jewish tradition already quite elaborate in Deuteronomy 28–30. The speaker sets before his audience two paths, between which they have to choose, or two prospects, one of which will be realized, depending on how they respond to the speaker's challenge. The classic Christian examples are Matt 7:13-14 and the early second-century church manual, *Didache* 1–6. Here the indicative terms are "later times" and "depart from" (4:1); "follow" (4:6); "train yourself" (4:7-8); "promise of life" (4:8); "strive," "hope" (4:10); "progress" (4:15); and "you will save" (4:16). The first alternative is characterized by talk of "deceitful spirits" and "demons" (4:1); "hypocrisy of liars" and "seared conscience" (4:2); "godless and silly myths" (4:7); and, by implication, general slackness and lack of discipline (4:7-8, 10, 15). The second alternative, to which the writer wishes to point his hearers, is characterized by "thanksgiving," "believing and knowing the truth" (4:3-4); "word of God and prayer" (4:5); "words of faith and of the good teaching" (4:6); "godliness" (4:7-8); "hope in God" and "believe" (4:10); "love, faith, purity" (4:12); "reading, encouraging, teaching" (4:13, 16); and "charism" (4:14). The contrast is stated sharply for effect, the former set out in pejorative terms, the latter in bland assertions; but sufficient detail is included to enable the reader to perceive that recognizable life-styles were in view.

4:1-5, The Wrong Way. The prospect of defection is held out as a certainty. It had been explicitly stated by the Spirit (v. 1). The reference is presumably either to the familiar scenario of immense suffering and persecution to be experienced by the faithful in the last days of the present age, or to a particular prophetic utterance elaborating the prospect in more detail. The prediction had been a feature in Jewish apocalyptic more or less since Dan 12:1-2. In Christian tradition, something similar is attributed to Jesus (Mark 13:5-6, 13, 19-22) and to Paul (Acts 20:29-30; 2 Thess 2:3-12), and the same foreboding is expressed in Revelation (e.g., Rev 2:5, 16; 14:9-12). The implication is that the writer understands his present as already "the last days."

The key word here, ἀφίστημι (*aphistēmi*), can be translated as "fall away," "become apostate," "desert" (NIV, "abandon"; NRSV, "renounce"), and is regularly used in the LXX of falling away from God (e.g., Deut 32:15; Jer 3:14; 1 Macc 1:15). There was a real choice to be made here, and given the volatility and lack of clear boundaries around the young churches, there would be considerable crossing of these boundaries, outward as well as inward (see Reflections on 1:1-11). The concern here, then, is to firm up the commitment and resolve of such recruits by painting the alternative in apocalyptic colors (cf. references to Daniel 12; Mark 13; 2 Thessalonians 2; and Revelation above).

The immediate contrast is between "the faith" and "deceitful spirits and teachings of demons." Presumably prophecies within or without the Christian assemblies are in view (cf. 2 Thess 2:2; 2 Pet 2:1; 1 John 4:1-3), promoting views that the writer saw as contrary to "the faith." The problem of false prophecy is an old one within the Judeo-Christian tradition (see, e.g., 1 Kings 22; Jeremiah 28; 1 Thess 5:19-22; *Didache* 11; Justin *Dialogue with Trypho* 82), though the earlier Paul was less disposed to attribute to false spirits and demons those prophecies that were to be rejected (see 1 Cor 10:20-21; 12:10). An example of such teaching supported by prophecy will be provided in 4:3, but it should be noted that the charismatic character of the earlier Pauline churches (1 Cor 14:26-32; 1 Thess 5:19-22) still persisted. The firmer structures of organization and formulation of "the faith" had presumably been found necessary, in part at least against the dangers of charismatic excess and false prophecy.

Verse 2 is a good example of polemical denigration. Those who depart from "the faith" for such reasons have simply succumbed to "the hypocritical preaching of liars whose own consciences have been seared" (lit., branded with a red-hot iron and thus desensitized).[66] The imagery evoked is vivid, but we should recall that it is coined by one who disagreed violently with the opinions expressed.

An example of such false teaching backed by prophetic utterance is the advocacy of an ascetic life-style: marriage forbidden and abstinence from certain foods advocated (v. 3). Similar issues had troubled the church in Corinth—regarding marriage (1 Cor 7:1)[67] and over the eating of meat offered to idols (1 Corinthians 8)—though in the latter case the principal problem was with those who thought it perfectly acceptable to eat such food (see Col 2:20-23). The advice here follows that in 1 Corinthians 7 and the theological logic of 1 Cor 10:25-26: Whatever has been created by God is good (Genesis 1).[68] The faithful, by definition, should know this truth, their consciences being instructed in the faith. The practical test is the same as in the nearest equivalent passage, Rom 14:6: Can the one who eats, acting in a way that seems overindulgent to others in the church, give thanks to God in doing so (v. 3)? The answer here is yes; the acceptability of a controversial life-style to God is more determinative than its acceptability to fellow church members.

The point is repeated in strong terms to reinforce it: "Everything created by God is fine and nothing need be rejected if it is received with thanksgiving, for then it is consecrated through the word of God and prayer" (vv. 4-5). That the rationale is essentially theological ("faith," "truth," "made by God," "word of God," "prayer"), and not simply freedom

---

66. Kelly, *The Pastoral Epistles*, 94-95, marginally prefers the sense "branded" as an owner would brand a slave—that is, by the "deceitful spirits" and "demons" of 4:2.

67. It is generally agreed that in 1 Cor 7:1*b* Paul quotes a letter he received from the Corinthians.

68. "A more powerful statement on the goodness of the created order would be hard to find," Johnson, *Letters to Paul's Delegates*, 164.

of the individual or liberty of opinion, should be noted.

4:6-10, The Right Way. The alternative is to be clearly taught by Timothy (v. 6). This is a primary responsibility of the "fine minister of Christ Jesus"; the term used is again διάκονος (*diakonos*, "minister," "one who serves"), underlining its still functional and not yet exclusively formal sense (as in 3:8-13; cf. 1:12; 2 Tim 4:5, 11; this was its more typical earlier use; cf. Rom 15:8; 1 Cor 3:5; 2 Cor 3:6; 6:4; 11:15, 23; Gal 2:17; 1 Thess 3:2). Here the idea of a way of discipleship comes more clearly to the fore, mingled with the earlier family imagery: Timothy has been "nourished, brought up"—that is, within "the household of God" (3:15)—and has "followed faithfully" (see Commentary on 2 Tim 3:10) "the words of the faith and the good teaching." The doubling up of two of the letters' most consistent terms to denote the body of teaching that had already been formulated as "Christian" (see footnote 9) makes clear the character and direction of the second alternative, the right way, being advocated. Again the impression is clearly given that within the relative amorphousness of the early Christian communities it soon became necessary to agree on and formulate more carefully defined statements of faith and more elaborate codes of acceptable conduct, presumably in order to give a sharper sense of Christian identity and a clearer boundary line over against wider society. In the Pastorals we see this process happening before our eyes.

In sharp contrast, the wrong-way alternative can be dismissed as "profane" (the same word appeared in the vice list in 1:9) and "old wives' tales [myths]" (v. 7), the latter phrase having the same disparaging overtone as today (see Commentary on 1:4). To avoid these requires strict self-discipline, which the writer clearly sees to be distinct from the asceticism of v. 3, in content, character, and goal.[69] The image now switches to the athlete's training (v. 8), an image much loved by Paul (1 Cor 9:24-25; Phil 3:13-14). If that is of some profit (as would be generally agreed), then training for "godliness" (the regular term of approbation in the Pastorals;

see the Commentary on 2:2) is of profit for everything. The promise is not simply of the victor's wreath in the games, but of life both now and in the age to come (cf. 1:16; 6:12, 19; 2 Tim 1:1, 10; Titus 1:2; 3:7). The writer is so confident of the truth of his conviction that he designates it also a "faithful saying and worthy of all acceptance" (v. 9). Some think "the faithful saying" refers to what follows, but v. 8*b* has the more formulaic character (see the Commentary on 1:15).

With the age-old religious instinct to set this present life and its circumstances into a long-term context, the writer reaffirms the goal of godliness: a hope that looks for a salvation beyond the limits of current experience (v. 10). The thought is still of the discipline required: "for this cause we work hard and exert ourselves" (ἀγωνιζόμεθα, *agōnizometha* as in the *agōn*, "athletic contest").[70] "Hope," as almost always in the NT, is the confident Hebrew assurance, rather than the tentative Greek aspiration (cf. Rom 5:2-5; 8:24; Gal 5:5; Col 1:5), the Hebrew character of the thought reinforced by a further reference to "the living God" (see Commentary on 3:15) as the guarantor of the hope.

The hope arises out of the conviction that God is "Savior" (v. 10). Elsewhere in the Pastorals (see Commentary on 1:1), the thought is always of "our Savior," whether in reference to God or to Christ Jesus. But here the note of universalism, first loudly struck in 2:4-6 (see also Titus 2:11), is sounded again: "Savior of everyone." The additional phrase, "especially believers," sounds odd and has occasioned much discussion: Does it qualify the note of universalism? Presumably it is intended primarily to underline the confidence of the writer's hope: If God is Savior of everyone, then those of faith in God can be all the more confident that they will share in God's salvation.

4:11-16, Timothy as an Example. The role envisaged for Timothy becomes clearer: He receives instruction from Paul and passes it on with authority to instruct and to teach (v. 11). How someone should be described who commands overseers and deacons is not made clear. The writer is content to leave the

---

69. It is unlikely that the "bodily training" was intended as a disparaging reference to the asceticism of 4:3. See J. M. Bassler, *1 Timothy, 2 Timothy, Titus,* ANTC (Nashville: Abingdon, 1996) 84. See also Kelly, *The Pastoral Epistles,* 100.

70. There is a variant reading: "suffer reproach." It is not very strongly attested, but since "exert ourselves" is more appropriate to the context, perhaps the former was replaced by the latter.

impression, here and elsewhere, that Timothy is Paul's personal representative and emissary. So the authority with which Timothy teaches is that of Paul himself, not that of a distinct rank or office.

The reference to Timothy's youth (v. 12) is somewhat surprising. At first encounter he is described in terms suggesting a fair degree of maturity (a disciple well spoken of, Acts 16:1-2). Since then he had functioned as Paul's chief aide for the rest of Paul's ministry (see Commentary on 1:2). That is, if the Pastorals do come from a late phase of Paul's ministry, then Timothy would have been Paul's chief coworker for about fifteen years. To call someone already into his thirties a "youth" would be unusual, and after such a period of training and responsibility, was anyone who respected Paul likely to question Timothy's authority? If, alternatively, the letter was written later, as seems more likely, and if Timothy himself was still in view, then he would probably have been in his fifties at least. It looks, then, as though the writer is working with an image of Timothy drawn from the earlier letters of Paul. Timothy, in other words, may here function as a representative model of the youthful leader, like the younger member of Paul's mission team of earlier years, someone whose charism or natural ability brought him to the forefront despite his youth. In an era that venerated the wisdom of age, such a one might well be "despised" (1 Cor 16:11, a different word, written at least ten years earlier). And though Paul never uses the word in reference to himself (cf. Rom 2:4; 1 Cor 11:22), there certainly were those operating within his churches who had scorned him in the past (e.g., 2 Cor 10:10).

The best way of answering such attacks would be for Timothy to show himself as a model worthy to be copied (v. 12). On several occasions Paul had put himself forward as an example (1 Cor 4:16; 11:1; Phil 3:17); it is interesting to note that in the first of these, Timothy is sent to remind the Corinthians of Paul's example (1 Cor 4:17). So now it is Timothy who is to provide exemplary leadership "in speech, in conduct, in love, in faith, in purity," the last probably with the sexual sense of "chastity" (cf. 5:2). Little is more destructive of community than authority of status not matched by quality of life.

With the instruction of v. 13, whether an epistolary characterization or a real visit in prospect, the function of the letter as the voice of the absent Paul is underlined. Paul's letters were often written to signal an imminent visit or a visit delayed (see Commentary on 3:14-16). "Until I come" can serve as a piece of advice that endures. "Reading" probably means public, rather than private, reading. This would certainly refer to the Scriptures,[71] but also to writings worthy to be read in church and probably already also readings of Christian documents—early collections of Jesus tradition and Paul's own letters (cf. Col 4:16; 2 Pet 3:15-16). It was in this way that their authority grew and spread. Worth noting is the implied content of a Christian assembly and its variety: the drawing upon ancient scriptural writings and newer writings of recognized worth; encouragement as well as teaching, presumably on the basis of the reading (see Luke 4:17-21; Acts 13:15).

Timothy's authority is underlined by reference back to what is considered a particular commissioning event (v. 14). It evidently had three elements: the giving of his "charism," that is, presumably, by the Spirit (1 Cor 12:4-7, 11); a "prophecy" (prophetic utterance; cf. 1:18); and "the laying on of hands by the presbytery." The event is referred to again in 2 Tim 1:6, and the nearest parallel is the commissioning of Barnabas and Saul by the leaders of the Antioch church at the behest of the Spirit, presumably through prophetic utterance (Acts 13:2-3; cf. Acts 14:23). The whole event, however, seems to be envisaged in more formal terms. The "charism" seems now to be conceived of as a permanent gift that Timothy can "neglect" (v. 14) or can "rekindle" (2 Tim 1:6), whereas Paul's earlier thought was more in terms of charism as the enactment of grace, coming to visible manifestation in a particular utterance or act (Rom 12:4-8; 1 Cor 12:4-11). The laying on of hands as an act of the presbytery (council of elders) sounds like a more formally conceived and structured act, though in 2 Tim 1:6 Paul refers only to his own action, and here the preposition "with" implies attendant circumstances rather than means ("through," as in

---

71. Kelly notes that "Public reading in the ancient world called for some technical accomplishment, for the words in the codex were not divided." See Kelly, *The Pastoral Epistles*, 105.

2 Tim 1:6; but see Commentary on 2 Tim 2:2). In v. 14, we appear to be on the way to a concept of "ordination" and of charism as "grace of office."

That commission ("these things") once given has to be thought about, carefully cultivated, and practiced (the first verb, μελετάω [meletaō], has this range of meaning); "these things" (v. 15) presumably embraces all that had been referred to in vv. 11-14. The charism that is not exercised will wither. "Be in them"; we might say, "Immerse yourself in them." The personal objective is "progress" in "these things"; the term "progress" (προκοπή prokopē) was popular in Stoic philosophy, and Paul had used it in Phil 1:25 (cf. Phil 1:12). The advice complements that of 1 Tim 4:12.

The most important yardstick is "the teaching" (v. 16): "Stick with that." It is that which will ensure salvation both for Timothy and for those whom he instructs in the teaching. Here again we see a deep concern to mark out and delimit the terms of the gospel, the faith, and to forge an exclusive link between that teaching and salvation. Down that track lies the old slogan, "Outside the church no salvation," with both its strengths and its weaknesses. The strength is that the teaching does encapsulate what Christians have found from the start to contain the words of life. The weakness is that salvation can be thought to be conditional on adherence to a particular set of words, first framed to meet certain historical challenges and interpreted in a narrow and insensitive way.

REFLECTIONS

The advantage of the "two ways" imagery is twofold. In the first place, it emphasizes that there is a choice to be made and that this choice will entail what may be lasting consequences. The vision of endless freedom and an infinite pluralism of "good" possibilities cloaks an uncomfortable fact, summed up in the old aphorism: We are free to choose, but we are not free to choose the consequences of our choice. Freedom to choose a particular career or to experiment with drugs or to throw off sexual restraint sets in motion a sequence of consequences from which it is impossible to escape and which will be character shaping as well as life-style constraining. And these are simply illustrations of the potentially far more momentous choice in regard to religion and faith, if indeed it is the case that a fundamental reality of human beings is that they are also spiritual beings made by God and for relationship with God.

This does not mean that such a momentous choice once made need never be made again. The reality is that there will always be some people, initially drawn to choose the best way, who will "fall away" by paying too much attention to what the writer calls "deceitful spirits" (the problem of false prophecy) and "hypocritical preaching of liars" (teaching proferred for factional or personal motives). Here as in other spheres, the price of liberty is eternal vigilance. In this often disturbing reality of enticing alternatives and clashing opinions, it is often vital to have a clear grasp of the basic principles and values on which the religion, the godly life, is built. In the case of the Pastorals, this means "the words of the faith and of the sound teaching." Few can live out of a faith outline as brief as "God is one; Jesus is Lord" (cf. Rom 10:9; 1 Cor 8:6). Most need something more. It is the task of leadership to indicate and define what that more should be, drawing not least from the reading of Scripture and previous tradition (4:13).

The danger on the other side is that such a statement of "the faith and the teaching" can become overdefined and too prescriptive. Here it is important to note the way the writer takes a firm stand on a principle of liberty in regard to one of the most contentious issues for the early churches: whether certain foods were prohibited to believers. In earlier days it had been a make-or-break issue; the very definition and status of "Jew" and "Christian" hung on it (1 Macc 2:62-63; Rom 14:3-4). In the light of such tradition, a cautious respondent would have been tempted to counsel, "If it's offensive to others, don't." But in this instance the writer follows the line of Paul's advice: "If you can give thanks to God in what you do and for what you do, then it is a consecrated act acceptable to God" (see 4:4-5; cf. Rom 14:6). In other words, the make-or-break issues for one need not be so for others or for the church as a whole. Discerning the difference is what marks out mature leadership.

In the second place, the image of a "way" is a reminder that the Christian life is not to be conceived as something static. This is often the hidden implication of alternative metaphors like "position" and "viewpoint." But the first formal title for Christianity seems to have been "the way" (Acts 9:2; 18:25-26; 19:9, 23; 22:4; 24:14, 22). And Paul's favorite image for Christian conduct is "walk," itself reflecting the traditional Jewish image הלך (*hālāk*, "walk"), from which the term *halakhah* ("rules for conduct") is derived. Here the point is evoked particularly by talk of "following" (v. 6) and "progress" (v. 15). The point is that the Christian life involves movement, growth (nurture, v. 6), development. Too often in Christian mission so much attention is given to conversion that the equally important development toward maturity is neglected.

The writer makes clear that such growth and development depend on training and the discipline involved (vv. 7-8); they involve hard work and sweat-inducing exertion (v. 10); they require cultivation of the gift given and committed personal involvement (v. 15). Here again a choice once made has to be repeatedly reaffirmed and lived out.

The imagery also provides another angle on "the faith" and "the teaching." The Pastorals can be too easily disparaged for their reliance upon a faith and teaching already formulated and prescribed. But it would be more fair to see this emphasis as a stage on the way to greater maturity (of individual and church). That is to say, "the faith/teaching" actually refers to the process of giving Christian identity greater clarity of definition. It is not an endpoint ("the faith" finally defined), but "faith seeking understanding."

Such progress in faith need not mean a steadily lengthening list of "what we believe and do" (even the more prescriptive tendency of rabbinic Judaism allowed for plenty of dissenting opinions). What it should mean is a greater appreciation of how faith responds to and impacts upon an increasing range of alternative ideologies and practical issues, a process that in turn should provide guidelines (not straitjackets) for future responses and objectives. To "do theology" is not simply to learn about past doctrines and classic statements of faith. It means still more to think through the reality of a living faith and to bring that reality (not just formulae and statements about faith) into dialogue with alternative views of reality, resulting in fresh formulations of the faith. A faith that does not grow and develop condemns itself to wither and die. *Tertium non datur:* There is no third alternative!

1 TIMOTHY 5:1–6:2, ON THE ELDERLY, WIDOWS, ELDERS, AND SLAVES

COMMENTARY

The thought returns to one of the writer's principal preoccupations: the good ordering of the church. But whereas the previous instructions were posed in third-person terms (3:1-13), now the talk is more in second-person terms, of the responsibilities as primarily Timothy's. As someone still relatively young (4:12), a test of Timothy's leadership would be how he handled himself in regard to those whose age would ordinarily command respect, as well as to those closer to his own age (5:1-12). This train of thought leads to acknowledgment of the significant body of elderly widows who would naturally be part of or attracted to such a community (5:3-8), and in turn to the younger widows who would be no less prominent (5:9-16). The elderly presumably included the elders whose responsibilities under Timothy required still greater sensitivity on the part of Timothy (5:17-22). The following exhortations seem to arise from concern for Timothy's ability to handle the strain (5:23-25), and the concerns for good management are rounded off quite naturally with conventional advice to slaves, again in third-person terms (6:1-2).

5:1-2, On Old and Young. A fascinating feature of this section of 1 Timothy is the use of πρεσβύτερος (*presbyteros*) three times within a few verses (vv. 1, 17, 19), where in the first case the word clearly means "older man," while in the other two it should probably be translated "elder." The former meaning is put beyond dispute by the contrast with "younger men" (v. 1) and the complementary reference to "older women/younger women" (v. 2). Although mortality rates were much higher then than today, many men and women did live to ripe old age; v. 9 envisages "pensionable" age as sixty. The concern here is not simply Timothy's youth, but no doubt reflects the general high regard for age, as the repository of experience and of the wisdom that (usually) came with it. The fact that the first thought is that Timothy might "rebuke" such a senior member of the church says much for the authority invested in him as here envisaged. The contrasting image of a father ("encourage him as a father"), given all the authority a father had over his son, simply reinforces the authority being claimed.

The counsel had respect for the older members primarily in view (vv. 3-10, 17-22); the reference to the younger men and women follows as a corollary (vv. 1-2). To be noted is the way in which the model of the family continues to provide guidelines. That the latter could also be used more generally for kinsfolk or fellow members of societies does not detract from the dominant family imagery here. Again, even more clearly than in 4:12, the writer recognizes that a still-young bachelor in a leadership role is likely to be vulnerable to thoughts of "impurity, unchastity" (see vv. 11-12).

5:3-8, Widows. A social feature of the time was the relatively high proportion of widows in any community. This was the result of a combination of factors. In particular, young girls beyond puberty were often married to much older men, and the mortality rate would often be high among men in military service. Unless well-to-do in her own right through inheritance, a widow's lack of legal status made her even more vulnerable; her legal (male) guardian might covet her wealth or abuse his authority.

Concern for the widow was a feature of Jewish legislation (e.g., Deut 14:29; 24:17-21; 26:12), and the prominence of widows in and around the early Christian churches is well enough indicated by the frequency of their mention in Luke–Acts (Luke 2:37; 4:25-26; 7:12; 18:3-5; 20:47; 21:2-3; Acts 6:1; 9:39-41). Their vulnerability made it all the more essential that a church that saw itself in direct continuity with the assembly of Israel (3:15) should take special measures to ensure that widows were properly cared for. Nothing is said explicitly, but the implication is that the churches would ordinarily administer some sort of social welfare fund (supplied by almsgiving; see Gal 2:10) on behalf of widows. The problem of caring adequately for widows arose already in the earliest days of the new movement (Acts 6:1) and had been dealt with in the same spirit as shown by Israel's ancient legislators (e.g., Deut 14:28-29; 24:19-21). Here it is clear that a formal register was already in operation (v. 9). The extensiveness of the treatment (vv. 3-16) may suggest that the policy was being clarified or extended, or even formulated for the first time.

The initial concern is that the communal funds be used only for those in genuine need—"real widows" (v. 3; the NIV's "really in need" in vv. 3, 5 says more than the Greek does). The term translated "honor" (τίμη *timē*) probably carries the connotation of "provide financial support for" (see also v. 17). The expectation was that a widow who had adult children or grandchildren should be looked after by them (v. 4). This is part of the basic "piety" that the writer both assumed and commended, as expected by and acceptable to God. Here "piety" is clearly defined by the fifth commandment (Exod 20:12), but the duty of children to parents was widely taught in the ancient world. A complementary consideration was the tradition of "favor" and "recompense" that governed acts of generosity by the gods or to a city, the honorific inscription as a way of returning the favor received. So provision for aged parents (here widowed mothers) is the "return" to be expected for their generosity in parenthood and upbringing. Here again it is to be noted how positive is the author's picture of the family; the family was expected to be the focus and model of care for the elderly.[72]

The "real" widow, in the sense of one who needs help not available to her from her immediate family, is the one "left alone" (v. 5). She has no one to hope in except God (an echo, perhaps, of Jer 49:11). Like Anna in Luke 2:37, she continues in prayer "night and day"—not, we may assume, simply out of a worry-free piety, but in her worry and distress the only one she can turn to is God (see Luke 18:2-7). The contrast is with the widow who has been left well off and can live luxuriously, in indulgence (v. 6).[73] The author's comment is dismissive and biting; such a one may be living it up, but she is so insensible to matters of true value that she is already as good as dead! It is Timothy's responsibility to make this plain to all widows (v. 7).

Significantly the thought returns to the responsibility of the family. It is the responsibility of the senior male member of a household to take forethought, to make provision for those in his care. Here we have a brief insight into the full sweep of responsibility of the *paterfamilias*. That responsibility included all his near relatives, whether living in his own immediate household or not, on whose behalf he had been appointed guardian. But he had a special responsibility for members of his immediate household, and here it is particularly his wife who is in view. The writer gives this responsibility the highest rank. To fail in it was tantamount to denying the faith. Such a one was "worse than an unbeliever." The importance of family and of family responsibilities as part of Christian faith and discipleship, and of the integration (not antithesis) of family and church responsibilities could hardly be more strongly stressed.

5:9-16, Younger Widows. The writer clearly expects that the churches written to would have a register of widows (v. 9). It is clearly enrollment that is in view and not admission to an order of ministry, as in 3:1-13 and 5:22.[74] The first rules had already been outlined: (1) Husbands ought to make provision for their wives in case they were widowed (v. 8); and (2) for a widow with adult children or grandchildren, the primary responsibility for her care lay with them (v. 4). A third and fourth rule are immediately added: (3) She should not be less than sixty years old (v. 9); and (4) she should have been married only once,[75] the assumption being that a woman widowed twice would have been provided for twice over.

A final criterion is that she should be attested by her (presumably earlier record of) "good deeds," "every good deed"—the regular phrase used by the author to indicate the actions or activities that would generally be commended as good (v. 10). In this case, we could put a colon after "good deeds" and treat the following list as indicating the sort of deeds the author had in mind. The list gives a quick glimpse of the responsibilities a woman might be expected to carry out within a household at the time. She should "bring up [her] children," a responsibility usually (but not necessarily) completed by the time of puberty for the sons. (Did a childless wife help in bringing up orphans?) She should welcome strangers, showing hospitality—again a reminder that the diaspora home played an important role in providing hospitality for kinsfolk and countrymen, and of the role of the woman in preparing or supervising preparation of meals (see Commentary on 3:2).

It is less clear whether "washing the feet of the saints" was conceived as a social courtesy or possibly a quasi-liturgical act (only the feet of the saints are mentioned). Either way, it is presumably significant that it is specified as a task undertaken by wives/widows. The humility expressed in the act is

---

72. See C. Osiek and D. Balch, *Families in the New Testament World: Households and House Churches* (Louisville: Westminster John Knox, 1997).

73. In *The Shepherd of Hermas* (mid 2nd cent. CE) the verb σπαταλάω (*spatalaō*) is used of sheep in rich pasture, perhaps in the sense "be frisky" (*Similitude* 6.1.6; 6.2.6). The only other NT occurrence, Jas 5:5, is more relevant.

74. Johnson provides a valuable discussion of the recent suggestion that "widows" were an order of women who practiced active ministry. See Johnson, *Letters to Paul's Delegates*, 177-83.

75. The NIV's "faithful to her husband" introduces an implication ("unfaithfulness" in the sense usually understood in relation to marriage) not present in the text. See Kelly, *The Pastoral Epistles*, 116.

clearly implied in John 13:6-8. That this was expected of wives/widows as a regular act tells us something of the relatively low social status widows enjoyed. More conventional and less jarring is the image of the woman "helping" the afflicted, comforting those in pain, tending the cuts or bruises of any who had been roughed up.

The reason why younger widows should not be enrolled is then explained. Unfortunately the reason immediately given is very confusing (vv. 11-12). First, it uses a verb (καταστρηνιάω *katastrēniaō*) that is otherwise unknown for this time. The verb is usually taken in the sense of "become wanton." How this governs the genitive phrase "[the] Christ," however, is unclear. Could it mean that they "feel sensuous impulses" in regard to Christ— that is, were they drawn to him sexually? Such a possibility, perhaps, should not be dismissed out of hand; the fact that in most churches the great majority of members are women presumably is not entirely to be divorced from the fact that the central figure of the Christian religion is male. But the phrase is usually taken in the sense "sensuous impulses that alienate them from Christ" (similarly NRSV and NIV).

The second puzzle is that they are condemned for wanting to marry, condemned for "rendering invalid their first faith." Does this refer to their Christian faith or to their first marriage? Either way, the writer's strong disapproval would presumably reflect his conviction that marriage should be for life— one life, one marriage (see Commentary on 3:2)—so that second marriage amounted to abandoning faith. But that would be odd in view of the subsequent advice that young widows should marry again (v. 14), unless the writer accepted this option unwillingly as a second best. Alternatively, is what was in view a "pledge" (NRSV, NIV) expected of widows when enrolled, as a commitment to the church or to Christ? That fits better with v. 14: the pledge of enrolled widow-hood would then not have to be abandoned in the event of a second marriage. But then why the reference to their "*first* pledge"?[76] The lack of clarity here is disappointing, since properly understood the verses would tell us much about the writer's attitude toward marriage and (young) widows.

The other reason for what seems to be the writer's disapproval of young widows as a group is that they have nothing to do and fill their time in inappropriate ways (v. 13). The sketch is vivid: They learn to be "idle, lazy, unproductive"; they go from house to house, gossiping, talking nonsense, bringing unjustified charges against others;[77] they pay attention to things that do not concern them; they are meddlesome busybodies (cf. 2 Thess 3:11).[78] These sweeping generalizations either suggest someone who has had bad experiences with such women or are stereotypical criticisms of "flighty young widows."[79] To the extent that it is an accurate portrayal, it reflects the very awkward position in which the death of a husband would usually leave a young wife. If she had no children (as implied by the contrast in v. 14) and few independent means, she would often be an awkward appendage in the household of a relative. Lacking a clear responsibility and obvious function, they would find time heavy on their hands. In such circumstances the tendency to spend time with others in similar positions would be hard to resist. The fault, in other words, was as much society's for leaving young widows to lead such pointless lives.

The obvious solution was for the younger widow to remarry (v. 14). In that way she would have a fulfilling role and make good use of her time. Here again we are given a brief indication of what would generally be regarded as the wife's space and sphere of responsibility: primarily to bear children (cf. 2:15), though presumably some nurture is also implied (v. 10), and to manage her household—a clear enough, but still limited, sphere, subordinate to the overall authority of her husband (see Commentary on 2:11-12). The implication is that such responsibilities would keep the younger wife busy enough and give no occasion for abusive accusations,

---

76. That virgins are in view, whose "first pledge" was to remain celibate (Bassler, *1 Timothy, 2 Timothy, Titus*, 92-97) is unlikely. The support for the equation here of "widow" = "virgin" is slight (see Ignatius *Smyrneans* 13:1). In the key text (5:9) it is taken for granted that the widow had formerly been married, and the author has already denounced the forbidding of marriage as a demonic lie (4:1-3).

77. The noun φλύαροι (*phlyaroi*) is *hapax*; the fuller rendering indicated here is suggested by its cognate verb φλυαρέω (*phlyareō*), as in its only occurrence in the NT, 3 John 10.

78. The note of inquisitiveness in the third term (περίεργος *periergos*) may carry the further overtone of curiosity about magic (cf. its only other occurrence in the NT, Acts 19:19).

79. See D. T. MacDonald, *The Legend and the Apostle: The Battle for Paul in Story and Canon* (Philadelphia: Westminster, 1983) 76-77.

such as may underlie not only v. 13 but also vv. 11-12. "The opponent" could be superhuman (cf. 2 Thess 2:4; *1 Clem* 51:1; and note 5:15), but here is probably human. The reason why the writer was so sensitive at this point is probably because young widows were themselves particularly vulnerable to the kind of gossip in which suspicion and rumor thrive. But he was also conscious (v. 15) that the pattern of daily life indicated in v. 13 had resulted in some turning away (see the Commentary on 1:6) after the satan (see the Commentary on 1:20).

But if widows, younger or older, would not or could not remarry, the primary responsibility for looking after them lay with their relatives (v. 16). The female believer who "has widows" should "help them" (the same word used in 5:10) just as the male relatives should do. The fact that the writer puts the responsibility on the "believing woman"[80] again tells us something about the woman's sphere of influence. Women who were single or widowed and had independent means could take in relatives left on their own, and women who were married still had the possibility of bringing such relatives within the domestic arrangements for which they were responsible. Again we see the importance of the family and its network of relations as still carrying primary responsibility for needy members of the family and providing occasion to meet that need. In that way, the church would be spared the (financial) "burden" (a rather negative word) of caring for widows and would be able to direct its resources to "helping" (the same word again) "real widows"—that is, those not otherwise provided for by husband or family (vv. 4-5, 8).

5:17-25, Elders. In view of the earlier usage (vv. 1-2), how should we now translate πρεσβύτεροι (*presbyteroi*, v. 17)? "The older men" as a translation would hardly do enough justice to the responsibilities referred to them—leadership" (see Commentary on 3:4-5), "laboring hard[81] in word [preaching?] and teaching." In fact, the writer seems to be thinking in terms of a sort of sequence of narrowing circles: the *presbyteroi* in general; within them the *presbyteroi* who give good leadership; within them those who work hard in speaking and teaching. The most obvious way to read this is that the widest circle is that of "the older men" (v. 1), those who by age and experience would naturally be looked to for leadership in any community. Within that circle some would stand out as more natural or gifted leaders. They are worthy of "double honor"—that is, both the veneration for their age and the acknowledgment of their leadership (cf. 6:1-2)—or double support from the common fund (as v. 18 implies).[82] Within that narrower circle some would be recognized for their labors in speaking and teaching. Should we limit the more formal term "elder" only to the second circle (cf. 4:14)? In short, do we see here the term πρεσβύτερος (*presbyteros*), "older man," becoming the technical term *presbyteros*, "elder"?[83] At any rate, we should note that they were expected to minister in speaking and teaching and that these functions were not limited to apostles, prophets and teachers, overseers, or deacons.

In a sudden burst of scripture quotations, almost unique in the Pastorals (vv. 18-19; otherwise only 2 Tim 2:19; but see also 2 Tim 3:8, 16), the scriptural authorization is given for this commendation of elders (v. 18). The first text cited more or less exactly causes little surprise: "You shall not muzzle an ox when threshing the grain" (Deut 25:4). The same text (in slightly variant form) had already been cited in 1 Cor 9:9, and the precedent was established for referring it to the rights of the preacher to receive benefit (financial support) from those to whom he preached.

More striking is the fact that the second text, still under the heading of "scripture," seems to come from the tradition of Jesus' own teaching, where Jesus sends out his disciples in mission and encourages them

---

80. Some scribes evidently found the reference only to a believing woman surprising and added "believing man or," reflecting the assumption that such important decisions would usually be made by men.

81. In the earlier Paulines this is a term he used several times to connote the hard work that marks out someone whose leadership qualities should be recognized. See esp. 1 Cor 15:10; 16:16; 1 Thess 5:12; but note also Rom 16:6; 12.

82. The Greek word for "honor" (μισθός *misthos*) can also mean "price," and so here "honorarium" or "stipend." But was there already such a range and ranking of different ministries ("single stipend, double stipend") that the churches supported with a regular salary? Or is the good elder's stipend double that of the widow (5:3)? The elder of a village would usually be an honorific position.

83. The ambivalence in the reference of *presbyteros* (5:1, 17) puts a question mark against the argument, most recently by J. T. Burtchaell, *From Synagogue to Church: Public Services and Offices in the Earliest Christian Communities* (Cambridge: Cambridge University Press, 1992), that the structure of church organization was taken over from the synagogue. See also R. A. Campbell, *The Elders: Seniority Within Earliest Christianity* (Edinburgh: T. & T. Clark, 1994).

to seek out and accept hospitality.[84] This is a very striking feature that must mean (a) that Jesus tradition circulated in the early churches before the Gospels as such were widely known and (b) that such tradition already had the status of "scripture"—that is, that the teaching of Jesus was prized as being of equivalent weight to the long-established scriptures of Israel (see also 6:3). The point is only slightly weakened if the Jesus tradition has been introduced here simply to elaborate the scriptural precept. It was evidently felt unnecessary to identify it as a saying of Jesus, probably suggesting that it would be well known as such and that its authority did not depend on explicit attribution. This single snatch of quotation, itself sandwiched within an isolated snatch of scripture quotation (vv. 18-19), can thus bear a substantial weight of inference about the use and value of Jesus tradition at this period.

Somewhat oddly, the advice turns abruptly to the question of disciplining an elder (v. 19)—a fact that strengthens the inference that this formal role was at an early stage of development and perhaps in danger of already falling into disrepute in Ephesus (hence the sustained emphasis in vv. 21-22, 24). Of course, any leadership role readily attracts criticism, though the actual advice here (v. 19) may reflect v. 13*b*, that unfounded accusations were arising out of gossip. Perhaps more to the point, however, is the complementary fact that the rest of the instruction focuses primarily on Timothy's authority in reference to elders, their discipline and appointment. Nothing like this is said of any other office in any Pauline letter (cf. 3:1-13); the implication again is of a lower-ranking function (under Timothy, himself under Paul), only beginning to take clearer and more recognized shape.

The first piece of counsel (v. 19) is a particular application of the traditional ruling that two or three witnesses were required if an accusation against a third party was to be sustained (Deut 19:15; cf. Matt 18:16; 2 Cor 13:1). Those who persisted in sin should be "reproved or corrected" (v. 20). The verb ἐλέγχω (*elegchō*) is used several times in the Pastorals (2 Tim 4:2; Titus 1:9, 13; 2:15), but here in context the more basic sense may be in mind: "bring to light," "expose." That is, a process seems to be in view: accusation investigated; if upheld, dealt with quietly; if conduct not discontinued, public exposure (cf. Matt 18:15-17). The purpose given is slightly disquieting—"in order that the rest might have fear"—but it is simply an application of the age-old rationale for punishment, that it should serve as an exemplary warning to others. In the context, "the others" must be other older men or elders.

A solemn charge follows: "before God, Christ Jesus and the elect angels" (v. 21; cf. Mark 13:32). As in *1 Enoch* 39:1, talk of the "elect" implies other angelic beings outside the sphere of God's favor. "The elect angels" presumably serve with God to form the heavenly court of judgment (cf. Job 1–2; Luke 12:8-9; 1 Cor 6:1-3). The charge is one that might be given, indeed perhaps was given, to a judge: to act "without prejudging the issue," without discrimination," and "not acting in accord with personal inclination, in a partisan way"; we are still in the ethos of the deuteronomic legislation (Deut 1:17; 16:19). Such is the role Timothy should expect to play and the authority he would have to exercise.

Timothy's responsibility in ensuring good order for the churches extends to commissioning and ordination (v. 22). It is not said that Timothy alone had this right or responsibility, but the impression is clearly given that a writ of authority is being passed down from Paul to Timothy to others that in itself would help to stabilize and give coherent identity to the churches in view. Such commissioning requires careful thought and perhaps also a period of probation (cf. 3:10); too hasty appointment could result in poor leadership.

The second piece of advice, in context, presumably reinforces the earlier advice: Failure to rebuke attested sin (vv. 19-20), partiality in judgment (v. 21), and overlooking shortcomings in a potential candidate (v. 22) would be to share in these sins. For the third time (also 4:12; 5:2), Timothy is urged to keep himself "pure, chaste" (similarly Titus 2:5).

The following sequence of exhortations (vv. 23-25) seems at first more disparate, but almost certainly they continue the line of thought. Timothy is envisaged as both somewhat ascetic (he drank only water) and

---

[84]. The wording is exactly that of Luke 10:7, slightly different from the parallel in Matt 10:10. The nearest OT texts are relatively remote: Num 18:31 and 2 Chr 15:7.

as suffering from "frequent or numerous ailments or weaknesses" (v. 23). It is a pity that more detail is not given, since such brevity encouraged ill-informed speculation. But in context we can perhaps imagine an unduly serious young man whose heavy responsibilities caused him considerable stress, manifested in stomach cramps and other ailments. The counsel recognizes the value of wine as a relaxant, though perhaps also because it purified the drinking water.

Verses 24-25 read as a kind of proverbial afterthought following the advice of the previous paragraph. The meaning of the second half of v. 24 is somewhat obscure, but the two sentences are obviously set out in parallel.[85] Some sins are "clear, known to all"— and so can (should) be easily enough dealt with. But in other cases the sins themselves or their consequences only become visible later—judgment should never be hasty. In contrast, "good deeds" are also "clear, known to all"; but even those that are not cannot be hidden—perhaps an encouragement to persevere in good deeds not so far acknowledged within the community. Such apparently trite proverbs are not atypical of proverbial, including Jewish, wisdom (Proverbs 10–24 provides many examples).

6:1-2, Slaves. The only obvious reason for adding this piece of counsel is that advice regarding slaves was part of the regular code for good household management.[86]

This became an established part of Christian paraenesis (i.e., practical instruction) with Col 3:18–4:1 (see also Eph 5:22–6:9; 1 Pet 2:18–3:7; Titus 2:1-10; *Did.* 4:9-11; Ignatius *Polycarp* 4:1–5:2; Polycarp *Philippians* 4:2-3). In this case it is almost a reflex reaction: No problem regarding slaves in Ephesus is envisaged[87] (cf. the relatively greater attention given in the other NT codes). The linking thought of "honor" (5:3, 17; 6:1) may be sufficient explanation. Otherwise, the teaching is fairly conventional. The writer did not think it necessary even to balance the counsel to slaves with corresponding counsel to masters (see Titus 2:9-10; 1 Pet 2:18-25; cf. Col 4:1; Eph 6:9). At the same time, the fact that slaves are addressed directly was unusual; even though slaves, they were full members of the Christian church and thus all the more, not less, responsible as such.

The advice is practical: Slaves should respect their (non-Christian) masters. A Christian slave who failed in his or her duty brought dishonor to God and to the teaching (6:1); note again that the good impression made on others is held up as a measure of Christian conduct (cf. Rom 2:24; 1 Thess 4:11-12; and see Commentary on 3:7). They should not disrespect their masters who were fellow Christians; on the contrary, as *brothers* they should be better *slaves* (cf. Phlm 15-16); in that way they would assist their masters to "devote themselves to doing good, benefactions" (6:2).[88]

---

85. Johnson prefers to read v. 25*b* as "even deeds which are not good [rather than which are not obvious] cannot remain hidden," but that translation ignores the parallelism. See Johnson, *Letters to Paul's Delegates,* 186.

86. Slavery was an established fact of life in the ancient world. As many as one-third of the inhabitants of a city like Ephesus would have been slaves; even relatively modest households would have had one or more slaves.

87. Otherwise, e.g., Fee, *1 and 2 Timothy, Titus,* 136-37.

88. This rendering follows the NRSV margin. Most prefer to take the clause as referring to the benefit the masters gain from their slaves (so NIV, NRSV); but the term εὐεργεσία (*euergesia*) is more naturally taken as denoting the generous act of a benefactor (εὐεργέτης *euergetēs*).

REFLECTIONS

Still on the theme of the well-ordered congregation, two further testing areas are dealt with: how the church should treat its more vulnerable and needy members and how discipline should be handled.

The linking theme is the elderly. It is regrettable that in many societies and churches the "elders/elderly" no longer have the status and respect that were recognized to be their due in former generations. The reason why such status and respect were accorded is obvious: Knowledge was accumulated through years of experience, no doubt frequently being tested and proved; out of such knowledge grew wisdom. The elderly were repositories of accumulated wisdom and had a crucial function in the village or community in giving advice on the basis of that accumulated wisdom.

The veneration still given to ancestors in a society like that of China is simply the extension of this insight, so fundamental in the good ordering of ancient society. But today there is a widespread assumption that such repositories of wisdom can be dispensed with; all we need is now contained in textbooks and computer disks.

The consequences are grave. For one thing, the elderly cease to have such a vital role in community; the very function for which they were valued has been taken from them; they become merely a burden and much less a blessing; they experience loneliness, along with loss of income, failing health, distance from family members and grandchildren, loss of friends. For developed countries, in which the retired are becoming a steadily larger proportion of the population, this is a fearful prospect, both for the societies and particularly for the less well-off retired people themselves. More hidden and, indeed, more serious is the loss of a sense of the character of and need for wisdom. Wisdom is being lost behind knowledge, and even knowledge is being submerged by mere information. It is imperative that knowledge, the ability to order and apply information, to discriminate between what is of relevance and what is not, should be given its proper place once again. But more important is that the still higher priority of wisdom, not least the wisdom of well-ordered human relations, be recovered. And then, we may hope, the vital role of the elderly as repositories and stewards of that wisdom may be restored, and with it more of the respect they are due.

Special attention is given in the text to widows. Somewhat surprisingly, they alone are mentioned of the four categories for whom welfare provision was specifically made in ancient Israel—widows, orphans, strangers, and the poor. The importance of hospitality toward strangers is taken for granted (5:10), but nothing is said of the other categories (though see 6:17-19). Presumably, we must assume that adequate provision was being made, not least through almsgiving, for others and that there were no problems needing to be addressed (cf. Jas 1:27). In terms of welfare provision, the only guidelines available to us relate to widows.

The principal point being made is that the primary responsibility belongs to the family: Children or grandchildren of a widow should make due return for all that had been done for them in childhood (5:4); the head of household is responsible to provide for needy relatives and particularly immediate kin (5:8); the woman of independent means should care for a needy relative who had been widowed (5:16). This responsibility is part of "the faith" (5:8); it should not be shifted to the church (5:16). Here again we see question marks to be lodged against more modern arguments that state or church can or should take over such family functions and responsibilities. Of course, in a more fragmented society in which families are often scattered, all kinds of support for caregivers may be needed and should be provided—by state and church; the loneliness of someone who cares for an aged parent with Alzheimer's, for example, is a burden that no one should be asked to bear alone. But the principle of the family as the primary network of supportive relationships is one that should not be lost. In contrast, the loss of family as the basic social unit, not least as the focus for nurture and the principal medium whereby the wisdom of the past is transferred through the generations, would be (is) disastrous for society.

The complementary notion of discipline is equally at threat—in this case the discipline required of younger widows (5:11-15) and in regard to elderly/elders from whom leadership was expected (5:19-22). Noteworthy is the fact that none of the matters in view in 1 Timothy 5 are items of doctrine or belief (cf. 1:19-20); the concern here is entirely over behavior. Contrast the laxer standards of postmodern society and the disparaging tone that now usually attaches to any talk of "good deeds." Here again a sense of "Christian character" needs to be recovered, of an ethos not narrowly defined by particular traditions of behavior, but illustrated as the writer does (5:10, 14, 17; 6:2), to bring out a more recognizable Christian identity by which claimants to the name "Christian" can measure themselves.

The threats to such Christian character will always include not only malicious gossip (5:13) and false accusation (5:19), but also accusations all too justified because of too hasty decisions (5:22) and irresponsible behavior (5:24). The wisdom and maturity of leadership will thus be evident in the way discipline is exercised. Good discipline will grow out of proper respect shown to others (5:1-2; 6:1-2), will thrive in a context where due responsibility is recognized (5:4, 8, 16) and undisciplined or unsocial behavior clearly criticized (5:6, 13, 24), and will be exercised by ignoring unsupported accusations (5:19), by forthright denunciation where that is needed (5:20), by maintaining strict impartiality overall (5:21), and by taking care in promoting people to leadership (5:22). Despite some unclarity (5:11-12) and suspicion that some criticisms are too sweeping and possibly even prejudiced (5:13), there is much here for any church council to reflect on.

So far as slavery is concerned (6:1-2), we should keep in mind that it was not at this time a moral issue (it took the slave trade to make it so). In the ancient world, slaves were simply the bottom rung of the economic ladder. We should not be surprised (or embarrassed), therefore, at the absence of any critique of slavery as such. The point of lasting note is that there are some basic circumstances of life that cannot be changed and that have to be accepted. The fruitful way forward is to work positively and creatively within them. The slave who constantly bemoaned his lot would benefit neither himself nor his master and would bring Christian teaching into disrepute. Even within such constraints there was opportunity to serve willingly and to honor the name of God. The teaching cannot be simply transferred to those at the bottom of the economic ladder today. The point is, rather, that where legitimate obligations exist, they should be carried out with goodwill and sincere dedication, as though to the master in heaven.

1 TIMOTHY 6:3-21, PUTTING WEALTH IN ITS PLACE

COMMENTARY

Chapter 6 is evidently structured as a conclusion that balances the introductory chapter 1, with a similar warning against other teaching (1:3-10; 6:3-10), a similar charge to Timothy, and a benediction (1:12-18; 6:11-16), a final exemplary warning (1:19-20; 6:17-21a), and a brief farewell (6:21b; cf. 1:1-2). In the first paragraph, contrary teaching is scorned (6:3-5) and is set in contrast with a description of "godliness" in terms of "contentment," which in turn is contrasted to the dangers of coveting riches (6:6-10). The godliness Timothy should pursue has very different motivation and imagery—"the good fight," "the good confession," in reference to Christ Jesus and the only God (6:11-16). This middle paragraph is bracketed by a further warning to the rich (6:17-19) and a final swipe at the "knowledge" pedaled by others (6:20-21).

6:3-10, Godliness as Contentment. The last four (Greek) words of v. 2 look as though they sum up and conclude the main body of teaching (2:1–6:2). That teaching is evidently what the writer means by "sound words" and "the teaching which accords with piety" (6:3), two phrases that encapsulate the forms, values, and standards that the writer so clearly cherished (see the Commentary on 1:10 and 2:2). The "sound words" are further identified as "of our Lord Jesus Christ" and may include reference to the church's store of Jesus tradition (see also 5:18). Anything opposed to this teaching is treated dismissively with a conventional vocabulary of vilification, which tells us next to nothing about the alternative teaching that is being attacked (6:4-5). Such a teacher is conceited or blinded (the same word as in 3:6); "he understands nothing"; "he is sick for controversy" (the same word appears in 2 Tim 2:23)⁸⁹ and "fighting over words" (the verb is used in 2 Tim 2:14) that produce "envy, strife, malicious talk, evil suspicions" (the equivalent verb is used in Acts 25:18) and constant irritations between people "wasted in mind" (cf. Rom 1:28) and "robbed of the truth" (cf. 2 Tim 4:4; Titus 1:14).

Only with the last phrase does a feature of substance emerge: "They think that godliness is a means to financial gain" (v. 5). In view are evidently those people, not uncommon in religious circles, who see their religious profession as a means of financial advantage (charging for their teaching) or of social advance.⁹⁰ This in itself is a reminder that the first Christian groups were not uniformly poor or successful in recruitment only among the disadvantaged. There were sufficient numbers of people of higher social status and some wealth for association with a church to provide such opportunities for "social climbing" (see also 2:9). But we should remember that the description is not necessarily unbiased.

In direct contrast, the real means of gain is "godliness with αὐτάρκεια [*autarkeia*]" (v. 6). The choice of this last word is striking (not least because the writer uses it to qualify or further define his favorite term, "godliness, piety"), for *autarkeia* was a favorite virtue of the Stoics and Cynics, the two main classical alternatives to Christianity.⁹¹ It denoted "self-sufficiency," "contentment" and characterized an attitude that cherished simplicity and a life lived in acceptance of the hand dealt out by nature or fortune. Here perhaps more clearly than anywhere else in the Pastorals we can see a pattern of Christianity in which specific Christian teaching and virtues like love are integrated with already acknowledged virtues cherished by others (cf. particularly Phil 4:8, 11).

The elaboration of such "contentment" is given in what seems like a proverbial form that can be set out in four lines (vv. 7-8).⁹² It is a classic statement of the contentment that finds value in life rather than possessions, and that looks for sufficiency rather than surfeit of food and clothing. It echoes a typically religious evaluation of possessions and wealth; in Jewish wisdom literature in particular the first two lines can be compared with Job 1:21 and Eccl 5:15, and the last two with Sir 29:21; nor should we forget Matt 6:25-34.

The point is elaborated in terms of the dangers of making the accumulation of wealth a goal to pursue (v. 9). The images are again conventional, but they resonate sufficiently with repeated examples in history for their force to be easily recognized: "falling into temptation," "snare," "senseless and harmful desires," "sink into ruin and destruction" (cf. Matt 7:13; Acts 8:20; Phil 3:19; 1 Thess 5:3). The warning is summed up in one of the most famous (and most misquoted) sayings in the Bible: "the root of all evils is the love of money" (v. 10; cf. Sir 27:1). It is directly to this craving that the writer attributes the fact that some "have wandered away or been led into error [the same word as in Mark 13:22] from the faith and have pierced themselves with many pains or woes." This is one of the most sustained critiques of desire for wealth in the NT, but it is easily paralleled by briefer allusions elsewhere (Mark 4:19; 10:25; Luke 1:53; 6:24; 12:15-21; 16:19-26; Jas 5:1-5; Rev 3:17-18). This emphasis undermines the argument that the Pastorals advocate a merely "bourgeois ethic."⁹³

6:11-16, Timothy's Goal. The contrast with those described in vv. 9-10 is Timothy, "God's person"—an ancient title for a prophet (e.g., Deut 33:1; 1 Sam 2:27; 9:6-7; 1 Kgs 13:1; 17:18). His appropriate response is posed in the antithetical imagery of "fleeing from" and "pursuing after" (v. 11). Paul earlier used the same counsel of flight in regard to the two great *bêtes noires* that had repeatedly proved so disastrous in Israel's history: illicit sexual relations and idolatry (1 Cor 6:18; 10:14; cf. 2 Tim 2:22). Evidently some threats to piety are so subtle and so powerful

---

89. The more usual translation is "morbid craving for controversy" (NRSV). Note the no-doubt deliberate contrast between other teaching as "sick" and the "sound/healthy" teaching (6:3) promoted by the author.

90. On the different kinds of support teachers of the day could expect or hope for, see R. F. Hock, *The Social Context of Paul's Ministry: Tentmaking and Apostleship* (Philadelphia: Fortress, 1980).

91. Illustrations can be found in A. Malherbe, *Moral Exhortation: A Greco-Roman Sourcebook* (Philadelphia: Westminster, 1986) 40, 112-14, 120.

92. The NRSV's "so that" at the beginning of the second line attempts to make sense of what appears to be a redundant ὅτι (*hoti*), which can mean "that," but by itself would be most simply translated "because." Early scribes resolved the question by inserting a further word to read either "it is true that" or "it is clear that." The NIV, in effect, ignores the problem.

93. Dibelius-Conzelmann's commentary is notably light in this section and on 6:17-19. See Dibelius and Conzelmann, *The Pastoral Epistles*.

that they can be dealt with only by running from them. The contrasting objects of pursuit are put in terms already classically Christian (cf. Titus 2:2, 12): righteousness, both of relationship with God (cf. Rom 9:30) and its social outworking (cf. 2 Cor 9:9-10); the writer's favorite "godliness," "piety"; "faith" merging into "faithfulness" (cf. Rom 14:22-23; Gal 5:22); "love," the highest Christian grace (see the Commentary on 1:5); "patience, endurance, fortitude," another much-prized grace (e.g., Rom 2:7; 5:3; 8:25); and "gentleness," a *hapax*, but understood at the time as a combination of "quietness" and "meekness," and less prized outside Christian circles.

"Fight the good fight" (v. 12) is the usual translation of the Greek in this passage, but the terms are broader. "Contest the good contest" does not read so well but is more accurate. The point is that maintaining "the faith" and living "the faith" require the energy and discipline of the good athlete (cf. 4:7). Eternal life is a gift of God's calling—a regular term for God's initiative in establishing the process of salvation (2 Tim 1:9; cf. Rom 4:17; 9:11, 24; 1 Cor 1:9; 1 Thess 5:24)—but they must "take hold of," "grasp" it. This is simply the outworking of the initial response to the divine "invitation" when Timothy "confessed the good confession" (see also v. 13), presumably at his baptism (cf. Rom 10:9-10) or ordination (4:14; 2 Tim 1:6), either way in public (see also 2 Tim 2:2).[94] Such emphasis on the complementarity of divine initiative and human commitment as characterizing the Christian life from first to last is characteristically Christian.

For the fourth time (v. 13; see also 1:3, 18; 5:21) the writer challenges Timothy in Paul's name, with the same solemnity as in 5:21. The epithets for God are honorific but have more immediate point. That God gives life to all things is the most basic statement of faith in God as Creator (cf. Neh 9:6; Wis 16:13; Rom 4:17; 1 Cor 15:22, 45; 1 Pet 3:18-19), but it is also the basis from which religious faith draws its strength. That Jesus "testified the good confession" is an unusual appeal within the NT letters (a reference back to Jesus as an example; cf. particularly 1 Pet 2:21-23), but it confirms how deeply embedded already within confessional faith was the memory of Christ's passion (including the name "Pontius Pilate").[95] "The good confession" evidently included public faithfulness to God in whatever was the commission given by God and not just a mouthing of a particular creed.

Verse 14 continues the imagery of a commission (here "commandment") that sums up the calling of God and its consequent responsibilities before God. That responsibility can be summed up in turn as "keeping" the commandment "without spot" (cf. Jas 1:27) or "blame" (cf. 3:2; 5:7). The negative imagery is not specified but complements the more positive imagery of vv. 11-12. The language here is a variation of a repeated aspiration in the Pauline letters (1 Cor 1:8; Eph 5:27; Phil 2:15-16; Col 1:22, 28; 1 Thess 3:13; 5:23; Jude 24). The endpoint in view is "the appearance of our Lord Jesus Christ," a regular referent in the Pastorals (see footnote 35); the term "epiphany" (ἐπιφάνεια *epiphaneia*) was commonly used in the religions of the time for the visible manifestation of a hidden deity.[96] That this will happen "in its own times" (the same phrase as in 2:6) may be partly a sign that the parousia was no longer expected imminently (cf. Rom 13:12; 1 Cor 7:29-31; Phil 4:5), but is principally an expression of confidence in God's ordering of the most significant events in human history.

As twice earlier (1:17; 2:4-6) the writer seems to take pains to set this faith with regard to Christ within a monotheistic framework (vv. 15-16). It is God who will "make known" this appearance of Christ "in its own times." The benediction that follows is, in effect, the more fundamental confession within which "the good confession" of Christ is to be integrated and understood. Its concepts and language are traditionally Jewish through and through, although they are usually shared with other religions. The "blessedness" of God (1:11) is particularly characteristic of the monotheistic faiths. That God was "alone" (vv. 15-16) is quintessentially Jewish (see Commentary on 1:17).

---

94. Others have suggested a public affirmation of faith made when put on trial, as with Jesus. But expectation of persecution by legal authorities is otherwise not in view in the Pastorals.

95. Kelly refers particularly to Acts 3:13; 4:27; 13:28 and to Ignatius *Magnesians* 11:1; *Trallians* 9:1; *Smyrneans* 1:2. See Kelly, *The Pastoral Epistles*, 143.

96. For details see Dibelius and Conzelmann, *The Pastoral Epistles*, 104.

"Ruler/sovereign" was an epithet used of God in early Judaism (Sir 46:5; 2 Macc 12:15). That God also was sovereign over all kings and masters is implicit in such passages as Psalm 2 and Dan 4:32 and explicit in 2 Macc 12:15 (cf. Deut 10:17; Ps 136:2-3); in Rev 17:14 the epithets are given to Christ (cf. Rom 10:12; 1 Cor 8:6). That God alone was immortal and invisible (v. 16) had already been affirmed in 1:17, but it is here elaborated, no doubt with allusion to such key precedents as Exod 33:20 and Isa 6:1-5.

6:17-21, Final Exhortations. It is striking that the writer should revert to his warnings about the hazards of wealth in this final paragraph (vv. 17-19). It is partly a stylistic feature (cf. the reversion to the initial theme in 1:3, 18; 5:1, 17). But here, the fact that it takes the place that might otherwise have been given to pleasantries and future plans underlines the seriousness with which the writer regarded the danger. In this, too, it is parallel to the abrupt launch into the initial warnings of 1:3-11: The seriousness of the concern overrode normal literary conventions.

The warning is more specific than in vv. 9-10. Riches tend to make people proud and haughty (cf. Rom 11:20), encouraging the thought that wealth either gives superiority or can simply buy what is wanted. Wealth tends to give the rich a sense of security for the future that others do not have (v. 17). The writer pricks the balloon with his adjectives: rich "in the present age" (cf. 2 Tim 4:10; Titus 2:12),[97] the "uncertainty of" riches. The wise person trusts in God, who provides all that is necessary for enjoyment; the basic thought is the same as vv. 6-8. The rich, it should be noted, are condemned not for being rich but for indulging in the attitudes toward God and others that riches breed. Their safeguard is to use their wealth in doing good, sharing generously and liberally (cf. Rom 12:8); in both cases the point is made twice for emphasis (v. 18). In this way they will store up for themselves a good foundation for the future (v. 19, an odd mixture of echoes of Matt 6:20 and 1 Cor 3:14) and attain the same goal set before Timothy in v. 12. The final phrase is similar to the one used of widows in 5:3, 5, 16: "real life" in contrast with the insubstantial nature of a life consisting of or based on riches.

The other concern the writer wanted to leave with his reader(s) was the contrast between the sound teaching he has emphasized throughout and the inferior or dangerous alternatives being put before them (vv. 20-21). The parting image is of a παραθήκη (*parathēkē*)—that is, "a deposit or goods entrusted to someone else"—which is to be guarded (the same imagery recurs in 2 Tim 1:12, 14). The image is not elaborated here but presumably has in view "the faith" and "sound teaching" as summarized in such passages as 1:15 and 3:16 (see further on 2 Tim 1:12).

This is set in sharp contrast to a teaching that is given a slightly clearer identity (v. 20). We have already met the dismissive descriptions "profane" (1:9; 4:7) and "empty talk" (cf. 1:6). Greater promise of information is given by the *hapax* "antitheses, objections, contradictions" and "knowledge" (falsely so called). The latter has suggested to many that an early form of Gnosticism is in view, and the former has been seen by a few as a reference to a work of Marcion that evidently set the teachings of the OT and of Paul in sharp antithesis. But without that very late association (Marcion thrived in the middle of the 2nd cent.) both words could refer to a wide variety of teachings. "Knowledge" was clearly their word, but all philosophies and religions prized knowledge (cf. Rom 2:20; 1 Cor 8:1; Phil 3:8; Col 2:3). And "antitheses" sounds more like the writer's caricature. The only other thing we are told is that "some" by "promising or professing" this knowledge "had missed the mark" (the same word as in 1:6; 2 Tim 2:18) concerning the faith (cf. 1:19-20).

The final benediction is typically Pauline in its focus on grace, but it is surprisingly abrupt (cf. Col 4:18; 2 Tim 4:22). The plural "you" presumably indicates that the letter, despite being addressed to Timothy alone, would have been read aloud in a church gathering (as still more clearly in Phlm 3, 22, 25).

---

97. The writer is assuming the Jewish perspective on time: The present age will be followed by a future/new age. The same perspective lies behind most of the NT writings—e.g., Jesus' teaching on the kingdom of God (see particularly Mark 13:1) and Revelation.

REFLECTIONS

The dominant impression left by this chapter is the concern regarding the dangers of wealth and of the attitudes of mind and habits of life that acquisition and possession of wealth encourage (6:5, 9-10, 17). It echoes earlier warnings to similar effect (2:9; 3:3, 8; 5:13). The writer evidently saw here a serious threat to Christian character and community. No one who is wealthy relative to others, other Christians or other nations, can sit wholly comfortably under teaching like this. As with Jesus' words in the Sermon on the Mount (Matt 6:19-21) or to the wealthy young man (Mark 10:23-25) or the fierce denunciation of James (Jas 5:1-5), the only appropriate response has to be: Is this me/us? Have I/we fallen into this temptation and trap? An affirmative answer or troubled conscience can then look to 6:18 for the appropriate guidance.

At the same time, the teaching of the chapter undercuts any kind of "prosperity gospel." "Godliness," the principal summary word for the character of the religion commended by the Pastorals, is set in clear and sharp antithesis to any desire for riches (6:6-9). And any thought that godliness might be a means of gain is totally abhorrent to the writer (6:5). The contrast of a godliness content with the provision of fairly modest necessities is striking (6:6-8). The point should not be overplayed: The writer was equally clear that those with means should make proper provision for family and relatives (5:8, 16); the wealthy are not told to sell all their riches (6:18). But the idea that Christian profession ensured prosperity in the wealth of this age (6:17) would certainly be disowned and denounced by the writer as a false priority with faith-threatening and life-threatening consequences.

A second strong impression given by the chapter is the readiness of the writer to draw on ideals and ideas that were common to other philosophies and religions. Thus he makes use of ideas more familiar among Stoics and Cynics (6:6-8), of widely shared concerns about the perils of wealth (6:9-10, 17), of the religious technical term "epiphany" (6:14), and of conventional epithets for the deity (6:15-16). He trod a clear line between syncretism (where language begins to change and corrupt the central idea) and communication of ideas central to his faith (here particularly "piety" and belief in God as one). That line has to be maintained, hard though it be at times to distinguish the alternatives. The key, presumably, is not to become overly definitive and overly prescriptive, but to get the essential points and principles right and to ensure that they are not compromised in particular cases. Jesus showed the way in his teaching on the law (Mark 12:23–34; cf. Mark 2:23–3:5; 7:1-23).

A third strong impression with which one is left at the close of this letter is the writer's repeated assumption of and (by repetition) insistence on Israel's traditional monotheism. No New Testament writing is more persistent on that point (1:17; 2:4-6; 6:15-16; cf. John 5:44; 17:3). This emphasis needs to be borne in mind whenever the christology of the Pastorals is assessed (particularly Titus 2:13), for with its high evaluation of Christ, Christianity looked as though it was redefining its belief in God, that it was linking Jesus with God in such a way as to question its own monotheistic credentials. In other words, some might say, at this point Christianity did not avoid syncretism and began to speak in terms close to a kind of polytheism (two gods). It still seems that way to Jews and Muslims. And Christians with too casual talk of Jesus as God and a too simplistic concept of God as Trinity (often closer to tritheism) continue to feed that suspicion. It is important, therefore, that the emphasis of the writer here not be lost to sight: Christian faith is still governed by Israel's fundamental insight of God's oneness, and those who confess Christ and confess with Christ (6:13) make this a part of their confession that God is one (the Jewish *Shema*). Those who await the appearance of the Lord Jesus Christ (6:14) do so as believers that the Blessed One is alone sovereign (6:15) and alone has immortality (6:16).

2 TIMOTHY 1:1–4:22

2 TIMOTHY 1:1-7, GREETINGS AND PERSONAL COMMENDATION

COMMENTARY

The introduction to 2 Timothy is more typically Pauline than either of the other Pastoral Epistles. The self-identification is formulated in characteristic Pauline terms, with typically Pauline elaboration (1:1); the greeting (1:2) has the same variation as in 1 Tim 1:2. More striking is the fact that 1:3-7, unlike 1 Timothy and Titus, follows (with variations) the characteristic Pauline pattern of an initial thanksgiving and prayer for the recipients, assurance of desire to see them, and expression of confidence in their good faith (1:3-6; cf. particularly Rom 1:9-13; Phil 1:3-8). More distinctive of the Pastorals is the initial charge to Timothy (1:6-7).

1:1. If any title was grasped by Paul and more or less insisted on, it was "apostle." Characteristic, too, was the conjunction of Christ Jesus and God in the determining of this identity: "apostle of Christ Jesus"; "through God's will" (1 Cor 1:1; 2 Cor 1:1; Gal 1:4; Eph 1:1; Col 1:1). That his commissioning by Christ should be in accordance with God's will was fundamental to both Paul's faith and his mission. The elaboration further specifies that his apostleship had in view the gospel (cf. Rom 1:1), here epitomized as "the promise of life that is in Christ Jesus" (cf. 1 Tim 4:8), again echoing strong Pauline themes: "promise" (e.g., Rom 4:13-16; Gal 3:14-29); "life" (e.g., Rom 5:17-21; 2 Cor 4:10-12); "in Christ," a favorite motif by which Paul indicated that the reality of the whole gospel and identity of believers as such was wholly bound up with Christ. The use of this motif in 2 Timothy (1:1, 9, 13; 2:1, 10; 3:12, 15) is more characteristically Pauline than in 1 Timothy (1 Tim 1:14; 3:13) and Titus (not used; though see the Commentary on 2:1).

1:2. The greeting is the same as in 1 Tim 1:1, except that Timothy is described as "beloved" rather than "legitimate, genuine." Paul used the term for fellow believers quite widely (e.g., Rom 1:7; 16:5, 8-9), but here it is the special relationship with Timothy (1 Cor 4:17) that is in view.

1:3. Paul's continuous resort to prayer is a feature of his letters (1 Cor 1:4; Phil 1:3-4; 1 Thess 1:2-3; the echo of Rom 1:8-9 is strong). However, the regularity of the pattern does not mean that the sentiments were merely conventional. Paul evidently lived his life as though in constant prayer dialogue with God. The reminder of his "service" serves a double purpose: The echo of its technical use (divine service in the Jerusalem Temple) strengthens the solemnity of the affirmation of regular prayer, and it implies continuity between Christian worship and the worship that had been focused in the Jerusalem Temple. The same point is reinforced by the reference to his "clean conscience" (a frequent motif in 1 Timothy; see 1 Tim 1:5). But the most striking feature is the assurance that Paul had thus served God "from my parents, ancestors," usually taken in the sense "as my parents, ancestors did." Either way the phrase underlines the conviction that the religion of his ancestors (not just the Judaism that he had previously practiced; see Gal 1:13-14) had sought to serve God in good faith and that Paul's apostolic ministry was in direct continuity with it. Since (pre-Christian) Judaism is regularly disparaged in Christian tradition (see Heb 8:13; or think of the bad overtones of the word "Pharisee" in English usage), the point is worth noting.

1:4. Paul's longing to see his readers is another characteristic theme of his letters (see Rom 1:11; Phil 1:8; 2:26; 1 Thess 3:6).

The talk of "tears" (here of Timothy) underscores the emotional intensity of the longing (cf. Acts 20:19, 31; 2 Cor 2:4). The inverse proportion of apostolic suffering and its outcome is another Pauline theme (cf. Rom 8:17-25; 2 Cor 4:12-18; Phil 1:12-14). But somewhat oddly, this is the only mention of "joy" in the Pastorals.

1:5. In a clearly parallel way, the emphasis on the continuity of Paul's service with that of his forebears (v. 3) is balanced in this verse by the memory that both his mother and his grandmother were precursors of Timothy's faith. The reference may be to his Christian faith (Acts 16:1); already with Timothy we are in third-generation Christianity! Alternatively, since Timothy was already a young adult by the time the gospel reached Lystra (Acts 14:6-7; 16:1), the implication may be, rather, that this (Christian) faith was in direct continuity with the typical piety of a Jewish home (cf. 3:15). As in 1 Tim 1:5, "faith" that is "sincere, without hypocrisy" is what really matters.

1:6. This re-call to honored precedents of service and faith becomes in turn the basis for the initial "reminder" to Timothy—a less strong word than the injunctions of 1 Tim 1:3, 18; 5:21; 6:14, more in keeping with the overall friendlier tone of 2 Timothy. The exhortation is to the same effect as 1 Tim 4:14, only the image is more positive ("rekindle" as of a fire); the image is of a campfire kept going for days on end and requiring to be fanned into fresh flame every morning. Here as in 1 Tim 4:14 the impression is of a "charism," which is now "in" Timothy; that the word is used in this way and only of Timothy inevitably raises the question of whether the earlier charismatic theology of Paul has been formalized (cf. 1 Cor 12:7, 11; 14:1). Again, as in 1 Tim 4:14, Timothy's possession of the charism is attributed to "the laying on of hands," raising the same question (though cf. Acts 8:18). In this case, only Paul's hands are mentioned. If the reference is to the same event as in 1 Tim 4:14, as seems most likely, then the implication is presumably that the formality of the act was more important than the question of who participated in it (see the Commentary on 1 Tim 4:14).

1:7. The writer points to the Spirit as the source of the charism (as in 1 Cor 12:4). Timothy's exercising of his charism should be in accordance with the character of the Spirit—a Spirit not of "cowardice, timidity" but of "power" (cf. 1:8; 3:5), of "love" (see Commentary on 1 Tim 1:5), and of "good judgment, moderation" (a variation of the virtue commended in 1 Tim 2:9, 15; see Commentary on 1 Tim 2:9). The form is modeled on Rom 8:15 (though here the statement is generalized), but the echoes are of Mark 13:11 and 1 Cor 2:3-5.

REFLECTIONS

Here again we see a fine blend of epistolary conventions and Christian adaptation. The Christianity of Paul and the Pastorals did not seek to subvert or revolt against such conventions; nor did it want to create wholly new structures of social communication. Rather, it took the forms of the day and infused them with Christian spirit—"in Christ Jesus," "grace" (see the Commentary on 1 Tim 1:2).

Even more striking here is the theological emphasis on continuity with what had gone before: "apostle of Christ Jesus through God's will"; the grace of Christ in conjunction with the mercy of God (see Commentary on 1 Tim 1:2); Paul's service in the gospel (Rom 1:9) in continuity with the cultic worship of his forebears; the sincere faith of Timothy inherited from mother and grandmother; the charism in character with the Spirit given earlier. The emphasis is in marked contrast with a considerable portion of Christian history wherein Christianity has found it necessary to establish its own identity by denigrating the Judaism that preceded it—Christianity as "gospel" to Judaism's "law." Denigration of predecessors is an unlovely way to advance one's own claims at any time, but in the case of Christianity and the religion of Second Temple Judaism the continuity of theology and ethos is too integral to Christianity's own identity for such disparagement to be carried through without risk to Christianity itself. Given Christianity's debt to the religion of Israel (not least for its Scriptures and its Messiah), Christians should be the last persons to be anti-Semitic.

The continuity between Spirit first given and ongoing obligation was no less important for Paul; we need recall only Rom 8:23 and Gal 3:3. Maintaining the "first love" (Rev 2:4) can be easily sentimentalized and become an excuse for failure to grow in faith (see 1 Cor 3:1-2; Heb 5:11-14), but Paul would not have re-called his converts so often to the beginnings of their lives as Christians unless he saw the decisiveness of that first commitment and yielding to God as somehow paradigmatic for the life of the committed in dependence on God. The implication of Gal 3:3 is that the continuing and the ending need to be in the same spirit/Spirit as the beginning. How can the freshness of first love and devotion be maintained without becoming overformalized and entrapped in rules and procedures? Not a few are still looking for the church that can answer that question effectively!

2 TIMOTHY 1:8-18, PAUL'S OWN TESTIMONY

COMMENTARY

Second Timothy stands out from the other two Pastoral Epistles as having more the form of a farewell address, with the characteristic hallmarks: reminder, warning, and charge (cf. Acts 20:18-35; 2 Peter). The actual "farewell" comes in 4:6-8, but 1:8-18 contains both charge (1:8-14) and reminder (1:15-18). The charge is further extended in 2:1-26 and 3:14–4:5, 9-21, and the reminder in 3:10-13, with 3:1-9 serving as the warning.

The appeal to the past is complemented by an appeal to Paul's own experience. The warrants for Timothy's ministry are the gospel entrusted to Paul (1:8-10), the ministry of Paul in discharging that trust (1:11-12), and the "sound words" that epitomize both (1:13-14). Equally paradigmatic for Timothy are the contrasting examples of those who abandoned Paul (1:15) as well as those who stood by him (1:16-18).

1:8. The appeal to Paul's own example parallels that in 1 Tim 1:12-20. But the distinctiveness of 2 Timothy within the Pastorals is heightened by the reference to Paul as a "prisoner" (only here in the Pastorals; but cf. Eph 3:1; 4:1; Phlm 1, 9). Even more striking is the use of the distinctive feature of Pauline theology: a σύν- (*syn*-) compound ("suffer *with*"; used again in 2:3 and 2:11-12, but only in 2 Timothy). Talk of "being ashamed" recalls Rom 1:16 and becomes a linking motif in this section (1:8, 12, 16). That the gospel involves suffering is another characteristic theme of Paul (e.g., Rom 8:17-23; 2 Cor 4:7-18), as also is the conviction that such suffering can only be endured by God's enabling and that such weakness is the necessary complement to any experience of God's power (see 2 Cor 4:7; 12:9-10).

1:9-10. The gospel is then summarized in what appears to be another creedal-type of statement, which the author quotes. It is not called a "faithful saying" but is very similar to the "faithful saying" in Titus 3:4-7. As with that statement, it functions as a confession of God (not of Christ): The gospel is an account not so much of what Christ has done as of what God has done through Christ. The consistent aorist tenses (describing what has already been accomplished) need not imply a changed perspective from the earlier Paulines (where salvation is essentially a future good, the goal of the saving process; see, e.g., Rom 5:9-10; 1 Cor 1:18); note, after all, 2:10. It could, rather, be intended to emphasize the decisiveness of the divine action, seen, as it were, from its endpoint (cf. Rom 8:24, 30). The language picks up the key Pastoral image of "salvation" (see footnote 34) and the different image of an effective invitation (cf. 1 Tim 6:12). "Called with a holy calling" is Hebraic in form and echoes Israel's understanding of itself as "called to be saints" (as also particularly in Rom 1:7; 8:27-28). Once again the continuity of identity with God's earlier purpose, of Israel as defined by the call of God (cf. Rom 9:7-11, 24), is implicit.

"Not according to our works" is an equally strong echo of a central Pauline statement of the gospel (Rom 3:20, 28; Gal 2:16), but there is a significant shift of emphasis. The concept of "works" seems to have broadened out from a more specific "works of the law" (Paul was usually thinking of the things the law required and that distinguished Israel from other nations) to "our works," "anything we have done" (NIV, meaning any attempt to secure our own righteousness; cf. Eph 2:8; Titus 3:5). At any rate, the bulk of the weight is again placed on the divine initiative and purpose: in accordance with God's "own will and grace"; "given [as a gift] in Christ Jesus"; "before time immemorial." The "in Christ Jesus" refers to the embodiment of God's saving act both on the cross (cf. Gal 1:4; 1 Tim 2:6) and in the gift of saving grace (1 Cor 1:4). "Before times eternal" refers to the eternal purpose of God, not to Christ (or "us") as pre-existent (cf. 1 Pet 1:20).[98]

This eternally planned grace has now been manifested through the appearing of Christ Jesus our Savior (v. 10). Here are brought together two of the Pastorals' most distinctive themes: the title "Savior," used for the only time in 2 Timothy, but now of Christ (see the Commentary on 1 Tim 1:1); and the term "appearing" (ἐπιφάνεια *epiphaneia*), usually used of Christ's (second) coming (1 Tim 6:14; 2 Tim 4:1, 8; Titus 2:13), but here of his first (cf. the verb in Titus 2:11; 3:4). The fact that salvation and "Savior" are attributed indiscriminately to God and to Christ presumably indicates that for the author the saving action was one and the same; a more carefully described attribution is given in the formulations in 1:9 ("in Christ Jesus") and Titus 3:6 ("through Jesus Christ"), and the dual use of the technical term "epiphany" (see the Commentary on 1 Tim 6:14) presumably indicates that the author saw a direct continuity between the first and the second appearances of Christ as both the manifestation and the enactment of the divine purpose and grace (see also Commentary on Titus 2:13).

Not insignificant is the fact that the achievement of this first appearing is summarized (v. 10) in terms of the destruction of death (cf. Heb 2:14) and the bringing to light of life and immortality (cf. 1 Cor 15:53-54). The overcoming of death is usually the most important function of religion. No wonder, then, that the gospel focused so much on the resurrection of Christ; and no doubt it was the centrality of the resurrection of Christ that gave the gospel such effective power in the ancient world. "Light" and "life" are as attractive a combination of images as one could imagine (cf. John 1:4; Acts 26:23). Note also that "through the gospel" parallels "through the appearing of Christ": Just as Christ was the embodiment of God's saving purpose, so also the gospel is the medium through which that saving purpose comes to particular effect.

1:11. This verse is a way of making the point that the gospel just summarized was Paul's gospel. The reinforcement is twofold: The gospel thus affirmed by the writer goes back to Paul, bearing the stamp of his authority; and Paul in turn (and his emissary) are validated by the gospel he proclaimed. The verse, in effect, repeats 1 Tim 2:7, with the unusual titles for Paul of "herald"[99] and "teacher."[100] The two terms bracket and embrace the more typical Pauline self-designation "apostle": The gospel of the Pastorals goes back to Paul's proclamation; the "teaching" so insisted on by the author goes back to Paul the "teacher."

1:12. In a well-rounded paragraph the writer returns to the theme of suffering and shame.[101] It is the same gospel that makes sense of Paul's suffering, particularly as a prisoner (v. 8). And over this gospel and the one it proclaims, Paul need not feel any cause for shame. As in Rom 1:16, which this verse echoes, there may well be a further echo of the Jesus tradition as contained in Mark 8:38 and Luke 9:26. The allusion is strengthened by the forward look once again "to that day." The image, then, is of a commission that

---

98. Despite Kelly, *The Pastoral Epistles*, 163.

99. See Epictetus *Discourses* 3.22.69, where he speaks of the Cynic preacher as "the messenger, the scout, the herald of the gods."
100. Some MSS read "teacher of the Gentiles," influenced, no doubt, by 1 Tim 2:7.
101. It is important to realize that honor and shame were pivotal values in the first-century Mediterranean world. See B. J. Malina, *The New Testament World: Insights from Cultural Anthropology* (Atlanta: John Knox, 1981) chap. 2.

others might well regard as a cause of shame: the proclamation of a crucified Christ (1 Cor 1:23). But the first appearing gives promise of a second, and the character and content of that first appearing—his words (Mark 8:38; Luke 9:26) and his death (1 Cor 1:23)—give sufficient ground that in the second appearing and the subsequent judgment belief in this Christ will be vindicated.

The theme of the faithfulness thus commended (v. 12) is summed up here and in v. 14 in the words παραθήκη (*parathēkē*), "deposit," "goods left in trust with someone else"—that is, presumably "the faith" (as in 1 Tim 6:20; see also on 1:13).[102] The image is rather static, and the complementary idea of "protecting" it (the same verb is used each time) encourages the picture of something retained and returned in the form in which it was first received. It is this image that probably above all gives the impression of a theology concerned more to preserve than to develop, a faith tied to earlier formulations and discouraged from seeking fresh expression. The Greek could be read as Paul's entrusting something to Christ (NIV, NRSV). And that makes good sense—entry upon the Christian life as a two-way commitment, of convert to Christ (v. 12) and of Christ to convert (v. 14). But in context the parallel is more between Paul and Timothy: not being ashamed (vv. 8, 12), sharing the same suffering (vv. 8, 12). So here we expect the parallel: Paul's deposit, Timothy's deposit (vv. 12, 14). The result might seem rather odd: Paul's confidence is in *Christ's* ability to guard what had been deposited with *Paul;* but that thought is itself very Pauline (e.g., Phil 4:13; Col 1:29).

1:13. Clearly Paul is being held up here as an example to be followed. This is precisely what the writer had said in 1 Tim 1:16, and he uses the same word here, the only two occurrences of the term in the NT. The implication is of a match between Paul's own life (as convert and apostle) and the gospel that converted him and that he preached. Both provide the "model/pattern/standard" in accordance with which others can both model and evaluate their own testimony and living. The "pattern" is here summed up in the familiar term "sound words" (ὑγιαινόντων λόγων *hygiainontōn logōn*; see footnote 9), presumably another way of saying the "gospel," another image for "the deposit." These, in turn, are correlated with the key Christian/Pauline terms "faith," "love," and "in Christ Jesus," as in 1 Tim 1:14.

1:14. In the parallel use of the *parathēkē* image (now "the fine deposit"),[103] it is Timothy who is to do the "guarding," as in 1 Tim 6:20. An important difference here (but no doubt assumed elsewhere) is that the indwelling Holy Spirit is the enabling power—the equivalent in v. 12 to Christ's guarding the deposit entrusted to Paul in v. 13. The Spirit does not appear much in the Pastorals; in fact, the Spirit hardly appears outside traditional formulations (1 Tim 3:16; Titus 3:5) or language modeled on an earlier distinctively Pauline formulation (2 Tim 1:7). First Timothy 4:1 could be regarded as an exception, but even that has the ring of an apocalyptic stereotype (the Spirit's predicting eschatological calamity and defection; see the Commentary on 1 Tim 4:1; cf. 2 Thess 2:2). Even 2 Tim 1:14 uses traditional Pauline language (cf. Rom 8:11: "the Spirit that dwells in you"). But the adaptation of the role of the indwelling Spirit to that of enabling Timothy to guard the deposit is distinctive of the Pastorals. We may compare the way Paul's much more liberal use of "charism" is limited now to a commissioning gift once given to Timothy (1 Tim 4:14; 2 Tim 1:6). Such features could be indicative of a changing pattern of experience of the Spirit and of the Spirit's engracing, but they could also be indicative of a community that was trying to live out of the spiritual resources of the past, cherishing the pattern of sound words as those that encapsulated the gospel's experience of grace and ensured its continuance into the present and the future (cf. 2:1-2).

1:15. If Paul is the positive model for Timothy's responsibility, there are other models that come directly from Paul's own experience. As at the end of 1 Timothy 1, two negative examples are cited. The news that "all in Asia had turned away from or repudiated" Paul carries a shocking overtone. "Turn away from" (ἀποστρέφω *apostrephō*)

---

102. Not the charism: that has to be "fanned into flame, rekindled"; this has to be "guarded, kept safe."

103. Both the NIV and the NRSV blur the fact that the same phrase is used in 1:12 and 1:14, but the NRSV's translation "treasure" obscures the point still further.

is one of several words used in the Pastorals to describe defection or apostasy from "the truth" (4:4; Titus 1:14). But "*all* in Asia"—could that be so? Did all the churches in the large province of Asia (modern western Turkey) defect? That could hardly be true, in view of Revelation 2–3 and the letters of Ignatius. Alternatively, did all (or most of) the Christians of Asia abandon Paul in some crisis? Is there an allusion here to the episode hinted at in 2 Cor 1:8? Of course, there is an element of hyperbole in the language, but the sense of betrayal and isolation is very strong. We know nothing more of Phygelus and Hermogenes, who are mentioned only here, or of why they in particular should be mentioned. One possibility is that they were delegates from the Asian churches who had been sent to Rome to support Paul, but who in the event had abandoned him.[104]

1:16-18. In contrast stands Onesiphorus, who evidently lived in Ephesus; his household is mentioned again in 4:19. It is noticeable that his household gets the credit, as it were, for Onesiphorus's kindness. It is a small reminder that the head of the household, the *paterfamilias,* represented the household as a whole, so that his decisions and actions would carry the whole household with him. But it sounds as though the household acted as a team in Christian service (cf. 1 Cor 16:15). He is remembered for having often "refreshed" Paul (ἀναψύχω *anapsychō*; lit., "renewed his soul"), and in contrast to "all in Asia," he is an example of "not being ashamed" (the third time the word ἐπαισχύνομαι [*epaischynomai*] appears in the chap.: 1:8, 12, 16). The particular act of kindness is spelled out—implying that Paul's whereabouts (in detention?) in Rome were not always well known (v. 17)—as well as the memory of much service earlier in Ephesus (v. 18). The repeated prayer wish is that Onesiphorus and his household should receive (v. 16) or find mercy from the Lord on that day (v. 18).[105] The idiom is Hebraic (cf. Gen 6:8; 19:19; Exod 33:16; Luke 1:30; Heb 4:16; 10:25), but "the Lord" here is presumably Jesus Christ (cf. Jude 21).

---

104. Hermogenes and Onesiphorus, however, are subsequently drawn into what we would call the "novel" known as *The Acts of Paul and Thecla.* See D. T. MacDonald, *The Legend and the Apostle: The Battle for Paul in Story and Canon* (Philadelphia: Westminster, 1983) 59-62.

105. Had Onesiphorus died? If so we have the first example of a Christian prayer-wish for someone who had died. See Kelly, *The Pastoral Epistles,* 171. Unfortunately the text is too ambiguous on the point for us to be sure. See Fee, *1 and 2 Timothy, Titus,* 237.

REFLECTIONS

There are two prominent themes in this passage: First, the repeated talk of not being ashamed (1:8, 12, 16), and, second, the image of faith as a "deposit" (1:14; cf. 1:12).

First-century Mediterranean society can be described as an honor/shame culture. This would have been brought home to the first readers of these letters every day, since the public places of every city, and particularly the capital of a province (like Ephesus), were filled with statues and honorific plaques and inscriptions. Typically, these commemorated favors and benefactions were made by leading citizens to the city or state. Social ethos encouraged the seeking and deserving of such honor as a worthy motivation and goal. The converse was the shame that one properly felt at failing to act in accordance with the obligations or expectations of one's position in society. The honor/shame mind-set is well illustrated by Jesus' parable in Luke 14:7-11 (it was customary to seat people at a banquet in order of rank; in Greco-Roman society the quality of food would usually be better for those of higher rank). Paul had used the language of shame in reference to women acting against the social convention of the time in 1 Cor 11:6 and 14:35. We saw 1 Timothy using the language of honor in 1 Tim 5:3, 17, and 6:1; and 2 Timothy uses it in obviously familiar imagery in 2:20-21.

Today we can see operative similar motivations among the well-to-do, for example, in the financing of a new student center or laboratory on a university campus—where the honor of a building named after the donor is the return for the benefaction. Again, many social conditions today carry the stigma of shame—for example, single parents, the homeless, welfare dependency. But overall, honor and shame are less powerful factors in determining the ethos of present-day society. There is not such a broad consensus of what society has a right to expect from its members, such that failure to fulfill the expectation would bring a sense of shame. Social embarrassment tends to follow a much more subtle code than being held up to public censure and ridicule. Whether this is a good or bad thing would be an appropriate subject for discussion. Also worth discussing is the extent to which effective codes of honor and shame depend on the cohesiveness of society and the degree to which it shares common values, and whether there are cultural codes that Christians stand out against.

Notable here, then, is the fact that the primary determinant of and ground for shame in the Christian is failure to live in accordance with gospel expectations. According to the conventions of the day, one might well have been ashamed of a gospel that gave such prominence to one who had died the most shameful of deaths, crucifixion (1:12; 1 Cor 1:18-31), and of the fact that one of its leading proponents was a jailbird (1:8, 16). But the gospel radically transformed these values and codes, because it changed priorities and relationships. The sort of questions that may emerge from this line of reflection are whether concerns to protect the "good name of the family" are always Christianly based, or whether "dishonorable" discharge from military service should necessarily be always regarded as shameful.

The second theme is not unrelated. In this passage we see the most forceful expression of a tendency apparent throughout the Pastorals. It is signaled particularly by talk of "the faith" and "the sound teaching," as well as in the quotation of what had already become treasured formulations from earlier days (the "faithful sayings"). Here it is expressed in the quotation of a summary gospel statement (1:9-10), by reference to the "pattern of sound words" (1:13), and particularly by the (double) reference to "guarding the deposit" (of faith) once given. It is difficult to avoid the conclusion that the Pastorals see faith in more formal terms than had Paul, that a significant shift had taken place from believing "in" to believing "that," that the process of definition and creedal formation was already well advanced.

Such a process was, of course, inevitable, and the location of the Pastorals, with their talk of "sound teaching" and "faithful sayings," within the New Testament canon authenticates and validates that process. At the same time, it is good to recognize a danger in this process— the danger of losing the substance in the form, the danger of putting more weight on the "that" than on the "in," the danger of confusing the creedal affirmation with the faith that it affirms. It must always be remembered that words spoken by humans will never be adequate to express divine reality, that they can serve only as metaphors for and windows onto an ultimately inexpressible reality. As icons and images they can easily become idols. When humans reciting the creeds think that the words are the thing itself, then the icon has become the idol. This is not to say that the writer(s) of the Pastorals has fallen into this trap. There are sufficient indications of a faith still living and personal. But the Pastorals have been taken to encourage such a formalization, and if they are taken to epitomize Paulinism, that tendency may be reinforced. It is important, therefore, that the emphasis of the Pastorals at this point be recognized as complementary to the gospel according to the earlier Paulines and not as the whole or the definitive portrayal of Pauline Christianity.

2 TIMOTHY 2:1-26, PAUL'S CHARGE TO TIMOTHY

COMMENTARY

This chapter contains the most sustained of the charges put to Timothy or Titus in these letters. It begins with the commission to ensure an effective succession for the deposit (1:14) entrusted to Timothy (2:1-2), followed by a sequence of vivid reminders of the discipline required (2:3-7). This leads naturally into the thought of the suffering and endurance indicated in the gospel (2:8, 11-13) and certainly entailed by its service (2:9-10). Further imagery contrasts the good worker and the sound foundation (2:15, 19) with alternatives of catastrophe, profane and empty talk, gangrene (2:14, 16-18), and again the contrast of expensive pottery with cheap pottery (2:20-21), to underline the importance of faithful maintenance of and dedication to the faith. The final paragraph rounds off the exhortation with a scattering of personal advice (2:22-23) aimed at winning back those who have apostatized (2:24-26).

2:1-2, Be Strong. The sequence begins on a tender and very personal note: "my son" (v. 1). The first thought is the need for the strength that comes from without, from Christ (cf. Eph 6:10), as with Paul himself (4:17; see the Commentary on 1 Tim 1:12). Here, significantly, the focus of that strength is "grace" (χάρις *charis*), the word that more than any other in the Pauline letters sums up the initiative and action of God for and in human beings to rescue and remake them.[106] Typical of the Pastorals is the fact that it is here described as "the grace that is in Christ Jesus" (cf. 1:9), like the "faith and love that are in Christ Jesus" (1 Tim 1:14; 3:13; 2 Tim 1:13; 3:15), the "life which is in Christ Jesus" (1:1), the "salvation that is in Christ Jesus" (2:10). In these phrases, the "in Christ Jesus" describes less the immediacy of the individual's personal involvement with Christ (see, e.g., Rom 6:11; 8:1; 16:3; 1 Cor 1:2, 30) and more the assurance that Christ embodies all the gifts and graces that the gospel holds forth (see, e.g., Rom 3:24; 6:23; 8:2, 39; 1 Cor 1:4).

Verse 2 is the nearest we have in the NT to an idea of apostolic succession (cf. Heb 2:3-4)—or, better, of gospel succession (the verb "entrust" [παρατίθημι *paratithēmi*] is the natural correlate to "deposit" [παραθήκη *parathēkē*] in 1:12, 14). What is envisaged is not only the transmission from Paul to Timothy—a regular theme in the Pastorals (particularly 1:13 and 3:14, but implied in the very character of the letters) and here given added *gravitas* by the allusion to a solemn act of transmission "through" or "in the presence of" many witnesses.[107] In addition, however, two further stages in transmission are envisaged—from Timothy to "faithful people, who will be competent to teach others also"—four stages, we may even say four generations, in all. It is hard to avoid the sense that a much longer time span is now intended than in the earlier Paulines, with the faithful transmission of the established tradition as the uppermost thought.

2:3-7, Share in Suffering. The following images all emphasize the thought of discipline and hard work. But the opening exhortation (v. 3) gives particular prominence to the thought of shared suffering—that is, shared with other believers (1:8) and with Christ (2:11). The theme is archetypically Pauline (see the Commentary on 1:8) and underlines the conviction (itself born of experience) that faithful witness to the gospel would inevitably bring suffering in its train. Paul did not hesitate to use the image of the soldier (cf. Phil 2:25; Phlm 2), or to encourage the implication that service of the gospel was a real warfare (cf. Eph 6:10-18; 1 Thess 5:8; see also the Commentary on 1 Tim 1:18). But here the primary thought is of the single-mindedness of the good soldier (v. 4). The image assumes the established

---

106. See Dunn, *The Theology of Paul the Apostle*, 13.2.

107. The διά (*dia*) could denote a further stage in the process of transmission: "through" Paul to many witnesses to Timothy. But that would run counter to the repeated impression of the directness of the link between Paul and Timothy. The preposition, therefore, is probably the *dia* of "attendant circumstances," denoting the presence and active approval or participation of the "many witnesses." Cf. the use of prepositions in 1 Tim 4:14 and 2 Tim 1:6. See also the Commentary on 1 Tim 4:14.

pattern of the professional conscript rather than the older idea of the citizen militia and echoes the pride in which the successful army held its general. In this case, the enlisting officer (or general) was Paul.

Two other pictures from common experience underline the point (vv. 5-6). Those who lived in the Greek cities fringing the Aegean would be familiar with the great athletic contests held regularly; for example, the Isthmian Games hosted by Corinth every two years. It is not surprising that it was in his first letter to Corinth that Paul first made use of the image (1 Cor 9:24-25). There as here, it is the link between faithful application and the winner's crown that is emphasized. Since many successful military veterans retired to farm land granted them by the state, the two images (soldier and farmer) went naturally together (as in 1 Cor 9:7). The latter metaphor uses ideas that were important for Paul elsewhere: work hard (see the Commentary on 1 Tim 5:17); "share [in benefit]" (Rom 15:27; 1 Cor 9:10; 10:16-18; Gal 6:6; Phlm 6). For Paul the same rule applied to the community of faith and the service of the gospel. The imagery need not imply a regular stipend for ministry (but see the Commentary on 1 Tim 5:17).

The little homily on lessons from daily life is applied in good teacher fashion (v. 7): "Don't just hear my words, but think about them" (an echo of Prov 2:6). The same rule applies: The words heard required some hard thought; only then would they yield their richest fruit. The teacher is confident in the truth of the lesson given, but at the same time he acknowledges that "understanding" is a gift from the Lord. The Christian pupil listens with one ear cocked to hear the new insight God may bring even from an age-old lesson.

2:8-13, Remember Jesus Christ. The focus and reason for the hard work is the gospel of Jesus Christ (v. 8). The exhortation is unique in the Pauline letters; where Paul talks of "remembering," it is usually something else he has in mind (see Gal 2:10; Col 4:18; 1 Thess 1:3). But it strikes a warmer personal note than the image of guarding a deposit (1:12, 14). The present tense may be rendered, "Keep on remembering."

On this occasion the gospel is summarized in a form that strongly echoes what looks to be an already established confessional formula cited by Paul in Rom 1:3-4. The two-liner focuses on the two earliest Christian claims that must have accounted for so much of the initial spread of the gospel among Jews: Jesus' qualification as the expected Davidic Messiah, and his having been raised from the dead. Evidently it was the importance of this double claim and the frequency with which it had to be asserted that established it as an early confession. In Paul's own ministry (among Gentiles) the Messianic claim was evidently less central because it was less controversial ("Christ" becomes more like a name than a title). It is the confession that this Jesus Christ had been "raised from the dead" that was more important and made the greater impact, as implied in the kerygmatic formula of 1 Cor 15:4, 12-17, 20 (note also the echoes in Rom 4:24-25; 6:4, 9; 7:4; 8:34; 2 Cor 5:15). "This is my gospel" (lit., "According to my gospel") echoes Rom 2:16 (and 16:25), not in the sense of being Paul's alone, but as indicating the gospel to which he had so tirelessly devoted himself. That the emphasis (for Gentiles as well as Jews, by faith alone) was characteristic, and to some extent distinctive, of Paul is balanced by the very basic nature of the gospel summary here.

Still in the mood of thinking about the physical consequences of Paul's commitment (vv. 3-6), the talk of resurrection from the dead prompts again the contrasting image of Paul in chains, like a criminal (v. 9). The thought is of a piece with the honor/shame contrast of 1:12. The linking preposition is usually translated as "for which," but the most obvious translation is "in which." The point presumably is, once again (see 1:8), that in Pauline theology suffering is not just a consequence of the gospel, but is itself part of the gospel—sharing in Christ's sufferings as the way in which and the means by which the resurrection from the dead comes to its full realization (see the discussion of v. 11). The contrast between his own imprisonment and ability to get about and the success of the gospel is one that gave delight to Paul elsewhere (Phil 1:7, 12-18).

Verse 10 simply elaborates the thought. Paul could endure his imprisonment and sufferings because they were in the service of the gospel. The gospel was the good news of Christ Jesus, in whom was salvation. The characterization of the beneficiaries as "the elect" was one of the terms Paul had carried over from his earlier Jewish self-understanding (e.g., Ps 105:6; Isa 42:1; 45:4; 65:9; Sir 47:22); it underpinned his claim that the salvation into which Gentiles were entering was the salvation promised to his own people by the God of Israel. The talk of "eternal glory" carries forward the honor/shame motif of the previous chapter and implicit in the contrasts of vv. 8-10: This glory comes not through great acts of heroism and civic honors, but through the rescue and wholeness offered by the gospel of the cross, proclaimed by a man in chains.

The theme is further elaborated by the fourth "faithful saying" (see the Commentary on 1 Tim 1:15) in vv. 11-13. Even more than the other gospel summaries (1 Tim 1:15; 2:6; 3:16; 2 Tim 1:9-10; Titus 3:4-7), it strikes a distinctively Pauline note, particularly at the beginning—so much so that it could be regarded as a formula or hymn crafted with the explicit purpose of keeping this emphasis of Paul's alive. The lines are obviously written to achieve effect by means of antithesis, but the theology is profound and the effect not merely rhetorical. The first-person plural "we" highlights the confessional nature of the sentiments.

The first line (v. 11) is almost a quotation of Rom 6:8, picking up Paul's distinctive *syn*-compound usage ("died *with*," "live *with*"). The thought is sufficiently familiar that there is no need to specify who the "with" refers to: Christ.[108] It thus sums up the strong double insight of Paul: The way of life is through death, and that death can only be so transformed (to become the forecourt to life) if the death they die is the death of Christ (see Rom 6:3-11; Phil 3:8-11). The depth of this insight is profound and has rarely been adequately plumbed.[109]

The thought of "enduring" (v. 12) coordinates well with the first line, since the endurance of suffering is the most immediate implication (v. 10; cf. particularly Rom 8:23-25; 12:12; see also the formula used in Matt 10:22 and 24:13). The counterpart is a third *syn*-compound: "reigning with" (Christ). The thought is clearly of a piece with v. 5, but it echoes the earlier Pauline language of Rom 5:17, 21, and 1 Cor 4:8.

The last three lines (vv. 12-13) are more coordinated, but create something of a puzzle. "If we deny him, he will also deny us" directly echoes one of Jesus' most disturbing sayings, in the form preserved in Matt 10:33. But there was a longer, more rooted tradition in Judaism that God remained faithful to the chosen people, even when they proved faithless time and time again (v. 13). It was a point that prophets like Second Isaiah and Hosea delighted in, and Paul had expressed himself clearly on the point in Rom 3:3-7, even before the lengthy exposition of Romans 9–11. The final line (v. 13) gives the reason for this confidence in classic theological terms: "He cannot deny himself." That is to say, the God here celebrated is the one committed to God's people (the foundational belief of Israel's covenant theology). This is the one God, a God faithful to creation (who wants all to be saved, 1 Tim 2:4) and to the chosen ones and concerned for their salvation, not arbitrary chance or blind fate. In this confidence, life can be lived confidently, whatever the suffering to be endured.

The problem is that lines three and four seem to run counter to each other: If denial of Christ brings denial by Christ in its train, how is it that unfaithfulness is not similarly punished? The answer will be partly that "denial" has a stronger tone of deliberate acting against and public renunciation, whereas "faithlessness" sounds more like failure to live up to one's profession. But it would surely be a mistake to press for any neat distinction. The point is presumably that the two lines serve different purposes: the first to warn the casual and to stiffen the resolve of the frightened, the second to comfort the broken and to give renewed hope to the despairing. However, it is of the nature of such epigrammatic summaries of Christian faith that they are open to different interpretations, intended to stimulate more than to teach.

2:14-21, Remind Them. The call to "remember" (v. 8) is matched by the call to "remind" ("keep reminding"). The

---

108. Some, however, prefer the thought of Timothy's being encouraged to share in Paul's sufferings. See Bassler, *1 Timothy, 2 Timothy, Titus*, 145-46.

109. It is inadequate, for example, to characterize Paul's language here in terms of "presenting Jesus as the supreme model for Christian behavior." See Johnson, *Letters to Paul's Delegates*, 67.

exhortation begins (vv. 14-15) by picking up the gospel just summarized (vv. 8-13); by adding a further image (the unashamed worker), it effectively links the thought back to both the earlier images (vv. 3-7) and the previous talk of being ashamed (1:8, 12, 16). All this provides a counter to alternatives again treated dismissively in another sequence of vilificatory imagery.

The other side of the faithful transmission of the gospel (vv. 1-2) is the encouragement of believers not to be distracted by arguments over mere words, verbal quibbles (v. 14; the same root [λογομαχέω *logomacheō*] as in 1 Tim 6:4 [λογομαχία *logomachia*]. Put like that, the warning has a much wider application than simply to teachers of what is obviously false doctrine. Even good and faithful believers can often stumble over particular terms or be distracted by attempts to overdefine or make the mistake of clinging to the word rather than to the substance (see Reflections at 1:8-18). But the sternness of the charge ("before God") indicates that the writer has in view a situation that, while it may have started in learned debate or word games, had now gone well beyond that, bringing "ruin," "destruction" (καταστροφή *katastrophē*; the word has given us the English term "catastrophe") to those who listened. What may have begun as debate about the meaning of "raised from the dead" (v. 8) had resulted in a teaching on the resurrection that had to be refuted (v. 18).

To counter the effects of ill-advised speculation, the teacher needs to be both approved by God and skilled in trade (v. 15). The first term ("approved" [δόκιμος *dokimos*]) has the connotation of "tried and tested" (cf. 2 Cor 10:18; 13:7), in contrast to "tried and failed" (3:8; 1 Cor 9:27; 2 Cor 13:5-7). The "unashamed workman" presumably is the one who has learned the trade well and who works consistently to good effect. The third image is of cutting a path straight across forested or rough country, so that travelers can go directly to their destination. So the thought presumably is either of cutting a straight path for the gospel or of leading the unwary through the thickets or uneven ground in the tradition that otherwise might cause them to lose their direction (given 2 Pet 3:16, the latter can hardly be dismissed). The gospel is sometimes described as "the word of salvation/righteousness/life"; here it is "the word of truth" (as in Eph 1:13; Col 1:5; Jas 1:18).

Alternatives are dismissed in familiar terms (v. 16): "profane" (1 Tim 1:9; 4:7; 6:20), "empty talk" (1 Tim 6:20), resulting in more and more "ungodliness" (Titus 2:12; the opposite of the Pastorals' favorite "piety," "godliness"). Their teaching will spread like gangrene (γάγγραινα *gangraina*, v. 17). Illustrative of the corrupting power of such teachers are Hymenaeus (mentioned already in 1 Tim 1:20) and Philetus (of whom we hear nothing more). And illustrative of the corrupting power of such teaching is their claim that "the resurrection has already happened" (v. 18).

What precisely is meant is unclear, but most infer a teaching that there was no future resurrection to look forward to (cf. 1 Cor 15:12). In this view, believers already shared in Christ's resurrection, and nothing more need be achieved so far as salvation was concerned. They already had resurrection life and would not die (cf. John 11:26).[110] If that is the case, we may further infer that Hymenaeus and Philetus set salvation and creation in antithesis (cf. 1 Tim 4:3), that salvation was seen as an escape from the body and from the material world, a denial that the created order would also participate in salvation (as Paul had taught, Rom 8:19-21). Whatever the precise teaching in view, the writer was convinced that in propounding it Hymenaeus and Philetus had "missed the mark, deviated from the truth" (ἀστοχέω *astocheō*; the same word as in 1 Tim 1:6; 6:21) and were "overturning, upsetting [as in Titus 1:11] the faith of some."

The counter and consoling thought is that "God's foundation is firm, solid, strong" (v. 19). The thought is probably prompted by Isa 28:16, a regularly cited text in early Christian apologetic (Rom 9:33; 10:11; 1 Pet 2:6; cf. Matt 21:42; Eph 2:20). In that case, the foundation is presumably Christ himself, or the gospel of his resurrection in particular (with the interpretation of it in 1 Corinthians 15 assumed). The image of a "seal" affixed to the foundation doubles the confidence-building imagery (see, e.g., 2 Cor 1:22;

---

110. This is how the later gnostic texts understand resurrection. See *Treatise on the Resurrection* 49; *Gospel of Philip* 56.

Eph 1:13; 4:30; Rev 7:2-8). The seal is identified with two scriptural quotations. The first is from Num 16:5, and with it an allusion to the classic case of presumption (Korah, Dathan, and Abiram) and its horrific outcome (Num 16:31-35; cf. Jude 11); those who were tempted to follow the teaching of Hymanaeus and Philetus were confronted by as serious a choice. The second seems to be no particular text as such but an amalgamation or summary of repeated exhortations in Jewish Scripture and writings (see Num 16:26; Job 36:10; Ps 6:8; Isa 26:13; 52:11; Sir 17:26). As elsewhere in the NT, "the Lord" who is named or called upon will be thought of here as Christ, but with the ambiguity of continuity implied, as in the equivalent use made of Joel 2:32 in Acts 2:17-21 and Rom 10:11-13.

The image of a foundation suggests the further image of the house built upon it (v. 20) and of the different pottery found in a great house—gold and silver, wood and earthenware (cf. 1 Cor 3:12). The expense of the former indicates that they were intended for occasions where their value would be recognized, where they would bring honor and respect to their owners (all this can be indicated by the word "honor"). The cheapness of the latter indicates humdrum or hidden use in kitchens and privies, such as no one would boast of and would bring no honor to the owner—literally "dishonor," but in a relative sense. The NIV tries to maintain the contrast by translating the Greek as "noble/ignoble"; the NRSV's "special use/ordinary use" is not so successful. The contrast had already been made in Rom 9:21.

Unlike Rom 9:19-24, however, the author breaks away from the predestinarian mold that the image of the potter encouraged—pottery as made for a particular use—and only the potter could make it afresh (see Isa 45:9; Jer 18:1-6). In this case he envisages the common pot as being able to scour itself clean and to become useful in public display (v. 21). Even so, he quickly corrects himself by switching to the passive: "consecrated [that is, by the owner], useful to the master of the house, made ready/prepared for every good work." The readiness to go beyond the image and to adapt it to the situation imagined should be noted, as also the attempt to hold the balance between human responsibility and divine initiative.

2:22-26, Flee Youthful Lusts. As in 1 Tim 6:11 the final burst of advice to Timothy begins with the reminder that there are some forces that work through his own nature that he needs resolutely to shun (v. 22). Here most explicitly "desires" are in view, the term clearly used in its negative sense of "lusts"; the sexual connotation should not be ignored. Earlier on, Paul had indicated that he shared the Jewish tradition that untutored "desire" is the root of sin (Rom 7:7-11; cf. Jas 1:15). Again, as in 1 Tim 6:11, the contrast to "flee from" is "pursue," with three of the same goals in view (see the Commentary on 1 Tim 6:11), plus "peace." This, it is assumed, is the common goal of fellow believers. The phrase and its context give us, in effect, two definitions or identity markers of Christians: "those who call on the Lord" (see also Rom 10:12-14; 1 Cor 1:2)—but he adds, "from a clean heart" (cf. 1 Tim 1:5; Matt 5:8)—and those who make "righteousness, faith[fulness], love and peace" their goal. The formulaic character of the language should not be allowed to cloak the fact that the writer did not define Christianity purely in formal terms, as though only those who could recite the "faithful sayings," for example, were to be regarded as Christians. The emphasis in v. 22*b* may be compared with Rom 2:7, 10.

The complementary call to "refuse," "reject," "avoid" (v. 23) is hardly more illuminating than the other dismissive rebuttals—"stupid" (Titus 3:9); "uninstructed," "controversies" (1 Tim 6:4; Titus 3:9), which only "breed quarrels/disputes" (Titus 3:9). The Lord's "slave/servant" ought to be quite the opposite (v. 24)—"not quarreling," but "gentle" (ἤπιος *ēpios*; the only other NT usage of this word, 1 Thess 2:7, evokes the image of the muse), "skillful in teaching" (1 Tim 3:2), "bearing evil without resentment." He will "correct his opponents with humility/considerateness" (cf. 1 Tim 3:3; Titus 3:2)—a fruit of the Spirit much prized by Paul (1 Cor 4:21; 2 Cor 10:1; Gal 5:23; 6:1; Eph 4:2; Col 3:12). The hope is that God may grant the repentance that will bring such people to the truth and make it possible for them to escape the snare of the devil (vv. 25-26; see also 1 Tim 3:7), in which they are held captive to do the devil's will.[111] Again we note the prejudicial language. But more to the point here is the mildness and pastoral sensitivity of the advice—in contrast to so much of the author's own dismissive language (1 Tim 1:4-7; 4:1-3, 7; 6:3-5, 20-21). Also to be noticed is the balance he attempts to maintain between human responsibility and the power experienced as operating from without, whether of God (v. 25) or of the devil (v. 26).

---

111. The Greek of the last clause is awkward, seeming to distinguish the one who captures from the one whose will is done. Hence the NRSV's margin: "may escape from the snare of the devil, having been held captive by him, to do his [that is, God's] will." Alternatively, both pronouns could be taken as referring to God: "snatched alive by God from the devil's snare, so that they can do God's will!" See Johnson, *Letters to Paul's Delegates,* 82.

REFLECTIONS

This passage is notable for several features. First we should note the variety, indeed, the kaleidoscope of images and metaphors on which it draws—soldier with commander, athlete with rule book, farmer with harvest, criminal in chains, catastrophe, worker, cutting a path, gangrene, foundation, seal, house, expensive and cheap pottery, snare. Such vivid imagery makes the attitude and message of the writer clear. Without metaphor and simile, parable and aphorism, communication is one-dimensional and rarely effective over a lengthy message. As Jesus knew well, it is the power of words to paint pictures, to enter the eye-gate as well as the ear-gate, that makes a speech memorable and effective. If that is so, then faith needs its metaphors as much as its creeds. The value of the metaphors in this chapter was presumably their relevance—they were drawn from the realities of everyday life as lived by both writer and readers. Presumably also it follows that contemporary attempts to convey the gospel have to draw on fresh metaphors. A metaphor that no longer "works" is a dead metaphor. It is like a dirty window; it needs to be cleaned or replaced.

Not least of importance here is the recognition that metaphorical speech is a richer way of communicating than is the teaching of algebraic or legal propositions. In metaphor the correlation between the word picture and its referent is not a simple one-to-one. The point of the metaphor is not simply to communicate data, but to tease the mind into fresh insights. The metaphor is a better teacher than the proposition: The proposition can be learned; the metaphor has to be pondered. That is why the lack of correlation between the different metaphors is not a problem. Metaphors like those in 2 Timothy 2 are not intended to cover every inch of truth like a carpet without holes. Rather, they overlap; they jostle against each other; they point in different directions. They are not hard around the edges, like a box or a sword, where overlap and incompatibility would be a problem; they are fuzzy, like a range of different light sources illuminating their immediate vicinity. They do not give definition; they give illumination.

In this chapter in particular we see how the writer can use this kaleidoscope of images to say what might seem otherwise contradictory things—not just the more familiar thought that divine initiative of the Creator (potter) and human responsibility somehow go hand in hand (2:20-21, 24-26), but also the more subtle balance between thought of the secure foundation and the seal confirming the faithfulness of God, over against the responsibility to avoid godless chatter, to name the name of the Lord, and to depart from iniquity (2:16-19). And not least for the Pastorals, the still more delicate ability to distinguish between Hymenaeus and Philetus on the one hand, and those who might yet be drawn back to the truth, and to adopt the appropriate pastoral tactic (2:17-18, 24-26) on the other hand.

This complexity of a gospel, spoken of in metaphors as well as proclaimed, has to be borne in mind when taking on board the initial exhortation that stands as a headline for the chapter as a whole (2:1-2). Metaphor cannot be transposed directly into proposition without serious loss. And the tradition Timothy had received from Paul and that he had in turn passed on to teachers who would pass it on to still others is made up of both. A teacher who took the injunction of 2:1-2 to apply only to creedal statements would be doing only half his job. There is also the whole ethos that is encapsulated in, or better, caught by, the kaleidoscope of metaphors. The counsel to pastor as well as to denounce has to be considered as well. That is the other half of Timothy's job as envisaged in this chapter—not just the teacher, but also the pastor sensitive to the complexity of the gospel imagery and the need to remint fresh metaphors and images for different contexts and new challenges.

The second main line of reflection is the tremendous basis the chapter gives for a positive theology of suffering. It is not simply a matter of using imagery like that of the good soldier, the knowledgeable athlete, the hardworking farmer, with the overtones of energy expended in disciplined and effective ways (2:3-6). Such images are fine where such energy can be expended to such good effect. But the writer also evokes the image of Paul, the prisoner held in chains against his will and unable to act with any freedom (2:9). This, too, is part of the theology of suffering. So also, later on, the writer will use the much more negative and frightening images of corruption eating into live flesh (2:17) and the animal caught helpless in a snare, unable to escape its captor (2:26). There is a suffering that warns of a plight from which only God can deliver.

But all these are taken up in the restatement of one of Paul's most powerful theological motifs: that of sharing with Christ in his death and enduring with him in his passion (2:11-12). For the writer, as for Paul earlier, it is this identification with Christ, the sense of a whole life caught up into Christ's destiny, that in the end is the only thing that gives hope of making sense of even the worst suffering—suffering sometimes as a signal of danger, suffering at other times as a trial to be borne, suffering at still other times as the discipline required of the dedicated soldier, athlete, farmer. In the darkest moments of disaster or deep personal loss, such thoughts provide little comfort. But as the sages of Israel had long ago learned, it is in such ways that God seeks to wean us from the world and to have us grow up mature; we need only think of Job and the psalms of suffering (particularly Psalms 22; 69). It is *through* suffering that the resurrection becomes a reality (see Rom 8:17-23; 2 Cor 4:16–5:5; Phil 3:8-11).

2 TIMOTHY 3:1-17, LESSONS FROM TRADITION

COMMENTARY

Further warnings follow as to the sort of evil people who may be expected "in the last days" (3:1-5), a malaise that will affect the Christian communities and be actively spread within them (3:5-7). The implication is that Timothy should already know to expect such, since the expectation itself is traditional. But Scripture gives specific prototypes in Jannes and Jambres (3:8-9). In direct contrast is the memory of Paul's own steadfastness under severe trial (3:10-13). The inference that previous history provides such valuable lessons is confirmed by the final appeal to the role of inspired Scripture in giving instruction to safeguard against repetition of the one precedent and to promote the other (3:14-17).

3:1-9, People to Avoid. As in 1 Tim 4:1-5, the writer draws on the well-established expectation (Jewish and Christian) that the final days of this age will be marked by a crescendo of evil (v. 1; see the Commentary on 1 Tim 4:1). The first Christians evidently believed that Christ's resurrection and the giving of the Spirit (cf. Acts 2:17) had ushered in the final sequence of events that would climax in "the last day" of general resurrection and judgment (see John 6:39-40; 12:48). Despite the regular comment that the delay of the end was a problem for the writer, the expectation seems to be little different from other expressions of it (cf. Jude 18 and the still later 2 Pet 3:3). As in 1 Tim 4:1-5, the implication is that the writer saw these expectations already being fulfilled in the situations confronting the churches of his day. What he had in view in speaking of such "difficult times," "times of stress," is indicated in the following catalog.

What follows in vv. 2-5 is a typical example of a vice list, the sort of behavior that would generally be regarded as such and that would be abhorred by most right-thinking people (typical examples elsewhere in the NT include Rom 1:29-31; 1 Cor 6:9-10; Gal 5:19-21; 1 Tim 1:9-10). The list should not be taken as a prediction of particular evils but as indicative and representative of a society's ethos breaking down under stresses too great for the principles and values it claims to espouse.[112] It is worth following the writer's lead in allowing the rapid array of character types that follow to build an impression of a type of society or community gone bad—"lovers of self/selfish," "lovers of money/avaricious" (Luke 16:14); "boasters/braggarts" (Rom 1:29); "arrogant/haughty" (Luke 1:51; Rom 1:30); "slanderous/blasphemers" (1 Tim 1:13); "disobedient to parents" (Rom 1:30); "ungrateful" (Luke 6:35); "unholy" (1 Tim 1:9); "unloving/lacking family affection" (Rom 1:31); "irreconcilable," "slanderers" (lit., "devils," as in 1 Tim 3:11; Titus 2:3); "without self-control/dissolute," "traitors/betrayers" (like Judas, Luke 6:16); "reckless/thoughtless" (Acts 19:36); "blinded or conceited" (1 Tim 3:6; 6:4); "lovers of pleasure rather than lovers of God."

The final description (v. 5) probably applies to all the preceding—"having the form of godliness [the Pastorals' favorite word; see footnote 10], but denying its power." The inference is clear: Those in view in the vice list of 3:2-4 are not outsiders; such people are also found within the church. The word used, "form" (μόρφωσις *morphōsis*), does not denote an appearance casually assumed or taken on to deceive, but a form that was appropriate to the reality—here the form that "godliness/piety" might well take (cf. Rom 2:20). The contrast, then, is with a godliness that really transforms a life and whose substance is displayed not simply in appearance but in useful service (2:21; cf. Titus 1:16).

An example of the subtlety of the self-deception here warned against would be the self-assumptions criticized in Rom 2:17-24. Such people are to be avoided—an exhortation easier to give than to enact, given the subtlety of the self-deceit just instanced.

The importance of this qualification becomes clearer in the light of the specific example given (vv. 6-7). Some of these people "creep into" or "worm their way into" households (the language is deliberately pejorative) and are successful in winning over those in the women's quarter. The picture is evidently drawn from experience, reflecting the fact that women were often effectively restricted within their households for large parts of the day and would often find time heavy on their hands; the door-to-door peddler of new religions and divergent sects has been a fact of life throughout Christian history and beyond (cf. 2 Cor 2:17). In the second century, Celsus made similar complaints regarding Christian evangelism.[113]

More disturbing for the modern reader are the disparaging terms with which the writer describes women who were enticed by such teaching (vv. 6-7). They are "little" women, a scornful diminutive, with the sense of "silly." They are filled up or overwhelmed by their sins, allowing themselves to be led astray by their desires, always trying to learn (cf. 1 Cor 14:35) and never able to come to a knowledge of the truth (cf. 1 Tim 2:4; Titus 1:1). There is a prejudice here, such as we see elsewhere in the Pastorals (particularly 1 Tim 4:7; 5:13), and it is difficult to know how much to discount for it, not least since it was one widely shared at the time.[114] At the same time, we should also recall the contrasting pictures of 1 Tim 5:10 and 2 Tim 1:5 and the disadvantaged state of the great majority of women, usually with little or no education and often hungry for knowledge, and so easy prey to the wandering teacher with good-looking credentials.

The description of such subversive teachers continues in familiar dismissive tones (v. 8): "they oppose the truth, people of corrupted mind, unfit, unapproved [the opposite of 2:15] concerning the faith." The writer is confident that he knows "the truth" and

---

112. The list shows some literary skill in its construction, particularly the almost unbroken sequence of eight words beginning with "a" in 3:2-3.

113. See Origen *Against Celsus* 3:55.
114. See Bassler, *1 Timothy, 2 Timothy, Titus*, 161.

firmly grasps "the faith," but otherwise such description tells us more of his attitude to alternative renderings of that truth and faith (recall that they "have the form of godliness") than of the alternative renderings (cf. 1 Tim 6:3-5).

In this case, however, he can cite a parallel or precedent—that of Jannes and Jambres (vv. 8-9).[115] The reference is to the episode in Exodus 7, when the Egyptian magicians attempted to counter Moses first, unsuccessfully, in the contest of staves becoming snakes (Exod 7:11-12) and then, apparently more successfully, in the contest of turning water into blood (Exod 7:22). The episodes attracted some speculation in later Jewish circles, and the two names given here were evidently already given to these magicians;[116] this is the way such traditions develop (cf. the story of the magi in Matthew 2, to whom later Western tradition gives the names of Balthasar, Melchior, and Gaspar). The reference to them, it should be noted, depends on the already developed tradition, since the brief account of Exodus 7 is inadequate in itself to support the suggestion that they were tricksters or deserving of comparison with those just described. The point, however, is that they represent an alternative religious standpoint, opposed to the truth and right of God (cf. Exod 9:27) and, therefore, can represent those against whom the writer warns here. More to the point, their failure in the face of the superior empowerment of Moses (note also Exod 9:11) provides an assurance that the truth of the faith will triumph in the end, exposing the folly of these other teachers in a similar way.

3:10-17, Precedents to Follow. Over against episodes in scriptural tradition such as that of Jannes and Jambres is set, not Moses, but Paul. Thus is picked up again an emphasis running through both letters to Timothy, where Paul is put forward, not only as Timothy's father and teacher in the faith, but also as a model for subsequent generations (1 Tim 1:12-16; 2:7; 2 Tim 1:11-12; 2:9-10; 3:10-12; 4:6-8). The point not to be missed here is that the reference to the traditions of Paul's mission work is sandwiched between references to the biblical precedent from Exodus 7 (3:8-9) and the fulsome affirmation of the role of Scripture (3:14-17). The implication is that the traditions of Paul (now preserved in Acts), like the traditions of Jesus' teaching (1 Tim 5:18, now preserved in the Gospels), already carry a paraenetical authority similar to that of the Hebrew (or Greek) Scriptures.

The appeal to Paul (vv. 10-11) is comprehensive: Timothy has "followed"—that is, he has "paid attention to" (precise translation is difficult, hence the NIV's "you have observed" and the NRSV's "you know all about"; it implies close attention to and learning from)—Paul's "teaching" (διδασκαλία *didaskalia*; one of the Pastorals' key terms), his way of life and conduct, his purpose and resolve (πρόθεσις *prothesis*; the same word as in 1:9), his faith or faithfulness (cf. 1 Tim 1:4-5; 4:12), his endurance or steadfastness (cf. 2 Cor 6:6; Gal 5:22), his love (see Commentary on 1 Tim 1:5), his patience (cf. 1 Tim 6:11; Titus 2:2), his persecutions, and his sufferings. The last two terms link in one of the dominant motifs in the preceding chapter (see 2:9-13) and introduce specific reminiscences of the hardships Paul endured in his mission. Clearly in view are the episodes vividly retold in Acts 13–14; even if this were a reminiscence between long-standing associates (see Acts 16:1), the fact that it is written with a view to a wider audience implies that such accounts of Paul's missionary work were familiar throughout the church founded by him. More to the point, Paul's history gave plenty of examples of the Lord's rescuing him from persecution—just the encouragement required for those enduring lesser troubles and pressures to stand firm. The language echoes Ps 34:19, evoking still earlier examples of steadfastness under trial and of God's deliverance.

The harsh reality is that such persecutions can be expected by "those who want to lead godly lives" (vv. 12-13; the adverb of his favorite "godliness" [εὐσέβεια *eusebeia*] is used here) in Christ Jesus (a usage that is closer to the earlier Pauline motif than others), while "wicked people and tricksters ["sorcerers" (γόητες *goētes*)] progress from bad to worse, deceiving and deceived." The recognition that followers of the crucified Christ were unlikely to escape persecution

---

115. An equivalent episode from Christian history is that of Elymas, also described as a magician. See Acts 13:8.
116. See *Damascus Document* 5:18-19. For further detail, see Dibelius and Conzelmann, *The Pastoral Epistles*, 117.

goes back to Jesus (particularly Matt 5:11; Mark 8:34). The use of *goētes* carries with it both the allusion to Jannes and Jambres (vv. 8-9) and the common suspicion that such "impostors" or "magicians" were more proficient at sleight of hand than they were mediums of supernatural power. At the same time, the recognition that such people can be self-deceived as well as deceivers, another common perception,[117] is a healthy qualification of the more regular cut-and-dried dismissal of contrary teaching. The contrast between the godly being persecuted and the wicked progressing in their wickedness is a variation on the regular theme in the psalms (e.g., Psalm 73), in which the righteous complain at the prosperity of the wicked.

The other secure guideline to wisdom and wholeness as recognized by God is the holy writings, which constituted Timothy's textbook from childhood (vv. 14-15); Timothy evidently owed much to his mother's and grandmother's teaching (see the Commentary on 1:5). Here we are reminded that the Torah, the Prophets, and the Writings provided the school curriculum for Jewish boys as well as Israel's law book and prayer book. Obviously implied is the continuity between Timothy's instruction from the Jewish Scriptures and his belief in Christ; it was because the two were so closely coordinated that Paul could defend and expound the gospel by referring to the Scriptures. So, too, the writer can take it for granted that the "holy writings" themselves are "able to make you wise for salvation through faith in Christ Jesus" (see 1 Tim 1:14; 3:13), without even referring to the gospel or to the teaching. Of course, the assumption is that the gospel is the outworking of Scripture, so that the wisdom, salvation, and faith held out in the gospel are continuous with that inculcated in the holy writings. That is also to say that the gospel's saving power is of a piece with the saving power of Scripture, or it is not the gospel.

The descriptions "sacred writings" (v. 15) and "every scripture" (v. 16) are obviously synonymous. Both terms, the latter singular as well as plural, had already been used by the Jewish philosopher Philo to refer more or less to what we call the Old Testament, the books of Moses in particular (see Rom 1:2). Their distinctive status is signaled by the striking term "God-breathed" (θεόπνευστος *theopneustos*), clearly indicating the writer's understanding of the process of inspiration (the word imagery is the same). To be noted is the fact that it is the scripture that is "God-breathed,"[118] and not merely the prophet who is "inspired," unless by that is meant inspired to speak particular words (cf. 2 Pet 1:20). It is for this reason that words of Scripture can be taken elsewhere in the NT to mean words spoken directly by God (explicit in Rom 9:15). This was the commonly understood phenomenon of prophetic inspiration—the speaking of words given not by the conscious mind but directly by the god possessing or the spirit inspiring.

At the same time, it is important to recognize that for the writer, the holy writings, Scripture, have a targeted purpose: "to make you wise for salvation" (v. 15); "useful/beneficial for teaching," for reproof,[119] for correction/improvement, for instruction/discipline (the regular term in Greek for "schooling" [ἐλεγμός *elegmos*]), that God's person (of whom Timothy was the type; see 1 Tim 6:11) might be capable/proficient (= able to meet all demands), "equipped for every good deed" (vv. 16-17). Presumably the two purposes are integrated: The purpose of Scripture is the purpose of good schooling—to produce the well-instructed and disciplined adult, proficient and well equipped in the graces and skills required for a positive role in church and society ("good work of every kind") and wise as to what makes for the wholeness of salvation. A similar rationale for Scripture and its continued usefulness is given in Rom 15:3-4 and 1 Cor 10:11.

---

117. "Deceived deceivers" was a commonly used phrase. See Dibelius and Conzelmann, *The Pastoral Epistles*, 119. The Alexandrian Jewish philosopher Philo draws a similar deduction from Exodus 7. See Philo *Migration of Abraham* 83.

118. This expression could be translated as, "Every God-breathed scripture is also useful . . ."; but it would be unjustified to deduce from such a translation that the writer thought there were some "scriptures" that were *not* God-breathed.

119. The word used here, *elegmos*, is hapax (see Sir 21:6; 32:17), but it is a close synonym with ἔλεγχος (*elegchos*), which is a less well-attested variant reading (see Prov 1:25, 30).

REFLECTIONS

Talk of "the last days" always tends to be somewhat embarrassing for Christians. One reason why is that the first Christians seem to have concluded that the last days had already begun in the first coming and resurrection of Jesus, and that time would soon climax in the coming again of Jesus. But that second coming has not happened and is still awaited. Another reason is that at scattered intervals ever since there have been groups of Christians who read the signs of the times to conclude that the final end was nigh. And it was not. Such repeated disappointments should make us extremely cautious about reading the signs of the times in the same way. At the same time, Christians should not be so embarrassed at thinking of all time since Jesus as "the last days," for thereby they are affirming that the first coming of Jesus has altered forever the way Christians view time. They belong to a new age that regards the resurrection of Christ as its starting point and the coming again of Christ as its climax. To view reality from that perspective gives a fresh perspective on Christian relationships with God, with others, and with the world, and on Christian responsibility in these "last days."

The linking theme in this passage seems to be learning from tradition and being realistic in the lessons learned. Traditional views of the "last days" warn repeatedly of times of stress to come (3:1); all desiring to live a godly life in Christ should expect persecution (3:12). The gospel, in other words, gives no promise of a quiet life or of escape from hard times. But if this point is taken, then when hard times do come the insight is confirmed and the faith may be strengthened rather than weakened. Tradition can then serve one of its principal purposes by providing practical lessons and further insights from the accounts of faith under stress in earlier hard times. To that extent the fact that "the last days" seem to have stretched out interminably becomes less of a problem, for so far as the good having a hard time at the hands of the bad is concerned, "the last days" are no different in character from the former times, only perhaps in degree.

From the history of tradition we learn also that the gradations of deception are almost infinite. The distinction between having the form of godliness and denying its power (3:5) may be very fine; those idle people who are captivated by the plausible alternative may deserve more sympathy than denunciation (see 3:6-7). Jannes and Jambres have moved from being moderately successful magicians, in one case matching Moses' prowess, to the epitome of trickery and sorcery (3:8-9). The imagery is clear, but the talk of those who are deceivers but also deceived (3:13), of those who are "blinded," is a further reminder that lessons to be applied are rarely clear and simple and that the most testing challenge is not that of the evil person (here the otherwise sweeping denunciation of 3:2-4 can be less rather than more helpful), but the person who is wholly sincere but whose instruction or praxis is beginning to diverge onto a track of its own.

Here again the diverse history of tradition, both Scripture and the lives of great heroes of the faith like Paul, provides fruitful instruction to those who pay it due heed. In view of this, it is inexpressibly sad, and to our own disadvantage, that so many Christian denominations have lost a sense of the importance of their history, of the saints and sages, the heroes and martyrs, as well as the failures and mistakes, that the history of Christianity provides. Just as the New Testament writers affirmed that sacred history was "written down to instruct us" (1 Cor 10:11; cf. Heb 11), so also we today need to recall the great men and women, and the wicked deeds and policies carried out in the name of Christ, of the last twenty centuries who also are there to instruct us. A very valuable exercise for many a congregation would be to ask who they might consider appropriate to count among their own particular canon of saints and what might count among the cautionary tales of their past, and so to remind one another of the lessons that might be drawn from both.

The need to be realistic about expectations regarding the Scriptures is not least of importance. Too many focus the whole of the teaching of 3:15-17 on the important term "God-inspired," and proceed to miss the point by making deductions directly from that term for the value of Scripture in describing, for example, creation and history (often signaled over the past century by the label "inerrant"). But the text is clear: The sacredness of the writings is directed to the end of "making wise for salvation"; the point of Scripture's inspiration was that the Scriptures should be beneficial for teaching and equipping the student believer for effective living as a Christian. Since this text is the most explicit biblical statement of what Scripture is *for*, the fact that it targets the purpose of Scripture so explicitly, and with a clearly delimited scope, should be given more weight, both in the doctrine and in the use of Scripture. Too much time is misspent asking of Scripture what it was not designed to answer. Better that Scripture itself should instruct us as to what its purpose is.

2 TIMOTHY 4:1-22, PAUL'S FINAL CHARGE AND REQUESTS TO TIMOTHY

COMMENTARY

The poignant final charge to Timothy serves as a bracket in parallel to chap. 1. It recapitulates both the previous charges (4:1-2, 5) and the previous warnings about likely defection (4:3-4). As elsewhere, Paul, now in his own final lap, is held up as the example to follow (4:6-8). The final spattering of instructions really continues the portrayal of Paul's final testimony (4:9-18). More typical of the greetings characteristic of the closures of Paul's earlier letters is the final paragraph (4:19-21), with a brief double benediction (4:22).

4:1-5, Paul's Final Charge. The opening words (v. 1) repeat those of 1 Tim 5:21 and 2 Tim 2:14. As in the former case, Christ Jesus is linked with God as joint witnesses to and authorities behind the commission. This time, however, the thought is given a triple elaboration in respect of Christ: (1) Reference is made particularly to his coming role as judge of the living and the dead. That the risen and exalted Christ had been appointed to this role was early on affirmed within Christianity (cf. Acts 10:42; 2 Cor 5:10), though we should recall that in Jewish reflection other old-time heroes like Abel and Enoch were given similar roles, as indeed are disciples and saints in Matt 19:28 and 1 Cor 6:2. (2) This will follow on Christ's "epiphany/appearing" (ἐπιφάνεια *epiphaneia*). Here the word certainly has his "appearing" again (second coming) in view (see the Commentary on 1 Tim 6:14). (3) Most distinctive is the talk of "his kingdom." Although it sounds familiar in Christian ears, the thought is actually very infrequent in the NT (Matt 13:41; 25:31; Col 1:13), particularly as measured against the more regular talk of God's kingdom. Perhaps the idea is implied of a royal rulership bestowed by God on Christ (in line with the influential Ps 110:1), whose climax would be the return of the kingdom to God so that God might be all in all (as in 1 Cor 15:24-28). At any rate, the final charge to Timothy has a strong eschatological bias: The responsibility placed on Timothy is to be carried out in the light of the future kingdom and will be validated and vindicated only in the final judgment.

The charge focuses on Timothy's preaching and teaching ministry (v. 2). "The word" stands as summary for the "word of God" (1 Tim 4:5; 2 Tim 2:9; Titus 2:5), "the word of truth" (2:15), "the sure word" (Titus 1:9), as also the gospel, the "sound teaching," and so on (cf. Gal 6:6; Col 4:3). The second imperative has the sense of "stand by"—that is, "be ready," "be on hand"—for opportunities and crises as they arise, whether the time is opportune or not. As so often in the Pastorals, the command to "expose, convict, reprove" (1 Tim 5:20; note the parallel in Matt 18:15) is nearly doubled by the overlapping "rebuke/warn" (ἐπιτιμάω *epitimaō*; the word used by the Lukan parallel, Luke 17:3), but then balanced by the more positive "encourage/comfort" (παρακαλέω *parakaleō*; as in 1 Tim 5:1; 6:2; Titus 2:15). Both (or all) should be aspects of the teaching, and both (or all) will require resilient "patience" (as in 3:10; cf. 2:24-25).

The need for such resoluteness is all the greater in view of what can be expected (vv. 3-4). Here is evident a clear sense that the "last days" (3:1) have still more unpleasant surprises to unfold (cf. 1 Tim 4:1); the eschatological horizon remains close (cf. Rom 13:11-12; 1 Cor 7:29-31; Phil 4:5) but still at some distance. A vivid little scenario is painted in three acts—the three stages of decline and defection. It begins with people "not putting up with, unwilling to listen to" (cf. Heb 13:22) "the sound teaching" (see the Commentary on 1 Tim 1:10). Instead, with "itching ears" (a well-known image for the curiosity that can be relieved only by scratching them with interesting and spicy bits of information), they "accumulate" teachers who appeal to their own interests and satisfy their desires. The outcome is that they "turn away" (1:15; Titus 1:14) from hearing "the truth" (see footnote 9) and "turn aside" (1 Tim 1:6; 5:15) to "the myths" (see the Commentary on 1 Tim 1:4). The writer uses his familiar praise and blame words, which tell us more of his attitude than of what it is he praises or blames. The double use of the image of "turning away/aside" provides a clear enough picture of how he conceived the errors he was concerned about.

Verse 5 in effect continues the commission of v. 2. "Be well-balanced, self-controlled" has been said elsewhere in complementary terms (e.g., 1:7; cf. 1 Pet 1:13). "Bear hardship patiently" uses the same word as in 2:9, evoking the same theological motif as in 2:3, 11-12. "Evangelist" (εὐαγγελιστής *euangelistēs*) was a recognized ministry, though it is less clear whether the term denoted a full-scale ministry, with the financial support that it would require (cf. Acts 21:8; Eph 4:11), or a function within a more diverse ministry (as here). "Your ministry" is obviously the more comprehensive term, with all the various functions implicit in it that 1 and 2 Timothy cover (the image is of a bowl or pitcher to be filled full).

4:6-8, Paul's Last Testimony. This is one of the most moving passages in the NT. Although the imagery is shared with (drawn directly from?) some of Paul's favorite imagery in his earlier letters,[120] it is hard to hear the passage as other than Paul's own words. Often neglected, however, is the way in which these verses act as a bracket with 1 Tim 1:15-16—the two letters held between Paul's own account of his beginning as a Christian and his imminent end. In fact, the various references back to Paul's ministry mean that the two letters effectively summarize his whole Christian life and ministry (1 Tim 1:15-16; 2 Tim 1:8, 11-13, 15-17; 2:2, 9-10; 3:10-11; 4:6-18). In other words, one of the purposes served by 1 and 2 Timothy seems to be to preserve the memory of the great apostle, illustrated by characteristic vignettes of his ministry. Whatever the origin of these passages, it is unlikely that this effect was unintended.

Paul drew on the imagery of priestly sacrifice (v. 6, "I am already being [or about to be] poured out as a libation/drink offering"; cf. Num 28:7) several times for his own ministry (see Rom 15:16). Here Paul himself is the sacrificial offering (σπένδω *spendō*; as in the other NT use of the verb, Phil 2:17). Clearly in view is Paul's death ("departure" [ἀνάλυσις *analysis*]; the verb is used in Phil 1:23), seen as imminent.

Equally characteristic of Paul is the imagery of the athletic contest or race (v. 7), but here again there seems to be almost a deliberate echo of 1 Cor 9:25-26, with the claim to have "completed the course" nicely answering to the sense of a race not yet finished in Phil 3:12-14 (not to mention 1 Tim 6:12). Precisely the same language is used in Paul's farewell speech in Acts 20:24. In context, since the metaphor runs on into v. 8, "I have kept the faith" should probably be understood as part of the same metaphor: I have competed as a good athlete, having kept the solemn promise or oath the athlete took at the beginning of the games to put out the utmost effort and to compete fairly (cf. 2:5).

That the imagery of 1 Cor 9:25 and Phil 3:14 was particularly in mind is suggested by the continuation of the metaphor in 4:8. The

---

120. The most obvious candidate would be Philippians, as the repeated references to Philippians in the Commentary might suggest.

prize in view is "the crown of righteousness" (cf. Phil 4:1; 1 Thess 2:19), presumably the righteousness of final acquittal (cf. Gal 5:5); the precise language may have been suggested by the prospect of vindication held out to the suffering righteous in Wis 5:15-16. In this case the imagery can be extended to the triumphal entry ("appearance") of the Lord of the games to take his throne on the final day of the games when the victors in the contests would be publicly honored—the day of judgment (as in 4:1).

That the final judgment would be "righteous," that absolute confidence could be placed in the fairness of the judge, was another fundamental conviction of Paul (Rom 3:3-6; cf. 2 Thess 1:5). And as with the use of "all" earlier (1 Tim 2:4-6), the open-endedness of the "all who have longed for his appearing" should not be lost to sight. The judgment of God may not be so closely correlated to the "sound teaching" as some may think. (Substance may be present without form, just as form is no proof of substance!) The God "who wants everyone to be saved" (1 Tim 2:4) may well recognize that "love of his appearing" is a more generous category than a narrow interpretation (which claims to be able, e.g., to specify the nature of that "appearing") allows. The mercy of God is always likely to be richer than even our best imaginings of it (cf. Rom 11:32-36).

4:9-18, Last Requests. The final exhortations, reminiscences, and personal requests are unique in the NT. They give the impression of a note-like communication, written under pressure of circumstances and time, where careful composition was impossible and the opportunity to communicate had to be seized. That it was a personal communication from the very last days of Paul's imprisonment, prior to his death (v. 6), is quite possible; it is just such a note that closely confined prisoners have managed to smuggle out in similar circumstances throughout history. If so, these could be the very last words penned by Paul—more poignant in the sense of abandonment and human aloneness than anything else he wrote, but confident in the Lord to the end.

Paul's close personal relationship with Timothy is a sustained feature of the letters (v. 9; cf. 1 Tim 1:2; 2 Tim 1:2). Little would bring more comfort to the failing Paul than to see and have Timothy with him for the last time. If this was a realistic request, it would take several months to fulfill, implying that Paul continued to hope for further delays before the second phase of his trial (v. 16); the end was not yet.

The plea is all the more affecting because of Paul's loneliness, caused partly by desertion and partly by the need to maintain contact with some supervisory role in relation to other churches (v. 10). Demas we hear of earlier in both Col 4:14 and Phlm 24, in not particularly warm terms. Evidently he had not been particularly close to Paul, but his defection (the sixth specifically identified in these letters; see 1 Tim 1:20; 2 Tim 1:15; 2:17) seems to have been more hurtful personally than the others. The verb "forsake/abandon" (ἐγκαταλείπω *egkataleipō*) is the one used in Jesus' "cry of dereliction" on the cross (Mark 15:34). The reason given ("having loved the present age") is unspecific but evocative (see other references to "the present age," Rom 12:2; 1 Cor 1:20; 2:6-8; 1 Tim 6:17; Titus 2:12). Crescens we hear of only here; the reference to Galatia strengthens the likelihood that Paul continued to have good links with the most easterly of the churches that remained within his sphere of mission (see 1 Cor 16:1).[121] On Titus, see Titus 1:4; Dalmatia, southern Illyricum (see Rom 15:19), was roughly equivalent to present-day Croatia;[122] there is perhaps here an echo of 2 Cor 2:13.

Luke (v. 11) is associated with Demas in both Col 4:14 and Phlm 24. (Had he been brought into the Pauline circles by Luke?) The reference here supports the inference of the "we" passages in Acts 16:10-17; 20:5-15; 21:8-18; 27:1–28:16 that Luke (the author of Luke–Acts) was a very close companion of Paul, not least in the final phase of his career. Mark appears in the same contexts in Col 4:10 and Phlm 24; that two men to whom tradition attributed the writing of two of the four Gospels were close companions of Paul is as intriguing as any of the notes in this section. Mark is also associated with Peter

---

121. A reading with some support has "Gaul" instead of "Galatia." It is probably a scribal error, though supported by Kelly. Even the possibility that Paul had missionary links farther west and north than Rome itself is intriguing. See Kelly, *The Pastoral Epistles,* 213.

122. On Dalmatia, see J. J. Wilkes, *Dalmatia* (Cambridge, Mass.: Harvard University Press, 1969).

(1 Pet 5:13) and in tradition is remembered as Peter's secretary whose Gospel was (based on) his own transcript of Peter's preaching. The positive affirmation of Mark ("he is useful to me for service") provides a pleasing sequel to the bruising breach recalled in Acts 15:36-40 (cf. the imagery of 2 Tim 2:21).

The impression that Paul continued to exercise pastoral oversight of his churches even while in prison is confirmed by v. 12. Next to Timothy and Titus, Tychicus was probably the most prominent of Paul's associate workers (note the commendatory epithets in Col 4:7 and Eph 6:21). According to Acts 20:4, Tychicus came from Asia, and in Eph 6:21-22 he is Paul's emissary to the region (or Ephesus in particular, as here). In Titus 3:12 he is to be sent to Crete.

The request for Paul's cloak, left with the otherwise unknown Carpus, and books, especially the parchments (v. 13), paints in a few strokes a graphic picture of Paul shivering in the winter nights and longing for reading material.[123] What would we give to know what these books were—quite possibly scrolls of particular biblical books (the word is used also, e.g., in Luke 4:17; John 20:30; Gal 3:10; Heb 10:7; Rev 22:7-19). And why were the parchments (μεμβράνα *membrana*) so special? Were there already biblical books in codex form? And were there already coherent collections (scrolls, codices) of Jesus tradition or even of (some of) Paul's own letters?[124]

The mention of Alexander (vv. 14-15) poses another intriguing puzzle. He is presumably not the same Alexander as in 1 Tim 1:20; this Alexander is remembered solely as an opponent. The suspicion that there is a mixed memory here of the episode in Acts 19 is given some support by the triple conjunction of Ephesus, a hostile metalworker (here coppersmith, but in Acts 19:24 the opponent is named as Demetrius, a silversmith), and the participation of an Alexander (a Jew) in the Ephesian riot (19:33; but he tries to calm the riot).[125] What the "great harm" was that he did to Paul is not otherwise indicated. At any rate, he is envisaged as still posing a threat to the Christian message (v. 15). The assurance that "the Lord will repay him according to his works" is not particularly vindictive; rather, it is an expression of the same confidence as at vv. 1 and 8 that God's judgment would be just (cf. Rom 2:6-16; 2 Cor 5:10), a confidence itself with deep scriptural roots (see Ps 62:12; Prov 24:12).

The sense of abandonment already prominent (v. 10) is reinforced by the pitiful complaint that in his first hearing (ἀπολογία *apologia*, "defense") no one had stood with him (v. 16), that all had abandoned him (the same word as used of Demas in v. 10). There need be no conflict here with v. 11 (Luke was with him). It is clear enough from the comings and goings indicated in vv. 10-12 that individuals came and went, often as much at Paul's behest as in accord with their own concerns and responsibilities. Nevertheless, the implication is clear that there were those who had been with him at the time and who had let him down. We gain something of the same flavor in Phil 1:15-17, and an echo of Jesus' abandonment (Mark 14:50; 15:34) may be deliberate. The thought that some Christians could have thus failed Paul is hardly encouraging, but Paul was a dominant personality who caused no little controversy within Christian circles. And we do not know how severe or serious was the outcome of the "first defense/hearing." The severity of Paul's state as indicated in this paragraph may also suggest that the hearing had gone badly and that Paul was being held in more restrictive captivity. The final prayer hope is less hostile than v. 14, but shows little desire for personal reconciliation (cf. Phil 1:18).

More characteristic of Paul is his unshakable confidence in his Lord (vv. 17-18). Unusual is the sense of the Lord's presence expressed in these terms ("stood beside me"), perhaps reflecting a sense of almost physical accompaniment, rather than Paul's more common mystical "in Christ" (but perhaps also reflecting the language and memory of Acts 23:11 and 27:23). More typical is the resulting sense of empowerment (see

---

123. The φαιλόνης (*phailonēs*; Latin *penula*) was a heavy outer garment. It has been suggested that the *phailonēs* could mean a cloth for wrapping books or a case for containing them. But why would Paul mention this before the books and parchments?

124. It is possible that the word denotes "parchment notebooks." See C. H. Roberts and T. C. Skeat, *The Birth of the Codex* (London: British Academy, 1983) 15-23. Paul may have used and kept notebooks in drafting his letters. Parchment was expensive, but presumably scraps of parchment unsuitable for more elaborate or finished works were available for purchase.

125. Still another Alexander appears in the late 2nd-cent. tract *Acts of Paul and Thecla* 26-36.

the Commentary on 1 Tim 1:12; 2 Tim 2:1). And still more characteristic is the conviction of a still-enduring commission to proclaim the gospel (here κήρυγμα *kērygma*) to all the Gentiles/nations (see the Commentary on 1 Tim 2:7).[126] This could still be fully discharged even in court (cf. Acts 26), but also through and not just despite his sufferings and circumstances (see Phil 1:12-18). The recollection of Daniel's deliverance from the lions, a story no doubt well known in every Jewish household (Dan 6:22, 27; 1 Macc 2:60; Heb 11:33; see also Ps 22:21), implies that Paul's peril had been every bit as serious as Daniel's had been.

And it still was (v. 18), but the same confidence that had proved true for the past held firm for the future. The image of eschatological rescue is a variation on the more common (in the Pastorals) "save"; in the earlier Paulines we can compare Rom 7:24; 11:26; 1 Thess 1:10 (not forgetting Matt 6:13). Here the thought is of rescue from "every evil attack," a phrase general enough to include all the negative factors already mentioned (from abandonment to legal judgment). The thought is not of escaping such circumstances (being declared innocent), but of being rescued through them to Christ's heavenly kingdom (see the Commentary on 4:1), the image of an age and society where only justice and mercy prevail. In typically Jewish fashion, the thought inspires an appropriate benediction (1 Tim 1:17; 6:16; cf. Rom 1:25; 11:36; 16:27; Gal 1:5; Phil 4:20).

4:19-22, Final Greetings. It was Paul's practice to close his letters with a number of personal greetings (e.g., Rom 16:3-16). Not surprisingly, Prisca and Aquila are first named (v. 19). They were probably Paul's favorite hosts, active with Paul not so much as companions on his missionary journeys, as were those who everywhere used their houses for hospitality and church gatherings (see Acts 18:2-3; Rom 16:4-5; 1 Cor 16:5). The implication is that they ran, and as Christians continued to run, a successful business with branches in several cities and that Prisca (named first, as more often than not) was the more dominant partner. It is presumed here that they were back in Ephesus. The household of Onesiphorus we have already met (1:16-18).

The additional information on the whereabouts of other of Paul's associates comes in here (v. 20; note v. 10) rather oddly. The name "Erastus" has caused a ripple of excitement, since we know from an inscription in Corinth that there had been a prominent official of that name in Corinth about this time. But whether the Erastus of Acts 19:22 and the one here can be identified with the Erastus of Rom 16:23 and then with the Erastus of the inscription is far from certain. According to Acts 20:4 and 21:29, Trophimus was from Ephesus; his presence with Paul in Jerusalem had been the trigger for the riot against Paul (Acts 21:27-30). Miletus was not too far from Ephesus (Acts 20:17) and was also a great seaport, a rival of Ephesus.

During the winter (November through March) sea travel virtually ceased (v. 21); hence, presumably, the request for speed (v. 9). The account in Acts 27:9-41 gives a good indication of the hazzards of winter travel. Of Eubulus, Pudens, Linus, and Claudia we know nothing more (the last three names are Latin), except, perhaps, the tradition first given by Irenaeus that Linus was Peter's successor as leader (bishop) of the Christian congregations in Rome.[127] Quite how the mention of these four, plus "all the brothers," squares with the sad plaint of v. 11 is hardly clear, but it may support the suggestion that vv. 9-18 and vv. 19-21 were quite different notes from Paul that were preserved separately.

The final benediction (v. 22) is a somewhat curious amalgam of Paul's more typical benedictions (cf. Rom 16:20; 1 Cor 16:23; Gal 6:18; Phil 4:23; 1 Thess 5:28; Phlm 25). As in 1 Tim 6:21, the "you" is plural.

---

126. J. Munck, *Paul and the Salvation of Mankind* (Richmond, Va.: John Knox, 1959) 332-34, suggested that when Paul stood before Nero, he would have understood (on the principle of the emperor's representative capacity) that he was fully proclaiming the gospel to "all the Gentiles."

127. Irenaeus *Against Heresies* III.3.3.

REFLECTIONS

The initial impact of this final section of 2 Timothy is the contrasting images of 4:1-5. On the one hand, there is the image of the committed preacher, teacher, and evangelist; on the other hand, the image of the kind of constituency or audience with which such a minister may well have to deal. The latter is particularly vivid; it conjures up the picture of interest groups, full of inquiry and eager to learn, but not finding their interest held by the church's preaching or teaching and seeking to satisfy their intellectual or spiritual curiosity in other arenas. What does a pastor do in such cases? Could it be that the preaching and teaching are not intellectually stimulating or spiritually satisfying? Could it be that the emphasis on "sound teaching" has become more emphatic on the "soundness" than on the "teaching"? Or are there more subtle and spiritually sophisticated approaches? The text gives no assurance that such situations (like those just envisaged) can be avoided. Pastors who find themselves asking such questions should not necessarily blame themselves—not necessarily. To ask such questions may be an essential stage in a congregation's growth toward maturity. At the same time, the balm that cures the itch (4:3) will probably not be the "sound teaching" itself, but the grace and skill with which it is explained and promoted (cf. 2:24-26).

The greater impact of this final chapter of 2 Timothy, however, is the portrayal of Paul, his final testimony and his last requests. It would be unfortunate if the value of the passage were restricted to the question of how it contributed to the debate on the authorship of the Pastorals. Whether it was penned by Paul or inserted into this part of the letter by a later writer, the effect is the same.

What we have in the first place is a moving self-testimony at the end of the career of one of the greatest of the world's movers and shakers—the Paul who effectively brought the gospel to Europe, who ensured its success as a universal religion, and who established in writing its theological character as a religion of grace and trust focused on the one God through the one Jesus Christ. We should allow the words of 4:6-8 to work on us in the way that the eulogy delivered at the funeral of a very fine person works on us—at the emotional level, to fire us not simply with admiration for that person, but with resolve to cherish the memory of that person and to allow it to influence and mold our own lives for the better.

This should be the value of Christian testimony, the value of "sharing" experience as well as faith in the way the earliest Methodist class meetings did so successfully. In these cases, "testimony" was not simply of one's conversion ("how I was saved"), but of one's continuing discipleship, of God's continuing dealings ("how I am being saved")—the low points as well as the high points. Such honest (not merely formal) testimony to the reality of grace in everyday life proved itself a powerful help to many a struggling Christian, both the testifier and the hearers. Sad to say, a society that has lost faith in priest and pastor now looks longingly to psychiatrist (or guru) for just that kind of role model and security in personal exposure. Sadder still, Christians often turn to that kind of help because they cannot find it in the fellowship of their own churches.

What we have in the second place is Paul's personal equivalent (4:9-18) of the psalms of complaint. What is so refreshing about even that final jumble of complaint and request is its honesty—the unashamed confession of reliance on others, the note of bitterness at betrayal, the concern for precious belongings that might seem trivial to others, the lament of the lonely. As with the honest prayer of the psalmist, Paul makes no attempt to impress or excuse; his relief at being able to pour it all out even in this intimate little note is almost tangible. When communication between Christians and in prayer can operate at that level, then real fellowship, healing, and wholeness can be experienced.

In the light of such honesty, the final expression of confidence (4:17-18) makes all the greater an impact. As again with the psalmist, it is the cathartic effect of such frank confession of human weakness that opens the one praying to the comforting and strengthening grace of God. It is a sad, but too often repeated, experience to be ignored, that the strength of Christ comes to its full expression only in the depth of human weakness. Prior to that, despite even best intentions, there is still the corrupting tendency to rely on one's own strength (abilities, success, family, and friends), to hold back from that complete reliance and trust that is faith. The lesson of this passage is that usually only *in extremis,* and only when that reality is accepted unconditionally, can there be that unconditional trust that remains confident in God through, as well as despite, everything.

TITUS 1:1–3:15

TITUS 1:1-4, GREETINGS AND REMINDER OF PAUL'S COMMISSION

COMMENTARY

The introduction takes the usual form of the writer's identifying first himself and then his recipients. In typical Pauline fashion, each element is elaborated with distinctive features (1:1-4a), possibly to give each letter its own personal quality. As with Rom 1:1-5 and Gal 1:1-2, the elaboration of Paul's authority and gospel (1:1-3) may indicate a sense that either or both were under some threat. The introduction concludes with the characteristic Pauline greeting (1:4b).

As in Rom 1:1 and Phil 1:1, Paul is described as "slave" (1:1), but whereas the normal usage is "slave of Jesus Christ," here it is "slave of God." This was language characteristic of Jewish worship (e.g., Neh 1:6, 11; Pss 19:11, 13; 27:9), and the great figures of Israel's history, particularly Moses and the prophets, were quite often referred to as Yahweh's slave (e.g., 2 Kgs 18:12; Ezra 9:11; Ps 105:26; Jer 7:25). The title, therefore, served several functions: It stressed the completeness of commitment (a slave by definition belonged to someone else); it was honorific (the greater the master, the greater the slave's authority); and it underscored the sense of continuity with Christianity's Jewish heritage.

More typical of Paul's earlier usage is the description "apostle of Jesus Christ" (as in 1 Tim 1:1). Typical also is the double attribution of Paul's status and authority to both God and Christ. The distinctive elaboration here is the purpose given for his appointment as (slave and) apostle "for the faith of God's elect"—that is, presumably, to bring about and to bring to greater maturity Christian faith and knowledge. The preposition κατά (*kata*) is somewhat surprising here and could be translated "in accordance with," but usage indicating goal or purpose is attested (cf. 2 Cor 11:21). The concern for "faith" is similar to that in 1 Tim 1:4-5. For "elect," see the Commentary on 2 Tim 2:10. "Knowledge of the truth" is the same goal as in 1 Tim 2:4 (see also 2 Tim 3:7). As typical in the Pastorals, the measure and proof of this faith and knowledge are "godliness/piety" (see 1 Tim 6:3).

The third member of the characteristic Pauline triad, "hope" (along with faith and knowledge), is instinctively drawn in 1:2—as always in Paul with the full confidence of Jewish usage rather than the tentativeness of Greek and modern usage (i.e., "I hope, but have no confidence that it will be so"; see also 2:13; 3:7). Again the preposition (ἐπί *epi*) leaves the precise correlation of the phrase with its context unclear. The NRSV leaves the ambiguity unresolved; the NIV opts to relate it directly to the faith and knowledge just mentioned, but "faith and knowledge" are not repeated in the Greek. Here the confidence is rooted in God's promise and the degree to which it has already been fulfilled. Again it is a question of the evident continuity between a divine original purpose (see the Commentary on 2 Tim 1:9), as revealed through prophet and Scripture, and its due fulfillment (see the Commentary on 1 Tim 2:6) announced in the preaching of the gospel (1:3). It was a fundamental feature of Paul's self-consciousness that he had been given a special commission to make this message known (as in 1 Tim 1:11). The confidence of Christian hope was thus rooted in the coherence of a divine purpose unfolding in history and the immediacy of the encounter with the divine in human experience.

As was Timothy (1 Tim 1:2), Titus, too, is addressed as Paul's "genuine child in faith" (1:4), here described as their "common" or "shared" faith. Although we have no other testimony to that effect, the language presumably indicates that Titus had been converted through Paul's ministry (cf. 1 Cor 4:15-17; Gal 4:19; Phlm 10); from Gal 2:1-10 we learn at least that he was regarded as a typical product of Paul's mission to Gentiles. The phrase combines the thought of Titus's dependence on Paul and of their mutual interdependence in the faith (cf. 2 Cor 8:23). The greeting itself is the typical Pauline one: "grace and peace" (unlike 1 and 2 Timothy). Characteristic of the coordination and balance Paul maintained in his greetings between God and Christ is the way both God and Christ are described as "our Savior" within three or four lines (1:3-4; see the Commentary on 1 Tim 1:1).

REFLECTIONS

Whether written by Paul himself or not, the Pastoral Epistles confirm a Pauline pastoral tradition of adapting regular forms to particularize and personalize each of his letters. Here not only do we have the characteristic Pauline christianizing of the Greek and Jewish greetings ("grace and peace"; see the Commentary on 1 Tim 1:2) and the intimacy of the address ("loyal child"), but also the elaborate self-description of Paul. Given the importance of traditional forms for the author(s) of the Pastorals, this maintenance of the Pauline tradition of adaptation is worth noting. In the sphere of pastoral practice every person and every church is unique, and the distinctive needs in each case cannot be handled simply in accordance with some ready formula. The personal character of Paul's involvement with his churches no doubt added immeasurably to the authority of his letters.

The purpose of Paul's apostleship was the promotion of faith, knowledge, and hope. The terms can be varied or added to, but these three have a balance that should be ever sought in preaching and pastoral instruction: trust of heart and knowledge of head—the blend of intellectual appreciation and commitment with deep emotional roots; knowledge informed from the past; faith in God and in Christ here and now; and hope for the future. Where these are well integrated, we can begin to speak of maturity of believer and church.

TITUS 1:5-16, THE CHURCH—ITS LEADERSHIP AND ENEMIES

COMMENTARY

The letter as a whole takes the form of a commission to Titus, and the typical thanksgiving (as in 2 Tim 1:3-4) is omitted. Notable is the fact that it begins with Titus's responsibility to appoint elders (1:5-6) and a summary description of the qualities looked for in an overseer (1:7-9). The emphasis is on the ability to refute false teaching (1:10-14). The description of such teachers is as dismissive as in the other two letters (1:10, 12, 15-16). But particular features suggest that Jewish or Jewish-Christian teaching is particularly in view (1:10, 14). That apart, the counsel here seems to summarize more lengthy instruction given particularly in 1 Timothy.

1:5-9, The Character of Christian Leadership. Just as Timothy had been left at Ephesus (1 Tim 1:3), so also Titus had been left in Crete (v. 5). We have no other indication of a Pauline mission to that island, unless the account of Paul's final journey (as in Acts 27:12) had been elaborated, perhaps along the lines of the related account of wintering in Malta (Acts 28:7-11).[128] The purpose

---

128. If, however, the letter was by Paul, then we would have to assume that Paul, following release from imprisonment in Rome, turned his attention back to the eastern Mediterranean (despite Rom 15:23-24, 28)—i.e., Crete, Ephesus, Troas, Macedonia, Nicopolos. Paul would have evangelized Crete at that time, leaving to Titus the organization of the young house churches on the island.

of thus leaving Titus was that he might "set right" (ἐπιδιορθόω *epidiorthoō*; the only occurrence of this word in early Christian literature, but its meaning is clear enough) what remains or is "lacking/falls short" (as in 3:13). This is not to be taken to imply that Paul's mission was defective, but simply that when Paul left there were still things to be done, as he himself had indicated (v. 5).

Chief among these tasks, or the principal way of remedying defects, would be the appointment of "elders." Clearly in view are men similar to those referred to in 1 Tim 5:17-22; as there, presumably the thought is that among the ranks of the πρεσβύτεροι (*presbyteroi*, "older men") there will be some who should be accorded special authority as *presbyteroi* ("elders"). Although the language is different ("appoint"), the thought is no doubt the same as in 1 Tim 5:22 ("laying on of hands"). Notable is the echo of Acts 14:23 and the assumption that there was a church in almost every town. Like Timothy, Titus is expected to exercise an authority like that of Paul (cf. Acts 14:23), as one superior to the elders and overseers whose appointment is in view.

The qualities of the elder (v. 6) closely resemble those listed in regard to the overseers and deacons in 1 Tim 3:2-4, 10-12. They are to be "blameless" (1 Tim 3:10), once married (1 Tim 3:2, 12), have faithful children (1 Tim 3:4, 12), and should not be open to accusations of debauchery (cf. 1 Tim 3:3, 8) or lack of personal discipline (cf. 1 Tim 3:2-3). The lack of any mention of deacons here may indicate that the structures of leadership were developing in different ways in different places.

The linkage of thought into v. 7 ("for an overseer must . . .") strongly suggests that πρεσβύτερος (*presbyteros*) and ἐπίσκοπος (*episkopos*) were regarded as near synonyms (cf. Acts 20:17, 28). We may deduce that just as the elder was appointed from among the older men, so also the more specific role of overseer emerged from that of the elders. We are not yet at the stage where the overseer was a single figure, quite distinct in office and status from other leaders; bishop had not yet become distinct from presbyter/elder. At the same time, the function of the overseer is made clearer by the further description, "God's steward" (cf. 1 Cor 4:1-2); just as the steward administered an estate on its owner's behalf (cf. Gal 4:1-2), so also the overseer had to exercise oversight over God's estate (cf. 1 Tim 3:5) or household (cf. 1 Tim 3:15).

The qualities of the overseer (vv. 7-8) pick up from those already listed (v. 6): "blameless"; "not self-willed, stubborn, arrogant" (elsewhere in the NT only in 2 Pet 2:10); "not inclined to anger/quick-tempered"; "not addicted to wine" (1 Tim 3:3); "not a bully" (1 Tim 3:3); "not greedy for money" (1 Tim 3:8), but "hospitable" (1 Tim 3:2); "a lover of what is good" (a *hapax*, but common in honorific inscriptions of the time); "prudent/moderate" (1 Tim 3:2); "just," "holy," "self-controlled." Again it is worth noting that most of these qualities would have been regarded as virtues within religious or philosophical circles of the time; two in particular (moderate and just) belonged to the four cardinal virtues in Greek philosophy (prudence, justice, temperance, fortitude).

The more specific and distinctive Christian criteria emerge in v. 9 in the familiar language of the Pastorals: "holding to the faithful word in accord with the teaching" (see the Commentary on 1 Tim 1:15), "able to encourage in the sound teaching and to reprove/correct those who speak against it" (cf. 1 Tim 5:20). The doubling of the language reinforces the impression of a teaching, not necessarily greatly elaborated, but set out in clear formulations that had already become the touchstones for the faith and soundness of profession (see the Commentary on 1 Tim 1:10). Without a clearer idea of what was being thus warned against, it is not possible to determine whether this was a faith-saving insistence on primary principles or merely a rather conservative unwillingness to allow alternative or exploratory formulations of the same basic faith.

1:10-16, The Character of False Teachers. Just as the description of the qualities of Christian leadership both emphasizes virtues that all would commend and highlights the importance of Christian teaching, so also the warning against false teaching both draws on the familiar rhetoric of vilification and opposes it to "the truth." Many are "lacking in personal discipline" (ἀνυπότακτοι *anypotaktoi*, v. 10; the same word as in 1:6; 1 Tim

1:9), "idle talkers" (cf. 1 Tim 1:6), "deceivers." Such terms tell us little or nothing about the teaching under attack. In view of the parallels with 1 Tim 4:1 and 2 Tim 3:1, the implication is that "the last days" are already upon them.

The next phrase, however, strikes a clearer note: "especially those of the circumcision" (v. 10). The phrase is the same as that in Acts 11:2; Gal 2:12;[129] and Col 4:11. It presumably, therefore, denotes Jews (only Jews regarded circumcision as a positive identity marker); but not Jews as such, rather Jews who, like Peter, Paul, and the others, had believed in Jesus as Messiah and continued to think as Jews—that is, they continued to assume that the way for Gentiles to share in Israel's covenant blessings (the Messiah!) was for them to be circumcised and become proselytes. Possibly this indicates that the letter had in view continuing opposition to the Pauline mission from (more) conservative Christian Jews (as in Galatians and Philippians 3:1). Or possibly this is simply a later picking up of a phrase that indicated opposition to Paul. This could mean, in turn, that the teaching generally resisted as false was that of conservative Jewish Christians or simply that such Christian Jews were one of several factions generally rubbished by the Pastorals. The alternative suggestion that circumcision was simply a Jewish element imported into a more amorphous syncretistic teaching is less likely; "those of the circumcision" indicates a group who espoused a distinctively Jewish identity; such people would not regard circumcision as a free-floating ritual easily combined with other, non-Jewish features.

This momentary illumination is lost again in the fierceness of the dismissal (v. 11). "Their mouths must be stopped"—the image of something being put into the mouth to prevent unwanted movement or speech is clear. That such an action was deemed possible suggests that those in view operated within the churches rather than from outside; but that may press the imagery too hard. "They upset [ἀνατρέπω *anatrepō*; the same word as in 2 Tim 2:18] whole households"; we are reminded of the importance put on the well-ordered household repeatedly in 1 Timothy (e.g., 1 Tim 2:11-15; 3:4-5, 12; 5:8, 10, 13-14), as again in Titus 2:1-10. "They teach for shameful gain what they ought not to teach" (cf. v. 7; 1 Tim 5:13); the distinction with teaching deserving of support (1 Tim 5:17-18) would again be clear by reference to the "teaching" itself.

The picture becomes rather more confused by use of the quotation from Epimenides (v. 12),[130] since it indicates that the opponents in view were themselves Cretans. There is evidence of several Jewish synagogues in Crete,[131] but the language here implies that such Jews could be regarded as native Cretans (cf. Acts 2:11). The quotation should not be regarded as a careful description, though Epimenides' low esteem for Cretans was widely shared;[132] it falls, rather, into the category of populist denigration, in which the inflated criticism primarily attests intercommunal rivalry or the reaction of a local boy made good looking back on his native place with a jaundiced eye (Epimenides was himself a Cretan). The fact that Epimenides is called a prophet reflects his reputation as a speaker of oracles;[133] it may mean that the writer understood the words to have been inspired (cf. John 11:51) or simply that he recognized in the social commentary a true insight into Cretan character (v. 13*a*). At any rate, he finds in the citation justification for advising Titus to take a strong line with such people. "That they might be sound in the faith" confirms both that those in view were within the Christian community and that the author was working with a well-defined form of faith ("the faith") and with a model of "soundness" (see footnote 9).

That Christian Jews (in this instance, at least) in particular were thus being targeted is confirmed by the double description of the alternative teaching being warned against (v. 14). "Jewish myths" tells us little more than did 1 Tim 1:4 (see the Commentary on

---

129. The correlation is interesting in view of Titus's involvement in the preceding incident see Gal 2:1-10.

130. For more information on Epimenides of Crete (6th–5th cents. BCE), see Dibelius and Conzelmann, *The Pastoral Epistles*, 136.

131. Of some interest is a 4th-cent. epitaph from Crete that describes a woman named Sophia as both a "presbyter" and an ἀρχισυνάγωγος (*archisynagōgos*, "leader of the synagogue"). See B. J. Brooten, *Women Leaders in the Ancient Synagogue*, BJS 36 (Chico, Calif.: Scholars Press, 1982) 11-12.

132. Cretans were often called liars because they claimed to have the grave of Zeus on their island. See Dibelius and Conzelmann, *The Pastoral Epistles*, 137.

133. See, e.g., Barrett, *The Pastoral Epistles*, 131. According to Plato, Epimenides predicted the failure of the Persian invasion. See Plato *Laws* 642D.

1 Tim 1:4), except that the "myths" in view were Jewish—that is, presumably the sort of speculations about legendary figures of the past, such as Adam and Abel, Enoch and Abraham, whom we know of from the OT pseudepigrapha.[134] The second description, "commands of human beings," carries a strong echo of earlier Christian polemic against Jewish preoccupation with tradition (Matt 15:9/ Mark 5:7-8, 13; Col 2:22; cf. Gal 1:14). In the Greek, "those who turn away from the truth" (the same phrase as in 2 Tim 4:4) refers to the "human beings." The implication is either that the Cretans were enamored of teachings from elsewhere that, by the measure of "the truth," had already lost the way, or that the Cretan Christian Jews were themselves too caught up in such speculations and Jewish traditions and as a result had turned away from a truth whose focus and measure were Christ.

The attack on the false teachers continues to use Jewish categories. "To the pure all things are pure" (v. 15) echoes Paul's counsel in Rom 14:14 and 20. The imagery is that of the laws of clean and unclean, which were so fundamental to Jewish identity (cf. 1 Macc 1:62-63; Mark 7:1-23; Acts 10:14). In the context of the Temple (on which the purity laws centered), all things were indeed clean/pure; they had to be. So the worshiper, on entering the Temple duly purified, could be confident that nothing and no one touched would render him or her impure. Paul had extended the principle: For the believer cleansed by faith (cf. Acts 15:9), the previous sharp distinction between sacred and secular had been broken down; all things given by God for human use (unclean food as well) could properly be regarded as clean (Rom 14:14, 20; cf. 1 Tim 4:4). The principle is that purity before God is primary: If God has accepted someone, the secondary human regulations about acceptable and unacceptable are irrelevant. In these circumstances, since God ignores such regulations, so can those accepted by God.

The opposite principle, which in fact underlays the laws of clean and unclean, is that impurity contaminates. "The corrupt" (μιαίνω *miainō*) uses a verb also drawn from the sphere of ceremonial impurity (as in John 18:28), though used here of moral defilement through sins and vices. Everything that such people touch is thereby rendered impure—here in particular their minds and conscience. If, indeed, the teachers under attack here were Christian Jews or those heavily influenced by Jewish tradition, the logic would likely have powerful effect.

The final dismissive attack is on their Christian profession (v. 16): "They profess to know God, but deny him by what they do." The thought is similar to that of 2 Tim 3:5. Is there a link to the claimed (higher) "knowledge" of 1 Tim 6:20? Not necessarily; the verb is different, and for Paul knowledge of God is the most fundamental description of true religion (Rom 1:21; 1 Cor 1:21; 1 Thess 4:5). It is not a higher knowledge of God that is disputed, but the basic claim to "know" God at all. Here, as in Matt 7:16, the fruit produced is evidence of the character of the tree; we might also note the echo of Ps 14:1. Implicit once again is the conviction that the writer's understanding of "godliness" is a measure of what is acceptable to God and what is not. The final clause reverts to vilification—"abominable," "detestable" (echoing the Jewish horror of idolatry; see Deut 29:17), "disobedient" (as in 3:3), "unfit [as in 2 Tim 3:8] for any good work."

---

134. See J. Charlesworth, ed., *The Old Testament Pseudepigrapha*, 2 vols. (Garden City, N.Y.: Doubleday, 1983–85).

REFLECTIONS

The sections of this paragraph are linked by the theme of development. Here we see more clearly than elsewhere how Christian ministry developed—how the role of overseer/bishop emerged from the broader role of presbyter/elder, just as that of elder had emerged from that of older man (1 Timothy 5). The development was natural. As Moses had realized centuries earlier (Exodus 18), heavy burdens of responsibility need to be defined and divided up; representative persons need to be appointed to represent both the unity and the diversity of the movement to each other. Thus the wisdom of age provided the obvious pool of leadership from which such representative roles could be drawn.

Interesting questions arise for those who regard the New Testament as canon—that is, as providing a rule for faith and life. Was this development once for all, so that its outcome (the increasing focus of representative ministry and authority in the bishop) should be regarded as determinative for all time? Or is the canonical force of a passage like this the character of ministry as *developing* to meet the emerging needs of the young churches? If the emergence of the episcopate was a natural development reflecting contemporary views of leadership (the older man as the elder, the overseer as steward of God's estate), to what extent should patterns of ministry continue to develop and to what extent should they draw on contemporary wisdom regarding management and leadership? We should not lightly turn our backs on the wisdom and lessons of the past; but neither should we assume that the church of tomorrow will take the same shape as the church of yesterday.

In the second half of the paragraph we are given an insight into the strains and tensions that were consequent on Christianity's development from within Judaism. The echoes of Jesus' critique of his contemporaries' overdependence on tradition (1:14-15) and of Paul's confrontation with "those of the circumcision" (1:10) are uncomfortable reminders that Christianity's claim on the heritage of Israel was neither so clearcut as the Pastorals would imply nor so uncontested as the Pastorals confirm. The resulting dialogue between the heirs of Israel's heritage (Jews and Christians), "God's elect" (1:1), was not completed with the sweeping dismissal of 1:15-16. Rather, the testimony of the New Testament is that this dialogue is constitutive of Christianity's identity. Reflection on the significance of the patriarchal narratives ("Jewish myths"?) is not an exclusively Jewish preoccupation. And the Pastorals are the clearest evidence within the New Testament that tradition became a matter of defining importance for Christianity as much as for Judaism. Despite its vilificatory language (typical of the day), the Pastorals are themselves evidence of the ongoing dialogue on such matters. It is not the sentiments of the Pastorals that should be our guide here, but the reality of a faith wrestling with its heritage and with other claimants to that heritage.

One of the guidelines is given in the epigram, "To the pure all things are pure" (1:15). It is one of those epigrams that can be easily cheapened or abused. At one level, it can connote a naïveté that, lacking all worldly experience or wisdom, simply fails to recognize that which corrupts or contaminates. At another level, it is a reminder of the subtlety of the link between inner purity and ritual purity, which can neither be simply assumed nor lightly dismissed. Here it sums up the priority of purity with God, of acceptability in the presence of God. All who claim the heritage of Israel would affirm the first priority of "knowing God" (1:16), but the passage (and the precedents it echoes) is a reminder that that priority can become so hedged around with qualifications and further traditions or regulations as to lose its primacy. When acceptability before God is an insufficient criterion for acceptability between those who claim the same religious heritage, then we know that profession is being denied by deeds.

TITUS 2:1-15, GOOD HOUSEHOLD MANAGEMENT AND ITS THEOLOGICAL RATIONALE

COMMENTARY

2:1-10, The Well-Ordered Household. The letter to Titus shares with 1 Timothy a concern for good household management, no doubt both as a test of leadership (cf. 1:6) and as a model for good church management (as in 1 Tim 3:4-5, 12). In its compactness, the outline here comes closer to the model *Haustafel* (guidelines for good household management) found in Col 3:18–4:1 than does any other in that all the elements of the typical household of the time are present: wives, husbands, children (vv. 4-5), slaves, and masters (vv. 9-10). The slant of this passage, however, reflects the same distinctive concern displayed in 1 Timothy 5 over the older men and women (vv. 2-3) and places the responsibility for counseling wives on the older women (vv. 4-5). The responsibilities of younger men, and of Titus, are likewise inserted (vv. 6-8). Unusually, no word of counsel is given to the primary male member of the household: the husband, father and master (cf. Col 3:19, 21; 4:1). The implication may be that in the household of the church that role is to be filled by Titus. Unlike 1 Tim 5:3-6, there seems to be no problem regarding the rights and responsibilities of widows.

The focus now switches to Titus's own positive teaching (v. 1). He must speak "what is fitting, appropriate to sound teaching." Once again we note that there is a criterion and measure of acceptable teaching, what we might call the agreed syllabus of confessional claims and acceptable conduct.

Somewhat surprisingly, the first example of such teaching is the advice of how older men should conduct themselves (v. 2; the word here is not πρεσβύτερος [*presbyteros*] but πρεσβύτης [*presbytēs*], denoting a man aged in the 50s or 60s). Also somewhat surprising is the fact that the commendatory virtues listed are so similar to those used in 1 Timothy 3, particularly in reference to the overseer; the older men are to be temperate (as in 1 Tim 3:2, 11); respectable, dignified, serious (as in 1 Tim 3:8); prudent, moderate (as in 1:8 and 1 Tim 3:2); sound (like the teaching, v. 1) in faith (cf. 1 Tim 3:9), in love (cf. 2 Tim 1:13), and in patience (lit., "as to the faith, the love, the patience," where "the" indicates "the well-known, characteristic"— i.e., themes familiar within the church's discourse; cf. 2 Tim 3:10). At the very least, the overlap confirms that the obvious place to look for leadership in the churches was from among the ranks of the older (more experienced, wiser) men.

As in 1 Tim 5:1-2, thought of responsibility toward the older men prompts a matching reflection on the role of older women (v. 3). What is striking here is the extent of the responsibility put upon them and the language used for them. Their "behavior/demeanor" should be "as befits a priest" (NIV and NRSV, "reverent"). The imagery would be surprising only if earliest Christianity had retained an office of priest and confined it to men. But Paul's language elsewhere indicates that he saw all ministry of the gospel as priestly in character (Rom 15:16; Phil 2:25); the "royal priesthood" of 1 Pet 2:9 was not gender related. So here, it evidently did not jar to associate the image of priest with the older women. They, too, could exercise a priestly ministry in serving the gospel (vv. 3-5; 1 Tim 5:3-10) or by their personal dedication (cf. Rom 12:1-2, the priestly task of offering their bodies as a sacrifice).

The following vices to be avoided give a more negative view of the women, but in fact accord with what was said regarding deacons in 1 Timothy 3: "not slanderers" (1 Tim 3:11), "not enslaved to much wine" (cf. 1 Tim 3:8). Perhaps most surprising of all, in view of 1 Tim 2:12, is the next criterion: They are to be "teachers of what is good." However, it becomes clear in vv. 4-5 that the teaching role of the older women is in reference to younger women. Nevertheless, the responsibility put upon the older women here is significantly larger than that envisaged in 1 Tim 5:5, 10. Here again the clear assumption is that the older person has a responsibility to pass on to the next generation the wisdom gained through the years.

The specific term σωφρονίζω (*sōphronizō*) can be translated quite strongly as "bring the younger women to their senses," but it may have the weaker sense of "encourage," "advise," "urge" (v. 4). Particularly in view is the role of the matriarch within the household: to encourage the wife of the household to "love her husband and love her children." That the wife's or the husband's mother should be given such respect within the household would be taken for granted; no hint is given of the pressures on the young wife under the authority of both her husband and her mother(-in-law), but they do not take much imaging.

Like the older men (v. 2) the younger women are to be encouraged to be prudent, moderate, perhaps here with the overtone of "chaste/modest/pure," like Timothy (1 Tim 5:22), "house-keepers" (οἰκουργούς *oikourgous*, "working at home."[135] More characteristic of the codes of good household management is the counsel that they should be "submissive" to their husbands (v. 5; see the Commentary on 1 Tim 2:11-12). As elsewhere the concern was lest the liberating message of the gospel might encourage Christian women to ignore or react against the patterns of sound household management and so bring the message of the gospel into disrepute as antisocial and destructive of the good order of society's basic unit (see 1 Tim 3:7).

If the responsibility for instructing the younger women was primarily that of the older women, the responsibility for instructing the younger men belongs to Titus himself (v. 6). They are to be "reasonable/sensible" (σώφρων *sōphrōn*; the same range of words denoting a highly prized virtue in Greek circles; both the NIV and the NRSV prefer "self-controlled"; the REB uses "temperate"). Titus has to present himself as a "model of good works" (v. 7, a favorite commendatory category in the Pastorals), in his teaching "incorrupt" (a *hapax*, but close in meaning to "sound"), "respectable," "dignified," "serious" (one of the Pastorals' favorite terms; see footnote 16), "sound" (the familiar term) in preaching that is "beyond reproach" (another *hapax*). The objective (but not the only one) is that "he who is opposed [another *hapax*] might be put to shame at having nothing bad to say about us" (v. 8). Worth noting, once again, is the concern for a good reputation and the assumption that behavior worthy of criticism on the part of Titus would reflect badly on the whole community ("us").

As in other household codes, the responsibility of slaves to their masters is given final prominent place (vv. 9-10; see the Commentary on 1 Tim 6:1-2). The fact that the same term (ὑποτάσσω, *hypotassō*, "submit") is used for the attitude of the slave to the master as for that of wife to husband (v. 5) reflects the legal authority of the *paterfamilias*. At the same time, in both cases the writer is careful to specify that they are to be submissive to their *own* husbands/masters. What is in view is not the submissiveness of women or slaves as a class, but, once again, the good order of each individual household—it being taken for granted that such depended on the authority of the *paterfamilias* being properly recognized. As in 1 Tim 6:1-2, nothing is said of the responsibility of the master (cf. Col 4:1), but here that is paralleled by nothing's being said about the responsibility of the husband or the father. For some reason the writer restricts his counsel to one side of each of the three relationships that made up the typical household.

The goal of the slave should be to please the master; "in everything" could be linked to the first instruction, thus "submissive in everything" (NIV), or to the second, thus "well-pleasing in everything" (NRSV). Since the adjective "well-pleasing," "acceptable" (εὐάρεστος *euarestos*) is usually used in reference to God, we may assume that what is in view is the ideal slave (not one who pleases an evil master). He or she should not speak against or contradict the master (again assuming the ideal master; cf. 1 Tim 2:11-12). Nor should the ideal slave misappropriate or pilfer (νοσφίζω *nosphizō*) anything from the master (the same word is used in Acts 5:2-3). These last two words give a sharp insight into the temptations typically confronting the slave

---

135. A few MSS read οἰκουρούς (*oikourous*) "staying at home," reflective of the common assumption that the home was the woman's proper place; the NRSV translates the "good" twice, both with *oikourgous*, "good managers of the household," and as "kind").

and to which, no doubt, many succumbed. The Christian alternative was to "show/demonstrate all faithfulness as good" (the NRSV takes the three words as a single phrase, "well-pleasing in everything"); the Christian slave should be the ideal slave. Such behavior would "adorn" (κοσμέω *kosmeō*; the same word as in 1 Tim 2:9) the teaching of the Savior in every way. Once again the concern is prominent that the Christian message should produce behavior that would commend it to others.

2:11-15, The Theological Rationale. What follows, in effect, is another faithful saying—that is, a summary of the gospel (vv. 11-14). It focuses on the coherence between the two appearings of Christ (vv. 11, 13), between what has already been accomplished (vv. 11, 14) and the hope for what is yet to happen (v. 13). It is this correlation that provides the rationale for godly living in the present (v.12), as illustrated by the preceding paragraph. The exposition is completed with a repetition of the commission to Titus (v. 15), the section as a whole (vv. 1-15) being held together by the two bracketing exhortations (v. 1 and v. 15).

The opening of the theological affirmation (v. 11) is very similar to that of 2 Tim 1:9-10, with the common talk of the generous "grace/favor" of God and its saving manifestation (see the Commentary on 2 Tim 1:9-10). The language echoes traditional talk of God's self-revelation (as at Bethel in Gen 35:7 and in the Temple in 2 Macc 3:30). Christ is not mentioned as such, and, unusually, it is the adjective (rather than verb or noun) that is used: "bringing salvation" (σωτήριος *sōterios*). But even if it is not clear enough here (see v. 14), the parallel between the two passages puts it beyond dispute that what is in view is the grace of God enacted in and through Christ in his first appearing.[136] As in 1 Tim 2:3-4 and 4:10, it is assumed that the purpose of God's gracious action in Christ is the salvation of *all*.

The immediate switch to first-person plural ("training us") is not a sudden diminution of that universal goal to the few who have responded. Rather, it is a reminder that the training of the few has in view the salvation of the whole (v. 12). Not that the few are envisaged as shock troops or as some elite squad charged to complete the saving purpose of God for all. Rather, the thought seems to be of the few as the first colony or circle of salvation, who by living as those on the way to complete salvation function as a representative sample of humanity, whose very lifestyle will be a witness to the quality of God's saving purpose. This is presumably why this final paragraph can function as the theological rationale for the seemingly mundane household rules of vv. 1-10. It is divine grace expressed in the quality of basic human relationships that will be the most effective witness to the character of God's saving purpose.

For the same reason, the point of the earlier manifestation of God's grace can be put in such simple terms as "educating," "training," "disciplining" (v. 12), the word παιδεύω (*paideuō*) embracing all that was involved in a good upbringing. The negative and positive goals of this education are both summed up in familiar Pastoral terms: "refusing/repudiating ungodliness" and "living a godly life in the present age." The former is elaborated in terms of worldly desires; there is a fine distinction involved here between κόσμιος (*kosmios*), denoting what society would respect (1 Tim 2:9), and κοσμικός (*kosmikos*), denoting what partook too much of the world in its opposition to God—that is, desires becoming lusts, desires for advancement and gain in the world. The latter is elaborated with the adverbial form of the term already used three times in the letter as an adjective (σώφρων *sōphrōn*), "soberly/moderately/displaying self-control," as well as with the adverbial form of its partner in 1:8 (δίκαιος *dikaios*), "justly." The appearance of three of the most highly prized virtues in Greek thought (piety, moderation, justice), following the classic Greek term for education, underlies the degree to which the Christianity of the Pastorals saw itself as complementary to the highest aspirations of Greek philosophical ethics.[137] The resulting picture is not very dynamic, but what is in view is the character of responsible living and relationships as the most potent forces of all.

---

136. As in 3:4, the verb ἐπιφαίνω (*epiphainō*), "appear," is equivalent to the more regular noun, ἐπιφάνεια (*epiphaneia*), "epiphany," which in the Pastorals usually refers to the still-future coming of Christ (as in 2:13), with 2 Tim 2:10 being the sole exception.

137. See S. C. Mott, "Greek Ethics and Christian Conversion: The Philonic Background of Titus 2:10-14 and 3:3-7," *NovT* 20 (1978) 22-35.

What gives the community its dynamism is more the hope of what is to come; the community literally lives in hope of the appearance of Christ (v. 13). Indicative of the character of Christian hope is the fact that the word is used here for what is hoped for (cf. Col 1:5). Hope does not depend on human feelings of hopefulness, but on the one in whom that hope is invested. This is the second "appearing" in view, and, as with the first (v. 11), the theme of "salvation" (here "Savior") is linked with it (see the Commentary on 2 Tim 1:10). Clearly implied, then, is the thought that salvation is a process from first to second, begun by Christ's saving act in the first (v. 14) and climaxed by his appearing again. This also helps to clarify why the title "Savior" can be used equally of God and of Christ, for it is the saving purpose of God (v. 11) that is brought to effect in both appearings.

Verse 13 is particularly interesting for its christology, for the blessed hope is expressed as "the appearance of the glory of our great God and Savior Jesus Christ." The interest is not just in the further example of Christ being called "Savior" (see the Commentary on 1 Tim 1:1). It focuses more on the preceding phrase. Almost certainly what is in view is not a double appearance (of God and of Christ)—that would be a less obvious rendering of the Greek, and the formula "God and Savior" was common in inscriptions of the time.[138] The point is, rather, that Christ is described by the whole phrase: "our great God and Savior." In other words, here we have one of very few instances in the NT where Christ is called "God" (otherwise only John 1:1, 18; 20:28; Heb 1:8; and possibly Rom 9:5). This is how most understand the phrase.[139] But it is also possible that it is the still fuller phrase that should be taken in apposition to Jesus Christ: "the glory of our great God and Savior"—that is, Christ described as the visible manifestation of divine glory (as in John 12:41, referring to Isa 6:10).[140] Either way, the passage becomes a clear measure of the amazing significance already recognized in or attributed to Christ, that in Christ Christians realize that God, insofar as God may be known to human beings, had been manifested.

Just as the hope of the second appearing rests on the first, so also the recognition of Christ's divine significance rests on what he has already done (v. 14). The language of v. 14a is that of already well-established summaries of the gospel and is very similar to that of 1 Tim 2:6 (see the Commentary on 1 Tim 2:6). There is a strong echo of Ps 130:8: The Lord "will redeem Israel from all his iniquities." That the echo is deliberate is confirmed by the talk of God's cleansing "a chosen people, a people of his own" (the phrase used of Israel in Exod 19:5; Deut 7:6; 14:2; note also the echo of the great vision of Israel's restoration in Ezek 37:23). Clearly, then, the thought is of these little Christian communities in Crete fulfilling God's purpose for Israel. As Israel was pledged to live as God's people, so these Christians should be "zealous for good works." Given the hostility to "those of the circumcision" and to "Jewish myths" (1:10, 14), this positive assertion of the continuity of Israel in the Christian churches of Crete should be noted. And since the thought is of a piece with that of God as Savior of all (2:11), the implication presumably is that the churches, like Israel, formed a representative people, chosen with a view to benefit all, to be a light to the nations (Isa 49:1-16).

This, it should be noted again, is the rationale for the preceding instruction on good household management (vv. 1-10): Israel's obligation to be a people dedicated to God, living lives and maintaining households of positive benefit to neighbor and community. The repetition of the opening command (v. 1) in the final sentence (v. 15) underscores the integration of the whole chapter, with the "sound teaching" (v. 1) now documented both in its theological rationale (vv. 11-14) and in its practical outworking (vv. 2-10), and providing Titus with the terms of reference for both encouragement and reproof, as also the authority behind both (cf. 1 Tim 4:12).

---

138. However, Johnson and Davies prefer to read the text as "the glory/splendor of our great God and of our Savior Jesus Christ/Christ Jesus." See Johnson, *Letters to Paul's Delegates*, 238; Davies, *The Pastoral Epistles*, 103. On "epiphany" as the appearance of deity see the Commentary on 1 Tim 6:14.

139. See M. J. Harris, "Titus 2:13 and the Deity of Christ," in *Pauline Studies: Essays Presented to F. F. Bruce*, ed. D. Hagner and M. J. Harris (Grand Rapids: Eerdmans, 1980) 262-77.

140. Favored by Fee, *1 and 2 Timothy, Titus*, 196.

REFLECTIONS

The logic of chapter 2 is indicated by the double bracket within which it operates. The first is the inclusio of 2:1 and 2:15, which rivets the whole chapter together. The detailed practicalities of 2:2-10 are thus held tightly together with the high theological reflection of 2:11-14. As the "for" at the beginning of 2:11 suggests, 2:11-14 provides the theological underpinning for the preceding instructions. Thus we can see that theology and ethics hang together and are mutually interdependent. In a highly pluralistic society, any ethical system needs to be justified; here such a justification is provided. Alternatively expressed, a theology is incomplete if it does not produce a coherent ethic. A theology may be profound and deeply challenging on its own account, but if it does not eventuate in a guide for right living, then there is something wrong with it. Here it is the humdrum ethics of family relationships—the responsibilities of the older members of the community, of the younger women and men, and of the slaves. For theology to come down to such a level is not a denigration of theology or an abandonment of its proper business; on the contrary, such practical ethical concern is a test of a theology's character and quality.

Any church, then, would be well advised to examine how its creedal affirmations correlate with its practical life-style and the social concerns of its people. Here the care taken that the life-style within the Christian household and family should accord with what was generally reckoned to be the best standards is to be noted. The respect of the wider community is something to be prized (2:5, 8, 10). At the same time, there are clearly indicated categories of behavior to be avoided—slander, excessive drink, disrespect for legitimate authority, dishonesty, impiety, and worldly lusts. The world does not set the agenda; the principles are provided by the theology.

The lesson to be derived from all this is not any slavish following of the precise advice given here, much of it conditioned to the values of the time. Rather, the lesson is that in the different circumstances of different times a similar strategy needs to be followed, an equivalent balance struck between what gains proper respect in the wider community and what is to be avoided, however acceptable to or even lauded by society's opinion formers. In some instances, the choice will be clear: Policies and practices that pander to our lower natures (what Paul calls the "flesh") are to be resisted (see Rom 8:5-8). Many would criticize the "prosperity gospel" at just this point (conformity to the world, Rom 12:2). But in other cases we will need to be ready to acknowledge and support what is "good," no matter who seeks to promote it (see Rom 2:7, 10). Luke 16:1-8 reminds us of how difficult it can be to recognize appropriate models of conduct. Here not least we need the gift of discernment to know (and do!) what is God's good and acceptable and perfect will (Rom 12:2; Phil 1:9-10; Col 1:9-10).

The second bracket shaping the chapter's theological rationale is that provided by the two appearances of Christ (2:11, 13), the first in the self-giving death as a ransom (2:14), the other as the appearing of divine glory (2:13). This reminds us of the character of the saving process "in the present age" between the two appearings—as a process begun, but not yet completed. This eschatological tension shapes all Christian ethics, indicating the starting point and resource for all conduct (God's grace and what God has done in Christ). But it also reminds us that all aspiration and conduct in the between-time will partake of the not yet incompleteness of God's "good work" (Phil 1:6), with its attendant failure and frustration. The relevance of this observation to the present chapter is the recognition that even good household management in first-century terms shared in the deficiences and inadequacies of the still-incomplete process of refashioning all too human beings into the body of Christ, but not yet measuring up to the full stature of Christ (Eph 4:13).

The bracketing of the two appearances of Christ also reinforces the strong sense that the little churches of Crete are in direct continuity with Israel of old and share in both Israel's privileges and Israel's responsibilities. Like Israel, they have been chosen to be "a people of his own" and in the time between Christ's appearances they should be "zealous for good works" (2:14). This provides a further resource for Christian ethics, not least in the ethical standards and principles of social welfare enshrined in Israel's Scriptures (e.g., Deuteronomy 24; Isa 1:12-17; Mic 6:6-8). But it also brings out other aspects of the eschatological tension: How are we to distinguish Israel's heritage from "Jewish myths" and "zeal for good works" from zeal for the law? How can an increasingly Gentile religion continue to affirm its destiny as Israel? And it sets up at the heart of Christianity that ambivalence between affirmation of God's choice of a people of God's own and affirmation of God's desire for the salvation of all (2:11). The question of how Christianity both affirms the Old Testament and appropriates that heritage without also denying it remains at the heart of Christian identity, a question that will not be finally resolved until that glorious appearing.

The reference to the double appearing helps as well to frame the Christian understanding of Christ and of God in/through Christ. Here an appreciation of the significance of Christ struggles to gain expression. It is not simply that he has acted on God's behalf; both Christ and God can be called "Savior" because it is the one salvation, one and the same grace of God. It is, rather, that in his appearing, here particularly his second appearing, Christ is spoken of as the manifestation of God in glory (2:13). The resulting tension between recognizing both "the man Christ Jesus" (1 Tim 2:5) and "the glory of our great God and Savior" (Titus 2:13), has been not only an awe-inspiring challenge but also an immensely fruitful dynamic at the heart of Christian theology. That Jesus, the man, the Jew of first-century Palestine, expresses and reveals the reality of God has been at the heart of all Christian thinking from the first. That his (re)appearing functions as a goal and motivation for a distinctively Christian way of living has been at the heart of all Christian ethics from the first. It is such depth and seriousness of theological reflection that lie behind and come to expression in the day-to-day ethic of Titus 2:1-10.

TITUS 3:1-15, OF GRACE AND WORKS

COMMENTARY

Following the advice on good household management, reinforced by weighty theological consideration (2:1-15), the same pattern is followed with regard to wider responsibilities. Counsel on the attitudes Christians should adopt toward authorities and on relationships with the wider community (3:1-2) is likewise reinforced by a reminder of what their former lives were like (3:3) and by the fullest restatement of the gospel in the last of the faithful sayings (3:4-8a). This is followed by a brief summary repetition of the advice given earlier in the Pastorals to the good church leader—what to teach (3:8b), what to avoid (3:9), and the limits of effective church discipline (3:10-11). Personal instructions (3:12-13) are capped by a final reminder of the importance of "good works," the linking term in the passage (3:1, 5, 8, 14). The chapter closes with a final farewell (3:15).

3:1-8a, Living Within the World and Its Rationale. The concern that lay behind the advice on good household management (2:1-10)—that is, to demonstrate that Christian households were/should be a major contributory factor to the good order of the city and the state—becomes more explicit in these next exhortations (vv. 1-2). Christians should be "submissive" (ὑποτάσσω *hypotassō*) to the legitimate authorities. The term is the same as that used in 2:5 and 9, and the concern is the same: the need for believers to respect and live within the legal system of the day, to acknowledge by their submissiveness and obedience where authority and power lay in the ordering of the society of which they were a part. The concern is the same as in Rom 13:1-7 and 1 Tim 2:1-2. In each case there is a sober appreciation of the realities of power in the ancient city and state and of the need to live within these realities. Here again it needs to be recalled that such small groups had no possibility of exercising political power on their own behalf. Since retreat into the desert was not yet conceived of as an option, the only alternative was to live within the system and within its terms. "Ready for every good work," however, indicates not a sullen acceptance of an unfavorable situation, but a keenness to identify and seize opportunities to do good whenever they arose. The "good works" are not identified, but the forward-looking, proactive attitude should be noted.

The concern for good relations with the wider community extends to practical advice (v. 2) on conduct with non-Christian neighbors in street and workplace (cf. the conjunction of 3:1-2 with Rom 12:9–13:10). There is to be no slanderous gossip (the same term as in 2:5), not quarrelsome but gentle (the same word contrast as in 1 Tim 3:3), showing all "gentleness, humility, courtesy, considerateness" (the same word is used in 2 Tim 2:25) to all. The picture is that of political weakness but of inner strength, of engagement with the wider community but displaying attractive qualities that would win the confidence of others and would, no doubt, provide opportunities for witness from time to time—though that would be a by-product of the policy, not its goal.

One encouragement to such positive engagement is the contrast with their pre-Christian attitudes and behavior (v. 3). The contrast is probably overdrawn (as is often the case in such before-and-after conversion contrasts; cf. such passages as 1 Cor 6:9-11; Col 3:5-10; 1 Pet 4:3). But even if v. 3 expresses a Christian perspective on non-Christian mores, it at least signifies how the early Christians perceived their lives before they came to faith—"foolish" (as in 1 Tim 6:9), "disobedient" (as in 1:16), "led astray, deceived" (as in 2 Tim 3:13), "enslaved to various lusts and pleasures" (similar to 1 Tim 6:9; 2 Tim 3:6), "spending our lives in malice/ill-will and envy/jealousy" (cf. 1 Tim 6:4), "hated and hating one another." The last three phrases in particular provide a vivid snapshot of the avaricious society of all times.

All this is a foil to the last and fullest of the faithful sayings (vv. 4-7; see the Commentary on 1 Tim 1:15), again an attempt to preserve important Pauline themes. As in 2:1-15, the praxis commended in vv. 1-2 is given theological underpinning by an appeal to first principles of the gospel. What has made the difference between former day-to-day living (v. 3) and what may now be expected (vv. 1-2) is the decisive intervention of the goodness (cf. Rom 2:4; 11:22) and loving kindness (φιλανθρωπία $philanthrōpia$) of God (v. 4). At once it should be noted that the saving action spoken of is entirely that of God; it is God who "saved us" and poured out on us the Spirit (vv. 5-6). Although both God and Christ are described as "our Savior" (vv. 4, 6), God is clearly understood as source and author, and Christ as agent of the divine action (cf. Eph 2:7).

Here again the verb ἐπιφαίνω ($epiphainō$, "appear") refers to the first appearance of divine grace (as in 2:11), but in this case the thought is not so immediately focused on the action of Christ as on the impact of saving grace in human experience.[141] In fact, what we have is one of the clearest statements in all the Bible that the implementation of God's saving purpose is wholly at the initiative of God—"not from works in righteousness which we have done, but according to his own mercy" (v. 5).

Several points call for comment here:

(1) It is not an anti-Jewish statement; the echo of Deut 9:5 is actually closer than that of, say, Rom 3:28. The principle of salvation by the initiative of divine grace is rooted in the original choice of a slave people to be God's people. The use of the term "mercy" (ἔλεος $eleos$) here is no accident, for, as we saw in 1 Tim 1:2, it is the usual Greek translation of the strong Hebrew term denoting God's "covenant love/loving kindness" (חסד $ḥesed$) so fundamental to Israel's self-understanding as God's chosen people (Exod 34:6-7).

---

141. For the use of "saved" as denoting an act already achieved, see the Commentary on 2 Tim 1:9.

(2) It is not a direct repetition of what Paul said; he spoke of righteousness as a gift from God (as in Rom 4:3) and of works of the law, not of righteous works. The more specific case made by Paul (that Gentile believers should not be required to take on a Jewish life-style/works) is broadened out into a restatement of the original principle behind God's saving act (as in Eph 2:8-9).

(3) It is not a disparagement of good works or of righteous deeds. That could hardly be the case in an author who commends good works so strongly (as consistently in this passage, see vv. 1, 8, 14; see also Eph 2:10). It is, rather, a reminder that neither human actions nor human goodness can provide an adequate basis for relationship with God, however good, however righteous. Only God can establish and sustain that relationship. Good works are necessary, but as the fruit, not the root, of the discipleship. Good works will be the inevitable expression (and proof) that the relationship is sound, not its basis. Getting and keeping that balance require constant watchfulness and honesty within the community of faith.

The implementation of God's saving act comes through three means (vv. 5*b*-6). (1) The "washing [or "bath"] of regeneration."[142] This may refer to spiritual cleansing (cf. 2:14) or to baptism or to both (cf. Eph 5:26). The absence of any mention of "faith" here (cf. Acts 15:9) is hardly significant in view of its prominence elsewhere in the letter (here vv. 8, 15). (2) "Renewal [ἀνακαίνωσις *anakainōsis*; the same word as in Rom 12:2] by the Holy Spirit." That the gift of the Spirit is the fundamental and decisive feature in conversion/initiation is a central feature in Pauline theology (see, e.g, Rom 8:9; Gal 3:2-3). Note that the two phrases are coordinated: The washing and the renewal form a kind of hendiadys (a single, complex idea) governed by the single preposition ("through"). The implication is either that the renewal by the Spirit happens in or through baptism or, more likely, that the spiritual cleansing is also renewal by the Spirit (cf. John 3:5; Acts 15:8-9; Heb 10:22). The echo of the Pentecost reference to Joel 2:28 (Acts 2:17, "poured out on us"; cf. Rom 5:5) implies that this initiating gift of the Spirit is the Pentecostal Spirit; the renewal is not only for personal salvation but also for witness. (3) "Jesus Christ our Savior."

This last phrase is given a double elaboration in v. 7: (a) "That we might be justified by his grace"—the saving goodness of God comes to expression in and as the saving grace of Christ, his redemptive death being primarily in view (cf. Rom 3:24). Note the taken-for-granted link between the act of the cross and the experience of saving grace subsequently in individual lives. Presumably it was because this experience came in the context of preaching on the cross and evinced the same character that the link was so much taken for granted. (b) "And become heirs in hope of eternal life" (see the Commentary on 1:2; cf. 1 Tim 1:16). The language echoes a familiar and central theme in Paul's theology. On the one hand, there is the theme of inheritance (absent in the rest of the Pastorals)—that is, of Christian believers as entering into a share of the inheritance promised to the seed of Abraham (Rom 4:13-14; Gal 3:29; cf. Col 1:12).[143] On the other hand, there is the idea that believers share with Christ both as son and heir to Abraham and as son and heir to God (Rom 8:17; Gal 4:7). The centrality and richness of the christology should not go unmarked: Christ embodies both the saving grace of God and the inheritance promised to Abraham and is the one through whom humans experience that grace.

3:8b-11, The Outworking of the Gospel. As in Eph 2:8-10, the most immediate outcome for a life predicated on this gospel is "good works" (v. 8); once again, theology leads at once to praxis. Titus is to "speak confidently, insist" on the gospel expressed in such terms in order that transformed lives should result. Worth noting is the description of those for whom this gospel is the basis of life: "those who have believed [in] God" (the tense implies a commitment once made, determining a continuing orientation of life).

---

142. The word translated "regeneration" (παλιγγενεσία *palingenesia*) is unusual; the only other usage is Matt 19:28. But the imagery is expressed in other terms elsewhere, particularly in the Johannine writings; see John 1:13; 3:5; 1 John 2:29; 3:9; 4:7; 5:1, 4, 18; see also Jas 1:18; 1 Pet 1:3, 23. It is unclear here whether the word was intended to carry the eschatological overtones of Matt 19:28. Equally uncertain is the relevance of other use of rebirth imagery. See Dibelius and Conzelmann, *The Pastoral Epistles*, 148-50.

143. Paul was not alone in broadening out the promise of the land (Canaan) to the idea of inheriting the earth (Rom 4:13; Sir 44:21) or the world to come (*2 Bar* 14:13; 51:3).

The definition of a Christian need not always include reference to Christ. They are to be "intent upon/careful about" "engaging in/busying themselves with" good works (the same phrase in v. 14). "These things are excellent and profitable to fellow human beings"; again the wider impact of the gospel as reflected in Christian behavior comes at once to the fore. Here is a classic statement of the social gospel: It is sufficient rationale for Christian "good works" that they are fine in themselves and benefit others.

It would not be one of the Pastoral Epistles if there was not a final swipe at competing teachings, dismissed, as usual, with a sequence of offhanded derogatory terms in v. 9: "stupid controversies" (as in 2 Tim 2:23), "genealogies" (see the Commentary on 1 Tim 1:4), "dissensions/strifes" (1 Tim 6:4), "fights over the law" (cf. 1 Tim 1:7-8), "unprofitable" and "futile/worthless." The reference to the law confirms the impression given in 1:10, 14 that Christian Jews are primarily in view. One of the issues, if not the issue, presumably was the continuation of the earlier question: To what extent do Gentile converts have to observe all of the law's injunctions?[144] Once again we see the tension between a claim to Jewish inheritance (implied in 3:7) and a denial that salvation required obedience to all the law.

Equally important in the final summary exhortation was the reminder of how persistent opponents should be dealt with (vv. 10-11). The initial phrase used could be translated "heretical person," but αἱρετικός (*hairetikos*; a *hapax*) does not have that more technical sense; rather, it denotes someone who persists in dissenting opinions, who promotes factions, or who causes actual divisions. Note once again, however, the clear implication that those in view are within rather than from outside the congregations; the implication of v. 9 is of tensions between Jewish and Gentile members of the same congregations. At an earlier point, Paul conceded that such factions had the value of demonstrating who the mature members of a congregation were (1 Cor 11:19). It is also worth noting that the closest parallel to the instruction given here is that regarding recalcitrant elders in 1 Tim 5:20; the discipline of withholding fellowship was already foreshadowed in 1 Cor 5:11 and 2 Thess 3:14-15. The logic of v. 11 is that persistence in such fractiousness is a sign that someone has turned from the way ("is perverted, warped") and continues to sin, and in consequence is self-condemned.

3:12-15, Final Instructions and Greetings. As typical of the Pauline letters, the final concern is with personal notes regarding travel plans (vv. 12-13). Whether these are derived from scrappy notes from Paul or indications of his own and in the letter as a whole or suggest, rather, a later author drawing on knowledge of the Pauline letter may be less important than the reminder that these early congregations enjoyed, and to some extent depended on, a regular interchange of visitors. Of Artemas we know nothing more. Tychicus we have already met (see 2 Tim 4:12). The reference to Paul's intention to winter at Nicopolis (probably in Epirus, on the Greek coast, south of Corfu) certainly strengthens the view that the passage was penned by Paul himself, since that kind of personal detail is less likely to have been contrived. The same is true of the commendation of Zenas the lawyer (of whom, once again, we know nothing more) and Apollos. The latter was one of the most influential of the secondary figures of whom we hear in connection with Paul, having taught both in Ephesus (Acts 18:24-26) and particularly in Corinth to great effect (Acts 18:27-28; 1 Cor 1:12; 3:4-6, 22; 4:6; 16:12). The reference here confirms that there was no hostility between the two, as some of the 1 Corinthian references might suggest. The request here is for financial assistance in their travels (cf. Rom 15:24; 1 Cor 16:6, 11; 2 Cor 1:16).

The final exhortation, making a bracket with v. 1 (as in chap. 2), is to "apply themselves to good works" (v. 14). Somewhat surprisingly, at this last gasp, we are given a clue as to what constitutes such good works. The primary outcome will be that those who are looking for ways to do good will be the better ready to recognize and meet urgent needs[145]

---

144. Justin Martyr indicates that there was still a range of views on the point among Jewish Christians in the middle of the second century. See Justin *Dialogue with Trypho* 47.

145. The phrase could signify "necessary needs" in the sense of the NIV's "daily necessities"; but the juxtaposition of two such close synonyms suggests, rather, that the two terms were intended to reinforce each other—"pressing needs." Cf. the sense of the noun ἀνάγκη (*anagkē*) as "distress," "calamity" in 1 Cor 7:26.

when they arise. Any society will need its emergency services; a Christian society will be forward in their provision. The secondary consequence will be that they live fruitful lives—fruitfulness here being understood not in terms of qualities of character (as in Gal 5:22-23) but in terms of actual help or benefit from one to another (see Eph 4:28-29).

As usual in the Pauline (as in most) letters the final word is one of greeting (v. 15; cf. 2 Tim 4:19-21). Interesting is the choice of the weaker term φιλέω (*phileō*, "love," "have affection for," "like") rather than the stronger ἀγαπάω (*agapaō*, "love [as Christ loved]"). Thus he tells them to "greet those who have affection for us in faith." Otherwise it reinforces the typical Pauline connection between love and faith (as in 2:2). The final benediction is as that of the other two Pastorals, though here the "all" is a reminder that the letter would be read aloud at a gathering of the whole congregation.

REFLECTIONS

The linking theme here is "good works" (see also 1:1, 5, 8, 14). This term has had an uncomfortable history within Christian thought. On the one hand, it is associated with the attitude of those who try or hope to work for their passage to heaven. The problem has been that this attitude embraces a diverse spectrum of conditions and individuals—from the humble, perhaps unsophisticated believers, who instinctively feel that they must be able to show something for their life in its final reckoning, to the arrogant figures of political or financial power who naturally assume that the hard work or market manipulation that has gained them their prestige must count for something in the heavenly account books as in the obituaries of the quality newspapers. Do they all come under equal condemnation? The principle is clear and needs constant restatement: No human being on his or her own can achieve acceptability before God; no human society can bring about or emulate the kingdom of God. Without the initiative of God—as in creation, so in salvation—no one can hope to experience in any fullness that quality of existence and life that is encapsulated in the expressions "eternal life" and "heaven." To that end, all dependence on human works needs, indeed, to be warned against as the most subtle as well as the most blatant attempt of the creature to claim rights before the Creator. Religion begins from and with humility, and without such humility it never begins at all.

On the other hand, of the four references to "[good] works" in this chapter, three are positive and commendatory, and only one (3:5) is treated dismissively. The danger, then, is that the one is allowed to overshadow and devalue the three, that because of the danger of "good works" the disparagement of 3:5 is extended to the other three references. This is implied in the dismissive and mocking tone often used, even in Christian circles, of "good works" and "do-gooders." That is unfortunate in the extreme—if the balance of chapter 3 is any guide. Apart from anything else, it encourages the idea that religion—or to use the favorite term of the Pastorals, "godliness"—is expressed only in prayer and worship, in the activities of the church and of Sunday, and not those of home and workplace and leisure time, of Monday to Friday (not to mention Saturday). But clearly this is not the view of the Pastorals, as their repeated commendation of good works shows beyond dispute. Good works are evidently understood as the way "godliness" expresses itself precisely in the wider world, and without good works, godliness has been cut off at the root.

To be noted in this passage is the elaboration of the theme, both at beginning and at end (3:1-3, 14). In view, in the first place, is an ethos expressed in good citizenship, the refusal to share in slanderous gossip or to pick fights, and in gentleness and courtesy toward neighbors, toward fellow workers, and toward acquaintances (3:1-2). This is in contrast to the ethos that promotes the satisfaction of desire and pleasure as the greatest good and that expresses itself in malice, envy, intercommunal suspicion, and hatred (3:3). The importance of good works, in other words, is not just in the works themselves, but in the attitudes and priorities they express. In the second place, good works come to expression particularly in sensitivity to the needs of others and the readiness to help when crisis or emergency strikes, and generally in the image of a fruitful life (3:14).

The trick is in being able to distinguish between the two kinds of works—or rather, the two kinds of attitudes expressed in works. In the end, the negative term always comes back to a degree of self-centeredness: a concern to achieve, a concern for one's own dignity and prestige, a concern to justify and prove oneself. Like a worm at the center of an apple, that concern can undermine even the most Christian of activities; Paul had already warned against this in 1 Cor 13:1-3. The self-knowledge that can alert the doers of good works to their peril is not easily gained. Blessed is the Christian community in which friends and counselors can signal that alert before the condition becomes serious. The key factor is the recognition that the "good works" that gain the author's commendation are always those that spring from the goodness and loving kindness of God, which consciously take their beginning and inspiration from the grace of God in Christ and the outpoured Spirit. Here, too, it is only the genuine humility of the doer that prevents the good works urged upon believers from deteriorating into the works that prevent the grace of God in Christ from having its full effect in and through a human life.

THE LETTER TO PHILEMON
INTRODUCTION, COMMENTARY, AND REFLECTIONS
BY
CAIN HOPE FELDER

THE LETTER TO
PHILEMON

INTRODUCTION

The Letter to Philemon is one of the seven letters that almost all biblical scholars hold were written by the apostle Paul. Having only twenty-five verses in its English rendering from the 335 words in the apostle's Greek original, Philemon is the shortest among the Pauline epistles. The textual integrity of the letter is complete (i.e., fully preserved) in twelve of the major uncial manuscripts, and there is a near-total word agreement among the Greek texts of the letter, with but few orthographical differences (in vv. 2, 6, 9, 12, 25).[1]

Most commentators agree that Philemon reflects Paul's spirit, theology, moral tone, language, and style, as do 1 Thessalonians, Galatians, 1 and 2 Corinthians, Romans, and Philippians, the six other undisputed letters. Ancient church tradition links the letter to Paul, and the major catalogs of the New Testament canon from the early centuries (e.g., the late second-century Muratorian Fragment and Bishop Athanasius's thirty-ninth Festal Letter to his clergy in 367 CE, among others) list it among Paul's writings.

DATE AND PLACE OF WRITING

The Letter to Philemon differs significantly from Paul's other writings in two ways. First, it is not addressed to a church but to specific persons. Second, it is a letter of mediation to foster reconciliation between two individuals to whom Paul bears common relation as their spiritual leader: Philemon, a slavemaster, and Onesimus, a slave who fled Philemon's household but who has returned, concerned to make things right. This letter was Paul's plea for a renewed relationship between the two, but one on better terms than before in the light of their mutual faith as Christians.

Three options are usually set forth regarding the place from which Paul wrote the letter: Caesarea, Ephesus, or Rome. These are the places where Paul was imprisoned for considerable

---

1. On the orthographical differences, see Bruce M. Metzger, *A Textual Commentary on the Greek New Testament* (London/New York: United Bible Societies, 1971) 657-58.

periods of time (although there were other occasions when he was taken into custody, as 2 Cor 11:23ff. reports). The dating of this letter depends in large measure on the location of its composition. If Paul wrote to Philemon from Rome, as seems most likely, then the letter was composed about 61 CE. If written during his imprisonment at Caesarea, the letter should be dated about 58 CE. If written from Ephesus, a date of 55 CE would be required.

The argument for Rome as the place of composition has particular merit. Since Philemon was the overseer of the Lycus Valley house churches at Colossae, in Asia Minor, Onesimus, his slave, would most likely not have remained within a short distance from the household he had fled but would have found his way to Rome, where other runaway slaves from the provinces tended to seek refuge. Although Rome sought to protect slave owners' rights and even encouraged bounty for assistance in returning fugitive slaves to their owners, it is not certain that Onesimus was, in fact, a runaway at all or, if he was, that he had become one without just cause.

Those who suggest Ephesus as the place of origin for this letter cite Paul's request that Philemon prepare lodging for his visit (v. 22) as an indication that Paul must have been imprisoned nearby. In addition to this, Ephesus was a provincial capital whose proximity to Colossae made it a more convenient destination for a slave without resources. Against this argument, however, is the fact, based on Col 4:7-9, that Onesimus and Tychicus were commissioned by Paul to carry letters from him to Ephesus, Laodicea, and Colossae. As for Caesarea as the place of writing, it is the most improbable choice of the three because of the difficulty in aligning events surrounding Paul's imprisonment there (see Acts 23–25) and the contents of this letter to Philemon.

The circumstance occasioning the letter to Philemon has strong bearing on Col 4:7-9, which mentions Tychicus ("beloved brother, a faithful minister, and a fellow servant in the Lord," Col 4:7) as someone who will update the Colossian church members concerning Paul's situation. The same text refers to Onesimus as traveling with him; Paul there described Onesimus as "the faithful and beloved brother, who is one of you" (Col 4:9). It is also instructive, and doubtless indicative, that this mention of Onesimus occurs just after the segment in Colossians that details the subordination codes pertaining to slaves and masters (Col 3:22–4:1; it should be noted that the injunction in Col 4:1, advising those who owned slaves to "treat your slaves justly and fairly, for you know that you also have a Master in heaven" is a unique principle for such stock codes).

FOCUS

At first glance, the Letter to Philemon seems to focus almost entirely on the issue of slavery. Paul was imprisoned or under house arrest (vv. 9, 13, 23) as he wrote; nevertheless, he was able to provide refuge for the slave Onesimus, who for some reason had fled the household of his master, Philemon. Paul appeals to Philemon as a friend and fellow Christian to take Onesimus back and to receive him without penalty or prejudice, in view of the slave's conversion and new life in Christ, their common Lord. Thus the reference to Onesimus as a "beloved brother"; Onesimus had become a Christian in the interim between leaving Philemon's household and the time the letter was written. Paul's description of Onesimus as "my child, whose father I have become during my imprisonment" (v. 10) can be understood to mean that Paul was the primary human agent in helping Onesimus to become a Christian.

The view widely held across many centuries is that this is a fairly straightforward personal letter in which Paul petitions his friend Philemon to forgive and restore his runaway slave, who was both a fugitive and a thief. Now, various questions can be raised about why Onesimus left Philemon's household and why he sought out Paul. Had he been abused by Philemon? Had he, in leaving Philemon, caused him to undergo some financial loss? However, although Paul recognized Philemon's "claim" upon Onesimus, nothing in the letter provides warrant for the notion that Onesimus was a criminal fugitive who had stolen something from his master.

The central meaning and purpose of the Letter to Philemon concern the difference the transforming power of the gospel can make in the lives and relationships of believers, regardless of class or other distinctions. However, the way slavery has figured so prominently in modern history has obscured this deeper, more essential meaning and veiled the perennial significance of the letter. During the period of the European and American slave trade, many slave owners and other defenders of the system who laid claim to Christian leadership appealed to the Letter to Philemon to justify the racial stereotypes they held and the compliance they believed that Scripture requires from those under the slavery system. To be sure, the institution of slavery in the Roman Empire during the first century, the legal infrastructure that supported it, and the various moral judgments given in the New Testament regarding its legitimacy are issues that must be considered in reading the letter. However, close study of the text makes clear that Paul's primary focus is not on the institution of slavery but on the power of the gospel to transform human relationships and bring about reconciliation. There is no basis whatsoever for thinking of Onesimus as a progenitor of the African American slave, especially since the Roman Empire did not have a race-based policy for the institution of slavery, neither in the first century nor at any other time.[2] All things considered, the way Paul's letter to Philemon is viewed provides excellent opportunity for a case study about the ways in which a person's social location can serve as a tacit rationale for reading inappropriate values into the text, distorting the document's original intent.

Quite apart from the fact that it was the work of Paul, the inclusion of the letter to Philemon in the New Testament canon would be justified on the basis of its message about reconciliation. Lloyd Lewis draws attention to Paul's use of "family language" in the letter: "brother" (vv. 1, 7, 16, 20), "sister" (v. 2), "my child . . . whose father I have become" (v. 10), and the like. The frequency of use of the terms is so pronounced that the communal-family emphasis cannot be viewed as coincidental. Lewis highlights Paul's noble intent expressed in those terms of endearment; the apostle exposes "an unwillingness to canonize the social roles found in his environment."[3]

In addition to the many published studies that report traditional interpretations of the Letter to Philemon, new studies have appeared seeking to buttress older views or to supply fresh perspective on how the letter should be viewed and explained. Sarah C. Winter has suggested that the Letter to Philemon was primarily written to a church and was only formally addressed to Philemon as the congregational overseer. The references to the situation between Philemon and Onesimus are explained as not so much dealing with personal matters as framing a paradigm for changing master/slave relationships into new opportunities for manumission and shared fellowship.[4]

Perhaps the most dramatic departure from the traditional understanding of the Letter to Philemon of late is found in the work of Allen D. Callahan.[5] Callahan seeks to dispel the idea that Onesimus was a slave at all, suggesting rather that he and Philemon were estranged biological brothers whom Paul sought to reconcile. Despite flashes of keen insight, Callahan's heavy reliance on "silences of the text" and his literal interpretation of Paul's words about Onesimus as "a beloved brother . . . in the flesh and in the Lord" (v. 16) as indicating a blood kinship between Onesimus and Philemon move the interpretive center of the letter too far from the more common and ancient understanding of Onesimus as a runaway slave.

Eduard Lohse calls attention to the interpretive center of the Letter to Philemon in his majesterial commentary, citing Martin Luther's influential evaluation of the Pauline writing:

> This epistle gives us a masterful and tender illustration of Christian love. For here we see how St. Paul takes the part of poor Onesimus and, to the best of his ability, advocates his cause with his master. He acts exactly as if he were himself Onesimus, who had done wrong. Yet, he does this

---

2. See, among other pertinent studies, Frank M. Snowden, Jr., *Before Color Prejudice: The Ancient View of Blacks* (Cambridge, Mass.: Harvard University Press, 1963) 63-64, 69-71; W.L. Westermann, *The Slave Systems of Greek and Roman Antiquity* (Philadelphia: American Philosophical Society, 1955) esp. 102-9. For a helpful study on how scorn and rivalry were expressed among the diversified peoples unified under Roamn imperialism, see A. N. Sherwin-White, *Racial Prejudice in Imperial Rome* (Cambridge: Cambridge University Press, 1970).

3. Lloyd A. Lewis, "An African American Appraisal of the Philemon-Paul-Onesimus Triangle," in *Stony the Road We Trod: African American Biblical Interpretation,* ed. Cain Hope Felder (Minneapolis: Fortress, 1991) 246.

4. S. C. Winter, "Methodical Observations of a New Interpretation of Paul's Letter to Philemon," *Union Seminary Quarterly Review* 39 (1984) 203-12. See also her study, "Paul's Letter to Philemon," *NTS* 33 (1987) 1-15.

5. Allen D. Callahan, *Embassy of Onesimus: The Letter of Paul to Philemon* (Valley Forge: Trinity Press International, 1997). See also Callahan's earlier article, "Paul's Epistle to Philemon: Toward an Alternative Argumentum," *HTR* 86:4 (1993) 357-76.

not with force or compulsion, as lay within his rights; but empties himself of his rights in order to compel Philemon to waive his rights.[6]

Luther's observation conveys his view that Onesimus had done something wrong, yet exactly who in the letter is the injured party or real victim has remained open to debate. It is quite possible, for example, that Onesimus's only offense was leaving the household of a master—Philemon—who had abused him in some way. There is greater warrant for such a scenario than for viewing Onesimus as a lazy or dishonest servant—the view found in the folklore that circulated among the ruling classes of the modern Western world, especially those who championed and benefited from the institution of slavery.

While Paul's letter to Philemon does not focus on the issue of slavery, it certainly offers clues that help to clarify the apostle's moral stance on the issue. Paul was aware of the provisions in the Hebrew Bible that sanctioned some forms of slavery despite the abhorence of the Hebrews for the long period of their own bondage in Egypt. And, as a Roman citizen, he certainly knew the legal warrants for the system as practiced across the empire. He was astute enough to recognize that the role of a pronounced abolitionist would not only have been foolhardy for himself, despite his Roman citizenship, but it would also have been disastrous to the nascent Christian missionary movement. Such factors make all the more astonishing texts like Gal 5:1, "For freedom Christ has set us free. Stand firm, therefore, and do not submit again to a yoke of slavery"; or 1 Cor 7:21, which suggests that slaves should use every opportunity to gain manumission;[7] or 2 Cor 11:20-21, which castigates those who let others enslave them. These statements, rightly viewed, are hardly the words of someone who approves of the institution of slavery. On the contrary, they reflect an attitude consistent with the appeal made in the Letter to Philemon, making the words found there all the more poignant and significant, for Paul is also the one who brought Philemon into the faith.

6. Cited by Eduard Lohse, *Colossians and Philemon*, Hermeneia (Philadelphia: Fortress, 1971) 188.
7. See, however, on the history of interpretation of the Greek wording in 1 Cor 7:21, S. Scott Batchy, ΜΑΛΛΟΝ ΧΡΗΣΑΙ: *First-Century Slavery and the Interpretation of 1 Corinthians 7:21*, SBLDS 11 (Missoula, Mont.: Scholars Press, 1973).

BIBLIOGRAPHY

Commentaries:

Bruce, F. F. *The Epistles to the Colossians, to Philemon, and to the Ephesians.* NIGNT. Grand Rapids: Eerdmans, 1984. A scholarly, evangelical commentary.

Caird, George B. *Paul's Letters from Prison.* NCIB. Oxford: Oxford University Press, 1976. A classic commentary that explores the theological meaning and historical background of Paul's letters.

Dunn, James D. G. *The Epistles to the Colossians and to Philemon: A Commentary on the Greek Text.* NIGNT. Grand Rapids: Eerdmans, 1996. A scholarly commentary, particularly helpful for study of the Greek text.

Knox, John. "The Epistle to Philemon: Introduction and Exegesis." *Interpreter's Bible.* Vol. 10. Nashville: Abingdon, 1955. A classic commentary for preachers and teachers.

Lohse, Eduard. *Colossians and Philemon.* Hermeneia. Philadelphia: Fortress, 1971. A scholarly commentary, with extensive notes and references.

Metzger, Bruce M. *A Textual Commentary on the Greek New Testament.* New York: United Bible Societies, 1971. An excellent overview of the textual variants of the NT writings.

O'Brien, Peter T. *Colossians, Philemon.* WBC. Waco, Tex.: Word, 1982. A critical, scholarly, evangelical commentary.

Osiek, Carolyn. *Philippians, Philemon.* ANTC. Nashville: Abingdon, 2000. A concise, critical commentary, particularly valuable for its analysis of rhetorical strategies and social realities.

Other Specialized Studies:

Bartchy, S. Scott. ΜΑΛΛΟΝ ΧΡΗΣΑΙ: *First Century Slavery and the Interpretation of 1 Corinthians 7:21.* SBLDS. Missoula, Mont.: Scholars Press, 1973. A detailed, scholarly analysis.

Bruce, F. F. *Paul: Apostle of the Heart Set Free.* Grand Rapids: Eerdmans, 1997. A study of Paul's life and thought from an outstanding evangelical scholar.

Callahan, Allen D. "Paul's Epistle to Philemon: Toward an Alternative Argumentum." *HTR* 86:4 (1993). An intriguing reading of the Letter to Philemon.

———. *Embassy of Onesimus: The Letter of Paul to Philemon.* Valley Forge, Pa.: Trinity Press International, 1997. A comprehensive statement of the author's provocative reading of the Letter to Philemon.

Lewis, Lloyd A. "An African American Appraisal of the Philemon-Paul-Onesimus Triangle." In *Stony the Road We Trod: African American Biblical Interpretation.* Edited by Cain Hope Felder. Minneapolis: Augsburg Fortress, 1991. An analysis of the Letter to Philemon from a contemporary African American perspective.

Martin, Ralph P. *Reconciliation: A Study of Paul's Theology.* Atlanta: John Knox, 1981. A comprehensive examination of Pauline theology, emphasizing reconciliation.

Meeks, Wayne A. *The First Urban Christians: The Social World of the Apostle Paul.* New Haven: Yale University Press, 1983. A classic study of the social environment of the early Christian movement.

Sampley, J. Paul. *Pauline Partnership in Christ: Christian Community and Commitment in Light of Roman Law.* Philadelphia: Fortress, 1980. A study of partnership in Paul's missionary work and writing as influenced by concepts in Roman law.

Winter, S. C. "Methodical Observations of a New Interpretation of Paul's Letter to Philemon." *Union Seminary Quarterly Review* 39 (1984).

OUTLINE OF PHILEMON

I. Philemon 1-3, Opening Greetings

II. Philemon 4-7, Philemon Is Commended for His Faith and Charity

III. Philemon 8-20, Paul's Request Regarding Onesimus

IV. Philemon 21-22, Paul's Expectation to Visit

V. Philemon 23-25, Concluding Words and Benediction

PHILEMON 1-3
OPENING GREETINGS

COMMENTARY

Following the conventional forms of letter writing of his time, Paul names himself first as the one writing; then Timothy, a known close associate who was with him as he wrote. Finally he names the intended recipients: Philemon; Apphia and Archippus, two presumably key persons within Philemon's circle, possibly even family members; and the "church in [Philemon's] house." Paul describes himself as a "prisoner" (δέσμιος *desmios*, vv. 1, 9), which was his current situation, being in custody. However, he wanted it clearly understood that he did not view himself as a battle casualty but as an obedient servant to Jesus Christ. Thus the full self-designation "prisoner of Christ Jesus," which could also mean "prisoner for Christ Jesus" (as the Greek was rendered previously in the RSV).

Paul's self-description here as "prisoner of Christ Jesus" deviates from his more customary self-reference in the undisputed letters as an "apostle of Jesus Christ" (see 1 Cor 1:1; 2 Cor 1:1; Gal 1:1; etc.); in the deutero-Pauline Eph 3:1 we find his self-reference as "prisoner for Christ Jesus"; at Eph 4:1, "prisoner in the Lord"; and at 2 Tim 1:8, "me his prisoner." It is clear that Paul always associated his imprisonments with having been obedient to his Lord. Callahan has suggested that "perhaps Paul's failure to claim his apostolic credentials here, which he so readily flashes before those congregations he has established personally, is better understood as a reflection of his rhetorical situation vis-à-vis churches in which his personal standing and relationship are less than certain."[8] Paul did sometimes assert his claims to apostolicity when his credentials were challenged by opponents; this is seen in his writing to the Corinthians and the Galatians. Yet it was not necessary for him to do so here; since he did not have to assert leadership priority in dealing with a house church that he did not plant, his apostleship is not being questioned. Paul is merely sending this particularly personal letter to Philemon, whom he addresses as his "dear friend and co-worker."

Philemon is not named elsewhere in the Pauline corpus or in the early Christian literature. Apart from his appearance by name in this letter, nothing more is known concerning him except that he was a slave owner, a head of a household, a leader of a church group that met within his properties, and, by inference, that he was engaged in some business that supported his status. (As for the name "Philemon," it was as common in the Greek-speaking culture as are "John" and "Joe" in English-speaking countries.)[9]

Paul addressed Philemon as "dear friend" (ἀγαπητός *agapētos*, "beloved one"); the abstract adjective seems appropriate because he and Paul had known each other in some settings as coworkers in the furtherance of the gospel. Κοινωνία (*Koinōnia*), or "fellowship," exists between them, and Paul highlights this fact as he addresses his friend. Callahan suggests that this was Paul's way of preparing Philemon for the claim this letter would press upon him as he read it, "coworker" being not only initially descriptive but finally prescriptive as well.

Apphia is traditionally assumed to have been Philemon's wife; that she was so is asserted by John Chrysostom (c. 344/354–407) in his first homily on the Letter to Philemon. Since Philemon is referred to as "beloved," some scribes added "the beloved" after her name as well in making copies of this letter, as many cursives (copies written in small cursive letters) reveal. As for Archippus,

---

8. Callahan, *Embassy of Onesimus*, 23.

9. See *A Greek-English Lexicon of the New Testament and Other Early Christian Literature*, ed. Walter Bauer, William F. Arndt, F. Wilbur Gingrich, and Frederick W. Danker (Chicago: University of Chicago Press, 1979) 859.

some commentators suggest that the person identified here by that name is the same person mentioned in Col 4:17. Indeed, many have promoted the view of Theodore of Mopsuestia (c. 350–428), influential Antiochene exegete and theologian, that the Archippus greeted here was a son of Philemon and Apphia. The paucity of information from that early period of church history has prompted the pressing of meager data into unwarranted and dubious constructions. Nevertheless, Paul's greeting—addressing them together with Philemon—indicates that both Apphia and Archippus were important figures in the house church headed by Philemon. Archippus is also addressed in loving terms, being greeted as "our fellow soldier" (συστρατιώτης *systratiōtēs*). F. F. Bruce has commented that "some personal association with Archippus in the work of the gospel is implied, but what it was is unknown to us."[10]

"The church in your house" is mentioned by way of extension. Paul acknowledges the work for which Philemon was responsible and shows concern for the welfare of the assembly. He was aware that Philemon and his family, so intimately related to the congregation for which Philemon had oversight, would appreciate a word that included the group's welfare. Moreover, Paul knew that the plea he was about to make to Philemon in this letter, no matter how it might be handled, would affect social relations within the assembly. So the formulaic close of the apostle's greetings, the implied prayer for continued "grace to you [plural] and peace from God our Father and the Lord Jesus Christ," is more than a simple expression of courtesy. The greetings and implied prayers found in Paul's correspondence always convey his pastoral concern.[11]

---

10. F. F. Bruce, *The Epistles to the Colossians, to Philemon, and to the Ephesians*, NICNT (Grand Rapids: Eerdmans, 1984) 206.

11. See Gordon P. Wiles, *Paul's Intercessory Prayers* (Cambridge: Cambridge University Press, 1974) esp. 217-18.

REFLECTIONS

1. A true soldier understands orders and obeys them, strengthened by trust in the cause and a disciplined will to fulfill a known duty. Paul understood himself as a soldier for Christ, a man under orders, so he had no shame in being a prisoner; he knew it was in the interest of the cause he served.

Imprisoned, with a Roman soldier always in his presence or within sight, Paul was reminded constantly of his own ties to authority. He viewed himself as a soldier sent out by his Lord under orders to deal with evil. Though confined for a time, he was content because he had been "captured" while "in battle." The soldier image must have been uppermost in his mind when, in greeting Philemon, Paul remembered his ties with Archippus (possibly Philemon's son) and greeted him as well, calling him "fellow soldier." Images from military life may not be as stimulating to the present generation as to those of the past, but it is not possible to understand the depth of Paul's commitment to Christ and his willingness to undergo his many periods of confinement in prison without taking into account the positive aspects of what it means to be "under orders" and to obey them despite the costs involved (cf. 2 Cor 9:16).

2. The church at Colossae, perhaps still in its early growth stage, was blessed by a hosting home where its members could meet. Stated church buildings would come only in the future (the third century, to be exact), but at that early time the nascent church realized itself and promoted its mission through gatherings in homes. The home was central to the tasks envisioned, the place where worship and learning could take place and fellowship could be experienced. Churches in our time have been discovering anew the importance of small-group life in teaching, in learning, and in community ministry.

With so much in our day that militates against quality time at home, there must be a commitment on the part of a family to provide space and time for church gatherings in the home setting. A church gains something vital when cells of believers can meet for prayer, Bible study, or fellowship in a home setting. Despite the conveniences afforded in other places available for congregational uses, it is in the home that openness beckons, love is promoted, unselfishness is modeled, intimacy deepens, encouragement is gained, and integrity is nurtured.

3. At the beginning of the third millennium, the phrase "church in your house" seems rather foreign; popular culture portrays the modern home as a secular institution. However, reflecting on that phrase takes us to the historical depths of church life—that is, the way particular congregations began and who assisted in their development. Many a vital church began when some person or family offered their dwelling place as a meeting site to help start a fellowship group. Providing space was a ministry that generated cooperation, cohesion, and growth—and that spawned other ministries.

A wise Christian fellowship will keep track of its life as it develops, teaching truths, marking trends, and charting timelines. And a caring church will honor those whose commitment encourages growth and ministry to happen. In modern consumer-oriented societies where so much is readily thrown away to make room for what is next, church leaders with vision will acquaint themselves and the other members of their congregation with information about their group's history, and they will inspire members to appreciate and add to that history through commitment to duties essential for a vital ministry.

PHILEMON 4-7

PHILEMON IS COMMENDED FOR HIS FAITH AND CHARITY

COMMENTARY

Paul's pastoral concern involved him regularly in prayers for the churches under his care, for his coworkers, and for those converted under his ministry. Philemon, one of Paul's own converts (v. 19) as well as his "dear friend and co-worker," here learns about the prayers offered to God by Paul on his behalf. Those prayers are filled with thanksgiving over reports from others that Philemon shows "love for all the saints" and a contagious "faith toward the Lord Jesus" (v. 5). But they also include intercession, with the apostle asking God to help Philemon share his faith, informed by the knowledge of all the good ways in which this can be done and with an increased effectiveness that honors Christ, his Lord.

These words show us something more than a customary thanksgiving section of a letter: They reveal a specific commendation from Paul to Philemon. Although Paul wrote with particular instances of Philemon's charity in mind, many of which were shared with him by Epaphras (who is named in v. 23) and perhaps by Onesimus as well, no such details appear in this letter. Paul is impressed by Philemon's charitable disposition and pays him tribute, acknowledging his deeds as having been done in love and inspired by his faith in the Lord Jesus. "Love" (ἀγάπη *agapē*) and "faith" (πίστις *pistis*) are highlighted here by Paul as they are in his other letters, but it is interesting that while "faith" is usually mentioned first elsewhere, "love" receives first mention here. It is likely that Paul was thinking strategically about the issue for which the letter was being sent, hoping that Philemon's charitable disposition would allow the forthcoming appeal regarding Onesimus to be received with understanding and acceptance.

Paul's words of tribute regarding Philemon's charity were not merely literary flourish or contrived flattery. They were an honest expression based on known facts regarding Philemon, knowledge gained, perhaps, from Paul's own previous experience with him, but surely from the good reports heard from others whose lives had been touched in helpful, meaningful ways by the man. Paul, therefore, adds a personal comment about his own emotion resulting from such good reports: "I have received much joy and encouragement from your love, because the hearts of the saints have been refreshed through you, my brother" (v. 7). Paul's words here are remarkably similar to those in 3 John 3, where John the Elder confesses his joy over reports about Gaius's "faithfulness to the truth, namely how you walk in the truth." Bruce has commented, "It is a pleasant coincidence that the two really personal letters in the NT should both be addressed to men so like-minded in their generosity."[12]

Paul's intercessory prayers for Philemon included concern regarding what the NIV translates as being "active in sharing your faith," but which the NRSV renders as "the sharing of your faith." All told, that "sharing" (κοινωνία *koinōnia*) would involve Philemon's witnessing to others about his faith as well as doing deeds that showed evidence of his faith. Generosity is the present focus, and that becomes clearly noted in v. 7 where Paul mentions how the "hearts of the saints have been refreshed [ἀναπέπαυται *anapepautai*, "calmed," "comforted," "relieved"]" through Philemon's charitable deeds. This commendation covers much about which we have no knowledge, but "the saints" did, and from personal experience.

---

12. Bruce, *The Epistles to the Colossians, to Philemon, and to the Ephesians*, see 210n. 43.

While this much is certainly understood from the commendation in vv. 4-5, the grammatical construction of v. 6 leaves us perplexed by translation difficulties and many alternative exegetical possibilities. The Greek wording in v. 6 is awkward in its phrasing; the intended meaning of the crucial term *koinōnia*, especially linked with *pistis*, remains unclear. The differences between the NIV and the NRSV in translating the Greek are readily noted; other translation options can be observed by comparing additional renderings of v. 6 in English:

The New English Bible: "My prayer is that your fellowship with us in our common faith may deepen the understanding of all the blessings that our union with Christ brings us [or "that bring us to Christ"]."

New American Standard: "And I pray that the fellowship of your faith may become effective through the knowledge of every good thing which is in you for Christ's sake."

The New King James Version: "... hat the sharing of your faith may become effective by the acknowledgment of every good thing which is in you in Christ Jesus."

Good News: "My prayer is that our fellowship with you as believers will bring about a deeper understanding of every blessing which we have in our life in Christ."

Paul's use of *koinōnia*, linked in the context with the genitive πίστεως (*pisteōs*) and the possessive σοῦ (*sou*), requires strict attention. While *koinōnia* primarily means "common participation" in something, as equal sharers, the question raised by linking that word in the verse with *pisteōs sou*, "your faith," is whether that "common participation" should be understood as objective—the fellowship or sharing that results from faith—or as subjective—one's experience of a commonly shared faith. If Paul intended the subjective meaning, then his prayer for Philemon was that God would make him increasingly knowledgeable and effective in the ways that good can be accomplished for, in, and through Christ. "To perceive (or understand) and appreciate all the good [ἐπιγνώσει παντὸς ἀγαθοῦ *epignōsei pantos agathou*]" no doubt refers ultimately to beneficial deeds and helpful relationships. As he wrote or dictated this passage of the letter, Paul was surely solicitous for Philemon to respond graciously to the request he was about to make on behalf of that leader's returning slave, Onesimus.

REFLECTIONS

1. Paul wrote with a quill dipped in the inkwell of grace. He offered thanksgiving to God for Philemon, and he confessed this to Philemon, thus complimenting him. Everyone has times of feeling misunderstood or unappreciated. And we are usually strengthened when appreciation for us is expressed or when good deeds we have done are acknowledged. At the same time, the person who expresses that appreciation is usually gladdened for having done so. While it may sometimes be vain to seek approval, the need for recognition is a basic human quality.

2. Paul knew of Philemon's social position and wealth. Paul did not commend him, however, for either his station or his possessions, but rather for his gracious and more just use of them. Not only had Philemon done good in "refreshing the hearts of the saints," but he also had done so in right ways and in the right spirit. The dignity of those who benefited from Philemon's largesse was not undermined but undergirded by the spirit he showed in sharing. No wonder Paul, like many others, no doubt, heard about Philemon's "love for all the saints." One is reminded of the line in William Shakespeare's *The Merchant of Venice:*

How far that little candle throws its beams!
So shines a good deed in a naughty world. (5.1.90)

Differences in status or financial condition should never get in the way of helping someone in distress, especially someone in the community of faith (see Gal 6:10). Christian love not only establishes new "familial" bonds, but also dictates timely action when needs are known.

PHILEMON 8-20

PAUL'S REQUEST REGARDING ONESIMUS

COMMENTARY

Having reiterated the basis for rapport between himself and Philemon (this being clear from the singular use of "you" in vv. 4-21), Paul now begins the primary message the letter is sent to convey. Thus the "therefore" (διό *dio*), which here is translated "for this reason" (v. 8).

The intercession for Onesimus begins, couched in carefully chosen terms but offered in frankness: "I . . . appeal to you" (v. 9). Paul was aware that his situation as intercessor was legally defensible, Roman law having provided for cases of advocacy on behalf of runaway slaves who returned to their master. He also knew that he had a right to intercede on behalf of the now-converted runaway slave as Christ's apostle (thus the use of πρεσβύτης [*presbytēs*, "ambassador"]). Paul surprises us, however, by choosing not to appeal to Philemon from either position of authority. He makes his appeal for Onesimus "on the basis of love."

The appeal Paul is about to make is prefaced by a statement of relationship with Onesimus that notifies Philemon about a new fact concerning his runaway slave: "I am appealing to you for my child, Onesimus, whose father I have become during my imprisonment" (v. 10). John Knox commented that "this clearly means that Onesimus has become a believer in Christ under Paul's influence."[13] Peter T. O'Brien has suggested that:

This was the first news Philemon had received of his slave since he ran away and he might be expected to react negatively to the mention of his name. So with delicate tact Paul first establishes the central fact that Onesimus has become a Christian, converted during Paul's imprisonment.[14]

The situation of Onesimus as a runaway slave returning to face Philemon, his master, raises many questions. Why did Onesimus leave in the first place? Where did he go, and where could he expect refuge? If Onesimus had committed some crime, had Philemon published a reward notice regarding him? If so, then how widely would that reward notice have been circulated and known? If there was a reward notice, then Onesimus would have had increased need to remove himself as far from the master's arena of influence (Colossae) as resources and opportunity would allow. If he traveled as far from Colossae as Rome, then perhaps he came to Paul's notice through some encounter with Christians there, Onesimus having sought them out for whatever initial reasons.

But it is also possible that Onesimus went looking for Paul, aware of Paul's influence on Philemon. Paul could be an advocate for him in resolving his situation as a runaway slave. Roman law regarding returning slaves did allow a friend of the master to advocate on the returning slave's behalf in the interest of his or her safety and well-being.[15]

There are still other questions. Had Philemon disappointed Onesimus, promising manumission and then delaying it? Had Onesimus reached thirty years of age, when freedom was sometimes granted to faithful and deserving slaves, and escaped because he had been denied it?[16]

---

13. John Knox, "The Epistle to Philemon: Introduction and Exegesis," *Interpreter's Bible*, 12 vols. (Nashville: Abingdon, 1955) 10:567.
14. Peter T. O'Brien, *Colossians, Philemon*, WBC (Waco, Tex.: Word, 1982), 290.
15. See P. Lampe, "Keine 'Slavenflucht' des Onesimus," *ZNW* 76 (1985) 135-37. On reward notices about runaway slaves, see examples cited by C. F. D. Moule, *The Epistles of Paul the Apostle to the Colossians and to Philemon*, CGT (Cambridge: Cambridge University Press, 1957) 34-37.
16. See S. Scott Bartchy: ΜΑΛΛΟΝ ΧΡΗΣΑΙ: First-Century Slavery and the Interpretation of 1 Corinthians 7:21, SBLDS (Missoula, Mont.: Scholars Press, 1973) esp. 87-91. See also Francis Lyall, *Slaves, Citizens, Sons: Legal Metaphors in the Epistles* (Grand Rapids: Zondervan, 1984) esp. 39-45.

There is all too little about Onesimus's situation that can be stated with certainty; too much is left for conjecture. But the little that is given in the Letter to Philemon is positive rather than negative. Onesimus has become converted, Paul's "child" (τέκνον *teknon*) in the faith (v. 10). He is now even more "useful" than before, since we must assume that he had served Philemon in some meaningful capacity before his decision to leave or escape Philemon's household. Paul's statement that "formerly he was useless [ἄχρηστος *achrēstos*] to you" (v. 11) could have been intended to cover only the period Onesimus was absent from Philemon and the problems associated with that absence, and, therefore, was not intended to mean that Onesimus was always a lazy or shiftless person. The notice that "now he is indeed useful [εὔχρηστος *euchrēstos*] both to you and to me" completes Paul's play on the meaning of the returning slave's name Ὀνήσιμος (*Onēsimos*), which in Greek means "useful," "profitable." This name was common among slaves, either bestowed in tribute or perhaps as an incentive to usefulness and a master's profit. Now, as a converted person, Onesimus was more useful than ever.

Paul had no doubt benefited from that usefulness during the time Onesimus had been with him, thus his words "useful both to you and to me." Because of that usefulness, and having become fond of the slave, Paul would have kept Onesimus with him (see v. 13); but a reconciliation needed to occur between the runaway and his master. The two, as Christians, needed to become friends—no longer one the master and the other a slave. So Paul writes: "I am sending him . . . back to you" (v. 12).

The appeal Paul makes, on the basis of love, not law, is for Philemon to receive Onesimus back "no longer as a slave but more than a slave, a beloved brother—especially to me but how much more to you, both in the flesh and in the Lord" (v. 16). Here is the substance of the appeal. Paul knew that this request might well test Philemon's heart, so Paul reveals his own emotion, confessing that Onesimus was linked with his heart: "I am sending him, that is, my own heart, back to you" (NIV, "[he] is my very heart").

Raymond E. Brown maintains that through appealing to Philemon's cooperativeness rather than censuring him, Paul challenged "a Christian slave owner to defy the conventions: To forgive and receive back into the household a runaway slave; to refuse financial reparation when it is offered, mindful of what one owes to Christ as proclaimed by Paul; to go farther in generosity by freeing the servant; and most important of all from a theological viewpoint to recognize in Onesimus a beloved brother and thus acknowledge his Christian transformation."[17]

Paul has already stated that he was not seeking to impose his own will (v. 14) or to use any authority he possessed (v. 8) to achieve the goal of his appeal; but some forcefulness is evident in his words in v. 17, when he invokes the rules of partnership: "So if you consider me your partner, welcome him as you would welcome me." Having earlier referred to himself as Christ's "ambassador" (*presbytēs*, v. 9), Paul here suggests that Philemon favorably honor his petition by accepting Onesimus with the same cordial diplomacy an envoy or ambassador expects and enjoys in representing the one who sends him or her. By introducing the concept of partnership, a mercantile image, Paul thereby invokes its terms, calling upon Philemon to honor all that partnership involves and implies: acceptance, trust, regard, divisions of responsibility in a common purpose, and equality of sharing (in profits and losses).[18] This explains in part why Paul could so readily move forward to accept as his own any debts owed Philemon by Onesimus: "If he has wronged you in any way, or owes you anything, charge that to my account" (v. 18).

It must be noted from Paul's wording that he has allowed for the possibility of wrongdoing by Onesimus, but he does not mention that he knows of any. His "if" is probably more than rhetorical; it allows Philemon to reckon any damages due him, since only he would know of these. Like Paul's worthy greeting at the beginning of the letter, this gesture of willingness to assume responsibility for Onesimus, debts and all, was carried out in good faith. Paul was thus honoring the

---

17. See Raymond E. Brown, *An Introduction to the New Testament*, ABRL (New York: Doubleday, 1997) 506.
18. On the terms of partnership in the Roman society, see Lyall, *Slaves, Citizens, Sons*, 143-45.

mutual dictates of partnership, and Philemon was being challenged to do the same. To authenticate that this was his own true pledge as Onesimus's guarantor, Paul did what was his custom when certifying his involvement in some special matter or action, signing his name in his own special way: "I, Paul, am writing this with my own hand: I will repay it" (v. 19*a*). (On Paul's custom of authenticating his presence and involvement in a letter, see 1 Cor 16:21; Gal 6:11; 2 Thess 3:17.)

Interestingly, if Colossians was written by Paul—and at about the same time as the letter to Philemon—Paul may have thought about the situation of Onesimus as he wrote the injunctions addressed in Col 3:22-25 to Christians who were slaves, particularly the warning Col 3:25: "For the wrongdoer will be paid back for whatever wrong has been done, and there is no partiality." But immediately thereafter, this stricture addressed to masters appears: "Masters, treat your slaves justly and fairly, for you know that you also have a Master in heaven" (Col 4:1). Although the injunctions to masters and slaves in some of Paul's letters reflect aspects of the social structure of the churches he addressed, it is natural to wonder whether in this case he had Onesimus and Philemon in mind. Given his stress on justice and fairness regarding slaves, one can reasonably argue that while Paul understood societal conventions and social groupings, he saw some of them ultimately as antithetical to Christian fulfillment through the κοινωνία (*koinōnia*) relationship made possible in Christ, as Col 3:11 and Gal 3:28 dramatically declare.

REFLECTIONS

1. Pastoral or ecclesiastical authority based on church law is often used as a warrant and resource in dealing with church problems. However, the more Christlike and creative approach calls for the spirit of persuasiveness, conditioned by love; and this usually yields a more peaceable and long-lasting harvest of harmony.

2. It is the work of divine grace to make "unprofitable" persons profitable. When apprehended by a sense that God's favor is being personally felt and known, every person can be changed into someone whose life offers profit (beneficial fruit) to God and to others. This is the triumph of Christ, his very reason for coming into the world; but it happens only through his "begetting" work in our lives.

Those who have been "born anew" must show others what that new birth means and can effect in everyday, practical terms. The highest and noblest service we believers can render is to reach beyond established barriers of human separation, social class, and ethnicity and touch the lives of persons who are considered "different" and "unprofitable" and, like Paul, help them in Christ to become "useful." However wasted anyone's life may seem to be, that person must never be written off. God's grace can intercept us, intervene in our particular situations, inspire hope in our hearts, and bring about needed change in our lives. There is a purpose for the life of each and all, and there is a service to be rendered by each of us in this world.

3. Written as a personal request, the Letter to Philemon could be considered a missive of "limited application." But in the light of the social problems of slavery and the repercussions of its existence and support in the centuries since Paul's day, the concern Paul expressed in this brief letter must be understood and valued as more than an ancient and isolated issue. The important theme in the letter was never highlighted in any of the great theological debates of the ancient church. Divine providence was at work in preserving this letter, for it speaks more forcefully in these later times to us, perhaps, than it did in the first century CE to Philemon, its initial primary reader.

Paul sent Onesimus, a runaway slave, back to his master, Philemon. Many modern readers bristle at Paul's action. They are influenced by modern notions of freedom and an abhorrence of all systems that delimit and circumscribe human dignity. Why did Paul not provide Onesimus with continued refuge? And why did he not overtly condemn the system of slavery within the Roman Empire at that time?

One explanation offered is that Paul did not view slavery as a wrongful institution. Being a Roman citizen, and hence someone who enjoyed the privileges associated with that social boon, he accepted the empire's customs and social systems as a given, and hence he felt no need, even as a Christian, to oppose slavery.

Another explanation put forward defends Paul's deed of returning Onesimus to Philemon by appealing to Paul's apocalyptic views as expressed in 1 Cor 7:29*a*, 31*b*. It suggests that because of Paul's view that "the appointed time has grown short" and that "the present form of this world is passing away," he was tolerant of the slavery system and content to live with it, informed by an interim-ethic. However, it must be pointed out that apocalyptic concerns have often served as a catalyst for radical action and protest, both within the Old Testament period and in New Testament times.

There is another more sensible way to answer the question, and it forms an explanation based on three pieces of evidence: this very letter to Philemon, Paul's steady emphasis on freedom in his writings, and a statement in 1 Cor 7:21. All of these passages underscore the personhood of slaves and thus grant us fresh perspective for viewing the socioeconomic arrangement of the master/slave relationship. When Paul made his plea to Philemon to "receive [Onesimus, now converted] back no longer as a slave but more than a slave, a beloved brother" (v. 16), it should be forcefully clear that Paul wanted Philemon to honor their new tie as Christians *above and beyond* any legal demands. Their relationship was to be conditioned by love, not law, now that they were linked by faith, and not fealty.

Surely Paul must have sensed what this stipulation could mean in the long run and on an even wider scale, not only within but also beyond the household of Philemon. Paul's action here was that of a true ambassador, which is how he earlier described himself (v. 9). In returning Onesimus to Philemon, Paul used a form of diplomacy that appears to ignore one aspect of the slavery problem while offering his rationale for a new social arrangement that would in time effect a deeper concern and wider results.

4. In the *Declaration of Independence* of the United States, the first among the truths held and listed as "self-evident" are these: "that all men are created equal, that they are endowed by their Creator with certain unalienable rights." (Interestingly, at the time these truths were declared in writing, the Negro slave was not included, being viewed, rather, as but "three-fifths" of a person!) The full truth is this: Every person is unique and of worth because every person is made in the image of God; so human relations are fundamental and crucial. We who preach and teach must be leading examples and instruments of God's will in reaching out to people, in regarding each and all, in responding to acknowledged need, and in working steadily for the human good of all.

Unlike Paul's setting, which was dominated by Rome's monolithic, worldwide system of rule, our surroundings are smaller pockets of organized life within which our voices and votes and personal vision can have some impact. Paul was a significant actor within the world of his time, and his wit and will brought results far beyond his calculation and time. We who serve "the present age" must look to the same Lord for guidance in meeting the demands of our time and place. Paul was convinced that God's "plan for the fullness of time, [is] to gather up all things in [Christ]" (Eph 1:10). Our rightful work falls within that plan, and it is ours to serve our Lord with faith, courage, and commitment. While mindful that human servants can never bring in God's kingdom, we—like Paul—must work in this world with kingdom values informing and influencing our lives and deeds.

PHILEMON 21-22

Paul's Expectation to Visit

COMMENTARY

Paul was intent to do all within his power to reconcile Philemon and Onesimus. The apostle volunteered to remove any stumbling blocks to that desired end, and his letter spells out his role in the process. With Onesimus having been sent back to him, the rest would be up to Philemon. Paul asserted, doubtless for Philemon's encouragement, that he was "confident of [Philemon's] obedience" (v. 21), presumably to the dictates of Christian love, and that he expected Philemon to "do even more" than he had suggested.

Paul may have hoped that, once Philemon and Onesimus were reconciled, Onesimus might be released by Philemon to assist Paul in ministry. The slave was now "a beloved brother" who had proved to be "indeed useful"; his service was viewed by Paul as a possible further expression of Philemon's generosity (through Onesimus's manumission?). Onesimus could by mutual agreement be of service to Paul (in Philemon's place) during the apostle's imprisonment (see v. 13).

Paul expected eventually to be freed from prison and, therefore, expresses his hope to visit Philemon. Thus the second and last request made in the letter: "One thing more—prepare a guest room for me, for I am hoping through your prayers to be restored to you" (v. 22). The apostle was eager to visit Philemon and the believers at Colossae. This request reflects a more relaxed mood on Paul's part, but it also reflects his knowledge about Philemon's resources as a householder with the means to provide hospitality and support for guests at times of need. It is interesting that in reporting that he expects "to be restored to you," Paul returns to the plural for the first time since v. 3. This might well imply his recognition that Apphia—or even the entire membership of the house church—should also be informed of his plan to visit. Meanwhile, he lives in hope (ἐλπίζω *elpizō*) for this event, trusting their prayers, along with his own, to be fulfilled in God's time.

PHILEMON 23-25

CONCLUDING WORDS AND BENEDICTION

COMMENTARY

The list of persons who sent greetings along with Paul is instructive, and their appearance in this letter provides a clue regarding the location of Philemon and his house church. Epaphras, mentioned first as Paul's "fellow prisoner in Christ Jesus" (v. 23), would surely have known Philemon at close range, since he was from Colossae (see Col 1:7-8; 4:12-13). Described as a "fellow prisoner," which should be understood literally, Epaphras was no doubt serving as a personal attendant to Paul, perhaps quartered with him along with the soldier holding authority over Paul. The kind of custody Paul experienced as a Roman citizen allowed him freedom to "conscript" volunteers to serve his outside interests while confined himself. It is possible that by adding "in Christ Jesus" to the description, Paul is really describing Epaphras as standing in close relation to him as a slave would be; a personal slave would have a freedom of access to an imprisoned "master" that others, even close friends, could not share.[19] Epaphras's role as a personal attendant, then, was something different in kind or extent than Timothy's, who is referred to as "our brother" (v. 1), while Mark, Aristarchus, Demas, and Luke are described as "my fellow workers" (v. 23).

Mark, here, is the same John Mark of the book of Acts (see Acts 12:12, 25; 15:37, 39; Col 4:10; 2 Tim 4:11; 1 Pet 5:13), and it is likely that the Aristarchus mentioned here is the same person spoken of in Acts 19:29; 20:44; 27:2; and Col 4:10. If the view is accepted that the Letter to Philemon was written from Rome, then one can harmonize the data in Acts and Colossians to locate Aristarchus with Paul during Paul's imprisonment there, and thus relate Colossians and Philemon as having been written at about the same time. Demas, also mentioned elsewhere as being among Paul's circle of workers (Col 4:14; 2 Tim 4:10), joined Paul, Luke "the beloved physician" (Col 4:14), and the others in a statement of greeting to Philemon as Paul prepared to close the letter.

The letter required no final instructions. Its message had been shared, its appeal made, and a confidence expressed that its purpose would be honored. So Paul concluded the letter with his customary, brief, but earnest, benediction: "The grace of the Lord Jesus Christ be with your spirit" (v. 25). F. F. Bruce, in his commentary on this letter, asked: "Was Paul's request granted? Yes; otherwise the letter to Philemon would not have survived. That it survived at all is a matter calling for comment, but if Philemon had hardened his heart and refused to pardon and welcome Onesimus, let alone send him back to Paul, he would certainly have suppressed the letter."[20]

---

19. On the terms of partnership in the Roman society, see Lyall, *Slaves, Citizens, Sons*, 143-45.

20. Bruce, *The Epistles to the Colossians, to Philemon, and to the Ephesians*, 200.

REFLECTIONS

A close look at the names of those who joined Paul in his final greeting to Philemon brings to view some treasured members of the apostle's circle. Those names, and the histories connected with them, also provide evidence of Paul's charisma as a person and as a leader.

Paul's personality involved something contagious that went far beyond any limitations to his physical appearance. Based on a legendary account of how he looked—the account being so plain and unflattering that the legend seems to embody some truth—Paul was "a man small of stature, with a balding head and crooked legs, in a good state of body, with eyebrows meeting and nose somewhat hooked, full of friendliness."[21] That phrase "full of friendliness"[22] tells much about how Paul was known as a person and as a leader.

Three among those named were Gentile Christians: Epaphras, Demas, and Luke; the other two were Hebrews. The New Testament records both their distinctiveness and their unity. Most important, they were vital and valued members of Paul's circle. They were with him because Paul was a dynamic, creative leader.

What were some of Paul's leadership traits?

(1) Paul led as he was being led: "Be imitators of me, as I am of Christ" (1 Cor 11:1). Enthralled by his Lord, that supreme person Christ Jesus, Paul was forever busy listening for Christ's voice, forever seeking to fulfill the vision laid out for his life by his Lord. Paul not only knew the name "Jesus," but also *he experienced the risen Jesus.*

(2) Paul appreciated, recognized, and encouraged others. The many gracious compliments found in his letters are genuine, and not merely contrived. He was not making verbal backslaps with political ends in mind. Leaders of integrity, leaders who value people as persons, avoid the semblance of friendship.

(3) Paul always kept "the big picture" in view as he planned and worked. Even in this letter, something larger remains in view than the reconciling of Onesimus and Philemon, as essential as that was. Paul was eager to see the Christian enterprise move forward with greater effectiveness (see v. 6).

(4) Paul knew how, when, and to whom to delegate responsibilities. He needed to enlist the help of others, to be sure, but he also trusted their help and complimented those who gave it.

(5) Paul observed protocol, doing what he sensed to be right at the right time and in the right way.

(6) Paul had goals and sought to reach them through strategic means: prayer, planning, and the help of others, providing honest and honorable incentives to those who assisted him. The Letter to Philemon well illustrates this.

(7) Paul's leadership was characterized by the *servant-leader attitude.* He was not self-centered. He aspired to live what Martin Buber referred to in another connection as an "unexalted life."[23] "Christ will be exlated now as always in my body, whether by life or by death" (Phil 1:20*b*).

These were some of the traits Paul's circle of friends were familiar with as they followed his lead. Small wonder, then, that he remained so influential and that his coterie of workers remained so loyal. Paul had that personal "power" about which Ralph Waldo Emerson commented in one of his essays: "Who shall set a limit to the influence of a human being? There are [leaders], who, by their sympathetic attractions, carry nations with them, and lead the activity of the human race."[24] While each of us has particular gifts with which to further the cause of Jesus Christ, we, too, would do well to follow Paul's lead as appropriate to our circumstances.

---

21. F. F. Bruce, *The Epistles to the Colossians, to Philemon, and to the Ephesians,* NIGNT (Grand Rapids: Eerdmans, 1984) 200.

22. Cited from *New Testament Apocrypha,* vol. II: *Writings Relating to the Apostles, Apocalypses, and Related Subjects,* ed. Edgar Hennecke, Wilhelm Schneemelcher, Eng. trans. ed. Robert McLachlan Wilson (London: Lutterworth, 1965) 353-54. The assessment of the account as embodying "a very early tradition" is that of W. M. Ramsay, *The Church in the Roman Empire: Before* A.D. 170 (New York: G. P. Putnam's Sons, 1893) 32.

23. See Maurice Friedman, *Encounter on the Narrow Ridge: A Life of Martin Buber* (New York: Paragon House, 1991) 44.

24. Ralph Waldo Emerson, "Power," in *Ralph Waldo Emerson: Essays and Lectures,* compiled by Joel Porter (New York: Library of America, 1983) 971.

THE LETTER TO THE HEBREWS
INTRODUCTION, COMMENTARY, AND REFLECTIONS
BY
FRED B. CRADDOCK

THE LETTER TO THE HEBREWS

INTRODUCTION

The Christian faith grows out of and is sustained by the conversation between the church and its Bible. From this engagement, generation after generation, come the beliefs, the ethics, the liturgy, the purposes, and the relationships that define the Christian faith. To be sure, other voices enter the conversation, invited and uninvited, affecting the language used and the conclusions reached; but the primary and most influential partners are the community and the book. Of course, not all persons in the community are equally engaged in the conversation; some prefer to be silent, and some are silenced. Neither do all the books of the Bible participate equally. The reasons for this unevenness usually lie in the contents of the writings themselves, but not always. Sometimes there is quite a distance between what a document has to say and the church's willingness or ability to hear it. The Letter to the Hebrews is a case in point.

Why has Hebrews not had a stronger and more influential voice in the conversation between the church and the Bible? This is not to imply that this letter has been silent or silenced. On the contrary, Hebrews has been called on to say a few words at quite a few assemblies of the church. Most commonly it is to offer the benediction:

> Now may the God of peace, who brought back from the dead our Lord Jesus, the great shepherd of the sheep, by the blood of the eternal covenant, make you complete in everything good so that you may do his will, working among us that which is pleasing in his sight, through Jesus Christ, to whom be the glory forever and ever. Amen. (13:20-21 NRSV)

However, there are other, and some would say more important, moments in the worship service at which Hebrews is invited to speak. Among churches that use the ecumenical lectionary, Hebrews provides the epistle reading every year on Good Friday as well as on Monday and Wednesday of Holy Week. Likewise, during the Christmas season, the prologue to Hebrews (Heb 1:1-4) always sings the praise of Christ in tandem voice with the prologue to the Gospel of John (John 1:1-14). Congregations that observe the Annunciation to Mary (March 25) and the Presentation of Jesus in the Temple (February 2) hear every year brief passages from Hebrews.

For two brief periods between Pentecost and Advent semi-continuous readings from this epistle give preachers and listeners opportunities for a bit more extended engagement with Hebrews. Interestingly, this letter, which speaks every year on Good Friday, never says a word during the Easter season or on Pentecost. Does this seasonal silence reveal something about the message of the book or merely the preferences of the conversation partner, the church? We may discover an answer as we engage the text.

The ecumenical lectionary reflects what is broadly true of the conversation between the church and the Bible; namely, that while Hebrews is invited to speak on occasion, the church is not as attentive to this voice as it is to others, such as Romans or 1 Corinthians. Scholars have intervened on behalf of Hebrews: The author demonstrates greater skill in the use of the Greek language than does any other New Testament writer, including Luke; Hebrews is the finest example of homiletical rhetoric available to us from the first century CE; this letter offers the most elaborate Christian reading of the Old Testament to be found in the New Testament; as a theologian, the writer of Hebrews is not inferior to Paul or John. These witnesses have been heard with appreciation, but the distance between the church and Hebrews remains. Why?

Before the search for reasons takes us inside the letter itself, a partial explanation may lie in the location of Hebrews within the canon. In a New Testament of 251 pages, Hebrews begins on page 208. Justified or not, a position near the end is read as a value judgment. The reader of the New Testament moves through the Gospels, Acts, and Paul's writings as a traveler on a well-lighted street, not quite familiar but providing enough names and addresses so as to remove the sense of one's being a stranger. However, once past Paul, the traveler finds the road uncertain, the houses dimly lit, and no familiar landmarks. The temptation is to stop and turn back to the Gospels, Acts, and Paul. After all, for these areas there are excellent maps.

In addition to its location in the canon, this letter suffers from a title that has a distancing effect on the reader. Granted, the title is a later scribal addition (more later), but still it is the first word the reader sees—large bold print over the entrance to whatever may await the one who enters. Other titles temporarily distance us—after all, we are not Galatians, Corinthians, or Philippians—but these are geographical designations. All of us have traveled enough to know that initial strangeness soon dissolves, and, once inside, we find ourselves more alike than different. But "Hebrews" is not a geographical term; it is ethnic, and ethnic distances are more complex, more difficult to negotiate, requiring more energy than some people are willing to expend.

Once inside, the reader never relaxes, never quite feels at home. The paragraphs are not written in such a way that they can easily be extracted for devotional or sermonic use; rather, they are carefully linked in one long sustained argument. The furniture seems permanently in place. As for the message of the argument, it is offered in an idiom strange to most readers. The writer is certainly not estranged from the Christian tradition that we meet elsewhere in the New Testament, nor is there any attempt to contradict it. Rather, that tradition is recast in categories and images that make vivid and vital what other writers were content to handle by allusion and implication. As a framework for understanding the redemptive work of Christ, the writer takes us inside the cultus of the tabernacle of Israel's wilderness journey. Priest, altar, sacrifice, atoning blood, and cleansing rituals—these are not the ancient and remote trappings of a people past but the stuff of the writer's presentation of what Christ has done and is doing for us now.

Most other New Testament writers, in making christological affirmations, use Ps 110:1: "The LORD says to my lord,/ 'Sit at my right hand/ until I make your enemies your footstool'" (NRSV). Only Hebrews compels us to look at v. 4 of that psalm: "The LORD has sworn and will not change his mind,/ 'You are a priest forever according to the order of Melchizedek'" (NRSV). Suddenly a shadowy figure, hardly holding a place in the margin of our memories, moves center stage in the explication of christology. Most readers are not in familiar country. The author assumes an audience familiar enough with the Old Testament to make detailed exegesis of its texts convincing, word studies delightful, and swift allusions powerful. Most congregations will acknowledge, "We are not that audience." Then can one argue that the theological and practical yield from the extra work required of the reader will make the effort well worth it? Without qualification, yes.

In this brief survey of reasons for the church's relative inattention to Hebrews, one other matter needs to be mentioned: the very stern nature of its imperatives. Even though the writer does not think the readers have reached the point of no return (Heb 6:9), that grim possibility is held up before them in very sharp language. Those who receive all the blessings of salvation and then fall away are beyond restoration (Heb 6:4-6). Those who willfully continue in sin face the fearful prospect of certain judgment (Heb 10:26-29): "It is a fearful thing to fall into the hands of the living God" (Heb 10:31 NRSV). Be warned by Esau, says the writer, who sold his birthright, then later sought to regain it but "found no chance to repent, even though he sought the blessing with tears" (Heb 12:17 NRSV). A letter containing such sentences is usually attractive only to those groups who deal easily in judgments and ultimatums. Certainly those churches that not only do not believe they are anywhere near such dangerous spiritual brinks but also do not believe that such brinks even exist will look to other writings for words more gentle and gracious. Especially for those who have luxuriated in a world of grace without ethical demand, who regard all moral urgings as quaint echoes of a puritan past, Hebrews is not welcome reading. Investigation into the situation of the letter's recipients will not dull these sharp warnings, but will very likely increase empathy and understanding for both the writer and the readers.

Perhaps this is the moment to caution all who read Hebrews, especially those who read with a view to teaching or preaching to others, to be patient. Be in no hurry to collapse the distance between the church and the text. Restrain the appetite for immediacy, for a "lesson for today." Trust that that will come in due season. Recall the reminder of Clement of Alexandria that the Bible does not yield its hard-won truths to every casual passerby. It is in the service of that needed patience that the following introductory considerations are offered.

HISTORICAL CONSIDERATIONS

Author. The King James Version answers the question of authorship quite clearly: "The Epistle of Paul the Apostle to the Hebrews." That heading does not simply reflect the opinion of English translators in 1611; that opinion has a long history. In a papyrus from the third century CE, designated P[46] in the Chester Beatty collection, Hebrews follows Romans among the letters of Paul. Both Clement and Origen, leaders in the great Christian intellectual center of Alexandria, judged the content of Hebrews to be from Paul. However, the style of the letter was so different from the remainder of the Pauline corpus that they concluded the actual writing to have been done by another, perhaps Luke or Clement of Rome. This uncertainty, growing out of the language and style of the letter, is preserved in a note at the end of Hebrews in the KJV: "Written to the Hebrews from Italy by Timothy."

In the Western church, early writers and lists do not include Hebrews among the letters of Paul. Tertullian, for example, suggested Barnabas, a candidate supported by three arguments: his close association with Paul (Acts 9:27; 13:2–15:39); his name, which Luke interprets as "son of encouragement" (Acts 4:36); Hebrews is called a "word of exhortation" (Heb 13:22; "encouragement" and "exhortation" translate the same Greek word [παράκλησις *paraklēsis*]; and the fact that Barnabas was a Levite (Acts 4:36). Hebrews exhibits a detailed knowledge of the Levitical priesthood. However, by the fifth century CE, under the strong influence of Augustine and Jerome, the Western church had accepted Pauline authorship, a position dominant until the Reformation.

The debate would not die. Students of both Paul and Hebrews found difficulty attributing to Paul the language and literary style of this epistle (if, indeed, it is an epistle), the centrality of the cultus, a priestly christology, and the admitted second-generation position of the writer. Would Paul, who insisted his gospel was not from any human source but from a revelation of Jesus Christ (Gal 1:11-12), have written: "It was declared at first through the Lord, and it was attested to us by those who heard him" (Heb 2:3 NRSV)? There has been no lack of other candidates, Silas, Priscilla, and Apollos among them. Luther's choice was Apollos, the Jewish Christian from Alexandria, eloquent and well versed in the Scriptures (Acts 18:24). Among recent scholars who have been interested to pursue the question of authorship, the most extended arguments have been in support of Apollos as well.[1]

There was a time when establishing the authorship of a book was vital in arguing for its canonicity. Today, concerns about authorship are almost totally related to the larger issue of interpreting the text. Knowing the author would be of some help, but neither canonical authority nor theological merit depends on having that knowledge. In the case of Hebrews, although the name is lacking, the writer does have some visibility. The author was a Christian who lived and thought within the apostolic tradition (Heb 2:3). Timothy had been a companion in ministry and might be again (Heb 13:23). The writer was temporarily distanced from the readers but expects to return to them soon (Heb 13:19, 23). Their situation is known in great detail, either through their leaders (Heb 13:7, 17, 24) or by direct association. The writer joined strong pastoral concern with the authority of either person or office. Both the instructions and the exhortations of the letter reveal a person well educated in Greek rhetoric as well as in Judaism, especially Hellenistic Judaism formed in part by the Septuagint, a Greek translation of the Old Testament. The Greek translation and not the Hebrew text provides the major lines and the subtler nuances of the writer's argument and appeal.

Date. As with most documents of the New Testament, establishing the time of writing of Hebrews cannot be done with precision or certainty. However, with the external and internal evidence available, a chronological frame can be ascertained. The primary external evidence is the letter of Clement of Rome to the church in Corinth. In chapter 36 of that letter, Clement quotes and paraphrases key passages from Hebrews 1:1–3. Clement's letter is generally, though not unanimously, dated 95–96 CE. Thus Hebrews must be dated earlier, but how much earlier? For an answer, we look for internal evidence.

It must be pointed out that three arguments for dating based on internal evidence that once held favor among commentators are now considered seriously flawed. First, the high christology of Hebrews (the pre-existence, incarnation, and exaltation of the Son of God) demands as late a date as possible. This evolutionary view of christology cannot be supported by the New Testament. For example, high christology can be found in Paul's writing (1 Cor 8:6; 2 Cor 8:9; Phil 2:5-11), and he quite possibly quoted from earlier sources. Second, since Hebrews describes the priestly activity and culture of Israel using the present tense (e.g., Heb 7:27-28; 8:3-5; 9:7-8), then the letter must be dated prior to the fall of the Temple in the year 70 CE. However, it is not the temple cultus but that of the wilderness tabernacle that is presented for comparison and contrast with the sacrificial work of Christ. As for the use of the present tense, this literary device is commonly used in the service of persuasion, and as we shall see, the writer was a skilled rhetorician. And finally, if the Temple no longer existed at the time of writing, the writer would have used that fact as a strong argument against the validity of Judaism's claims. The fault of this argument is not only that it is based on silence but also that it fails to understand the author's perspective toward Judaism and the Old Testament. The writer appeals to the Old Testament as a living Word of God and presents his case for the Christian faith as being in continuity with that Word. To read Hebrews as an attack on Judaism is to misread Hebrews.

What, then, can we say about internal evidence for dating? Concerning his message, the writer says: "It was declared at first through the Lord, and it was attested to us by those who heard him" (Heb 2:3 NRSV). This statement seems to place the author in the generation following the apostles. In addition, we are told that Timothy was still active in ministry (Heb 13:23). If this is the same Timothy who was a young companion to Paul, a date between 60 and 90 CE would likely be appropriate. Since Clement knew the letter by the year 95, then we may consider the years 60–95 CE as the chronological frame for Hebrews. Obviously, we lack precision, but fortunately, precision in fixing the date of writing is not essential for understanding the message of the letter.

Intended Audience. For interpreters of this letter, more helpful than knowledge of author or date would be the identification of the intended readers. Who were they? Where were they?

---

1. Anyone wishing to follow this matter further will be well informed by H. W. Montefiore, *A Commentary on the Epistle to the Hebrews* (London: A and C Black, 1964) 9-16; and Luke T. Johnson, *The Writings of the New Testament* (Philadelphia: Fortress, 1986) 215-16.

Quite early the addressees were identified as "Hebrews" in a scribal conjecture that gave to the document the heading "To Hebrews." It is with this "title" that the writing appears in the earliest manuscript evidence of its existence, a papyrus (P^{46}) from the beginning of the third century CE. But the heading raises more questions than it answers. Quite likely the scribe who made the designation did so on the basis of the content of the letter itself. Let us do the same: Allow the letter to characterize its recipients, and then determine if we can give them a name and an address.

It must be said at the outset that the intended readers are Christian (Heb 3:6, 14; 4:14; 10:23), lest the heading to the letter lead someone to think the writing was addressed to Jews in order to convert them. The work is not polemical but a strong pastoral exhortation to a church in crisis. The writer knew the readers, having been with them earlier and now hopeful of a return soon (Heb 13:19, 22-23). The relationship between the author and the addressees is not clear. Urging the church to obey their leaders (Heb 13:17) implies that the writer is one in a position of even greater authority, either by reason of office or long relationship. The entire letter carries a tone of authority, of one who has the right and the obligation to remind, to instruct, to warn, and to encourage.

The readers along with the writer were second-generation believers (Heb 2:3-4), having been baptized (Heb 6:4-5; 10:22) and fully instructed (Heb 6:1-2). In fact, they had been believers long enough to have become teachers (Heb 5:12), but had been stunted in their growth. In a vigorous pastoral move, the writer on the one hand chastises them for their infantile spiritual state (Heb 5:11-14) and on the other hand assumes that they are capable of following a lengthy and complex christological argument (6:9–10:39). Their earlier instruction not only focused on their "confession" (Heb 3:1; 4:14; 10:23), perhaps a digest of the faith (is Heb 1:1-4 that confession?), but also included extended engagement with the text of the Greek Old Testament. The author's freedom to argue from nuances of the Greek translation of the Hebrew text and to make allusions to persons and events in Israel's history certainly implies a familiarity with that material on the part of the addressees.

But the readers are a faith community in crisis. Some members have grown lax in attendance at their assemblies (Heb 10:25), and commitment is waning. If the writer's urgings are problem specific, then we have in the letter a painfully clear image of their condition. Listen:

Let us hold fast to our confession. (Heb 4:14 NRSV)

Therefore lift your drooping hands and strengthen your weak knees, and make straight paths for your feet, so that what is lame may not be put out of joint, but rather be healed. (Heb 12:12-13 NRSV)

See that you do not refuse the one who is speaking; for if they did not escape when they refused the one who warned them on earth, how much less will we escape if we reject the one who warns from heaven! (Heb 12:25 NRSV)

Anyone who has violated the law of Moses dies without mercy "on the testimony of two or three witnesses." How much worse punishment do you think will be deserved by those who have spurned the Son of God, profaned the blood of the covenant by which they were sanctified, and outraged the Spirit of grace? (Heb 10:28-29 NRSV)

The writer does not think the addressees have already fallen away (Heb 6:4-8) or are yet in the condition of Esau, who "found no chance to repent, even though he sought the blessing with tears" (Heb 12:17 NRSV). In fact, better things are expected of these believers in view of their past record of love and good works, a record that has not totally come to an end (Heb 6:9-10). The author recalls that past during which they were cheerful, generous, and caring under most difficult circumstances and asks them not to abandon what they possessed as dearer than life itself (Heb 10:32-39).

What is the root cause of this crisis in the church? The text of Hebrews reflects not one but a number of factors. The delay of the final return of Christ may have had a demoralizing effect in the community (10:25, 35-39). It has been speculated by some that all the attention on the cultus in this letter implies a felt need among the readers for a more adequate liturgical and ritual life. The long-held theory that Hebrews addresses the problem of Jewish Christians returning to Judaism has been argued in terms of a more attractive cultus or of the security of a long and established tradition or of government protection from persecution, a privilege enjoyed within Judaism at various times and places. There is no doubt that the addressees had been under extreme external pressure. Some members had been imprisoned, and others suffered the confiscation of their property (Heb 10:34). They had not yet shed blood for their faith (Heb 12:4), but the writer does use the words "persecution" (Heb 10:33), "hostility" (Heb 12:3), and "torture" (Heb 13:3 NRSV). By no means the least painful form of pressure was public abuse and ridicule (Heb 10:33). More recent cultural and sociological studies of the New Testament have opened our eyes to social, political, and economic values that governed life in the Mediterranean world. Chief among those values were honor and shame. It is difficult to imagine that the Christians addressed in Hebrews were not facing daily the problem of suffering dishonor as followers of one who endured the shame of the cross (Heb 12:2).[2]

Whatever may have been the external factors contributing to the crisis of the community of readers, the fact that the writer responds to them with a lengthy and carefully argued christological presentation strongly implies that at the heart of the crisis was a christology inadequate for their social context. Perhaps they had a christology that was long on divinity but short on humanity, providing no way to fit the flesh and blood, lower than angels, tempted, crying and praying, suffering and dying Jesus into the larger scheme of God's redemption. Or perhaps their christology ended with the exaltation and enthronement of the Son and offered no good news of his continuing ministry of intercession for the saints. At least in the writer's view, the crisis can best be met not with improved structures or social strategies but with a more complete christology.

Can we, from the text of Hebrews, name and locate the addressees? Not with any confidence. Focus on the cultus does not necessarily place the readers in Jerusalem, nor does an assumption of the readers' knowledge of the Greek Old Testament argue conclusively for a Jewish past. Paul made heavy use of the Old Testament in exhorting the Corinthians, who were presumably of Gentile background. Jewish and Hellenistic thought had been long blended as evident in such writings as the Wisdom of Solomon and the vast religious-philosophical works of Philo of Alexandria. The clues in the text have been too many and too few, prompting theories of identification ranging from Christian Zionists on their way to Jerusalem to Gnostic spiritualists, pilgrims moving through this alien world to the eternal realms from which they came.[3]

If we broadly identify the readers as Hellenistic Jewish Christians, perhaps the best guess for their location is Rome. When the writer says, "those from Italy send you greetings" (Heb 13:24 NRSV), it is not clear whether the expression locates the writer or the readers in Italy. Similarities to 1 Peter, a letter written from Rome (1 Pet 5:13), argue for a Roman origin. However, early knowledge of Hebrews by Clement of Rome indicates a Roman destination, and what we know of the house churches in Rome makes that city a likely candidate as the location of the addressees.[4]

THEOLOGICAL CONSIDERATIONS

Any overview of the theology of Hebrews must be prefaced with two observations: (1) The theology of the epistle is woven into a lengthy argument and can be extracted only at the risk of

---

2. A strong case has been made for understanding Hebrews in these categories by David DeSilva, *Despising Shame: A Cultural-Anthropological Investigation of the Epistle to the Hebrews*, SBLDS 152 (Atlanta: Scholars Press, 1995).

3. For anyone wishing to pursue further these various views, W. L. Lane, *Hebrews 1–8*, WBC 47A (Waco, Tex.: Word, 1991) li-lx, provides a brief but clear discussion along with a thorough bibliography.

4. For anyone wishing to pursue further these various views, Lane, *Hebrews 1–8*, lviii-lx.

the loss of its vitality, and (2) the theology of the epistle is rhetorically presented in the service of urgent pastoral exhortations and can be extracted only at the risk of the loss of its purpose. With these cautions in mind, the reader of Hebrews might benefit from a brief sketch of its major theological tenets, most of which the writer and readers have in common, and some of which represents the writer's imaginative elaboration of elements within that common tradition of belief.

God. This is not a Christian writing so preoccupied with the person of Jesus or the work of the Holy Spirit that God is pushed into the background as a silent assumption. On the contrary, God is the subject of the opening sentence, the closing benediction, and the narrative of redemption in between. God created and maintains the world through the Son (Heb 1:2-3, 10; 2:10; 3:3-4; 11:3). The entire redemptive career of Jesus, from incarnation to exaltation, was according to God's will (Heb 10:7). It is God who offered the promise of rest to Israel (Heb 3:7-11) and continues to hold out that promise today (Heb 4:1-11). God enters into covenants with those who trust (Heb 8:8-12) and holds always before us not only the prospect of judgment (Heb 9:27; 10:30-31; 12:23) but also the promise of a better home, an abiding place, a heavenly city of God's own building (Heb 11:10, 13-16; 13:4). To describe God's work of love toward believers, the writer uses categories of cosmic proportions. The category of time stretches from creation to consummation; the category of space reaches from the real and abiding world above (Heb 8:4-6; 10:1) to this temporary world of shadows, not substance.

The single most recurring characteristic of God as portrayed in this letter is that God speaks. God spoke through the prophets (Heb 1:1), speaks through a Son (Heb 1:2), speaks through the Old Testament (Heb 1:5-12; 4:3, 7; 7:21; 8:8-12) and through the Holy Spirit (Heb 10:15-17). Important to notice is the frequent use of the present tense; God's voice is a living voice, whatever the medium through which it comes.

Jesus Christ. No New Testament writer presents a more human Jesus than does the author of Hebrews. In fact, among all the titles used to refer to the Christ, the writer's preference seems to be "Jesus." That Jesus was one of us (Heb 2:11), tempted as we are (Heb 4:15), that he submitted to God in tearful and prayerful obedience (Heb 5:7-8), and was subject to death (Heb 2:14) constituted for some within and without the church a flaw in the Christian faith, an offense to the human quest for honor and place. But the writer of Hebrews, rather than denying or subordinating such a portrayal of Jesus, accents it as essential in the larger scheme of redemption. As a priest, Jesus had to be chosen from among the people (Heb 5:1) in order to be able to sympathize with their weakness (Heb 4:15) and to "deal gently with the ignorant and wayward" (Heb 5:2 NRSV). As we shall see, establishing that Jesus was a priest, even though not a Levite, is the extraordinary theological achievement at the heart of the letter. Being one of us not only qualified Jesus to be a merciful priest, but also equipped him to be the model to whom believers look. He is the pioneer and perfecter of the faith pilgrimage, showing his followers how to bear suffering, endure hostility, and disregard shame (Heb 12:1-3). Believers could not be expected to walk in the steps of one who had not walked in theirs.

However, this is not the total picture; Hebrews rivals the Gospel of John in moving beyond the historical evidence to declare who Jesus really is in the grand sweep of God's saving purpose. Anyone who charges that the writer of Hebrews has reduced christology in order to portray Jesus as a model and guide to a church in crisis has not read the entire book.[5] Jesus was lower than the angels "for a little while" (Heb 2:9), incarnate (Heb 1:6; 2:14-18; 10:5-7) to make purification for sins (Heb 1:3), but is now seated at God's right hand (Heb 1:3), a high priest forever, making intercession for the saints (Heb 4:14–5:10; 7:23-25; 8:1-2). In a related but slightly different line of reasoning, the writer presents Jesus as the mediator of a new and better covenant (Heb 9:15–10:18). At the end of the age, Christ will return "to save those who are eagerly waiting for him" (Heb 9:28 NRSV; 10:37). These can be the achievements only of one who was not only of the people but also of God, and that he was of God the writer leaves no doubt. Jesus' divinity is anchored in his pre-existence as God's Son, heir of all things, agent of creation, sustainer of all things, the very mirror image of God's glory and character (Heb 1:2-3).

---

5. E. Käsemann almost makes such a charge against Hebrews in *Jesus Means Freedom* (Philadelphia: Fortress, 1970) 101-16.

In their assemblies the readers most likely recited as a confession this inclusive, embracing Christ's pre-existence, incarnation, and exaltation.

Holy Spirit. Hebrews does not contain any trinitarian formulas. God is the primary character in the narrative, and the person and work of Jesus Christ occupy the central place in the argument developed. However, the role of the Holy Spirit is of such significance as to merit our attention. The Holy Spirit is a revealer, with words of the Old Testament being attributed to the Spirit (Heb 3:7-11; 10:15-17), although some of the same words are also attributed to God (Heb 4:3). The Spirit is also an interpreter of the Scriptures (Heb 9:8). In relation to Christ, it was through the Spirit that he offered himself as a sacrifice without blemish to God (Heb 9:14). In relation to the church, the Holy Spirit comes as gifts to the members, distributed according to the will of God (Heb 2:4; 6:4). Because Christians share in the Holy Spirit, any willful persistence in sin constitutes a grave sin against the Spirit, called by the writer an "outrage" (Heb 10:29). It may also be said of the Spirit in Hebrews that along with God and Christ, the Holy Spirit provides continuity in revelation and in redemptive activity between Israel and the church.

Church. Even though the word usually translated "church" (ἐκκλησία *ekklesia*) occurs only twice in Hebrews (Heb 2:12; 12:23), it is quite clear that the writer is addressing a congregation, a group identified by a confession of faith (Heb 4:14), having been called together as a fellowship of brothers and sisters, of each other and of Christ (Heb 2:11-17). They assemble regularly to offer the sacrifice of praise to God (Heb 13:13), to provoke one another to love and good deeds (Heb 10:24), and to identify through compassion and sharing with those members who are imprisoned and tortured (Heb 13:3). In addition to love for one another, they are obliged to love strangers, showing hospitality (Heb 13:1-2), and to make every effort to be at peace with everyone (Heb 12:4). In the two modes of the Christian life, tenacious faithfulness and continuous pilgrimage toward the city that is to come—that is, possessing both stability and flexibility—Christ is the model. He was unwavering in faithfulness to God and undeterred as the pioneer leading his people to glory.

Scripture. The Scripture for the writer of Hebrews is the Old Testament in Greek translation, hereafter referred to as the Septuagint (LXX), even though points at which the writer varies from the LXX as we have it will be noted. Even though the author holds in common with the readers a Christian tradition, no writings from that tradition known to us are quoted as Scripture. The only words of Jesus that appear in Hebrews are at 2:12-13 and 10:5-7, where words from Psalms and Isaiah are attributed not to the writers of those passages but to Christ. The Old Testament comes to the reader in direct quotations, paraphrases, and allusions. Sometimes the original historical context is preserved; sometimes a passage is set in a new context. Interestingly, the writer's appropriation of the life and faith of Israel is drawn from an earlier appropriation by the psalmist.

Why does the author draw so heavily on the retelling of Israel's narrative in the psalms? Is the reason hermeneutical? That is to say, is the writer's use of Scripture simply a continuation of what the psalmist had done, putting an old story in a new setting? Or is the reason liturgical, using Israel's worship materials to interpret and enrich the culture and liturgy of the church? Of course, the reason may be more practical: the psalms best provide the grounds for the author's own theological and christological construction. In any case, in this rich and imaginative engagement with Scripture, the Old Testament never ceases to be the living voice of God. In fact, the authority of the Old Testament is enhanced for the readers by the writer's practice of introducing quotations from it with the phrases "God says," "Christ says," and "the Holy Spirit says." As we shall see, the writer of the epistle does not, in an act of interpretive tyranny, simply make irresponsible raids on the Old Testament to construct his own theological house, leaving among his scriptural sources not one stone upon another. Hebrews is not only the most extended treatment of the Old Testament in the New, but is also, along with Luke, the most respectful of continuity. The Bible tells one story, not two, and it is the story of God's saving initiative toward humankind. This metanarrative is carried forward through many subnarratives.

LITERARY CONSIDERATIONS

Those who teach and preach the Bible are increasingly aware that literary factors no less than historical and theological ones demand attention in an honest and fruitful hearing of the texts. Every writer wants both to say something and to do something, and therefore employs available literary devices and rhetorical strategies in order to be clear and to be effective. The careful reader of Hebrews will, therefore, want to attend to the manner as well as the matter of this work. To alert us to the literary and rhetorical skills of this writer and to prepare us for a fuller experience of reading and hearing, we here attend briefly to three matters: integrity, genre, and structure.

Integrity. Keep in mind that the word *integrity* used in a literary discussion refers only to the unity of a writing and not to the merits of its content. In other words, is any part of the text from a different hand or from the same hand but not intended by the writer to be a part of this document? The question arises with Hebrews only with reference to chapter 13.

Doubts as to whether chapter 13 was originally a part of Hebrews have been prompted by two observations, one minor and one major. The minor observation is that there is a noticeable shift in both mood and content between chapters 12 and 13. Such a break, however, is not uncommon at that point where a writer concludes an argument and then moves to a list of practical admonitions, usually rather standard, along with words of a personal nature (note Gal 6:11; Rom 15:14; 16:1). There is no Greek manuscript of Hebrews that concludes at chapter 12. The major observation concerns the contrast between the epistolary ending (Heb 13:18-25) and the non-epistolary beginning. In its opening Hebrews is similar to 1 John alone among New Testament epistles, the others having the customary address, signature, and greeting. This seeming discrepancy has prompted, among other theories, speculation that chapter 13 was added by another person, perhaps a secretary or a disciple or someone imitating Pauline conclusions in an effort to get Hebrews accepted into the Pauline corpus. Analyses of vocabulary and themes in chapter 13 have not supported such theories. In fact, the unity between this chapter and the main body of the letter has been so convincingly argued that very few voices are raised to the contrary.[6]

Genre. Accepting chapter 13 as integral to the entire writing does, however, pose another question: What does one call a document that ends as a letter but begins as an oration? I have in these introductory comments continued to use the traditional designation "epistle," and there are some students of Hebrews who do not find sufficient reasons to abandon it. After all, in the ancient Mediterranean world, "epistle" (ἐπιστολή *epistolē*) could be used to refer to writings ranging from private correspondence to public statements sometimes posted on bulletin boards. As for the difference between the beginning and the ending, Hebrews is not alone in that feature. For example, James is like Hebrews, but in reverse: It begins as a letter but ends as an oration. Nor can one argue conclusively that the content of Hebrews is not epistolary. Writings indisputably epistolary contain expositions of Scripture with application (1 Cor 10:1-14), moral instruction (Gal 5:13–6:10), and even strong exhortations that seem to interrupt the context (2 Cor 6:14–7:1). Even so, there is no major gain or loss to the interpreter in proving Hebrews is or is not a letter in any formal sense.

However, when a writing bears a self-designation the author has provided a category that helps the reader to understand both the purpose of the communication and the literary strategies employed to achieve it. Hebrews is, says the writer, a "word of exhortation" (Heb 13:22 NRSV). This expression occurs at Acts 13:15 to refer to Paul's speech in Acts 13:16-41, a speech noticeably similar to Hebrews. Harold Attridge thinks "word of exhortation" is "probably a technical literary designation for a certain kind of oratorical performance."[7] Whether or not there is sufficient evidence to support such a claim, the term does alert the reader to what the writer is doing. For example, every reader of Hebrews observes the alternation between exposition and application throughout the work. But to the question of whether applications are simply postscripts to a major expository argument or exposition of Scripture serves the application, the

---

6. See Floyd V. Filson, *"Yesterday": A Study of Hebrews in the Light of Chapter 13* (Naperville, Ill.: Alec R. Allenson, 1967).
7. Harold Attridge, "Paraenesis in a Homily," *Semeia* 50 (1990) 217.

writer gives an answer: This is not a word of exposition but a word of exhortation. Even the most elaborate expository sections serve as fuel to keep alive a fire that seems to be flickering out. The writer rushes forward after each phase of the argument, eager to press home the lessons from every Old Testament text cited.

In the expression "word of exhortation" a host of literary devices and rhetorical strategies find their reason. Notice the force of an argument expressed in double negatives (Heb 4:15; 6:10; 7:20); the energy of words joined without the homogenizing effect of conjunctions (Heb 7:3, 26; 11:32-34, 37; 12:25); the sharp edges of vivid contrasts (Heb 7:18-20, 23-24, 28; 10:11-12); the cumulative effect of repeated phrases, such as "by faith" in chapter 11; and the pleasant attention-getting sounds of alliteration (Heb 1:1; 2:1-4; 4:16; 10:11). Metaphors abound, drawn from athletics, agriculture, education, architecture, seafaring, courts of law, and more. Verbs are noticeably in the present tense, and the language of speaking prevails over that of writing (Heb 2:5; 5:11; 6:9). Greek and Latin rhetoricians had long urged these and other strategies in the service of persuasion. There is no question that the writer is preaching.

However, simply to call Hebrews a homily seems not sufficiently to acknowledge its magnitude and complexity. After all, a homily, at least in the early days of the church, was an informal discussion or conversation about a topic (Luke uses the word in his Gospel at 24:14-15), and Hebrews exhibits the formal qualities of a carefully constructed piece of rhetoric. And a homily lacks the complexity of Hebrews, which is not solely a sermon but a sermon containing sermons (e.g., Heb 1:5–2:4; 2:5–3:1; 8:1–10:25). In this respect, Hebrews resembles Deuteronomy, which is Moses' final sermon to Israel but also is a collection of sermons within the sermon. If, then, in the commentary to follow Hebrews is sometimes called a letter and sometimes a sermon, the reader will understand why both are true but neither is fully true.

Structure. While there is broad agreement about the rhetorical skills of the writer of Hebrews, there is no consensus about the structure of this sermon. Some analyses fail because they try to fit Hebrews into one of the three major types of ancient rhetoric: Is it forensic, persuasion concerning the truth of a past event; or deliberative, persuasion concerning a future decision or course of action; or epideictic (ceremonial), persuasion concerning the virtues of one whose life is worthy of emulation? The fact is that Hebrews contains some of all three. Other analyses prove inadequate because they locate focal points in the expositions or doctrinal portions and merely attach the exhortations as subordinate to the argumentation. The location and extent of hortatory materials make it clear that for the writer these sections are of equal if not greater importance for the purpose of the sermon. At the risk of making oversimplified divisions, the following broad outline may give some perspective:

Exposition 1:1-14
Exhortation 2:1-4
Exposition 2:5–3:6
Exhortation 3:7–4:16
Exposition 5:1-10
Exhortation 5:11–6:20
Exposition 7:1–10:18
Exhortation 10:19–13:25

Such a flat list does not register the cumulative effect of sections tumbling one upon the other. No analysis focusing on exposition alone can be fair to the whole. Perhaps all structural displays fail to the extent that they lose sight of the extremely urgent pastoral situation that prompted Hebrews. A concerned leader seeks to persuade a church from its path of decline in faith and communal love before it is too late. Every communication skill must be called into service because the end is to save a church, not to please an instructor in a rhetoric class. Perhaps this accounts for there being too many rather than too few clues to the structure of Hebrews within the composition; the writer speaks to a crisis.

All recent attempts to discern the structure of Hebrews have had to respond to the lifelong studies of A. Vanhoye.[8] He was impressed by the remarkable symmetry of the work and came to the conclusion that it was structured concentrically, moving toward and away from the central argument. This literary form is called a chiasmus, fairly common in briefer units in the New Testament. In this case, the chiasmus consisted of five parts: 1:1–2:18; 3:1–5:10; 5:11–10:39; 11:1–12:13; 12:14–13:25, on the pattern of ABCB´A´. This means that parts one and five are parallel, parts two and four are parallel, and part three is the centerpiece. Support for Vanhoye's analysis has been only partial; but reading Hebrews in this pattern has been stimulating, and modifications of his conclusions have found their way into much of the literature on Hebrews.[9]

A major problem with Vanhoye's and other similar analyses, however, is a practical one. Granted, Heb 7:1–10:18 is a major and complex section for which the writer gradually prepares the reader, but is it the climax? If so, one would expect that after Heb 10:18 the arguments and exhortations would draw heavily from the theological achievement of that central section; otherwise, why have the climax in the center of the composition? But such is not the case. Chapters 11–13 make only minimal use of the lengthy argument about Christ's priesthood. The final three chapters move the reader to a climax of intellectual, emotional, and volitional energy at the point where homiletically it belongs: at the end.

Therefore, the outline offered below as a framework for the commentary is not concentric but rather cumulative. The final exhortation in Heb 12:12–13:19 is the end toward which the writer moves from the very beginning, where the faith held in common with the readers is recited.

8. Vanhoye's literary analyses of Hebrews began in the early 1960s, and his publications have been in French. However, the fruit of his work is available in English in A. Vanhoye, *Structure and Message of the Epistle to the Hebrews* (Rome: Pontifical Biblical Institute, 1989).

9. For a review of various structural analyses and their justifications, see Lane, *Hebrews 1–8*, lxxv-ciii.

BIBLIOGRAPHY

Commentaries:

Attridge, H. W. *A Commentary on the Epistle to the Hebrews.* Hermeneia. Philadelphia: Fortress, 1989. Detailed and scholarly treatment of the text with citations of pertinent primary sources and in conversation with other students of Hebrews.

Bruce, F. F. *The Epistle to the Hebrews.* NICNT. Rev. ed. Grand Rapids: Eerdmans, 1990. Solid evangelical scholarship made available to serious students of the Bible, both lay and clergy.

Buchanan, G. W. *Hebrews.* AB 36. Garden City, N.Y.: Doubleday, 1972. An unusual interpretation of Hebrews as a document of early Christian Zionism.

Ellingworth, P. *The Epistle to the Hebrews: A Commentary on the Greek Text.* NIGTC. Grand Rapids: Eerdmans, 1993. Studies of words and phrases of the original language of the text, helpful to persons unfamiliar with Greek.

Jewett, R. *Letter to Pilgrims.* New York: Pilgrim, 1981. An interpretation of Hebrews in the light of the heresy addressed in Colossians.

Lane, W. L. *Hebrews 1:1–8; Hebrews 9:1–13.* WBC 47A and 47B. Dallas: Word, 1991. Detailed treatment of the text accompanied by a full bibliography and strong theological reflections.

Montefiore, H. W. *A Commentary on the Epistle to the Hebrews.* Harper's NT Commentary. New York: Harpers, 1964. Sound scholarship available to non-specialists, often differing from traditional views.

Williamson, R. *The Epistle to the Hebrews.* London: Epworth, 1965. An interpretation of Hebrews in the light of Greek philosophy mediated through Judaism.

Wilson, R. M. *Hebrews.* NCBC. Grand Rapids: Eerdmans, 1987. Results of scholarship offered to non-specialists with brevity and clarity.

The following special studies in Hebrews will enrich one's understanding of the letter, its theology, literary form, interpretive method, and use of the OT.

Hay, David M. *Glory at the Right Hand: Psalm 110 in Early Christianity.* SBLMS. Nashville: Abingdon, 1973. An examination of the uses of Psalm 110 in the NT and other early Christian literature.

Hughes, Graham. *Hebrews and Hermeneutics.* SNTSMS. Cambridge: Cambridge University Press, 1979. An analysis of Hebrews as a Christian interpretation of OT texts.

Hurst, L. D. *The Epistle to the Hebrews: Its Background of Thought.* SNTSMS. Cambridge: Cambridge University Press, 1990. An interpretation of Hebrews in the philosophical and religious contexts of the first century.

Käsemann, E. *The Wandering People of God.* Translated by R. Harresville and I. Sandberg. Minneapolis: Augsburg, 1984. A commentary on the major sections of Hebrews in relation to the religious syncretism called Gnosticism.

Lindars, Barnabas. *The Theology of the Letter to the Hebrews.* Cambridge: Cambridge University Press, 1991. An exploration of the major theological themes in Hebrews.

In addition, the reader's attention is called to articles cited in the Commentary that may offer further help in preaching and teaching Hebrews.

OUTLINE OF HEBREWS

I. Hebrews 1:1-4, Introductory Statement of Faith

II. Hebrews 1:5–2:18, The Son and the Angels

    A. 1:5-14, The Son Superior to Angels
    B. 2:1-4, Therefore Listen Carefully
    C. 2:5-18, The Son Lower Than Angels
        2:5-9, He Became as We Are
        2:10-18, A Faithful and Merciful High Priest

III. Hebrews 3:1–5:10, Christ, the Faithful and Merciful High Priest

    A. 3:1–4:13, Christ the Faithful
        3:1-6, Christ and Moses Compared
        3:7-11, The Faithless People
        3:12-19, Failure to Enter God's Rest
        4:1-11, God's Rest Still Available
        4:12-13, God's Word Still Active
    B. 4:14–5:10, Christ the Merciful
        4:14-16, Hold Fast; Draw Near
        5:1-10, Christ Qualified as High Priest

IV. Hebrews 5:11–6:20, Preparation for the Difficult Discussion

    A. 5:11–6:3, A Call for Maturity
    B. 6:4-12, Stern Warning with Hope
    C. 6:13-20, The Ground Hope

Hebrews—Introduction

V. Hebrews 7:1–10:39, The Difficult Discussion

    A. 7:1-28, Christ and Melchizedek
        7:1-3, Melchizedek, King and Priest
        7:4-10, Melchizedek Is Superior to Levites
        7:11-19, A New Priesthood
        7:20-25, Confirmed by God's Oath
        7:26-28, Christ, Our Eternal High Priest
    B. 8:1–10:18, The High Priestly Ministry of Christ
        8:1-5, Christ's Sanctuary
        8:6-13, Christ's Covenant
        9:1–10:18, Christ's Sacrifice
        9:1-14, The Old and the New Sacrifice
        9:15-22, Sacrifice and the New Covenant
        9:23–10:18, The New and Final Sacrifice
    C. 10:19-39, Life in Response to This Ministry of Christ
        10:19-25, A Threefold Admonition
        10:26-31, Warning About the Future
        10:32-39, Encouragement from the Past

VI. Hebrews 11:1–12:17, A Call to Fidelity and Mutuality

    A. 11:1-40, Learning from Our Forebears in Faith
        11:1-2, The Meaning of Faith
        11:3-7, Faith: From Creation to Noah
        11:8-22, Faith: From Sarah and Abraham to Joseph
        11:23-31, Faith: Moses and Israel
        11:32-38, Faith: Prophets and Martyrs
        11:39-40, Faith: Fulfilled in Christians
    B. 12:1-17, A Call to Continue in Faith
        12:1-3, Look to Jesus
        12:4-11, Regard Suffering as Discipline
        12:12-13, Regain Your Strength
        12:14-17, Again, Be Warned

VII. Hebrews 12:18–13:19, Final Exhortations

    A. 12:18-29, Zion, the Unshakable Kingdom
    B. 13:1-19, Life in the Faith Community
        13:1-6, Mutual Duties
        13:7-8, Examples to Follow
        13:9-16, Christ's Sacrifice Revisited
        13:17-19, Concerning Your Leaders

VIII. Hebrews 13:20-25, Benediction and Greetings

    A. 13:20-21, Benediction with Doxology
    B. 13:22-25, Greetings and Farewell

HEBREWS 1:1-4

INTRODUCTORY STATEMENT OF FAITH

COMMENTARY

With a literary artistry unmatched in the NT, the writer of Hebrews begins addressing the readers. Verses 1-4 consist of one carefully composed sentence called a "period"—that is, a sentence that makes a complete circle around the track (περίοδος *periodos*). So rich and full is this sentence that it is understandable why English translations would aid the reader by making of it three (NRSV) or four (NIV) more manageable statements. Before attending to its details, let us appreciate the author's remarkable achievement in this one sentence. The reader's attention is captured and held by a number of rhetorical devices: alliteration (five words in verse 1 begin with the letter π (*p*); contrast (long ago/in these last days; to our ancestors/to us; by the prophets/by a son); repetition (of relative pronouns and participles); and temporal sequence (pre-existence, incarnation, exaltation). But artistry also serves substance; the sentence expresses the faith held in common with the readers. The passage is not at all polemic, seeking to correct errant views, or pedagogical, pressing new and additional ideas on the recipients. In fact, the writer may be quoting, in entirety or in part, from the liturgy of the church addressed. Whether these verses contain the "confession" often mentioned (3:1; 4:14; 10:23) cannot be determined. We can, however, appreciate the strategic importance of creating an atmosphere of trust by beginning on common ground. And finally, the writer accomplishes several practical ends in the opening sentence: (1) With a theocentric beginning, arguments of both continuity and discontinuity between Judaism and Christianity have room. God is the subject of both testaments. (2) The categories of speaking and hearing are appropriate to a "word of exhortation" (13:22) and anticipate the oral quality of the entire discourse. (3) The opening sentence is also programmatic in that it introduces most of the major themes to be developed in the "sermon," even using the language of two OT texts very central to all that follows, Psalm 2 and Psalm 110. And (4) the final clause (v. 4) allows the author to introduce the subject of the first major unit (1:5–2:18), Christ and the angels.

Many commentators divide vv. 1-4 into two parts: vv. 1-2, in which God is the actor, and vv. 3-4, in which the Son is the actor. However, this discussion will separate v. 3 and v. 4, reasons for which should be apparent.

1:1-2. The sermon that we call Hebrews is predicated on the affirmation that God speaks (1:5-13; 3:7; 4:3; 5:5-6; 7:21; 8:8-13) and on the injunction, "See that you do not refuse the one who is speaking" (12:25 NRSV). This foundational conviction is broadly framed in vv. 1-2 in a balanced statement. God:

spoke	has spoken
in the past	in these last days
to our ancestors	to us
by the prophets	by a Son

God's speaking in the past was "in many parts or segments" and "in many forms." Such sweeping introductory statements characterizing the past were fairly common among Greek rhetoricians.[10] Here the writer describes God's past revelation in three ways. First, it was in segments or episodes, not continuous. Second, God's speaking took many forms, and the OT bears witness to these forms: voices, events, visions, dreams,

---
10. For examples, see H. W. Attridge, *A Commentary on the Epistle to the Hebrews*, Hermeneia (Philadelphia: Fortress, 1989) 37nn. 17-18.

stories, and theophanies, among others. Third, revelation came through the prophets. There is no reason to understand prophets here in a restrictive sense, as distinct from the Law and the Writings. In the broader sense, the term "prophets" was used to refer to those who spoke for God, and for the writer of Hebrews certainly included Moses and David. God's speaking begins in Genesis (Heb 11:3).

Continuous with and yet distinctly different from past revelation is that which is "to us." God's speaking is here presented with two strong qualifying phrases. First, it comes "in these last days." The expression is not so much chronological as it is eschatological. Such was the accepted meaning among the prophets (Isa 2:2; Dan 10:14; Hos 3:5; Mic 4:1), and for early Christians, the eschaton was inaugurated by the advent of Jesus Christ. Second, God has spoken "by a Son." There is no need to add "the" Son or "his" Son as some translations do, as though there were a need to specify to whom the writer refers. About that there is no doubt. In the present instance, the absence of the definite article seems quite purposeful. As a general rule, in Greek the presence of the definite article serves to identify, and its absence serves to qualify. In other words, what is the quality or nature of God's speaking? It is through the person of a Son and through the relationship of that Son to God. Past segments and forms of revelation are neither minimized nor negated, but the writer's conviction is clear: In a Son God has spoken the culminating Word.

Although God continues to be the subject of the verbs in v. 2 ("appointed," "created"), the reader's attention is now being drawn to the Son. In two strong assertions the writer presents the credentials qualifying the Son to be the speech of God. In the first, Psalm 2, which provided the title "Son," is drawn upon again for the title "heir of all things."

"You are my Son;
today I have begotten you"?

Ask of me, and I will make the
nations your heritage,
and the ends of the earth your possession.
(Ps 2:7-8 NRSV)

This psalm will be one of the major sources for developing the christology of Hebrews. In good rhetorical style, the author introduces early texts and themes that will be addressed fully at a later point. The same is true of the metaphor of inheriting; it will be a favorite term to speak not only of the Son but also of the promised future of the faithful (1:14; 6:12, 17; 9:15; 11:7, 8; 12:17). As for the Son, "heir of all things" describes his pre-existent life with God. Perhaps it is not too soon to become alert to a tension in the christology of Hebrews (which the author does not attempt to resolve) between what the Son has in pre-existence and what the Son gains by reason of his work of redemption and exaltation to God's right hand. In other words, is his last state a return to the first or is the last greater than the first? As for the "all things," the writer likely includes, but is not limited to, the inheritance granted the Son-King of Psalm 2. It is enough to say that nothing of God's is withheld from the Son.

The second assertion in v. 2 adds further to the Son's qualifications to be the eschatological Word of God: The Son was God's agent of creation. That God worked through an intermediary in creating is an idea that developed in Jewish theology (Prov 8:22-31; Wis 7:22), the intermediary being called Sophia ("Wisdom" [σοφία *sophia*]) or Logos ("Word" [λόγος *logos*]). The church appropriated these terms in developing its understanding of the relation of Christ to God, and praise of Christ as agent of creation entered quite early into hymn and creed (John 1:3, 10; Rom 11:36; 1 Cor 8:6; Col 1:16). The "worlds" (NRSV) and "universe" (NIV) translate αἰῶνας (*aiōnas*), "aeons" or "ages." The word came to have both a temporal and a spatial meaning. As will be noted later, categories of time and movement toward the future are more important for this writer than are categories of space and distance.

1:3. Here the opening statement takes a noticeable turn, as registered by the translators' decision to begin a new sentence. Verse 2 spoke of God's relation to the Son; v. 3 speaks of the Son's relation to God. Some scholars account for the shift by seeing this verse as all or part of an early christological hymn that has been skillfully incorporated by the writer.[11] Certainly elements found in passages widely accepted as hymns (Phil 2:6-11; Col 1:15-20; 1 Tim 3:16) are here: the relative pronoun ὅς (*hos,* "who," translated here as "he"), balanced phrasing (being, sustaining, having made), and a full display of the Son's sojourn (pre-existence, humiliation, exaltation). If the author is quoting a hymn, he has woven it well into the larger affirmation.

The last two affirmations about the Son move away from the wisdom source and into the christological theme that will be the major burden of the letter. It is not enough to summarize these two final clauses of v. 3 as the humiliation and exaltation of the Son. The humiliation is cast in sacerdotal and priestly terms: He made purification for sins (cleansing of sins, here and at 2 Pet 1:9). The whole of the Son's earthly career is gathered up in one image: a priest at the altar making purification for sins. The brief depiction anticipates and begs for the elaboration soon forthcoming. And then in the only finite verb in v. 3 the writer sums up both the completion of the Son's work on earth and his elevation to the highest station: He sat down at the right hand of the Majesty (a reverential substitute for God). The Son-Priest is enthroned. The source of this portrayal of the Son is Psalm 110, the most significant psalm in the development of New Testament christology[12] and the key text for Hebrews. Peculiar to Hebrews, however, is the use of both v. 1 and v. 4 of Psalm 110 to join king and priest in the presentation of Jesus Christ. Son-Priest-King—already the writer has set out the themes of his sermon and the burden of his argumentation.

1:4. This final affirmation about the Son in the introductory statement of faith serves as a transition to the first major unit of the text, 1:5–2:16, in which the subject is the Son's relationship to angels. The declaration of the superiority of the Son over the angels seems abrupt and polemic in a way that the difference between God's speaking through the prophets and through a Son did not. Until v. 4 one feels no debate, but rather a confession held in common between the writer and the readers. But now to say that the Son is greater than the angels is to give the impression that some persons of a contrary view are in the audience or are known to the audience. The phrase "superior to" or "greater than" will occur thirteen times in the writer's presentation of his christology. It can be argued, therefore, that v. 4 was not a part of the confession of faith but has been added by the author to introduce the first major theme. But not necessarily. The statement of faith in 1:1-4 may have been framed in its entirety in a community of faith where angels functioned in their theology either as a threat to the superior place of Christ or simply as a foil against which the lofty status of Christ was played. The reader will have to devote attention in the next unit to this question, Why introduce angels into the discussion? As for the "more excellent name" the Son inherited (again, a favorite expression of the writer's; see Commentary on 1:2), that name is most likely "Son" whether the inheriting was in pre-existence (v. 2) or after his humiliation and exaltation. For Paul the name given above every other name was "Lord," bestowed on Christ after God had exalted him (Phil 2:9-11). Thus far, the writer has not used the designations "Christ" or "Lord," or the name "Jesus."

---

11. See J. T. Sanders, *New Testament Christological Hymns* (Cambridge: Cambridge University Press, 1971) 19-20, who follows suggestions of earlier scholars. The writer of Hebrews is indebted to Jewish wisdom theology for the first two of the four statements concerning the Son. As noted earlier, wisdom was God's agent in relating to the world in creation, providence, revelation, and reconciliation. According to Wisd Sol 7:24-27, Sophia is the mirrored reflection (radiance) and exact imprint (representation) of God's being. These two terms are found nowhere else in the NT. God's being is here ὑπόστασις (*hypostasis*), "essence" or "substance." An interesting use of the word occurs at Heb 11:1: Faith is the *hypostasis* of things hoped for. At Heb 1:3 the writer is saying that what God is, the Son is (cf. John 1:1). The author also appropriates for the Son wisdom's providential and sustaining relation to the created order. The Son's word, which will also be in Hebrews God's word and the Holy Spirit's word, not only speaks life into being but also sustains it continually. As Paul puts it, "one Lord, Jesus Christ, through whom are all things and through whom we exist" (1 Cor 8:6 NRSV); and again, "in him all things hold together" (Col 1:17 NRSV). The term "all things" (τὰ πάντα *ta panta*) was in Hellenistic philosophy a technical term for the universe, the totality, visible and invisible. Christian writers, and especially Paul, adopted the expression to announce the cosmic dimensions of Christ's work. Nothing and no one lies beyond the reach of God's activity through the Son.

12. The subtitle of David Hay's *Glory at the Right Hand* (Nashville: Abingdon, 1973) is Psalm 110 in Early Christianity. He traces the role of the psalm in the christologies of the NT and non-canonical writers.

REFLECTIONS

1. From the outset the reader is reminded that the subject of the Christian faith is God. It is a regrettable fact that theocentricity is absent from much Christian teaching and preaching. To be sure, writing and speaking about Jesus Christ in a community already firm in its faith in God as Creator, Sustainer, and Redeemer is appropriate. Such is the case with early Christian documents written from within or addressing Judaism in which faith in God lay at the heart of a long history. But when those writings are taught or preached in cultures for whom faith in God may not already be present, beginning with christology is beginning too late. The appropriate starting point is "In the beginning, God . . ." even if the discussion will eventually focus on Christ or the Holy Spirit or the church. The writer of Hebrews does not forget this, and by stating rather than assuming the centerpiece of Christian faith reminds the church to be discerning in what it can and cannot assume about the culture to which it speaks. It could be calamitous to get people attached to Jesus without any faith in God.

2. God speaks—never so loudly that every casual passerby hears, but God speaks nevertheless. God's self-revelation is the cornerstone of both Judaism and Christianity. That creation is a medium of revelation is affirmed in both Testaments, especially in wisdom literature, but the weightier freight of revelation is carried by persons, by relationships, and by events. If God did not speak to us, we would be left with a painfully vague yearning for God, a hunger still unsatisfied after a feast of sunsets and songbirds.

3. This introductory statement of faith is so worded as to lead the reader to anticipate either a discussion or a demonstration of the continuity and discontinuity between Christianity and Judaism. Every major New Testament writer struggled in some way with this issue, but none opted for discontinuity alone. Later there were voices such as Marcion's, who called for a Bible stripped of all Jewish writings; but those voices did not prevail. The composition of the Christian Bible testifies to that and calls upon every generation of Christians to deal with the problems of continuity and discontinuity in the formation of its own faith. How will the author of Hebrews deal with this important matter? That it will be dealt with is announced in 1:1.

4. The old sentimental image of the early church as a huddle of the poor and unlettered at the margins of society is shattered by the artistry and sophistication of Heb 1:1-4. Here is a creedal formula, perhaps framed for the liturgy of the congregation to be sung long before it became official dogma, in which is distilled the heart of the Christian faith. Within it is a christological hymn not unlike others in the New Testament (v. 3).[13]

---

13. See J. T. Sanders, *New Testament Christological Hymns* (Cambridge: Cambridge University Press, 1971).

HEBREWS 1:5–2:18

THE SON AND THE ANGELS

OVERVIEW

The confession of faith in 1:1-4, which contains in digest the major affirmations of the entire letter, concludes with the declaration that the Son is superior to the angels. Most modern readers would have been content with a reference to the exaltation and enthronement of the Son, with no mention of angels. Angels seldom if ever appear in the theologies and christologies of Christian communities today. In Hebrews, however, the author not only introduces them in 1:4 but also discusses them at length in 1:5–2:16. Undoubtedly there are strong reasons for doing so, the discovery of which is a primary task of the investigation of this unit. And it must be done here; angels appear elsewhere in Hebrews only at 12:22 and 13:2 in brief references to the assumed world of the readers and not as factors in any substantive discussion. Before moving to the subject of angels, however, it would be helpful to note the ways this unit contributes to an understanding of the method and the content of the epistle as a whole.

First, the reader is immediately immersed in citations from the OT. Scriptural allusions appeared earlier (Ps 110:1 and Wis 7:25-26 at 1:3), but beginning at 1:5 direct quotations begin and continue with great frequency until the end of the letter. Between thirty and thirty-five (depending on whether one counts verse fragments) OT passages are explicitly cited, most of them from the psalms. Some are repeated, bearing the weight of lengthy argumentation; others appear only once but are no less vital to the unfolding message of the writer. No generalizations can be drawn about the author's principles of interpretation until specific uses of Scripture are examined.

Second, in this early unit the reader meets the writer's habit of introducing biblical quotations with verbs of speaking ("God says") rather than of writing ("it is written"). This pattern is not surprising, given the portrayal of God at the outset as having spoken and continuing to speak (1:1-2). Nor is this way of introducing Scripture passages unique to Hebrews; the writer of Matthew (Matt 1:22; 5:21, 27, 31, 37, 38, 43) and Paul (Rom 10:11-13; 15:10; 1 Cor 6:16), among others, do the same. However, both Matthew and Paul easily alternate between "speaking" and "writing," while in Hebrews the introductory formula, "it is written," occurs only once in a direct citation (10:7) and the noun form (γραφαί *graphai*, "writings" or "scripture") not at all. While the speaker of the biblical citations may vary (God, the Son, the Spirit, or "someone somewhere") the author's preference for this method of presenting Scripture is abundantly clear.

What does this phenomenon mean for the reader? Hearing the OT being "said" to them has significance at two levels for the reader. On one level is the rhetorical impact. After all, Hebrews is a sermon (13:22), and, therefore, we should expect the author to employ rhetorical strategies. Fundamental to the art of persuasion is the task of making what is absent, by time or by space, present to the hearer or reader. A direct quotation accomplishes that far more effectively than does a paraphrase or a summary, and if that quotation is presented as the speech of God, presence is achieved most dramatically. In addition, if such formulations are kept relatively free of the writer's comments, they are regarded by the reader as far more reliable. As a case in point, notice how minimal is the author's involvement in 1:5-14—only brief phrases joining seven OT quotations. On the theological level, the implications of the author's rhetorical style are unmistakable: The OT is the very speech of God. The words of Scripture are not past speech being dragged into the present by means of hermeneutical maneuvers on the part of the writer; they are God's words to the present. The modern reader is, of course, nervous. What appears to be an uncritical transfer of content from past to present seems too easy a purchase of continuity between the OT and the NT. The questions are many, but at this point it is enough that we observe the writer's method and sense something of the rhetorical and theological force.[14]

A third and final observation prompted by this unit and helpful toward understanding the entire epistle concerns the structure of 1:5–2:18. Notice two features, the form and the movement. The form is quite clear: exposition (1:5-14); exhortation (2:1-4); exposition (2:5-18). This pattern of alternating exposition and exhortation will be sustained until the writer's closing remarks. However, that the exposition serves the exhortation will be increasingly clear as the reader moves to the later chapters. At 13:22 all debate ceases; the writer identifies his work as "my word of exhortation." The movement of the unit, and of the epistle, however, is less obvious but certainly discernible and no less impressive.

One example of the way the author moves a subject or theme into the reader's thinking is 1:3. In a most concise way, the Son is presented as priest and king; he makes purification for sins and is seated at God's right hand. The scriptural allusion is to Psalm 110, but that text is neither quoted nor discussed further—that is, until 1:13. At that point only v. 1 of Psalm 110 is quoted, apparently solely in the service of the immediate issue, the superiority of the Son over the angels. The reader remembers 1:3, the kingly enthronement of the Son at God's right hand, but what about the other half of the affirmation of 1:3, the Son as priest? That reappears at 2:17 in a fuller statement: The Son is "a merciful and faithful high priest." This statement anticipates, but does not yet make use of, v. 4 of Psalm 110. The writer plants the seed and further cultivates the idea at 4:14, but then only gradually. Finally, Ps 110:4 is quoted at 5:6, the reader being reminded of its affirmation at 5:10, again at 6:20, and then finally its full exposition beginning at 7:1. And so the author has led the reader to the very difficult central argument of the epistle, and by what path? First an allusion to the priest-king of Psalm 110, the gradual unfolding of one-half of the affirmation, and then the ever so gradual unfolding of the other. Such movement of ideas is not only artistic but is pedagogically and rhetorically sound as well.

We return now to the central subject of 1:5–2:16, Christ and the angels, and to the question prompted by that subject: Why all this attention to angels? We have to assume that asserting Christ's superiority over angels is important for both the writer and his readers. It is not a matter of debating the existence or non-existence of angels; these beings were common to the assumed worlds of late Judaism, Christianity, and other religions of the Near East. Angels (the word ἄγγελοι [*angeloi*] means "messengers") were commonly portrayed as God's intermediaries in all the ways God relates to creation and to humanity in particular. In some quarters angelologies were very complex, even including angels who revolted against God and devoted themselves to thwarting God's purposes (Matt 25:41; Rom 8:38; Gal 4:3).[15] Are we to assume such a backdrop to Hebrews?

Judgment as to why the writer of Hebrews develops a christology over against angels in 1:5–2:16 should be reserved until investigation of the passage is complete. However, it might be helpful to place the best options before us as we proceed. One option maintains that the writer felt the need to elaborate on the reference to angels in the creedal formula in 1:1-4. All items in the opening confession are developed in the letter, but this one, that the Son is superior to angels, is the least important to the writer and readers and, therefore, is treated first and dismissed. The procedure might be compared to dealing early with "he descended into hell" in a discussion of the Apostles' Creed in order to give primary attention to its other affirmations. A second view holds that the nature and role of angels was not a live issue for the readers and, therefore, provided a perfect foil for a recital of the greatness of Christ. No debate, no polemic, is involved here. A third position takes the

---

14. For anyone interested in further study of this form of argumentation, I recommend G. W. Savran, *Telling and Re-telling,* Quotation in Biblical Narrative (Bloomington: Indiana University Press, 1988).

15. Anyone wishing to review the whole subject of angels will find quite thorough and fair the article "Angel," Theodor Gaster, *Interpreter's Dictionary of the Bible,* 6 vols. (Nashville: Abingdon, 1962) 1:128-34.

subject of angels more seriously. Two issues are engaged. First, since it was believed that the law was given through angels (2:2), any adequate defense of the superiority of Christianity to an audience steeped in or attracted to Judaism must establish that Christ is superior to angels. Second, since Christ suffered and died, how can he be superior to angels? That apparent contradiction must be addressed. Some commentators have conjectured that some of the readers may have resolved the problem by holding to an angel christology in which Christ only seemed to suffer and die but in reality was an angel on a mission for our salvation.

A fourth and final position on the question of why the writer argues that Christ is superior to angels insists that the writer is confronting the problem of angel worship in the church of his readers. The most recent advocate of this view, Robert Jewett, interprets Hebrews by means of Colossians.[16] To be sure, within the complex and somewhat obscure heresy at Colossae was the practice of the adoration of angels (Col 2:8-19),[17] but to find in Colossians the key to understanding Hebrews is a questionable hermeneutical move. It will be the interpretive task of this commentary to make a judgment as to whether the text best supports this or one of the other options on the subject of Christ and the angels.

---

16. Robert Jewett, *Letters to Pilgrims* (New York: Pilgrim, 1981).
17. Revelation also seems to carry evidence of a problem of angel worship (19:9-10; 22:8-9).

HEBREWS 1:5-14, THE SON SUPERIOR TO ANGELS

COMMENTARY

Except for the writer's connecting comments and closing remark in v. 14, this unit consists of seven quotations from the OT: five from the psalms, one from Deuteronomy, and one from 2 Samuel. All citations are from the LXX; where slight variations occur, it is not always possible to determine whether the differences are the author's own work or whether they existed in the particular text of the Greek translation being used. Such a pattern of joining a number of quotations is sometimes called a *catena* (a chain of related expressions or ideas) and sometimes a *florilegium* (a gathering of expressions on the analogy of a bunch of flowers). One can find parallel arrangements of texts in the *mashalim* (narratives formed by joining a number of texts) of the rabbis and in writings from Qumran. This particular catena may have been in a Christian tradition prior to Hebrews and was employed here by the writer to address the relation of Christ and angels. The scarcity of commentary by the author and the absence of polemic elaboration may indicate that the readers were already familiar with the catena from another context. Whether the early church had a collection of OT texts suitable for Christian preaching (called "Testimonia") has been debated since the work of J. Rendell Harris on this subject.[18] Certainly some texts were used widely by NT writers, Pss 2:7 and 110:1 being prominent among them. But whether an original arrangement or borrowed, it is the writer of Hebrews who makes 1:5-13 an inclusio (a passage that ends as it begins) by beginning and ending with the rhetorical question, "To which of the angels did God ever say?"

1:5. This verse flows directly from two affirmations in the opening confession of faith: God has spoken through a Son (v. 2), and the name "Son" excels that of the angels (v. 4). It is the name "Son" that joins the two quotations, the one from a royal psalm idealizing the king as God's Son (Ps 2:7), the other from Nathan's prophecy, not only establishing David's house forever but also announcing that David's son would be God's Son (2 Sam 7:14). The joining of these two texts was not unique to the early church, in which they were important foundation texts in developing christology; they were also linked in

---

18. J. Rendell Harris, *Testimonies*, 2 vols. (Cambridge: Cambridge University Press, 1916, 1920).

messianic thinking at Qumran.[19] Elsewhere in the NT, Ps 2:7 is used in accounts of Jesus' baptism (Mark 1:10-11 and par.) and as a prophecy fulfilled in God's raising of Jesus from the dead (Acts 13:33-34).

That Ps 2:7 would be used by Christians as appropriate at Jesus' baptism and at his resurrection raised for some the question, When did Jesus become Son of God? At birth, at baptism, or at resurrection? John and Paul would join the Hebrews writer in adding, Or in pre-existence? New Testament writers show no interest in the question; rather, they employ a number of available categories and images to affirm the unique relation between Christ and God. For example, the writer of Hebrews has just declared the Son pre-existent, the one through whom God created the worlds (v. 2), and now he uses a text portraying the Son as begotten. We may feel christological discontinuity here, but apparently the writer did not. Perhaps it should be said here that of the several ways to express Christ's sonship, the one most recurring in Hebrews is pre-existence, the essential first phase of the formula: pre-existence, humiliation, exaltation (2:8-13; 7:3; 10:5; 11:26).

Two general observations about this verse need now to be made. First, any discussion of the christology expressed here needs to be subordinated to the primary assertion of Hebrews—namely, God is the initiator of all that follows. God speaks, and the king is "Son"; God speaks, and David's son is God's own Son. Christology must flow out of theology. Second, if there is among the readers any serious angel worship, then the writer missed an excellent opportunity to counter it with Psalm 2. The context for Ps 2:7 is intermonarchical rivalry in which kings and rulers conspired against God's anointed, but to no avail. Israel's king is God's Son, and all other rulers will be subordinated to him. This context of the quoted Ps 2:7 would have been a sure weapon against any angels pretending rivalry with God's Son, were such thinking a problem among the readers.

1:6. This verse consists of two parts: the writer's introductory comment and the quotation of Deut 32:43, each full of ambiguities.

For the author to speak of the Son as "firstborn" is not awkward here; he has already spoken of him as begotten (1:5) and as heir (1:2). The term "firstborn" (πρωτότοκος *prōtotokos*), implying authority, privilege, and inheritance, had been used of David (Ps 89:27), of Israel (Num 11:12; Hos 2:1), and elsewhere of Christ (Rom 8:29; Col 1:15, 18). But to what event or christological moment does the writer refer with the expression "when he [God] brings the firstborn into the world"? Technically the adverb "again" may modify the verb, hence "bring again" could refer to the parousia, the Second Coming. Some interpreters prefer this reading, but it is more likely that "again" is simply a connective (as at 1:5; 2:13; 4:5; 10:30). Thus understood, the bringing of the firstborn into the world is without chronological clues and, therefore, may refer to the incarnation, to the parousia, to the world to come (2:5), or to the exaltation into the "world" of the angels, who are commanded to worship him.

The quotation itself speaks directly to the subject of the unit: Christ and the angels. Although the citation is very similar to Ps 97:7 ("all gods bow down before him" ["angels," LXX]), most likely the writer has in mind Deut 32:43. Originally the text called for all the sons of God to worship God. A version of the LXX changed "sons" to "angels," obviously preferred by the writer. The other alteration, directing angelic praise to the Son rather than to God, is the writer's own modification. However, the author may be citing Deut 32:43 not directly but from the odes attached to the psalter in some manuscripts of the LXX or from a Christian liturgy that made use of the Song of Moses in its own worship (Rev 15:3).

1:7. The fourth of the seven quotations is Ps 104:4, and again the writer uses the LXX translation. The Hebrew reads, "who makes winds to be his messengers and fire and flame his servants," while the LXX reverses the expressions: "who makes his messengers [angels] to be winds and his servants to be fire and flame." The writer's point about angels is clear only when read in conjunction with vv. 8-9. The point is not that God harnesses the forces of nature to serve the Creator's purpose (Heb. text) but that angels are as transient and temporary as wind and fire (LXX text).

---

19. Attridge, *A Commentary on the Epistle to the Hebrews*, 53n. 39. 2 Sam 7:11-14 is cited in 4Q Flor 1.10-11; Ps 2:1-2 is cited in 4Q Flor 1.18-19.

This will be abundantly clear momentarily. As to the identity of the "who" ("he" in Eng. text) in the phrase "who makes" (ὁ ποιῶν *ho poiōn*), it is not necessary to assume the writer has Christ, and not God, in mind. Even though the Son is agent of creation (1:2), the contrast between Christ and the angels is not that of creator/creature but of permanent/transient.

1:8-9. The writer introduces Ps 45:6-7 by saying that what follows applies to the Son. Psalm 45 is a marriage song praising the king as bridegroom and calling on the bride, a princess from Tyre, to abandon all former loyalties in recognition of the superior status of the groom. The Hebrews writer does not develop the marriage theme, which would have served well in another context (e.g., Christ and the church). Rather, Psalm 45 yields other themes appropriate to the Christ/angels discussion. First, as the adversative "but" indicates, there is a sharp contrast with the portrayal of the angels in the preceding verse. The angels are changing and transient; the throne of the Son is forever and ever (13:8). Second, because the Son is a king whose reign is marked by righteousness, the writer anticipates the discussion of Melchizedek, king of righteousness, beginning at 7:1. Third, that God "has set you above your companions" has clear implications for the issue of Christ's relation to the angels.

It is striking that the writer gives no special attention to the most shocking feature of the quotation: the king, and hence the Son, is called *God*. Although many interpreters have devised ways to avoid the direct address, "Your throne, O God, is forever and ever" seems to be the unavoidable sense. As awkward as it is to many Christians, references to the Son as God can be found in early liturgical texts (John 1:1; 20:28; Rom 9:5; Titus 2:13; 2 Pet 1:1). The second apparent reference to the king (Son) as God is not so persuasive: "therefore God, your God, has anointed you" could be read as a nominative, not a vocative. This is to say, it could be read, "God; that is, your God has anointed you." But, as stated above, referring to the Son as God seems not to have been the reason for the author's attraction to this psalm. And so, almost incidentally and from a text not listed among the messianic psalms, comes the strongest attribution of divinity to the Son, even stronger than 1:1-4. If any doubt remained of the Son's superiority to angels, that doubt has surely been removed.

1:10-12. Psalm 102 is a lament of a person ill and dying, reflecting on the brevity of life, mortality, and vulnerability. The psalmist then contrasts his own condition with the abiding nature of a never-changing God. The Hebrews writer presents this description of God as God's words concerning the Son. There is no doubt, therefore, that the one addressed as Lord is the Son. What, then, does the quotation of Ps 102:25-27 contribute to the discussion concerning Christ and the angels? Several themes are underscored. The role of the Son as creator and sustainer of the universe (1:2-3) is here elaborated to highlight the contrast between Christ as creator and angels as creatures. This leads to a second contrast between the Son, who never changes, and creation, which perishes. In vivid imagery the psalmist pictures creation as old clothes that wear out, as a cloak rolled up and put away. In addition, Ps 102:25-27 contributes beyond this unit to discussions yet to be developed. One observes here the writer's practice of anticipating future ideas by dropping words and phrases that will receive fuller attention later. For example, just as creation grows old and wears out like clothing, so also the old covenant grows old, soon to disappear (8:13). Again, just as the Son remains the same forever, so also will this unchanging quality characterize Christ's priesthood (5:6; 6:20; 7:3, 17). Or again, just as creation perishes, so also will there be a shaking and an end to all things in the eschaton, leaving only the kingdom that cannot be shaken (12:26-28). Telegraphing ahead themes yet to be developed is sound rhetoric and effective pedagogy.

1:13. The catena in vv. 5-13 ends as it began, with a rhetorical question: "To which of the angels has God ever said?" The writer now quotes the text to which he alluded in v. 3, Ps 110:1. Only its contribution to this immediate context will be considered here. To do more would be to discuss the remainder of the epistle, because not only are portions of this psalm quoted later (5:6; 7:17, 21) but it also provides the scriptural authorization for the unique christology of Hebrews.

George Buchanan's commentary is based on the view that Hebrews is an extended homiletical midrash on Psalm 110.[20] This psalm is also frequently employed elsewhere in the NT; in quotation and clear allusion it appears in christological debate, in proofs of the resurrection and exaltation of Christ, and in prophecies of the parousia (e.g., Mark 12:35-37; 14:62; Acts 2:34; 1 Cor 15:25).

Psalm 110 is God's address to the king, and it contains two oracles: the offer of a place of power at God's right hand (Ps 110) and the declaration of the king's priestly office after the order of Melchizedek (Ps 110:4). Only Hebrews in the NT develops Ps 110:4 as a christological text. In fact, later in the epistle the writer drew upon more of the psalm than these two verses. In the present context, only Ps 110:1 is quoted, and it is presented as the words of God to the Son. For what immediate purpose? In addition to the affirmation of the supremacy of the Son, the psalm predicts the final subordination of all enemies of the Son. Later in the epistle the writer will discuss the Son's victory over the two great enemies, sin and death (2:14-15; 10:27). But within 1:5–2:18 are the enemies the angels? This is very strong language, much stronger than that of Ps 45:7 in 1:9: God "has set you above your companions" (NIV). If angels are Christ's enemies, then the language here is reminiscent of Paul, who regarded angels among the principalities and powers finally to be brought under subjection to Christ (1 Cor 15:24-28; Phil 2:9-11). Apparently, however, the writer realized that the quotation, while serving his purpose, said more than he wanted to say. Therefore, in his own words, without further quotation, he softens, in fact alters, the impact of Ps 110 by appending a concluding statement.

1:14. No further word needs to be said at this point concerning the Son; his position has been adequately presented. However, the writer feels the need for one more clarifying statement about the angels, especially in view of the implication that they are enemies of Christ (v. 13). This statement is in the form of a question, but the syntax of the Greek text makes it clear that an affirmative answer is expected: "The angels are ministering spirits, are they not?" For this conclusion, the writer returns to Ps 104:4 (quoted in v. 7), not only for the idea that angels are ministers or servants but also for the language, "minister" (λειτουργός *leitourgos*) and "spirit" or "wind" (πνεῦμα *pneuma*). The word translated "minister," which gives us the word "liturgy," prompted the NRSV to translate the expression "in the divine service." The author's meaning is very clear: Angels are spirits who minister in God's service. Unlike the Son, who sits at God's right hand, angels are sent out on mission, and the beneficiaries of their service are those soon to inherit salvation. Who these persons are and of what their salvation consists are questions yet to be answered by the writer.

Verse 14 serves, then, as an important transition. It speaks positively of the work of angels, providing an opening for a statement about one of the significant tasks of angels, the giving of the law (2:2). In addition, it announces salvation, a subject soon to be developed (2:3-4). And finally, v. 14 introduces those who will inherit salvation, the group to be strongly admonished in 2:1-4.

---

20. George W. Buchanan, *Hebrews*, AB 36 (Garden City, N.Y.: Doubleday, 1972) xix. For a detailed study of early Christian uses of Psalm 110, see Hay, *Glory at the Right Hand*.

REFLECTIONS

1. It may first appear to teachers and preachers that a text preoccupied with angels bears little yield to nourish the church. Angels have, it is true, always lain at the edge of Christian faith, and not at its center; the creeds do not include them. Very likely they were not vital to the faith of the writer of Hebrews; they disappear when he moves to the central substance of his christology. However, for some of the readers angels have moved from the edge toward the center. We do not know how important they were, in what ways they functioned for the believers, or if the Christians addressed sought

to worship them, appease them, or simply talk about them a great deal. We cannot borrow from Paul's churches to clarify Hebrews.

What we do know is that the writer was a Christian leader and as such did not confine his interests to the items in his own personal faith. If angels concern the church, they concern him. Moving angels from the margins to a more prominent place demands attention; after all, faith is often a matter of proportion. What does it say about the health of a believing community if it begins to give large attention to angels or, for that matter, to demons, to the Second Coming, to the millennium, to the rapture, or to the pre-resurrection state of the dead? Has curiosity replaced faith? Has the gospel become boring and in need of some new mystery? Maybe the gospel or christology suffers from inattention and so items from the edge are drawn into the vacuum. It may be that faith in Christ is so weak that the church is looking for supplements, for backup. Add a few angels. Whatever the condition in the church addressed by Hebrews, the writer responds with a strong christology, the fully adequate and final word from the God who has always spoken. Having said that, it should be noted that the author is not hesitant to remind the readers of the positive role of angels in their salvation (1:14).

2. The writer's use of the Old Testament will be a continuing part of the investigation of Hebrews. However, it is already clear that for the writer and the readers the Old Testament is God's Word. The author does not dismiss the ancient texts with some dispensational argument so that he may construct Christianity with entirely new material. The continuity between old and new is real because it is one God who speaks, who sustains, who redeems. To be sure, the Old Testament is a book of promise and anticipation, looking beyond itself—but so is the New. Both Israel and the church are self-declared pilgrims, looking for the city that has foundations. Of course, the author affirms Christ as God's Son whose person and work fulfills hope, but his case is not made by dancing on the graves of the prophets. The writer's methods of interpretation are not ours; they belong to him and to the teachers of his time and place. But at the heart of his hermeneutics are two principles of abiding value. One is respect for the text as revelatory. The other is the sense that the text belongs to the entire believing community. Hebrews does not present a private interpreter playing with biblical texts to persuade an uninformed church to his view. Rather, it is abundantly clear by the writer's lack of argumentation that the readers are informed and in agreement with the affirmations expressed in the quoted texts. The writer will soon lead them into difficult and unfamiliar exegetical territory, but at the end of this chapter the readers are responding with both understanding and agreement.

HEBREWS 2:1-4, THEREFORE LISTEN CAREFULLY

COMMENTARY

The writer has not finished with the subject of Christ and the angels. That matter will be resumed at 2:5 with the exegesis of a critical text. He pauses here, however, to drive home the vital importance of what has been said and will be said. The entire epistle is called a "word of encouragement" or a "word of exhortation" (13:22); either translation is acceptable, and the content of the letter supports both. At 2:1-4 the hortatory portion begins and will reappear from time to time (3:12–4:13; 5:11–6:12; 10:19-39; 12:14-29). The balance between 1:1-4 and 2:1-4 is apparent. Having begun with the one who speaks, the writer now turns to those who hear what has been spoken. The author does not separate himself from the readers in an accusing tone but uses the inclusive "we" throughout. Moving through the lines, one will notice how tightly woven the argument, how vivid the imagery, and how rhetorically skilled the writer is.

2:1. It is understandable that one might regard 2:1-4 as an interpolation into the text.[21] The argument at 1:14 seems to resume at 2:5, as though 2:1-4 were not there; there are no quotations from the LXX; and the vocabulary seems different, consisting of several rare words. But exhortations often are literarily and substantively different from exposition; such is their nature, and this is but the first of many alternations between exposition and exhortation. It must also be observed that the subject of angels does not resume at 2:5; it is central to 2:1-4 as well. In addition, 2:1 recalls 1:1 phonetically. Both display the rhetorician's use of alliteration, in each case the repetition of π (Eng. p), an explosive consonant that, when repeated, impresses an audience. Further, the "Therefore" of 2:1 clearly links the exhortation to what precedes it, not to 1:14 specifically but to the entire presentation of the Son's superiority to angels.

The injunction to "pay greatest [the comparative probably carries the force of the superlative here] attention" uses a word rare in Hebrews (προσέχω *prosechō*; used elsewhere only at 7:13) but rather common in other NT texts. Matthew uses it repeatedly (e.g., Matt 6:1; 7:15; 10:17; 16:6) as a term of strong warning: "Beware, watch out!" The danger is not that of willful engagement in ethical or doctrinal error but that of drifting or slipping past one's mooring. This second key word may be a nautical term, appearing nowhere else in the NT and only twice in the LXX (Prov 3:21; Isa 44:4). The condition addressed is a serious one. Toward the message they have heard (its content is not specified; its certainty is the present focus), the readers are displaying a laxity, a carelessness, a loss of attention. This warning comes early, and appropriately so, lest it also fall on indifferent ears.

2:2-3. Verse 2 begins a rather lengthy and complex sentence concluding at v. 4, which, in the service of clarity of translation, has been divided into two (NRSV) or three (NIV) concise statements. The sentence is a conditional clause consisting of an "if" (*protasis*) and a "then" (*apodosis*). The "if" here does not express an uncertainty but a certainty and, therefore, could be translated "since" (cf. Phil 2:1). The "then" is rather unusual, consisting of a rhetorical question, the answer to which is already known to both speaker and hearer, and it is inescapably clear. The argument is from the lesser ("If the word spoken through angels") to the greater ("spoken through the Lord"). This form of argumentation (*a fortiori*) is a favorite of the writer (7:20-22; 9:13-15; 10:28-29). The sentence continues the language of speaking begun at 1:1, and since both angels and the Lord are referred to as agents, the assumed speaker is God. This assures that even though lesser and greater describe the revelations, in both the word is from God.

Even though Exod 20:1 gives no indication of the presence of mediating angels at Sinai, later on the belief came to be held among both Jews and Christians. For example, in the book of *Jubilees* (*Jub.* 1:27, 29) an angel dictated the Torah to Moses, and among Christians the belief that the law came through angels is expressed here, at Acts 7:38, 53, and at Gal 3:19. The theological process by which angels made their way into the narrative is not clear. Since wind and fire were spoken of as angels (Ps 104:4), perhaps the meteorological elements at Sinai came to be viewed as angelic agents. In the LXX, angels are present in the final blessing of Moses: "The LORD came from Sinai/... With him were myriads of holy ones;/ at his right, a host of his own" (Deut 33:2 NRSV; "At his right hand angels were with him," LXX). Some have suggested that angels became a theological necessity as the distance between a transcendent God and frail humanity came increasingly to be accented. Whatever the origin, angels as mediators of Torah are not portrayed here as rebels against God or as harbingers of what is antithetical to the gospel. On the contrary, the word through angels was "binding" or "valid" (βέβαιος *bebaios*), very likely intended here as a legal term (as at 9:17), given the use of other such vocabulary in the sentence. The compound "transgression [violation, NIV] and disobedience" (not

---

21. As does F. C. Synge, *Hebrews and the Scriptures* (London: SPCK, 1959) 44-52.

or disobedience, NRSV) serves to underscore the seriousness of any breach of Torah, and the word "disobedience" ("refusal to listen" [παρακοή *parakoē*]) keeps intact the language of speaking and hearing. Every act of disobedience had as a sure consequence a "just ἔνδικος [(*endikos*), a rare word in the NT; cf. Rom 3:8] recompense" (μισθαποδοσία *misthapodosia*; only in Hebrews in the NT). The translation "penalty" or "punishment" is justified here, given the context, but in a positive setting the word can mean "reward" (10:35; 11:26).

It is the backdrop of a Torah without legal uncertainties and with careful administration that gives the question, "How shall we escape?" much of its gravity. The greater seriousness, however, is carried by the phrase "spoken through the Lord." Since the Son is greater than angels, the word of the Son is greater than the message delivered through angels. At this point, exactly what will not be escaped is not spelled out, but it will soon be clear that the writer has in mind eschatological punishment (6:8; 10:27, 31; see also Luke 21:36; Rom 2:3; 1 Thess 5:3). Again the writer is specific: The danger among the readers is neglect (2:1) or indifference. Jeremiah had warned that such behavior could result in God's neglecting (8:9; "no concern," NRSV; "turned away," NIV) Israel. At stake is a "great salvation" (1:14), which, interestingly enough, is portrayed as something *spoken*. Its reality and certainty are secured in God's having said so. That is enough. As a minimum this salvation means exemption from eschatological punishment (9:28; 10:25), but the epistle will also detail present benefits (4:16; 6:5; 8:7-12; 9:13-14, 26-28; 10:2, 15-18, 22).

That this salvation was first spoken through the Lord raises the question, "When?" Since the writer uses "Lord" and not "Son," this influence from Ps 110:1 may imply that the announcement occurred at the exaltation. However, since much attention is also given the incarnation (2:5-18; 5:7-8; 10:1-10), the author could well have had in mind a recital such as is found in Acts 10:36-39 or Luke 4:16-21 or Mark 1:14-15. That the message was confirmed (attested, validated) to us by those who heard him implies more likely a historical occasion rather than an announcement from the heavenly throne. But the question, "When?" is more ours than the writer's. Neither is the author seeking to argue for a particular tradition by the formula: from God, through the Lord, to those who heard, to us. It could be that the author is anticipating 13:7: "your leaders, those who spoke the word of God to you" (NRSV). For one who admittedly was not among the Lord's hearers, it was important, of course, to state the unbroken continuity of the word (cf. 2 Pet 3:2), but one does not sense that the affirmation is intended to counter another tradition. Rather, the strength of the statement depends on the writer and the readers having had common access and common agreement as to the great salvation about which they had heard.

2:4. The conditional sentence begun at v. 2 concludes with a phrase called an absolute, a grammatical construction important to the sentence but having its own subject and verb and, therefore, making its own statement. God, the sometimes stated, sometimes implied speaker from 1:1 through 2:3 now becomes the actor, the one who through signs, wonders, powerful deeds, and distributions of the Holy Spirit offers supporting testimony to the word spoken (see also 6:5). Signs and wonders had long been joined (Exod 7:3; Deut 4:34; 6:22; Ps 135:9; Jer 32:20-21; Neh 9:10), and early Christians often added "deeds of power" (Acts 2:22; Rom 15:19; 2 Cor 12:12). These expressions, along with "distributions of the Holy Spirit" (1 Cor 12:11; Gal 3:5), clearly set the church of both writer and reader within the mainstream of the Christian community portrayed in the NT. It is too easy, because of the unique presentation of Christ as high priest, to think of the church of Hebrews as peripheral or isolated and, therefore, less significant than in Acts or the Pauline epistles as a witness to early Christianity.

The signs, wonders, miracles, and gifts of the Holy Spirit are set between two modifiers of major importance. First, these acts of God in confirming support of the spoken word are described as testimony or witness. The fact that they are acts of God does not mean that these acts are overwhelming and incontrovertible proof. God does not coerce faith but joins the rest of us. This means that the signs and wonders may be interpreted as other than acts of God. In the biblical world the question was not simply whether these wonders really occurred but, Who did them? In both the ministry of Jesus (Mark 3:21-27) and the churches of Paul (2 Thess 2:9), deeds of power were also attributed to Satan. Faith always involves making a decision. Second, all these acts of testimony are according to God's will. Signs, wonders, and gifts of the Spirit are received from God, precluding all human possession of these powers for purposes of control, manipulation, or persuasion.

REFLECTIONS

1. The many-splendored portrayal of the superiority of the Son in 1:5-14 is a clear reminder that Christian life and thought begin in doxology. But following the liturgy comes the "Therefore," and 2:1-4 supplies the first of many in Hebrews. In this regard the writer is not unlike Paul, who, having concluded Romans 1–11 with a burst of praise (Rom 11:33-36), begins chap. 12 with "Therefore." There is always a "Therefore."

2. One has to be impressed by the strength of the writer's case for the message of the "great salvation." Note the source of the message (God); the superiority of the messenger (Christ); the unbroken tradition of the word (God-Christ-his hearers-us); and the corroborating testimony from God (signs, wonders, miracles, gifts of the Holy Spirit). And in view of this forceful reminder of what was theirs as inheritors of salvation (1:14), one has to be a bit surprised that the condition addressed was that of inattention, neglect, indifference, drifting. That there could be apathy toward the gospel may seem unbelievable to the newly baptized, but the fact is that this condition has plagued the church from the first century. Among the seven deadly sins, the ancients saw fit to list ἀκηδία *akēdia*, usually translated "sloth." The word means "unconcerned," "uncaring," "disinterested." The writer will mount repeated campaigns against this passivity; with what success, we do not know.

HEBREWS 2:5-18, THE SON LOWER THAN ANGELS

OVERVIEW

By means of a tapestry of biblical texts the case for the superiority of the Son over angels has moved along beautifully. The catena of 1:5-14 has been haunted by the line "When he had made purification for sins" (1:3 NRSV), but until now its implications have been unaddressed. The writer turns now to do just that, to face the fact that may have prompted interest in angels: The Son became incarnate, subject to all the conditions flesh is heir to, including death. The writer, then, returns to exposition and to the interpretation of biblical texts. The thought of 1:13 (Ps 110:1) is resumed, but the line of reasoning takes a significant turn. Instead of continuing the comparison of the Son and angels, the author now argues that just as angels were not the means of redemption, so also they are not the recipients, the beneficiaries of it. With this new orientation toward humanity, toward those "who are to inherit salvation" (1:14), the primary consideration of the epistle will have been established. After 2:16 angels will no longer be a factor in either exposition or exhortation.

This unit falls easily into two parts: 2:5-9, which consists primarily of a christological exegesis of Ps 8:4-6[8:5-7 LXX], and 2:10-18, which elaborates on that exegesis soteriologically and anticipates the fuller development of the high priesthood of Christ. Portions of Psalm 22 and Isaiah 8 support the argumentation.

Hebrews 2:5-9, He Became as We Are

COMMENTARY

2:6. The discussion beginning at v. 5 seems so loosely connected to what precedes it that the conjunction "for" (γάρ *gar*) in the Greek text is dropped in the NIV and translated with the rather noncommittal "now" in the NRSV. However, v. 5 does continue an earlier line of thinking, not in the exhortation of 2:1-4 but in 1:13. In fact, v. 5 looks in two directions: back to 1:13, which declares through Ps 110:1 the ultimate sovereignty of the Son, and ahead to 2:8, where Psalm 8 provides the vocabulary of "subjection." But first the writer wants it clear: The subject about which he is speaking is the world to come, the eschatological age of messianic rule (6:5). If that was not clear at 1:13, it must be clear now, because what follows is an interpretation of Psalm 8 in which the future and final reign of Christ is central. From the statement that the world to come was not subjected to angels it may be implied that angels do have some governance in this present age. Such a view was at least available to the author (e.g., Deut 32:8; Dan 10:13; Sir 17:17; 1 Enoch 60:15-21; 89:70-76).

Psalm 8:4-6, the centerpiece of Heb 2:5-9, is introduced as speech of indefinite citation: "someone has testified somewhere" (cf. 4:4; 7:17; 12:5-6). Attridge has found parallels in Philo and concludes that it may have been a common homiletic practice.[22] Sometimes specific citations are unhelpful, sometimes awkward, and sometimes they complicate the discussion. Public speakers know that undivided attention on content can often best be served by indefinite referencing. Certainly in Hebrews this practice does not justify the view that the writer was cavalier in his attitude toward the OT; too many quotations are introduced as the speech of God or of Christ or of the Holy Spirit. As for the quotation itself, several features should be noted. First, the Hebrews text (vv. 6-8*a*) follows Ps 8:4-6 closely except for the omission of one line: "You have given them dominion over the works of your hands" (Ps 8:6*a* NRSV). This expression apparently was not useful to the writer in the christological interpretation of the psalm. However, we must use terms such as "omitted," "added," or "modified" with some caution, since we are not always sure which recension of the OT text lay before the writer.[23] Second, the author uses the Greek text (LXX) of the psalm, which had rendered the Hebrew "a little lower than gods " as "a little lower than angels." Third, the expression "a little [βραχύ τι *brachy ti*]" may have a temporal meaning, "a little while." This seems to be the writer's sense in the exegesis (v. 9), and so the NRSV translates it (vv. 7, 9). The NIV keeps the qualitative meaning in its rendering, "a little lower." On the matter of translation, the NRSV has honored its commitment to more inclusive language by translating "man" and "son of man" (synonymous parallels) as "human beings" and "mortals." The meaning of the psalm in its own context is not violated by this translation, but the shift from plural to singular in the application of the psalm to Christ is made awkward. Similarly, the phrase "son of man" is lost, and it is possible that this phrase first attracted christological interpretations of the psalm by the early church.

The psalm offers praise to God and contrasts the power and majesty of God with the relative insignificance of human beings. It ponders why God would think of or care for humans. The psalmist does not lament human frailty but reaffirms the unique place of humanity in relation to God and to the rest of creation (Gen 1:26-28). That the psalm is anthropological in original intent is fully clear. What is not clear is the point in the author's exegesis of it (beginning at v. 8*b*) at which the reader's attention is shifted from man(kind) to Christ. Jesus is not specifically mentioned until v. 9, but is the author already thinking of him in v. 8*b*: "In putting everything under him, God left nothing that is not subject to him. Yet at present we do not see everything subject to him"? The question is interesting

---

22. Attridge, *A Commentary on the Epistle to the Hebrew*, 70-71.

23. J. C. McCullough, "The Old Testament Quotations in Hebrews," *NTS* 26 (1980) 263-79.

but not crucial. If at this point the writer is thinking of man(kind), then it is obvious that humanity has not succeeded in holding dominion over all else in creation. Nor is the author moving toward the point that in some future time humanity will complete that assignment from God. If it was not to angels that God subjected the world to come, neither is it to humanity. If the writer is already thinking of Christ, then it is likewise clear that the full subjection of the world to come is not yet. The "until" of Ps 110:1 is still in effect: "until I make your enemies your footstool" (NRSV)—even though, as at 2:3, there are ample present benefits of the eschatological age.

Perhaps we can safely regard v. 8*b* as a swing statement, a point at which the writer turns the reader away from any lingering thoughts of the original intent of the psalm toward its present use as a proclamation of the humiliation and coronation of Christ. It does not seem appropriate here to elaborate on possible second Adam or Son of man christologies embedded in the text.[24] Neither is developed in Hebrews and, therefore, would require heavy borrowings from the Gospels and Paul.

The author concludes his exegesis of Ps 8:4-6 with a bold statement. Having spoken of what we do not see (v. 8*b*) he now announces what we do see (v. 9). The Greek construction is especially impressive. Between two expressions from the psalm ("the one made for a little while lower than the angels" and "the one with honor and glory crowned") is placed the principal clause, "we see Jesus." It was important that the two expressions that had been joined as a description of the station of humanity now be separated as two phases of the temporal journey of the Son: lower than angels for a little while, crowned with glory and honor forever. There is no shrinking back from or minimizing what happened to Jesus during that "little while." In fact, at this point, where the author first mentions the name "Jesus," two strong assertions are made: (1) It was because he suffered death that Jesus was crowned with glory and honor (the exaltation). (2) In his dying, Jesus "tasted death" (Matt 16:28; John 8:52) for everyone. This statement anticipates the theological elaboration of 2:10-18 in which the author will take what may have been for some a theological embarrassment, the suffering and death of Jesus, and demonstrate its central importance for the priestly ministry of Christ. If any preferred passionless angels over a suffering Jesus, they will now hear strong reasons to reconsider.

One final word on the text. In some early versions and in some Greek MSS of Hebrews (beginning in the third century), instead of "by the grace of God" (v. 9) is the reading "apart from God." Careless copying may account for the difference (χωρὶς θεοῦ *chōris theou* instead of χάριτι θεοῦ *chariti theou*). Or perhaps a scribe wanted to follow 1 Cor 15:27 and assure the reader that Christ's subjection of "all" or his death for "all" did not include God. And, of course, the phrase "apart from God" might have been motivated by a view of the atonement; that is, for Christ to die, God had to abandon him. This alternate reading, however prompted, hardly fits the immediate context of Hebrews or the affirmations made thus far concerning the relation of God to the Son. (See Reflections at 2:10-18.)

24. Anyone wishing to pursue these christologies further or wishing to be further persuaded that such pursuits are not justified here is referred to Attridge, *A Commentary on the Epistle to the Hebrews*, 73-75.

Hebrews 2:10-18, A Faithful and Merciful High Priest

COMMENTARY

2:10. It quickly becomes clear that the writer's use of Psalm 8 to acknowledge that "for a little while" Christ was lower than the angels is in no way a concession, a willingness to lose a point in the process of winning an argument. On the contrary, during that "little while" the drama of redemption was played out. The essential vocabulary of that drama has already been introduced: suffering, death, grace of God, for everyone (v. 9); now, consistent with a literary pattern already employed, the writer will elaborate on that vocabulary. Before stating what is achieved by the suffering and death of Jesus, two affirmations are underscored for the reader. First, what occurred during the "little while" of Christ's incarnation was at the initiative of God. The use of an omnipotence formula (for whom and through whom all things exist, v. 10) removes even a hint of accident, coincidence, or historical contingency. This formula is like Rom 11:36 in its theocentricity; any mention of agency (through the Son) as at 1:2-3 would here be awkward, because in what follows the Son is the object of God's activity. Second, this activity of God is totally appropriate to the character of God and to God's relationship to humankind. Speaking of what is proper behavior for God is unique to Hebrews in the NT. Other writers refer to what is proper conduct for John the Baptist (Matt 3:15), for women in the church (1 Cor 11:13), for believers in general (Eph 5:3), or for a young minister (Titus 2:1), but not for God. For this writer to be so audacious clearly indicates how crucial the point is.

And what is it that God is doing? According to v. 10, God's purpose is to lead many children (the word is "sons" (υἱοί *huioi*), but is unquestionably inclusive) to glory. Honor and glory belong to Jesus (v. 9), but now many others will share in that glory (cf. John 12:28-32). The glory with which Jesus is crowned is "because of the suffering of death"; that same suffering will be the means by which Jesus becomes the leader of salvation for many. By his suffering and death, Christ gains glory not only for himself but also for "many children." In this service he is called "pioneer" (NRSV) or "author" (NIV). The word ἀρχηγός (*archēgos*) is rare in the NT (Acts 3:15; 5:31; Heb 12:2) but very important in Hebrews. While the word can be translated as "founder," "author," or "leader," here and at 12:2 Jesus is portrayed as the one who in himself creates the path for his followers.

For that work he is made "perfect" (τελειόω *teleioō*) through suffering. Perfection is not a term for moral flawlessness; that quality of blamelessness is otherwise stated in 4:15; 7:26; and 9:14. Rather, it refers to the completeness of Jesus' preparation for his priestly ministry. Any life short of suffering and death would have been less than an identification with humankind and, therefore, less than a full understanding of the human condition. In the LXX, "to perfect" is used to describe the consecration of the priest (Exod 29:9; Lev 16:32; Num 3:3), and in view of the movement of Hebrews 2 toward the presentation of Jesus as high priest, the cultic use of the term in the LXX must lie close to the writer's intention. Two of the key words in 2:10, "pioneer" and "perfect," will again be joined in a summary description of Jesus at 12:2.

2:11. If "to perfect" implies sacerdotal activity, the language of sanctifying or making holy clearly brings the reader to the altar of priestly service. In the OT, God is the one who sanctifies (Exod 31:13; Lev 20:8; Ezek 20:12), but here the reference is to Jesus. Later the writer will associate sanctifying with the shedding of blood (9:13; 10:10; 13:12), but at this point the unity of the sanctifier and the sanctified is the message. The expression that they are "from one" is variously understood, the "one" being interpreted as Adam or humanity or God. This could be a reference to a common humanity (v. 14), but "the children God has given me" of v. 13 makes it more likely that the writer has in mind one family (NIV) in the sense of both the sanctifier and the sanctified being children of God (NRSV). Since, therefore, the incarnation and its conditions of suffering and death are appropriate to God's purpose, and that purpose is to lead many to glory, Jesus is not ashamed to be identified with us. His "for a little while" is not an embarrassment to God, to Jesus, or to the church.

2:12-13. In support of the closing affirmation of v. 11, the writer quotes the OT three times, but all three citations are presented as words of Jesus. Because the Scripture is the living Word of God, for the Hebrews writer any passage may be spoken of as words of God, or as words of the Son through whom God speaks. A pre-existent christology makes it possible to move across chronological and historical distinctions.

The citations are Ps 22:22 and Isa 8:17-18, treated as separate quotations. They are joined by the familiar literary link "again" (1:5-6). Psalm 22 is much employed by NT writers (more than twenty times) in portrayals of the crucifixion, but the Hebrews writer dips into the latter portion of the psalm after the radical shift of mood (Ps 22:21). The psalmist proposes a banquet for all the beneficiaries of God's deliverance: himself, the poor, the sick, the deceased, foreigners, and future generations. They are all brothers and sisters by virtue of both affliction and deliverance. Isaiah 8 is a message of hope in a time of despair. Isaiah expresses hope by his own affirmation of trust or faithfulness (Isa 8:17) and through his children, who are symbols of God's faithfulness (Isa 8:18). If these three citations strike the reader as saying more than is needed to support v. 11 b, a closer look will show how vital all three are to the writer's developing discussion. The third (Isa 8:18), with the theme of children, moves immediately into v. 14. The first (Ps 22:22) and second (Isa 8:17) feed into v. 17 with the themes of brothers and sisters and of faithfulness.

2:14-15. The transition at v. 14, "Since, therefore," announces the gathering up of what has been said thus far and the projection of lines of thought stated here but to be developed later. The summary: Since all human beings share (κεκοινώνηκεν *kekoinōnēken*; perfect tense, indicating an abiding condition) blood and flesh, Jesus in every way participated (μετέσχεν *meteschen*; aorist tense, indicating a completed act in the past) in the same things. The language is clear: He was as we are, no pretensions, no appearances, no exemptions. "Flesh and blood" (here "blood and flesh"; see John 1:13) was a common way to summarize the human condition (Matt 16:17; 1 Cor 15:50; Gal 1:16). The first projected implication of that summary: Through his death, Jesus destroys the one having the power of death; that is, the devil. To say that Jesus "destroys" (καταργέω *katargeō*) the devil very likely means "to break the power of." Paul uses the same word in the same way to speak of Christ's victory over the principalities and powers (1 Cor 15:24); they are not destroyed but subdued and put in subjection to Christ. So here the devil, who holds death's power (John 8:44; 1 Cor 5:5; 10:10), is defeated. And what is the power of death? To hold people in bondage to the fear of it. By his death Christ has broken the chains of that fear. How that victory is actually accomplished is not stated. Perhaps the idea was commonplace among the readers and needed no elaboration. Myths of heroes and champions who faced death and through dying set the people free abounded in that culture,[25] perhaps providing the church a way of understanding one of the benefits of Christ's death. Later the writer will present Jesus as a model for those facing suffering and death, and thereby may indicate one way Jesus liberates us from bondage to fear of death (12:2-3). And, of course, his resurrection and exaltation, opening access to God, grant confidence and freedom to the believer (10:19-20; 13:20-21).

2:16. Before continuing to state the benefits of Christ's incarnation and death, the author pauses to discuss the angels, who have thus far remained on stage since 1:4. This verse is almost parenthetical, but yet essential for the progress of the argument. With a construction found only here in the NT, meaning "of course not" or "certainly not," the reader is reminded of the obvious: that the discussion here concerns believers, those who by faith are children of Abraham, and not angels. The drama of salvation, which hinges on incarnation, suffering, and death, is not an angel story. While angels are in divine service for the benefit of those who inherit salvation (1:14), they are neither the agents nor the beneficiaries of that salvation. With this sentence angels leave the stage of Hebrews, but they leave honorably. They have their place in God's work (2:2), but it is not the central place. They enjoy God's presence, but they do not sit at God's right hand. Nor are they portrayed as competitors and enemies of Christ, as apparently angels were at Colossae. While we do not know how firmly they were fixed, if at all, in the church addressed by Hebrews, it hardly seems justified to borrow from Colossians and from heterodox Judaism in order to fill in the blanks. They leave as they entered, suddenly and mysteriously, as the writer turns to his principal subject: the high priesthood of Christ.

2:17-18. These verses continue the writer's presentation of the purpose and benefits of Christ's incarnation and death. The imagery shifts from that of vv. 14-15, where Christ defeats the devil and breaks the bondage of fear of death, to that of a high priest in God's

---

25. For example, see Seneca *Hercules Furens* 858-92; *2 Enoch* 22:8-10. Variations on this theme occur at Eph 4:8-10 and 1 Pet 3:18-22. For a detailed investigation, see Ragnar Leivestad, *Christ the Conqueror: Ideas of Conflict and Victory in the NT* (New York: Macmillan, 1954).

service. We should remind ourselves, however, that the difference between a champion who destroys the devil for our sakes and a high priest who ministers in our behalf may be greater for us than it was for the first readers. Lane has located the following passage in the pseudepigraphal *Testament of Levi* (18:10-12), which joins the two images:

Then shall the Lord raise up a new priest. . . .
  And he shall execute a righteous judgment
    upon the earth.
  And he shall open the gates of paradise
    and shall remove the threatening sword
      against Adam.
And Beliar shall be bound by him,
  and he shall give power to his children to
    tread upon evil spirits.[26]

In addition, the priest-kings of the Hasmonean dynasty (142–63 BCE) provide a historical antecedent for this double portrait of Christ in Hebrews. And, of course, there is Psalm 110, the writer's primary text for developing the priesthood of Christ. While Ps 110:1, 4 is the direct citation, the remainder of the psalm speaks of the conquering power of the priest at God's right hand.

Although priestly language was implicit at 1:3 and explicit at 2:11, here at 2:17 the first application of the title "high priest" to Jesus occurs, and to speak of Jesus as high priest is unique to Hebrews in the NT. There will be occasion in discussing the statement "You are a priest forever,/ according to the order of Melchizedek" (5:6 NRSV) to explore the questions of possible sources for this image of Christ and of its possible uniqueness to the Hebrews community. In this almost abrupt introduction of the title, the author distills into four compact statements the matters for exposition in chaps. 3–10. First, it was necessary that Jesus be in every respect like his brothers and sisters. Note the strong language. Full and complete identification with us was an essential precondition for his ministry. In fact, says the author in the second statement, Christ's being totally like us was for the purpose of (in order that) being a merciful and faithful high priest in the service of (concerning the things of) God. The two adjectives describing the high priest are deliberately chosen and important. That he is faithful will be presented in 3:1–4:14; that he is merciful, in 4:15–5:10. And no less important, these two qualities will be urged on the readers as essential for all who benefit from Christ's priesthood.

The third statement about Jesus as high priest continues the purposive language: He became a priest in order to make atonement (NIV)/to make a sacrifice of atonement (NRSV)/to make expiation (REB) for the sins of the people. The word translated "atone" or "expiate" (ἰλάσκομαι *hilaskomai*) is rare in the NT. A form of the word in Luke 18:13 can be translated "be merciful," and at 1 John 2:2 and 4:10 the usage is the same as found here in v. 17. At Heb 9:5 the word occurs as a noun of place in a description of the "mercy seat," an altar in the Temple's holy of holies on which blood was sprinkled on the Day of Atonement. In Rom 3:25 it is used in a reference to Christ as our "mercy seat." In the LXX, the primary uses express the mercy of God in the provisions for the removal of human sin in order to restore divine-human relations.[27] This removal or covering of sin, usually by blood sacrifice, is often called "expiation," a term no longer familiar to most believers. Neither in the LXX nor in the NT does the word mean "propitiate" in the sense of placating or appeasing God, since it is not human but divine initiative that effects mercy and atonement. Human beings do not act or speak so as to make God gracious; we have already been alerted that the drama unfolding is "by the grace of God" (2:9).

The fourth and final statement concerning the priestly ministry of Jesus has to do with his capacity and willingness to help those being tested. A priest not only offers sacrifice for sins but also makes intercession for those in need. No doubt the readers share the common human lot of multiple temptations, but the writer is not speaking generally but rather specifically. Those being addressed have endured suffering, public abuse, persecution, imprisonment, and the confiscation of property (10:32-34). Although none of them has yet been killed for the faith (12:4), that does not seem too distant a prospect. To

---

26. Lane, *Hebrews 1–8*, 65.

27. See the articles on ἵλεως and derivative terms by H. Buchsel and J. Herrmann in Kittel, *TDNT*, 3:300-323.

them Jesus ministers not only as the pioneer and model who "endured the cross, disregarding its shame" (12:2 NRSV), but also as the high priest making intercession for them from his place at the right hand of God (4:15-16). On these four statements the author will begin to elaborate in the next section, 3:1–5:10.

REFLECTIONS

1. The author of Hebrews reminded us quite early that the beginning and ending of all Christian thinking and living is God. God is the subject of the New Testament as well as of the Old. Having said that, the writer moves us to the primary consideration within *theo*logy, and that is *christ*ology. Christology is not bragging on Jesus in public; it is thinking about who Jesus is in relation to God and to us. Some pursue this study through the titles used of Jesus; this is important and can be fruitful. The Hebrews writer certainly chooses such terms carefully and introduces them appropriately: Son, Jesus, high priest. But this letter teaches us how important it is to understand the shape of the christology of a given writing. The shape of the christology of Hebrews is clear: pre-existence with God, existence on earth, post-existence in exaltation to God's right hand. All that is said about Jesus Christ in the letter, and, therefore, all that can be said in lessons and sermons on Hebrews, is conscious of this framework. This pattern, sometimes called descent-ascent christology, is found in the writings of Paul and John, but with major differences. For example, in John the "existence on earth" phase is presented as a full ministry with crucifixion and resurrection, whereas in Paul, Christ's existence on earth is almost totally condensed into crucifixion and resurrection. As we shall see, Hebrews lies somewhere between the two, but clearly with the focus on suffering, death, and exaltation. Contrast the shape of this christology with that of the synoptic gospels, which frame their christologies on a horizontal line—birth, life and work, death, and resurrection—without any presentation of his pre- and post-existent activities. Preaching and teaching on biblical texts should honor the shapes of the christologies of those texts lest listeners be confused by messages that pour everything every writer says about Christ into every passage.

2. Hebrews interprets Psalm 8 christologically, but not in such a way as to rob it of its original meaning. Rather, it affirms it. The psalm sings of human life as but little lower than angels, crowned with glory and honor, holding dominion over all other creatures. It is this expression of the human estate that attracts the writer of Hebrews to say, "Yes, this is who Jesus is: lower than angels for a little while, crowned with glory and honor with all things subjected to him." The christological use of the psalm blesses it rather than consuming it; Psalm 8 retains its own message. It is not necessary, then, to assume that one honors Christ by having the truth of the psalm apply to him alone, underscoring this opinion by lamenting the human condition after the fall with long paragraphs on sin, degradation, and death. Christ does not shine brighter by casting him against the dark background of Genesis 3. Sin and death have entered the world, to be sure, and God's high aspirations for humankind still await fulfillment; else why God's gracious act in Jesus? But if nothing of Genesis 1 survived the crash of Genesis 3, then why God's gracious act in Jesus? The psalmist sang his song in a world much like ours, full of sin and death. Was he softened into sentimentality on a beautiful starry night? Perhaps, but the stars did not amaze him so much as did human beings. Let us not be guilty of the charge that Christians steal Old Testament texts and use them up for their own purposes. These texts are not used up; they still carry their own truth

3. The church has always struggled with the insistence of Hebrews that Jesus "had to become like his brothers and sisters *in every respect.*" We know what we are like, and we hesitate to admit him into our ranks. We feel the need to add lengthy footnotes (the writer himself will drop one at 4:15) to explain what "in every respect" does not mean. Some early Christians fell into the heresy of denying Jesus' humanity, saying he only "seemed" to be fully human. He did not really die, some said; on the cross he was given a strong potion in a sponge, fell into a death-like sleep, and awakened three days later, some said. And on and on. It was against such theories, spun to protect Jesus from our common life, that the Apostles' Creed declared: born of the virgin Mary, suffered under Pontius Pilate, crucified, dead, and buried. No New Testament writer takes the humanity of Jesus Christ more seriously or more purposefully than does the author of Hebrews.

4. It is evident, after only two chapters, that the writer of Hebrews is a pastor, writing a word of encouragement (13:22). For example, in 2:5-18, Christ is presented to the readers as a pioneer, the one who goes before them not only showing the way but also creating a path. Christ is also our champion, defeating the devil and setting us free from the fear of death. In addition, Christ is our high priest, offering a sacrifice of atonement for our sins. And finally, Christ is our representative before God, our advocate, intercessor for all who are being put to the test. "For us and our salvation" runs through the passage like a refrain. But E. Käsemann says that perhaps the writer has gone too far.[28] So strong are the pastoral concerns, so pressing are the needs that the author bends christology to fit the crisis of the church. By subsuming christology under pastoral preaching, the offense and integrity of christology are consumed without remainder. Christology made to be so functional ceases to be christology and becomes another item in one's homiletical arsenal.

This is a tough one. If christology is not functional, of what value is it? If it is too functional, of what value is it? Before we finish Hebrews, we probably will discover Käsemann overstated his case. In the meantime, the church would do well to ponder the difference, if any, between "Christ" and "Christ for us."

28. Käsemann, *Jesus Means Freedom*, 101-16.

HEBREWS 3:1–5:10

CHRIST, THE FAITHFUL AND MERCIFUL HIGH PRIEST

OVERVIEW

As we have come to expect of the writer of Hebrews, the essential content of the next section is announced in the preceding one by means of a phrase or concise statement. So at 2:17, "so that he might be a merciful and faithful high priest in the service of God" (NRSV), introduces the primary subject matter of 3:1–5:10. The modifiers "merciful" and "faithful" will now be developed, but in reverse order, the last one mentioned being the first for consideration. In method of development, this unit will parallel 1:5–2:18 in three important respects. First, at the base of the argument lies a comparison: Christ and the angels, and now Christ and Moses. However, in the first section, the comparison of Christ with angels was sustained throughout, whereas the comparison with Moses quickly recedes (3:1-6a) in favor of a rather lengthy treatment of faithfulness (3:6b–4:13). Second, like 1:5–2:18, this section will consist of alternating exposition and exhortation. Again, however, there is a noticeable difference. In the first section, a brief hortatory unit (2:1-4) divided two rather lengthy expository units (1:5-14; 2:5-18). Here, exhortation occupies a much larger place: exhortation, 3:1-2a; exposition, 3:2b-6a; exhortation, 3:6b–4:16; exposition, 5:1-10. Whether this increase of exhortation signals the presence of a larger pastoral problem remains to be seen. Finally, the two sections are parallel in the use of quoted Scripture to ground the argument.[29] Both Gen 2:2 and Ps 95:7-11 supply proof for the writer's argument in 3:1–4:13, but especially Ps 95:7-11, which is not only quoted (3:7-11) but also reappears in part at 3:15; 4:3, 5, 7. In 4:14–5:10, Ps 2:7 and Ps 110:4 are quoted for use in an argument delayed until 7:1.

Within this section, therefore, we will follow two major considerations: Christ the faithful high priest (3:1–4:13) and Christ the merciful high priest (4:14–5:10). Each line of thought will begin with exhortation, move to exposition, and return to exhortation (although the closing exhortation of part two lies outside this section, 5:11–6:20).

---

29. There are allusions to certain OT texts in 3:1-6, but allusions function quite differently from direct quotations. Allusions to earlier texts are woven into the argument or narrative they serve in an indirect manner, sometimes seemingly casual, even unconscious on the part of the writer. The reader's familiarity with texts so employed is assumed, whether or not that assumption is correct. This indirection is effective, avoiding as it does the delays and obstacles often encountered in direct citation and argument.

HEBREWS 3:1–4:13, CHRIST THE FAITHFUL

OVERVIEW

Notice that the expected "high priest" has been omitted from the heading above, just as it has been from the heading to 4:14-10. This is not to deny or to obscure the author's clear use of the term at the beginning of each unit (3:1; 4:14). That Christ is our high priest will be developed in great detail later. The immediate concern is to present to the reader these two qualities of the high priest, faithfulness and mercy, and the wording of the two headings is intended to underscore that fact. In 3:1–4:13, the reader will be impressed with the dominating and pervasive use of vocabulary developed from the stem word "faith" (πίστις *pistis*): "faithful," "faithfulness," "obedience," "unfaithful," "faithlessness," "disobedience."

Hebrews 3:1-6, Christ and Moses Compared

COMMENTARY

3:1. In an "epistle" lacking the characteristic opening salutation, the writer directly addresses the readers for the first time. The rhetorical flourish, "brothers and sisters, holy partners in a heavenly calling," is more than oratory; the terms are appropriate to what has been and will be said. The readers have already been called brothers and sisters (2:11-12, 17), those who are sanctified (2:11), and partners with Christ in the human condition (2:14); but now they are called partners (3:1; also 3:14; 6:4) in a heavenly calling. That the calling is heavenly points not only to its source but also to its goal (2:10). The readers are addressed directly in order to urge them to think carefully, to "give attention to" (Luke 12:24, 27; Acts 7:31-32) Jesus in his unique role in their salvation. This insistence on focused attention is understandable, given the tendency among them to drift, to neglect, to be distracted (2:1-4). The role of Jesus is captured in two terms: "apostle" (ἀπόστολος *apostolos*) and "high priest" (ἀρχιερεύς *archiereus*), both of which gather up previous discussions. That Jesus is high priest has been stated (2:17) and will be discussed. That Jesus is apostle has been stated in function, as he is the envoy of God's Word (1:2) and work (1:3; 2:12, 16). The title "apostle" is applied to Jesus only here in the NT, but that he was "sent" of God is the testimony of many (e.g., Matt 10:40; Mark 9:37; Luke 10:16; Gal 4:4; John 3:17, 34; 5:36). God had many messengers and intermediaries, but Jesus alone is apostle and high priest of "our confession." Confession may refer to both the act of confessing and the content of the community's faith (cf. also 4:14; 10:23). We cannot know with certainty the content of the confession (1:1-4 is a possibility) or the occasions on which the community confessed its faith, although the priestly language of Hebrews favors liturgical settings such as baptism or the eucharist.[30]

3:2-6. The single quality of Jesus as apostle and high priest underscored here is fidelity to God (v. 2), and it is this fidelity that joins Jesus and Moses. Notice that there is no putdown of Moses in this comparison, as though Jesus were faithful but Moses unfaithful. On the contrary, the author twice alludes to Num 12:7: "my servant Moses; in all my house he is faithful" (LXX). Very likely "house" here refers to the people of Israel, but it is not yet clear how the author of Hebrews is using the term.[31] Even though Moses and Jesus were both faithful, they differ in station: Moses is a servant (the word for "servant" [θεράπων *therapōn*] occurs only here in the NT, but is taken from Num 12:7 LXX), while Jesus is a "son" (1:2, and frequently thereafter). They differ also in function: Moses serves in God's house, while Jesus as Son is over God's house (vv. 5-6). That Moses is a servant in God's house does not diminish him; Num 12:7-8 makes that clear. Having declared that prophets receive God's Word in visions and dreams, God says:

Not so with my servant Moses;
   he is entrusted with all my house.
With him I speak face to face—
   clearly, not in riddles;
   and he beholds the form of the Lord. (NRSV)

This otherwise clear comparison between Christ (used for the first time in Heb at 3:6) and Moses is complicated by two somewhat parenthetical statements, obviously intended to clarify. First, Jesus has more glory than

---

30. E. Käsemann, *The Wandering People of God,* trans. R. Harresville and I. Sandberg (Minneapolis: Augsburg, 1984) 167-73.
31. The range of possibilities for the meaning of οἰκία (*oikia*) in Hebrews is immense: "temple," "Israel," "family," "community," "heaven," "Davidic dynasty," or "creation," with variations on some of these.

Moses did, just as a builder has more glory than the building. It is not necessary to press this analogy to say that Moses is the building or that Jesus is the builder in the sense of being the one through whom God made the worlds (1:2). Like any good analogy, this one's service is completed in the clarity of its own appropriateness.

Second, the reader is reminded that while every house has a builder, the builder of the universe is God (v. 4). This unusual note serves to set in perspective both servant and son. However, it complicates the exposition by adding yet another meaning to the metaphor "house." The word οἰκία (*oikia*), used six times in this brief passage, means "Israel" (vv. 2, 5), a "building" in the ordinary sense (vv. 3*b*, 4), and "the universe" (v. 4). The author of Hebrews, however, draws once more on the metaphor and makes specific its meaning for both exposition and exhortation: "we are his house" (v. 6). There is no attempt here to argue that the Christian community and not Moses' Israel is the true house of God. In fact, the writer will later include in God's house Moses and many in Israel who were faithful (esp. 11:40). Rather, "we are his house" is intended to hold the attention of the readers on what they have been urged to consider (v. 1). In other words, "I am talking to you." This is evident in the conditional clause, "if we hold on to our courage and the hope of which we boast" (v. 6*b*). Courage or boldness is common in descriptions of early Christian witnessing (Mark 8:32; John 7:13; Acts 2:29; Phil 1:20), and in Hebrews it applies both to prayer (4:16; 10:19) and to public statements of faith (10:35). So also is the admonition to "hold on" or to "hold firm" (cf. Luke 8:15; 1 Cor 15:2; 1 Thess 5:21). The expression "the hope of which we boast" (lit., "the boast of hope") has parallels in Paul (Rom 5:2; 2 Cor 3:12) and probably refers not only to the exaltation of the crucified Jesus but also to the final victory of the saints.

As for the comparison between Jesus and Moses, it was almost inevitable that it be addressed; the writer could hardly deal with any aspect of Judaism, its law, its covenants, or its cult, without dealing with Moses. Of all the greats of the OT, Moses alone talked with God face to face. However, since Jesus is presented as a priest, is he being compared to Moses as priest? Not explicitly. Moses was a Levite (Exod 2:1-10), on occasion served at an altar (Exod 24:4-8), and, in fact, was called a priest in the OT (Ps 99:6) and in certain traditions of Judaism.[32] But here the comparison is not of an old and a new priesthood; that discussion is yet to come, and it will compare Christ and Aaron, not Moses. Moses in 3:1-6 is a servant in God's house whose greatness lay in his faithfulness and in his witness to God's Word, which continues to be spoken (3:5). And the discussion of Moses is here too brief and too embracing to support claims that the writer is engaged in a polemic with readers who hold a Moses christology.[33] There are reflections of a Moses christology in the NT (John 6:14; Acts 3:22; 7:37), but not in Hebrews; at least no more than there is an angel christology or a Joshua christology or an Aaron christology. (See Reflections at 4:12-13.)

32. Philo *The Life of Moses* 2:66-186.
33. Buchanan, *Hebrews*, 54, 255. For a quite different view, see M. R. D'Angelo, *Moses in the Letter to the Hebrews*, SBLDS 42 (Missoula, Mont.: Scholars Press, 1979) 65-199.

Hebrews 3:7-11, The Faithless People

COMMENTARY

This unit consists entirely of a quotation of Ps 95:7*b*-11 LXX. The writer provides commentary in 3:12–4:11, and therefore further commentary at this point would be premature and inappropriate. However, a number of observations about the quotation may be helpful preparation for the commentary. First, the introductory "therefore" joins the quotation to the conditional clause in v. 6*b*, "if we hold firm." The writer thus telegraphs ahead that the quotation from Psalm 95 will be in the service of paraenesis (exhortation to Christian living), and specifically the matter of holding firm, or fidelity. Second, the quotation is introduced as the words of the Holy Spirit (v. 7). Earlier, scriptural citations were presented as speeches of God (1:5-9, 13) or of Christ (2:12-13). The effect of such attribution is to allow no discontinuity between past and present people of God. The application of Psalm 95 to the present readers assumes the correspondence between the situations of Israel and the church as the pilgrim people of God, and the phrase "the Holy Spirit says" rather than "the psalmist says" or "the Scripture says" removes the distance between past and present. The verb "says" (λέγω *legō*) continues the use of verbs of speaking, which began at 1:1 and is appropriate to the homiletical nature of Hebrews.

As for the quotation itself, the LXX is followed rather closely, with a few variations. We do not know whether these variations are the work of the writer of Hebrews or due to the carelessness of scribes or whether they are to be accounted for by the writer's use of a different recension of the LXX text. Only two textual notes need to be made here, one having to do with a difference between the LXX and the Hebrew original, and the other with a difference between the LXX and its use by the author of Hebrews. The Hebrew text of Ps 95:8 refers to Meribah and Massah as geographical places where Israel quarreled and tested God (cf. Exod 17:7; Num 20:13). In the LXX, the place names have become experiences: rebellion and testing. One will see the difference by reading Ps 95:8 as quoted here and as it appears in the OT. The second textual note has to do with Ps 95:9-10. In the LXX, the forty years refers to God's anger: "For forty years I was angry with that generation." The writer of Hebrews has inserted a "therefore" before the expression "I was angry with that generation," leaving the forty years to be attached to the preceding statement, "though they had seen my works for forty years." One might think that this alteration had been motivated by a desire to portray God as acting providentially and graciously for forty years and then becoming angry. However, at 3:17 the author reads the LXX correctly: God is angry for forty years. Apparently both statements stand: The ancestors observed God's providential activity forty years; God was angry forty years, doubtless the same forty years.

One final observation: It is significant that the writer of Hebrews did not return immediately to the historical books (Exod 17:1-17; Num 14:20-23, 28-35; 20:2-13) to recall Israel's rebellion and testing of God, and God's oath that they would never see the land of promise. Rather, the author uses the memory of those events as preserved in Ps 95:7-11, returning later (3:16-18) to Numbers 14 to use the fate of Israel at Kadesh as a stern warning to the readers.

To what benefit is the psalmist's account employed? There are at least three. First, the psalmist has provided a model for appropriating the past for present purposes. In other words, the psalmist did for his generation what the Hebrews writer is doing for the readers addressed: making a past word a present word. Second, the account of Israel's failure as presented in Psalm 95 begins with the word "today." With that word the writer can transfer the entire exhortation of Ps 95:7-11 to the congregation as direct and immediate address: "This is what the Holy Spirit is saying to you here and now." And finally, by using the psalmist's account and not that of the historical books themselves, the author has appropriated a piece of liturgy for a homily that is liturgical in nature. Psalm 95 is a call to enter God's presence with praise, and in that setting it urges the people to fidelity, avoiding Israel's ancient failure. The sermon we call Hebrews is a call to come into God's presence (e.g., 4:16; 10:22), and within that setting is this exhortation to fidelity, likewise avoiding Israel's ancient failure. If Hebrews was read in a worship assembly of the church, and if some of the members recalled the frequent use of Psalm 95 in synagogue services, the words heard and the words remembered would have compounded effect. (See Reflections at 4:12-13.)

Hebrews 3:12-19, Failure to Enter God's Rest

COMMENTARY

At 3:12 the author begins the commentary on Ps 95:7-11 in the form of a homiletical midrash; that is, an interpretation of a passage of Scripture for a particular audience in a situation sufficiently similar to that of the text so as to make the application reasonable. Key words and phrases of the text ("today," "turn away," "rebel," "unbelief," "listen," "harden," "disobey," "rest") are brought directly to bear on the reader's spiritual condition. Of course, back of Psalm 95 stands Numbers 14, the account of Israel's unbelief and disobedience at Kadesh. Poised to enter the promised land, the Israelites were discouraged by the report of the spies, refused to move forward, and threatened to choose new leaders and return to Egypt. Angered by their rebellion, God swore that Israel would not enter "my rest." The commentary on the quoted psalm assumes that the readers of Hebrews are now at their own spiritual Kadesh and must learn from Israel's failure. There are three units in the commentary (3:12-19; 4:1-5; 4:6-11), each unit being built around a quoted portion of the psalm. The first unit (3:12-19) is an inclusio, a rather common rhetorical form that concludes with words, phrases, and ideas with which it began. In both v. 12 and v. 19 are the key words βλέπω (*blepō*, "see," "see to it," "take care") and ἀπιστία (*apistia*, "unbelief"), which occurs only here in Hebrews.

3:12. This verse repeats v. 1 in addressing the brothers and sisters, but strengthens the verb from "consider" to the word of warning, "Be alert to the danger" (cf. Matt 24:4; Acts 13:40; 1 Cor 10:18). The danger is presented in a grammatical construction that indicates a possibility very real and present (cf. Col 2:8). The community of believers is to be so alert as to see that not a single one of their number turns away from God. The "evil heart" is characterized by faithlessness and turning away from God; that is, disobedience. The words are taken from Num 14:22, 29, 32; Ps 95:7; and Jer 16:12; 18:12, and, therefore, do not refer to agnosticism or atheism but rebellion against God. What is involved in turning away (apostasy) the writer spells out in 6:4-8; 10:26-31; 12:15-17, 25. It is quite clear from v. 13 that abandoning God involves abandoning the community of faith.

3:13. Such a grim prospect can be avoided by daily exhorting (encouraging) each other, an activity that may imply preaching (Luke 3:18; Acts 14:22; 2 Cor 1:4) as well as admonitions on specific matters (Rom 12:1; 16:17; 1 Cor 16:15; Phil 4:2). The "today" of this verse and Ps 95:7 remains open, and the invitation to hear God's word still stands; but the implication is that the door of salvation could close. God's offer is available, but so is the deceptive sin that hardens the heart toward God. The language is borrowed from Ps 95:8 and seems rather general and widely used (Rom 7:11; 2 Cor 11:3; 2 Thess 2:10). Again, sin here seems to refer to faithlessness and apostasy and not to particular moral disorders that often follow turning away from God.

3:14. The epistle here repeats what has been said earlier in chap. 3 but with new emphasis. For example, the affirmation that we have become partners of Christ (v. 1) is followed by a strong conditional conjunction, "if indeed." Or again, the "confidence" of v. 6*b* is here expressed with a stronger and more unusual term. The word ὑπόστασις (*hypostasis*) may be translated "resolution," "standing firm," or "the very essence of a matter."[34] It appears in 1:3 as the "very being" of God and in 11:1 as the very "reality" of what is hoped for. The word must not get lost in subjectivity here. Apparently the author is saying that the fundamental core of one's faith commitment must be as securely held at the end as at the beginning. By "the end" reference is being made not so much to one's own death as to the final consummation of the Christian hope.

3:15. The direct address to the readers in straightforward exhortation ends temporarily at v. 14 as the writer again quotes the opening lines of Ps 95:7*b*-11. There seems to be a shift from exhortation to exposition through v. 19,

---
34. H. Koester, *TDNT*, 8:572-89.

but this only appears to be the case. Both the quotation and the comments that follow are clearly hortatory; the move is simply from direct to indirect. The writer is speaking *about* Israel but in so doing is speaking *to* the readers. Rhetoricians understood that relief from a confrontational style was often more effective than continuous confrontation. As was said of some in Jesus' audience, "They perceived he was talking to them." There is, however, some grammatical awkwardness in the shift at this verse. Some commentators find it helpful to link this verse with what precedes it. Attridge suggests that this quotation provides the actual words with which the members are daily to exhort one another (v. 13).[35] Others join v. 15 to what follows, noting the connection between "rebellion" (v. 15) and "rebellious" (v. 16). The real structural difficulty occurs at the beginning of v. 16 with the conjunction "for," which seems to continue a line of thought that, in fact, is just being introduced. The NRSV smoothes the sentence by translating the conjunction as "now"; the NIV just omits it altogether.

3:16-19. The quotation is inescapably appropriate to the readers; after all, it is the word of the Holy Spirit (v. 7), and it is a word for "today." But the situation of the believers being addressed is too critical to allow them to assimilate Ps 95:7*b*-8*a* on their own; the writer drives it home with three rhetorical questions and answers (vv. 16-18). The questions draw upon the language of Psalm 95, the answers from what happened to Israel at Kadesh according to Numbers 14. In pressing his point, the writer inserts no exemptions or qualifiers. For example, in v. 16, "all" rebelled. Numbers 14:22 does so state the case, but later exempts Joshua and Caleb (Num 14:30, 38).[36] Or again, in v. 17, the forty years is the period of God's wrath (as in Ps 95:10), whereas the writer had earlier (vv. 9-10) referred to it as the time of God's gracious providence. The OT views the forty years both ways (cf. Ps 95:10 with Deut 2:7), but mercy and judgment are never far from each other. God made clothes for the guilty pair exiled from Eden and protected the fugitive Cain east of Eden. When the writer concludes with "So we see that they were unable to enter" (v. 19), it is likely that the sad ending to Numbers 14 is in mind. When the Israelites realized their sin, they sought to prove their repentance by attempting to enter the land in spite of warnings that God was not with them. The result was tragic defeat at the hands of the occupants of the land (Num 14:39-45). Perhaps the preacher of Hebrews is preparing the readers for the strong language concerning second chances in 6:4-8; 10:26-31; 12:16-17. As for the shift from "disobedient" in v. 18 to "unbelief" in v. 19, the awkwardness exists in the English and not in the Greek text. The two words are derived from the same root (ἀπιστέω *apisteō*) and so will often be used interchangeably. (See Reflections at 4:12-13.)

---

35. Attridge, *A Commentary on the Epistle to the Hebrews*, 119-20.

36. In 1 Corinthians 10, Paul exhorts and warns the church using Numbers 14, but he repeatedly uses a qualifier, "as did some of them" (see 1 Cor 10:7-10).

Hebrews 4:1-11, God's Rest Still Available

COMMENTARY

The author continues and concludes the exposition-exhortation begun at 3:7, which consists almost entirely of an interpretation of Ps 95:7*b*, with Israel's failure at Kadesh and God's oath as recorded in Numbers 14 always near the surface. However, in several ways 4:1 does mark a transition. Besides the conjunction "therefore," which is itself transitional, the text shifts from exhorting by means of talking *about* Israel (3:15-19) to exhorting by means of direct address *to* the hearers. In addition, v. 1 begins an inclusio, which ends at v. 11. In other words, 4:1-11 is a unit, beginning and ending with strong imperatives ("let us be careful"; "let us make every effort") and strong warnings ("that none of you should seem to have failed to reach it"; "that no one may fall"). Within the unit can be discerned two sub-units, vv. 1-5 and vv. 6-11. Psalm 95:7*b*, 11 is fundamental to this passage, and through it all runs the often-repeated word "rest" (κατάπαυσις *katapausis*).

In 3:7-19 the writer assumed the propriety of applying Psalm 95 to the church of the readers, an assumption perhaps based on the introductory assertion, "as the Holy Spirit says" (3:7). In other words, the words of Scripture are the living voice of the Spirit addressed to us. In 4:1-11, however, it is as though the author realized that some might not be persuaded by this uncritical transfer of a text (Psalm 95) from one time and place to another, and, therefore, the distance between Israel's history and the Hebrews congregation needs to be negotiated more deliberately. The distance is of two kinds: geographical, in that entering Canaan and entering rest cannot be synonymous, and chronological, in that the rest promised to ancient Israel cannot be assumed as being available to readers centuries later. The author handles the first by recourse to Gen 2:2, the second by a final return to Psalm 95.

Overall, the line of thought is clear. Since the promised rest of God is still available (keep in mind the "today" of the offer, Ps 95:7*b*), we must take care (lit., "let us be afraid," v. 1) that no one fail to enter. Our situation and Israel's are parallel in that all of us heard the good news (lit., "were evangelized," v. 2), but we differ from Israel in that we received the good news in faith and are entering that rest. Notice the present tense (v. 3); rest is not only an eschatological future but also a present favorable state, as the sermon will unfold later. But what is this rest? For Israel it was initially a place, a land of their own, but the writer here (vv. 3-5) finds quite a different meaning to "rest."[37] By interpreting the noun "rest" in Ps 95:11 and by citing the verb form of the same word in Gen 2:2 (LXX), "God rested," the author moves beyond the idea of a land to that of a condition in that we participate with God. The author made this same kind of interpretive move in treating the word "house" in 3:1-6. "Rest" now becomes a synonym for salvation, the presence of God now and in the future. To the matter of sabbath rest, we shall return shortly. As for the writer's indefinite reference to Gen 2:2, "For somewhere he has spoken" (v. 4, NIV preferred over NRSV here; see Commentary on 2:6).

Having dealt with the shift from Canaan to sabbath rest in vv. 1-5, the author turns in vv. 6-11 to the chronological problem: How can an ancient offer to Israel be understood as an offer to believers in the present? The writer's reasoning is as follows: God's offer of rest was not accepted because of disobedience, and, therefore, it remains open to those of faithful obedience. This is underscored by the use of the word "today." This "today," says the author, was spoken by God through David in Psalm 95, and David lived much later than the wilderness generation led by Joshua. This clearly means that the offer in Joshua's day, having been rejected, was at a later day still open. And the offer is to rest from labor, the sabbath rest in which God also participates. Therefore, while the readers are like the Israelites in that they are on a journey and are invited to enter God's rest, they must be diligent to be unlike the Israelites in the matter of falling short due to disobedience.

Such is the general flow of thought in 4:1-11, but we must now return to the passage and face three thorny problems in the text itself. The first appears in v. 1. What is it about which the readers are to "take care," or more literally, "be afraid"? The word translated "seem" (NRSV) can also mean "judged to be" or "reckoned as" (cf. Prov 17:28; 27:14, where the same word appears), and this stronger meaning fits well with the warning, "Be afraid that." To seem to be or to appear to be is too weak. The infinitive translated "failed to reach" (NRSV) or "fall short of" (NIV) can also have the meaning "to arrive too late." With this translation the warning would be "not to think you have arrived too late" to enter God's rest; that is, the past offer is now closed, and Christians cannot enter. So some commentators prefer,[38] but there is nothing in this passage or elsewhere in the letter to suggest that this was a fear of the writer or the reader. On the contrary, they are the heirs of salvation (1:14).

---

37. Buchanan has argued that "rest" does not have a different meaning for Hebrews, but that "the author expected the promised heritage of the land of Canaan under the rule of the Messiah to be fulfilled for Jesus and his followers." See Buchanan, *Hebrews*, 65. The writer of Hebrews understands "rest" differently.

38. E.g., Montefiore, *A Commentary on the Epistle to the Hebrews*, 80-81.

The second problem occurs in v. 2 and is rooted in the variations among Greek manuscripts. According to some texts, the sense would be, "the word heard did not benefit them because it met with no faith in those who heard it." This is perfectly clear and appropriate to the argument, but the best attested manuscripts have the more difficult reading: "the word heard did not benefit them because they were not united by faith with those who listened." Who were those who listened? Historically Joshua and Caleb, but it is possible the writer refers to himself and his readers. This is the view that will be expressed later (11:40).

The third and final problem is not one of text or translation, but of interpretation: What is the rest of God, the sabbath rest? Just as we noted earlier that the political understanding—that is, the conquest of the land by the new Israel (Jesus and his disciples)—is inappropriate to Hebrews, so also is the gnostic.[39] That the soul, pre-existent and eternal, enters a body, journeys homeless in the world, and returns to its home is a cyclical view of life that does not blend easily with the biblical view of creation and history. This is not to say that echoes and fragments of such views do not exist in some Jewish and early Christian groups. Philo of Alexandria had allegorized Israel's history into a narrative of the soul's wandering toward a spiritual rest. The *Gospel of Thomas* psychologizes "rest," making it a subjective possession.[40] And in the canonical NT apart from Hebrews, rest is spoken of quite apart from notions of the land or the seventh day (Matt 11:28-30). All this is to say that the writer of Hebrews is not creating *de novo* the view that rest transcends place and history, while being experienced here and now (vv. 3, 10). It is an eschatological reality in the sense of being grounded in the ultimate purpose of God for God's people. It neither began nor ended at Kadesh (Numbers 14). Rest is a primordial reality, existing from "the foundation of the world" (v. 3). This fairly common expression for designating true and non-contingent things of God (Matt 13:35; 25:34; John 17:24; Eph 1:4; Rev 13:8) does not refer to pre-creation activity of God, but to post-creation. God "rested on the seventh day from all the work that he had done" (Gen 2:2 NRSV), just as those who enter God's rest will do (4:10). While the sabbath was later justified on humanitarian grounds (rest for all creation), for historical reasons (remember the exodus), and for liturgical purposes (the praise of God), Gen 2:2 is its birthplace. The sabbath but institutionalized a central truth: God rested and invites others into that rest with all the blessings attendant to the presence of God. The book of *Jubilees,* a second-century BCE Jewish writing, sings of God's invitation to the angels to join God's people on earth in a festive day of rest, a celebration in heaven and on earth of God's rest from work.[41] The church of Hebrews must have been aware of such traditions about "rest." (See Reflections at 4:12-13.)

39. Käsemann, *The Wandering People of God,* 74-75.
40. Cf. Philo *Sayings* 51, 52, 60.
41. *Jub.* 2:18-21.

Hebrews 4:12-13, God's Word Still Active

COMMENTARY

The writer-preacher concludes the section begun at 3:1, and especially the exhortation of 3:7–4:11, with a rhetorical flourish on the Word of God. Although 4:12-13 contains the marks of conscious literary artistry, and is in a sense a self-contained unit (an inclusio, beginning and ending with Logos, the Word), it is not necessary to conclude that the passage was borrowed or was composed for another setting. It forms a perfect conclusion to the argument based on Ps 95:7*b*-11, which was introduced as the message of the Holy Spirit (3:7). This forceful reminder of the nature and work of God's Word is a fitting underscoring of the strong imperatives of the preceding section: "See to it" (3:12); "let us be afraid" (4:1); "let us be eagerly diligent" (4:11).

One can find a rhetorical context for 4:12-13 in the larger world of Hellenistic Judaism, with its descriptive phrases concerning Word,

Wisdom, and Torah, which are at times used interchangeably. And since this was most likely the thought world of the writer of Hebrews, echoes and allusions may well join these verses to that culture. For example, Wisdom "pervades and penetrates all things" (Wis 7:24 NRSV); or the Word of God has the power "to cut";[42] or Torah was created before the world was made and was God's instrument in making all things, including humankind.[43] But one can find resources aplenty in the OT for all the affirmations made here about the Word of God. In fact, the writer is primarily gathering up and reasserting what has been said already in Hebrews: The God who spoke still speaks, and that word is inescapably valid (2:2-4). In the writer's theology, words of Scripture are words of God to us today. Hence, the Word is living and active (cf. Isa 55:11), sharper than any two-edged sword (cf. Isa 49:2; Eph 6:17; Rev 19:15). The word that creates is also able to discern and judge (Ps 51:6; Amos 1:2). One should not tarry too long over "soul and spirit, bone and marrow"; these terms, drawn from the anthropology of the day, are simply a forceful way of saying that no part of the human life is beyond the knowing gaze of God. The Word of God serves as the eyes of God, seeing everything the heart devises and feels. These two verses could be read as a digest of Psalm 139: "O LORD, you have searched me and known me./ You know when I sit down and when I rise up. . . . Even before a word is on my tongue, / O LORD, you know it completely. . . . Where can I go from your spirit?/ Or where can I flee from your presence? . . . For it was you who formed my inward parts;/ you knit me together in my mother's womb" (Ps 139:1-3, 7, 13 NRSV). As the Hebrews writer puts it: "all are naked and laid bare to the eyes of the one to whom we must render an account" (v. 13; see also Rom 8:27; 1 Cor 4:5).

The passage ends as it began, with Logos, but here it is not God's Word but ours, hence the translation "account" (as in 13:17; see also Luke 16:2; 1 Pet 4:5). It is as though the writer were a liturgist who concludes the reading of Scripture with, "This is the word of God," with the expectation that the readers will respond, not with "Amen" but with their lives.

---

42. Philo *Who Is the Heir of Divine Things?* 130.
43. For a concise treatment of Jewish speculations on Torah, Word, and Wisdom, see Fred Craddock, *The Pre-existence of Christ in the NT* (Nashville: Abingdon, 1968) 31-53.

REFLECTIONS

1. It is somewhat surprising that the author of Hebrews does not introduce the word "faith" until 4:2, a word that will later serve as the key to understanding salvation history from creation to the eschaton (chap. 11). Faith, the writer will say, is the means of apprehending as present that for which we hope, the ability to see as real that which to human eyes is invisible (11:1). The delay until 4:2 cannot be taken, therefore, as a kind of indifference toward the word. On the contrary, the readers have been prepared to hear the word by the writer's frequent use of terms drawn from the same root, words such as "faithful," "faithless," "obedient," and "disobedient." By such preparation the readers are helped to see how muscular and active faith is. Faith is tough and tenacious; it holds fast. It stands firm. It is a "to the end" (3:14) quality. Faith generates companion words: "courage," "boldness," and "confidence," all of which are used in this epistle-sermon. Faith is not mentioned at quiet times, accompanied by sonnets, but in the story of a people struggling in the desert, accompanied by grumbling and rebellion. And faith has content, as the text makes clear by reference to our confession (3:1). In other words, faith is more than an orientation of the heart toward God, although it is that. Faith has something to say about God, and it does so with boldness (3:6) and confidence (3:14).

2. Hebrews speaks about a community (Israel) and to a community (the church). In reciting the story of Israel in the wilderness, the writer clearly understands that the desert journey was a group experience, the behavior of some affecting the behavior of all. There was no subjective captivity of the good news of God's promise; they heard it together (4:2). Likewise, the message of this letter-sermon is addressed to the whole congregation, and most likely was read at an assembly of the church, a fact we may forget now that we all have our own Bibles. The preacher says repeatedly "us," "we," and "you" (plural). There is concern for the individual, but it is a community concern: "that none of you may be hardened" (3:13 NRSV); "let us take care that none of you should seem to have failed to reach it" (4:1 NRSV). Shepherding was a congregational responsibility. And so was preaching: "But exhort [encourage] one another every day" (3:13 NRSV). It is very difficult to reclaim ministries once surrendered, but it can be done if those few who now own those ministries are willing to share them again.

3. Since teachers and preachers always struggle with the hermeneutical issues related to the meaning of texts of one time and place for persons of another time and place, it might be instructive to compare the methods in Heb 3:7–4:11 and 1 Cor 10:1-13. A comparison is possible because of a number of remarkable similarities: Both draw on the failure of Israel in the desert, with Numbers 14 being central to the story; both characterize the life of faith as a pilgrimage, beset with tests and struggles; both speak of God's providence on the way to the promised future; both draw lessons and warnings from Israel's fall in the desert. It is important also that neither writer evaporates Israel's history in some grand allegory of the pilgrimage of the soul. History remains history; neither past nor present is consumed by the other. However, the writers move into the present differently. Paul more directly makes the past serve the present by referring to Israel's experiences as examples (types): "These things happened to them to serve as an example, and they were written down to instruct us" (1 Cor 10:11 NRSV). Paul thus robs the past of some of its own integrity by viewing it as "for us." The writer of Hebrews negotiates the distance between past and present without making yesterday the servant of today. This is achieved by mediating Israel's desert history through Psalm 95. Two interpretive advantages are thus taken: The psalmist stands chronologically between Numbers 14 and the present and hence is able to move the story forward toward the readers; and the introductory "Today" of Ps 95:7*b* sets the ancient record directly before the Hebrews church as a word spoken to them. As the writer puts it: "The Holy Spirit says" (3:7 NRSV). In other words, every time and place is the "present" of God's Word. Neither method need be imitated by today's preacher but should serve to instruct and to urge thoughtful intentionality in one's own interpretive methods.

4. The introduction of the theme of "rest" into the presentation of the Christian life as that of a pilgrimage provides a striking image of the rhythm of faith: movement and rest. Psychologists and counselors have long understood this rhythm as basic to a healthy life, and leaders of organizations, including churches, are using it to design programming. But Hebrews can be additionally helpful in the reminder that the life of faith is not simply scheduled as periods of movement and periods of rest. Rest, says the text, does not just follow pilgrimage but occurs during pilgrimage as well (4:3). The rest of God is both present and future. Therefore, just as the Near Eastern proverb says, "There is going in my staying and staying in my going," so also does the preacher in Hebrews say, "There is rest in movement and movement in rest."

5. Every now and then we should pause to appreciate the rhetorical skill of the writer-preacher of Hebrews and reflect on its significance. Rhetoric is the art of persuasion, and that primary purpose undoubtedly fuels all that is being done here. The interplay of exposition and exhortation; alliteration; repetition of words and sounds; perfectly rounded inclusios; the rhythm of direct and indirect discourse; anticipation and restraint—these and other techniques are in the service of persuasion. But rhetoric is an art, and like all art it gives pleasure to the reader or hearer. The skillful writer or speaker, no matter how weighty the issue, how noble the cause, gives pleasure, and that pleasure is not for the purpose of sedating or seducing, or simply to curry the favor of an audience. Pleasure is a fundamental force in human history. Biological continuity, cultural continuity, intellectual continuity—all are indebted more to pleasure than to logic. The ancient Greeks understood that, and so do many African American preachers today. And the Word of God continues in the world, thanks to those who delight in the law of the Lord and to the enjoyment of Scripture by those who speak and those who listen.

6. One can assume that when the Hebrews preacher speaks of the living and active Word of God, probing, penetrating, and revealing, the expectation is that the readers/hearers will associate that word with what has been said (esp. 3:7–4:11). But the Word of God is not being *defined;* that is, the writer is not saying that Scripture *is* the Word of God, or Scripture *contains* the word of God, or Scripture *becomes* the word of God. Rather, the Word of God is being characterized as to what it *does.* No claim is being made for the message presented, as if to say, "My sermon is the word of God." From the beginning at 1:1 it has been abundantly clear that the word is *God's* word and any attempts to locate it or define it would be inappropriate. What the author does is appeal to Scripture in such a way as to assume that the readers accept that tradition as normative, and then interpret that Scripture so as to address the readers in their own circumstance. This, too, is done in such a way as to assume that the readers accept interpretation of Scripture as the regular activity of the community. The book and the community are brought face to face by the preacher with the expectation that the community will hear God's voice speaking to them. As both promise and warning, what they are told is that when God speaks, the word is incisive, revealing what is hidden and giving its hearers the experience of being exposed before God with full accounts to be rendered. To be more precise than that would be to violate God's freedom to speak or to be silent and the listeners' freedom to hear or not to hear.

HEBREWS 4:14–5:10, CHRIST THE MERCIFUL

OVERVIEW

That 4:14–5:10 is a distinct unit is widely recognized, although it has been argued that 4:14 should be joined with what precedes it, returning as it does to the theme expressed in 3:1.[44] However, such an arrangement must account for the abrupt shift from 4:12-13 and for the fact that 4:14 does not so much return to 3:1 as it does to 2:17-18, the very vocabulary of which is repeated in 4:14-16. This unit is a transition passage, concluding what has been said and introducing what is yet to be said. The reader will recognize in the elaborated themes here the hints, intimations, and brief references in 1:3, 13; 2:17-18; and 3:1.

But it was the description of Christ as a merciful and faithful high priest at 2:17 that provided the structure for 3:1–5:10. Taking the two characteristics in reverse order, as is the writer's custom, 3:1–4:12 developed Christ's (and our) faithfulness; 4:14–5:10 will focus on his mercy. As in previous units in which Christ was presented in a contrast, first with angels and then with Moses, so here he is portrayed as being like and yet very unlike Aaron. The twin credentials of a priest, to be of the people and to be of God—qualities

---
44. Among those favoring this view, Lane, *Hebrews 1–8*, 96, provides the strongest support.

already and repeatedly claimed for Christ—are now treated more extensively. Notice the flow of thought: of the people (4:14–5:3); of God (5:4-6); of the people (5:7-9); of God (5:10). Of key interest in this unit are two moves by the writer: the joining of Ps 2:7 and Ps 110:4 and the introduction of the scriptural ground for presenting Jesus as a priest when genealogically and liturgically he was not. The exposition of "according to the order of Melchizedek" will, however, be delayed until 7:1.

Hebrews 4:14-16, Hold Fast; Draw Near

COMMENTARY

Just as the preceding unit was framed on movement and rest, so also here the message joins holding fast and drawing near. These three verses hang on the two exhortations: to get a firm grip (stronger than 3:6) on our confession (cf. Commentary on 3:1) and to approach (as in prayer) the throne of grace. The ground for both appeals is the nature of our high priest. By joining "Jesus" and "Son of God" the writer may be drawing on the language of the confession; we do not know. But we do know that the two terms join the two qualifications of a priest: to be made like his brothers and sisters (Jesus), and to be appointed of God (Son of God). The writer has stated this before (2:9-18), but now the presentation of Jesus as one who shares our lot and who also bears a special relation to God is made especially important, for two reasons. First, it is essential as a basis for assurance that our approach to God will be met with sympathy and understanding; he has been tested as we are tested. That Jesus experienced completely the human condition gives confidence to a prayer life that fully expects both mercy and help. Not forgiveness alone, but forgiveness and help for the improvement of one's lot. And since Jesus, having been as we are in every respect, passed through the heavens—that is, entered into God's presence—access to God has been opened for us, with Jesus already there interceding on our behalf (7:25; 9:24). Second, this presentation of Jesus as being both of the people and of God is a clear anticipation of 5:1-10, where the writer begins the difficult task of establishing that Jesus was and is a priest. Several times now the author has referred to Jesus as high priest, but early Christian documents do not reveal this characterization of Jesus as widespread or well known. By the time the readers reach 5:1, their hands are in the air with a question: How could Jesus be a high priest, given his genealogy, the geographical location of his ministry, and the adversarial nature of his relationship with temple authorities? It is time to establish credentials.

Before moving to 5:1-10, however, we need to attend to several significant phrases in 4:14-16. That our high priest "has passed through the heavens" (v. 14) evokes the image of the Jewish high priest on the Day of Atonement, passing through the veil of the Temple and entering the holy of holies, the place of God's presence as symbolized by the ark of the covenant, which rested in the inner chamber of the tabernacle. That Jesus has entered God's presence was implied at 1:3, 13, but is now stated with the obvious intention of recalling the imagery of the wilderness tent of meeting as well as of anticipating more detailed discussion of Jesus' passing beyond the veil (6:19-20; 8:1-2; 9:11; 10:20). As for the source of the idea of passing through the heavens, antecedents are available in the ancient figures of Enoch (Gen 5:24) and Elijah (2 Kgs 2:11), with ascension stories becoming more elaborate in apocalyptic texts of late Judaism.[45] In gnostic redeemer myths, the savior of human souls had to pass from God through a succession of heavens filled with hostile powers to reach the earth and then return the same way. However, there is nothing here to suggest that hostile angelic forces sought to impede Jesus in his journey to God.[46]

In saying that Jesus is able "to sympathize with our weaknesses" (v. 15), the writer surely does not refer to physical weakness or

---

45. As held by Jewett, *Letter to Pilgrims*, 81
46. E.g., *Ascension of Isaiah* 6–7; *1 Enoch* 14–19; 70–71.

illness, although the word often carries that meaning and may be translated "diseases" (Luke 5:15; 8:2; John 5:5). Paul used the word to describe the general inclination of the flesh (Rom 6:19; 1 Cor 15:43), and the moral force of "weakness" is undoubtedly present here as well as at 5:2 and 7:28. This is made evident in the description of Jesus as being sympathetic and yet "without sin." That Jesus was without sin was variously expressed by early Christian writers (John 7:18; 8:46; 1 Pet 1:19; 2:22; 1 John 3:5), in each case with a particular understanding of sin. It is not necessary here to flood the mind with a lengthy catalog of sins and then excuse Jesus from all of them. In the context of 4:14-16, being without sin refers to Jesus' unwavering firmness in his faithfulness to God. Neither is it necessary to argue that his being without sin somehow lessens his capacity to sympathize with us. It is not by sinning that one is made sympathetic but by being tested as we are tested. As the ancients expressed it, he was as we are, and therefore he will help; he was not as we are, and therefore he can.

A closing note on the rhetorical form of 4:15: Notice the use of the double negative and the adversative conjunction. To say that "we do not have a high priest who is not able" is much more forceful than "we have a high priest who is able." In addition, the negative statement of the positive sets up the conjunction "but," sharpening even further the affirmation about the priestly ministry of Jesus. Both double negatives and contrasts were rhetorical devices used by skilled communicators of the time. (See Reflections at 5:1-10.)

Hebrews 5:1-10, Christ Qualified as High Priest

COMMENTARY

It is difficult to explore the concept of Christ as high priest without engaging the question of the source or sources. Answers, however, are not quickly forthcoming, because lines of influence are not clearly discernible. Fragments of related ideas are found in the New Testament outside Hebrews: the tearing of the temple veil at the death of Jesus (Mark 15:38), Jesus' words, "Destroy this temple, and in three days I will raise it up" (John 2:19 NRSV); Jesus gave his life as a sacrifice and, therefore, functioned as a priest; Jesus is the place of atonement (mercy seat) for our sins (Rom 3:25); and other hints and intimations. But the sum of these hardly adds up to a satisfactory answer. The concept may have developed out of the church's wide use of Psalm 110. Although it is Ps 110:1 that is so much employed, Ps 110:4, which declares "You are a priest forever," lies close at hand. Other possible influences have been found in the Logos-Priest of Philo of Alexandria, the Messiah-Priest of Qumran, or the priest of late Jewish apocalyptic visions.[47] Of course, it is quite possible that a church that re-read and reappropriated its own sacred texts and heritage in Judaism created a liturgy out of a Christian interpretation of the Day of Atonement. If the exodus and wilderness experiences of Israel were so instructive for the church's self-understanding, why not also find in the rituals of the wilderness tabernacle precursors of its own view of Christ and the liturgies that enshrine and proclaim his saving activity? We have in common with the congregation of Hebrews the need to follow the writer carefully in the treatment of this concept, which admittedly is "difficult to explain" (5:11).

In vv. 1-4 the writer presents the essential qualities of any high priest before moving to the consideration of Christ as high priest in vv. 5-10.

Of course, not just any high priest is in the writer's mind; the Aaronic priesthood will lead to the portrayal of Christ's priesthood. At least logically this is the movement of thought, but theologically, the movement is from Christ to Aaron. This is to say, the writer is very selective in sketching the qualities of a priest, choosing to discuss only those features appropriate to the comparison with Christ. In this sense the writer begins with Christ. Of

---

47. Käsemann, *The Wandering People of God*, 195-217, reviews a range of possibilities arriving at his own view of a gnostic redeemer myth as the source.

any priest it must be the case that the person be chosen from among persons whom the priest will represent before God. But the priest must also be chosen of God, to represent God to the people. When the discussion turns to Christ, these two qualifications will be discussed, but in reverse order.

5:1-4. The first qualification, that the high priest be one of the people, enables the one so serving to minister in two ways: to "offer gifts and sacrifices for sins" (v. 1) and to "deal gently" (v. 2). One should not try to be careful in distinguishing gifts and sacrifices; the expression came to be something of a stock phrase (8:3; 1 Kgs 8:64) to refer to the whole sacerdotal activity of the high priest. It will become clear that the writer has in mind the blood sacrifice of the Day of Atonement (9:12).

As for "dealing gently" with the people, this was not in the list of credentials for Aaronic priests, but can be inferred from their duties. Forbearance and humility were evident in both Aaron and Moses (Num 12:3; 14:5), but very likely the author is reading backward from qualities of Christ to qualities of the Aaronic high priest. The word translated "deal gently" (μετριοπαθέω *metriopatheō*) occurs only here in the New Testament and means "to moderate" or "control" emotion. In extracanonical literature the word was used most often in relation to anger. This is not a quality synonymous with sympathy, the capacity to be one with others, attributed to Christ at 4:15. Here the high priest is to behave with restraint toward the ignorant and wayward, a restraint born of the priest's awareness of his own weakness.

Sacrifices for sin were efficacious under circumstances of unwilling or unintentional errors and breaches of God's law due to ignorance (Lev 4:13; Ezek 45:20). Luke likewise extends God's offer of forgiveness to those who acted in ignorance (Luke 23:34; Acts 3:17; 17:30), and according to 1 Tim 1:13, Paul received mercy "because I had acted ignorantly in unbelief" (NRSV). Such sins, according to the Hebrews author, are viewed quite differently from those committed willfully (6:4-8; 10:26-31; 12:17). The high priest behaved with moderation toward ignorantly erring people because he was himself subject to weakness (lit., "clothed with weakness"). In fact, his own sins made it necessary for him to offer first a sacrifice for himself and then a sacrifice on behalf of the people (v. 3), as it is written: "Aaron shall present the bull as a sin offering for himself, and shall make atonement for himself and for his house," then he shall make atonement "for all the assembly of Israel" (Lev 16:11, 17 NRSV). This difference between the Aaronic high priest and Christ will be noted later.

The second qualification, that the high priest be chosen of God, is to the writer so self-evident that the writer feels no need to elaborate beyond the simplest statement of it (v. 4). That Aaron was so qualified has triple attestation in Scripture: at his call (Exod 28:1); at his public ordination (Lev 8:1-36); and at God's reaffirmation of Aaron's priesthood following the rebellion of Korah (Numbers 16–18). Notice that there is no putdown or criticism of Aaron. As the writer did not find it necessary, in the development of christology, to speak disparagingly of angels or Moses or Joshua, so here the flaws of Aaron's person or ministry are not exhibited, as though Christ would shine brighter by comparison. It is enough to say that a priest ministers only when called of God, "as Aaron was."

5:5-10. In these verses the writer turns to Christ as high priest, addressing the same two considerations: that he was of the people and of God. Now, however, the two themes are treated in reverse order, forming with vv. 1-4 a small chiasm (a literary form of inverted parallels; that is, ABB´A´) The Aaronic priesthood is:

of the people (vv. 1-3)   A
of God (v. 4)   B

Christ's priesthood is:

of God (vv. 5-6)   B´
of the people (vv. 7-9)   A´

Verse 10 paraphrases v. 6, reaffirming that Christ is a priest *of God*.

5:5-6. Christ's priesthood is by divine appointment. Just as the Aaronic priesthood was not by human initiative but by the call of God (v. 4), so also Christ did not glorify himself. On the contrary, glory and honor were bestowed on him by God (2:9). In support of this affirmation the writer does not argue but rather quotes Psalms 2 and 110. These citations are not introduced here but are repeated from the catena of biblical quotations in 1:5-13. At that point, Psalm 2 opened the catena and Psalm 110 closed it. However, while Ps 2:7 is repeated, from Psalm 110, not v. 1 but v. 4 is here cited, and for the first time. The NT bears abundant testimony to the early church's use of Ps 110:1 in christological formulations, but only in Hebrews is Ps 110:4 used. This appropriation of the psalm may be original with this author; in fact, the gradual and detailed introduction and development of this theme (5:6; 5:10; 6:20; 7:1) indicates that it is not familiar to the readers. More familiar is the application of Ps 2:7 to Christ; "You are my son;/ today I have begotten you" (NRSV) needs only to be quoted, without supporting argument.

The title "Son," introduced at 1:2, is the constant term for referring to Jesus Christ in chapters 1–4. It would be to deviate from the writer's point to let the word "begotten" lead to discussion of Jesus' birth. Here the term is from the language of appointment, not parentage, just as it is in the psalm's original sense: God appointed or designated Israel's king as God's son. Being "God's son" has roots in royal ideology. Interestingly, neither Matthew nor Luke uses Ps 2:7 in the nativity story. Equally unfruitful would be efforts to define "today" with precision. Adoptionist christologies found support in the use of a portion of Ps 2:7 in the stories of Jesus' baptism (Mark 1:11; Luke 3:22), but this verse is also used to argue the resurrection of Jesus (Acts 13:33). And Hebrews places "today" in eternity, prior to creation (1:2). So when is "today"? Pre-existence? Baptism? Resurrection? Exaltation? Precision here is limiting. It is better to be guided by the psalm's own meaning: God grants to the king a place above all other monarchs and princes. Let the attention be given to God, whose appointment is sure and final.

Of greater significance is the joining of these two psalms, which offer in support of God's appointment two apparently quite different proclamations: "You are my son" and "You are a priest forever." These texts, united by "as" or "likewise" (v. 6; the NIV inexplicably omits the word and thus loses the direct comparison), join two christological motifs: kingship and priesthood. This is not an original conjunction; the figure of Melchizedek unites in himself both king and priest (7:1-3). Nor is there any inherent tension between the two. The misuses of power during the reign of the Hasmoneans were not the inevitable result of combining in one person both political and religious authority. According to 5:5-6, Son, King, and High Priest are joined in Jesus Christ in ways to be explicated later (beginning at 7:1).

Some interpreters, however, find more meaning in the union of these two psalm citations. For example, it has been argued that Ps 2:7 and Ps 110:4 serve to present Christ as both pre-existent (Son) and post-existent (Priest). But that affirmation has been well made more than once in chapters 1–2. In addition, it presumes that Christ's priesthood is a post-incarnation activity. It is that, of course, in that he is continually in God's presence, making intercession for us (2:18; 4:14-16; 6:20; 7:23-26; 8:1-2); but prior to entering God's presence beyond the veil, the high priest makes sacrifice for sin. This Jesus did in the offering of himself (2:17; 9:14, 26; 10:10). His priestly service, therefore, cannot be confined to his post-exaltation ministry. F. F. Bruce, in his search to explain the union of the two psalm citations, suggests that it may be a response to messianic expectations at Qumran. In that community, two messiahs were anticipated, the one royal, from the house of David, the other priestly, from the house of Aaron. According to Bruce, the writer is saying that there are not two messiahs but one, and it is Jesus Christ who is both King and High Priest.[48] However, it would seem that such an important apologetic would be more fully argued rather than so subtly presented. Perhaps it is enough here to say that vv. 5-6 have a double function: to recall what has been said (1:5, 13) and to prepare the reader for an argument yet to be made (7:1ff.). We have come to expect of the writer such rhetorical moves.

5:7. Having dealt with the qualification that Jesus is of God, the writer now turns to the second essential for being a high priest: Jesus is one of the people. That he shares the common human condition is not introduced

---

48. F. F. Bruce, *The Epistle to the Hebrews*, rev. ed., NICNT (Grand Rapids: Eerdmans, 1990) 94-97. See especially notes 26, 27.

here; that characteristic has been stated in 2:9-18 and 4:15, but in 5:7-9 the reader is given an elaboration of those statements. The "for a little while was made lower than the angels" (2:9 NRSV) is elongated into a vivid description of life "in the days of his flesh." This portrait of Jesus' earthly life is not, of course, as extended as that of the Gospels, but then it is not so abbreviated as that of Paul. Paul's gospel concerned a Christ who died for our sins according to the Scriptures, was buried, was raised on the third day according to the scriptures, and made appearances to his followers (1 Cor 15:3-8). There is no presentation of Jesus' words and work, just as there is not in the Apostles' Creed: conceived by the Holy Spirit, born of the virgin Mary, and then immediately "suffered under Pontius Pilate," without a single reference to the years between birth and death. Such silence about Jesus' life cannot serve the present writer, whose task it is to show that Jesus was a high priest "chosen from among mortals" (v. 1) and "able to deal gently with the ignorant and wayward" (v. 2).

The literary form of vv. 7-10 is striking. The similarity between the structure of christology in Hebrews and that of Phil 2:6-11 (pre-existence, humiliation, exaltation) is evident, but there may be other resemblances. Like Phil 2:6-11, Heb 5:7-10 contains hymnic qualities. For example, v. 7 begins not with the name "Jesus" or even with the personal pronoun "he" but rather with the relative pronoun "who" (ὅς *hos*): "who in the days of his flesh." Hymnic or poetic expressions in praise of a person or god in Greek literature of the time often opened with the relative pronoun.[49] Note, as examples, Phil 2:6-11; Col 1:15-20; and 1 Tim 3:16. In addition, the sentence (translators divide vv. 7-10 for purposes of clarity) is carefully balanced with a series of participles leading to and away from the finite verbs that control the passage: "learned," "suffered," "became." These verses also give the impression of being a summary or a digest of a larger body of material, another characteristic of early Christian hymns and faith formulae. And finally, the phrases, especially in v. 7, are unique in Hebrews, and may be so because they are quoted from a source familiar to the writer and perhaps to the reader. However, nothing substantive to the discourse hinges on proving or disproving the hymnic nature of the passage, even though curiosity is raised about the nature of Christian sources available to the writer. Whether hymn or not, statements about "the days of his flesh" have been so woven into the broader movement of thought that they do not at all distract or divert attention.

The image of Jesus in fervent prayer, with loud cries and tears appealing to the One able to save him from death, brings to mind Jesus in Gethsemane (Matt 26:36-46; Mark 14:32-42; Luke 22:40-46). However, the writer's familiarity with the synoptic accounts, as some have argued,[50] is not easily established. The author may be drawing on another tradition, or possibly summarizing the entire passion experience. The language of v. 7 carries echoes of Psalms 22; 39; 116; Isaiah 65; and Job 40, but clearly fits the context. For example, Jesus "offered up" prayers, a term used to describe the sacrificial activity of a priest (5:1, 3). That Jesus' prayers were heard and yet he still suffered poses no theological problem; rather, it locates Jesus more firmly among his brothers and sisters whose experiences are precisely the same. The posture of Jesus is that of one facing death. Even though the expression "from death" (v. 7) can be translated "out of" death, making his prayer a petition for resurrection, there is no reason not to take it in its plainest sense; like the rest of us, he cries out to God in the face of the immediate prospect of death. That he was heard because of "reverent submission" (v. 7) has generated many questions, not so much translational as christological. What is being said about Christ? That he was worshipful, filled with awe, reverent, devout, in fear of God? When the word is an adjective describing a virtue in a person, it can be translated "devout" (as in Luke 2:25; Acts 2:5; 8:2; 22:12). However, here at 5:7 and at 12:28, the author's only other use of the word, it is in a context of priestly service before God and, therefore, describes the attitude or behavior appropriate to that service: bowing in reverence.

---

49. An observation developed at length, with many examples, by E. Norden, *Agnostos Theos* (Leipzig: B. G. Teubner, 1913) 253, 383-87.

50. Montefiore, *A Commentary on the Epistle to the Hebrews*, 97-8; Bruce, *The Epistle to the Hebrews*, 98-100; J. Moffatt, *A Critical and Exegetical Commentary on the Epistle to the Hebrews* (New York: Scribner's, 1964) 66.

5:8. While the adversative phrase "although he was a Son," which opens this verse may be read as the conclusion of v. 7, it seems to serve best as the introduction to the statements that follow. This is to say, being God's Son did not exempt Jesus from learning, from obedience, from suffering, so complete was his identification with all who share flesh and blood. And strikingly, learning is joined to obedience and obedience to suffering. "Learning" (μαθεῖν *mathein*) and "suffering" (παθεῖν *pathein*) were joined in popular wordplays, and the usual sense was, "we learn from our mistakes." That meaning is foreign here. The writer clearly has in mind the readers who must learn that old proverbs that join obedience with bliss and disobedience with suffering are broken both by the experience of Christ and their own. That the obedient suffer is a lesson difficult to learn, as the author will point out later (12:4-11). The writer cannot discuss Christ without thinking of the church, nor can he discuss the church without thinking of Christ. By learning obedience through suffering, Jesus is qualified as both intercessor and model.

5:9. This verse gathers up in summary fashion what has been said thus far about Christ's preparation for and fulfillment of his ministry as our high priest. This statement is, however, little more than what was said at 2:10, and the reader is urged to review comments at that point. One matter deserves repeating: The perfection of Christ is not a reference to moral achievement but to the "completion" or to the "finishing" of his preparation as high priest, and that was through testing, suffering, and death. No doubt the author is using the word "make perfect" in its cultic sense, borrowing the term from its use in the LXX to describe the priest of Israel's tabernacle. There the word is translated "consecrated" or "ordained" (Lev 4:5; 8:33; 16:32; 21:10; Num 3:3).

In 2:10 Christ is the "pioneer" of our salvation; here he is the "source." It is not necessary to attempt to be specific as to a particular aspect of Christ's salvific work; his being a model of obedient suffering, his role as the one offering sacrifice for sin, and his interceding for us in God's presence are all involved. The expression "eternal salvation" occurs only here in the NT (it is found in the OT at Isa 45:17). The writer shows a fondness for the adjective "eternal" (6:2; 9:12, 14-15; 13:20), perhaps as a way of asserting the once-and-for-all finality of Christ's work and of assuring pilgrims who otherwise might be discouraged by the transient nature of life. As for the phrase "for all who obey him," the writer assumes by now that obedience as an ingredient to faith has been amply established in the portraits of Moses, Joshua, Israel, Christ, and Christ's followers. It is helpful to notice that the word for "obey" is here (and widely in both testaments) a form of the word "to hear," recalling the repeated references to speaking and hearing so characteristic of Hebrews.

5:10. This verse does not advance the discussion but holds it in place until it is resumed in 7:1. In other words, the writer knows that the quotation of Ps 110:4 at v. 6 is the key to the difficult discussion upcoming in 7:1–10:25, and it is important that what is said in vv. 7-9 not erase from the reader's mind the affirmation that God has designated Christ a high priest forever after the order of Melchizedek. So the statement is repeated, as if to say, "I must now make preparatory comments of a serious nature before continuing, but hold this thought." From a rhetorical point of view, this strategy both builds anticipation and prepares the soil of the reader's mind for what is to come.

REFLECTIONS

1. Hebrews takes very seriously the historical career of Jesus. Nowhere in the sermon is this more evident than in 4:14–5:10. Whether or not the writer was familiar with the gospel narratives is a question prompted by historical curiosity, but it is not the primary issue. The more significant question has to do with the function of the life of Jesus of Nazareth for the life of the church and for Christian faith. Hebrews has thus far drawn from the life of Jesus two central meanings: As one in every respect like us, his brothers and sisters, he is able to serve as our priest with sympathy and patience; and as one who experienced life as we know it with faithfulness and full obedience, he is the pioneer and model for the Christian pilgrimage. As priest, his sympathy flows out of his being tested, not out of failing the test; therefore, his being without sin is not erosive of his capacity to be touched by our weaknesses. As model, his faithful obedience through suffering qualifies him. This is to say, he lived his own life and faced his own struggles, and hence can be a model. But to say that he acted and spoke as he did *in order to be a model* is to rob his life of meaning in itself and, therefore, to remove him as a good model. For example, if he prayed in order to be a model of prayer life, then he is not a model of prayer life. This is not to imply that the writer of Hebrews thus evacuates meaning from Jesus' life. On the contrary, his Jesus prayed with loud cries and tears, was heard for his reverence, and learned obedience through suffering, but the church's Jesus has sometimes been portrayed as moving through his life as a self-conscious example for others. Why was he baptized? As an example. Why was he tempted? As an example. Why did he pray? As an example. This is a gross misunderstanding of Jesus and a mishandling of the biblical texts. One finds meaning in Jesus' life only if that meaning is already there.

The two interpretations of Jesus' life offered by Hebrews do not, of course, exhaust the interpretive potential, but they do prompt the church to understand that life in ways appropriate to its time and place. From Advent through Easter, lectionaries place gospel narratives about Jesus at the center of the worship and preaching of the church, but these texts can be used week by week without dealing with the overarching question: What does the life of Jesus mean for the life of faith? If the gospel is the death and resurrection of Jesus, as Paul insists, is all that precedes his death not gospel but preface to the gospel? Or are Jesus' healing, feeding, receiving, forgiving, loving, and caring also gospel? The author of Hebrews not only offers a way of reading texts about Jesus but by so doing also presses us to think through again this vital question.

2. Assuming that the writer of Hebrews had access to oral or written traditions about Jesus, then it is safe also to assume that there were choices available for locating within Jesus' life that event or those events that would present both who he was and his significance for the readers. It is striking that, while several summary statements are made about his learning, his being tested, his suffering, and his faithfulness, the strong governing image is that of Jesus in fervent and agonizing prayer. That portrait in 5:7-8 is inescapably gripping, and one can expect that from it the writer will, in the chapters to follow, draw energy and exhortation. The readers will likely be led to see themselves before God in the posture of prayer, offering supplications in submissive reverence. This is the task of the writer as pastor, to join the life of Jesus to the lives of the readers at a point of crucial relevance. This does not mean that subsequent readers of Hebrews must make the same choice, and make the same connections to the church. What it does mean is that subsequent readers must (1) be honest in identifying the writer's choice with as much justifying support as the text will yield, and (2) be so bold as to identify from the life of Jesus that which most relevantly addresses the church of their own time and place, with as much justifying support as biblical text and congregational context will yield. All interpreters of the Jesus traditions pass a magnet over the texts to draw out the message most needed for the hour, but not all interpreters admit to doing so, claiming instead a disinterested objectivity. Even if such neutral readings were possible, they are never an option for such a pastor as one meets in Hebrews.

3. Even though extensive commentary on the relationship between Judaism and Christianity waits on further reading in Hebrews, the occasion of the writer's brief discussion of the priesthood of Aaron and of Christ (5:1-6) provides opportunity for some reflection on the issue. It is distressing how much secondary literature and how many sermons on Hebrews underscore only the discontinuity between Judaism and

Christianity with little attention to the lines of continuity. Certainly there is discontinuity. Claims about Jesus Christ, even in low christologies, state or imply that God has done a new thing in Jesus of Nazareth, but something new has little meaning unless it rests on a broad base of the familiar and the commonly accepted. The writer of Hebrews knows this and develops its themes accordingly, never trashing the history, the institutions, or the rituals of Judaism. It is regrettable, therefore, that the word "antithesis" is used to characterize the entire relationship, producing a kind of dispensationalism that honors neither Judaism nor Christianity and portrays God in trial-and-error activity. Much of such a reading of Hebrews, and indeed of much of the New Testament, very likely proceeds from conversionist theology. Such theology thinks in terms of "old" and "new" separated decisively and totally by the event of Jesus Christ, much as a watermelon responds to a knife. When one's personal experience is so understood, it often follows that Scripture is so understood. This perspective looks unfavorably on continuities, in life and in Scripture, as though they represented something less than a clean and full break with the past. Such thinking needs assurance that neither personal faith nor christology is compromised by the discovery of continuities in the story of God's active love from creation to eschaton. Hebrews offers such assurance.

HEBREWS 5:11–6:20

PREPARATION FOR THE DIFFICULT DISCUSSION

OVERVIEW

What 5:11–6:20 is a discrete unit is clear both by reason of its content and by the literary signals that mark the beginning and ending of the passage. The expression "a high priest according to the order of Melchizedek" at 5:10 and 6:20 alerts the reader to the distinct nature of the material between those markers. In fact, one can read the text smoothly moving from 5:10 directly to 7:1. This is not to imply that 5:11–6:20 is an insertion, either by the author or a later scribe; no manuscript evidence supports such an opinion. Neither is it totally correct to label this unit a hortatory digression as some have done. A portion of this unit (6:13-20) consists primarily of exposition of Gen 22:17 as a sure ground for exhortation and encouragement. And "digression" is too disjunctive to describe this passage. Lane is on target with the characterization "appropriate preamble,"[51] since, unlike most exhortations that follow exposition, 5:11–6:20 precedes and anticipates exposition. The readers need to be forewarned and prepared for the very difficult discussion to follow (7:1–10:25) in which the preacher will seek to establish what retrievable history does not establish: that Jesus was and is a priest.

The unit before us falls naturally into three sub-units: 5:11–6:3, A Call for Maturity; 6:4-12, A Stern Warning with Hope; 6:13-20, The Ground for Hope. In terms of the movement of its thought, 5:11–6:20 will be paralleled at 10:19-39 (exhortation, stern warning, and encouragement), and the two passages together shed most of the little light we have on the pastoral situation of the church to which the Hebrews sermon was addressed.

The writer of Hebrews, along with other writers of New Testament documents, was moved by two strong impulses. The first impulse was to be inclusive, to invite all persons into the fellowship, to extend hospitality to strangers (13:2), and to implement in every way the "whosoever will" of Jesus' life and work. This impulse had its opponents, as Acts and the letters of Paul testify, and it may have been that the conditions of persecution and public abuse were persuading some in the Hebrews church to pull back from this open-door policy (10:39; 13:2, 13). The second impulse might be called "quality control"—that is, holding before the membership the standards of conduct and of relationships appropriate to a community of Jesus' followers. Inattention to quality of life together brought strong words from Matthew (Matt 18:6-35; 22:1-14), from Paul (Rom 14:1–15:7; 1 Cor 5:1–6:11; Gal 6:1-5), and from others, but none more sobering and stern than from the author of Hebrews. We have already heard from the writer rather strong admonitions (2:1-4; 3:12-15; 4:1-11), but the passage before us now will introduce a question that disturbed the early church for generations: the question of post-baptismal sins and the possibility of a second repentance.

---
51. Lane, *Hebrews 1–8*, 134.

HEBREWS 5:11–6:3, A CALL FOR MATURITY COMMENTARY

It is clear to the writer of Hebrews that further discussion of the high priesthood of Christ will not only contribute to the maturity of the readers (6:1) but also require a degree of maturity for its progress (5:14). Therein lies the tension in 5:11–6:3. Are the readers capable of moving on with the difficult subject matter? According to 6:1-3, apparently they are. Are the readers too dull, too immature, too unskilled in the word to continue? According to 5:11-14, apparently they are. It is obvious that before we can accept the writer's invitation to move beyond the basics to more profound reflection (6:1-3), we must come to some clarity about the apparent indictment in 5:11-14.

5:11-14. In v. 11, the subject soon to be presented is identified: It is "about this." Since the pronoun οὗ (*hou*) may be neuter ("this") or masculine ("him"), the writer may be referring to the whole matter introduced in v. 10 (Christ's high priesthood after the order of Melchizedek) or more specifically to "him"—that is, to Christ or to Melchizedek. In either case, the subject is hard to explain (more literally, "hermeneutically difficult"). The expression "we have much to say," while an acceptable translation, gives the impression that the communication problem lies between the preacher and the readers and thus obscures the word-centered nature of v. 11. If we would tolerate for a moment the awkwardness of a literal rendering, an important point might come clear: "the word [λόγος *logos*] has much to say to us difficult to interpret." It is with "the word" that both writer and reader must struggle, for, as Clement of Alexandria has reminded us, the Word of God does not yield its message easily to every casual passerby. By keeping the term "the word" before us, the passage, far from being a hortatory digression, joins the remainder of the letter at many points. The accent on God's speaking, from 1:1 onward, is recalled, as is the lyrical prose in praise of the living, active Word of God in 4:12-13. In addition, the phrase "dull in understanding" (NRSV; "slow to learn," NIV) is clarified. Literally, the readers are accused of being "dull or sluggish of *hearing.*" This has been the charge all along (note especially 2:1; 3:7-8, 15; 4:2, 7). And what is not being heard clearly is not the preacher's sermon but the Word. To think that the issue here is simply a case of an inattentive congregation's not being able to follow substantive sermons is to miss the gravity of the indictment. It is toward the word already preached and the word now to be further explored that the readers have become dull or sluggish (νωθρός *nōthros*; a word used only here and at 6:12 in all the NT).

In vv. 12-14, the statement in v. 11 receives elaboration by means of vocabulary and analogies drawn from educational circles of the Hellenistic world. Anyone moving normally through the stages of education available would be expected to progress from the basic elements to the point of being able to communicate with others in discourses of some complexity. The term "teachers" (διδάσκαλοι *didaskaloi*) need not be taken as being addressed solely to the leaders of the church; this was an expectation of the congregation generally, an expectation based on time spent in the faith and in the fellowship. In other words, "You have been Christians long enough to be informed and bold witnesses." Instead, says the author, "You need to be enrolled in a class on the most rudimentary elements of the oracles of God." In v. 12 may be an allusion to formal catechetical instruction that later was institutionalized as lengthy (1-3 years) preparation for baptism. We do not know how structured such education was at this time and place, or whether it preceded or followed baptism. The content of such instruction is "the oracles of God," a familiar designation for the Jewish Scriptures (Num 24:16; Ps 107:11; Acts 7:38; Rom 3:2); but given the author's Christian reading of those texts, very likely specific content about God and Christ was included. For example, 1:1-4 might be found among such "oracles."

Continuing with the educational vocabulary of the day, the writer says, "You need milk, not solid food" (v. 12). That this language appears in 1 Cor 3:1-3 does not prove a literary relationship between Paul and Hebrews; "milk" and "solid food" were common terms for referring to levels of educational development.[52] Here milk is an image for "the basic elements of the oracles of God," while solid food is "the word of righteousness," which is the capacity in the believer "to distinguish good from evil." Much more is likely involved in the phrase "word of righteousness," but here the writer focuses only on moral and ethical discernment. Not necessary for purposes of clarity but rhetorically effective is the further multiplication of contrasts: infant and mature; unskilled (inexperienced) and trained by habitual practice. Having one's faculties (senses) trained by practice is athletic imagery and is common in the NT (1 Tim 4:7; Heb 12:11; 2 Pet 2:14), although some of the vocabulary here is unique in the NT ("faculties" and "practice" or "habit"). The writer will soon provide the readers with some of this exercise by leading them through a larger and deeper understanding of Christ's person and his salvific work.

Perhaps this is the place to pause and note the importance of the word "perfect" (τελειόω teleioō) for the writer of Hebrews and to observe in a preliminary way the variety of uses of the word. The term was used earlier in descriptions of Christ as one who was made perfect through full identification with humankind, including suffering and death (2:10; 5:9). In our theological vocabulary, his incarnation, humiliation, and exaltation perfected or completed his redemptive work, and hence he is "perfect forever" (7:28). There was no reason to translate the word as "mature," since nothing of moral growth or achievement was involved in these characterizations of Christ as perfect. However, in these verses, at 5:14, and again at 6:1, the term is used to describe the moral, ethical, intellectual, and spiritual goal of the believer's life—a goal achieved by learning, practice, and teaching others, a goal expected of all who submit themselves to the resources for Christian growth. In the discussion of 5:11–6:20, it is, therefore, appropriate to translate the word as "mature" or, in its noun form at 6:1, "maturity." Both the NIV and the REB are consistent in the translation at 5:14 and 6:1.

For some reason the NRSV reverts to "perfection" at 6:1, blurring the distinction between Christ's being perfected and believers' becoming mature. Perhaps the NRSV is anticipating yet a third use of the word in Hebrews, and that is the sense in which Christ perfects his followers (10:14; 12:2, 23). In other words, the Christian life is not completely a matter of spiritual and intellectual growth and ethical achievement, as vital as that is. Christ's redemptive act and his continual intercession perfect his followers in that it is he who brings the believers into his own perfection in the presence of God, a foretaste of which is even now experienced by those who trust his grace. Hence, three uses of "perfection" already impress themselves on us: the perfection of Christ through suffering, death, and exaltation; the maturing of believers through the disciplines of growth; and the perfecting of believers through the redeeming grace of Christ. The reader should remain open to even further nuances of this word as we move through Hebrews.[53]

In all fairness it should be pointed out that a radically different reading of "perfection" in Hebrews has been offered by Käsemann.[54] He regards Hebrews as an interpretation of Christianity on the philosophical framework of what we broadly call Gnosticism, by which we designate a number of systems of speculation about how eternal spirits fell into this world of matter and by what means they can be extricated from this world and return to the eternal realm of the spirit. Basically, salvation comes by possessing the secret knowledge of who we are, whence we came, and whither we go. Not all have or can have this knowledge. Those who are carnal cannot; those who are intellectual may with effort attain it; the spiritual ones can receive it and be saved, gathered to the gnostic redeemer, Christ.

Käsemann identifies the perfect or mature ones in 5:14 and 6:1 as those who are spiritual, capable of receiving the secret knowledge. That the concepts and vocabulary of

---

52. Attridge, *A Commentary on the Epistle to the Hebrews*, 159n. 59, gives examples of such use in Philo and in Epictetus.

53. These uses of the term will be noted as they appear in the text, but for anyone seeking to engage in a thematic study of "perfection" in Hebrews, David Peterson's *Hebrews and Perfection* (London: Cambridge University Press, 1982), will be helpful.

54. Käsemann, *The Wandering People of God*, esp. 187-92.

such philosophies were known to some early Christian communities and were here and there embraced in varying degrees is clear. The epistle to the Colossians, the *Gospel of Thomas,* the *Gospel of Truth,* the *Epistle of Barnabas,* the writings of Clement of Alexandria and of Origen, among others, make this evident. But one is hard pressed to identify the kind of Gnosticism Käsemann describes as existing in the time and place of Hebrews and to find in the letter evidence that the spiritually elite possessed the secrets to a heavenly return. That the resources for Christian maturity were available to all and that all were expected to "grow up" account quite adequately for the discussion in 5:11–6:20.

We return now to the question raised earlier: Is the indictment of the readers as immature milk drinkers a serious one? It would seem so, given the repetition of it in 5:11-14, using a number of sharp images and analogies. And yet it seems not to be so, given the call to move on to maturity (6:1), the complimentary and encouraging words in 6:9-12, and the writer's reason for speaking in this manner, "so that you may not become sluggish" (6:12 NRSV), even though the readers have already been accused of being "sluggish in understanding" (5:11). Several things are clear. Given earlier warnings about neglect, drifting, inattention, hardening, and falling short, 5:11-14 must be taken as reflecting a real malaise among some if not all the members of the church being addressed. A lethargy has overtaken a community once healthy, active, and courageous (6:9-11; 10:32-36). But the readers are not infants; 1:1–5:10 is not addressed to the immature. And it is clear that the writer intends to proceed in serving solid food, demanding more and more of them in digesting the profound message of Christ's high priestly work. Apparently the recipients have been receding, slipping, or perhaps shrinking back from earlier service and witness, for reasons that may come clearer as we proceed. How does a preacher get through to them and halt the regression? Irony? Perhaps. Exaggeration? Perhaps. We can recognize a rhetorical strategy in shocking confrontation followed by softer words of encouragement (5:11-14 and 6:1-3; 6:4-8 and 9-12; 10:26-31 and 32-39). The writer will later urge the readers to "provoke" (παροξυσμός *paroxysmos*; "irritate," "distress," "pester," "cut") each other back to life and faithfulness again (10:24). Because the situation is critical, the preacher has done just that in 5:11-14.

6:1-3. When the author issues the call to maturity at v. 1, it is important to notice that the connection with what precedes is not "however," as if to say, "Even though you are immature and cannot grasp what follows, I must continue even if it falls on dull ears." Rather, the conjunction is "therefore" or "so then" as if to say, "Of course, you can follow this complex discussion, and I expect you to do so." The preacher has upbraided the readers but still does not anticipate that the sermon will fall to the ground unheard.

In the discussion of the several meanings of "perfection" in the commentary on 5:11-14, the expressed preference was for the translation "maturity" at 6:1, continuing the sense of the adjective "mature" at 5:14. However, in the pilgrimage language of 6:1 ("leaving behind . . . going on"), the eschatological flavor of the word should be kept in mind. This is to say, believers not only practice the disciplines of Christian living that lead to maturity, but also receive a completeness or perfection granted by the perfection of Christ. The serious and sometimes difficult exercises of the Christian life are always performed under the benediction of grace. This awareness may be implied in the writer's choice of the passive "let us be carried" (φερώμεθα *pherōmetha,* trans. "let us go on"). We not only move on toward maturity; we are carried along toward perfection. Such a pilgrimage requires "leaving behind" the elementary teachings, but not in the sense of rejecting. After all, such instruction constitutes the "foundation," says the author, shifting momentarily to an architectural metaphor to underscore the fundamental importance of their primary education in the faith.

The phrase translated "the basic [elementary, NIV] teaching about Christ" is problematic both in translation and in reference. Literally, the expression is "the teaching of the beginning of Christ." If "Christ" is read as subjective, then the writer has in mind Christ's own basic or primary teaching. The following phrase, "repentance from dead works and faith toward God," seems to support this interpretation, since, according to the Gospels, Jesus came preaching, "Repent, and believe in the good news" (Mark 1:15 NRSV). In addition, the author assumes a knowledge of the historical Jesus (5:7-8), further supporting the view that the basic instruction of Christians involved teaching what Christ himself taught. If, however, "Christ" is read as objective, then the instruction here referred to was about Christ and may well have included material such as is found in 1:1–5:10. We prefer precision of reference, but in its absence there is no reason not to accept both interpretations of "the basic teaching of Christ." When the canon of the NT was determined, both teachings by Christ and about Christ were included. Whether the author intended "the basic teaching of Christ" (6:1) to be synonymous with "the basic elements of the oracles of God" (5:12) is not clear.

What follows in vv. 1b-2 may be read in either of two ways. One reading elaborates on "the foundation" with three paired expressions:

repentance from dead works — faith toward God
instruction about baptisms — laying on of hands
resurrection of the dead — eternal judgment

The other reading makes two segments of the passage: "the foundation of repentance from dead works and of faith toward God," followed by an elaboration in two paired expressions. One could translate this portion: "that is [referring to the foundation], instruction."

about baptisms — laying on of hands
resurrection of the dead — eternal judgment

In the second reading, the foundation is one of repentance and faith, further defined as teaching in four subject areas. The difference lies in textual variants among the Greek manuscripts concerning the word "instruction"—if in the genitive case, it belongs on the list of six items (first reading); if in the accusative, "instruction" is simply a repetition of "foundation" (second reading).

Commentators are divided, and there would be no reason to pause over the difference except for interest in the elements constituting catechetical instruction of believers in the time and place of Hebrews. There seems to be here a formula or portion of a formula for the catechizing of new members. The choice of reading in these comments is the second. This is to say, the foundation laid in the lives of the readers is characterized broadly as consisting of "repentance from dead works and faith toward God." This expression summarizes the entire movement from the former life to the present life. The "dead works" from which the readers have turned need not evoke Paul's treatments of works versus grace. The writer uses the phrase here and at 9:14 as a general characterization of the activities and rituals of the reader's former life, whether in Judaism or some Hellenistic religion. If anyone expected "faith toward Christ" rather than "faith toward God," that expectation can be corrected by the letter to Hebrews itself. God is the source of revelation and of salvation; God is the one who sends Jesus (1:1–5:10). For Christianity to distance itself so far from Judaism that this primary tenet of faith, commonly held, is overlooked, is to allow the effort to be unique to cripple both tradition and faith.

The four items of instruction listed as constituents of the foundational instruction may be only a selection from a longer list that provided a catechetical curriculum. If so, these four may be mentioned because they were either unusually significant or problematic for this particular congregation. In any case, the writer has only to mention them without comment, both because they were already familiar to the readers and because to tarry with explanations would contradict the exhortation to leave these matters behind and move on. The modern reader is, of course, curious to know more. As for "baptisms," the word βαπτισμῶν (*baptismōn*) is better rendered "washings"; another form of the word is used regularly in the NT to speak of Christian baptism. Just as Paul had to distinguish between the eucharistic meal and pagan ritual meals (1 Corinthians 10–11), so also perhaps new Christians needed to understand differences between ritual washings of other groups (Traditional Judaism? Qumran? The movement following John the Baptist? Pagan ablutions?) and the baptism of the church. The same is true of the "laying on of hands," associated with commissioning, healing, ordination, confirmation, and the gift of the Holy Spirit. The twin teachings of resurrection and judgment were certainly basic to the community's faith, being firmly fixed in Pharisaic Judaism, the teaching of Jesus, and apostolic preaching in the church after Jesus. Some students of Hebrews have noted that the items in the curriculum cited here could as easily have been used in a synagogue of the time. Quite true. But the search for differences between synagogue and church should not be pursued too diligently; to find a practice or belief in one is not automatically to remove it from the other. Similarities provided both the ground and the necessity of instruction in order that new believers understand the "of Christ" dimension of basic Christian teaching, especially if that teaching grew out of Judaism.

This first of three sub-units within 5:11–6:20 concludes with a common (Acts 18:21; 1 Cor 4:19; 16:7; Jas 4:15), but not empty expression of the need for God's blessing: "if God permits." What the author says "we will do" refers to the earlier expression using the first-person plural: "Let us go on." What "we will do" is to move on toward maturity (perfection), engaging in the rigorous exercise of discussing the person and the work of Jesus as a high priest after the order of Melchizedek. Thus the author positions the reader on the edge of what will prove both demanding and rewarding.

REFLECTIONS

1. Some may raise questions about the appropriateness or the effectiveness of the writer's rhetorical strategy: stern charges and warnings followed by words of encouragement and hope. And, of course, we have no way of knowing how this sermon was received or to what effect. We can appreciate, however, the concentration of knowledge and skill in response to one clear and undeniable fact: Hearing is difficult, not only for this audience but also for any audience. The Scriptures honor hearing: "Hear, O Israel; The LORD is our God, the LORD alone. You shall love the LORD your God with all your heart, and with all your soul, and with all your might" (Deut 6:4-5 NRSV). Or again, "So faith comes from what is heard, and what is heard comes through the word of Christ" (Rom 10:17 NRSV). The verb "to hear" (ἀκούω *akouō*) provides the root for the verb "to obey" (ὑπακούω *hypakouō*). But the Scriptures also understand the difficulty of hearing: "Morning by morning God wakens—/ wakens my ear/ to listen as those who are taught./ The Lord GOD has opened [lit., "dug out"] my ear" (Isa 50:4-5 NRSV).

We know some reasons for this difficulty, hardly overcome except by an act of God: distractions, pre-occupations, physical problems, no confidence in the speaker, old memories awakened, and refusal to listen to that which may alter one's life. But the Hebrews preacher knows another: a dullness or sluggishness brought on by lack of exercise in communication. The readers have apparently pulled back from bold witness to outsiders and from exhorting and encouraging one another. The loss of a congregational conversation means a loss of hearing. Through lack of use faculties grow dull and the members regress to a former condition of immaturity. Persons who do not contribute to a group's discussion often say, "But I am listening." Perhaps so, but not as well.

2. One is impressed by the fact that the preacher of Hebrews shares with the readers difficult and demanding material. The message, deep and complex as it is, belongs to the whole church, and they are trusted with it. From the beginning of their faith pilgrimage this has been so, as evidenced by the foundational instruction previously received. Had the writer chosen to do so, dozens of reasons could have been found in the condition of the readers to justify withholding from them all but the simplest and most easily digested elements of the faith, saying privately, "The weightier matters are

to be reserved for discussions among the clergy." The writer understood, however, that to have done so would have further contributed to the weakened and sluggish condition of the readers. Many pastors have yet to appreciate the levels of maturity that laity can attain when the resources for growth are shared patiently and pastorally, and when the withholding of matters theological, christological, and ethical, no matter how complex or controversial, is recognized for what it is: a means of control.

3. According to 5:14, a mark of Christian maturity is the capacity "to distinguish good from evil." As much as most of us enjoy an informed theological conversation, maturity for the writer of Hebrews is something much more practical: a discerning spirit able to make its way among the paths that seem right, paths often made more attractive by the apparent support of selected biblical texts, without becoming lost. Being able to distinguish between good and evil implies at least three things. First, the Christian faith, like its parent Judaism, is morally and ethically serious. All relationships and patterns of behavior in daily situations are the subject matter of discipleship and are to be informed by one's theology. Second, distinctions between good and evil are not always easily made. It is one thing to urge that we do God's will; it is quite another to discern what that is. To think that between vice and virtue is a line clear and unmistakable is to embrace an illusion. And finally, as the writer says, this capacity to discern comes only by practice and exercise. As everyone knows, practice and exercise often involve falling, being hurt, trying again. The room where this takes place with support and encouragement is the church, where beginners and long-time practitioners are given both resources and opportunity to "move on toward maturity."

HEBREWS 6:4-12, STERN WARNING WITH HOPE

COMMENTARY

Several preliminary comments need to be made before investigating the details of this most sobering passage. First, it is important to notice that 6:4-12 fits a rhetorical pattern now familiar in Hebrews: a stern warning (vv. 4-8), followed by words of encouragement and hope (vv. 9-12; cf. 2:1-9; 4:1-16). In fact, since the strong words of 6:4-8 follow immediately the encouragement portion of the preceding unit (6:1-3), the net effect is that the sober warning of 6:4-8 is surrounded by positive and affirming words. This observation is not intended to soften the blow of vv. 4-8; on the contrary, the context of pastoral encouragement makes these verses seem even more stark by contrast.

This observation leads to a second comment. The writer clearly wants the reader to hear the words about the impossibility of restoring certain persons to a second repentance as part of the larger message of pastoral encouragement. At v. 4, the conjunction "for" or "because" says, in effect, "We will move on to maturity because the alternative condition is that of falling away, without the possibility of renewal." At v. 9, the adversative conjunction "but" (δέ *de*, trans. "even though") says, in effect, "But having been persuaded otherwise in your case." In other words, the harsh warning of vv. 4-8 is not being spoken to persons to whom it presently applies. It looms on their horizon, to be sure, but were it descriptive of their current condition, the message would be wasted on persons unable any longer to hear it.

A third and final preliminary comment is a reminder to ourselves to resist letting 6:4-8 become a magnet drawing into its interpretive orbit all the NT passages with dire words about certain sins among believers or about post-baptismal sins in general. In other words, the expression "it is impossible to restore again to repentance," both in its internal meaning and its application to "those who," must be understood in its context in Hebrews and not as one among many rigorous statements concerning sin within the Christian community. It is easy to see why some commentators[55] subsume 6:4-6 under the general topic of post-baptismal sin; in one way or another, most NT as well as extra-canonical Christian writings had to deal with the reality of continuing sin in the church. In spite of the ideal that those born of God do not sin (1 John 5:18) or, in Paul's image, are dead to sin (Rom 6:1-11), the fact is that not only did sin in many forms among the believers need to be addressed but also instructions needed to be given for punishment (1 Cor 5:1-8), or resolution (Matt 18:15-20), or restoration (Gal 6:1-2; Jas 5:19-20). At least one writer dealt with the problem by classifying sins according to seriousness, placing the sin that is mortal ("unto death") beyond the reach of any restoration (1 John 5:16-17). The Gospel writers report from the lips of Jesus one sin more serious than all others: "But whoever blasphemes against the Holy Spirit can never have forgiveness, but is guilty of an eternal sin" (Mark 3:29 NRSV; see also Matt 12:32; Luke 12:10)—a statement so dramatically final that the church has long sought to identify that sin lest some member be guilty of it.[56]

This brief rehearsal is enough to show that matching texts that are similar in rigor can lead one away from the issue of substance: What is the condition of those who are, in the mind of the writer of Hebrews, beyond the possibility of restoring again to repentance? What is meant by "falling away" (v. 6)? One senses, in advance of further examination of the text, that moral irregularities such as fornication, anger, or sloth, no matter how gravely regarded, do not at all identify the issue of Heb 6:4-8.

The unit falls naturally into three parts: vv. 4-6, the warning; vv. 7-8, the analogy from agriculture; vv. 9-12, the words of encouragement.

6:4-6. The warning itself is framed to achieve maximum rhetorical force. The first word is "impossible" (ἀδύνατος *adynatos*), which is completed with the infinitive "to renew" (ἀνακαινίζω *anakainizō*), which does not appear until v. 6. The descriptions of "those who" in vv. 4-5 come between these two anchoring words. The NRSV obscures this dramatic word order, while the NIV preserves it. There is no finite verb in vv. 4-6; "it is" is supplied by translators to make a complete sentence of the stark, verbless warning.

The emphatic "impossible" governs the three verses, but the writer does not specify with whom the impossibility lies: God cannot? The preacher cannot? The listener cannot? One hesitates to say that God cannot, since with God all things are possible. Likewise, it seems inappropriate to lay such a critical burden on the skills or lack of skills of the preacher. As for the listener, here as elsewhere in Scripture psychological probing is an uncertain business and should be kept to a minimum. One can cite case after case in support of the proverb, "The heated iron, once cooled, is difficult to heat again," but the text is not about what is "difficult."[57] Nor is it about how anyone feels concerning the gospel. The impossibility lies in the writer's understanding of the once-for-all act of God in Jesus Christ. The author repeatedly finds the expression "impossible" useful in clearing away from the christology of the letter any modifiers, any alternatives, any exceptions. Note: "through two unchangeable things, in which it is impossible that God would prove false" (6:18 NRSV); "it is impossible for the blood of bulls and goats to take away sins" (10:4 NRSV); "gifts and sacrifices are offered that cannot perfect the conscience of the worshiper" (9:9 NRSV); "the law . . . can never, by the same sacrifices that are continually offered year after year, make perfect those who approach" (10:1 NRSV); "offering again and again the same sacrifices that can never take away sins" (10:11 NRSV); "without faith it is impossible to please God" (11:6 NRSV). For Hebrews, impossibilities are implied in the writer's affirmation: "And it is by God's will that we have been sanctified through the offering of the body of Jesus Christ *once for all*" (10:10 NRSV, italics added). At 6:4-6 the impossibility is in restoring (renewing) again

---

55. E.g., Montefiore, *A Commentary on the Epistle to the Hebrews*, 107-9.
56. Variously identified as adultery, or any one of the seven deadly sins, or cowardly hiding from persecutors of Christians. A very early interpretation of this sin was testing or questioning a Christian prophet who "speaks in a spirit" (*Did.* XI. 7.).
57. A translation, softening the text and preferred by Erasmus and a few others, lacks MSS support.

to repentance—that is, one does not lay again the foundation that begins with repentance (6:1), an act that would contradict the once-for-all christology.

The persons addressed by the warning are simply identified as "those who" (v. 4). However, they are described in a series of participles that depict with an extraordinary flourish the experience of entering and participating in the life of the Christian community.

6:4a, "Having once been enlightened." The adverb "once" (ἅπαξ *hapax*) commonly refers to that which occurs only once, that which is thus unique, "once and for all." It occurs in Hebrews in references to the salvific act of Christ (7:27; 9:12, 26; 10:12, 14), and quite likely the writer hopes the connection between their experience and the saving act of Christ will not be lost on the readers. Being "enlightened," moving out of darkness into light, was a widely used metaphor for the trustful reception of the message about Christ (John 1:9; 2 Cor 4:4-6; Eph 1:18; 2 Tim 1:10; 1 Pet 2:9). The author uses the expression again at 10:32 in recalling the readers' firm stand in their confession. Whether the enlightenment was related to the rite of baptism is not certain at the time and place of Hebrews.[58]

6:4b, "Having tasted the heavenly gift." The vivid metaphor "to taste" has already been used by the author (Christ tasted death for everyone, 2:9), and it will be repeated in v. 5. It refers to direct personal experience (Ps 34:8; 1 Pet 2:3). The heavenly gift is most likely a reference to God's grace. That which is "heavenly" is for Hebrews that which is ultimate, true, and from God (3:1; 8:5; 9:23; 11:16; 12:22). Those who argue that "having tasted the heavenly gift" refers to the eucharist usually do so on two grounds: (1) the verb "taste" and (2) the experiential sequence of baptism (enlightened) and then sharing at the table (tasting the heavenly gift). The persuasiveness of the case depends very much on drawing from sources (e.g., the bread from heaven of John 6) with which we have no knowledge that the writer of Hebrews was familiar.[59]

6:4c, "Having become sharers of the Holy Spirit." The language of partnership has already been used in relation to the heavenly calling (3:1) and to Christ himself (3:14). Likewise, God's distribution of the Holy Spirit in the community was assumed by the author as both the understanding and the experience of the readers (2:4). Hebrews thus confirms what is clear from other NT writers, that the presence and activity of the Holy Spirit are the hallmark of the early church and clearly identify the audience as Christians.

6:5, "Having tasted the goodness of the word of God and the powers of the age to come." The first four chapters have repeatedly asserted not only the power and certainty of God's speech but also its goodness; that is, God is for us and our salvation. No provision necessary for the believers to enter God's rest is lacking. In confirmation of this promise, the qualities of that age to come break in upon the present as "signs and wonders and various miracles" (2:4 NRSV), providing what Paul would call an earnest or foretaste of what is yet to be (2 Cor 1:22; Eph 1:14). In this and the three preceding participles, the writer withholds nothing in reminding the addressees of the abundance of God's investment in them. Upon them God has poured out more than they could ever have asked for or imagined.

6:6. It is against this flourish of God's favor, which has been in the community's experience both pleasure and power, that the fifth participle tosses an almost incomprehensible response: "and then have fallen away." The author has here chosen a verb (παραπίπτω *parapiptō*) that appears nowhere else in the NT. In the Septuagint the word occurs, being variously translated: "acting faithlessly" (Ezek 14:13 NRSV; "breaking faith," REB); "dealing treacherously" (Ezek 20:27 NRSV). Although the root of the verb means "to fall," the usage here by no means is to be taken as "carelessly slipping"; the sense is that of rejection, violation of a relationship, breach of faith, abandonment. At 3:12 a similar word was used (ἀποστῆναι *apostēnai*, "to turn away," "abandon") to express a turning away from God. Neither at 3:12 nor at 6:6 is the issue simply doctrinal, as though someone were rejecting a tenet of the creed. The act of falling away is not so much against a dogma as

---

58. Käsemann, *The Wandering People of God*, 187-88, thinks the adverb "once" implies that the writer has in mind the specific act of baptism.
59. For a full presentation of the case for and against the eucharist, see R. Williamson, "The Eucharist and the Epistle to the Hebrews," *NTS* 21 (Jan. 1975) 300-312.

against a person, at 3:12 against God, at 6:6 against the Son of God. The remainder of v. 6, crucifying again the Son of God and holding him up to ridicule, makes this abundantly clear. Apostasy, yes, but not as a charge of one side of a debate against the other; rather, it is the sin of abandoning God, Christ, and the fellowship of believers (cf. 10:25). This act is far too grave and all-encompassing to be handled adequately by Tertullian's use of this text to declare that there is no second repentance for the adulterer and fornicator.[60] Tertullian is writing in response to Hermas, a Christian of the midsecond century, whose apocalyptic work, *The Shepherd of Hermas,* was very influential. In *The Shepherd,* Hermas agrees with the teaching that there is no second repentance after baptism. However, he claims that through a revelation God had granted him the ministry of announcing one repentance after baptism. This offer, he said, was not for all time and thus to be calculated by believers, but was a dispensation for his own time. Hermas makes these statements in the context of discussing marriage, remarriage, and adultery.[61] It is clear, therefore, that while Hermas is generally regarded as the earliest interpreter of Heb 6:4-6, he has moved the issue from falling away or abandoning Christ to that of committing particular sins after baptism. The difference is major.

As stated above in comments on v. 4, the "those who" of this warning are not the readers, except in a potential sense. Is the entirety of 6:4-6 merely theoretical, a grim prospect sketched out to frighten the believers into more acceptable behavior? We cannot know, of course, if the writer was thinking of particular persons somewhere when this warning was framed, but it would be a mistake to call it theoretical in the sense of being less serious or less real. The sin portrayed so vividly here was not only a possibility but a documented actuality as well. The Emperor Trajan sent Pliny to the provinces of Bithynia and Pontus to investigate suspected irregularities in the handling of government funds and to bring to justice persons and groups guilty of treason or sedition. In the years 111–113 CE, letters between the two were exchanged. The subject in some of this correspondence was the Christians, a group heretofore unknown to Pliny. In his investigations, Pliny interrogated some who "said that they had ceased to be Christians two or more years previously, and some of them even twenty years ago. They all did reverence to your [Trajan's] statue and the images of the gods in the same way as the others, and reviled the name of Christ."[62] Pliny's description of those who turn away from Christ, embrace the imperial gods, acknowledge the emperor as lord, and revile the name of Christ is not unlike that of v. 6: "They are crucifying again the Son of God and are holding him up to contempt." This is to say, the apostates take it upon themselves to join in the shameful rejection of Christ expressed in the crucifixion and voluntarily join in heaping upon him the ridicule and verbal abuse frequently heard at public executions. The contrast with the life they had experienced within the community of grace could not be more stark. The church has heard this harsh and painful warning, and yet has never ceased to struggle with it in the light of its central proclamation of the unceasing and unrelenting grace of God.

6:7-8. This second of the three sub-units of 6:4-12 continues the discussion as evidenced by the conjunction "for," the same word beginning v. 4. These verses consist entirely of an illustration from agriculture, a common source for both Jewish and Christian preaching (Isa 5:1-7; Ezek 19:10-14; Matt 3:10; 7:16; Mark 4:3-9; Luke 13:6-9). Like any good illustration, the analogy does not draw attention to itself with distracting internal complexities, but in its simplicity serves to drive home with unfailing clarity the point being made. It does carry echoes of OT texts doubtless familiar to the readers: thorns and thistles of Gen 3:17-18, blessing and curse of Deut 11:26-28, and perhaps the fruitless vineyard of Isa 5:1-7. These echoes serve to support the message: Ground cultivated and receiving rain that produces a crop is blessed by God; ground cultivated and receiving rain that produces thorns and thistles is under a curse and destined for burning. The burning is not for the purpose of restoring and renewing the soil but is clearly the deserved "end," the final punishment (10:27). The illustration looks back to vv. 4-6: the fruitful ground

---

60. Tertullian *On Modesty* 20.
61. *The Shepherd of Hermas* Mandate IV.1-4.
62. Pliny *The Letters of Pliny,* LCL ed., Bk X, 96.

recalling vv. 4-5, the fruitless ground recalling v. 6. But the illustration also looks ahead. The "blessing" anticipates the discussion about Abraham in vv. 13-20, and the "fire" prophesies the severity of the final judgment for apostates (10:27). The illustration functions well; the reader is not allowed to forget the rigorous warning about the impossibility of a second repentance.

6:9-12. This third and final sub-unit returns the reader to a positive mode with a message that is emphatic in its confidence and hope. The adversative conjunction "but" signals a radical turn in thought. The readers are addressed affectionately as "beloved" (v. 9), the only time they are so greeted in the sermon. The preacher softens the voice with "Even though we speak in this way" (v. 9; that is, referring to the rigor of the preceding warning; in the Greek text this clause closes rather than opens v. 9, sustaining the positive mode through the entire sentence). However, the strongest signal that salvation and not damnation lies before the congregation is in the opening word: "We are confident [certain/sure/persuaded]." This rhetorical flourish is familiar to readers of Paul, who, after demanding instruction and exhortation, sounded a note of confidence in the readers (e.g., Rom 15:14; Gal 5:10). Repeatedly the writer uses the editorial "we" (*we* speak; *we* are confident; *we* want), enlarging the company of concern beyond the private but without losing the personal relationship. The "those who" of the warning (v. 4) has given way to the pronoun of direct address, "you," used in every statement of vv. 9-12. That the author is confident of "better things" (a favorite expression of this writer; 1:4; 7:7, 19, 22; 8:6; 9:23; 10:34; 11:16, 35, 40) of the reader—that is, that they will produce a fruitful crop (v. 7)—is in no way to be taken as an apology for the harsh warning. The warning was appropriate; there were clear signs that some were slipping away ("drift"; "neglect"; "inattention"; "dullness of understanding"; see 2:1-3; 5:11-12). Nor is the writer simply trying to put a happy face on a sad situation. The preacher knows the congregation and has firm ground for projecting a hopeful future.

According to v. 10, two factors have persuaded the preacher of better things from the congregation. One is the justice or faithfulness of God. That God has been at work among them has been amply stated (2:4; 6:4-5). The second factor is that God's investment in them has borne fruit in their love and service in God's name toward the saints (fellow believers). It is not only their past record of serving that gives confidence to the preacher but also the fact that they continue to do so. The word for "serve" here (διακονέω *diakoneō*) appears nowhere else in Hebrews but was used widely in the early church to refer to a wide range of ministries (Matt 20:28; Rom 15:25; Acts 6:1-3; 2 Cor 9:1; 1 Pet 1:12). Here the writer probably has in mind the behavior of the believers spelled out in 10:32-34: endurance of suffering, bearing public ridicule and verbal abuse, being empathetic partners with those subjected to such persecution, showing compassion on imprisoned brothers and sisters, and cheerfully accepting the destruction and confiscation of property.

This record and the faithfulness of a God who does not forget prompts the preacher, not to further warning, but to gentle urging. Here (vv. 11-12) the words are even more personal ("each of you"; see also 3:12-13; 4:1, 11). Every member of the community is to be diligent, persistent, and to realize the fullness of hope to the end. Here the words not only recall 3:14 and anticipate 9:28 but also join in the New Testament's admonition to all who cling to faith under great duress (Mark 13:13; Rev 2:10). Such faithfulness enables them to throw off the sluggishness (dullness) that had overtaken them (5:11). This, says the preacher, is what "we want" (v. 11). The word ἐπιθυμοῦμεν (*epithymoumen*, "want") is a strong one, indicating passion or desire. When the object of such feeling is less noble, the word is translated "covet" or "lust." The intensity of emotion was not only persuasive but no doubt also appreciated by those hearing it as deep pastoral affection.

The expression "imitators of those who through faith and patience inherit the promises" (v. 12) reminds the readers of the discussion of entrance into the rest of God, a promise that remains open (4:1, 8). More immediately, however, the writer is preparing for the exposition of God's promise to

Abraham, a promise obtained through faith and patience (vv. 13-20). Although Abraham is the example to be imitated in the upcoming discussion, the theme of imitating those who persevere in faith will be repeated (13:7) and enlarged (11:4-38). In chap. 11, the writer will be careful to point out that the faithful of the past did not, in fact, receive "what was promised, since God had provided something better" (11:39 NRSV), a something that had its fulfillment in the Son. But that is an argument for a later time; it is sufficient at the moment to see the faithfulness of God toward those who live in patient trust. Scripture yields no clearer model than that of the covenant between God and Abraham.

REFLECTIONS

1. The preacher or teacher in today's church should not be surprised to find that a discussion of the impossibility of restoring to repentance those who have fallen away does not carry for many parishioners the force of a stern warning. More likely it will sound antiquated or fanatical or foreign. The reasons are several. (1) Repentance has not been understood or experienced as a condition for entering or remaining in the Christian community. (2) The grace of God is commonly viewed as being without ethical or moral expectation but is rather like a giant grading curve on which everyone passes automatically. (3) Both apostasy and heresy are inconceivable to persons who reduce the response to all that God has done and is doing to simply "joining a church." Under such a circumstance, apostasy is no more than becoming inactive or irregular in attendance. It is only when coming to faith in Christ is experienced as receiving all the gifts of God listed in vv. 4-5 that "falling away" can be seen in all its ugliness and danger. Anyone who takes lightly entrance into the community of faith will not likely be deterred from easy departure by pulpit threats based on 6:4-8.

2. In the history of Christian preaching the sober warning of 6:4-8 has been employed as a weapon against any sin in the church membership regarded as most offensive. Although Hermas was more yielding than Tertullian, both used this text to address fornication, adultery, and remarriage. Single-issue pulpits seem most susceptible to this error, but all of us need to be warned against irresponsible employment of this text in times of anger or disappointment or frustration with the congregation. The message marked "Ultimatum" should be reserved for the appropriate occasion, which most likely will never arise. In the meantime, the difference between the "those who" of the warning (vv. 4-8) and the "you" of encouragement (vv. 9-12) deserves reflection, holding promise for both preaching and pastoral care.

3. When the writer of Hebrews encourages the readers (6:9-12), there is no departure from or lessening of theological seriousness. The preacher does not resort to non-substantive tactics, painting smiling faces on everything and otherwise trying to manufacture good cheer. There is a prejudice in our culture to the effect that everything negative or critical or stern in its expression is somehow deep or profound or substantive, whereas the positive or affirming or encouraging is regarded as shallow and lacking in thought. Preachers are often seduced by this unjustified perception and hence do not support words of hope and encouragement with the same degree of theological reflection as used to undergird other pulpit discourse. In this regard, 6:9-12 is instructive. Here the encouragement of the church is firmly grounded theologically in the justice or fairness or faithfulness of God. God is aware, says the writer, of our excellent record of love and service, a record that we continue to maintain. Not only is God aware, but also God is just and dependable. Hence the congregation can expect continued favor and the support necessary for their diligence to the very end. God is true to God's own self; therefore, they will not be abandoned on their way to inherit the promises. As Paul expressed it, human faithlessness does not nullify the faithfulness of God (Rom 3:3-4). The relationships of love and service within the congregation are grounds for encouragement, it is true, and the models of faith and patience among those who have gone before likewise spur the members on in spite of severe difficulties. But the solid and unshakable foundation for all their hope is the character of God. So important is this consideration that the writer will develop it further in vv. 13-20.

HEBREWS 6:13-20, THE GROUND FOR HOPE

COMMENTARY

In this third and final unit of the section 5:11–6:20, the writer turns again from exhortation to exposition. It is clear, however, that the exposition is in the service of the word of encouragement offered in the preceding unit (vv. 9-12). In fact, this unit elaborates on words already introduced: "blessing" (v. 7), "promises" (v. 12), "faith and patience" (v. 12), and, further could be understood as a development of the affirmation in v. 10, "God is not unjust." There are three discernible parts to this unit: vv. 13-15, which deal with God and Abraham; v. 16, which enlarges on God's sworn promise to Abraham to a principle common to human relations; and vv. 17-20, which apply the sworn promise to us as the ground of our encouragement and hope. Verse 20 closes with a repeat of the ending of 5:10, "a high priest according to the order of Melchizedek," thus returning the reader to the subject temporarily delayed while the author addressed the question of the readers' capacity to understand so difficult a discussion.

6:13-15. These verses develop two themes: Abraham as a prototype of those who trust in God's promises and God's promise, guaranteed by an oath. The first theme is familiar not only from the treatments of Abraham in biblical and Jewish literature but also from his frequent appearance in this role in the NT (Rom 4:3; Gal 3:6; Heb 11:8-19; Jas 2:21-23, which puts a different accent on the story). The brevity of the treatment of Abraham's faith, patience, and endurance at this point is probably due in part to the assumption of the reader's familiarity with the story (cf. 12:17, "afterwards, as you know"), in part to the fact that Abraham will reappear in chap. 11 as the model faith pilgrim, and in part to the adequacy of such a brief statement to make specific the general exhortation to imitate "those who through faith and patience inherit the promises" (v. 12). The other theme, God's promise guaranteed by an oath, receives extended treatment, not simply because it is less familiar but rather because it is God's promise and not our faith or endurance that is the ground of all encouragement and hope (see also 7:20-22, 28).

God's promise to Abraham was twofold: the multiplying of his offspring (Gen 12:2; 15:5; 22:17) and the possession of the land (Gen 12:7; 13:14-17). Abraham's relation to the land, which he sought in faith, will receive attention in 11:8-16; here the writer is concerned only with the promise of many descendants. The apparent quotation in v. 14, "I will surely bless you and multiply you," is not really a quotation but rather a sharpened summary of Gen 22:17: "I will indeed bless you, and I will make your offspring as numerous as the stars of heaven and as the sand that is on the seashore" (NRSV). What gives this promise unusual significance is that it follows the most severe trial of Abraham's faith, the offering of his son Isaac (Gen 22:1-14). God had promised earlier, but now, in view of Abraham's trust beyond comprehension, a trust that was willing to give up the only conceivable means for gaining that promise of descendants, God undergirds the promise with an oath:

"By myself I have sworn, says the Lord: Because you have done this, and have not withheld your son, your only son, I will indeed bless you, and I will make your offspring as numerous as the stars of heaven and as the sand that is on the seashore." (Gen 22:16-17 NRSV)

The author of Hebrews may be anticipating another oath of God concerning Melchizedek (7:21, quoting Ps 110:4), but in this context the reference to God's oath has one clear purpose: to undergird further the reader's confidence in the dependability of God.

Much is at stake for both the writer and the church addressed. If the drifting neglect, the sluggish inattention of the church members, has a portion of its cause in the hardships the people are enduring, then they need to look to Abraham, whose faith endured the offering of an only son. If their behavior has a portion of its cause in a faltering trust in God's dependability, then they need to remember not only the promise but its confirmation in the oath as well. That the preacher is trying seriously to persuade the congregation is reflected in the use of the forensic language of the courtroom: "swear," "oath," "to end debate," "surely [with certainty]," "provide a guarantee," "give proof," "impossible to falsify," "unchangeable [irrevocable]," "secure an oath" (vv. 13-18).

Critical situations call for strong language, and both Abraham and the recipients of Hebrews were in critical situations. That God would make a promise and then confirm it by an oath, swearing by God's own name and nature, having no one and nothing greater by which to secure the oath, is strong language. Some Jewish commentators on Gen 22:17 discussed the appropriateness of speaking of God's swearing. Philo, a Jewish philosopher, historian, and biblical interpreter in Alexandria early in the first Christian century, reported that some were offended by the idea, but in his own opinion:

There is nothing amiss in God's bearing witness to himself. For who else would be capable of bearing witness to him? . . . God alone therefore is the strongest security first for himself, and in the next place for his deeds also, so that he naturally swore by himself when giving assurance regarding himself, a thing impossible for anyone else.[63]

The language may have had its origin in oath ceremonies that Israel adopted and adapted from neighboring religions. In systems of polytheism, the lesser beings swore by the greater, but in monotheism, there are no lesser and greater gods. Therefore, God's own name is the guarantee of a promise God would swear to keep.[64]

6:16. As indicated above, this verse moves away from the God-Abraham encounter per se and enlarges on the function of oaths in society familiar to the readers, whether that society be Jewish or Hellenistic or a mixture of the two. As in our own culture, an oath raises ordinary human speech to another level of responsibility, for once the oath is given ("I do solemnly swear"), the one swearing comes under the laws of perjury. The oath is thus taken as confirmation of the truth of statements made; therefore, debate about those statements ends. If, however, it is established that a person lied under oath, debate resumes and the one so sworn is punished. In this formal sense, oaths functioned similarly then and now.

6:17-20. Drawing on this analogy from human discourse, the author now explains the meaning of God's oath for "the heirs of the promise." God's words do not, of course, require confirmation, but God wanted to "show even more clearly" (demonstrate more abundantly) the unchanging nature of God's purpose. Hence the oath, to confirm even more assuredly to the ones addressed the trustworthiness of God. The writer of Hebrews knows, and the readers must not forget, that this certain truth about God underlies not only the entire message of the sermon but also their lives, individually and as a community of faith. It is to underscore this truth that God does what was really not necessary but was an accommodation to human need; that is, God guarantees a promise.

The word translated "guaranteed" (μεσιτεύω *mesiteuō*, "confirmed," NIV) is literally "interposed" or "mediated," but in the legal language of the passage refers to the act of an intermediary in offering security or a guarantee. It is difficult not to hear in the word the description of Christ as mediator in passages yet to come (8:6; 9:15; 12:24). As for the identity of "the heirs of the promise," the writer is at this point non-specific. At v. 12, those who "inherit the promises" refers obviously to patriarchs and matriarchs whose

---

63. Philo *Allegorical Interpretations* III. 205-6.

64. Hugh White, "The Divine Oath in Genesis," *JBL* 92 (1973) 165-79, esp. 172-79.

faith was worthy of emulating. At 2:16, "the descendants of Abraham" clearly are those who are to inherit salvation, and no doubt the readers will embrace the expression as including themselves as being by faith the children of Abraham and heirs of God's promise.

The promise and the oath, both unchangeable, immutable, irrevocable, are the pillars underneath the strong encouragement provided the believers (v. 18). That God could lie is "impossible" (see Commentary on 6:4 for the author's fondness for this word). In this context, "encouraged" is the translation preferred over "exhorted," even though both are possible (12:5; 13:22). However, even when taken as "exhort," παρακαλέω (parakaleō) never loses its intrinsic sense of comfort and support. Those who are thus encouraged are identified as "we who have fled" (NIV; "taken refuge," NRSV). We cannot know for sure what particular image the writer intended to evoke by portraying the Christians as those who have fled, those who are refugees. The flight from Egypt comes to mind (the exodus theme was developed earlier in chaps. 3–4). Then again, in ancient times persons fleeing for their lives could run to the place of worship and lay hold of the altar, where they would be safe from pursuers (cf. 1 Kgs 1:50-51; 2:28-30). The writer may be recalling the LXX, where the Greek word used here for "those who flee" (καταφυγόντες *kataphygontes*) is used to describe persons fleeing from avengers to designated cities of refuge for asylum (Deut 4:42; 19:5; Josh 20:9). The NRSV seems to favor this last possibility with the translation "we who have taken refuge." Since the author does not develop the image, perhaps it is best to leave open the possibility of association with exodus and pilgrimage language, so important and richly suggestive in Hebrews.

In any case, we who flee are not scattered aimlessly by fear; rather, we move deliberately toward the hope lying before us. Here "hope" is not a subjective quality describing us but is an objective reality, synonymous with "promise," what we have been and will be given through the redemptive act of Christ. Then hope is present as assurance (6:11), but it is also eschatological. The participle "set before us" permits both present and future reference.

Verses 19-20 not only continue the description of "hope" but also turn the reader's attention to the work of Jesus as high priest, the major subject next to be developed. In v. 18, "hope" was the goal set before fleeing refugees; in v. 19, "hope" is an anchor of the soul. This nautical metaphor for stability was rather common in Greek literature,[65] but is absent elsewhere in biblical writings. Its meaning is clear, however, especially with the modifiers "firm" and "secure." The word "secure" or "steadfast" (βέβαιος *bebaios*), sometimes translated "valid" or "in effect," is a favorite of this writer (2:2; 3:6, 14; 9:17) and a most important one for persons who are refugees or pilgrims in the world. The writer now moves from the nautical metaphor to what is almost a personified image of "hope": It "enters the inner shrine behind the curtain." The subject is hope, but one can see how easily the writer can move in v. 20 to Jesus, for only the high priest entered the holy of holies, the inner sanctuary, and then only on the Day of Atonement. About this much will soon be said, but for the present the writer's presentation of hope needs to be heard. Hope is the goal lying before the refugees; hope is the firm and steady anchor of the soul; hope is in the very presence of God, in whom is our assurance and toward whom we move.

By introducing the imagery of the tabernacle and the scene of the mediating work of the high priest, the author returns to the subject briefly delayed at 5:10: Jesus as our high priest. At this point three affirmations about Jesus in this role are made: (1) He has entered the inner sanctuary behind the curtain; (2) he is a forerunner; and (3) he has entered "on our behalf" (v. 20). The curtain or veil mentioned here refers to the partition between the holy place and the most holy place in the desert tabernacle (Lev 16:2, 12, 15; Exod 26:31-35). It was this corresponding curtain in the Temple that was torn from top to bottom when Jesus died (Matt 27:51; Mark 15:38). That Jesus went inside this curtain specifically recalls the entry into the inner shrine by the high priest on the Day of Atonement (Lev 16:2). The work of Jesus presented in terms of this cultic activity will be developed later in Hebrews (9:3, 8,

---

65. For examples, see Lane, *Hebrews 1–8*, 153.

11; 10:19-20). It is enough at this point that the imagery be evoked and that it begin its own impact on the readers in preparation for that discussion.

Very likely the recipients were already familiar with symbolic interpretations of the structure, the furniture, and the activity of the tabernacle and its successor, the Temple. For example, in some intertestamental Jewish literature, the curtain represented the division between the lower heavens, where angels dwelled, and the highest heaven, the dwelling place of God. The saints of old who experienced ascensions encountered this division of the heavens.[66] Some forms of Gnosticism that may have influenced early Christianity (still an open debate) understood the curtain to represent the barrier between earth and heaven, between the material and the spirit worlds. According to such a reading of Hebrews, Christ, by his descent, penetrated this barrier and by his ascent penetrated it once more, opening the way for his followers to leave the material world and enter the sanctuary of God's presence. Käsemann has been a strong advocate of locating Hebrews in such a gnostic milieu, but with few in agreement.[67] At 8:1-6, the heavenly counterpart to an earthly sanctuary will receive more extensive treatment.

The second affirmation in v. 20 about Jesus as high priest is that Jesus entered behind the veil into God's presence as a "forerunner" (πρόδρομος *prodromos*). This is the only use of the word in the NT, although it occurs in the LXX and in Greek literature in various contexts: the runner out in front in an athletic event; a herald announcing the approach of an important person or group; a scout in advance of an army; or even the early fruit that promised the arrival of the harvest. In the culture of the tabernacle or Temple, the high priest was not a forerunner. No others, not even priests, followed him into the holy of holies; he went alone. By contrast, Christ, even though his salvific work of offering himself was peculiar to him alone, was a forerunner; that is, he prepared for others to follow. This interprets in part the third affirmation: Christ entered "on our behalf." Just as his earthly ministry of death on the cross was on our behalf, so also is his continuing ministry in God's presence, not solely as intercessor but as the one who makes possible our entry into the heavenly sanctuary. But first the author must find a ground for the claim that Christ is a high priest. That ground is Melchizedek.

66. *Testament of Levi* 3:2-4; *1 Enoch* 14:10-20.
67. Käsemann, *The Wandering People of God,* 223-25.

REFLECTIONS

1. When the writer of Hebrews develops the twin themes of God's faithfulness and Abraham's (and our) faith, it is both striking and refreshing that the theme of God's faithfulness receives the extended treatment. This is not to say that faith as the acceptable human response to God is neglected in the Hebrews sermon. By no means; faith is a note sounded repeatedly, reaching a crescendo in chap. 11. But prior to faith is God's faithfulness, and unless the church hears this and says this, faith can be urged upon the frustrated, who, lacking a clear object of trust, are left to have faith in faith. Without a clear "whom" or "what," faith becomes another exercise in self-help. Let the pulpit not cease saying that God is dependable, that God does not break promises, that God does not abandon.

2. Like faith, hope is a primary ingredient of a life healthy and alive toward God. But the contribution of 6:18-20 to our thinking about hope is that it is presented not so much as our posture toward God and the future as it is a quality of the Christian message, real and certain in itself, however we may happen to feel on any given day. Hope is out in front of the refugees, beckoning them. Hope is an anchor firm and secure in the very place where God is. Hope has already entered the inner sanctuary, where the act of atonement is offered and received. We must have hope, to be sure, but on occasions when we feel no hope, hope still exists. There is hope beyond hope; therefore, the Christian life is not held hostage to feelings. Hebrews 6:18-20 breaks the subjective captivity of the gospel.

3. Hebrews 6:13-15 dips into Genesis 22 to draw upon God's promise and oath to Abraham as a resource for the encouragement of the believers. That promise and oath follow immediately the story of Abraham's offering his son Isaac, but there is no mention of that story to the readers. The writer knows that they know it and that the memory of it will do its own appropriate work in their minds. A lesser preacher would have milked that story for all kinds of hortatory urgings. "You think you have it rough? You think your faith is being tested? You think you are making sacrifices? Look at Abraham, giving up his only son, etc., etc., etc." There is neither encouragement or effective exhortation in telling those who are suffering that others have suffered more, in telling those grieving that others have lost more, in telling the hungry that others have actually starved. Such spoutings produce feelings of guilt, shame, and anger—all of which are not only unproductive but also destructive of the faith that was already only barely clinging to the altar.

HEBREWS 7:1–10:39

THE DIFFICULT DISCUSSION

OVERVIEW

The writer of Hebrews comes now to the subject repeatedly anticipated but delayed at 5:10 because it was a matter about which "we have much to say that is hard to explain" (5:11 NRSV). The subject is the high priestly ministry of Christ. The reader has known since 1:3 that at some point this christological development was coming. Tantalizingly brief references to the effect that Christ functions for us as priest were sprinkled through the discussion (1:3; 2:17-18; 3:1; 4:14-16) until finally, at 5:6, the full assertion is made by means of Ps 110:4: Christ is a high priest forever after the order of Melchizedek, an assertion repeated at 5:10 and 6:20. The figure of Melchizedek (Gen 14:17-20) will occupy the writer only at 7:1-10, but "the order of Melchizedek" will directly and indirectly undergird the christological argument of this entire section. Therefore, Ps 110:4 is absolutely pivotal for the writer's portrayal of Christ.

In 5:7-9 it was evident that the author had access to traditions about the earthly life of Jesus, whether or not those traditions were mediated through the synoptic Gospels. However, nothing in those traditions (at least in the ones available to us) of the preacher, teacher, exorcist Jesus provides a biblical basis adequate to support a high priestly christology. After all, Jesus was not a Levite, and never in his visits to the Temple in Jerusalem was he there in the role of a priest. On the contrary, according to the Gospel accounts he was opposed by the priests. The writer looks, then, not to those accounts but to Ps 110:4 for an exegetical foundation. Just as Paul countered Mosaic legalism in the church by going back to Abraham (430 years earlier, Gal 3:17) for the faith covenant that provided continuity between Judaism and Christianity, so also the author of Hebrews went back of the levitical priesthood to Melchizedek to ground a priestly christology in Jewish Scriptures and, most important, in the plan of God before there ever was a tabernacle or a levitical priest.

The section before us, 7:1–10:39, is clearly the central movement of the epistle-sermon. Vanhoye, whose detailed (and sometimes strained) literary analysis of Hebrews as an elaborate concentric composition has influenced most subsequent analyses, regarded 7:1–10:39 as the third of five movements in the argument of the text.[68] Two movements (1:5–2:18; 3:1–5:10) lead to this section, and two (11:1–12:13; 12:14–13:19) flow from it. His schema differs, however, from what is offered here in that he includes 5:11–6:20 as a preliminary exhortation and 10:19-39 as a final exhortation, both within the section. He is correct in observing the close parallels between these two exhortations (warning and encouragement), but is not persuasive in arguing for their inclusion in the section. This commentary separates 5:11–6:20 as preparation for the difficult discussion and joins 10:26-39 to 11:1–12:17 as a part of the call to fidelity and mutuality based on the argument of 7:1–10:39. Various commentators use slightly different outlines, but all are offered in the service of the writer's argument and the reader's understanding.

There are within this section three major divisions: 7:1-28; 8:1–10:18; and 10:19-39. The first establishes Christ's priesthood according to the order of Melchizedek; the second develops the high priestly ministry of Christ in terms of sanctuary, covenant, and sacrifice; the third speaks briefly of life individually and communally in response to this ministry of Christ.

---

68. A. Vanhoye, *La structure litt'raire de l'Épître aux Hébreux* (Paris: Descl'e de Brouwer, 1963). For his influence on most subsequent analyses, see Lane, *Hebrews 1–8*, lxxxvii-lxxxviii.

HEBREWS 7:1-28, CHRIST AND MELCHIZEDEK

OVERVIEW

Obscure figures of the Old Testament whose portraits are very briefly sketched or whose stories contain elements of mystery attracted great interest in subsequent generations. Enoch vanished from the earth because God took him (Gen 5:24); Moses' grave was never found (Deut 34:6); Elijah ascended in a whirlwind (2 Kgs 2:11). It was not simply curiosity that drew poets and scholars to these characters; the gaps and ambiguities provided room for traditions to develop around these figures in support of various theologies and institutions.

The shadowy and mysterious Melchizedek belongs in this company. His sudden appearance and disappearance (Gen 14:17-20) are an invitation to all who would find in antiquity a precedent or the origin of their own traditions. In rabbinic literature, the account in Gen 14:17-20 is interpreted as the transfer of the priesthood from Melchizedek to Abraham and his descendants. Psalm 110:4, "You are a priest forever according to the order of Melchizedek" (NRSV), was thus understood as having been spoken to Abraham.[69] Of course, anyone "having neither beginning of days nor end of life" (Heb 7:3) would have a place in the visions of apocalyptic writings and in those speculations perhaps spawned by apocalypticism, which we refer to as Gnosticism. Along this line, Käsemann identifies Melchizedek as one of several incarnations of the primal Adam who was a priest,[70] but Käsemann's case for such speculation's being pre-Christian and influential in Hebrews is not very strong. Philo of Alexandria allegorically interpreted Melchizedek in Gen 14:18-20 as "the right word or principle"[71] in each of us. Chronologically, Philo could have been available to the writer of Hebrews, but on this matter they seem worlds apart. In 1956 in Qumran Cave 11 manuscript fragments were discovered that bear witness to one Melchizedek tradition in at least one Palestinian Jewish community early in the first Christian century. According to this very fragmented document (11Q Melch), Melchizedek held a position above other heavenly beings, was an agent of divine judgment associated with the final year of Jubilee, and had a significant role on the Day of Atonement. While 11Q Melch comments on several isolated scriptures, there is no mention of either Gen 14:17-20 or Ps 110:4.[72] These brief comments are sufficient to instruct us that the writer of Hebrews was not alone in commenting on Melchizedek in support of a theological position. Hebrews is alone, however, in its line of thought: from Jesus Christ to Ps 110:4 to Gen 14:17-20.

---

69. F. L. Horton, Jr., *The Melchizedek Tradition* (Cambridge: Cambridge University Press, 1976) 114-30.
70. Käsemann, *The Wandering People of God*, 202-5.
71. Philo *Allegorical Interpretation* III.79.
72. J. A. Fitzmyer, "Further Light on Melchizedek from Qumran Cave 11," *JBL* 86 (1967) 25-41.

Hebrews 7:1-3, Melchizedek, King and Priest

COMMENTARY

Two brief paragraphs are devoted to the person of Melchizedek and his meeting with Abraham (Gen 14:17-20). The first (vv. 1-3) consists of a paraphrase of Gen 14:18-20 and an interpretation of what the text does *not* say; the second (vv. 4-10) interprets the significance of the Genesis account. Verse 10 returns to v. 1: Melchizedek met Abraham, a statement that forms the inclusio. In the Greek text, vv. 1-3 constitute one elaborate sentence ("For this Melchizedek... remains a priest forever") that has been divided to accommodate English style. The poetic or hymnic qualities of the sentence have been noted by commentators, leading some to theorize that an early Melchizedek hymn lay back of vv. 1-3 and perhaps vv. 1-10.[73] Perhaps that is true, but for the Hebrews writer's purposes, Gen 14:17-20 is viewed through the lens of Ps 110:4, and it is the declaration of the psalm that determines what is and what is not to be interpreted in the Genesis text.

Genesis 14 records the victory of Abraham over a coalition of five kings, the rescue of Lot, and Abraham's meeting with the king of Sodom on his return from the war. During their meeting, King Melchizedek appears, offering bread and wine, but not until Gen 14:18*b* does Hebrews 7 pick up the story: Melchizedek was a priest of God Most High. That Melchizedek was a king is also important for Hebrews, because Psalm 110, the central text for the christology of the letter, joins kingship (Ps 110:1) and priesthood (Ps 110:4). In fact, at 7:2 the writer elaborates on Melchizedek's kingship, first etymologically (his name in Hebrew means "king of righteousness") and then geographically ("king of Salem" means "king of peace"). Even so, of primary importance here is his priesthood; he blessed Abraham and from Abraham received a tithe of all Abraham had (Gen 14:19-20).

Thus far, the author of Hebrews has drawn his message from what is stated in Genesis 14, but the interpretive burden increases in v. 3 with the most important assertion of the passage, "resembling [like, in like form] the Son of God, he remains a priest forever." How can such a conclusion be drawn from Gen 14:17-20? Using an accepted method of rabbinic exegesis, the writer interprets the silences of the text. According to Genesis 14, Melchizedek suddenly appears, performs a priestly function, and disappears. The text's silences about whence and whither are interpreted: motherless, fatherless, no genealogy, no beginning, no end. Verse 3 is a classic example of terse, condensed language for rhetorical effect. The writer is not arguing but is giving the recipients an impressive way of reading the text. And why this reading? Because it supports the primary text, Ps 110:4: "You are a priest forever according to the order of Melchizedek" (NRSV). If Christ's priesthood is forever, like that of Melchizedek, then Melchizedek's had to be forever. The "forever" is derived from the silence of his coming and going. "From nowhere to nowhere" is translated "from eternity to eternity." While the argument seems to be from Melchizedek to the Son of God, it is, in fact, from the Son of God to Melchizedek. The conviction that Christ is our eternal high priest finds its support in Psalm 110, which then becomes the key for interpreting Genesis 14.

It is not enough, however, simply to declare Melchizedek an eternal priest; the author wants to express it in a way that will anticipate the coming argument as to the superiority of Melchizedek's priesthood over levitical priesthood. Since the levitical priesthood depended on the record of parentage and an approved genealogy and since it passed from generation to generation because of the fact of death, v. 3 is more than a rhetorical flourish. In its poetic description of Melchizedek's eternality is a distilled statement of the inferiority of the levitical priesthood, its dependence on the contingencies of parents, genealogy, and death. But the writer will not leave these subtleties to be caught by a few; they will be spelled out so that no one will fail to understand. (See Reflections at 7:26-28.)

73. Jewett, *Letter to Pilgrims*, 117-18.

Hebrews 7:4-10, Melchizedek Is Superior to Levites

COMMENTARY

The writer extols the greatness of Melchizedek through several lines of thought, beginning with the matter of the tithe. Although the levitical priests also received a tithe, on several counts Melchizedek is greater. First, he received a tenth of the spoils or booty of war (v. 4). The spoils consisted of the most prized and valuable materials taken from an enemy (gold, silver, ornate furniture and clothing, fine horses, etc). In other words,

Melchizedek received a tithe of the very best. Second, he collected a tithe from Abraham, and it is the greatness of Abraham that argues for an even greater Melchizedek. Abraham is the patriarch (v. 4), which is to say that he is the progenitor of all Israel—he *is* Israel in prospect and promise. When one thinks in terms of corporate personality or community rather than individuals, then it becomes clear that the primacy of Abraham is more than chronological. In addition, Abraham is the one who received the promises from God (v. 6; 6:13-15). The promises, confirmed by an oath (Gen 22:17), are superior to the law of Moses, by which the Levites operate (v. 5). The law states that levitical priests are to receive from all non-priestly Israelites a tithe (Num 18:21-32), but Melchizedek received a tithe from the one with the promises. The writer does not at this point develop arguments for the superiority of promise over law as did Paul in Romans and Galatians, but it is clear and will become clearer that this is the writer's position. Third, Melchizedek blessed Abraham, and, in the writer's value system, the one who blesses is always greater than the one who is blessed (vv. 6-7). Fourth, Melchizedek received a tithe as one who was totally apart from a genealogical record, since he was a priest "in perpetuity" (v. 3), while levitical priests were mortal (ἀποθνήσκοντες ἄνθρωποι *apothnēskontes anthrōpoi*; lit., "dying men," v. 8) and hence had to be replaced. And finally, Levi himself paid tithes to Abraham in the sense that he was "still in the loins" of Abraham when Abraham paid tithes (vv. 9-10). In other words, the one who received tithes paid a tithe. The writer seems to recognize a difference in the weight or duality of this final argument, prefacing it with the qualifier, "one might even say" or "so to speak" (v. 9). The line of argument is to our ears unusual and perhaps unpersuasive, but within the writer's available methods of interpretation and in a culture that thought in terms of the solidarity of the race, both living and dead, the yet unborn Levi could be understood as being represented in his ancestor Abraham. Viewing vv. 9-10 as "artificial" and "playful"[74] may be taking the writer's reasoning too lightly. (See Reflections at 7:26-28.)

74. Attridge, *A Commentary on the Epistle to the Hebrews*, 197.

Hebrews 7:11-19, A New Priesthood

COMMENTARY

The homiletical commentary (midrash) continues, but the person of Melchizedek and Gen 14:17-20 are left behind and in their place are "the order of Melchizedek" and Ps 110:4. Unlike the historical narrative of Genesis 14, Psalm 110 is an oracle of God—that is, a direct declaration of God's will and word. In form, vv. 11-19 constitute an inclusio, as did 1-10; that is, the writer returns in v. 19 to references to perfection and law, introduced in v. 11.

7:11-12. This unit of the argument opens with a rhetorical question of a standard variety: If this were the case (but it is not; the Greek text presents a condition contrary to fact), then why would the following be said? The question is based on a deduction from Ps 110:4, which speaks of another (of a different kind of) priesthood to the effect that the psalmist would not have spoken thus if the levitical priesthood had been fully effective. The ineffectiveness of the levitical priesthood lay in its inability to "perfect" the people (v. 11). The writer's fondness for the word "perfection" and the range of meanings in its usage were noted earlier (see Commentary on 2:10; 5:9, 14; 6:1): The Son is perfected through suffering, and the believers are to grow into perfection (maturity). But here the writer introduces yet another use of the term: the perfecting of the people through priestly activity. As is the habit of the writer, an idea is introduced without comment, telegraphing ahead to a discussion yet to come. At this point we may assume that the perfection of the people through priestly activity refers to that right and complete relation to God effected through the priestly sacrifice of Christ. Perfection, then, has both present and eschatological dimensions. The writer will return us to this subject.

Important to the argument here is the writer's joining of the priesthood and the law (Mosaic), first in a parenthetical comment in v. 11 and again in v. 12. The NRSV inadequately translates "for the people received the law *under* this priesthood" (v. 11). To say "under" might convey simply a temporal sense: The people received the law *during the time of* this (levitical) priesthood. The NIV more correctly captures the strength of the prepositional phrase: The people were given the law "on the basis of" this priesthood. This is to say not only that the relation between the law and the priestly system is inseparable, but also that the law was based on the cultus. It is now quite clear that the Hebrews writer has a cultic understanding of Mosaic legislation, as stated in v. 12: "For when there is a change in the priesthood, there is necessarily a change in the law as well." In other words, the entire system under which Israel lived would change with the arrival of the "different" priest, the priest after the order of Melchizedek. The inability to perfect the people was the flaw of the entire system and not of the priests themselves. The levitical (Aaronic) priests were called and appointed of God (5:1-4), but they functioned, says the author, in a system that was incomplete, unable to fulfill its adherents. As the argument unfolds, it will be important to keep this writer's perspective on the law through the rituals of the tabernacle (temple) free from the predominating influence of Paul, whose extensive treatment of the law as a system of works and merit is quite different.

7:13-14. The author finally addresses the objection that has hovered over every reference to Christ as a priest: He was not of the tribe of Levi, but of the tribe of Judah (Matt 1:1; Acts 13:22-23; Rom 1:3). So how could he be a priest? In an interesting move, the writer turns this objection into an affirmation, saying, in effect, "Of course, Christ was not a Levite; that is my point. He was a different (ἕτερος *heteros*; trans. "another") priest from a different (translated "another") tribe; he was of a different order, the order of Melchizedek." That Christ was of Judah rather than Levi is not, therefore, a grudging concession but a truth that is obvious (v. 14) and in support of the claim that Christ is a priest like Melchizedek.

7:15-16. What is even more obvious is the superiority of the priest resembling Melchizedek over those of the line of Levi (v. 15). Notice that the writer substitutes "resembling" (v. 15; also v. 3) for "order," making it clear that Christ's being a Melchizedek priest is not a matter of lineage or tradition or succession but of likeness or similarity to Melchizedek. That similarity lies in "the power of an indestructible life" (v. 16). The resurrection of Jesus is likely in the author's mind here. The power or authority of Jesus' work comes from his eternal nature and the life he has, exalted at God's right hand (Ps 110:1). This eternality had been attributed to Melchizedek (v. 3), and in this respect Christ is a priest "after the likeness" of Melchizedek. In sharp contrast is the authorization of levitical priests by "legal requirement concerning physical descent" (v. 16), recalling statements made about the law in vv. 5 and 11-12. Literally, v. 16 says, "according to a law of a fleshy commandment." The word "fleshy" (σάρκινος *sarkinos*) does not here carry all the pejorative meanings attached to it in Paul's letters, but it does speak of the genealogical ground of the levitical priesthood, of the attention given to physical matters in laws regarding priests and their functions, and of the transient nature of both the regulations and the priestly system itself.

7:17. Psalm 110:4 is quoted again, one of three such direct citations in Hebrews (cf. 5:6; 7:21). In 5:6, the quotation is employed to show that just as the levitical priests were appointed by God (5:4), so also was Christ. The words of Ps 110:4 are understood as God's words addressed to Christ, establishing that he was appointed by God to be a priest. But while Ps 110:4 in Heb 5:6 was used to show that Christ was *like* levitical priests in divine appointment, at 7:17, 21 the same text serves the argument that Christ's priesthood is *superior* to that of the Levites. This argument, that Christ's priesthood is superior to or better than that of Aaron, is the burden of Hebrews 7, and Ps 110:4 carries that burden.

Of the ten allusions to or quotations of Ps 110:4 in Hebrews, seven occur in this chapter.[75] In v. 17, the citation is introduced with the language of witnessing: "For it is attested [NRSV; "declared," NIV; lit., "it is witnessed" (μαρτυρεῖται *martyreitai*)] of him." And the witness is that his priesthood is "forever," or perhaps more appropriately, "unending." Hence the psalm is offered as proof of the preceding assertion that Christ's life, unlike that of a levitical priest, was "indestructible." The resurrection-exaltation of Christ is surely in the writer's mind here. Whether one argues that Ps 110:4 led the writer to a priestly interpretation of Easter or that Easter turned the writer to Ps 110:4,[76] the conclusion is the same: At 7:17 the two are joined in the word "forever." As we will see, at v. 21, Ps 110:4 will be introduced not with the language of witnessing but with that of swearing, and it will be used in the service of another point altogether.

7:18-19. These verses are framed on the familiar pattern "On the one hand . . . but on the other," with the second half of the construction carrying the stronger or more important message. The first half announces the abrogation (annulment) of law. This is legal terminology, much stronger than "change" of law at v. 12. But how does the replacement of a transient priesthood based on genealogy with an unending one based on a life without genealogy (v. 3) annul law? For the writer, law and priesthood are inseparably joined (7:5, 11-12, 16); the replacement of one means the replacement of the other. In addition, the law that established the levitical priesthood was "earlier"; that is, the declaration of priesthood in Ps 110:4 was, in the writer's view, chronologically later than the law of Moses and, therefore, announced a successor to the levitical priesthood (argument from chronology appears earlier at 4:6-9). It is interesting that in 7:1-10 the writer argues that Melchizedek, being *historically prior* to Levi (Gen 14:17-20), is superior, while here God's declaration about the order of Melchizedek is *subsequent to* Levi (Ps 110:4) and, therefore, superior. And finally, the law is annulled because it was "weak and ineffectual" (unprofitable, useless). While the author of Hebrews might well agree with Paul that the law is "holy and just and good" (Rom 7:12 NRSV) and that weakness lay not in the law but in the flesh (Rom 8:3), the fact is that the writer is here pursuing another line of thought. In the language of Hebrews, the ineffectiveness of the law lay in its inability to "make perfect" (v. 19; see also v. 11); this is to say, it was not able to bring God's people to their intended end. The writer thus looks to Christ, a priest like Melchizedek, to fulfill this eschatological expectation of being in God's presence, since he is, on our behalf, at the right hand of God (Ps 110:1).

This access or approach to God is present through our prayer and Christ's intercession (4:14-16), but is also a hope (7:19). That this hope is "better" is no surprise to the reader, given the writer's demonstrated fondness for this word (1:4; 6:9; 7:7, 22; 8:6; 9:23; 10:34; 11:16, 35, 40; 12:24). As for the nature and ground of this hope, see the Commentary on 6:18-20 especially, but also at 3:6 and 6:11. In 7:19, it is this hope that encourages and emboldens the believing community to approach God. Even though drawing near or approaching God has at times a cultic meaning (Exod 24:2; Lev 10:3), it is best here to take the expression in its broader sense of worshipers coming into the presence of God (Isa 29:13; 58:2; Hos 12:6). (See Reflections at 7:26-28.)

---

75. Since only Hebrews in the NT uses Ps 110:4, it seems unlikely that this verse would have appeared in a list of OT passages useful for Christian preaching. Such lists are referred to as testimony books, although their existence is unproven. Psalm 110:1, however, is quoted or alluded to in eleven NT documents and seems to have circulated widely as useful OT testimony to Christ as Messiah-King. Cf. the chart of citations in Hay, *Glory at the Right Hand*, 163-66.

76. In arguing against the popular position that Philo strongly influenced Hebrews, Williamson finds the resurrection of Jesus a sufficient magnet to draw texts directly from the OT without mediation through Philo. See R. Williamson, *Philo and the Epistle to the Hebrews* (Leiden: E. J. Brill, 1970) esp. 443-49.

Hebrews 7:20-25, Confirmed by God's Oath

COMMENTARY

These six verses fall naturally into two sub-units: vv. 20-22 and vv. 23-25. Verses 26-28 could easily be included here as a third sub-unit, all three being bound as an inclusio, beginning (v. 20) and ending (v. 28) with the unusual word translated "taking an oath" (ὀρκωμοσία *horkōmosia*). Since, however, vv. 26-28 are a rhetorical flourish serving as a conclusion to the entire chapter, that sub-unit will be discussed separately.

Verses 20-25 contain two arguments for the superiority of Christ's priesthood over that of Aaron's line, neither of which is surprising. In fact, both have been so fully anticipated as to seem repetitious. It is the conclusions drawn from them that grab the reader's attention. Both arguments are, like the one in vv. 18-19, framed on the "On the one hand . . . but on the other" pattern, but translators obscure the form in favor of diversity of expression, thereby losing the cumulative force of repetition in argumentation.

7:20-22. The first argument, simply stated, is that priesthood confirmed by an oath (Christ's) is superior to priesthood without an oath (levitical, Exod 28:1). This argument is a straightforward interpretation of Ps 110:4a, taken to be the direct speech of God to Christ: "You are a priest forever." In v. 17, that Christ's priesthood was unending was argued from his indestructible life; here it is established by God's oath. Earlier statements about God's making oaths (3:11–4:3; 6:13-18) have prepared the reader to receive this unusual language about God. But as though God's swearing was not emphatic enough, the writer underscores it with the rhetorically forceful double negative: "And it was not without an oath!" (preserved in the NIV, lost in the NRSV; for an earlier example of the double negative, see 4:15).

The unexpected conclusion to this argument involves a move in thought from priesthood to covenant (v. 22). This is the first use of this word in Hebrews, but its introduction follows a familiar pattern of the anticipatory use of important terms to be developed later (8:6–9:20; 10:16, 29; 12:24; 13:20). Therefore discussion of "covenant" (διαθήκη *diathēkē*) will be reserved until discussion of chap. 8. However, it is important to notice here two features of this covenant. First, "a better covenant" is an extension of the earlier reference to "a better hope" (v. 19). This is to say that the hope of which the writer speaks will have its implementation within a covenant relationship between God and the believing community. Second, of this better covenant Jesus is the "guarantee" or "surety" (ἔγγυος *engyos*).[77] The word is quite different from "mediator," which will be employed later (8:6). One who is a "surety" guarantees the work or commitments of another, even at the risk of property and even life itself. The LXX uses the word at Sir 29:15: "Do not forget the kindness of your guarantor,/ for he has given his life for you" (NRSV). While it is possible to interpret the expression to mean that Christ offers his life as our surety toward God, the context argues for the opposite meaning: The God who promises and makes oaths also guarantees the covenant with Christ's priestly offering of himself for us.

7:23-25. The second argument of this sub-unit turns on the "transient-permanent" contrast, already familiar from 7:3, 16-17. Here the difference between the levitical priesthood and that of Christ is reframed in terms of "many" and "one." The Levites are many—that is, generation after generation—because they are subject to death. Christ, however, is one, because he continues forever. He has no successor but "remains" (v. 24; recall the frequency of this word in the christology of John's Gospel, e.g., John 1:32-33, 38-39; 4:40; 6:27; 8:31; 12:34; 14:10). This line of argument proceeds from Ps 110:4b just as the argument in vv. 20-21 proceeded from Ps 110:4a. And again, the writer draws a conclusion: "Consequently" or "Therefore" (v. 25) Christ is able to save for all time (NRSV) or completely (NIV). The adverbial phrase can be taken either way, but given a context filled with terms like "eternal," "unending," and "always," the temporal sense is to be preferred, but with no loss of meaning if translated "completely." The beneficiaries of this salvation are those who approach God through Christ the high priest. This metaphor of "drawing near" to God is a favorite of the writer, who is mindful of its cultic base but expands on it to refer to the whole of a Christian's relation to God (see Commentary on 7:19).

The "complete" or "for all time" quality of this salvation rests on two affirmations about Christ. First, he continues alive forever, and therefore his priestly endeavors for

---

77. It would be instructive to review the points at which the author has previously introduced the name "Jesus" (2:9; 3:1; 4:14; 6:20).

his followers never cease. Second, priestly ministry involves making intercession. His sympathy for us because he was one of us (4:15; 5:1; 5:7-9) and his access to God as one appointed of God (5:5-6) and who is now at God's right hand (1:8, 13) join as the twin credentials qualifying him to intercede on our behalf (4:14-16). The writer is not at this point careful to specify the intercession as forgiveness and, therefore, an extension of the benefits of the cross or as more general intercession for the saints, involving occasions of trial and persecution as well as commission of sin.[78]

[78]. Attridge, *A Commentary on the Epistle to the Hebrews*, 211-12, summarizes a range of views on the nature of Christ's intercession.

But if his salvation is "complete," it is difficult to imagine the favor of intercession being episodic or reserved for only certain conditions. The word here translated "make intercession" (ἐντυγχάνω *entygchanō*) occurs elsewhere in the NT four times, all with this sense of petitioning or pleading on behalf of another (Acts 25:24; Rom 8:27, 34; 11:2). The image of Christ alive in God's presence, ministering on behalf of believers, is a major contribution to the church's struggle with the question, How do the blessings of Christ's life, death, and resurrection survive the constraints of time and place in history? (See Reflections at 7:26-28.)

Hebrews 7:26-28, Christ, Our Eternal High Priest

COMMENTARY

This final sub-unit of the chapter is a rhetorical flourish on the eternal high priest, recalling the burst of praise of Melchizedek with which the chapter began (v. 3) and, more distantly, the hymn to the Word of God at 4:12-13. Like the other two, five characteristics are listed, and like v. 3, the traits are listed without conjunctions, a well-known rhetorical device for accenting by eliminating the dulling effect of repeated conjunctions. The majestic nature of the passage suggests that a fragment of a hymn or poem is embedded here, but efforts to extract it are inconclusive. In content, vv. 26-28 function not only as a summary of vv. 1-25 but also to anticipate the continuation of the argument in 8:1–10:18. The reader will notice that just as the argument moved from Melchizedek (Gen 14:17-20) to the order of Melchizedek (Ps 110:4), so also now it moves to Christ as high priest without need for repeated authorization from Psalm 110. In other words, the writer believes the case has been made. In these three verses, Christ as high priest will be presented in terms of character, achievement, and status.

7:26. Both the character and the self-giving of Christ are, says the writer, "fitting" or "appropriate" (πρέπω *prepō*, v. 26). This expression was used at 2:10 to speak of God's making the pioneer of our salvation perfect through suffering. Here the appropriateness seems to have us in mind ("fitting that we should have such a high priest"), although the distinction should not be too sharply drawn. Whether from the perspective of God's activity or of our need, the fittingness lies in God's purpose. The three adjectives characterizing our high priest are not common in either the LXX or the NT. The word "holy" (ὅσιος *hosios*) is not the one most frequently used but does occur in reference to God (Rev 15:4; 16:5), to Christ (Acts 2:27; 13:35), and to believers (1 Tim 2:8; Titus 1:8). "Blameless" (ἄκακος *akakos*) is found elsewhere in the NT only at Rom 16:18. The most cultic of the three, "undefiled" (ἀμίαντος *amiantos*) appears at Jas 1:27 and 1 Pet 1:4 and again at Heb 13:4, but with a clearly ethical sense. The three words together echo 4:15, but this vivid elaboration adds little to the sense expressed at 4:15. The two participial phrases, "having been separated from sinners" and "having become exalted above the heavens" refer essentially to the same event, the elevation of Christ to the presence of God. It is in this sense that he is apart from sinners and not in any way that would diminish his capacity for human sympathy, a point the writer has taken great pains to make repeatedly (2:10-18; 4:14-16; 5:1-2, 7-8). The one who passed through the heavens (4:14) is now "above the heavens"—that is, in the presence of God Most High (1:3), who occupies the heaven beyond the heavens. In the cosmology of the time, "heavens" (οὐρανοί *ouranoi*) was commonly a plural word referring to regions above the earth occupied by spirit beings, a view reflected especially in Paul's affirmations of the cosmic scope of Christ's redemptive work (Phil 2:10-11; Col 1:15-20). In expressions of praise, "heavens" is a plural of "majesty."

7:27. Here it becomes clear why the writer has presented the unique character of Christ in v. 26: He is unlike other high priests who (1) offer sacrifices repeatedly and (2) first for their own sins (5:1-3). In contrast to other high priests, he (1) made one sacrifice once and for all and (2) had no need to offer a sacrifice for himself, being without sin (4:15). In speaking of "daily" sacrifices by the high priest, the writer seems to have collapsed into a single image the entire sacrificial system, both the daily offerings of priests and the annual sacrifice by the high priest (Yom Kippur). Had the writer said "yearly" rather than "daily," the statement would have been historically correct, but perhaps "daily" was chosen to sharpen the contrast between the repetition of the levitical system and the once-for-all sacrifice of Christ.[79]

Here in this verse is the author's first use of the expression "he offered himself." Whether Isa 53:10 lay in the immediate background of the writer's thought is uncertain; certainly many NT writers expressed in a variety of ways that Christ gave himself for us. However, it is only in Hebrews that the idea and its many inferences are developed into the image of a high priest offering himself as a sacrifice for sin. Up to this point the writer has spoken of Christ's high priestly work as primarily that of intercessor (2:18; 4:14-16; 7:24-25); his sacrifice of himself for sin is a theme yet to be developed. It is interesting that the discussion moves from intercession to sacrifice when chronologically one would have expected first the sacrifice and then the move into God's presence as intercessor. Perhaps this is a case of arguing from the matter of lesser difficulty to the greater or, more likely, from the point established by Psalm 110 (at God's right hand, intercessor), a text widely used in the early church, to texts not commonly cited to establish that Christ's death was also a high priestly act. We anticipate more clarity to come.

7:28. The chapter closes with a summary framed as contrasts between the levitical high priest and Christ, again referred to as Son (recalling 1:2; 3:6; 4:14; 5:5, 8). The appointment of the high priest is in the one case by law (vv. 11-12, 18-19), in the other by an oath (vv. 20-22). The high priest appointed by law is subject to weakness (i.e., death, vv. 8, 23); the one appointed by an oath is eternal (6:20; 7:3, 21, 25). The oath came later than the law, replacing the weak and ineffectual commandment (v. 18). The law made nothing perfect (v. 19), but the Son "has been made perfect forever" (v. 28). Perfection here carries the force of permanence and finality, clear implications of the exaltation of the Son to the right hand of God (Ps 110:1, 4).

---

79. Lane, *Hebrews 1–8*, 194, summarizes scholarly opinions about the writer's apparent misstatement.

REFLECTIONS

1. Hebrews 7 contains some of the most interesting examples of rabbinic exegesis to be found in the New Testament. There are interpretations of silence (the sudden appearance and disappearance of Melchizedek = motherless, fatherless, without beginning or end), of chronology (Melchizedek is earlier than Levi, therefore greater; Ps 110:4 is later than the law, therefore superior), of the power of oath to abrogate law, and others. These methods should not merely satisfy historical curiosity or serve as models uncritically embraced; rather, they should prompt critical examination of one's own methods. One of the more interesting of the writer's arguments, that Levi paid a tithe to Melchizedek because Levi was in Abraham's loins when Abraham paid the tithe (vv. 9-10), deserves special attention because it is predicated on a biblical perspective much larger than Hebrews 7. That perspective is sometimes called "corporate personality," a conviction that the many are really one, that community is primary, including the departed, the living, and the yet-to-be born. Generations after the exodus, Israelites recited before God: "A wandering Aramean was *my* ancestor. . . . when the Egyptians treated *us* harshly and afflicted *us* . . . *we* cried to the Lord" (see Deut 26:5-10). Notice the collapse of historical distance before the greater belief that Israel is one. Persons caught in individualism and subjectivism have difficulty not only interpreting such texts but also forming strong communities of faith.

2. If there were uncertainties earlier, chapter 7 makes it abundantly clear that the cultus provides the writer's perspective on the faith and practices of both Judaism and Christianity. Both law and covenant are discussed, but only in their relation to the sacerdotal system. Paul's categories of works and faith are not here. The reader of Hebrews is addressed as a worshiper whose life is fulfilled in drawing near to God (4:16; 6:19-20; 7:19, 25). To be sure, Paul had a strong sense of worship, viewing life (Rom 12:1) and work (Rom 15:16) liturgically and often quoting hymns and confessions in his letters. However, it is the writer of Hebrews who makes the case for God, whose presence is the goal of the faith pilgrim, and for Christ, whose life, death, and exaltation make access to God possible. The one perfected through suffering is able to perfect those who look to God through him. Hebrews would, therefore, urge the church not only to take worship seriously but also to take it theologically and christologically. Gatherings of the church to massage the self hardly qualify according to the standards of Hebrews.

3. Closely tied to the preceding reflection is the work of Christ as intercessor with God on our behalf (4:14-15; 7:24-25). This dimension of Christ's saving work is generally neglected, although Hebrews has the support of Paul (the Spirit intercedes, Rom 8:26-27) and John, who deals more lengthily than does any other New Testament writer with the crisis created by the departure of Christ, addressing such questions as, Where is Christ now? and What is his relation to us? (John 13–17). Without this vital doctrine, the church lives in a barren desert between "Christ was here" and "Christ will be here again." Meanwhile, back at the church, Christian faith consists of believing in an extraordinary past and an extraordinary future. Christ as intercessor transcends the constraints of time and place and restores "today" to the relationship between God and the believer. Many conclude their prayers with "in the name of Christ" with little or no awareness of the christological foundation for the phrase or of the immense encouragement available in the understanding that Christ is continually in God's presence on our behalf. The study of Hebrews should yield to the reader the sure benefit of this conviction, even to the one who otherwise finds in this sermon-epistle much that is difficult to understand (5:11).

HEBREWS 8:1–10:18, THE HIGH PRIESTLY MINISTRY OF CHRIST

OVERVIEW

The writer has now established firmly the rank or status of Jesus Christ, and in doing so has employed the titles on which all further argument will depend. He is Son (Ps 2:7; Heb 5:5), King (Ps 110:1; Heb 1:3, 13), and High Priest (Ps 110:4; Heb 2:17; 3:1; 4:14; 5:5, 10; 6:20; 7:26, 28). "High Priest" will be the title most prominent in what follows, but the other two are essential to the portrayal of Christ as high priest and, therefore, should not leave the reader's awareness. Rank, then, is no longer the argument; now the writer-preacher will develop the ministry of "such a high priest." To do so, it must be established that this high priest had the essentials of a priestly ministry: a sanctuary, a covenant between God and humanity within which a priestly ministry has its efficacy, and something to offer: a sacrifice.

But a major question will haunt the discussion until it is resolved: Since Christ's is a ministry in heaven, eternal and in God's presence, when and where is his sacrifice of himself to be located? If on earth, on the cross, then it could hardly qualify as a high priestly act, since the writer has made it clear that on earth Christ was not a priest (7:14; 8:4). If in heaven, how is one to understand his offering himself as an eternal, heavenly sacrifice? How does one give one's life for others in a realm "above the heavens"? If his sacrifice is understood as a heavenly act, then what happens to the cross? Does it evaporate in allegorical and spiritual interpretation, or is it reduced to the status of precondition or preface to Christ's high priestly work?

It would be simple enough if the chronology were thus: Jesus, one of us in every respect and yet appointed of God, gave his life for us and is now engaged in the high priestly work of intercession. But that is not the whole story, since Christ's high priestly ministry requires also a sacrifice in the presence of God. It seems most unlikely that the author will make the case for Jesus' heavenly ministry by simply jettisoning the earth and all the ugly historical contingencies that Jesus endured "for a little while" (cf. 2:9; 12:2-3). The earth is God's creation, the arena for Israel's faith, the locus of Christ's perfection through suffering, and the inescapable circumstance in which the readers are to be faithful. The burden on the writer is to separate heaven and earth in order to affirm what is better and superior, and yet hold heaven and earth together as the single object of God's love in Christ "through whom he also created the worlds" (1:2 NRSV). The reader can expect, therefore, not only the continuation and even increase of contrasts (earth/heaven, flesh/spirit, many/one, transient/eternal, old/new, external/internal), but also a presentation of the high priestly work of Christ, which transcends and relativizes all contrasts.

The centerpiece for the section is Jeremiah 31. In fact, the preacher will not only quote the relevant portion of that text but will also draw on it, directly and indirectly, to authorize an exegetical homily on covenant and atoning sacrifice. The entire section is exposition; exhortation will follow, beginning at 10:19.

Hebrews 8:1-5, Christ's Sanctuary

COMMENTARY

So much was said in chap. 7 that the discussion could continue in any one of a number of directions. The writer, therefore, immediately focuses attention: "The main point is this." The word translated "the main point" (κεφάλαιον *kephalaion*) is the very first word and could be translated "the sum" (as in the only other NT use of the word at Acts 22:28); but here the clear meaning is not so much "summary" as "focus."

8:1-2. These verses state what the focus is: that we have "such a high priest" (7:26) who is identified by location and by function. His location is "at the right hand of the throne of the Majesty in the heavens." This paraphrase of Ps 110:1 recalls 1:3 (Ps 110:1*b* was quoted at 1:13). The image of a heavenly throne was deeply embedded in Judaism (Pss 11:4; 47:8; Isa 6:1; 66:1; Ezek 1:26) and abundantly used in apocalyptic literature, including the Apocalypse of John (Revelation 4–5; 7:15-17). The affirmation that Christ is seated at God's right hand does not serve at this point to declare Christ's lordship but rather to establish the location of his ministry as high priest. This is to say, Ps 110:4 (that he is a high priest) is joined to Ps 110:1 (his ascension to God's right hand) to make clear that Christ's high priestly work will be performed in heaven. (In addition to the explicit use of Psalm 110, there may be an echo of

Zech 6:13, where throne and priesthood are joined.)

Just as v. 1 identifies the high priest by location, so also v. 2 identifies him by function: He is a minister in the sacred place and tabernacle set up by the Lord, not any mortal. This distinction between the sanctuary and the tent as a whole not only reflects the structure of the desert tent of meeting (Lev 16:16, 20, 33) but also anticipates Christ's ministry in the inner sanctuary, where only the high priest enters. The tabernacle the Lord has pitched (πήγνυμι *pēgnymi*, a verb used only here in the NT) is the "true" one—that is, the real, genuine, lasting one (also 9:24; 10:22; recall the frequent use of this word in the Gospel of John to distinguish the real from the apparent, John 1:9; 4:23; 6:32). Commentary on 8:5 will include detailed discussion of the heavenly sanctuary.

8:3-4. These verses do not add substantively to the argument but function to set up the many contrasts between the levitical high priest and Christ that will follow. Verse 3 might easily have been framed as a question: Since all high priests are appointed in order to offer gifts and sacrifices (5:1), what will this high priest offer? It is not that the question has not yet been answered; 7:27 tells us that "he offered himself." But that statement is too sketchy, too ambiguous, open to a range of interpretations. What lies ahead are the details of method and meaning. One thing is sure: His offering will not be "on earth," because on earth he was not a priest, either by genealogy (7:14) or by law. On earth the levitical priests are the legal appointees (v. 4; 7:16, 18).

8:5. The closing verse of this unit is critical for everything yet to be said, for here the writer states the two-sanctuary position essential for presenting Christ's heavenly ministry and supports it with God's instruction to Moses according to Exod 25:40 (Acts 7:44). Perhaps this crucial and extraordinary verse can best be handled in a series of statements.

(1) The earthly tent that served Israel in its desert journey was of God, not simply in a general sense but with specific instructions to Moses. The divine communication ("was warned" [χρηματίζω *chrēmatizō*]) is expressed with the same word used to speak of God's warning the magi (Matt 2:12) and Joseph (Matt 2:22), revealing to Simeon that he would see the Messiah (Luke 2:26), and directing Cornelius to send for Peter (Acts 10:22). All this is to say that the earthly tabernacle was not of human origin and, therefore, is not deserving of general indictments. Its limitations and inabilities lay in its transient nature and defined purposes, unable to do what it was not intended to do. As Paul said of the law, it "is holy and just and good" (Rom 7:12 NRSV), but. . . .

(2) However, the earthly tabernacle is a copy and shadow of the heavenly one. This is the author's interpretation of Exod 25:40: "See that you make everything according to the pattern that was shown you on the mountain."[80] Five texts state that Moses was given a pattern or type (Exod 25:9, 40; 26:30; 27:8; Num 8:4). In their contexts, all these references serve to enhance the nature of the desert tabernacle; that is, it was not of circumstantial or even Mosaic origin, but everything about it was of God's design. However, at Heb 8:5 the use of Exod 25:40 is pejorative; the earthly tabernacle was but a shadow of the real tabernacle, the one in heaven.

(3) That there is a heavenly sanctuary and that there are correspondences between it and earthly ones is an idea rather widespread in both Jewish and Hellenistic sources. In Greek literature the heavenly or true temple was the cosmos, but it bore no resemblance to the temples of the various cults in the Greek world. On the contrary, the cosmos as temple was the principal ground for attacking earthly temples as centers of deception and superstition. It is unlikely that such literature served as a resource for Heb 8:5. In Judaism, the idea of a heavenly sanctuary found broad and varied expressions, from simple to a sanctuary with two sacred spaces to the grandly elaborate temple of apocalyptic and mystic writers.[81] Among those perhaps most immediately in the background of Hebrews was Philo, who reinterpreted Judaism for the cultured and philosophical minds of Hellenized

---

80. This is not an exact quotation of the LXX. A verb form is different, and "everything" is added, perhaps borrowed from Exod 25:9. It is not clear whether the author of Hebrews was following a different Greek text or was responsible for the changes. It is interesting that Philo, when citing Exod 25:40, also adds "everything" (Philo *Allegorical Interpretation* III.102). Some commentators see here a direct influence of Philo on Hebrews. See K. J. Thomas, "The OT Citations in Hebrews," *NTS* 11 (1965) 309.

81. For an excellent survey, see Aelred Cody, *Heavenly Sanctuary and Liturgy in the Epistle to the Hebrews* (St. Meinrad, Ind.: Grail, 1960) 9-46.

Alexandria. He found Plato immensely helpful for this purpose. Plato contended that the real consisted of invisible forms and ideas of which the earthly and material is but a shadow. Hence the dualistic metaphysics of the real and the shadow. According to this metaphysics, Philo developed elaborate allegorical interpretations of the LXX. In fact, he interpreted the same text cited in Heb 8:5 (Exod 25:40) on the real/shadow schemes.[82] Whether the writer of Hebrews read Philo or was a product of Hellenistic Judaism and, therefore, worked with similar vocabulary and thought patterns is much debated.[83] In either case, the Hebrews writer's incarnational christology and eschatology signal the degree of modification such dualistic thinking had to undergo to serve the gospel, whatever may have been the sources.

(4) As helpful as possible associations between Hebrews and Philo, Qumran, apocalyptists, rabbis, OT writers, or Greek philosophers may be in understanding this epistle, the debate revolving around 8:5 is much larger than that of sources. The question is this: Has the writer, in developing the thesis that the true sanctuary is in heaven, with the one on earth its copy or shadow, abandoned the categories of time and history? The heavenly and the earthly, the real and the copy constitute a spatial framework, whereas the dominant perspective of Scripture as a whole is temporal, portraying God at work through the processes of history, from creation to eschaton. Taken alone, spatial categories (above/below) have no place for salvation history, at least not in any serious way. Do they, therefore, replace the old/new framework?

On the one hand are interpreters, such as Käsemann,[84] who regard the heavenly/earthly language fully adequate for understanding the whole of Hebrews. On the other hand are those, like Williamson,[85] who admit the presence of a modicum of such language but not of such significance as to modify or reduce the dominant role of eschatology in the letter. Closer to the truth than either extreme position is the plain fact that the writer has employed the categories both of time and of space. Without reference to former and latter, old and new, former times, these last days, faith pilgrimages, and the judgment to come, the readers of Hebrews could feel abandoned to the conditions of history while God and Christ were busy with important things somewhere above their heads. And without a christology that could more adequately be expressed by heavenly and earthly, by pre-existence, existence, and post-existence, the readers could feel that Christ, indeed, was one of them and even died as they do. But where is the relief from history? For the writer to employ both time and space to frame the message for a church living in a culture with both categories is certainly not unique in the New Testament. Paul could find many continuities with the history of Israel (Rom 9:1-5) and hold great hope for the fulfillment of that history (Romans 11), and he could still speak of a Christ who not only came from Israel but also descended from heaven and ascended to heaven (2 Cor 8:9; Phil 2:6-11). To reduce the both-and of Hebrews to either-or would be to oversimplify its message at great loss to the readers. (See Reflections at 9:23–10:18.)

---

82. Philo *On the Life of Moses* 2:74.
83. Williamson, *Philo and the Epistle to the Hebrews*, 142-59, traces the debate but with a strong position of his own.
84. Käsemann, *The Wandering People of God*.
85. Williamson, *Philo and the Epistle to the Hebrews*.

Hebrews 8:6-13, Christ's Covenant

COMMENTARY

At v. 4 the author used a particle (μέν *men*) that alerts the reader to anticipate in a subsequent clause a particular conjunction (δέ *de*). If *de* occurs (it may not), then the entire thought can be framed as an "on the one hand . . . but on the other hand" construction. Such is the case with vv. 4-6. The text says: "On the one hand, if this high priest were on earth he would not be a priest at all. There are on earth those who by law minister in a tabernacle that is a copy and shadow of the heavenly one. Exodus 25:40 confirms this understanding. But on the other hand (v. 6), "Christ has obtained a better ministry." One can thus understand why many commentators include v. 6 with vv. 1-5. The decision to join v. 6 with what follows is based on the shift in content, a consideration weightier than syntax.

The ministry (cf. Commentary on 8:1-2) Christ has obtained is a permanent one (the perfect tense of the verb τυγχάνω [tygchanō]), conveying that sense. He entered into the heavenly sanctuary to minister on our behalf, and he is still there. His ministry is "more excellent" in that he mediates a better covenant, enacted on better promises. The only other use of the verb expressing the idea of "enacting" in the NT occurs in 7:11. Notice the writer's continued fondness for the word "better" (κρείττων kreittōn, 1:4; 6:9; 7:7, 19, 22), a comparative that carries the weight of a superlative. The better covenant, introduced at 7:22, will be the subject matter of the quotation of Jer 31:31-34 and the discussion that follows. Christ serves this better covenant as mediator (μεσίτης mesitēs, 8:6; 9:15; 12:24; unlike "guarantee" at 7:22). Although the writer will more specifically link priesthood to covenant in 10:15-18, it is important to remind ourselves that the author views the whole of religion through the cultus. When discussing priestly ministry, the introductions of "law" and "covenant" are not abrupt shifts of subject; each is inseparably bound to the sanctuary. As for the better promises, nothing is as yet spelled out. We can surmise that what the author has in mind will include inheriting salvation (1:14), entering the promised rest (4:1), and approaching God (7:25), but we wait for further details.

Verses 7-8a introduce the quotation of Jer 31:31-34. The function of the introduction is not to draw out the benefits of the new covenant but to underscore the need for it. Had the first been without fault, "no place ["room," "opportunity"; see Acts 25:16; Rom 12:19] would have been sought for another" (the NIV is preferred here). The fault lies both in the covenant (v. 7) and in the people (v. 8a). In other words, the first covenant is not working to effect the relationship between God and Israel that God desired.

Before moving to the quotation about a new covenant, two observations need to be made. First, it is God who gave the old and promises the new; both are God's doing. This realization should give pause to impulses to attack the old covenant as a preface to extolling the benefits of the new. Unless continuity and discontinuity are kept in tension, both covenants may be misrepresented. Second, since the promise of a new covenant comes within the old, Jeremiah 31 is, in fact, a case of the old critiquing itself. It is important to keep in mind that the Hebrews writer is appropriating a process that is going on within Israel and not between Israel and Christianity. The discontinuity here is to be located within the old and not between the old and the new. The neat division of the Bible into Old and New Covenants (Testaments) makes it too easy to locate discontinuities between the two rather than to be more careful to see tensions within the Old, within the New, as well as between them.

The oracle in Jer 31:31-34 is introduced with "God says," recalling the pattern in Hebrews of using verbs of speaking rather than "it is written," and in the present tense, as though directly addressing the readers (e.g., 1:5-8; 2:12; 3:7). This is the lengthiest quotation in the entire New Testament. This passage comes from the series of oracles in Jeremiah 30–33 offering Israel of the exilic period the hope of restoration to the homeland. But the return will not mean simply a return to the covenant made at Sinai; there will be a new covenant relationship between God and Israel that will be qualitatively different. Hebrews reproduces exactly the opening words of Jeremiah's prophecies: "The days are surely coming" (lit., "Behold, the days are coming"; see Jer 7:32; 9:25; 16:14; 23:5, 7). As for the remainder of the quotation, there are some variations from the LXX, mostly stylistic, that may have existed in the text used by the writer or may have been made by the writer. One should be cautious about reading into these modifications an attempt by the author to speak more negatively of the first covenant and more positively of the second.[86]

It would be inappropriate at this point to offer a running commentary on Jer 31:31-34;

---

86. J. C. McCullough, "The OT Quotations in Hebrews," *NTS* 26 (1980) 364-67.

the writer of Hebrews will draw from it what is useful for the immediate purpose and interpret it according to that purpose. It is enough here to observe that the new covenant promises the inscribing of God's law on the hearts of believers and the forgiveness of sins. There is no offer of new content but a new manner of the law's being presented and being appropriated. The relationship between God and the people will be restored and all past iniquities removed forever. It was the fault (v. 7) of the first covenant that this relationship had not been effected. But even these central affirmations are not the immediate concern of the author, as v. 13 shows. It is enough at this point to observe that the very phrase "a new covenant" makes the first one old (obsolete). In fact, the obsolete and antiquated (1:11) is near the point of vanishing. To say that it is "near vanishing" should not be taken to mean that the Temple in Jerusalem is still standing but soon to be destroyed. The earthly sanctuary of Hebrews is the desert tabernacle, not the Temple. The phrase "near vanishing" portends the end of the old covenant effected by the inauguration of the new by Christ's high priestly act, now to be described. (See Reflections at 9:23–10:18.)

Hebrews 9:1–10:18, Christ's Sacrifice

OVERVIEW

This is by far the largest of the the divisions of 8:1–10:18, and it could well be argued that it should not be regarded as a single division, but broken into smaller, more manageable units.[87] However, since the whole of 9:1–10:18 is an exegetical commentary on Jer 31:31-34, it seems wise to keep the reader's eye on the whole, especially since the passage is so full of details about tabernacles, altars, and offerings that the trees could obscure the forest. Additionally, keeping the sweep of the entire movement in mind is important, because it will seem for a time that, except for the word "covenant," the writer has lost touch with the textual centerpiece, Jer 31:31-34. That is only apparently the case, because the homily will not only return to Jeremiah 31 in 10:15-18, but also will never take its eye off the two primary theses of Jer 31:31-34: the location of the new covenent in the heart and the promise of forgiveness of sin. The contours of the argument in 9:1–10:18 permit discussion to fall into three sub-units: 9:1-14; 9:15-22; and 9:23–10:18. Even within these sub-units, the writer's literary signals will be observed, permitting focus on even smaller, discrete parts, some of which may have been taken from the church's liturgical and confessional tradition.

Again we need to be reminded that since in Hebrews the desert tabernacle and not the Temple provides the antithesis to the heavenly sanctuary, the present-tense verbs should not be taken as references to what is going on at the time of the writing of Hebrews. Rather, these present tenses are historical presents; that is, in the time and place of the desert tent, these things "are happening." As for the appropriateness of discussing Christ's priestly ministry vis-á-vis the tabernacle rather than the Temple, it need only be said that it is the tabernacle that is the copy and shadow of the heavenly sanctuary (8:5), it was the tabernacle that Moses was commanded to build, and it is the tabernacle that is associated with the old covenant. And, homiletically speaking, a movable desert tabernacle is much more suggestive of pilgrimage, a governing metaphor in the writer's understanding of the Christian life.

---

87. See, e.g., Lane, *Hebrews 1–8*; W. L. Lane, *Hebrews 9–13*, WBC 47B (Dallas: Word, 1991); Attridge, *A Commentary on the Epistle to the Hebrews*.

Hebrews 9:1-14, The Old and the New Sacrifice

COMMENTARY

Verses 1-14 fall naturally into two parts: vv. 1-10 describe the cultic practices of the levitical priests in the earthly sanctuary; vv. 11-14 present Christ's high priestly offering of himself. The two parts constitute an "on the one hand . . . but on the other hand" construction, common to the series of antitheses in the argumentation of Hebrews. Verse 1 begins a cultic recital growing out of 8:13, implicit in the reference to the first covenant. Thus translators are justified in adding the word "covenant" in v. 1: "Now even the first. . . ." Provisions in the first covenant for cultic practices were in two categories: regulations (ordinances, requirements) and a place, a sanctuary. The writer discusses them in reverse order (chiastic), a pattern now familiar to the reader.

9:1-10. 9:1-5. The "sanctuary" is here designated by the word ἅγιον (*hagion*), which refers to the entire tabernacle and not to a particular part of it. The adjective "earthly" ("worldly" [κοσμικός *kosmikos*]) anticipates its opposite, the heavenly sanctuary. Verses 2-5 are simply descriptive, and as the author states (v. 5), there is no intent to pursue details beyond what is appropriate for the immediate purpose. Anyone interested in further information about the desert tabernacle can find in Exod 25–31:11 God's instructions to Moses, in Exod 36:2–39:43 the account of its construction, and in Exod 40:1-38 the story of Moses pitching the tabernacle. There are, of course, other references, canonical and extra-canonical, to the building, its furnishings, and its services with some differences in terminology and in the location of furniture.

The descriptions in Hebrews, while generally in accord with Exodus 25–31, may reflect a different liturgical tradition and a knowledge of other texts pertaining to tabernacle and temple services.[88] One would get the impression from vv. 2-3 that there were two tents or tabernacles, but it is evident that the writer's references to two tents are actually to be understood as two compartments or distinct areas of the one tabernacle. In this matter, Hebrews is in full agreement with Exodus. In the first compartment or sanctuary, called the holy place (ἅγια *hagia*), were the lampstand (menorah) and the table, and on the table were twelve loaves of the presentation (show bread or bread of the Presence). Behind a curtain was a second sanctuary, called the holy of holies (ἅγια ἁγίων *hagia hagiōn*), or Most Holy Place. In this area, says the writer of Hebrews, was the golden altar of incense (v. 4). The strongest traditions locate the altar of incense at the rear of the holy place near the curtain. Priests, who were allowed into the holy place, burned incense on this altar daily (e.g., Luke 1:8-11). However, biblical references to the location of this altar are not exactly clear (Exod 30:1-10; 37:25-28; 40:5, 26; Lev 16:18; 1 Kgs 6:20, 22). Of central importance within the holy of holies is the ark of the covenant, an ornate chest containing the stone tablets from Sinai. According to Exod 16:32-34 and Num 17:10-11, a pot of manna and Aaron's rod, which budded, were placed "before the covenant." Among all references, only Hebrews places them inside the ark with the stone tablets. On top of the ark were cherubim of glory, indicating this place as the throne of divine glory. Between the cherubim was the atonement place, or mercy seat (ἱλαστήριον *hilastērion*; Exod 25:17, 21), the focal point of the activity of the high priest on the Day of Atonement (Lev 16:14-15; for detailed descriptions of the tabernacle furnishings, see Exodus 25–31). In fact, as the writer says (v. 5), no more details are needed; the holy of holies and mercy seat within it locate the ritual soon to be described.

9:6. At v. 1 the author gathered up the cultic expressions of the first covenant in two categories: regulations and sanctuary. Having described the sanctuary (vv. 1-5), the author turns now to the regulations or rituals (vv. 6-10). Verse 6 presents briefly

---

88. See the excursus in Attridge, *A Commentary on the Epistle to the Hebrews*, 236-38, for a detailed discussion of attempts to account for the differences between Hebrews and Exodus/Leviticus on terminology and the placing of the tabernacle furnishings.

the priestly activity in the first tent (compartment of the tabernacle), the holy place. Into the holy place the regular priests "are always entering" (note the accent on the continual and repetitive functioning) to attend to their ritual duties. The routine activity included trimming the lamp (Exod 27:21), replacing the bread on the table every seven days (Lev 24:5), burning incense (Exod 30:7), and offering the scheduled sacrifices (Lev 6:8, 30; Num 28:1-10). But the writer goes into no detail because no immediate purpose would be served.

9:7. Into the second tent, the holy of holies, goes not any priest but only the high priest. He enters alone, only once a year, and then "not without blood" (v. 7). Notice the writer's fondness for the double negative for expressing the very important and essential (4:15; 6:10; 7:20; 9:18, 22). The high priest's entering alone anticipates the priestly act of Christ, as does the "once a year," which, while in contrast with the daily service of the priests, will itself contrast with Christ's offering "once for all." The word "offers" (προσφέρω *prospherō*) also anticipates the way the writer will refer to the self-giving of Christ (9:14, 25, 28; 10:12). In fact, even though it is proper to speak of v. 7 as anticipating the high priestly ministry of Christ, the reality is that it was the high priestly ministry of Christ that guided the presentation of the activity of the levitical high priest.[89] The event sketched in v. 7 is the Day of Atonement (Yom Kippur). The writer selects appropriate details from what was an elaborate day of rituals (Lev 16:29-31). For present purposes, it is enough to recall that the high priest first sacrificed a bull and sprinkled its blood on the ark of the covenant for his sins and those of his family (Lev 16:6, 11, 14), quite unlike Christ, who had no need to offer a sacrifice for himself (5:3; 7:27). Then the high priest sacrificed a goat and offered its blood for the sins of the people (Lev 16:15, 30). Hebrews qualifies this sacrifice as being effective for inadvertent sins, a distinction quite important to the writer (10:26; cf. Num 15:22, 30).

9:8-10. These verses offer an unusual interpretation of vv. 1-7. The description of the desert tabernacle and its rituals has not been offered as a story of ineffectiveness against which to lay the effective priestly ministry of Christ. On the contrary, the very existence of the first tent (holy place) and its cultus offers a revelatory and prophetic word, although that word can be known only through the Holy Spirit. For Hebrews, the role of the Holy Spirit is not solely that of inspiring Scripture so that biblical quotations can be introduced "The Holy Spirit says" (3:7). The Holy Spirit makes God's Word present "today," and discloses (makes clear, reveals; see 1 Cor 3:13; 2 Pet 1:14) what had not been understood. And what is here disclosed by the Holy Spirit? That as long as the first compartment of the tabernacle (holy place) "has standing" (used in both a structural and a normative sense), the way into the holy of holies—that is, the presence of God—is not yet manifest. The holy of holies is closed to both priests and laity. That the high priest enters alone and only once a year, and never without blood to offer, testifies more to its inaccessibility than to its accessibility. The way into the holy of holies will be made open by the priestly act of Christ (2:10; 4:16; 10:19-20).[90] The first tent—the holy place (clearly the antecedent of "this," v. 9)—is a symbol, a figure, a parable of the present time. Apart from two appearances in Hebrews (9:9; 11:19) the word "parable" (παραβολή *parabolē*) occurs in the NT only in the synoptic Gospels, where it refers quite often to extended metaphors. While the word may designate a straightforward comparison, it often refers to a comparison not readily apparent; that is, figurative speech.[91] Both uses in Hebrews carry this meaning; in fact, in 9:9 that the holy place is a parable of the present time is a disclosure effected by the Holy Spirit.

Key to the meaning of vv. 9-10 is the expression "the present time." Since the writer is discussing the cultus of the first covenant, it would be easy enough to think only in temporal terms and interpret "the present time" as "past time." Dispensational thinking could take over and the image would be a simple one: an old cultus replaced by a new one. And the teasing truth is that temporal categories are important in Hebrews

---

89. N. H. Young, "The Gospel According to Hebrews 9," *NTS* 27 (1980-81) 198-210, esp. 209.

90. There is no need to read into "the way" the gnostic myth of the flight of the soul from the physical world to the spiritual and finally to God, as does Käsemann, *The Wandering People of God*, 75-96.

91. F. Hauk, "παραβολή," *TDNT*, 5:744-61.

(see Commentary on 8:5) and should never be abandoned. However, in 9:9 the holy place is a parable of the present, not the past. Perhaps, then, the category of space might be helpful. At 8:5 the writer spoke of a heavenly and an earthly tabernacle, the real and the shadow. The difference is not one of time but of nature or quality. The difference between the levitical cultus and that of Christ is not so much one of time but of nature.

Ministry in the holy place can be going on even while the ministry of Christ has accomplished what could never be accomplished in the earthly tabernacle. Therefore, a chronology of past, present, and future does not adequately frame the message of priestly ministries that differ more in kind than in time. Perhaps this is why the writer uses καιρός (*kairos*, time in the sense of opportunity or meaningful time) rather than χρόνος *chronos*, measurable time). The holy place is, therefore, a figure for a prevailing condition in which the way to God is not open even though gifts and sacrifices are repetitively offered. The condition cries out for the high priestly ministry of Christ, which is also at the present time, but also eschatological and heavenly. Perhaps the best commentary on 9:9-10 is 10:1-2 in that the "symbolic" nature of the gifts and sacrifices of the levitical system corresponds to the "shadow" rather than the reality (cf. 8:5).

The author understands that the sacrificial system of the first tent serves a purpose: the ritual cleansing of persons who had been in violation of regulations concerning food, drink, the body, and the essential utensils for daily living. Laws of purity were many, and breaches of those laws called for rituals of restoration. But none of this priestly activity could "perfect" the worshiper (see Commentary on 5:9; 7:11-19). Here the author introduces the word "conscience" (συνείδησις *syneidēsis*), since it is the conscience that is purged and restored by the offering of Christ. It stands in contrast to "body" (σάρξ *sarx*, v. 10), the area of benefit from the sacrifices in the first tent, and also renews attention on the inwardness of the new covenant (8:8-12), which is inaugurated by the high priestly act of Christ. The term "conscience" entered biblical literature from the Hellenistic world, where it meant "awareness of oneself" and was used in both moral and non-moral senses. In the LXX the word is lodged in the wisdom literature, where it conveys the idea of being aware of sin or wrong in one's life and can be translated "inner thoughts" or "heart of hearts" (see Job 27:6; Eccl 10:20; Wis 17:11; Sir 42:18). To be perfected in conscience is to be both cleansed of and freed from any hindrance preventing one's entering into God's presence. It is to have fulfilled the promise of the new covenant: "I will put my laws in their minds,/ and write them on their hearts" (8:10 NRSV).[92] But the "regulations of the body" ("flesh," v. 10) operative in the first tent, the holy place, could not achieve this, and therefore were marked for a "time of correction," a "time for setting things straight," a "time of amendment" (v. 10).

Like "the present time" of v. 9, "the time of correction" is also a *kairos*, the right time, the opportune moment in the purposes of God. Both times, therefore, are to be viewed not simply chronologically, as though one time has ended and another has begun. Although time in the usual historical sense is always a consideration in both Judaism and Christianity, in 9:9-10 the references are similar in meaning to "this age" and "the age to come." The difference is not so much one of present and future as it is of values, orientation, and meaning. Both "this age" and "the age to come" are here now, but they are qualitatively different realms of being. The same is true of "the present time" and "the time of correction."

9:11-14. Verses 1-10 presented that which exists "on the one hand"; these verses announce, "But on the other hand." The adversative conjunction makes it clear that the discussion moves in a new direction, that of Christ's high priestly offering of a new sacrifice. What follows in this paragraph is a development of what was introduced at 8:1-5.

9:11-12. These two verses constitute one sentence, "Christ . . . entered," containing several modifying clauses and phrases. The sentence follows the structure of vv. 1-10, where the place and the rituals of the earthly tabernacle were treated, in that order. Here the place is described in positive and

---

92. Cf. the use of "conscience" at 9:14; 10:2, 22; 13:18. For more on the term, see R. Jewett, *Paul's Anthropological Terms* (Leiden: E. J. Brill, 1971) 402-46.

then negative terms—the ritual in negative, then positive terms (ABB´A´, a chiasm). "But Christ having come as a high priest of the good things that have come" identifies the time of setting things right (v. 10) and states it as present and accomplished. The "good things" are not specified, but two were mentioned earlier: access to God and the perfecting of the conscience (vv. 8-9).

A number of MSS have "good things to come" rather than "good things that have come." This variant reading has probably been influenced by 10:1, but even there "to come" is not futuristic but refers to that which was yet to come from the perspective of the old law, which foreshadowed a future that in Christ is now present. These temporal expressions should not, however, be allowed to flatten out the passage into a past/present scheme only; the spatial categories of earthly/heavenly, shadow/real are still essential to the argument (see Commentary on 9:10).[93] In fact, the "greater and perfect [μείζονος καὶ τελειοτέρας *meizonos kai teleioteras*; lit., "more perfect"] tent" is but another way of referring to the heavenly sanctuary of 8:1-2 (also 6:19-20).

There is no strong reason to interpret "through the greater and more perfect tent" as instrumental; that is, "by means of the greater. . . ." This possible, but strained, reading would then understand "tent" in a metaphorical sense as "body," meaning "by means of Christ's body." This interpretation contradicts the use of "tent" (σκηνή *skēnē*) throughout this section as it does the following phrase, "not made with hands, that is, not of this creation." The author has made it clear that Christ's body was material and of this creation (2:14-18). It is better to take the expression in its straightforward, local sense: Christ went through the tent, entering the Most Holy Place (holy of holies)—the presence of God. That this tent is greater, more perfect (the comparative of "perfect" is not used in English), and not of human construction recalls earlier terminology (8:2, 5; 9:24). The NRSV, by using "he entered once for all into the Holy Place" (v. 12), translates correctly but confuses the image. The Holy Place often refers to the first compartment of the tabernacle (v. 2), but here it obviously refers to the Most Holy Place, the holy of holies (v. 3), the inner compartment, which the high priest alone entered to sprinkle blood on the mercy seat. The NIV properly conveys this image.

That Christ's high priestly ministry on our behalf involved not only intercession but also sacrifice was anticipated at 5:1; 7:27; and 8:3, but now at 9:12 it is boldly stated. The interpreter must move away from the courtroom forensics and judicial language, made familiar by Paul, and focus completely on the cultus. The writer has set the scene in vv. 1-10: The place is the holy of holies, the sole liturgist is the high priest, the central act is the sprinkling of blood on the seat of mercy, and the time is the Day of Atonement. The one essential element is blood; in the language of Hebrews, the effective entrance into God's presence is "not without taking the blood" (v. 7). The distance from "blood" language an interpreter may experience might be lessened by his or her entering into the thought world of the community for which this ritual was central. Offering the blood was offering the life (Lev 17:11-14), and instructions about the use and disposition of blood were many and very specific:

Only be sure that you do not eat the blood; for the blood is the life, and you shall not eat the life with the meat. (Deut 12:23 NRSV)

For the life of the flesh is in the blood; and I have given it to you for making atonement for your lives on the altar; for, as life, it is the blood that makes atonement. (Lev 17:11 NRSV)

Four statements can now be made that elaborate the condensed but crucial presentation of Christ's high priestly act in v. 12. (1) Christ entered the heavenly sanctuary, the true and perfect tabernacle, into the presence of God. (2) Christ entered once and for all. This affirmation stands in sharp contrast to the daily repetition of the activities of the levitical priests and the annual ritual by the high priest on the Day of Atonement. (3) Christ offered his own blood, not that of goats and calves (see Commentary on 9:7). Christ offered his own life to God on our behalf, to make atonement, to relate us fully and finally to God, to

---

93. See Lane, *Hebrews 9–13*, 236, for an interpretation of 9:10-11 in temporal terms.

enact the new covenant, which clearly promises, "I will be their God,/ and they shall be my people. . . ./ For I will be merciful toward their iniquities,/ and I will remember their sins no more" (8:10, 12 NRSV, quoting Jer 31:33-34). And finally, (4) Christ secures redemption that is eternal; that is, it is not repeated (v. 9) but possesses eschatological finality (5:9). While the word "redemption" (λύτρωσις *lytrōsis*) is rather rare in the NT (9:12, 15; Luke 1:68; 2:38), this metaphor for salvation is common in both Judaism and Christianity, sometimes referring to freedom from slavery, sometimes from prison, sometimes from death, sometimes from sin. The writer does not press the metaphor to refer to any particular transaction, and so it seems best to leave it as open as it is in the text.

The sacrifice of Christ is, therefore, consummated in heaven. Some interpreters have argued that Christ's high priestly work was not *consummated* in heaven but *began* in heaven. This is to say that the efficacious act of the high priest was not the killing of the animal but the offering of the blood in the inner sanctuary. Therefore, the atoning work of Christ was not his death on the cross but his once and for all entrance into God's presence, where he continually intercedes for us.[94] Taken alone, 9:11-14 can be so read, but the whole of Hebrews will not tolerate this separation of the death from the heavenly installment of Christ. Too much has already been made of Christ's identification with his brothers and sisters in the flesh, his being tested, and his suffering of death (2:9-18; 4:14-16; 5:7-10) to jettison all that as but a preface to ministry or as pre-priestly. In 10:1-10 the writer will return to the subject of sacrifice, and there the accent will be on the offering of the body of Jesus. More appropriate to Hebrews, therefore, is the understanding that death on the cross, ascension, and entrance into the sanctuary of God's presence constitute one redemptive movement.

9:13-14. With these verses the author concludes this sub-unit on the old and new sacrifice. Here the meaning of vv. 11-12 is expanded and enriched in the form of an argument *a fortiori* (from lesser to greater), a type of argument already familiar from 2:2-3. The "lesser" half of the argument refers again to the rituals of the Day of Atonement, but with the addition of the ritual of the red heifer (for its details and purpose, see Numbers 19). Why there is the reference to this ceremony is not clear. That the heifer was slaughtered and burned "outside the camp" may anticipate 13:12, 13. Even though exegetical traditions differ as to whether the high priest was involved, certain elements in the ritual of the heifer do serve to set up the contrasting sacrifice of Christ: The blood is sprinkled on the outside of the tabernacle, reminding the reader of the external efficacy of the levitical system; the heifer is referred to as a sin offering; and the ashes of the heifer in the water of purification cleanse the bodies (flesh) of those being sprinkled. These rituals have to do only with ceremonial cleansing (vv. 10, 13) from the range of defiling activities and relationships in which the people engaged, such as touching a corpse or being in contact with a foreigner. To be sanctified or made holy is familiar to NT readers as referring to Christ's gracious act toward believers, with spiritual and moral implications, but here it refers to the effects of a ritual system that purified human bodies as well as buildings, cooking utensils, furniture, and all other materials involved in a life ceremonially acceptable in the community of Israel.

The "greater" and concluding half of the argument presents the "how much more" of Christ's high priestly sacrifice. Four affirmations underscore the superiority of his sacrifice. First, his sacrifice is the offering of his own blood, not the blood of another. By speaking of Christ's blood, the writer maintains the language of the cultus, but what is meant by it is given in the expression "offered himself." Second, Christ's offering is "through the eternal Spirit." This way of referring to the Holy Spirit occurs nowhere else in the NT, but is especially appropriate here. The writer uses the term "eternal" (αἰώνιος *aiōnios*) as a contrast to the daily and annual repetition of levitical sacrifices (5:9; 6:2; 9:12, 15; 13:20). As for the Holy Spirit, the term has already been employed in a variety of ways (2:4; 3:7; 6:4; 9:8), but here probably serves double duty: as a contrast to bodily rituals of the old system and as a term to locate Christ's

---

94. Argued by W. E. Brooks, among others, but with dissenting voices represented, in "The Perpetuity of Christ's Sacrifice in the Epistle to the Hebrews," *JBL* 89 (1970) 205-14.

offer of himself; it is in the realm of the Spirit, in God's own presence. (Associating the Spirit with Christ's death and exaltation is not uncommon in the NT; see Rom 1:4; 1 Cor 15:45; 1 Tim 3:16; 1 Pet 3:18.) Third, Christ as the sacrifice is "blameless" or "without blemish," again preserving the terminology of cultic sacrifices (Exod 29:2; Lev 1:3, 10; 4:3; Num 6:14; as applied to Christ, see Heb 4:15; 7:27). And finally, Christ's offer of himself purifies the inner self, the conscience (see Commentary on 9:9), from dead works.

In other words, rather than cleansing from the defilement of contact with dead bodies, Christ cleanses from the dead works of which believers repent (6:1). The end and purpose of Christ's sacrifice for us is in order that we may worship ("serve," NIV) the living God. The verb "to serve" (λατρεύω *latreuō*) comes from the cultus and has the immediate sense of worship, but throughout the NT it includes service to God much more broadly (12:28; Luke 1:74; Acts 27:23; Rom 1:9; Phil 3:3). (See Reflections at 9:23–10:18).

Hebrews 9:15-22, Sacrifice and the New Covenant

COMMENTARY

The writer now returns to the theme of covenant and to the language of Jeremiah 31, the basic text being expounded in 8:1–10:18. It may seem to the reader that the author has strayed from the old and new covenant of Jeremiah 31 with discussions of two high priests, two sacrifices, and two tabernacles, but that is far from the case. Covenant, law, and cultus were earlier joined (see Commentary on 7:11-12, 22; 8:6-7, 13; 9:1); in fact, covenant and law have been understood as inextricably bound to cultus, and a change in cultus meant a change in covenant and law. In the plenitude of meanings explored in the discussion of Christ's purifying and atoning offer of himself, yet one more is now to be unfolded: the death of Christ as the inauguration of the new covenant. The discussion in vv. 15-22 proceeds in this way: Verse 15 summarizes the act and the benefits of the act of Christ mediating a new covenant; vv. 16-17 make a theoretical argument for the truth of v. 15; vv. 18-21 repeat the argument in practical and historical terms; and v. 22 states an axiom, a general truth that has been both implicit and explicit in the entirety of chap. 9.

9:15-17. Verse 15 not only connects with vv. 11-14 as the phrase "for this reason" (because of this) indicates, but also continues the thought established at 8:6: "He is the mediator of a better covenant, which has been enacted through better promises" (NRSV). Before developing further the theme of covenant, two benefits of Christ's death are stated. First, his death provided an inheritance for those who are called—that is, for his brothers and sisters who were to inherit salvation (1:14; 4:1; 6:17). Here salvation is cast in terms of the promised inheritance developed earlier (4:1-11; 6:12-20). How Christ's death makes this inheritance available will become evident in the writer's play on the word "covenant" as also meaning "will" (vv. 16-17). Second, Christ's death sets us free from transgressions under the first covenant. The metaphor of redeeming occurred at v. 12 and has enjoyed wide employment in Christian circles outside Hebrews (e.g., Rom 3:24-26; Eph 1:7). That these transgressions occurred under the first covenant is simply a restatement of vv. 9-10 and refers to the impotence of the levitical cultus to remove sin. No complicated relationship between cultus and sin similar to Paul's argument about law and sin (Romans 7) is here implied.

In vv. 16-17 the writer proceeds to argue the necessity of Christ's death for the inauguration of the new covenant, and the argument is based on the principle that a covenant takes effect only at death. What is not altogether clear is the author's meaning when using the word "covenant." The term διαθήκη (*diathēkē*) may be translated both "covenant" and "will."[95] If the writer is here playing on the ambiguity of the word and means "will" (as both the NRSV and the NIV have it), then vv. 16-17 are clear

---

95. The word is used in the title for the Christian Scriptures: the New Covenant or the New Testament (Will).

and straightforward: A will does not go into effect until the death of the one making the will. The application to Christ's death is self-evident. Such a wordplay is possible here;[96] the author has already proved to be quite a rhetorician and certainly wordplays were not only permitted but encouraged by teachers of rhetoric.[97] It is not necessary to argue that in Hebrews a word has only a single meaning (cf. the range of meanings in the word "perfect," noted earlier). However, the difficulty with shifting the meaning of the word from "covenant" to "will" is that while making a clear and self-contained argument for the necessity of Christ's death, the change of translation interrupts rather than contributes to the flow of the discussion. The word is clearly "covenant" in v. 15, and when the writer proceeds to give an example in vv. 18-21, the word is again "covenant." The question is this: Do vv. 16-17 make sense if the key term keeps the sense of "covenant"? Yes, if one assumes the writer is arguing on the basis of ancient rites of covenant making in which the slaughter of an animal symbolically represented the parties who pledged with their lives the keeping of the covenant.[98] The person or persons ratifying the covenant have thus in a figure given their lives. This may be implied in v. 17, where the expression "takes effect at death" is literally "takes effect on dead bodies." In support of this interpretation one may recall the dividing of slaughtered animals on the occasion of God's covenant with Abraham (Gen 15:6-21) and God's words to an Israel that had not kept the covenant, "I will make like the calf when they cut it in two and passed between its parts" (Jer 34:18 NRSV). In other words, God accepted the blood of the animal as a substitute for the people's blood, but now that they had broken the covenant, the pledge of their blood (lives) will be collected (cf. also Ps 50:5). One may understand death, therefore, as necessary for the effectiveness of a "covenant" as well as for a "will."

9:18-21. If vv. 16-17 provide the argument in principle, these verses provide the example of the shedding of blood as essential in the inauguration of a covenant. The writer draws on the tradition of the covenant at Sinai to make the point. The reader who turns to Exodus 24 to read in full the account of the ritual recalled in vv. 19-20 may be surprised to find noticeable differences. Apparently the writer of Hebrews is either following a tradition other than Exodus 24 or is taking the "first covenant" in a general sense and hence feels free to amalgamate various rituals performed "under the law" (v. 22). To the Sinai ceremonies, goats are added from the Day of Atonement, and water, scarlet wool, and hyssop from the ceremony of the red heifer. Other embellishments may be the author's own or drawn from liturgies unavailable to us.[99] But for all the complexity of the Sinai covenant ritual and in spite of all the substances used, the writer draws the reader's attention to one element only: "This is the blood of the covenant that God has ordained for you" (v. 20; cf. Exod 24:8). The writer may have used a slightly different translation of Exod 24:8, may have quoted from a liturgy, or may have been paraphrasing.

9:22. At this point the author feels justified in stating a general truth. The maxim-like affirmation consists of two parts. First, "under the law almost everything is purified with blood" (v. 22a). The qualifier "almost" is an acknowledgment that in the levitical system there were some rituals of cleansing using substances other than blood. Second, "without the shedding of blood" there is no "putting away" or "removal" of sins (v. 22b; the Greek text does not have "of sins" as in the NRSV). As this statement looks backward, it refers to the removal of impurities and uncleanness of the body (vv. 10, 13). Such was the limited efficacy of the old system. As this statement looks forward, it anticipates Christ's atoning work and his mediation of a new covenant under which "I will remember their sins no more" (8:12 NRSV). As a whole the statement is a fitting summary of the claims made about blood thus far in this chapter: Blood provides entrance before God (v. 7), purification of the conscience (v. 14), inauguration of a covenant (v. 18), cleansing of those entering a covenant (v. 19), and purifying of almost everything (v. 22). Not surprisingly, then, the writer repeats the phrase already twice used (vv. 7, 18), a phrase cast as a double negative

---

96. So argues Attridge, *A Commentary on the Epistle to the Hebrews*, 253-56.
97. See discussion and examples in Cornificius *Ad Herennium* IV. 14. 20-21.
98. Lane, *Hebrews 9–13*, 242-43, defends this position.
99. Young, "The Gospel According to Hebrews 9," 205.

for emphasis: "not without" or, as best translated here, "without blood shedding, there is no forgiveness." Again, let it be said to the reader whose confession and piety do not include the language of blood sacrifice that both the understanding and the appreciation of the message of Hebrews requires placing oneself within a cultus in which the above-mentioned vocabulary and actions were integral to rituals of cleansing, renewal, approaching God, and community forming. The writer is presenting the benefits of Christ for believers in these same images, obviously with hope for the same effects: cleansing, renewal, approaching God, and community formation. (See Reflections at 9:23–10:18.)

Hebrews 9:23–10:18, The New and Final Sacrifice

COMMENTARY

The argument now moves away from the focus on sacrificial victims and blood and back to the discussion in vv. 11-14. The occasion is the Day of Atonement, the officiant is the high priest, and the setting is the inner sanctuary. However, as at vv. 11-14, the reader is asked to think again in the Platonic categories of the real or true heavenly sanctuary and its earthly shadow or sketch; that is, the one Moses built (see Commentary on 8:1-6). The rites described earlier (vv. 18-21) purified the building, vessels, and people related to the tabernacle, which was but a copy of the heavenly one, but the heavenly sanctuary itself requires a better sacrifice (v. 23). The use of the plural "better sacrifices" is not meant to imply more than one (the writer is adamant about that!) but simply to parallel "these rites."

9:23-26. Interpreters are divided as to how far to press the analogy in v. 23. Animal sacrifices purify the earthly sanctuary (Lev 16:16; 20:3; 21:23; Num 19:20). Does this mean that the better sacrifice of Christ purifies the heavenly sanctuary? If thus pressed, then there is sin or impurity in the heavenly realm in need of cleansing. Some proponents of this view draw from Revelation 12 (Satan in heaven) and from the belief in hostile principalities and powers in heavenly places, familiar from the Pauline circle (e.g., Rom 8:38; Eph 3:10). However, such excursions take us far afield from the thought world of Hebrews. It seems wiser to take the analogy in a broad and general sense, to understand that Christ has entered the heavenly sanctuary with a better sacrifice—that is, himself—but to draw no more detailed comparisons than the writer does in the verses that follow (vv. 24-26). As for the purging or cleansing in the heavenly or spiritual world, the writer has spoken only of the purifying or perfecting of the conscience of the believers (vv. 9, 14). Whether identifying the cleansing of the heavenly tabernacle with the purifying of the conscience is an interpretation too subjective is a judgment withheld until further discussion by the writer.[100] For the present, it is important to maintain the contrasts between Christ and the levitical high priest and to underline elements in the contrasts appropriate to the argument.

Maintaining the contrasts involves repetition: Christ appeared in heaven itself, not in an earthly copy (8:2-6); Christ offered himself, not the blood of another sacrifice; Christ entered the presence of God, not the inner tent with only symbols of God's presence; Christ offered himself once for all, not again and again; Christ removed sin, not bodily impurities (vv. 10, 13). Within these contrasts, the writer calls attention to several aspects of Christ's high priestly ministry. That Christ's appearance in God's presence was "on our behalf" recalls the intercessory function of his ministry (2:18; 4:15; 7:25). This accent must not, however, diminish the importance of his act of sacrifice for the removal of sin. The intercession before God is not to be separated from the cross, which preceded it. In fact, the expression "to suffer" (v. 26) is clearly a reference to the death on the cross. That Christ's sacrifice was "once for all" (7:27; 9:12) is underscored by the absurd alternative: Otherwise it would be necessary

---

100. See Lane, *Hebrews 9–13*, 247-48, for an alternative interpretation.

for him to die repeatedly "from the foundation of the world"—that is, from the very inception of God's purpose (4:3).

A third and final accent amid the repetitions of vv. 24-26 is the portrayal of Christ's sacrifice of himself as an eschatological event: "He has appeared once for all at the end of the age" (v. 26). The phrase here translated "the end of the age" is found elsewhere in the NT in Matthew (Matt 13:39, 40, 49; 24:3; 28:20), but the view of Christ as the central eschatological event is more widely expressed (1 Cor 10:11; Gal 4:4; 1 Pet 1:20). That his coming was called an "appearing" or "manifestation" seems to have become lodged in liturgy (1 Tim 3:16; 2 Tim 1:9-10; Titus 2:11; 1 Pet 1:20; 1 John 1:2). The affinity of v. 26 with 1 Pet 1:20 is striking: "He was destined before the foundation of the world, but was revealed at the end of the ages for your sake" (NRSV).

9:27-28. Quite possibly these verses contain lines drawn from the catechesis the readers had received at baptism (6:1-2). The comparison between the common human experience (to die only once and then to be judged) and Christ's salvific work (offered for sins only once and then to appear again to save) is formally balanced, perhaps an excerpt. In content, the comparison joins a popular truism (one death is ordained for each person), an allusion to the Suffering Servant of Isaiah (bearing the sins of many, Isa 53:12), and the cultic imagery common to this epistle (offered for sin). But whether from a catechism or original, the central point is not our death and judgment; these serve as analogies to underscore the emphasis on the once-for-all nature of Christ's high priestly ministry. The cross and Christ's entry into God's presence happened once, are effective for "many," and will not be repeated.

What will happen a second time is his appearing, but this time it will be "apart from sin"; that is, his second appearance will not be to deal with sin, since that work was done once for all. Rather, the Second Coming (that this is a reference to the parousia is clear) will be for the consummation of salvation for those eagerly awaiting his coming. Verse 28*b* could be translated, "He will be seen by those eagerly expecting him for salvation" (cf. Sir 50:5-10). The writer may here be returning to the image of the Day of Atonement ritual. While all the worshipers waited outside, the high priest entered the Most Holy Place to sprinkle blood on the mercy seat, in the very presence of God. Will the high priest reappear, or is it too audacious for any person to approach God? The people eagerly await his "second coming."

10:1-18. With this passage the exposition of the high priestly ministry of Christ comes to a close (8:1–10:18); exhortation is resumed at v. 19. At v. 18 the writer will also conclude the interpretation of Jeremiah 31 (8:8-12) and the new covenant, the centerpiece text for the entire argument of 8:1–10:18. The discussion in 10:1-18 falls naturally into two parts: vv. 1-10 and vv. 11-18.

10:1-10. The reader of these verses will need to be careful, lest the high degree of repetition lull the mind into missing what is strikingly new here. For example, vv. 1-4 seem at first merely a summary of what has been said since 9:1. However, a closer reading reveals a new perspective and a new accent. The new perspective has to do with the use of the "shadow/substance" schema associated with Plato's philosophy and introduced into Hebrews at 8:2-6 (see Commentary on 8:5). In chaps. 8–9 the schema used spatial categories; that is, the earthly tabernacle was but a shadow of the true and real heavenly tabernacle. At 10:1, however, the "shadow" and the "true form"[101] are temporal categories referring to what the law "foreshadows" and the "good things to come" in Christ. That the benefits in Christ are "to come" does not mean that they are totally futuristic from the believer's perspective but that from the perspective of the law they were "to come." By returning to the temporal categories (past, present, future), the writer can again discuss the historical dimension of Christ's high priestly ministry—namely, his death on the cross. With spatial categories, the ministry of Christ was presented as heavenly, in the true tabernacle, while the levitical ministrations were earthly. Now both Levites and Christ are historically portrayed as anticipation and fulfillment. It would be difficult to overestimate the importance of this shift to temporal

---

101. Use of the term "form" (εἰκών *eikōn*) does not imply three levels of being: shadow, form, and reality. Here the "true form" (or lit., "the form itself") refers to the reality itself. This is not an unusual use of the term. See the articles by G. von Rad, G. Kittel, and H. Kleinknecht in *TDNT,* 2:381-97.

categories, without which the death on the cross (historical) would not be an integral part of Christ's high priestly service. Christ's ministry as our high priest would be limited to the heavenly work of intercession in the presence of God. If the death on the cross were but a preface to Christ's ministry and not part of that ministry, the evaporation of the Christian religion into a gnostic myth could be more easily achieved.

It was stated above that with 10:1 came a new perspective (not really new but a return to the perspective of Hebrews prior to 8:2) and a new accent. The new perspective is a move away from the spatial categories (above, below) and a return to the temporal categories (old, new). The new accent is the impact of the high priestly ministry of Christ on the believer. Again, the subject is not new (cf. 9:14, even though most of 9:11-28 focuses on the objective rather than the subjective side of Christ's sacrifice), but attention to the spiritual gain for the Christian is increased. No doubt, the writer is now responding to the inwardness of the new covenant (mind, heart, knowing without instruction, favored with God's mercy and forgiveness) of Jeremiah 31, quoted at 8:8-12 and repeated in part at 10:16-17. A key term in the discussions of the subjective side of Christ's sacrifice for sin is "conscience." The reader met the word at 9:9, at which point an unperfected or unpurified conscience was presented as a hindrance to worship—that is, to access to God. At 9:14 it is clear that the benefit of Christ's self-sacrifice is the purifying of the conscience from dead works (see Commentary on 6:1) in order that worship of God may follow. The major inadequacy of the system of animal offerings was not only the inability to remove the "conscience of sins" ("consciousness of sin," NRSV; "felt guilty for their sins," NIV), but also a reminder, by the fact of constant repetition, of the very sin that could not be erased by the process (vv. 2-3). Of the five occurrences of the term "conscience" in Hebrews, the remaining two will be at 10:22 and 13:18, in each case consistent with the uses at 9:9, 14 and 10:2. Thus this ancient word, variously used in Hellenistic, Jewish, and Christian writers to refer to the human capacity for self-knowing, self-accusing, and when liberated, self-affirming,[102] is the writer's term of choice for locating the place where the "objective" act of Christ's sacrifice meets the "subjective" self of the believer.

Nearing the end of the discussion of the new and final sacrifice of Christ, the writer now seeks to show more convincingly the contrast between the levitical priesthood and Christ's by citing a psalm text that will demonstrate that within the old system itself could be found declarations of its own failing. Such is the focus of vv. 5-10, which consist of a biblical quotation with a brief midrash or commentary. Psalm 40:6-8 is introduced as words of Christ at the time of his incarnation, his coming into the world (cosmos). Attributing OT citations to Christ is fully in accord with Hebrews christology (1:1-4) and has been done previously at 2:12-13. Also consistent with the writer's practice is the use of verbs of speaking ("he says") rather than "it is written." In its own context, Ps 40:6-8 is a familiar prophetic warning against excessive dependence on ritual and a testimony to God's preference for obedience and observance of the law within the heart (1 Sam 15:22; Ps 50:8-10; Isa 1:10-13; Jer 7:21-24; Hos 6:6; Amos 5:21-26). This particular citation, however, fits extremely well the writer's purpose in a number of ways: the sharp contrast between the levitical cultus and Christ's willing obedience; the contrast between animal offerings and Christ's offering of his body; the contrast between ritual and the law in the heart. All of these accents serve well the author's use of Jeremiah 31 with its description of the qualities that prevail under the new covenant. The sacrifice of his own will to God's and the inwardness of God's law mark the high priestly ministry of Christ.

Between Ps 40:6-8 LXX and its quotation in Heb 10:5-7 there are a number of minor alterations (perhaps made by the writer of Hebrews), but one difference is both noticeable and important: In the Hebrew text and in some texts of the LXX, Ps 40:6 reads, "Ears you have dug for me" (NRSV, "You have given me an open ear"). The image is of one prepared to listen and to obey (as at Isa 50:5 in the description of God's servant). However,

---

102. See C. A. Pierce, *Conscience in the New Testament* (Chicago: Alec Allenson, 1955) esp. 40-53, 99-103.

the writer of Heb 10:5 uses a variant reading of the LXX text of Ps 40:6 that replaces "ear" (ὠτίον *ōtion*) with "body" (σῶμα *sōma*). This alternate reading fits perfectly the argument now being brought to a close; that is, not through the repeated rituals of the law's system, but "through the offering of the body of Jesus once for all" (v. 10) we have been sanctified (2:11; 9:13; 10:10, 14, 29; 13:12). This sanctification is another way of saying what is expressed elsewhere as the cleansing or perfecting of the conscience. Here the writer is underscoring the interiority of both Christ's act (a delighted willingness to do God's will) and its benefit (our sanctification). Without directly saying so, the writer is commenting on the inwardness of the new covenant (on the mind, in the heart, mercy and forgiveness). But the word "body," so important in 10:5-10, stands firm to prevent a totally subjective reading of Christ's redemptive work.

Thus it is a citation from the OT itself, Ps 40:6-8, that authorizes for the writer a bold conclusion: "He abolishes the first in order to establish the second" (v. 9; also 8:13). It is important to note that this conclusion is based on the OT's self-criticism and attempt to correct itself (Ps 40:6-8 is but one example) rather than a Christian critique of the OT. Just as Jeremiah saw a new covenant replacing the old (31:31-35), so also the psalmist saw the end of the old sacrificial system and the inauguration of the new. The Christian contribution to the thought here is in hearing in Ps 40:6-8 the voice of Christ himself as the one through whom the old ends and the new begins. The reader is now ready to move on to vv. 11-18—except for the nagging uncertainty of the meaning of the rather parenthetical ending of the quotation: "in the scroll of the book it is written of me" (v. 7). For the psalmist, two possible meanings suggest themselves. The line could refer to the common notion of God's making entries in a book about each of us, what we are to do and what we do (Pss 56:8; 139:16). Or the psalmist may have had in mind the book of the laws governing the conduct of the king (Deut 17:18). For the Christian reader, the statement may be taken as a general reference to all in the OT that points to Christ. Such a view permits the kind of christological reading we find in Hebrews.

10:11-18. These verses conclude the exposition that constitutes the central section of Hebrews (8:1–10:18). As a conclusion, these verses offer a summary of points already made rather than new material. From a rhetorical point of view, however, this conclusion is worthy of investigation. For example, notice the contrast between other priests and Christ. They stand, because their work never ends but is, rather, a day-after-day-after-day tedium of ineffectiveness; Christ sits, because his single offering once for all has been completed, and he has only to wait until all its effects are brought to fruition. Citing Ps 110:1, with which this section began (8:1), the author relates that the eschatological consummation of Christ's sacrifice will see all his enemies become a footstool for his feet. The language of "enemies" is preserved but without identification of who or what they are. The one benefit of Christ's priestly work that is specified is the perfection of the ones "being sanctified" (ἁγιάζω *hagiazō*, v. 14, present tense, indicating "in process"). The statement combines the idea of finished work with the acknowledgment that the believers are still moving toward that completion. (For the different meanings of the word "perfection" in Hebrews, see Commentary on 2:10; 5:9, 14; 7:19, 28; 9:9; 10:1.)

At this point the writer returns to Jeremiah 31, having come full circle since introducing this classic text on the new covenant (8:8-12). Only two features of that covenant are here repeated: its inwardness and God's remembering sin no more (Jer 31:33*a*, 34*b*). At 8:8 the citation of Jeremiah 31 was introduced as God's words; here "the Holy Spirit testifies" (3:7). The writer is comfortable attributing words of Scripture to God, to Christ, or to the Holy Spirit. And given the unified vision of what God is doing from the beginning up to and including these last days in which the Son acts finally and sufficiently, the writer is also comfortable in saying that the words of Jeremiah 31 are "to us" (v. 15).

The new covenant is now in place, and its benefits are ours. This is the last word. And the *very* last word is *no more*—no more remembrance of sin—and *no longer*—no longer any need for the continuation of cultic acts that by their very repetition testified to their ineffectiveness. Christ, our high priest, has effected forgiveness of sin.

REFLECTIONS

1. The teacher or preacher who leads a group of reader-listeners into 8:1–10:18 will want to think through in advance what may be major obstacles not simply to understanding this section but to appreciating it and to appropriating it as a meaningful way of entering into and being sustained by God's behavior toward us in Jesus Christ. The density of the text and its unfamiliar vocabulary will be somewhat daunting. The frequent repetition of points already made may dull interest. But perhaps most critical for fruitful engagements with this material will be introducing participants to a world of ritual, for many a strange and new world. There is a tent or tabernacle that is a "tent of meeting," a place for meeting, not other persons for fellowship and conviviality, but God. In the tabernacle are pieces of furniture, each with historical and theological significance. There are special persons who minister as priests at the tabernacle, with clear regulations as to appointed days and appointed rituals. On the appointed Day of Atonement the high priest enters alone, beyond the chamber where priests serve into the Most Holy Place to minister before the Mercy Seat, the place of meeting between God and persons who wait anxiously outside for the return of the high priest, who has approached God on their behalf. It is on this analogy, by careful comparisons and contrasts, that the writer of Hebrews frames Christ's redemptive activity on our behalf. Why so much preparatory work by the teacher or preacher? Because many people have no significant ritual life, religious, political, or cultural, from which to draw analogies. There is a sharp decline in those commemorative events, bodily practices, and public recitals by which people remember and participate in their own history. But this effort with persons lacking memory, theological vocabulary, and significant ceremonies can prove not only satisfying but also life changing. If creating liturgical memories needs explanation or justification, one can begin by pointing out how integral to the experience of a baseball or football game are certain always-repeated sights, sounds, and even smells.

2. At 8:1-5 the writer introduces into christology the spatial categories of the heavenly and real and the earthly, which is a shadow or sketch of the real. Temporal categories, by which the writer presents God's activity in history, culminating in Jesus Christ, have been and will continue to be used. This heavenly/earthly schema is somewhat different from Paul's descent/ascent christological pattern, but both testify to the early church's struggle to find categories adequate to carry the weight of a message reaching into all time and space. In every generation the church seeks in its cultural context vehicles for conveying the gospel. In the case of Heb 8:1-5, the source seems to be Plato, mediated through Philo and certain rabbinic exegetes. Identifying sources then and now is important for understanding. However, one wants to avoid the genetic fallacy of thinking that by identifying a source one has explained a concept or image. Oral footnotes, like written ones, often seduce both speaker and listener into thinking a matter has been explained when actually it has only been surrounded.

3. The writer follows the portrayal of Moses' desert tabernacle as a shadow or sketch of the true heavenly one with repeated discussions of the inabilities of its ritual system (9:1-15, 23-28; 10:1-4). Neither the blood of calves and goats nor the countless other offerings of its priests take away sin. It is very likely that many worshipers before that tabernacle would agree. Prophets warned against excessive dependence on the prescribed rituals (10:5-6, citing Ps 40:6-7), but they did not call for an abolition of tabernacle or temple services. An institution and its ceremonies, which do not provide the ultimate benefit, forgiveness and access to God, can still be of immense value to a community. One should not, therefore, take the designation "sketch" or "shadow" as occasion to speak pejoratively of the tabernacle of Israel beyond such speaking in the text itself.

That the desert tent was a copy of the heavenly one (8:5) is not altogether a negative appraisal. And Moses built it according to God's instruction! Already there is reason enough to reflect on its values. Neither the church nor its several ceremonies assure forgiveness of sin and access to God, but that does not disqualify them as valueless. God can be the source of and authorization for activities, places, persons, and rituals that are not finally salvific but are quite providential in the forming and sustaining of a people. As long as the provisional is not elevated to become the ultimate and absolute, both law and cultus can be held in high and healthy regard as gifts of God. Such a caution also includes the church.

4. The argument of 8:1–10:18 is in large measure an exegesis of Jeremiah 31 (Heb 8:8-12; 10:16-17). Because the new covenant of Jeremiah 31 is discussed in a Christian document, it is easy to forget that the new covenant was God's promise to Israel through one of Israel's prophets. A strength of vital religion is its willingness to be self-reflective, to balance calls to remember with calls to move beyond former things, to interpret afresh its own texts and institutions. Jeremiah's message was not a call to return to Sinai but to accept a new covenantal relationship with God, a relationship characterized as God-centered, relational, inward, and with forgiveness that frees persons to move forward. Hebrews tells the church to overhear Jeremiah's word from God, to accept it and become heirs of its promises through the mediating act of Christ, but not to become so possessive of it as to forget that it is the offer of a God who is always doing a new thing. Above all, God is a God who enters into covenants with human beings and in those covenants remains faithful.

5. The inwardness of which Jeremiah 31 speaks is characterized by the words "mind" and "heart"; a favorite term for the writer of Hebrews is "conscience" (9:9, 14; 10:2, 22; 13:18). This word has had an ambiguous history among Greeks, Jews, and Christians,[103] but in Hebrews it refers at least to the center of our being, doing, and valuing, the "place" in us where the self-giving of Christ meets us and perfects or completes us, and the seat of all conduct and relationships. But two reminders about inwardness are in order. First, the interiority of our faith has its origin and prompting in the interiority of Christ's own ministry—the sacrifice of his will to the will of God and his delight in doing God's will (10:5-7). Second, the whole redemptive work of Christ cannot be written without remainder on the human mind or heart or conscience. Out there, historically and objectively, are the person of Jesus, who lived among us as one like us, the cross on which was offered the body of Jesus, the community with whom and among whom the benefits of Christ's ministry are shared, and the world, created and upheld by the word of his power (1:2-3).

6. We have had occasion to observe that "blood" is in the ancient texts the equivalent of "life" and that the writer of Hebrews at times makes the exchange so that Christ's sacrifice is the offering of himself (as at 9:14), presenting to God his life. While modern readers may find this expression more palatable than "shedding blood," it also moves the act of Christ within the circle of response and responsibility by his followers. This is to say, Christ's offering of his life to God was the ultimate act of worship in order that we, with purified consciences, may "worship the living God." What, then, is this worship if it is not the offering of ourselves to God in ways appropriate to the nature of God and the needs that present themselves to us? On this matter, the word of Hebrews is not unlike the urging of Paul to the Roman Christians: "Present your bodies as a living sacrifice, holy and acceptable to God, which is your spiritual worship" (Rom 12:1 NRSV).

---

103. See Pierce, *Conscience in the New Testament*, esp. 40-53, 99-103.

7. At 10:15 the writer says that the words of Jeremiah 31 are "to us." How can that be, given the historical location of Jeremiah and his audience? Paul also spoke of ancient texts as having been written "to instruct us" (1 Cor 10:11 NRSV). He found a linkage in the parallels between the wilderness experiences of Israel and the "wilderness" experiences of the Corinthian church. The writer of Hebrews spoke similarly in discussing the available sabbath rest (Heb 3:7–4:11). But here the words are "to us" by virtue of being words of the Holy Spirit, which makes the past present. Instead of "It is written . . . ," which then requires a hermeneutical move from past to present, from "meant" to "means," the writer's use of "The Holy Spirit says . . ." implies that distances between past and present are dissolved. When words of Scripture are presented as words of the Spirit, every generation is in turn addressed; all can say the words are "to us." This does not mean the writer has made an uncritical argument by proof text. In the exegesis of Jeremiah 31, the case has been made that the promised new covenant is inaugurated by the covenant-sealing death of Christ. The benefits of that covenant are now in effect: The word is "to us."

8. In the struggle to understand and communicate the content of 8:1–10:18, the preacher will not want to miss the forceful rhetoric of this epistle-sermon. The two most operative rhetorical devices of this section are repetition and contrast. Under the cultural pressure to say something new in a new way, the preacher may too easily abandon the time-tested value of repetition used in the service of memory, clarity, and cumulative impact. As for contrasts, rhetoricians have long known the persuasiveness of sharp, clear, bold presentations framed as old/new, dead/alive, ineffective/effective, apparent/real, endless repetition/once for all, shadow/substance. Consider one example among many. At 10:11-12, two images are offered. One is of a priest, standing, working in the relentless cycle of the day-after-day repetition of the same words and actions. It is the picture of futility. The other image is of a priest who has made a single offering, a one-time-only act, and is now seated, waiting for the full harvest of benefits from that never-to-be-repeated sacrifice. It is the picture of finality. Much that is presented from desk and pulpit is, of course, properly framed as "both-and." However, in most recitals of events and relationships there are also discontinuities that beg for crispness and clarity. The writer of Hebrews offers a model for casting such material "on the one hand/but on the other hand."

HEBREWS 10:19-39, LIFE IN RESPONSE TO THIS MINISTRY OF CHRIST

OVERVIEW

With this unit the "difficult" discussion comes to a close. Perhaps more correctly, the discussion of Christ's high priestly ministry (7:1–10:18) is now followed with the kind of hortatory material that preceded it. The larger arrangement looks something like this: 5:11–6:20, exhortation; 7:1–10:18, exposition; 10:19-39, exhortation. Upon closer examination it is clear that the hortatory material in 10:19-39 parallels in form that which preceded the exposition. In 5:11–6:20, the author provides admonition (5:11–6:3), stern warning (6:4-8), and encouragement based on the church's history of performance (6:9-20). Likewise, here the exhortation consists of admonition (10:19-25), stern warning (10:26-31), and encouragement based on the church's previous performances (10:32-39). This symmetry is not accidental and testifies to the considerable rhetorical skills of the writer-preacher.

Hebrews 10:19-25, A Threefold Admonition

COMMENTARY

In this first of the three distinct paragraphs of this unit, the writer begins to develop the implications of what has been said for the lives of the readers ("therefore"). They are directly addressed ("Brothers and sisters," trans. "friends" in the NRSV for variety; cf. 3:1, 12), and the admonitions again include the writer along with the addressees ("Let us"). The paragraph is, in the Greek text, one extended sentence consisting of a statement of the christological grounds for the admonition (vv. 19-21) and the admonition itself (vv. 22-25). The christological grounds are two: "having boldness or confidence" and "having a great priest." The translation "since we have" alerts the reader that conclusions are soon to be drawn. The conclusions consist of a threefold admonition, each portion beginning with the hortatory formula "let us": Let us approach God; let us hold fast; and let us help one another. The first admonition centers on faith, the second on hope, and the third on love, giving the paragraph the balanced and rounded-off quality of a homily.

10:19-21. Not surprisingly, these verses are filled with words and phrases used earlier; after all, subsequent injunctions will depend on and flow out of earlier discussions. The confidence or boldness of which the writer has previously spoken in a strongly subjective sense (3:6; 4:16) now carries more objective weight in that the believer's boldness has been given firm footing, "authorization,"[104] by the entrance of our pioneer, our forerunner (2:10; 6:20) Jesus, who did so in the offering of his own blood. The "on our behalf" quality of his act is implicit in the statement "we enter in the blood of Jesus." Our entrance is into the sanctuary, the Most Holy Place, where God dwells and where Christ now is (2:10; 4:3, 10; 6:19). The high priestly act of Christ's self-giving does not leave us outside, as the ancient worshipers stood anxiously awaiting the exit of the high priest, but removes all obstacles to our own access to God. In the vivid metaphor of the Synoptics, the veil has been rent from top to bottom (Mark 15:38 and par.). The cultic language ("by the blood of Jesus") is preserved, but there is no question, as unique as his act was, that our entry by the "new" (πρόσφατος *prosphatos*, a rare word used only here in the NT) and "living" (4:12; 7:25; 10:31) way will be after the manner of his—and that is by obedience to God's will (10:5-10). That fact will be spelled out in the remainder of the letter. The translation of ἡμῖν ἐνεκαίνισεν (*hēmin enekainisen*) as "he opened for us" (v. 20) does not quite carry the freight of meaning. More literally, the writer says, "He inaugurated for us," language that echoes the entire new covenant discussion (cf. 9:18) and sets the reader in that theological context.

There has been much debate over the ambiguous phrase "through the curtain [that is, through his flesh]" (v. 20). Essentially the issue is whether the reader is to take "flesh" (σάρξ *sarx*) as appositional to "curtain," (καταπέτασμα *katapetasma*) thereby identifying his flesh as the curtain or veil. Such a strict equation raises for many some uneasy questions.[105] For example, since the curtain is a barrier, an obstacle to access to God, does this imply that in his lifetime, "in the days of his flesh," Jesus posed a barrier to God, a barrier that had to be removed if we were to be able to approach God? Certainly nothing in Hebrews about the historical Jesus can be so construed; quite the contrary, his life among us as one who identified in sympathy with his brothers and sisters is most positively portrayed. In addition, nowhere else in Hebrews, with all its discussion of the veil of the tabernacle, is the veil identified as Christ's body. The REB breaks up the identification of veil and body with the translation, "the way of his flesh." This rendering may not be justified, but the interpretive attempt is welcomed. This is to say that "his flesh" should be understood in the movement of the entire passage; the way through the veil has been provided by the offering of himself, by his death, by his

---

104. Lane, *Hebrews 9–13*, 279.

105. The alternative views are clearly presented in Bruce, *The Epistle to the Hebrews*, 247-49.

own blood. Such an understanding is fully in accord with the entire context and says anew what was stated at 9:12-14 (see also 10:10).

The first ground, therefore, on which subsequent admonitions will rest is our confidence to approach God, because Christ's self-offering has made the way available (vv. 19-20). The second is more briefly stated: "and since we have a great priest over the house of God" (v. 21). The writer is not adding anything to the discussion, but is, rather, employing two phrases to evoke for the reader key presentations made earlier; "great priest" recalls 4:14-16 and "house of God" brings to mind 3:1-6. Those passages are clearer and richer in meaning given the discussion of 7:1–10:18. Having laid this foundation, the author proceeds directly to three admonitions.

10:22-25. First, "let us approach with a true heart in full assurance of faith." Our approach to God, of which the writer has already spoken (4:16; 7:19), does not have here a stated purpose, but undoubtedly it is "to worship the living God!" (9:14 NRSV). As will be unfolded, worship has communal and moral, as well as liturgical, implications. The writer feels the need to say here what should be assumed without being stated: Our approach should be with sincerity and integrity ("true heart," Isa 38:3) and with abundant faith (6:11). These qualities are born of the confidence (recall both its subjective and objective sides) granted by the act of Christ on our behalf.

As preparation for this worshipful approach to God, we will have been granted that total cleansing not achieved under the old cultus. Bringing forward the now familiar image of sprinkling (9:13), the inward purification is of heart and conscience, also familiar terms for the interiority of life under the new covenant (8:10; 10:2). Somewhat surprisingly, the writer adds the washing of the body with pure water. This obvious reference to baptism not only recalls Israel's cultic practice (Lev 16:4; Ezek 36:25-26), but also testifies to the early church's joining of baptism to inward changes in the person being baptized. The language here may be liturgical. The similarity to 1 Pet 3:21 is striking: "And baptism, which this prefigured, now saves you—not as a removal of dirt from the body, but as an appeal to God for a good conscience, through the resurrection of Jesus Christ" (NRSV).

Second, "let us hold fast to the confession of our hope without wavering" (v. 23). Here is the second half of a rhythm recurring throughout the sermon: Let us approach (move forward); let us hold fast. Already the writer has urged this tenacity (3:6, 14; 4:14) and with special reference to hope, the "sure and steadfast anchor of the soul, a hope that enters the inner shrine behind the curtain" (6:19 NRSV). Confidence and firmness to the end must characterize hope, because the final results of Christ's work are not yet in and there are many enemies (10:13). This confidence is grounded, finally, not in the strength of our grasp but in the trustworthiness, the faithfulness of the one who keeps promises (6:13-18). Hence, "confidence" is never solely a subjective state of the believer.

Third, "let us consider how to provoke one another to love and good deeds" (v. 24). This is now the second time the writer has called on his readers to "consider," "to think mutually about a matter" (3:1). What is to be considered are ways to "provoke" or "irritate" one another. The word παροξυσμός (*paroxysmos*) can also be translated "pester." Provocation can, of course, have a negative sense (Num 14:11; Deut 1:34; Acts 15:39; 1 Cor 13:5), but the word also had a positive use in the sense of disturbing the apathetic or fearful person into activity. Such is its present use: to produce love and good works. The expression is strong but necessary for a community earlier characterized as inattentive, neglectful, and drifting.

To this third admonition, like the first, are attached two participial expressions. The first is negative, indicating that some members of the community are neglecting ("abandoning"; cf. Matt 27:46; 2 Tim 4:10, 16) the assembly, the gathering for worship, and acts of mutual support. The reason for this desertion is not stated; later chapters will suggest possibilities: fear of persecution, heresy, feeling the group is not essential to personal faith, leadership tensions, discouragement over the delay of the parousia. This last possibility is suggested by the second participial addition: "encouraging one another, and all the more as you see the Day approaching" (v. 25*b*). This call for mutual encouragement recalls 3:13, at which point the NRSV chose to use the other sense of the verb, "exhort one another." Given the condition of the church reflected in vv. 24-25, "exhorting" may be the better translation here. References to the day of the Lord, the day of judgment, or the day of Christ's coming were so frequent and familiar that the writer needed only to say "the Day." Reminders that the day was near (Rev 1:3) were integral to sustaining the eschatological expectation of the community, but with the passing of time and the increase of hardship, in some quarters these reminders suffered declining influence. (See Reflections at 10:32-39.)

Hebrews 10:26-31, Warning About the Future

COMMENTARY

Warnings to the readers have appeared in hortatory passages with some frequency (2:1-4; 3:12; 4:1), but by far the most severe occurred at 6:4-8. The warning here in 10:26-31 parallels 6:4-8 in both form and function. Each consists essentially of four statements: the previous experience of the believers; the apostasy; the impossibility of renewal; and the final fate.[106] A major difference between the two is that 10:26-31 is framed in the cultic language of the preceding exposition. It might be helpful to review 6:4-8 and commentary as preparation for reading 10:26-31.

10:26-27. The introductory "for" joins what follows to the exhortations immediately preceding (vv. 22-25). More specifically it is likely that v. 25 triggered this warning, because the writer has just referred to neglectful absence from church assemblies and the approach of the day of reckoning. In fact, the first-person plural of vv. 19-25, joining writer and readers in the same community of grace and duty, continues in vv. 26-31. No one, not even the author-preacher, is exempt from the warning. The very first word in the Greek text (ἑκουσίως *hekousiōs*) is "willfully" ("deliberately," "intentionally"), its position of prominence announcing that it is the key term in the warning. Note also the use of the present tense of continuing action ("keep on sinning," NIV; "persist in," NRSV), making it clear that the violation and its penalty consist of sin that is intentional and continuous. In speaking of intentional or willful sin, the author is recalling the language of Num 15:22-31, where it is stipulated repeatedly that atonement ceremonies under the first covenant dealt with "unintentional" sins. The superiority of the new covenant to the old, as has been argued in 8:1–10:18, gives to the words "willful" and "continuous" a special gravity.

That the warning is to those living within the new covenant is expressed in the phrase "after having received the knowledge of the truth" (v. 26). Here in digest is a reference to the benefits of the new covenant presented more elaborately in 6:4-5. Having "knowledge of the truth" seems to have been a rather broadly used way by which early Christians referred to their faith experience (John 8:32; 17:3; 1 Tim 2:4; 4:3). It comes as no surprise to the reader that for those who thus repudiate the covenant with its benefits, which they had enjoyed, Christ's sacrifice cannot be repeated (v. 26); that his self-offering was once for all has been repeatedly stated (10:10, 12, 14, 18). Instead of another sacrifice for sin, there awaits a certain judgment of fire (v. 27). While a general conflagration was widely associated with God's final judgment (Isa 26:11; Zeph 1:18; Matt 25:41; 2 Pet 3:7, 12), the language here seems more reminiscent of the fiery punishment of the rebellious Levites under Korah's leadership (Num 16, esp. v. 35). Those to be punished with raging fire are characterized as "adversaries," persons who "stand over against" God. The writer may have in mind the enemies to be put underfoot, the image in Ps 110:1 (Heb 1:13; 10:13).

10:28-29. The argument here is on the pattern of "lesser to greater" (*a fortiori*), used also at 2:2-3. Under the law of Moses, the death penalty was stipulated for murder (Lev 24:17), for blasphemy (Lev 24:14-16), and for idolatry (Deut 17:2-7). This last violation

---

106. See Lane, *Hebrews 9–13*, 296-97, for a clear display of the parallels, not only between the two warnings but also between the encouragement passages that follow (6:9-12; 10:32-36).

is the one in the writer's mind, since it constituted a breach of covenant, required the testimony of two or three witnesses (Deut 17:2-7), and for it punishment was to be administered "without pity" (Deut 13:8), even if the guilty person were a relative or friend. The writer's logic moves forward without wavering: If this sequence held for those who violated the old covenant, those who reject life under the new can expect even more severity. Greater blessings imply greater judgment; the measure of height is the measure of depth.

In three participial phrases the violation of the apostates from the new covenant is graphically presented. First, they have trampled underfoot the Son of God (the NIV is more literally correct here). The verb "to trample" (καταπατέω *katapateō*) is used elsewhere to describe what happens to salt that has lost its savor (Matt 5:13), to pearls cast before swine (Matt 7:6), and to seed scattered on a path (Luke 8:5). One can hardly imagine a metaphor of greater contempt. The use of the title "Son of God" further underscores the depravity of the act. Second, they have treated as "common"/ "vulgar"/"profane" (κοινός *koinos*) the blood of the covenant. Although the phrase "blood of the covenant" recalls for Christians the eucharist (Mark 14:24 and par.; 1 Cor 11:25), there is no evidence that the writer is referring to a sacramental dispute that occupied a later generation.[107] Here the term refers straightforwardly to Christ's act of giving himself for our sins (9:12, 14; 10:19). And finally, the violators have "outraged" (ἐνυβρίζω *enybrizō*; "insulted," NIV) the Spirit of grace. The participle is a form of the word transliterated *hybris*, used in the Hellenistic culture to refer to a haughty arrogance that belittles others.[108] At Matt 22:6 the word is translated "mistreated" (servants); at Luke 11:45, "insult"; and at 1 Thess 2:2, "shamefully mistreated." These who have "shared in the Holy Spirit" (6:4) now behave toward that Spirit, which had made specific in their lives the grace of God, with words, conduct, and attitude borne of cynical self-importance. That the writer framed this strong sentence as a question ("What do you think these perpetrators deserve?") does not reflect.

---

107. Ignatius *To the Smyrneans* VII.
108. See G. Bertram, "ὕβρις *hybris*," *Theological Dictionary of the NT,* 8:295-307. The opposite of *Hybris* is described by Philo *Concerning God* 10.5 as the character of God.

uncertainty but calls on the readers themselves to pronounce the sentence of judgment

10:30-31. However, that judgment is not theirs to make. Judgment, like salvation, is God's work, not the readers', not their leaders', and not the writer's. And lest anyone think that the writer is making the judgment or is calling on the readers to do so, two texts are cited that remind everyone that judgment belongs to God alone (Deut 32:35*a* with a slight variation from the LXX, and Deut 32:36; also Rom 12:19). While judgment often involves the vindication of God's people, at v. 30 the accent is clearly on the punishment of apostates. In closing the warning, the writer gathers up all that has been said in vv. 26-30 in a sentence that has the ring of holy law or prophetic pronouncement: "Fearful it is ['Fearful' is emphasized by being placed first in the sentence] to fall into the hands of the living God." While falling into God's hands can be an experience of comfort and rescue (2 Sam 24:14), it is not so here. The living God is held before apostates as "a consuming fire" (12:24). At stake is the majesty and holiness of God.

The behavior described here and at 6:4-8, which the author regards as beyond the restoration of repentance and without forgiveness because there is no more sacrifice for sin, can be understood through the language of covenant. Throwing off the bond of covenant, old or new, was seen as final and fatal. However, an alternative way of understanding apostasy has been offered by a probing of the patron/client relationships that were prevalent in the first-century Mediterranean world. From correspondence and other documents of the time, we have learned that persons in position to bestow favors (freedom, money, political advantage, etc.) entered into relationships, directly or through a mediator (broker), with persons needing and seeking those favors. In return the clients gave to their patrons gratitude and honor. If a client were ever to violate that relationship, either by public denial or gradually drifting away, the affront to the person and honor of the patron would be of such gravity that the patron and client would become adversaries. The position and public esteem of the patron would require severe punishment of the former client. This social, rather than cultic, interpretation of Hebrews views God as patron, Christians as clients, and Christ as the mediator-broker. Any Christian who violated this relationship, either by neglect or by public words and behavior, would thereby be guilty of holding up the patron to ridicule and shame, while trampling underfoot the benefits previously enjoyed. Such persons would be apostates, and since the honor and majesty of God was at stake, would have to be punished, severely and finally. Whether this cultural analysis provides an adequate rationale for the vocabulary, theology, and argumentation concerning apostasy in Hebrews is a judgment needing further reflection.[109] (See Reflections at 10:32-39.)

109. For the best case for this cultural analysis (thus far), see deSilva, *Despising Shame.*

Hebrews 10:32-39, Encouragement from the Past

COMMENTARY

Again, returning to the parallel passage at 6:9-12 might be helpful. It and the present passage are texts of encouragement, recalling former days of faithfulness in the congregation, urging that such behavior be sustained in the present, and anticipating eschatological confirmation and reward. At 10:32-39, however, we are given more details about the recent history of the church.

10:32. The adversative conjunction "but" alerts the reader to a radical shift from vv. 26-31. The fundamental ground for encouragement is in remembering former days. The activation of memory was basic to preaching in both synagogue and church (Lev 19:33-34; the entirety of Deuteronomy; 1 Cor 15:1; 2 Tim 1:6; 2 Pet 3:2), and those days to be remembered were not necessarily "the good times." For example, the Israelites were urged to embrace the stranger among them, remembering their own bitter experiences as strangers in Egypt (Lev 19:33-34). So here, the recollection is of times of verbal and physical abuse, but times, nevertheless, when they were firm, bold, and sympathetic. The writer need only briefly remind the readers that their "contest with sufferings" (an athletic image to be developed later in chap. 12) came "after you had been enlightened" (v. 26; 6:4). Becoming followers of Christ did not end hardship but began it in new and intense ways.

10:33-34. These verses lay out in four expressions, framed in the now familiar form of a chiasm, the former experiences to be remembered:

A	publicly exposed to abuse and persecution
B	being partners with those so treated
B´	having compassion for those in prison
A´	cheerfully accepting the plundering of possessions

This presentation makes clear the two aspects of the congregation's sufferings: those endured directly and those endured in sympathy with others. Those directly endured were of two kinds: verbal abuse (reproach, derision, taunt [Jer 20:8; 24:9]) and physical abuse (a general term for all kinds of affliction [Mark 13:19; Acts 20:23; Rom 5:3]). Added to the pain was its public nature, the believers being made a "spectacle" ("theatrical display," 1 Cor 4:9). But under such humiliating conditions the faithful did not avoid further disgrace by abandoning fellow believers in their times of trial; rather, they entered into their sufferings as partners, as sharers in a common lot.

This description is in sharp contrast to the tendency of some to absent themselves from the church assemblies (v. 25). Demonstrating sympathy for those imprisoned involved more than a feeling of sadness or regret; rather, it meant visits, providing food, running errands, and perhaps interceding (Matt 25:36; Phil 2:25). All of these activities meant risking further verbal and physical abuse. The plundering of the property of Christians may refer to official seizure, mob violence, or perhaps to the burglarizing of the homes of believers who were taken to prison.[110] Citizens of the many provinces of the Roman Empire did not wait for imperial edicts to make life miserable for minority groups, ethnic or religious. However, the Christians were able to endure the loss of one kind of property because they were sustained by the certainty that they had another kind of possession, "better" (1:4; 7:19; 8:6) and "permanent" (7:3; 11:14-16; 13:14). In fact, the Christians not only endured such treatment, but they also "cheerfully anticipated" it, embracing a perspective traced back to Jesus himself (Matt 5:12; Luke 6:22; Rom 5:3; Acts 5:41).

10:35-39. Words of encouragement conclude by urging three qualities that the congregation already possesses, as demonstrated by past performances: boldness, endurance, and faith. In urging that the readers not throw away their boldness, the writer is speaking not only of a quality of tenacity (3:6) but also of the confidence granted them by the high priestly ministry of Christ (4:16; 10:19). What is at stake is the final reward, the lasting possession, that God will give in the day of judgment, since judgment includes not only punishment but also God's favorable response to their work and love (6:10). Likewise, the endurance the congregation needs now as much as ever was formerly a principal quality of the membership (v. 32). Whether the implied loosening of their grip was due to a worsening of afflictions endured or to attrition is not evident. To the "very end" (6:11) can be a long time, but for them "endurance" was the very definition of God's will (v. 36). At the end of endurance lies the "promise" (ἐπαγγελία *epangelia*), a term already familiar as a reference to the salvation provided by Christ (4:1, 8; 6:12, 17; 8:6), which will reappear frequently in chap. 11 (11:13, 17, 33, 39).

The final quality urged on the readers, faith, is introduced by a composite quotation of Scripture (vv. 37-38) to which the writer adds a brief homiletical application (v. 39). Noticeably absent is the author's usual introduction of a quotation: God says, Christ says, or the Holy Spirit says. That omission might have been for rhetorical effect in order to follow the general eschatological remark in v. 36 with the sharp and sudden "a little while." The brief citation (three words) is from Isa 26:20, and it may have been detached from the remainder of Isa 26:20 in early Christian liturgy to serve an eschatological accent. The whole of the verse says,

Come, my people, enter your chambers,
    and shut your doors behind you;
hide yourselves for a little while
    until the wrath is past. (Isa 26:20 NRSV)

Is the Hebrews writer citing this verse and then "correcting" it with the use of Hab 2:3, 4 because the church addressed had adopted Isa 26:20 as its scriptural support for a pattern of retreat and withdrawal from public life? At least one commentator thinks so.[111] But the general portrait of the congregation (drifting, slipping, neglecting, forgetting, waning) hardly fits the image of a church that has deliberately taken a position of acquiescence, which it supported with Scripture. It is more reasonable to understand "in a very little while" as the author's way of introducing the Habakkuk citation on a note of urgency and perhaps addressing a lethargy born of the delay of the parousia.

In the citation of Hab 2:3c-4, the writer again uses the LXX and not the Hebrew text, and again there are variations from the LXX text. The writer may be following a different text of the LXX or, given the importance of Hab 2:3-4 for the early church, may be using a form of the citation already adapted for Christian use.[112] More likely, however, at least some of the modifications are the work of the writer of Hebrews. Other than stylistic differences, Heb 10:37-38 varies from Hab 2:3c-4 LXX in three significant ways: (1) The definite article is added to the participle "coming" (referring to the vision in Hab 2:3c) to make it read ὁ ἐρχόμενος (*ho erchomenos*), "the one coming" and, therefore, messianic; (2) the "my" of Hab 2:4 is moved from "my faith" ("my faithfulness") to "my righteous one" (i.e., the reader); and (3) the order of

---

110. Lane, *Hebrews 9–13*, 300, cites Philo's description of the violence against Jews in Alexandria in 38 CE: "Their enemies overran the houses now left vacant and began to loot them, dividing up the contents like spoils of war" (*Against Flaccus* 56). Of course, pogroms against Jews in any city would also affect Jewish Christians (Acts 18:1-2).

111. T. W. Lewis, "'. . . And If He Shrinks Back' (Heb 10:38b)," *NTS* 22 (1975) 88-94.

112. J. A. Fitzmyer, "Hab 2:3-4 and the NT," in *To Advance the Gospel: New Testament Studies* (New York: Crossroads, 1981) 236-46.

the two clauses in Hab 2:4 has been inverted so that "My soul takes no pleasure in anyone who shrinks back" (v. 38) follows rather than precedes "but my righteous one will live by faith." The reasons for this inversion of clauses are probably two: (1) In its new location the reference to one who shrinks back clearly refers to the believer ("my righteous one") and not to the Messiah ("the one who is coming"); (2) by ending with the line about anyone who shrinks back, the writer is able to conclude with an exhortation that both repeats the previous warning ("Do not throw away your confidence," v. 35) and anticipates the discussion of faith that follows. This is to say, vv. 38*b*-39 are perfectly fitted as transitional.

From a rhetorical point of view, vv. 38-39 contain two familiar and forceful moves. First, the two verses form a chiasm:

A	live by faith
B	not shrink back
B´	not shrink back
A´	have faith

This construction both aids the hearer's memory and makes the impact of emphasis by repetition.

Second, the writer's arrangement of the material makes possible a more effective final exhortation, "not this . . . but this," which denies the negative and affirms the positive: We are not those who shrink back and are lost (destroyed) but those who have faith and are saved (preserve the soul). By saying that we are not of or among the shrinkers but of or among the faithful, the writer anticipates a roll call of those among whom we live, men and women who did not shrink back but who held firmly to their faith in God. Such will be the content of chap. 11.

REFLECTIONS

1. We have learned by this time that the author of Hebrews is a skillful preacher, and nowhere is that fact more evident than in the hortatory portions of this epistle-sermon. Some of the rhetorical strategies have been noted in the commentary. For example, the balanced admonitions to faith, hope, and love in 10:19-25 are given to the reader in the symmetry of homiletical form. Preachers are warned, however, to beware of pre-packaged sermons, even if they are presented in the biblical text itself. Rather than be seduced into shortened preparation when faced with a text that is preaching itself, one is well advised to dig into the problems addressed by the writer's homily. The congregation of readers is suffering waning zeal and a noticeable decline in attendance at its assemblies. Why? Is it the problem of individualism? Is nothing significant being said or done? Do those attending face public ridicule? What more likely produces a debilitating lethargy: persecution, lack of attention from the culture, or cultural favor? Perhaps this church has allowed itself to be defined by its opposition and has not really defined itself by God's gracious act in Christ. Since the time of Socrates, philosophers and theologians have observed a condition that afflicts persons and communities, sometimes without causes known to themselves, called *ennui*. Sails hang limp, but not for lack of a breeze. In the church the condition is labeled *akedia*, often translated "sloth" and listed among the seven deadly sins. How is it to be addressed?

2. If the writer of Hebrews thinks the church being addressed is even approaching ennui, then one can better understand the intensity of the warning against apostasy (vv. 26-31). There is a passion in the warning that burns with a fire rarely seen or heard. In the writer's case it is borne both out of concern for the church and out of a theology that has a once-and-for-all quality. It is covenant theology, which sees God's gracious act toward us in Christ as sufficient for the human condition of sin. The author cannot imagine anyone experiencing its benefits and then willfully breaking the covenant. Language is strained to describe such an act: The Son of God is trampled underfoot, the blood of the covenant is treated as profane and vulgar, and the Spirit

of grace is regarded with haughty contempt. It takes a high view of the Christian faith to make such a "low" possible. For Christians who regard all matters of religion as optional, as opinions of only private merit, and as unworthy of such passion, the language of 10:26-31 must, indeed, sound primitive and unenlightened. Perhaps the readers of Hebrews, drifting and neglectful as they were, saw nothing in the life of their congregation remotely deserving of such a warning. Maybe that is just the point.

3. The readers are reminded (10:32-39) that their sufferings, their verbal and physical abuse, began "after you had been enlightened." One wonders if these believers were alerted before baptism to the real possibility that discipleship would bring hardship. So easy it is to say that one has pain and troubles in the world, but if one trusts in the grace of Christ, pain and troubles are carried away. Perhaps the old problems do depart, but they are often replaced by large, unexpected ones, known only to, borne only by, those who speak and act for God in the world. Faith and love and hope and generosity and forgiveness have enemies out there, enemies not yet put underfoot. Until they are, candidates for baptism need to be informed: It is not only disobedience but also obedience that exacts a price.

4. In 10:32-39, the writer turns to the faculty of memory to nourish faith and encourage those who believe. Memory is essential to the life and vitality of both Judaism and Christianity. The exodus continues to be a resource for those who remember; the self-offering of Christ continues as a reality for those who share the sacrament of remembrance. For both synagogue and church memory is of two kinds: the memory of what God has done prior to our own lives, and the memory of what God has done within the span of our own years. It is this second kind that is being activated in Heb 10:32-39. The congregation is urged to turn the pages of its own history, to remember the difficult times, and to recall especially how boldly and graciously they responded to those hardships. The young can borrow these memories and claim them as their own; the ones who lived those memories can be continually refreshed by them. Blessed is the congregation that can call up its own record of love and good works as a resource for times of discouragement.

HEBREWS 11:1–12:17

A CALL TO FIDELITY AND MUTUALITY

OVERVIEW

That a new section begins at 11:1 is clear, for reasons to be elaborated, but not so clear is the terminus. On the basis of common vocabulary and the themes of faith, endurance, and discipline, one could end the section at 12:11. However, 12:12-13 flow naturally enough out of 12:1-11 to argue for 12:13 as the close of the section. As for 12:14-17, the decision is to join them either with what precedes or with what follows. Since 12:18 brings such a dramatic shift in thought and image, it was decided to attach 12:14-17 with the preceding paragraph. No real exegetical gain or loss is at stake; it is in the nature of hortatory material that the subjects treated are multiple and shift easily from one to another.

What is quite clear is that 11:1-40 is a unit in form, function, and theme. Technically this unit is exposition, but it functions as exhortation, while 12:1-17 is directly hortatory. The twin themes of faith and endurance in 11:1-40 were introduced in the immediately preceding 10:36-39, joining this unit to the context smoothly. In fact, these themes have been anticipated since 6:12-15. "Endurance" (ὑπομονή *hypomonē*) as a noun occurs only at 10:36 and 12:1, but it is used as a verb at 10:32; 12:2-3, 7. The transition into 12:1-17, therefore, is natural, although 11:40 ("they would not, apart from us, be made perfect") makes it evident that at 12:1 the subject will shift from faith examples of the past to the present; that is, to Jesus and his followers.

The movement, then, is from the earlier experiences of faithful endurance by the readers (10:32-39), to those examples from redemptive history (11:1-40), to Jesus and the Christian community (12:1-17). But this flow of the material toward the future is more than the author's literary creation. It is chronological in that the sketches of God's faithful begin at Genesis 1 and continue through Joshua 6, followed by a swift summary of many others. It is theological in that faith's endurance and God's approval are one continuous story of the reliability of God (11:11). It is christological in that the story moves toward Christ, in whom the narrative has its completion and the past faithful their fulfillment. Hence faith is never very different from hope (11:1, 10, 13, 16, 26, 39-40). Enough has been said previously about Christ, in whom God has spoken "in these last days" (1:2), and about those who have entered into the new covenant inaugurated by him to anticipate very clearly the level of expectation in terms of faithful endurance, which will be spelled out in the exhortations to follow (12:1-17).

HEBREWS 11:1-40, LEARNING FROM OUR FOREBEARS IN FAITH

OVERVIEW

Because 11:1-40 is so obviously a unit in form, function, and theme, and because the reader can move rather smoothly from 10:39 to 12:1, the question has naturally arisen as to whether this chapter once had a separate existence but has been inserted here by the author or a later hand. In response, let it be said that no extant manuscript of Hebrews is without 11:1-40. In addition, as has been noted, the themes of faith and endurance were introduced in 10:32-36, and the whole of chap. 11 is well joined to that context. Furthermore, the author has already demonstrated the use of exposition of Scripture for purposes of exhortation (3:7–4:11; 10:30-31, 37-39), which is the nature of 11:1-40. And finally, the theology of this unit is fully consonant with that of the remainder of the epistle. It can be concluded, therefore, that 11:1-40 is the author's own, and if composed separately, it has certainly been well woven into the fabric of this "word of exhortation" (13:22).[113]

With that in mind, the reader would do well to reflect briefly on this remarkable composition as a single literary piece. Verses 2 and 39 form an inclusio by the use of the unusual passive form of μαρτυρέω (*martyreō*), "to witness." When so used, it is variously translated "received approval," "was attested," "were commended" (vv. 2, 4-5, 39). Throughout the recital of actions by the faithful men and women of old, some form of the word "faith" appears twenty-four times. If one returns to the accounts of these characters in Scripture, one notices that often there is no reference to faith as the moving force in their lives, even though it may be strongly implied. The phrase "by faith" names the perspective of the writer's rereading of the OT. The eighteen appearances of the phrase "by faith" constitute *anaphora*, a rhetorical device in which a word or phrase is repeated at the beginning of successive clauses, or verses if used in a poem. Anaphora makes an impact on memory when used to teach, impresses listeners when used in an encomium, and has cumulative effect when employed in argumentation. But with or without anaphora, the rhetorical use of lists, often constructed from a selective reading of a people's past, was widespread in the Mediterranean world.[114]

Aristotle, in his *Rhetoric* (Book I) discussed the nature and role, strengths and weaknesses, of "examples" in public speaking. He defended their use as both impressive and persuasive when carefully located and arranged in an address. By "examples" he referred not only to persons but also to events, places, relationships, things, etc. Among Jews and Christians who drew heavily on sacred history for homiletical purposes, lists of persons and their deeds are not uncommon. Brief lists with sermonic functions can be found at Josh 24:2-13 and 1 Sam 12:6-15. In Wis 10:1–11:1, wisdom functions in the recital very much as faith does in Hebrews 11. However, in an apparent effort to underscore that all commendable behavior was made possible only by the wisdom of God, names are withheld, even though the persons, beginning with Adam, are easily identifiable. The hymn to the ancestors ("Let us now praise famous men") in Sir 44:1–49:16 has much in common with Hebrews 11, but the closest parallel to this text is in the Christian epistle *1 Clement* (*1 Clem* 17:1–19:3).[115] However, for Clement the virtue being extolled is not faith but humility. But among these and many other antecedents and parallels, Greco-Roman, Jewish, and Christian, Hebrews 11 remains a composition more properly understood in its own form, function, and context than in relation to possible sources.

---

113. Buchanan, *Hebrews*, 184.

114. Michael Cosby, *The Rhetorical Composition and Function of Hebrews 11* (Macon, Ga.: Mercer University Press, 1988) esp. 1-24, 93-109.

115. The relationship between *1 Clement* and Hebrews is much debated. However, that there is a relationship and that *1 Clement* is from Rome has persuaded many that either the provenance or the destination of Hebrews was also Rome.

Hebrews 11:1-2, The Meaning of Faith

COMMENTARY

In this brief introduction, the writer makes the two affirmations that inform and focus the recital that follows: the nature of faith and the approval of God on the life that was determined by such faith. One can argue that v. 1 does not "define" faith; after all, the word πίστις (*pistis*, "faith") will sometimes indicate trust or belief and sometimes refer to the quality of loyalty or faithfulness. Rather than offering a definition, the author focuses and gives thematic unity to the discussion. In 10:36-39, faith is presented in a context of related words: "assurance," "endurance," "firm hope in the promises from which we do not shrink back." The orientation is eschatological, and that perspective will prevail through v. 40. As used here, faith cannot be severed from hope. The vocabulary of v. 1 will not be carried through the chapter, but were v. 1 to be read as a refrain following each episode of faith, it would fit naturally.

Translators of v. 1 are never satisfied even with their own renderings of the two key but very complex terms, ὑπόστασις (*hypostasis*) and ἔλεγχος (*elegchos*). Both the NRSV and the NIV treat these words subjectively in terms of "assurance"/"being sure" and "the conviction"/"certain." The REB is almost objective in translating the first as "gives substance to" and subjective in the second, "convinces us." There is no question that faith strongly involves the quality of human embrace and trust and tenacity, but this does not handle adequately these two words; that is, it is not a case of "believing it makes it so." The first term is used at 3:14 with the obvious sense of "confidence" on our part, but at 1:3 the meaning is more philosophical, referring to the very essence or substance or being of God. This is to say, the word points to a reality that does not owe its existence to human awareness. Faith, then, joins the subjective and the objective: "Faith is the assurance of things hoped for." Interestingly, *hypostasis* is used in the LXX at Ruth 1:12; Ps 39:7; and Ezek 19:5 to translate the Hebrew word for "hope" (תקוה *tiqwâ*). Hence, in this unusual clause, the certainty both of faith and of faith's object is asserted. This certainty was earlier anticipated in the image of the anchor behind the veil (6:19).

The second key word (*elegchos*) is more at home in a court of law and can properly be translated "proof" or "demonstration": "Faith is proof of the unseen." That which is not seen may be a spatial reference pointing to the Platonic realm of the true and real, encountered earlier in discussions of the heavenly sanctuary (see Commentary on 8:1-5; 9:11, 24). However, it may also be a temporal reference pointing to the future, and given the orientation of the entire chapter toward what lay in promise for all the faithful, the latter sense is the dominant one.

Hope (3:6; 6:11, 18; 7:19; 10:23; 11:1) and promises to be inherited (4:1; 6:12, 17; 7:6; 8:6; 9:15; 10:36; 11:11, 13, 39-40) are accents too strong to be abandoned at this critical point in the message. In fact, it was this quality of faith as the substance of hope, the proof of what was yet to come, that brought approval (confirmation) to the ancients, our ancestors in the long narrative of trust in God. The persons referred to (v. 2) are called "elders," but not in any technical sense (as at Mark 7:3, 5); they are the characters in the recital soon to begin (v. 4). The approval they received is literally "received testimony"; this is to say, their lives are in the biblical record as lives of faith. That the Scripture bears witness to them (7:8, 17; 10:15) is the equivalent of saying that God testifies to their faithfulness. The brief sketches in the roll call that follows are thus to be read as God's testimony about their lives. (See Reflections at 11:39-40.)

Hebrews 11:3-7, Faith: From Creation to Noah

COMMENTARY

11:3. Verse 3 seems to lie on the border between vv. 1-2 and vv. 4-31, prompting some interpreters to consider it as a part of the introduction (vv. 1-3), while others place it as it appears here. The repeated "by faith" appears here in the first of eighteen times, but uncharacteristically the subject is "we" rather than one of the ancestors mentioned in v. 2. The effort to relieve the sentence of this awkwardness by making "we understand" parenthetical ("By faith, we understand, the worlds were prepared,") creates greater difficulty by raising the question, Whose faith? God's? The preparing (ordering) of the worlds was "by the word of God," not "by faith." This affirmation essentially repeats 1:2-3, without the christology. The sense of the passage is better served by preserving the pattern of the entire recital, following the phrase "by faith" with the subject of that faith: "By faith, we." By beginning with his own and the reader's Christian witness, the writer begins the narrative as it ends, in the first person (vv. 39-40). This is to say, the roll call of the faithful springs from the earlier word, we are "among those who have faith" (10:39 NRSV), and moves toward the conviction that "they would not, apart from us, be made perfect" (11:40).

As to the particular point at which our faith is demonstrated, the narrative itself, following the order of the OT, dictates that it concern creation. The perspective on creation is based on one of the definitions of "faith" in v. 1: "faith is the proof of what is not seen." This faith enables the understanding that the creation, which is seen, was made from what is unseen—that is, the Word of God. The NIV's "what is seen was not made out of what was visible" is preferred over the NRSV's "what is seen was made from things that are not visible." Although both renderings are possible, the NIV opens the door to the doctrine of creation *ex nihilo,* which entered Hellenistic Judaism (Wis 11:17; Philo *Life of Moses* II.267); the NRSV suggests that God made the world from some invisible material. This difference has been much debated among Christians. Plato's theory of visible and invisible worlds lies back of that debate and may lie in the background of this statement in Hebrews, but the writer's point does not come within that argument. The assertion here is that the visible came from the invisible, and the invisible is the Word of God. This is the writer's point; whether God worked with invisible "stuff" is not at issue here. That the Word of God brought into being the universe is a tenet of faith, which is proof of the unseen.

11:4. Verses 4-7 begin the roll call with the names of three ancestors who lived "by faith": Abel, Enoch, and Noah. Again, it must be remembered that the reading of these vignettes from the OT as actions "by faith" is the author's own, whether faith is present implicitly or explicitly in the ancient account. Similarly, to what extent the Hebrews writer is commenting on the biblical text alone or is influenced by Jewish and Christian traditions about the biblical accounts is not always clear.

The interest in Abel is as focused as the very sparse record in Gen 4:4. His life is distilled into a single act, the offering of a sacrifice to God, which, in comparison with his brother's, was "better" or "greater." But in what sense or on what grounds was it "more acceptable" (Gen 4:4 NRSV)? Quantitatively? Qualitatively? The writer does not speculate; it is enough that it was offered by faith and that God testified (approved, attested) that through that faith Abel was righteous (Hab 2:4 at Heb 10:38; also Matt 23:35; 1 John 3:12). Whether the author knew the tradition asserting that God's approval took the form of a fire that consumed Abel's sacrifice[116] is not evident. What is clear, however, is the message that Abel continues to speak. It is not the cry for vengeance that rises from the ground (Gen 4:10; Rev 6:9-10); that certainly is not the message the writer wants the readers to hear. Rather, "through *it*"—that is, "through faith"—Abel still speaks. It is his

---

116. As later preserved in Theodotion's Greek translation of Gen 4:4-5. See Lane, *Hebrews 9–13,* 334. Recall God's response to Elijah's sacrifice at 1 Kgs 18:38.

faith, accepted and approved by God, that is held up as worthy of emulation.

11:5-6. One has to admire the Hebrews writer's restraint in the treatment of Enoch, since few biblical characters have been so embellished with traditions and legends. Out of a single verse (Gen 5:24) grew apocalypses (*1–2 Enoch*) as well as stories of his piety. Enoch was represented as a model of repentance (Sir 44:16), of purity (Wis 4:10-11), and of obedience (*1 Clem* 9:2-3), as well as a prophet of the final judgment (Jude 14-15). For the present writer, the slightly elaborated translation of Gen 5:25 LXX is sufficient as a comment on "By faith, Enoch": "And Enoch pleased God and he was not found, because God translated him."

It was the affirmation that "Enoch pleased God" that not only earned him a place on the list of heroes of faith but also provided the author an exegetical base for a general principle regarding faith. The argument unfolds in this way: If Enoch pleased God, then Enoch was a person of faith, because "without faith it is impossible to please God" (v. 6). Both the reference to what is impossible (6:4, 18; 10:4) and the form of the argument (6:16; 7:12; 9:22) are familiar in Hebrews. The brief argument is then elaborated into a two-part formula concerning faith. First, anyone approaching God (in worship, in petition) must believe that God exists. This is not a bland and general belief that there is a God but a focused faith that "draws near." This rare expression "that God exists" may have developed in Judaism's missionary contact with Hellenistic culture.[117] That God exists was, in that context, necessary preface to the further argument that God is one (Deut 6:4). The second part of the formula is stronger: Anyone approaching God (in worship, in petition) must believe that God is a "rewarder" (μισθαποδότης *misthapodotēs*; only occurrence in Scripture) of those who seek after God, an image of persistent trust familiar from devotional texts (Pss 14:2; 22:27; 119:2).

That God rewards faith is a clear conviction of Hebrews (10:35) and an important feature of the recital in chap. 11 (e.g., 11:26).

11:7. The third and final example from this first group of faith heroes is Noah, whose story in the OT is rather lengthily told (Gen 6:8–9:17) but is here condensed around the theme of faith. Noah's faith is of the character described in v. 1*b* ("the proof of things unseen") in that he trusted God's warning (8:5; 12:25) about what was not yet apparent, the flood. He acted in "holy fear" (NIV, preferred over "respected the warning," NRSV) when he built the ark to save his own household (Gen 6:18; "a remnant," Sir 44:17). There is some ambiguity in the expression "by this he condemned the world." The antecedent of "this" can be either "faith" or "ark." While a few interpreters consider the ark itself to have been a judgment on Noah's generation, more likely it was his faith that served to judge the world.

Those traditions that present Noah as a preacher of repentance (2 Pet 2:5; *1 Clem* 7:6; 9:4) understand his judgment to have been sermonic. However, the judgment could have been indirect in the way that a person of faith is a judgment on unbelieving contemporaries. Just so does the Fourth Gospel present Jesus as a judgment of the world, even though he did not come to judge (John 3:17-19). That Noah was righteous is repeatedly affirmed in Scripture (Gen 6:9; 7:1; Ezek 14:14, 20; Sir 44:17; Wis 10:4), but in this verse his righteousness is joined to faith. That he is righteous by faith not only accords with the theme of faith, which governs all the sketches in Hebrews 11, but also with Hab 2:4 (quoted at 10:38). And, of course, both Heb 11:7 and Hab 2:4 recall the tradition of Abraham, next to be discussed: "And he believed the LORD; and the LORD reckoned it to him as righteousness" (Gen 15:6 NRSV). That Noah was "heir" to this righteousness underscores God's grace rather than Noah's merit, an accent made elsewhere in Hebrews in other contexts (6:12, 17; 9:15). (See Reflections at 11:39-40.)

---

117. Note Exod 3:14 LXX: "I am the one who is (exists)."

Hebrews 11:8-22, Faith: From Sarah and Abraham to Joseph

COMMENTARY

This unit of the recital on faith and its heroes is the heart of the narrative, and Abraham, with Sarah, is its central figure. The story of Abraham's life of faith recalls in a clear and rather simple way the biblical account (Genesis 12–22). There are three foci in the story: Abraham's response to God's call to the life of a stranger in the land of promise (vv. 8-10); Abraham's and Sarah's receiving of the promised heirs (vv. 11-12); and Abraham's offer of Isaac (vv. 17-19). Between the second and third foci is a reflection on the life of faith as that of an alien sojourner (vv. 13-16). It becomes more apparent in this narrative that faith is forward looking, oriented toward the future, trusting that God will keep promises made to those who believe. In other words, faith and hope are one, and life is pilgrimage. Larger place is also given in this unit to the characterization of God as one who makes promises and keeps them (recall 6:18-20), regardless of the time that passes and the circumstances, which seem hopeless.

The author of Hebrews joins other writers, Jewish and Christian, in a rich exegetical and homiletical tradition that presents Abraham as the ideal figure.[118] The differences between the account in Hebrews and the narrative in Gen 12:1–25:11, other than those that belong to any condensation of a longer story, are of two kinds: those that represent purposeful selectivity and those that are modifications and commentary appropriate to the immediate purpose. The writer's selection of three episodes (although the first is in two parts, going and staying) from Abraham's life was noted above. The modifications and commentary deserve careful attention.

11:8. Attention is fixed immediately on Abraham rather than on God's call (Gen 12:1-3), since faith is the subject under consideration. And Abraham's faith is expressed in obedience, implied in Genesis 12 but explicitly stated here, a quality Abraham shares not only with Christians (5:9) but also with Christ himself (5:7). The substitution of "place" for "land" (Gen 12:1) seems also deliberate, opening the door to a new interpretation of Abraham's destination (vv. 10, 13-16), an interpretation already suggested at 4:8 and 8:15. That the place Abraham was to receive was an inheritance is clearly implied in the Genesis story (Gen 15:7; 22:17; 28:4), but the word "place" is used here to attract the positive associations of that term already presented to the reader (1:2, 4, 14; 6:12, 17; 9:15; 11:7).

11:9. That Abraham did not know where he was going accords with Gen 12:7 and 13:14, since it was not until his arrival in Canaan that he was told the place of inheritance. In this land he lived temporarily ("living in tents," v. 9) as in the home of another. His faith was in reality hope, as indicated by the reference that his son Isaac and his grandson Jacob shared in the same experience of sojourning as foreigners in "the land of promise" (an expression found only here in Scripture). The terminology in v. 9 recalls not only the experience in Canaan (Gen 17:8; 23:4; 37:1) but also the time in Egypt (Gen 12:10; 15:13; Acts 7:6). Some Christians found this language also appropriate to characterize their life in the world (Eph 2:19; 1 Pet 1:17; 2:11).

11:10. In this verse the author departs from the Genesis account and gives his Christian interpretation of vv. 8-9, an interpretation extended in vv. 13-16. Abraham's hope, says the writer, is eschatological, not to be fulfilled by possession of a piece of real estate. For a sense of the intensity of his "looking forward," see the same word at 10:13 (see also Acts 17:16; 1 Cor 16:11; Jas 5:7). In contrast to the tent home, the image of life that is temporary and vulnerable, Abraham anticipated a city, permanent and with sure foundation; that is, the heavenly

---

[118]. Among them are Sir 44:19-21; Wis 10:5; 1 Macc 2:52; Philo *On Abraham* and *The Migration of Abraham*; Gal 3:6-9; Romans 4:1; Acts 7:2-8; *1 Clem* 10:1-7.

Jerusalem (v. 16; 12:22, 28; 13:14).[119] Here the writer draws on familiar images of the secure and permanent Holy City, which God founded (Ps 87:1; Isa 33:20; 54:11). The terms used to speak of God as "architect" and "builder" ("designer" and "creator") are unique in the NT, although they can be found in Philo and his sources in Hellenistic philosophy. This city of God is the hope and goal of all pilgrims of faith, including the readers (vv. 14-16).

11:11-12. The second movement of the Abraham story centers on the birth of Isaac and through Isaac a promised progeny beyond number. This brief faith summary gathers up all that the Genesis accounts say about both Abraham and Sarah with reference to advanced age, sexual inactivity, and barrenness (Gen 15:1-6; 17:15-22; 18:9-15; Rom 4:19). A problem of translation exists, however, in v. 11, due to the unusual awkwardness of the sentence. Variations in the Greek MSS testify to scribal attempts to clarify the meaning. Without chasing all the possibilities,[120] one gets a sense of the difficulty by attending to the role of Sarah. Both the NRSV and the NIV keep the focus on Abraham by treating the statement about Sarah as circumstantial or parenthetical: "and Sarah herself was barren." However, an alternate reading, preserved in a footnote, has been accepted as the text of v. 11 by the REB: "By faith even Sarah herself was enabled to conceive, though she was past the age, because she judged that God who had promised would keep faith." While this rendering is possible, the NRSV and the NIV are to be preferred, since Abraham is the subject in the preceding and following verses, and it is his story that continues after the interpretive break at vv. 13-16. In addition, the phrase translated "received power of procreation" is literally "received power for casting seed," the male activity in conception. And so from Abraham, from one person who was "as good as dead" (recall Paul at Rom 4:19), came a multitude of descendants. That the number is as many as the stars and as the grains of sand by the sea is biblical language, paraphrasing but not quoting Gen 22:17. This extraordinary consequence flowed from a faith that trusted God as a keeper of promises.

11:13-16. The recital of ancient models of faith is temporarily halted in order to reflect on its meaning. The reflection is on "all of these," likely a reference to Abraham, Isaac, and Jacob (v. 9), the pilgrim patriarchs. Of the persons mentioned earlier (Abel, Enoch, Noah), Enoch at least could not be included, since he did not die. The promises not received do not, of course, include progeny, because that promise had been fulfilled.

The context makes it clear that the promise not received was a "homeland" (v. 14). This was true in the literal sense as a reference to Canaan, but in the present discussion the homeland is the "better country, that is, a heavenly one" (v. 16). It was not Abraham alone but Isaac and Jacob as well who "looked forward to the city that has foundations, whose architect and builder is God" (v. 10). That they saw it from a distance and greeted it as a pilgrim would greet a destination coming into view is an image borrowed from the account of Moses on Mt. Nebo (Deut 32:48; 34:4). The homeland they see from a distance is one seen with eyes of faith. It was this vision by faith that empowered them not only to live as "strangers and foreigners on the earth" (v. 13) but to confess publicly that such was their life. The homeland toward which they moved made relative all the goals, values, and relationships pertaining to the society in which they were resident aliens. If by "homeland" they had in mind Mesopotamia, from which they had come, opportunities to return were there. Here again the writer is speaking in symbolic terms; they could have abandoned the pilgrimage to the better country and settled into the values, goals, and relationships of the land in which they now lived as strangers. That option was always available to them (v. 15).

The concept of being a stranger on earth and having elsewhere a homeland is not original with the writer of Hebrews; such thinking belonged to the Greco-Roman culture and had been embraced, with modification, by Hellenistic Judaism. Plato had spoken of the human soul as having come from the noumenal "real" world into the phenomenal "shadow" world. This idea of the soul's sojourning on earth and returning to the

---

119. Buchanan, *Hebrews*, 188-89, is a minority voice interpreting Hebrews as an expression of hope for repossessing the land and rebuilding the earthly Jerusalem.

120. Jas Swetnam, *Jesus and Isaac* (Rome: Pontifical Biblical Institute, 1981) 98-101, gives a summary of the various opinions.

invisible and eternal realm was adopted by some forms of mystical Judaism and gnostic Christianity. Philo used the basic idea to allegorize such stories as that of Abraham, whose pilgrimage was interpreted as the passing of the soul through this alien world.

The writer of Hebrews does not follow Philo in such spiritualizing of history. Abraham and his descendants were in fact strangers and foreigners in the land of Canaan (Gen 23:4; Ps 39:12) and so understood themselves. Rather than evaporating that history by allegorizing, the writer here understands that history in a larger context of God's purpose brought to fulfillment in Jesus Christ. The history of the pilgrim forebears thus became a type of the writer's larger narrative: All the ancients of faith were anticipating and moving toward a homeland, a better country, which made only relatively important the actual land in which they lived.

Those who interpret the NT in the context of the social and cultural structures and values of the Mediterranean world help us to understand the status of those who are "strangers and foreigners on the earth."[121] The stranger or alien in that culture had to endure the verbal abuse, the disgrace, and often the economic mistreatment heaped on persons of lower social status (see Commentary on 10:32-39). In a sociological sense, "the land that they had left behind" (v. 15) would have been a life of accommodation to the values and mores of the culture within which they lived. Perhaps the writer is here addressing indirectly the reader's attraction to the favors of social acceptance that would come with abandoning the life of an alien with its abuse and shame. For them, "apostasy would provide the surest route back to favor within the unbelieving society."[122] Because the faithful pilgrims chose God's approval over that of the society about them, "God is not ashamed to be called their God" (v. 16). This is clearly an echo of references to God as the God of Abraham, Isaac, and Jacob (Gen 28:13; Exod 3:6; Matt 22:32), and a reminder to the reader of Heb 2:11: Christ is not ashamed to call us brothers and sisters. Whether or not social considerations of shame and acceptance were primary factors in the configuration of problems in the congregation of hearers, they were doubtless present and contributed to the "near falling away" state of the church.

The "better country" that the resident aliens "desired" (a strong word for "yearning" (ὀρέγομαι *oregomai*), used only here and at 1 Tim 3:1; 6:10) is "better" by reason of being heavenly rather than earthly (v. 16). The writer speaks often of that which is better, the precise nature of that favorable comparison being defined in each case by the context (6:9; 7:7, 19, 22; 8:6; 9:23; 10:34; 11:35, 40; 12:24). And again, as at v. 10, the better country is imaged as a city that God has built. With the occupation of that city in God's promised future, the pilgrims will enjoy the honor and esteem that come with citizenship in a great city,[123] and will finally know the permanence tent life never afforded.

11:17-19. The third and final movement in the recital of Abraham's faith recalls Gen 22:1-8, the offering, or as expressed in Jewish tradition, the binding (Aqedah) of Isaac. In the space of these verses the writer not only captures the longer account in Genesis 22, but also reveals some familiarity with the rich traditions that grew out of this story (a portion of which can be found in Sir 44:20; Jdt 8:25-26; 1 Macc 2:52; 4 Macc 16:20; Jas 2:21-24). A prominent feature of the Genesis 22:1 account and of the tradition is the introductory statement, "God tested Abraham" (Gen 22:1; Heb 11:17). None of the other exemplars of faith presented in Hebrews 11 is so portrayed.

The extraordinary nature of Abraham's act of faith is underscored in several ways. First, Abraham "offered" (προσφέρω *prospherō*) Isaac (v. 17). The verb here is in the perfect tense to indicate an accomplished fact. In Abraham's faith it was so, even though later in the same verse the writer uses the imperfect tense ("ready to offer," NRSV; "about to offer," NIV) to describe the act itself. This use of the imperfect is called inchoate or conative (cf. Rom 9:3, "I could wish"). In other words, by faith Abraham offered his son to God and was in the process of doing so when the act was interrupted. Second, the

---

121. J. H. Elliott, *A Home for the Homeless: A Sociological Exegesis of 1 Peter* (Philadelphia: Fortress, 1981). The image of early Christians as strangers and foreigners in 1 Peter is not unlike Heb 11:13-16.
122. deSilva, *Despising Shame*, 186.

123. See deSilva, *Despising Sham*, 187, especially the citation from Quintilian (*Institutio Oratoria* 3.7.26) concerning the advantages of a great city for its inhabitants.

unusual nature of Abraham's faith is accented by contrasting the promise and the test. The promise of progeny was tied to the birth of Isaac (vv. 11-12); the test calls for the end of Isaac's life. The writer not only refers to the fact that Abraham had received this promise but emphasizes it by quoting Gen 21:22: "It is through Isaac that descendants shall be named for you" (Heb 11:18). Third, Isaac is referred to as Abraham's "only son" (v. 17; "beloved son," LXX), expressing in dramatic fashion the indispensability of Isaac for the fulfillment of the promise. The testing of Abraham thus seems to contradict his faith, the promise, and the character of the God in whom he trusted. The offering of Isaac is, in Kierkegaard's famous expression, "the suspension of the ethical" in the service of one's faith.[124]

How, then, was Abraham able to comply with this command as an act of faith rather than as a denial of faith? The fourth and final expression of the extraordinary nature of his faith is in v. 19: "He considered the fact that God is able even to raise someone from the dead." Neither this statement nor the phrase "only son" should send the reader rushing ahead to christology; such is not the writer's use of the Abraham-Isaac story. The present point is that Abraham believed that God is not only faithful but also powerful. Even the death of Isaac would not finally impede God's keeping a promise, because God is able to give life to the dead. Such faith may have been borne of reflection on his and Sarah's capacity to have a child in the first place; that was, in effect, life from the dead. In fact, Paul so refers to the birth of Isaac as life from the dead (Rom 4:17-21). That Abraham so reasoned is not, of course, clear to us. Faith that God is able to raise someone from the dead is not a part of the Genesis 22 story. However, it is in the tradition. Of the Eighteen Benedictions of the synagogue service, the second concludes, "Blessed are you, O God, who raises the dead." And, says the writer, "figuratively speaking, he did receive him back" (v. 19).

It is unusual that the author would say "figuratively" (ἐν παραβολῇ *en parabolē*; lit., "in a parable" or "parabolically speaking") since Abraham did in fact receive back Isaac and the two descended Mt. Moriah together. Some interpretive help comes by recalling the writer's earlier use of the word "parable" at 9:9. In that instance, the first tabernacle was called a "parable" or a "symbol" of the true tabernacle yet to be. This is to say, "parable" was used eschatologically to point to a future reality, and its function in v. 19 is very likely the same. For this reason, Lane feels justified in the translation, "in a foreshadowing."[125] That which is foreshadowed is not only the resurrection of Christ, although that is included (13:20), but also the vindication, the deliverance of all God's faithful. The readers of the epistle, in threatening and painful circumstances, should have heard this word of assurance without its being directly applied to them.

11:20-22. In much briefer sketches, the list of heroes of faith continues with Isaac, Jacob, and Joseph. These three have in common the future orientation of faith; that is, faith is in large measure hope. In the cases of Isaac and Jacob, this hope-filled faith is expressed in the blessing of descendants; with Joseph it is evident in prophetic words about the future of his people, a future in which he wanted to share even as a corpse. In Isaac's blessing of Jacob and Esau (Gen 27:27-40), none of the details of that story of intrigue and deception are pertinent. The single focus is that the blessing concerned the future, or more literally, "things to come." This expression, a favorite of the writer of Hebrews (1:14; 2:5; 6:5; 10:1; 13:14), keeps the history of salvation moving forward without having to pause each time to supply details about the nature of the salvation viewed now in prospect.

Jacob's blessing of the sons of Joseph, Ephraim and Manasseh, is recorded in Gen 48:1-22. That he did so "when dying" recalls Gen 47:29; 48:1, 21, and "bowing in worship over the top of his staff" quotes Gen 47:31 LXX (the Hebrew text has "head of his bed"). The image is not simply that of a weakened old man approaching death but of a man of faith worshiping the God of promises and reaffirming faith in those promises by blessing his grandsons. The staff may here be a symbol of pilgrimage as in the instruction to Israel for observing the exodus: "your staff in your

---

124. Søren Kierkegaard, *Fear and Trembling*, Problem I.

125. Lane, *Hebrews 9–13*, 362-63.

hand" (Exod 12:11 NRSV). This interpretation is supported by Jacob's request of Joseph that he not be buried in Egypt but in Canaan, the land of promise (Gen 47:28-31; 49:29-32; 50:4-13). By faith, Jacob joined the exodus and even in death claimed the promise.

Likewise Joseph, having buried his father in Canaan (Gen 50:4-13), spoke to his brothers about the exodus from Egypt to the land promised to Abraham, Isaac, and Jacob. In anticipation of that future, he made the Israelites swear that they would carry his bones with them (Gen 50:24-26). His choice of Canaan as his burial place was a witness to his faith that God would keep the promise, much as Jeremiah's purchase of property in Anathoth prior to the exile was testimony that God would again bring the people to their homeland (Jer 32:6-15). Thus Joseph's prophecy of the exodus and his desire to participate in it, even in death, moves the narrative forward to the exodus itself. (See Reflections at 11:39-40.)

Hebrews 11:23-31, Faith: Moses and Israel

COMMENTARY

Abraham and Moses are clearly the principal figures in the recital of heroic faith, each being treated at much greater length than the others. In this unit, the writer recalls the faith of Moses (vv. 23-28), followed by three events spawned by his faith in God: crossing the Red Sea (v. 29), the conquest of Jericho (v. 30), and Rahab's hospitality (v. 31). The movements of Moses' own life of faith are four, each preceded by the anaphoric "By faith": his being hidden as a child (v. 23); his identification with his own people rather than with the Egyptians (vv. 24-26); his flight from Egypt (v. 27); and his institution of the Passover (v. 28). This structure parallels the Abraham story, which also specifies four particular acts of faith (the first two are treated as one), followed by three faith sketches indirectly related to Abraham.

11:23. The first of the four episodes of Moses' faith, while beginning "By faith Moses," is in fact a witness to his parents' faith. They (Exod 2:2 LXX; the Heb text mentions only the mother) hid him for three months because he was "beautiful." This is not to imply that an ugly baby would have been given up to Pharaoh's sword, but that the child's comeliness was taken as a sign of God's favor. In Stephen's speech rehearsing Israel's history, Moses is said to have been "beautiful before God" (Acts 7:20 NRSV). The parents' faith is expressed in their boldness or courage in the face of the Egyptian king's edict. Faith that fears God (5:7; 10:31; 12:28) rather than human opponents has the approval of the author of Hebrews. In the biblical text it is the midwives who fear God rather than the pharaoh (Gen 1:17, 21). Perhaps the writer here felt that such a characterization of the parents was a justifiable inference, given their bold and risky behavior.

11:24-26. The faith activity of Moses when he was grown up (see Exod 2:11; Acts 7:23), is his identification with his own people rather than enjoying the luxury and power of Pharaoh's house. That Moses had become "a son of Pharaoh's daughter" is based on the statement of Exod 2:10, "He became her son." This clearly implies that Moses would be an heir of the monarch's house, a fact that sharpens the nature of his choice to return to his own people with the ill-treatment, abuse, and shame that followed such a choice. Moses' refusal to be a son of Pharaoh's daughter is not detailed as to manner, here or in Exodus 2. Very likely it did not involve any formal legal action but was the consequence of his killing the Egyptian who was beating a Hebrew (Exod 2:11-15). In fact, the statement that "after Moses had grown up, he went out to his people and saw their forced labor" (Exod 2:11 NRSV) may be the basis for the Hebrews writer's more dramatic presentation of Moses' choice: He turned his back on the palace life, with its fleeting pleasures of sin, and joined his own oppressed people (vv. 24-25).

A few Greek manuscripts make this connection more specific by inserting between v. 23 and v. 24, "By faith Moses, when he was grown up, killed the Egyptian, because he observed the humiliation of his people." In his more "homiletical" portrayal of Moses, the writer may reveal awareness of some of the elaborations of the Moses tradition available at the time of writing.[126] However, the major influence on the author's shaping of the story was likely the circumstance and condition of the readers. Moses' choice, like Abraham's before him, was to act out of faith in God knowing the hardships that would follow such a choice. Given the readers' social and economic situation (10:32-34), the lesson from Moses' faith could hardly be missed. The sinful pleasures that Moses rejects are temporary, a description recalling the reminder to the persecuted readers: "knowing that you yourselves possessed something better and more lasting" (10:34 NRSV). Choosing the permanent over the temporary was a staple in the advice of sages, including Jesus (Job 15:29-35; 18:5-21; Matt 6:19-21; 7:24-27).

In v. 26, the choice of Moses is expressed again, but in a different and quite vivid image: He preferred over the treasures of Egypt[127] a greater wealth. The greater wealth is the "reproach" ("abuse suffered," 10:33; 13:13; "disgrace," 1 Tim 3:7; "insult," Rom 15:3) of Christ. The striking contrast is dulled somewhat by the enigmatic expression "the reproach of Christ." Who or what is the Christ, the Anointed One? There is ample testimony in Scripture to the effect that faith in and service to God brought reproach or stigma (e.g., Ps 69:7, 9-12, 19-20) from the general culture. Paul applied Ps 69:7 to Christ: "The insults of those who insult you have fallen on me" (Rom 15:3 NRSV). The language of v. 26, however, seems to be that of Ps 88:51-52 LXX: "Remember, O Lord, the reproach of your servants which I have borne in my breast from many nations, with which your enemies, O Lord, have reproached [me (?)], with which they have reproached your anointed one by way of recompense."[128] This psalm gives to the writer of Hebrews the key terms "reproach," "anointed one" (Christ), and "reward" ("recompense"), and it is as appropriate to this epistle's view of Scripture to attribute these words to Moses as it was for Paul to attribute Ps 69:7 to Christ.

However, is the writer of Hebrews saying that Moses envisioned the day of Jesus Christ and cast his lot with Christ and his followers? Montefiore is uneasy with the idea and interprets "the Anointed One" as a reference to the whole people of God,[129] but such a position is unnecessary. Given the writer's understanding of redemptive history as one single narrative oriented toward a future completed in Jesus Christ, and given the portrait of Abraham as one who looked beyond the land to the heavenly city (v. 10), it is easily conceivable that Moses be presented as looking to Christ and participating in his shame and reproach. After all, says the writer, "he was looking ahead to the reward" (v. 26; cf. 10:35). In reading Christ into an OT story, this writer is not alone. In a classic bit of typological exegesis, Paul described Israel's wilderness journey, saying, "For they drank from the spiritual rock that followed them, and the rock was Christ" (1 Cor 10:4 NRSV).

11:27. The third episode in the recital of Moses' faith, "he left Egypt," parallels the first movement of Abraham's faith: He "set out for a place that he was to receive as an inheritance" (v. 8). However, Moses left Egypt under circumstances far different from those prompting Abraham to leave Mesopotamia. Moses had killed the Egyptian who was beating a Hebrew, and "when Pharaoh heard of it, he sought to kill Moses" (Exod 2:15 NRSV). Because he was afraid (Exod 2:14), Moses fled Pharaoh and settled in Midian. This verse contradicts Exod 2:14, saying that Moses was not afraid of the fury of the king. The writer seems to be aware of the tradition that spoke of the fearlessness of Moses in relation to Pharaoh.[130]

There have been numerous efforts to resolve the apparent contradiction, even suggesting that the reference to Moses' leaving Egypt was to the exodus. However, that violates the sequence, since the next verse speaks of the Passover (v. 28), which preceded the exodus (v. 29). The best solution is to regard Moses' fearlessness as an overall

---

126. Cf. Philo *Life of Moses* 1; Josephus *Antiquities of the Jews* 2.
127. Gold? Granaries? Tribute of subject peoples? The treasures of Egypt that Moses rejected are unspecified. Philo elaborates on the luxury and wealth Moses rejected. See Philo *Life of Moses* 1.29, 47, 135, 149, 152, 154.
128. Translated in Lane, *Hebrews 9–13*, 373.
129. Montefiore, *A Commentary on the Epistle to the Hebrews*, 203.
130. Philo *Life of Moses* 1.49-50; Josephus *Antiquities of the Jews* 2.254-56. And, of course, upon his return to Egypt forty years later, Moses was fearless before Pharaoh.

trait of his life, even though his impulse after killing the Egyptian was to run. Faith overcame fear, for Moses as for his parents (v. 23), the two examples underscoring an important lesson for the readers. Likewise, vital to faith is perseverance (endurance), obviously another quality drawn from Moses' life because it addressed a need of the readers (6:11). In so describing Moses, the writer provides the key to understanding his faith: He was one who kept his eyes on the "invisible one" (ἀόρατος *aoratos*, v. 27*b*). It is this keeping the invisible one continually before him that constitutes Moses' perseverance. This term for God, not found in the LXX, apparently arose in Hellenistic Judaism and was adopted by early Christians (Rom 1:20; Col 1:15; 1 Tim 1:17). This way of referring to God is especially appropriate here, because it confirms the writer's definition of faith as laying hold of the hoped for and the unseen (v. 1), because it reaffirms Moses' faith as "looking ahead to the reward" (v. 26), and because it places Moses in the tradition of Abraham, who left the land of his birth in search of the city whose architect and builder is God (v. 10).

11:28. The fourth and final movement in the recital of Moses' faith centers on the Passover and the sprinkling of blood (v. 28; Exod 12:1-13). The vocabulary and phrasing of Exodus 12 are preserved even in this brief condensation of the narrative. The statement is straightforward, with no suggestion that the Passover or the pouring of blood was to be taken figuratively or symbolically, as was the case in the offering of Isaac (v. 19). In fact, one admires the writer's restraint at a point when christological implications and foreshadowings come so easily to mind. Of course, it could be that the writer knew the reader would make such connections, especially with the sprinkling of blood (9:12-14, 18-22) and, therefore, felt no need to be explicit. If readers think it without the writer's saying it, the communication is all the more effective.

11:29-31. The mention of the people (v. 28) moves the story forward to the exodus and vignettes from the conquest of the land. From the narratives of Exodus and Joshua the writer selects three events as having occurred "by faith": the Israelites' passing through the Red Sea (the LXX expression for "Sea of Reeds," Exod 10:19; 13:18; 15:4, 22; 23:31) as on dry land (Exod 14:19-29); the conquest of Jericho (Josh 6:1-21); and the sparing of Rahab the prostitute (Josh 2:1-21; 6:22-25). In each of these three episodes the contrast is made between the faith of Israel and the unbelief of Israel's opponents, with predictable consequences in each case. Believing, the Israelites walked through the sea as on dry ground; the Egyptians drowned. Believing, the Israelites captured Jericho; the inhabitants perished. Believing, Rahab, along with her family, was rescued; the disobedient (unbelieving) inhabitants of Jericho were destroyed. By her act of hospitality, Rahab cast her lot with Israel; therefore, Israel's faith was hers as well. The only woman besides Sarah mentioned in the list of exemplars of faith, Rahab was immortalized as a symbol of hospitality (Jas 2:25), as was Abraham (Heb 13:2). In the present context, her faith is important in that she believed that the future belonged to Israel's God and, therefore, to Israel; to join herself to Israel was to trust in what was yet only hoped for, that which was yet unseen (v. 1). (See Reflections at 11:39-40.)

Hebrews 11:32-38, Faith: Prophets and Martyrs

COMMENTARY

11:32-35a. At v. 32 the form of the narrative changes. The anaphora ("by faith"), the rhetorical device by which discrete and quite different units of material are held together, is now abandoned, even though "through faith" occurs at v. 33 and will occur again at v. 39. This does not mean that the author no longer employs rhetorical skills. On the contrary, such skills become even more evident. Verse 32 opens with a rhetorical question followed by a common rhetorical device for moving to a close: "Time would fail me to speak of," which in turn introduces a rapid survey of that which cannot be treated here and now.

Six names are mentioned, assuming the reader's familiarity with their stories; they appear out of chronological order (Gideon, Judges 6–8; Barak, Judges 4–5; Samson, Judges 13–16; Jephthah, Judges 11–12; David, 1 Samuel 16; Samuel, 1 Samuel 1), highlighting the fact that the preceding narrative is not being sustained but is now replaced by dipping here and there into the story of salvation history. Why the writer selected these four judges, one king, one prophet-priest, followed by "the prophets" is not evident, although the choices are probably not random; the sub-unit is too carefully executed rhetorically. These may have been popular heroes of faith among the readers. What follows in vv. 33-34 is definitely not random or hastily conceived. Even though the passage may not qualify as a poem,[131] it certainly bears the marks of carefully constructed prose, with an appreciative audience in mind. The nine short clauses in these two verses seem to fall into three groups of three clauses each. The introductory relative pronoun "who" (plural) would lead one to assume that the nine activities refer to the persons listed in v. 32, but as the list unfolds the fact that other persons from Israel's history are in the writer's mind is evident.

The first three activities (conquered kingdoms, practiced [or administered] justice [righteousness], and obtained promises) can be attributed to all or at least some of the six persons named. All four judges engaged in warfare and hence conquered kingdoms, and of David it is said that he administered justice to all the people (2 Sam 8:15). All six persons obtained promises, but perhaps David was foremost in mind, since he enlarged Israel's territory, brought peace, and through him came the promise of a house forever (2 Sam 7:11). The next three clauses speak of divine rescues gained through faith. Samson (Judg 14:5-6), David (1 Sam 17:34-37), and Daniel (Dan 6:23) "shut the mouths of lions," but most likely Daniel is the one in the author's mind. Through faith Daniel's three friends survived the fiery furnace (Dan 3:19-28, 49-50), and those who escaped the edge of the sword were many, including David (1 Sam 17:45-47), Elijah (1 Kgs 19:1-3), and Jeremiah (Jer 26:7-24). The final group of three clauses is oriented toward military victories, although the sense in which the writer speaks of "becoming strong out of weakness" is unclear. The expression may refer to anything from David's defeat of Goliath to the victory of Gideon's small army to the numerous women, such as Deborah and Judith, who defeated stronger forces. As for being mighty in war and putting foreign armies to flight, the possible references are too many to list.

The nine clauses in vv. 33-34 describing achievements "through faith" have in common the triumphant, successful outcome of faith. There will follow in vv. 35*b*-38 the experiences of others whose faith brought persecution, prison, public abuse, poverty, ostracism, and death. Between the sketches of victories and sufferings is a transition statement that participates in both, in life and death: "Women received their dead by resurrection" (v. 35*a*). This is surely an allusion to the widow of Zarephath (1 Kgs 17:17-24) and to the Shunammite woman (2 Kgs 4:32-37).

11:35b-38. The writer now turns to a catalog of cases involving persons unnamed whose faith brought them hardship and mistreatment, often of the most cruel kind imaginable. For these persons, faith is faithfulness, a tenacity with hope of something better (v. 35*b*). The torture some endured is not a general reference to physical abuse; the word τυμπανίζω (*tympanizō*, "torture") derives from the term for "drum," hence to beat as one would a drum. The victim was often stretched on a stake or wheel. The reference may be to the mother and her seven sons, who, during the Maccabean period, refused to deny their faith ("refusing to accept release") in the hope of "a better resurrection" (2 Maccabees 7). As one of the sons expressed the hope in the hour of his death: "One cannot but choose to die at the hands of mortals and to cherish the hope God gives of being raised again by him" (2 Macc 7:14 NRSV). At v. 35 the writer recalls the women whose sons were raised to continue a mortal life; this mother and sons hope for a better resurrection, a hope that is faith turned to the future. For others, faith that refused to capitulate brought verbal abuse, the pain and disgrace of public flogging, and the countless indignities of prison (v. 36). The readers could probably provide a roll call of such sufferers,

---

131. As Buchanan regards it. See Buchanan, *Hebrews*, 201.

and no doubt they identified with them (10:32-34).

At vv. 37-38, as at vv. 33-34, the writer employs the rhetorical device called *asyndeton* (omission of conjunctions) in order for each mode of suffering to keep its harshness as though not part of a list while still contributing to the cumulative effect of the whole. The descriptive terms seem to come from a martyrology, and both ancient Jewish history and the more recent Maccabean revolt provided cases of such suffering. One such case was that of Isaiah, who, according to tradition, was sawn in two.[132] Every period of revolt in Israel's history produced guerrilla warriors who hid out in the deserts and in mountain caves, surviving almost like animals in order to strike another blow against the enemy. Greek tyrants, Herod the Great, the Romans—all had conducted extended harsh campaigns against rebels and freedom fighters. Of all these tenacious heroes of faith, the writer says, "The world was not worthy." Living by values and a hope beyond the understanding of their contemporaries, these homeless and pursued faithful were not only an enigma to the world, but they were beyond its deserving as well. (See Reflections at 11:39-40.)

132. *Ascension of Isaiah* 5:1-14.

Hebrews 11:39-40, Faith: Fulfilled in Christians

COMMENTARY

The writer now gathers up in a conclusion what has been said since v. 1 and points the discussion ahead. Verse 39 is the conclusion, expressed in three ways. First, the phrase "all these" puts into one category all the exemplars of faith, from Abel to all those nameless ones since Eden "of whom the world was not worthy." Second, all these persons "were commended for their faith." This expression, translated "received approval" (vv. 2, 4) and "it was attested" (μαρτυρέω *martyreō*, v. 5) returns the reader to the important affirmation at the outset: God testified to the faithfulness of these figures in salvation history. Third, none of these persons received "what was promised." This statement essentially repeats what was said of Abraham (v. 13). Of course, in an immediate and short-term sense, they did receive promises (6:15; 11:33), but by this time in the discussion the reader is aware of the larger eschatological use of "promise" (see Commentary on 6:17; 8:6; 9:15; 10:36). The writer has repeatedly asserted that all the faithful had this eschatological perspective (vv. 10, 13, 26, 35).

That they did not receive the promise is not due to any flaw in their faith; rather, it was due to the unfolding purpose of God. The statement of that purpose in v. 40 is somewhat difficult to translate. It reads literally, "God having foreseen [provided] something better concerning us, in order that apart from us they would not be perfected." The NRSV chose to omit "concerning us"; the NIV has "for us"; and the REB translates the phrase "with us in mind." Both the NIV and the REB try to soften the seeming triumphalism in "apart from us they would not be perfected" by saying "with us" they should be made perfect. The writer is not arguing that one faith community supersedes another; rather, the point is that the promises that moved forward all God's faithful are fulfilled in these last days through the sacrifice and priestly intercession of the Son. That in which we share they also share, the "something better" that God has provided (foreseen). What is "better" (7:19, 22; 8:6; 10:34; 11:16) is completion of one's pilgrimage toward God; that is, the very presence of God, the gracious gift of Christ's act on our behalf, "for by a single offering he has perfected for all time those who are sanctified" (10:14).

The recital is over; the writer has in v. 40 twice used the pronoun "us," returning to the direct address of the readers for the first time since 10:39 (the "we" of 11:3 is somewhat parenthetical). The way is thus prepared to return to exhortation and encouragement.

REFLECTIONS

1. Our reflections on this unit can well begin with a brief consideration of the rhetorical skills employed within it. The author is a teacher of the "how" as well as of the "what." Attention has been drawn to several of the rhetorical devices in the commentary: anaphora, asyndeton, multiple examples, and the formalized rhetorical question and answer. All these are proven methods and portable beyond Hebrews. Among them, the use of examples is most subject to misuse. The use of a life or an act as an example must always be a reflection on a life or an act that was not intended to be an example but had its own reasons, its own integrity. No one in the list of exemplars of faith lived his or her life as an example to anyone; their having done so would have disqualified them as good examples. It is because they lived out of their own faith without an eye for an audience that they are examples to us.

Notice also the use of contrasts for vividness and impact. For example, tent life is contrasted with the city with foundations (vv. 9-10), and the choice of ill-treatment is contrasted with the people of God over the fleeting pleasures of the palace (vv. 24-26). Notice also the writer's restraint and economy of words in each case. Such brevity is not solely a result of time constraints; it is a characteristic of most of the Bible. Later legends and traditions elaborated in detail on the translation of Enoch, the offering of Isaac, the beauty of Moses, the luxury of Pharaoh's house, often drawing lessons and morals typologically and allegorically. The writer of Hebrews 11 is not only terse in narration but also remarkably restrained in making applications to the readers. The exposition itself, focused and appropriate to the reader's situation, serves as the exhortation. Of course, the writer assumes the reader's familiarity with the biblical stories, an assumption that cannot always be made.

2. Hebrews 11 provides the raw material for drawing a profile of faith as it has characterized the people of God throughout salvation history. Faith is not simply belief that there is a God but trust that God "rewards those who seek him" (v. 6). Faith has a long memory and profits from the experiences of our forebears. Faith also hopes (v. 1), looking beyond the immediate to God's future (vv. 10, 13, 26, 35, 40). Faith is tenacious and enduring, able to accept promises deferred in the conviction that death itself does not annul God's promises (vv. 8-10, 13, 16, 29-40). Faith is not coerced; believers always have the option of returning to "the land that they had left behind" (v. 15). Faith is courageous, acting often in the face of kingly edicts (v. 23) and royal fury (v. 27). Faith is subjective, to be sure, a conviction firmly held (v. 1); but it is not solely subjective, since it is the substance, the essence, the very being of things hoped for (v. 1).

3. This chapter, along with Ephesians 2 and 1 Peter 1, prompts Christians to think through again what it means to be a community of "strangers and foreigners on the earth" (v. 13). The communities addressed by Hebrews, Ephesians, and 1 Peter were different and, therefore, had different understandings of life as "resident aliens." Christians in each time and place must deal with this perspective in ways appropriate both to Christian existence and to the conditions of the culture, which not only is the context of the community but also in many ways is part of the church's self-understanding. Certain questions persist from Abraham's time to the present: Is the metaphor of stranger and foreigner still an appropriate one? Does too much separation from culture distance the church from the world God created and through which God may address the church? Can one be both a resident alien and a responsible member of the human race, caring for the people and the environment? Do "church" and "culture" really refer to the same people but in different settings? What is lost by immersion in culture? What is gained by isolation? Whether or not one uses the image of stranger, sojourner, or exile, these questions will not go away.

4. Hebrews 11 offers two portraits of the life of faith. One image is filled with triumph and victory over all enemies, with dramatic deliverances from all threats and dangers, even death (vv. 32-35*a*); the other is marked by torture, public mocking, imprisonment, beatings, stonings, homelessness, destitution, hiding in caves, and violent death (vv. 35*b*-38). Popular names for the two conditions are "triumph" and "tragedy," "success" and "failure"; and yet both are descriptions of the life of trust in God. The one group would likely draw new adherents to faith in order to share in its remarkable benefits; the other would likely evoke mocking and jeers, "Where is your God? Why does your God not come to rescue you?" To those who always draw a direct correlation between faith and one's circumstances, the second portrait is not of faith but of unbelief; else why would they suffer? To those who always draw a direct correlation between faith and hardship, the first portrait is not of faith but of compromise; else why would they fare so well?

Hebrews simply entitles both portraits "faith." Faith does not calculate results and so believe, nor can an observer look at one's lot in life and thereby measure the depth of one's faith. The writer is simply reporting on what has always been true among God's believers, and the reasons for the differences are hidden in the purposes of God. To offer both examples to the readers is in the service not only of truth but also of encouragement. The readers have suffered a great deal (10:32-34). To offer them only examples of suffering faith could add to their discouragement; to offer only examples of victorious faith could produce feelings of guilt and self-doubt. But both are presented, and the readers must locate themselves among them.

5. "God had provided something better so that they would not, apart from us, be made perfect" (Heb 11:40 NRSV). There are at least two ways to read this statement. It may be read triumphally, pointing out the incomplete and unfulfilled nature of faith among our forebears in contrast to those who through Christ's priestly ministry have perfected faith. Or it may be read humbly, recognizing that our faithful forebears lived the earlier chapters of one continuous story and that the last chapter is not to be separated from all that preceded. The "something better" has been prepared for them as well as for us. In fact, we can be grateful that God's story is a lengthy one, a sign of God's patience, not wanting any to perish (2 Pet 3:9). The deferral of God's promises may thus be understood as being for our sakes in order that we, too, might be included among those who believed but who died "without having received the promises, but from a distance they saw and greeted them.... Therefore God ... has prepared a city for them" (Heb 11:13, 16 NRSV).

HEBREWS 12:1-17, A CALL TO CONTINUE IN FAITH

OVERVIEW

Of the many faces of faith presented in chap. 11, the one that now comes to the fore as the writer returns to exhorting the readers is endurance. Faith as endurance was very evident in the recital of the lives and exploits of exemplars of the past, especially toward the end of chap. 11, and the present aim of the writer is to encourage the readers to endure in their sufferings (10:32-34). Although some of the persons described were martyrs, likely from the Maccabean era, and although Jesus' death will be cited, neither they nor he will be held up as a martyr to be imitated. The call is not for death but for endurance. In fact, the cross will be spoken of as something Jesus endured (12:2). This theme will be developed in two parts: Jesus as an example (vv. 1-3) and the interpretation of suffering as divine discipline (vv. 4-13). As pointed out in the introduction to this section (11:1–12:17), vv. 14-17 are not closely joined to either vv. 1-13 or vv. 18-29, but they are placed in this unit because the break between v. 17 and v. 18 seems more disjunctive than that between v. 13 and v. 14.

Hebrews 12:1-3, Look to Jesus

COMMENTARY

12:1. The doubly strong conjunction translated "therefore" (τοιγαροῦν *toigaroun*) not only marks a transition but also indicates that the preceding material will be drawn on for the exhortations to follow. The writer does just that in v. 1: The ancient exemplars are gathered about the Christian community as "a cloud of witnesses." That the word "cloud" (νέφος *nephos*) was a fairly common metaphor for a great crowd of people is well attested.[133] The witnesses are the persons named and unnamed in chap. 11, here gathered as spectators at the athletic event in which we all are runners. But they are a special group of spectators. The word "witness" has already occurred four times in chap. 11 (vv. 2, 4, 5, 39) as a verb in the passive voice, used to speak of these persons of faith as "being witnessed to" by God. That is, God has already approved or confirmed their faithfulness, and they now gather around us for whom the race is not finished. They are spectators whose presence exercises a strong positive influence on the runners.

The athletic imagery continues with the preparation of the participants: "having put off every weight and the sin which so easily clings" ("surrounds"/"besets"/"distracts"; this unusual word [εὐπερίστατος *euperistatos*] occurs nowhere else in the Bible). The images are non-specific; they may refer to any encumbrances, including body fat and clothing. None of the literature of the time yields the idea of weights used in training. Neither does the writer specify the sin, perhaps intentionally so; the readers could supply that. The overall picture is the usual one of preparing to run a race. Although ἀγών (*agōn*) may refer to any athletic event, here clearly the event is a race. The *agōn* (from which we get such words as "agonize") easily lent itself as a metaphor for moral and ethical struggle, involving as it did rigorous training, self-discipline, and intense effort; and so it was widely used in Hellenistic literature, including Jewish and Christian.[134] Whether on the athletic field or in the struggle over difficult moral choices or when facing martyrdom (4 Macc 17:11-16), a primary virtue is endurance, the writer's theme in 12:1-13.

While the word ὑπομονή (*hypomonē*) may mean "patience," and is often so used in the OT (as in "waiting patiently for the LORD") the preponderance of its uses in the NT and among the Greek moralists carries a more active sense, more appropriately translated "perseverance," enduring in the face of hostile forces.[135] The race, says the writer, is set before us in the sense of being a course laid out, a course that the entire epistle has described and that should come as no surprise to the readers. There are many examples in Greek literature of the use of the expression "being set before us" in connection with a contest, athletic or otherwise.[136]

12:2. The race is to be run "looking to Jesus" (v. 2). Literally, the participle says, "looking away to," which implies looking away from everyone and everything else and concentrating on a single object. The same word described the Maccabean martyr as looking away to God while enduring torments (4 Macc 17:10). The Christian readers of Hebrews are to look away to Jesus, who is not only the focus of their attention but

---

133. Lane, *Hebrews 9–13*, 408.
134. V. C. Pfitzner, *Paul and the Agon Motif* (Leiden: Brill, 1967), informs Hebrews as well as Paul's work.
135. F. Hauck, "ὑπομονή *hypomonē*," *Theological Dictionary of the NT*, 4:581-88.
136. Attridge, *A Commentary on the Epistle to the Hebrews*, 355.

also the one they "look to" in the sense of guidance and aid. Notice the name "Jesus" here. The writer has in mind the historical Jesus, who was one of us, tested as we are, subject to suffering and death (2:9-18; 4:15; 5:7-9). He is for the believers an example in ways that faithful forebears could not be. Two descriptive titles make that clear. He is the pioneer, originator, founder of the faith (2:10), and he is the perfecter of faith. Apart from him the forward-looking faith of the ancient exemplars could not be made perfect ("complete," "fulfilled," 11:39-40). Jesus is the first to attain faith's goal—the presence of God—and he is the one who makes it possible for others to have that access. The language of perfection is frequent in Hebrews (2:10; 5:9; 7:19, 28; 9:9; 10:1, 14), but the noun "perfecter" (τελειωτής *teleiōtēs*) occurs only here in the epistle and nowhere else in Scripture.

By far the most critical point in the author's presentation of Jesus as the primary example of endurance in suffering lies in the relative clause in v. 2: "who for the joy that was set before him endured the cross, disregarding its shame, and has taken his seat at the right hand of the throne of God." The key term is the preposition ἀντί (*anti*), variously translated "for," "for the sake of," "instead of." Until the Protestant Reformation, the most common translation was "instead of." This rendering accords with a frequent meaning of the word, it avoids the moral ambiguities embedded in the alternate view (Jesus suffered for the sake of or in order to obtain the reward), and it presents Jesus as self-consciously choosing to suffer (10:5-7) instead of maintaining the joy of his pre-incarnate life (1:2). In favor of the alternate view—that is, that the joy was not already his but lay in prospect and "for the sake of" which he suffered—is that this is an acceptable translation of *anti*; it offers a meaning of "set before him" that parallels the same expression in v. 1, "set before us," which at that point clearly refers to what is in prospect rather than in possession; it accords with the one other use of *anti* in Hebrews (12:16), it continues the forward-looking nature of faith presented in chap. 11 in that Jesus looks forward to the joy; and it acknowledges reward as the consummation of faith, a tenet already expressed by the author (11:6, 26). Most English translations prefer "for the sake of" rather than "instead of," and so do most commentators.[137]

It may be that the ambiguities arise from the possibility that the writer is quoting a christological fragment, the original meaning of which is lost by its being pressed into hortatory service and hence given a new meaning. It was rather common for christological hymns to begin with the relative pronoun "who" (Phil 2:6-11; Col 1:15-20; 1 Tim 3:16) and then present Christ in his two states, in heaven, on earth, and then again in heaven. A literary form lending itself to this kind of affirmation is the chiasm, or inverted parallelism. Perhaps the writer is quoting thus:

"Who (A) instead of the joy set
before him (heaven)
(B) endured the cross, (earth)
(B') disregarding its
shame, (earth)
(A') and is seated at the right
hand of the throne of God" (heaven)

This is but conjecture, but it might help to explain the ambiguity created when a former meaning lingers over a text now used to say something more fitting to the reader's circumstance: Jesus also suffered, but he endured by looking ahead to the joy of God's right hand (Ps 110:1). But in any case, the key term is "endurance." Here the cross is the scene not solely of death but of ignominy and shame, which Jesus endured. (See Commentary on 10:32-34; 11:13-16 on the subject of shame in the culture of the time.)

12:3. For persons who have not yet resisted to the point of shedding blood (v. 4), this model of endurance, not martyrdom, is the urgent message. In fact, it is this element alone of the christological assertion in v. 2 that the writer underscores by elaborating on it in v. 3. The readers need to "consider," to reflect seriously on this experience of Jesus. He endured (the perfect tense may indicate a condition over a long period and not the singular experience of the cross) the hostility of sinners.[138] The circumstances

---

137. Lane, *Hebrews 9–13*, is a notable exception.
138. The plural "against themselves" rather than "against himself" has strong support in the Greek MSS (see footnote in NRSV). If so rendered, αὐτούς ("themselves") doubtless would refer to the self-destructive nature of opposition to Jesus.

of the congregation had earlier prompted a similar word: "You have need of endurance" (10:36). The word translated "hostility" (ἀντιλογία *antilogia*) refers to verbal opposition and abuse, referring back to the shame and disgrace of v. 2 and recalling a major element of the reader's own suffering (10:33). The encouragement lies in Jesus' identification with them, not simply in suffering but in the specific nature of that suffering. The benefit of "looking to Jesus" (v. 2) and "considering him who endured" (v. 3) is that the readers not grow weary and faint. The writer has returned to the athletic metaphor to alert the church to what can happen to runners without endurance. In summary, it should be noted that vv. 1-3 do something surprisingly rare in the New Testament: They argue for Christian conduct by presenting Jesus as an example. There have been earlier occasions (esp. chaps. 2 and 5) and there will be a subsequent one (13:13) for noting the importance of the historical Jesus in the message of Hebrews. (See Reflections at 12:14-17.)

Hebrews 12:4-11, Regard Suffering as Discipline

COMMENTARY

12:4-6. Whether or not one considers v. 4 as beginning a new paragraph (as does the NIV, following major editions of the Greek NT), it is clear that the author now turns from the example of Jesus to the second ground for exhortation: suffering as divine discipline. In fact, in vv. 4-11 Jesus is not at all a factor in the discussion; rather, the argument centers on God and human suffering, with suffering interpreted as "the discipline of the Lord" (v. 5). The appropriateness of this argument depends, of course, on the fact that the addressees "have not yet resisted to the point of shedding your blood" (v. 4). Martyrdom can hardly be understood as discipline. Endurance continues to be the theme (v. 7), the need of the readers that prompted the writer to interpret even the cross as an example of endurance (v. 2). It is important to notice that the writer is not being judgmental in reminding the readers that they have not shed blood for their faith. Even if there is a mild rebuke in v. 4, it certainly is not as though they were being told, "Your sufferings are nothing compared to those of Jesus." Jesus is a model, not a judgment.

A slightly stronger rebuke is expressed in v. 5: "And you have forgotten the exhortation that addresses you as children." In citing Scripture, the writer does what has been done often in the epistle: He assumes that the Scriptures are authoritative, that they are addressed to the readers of the epistle, and that they contain an appropriate word for the present situation, in this case an "exhortation" ("encouragement"; cf. 6:18; 10:25; 13:22; cf. Rom 15:4, where Paul speaks of "the endurance of Scripture"). Also, the writer follows the citation (vv. 5-6) with an exposition (vv. 7-11). The citation is Prov 3:11-12 LXX (except for the addition of "my"). By applying this text directly to the readers, the writer is, in effect, calling them children (lit. "sons") of God. Perhaps the writer hopes that they will recall 5:8 ("Although he was a Son, he learned obedience through what he suffered") and make the connection to themselves. At any rate, it is very important that the congregation understand their experiences in the context of the parent-child relationship. The wisdom tradition was full of advice for parents and children in the family and larger community relationships, but much less frequently dealt with God as a parent disciplining children (Wis 11:10; 12:20-22; Sir 23:1-2; see also Deut 8:2-5).

The central question in both the citation and the exposition that follows has to do with the purpose of God's discipline. Is it punitive and corrective, or is it formative and educational? In the quotation from Proverbs 3, v. 11 contains parallel expressions that link the noun "discipline" (παιδεία *paideia*) with "punish" (μαστιγόω *mastigoō*; in the sense of "rebuke" [NIV] or "correct"). Verse 12 of the quotation contains parallel expressions that link the verb "disciplines" with "chastises" (from παιδεύω [*paideuō*], a verb that means lit. "to flog"; Luke 23:16, 22). There is no doubt that in Proverbs 3 the discipline described involves punishment and correction. In other words, discipline is punitive, as has been observed by writers Christian and Jewish who have commented on Prov 3:11-12.[139]

But does the writer of Hebrews accept and continue this view of suffering as punitive discipline, or does the context in which Prov 3:11-12 is quoted imply—indeed, call for—a different perspective on God's discipline? Ample uses of παιδεία (*paideia*) in a non-punitive sense of education and character formation were available to the writer, especially in the Hellenistic culture and in Jewish writings strongly influenced by that culture (e.g., 4 Macc 1:17; 5:24; 10:10; 13:22). And in the context of Hebrews 12 there is no indication that the readers are involved in sin that is being punished and corrected by God-sent suffering. The "sinners" and "sin" of vv. 3-4 refer to those hostile forces that opposed Jesus and now beset the church. This is not to imply that the members were sinless; certainly not, plagued as they were by apathy and loss of zeal. But the immediate battle being waged does not prompt the writer to say, "Put to death the sins within you." Rather, he says, "Endure in the face of hostility, verbal abuse, and public shame."

12:7-11. These verses open with the imperative, "Continue enduring for the purpose of discipline." While the writer is by no means offering a broad theology of suffering, there certainly is an attempt to provide a way of interpreting the present hardships of the readers. When their suffering is understood as discipline from God, then it can be seen, not as evidence of God's rejection, but as a sign of God's embrace. After all, discipline is an ingredient to the parent-child relationship and all children share in this experience. In fact, children without parental discipline are bastard children (v. 8). Notice the use of the pronouns "you" and "we"; the exposition is not simply an exegesis of Prov 3:11-12 but is rather a homiletical midrash or commentary. The sermonic commentary continues in vv. 9-10 with an analogy between human parents and God, arguing from the lesser to the greater (recall 2:2-3). The comparison is in two parts. First, human parents discipline us and we respond with respect for them. Should we not, then, respond to the "Father of spirits"[140] with submission (stronger than "respect"), the fruitful end of which is life, both now and eschatologically (10:36-38)? Second, the discipline of human parents and of God is compared in terms of duration and of criteria. As for duration, human parents discipline for a short time because of the brevity of a child's minority; but God's discipline is not given a time frame, because we do not outgrow the need, and the race that is set before us has no time limit. As for criteria, human parents are guided by what seems best to them, implying both good intention and fallibility. God, however, disciplines for our benefit, which is for the explicit purpose of "sharing in God's holiness." This rare expression has strong moral overtones (v. 11; 12:15-17; 13:1-5) but recalls as well the epistle's emphasis on the final access to God made available to us by the high priestly ministry of Christ.

The exposition proper concludes at v. 11 with a final comparison, not between human and divine discipline but between discipline's present pain and future joy. This contrast was commonly expressed by both Greek and Latin philosophers and moralists, whether speaking of athletic training, military activity, education, or life itself; but the writer here has other values and goals in mind. In this final statement, discipline gathers up themes developed earlier. The "training" (γυμνάζω *gymnazō*, giving us our word "gymnastics") returns to the athletic imagery (vv. 1-2) and recalls 5:14, the only other occurrence of the word in Hebrews: "But solid food is for the mature, for those whose faculties have been trained by practice to distinguish good from evil." The thought is similar to Paul's "suffering produces endurance, and endurance produces character" (Rom 5:3-4). The expression "peaceful fruit," or perhaps better translated "fruit of peace,"[141] introduces a quality in the community of faith, "peace," which will be more directly treated at v. 14. The mention of joy (translated "pleasant") recalls a key

---

139. See the article "παιδεύω *paideuō*" by G. Bertram in *TDNT*, 5:596-625, for the range of meanings of παιδεία (*paideia*) in Greco-Roman, Jewish, and Christian writings.

140. This expression seems to belong to this writer, even though similar phrases such as "God of spirits" and "Lord of spirits" appear elsewhere (Num 16:22; 27:16; 2 Macc 3:24; Rev 22:6; *1 Clem* 59:3).

141. Lane, *Hebrews 9–13*, 425.

word at v. 2 and reminds the reader that joy can be experienced not only within suffering (10:34) but finally as an eschatological gift. (See Reflections at 12:14-17.)

Hebrews 12:12-13, Regain Your Strength

COMMENTARY

With "therefore" the writer moves from the exposition, which was indirectly hortatory, to direct exhortation. The language is again athletic but not precisely so. For example, the condition of the hands seems not to bear directly on running a race, and in an athletic contest the track is provided; the runner does not have to make a straight path. Apparently the writer has chosen to do what is customary in the letter, and that is to couch exhortation in language from the reader's own Bible, the familiar voice of authority reinforcing the writer's urging. Drawing on the familiar and directly addressing a condition take precedence over precision of analogy. In this exhortation, therefore, the readers probably heard Isa 35:3, "Strengthen the weak hands, and make firm the feeble knees," and Prov 4:26, "Keep straight the path of your feet, and all your ways will be sure." And certainly they heard their own condition being addressed, a congregation stumbling and faltering, with some of them on the verge of dropping out of the race altogether. To them the word was clear: Recover your strength, stay on course, avoid careless worsening of your condition, and accept the healing that will enable you to finish the race. (See Reflections at 12:14-17.)

Hebrews 12:14-17, Again, Be Warned

COMMENTARY

As stated in the Overview to 11:1–12:17, 12:14-17 sits awkwardly between 12:1-13 and 12:18-29. Among those who join vv. 14-17 as an introduction to vv. 18-29, Lane makes the best case, seeing affinities between the two passages not only in mood but also in the concepts of holiness and seeing God, both of which figure prominently in vv. 18-29.[142] However, the separation of the two passages in these comments should not obscure the meaning of either. Verses 14-17 contain exhortation (v. 14), stern warnings (vv. 15-16), and a brief exposition extending the third warning in order to underscore its severity (v. 17).

12:14. If any of the readers are still behaving as though the pilgrimage toward God and the heavenly city were but a saunter, this verse should provide a double jolt. First, it reminds the congregation that they are to be involved in aggressive initiatives toward peace and holiness. To "pursue peace" is a biblical expression (Ps 34:14; 1 Pet 3:11) that echoes v. 11*b*, and the effort to attain holiness continues a thought from v. 10*b*. Both peace and holiness are here represented as realities out in front of the readers and not simply internal feelings. While each is to be pursued with effort, both writer and readers know that peace and holiness are gifts of God. Holiness has moral overtones, to be sure, but it has already been made clear that to be holy is to be sanctified by the self-giving of Christ (2:11; 9:13-14; 10:14). Second, v. 14 reminds the readers of the communal nature of the Christian life. If the analogy of the race tended to nourish individualism, that perception is now balanced with mutuality. The pursuit of peace "with all" is a congregational reference and not an injunction regarding their relationship with the larger society (contra NIV). The entire sermon has made it clear that some members of the congregation are lagging behind and beginning to absent themselves from the

142. Lane, *Hebrews 9–13*, 444.

assembly (10:25). Toward these the others are to assume some responsibility (3:12-14; 10:24). Such mutuality and not simply one's own spiritual state is essential for ultimately "seeing God," a traditional expression for the final goal of one's life of faith (Matt 5:9; 1 Cor 13:12; 1 John 3:2; Rev 22:4).

12:15-16. These warnings consist of an overall participle, "being watchful" (ἐπισκοπέω *episkopeō*; 1 Pet 5:2), followed by three parallel clauses, each beginning with "lest anyone." Each warning calls attention to the condition of fellow members and does not simply urge self-examination. The first warning alerts the readers to the possibility that one or more of their number may "fall short" (ὑστερέω *hystereō*; the same verb as at 4:1) of God's grace. It has already been made clear that such a failure is a real possibility, not for humanity in general but for the community of believers (6:4-8; 10:26-31).

The second warning centers in a citation of Deut 29:18*b* [17*b*], but the wording varies somewhat from the LXX text usually followed by the writer,[143] leaving one to speculate as to whether the differences are the writer's own doing or belonged to the particular text being quoted. What is clear, however, is that Deuteronomy 29 deals with covenant relationships and warns against breaking covenant with the community. The one who does so is not a single fatality; such a person is a "root" (a metaphor for a dangerous element in a society, 1 Macc 1:10), a source of community disruption, in this case, bitterness. The bitterness may arise as a response to persecution, but more likely from resentment in the membership over tensions between those who are beginning to drift away and those still bearing the abuse heaped on the faithful. If unchecked the bitterness can spread to the entire church, with the result that "many become defiled." The term "defiled" (μιαίνω *miainō*) is cultic, the opposite of "sanctified" (ἁγιάζω *hagiazō*; cf. John 18:28; Titus 1:15).

The third and final warning is to be watchful lest anyone become "a fornicator and profane person, as was Esau." The NIV is literally correct in translating the first adjective as "sexually immoral" rather than simply "immoral" (NRSV); sexual issues may have been a cause for concern among the readers (13:4). However, fornication was a metaphor for all kinds of unfaithfulness, especially idolatry (Deut 31:16; Judg 2:17; Jer 2:20). The story of Esau in Genesis does not include accounts of fornication, although he did marry Hittite women who were a thorn in the side of his parents (Gen 26:34-35). That he was "profane" is reflected in his giving up his rights as the firstborn son in exchange for a single meal. While food in particular may not be a problem for the readers (13:9), the primary thrust of the warning is inescapable: Some of those who are in line to inherit salvation and all the promises of God (1:14; 6:12, 17; 9:15; 11:7-8) are in danger of relinquishing it all for something worthless by comparison.

12:17. Here the warning centering around the tragic case of Esau is extended beyond his bartering away his birthright to his second great loss, the blessing of his father, Isaac (Gen 27:30-40). That this is a separate episode is implied in the writer's use of the word "later." The writer uses the important word "inherit," although it does not appear in the biblical record, because it is so appropriate to the reader's situation (see Commentary on 12:16). Esau's attempt to persuade his father to reverse the earlier act of giving the blessing to Jacob was futile. He "found no place of repentance."[144] Although the expression could be read "he could bring about no change of mind" (NIV; that is, he could not get his father to change his mind, NRSV footnote), it is more likely that repentance here refers to Esau: "he found no chance to repent" (NRSV). The account in Genesis 27 speaks of Esau's weeping (vv. 34, 38), but there is no word about attempts to repent. This is the writer's extension of the story in order more directly to address the church to whom it has already been said, "It is impossible to renew again to repentance" (6:4). The final clause, "he sought it with tears" leaves open the antecedent of "it"; both "blessing" and "repentance" are possible. Both the NRSV and the NIV render it "blessing," but "repentance" is not out of the question, given the writer's strong stand that a second repentance is not an option for the people of God.[145]

---

143. See Attridge, *A Commentary on the Epistle to the Hebrews*, 368, for the various possible explanations.

144. An idiom meaning "no opportunity to repent"; cf. Wis 12:10; *1 Clem* 7:5.

145. Attridge, *A Commentary on the Epistle to the Hebrews*, 370, holds this position.

REFLECTIONS

1. The role of the historical Jesus in the life and faith of the Christian community presents itself again in 12:1-3. Earlier at 2:9-18; 4:15; 5:7-9, this important consideration was brought to the reader's attention. At those points the writer made it clear that for Christ to be an effective high priest on our behalf, it was essential that he be not only "of God" but also "of us." His capacity for sympathy and the efficacy of his intercession depended on his experiencing our flesh and blood, our trials, our suffering, and our death. To that discussion the writer now adds what was implied but not so directly stated: the role of Jesus as example. To be sure, Jesus as example does not consume without remainder the writer's christology: Jesus Christ is the pre-existent agent of creation, God's revelation in these last days, God's Son, and our High Priest, whose offering of himself and continuing intercession make possible our salvation and access to God. Even so, to look to Jesus as the model of endurance in the face of hostility, verbal abuse, and shame is no small dimension of New Testament christology. Of course, the dominant voice has been that of Paul, whose gospel of Jesus' death, burial, and resurrection (1 Cor 15:3-8) has so influenced subsequent preaching that even the four Gospels have been viewed in many quarters as but a preface to the "real" message. Even the Apostles' Creed has no word about Jesus between "born of the virgin Mary" and "suffered under Pontius Pilate." Hebrews insists that the Jesus between birth and death is vital for the life of the church.

2. The teacher or preacher will want to reflect carefully on the dominant theme of 12:1-13: endurance. Like self-control, endurance is among those virtues almost totally silenced by the triumph of intuition, feeling, freedom, immediate gratification, and self-expression. Whether endurance has been permanently replaced on the church's virtue list, and with the minister's blessing, or whether the church has too long been held hostage to feelings is a matter for the preacher to ponder. If it is determined that endurance should be reactivated, then the one who attempts to do so must be willing to "endure." For a time the word will strike the ears of many as antiquated, as old as the Bible and no newer than the Great Depression of the 1930s. But, of course, the rehabilitation of endurance will require much more than pronouncing the word several times in a sermon. For the word to have life and meaning again it will be essential for the Christian life to be so portrayed that endurance will be called for. To this presentation of the life of faith as making its way in the world and for the world, Jesus will speak, as will the cloud of witnesses who preceded him.

3. Hebrews 12:4-11 interprets the suffering of the readers as God's discipline, painful, to be sure, but to be understood within the relationship of parent and child. Discipline is an ingredient to parental love, says the writer, having as its goal education, character formation, and growth. This passage is an important piece in Scripture's attempts to address the problem of suffering. However, it is important to understand that this text is but one of many voices in Scripture and should be presented as such. The writer of Hebrews is not offering an overarching theology of suffering. Not all suffering, but the particular kind of suffering being experienced by one congregation is being addressed; not all interpretations of human suffering, but one way of understanding their suffering is being offered. When or where or if this understanding is presented to another congregation is a matter of appropriateness that is usually the minister's responsibility to determine.

HEBREWS 12:18–13:19
FINAL EXHORTATIONS

OVERVIEW

The final section of Hebrews consists of two units, 12:18-29 and 13:1-19. In the first, the writer gathers up themes and motifs from the body of the epistle in a rhetorical flourish that is in many ways the climax of the entire message. The flourish is substantive, not decorative or emptily dramatic. It involves two extended metaphors, Mount Sinai and Mount Zion, sharply contrasted under two verbs: "you have not come" (v. 18) and "you have come" (v. 22). The homiletical style is reminiscent of Paul's allegory of Hagar and Sarah, slavery and freedom, the earthly Jerusalem and the Jerusalem that is above (Gal 4:21-31).

Here Mount Sinai recalls all that has been said in the letter about the exodus, the wilderness wanderings, the levitical cultus, the first covenant, and unfulfilled longings. Drawing on descriptions of the theophany at Sinai (Exodus 19–20; Deuteronomy 4–5) and theologically recasting them in the light of life under the new covenant, the writer pictures Israel's experience of God at Sinai as an experience of the distant and inaccessible. The terrifying and dreadful nature of the occasion is underscored by natural disasters, trumpet blasts, and a frightening voice without face or form. The readers, however, are as pilgrims who have come to Zion, the heavenly Jerusalem in festive assembly with God, with Jesus, whose self-offering has made possible this accessibility to God's presence, with all the saints, and with angels in joyful song. But again the church is warned by means of the familiar argument of lesser to greater (12:25-29; cf. 2:2-3; 12:9-10). Christians have not arrived at a soft and permissive place; the proper posture is not chumminess with God but worship in reverence and awe. God remains "a consuming fire" (v. 29).

The second unit (13:1-19) consists of a collection of exhortations touching on, without elaboration, a range of subjects that together sketch the life-style that is appropriate to those engaged in "acceptable worship" (v. 28). Because these exhortations are presented in the traditional form of moral and ethical instruction, such as one finds in Pauline and other epistles, and because they seem "attached" to chaps. 1–12 without so much as a transitional sentence or phrase, various theories about later editorial hands have been spawned. For example, did a later scribe, in order to get this homily accepted in the larger church, add to it a Pauline-like ending? The fact remains, however, that this material is there and we have no manuscript of Hebrews without it. There is no reason why the preacher, unable to be present for the delivery of this "word of exhortation" (13:22), did not do what absent preachers do—that is, make the homily a letter to be read to the church, concluding with appropriate remarks pastoral and personal. None of the exhortations is out of line with the message of the epistle; in fact, 13:10-19 recalls again the essential language and imagery of the central argument of the sermon.[146]

---

146. For a discussion of chap. 13 as part of the letter, see the Introduction and the excellent study by Filson, *"Yesterday," A Study of Hebrews in the Light of Chapter 13*.

HEBREWS 12:18-29, ZION, THE UNSHAKABLE KINGDOM

COMMENTARY

Chapter 12 concludes with two sharp contrasts, that which is palpable (can be touched) and that which is heavenly (vv. 18-24), and that which is shaken and that which cannot be shaken (vv. 25-29).

12:18-21. The first contrast is between Mount Sinai and Mount Zion, even though Mount Sinai is not named (some MSS have "mountain" in v. 18). Details of the description of the theophany at Sinai are taken primarily from Exod 19:16-22; 20:18-21; Deut 4:11-12; 5:22-27; 9:19, although "gloom" is probably the writer's contribution to the scene, and "palpable" is borrowed from the description of the plague of darkness in Egypt (Exod 10:21; cf. Luke 24:39; 1 John 1:1). The condensation of the several accounts into one sentence (Greek text, vv. 18-21) makes the event even more terrifying. Of course, this is the effect desired by the writer. The traditional symbols of God's presence are all here—wind, fire, and thick darkness—but the net effect is that the people cannot bear it: "Do not let God speak to us or we shall die" (Exod 20:19). If even an animal barely touched the mountain, it would be stoned to death (Exod 19:13); the reader can conclude what the fate of a person would be. The writer's point is unavoidable: The conditions under which the old covenant was given were dread, fear, distance, and exclusion (Exod 19:23). The old tabernacle, with its curtain, preserved the features of distance, exclusion, and inaccessibility.

12:22-24. The second half of this first contrast opens with an expression parallel to v. 18: "You have not come. You have come." The verb "come" (προσέρχομαι *prosercho-mai*) is cultic, referring to one's approach in worship, and its tense is perfect, implying an action begun and continuing. If worship is the means of drawing near, no details of the modes or elements of worship are provided.

As impressive, however, as were the details of the description of Mount Sinai are the details of the destination of the pilgrim Christians. Mount Zion, the city of the living God, and heavenly Jerusalem are in reality a single eschatological reference. Since the time of David, Zion and Jerusalem were regarded as the location of God's presence, sometimes both being named, sometimes one or the other (Ps 2:6; Isa 8:18; Mic 4:1; Joel 2:32; 3:16-17). Of course, the writer has in mind the heavenly Jerusalem, the city for which the faithful long (11:10, 16). Within the heavenly city are "myriads of angels," the thousands upon thousands of angels who fill God's court and attend God's self-disclosures (Deut 33:2; Ps 68:17-18; Dan 7:10; Rev 5:11). The angels are in "festal gathering;"[147] that is, in joyous celebration (festivals were a staple in Israel's worship, Hos 9:5; Amos 5:21). The term "panegyric" (πανήγυρις *panēgyris*) occurs only here in the NT. The assembly ("congregation," "church" 2:12) of the "firstborn" has two strong connotations: The firstborn receive the inheritance (12:16), an important theme in Hebrews; and they share in the benefits of him who is the Firstborn of God (1:6; cf. Col 1:15, 18). That they have been entered in God's registry is a familiar biblical image (Exod 32:32; Dan 12:1; Luke 10:20; Rev 13:18; 17:8). That "you have come" to "a judge, God of all" (a better rendering of the word order than "God, judge of all") is in this context a positive and welcome experience. The judge is the God of all, and, therefore, the believers can anticipate fairness, impartiality, and vindication as well as condemnation. Those who trust God do not fear the day of judgment.

The spirits of the righteous being in the presence of God is a traditional figure (Wis 3:1; Rev 6:9-10), but to it the writer joins a familiar theme: perfection. This means the righteous dead have completed their pilgrimage, to be joined by the faithful readers who have been given access to God through the

---

147. Whether "festal gathering" is to be joined to the angels, to the assembly of the firstborn, or is to stand alone is not clear. See the footnote in the NRSV.

self-offering of Christ (10:14; 11:40), who was himself perfected through what he suffered (2:10). The final image in the list of the blessings to which the readers "have come" is that of Jesus and his sprinkled blood. The use of the name "Jesus" recalls his suffering humanity (2:9; 12:2); the entire expression evokes the imagery and argument of chaps. 8–9, where Jesus is portrayed as the mediator of the new covenant whose sprinkled blood cleanses our hearts (10:22) and completes the new covenant with God. That the blood of Jesus speaks a better word than that of Abel should not be read as a contrast but as a comparison. This is to say, the reference to Abel recalls 11:4, which refers to his acceptable sacrifice of an animal (Gen 4:4) rather than to Gen 4:10, which says that Abel's own spilled blood cried out for revenge against Cain. In this sense, the message of Christ's blood is "better than" (a favorite phrase of Hebrews) rather than "different from" Abel's.

12:25. The vivid language of vv. 18-24 becomes the basis from which to launch a strong warning ("see to it," "watch it"). The contrast between Sinai and Zion continues as a contrast between earth and heaven, between what will be shaken and what cannot be shaken. Such a warning is not new to Hebrews (3:12; and with a different word for "be watchful," 12:15-16). At v. 19, Israel at Sinai begged that God speak no more to them; at v. 25, they reject the one speaking. The seriousness of that refusal and its warning to the readers is made even more clear by the recollection that the God of Hebrews is the One who speaks (1:1; 2:1-4; 3:7-8a; 4:12-13). In a now familiar argument from lesser to greater (2:2-4; 10:26-29), the author again contrasts Israel and the readers. The writer has earlier made it abundantly clear that the unbelieving and disobedient people did not escape God's punishment (2:3; 3:16-18; 4:11; 10:27-28). How unreasonable, then, to think that we will escape if we refuse the voice from heaven. In both cases the voice is God's, but the writer does not think it necessary to repeat the differences, both in benefits and in obligations, between the old and earthly and the new and heavenly (9:1-14, 23-28). To reject, to refuse, to turn away from recalls the warnings about apostasy in 6:6-8, 10:26-31, and perhaps 12:15-17.

12:26-27. The earth/heaven contrast becomes a then/now contrast, introducing the quotation of Hag 2:6. The theophany at Sinai caused the earth to shake (though not in Exodus 19–20; other references to the event include the language, Judg 5:4; Ps 68:8). The shaking of the earth became a common feature of descriptions of theophanies (Ps 18:7; Isa 6:4; Amos 9:5; Matt 27:51). Thus the language of "shaking," used to introduce Hag 2:6, then found within the quotation itself, and finally in the homiletical exposition of the quotation, governs the closing lines of chap. 12. Haggai 2:6 was the prophet's word of assurance concerning the future splendor of the Temple in a time of great confusion and disappointment. The writer of Hebrews quotes only one-half of the verse, from the LXX and with slight modifications, to point to an eschatological shaking of the old universe, its totality being expressed as "not only the earth but also the heaven."[148] This, says the writer, is what God has "promised," extending the meaning of Hag 2:6 beyond the shaking of the nations to the shaking of all creation (v. 27). To support this interpretation, the adverbial "yet once more" of the quotation is cited.

In the eschatological convulsion, all created things will be removed. Creation is here portrayed, not as evil or corrupt, but as temporal and transient, just as heaven and earth were portrayed in 1:10-12, in contrast to the eternality of God and God's Son. All that will remain will be that which cannot be shaken. Verses 26-27 do not seem to present the sequence of the end of the old heaven and earth and the beginning of the new as in some biblical writings (Isa 65:17; 1 Cor 7:21; 2 Pet 3:10; Rev 21:1). What is unshakable has been there all along but will be fully and finally evident after the removal of all that is temporary. This contrast again echoes Ps 102:25-27, cited at 1:10-12 and implied in the contrasts running through the central argument of the epistle. Those things that "remain" (v. 27), that are constant and unshakable, are God's Son (1:11), Christ the high priest like Melchizedek (5:6; 6:20; 7:3; 10:13-14), the lasting possession of those

---

148. "Heaven" here is used in the sense of the far reaches of creation, as in 1:10, and not the heaven of God's throne, the true tabernacle, and Christ's continuing presence (9:24).

who remain faithful (10:34), and the city that abides forever (11:10, 16; 13:14). Christ's continuing priesthood and the benefits of that priesthood, which will accrue to those who endure, are unshakable because they are established in the unchangeable character and purpose of God (6:17-19).

12:28. The quotation of Hag 2:6 with homiletical commentary leads naturally into an exhortation: "Since we are receiving a kingdom [a phrase from Dan 7:10] that cannot be shaken" (ἀσάλευτος *asaleutos*; strikingly the verb "are receiving" (παραλαμβάνοντες *paralambanontes*) is present tense). Again the future is balanced with the present, because the event that determines the eschaton has already occurred and the community of faith is already participating in its benefits (4:14-16; 9:14; 10:19-22). From the community's perspective the access to God already available is lived out in their worship, and worship that pleases God (13:16, 21; recall Enoch, 11:5) is marked by gratitude, reverence, and awe. Giving thanks (ἔχωμεν χάριν *echōmen charin*; lit., "have gratitude"; cf. Luke 17:9; 1 Tim 1:12; 2 Tim 1:3) is the overall framework for "offering service" (liturgical), an expression already familiar (8:5; 9:9; 10:2). Reverence and awe inject into Christian worship reminders that it is God whom we approach. It was with reverence that Noah received the warning of a flood to come (11:7), and it was with reverence that Jesus cried out to the God who could save him from death (5:7). The word "awe" (δεός *deos*) is even more sobering. It appears only here in the NT, but it occurs in the LXX in scenes of terror and trembling (2 Macc 3:17, 30; 12:22; 13:16; 15:23). Obviously the writer is thinking ahead to the next statement (v. 29), which reminds the reader that the reason for reverence and awe lies in an ancient portrayal of God that is not lightly to be dismissed on the grounds that we are Christians and not Israelites.

12:29. This verse is a quotation of Deut 4:24*a*, modified so as to address the present audience, among whom the writer is included ("our God" for "your God"). In biblical texts, fire is often associated with the presence of God (1:7; 12:18; Acts 2:3; Joel 2:3; Sir 45:19), and especially in scenes of judgment (6:8; Matt 25:41; 1 Cor 3:13; 2 Thess 1:7-8; 2 Pet 3:7). The writer apparently thought it appropriate to conclude this exhortation with the same stern voice with which 10:26-31 ended, not simply because of the nature of worship that reveres the awesomeness of God, but because of pastoral concern for a church plagued by neglect, apathy, absenteeism, retreat, and near the point of apostasy. But as is this preacher's custom, stern warnings are followed by more positive words of instruction and encouragement.

REFLECTIONS

1. Rhetoricians have long known that vivid contrasts are more effective as a communication strategy than are coordinated words and phrases. Contrasts can be dangerous, however, in that they invite overextension and loss of precision in the effort to have the greatest possible effect on the audience. Therefore, in dealing with passages, such as Heb 12:18-29, that are structured on a series of contrasts, the preacher will want to be careful. First, it is important to be reminded that both Sinai and Zion, the earthly and the heavenly, the then and the now, the shakable and the unshakable, have their source in God. This realization will serve as a guard against improper value judgments, such as evil and good, false and true, corrupt and pure. Second, one wants to locate the true points of contrast. For example, the author does not place in opposition the objective and the subjective, as though Israel's law and cultus were concerned only with things and with activities while the Christians attend to the heart. Nothing could be farther from the writer's message.

The author does sharply contrast the transient and the permanent. There is a transiency about all the order of creation, but there is another order of reality, apprehended by faith (11:1), that has its center in God and in God's Son, who has made available the believer's access to God. And the writer does sharply contrast those who have refused to listen to God and those who do listen. This contrast is presented, not to blame and to praise but to warn. Obstinacy is not confined to the past, nor is it a trait peculiar to persons at whom the finger can be pointed. The readers, therefore, are not to be proud by reason of some advantage; rather, they are to be humbled by the realization of greater responsibility borne by those to whom much is given.

2. The present and practical side to the grand eschatological image of God's dwelling place is the worship of the Christian community (v. 28). Worship is the means by which the church in its present life draws near to God. Worshipers approach God with confidence, knowing that in Jesus our priest we will find mercy and grace to help (4:14-16). This understanding infuses every word and act of worship with gratitude (v. 28). But never does the worshiper forget that it is God whom we approach and that, therefore, the service is offered in reverence and awe (v. 28). A service of worship is designed and implemented so as to be appropriate to the nature of God. Unless worshipers are informed and led in ways that have their reasons in theology and christology, preferences in music, texts, and preaching, while satisfying certain appetites, may fall short of "acceptable worship." The image of "a consuming fire" (v. 29), while jolting and distancing at first, reminds a congregation that has grown neglectful, apathetic, dull of hearing, and indifferent toward its own gatherings (10:25) that its life of worship is not to sink into that same carelessness. In fact, 12:28-29 may also be understood to imply that designing worship that abandons gratitude, reverence, and awe in order to please passing tastes may meet with some applause but fail in what is acceptable to God.

HEBREWS 13:1-19, LIFE IN THE FAITH COMMUNITY

OVERVIEW

Chapter 13 has long presented readers of Hebrews two literary problems: the relationship between this chapter and chapters 1–12, and the internal unity of 13:1-25. As for the first problem, that 13:1 represents a noticeable shift in style, is without question. In fact, one would hardly be justified in calling Hebrews an epistle were it not for chapter 13. Here alone are epistolary traits to be found: traditional parenesis (moral imperatives and instructions), benediction, and farewell. But these characteristics do not argue persuasively for a different author or, as Buchanan contends,[149] a different author and a different audience. The author of chaps. 1–12, unable to be present to deliver the sermon, may well have concluded it as a letter to be read to the congregation. Since many epistolary features are traditional, it is to be expected that 13:1-25 would bear resemblances to letters of Paul, resemblances that have through the centuries persuaded some that Hebrews was written by Paul or by a scribe imitating Paul in order to win for Hebrews a place in the canon. Such theories have not been finally convincing to most students of Hebrews. See comments on this literary problem in the introduction to this section (12:18–13:19) and the Introduction to the entire epistle.

The second literary problem, the internal unity of 13:1-25, is one that arises out of all traditional parenetic material, which consists of a series of discrete admonitions that seem unrelated to each other and easily portable to

149. Buchanan, *Hebrews*, 267.

a variety of congregations. The same is true of benedictions and blessings, some of which became embedded early in Christian liturgy. And the presence of exposition (vv. 10-16) within parenesis does not fragment the chapter. The writer has repeatedly used exegesis and exposition for hortatory purposes. The numerous attempts to discover a format or rhythm by which to make a unit of 13:1-25[150] are to varying degrees attractive but actually unnecessary, given the nature of epistolary conclusions. The commentary will treat vv. 1-19 in four parts: vv. 1-6; vv. 7-8; vv. 9-16; and vv. 17-19.

150. Fairly presented and clearly displayed by Lane, *Hebrews 9–13*, 499-505.

Hebrews 13:1-6, Mutual Duties

COMMENTARY

These six verses consist of four couplets, each stating a pair of related exhortations with comments interspersed that provide support and motive for the action enjoined.

13:1-2. The first set of twin injunctions have to do with love of brothers and sisters and love of strangers. Here the writer joins related words that are often seen transliterated into English as *philadelphia* (φιλαδελφία) and *philoxenia* (φιλοξενία). Familial language had been used earlier to characterize the relationships of the church members to each other (3:1, 12; 10:19) and in so doing reflects the practice of the larger Christian community (Rom 12:10; 1 Thess 4:9; 1 Pet 1:22). That love of brothers and sisters is to "remain" ("continue," NRSV) recalls 12:27 and gently reminds the reader that among those things that cannot be shaken is the mutual love within the covenant community. But this mutuality is not a closed circle; love of strangers is not to be "forgotten" (NIV; "neglected," NRSV).

The strangers in mind here are most likely the itinerant Christians who depended on local Christian communities for hospitality (Matt 25:35; Rom 12:13; 1 Tim 3:2; 1 Pet 4:9). It is understandable, however, why some house churches, either living in an atmosphere of suspicion due to opposition and persecution from society or facing the upheavals created by traveling heretics, would become reticent about extending hospitality. Some even used certain criteria for testing strangers before welcoming them (3 John 9-10; *Didache* 11).[151] These injunctions to love fellow members and strangers should not be taken automatically as implying that these were problem areas for this congregation. Closing parenesis was too traditional and too broad in its address to provide such specific indicators, unless the document elsewhere confirmed them. The neglect of the church assemblies by some (10:25) hardly provides that evidence.

The exhortation to hospitality is supported by an encouraging reminder that in the past some who practiced hospitality had, without being aware of it, welcomed angels. The implication is that such a pleasant and blessed possibility existed for the readers. The allusion is most likely to Abraham and Sarah's welcoming of three visitors who brought the good news of a promised son (Gen 18:1-21), but there are other stories of hospitality to mysterious strangers (Gen 19:1-14; Judg 6:11-18; 13:3-22; Tob 12:1-20). It is regrettable that translations of vv. 1-2 are unable to reflect the remarkable kinship among key words in the passage; in addition to the twin terms for "love of brothers and sisters" and "love of strangers" (noted above), the words φιλοξενία (*philoxenia*) and ξενίζω (*xenizō*), translated "hospitality" and "entertained," have the same stem, as do the expressions "neglect" ("forget," ἐπιλάνθανομαι *epilanthanomai*) and "without knowing it" (λανθάνω *lanthanō*). The rhetorical pleasure provided by the passage in no way dulls the edge of its imperatives.

13:3. Just as the latter half of the first couplet is driven by the directive "Do not forget," so also the second couplet begins with the directive "Remember." To be remembered

151. For further study, see John Koenig, *New Testament Hospitality* (Philadelphia: Fortress, 1985).

are those of their number in prison[152] and those being mistreated. This imperative is not satisfied by a moment of silence in the assembly, or solely by intercessory prayer, although that would certainly be expected. Rather, remembering involves full solidarity with those imprisoned and those suffering at the hands of others. The author had spoken with appreciation earlier of the readers' partnership with those suffering public abuse (10:33) and compassion for the imprisoned (10:34). Here the language of solidarity is even stronger: Behave as though you yourselves were in prison with them, as though you yourselves were being mistreated. Literally, this last phrase is "as though you yourselves were in the body." Although "the body" (σῶμα *sōma*) conjures up Paul's metaphor for the church, it is not likely that the writer has that in mind. The meaning parallels the first half of the couplet: As you are to join those in prison, so you are to be in the body of those being made to suffer. To do so requires more than a sympathetic ache; it means refusing to distance oneself from those suffering out of fear of becoming the target of the same mistreatment, providing for the needs of prisoners (prisoners depended on those outside for food, clothing, and all other needs), even though this meant exposing oneself as a fellow Christian, and being present with the sufferers in every way that might encourage and give relief. Even intercession with local authorities would not be out of the question. The word translated "tortured" (κακοήθεια *kakoētheia*) was used earlier at 11:25 and 37 and hence serves as a reminder to the readers that they are in the good company of Moses, who shared the sufferings of the people of God, and of the forebears in faith, "of whom the world was not worthy" (11:38).

13:4. The third couplet focuses on marriage and, in particular, on the sexual relationship within marriage ("the marriage bed"). There are no reasons within the text of Hebrews for assuming that there were strong advocates of celibacy within the congregation (as reflected in 1 Tim 4:3), or that the mutual love urged in v. 1 in some way threatened marriage vows. The Christian community continued Judaism's high regard for marriage and its strong prohibition against adultery, the violation of the marriage vow (Exod 20:14). The Roman governor Pliny, investigating the Christian community in Bithynia early in the second century, reported to Emperor Trajan that Christians bound themselves with an oath that included, among other things, abstaining from adultery.[153] In this virtue the Jews and Christians had the support of Greek moralists.

In saying that the marriage relationship should be "undefiled" the writer reverts to the cultic language so pervasive in Hebrews. By so doing, the author brings marriage into the circle of sanctification essential to worship that is acceptable to God (12:28). This directive about marriage is given support by a reminder that God judges fornicators (a general reference to sexual immorality) as well as adulterers (a specific reference to a breach of marriage vows). Fornication seems to have been a widespread concern in the early church, perhaps because of a lack of clear instructions about sex among the unmarried (Acts 15:28-29; 1 Cor 5:9-11; Eph 5:3, 5; 1 Thess 4:3-7; 1 Tim 1:10; Rev 21:8; 22:15).

13:5-6. The fourth and final couplet in vv. 1-6 concerns money, or more accurately the love of money. The accents fall on two terms: "without love of money" (the negative form of the word used in 1 Tim 6:10, "the love of money is a root of all kinds of evil" [NRSV]) and "be content." Contentment with what one had was a commonplace in Greek morality and was embraced by early Christians (Luke 3:14; Phil 4:11; 1 Tim 6:8). These exhortations fall within the general instructions to Christians concerning material possessions, instructions traced back to Jesus himself (Matt 6:19-21, 24-34; Luke 10:22-34) and echoed in many warnings to the churches about greed (Eph 5:3, 5; 1 Cor 5:10 among many). The writer's addressing the problems of sexual misconduct and greed together is probably due not so much to the frequent companionship between these two vices in society but to the prohibitions against them in the seventh and eighth of the Ten Commandments (Exod 20:14-15), setting the pattern for subsequent treatments of the subjects.

---

152. Whether or not regard for strangers (v. 2) and prisoners echoes Matt 25:35-36, the exhortations here are fully consistent with the teaching of Jesus in Matthew 25 and elsewhere.

153. Pliny *Letters of Pliny* X.96.

The twin injunctions against greed are supported by two Scripture citations that combine to say that the believer's trust in God makes trust in money not only misplaced but a contradiction of faith as well (recall Matt 6:24-34). The first citation is very likely from Deut 31:6, although similar expressions are found in Gen 28:15; Deut 31:8; Josh 1:5; and 1 Chr 28:20. Hebrews 13:5 does not conform exactly to the LXX in any of these passages. That the same form of the citation is in Philo[154] may indicate a standardizing of the divine promise for synagogue worship. As is typical of the writer of Hebrews, words of Scripture are taken as God's direct word to the readers. The second citation, a quotation of Ps 118:6 (v. 6), appears as the believer's response to God's promise in v. 5. God's promise never to abandon the people gives boldness or confidence (cf. 3:6; 4:16; 10:19, 35) to burst into an affirmation of God-given fearlessness. The words of the psalmist, reciting occasions of God's help in times of great distress, become the church's words, dwelling in its own context of imprisonment and persecution. Thus v. 6 speaks not solely to the issue of dependence on money but to the larger condition of the church's life as described particularly in 10:32-36. In fact, 10:32-36 was also followed immediately with an encouraging quotation of Scripture (10:37-38). (See Reflections at 13:17-19.)

154. Philo *On the Confusion of Tongues* 166.

Hebrews 13:7-8, Examples to Follow

COMMENTARY

The writer's urgings not to forget and to remember, so central in vv. 1-6, continue in v. 7. Benefit for life and fidelity is to be derived from remembering former leaders. Good examples are good teachers, as chap. 11 argued abundantly. There is no indication that these leaders held particular offices or had specific titles, the term used here for "leaders" (ἡγουμένων *hēgoumenōn*) being a general one used not only in religion but also in politics and the military (Luke 22:26; Acts 15:22; Sir 17:17; 1 Macc 9:30). They are identified only by their function: They spoke the Word of God—that is, they preached the gospel (Acts 4:29, 31; Phil 1:14; 1 Pet 4:11). These leaders may have been the founders of the congregation, belonging to the tradition of the word from God, to Jesus, through the apostles, to the community (2:3-4). What is to be considered ("contemplated," "focused upon") is the "outcome" ("result," "end") of their conduct. Obviously, there is some uncertainty here as to precise meaning. The outcome could be the result of their preaching, or it could be a reference to their deaths. Martyrdom may be implied, but more likely the sense is that they were faithful to the end (6:11-12; 10:39). It is their fidelity that is to be imitated. Imitating the faithful had earlier been urged (6:12) and shares in the widespread pattern of instruction by example (1 Cor 11:1; Phil 3:17; 1 Thess 1:6; 2 Thess 3:7-9). This discipleship motif is quite distinctive of Hebrews.

The acclamation of Jesus Christ (on the compound name, see 10:10; 13:21) in v. 8 may be a traditional formula drawn from elsewhere, perhaps from a confession of faith. It echoes the affirmation of Christ's eternal sameness in chap. 1 (1:8, 10-12) but draws upon other liturgical language for its expression here (e.g., Rev 1:4, 8; 4:8; "forever" ["to the ages"] is common in early Christian praise, see Luke 1:33; Rom 1:25; 9:5; 11:36; Phil 4:20; Heb 13:21). The point of the acclamation is the sameness of Christ, which can anchor the fidelity of the church. However, some commentators break the expression into three parts, finding in it three phases of the christology of Hebrews,[155] an analysis interesting but unnecessary to the function of the formula at 13:8. The function seems to be a double one. In relation to v. 7, it says that the faithful leaders whose fidelity was exemplary have passed on, but Jesus Christ, whom they preached, has not; he remains eternally the same. This

155. As does Bruce, *The Epistle to the Hebrews*, 396: yesterday (5:7), today (4:14-16), and forever (7:25).

connection with the preceding verse recalls the sequence of chap. 11 and 12:1-2: Faithful models have died in faith, but Jesus Christ is the one to whom we look. The other function of v. 8 is to prepare for v. 9 by way of sharp contrast. The eternal sameness of Jesus Christ is the place to stand when the congregation is called on to deal with "all kinds of strange teachings." (See Reflections at 13:17-19.)

Hebrews 13:9-16, Christ's Sacrifice Revisited

COMMENTARY

13:9. In vv. 7-8 the writer presented a clear and strong image of unity, stability, and certainty. Now the very opposite picture appears: Teachings are being held before the readers that are "multiple" (the only occurrence of this word in the plural in the NT), "diverse" (Titus 3:3), and "strange" ("foreign"). The warning not to be "carried away" (Jude 12) by such teaching became a rather standard warning in battles against heresy (Eph 4:14-16; Col 2:8; 1 Tim 1:3-7). The assumption is that the congregation has been grounded in a body of traditional instruction (6:1-2) and that what is being offered from unnamed, unidentified sources is contrary to that instruction. All that is said specifically is that these teachings have to do with foods, the eating of which is promoted as a substitute for or as a vital supplement to the grace by which they are saved. The author flatly denies that any benefit accrues to those who participate in such meals. The issue for the interpreter is the identification of those meals.

That problems arose in some congregations over meals (what to eat, who is to eat, and the manner of eating) is evident from other writings (Acts 11:3; 15:20; Romans 14; 1 Corinthians 8; 10–11), but those references assure no clear meaning here in Hebrews. There were ritual meals in Hellenistic religions that held some attraction, as well as confusion, for some Christians (1 Corinthians 10). All Jewish meals have a ritual and numinous meaning, but the writer has already made it clear that food and drink and practices of the body "cannot perfect the conscience of the worshiper" (9:9-10). It could have been that some members of the congregation with a background in Judaism continued certain ritual meals, finding them at least supplementally efficacious. Of course, for the author such exercises had no place among people of the new covenant. Another possibility is that the issue over food was due to an interpretation of the Lord's supper that the writer regarded as a contradiction of the grace extended by the sacrifice of Christ. If some were making the Lord's supper a sacrificial meal with meanings drawn from either Jewish or Hellenistic influences, then perhaps the author regarded such an interpretation a contradiction of the once-and-for-all nature of Christ's sacrifice.[156] At any rate, it is important to note that the statement in v. 9 is not polemical, as though there were a heretical intrusion threatening the congregation, but is rather pastoral exhortation, instructing and correcting. Whatever the nature and the extent of the influence of these diverse and foreign teachings, the writer apparently believes the best response is a brief revisit to the sacrifice of Christ, from which new implications for the lives of the readers can be drawn (vv. 10-16).

13:10-12. As has been done frequently throughout the sermon, the preacher shifts to exposition, but it is exposition in the service of exhortation. This brief exposition is centered by the opening affirmation, "We have an altar." The expression "we have" (ἔχομεν *echomen*) is used frequently in Hebrews and has a confessional quality (4:15; 6:19; 8:1; 10:19). Verse 10 raises two questions for the interpreter: What is the altar? And who are they who have no right to eat? On either question there is no unanimity among students of Hebrews. From the second century the tradition that the altar is the eucharistic table has persisted, embraced primarily by the Roman Catholic Church. However, v. 9 and the whole of Hebrews make it difficult

---

156. For a discussion of the alternative views, see Filson, *"Yesterday," A Study of Hebrews in the Light of Chapter 13*, 50-54, and the excursus in Attridge, *A Commentary on the Epistle to the Hebrews*, 394-96.

to support the idea of a sacrificial table in the church addressed. Other views include the cross and the heavenly sanctuary. These two interpretations are not totally separate, since the writer has been careful throughout to make clear that the priestly work of Christ includes both his death on the cross and his continuing intercession before God on our behalf.

Given the lengthy argument distinguishing old covenant from new, old priesthood from new, earthly tent from heavenly one in 7:1–10:18, it seems wisest to understand our "altar" in a metaphorical sense; that is, as the place of our having received and continuing to receive the grace of God through the high priesthood of Christ. The writer does not support any practice in the congregation that either continues levitical rituals or seeks to imitate them. Our altar is in the heavenly sanctuary where Christ is, having gained for us access to God. That the author is sustaining the contrasts of 7:1–10:18 is evident in the description of those who have no right to "our altar": "those who serve in the tent [tabernacle]." The author is recalling 8:5 and 9:1-10, and as the following verses further clarify, the Day of Atonement serves as the specific place of contrast. To say that the writer is antisacramental is hardly justified, but the return to the language of contrast does show, as v. 9 indicates, opposition to some practices or views to which the congregation is exposed that either continue Jewish ritual meals or confuse Christian meals by giving them old levitical interpretations.

In vv. 11-12, the readers are asked again to recall the Day of Atonement (9:1-14; Leviticus 16). The central figure is the high priest, the place is the sanctuary (the writer again uses the term that refers to the inner chamber of the tabernacle), and the act is the sprinkling of blood on the mercy seat as a sacrifice for sin. But the writer has dealt with this earlier and needs to discuss it no further. The present point is that the bodies of the sacrificial animals were not eaten by the high priest but were burned outside the camp (Lev 16:27). In other words, not even the sacrifices under the old system were eaten, so, by implication, why would Christians interpret their participation in the sacrifice of Christ as a ritual meal in which Christ is regarded as a food? If some are attempting to bring into the congregation an interpretation borrowed from the levitical system, they need to read again Leviticus 16; there was no meal of the sacrifices. That Jesus sanctified others (2:11; 9:13-14; 10:10, 14, 29) by his own blood is here a reminder of a previous argument and not a new one. The new element here is that Jesus fulfilled the service of the Day of Atonement in one other regard: He suffered "outside the city gate," the equivalent of "outside the camp." The writer again reveals some knowledge of the tradition about the historical Jesus (John 19:20 and at least implied at Matt 27:32; Mark 15:20; John 19:17). On this unusual historical note the author concludes the exposition (vv. 10-12), resuming the exhortation at v. 13, and drawing on the exposition for the focus of the paraenesis.

13:13-16. The writer draws three injunctions: "Let us" (v. 13), "Let us" (v. 15), and "Do not forget" (v. 16), the last being the very verb used at v. 2 to launch this hortatory unit. Concluding on a note sounded at a beginning (called an inclusio) is a common literary pattern for this author. All three injunctions employ the language of the cultus reintroduced at v. 10 (perhaps at v. 9). The first draws directly on the reference from the ceremony of the Day of Atonement analogy; that is, Jesus died "outside the camp," outside the sacred precinct. It was outside that animal carcasses were destroyed and criminals were executed (Lev 24:14, 23; Num 15:35-36; Deut 22:24). Just as the writer had earlier spoken of the manner of Jesus' death as one of shame and disgrace (12:2), so here the place of his death is one of "abuse" ("reproach," "disgrace"; used of Moses at 11:26). And just as the readers were called on to "look to" the Jesus on the cross of shame (12:2), so here they are called on to "go to him" and bear his abuse outside the camp (v. 13).

Going to Jesus outside the camp has been variously interpreted. Some commentators take it in its immediate contextual sense as leaving all attachment to the rituals and places of Judaism, as some of the members seem loathe to do (vv. 9-10). Others find here a larger application, and that is to turn loose of all the securities and certainties offered by those institutions that cushion believers from the risk taking that discipleship involves.

This view is roughly equivalent to the calls for cross bearing and losing one's life that are found in the Gospels (Matt 10:38; Mark 8:34; Luke 14:26-27).[157]

It is likely that v. 14 supplies a sufficient interpretation. To go to Jesus outside the camp is to join Abraham and all the company of faith pilgrims who left a homeland in search of the homeland, who left a city in search of the city (11:8-16). By declaring themselves strangers and aliens on the earth (11:13), they took on the abuse that goes with the life of a pilgrim, which is to be without identity, without status, without place in the world. In other words, they suffered shame and public abuse (see Commentary on 11:13-16). It is evident that the readers have already experienced such treatment (10:32-34; 13:3). What is not evident is whether they will endure to the end.

The second injunction (v. 15) drawing on the rich cultic language of both the immediate and larger contexts calls on the readers not to allow the abuse and shame heaped on them to define who they are and to sever their relation to God. On the contrary, through the one who calls out the church to the pilgrim life, a continual sacrifice of praise is to be offered to God. Both "sacrifice" and "fruit of lips" were expressions used in Judaism to characterize genuine worship of God, which did not always rely on material offerings (Hos 14:3; Pss 50:14, 23; 107:22; see also Pss 34:1; 71:8; 145:21). Here such unending praise is characterized as being "through him" (Christ) and "confessing his name" (3:1; 4:14; 10:23). In the context of public abuse and ridicule, confessing the name of the one who has through similar suffering provided access to God and there established our altar is a clear demonstration of the boldness and confidence appropriate to the people of God.

The third and final admonition of this unit (v. 16) enlarges on the cultic image of sacrifice to include non-cultic activities in the congregation: doing good (εὐποιΐα *eupoiia*; the only use of this word in the Scriptures) and fellowship or sharing (κοινωνία *koinōnia*). This sharing was as total as love of brothers and sisters and the embrace of strangers implied: goods, ministry, worship (Acts 2:42; Rom 15:26; 1 Cor 10:16; 2 Cor 9:13; Phil 1:5; 1 John 1:3, 7). Paul viewed the Christian life itself as an act of worship (Rom 12:1) as he did his ministry among the Gentiles (Rom 15:16). In summary, the life of continual praise (v. 15), of doing what benefits others, and of sharing with the other members of the congregation in full partnership (v. 16) is an elaboration on the author's expression at 12:28: "We offer to God an acceptable [pleasing] worship with reverence and awe." (See Reflections at 13:17-19.)

---

157. For a summary of views, see Lane, *Hebrews 9–13*, 344-46.

Hebrews 13:17-19, Concerning Your Leaders

COMMENTARY

13:17. Three times "your leaders" are brought to the readers' attention with clear admonitions: remember your leaders who are now deceased (v. 7); greet your leaders (v. 24); and obey your leaders and submit (ὑπείκω *hypeikō*, the only use of this word in the NT) to them. Interestingly, the congregation is always addressed concerning the leaders; the leaders are never addressed concerning the congregation (as in 1 Pet 5:1-5). Again no titles are used, nor is there any indication as to the manner of their assuming roles of leadership. Instructions to congregations concerning their leaders appear early (1 Cor 16:15-18) but not with the directives to be subordinate and obedient, which became commonplace in the generations after the apostles.[158] Clement (c. 100 CE) even uses a military analogy and refers to leaders as "generals."[159] One cannot argue well from silence, but Hebrews seems to be addressed to a time and place that either was unfamiliar with ecclesiastical titles and offices or did not need appeals to such in order to present the congregation's proper relationship to its leaders.

---

158. E.g., *1 Clem* 42:2; Ignatius *To the Trallians* 2:1.
159. *1 Clem* 37:1-5.

There is no indication in these brief notes about leaders that tensions existed or that there was any rebellion against authority. On the contrary, the admonition to obedience and submission is supported by three positive reasons. First, your leaders are keeping sentinel watch ("staying alert," Mark 13:33; Luke 21:36; Eph 6:18) over your souls. The vocabulary is different, but the message is reminiscent of Paul's exhortation to the Ephesian elders (Acts 20:28-31). The writer may have in mind the threat of "strange teachings" (v. 9) as a reason for their keeping alert. Second, your leaders will give account to God for their conduct on your behalf. The expression rendered "give an account" (λόγον ἀποδώσοντες *logon apodōsontes*) is the same as used in Jesus' parable of the clever steward (Luke 16:2; see also Acts 19:40). The accountability of leaders is more forcefully stated in the warning in Jas 3:1 to the effect that teachers will be judged with greater strictness. And finally, your leaders can, with your help, do their work with joy (10:34; 12:2, 11) rather than with groaning (στενάζω *stenazō*; the NRSV's "sighing" is not quite strong enough; cf. this word at Mark 7:34; Rom 8:23; and Jas 5:9, where it means "grumbling"). Hermas may have been echoing Heb 13:17b in the admonition, "Correct therefore one another and be at peace among yourselves, that I also may stand joyfully before the Father, and give an account of you all to the Lord."[160] To behave in such a way as to bring groans and grief to the leaders would be "unprofitable," or more strongly, "harmful" (ἀλυσιτελής *alysitelēs*) to the membership. The word occurs nowhere else in the NT; here it seems a soft way of saying that they, too, would give account and such behavior would be on their record as a loss, not a gain.

13:18. The writer is included among the leaders in the request for prayer. One could take "us" as the editorial plural, as in the author's earlier uses (5:11; 6:9), but the use of "I" in the next verse seems to indicate a literal use of "us" here. This does not necessarily mean that the writer is one of a formal body of leaders. All that can safely be said is that the writer is among those who have responsibility for the congregation and, therefore, will have to give account.

To pray for leaders was a standing petition among the churches (Rom 15:30; Col 4:3; 1 Thess 5:25; 2 Thess 3:1) and need not imply a crisis. If there had been among the readers a perception of crisis, in conduct or relationship, the writer assures them that "we are sure [persuaded] that we have a good conscience." This could be a general expression of self-affirmation, or it could be made with reference to a particular issue known to the readers but not to us. In earlier comments, the author spoke of the conscience as the center of conduct and relationship to God (see Commentary on 9:9, 14; 10:2, 22), and the conscience is cleansed by the sacrificial act of Christ. Here, however, the claim of a clear conscience has to do with the will or the motive of the leaders. It is their desire to act honorably in everything. The verb "to act" or "to conduct themselves" (ἀναστρέφω *anastrephō*) appeared in the noun form in v. 7 with reference to former leaders. The implication may be that our conduct is equally as deserving of respect and emulation.

13:19. The shift at this verse is from the plural "we" to the singular "I" and from self-affirmation by the leaders to a personal petition by the writer. The general request for prayer for the leaders is now personalized and made a more urgent appeal: "I urge/request/beseech" (παρακαλέω *parakaleō*; the noun form has been used in the epistle as "exhortation" or "encouragement"). The request is specific: that the writer may be restored to them sooner. This appeal does not tell us where the author is, the reason for the absence, or the length of it. Neither does it tell us the nature of the former relationship between writer and readers. What is revealed is a relationship that is personal and that draws the writer toward the church again with great urgency. No doubt, had it been possible, the sermon now completed would have been spoken rather than written. This reference to travel plans, although brief (vv. 19, 23), was a commonplace in early Christian correspondence.[161]

---

160. *The Shepherd of Hermas* Vision III, 9, 10.

161. W. G. Doty, *Letters in Primitive Christianity* (Philadelphia: Fortress, 1973) 36-37.

REFLECTIONS

Material such as 13:1-19 presents a special problem for the teacher and preacher (esp. the preacher), because it is already framed as exhortations and admonitions, and the temptation is to transfer these urgings directly and uncritically to a present audience. Such texts seem to preach themselves with little further work, being sharpened and aimed as they are. This temptation must be resisted; the portability of these texts must be established with the same careful historical reconstruction and hermeneutical honesty as any other. In fact, texts such as 13:1-19 are in some ways more difficult of application simply because much traditional parenetic material lacks specificity of audience, and that which speaks generally does not have the concreteness needed when seeking to be appropriate. One will want, therefore, to beware of being seduced by texts that seem "pulpit ready."

1. Being thus warned, the preacher can find here concerns expressed that have long histories extending into the present. For example, love of the stranger ("hospitality," v. 2) has been urged on the people of God since the time of Moses: "The alien who resides with you shall be to you as the citizen among you; you shall love the alien as yourself, for you were aliens in the land of Egypt" (Lev 19:34). Jesus repeatedly underscored hospitality to the stranger as an essential characteristic of disciples (e.g., Matt 10:40-42; 25:31-46). The frequency of this admonition testifies not only to its importance but also to the tenacity of xenophobia (fear of strangers) in society and among the people of God. Likewise, warnings about abuses of sex and money fill both testaments and very often these are treated as twin dangers (vv. 4-6). It is not enough to rail against these abuses as symptoms of personal degradation; they are also lodged in the value systems of society. In the Mediterranean world both sex and money were avenues to and expressions of power and position and, in many eyes, honor. For the church's teachings regarding both to be met with public ridicule made them even more difficult to observe. To address these issues as private matters was and is inadequate.

2. Hebrews 13:13 urges the readers to go to Jesus outside the camp and bear his abuse. At that time and place, the church was a pilgrim minority outside the structures, social and political, that provided identity, values, and place. Today in many places, the church is inside, not outside, embraced and endowed with money and favor. The preacher must decide whether the call to the pilgrim life was contingent on circumstances of time and place that no longer exist or whether there is in the image of the faith pilgrim something integral to Christianity and, therefore, never to be abandoned, regardless of public favor or disfavor. If the call of 13:13 is a continuing one, then its implications for the church in situations now radically altered will need to be spelled out. The teacher and preacher can properly recall here the familiar call to discipleship in terms of cross bearing (Matt 10:38; 16:24; Mark 8:34; Luke 14:27).

3. Hebrews 13:15-16 joins words of praise and acts of kindness and generosity as together constituting worship that is pleasing to God. To understand conduct and relationships as liturgical is itself informative and encouraging, but to unite words and deeds in this way is especially instructive. For some reason it has seemed difficult for the people of God to embrace both as a single offering to God. There are the voices full of references to God, to Christ, to the Spirit, and often to their own experiences of divine visitations, but whose hands and purses are less than fully employed in the lives of those in need. And there are the donors and volunteers who put at the disposal of the world's helpless both purse and energy, but who remain reticent and silent about the faith. These things ought to be done but without leaving the other undone. Words are not "only words," and deeds are not "only deeds"; together they are "sacrifices pleasing to God."

HEBREWS 13:20-25
BENEDICTION AND GREETINGS

OVERVIEW

Several epistolary characteristics of chap. 13 have already been noted: the closing paraenesis (vv. 1-17), a request for prayer (vv. 18-19), and a brief note on travel plans (v. 19). These characteristics continue through the remainder of the chapter: a benediction with doxology (vv. 20-21), a brief reflection on what has been written (v. 22), a further word on travel plans (v. 23), greetings (v. 24), and farewell (v. 25). Many of these features can be found in the letters of Paul, the Pastorals, 1 Peter, and the letters of Clement and Ignatius.

Paul is usually credited with modifying letter writing in the Greco-Roman world in order to make it an extension of his ministry, and Hebrews is but one example of a modification of Paul's modification, with the same purpose in mind. The epistle form permitted the writer to do many things other than pass along information.[162] By concluding this sermon as an epistle, the author was able to achieve many purposes integral to the leader-congregation relationship: nourishing, guiding, renewing, adding anticipation, and providing self-disclosure, sketchy as it is. The formal kinship of Hebrews 13 to other early Christian correspondence does not argue for direct literary dependence or for the presence of a hand other than that which wrote Hebrews 1–12. The author is simply participating in what had become by this time a literary tradition.

162. S. K. Stowers, *Letter Writing in Greco-Roman Antiquity* (Philadelphia: Westminster, 1986) esp. 15-16.

HEBREWS 13:20-21, BENEDICTION WITH DOXOLOGY

COMMENTARY

The benediction picks up on several theological and christological themes of the sermon. As at the beginning of chap. 1, God is the first and principal actor in the drama of salvation. The title "God of peace," common in Pauline benedictions (Rom 15:33; 16:20; 2 Cor 13:11; Phil 4:9; 1 Thess 5:23), recalls the call to pursue peace (12:14) and the instructions on how to achieve it (13:1-2, 7, 17-18). That God raised Jesus from the dead is foundational and almost universally stated in early Christian literature. In Hebrews, this affirmation is implied and assumed but is here directly said for the first time. And even here the usual word for "raise up" is not used. The writer may be echoing Isa 63:11 LXX, which speaks of God's "bringing up" Moses as shepherd of the flock. The frequent statements concerning Christ's exaltation to God's right hand have resurrection embedded in them. The metaphor "Jesus, the great shepherd of the sheep" is at 13:20 new to Hebrews, although "great" has been used in speaking of Jesus as high priest (4:14; 10:21). The closest parallel is at 1 Pet 5:4, where Jesus is called "the chief shepherd," but the image was widely used of God in relation to Israel and of Christ in relation to the church (cf. John 10:10, 14; *The Shepherd of Hermas*). The phrase "blood of an eternal covenant" is more at home in Hebrews than in other NT works, here reviving in the reader's mind the heart of the sermon (esp. 2:14; 9:12, 14-15, 18-20; 10:19, 29).

Like many benedictions, this one includes a prayer for the addressees: May God "provide"/"equip" ("prepare" [καταρτίζω *katartizō*] at 10:5; 11:3) you with everything necessary to do God's will. The reader may recall 10:5-7, where Christ was provided with a body in order to do God's will. It is not only God who equips for obedience, but it is also God who works in (among) us to accomplish what is pleasing to God. This double role as both provider and enabler is equivalent to Paul's directive to work out your salvation, for it is God who is at work in you both to will and to work that which is God's pleasure (Phil 2:12-13). In Hebrews, what pleases God is faith (11:5), worship in reverence and awe (12:28), doing good, and sharing what one has (13:16). In the doxological closing to the benediction, the ascription of praise (glory) seems to be to Jesus Christ, since his name is the closest antecedent. This could well be the correct interpretation,[163] but if the benediction is looked at as a whole, one sees that the ending may have returned to its beginning: God. Such a concentric movement of thought, already familiar in Hebrews, may be the case here. The God announced at 1:1 as the subject of this sermon-letter is the governing thought in the framing of the final benediction. One is reminded of Paul's doxological benediction: from God, through God, to God (Rom 11:36).

163. See Attridge, *A Commentary on the Epistle to the Hebrews*, 407-8.

HEBREWS 13:22-25, GREETINGS AND FAREWELL

COMMENTARY

It is evident that the letter-sermon was a second choice to being present with the congregation, but it is the writer's clear expectation to remedy that very soon. The same sentiment is expressed in Phlm 21-22; 2 John 12; and 3 John 13. In the meantime, the writer appeals ("urges"; cf. v. 19) to them to bear with "my word of exhortation [encouragement]." Here the word παράκλησις (*paraklēsis*) is the noun form of the verb "to appeal/urge/beseech/encourage/exhort," which was used to open this sentence. "Word of exhortation" may be a semi-technical term for "sermon" (cf. Acts 13:15; at 1 Pet 5:12 a form of this word is used to describe the content and intent of that letter).[164] The ground for the writer's appeal that they bear with the letter-sermon is that it is brief. A similar expression at 1 Pet 5:12 may indicate that the writer is using a conventional phrase. As for the request itself, that they "bear with" his epistle, meaning is dependent on mood, and mood is almost irretrievable. The word appears in Matt 17:17: "You faithless and perverse generation. . . . How much longer must I *put up* with you?" (NRSV, italics added). The meaning is "to tolerate but patience is wearing thin." Paul uses the word sarcastically in asking the Corinthians to *put up* with him as they would a fool (2 Cor 11:1, 4, 19-20). Perhaps here at v. 22 there is rhetorical irony in the understated appeal, just as there may be in saying that he has written "briefly" ("a short letter," NIV). In the NT only Romans and 1 Corinthians are longer. Although to say that one has written "briefly" may be a literary convention (1 Pet 5:12), the author may simply mean, "I have so much more to tell you."

In v. 23, the author provides information about Timothy that is not entirely clear to us. That this is the Timothy who was Paul's companion and co-worker there is no reason to doubt, but the meaning of his being set free is unclear. The verb "set free" (ἀπολύω *apolyō*) was commonly used in referring to release from prison (Matt 27:15; John 18:39; Acts 3:13; 16:35-36) and could well have that meaning here. Imprisonment was among the abuses endured by the Hebrews congregation

164. Attridge, "Paraenesis in a Homily," 211-26.

(10:34; 13:3). We do not know where or on what charge Timothy was in prison, nor do we know the reasons for his release. To try to answer these questions from Acts and Paul would not really satisfy inquiries addressed to Hebrews. The writer's travel plans are to come to the congregation very soon (v. 19). Those plans include Timothy, with whom, "if he comes in time, he will be with me when I see you" (v. 23).

The sending of greetings, first from the writer and then from others in the writer's presence, was a rather common way of attending to this standard feature of a letter (2 Cor 13:12; Phil 4:21-22; 2 Tim 4:19, 21). To greet "all the leaders" and "all the saints" need not be taken to imply that the recipients are but a small group within a larger fellowship or that there are divisions between the writer and some of the congregation or within the congregation. It is enough to understand v. 24a as an attempt to be inclusive and manifest the same harmony that was urged on the membership. The identity of "those from Italy" is difficult if not impossible to determine. Are Italians away from home sending greetings back to Rome, the destination of the letter according to some commentators? Are Italian Christians in Rome sending greetings to this congregation, making Rome the place of origin for the letter? We do not know. (See the Introduction, where v. 24b is discussed in the attempt to ascertain the places of origin and destination of Hebrews.) A preferred reading is that greetings are sent to the church from a group of Italians who are away from home and who are within the vicinity of the writer, who also seems to be away from home.

The farewell blessing, "Grace be with all of you," puts Hebrews in the company of most of the letters of the NT. The expression may have already become a part of the church's liturgy, although the forms of the blessing vary slightly. The form here is exactly the same as in Titus 3:15. The word "grace" (χάρις *charis*) appears but eight times in Hebrews, but it is used as descriptive of God, of Christ, and of the Spirit. The readers are never given reason to doubt that all God's actions toward them have been and are "gracious."

THE LETTER OF JAMES

INTRODUCTION, COMMENTARY, AND REFLECTIONS
BY
LUKE TIMOTHY JOHNSON

THE LETTER OF
JAMES

INTRODUCTION

Traditionally included as the first of the "general" or "catholic" epistles, the Letter of James is as clear and forceful in its moral exhortations as it is difficult to place within the development of earliest Christianity. Although its formal canonization was relatively late, there are signs that James was used by some writings (e.g., *1 Clement* and the *Shepherd of Hermas*) before the middle of the second century CE. Largely through the enthusiastic endorsement of Origen, it became part of the church's collection, first in the East and, by the end of the fourth century, in the West. Martin Luther's distaste for James is well known, but was not widely shared by other reformers. Luther considered that Jas 2:24 ("You see that a person is justified by works and not by faith alone" [NRSV]) contradicted Paul's teaching on righteousness in Gal 2:16 ("a person is justified not by the works of the law but through faith in Jesus Christ" [NRSV]). Luther's view dominated much of the scholarly approach to the letter until very recently. Most readers through the ages, however, reached a position like that of patristic interpreters, and the opposite of Luther's: (1) James and Paul do not contradict each other, because they are not addressing the same point; (2) when read on its own terms, James is a powerful witness to both the diversity in early Christianity and the moral imperative of Christian identity in every age.

CHARACTER OF THE COMPOSITION

Before considering the circumstances of composition, which are a matter of considerable debate, the distinctive voice of the composition itself should be appreciated. James is written in a clear and even somewhat elegant *koine* Greek that shows the influence of the Septuagint (LXX) not only in its explicit citations and allusions but also in its diction. The style does not lack adornment or rhetorical force. Its short sentences adhere to the ancient ideal of brevity, and although to some readers they appear disconnected, closer analysis reveals careful construction and vigorous argument.

James presents itself as a letter, although after the greeting (1:1) it lacks specifically epistolary elements (for instance, there is no prayer for grace and peace, no declaration of thanksgiving or pronouncement of a blessing on God). The determination of whether it was a "real" letter depends to a considerable extent on the decision concerning authenticity. In any case, the readership is a general one, and the situations portrayed in the letter are better thought of as general and typical rather than actual and local. It is widely agreed that James is a form of moral exhortation, but refining that definition has proved more difficult. James has appropriately been compared to the Greco-Roman diatribe because of its lively, dialogical style, especially in the essays of 2:1–5:20 (see, e.g., 2:14-26). Because it conveys traditional moral instruction, it has also been thought of as paraenesis. It is, however, best understood as a form of protreptic discourse in the form of a letter: James seeks to persuade the readers to live up to the profession to which they have committed themselves—namely, the faith "in our glorious Lord Jesus Christ" (2:1 NRSV).[1]

The structure of James's moral discourse is also difficult to determine with precision. One influential position argues that James has no real compositional structure, but is a collection of separate traditions only loosely joined together. The exegetical implication of this position is that each verse must be interpreted separately without reference to its immediate context. At the opposite extreme, a variety of complex—and not easily visible—structures have been suggested. Most scholars have preferred a less radical position. They recognize that James contains a number of easily identifiable and coherent "essays," although the precise delimitation of these is debated (e.g., 2:1-11 on the incompatibility of faith and discrimination; 2:14-26 on the inadequacy of faith without deeds; 3:1-12 on the misuse of speech; 3:13–4:10 on the contrast between friendship with the world and friendship with God; see also 4:13–5:6; 5:7-11, 13-18). Analysis from the perspective of ancient rhetoric demonstrates that these essays follow the conventions of argumentation in the Hellenistic world. The biggest problem is the relationship of chapter 1, which is far less obviously coherent and far more aphoristic in character, with these later and longer essays. It is clear that themes that are touched on in chapter 1 by way of aphorism are also found developed in the essays: The prayer of faith in 1:5-7 is advocated more elaborately in 5:13-18; the reversal of fortunes of the rich and poor in 1:9-10 is developed by 2:1-6 and 4:13–5:6; the theme of enduring testing in 1:2-4, 12 is found further in 5:7-11; the contrast between wicked desire and God's gift in 1:12-18 is argued more extensively in 3:13–4:10; the use of the tongue in 1:19-20 is picked up by the essay in 3:1-12; the necessity of acting out religious convictions in 1:22-27 is elaborated by the essay in 2:14-26. In effect, then, 1:2-27 serves as an *epitome* of the entire composition, setting out in concentrated form the themes to be developed by the essays. As for the final statement in 5:19-20, it serves as an excellent conclusion, recommending that the reader do for others what the author has tried to do for the readers.

JAMES AS WISDOM WRITING

As moral exhortation (there are some 59 imperatives in its 108 verses), James can be compared to other ancient writings whose concern is the practical wisdom of right behavior. James resembles the popular moral philosophy of the Greco-Roman world in its insistence on control of the passions and of speech and on the demonstration of verbal profession in practice, as well as in its perception of envy and arrogance as destructive vices.[2] The specific symbolic world of James, however, is that of Torah. James appropriates the multiple dimensions of Torah in a way distinctive among New Testament writings. First, James has a positive view of the *law,* not as a set of ritual obligations but as moral commandment expressed most perfectly by what it calls "the law of the kingdom" or "royal law"—namely, the law of love of neighbor from Lev 19:18 (Jas 2:8-13). Second, James appropriates the voice of the *prophets* in its understanding of human life as fundamentally covenantal and relational and in its harsh condemnation of those whose desire for self-aggrandizement leads them to oppress and defraud others (4:13–5:6).

---

1. See Robert W. Wall, "Introduction to Epistolary Literature," in Vol. 9, *The New Interpreter's Bible Commentary,* 10 vols. (Nashville: Abingdon, 2015).
2. See Abraham J. Malherbe, "The Cultural Context of the New Testament: The Greco-Roman World," in *The New Interpreter's Bible,* 12 vols. (Nashville: Abingdon, 1995) 8:12-26.

Third, James represents the *wisdom* tradition of Torah, not only in its liberal use of proverb and maxim, but also by understanding human freedom in terms of an allegiance either to a "wisdom from above" or to a "wisdom from below" (1:5; 3:13-18).

As a kind of wisdom literature, James naturally bears a certain resemblance to the wide range of wisdom writings that were produced in the ancient Near East. Wisdom has an international character, not only because human behavior does show some constants across cultures, but also because wisdom literature was produced by scribes in ancient bureaucracies who borrowed freely from other cultures in shaping wisdom for their own. James most resembles certain Jewish writings that shared its commitment to the world of Torah within the wider cultural setting of Hellenism, such as the *Sentences of Pseudo-Phocylides* and the *Testaments of the Twelve Patriarchs*.[3] When a thorough comparison is made between James and all these other wisdom writings, however, the distinctiveness of James emerges more clearly.

There are four ways in which James stands out among all ancient moral literature. First, James's concern is with morals rather than manners. Much of the moral exhortation of antiquity dealt with finding and keeping one's place in the world as a means to success and honor. James has none of those concerns, but deals exclusively with moral attitudes and behavior. Second, James addresses an intentional community rather than a household. It has nothing about obligations within the household or the state, nothing about duties owed by parents to children or slaves to masters. It says nothing about sexual morality. Its attention is exclusively devoted to an *ekklēsia* gathered by common values and convictions, summarized by faith in Jesus Christ (2:1). Third, James is egalitarian rather than hierarchical. Much of ancient wisdom assumes and reinforces the differences in status, especially between parents and children. In James, the only kinship language is that of "brother" and "sister," with even the author presenting himself as a "slave" rather than as an authority. God is the only "father" in this community (1:17-18, 27). The egalitarian outlook of James is shown as well in its condemnation of favoritism in judging (2:1, 9) and every form of boasting (3:14-15) and arrogance (4:6), slander and judging (4:11-12). Fourth, James is communitarian rather than individualistic. Against every form of self-assertion that seeks advantage at the expense of another, James calls for attitudes of solidarity, mercy, and compassion. In contrast to the logic of envy that leads to oppression and "killing the righteous one" (5:6), James calls for a community that rallies around the sick and sinful in order to heal/save them (5:14-16).

JAMES AS A CHRISTIAN WRITING

Despite such noteworthy points of connection to the broader world of ancient wisdom literature, James is unmistakably a Christian writing.[4] Recent scholarship has properly abandoned the once-popular view that James originated as a Jewish composition that was subsequently lightly baptized. It is true that the name of Jesus is mentioned only twice (1:1; 2:1) and that the composition lacks the characteristic themes associated explicitly with Jesus. It makes no mention of his earthly life or miracles, does not explicitly speak of his death and resurrection, and never adverts to baptism, the Holy Spirit, or the Lord's supper. Yet the language and perceptions of the composition are without question those of the nascent messianic movement, with its sense of an inheritance according to promise, of belonging to a kingdom proclaimed by Jesus, and of a life normed by faith and love.

Of all the compositions from the first-century Mediterranean world, in fact, James most resembles the letters of Paul in its style and outlook. The resemblance is not restricted to the disputed lines in 2:14-26, nor is it due to the dependence of one writer on the other. Rather, despite the obvious differences between the extant literature of each author, James and Paul share a range of convictions and perceptions that is best explained by the hypothesis that both are first-century Jewish members of the messianic movement with significant roots in the world

---

3. These can be found in J. H. Charlesworth, ed., *The Old Testament Pseudepigrapha*, 2 vols. (New York: Doubleday, 1983; 1985).
4. For a full discussion, see L. T. Johnson, *The Letter of James*, AB 37A (New York: Doubleday, 1995) 48-64.

of Palestinian Judaism. James has its own distinctive christology, based less in the deeds of Jesus than in Jesus' words. In James 1:5-6, 12; 2:5, 13; 4:8, 11-12; 5:9, 12, we find language that appears to be derived from the tradition of Jesus' sayings at a stage prior to their incorporation into the synoptic Gospels.[5] For James, then, "the faith of Jesus" means living before God in a manner shaped by the words of Jesus, and above all by his declaration that loving the neighbor as oneself is the "royal law" (2:8 NRSV).

Nevertheless, James is clearly less christocentric than theocentric. It would be difficult to find a New Testament writing with as rich a collection of statements concerning the nature and activity of God. James begins with the confession that God is one (2:19), but scarcely stops there. God is the living God, who makes "even the demons believe—and shudder" (2:19 NRSV) and is the "Lord of hosts" (5:4 NRSV). God is constant and without change (1:17) and has nothing to do with evil (1:13) or human anger (1:20). God is the creator of all (1:17), who, by a "word of truth," has "given birth" to humans as a first fruits of all creatures (1:18) and has created them in God's own likeness (3:9). God has revealed the "perfect law of liberty" (see 2:8-12) and will judge humans on the basis of that revelation (2:12; 4:12). God is fit to judge because God alone is able "to save and to destroy" (4:12 NRSV). God has implanted a word within humans that is able to save them (1:21) and has made a spirit to dwell in them (4:5). God directs human affairs (4:15) and declares righteous those who have faith (2:23). Above all, God is defined by the giving of gifts (1:5, 17; 4:6), especially those of mercy and compassion (5:11). God has promised the crown of life to those who love God (1:12; 2:5), has chosen the world's poor to be rich in faith and heirs of the kingdom (2:5), considers true religion to include the visiting of orphans and widows (1:27), hears the cries of the oppressed (5:4), raises up the sick (5:15), listens to the prayers made in faith (1:5-6; 5:17-18) rather than wickedly (4:3), and forgives the sins of those who confess them (5:15). This is a God who approaches those who approach (4:10) and enters into friendship with humans (2:23; 4:4), even while resisting the arrogance and pride of those who oppress others (4:6; 5:6).

JAMES'S THEOLOGICAL ETHICS

Such characterizations are not random but fit within a coherent understanding of God as the source of all reality ("the giver of every good and perfect gift") who calls humans into a life shaped according to the gifts given them and a community of mutual gift-giving and support rather than of rivalry and competition. In a word, James's theological statements serve as warrants for his moral exhortations.

James's ethical dualism is consistent and based on a contrast between the measure of reality offered by "the world," on the one hand, and "God," on the other. The "wisdom from below" is the wisdom of the world, which is based in desire and envy and leads to every form of competition, violence, and eventually murder and war (3:13–4:3). In contrast, the "wisdom from above" is that given by God through the "implanted word," a wisdom that measures reality according to God's gifts rather than according to human possessions, and that leads to a life lived in cooperation and peace (3:13-18). James expresses this dualism in terms of friendship, which in the ancient world was regarded as a particularly profound form of sharing all things: Friends share not only their material things but above all their view of the world. Friends were of "one mind" (see Commentary on 2:14-26). In 4:4, James reminds his readers (and thus assumes their previous grasp of the point) that they cannot be "friends of the world" and also "friends of God," because God and "the world" represent entirely different and opposed measures of reality. Thus one who is a "friend of the world" seeks to kill a righteous person in order to gain more possessions, convinced that life must be seized. But Abraham is called a "friend of God," because he is willing to offer his son Isaac on the altar, recognizing that God is the constant giver of gifts (2:21-23).

---

5. For treatment of the Jesus tradition assumed in James, see P. J. Hartis, *James and the Sayings of Jesus*, JSNT 47 (Sheffield: JSOT, 1991).

James's particular targets, however, are those of his readers, who may understand these things theoretically, but whose practice does not match their profession. They want to be friends of God, yes, but also friends of the world. James calls them "double-minded" (1:8; 4:8), because they want to live by two measures simultaneously. Much of James's instruction is intended to show the moral illogic and self-deception involved in such vacillation. The heart of the composition is 3:13–4:10, a call to conversion from double-mindedness to that "purity of heart" which is to will one thing.

CIRCUMSTANCES OF COMPOSITION

The circumstances of James's composition are the most difficult to determine and have been the cause of considerable debate within critical scholarship. The letter does not offer many clues to the circumstances of the readers (but see, e.g., 2:2, 6-7; 5:4). If taken literally, "the twelve tribes in the dispersion" in the greeting would refer to Jewish Christians outside Palestine; if taken metaphorically, the original readers could be regarded as those who are spiritual heirs to Israel and sojourning away from their heavenly homeland. In either case, we learn nothing about the specific circumstances of the first readers. The situations portrayed by the composition are also, as noted above, typical in character. It is probably safe to assert, however, that the readers either are, or perceive themselves to be, among "the poor" who are called into God's kingdom and are persecuted and oppressed by the rich (see esp. 2:1-6; 5:1-6).

As for the inscribed author, the best candidate is "James the brother of the Lord," who figured prominently in the first generation of the Christian movement as one of the leaders of the church in Jerusalem (see Mark 6:3; Acts 12:17; 15:23-29; 21:20-25; 1 Cor 15:7; Gal 1:19; 2:9, 11-14). If this James actually wrote the letter, then the composition would be important evidence for Jewish Christianity within Palestine before the year 62.[6] The traditional attribution to James has vigorously been challenged on two basic counts. The first is that Jas 2:14-26 appears to presuppose the Pauline teaching in Galatians and Romans, and thus must come from a time after the first generation. The second is that the Greek style is too fine for a Palestinian Jew to have written. Many scholars, therefore, consider James to be a pseudonymous composition. Once the tie to James is broken, even less can be said about the time and place of writing, and it has been dated variously between the beginning and the middle of the second century.

Many other scholars—even a majority until recent years—consider the traditional attribution reasonable. Some have dealt with the critical problems by proposing that Paul was responding to James, rather than the reverse, and that the Greek style of the letter might be accounted for by a translation of an Aramaic original. These expedients, however, are not necessary in order to hold that James the brother of the Lord may well have been the author of this letter. In the first place, as was recognized already by patristic interpreters, James in 2:14-26 is simply not addressing the same topic as Paul does in Galatians and Romans. When James declares that faith co-works the works of Abraham and that faith is perfected by those works (2:22), he simply addresses the necessity of convictions to be translated into action, a position also held by Paul (see Gal 5:6). As for the Greek style, research over the past thirty years has decisively demonstrated that Palestine was as thoroughly Hellenized with regard to language as was the diaspora, and there is no reason why a Christian of the first generation who grew up in Galilee and wrote from Jerusalem should not have a style as good as that revealed in this composition.

The position that James is a first-generation writing has much to recommend it. First, it lacks any of the signs usually associated with pseudonymous authorship, such as the fictional elaboration of the author's identity, and shows none of the characteristics of institutional development. Second, James reveals the social situations and perspectives appropriate to a sect in the early stages of its life, with no attention to generational changes, and an active anticipation of an imminent judgment. Third, James makes use of Jesus traditions at a stage earlier than their

---

6. When, according to Josephus's *Antiquities of the Jews* 20:200, James was martyred.

incorporation into the synoptic Gospels.[7] Fourth, James closely resembles in its language and outlook our earliest datable Christian writer, the apostle Paul. The best way to account for the similarity is to view both as first-generation Christians deeply affected by Greco-Roman moral traditions, yet fundamentally defined by an allegiance to the symbols and story of Torah. Even if the writing is from the first generation, it need not necessarily have been written by James, the brother of the Lord, but that hypothesis remains as convincing as any other that has been offered in the history of scholarship. The value of James's witness, in any case, is not determined by a decision concerning its authorship or date or circumstances of composition.

There are at least three ways in which James speaks to every generation of Christianity with unparalleled clarity and conviction. First, it is uncompromising in its demand for a clear rejection of "the world," together with a consistent commitment to an understanding of reality as measured by God. Second, because its teaching is rooted less in christology than in theology, it is among the most ecumenical writings in the New Testament, able to speak also to those who do not confess Jesus as Lord but who share the faith of Abraham. Third, it is the New Testament writing that most clearly yields a social ethics grounded in the perception of the world as created and gifted by God.

---

7. See Johnson, *The Letter of James*, 55-57.

BIBLIOGRAPHY

Adamson, J. B. *The Epistle of James.* NICNT. Grand Rapids: Eerdmans, 1976.

———. *James: The Man and the Message.* Grand Rapids: Eerdmans, 1989.

Baker, W. R. *Personal Speech-Ethics in the Epistle of James.* WUZNT 2.68. Tübingen: J. C. B. Mohr (Siebeck), 1995.

Cargal, T. B. *Restoring the Diaspora: Discursive Structure and Purpose in the Epistle of James.* SBLDS 144. Atlanta: Scholars Press, 1993.

Davids, P. H. *Commentary on James.* NIGTC. Grand Rapids: Eerdmans, 1982.

Dibelius, M. *James: A Commentary on the Epistle of James.* Edited by H. Greeven. Translated by M. A. Williams. Hermeneia. Philadelphia: Fortress, 1975.

Hartin, P. J. *James and the Sayings of Jesus.* JSNT 47. Sheffield: JSOT, 1991.

Johnson, L. T. "Friendship with the World/Friendship with God: A Study of Discipleship in James." In *Discipleship in the New Testament.* Edited by F. Segovia. Philadelphia: Fortress, 1985.

———. *The Letter of James.* AB 37A. New York: Doubleday, 1995.

Laws, S. *A Commentary on the Epistle of James.* HNTC. San Francisco: Harper & Row, 1980.

Lodge, J. C. "James and Paul at Cross-Purposes? James 2:22." *Biblica* 62 (1981) 195-213.

Martin, R. P. *James.* WBC 48. Waco, Tex.: Word, 1988.

Via, D. O. "The Right Strawy Epistle Reconsidered: A Study in Biblical Ethics and Hermeneutics." *Journal of Religion* 49 (1969) 253-67.

Wall, R. W. *Community of the Wise: The Letter of James.* The New Testament in Context. Valley Forge, Pa.: Trinity Press International, 1997.

Ward, R. B. "The Communal Concern of the Epistle of James." Ph.D. diss., Harvard University, 1966.

Outline of James

I. James 1:1-27, Greeting and Epitome of Exhortation

II. James 2:1-13, Active Faith, Consistent Love

III. James 2:14-26, The Deeds of Faith

IV. James 3:1-12, On the Perils of Speech

V. James 3:13–4:10, Call to Conversion

VI. James 4:11–5:6, Examples of Arrogance

VII. James 5:7-20, A Community of Solidarity

JAMES 1:1-27

GREETING AND EPITOME OF EXHORTATION

COMMENTARY

1:1. The greeting follows the classic form of the Hellenistic letter. Two positions can be adopted concerning the identification of author and recipients. If the letter was written by James, the brother of the Lord, before the year 62, then the self-designation "servant" (δοῦλος *doulos*; lit., "slave") of God and of the Lord Jesus Christ would suggest the confident and understated authority of a teacher (see 3:1), and those "in the Dispersion" would signify Jewish Christians outside Palestine, perhaps in those regions of Antioch, Syria, and Cilicia that were clearly within Jerusalem's sphere of influence in the first generation (see Acts 15:23). If the letter is regarded as pseudonymous, then "James" is assumed to have been sufficiently important in the first generation for later readers to recognize his authority with no further elaboration, and "the twelve tribes in the Dispersion" would simply refer to all Christians, including Gentile Christians, who were far from their heavenly homeland (see 1 Pet 1:1; 2:11). Whatever historical data the greeting may supply, its compositional function is to make readers of every age the recipients of a "letter" from the earliest days of the Christian movement and, therefore, challenged by the freshness and vigor of that first generation.

1:2-27. This passage challenges any reading of James as a coherent literary composition. It seems, at first sight, to be made up of disparate statements that are joined more by word linkage than by logic or theme. In the Greek text, for example, it is obvious that the ending of each phrase between v. 1 and v. 6 is picked up by the beginning of the next. Likewise, the very same word (πειρασμός *peirasmos*) appears to mean "trial" in v. 12 and "temptation" in v. 13. Such word linkages can sometimes indicate traditional material drawn together by a later editor on the basis of mnemonics (or catchword association). But they are also a feature of ancient rhetoric and can be seen as the deliberate construction of the author.

The separate statements in vv. 2-27, as stated in the Introduction, anticipate themes that are developed more fully later in the composition and serve as an epitome of the exhortation as a whole. But is this first chapter simply a jumbled table of contents, or does it have a distinctive literary character of its own? Two features of this chapter give it a special character: First, it establishes the ethical and religious dualism that structures the composition as a whole; second, it emphasizes the need to properly understand the perception of reality within which such a dualism makes sense.

James places in opposition the measure of reality that comes from God and that associated with the world (v. 27). The outlook of the world is duplicitous and envious. But God gives to all simply and without grudging (v. 5). God can, indeed, be defined as the giver of every good and perfect gift (v. 17). Worldly desire conceives sin, and sin, when it reaches term, gives birth to death (v. 15). But God gives genuine birth to humans by a word of truth and makes them the firstfruits of the creatures (v. 18). James also contrasts the attitudes and behavior that correspond to each measure. To live by God's word of truth means being meek rather than angry, for "anger does not produce God's righteousness" (v. 20); it means reversing the estimation of wealth and poverty, since the poor are exalted by God and the rich are humbled (v. 9); it means being driven not by evil desires (v. 14) but by the search for the wisdom that comes from God (vv. 5-6). Most paradoxically, it means counting trials completely as joy (v. 2), an attitude possible only to those who believe in a God who gives the crown of life to those who endure such trials because of their love of God (v. 12). These contrasts can be summarized in the final verse as one between the sham and self-deceived religiosity of speech and appearance, and authentic religion "pure and undefiled before God," expressed by care for the world's needy (vv. 26-27).

The opening verses in James are noteworthy also for the emphasis they place on *understanding*. The very first exhortation is cognitive: They are to "reckon/calculate/consider" trials in one way rather than another (v. 2). In the first twenty-seven verses, James uses terms of knowing or perceiving some seventeen times, and in the remaining eighty-one verses only seven times (2:20; 3:1; 4:4, 5, 14, 17; 5:20). Prior to speech or action, in other words, is proper perception.

1:2-8. Once the literary coherence of the chapter is taken seriously, it is possible to detect the flow of an argument. Verses 2-8, for example, can be seen as a loose agglomeration of statements joined by word linkage, forming the trope called *sorites* (or climax), but they also hold together logically; the commands are grounded in warrants and lead to specific results. In fact, this opening exhortation states the basic thesis that is then worked out in this chapter and throughout the composition. The theme is faith and how it reaches perfection. Despite a variety of "testings" presented by a world actively hostile to God, it reaches its perfection through "deeds of faith" like those of Abraham and Rahab (2:20-25), through the "endurance of faith" like Job's (5:10-11), and through the "prayer of faith" like Elijah's (5:17-18). This opening exhortation contains in compressed form each of these expressions: faith's perfect work/product, endurance, and prayer.

In the Greco-Roman world it was something of a commonplace that the testing of virtue strengthens character (see Rom 5:2-4; 1 Pet 1:6-7).[8] James, however, speaks not of the virtue of an individual but of a community's faith. What makes his exhortation more than a moral anodyne is the breathtaking assertion that human existence is not located in a closed system of competition (even for virtue or excellence) but in an open system ordered by and to a God who gives gifts to humanity. This is the theological perspective of faith that grounds a positive assessment of testing. Endurance is not the demonstration of an individual's moral character but of a community's fidelity to God as its source of being and worth. This is why the command to *pray* is fundamental (1:5), for prayer is itself an opening to the understanding of reality as one drenched with grace given by God the giver of every perfect gift (1:17). The warning against being "double-minded" in prayer (1:8) identifies the specific audience for James's exhortations, namely, those who "know" the construal of reality given by faith but want also to live by the measure of the world.

1:9-12. If vv. 2-8 exhort readers to a certain perception of testing based on what they "know" (v. 3), vv. 9-12 provide the content of that knowledge. James presents the world as being open to God and human existence as ordered by relationship to God. This measure affects everything, above all the understanding of human destiny. In v. 12, James declares clearly that the future for those who have endured testing because of their love for God will receive the reward that is life ("the crown of life"). This promise is the premise underlying the exhortation in v. 2.

Understanding vv. 9-11 is difficult. If they make the same point as v. 12, they do so allusively. The main problem is understanding the identity of the rich person. The exalting of the lowly brother makes sense when correlated with v. 12: The world may see poverty only in negative terms, but from the side of God, it is a sign of election (which 2:5 will make explicit). The exaltation of the poor corresponds to the crown of life (1:12) or kingdom (2:5) promised to those who love God. The poor, therefore, can exult both in their present status and their future hope. But what about the rich? The main difficulty is deciding whether the rich person is a member of the community or an outsider. If the rich person is one who oppresses the community (see 2:6; 5:1-6), then James's tone here must be ironic. People like this boast, even though God's reversal of status will destroy them and their riches! The structure of the sentence in vv. 9-10, however, seems to demand considering the rich person

---
8. See also Seneca *On Providence* 2:1-6.

also as a "brother" in the community. In this case, the character of this person's exaltation and the point of passing away are less clear. There are two possibilities. One is to read the sentence prophetically: Rich members of the community are not truly so, for they live by the world's values. They will be humbled for giving in to the "testing" of wealth and placing reliance on it. This fits James's position in 5:1-6. Another possibility is that James is making a sapiential point: The rich person is humbled within a community of the poor that does not give wealth a special status, but honors the poor instead. This fits James's argument in 4:13-17.

More important is to understand that James is not here making an exhortation, but *stating basic principles* concerning the human condition before God. In that light, the harsher reading is more likely, for it makes the contrast clearer. This reading is strengthened further by James's allusion to Isa 40:7 in v. 11, which suggests a contrast between reliance on appearances and on "the word of our God will stand forever" (Isa 40:8 NRSV). Humans live, say vv. 9-12, before a God who exalts those who are lowly and resists those who are proud. This theme will recur (see, e.g., 4:6).

1:13-21. If God is so intimately involved in human destiny, can God be blamed for human failure? This is the import of the issue in v. 13. James's first response is simply to remove God from the realm of evil entirely: God neither is tested by evil nor tests anyone. This short rejoinder is not sufficient, so in vv. 14-19a, James provides the proper understanding of the roots of temptation and of God's relations to humans ("Do not be deceived," v. 16), and then in vv. 19b-21, sketches the right and wrong responses of humans to this relationship.

Critical to this discussion is the shift in meaning of the terms πειρασμός (*peirasmos*) and πειράζω (*peirazō*) in v. 13 from "testing" to "tempting," for what James now deals with are not things that befall people from the outside, but the results of their own desires. Indeed, "desire"—understood not as legitimate wanting but as disordered passion—is here personified, and James uses the feminine gender of the noun to develop a grisly sequence of conception, birth, and death (v. 15; see 4:1-4; 5:1-6). In contrast, God is defined in terms of complete and generous goodness in vv. 17-18. God is associated with light rather than darkness, with stability and consistency rather than change and alteration, with the giving of gifts rather than with the grasping characteristic of desire. Patristic writers recognized in v. 17 one of the noblest theological statements in the NT, and it continues to be recited at the conclusion of the *Divine Liturgy of St. John Chrysostom* in the Orthodox tradition.

In a daring appropriation of the language of sexual generation, which he used for desire/sin in v. 15, James says that God "gave birth" to humans "by the word of truth" (v. 18). This could refer to creation itself, to the giving of the law, or—most probably—to the word of the gospel (cf. 2 Cor 6:7; Col 1:5). Humans are meant to be a certain "first fruits of his creatures"—that is, they are to represent all creatures before God. In vv. 19b-21, James describes the first stage of response to the call implied by God's gift. The "implanted word" can only save them if it is truly received. The moral life of Christians begins, then, with "putting aside" all those qualities of arrogance and desire and rage that oppose "God's righteousness" (v. 20), and "putting on" the qualities of meekness and hearing that will enable them to be reshaped according to "the word of truth."

1:22-27. The last section of argument in vv. 22-27 is clear in meaning, although its mode of expression may be obscure to present-day readers. The basic point is one that has been implicit from James's statement that faith can produce a perfect effect (v. 4): For faith to be real, it must be translated into deeds. It is not enough to be a "hearer of the word"; one must become a "doer of the word" as well. Otherwise, one's faith is only self-deception (v. 22). James here agrees with ancient moralists that theoretical correctness matters little if one's life does not conform to the ideas one espouses (see 1 Cor 13:12).[9]

To make his point, James uses a common image in ancient paraenetic literature: gazing into a mirror for self-improvement (see also 1 Cor 13:12).[10] In this case, however, the

---

9. See also, e.g., Seneca *Moral Epistles* 20:1; Plutarch *Progress in Virtue* 14.
10. See, e.g., Epictetus *Discourses* II.14.17-23.

person who gazes simply at his or her "natural" face and forgets what was seen is like the one who only "hears and does not do." This person gains no benefit from instruction. In contrast, the person who gazes into the perfect law of liberty is the one who learns from the examples presented by Torah (Abraham, Rahab, Job, Elijah) on how to turn faith into deeds and is blessed (vv. 24-25). James here makes "the word of truth" (v. 18) and "the perfect law, the law of liberty" (v. 25) virtually synonymous. In this composition, faith, word, law, and wisdom are not dialectically opposed, but are seen as mutually reinforcing gifts from God.

Verses 26-27 close the first chapter and provide the transition to the essays that follow. Once more, we see the basic contrast between the measure of the world, revealed by a foolish religion that fails to control the tongue and indulges or deceives the heart, and the measure of God, revealed by a pure and undefiled religion that resists the measure of the world and shows its authenticity by giving gifts to the needy in the same way God gives them to all creatures. The first chapter of James not only anticipates the themes to be developed by the essays to follow, but also weaves them into a coherent epitome of the composition's basic point: Live as a friend of God and not as a friend of the world.

REFLECTIONS

As wisdom literature, James challenges readers —who now occupy the place of "the twelve tribes in the Dispersion"—more directly than do narratives about Jesus or discussions by Paul. Readers are presented with commands that are supported by warrants. Their response cannot stop with an analysis of what the command might have *meant* back then. They must ask, "Do we really think this warrant to be true? Is this how we view reality?" And then, more than that, readers must go beyond the testing of the text against theory to the testing of their lives against the text: "Will we now see and think and speak and act in this way?" Readers who so respond to Jas 1:2-27 should experience some real difficulty, for James is so uncompromising in forcing a choice where most people would prefer a compromise. James's call to consider all the various trials into which people fall as a matter "entirely of joy" flies in the face of a hedonistic culture that equates suffering with evil and seeks every means possible either to avoid trials or to anesthetize the self against them. It also challenges a longing for a faith that is secure from trial and test, by insisting that faith only matures by what it endures.

The contrasting evaluations of suffering derive from fundamentally opposing perceptions of reality, and it is here, above all, that James challenges present-day readers. For those living under the influence of modernity, the intellectual atmosphere shaped by the Enlightenment, "the world" is what is most real and obvious. It is a closed system of cause and effect and of limited resources. Humans are defined by their place in this system, and the system is defined by the capacity of human reason to measure it. What seems least real or obvious is "God," a name that has increasingly been reduced to a concept, and one that people must struggle to take seriously.

For James, the opposite is the case. "God" appears as the subject in these verses some eight times, not as a remote or remnant concept, but as the One who is most real and defines reality. God creates humans, listens to their prayers, rewards their fidelity. Above all, reality itself is defined by the God who gives to all generously and without reproach (1:5), and who is the source of every good and perfect gift (1:17). If reality is defined by the endless bestowal of gifts, then it is not a closed system but an open one, not a world of limited resources, but of infinitely renewable resources. And if God defines reality, then humans are not in competition with each other for their very being, so that their desires must lead ultimately to murder; rather, humans can gift each other as God gifts them (1:27).

The real challenge of chapter 1 to the readers of James is whether this view of reality is really one they "know" (1:3, 19) and seek to live by (1:22-25), or whether they are "self-deceived" (1:22, 26) by trying to live with a divided consciousness (1:8). Do they really believe that those who endure in faith until death will receive a crown that is life (1:12)? If so, then they can, with simple hearts, dispose of themselves joyfully in generous giving. But if they do not, then it makes sense for them to be self-protective, to husband their resources. Do they really think that God's implanted word is able to save their lives (1:21)? If they do, then they will turn in every circumstance to pray for the wisdom so to live by that word (1:5). But if they do not, then they should abandon humility and meekness in favor of a "human anger" by which they can gain security for themselves. It is almost as though, before developing the implications of these convictions, James insists that readers pause and ask: Do we really believe this? Is this the understanding of reality to which we are committed?

JAMES 2:1-13

ACTIVE FAITH, CONSISTENT LOVE

COMMENTARY

James 2:1-26 forms a single argument concerning the necessity of translating convictions into action, or the faith of "our glorious Lord Jesus Christ" (2:1) into the "works of faith." This coherent essay picks up from 1:26-27, which identifies authentic religion as one of rejecting the standard of the world and living by God's standard in helping the needy. James now considers those who profess the faith of Jesus yet do not live up to it. In 2:1-13, he shows how preference for the rich rather than the poor is a betrayal of the law of love. In 2:14-16, he shows how the refusal of help to those in need is an empty faith. The richness of the essay makes separate treatment of the two sections desirable, but readers should recognize that they form part of the same argument.

James 2:1-13, in turn, can be divided into vv. 1-7, which present a vivid example of how a community acts in opposition to its professed ideal, and vv. 8-13, which show how such behavior is inconsistent with the claim to live by the law of love taught by Jesus. The two parts are linked by the notion of favoritism, which is declared incompatible with the faith of Jesus in 2:1, and which is declared incompatible with the law of love in 2:9.

2:1-7. With remarkable conciseness, James sketches a situation that makes the readers' double-mindedness apparent. He pictures them gathered in the assembly, interestingly called "synagogue" (συναγωγή *synagōgē*, vv. 2-3). It is not clear whether they are meeting for worship or for purposes of deciding disputes (cf. 1 Cor 6:4-6). Neither is it clear whether the two people who enter the assembly are members of the community. Certainly the evidence from 1 Corinthians suggests the possibility of some members being considerably better off than others (see Rom 16:1-2, 23; 1 Cor 16:15-18). In any case, the behavior here described applies to virtually every human group. The community treats the richly attired person with every mark of worldly honor: This person is invited to come close, to sit, and to be comfortable. The shabbily dressed person is treated with scorn and degradation, put at a distance and made to stand—or worse, made to sit in a position of submission. The behavior of these members of the community has already answered James's rhetorical question in the affirmative; they have shown discrimination and become like unjust judges. The question is more complex than it first appears. The term James uses could also mean that they are divided within themselves, even as they make discriminations among themselves; in other words, they are double-minded (1:7-8). And by implying that they are corrupt judges, James alerts us to the original biblical context for language about impartiality; in Lev 19:15, judges are forbidden to discriminate between the rich and poor on the basis of appearance, but are to decide cases impartially.

James's question gains its real force, however, when placed against 2:5-7, which shows how clearly the community's behavior betrays the measure by which it claims to live. Here James invokes the most basic premise of the community's life. In language that strongly echoes the beatitudes of Jesus (Matt 5:3; Luke 6:20), he reminds them that God has chosen those who are poor in the world's eyes to be rich with respect to faith, and to be heirs of the kingdom, promised to those who love God (2:5). Notice that James again opposes two measures: The view of "the world" is antithetical to that of "God." Within the community of "the faith of Jesus Christ"—that is, within a community measured by the preaching and teaching of Jesus—the poor should hold a position of honor, since they have been honored by God. Remember 1:9, which declared that the lowly member should exalt in his or her exaltation, while the rich person should exalt in being lowered. But the assembly pictured by James acts in opposition to God's measure. It meets as a community of faith, but it acts according to the ancient world's measure of values in which the rich and powerful are shown honor in the hopes of receiving from them a benefaction in return. Employing the language that fits within that world of honor and shame, James observes tersely that they have dishonored the poor person (2:6).[11]

James sharpens his attack on this double-mindedness even further by showing his readers that their behavior contradicts not only the faith of Jesus but also their own experience! They are, in fact, a community that is being oppressed by the rich by means of legal fraud. James's language is emphatic: The rich are the very ones who are dragging community members into court! This activity of the oppressive rich will be described even more graphically in 5:1-6. James adds that (again emphatically) the rich are "the very ones" who blaspheme the noble name that is invoked over the community (2:7), by which he surely means the name of Jesus.

His skewering of these double-minded Christians could not be more precise. They have gathered in the name of Jesus, who proclaimed the poor to be blessed. They are a community that is itself oppressed by the rich. Yet when a poor person enters the assembly, they act toward a community member the same way the rich act toward them!

2:8-13. When James begins speaking of the law in v. 8, it appears at first that he might be changing the subject. Closer analysis, however, shows that this is not the case. What does James mean by "the royal law" after all? The term βασιλικός (*basilikos*) is used in ancient literature for anything having to do with a king, and in some contexts, such as this one, it can refer to a king's rule or kingdom. James has just spoken of the poor as those who were to inherit "the kingdom" (v. 5). When he refers to the royal law, therefore, he means the law that obtains in the kingdom of God as proclaimed by Jesus. This becomes even more evident when he quotes Lev 19:18, "You shall love your neighbor as yourself" (NRSV), as that "law of the kingdom."

We know from the gospel tradition as well as from other early Christian writings that this commandment held a privileged place and probably went back to the teaching of Jesus himself (see Matt 19:19; 22:39; Mark 12:31; Luke 10:27; Rom 13:9; Gal 5:14). With the expression "those who love [God]" in 1:12 and 2:5, the citation from Lev 19:18 completes the combination of love of God and love of neighbor, isolated by Jesus as the central commandments.

The connection to Jesus' proclamation of the kingdom of God (and therefore to "the faith of Jesus Christ") is one reason for citing Lev 19:18 with reference to behavior in the assembly. There is also another. James's phrasing in 2:8 is peculiar. He says that if they "really" fulfill the royal law of love, they do well. But his phrasing suggests that this fulfillment must be "according to the scripture." Neither the NRSV nor the NIV captures this nuance in translation. What James means becomes clear when he says that if they practice discrimination, then they are sinners and are convicted by the law as transgressors (v. 9). The prohibition of partiality in judgment, as we saw in the discussion of 2:1-4, is found in Lev 19:15, in the immediate context of the "royal commandment" of love (Lev 19:18). For James, then, "love of neighbor" is not a vague or undefined ideal. It is spelled out by Torah itself. Indeed, we find that throughout the composition, James alludes to the text of Leviticus 19:1 in order to fill out what is meant by loving the neighbor (Lev 19:12 = Jas 5:12; Lev 19:13 = Jas 5:4; Lev 19:15 = Jas 2:1, 9; Lev 19:16 = Jas 4:11; Lev 19:17*b* = Jas 5:20; Lev 19:18*a* = Jas 5:9; Lev 19:18*b* = Jas 2:8).

James's statement in v. 10 that a person who fails in one commandment is liable for the whole law must be seen in this context. He is not speaking theoretically but practically. The person who claims to live by the law of love, yet practices the sort of discrimination that the law of love itself forbids has broken the law of love entirely. The reason, as James then goes on to show, is that transgression is not against a "commandment" but against the lawgiver. The unity of the law is found in the will of the legislator. To make this point, James quotes from the Decalogue according to the order of commandments in the LXX

---

11. For a guide to honor/shame values in the NT world, see D. A. deSilva, *Despising Shame: Honor Discourse and Community Maintenance in the Epistle to the Hebrews*, SBLDS 152 (Atlanta: Scholars Press, 1995).

(2:11). The same God forbade both murder and adultery; if one avoids adultery but commits murder, one is still a "transgressor of the law." This example is meant to confirm James's judgment concerning partiality in the assembly. If they have discriminated among themselves on the basis of appearance, then they have entirely missed the meaning of the law of love.

This passage gives us some sense of James's distinctive appropriation of Torah. We notice first that "faith" and "law" are not opposed but are seen as complementary. Second, we see that "law" is not spelled out in terms of the ritual commandments of Torah, such as circumcision or the observance of feasts or purity and dietary regulations. There is no trace of such a Judaizing tendency in James. Rather, the law includes the moral heart of Torah—namely, the Ten Commandments and the law of love (a combination attested also in Rom 13:9). Finally, James uses the teaching of Jesus to identify the love of neighbor as "the law of the kingdom."

It is in this light that James's next statement should be read; his readers should "so speak and so act" as people who are to be judged by the "law of freedom" (v. 12). The reality of a future judgment by God is, of course, as standard in early Christianity as it was in Judaism. Such a judgment is assumed by James's assurance of reward for those who are faithful to God (1:12). That the keeping of God's law will be a criterion of judgment is also taken as obvious by Paul in Rom 2:6-16. The only issue here is what James means by the "law of freedom." James used the expression "the perfect law, the law of liberty" in 1:25 (NRSV) as that glass into which people should gaze in order to be "not hearers who forget but doers who act" (NRSV). This perfect law of freedom has now been identified as the "law of the kingdom," which is given succinct expression by the commandment of love for neighbor. Those, then, who look on their neighbors in the assembly should not act as judges with evil designs (v. 4) by practicing partiality and discrimination, but should remember that they themselves will be judged by the One "who is able to save and to destroy" (4:12 NRSV). In v. 13, James begins by stating the same sort of equation that we find in the Lord's prayer: Judgment is without mercy to those who are merciless. Actually, the phrase James uses is "to the one who has not done mercy." The Greek is evocative. Greek patristic commentators picked up here an allusion to the "doing of mercy" that was almsgiving (see, e.g., Sir 29:1). And they interpreted this passage in the light of the parable of Lazarus and Dives in Luke 16:19-31; if the rich man there had given alms, God would have shown him mercy, but since he did not help Lazarus, his own judgment was "without mercy."[12] Such an interpretation may seem at first to be fanciful, but when we place v. 13 in context, we see that it does, in fact, serve as a transitional verse between vv. 1-12 and vv. 14-26. Is it any surprise, then, that we should immediately find the negative example of those who refuse help and hospitality to the poor in vv. 14-16, followed by the positive examples of faith and hospitality provided by Abraham and Rahab in vv. 20-25? These examples help to show how "mercy triumphs over judgment" (2:13b). James's argument, then, continues past this point into an elaboration in more general terms of the necessity of acting out one's convictions. But that development remains rooted in the practical life of the community, and above all in the way the poor are either honored or scorned within this community that claims to live by the faith of Jesus. On the basis of this very specific application of the law of love, James suggests, the community will be judged by God.

12. See, e.g., Niles the Abbot *Peristeria* IV.15.

REFLECTIONS

James enjoys not a little of its reputation for vividness and power from this part of his composition. At one level, one can see this as effective rhetoric; the techniques of the diatribe (e.g., addressing an imaginary opponent) are here put to good effect. At another level, however, it is impossible to miss the tone of prophetic outrage, as James lashes members of the community of faith whose behavior in the assembly "with the noble name invoked over them" so contradicts their professed identity.

Although the scene described in 2:1-4 bears some of the marks of its own period (the specific implications of rank attached to wearing gold rings, the symbolism of being seated in one place rather than another), its stark simplicity transcends cultural particularity and locates a pattern attested among virtually all groups. It speaks directly, therefore, to all forms of discrimination on the basis of appearance practiced within communities. The form of partiality most obviously opposed is that which excludes or marginalizes another on the basis of appearance. It does not take long to compile a list of the kinds of appearances that have led to such marginalization. In contemporary America, the "appearances" of race and gender are instantly recognizable, for they have, through titanic struggles, finally been brought to general consciousness. On these fronts, the church's record has been mixed; despite some strong efforts toward genuine inclusiveness, racial and gender discrimination is still a reality within most denominations. The sort of discrimination of the poor person that James describes is less easy to see, partially because denominations tend to sort themselves out along socioeconomic lines. But to imagine a dirty and bewildered street person wandering into a Sunday morning fellowship seeking warmth and coffee is in most cases also to imagine a deeply uncomfortable fellowship. Such instances—and it is easy to multiply the ways in which people can, because of appearance, size, gender, sexual orientation, and status, seem to be "poor by the world's standards"—challenge the church's recollection that it is supposed to be a "kingdom" made up of just such inconvenient and unacceptable persons. When the poor cannot find a place in a Christian church, that church no longer has any connection to Jesus.

Perhaps an even more frequent form of partiality takes place when the rich or famous or powerful are shown disproportionate attention and honor in the assembly. The pastoral problem presented by a rich church donor who also wants to receive deference as well as the power to direct the church's affairs is not new. The evidence is that the very first Christian communities faced the same tension; they needed the financial support of the rich, yet they lived within a value system that rejected the honor that patronage assumed as its due. Pastors in small and great churches alike recognize immediately the powerful urge to cater to those few wealthy members on whom the financial stability or success of their particular congregation seems to rest. James's vignette suggests how the wisdom of the world operates even within the community of faith, and how easy it is for communities to become double-minded, not only in their marginalization of those whose appearance it finds uncomfortable, but also in their cultivation of those whose patronage it seeks.

James's privileging of the poor within the community of faith is startlingly close to Jesus' own proclamation to the poor that "yours is the kingdom of God" (Luke 6:20 NRSV). And when he declares the love of neighbor to be "the law of the kingdom," he once more echoes teaching that without question goes back to Jesus himself. James is also a valuable witness to the meaning of that central Christian law. A Christian ethics based on love can often appear to be both idealistic and lacking in content. Who, after all, is one's neighbor, and what does it mean to love? By placing the commandment of love where he does, James makes clear that "the neighbor" must include all who enter our space, not only those whom we find attractive or even valuable to us, but above all those whom we find alien and, therefore, threatening.

The commandment of love is, in James, neither abstract nor lacking in content. It is as real as the assembly that gathers together every week and is as specific as the question of where people are to be seated. As for content, James's insistence that love must be "according to the scripture" and his citation of the Decalogue show that anyone who murders or commits adultery or breaks any of the other of these commandments cannot claim to love the neighbor. More than that, his use of Lev 19:13-18 to fill out the demands of love provides Christians with some sense of what other behaviors clearly contradict this command. Discrimination is incompatible with love (2:1, 9); so are slander and judging a neighbor (4:11); so is grumbling against a neighbor (5:9); so is oppressing the poor (5:4); so is taking oaths (5:12); so is failing to reprove a neighbor who does wrong (5:20). For James, both "faith" and "love" have a strong and compelling moral urgency; faith in God and love for God cannot be separated from the way the neighbor is treated.

And just as his definition of authentic religion in 1:27 had nothing to do with proper theology and everything to do with the visiting of orphans and widows in their affliction, so also it cannot be by accident that his illustration of faith and love also involves precisely those who are, in the eyes of the world, most negligible and disposable: the poor, who in virtually every age include most of all women and their children. The assembly gathered *by* faith, says James, must act on the basis of another set of values. Those whom the world most despises are to be regarded, *in* faith, as heirs of the kingdom and, therefore, honored by the specific hospitality of the community: its greeting, its body language, its space. It is by this measure that the community is to be judged (2:12). Woe to the church that does not meet this measure of mercy, for it will face merciless judgment (2:13).

JAMES 2:14-26

THE DEEDS OF FAITH

COMMENTARY

James had insisted in 1:22-25 that his readers be not only hearers of the word but also doers. Now he insists that "faith alone" is not adequate without the deeds of faith (2:18-26). Likewise, in 1:27, James identified the care for those in need as the mark of true religion. Now in 2:14-16 he shows how false is a faith that refuses help to those in need.

Connections to the first part of chapter 2 are also obvious. The rhetorical question in 2:14 poses the same sort of opposition as in 2:1. James then provides a similar vivid hypothetical case (2:15-16; see 2:2-3) that ends in a rhetorical question (2:16; see 2:4). In 2:5-7, readers were shown the logical inconsistency of their behavior. Now in 2:18-19 the claim that faith and deeds are separable is refuted by a *reductio ad absurdum*. In 2:8-11, James argued from Scripture for the unitary character of obedience to the law of love. In 2:20-25, he argues from Scripture for the unitary character of faith and faith's deeds. Finally, just as 2:12 provided an aphoristic conclusion to the first section, so also does 2:26 conclude the entire essay with an aphorism. The main literary difference between the two parts of the chapter is the introduction of an imaginary interlocutor in 2:18, whom James—in typical diatribal style—uses to advance the argument.

Attention to these internal literary connections and the logic of James's argument is important here above all because this section of the letter, which has by far received the most attention in the history of interpretation, has been taken out of context for purposes of comparison with Paul, and as a consequence has been distorted. Because Paul and James use a range of similar vocabulary (faith/saving/works/righteousness) and employ the same scriptural example (Abraham), it was natural enough to compare this section to Paul's discussions in Galatians 3 and Romans 4.

It is obvious to every reader that James is saying something different from what Paul said. The question is, how different? Patristic authors, and even Reformers like Calvin, read James and Paul as applying the same convictions to different circumstances.[13] The real problem began when Luther concluded that difference in this case was a contradiction. Since Luther regarded Paul as the true apostle, he demoted James; and since Luther had such enormous influence on the development of NT scholarship, his opinion sustained the marginalization of James. Enormous amounts of scholarship have been devoted to supporting and refuting Luther's charge that James "drives us back to the law." Perhaps the biggest loss has been that such obsessive attention to one passage has led to the neglect of the rest of James as well as to the neglect of the broad range of agreement between James and Paul not only on this but on other points as well. It is very unlikely that James was responding to Paul or that Paul was responding to James. Like other NT writings (e.g., John 8:34-59; Acts 3:25; 7:2-8; Heb 11:8-19), Paul and James use the figure of Abraham to make their respective arguments concerning the good news to the Gentiles and the necessity of acting out faith, with language that converges enticingly at the semantic level yet diverges just as decisively at the conceptual level.

2:14-17. Despite the difficulties posed by 2:18 (see below), the basic point made here is simple. James starts with the question of "usefulness" (2:14). How can faith that is professed but is not manifested in deeds ("works") be authentic? Even though he uses the term "save" in the question, "Can faith

---

13. See, e.g., John Damascene *The Orthodox Faith* IV.9; Calvin, *Commentary on James* 2:21.

save you?" (2:14), James's topic is not really soteriology; he has already declared that it is the "implanted word" from God that "is able to save your souls" (1:21). The issue is, rather, how to be a "doer" of that word. Notice furthermore that James does not talk here about the "works of the law" but specifically about the "works of faith." His topic is the necessary unity between attitude and action that preoccupies the moralists of his and virtually every age. The point is certainly not that the actions substitute for the attitude! It is, rather, that the actions reveal the attitude and make it "alive." As interpreters from Origen to Calvin recognized, James's position is precisely that expressed by Paul in Gal 5:6, "neither circumcision nor uncircumcision counts for anything; the only thing that counts is *faith working through love*" (NRSV).

It is within such a moral framework that this section of James should be understood. His opening illustration provides the negative example and bears strong resemblance to the admonition in 1 John 3:17-18. The "brother and sister" are obviously among the poorest of the poor, lacking both clothes and daily food. Furthermore, their condition cannot be missed; the believer sees them and speaks to them. But they are dismissed with kind wishes and religious jargon (2:15-16). This is the perfect illustration of the "empty religion" that James rejects, combining self-indulgence, failure to control the tongue, and a refusal to care for orphans and widows (1:27). It is, therefore, not "unstained by the world" or "pure and undefiled before God." James declares such purported faith to be, simply, "dead" (2:17).

2:18-19. At this point James has his fictional dialogue partner say his piece. Verse 18 is, however, infamously difficult to interpret, largely because it appears as though the objector actually holds the position of the author! The best solution of a hard problem is to take the objection as advancing the divisibility of faith and deeds (or "works"), as though one person could have one and another, the other. Read this way, James's response is an insistence on the indivisibility of the two: One can "show" faith by pointing to the deeds of faith. But what would faith look like without any deeds? James suggests that it would be simply "belief," as an intellectual assent: There is one God. His response is ironic: Good for you! But the inadequacy of such "faith" is obvious when one considers that even those forces that oppose God have *that* level of belief, without responding to God positively at all (2:19). This is a parody of faith rather than the response of those who love God (1:12; 2:5).

2:20-26. James's response to the interlocutor shows his use of the diatribal style of argumentation and something of his stylistic flair. In 2:20 he uses apostrophe and a rhetorical question with a fine sense of irony. His interlocutor is an "empty fellow" (NIV, "foolish man"; NRSV, "senseless person"), who will be shown how faith "apart from works [ἔργα *erga*] is empty [ἀργή *argē*, lit., "without work," *a + erga*]." His own understanding of genuine ("perfect") faith is found in the examples he cites from Torah (2:20-25). Both Abraham and Rahab had faith that was *demonstrated* by their actions. James's choice of the testing of Abraham (in the call to sacrifice his son Isaac; see Gen 22:1-18) is particularly appropriate, for Abraham's obedience was precisely an *act of faith*. In a sentence whose Greek is much clearer than either the NIV or the NRSV translation, James insists that the faith "co-worked the work" and that faith was "brought to perfection/fulfillment" by the deed (2:22; cf. 1:4). In other words, faith is the subject from beginning to end. Deeds do not replace faith; they complete it.

Like Paul, James cites Gen 15:6, which declares Abraham righteous because of his faith. But James's way of understanding that verse is a bit different; for James, Abraham's willingness to sacrifice his son in obedience to God was itself the "fulfillment" of the text in Gen 15:6. Thus the translation of 2:21 might better be that Abraham was "shown to be righteous," since the entire line of argumentation has involved demonstration (see v. 18). And it is in the light of James's own demonstration—rather than as a response to Paul on a completely different controversy—that his declaration in v. 24 should be understood. If "works" are understood as the "works/deeds" of faith itself—that is, as the expression of faith itself in acts of obedience—then it seems plainly the case that, as he says, a person is declared righteous on the basis of deeds and not only on faith. (It remains one of the peculiar aspects of the history of theology that Luther's *sola fide* must be derived from this passage in James, since it is certainly not found in Gal 2:16.)

Distinctive to James's treatment of Abraham is his designation of him as "friend of God." This is not part of the Genesis citation, but seems to derive from a merging of the statements in 2 Chr 20:7 and Isa 41:8 that God "loved" Abraham and the Hellenistic understanding of friendship as a peculiarly close sharing of all material and spiritual things. "Friends," said the Greeks, "are of one mind."[14] For James to call Abraham "friend of God" because of his offering of Isaac fits within the dualistic framework of his composition. We have seen him opposing the measure/wisdom of the world with that from God (see 2:5). This opposition reaches its most explicit form in 4:4, where James will contrast "friendship with the world" and "friendship with God" as antithetical options.

Abraham represents the person who is not double-minded and truly "wills one thing." He thinks and acts according to the measure of God. If Abraham had been a "friend of the world," then he would not have been willing to sacrifice his son. He would have viewed reality as a closed system in which his future was determined by what he could possess and control. Even though Isaac was a gift from God, he was now "Abraham's" and his way of securing the promise. Thinking in worldly terms, Abraham's killing his son when he had no human hope for another would be folly. But Abraham showed he was a friend of God, because he considered God to be One who gives to all generously and without grudging (1:5), the giver of every good and perfect gift (1:17), who gives to the humble a greater gift (4:6). Abraham saw things God's way: If God could give Isaac as a gift, then God could give another gift also. Abraham's willingness to give back to God what God had gifted him with demonstrates and perfects his faith and shows what "friendship with God" means.

The example of Rahab takes only one verse (2:25), but is noteworthy first of all because it provides a straightforward female exemplar from Torah—a woman who is to be imitated for her own behavior and not because of her relationship to a patriarch. Rahab's story is recounted in Josh 2:2-21, and in Jewish lore she was celebrated above all as a proselyte and as an example of hospitality.[15] The combination of faith and hospitality is picked up by James. In contrast to Heb 11:31, James does not mention her faith explicitly, but readers would remember that Rahab made a confession of the Lord as the one God in Josh 2:16. James focuses on her reception of the Israelite scouts as an *expression* of that faith.

The question arises as to why Rahab is included at all, if her example is so unelaborated. This question attaches itself also to James's odd use of the plural "works" with reference to Abraham in 2:21-22—odd, because only one "work" (the binding of Isaac) is mentioned. It is possible that this plural is the clue to the subtler midrashic implications of James's inclusion of Rahab and Abraham. In the Jewish tradition, both figures were renowned above all for their hospitality.[16] It is certainly possible that James intended the reader to catch not only that Rahab's faith was demonstrated by hospitality but that Abraham's was as well. This possibility is intriguing on two counts. First, it provides a male and a female figure to correspond to the "brother and sister" in dire need of hospitality (2:14-16) and who are turned away by the pious but unmerciful believer. Second, it makes the "deeds" of Abraham and Rahab fit the specific argument that James has been developing throughout chapter 2. The first vignette in vv. 1-4 showed the poor being marginalized within the community by a lack of hospitality; the second showed the desperately needy deprived of assistance by community members. Perhaps the combined examples of Abraham and Rahab provide a response, showing how active faith demands a sharing of gifts that God has given and a providing of space to those whom God sends unexpectedly. It is significant that whereas James portrays the "wicked judges" (vv. 2-4) as speaking, the callous believers (vv. 15-16) as speaking, and the dense interlocutor (v. 18) as speaking, Abraham and Rahab do not speak. Their faith is shown in *action.* James concludes this discussion with a final aphorism in v. 26 that repeats v. 17: Faith without deeds is dead.

---

14. See, e.g., Euripides *Orestes* 1046; Aristotle *Nicomachean Ethics* 1168B.

15. See, e.g., *Deuteronomy Rabbah* 2:26-27; *Ruth Rabbah* 2:1.
16. See Philo *On Abraham* 167; *Aboth de Rabbi Nathan* 7.

REFLECTIONS

James's passionate insistence in this section that faith must be translated into practice seems like the most obvious good sense. We might wonder why it needs saying. Yet the evidence is overwhelming that precisely this reminder above all needs to be made repeatedly and urgently. There is something deep inside humans that leads them to presume that knowing the right truth or holding the right position is enough to make them righteous. The ancient Greco-Roman philosophers knew this. The *Discourses* of Epictetus are filled with remonstrances against students of philosophy who can quote their textbooks concerning self-control and reasonableness, yet whose lives exemplify neither.[17] Indeed, even among philosophers, the gap between profession and performance was often so prominent as to encourage the popular stereotype of the daytime philosopher, dignified and sober, who was also the nighttime carouser, lewd and drunk.[18] The earliest Christian movement was not free from this same tendency, as the moral exhortations in Paul's letters make plain. Among James's readers, as well, there were clearly some who considered that believing "that God is one" (2:19) qualified them to be considered among God's people, or that believing in "our glorious Lord Jesus Christ" (2:1) was itself sufficient to consider themselves members of the kingdom proclaimed by Jesus. The propensity to find a refuge in religion and a resting place within a community of faith remains constant and keeps James's exhortation perennially relevant.

The tendency can take the form of compulsive doctrinal correctness or ritual conformity. The mark of a "good" Christian can become the fervent affirmation of the right confessional formulae or a pledge of allegiance to the inspiration of Scripture or an insistence on the inerrancy of a leader or the dedication to the proper liturgical forms. It can also take the form of an obsessive use of religious language, as though faith were a matter of a style of speech, and that devotion to a person could best be demonstrated by the number of times his name was mentioned. The mark of a "good" Christian can become the constant invocation of the Lord in every conversation.

These postures of piety, James reminds us, can coexist with behavior that is deeply inconsonant with true faith. To sit in an assembly of worship "in the name of Jesus" and to scorn the very poor whom Jesus embraced is to confuse correct liturgy with authentic faith. To dismiss the needy on the street with the pious wish, "Go in peace," is to corrupt religious language.

There is certainly not a congregation in the world today that would declare Jas 2:14-26 wrong. All Christians would agree that faith needs to be demonstrated in action. The issue is precisely whether that theoretical agreement is met in such congregations with corresponding attention to action, and, furthermore, what sort of action the community considers to be a priority. One way to test this is to ask whether the content of sermons, the subject matter of meetings, or the line items of budgets reflect the consciousness of the community that the "faith of Jesus Christ" is not a matter of doctrine or ritual, but a matter of sustained moral presence in the world.

An even more pertinent question—especially to churches in North America—is the extent to which churches would, as James does, make the community's response to the poor a touchstone for testing the authenticity of its faith. Insofar as contemporary Christianity has aligned itself unthinkingly with the individualistic and competitive ethos of capitalism, or allowed itself to be seduced into equating financial success with God's blessing, it has, by James's standards, become a friend of the world and not a friend of God. The obsession of many congregations—and most televangelists—with money must be regarded as an obscene perversion of Christianity.

17. See, e.g., Epictetus *Discourses* II.1.31; III.22.9.
18. See Lucian of Samosata *Timon*.

It is to the credit of liberation theologians—for many of whom James is a most important text—that they have reminded Christians of the central place of the poor in Jesus' preaching and in the call of the church. Insofar as liberation thought has worked to empower the poor by encouraging communities of solidarity, it has been an extremely beneficial development in Christian theology and practice. Insofar as it has aligned itself with Marxist class theory, however, it has also tended to distort both the concrete realities of poverty and the character of Christian hope by locating evil entirely in alienating social structures, and not also in the depths of human freedom.

James does not rail against an economic system that oppresses the poor. Instead, he calls precisely for the formation of communities gathered by the faith of Jesus in which the poor are honored and cared for by others who are themselves "poor" in the eyes of the world. Nor does James suggest that those who are impoverished need to be relieved of their poverty before they can claim human dignity. Just the opposite: The poor have been chosen by God to be heirs of the kingdom. To say that the poor need to get possessions to become more fully human is to accept the equation of being and having characteristic of the world. For James, the hope of the poor is in the God who gives every perfect gift to all without grudging, and a crown of glory to those who love God (1:12).

James demands that we pay attention to the ragged homeless person who wanders into our assembly, to the desperately needy man or woman we meet on our city streets, to the orphans and widows who make up so much of the world's perennially impoverished population. And he asks us: Have you scorned this ragged person in your assembly by seeking to remove him from your sight and that of the rich person you have placed in prominence? Have you covered over your neglect of the famished and ill-clad by good wishes and pious language? Have you clung to your safe orthodoxy and ritual rather than, like Abraham and Rahab, opened your hearts and your spaces for those who are different and threatening? If our answer to these questions is yes, then, by James's standard, we cannot claim to live by the faith of Jesus Christ or the law of love, which is the law of his kingdom.

JAMES 3:1-12

ON THE PERILS OF SPEECH

COMMENTARY

This is a self-contained essay, beginning with a prohibition (like that in 2:1) to "my brothers" and concluding with a short aphorism (like 2:26) to "my brothers." The Greek is exceptionally well crafted, with a high incidence of alliteration and balanced clauses (3:5, 9). The use of particles shows that James has done more than string together a number of aphorisms; he has constructed an argument. Its direction is announced in 3:1-2. On one side, 3:2 seems to suggest that human perfection is possible and that control of speech represents the height of perfection. On the other side, 3:1 contains a harsher perception: Speech is a dangerous thing, and the role of a teacher is hazardous.

Following this opening set of ambiguous statements, 3:3-4 develops the optimistic side, using the typical Hellenistic commonplaces concerning the control of speech. But 3:5-6 moves in a more pessimistic direction, emphasizing both the power of the tongue and its destructive character. This pessimism is given most explicit expression in 3:7-8, which contrasts human control over creation to the human inability to control speech. The example in 3:9-10 is explicitly theological. It draws the discussion of speech into the ethical and religious dualism of the letter as a whole. Nothing so reveals the destructive power of speech than the cursing of another human. Nothing so vividly reveals double-mindedness than to have that curse proceed from the same mouth that blesses God. The theme of "doubleness" is then developed by a rapid series of contrasts in 3:11-12, all of which have the simple point: This ought not to be so!

It is typical for James to announce themes in chapter 1 that are elaborated by later passages. James 3:1-12 obviously develops the statements found in 1:19 that everyone should be quick to hear but slow to speak, and in 1:26 that a pretense of religion without control of the tongue is worthless. The essay also pulls together a thematic interest in the proper and improper uses of speech. Before this section, we have seen several negative examples of speech: the claim that one's temptations come from God (1:13), the greetings that are flattering to the rich and scornful of the poor (2:3-6), the careless religious discourse of those who wish well for the poor but do not help them (2:16), the superficial speech of those who claim to have faith even without deeds (2:18). After 3:1-12, we shall see other examples: judging and slandering a brother (4:11), boasting of one's plans (4:13), grumbling against a brother (5:9). Against these negative examples, James will show the positive functions of speech in the faith community (5:12-20).

All of the wisdom of the ancient Mediterranean world, both Greco-Roman and Jewish, agreed on certain points concerning the power and perils of speech. From the sages of ancient Egypt, through the biblical books of Proverbs and Sirach, to the essays of Plutarch and Seneca, there is a consensus that silence is better than speech, that hearing, not speaking, is the pathway to wisdom, that speech when necessary should be brief, that above all speech should be under control and never the expression of rage or envy. The mark of the wise person was above all control of speech (see Sir 5:13).[19]

James's miniature essay in chap. 3 would recommend itself to the moralists of his world, not least because it so markedly demonstrates the rhetorical ideal of brevity; he manages to say a great deal in a remarkably short span of statements. His essay also contains a number of the commonplaces of his cultural context concerning speech. First among these is the importance of controlled speech for the sage or teacher (v. 1). It is striking that for the only

---

19. See also *Pirke Aboth* 5:7; Philo *On Dreams* 2:42.

time in this letter, James uses the first-person plural with reference to teachers, "we who teach will be judged with greater strictness." Not only are teachers people who use speech more frequently, as public persons who have control over others, but also they are subject to temptations with regard to speech that others are not: arrogance and domination over students, anger at contradiction or opposition, slander and abuse directed toward rivals, flattery of students for the sake of popularity. Such failures were especially grievous in a culture that took teaching seriously as the modeling of virtue.

Also staples of Greco-Roman moral discourse on speech are the images of the bridle, which controls the horse by controlling the horse's mouth (v. 3), and the rudder, which enables a pilot to control by his will a mighty ship.[20] In each of these cases, there is the contrast between the smallness of the instrument and the power it exercises. The comparison between taming wild animals and taming the tongue is also attested in this literature (vv. 7-8).[21] And throughout these writings, we find a similar emphasis on the tongue's power to effect both good and bad (vv. 5-6).

In other ways, James's essay diverges from the standard treatment of speech in his cultural context. In the first place, he is much more pessimistic in his evaluation of human speech. Hellenistic moralists are aware how difficult control of the tongue is, but they are fundamentally sanguine about the possibility of bringing speech into line with reason and virtue. James is not. He flatly asserts that no one can control speech (v. 8). Indeed, he personifies the tongue, as though it were an independent agent outside anyone's control: "It makes great boasts" (v. 5 NIV; NRSV, "it boasts of great exploits"). Following the logic of v. 2—if anyone controls speech, that is a perfect person—James does not regard human perfection as possible.

James also heightens the capacity of speech to do evil. His characterization of it as "a restless evil, full of deadly poison" (v. 8) is entirely negative. In James's treatment, the tongue is almost a cosmic force set on evil. Verse 6 is very difficult to translate, but the meaning is that the tongue within our body in effect represents or constitutes the "world" that for James is inimical to God. And in a touch that will be repeated in 3:13–4:8, this opposition is seen as more than human. The tongue is a fire that is "lit from Gehenna" (NRSV and NIV, "from hell") and itself "sets aflame the cycle of life." As the alternative translation of the NIV and the NRSV suggests, the translation of this last part of v. 6 is difficult and disputed; the idea seems to be that the power of wicked speech can spread evil through everything in human existence. When compared to similar discourses in the Greco-Roman world,[22] James's discussion of speech is also more fundamentally and pervasively religious. In the Hellenistic world, silence was sometimes connected to the religious awe associated with the mysteries;[23] but for the most part, attention to speech was a matter of cultivating individual virtue. Although it was recognized that speech could do harm to others, more emphasis was placed on the ridicule and shame that uncontrolled speech brought upon the loquacious person. In contrast, James makes failure to control speech the very antithesis of authentic religion (1:26). His religious framework is that of Torah. He evaluates speech in relational—that is, covenantal—terms. Human speech and action must be normed by the speech and action of God, who has chosen to become involved with humans. Human behavior, therefore, is judged not only on its capacity to perfect or to flaw an individual's character, but above all on the way it manifests right or wrong relationships.

Several aspects of James's religious emphasis are evident in 3:1-12. The theme of double-mindedness (1:8; 4:8), for example, here takes the form of being "double-tongued." For James, this is not merely a matter of saying one thing and doing another. When the same tongue is used both to bless God and to curse a human person who is created in the likeness of God (3:9), the allegiance by which one claims to live is betrayed in a fundamental way. There is not only moral failure here, but also sin. The theological warrant that humans are created according to God's likeness is not derived from observation of

---

20. See Philo *On the Confusion of Tongues* 115; Dio Chrysostom *Oration* 12:34.
21. See Philo *On the Creation* 58.

22. E.g., Plutarch *On Garrulousness*.
23. E.g., Plutarch *On Garrulousness*, 10.

human behavior; such an empirical survey might lead to quite different conclusions! It is rooted in the tradition and teaching of Torah (see Gen 1:26-28). Something more is at stake here than the perfection of the human sage; what is at issue is the proper mode of responding to God's creation.

When James characterizes the tongue as "inflamed by Gehenna" (3:6 NRSV note), in turn, he is saying something more than that speech is a problem to be solved. He points to the cosmic dualism that underlies the two ways of directing human freedom. In the call to conversion of 3:13–4:10, these options will be developed more fully. The power at work in the tongue is not simply one of human vice, but of a system of values that is positively at enmity with God (4:4), and can be called "demonic" (3:15). There is a larger battle here than that of an individual's struggle for self-control; it is a battle involving spiritual allegiances. Thus when James says that his readers should be "quick to listen, slow to speak, slow to anger" (1:19 NRSV), he is not saying anything more than a Hellenistic philosopher would have said. But when he adds, "for [*human*] anger does not produce *God's* righteousness" (NRSV), he adds a level of religious complexity not found in the Hellenistic literature.

For James, human speech must be placed in the context of God's Word. The readers have been told in 1:18 that they were given birth as a kind of "first fruits of his creatures" (NRSV) by "the word of truth." Such creation imagery is found also in the present passage, with its references to the taming of the beasts and humans' having been created in the likeness of God. They were also told in 1:21 that they were to receive the implanted word that is able to save their souls "with meekness." Human speech is qualified by reference to the creative and saving Word of God, which is different from the wisdom of the world.

To curse a fellow human being is to break out of the frame of God's creation and God's wisdom. It is to place oneself in the frame of competition and envy and violence and murder, which for James means to betray the purpose of creation: "From the same mouth come blessing and cursing. My brothers and sisters, this ought not to be so" (3:10). These last words convey almost a sense of despair at the human drive to distort God's creative will. And so James concludes with a series of rhetorical questions demanding the response, "No!" All of the examples are, in fact, drawn from the order of creation. Surely no one could deny the truth that a fig tree does not yield olives (3:12). But then how could anyone endure the unnaturalness of a mouth that blesses God yet also curses a neighbor?

The explicitly theological framework for James's exhortation enables us to better understand his insistence in 3:1 that teachers would receive "greater judgment." It is clear that he does not have in mind simply the worse shame they must suffer before human eyes if they fail in speech. He means that those who, as teachers within the Christian community, fail in the fashion he has described will receive a more severe judgment from God. This is the frame of reference for James's readers: "So speak and so act as those who are to be judged by the law of liberty" (2:12 NRSV).[24]

---

24. For sayings of Jesus about speech, see, e.g., Matt 5:22, 33-37; 12:36-37.

REFLECTIONS

James's discourse on speech is so direct and forceful that little effort is required to apply it to the specific death-dealing acts of speech within communities. James himself has already mentioned some, and he will shortly catalog others. As with so much hortatory literature, the proper response to a composition seems less reflection than confession, an acknowledgment of the many ways in which the disease so brilliantly diagnosed has infected our lives.

We are, however, invited to a deeper reflection on the role of language in human double-mindedness by James's fascinating connection between speech and creation. The clearest indication that the reader should be thinking in terms of the Genesis account is James's reminder that humans are created according to the likeness of God

(3:9), which recalls the first creation story (Gen 1:26). The mention in 3:7 of "beast and bird, of reptile and sea creature" (NRSV) that are tamed by humans also echoes Gen 1:27-28. In the second creation account, the human person is given the power of speech to name all of the living creatures (Gen 2:19). The first and most important gift distinctive to humans is this power to name, to create language, and by creating language also to continue God's own creative activity in the world.

When we realize that language is a world-creating capacity, then we begin to appreciate James's cosmic imagery in describing its power and its peril. Even the world as it emerges moment by moment from God's creative energy—the "given" world of natural forces and juices—is reshaped and given its meaning by human language, whose symbols enable us both to apprehend the world as meaningful and to interpret it. The power of language, then, is awesome, for it gives humans the freedom to structure human life according to "the word of truth" so that humans are "a kind of first fruits of his creatures" (1:18 NRSV), or to create a universe of meaning in which God is omitted or ignored. The real peril of the tongue is not found in the passing angry word or the incidental oath or the petty bit of slander. It is found in the creation of distorted worlds of meaning within which the word of truth is suppressed. One of the most distinctive and disturbing features of contemporary culture is the way in which language serves precisely such distorting functions. We dwell in a virtual Babel of linguistic confusion and misdirection. One need think only of the advertising industry to appreciate how pervasive is the use of language to at once deceive and seduce, to consciously create by means of words and images multiple illusions in pursuit of which other humans can spend their fortunes and their energies. Such language weaves its deceptive web with a cunning awareness of how desire, avarice, and envy can "seduce the heart" (see 1:26).

We are aware as well how the slippery half-truths of advertising have become the common language of politics, where messages to the public are crafted precisely according to their ability to "sell" a candidate, where lying about and slandering opponents have become recognized as the most effective of all campaigning devices, and where political agendas are advanced by appeals to the electorate's most primitive fears and most unworthy cravings.

The language of various post-Enlightenment ideologies has also worked to flatten reality by eliminating the possibility for transcendence. The language of the so-called social sciences in particular has shaped a world in which human freedom is reduced to a statistical coefficient and the human spirit is reduced to a function of brain chemistry or social forces. But if language shapes reality, the result of such reductionism is a world in which transcendence is matter-of-factly denied, and in which God's claim on the world appears as ludicrous as tales of UFOs.

Indeed, more than at any previous time, we have become conscious of the power of speech to shape the world we inhabit and thereby also to shape human experience. The emergence of feminism within Christian communities has heightened such consciousness. Women are increasingly aware of how, in the Genesis story, it is "Adam" who is given the power to name, not only the animals but even his female partner. With the power to name comes the power to control, and men have shaped by language a world that in many ways has excluded women and their experience. Now women claim their legitimate share in the "image of God" that is the power to speak. They insist that just as all humans bear God's image, so also should language itself be broad and flexible enough to include all human experience. Although during the present period of transition relations between the genders are understandably stressful, the opening of language—and thereby of the world—to the creative and powerful contributions of half the human population must surely be regarded as a blessing and a positive receiving "with meekness" of the "implanted word" given to humans by God (1:21). And although communities may in the present period find themselves divided over the legitimacy or propriety of using inclusive language in texts and worship and even in speech to and about God, it must be said that, however painful, this linguistic stretching represents the positive suffering that results from growth rather than the negative suffering that results from suppression.

If, as James has led us to reflect, human language is such a potent instrument for the continuation of God's creative work, as well as for the misshaping of God's purpose for humanity, several corollaries suggest themselves. The first is that we have an obligation to pay attention to the language we use. The language of faith is not something that can be taken for granted, but must be nurtured. The second is that, even as we preserve the language of faith against those tendencies of the world that seek to shape reality apart from God, so must we work to keep our language open to the mystery of God's self-disclosure, which never ceases and which encounters us above all in human experience. Our awareness that language can both enable and suppress human creativity is a call to maintain freshness, flexibility, and poetic power within the language of faith, so that all God's people can find its experience of God reflected within it.

Finally, as James 3:1 insists, those who have the special task of shaping theological language within the church—not only the academic theologian but above all the preacher and teacher in each community—also bear the greater responsibility for keeping the language of faith alive. If, on the one hand, their preaching is little more than a lightly baptized form of psychobabble, then they have simply taken into the pulpit the language of the world, which rejects God's measure. But if, on the other hand, their language is nothing more than a rigid and doctrinaire biblicism, then they run the risk of deadening the language by closing it from the experience of God in human experience. The maintenance of the language is a difficult but necessary responsibility of Christian teachers. Those who cannot bear this greater judgment should not take on the role.

JAMES 3:13–4:10

CALL TO CONVERSION

COMMENTARY

Taking 3:13–4:10 as a single literary unit requires some justification, since other commentaries tend to separate it into smaller sections: 3:13-17 is taken as a statement on wisdom, 3:18 as a distinct aphorism, 4:1-6 as a warning against violence, and 4:7-10 as a call to repentance.[25] Such segmentation both follows from the premise and strengthens the perception that James has little thematic coherence. Analysis of earlier portions of this composition, however, gives us confidence that if James is granted literary coherence, his argument becomes much easier to detect.

In the present case, there are far more obvious links with the previous essay on speech (3:1-12) than with the verses following 4:10, although there, too, James creates a subtle and substantive connection. Most striking is the question in 3:13, "Who is wise and understanding among you?" which picks up so naturally the warning against becoming teachers in 3:1. There is also the word linkage between "bitter" in 3:11, 14; the phrase "in your members" in 3:6 and 4:1; and the repetition of "restless" in 3:8, 16. It is possible to detect a natural transition from the two sources of water and their fruits in 3:11-12 and the two sources of wisdom and their fruits in 3:13-18. Finally, there is the implied violence of cursing one's neighbor in 3:9 and going to war against others in 4:1. These links to the passages before and after it only serve to highlight how distinctive the literary structure of 3:13–4:10 is when taken as a unit.

The section is, first of all, intensely sermonic. It contains a generous portion of those stylistic features associated with the diatribe: rhetorical questions (3:13; 4:1, 5), abusive epithets (4:4, 8), vivid imagery (4:1, 9), virtue and vice lists (3:14-15, 17), sharp contrasts (3:14-17; 4:4, 6, 10), and the citation of authoritative texts (4:6). These stylistic features, however, are fitted into a rhetorical structure that forms the two parts of a call to conversion; 3:13–4:6 sets up an indictment, to which 4:7-10 is the response.

The series of imperatives and assurances in 4:7-10 is clearly shown to be answering the section preceding it by the use of the connective "therefore" in 4:7. The terms of the exhortation, furthermore, mirror those in the preceding indictment. Thus the purification of the heart in 4:8 corresponds to the "selfish ambition in your hearts" in 3:14, as well as to the "purity" attached to the wisdom from above in 3:17. The double-minded persons in 4:8 respond to the "undivided" (ἀδιάκριτος *adiakritos*) in 3:17. Most obviously, the command to humble oneself before the Lord with the expectation of being exalted (4:10) picks up from the statement that the Lord resists the proud and gives grace to the humble (4:6) as well as the above/below pattern associated with wisdom in 3:13-17. The content of 4:7-10 is that of a call to repentance: approaching God and fleeing the devil (4:8), moral purification and mourning (4:8-9), submitting to God (4:10).

The call to conversion is set up by a more complex indictment, which is structured primarily by a series of rhetorical questions in 3:13; 4:1, 4-5. The first and second of these questions are joined: 3:13 asks about the wise and understanding "among you," and 4:1 asks about the source of wars and battles "among you." Each rhetorical question is followed by exposition or accusation. In 3:13-14, the initial contrast between wisdom from above and bitter jealousy is explained by a second set of antithetical statements in 3:15-16. Then 3:17-18 picks up from 3:13 the conviction that true wisdom manifests itself in mild and peaceful behavior. The second

---

25. See M. Dibelius, *James: A Commentary on the Epistle of James*, Hermeneia (Philadelphia: Fortress, 1976); S. Laws, *A Commentary on the Epistle of James*, HNTC (San Francisco: Harper & Row, 1981)

set of rhetorical questions forms an antithesis to 3:17-18. The bitter jealousy that in 3:14-15 leads to social unrest now is expressed in terms of wars and battles (4:1). Accusations rather than exposition follow this set of questions: Their desire leads to murder (4:1-2). James then tells them why their prayers do not get answered: They pray only to fulfill their own desires (4:3). This is followed by still another rhetorical question, reminding them of a traditional understanding of the irreconcilability of friendship with God and the world (4:4).

The climax of the indictment comes in 4:5-6. Notoriously difficult to translate, the rhetorical purpose of these verses is plain. The entire exposition comes down to the question of the validity of the scriptural witness concerning the way God works in the world: Is all that Scripture says in vain? Is envy really the proper sort of longing for the spirit God made to dwell in humans? The citation of Prov 3:34 answers the question in the negative and sets up James's explicit call to conversion.

The preceding analysis shows that 3:13–4:10 makes sense as a literary unit. Before turning to the specific theme James develops in these verses, it is necessary to acknowledge that two notorious problems in the text have here been solved in a manner that differs in each case from at least one of the translations provided. The first occurs in 4:2, where the major questions are whether James could actually accuse his readers of killing and, if so, how the sentence should be punctuated. In this case, both translations correctly include the charge "you kill," but only the NRSV follows the best scholarship in its punctuation by constructing two sentences, each of which begins with frustrated desire and ends in violence.

The second problem is much more difficult and has led to a variety of attempts at a solution. Is 4:5 a statement or a rhetorical question or two rhetorical questions? Does the Greek phrase πρὸς φθόνον (*pros phthonon*; lit., "toward envy") refer to God as its subject or to the spirit God made to dwell in humans? And what does James mean by "the scripture" that speaks in vain? There are no texts in the LXX close to the contents of 4:5. Is he then making a vague allusion to some specific text, or perhaps to an apocryphal text? Does he intend his question/statement to refer to his citation of Prov 3:34 in 4:6? Or is he referring to Scripture in general? The NIV takes 4:5 as one question and refers the envy to the human spirit, but then adds two other possibilities in its notes. The NRSV, in contrast, makes God the subject and takes the phrase *pros phthonon* as indicating God's "yearning jealously" over the spirit placed in humans. The difficulty with this last solution, however, is that the noun φθόνος (*phthonos*) is never applied to God in the LXX, and in Greek usage it is always used for the human vice of envy, with which God has nothing to do.[26] The best solution is to read 4:5 as a double rhetorical question: "Does the scripture speak in vain? Is the spirit God made to dwell in us for envy?" The expected answer to these questions is negative. James then introduces Prov 3:34 with the introduction, "but he gives all the more grace." This solution is not perfect, but it covers the textual evidence better than the others offered, and it fits the thematic argument James is making in this section, to which we can now turn.

As in chapter 1, James establishes a spatial contrast between above and below, exaltation and humiliation. There is first a "wisdom from below," which is earthly, unspiritual, and demonic and stands in opposition to a "wisdom from above" (3:15-17). The reader recognizes that this wisdom from above is the one that comes from God (see 1:5, 17) as the "word of truth" and the "implanted word" that is to be received with meekness (1:18, 21). Connected to these two sources of wisdom is a second contrast between the "arrogant" (or "proud," NIV, NRSV), whom God resists, and the "lowly" (or "humble") to whom God gives gifts (4:6). This language bears within it a spatial imagery: The arrogant person moves upward in self-aggrandizement; the humble person is lowly. Finally, the passage contains a double command (4:7, 10) to "submit" and to "humble oneself" before the Lord, with the assurance that the Lord will respond in kind: "he will lift you up" (4:10).

The spatial opposition between lower and higher, being raised up and being put down, helps to define the religious framework for James's moral exhortation. Human behavior

---

26. See, e.g., Plato *Phaedrus* 247A; *Timaeus* 29E.

operates within an overall perception of reality that can be called a "wisdom." For James, however, only one "wisdom" is true: the one that "comes from above" and measures reality by the God who is the giver of all good gifts (1:5, 17) and alone is able to save and destroy (1:21; 4:12). This is the God who made a "spirit" (πνεῦμα *pneuma*) to dwell in humans (4:5). The question posed by James, then, is whether the human spirit will live by the wisdom that comes from God or according to an earthbound, unspiritual, "demonic" wisdom that he identifies explicitly with the power of the devil (3:15; 4:7). The moral choice facing humans is also a choice between religious allegiances.

The real key to understanding this passage, however, is the recognition that James describes the wisdom from below in terms that would be instantly recognizable to ancient readers but is not visible to present-day readers dependent on translations. In 3:14, 16, and 4:2, James uses terms meaning "jealousy" (ζῆλος *zēlos*) or "envy" (φθόνος *phthonos*), and he associates with those terms all the characteristics that ancient moralists connected to the vice of envy. Once we realize that James is using rhetorical commonplaces, we are able to see that topics that at first appear to us as disparate are actually part of a single argument.

Greco-Roman moralists defined virtue in terms of health and vice in terms of sickness.[27] The loathsome reputation of envy among the vices is suggested by a saying attributed to Socrates that envy is the "ulcer of the soul," a description that nicely captures the gnawing character of what Aristotle called a "certain sorrow" experienced because someone has something that we do not.[28] Why sorrow? Because envy derives from the "wisdom from below" that identifies being with having. A person's identity and worth derive from what can be acquired and possessed. In such a view, to have less is to be less real, less worthy, less important. Therefore, one feels a sense of loss and, therefore, of grief or sorrow. Conversely, to have more is to be more real, more worthy, and more important. According to the wisdom from below, humans live in a closed system of limited resources and are, therefore, fundamentally in competition with each other. In the realm of material things, for one to have more means that another must have less. The logic of envy demands competition for scarce resources.

When ancient moralists observed the vice of envy as it manifested itself in real human behavior, they saw that it lay behind all sorts of rivalry, party spirit, and competition (see 3:14, 16).[29] In this moral literature, as in James, envy is consistently associated with hatred, boorishness, faithlessness, tyranny, malice, hubris, ill will, ambition, and above all, arrogance (ὑπερηφανία *hyperēphania*), the word that James uses in 4:6, and that the NRSV and NIV translate as "proud." The term "arrogance" is better, because it conveys the nuance of competition and implicit violence that "pride" does not. Arrogance is the self-aggrandizing manifestation of envy that creates the desire to have that will stop at nothing to acquire what it seeks (4:2). The ancients perceived that there is no boundary to such craving and that the logic of envy leads inevitably to social unrest (3:16), battles, and wars (4:1). Ultimately, envy leads to murder (4:2).[30] Killing the competition is the ultimate expression of envy. This is the true face of the arrogance that God resists (4:6). This is the wisdom of the world that turns even prayer into something wicked, because it uses God simply as a means of fulfilling envy's incessant cravings (4:3). In 4:4, James opposes the two measures in the sharpest possible terms. His readers are not those who live completely by the measure of the world. They are not literally killing each other in order to gain possessions. But they are "double-minded" (4:8). They want to live by another measure, another wisdom, even as they claim God's measure as their own. James employs the language of the Israelite prophets when he calls them "adulteresses" (the NIV and NRSV attempt to be more inclusive, but they miss the fact that the feminine here is part of the symbolism for covenantal loyalty in the prophets, wherein God plays the role of husband and Israel that of the wife, as in Isa 54:4-8; Jer 3:6-10; Ezek 16:38; Hos 3:1; 9:1). James rebukes them for failing to live

---

27. See Plutarch *On Virtue and Vice*.
28. Aristotle *Rhetoric* 1387B.
29. Cf. Plutarch *On Brotherly Love* 17.
30. Cf. Plato *Laws* 869E-870A; Philo *On Joseph* 5-12.

by what he regards as a shared understanding ("do you not know") that friendship with the world means enmity with God (4:4). To fully appreciate James's stark contrast in 4:4, it is necessary first to remember that in this composition, "the world" is not a neutral term, but is used precisely in contrast to God (1:27) and to faith (2:5; see 3:6). The "world," in other words, represents the wisdom from below. It is also helpful to know the nuances attached to friendship in the ancient world. These have been examined already in the discussion of James's designation of Abraham as a "friend of God" (2:23). For the ancients, to be friends with another meant to see things the same way, to share the same outlook.[31] To be "friends of the world," therefore, means for James that one chooses to live by the logic of envy, rivalry, competition, violence, and murder. James's dualism is complete and unequivocal. Even to "wish" (NRSV) or to "choose" (NIV) to be a friend of the world in this sense is to be "established as an enemy of God." James's call to conversion, then, is aimed at those who want not to have to choose, who seek to be friends with everyone, living by God's measure but simultaneously acting according to the world's measure. James will not have it. The one who is "wise and understanding" must "show it by his good life, by deeds done in the humility that comes from wisdom" (3:13 NIV), not by the violence inherent in the competition generated by envy.

James's exhortation uses the language of Hellenistic moral teaching, but is rooted in the symbolic world of Torah. Those who seek to have two allegiances at once are called "adulteresses" (4:4) precisely because that is the prophetic language for those in covenant with the one God who also seek after idols. And at the climax of his indictment, James explicitly invokes the voice of Scripture. Scripture does not portray the spirit God made to dwell in humans as being for envy. Rather, as Prov 3:34 makes clear, God resists the arrogant and gives gifts to the lowly. The verse cited by James points to that entirely different understanding of reality given by the "wisdom from above" found in Scripture: Life is not about competition for possessions; it is about the receiving of gifts from a God who "gives all the more grace" (4:6).

James's scriptural heritage is obvious as well in the language he uses in the call to repentance (4:7-10). The images of purifying and cleansing derive primarily from Israel's cultic tradition; people needed to be "purified" to "approach God" in ritual or worship (see Lev 16:19-20). Here James uses the language for moral conversion: They are to "purify their hearts," which means to become single-minded rather than double-minded. The language of grieving, mourning, wailing, and gloom comes from the prophets, who use such terms for the response of people at the visitation of God (4:9; cf. Jer 4:13-28). But although the language is complex, the message is clear. In a statement of breathtaking simplicity, James tells them to approach God, and God will approach them (4:8). How do they approach? By humbling themselves and being receptive to God's gifts. How will God approach them? By "giving still more grace" and lifting them up (4:10; see 1:9).

---

31. See Plutarch *On Having Many Friends* 8; *On Brotherly Love* 8.

REFLECTIONS

This section of James is not only of pivotal importance for the understanding of the composition, containing as it does the essential theological framework for James's exhortation, but it also provokes reflection on a number of points.

It reminds us that conversion is a continuing process and an essential element in spiritual transformation. James is not writing to those "in the world" who explicitly embrace the logic of envy and whose competitive desires lead them to violence, war, and murder. Scholars who imagine that James is warning against some ancient zealot activity miss the mark entirely. He is addressing members of the Christian community who gather in the name of Jesus and profess the faith of the glorious Lord Jesus Christ, but whose attitudes and actions are not yet fully in friendship with God. Too often, conversion is seen as a once-for-all thing. Turning to Christ is thought to be the final answer. Everything in a person's life before that turning is seen as darkness, and everything after it must, therefore, be cast in light. Such an understanding, however, demands an artificial removal of all ambiguity from Christian life. But James sees that conversion is never complete. There is always double-mindedness, even among those who truly want to be friends of God. The wisdom from below is not easy to abandon or avoid, precisely because it is the "way of the world," inscribed not only in the language and literature of our surrounding culture but also in our very hearts. Those who recognize this are better able to deal with the continuing ambiguity experienced by all believers, even after an initial conversion to faith. Complete consistency in life is not given by a first commitment. It is slowly and painfully won through many conversions. This realization gives us deeper insight into what James means by faith's being tested through many trials (1:2-3), and why it should be counted as all joy when such trials occur. Each such test is a possibility for growth and for a new conversion from the measure of the world to the measure of God. It was just so that, when asked to offer Isaac, Abraham's recognition that God gives a greater gift enabled him to express his faith through his deeds and show that he was a "friend of God" (2:21-23).

This passage is a reminder also that the evil we experience in the world through social upheaval and violence and war and murder is not simply the result of inadequate social structures, but is above all the result of a diseased human freedom that has committed itself to a wisdom from below, which distorts reality—and which finds expression in social structures that make such distortions systemic. James's analysis of envy and the way it leads to murder is the most explicit and powerful in the New Testament, providing dramatic evidence for the earlier proposition that desire gives birth to sin; and when sin comes to full term, it brings forth death (1:15). No analysis is more pertinent to contemporary North American culture, which is virtually based on the logic of envy. In the Reflections on 3:1-12, we considered how the language of advertising creates a world of values in which "to be" means "to have," and to have more means to be more, a mechanism that is aimed directly at generating "a certain sorrow" when someone has something that one does not, together with the desire to do anything to acquire that which is sought. Every day on city school grounds, we see the accuracy of James's analysis, as children murder each other in order to acquire that specific pair of sports shoes or athletic jacket that will make them "someone." But the logic that envy leads to murder spirals beyond the inner city to the highest reaches of society; indeed, it is the engine generating global conflict and war. Why, asks James, are there wars and battles among you (4:1)? It is because of envy, because of the craving—not only in individuals but also in corporations and states—that demands seizing what belongs to another in order that one might become greater.

Because James's analysis makes use of what is best in Greco-Roman moral philosophy as well as in the tradition of Torah, but is not explicitly attached to christology, it is available to a genuinely ecumenical appropriation. James is virtually unique among the New Testament writings in providing the possibility for a social ethics, not only because of the obvious social dimension of reality that it considers, but also because it locates its moral demands within the framework of faith in the living God rather than specifically in the mystery of Jesus' death and resurrection.

Because James attributes social disruption and violence to a disease of the human heart, he does not propose any healing for it except through a turning to God that is explicit and wholehearted. In an age when religious belief does as much to divide as it does to unite, James points to a way of thinking about social ethics that can be engaged by all those who regard human freedom as deriving from and responsible to the God "who gives to all generously and ungrudgingly" (1:5 NRSV). But what James demands of those who think this way is a commitment to simplicity of heart and integrity of purpose that is extraordinarily rigorous. Kierkegaard, who was a lover of this letter, declared that purity of heart means to will one thing. James's analysis shows how hard that is, and how necessary it is to "approach God" if humans are to avoid that demonic wisdom that makes even prayer a means of manipulating God (4:3). Perhaps that is why the Shaker hymn says, "'Tis a gift to be simple, a gift to be free."

JAMES 4:11–5:6

EXAMPLES OF ARROGANCE

COMMENTARY

This section of James again challenges the reader who seeks an obvious literary coherence. James 4:11 certainly seems to represent a starting point, since 4:10 rounds off the call to conversion in 3:13–4:10, and since 4:11 takes the form of a negative command such as we find at other transition points in the composition (see 2:1; 3:1; 5:12). But should 4:11-12 be read as a discrete command and warrant, disconnected from any larger argument? At first glance, it would appear so, for 4:13 has its own distinctive introduction ("come now!"), which is repeated in 5:1. Some commentators divide these verses into three discrete sections (4:11-12, 13-17; 5:1-6), which is, in effect, to despair of detecting any overall argument.[32] For that matter, neither is it easy to decide where the section ends. On the one hand, 5:7 seems to respond to what precedes it, since, like 4:7, it uses the connective "therefore" (οὖν *oun*). On the other hand, 5:7-20 has a positive focus on community attitudes in contrast to the harsh attacks that pervade 3:13–5:6.

Despite the literary problems, it is appropriate to consider 4:11–5:6 as a single unit, primarily because it is unified by a single theme. Whether those being addressed are "brothers" (4:11) or "those who say" (4:13) or "the rich" (5:1), their behavior is attacked by the author. More significant, their behavior is in each case identifiably a form of arrogance (ὑπερηφανία *hyperēphania*), such as God is said to oppose in 4:6. This section, then, follows James's call to conversion with three specific examples of arrogance, and it is connected to the preceding section by his final rhetorical question in 5:6, "Does not [God] oppose you?" (see below for the justification of this translation, which differs from both the NRSV and the NIV).

The examples move progressively from the "brothers," whom we assume to be within the community, to "the rich," who are preeminently the outsiders for these readers (see 2:2-7). There is also a progression in the degree of arrogance revealed, from the slander that judges another in secret, through the public boasting that accompanies public projects, to the systemic corruption of society and the destruction of the innocent by oppression. Corresponding to these degrees of impact is the respective weight of condemnation, from the reminder of who is judge and lawgiver, through the identification of arrogance as sin, to the threat of destruction in the day of judgment.

4:11-12. Beneath such obvious differences in the three examples, however, a single point is being made, which further examination of each case reveals. The basic shape of James's argument is laid out by 4:11-12. He begins with a direct prohibition of slander (lit., "evil speech" [καταλαλιά *katalalia*]). This may, at first glance, seem to be simply one more example of loose speech that James singles out for attention (see 3:1-12). But the next statement is tantalizing: The one who slanders a brother also slanders the law and judges the law (4:11)! There are several unstated premises here. The first is that slander, by its very nature, involves a secret judging (and condemnation) of an associate. It is clear that to assume the right to judge and condemn another is to claim a privileged position of superiority over that person. Second, James considers such superiority to be false. No one has appointed one person to be the judge of another. Then why is that superiority assumed? Here the logic of envy comes into view once more. Slander serves both to lower the neighbor and to elevate the self; it takes away status from another and ascribes it to

---
32. See Dibelius, *James*; J. B. Adamson, *The Epistle of James*, NICNT (Grand Rapids: Eerdmans, 1976).

the one doing the slandering, who poses as the superior judge. It is, in microcosm and in secret, the perfect exemplar of life as competition. Slander, therefore, is a form of arrogance that seeks to assert the self by destroying another. It can thrive between those calling each other "brother," because it is evil speech carried out in secret.

But how does such speech also represent a slandering and judging of the law? To appreciate this connection, we must remember how James has used Lev 19:13-18 thematically throughout this composition. Leviticus 19:16 prohibits slander against a neighbor. To disobey the prohibition against slander, therefore, is to place oneself in a position of superiority to the law; it assumes the right of picking and choosing which of the commandments are to be taken seriously. Just as claiming to live by the law of love yet discriminating against a neighbor is not to "truly" live by it "according to the scripture" (2:8), so also is claiming to live by love while slandering a neighbor a form of falsehood. James identifies the form of arrogance precisely when he tells the people that they are acting as judges of the law rather than as doers of it. He then counters such pretension with the sharp reminder that the One who gave the law is also the only judge of all humans. The final contrast in 4:12 serves to reveal the reality that slander suppresses: The God who gives the law and who judges according to the law of love (2:12-13) is alone "able to save and to destroy." Over against this power, James asks, "Who are you?"

4:13-17. The form of arrogance shown in these verses is not subtle. James characterizes it as ἀλαζονεία (*alazoneia*), a term that is widely used in Hellenistic literature as the specific quality of the braggart, the boaster, the foolish loudmouth.[33] James summons the people ("come now") to a consideration of their lack of wisdom from above. Once more, they are given speech to express their plans of future travel, trade, and profit. At the most obvious level, the traders are criticized for their arrogant assumption that they can depend on the future as though it were secure. But at a deeper level, they show that they operate by the wisdom of the world, which is the logic of envy; by selling and getting a profit, they will secure their own future. James responds to them first in the way that Qohelet would, by reminding them of the evanescent quality of human life (4:14; see Eccl 12:1-8).[34] How can they plan for the next year when they cannot guarantee that they will even see tomorrow? The awareness that human existence itself is a "mist that is here and gone" encourages modesty concerning human plans and projects.

James also challenges the very view of reality assumed by such friends of the world. Their speech shows that they see the world as a closed system of limited resources, available to their control and manipulation, yielding to their market analysis and sales campaigns. When James tells them that they should say, "If it is the Lord's will, we will live and do this or that" (4:15), he is not simply recommending a more pious form of speech. Rather, he calls for a profoundly different perception of reality. He is recommending the view provided by faith and friendship with God that the world is an open system, created by God at every moment and infinitely rich in resources provided by God for humans to exist and to prosper, in cooperation rather than in competition and mutual elimination. Within *this* perspective, their pretentiousness and boasting are more than foolishness; they are symptoms of something evil (4:16).

When James spelled out faith's perception of wealth and poverty, suffering and success in 1:9-12, he did so in terms of paradox and reversal; the lowly were to boast in their exaltation, and the rich in their humbling; those who relied on their wealth would pass away in the midst of their affairs, while those who endured testing would gain the crown that is life. In the present passage, the traders' failure so to think about their lives and so to speak with reference to God's will is, for those living in the community of faith, to know the right thing to do and fail to do it. For James, this is not simply a moral failure, but a sin (4:17). This statement on the "sin of omission" is a hinge between the preceding example and the one following. If it applies to entrepreneurs who pursue profit without reference to God, it refers even more directly to those who fail to do what the law specifically demands—namely, to provide wages for their workers.

---

33. See Plato *Republic* 560C; Plutarch *On Love of Wealth* 1.

34. See also Seneca *On the Shortness of Life* 1:1-4.

5:1-6. James's final example of arrogance is the most blatant and evil (5:1-6). Adopting once more the rhythms of the great social prophets Isaiah and Amos, he uses some of his most vivid language in attacking the oppressive rich. In this example, he goes into much greater detail concerning their behavior and the consequences they must face. A distinctive feature of his treatment is the way he weaves those two aspects together, which gives his every statement a harshly ironic dimension.

The energy and force of James's opening words in 5:1 are startling. The rich are to "weep" and to "wail" over the miseries that are coming upon them. Note that what those charged in 3:13–4:6 were supposed to do by way of repentance (4:7-10) is now happening to the rich by way of judgment. Rather than focus on their misery, however, James describes the fate of their wealth itself: It has become rotten, moth-eaten, rusted (5:2). According to the logic of envy, they had identified their being with their having and thus had been willing to do anything to get more wealth, including fraud, violence, and murder (5:6). They apparently thought that by so doing they were building up treasure for their last days. With bitter irony, James agrees that they have done so (5:3), but it is not a retirement fund: They have prepared themselves for a day of slaughter (5:5). The very possessions in which the wealthy had sought security eloquently proclaim their own fate: Their precious metals have rusted, and "their rust will be evidence against you and it will eat your flesh like fire" (5:3 NRSV).

These rich people perfectly exemplify in their attitudes and actions the logic of envy and arrogance James sketched in 3:13–4:10. They have devoted themselves to an exploitative manipulation of the earth, living to fulfill their own desires for pleasure (5:5; see also 4:1-3). In order to reach their desires, they have been willing to deprive their hired laborers of the wages that are owed them (5:4). Once more, James appears to be making an allusion to the scriptural context of the law of love in Leviticus, for Lev 19:13 contains a clear prohibition of just such withholding of wages from the laborer. The language used in Jas 5:6 ("you have condemned the righteous one," NRSV), furthermore, suggests the sort of judicial procedure James had mentioned in 2:6: The rich use the law courts to perpetuate their fraud and to "condemn" the poor. By the "righteous one" here, James does not have any specific individual in mind (patristic writers thought perhaps that he was referring to Jesus; see Acts 7:52); rather, those oppressed in such fashion are "innocent/righteous" in that they have committed no offense and have suffered the loss of what was owed them for their service. Consistent with the entire biblical tradition, James recognizes that such fraud is a form of legalized violence and murder. To withhold from the poor their daily wages is literally to deprive them of the means of life: "to deprive an employee of his wage is to shed blood" (Sir 34:22).

Here the logic of envy that James sketched in 4:2 is carried out in action: "You want something and do not have it; so you commit murder" (NRSV). Here also is the ultimate arrogance of the rich, who assume the divine power to judge and do so unjustly ("you have condemned the righteous one"), and who arrogate to themselves the divine power to "save and destroy" (4:12); "you have killed the righteous one."

This brings us to the last clause in 5:6. Like most other contemporary translations, both the NRSV and the NIV translate the Greek as an indicative whose subject is the righteous person oppressed by the rich, thus "who does not resist you" (NRSV) or "who were not opposing you" (NIV). There are good reasons, however, for understanding this last clause as a question with God as its implied subject, thus, "Does he [God] not oppose you?" The reasons for such an interpretation are basically twofold. First, 5:1-6 has alternated the actions of the rich with the response to those actions by God. The statement that the rich had condemned and murdered the righteous person, the supreme act of arrogance, would appropriately lead to the response that God opposes them. Second, the verb "resist/oppose" (ἀντιτάσσω *antitassō*) is identical to that used in 4:6, where it is used to state that God resists the proud ("arrogant") but gives grace to the lowly. The use of the same verse here after the recitation of three examples of arrogance seems logically to point to God as the subject.

If 5:6b is read this way, then James matches the violence of the rich with force from the side of God, who has heard "the cries of the harvesters" (5:4). The willful denial of this righteous God's election of the poor to be heirs of God's kingdom has enabled the rich to make friends of the world and to exploit its systems to their own advantage. But in the perspective of faith, James asserts, God's power is, if not obvious, nevertheless more real. The world is not, as the arrogant suppose, a closed system whose prize goes to the most ruthless. It is an open system answerable to the God who creates it. In contrast to those who are judges with evil designs (2:4), God judges without partiality and on the basis of human deeds (2:12). The rich who have oppressed the poor will experience in their own flesh how God opposes them (5:3, 6). They will discover in the "last days" how judgment can be merciless to the ones who have not shown mercy (2:13).

REFLECTIONS

The more it becomes clear that James consists not simply of discrete exhortations but is making an interconnected argument, the more readers are challenged to engage the text at a deeper level, thinking through some of the connections that James asserts. It is certainly not obvious on the surface that arrogance is the theme of the present section, just as most readers would probably not identify arrogance as the spiritual or moral attitude most problematic for their world or their own lives. For that matter, neither would many present-day Christians think of themselves as living with half of their minds and hearts within the logic of envy. What is the real connection between envy and arrogance? And how can the process of thinking through these connections begin to locate the fundamental moral and religious issue with which readers in James's day and in our own are obliged to struggle?

If we go back to the definition of envy as a sorrow for something we do not have, we can begin to see how this most "needy" of vices lies at the root of arrogance. The logic of envy, as James has shown us, is based on the perception of the world as a closed system of limited resources for which humans are in competition. Envy and arrogance are the two sides of this competitive battle. It is envy that spurs the "have-nots" to violence against those who have what they want; it is arrogance that spurs the "haves" to boast over those from whom they have taken in order to "be" who they are. The value of the examples that James provides is that they show how subtle and pervasive the manifestations of arrogance can be. We may think of it primarily in its overt form of "king of the mountain," with the temporary childish victor, chest thrown back, arms akimbo, crowing loudly over the vanquished. James shows us that it is often a more secret and sneaky vice whose violence, though covert, is no less real.

James's first example, that of slander, makes the point beautifully. Once we think about it, we can agree that this "evil speech done in secret," which seeks specifically to tear down another so that I can appear to be superior (as critic, as judge), is driven by envy. Whatever it is that I think my target now possesses that I do not (status, reputation), my intention is to take it away, at least in the perception of my hearers. When we think a bit further, we can also agree to James's placing this as a form of arrogance not only against the neighbor but also even against God's law, which forbids such slander: "Who are you," says James, "to judge another?" Slander arrogates to oneself divine powers of knowing the hearts of others and of being able to condemn them. Only a bit more reflection is required for us to reach another agreement: that slander is one of the most pervasive and destructive forms of arrogance. It operates so consistently that we may not even be aware any longer of its nature, from the whispered remark behind the hand in the pew or at a board meeting, through the screaming tabloid headlines, to the gossip of television talk shows. The willingness to use speech to destroy others simply in order to realize a temporary sense of superiority has become a manifestation of arrogance so widespread it has become normalized. James reminds us that it is a form of speech that is "death-dealing poison" (see 3:8).

With the second example, as well, it is not difficult to find the contemporary analogy to the ancient entrepreneurs who planned their trips and anticipated the profits they might make from trade. James challenges them because of their assumption that their world is predictable and controllable, and that they can define their being in terms of their having. In the present-day world of commercialism and conglomerates and multinational corporations, the logic of envy and arrogance is the connective tissue. And within this world, the bottom line of profit or loss is the only measure worth considering. The commercial apprehension of reality is the perfect expression of the outlook of "the world" closed to God as giver of every perfect gift; success is measured by the amount of "goods" (whichever they are) that can be accumulated. Perhaps the most serious question for Christianity in the present cirumstance is whether it is any longer in a position to exercise the kind of prophetic critique of that outlook such as enunciated by James. Is it not the case that many churches are themselves so co-opted by the logic of envy and arrogance—if not in strictly monetary terms, then in terms of membership and influence—that they cannot perceive that such is the way of the wisdom from below, which is earthbound, unspiritual, and demonic?

Being heedless of anything else but making a profit is one thing; committing actual violence against others in order to live luxuriously on the earth is another and far more perverted form of arrogance. Once more, we see the way in which James is able to connect the diseases of the human heart to the distortions of the social order. Envy and arrogance can take, do take, a public form in economic and political systems that privilege the few and punish the many, that exploit the resources of the earth for the extravagant lifestyle of those privileged to live in the first world rather than the third, that reduce the laborers in the fields (and factories and sweatshops and fast-food eateries) to slaves by systems of reward and taxation that perpetuate inequity, that so marginalize major portions of the population that they are unable to sustain their existence at a meaningful human level, that commit legal murder against the innocent by means of litigation and the corruption of the courts. Liberation theology has used this passage in James appropriately to challenge the obvious oppressive systems of government and finance that marginalize and abuse the poor peoples of third world countries. Churches in the first world have been much slower (perhaps because of being co-opted by the logic of envy and arrogance) to challenge the systems of meaning that perpetuate such abuses and generate them from within the comfortable corporate headquarters down the street from the local suburban congregation. But James tells us that we cannot close our eyes to these realities, that even if we cannot by ourselves change them, somehow we must by our own lives challenge them and that, in our own envy and arrogance, we stand within that same distorted view of the world and, therefore, under the same judgment of God.

JAMES 5:7-20

A COMMUNITY OF SOLIDARITY

COMMENTARY

The last part of James makes a decisive turn inward to the members of the community of faith with exhortations that are positive and encouraging. It is possible to subdivide the section further. Verses 7-11, for example, have a distinctive eschatological character, and vv. 12-20 can be seen as devoted to speech acts within the assembly. But what joins the entire section together is the turn from condemnation to edification. With the three examples of arrogance in 4:11–5:6, James brought his call to conversion to a conclusion, as well as his depiction of the wisdom from below, which operated in envy and arrogance and led to a world divided by competition and violence. Now James turns to those gathered in "the faith of our glorious Lord Jesus Christ" (2:1) with instructions on how to build a community unlike that of "the world." What does a community governed by Jesus' faith and the law of love look like? How does "friendship" with God affect the way persons speak and act toward each other? James sets out to show how friendship with God leads to solidarity in gift giving and life, just as friendship with the world leads to competition for possessions and murder.

5:7-9. He begins by placing his readers within the context of eschatological judgment. James's expectation of this judgment—to vindicate the righteous/poor and to punish the oppressive/rich—is neither abstract nor distant. The language James uses makes it clear that the "Lord" whom he expects to come in judgment is Jesus; the expression "the return of the Lord" (παρουσία τοῦ κυρίου *parousia tou kyriou*), which James uses here twice, is not found in the LXX, yet is virtually a technical term for the return of Jesus in the New Testament (see 1 Cor 15:23; 1 Thess 2:19; 2 Pet 3:4; 1 John 2:28). His coming, furthermore, is "near" (5:8); in a statement remarkably close to Rev 3:20, James declares that the judge is "standing at the door" (5:9 NIV). Nevertheless, their present experience is more like those who await "the precious crop from the earth" (NRSV); what they most desire is not yet here.

How are those who await this judgment to act? James tells them that they must "strengthen their hearts" (5:8). As always in this composition, the heart refers to human intentionality; in effect he is instructing his readers to stay focused. This means first that they must be patient. By this, he means more than that they should endure, for the word he chooses (μακροθυμία *makrothymia*), is used for the attitude of "long-suffering" judges. Until the Lord comes, oppression by the rich and powerful will continue. In such circumstances, it would be natural for people to turn on each other. In fact, oppression typically fosters such internal divisions among those under stress. James, therefore, forbids them to "grumble against one another" (5:9). Like the people of Israel oppressed in Egypt, their "complaint" (στεναγμός *stenagmos*) should be turned to the Lord, who can hear them, and not turned against each other (see Exod 2:23-24). If they turn such grumbling against each other, the community itself will become a realm of competition rather than cooperation.

5:10-11. Their patience needs this quality of long-suffering to put up with affliction until the Lord can exercise judgment. James proposes as the model for such endurance the prophets who spoke in the name of the Lord (v. 10; cf. Matt 5:12; Luke 6:23; 11:49-51). It is startling, perhaps, to see that Job is not only included among the prophets, but is also recommended as the example of endurance. This is not the picture of Job that the dialogues in the biblical book suggest. (Together with the apocryphal *Testament of Job,* James seems to be the source for the tradition of the patient Job.) But his reading is not completely off the mark. Job, after all, argued with God even as he looked to God for vindication, but he did not turn in spite against his fellows. And when James reminds his readers that they have seen "the purpose of the Lord," he reminds them that Job's endurance was rewarded. The phrase is a difficult one; the NIV translates it as "what the Lord finally brought about," emphasizing Job's reward at the end of the biblical story. The macarism of v. 11, "we call blessed those who showed endurance" (NRSV), clearly echoes that in 1:12, "blessed is anyone who endures temptation" (NRSV), showing the connection between this miniature essay and the aphorisms of chap. 1. The statement that God is compassionate and merciful (v. 11) reiterates the theme of God as constant gift giver (1:5, 17; 4:6; see also 2:13).

Throughout his composition, James has focused on speech as the indicator of the human heart. Up to this point, his portrayal of speech has been almost entirely negative, as he showed how the tongue revealed that friendship with the world is enmity with God, or revealed a person who was double-minded rather than simple in friendship with God. In this last section, he devotes particular attention to the positive functions of speech within the community.

5:12. Appropriately, he begins with a condemnation of oaths. The instruction echoes the context of the "law of love," since Lev 19:12 reads (in the LXX): "You shall not swear in my name wickedly and you shall not profane the name of your God." The prohibition here, however, is absolute, and it resembles most of all the saying attributed to Jesus in Matt 5:34-37. James's version is somewhat simpler, suggesting that it represents a stage of the saying prior to its incorporation into the synoptic tradition.

The prohibition of oaths is in reality the encouragement of plain speech within the community of faith. It is a call to simplicity in speech as well as in heart. If one's yes can reliably be depended on to be a yes, and one's no truthfully communicates no, then speech can be trusted. James introduces this commandment with "above all" because such simplicity in speech is fundamental to every other sort of speech and action within the community. Otherwise, the prayer of one in distress, the song of praise, the call for help, the confession of sins, the correction of the neighbor can all be deceptive and destructive, instruments of manipulation and competition rather than cooperation. James forbids oaths, because he desires a community of solidarity based in mutual trust. Such trust is possible only where speech is simple and unadorned with false religiosity.

5:13-16. James turns next to prayer within the community as an expression of truth. The person who is suffering should not say, "I am being tempted by God" (1:13), or seek to retaliate against the source of distress (5:7). Instead one should let one's cries reach "the ears of the Lord of hosts" (v. 4), for the Lord is the one who "gives more grace" to the lowly (4:6). The person who is feeling good should give expression to that truth in song, recognizing God as the generous giver (1:5) of every good and perfect gift (1:17), as the one who is above all compassionate and merciful (5:11), and the source of authentic human blessedness (1:12; 5:11).

The next part of James's discourse on speech deals with the sick and the response to those who are ill within the community. Like 2:14-26, this passage has received disproportionate attention in the history of interpretation because of debates concerning the sacrament of extreme unction, or anointing of the sick. More recent interpretations have sought to locate the custom of visiting, praying for, and anointing the sick within the life of Jewish communities. Each of these activities is attested, although seldom together as here.[35]

It is probably not by accident that James here uses the word ἐκκλησία (*ekklēsia*, "church"/"assembly") for the first time in the composition, for it is the community as such that is threatened by sickness. Will the community rally in support of the sick and show itself to be in solidarity, or will it isolate those who threaten its possession of health and security? We notice that James empowers the sick themselves with regard to the assembly. They are to "summon" the elders, a word that has a definite connotation of official demand (v. 14). The elders are to pray over and anoint the sick person in the name of the Lord (note again the typical early Christian

---

35. See, e.g., *b.B.Bat.* 116a; *b.Hag* 3a; *Testament of Solomon* 18:34.

usage, as in Acts 3:6; 4:10). The elders represent the community's willingness to overcome the alienation that sickness imposes on the sick. The oil they use for anointing was widely used for medicinal purposes in the Greco-Roman world. There is no gap here between physical and spiritual healing. They happen together. The oil gains its power from the human hands that apply it and that, by reaching across pain and loneliness, reestablish the solidarity of the community. The prayer, likewise, is said "over" the sick person as a sign of the community's commitment and support in the time of crisis.

We recognize in these gestures the practices of the early Christians rooted both in the traditions of Israel and in the ministry of Jesus. James's language contains two remarkable parallels to the Gospel accounts of Jesus' healings. The first is the connection between healing and the forgiveness of sins: "anyone who has committed sins will be forgiven" (v. 15). What makes James particularly intriguing on this point is that he applies the healing not only to the sick individual but also to the community as such: "confess your sins to one another, and pray for one another, so that you may be healed" (v. 16). James also shares the gospel tradition's confidence in the power of prayer to heal individuals from their illness and communities from their alienation. The prayer of faith will save the sick person, and the Lord will raise that person up (5:15), recalling the Gospel accounts of Jesus' healings (e.g., Matt 9:5-7; Mark 3:8; Luke 7:14; John 5:8) and suggesting the continuum between healing and salvation. James makes no great distinction between saving the soul and saving the life, between being "raised up out of the sickbed" and "raised up" in resurrection. His confidence in prayer resembles Jesus' own: "Ask and it will be given to you" (Matt 7:7; see Jas 1:5-6).

5:17-18. It is in connection with such confidence concerning prayer that James advances his fourth and final example from Torah: the prophet Elijah. Elijah shows that a righteous person's prayer has great power (v. 16). James refers to the account of Elijah's "closing and opening of the heavens" in 1 Kgs 17:1–18:45. It is natural that a prophet should have such power, since a prophet's business is the traffic between God and humans. But James bridges the gap between Elijah and his readers by means of two small, but important, details.

The first is that Elijah is called "a human being like us" (NIV, "man just like us"). The Greek is literally, "of like feeling" and, as in passages such as Acts 14:15, serves to link Elijah's simple humanity to that of the readers: If he could do it, so can they. The second small touch is the implication that Elijah is a "righteous one" (δίκαιος *dikaios*, v. 16*b*), whose prayer is powerful. This connects him also to the experience of the community that is being set upon by oppressors (v. 6), yet whose prayers will reach the ears of the Lord of hosts (v. 4). Just as in response to his prayers the "earth yielded its harvest," James implies, so also the Lord will respond to their prayers as they wait for that "precious crop from the earth," which is the coming of the Lord (v. 7). The prayer of the community that gathers in solidarity to support its sick and, by confessing sins one to another, also strengthens its spiritual weakness is already a victory over the world, which defines itself by envy and competition.

5:19-20. James concludes this section and the letter with an encouragement to mutual correction. Such correction was a staple of ancient moral teaching, both in Hellenism and in Judaism (see Ezek 3:1-11; 18:1-32; Dio Chrysostom *Oration* 77/78:37-45). It is not a manifestation of that sort of judging or slandering of a neighbor that James condemns in 4:11, for that was the expression of envy. Mutual correction is a form of edification that takes the construction of a community of character seriously. It is a gesture of solidarity for those who have been given birth by the word of truth to seek to keep each other on the path of truth. Once more, we can detect here an echo of Lev 19:17 ("you will earnestly reprove your neighbor and will not bear sin on his account"), which for James is an expression of the "royal law" of love (2:8).

The precise meaning of the final clause is unclear. Is it the brother's or the sister's soul that is saved, or is it that of the one who does the correcting? And what is meant by "covering a multitude of sins" (v. 20)? The latter phrase may be an allusion to Prov 10:12 LXX, but it is not a clear one (see also 1 Pet 4:8). The best interpretation is that the one doing the correcting will save the other person's soul from death and that the sins that are covered over (or suppressed/prevented) are the ones the associate might have committed if not corrected.

James has sketched how speech can build an alternative community based in solidarity and cooperation rather than in envy and arrogance. It is speech characterized by simplicity and directness, prayer, mutual confession, and mutual correction. And at the end, James tells his readers to do for each other what he has tried to do for them.

REFLECTIONS

This last section of James is a rich source of reflection for any community that claims to live in the faith of Jesus Christ or in friendship with God. As has been obvious from the beginning, such a commitment to an alternative "wisdom," especially when expressed in a communal mode of life, will inevitably come into conflict with the dominant wisdom of the world. Sometimes this conflict will take the form of direct oppression, such as James describes in 5:1-6. More often, it takes the form of internal stress, as the community seeks to build its own distinctive identity even as many of its members are "double-minded," divided in their loyalties. Such stress might lead naturally to slander and condemnation of one another (4:11), or of "grumbling against one another" (5:9)—modes of speech that bring the competitiveness of worldly wisdom within the community. These are examples of "armored" speech, which seeks to harm the other while protecting the self. In contrast, James offers speech that makes the self vulnerable to others.

Note, for example, how the prohibition of oaths in 5:12 actually encourages speech that is simple, unadorned, and unarmored. When one's yes can be trusted as yes, and when one's no can truly be heard as no, then members of the community are exposed to one another in truth. The same sort of vulnerability characterizes genuine mutual correction as opposed to slander and condemnation. The proof is how difficult such reproof is to carry out. Most people prefer a form of secret slander to the open and candid correction of another in love. To risk correction is to risk looking foolish in the eyes of others as well as exposure to a colleague's anger or rejection.

James's most provocative example, however, is the speech of the sick within the community, as well as the speech that should be used with those who are sick. This is because sickness is a profound threat to the identity and stability of any community. Sickness is not the same thing as sin, nor does James suggest that sickness derives from sin. Yet, sin and sickness are analogous in their social effects. The healing of the sick person, therefore, like the restoration of the community after sin, must take into account the spiritual dimensions of this threat. The way James correlates the healing of illness and the forgiveness of sins testifies to his grasp of this reality.

The challenge of physical or emotional or mental illness to the community of faith is to test whether it will behave like friends of God or friends of the world. According to worldly wisdom, the logical response to any form of threat is self-defense. Only the fittest should survive, and competition exists precisely to identify them. Envy seeks strength at the expense of others and, as James has shown, leads inevitably to murder. Has someone we know fallen sick? Then that person is weak and should be left behind. The elimination of the sick person leaves more resources for those who are left. Having to share our attention and resources with those who are weak distracts us from our own growth and weakens us in our own struggle for survival and supremacy.

The logic of the world, therefore, is to isolate the sick from the healthy. The healthy organism recoils from what is sick in order to protect itself. Sickness, then, becomes the occasion for social isolation and alienation. This "natural reflex" of survival, however, also becomes a form of sin when it leads to the deliberate exclusion of the sick from the community's care and support, when the physical distance imposed by sickness is embraced as a spiritual alienation from those who are sick and a rejection of them from community.

In James, the sick are empowered to summon the community's elders. This is as remarkable a reversal of the logic of envy as is the way the community is to honor rather than scorn the poor (2:5). Not those who are well, but those who are sick are to define the truth of the situation. And in the speech of those gathered around the sick, James explicitly calls for the recognition of the weakness and failure of all, so that not only the person manifestly ill but all those in the community might be "healed" or "saved" by the confession of sins and the prayer of faith.

This entire scenario of an intentional community structured according to principles of solidarity and mutual cooperation not only provides the most direct challenge to the practice of our culture concerning the care of the sick, but it also invites us to engage in self-examination concerning all those among us who are in any fashion weak and alienated. It is obvious that the larger society today is based on envy and competition. The sick and the poor (often the same) represent a threat to survival that must be repelled by at best neglect and at worst fraud, oppression, and murder.

The harder issue is the extent to which Christianity colludes in an understanding of reality that is based on envy and competition. There is no more visible and obvious indicator than the way churches themselves work with and for the care of children, the poor, the ill, the elderly, the dying. Does the church, like the world, seek its own survival by defending itself against the threat of weakness? Or does the church seek friendship with God by embracing in the same spirit of open gift giving all of God's creatures, so that the strength of each one is gathered from the shared strength of all?

From its opening words to its last, James witnesses to a way of life that is truly radical in its implications. It not only challenges Christians to an integrity in thought, speech, and action, but also, by sketching a vision of the world opposite the one offered by the logic of envy, it offers the possibility for Christians to enter into conversation with others who view the world as defined by a gift-giving God, a conversation in which the insights and clarity of James can contribute toward a genuine social ethics based in solidarity and peace rather than competition and violence.

THE FIRST LETTER OF PETER
INTRODUCTION, COMMENTARY, AND REFLECTIONS
BY
DAVID L. BARTLETT

THE FIRST LETTER OF PETER

INTRODUCTION

First Peter is one of the general or catholic epistles, along with Hebrews; James; 1, 2, 3 John; 2 Peter; and Jude. The general epistles are distinguished from other letters in the New Testament in two ways. First, they are not attributed to Paul. Second, they are (for the most part) addressed not to a particular church but to a group of churches—they are general and, in that sense, catholic.[1] First Peter is also "catholic" in a larger sense: It speaks to the condition of the churches across the traditional lines of time and place. A letter written for churches that are alienated from the surrounding society and for Christians who are slandered for their faith, it has provided comfort for believers in troubled times from the end of the first century to the beginning of the third millennium. Using the imagery of baptism, it provides a reminder for the baptized of what it means to live out of the sacrament and to live out the sacrament in their lives as individuals and as a community. As early as Polycarp's *Letter to the Philippians,* there is evidence that Christian writers found in 1 Peter words of encouragement that were worth cherishing, repeating, and interpreting. Polycarp alludes to 1 Pet 1:8 as he recalls the suffering and resurrection of Christ, "in whom, though you did not see him, you believed in unspeakable and glorified joy."[2] This brings to mind also 1 Peter's, "Although you have not seen him, you love him; and even though you do not see him now, you believe in him and rejoice with an indescribable and glorious joy" (NRSV).[3] So, too, Polycarp's *Letter to the Philippians* 8:1 reflects 1 Pet 2:22, 24, while both texts also interpret Isaiah 53.[4]

From 1 Peter churches in Europe and America may find clues to faithful living as Christendom fades and Christians again feel like sojourners and aliens. Churches in developing countries will find reminders of like-minded Christians, bearing witness to a faith that is still professed by a small minority, but that history shows will hold fast, grow, and flourish.

---

1. The designation of 1 Peter as a catholic epistle is found as early as Eusebius (c. 300 CE). See Pheme Perkins, *First and Second Peter, James, and Jude,* Interpretation (Louisville: Westminster John Knox, 1995) 1.
2. Polycarp *Letter to the Philippians* 1:3. See Kirsopp Lake, trans. *The Apostolic Fathers,* LCL (Cambridge, Mass.: Harvard University Press, 1969) 1:283-85.
3. The word for "glorified" or "glorious" (δοξάζω *doxazō*) in the two quotations is the same.
4. See Paul J. Achtemeier, *1 Peter,* Hermeneia (Minneapolis: Fortress, 1996) 44. Polycarp was martyred in 155 CE.

AUTHOR, DATE, AND AUDIENCE

First Peter begins straightforwardly enough: "Peter, an apostle of Jesus Christ." An early Christian audience would think what we might: that this was a letter written by Simon Peter, one of the first disciples called by Jesus (Mark 1:16-20 par.), designated by Acts as one of the apostles. Peter was recognized by Paul both as a fellow apostle with special responsibility for the mission to the Jews and as an antagonist on issues relating to the obligation of Gentile Christians in regard to observing the Jewish Law (see 1 Cor 9:4; Gal 2:7-14). Yet in more recent years scholars have raised a number of questions to challenge Simon Peter's authorship of the first letter that bears his name.[5]

First there is the question of style. The Greek prose of 1 Peter is fairly sophisticated and the syntax fairly complicated. Is it likely that Simon, the Galilean fisherman, would be capable of writing Greek of this sophistication (see Acts 4:13)?[6]

Related to this issue is the fairly clear indication that when the writer of 1 Peter quotes Scripture (the Old Testament), it is the Greek version of the Old Testament that he uses. Usually the citations are very close to the Septuagint. Again, recognizing Peter's background as one who almost certainly would have known Scripture either in Hebrew or in Aramaic, is this familiarity with the Greek text plausible? Furthermore "Peter" uses the Greek form of his own name, whereas even in writing to Gentiles Paul always refers to Peter by the Aramaic name "Cephas."[7]

Further, there is the issue of theological development. All our guesses about the way that doctrine developed in the first century and a half of the church's existence are in large measure conjectural, but on one fairly plausible reading of doctrinal development, 1 Peter already presupposes conditions that might seem to be later than the time of the apostle. In theology the Jewish/Gentile controversies so central to Paul seem to have faded to the background, and motifs seem closer to those in letters by Paul's disciples (Colossians, Ephesians, and the Pastorals).[8]

Indeed, while there is no clear evidence that the author of 1 Peter knew or used Paul's letters, there are themes and motifs within it that suggest this epistle was written after the ministry of Paul. Parallels most often cited are between 1 Peter and Romans, on the one hand, and between 1 Peter and Ephesians, on the other hand. For instance, 1 Pet 3:8-9 uses language reminiscent of Rom 12:16-17:

Finally, all of you, have unity of spirit, sympathy, love for one another, a tender heart, and a humble mind. Do not repay evil for evil or abuse for abuse; but, on the contrary, repay with a blessing. It is for this that you were called—that you might inherit a blessing. (1 Pet 3:8-9 NRSV)	Live in harmony with one another; do not be haughty, but associate with the lowly; do not claim to be wiser than you are. Do not repay anyone evil for evil, but take thought for what is noble in the sight of all. If it is possible, so far as it depends on you, live peaceably with all. (Rom 12:16-18 NRSV)

It is certainly possible that 1 Peter depends on a recollection of Romans here, but it is also possible that each reflects a growing Christian tradition about non-retaliation, a tradition also reflected in other early Christian literature, such as Matt 6:39.

So, too, the close correspondence to some material in Ephesians may reflect the widespread development of particular themes and motifs rather than any direct dependence of 1 Peter on this (deutero-)Pauline letter:

Blessed be the God and Father of our Lord Jesus Christ! By his great mercy	Blessed be the God and Father of our Lord Jesus Christ, who has blessed

---

5. A clear summary of many of these points is found in Norbert Brox, *Der erste Petrusbrief, Evangelisch-Katholischer Kommentar zum Neuen Testament* (Zurich: Benziger Verlag and Neukirchener Verlag, 1979) 44-46.
6. See A clear summary of many of these points is found in Brox, *Der erste Petrusbrief,* 44.
7. See Perkins, *First and Second Peter, James, and Jude,* 10.
8. So Brox, *Der erste Petrusbrief,* 51.

he has given us a new birth into a living hope through the resurrection of Jesus Christ from the dead. (1 Pet 1:3 NRSV)	us in Christ with every spiritual blessing in the heavenly places. (Eph 1:3 NRSV)

The strong similiarity between the two doxologies results in part from the fact that both are doxologies and share similar, perhaps liturgical, language to declare the thanksgiving that frequently follows the salutation in early Christian letters.

Paul Achtemeier judiciously sums up the evidence for the relationship of 1 Peter to the Pauline letters:

> While the relationship of 1 Peter to the Pauline way of theological reflection cannot be denied, how much of the "Pauline" flavor of 1 Peter is the result of a common use of early liturgical or confessional material is difficult to say with precision. Similarly, whether the author of 1 Peter was aware of the Pauline letters, or had read them, or whether the "Pauline" material in 1 Peter had already passed into common tradition by the time 1 Peter was written is equally difficult to demonstrate.[9]

In either case, the probable trajectory of influence suggests that 1 Peter was written later than the Pauline letters, and perhaps even later than a probable deutero-Pauline book like Ephesians. If this is true, then it is all the more clear that this epistle is pseudonymous.

In terms of the social strictures of the letter, the concern for the fixed orders of house or church seem more likely contemporary to letters thought of as deutero-pauline than to Paul himself. The closest analogies are found in Colossians, Ephesians, and the Pastoral Epistles.[10]

In terms of the spread of Christianity, one has to assume a quite rapid expansion to the churches of Asia Minor so that before Peter's death (traditionally held to be in the 60s of the common era) there were already churches established in a number of towns in Asia Minor, with their own leaders and nascent structures.

On the other hand, none of these doubts provides indisputable evidence that Peter could not have written the letter. They raise a complex of issues that have caused a number of students of the epistle to say that the probability rests with the claim that the letter was written after Peter's death but in Peter's name.

There are mediating positions that try to find a place between the claim that Peter wrote or dictated this epistle word for word and the claim that a later Christian penned the whole thing, using Peter's name to give weight to its affirmations and prescriptions. One position interprets the epistle in the light of 1 Pet 5:12: "Through Silvanus our faithful brother, as I reckon, I have written to you briefly, exhorting (you) and bearing witness to the true grace of God" (author's trans.). While it is logically possible that "I have written you through Silvanus" could mean, "I have written this letter and am sending it through Silvanus," the fact that "Peter" says, "I have written briefly through Silvanus" makes it more likely the impression the reader is to gain is that Silvanus was the scribe who took down Peter's dictation.[11]

There is ample precedent in the New Testament for letters whose author acknowledges a helper. In 1 Cor 1:3, the address is from Paul and Sosthenes, and in 1 Cor 15:21 Paul insists that the final greeting is in his own hand, indicating that the letter up until that point had been dictated. Second Corinthians 1:1 addresses the Corinthian church from Paul and Timothy. Galatians ends with the indication that Paul is (now) writing with his own hand (Gal 5:11) (cf. Col 4:18). Philippians is from Paul and Timothy (Phil 1:1). First Thessalonians is from Paul, Silvanus, and Timothy (1 Thess 1:1) and also ends with Paul's handwritten greeting (2 Thess 3:17), emphasized perhaps to contrast it with pseudonymous letters written in Paul's name.

---

9. Achtemeier, *1 Peter*, 18-19.
10. It is obvious that if one takes Colossians, Ephesians, and the Pastoral Epistles to be Pauline, then the kind of social development 1 Peter reflects may have been taking place in Peter's lifetime.
11. Leonhard Goppelt thinks that Silvanus helped with the writing. See L. Goppelt, *A Commentary on I Peter*, ed. Ferdinand Hahn, trans. John E. Alsup (Grand Rapids: Eerdmans, 1993) 369. Achtemeier cites the use of similar formulas for the one who carries the letter and argues that this is Silvanus's role. See Achtemeier, *1 Peter*, 350n. 56.

Some have thought that the Silvanus mentioned in this epistle is more redactor than scribe, taking Peter's general themes or fragmentary exhortations and shaping them into a fuller and more coherent letter. If this Silvanus is the Silvanus of 1 Thessalonians and Acts, he was Paul's companion and might well have been versed in Greek and in the Greek version of the Old Testament; and he would have used that knowledge to present Peter's themes in a form accessible to the Gentile, Greek-speaking Christians of Asia Minor.[12] Still another position suggests that 1 Peter is a letter from the church at Rome to the churches in Asia Minor. The church at Rome honored Peter and remembered much of his teaching, and, therefore, it was bold to write in his name to the other churches in the East without making any direct claim that Peter penned or dictated the letter himself.[13] Each of these mediating positions represents an attempt to maintain the integrity of the claim that Peter was responsible for the epistle while acknowledging the doubts that its every word was written or dictated by the fisherman apostle.

Obviously, no one has solved the problem of authorship to the satisfaction of every other interpreter. Not surprisingly, there is a congruence between the interpreter's understanding of scriptural authority and the claims about authorship. Interpreters for whom scriptural authenticity depends in large measure on its factual accuracy are inclined to support authenticity, either outright or in one of the mediating positions. Interpreters who are more skeptical about the factual accuracy of other parts of the New Testament (the authorship of the Pastorals, for example, or the possibility of harmonizing the events of the Gospels into a single synopsis) are more skeptical of Peter's authorship.

In terms of the theological claims of the epistle, the answer one gives to the question of authorship may make surprisingly little difference. Whether it was written by Peter or by a later Christian in his name, the epistle helps to strengthen Christians in times of distress; sets their lives within the history of God's activity, which moves from creation to consummation; holds up the atoning death of Jesus Christ; and encourages mutual love among Christian people and forbearance of enemies. Nothing in this list would be impossible for the historical Peter to enjoin; nothing loses its power to shape faith if the words were written by some later Christian in his name.

The one difficult interpretive issue, however, is the question of the relationship between authorial integrity and doctrinal authority. There are benign and less benign theories of pseudonymity. On the benign theory, the disciple of an apostle writes a letter in the apostle's name to say what the disciples believe the apostle would want to have said in a particular situation. Whether or not readers were deceived into believing the letter to be authentic, deception was not the point.[14] On the more suspicious theory of pseudonymity, the whole purpose of writing a pseudonymous letter was to mislead readers into believing that the words of some anonymous Christian carry the authority of the apostle. So, for instance, the author(s) of the Pastoral Epistles tries to correct what he thinks is a wrong interpretation of Pauline doctrine by forging a letter, or letters, purporting to be from Paul and throwing in some false memorabilia about fellow Christians, cloaks, and books, deliberately to throw suspicious readers off the scent.[15]

The question of the authorship of 1 Peter is probably unanswerable. The question of its usefulness to the church is not. We have every scriptural treasure in earthen vessels, and the historical question about the intention of the original author may be less important than the question of what the letter enjoined of its first readers and how it might have brought comfort to them and, by extension, to their successors in every generation, including our own.[16]

One's guess about the date for 1 Peter, of course, is closely related to one's guess about its authorship. If Peter wrote the epistle, and if the tradition that places his death in the 60s is accurate, then the epistle was probably written toward the close of his life. If the letter is

---

12. This is the position of E. G. Selwyn, *The First Epistle of Peter* (London: Macmillan, 1958) 9-17.

13. This seems to be Goppelt's position. See Goppelt, *A Commentary on I Peter,* 51-52. J. Ramsey Michaels finds a mediating position between this one and the claim of Petrine authorship. See Michaels, *1 Peter,* WBC (Waco, Tex.: Word, 1988) lxvi.

14. I take this position to be close to the consensus of the contributors to *Peter in the New Testament,* ed. Raymond E. Brown, Karl P. Donfried, John Reumann (Minneapolis and Paramus: Augsburg and Paulist) 149-50.

15. This is a simplification, but not an unfair one, of Lewis Donelson's reading of pseudonymity in the Pastorals. See Donelson, *Pseudepigraphy and Ethical Argument in the Pastoral Epistles* (Tübingen: J.C.B. Mohr [Paul Siebeck], 1986) esp. 54-66.

16. Goppelt puts this argument more elegantly. See Goppelt, *A Commentary on I Peter,* 52.

pseudonymous, the range of possibilities grows accordingly, and one's hypothesis is based largely on one's reading of the historical circumstances of the epistle.

From the perspective of the pseudonymous theory, this letter was written long enough after the deaths of Peter and Paul for Christianity to have spread and received some institutional shape in Asia Minor, and long enough for Pauline motifs to have entered into the broader stream of Christian tradition. On this hypothesis, it is appropriate to suggest that the epistle be dated toward the end of the first century.

The other clue that might help with dating the epistle is its references to suffering and trouble for the Christians of Asia Minor. Nero's persecution of the Christians would have been confined largely to Rome and would have been too early for this letter if it was written in the generation after the death of Simon Peter. The emperor worship that seems to have been instituted under Domitian and carried on by his successors is not mentioned in 1 Peter. On the contrary, the emperor is worthy of honor (1 Pet 2:13). Nor is 1 Peter driven by the intense hatred of empire that drives Revelation, written probably around the turn of the first century. Furthermore, the troubles that seem to be bothering the recipients of the letter may be more aptly described as local harassments than as systematic persecution. The people are being slandered and perhaps even accused, but there is no sense that the government has turned against them.

All this suggests a date toward the end of the first century, when a growing Christian movement had already stirred up trouble among its neighbors but had not yet attracted the attention of the emperor or been forced to choose between allegiance to him and allegiance to Christ. About 110 CE, Pliny the Younger, writing from Asia Minor, asked the emperor Trajan for advice about how to deal with people accused of being Christians. The correspondence between Pliny and Trajan reflects developments somewhat later than the situation in 1 Peter; emperor worship was now prescribed, and the Christian movement was growing so fast that Pliny thought it needed to be checked.

However, the atmosphere of accusation, charge, and slander that 1 Peter reflects was still present in this somewhat later period. Trajan's response to Pliny shows something of the circumstances of the growing Christian movement in Asia Minor:

> You have followed the right course of procedure, my dear Pliny, in your examination of the cases of persons charged with being Christians, for it is impossible to lay down a general rule to a fixed formula. These people must not be hunted out; if they are brought before you and the charge against them is proved, they must be punished, but in the case of anyone who denies that he is a Christian, and makes it clear that he is not by offering prayers to our gods, he is to be pardoned as a result of his repentance however suspect his past conduct may be. But pamphlets circulating anonymously must play no part in any accusation. They create the worst sort of precedent and are quite out of keeping with the spirit of our age.[17]

Already in 1 Peter, the label "Christian" was making life difficult if not dangerous (see 4:14, 16), and already in 1 Peter there are hints of anonymous accusations and slanderous insults (see 2:12; 3:9, 16).

The evidence seems to point to a letter written between Paul's letters to the Gentile churches and Pliny's and Trajan's letters to each other. Given the evidence of emperor worship as a problem for John of Patmos and not for the writer of 1 Peter, we can also put this letter before Revelation. One might guess that the letter was written sometime around 90 CE, knowing that one speaks at best of probabilities.

The evidence that helps to date the letter also helps us to understand the situation of the audience. First Peter 1:1 gives us much of the crucial information. The letter is written to churches of Asia Minor, and they are probably listed in the order in which the letter might be circulated from one church to the next. The recipients are "exiles," as later they are both "resident aliens" and "exiles." The author is also presumably an exile, since his word for Rome, from which he writes, is "Babylon," not only a cipher for an enemy of God's people (as in Revelation), but also

---

17. Pliny *Letters* 10, 97, from *Pliny, Letters and Panegyricus*, trans. Betty Radice (Cambridge, Mass.: Harvard University Press, 1969) 291-93.

the reminder that Rome itself is a place of exile (see Commentary on 1 Pet 5:13). Recent work in sociological theory has debated whether these Christians can also be described according to their socioeconomic setting—that is, members of a class of resident aliens, living as guest workers in communities where they had no citizenship and no power.[18] More traditional interpretations have seen the language of exile as a metaphorical reminder to these Christians that on this earth they have no lasting home; their citizenship is in heaven.[19] Careful study of the letter suggests a third possibility, one that does not necessarily contradict the other two (anymore than they necessarily contradict each other). Language of exile and alienation is language that distinguishes the Christians who received this letter from the larger culture around them. It is that culture from which they emerged, but now they are a slandered minority, exiled as Israel was exiled in Babylon, strangers in a strange land (all the more strange because it used to be home).

It is also quite clear that the recipients of the letter were Gentiles who formerly shared the paganism of the neighbors who now reject them (see 4:3-4). As is so often the case with early Christians, these former pagans, who were ethnically Gentiles, took on the identity of Israel, no people become a people (2:10). "Gentiles" in the epistle refers to those friends and neighbors who had not left their old ways in order to join this Israel in exile, this community of faith.

If we can judge the social setting of the recipients of the letter from the rhetoric of its specific advice (2:18–3:7), we can also guess that there were more slaves than masters among these Christians, and more believing wives with pagan husbands than vice versa. No advice is given to masters, but much to slaves. Women are told how to get along with their unbelieving husbands, but husbands (who presumably set the religious rules for the household) receive shorter instructions, all of which presume that their wives are believers, too.

THE USE OF THE OLD TESTAMENT IN 1 PETER

This epistle is steeped in Old Testament themes, quotations, and allusions. Although the recipients of the letter are mostly Gentiles, the epistle assumes that the Old Testament had become their Scripture. Several features of the use of the Old Testament are noteworthy.

(1) As Paul Achtemeier points out, the letter is permeated by a governing metaphor: the image of the church as Israel. "In a way virtually unique among Christian canonical writings, 1 Peter has appropriated the language of Israel for the church in such a way that Israel as a totality has become for this letter the controlling metaphor in terms of which its theology is expressed."[20] Unlike such New Testament writings as Romans and the Gospel of Matthew, 1 Peter does not attend to the relationship between Christians and Jews as possible heirs to Israel. The epistle simply takes over images and phrases that the Old Testament applies to Israel and applies them to the church. Christians are now the people who were once no people; the church is the community of those who were without mercy but have now received mercy (1 Pet 2:10, quoting Hos 2:23).

One image in particular from Israel's story is crucial to 1 Peter's claims about the Christians of Asia Minor. Just as God's people were once exiled in Babylon, so also the recipients of this letter are exiles in Asia Minor (1:1). Just as Abraham was a stranger among the Hittites, so also Christians are strangers within the dominant pagan culture (Gen 23:4; 1 Pet 2:11).[21] Non-Christians are referred to as "Gentiles," implying that the Christians are "Israel," though ethnically most of those who would hear this letter were Gentiles, too (2:12). The author hints that he, too, knows what it means to live in exile, since his code name for the city from which he writes is "Babylon" (5:13).

The story of Jesus, too, is foretold by Israel's story. In particular the Servant Songs of Isaiah provide the explicit and implicit background for 1 Pet 2:22-25 (see Isa 53:4-9). First Peter 2:21

---

18. See John H. Elliot, *A Home for the Homeless* (Philadelphia: Fortress, 1981), and the essays by Elliot and David Balch in Charles H. Talbert, ed., *Perspectives on First Peter* (Macon, Ga.: Mercer University Press, 1986).
19. See C. Spicq, *Les Épitres de Saint Pierre* (Paris: Librarie Lecoffre, 1966) 40.
20. Achtemeier, *1 Peter*, 69; the whole discussion is found on 69-72.
21. Achtemeier, *1 Peter*, 69; the whole discussion is found on 71.

introduces this passage on suffering, in a word to Christian slaves: "For to this you have been called, because Christ also suffered for you, leaving you an example, so that you should follow in his steps" (NRSV). The epistle thus presents a threefold typology. The suffering servant foreshadows the suffering of Christ; Christ foreshadows the suffering of Christian slaves; and slaves model appropriate behavior for all Christians in the face of suffering.

(2) Also pervasive in 1 Peter is the use of passages bound together by key words or images, images that link the passages to each other and also to the situation of the first-century Christians (for other instances in the NT see, e.g., Rom 9:14-21; Heb 1:5-13). In this epistle, the most striking examples are found in chap. 2. In 2:4-8, "stone" is the central image, with allusions or quotations from Ps 118:22; Isa 28:16; and Exod 19:6 with Isa 61:6. Christ is the stone, and Christians are the stone; the stones together build a house or temple. Christ is the cornerstone, the stone the builders rejected, the stumbling block.

Similarly, in 1 Pet 2:9-11 a host of OT images and phrases related to being a people are built one on top of the other, leading up to the climactic quotation from Hos 2:23 (in these three verses there are allusions to Exod 19:6; Deut 4:20; 7:6; 14:2; Isa 43:20-21 LXX; 61:6—all woven together).

(3) First Peter provides a rationale for its own use of Scripture:

Concerning this salvation, the prophets, who spoke of the grace that was to come to you, searched intently and with the greatest care, trying to find out the time and circumstances to which the Spirit of Christ in them was pointing when he predicted the sufferings of Christ and the glories that would follow. It was revealed to them that they were not serving themselves but you, when they spoke of the things that have now been told you by those who have preached the gospel to you by the Holy Spirit sent from heaven. (1 Pet 1:10-12 NIV)

For 1 Peter, the OT was not written to point to Israel but to point to Christ and through Christ to point ahead to the life of the church. The Holy Spirit, who inspired the prophets (and was instrumental in Christ's resurrection, 3:18), also speaks among contemporary Christian preachers. Indeed, the OT was written for the sake of those preachers and the Christian congregations to whom they speak.

(4) At some points, at least, the context of the passage 1 Peter quotes adds further light on the significance of that passage in the argument of the letter. For example, 1 Pet 1:24-25 quotes Isa 40:6-8. These verses are immediately pertinent to the epistle's claim that God's Word lives and endures. More than that, the larger context in Isaiah reinforces themes found elsewhere in 1 Peter. Isaiah 40:5 declares the revelation of God's glory, a theme evident in 1 Pet 1:7; 2:12; 4:11; 5:1, 10. Isaiah 40:9 calls for a herald of "good news" to speak to Zion. The verb in the Septuagint of Isa 40:9 is εὐαγγελίζω (*euangelizō*), the same as in 1 Pet 1:12, 25. The larger context of the quotation echoes other themes in the epistle.

(5) The "scriptural" resources on which 1 Peter draws may be larger than our own version of the OT canon. At least in the complicated claim about Christ's proclamation to the spirits after his resurrection, 1 Peter seems to draw on traditions from *1 Enoch*.[22] While the epistle never explicitly says that this extra-biblical material counts as Scripture, the author relies on those traditions in much the same way that he elsewhere draws on canonical OT themes.

(6) Finally, 1 Peter implies that the life of Scripture—and its power—lives on in the community of faith. In 1 Pet 1:12, the very purpose of OT Scripture is to provide the good news for Christian preachers. In 1 Pet 4:11, the author is writing about mutual service in the community of faith: "Whoever speaks must do so as one speaking the very words of God" (NRSV). This may imply a reliance on Scripture as the basis for preaching.[23] More likely, it claims for preaching a representation of that authority found in Scripture; like the prophets of old, Christian preachers speak of Christ for the sake of Christ's people.

---

22. See William Joseph Dalton, *Christ's Proclamation to the Spirits: A Study of 1 Peter 3:18–4:6*, 2nd ed., AnBib (Rome: Pontifical Biblical Institute, 1989) 166-71. See also Commentary on 1 Pet 3:18-22.

23. Achtemeier acknowledges this possibility. See Achtemeier, *1 Peter*, 298-99.

SOCIAL SETTING AND THE LIFE OF FAITH

Social context shapes faith, and faith reshapes the social context. The clearest evidence for the nature of the communities for which this letter was written is 1 Peter itself. Yet on the basis of this epistle one can present reasonable hypotheses about the Christians of Asia Minor, and then, of course, use the hypotheses to help interpret the letter. Study of 1 Peter suggests that the Christians for whom it was written had an ambivalent relationship to the larger society around them.

The references to being sojourners, aliens, strangers indicate the distance of these Christians from the society around them. They were not rescued *from* exile; they were rescued *into* exile. Their alienation is a mark of their faithfulness: "Live in reverent fear during the time of your exile. You know that you were ransomed from the futile ways inherited from your ancestors" (1:17-18 NRSV).

On the other hand, it is clear that the approval of the larger society is crucial not only to the Christians' safety but also to their self-esteem: "Beloved, I urge you as aliens and exiles to abstain from the desires of the flesh that wage war against the soul" (2:11 NRSV). Here we might expect an exhortation to shun those pagans whose standards are unworthy of the faithful, but the exhortation continues: "Conduct yourselves honorably among the Gentiles, so that, though they malign you as evildoers, they may see your honorable deeds and glorify God when he comes to judge" (2:12 NRSV).

There is intense concern for the internal life of the Christian community, but the "world" is not roundly condemned (as in the Johannine epistles) except as it represents a set of practices that the Christians have left behind (1:18; 4:3-4). Indeed, the hope of 2:12 that the "Gentiles" might in the end glorify God implies a hope for redemption that extends beyond the community of faith. There is an absolute devotion to God as the only God; honoring the emperor is not only allowed but is commended as well (2:13, 17). It is probably the case that the emperor did not yet make the idolatrous demands that lie behind the book of Revelation, but it is also the case that the reverence for authority in 1 Peter lies very far from the suspicion of authority in the later book. Yet 1 Peter 2 is also quite different from Romans 13; the emperor is merely a human figure, one more authority within the created order. There is no sense that the authority is itself divine (unlike Rom 13:1-2). The behavior enjoined in 1 Peter 2 and Romans 13 is very similar, but there are important distinctions between the warrants given for that behavior.

First Peter is, therefore, sectarian without being countercultural.[24] It raises problems for contemporary Christian obedience. In a time when Christian social action seems to many an essential element in discipleship, is 1 Peter too sectarian and passive to be a guide for Christians in society? On the other hand, does the epistle's too easy acceptance of the larger society prevent the author from seeing how profoundly Christians must stand against culture? Does the epistle fail to recognize that Christians, who are resident aliens, must be alien, indeed?

Study of 1 Peter further suggests that the Christians for whom it was written lived or were enjoined to live uncomplainingly in social structures that were both hierarchical and patriarchal. Pauline churches never fully worked out the implications of Paul's gospel in Gal 3:28 that "there is no longer Jew or Greek, there is no longer slave or free, there is no longer male and female; for all of you are one in Christ Jesus" (NRSV). For the churches of 1 Peter, such a radical claim barely appeared on the horizon.

This study will suggest that the strong attention to right behavior on the part of slaves and wives (with no attention to masters and slight attention to husbands) probably reflects churches still dominated by slaves and non-slave owners and marked by the Christian wives of pagan husbands. Nonetheless, the demand that slaves and wives be properly subject to masters and husbands enforces a picture of Christianity as meekly submissive—and stands over against quite different visions, such as Mary's magnificat in Luke 1:46-55.

The strongest christological warrants are brought forth to remind slaves to "accept the authority of your masters with all deference, not only those who are kind and gentle but also those

---

24. A phrase suggested by Marion Soards in editorial correspondence.

1 PETER—INTRODUCTION

who are harsh" (2:18 NRSV). Christ's suffering becomes a model for the suffering of slaves, and the suffering of slaves becomes a model for all Christians who suffer unjustly for their faith or for doing good. Therefore, the appeal to submissive behavior colors the christology. Not only does Christ become a model for slaves, but also slavery becomes the lens through which the epistle views christology and enjoins discipleship.

Furthermore, wives are urged to be quiet about their faith in order to entice their husbands toward believing, not by explicit profession of faith, but by modest and gentle demeanor. The letter—almost—unquestioningly takes up the androcentric assumptions of the larger society. There is one notable exception. There is no claim that Christian wives should give up their faith in order to conform to their husbands' religion; in this way, 1 Peter stands against the norms of its larger society.

Nonetheless, in our time, when the gospel is rightly seen as including a profound concern for liberation, 1 Peter can be seen as profoundly unliberating. And for churches that urgently need to hear women's voices, the injunctions to quiet demeanor can be seen as profoundly unfaithful.

This study will seek to acknowledge the specificity and otherness of the world for which this epistle was written. It will also suggest that across barriers of culture and time, the epistle has a message that is still good news for Christians.

THEOLOGICAL THEMES

The motifs of the epistle are best understood in their context, as one reads through its argument and allusions. Several motifs, however, can be extracted as guides to a more thorough reading.

God. Only in 1 Peter in the New Testament is God explicitly designated by the noun "Creator" (κτίστης *ktistēs*; 4:19). The whole epistle presupposes that history is in God's hands, from beginning to end. From the beginning God has created the earth and called Christians to be God's own people. At the end, God will provide the imperishable award granted to those who have proved faithful. In between times, God provides the Spirit to encourage believers and to inspire appropriate—and joyful—worship.

Christ. Christ is the one who brings believers to God (3:18). He does this especially through his crucifixion and resurrection. His suffering is both the example and the ground for the faithfulness of Christians who also face suffering. His resurrection is the vindication that makes faith possible and prefigures the final victory, when God, having judged the living and the dead, will be glorified forever (4:11).

Suffering. In 5:12, the author says that he has written a letter of encouragement, and certainly a major purpose of the epistle is to strengthen the Christians of Asia Minor in their time of distress. Whatever the nature of that distress, it serves to strengthen their faith for the last days and to bring them into communion with Christ, whose suffering prefigures and validates their own.[25]

Baptism. The only explicit reference to baptism is in 1 Pet 3:18-21, where Christian baptism is an antitype to Noah's escape in the flood and a laying hold of the assurance made possible through Christ's resurrection. Yet much of the epistle plays on themes that are appropriate to new Christians, whether explicitly growing out of baptismal traditions or otherwise.

First Peter deals with two contrasts appropriate to baptismal reflection. There are the temporal contrasts between then and now. In some cases, "then" is what the Christians used to be when they were among the Gentiles. "Now" is what they are as resident aliens in a Gentile world (see 4:1-4). In some cases, now is the era in which Christians live by faith even in the midst of suffering, and then is what will happen in the future, when their opponents will be surprised by God's judgment and Christians will be given their everlasting inheritance (see 1:4-8;

---

25. Brox thinks that 1 Pet 5:12 is the key to the whole epistle, and he uses that as a criticism of a too great emphasis on baptismal themes. See Brox, *Der erste Petrusbrief,* 18-19.

4:7, 12). Now is the time when Christians live by faith; then is the time when that faith will issue in salvation (see 1:5, 9).

There is also the contrast between "us" and "them." They are the Gentiles who represent the life that Christians have left behind. But within the theology of 1 Peter, there is hope even for them, who may be shamed or astonished into the final redemption (see 3:12).

Furthermore, appropriate to the life of new Christians is the assumption, also evident elsewhere in the New Testament, that the gifts of the faithful life will be shown in faithful conduct—in traditional terms, the combination of indicative and imperative (see 1:14-15; 2:1-3, which is explicit in its reference to rebirth and implicit in its allusion to baptism).

The new life is life in community, with emphasis on shared responsibility, shared worship, and shared identity as a "chosen race, a royal priesthood, a holy nation, God's own people" (2:9 NRSV). Those who seem to outsiders to be barely legal immigrants, sneaked over the border to stir up trouble, are really citizens in the only country that counts and members of the family that nurtures and endures.

Life in Exile. Finally, Christians are exhorted to be exemplary aliens in the land that does not welcome them. This means that they are to be as upright as the most upright of their neighbors. More than that, they are to forge for themselves an identity that sets them apart without necessarily setting them in conflict with the pagans around them. They are to return good for evil, blessing for slander—hoping, perhaps against hope, that in the judgment their very fidelity may shame their slanderers into believing.

LITERARY FORM

It seems obvious that 1 Peter is a letter, with the style of address and final salutation, the thanksgiving or blessing, and the exhortation that are typical of Hellenistic letters of the first centuries CE and quite analogous to other letters in the New Testament. It has also been noticed for many years that there seems to be a kind of break between 1 Peter 4:11 and 4:12, representing either a new subject or a new intensity of interest in subjects already raised. Early in the twentieth century it was proposed that the letter really consisted of two separate pieces joined together. First Peter 1:3–4:11 was a baptismal homily full of the joy of the new life in Christ, and 4:12–5:14 was a word of encouragement in a time where persecution had moved from possibility to reality.[26] While this is a possible explanation for the text as we have it, like all such literary constructions, it remains unprovable. This study will affirm that there is clear evidence of themes appropriate to baptism in the first part of the letter, but it will suggest that the last part (beginning with 4:12) is an appropriate expansion and application of themes already introduced, brought to deeper intensity because 4:12 begins the closing exhortation. Whatever the truth about the sources of 1 Peter, the letter as we have it makes its own literary and theological sense, and we shall read it as one document read or heard by its intended audience from 1:1 through 5:14.

Beyond the obvious fact that the epistle moves from salutation to thanksgiving to body to closing salutation, the analysis of the structure of the letter depends in part on one's interpretation of how the argument or exhortation of the epistle moves. One can detect a continuing alternation between claim and exegetical grounding (cf., e.g., 1:22-23 with 1:24-25; 2:4-5 with 2:6-8). And one can find an alternation between indicative claims and imperative applications (1:1-12 leads to 1:13-16; 2:9-10 grounds 1:24-25 [which validates 1:22-23] and also grounds 2:1-30).

David Balch has found helpful internal clues for dividing the body of the letter (1:13–5:11). First Peter 1:13–2:10 works out the themes of the introductory blessing (1:3-12); therefore, these verses form a unit. First Peter 2:11–4:11 is marked by the recurrence of a number of themes—slander, suffering, the contrast between doing good and doing evil, judgment and

---

26. See the discussions in Goppelt, *A Commentary on I Peter*, 15-17; and Achtemeier, *1 Peter*, 58-59.

justice.[27] There is also a repetition of themes in the beginning and end of this section, in the stress on God's coming judgment on believers and unbelievers alike (2:12; 4:5) and the stress on glorifying God (2:12; 4:11). First Peter 4:12, with its renewed address ("Beloved") and its renewed urgency, begins the final section of the main body of the epistle.

---

27. David L. Balch, *Let Wives Be Submissive: The Domestic Code in 1 Peter*, SBLMS (Chico, Calif.: Scholars Press, 1981) 123-29.

BIBLIOGRAPHY

Commentaries:

Achtemeier, Paul. *1 Peter.* Hermeneia. Minneapolis: Fortress, 1996. A wonderfully thorough and judicious study of the epistle. The most technical of the works here listed.

Craddock, Fred B. *First and Second Peter and Jude.* Westminster Bible Companion. Louisville: Westminster John Knox, 1995. An excellent, less technical study, especially useful for laypeople and adult Bible classes.

Goppelt, Leonhard. *A Commentary on 1 Peter.* Edited by Ferdinand Hahn. Translated and augmented by John E. Alsup. Grand Rapids: Eerdmans, 1993. A very clear discussion of the issues, especially helpful in looking at pertinent extra-canonical material.

Michaels, J. Ramsey. *1 Peter.* WBC. Waco, Tex.: Word, 1988. A study of the Greek text with commentary; balanced and useful.

Perkins, Pheme. *First and Second Peter, James, and Jude.* Interpretation. Louisville: Westminster John Knox, 1995. Along with Craddock, the most widely accessible of these commentaries, especially helpful for preaching.

Other suggested studies:

Balch, David L. *Let Wives Be Submissive: The Domestic Code in 1 Peter.* SBLMS. Chico, Calif.: Scholars Press, 1981. Sets the domestic code in the context of other Hellenistic and Hellenistic-Jewish literature and uses the code as a clue to the setting and themes of the epistle.

Dalton, William Joseph. *Christ's Proclamation to the Spirits: A Study of 1 Peter 3:18–4:6.* 2nd ed. Rome: Pontifical Biblical Institute, 1989. A remarkably thorough and influential exegesis of the most puzzling passages in 1 Peter.

Elliott, John H. *A Home for the Homeless: A Sociological Exegesis of 1 Peter, Its Situation and Strategy.* Philadelphia: Fortress, 1981. Understands the readers of 1 Peter as "resident aliens" in a social and political as well as a theological sense, and reads the letter in that light.

THE NEW INTERPRETER'S BIBLE COMMENTARY

OUTLINE OF 1 PETER

I. 1 Peter 1:1-2, Greetings

II. 1 Peter 1:3-12, Praise to God

III. 1 Peter 1:13–2:10, God's Holy People

    A. 1:13-25, Being Holy
    B. 2:1-10, Being God's People

IV. 1 Peter 2:11–4:11, Life in Exile

    A. 2:11-17, Living Honorably Among the Gentiles
    B. 2:18–3:7, Living Honorably in the Household
    C. 3:8-22, Faithful Suffering
    D. 4:1-11, Living Out Salvation

V. 1 Peter 4:12–5:11, Steadfast in Faith

    A. 4:12-19, The Impending Crisis
    B. 5:1-11, Caring for the Household of God

VI. 1 Peter 5:12-14, Final Greetings

1 PETER 1:1-2

GREETINGS

COMMENTARY

First Peter is written in Greek, and Greek letters of the first century typically began with a salutation: "From X to Y, greetings." Sometimes the salutation was expanded so that letter writers could give some information about themselves and suggest their concerns for those to whom the letter was addressed.[28] For Christian writers, the salutation provided the opportunity to begin to present the pastoral and theological motifs of the epistle.[29] First Peter 1:1-2 represents the salutation for this epistle.

1:1. The writer introduces himself as Peter. He does not use his proper name, Simon, as recorded in the four Gospels (see, e.g., Matt 1:30; Mark 1:16, 30; Luke 5:8; John 1:40), but only his nickname, "Petros," Greek for the original Aramaic "Cephas." Some have seen this as a sign that the letter is late and implies the later church's devotion to the figure of Peter, leaving aside his probable self-designation as Simon. However, already in 1 Cor 1:12 and Gal 2:11 and six other times (1 Cor 3:22; 9:5; 15:5; Gal 1:18; 2:9, 14), Paul refers to Simon only as "Cephas" (κηφᾶς *kēphas*), and in Gal 2:7-8 Paul refers to him simply as "Peter." Therefore, very early in the Christian community Simon Peter had become Cephas or Peter. The term "Cephas," or "Peter," can be translated "rock," and different Gospels give somewhat different accounts of how Simon the son of Jonah received this name. In Mark 3:16, Jesus seems to designate Simon as Peter at the time that Jesus appoints the Twelve to proclaim the gospel and to cast out demons. The account in Luke 6:14 is similar. (It is possible that Mark and Luke simply record here the fact that at some other time Jesus designated Simon as Peter, but it seems more likely that they thought the naming and the appointment went together.) In Matthew, Simon receives the name "Peter" after his confession of Jesus as Christ, son of the living God, at Caesarea Philippi (Matt 16:18); however, Peter is called Simon Peter by the narrator before that incident. At the story of the call of Simon in Matt 4:18, Matthew seems to indicate that Christians at the time of the writing of the Gospel called Simon "Peter," but that he was not yet known as Peter within the time of the narrative itself. At any rate, there can be no question that the author of the letter signifies himself to be Simon Peter, Jonah's son and one of the earliest circle of Jesus' disciples.

The writer calls himself an apostle of Jesus Christ. "Apostle" is also Paul's favorite self-designation at the beginning of letters (see Rom 1:1; 1 Cor 1:1; 2 Cor 1:1; Gal 1:1). Even if Ephesians and Colossians were written by persons other than Paul, they use the designation "apostle" for Paul himself, as do 1 and 2 Timothy and Titus. Paul, too, certainly thinks of Peter as one of the apostles (see 1 Cor 9:5).

In Luke and Acts, the term "apostle" is the official designation for the twelve who followed Jesus in his earthly ministry and were chosen by him to establish the church in the power of the Holy Spirit.[30] First Peter does not elaborate on the call or function of an apostle, as Paul's letters do. On the one hand, we can assume that for this letter, as for Acts, Peter is self-evidently one of the circle of those who witnessed Jesus' earthly ministry and resurrection and who bore witness to Jesus in the church's early proclamation. In its root form, the term "apostle" comes from the Greek verb "to send" (ἀποστέλλω *apostellō*) and may go back to the Hebrew notion of the שליח (*šālîaḥ*). The *šālîaḥ* was an emissary sent with the authority, commission, and message

---

28. See John L. White, *The Form and Function of the Body of the Greek Letter: A Study of the Letter-Body in the Non-literary Papyri and in Paul the Apostle*, SBLDS (Missoula: SBL, 1972) 7-8.
29. See Brox, *Der erste Petrusbrief*, 55.
30. In Acts, Paul is usually not counted as an apostle, but see Acts 14:14.

of the sender.³¹ Therefore, for Peter to be an apostle of Jesus Christ was for Peter to speak with authority given by Jesus Christ and to speak a word that Jesus Christ commissioned him to bring.

It was noted in the Introduction that different interpreters have different understandings of the term "exile" (παρεπίδημος *parepidēmos*) in the part of the greeting that designates the recipients of the letter. Some scholars think that the Christians who received the letter were "exiled" because they had departed their homelands to become resident aliens in Asia Minor. Other scholars think that all Christians are "exiled" because they are separated for a time from their eternal home.³² Language about exile in 1 Peter seems to show an analogy between the Christians of Asia Minor and the Jews who were exiled to Babylon. The stress is not so much on the fact that they are far from home (whether an earthly home or a heavenly one). The designation emphasizes the fact that they are surrounded and outnumbered by the citizens, the natives, who misunderstand them and who constantly test their faith.

One biblical paradigm for these Christians is Abraham. In Gen 23:4 he makes an appeal to the Hittites among whom he lives: "I am a stranger and an alien residing among you; give me property among you for a burying place" (NRSV).³³ Just as Abraham had gone forth from his father's house, so also the Christians of Asia Minor had left behind the practices of their pagan fathers and mothers to find themselves aliens and strangers in the land that used to be their home.

Furthermore, for this letter the exile in Babylon would have been a foretaste of the later dispersion of Jews throughout the known world and their status as a sometimes troubled minority. Again 1 Peter takes a term familiar in its application to Judaism outside of Palestine and applies it by extension to Christians. Followers of Christ in Asia Minor are the new dispersion, scattered among opposing Gentiles, the majority community of the pagans. As noted, of course, most of these Christians to whom the letter was written were themselves pagans before they were called by God to Christian belief. A possible forerunner of 1 Peter is found in the letter that Jeremiah wrote to the exiles in Babylon (Jer 29:4-23):³⁴

Thus says the LORD of hosts, the God of Israel, to all the exiles whom I have sent into exile from Jerusalem to Babylon: Build houses and live in them; plant gardens and eat what they produce. Take wives and have sons and daughters. . . . But seek the welfare of the city where I have sent you into exile, and pray to the LORD on its behalf. (Jer 29:4-7 NRSV)

This portion of Jeremiah's letter foreshadows the call of 1 Peter to its readers. They are to find their identity among the pagans where they are exiled. In part this means being exemplary citizens of a society that abuses them and honoring the authorities that rule this alien land (see 2:13-17).

The order of the Greek text is rather different from that of the NRSV. In Greek the greeting is literally "to the chosen exiles of the diaspora," not "to the exiles of the Dispersion . . . who have been chosen" (the NIV is more accurate here). It may be that for the writer the election and the exile go together. To be chosen is to be exiled from those around you who have not been chosen in the same way and for the same destiny. This would echo Jeremiah's letter to the exiles of his time. They are the exiles God has sent into exile. Their exile is a part of their calling and their election (Jer 29:4).

The letter was addressed to Christians in five provinces of Asia Minor (see Introduction). If there is any reason for the order in which the provinces are listed, it may be that the letter circulated among the provinces in the order listed, though this remains conjecture.³⁵

1:2. The NRSV translation includes part of the Greek of v. 1 in this verse. The Greek text more literally reads: "To the chosen exiles of the Dispersion . . . destined by God."

---

31. See Karl H. Rengstorf, "Apostolos," in *TDNT*, 1:407-46, esp. 414-18.
32. For the first option, see John H. Elliott, *A Home for the Homeless: A Sociological Exegesis of 1 Peter, Its Situation and Strategy* (Philadelphia: Fortress, 1981). For the second option see Selwyn, *The First Epistle of Peter*, 118; and Spicq, *Les Ŝpitres de Saint Pierre*, 40.
33. See Achtemeier, *1 Peter*, 81-82.
34. See Michaels, *1 Peter*, xlvi. Michaels also cites other examples of the genre.
35. See Peter H. Davids, *The First Epistle of Peter* (Grand Rapids: Eerdmans, 1990) 8. For reservations about this theory, see Goppelt, *A Commentary on 1 Peter*, 4-5.

The Greek term that the NRSV translates as "destined" (πρόγνωσιν *prognōsin*) refers to God's foreknowledge, closely related to the sense of divine destiny but perhaps not simply to be equated with God's destining. What Peter says is that from the beginning God has elected the exiles in accordance with God's foreknowledge. This reference suggests not only that the God who elects these exiles has known them from the beginning, but also that God already knew of the whole drama of salvation in which they have a place.

The verse refers to the activity of God the Father, of the Spirit, and of Jesus Christ. Goppelt is surely right in suggesting that in the Greek the activity of Father, Spirit, and Jesus Christ all explain the way in which these Christians have been chosen, elected.[36] The NIV captures this nuance more clearly than does the NRSV by reiterating the "elect" (ἐκλεκτός *eklektos*) of v. 1 in the "chosen" (*prognōsin*) of v. 2, preceding the explanation of how it is that Christians are elected or chosen.

The Father is the one who has known the Christians and their story from the beginning. In the context of this letter, God is Father of both the Christians and Jesus Christ.[37] The Spirit is the one who strengthens Christians in holiness and sanctifies them in their walk. Jesus Christ is both servant and served. The purpose for which the Christians of Asia Minor were chosen was to be obedient to Christ. What makes their obedience possible is the gift of his blood. The phrase probably recalls Leviticus 16, where Aaron is to slaughter a bull and a goat and to sprinkle their blood on the mercy seat in the sanctuary, "because of the uncleannesses of the people of Israel, and because of their transgressions, all their sins" (Lev 16:16 NRSV; see also Exod 24:1-9).

The theme is similar to that in Heb 12:24. It points the way to one of the great themes of the epistle: Christ's suffering for the sake of the faithful and as an example of faithfulness. The fact that the first sprinkling took place while the children of Israel were wandering in the wilderness may also underline the theme that they were exiles—not really at home but nonetheless blessed by God's mercy. There may also be here a hint of the theme of initiation; the author recalls for the Christians the new beginning made possible for them in Christ's blood.

The common salutation of Greek letters was the word χαίρειν (*chairein*), "greeting." In early Christian letters, a slightly different word was frequently used, χάρις (*charis*), "grace." The coupling of this word with "peace" (εἰρήνη *eirēnē*) is also typical (see, e.g., Rom 1:7; 1 Cor 1:3; 2 Thess 1:2; Titus 1:4). For Paul, "grace" is the word that defines the right relationship of God to humankind, God's total self-giving in Jesus Christ. In 1 Peter the word seems to have less fundamental and less rich connotations, to represent one of the gifts God provides more than the underlying presupposition of all gifts. "Peace" is the translation of the Greek translation of the Hebrew שלום (*šālôm*), connoting not only peacefulness but wholeness, health, and well-being as well. The prayer that grace and peace might grow, multiply, abound suggests a rather different understanding from Paul's sense that grace is the reality in which Christians stand, so all-encompassing that nothing can add to its immeasurable depth.

As Norbert Brox points out, however, already in these verses we see great themes of the writer's affirmation and exhortation to a people in trouble. They are "chosen, destined, sanctified, sprinkled with Christ's blood, and brought into the realm where grace and peace will grow."[38]

36. Goppelt, *A Commentary on I Peter*, 70.
37. See Michaels, *1 Peter*, 10.
38. Brox, *Der erste Petrusbrief*, 59.

REFLECTIONS

1. A theme struck immediately by the letter resonates with many contemporary Christians. Are we exiles in the world(s) in which we live? The notion that Christians are "resident aliens," not really belonging to the troubled and troubling world around us, has from early on had an immense appeal for the faithful. If we understand

ourselves to be outsiders, then faithful obedience will require careful attention to what it means to be *in* the world but not *of* it. Hauerwas and Willimon have written a book called *Resident Aliens*.[39] Drawing on the image from 1 Peter, they ask what is to happen to American Christianity now that American Christendom has come to an end. Only somewhat facetiously they point to the Sunday in 1963 when the Fox Movie Theater stayed open on the Lord's Day for the first time as the end of the time when Christians could take their hegemony in the United States for granted. On the whole, they argue that the church will find its mission best as a colony rather than an empire. Preaching on 1 Peter in the light of this analysis, we have to ask whether they got 1 Peter right (Is it as countercultural as their use of the image would imply?) and whether they have the United States right as we move into the twenty-first century. Do Christians still have more power than the first-century Christians of Asia Minor could have envisioned? If so, what responsibility do we have for the world as well as over against it? These are difficult questions, and 1 Peter may help us best by forcing us to raise them.

2. Like the rest of the New Testament, 1 Peter does not present a fully developed doctrine of the Trinity. Yet the letter does claim that the exiles who received this letter have been chosen, elected, in three ways: (1) They have been elected by the foreknowledge of God the Father. (2) They have been elected by the Spirit, who trains them in holiness. (3) They have been elected by Christ, whose blood atones for sins and brings them to God's mercy seat. If not a doctrine of the triune God, there is at least a threefold understanding of the way in which God acts for believers and in the whole human story.

3. In one sense, the salutation "let grace and peace abound" is highly conventional, the standard stuff of Christian discourse. Yet, what does it mean that already by the end of the first century it was conventional for Christians to greet one another as those whose lives are marked both by grace and by *shalom?* Perhaps as interesting as the theological insights of the New Testament writers are the signs of the fundamental understandings that marked the life of everyday Christians. If the claim that we live under God's grace and seek God's peace is conventional, it is a convention that contemporary Christians could gladly emulate. We sing "Amazing Grace" and sign our letters "Shalom" almost too perfunctorily, too easily. These first-century Christians had left an old world behind to live in a new world marked by God's graciousness; and the *shalom* they found they knew was bought at a price—Christ's suffering and perhaps their own. We seek to find in our worship and our practice the gifts that will enable us to be surprised by the familiar, to claim the traditions as still good news.

---

39. Stanley Hauerwas and William H. Willimon, *Resident Aliens* (Nashville: Abingdon, 1989).

1 PETER 1:3-12

PRAISE TO GOD

COMMENTARY

Norbert Brox suggests that the theme of 1 Peter can be discerned in the words of 5:12b. It is a letter of encouragement,[40] a motif that is evident from the beginning of the epistle.

Letters written around the time of 1 Peter often opened with thanksgivings or blessings, and the themes of those letters can sometimes be discerned in the motifs of the thanksgiving.[41] Such is certainly the case here, where themes of suffering and hope come together, themes that will permeate the entire letter.

1:3-5. God is praised here for the ways in which Christians have been elected and redeemed. God, who is "Father" in v. 2, is now explicitly acknowledged as (above all) the Father of Jesus Christ. The writer, who prayed grace and peace for the readers, now insists that God has already provided mercy to those who are chosen. In the face of distress and suffering, what God's mercy provides is "new birth" and "living hope."

For the earliest generations of Christians, it was clear that Christian life was "new birth." One was not born into the faithful community, but chose it, often leaving behind the security or the good reputation of the old life for the insecurity—and blessing—of the new (see 2:2, 10 for the blessing; for the difficulty, see 3:16; 4:4). Goppelt points out that the word for "born again" (ἀναγεννάω *anagennaō*) occurs only here in the New Testament, although the motif is obvious elsewhere (e.g., John 3:3, 5, 7; Titus 3:5; Jas 1:18).[42] Hope lives because it is based in Jesus' resurrection from the dead, his triumph over death. Hope lives because death cannot overcome it. Hope lives because even in the face of tribulation it does not back down or grow faint. Living hope is hope that gives life.

There is a clear parallel here between the new birth of Christians and the resurrection of Jesus Christ. Both move from death to life; thus the resurrection of Jesus is the grounds for the new life of the believer. It may be that there is an allusion to baptism here as well, with something like the reminder of Rom 6:4: "Therefore we have been buried with him by baptism into death, so that, just as Christ was raised from the dead by the glory of the Father, so we too might walk in newness of life" (NRSV). Verses 4-5 spell out the twofold shape of Christian hope. On the one hand, Christians lay hold of a promise that is already kept in the heavens (see Eph 1:11-14; Col 1:5). That is, however difficult earthly life may seem, God's promise is signed and sealed and guaranteed. On the other hand, the fullness of that salvation has not yet been revealed and will not be so until the last day. The writer here demonstrates two rather different ways of understanding the relationship of the present to the promises of the transcendent God. On the one hand, there is the reality of God's present rule "in heaven," where God's promises are stored up, treasured, preserved, almost as if believers had a divine safety deposit box. On the other hand, there is the promise that God will one day rule fully on earth, and the salvation kept in heaven almost as a secret will be made manifest to the whole creation. Since the original readers of 1 Peter seemed acutely aware that to the larger world they looked foolish and misled, there will be a kind of justice at that last time when God's true salvation will be revealed and the foolish will prove to be wise, the wise foolish.

The claim that Christians have an inheritance in heaven has a rich background in the Old Testament and is also attested elsewhere in Christian literature (see, e.g., Ps 16:5; Rom 8:17; Gal 4:7). It may be that the notion of rebirth in v. 3 leads to the promise of an inheritance, since those who are born

---

40. See Brox, *Der erste Petrusbrief*, 16.
41. See Paul Schubert, *The Form and Function of Pauline Thanksgivings* (Berlin: A. Töpelmann, 1939).
42. Goppelt, *A Commentary on I Peter*, 81.

as children of God with that rebirth become "legally" heirs of God's promises.[43]

Notice, too, the shift in the use of pronouns from v. 3 to v. 4. In v. 3 God has given "us" new birth, and in v. 4 God keeps an inheritance for "you." Rhetorically this is a shift from the confessional to the homiletic, from the testimony about shared faith to the hortatory reminder to the "you" who read of what this shared faith means in their lives.

The qualities of this heavenly inheritance, that it "can never perish, spoil or fade" (NIV), suggest what it means to say that Christians are born anew to a living hope. It is a hope that no power can destroy, tarnish, or mar. What can keep believers steadfast while they await their heavenly inheritance is faith. Faith is, in part, the confidence that believers do have a treasure laid up for them that neither moth nor rust can corrupt. The letter throughout helps its readers to find what does not perish in a perishable and perishing world.

1:6-7. The verb with which v. 4 began, "rejoice" (ἀγαλλιάω *agalliaō*) can be either indicative or imperative—either "you do rejoice in this salvation" or "you should rejoice in this salvation." Even if the verse is descriptive, the implication is clear that despite all odds the Christians of Asia Minor are to find joy even in difficult circumstances.

"In this" can mean either "in this promise" or "in God" or "in all these circumstances"— i.e., "in the light of everything we have said." It might also refer to the preceding promise of the last day. In that case, the verb (though strictly in the present) would have to be understood as future: "on that day you will rejoice."[44] The NRSV and the NIV both opt for the more general understanding of this clause, and this reading seems to make clearest sense of the movement of the passage.

The Introduction suggested that the nature of the various trials is not clearly specified. First Peter is more likely addressed to churches that know local harassment than to churches that are part of any systematic imperial persecution. The "little while" reminds the Christians that they live in the time between Christ's resurrection and his return and that the "last time" of v. 6 will not be a long time coming. That is to say, the fundamental realities with which they live are with the guarantee of their redemption, stored in heaven, and the promise of their redemption soon to come to earth. The present difficulties are bracketed and made relative by the abiding promises.

Verse 7 suggests either the *reason* for the present difficulties or the *result* of those difficulties. It may be that the trials are sent in order to prove the genuineness of the readers' faith; or it may be that, however trials arise, the result is that the genuineness of that faith will be proved. One's reading of this verse depends in part on one's interpretation of v. 2, where the author refers to the "foreknowledge" (NIV) or "destining" (NRSV) of God in the lives of the believers. Also pertinent is the reading of v. 6. If the believers have had to suffer trials, is that because circumstances have made such suffering necessary or because God has prepared such a destiny?[45]

The image in the verse is quite clear. Just as gold is refined through fire, so also genuine faith is refined through suffering (cf. Ps 66:10; Mal 3:3). Further, genuine faith is more precious than gold, because genuine faith is imperishable, while even the most precious gold will one day perish. Notice how often the epistle suggests that the gifts of the Christian life have two qualities that set faith apart from the values of the larger world. Christian gifts are immeasurably precious, and Christian gifts are unfading and imperishable. We recall from this verse, too, that genuine faith is absolutely essential, because through faith God's power preserves the faithful—in their faith—until the last day (v. 3)

It is equally clear that this whole test is set in an eschatological framework. The genuineness of faith (faith as genuine) will be made clear at the last day when Jesus Christ is revealed, at the end of this "little while" wherein the faithful now suffer. To whose praise, glory, and honor will faith's reality redound? Perhaps to the praise, glory, and honor of the Christians, but most certainly to the praise, glory, and honor of God as God is revealed in Jesus Christ.

---

43. See J. N. D. Kelly, *The Epistles of Peter and Jude*, Black's New Testament Commentaries (London: Adam and Charles Black, 1969) 51-52.
44. See Michaels, *1 Peter*, 27; Goppelt, *A Commentary on 1 Peter*, 88-89.
45. Brox suggests that the very use of the term "trial" (πειρασμός *peirasmos*) suggests that God is, indeed, the one who sets the tests for the sake of proving the faith and refining the gold. See Brox, *Der erste Petrusbrief*, 65. Davids nuances the argument to say that while suffering is not part of God's desire, it is not outside God's sovereignty. See Davids, *The First Epistle of Peter*, 56.

Excursus: Suffering in 1 Peter

There are four key sets of references to unjust suffering in this epistle. First is the passage about "unjust trials" (vv. 6-7). Second is the long section on slaves who have to suffer unjustly (2:18-25). Third is the encouragement for those who apparently suffer for their open confession of their Christian faith (3:17-18). Fourth is the reference to the "fiery ordeal" in 4:12-19.

The material in chaps. 1, 3, and 4 may deal with the suffering that comes to Christians for maintaining their faith in the face of opposition. The reminder to slaves is explicitly encouragement to suffer courageously unjust treatment at the hands of their masters, though implicitly this too may include mistreatment precisely because of their Christian faith. Because slaves suffer unjustly, as Christ suffered, they become a paradigm and example for all Christians, slave and free, who suffer unjustly at the hands of their masters or at the hands of society.

We cannot be sure whether the suffering that Christians undergo includes actual judicial proceedings, but certainly it includes slander, innuendo, and abuse (see 2:12; 3:17; 4:14). We also cannot be sure whether the "fiery ordeal" of 4:12 is a new and more threatening example of opposition that calls forth the strong response to be brave and to rejoice or whether, as the letter draws to a close, the rhetoric takes on even greater passion.

What is clear is that in this epistle the issue is not why bad things happen to good people. Rather, the issue is how to interpret the suffering Christians undergo as a result of their conviction and confession. First Peter interprets the suffering of Christians in at least these ways:

(1) Suffering can provide for the refining of faith. As Achtemeier suggests, in 1 Pet 1:6-7 there is a comparison between the lesser and the greater: If fire can purify gold, then how much more can the fire of suffering purify the faith of those who are steadfast?[46] There is the implication that the suffering may be sent from God and the promise that the value of faith tested by hardship will be revealed at the end (see also Matt 5:11-12).

(2) The one who suffers imitates Christ, who also suffered unjustly, not only as Christians' redeemer but also as their example (2:21-25; 3:17-18; 4:13; 5:13).

(3) Suffering is not only the result of human bad will but also is a consequence of the power of the devil (5:8).

(4) Nonetheless, part of the power of Christ's resurrection was his power to proclaim victory over the forces of evil (3:18-20). Therefore, by implication, Christians know that those who cause their suffering will also finally be judged and defeated.

(5) Suffering for being a Christian is itself a sign that the end of history is at hand (4:12-16).

(6) When Christ does return, those who have suffered for their faith will receive the reward of eternal glory, and the Spirit, which is the firstfruits of that glory, already is given to the faithful who suffer (1:7; 2:11; 4:13; 5:4, 10-11).

---

46. See Achtemeier, *1 Peter*, 100. Cf. Rom 5:3-4; Jas 1:2-4, as cited in Goppelt, *A Commentary on I Peter*, 91.

1:8-9. Some texts suggest a different reading for the first clause, "Although you do not know him," suggesting a scribal slip or that the two references in this verse to "see" (using different forms of the Greek verb ὁράω [*horaō*]) seem redundant. As both the NIV and the NRSV suggest, however, "see" seems the more likely reading.[47]

What vv. 8-9 show forth is the present reality of the salvation provided the faithful in Jesus Christ. Although the fullness of Christ's glory is yet to be revealed, those who are reborn to a living hope even now have the privilege of loving Christ, being faithful to Christ, and rejoicing in him. The doxological emphasis suggests that in v. 7 as here the clearest emphasis is on the way in which the work of salvation redounds to Christ's praise. It is not clear what distinction is being made when the author says that the readers "have not seen" Christ and "do not see him now." Perhaps it is simply a way of saying that they were not eyewitnesses to his ministry and that even in the present they know him by faith and not by sight.

We notice, too, that the term for "believing" or "faith" has occurred four times in the seven verses of this prayer. Faith is what protects Christians as they await their final salvation (v. 5), but faith is also the way in which Christians relate in the present to the Christ they will see only in the future. Even in the present, faith has its result: the salvation of souls.

Therefore, for 1 Peter the Christian promise has at least three elements. It includes (1) the inheritance being kept safe in heaven; (2) the glorious revelation and judgment of Christ on the last day; and (3) the salvation that is present for believers now as they await that last day. In all these ways, the faith that 1 Peter describes is very much like the "living hope" into which Christians have been reborn.

When the letter refers to "the salvation of your souls," it does not distinguish the soul from the body, but uses the term ψυχή (*psychē*), as the NT often does, to refer to the person, the salvation of the self.[48]

1:10-12. These verses stress the particular blessedness of the Christians to whom the letter is addressed. True, they may be undergoing various trials, but the prophets of the OT knew themselves to be servants of these small bands of Christian believers, and the very angels wish that they could know the gospel as these faithful mortals do.

One can see both themes present in the Epistle to the Hebrews. In Heb 11:39-40, after the author has brought out the whole roll call of the OT heroes, he adds: "Yet all these, though they were commended for their faith, did not receive what was promised, since God had provided something better, so that they would not, apart from us, be made perfect" (NRSV). And Heb 2:16 states: "It is clear that [Christ] did not come to help angels, but the descendants of Abraham" (NRSV). As Achtemeier suggests, this passage "seems to reflect [a] tradition of the angels' lack of knowledge and of their resultant inferiority to human beings. Hence they desire merely to glimpse what is now openly proclaimed in the gospel."[49]

It is evident from the context of these verses that the prophets mentioned here are those of the Old Testament. The purpose of prophecy for the writer of 1 Peter was to foretell Christ's advent, suffering, and glory. The efficacy of prophecy depended on Christ's own Spirit, which spoke to the prophets. Clearly for the writer of 1 Peter the Holy Spirit who inspired prophecy could not be other than the Spirit of Christ. Perhaps this reference simply communicates the New Testament idea that it is Christ who sends the Spirit; therefore, one can refer, however anachronistically, to the Spirit of Christ.[50] Perhaps, however, the epistle claims that the pre-existent Christ was present in the Spirit to the prophets, bearing witness to himself long before his earthly ministry (see 1:20).[51]

In any case, what is clearly underlined is that the same Spirit who inspired the prophets also inspired the preachers who brought the good news (the Greek word is εὐαγγελίζω [*euangelizō*], "to preach the gospel") to these

---

47. See Bruce M. Metzger, *A Textual Commentary on the New Testament* (New York: United Bible Societies, 1971) 687.
48. See, e.g., Davids, *The First Epistle of Peter*, 60; Spicq, *Les Spitres de Saint Pierre*, 53.
49. Achtemeier, *1 Peter*, 112.
50. So the note in Kenneth Barker, ed., *The NIV Study Bible* (Grand Rapids: Zondervan, 1985) 1888.
51. So, e.g., Brox, *Der erste Petrusbrief*, 70; Kelly, *The Epistles of Peter and Jude*, 60-61, who cites references from the Church Fathers and recalls 1 Cor 10:4.

troubled Christians (see also 1:25). Both prophecy and gospel bear witness to Christ's sufferings and to the glories that follow those sufferings. Both prophecy and gospel, therefore, also foreshadow the story of these Christians who now suffer in the hope of glory.[52] The "grace" (v. 10) that comes to these Christians is at least in part the encouragement that comes from that gospel, from that story.

First Peter uses the OT in the way that the description of the prophets would suggest.

52. So Kelly, *The Epistles of Peter and Jude,* 61.

Throughout, as we shall see, OT passages are read as predicting, testifying in advance to Christ's story. And the function of these OT passages is precisely to serve first-century Christians as they seek encouragement.

The blessing of 1 Pet 1:3-12 has a double focus: It is a prayer directed to God, and it is an exhortation directed to the reader. God is praised for precisely those gifts in which the readers are called to rejoice. The God who gives hope is blessed in part so that Christians can take the hope they need for the trials through which they live.

REFLECTIONS

1. The claim that Christians are born anew raises some of the same issues as does the image of Christians as "strangers in the world" (NIV) or "exiles" (NRSV) in 1 Pet 1:1. For the Christians to whom the author of 1 Peter writes, it is quite clear that Christian faith represented a conscious and difficult decision to move away from their old lives and from the predominant culture in which they lived. Today "born-again" Christianity can sometimes refer to a particular spiritual experience without radical social or ethical implications. For Christians of Peter's time, however, it was clear that being born again not only meant adding joy to one's life, but also leaving behind one's congenial relationship with neighbors and community. Being born again hurt.

2. Like virtually every New Testament writing, 1 Peter entices us to think about the relationship between present and future in the Christian story. The writer of 1 Peter believes strongly that the fullness of salvation will not be available until God consummates the story that began in creation and will reach its focus in Jesus Christ. The end of the story will be salvation for the faithful and praise and glory for God, but the readers of 1 Peter are not at the end of the story yet; they await that ending with hope.

Yet salvation is also a present reality, laid hold of by faith in God and by love for Christ. For Peter as for the rest of the New Testament, we walk by faith and not by sight, but that faith includes the unquenchable hope that one day we will see the one for whom we hope. And that hope is embodied in faith that trusts that God is with the faithful in the present, too.

Jonathan Kozol has written a moving book on the life of poor people in the Bronx, New York. The book is called *Amazing Grace,* because that is the favorite hymn of many of the residents of that neighborhood and, one suspects, because Kozol is amazed at the grace and courage he found there.[53] The verse of the hymn that is most deeply loved by the people whom Kozol met catches both sides of 1 Peter's eschatological reality: final hope and present comfort.

> Through many dangers, toils, and snares
> I have already come;
> 'Tis grace that brought me safe thus far,
> And grace will lead me home.

3. The tension between present and future redemption is particularly appropriate in the use of 1 Pet 1:3-9 as a lection for the second Sunday of Easter (Cycle A). The

53. Jonathan Kozol, *Amazing Grace: The Lives of Children and the Conscience of a Nation* (New York: Crown, 1995) 82.

resurrection of Christ provides hope for the future and strength for the present. Christ risen from the dead is both the guarantor of final glory for the faithful and the ground of present Christian joy—even in suffering. Acts 2:22-31, the portion of Peter's pentecost sermon also assigned for the second Sunday of Easter, plays on a similar combination of present joy and hope for the future. Especially in Peter's quotation of Ps 16:8-11, the sermon grounds the joy of believers and their hope for ransom from Sheol in the fact that God freed Jesus from death (Acts 2:24).

4. Another theme in 1 Pet 1:3-9 echoes the Gospel lesson for the second Sunday of Easter (Cycle A). The risen Christ assures Thomas, after his bout with doubt, that the greatest blessing is given those who have faith without actually having seen the risen Lord. It is just this blessing that 1 Peter pronounces upon the faithful of its generation: "Although you have not seen him, you love him; and even though you do not see him now, you believe in him and rejoice with an indescribable and glorious joy" (1 Pet 1:8 NRSV). Despite all the movies that try to entice us with technicolor portraits of Jesus walking through the Galilee, it is false romanticism to think that our commitment would be improved had we been there to experience his ministry or, like the apostles, seen the risen Lord. Then and now it is finally by faith that we lay hold of the promise that provides hope for our final end and joy for the days until then.

5. A theme emerges here that is as inescapable for contemporary Christians as it was for first-century ones. How do we understand suffering? Commentators read 1 Pet 1:6-7 in quite diverse ways. Is suffering part of God's plan for believers and for human history, or is it a happenstance whose origin we cannot really discern? Does God send tests in order to refine us, or is it, rather, that when tests come, God uses those tests for the strengthening of our faith? Whether it is the purpose of suffering or only its outcome, what 1 Peter does insist is that for Christians trials can purge and refine and purify faith. Of course, the trials 1 Peter has in mind are those that result from confessing Christ. But Christians in our own time generalize the question. The puzzle that not even this epistle addresses is what most Christians have observed—namely, that the same trials that strengthen some believers destroy others. Persecution can establish faith or destroy it, but even more mundane matters like debilitating illness can lead some to God and others away—and there is no predicting who will turn which way. That truth may be a mystery beyond the purview of the author of 1 Peter and beyond even the most careful discussions of tribulation as refining.

6. No critical biblical scholar is likely to be satisfied with 1 Peter's description of prophecy—at least not without considerable qualification. Historical-critical studies lead us to doubt that the Hebrew prophets were searching for the date and circumstances of Christ's life, death, and resurrection. Yet this strong statement from a first-century Christian to other first-century Christians reminds us that the Hebrew Bible did not become scripture for the church simply because Christians loved the old, old story or were delighted that Isaiah predicted the birth of a child to King Ahaz (in one interpretation of the historical context of Isa 7:14). As 1 Peter and Paul's epistles and Hebrews and the Gospel according to Matthew especially show, whatever the prophets had in mind, what Christians found in prophecy was the foreshadowing of that great story that "evangelized" them, the story of Christ crucified and risen again. So for contemporary Christian faith, preaching, and theology, it is not enough to place each passage in its original context without asking how the early church might have found Jesus prefigured in the Old Testament, and how we might find him foreshadowed or adumbrated there, too. Put differently, we are still called to ask how we understand Christ better in the light of those texts whose story provided the indispensable context of his story. For 1 Peter, apparently, the same Spirit preaches the gospel from Gen 1:1 through to the Christian preachers. We are invited to find ways to lay hold of that promise, with integrity but without apology.

1 PETER 1:13–2:10

GOD'S HOLY PEOPLE

OVERVIEW

This first section of the body of the epistle works out the themes of the thanksgiving: How does doxology work out in obedient living? The whole section is grounded in two passages from the Old Testament: the call from Leviticus to be holy as God is holy (Lev 11:44-45) and the promise from Hosea that those who have been no people are now God's people (Hos 2:23). This call to obedience, however, is not merely a command without promise. The obedience is grounded in the goodness of Christ, whose blood is like that of a lamb without blemish (1:19), the cornerstone of God's house (2:7). Obedience will find its reward at the final revelation of Christ in glory (1:13). And obedience is nourished by the good gift of God's own Word as preached to God's people (1:22-23).

1 PETER 1:13-25, BEING HOLY

COMMENTARY

First Peter 1:3-12 praises God for the gifts that God bestows upon faithful people. First Peter 1:13-25 shows Christians the responsibility that goes with these gifts. The holy God requires a holy people.

1:13-16. The section begins with "therefore," indicating that the calls to hopeful life that follow are based precisely in the nature of the God who has been praised in 1:3-12. Because you are called by such a God, therefore. . . . Further, in the immediate context of 1:12, because you have heard such good news, therefore. . . .

1:13. The writer of 1 Peter frequently uses participles in ways that are ambiguous. The main verb of this verse is "hope" or "set your hope" (ἐλπίσατε *elpisate*), and the other terms that both the NRSV and the NIV translate as imperatives are actually participles. Participles can be used with imperative force, but since the letter gives us only the one imperative, one might think that the participles serve in an adverbial way, to show the conditions under which the readers live as they are called to "set their hope."[54] A somewhat wooden, but perhaps helpful translation would be this: "Therefore having girded the loins of your understanding, and being sober, set your hope entirely on the grace to be given you at the revelation of Jesus Christ." This translation underlines the emphasis that connects the first twelve verses of this chapter with the last thirteen: You have been born to a living hope; therefore hope. Live out your call.

This translation also suggests that metaphors lie behind the descriptions of the lives of those who are called to hope. What the NIV and the NRSV translate as "prepare your minds for action" is more literally "gird the loins of your mind," as a worker might roll up a gown in order to work or a pilgrim might roll up his or her garment for the journey. "Be self-controlled" or "be disciplined" (νήφω *nēphō*)

---

54. For a thorough discussion of ambiguous phrases, especially participial phrases, in 1 Peter, see Lauri Thuren, *The Rhetorical Strategy of 1 Peter with Special Regard to Ambiguous Expressions* (Åbo, Finland: Åbo Academy Press, 1990). Achtemeier thinks that most participles in 1 Peter can be interpreted without resorting to the rare imperatival participle. See Achtemeier, *1 Peter*, 117.

more literally means "be sober" as opposed to drunk. (The adverb "entirely" [τελείως *teleiōs*] might go with "be sober" rather than with "set your hope.") Certainly the phrases are already traditional and the translations capture much of their meaning, but the metaphors may be richer than the more prosaic paraphrases suggest (on the girding, see John 21:18; Eph 6:14; on being sober, see 1 Thess 5:8, which combines images of sobriety and right clothing; 1 Pet 4:7; in Rom 13:13 the call to sobriety is not merely metaphorical). As elsewhere in the NT, these images are invoked in the light of the impending coming of Jesus in glory (see 1 Thess 5:8).

"Grace" (χάρις *charis*) here seems to have yet a slightly different meaning from the earlier use in this epistle. Here "grace" is the salvation that will be granted only at the parousia. The whole verse is an exhortation to have hope in the light of Jesus' impending revelation. As people who are sober, as people who are ready for action, Christians are to live in hope.

1:14-16. Verses 14-15 also have one main thought in the imperative clause: "Be holy" (v. 15). Again the participle describes the state of those who are called to be holy. They do not conform to their former evil desires. (The description of their former lives is more complete in 4:3. The reference to "not conforming" recalls Rom 12:2.) But it is not enough to leave behind the blandishments of the old life. The readers are positively to embrace the possibilities of the new: "Be holy in all you do" (v. 15, NIV). Thus to be a "child" of obedience is both to leave behind the former pagan ways and to embrace the new ways of holiness. That these Christians are children of *obedience* speaks primarily of their status as those who obey God, but that they are *children* may also remind us that they are only recently born anew (see also 1:3, 23; 2:2).[55] The reference to their former pagan days as times of "ignorance" recalls Acts 17:23, 30 and Eph 4:18.[56]

The point of these verses is to compare the one who calls to the Christians who are called. A holy God demands a holy people, just as a God of hope creates a hopeful people. The quotation is from Leviticus (see Lev 11:44-45; 20:7; 29:2). One of the dominant themes of Leviticus is the claim that the holy God demands holiness of God's own people. Here 1 Peter, like much early Christian writing, takes the words that Moses addressed to the children of Israel and applies them unapologetically to the early Christians. It is significant, perhaps, that Moses spoke these words to Israelites still in the wilderness, in exile, as they awaited the entrance to the promised land. So in the next verse we are reminded that these early Christians live in exile.

1:1:17. The ambiguity of this verse provides for two possible interpretations, not necessarily mutually exclusive. The point may be, "Since the one you already call 'Father' is also an impeccably fair judge, be sure that you live in appropriate fear of God's judgment." The point may equally well be, "Since the one who judges all impartially is the one you are invited to call 'Father,' though you rightly fear God, your fear can include confident reverence." This would be rather like Paul's confident assurance in Rom 8:15-17 (see also Gal 4:6). The NIV shades toward the first reading, the NRSV toward the second. What is clear in either case is that the claim that God is "Father" is directly related to the call in v. 14 for the readers to be "obedient children." This is not just a vague general claim that all Christians are God's children. Like much Christian exhortation, the verse includes both the reminder of God's gracious relationship to the Christians and the call to responsible living in the light of that relationship. In this context, the exile seems to be the time of waiting for the full salvation that will come "when Jesus Christ is revealed" (v. 13 NIV).

1:18-19. Verse 18 begins with a participle, the force of which is caught better by the NIV than by the NRSV. This statement is not a new idea but a modification of v. 17: "Live in reverent fear, since you know. . . ." Verses 18-19 present one of the great contrasts that underlie the argument of the entire epistle. Christians base their lives not on what is perishable but on what is imperishable; not on what is base but on what is precious. In v. 7 it was the faith of Christians that is precious and imperishable; in vv. 18-19 it is the blood of Christ. Much of 1 Peter is based on

---

55. See Michaels, *1 Peter*, 6.
56. See Michaels, *1 Peter*, 58. Note that here, too, the reference is to the behavior of Gentiles.

these analogies between the life of faith and the gifts of the faithful God. God's holiness requires the holiness of Christians. Christ's precious blood evokes the believers' precious faith. (For other images of gifts that are precious or imperishable, see 1:23, 25; 2:4, 6-7; 3:3-4; 5:4.) Christ the living stone forms Christians as living stones (2:4-5).

The reference to Christ's blood as being like that of a perfect lamb recalls v. 2 and the reminder that Christians have been sprinkled with Christ's blood in their initiation into faith and obedience. The reference to the unblemished lamb probably recalls Lev 22:21. The perfection of the lamb may be another reminder from Leviticus: Now just as Christ is holy, so also Christians are to be holy (see v. 16). The claim that Christ is himself the sacrificial lamb is found also in 1 Cor 5:7 and Heb 9:5 (and these references may recall Isa 53:7).[57] The stress on Christ's sacrificial gift of himself begins to point to a major theme of the epistle: Christians, too, will be called to courageous sacrifice.

1:20. This verse captures the temporal framework of the whole epistle. The time in which the readers live is the end of time, but Christ has been known by God from before the beginning of time. Here God's work in Christ is analogous to God's work in Christians. The faithful, too, have been foreknown, destined for their calling of faithfulness (v. 2). Not only does God's purpose in Christ foreshadow God's purpose in Christians, but also God's great act in Jesus Christ is for the sake of this little band of believers in Asia Minor. Just as the prophets serve not themselves but Christian faithful, so also Christ comes not to serve himself but to serve those who believe in him (cf. v. 12). Since this is a letter of encouragement, we can see how the author strives to encourage these faltering Christians by reminding them that from the foundation of the world God has destined them to be God's people. From the foundation of the world, God has destined Jesus Christ to redeem them through his blood. And God has sent prophets to interpret God's work in Jesus—for the sake of these same Christian believers.

1:21. The strong analogy between Christ and Christians prepares the readers for the affirmations of this verse. God has done a great work in Jesus Christ: his resurrection and his ascension to glory (see Commentary on 3:22). God has done this great work for the sake of Christians. Because of Jesus Christ, Christians are given the gifts of faith and hope. Faith sustains Christians' relationship to God in this present time (at the beginning of the end of the age), and hope lays hold of the promise of glory that is soon to be revealed in Christ's return. (Both the NRSV and the NIV miss the repetition in vv. 21a and 21c of forms of the Greek word for "faith" [πίστις *pistis*]: "to you who through Christ, [are] faithful to the one who raised him from the dead and gave him glory, so that your faith and hope are in God" [author's trans.]) Then Christ's glory will be the glory of the faithful.

Now is the time of exile, but exile is framed by God's intention from before the beginning of time and by Christ's imminent return at the end of time. In the meantime, Christians live by faith and look ahead in hope.

1:22. Obedience is a major concern of this epistle. Faith shows itself and hope realizes itself through obedience (in this sense, 1:2 states the theme of the whole epistle). The first manifestation of obedience is love for other believers. However one understands the social and political situation of the recipients of this letter, they surely found themselves to be a threatened minority in a disbelieving and sometimes hostile world. Not only the demands of the gospel but also the dictates of prudence suggest the importance of mutual love. Benjamin Franklin's word to John Hancock, spoken under threat of persecution, applies well here: "We must indeed all hang together or, most assuredly, we shall all hang separately."

This sentence is also full of participles, which can be taken as either imperatives or adverbial modifiers.[58] The main verb, in the imperative, is "love one another" (ἀγαπήσατε *agapēsate*). The verse could begin "Purify yourselves" or "Since you have purified yourselves." The purifying may also be related to the sprinkling of v. 2 in a reference to the readers' baptism.[59] (Both the NIV and the NRSV take the latter meaning.) The purifying by

---

57. See Michaels, *1 Peter*, 66.
58. See Thuren, *The Rhetorical Strategy of 1 Peter with Special Regard to Ambiguous Expressions*.
59. So Davids, *The First Epistle of Peter*, 76.

obedience may refer the readers to both the purity of the unblemished lamb and the quotation from Leviticus, "Be holy as I am holy." Although the Greek word for "purify" (ἀγνίζω *hagnizō*) is here introduced to the letter for the first time, there remains something of that sense that the life of the Christian reflects the purity of God's life and of Christ's sacrifice. Two words are used for "love." In the participial phrase, the term is φιλαδελφία (*philadelphia*), the love of the brethren ("mutual love," NRSV; "love for your brothers," NIV). The adjective ἀνυπόκριτος (*anypokritos*), which the NRSV translates as "genuine" and the NIV as "sincere," is more literally, "not hypocritical," "not feigned." In a situation where one Christian may betray another to local authorities, unfeigned love is both virtue and necessity. The second reference to love, in the main verb of the sentence, is ἀγαπάω (*agapaō*), the most frequently used term for "love" in the New Testament. The whole movement of the verse reminds us of the old summary of early Christian (especially Pauline) ethics: "Be what you are." Since you have been purified, since you do have genuine love for one another, well, act that out in heartfelt devotion. For v. 22, there is also good textual evidence for the reading, "love one another deeply from a pure heart," a reading found in papyrus 72 and some other ancient sources. The reading elaborates but does not change the import of the translation.[60]

The motivation for this love is obedience to the truth. The truth that 1 Peter proclaims requires obedience, not just assent, and is manifested in love, not just in knowledge.

1:23. This verse echoes v. 3 and the writer's thanks to God for the new birth provided Christian believers through Christ's resurrection. Now, just as Christ's resurrection is to eternal life, so also the new life of believers is grounded in an eternal gift. The imperishable seed here is apparently the Word itself, which along with faith and Christ's sacrifice is another of those imperishable gifts on which these early Christians could found their life and practice.[61] As the NRSV points out, the verse could also read "through the word of the living and enduring God," but the contrast between perishable and imperishable seed and the following quotation from Isaiah 40 strongly suggest that it is God's Word that lives and endures. Notice the close connection between the living hope of v. 3 and the living word of v. 23. Like the living hope, the living word is itself alive, lively, and life-giving. Notice the close connection between the imperishable salvation of the heavenly inheritance in v. 4 and the abiding word of v. 23. Both God's gracious activity and the word of the gospel that proclaims that activity endure eternally. By implication, the blood of v. 19 is also imperishable as well as precious.

If the references to new birth in 1 Peter go back to a baptismal homily or liturgy, then here word and rite come together as signs of the new life in Christ. Christians are born anew through the ceremony of baptism, but it is the Word that brings them to that new birth.

1:24-25. In accordance with v. 12, the prophecy from Isa 40:6-8 is understood to be a reminder for first-century Christian believers. The contrast between the perishable flesh and the eternal Word not only looks back to the references to imperishability, but also looks ahead to the concern that faithful people not be held captive to the flesh—that which is bound to pass away (2:11; see also Commentary on 3:18; 4:1-2).

Not only these verses themselves but also their context in Isaiah help to provide the themes for the epistle. Immediately prior to the verses quoted, Isaiah declares the revealing of God's glory, as 1 Peter looks to the final revelation of God's glory in 1:5-7 (Isa 40:5). Immediately following these verses, Isaiah calls for a herald of "good news" to speak to Zion (Isa 40:9; the verb in the Septuagint is εὐαγγελίζω [*euangelizō*], as in 1 Pet 1:12, 25).

Now it is clear for Peter that the good news predicted by Isaiah is precisely that good news that the Christians of Asia Minor have heard, and Isaiah's prophecy fulfills the description of prophecy in 1:2. Isaiah looks forward to the gospel; the Christian preachers preach that gospel; these little bands of Christians have heard that gospel. The gospel they have heard is the word of which Isaiah spoke—it is the word that lives and endures, gives life and stays alive—eternally (for a different application of the Isaiah passage, cf. Jas 1:10-11).

---

60. See Metzger, *A Textual Commentary on the New Testament*, 688-89; Achtemeier, *1 Peter*, 135. See also the NRSV and NIV notes.

61. See Kelly, *The Epistles of Peter and Jude*, 80.

REFLECTIONS

1. From the admonition of Paul through the meditation of Thomas Kempis, Christians have sought to engage in the imitation of Christ (see 1 Cor 11:1). Drawing on the themes of the holiness code of Leviticus, 1 Peter encourages the faithful to imitate God, to be holy as God is holy. Perhaps *imitation* is not the best word for this relationship. In the covenant there is not equality between the partners but recognition of reciprocal responsibilities: God's holiness demands the holiness of the faithful.

2. Here as throughout 1 Peter there is a contrast between two ways of living, two directions of the self. The self can be directed toward perishable things—like silver and gold—or toward the imperishable realities—Christ's redeeming act on the cross and the Word that proclaims that act. This portion of the epistle implies what the whole letter will make clear: Those who set their hearts on the perishable will perish; those who set their hearts on what endures will endure. In his book on the people of the Bronx, Jonathan Kozol contrasts two citizens of New York. One is a newspaper columnist who has given up on invisible realities and divinely driven hopes. She writes:

> "All right. . . . Out there, someone is sleeping on a grate. . . . and the emergency rooms are full of people. . . . [Still] cruelty is as natural to the city as fresh air is to the country. . . . I used to feel this cruelty was wrong, immoral. . . . Now I don't know. Maybe it's the fuel that powers the palace."[62]

While this woman rejoices in the cruelty-fueled palace, a boy named Anthony grows up with not a fraction of her security and worldly wealth. Anthony has his heart set on another vision; aspiring to be a writer, he writes his hope for God's kingdom:

> "God's Kingdom. . . . God will be there. He'll be happy that we have arrived.
> "People shall come hand-in-hand. . . .
> "God will be fond of you."[63]

3. The holiness of God's holy people is not centered in God alone or in one's own devotional life. Holiness builds community, the community of mutual love and support. Just as the holiness code of Leviticus sets a people apart from the unholy nations around them, so also the holiness code of 1 Peter builds a community of brotherly and sisterly love. Love for God, purity of self, love for the brother and sister in Christ are all essential ingredients of the community of living hope that 1 Peter seeks to build. In a nation committed to individualism and a time devoted to consumerism, Americans go church shopping. "What can I get out of it?" they ask. This is far from the God who calls us to be a people, who speaks to *us* far more often than to *me*. Perhaps the renewal of the church will come when we begin the "Our Father . . . " remembering the absolutely essential plural of the pronoun.

4. The immediate history of the Christians of Asia Minor is set in a much larger eschatological framework. Their story was destined by God from the beginning and moves toward God at the end. They have been called; they will be judged. The time between these times looks back to that foundation and forward to that consummation. Any reading of 1 Peter that looks only to the daily life of those Christians (or to ours) misses the depth and scope of the hope Peter proclaims. Some years ago an American graduate student returned from studying with the German New Testament scholar

---

62. Kozol, *Amazing Grace*, 113-14.
63. Kozol, *Amazing Grace*, 237-38.

Ernst Käsemann. After listening to one of Käsemann's particularly impassioned lectures, the student complained, "But Professor, that wasn't a lecture, it was a sermon." "Of course," said Käsemann, "there's no time left for anything else."

5. Christian proclamation is held in very high regard in these verses. It is the fulfillment of Isaiah's prophecy and the means by which Christians lay hold of new life. Preaching is a primary way in which faithful people can appropriate what God has done in the cross of Christ. Preaching provides what the whole letter provides, encouragement and witness to the true grace of God (see 1 Pet 5:7). One doubts that the author of 1 Peter would be encouraged to attend Christian worship and hear the preacher begin, "I have a few thoughts to share" or "I know this is only a matter of opinion." Karl Barth's great book *The Word of God and the Word of Man* shook preaching in this country with the claim that in preaching the two words come together.[64] For several decades most of us have been retreating from that claim. We suspect that no one out there believes it; of course, that may be because we have stopped believing it ourselves.

6. Since Easter is the presupposition of Christian faith, the whole New Testament can be read as a commentary on the significance of Easter. Yet it is perhaps especially appropriate that the *Revised Common Lectionary* turns to 1 Peter during the Easter season. For all its appropriate emphasis on the suffering example of Christ crucified, 1 Peter founds its hope and bases its joy on absolute confidence in the resurrection as the event in which both Christian hope and conduct are grounded. On the third Sunday of Easter (Cycle A), 1 Pet 1:17-23 is linked to the conclusion and response to Peter's Pentecost sermon (Acts 2:36-41). In the epistle, the author reminds the Christians of Asia Minor that the Word of God preached to them has been the instrument by which God has given them new birth. Quite possibly the author re-calls them to their baptism; certainly he re-calls them to the faith that made them a new people, marked by God's mercy. Acts enacts what 1 Peter claims. Hearing the word preached by Peter, three thousand people were "cut to the heart" and were baptized. The message of the risen Christ convicts and redeems; born-anew Christians at Pentecost and a generation later in Asia Minor turned from their old patterns of life to devote themselves to the pattern of the apostles. (If I were to preach the two texts, I would certainly sneak in Acts 2:42.)

64. Karl Barth, *The Word of God and the Word of Man,* trans. Douglas Horton (Boston: Pilgrim, 1928).

1 PETER 2:1-10, BEING GOD'S PEOPLE

COMMENTARY

The letter alternates between affirmation and exhortation. The readers are reminded of the good news they have heard. Then they are called to live responsibly in the light of that good news. Then they are comforted again by the reminder of God's election and call. This section provides affirmation and comfort.

2:1-3. Like so much of 1 Peter, this passage represents a contrast between the old life and the new. Perhaps it re-calls the Christians to their baptism. Certainly it reminds them that they are called to live lives very different from what they left behind. If the author is re-calling them to their baptism, then perhaps they remember leaving behind their old clothes and being clothed anew in white baptismal gowns. Leaving behind their old clothes, they left behind their old lives of malice, guile, insincerity, envy, and slander (NRSV).

2:1. Both the NIV and the NRSV translate the opening word as an imperative, "Rid yourselves," but in the Greek it is another participle (ἀποθέμενοι *apothemenoi*). It may well have imperative force, but it could also describe the circumstances of the readers, "As you rid yourselves of all malice." In that case, the verses drive toward the main verb "crave" or "long for pure, spiritual milk."

Malice, guile, insincerity, envy, and slander are those habits that are most apt to destroy the mutual love to which 1 Peter calls believers (1:22). Once again we see that a major feature of the new life in which the faithful live is the mutuality and trust that Christians have with one another. That mutuality and trust require shedding the comfortable old garb of familiar selfishness (cf. Gal 5:19-23; the pattern here, in fact, is much more like 1 Cor 6:9-10, with its explicit reference to baptism as the place where these vices are left behind).[65]

2:2. The epistle here uses a different term to remind believers that they are living a brand-new life. In 1:3 and 1:23 the author tells them that they have been begotten anew or born anew. Here he says that they are "just born" or "newborn" (ἀρτιγέννητος *artigennētos*), the emphasis not so much on being born again as being freshly born. The reminder that the world of faith is a brand-new world for them leads to the image of the infant drinking milk, food both good and necessary.

There is no implication here that the "milk" newborn Christians drink is somehow inferior to the solid food they will get later on. In 1 Cor 3:2, Paul associates milk with immaturity and with a life still burdened by the cares of the flesh, still lived with one foot in the old age (see also Heb 5:13).[66] Here, however, milk is gift and grace. It is of the spiritual realm, not of the flesh. Both the NRSV and the NIV call this "spiritual" milk, but the Greek adjective λογικός (*logikos*) is not derived from the word for "spirit" (πνεῦμα *pneuma*) but from λόγος (*logos*), "reasonable," "rightly ordered." It is the same term Paul uses in Rom 12:2 for "a reasonable worship." "Spiritual" is a fair enough translation, but the Pauline contrast between flesh and spirit, which also has its place in parts of 1 Peter, is not in the forefront here. Brox, who translates the term "spiritual," also points to the other uses of *logos* in 1 Pet 1:23; 2:8; 3:1.[67] Achtemeier suggests that the derivation of the adjective should be directly related to the word of preaching (as in 1 Pet 1:23) and translates the phrase, "the milk of God's word."[68] Just as the promised land flowed with milk and honey for the children of Israel, so also Christian believers receive milk as a foretaste of the fuller salvation yet to come.

That is why spiritual milk grows newborn Christians toward salvation as mother's milk nurtures newborn infants toward maturity. The NRSV translates the last part of v. 2 as "growing into salvation," the NIV as "growing up in your salvation." The former translation stresses salvation as goal; the latter stresses salvation as gift. For 1 Peter, Christians live with the promise of the fullness of God's mercy and have a foretaste of what that mercy will be. The two translations capture those two aspects of the epistle's hope, although the NSRV seems somewhat more accurately to reflect the Greek text and the usual meaning of the preposition "into" (εἰς *eis*).

"Milk" is here an image for the whole range of gifts provided to newborn Christians and should probably not be more narrowly specified as scripture or right doctrine. In this context, pure milk is the opposite of guile and slander. The selfishness of the flesh is what believers leave behind for the purity of the new life in Christ.

2:3. The exhortation ends with an allusion to the OT that sums up these verses and provides the beginning for a section of the epistle that piles up scriptural citations to remind the readers of the promises of this life into which they have just been born: "O taste and see that the LORD is good" (Ps 34:8*a* NRSV). Now the milk that the believers drink is not only the gift but also the giver; what tastes good is Christ's own self. The construction of the sentence, beginning with "if indeed you have tasted" (NRSV) or "now that you have tasted" (NIV, perhaps somewhat better) may indicate that there is an indirect reference to eucharist or the Lord's supper, just as v. 1 may

---

65. Davids notes that instead of the list of virtues we might expect in contrast to the vices Christians leave behind, "we discover a call to dependence on God." See Davids, *The First Epistle of Peter*, 81.
66. See the discussion of the image of milk in Goppelt, *A Commentary on I Peter*, 129-30.
67. Brox, *Der erste Petrusbrief*, 92.
68. Achtemeier, *1 Peter*, 143, 147.

include an indirect reference to baptism.⁶⁹ In baptism, one puts off the old self; in eucharist, one tastes that the Lord is good. These sacraments shape the wholeness of our lives as individuals and as a people.

The continuation of the exhortation in v. 4 suggests that the Lord whom Christians taste and the living stone to whom they come is Christ. In Psalm 34, the psalmist praises God for deliverance from distress, and therefore the whole psalm foreshadows themes that will be increasingly important to 1 Peter's assurances to people under threat.

2:4-8. Now the image for Christ shifts. Instead of being like milk, life-giving and good to taste, now Christ is like a stone, a foundation on which to build one's life.⁷⁰ But Christ is also a living stone. Christ is not static or staid; Christ is alive. Christ is not barren or cold; Christ is life-giving.

The whole section is built on a collection of OT passages dealing with stones, almost as if there were ready-made a kind of compendium of OT references to stones that early Christians thought could be applied to Christ.⁷¹ The OT texts on which the letter draws are Ps 118:22; Isa 8:14; 28:16.

2:4. This verse begins with another participle, a form of the verb "to come" (προσέρχομαι *proserchomai*). The NIV keeps something of the adverbial reading of the participle; "as you come" represents the circumstances under which believers are being built into a spiritual house. The NRSV interprets the participle as an imperative, "Come to him." The main verb for this clause is found in v. 5 "you are being built" or "let yourselves be built" (οἰκοδομεῖσθε [*oikodomeisthe*] can equally well mean either one).

The verse uses two adjectives for Christ as a stone that are typical of 1 Peter's terms for evaluating the worth of the gifts God gives in Jesus Christ. The stone that is Christ is both living and precious. So in 1:3 the hope into which Christians are born anew is living hope, and in 1:7 the faith Christians show is "more precious than gold." Verse 4 shows the contrast between human valuings and God's valuing. Humans have rejected this stone as if it were dead and worthless. God has chosen this stone as living and valuable. The stone is also "chosen," "elect," as the Christians to whom the letter is written are elect as exiles (1:1); that is to say that the Christians, like Christ, are rejected by humans—their pagan neighbors—but are elected and precious in the sight of God. The "precious" and the "elect" quality of the stone is there in the OT source, Isa 28:16, which is here combined with an allusion to Ps 118:22. The adjective "living" is apparently the epistle writer's own contribution.

Christians, therefore, participate in the life of Christ, with both its threat and its blessing. We have already seen how Christians are asked to live in imitation of God: "You shall be holy, for I am holy" (1:16 NRSV). Now the implication is that Christian life imitates or partakes of the reality of Christ's own life. He is a living stone, and Christians are living stones as well, full of life and life-giving.

2:5. This verse provides the main verb of this sentence and either reminds the believers that they are being built into a spiritual house (NIV) or exhorts them to let themselves be built into a spiritual house (NRSV). The images pile together. Stones are built into houses, but houses are also temples; and in temples holy priests offer spiritual sacrifices.⁷² Spiritual sacrifice is surely a reference to the whole shape of the faithful life—the life of holiness.

The packed sentence begins to point to one of the main themes of this section of 1 Peter. The gracious God who has sent Jesus Christ through him has called and blessed a new people: God's people, God's household, God's new priesthood. The verse, therefore, serves several functions. It underlines the close relationship between what God has done in Jesus Christ and what God is doing in these Christians. It reminds the Christians that despite their apparent disgrace in the eyes of the world they are precious in God's sight. It calls them, in somewhat different

---

69. On the possible reference to eucharist, see Kelly, *The Epistles of Peter and Jude*, 87. Brox thinks we may have here catechetical material on the new life in Christ. See Brox, *Der erste Petrusbrief*, 91. In either case, the stress is on the transition from the old ways to the new.

70. For this image see John H. Elliott, *The Elect and the Holy* (Leiden: E. J. Brill, 1966) 26-33.

71. Notice at least the combination of references similiar to 1 Pet 2:6-8 and Matt 21:42, 44 and themes like 1 Pet 2:6, 8 in Rom 9:33. For the claim that this is traditional material that antedates 1 Peter, see Brox, *Der erste Petrusbrief*, 100; Davids, *The First Epistle of Peter*, 89.

72. Brox points out that the "holy priesthood" of v. 4 is picked up in the "royal" priesthood of v. 9. Since the whole imagery of these verses is so closely interwoven, he argues that the spiritual house is also the royal house and that the imagery, which is somewhat elusive, suggests that Christians are built into a holy temple. See Brox, *Der erste Petrusbrief*, 98.

words, once again to live out their calling, to be holy even as God is holy. (The verses may also point ahead to the reminder of 4:17, that judgment begins "from the house of God." It is not just that these believers worship in the house of God; they *are* the house of God.)

2:6-8. Now the two references that are combined in v. 4 are cited more fully in vv. 6-7. The introductory "therefore" indicates again that 1 Peter finds confirmation for its Christian claims in the prophetic affirmations of the OT (see 1:10-12).

The image from Isa 28:16 fits beautifully the epistle's picture of the household of God. All Christians are living stones, built into the edifice. But the cornerstone is Jesus Christ. He is the cornerstone because the whole building rests on him. He is the cornerstone because the building takes its design from him. No Christ; no building. (The citation of Isa 28:16 does not correspond exactly to either the MT or the LXX. The notion that those who stumble shall be put to shame does represent the LXX; in the MT they scurry about or away, hence the NRSV translation of Isa 28:16, "One who trusts will not panic.") The "chosen and precious cornerstone" turns the allusion of v. 4 into an explicit citation. That Christ is chosen reminds the readers that the whole pattern of salvation is part of God's electing plan from the beginning—centering in Christ but including all believers. That Christ is precious reminds the readers of the pervasive distinction between valuable and tawdry goods, the things of heaven and the things of this world. It is also possible that the reference to the stone established in Zion reminded some readers that in Christ they will come "home" to the holy city, Zion—home from their exile and dispersion.

Verses 7-8 use two other quotations to make a key point: God's faithfulness requires responding faith. Those who have faith know that the stone is precious, but to those who do not have faith the same stone is not a cornerstone. On the one hand, unbelievers reject the stone; they lay it aside as worthless. On the other hand, the "stone" rejects them. It causes them to trip and fall. Those who know who Christ is build their lives on him; those who do not accept him stumble and fall. In a way people pronounce judgment on themselves. See Christ aright, and you are built into God's household; see Christ wrong, and you stumble, trip, fall.

There is another possible interpretation of v. 7*a*: "Honor" is given to those who believe. This means that believers partake in the honor of the "honored" stone, Jesus Christ. It also distinguishes them from the unbelievers, who, far from being honored, will be "put to shame."[73] The OT references are Ps 18:22 (again the allusion of 1 Pet 2:4 becomes an explicit citation) and Isa 8:14. There is a very similar use of Isa 8:14 in Rom 9:33, where Paul talks about the destiny of Israel. Again the distinction is between the faithful, who receive God's righteousness, and the unfaithful, who stumble. In Romans, however, the stumbling stone is not so directly identified with Jesus Christ.

Again in v. 8 it is clear that faith is not just a matter of believing; it is also a matter of obedience. Just as faithful Christians have been chosen and destined for obedience (1:2), so also the unfaithful outsiders have been chosen and destined for disobedience (see 1:14, 22). What they disobey is the word, presumably the word of preaching that has been good news and salvation to believers (1:25), the word that endures forever, while those who disobey that word stumble and fall away, like flesh, like the grass. The epistle is like a tapestry with recurring motifs and colors or like a symphony in which a theme recurs again and again in slightly different form. To read one verse is almost always to recall others.

Although 1 Peter does not begin to present any full-fledged discussion of providence, call, and predestination, what is clear throughout is that God is in charge of the story of Jesus Christ, of the world's story, and of the story of individual believers. If some believe, that is because God has chosen them; if some do not believe, that disbelief also lies in the plan and providence of God.

2:9-10. These verses are woven carefully together. Verse 9 represents an array of images drawn from the OT that contrast the believers from the stumbling unbelievers of v. 8. Verse 10 sums up the promise to the faithful as it is found in the passage from Hos 2:23.

The two verses make a stunning claim. To unbelievers it seems that the Christian

---

73. See Goppelt, *A Commentary on 1 Peter*, 145; Achtemeier, *1 Peter*, 149, 160-61.

believers have been rejected, as Christ was rejected; they are aliens and exiles, foolish and straying. To the eyes of faith it is clear that Christians are chosen exactly as Christ the cornerstone is chosen, precious and beloved of God. From the perspective of faith, the world is turned upside down. Pagan unbelievers, who seem secure in their positions and their prestige, are stumbling and falling. Christian believers, who seem foolish and useless, are God's own people—holy, blessed, royal.

Verse 9 shows the ingenuity of the author in drawing his images from two OT passages.[74] The basic passage, which the others seem to interpret, is Isa 43:20-21:

The wild animals will honor me,
    the jackals and the ostriches,
for I give water in the wilderness,
    rivers in the desert,
to give drink to my chosen people,
    the people whom I formed for myself
so that they might declare my praise. (NRSV)

The Septuagintal phrase for the last line is more like "so that they might narrate my praiseworthy deeds"; 1 Peter instead suggests that the faithful celebrate God's praise in doxology.

In the context of Isaiah we are reminded that the chosen people are in the wilderness, exiles, yet even in the desert God shows them to be God's own and cares for them tenderly. Three phrases in v. 9 are drawn from the Isaiah passage: "chosen people," "people belonging to God," and "declare the praises of him" (NIV). Michaels suggests that the addition of εἰς (*eis*, "for") to the LXX's "a people of possession" reminds the readers that the fullness of their belonging to God is still reserved for the eschatological future.[75]

The references to "royal priesthood" and "holy nation" are apparently drawn from Exod 19:6 (Exod 23:22 LXX). Again the setting is the wilderness, as Moses speaks to the people still waiting to enter the promised land. The context in Exodus as a whole foreshadows these assurances in 1 Peter:

"You have seen what I did to the Egyptians, and how I bore you on eagles' wings and brought you to myself. Now therefore, if you obey my voice and keep my covenant, you shall be my treasured possession out of all the peoples. Indeed, the whole earth is mine, but you shall be for me a priestly kingdom [1 Peter's "royal priesthood"] and a holy nation." (Exod 19:4-6a NRSV)[76]

The issue for the people of 1 Peter is their status in the eyes of God versus their status in the eyes of the larger world in which they are despised exiles. The story of the exodus, recalled by these verses, reminds them once again that God delivered the despised people of Israel from their enemies, and after the time of their wandering brought them to the promised land. Surely those who read and hear 1 Peter are to find comfort in this story themselves. The claim that they are a holy people also recalls 1:15-16. They are not only commended as holy but also called to holiness. The blessing carries further responsibility.

First Peter builds its claims on two fundamental distinctions: the distinctions between the larger world and the community of the faithful, and the distinction between then and now. The first part of 2:9 reinforces the distinction between outsiders and insiders, those who appear to prosper (outsiders) and those who have really received the promises of God's own people (insiders.) The allusion to Exodus 19 draws a distinction between then and now. Then you were in Egypt; now I have brought you out on eagles' wings. This distinction builds to the climax of the verse. Once the believers were in darkness, and now they are in light (see the close parallels in Eph 5:8; Col 1:12-13). What brings them into the light is the call of God. The Christians have already learned that God calls them to holiness (1:15). They will learn that God calls them to obedient suffering, if faith requires suffering, and that God calls them into God's eternal glory in Christ (5:10). Holiness, obedient faithfulness—even if it requires suffering—and eternal glory are all aspects of that

---

74. Brox seems basically correct in suggesting that this is not typological exegesis. The author is not saying that these passages applied first to Israel as type, and then to the church as antitype. He simply reads the OT as applying to believers (as 1 Pet 1:12 would indicate). See Brox, *Der erste Petrusbrief*, 103.

75. Michaels, *1 Peter*, 109.

76. Selwyn, *The First Epistle of Peter*, 165-66.

light in which the faithful now live and in which they will live forever.

In the light of what God has done for them and in the light of Isa 43:21, believers are not only to obey but also to declare God's praises. In the context of both Isaiah and 1 Peter, this probably means that Christians are to praise God in worship and thanksgiving.[77] The response to being insiders and not outsiders is praise; the response to having been in darkness and now being in light is praise as well.

Verse 10 draws on Hosea to bring together the two contrasts that are central to this passage and to the whole epistle—outside/inside; then/now. Once no people; now a people. Once outside; now inside. The citation is from Hos 2:23. God has told Hosea as a sign of judgment to name Hosea's own children "not pitied" and "not my people." Now in a prophecy of hope, God tells Hosea that his children, and the children of Israel, will again know God's pity and will again be God's people. Just as Hosea's children changed their names, so also the Christians of 1 Peter know a new reality in Jesus Christ. They are those on whom God has had mercy. They are God's own people.

Again it is possible that the references to new names and to new reality recall the readers to their baptism; certainly they are part of a new community. Certainly the passage is a reminder of that new life that baptism represents, a life in which old ways and worldly expectations are entirely reversed and undone.

---

77. Part of the debate between Balch and Elliot is over the question of whether the believers in 1 Peter are called to evangelize or only to "thank God." The issue rests partly on the understanding of "declare" (καλέω *kaleo*) in this passage. See John H. Elliott, *The Elect and the Holy* (Leiden: E. J. Brill, 1966) 41-43; Balch, *Let Wives Be Submissive*, 132-33; Achtemeier, *1 Peter*, 166. See also Michaels, *1 Peter*, 110, who says that lexically either interpretation is possible.

REFLECTIONS

1. First Peter 1:1-10 reminds us that the difference between Christians and non-Christians is not that we see different things but that we see the same things differently. Those who believe and those who do not believe both see Jesus Christ, the rock. For believers, that rock is the cornerstone or the capstone of their lives as individuals and in community. For unbelievers, that rock is simply to be rejected. What makes the difference between the two ways of seeing is faith.

Today two quite different views of the role of Christian theology vie for preeminence in the church. Some maintain that faith and the theology that explains it are the property of faith communities. We teach and learn the language and stories of faith with each other, and it is in the context of that communal language and practice that the stories touch us and direct us. Others are eager that Christian theology go public, that we find claims and suppositions that can be presented and defended outside the confines of the church.

First Peter, like much of the New Testament, presents a view of faith rather different from either of these current claims. For this epistle, the great story that feeds faith is absolutely public. It is a word declared aloud about deeds seen clearly. The story of Jesus is not hidden. The language about Jesus is not esoteric, confined to insiders, like the secret language of lodges and clubs.

Yet the fact remains that when different people hear that very public story, each responds very differently. Some hear the story and find in it the narrative of the way God has had mercy on those who had found no mercy and draws forth a people from those who had no sense of belonging. Jesus is Christ and Lord, cornerstone of the lives they build and the communities they build. Other people hear the same story and find it dull or pointless. The dispute is not about whether Jesus ever lived or about the reports of his words and deeds. They dispute what God did through Jesus, if God did anything at all. Those who hear the story in faith praise God for God's wonderful deeds. Those who do not hear the story in faith laugh and stumble.

It complicates this discussion that, for 1 Peter as for much of the New Testament, the distinction between those who have faith and those who do not is found in the call and predestining of God. But the Christian testimony from the beginning has been something like that. It is not the smartest, the most pious, the most virtuous who know that Christ is cornerstone and not stumbling block. Rather those who have faith know Christ this way—and that faith is always gift, not achievement. One way to insist that faith is a gift is to say that it is destiny and not achievement that makes faith possible.

2. The powerful claim of 2:5, 9 that in Christ Christians have become a royal priesthood is not directly a claim about the orders or offices of church life (any more than the claim that believers are "kingly" is directly a prescription for ordering the political realm). Luther's strong affirmation of the priesthood of all believers may rest in part on a reading of this text, and from the earliest days of the church the richest theological claims have often been based on re-reading Scripture in the light of one's own time and under the direction of God's Spirit.[78] The claim here, however, is not about how believers function in relationship to each other. The claim, based on Exodus, is that as God chose Aaron to be a priest for the sake of God's glory, so now all Christian people are called by God and all are called to offer sacrifices—not the sacrifice of the altar (neither animal sacrifice nor eucharist is in view here) but the sacrifice of faithful obedience and the life of love that goes with that. The sacrifice these Christians were called to live—and we are called to live as well—is a life without malice, guile, insincerity, envy, or slander, which 1 Peter says we have put off with our faith.

A traditional communion prayer captures this motif from the epistle beautifully: "Here we offer ourselves in obedience to you, through the perfect offering of your Son, Jesus Christ, giving you thanks that you have called us to be a royal priesthood, a holy nation, your own people; and to you, O God, Creator, Redeemer, and Sanctifier, be ascribed blessing and honor and glory and power for ever and ever. Amen."

3. In the history of Christian faith there has often been a tension between ecclesiology and eschatology—the doctrine of the church and the hope for God's final reign. First Peter describes the polarity of the Christian life in terms that embrace both ecclesiology and eschatology. On the one hand, there is the language of community, often expressed in the distinction between insiders and outsiders. *We* are the chosen race, the royal priesthood (or holy palace), God's own people. Those others are chosen only for stumbling and are separate from God.

On the other hand, there is the language of eschatology, the sharp distinction between then and now or between now and the reign of God not yet fully come. Once we were in darkness, but God has called us to light; once (like Hosea's children), we were without mercy and were no people, now as God's own people we live in utter mercy. Once we carried those old vices; now we have put them off and taste of God's own goodness, rich and life-giving as a mother's milk.

The eschatological language tempers the ecclesiastical language. To be sure, some are in and some are out. But every Christian remembers that only yesterday he or she was out and that only by God's grace has been brought in, received mercy, made a member of God's people. In the great story God has authored and continues to author, who knows who will find mercy and light tomorrow, who will next be included in God's dear people?

4. Whatever our reaction to the exclusiveness of the claim that Christians are God's own (only?) people—by no means unique to 1 Peter in Christian literature—the

---

78. See the helpful excursus by Brox on the post–New Testament history of the concept of general priesthood. Brox, *Der erste Petrusbrief*, 108-10.

positive side makes its claim in our generation as in the generation for which the epistle was written. For believers, Christian identity *is* our identity. Christian community is our community, and Christian family our family. Especially in a time of ongoing racial tension Christians rightly recall that as Christians (not as Caucasian, African American, Hispanic, or Asian people) we are a chosen race. For Christians who take 1 Peter seriously, the line on the application that asks for race ought to be filled in: "Christian."

1 PETER 2:11–4:11

LIFE IN EXILE

OVERVIEW

Having been comforted by the reminder of their identity as God's people, the readers are now instructed how to live as God's people in the midst of indifference and even opposition.

Both structurally and morally the exhortation to honorable living in 2:11–4:11 is the center of 1 Peter. It represents the author's most elaborate discussion of the shape of Christian life in a hostile world. The section is a mixture of fairly traditional Greek and Roman exhortation and of a vision of life seen through the Christian story of the cross. Perhaps more accurately, the epistle uses the story of Christ's passion as a lens through which to view the traditional injunctions in a new way.[79] For contemporary Christians, the section is difficult in part because structures that seemed to the author commonplace and appropriate seem to contemporary readers antiquated and oppressive. We can understand the import of these verses for contemporary practice, however, only when we give them their due as part of a program for first-century Christian behavior.

Significant contemporary interpretations of these verses of 1 Peter have drawn upon social-scientific models to provide hypotheses about the situation of the earliest readers of this letter. Not surprisingly, different commentators have drawn rather different conclusions.

John H. Elliott, in his book *A Home for the Homeless,* has maintained that the Christians who received this letter were sociologically, and not only spiritually, sojourners and exiles.[80] They were among the marginalized people of Asia Minor, living at the edges of power and prestige. As Christians, too, these believers were divorced from acceptable communities of belief and authority. In sociological terms, the Christians who first read 1 Peter were part of a sectarian movement. As with sects in our own time, argues Elliott, one of their concerns was to form a strong group identity, and the way in which they did that was to adopt standards for the ethical life that set them apart from their non-Christian neighbors.

For the Christian community, in other words, there exists a different standard of values, namely the will of God and the exemplary obedience of Jesus Christ, which distinguishes it from outside society. In the estimation of the Gentiles the Christians amount only to a motley collection of lowly aliens, ignoble slaves, religious fanatics and "Christ-lackeys" obsessed with self-humiliation. Within the family of God, however, and in God's estimation, Christians enjoy a new status which can only be retained by avoiding conformity to the degrading social norms of the Gentiles. . . . Over against the futile world of the Gentiles the Christians constitute an alternative and superior form of social and religious organization.[81]

David L. Balch, who has studied 1 Peter by paying special attention to the codes of behavior in the household (2:13–3:7), also recognizes that new Christian believers are cut off from some aspects of the predominant "Gentile" society. He argues, however, that the main purpose of the exhortations to humble behavior is not to set up a superior and unique set of Christian practices but to help Christians live as exemplary citizens, citizens who outdo the Gentiles precisely in

---

79. This point is made well and repeatedly in Ferdinand-Rupert Prostmeier, *Handlungsmodelle im ersten Petrusbrief: Forschung zur Bibel* (Würzburg: Echter Verlag, 1990) esp. 53-55, 420.

80. Elliott, *A Home for the Homeless.* On the social location of these early readers, 23-26.

81. Elliott, *A Home for the Homeless*, 128.

living according to the highest standards of the larger society.[82]

We shall need to return to these different hypotheses as we look at particular verses in this section of the letter. Both a careful reading of 1 Peter and attention to the nature of minority believing communities suggest that "sectarian" communities do not necessarily choose between a strong sense of their unique identity and a desperate concern to be approved by the larger society.[83] The Pastoral Epistles in the New Testament and any number of contemporary "marginalized" Christian communities show considerable evidence of both strategies. On the one hand, sectarian Christians stress the unique and special gifts of their community; on the other hand, they make perfectly clear that their community can trump the larger society in the very values it most espouses. Thus some contemporary Christians may feel embattled in an increasingly secular society. They deride the society for its values, yet they try to outdo "outsiders" by their zeal for other societal values. They may abhor what they see as sexual leniency but cling fervently to patriotism. They may deplore the popular media but borrow extensively from the strategies of popular entertainment. The mix of separation and accommodation is not confined to either the "left" or the "right" among contemporary Christians. Some Christians argue vehemently against abortion but show strong support for the death penalty. Other Christians staunchly oppose executions, while their position on abortion is indistinguishable from that of other more "liberal" Westerners.[84]

To be entirely anachronistic, the debate between Elliott and Balch represents an argument over whether the community to which 1 Peter was written is more like the Amish or more like the Seventh-Day Adventists in our own time. Both stand apart from the majority society in their theology and in some of their values, but Adventists tend to participate fully in commerce and comity, while the Amish stand more apart.[85]

However one hypothesizes about the communities for which 1 Peter was written, the fourfold movement of this section of the epistle is fairly clear. In the first subsection (2:11-17) the issue is how Christians should interact with those outside their own households and outside the community of faith, and in particular how they relate to governmental authorities. In the second subsection (2:18–3:7) the issue is how Christians should relate to others, particularly non-Christians, in their own households. Again the question is how to bear faithful witness in a predominantly non-Christian environment. The third subsection (3:8-22) deals with a particular problem in relation to the pagan environment: the problem of suffering. The final section (4:1-11) places the whole issue of faithful Christian behavior in the larger context of the new life Christians have received through Christ and the reminder that they will be called to account at the last judgment.

---

82. See Balch, *Let Wives Be Submissive*, 87-88. Elliott argues that Balch relies too exclusively on the household codes in interpreting the overall social strategy of the epistle. See John H. Elliott, "1 Peter, Its Situation and Strategy," in Talbert, *Perspectives on First Peter*, 61-78. Balch responds that the household codes in 1 Peter are better understood by sociological theories of acculturation than by those of conflict and that part of the strategy is to counter the Roman fear that foreign cults threaten both the domestic and the civic order. See David L. Balch, "Hellenization/Acculturation in 1 Peter," in Talbert, *Perspectives on First Peter*, 79-101.

83. Elliott at some points suggests that it is the motivation more than the shape of Christian behavior that marks it off from that of the respectable "Gentiles." See Elliott, "1 Peter, Its Situation and Strategy," 66. He sees the stress on mutual humility of all Christians as also being different from Hellenistic household codes.

84. Balch, in fact, argues at one point for this twofold aspect of sectarian development. See Balch, "Hellenization/Acculturation in 1 Peter," esp. 86-96. Elliott's contribution to the discussion is Elliott, "1 Peter, Its Situation and Strategy," 61-78.

85. See especially Balch, "Hellenization/Acculturation in 1 Peter," 74. He further suggests that the themes of missionary concern in 1 Peter do not fit with Elliott's strongly sectarian hypothesis.

1 PETER 2:11-17, LIVING HONORABLY AMONG THE GENTILES

COMMENTARY

2:11. These verses set the focus for the long discussion of proper behavior that follows. The address to the audience, "beloved," and the direct exhortation, "I urge you," indicate the beginning of a new major section of the epistle. The verb "I urge" (παρακαλέω *parakaleō*) is typical of the introduction to paraenetic material in Paul's letters but is also a standard term for moral exhortation in other Greco-Roman writings.[86] It stresses the urgency of the exhortation and the authority of the writer to beseech, if not to direct, the readers.

The address to the readers as "beloved" recalls both their love for one another (1:22) and the fact that they are called and chosen by God (1:2).[87] The NIV translation "dear friends" leaves out the second aspect of this and undervalues the first. The stress is rather on the readers as "beloved" of the author. The salutation also sets up a contrast between the truth of faith and the appearances of this world. In the light of faith this band of Christians are the beloved; in the light of the world they are exiles and aliens.[88] As the verse will further suggest, they are aliens to the world of fleshly desires and at home in the sphere of the soul.

It has already been suggested that the readers are aliens and exiles ("strangers," NIV), not so much because of their social status as marginalized people or because they are separate from their heavenly home. They are aliens and exiles because they are believers amid an unbelieving community; they are a diaspora among a vast majority of "Gentiles" (see 1:1).

The NRSV translates v. 11 more literally than does the NIV: "I urge you . . . to abstain from the desires of the flesh that wage war against the soul." The verse sets up a kind of parallel. The dominant pagans are associated with the values of the flesh; the "exiled" Christians are associated with the values of the soul. The tension between Christian outsiders and pagan insiders is not merely the struggle between two social groups; rather, it is part of the battle of two different spheres, two kinds of desires, two longings. Pagans long for the things of the flesh; Christians long for the gifts that strengthen the soul. As we shall see, the struggle between flesh and spirit is part of the struggle between God and Satan (see 5:6-11). Here again the NRSV has the more literal translation; "flesh" (σαρκικός *sarkikos*) wages war against "soul" (ψυχή *psychē*), not against "your soul." This is not only a battle within the life of each Christian but a battle within the cosmos between opposing forces. Furthermore, the outcome of that battle is not really in doubt. Those who listen to 1 Peter remember that the author has already assured them using the words of Isaiah:

"All flesh is like grass
 and all its glory like the flower of grass.
The grass withers,
 and the flower falls,
but the word of the Lord endures forever,"
(1:24-25a NRSV; cf. Isa 40:6-8)

Although the NIV misses the connection between 2:11 and 1:24, it does catch something of the meaning that 1 Peter gives to the term "flesh": "I urge you . . . to abstain from sinful desires." Whether or not the author of 1 Peter knew Paul's letters, he certainly picks up something of Paul's anthropology here. For Paul, "flesh" was the realm of selfishness, the power that worked destruction both within the individual believer and in the life of the church. While "fleshly" behavior for Paul sometimes referred to unacceptable sexual conduct, in its broader meaning "flesh" was the power that turned people in upon themselves, away from the neighbor and away from God (see, e.g., Rom 7:14-20; Gal 5:16-21).[89] For the writer of 1 Peter, the self-centered behavior of the pagans is what Christians have left behind, and yet Christians constantly fight a rear-guard action against the very forces they have defeated in their baptism and rebirth.

2:12. Here the author continues to draw the contrast between Christians and the world in which they find themselves as strangers. The behavior that outsiders malign is, in fact, behavior that is honorable and that honors God, and in the day of God's visitation the true values of the Christians will be

---

86. See Michaels, *1 Peter*, 115.
87. See Goppelt, *A Commentary on I Peter*, 155.
88. See Brox, *Der erste Petrusbrief*; Ferdinand-Rupert Prostmaier, *Handlungsmodelle im ersten Petrusbref, Forschung zur Bibel 63* (Würzburg: Echter Verlag, 1990) 141-42.
89. The classic and still instructive discussion of these categories is found in Rudolf Bultmann, *Theology of the New Testament*, trans. Kendrick Grobel (New York: Macmillan) 1:205-10, 232-39. Goppelt suggests that because the contrast between flesh and soul/life (*psyche*) is not Pauline, 1 Peter draws on general Christian tradition, not on the Pauline corpus. See Goppelt, *A Commentary on I Peter*, 156-57n. 10.

confirmed—even in the eyes of the "Gentiles." Note how closely 1 Peter identifies the readers with Israel and the non-Christians with Gentiles, though we have seen that most of the readers certainly were ethnically Gentiles, too. "Gentile" here is a description of one's faith community, not of one's ethnic origin. The Christians who were once "no people" are now "the people"—Israel (see 2:10).

The verb ἀναστρέφω (*anastrephō*), which the NIV translates as "live" and the NRSV as "conduct," is another of those participles that may be translated in the imperative. If, however, one reads it as modifying the main verb, then the verb it qualifies is "refrain" in v. 11: "Refrain from fleshly desires . . . as you live honorably among the Gentiles." However the word is translated, it is clear that living honorably and refraining from evil desires are two sides of the same coin. To live honorably among the Gentiles is to live according to standards more honorable even than those the Gentiles hold in honor.

There is some evidence from non-Christian sources that what appeared to Christians to be virtues were seen by their detractors as vices, signs of wickedness, or superstition. "It was often the very abstaining 'from fleshly desires' that caused pagans to despise Christians. . . . Thus Tacitus claimed that 'they were hated because of their vices' *(Ann.* 15:44), and Suetonius refers to them as 'a class of people animated by a novel and dangerous superstition' (*Nero* 16:2)."[90]

The stress on the undeserved slander received by the Christians foreshadows the retelling of the story of Christ, whose passion places the suffering of each Christian in perspective: "When they hurled their insults at him, he did not retaliate; when he suffered, he made no threats. Instead, he entrusted himself to him who judges justly" (2:23 NIV).

In v. 12 it is Christians who are called to entrust themselves to God, who will judge justly in the day of visitation. Christian hope in the midst of slander and suffering is sustained by the eschatological faith—that God will give victory to God's people. The battle Christians wage for the soul against all fleshly desires foreshadows the victory God will consummate on the day of visitation. Here the NIV translates more strictly and, therefore, more helpfully than does the NRSV; this is a visitation not only of judgment but also, of course, of grace (cf. Luke 19:44).

While there is a kind of missionary appeal here, the hope that the Gentiles will be impressed by the honorable behavior of the Christians, hope is still eschatological hope. There is no easy assumption that faithful behavior will win admiration in this world; rather, at history's end, when God comes to visit, the outsiders will behold the good deeds of the faithful. Then, at last, at *the* last, they will glorify God. This is the judgment toward which the epistle already pointed in 1:17, reminding the readers that God is both Father and impartial judge.

It is God whom the Gentiles will glorify, however, not the Christians themselves. The verse keeps the same balance as that of the Sermon on the Mount: "Let your light shine before others, so that they may see your good works and give glory to your Father in heaven" (Matt 5:16 NRSV). The good deeds of believers do not redound to the glory of believers; they redound to the glory of God.

Psychologically as well as theologically it is striking that the epistle here at least resists the temptation to assume that the day of visitation will mean wrath and destruction for those who have acted destructively and wrathfully against Christians. Instead, the hope is that those who have not understood the good conduct of the faithful in the everyday world will at the final transformation also be transformed—from unbelief to faith (contrast Revelation 18).

2:13-17. Beginning with v. 13 and continuing at least through 3:22, 1 Peter spells out what it means for Christians to "conduct themselves honorably" among the Gentiles. The author writes with a twofold hope. First, there is the hope that the Christians of Asia Minor may be spared unjust slander and may indeed impress their accusers with the excellence of their behavior. Second, and even more basic, there is the hope that these Christians will live a life that honors God, who has chosen them in Jesus Christ.

2:13-14. It is unclear whether v. 13 is the introductory sentence for only the immediately succeeding verses on the relationship of Christians to government or whether it is,

---

90. Davids, *The First Epistle of Peter*, 97.

rather, an introduction to the whole series of injunctions regarding proper obedience. Certainly the verb that begins this section, "Be subject" (ὑποτάσσω *hypotassō*), provides the basic command that shapes a whole series of proper relationships for Christian people.[91]

Already in v. 13a we see a juxtaposition or a tension that informs the whole discussion of proper Christian behavior. Christians are supposed to "accept the authority of every human institution" (NRSV) or to submit "to every authority instituted among men" (NIV); but they are to do this "on account of the Lord." The tension is even clearer if the first phrase is translated more literally "be subject to every human creature."[92] If the "Lord" in the second part of the phrase is the sovereign God, then Christians are enjoined to be subject to created authorities for the sake of the Creator. If the "Lord"—as is often the case— is Jesus, then Christians are admonished to follow his example of humble subjection.[93]

It is possible that the kinds of behavior here encouraged give clues to the accusations that outsiders brought against the Christians.[94] What the letter urges them to do is to show the accusers to be hopelessly false and misguided. It must also be admitted that much of this advice seems to represent a fairly standard adaptation of approved cultural standards of behavior to the particular case of Christians. There are some important differences, but also considerable family resemblance between this passage and Rom 13:1-7 (see also Titus 3:1 and, a little farther afield, 1 Tim 2:1-3).

Certainly one concern for early Christians was that they not be accused of being unpatriotic, and the first concern to appear in the list of injunctions speaks to that issue. The contrast between 1 Pet 2:13-14 and Rom 13:1-2 is instructive. In Romans, Paul writes: "Let every person be subject to the governing authorities; for there is no authority except from God, and those authorities that exist have been instituted by God. Therefore whoever resists authority resists what God has appointed, and those who resist will incur judgment" (Rom 13:1-2 NRSV). Here the reasons for loyalty are much more simply pragmatic. Emperors and governors are one example of those "human creatures" to whom Christians are called to show humble honor. Moreover they are useful because they uphold at least minimal standards of behavior. The description of the relationship of God to emperor to governors does not imply any divine chain of command, as if God authorizes the emperor, who then authorizes the governors. Rather, God creates the emperor and the governors, and the emperor gives authority to the governors for the sake of good order.

2:15. As this verse makes clear, Christians should support good order because they want to silence their detractors. Since emperors and governors promote good order, it is to the advantage of Christians to be subject to them.[95] This verse beautifully conjoins the two major reasons 1 Peter stresses for proper behavior: to put to shame your accusers in their foolishness, and because it is the will of God, and not just for the sake of self-satisfaction.

A similar combination of sanctions for right behavior is presented in 1 Timothy: "First of all, then, I urge that supplications, prayers, intercessions, and thanksgivings be made for everyone, for kings and for all who are in high positions, so that we may lead a quiet and peaceable life in all godliness and dignity. This is right and is acceptable in the sight of God our Savior" (1 Tim 2:1-3 NRSV).

2:16. Clearly for the author of 1 Peter, "honorable conduct" means not only honoring those with governing authority, but also doing nothing to draw the wrath—or the attention—of governors. The verse captures the almost paradoxical vision of civic behavior that 1 Peter—and other early Christian writings—commends. Because Christians are servants (slaves) of God—only!—they are free

---

91. Kelly argues that, indeed, this verse is the topic sentence for the whole section concluding with 3:22. See Kelly, *The Epistles of Peter and Jude*, 108. Similarly, Michaels suggests that the injunctions that follow 2:13 are "case studies" of proper subjection. See Michaels, *1 Peter*, 123.

92. So Michaels translates ὑποτάγητε πάσῃ ἀνθρωπίνῃ κτίσει (*hypotagēte pasē anthrōpinē ktisei*). See Michaels, *1 Peter*, 121.

93. Davids argues for the second interpretation; see Davids, *The First Epistle of Peter*, 99. Spicq thinks there may be an implicit argument against idolatrous worship of the emperor, who is, after all, only a creature. See Spicq, *Les Epitres de Saint Pierre*, 101.

94. See Balch, *Let Wives Be Submissive*, 82.

95. All this tends to confirm Balch's perspective on the social context and values of these early Christians as 1 Peter understands them. Balch's argument in part is that for both Hellenized Romans and Hellenistic Jews there is a correlation between the good order of the household and the good order of the state. See Balch, *Let Wives Be Submissive*, 76. First Peter at least asserts the importance of good household order as an apologetic device against accusations of civic disruption. See Balch, *Let Wives Be Submissive*, chap. 6.

in their relationships to political authorities. In himself the emperor has no authority over the Christian; in themselves, the governors are owed no allegiance by Christians. Authority and allegiance belong to God alone. Nonetheless, Christian freedom is freedom to do what is right, not what is wrong. And doing what is right includes being properly submissive to governing authorities.

Therefore, the evil that Christians are to avoid is the evil that authorities are instituted to punish: the violations of moral behavior that even non-believers would condemn. And the evil that Christians should avoid is the evil of failing to give proper submission to those authorities who punish immoral behavior. To avoid such evil is to act honorably among the Gentiles, to avoid slander for Christians, and, more important, at the last day to lead the Gentiles to glorify God (v. 12).

2:17. This verse is a chiasm, a rhetorical figure in which the two outer members are linked thematically to each other and the two inner members are linked thematically to each other as well: A B B´ A´.

A   Honor everyone
  B   Love the brotherhood
  B´ Fear God
A´ Honor the king

The B and B´ phrases are internal not only to the figure of speech but also to the life of the Christian community. As insiders, Christians have two responsibilities: to love their Christian brothers and sisters and to fear God. As "outsiders" in dealing with the outside world, Christians are to honor everyone (every created human person or institution, v. 13*a*), in particular the emperor (v. 13*b*). The verse may be partly drawn from Prov 24:21: "My son, fear the Lord and the king, and do not disobey either of them" (author's trans.). If so, it is particularly striking that 1 Peter shifts the injunction: Fear the Lord, but (only) honor the king.[96]

Recall the twofold address with which this whole section began: Christians are "beloved," insiders called to love one another and to fear God. Christians are "aliens and strangers," outsiders directed to honor every creature, even their pagan opponents, and in particular to honor the emperor (see v. 11).

It is also striking that the injunctions for "inside" behavior are stronger than are those for "outside" behavior. Outsiders and rulers are to be honored. Christians are to be loved, and God is to be reverenced with godly fear.

In many ways this chiastic injunction not only wraps up the first verses of this "station table"[97] but it also provides a transition to the further discussion of proper honoring and loving in the verses that follow.

---

96. Balch cites Danker's suggestion that the Proverbs verse may be altered in the light of Mal 1:14, and the whole following section shaped by Malachi's stress on Israel as God's servant. See Balch, *Let Wives Be Submissive*, 96.

97. Goppelt's term; see his excursus in Goppelt, *A Commentary on I Peter*, 162-79.

REFLECTIONS

1. Eschatology shapes the whole letter. These Christians have been called from the beginning, and they will be judged at the end. An unfading and precious inheritance has been laid up for them in heaven. The time in which they now live is the meantime. It is important, a field for faithfulness, but it is made relative by the decision that chose them from the beginning and by the judgment that will determine their end. Everyone who reads the New Testament carefully has to deal with eschatology, because Matthew awaits Christ's coming in glory and Revelation proclaims God's apocalyptic victory and every book in between deals one way or another with Christ, the alpha and the omega. To think aright about 1 Peter is to think about how we live in the meantime. Sometimes we envision the eschaton best as history's end. Sometimes we envision the eschaton best as history's depth, present as well as hoped for. Commenting on 1 Pet 2:12, E. G. Selwyn quotes Cranmer's prayer as a reminder for those times when eschatology not only draws us to the future but also permeates the present: "Lord, we beseech thee, give ear unto our prayers, and by thy gracious visitation lighten the darkness of our hearts through Jesus Christ our Lord."[98]

2. If not baptism, at least the insistence that Christian commitment requires new beginning, new birth, shapes 1 Peter from beginning to end. In the light of Easter, the *Revised Common Lectionary* includes 1 Pet 2:2-10 as a reading for the fifth Sunday of Easter (Cycle A). Oddly, the lectionary omits the first verse of the chapter and of the paragraph. In this reading, Christians are enjoined to act like newborn infants, without any notice of what we must leave behind to be "born again": "Rid yourselves, therefore, of all malice, and all guile, insincerity, envy, and all slander" (1 Pet 2:1 NRSV). Like too many sermons on the Nicodemus story, this truncated lectionary reading runs the danger of emphasizing how nice it is to be born anew without recalling how painful it is, how much of the old life must be left behind. For Nicodemus, what needed to be left behind was his status in the synagogue; for the readers of 1 Peter, it was the comfortable co-existence with pagans. No one who thinks very hard about the human comedy will doubt that sometimes malice, guile, insincerity, envy, and slander are just as hard to leave behind as are prestige and power. Giving up gossip may be as hard as giving up clout.

The lectionary does hold on to the great affirmations of the text—what it means to be born anew, not just to be an individual with a warm relationship to Jesus, to be part of a race, a nation, a people. The risen Christ does not live only, or even primarily, in the hearts of each believer; he lives triumphant with the God who sent him and in the community that serves him.

3. Our understanding of the social location of the recipients of 1 Peter (at least as the letter implies that location) helps us to interpret the significance of the epistle. Our understanding of our own social location will help to determine how we appropriate the epistle for our own time. Are we strangers and aliens, so radically divorced from the culture around us that we are called to stand over against the values of the larger society and to build enclaves of Christian fidelity? Are we the happy citizens of a society in which Christian values generally win out, so that our proper function is to lend the blessings of the church to the successes of the culture? Or are we (like the implied hearers of the epistle) caught somewhere in the middle—citizens of a society in which we are never entirely at home, but which is still created by God and where good things sometimes happen to good people? Do we want at the same time to strengthen our place as a peculiar people and to be in conversation and community with all neighbors who are a part of other peculiar communities? We will answer that question in part out of our denominational as well as out of our theological convictions. First Peter points us to a Christianity that is sectarian enough to know what it stands for, "churchy" enough to promote good citizenship, and "universalist" enough to hope that in the last day even those who have scoffed at our pious silliness will see the light and glorify the God who created us all.

4. Even today the general outline of the appropriate relationship between the Christian community and the larger world that we find sketched in 1 Peter seems appropriate. On the one hand, there are those standards of behavior and commitment that are internal to the Christian community, that set us apart from the larger world, and that we hold to as being the signs of the holiness to which God calls us. On the other hand, there is a whole host of secular goods that do not conflict with our Christian convictions—marks of good citizenship, neighborliness, even social zeal, that may not be rooted directly in the Christian story, but that help us to live as Christians in a pluralistic world. Otherwise how could we vote, run for city council, or join the P.T.A.?

---

98. Selwyn, *The First Epistle of Peter*, 171.

There is a tougher question. Is it possible that some worldly values might actually enrich the faithfulness of our commitment to God and to our neighbor? Much rhetoric about the distinctive fidelity of Israel in the midst of a pagan world misses the fact that monogamous marriage, for example, entered Judaism and then Christianity from the "pagan" Greco-Roman environment. Much contemporary Christian rhetoric bemoans the Enlightenment and its stress on rationality and toleration as a falling away from the purer faith of a more theocentric age. But along with the undeniable loss, was there not also some gain in the emergence of sufficient toleration to dampen our ancestors' enthusiasm for going to war in the name of denominational purity? Much of the contemporary debate on sexuality insists that the secular world should not distract the church from what Bible and tradition have taught. But is it possible that secular studies of the genesis and social location of sexuality have something to teach us that we might incorporate into the enrichment of our faithfulness? If for the Lord's sake we are to honor "every human creature or creation," might that at least mean that we are invited to pay some attention to insights that emerge from Athens as well as those originating in Jerusalem?

5. In some ways, our social location is very different from that of the recipients of this letter. In ways that the Christians of Asia Minor could not have dreamed, Christian people now often are the "human authorities" of whom 1 Peter speaks. We have the power that those Christians were told to honor. What does Christian fidelity look like when we not only are called to obey the laws but also to make the laws? How does one move from an ethic for a small minority in an empire to an ethic for at least a nominal majority in at least a nominal democracy?

There are at least a couple of clues in 1 Peter. The right role of government is still to "punish those who do wrong and to praise those who do right." Christian people need to think about the relationship of punishment to praise and the distinction between right and wrong. Obviously neither of those relationships can be spelled out simply or simplemindedly. In a pluralistic society, Christians will want to argue for the right but not to impose our understanding of the right as if from above. For people whose social agenda is set in large measure by the New Testament, there will always be the question of whether there are modes of punishment and praise that might entice evildoers to become doers of good, that might bring slanderers to the point where they can praise God in the day of God's visitation.

Furthermore, the Christian freedom to which this letter points includes at least implicitly the freedom to dissent from the mandates of society—not only of the emperor but also of the republic—if there is a conflict between being God's slave and being slave to the state. We are called to honor the emperor, but to fear God; and on those occasions when we must choose whether to serve the one we honor or the one we revere, the choice should not be too difficult to make—though often incredibly difficult to carry out.

Dietrich Bonhoeffer, Rosa Parks, Martin Luther King, Jr., and a host of the less famous stand as constant reminders that sometimes Christian freedom means freedom from society's rules, and not merely freedom to obey willingly.

❖ ❖ ❖ ❖

EXCURSUS: THE HOUSEHOLD TABLES

The material in 1 Pet 2:18–3:7 is formally very like the sets of exhortations on household order in Col 3:18–4:1 and Eph 5:21–6:9, and it is quite similar to material found more dispersed through the Pastoral Epistles (1 Tim 2:8-15; 5:1-2; 6:1-2; Titus 2:1-10; see also *Did.* 4:10-11; Ignatius to Polycarp, 4:3–5:2). The concern for proper order within Christian community and family appears again in 1 Pet 5:1-5. Further, the concern for proper submission within the household is closely related in 1 Peter to proper submission to governmental authorities (as also in 1 Tim 2:1-2; Titus 3:1). David Balch argues persuasively that the antecedents for these household codes are to be found as early as Plato and Aristotle and are continued among Stoics and the Hellenistic Jews Philo and Josephus.[99] In these non-Christian writings there was great concern for the proper management of the household, with some sense that the security and unity of the state depended on the security and unity of the families within that state.[100] So, too, in 1 Peter the overall injunction to orderly behavior begins with the appeal to obey human authorities, starting with the emperor. Governors, masters, and husbands are all examples of the general category of those people who have special authority.

Balch argues that the social context for the code in 1 Peter is to be found in 3:15: "Always be ready to make your defense" (NRSV). Part of what Christians have to defend is the accusation that their religion overturns the approved social order. Following the household code is a way of making sure that there is no substance to these pagan accusations.[101]

The following interpretation will acknowledge much truth to Balch's claims, but the close parallels to Colossians and Ephesians (where there is not the same concern with confounding pagan opponents) suggest that—whatever its origins—the household code now seemed an appropriate way of encouraging social order within the Christian community. Indeed, in the case of slavery, for 1 Peter the right domestic order is an enfolding of right christology. Slaves suffer unjustly, as did their Lord (2:20-25).

99. Balch, *Let Wives Be Submissive*, 14-15, 25-56.
100. Balch, *Let Wives Be Submissive*, 14-15, citing Friedrich Wilhelm, 14.
101. See Balch, *Let Wives Be Submissive*, 14-15, 90.

❖ ❖ ❖ ❖

1 PETER 2:18–3:7, LIVING HONORABLY IN THE HOUSEHOLD

COMMENTARY

Both formally and materially these verses comprise the center of the exhortation for Christians to exhibit good behavior in the midst of an unbelieving society. The exhortation to slaves is so shaped by the author's christology that it becomes evident that these verses are intended directly as an admonition to household slaves and indirectly as an admonition to all Christians who serve Christ, the suffering servant.

Unlike the exhortations in Col 3:22–4:1 and Eph 6:5-9, 1 Peter addresses only household servants and not their masters. In part this probably reflects the reality of the churches of Asia Minor; they were composed far more heavily of servants than of masters.[102] Furthermore, the attempt to show "good behavior" before pagans may be a response to the accusation on the part of non-Christian masters that Christianity was inciting newly converted slaves to insubordination.[103] It is also clear that the household slaves are examples and paradigms for Christians and, as Elliott points out, that the "household" is a ruling metaphor for the Christian community. It is, perhaps, also for this reason that servants are addressed as "household servants," not (as in Colossians and Ephesians) as "slaves," and that the admonition to them is the first of the household injunctions, not (as in the other epistles) the last.[104]

It may also be that for 1 Peter Christians are slaves (οἰκέται *oiketai*) only of God, while they may very well be household servants of earthly masters. So they are slaves of the God whom they fear, but household servants of the masters whom they obey—for the Lord's sake.[105]

2:18-20. These verses begin the section that is often characterized as a *Haustafel*, a "table" of rules for the household. Yet it is clear that the concern for a right order within the house is not divorced from the concern for right order within the community and even the empire. For this reason, Goppelt notes how closely this material is tied to the preceding section and says that all would be better designated "station code" rather than "household code." The issue is, in the whole of society, how Christians should live out their own "station" in relationship to those with other stations.[106]

2:18. The exhortation begins again with a participle that can probably best be interpreted as an imperative (as both the NRSV and the NIV do). It reprises the verb with which 1 Peter urges believers to be subject to every created human being or institution (v. 13).[107] Masters (δεσπόται *despotai*), like the emperor and the governors, are among those created powers to whom Christians are properly subject. But the readers recall the larger claim of v. 13: They are subject only on account of the Lord. When the author tells them to be subject "in fear" (NIV, "with all respect"; NRSV, "with all deference"), he probably continues to keep the injunction in this larger theological framework. They are to be subject to earthly masters because, as v. 17 has enjoined, they fear God.[108]

The assumption of v. 18 is that it is no test of Christian fidelity to be subject to good masters; the test is what a Christian does in the face of treatment that is cruel. In this sense, the issue is more complicated than that of obedience to the emperor. There the author assumes that the function of the emperor is to reward right behavior and to punish wrong behavior. Now Christians are enjoined to be subject to masters—even when they behave harshly.

One can say that the dilemma of Christian servants suffering unjustly drives the author to the affirmation of Christ's suffering as comfort and example. But one could equally well say that the story of Christ's passion as seen through Isaiah 53 shapes 1 Peter's description of the proper life of the household servant. The unjust suffering of Christ provides the paradigmatic image that allows the author to interpret the meaning of the unjust suffering of Christian household slaves. By extension, the unjust suffering of Christ provides the image that allows the author to interpret the unjust suffering of any of his first readers. "If you suffer for doing good and you endure it, this is commendable before God" (NIV). This is an injunction not only for household slaves but also for all those whom the author assumes find themselves suffering unjustly.[109]

---

102. See Kelly, *The Epistles of Peter and Jude*, 114-15; Michaels, *1 Peter*, 138. Achtemeier, however, is skeptical of drawing any social implications from this lack. He stresses, rather, the paradigmatic role of slaves as examples for the obedience of all Christians. See Achtemeier, *1 Peter*, 192.
103. Balch proposes this possibility, *Let Wives Be Submissive*, 95.
104. See the helpful discussion in Elliott, *A Home for the Homeless*, 205-7.
105. See Goppelt, *A Commentary on 1 Peter*, 194, for a similar suggestion.
106. See Goppelt, *A Commentary on 1 Peter*, 194, for a similar suggestion, 165.
107. On participles functioning as imperatives, see footnote number 54, above.
108. See Michaels, *1 Peter*, 138.
109. This reading is influenced by Prostmeier's thoughtful interpretation of these verses. See Ferdinand-Rupert Prostmeier, *Handlungsmodelle im ersten Petrusbref, Forschung zur Bibel* 63 (Würzburg: Echter Verlag, 1990) 155-58.

2:19-20. The concern with the Christian's right conduct before God reminds us that two theological premises introduced this whole section on right conduct: the eschatological hope that Christians' behavior would convince unbelievers of the rightness of their cause at the time of God's visitation and the reminder that all Christian submission is undertaken, not for the sake of the created authorities, but for the sake of the God who created them (vv. 12-13). Furthermore, the conduct of slaves is a particularly pointed working out of the larger claim about Christian freedom that 1 Peter makes in direct relation to obedience to governing authorities: "As servants of God, live as free people, yet do not use your freedom as a pretext for evil" (2:16 NRSV). These household slaves, too, are *really* God's slaves, not the master's. Therefore, they are free; and yet precisely for God's sake they are to use that freedom to do what is right—even when what is right includes totally unwarranted suffering.

Two terms in v. 19 are familiar in NT literature, and each is used here somewhat differently from the manner usually expected. The term that the NIV translates "it is commendable" and that the NRSV translates "it is a credit" is often translated "grace" (χάρις *charis*), although here it seems not to carry the rich connotations of the term when it is used by Paul or in Ephesians. "It adds to your account" would be a more literal translation. This reading is confirmed when the term is used again at the end of v. 20. Suffering for the sake of righteousness represents a credit—with God. Again the immediate concern for impressing the neighbors by correct behavior is set in the larger context: Christians do this for God's sake. (The writer of 1 Peter also uses the term *charis* in 1:2, 10, 13; 4:10; 5:10, 12. In these cases, the word carries richer theological meaning than it does here, though the implications are somewhat different from those of Paul's use of the term.)

The term συνείδησιν θεοῦ (*syneidēsin theou*) in v. 19, which the NIV translates as "conscious of God" and the NRSV translates as "being aware of God," sometimes means "consciousness" or "awareness," and also sometimes means "conscience" (as it apparently does in 3:16, 21). Selwyn affirms this interpretation: "The conscience of the Christian slave provides a fortifying motive for the patient endurance of injustice, and is also satisfied in it."[110]

Whatever the details of particular vocabulary, the general thrust of these verses is clear. As part of the call to be subject to human creations for the sake of the Creator, household slaves are to be subject to their householders—not only when the masters' demands are just, but also when they are unjust—for such obedience is pleasing and acceptable to God. In this concern for the approval of God, the sense of God's immediate presence (the consciousness of God) and God's final judgment (the visitation of God) come together.

2:21-25. Now this injunction to submissive behavior is grounded in the story of Christ's passion, a paradigm not just for household servants but for all Christians who suffer injustice. Verse 21, in remarkably compact terms, sketches both an ethic and a christology.[111] The first readers of this epistle were those who had been "called." From the opening salutation throughout the letter, the author has reminded the Christians that their status is a matter neither of historical accident nor of their own decision. They have been called to be who they are, written into a story by God, who is the author of their story and of all history. Now it is clear what their role is, what part they have been called to play. They were called to suffer for righteousness' sake. This is not bad luck or ill fate; it is their vocation. If we are right in seeing the letter as being shaped in part around themes of baptism and rebirth, then Christians are asked to remember their baptism as a mark of their call.

This vocation is grounded not only in God's call but also in Christ's passion. Christ's passion establishes the vocation in two ways: (1) Christ suffered for the Christians (some early MSS read "Christ died on your behalf"; that reading is most likely an assimilation of 1 Peter to the more familiar Pauline formula, or to 1 Pet 3:18).[112] (2) Christ's suffering serves as the example for the appropriate behavior of the Christians. The Greek word

---

110. Selwyn, *The First Epistle of Peter*, 177. Spicq also translates συνείδεις (*syneideis*) as "conscience" which the slave has from God. Spicq, *Les Ŝpitres de Saint Pierre*, 108.
111. Michaels suggests that the reference to the "grace" Christians have before God recalls the whole "grace" that God provides in Jesus Christ; this may be a stretch. See Michaels, *1 Peter,* 108.
112. See Metzger, *A Textual Commentary on the New Testament,* 690; Davids, *The First Epistle of Peter,* 109n. 10.

for "example" is ὑπογραμμός (*hypogrammos*), which more literally means the pattern that a child, learning to write, traces over.[113] The idea of "walking in his steps" follows the same motif. Christ's passion is the path Christians take; they trace his pattern, walk in his steps.

Verses 22-25 draw very heavily on motifs from Isaiah 53; it may even be possible to say that they are a kind of homiletical elaboration on themes from Isaiah's great Servant Song. Here are the verses that 1 Peter draws from as found in the Septuagint:

He bears our sins
    and suffers pain for us,
yet we accounted him to be in distress,
    and in suffering, and in affliction.
But he was wounded for our sins,
    wounded for our iniquities;
the chastisement [παιδεία *paideia*] of our
        peace was upon him,
    and by his bruises we are healed.
We have all gone astray like sheep;
    every person has gone astray on his
        own path,
and the Lord has handed him over
    for our sins.
Yet on account of the evil that was
        done him,
    he does not open his mouth.
He was led like a lamb to the slaughter
    and as a sheep that before its shearers
        is silent;
so he does not open his mouth.
. . . .
And I shall give the wicked for his grave
    and the rich for his death,
because he did nothing unlawful
and no deceit was found in his mouth.
(Isa 53:4-7, 9, author's trans.)

The first two verses of this reading of Isaiah 53 (in 1 Pet 2:22-23) shed light on the second claim of 2:21: Christ is the example, the paradigm for Christians. The second two verses explicate the first claim to the readers in v. 21, that Christ suffered "for you."

In elaborating on the promise that Christ is a paradigm, v. 22 quotes directly from Isa 53:9, and the rest of the passage presents themes from Isaiah's passage to illuminate ways in which Christ served as an example for suffering household servants and for all suffering Christians in the communities to which 1 Peter was written.

The reminder from Isa 53:9 that Christ "committed no sin,/ and no deceit was found in his mouth" (v. 22) makes Christ the forerunner of those household servants who "suffer for doing good and you endure it" (v. 20). Therefore, by extension Christ becomes the forerunner of all Christians who suffer unjustly, those who "now for a little while you may have had to suffer grief in all kinds of trials" (1:6 NIV). Christ lived out his calling as predicted by the prophets, that he should suffer (1:11). Now Christian servants and all Christians undergoing trials live out their calling too (2:21).

For Christ, for household servants suffering injustice, for all Christians undergoing tribulation for their faith the end of suffering is glory that comes from God. That glory has already been granted to Jesus Christ (1:11). It relates directly to the eschatological promise to those household servants who were suffering unjustly when 1 Peter was written, who "have God's approval" (v. 20), and it is the promise for all the suffering Christians who read or hear 1 Peter. Just as Christ's sufferings led to his glory, so also their suffering tests that faith that "may be found to result in praise and glory and honor when Jesus Christ is revealed" (1:7 NRSV). An additional benefit of this faithfulness, even in the midst of suffering, is that when Christ is revealed, at least some of those who malign the Christians will "see [their] honorable deeds and glorify God when he comes to judge" (2:12). One can assume that among the slanderers are slavemasters who were anxious about their house slaves' new religion and that among those slandered are the slaves who suffered reproach precisely for their newfound faith.

Verses 22-23 show what suffering slaves and all suffering Christians are to do in the meantime, before God's glorious visitation. They are not to give slander in return for slander received, but they are to be like their Lord as he is foreseen in Isa 53:7, 9. The echoes of some of the gospel material are very strong here as well. The passage recalls Mark 14:53-61, Jesus' silence before false accusations,

---

113. See Davids, *The First Epistle of Peter*, 109-10; Selwyn, *The First Epistle of Peter*, 179.

and Mark 15:19, where Jesus is silent before his taunters. For slandered Christians, the passage recalls Matt 6:43-44 and Luke 6:28. So for 1 Peter, Christians, like Jesus Christ, are to trust their lives to God, who they have already been told is both Father and a just judge (1:17; again the gospel tradition suggests a kind of parallel in Luke 23:46).[114] Here the author reminds Christians to do what he has already assured them they are able to do in Christ Jesus: "Through him you have come to trust in God, who raised him from the dead and gave him glory" (1:21 NRSV).

Now in vv. 24-25—still drawing on Isaiah 53—1 Peter elaborates on the already traditional Christian claim that Christ suffered "for you." The passage makes two claims about the ways in which Christ represents the believers, or stands as substitute for the believers, in bringing them safely before the one who judges justly. Explicitly 1 Peter says that Jesus took believers' sins to the cross, thereby delivering them from sin. In theological terms, this could represent either substitutionary atonement wherein Christ, though sinless, took upon himself the punishment for human sin on behalf of believers, or an atonement of victory wherein Christ vanquished sin through his fidelity on the cross (for images closer to the first option, see 2 Cor 5:21; for the second, see Col 2:13-15). Both the NRSV and the NIV may overinterpret (or misinterpret) the phrase about getting rid of sin. The Greek phrase translated quite literally means "in order that having departed from sins we might live in righteousness."[115] This is not an explicit statement about Christian freedom (as in the NRSV) or about "dying" to sin (as in the NIV).

Implicitly 1 Peter says that as the lamb of God, Jesus suffered for those Christians who before their conversion had themselves been straying sheep. Surely the reference from Isa 53:6 in v. 25 recalls for the readers Christ himself as the sacrificial lamb in 1:19. And there is yet another image of the salvation worked in Christ in the citation from Isa 53:5 in v. 24. Now Jesus is the wounded surgeon whose wounds heal the wounded believers.[116]

At the conclusion of this rich meditation on Isaiah 53, the author draws on another prophet, Ezekiel, for whom the word of the Lord is: "So they were scattered, because there was no shepherd.... My sheep were scattered, they wandered... over all the face of the earth, with no one to search or seek for them" (Ezek 34:5-6 NRSV). The oracle moves, however, to promise, as the author, and perhaps his readers also, knew: "I myself will be the shepherd of my sheep... says the Lord GOD" (Ezek 34:15 NRSV). In 1 Peter, Jesus has become the true shepherd; the words are fulfilled in him. The Christians, who before coming to faith were wandering far and wide, have now returned to him—shepherd and guardian, overseer, bishop of their souls. Though to the world the Christians look like wandering sheep (aliens and exiles, 2:11), they know that they are at home in the shepherd's fold (the "beloved," 2:11). The image of the shepherd will recur in 5:4, where Peter and the elders are implicitly deputy shepherds as well. As with so much of the NT, these verses are not a full-fledged doctrine of the atonement at all. Rather, they give us a rich mix of images and allusion, drawn largely from Isaiah 53:1 and from Christian formulas ("he suffered for you") and from elsewhere in this epistle. The strategy is homiletical rather than systematic. The purpose of the rhetoric seems clear: to strengthen Christian believers, especially household slaves, in faith and in obedient behavior. They are strengthened because they look to Christ as example and as redeemer; through his silence, obedience, and trust he has opened to them the imperishable inheritance that no earthly master can tarnish or destroy.

Notice that the whole use of Isaiah 53 in these verses demonstrates precisely that understanding of Hebrew Scripture that 1 Peter has praised in 1:10-11: "Concerning this salvation, the prophets who prophesied of the grace that was to be yours made careful search and inquiry... [concerning] the sufferings destined for Christ and the subsequent glory" (NRSV).

3:1-7. Now the author turns to husbands and wives. As in Ephesians 5 and Colossians 3, wives are addressed first, but in 1 Peter, the heavier weight of both words and argument rests with the injunction to the wives.

---

114. See Spicq, *Les Epitres de Saint Pierre*, 111.
115. See Selwyn, *The First Epistle of Peter*, 181.
116. For a powerful poetic reference to Christ as wounded healer, see T. S. Eliot, *The Four Quartets*, "East Coker," canto IV, line 1, in *The Complete Poems and Plays* (New York: Harcourt, Brace & World, 1962) 127.

Comparing 1 Peter to other Greco-Roman literature on the household, David Balch suggests that "slaves and wives are addressed first by these early Christian moralists because they were the focus of an intense social problem between the church and Roman society. Romans frowned on their wives and slaves being seduced by bizarre foreign cults, and this led the author of 1 Peter to address the household code to those who were the focus of the tension."[117]

3:1-2. The introductory "in the same way" provides a rhetorical transition; but more than that it suggests that the willing subjection of wives to their husbands follows the same pattern that the letter prescribes for household servants in relation to their masters and for all believers in relation to governmental authorities. Indeed, the participle that both the NIV and the NRSV render as an imperative, "accept the authority of your husbands" (NRSV) and "be submissive to your husbands" (NIV), is another form of the verb in 2:13, where the author enjoins the readers to be subject to every "created authority for the Lord's sake." Among the created authorities are not only emperors and householders but also husbands. Here again, wives are to be obedient not for the sake of the husband but for the sake of the Lord, serving the created human authority for the sake of the Creator.

The letter is more explicit about how serving the husband might mean serving the Lord. Service can provide a means to witness. Husbands who have not been persuaded "by the word"—who may even oppose the word— might be convinced "without a word" (the wordplay occurs in the Greek, as well as in the English translations) by the behavior of their wives. Achtemeier persuasively argues that this represents an admonition to Christian wives to avoid speaking explicitly about their faith, not to avoid speaking altogether.[118] The word for "conduct" (ἀναστροφη *anastrophē*) is the same word used in 2:12, and the hope that wives will bear witness to their husbands by their good conduct becomes a concrete example of the broader eschatological hope that the Gentiles may see the honorable deeds of believers and glorify God at God's visitation (2:12). While these verses attempt to indicate that Christian women are upholding the orders of the household, there is quiet subversion here, since the assumption within that social setting was that wives would follow the religious practices of their husbands and that the unbelieving husbands would be among those Gentiles who maligned their own believing spouses as evildoers (2:12).[119]

Verse 2 can be translated more woodenly as "when they see the pure conduct in fear [or reverence] of your lives." In the light of 2:17, the NIV and the NRSV rightly understand the fear as being fear of God. Again wives are obedient to their husbands, not for the sake of their husbands or out of fear of their authority, but "for the Lord's sake" (2:13). Pheme Perkins helpfully points out that, unlike in the case of household slaves, this passage does not presume that the husbands are behaving abusively, but only that they are unbelieving or even refusing to believe.[120]

3:3-4. These verses describe the appearance of such pure and reverent lives.[121] The adornment of the "quiet spirit" reminds us that Christian women are to win their husbands "without a word" (v. 1). That is, it is not merely the case that conduct speaks louder than words in winning recalcitrant husbands; more than that, the appropriate conduct includes demure silence. Wives are not to argue their husbands toward faith. As is so often the case in this epistle, these verses echo an earlier claim. The quiet behavior of the Christian wives is "unfading beauty . . . in God's sight"(NIV)—just as the inheritance of Christians is "unfading" (1:4) and the seed of God's Word is "imperishable" (1:23). Their behavior is "precious" (πολυτελής *polyteles*; 3:4) as their faith is "precious" (*polyteles*; 1:7). The reminder that true adornment is spiritual and not cosmetic is similar to 1 Tim 2:9. In that epistle, there is some sense that the adornment of physical beauty is itself licentious and demeaning. Here it seems rather that Christian women are called to choose between the lesser and the greater—the perishable beauty of physical adornment and the imperishable beauty of a gentle spirit.[122]

---

117. Balch, *Let Wives Be Submissive*, 96-97.
118. Achtemeier, *1 Peter*, 210.
119. See Balch, *Let Wives Be Submissive*, 99.
120. Perkins, *First and Second Peter, James, and Jude*, 56-57.
121. Balch, *Let Wives Be Submissive*, 101-2, presents a number of near parallels from Greco-Roman literature.
122. Goppelt, *A Commentary on I Peter*, 218, lists a number of close non-Christian parallels from Greco-Roman writing; Michaels, *1 Peter*, 159, lists Jewish and Hellenistic parallels.

3:5-6. The "holy women of old" become examples for Christian wives as Christ is an example for Christian slaves. Obviously the examples of Sarah and the other wives provide nothing like the rich christological reflection of the passion story, but the rhetorical strategy is similar: Encourage faithful behavior by recalling exemplars from the heritage of faith. The description of the faithfulness of these women, that they were submissive to their own husbands, exactly recapitulates the exhortation to the Christian wives to be "submissive to their husbands" (v. 1 NIV; the NRSV makes the two phrases exactly parallel).

That the women in the OT story were "holy" recalls the earlier exhortation to all Christian women and men to imitate the holiness of God and the reminder that Christian people are now a holy nation (see 1:16; 2:9). According to 1:14-16, Christians show their holiness by acting like "obedient children." Now Sarah is held up as an example of obedience; her obedience to her husband is by extension also an instance of obedience to God. Pheme Perkins points out that the analogy can only go so far. Sarah shared in the faith of her husband; Christian wives are encouraged to stand fast—quietly but firmly—in their own convictions.[123]

Sarah calls Abraham "lord" in the Septuagintal version of Gen 18:12, though the larger context of Sarah's disbelief in the light of the angel's announcement is not a noteworthy example of obedience either to her husband or to God. In 1 Pet 3:6, Sarah has become a model of the whole range of right Christian conduct, and Christian women are her daughters because they imitate her behavior (cf. Paul's different understanding of Christian men and women as Abraham's children, Rom 4:13-25).

The final exhortation to the women not to "give way to fear" echoes Prov 3:25 and is probably an encouragement to hold fast their faith even while being submissive and obedient to their husbands.[124] The Proverbs injunction is preceded in Prov 3:21-22 by the plea to let wisdom and prudence be "adornment for the neck," a theme echoed in 1 Pet 3:3-4.

3:7. Here the husbands are addressed briefly.[125] Of course, the assumption is that believing husbands will have believing wives and households, so the issue of the relationship to an unbelieving spouse does not arise. What does come to the fore is the obligation of the husbands to behave lovingly to the wives, not in submission (or even mutual submission as in Eph 5:22) but in "respect" (NIV) or "honor" (NRSV). The term "honor" (τιμή *timē*) is the same term used to tell Christians what is due the king in 2:17. The phrase "in the same way" may hint at a fuller mutuality between husband and wife, a mutuality expressed differently because of their different stations. That wives are weaker "vessels" probably refers only to their physical strength, and perhaps also to their vulnerability—a warning against any possible abuse.[126] There is no indication here, as in the Pastoral Epistles, that women are somehow more subject than men to false faith or mistaken beliefs; on the contrary, the apparent assumption that there are more believing wives than husbands in this community indicates that women can be equally strong in faith. Husbands are to behave toward them with "knowledge," the understanding that recognizes their vulnerability but also honors their gifts. Indeed, the fundamental equality of men and women in the light of God's coming reign is underlined by the reminder that they are "joint heirs of the grace of life." Since 1 Peter so strongly stresses the imperishable inheritance given the faithful (1:4), the implication here is that whatever the relative social standing of men and women in this perishable world, in the indestructible realm of grace they are equal.

The notion that failing to give due respect to one's spouse might hinder one's prayers apparently plays on the assumption of much early Christian writing that the life of prayer is nourished by faithful behavior and hindered by behavior that violates the neighbor or the spouse (see also Jas 4:3).[127] In 1 Pet 4:7, the author calls for the discipline and right behavior that engender right prayer (note that the exhortations to children and parents in

---

123. See Perkins, *First and Second Peter, James, and Jude*, 58.
124. So Kelly, *The Epistles of Peter and Jude*, 132.
125. Achtemeier, *1 Peter*, 217, suggests that all males in the Christian community are addressed.
126. On the issue of what "weaker vessel" might mean, see Davids, *The First Epistle of Peter*, 122-23.
127. So Brox, *Der erste Petrusbrief*, 149. Kelly, *The Epistles of Peter and Jude*, 134, thinks the last injunction applies to both wives and husbands.

Eph 6:1-4 are missing in this section of 1 Peter, yet a somewhat analogous concern for intergenerational order is found in 1 Pet 5:1-5).

REFLECTIONS

1. With good reason we are glad to be beyond a society in which slavery is part of the social order. Toni Morrison's novel *Beloved* is the irrefutable rejoinder to any who still try to romanticize American slavery or to make a distinction between benevolent and malevolent ownership of other humans. The mysterious "Beloved" comes to represent all those whose identity disappears in slavery: "Everybody knew what she was called, but nobody knew her name. Disremembered and unaccounted for, she cannot be lost because no one is looking for her, and even if they were how can they call her if they don't know her name? Although she has claim, she is not claimed."[128] Finally for all the difference between first-century and nineteenth-century slavery, the refusal to condone any slavery is now an established Christian principle, indicating that to be Christian in our time is not simply to accept the values of our honored and faithful forebears in the faith. Yet in 1 Peter the household slave in his or her obedience is a paradigm of faithful Christian behavior, modeled on Christ's fidelity and modeling fidelity for other believers. In many ways, 1 Pet 2:16 provides the basic guideline not only for the behavior of these household slaves but for all Christians as well: "As slaves of God, live as free people, yet do not use your freedom as a pretext for evil" (NRSV margin). Christian freedom lives out Christ's freedom, and Christ's freedom did not include the freedom to repay evil for evil, but the freedom to repay good for evil.

For a host of reasons, we cannot simply take 1 Peter as a clear and infallible guide to contemporary faithful behavior. Our understanding of slavery has unalterably changed. Our sense of the power and the intractability of social forces is mitigated by the knowledge that as citizens and Christians we have the power to make changes in those structures.

Yet the difficult and paradoxical shape of Christian life as here delineated stands over us as a challenge and even a possibility. No one can take my freedom from me; but because I am God's slave, I am free not to resist violence with violence, not to fight fire with fire or to oppose the lies of the oppressive with my own list of persuasive exaggerations and caricatures.

2. The *Revised Common Lectionary* turns to 1 Peter 2 as a reading for the fourth Sunday of Easter (Cycle A), but evasively assigns the passage 2:19-25. Thus the lectionary manages to hold on to the christological and soteriological affirmation without the sociological context to which it was addressed. The hard task of preaching is to be as honest as we can about both the concrete context for a biblical passage and our own, sometimes quite different, context. In 1 Peter slavery represents both a social reality and a metaphor for Christ's obedience and for the obedience of Christians. The brave (and honest) interpreter will not look at this passage apart from attention to the tough question of this epistle's attitude toward slavery. If our social context is entirely different, do 1 Peter's metaphors function faithfully for our time? If they can do so, it will not be because we have abstracted them from the real world of social relationships.

In the lectionary reading, 1 Peter is linked with Psalm 23 and John 10. We find the image of believers as sheep more comfortable than the image of believers as slaves. Yet perhaps both pictures are more problematic than we are wont to admit; or perhaps in the interplay of the two images we can find clues to what it might mean in our time to be faithful to the One who was both our shepherd and the lamb who was slain (1:18-19; 2:25).

---

128. Toni Morrison, *Beloved* (New York: Alfred A. Knopf, 1987) 274.

3. With good reason Christians find godly and humane grounds to resist images of the household that depend on the submissiveness of wives to husbands. Contemporary feminist concerns for restructuring relationships—including marriage—are not merely a reflection of the triumph of secular values or the enticements of modern egalitarian political thought. From the clear fact that women were among Jesus' closest followers to Paul's bold call that in Christ there is neither male nor female, the New Testament provides its own powerful counterpoint to images of subordination in relationships between men and women (see Gal 3:28).

Indeed, one should not underestimate the countercultural implications of this passage from 1 Peter. While the author advises Christian women to behave honorably among unbelievers so as not to stir up unnecessary trouble, he holds firm in the conviction that the wife has the right to her own Christian faith, whether the husband believes or not. In the Roman Empire of 1 Peter's time, that was a subversive claim, however clothed in modesty and silence.[129] Furthermore, the fact that both wives and husbands are addressed and their responsibilities to each other explicated suggests mutuality, if not equality, in their relationship.[130] And while as aliens and strangers in the world there is a distinction between the power and authority of wife and husband as God's beloved, they are both—equally—"heirs of the gracious gift of life" (3:7 NIV).

Nevertheless, as with the question of slavery, Christian perspectives on the relationships between women and men are appropriately subject to reevaluation as circumstances and knowledge change. Our study has recognized that the Christian household codes were profoundly affected by the best "pagan" wisdom of their time, and it would require a fantastic feat of intellectual isolationism for contemporary Christians to ignore the discussions of our own time about gender, patriarchy, and the possibilities and limitations of "liberation."

Different Christians will come to different understandings of marriage and family, and they will do so out of faith. It seems implausible to assume that as we move into the twenty-first century faithful Christian marriage will precisely replicate faithful Christian marriage in first-century Asia Minor any more than faithful Christian citizenship would simply honor the emperor. Obedience to God in our time and place will not look exactly like obedience in 1 Peter's time and place. Christian freedom is not so simple or so simpleminded as that. We will learn from 1 Peter that Christian marriage includes real mutuality, a gentle spirit—for men and for women alike—and constant communion with one another and with God in the gift of prayer.

4. The relationship between the life of prayer and the life of charity is attested throughout the canon. In Amos, God despises the feasts and solemn assemblies of those who do not do justice (Amos 5:21-24); and in Matthew Jesus tells us that we should not come to the altar until we have sought reconciliation with our brothers and sisters (Matt 5:23-24). In 1 Corinthians, Paul tells the Corinthians that if they take the Lord's supper without discerning the "body" they eat and drink judgment on themselves (1 Cor 11:29). In part, at least, this is an exhortation to attend to other Christians who are members of the body with ἀγάπη (*agapē*, 1 Cor 11:29). James insists that prayers are not answered if they do not derive from selfless motives (Jas 4:3) and that it is the prayers of the righteous that are "powerful and effective" (Jas 5:16). Of course, one great stream of biblical faith insists that the sinner's prayer for mercy is blessed in God's sight, but we note that it is the prayer for mercy that is blessed—not prayers that presume on God's favor for the unrepentant. (As Matt 18:23-35 reminds us, even the prayer for mercy presupposes our willingness to be merciful.) The life of

---

129. See Balch, *Let Wives Be Submissive*, 84-85.
130. See Balch, *Let Wives Be Submissive*, Appendix V, 142-49, for a persuasive discussion of the basic similarity between the most "enlightened" pagans and Christian household codes on the mix of honor and submission assigned to wives. Overall, Eph 5:21 advocates a somewhat more inclusive notion of mutual subjection than is found in 1 Peter.

prayer informs the life of action; but active obedience also enriches the life of prayer. We pray that we might act graciously, but we act graciously in order that we might learn to pray.

5. Interpreters assume that behind much of the christology of the New Testament is the influence of the Servant Songs of Isaiah. In this section of 1 Peter that influence is evident and pervasive. Using Isaiah 53 as the basis for his reflection, the author claims both that Christ suffered for us and that Christ suffered *before* us. He suffers for our sake and thereby provides present grace and eternal redemption; but he is also our forerunner and paradigm. Our faith in him will not deliver us from the responsibility to follow "in his steps" (1 Pet 2:21). And following in his steps does not simply mean being nice or having integrity or strengthening one's devotional life. Following in his steps means following to Golgotha. We are only strengthened to go to Golgotha because he has gone before us; but because he has gone before us, there is no pretending that we can escape that terrifying pilgrimage. Despite the comfortably "Christian" culture in which we live, we know people who took up their own crosses. A young man quit a lucrative job in a major merchandising chain because it was involved in shady marketing practice and wanted him to acquiesce. A Chinese student who came to the United States to study law found an apartment at the divinity school and was invited to join in the community Bible study. She has now become a Christian, but because of her outspoken views can probably never return to China and her family again. A congregation made explicit the fact that it will welcome gay and lesbian members, and its denominational association severed all ties. Christ's cross does not always protect us from our own crosses.

6. In the larger context of 1 Pet 2:11–3:7 Christians in general (2:12) and wives in particular (3:1-2) are urged to practice evangelism by evangelical practice. Wives are explicitly told that it is better to be quiet about their faith and to convince their unbelieving husbands by their excellent behavior. The whole community is not necessarily enjoined to silence, but there is the clear implication that deeds speak at least as loudly as words and that, from an eschatological point of view, good behavior will reap the harvest of conversions. In part this is a counsel of prudence. Women will not get in trouble for acting decorously, while constant verbal plugs for the gospel may make for marital strain. Household slaves are probably not in the position to argue with their masters, but they are in an excellent position to live in ways that elicit admiration. In our own time, when the worst consequence of outspoken evangelism is usually that we feel a little foolish, we may need to be reminded of the power of speaking Christ's name aloud, and in unfamiliar places. Nonetheless, part of Christian fidelity in our day as in the time of 1 Peter is the life lived obediently—sometimes decorously, sometimes outrageously, but always faithfully, visibly.

1 PETER 3:8-22, FAITHFUL SUFFERING

COMMENTARY

3:8-12. This section concludes the discussion of appropriate social relations for Christians and provides the introduction to the discussion of the Christian relationship to the larger society, where the faithful often must suffer for their faith.

3:8. This verse clearly refers to relationships within the church community. "All" Christians—slaves and masters, husbands and wives—are to live according to the virtues set forth in this verse and, by their appropriate behavior within their station, show forth harmony, sympathy, brotherly love, compassion, and humility. The NIV and NRSV translations are probably right to render this verse as a series of imperatives, although it is written as a series of participles and might almost as well be descriptive as prescriptive: Here is who you are as Christian people (similar to 1 Corinthians 13, which Paul wrote to exhort the Corinthians to love but did so by describing that love).[131]

3:9. This verse continues the theme of faithful Christian behavior but begins to shift the focus from Christians' behavior toward each other to their actions toward the larger (hostile) society. This, too, represents a further application of the station tables, since by implication both slaves and wives are enjoined there to repay the opposition of their masters/husbands with obedience and kindness (2:18; 3:1-2). The exhortation to non-retaliation is congruent with demands we find in other early Christian literature (see Matt 5:38-42; Luke 6:29-31; Rom 12:19-21).

The correlation between blessing one's enemies and receiving a blessing also fits a major theme within the eschatological understanding of the early church: "For if you forgive others their trespasses, your heavenly Father will also forgive you; but if you do not forgive others, neither will your Father forgive your trespasses" (Matt 6:14-15 NRSV; see Luke 6:35). First Peter has noted this theme in its description of Christ's own suffering (2:23).[132] As so often in 1 Peter, the ethical injunction is set within the providential context of a call. Christians have been called both to bless and to receive a blessing. That call includes a present obligation and an eschatological promise (see 1:15; 2:9, 21; 5:10). Although the language is different, 1:1-9 has a similar combination of stressing God's choice, suffering in the present, and a future blessing for the faithful.

3:10-12. The quotation from Ps 34:12-16 provides not only a warrant but also a further elaboration of the shape of the faithful Christian community. There is an allusion to Ps 34:8 in 2 Pet 2:3 as well.[133]

The "life" and "good days" to which the psalm points are interpreted as marks of the eschatological promise, of the blessing that those who bless will receive. (For "life" as an eschatological gift, see also 3:7.) The injunction to be careful in speaking, and especially the reminder to avoid deceit, recalls 2:22, where under the most difficult circumstances no deceit was found in Christ's mouth. In following the direction of the psalm, Christians continue to walk "in his steps" (2:21). (The concern with the proper use of the tongue is also found in Jas 3:1-12.)

Balch points out that the call in 3:11 to "seek peace" is a summary of the themes of the preceding household rules.[134] And the reminder that God's ears are open to the prayers of the righteous becomes a further explanation of the warning that the prayers of Christian husbands would be hindered unless they behaved uprightly toward their wives (3:7).[135]

In all these ways, the psalm citation provides a rich and compelling summation of the themes of the preceding verses. In the contrast between the righteous, whom the Lord hears, and the evil, whom the Lord ignores, the psalm also moves the argument of 1 Peter toward the fuller discussion of unjust suffering at the hands of those who are evil. On the one hand, the psalm warns Christians not to practice evil, but it also inevitably draws toward the discussion of those who practice evil toward Christians.

3:13-22. These verses remind us of what our whole study of the epistle has shown: First Peter was written for a community that was suffering slander, if not persecution, from an unbelieving world. The question Christians face is how to hold fast to the promise of God's blessing and at the same time act appropriately toward those who are hostile to the faith.

3:13-15a. These verses suggest that on the whole Christians need not fear harm if they are zealous for the good—but the possibility of unjust suffering is not to be ruled out. (They are warned against offenses that deserve punishment in 4:15.) The "blessedness" pronounced on those who suffer for

---

131. Achtemeier keeps the adverbial force of the participles, with the main verb only implied; see Achtemeier, *1 Peter*, 220. Michaels points out that the virtues enjoined are quite similar to those in Rom 12:9-13. There Paul also writes descriptively, implying the imperative. See Michaels, *1 Peter*, 173.
132. See Perkins, *First and Second Peter, James, and Jude*, 60.
133. See Kelly, *The Epistles of Peter and Jude*, 138.

134. Balch, "Hellenization/Acculturation in 1 Peter," 94-95. Balch also notes the similar use of the phrase (from Ps 34:15b) in Heb 12:14 and *1 Clement* 22.
135. See Perkins, *First and Second Peter, James, and Jude*, 60.

righteousness recalls both the claim of v. 9 that those who do not return evil for evil will receive blessing at the end and the promise of the psalm cited in v. 12 that God's eyes are on "the righteous." The term "blessed" (μακάριος *makarios*), however, is not the same term as that found in v. 9 (εὐλογία *eulogia*). It is, rather, the "blessedness" pronounced in the beatitudes of the Sermon on the Mount. Indeed, the passage is reminiscent of Matt 5:11-12*a*: "Blessed are you when people revile you and persecute you and utter all kinds of evil against you falsely on my account. Rejoice and be glad, for your reward is great in heaven" (see also 1 Pet 2:20; 4:14; Luke 6:22). We remember that the injunction to slaves in chap. 2 becomes paradigmatic for all Christians who have to suffer for their faith.

The exhortation "Do not fear what they fear" is a quotation from Isa 8:12-13, where the prophet is told to take his cue from his faith and not from public opinion. We should not fear what everyone else fears but "the Lord God of hosts . . . let him be your fear" (NRSV).[136] First Peter takes the reference to the Lord God as the one to be feared and sanctified in Isaiah and applies that word to the Lord Christ. Let Christ be the object of your godly fear; let him be the one you sanctify in your hearts. "Sanctify" (ἁγιάζω *hagiazō*) is the same verb as that in the Lord's prayer: "Your name be sanctified" (Matt 6:9, author's trans.). The epistle has already quoted the next verse from Isa 8:14 in the context of the judgment against unbelievers who stumble on the rock that the builder rejected (2:8). Perhaps it is not too long a stretch to suggest that in the overall context of 1 Peter and of Isaiah 8, Christians are here reminded that the rock in whom they put their trust is the rock on whom unbelievers stumble and fall. Again we have the exegetical method that the writer of 1 Peter commends in 1:10-11, to find in the prophets those words that point to the present salvation of 1 Peter's readers and hearers.

3:15b-16. Here the writer spells out the way in which Christians, even when they suffer evil for doing good, may fear Christ and sanctify him in their hearts. The defense that the faithful are called to make might include defense in a legal proceeding, but more likely it means simply to give an account in the face of those who slander and abuse, as v. 16 would suggest.[137] Notice that those to whom Christians give an account will themselves have to give an account to God on the judgment day (4:5). That such a defense is to be made "always" and to "everyone" indicates that Christian witness is offered eagerly, and not just under compulsion. For 1 Peter, the whole content of the Christian faith can be summed up as "hope"—a motive and motif that runs through the whole epistle (see explicitly 1:3, 13, 21[3:5]; implicitly 1:8-9; 2:12; 4:13; 5:4, 6, 10). The gentleness and reverence that Christians show to outsiders in defending their hope mirror the sympathy and humility they show to one another in their communal life (v. 8). The appeal to a clear conscience is an appeal again to make sure that any charges brought against Christians are for their goodness, and not for their participation in evil (on conscience or consciousness, cf. Commentary on 2:19). The shame that their slanderers may face is probably both the immediate shame of bringing false accusations and the ultimate shame of standing before the God who judges and may yet redeem them (see 2:12; 4:5).[138]

3:17-18. In discussing these verses, Brox points out that v. 17 has something of the same tenor as 3:14 and 4:14. It is a description of the blessedness that is part of God's will for those who are faithful.[139] Kelly elaborates: "When well-doers suffer, they have the satisfaction of knowing that their suffering is not the moral consequence of their well-doing, even if it is their good actions which have brought their enemies' hostility down upon them. Indeed, in so far as they can

---

136. Selwyn thinks that the subjective genitive of the LXX has been interpreted here as an objective genitive—not "do not fear what they fear" but "do not fear with the fear of them." He cites Ps 64:2. See Selwyn, *The First Epistle of Peter*, 192. Brox points out that the situation of Israel before Assyria has become an example for Christians before their unbelieving opponents. See Brox, *Der erste Petrusbrief*, 159.

137. Selwyn lists other NT instances of ἀπολογία (*apologia*) or the root verb ἀπολογέομαι (*apologeomai*) with similar meaning: Luke 12:11; 21:14; Acts 19:33; 22:1; 26:1-2, 24. See Selwyn, *The First Epistle of Peter*, 193.

138. On the eschatological implications, see Michaels, *1 Peter*, 190-91. He also shows the resemblance of the whole purpose clause to 1 Pet 2:12*b*, both grammatically and theologically.

139. Brox, *Der erste Petrusbrief*, 162.

discern God's hand in their afflictions, Christians have grounds for rejoicing."[140]

Verse 18 presents the underlying christological grounding for the blessedness of Christian suffering. There is a remarkable range of variant readings for the first phrase of the verse. The *Textual Commentary on the New Testament* chose the text used by the NRSV rather than that used by the NIV—"Christ suffered for sins" (Χριστὸς περὶ ἁμαρτιῶν ἔπαθεν *Christos peri hamartiōn epathen*) rather than "Christ died for sins" (Χριστὸς περὶ ἁμαρτιῶν ἀπέθανεν *Christos peri hamartiōn apethanen*). The phrase seems more consistent with the argument of the epistle, and it is easier to see why later scribes would substitute the traditional phrase "he died" for the less traditional "he suffered" in conjunction with "for sins." In either case, the notion of suffering clearly means "suffering unto death" in the context of the reference to Christ's passion, resurrection, and ascension.[141] It is not only that such suffering will receive vindication in the last judgment, but that by such suffering Christians imitate the redemptive suffering of Christ himself. This is a pattern already seen in the discussion of the obligation of Christian slaves to suffer unjust treatment (see 2:21-25).

Indeed, the whole pattern of 2:18-25 is very like the pattern of 3:13-18. This suggests again that the relationship of slave to (unbelieving) master has become paradigmatic for the relationship of Christian to (unbelieving) opponent.

"If you endure when you do right and suffer for it, you have God's approval." (2:20 NRSV)

"If you do suffer for doing what is right, you are blessed." (3:14 NRSV)

"For to this you have been called, because [ὅτι *hoti*] Christ also suffered for you . . . so that you should follow in his steps." (2:21 NRSV)

"For [*hoti*] Christ also suffered for sins once for all, the righteous for the unrighteous, in order to bring you to God." (3:18 NRSV)

---
140. Kelly, *The Epistles of Peter and Jude*, 145.
141. See Metzger, *A Textual Commentary on the New Testament*, 692.

In chap. 2 the suffering of Christ first represents an example for maligned slaves to follow (2:21), but then it also becomes clear that his suffering is the grounds of their righteousness. Apart from Christ's suffering it would not be possible to follow him in obedience. In chap. 3, likewise, it becomes clear, in general scope if not in detail, that Christ's suffering, death, and resurrection are not only the example and motivation for Christian hope in suffering, but also are the grounding for Christian baptism, which makes possible the good conscience in which fidelity—even faithful suffering—is exercised. (There is a somewhat similar pattern in 4:12-14.) In fact, it is the parallel between these two passages, with their balance between the suffering of Christians and the redemption accomplished in Christ's suffering, that may help us to make sense of one of the most puzzling passages in 1 Peter, the claim that Christ preached to the spirits (3:19-20).

We can perhaps best understand this passage by going through it verse by verse. Verse 18 depends on the antitheses that in dramatic form show the astonishing nature of Christian redemption. Christ suffered once for all (as opposed to the ongoing suffering of Christian followers). Christ suffered as the righteous one (for the unrighteous). Christ died in the flesh (but was made alive in or by the Spirit). The first and second of these affirmations are powerful, but no longer surprising. In a context in which Christian slaves in particular and the whole community of believers in Asia Minor in general are being encouraged to stand fast in hope, there is comfort in the claim that the daily slanders that Christians suffer are finally overcome by the one great passion of Jesus Christ for the sake of the world. For all believers who know that they are also sinners (see 4:3), there is comfort in the realization that the death of the righteous Christ frees repentant sinners and "brings them to God."

The puzzling phrase is that Christ was "put to death in the body but made alive by the Spirit" (NIV) or "put to death in the flesh but made alive in the spirit" (NRSV). While resurrection throughout the NT is a great mystery, there is not generally the sense that some part of Christ died and some other part was brought to life, as if the body died and the soul lived. There are somewhat similar phrases in Rom 1:3 and 1 Tim 3:16, both formulas perhaps adapted by the letter writers to their circumstances.[142] We have already seen in 1:24 that the flesh is associated with the perishable, on the basis of Isa 40:6-8. Michaels's suggestion that the flesh represents Christ in his earthly limitation and the Spirit in his resurrected glory is as plausible as any: "If 'flesh' is the sphere of human limitations, of suffering, and of death (cf. 4:1), 'Spirit' is the sphere of power, vindication, and a new life."[143] In the larger context of chaps. 3–4, "flesh" also might be the realm of human passions and intentions, those misdirected volitions that put Christ to death; if so, he was put to death "by the flesh" but raised "by the Spirit." This is also a possible translation of the Greek.[144]

3:19-21. In part one suspects the reference to "Spirit" here provides the transition to the claim in vv. 19-20 that Christ preached "to the spirits." The ἐν ᾧ (*en hō*) with which v. 19 begins may not be a direct reference to the Spirit (as in their different ways the NIV and the NRSV both take it), but rather a circumstantial adverb, "in which circumstances" or "when" (cf. 1:16).[145] Verse 19*b* is the subject of much scholarly discussion. When did Christ do this? What spirits? How does this verse relate to 4:6 (if at all)?[146] While trying to adjudicate the various claims, two disclaimers should be kept in mind. First, the material is complicated, its historical and religious background uncertain, and its meaning unclear. This statement is one of those NT passages from which contemporary readers realize that the first Christians lived in a world with radically different presuppositions from their own—some of them so different that they cannot be reconstructed with any confidence. Second, the way in which one interprets the meaning of vv. 19-20 is not particularly crucial for understanding the larger argument of the epistle or even of the chapter. What the epistle here affirms is that the saving act of Christ's suffering, death,

resurrection, and ascension is laid hold of by believers in their baptism. His saving act and their baptism together "bring [the faithful] to God" (3:18). That the nature of one moment in that saving act is hard to reconstruct does not make the basic thrust of the letter's claim any less clear or any less powerful.

There are three basic interpretations of the claim that Jesus preached to the spirits in prison. The third interpretation is the most persuasive, but questions remain. The three options noted here are nicely outlined in the NIV study Bible. (1) Before his incarnation, Jesus preached to the disobedient people of Noah's time, perhaps through Noah himself. (2) Between his death and resurrection, Jesus descended to the place of the dead and preached to the spirits of the evil people of Noah's time. (3) Between his death and resurrection, Jesus ascended to the realm of the wicked angels (sons of God) who are mentioned in Gen 6:2, 4 as forerunners of Noah and the wickedness of Noah's time. There Jesus proclaimed God's victory over all principalities and powers.

In deciding which interpretation is most likely, one should begin by noting that it may not be the case that this claim about the risen Christ's preaching to the spirits represents the same affirmation as 4:6, where the gospel is proclaimed even (or also) to the dead. For instance, in 3:19 the spirits receive some kind of proclamation (the verb is κηρύσσω [*kēryssō*]), while in 4:6 the dead have clearly received the proclamation of the gospel (εὐαγγελίζω *euangelizō*). We need to begin by trying to understand 3:19, and then in studying 4:6 see whether the affirmations are really the same.

In 3:19 it is clear that the proclamation described took place after the resurrection, and it is the risen Lord who did the proclaiming. The puzzle is, Who were the spirits to whom such proclamation was made? The epistle tells us that they are spirits who did not obey during the time of Noah. This suggests two possibilities. Either these are the spirits of the people whose disobedience is contrasted to Noah's obedience, and who perished in the flood. Or these spirits are the offspring of the intercourse between the "sons of God" and mortal women, described in the puzzling passage Gen 6:1-4, a passage that precedes the story of Noah and also leads into it. (Genesis 6:5 seems to be a comment

---

142. See Selwyn, *The First Epistle of Peter*, 196-97.
143. Michaels, *1 Peter*, 205.
144. This is close to Achtemeier's proposal, Achtemeier, *1 Peter*, 239.
145. See Selwyn, *The First Epistle of Peter*, 197.
146. For discussions, see Michaels, *1 Peter*, 196-211; Selwyn, *The First Epistle of Peter*, 314-62; Bo Reicke, *The Epistles of James, Peter, and Jude*, AB 37 (New York: Doubleday, 1964) 109-15; Achtemeier, *1 Peter*, 244-46.

on Gen 6:1-4; the behavior of the sons of God and the mortal women is part of the wickedness God condemns.)

William Joseph Dalton, in a thorough and largely persuasive discussion of this passage, has searched other literature roughly contemporaneous with 1 Peter and found evidence that there was considerable speculation about the offspring of the angels discussed in Gen 6:1-4.[147] He judiciously set this passage in the context of the whole epistle:

The strategy of the letter is not to fire the addressees with new enthusiasm for the conversion of the pagan world, but to enable them to reflect on their Christian calling and the value of suffering for Christ's sake, so that they can stand firm and faithful despite their experience of alienation. This last point is particularly important for the understanding of 1 Peter 3:19: Christians are not being called on to imitate the example of Christ by going out and heroically proclaiming the gospel to the most notorious sinners. On the contrary, the strategy of 1 Peter is the strategy of survival.[148]

In searching comparative literature for an understanding of who the spirits might be, Dalton focuses especially on the book of Enoch, in which spirits (as usually in the NT) are supernatural spirits and not the souls of dead persons.[149] Furthermore, in *1 Enoch* 10:4-13, the warning for Noah to prepare for the flood is closely connected with the "binding" of the angels in Gen 6:1-4. These angels were blamed for leading people astray in the rebellion that led to the flood.[150]

Dalton further thinks that the prison in which the spirits were imprisoned was for the wicked spirits awaiting judgment and that it was probably located in the lower heavens, between earth and the throne of God.[151] While the verb κηρύσσω (*kēryssō*) can refer to preaching the gospel, both in the NT it often has the more general meaning of "proclaiming" or "declaring." In this context, it refers to a declaration of victory.[152] Dalton also says that when the NT writers refer to Christ's descent into the realm of the dead, they always explicitly say that Christ went "down": "The verb πορεύομαι *poreuomai* [I go] found in 1 Pet. 3:19, is never used. On the contrary it is commonly used for the ascent of Jesus into heaven."[153] Selwyn points out that "in the Patristic evidence before A.D. 190 . . . despite the popularity of the doctrine of Christ's 'harrowing of hell,' 1 Pet. iii 18ff. is never quoted as authority for it."[154] According to Dalton, the purpose of 3:19 is to provide encouragement for the exhortation of 3:14, "Do not fear what they fear, and do not be intimidated."[155] Encouragement is given in the memory of the risen Christ, who, vindicated by God, ascended to the presence of God. On the way to God's throne, he stopped at the prison of the evil spirits of Genesis 6 and there declared his victory over them and over evil.

Other "ascension" material in the NT may be pertinent. The hymn in Phil 2:6-11 suggests Christ's victory over powers "underneath the earth" as well as in heaven. Ephesians 1:20-21 notes that Christ's ascension places him over all subordinate spirits but with no reference to their location. First Timothy 3:16 includes the distinction between the realms of flesh and spirit, the idea of vindication, and ascension to glory. It may also reflect something of the same thought world as 1 Pet 3:19-21.

While I am largely persuaded by Dalton's extensive argument, other interpreters are more inclined to believe that Christ preached to the souls of those people who were destroyed in Noah's flood. Others maintain that the prison of evil spirits was to be found in the underworld and not in the mid-heavens.[156] Given our present state of

---

147. Dalton, *Christ's Proclamation to the Spirits*.
148. Dalton, *Christ's Proclamation to the Spirits*, 23. Dalton also argues that vv. 19-21 are a baptismal catechesis inserted within a hymn fragment (3:18-22), but this source-critical claim is not crucial to his argument. See Dalton, *Christ's Proclamation to the Spirits*, esp. 26.
149. Dalton, *Christ's Proclamation to the Spirits*, 153-54.
150. Dalton, *Christ's Proclamation to the Spirits*, 167-68. These are apparently the same spirits mentioned in 2 Pet 2:4 and Jude 6:1.
151. Dalton, *Christ's Proclamation to the Spirits*, 159-61.
152. Dalton, *Christ's Proclamation to the Spirits*, 153-59.
153. Dalton, *Christ's Proclamation to the Spirits*, 162. See also Acts 1:10-11. Dalton does not here list any examples. The verb is also used in 3:22, with clear reference to the ascension. See Dalton, *Christ's Proclamation to the Spirits*, 162n. 73.
154. Selwyn, *The First Epistle of Peter*, 340.
155. Dalton, *Christ's Proclamation to the Spirits*, 124, 127.
156. For the first argument, see Perkins, *First and Second Peter, James, and Jude*, 65; Goppelt, *A Commentary on I Peter*, 259, who thinks Christ preached the gospel, not victory, there. On the second argument, see Reicke, *The Epistles of James, Peter, and Jude*, 109-11, who thinks the "spirits" may have included the disobedient people of Noah's time as well as the angels, that the location of their prison may be in the underworld, and that Christ preached the gospel to them in prison, an example to the readers of 1 Peter to be forthright in declaring the gospel to their pagan opponents (109-11). Kelly, *The Epistles of Peter and Jude*, 155-57, reads the text much as Dalton does. Brox, *Der erste Petrusbrief*, 181, acknowledges our distance from this tradition and remains agnostic about its details.

knowledge, it is hard to see how these issues can be finally resolved.

What is clear is that v. 19 takes its place in the whole movement of 3:18-22, wherein Christ's suffering, death, resurrection, and ascension comprise the normative narrative that gives courage and significance to the suffering Christians of Asia Minor. Christ's suffering gives meaning to their suffering, and his victory provides them the promise of eschatological victory as well. (The passage also recapitulates and expands on the description of the work God does in Christ, which consists of Christ's suffering and subsequent glory, 1:11-12.)

Just as the reference to Christ's resurrection "in the Spirit" led directly into the reminder of his proclamation to the spirits (v. 19), so also the reference to the disobedient spirits of Noah's time leads into the description of Noah as prefiguring Christian baptism (vv. 20-21). Using the flood as a type for Christian baptism requires some metaphorical athleticism, since Noah's family was saved from the water and Christians are saved through the water—though one can say that the water that destroyed the disobedient provided safety for the obedient (ἀντίτυπος *antitypos*; cf. Heb 9:24; for τύπος [*typos*], see Rom 5:14; Heb 8:5). The few who are saved are Noah and his family. There is certainly the implication that the Christians of Asia Minor, though few in number, are saved, while the far more numerous host of the disobedient are destined for destruction—unless, of course, they are shamed into repentance. In this regard the reference to God's patience also has typological force.[157] The God who was patient in the time of Noah is also patient now in the time of 1 Peter. The end is coming, but has not yet come. There is still hope that the disobedient "Gentiles" may be shamed into believing (as in 3:16).[158] Verses 21-22 comprise the one passage in 1 Peter in which baptism is mentioned explicitly, though, as noted above, remembrance of baptism provides an implicit background for many of the letter's themes.

The contrast between the washing that removes dirt from the body and the baptism that appeals (or makes a pledge) to God may be simply a rhetorical play on the ways water is used (see Eph 5:26). It may, however, as Dalton suggests, represent a contrast between baptism and circumcision, which removes the unseemly foreskin from the body without working the salvation that is available in baptism. The clearest analogy would be Col 2:11-12: "In him also you were circumcised with a circumcision made without hands, by putting off the body of the flesh in the circumcision of Christ; when you were buried with him in baptism you were also raised with him through faith in the power of God, who raised him from the dead" (NRSV, using the marginal reading for v. 11). Here the "putting off" of baptism is implicitly contrasted with the "putting off" of the circumcision that is made "with hands," the physical removal of the foreskin.[159] Dalton also points out that the syntax of this verse implies a strong contrast between what baptism is and what it is not. Were the reference to washing, the epistle would more likely read "Not only through the removal of dirt from the body, but also as a appeal."[160] Further clarity about the meaning of this passage depends in part on how far one would think either the author or the recipients of this letter would be sensitive to distinctions between circumcision and baptism.

Even harder than understanding the first part of this contrast is understanding the second part. The NRSV understands baptism here as "an appeal to God for a good conscience," or as in the marginal note, "a pledge to God from a good conscience." The NIV translates the phrase "the pledge of a good conscience toward God." The NIV study Bible interprets the translation as: "The act of baptism is a

---

157. Kelly, *The Epistles of Peter and Jude*, 158, sees the reference to God's patience as a reading of Gen 6:3.

158. Dalton agrees with the typological and eschatological force of the reference but doubts that it has much to do with hope for the pagans. This is in keeping with his insistence that Christ's preaching to the spirits did not include any hope of their repentance. See Dalton, *Christ's Proclamation to the Spirits*, 191.

159. The term for "putting off" is different in Colossians (ἀπέκδυσις *apekdysis*) from that in 1 Peter (ἀπόθεσις *apothesis*). Dalton, who makes the argument for a reference to circumcision, shows other places in the NT where "putting off" refers to those practices that the (newly baptized) Christian leaves behind. See Dalton, *Christ's Proclamation to the Spirits*, 200-202.

160. The term for "putting off" is different in Colossians (ἀπέκδυσις *apekdysis*) from that in 1 Peter (ἀπόθεσις *apothesis*). Dalton, who makes the argument for a reference to circumcision, shows other places in the NT where "putting off" refers to those practices that the (newly baptized) Christian leaves behind. See Dalton, *Christ's Proclamation to the Spirits*, 203. The discussion of the foreskin as "filth" in Jewish and early Christian writing is less persuasive, as is the comparison with Jas 1:21. One needs to be persuaded of the reference in the James passage to make it work in 1 Peter. See Dalton, *Christ's Proclamation to the Spirits*, 203-6.

commitment on the part of the believer in all good conscience to make sure that what baptism symbolizes becomes a reality in his life."

The word variously translated as "appeal" or "pledge" is ἐπερώτημα (*eperōtēma*). Dalton shows how seldom the term is used to mean "request" or "appeal" in other Greek literature, though his own preference for "pledge" relies largely on literature considerably later than 1 Peter.

The writer of 1 Peter uses the word "conscience" (συνείδησις *syneidēsis*) also in 2:19 and 3:16. In each case the term seems to refer not so much to a subjective attitude as to an orientation of the person toward God. In 2:19 it is the conscientious relationship toward God that makes suffering endurable and worthy. In 3:16 it is conscientious confession that will help shame the opponents before the judgment of God. Suffering and confession grounded confidently in God show forth "good conscience" and bear the fruits of faithfulness. Just as faithful suffering and faithful confession are grounded in God and directed toward God, so also conscientious baptism puts off what is fleshly and cleaves wholeheartedly to God, who is Spirit. It is that wholehearted binding to God that is either pledged or (less likely) besought in whatever words the baptized person professes.

The power of God as Spirit, the power that saves the baptized, is manifested in Christ's resurrection, which is the Spirit's work or occurs within the sphere of the Spirit's power (see 3:18). Perhaps the best parallel is Heb 10:22-23: "Let us approach with a true heart in full assurance of faith, with our hearts sprinkled clean from an evil conscience and our bodies washed with pure water. Let us hold fast to the confession of our hope without wavering" (NRSV).[161]

The key question is what interpretation makes most sense in the light of the larger movement of 1 Peter's discussion of Christ's passion and victory and of the believers' baptism and faith. In this context it seems most likely that the "conscience" to which the letter refers is that assurance by which believers lay hold in baptism of the victory Christ has attained on their behalf.

3:22. This verse is very close to 1 Tim 3:16 in its affirmation.[162] It brings the passage on baptism full circle to a reminder that the shape and significance of the Christian life are grounded in the story of Jesus' suffering and victory. It is not, finally, baptism that saves, but the resurrection of the Christ into whom the faithful are baptized. In baptism, Christians with good conscience and full assurance lay hold of that victory that Christ achieved over his sufferings and that he promises over their sufferings as well.

---

161. See Dalton, *Christ's Proclamation to the Spirits*, 211. Much of Dalton's discussion of the "pledge" involved in baptism refers to uses of ἐπερώτημα (*eperōtēma*) and to baptismal practices from the late second century and later.

162. This again lends some credence to Dalton's reconstruction of the basic shape of this passage and its affirmation of Christ's subordination of the spirits by his resurrection and ascension.

REFLECTIONS

1. This section of 1 Peter raises an issue for contemporary Christians that is central to much early Christian literature: the issue of non-retaliation in the face of evil. The call to endure suffering rather than to return it in kind is set here as elsewhere in the context of the eschatological promise: The one who blesses now, and perhaps especially the one who blesses the enemy, will "inherit a blessing" when the full inheritance promised in Christ comes to fruition at the last days.

Among Christians who are or have been the victims of abuse and oppression, the call to non-retaliation has of late had a bad reputation. Cannot this represent the means by which oppressors play on the piety of the oppressed simply to prolong evildoing? As usual it is easy for those of us who are relatively powerful in our society to urge non-retaliation on those who are relatively powerless. Nonetheless the larger context nuances the claim that Christians are to suffer for doing right rather than to return evil for evil. Within the context of 1 Peter, Christians are to suffer if need be, but not to suffer silently. They join the struggle against oppression by speaking honestly and powerfully of what they hold dear, making their defense unapologetically. Christ himself becomes an example of this activity, of course, and when we read the Gospel accounts of his passion we note that he was by no means altogether passive. His silence and his speeches manifest power in weakness, and that power is as clear as the weakness. Thus for Christians the unwillingness to abuse and to slander does not mean the willingness to take abuse and slander without speaking the word that might convict or even convince those who do the abusing and slandering.

In twentieth-century America, the great example of non-retaliation is Martin Luther King, Jr. But his nonviolence was not non-resistance. On the contrary, the courage he and his followers showed was the courage of active, and risky, faith.

Further, the claim that those who suffer unjustly will inherit a blessing is not simply a promise of pie in the sky. It sets the hope that informs the whole context of 1 Peter—that Christ's resurrection and ascension are the guarantee of the victory of his cause over the forces of evil. Christians can refuse to do violence to those who oppress them because Christians are biding their time, or biding God's time, until the (near) moment when they will be vindicated and their oppressors shamed.

2. It is, perhaps, in this context that we can make the best sense of the passage about Jesus' declaring or preaching to the "spirits in prison." That the evil spirits who led people astray in Noah's time are in prison is itself a sign of hope. That Christ preached victory over them (as Dalton interprets this event) makes clear that the fulfillment of that hope is accomplished in Jesus Christ. The christological image of Christ as victor lies just beneath the surface here. To be sure, Christ suffered as Christians suffer, but in his resurrection he not only overcame suffering but he also raised his flag of victory over the evil forces that bring suffering on the just and the faithful. The recounting of this proclamation is itself a way of grounding hope; so contemporary Christians, too, need to live with the promise that the apparent victories of this world are not the final victories—that the final victory is in God's hand and is foreshadowed by Christ's resurrection.

It is this theme of Christ's victory over suffering and evil that makes 1 Pet 3:13-22 an especially appropriate passage for Easter (Cycle A, Easter 6 in the *Revised Common Lectionary*). Any occasional annoyance at the tendency of the lectionary to avoid tough verses fades before the assignment of this text on preaching to the spirits. Surely the lectionary rightly sees this as a passage grounded in the triumph of Easter, in many ways similar to the great hymn in Phil 2:6-11. As with Philippians, the christological affirmation has ethical implications. Here, in the light of Christ's triumph, Christians can stand fast in the face of opposition. So, too, the text fits well with the assigned text of Paul's speech at the Areopagus (Acts 17:22-31). Paul begins his sermon with an appeal to the common religious experience of his audience but ends with the shocking and difficult claim that the God in whom we live and move and have our being is also—and above all—the God who has raised Jesus Christ from the dead. This is the promise Dionysius the Areopagite and the woman named Damaris heard and believed, as have all the believers to whom 1 Peter was written, all of whom turned from the worship of many idols to serve the true God, who has made "angels, authorities and powers" subject to the risen Lord.

3. First Peter 3:18-22 is again assigned as the epistle reading for the first Sunday in Lent in Cycle B. By beginning with v. 18, the reading moves away from the stress on Christian courage in the face of opposition to the appropriate Lenten stress on Christ's passion for the sake of sinners. The Old Testament reading, Gen 9:18-19, provides the data for 1 Peter's claim that eight persons were on Noah's ark. The Gospel lesson, Mark 1:9-15, provides an example of proclamation from Jesus' ministry, perhaps to balance the proclamation to the spirits after his death and resurrection—though if this interpretation is right the content and purpose of proclamation in the two instances were strikingly different.

4. The injunction to "not fear what they fear" (3:14 NRSV) represents an insightful reading of the nature of idolatry. Idolatry is not only worship of the wrong god, but also it is fear of the wrong power. It is to give the non-gods the power that should belong only to God—to frighten us, to make us awe-struck. The antidote to false fear is right worship: "But in your hearts set apart Christ as Lord." Paul reminds us that "whatever does not proceed from faith is sin" (Rom 14:23 NRSV). In the context of 1 Peter, all action that is based on fear of powers less than God is also sin.

Excessive nationalism may be the other face of excessive fear of others. Egotism is the game we play to fend off the fear of our own insignificance. The need constantly to assert the superiority of our race or our faith or our way of living poorly masquerades our fear of others—that they may take away what we hold most dear, that what they hold most dear is better than what we have.

For the people to whom Isaiah spoke in the passage quoted in 1 Peter, what they feared was Assyria and its power. All of us have constructed Assyrias in our imaginations, dreaded forces so threatening that we cower in fear. Isaiah's strong word is still a word for us:

> For the LORD spoke thus to me . . . and warned me not to walk in the way of this people saying: Do not call conspiracy all that this people calls conspiracy, and do not fear what it fears, or be in dread. But the LORD of hosts, him you shall regard as holy. (Isa 8:11-13 NRSV)

First Peter simply underlines and elaborates that claim by reminding us that the one we hallow in our hearts is the Lord Christ, who alone brings us to the holy God.

5. There is a rich understanding of the meaning of baptism in this passage. According to 1 Peter, the waters of baptism have symbolic or sacramental power. But that power is confirmed through the conscience or intention of the believer; and yet the believers can only lay hold of the victory God has already won in Jesus Christ.

The waters are prefigured by the waters of the flood, and just as those waters had tremendous power to destroy the sinful (and to save the righteous), so also baptism has tremendous power. It does not work superficially, like washing your hands—or on another reading, like circumcision—but it works to bring the whole person into a lasting relationship with God.

Baptism also requires the "conscience" or "intention" or "pledge" of the person being baptized. There is no sense here that baptism operates outside of the determination of the person being baptized. Precisely what the difficult phrase in 3:21*b* means is very hard to determine, but we can be quite sure that baptism involves the volition of the one who chooses to lay hold of God in Christ. (Of course, we have seen from the beginning of this epistle that the antecedent act is always God's call and election of the faithful.)

But, above all, baptism enacts the power of Jesus Christ, who, in his resurrection, ascension, and power over all the lesser authorities, also has the power that baptism requires; he has the ability to bring us to God. (Note that the stress here, unlike in Romans 6, is on Christ's resurrection and victory, not on his dying and rising.)

This passage says nothing explicit about the means of baptism or the required age of the person being baptized. It does point to a theology of baptism in which the sacrament, the intention, and the work of God in Christ are conjoined. In our time, when baptism has too often become the ecclesiastical equivalent of the baby shower (for infant baptism) or of getting a driver's license (for adolescent "believers'" baptism), 1 Peter calls us again to the utter seriousness of the sacrament—the mystery of faith conjoined with the mystery of Christ, gifts that lie too deep for words.

1 PETER 4:1-11, LIVING OUT SALVATION COMMENTARY

There is an almost circular movement from 1 Pet 3:8 to 1 Pet 4:11. In 3:8-17, the Christians of Asia Minor are encouraged to live lives that are faithful and mutually upbuilding. In 3:18-22, this behavior is grounded in the suffering, resurrection, and ascension of Jesus Christ. In 4:1-11, the christological claims of the epistle again become the grounds for moral exhortation—for directions for the faithful life.

4:1-2. The epistle makes clear that it is the story of Christ's suffering, death, resurrection, and ascension that provides motive and measure for the life of faithful Christians, "since, therefore Christ suffered . . . arm yourselves."

The difficult part of the first verse of this chapter is the reference to life in the flesh and the relationship of that description to the larger claim that those who suffer in the flesh have somehow "finished with sin." We have already seen the clue to the claim that Christ suffered in the flesh in the discussion of 3:18. The claim that Christ died in the flesh or suffered in the flesh is not simply the claim that his body suffered and died. In this verse even more than in 3:18 it seems clear that (as is often the case for Paul) the flesh is not only the realm of mortality but also the realm of selfish desire that stands in opposition to the will of God. The term "flesh" here is closely parallel to the words of v. 2: "human desires." In the realm of human desires, Christ suffered and died in order to triumph over those human desires in the power of the Spirit.[163]

When the readers of the epistle are told to "arm" themselves, it is presumably to do battle against those same fleshly powers that provided the context for Christ's suffering. The metaphor is military and looks ahead to the battle against Satan, the roaring lion of 5:8.[164] It seems plausible to suggest that the realm of the flesh is the realm where Satan can tempt and hurt the faithful, though it is not necessarily the realm under his control. The "same" understanding presumably means the "same" understanding that Christ had and corresponds to the intention or understanding of v. 2, "the will of God." (Cf. Phil 2:2 where the Philippians are told to have "the same love." Does that mean mutual love, or does it mean love like the love that is "in Christ" in 2:1?)

In this context, the claim that "whoever suffers in the flesh has ceased from sin" makes rather more sense. This must be a parenthetical application of the story of Jesus to that of believers. It is not a further explication of the meaning of Christ's death, since he did not have to "cease from sin."[165] Suffering in the flesh does not mean having bodily pain; it means doing fierce battle against the forces of human desire—the realm of the flesh—and bearing the suffering that comes with that battle.[166] When one does battle against the realm of the flesh, one has already enlisted on the other side: the side of righteousness against sin; the side of the Spirit against the flesh. Choosing life rather than death, the faithful Christian has "ceased from sin," moved from the realm of the old into the new. This contrast will continue to control this section through its conclusion in v. 6.

We can schematize the contrasts of these two verses. To the world against which Christians do battle belong the "flesh" and "sin" (v. 1) and "human desires" (v. 2). To the realm in which faithful Christians live belong "the same intention" as Christ's and "the will of God." The contrast recalls Jesus' words to Peter in Mark 8:33: "You are setting your mind not on the things of God but on the

---

163. Goppelt, *A Commentary on I Peter*, 276-77, correctly points out that the christological formula "flesh/spirit" is here applied anthropologically. Perhaps more accurately, the anthropological implications of the christology are spelled out.

164. Goppelt lists a number of uses of the military image for faithful Christian life. See Goppelt, *A Commentary on I Peter*, 179n. 13.

165. For a Pauline reading in which Christ has taken on sin, though without being sinful, see Kelly, *The Epistles of Peter and Jude*, 166.

166. This is somewhat different from Goppelt's reading that the suffering unto death of Christian people is a necessary part of the conquest of sin (Goppelt, *A Commentary on I Peter*, 281-82), and from Perkins's more direct tie to baptismal language about dying and living again in Christ (Perkins, *First and Second Peter, James, and Jude*, 68). Kelly presents both a christological (Christ brought sin to a halt) and a baptismal (Christians have died to sin) interpretation as possibilities (Kelly, *The Epistles of Peter and Jude*, 167-68). First Peter 2:24 lends some weight to the christological proposal. Davids examines several proposals, none of them precisely like the one suggested here. See Davids, *The First Epistle of Peter*, 148-50.

things of humankind" (author's trans.). Christians in both texts are seen as living in a battle between two realms.

Of course, until Christ returns the realm in which we live (as in v. 2*b*) is "the realm of the flesh," so that even though Christians have suffered in the fleshly realm and put sin to rout, it is still within the realm of the flesh that they are bound to live. The NRSV marginal note, therefore, is much more helpful than the translation "earthly life." The realm of the flesh is under sentence and will be undone, but as yet it provides the sphere for Christian living.

4:3-4. These verses characterize the nature of the realm of the flesh and the shape of its opposition to the faithful. What is particularly striking is that the realm of the flesh is also the realm of the Gentiles. All the more obvious, therefore, is the reason why the realm of the flesh is both the realm the faithful have left behind and the realm in which they have to live out the rest of their earthly days. They are in the world, but not of it; among the Gentiles, but not of their number. (One needs to remember that "Gentiles" are "non-Christians," and not "non-Jews" in 1 Peter.) Kelly is certainly right in seeing rhetorical sarcasm in v. 3. "You have already spent time enough" means that you have already spent more than enough time.[167] The phrase the NRSV translates as "what the Gentiles like to do" represents the Greek term βούλημα (*boulēma*). *Boulēma* means "the intention" or "the will" or "the disposition" of the Gentiles, so that the will of the Gentiles is contrasted with the will of God (using another Greek term, θέλημα [*thelēma*]) in v. 2*b* (in Rom 9:19, *boulēma* is used for the will or intention of God). The phrase "will of the Gentiles," therefore, is directly parallel to "passions of humans" in v. 2*a*; the term for "passions" (ἐπιθυμίαι *epithymiai*) recurs in the catalogues of vices in v. 3. These Christians had formerly lived according to human passions and Gentile intentions; now they will live according to the will of God. (The whole "then" but "now" pattern was anticipated in 1:14-15.)

The catalogues of vices here recall other NT lists and, therefore, may be seen as fairly standard rather than as representing some particular insight into the unique vices of the pagans of Asia Minor. See Rom 13:13-14 and Gal 5:19-21, cited by Kelly,[168] but also 1 Cor 6:9-11, which shows the same temporal distinctions between what these Gentile Christians used to be and what they are now. The old ways are the "futile ways inherited from your ancestors" (1:18 NRSV). Selwyn gives the most thorough discussion of each of the offenses listed, along with appropriate parallels from non-Christian literature.[169] The fact that the list climaxes and concludes with the reference to lawless idolatry recalls Rom 1:18-27. In 1 Peter, as in Romans, idolatry is the fundamental mistake of the pagan, and the other vices are manifestations of that profoundly erroneous orientation.

The epistle now returns to a familiar theme, the way in which pagans slander the Christians. Now this description is given a particular motivation and a theologically loaded description. The motivation for the "Gentiles" to slander the Christians is that the believers had formerly joined in the dissipation the pagans still enjoy. The pagans are astonished that their former partners in dissolution now stand aside, and—jealous or angry or appalled—the pagans speak evil against them.

The description of this slander is not only that it is untrue and vicious but also that it is blasphemous (for earlier descriptions of the pagans' slandering of Christians, see 2:12; 3:9, 16; for Christ as an example of one suffering such slander, see 2:22-23). The most obvious and probably the most persuasive explanation for this slander against Christians is that for pagans to speak against those who are faithful is to speak against the one in whom they have faith—and that is blasphemy.[170] Certainly in Mark 3:28-30, the false accusation against Jesus—that he acts under the authority of Satan—is blasphemy, because it slanders the Spirit of God, which empowers and validates his ministry. We have already seen here that the suffering of Christians replicates the suffering work of Jesus, and that slander against Christians recalls slander against Christ. So

---

167. Kelly, *The Epistles of Peter and Jude,* 179.
168. Kelly, *The Epistles of Peter and Jude,* 170.
169. Selwyn, *The First Epistle of Peter,* 211-12.
170. See Goppelt, *A Commentary on I Peter,* 287, for a similar reading. Selwyn points out that βλασφημέω (*blasphēmeō*) can also be used of slandering other people without the theological overtones, but reading Matt 12:31-36 (some of it par. Mark 3:1), he comes to a suggestion much like that in this study.

perhaps it is not inappropriate to say that when the faithful are maligned, the God they worship is maligned—and that is blasphemy.

4:5-6. These verses place the distinction between then and now and between Gentiles and believers into the even larger eschatological framework, in the perspective that informs the whole epistle (see 1:5, 7, 13; 4:13, 17; 5:4). Then (formerly) those who are now Christian joined the pagans in their dissipation. Now the pagans judge and misjudge the Christians for their faithfulness. Then (finally) the pagans will themselves be judged by the One who judges the living and the dead. There is a nice verbal echo in this passage. In 3:15, Christians are always to be ready to "make a defense" or to "give an account" to those pagans who demand it of them. In 4:5, it is the pagans who will need to give an account to the God who even now "stands ready" to judge them. One may recall that this final judgment may not lead only to condemnation, but instead, for some at least, to shame and perhaps—by implication—to repentance (see 3:16).

The reminder that God is judge of both the living and the dead leads to the much interpreted and much disputed claim of v. 6. Before attempting a provisional solution to its problems, we note two things. First, it is the claim of v. 5 that is central to the argument in this portion of 1 Peter; v. 6 is an expansion and elaboration on that verse, and one need not be clear about the meaning of the elaboration in order to understand the fundamental claim that God is judge of all. In other words, the amount of exegetical ink used on this passage is not proportional to its centrality to the purposes of the letter. The issues are fascinating as we try to reconstruct the thought world of some early Christians, but it is not central to either the kerygmatic or the paraenetic strategies of 1 Peter. Second, 4:6 has often been combined with 3:19 as if these were clearly descriptions of one event. However, the language and function of the two passages are rather different, and v. 6 needs to be interpreted on its own terms.

There are two possible interpretations of the claim that the gospel was proclaimed to the dead. The first is that the gospel was proclaimed to those who had died prior to Christ's coming—either in Hades or wherever was understood to be the abode of the dead. The second is that the gospel was proclaimed to those Christian believers who had died after Christ's coming but before the writing of 1 Peter and, therefore, before the final judgment. Though they are not now alive, their previous sins (in the flesh) have been judged, and they will—with the Christians of 1 Peter's time—live forever with God in spirit.

There are persuasive arguments to be made for each of these claims, and the evidence for each claim consists in large measure in evidence against the other. Thus the discussion of the meaning of the passage can begin by noting that the "event" of 1 Pet 4:6 needs to be distinguished from the "event" of 1 Pet 3:19-20. It was suggested in the commentary on chap. 3 that the "spirits" to whom Christ preached were not the spirits of the departed dead, not even the spirits of those people who had disobeyed in the time of Moses. They were, rather, spiritual beings, either the angels of Gen 6:1-4 or their offspring, who dwelt in some abode below the heavenly home of God, and to them Christ declared victory as he ascended to heaven.[171]

In v. 6 the reference is clearly to the proclamation to "dead" human beings, and what is proclaimed is not victory; it is explicitly the gospel. The point of the verse is twofold: First, it emphasizes the universality of judgment—God judges both the living and the dead. Second, it provides hope for the Christians of Asia Minor as they think about these dead persons, hope that they, too, may be heirs of life through the Spirit.

Notice, too, that the contrast between flesh and spirit, which has permeated vv. 1-6, plays a crucial role in this climactic verse as well. Like the living, the dead have been judged in the realm of the flesh, but as with the living there is hope that they may live in the Spirit.

Many interpreters think that the function of this passage is to declare that judgment and salvation extend to those who lived before Christ's coming, to whom he declared the gospel after his crucifixion and resurrection. Goppelt thinks the affirmation is an expansion

---

[171]. Perkins thinks that the two passages refer to the same event, in both cases to preaching to the spirits of departed persons. See Perkins, *First and Second Peter, James, and Jude,* 68-69.

of the claims of 3:18-19 and a kind of affirmation of what Paul wrote in Rom 14:9: "For to this end Christ died and lived again, so that he might be Lord both of the dead and the living" (NRSV). Just as after his resurrection Christ preached to the rebellious spirits, so also he declared good news to those who had already suffered death as a consequence of their sins in the flesh. Perhaps he declared good news only to those whose behavior had already marked them as righteous. Perhaps he preached good news to all, so that the possibility of repentance and new life extended to all who had died before Christ's coming.[172]

An alternative explanation for this verse is provided by Dalton. He also finds a Pauline parallel, not in Romans but in 1 Thess 4:13-17:

But we do not want you to be uninformed, brothers and sisters, about those who have died, so that you may not grieve as others do who have no hope.... For the Lord himself, with a cry of command, with the archangel's call and with the sound of God's trumpet, will descend from heaven, and the dead in Christ will rise first. Then we who are alive, who are left. (NRSV)

The context of 1 Peter 4 is the eschatological judgment, when the dead will rise and the living and the dead will be judged. There is no reason given in this passage to think that it was Christ who proclaimed the gospel to the "dead." Rather, he was the subject of the gospel that was preached while they were still living.

Dalton suggests that this also makes the best sense of the conclusion of the verse, which he translates, "In order that, though judged in the flesh in the eyes of people, they might live in the spirit in the eyes of God."[173] The verse has a double contrast again: on the one side, judgment in the realm of the flesh, according to human standards; on the other side, vindication in the spirit according to God's standards (see Commentary on 4:2-3). That is, although the pagan slanderers might think the death of Christian believers is proof that their claims about God's vindication are false, in fact God will vindicate believers by bringing them at last to salvation.[174] How can we decide between these options? Certainly Dalton is right to see a parallel (an inclusio) between 3:18 and 4:6: "He was put to death in the flesh but made alive in the spirit" // "they have been judged in the flesh... (but will) live in the spirit."[175] The overall claim again is the correspondence between Christ's suffering, death, and consequent victory and the suffering, death, and consequent victory of believers. In this context, 1 Peter is read most consistently if the issue in 4:6 is the fate of believers who (like Christ) have suffered unto death and who, like him, will be vindicated in the spirit.[176]

Nonetheless, whichever way one interprets this verse the overall claim of this section of the epistle is that God is the righteous judge of all and that, therefore, Christians are to stand firm in their resistance to their old idolatry—despite the slander of their former fellow carousers—trusting to God, who will judge them justly and give them life in the Spirit. The phrase κατὰ θεόν (*kata theon*) might mean that Christians are to live in the Spirit "as God does" (NRSV), that they will live "by God's standard," or that their life is "in God's sphere" as opposed to the human sphere.[177] The whole claim is set in the contrast between the sphere of the flesh, where Christians suffer and are slandered, and the sphere of the spirit, in which they will be vindicated and will have life.

4:7. The eschatological basis for this epistle's hortatory emphasis comes to the foreground again. Christians need to live in the sphere of God, into which they have entered through baptism, because the judgment of God is not some distant possibility. It is at hand, at the door, drawing near. The two imperatives become another way of summing up what the epistle has said about standing fast in the midst of the Gentile world. "Think

---

172. See Goppelt, *A Commentary on I Peter*, 288-91. His reading depends in part on a somewhat different interpretation of 1 Pet 4:1 than given here. Death in the flesh is the necessary precondition for salvation p. 290).
173. Dalton, *Christ's Proclamation to the Spirits*.
174. Dalton finds a close parallel here in Wis 3:4. See Dalton, *Christ's Proclamation to the Spirits*, 238; the whole argument is found on 230-41.
175. Dalton finds a close parallel here in Wis 3:4. See Dalton, *Christ's Proclamation to the Spirits*, 238; the whole argument is found on 240-41.
176. The NIV translation basically reads the text Dalton's way by inserting "now" before "dead." Kelly, *The Epistles of Peter and Jude*, 273-76, also reads the text largely as Dalton does. See also Davids, *The First Epistle of Peter*, 153-55; and Achtemeier, *1 Peter*, 291. Brox remains agnostic about whether the dead hear the gospel when they are dead or heard it during their lives; the overall point of God's vindication of those who are faithful remains. See Brox, *Der erste Petrusbrief*, 195-201.
177. For the second alternative, see Davids, *The First Epistle of Peter*, 147.

wisely" (σωφρονέω *sōphroneō*) as opposed to the foolishness of your former life. "Be sober" (νήφω *nēphō*) as opposed to the various forms of excess in which your neighbors revel. The call to sobriety reminds the readers of 1:13, where the author also uses the term *nēphō* ("be sober") as an exhortation in the light of Christ's impending final revelation, and it points ahead to 5:8, where sobriety arms the believer against the weapons of the devil. It also contrasts with the third verse of this chapter, the reminder that the Gentiles prefer drunkenness to sobriety, and the implicit reminder that not so long ago, so did the hearers of this letter.[178] The writer provides the two exhortations to "think wisely" and to "be sober" and then closes the verse with a bare prepositional phrase, "for prayers." Does this mean that wisdom and sobriety are the preconditions for right prayer, as both the NRSV and the NIV translations seem to assume? (A possible parallel would be the exhortation to husbands about proper living in 3:7; see 3:12.)[179] Or does it mean that thinking wisely and keeping sober prepare the Christian for prayer?[180] Or is prayer itself the primary means of thinking rightly and staying sober?

4:8. "Above all" echoes directly the "end of all" of v. 7. As all things come to an end, above all things hold fast to love. Love here is love for the other members of the community and brings us back to the strong stress on upbuilding community life we have already seen in 3:8. The difficult part of the verse is the second half: "Love covers [over] a multitude of sins." What can this mean? The phrase may already have been almost proverbial for early Christians. It occurs in Jas 5:20, where the particular manifestation of love—bringing back a straying Christian—covers a multitude of sins. Behind it lies Prov 10:12, and in various forms it is found in a number of early Christian sources.[181] Selwyn cites those who interpret this declaration as meaning that love covers over the sins of unbelievers and opponents.[182] In the context of this epistle, however, the concern about covering sins seems to be a concern about the life of believers, not of those who are hostile to them. The statement cannot mean that sins are excused by love, since the sphere of sin is the sphere that is judged by God and left behind by believers (4:2-4). It cannot mean that love hides the multitude of sins, since the all-judging God sees with eyes that miss nothing (4:5-6).[183] Rather, the point seems to be that as suffering causes sin to pause by moving the faithful Christian out of the realm of sin, love (which is the manifestation of faith) is a sign and fruit of the move from the old sphere, where sin had power, to the new sphere, marked by sobriety, faith, and love. It is a sign not of the flesh but of the spirit and, therefore, of life according to God's purposes (4:6).[184] Just as faithful suffering in the flesh brings sin to a halt (4:1*b*), so also faithful loving covers sin over, puts it finally in the past.

4:9-11. These verses show what this love looks like in the community of faith. Hospitality was an important Christian virtue. Hospitality included both the willingness to serve as host for one's fellow Christians in worship and fellowship and the willingness of the local community to serve as host for itinerant prophets and preachers.[185] In 1 Peter, the context seems to be especially hospitality within the community of one's fellow Christians. But what does it mean to be in community according to the love that covers sins? The reminder that Christians are to be hospitable without complaining is a word pertinent enough in every generation that it needs no further comment. Verses 10-11*a* are similar to the discussions of spiritual gifts in 1 Corinthians and in Ephesians 4. The three key words of v. 10 in remarkably short compass show forth the epistle's understanding of charisms and responsibilities in the church. Christians

---

178. For other uses of the first verb see Rom 12:3 in the eschatological context of the Christian transformation, and Mark 5:15, where the man who has been driven by demons when released by Christ is in his "right mind." For the second see in addition to 1 Pet 1:13 and 5:8, 1 Thess 5:6, 8, where the term is used in a very similar eschatological setting, and 2 Tim 4:1, where Timothy is urged to be sober "in the presence of God and of Christ Jesus, who is to judge the living and the dead, and in view of his appearing and coming" (NRSV).
179. Selwyn, *The First Epistle of Peter*, 216, makes this connection.
180. So Davids, *The First Epistle of Peter*, 156-57.
181. For a list see Kelly, *The Epistles of Peter and Jude*, 178.

182. See Selwyn, *The First Epistle of Peter*, 217.
183. Though this seems to be the meaning Selwyn finds most likely. See Selwyn, *The First Epistle of Peter*, 217.
184. Kelly's interpretation is rather close to this. See Kelly, *The Epistles of Peter and Jude*, 178. Davids, *The First Epistle of Peter*, 157-58, notes that in Proverbs the phrase refers to "covering over" another's sins without exacerbating a bad situation, though he acknowledges that may not be the meaning here. Michaels, *1 Peter*, 247, argues that "sin" is primarily a social phenomenon and that the love of the community can virtually blot it out.
185. For examples of other pertinent texts, see Michaels, *1 Peter*, 247-48.

are "gifted"; Christians are "stewards"; Christians "serve." Christians are gifted; their roles in the church are not their own accomplishments but are entirely from God. Christians are stewards; they are responsible for the faithful use of those gifts.[186] Christians serve; the right use of the gifts God has given is for mutual upbuilding, for the sake of other Christians.

The gifts God has given are also "manifold," so the examples in v. 11 must stand for a larger list of ministries. The two examples given, however, are exemplary as well as illustrative. God gifts Christians to speak, and God gifts Christians to act on behalf of one another.

In a brief phrase, 1 Peter provides a very high doctrine of proclamation, though of course there is no indication that preachers are a particular subgroup of Christians. One suspects the model is more like 1 Corinthians 14, with various Christians speaking in worship. Of course, this is both a promise and a warning. When one speaks, the promise is that the words may be God's own words to the people. Therefore, Christians should pay heed to what they say; they should live up to the high calling of faithful speaking. The exhortation recalls the strong view of proclamation in 1:12, that through the Holy Spirit, Christian preachers have brought to their congregations mysteries so mighty that angels fear to look upon them.

Serving, which is a gift in the first place, is not possible through the strength of the server, but only through the strength that God provides. So, then, God gives gifts; God gives words; God gives strength.

Verse 11 moves toward doxology. Since it is God who gives the gifts, gives the words, and gives the strength, then in all these things—in all things indeed—it is God who is to be glorified. That glorification is through Jesus Christ, whom the whole epistle has shown to be the One who brings Christians to God (3:18).

One may notice in these few verses the repetition of forms of the noun "all things" (πᾶς pas). The end of "all things" is near. Above "all things" have profound love for one another. In "all things" let God be glorified. This is not conversation about middling matters or modest steps. This is the one God claiming the glory due to God through Jesus Christ. Soon that glory will be made manifest as all things come to an end. Now above all things (all those things that are passing away) that glory is served through the love that Christians show to one another.

Because God is both the source and the end of all things, giver of gifts and words and strength through Jesus Christ, therefore the exhortation is bound to end in praise.[187]

---

186. Kelly points out that the word "steward" (οἰκονόμος *oikonomos*) is usually a technical word for the slave entrusted with management of the master's property. See Kelly, *The Epistles of Peter and Jude*, 180. The NRSV makes it sound more like a simile than a job description: "like stewards" rather than "as stewards."

187. The doxological delight that God has glory forever becomes again a comfort to Christians who now live "in the spirit as God does" (4:6). Selwyn, *The First Epistle of Peter*, 220, has a thorough discussion of doxologies in the NT.

REFLECTIONS

1. E. G. Selwyn (whose book of grammatical notes contains a hidden wealth of homiletical hints) quotes Lancelot Andrewes, who reads 1 Pet 4:1 along with Romans 6:

> To cease from sin, I say, understanding by sin, not from sin altogether—that is a higher perfection than this life will bear but as the Apostle expoundeth in the very next words (Romans 6:13) . . . from the dominion of sin to cease. For till we be free from death itself, which in this life we are not, we shall not be free from sin altogether; only we may come thus far . . . that sign "reign not," wear not a crown, sit not in a throne, hold no parliament within us, give us no laws; in a word . . . that we serve it not.[188]

---

188. Lancelot Andrewes, *Sermons*, vol. ii, pp. 202ff.; quoted in Selwyn, *The First Epistle of Peter*, 210.

2. The NIV translation of 4:4 ("they think it strange that you do not plunge with them into the same flood of dissipation") probably rests on a text from Strago cited by Selwyn and referring to rock pools filled to overflowing at high tide. This may be something of an etymological stretch as a translation, but it has the homiletical payoff of finding in the situation of the first-century pagans a striking analogy to the situation of Noah's contemporaries, who drowned in their own flood.[189]

3. This section of the letter draws heavily on a polarity or dialectic that can be characterized as the contrast between living in the sphere of the flesh and living in the sphere of the spirit. On the one hand, that contrast is between unbelievers and believers; on the other hand, it is a contrast between the past and the present.

For the writer of 1 Peter, the unbelievers are those who live by "human desires" rather than by "the will of God" (4:2). Those human desires stem from idolatry and result in all manner of licentiousness. To be Christian for this epistle is, as we have seen, to be a sojourner or resident alien; and one way to define a faithful person is to say that he or she stands against the fleshly devices and desires of the pagan outsiders. However, for 1 Peter even those who live in the fleshly sphere have not been entirely excluded from the possibility of mercy. In 3:16 there is the hope that at the judgment day those who have reviled the Christians may yet be shamed (to repentance), and so the judgment declared in 4:5 may not mean the end of hope even for those who have lived according to the flesh. (See Commentary on 2:12.)

The discussion of insiders and outsiders in this epistle is finely nuanced. On the one hand, Christians find their identity in their distinction from the larger world of pagan dissipation. On the other hand, they do not declare the pagans hopelessly lost to salvation, and they surely remember that those who now celebrate Christ's goodness were themselves also the "unrighteous" whom Christ has brought to God (3:18).

Therefore, the contrast between the sphere of the flesh and that of the spirit is also a contrast between past and present. The "sins" of the pagans are the very sins in which the readers have themselves spent time aplenty. Now in the present they can live by the will of God and in the hope of glory at the end of all things, but they also know that they have not long been free from the reign of flesh.

In this contrast, therefore, there may be a model for an understanding of the relationship of Christians to the larger unbelieving, or pagan, society. On the one hand, we find our identity in part over against them, praying to desire the things of God and not to be captive to human and fleshly passions and desires. On the other hand, we know that just yesterday we were subject to the very same forces we now condemn in the world around us, and therefore it may well be that tomorrow other pagans will find the judgment and mercy of God. As Christians we stand apart from the world and its tests; but we have not been apart from that world for long, and our hope and sympathy for those who are still bound by the flesh should reflect honesty about our own recent and narrow escape.

4. Kierkegaard wrote a masterful sermon on 1 Pet 4:8 and the love that covers a multitude of sins. He interpreted the text as meaning that the love of the faithful covers over the sins of others, and does it with such power that it makes one want to rethink the interpretation of the passage suggested by this commentary. Kierkegaard wrote first of the power of love to cover over sins, and then of the fact that it takes multifaceted love to find the many ways necessary to cover the multitude of sins. The sermon ends with an interpretation of a familiar gospel passage—as a story about 1 Pet 4:8.

> When the scribes and the Pharisees had taken a woman in open sin, they brought her into the midst of the temple before the face of the Saviour; but Jesus bowed down and

---

189. See Selwyn, *The First Epistle of Peter*, 212, who is not sure that the tidepool example is pertinent.

wrote with His finger in the ground. He who knew everything, knew also what the scribes and the Pharisees knew, before they told Him. The scribes and the Pharisees soon discovered her guilt, which was indeed easy since her sin was open. They also discovered a new sin, one of which they made themselves guilty, when they artfully laid snares for the Lord. But Jesus bowed down and wrote with His finger upon the ground. Why, I wonder, did He bow down; why, I wonder, did He write with His finger upon the ground? Did He sit there like a judge who listens attentively to the story of the accusers, who, listening, bows down and jots down the principal points so that he may not forget them, and may judge strictly; was the woman's guilt the only thing which was noted by the Lord? Or did not He who wrote with His finger on the ground, rather write it down in order to erase it and forget it? There stood the sinner, surrounded perhaps by those even more guilty, who loudly accused her, but love bowed down and did not hear the accusation, which passed over His head into the air; He wrote with His finger in order to blot out what He himself knew; for sin discovers a multitude of sins, but love covers the multitude of sins. Yes, even in the sight of the sinner, love covers a multitude of sins. For by one word from the Master the Pharisees and the scribes were struck dumb, and there was no longer an accuser, no one who condemned her. But Jesus said to her: "Neither do I condemn thee, go and sin no more," for the punishment of sin breeds new sin, but love covers a multitude of sins.[190]

5. In remarkably brief compass, 4:10-11 gives a picture of the mutuality of church life the author envisions for the churches in Asia Minor. The promise of 4:6 is that those who have died and will be resurrected will live "in the spirit as God does" (NRSV). In striking ways the community of faith already lives in the spirit and Christians represent the life of God to one another. Those who proclaim—whether through sermon or spiritual saying or prophecy—speak as those entrusted with God's oracles. They become God's voice to one another. Those who minister or administer are servants of God's strength. So God's power and God's strength are manifested in the church through the service of Christians toward one another. The gifts that come from God are returned to God through praise. Like the creation itself, the church comes from God and returns to God; its life from source to goal is doxology, and that doxology is lived out in the love Christians show to each other. Pheme Perkins spells out the practical implications of this: "Passages like this one remind Christians today that faith requires community. Believers should be active members of local churches that are gathered for prayer, for mutual support, for celebration. They are also reminded that local churches should be places in which all members of the church share the particular gifts that God has given them."[191]

---

190. Søren Kierkegaard, "Love Covers a Multitude of Sins," in *Edifying Discourses: A Selection,* ed. Paul Holmer, trans. D. and L. Swenson (London: Collins, Fontana, 1958) 78-79. The whole sermon is found on 63-79.
191. Perkins, *First and Second Peter, James, and Jude,* 71.

1 PETER 4:12–5:11

STEADFAST IN FAITH

OVERVIEW

First Peter 4:12 marks the break that some commentators think indicates that the author or compiler of the epistle now moves from a baptismal homily to a more direct letter of exhortation and injunction. Reasons for skepticism about the "two part" theory of the composition of the epistle are indicated in the Introduction. It is argued there that there is not an evident break in the occasion for the epistle between 4:11 and 4:12. Three further comments may be added.

First, the reconstruction of hypothetical sources behind extant writings is notoriously tricky. Suggestions about the editorial policy behind 1 Peter may be suggestive or even plausible, but given the limits of available evidence they can hardly be compelling. Second, even if it is the case that the author of this epistle joined together two disparate sources, or one source and his own later letter, the document that he wrote is the document that extends from 1:1 through 5:14; therefore, he presumably found continuity between the earlier and the later parts of his epistle. The job of the exegete is to try to seek the basis for that unity, both in the history behind the letter and in the literature of the letter itself. Third, to shift from the perspective of the author to the perspective of the readers, both original and modern, the document we read or hear is 1 Peter, and it needs to be understood as one piece of literature, however many literary sources may lie behind it. It has its own integrity and moves toward its own purposes. As we both try to understand how first-century congregations may have heard this letter and try to understand its significance for faithful people today, we need to attend to the letter as a whole.

Therefore, we can consider the section from 4:12–5:11 as an expansion and intensification of themes already apparent in this epistle. The subsection 4:12-19 reinforces the author's reminder that suffering is an inescapable part of the life of his hearers. Such suffering shares in the suffering of Christ himself, and it carries with it the promise of final glory. Indeed, the very fact of suffering shows that the final judgment and blessing draw near. Verse 19 draws the hortatory conclusion from this analysis of suffering and provides the transition to 5:1-11: "So then, those who suffer according to God's will should commit themselves to their faithful Creator and continue to do good" (NIV).

First Peter 5:1-11 (as with other passages in this epistle) specifies what doing good might include. In a pattern rather like the household or station codes of 2:18–3:7, the household of faith is now addressed. Elders are reminded of their responsibilities for those under their care, and those under their care are reminded of their proper deference to their elders. All of the Christians who hear or read this letter are called to stand fast and faithful under the stress of opposition. All are assured that the outcome of this difficulty lies in the hands of a gracious God.

1 PETER 4:12-19, THE IMPENDING CRISIS

COMMENTARY

4:12-16. Because Christians know that the glory and power belong forever to God through Christ, they are able to face the ordeals imposed upon them during the passing age in which they live. In many ways the whole section of 4:12–5:9 drives toward the benediction of 5:10-11. It is in that confidence that Christians are able to live faithfully. We have no way of knowing whether the "fiery ordeal" of which the author writes is some cataclysmic event more dramatic than the obvious opposition and slander that the first part of the letter has presupposed. The "ordeal" may represent the visible sign of the eschatological claim of 4:7, "The end of all things is near" (NRSV). In this way, the author has prepared the readers for this climactic exhortation, and the passage itself is set within a strong sense of eschatological expectation (see 4:13). On the one hand, there may be some further outbreak of opposition that warrants this apparently more energetic response. On the other hand, this may be a rhetorical move as the letter draws to its close, rehearsing the themes of the epistle but modulating into a new key. Goppelt writes: "What is new is not the situation but the parenetic interpretation that is now given for this situation of permanent social discrimination and legal uncertainty. . . . To this point the readers have been admonished to refute discrimination by just behavior in order to avoid conflicts. . . . Here it is not the occurrence of suffering but the fundamental necessity of suffering that is addressed."[192]

"Beloved" (ἀγαπητοί *agapētoi*) is a reprise of the address of 2:11. As in that case, this address marks the beginning of a section of direct and quite personal exhortation and carries with it a kind of urgency. Also as in 2:11 the first readers are invited to think of themselves both as "beloved" of the author and as loved by God in Christ (see 1:3-4, 9-10). The imperative to not be "surprised" (ξενίζεσθε *xenizesthe*) uses the same word as 4:4 where the Gentiles are "surprised" by the faithfulness of the Christians. One does not need to be surprised if one reads what is going on in the light of God's providence. The pagans, who have no clue, are astonished; Christians, who have every clue they need, should not be astonished at all.

That the "fiery ordeal" is also a test or temptation brings the readers back to 1:6-7. There they were reminded that for a little while they may suffer various "tests" so that the genuineness of their faith may be proven "as through fire." The root word for "fire" (πῦρ *pyr*) is the same used in 1:7 and 4:12. Now the fire is burning, and the faith is under trial.

Verse 13 states with great clarity and intensity one of the main themes of the epistle. The readers have already been reminded that Christ's suffering was both the example for their suffering and the grounds of their salvation (3:18; see also 2:21-25, addressed specifically to slaves but clearly with implications for all believers who undergo suffering). Now they participate, share in, have the communion of Christ's suffering. The verb form of κοινωνία (*koinōnia*) is used here, a word that can represent mutuality, communion, or fellowship. In 1 Corinthians 10 the fellowship also includes the communion of the Lord's supper, where Christians participate in Christ's suffering in a somewhat different way (see 1 Cor 10:16).

Again 1 Peter presents the "already" and the "to be completed" vision of salvation in Jesus Christ. Because Christians share in his suffering, they can already rejoice; but when his glory is revealed they will rejoice exceedingly. Put in other words, now suffering and joy combine; then there will be only joy. The pattern is one we have seen throughout 1 Peter. Christ suffered and was raised in glory; now you suffer, but when he returns you will share that glory.

Verses 14-16 remind the readers that the life that shares Christ's victory is a life marked by the power of the Spirit (see 3:18; 4:6; on the role of the Spirit in the life of the congregation, see also 1:2, 12; on the relationship of "spirit" and "glory," see 2 Cor 3:18; on the promise of glory, see 2 Cor 4:17; Col 3:4).[19] The Spirit is explicitly presented as the first fruits of the eschatological promise, because as Christians await glory in (4:13), the Spirit of glory already rests upon them (4:14).[194] Because the Spirit rests upon them and is a foretaste of glory, Christians who are "insulted" because they carry the name

---

192. Goppelt, *A Commentary on I Peter*, 311. Brox, *Der erste Petrusbrief*, 211, calls it an "escalation."

193. Goppelt, *A Commentary on I Peter*, 323.
194. Does the Spirit's "resting" upon believers recall the Spirit's descending on Christ at his baptism and resting on him (Matt 3:16, with another term for "resting")? See also Isa 11:2, which could obviously be read messianically but here is interpreted as pointing toward believers. Michaels, *1 Peter*, 264. Goppelt, *A Commentary on I Peter*, 324n. 32, thinks that Num 11:25 and the spirit given the elders is the closer parallel.

of Christ (NIV) are also "blessed." Here as in 3:14 the term for "blessed" is μακάριος (*makarios*). In both cases blessedness, the eschatological gift, is pronounced on those who suffer unjustly. In 3:14, Christians suffer for doing what is right. Here the christological definition of what counts as right is made explicit; the blessing is pronounced on those who suffer in Christ's name. This suggests that something of what it means to share in the sufferings of Christ (v. 13) is to suffer for Christ's sake. In both cases the phrase is closely parallel to Matt 5:11-12.[195] The claim that Christians are being reviled for being Christian is a theme that recurs throughout 1 Peter—not so much a sense of physical persecution but a sense of insult, slander, accusation.

As in the earlier admonition to slaves (2:20) and to the entire Christian community (3:17), the epistle reminds the readers that in suffering the Christian participates in Christ's suffering, only if the one who suffers does so unjustly, as Christ did. The list of possible offenses for which Christians might suffer recalls the list of their former behaviors in 4:3-4.[196] What surprises the pagan opposition is that Christians no longer act in such ways; and Christians need not be surprised if they suffer the consequences of their neighbors' astonishment.

The term "Christian" (χριστιανός *christianos*) in v. 16 was not yet widely used of Christ's followers in the New Testament. The use of the term in Acts 11:26 and 26:28 by non-believers may suggest that the term was coined by outsiders.[197] The use of the term here may also indicate that 1 Peter was written somewhat late in the first century, when the phrase had become more commonplace. The claim that one should glorify God "for that name" or "by means of that name" calls us back immediately to v. 14. Those who are insulted "in the name of Christ" should rather glorify God "by the name of Christ(ian)." Again it is a matter of "glory." Those who suffer unjustly for Christ's sake *will* participate in Christ's glory at the eschaton (4:13). In the meantime they can be encouraged because the spirit of glory rests upon them (4:14), and, therefore, they should glorify God (4:16). The NRSV catches and the NIV misses the threefold use of terms related to "glory" in vv. 13-14, 16. The whole passage also echoes v. 11.

One does wonder whether here we have gone beyond the neighborly insult and abuse to the implication that Christians are sometimes being turned in and tried precisely for being Christian. Pliny's letter to Trajan probably comes from a somewhat later time than 1 Peter, when Christianity was growing apace in Asia Minor and when opposition was more organized and more widespread. Nonetheless, Pliny's words suggest further developments of a pattern already nascent in the situation 1 Peter addresses:

I have never been present at an examination of Christians. Consequently I do not know the nature or the extent of the punishments usually meted out to them, nor the grounds for starting an investigation and how far it should be pressed. Nor am I at all sure . . . whether a pardon ought to be granted to anyone retracting his beliefs, or if he has once professed Christianity, he shall gain nothing by renouncing it; and whether it is the mere name of Christian which is punishable, even if innocent of crime, or rather the crimes associated with the name.

For the moment this is the line I have taken with all persons brought before me on the charge of being Christians. I have asked them in person if they are Christians, and if they admit it, I repeat the question a second and third time, with a warning of the punishment awaiting them. If they persist, I order them to be led away for execution; for, whatever the nature of their admission, I am convinced that their stubbornness and unshakeable obstinacy ought not to go unpunished.[198]

4:17-19. These verses again place the "fiery ordeal" in its appropriate eschatological context. This difficulty is not merely

---

195. Some texts add to 4:14, "On their part he is blasphemed but on your part he is glorified." See NRSV note. Metzger notes the lateness of the texts, and his committee thinks the phrase is an explanatory gloss, though the theme fits well enough with the rest of 1 Peter. See Metzger, *A Textual Commentary on the New Testament*, 695.

196. In the Commentary on 4:3-4 the similarities to 1 Cor 6:9-11 were noted. The term ἀλλοτριεπίσκοπος (*allotriepiskopos*), translated by the NIV as "meddler" and by the NRSV as "mischief maker," occurs only here in Greek literature of this era. Achtemeier translates it as one who "defrauds others" and provides an excursus explaining his interpretation. See Achtemeier, *1 Peter*, 302, 311-12.

197. See Achtemeier, *1 Peter*, 313. Other early Christian and non-Christian references are cited in Goppelt, *A Commentary on I Peter*, 327n. 41.

198. Pliny *Letters* x.96. Trajan's response is x.97. See LCL 285-87.

trouble; it is the prologue to judgment day. Thus in v. 17 the author makes the eschatological claim in yet another way. While distinctions between καιρός (*kairos*), meaning time as the significant moment, and χρονός (*chronos*), meaning time as it ticks on, may be overdrawn, the use of *kairos* here is congruent with the eventful use of the term in other NT passages, like Mark 1:15. The passage from 1 Peter, too, is about time that is fulfilled and comes to its climax in the mercy of God. *Fulfilled* time includes judgment, as the whole letter has affirmed. The passage says that judgment begins with the house or household of God, that is with the Christian community, and apparently includes the suggestion that the present suffering may be part of that judgment, the sign of the movement toward history's climax. Achtemeier catches the nuance of the passage: "The judgment ... is the final judgment of which the present suffering of the Christians is not so much a harbinger or proleptic participation as it is part of it, indeed the beginning of it."[199]

The picture of the church as God's house has been underlined by the injunctions of 2:18–3:12, where the instructions for particular Christian households are generalized into a reminder of the mutual sympathy that should mark the shared household of believers—the church. The image of the household for the body of believers takes us back to 2:5, where Christians are reminded that they are to be built "into a spiritual house." The house is marked by Christ's being its cornerstone and by its distinction from the larger world outside—those who are not yet, at least, part of the "royal priesthood" and "holy nation." The same contrast between insiders and outsiders is still at issue in this verse with the comparison between the appropriate judgment for believers and the even greater judgment for those who disbelieve (see also 2:17 for Christians as the "family of believers").[200]

The contrast drives toward, or is driven by, the quotation from the LXX version of Prov 11:31, quoted in v. 18. Both v. 17*b* and v. 18 draw on the traditional rhetorical move from the lighter to the heavier, or from the lesser to the greater. If judgment on those who are faithful will be fearsome, how much more terrible will be judgment on those who do not have faith? Nonetheless, the purpose of the warning here is not to pronounce God's judgment on the outsiders but to remind insiders that they, too, continue to stand under judgment as well as mercy. Even though those who have suffered in the flesh "have finished with sin," temptations to sin remain—and the one who stands ready to judge the living and the dead does not exempt believers from that judgment (see 4:1, 5).

The "therefore" of v. 19 makes clear where this whole passage, beginning with 4:12, is meant to direct the readers. In the face of present persecution and coming judgment, faithful people are called to do two things. First, they are to trust in God, who will judge, but who will do so with justice and mercy. That God is here called "faithful Creator" reminds the Christians of Asia Minor that from the beginning of time to the end of time they live under the providential power of God (see, e.g., 1:5). This is the only place in the NT where God is referred to by precisely the term "creator" (κτιστής *ktistēs*).[201] Second, because they trust in God's mercy and acknowledge God's judgment, they are to continue to do good. The whole epistle has spelled out in considerable detail what "doing good" means (the term ἀγαθοποιέω [*agathopoieō*] is used also at 2:14-15, 20; 3:6, 17).[202]

When the author says that the faithful readers are "suffering in accordance with God's will" (NRSV), he probably does not mean that it is God's will that these people should suffer. Rather, he is saying that given suffering, one should respond according to God's will and not lose heart or return evil for evil.

---

199. Achtemeier, *1 Peter*, 315. For a discussion of the background for the joining of suffering and judgment, see Goppelt, *A Commentary on 1 Peter*, 330-32. The background for the claim about the household of God may be Ezek 9:6 or Jer 25:29. See Brox, *Der erste Petrusbrief*, 222.

200. Goppelt thinks that those who will receive greater judgment are not simply those who disbelieve, but those who disobey the gospel by opposing Christians. See Goppelt, *A Commentary on 1 Peter*, 332.

201. Goppelt thinks that those who will receive greater judgment are not simply those who disbelieve, but those who disobey the gospel by opposing Christians. See Goppelt, *A Commentary on 1 Peter*, 335.

202. Goppelt thinks that those who will receive greater judgment are not simply those who disbelieve, but those who disobey the gospel by opposing Christians. See Goppelt, *A Commentary on 1 Peter*, 336.

REFLECTIONS

1. The great challenge of interpreting the New Testament for contemporary Christians is not dealing with mythology but with eschatology. These verses simply bring front and center what is the background of the whole epistle. History moves toward God's final judgment and mercy in Jesus Christ, and for 1 Peter history is moving toward that final day at amazing speed. The suffering that Christians undergo is in part a further sign that judgment time is already under way and will soon reach its consummation.

By the time of the writing of 2 Peter it was already clear that the expectations of the earlier Christian church had not been met as expected: "But do not ignore this one fact, beloved, that with the Lord one day is like a thousand years, and a thousand years are like one day. The Lord is not slow about his promise, as some think of slowness, but is patient with you, not wanting any to perish, but all to come to repentance" (2 Pet 3:8-9 NRSV). In our time it is not only that the final judgment has been delayed, but also that we cannot simply think about that event in traditional terms, where Christ comes from "on high" to signal the beginning of final judgment.

The solution to the puzzle of how to understand eschatology for contemporary Christians is beyond the scope of these reflections or their author. Yet two familiar reminders still seem helpful.

First, in part, talk about eschatology is a reminder of the transcendent significance of our lives. Decisions we make are not only our business but also stand within the providence and judgment of God. Our acts have consequences beyond the visible and measurable—consequences that are invisible and eternal.

Second, the eschatological framework of 1 Peter declares what we can still lay hold of only through hope: that not only individual lives and decisions but also the movement of history is shaped by God from creation to consummation. The fullness of that consummation is beyond either our predicting or our imagining. But that consummation is foreshadowed in the victory we have seen—the victory of Jesus Christ over sin and death. That affirmation (declared, e.g., in 1 Pet 3:18-22) provides the sign that enables us to lay hold of God's future in confidence. Jonathan Kozol, visiting the poverty-stricken people of the Bronx, New York, found that their faith was too simple or too deep to lend itself to easy demythologizing of final promises. In a neighborhood full of the ugliness of poverty and drugs and despair, Kozol visited P.S. 65:

> I ask the children to tell me something they consider beautiful.
> Virtually every child answers, "Heaven."[203]

2. As with so much of 1 Peter, and as with so much of our lives, we are faced in these verses with the question of how to understand the suffering of faithful people. The passage makes three suggestions that by no means exhaust or solve the issue but are helpful encouragements to those who suffer. First, suffering may, indeed, provide the test by which our faith and convictions are strengthened. Second, suffering provides the opportunity for us to participate in Jesus' own story, not only his passion but also the promise of glory that is at the end of that story. Third, as we have seen in 1 Pet 4:19, faithful people are invited to suffer "in accordance with God's will." This does not mean that God wills each individual his or her suffering, but that when suffering comes it provides the opportunity for us to live according to God's will, in trust and in doing good.

No one, of course, should take these verses as encouraging Christians to seek suffering in a misguided attempt to imitate Christ. Rather, these verses assure us that

---

203. Kozol, *Amazing Grace*, 123.

as suffering came to Jesus unbidden, it may also come to us, and from his story we can take comfort.

No one, as well, can simply take these assurances as sufficient solution to the enormous issues of theodicy. Rather, they provide practical intermediate steps to help Christians get through the sufferings that are sometimes inescapable without losing either hope or charity.

1 PETER 5:1-11, CARING FOR THE HOUSEHOLD OF GOD

COMMENTARY

The word translated "I appeal" (NIV) or "I exhort" (NRSV; παρακαλέω *parakaleō*) in v. 1 is often used in epistles to mark the beginning of final remarks (see Rom 15:30; 1 Cor 16:15; Heb 13:22).

Perhaps in the light of the preceding eschatological exhortation, the author returns to a kind of station code. Now he speaks not of the right order within the households of Christian people, but of right order within the church, within the spiritual household where judgment has already begun.[204]

5:1-5. In these verses, "elders" are clearly church leaders, but the more literal connotation of their designation as "older Christians" also enters into the balanced exhortation to the "younger" in v. 5. The pattern of balanced exhortation reminds one of the balance between wives and husbands in 3:1-7 (in each case, there is more elaboration of the responsibilities of the first member of the set).

5:1-4. Throughout the epistle, Christ has been set forth as an example for those who read or hear this letter. Now the author sets himself (or his fictional self) forward as the exemplary figure. As a fellow elder he is an example for the elders. The Greek for "fellow elder" is one word (συμπρεσβύτερος *sympresbyteros*), like the English "co-elder" or "co-pastor." As one who knows Christ's sufferings and Christ's glory, the epistle writer is an example to all the Christians to whom he writes. Of course, the author's claim that he was a witness to Christ's suffering is in part an attempt to establish his apostolic authority.[205]

The term for "witness" (μαρτύς *martys*) may by this time already have taken on something of the meaning of "martyr," one who not only witnesses but also shares in that suffering. In that sense, the author is a follower of Christ and a forerunner of the Christians of Asia Minor who faced their own more modest martyrdoms. Moreover, as one who now shares in the glory that will be revealed, the author lives in that eschatological "between the times" where he has placed his readers, waiting for a consummation that is not yet complete but already manifest (see, e.g., 1:3-5, 8-9, 23; 4:13-14).

The exhortation to the elders rings familiar in other exhortations to church leaders of the first century. The passage is particularly reminiscent of Paul's exhortations to the Ephesian elders in Acts 20, where elders are also designated as shepherds and as overseers and where they are also warned against using their ministry for gain. In that chapter, Paul uses himself as an example of pecuniary restraint (Acts 20:33-34). The qualifications for bishops in 1 Tim 3:1-7 and for elders in Titus 1:5-9 also show parallels with this passage.[206]

The phrase that the NRSV translates "to tend the flock of God" more literally means "to shepherd the flock of God"; it points ahead to the call to await the chief shepherd in 5:4 and back to the reference to Christ as shepherd and guardian of souls in 2:25. "Guardian" in 2:25 translates ἐπίσκοπος (*episkopos*, NRSV). The verbal form of that noun is found in 5:2 as "serving as overseers"

---

204. See Ferdinand-Rupert Prostmeier, *Handlungsmodelle im ersten Petrusbref*, Forschung zur Bibel 63 (Würzburg: Echter Verlag, 1990) 178.
205. See Selwyn, *The First Epistle of Peter*, 228.

206. On the shepherd image, see also *1 Clem* 4:43 cited in Goppelt, *A Commentary on I Peter*, 344.

(NIV). In a tradition that the author and his audience may have known, the risen Christ appointed Peter to shepherd his sheep (John 21:16). In the larger context of the letter, and perhaps the even larger context of early Christian tradition, therefore, the elders stand in a line of precedence. Christ is the chief shepherd and overseer. Peter also gives an example of tending and overseeing the flock. Now these elders of Asia Minor are to follow in these apostles' footsteps.

The fundamental reminder to the elders is that the flock to which they tend is God's flock, and they are its caretakers, not its masters. Within that understanding the specific responsibilities of the elders are sketched out briefly. They are to serve ungrudgingly (not under compulsion) and gladly, not for personal gain but so that others might gain, not by haughtiness but in humility. (The reminder that Christian leaders should not "lord it over others" is also found in Matt 20:25; Mark 10:42.) The great chain of exemplary behavior continues. Christ is the example for Peter; Peter is the example for the elders; the elders are the example for the flock.

5:5. As is so often the case in 1 Peter, this injunction has an eschatological sanction. The good shepherds will be rewarded by the Good Shepherd at the time of his appearing. The crown of glory they will receive is another of those "unfading" gifts that 1 Peter promises to those who have faith (see 1:4 for a variant of the same term; for a similar theme, see 1:23). This verse is the balancing exhortation to the "younger"—presumably both younger members of the church and members of the church who are not leaders, not "elders." The "likewise" is the mark of reciprocity of Christian life as the epistle commends mutual respect (see 3:1, 7; similarly 1 Cor 7:3-4). The instruction to the youths is brief: "be subject to the elders." The verb "be subject" (ὑποτάσσω *hypotassō*) is the same word used in 1 Pet 2:13, 18; 3:1, 5, and (for angelic powers) 22.

Verse 5*b* presents the more general exhortation that includes elders and younger Christians alike, so that while the younger Christians are called to submission, no Christian is exempt from humility. The "all" of v. 5*b* recalls the "all" of 3:8 where the specific "station" exhortations are now generalized to the claims of faithfulness upon all Christian people.[207] The quotation is again from the LXX version of Proverbs (here Prov 3:34). The preceding proverb reads, "The LORD's curse is on the house of the wicked, but he blesses the abode of the righteous" (Prov 3:33 NRSV). If the readers knew their Scripture well enough to know the context, this would echo the concern for God's house in 1 Pet 4:17. The proverb that the author quotes here places the issue of human reciprocal respect in the context of the greater issue of the will and judgment of God. It also recalls the hope that Christians are to have for the last day and "the grace that Jesus Christ will bring you when he is revealed" (1:13 NRSV).

5:6. This verse sums up the instructions to elders and youths and provides a transition to the closing encouragement in the face of suffering. The quotation from Proverbs has already given the call to humility its proper grounding in the intention of God. Now the author reminds the reader that the fundamental humility that marks Christian life is precisely humility before God. The pattern of humility now and exaltation to come states in new words the tension or dialectic of the whole epistle. Now humility, then exaltation; now suffering, but then glory. The whole pattern was introduced in 1:3-10, is now reiterated toward the end of the epistle, and really governs all the comforts and injunctions in between.

5:7. Here the readers are reminded that the power of God that humbles them also comforts them; God, who is strong, is also strong to save. The NRSV play on words, "Cast all your anxieties on him, because he cares for you," unfortunately is not found in the Greek, but nicely catches the theological balance anyway.

The comfort moves to warning and then will move to comfort once again. God's mighty hand is opposed by a power weaker than God, but it is a real power nonetheless.

5:8. This verse begins with two bare imperatives summing up the appropriate response of faithful people in the face of present danger and coming judgment. Twice already we have encountered the call to sobriety (1:13; 4:7). This behavior is the appropriate response in the light of the

---

207. See Prostmeier, *Handlungsmodelle im ersten Petrusbref,* 173.

dangers of Satan and the powers of God, and it stands in contrast to the licentiousness of the readers' former behavior (see 4:3-4). The call to be alert is characteristic of apocalyptic warnings, as in Mark 13:34. The two verbs occur together in 1 Thess 5:6.

Pheme Perkins points out that the image of the lion as an instrument of affliction can be found as well in Ps 22:13.[208] In the psalm the lion is a symbol for human enemies; here Satan is the enemy, though we have seen through the whole epistle that it is humans who are the instruments of opposition to the church.

5:9. The exhortation to stand firm in v. 8 now finds a new grounding and reason. Not only has Christ suffered, but other Christians throughout the world are also suffering; the *koinonia* of persecution includes Christ and the company of Christians throughout the world (see 4:14).

5:10-11. After the exhortation comes comfort again—eschatological comfort to overcome eschatological suffering. The author invokes God and attributes to God some of those gifts that the epistle has already stressed. God is the one who provides grace (1:2, 10, 13; 5:5). God is the one who calls the faithful (1:15; 2:9, 21; 3:9). God is the one who is glorified and who brings the faithful to glory (1:7, 11, 21; 4:11, 13-14, 16; 5:1, 4). God does all this through Jesus Christ.

The present is the time between, the short time of suffering. But there is a great time coming in which God will put Satan to rout and bring final judgment and grace. Because all power can rightly be ascribed to God, Christians can rightly trust that God will show that power by strengthening them and establishing them.

208. Perkins, *First and Second Peter, James, and Jude*, 80.

REFLECTIONS

1. Questions of the appropriate role of church leaders endure from the first century until now. While there is no sense in 1 Peter that particular persons are ordained, and while it is highly unlikely that any of these local church leaders would be "full-time," it is clear that already a cadre of leadership had emerged in the churches. The signs of appropriate leadership still provide a powerful lure and criticism against many contemporary forms of ministry. In our time, ministry carries with it more authority than we often recognize or own, and the temptations to be authoritarian are no less dangerous because they are subconscious. Given the salaries of many church leaders today, one would hardly think that greed would be an issue. But it remains hard to resist the temptation to mark one's success and chart one's career path on the basis of ever-increasing take-home pay. Indeed, the enjoinder that ministers serve freely and not out of compunction is a good reminder that when we find ourselves grumbling about "those people" for the third straight day, it is time to remember our call or rethink it or return to whatever streams provide God's living water for our own souls' sake and for the sake of God's flock whom we serve.

2. In his autobiography Benjamin Franklin told of his youthful attempts at virtue. He listed the qualities he intended for himself and ended with this listing: "Humility: Imitate Jesus and Socrates."[209] The irony of thinking one could humble oneself by being Christlike or even Socrates-like seems to have escaped the sage from Philadelphia. But sermons admonishing humility are hard to preach, and they often carry the implicit promise that if you are humble enough you will truly be great. First Peter puts the issue of humility in a different context: Humility is ultimately not a matter of our relationships to one another, but of our stance before God. Under God's mighty hand no one can stand on his or her own power or boast in his or her credentials. At the end, says Peter, there will be glory to be sure. It will not be the glory of rank or status, however, but the glory of all the saints joined together in the presence of the One who alone is worthy of status, rank, and praise.

209. Benjamin Franklin, *Autobiography*, 327-28, quoted in Carl Van Doren, *Benjamin Franklin* (Cleveland: World, c. 1938) 88.

3. In a motion picture that seeks to make visible the reality and elusiveness of evil, one of the main characters says, "The devil's cleverest trick is this; to persuade people that he does not exist. Then he is free to do anything." However one seeks to understand the personality of evil, the reality of evil is an undeniable feature of the Christian understanding of the world. We do not have to deal with only human error or bad intentions or misfortune. There are powers of evil that transcend both the individual actors and their actions. Racism is deeper and tougher than the sum total of people who display prejudice. Greed can be institutionalized and take on a life of its own. Sometimes the only viable description of the woes of the world is to say that evil is both real and strong. God, of course, is stronger, but Christians are still called and strengthened to engage in a genuine struggle with forces whose ultimate defeat we know, but who in the meantime are just as ravenous, ambulatory, and dangerous as the lion 1 Peter warns us to fear.

1 PETER 5:12-14

FINAL GREETINGS

COMMENTARY

In the Introduction to this epistle, the role of Silvanus in the writing of this letter is discussed. Here we only need note again that the phrase "through Silvanus" almost certainly means that Silvanus was described as the scribe, not as the carrier of this epistle.[210] The "short letter" is the letter that Peter dictated to Silvanus, perhaps in fact or perhaps as part of the fiction of apostolic authorship.

In many ways v. 12b gives the clearest statement of the purpose of the letter. The aim of the letter is to provide encouragement for Christians who are facing some kind of distress. That encouragement has included exhortation—directions for standing fast in courage even in difficult times.

"The true grace" of God is a brief description of the whole content of the letter. Christians who are suffering suffer in the company of Jesus Christ and will come into his glory. In the meantime, they are to turn to one another in mutual upbuilding and humility. God's true grace is given in Jesus Christ, is shared among believers, and will be consummated at Christ's coming in glory. The readers are invited and encouraged to stand fast in that grace.

"She who is in Babylon" almost certainly refers to the church in Rome. Babylon became a code word for Rome for early Christians, as it was in some Jewish literature of the time.[211] The use of the term here also reminds us that it is not just the Christians in Asia Minor who are aliens and exiles. Babylon was the place of Judah's exile, and in Babylon as in Asia Minor, Christians are still outsiders, exiles, until Christ returns in glory.[212]

Mark is usually associated with Paul's mission, but later Eusebius wrote that Mark drew upon Peter for the writing of his Gospel.[213] As with Silvanus, Mark was either a companion of Peter who wrote this epistle, or his name was used by the pseudepigraphical writer to lend veracity and specificity to his epistle.

The letter ends with the granting of peace—to "all," again. Peace is not merely a gift for the individual Christian, but also a gift to the community that lives together in humility and mutual love, even under duress, until the consummation of God's glory.

---

210. But see Achtemeier, *1 Peter,* 350, for citations of the other usage. The grammatical problem still seems to be that "through Silvanus" modifies "I have written briefly."
211. Achtemeier cites not only Rev 14:8; 16:19; 17:5, 18; and 18:2 but also 2 Bar 11:1-2; 4 Ezra 3:1-2, 28. See Achtemeier, *1 Peter,* 354n. 81.
212. See Goppelt, *A Commentary on 1 Peter,* 374-75.
213. See Introduction. See also Eusebius *Ecclesiastical History* 2.15.1-2; 3.39.15; 6.25.5; cited by Achtemeier, *1 Peter,* 354n. 89.

REFLECTIONS

1. The most difficult hermeneutical question about this epistle is whether its authority depends on its authenticity. If the references to Silvanus and Mark are not accurate historical clues but are deliberate attempts by the author to make the letter sound authentic, what does this do for the epistle's standing as a guide to faith?

The quick answer, and perhaps the most appropriate one, is that the church and faithful Christians therein have found in this epistle strong and reliable comfort especially in times of suffering. It offers guidance for the way the church is to live in a sometimes hostile world. Since the question of authorship will probably remain unanswerable, we are perhaps allowed to take comfort in the wisdom of the writing, leaving the question of its authenticity for that day when Christ will come to judge the quick and the dead, when presumably we will have more important things to ask about anyway.

2. It is trite but true to affirm that the letter ends with peace *to all* and with peace *in Christ.* Christ is the ground of Christian peace, and the whole epistle is a reaffirmation of the story of his passion and resurrection as the informing narrative for every Christian life.

The peace Christ brings he brings to all, but in the beginning he brings it to the community of faith. To be in him is to be at peace with one another, and the depth of our divisiveness is a mark of our distance from him and the reconciliation that he brings. Theologian Mark Heim reminds us that as we move into the twenty-first century the deepest divisions within Christendom are not among denominations but between worldviews, cultures, across denominational lines, and he calls for a new ecumenical movement that acknowledges these difficult divisions: "The rationale of the modern ecumenical movement still holds: there is a scriptural and intrinsic mandate for unity."[214] Furthermore, because we are not only "aliens" in our society but "resident" aliens as well, we have a particular responsibility:

> If Christians are serious that Christian unity is to serve the whole human community, then a new ecumenical movement is the greatest contribution Christians could make to their society. The issues that divided U.S. Christians are, in large measure, the issues that divide the U.S. We need not believe that Christians have the answers to our social crises to know that even a small measure of Christian unity, civility and forbearance would go far to creating an environment in which our nation's crises could be addressed more honestly and effectively.[215]

The calling of Christians is not just to live faithfully as resident aliens of an unbelieving world. The almost tougher calling is to live as brothers and sisters with our fellow believers in the world that God created and that God alone can judge—and redeem.

---

214. Mark Heim, "The Next Ecumenical Movement," *The Christian Century* 113 (1996) 782.
215. Heim, "The Next Ecumenical Movement," 782-83.

THE SECOND LETTER OF PETER
INTRODUCTION, COMMENTARY, AND REFLECTIONS
BY
DUANE F. WATSON

THE SECOND LETTER OF
PETER

INTRODUCTION

AUTHORSHIP, ORIGIN, AND DATE

Although 2 Peter is presented as the work of "Simeon Peter, a servant and apostle of Jesus Christ" (NRSV), most scholars ascribe the book to an unknown author writing under the name of the apostle Peter.[1] Scholars consider 2 Peter to be pseudonymous for several important reasons:

(1) Second Peter is a farewell address, a literary genre in Jewish literature that was predominantly pseudonymous.

(2) Regardless of opinion reached about the authorship of 1 Peter, there are no indications that 1 Peter and 2 Peter were written by the same author. The books differ significantly in style and do not share a distinctive vocabulary or theological terminology. For example, in 1 Peter the Second Coming is a "revelation" (ἀποκάλυψις *apokalypsis*; 1 Pet 1:7, 13; 4:13), and in 2 Peter it is a "coming" or "advent" (παρουσία *parousia*; 2 Pet 1:16; 3:4).

(3) The picture of the author derived from the letter does not conform to what we know of the apostle Peter, a rural fisherman from Galilee whose native language was Aramaic. The author of 2 Peter was highly educated, perhaps of a scribal background. He was highly literate, exhibiting a rich Greek vocabulary complete with Hellenistic terminology. He was skilled in the art of Greco-Roman rhetoric, especially Asiatic rhetoric, a flowery, verbose, and excessive rhetoric popular in the late first-century CE. Greek, Jewish, and Christian traditions were familiar to him. These characteristics indicate a man (education was typically the prerogative of males in ancient society) raised in an urban setting where formal education was available. The writer's extensive knowledge of the Old Testament, Jewish tradition, and Hellenistic terminology suggests that he was a strongly Hellenized Jewish Christian.[2]

---

1. On the textual reading "Simon" or "Simeon," see Commentary on 1:1. For a discussion of the introductory issues, see R. J. Bauckham, "2 Peter: An Account of Research," in *Aufstieg und Niedergang der r"mischen Welt*, ed. W. Haase and H. Temporini (Berlin: Walter de Gruyter, 1988) II.25.5, 3713-52; T. Fornberg, *An Early Church in a Pluralistic Society: A Study of 2 Peter*, ConBNT (Lund: CWK Gleerup, 1980).
2. For the social location of the author, see J. H. Neyrey, *2 Peter, Jude,* AB 37C (New York: Doubleday, 1993) 128-42.

(4) The author was conscious of the fact that he was living in the post-apostolic era. The scoffers whom the apostles had predicted would appear in the end times had now appeared (2:1-3*a;* 3:3-4). All the apostles are considered to have taught the same message, and apostolic tradition is the norm to be defended (1:12, 16-18; 3:1-2, 15-16).

Being a letter to churches once addressed by the writer of 1 Peter from Rome (3:1; 1 Pet 1:1; 5:13), and being similar to early Christian literature from Rome, 2 Peter also may have originated from that city. The author may have been a member of the Roman "Petrine circle," composed of close associates and disciples of Peter. Perhaps one of these associates felt that he knew enough of the teaching of the apostle Peter to write an epistle in Peter's name after Peter's death, in essence giving Peter a new voice in the next generation. He would have been writing as a representative of the Roman church under the name of its most prominent leader. In fact, however, the letter was accepted into the canon as a product of the apostle Peter, but that conclusion was based in part on the assessment that it contained apostolic doctrine.[3]

Dating 2 Peter cannot be done with any certainty. Dates given range from the 60s (if written by the apostle Peter) to the mid-second century (if pseudonymous). Often the documents that have been used in the construction of 2 Peter (e.g., Jude) or those citing the letter (e.g., *Apocalypse of Peter*) are dated, and then a probable date for 2 Peter is surmised. However, those documents themselves cannot be dated with any certainty. Bauckham offers a helpful hypothetical approach.[4] He notes that the death of the first Christian generation was the impetus for the eschatological skepticism of the false teachers (3:4). The early church expected the parousia within the lifetime of the first generation of Christians, and the death of this generation created a crisis of belief. Bauckham calculates that this generation would have been born no later than 10 CE and would have lived about seventy years, thus arriving at a date of 80–90 CE as the earliest probable time for the writing of 2 Peter.

THE RECIPIENTS, THEIR OPPONENTS, AND THE HISTORICAL SITUATION

The recipients of 2 Peter were undesignated churches once addressed by 1 Peter (2 Pet 3:1) and by some of the Pauline Epistles (2 Pet 3:15-16). That would include, in Asia Minor, churches in Pontus, Galatia, Cappadocia, Asia, and Bithynia (1 Pet 1:1). The historical situation that prompted the author to write is the presence in the church of false teachers (2:1) who apparently were backslidden Christians (2:15, 20-22). These false teachers had convinced some, particularly spiritually weak or new Christians, to accept their doctrine and practice (2:1-3*a*, 14, 18). They even posed a danger to those mature in faith who as yet had remained unconvinced by them (1:12; 3:17).

The doctrine of the false teachers was based on eschatological skepticism (2:3*b;* 3:4, 9). They, as well as many other early Christians, anticipated that the parousia of Christ would transpire during the lifetime of the first generation of Christians. But that generation died without the parousia's materializing. As a result, they claimed that the apostolic proclamation of the parousia was a myth (1:16). Old Testament prophecies thought to support the apostolic proclamation were not inspired, they claimed, but were the result of the prophets' misguided personal interpretations of their own prophetic visions (1:20-21).[5]

Naturally the false teachers also denied the judgment that will accompany the parousia (2:3*b;* 3:5-7). Disregarding the constraint of judgment, they justified a moral libertinism that the author of 2 Peter details in a striking denunciation (2:10*b*-22). The false teachers denied the true freedom that lies in obedience to the moral commands of God and knowing Christ, and they returned to the bondage of sin (2:2, 15, 19-22). This antinomianism was attractive because

---

3. See R. J. Bauckham, *Jude, 2 Peter*, WBC 50 (Waco, Tex.: Word, 1983) 158-62; T. V. Smith, *Petrine Controversies in Early Christianity: Attitudes Towards Peter in Christian Writings of the First Two Centuries*, WUNT 15 (Tubingen: J. C. B. Mohr [Paul Siebeck], 1985) 65-101; M. L. Soards, "1 Peter, 2 Peter, and Jude as Evidence for a Petrine School," in *Aufstieg und Niedergang der römischen Welt* (with addenda by V. O. Ward), ed. W. Haase and H. Temporini (Berlin: Walter de Gruyter, 1988) II.25.5, 3827-49.
4. Bauckham, *Jude, 2 Peter*, 157-58.
5. See C. H. Talbert, "II Peter and the Delay of the Parousia," *VC* 20 (1966) 137-45.

Christian morality excluded the early Christians from many aspects of business and social life. Businesses and social clubs often held meetings in temples associated with the worship of pagan gods. The idolatry and sexual immorality associated with this kind of worship precluded Christians from participating in such meetings. Any teaching justifying a Christian's renewed participation in these activities would have been tempting to new converts who were accustomed to the benefits of these social events.

Since Paul's letters were known in these churches, this antinomianism might also have arisen from a misinterpretation of the Pauline doctrine of freedom in Christ (3:15-16; cf. 2:19). However, it seems to be rooted more in eschatological skepticism, which denied judgment, than in a perversion of the understanding of grace. Also, the false teachers were not gnostics, for the antinomianism is not based in a cosmic dualism that denigrated the flesh; rather, it was based on the delay of the parousia.

The situation was serious, because the doctrine and practice of the false teachers were contrary to those taught by the apostles. Apostolic doctrine defined the Christian life as one of living a "holy" life while awaiting the parousia (1:3-11; 3:11, 14-15*a*, 18). Believing and acting as they did, the false teachers and their followers would not be spiritually prepared when the parousia arrives, and they will suffer judgment (2:1, 3*b*, 4-10*a*, 12; 3:7, 16; cf. 2:17). The author's urgency stems from the conviction that the parousia would occur in the lifetime of the Christians addressed (3:11-18). Since the appearance of false teachers and their scoffing is a precursor or sign of the parousia of Christ and the judgment of the world (3:3-4), the author believed that the parousia was near.

Neyrey suggests that the false teachers' doctrine is similar to that usually associated with Epicureans.[6] The Epicureans affirmed the complete transcendence of God. God was not troubled by the goings-on of humanity. As a corollary, they also denied the providence of God, the prevailing understanding of God at the time. According to them, God is not provident. God does not work in the world according to a divine plan. The world was made by chance; humanity has freedom of choice; there is a delay of justice upon the wicked; and prophecy goes unfulfilled. A denial of the providence of God led likewise to a denial of the afterlife and its rewards and punishments. Epicurean thought filtered down into Jewish and Greek thinking in more popular forms and certainly could have influenced the audience of 2 Peter.

Noting the delay of divine judgment, the false teachers deny the intervention of God in the world and deny judgment altogether (2:3*b*; 3:4, 9). They consider important prophecies to be "cleverly devised myths" (1:16 NRSV) and "one's own interpretation" (1:20 NRSV), and they scoff at apostolic prophecy (3:3-4). They promise their followers freedom (2:19). The author of 2 Peter employs topics typically used in polemics against Epicureanism. He affirms the providence of God in judgment, both past and future (2:3*b*-10*a*; 3:5-13), and the truth of the prophecies that undergird it (1:16-21).

THE STANCE AND RHETORICAL APPROACH OF THE LETTER

Many interpreters have classified 2 Peter as an "early catholic" document. This designation refers to a now-questionable reconstruction of early Christianity that postulates that beginning with the second generation of Christians there was a movement toward institutionalization of offices in the church and toward "faith" denoting a body of doctrine and practice rather than a personal commitment. This movement was fostered by delay of the parousia and an encounter with heresy, which necessitated the creation of church offices to centralize authority and the clear articulation of doctrine.[7]

Yet 2 Peter should not be classified as early catholic. Although the delay of the parousia underlies the eschatological skepticism of the false teachers (2:3*b*; 3:4, 9), the author expects both the churches and the false teachers to be alive when the parousia does arrive (1:19; 2:12;

---

6. Neyrey, *2 Peter, Jude*, 122-28; "The Form and Background of the Polemic in 2 Peter," *JBL* 99 (1980) 407-31.
7. E. Käsemann, "An Apologia for Primitive Christian Eschatology," in *Essays on New Testament Themes*, trans. W. J. Montague, SBT 41 (London: SCM, 1964) 169-95.

3:14). The judgment of the false teachers at the parousia will not forever be delayed, and when it comes it will be swift (2:1-3a). The author does not address any church officers (unless the false teachers of 2:1 hold an office), but assumes that the churches will understand the situation and respond as desired. Also, faith is not understood as a set body of orthodox doctrine. The author is defending apostolic tradition against perversion of its eschatological and ethical teachings, but there is no indication that these are encapsulated in creedal formulae and governed by church authorities.[8]

Second Peter is predominantly deliberative rhetoric that, by proofs and advice, tries to persuade an audience to do what is advantageous, necessary, and expedient and to dissuade it from what is the opposite. The letter is explicit that its aim is to remind the audience of the apostolic tradition on eschatology and ethics (1:12-15; 3:1-2). Its aim, therefore, is not to heed the false teachers' doctrine and practice, and thus come under like judgment at the encroaching parousia. However, 2 Peter also contains sections of judicial and epideictic rhetoric. Judicial rhetoric, rhetoric of accusation and defense, comprises portions in which the author refutes and counter-accuses the false teachers (1:16–2:10a; 3:1-13). Epideictic rhetoric, the rhetoric of praise and blame for the purpose of uplifting what is honorable and casting down what is dishonorable, is found in 2:10b-22. Here the author denounces and negatively characterizes the false teachers and their doctrine and practice by comparing them with great sinners and sins of the past. He does so in order to increase the churches' assent to the received faith and preserve them from impending judgment.[9]

To minimize the influence of the false teachers, the author urges the faithful to strive for Christian maturity and godliness in accordance with apostolic doctrine (1:3-11; 3:11-18). He refutes the false teachers' denial of Christ's parousia and prophecies that support its proclamation (1:16-21; 3:1-13) and their denial of judgment (2:3b-10a; 3:1-13). He exposes their doctrine and practice for the evil they really are (2:1-22). He brings to bear the authority of the Old Testament and Jewish tradition (2:3b-10, 15-16, 22; 3:5-6), the Old Testament prophets (1:19-21; 3:2), the New Testament apostles (1:3-11, 16-19; 3:1-4), the Epistle of 1 Peter (3:1), Paul (3:15-16), the Letter of Jude (2:1-18; 3:1-3), and Jesus (3:2).

LITERARY GENRE, COMPOSITION, AND CONTENT

Second Peter is a blend of two literary genres. As indicated by its opening (1:1-2), one genre is that of the letter. The other genre is the farewell speech or testament. The testament was popular in Judaism and was used to relate the last words of dying men of renown, both within and beyond the Old Testament (Genesis 49; Deuteronomy 33), and was borrowed by early Christian writers (John 13–17; Acts 20:17-34; 2 Timothy). In a testament, the dying leader announces his death and rehearses ethical teachings and traditions central to the community that he wants them to continue to observe after his death. Thinking that a dying individual was given prophetic powers just prior to death, people understood the testament to provide revelation about the future of the community, and this future provided a basis for the particular emphasis of the ethical instruction.

In 2 Peter, "Peter" gives ethical instruction to remind the churches of their heritage (1:3-11), announcing his death and wishing that his instructions be remembered (1:12-15; 3:1-2). He reveals that after his death there will be a rise of false teachers in the last days who will deny eschatological expectation and will corrupt ethical practice (2:1-3a; 3:1-4). The remainder of the letter defends the apostolic teaching on eschatology and ethics. The testament is not usually in the form of a letter, but when it was to be sent to a specific congregation, the letter genre was a natural adaptation.[10]

When comparing the prophecies of "Peter" with the current situation of the churches, the author shifts from the perspective of a testament, often in future or past tense (2:1-3a; 3:1-4),

---

8. Bauckham, *Jude, 2 Peter*, 151-54.
9. See D. F. Watson, *Invention, Arrangement, and Style: Rhetorical Criticism of Jude and 2 Peter*, SBLDS 104 (Atlanta: Scholars Press, 1988) 81-146.
10. E.g., *2 Apoc. Bar.* 78-86.

to the perspective of the churches, addressed in the present tense (2:3b-22; 3:5-10, 16b). These tense shifts are not the result of forgetting that he was presenting a testament that prophesies events in the future; nor is it the futuristic use of the present tense, which substitutes the present tense for the future when there is great confidence about future events. This juxtaposition of past prophecies of false teachers and their teaching with their present manifestation in the churches is a teaching tool that helps the churches to understand that what has been prophesied about false teachers in the past is being fulfilled in their present.

The author of 2 Peter is familiar with a variety of literature. He quotes the Old Testament (LXX) three times (2 Pet 2:22 = Prov 26:11; 2 Pet 3:8 = Ps 89:4[90:4 MT]; 2 Pet 3:13 = Isa 65:17; 66:2) and alludes to it many other times (e.g., 2 Pet 1:17-18 = Ps 2:6-7). He uses extra-biblical Jewish haggadic traditions (2:4-5, 7-8, 15-16) and a Jewish apocalypse (3:4-13). His letter exhibits many similarities with Hellenistic Jewish literature (like the works of Philo and Josephus). Gospel tradition that is independent of the canonical Gospels is also present (1:14, John 21:18; 1:16-18, Transfiguration; 3:10, Matt 24:43-44, Luke 12:39-40). He knows a partial or complete collection of Pauline letters, which he regards as inspired and authoritative (3:15-16), but does not seem to be influenced by them. He also knows of 1 Peter, but does not use it (3:1). This independence of 1 Peter is unusual because pseudonymous authors usually tried to emulate known works by the person in whose name they were writing. Parallels in language and tradition with *1 Clement, 2 Clement,* and the *Shepherd of Hermas* are present, and their presence can be explained only if 2 Peter derives from the same Christian community in Rome.

Second Peter is most noted for dependence upon the Letter of Jude (2 Pet 2:1-18 = Jude 4-13; 2 Pet 3:1-3 = Jude 16-18). The verbal resemblances are not as close as those between Matthew and Mark, for example, but redaction criticism indicates that the author of 2 Peter used Jude in his composition. Jude is a carefully crafted letter, and the corresponding portions of 2 Peter are scattered throughout a denunciation of the false teachers. It is easier to see the author of 2 Peter mining the Epistle of Jude for images and examples helpful in building a denunciation than it is to see the writer of Jude using scattered portions of 2 Peter to write a carefully constructed letter aimed at the problems of a specific community. In his use of Jude, the writer of 2 Peter omits allusions and quotations to *1 Enoch* (Jude 14-15) and the *Testament of Moses* (Jude 9). This may be because these works were not well-known outside Palestinian Judaism, the community in which Jude was written, and not because the author of 2 Peter was working with a growing sense of canon, as claimed by those classifying it as an early catholic epistle.

The letter begins with a typical prescript (1:1-2), followed by a miniature homily that outlines apostolic teaching on the nature of the Christian life and provides the basis for the argumentation to follow (1:3-11). The homily is followed by a statement of the purpose of the letter as being a reminder of apostolic teaching, an element central to the testament genre (1:12-15). The body of the letter is composed of 1:16–3:13. It refutes the proposition of the false teachers that the apostolic preaching of the parousia is a myth supported by Old Testament prophecies that are not inspired (1:16-21). In turn, the author counteraccuses the false teachers of standing in the tradition of the false prophets (2:1-3a) and refutes their denial of the parousia judgment based on its delay (2:3b-10a). Breaking up the refutation is a strong denunciation of the false teachers, aimed at destroying their credibility (2:10b-22). The body of the letter closes with an apology for the delay of the parousia, refuting the false teachers' denial of the parousia and the belief that God has not acted in judgment in history on a cosmic scale (3:1-13). The letter closes with moral exhortation and a doxology (3:14-18).

THE THEOLOGY OF 2 PETER

The false teachers charged that the apostolic teaching about the parousia and its accompanying judgment was a "cleverly devised myth" based on uninspired prophecies in the Old Testament (1:16-21). Their eschatological skepticism was fueled by the delay of the parousia, which they expected in the first Christian generation (3:3-4), and their denial that God had or ever would intervene in history with judgment (2:3b, 9-10a; 3:3-4). The author's theological approach is conditioned by the needs of refuting this eschatological skepticism. He emphasizes apostolic tradition, which affirms the parousia and its judgment. This tradition is founded on the teachings of Peter (1:12-18), Paul (3:15b-16), the other apostles (1:16-18; 3:1-2), and the Old Testament prophetic witness (1:20-21; 3:2).[11]

The Nature of Scripture. In his appeal to apostolic tradition, the author of 2 Peter makes several comments about the nature of Scripture. Old Testament prophecies are the prophets' inspired interpretations of the signs, dreams, and visions they received from God. These prophecies provide preliminary revelation into the future purposes of God (1:19-21; 3:2). The author regards a collection of Paul's letters (the letters involved are unknown) as inspired Scripture, a designation that includes the Old Testament and perhaps other writings in the New Testament. Paul is said to have written with the wisdom given him, just as the Old Testament prophets were moved by the Holy Spirit to give their prophecies (3:15b-16; cf. 1:20-21).

The Parousia and Judgment. In contrast to the false teachers' denial of the parousia and its accompanying judgment, the author affirms both. God's perspective of time is different from our own, and what seems to us to be a delay is not so for God (3:8). The parousia and judgment have been delayed because God is allowing time for the ungodly to repent; but Christ will eventually return at an unexpected time, and all the works of humanity will be exposed and subjected to judgment (3:9-10). The ungodly will be destroyed at the judgment (2:1, 3b, 9-10a, 12; 3:7, 16), whereas the godly will share the incorruptibility and immortality that characterizes God's nature (1:4; 2:19-20); they will be given entrance into the eternal kingdom (1:11) and provided a place in the new heaven and new earth (3:13).

The false teachers' denial of God's intervention in judgment is countered by the author's stressing the interrelated roles of God as Creator and Judge. As is understood from Genesis 1, God created the heavens and earth by God's Word, or divine fiat. God's Word separated the waters of the cosmic sea both above and below to form land (3:5). It was by God's same Word that the waters above and below the earth were released to produce the judgment of the flood (3:6). It will also be by God's Word that the heavens and the earth will be judged with destruction by fire (3:7). It is presumed that this same Word will create the new heavens and the new earth, where only righteousness can dwell (3:11-13). Examples of God's judgment from the past are used to prove that God intervenes in history for judgment and thus will do so again (2:3b-10a; 3:3-7).

The Christian Life Under Christ's Lordship. The denial of the parousia and judgment led the false teachers to disregard the moral implications of the gospel. Thus the author of 2 Peter emphasizes the Lordship of Christ. Jesus is both Lord and Savior (1:11; 2:20; 3:2, 18). The title "Lord" (κύριος *kyrios*) indicates Jesus' authority at God's right hand to rule both people and the cosmos. The title "Savior" (σωτήρ *sōtēr*) is used in conjunction with "Lord," indicating that by his redemptive work as Savior, Jesus is now Lord, particularly of those he has redeemed. He is the Master who bought them from slavery to sin (2:1), and knowledge of him enables release from slavery to corruption, decay, and mortality (1:4; 2:19-20).

Christ's gift of salvation and everything needed for the moral life is grounded in the knowledge of him (1:3-4). Christians must make every effort to grow in righteousness in order to confirm Christ's call and election (1:3, 11; 3:18). Such moral effort rooted in the knowledge of Jesus Christ is needed in order to escape corruption and mortality (1:4; 2:19-20) and to be able to enter the eternal kingdom (1:11). This moral effort includes nurturing virtues (1:5-7) and following the way of righteousness established by Christ through the holy commandment to love God with all our being and to love other people as we love ourselves (2:21). Christians are to live with vital eschatological expectation that the parousia will come "like a thief" (3:10 NRSV). They are to be morally blameless in the interim in order to be ready to become citizens of the new heavens and the new earth, which are characterized by righteousness (3:11-14). The righteous will be rescued from the world and its corruption only if they remain righteous (2:5, 8-9).

---

11. For the theology of 2 Peter, see Bauckham, *Jude, 2 Peter,* 39-107; A. Chester and R. P. Martin, *The Theology of the Letters of James, Peter, and Jude,* New Testament Theology (Cambridge: Cambridge University Press, 1994) 134-63.

Immoral behavior is an affront to Christ's status as Lord and Savior. It amounts to denying his authority and maligning the way of truth (2:1-2), departing from the way of righteousness and the holy commandment (2:15, 20-21), and returning to slavery to corruption under the pretense of freedom from moral constraint and judgment (2:19-20). It is to be unfruitful in the knowledge of Christ and not confirm Christ's call and election (1:8-9), to stumble in the moral walk and forfeit salvation (1:10-11).

BIBLIOGRAPHY

Bauckham, R. J. *Jude, 2 Peter.* WBC 50. Waco, Tex.: Word, 1983. The most comprehensive commentary in English that both summarizes previous scholarship and makes many new and helpful advances. It places Jude within its Jewish, Christian, and Greco-Roman literary and theological contexts.

———. *Jude, 2 Peter.* WBT. Waco, Tex.: Word, 1990. A companion to the preceding commentary; discusses the theological themes of 2 Peter.

Chester, A., and R. Martin. *The Theology of the Letters of James, Peter, and Jude.* New Testament Theology. Cambridge: Cambridge University Press, 1994. One of the finest discussions available of the theology of 2 Peter within its context.

Neyrey, J. H. *2 Peter, Jude.* AB 37C. New York: Doubleday, 1993. An excellent commentary that breaks new ground by incorporating a social-science perspective. It places the authors and audiences of these letters within their social world by using various social-science models or perspectives.

Perkins, Pheme. *Peter: Apostle for the Whole Church.* Studies on Personalities of the New Testament. Columbia: University of South Carolina Press, 1994. A thorough, readable investigation of Peter in the NT and Christian tradition.

Watson, Duane F. *Invention, Arrangement, and Style: Rhetorical Criticism of Jude and 2 Peter.* SBLDS 104. Atlanta: Scholars Press, 1988. Demonstrates how the author of 2 Peter used Greco-Roman rhetorical conventions to persuade his audience to take a course of action deemed necessary to remain faithful in the light of the influence of false teachers.

OUTLINE OF 2 PETER

I. 2 Peter 1:1-2, Letter Prescript

II. 2 Peter 1:3-11, The Christian Life in Brief

III. 2 Peter 1:12-15, A Reminder of the Christian Life

IV. 2 Peter 1:16–3:13, Refutation of the Accusations of the False Teachers

    A. 1:16-21, The Apostolic Preaching of the Parousia Is Not a "Cleverly Devised Myth"
    B. 2:1-3a, Prophecy of the Appearance of False Teachers
    C. 2:3b-10a, The Judgment of God Is Not Idle or Asleep
    D. 2:10b-22, A Denunciation of the False Teachers
    E. 3:1-13, An Apology for the Delay of the Parousia

V. 2 Peter 3:14-18, Exhortation to Stability

2 PETER 1:1-2

LETTER PRESCRIPT

COMMENTARY

The Epistle of 2 Peter begins with a three-part prescript common to Jewish and early Christian letters: identification of (1) the sender and (2) the addressee(s), both often described theologically in their relationship to God, to Christ, and to each other, and (3) a greeting (here a blessing) that originated in the Jewish wish for peace and prosperity for the recipients. Through the theological description and greeting, the letter prescript functions rhetorically to establish the authority of the sender to address the addressee(s) and to obtain the goodwill of the addressee(s) so that the content of the letter may be heard (the letter would have been read aloud to the churches).

The author is identified as "Simeon" (NRSV), a less typical Greek transliteration of the Hebrew name "Simon," which was how Peter was known in Palestinian circles (Acts 15:14). Some Greek MSS read "Simon" (NIV), the more typical Greek transliteration of the Hebrew name. The author is identified theologically as "a servant and apostle of Jesus Christ." "Servant" (δοῦλος *doulos*) is a title for any Christian as one whom Christ, through his work in redemption, bought out of slavery to sin and who now serves him (1 Cor 7:22-23; Eph 6:6; 1 Pet 2:16). As a self-designation, "servant" also denotes a Christian leader, especially in letter openings (Phil 1:1; Jas 1:1; Jude 1). In this regard, "servant" is an adaptation of "servants of God," used of the great leaders of Israel (Exod 32:13; Deut 9:27; 34:5; Ps 89:3). The extended title "servant of Jesus Christ" implies that the leader exhibits the qualities of servant leadership, exemplified by Christ. "Apostle" (ἀπόστολος *apostolos*) establishes the leadership and authority of Peter as a member of the twelve apostles called by Christ, among whom Peter was the leader (Matt 16:18-19; Mark 3:13-16). Paul as well used "servant" and "apostle" together at the beginning of his letters to establish his authority (Rom 1:1).

The recipients of the letter are given the theological identification "those who have received a faith as precious as ours through the righteousness of our God and Savior Jesus Christ." The last phrase can also be translated "of God and of Jesus our Lord," a rendering that does not call Jesus "God." This is preferred over the NRSV or the NIV reading, "God and Savior Jesus Christ." In v. 2, which is in parallelism with v. 1, God and Jesus are distinguished from each other; it is rare to find Jesus called "God" in the New Testament (e.g., John 1:1-3; 20:28). In any case, this identification establishes common ground with the letter's recipients, and it is included in part to obtain their goodwill. They have received a faith as precious as that of the apostles through the righteousness (or justice) of God and Jesus Christ, who show no partiality in bestowing the benefits of redemption upon Christians. Persuading the recipients to uphold their righteousness in spite of the challenge posed by the unrighteous false teachers is central to the author's deliberation.

The blessing of v. 2 also increases the recipients' goodwill. Grace and peace are rooted in the personal knowledge (ἐπίγνωσις *epignōsis*) of God and Jesus, gained at conversion (1:2-3, 8; 2:20). This contrasts knowledge (γνῶσις *gnōsis*) that can be gained of God after conversion (1:5-6; 3:18).[12]

---

12. R. E. Picirelli, "The Meaning of 'Epignosis,'" *Evangelical Quarterly* 47 (1975) 85-93.

REFLECTIONS

1. The faith we have received through the righteousness of Jesus Christ is not the privilege of a few but for all who believe. It is of the same kind and precious caliber as that which the apostles themselves experienced and convinced others to receive. At the basic level of faith, all people are equally blessed. Partly as an outgrowth of the righteousness that is their nature, there is no elitism or partiality in God's and Christ's distribution of the gift of faith. Christ's redemptive work was for all who desire to avail themselves of it. Christ gives faith as a gift, thus depriving anyone of the temptation to claim any special status among other believers in Christ.

2. Grace and peace are rooted in relationship with Christ, in personal knowledge of him gained through conversion and service to him. They are not rooted in viewing Christianity as an abstract set of rules to be obeyed or in trying to be a moral person as described and measured by a moral code. Rather, they are rooted in relationship. It is only when we live righteously according to personal and communal knowledge of Christ that we will have grace and peace. Grace and peace may be part of our lives simply by coming to a knowledge of Christ, but they will not become ours in abundance unless that knowledge is expressed in acts that promote righteousness (1:3-11).

2 PETER 1:3-11

THE CHRISTIAN LIFE IN BRIEF

COMMENTARY

Second Peter 1:3-11 is the letter opening, or, from a rhetorical perspective, the *exordium*, an introduction that establishes common ground with the audience and introduces the reasons for writing. The common ground is given in the tradition outlined in vv. 3-11; and as stated in vv. 12-15, the reason for writing is that the churches can read the letter and be reminded of the tradition. Usually after the letter opening in Christian letters there is a thanksgiving to God, which incorporates prayers and blessings and introduces some of the topics to be addressed. Although 1:3-11 is not a thanksgiving, it performs these functions.

The *exordium* is a miniature homily presenting the essence of apostolic preaching. It conforms to the standard homiletic pattern found in Jewish and early Christian literature. First there is a historical and theological section that reiterates the acts of God in salvation history (1:3-4). Second, there are ethical exhortations based on the preceding section that anticipate what is to come (1:5-10). Finally, there is an eschatological section that either promises salvation or threatens judgment (1:11).[13] Within this farewell address the homily is intended to present the dying individual's message as he or she intended it to be remembered after death (cf. 1:12, 15). In 2 Peter, the ethical and eschatological teaching of the homily form a theological and ethical standard by which to measure the doctrine and practice of the false teachers.

1:3. It is through Christ's power—power that he shares with God—that Christians have everything needed to live a godly life. "Godliness" (εὐσέβεια *eusebeia*) means having the proper attitude of piety toward God, expressed in obedience to the will of God, and walking according to God's moral standards. It is a mark of Christian maturity (1:6-7) that confirms being called by Jesus (1:3, 10). The eschatological reality that in the new heavens and earth only righteousness will be found makes godliness essential for a share in it (3:11-13) and necessitates being "without spot or blemish" (godly) at the parousia (3:14).

This gift of possessing everything necessary for a godly life comes with the personal knowledge of Jesus Christ obtained at conversion, when the Christian responds to Christ's call through his glory and goodness (i.e., divine power). The knowledge (ἐπίγνωσις *epignōsis*; ἐπιγινώσκω *epiginōskō*) of Jesus is both central for conversion and subsequently derived from conversion. It forms the basis of Christian growth, enabling the Christian to escape the defilements of the world (1:2-4, 8-9; 2:20-21). It is contrasted throughout 2 Peter with the knowledge (γνῶσις *gnōsis*; γινώσκω *ginōskō*) gained from living the Christian life (1:5-6; 2:20; 3:18).

1:4. Through his divine power and knowledge of him, Christ has given us precious and very great promises. By living a godly life, which this power and knowledge enable, Christians can look forward to the fulfillment of the promises of Christ. Elsewhere in 2 Peter the promises are eschatological and refer to the parousia (3:4, 9) and the new heavens and new earth (3:13). The promises are eschatological here, too. The promise of Christ is that Christians will "escape from the corruption that is in the world because of lust, and may become participants of the divine nature." This does not refer to escaping moral evil in this life by avoiding sin; nor does it refer to the soul's uniting with God at death or in any sense becoming a part of God's very essence. Rather, it is an idea

---

13. Bauckham, *Jude, 2 Peter*, 173-75; Klaus Baltzer, *The Covenant Formulary*, trans. D. E. Green (Oxford: Basil Blackwell, 1971) 173-75. Other farewell discourses exhibiting this pattern are 4 Ezra 14:28-36 and the *Acts of John* 106-107.

borrowed from Hellenistic Judaism that the soul, having escaped the material world, which is subject to corruption because of lust (evil desires; 2:10, 18-19), either at the parousia or through death, attains immortality and incorruptibility, which characterize God's nature and the heavenly realm (e.g., 4 Macc 18:3; Wis 2:23; a similar idea is found in Rom 8:18-25; 1 Cor 15:42-57). Thus Christians are saved from the destruction reserved for the corrupted world and its corrupted inhabitants (2:4-10*b,* 12-13; 3:5-13), including the false teachers who misuse their freedom and become prey to worldly corruption through lust (2:10*a,* 12-13, 19-22; 3:3-7).

1:5-7. The benefits afforded Christians by divine power through knowledge of Christ enable them to live godly lives and to be blessed with the promise of immortality (vv. 3-4). Christians cannot expect to have that promised immortality unless they make every moral effort possible to overcome sin (1:5, 10; 3:14) and obtain the virtues, seven of which are listed in these verses. Lists of virtues and vices were popular in the NT for exhortation and instruction. They appear in several forms and are tailored to the situation of the letter and the needs of its audience (e.g., Gal 5:19-23). One form, found here, uses climax, a figure of speech in which a word is repeated before passing on to the next. This form of a virtue-and-vice list was a Jewish and Christian convention, adapted from Hellenistic moral philosophy, to describe the good or bad life and its eschatological goal (Rom 5:3-5; *Shepherd of Hermas,* Visions 3.8.7). Such lists lay out the virtues that characterize the Christian life, beginning with faith and ending with love. Each virtue is supported by all those that precede. Faith, being first, is the grounding of all the virtues. Knowledge of Christ gained by faith provides all that is necessary for a godly life (v. 3). Since love (ἀγάπη *agapē*), the chief virtue in such lists of Christian virtues, concludes the list it ultimately includes all the other virtues as well.[14]

The other virtues are presented at random. "Goodness," or "virtue" (ἀρετή *aretē*), is moral excellence, to which the Christian is called (v. 3). "Knowledge" (γνῶσις *gnōsis*) is the knowledge of Christ gradually acquired throughout the Christian walk. "Self-control" (ἐγκράτεια *egkrateia*) is restraint from the excesses of physical desires, especially sexual desires, which have brought corruption to the world. To exercise self-control is to resist the false teachers who indulge their lusts, become corrupt, and entice others to do the same (2:18-22; 3:3). "Endurance" (NRSV) or "perseverance" (NIV; ὑπομονή *hypomonē*) is continuation in right thinking and practice in spite of temptation, suffering, or evil. To show endurance is to trust in God and the fulfillment of God's promises. "Godliness" (εὐσέβεια *eusebeia*) is the attitude of honoring God, acknowledging God's authority, and obeying the will of God. "Mutual affection" (φιλαδελφία *philadelphia*; lit., "brotherly kindness," NIV) is affection for other Christians as brothers and sisters in Christ.

1:8-9. These verses give further reasons for heeding the exhortation of vv. 5-7. Knowledge of Christ gives Christians everything needed for living a godly life (v. 3). Supporting faith with virtues keeps Christians from being ineffective and unfruitful (NRSV) or unproductive (NIV) in this knowledge of Christ (not possessing ethical qualities and exhibiting good works; Gal 5:22-23; Col 1:9-10; Titus 3:14; Jas 2:20). Leaving faith unsupported leaves Christians "nearsighted" and "blind," metaphors for the inability or unwillingness to perceive the truth (1 John 2:11; Rev 3:17). Such faith has forgotten the cleansing of past sin at baptism (Eph 5:26), which opens eyes blinded by sin. Leaving faith unsupported is to return to sin and blindness (Heb 6:4; 10:32).

1:10. This verse presents the conclusion of all of vv. 3-9. Its content echoes v. 5 in emphasizing that all effort possible needs to be expended toward maturing as a Christian, an emphasis that recurs in the letter closing (3:14). Here the churches are urged to "confirm your call and election" (NRSV) or "make your calling and election sure" (NIV). "Call" (κλῆσις *klēsis*) and "election" (ἐκλογή *eklogē*) are synonymous terms for Christ's summons of the Christian to repent, to be saved, to serve God in accomplishing God's purposes, and to enter into the kingdom and partake of its blessings. Christ has called Christians and given them everything

---

14. Bauckham, *Jude, 2 Peter,* 174-76; H. A. Fischel, "The Uses of Sorites (Climax, Gradatio) in the Tannaitic Period," *HUCA* 44 (1973) 119-51.

needed for a godly life (v. 3), but moral effort (as outlined in vv. 5-7) is necessary in order to obtain the promise of immortality (v. 4). Such effort guarantees that Christians will not stumble or fall, which in this context means not only not to sin, but also not to lose salvation (cf. v. 11; Jude 24). Stumbling or falling is the likely outcome of being nearsighted or blind (v. 9)—that is, to neglect cleansing from sin is to lose one's salvation.

1:11. This verse amplifies vv. 3-10. It is a climax that holds out the ultimate hope of every Christian: entrance into the eternal kingdom. To the Christians who provide their faith with virtues (v. 5), Christ will richly provide "entrance" (NRSV) or "welcome" (NIV) into his kingdom, the reign of God in the new heavens and earth (3:13). Christians make the moral effort using gifts Christ has given to them, and he in turn provides a lavish entrance into his kingdom. Although Christians must expend effort in their spiritual lives, salvation and all that is needed to grow spiritually, as well as the eschatological promises, remain gifts.

REFLECTIONS

1. Knowledge of Christ is gained at conversion and through the communion with and service to him that follow. Knowing Christ places one in a relationship and gives a new perspective that demands a whole new way of living conducted according to Christ's nature (1:3-11). Knowledge of Christ is a lifelong process, learned through living the godly life in relationship with him (1:5-7; 3:18). This knowledge can also be described as having "known the way of righteousness" (2:21 NRSV), which Christ's life exemplifies. Knowledge of Christ frees us from the corruption of sin (1:2-4, 8-9; 2:20-21) so that our call and election can be confirmed through our spiritual growth (1:5-10).

2. To be a Christian and live a godly life through the knowledge and power of Christ is to be the recipient of great promises. These promises include becoming immortal and incorruptible like God (1:4), escaping judgment at the parousia or at death (3:4, 9), and having life in the new heavens and new earth (3:13). To be a Christian is to escape the world, corrupted by sin and lust (2:10, 18-19), which only leads to destruction (2:4b-10b, 12-13; 3:5-13).

3. Christian virtues are not something to decorate or enhance our Christian faith, but are the very means by which we exercise the power and knowledge of Christ to escape the corruption of the world and experience eternal life. Faith is the grounding of all Christian virtues because it provides the knowledge of Christ needed for a godly life (1:3). Love is the apex of the virtuous walk. When *agape* love is in evidence, all other virtues are present as well. The relationship between the virtues also reminds us that individual Christian virtues, while good in themselves, should be exercised in relationship to the others, with the goal's being *agape* love. The supreme goal of the Christian life is to be as perfect as God, and love is central to God's being (1 John 4:16). Love of others is motivated by God's love for us as expressed in the sacrifice of Christ for sin. Love for others perfects God's love in us (Matt 5:43-48; 1 John 4:7-11).

4. Supporting faith with virtues makes our faith productive for the kingdom of God. Not supporting faith with virtues returns us to the blindness of sin, and we forget our cleansing from sin (1:8-9). Continued effort to confirm our call and election through discipline and self-control will help to prevent us from slipping back into sin and corruption and thereby losing salvation (v. 10). Making every effort to support faith and to be godly through the power that Christ provides leads us to a rich provision in the eternal kingdom (1:11).

5. All the Christian life is a gift. The initial gift of everything needed for living the Christian life and godliness comes through knowledge of Christ and his power, gained at conversion. Escape from the corruption of sin and confirmation of our calling through godly living are made possible through the exercise of the gifts he has given us. Entrance into the eternal kingdom can be richly provided because his powers are available to allow us to be fruitful and effective in our Christian lives and not to return to sin and corruption.

2 PETER 1:12-15

A REMINDER OF THE CHRISTIAN LIFE

COMMENTARY

The opening of the body of 2 Peter is 1:12-15. This is indicated by the "reminder" topic, which is related to the full-disclosure formula, often used in letters: "I wish you to know that. . . ." In the body opening, the sender establishes common ground with the recipients and informs them of the reason for writing. The reason for writing the Epistle of 2 Peter is to provide a reminder of apostolic teaching, which is the common ground shared by the author and the churches to whom he wrote (cf. 3:1-2).

Farewell addresses remind their recipients of a common heritage to be preserved in the future, when death will have silenced the voice of the testator. The testament genre allows the author to use Peter's apostolic authority and teaching to address the situation of false teachers in his own time, as though Peter himself were speaking to the future—a future that is the present of the author and the letter's recipients. As a farewell address in the form of a letter, 2 Peter can keep on reminding the recipients of their common heritage (v. 12), because they can read the letter many times (v. 15). The apostolic teaching in 1:3-11 is initially the subject of reminder; but as the letter is read in the churches, the entire letter and its defense of apostolic teaching against the false teachers becomes the subject of reminding (1:15; 3:1-2).

Reminding is important because the Christians' lavish welcome into the kingdom depends upon their confirming their call and election by following the teachings of vv. 3-11. The churches know the tradition of which they are reminded because it is the basic Christian instruction, "the truth that has come to you" (v. 12). The author understands this truth as the message that Peter (3:1), Paul (3:15-16), and all the apostles preached (1:16-18; 3:1-4). The churches are established (στηρίζω *sterizō*) in this truth (v. 12), a common metaphor for stability in the Christian life (cf. Rom 16:25). In contrast, the false teachers have conveniently ignored the truth (3:5, 8) and are unstable (3:16). They entice unstable souls (2:14) and pose a threat to the stability of the hearers of this letter (3:17).

Peter is portrayed as being about to die, expressed in two analogies: that of getting rid of a tent being similar to the soul's leaving behind the temporary shelter of the body at death ("tent of the body," NIV; "body," NRSV; vv. 13-14; cf. 2 Cor 5:1-5), and that of an exodus ("departure," NRSV, NIV) from earth (v. 15), which precedes entry into the eternal kingdom (v. 11). The author portrays Peter as knowing of his impending death, not just because of Christ's prophecy about his martyrdom (e.g., John 21:18) as implied in the NRSV and NIV (v. 14), but also from revelation at the time of the writing of this letter. The testator was often portrayed as having had a revelation of his impending death, which prompts the writing of his farewell letter.

REFLECTIONS

1. This reminder is an element of the testament genre and contains few specifics upon which to reflect. However, the overall approach the author takes to help these churches is informative. This church leader continues to remind his churches of the apostolic teachings upon which they have based their faith and life together as a community. He also reminds them of their hope for the future as it impinges upon the way they live in the present. The churches are reminded of the gifts of Christ for the spiritual life, the need to mature in the faith, the need to confirm their call and election, and the promises of escaping corruption and entering into the eternal kingdom. The core gospel is not relegated to the confirmation class or the occasional evangelistic sermon, but remains the vital core of the church community, providing self-understanding, enunciation of purpose, direction to mission, hope for endurance, and, as the author of 2 Peter reminds us, spiritual stability.

2. This portion of the testament also reminds us that as each generation passes away, it needs to be sure that succeeding generations are aware of their traditions and will have opportunities to hear these traditions. Herein lies the importance of Christian education, preaching, and teaching in the church, as well as the need systematically and consciously to inform congregations of their heritage. In our post-Christian world, the social values and assumptions of our neighbors, popular culture, and mass media are decreasingly based on Christian values. So it is increasingly important that Christian tradition be a conscious part of our lives. We need that tradition in order to know how to live faithfully in an environment that does not necessarily uphold these virtues and values.

2 PETER 1:16–3:13

REFUTATION OF THE ACCUSATIONS OF THE FALSE TEACHERS

OVERVIEW

Second Peter 1:16–3:13 is the middle of the body of the letter and develops the material of the body opening. It corresponds to the rhetorical *probatio* in which the author presents propositions and corresponding proofs to support the reasons for the address as mentioned in the *exordium*. In 2 Peter, the body middle defends the apostolic tradition of the parousia and judgment, and the ethics that are appropriate in the light of it. The body middle also counterattacks the doctrine and practice of the false teachers, which stand in opposition to that of their apostolic counterparts.

2 PETER 1:16-21, THE APOSTOLIC PREACHING OF THE PAROUSIA IS NOT A "CLEVERLY DEVISED MYTH"

COMMENTARY

1:16a. The body of the letter begins with an implicit accusation of the false teachers, followed by the author's refutation of it (vv. 16*b*-19). The author uses the formula "not . . . but" (οὐ . . . ἀλλά *ou . . . alla*) to reject the false teachers' accusations (as in 1:21; 3:9). The false teachers charged that the apostolic proclamation of the "power and coming" or "coming in power" of Christ (parousia) was based on "cleverly devised myths" (NRSV) or "cleverly invented stories" (NIV). "Parousia" (παρουσία *parousia*) was a technical term for a visit to a city by a god, a ruler, or an important person to dispense rewards or mete out judgment. In Christianity, parousia came to refer to the return of Jesus Christ to judge the living and the dead (Matt 24:3; 1 Thess 2:19). The false teachers question this doctrine because of the apparent delay of the Second Coming (2:3*b*; 3:4). "Cleverly devised" (σοφίζω *sophizō*) implies that the doctrine of the parousia was concocted by deceit and ingenuity. Using the term "myth" (μῦθος *mythos*) to describe a narrative or prophecy connotes that it is untrue or lacks historical veracity. The Epicureans, for instance, to whom the false teachers bear some resemblance, considered the doctrines of providence and judgment of the wicked after death to be myths devised for social control.[15]

1:16b-18. Refutation of accusations against Christian doctrine often emphasized apostolic eyewitness testimony to historical events (1 Cor 15:3-8; 1 John 1:1-3). The author of 2 Peter begins to refute this accusation against the parousia with a proof from eyewitness testimony. Peter, James, and John witnessed Jesus' transfiguration, which was an apocalyptic revelation or proleptic vision of God's installation of Jesus as God's eschatological viceroy (Mark 9:2-8 par. Matt 17:1-8 par. Luke 9:28-36).[16] In v. 17, God's (the "Majestic Glory") quotation of

---

15. J. Neyrey, "The Form and Background of the Polemic in 2 Peter" (Ph.D. diss., Yale University, 1977) 185, 194-95.
16. H. C. Kee, "The Transfiguration in Mark: Epiphany or Apocalyptic Vision?," in *Understanding the Sacred Text*, (Valley Forge: Judson, 1972) 149; Bauckham, *Jude, 2 Peter,* 210-12.

Ps 2:7 at the transfiguration, originally spoken to install a king of Israel (later interpreted as the Messiah), indicates that God was not simply revealing Jesus' kingship, but installing him as king-Messiah. The transfiguration provided the historical basis for the proclamation of the parousia, when Jesus returns as eschatological king. The parousia hope is not false. It only remains for Jesus to exercise his authority, which already has been bestowed upon him by God at the parousia. The shift to the first-person "we" in vv. 16-18 groups Peter with the other apostles, the underlying assumption being that all the apostles preached the message of the parousia based on the transfiguration as related by the three eyewitnesses.

1:19. The author continues his refutation with a proof from a document, the "prophetic word." This phrase usually refers to the Old Testament, either as a whole or specific portions, and the false prophets mentioned in 2:1 make OT prophecies (probably interpreted as relating to the parousia) the likely reference. Apostolic teaching of the parousia is dependable because it relies on OT prophecy. The comparative adjective βεβαιότερον (*bebaioteron*) may be translated as a true comparative, "more fully confirmed" (NRSV) or "more certain" (NIV), and mean that OT prophecy has been made more reliable by the transfiguration. However, it is legitimate and probably better to translate it as a superlative, "very firm," which gives the meaning that OT prophecy provides firm support for the apostolic doctrine of the parousia. The author is refuting an attack on the doctrine of the parousia, not the reliability of OT prophecy, as the comparative sense implies.

The author is confident enough in the reality of the parousia to offer its imminence as a proof of the truth of the apostolic proclamation about it (v. 19). The importance of being attentive to this proclamation is amplified by the statement "You will do well to be attentive to this as to a lamp shining in a dark place" (NRSV). By being attentive to the parousia and all it entails, the churches will be ready when the true light of Christ, to which prophecy points, comes (cf. 1:10).

That coming light is expressed in two images. The first image, the "day dawns," refers to the coming of the eschatological age (cf. 3:18; Rom 13:12), the day of the Lord, the parousia (3:10), a day of judgment (2:9; 3:7; cf. 3:12). The second image, the "morning star rises in your hearts," has several referents. It alludes to Num 24:17 LXX, "a star will rise out of Jacob," which Judaism interpreted as the coming of the Messiah. The "morning star" is also the star seen at dawn, heralding approaching daylight. In Revelation, Jesus is called the "morning star" (Rev 2:28) and the "bright morning star" (Rev 22:16), the latter in the context of his being a descendant of David. All this material indicates that in 2 Peter "bright morning star" refers to the second coming of Jesus as Messiah to inaugurate an age of light, which our hearts can only believe now by faith, but will then experience in full.

1:20-21. The second accusation of the false teachers, in combination with 2 Peter's refutation, is provided in these verses. The accusation implicit here is that the OT prophecies upon which the apostles based their teaching of the parousia "came about by the prophet's own interpretation" of their dreams and visions, and not by revelation from God through the inspiration of the Holy Spirit. The author argues that no OT prophecy was a product of human will because the prophets were, indeed, inspired by the Spirit.

The NRSV's translation implies that the false teachers are claiming that they can interpret prophecy themselves without having to rely on apostolic interpretation. It is a matter of one's own interpretation, they seem to say. However, the type of argumentation and the words and phrases used in vv. 20-21 had become standard in Hellenistic Judaism and early Christian discussion of the human versus the divine origin and interpretation of OT prophecy[17] and of the prophets' interpretations of their dreams and visions as being divinely inspired (e.g., "intepretation" [ἐπίλυσις *epilysis*], Gen 40:8 [Aquila], 4 Ezra 10:43 [Gk]). The author's refutation of these false teachers is reminiscent of OT polemic that true prophets, as opposed to false prophets, do not speak their own words, but the Word of God (Jer 23:16-22; Ezek 13:1-7).[18]

---

17. E.g., "one's own" (ἴδιος *idios*); see Philo *Who is the Heir of Divine Things?* 259; *Moses* 1.281, 286.
18. Bauckham, *Jude, 2 Peter*, 228-35.

REFLECTIONS

1. God's delay in fulfilling prophecies and promises of Christ's return can make them seem like myths. Often we wonder about the truth of the promised parousia because God has not acted to fulfill that promise in nearly two millennia. Our doubt may be subtly expressed in attitudes and behavior that do not exhibit a concern for being found morally blameless when Christ does return. Our doubts surface in times of personal crisis. They are fueled by growing public problems that seem to threaten the very fabric of life on this planet, problems like the depletion of natural resources at an alarming rate, the continual outbreak of wars and ethnic violence, the emergence of super viruses, and the complexities involved in making even small steps forward in eradicating crime, poverty, and a host of other pervasive problems. Yet we can put our trust in the inspired apostolic eyewitness testimony to the transfiguration as it is now found in the New Testament and in the Old Testament prophecies that support the proclamation of the parousia. We can endeavor to live in the light radiated by this small lamp of proclamation until fully radiated by Christ at his return.

2. We are given an insight here into the ways prophets received their prophecies. One model for receiving the prophecy is that it was spoken directly from God (Amos 3:8). Another model is the prophet's receiving a sign (Jer 1:11, 13), a dream (Zech 1:8–6:15), or a vision (Ezek 37:1-14), which later must be interpreted through the power of the Holy Spirit (Amos 7:8-9). False prophecy or misinterpretation arises when personal interpretation of the dream or vision replaces that of the Holy Spirit (Jer 23:16), or even when the dream or vision itself and its interpretation arise from the prophet (Ezek 13:2-3). Such misinterpretation results from excessive personal ambition and the desire to please the crowd by telling the people what they want to hear (Jer 23:25-26), lack of trust in God to fulfill the prophecy because it stands in too great a contrast to current conditions to be believed, or deciding for ourselves that God should not or certainly would not act in the fashion revealed in the prophecy. Such were the roots of false prophecy and misinterpretation in the Old Testament (just what Jeremiah said about his opponents or the author of 2 Peter says about his!). Such are also the roots of misinterpretation in the church today when God's message is qualified and muffled because it is disquieting to special interests, does not seem possible because God has not acted that way in some time, or does not conform to our scenarios of a comfortable future.

2 PETER 2:1-3*a*, PROPHECY OF THE APPEARANCE OF FALSE TEACHERS

COMMENTARY

The testament genre in Judaism usually included prophecy about the last days. In early Christian testaments the appearance of false teachers in the church in the last days is the focal point of such prophecy (Acts 20:29-30; 2 Tim 3:1-9; 4:3-4). The author of 2 Peter provides such a prophecy in 2:1-3*a*. His message depends on the preaching of Jesus and the apostles, which include prophecies of false teachers in the last days (Matt 24:11, 24; 1 Tim 4:1-5; 1 John 4:1-3; Jude 17-18). The switch within the prophecy from "false prophets" to "false teachers" (v. 1) indicates that the opponents did not claim prophetic inspiration for their teaching. However, their teaching did warrant their classification as false teachers motivated by greed (vv. 3*a*, 14-15).

In this prophecy, the author turns from refuting the false teachers' accusations against apostolic teaching (1:16-21) to counteraccusing them of similar behavior. Using Jude 4, in 2:1 the author claims that, rather than the apostles, it is the false teachers who stand in the succession of the false prophets of Israel. Their teaching is to "secretly bring in destructive opinions" (NRSV) or to "secretly introduce destructive heresies" (NIV). The verb "bring in" (παρεισάγω *pareisagō*) often connotes something underhanded. "Destructive opinions" (αἵρεσις *hairesis*) refers to a school of thought or a particular teaching of that school (later the word was given the negative meaning "heresy" or "wrong doctrine"; cf. NIV). These opinions are destructive because they lead to destruction at the parousia. In v. 3*a* the teaching of the false teachers is also described as "deceptive words" (NRSV) or "stories they have made up" (NIV; πλαστοῖς λόγοις *plastois logois*). The false teachers' claim that the apostles preached a myth (1:16) has been turned back upon them.

The height of erroneous teaching is expressed in a common Christian metaphor: The false teachers even "deny the Master" (NRSV) or "sovereign Lord" (NIV) who bought them (v. 1). A master (δεσπότης *despotēs*) was the head of a household (or ruler) who was due great honor (1 Tim 6:1; 2 Tim 2:21; Titus 2:9; 1 Pet 2:18). Like masters who acted as patrons and purchased slaves out of slavery in order to set them free (sacral manumission), Christ offered his blood as a purchase price to buy sinners from slavery to sin and death to set them free to serve him (1 Cor 6:20; 7:23; 1 Pet 1:18-19; Rev 5:9; 14:3-4). Any master who acted as a patron for a slave in this capacity was due lifetime gratitude and honor. Redemption by Christ should lead to slavery to him and a life of righteousness that honors him and expresses the loyalty due him (Rom 6:15-23). The false teachers probably do not deny Christ's authority with some doctrinal statement, but with the sinful conduct of their moral life that is an outgrowth of their denial of judgment. They are disobedient, renegade slaves who do not obey their Master's instruction and, therefore, shame him.

By following the false teachers' denial of the Master and of final judgment, some persons in the church have backslidden into the accompanying behavior of "licentious" and "shameful" ways of pagan immorality (v. 2). As a result of denying Christ through ethical misconduct "the way of truth will be maligned" (NRSV), an allusion to Isa 52:5 LXX: "Because of you my name is continually reviled among the nations." This text was commonly alluded to or quoted in early Christian exhortation not to live immorally and give Gentiles cause to revile God and God's truth—truth that should be guiding the ethical life (Rom 2:23-24; 1 Tim 6:1; Titus 2:5). The ethical life that God demands is described with the common Jewish-Christian metaphor of the "way." Christianity is not defined as a person's simply cognitively adopting doctrines for one's own, but adopting a disciplined way of life (Acts 9:2). Besides maligning the way of truth, elsewhere the false teachers are said to have forsaken the straight way (v. 15), having once known "the way of righteousness" (v. 21).

In his counteraccusation the author makes the additional point that these false teachers will be judged with "swift [or imminent] destruction" (v. 1). Describing their judgment this way anticipates their accusation that destruction is asleep (v. 3*b*) and that Christ is slow about coming in judgment (3:4, 9). Ironically, the "slow" coming is really "imminent" destruction (cf. 1 Thess 5:3)! The very judgment that the false teachers deny is the judgment they will incur for their "destructive opinions" (v. 1).

REFLECTIONS

1. The contrast between the false teachers of 2 Peter and the false prophets of the Old Testament is more accusatory than is immediately evident. Like the false prophets, the false teachers do not speak with divine authority. Rather, they proclaim a false message of peace and security against the true prophetic (and apostolic) message of judgment upon sin on the day of the Lord. Like the false prophets, the false teachers will be subject to the very judgment of God that they have denied (Deut 18:20; Jer 14:13-16; 23:9-40; 28:16-17; Ezek 13:1-16).

2. We are reminded by 2 Peter that within the confines of Christianity are interpretations, doctrine, and practices that are not acceptable to God and the church because they are at variance with the revealed nature of God, with traditions from Jewish heritage, with the apostolic proclamation of the gospel, and with subsequent Christian tradition. Belief and behavior incongruous with God's revealed nature and revealed will for us, which maligns the witness of Christianity, lead to God's judgment and to destruction at the parousia (e.g., abandonment to lust or denial of Christ's Lordship in our lives).

3. We need to see the Christian life as obedience to Jesus Christ as our Master. The Christian way is a lifetime of gratitude for his redemption of us from slavery to sin, a gratitude lived out in voluntary servanthood to him. Like slaves so redeemed in antiquity, we live in order to honor the Master. But we have been given a choice: We can be grateful slaves who honor the Master by obeying him, or ungrateful slaves who shame our Master by disobeying him. Desire to honor Christ the Master can be a powerful motivation for our ethical walk. Fear of shaming Christ the Master can likewise be a powerful motivation to live morally upright lives.

4. Christianity is not defined as merely intellectually embracing a right doctrine. One needs also to adopt a morally disciplined walk, a way of life and truth. The truth of the doctrines we accept is made known and exemplified by the way we live our lives. Acts of kindness that exemplify the life to which Christ calls us do get noticed. We may be surprised that a small part of our life, lived according to the truth, can influence someone to place his or her trust in Christ. But the truth can also be maligned by the way we choose to live and can become a source of ridicule for those who have yet to accept the way of truth. Who knows how many persons have rejected Christ because of the poor example of unfaithful Christians?

2 PETER 2:3b-10a, THE JUDGMENT OF GOD IS NOT IDLE OR ASLEEP

COMMENTARY

2:3b. In vv. 3b-10a, the author refutes another accusation of the false teachers. First, though, he gives a proposition that is really a denial of the accusation that divine condemnation is idle, and divine destruction is asleep, a charge underlying 3:4, 9 as well. The accusation is similar to that of pagan skeptics who mocked the gods for their inactivity in the world; it is similar as well to several OT passages in which God or a god is accused of being ineffective or not acting in judgment (e.g., 1 Kgs 18:27; Ps 44:23-26).

2:4-10a. This passage is an elaborate one-sentence proof for the proposition of v. 3b that the condemnation and destruction of judgment, pronounced long ago, have not been idle or asleep. The proof is based on three OT examples of sinners who were judged: the watchers, the generation of the flood, and the inhabitants of Sodom and Gomorrah. The two examples of the destruction by water at the flood and by fire at Sodom and Gomorrah are sometimes linked together in tradition as the two prime examples of divine judgment[19] or the two prototypes of eschatological judgment (Luke 17:26-30). In the ancient world

19. *Jub.* 20:5.

there was a tradition that divine judgment was manifested by the means of destruction by water and fire.[20]

These three examples are part of a traditional scheme used to affirm the judgment of the wicked and the salvation of the righteous (Sir 16:6-23). The author of 2 Peter depends on Jude 6-8, but he substitutes the flood generation for the wilderness generation. He also adds examples of the righteous who were spared judgment, perhaps to reassure the faithful in the churches to whom he is writing of their ultimate deliverance from the sin of the world. These examples are prophetic types or acted prophecies of the eschatological judgment awaiting the ungodly and of the salvation awaiting the faithful. It is the fate of the false teachers and the faithful in the churches respectively.

2:4. The first example of judgment comes from Jewish tradition about the watchers. The watchers are the angels referred to in Gen 6:1-4, who are portrayed as having had sex with human women. In Jewish tradition, these angels were cast into hell and confined to chains of deepest darkness until judgment for their sexual sins.[21] "Hell" is literally the Tartarus of Greek mythology, the lowest part of the underworld, where the titans (giants) were kept in chains by the Greek gods for their rebellion against them. In Jewish apocalyptic literature, Tartarus became the lowest place in Hades (Gehenna), where divine punishment of the wicked was dispensed.[22] For the false teachers, the deepest darkness has also been reserved (2:17).

2:5. The second example of judgment is the flood, which was necessitated by the corruption of humanity by the watchers and their offspring (Gen 6:5–8:22). In Judeo-Christian tradition, the flood is considered a prototype of the eschatological judgment (*1 Enoch* 6-16; Matt 24:37-39). The author of 2 Peter later reintroduces the example of the judgment of the ungodly by water as a prelude to the eschatological judgment of the wicked by fire (3:5-7). He also uses the righteous Noah and his family, the sole survivors of the flood, as types of the faithful Christians who will survive the judgment in the parousia. In Jewish tradition, Noah proclaimed repentance to his ungodly neighbors—unfortunately with no success. We may surmise that the faithful in the churches that received this letter were making similar proclamations, or were being urged by Noah's example to do so, with the promise that they, too, will be saved when the ungodly are destroyed.

2:6-8. The third example of judgment is the destruction of Sodom and Gomorrah (Gen 19:1-29). This judgment is often described as a warning example, as it is here (cf. Deut 29:22-28; Wis 10:6-8; Matt 10:15; 11:23-24). This example would be particularly effective if the author of 2 Peter and his audience believed, as did many at that time, that the hot springs and sulfurous gases of the region south of the Dead Sea were the smoldering ruins of Sodom and Gomorrah.[23] This judgment is a prophetic type of the eschatological judgment by fire (3:7; for more on the sin of Sodom and Gomorrah, see Commentary and Reflections at Jude 5-10). This extended description of the righteous Lot and his spiritual distress over the licentiousness of his neighbors portrays his situation in a way that the author's churches could empathize, for they, too, were probably distressed at the evil surrounding them.

2:9. The proposition that the examples of vv. 4-8 prove that judgment is not idle and that destruction is not asleep (v. 3*b*) is restated: "The Lord knows how to rescue the godly from trial, and to keep the unrighteous under punishment until the day of judgment." The antithesis in the proposition juxtaposes and emphasizes the fates of the righteous and the ungodly. The trial from which the righteous will be rescued is the afflictions that the righteous suffer in an evil world; trials with which the audience can probably identify (Luke 8:13; Jas 1:2-3; 1 Pet 1:6). This trial is not necessarily the tribulation of the last days (1 Pet 4:12; Rev 3:10); but for the author of 2 Peter the presence of the false teachers is indicative of the end times (3:3-4), and he may have final tribulation in mind. Keeping the unrighteous under punishment until the judgment probably does not refer to preliminary punishment in some intermediate state

---

20. Plato *Timaeus* 22B-C; Lucretius *On the Nature of Things* 5.341-44, 383-415; 6.660-737.
21. Rather than "chains" (σειρά *seira*), some MSS read "pits" (σειρός *seiros*), which the NIV translates as "dungeons."
22. *Sib. Or.* 2.302; 4:186.
23. Philo *Moses* 2.56; Josephus *The Jewish War* 4.483.

prior to judgment, but to the punishment awaiting the unrighteous at the parousia.

2:10a. The proposition of v. 9 is emphasized by the phrase in the first part of this verse, which mentions for the first time the sins of the three examples of vv. 4-8: indulging their lust and despising authority as outlined in the counteraccusation of v. 1-3a. These two sins are related, for to engage in any misconduct is by nature to despise divine authority. "Indulge their flesh in depraved lust" (NRSV) or "follow the corrupt desire of the sinful nature" (NIV) implies that the flesh is the master or god that the false teachers follow (Deut 4:3; 6:14 LXX), not Christ (cf. 2:1).

REFLECTIONS

1. Noah and Lot are representative of the situation of the righteous, who must live within contexts in which moral authority is dismissed and the flesh is indulged. In Jewish tradition, these two men did not simply choose to ignore the rebellion against God that was being waged around them. Noah actively proclaimed repentance, and Lot was deeply distressed by the lawlessness encompassing him. Although Noah's preaching did not change the ways of his neighbors, he was found faithful and was spared the judgment of the flood. His reward was based on his righteousness, not on the response of his neighbors. This is an encouragement to us that even when our best efforts fail to lead someone to repentance, we are still rewarded for having tried.

2. This section reminds us that sometimes our perspective on a situation may be too limited. Often there are times when God does not seem to be actively working for us, when it appears that the world is riding roughshod over us and no one cares. The righteous suffer trials in an evil world, for righteous living angers the world by reminding it of its fallen state and its capitulation to sin and the flesh. The righteous suffer because they refuse to take unethical shortcuts and will not put themselves above others—characteristics that may let the unrighteous beat them to goals. The author of 2 Peter assures us that God is always actively working for the salvation of the righteous, even when they are in the midst of trial. God's work is evident when we use the gifts that Christ has given to live a godly life and escape corruption (1:3-4); and when such trials produce endurance and spiritual maturity (Jas 1:3-4).

3. From time immemorial it has seemed to those striving to live an honest and righteous life that the liars and cheaters rarely get caught and seem to benefit without any negative consequences. The author of 2 Peter reminds us that the judgment of God, ultimate justice, is quite capable of sorting out the righteous for reward and the unrighteous for destruction, even if it does not occur in this life.

2 PETER 2:10b-22, A DENUNCIATION OF THE FALSE TEACHERS

COMMENTARY

At this juncture the author digresses from the main flow of the body of the letter to supply a loosely structured denunciation based in part on Jude 8-13, 16. The denunciation negatively characterizes the false teachers as ungodly, castigates their doctrine, and alerts the audience to the dire consequences of following that doctrine.

2:10b-11. The denunciation begins abruptly with two accusations. The false teachers are "bold"—that is, they have an unwarranted presumption of power and status (cf. Jude 9)—and they are "willful"/"arrogant." These accusations are substantiated by the false teachers' slandering of the "glorious ones" (NRSV) or "celestial beings" (NIV), a reference to angels (v. 11).[24] Some commentators envision the false teachers as slandering good angels involved in judgment (Matt 24:31; Rev 14:15-16), with the point of v. 11 being that good angels, even though more powerful, will not in turn bring a slanderous judgment from the Lord against the false teachers.

However, the false teachers are probably slandering evil angels. Perhaps because of their immorality, which they justify as an expression of freedom in Christ (v. 19), the false teachers have slandered the evil angels as having no power over them. The audacity of this action is emphasized by contrast to good angels, who are more powerful than the evil angels (and certainly more powerful than the false teachers), but are not so bold as to slander them. In Jude 8-9, upon which this section is based, it is the good angel Michael who will not pronounce judgment upon the evil angel Satan.

2:12-13a. In v. 12 the false teachers are said to slander those (the evil angels) whom they do not understand. Such ignorance shows them to be functioning like irrational animals, which act on instinct, born to be captured and destroyed. Most commentators (e.g., NRSV, NIV) understand the concluding phrase of v. 12, "will be destroyed" in their destruction, as an indication that the false teachers will be either destroyed like animals, which are intended to be destroyed for food, as just described as the reason that animals are born, or destroyed like animals with the future judgment by fire (3:11-13), just as ungodly humans and animals were destroyed together in the flood (2:5). However, if one understands the continued focus here to be on the evil angels, then this reference is to the false teachers' sharing the destruction of the evil angels, whom they slander! This destruction is emphasized in v. 13a, for the false teachers, like the evil angels, will be "suffering the penalty for doing wrong"—that is, eschatological judgment.

2:13b. The theme of the false teachers' having led some in the churches into licentious ways for reasons of greed, originally expressed in the counteraccusation of vv. 1-3a, is developed in vv. 13b-16. The false teachers find pleasure to "revel" (NRSV) or "carouse" (NIV) in the daytime (v. 13b). Such behavior was considered a standard mark of moral degeneration (Eccl 10:16; Isa 5:11-12). The false teachers have carried this "reveling in their pleasures" (NIV) or "dissipation" (NRSV; usually of a sinful nature) into the love feasts of the churches, where it has no place. Such activity makes the false teachers "blots and blemishes" (morally corrupt), which is contrary to the desirable state of being without spot or blemish (morally incorrupt) at the parousia (3:14).

2:14. The author accuses the false teachers of having "eyes full of adultery, insatiable for sin," of always looking for someone with whom to commit adultery. The author may be relying on a well-known maxim that a shameless man does not have κοραί (*korai*), "pupils" or "maidens"—a pun—in his eyes, but πορναί (*pornai*), "harlots."[25] Another accusation is that the false teachers "ensnare unsteady souls" or "seduce the unstable." This accusation relies on fishing and snaring with bait as a metaphor for enticing a person to commit a vice, and it portrays the false teachers as fishing for the unstable, probably new converts whom they ensnare (v. 18), like unsuspecting fish. The false teachers also possess "hearts trained in greed." They are "experts in greed." This accusation relies on athletic training as a metaphor for the effort expended and practice performed to become effective in greed. Whereas the victims of the false teachers are unsteady, the false teachers themselves are thoroughly trained in and dedicated to greed and know how to exploit the unsteady. The exclamation "accursed children!" effectively summarizes the consequences of the false teachers' behavior—coming under God's judgment (Isa 57:4; Eph 2:3).

2:15-16. Here the author relies on the comparison of the two ways Judaism used to describe the ethical walk: the righteous way

---

24. Some MSS have "from the Lord" (NRSV), and others "to" or "before the Lord," as if the angels come into God's presence to make the accusation (NIV). The use of Jude favors the former reading, for the archangel Michael deferred slanderous judgment to the Lord (Jude 9).

25. Plutarch *Moralia* 528E. Bauckham, *Jude, 2 Peter*, 266.

of obedience to God and the wicked way of disobedience to God (e.g., Prov 28:18). First he accuses the false teachers of having "left the straight [way] and have gone astray." "Straight way" (εὐθεῖαν ὁδὸν *eutheian hodon*) is a common metaphor for obedience to God (Prov 2:16 LXX; Isa 33:15 LXX) and "leaving" and "going astray" (or "wandered off," NIV) are complementary metaphors for disobedience to God (Deut 11:28 LXX; Prov 21:16 LXX). This accusation is amplified in vv. 15*b*-16 with the example of Balaam, son of Bosor, who left the straight way because of greed (Num 22:21-35). "Bosor" is an unattested form of the name "Beor," and is probably a play on the Hebrew word בשׂר (*bāśār*, "flesh"; Βοσόρ *Bosor*), which in effect calls Balaam "son of the flesh."[26]

The description "loved the wages of doing wrong" or "wages of wickedness" refers to the monetary gain that Balaam hoped to receive from Balak for cursing Israel (cf. Acts 1:18, where the same phrase refers to the wages Judas received for betraying Jesus). It may also be ironical, referring to the reward of judgment Balaam received from Israel's God. Tradition says that Balaam's reward was death by the sword of Israel's army when he was caught with the Midianites (Num 31:8).[27] These wages refer to the penalty or payback of judgment the false teachers will experience for their sin (v. 13*a*).

Although in the text of Num 22:21-25 the ass only rebukes Balaam for striking her, and it is the angel who makes the full rebuke, the author of 2 Peter relies on Jewish haggadic tradition in which the ass does speak against Balaam's madness in attempting to curse Israel for monetary gain, against the will of God (targums to Num 22:30). Having compared the false teachers to irrational animals (v. 12), having identified the false teachers as followers of the way of Balaam in greed (v. 15; cf. v. 3*a*), and now having mentioned that Balaam's madness in attempting to curse Israel was refuted by an ass that proved more rational than he, the author leads his audience to conclude that the false teachers, like Balaam, are less rational than an irrational ass.

26. Bauckham, *Jude, 2 Peter,* 267-68.
27. Bauckham, *Jude, 2 Peter,* 268; J. Neyrey, "Polemic in 2 Peter" (1977) 91-94; *b. Sanh.* 106a; *Num. Rab.* 22:5.

2:17. In this verse the false teachers are called "waterless springs" and "mists driven by a storm." These metaphors rely on the traditional imagery of religious teaching as being the sustainer of the spiritual life just as water is the sustainer of the natural life (Prov 13:14; Sir 24:23-34). Both metaphors emphasize that although the doctrine of the false teachers seems to promise spiritual life, in reality it proves to be empty. Also, like the mists, which have no will of their own but are subject to the wind, the false teachers are not free. They are slaves to corruption and defilement by the world (vv. 19-20). The judgment of "deepest darkness" ("blackest darkness," NIV), the "holding cell" of the watchers (2:4, 9), is the eschatological fate of the false teachers (cf. Jude 13).

2:18. The false teachers can be characterized as spiritually empty of promise, lacking freedom, and headed for deepest darkness for reasons given in vv. 18-22. Here they are said to speak "empty, boastful words" ("bombastic nonsense," NRSV) that entice with "licentious desires of the flesh" ("lustful desires of sinful human nature," NIV). The victims of the false teachers' proselyting are new converts, a portion of the unsteady souls enticed by the sinful living of the false teachers (vv. 2, 14), those not established in the faith (1:12). They have escaped error (πλάνη *planē*), a typical designation for the turning away from the pagan, non-Christian life-style that strays from the moral way established by God (v. 15). It is the error of the lawless that the established Christians being addressed are exhorted to beware of as a threat to their stability (3:17).

2:19. This verse conveys the empty message with which the false teachers ensnare the new Christians (v. 18) and renders them liable to judgment (v. 17): promise of freedom from judgment and moral restraint. Ironically, this kind of freedom enslaves the false teachers to the corruption ("depravity," NIV) that such "freedom" generates (cf. Rom 8:21). Corruption is mortality, the consequence of sin and God's judgment (v. 12). Corruption is the consequence of indulging in lust and failing to become a participant in the divine nature (1:4). Corruption is personified and portrayed in the image of a victor in war who seizes the defeated as slaves and booty. This personification is underscored by the ancient maxim, "People are slaves to whatever masters them." The false teachers promise freedom, but scoff that Christ's promise of the parousia is unfulfilled (3:4, 9). The author points out that it is the false teachers who are guilty of making promises that will go unfulfilled.

2:20-22. Serving as a strong deterrent to those who would follow or have followed the false teachers, these verses describe how drastic a mistake that would be. Whereas becoming a Christian means escaping the corruption in the world (1:3-4), leaving this state is more tragic than never having escaped the world's corruption ("defilement," NRSV) at all. This assertion is supported by a saying of Jesus (from either Matt 12:45 par. Luke 11:26, Q, or oral tradition) concerning the state of one who experiences the return of the unclean spirit with seven others (v. 20).

In 1:3-4, the essential content of Christianity is presented, and in 2:18-20 this content is contrasted with the apostasy of the false teachers. The knowledge of Christ (ἐπίγνωσις *epignōsis*, 1:3) is a divine gift that enables a godly life. The promises of Christ (ἐπάγγελμα *epangelma*, 1:4) enable escape (ἀποφεύγω *apopheugō*, 1:4) from corruption in the world (ἐν τῷ κόσμῳ . . . φθορᾶς *en tō kosmō . . . phthoras*, 1:4) because of passion (ἐπιθυμία *epithymia*, 1:4). The knowledge of Christ (*epignōis*, 2:20) that enables escape (*apopheugō*, 2:20) from defilements of the world (τὰ μιάσματα τοῦ κόσμου *ta miasmata tou kosmou*) does not prevent one from becoming a slave to those defilements once more. Those who have such knowledge and have escaped can be lured away by what the false teachers promise (2:19) to become slaves of corruption (δοῦλοι τῆς φθορᾶς *douloi tēs phthoras*, 2:19) by licentious desires of the flesh (ἐν ἐπιθυμίαις σαρκὸς ἀσελγείαις *en epithymiais sarkos aselgeiais*, 2:18; cf. 2:10).

Verse 21 repeats v. 20 in the form of a *Tobspruch,* a proverbial form expressing the idea of one state's being better than another. This form was borrowed from Judaism and was used widely in early Christian writing to emphasize how terrible are certain behaviors (Matt 5:29, 30; 12:45; 1 Pet 3:17). It is worse to turn away from the way of righteousness, a common metaphor of the ethical life (Prov 21:16, 21 LXX; Matt 21:32), and its equivalent "holy commandment" ("sacred command," NIV), than never to have known it at all. Such turning from the way of truth (2:2) and the straight way (2:15) is to follow the way of Balaam (2:15). The verb "delivered"/"passed on" (παραδίδωμι *paradidōmi*) is a technical term for passing on tradition, and its use should remind the churches that the Christian instruction in question was delivered to them by the apostles. It is not something to be spurned, but should be held in authority (as assumed in 3:2).

The denunciation of the false teachers ends in v. 22 with a proverb that underscores their return to soil themselves in the filth of immorality after having been cleansed from sin (cf. 1:9). They are like a dog that returns to ingest the impurity of its own vomit and the pig that returns to the mud once it has been cleaned. Dogs and pigs, despised animals in the ancient Near East, were often joined in proverbs to symbolize the immorality of the Gentiles (Matt 7:6; Rev 22:15). The first half of the proverb is derived from Prov 26:11, and the second half is traditional to the ancient world.[28]

28. *Ahiqar* 8:18 [Syriac], 8:15 [Arabic].

REFLECTIONS

1. The author's denunciation of other Christians in 2:10*b*-22 (esp. vv. 10*b*-16) may seem harsh and unchristian to us. Obviously it was his firm belief that teachers of non-apostolic doctrine, a denial of judgment that leads to immorality, should be negatively characterized. It was the practice of the author's time to portray one's opponents in the worst possible light—as greedy, immoral, rebellious, lustful, and taking advantage of others for personal gain. It was acceptable to associate one's opponents with all kinds of negative images in order to destroy their reputation and thus to lessen the proclivity of others to accept their doctrine and practice. We still must speak out against aberrations of doctrine in our day, but we must be sure to do so in ways that are effective in our culture. Bombast directed at someone may not be one of the ways we would choose today. Even the ancient orators warned that if you attack your opponents too harshly, the audience will begin to sympathize with them instead of with you.

2. The author reminds us of the serious responsibility Christian leaders have of remaining faithful stewards of Christian tradition. Misleading converts with doctrine and practice that vary from what is taught by Scripture and tradition or not delivering what is needed for spiritual growth and sustenance have serious negative consequences. He also reminds us that our own spiritual life, our own understanding of doctrine and its outworking in practice, affect those whom we are seeking to lead.

3. This digression in 2 Peter raises the need to discuss the serious attitude that the early church took toward post-baptismal sin. Persistent sin after conversion is a conscious rejection of salvation by Christ. Persistent sin leaves Christians without recourse to divine grace (1 Cor 3:16-17; Heb 6:4-8), without a sacrifice for sin (Heb 10:26). Hebrews describes this state as "crucifying again the Son of God," "holding him up to contempt" (Heb 6:6 NRSV), and having "spurned the Son of God, profaned the blood of the covenant by which they were sanctified, and outraged the Spirit of grace" (Heb 10:29 NRSV). Rejecting Christ's redemptive work on the cross through continuing in sin is a state worse than never having availed upon his offer of salvation, because that offer has been irrevocably rejected. To return to the corruption of the flesh (1:4; 2:19) is to reject the lordship of Christ and to be led instead by instinct (2:1, 12).

Post-baptismal sin is a reality in the life of every Christian. It has many roots. Sometimes such sin is rooted in ignorance of what the Christian life is all about. Maybe we simply did not know that a certain attitude or behavior was inappropriate for a Christian. Sometimes sin derives from personality patterns so ingrained that we simply cannot shake them off quickly. Sin can be an addictive behavior that may need professional help to dispell. The author of 2 Peter raises the issue of the sources of sin here because it needs to be stressed that God knows the difficulty that sin can pose to us and how strong its roots can sometimes be. The author points out that the greater problem is indulging sin rather than striving "to be found by him at peace, without spot or blemish" (2 Pet 3:14 NRSV) and growing "in the grace and knowledge of our Lord and Savior Jesus Christ" (2 Pet 3:18 NRSV). The greater problem is capitulation to sin rather than striving for spiritual growth. Be encouraged: God knows that our spiritual walk will have slipups in spite of our attempt to obey and that digging out the roots of sin may take some time.

2 PETER 3:1-13, AN APOLOGY FOR THE DELAY OF THE PAROUSIA

COMMENTARY

3:1-2. After the digression of 2:10*b*-22, the author returns to the main argument of the letter body with a transition in these verses (based on Jude 17). Whereas the digression describes the false teachers in the present tense, the reference in v. 1 to this being the second letter intended as a reminder recalls 1 Peter and reestablishes that the letter is a testament of Peter regarding the future. The transition prepares the churches for "Peter's" prediction in vv. 3-4 that false teachers will arise after his death (cf. 1:12-15), a common theme in farewell addresses.

The author exhorts the churches to remember OT prophecy and Jesus' commandment (ethical teachings), given through the apostles who founded the churches in faith (i.e., "your apostles"), concerning the parousia and its accompanying judgment. Reminding the audience of these teachings and appealing to the OT, to Jesus, and to the apostles is the same strategy the author used in 1:12-21. By referring to the audience as having "pure thinking" in a moral sense (εἰλικρινής διάνοια *eilikrinēs dianoia*; "sincere intention," NRSV; "wholesome thinking," NIV) and by reminding them of Jesus' commandment, the author distinguishes the audience from the false teachers who have forgotten the commandment (2:21) and who follow after their own lusts (3:3).

3:3-4. As mentioned in vv. 1-2, there were OT prophecies of scoffers who mocked the delay of divine judgment (Amos 9:10; Mal 2:17) and early Christian prophecies of the arrival of false teachers in the last days. These Christian prophecies are attributed to Jesus (Matt 7:15; 24:11, 24; Mark 13:22), to Paul (Acts 20:29-30; 1 Tim 4:1-3; 2 Tim 4:3-4), and to others (1 John 4:1-3; *Did.* 16:3). However, these prophecies are not merely reiterated here; rather, Peter is portrayed as giving an analogous prophecy of scoffers of the parousia and judgment. In v. 3, "scoffer" (ἐμπαίκτης *empaiktēs*) is a derogatory term for someone who despises and ignores religion and morality. It is partially defined as "indulging their own lusts" (NRSV) or "following their own evil desires" (NIV; ἐπιθυμία *epithymia*)—that is, to follow the flesh rather than God's direction (2:10a, 18). The words and deeds of the false teachers will indicate to the churches that they are the scoffers who were predicted to come in the last days.

In v. 4 the author presents the accusation of the false teachers as part of the prophecy of Peter: "Where is the promise of his coming? For ever since our ancestors [lit., "fathers"] died [lit., "fell asleep"], all things continue as they were from the beginning of creation!" (cf. 2:3b). This accusation is in the form of a rhetorical question, reminiscent of such questions raised by scoffers of God in the OT (beginning with "where is" [ποῦ ἐστιν *pou estin*]), including questioning of God's intervention in judgment (Jer 17:15; Mal 2:17 LXX). The promise mentioned is part to those of Jesus referred to in 1:4, including some which seem to limit the parousia to the lifetime of Jesus' contemporaries (cf. 3:13; Matt 16:28 par. Mark 9:1 par. Luke 9:27; Matt. 24:34 par. Mark 13:30 par. Luke 21:32; John 21:22-23; cf. Matt 10:23). The false teachers are denying the parousia because, according to apostolic proclamation, the fathers, the first generation of Christians, were to have experienced the parousia, but died without its materialization.

3:5-13. Besides the death of the first Christian generation, the false teachers seem to be basing their scoffing and denial of the parousia on the premise that the world has not experienced judgment of cosmic magnitude like that expected to accompany the parousia (cf. vv. 10, 12). This is the argument the author refutes in vv. 5-7. The denial of the false teachers has parallels in the Epicurean denial of providence, or divine intervention, in the world in both creation and judgment. The Epicureans denied God's providence and the reality of judgment on the basis of the delay or slowness of divine judgment.[29]

In vv. 5-13 the author refutes the false teachers' two-pronged accusation of v. 4. Refutation is indicated by the shift from the prophecy of false teachers and their accusation given in the future tense in vv. 3-4, to the author's refutation of the accusation in the present tense in vv. 5-13. The accusation that the world has continued without judgment is refuted in vv. 5-7 (as in 2:3b-10a), and the accusation that the promise of the parousia is false because it did not come during the lifetime of the first Christian generation is refuted in vv. 8-13. This defense in vv. 4-13 is partially derived from a Jewish apocalyptic source or argumentative scheme that, in spite of its delay, defended the doctrine of God's intervention with judgment in history.[30]

3:5-7. The opening phrase of v. 5, "they deliberately ignore this fact," implies that the false teachers can make their accusation only by ignoring the facts of the creation, the flood, and the fiery judgment described in these verses. As in Genesis 1, the author of

---

29. See Neyrey, "The Form and Background of the Polemic in 2 Peter," 203-5; "The Form and Background of the Polemic in 2 Peter," *JBL* 99 (1980) 420.
30. A source or scheme also used to explain the delay of the parousia in *1 Clem.* 23:3-4 and *2 Clem.* 11:2-4. Bauckham, *Jude, 2 Peter,* 283-84.

2 Peter here stresses the role of God's Word in creation. By God's Word the heavens and the earth were created (v. 5); by God's Word water was stored up for world judgment at the flood (v. 6); and by God's Word fire is stored up for cosmic judgment at the parousia (v. 7).[31] The unexpressed conclusion is that God clearly has and can intervene for judgment by the same Word that underlies creation itself. The affirmation in v. 7 that the present heavens and earth have been stored up for destruction by fire "by the same word" underlying the flood indicates that the author believed he was drawing this information from prophecy. This prophecy may have been the Jewish apocalyptic source he was using or OT texts (e.g., Deut 32:22; Isa 66:15-16; Zeph 1:18).

The argumentation of vv. 5-7 is tied to that of 2:3b-10a. The example of the flood affirms that God's judgment is active in history (2:5-6). The example of Sodom and Gomorrah affirms that the judgment of the ungodly will be by fire (2:6). Like the watchers, the unrighteous are kept for judgment (2:4, 9). Now it is affirmed that the heavens and the earth are kept for the judgment of destruction by fire and the destruction of the godless.

3:8-13. Whereas vv. 5-7 refute the false teachers' accusation that the world has continued without judgment (v. 4), these verses refute the accusation that the promise of the parousia is false because it did not occur during the first Christian generation. That v. 8 begins further refutation is indicated by the opening phrase, "do not ignore this one fact," which is similar to the opening phrase of v. 5. Whereas in v. 5 the false teachers are accused of overlooking God's Word in judgment, in v. 8 the churches are urged not to overlook God's forbearance.

In v. 8 the author reworks Ps 90:4: "For a thousand years in your sight/ are like yesterday when it is past,/ or like a watch in the night" (NRSV). This verse was used to prove that human life is transient, while God is everlasting (Sir 18:9-11) and that the period before the eschatological end would seem long to humanity, but not to God.[32] The author affirms that what may seem like a delay of the parousia is not a delay from God's perspective, and the author still expects the parousia to come in the lifetime of those whom he addresses (1:19; 3:14).

The formula "not . . . but" (οὐ . . . ἀλλά *ou . . . alla*), which the author uses to reject the false teachers' accusations, begins v. 9 (as also 1:16, 21). This verse explicitly refutes the main point of the accusation that the promise of the parousia is false because it was temporally limited to the lifetime of the apostolic generation. The author does not address the problem of the failure of the parousia to occur within this limited time. Rather, he admits the delay and affirms the eventual fulfillment of the promised parousia. He alludes to Hab 2:13, a central passage in Judaism's reflection on the problem of the delay of God's judgment.[33] The delay does not indicate a false promise, but God's forbearance as provision for the repentance of sinners. The argument that God's judgment is delayed due to God's forbearance was traditional (Joel 2:12-14; Jonah 4:2; Rom 2:4; *Shepherd of Hermas,* Visions 8:11:1), and it was often used to explain the delay of eschatological judgment.[34]

The parousia and judgment are affirmed in v. 10. The affirmation opens with the verb "will come" (ἔχω *echō*) to emphasize that, although God's patience delays the parousia, surely it will come. It refutes the false teachers' accusation underlying vv. 4 and 9 that the Lord's delay in fulfilling this promise voids that promise. The simile of the thief probably comes from Jesus' parable of the thief in gospel tradition (Matt 24:43-44 par. Luke 12:39-40; 1 Thess 5:2; Rev 3:3; 16:15). The simile is quite effective in conveying both the unexpectedness of the parousia and the threat of judgment it brings to those who impose on the patience of God by delaying their own repentance.

At the parousia the heavens will pass away and then the elements will dissolve with fire. Here "elements" (στοιχεῖα *stoicheia*) may denote either what constitutes things in creation (earth, air, fire, and water) or heavenly

---

31. Whereas the NRSV leaves it ambiguous, the NIV takes the referent beginning v. 6, "by means of which" (δι ὧν *di hōn*), to be the waters of v. 5. It is the waters of creation that were the means of the flood. However, the referent is more likely to be the waters and the Word of God of v. 5. This understanding assumes that there is parallelism in 3:5-7, with all three verses assuming that God's Word is the means of accomplishing judgment.

32. *2 Apoc. Bar.* 48:12-13; Pseudo-Philo *Biblical Antiquities* 19:13a.
33. See 1QpHab 7:5-12; Heb 10:37; *2 Apoc. Bar.* 20:6; 48:39.
34. See *1 Enoch* 60:5; Ignatius *To the Ephesians* 11:1.

bodies (sun, moon, stars). The author's dependence on Isa 34:4 LXX indicates that the elements are not primarily those of creation, but are the heavenly bodies instead. However, since the earth is preserved for a fiery judgment (v. 7) and since a new heaven and earth will be coming (v. 13), whatever constitutes things in creation, including the earth, will be dissolved as well. This scenario corresponds to the picture of the end times that is found in early Christian eschatology in which both the earth and the heavens pass away (Mark 13:31 par. Matt 24:35 par. Luke 21:33; Matt 5:17-18; Luke 16:17; Rev 21:1).

The resulting state of the earth and the deeds done upon it are described as "found" (εὑρεθήσεται heurethēsetai; "disclosed," NRSV; "laid bare," NIV).[35] Without the obstruction of the heavens, which are now burned away, the works of humanity will become visible to God and vulnerable to judgment.[36] This is the destruction of the ungodly, when the earth is destroyed by fire (v. 7), and why the faithful are exhorted to be "found" (heurethēsetai) at peace and without spot or blemish at the parousia (v. 14). This state is one aspect of the biblical image of the wicked's trying in vain to hide from God's eschatological judgment (Isa 2:19; Hos 10:8; Amos 9:1-6; Rev 6:15-17).

As was common to epistles and testaments, the author ends his refutation (3:1-10) by exhorting the churches about behavior appropriate in the light of the certainty of the parousia and judgment (3:11-13). The new heavens and earth are the home of righteousness, and righteousness will characterize its citizens as well. The author assumes that while Christians are waiting for the parousia, living godly lives (being morally vigilant, 1 Cor 16:13; Col 4:2; 1 Pet 5:8) will hasten its coming (here expressed as "the day of God"). This is a corollary of v. 9, which claims that God delays the parousia to allow for repentance, and it stands in contrast to the false teachers' assumption that its delay makes the parousia void and ungodly behavior inconsequential.

Verse 13 is a positive affirmation of the parousia and a new heaven and earth based on the promises of Christ (1:4), which contrasts its denial by the false teachers (3:9). Common to Jewish apocalyptic,[37] the content of the promise is derived from Isa 65:17; 66:22 and was adopted by early Christianity (Matt 19:28; Rom 8:21; Rev 21:1). The fire of judgment will return creation to chaos so that a new creation may emerge.

---

35. There are several textual variants here. "Will be found" (εὑρεθήσεται heurethēsetai) and "will be found destroyed" (εὑρεθήσεται λυόμενα heurethēsetai lyomena) are the two major variants. In the context of cosmic conflagration, the latter reading makes better initial sense. The former reading is usually questioned on the grounds of internal evidence. How can the world "be found"? However, "found" (heurethēsetai) is the preferred reading because it has the superior external evidence, and internally it is used of the faithful Christians' being "found" at the parousia (3:14). Bauckham, Jude, 2 Peter, 316-21.
36. Cf. 2 Clem. 16:3.
37. See 1 Enoch 45:4-5; 72:1; 2 Apoc. Bar. 32:6; 44:12; 57:2; 4 Ezra 7:75.

REFLECTIONS

1. It is noteworthy that one way of remaining faithful in our Christian doctrine and ethical walk is to continually remind ourselves of the teachings of Scripture and tradition that have been handed down to us. It is not enough to read them for confirmation or church membership classes and then put them aside. Our Christian heritage needs to be celebrated and brought back to our consciousness continually in new and exciting ways in order for it to remain a vital part of our lives. This heritage needs to be incorporated into preaching, teaching, and liturgy and become a continual reminder of the purposes and promises of God.

2. The scoffers are indicative of our tendency to despair of the promises of God when God does not respond to our pleas within the time span we have set as reasonable or convenient. We would like God's help, insight, power, and strength when we want it, not when God in sovereignty deems it appropriate. We may not scoff verbally, but our prayer life, church attendance, and overall life-style may begin to suffer as we despair of God's promises. However, based on God's work, God's timetable, and God's mercy, we can affirm that God will act on promises given.

3. The argumentation in 3:5-7 leaves lingering questions about creation. It does not teach that the heavens were created long before the earth ("heavens existed long ago and an earth was formed . . ." NRSV); rather, like Gen 1:1, it teaches us that both the heavens and the earth were created long ago. As in Genesis, the understanding of creation is Near Eastern—the earth and sky were created by the pushing back of the waters of a primeval ocean above, below, and around the earth (Gen 1:2, 6-10). At the flood this primeval ocean was released from the bounds imposed by creation, and the world returned to chaos (Gen 7:11).

4. Patience ("slow to anger," 3:9) is often cited as a character trait of God (Pss 86:15; 145:8), based on God's self-revelation in Exod 34:6-7. This mercy is an outgrowth of God's love in putting up with sins of sinners and withholding the judgment the sin deserves at the time it is committed. This gives the sinner time to repent; but this time of mercy is not unlimited. Judgment will eventually come for the unrepentant, and the time of its coming is as unpredictable as the coming of a thief. Thus we should not take so much comfort in the patience of God that we do not immediately repent when we stray from the way of righteousness or ignore our obligations to evangelism with a false sense that there is plenty of time to attend to the unrepentant.

5. In the light of the eventual destruction of all creation and the evil within it, and the fact that the new heavens and earth are the home of righteousness, we are advised to live "lives of holiness and godliness" (3:11 NRSV). Such a life-style is partially defined by 1:5-7. Our call to right living is partially motivated by our desire to live eternally in righteousness with God when all that is subject to corruption is destroyed.

6. In 3:9, 12 the churches addressed by the author of the epistle are the ones whom God is patiently waiting to repent, especially those whom the false teachers have led into sin (2:14, 18; 3:17). The author is not saying that the time of the parousia depends on the action of the church—delayed for unrepentance and lack of evangelism (3:9) and hastened for godly living (3:12)—as though God had no say in the matter. Rather, in God's sovereignty and by God's mercy and love there is allowance for the spiritual state of the church and the world to which the church is to proclaim God's love and mercy. God's forbearance is also motivated by the desire that all people repent (Ezek 18:23, 32; 33:11; 1 Tim 2:3-6), and such forbearance alerts us to the fact that the time to evangelize is limited.

2 PETER 3:14-18

EXHORTATION TO STABILITY

COMMENTARY

3:14-16. These verses comprise the closing of the body of the letter, beginning with direct address. The body closing reiterates and emphasizes what has been said and urges attending to, and taking responsibility for, the matters discussed. It corresponds to the rhetorical *peroratio,* which reiterates the main points of the *probatio* and appeals to the audience's emotions to persuade them to respond as desired.

Exhortation based on the promise of the parousia and the assurance of judgment, begun in v. 11, continues in vv. 14-16. This section reiterates topics from vv. 8-13 as it instructs the churches in how to live while awaiting the parousia. In v. 9, the Lord's patience is to allow for repentance, and here this patience is expressed as salvation (v. 15). In v. 10, the Lord is said to come as a thief, and the earth and everything done on it are "found"; and the churches are to strive to be "found" by God at peace (reconciled with God), without spot or blemish (morally blameless; v. 14). "Found by him at peace" (NRSV) is probably a better understanding than "found at peace with him" (NIV). As 3:10 indicates, what is primarily being described is the act of Christ's finding the Christian at the parousia and, secondarily, the state in which the Christian is actually found.

This state of being "found" by God at peace is opposite that of the false teachers, who are blots and blemishes on the love feast (2:13). Christians are often expected to be without spot or blemish at the time of the parousia (Eph 1:4; 5:27; Phil 1:10; 2:15; Col 1:22; 1 Thess 3:13; 5:23; Jude 24). Striving for this state is part of the Christian's walk, making every effort to support the faith (1:5) and being "very eager" to confirm their call and election (1:10).

In vv. 15*b*-16 the author bolsters the entire message with his portrayal of Peter. Peter is an apostle; the use of "our" in "our beloved brother Paul" probably refers to the apostles as a whole, with whom Peter is identified (1:1, 16-19). The author points out that both Peter and Paul have the same inspired message for the churches, Paul's being written "according to the wisdom given him"—that is, by inspiration (like the OT prophets, 1:20-21). Paul sent his message to the churches in letters, which specific ones we do not know. Paul's letters contain some things hard to understand (as the history of scholarship attests!), but it is implied that Peter can interpret them and that so can those with knowledge and stability, like the churches addressed. It is the "ignorant and unstable," like the false teachers, who twist Paul's revelation to their own destruction, as they do with the OT (1:20-21) and other sacred writings, the "other scriptures," as well. Here the author is referring to the false teachers' destructive opinions (2:1) and deceptive words (2:3)—that is, doctrine supporting behavior that leads to loss of salvation and destruction at judgment (2:1, 3, 12; 3:7). They may have misinterpreted (or even rejected) Paul's teaching on the imminence of the parousia (Rom 13:11-12; Phil 4:5; 1 Thess 4:15) or understood some passages as being supportive of antinomianism, the teaching that moral laws are nullified by faith (2:19, "promise of freedom"; Rom 4:15; 5:20; 8:1; 1 Cor 6:12), a problem Paul himself faced (Rom 3:8; 6:15; Gal 5:13). Perhaps both notions are in view, since the eschatological stance that people take influences their ethical stance.

3:17-18. The letter closing functions like the *peroratio* in reiterating topics and appealing to emotion. The closing begins with a warning, "You are forewarned" or "already know." This warning resumes the fiction of Peter's prophecy (2:1-3; 3:3-4) and is a main feature of the testament genre—to forewarn the community of false teachers who will come after the death of the testator. Whereas the churches are stable in the truth (1:12), the false teachers and their followers are unstable (2:14, 3:16) and threaten the stability of the churches (3:17). There is the threat that the church will be carried away by the error of following these false teachers as others have done before them (2:15, 18).

The letter ends with a doxology (cf. Jude 24-25), which is unusual because it is addressed to Christ, and not to God. The ending may be a doxology because the personal greetings of the typical epistolary ending would be difficult to construct for a pseudepigraph—that is, a work written as if someone other than its author wrote it. The author is mainly interested in being "Peter" to give instruction, not to elaborate a fiction. Christ's glory is not and to the "day of eternity" (NRSV) or "forever" (NIV), the unending eschatological future to be ushered in at the parousia. It is the day dawning (1:19), the day of God (3:12).

REFLECTIONS

1. Paul's letters are sometimes hard to understand. This assessment by the author of 2 Peter is unsettling to some modern Christians. How can we say that about inspired Scripture written by an apostle? Lack of clarity results from several things. Paul was addressing the specific situations of his churches. They were familiar with the details of these situations and did not require Paul to provide explanation, even though we would like to have it today. (Just what was the Colossian heresy?) Paul and his churches shared social, cultural, and ideological assumptions and corresponding practices that are unfamiliar to us (e.g., honor and shame as a basis of social interaction). Thus Paul's approach and advice to his congregations puzzles us. Finally, Paul's approach to argumentation and persuasion are Jewish and Greco-Roman. The "logic" of his approach to a problem in a letter may elude us 2,000 years later (e.g., his argument for the resurrection in 1 Corinthians 15).

2. Our eschatological expectation has a bearing on our ethics. Lack of any real expectation of the return of Christ in judgment can diminish our resolve to live a Christ-like life. However, a vital expectation can motivate us to set our ethical walk in order, to renounce immorality in every form, to repent of sin, and to be reconciled in every way with God. This is not only for the negative reason of the fear of losing our salvation, but for the positive reason of wanting to be the kind of righteous person who can inhabit the new heavens and new earth.

3. When we are not properly conducting our lives as Christians we can tend to misinterpret Scripture to support our perversion of the faith. Sin blinds us to the truth. Rather than let truth change us, we change the truth so that we do not have to change to conform to it. We then live in a delusion that we think justifies our thinking. We do not want to examine this delusion too carefully for fear that its weaknesses will become all too apparent in the light of the truth.

4. The danger always exists that we can lose our spiritual stability by being carried away by false doctrine and practices. We cannot take our spiritual stability for granted. We should grow in the grace and knowledge of Jesus Christ, who is our Lord. It is knowledge of him and his grace freely given that has granted us everything necessary for life and godliness and supports the development of virtues and spiritual fruit in our lives, keeping us free from corruption. This growing or sanctification process is the antithesis of being carried away by wrong thinking and behavior, becoming ineffective in faith, forgetting cleansing from sin, and losing salvation (1:3-11).

THE FIRST, SECOND, AND THIRD LETTERS OF JOHN

INTRODUCTION, COMMENTARY, AND REFLECTIONS
BY
C. CLIFTON BLACK

THE FIRST, SECOND, AND THIRD LETTERS OF
JOHN

INTRODUCTION

"How plain, how full, and how deep a compendium of genuine Christianity!"[1] Thus did John Wesley (1703–91) estimate the First Epistle of John. As three of the canon's catholic or general epistles (along with James, 1 and 2 Peter, and Jude), the Johannine letters have justly enjoyed esteem disproportionate to their size. As well as rewards, these texts offer their interpreters some mysteries.

THE AUTHORSHIP OF 1, 2, AND 3 JOHN AND THEIR ATTRIBUTION IN THE EARLY CHURCH

Very little can be said with confidence about the author of these documents. Like the Fourth Gospel, the First Epistle of John is anonymous. The sender of 2 John (v. 1) and 3 John (v. 1) identifies himself, not as "John," but as ὁ πρεσβύτερος (*ho presbyteros*, "the elder"), a designation patient of alternative interpretations (see the Commentary on 2 John 1). While the matter is beyond knockdown proof, the Second and Third Epistles are sufficiently similar to 1 John, stylistically and substantively, to suggest that "the elder" authored all three letters (cf. 1 John 2:7; 3:11/2 John 5-6; 1 John 3:6/3 John 11). This commentary will proceed from the assumption that the Johannine letters were composed by the same author, who, for the sake of convenience, will be referred to as "the elder."

For its first seven centuries the church's reception of the Johannine epistles was fitful and heavily dependent on assumptions about their authorship. First John is the earliest and consistently best attested of the three; its wording is echoed as early as 135 CE in Polycarp's *Letters to the Philippians* (cf. 7.1 with 1 John 2:24; 3:8; 4:2-3). Along with 2 John, 1 John is indisputably quoted around the year 180 in Irenaeus's *Against Heresies* (cf. 1.16.3 with 2 John 11; 3.16.5 with 1 John 2:18-19, 21-22; 3.16.8 with 2 John 7-8 and 1 John 4:1-2; 5:1). From the third

---

1. John Wesley, *The Works of John Wesley*, vol. 21: *Journal and Diaries IV (1755–65)*, ed. W. Reginald Ward and Richard P. Heitzenrater (Nashville: Abingdon, 1992) 427 (journal entry for Thursday, September 1, 1763).

century onward, acceptance of the First Epistle was secure and widespread, owing mainly to its ascription to John the son of Zebedee, whom the early church came to identify as the "disciple whom Jesus loved" (John 13:23; 19:26-27; 20:1-10; 21:7, 20-24) and the author of the Fourth Gospel. Furthermore, 1 John's content was found congenial with several religious and theological interests of the patristic church, such as refinements in the doctrine of sin and the refutation of heresy.[2] Doubtful apostolic authorship and sparseness of content probably account for the slight use, neglect, or rejection of the Second and Third Epistles during the same period.[3] Third John is unattested until the mid–third century.[4] It appears to have been carried into scriptural recognition on the coattails of 2 John, just as the popularity of the Second Epistle derived from the church's recognition of the First. By the late fourth century, in some regions, the three epistles were regarded to be a unit and were circulated as such. As confirmed by the Venerable Bede (672/73–735), their collective acceptance into the canon was ultimately based on the medieval church's consensus that the apostle John had authored all three epistles.[5]

Nevertheless, there is no hard evidence to support the composition of 1, 2, or 3 John by John the apostle and son of Zebedee, an inference challenged as early as 130 CE by Papias of Hierapolis.[6] Likewise, Dionysius of Alexandria (d. c. 264) expressed doubt that John of Patmos, the author of Revelation (Rev 1:9; cf. Rev 1:1, 4; 22:8), had written either John's epistles or the Gospel of John.[7] The authorship of the Johannine letters remains a mystery. Unlike many patristic interpreters, however, we may safely regard these letters' continuing benefit for the church as both logically and theologically independent of their authorship. If "the elder" did not consider the verification of his identity crucial for his message's validity, then neither need we.

THE RELATION OF THE EPISTLES TO THE GOSPEL OF JOHN

Most interpreters, ancient and modern, have recognized an appreciable resemblance in the ideas and phraseology of the Fourth Gospel and the Johannine letters: among others, "to know [or walk in] the truth" (see John 8:32; 1 John 2:21; 2 John 1, 4; 3 John 3); "a commandment" to "love one another" (John 13:34; 15:12, 17; 1 John 3:23; 2 John 5); the completion of joy among believers (John 15:11; 16:24; 17:13; 1 John 1:4; 2 John 12). The likenesses between the Gospel of John and 1 John are especially abundant; for instance, the address to believers as little children (John 13:33; 21:5; 1 John 2:1, 12, 14, 18, 24); the presentation of Jesus as advocate, or "Paraclete" (John 14:16; 1 John 2:1); the world as the realm of disbelief or hostility (John 7:7; 8:23; 15:18, 19; 17:16, 25; 1 John 2:16; 3:1, 13; 4:5); the importance of "abiding" in God or in Christ (John 6:56; 15:4, 5, 6, 7; 1 John 2:6, 27, 28; 3:6, 24; 4:13, 15, 16). Such resemblances as these would seem to support the composition of 1, 2, and 3 John by the Fourth Evangelist, a position held by some scholars.[8] Their equally impressive differences, some of which will be detailed below, lead most interpreters (including me) to think that the Gospel and the epistles were probably composed by different authors within a circle of communities that shared a common Johannine tradition.[9]

Heavier debate swirls around the letters' dating. Which came first: one or all of the epistles or John's Gospel? The question of chronology usually turns on the interpretation of perceived divergences, between the letters and the Gospel, in their social situation and theological point of

---

2. Cf. Tertullian *On Modesty* (c. 220) 19.10, 26-28 with 1 John 4:2; 5:16-17.
3. See Eusebius *Ecclesiastical History* 3.24.17-18; 3.25.2-3.
4. See Eusebius *Ecclesiastical History* 6.25.10, citing Origen (c. 185–254).
5. Bede, *Commentary on 2 John* 1, in *The Commentary on the Seven Catholic Epistles of Bede the Venerable*, Cistercian Studies Series 82 (Kalamazoo, Mich.: Cistercian Publications, 1985) 231.
6. See Eusebius *Ecclesiastical History* 3.39-3-4.
7. See Eusebius *Ecclesiastical History*, 7.25.18-23. See R. Alan Culpepper, *John, the Son of Zebedee: The Life of a Legend*, Studies on Personalities of the New Testament (Columbia: University of South Carolina Press, 1994). This work is a definitive study of the figure of John in Christian antiquity. On traditions related to the Johannine letters, see 89-95.
8. See, for instance, A. E. Brooke, *A Critical and Exegetical Commentary on the Johannine Epistles*, ICC (Edinburgh: T. & T. Clark, 1912) i-xix; Werner Georg Kümmel, *Introduction to the New Testament*, rev. ed. (Nashville: Abingdon, 1975) 442-45, 449-51.
9. Among others, C. H. Dodd, "The First Epistle of John and the Fourth Gospel," *BJRL* 21 (1937) 129-56, which is presupposed by the same author's *The Johannine Epistles*, MNTC (New York: Harper and Bros., 1946); Judith Lieu, *The Second and Third Epistles of John: History and Background*, Studies of the New Testament and Its World (Edinburgh: T. & T. Clark, 1986) 205-22; Hans-Josef Klauck, *Der erste Johannesbrief*, EKKNT 23 (Zürich: Benziger/ Neukirchener, 1991) 42-47; Rudolf Schnackenburg, *The Johannine Epistles: Introduction and Commentary* (New York: Crossroad, 1992) 34-39.

view. Commentators' assessments of the evidence split into roughly four groups: (1) those who believe that one or more of the letters antedated the Gospel; (2) those who think that John was written before 1, 2, or 3 John; (3) those who hypothesize a more fluid, mutually contemporary process of composition, in which the characteristics of one or more of the epistles are in some way presupposed by parts of the Gospel; and (4) those who find the evidence too ambiguous to invest confidence in any proposed sequence for the creation of these writings.[10] The complexity implied by alternative (3) is plausible, though by its nature impossible to reconstruct without considerable speculation. Option (4) is laudable for its candor and (1) for its inclination to treat the letters on their own terms; still, it is difficult to interpret the vagaries of 2, 3, and especially 1 John apart from the Fourth Gospel.[11]

Less problematic is a modified version of possibility (2): if the letters do not rely on John in its finished form, they manifestly draw from a Johannine tradition whose most extensive extant deposit is that Gospel. Such an assessment comports with a date for the epistles' composition around the turn of the first century CE, as most commentators suggest and the evidence of Polycarp supports.[12] We cannot be sure that these letters were composed in the order that they were canonized. Working from the assumption that all three were written at about the same time, in practice most interpreters have found 2 and 3 John more intelligible in the light of 1 John. Since Smyrna's Bishop Polycarp knew 1 John, Asia Minor (modern-day Turkey) is a possible provenance for the letters; of late, however, scholars have tended to locate the Johannine literature closer to Palestine, perhaps in Syria. It is impossible, in any case, to confirm the epistles' original locale. Also beyond verification is their composition after the Fourth Gospel. Nevertheless, 1 John appears to know at least the tradition on which that Gospel was based. Accordingly, the present commentary will interpret the letters of John within the context of the Gospel of John.

THE SETTING OF THE JOHANNINE LETTERS IN RELIGIOUS ANTIQUITY

Introducing his exegesis of the Johannine epistles in *The Interpreter's Bible,* Amos N. Wilder observed that, in contrast to John's Gospel, 1 John "lacks evidence of Semitic style. It reflects more directly than John a Hellenistic milieu . . . not Greek, properly speaking, but Oriental-Gnostic."[13] Wilder's appraisal conformed with Rudolf Bultmann's analysis of the First Epistle, which hypothesized a source with oriental, non-Christian gnostic tendencies, used but corrected by the author of 1 John.[14] Especially in Germany there is continuing support for the view that John's Gospel and letters are at home within gnosticism (a syncretistic movement, characterized by a radically dualistic worldview, which proposed salvation by revealed, esoteric knowledge). Such a theory is by no means impossible; nevertheless, it runs up against substantial problems. The correspondence between gnostic and Johannine conceptuality is not as precise as sometimes alleged, and the literature of gnosticism, though indebted to older traditions, is considerably later than any of the NT documents. At present many scholars speak with less certitude than Bultmann or Wilder of a gnostic background for the Johannine letters. They are more inclined to regard Johannine Christianity as a part of the background for gnosticism as it evolved in the second century and beyond.

An important reassessment of Johannine literature has occurred with the discovery of the Dead Sea Scrolls, which can be confidently dated to the century before the NT. Understandably, Wilder's treatment of 1 John's background does not engage the Qumran texts, the first of which

---

10. Each of these alternatives is exemplified, respectively, by Georg Strecker, *The Johannine Letters: A Commentary on 1, 2, and 3 John,* Hermeneia (Minneapolis: Fortress, 1995) xxxv-xliii; Stephen S. Smalley, *1, 2, 3 John,* WBC (Waco, Tex.: Word, 1984) xxxv-xliii; Charles H. Talbert, *Reading John: A Literary and Theological Commentary on the Fourth Gospel and the Johannine Epistles,* Reading the New Testament (New York: Crossroad, 1992); and Judith M. Lieu, *The Theology of the Johannine Epistles,* New Testament Theology (Cambridge: Cambridge University Press, 1992).
11. Similarly, see D. Moody Smith, *First, Second, and Third John,* Interpretation (Louisville: John Knox, 1991) esp. 14, 28, 32, 36.
12. Polycarp *Letter to the Philippians* 7.1.
13. Amos N. Wilder, "The First, Second, and Third Epistles of John," in *IB,* ed. George Buttrick et al., 12 vols. (Nashville: Abingdon, 1957) 12:213.
14. Rudolf Bultmann, "Analyse des ersten Johannesbriefes," *Festgabe für Adolf Jülicher zum 70. Geburtstag* (Tübingen: Mohr [Siebeck], 1927) 138-58. Bultmann's theory, refined to posit an "ecclesiastical redaction" of the First Epistle, was presupposed for his commentary *The Johannine Epistles: A Commentary on the Johannine Epistles,* Hermeneia (Philadelphia: Fortress, 1973).

had been found less than ten years before he penned his introduction. The parallels between the scrolls and John's epistles should not be exaggerated. To take but one example, Qumran's radically pious devotion to the law of Moses[15] is obviously different from 1 John's radical obedience to the commandments of Jesus Christ (2:3; 3:23). Yet the affinities between Johannine and Qumran language are equally hard to deny; among others, "doing the truth" (1 John 1:6 [also John 3:21]/1QS 1:5; 5:3; 8:2) and "walking in light" or "in darkness" (1 John 1:6-7; 2:9-11 [also John 12:35-36]/1QS 3:20-25). Although the nature of the relationship between John and Qumran remains a debated question, the discovery of the scrolls has indisputably enhanced scholars' appreciation of Jewish influence, beyond the OT, on the Johannine writings.[16] As a result, John's vocabulary and ideas, which at one time seemed closely akin to Greco-Roman mysticism or "higher paganism,"[17] have been largely reconceived within the contexts of Palestinian and Hellenistic Judaism.

More conspicuous in the religious background of John's letters, especially 1 John, are basic confessions within early Christianity about God, Christ, and Christian responsibility.[18] The claim that God sent the Son into the world (1 John 4:9) to accomplish, by his sacrificial death, atonement for sin (2:2; 4:10), salvation (4:14), and familial fellowship with God (1:3) lies at, or very near, the core of the proclamation of other New Testament witnesses (cf. Matt 11:25-27/ Luke 10:21-22; Acts 3:19; Rom 3:25; 8:15-17; Gal 4:4; Eph 2:1-10; Heb 4:15–5:10; 9:11–10:18). While nuanced in a distinctively Johannine idiom (cf. John 7:17; 13:34; 16:8, 10), the importance of doing God's will (1 John 2:17), the performance of righteousness (1 John 3:7, 17), and the commandment to love God and neighbor (1 John 4:21) are closely paralleled in the synoptic Gospels (Matt 7:21; Mark 3:35 par.; 12:28-34 par.; Luke 6:46; 13:25-27), in Paul (Rom 12:2; 13:9-10; Gal 5:14), and in James (Jas 2:15-16). Like Paul (1 Cor 15:3-11), the author of 1 John (1:1-4; 2:7; 3:11) underscores the indebtedness of his preaching to Christian tradition shared with his readers.

Close verbal and conceptual similarities that obtain between the Gospel and epistles of John were noted earlier in this introduction. The letters of John apparently drew from, and exemplify, a discrete Johannine tradition within primitive Christianity. Whether this tradition manifested itself sociologically as a "sect" or a "school" has been much discussed in the past twenty-five years; predictably, judgments in that matter depend greatly on how those terms are defined.[19] For the purpose of this commentary one need only observe that 1 John implies, and 2 John (v. 1) and 3 John (v. 1) expressly indicate, the existence of different Christian congregations within a Johannine network, for which those letters' author assumes an advisory and perhaps supervisory responsibility. The situation seems similar to that in Revelation 1–3, where John of Patmos issues encouragement and warning to a nearby circle of seven churches in Asia Minor. At the time of the composition of the Johannine epistles, the communities addressed by the elder showed signs of disintegrating (on which, see below).

THE GENRE OF 1, 2, AND 3 JOHN

On at least one feature of the Johannine epistles there is practically universal agreement: Second and Third John are real letters, adhering as closely to the epistolary conventions of antiquity as any such literature in the NT. Second John contains petitions addressed to a community.

---

15. See 1QS 5:8, 21; 6:6; 8:15; 1QpHab 7:10-11.

16. See Marie-Émile Boismard, "The First Epistle of John and the Writings of Qumran," in *John and the Dead Sea Scrolls*, ed. J. H. Charlesworth (New York: Crossroad, 1991) 156-65. The influence on 1 John of OT narratives (like that of Cain and Abel, 1 John 3:12; cf. Gen 4:1-16) and ideas (notably sin and its atonement, 1 John 2:2, cf. Lev 16:1-34) is real, though apparently minimal. The question of Scripture's bearing on the Johannine letters has been usefully reopened by Judith M. Lieu, "What Was from the Beginning: Scripture and Tradition in the Johannine Epistles," *NTS* 39 (1993) 458-77.

17. Notably, Dodd, *The Johannine Epistles*, xvi-xxi, which anticipated his more extensive account in *The Interpretation of the Fourth Gospel* (Cambridge: Cambridge University Press, 1953) 3-130.

18. On this subject Otto A. Piper, "I John and the Didache of the Primitive Church," *JBL* 66 (1947) 437-51, remains well worth consulting.

19. Noteworthy are the studies by Wayne A. Meeks, "The Man from Heaven in Johannine Sectarianism," *JBL* 91 (1972) 44-72; R. Alan Culpepper, *The Johannine School: An Evaluation of the Johannine-School Hypothesis Based on an Investigation of the Nature of Ancient Schools*, SBLDS 26 (Missoula, Mont.: Scholars Press, 1975); and D. Moody Smith, "Johannine Christianity: Some Reflections on Its Character and Delineation," *NTS* 21 (1976) 222-48.

Third John is a more private communication (v. 1), adopting the form of a letter of recommendation (v. 12).

Identifying the genre of the First Epistle, however, has proved vexing, both for what it contains and for what it lacks. In comparison with ancient letters, 1 John has neither a formal salutation nor a formal conclusion. While epistolary material may stand without the former (Hebrews) or the latter (James), it is unusual for an epistle to omit both. Most commentators concur that the form of 1 John does not clearly register as that of an epistle, but there is no consensus on how this document should be classified—whether as an essay, or a treatise, a sermon or a manifesto, an encyclical or a circular letter, to name but a few proposals. Functionally at least, some of these alternatives (sermon or essay) are more closely analogous to documents contemporaneous with 1 John than are others (encyclical). Furthermore, many scholars judge 1 John to be a commentary on, or in some sense an application of, the Johannine tradition, perhaps even to the extent of being modeled after the Fourth Gospel's general framework.[20]

If these questions cannot be resolved, they can be clarified. Whatever its genre, 1 John is a written communication (1:4; 2:1, 7-8, 12-14, 21, 26; 5:13), which does not preclude its having been experienced orally or aurally by its first readers. It is unwise to force 1 John into a single generic pigeonhole. In antiquity literary categories—letters, in particular—were often conflated with other genres (as we can witness throughout the canon). In the NT, form typically follows function; it is more important that we understand what 1 John does, less crucial that we agree on the right tag with which to label it.

On the face of the evidence, 1 John is concerned with proclamation (1:1-3), exhortation (2:7-11), and encouragement (2:12-14). Frequently, all three activities are tightly entwined (e.g., 1:5–2:6). Like Hebrews, 1 John functions as a "word of exhortation" (λόγος τῆς παρακλήσεως *logos tēs paraklēseōs*; Heb 13:22; cf. Acts 13:15), though that term appears in none of the Johannine writings and should not be pressed as a hard-and-fast classification of 1 John. Provided that we bear in mind the limits of the traditional characterization, there is no harm in our calling 1 John a "letter" or an "epistle," as a matter of convenience and responsible alignment of that document with 2 and 3 John. Finally, while the Johannine letters manifest an appropriation of the Johannine tradition, it is less clear that 1 John is so closely patterned after the Gospel of John that the First Epistle was intended to serve as an extended commentary on the Fourth Gospel. First John's affinities with John might be better conceived as functionally akin to those reflections on the biblical witness that are integral components of *The New Interpreter's Bible Commentary*. That is to say, the elder engages his community's tradition, drawing out some of its theological implications for the life of the church in a new day.

THE STRUCTURE AND STYLE OF THE JOHANNINE LETTERS

Exhortations to communal life in Christian love and truth lie at the heart of the more general Second Epistle of John and the more pointed Third. Combined with the letters' brevity, this hortatory core has made it rather easy for interpreters to articulate the structure of 2 and 3 John. Again, however, the First Epistle is more difficult to analyze. Thoughtful interpreters have long disagreed on this document's organization. Some perceive in 1 John an intricately woven structure; others a pattern no more discernible than "the waves of the sea."[21]

Describing the argument of the First Epistle, John Calvin (1509–64) noted that "it contains teaching mixed with exhortations." Many modern interpreters concur that an oscillation of proclamation with paraenesis (moral exhortation) distinguishes the framework of 1 John.[22] Most commentators agree, further, that its thought does not adhere to a single, tightly reasoned line of

---

20. For two very different hypotheses in this vein, see Raymond E. Brown, *The Epistles of John: Translated with Introduction, Notes, and Commentary*, AB 30 (Garden City, N.Y.: Doubleday, 1982) 116-29, and Kenneth Grayston, *The Johannine Epistles*, NCB (Grand Rapids: Eerdmans, 1984) 3-4.

21. Friedrich Hauck, *Die Briefe des Jakobus, Petrus, Judas und Johannes: Kirchenbriefe*, 5th ed., NTD (Göttingen: Vandenhoeck & Ruprecht, 1949) 115. Brown tabulates over four dozen discrepant divisions of 1 John, proposed by as many commentators. See Brown, *The Epistles of John*, 117n. 269, 764.

22. Along this line, Theodor Häring, "Gedankengang und Grundgedanke des ersten Johannesbriefes," in *Theologisches Abhandlungen*, ed. Carl von Weizsäcker (Freiburg im Breisgau: Mohr, 1892) 171-200, has proved influential. Cf. John Calvin, *The Gospel According to St John 11–21 and the First Epistle of John*, ed. David W. Torrance and Thomas F. Torrance (Grand Rapids: Eerdmans, 1961) 231.

argument. In musical terms, 1 John is not a *Brandenburg Concerto* that chugs relentlessly along a straight line from start to finish. The First Epistle is more like Ravel's vertiginous *Bolero,* which repeats a few themes with increasingly complex orchestration. "The writer 'thinks around' a succession of related topics," as C. H. Dodd observed. "The development of a theme brings us back almost to the starting-point; almost, but not quite, for there is a slight shift which provides a transition to a fresh theme; or it may be to a theme which had apparently been dismissed at an earlier point, and now comes up for consideration from a slightly different angle.[23]

The movements of thought within 1 John are held together by at least two devices. The author uses particular words or phrases to link clusters of thought—e.g., "sin" or "walks in darkness" (1:5–2:11/2:12-17); "born of God" and "children of God" (2:18-29/3:1-24); to "know the spirit of truth" and to "know God" (4:1-6/4:7–5:5). The elder also employs "hinge verses" whose themes pivot between the letter's parts—e.g., 2:28-29 ("abide in him"/"born of him") and 5:12-13 ("the Son of God"/"have [eternal] life"). Many commentators are less inclined than some of their early twentieth-century predecessors to regard conceptual tensions within 1 John as vestiges of a complex redaction of traditions or sources. While not inconceivable, such a process is largely if not entirely untraceable.[24]

In pointing up its convoluted structure, an important and pervasive aspect of 1 John's style comes into focus. The technical term for its circular redundancy is "amplification": a rhetorical technique, based on patterns of parallelism, that suggested to ancient listeners a grandeur appropriate for the consideration of lofty, even divine, matters. Even to modern ears 1 John's famous disquisition on love (4:7-21) registers with extraordinary gravity because of what the elder says and the sonority with which he says it. Yet the elder is not merely an accomplished stylist. His manner has a theological point, for the discourse in 1 John is unmistakably redolent of Jesus in the Fourth Gospel (cf. John 17:20-26). The rhetoric of 1 John "abides" in the speech of the Johannine Jesus, enacting the elder's assurance, "This is the message we have heard from him and proclaim to you" (1 John 1:5*a* NRSV; cf. John 17:7-8).[25]

THE ADVERSARIAL CHARACTER OF 1, 2, AND 3 JOHN

Who is the liar but the one who denies that Jesus is the Christ? (1 John 2:22*a* NRSV)

Many deceivers have gone out into world . . . any such person is the deceiver and the antichrist! (2 John 7 NRSV)

Whoever does good is of God; whoever does evil has not seen God. (3 John 11*b* NRSV)

Since the Middle Ages most commentators have detected a polemical edge in John's epistles. There has been considerably less agreement on the nature of the opposition challenged by the elder. Such a question is still worth pondering, for if we grossly misunderstand the elder's points of resistance, we may vastly misconstrue the letters' implications in our own day. Only broad dimensions of this critical issue can be sketched here, along with some reasons for the approach adopted in this commentary.

The Third Epistle patently revolves around the offer and refusal of hospitality among communities within the Johannine circle (see 3 John 3, 5-8, 10*b*, 12). As shall be considered in the Commentary and Reflections on 3 John, larger issues of authority may underlie this controversy (3 John 4, 9). The elder's brush across theologically charged topics within Johannine tradition ("love," 3 John 1, 6; "truth," 3 John 1, 3-4, 8, 12) has prompted many interpreters to imagine a

---

23. Dodd, *The Johannine Epistles.*
24. Nevertheless, Kysar considers 1 John "a hurried union of disparate pieces . . . a kind of anthology of bits of sermons patched together and rendered into a written form for circulation." See Robert Kysar, *I, II, III John,* Augsburg Commentary on the New Testament (Minneapolis: Augsburg, 1986) 16.
25. See C. Clifton Black, "'The Words That You Gave to Me I Have Given to Them': The Grandeur of Johannine Rhetoric," in *Exploring the Gospel of John in Honor of D. Moody Smith,* ed. R. Alan Culpepper and C. Clifton Black (Louisville: Westminster John Knox, 1996) 220-39.

doctrinal component in this letter's dispute over jurisdiction. The elder, however, neither makes that connection explicit nor elaborates any theological terms in 3 John. The issue of hospitality, particularly the basis for its denial, recurs in 2 John (vv. 10-11), though here the topic is eclipsed by a more obviously theological concern: the teaching of many deceivers that Jesus Christ has not come in the flesh (2 John 7-9).

Similar worries apparently motivate some comments in the First Epistle. The nub of the dispute alluded to in 2 John 7 is echoed in 1 John 4:2*b*-3. The elder insists, in addition, that Jesus is the Christ (1 John 2:22), belief in which assures that one is born of God (1 John 5:1). Those who confess Jesus as the Son of God abide in God (1 John 4:15) and conquer the world (1 John 5:5). Jesus Christ came, not with the water only, but with the water and the blood (1 John 5:6). The denial of such claims is associated with "many antichrists," "false prophets," and "liars" (1 John 2:18-19, 22; 4:1, 3*b*, 5; 5:10). Also considered a "liar" is one who claims sinlessness but disobeys the commandments (1 John 1:10; 2:4), who professes love for God but hates other Christians (1 John 4:20). First John indicates, furthermore, that certain dissidents have broken off relations with the elder and his audience (1 John 2:18-19; 4:1-3). On its face the evidence suggests that 1 John, like 2 and 3 John, has arisen from an adversial situation.

Beyond this point any assessment of the elder's opponents becomes deeply conjectural and impossible to verify with confidence. The position challenged by the elder appears to have an affinity with docetism (δοκεῖν *dokein*, "to seem"), a second-century theological trend that, according to Ignatius (d. c. 110 CE), disavowed Jesus Christ as "flesh-bearing,"[26] claimed that Christ "merely seemed to suffer,"[27] and rejected the saving significance of Christ's death.[28] In spite of ingenious attempts by some commentators to fill the gap,[29] the elder himself does not clarify the connection, if any, between his adversaries' docetic leanings and their dubious conduct.

While the Johannine letters bear real marks of contentious literature, we should beware of overinterpreting the evidence. Of the elder's opponents we have no direct knowledge independent of his imputations, which are scant, vague, and partial. Moreover, some of 1 John's refutations probably reflect their author's dialectical style; he is not always rebutting adversaries, but sometimes provoking friends to self-examination (see 1 John 1:6-7; 2:9-11; 4:7-8, 19-21; 5:12).[30] One's perception of these epistles' whispered quarrels should be balanced, therefore, by confessing one's ignorance of their depth, coherence, and precise profile. "The work of reconstruction is always fascinating," A. E. Brooke mused. "But we have to remember how few of the necessary bricks are supplied to us, and how large a proportion of the building material we have to fashion for ourselves."[31]

MAJOR THEMES OF THE JOHANNINE EPISTLES

The primary subjects to which the elder returns are tightly interwoven, though no more systematically coordinated than those of any NT author. Before engaging in commentary, it is vital that we take our bearings on these letters' theology, with attention to its development beyond the Gospel of John.

1. "God is Light and in Him There is no Darkness At All": The Nature of God. C. K. Barrett's assessment of the Fourth Evangelist may also be pertinent to the author of the Johannine epistles: "There could hardly be a more Christocentric writer than John, yet his very Christocentricity is theocentric."[32] If anything, this "theocentric Christocentricity" is clearer in

---

26. Ignatius *Smyrn.* 5.2.
27. Ignatius *Trall.* 9.1; 10.
28. Ignatius *Smyrn.* 7.1; *Magn.* 11.
29. See, e.g., John Painter, "The 'Opponents' in 1 John," *NTS* 32 (1986) 48-71. Brown's magisterial commentary (Brown, *The Epistles of John*, esp. 69-115) is predicated on his subtle reconstruction of contesting interpretations of Johannine thought and practice: Raymond E. Brown, *The Community of the Beloved Disciple* (New York: Paulist, 1979) esp. 93-167.
30. See Pheme Perkins, *The Johannine Letters*, New Testament Message 21 (Wilmington, Del.: Michael Glazier, 1979) xvi-xxiii; Judith M. Lieu, "'Authority to Become Children of God': A Study of 1 John," *NovT* 23 (1981) 210-28.
31. Brooke, *A Critical and Exegetical Commentary on the Johannine Epistles*, xxxix-xl.
32. "'The Father Is Greater Than I' John 14:28: Subordinationist Christology in the New Testament," in C. K. Barrett, *Essays on John* (Philadelphia: Westminster, 1982) 32. See also the finely nuanced treatment by Paul W. Meyer, "'The Father': The Presentation of God in the Fourth Gospel," in Culpepper and Black, *Exploring the Gospel of John in Honor of D. Moody Smith*, 255-73.

the letters. For the elder, God is the standard of fidelity, of righteousness (1 John 1:9; 3:7), and of goodness (3 John 11), the agent of forgiveness (1 John 1:9; 2:12) whose essential character is light (1 John 1:5, 7), purity (1 John 3:3), truth (1 John 5:20), and, most especially, prevenient love (1 John 4:7-12, 16, 19). From this central understanding of God radiate most of the letters' other themes. Jesus, God's Son, has been sent by the Father as the Savior of the world (1 John 4:14). Through the Son (1 John 2:23; 5:20), who enables obedience to his commandments (1 John 2:3-5), all believers "have" or "know" God (1 John 2:23; 4:7-8; 2 John 9). They abide in or experience a fully reciprocal relationship with God (1 John 1:3; 2:24; 3:24; 4:13-16). Throughout the Johannine epistles (1 John 1:2-3; 2:1, 15-16, 22-24; 3:1; 4:14; 2 John 3-4, 9), the image of God as father is adopted by the elder to convey God's personal and caring nature, not God's gender. Much like John Wesley centuries later, the elder favors a model of God as provider and loving parent.[33]

2. "What we have seen and heard we proclaim to you": The Traditional Context for Theological Understanding. If God is the magnetic north of the elder's theological compass, then the Johannine *kerygma* ("proclamation") shared with his readers is one pole of that magnetic field. Incisive interpretations of this tradition are not the elder's forte, and its innovative reformulation is not his aim (cf. 2 John 9). Instead, the believing community is repeatedly driven back to "that which was heard from the beginning," a primordial declaration of faith that still impinges forcefully on the church's present experience (1 John 1:1-5; 2:7, 24; 3:11; 2 John 5-6). Although less overtly engaged with Scripture than is the Fourth Gospel (John 5:39, 45-47; 7:23), "the message we have heard and declare" remains wedded in 1 John with OT precept and example (1 John 2:2/Lev 16:16, 30; 1 John 3:12/Gen 4:1-6). The community's faith is crystallized in remembered commandments of Christ (1 John 2:7-8; 2 John 5-6), the example of Jesus (1 John 2:6; 3:16-17), and Christian creedal affirmations (1 John 4:2; 5:6). For proper interpretations of that tradition, the elder recognizes the church's experience of being anointed as "children of God" (1 John 2:20, 27; 3:1-2) and the necessity of "test[ing] the spirits" for their authenticity (1 John 4:1-6).

3. "Children, it is the last hour!" The Eschatological Context for Theological Understanding. The elder's retrospection should not mislead us to think that he and his readers are stuck in the past. To the contrary, the Johannine epistles are attracted to an apocalyptically charged expectation. In this view—played down in the Fourth Gospel (cf. John 3:36; 5:24-29; 6:39-40; 11:23-26) though prevalent in NT documents early (1 Thess 4:13–5:11) and late (2 Peter 3:1-18)—history is hurtling toward its divinely appointed end. Confirmation of this belief lies, for the elder, in the coming of "antichrist" (1 John 2:18, 22; 4:3; 2 John 7). This expression, unique to the Johannine letters, personifies a cataclysmic evil that some expected to flare up before God's final victory (cf. Dan 11:36–12:13; 2 Thess 2:3-9). Not fear, but confidence (παρρησία *parrēsia*), encouragement, and hope for the church flow from the prospect of Christ's coming (παρουσία *parousia*; 1 John 2:28; 3:2-3; 4:17-18; 2 John 8). This apocalyptic view of the future provides a lens through which the community's present experience is viewed; the elder regards both confession and schism within the church, not as theologically neutral, but as indicators of a cosmic drama, played out under the direction of a provident God.

4. "Jesus Christ has come in the flesh": Who Jesus Is. Since the christology of the Johannine epistles is not systematically presented, one can safely speak only of emphases in the elder's portrayal of Jesus. Undeniably, Jesus is the Christ, "the anointed one" (1 John 2:22; 5:1). That identification of Jesus is exceeded by another: the Son of God (2:22-23; 4:15; 5:5, 10, 20), which, though apparently interchangeable with Christ (5:1, 5), accents his intimate relation with God the Father (1:3; 2:23-24; 4:13). This conjunction is so close that at many points in 1 John it is impossible to tell whether the pronouns "he" or "him" refer to Jesus or to God (see 1 John 1:9-10; 2:3-6, 27-28; 3:23-24; 4:17). This ambiguity may suggest a high christology, effectively equating Jesus with God; or it may simply betoken a lack of precision in the elder's

---

33. On the language of God's fatherhood in the Johannine tradition, see B. F. Westcott, *The Epistles of St John: The Greek Text with Notes and Essays* (London: Macmillan, 1909) 27-34; on the appropriation of that language in our day, see Gail R. O'Day, "John," in *The Women's Bible Commentary*, ed. Carol A. Newsom and Sharon H. Ringe (Louisville: Westminster/John Knox, 1992) 303-4. On Wesley's characterizations of God, consult Randy L. Maddox, *Responsible Grace: John Wesley's Practical Theology* (Nashville: Kingswood, 1994) 48-64.

wording. "Jesus Christ has come in the flesh" (1 John 4:2 NRSV) is a confession that, for the elder, appears to have acquired the status of proper doctrine (διδαχή *didachē*; 2 John 7-10). That a claim so unobjectionable on its face requires such emphasis, and elicits such sharp repudiation of those who deny it, suggests that Christ's incarnation had become a disputed point within Johannine Christianity at the time of these letters.[34]

5. "He is the expiation for our sins": What Jesus Does. In general, Jesus in 1 John deals with sin and its consequences. By his blood, believers are cleansed from all unrighteousness (1 John 1:7b, 9), their sins forgiven for his sake (1 John 1:9; 2:12). Indeed, Jesus expunges the sins of the whole world (1 John 2:2; 3:5; cf. John 1:29). These claims are related to the depiction of Jesus as a ἱλασμός (*hilasmos*), an "atoning sacrifice" for sins (1 John 2:2; 4:10). This term is unique to 1 John in the NT, although Romans (Rom 3:25) and Hebrews (Heb 2:17; 9:5) contain cognates. Antecedents for the concept of vicarious expiation by one who is pure or without sin can be found in OT descriptions of cultic sacrifice (cf. Lev 4:1-35; 16:1-34 with 1 John 3:3, 5; 1 Pet 1:18-19), which later were broadened in reference to pious martyrs for the Jewish nation (4 Macc 6:28-29; 17:21-22). For any believer who sins, Jesus Christ the righteous is an advocate (παράκλητος *paraklētos*) before the Father (1 John 2:1; cf. John 14:16, 26; 15:26; 16:7, where intercession is performed by the Holy Spirit). "Anointing" by "the Holy One," which instructs the church and verifies its knowledge, is yet another expression of Christ's (or the Spirit's) benefits (1 John 2:20, 27). An interesting feature of all these models of salvation is that they are confined neither to Jesus' past death nor to his future coming, but are considered perpetually effective in the church's present experience.

6. "Beloved, let us love one another": The Shape of Christian Existence. God's activity in Christ establishes the context for Christian life and self-critical discernment. First John insists on the inseparability of religious experience from moral conduct, with reciprocal testing of the one's soundness by the other's vitality (1 John 1:6-7; 2:3-6, 9-11; 3:6-18, 24; 4:7-12, 20-21). Thus, being "born" of God (1 John 2:29; 3:9; 4:7; 5:1, 4, 18) or a "child" of God (1 John 3:1, 2, 10; 5:2), "knowing" God (1 John 2:3; 3:6) or "abid[ing] in him" (1 John 2:6, 10, 17; 3:6-10, 24; 4:16), do not describe an inward, mystical state but are concretely manifested by "doing what is right," "keeping his commandments," or "walk[ing] just as he walked" (1 John 2:3, 6; 3:10, 14a, 22; 5:3). By contrast, "the children of the devil," who "abide in death" and falsehood, are recognizable by their unrighteousness, disobedience, and lack of love (1 John 2:4; 3:10, 14b; cf. 3 John 11). Pulsing throughout the First Epistle is a tension, if not contradiction, between candid acknowledgment of persistent sin within the church (1 John 1:8–2:1; 5:16-17) and categorical denial that one begotten of God can sin (1 John 3:6, 9; 5:18). If 1 John does not resolve this theological dilemma, it effectively crystallizes it as a pressing question for subsequent Christian theology.

The observation of Augustine (354–430) that 1 John commends nothing else but love is only slightly exaggerated.[35] More than any other concept, love (ἀγάπη *agapē*) expresses the abiding nature of the unseen God (1 John 4:7b, 8b, 12, 16), whose initiative in sending his Son reveals that love (1 John 3:16; 4:9-10), evokes love as a possibility among us (1 John 4:11, 19), and specifies the practical pattern to which our responsive love should conform (1 John 3:17-18; 5:3; 2 John 6). God's love for us (1 John 2:5; 3:1; 4:16-17) and our love for God (1 John 4:20-21; 5:1) are perfected in our sibling love for one another (1 John 2:10; 3:10-11, 14, 23; 4:7, 11-12, 20-21; 5:2; 2 John 5; see also John 13:34; 15:12, 17). While the world's hatred belongs to the sphere of darkness and is not to be reciprocated (1 John 2:9-11; 3:13-15), the elder's attention to love does appear intramurally preoccupied, the universal potential of the Johannine love command recognized (1 John 2:2; 4:14), yet left undeveloped.

---

34. See M. de Jonge, "The Use of the Word ΧΡΙΣΤΟΣ in the Johannine Epistles," in *Studies in John Presented to Professor Dr. J. N. Sevenster*, NovTSup 24 (Leiden: Brill, 1970) 66-74.

35. Augustine, "Ten Homilies on the First Epistle of St. John," in *Augustine: Later Works*, selected and trans. John Burnaby, The Library of Christian Classics (Philadelphia: Westminster, 1955) 259-348, esp. 329.

THE LETTERS OF JOHN IN THE LIFE OF THE CHURCH

Just as for the rest of the NT, the church is the native habitat for 1, 2, and 3 John. These documents offer us, as it were, blurred snapshots of primitive Christian communities—congregations that grappled with some implications of their own religious tradition, appealing to doctrine, policy, and authority that were all at an embryonic stage. These epistles adapted the legacy of John for a new day, much as 1 and 2 Timothy and Titus appropriated the Pauline tradition. To characterize 1, 2, and 3 John as "Johannine Pastorals" thus captures something essentially true to their aims and theological temperament.[36]

In our own era John's epistles have not wanted for scholarly commentary. The depth of their appropriation within the church is harder to gauge. The *Revised Common Lectionary* (1992) assigns six excerpts from 1 John (1:1–2:2; 3:1-7; 3:16-24; 4:7-21; 5:1-6; 5:9-13) as the epistle readings for the second through seventh Sundays of Easter (Year B), as well as 1 John 3:1-3 for All Saints (Year A). Neither 2 John nor 3 John appears in the *Common Lectionary,* which is not surprising; also missing are other NT passages that blaze with controversy, such as John 8:12-59; 1 Cor 4:6–5:5; Gal 2:1-14; 1 John 2:18-27; 4:1-6; and Jude. Regrettably, pitched conflict is as much a part of our past as it is of our present, no less in Christianity than in other religions. However we assess the responses of early Johannine Christians, the issues that these letters raise—among others, the maintenance of confessional integrity and the potential for congregational self-destruction—must be faced by Christians in every age.

Finally, this literature does not invite rendition in a minor key. The Johannine letters assure Christians of their calling, grounded not in their own ability under stress but in God's enduring, self-sacrificial love for them. First John's confidence was abundantly clear to Martin Luther (1483–1546): "This is an outstanding epistle. It can buoy up afflicted hearts. Furthermore, it has John's style and manner of expression, so beautifully and gently does it picture Christ to us."[37] What Luther implies, Wesley states outright in a comment that for many readers of these epistles still rings true: "And in [addressing his contemporaries, the elder] speaks to the whole Christian church in all succeeding ages."[38]

---

36. The landmark statement of this idea is Hans Conzelmann, "'Was von Anfang War,'" in *Neutestamentliche Studien für Rudolf Bultmann zu seinem 70. Geburtstag,* ed. Walther Eltester, BZNW 21 (Berlin: Töpelmann, 1954) 194-201. The polychromatic picture of the church emerging from these documents is examined in C. Clifton Black, "The Johannine Epistles and the Question of Early Catholicism," *NovT* 28 (1986) 131-58.

37. Martin Luther, "Lectures on the First Epistle of St. John," *Luther's Works,* vol. 10. *The Catholic Epistles,* ed. Jaroslav Pelikan and Walter A. Hansen (St. Louis: Concordia, 1967) 219.

38. John Wesley, "Spiritual Worship" (sermon 77), in *The Works of John Wesley,* vol. 3: *Sermons 71-114,* ed. Albert C. Outler (Nashville: Abingdon, 1986) 89.

BIBLIOGRAPHY

Commentaries:

Brown, Raymond E. *The Epistles of John.* AB 30. Garden City, N.Y.: Doubleday, 1982. Comprehensive in scope, meticulous in detail. A benchmark in Johannine study.

Bultmann, Rudolf. *The Johannine Epistles: A Commentary on the Johannine Epistles.* Edited by Robert W. Funk. Hermeneia. Philadelphia: Fortress, 1973. A slender, somewhat idiosyncratic treatment by the twentieth century's foremost Johannine interpreter.

Dodd, C. H. *The Johannine Epistles.* MNTC. New York: Harper and Bros, 1946. Inevitably dated in its scholarship, but still glistening with theological discernment.

Kysar, Robert. *I, II, III John.* Augsburg Commentary on the New Testament. Minneapolis: Augsburg, 1986. Based on sound scholarship, a clear introduction from which laity may profit handsomely.

Schnackenburg, Rudolf. *The Johannine Epistles: Introduction and Commentary.* New York: Crossroad, 1992. A standard treatment since 1953, now in its seventh edition (German original, 1984). Unusually rich in theological exposition.

Smalley, Stephen S. *1, 2, 3 John.* WBC 51. Waco, Tex.: Word, 1984. A technical commentary on the Greek text, written from a British evangelical perspective.

Smith, D. Moody. *First, Second, and Third John.* Interpretation. Louisville: John Knox, 1991. Concise, balanced, and acute; aimed at teaching and preaching within the church.

Strecker, Georg. *The Johannine Letters: A Commentary on 1, 2, and 3 John.* Edited by Harold Attridge. Hermeneia. Minneapolis: Fortress, 1996; German original, 1989. Thorough, technical scholarship in the German tradition, closely attentive to the epistles' syntax and religious background.

Other Studies:

Brown, Raymond E. *The Community of the Beloved Disciple.* New York: Paulist, 1979. An ingenious reconstruction of the history of the Johannine community.

Calvin, John. *The Gospel According to John 11–21 and The First Epistle of John.* Edited by David W. Torrance and Thomas F. Torrance. Grand Rapids: Eerdmans, 1961. A classic specimen of theological interpretation in the Reformed tradition.

Lieu, Judith. *The Second and Third Epistles of John: History and Background.* Studies of the New Testament and Its World. Edinburgh: T. & T. Clark, 1986. The two often-neglected letters receive careful scrutiny.

———. *The Theology of the Johannine Epistles.* New Testament Theology. Cambridge: Cambridge University Press, 1991. A synthetic account, based on perceptive and judicious exegesis.

OUTLINE OF 1, 2, AND 3 JOHN

I. 1 John 1:1–5:21, The First Letter

    A. 1:1–2:6, Introit for Eternal Life
        1:1-4, What Was from the Beginning
        1:5-10, Walking in Darkness or in Light
        2:1-6, Walking Just as He Walked
    B. 2:7-14, What I Am Writing
        2:7-11, A Commandment Old Yet New
        2:12-14, The Family Restored
    C. 2:15–3:10, Children, It Is the Last Hour
        2:15-17, The World Versus the Will of God
        2:18-25, Endurance Amid Antichrist's Coming
        2:26-27, Anointing in Truth
        2:28–3:3, Confidence at Christ's Coming
        3:4-10, Children of God, Children of the Devil
    D. 3:11–5:12, The Message You Have Heard from the Beginning
        3:11-18, By This We Know Love
        3:19-24, By This We Shall Know That We Are of the Truth
        4:1-6, By This You Know the Spirit of God
        4:7-12, By This God's Love Was Manifested Among Us
        4:13-21, By This We Know That We Abide in God and God in Us
        5:1-5, By This We Know That We Love God's Children
        5:6-12, The Testimony That God Has Borne to the Son

E. 5:13-21, Refrain: That You May Know That You Have Eternal Life
   5:13-17, The Boldness in Our Asking
   5:18-21, What We Know

II. 2 John 1-13, The Second Letter

   A. Verses 1-3, Saluting the Elect Lady and Her Children
   B. Verses 4-11, Requests, Benefits, and Cautions
      Verse 4, Rejoicing in Truth
      Verses 5-8, Follow Love and Spurn Deception
      Verses 9-11, Abide in the Teaching
   C. Verses 12-13, Regrets, Hopes, and Greetings

III. 3 John 1-15, The Third Letter

   A. Verses 1-4, Salutation, Prayer, Rejoicing
      Verse 1, Saluting Gaius
      Verses 2-4, Praying for Health, Rejoicing in Truth
   B. Verses 5-12, The Elder's Recommendations
      Verses 5-8, Supporting God's Missionaries
      Verses 9-10, Condemning Diotrephes
      Verses 11-12, Commending Demetrius
   C. Verses 13-15, Regrets, Hopes, and Greetings

1 JOHN 1:1–5:21

THE FIRST LETTER

1 JOHN 1:1–2:6, INTROIT FOR ETERNAL LIFE

OVERVIEW

We expect a letter, whether modern or ancient, to open with a clear salutation to a designated addressee. Yet nothing so pedestrian awaits us in the introduction to the First Epistle of John. Instead, we are thrown headlong into the symphony of salvation, arranged and conducted by God. Stamped into our lives are the great Johannine themes, announced here for later development: the contest between sinful deceit and righteous truth, the triumph of light over darkness, the manifestation of eternal life, the realization of joy, the perfection of love. At first, in 1:1-4, the author of 1 John sets us on a promontory and turns us to look backward, to scan the expanse of the church's proclamation "from the beginnning." Immediately, in 1:5-10, we are carried up to the community's life in the present, to consider the moral implications of what the church has heard and proclaimed. Then 2:1-6 tightly knots the congregation's proclamation and paraenesis—its message about Jesus Christ and its enactment of his way of life. The church lives what it preaches; it preaches what it has heard.

1 John 1:1-4, What Was from the Beginning

COMMENTARY

1:1-2. Rumbling within the prologue of 1 John (vv. 1-4) are echoes from the prologue of John's Gospel (John 1:1-18):

1 John	John 1
"from the beginning" (v. 1)	"in the beginning" (vv. 1-2)
"what we have looked at [ἐθεασάμεθα, *etheasametha*]" (v. 1)	"we have seen [ἐθεασάμεθα *etheasametha*] his glory" (v. 14)
"the word" (λόγος *logos*, v. 1)	"the word" (λόγος *logos*, v. 1)
"life" (v. 1)	"life" (v. 4)
"with [πρός *pros*] the Father" (v. 2)	"with [πρός *pros*] God" (v. 1)

The resonance between these books is in fact deeper than these points of correspondence suggest. The first four verses of 1 John seem to assume a reader's intimate acquaintance with ideas and terminology that chime in distinctively Johannine ways. "What was from the beginning" (v. 1) vaguely recalls Jesus' various descriptions of himself, the devil, and witnesses to Jesus "from the beginning" (John 8:25, 44; 15:27). Eternal life (1 John 1:2) and the fulfillment of joy (v. 4) are associated with Jesus throughout the Gospel of John (John 3:15-16, 29, 36; 5:24; 6:24, 68; 15:11; 16:22, 24; 17:2-3, 13). The Gospel of John also underscores the importance of testimony, to Jesus or to God, on the basis of what is "heard" and "seen" (1 John 1:1-3; cf. John 3:11, 32; 4:42; 19:35). That we should be launched so quickly and so tightly into a Johannine orbit at vv. 1-4 is consistent with the elder's express concern for fidelity to the community's origins. Without the Fourth Gospel's more explicit articulation of Johannine Christianity's basic testimony to Jesus, a modern reader might find the First Epistle's roundabout, densely worded introduction nearly impenetrable.

Equally perceptible here, however, is a refocusing of that Johannine tradition. For one thing, "the beginning" to which the two prologues refer seems to be different. Whereas John transports the listener out of time and space, to the beginning of creation (John 1:1-3; cf. 1 John 2:13-14; Gen 1:1), 1 John obliquely directs the reader to the One in whom the church's message (ἀγγελία *angelia*, v. 5) originates: Jesus, the font of that community's tradition, to whom the church bears witness and in whom the church finds the springs for its continued existence (1 John 1:1-3; cf. 2:7, 24; 3:11). In this regard "the word of life" (v. 1) is ambiguous, possibly multivalent. While those who know the Gospel may be reminded of its presentation of Jesus, who is life (John 14:6) and whose word gives life (John 5:24), "the word" in 1 John seems at least as closely associated with the preached word—proclamation, by the author and others, of that life "that was with the Father and was made revealed to us" (vv. 2-3; cf. John 6:68; Acts 5:20; Phil 2:16; Col 1:5; 2 Tim 1:1). Both prologues speak in allusive language about Jesus Christ, but with different accents. Whereas John highlights the pre-existent glory of the Word who indeed became flesh (John 1:1-3, 14-18; cf. John 6:51-58; 20:27-28), 1 John stresses the empirically verifiable reality of the Son, "which we have heard, which we have seen with our eyes, which we have looked at and our hands have touched" (v. 1 NIV). Both of these shifts in Johannine focus—an emphasis on Jesus' humanity and the movement of the church's self-understanding into the theological foreground—are noteworthy throughout John's letters.

Some features of the internal syntax of 1 John 1:1-4 invite special comment. The main verb of the letter's opening sentence, "we proclaim" (ἀπαγγέλλομεν *apangellomen*), is delayed until v. 3 (as suggested in the RSV but obscured, in different ways, in both the NRSV and the NIV). In Greek, unlike English, the emphasized element tends to gravitate to the beginning of the sentence. Front-loaded in 1 John's serpentine introduction, therefore, is not "we who have declared" but the *object* of that declaration: "*what* was from the beginning, *what* we have heard, *what* we have seen with our eyes." Structure and content are thus perfectly married; the one in whom indestructible life was tangibly revealed from the beginning is the one proclaimed here, at the start of every clause.

The author appears to have chosen with care the tenses of verbs in his opening remarks. The aorist (punctiliar past) tense is used to predicate "the life [that] appeared," "which we looked at and ... touched" (vv. 1-2) at a particular point in history. What "we have heard" and "we have seen" (vv. 1-3) is cast in the perfect tense, which typically expresses an action in the past whose effects still obtain in the present. In this proclamation, therefore, two claims are being fused together: This life, which appeared at a precise moment in history, molds the audition and vision of those who currently testify to that life as eternally significant.

Also in vv. 1-4 is the first of many instances of that letter's chainlink unfolding of thought. Words are introduced, then repeatedly developed: among others, what "we have seen" (vv. 1*c*, 2*b*, 3*a*), the "life" (vv. 1*f*, 2*a*, 2*d*), "we proclaim [and write] to you" (vv. 2*c*, 3*b*, 4*a*). In effect, verbal batons are transferred from one clause or sentence to the next. The style is similar to that displayed in the Fourth Gospel's prologue. Such a technique is especially apt for 1 John, whose author locates himself among those who are handing over primal testimony "to you," the letter's recipients (vv. 2*c*, 3*b*).

1:3. In the first half of v. 3, the purpose of the elder's declaration is expressed: "that you also may have fellowship with us." The theological foundation of this fellowship is immediately pointed up: "and truly our fellowship is with the Father and with his Son Jesus Christ." While rare in the NT's Johannine tradition (only here and in 1 John 1:6-7), κοινωνία (*koinōnia*) is used of "active [Christian] participation" in much the way that we find in Paul's letters (e.g., 1 Cor 1:9; 10:16;

2 Cor 9:13; 13:13; Phil 1:5; 2:1; Phlm 6; the Greek term basically denotes partnership in a venture or joint ownership of a concern). Already in 1 John 1:3 there may be a whisper of an idea given forceful enunciation later (cf. 2:18-19): Christian fellowship is not only grounded in God's activity through Christ but is itself proof of that grounding as well. With good reason John Wesley located Christian fellowship at the center of 1 John's "apparent aim": "to confirm the happy and holy communion of the faithful with God and Christ, by describing the marks of that blessed state."[39]

1:4. Some ancient texts of this verse read, "And these things we write *to you,* that *your* joy may be complete" (cf. John 15:11; 16:24).

The manuscript evidence for these alternative readings is well supported and widely scattered; more likely original, however, is the well-attested, shorter, and somewhat more difficult reading favored by both the NIV and the NRSV. Interestingly, this verse inverts the sentiment, conventional in antiquity and expressed in 2 John (v. 12) and 3 John (vv. 13-14), that words on a page are a poor substitute for face-to-face communication. Here, the author's joy is not frustrated but fulfilled by writing. And given the defensive posture adopted later in this document, we should note the vibrantly positive and edifying note on which its prologue ends: the fulfillment of joy in the declaration of that fellowship that demonstrably begins "with the Father and with his Son Jesus Christ" (cf. Paul's kindred comments in Phil 1:2-7; 2:1-2).

---

39. John Wesley, *Explanatory Notes Upon the New Testament* (1755) (London: Epworth, 1950) 902.

REFLECTIONS

1. First John 1:1-4 offers a cornucopia of theological considerations for those who "proclaim [to others] concerning the word of life." For the elder, what shape does Christian preaching take? To declare to others ("the eternal life that was with the Father and revealed to us" (1 John 1:2) means, in the first place, faithful restatement of the Christian heritage, creatively addressed to the church that lives in a new situation. By adapting the Johannine tradition to the altered needs of Johannine Christians, the elder displays considerably more freedom than do some contemporary Christians who are not supple enough to bend. Yet he remains faithful to "that which was from the beginning." By emphasizing the church's durable fellowship with the God who has been revealed to us in Jesus Christ, the elder proves himself wiser than those in our day who idolize novelty.

The gospel requires creative presentation and imaginative interpretation, if its intent is to be realized in a new day. But the gospel itself is not created anew every morning. As David C. Steinmetz wisely observes, the church's teachers are not inventors but *couriers:*

> To be a minister is, to put it bluntly, to be a servant and the virtue most highly prized in a servant is not originality, but fidelity. Ministers have been ordained to transmit a message that they did not compose and that they dare not alter. They have been called, not to improvise their assignment, but to fulfill a role prescribed for them by someone else.[40]

2. Also noteworthy in 1 John 1:1-4 is its language, exquisitely balanced and pitch-perfect for its proclamation. To declare nothing less than "the eternal life that was with the Father" (1:2 NRSV) invites, as Amos Wilder puts it, "an august exordium, and one which takes the reader immediately into the secrets of the divine counsels and the sharing of the divine life."[41] The preacher of 1 John 1:1-4 will want to avoid muffling the loftiness of its cadence and phrasing, which still have power to penetrate

---

40. David C. Steinmetz, *Memory and Mission: Theological Reflections on the Christian Past* (Nashville: Abingdon, 1988) 72.
41. Wilder, "The First, Second, and Third Epistles of John," 12:217.

the coarseness in which modern congregations live and to lift them beyond the banality of their everyday lives. Yet the style of this prologue does not encourage its listeners in flight from this world, for the very grandeur of 1 John's discourse reminds the listening church of the voice of its Lord while on earth, as he is remembered in the Johannine tradition (cf. John 14–17). In other words, 1 John 1:1-4 spurs modern preachers to reach for a rhetoric that is at once supernal yet down to earth, a form of communication that meets congregations where they really are—the world into which Christ came—while at the same time inviting them to regard those circumstances from within the gospel's liberating frame of reference. One way of approaching this challenge might be to align 1 John 1:1-4 with John 20:19-31, the Gospel lection with which 1 John 1:1–2:2 is paired for the Second Sunday of Easter (Year B). Like the risen Jesus in the Fourth Gospel, the prelude of 1 John evokes in its proclaimers and listeners a multidimensional faith that remembers what the church has heard, seen, gazed upon, and touched—a peculiar memory of the Son of God who transcended death without sloughing off the wounds of crucifixion.

3. The prologue does much more than express the church's christological reflection. It *re-presents* Jesus Christ; that is to say, by 1 John's proclamation, *Christ is made present* to a generation of Christians who no longer can see or hear him, except by the eyes and ears of faith (cf. John 20:29). Here the elder seems to anticipate Dietrich Bonhoeffer: "Christ is not only present *in* the word of the church but also *as* the word of the church, i. e., as the spoken word of preaching. . . . Christ's presence is his existence as preaching. In preaching the whole Christ is present, [Christ] humiliated and [Christ] exalted. . . . It is the form of the presence of Christ in which we are found and to which we must keep."[42]

That this is consistent with 1 John's understanding is suggested by the reason given for writing and the result expected from proclamation: the formation of communion and the completion of joy (1:3-4). The elder believes that the church is not merely "a human association (such as a club or party, which might get over its difficulties by a little politic give-and-take); it exists by sharing the divine life embodied in Christ."[43] Nor does that existence depend on a coterie of seriously religious people who yearn for eternal life or who think that by their devotion they can make it happen. Authentic fellowship occurs only by declaration, by voice and in deed, of that "word of life" to which 1 John bears witness; it is sustained only by the church that lives by that word and allows itself to be acclimatized into a new environment that is conditioned by Christ (cf. 2 Cor 5:17). Therein lies the possibility of joy, which in the Johannine tradition should not be confused with momentary delight or contented resignation or wishful thinking. Joy is the beforehand experience of that communion with God and Christ, which is to be consummated in eternity (John 15:11; 16:20-24; 17:13), confident that Christ has already prevailed over this world's tribulations (John 16:33).

42. Dietrich Bonhoeffer, *Christologie* (Munich: Kaiser, 1981) 30.
43. Dodd, *The Johannine Epistles*, 8.

1 John 1:5-10, Walking in Darkness or in Light

COMMENTARY

1:5. To this point, exactly what has been heard and proclaimed (vv. 1-4) has been left rather vague. In v. 5 "the message" is given greater content: "God is light and in him there is no darkness at all," which is conceptually close to James's claim of God's constancy as "the Father of lights, with whom there is no variation or shadow due to change" (Jas

1:17 NRSV; see also Pss 27:1; 36:9).[44] As vv. 6-10 verify, the author of 1 John construes light and darkness within a *moral* context (cf. 1 Cor 4:5; 2 Cor 6:14), in accordance with a broad biblical tendency to regard darkness as the habitat of such sins as adultery and murder, the hiding place of the wicked, who think that their evil is thereby concealed from God (Job 24:13-17; Isa 29:15; Sir 23:18-19). By contrast, light is the Lord's raiment (Ps 104:2). With light the Lord exposes evil (Job 38:12-13)—a function that the Fourth Evangelist ascribes to Christ as "the light of the world" (John 8:12 NRSV; 9:5; cf. 1 Tim 6:15-16).

The "handed-down," traditional character of this message is patent: "we have heard . . . and declare to you" (cf. 1 Cor 11:23; 15:3). Murkier is the identity of the message's sender. Is it from Jesus Christ (v. 4) or from God (v. 5)? Here as elsewhere (most immediately, see vv. 6-7), a third singular masculine pronoun is used without precise referent, an ambiguity that may indicate the author's internalization of the Johannine confession that the Father is visible in and authentically revealed by the Son (John 1:18; 6:46; 8:19; 12:44-45; 14:9-10).

1:6-10. In v. 6 the author introduces a series of observations that are tailored to the formula "If we profess certain things under particular conditions, then some disturbing consequences will follow." The author may be thinking of real instances of moral failure in the community to which he is writing.[45] Here, nevertheless, the elder speaks universally, implicitly including himself among "we [who may] say" (vv. 6, 8, 10; cf. vv. 3, 5). In vv. 6-10 the *potential* for breakdown and its repair appears to be primarily in view—although anyone familiar with everyday life in the church knows that collapse and restoration do not remain merely hypothetical possibilities for long.

Structurally, vv. 6-10 express variations on an antiphonal theme of sin (vv. 6, 8, 10) and restoration (vv. 7, 9). Although seemingly interchangeable, the passage's constituent claims about sin mount to a climax: from lying (v. 6), to deep self-deception (v. 8), to gross misrepresentation of God (v. 10). Moreover, these assertions, like those in vv. 1-4, are intricately interconnected. The first pair of claims (vv. 6-7), formulated in the imagery of "darkness" and "light" (v. 5), picks up from v. 3 the desire for "fellowship" and ends on the confession of "sin," around which the next series of claims revolves (vv. 8-10). Another thread that runs through these comments is the dichotomy between "deception" or "lying," whether to others (vv. 6, 10) or to oneself (v. 8), and "the truth" (vv. 6, 8) or "his word" (v. 10), which in context implies truthful exposure of sin and the promise of forgiveness (resumptive of v. 1, "concerning the word of life"). This interlocking pattern is more than aesthetically satisfying. It formally conveys the passage's presiding concern for Christian *integrity*, within the believing community as well as between it and God.[46]

If the prologue (vv. 1-4) sets forth the traditional basis for communion with God and with one another, vv. 5-10 probe the proper understanding of that fellowship and unfold some of its practical conditions. Notably, communion with God is not described as a mystical experience. Nor is it portrayed by the elder as some sterile, intellectual exercise, as though one could accept "the proclamation proclaimed" (v. 5) without further obligation. Such constructions tend toward a compartmentalized individualism that is foreign to the approach of this author for whom communion with God is proved by the quality of one's communion with others (v. 7; cf. Lev 19:18; Deut 6:4-5; Mark 12:29-31). Both forms of fellowship are concretely manifested in conduct, by the way in which one "walks" (v. 6 [περιπατεῖν *peripatein*; הלך *hālak*]; cf. Prov 8:20; Eccl 11:9; Isa 2:3; Mic 2:7; 4:2; 6:8; Rom 6:4; 8:4; 14:15; 2 Cor 4:2; Gal 5:16; 1 Thess 2:12; *Barn.* 18.1–21.9; *Did.* 1.1–6.2).

First John is by no means the only NT book that stresses the importance of "walking in the light" (see also John 8:12; 11:9-10; 12:35-36; Rom 13:13; Eph 5:8-9; Rev 21:24;

---

44. Associations of "light" with "life" are commonplace in religious antiquity (note also 1QS 1:9-10; 3:3, 20; 4:2-6, 9, 11; Philo *On Dreams* 1.75; *T. Levi* 19:1). See the discussion in Peder Borgen, "The Gospel of John and Hellenism: Some Observations," in Culpepper and Black, *Exploring the Gospel of John in Honor of D. Moody Smith*, 98-122, esp. 114-16.

45. See, among others, Pheme Perkins, "*Konōnia* in 1 John 1:3-7: The Social Context of Division in the Johannine Letters," *CBQ* 45 (1983) 631-41.

46. Similarly, Duane F. Watson argues that the repetitive style of 1 John bolsters the fellowship for which its author appeals. See Watson, "Amplification Techniques in 1 John: The Interaction of Rhetorical Style and Invention," *JSNT* 51 (1993) 99-123.

cf. Ps 89:14-16; Isa 2:5; *1 Enoch* 92:4-5). It is more pointed than most in explaining the implications of that injunction; to "walk in the light as he himself is in the light" (v. 7) is not to pretend to flawlessness, but to own up to sins that rupture communion, both divine and human (vv. 8-9), and to acknowledge God's Son as the agent of reconciliation (vv. 7, 9). Likewise, "truth" is not abstractly propositional; truth (v. 6), for the elder, is to be done (NRSV) or to be lived by (NIV; see also John 3:19-21; 2 John 4; 3 John 3-4; cf. Tob 4:5-6). Precisely because the elder construes truth as *activated integrity,* truth's opposite is not incorrectness stemming from ignorance, but lying, a deceit for which those who do not live the truth are culpable and accountable (vv. 6, 8; cf. Prov 20:9; John 9:41; 15:22, 24). And because our deluded denial of sin effectively precludes our acknowledgment of the need and possibility for forgiveness, the logical if heinous outcome of such radical inauthenticity is to make God (or Jesus) out to be a liar (v. 10).

By contrast, the integrity of that One who "is in the light" (v. 7), "he who is faithful [πιστός *pistos*] and just [δίκαιος *dikaios*]" (v. 9; cf. Deut 7:9; Pss 36:5-6; 119:137-38; Heb 10:23), is demonstrated by his willingness to cancel the debts that we confess (v. 9) and by his making good on his promise to cleanse the full extent of our injustice (ἀδικία *adikia*), or moral disintegration (vv. 7, 9; cf. Exod 34:6; Ps 32:5; Prov 28:13; Jer 33:8; Mic 7:18-20; John 13:10-11). "Cleansing" is the first of 1 John's several metaphors to describe what, for those in Christ's fellowship, has been done to sin; it has also been "forgiven" (v. 9; 2:12; cf. John 20:23), "expiated" (2:2; 4:10), and "taken away" (3:5; cf. John 1:29). In v. 7 the means by which purification from sin is accomplished is "the blood of Jesus his Son," a claim that harks back to the cultic imagery of Exodus (Exod 30:10) and Leviticus (Lev 16:15-19). The purifying power of Jesus' blood is not explained here or elsewhere in 1 John. In the light of the elder's imminent description of Jesus Christ as "the atoning sacrifice for our sins" (2:2 NRSV), the significance of Jesus' blood most likely lies in the giving of his life for the lives of others. This corresponds with the levitical understanding of blood as the seat of life and, for that reason, the appropriate offering for atonement of sin (Lev 17:11; cf. 1 Pet 1:18-19; Rev 1:5; 7:14), as well as with the thought, which found expression in intertestamental Judaism, that the self-sacrifice of devout martyrs had atoning value for Israel (2 Macc 7:37-38). More immediately, it squares with the elder's own inextricable association of Jesus with the light, fidelity, and integrity of God (vv. 3, 5, 7, 9). On the meaning of sin in 1 John, see the Commentary on 3:4-10. (See Reflections at 1 John 2:1-6.)

1 John 2:1-6, Walking Just as He Walked

COMMENTARY

In the preceding pericope a pair of disturbing possibilities for our estrangement from God (vv. 6, 8) was immediately answered by a pair of comforting alternatives for our reconciliation (vv. 7, 9). Verse 10 abruptly broke this pattern by conjecturing a negative possibility without its positive reversal. This formal asymmetry jolts readers or listeners of the text into contemplation of the depth of delusion, falsehood, and vapidity of which, according to the author, we are capable. The segment beginning at 2:1 reestablishes a theological equilibrium by wedding the confessional and ethical emphases of the preceding segments in a carefully balanced way. Thus 2:1-2 develop the christological claims of 1:3, 7, and 9; 2:4-5, the moral gravity of 1:6, 8, and 10. Both of the concerns are bridged in 2:3, 6 by the elder's linkage of knowledge of Christ (= abiding in him) with obedience to his commandments (= walking the very way that he walked).

2:1-2. Sin is a besetting reality for the church, but it is certainly not the author's objective to instill within his readers a sense of paralysis by their abysmal potential for depravity. Rather, he writes these things "so that you may not [commit] sin" (v. 1), much as Sirach cautions against compounding sin by presuming on God's mercy (Sir 5:5-6) and Paul rebuts any license to sin in his elaboration of abounding grace (Rom 6:1-2). "God certainly forgives freely, but in such a way that the easiness of mercy does not become an enticement to sin."[47] Addressed to the elder's "little children" (τεκνία *teknia*), which in 1 John is consistently a term of endearment (2:12, 28; 3:7, 18; 4:4; 5:21; cf. Jesus' address to his disciples in John 13:33), the tenor is tender, not reprimanding.

Jesus' ability to deal with sin, an idea broached in 1:7, 9, is further explored in 2:1-2. Jesus is described as (a) an "advocate" (NRSV); (b) Christ, the righteous (one); and (c) the atoning sacrifice. Expressed as a title without additional comment, "Jesus Christ [the] righteous" appears to be a traditional formula (cf. Acts 3:14; 7:52; 22:14). The reassertion of Christ's justice (δίκαιον *dikaion*; cf. 1:9) aptly bespeaks a necessary qualification of the One who restores a radically deviant humanity to the norm of a just God (1:9; cf. *1 Enoch* 38:2; 53:6, which attributes righteousness to the Messiah). This forensic imagery is extended by the claim that in Jesus "we have one who *speaks* to the Father *in our defense*" (NIV). The Greek term translated in this way is παράκλητος (*paraklētos* lit., one "called to [a friend's] side"). In ancient jurisprudence the "advocate" was counsel for the defense before the court.[48] In the Fourth Gospel that intercession is provided by the Holy Spirit, expressly described as "another Advocate" (John 14:16-17 NRSV), who is sent by the Father or by Christ (John 16:7) to remind the church of Jesus' instruction (John 14:26), to bear witness to Jesus (John 15:26), and to execute judgment of the world (John 16:7-11). Within the New Testament only the Johannine tradition depicts Jesus (and the Spirit) as "advocate"; yet the image of Christ as intercessor between humanity and God is employed by both Paul (Rom 8:34) and the author of Hebrews (Heb 7:25; 9:24).

The image of Christ's cultic intercession in Hebrews may offer a clue for the elder's conceptual move from Jesus as our advocate with the Father to Jesus as "the atoning sacrifice for our sins" (1 John 2:2). Common to the tasks of both the legal advocate and the priest is mediation. Whereas Hebrews develops dual understandings of Jesus as both the superlative high priest (Heb 4:14–5:10; 7:1-28) and superior sacrifice (Heb 9:11–10:18), 1 John zeros in on the second of these claims by characterizing Jesus as an expiation (ἱλασμός *hilasmos*), a sacrifice of atonement ("at-one-ment" or reconciliation) between human beings and God, by which sinners are cleansed of their sins (1:7, 9; cf. 2:12; 1 Tim 2:5-6; Heb 9:14-15). The implied disposition of God toward human beings is one of merciful love, not displeasure that must be placated. This is suggested not only by the context of 1 John (2:5; 4:9-10), but also by the connotation of the term ἱλασμός; its verbal cognates ἱλάσθητι (*hilasthēti*; in Luke 18:13) and ἱλάσκεσθαι (*hilaskesthai*; in Heb 2:17) appear in contexts that emphasize God's mercy toward sinners. It is not God's anger with us that must be turned away, but our rebellion against God. Accordingly, expiation is not a human maneuver that changes God from furious to loving; expiation is an expression of God's love, which removes sin from the sinner. The elder emphasizes that Jesus' sacrifice is "not for ours [sins] only but also for the sins of the whole world" (2:2 NRSV; see also 4:14). For all of his preoccupation with the church, the elder's vision of Christ's saving sacrifice is universal, not parochial, in its intended effect. In this respect 1 John agrees with the Gospel of John (John 1:29; 3:16), with Colossians (Col 1:20), and with John Wesley: "Just as wide as sin extends, the propitiation extends also."[49]

2:3. Two senses of "knowing" (γινώσκειν *ginōskein*) are detectable throughout 1 John, both of which are evident in this verse: "certainty" or "assurance" (see also 2:5, 18, 29; 3:19, 24; 4:2, 12-13, 16; 5:2) and "relationship," usually with God or with Christ (see also 2:4, 13-14; 3:1, 6, 16, 20; 4:6-8; 5:20).[50]

---

47. Calvin, *The Gospel According to St John 11–21 and the First Epistle of John*, 241.
48. Brooke, *A Critical and Exegetical Commentary on the Johannine Epistles*, 23-27, documents a broad range of nuances for παράκλητος in classical, Jewish, and Christian literature.
49. Wesley, *Explanatory Notes Upon the New Testament* (1755), 905. Contrary to the suggestion offered above, but in line with the exegetical tradition of his day, Wesley interpreted "the atoning sacrifice" of 1 John 2:2 as that "by which the wrath of God is appeased," a nuance retained by some modern commentators (e.g., I. Howard Marshall, *The Epistles of John*, NICNT [Grand Rapids: Eerdmans, 1978] 117-18).
50. See B. A. du Toit, "The Role and Meaning of Statements of 'Certainty' in the Structural Composition of 1 John," *Studies in the Johannine Letters: Neot* 13 (1979) 84-100.

Again, however, the elder refuses to leave theological claims at the level of mere intellectualization. Even as truth is to be done (1:6), knowledge of Christ is demonstrated by obedience to his commandments (cf. Matt 5:19; 7:21). This point is pressed both positively (2:3) and negatively (2:4). The latter assertion recalls the hypothetical statements in 1:6, 8, and 10, their sharp distinctions between truth and lie, and the tests by which "the truth" or "his word" may be found within us.

2:4. Interpretation of this verse is complicated by at least two things. First, compared with the conditional wording of 1:6, 8, and 10 ("if we say"), this verse indicates a possibility that is slightly more precise (lit., "the one who says"; see also 2:6). This may suggest that the elder has in mind a particular person whose words and deeds are incompatible; that suggestion is rendered less likely, however, by the indefinitely formulated rebuttal in v. 5: "but whoever keeps his word" ("obeys his word," NIV, NRSV). A second difficulty presented by v. 4 is the unnamed content of the commandments to be kept. The parallel comment in v. 5—that obedience to his word is completed in love—suggests that in view here is the primary commandment to love (see also 3:23; 4:21; 5:2-3). This interpretation jibes with the teaching of the Johannine Jesus, who defines his disciples' love for him as the keeping of his commandments (John 14:15, 21, 23) and who repeatedly commands them to love one another as he has loved them (John 13:34-35; 15:9-10, 12-13, 17). For the elder, as for the prophets Hosea (Hos 4:1-6) and Jeremiah (Jer 31:31-34), knowledge of God is assured only through obedience to God.

2:5-6. Verse 5 marks the first of fifty-two references to "love" (ἀγάπη *agapē*) within 1 John (with ten additional occurrences in the even briefer 2 and 3 John). Although obviously important to this author, the topic of love is not always treated with the clarity that we might wish, of which this first instance is a good example. What is perfected by obedience to his word: God's own love (NIV)? Love for God (RSV)? Or "the divine love" (NEB)? "The love of God" (NRSV) may be the most apt translation, since it allows for multiple nuances in the Greek phrase and captures in English the ambiguity that grammar alone cannot decide. The elder's comment in v. 5 obviously stands in balanced contrast to v. 4, which exposes as a liar the disobedient one who claims to know God (or Christ). Thus the immediate context may favor construing "the love of God" in v. 5*a* as the fulfillment, through obedience, of our love for God (see also 4:21; cf. John 14:15, 21, 24). The reciprocity of love in Johannine thought (4:12, 16; John 14:23) should restrain us, however, from pressing a distinction too rigorously here, even as the elder will later make abundantly clear that human love is essentially derivative of God's initiatory love for us (4:7, 10-11, 19; cf. John 15:9-10; 17:26). Another aspect of v. 5 registers with much greater clarity and consistency: a concern for the conditions under which love, and love alone, is perfected or reaches maturity (see also 4:12, 17-18).[51]

"By this" (ἐν τούτῳ *en toutō*, v. 5c) is a favorite connecting phrase of the elder, occurring in 1 John a dozen times. Grammatically, it can point backward or—as it does here and in v. 3a—to the comment that follows (so NIV and NRSV). Verbally linking vv. 5-6 are two formulas of "immanence" or "indwelling": "in him" (twice in v. 5) and "to abide in him" (v. 6).[52] In Johannine thought the phrases "in the Son" (ἐν τῷ υἱῷ *en tō hyiō*, 5:20) and "in him" (ἐν αὐτῷ *en autō*, 2:5, 8; 5:20) usually function as metaphors of domain, referring to that sphere of divine truth or love, characteristic of God and of Christ, that anchors and gives shape to the believer's life. As such, these formulas are akin to the elder's previous mention of "fellowship with the Father and with his Son Jesus Christ" (1:3, 6 NRSV) but richer in implication. They seem to approximate Paul's conception of Christian existence "in the Spirit" (Rom 7:6; 8:9; 14:17) or, more often, "in Christ [Jesus]" (Rom 3:24; 6:23; 8:1-2, 39; 12:5; 16:3; 1 Cor 1:2; 3:1; 4:17; 15:18, 22; 2 Cor 5:17; 12:19; Gal 2:4, 17; 3:26, 28; 5:6; Phil 2:5; 4:7, 19, 21; 1 Thess 4:16; Phlm 8). The closely related Johannine expression "to abide in him" ("to continue" or "to remain" [μένω *menō*]) adds

---

51. By comparison, the Fourth Gospel speaks of the perfection or fulfillment of various things in addition to love (John 13:1): works (John 4:34; 5:36; 17:4), unity (John 17:23), and Scripture (John 19:28).

52. For more detailed examination, see Edward Malatesta, *Interiority and Covenant: A Study of* εἶναι ἐν *and* μένειν ἐν *in the First Letter of Saint John*, AnBib 69 (Rome: Pontifical Biblical Institute Press, 1978).

a durative nuance to the metaphor, connoting the believer's persistence in that realm defined by the character of God (1 John 2:24, 27-28; 3:6; 4:13; the number of occurrences of μένω in the Johannine corpus bespeaks its importance: forty in John, twenty-four in 1 John, three in 2 John, one in Revelation). Characteristic of this abiding is a reciprocity between the believer and God, as 1 John 2:4-5 suggests: The truth that is God, or the love of God, is in the believer who keeps the commandments; that believer is also said to be in God, or to abide in God (similarly, 2:24; 3:24; 4:13, 15-16; John 6:56; 14:20; 15:4-7, 16; 17:21-23; cf. Rom 8:9; Gal 4:19). Such reciprocity does not imply any dissolving or mystical interpenetration of God and the believer; though intimately bonded, those personalities remain distinct. Indeed, there exists within this abiding a definite "gravitational pull": It is the Father or the Son who attracts the believer, not the other way around (4:13-19; cf. John 15:1-11).

Finally, as v. 6 makes clear, the criterion for the believer's endurance in the truth and love of God is irreducibly ethical. Returning to the metaphor of "walking" as moral conduct, introduced in 1:6-7, the elder amplifies the path that the believer should take: "Whoever says, 'I abide in him,' ought to walk just as he [lit., "that one"] walked" (cf. 3:16; 5:2-3; John 13:15; 14:21, 23; 15:9-10; 1 Cor 11:1; Phil 2:1-11; 1 Thess 1:6; 1 Pet 2:21). In this single, masterly stroke, the author does two things. First, he grounds the believer's abiding in practical love. Second, the elder delineates the contours of love, not in the believer's natural sympathies or inclinations, but in Jesus, whose life epitomizes fidelity and righteousness (1:9; 2:1; cf. 3:7), the very one who has visibly trod the way before us (1:1-3).

REFLECTIONS

1. The loftiness of the elder's introductory claims (1:1-4) is matched by his down-to-earth recognition of sin within the church (1:6, 8, 10; 2:1, 4). For those whose ecclesiology is troubled by this reality, 1 John offers sound assessment and straight thinking. Whether in the elder's century or our own, the church is not an assemblage of spiritually healthy people; the church is where the sick gather to be healed from the disease of sin. Notably within the Anabaptist movement of the Radical Reformation, but also in every era, Christians have been tempted to regard the early church as a golden age of purity, which, were it only recovered, could restore Christianity to its original flawlessness. Such nostalgic myopia is corrected by the Johannine letters and, indeed, by the NT in its entirety. "The primitive church," Luther dryly commented, "wasn't as holy as we believed it to be."[53] It is not that we are so lamentably different from our forebears in faith; in fact, we resemble them far too closely.

In the creedal affirmation of the holy catholic church, "the communion of saints" stands beside "the forgiveness of sins." That conjunction is not accidental. The measure of sainthood is not human sinlessness but divine vocation. The community set apart in Christ lives continually by the gospel of God's forgiveness, precisely because we are sick and need a physician (Mark 2:17).

2. Nevertheless, 1 John's candor about sin may be more vinegary than most of us can swallow. From a survey of Christians across denominations in a Midwestern state, these interesting statistics emerged: "Although 98% said they believe in personal sin, only 57% accepted the traditional notion that all people are sinful and fully one-third allowed that they 'make many mistakes but are not sinful themselves.'"[54] The elder protests: "If we claim to be without sin, we deceive ourselves and the truth is not in us" (1:8 NIV). In desperate flight from responsibility to God, the guilty heart will suborn a terrified mind into almost any sophisticated casuistry, self-serving rationalization,

---

53. Luther, "Lectures on the First Epistle of St. John," 230.
54. Cited by Marianne Meye Thompson, *1–3 John*, IVP New Testament Commentary (Downers Grove, Ill.: InterVarsity, 1992) 46.

or conceptual incoherence, rather than admit to the sin at its seat. Much on 1 John's wavelength, Søren Kierkegaard (1813–55) located the root of the gospel's rejection in humanity's denial of its own contingency, our refusal to acknowledge God as God:

> People try to persuade us that the objections against Christianity spring from doubt. That is a complete misunderstanding. The objections against Christianity spring from insubordination, the dislike of obedience, rebellion against all authority. As a result people have hitherto been beating the air in their struggle against objections, because they have fought intellectually with doubt instead of fighting morally with rebellion.[55]

Unchecked, warns the elder, a headlong plunge into darkness sets the moral compass spinning without possibility of orientation. By denying the truth about ourselves, we criminally make into a liar the One who *is* truth (1 John 1:10; cf. John 8:44; Rom 1:18-32).

Truth to tell, God is no vindictive tyrant, eager to punish, but the loving heavenly Father to whom self-acknowledged sinners may repair. "It is very important," said Calvin, "to be quite sure that when we have sinned there is a reconciliation with God ready and prepared for us. Otherwise we shall always carry hell about within . . . [for] hell reigns where there is no peace with God."[56] Unlike human beings, who can be either heartlessly rigorous or loyal to a fault, in God fidelity and justice are one; forgiveness is offered us, not because we prove ourselves humble or well intentioned, but because mercy has been built into the structure of reality by its Creator and Judge, whose kindness toward us is utterly reliable (see 2 Tim 2:13).

In this context the elder's remarks about expiation (1 John 2:2; cf. 1:9; 4:10) fall into place, as well as pose for us some questions. First John joins with other NT documents, early (1 Cor 15:3) and late (Rev 1:5; 5:9), in articulating the belief that Jesus' death atones for sins. In 1 John the cultic practice of sacrifice, familiar to the elder and his audience, is assumed, not explained.[57] The underpinnings on which the elder's conviction rests are that (a) in a moral universe sin is real and lethally toxic; (b) the rupture created between sinners and God is real and in some sense demands the giving of our lives for its repair; and (c) Jesus' merciful giving of his life for our own heals our estrangement from God.

Owing to many religious and cultural influences, modern Christians appropriate such an understanding of atonement with varying degrees of ease. It is unquestionably the case, furthermore, that the NT incorporates a variety of views of Jesus' death and its redemptive consequences.[58] Still, it is worth pondering what may be lost from a Christian theology that has no room for an understanding of expiation such as that which 1 John suggests. An ability to perceive among a sanctuary's furnishings an altar, where sacrifice is offered, and not just a table for the Supper? A place for Golgotha beside the Sermon's Mount? Perhaps one of the sins that the church needs perennially to confess is the assumption, often unvoiced, that we have within ourselves the capacity to mend our estrangement from God and to put the world to rights. By 1 John's lights, that is nonsense of a very dangerous sort. When we delude ourselves into thinking that we can stand before God as our own advocate, when we believe and act as though human sin and divine reconciliation were no longer in the picture, we drive ourselves on a fast highway to despair and self-destruction. As Reinhold Niebuhr

---

55. *The Journals of Søren Kierkegaard*, ed. and trans. Alexander Dru (London: Oxford University Press, 1938) 193.
56. Calvin, *The Gospel According to St John 11–21 and the First Epistle of John*, 240.
57. *How* Jesus' death corresponds to, and supersedes, levitical regulations for sacrifice is a primary concern in the Epistle to the Hebrews; *why* his death atones for sin becomes a pressing issue for medieval Christian theologians. See Walter C. Kaiser, Jr., "The Meaning of Sacrifice," in the introduction to Leviticus (*The New Interpreter's Bible Commentary*, vol. 1); Barnabas Lindars, *The Theology of the Letter to the Hebrews*, New Testament Theology (Cambridge: Cambridge University Press, 1991) 86-98; and Colin E. Gunton, *The Actuality of Atonement: A Study of Metaphor, Rationality, and the Christian Tradition* (Grand Rapids: Eerdmans, 1989).
58. G. B. Caird, *New Testament Theology*, ed. and completed by L. D. Hurst (Oxford: Clarendon, 1994) 136-78, provides an instructive overview.

observed, "The sinner who justifies himself does not know God as judge and does not need God as Saviour."[59]

3. Finally, a question to which 1 John and its readers shall repeatedly return: How do we know God? The answer, in this letter, is not the property of some 'lite corps of spiritual athletes. Its criterion is not intensity of religious experience or better education, even of a theological kind. The acid-test for our life in God is its conformity with the gospel's moral imperatives and their fruition in love.

Austrian zoologist Konrad Lorenz became famous for his demonstration of the process known as imprinting. By imitating the quacks of a mother mallard, he taught newly hatched ducklings to follow him as their foster parent. Put metaphorically, 1 John 2:5-6 asks: Do we bear the imprint of Christ? Is his stamp on us evident in the way we walk?

59. Reinhold Niebuhr, *The Nature and Destiny of Man*, vol. 1: *Human Nature* (New York: Charles Scribner's Sons, 1941) 200.

1 JOHN 2:7-14, WHAT I AM WRITING

OVERVIEW

This segment of 1 John offers much of what one might have expected to find at the top of the epistle: a thumbnail description of what its sender is writing (vv. 7-11) and of those whom he is addressing (vv. 12-14). Why have these matters been deferred until now? The answer lies within the material itself; no new commandment but rather an old one is being written (v. 7). "That which was from the beginning" (1:1) had to be recapitulated, at the letter's beginning, before it could be properly epitomized here and considered in a fresh light. Similarly, the epistle's addressees are identified, not by name, but as beloved members of God's family (see 2:1: "my little children"; "the Father"), whose lives bear witness to those very aspects of salvation that have just been proclaimed: forgiveness of sins (also 1:7-9; 2:2), knowledge of the Father (1:2-3; 2:1, 3-4), persistent endurance of the word of God (1:1, 10; 2:5-6).

1 John 2:7-11, A Commandment Old Yet New

COMMENTARY

The swing between affirmation and exhortation, begun in 1:5-10 and repeated in 2:1-6, is reestablished in 2:7-11. This pericope also returns to the parallel metaphors of "light" and "darkness," introduced in 1:5-10. As in 2:1-6, the opening of 2:7-11 sets the stage with a built-in contrast ("no new commandment"/ "yet a new commandment," vv. 7-8; cf. "so that you may not sin"/"if anyone does sin," v. 1). Then follow three contrastive generalizations pertaining to hatred (vv. 9, 11) and love (v. 10) of one's fellow Christian, "the brother" (τὸν ἀδελφόν *ton adelphon*, an inclusive term used with reference to a disciple, either male or female, in Hellenistic Judaism, Christianity, and other religions of that era). Like 1:6, 8, 10, and 2:4, 2:9 envisions a situation in which a claim of religious status ("if we say"; "the one who says") is contradicted by the claimant's moral failing (cf. 2:6 for a positive exhortation based on the same formula). The alternating current of indicative and imperative, which has pulsed throughout 1:1-4, 1:5-10, and 2:1-6, flows fully throughout 2:7-11. Every assertion in this passage is at once theological and ethical.

Indeed, the author's primary aim in this brief section is to insist that adherence to the commandment and dwelling "in the light" are inseparable sides of a single coin.

2:7-8. Once again (cf. v. 1), firm counsel is prefaced with tender address: Ἀγαπητοί (*agapētoi*, "beloved" [NRSV] or "dear friends" [NIV]), a vocative that occurs ten times in the Johannine epistles (1 John 2:7; 3:2, 21; 4:1, 7, 11; 3 John 1, 3, 5, 11). Here it is especially appropriate for introducing the author's initial reflections on Christian love.[60] For the careful reader, vv. 7-8 raise at least three questions. What is the commandment to which the elder refers (cf. vv. 3-4, "the commandments")? Why does the elder say that this commandment is not new but old (v. 7), then apparently reverse himself in the very next sentence (v. 8)? What is meant by the comment that this commandment "is true in him and in you" (v. 8)?

The first of these questions may be the easiest to answer. As in vv. 4-5, in view here is the command that Christians love one another (see v. 10), the primary directive that embraces all other commandments in the Johannine tradition (3:22-24; 2 John 4-6; John 13:34; 15:10, 12, 17). The *truth* of that commandment is brought into the open (and thereby "seen," NIV) "in him and in you" (v. 8; see also 2:4-6). In Christ (John 1:17; 14:6), who has issued the command (John 13:34; 15:12) and has patterned the way in which Christians walk (v. 6), the divine reality or authenticity of the love command is actualized.

The love commandment's realization in Christ accounts for its ambivalent description as both old and new. It is old because it harks back to the primal testimony of Jesus, "the word" that the church has heard "from the beginning" (v. 7; see also 1:1; 2:24; 3:11; 2 John 5-6).[61] Whether the author refers to the beginning of Jesus' ministry, to the community's original formation, or to the first stirrings of faith among its individual members is not clear. For the elder these alternatives would probably not be mutually exclusive. Throughout the Greco-Roman world, old religious precepts were typically regarded as venerable, not obsolete;[62] and the elder evidently thinks that he has good reason to distrust religious innovation (see 2 John 9).

Yet because it crystallizes the ethic of an era newly inaugurated by God through Christ (4:9-10)—marked by the fading of darkness and the dawning of "the true light"—the love command may be viewed in another sense as fresh, much as Jesus characterized it (v. 8; see also 3:14; John 13:34; cf. 2 Cor 5:17; Eph 5:8-14).[63] The commandment is "not new as a phenomenon in the history of ideas, but rather as an eschatological reality."[64] In comparison to other eschatological literature of this era, including the Fourth Gospel, 1 John views the light of the new age neither as unseen but awaited,[65] nor as fully ablaze (John 1:9; 3:19; *1 Enoch* 58:5), nor as liable to recession (John 12:35-36), but as "now shining in the world . . . for the darkness is beginning to lift" (JBP; see also 2:17; similarly, Rom 13:11-13).[66]

2:9-11. By framing a positive possibility of intramural Christian conduct (v. 10) with negative alternatives (vv. 9, 11), these verses recall the construction and thought of 1:5-10. Compared with that earlier statement, the present unit is, however, both more explicit and more pointed, announcing a major theme to which the epistle will frequently return: the command to love within the household of Christian faith (see 3:10-18, 23; 4:7-21; 5:1-2). As in 3:15 and 4:20, a firm distinction is drawn here between "the one who loves" and "the one who hates" (a sharpness slightly

---

60. Some later MSS, including the "Received Text" on which the KJV is based, read "brothers" instead of "beloved." The latter reading, however, appears in the earliest and best Greek texts of 1 John. "Beloved" is a frequent mode of address in the Pauline and Catholic letters (Rom 12:19; 1 Cor 10:14; 2 Cor 7:1; 12:19; Phil 2:12; 4:1; Heb 6:9; 1 Pet 2:11; 4:12; 2 Pet 3:1, 8, 14, 17; Jude 3:1, 17, 20).

61. Most of the later MSS, referred to in note 60, repeat the words "from the beginning" after "that you have heard" in 1 John 2:7 (so KJV). Absent from the oldest and best texts, this phrase is probably a scribal addition intended to balance the clause "that you have had from the beginning," earlier in the verse, and to echo the elder's phraseology elsewhere (1:1; 2:4; 3:11).

62. Robert W. Wilken, *The Christians as the Romans Saw Them* (New Haven, Conn.: Yale University Press, 1984) esp. 94-125.

63. The Greek relative clause in 1 John 2:8 (ὅ ἐστιν ἀληθές *ho estin alēthes*, "which is true," with pronoun and adjective in the gramatically neuter gender) is rendered with precision in neither the NIV ("its truth is seen in him and you") nor the NRSV ("a new commandment that is true in him and in you"), both of which predicate truth of the "commandment" (ἐντολή *entolē*, a feminine noun). The clause "which is true" apparently modifies the preceding concept as a whole.

64. Rudolf Bultmann, *The Johannine Epistles: A Commentary on the Johannine Epistles,* Hermeneia (Philadelphia: Fortress, 1973) 27.

65. *T. Levi* 18:3-4.

66. Although regrettably unavailable in English translation, an important article by Günter Klein, "'Das wahre Licht scheint schon': Beobachtungen zur Zeit- und Geschichtserfahrung einer uncristlichen Schule," *ZTK* 68 (1971) 261-326, remains helpful in clarifying this sequential aspect of 1 John's eschatology.

dulled by the NIV and NRSV translations, "whoever loves"/"whoever hates"). Furthermore, the elder tightens the knot of ethical responsibility in an eschatological age, which was suggested in 1:6-7. The fundamental criterion for "living" or "perseverance" (μένω *menō*; see the comments on 2:6) in the light, which is analogous to persistence in God's domain (2:27-28; 3:6, 24), is nothing other than love of the Christian brother or sister (see also 4:13, 16). Merely having the religious vocabulary down pat is no assurance of abiding in God's radiance; as in 1:6-7, darkness is a moral condition to which a believer is susceptible "even yet" (2:9; similarly, see Rom 13:12; 1 Thess 5:4-8). Hatred is a stumbling block (σκάνδαλον *skandalon*; cf. Lev 19:14; Ps 119:165; Hos 4:17; Rom 14:13), an entrapment of oneself (NIV, NEB, REB) or of others that properly has no place either in the light (RSV) or in the believer who loves (NRSV). (Obscure in Greek, the wording of v. 10 permits all of the alternative interpretations in the preceding sentence.) The elder's comments here may be clarified by comparison with the Fourth Gospel. In John, "light" usually refers to Jesus' gift of divine revelation, and "darkness" to human rejection of that gift and the refusal to follow Jesus (John 8:12; 11:9-10; 12:46). In other words, John uses the idiom of light and darkness to express a statement about the nature of faith and disbelief. In 1 John, by contrast, these metaphors are reworked to point up the dynamic, moral dimensions of that spiritual reality. Thus in v. 11, hatred so darkens the way to be walked that a benighted church literally cannot see where it is going (cf. 2:6; 3:10, 15; 4:20; Isa 6:10; John 12:35, 40).

REFLECTIONS

1. Modern readers may be troubled by the razor-edged distinction, whetted by the elder, between loving and hating. Many of us would prefer to soften that starkness with subtleties, to allow for emotional nuances between the extremes—from cordiality to indifference to dislike, and so forth. Such a reaction reveals some notable things about the elder's point of view and our own. First John, like the Fourth Gospel, inclines toward a radical dualism that resists gradations. There is light, there is darkness, and between them there is no place to hide. To love is to live in clear-eyed embrace of the light; to hate is to stagger blindly in the dark, cursing the light. In such a scheme a twilight zone of neutrality, whether in personal or societal relations, is not admissible. Although 1 John's understanding has probably been influenced by hostility in the church's environment (see 1 John 2:18-27), its theological basis lies ultimately in the elder's view of God: God *is* light and love, and in God there is no darkness or hatred whatever (1:5; 4:8).

Just here the Johannine perspective may clarify some differences in our own. Whereas we may almost reflexively reduce the essence of love to a feeling, whether of passion or of friendliness,[67] 1 John construes love *eschatologically.* Those who abide in God's love live in a dynamic realm, a domain animated by the power of light, which struggles against the demonic power of hatred and darkness (see also John 3:19-21; 15:17-19). In 1 John 2:7-11, love and hate are not emotional states that can be triggered by sentimental greeting cards or demagogic propaganda. They are, rather, forms of characteristic conduct that reveal which of two radically discontinuous spheres humanity inhabits (cf. Matt 6:24 = Luke 16:13; Luke 14:26). "The polar alternatives with which the Johannine writings sketch the world should remind all of us who perceive the world in grays and shadows from the soft, indirect lighting of our comfortable dwellings that there are serious moral alternatives . . . which can make differences between life and death."[68] Like Paul (Rom 5:5; Gal 5:6) and John

---

67. Such interpretations, of course, have their ancient counterparts (ἔρως *erōs* [cf. Plato *Phaedrus* 237, 242]; φιλία *philia* [cf. Sophocles *Antigone* 523]), which differ from 1 John's understanding of love.
68. R. Alan Culpepper, *1 John, 2 John, 3 John,* Knox Preaching Guides (Atlanta: John Knox, 1985) 37.

(John 13:31-38; 14:12-24), 1 John asserts that love is an aggressive expression of Christian faith, symptomatic of life that is renewed not by our own power but by God's.

2. The preacher or teacher may join with commentators in debating whether the elder (like the Fourth Evangelist) has too narrowly circumscribed the arena of Christian love.[69] In contrast to Paul (Rom 13:9-10; Gal 5:14; cf. Lev 19:18) and Jesus of the synoptic Gospels (Matt 5:43-45; Mark 12:28-31; Luke 10:27-28, 36), John and 1 John do not counsel the love of neighbor or of enemies but, rather, love for one another within the Johannine community (e.g., John 13:34-35; 15:13, 17; 1 John 2:10; 3:11, 23; 4:7).

The question is not easily settled. On one side, the Fourth Gospel and the First Epistle are not the only documents in early Christianity, or in religious antiquity generally, for which intramural love is a salient concern (see Rom 12:10; Gal 6:10; 1 Thess 3:11-12; 5:15). Viewed from another angle, the Johannine letters stand at a considerable remove from the Dead Sea Scrolls, some of which counsel hatred of the Qumran community's adversaries[70] in ways that the Johannine literature does not (although Rev 2:6 and 17:16 veer perceptibly in that direction). John and 1 John consistently speak of their audience's being hated by others and not reciprocating that hatred (John 15:18-19; 17:14; 1 John 2:9, 11; 3:13, 15; 4:20). Still another factor to be considered, however, is 1 John's ambivalence toward "the world" (shared with the Gospel though articulated differently there; see John 1:10, 29; 3:16-17; 4:42; 8:23; 12:25, 47; 15:19; 17:9, 14-18). Christ is the Savior and expiation for the whole world's sins, not just for those of Johannine Christians (1 John 2:2; 4:14). Yet the things of the world are not to be loved (1 John 2:15-16); the world is diabolically hostile toward the community (1 John 3:1, 17; 4:1; 5:19; cf. John 15:18-19, 23-25) and is something to be overcome (1 John 5:4; cf. John 16:33; Rev 11:15). Given the sharp distinction between love and hate in 1 John 2:9-11, 15, it is hard to conceive of how "not loving" could ultimately be for the elder anything other than "hating," even though the First Epistle itself never makes that equation.

At this point it may be that the First Epistle, like the Fourth Gospel, contains some theological tensions that, even if logically compatible, have not been explicitly reconciled by the elder and the Fourth Evangelist within their respective works. What is clear, positive, and valid on its own terms is the Johannine stress on *love within the circle of Jesus' disciples,* an emphasis that neither intentionally nor effectively repudiates the more general command to love the neighbor so much as it refocuses that commandment in a special and important way. If 1 John's intense concentration on love within the church tends to leave undeveloped other necessary considerations of love for moral theology, those aspects may be informed by Paul, the synoptic evangelists, and other witnesses within both the OT and the NT. Assessed within its canonical context, 1 John offers an analysis of Christian love that, while perhaps incomplete, is nonetheless vital in our own day as much as in the elder's.[71]

3. Often underestimated in the debate on the character of love in 1 John is the very thing the elder underlines in 2:7-11: that one's fellows in the Christian congregation are to be loved as sisters and brothers. The unstated presupposition among some interpreters seems to be that, if 1 John does not speak of loving neighbors or enemies, then its formulation of the love command must be "soft." This assumption is naïve. It minimizes or overlooks the fact that most churches in the first century were not homogeneous associations for the religiously like-minded, having access to the myriad

---

69. Cf. Schnackenburg, *The Johannine Epistles,* 110-14, 178-79, who perceives in 1 John no constriction of scope for Christian love, and Wolfgang Schrage, *The Ethics of the New Testament* (Philadelphia: Fortress, 1988) 316-18, who arrives at precisely the opposite conclusion.
70. 1QS 1:2-4, 8-11; 9:16, 21-23; CD 2:14-15; 1QH 4:24; cf. also Ps 139:19-22.
71. See D. Moody Smith, "The Love Command: John and Paul?" in *Theology and Ethics in Paul and His Interpreters: Essays in Honor of Victor Paul Furnish,* ed. Eugene H. Lovering, Jr., and Jerry L. Sumney (Nashville: Abingdon, 1996) 207-17.

support systems of modern Western society. As Paul, James, and John remind us, the membership of early Christian communities was remarkably diverse, prone to factions, yet heavily dependent on one another for the fulfillment of basic needs (John 10:16; 21:15-17; 1 Cor 1:26; 11:17-22; 2 Cor 8:1–9:15; Jas 2:14-17). For the members of such churches to assume familial responsibilities for one another entailed considerable commitment.

It still does. As anyone knows from experience with the wear and tear of real-life Christian community, to regard one's neighbors within the church as Christ's sisters and brothers, and to respond to them as God's children (1 John 3:9-10; 5:2), is scarcely soft and rarely easy. In some churches, just as in some families, it can be much easier to love the homeless and the stranger, those with whom we have brief encounters, than to love those whom we know well and have promised to uphold over the long haul. "I could never understand," mused Ivan Karamazov, "how one can love one's neighbours. It's just one's neighbours, to my mind, that one can't love, though one might love those at a distance.... One can love one's neighbours in the abstract, or even at a distance, but at close quarters it's almost impossible."[72] Ivan's analysis is not overstated. Just ask the church that has fallen apart along any one of a hundred ideological fault lines.

Maturation in Christian faith happens at close quarters, amid the church's motley messiness and unredeemed sin. It is, as Augustine understood, "the walls of the church that make the Christian."[73] First John invites us to view the church as the place where family is redefined and extended, where this world's darkness is being illumined afresh, and often surprisingly, by God's light.

72. Fyodor Dostoevsky, *The Brothers Karamzaov*, The Novels of Fyodor Dostoevsky, vol. 1, trans. Constance Black Garnett (London: Heinemann, 1912) 248-49.
73. *Saint Augustine: Confessions*, trans. R. S. Pine-Coffin, (New York: Penguin, 1961) 160 (8.2).

1 John 2:12-14, The Family Restored

COMMENTARY

Interpreters have long been puzzled by this brief passage, which bristles with questions that are to some degree masked by the NIV, the NRSV, and other English translations. We may deal with these problems under three headings.

(1) *The section's relationship to its context.* First John 2:12-14 seems to interrupt the letter's flow of thought. Admittedly, as observed up to this point, an argument fashioned with stairstep logic is hardly this author's forte; on the other hand, the intrusiveness of 2:12-14 should not be exaggerated. This passage explicitly recalls much of the language and concerns of 2:1-6: the introductory clause, "I am writing" (vv. 1, 12-13); the elder's address to his "little children," followed by acknowledgment of their sin and its repair (vv. 1-2, 12); a concern for the knowledge of God (vv. 4, 6, 13-14) and the maintenance of his word (vv. 5, 14). This similarity is a clue to the function of 1 John 2:12-14. Like 2:1-6, it offers a positive, consolatory counterweight to some negative possibilities that have been raised in a pericope immediately preceding (cf. 1:5-10 with 2:7-11).

(2) *Structural and grammatical peculiarities of 1 John 2:12-14.* The structure of 1 John 2:12-14 rhythmically balances two units, each including three statements with parallel forms of address:

| Unit 1: | Unit 2: |
1 John 2:12-13	1 John 2:14
"to you, little children" (v. 12)	"to you, children" (v. 14a)
"to you, fathers" (v. 13a)	"to you, fathers" (v. 14b)
"to you, young people" (v. 13b)	"to you, young people" (v. 14c)

With minor modifications, the second unit of comments basically repeats ideas expressed in the first. (Note especially 2:14b, which reiterates almost verbatim the address to "the fathers" in 2:13a.) Judged by the stylistic conventions of its day, such repetition probably intends to amplify, with vividness, the elder's reassurance of his readers.[74]

Less obvious in English translation is a change of the verb "to write" from the present (γράφω *graphō*, vv. 12-13) to the aorist (past) tense (ἔγραψα *egrapsa*, v. 14). This shift is clearer in the KJV ("I write"/"I have written"), more subtle in the NRSV ("I am writing"/"I write"), and imperceptible in the NIV. The difference may be more stylistic than substantive. If a distinction between these tenses is registered, perhaps it should be one of emphasis, as though the author were saying, in v. 14, "What I just wrote [in vv. 12-13] I say to you again."

In the six subordinate clauses within vv. 12-14, the NIV and the NRSV agree with most English versions in translating the conjunction ὅτι (*hoti*) as "because" (e.g., "because your sins have been forgiven"; "because you have known him who is from the beginning"). This rendering is supported by a similar use of that conjunction elsewhere in 1 John (e.g., 2:8, 21). If we accept this translation, the sense of vv. 12-14 would be that the church's forgiveness, knowledge, conquest, and strength were the *occasion* or *reasons* for the elder's writing to them. Yet *hoti* can also be translated as "that." If we adopt that rendering here, the effect of these verses is to bolster the readers' confidence; accordingly, the elder writes (or declares) to the church's members *that* their sins are forgiven, *that* they know (and so on). Although a minority option among modern versions (thus JB), this "declarative" rendering fits the substance and spirit of 1 John 2:12-14 very well, perhaps more logically than does the "causal" translation.[75]

(3) *Exactly who is addressed in this passage?* Verses 12-14 are aimed at "[little] children" (τεκνία *teknia*, v. 12; παιδία *paidia*, v. 14a), "fathers" (πατέρες *pateres*, vv. 13a, 14b), and "young people" (νεανίσκοι *neaniskoi*, vv. 13b, 14c).[76] This mode of address faintly echoes the familiar household codes of Ephesians (Eph 5:21–6:9), Colossians (Col 3:18–4:1), and 1 Peter (1 Pet 2:18–3:7), and the instructions to various church leaders in 1 Timothy (1 Tim 3:1–6:2) and Titus (Titus 1:5-9; 2:2-10). Unlike those epistles, however, 1 John does not set forth detailed instructions for the conduct of discrete social groupings within the church, much less ascribe to them particular ministerial functions or duties. Rather, this form of address is an affectionate reminder of the *familial* character of the Johannine church. It is a community of the old and of the young, each group enjoying characteristic resources (the fathers, knowledge; young people, strength) but all regarded by the author as "dear children" (see also 2:1, 28; 3:7, 18; 4:4; 5:21), "beloved" (2:7; 3:2, 21; 4:1, 7, 11), "brothers and sisters" (2:9-11; 3:13-14, 16-17; 4:20-21; 5:16), who universally share the blessings of a new age (see also 2:8). No image of the church is more dominant in 1 John than that of "the family of God."[77]

In vv. 12-14 the elder does not precisely differentiate these groups; "knowledge of the Father [i.e., God]," tantamount to knowledge of him who is "from the beginning" (cf. 1:1), is expressly attributed to both "fathers" (vv. 13a, 14b) and "children" (v. 14a; cf. Matt 11:25; Luke 10:21). Neither does 1 John elevate one group over another or play one off the others. None of them is *inherently* significant. The importance of each group derives from its members' adherence to "him" (whether God or Jesus). Thus the "fathers" are commendable because they, like the "children," have known *the Father,* a relational knowledge implying that both groups are keeping *God's* commandments

---

74. Thus Calvin, *The Gospel According to St John 11–21 and the First Epistle of John*, 253; see also Duane F. Watson, "1 John 2:12-14 as *Distributio, Conduplicatio,* and *Expolito*: A Rhetorical Understanding," *JSNT* 35 (1989) 97-110.

75. See Bent Noack, "On I John ii.12–14," *NTS* 6 (1959–60) 236-41.

76. Worth noting, though not belaboring, is the debate, as old as Augustine ("Second Homily: I John 2:12-17," 4-7), over how many groups are being addressed in 1 John 2:12-14. Is it one, designated by three names ("children," "fathers," "young people")? Two ("fathers" and "young people") as parts of a whole ("children")? Or three at different stages of maturity? In the opinion of most commentators (e.g., Brown, *The Epistles of John*, 297-300), the second possibility seems less speculative and in conformity with the elder's mode of address throughout 1 John. Following Hippocrates, Philo (*On the Creation* 105) reckoned seven seasons in a man's life: the infant (παιδίου *paidiou*), the boy (παιδός *paidos*), the lad (μειρακίου *meirakiou*), the young man (νεανίσκου *neaniskou*), the man (ἀνδρός *andros*), the elderly man (πρεσβύτου *presbytou*), and the old man (γέροντος *gerontos*).

77. This point is explored by Dietrich Rusam, *Die Gemeinschaft der Kinder Gottes: Das Motiv der Gotteskindschaft und die Gemeinden der johanneischen Briefe*, BWANT 133 (Stuttgart: Kohlhammer, 1993).

(see 2:3). The sins of these "little children" have been and continue to be forgiven for *his* name's sake—that is, for his own sake (cf. 3:23; 5:13; Ps 25:11; Ezek 20:8-9; 36:22; John 1:12; 3 John 7; Rev 2:3). The strength of the young, which prevails over personified evil (i.e., the devil; cf. 3:8, 10, 12; 5:18-19; John 6:70; 8:44; 12:31; 13:2; 17:15; Eph 6:16; 2 Thess 3:3), is linked with their abiding in the word *of God* (see also 1:1; 2:5-6, 10, 24, 27; 3:9). Although 1 John is not shy of reminders that the family of faith ought to abide in God or in Christ (2:5*b*-6), here the elder encourages the church by acknowledging that its members do indeed live in that light and walk in that way—not because they have successfully worked their way through a striver's manual, but because their victory over evil is even now assured (see also 4:4; 5:4-5; cf. Isa 11:4; John 12:31; the conquest of evil forces by Christians in the present is a recurrent theme in Revelation; see Rev 2:7, 11, 17, 26; 3:5, 12, 21; 12:11; 21:7; cf. Rev 11:7; 13:7). Even now the community's knowledge of God is restored (e.g., 3:24; 4:7; cf. Isa 11:2, 9; 52:3-6; Jer 31:31-34).

REFLECTIONS

1. Beyond dispute, the church is a flawed community, whose members too often do things that they should not and leave undone things that they should do. In such cases, reproof and correction in love are called for. But prophetic censure of the church's sin deteriorates into a shrill, heartless harangue when unaccompanied by acknowledgment of the church's identity as the restored family of God, with commendation for its "jobs well done" in keeping his commandments and overcoming evil. First John 2:12-14 reminds us that Christians grow into maturity, not by repeated verbal spankings or by being driven up a new wall every week, but through tender nurturance, with due praise, openhearted encouragement, and generous reminders of what they already know (see also 2:7). The church, after all, is *God's* family. Its identity and security are assured by God's action; it lives by the strength of God's love. The church is the community of those who adhere to the proclamation of eternal life (1:2), and by that adherence are no longer victimized or captivated by evil (2:13-14).

2. That family is an intergenerational entity. It is easy for us to misconstrue 1 John's sensitivity to this point, for in all likelihood the elder would be unimpressed by our ecclesiastical establishment's facile recruitment of "baby-boomers" and patronization of their elders. While sensitive to social pressures (see 2:15-17), 1 John is not animated by the kind of sociological insecurities that tempt the modern church to forgo catechesis and to confuse worship with entertainment. In the Johannine community youth and age were not considered virtuous in themselves (cf. Job 13:26; Ps 25:7), much less institutionally beneficial. Both the young and the old occupied places of real importance in the Johannine church, because its youth were perceived to be vitally interrelated with their elders—both groups having known "him who is from the beginning" (2:13-14), for the sake of whose name their sins had been forgiven (2:12). Can Christian communities in our day move beyond both idolization of youth and repentance from ageism to the profundity of this very different kind of claim? In an age scarred by widespread rupture within natural families, can the church recover its blessedly integral experience as Christian children, youth, mothers, and fathers? With 1 John's help, are we willing to reclaim our common birthright as forgiven children in the family of God?

1 JOHN 2:15–3:10, CHILDREN, IT IS THE LAST HOUR

OVERVIEW

What might be considered 1 John's third movement is, like the letter's other sections, constructed from characteristic motifs (love, truth, righteousness, sin, the world, eternal life, abiding, "from the beginning," being of God or born of God). Yet this entire section's keynote, setting the tone for everything else, may be expressed most clearly in 2:18: "Children, it is the last hour!" This portion of the First Epistle is obviously eschatological in tenor, filled with a sense that ultimate stakes have been raised. The world is to be rebuffed, because it is passing away (2:15-17). Now many antichrists have come (2:18-25). The anointing received by the church preserves it against "the big lie" (2:26-27). Though what we shall be is not yet manifest, the church may be confident at Christ's coming (2:28–3:3). Firm lines of demarcation must be drawn between sin and righteousness, between the devil and God (3:4-10). As in 2:7-14, the placement of 2:15–3:10 appears to be an important indicator of the author's theological perspective; the "last things" are not to be talked about last of all, because they have *already* commenced and shape the reality in which the church now lives and leans into God's future. The same point was made more concisely and more powerfully in 2:8: "the darkness is passing away and the true light is already shining."

1 John 2:15-17, The World Versus the Will of God

COMMENTARY

Having reiterated confidence in his readers' knowledge of the Father (2:12-14), the elder moves abruptly to his first explicit directive: Do not love the world or anything in it. By this the author is surely not commending retreat from everyday life into self-preoccupation. If that were his intent, it would be practically impossible to fulfill the old, yet new, commandment to love one's brother or sister (2:7-8, 10). So against what does 1 John 2:15-17 inveigh?

2:15. This passage itself indicates what, in the elder's view, is problematic about the world. We can locate those comments within a larger context provided by the Fourth Gospel. By setting in mutual opposition "love for the world" and "the love of the Father,"[78] 1 John recalls the Gospel's view of the world (κοσμός *kosmos*) as, at once, the theater of God's salvation (John 3:16-17; 4:14; 11:27; 12:47; 17:18; 18:37) and a deluded realm that is enslaved to wickedness (John 12:31; 14:30; 16:11; 1 John 5:19) as well as radically opposed to Christ, the world's illuminator, judge, and redeemer (John 7:7; 8:12; 9:5; 12:46-48; 15:18). In Johannine thought the world was created by God through the Word, which ultimately became flesh. Because the world did not recognize Jesus as God's agent for its salvation (John 1:10-11), the world thereby showed that it did not know God (John 17:25). As Jesus has been sent *into* the world by God (John 3:17; 10:36; 12:46; 16:28), his believers are sent *into* the world by Jesus (John 17:11, 18). But neither Jesus nor his disciples are *of* the world in the sense of belonging to it or deriving from it their identity or existence (John 8:23; 15:19; 17:14, 16; cf. 1:12-13). In Johannine perspective, to love the world (1 John 2:15) is to embrace an illusion that has rejected Christ

---

78. As rendered in the NIV and the NRSV, "the love of the Father [ἡ ἀγάπη τοῦ πατρός *hē agapē tou patros*]" preserves the ambiguity of the Greek phrase, which suggests "the Father's love" (NEB), "love [for] the Father" (REB), or both.

and, therefore, to show oneself hostile to God (cf. Jas 4:4).

2:16-17. These verses underscore the kind of distance that, in the elder's opinion, should exist between the believer and the world. From the world there bubbles up a boiling desire for things "of the flesh" (2:16; see also Prov 27:20). In Johannine thought, as elsewhere in the NT (Rom 13:14; Gal 5:17; Eph 2:3; 1 Pet 2:11), "flesh" (σάρξ *sarx*) does not equal sex. It refers, rather, to the entire domain of humanity, which is distinct from God (see John 3:5-6; 8:15). Not from God, but from the world originates an arrogant pretension (ἀλαζονεία *alazoneia*), inflated by the conspicuous consumption of worldly goods (see also Wis 5:8; Jas 4:16; Philo *On the Virtues* 162). The elder is not counseling rejection of material experience as such or an ascetic denial of normal appetites (to the contrary, see 1:1-2; 3:17; 4:2). What he rejects is an absorption with things "of the flesh" and visible "to the eyes": a preoccupation with matters of "everyday life" (βίος *bios*) that runs counter to the Spirit, undermines seeing by faith, and is hostile to eternal life. What he repudiates are lust and boastful presumption *alazoneia*—impulsive, self-aggrandizing desire for this world's ephemeral allurements that would unseat God as the sovereign center of one's existence (cf. Matt 6:24 = Luke 16:13; Rom 8:7). Such cravings are as ridiculous as they are wrongheaded, for their object, this world, is passing away (1 John 2:17; cf. Rom 12:2; 1 Cor 7:31; 15:50). Only the fulfillment of God's will is eternally enduring (1 John 2:17; cf. Matt 7:21; 4 Ezra 4:11; 6:20; 7:96; *2 Apoc. Bar.* 21:19; 31:5; 40:3).

REFLECTIONS

Where does the Christian self find its center?

Worldly wisdom proposes for each of us a triumphant autonomy, of the sort immortalized by William Ernest Henley:

> It matters not how strait the gate,
> How charged with punishments the scroll,
> I am the master of my fate;
> I am the captain of my soul.[79]

Here is a stalwart courage that most of us would admire—but also a boastful presumption of which we should beware. Lacking from such a credo is any acknowledgment of our dependence on a power beyond ourselves to whom we are accountable. What is missing, in a word, is God, whose captaincy outranks our own and claims final disposition of our destiny and souls. As the elder recognizes, the relationship between boastful presumption and lust is intimate, for when we forget or deny that God is God and we are not, invariably we relocate our identity in "all that is in the world" (1 John 2:16 NRSV). And because the core of the human self is neither independent nor incorruptible, as we may delude ourselves into thinking, we end up *being defined by* "the world." When God is factored out of our life's equation or relegated to the extraneous role of a cosmic coach, our identity becomes radically confused. We become what we do and how much we earn. We become the clothes we wear and the baubles we buy. We become the neighborhoods we live in, the schools our children attend, and the clubs we belong to. But an identity constructed from our ravenous cravings for the transitory is hopelessly unstable and doomed to disappointment. "You can in no manner be satisfied with temporal goods," said Thomas à Kempis (1379/80–1471), "for you were not created to find your rest in them."[80] Was Thomas correct? Ask anyone who has ever lost a job.

---

79. "Invictus" (1888), in *The New Oxford Book of English Verse, 1250–1950,* ed. Helen Gardner (New York: Oxford University Press, 1972) 792.
80. Thomas à Kempis, *The Imitation of Christ,* ed. Harold C. Gardiner, S.J. (Garden City, N.Y.: Doubleday, 1955) 128.

First John denies the commonplace assumption that human beings create themselves or are competent to assume final responsibility for their individual and collective well-being. In the elder's view, we are *radically contingent* beings whose loyalties and identities are molded by our inhabitation of one sphere or another. We are either "of the world" or "of God." Ultimately we do not define ourselves; ultimately our selves are defined by the domain in which we live. Either we are defined by our materialism and delusions of grandeur, or we are defined by our obedience to God's will, formed by God's affections rather than by our own egoism (cf. Deut 6:4-5; Mark 12:29-30 par.; John 3:5-6).[81]

To what do we ultimately entrust ourselves? To this world's bogus promises of salvation by beauty, financial security, and creature comfort? Or to God's guarantee of our full restoration through the love of Jesus Christ? First John 2:15-17 is a passage of admonition, a barbed reminder that we have to make this radical choice on which hinges nothing less than our eternal destiny. But the elder's exhortation has been immediately prefaced by encouragement (2:12-14), unmitigated assurance that we are empowered to decide wisely and to stick to that decision. On what does that consolation rest? On nothing less than the confidence that *we have already been chosen* as God's beloved children. Our desire to know the God who is our selves' genuine center, our will to commit our lives to God, is more than matched—indeed, is energized—by God's powerful desire to claim us with a love that will never let us go. In that light the bulk of 1 John could be considered an extended meditation on what it means to have been given "power to become children of God . . . who were born, not of blood or of the will of the flesh or of the will of man, but of God" (John 1:12-13 NRSV).

---

81. See Leander E. Keck, "Derivation as Destiny: 'Of-ness' in Johannine Christology, Anthropology, and Soteriology," in Culpepper and Black, *Exploring the Gospel of John in Honor of D. Moody Smith*, 274-88.

1 John 2:18-25, Endurance Amid Antichrist's Coming

COMMENTARY

Perhaps no segment of 1 John is more troubled than 2:18-25. Troublesome to clarify and somewhat troubling in its implications, this pericope bespeaks a Christian community undergoing deep disturbance.

2:18. From the passage's opening its language is portentous, like lowering clouds over a rocky landscape. The elder's "children" have heard of antichrist's coming, which suggests that ἀντίχριστος (*antichristos*; lit., a "counterchrist" or "opposing christ") was some figure expected within the community addressed in 1 John. It is remarkable to learn from the elder that antichrist has come— more than one, in fact. Thus described, this figure is unprecedented in the apocalyptic literature of 1 John's day, surprisingly absent from the Revelation to John, and rare in early Christian writings.[82] Most commentators assume a conceptual kinship between antichrist and "the lawless one," or "man of sin," in 2 Thess 2:3-9 and "the abomination that makes desolate" in Dan 9:27; 11:31; 12:11; 1 Macc 1:54; and the synoptic Gospels (Mark 13:14 par.). All of these anonymous images are associated with evil's last massive assault before God's final victory. Likewise, in 1 John the coming of antichrist confirms that the church is living in a final hour (v. 18; cf. John 5:28; Mark 13:32; Luke 12:40, 46; Rom 13:11; Rev 3:3). Lying, attributed by the elder to this counterchrist (1 John 2:22), recalls the Fourth Gospel's characterization of

---

82. See Polycarp *Letter to the Philippians* 7.1, which refers to 1 John 4:2-3 and 2 John 7.

the devil as "a liar and the father of lies" (John 8:44 NRSV). Deceit, perpetrated by "false Christs and false prophets" in the last days, is also forecast by Jesus in the Olivet Discourse (Matt 24:5, 23-24; Mark 13:6, 21-22; Luke 21:8; cf. Acts 20:29-30; Rev 16:13; 19:20; 20:10).[83]

2:19. According to 1 John, exactly what does this opposing christ do? Although two other comments in these epistles supply a bit more information (1 John 4:3; 2 John 7), here antichrist's coming is evidenced by only two things: a secession of some Christians from the Johannine community and a denial of Jesus that entails a denial of God. The first of these activities appears clearer than the second: A schism has occurred within the Johannine fellowship shared by the author and his readers (1:3; see Introduction, "The Adversarial Character of 1, 2, and 3 John"). From the elder's point of view, the secessionists were not expelled (contrary to the reading of Augustine, who likened them to "bad humors" whose vomiting out relieved the body of Christ).[84] It appears, rather, that the dissidents voluntarily walked out (cf. John 6:66-67; 13:30).

2:22-23. The second indication of antichrist is much harder to interpret: "the one who denies that Jesus is the Christ" and by so doing "denies the Father." The problem lies in ascertaining precisely what was being denied. Did some conclude that not Jesus, but rather someone else, is God's anointed agent, the Messiah? It is hard to imagine how such a conclusion could have been drawn by a party within Johannine Christianity, sharing with the elder the same traditions that we know from the Fourth Gospel (see John 1:17, 41; 11:27; 17:3; 20:31). Could some have denied that (the incarnate, earthly) Jesus is the (exalted, heavenly) Christ? This possibility seems more likely in the light of 1 John 4:2 and 2 John 7, both of which attribute a repudiation of Jesus' coming *in the flesh* to the deception of antichrist. Nevertheless, the controversy underlying v. 22 remains ill-defined, because the author does not clarify it. Whatever its causes, a chasm of some kind has opened up between the schismatics' understanding of Jesus and their construal of him as the Christ, a rupture that for the elder is all the same as a lie that "denies the Son." If the Son is denied, so too is the Father who sent him, since, in Johannine thought, one's response to Jesus is equivalent to one's response to God (v. 23; see also 1 John 4:15; 5:1; 2 John 9; John 5:23; 12:44-45; 14:6-9; 15:23; cf. Matt 10:32-33; 11:27 and par.).[85]

2:20-21, 24-25. How does the elder advise those left behind to regard the church's breakup? (1) He identifies the trauma as an expected, critical moment of decision: "Children, it is the last hour! As you have heard . . . " (2:18). This is the only occurrence of "last hour" (ἐσχάτη ὥρα *eschatē hōra*) in the NT. John's Gospel, however, refers to Jesus' crucifixion and resurrection/ascension as the eschatological "hour" of his glorious return to the Father (John 2:4; 7:30; 12:23, 27). Although 1 John may imply a link between the victorious hour of Jesus' glorification and the climactic hour of schism within the Johannine church, the elder does not clarify or develop that connection. Rather, he interprets the character of the Johannine community in the light of its fracture. The split now reveals those who have really belonged to the church from the beginning and exposes those who have not (2:19; cf. John 3:19-21; 1 Cor 11:19).

(2) The elder writes not for the purpose of reproving his readers, but of ratifying the soundness and basis of their own judgment. Here his comments are couched in language associated with ancient Jewish rituals of consecration and authorization for a task (see Exod 24:7; 1 Sam 9:16; 1 Kgs 19:16). Specifically, "an anointing from the Holy One"— which may refer either to God (Hab 3:3) or to Christ (John 6:69)—has endowed all of the church with the capacity to discern the truth (v. 20; cf. 2 John 1).[86] That anointing,

---

83. On the notion of "antichrist" in antiquity, see Brooke, *A Critical and Exegetical Commentary on the Johannine Epistles*, 69-79, and Schnackenburg, *The Johannine Epistles*, 135-39. On the concept's evolution in the history of Christian thought, see Bernard McGinn, *Antichrist: Two Thousand Years of the Human Fascination with Evil* (San Francisco: HarperCollins, 1994).

84. Augustine "Third Homily: I John 2:18-27," §5.

85. Some later MSS omit, apparently by accident, the second half of 1 John 2:23: "Everyone who confesses the Son has the Father also" (NRSV; cf. KJV). In this verse, as in 2 John 9 (cf. 1 John 5:12), "having God" suggests, not ownership, but the believer's firm connection with God (cf. 3 Macc 7:16; *T. Iss.* 7:7).

86. The Greek MSS evidence for 1 John 2:20 is evenly divided between two readings: "you know all things [πάντα *panta*]" (KJV), and "you all [πάντες *pantes*] know" (GNB, JB, NAB, NEB, NIV, NRSV, REB, RSV). The second alternative best fits the context: The author affirms the truth that all his readers know. He has nothing to add to it (2:21), and neither do the schismatics, whose claims are fraudulent (2:19, 22). The first alternative may have been created by scribes who thought the clause "you know" needed an object.

moreover, enables Christians to distinguish the truth from a lie (v. 21) and to utter truthful confession about both the Son and the Father (v. 23; "anointing" will be discussed in the Commentary on 2:26-27).

(3) The elder urges his readers to do exactly what the secessionists have not: allow the community's original proclamation (see 1 John 1:1; 2:7, 13-14; 3:11; 2 John 5-6) to "persist" (μενέτω *menetō*) among them, that they may also continue in the Son and in the Father (v. 24; the root verb μένω [*menō*] prominently refers in John's Gospel to the mutual indwelling of God, Christ, and the Christian believer [John 6:56-58; 15:1-10; 17:21-23]; see also Commentary on 1 John 1:3; 2:5-6). The outcome promised "to us"[87] by him (probably Christ; cf. John 3:15; 6:40) is "eternal life." Such life is not of infinite duration in some utopian future. It is, instead, life possessing a radically indestructible quality that even now transcends this world's evanescence (see also 1:2; 3:15; 5:11, 13, 20; John 3:36; 6:47; 10:10, 28; 17:3).

[87] A varied and considerable majority of MSS read "to us" (ἡμῖν *hēmin*) in 1 John 2:25, though a few have "to you" (ὑμῖν *hymin*, pl.). The word ἡμῖν, which in Greek sounds very similar to ὑμῖν, may have been copied into this verse by scribes thinking of the pronouns in 2:24 and the phraseology of 1:2-3.

REFLECTIONS

Some preachers or teachers of 1 John 2:18-25 may find aspects of this material disquieting, even repulsive. Images like "antichrist" and "the last hour" enjoy a more receptive hearing in some modern congregations than in others. A few commentators argue, with more tenacity than persuasion, that 1 John has already begun the process of "demythologizing" those images.[88] Moreover, the elder's branding of his opponents as liars and antichrists may strike some readers as exemplifying the tendency of a lamentable kind of religious behavior: the demonization of those with whom we disagree. An early and important step in reflecting on this material, therefore, is a candid acknowledgment of its difficulty.

Compounding these troubles are the intensity of the controversy in which the elder was embroiled and our distance from it. Behind the pained rhetoric of 1 John 2:18-25 is a harrowing reality: For the first time in the NT record, a church has fallen apart over a matter of critical importance, a division that must surely have been experienced with shock by those whose tradition accentuated the church's unity in Christ (John 10:16; 17:11, 21-23; 1 John 1:3). At the time of this letter's composition, that wound was fresh, gaping, and raw. To expect the elder's comments to be evenhanded under these circumstances would be as unrealistic as to generalize the relevance of a *cri de coeur* in all times and places. The wail of betrayal in 1 John 2:18-25 is very likely proportionate to just how much the elder and the secessionists once shared; had they not been so close, he could have regarded their departure with indifference. If we were fully able to appreciate the factors precipitating that congregation's collapse, we might be surprised by the coolness with which the author was trying to lead his readers in reasoning their way through it. Jane Austen wrote wisely, "Nobody, who has not been in the interior of a family, can say what the difficulties of any individual of that family may be."[89] That observation is acutely pertinent to the families in the Bible, whose affections and quarrels are so remote from us in time and culture.

It is especially illuminating to read the elder's rhetoric within the ancient context of slander, which was commonly used by the adherents of other Hellenistic religions. Colotes, a student of the Epicurean school, assailed rival philosophers as "buffoons, charlatans, assassins, prostitutes, nincompoops."[90] The Jewish historian Josephus castigated hostile Gentiles as "frivolous and utterly senseless specimens of humanity . . .

---

88. See, among others, Dodd, *The Johannine Epistles*, 49-50, and Bultmann, *The Johannine Epistles*, 36-38.
89. Jane Austen, *Emma*, in *The Complete Novels of Jane Austen*, vol. 2 (New York: Modern Library, 1992) 107.
90. Plutarch *Moralia* 1086E.

filled with envy . . . folly and narrow-mindedness."[91] Priests at Qumran prayed that the wicked—Jews as well as Gentiles—"be accursed, without mercy . . . and sentenced to the gloom of everlasting fire."[92] Such examples could be multiplied, but the point should be clear: The author of 1 John wrote in an era when polemic—hurled by both Gentiles and Jews against each other and even among one another—had assumed a conventionally strident, typically overwrought character that makes the occasionally harsh language of the Johannine epistles seem, by comparison, surprisingly mild.[93]

None of these reflections suggests that 1 John 2:18-25 should be written off as a museum piece or disdainfully ignored. After we have raised hard questions about this text, it responds with some others aimed straight at us.

1. Does the way in which Christians regard Jesus matter as much as the elder thinks? Modern congregations that lean toward social activism, readily approving of 1 John's insistence on practical love for the sister and brother, may find quaint or puzzling the same letter's commitment to orthodoxy ("straight thinking"; see also 2 Tim 4:3-4). But for 1 John there can be no distinction between "obedience to the commandment" and "abiding in the word," no separate compartments for morality and theology. God's truth requires of Christians confession in faith and activation in love. Failure to proceed both morally and confessionally in the light of that truth is, as the elder baldly puts it, lying—whether to others, to ourselves, or to God (1 John 1:6, 10; 2:4, 21-22, 27; 4:20; 5:10). That last possibility is the most frightening of all, for in 1 John 2:18-25 the elder's primary point is that if we get Jesus wrong, then we shall surely misconstrue the God who saves us; and if our understanding of God is corrupted, then the way we live will inevitably be deformed. The old saw, "It doesn't matter what you believe, so long as you're sincere," is an idea far more naïve and dangerous than any the elder puts forward. It is also more cowardly, for, as Richard Lischer has perceptively observed, "What often passes for 'tolerance' in the modern congregation is in reality excommunication through indifference."[94] First John compels us to consider that some beliefs we may hold about Jesus are intolerably divergent from God's norm, that some activities in which we may engage are inescapably at odds with the One in whom Christians have known atonement.

2. For all the gloom of 1 John 2:18-25, the elder writes with remarkable conviction (see also 3:21; 4:17; 5:14). Although his tone is sure, he never pretends to possess any truth that his readers do not also enjoy. The author confidently attests to the knowledge that Christians already have as the result of their own anointing (1 John 2:20-21). We know what we need to know, not merely to hang on but to thrive faithfully in this troubled world. Our hope rests not in ourselves but in God, who is master over every hour, from first to last (1 John 2:14, 24). The elder is certain that those who persevere in the community's originating affirmation of faith will remain united with Christ and with God (1 John 2:24).

Amid excruciating breakdowns within and beyond the church, in what does our own Christian assurance rest? In a skeptical and often cynical age, does the modern church believe that its witness receives what for Calvin was "the highest commendation": "that it unites us to God and contains whatever belongs to the true enjoying of God"?[95] Do our ministries, in substance and style, express the elder's hope that, despite all appearances to the contrary, God can and will make good on the promise to us of an indestructible life (1 John 2:25)?

---

91. Josephus *Against Apion* 1.25.225-26.
92. 1QS 2:7-8.
93. For a perceptive, richly documented survey, see Luke T. Johnson, "The New Testament's Anti-Jewish Slander and the Conventions of Ancient Polemic," *JBL* 108 (1989) 419-41.
94. Richard Lischer, "The Sermon on the Mount as Radical Pastoral Care," *Int* 41 (1987) 157-69; see esp. 166.
95. Calvin, *The Gospel According to St John 11–21 and the First Epistle of John*, 262.

1 John 2:26-27, Anointing in Truth

COMMENTARY

Once more (cf. 2:7, 12-14, 21) the author stresses that he has not written[96] to inform his readers of new matters or to correct their mistakes, but to clarify the threat posed by "those who are trying to lead you astray" (τῶν πλανώντων *tōn planōntōn*, a participle whose root idea is that of "wandering"). The elder's thought returns to "the anointing [χρῖσμα *chrisma*] that you received from him" (see v. 20), which keeps the congregation from straying.

Tightly compressed within v. 27 are six claims about this anointing:

(1) It is something given to the elder's readers ("as for you"). A contrast between them and their potential deceivers is implied.

(2) The readers have received this anointing (*chrisma*) "from him": either from God or from Christ, God's anointed one (Χριστός *Christos*).

(3) Their anointing "abides" or "dwells" (μένει *menei*) in them (cf. 2:14).

(4) The community's anointing by him[97] teaches its members as regards all things. They need no one to teach them. They certainly need no instruction from those who would mislead them or even, by implication, from the elder himself (see also vv. 20-21; cf. Rom 15:14-15; 1 Thess 4:9).

(5) That anointing is "real, not counterfeit" (NIV). It is thus, by implication, as utterly reliable as instructions from would-be misleaders would confuse.

(6) Because Johannine Christians are directed by this anointing, they are encouraged by the elder to reciprocate its persistence in them, not by straying, but by abiding (μένετε *menete*) in it or in him. (The grammar permits either interpretation, or both; see also 2:6, 10, 24.)

These comments do not specify what this *chrisma* is or under what circumstances the elder envisions its bestowal on his readers. They would surely have known to what he was referring and would have needed no explanation. For us, however, vv. 26-27 are almost as obscure as they are illuminating. Medicinal anointing of the sick with oil was widely practiced in antiquity (see Mark 6:13; Jas 4:14-15; Josephus *The Jewish War* 1.657; *Antiquities of the Jews* 17.172), but in 1 John there is no hint of such a *chrisma*. A more plausible suggestion is that anointing refers here either to baptism (cf. Acts 10:38) or to the community's tradition affirmed at baptism.[98] That interpretation is not, however, problem free; while we find some heavily veiled allusions in 5:6-8 (perhaps also in 1:9), 1 John makes no explicit reference to baptism. Moreover, the author speaks of this anointing as something experienced only by his readers, those who have not broken away from the community. Presumably, however, the Johannine secessionists (2:18-19), who appear to be "the deceivers" in v. 26, would also have been baptized.

A third possibility is grounded less securely in 1 John than in the Gospel of John: The anointing to which the elder refers is the coming of the Holy Spirit.[99] In John, Jesus speaks of the Spirit in many of the same terms that the elder in 1 John uses to express the church's anointing. The Spirit, which is of truth (John 14:17; 15:26; 16:13), is bestowed by God (John 14:16, 26) and by Jesus (John 16:7; 15:26) upon his disciples, in order that the Spirit may abide (μένω *menō*) among them forever (John 14:16-17). Of particular relevance to 1 John 2:26-27, the Spirit sent by God in Jesus' name will teach the disciples all things, reminding them of all that Jesus said to them (John 14:26; 15:26; 16:14-15). Although 1 John does not expressly connect

---

96. Although conjugated in the past tense (an "epistolary aorist"), the verb in 2:26 refers to the present letter (so NIV and NRSV), whose composition would have been completed by the time the original readers received and read it.

97. Weakly supported in the Greek textual tradition of 1 John 2:27 is the phrasing "but as his anointing *itself* teaches you" (NRSV; cf. KJV: "but as the same anointing teacheth you"). While appropriate in the present context, this wording is uncharacteristic of both the Fourth Gospel and the Johannine letters.

98. Thus Dodd, *The Johannine Epistles*, 62-63; Grayston, *The Johannine Epistles*, 87-88.

99. At least as old as John Calvin (*The Gospel According to St John 11–21 and the First Epistle of John*, 263), this interpretation is proposed by a majority of interpreters; see especially J. C. Coetzee, "The Holy Spirit in 1 John," in *Studies in the Johannine Letters*, *Neot* 13 (1979) 43-67.

the sending of the Spirit with the church's anointing, consecration with "the spirit of the Lord" is a venerable biblical image (1 Sam 16:13; Isa 61:1; cf. 2 Cor 1:21-22), and the elder does comment directly on the Spirit later in 1 John (3:24; 4:1-3, 6, 13; 5:6, 8). The Spirit's presupposition in 2:26-27 is not, therefore, unreasonable. Like the Fourth Gospel, the First Epistle assumes the closest possible relationship among the Father, the Son, and the Spirit sent by them to dwell among those who believe in Jesus (see 1 John 3:24; 4:1-6, 13; 5:7-8). Both John (John 15:1-11) and 1 John (2:20, 27) also assume the unmediated access of every believer to that Spirit and to Christ, to whom the Spirit bears authentic witness. By its own anointing, the Johannine church is and should remain bonded to Christ, the anointed one.

REFLECTIONS

1. Except for communities in the Pentecostal tradition, pneumatology (reflection on the character and activity of the Spirit) may be one of the most undernourished elements of theological reflection in the modern church. Across denominational lines, within local congregations as well as seminaries, spiritual formation is earnestly sought, though with little consensus among the seekers on what it means to be spiritually formed. First John 2:26-27 offers help in allaying the hunger of present-day Christians as they consider the Spirit's role in their life as the church. For instance, the elder's insistence that the community's anointing is God's *gift*, not the church's attainment, ought to relax Christians' anxious tension to "make it" in a driven culture that grinds by the rule of salvation by works. In many churches language about the Spirit sprawls across the religious map, from investigation of different forms of prayer, to demonstration of extraordinary speech or other abilities, to cultivation of artistic tastes or social responsibilities. Into this conversation 1 John injects a critical factor that all of these approaches may overlook: a concern for the lasting integrity of the church's witness to God's restorative activity in Jesus Christ. The community that joins with 1 John in claiming that God has anointed the whole church, the laity as well as its ordained leaders, is liberated for robust cooperation with its pastor or priest. The leader who shares that confidence is freed from the tyranny of a dysfunctional congregation.

2. Radically egalitarian by inclination, the elder's view of the church's anointing has been sharpened by a dire threat of deception. Some acute questions linger: What happens when the anointed Christian fails to "abide in him"? Although the believer should know all and need no instruction from anyone, may not one's anointing become tainted? And if so, how will it be restored, if not with the help of one's sisters and brothers—including the assistance of Scripture and tradition, the record of the family of faith? Without some objective standard beyond ourselves, how can we confirm that the instructional voice we hear is indeed the Spirit's and not merely the echo of our own? In reply, the elder—who in 1 John is plainly offering counsel—would ultimately point his readers back to "what you heard from the beginning" (2:24) as well as to those practical tests of religious experience that dot the landscape of 1 John (1:6; 2:3-6, 9-11; 3:4, 7-10, 14-15; 4:7-8, 20; 5:2).[100] Without working out the problem of spiritual confirmation, 1 John does suggest a pattern for deliberation within the church that remains well worth pondering: a dynamic interaction between the community's verbal witness to the word and the practical appropriation of that word by every believer, at the Spirit's prompting.[101]

---

100. The classic study of this subject is Robert Law, *The Tests of Life: A Study of the First Epistle of St. John* (Edinburgh: T. & T. Clark, 1909).

101. For further discussion, see Ignace de la Potterie, "Anointing of the Christian by Faith," in *The Christian Lives by the Spirit,* ed. Ignace de la Potterie and Stanislas Lyonnet (Staten Island, N.Y.: Alba House, 1971) 79-143.

1 John 2:28–3:3, Confidence at Christ's Coming

COMMENTARY

Although its train of thought moves in no clearly deductive fashion, this segment recapitulates many ideas previously announced: the elder's encouragement of those "beloved" (3:1, 2; see also 2:5, 7, 10, 15) to "abide in him" (i.e., God or Christ; 2:28; see also 2:6, 10, 14, 17, 24, 27) who is "righteous" (2:29; see also 2:1); the church's assured knowledge (2:29; see also 2:3, 5, 13-14, 18) and its separation from the unknowing world (3:1; see also 2:15-17). First John 2:28–3:3 differs from what has preceded in its decided look ahead. To this point the elder has spoken of the church's heritage (1:1-3) or current condition; here he points his readers forward to the future, to the time of Christ's return (2:28; 3:2). This adjustment of perspective is consistent with the eschatological shading of the author's remarks in 2:18-25. The community's present experience of the coming of Christ's opponents is now placed alongside the sure expectation of Christ's own appearance.

All of the preceding ideas are melded in several closely related themes:

Present Endurance as Preparation for the Future. In comparison to the Gospel of John, which places heavier stress on the present realization of eternal life in Christ (John 3:36; 5:24; 6:47, 54; 17:3; cf. John 5:28-29; 6:39-40, 54), 1 John's eschatological vision is more obviously bifocal. The community of faith is encouraged to dwell for now in that domain that has been climactically defined by Christ, so that later, when he is revealed at his (or God's) regal coming (παρουσία *parousia*), the church may stand before him, boldly confident (παρρησίαν *parrēsian*) and unashamed (1 John 2:28; 4:17; cf. Mark 8:38; Luke 9:26; 1 Thess 3:13; 5:23; Jas 5:8; 1 Pet 4:16). Throughout 1 John 2:28–3:3 the author's use of third-person singular pronouns is imprecise; thus it is unclear whether God or Christ is to be manifested as the standard to which believers will be conformed. Either way, in Hellenistic inscriptions of the era before Jesus, *parousia* typically refers to the arrival of a potentate; the term was adopted by early Christians to depict Christ's second coming (see Matt 24:3; 1 Cor 15:23; 1 Thess 2:19). First John balances a promise of its readers' status as God's children now with a reminder that the future into which they are growing has not been revealed. What the church will be when he (or that reality) appears is not yet clear (3:2; cf. 2 Cor 5:10; Col 3:3-4). The fact that all is yet to be resolved no more jeopardizes believers' assurance of their identity in 1 John than love is undermined in 1 Corinthians because the church's vision is now obscured (1 Cor 13:12). In both letters a sense of incompletion spurs Christians' persistence in Christ (see also Phil 3:20–4:1) and reminds them that their perception of God (or of Christ) will someday be perfected (see also Matt 5:8; 2 Cor 3:18; Rev 22:4).

Kinship with God. John's Gospel dwells on Jesus' oneness with God (John 5:19; 10:30, 38; 14:6, 11, 20; 16:15; 17:21), drawing out the implications of that unity for disciples who abide in Jesus (John 15:1-11; 17:11, 20-26). The emphasis is readjusted in 1 John. While assuming the Son's unity with the Father (1 John 1:3; 2:23-24; 4:13), in 2:28–3:3 and elsewhere the First Epistle accents the affinity of believers with God and with Christ. The elder favors the language of kinship to express this conviction: "we are God's children now" (3:2 NRSV; see also 3:1, 9-10; 4:7; 5:1-2, 4, 18; cf. Jer 31:9; Hos 11:1; Rom 8:14-17; Gal 3:26-27; 4:4-7; Rev 21:7). The one who is "begotten of him" (2:29; see also John 1:13; 3:3-8; 1 John 3:9; 4:7; 5:1, 4, 18; cf. Deut 32:18) demonstrates a family resemblance through conduct that is characteristic of the Father: "as he is, so are we in this world" (1 John 4:17 NRSV; see also 2:6; 3:17). Later gnostic writings, like the *Corpus Hermeticum* (3rd cent. CE), develop the concept of birth from God in terms of the soul's experiences and recovery of its original divinity. Such ideas are foreign to 1 John.

In 1 John 2:28–3:3, two "family traits" of God's children are highlighted. First, "doing righteousness" (2:29)—that is, assisting in that comprehensive rectification (δικαιοσύνη *dikaiosynē*) whose norm is God's own justice, which Jewish and Christian apocalypticism considered a primary ingredient of God's "new world order" (*Jub.* 1:15; 31:25; Matt 13:43, 49; 25:46; Rom 5:21). Second, "purity" (ἁγνός *hagnos*), which in 3:3 may be understood in the sense of "unimpeachable sincerity" or "moral uprightness" (thus Phil 1:17; 4:8; 1 Tim 5:22; Titus 2:5; Jas 4:8; 1 Pet 1:22; 3:2; Euripides, *Orestes* 1604). For the elder, the resemblance between God and the children of God is verified by the world's attitude toward Johannine Christians; the world knows neither them nor God (1 John 3:1*b;* cf. John 15:18-21; 17:14).

Calling and Responsibility. As in previous passages (1:6-10; 2:3-6, 10-11, 15-17, 24, 27), 2:28–3:3 accent the Christian's walk in the way of Christ. Yet the elder is equally insistent that human acts of justice (2:29) or purity (3:3) are not the precondition for God's favor. Such conduct is an apt *response* to God's prior action, since the initiative for creating children of God belongs entirely with the God of gratuitous love (3:1*a;* see also 3:16; 4:11, 19). Children do not give birth to themselves! Nor does our self-purification stem from misplaced confidence in ourselves; it arises instead from "this hope in him" (3:3). We abide in him, not out of dread that our identity as God's children will be stripped from us, but in order that our confidence may be bolstered, that at his coming we may not shrink from him in shame (2:28; cf. Phil 1:20). What we shall be has not yet been revealed; but that in no way overturns the reality that we are God's beloved children *now* (3:2; cf. *Jub.* 1:24-25, in which that status for the faithful is reserved for the future). The child of God is a responsible agent and is response*able*—enabled to respond—by the endowment of God's prevenient love.

REFLECTIONS

1. If 1 John 2:26-27 challenges the church to revisit its understanding of the Spirit, 2:28–3:3 incisively poses the question of eschatology, reflection on the "last things" or matters of final consequence along the horizon of God's intent. In American Christianity, eschatology has too often been abandoned to feverish imaginations among the radical right and left, with no alternative voiced by Christians occupying the theological center. Here we might take some cues from the elder, whose eschatological view deftly dodges many of the snares into which we might tumble. His thought is neither wistfully wedded to a past that never was nor fixated on someday's heavenly meringue. The elder does not tritely counsel Christians to live "in the moment," hermetically sealed off from the claims of history or the future's prospects. According to 1 John, the church lives in eschatological time—a fluid chronology, calibrated by God, that embraces all that has been and will be.

> Time present and time past
> Are both perhaps present in time future,
> And time future contained in time past.[102]

If the church abides as God's beloved children now, its everyday life indelibly stamped by "the anointing that you received from him" (1 John 2:27 NRSV), then that reality makes a difference in the ways that the church conducts its meetings and spends its money. Regarded from the vista of God's eternity, the church is a family with an open heart, not a business with a bottom line. If Christians know that they are growing into a future whose form resembles him in whom they dwell, then they can withstand uncertainty and loss—even death—with vigor and hope, continually replenished by God (see Rom 8:31-39; 2 Cor 4:7-12). When we center ourselves,

---

102. T. S. Eliot, *Four Quartets*: "Burnt Norton" I (1935), in *The Complete Poems and Plays, 1909–1950* (New York: Harcourt Brace & World, 1943).

not in secular society's immediate interests or anxious fears, but in God's claims and intentions for us, we remember the One to whom we are finally accountable and from whom we draw our strength.

2. By convention the Johannine letters are classified as a subset of the NT's catholic epistles, whose theological views are often regarded as a collective "falling off" from Paul's radical proclamation of God's grace. While it is true that the word χάρις (*charis*) does not appear in the sense of "grace" in 1 John (cf. 3:12; 2 John 3), it is false to conclude from that datum that the *concept* of grace as considered by Paul, Luke, and other NT authors is absent from 1 John. To the contrary, as the Venerable Bede recognized, the reality of grace is vigorously attested in this epistle. God's love is freely bestowed on believers "so that we both know how and are able to love him—to love him as children love their father," not merely as "lowly, faithful hired servants love their masters."[103] There is nothing that we have done or can do to earn the status of children of God. This is not an entitlement. It is, however, a reality grasped by faith, which contradicts the ultimacy of this life's miseries and deathward slouch.

Can it really be doubted that a hunger for assurance that they are "children of God" persists among many of our society's children, whose destruction of self and of others stems largely from never having known the love of even a human parent, much less the love of a heavenly one? Does not a deep yearning for this assurance gnaw even at the soul of the church, which, as much as any community in our day, is beset by the alluring but finally heartbreaking promises of fulfillment in our jobs, our wealth, and our politics? Such promises are bound to disappoint for the simple reason that doing what is right does not come naturally to human beings, nor does it move us a step closer to spiritual rebirth. For 1 John, this gets the matter entirely backward; doing what is right is the *verification* that one has already been "begotten of God" (1 John 2:29). Of all people, Christians should know that they live out of a faith that does not rest on a strict system of merits and rewards, but on the confidence that God continues to love us with an unearned love, which we are now empowered to reciprocate through just deeds in this bristly, tormented world.

103. Bede *Commentary on 1 John* 3:1.

1 John 3:4-10, Children of God, Children of the Devil

COMMENTARY

Worded in ways that are hard to penetrate, 1 John 3:4-10 presents nettlesome problems. The segment's greatest challenge, however, lies in reconciling some of its ideas with statements made elsewhere by the elder.

Nowhere in this letter is the context of a pericope more important for interpretation than here. In its literary context, 3:4-10 looks backward and forward. Retrospectively, the character of "everyone who commits sin" (v. 4) is immediately contrasted with the destiny of "all who have this hope" (v. 3). Looking ahead, the disparity between righteousness and sin in vv. 4-10 anticipates the division of love from hate in vv. 11-18. Furthermore, the terminology of vv. 4-10 heightens the eschatological coloring of the elder's comments as far back as 2:15. Basic in the literature of Jewish apocalypticism is the conflict between "lawlessness" (ἀνομία *anomia*, v. 4) and "righteousness" (δικαιοσύνη *dikaiosynē*, vv. 7, 10; see also 2 Cor 6:14–7:1). Elsewhere in the NT, *anomia* is depicted as an end-time cosmic power, a prevalent iniquity governed by the devil (ὁ διάβολος *ho diabolos*, vv. 8, 10; cf. Matt 7:23; 24:11-12; 2 Cor 6:14-15; 2 Thess 2:3, 7; Rev 12:9, 12). Justice or righteousness is the form in which God's sovereignty over creation has been revealed (ἐφανερώθη *ephanerōthē*, vv. 5, 8; φανερά *phanera*, v. 10; cf. Col 3:4; Heb 9:26). Some apocalyptic documents attribute to God's new age a liberation from the power of sin and the destruction of diabolical works (vv. 6, 8-9; cf. 1QS 4:21-22; *T. Levi* 19:9). The rhetoric in vv. 4-10 is an expression, therefore, of the elder's tendency to view the church's crisis of his day within an apocalyptic framework.

As in 2:18-25, apocalyptic language is used in 3:4-10 for patently controversial purposes: "Little children, let no one deceive [πλανάτω *planatō*] you" (3:7*a*). This Greek verb is a cognate of that used in 2:26 to characterize those who would lead the Johannine community astray (τῶν πλανώντων *tōn planōntōn*). The adversarial character of 3:4-10 is thus another important matter for the interpreter to bear in mind. The author is not spinning some end-time vision in the abstract. He is challenging the claims of opponents who, in his judgment, would tempt the Johannine church to wander off the way to which they should be firmly adhering (see 3:6, 9).

3:4, 7, 10. To imagine that the would-be deceivers in v. 7*a* are identical to those in 2:16, who in turn were associated with the "counterchrist" and "liar" in 2:18, 22, is attractive in its simplicity. The elder, however, does not clearly make that identification, nor does he correlate the views that he refutes in 3:4-10 with those he opposes in 2:18-25. The debating point in the earlier passage concerns some kind of denial that Jesus is the Christ (2:22). The problem suggested by 3:4-10 is rather different: a profound confusion of sinful conduct with righteousness, the sort of heinous sophistry that Paul spurns in Rom 6:1-2: "Should we continue in sin in order that grace may abound? By no means!" (NRSV). The author of 1 John evidently thinks it necessary to make assertions that seem self-evident, even tautologous: "Everyone who commits sin is guilty of lawlessness; sin is lawlessness" (v. 4; cf. Ps 32:1-2; Jer 31:34); "everyone who does what is right is righteous" (v. 7; cf. 2:29); "all who do not do what is right are not [of] God" (v. 10). The implication, perhaps, is that someone had attempted to persuade the Johannine community that the act of sinning was somehow compatible with being "born of God" and "abiding with God." Such guesswork is not fanciful; the *Didache,* another Christian document from the same period as 1 John, speaks of profound moral confusion in the last days, when "sheep shall be turned into wolves, and love shall change to hate" (*Did.* 16.3-4).

Exactly what the elder means by "sin" is hard to say, for he never works out a theory of sin, such as Paul offers in Rom 1:18–3:20. In the Gospel of John, sin is described as a fundamental and fatal opposition to God, revealed by the refusal to believe in Jesus (John 3:16-21; 8:21, 31-36; 15:24). In 1 John, as we have seen, sin is generally identified as lawlessness (ἀνομία *anomia*, 3:4), associated with not doing what is right. The elder does not correlate his view of sin with the transgression of moral norms outside the Christian community; instead, sin is epitomized as the failure to love one's siblings in the household of faith (v. 10). Nevertheless, sin in 1 John is not merely a parochial matter; in 3:4-10 the elder views local hatred apocalyptically, as a local manifestation of an archetypal evil.

3:5-6, 8-9. A divergence among Greek MSS of v. 5 is captured in the different renderings by the NRSV ("take away sins") and the NIV ("take away *our* sins"). Although the textual tradition underlying the NIV is well supported, it is hard to imagine why scribes would have deleted the possessive pronoun, had it been authentic (cf. 2:2; 4:10). The NRSV probably preserves the original reading.

If sin is considered no real problem, then there is no real need for a Christ competent to eradicate sin or to detoxify its effects. Just such claims are implicitly refuted by the elder: "You know that he was revealed to take away sins, and in him there is no sin" (v. 5; see also 4:10; cf. John 1:29; 8:46; 2 Cor 5:21; Heb 4:15; 9:14; 1 Pet 2:22; 3:18); "the Son of God was revealed for this purpose, to destroy the works of the devil" (v. 8; cf. John 12:31; Col 2:15). If sin were assumed to be congenial with Christian existence, then one's persistence in sin could be erroneously viewed as essential to a godly life. The elder swiftly rejoins: "No one who abides in him sins; no one who sins has either seen him or known him" (v. 6); "Those who have been born of God do not sin" (v. 9); "Everyone who commits sin is a child of the devil; for the devil has been sinning from the beginning" (v. 8; cf. John 8:44; 1QS 3:13–4:26; CD 12:2; 1QM 13:12).

Because we have no direct access to the position that the elder disputes, we cannot be sure that he has accurately framed his adversaries' views, or even that we have properly understood his own comments. We have hypothesized that the elder is challenging some confusion within the community that may have implied a warrant for sin in the Christian life (cf. the position challenged by Paul in Rom 6:1-2). If this conjecture approximates the crisis confronted by the elder, the flow of thought in 1 John 3:4-10 makes sense. So would some of its turbocharged rhetorical features. Thus "the one born of God cannot sin" (see v. 9b) would be understood—within *this* debate—not as an absolute pronouncement of a Christian's sinlessness, but as the strongest, most principled denial that sinfulness could ever be reckoned a birth certificate of godliness.

Even if our general approach to this material seems viable, it needs to take into account at least two interpretive problems. One pertains to the meaning of God's "seed" (σπέρμα *sperma*) in 3:9. The word appears nowhere else in the Johannine epistles, though it occurs in John (John 7:42; 8:33, 37), in Revelation (Rev 12:17), and in some other NT documents in the conventional sense of a descendant. Some translations of 1 John 3:9 assume of "seed" the connotation "for the offspring [children] of God remain in Him" (thus Moffatt and the alternative rendering in the NRSV footnote). Another nuance may be present here, that of "a divine seed" (NEB) or an "immanent divine principle," much as Philo of Alexandria speaks of a "seed of wisdom"[104] or "of hope"[105] and as the Stoics imagined a distribution of "seminal reason" throughout the created order, especially among human beings. Precisely what is signified by the "seed" in 3:9 is not clear and much debated. Many interpreters infer a reference to the Holy Spirit (cf. 2:27; 3:24; 4:13; John 3:5-8; 14:6-7) or to the gospel, to which the Spirit bears witness (cf. 1:1-4; 2:14; 1 Pet 1:22-25).[106] Either way,

the elder's point, conveyed in metaphorical—not scientific—language, seems simple enough. In his view, birth from God is not merely a one-shot occurrence; it has *longitudinal* effects (as does "anointing" in 2:27). "Those who are begotten of God" have within them, by God's insemination as it were, the permanent evidence of their recognizable character as children of God. To translate the metaphor of "seed" into modern, though equally figurative, terms: Righteous conduct is the genetic imprint that distinguishes a child of God (3:10; cf. 3:1; John 1:12-13). Thus the reproductive imagery in the Fourth Gospel is present in the First Epistle, but with differences in emphasis. In John, those begotten "of God" (John 1:12-13), or of water and of Spirit from above (John 3:3, 5-8), are those persons who have decided to accept the gift of faith. First John does not stress this initial decision for faith; rather, it emphasizes the ongoing implications of Christians' divine origin—their ability to act justly, without sin, because they are begotten of God.

This leads us directly to a thornier question, which has been "putting [commentators'] minds on the stretch" as far back as Augustine.[107] Do the claims in 3:6-9 cohere with those in 1:8–2:2? How can the elder affirm that those born of God and abiding in God do not and cannot sin (see also 5:18), while cautioning the community that denial of its sins amounts to self-deception and lying about God (see also 5:16-17)? Suggested reconciliations of this paradox are legion, though none has proved completely convincing. Some think, for instance, that the elder differentiates occasional sinning, momentary lapses that require expiation by Christ (2:1-2), from a life that is "habitually sinful" (JBP; note the NIV's rendering of 3:6, 9; 5:18).[108] We recognize such a difference when, in another context, we hear the president of the United States say of something, "That's not the American way," while being fully aware that such a course of action is regularly adopted by many Americans. That distinction, however

---

104. Philo *On the Posterity of Cain* 135.
105. Philo *On Rewards and Punishments* 12.
106. Favoring "the word" (= "the gospel"): Augustine "Fifth Homily: I John 3:9-18," '3; Dodd, *The Johannine Epistles*, 75-78; Judith Lieu, *The Theology of the Johannine Epistles*, New Testament Theology (Cambridge: Cambridge University Press, 1991) 35. Preferring "Spirit": Brooke, *A Critical and Exegetical Commentary on the Johannine Epistles*, 89; Schnackenburg, *The Johannine Epistles*, 175; Brown, *The Epistles of John*, 410-11. Smalley, *1, 2, 3 John*, 173, thinks that both interpretations are defensible here.

107. Augustine "Fifth Homily: I John 3:9-18," 2.
108. So John R. W. Stott, *The Epistles of John: An Introduction and Commentary*, Tyndale New Testament Commentaries (Grand Rapids: Eerdmans, 1964) 130-36. For J. L. Houlden, "what appears [in 1 John 3:9] as a statement of fact is in truth an expression of hope." See Houlden, *A Commentary on the Johannine Epistles*, HNTC (New York: Harper & Row, 1973) 94.

meaningful, is not clearly drawn in this letter. A similar proposal ascribes to 1 John the Reformation principle *simul justus et peccator* ("at once justified and a sinner"). The Christian is at once decisively justified by Christ and constantly in need of forgiveness.[109] Although theologically perceptive, such an explanation obviously owes more to Martin Luther than to the writer of 1 John. Others believe that the sin targeted in 3:4-10, which is by definition impossible for a Johannine Christian, is the refusal to accept the revelation of God that Jesus offers and, indeed, is.[110] While that understanding of sin certainly fits John's Gospel (John 8:24; 15:22, 24; 16:9) and may underlie later comments in 1 John (see Commentary on 5:13-17), here the explicit emphasis is on deeds of lawlessness that the righteous Son of God was revealed in order to destroy (1 John 3:4, 8*b*). Others find the contradiction between the elder's comments on sin impossible to explain, except on the theory that they derive from different sources and authors.[111] But if that is the answer, why did the editor of these fairly glaring discrepancies not recognize and eliminate them?

Perhaps no resolution of this dilemma is completely satisfying. The problem, in part, may stem from the author's dualistic worldview, which is not easily accommodated to a community's sometimes surprising conduct. (This unresolved tension is evident in the Fourth Gospel as well: The casting out of "the ruler of this world" [John 12:31] does not prevent Satan's entering the heart of Judas [John 13:27].) Yet the picture in 1 John is even more complicated than that, for in 1:8–2:2 and in 3:4-10 the author rebuts two equally faulty but rather different positions. First John 1:8–2:2 confronts a temptation within the community to grant the reality of sin but to deny that it has been committed. In response to this misjudgment, the elder insists on candid self-assessment, confession, and the possibility of sin's remedy by Christ. First John 3:4-10 challenges a view, associated with unidentified deceivers, that is even more perverse: a refusal to acknowledge sin as sin, draping lawless behavior with pretensions to godliness. To this the elder replies that sin is inherently alien to the character of God and of those who abide in God (cf. 5:17; Matt 7:16-20; Gal 5:25). In 1 John the elder seems to be concentrating on different problems at various points and appears less interested than one might wish in harmonizing his rebuttals. However, he does offer a theological lever that can be applied to rectify his apparent inconsistencies (see Reflections).

---

109. See Bultmann, *The Johannine Epistles*, 51-53. Smalley (*1, 2, 3 John*, 163-64) settles on this interpretation, following a reasoned account of all the alternatives. See Smalley, *1, 2, 3 John*, 158-65.

110. John Bogart, *Orthodox and Heretical Perfectionism in the Johannine Community as Evident in the First Epistle of John*, SBLDS 33 (Missoula, Mont.: Scholars Press, 1977), 51-91. Augustine's solution is similar: Since the Christian cannot do other than love, "Love is the only final distinction between the children of God and the children of the devil" ("Fifth Homily: I John 3:9-18," 17). Thus also John Wesley, "The Great Privilege of those that Are Born of God," in *The Works of John Wesley*, vol. 1: *Sermons I, 1-33*, ed. Albert C. Outler (Nashville: Abingdon, 1984) 436-41.

111. Henry C. Swadling, "Sin and Sinlessness in I John," *SJT* 35 (1982) 205-11.

REFLECTIONS

As elsewhere in 1 John, here the modern reader encounters some startling claims about just and unjust conduct, their origins and expressions. Discomfort with the stridency of the elder's language is a typical reaction. This may explain the *Revised Common Lectionary's* decision (for the Third Sunday of Easter, Year B) to frame the pericope as 3:1-7. With the inclusion of vv. 1-3, the asperity of the comments about sin (vv. 4-7) is cushioned by encouragement (a move with which the elder would likely sympathize); by quitting at v. 7, sin's diabolical character drops from sight (a result that the elder would surely disapprove of). One commentator has confessed the reaction of many to 1 John 3:4-10: "Perhaps the preacher should take a hint from the Lectionary and take a vacation from this text."[112]

---

112. Smith, *First, Second, and Third John*, 87.

1 JOHN 3:4-10 REFLECTIONS

1. To yield to that temptation would be a serious mistake. Precisely in its stark formulation, 1 John 3:4-10 demands that its interpreter come to grips with basic issues. The elder insists that sin be regarded with a seriousness that cannot come easily in a Western culture more comfortable in speaking of crimes and misdemeanors, inappropriate behavior, and "no fault" in almost everything from divorce to driving a car. The social effect of our widespread mitigation of responsibility is, as Daniel Patrick Moynihan has styled it, "defining deviancy down": As a society we inoculate ourselves to the injustice of injuries small and great by tolerating increasingly wide variance from a just and healthy norm.[113] The spiritual consequences are graver yet. By playing down or denying our culpability for unrighteousness, we repudiate God, who has established the primary norms from which all social contracts derive, and drive ourselves more deeply into the delusion that we have no sins to be expiated and certainly no failings that we are unable to correct. The fact that many in our world refuse to regard sin *as* sin—not as inappropriate behavior but as offensiveness to a just God—demonstrates the devilishness of this world's affections. That such critics would dismiss 1 John's analysis merely validates its point. While a fair-minded Christian might wish that the elder's assessment were more temperately nuanced, it is hard to evade a view of sin so uncompromisingly thrust in your face.

2. It may be equally difficult for us to accept the sunnier flipside of the elder's analysis: the good that we do flowers from the supernatural event of birth from God and our maturation as God's children. Modern Christians may fall afoul of this claim for various reasons. Some may think so highly of themselves that they mistake the stirrings of God within them for their natural dispositions and aptitudes. Some may suffer from such low self-esteem that they cannot easily acknowledge their supremely honored status as God's own children. Others find it hard to accept the image of God as a parent who endows us with a legacy of flawless, permanent love, because their treatment by human fathers and mothers has been warped by lovelessness. Still others cling to a self-interested piety that focuses their attention on private salvation that excludes the social obligations that inevitably flow from their parentage. All such misreadings of self and of God are challenged by 1 John 3:4-10, which offers Christians the assurance of their dignity and the test of their spiritual parentage—which, like its human counterpart, cannot be reversed, overthrown, or improved upon. "Birth cannot be reversed, neither does it happen by stages or in degrees!"[114]

3. First John 3:4-10 also evokes questions without answers. By their fruits one can distinguish "the children of God" from "the children of the devil" (3:7-8, 10), but why the children of both parents are found *within* the church remains a mystery. In this respect the elder seems to veer away from the Fourth Evangelist's viewpoint, which tends to identify as the devil's children those Jews outside the community of disciples who do not believe in Jesus (John 8:44). By contrast, in 1 John, as in Matthew, the wheat and the tares have been sown together (see Matt 13:36-43). The theologically prior question—why some are "begotten" of God, yet others of the devil—remains as obscure to believers as the origin of genetic processes confounds biochemists. Both kinds of interpretation, the religious and the scientific, arrange pieces of our experience into sensible patterns that leave gaps. The friction between 1 John's statements about sin (1 John 1:8–2:2) and sinlessness (1 John 3:6, 9) is reminiscent of modern debates among psychologists on the relative importance of nurture and nature. An inherited genetic makeup determines much that is fundamental in a child's personality, but who would deny that that biological inheritance is modified by the culture in which the child is reared? Similarly, for the elder, "we are God's children now" (3:2 NRSV); as

---

113. Daniel Patrick Moynihan, "Defining Deviancy Down," *The American Scholar* 62 (1993) 17-30.
114. Lieu, *The Theology of the Johannine Epistles*, 34.

Christians, our nature has been decided. Nevertheless, critical character formation takes place, for us and for the world to see, within the culture of the church.

If 1 John does not resolve the tension between the sinlessness of those born of God (1 John 3:9-10) and their need for confession of sin (1 John 1:8-10), it does admit the reality of both dimensions of Christian existence. An indirect response to this paradox is suggested by the elder's complex assertion in 3:2*a:* We are God's children *now,* though it is *not yet* manifest what we shall be. Without the consolation of the first claim, we might forget our true parentage and nosedive into despair. Lacking a reminder of the second, we might presume upon our inheritance and lapse into complacency. Those who deplore the elder's unsystematic handling of sin and sinlessness within the church should at least acknowledge his astute recognition of the need for speaking both words to Christians about the Christian life, not the half-truth of only one. Whatever revisions it may elicit in our own theological imaginations, 1 John offers us a distinctive vocabulary and repertoire of images, at considerable variance from those of popular culture, with which we can begin to think about our life before God.

1 JOHN 3:11–5:12, THE MESSAGE YOU HAVE HEARD FROM THE BEGINNING

OVERVIEW

In the fourth major movement of 1 John, we come to the letter's climax. The introduction of this section reprises the theme with which the epistle opened: "the message you have heard from the beginning" (3:11; cf. 1:1, 3, 5). That message—summarized in 1:1–2:6, aimed in 2:7-14, contextualized in 2:15–3:10—is unfolded by 3:11–5:12 in a series of interlocking subunits, most of which are accented with the consoling clarification "by this we/you know" (3:16, 24; 4:2, 6, 13; 5:2). As throughout 1 John, the membranes between these subsections are highly permeable. Cognate themes tumble upon one another, amplifying and deepening the church's reassurance of its indestructible life with God: love for one another (3:11-18), the criterion of truth (3:19-24), the Spirit of God (4:1-6), the manifestation of God's love among us (4:7-12), the mutual dwelling of God and the believer (4:13-21), love for God's children (5:1-5), God's testimony to the Son (5:6-12). These are but points of orientation for the commentary that follows. No schematization can do justice to the elder's achievement in this portion of 1 John.

1 John 3:11-18, By This We Know Love

COMMENTARY

In 3:11-18 the elder picks up some familiar threads: a reminder of the message that the community has heard "from the beginning" (v. 11; cf. 1:1, 5; 2:7, 13-14, 24), the church's estrangement from the world beyond its walls (v. 13; cf. 2:15-17; 3:1), an emphasis on upright conduct (v. 12; cf. 2:29; 3:7), a warning against intramural hatred (v. 15; cf. 2:9, 11), the reinforcement of intramural love (vv. 11, 13, 16; cf. 2:10), and the presentation of Christ as paradigmatic of righteousness and love (v. 16; cf. 2:1, 6). These verses are also an extended meditation on the verse immediately preceding (v. 10)—concrete examples of how the conduct of different "children" reveals their spiritual parentage.

Nevertheless, this segment's train of thought is hard to follow. This is partly due to the author's penchant for wide conceptual swings: between deeds evil and righteous (v. 12*b*), between brothers murderous and loving (vv. 12*a*, 14), between death and life (v. 14). The thought of vv. 11-18 does not clearly advance in a straight line. Instead, as in 2:28–3:3, the elder tightly interweaves different topics, each of which is succinctly treated before being curlicued into the others.

3:11-14a, The Association of Hatred with Evil and Murder. The representative figure for this constellation of motifs is Cain, who, devoured by sin crouching at his door, slew his brother Abel (Gen 4:1-16). While this is the most obvious allusion to the OT in 1 John, it is not the only one (cf. v. 17 with Deut 15:7-11; 1 John 1:9–2:2 with Exod 34:6; 1 John 2:11 with Isa 6:9-10). The elder is no more interested than the narrator of Genesis in exploring the reasons for Cain's murder of his brother. For John, as for Josephus[115] and Philo,[116] it suffices to say that Cain was motivated by evil (πονηρά *ponēra*); his brother, by righteousness (δίκαια *dikaia*; Heb 11:4; Jude 11).

The elder is more interested in other connections that this OT story allows him to make. First, the story of Cain is appropriate to the Johannine church because it pictures a devastating rupture within a family, between *brothers*—a matter very much on the author's mind here and elsewhere (see 2:9-11, 19; 3:10; this parallel is slightly obscured in the NRSV, which includes "sisters" in its translation of "brothers" [ἀδελφοί *adelphoi*]). Second, the elder draws a conclusion never reached in the Yahwist tradition of Genesis 4: Cain's butchery was derivative of "the evil one" (the devil; see also 1 John 2:13-14; 3:8).[117] This elaborates the point made in 3:10: By their conduct, children resemble their parents, for good and for ill (see also 2:29; 3:7; John 3:19-21). Third, by generalizing the implications of Cain's lethal conduct, 1 John raises the stakes in assessing intra-church breakdowns: hatred (v. 15) and indifference to need (v. 17) are considered equivalent to murder itself.

At this point a comparison of the First Epistle with the Fourth Gospel is instructive. Mirroring a Jewish and Jewish-Christian split that was probably occurring at the time of the Gospel's composition, Jesus in John slams "the Jews" who do not believe in him as "the devil's children," whose will is twisted by their spiritual father's murderous and duplicitous desires (John 8:39-47). By the time of 1 John the circumstances of the Johannine church have radically altered; now the threat to the community comes from within, and it is the conduct of certain Christians that is perceived as false, hateful, and diabolical.

The acrimony of 1 John's assessment should be weighed against several considerations. First, we cannot accurately measure the nature and degree of the offense that the elder and his readers have (recently) suffered. This should temper a rush to judgment of the letter's pained rhetoric. Second, as we have witnessed previously (2:18-25), 1 John does not advocate revenge on those who hate the community. Instead, their hatred becomes the foil against which love for one another within the church should more brilliantly gleam (see Commentary on 3:17-18; also John 15:18-19; 17:14). The elder's view is similar to that of *The Testament of Gad* 4:6 (c. 150 BCE): "Just as love wants to bring the dead back to life and to recall those under sentence of death, so hate wants to kill the living and does not wish to preserve alive those who have committed the slightest sin."[118] Third, the elder recognizes that profound threats to the church's stability may and sometimes do come from within the church itself. If that awareness is more clearly expressed in 1 John than in the Gospel of John, it is probably because the community for which the Gospel was written experienced a greater threat to its existence from outside than from inside its own walls (John 9:22; 12:42-43; 15:18-21; 16:2-3; cf. 6:66-71).

3:14b-16, Rethinking the Nature of Life and of Death. From the story of Cain, whose climax is reached with his murder of Abel, the elder zeros in on the character

---

115. Josephus *Antiquities of the Jews* 1.21.1.
116. Philo *Questions and Answers on Genesis* 1.59.
117. Cf. the assessment in the later gnostic work *A Valentinian Exposition* 11.22.38: "[And] Cain [killed] Abel his brother, for [the Demiurge] breathed into [them] his spirit. And there [took place] the struggle with the apostasy of the angels and mankind . . . the spirits with the carnal, and the Devil against God." Translated by Elaine H. Pagels and John D. Turner in *The Nag Hammadi Library in English*, ed. James M. Robinson (San Francisco: Harper & Row, 1977) 440.
118. Translated by H. C. Kee in *The Old Testament Pseudepigrapha*, vol. 1: *Apocalyptic Literature and Testaments*, ed. James H. Charlesworth (Garden City, N.Y.: Doubleday, 1983) 815.

of life and death from different angles. To begin, he redefines death, a biological state, as an existential condition: "Whoever does not love abides in death" (v. 14b; see also John 3:17; 6:51; 11:25-26; cf. 1 John 2:7-11, where an analogous contrast is developed between abiding in light and abiding in darkness).[119] Though unexpressed, the implication is clear: By hating his brother, Cain spiritually predeceased Abel—and so do all others who hate their siblings. The converse of this axiom also holds true: "Eternal life" is not future survival beyond the grave, but an accomplished reality for those within the community whose love for one another demonstrates their crossover into life that is real and indestructible (see also 1:2; 2:25; 5:11, 13, 20; cf. John 5:24; 1 Pet 1:22). If any doubt should linger about what such love looks like, it is erased by remembrance of Jesus: "By this we have known love: he laid down his life for us. So we ought to lay down our lives for our brothers" (v. 16; see also 1:7; 2:6; John 10:11-18; 15:12-13; cf. Rom 5:8; Gal 2:20; Titus 2:14; 1 Pet 3:18; Rev 1:5b). Christ's loving sacrifice of himself for us amounts to an antitype or mirror image of Cain, who hatefully deprived another of his life.

(This contrast is lost in the *Revised Common Lectionary's* truncation of 1 John 3:16-24 for the Fourth Sunday of Easter, Year B.)

3:17-18, The Concreteness of Everyday Love. Laying down one's life for sisters and brothers seems by definition to be once-in-a-lifetime heroism at best. Perhaps for that reason the elder offers a matter-of-fact example of what he has in mind: practical attention to those lacking life's basic necessities, paid by those with means of livelihood (τὸν βίον *ton bion*, translated "riches" in 2:16 NRSV; cf. Mark 13:44; 2 Tim 2:4). Such a conclusion for vv. 11-18 may seem anticlimactic and more obviously appropriate to the Letter of James (Jas 1:22; 2:1-17). Yet it plays a crucial role at this stage in the elder's discussion. The readers' attention is thereby concentrated, not on the hatred they have received from the "Cains" in their midst or from the world outside (v. 13; see also John 15:18-19; 17:14), but on the durable responsibility of love that members of the church owe one another (see also John 13:34-35; 2 John 5). The image of shutting or opening the heart (lit., one's "bowels" [σπλάγχνα *splagchna*; cf. Prov 12:10, רחמים *raḥămîm*]) is clearer in the RSV, obscured in both the NIV and the NRSV. The community is not to be stifled by bitterness or self-interest, but galvanized for compassion toward others.

The church is also reminded that such love is not a self-generated project or human attainment; it is, rather, *God's* love, which persists among those who remember that Christ "laid down his life for us" (v. 16; cf. 2 Cor 5:14-15). As rendered in the NIV, the JB, and the REB, the phrase "the love of God" (ἡ ἀγάπη τοῦ θεοῦ *hē agapē tou theou*) is as ambiguous in v. 17 as it is in 2:5, 15. It could be rendered "God's love" (RSV, NRSV), "love for God" (GNB), or "the divine love" (NEB). While all of these nuances are probably intermingled, a slight stress on God as the agent of love ("God's love") is suggested in v. 17 by the author's contextual remarks in vv. 1 and 16. The elder's moral conclusion spells out—forcefully, clearly, and inescapably—the claim that opened this section: Love for one another not only has been voiced and heard (v. 11) but also must be truthfully enacted (v. 18; cf. Deut 15:7; Rom 12:9-10; Ign. *Smyrn.* 6.2).

---

119. Some Greek MSS include an object in the relative clause in 3:14b: "the one who does not love *his brother* abides in death" (thus KJV, Moffat, Phillips). Scribes tended to clarify textual meaning by adding rather than subtracting words; accordingly, the shorter reading, which is attested in the earliest and best MSS of 1 John, is more likely to have been the original.

REFLECTIONS

1. If we assume that the Fourth Gospel was composed before the First Epistle, then 1 John 3:11-18 offers interesting instances of consistency and development within a particular Christian tradition. One case in point has been noted: the adoption of a critical outlook, previously articulated against outsiders (John 8:44) but now redirected within the church itself (1 John 3:11-15). To refocus a charge of devilish parentage may not appear to be a giant stride toward religious maturity. But when subjected to different pressures, the elder proves able to head in a different direction, anticipating the sad but sage appraisal of Walt Kelly's comic-strip possum, Pogo: "We have met the enemy and he is us." A happier example of 1 John's retrieval and extension of resources within the Johannine tradition occurs in 3:14a, with the elder's observation that intramural love is a sign of passage from death into eternal life. In John's Gospel (John 5:24) that same transfer is effected by hearing Jesus' word and believing the One who sent him. The elder does not repudiate the christological impulse of his tradition (see 1 John 3:23-24); under different circumstances he does, however, modulate that claim so that its moral implications are sharpened.[120] The challenge for today's church, as it was for the elder's, is not merely to mimic a Johannine viewpoint but to engage in the kind of intracongregational reflection evidenced in 1 John: working out fresh implications of the Christian heritage in conversation with new challenges.[121] In that enterprise we enjoy greater advantages than did the elder: a canon that consists not merely of Johannine literature but of multiple, complementary traditions that have been continuously interpreted and refined over twenty centuries of Christian thought and practice.

2. Like Matt 5:21-22, 1 John 3:11-18 pushes us to take a hard look at the violence in our world, and to look through that violence to its root in lovelessness. The elder's assertion that hatred is tantamount to murder (3:15) may seem exaggerated to some. In fact, it could not be more clear-sighted or on target. Warp love, and hate thrives. Hand hate a gun, and someone gets murdered. Blood from a hundred murders stains every hour of every day in the United States and throughout the world. As the elder could have predicted, most of the murderers are not strangers to their victims but members of the same family. Husbands knife their wives; wives shoot their husbands; children and parents slay each other. That horrifying pattern is magnified among the world's religions, whose adherents slaughter their kin: Buddhists and Hindus in Sri Lanka, Jews and Muslims in Palestine, Catholics and Protestants in Northern Ireland. Violence has become so commonplace that many Christians have grown callous to malice, accustomed to murder, and mute on this rampant obscenity. And so we are judged by a text like this one, which exposes our indifference to evil and the circumscription of our own love.[122]

3. A sermon on 1 John 3:11-18 must *begin* from the pulpit, within the framework of "the message you have heard from the beginning" (3:11 NRSV), for in a world like ours, we cannot possibly find within us the power to give ourselves for others. God alone has made love a reality for us. Without the assurance of that gospel, we would remain trapped in hate and paralyzed by fear. But a sermon on this text must *end* somewhere beyond the pew: on the streets or at home, in a prison or playground, a workplace or soup kitchen—wherever God's children find themselves among those in need. "We do not have two histories . . . one by which we become children of God and the other by which we become each other's brothers."[123] We have one history, aptly captured in the Cotton Patch Version of 1 John 3:18: "My little ones, let's not *talk* about love. Let's not *sing* about love. Let's put love into *action* and make it *real.*"[124] Without such responsible love, the distance between miserliness and murder is, as 1 John cautions us, considerably shorter than we may think. Thanks be to God, who, through Jesus Christ and disciples in his Spirit, gives us the vision, the energy, and the resources to nurture life, not to take it away.

---

120. The theological foundation of Christian ethics is also apparent in the Farewell Discourse of John's Gospel (esp. John 13:31-38; 14:12-24; 15:1-17).
121. For astute musings in this vein, see Robert Kysar, "Preaching as Biblical Theology: A Proposal for a Homiletical Method," in *The Promise and Practice of Biblical Theology,* ed. John Reumann (Minneapolis: Fortress, 1991) 143-56.
122. I am indebted to Moody Smith (*First, Second, and Third John,* 92) and to Patrick Willson for sharpening some of the points made here.
123. Gustavo Guti'rrez, "Faith as Freedom: Solidarity with the Alienated and Confidence in the Future," in *Living with Change, Experience, Faith,* ed. Francis A. Eigo, O.S.A. (Villanova, Pa.: Villanova University Press, 1976) 43.
124. Clarence Jordan, *The Cotton Patch Version of Hebrews and the General Epistles* (New York: Association Press, 1973) 79. Jordan, whose legacy continues in Koinonia Farm in Americus, Georgia, as well as through Habitat for Humanity International, translated 1 John into colloquial American English.

1 John 3:19-24, By This We Shall Know That We Are of the Truth

COMMENTARY

Typically in 1 John, a passage of exhortation (1:5-10; 2:15-17) precedes one of encouragement (2:1-6, 18-27). Likewise, the gentle 3:19-24 follows the stern 3:11-18. The latter passage ended by urging the church's manifestation of love in word and deed, in speech and truth. But how does one verify a life lived "in truth"? The primary burden of 1 John 3:19-24 is to answer that question.

3:19-21. While the ambiguous phrase "by this" (v. 19) can point forward or backward in 1 John, depending on the context (see Commentary on 2:5), it is natural to take the exhortation in v. 18 as a form of empirical evidence of the truthfulness of one's life. If one's conduct manifests "truth" (ἀλήθεια *alētheia*), which in 1 John is the activated integrity of word *and* deed (see Commentary on 1:6), then by such conduct the authenticity of one's life is thereby "known," in the sense of being certified (2:3, 5, 18, 25), not only by others but also by oneself. The latter consideration is important, since the believer needs the sort of reassurance that will satisfy a potentially condemnatory "heart" (vv. 19-20a). Throughout the Bible the heart (לבב *lēbāb*; καρδία *kardia*) is used to refer to the seat of religious and moral conduct within human beings (see, e.g., 1 Sam 12:20; 24:6; Ps 24:4; Luke 16:15; Acts 2:37; Rom 8:27; 1 Thess 2:4; Rev 2:23).[125] Here, with regard to the hearts of his "beloved" readers (v. 21; see also 2:7; 3:2), the elder imagines two possibilities. One is that our hearts might condemn us without full account of the evidence. In that event, the verdict in our case is overruled by a higher court: God, who, unlike our fallible scruples, knows everything necessary to render a valid judgment (v. 20; cf. 4:4; John 21:17; 1 Cor 4:3-5).[126] Another, simpler possibility is that "our hearts do not condemn us," so that we may stand with assurance (παρρησία *parrēsia*; "confidence," NIV; "boldness," NRSV) before the Judge (v. 21; see also 2:28-29; 5:14; Eph 3:11-12).

3:22. Whether we are vindicated by our own hearts or by God, who hears our case "on appeal," we are positioned to receive from God whatever we ask—provided that an important condition is met: "that we keep his commandments and do what is pleasing before him." Here, as elsewhere (2:3-4, 7-8), unspecified commandments are resolved into the primary commandment of love for one another (vv. 11-18, 23). While reminiscent of a venerable biblical dictum (see also Sir 48:22; Eph 5:10; Col 3:20; Heb 13:21), the corollary qualification of doing the things that are pleasing (τὰ ἀρεστά *ta aresta*) before him vividly evokes the Johannine Jesus, whose perpetual intimacy with God stems from his doing nothing on his own authority, from his speaking only as God had taught him, and for always doing what is pleasing to God (John 8:28-29). In this respect, and not for the first time in 1 John (1:7; 2:6; 3:3, 16; 4:11), the elder's readers are implicitly encouraged to imitate Jesus. To do so carries great cost. Just as Jesus' assertion of his divinely pleasing activity confronted a murderous world bent on his destruction (John 5:18; 8:37-38, 40; 11:53), so also the church should not be surprised by the world's hatred toward Christians (v. 13). To do what is pleasing to God carries, however, a benefit more than compensatory for that peril: receiving from God whatever the church asks (v. 22; see also 5:14-16), just as Jesus had promised his disciples (John 15:7, 16; 16:23*b*-24).

---

125. As presupposed by the translations of 3:19-21 in the JBP, the NEB, and the REB, 1 John's concept of "the heart" approximates the view of bad or clear conscience (συνείδησις *syneidēsis*) in Paul (e.g., Rom 13:5; 1 Cor 8:7; 10:25) and elsewhere in the NT (Acts 23:1; 24:16; 1 Tim 1:5, 19; 3:9; 2 Tim 1:3; 1 Pet 3:16, 21; Heb 10:22). See Christian Maurer, "σύνοιδα, συνείδησις," *TDNT* 7 (1971) 898-919.

126. Complicated by extraordinarily obscure Greek grammar, 1 John 3:19-21 is patient of the opposite interpretation, popular in medieval exegesis—namely, that God's *severity* is greater than our own heart's. See also Grayston, *The Johannine Epistles*, 115. Most modern commentators doubt that this understanding fits these verses' context and the elder's general outlook. See Brown, *The Epistles of John*, 453-60.

The critical point underscored by the elder is that the community's requests of God are not capricious or self-interested. They flow directly from obedience to the love command of Jesus and dedication to God's pleasure, not the church's own. First John's outlook harmonizes with the melody of prayer that runs throughout the NT; while all things are possible for God, petitions are offered in the name of Jesus (John 14:13-14; 16:26-27), the one who instructed his disciples to pray first that God's will be done (Matt 6:10; Mark 14:36; cf. Jas 5:16-18).

3:23. Here we find 1 John's most explicit definition of God's commandment. It is double-pronged. First, that we "believe in the name of his son Jesus Christ" (cf. John 6:29). The verb πιστεύω (*pisteuō*, "to believe") makes its first of nine appearances here in 1 John (see also 4:1, 16; 5:1, 5, 10 [3x], 13; cf. 98 occurrences of the verb in John). Because the cognate adjective "faithful" (πιστός *pistos*) and the noun "faith" (πίστις *pistis*) appear only once in 1 John (respectively, at 1:9 and 5:4; cf. 3 John 5), it is hard to determine a precise nuance for the verb in v. 23. Here the simplest meaning would be "to accept and confess the basic Christian proclamation" about Jesus as God's Son and Christ (cf. 2:23; 5:1). If a cue may be taken from 1:9, which ascribes fidelity (πιστός *pistos*) and justice (δίκαιος *dikaios*) to God (cf. 1:5) or to Jesus (cf. 1:7), v. 23 may further imply the responsibility of Christians to entrust themselves as fully to Christ as he has entrusted himself to them. The Christian's investment in Christ is far more than nominal. Drawing on the ancient understanding of one's name as an essential part of one's personality (Gen 32:29; Exod 33:19; 1 Sam 25:25), belief "in the name" suggests the believer's unreserved commitment to the sphere of power defined by Jesus, who manifested his holy Father's name to those disciples given by God to the Son (cf. 1:3; 2:12; 5:10, 13; John 3:18; 17:6, 11-12, 26; 20:31; Acts 4:12; 1 Cor 6:11; Col 3:17).

The second prong of God's command is ethical in tenor, derives from Jesus, and recapitulates a fundamental theme in both the Fourth Gospel and the First Epistle: "love [for] one another, just as he has commanded us" (1 John 2:10; 3:10-14; 4:7-21; 5:3; 2 John 6; John 13:34; 15:12, 17). The commandment's theological and ethical components are inseparable: "For without faith in Christ we are not able to love one another properly nor can we truly believe in the name of Jesus Christ without brotherly love"[127] (cf. Paul's insistence upon "faith working through love" [Gal 5:6 NRSV]). Yet the construction of v. 23 suggests that the confessional claim precedes its practical fulfillment. Love fills out our deepest belief, not vice versa (see also Mark 12:28-31).

3:24. The unit (vv. 19-24) concludes by effectively circling back to its starting point: keeping the commandments verifies the mutual indwelling (μένω *menō*) of the believer and Christ or God (v. 24*a*; cf. Rom 8:10; 2 Cor 13:5; Gal 2:20; see also Commentary on 1 John 2:6 and 4:13). "Being of the truth" and "abiding in him" are essentially synonymous (as suggested by 2:4-6, which correlates truth's internalization with keeping the commandment and abiding in Christ; cf. 2 John 2). "Being of the truth" or "abiding in him" is also interchangeable with "abiding in the light" (2:10) or "eternal life abiding in" one (3:15), since "God is light" (1:5) and the origin of eternal life (1:21; 2:25; 5:11, 16, 20).

By what do we "know that he abides in us"? The elder may be referring backward, redundantly, to "the keeping of his commandments" (v. 23). Alternatively, the confirmation for this abiding may lie just ahead in v. 24*b*: "by the Spirit that he has given us" (NIV, NRSV; see also 4:13). This is 1 John's first explicit reference to the Spirit, although the concept may have been implied in the elder's earlier remarks about the church's anointing (see 2:26-27). The elder's view of the Spirit will be developed at length in the next section of the epistle (4:1-6; also 4:13; 5:6, 8). The overt introduction of the Spirit here seems mysterious, until one recalls that the Spirit in the Gospel of John is closely associated with life (John 6:63) and truth (John 4:23-24). Indeed, John refers to the Paraclete, the successor of Jesus and continuator of his revelatory work, as "the Spirit of truth" (John 14:16-17; 15:26; 16:7, 13; cf. 1QS 4:21-22). Thus, in addition to self-giving love for others (1 John 3:11-18) and adherence

---

127. Bede *Commentary on 1 John* 3:23.

to the commandment (1 John 3:19-23), we find in v. 24 another instrument by which the church may verify its persistence in God's life: corroboration by the Spirit, itself a gift from God (cf. Ezek 36:27). Naturally, this claim does not settle the matter; rather, it opens another avenue of investigation: the validation of inspiration (4:1-6).

REFLECTIONS

1. First John 3:19-24 is a rich lode for what we would call pastoral care, an area of ministry that requires an equilibrium of consolation and discipline. Like all religious people, Christians are beset by the peril of arrogance, against which some of the elder's comments elsewhere serve as a potent antidote (1:6-10; 3:4-10). In 3:19-24, however, the implied problem within the community is quite different: the insecurity of devout Christians whose hearts may convict them of failure to do those things that they ought (3:17-18). We understand that fear of inadequacy. If taken seriously, a willingness to lay down one's life for others (3:16) is, to say the least, a formidable challenge. Outside the moment of crisis, who among us will lay claim for our ability to scale that pinnacle of discipleship? The summons to share one's abundance with Christians in want, the elder's down-to-earth example of self-sacrifice (3:17), triggers pangs of conscience among middle-class congregations that feel sucked into the vortex of upward mobility and guilt for their affluence. Over against this anxiety stands the solace in knowing that "God is greater than our hearts, and he knows everything" (1 John 3:20 NRSV). Because we are not God, we are neither the norm nor the final arbiter of our activity as Christians. The norm has been set by Christ, "the atoning sacrifice for our sins" (1 John 2:2 NIV, NRSV), who loved us so much that he "laid down his life for us" (1 John 3:16 NIV, NRSV). Our supreme court is not the human heart, whose feelings are fickle and manipulable by fear to self-condemnation. Our court of final appeal is God, whose antecedent love for us makes possible our own love (4:19) and in whom we invest complete confidence (3:21; see also 2:12-14; 4:4, 18; 5:4). "Conscience is one drop," mused Luther, "the reconciled God is a sea of comfort."[128] Centrally located in a letter that is earnest about moral responsibility, 1 John 3:19-24 amounts to a repudiation of any attempt by any Christian to lay a cheap guilt trip on anyone.

2. The elder's conviction that "we receive from him whatever we ask" (1 John 3:22a NRSV) is equally reassuring. It is also complex. We have not been abandoned, dependent only on our own resources—a prospect that ultimately would drive any of us to the brink of despair. As beloved children, we make petitions to God, who responds in ways that occasionally accord with our expectations, but that at other times seem to us strange. The elder is no sentimentalist. He understands that the world's hatred is a genuine accompaniment of eternal life (3:13-14). A church captured by the gospel finds in prayer the solutions for some of its problems. It is also given other problems that it never had and would happily dodge.

The promise of answered prayer is balanced against another consideration: "we keep his commandments and do before him what is pleasing" (3:22b, author's trans.). This qualification reminds us that submission to God is salutary for the children of God. Obedience is the environment from which our petitions flow. "Ask whatever you will, and it shall be done for you"—this is "almost Bible," a cruel half-truth that elevates illusions doomed to crash. *"If you abide in me, and my words abide in you,* ask for whatever you wish, and it will be done for you" (John 15:7 NRSV, italics added; cf. 1 John 3:22; Job 22:21-27; Mark 11:22-26)—this is the indispensable premise of Jesus' promise that our heavenly Father upholds us, even in the flames.

---

128. *Luther's Works* 10 (1967) 280.

As God's children, our first and last concern is that God be pleased. In the elder's judgment, it pleases God that we commit ourselves in faith to Jesus Christ and love one another as he commanded. The *whole* commandment is not fulfilled by doing one and doing without the other, as though Christianity could be reduced either to an orthodox proposition or to an improved social condition. The church's ethical imperative to love is rooted in its confession of Jesus as Christ and Son of God; otherwise, as Paul Ramsey perceptively observed, "we judge Christ by our composite notions of maturity, and fail to compose our ideas of maturity by decisive reference to him."[129] Stirred by the Spirit (1 John 3:24), our dedication to do what pleases God shapes, informs, and defines the petitions we make. That kind of commitment, which Jesus demonstrated with compelling clarity, prevents the degradation of our requests into self-aggrandizement and assures their fulfillment by a merciful God.

129. Paul Ramsey, *Basic Christian Ethics* (Chicago: University of Chicago Press, 1950) 199.

1 John 4:1-6, By This You Know the Spirit of God

COMMENTARY

While this pericope could be reckoned a digression from the author's overarching consideration of Christian love (3:10-18, 23; 4:7–5:3), the elder's address to those "beloved" (Ἀγαπητοί *Agapētoi*, 4:1; see also 2:7; 3:2, 21; 4:7, 11; 3 John 1-2, 5, 11) keeps that agenda in clear view. The principal concerns of 1 John 4:1-6 are related to at least two matters mentioned near the end of 3:19-24. First, the elder invokes caution about what the church should "believe" (4:1; cf. 3:23). Second, at greater length, he injects critical qualifications about "the Spirit" in comparison to other "spirits" (4:1-3, 6; cf. 3:24*b*). The elder formulates these comments with the use of some familiar, contrastive concepts:

Existence that is "of God"
(4:1-4, 6; see also 3:9-10; 5:1, 4, 18-19; 3 John 11)

Being "in the world"
(4:1, 3, 4-5; see also 2:15-16; 4:9, 17; 2 John 7)

The confession of Jesus Christ
(1 John 4:2-3; see also 1:9; 2:23; 4:15; 2 John 7)

The coming of "Antichrist"
(1 John 4:3; see also 2 John 7)

Truth
(1 John 4:6; see also 1:6, 8; 2:4, 21; 3:18-19; 5:6; 2 John 1-4; 3 John 1, 3-4, 8, 12)

Error
(1 John 4:6; see also 1:8; 2:26; 3:7; 2 John 7)

Also restated is the church's victory over its antagonists (1 John 4:4; see 2:13-14; 5:4-5), as well as the importance of acute knowledge (4:2, 6; see 2:3-5, 13-14, 18, 29; 3:1, 6, 16, 19-20, 24; 4:7-8, 13, 16; 5:2, 20; 2 John 1) and proper "hearing" (1 John 4:3, 5-6; see 1:3, 5; 2:7, 18, 24; 3:11; 5:14, 15; 2 John 6; 3 John 4). If 1 John 4:1-6 veers from the elder's main argument, it does so in ways consistent with the fabric of the First Epistle and other letters of John.

4:1. Following mention of the Spirit in 3:24, the author introduces the theme of "testing the spirits," with which 4:1-6 is generally concerned. This pericope presents difficulties similar to those encountered in 2:18-25. In both cases a rift within the church provokes the elder's comments: "for many false prophets have gone out into the world" (cf. 2:19: "[many antichrists] went out from us"). First John is not the only biblical book alert to the danger of false prophets (among others, Deut 13:1-5; 18:20-22; Jer 14:13-16;

Matt 7:15-23; Mark 13:5-6, 21-22; 2 Pet 2:1-3; Rev 16:13-14). In 1 John pseudoprophecy appears not as a hypothetical possibility, but as a real infection to be combatted. This accounts for the "us-versus-them" tenor of the elder's remarks in this passage, a stridency that exceeds the characteristic dualism of Johannine language.

First John does not offer an interpretation of the Spirit (pneumatology) as developed as that found elsewhere in the NT, especially in Paul's letters (Rom 8:1-27; 1 Cor 12:1–14:40) and the Fourth Gospel (John 14:15–15:11; 16:4b-15). The elder's reticence on this subject doubtless bespeaks the terms under which his church fell apart. If the schismatics claimed God's inspiration for their beliefs and conduct, the elder's appeal to the same warrant would prove nothing. First John pays minimal attention to the Spirit and shifts the discussion to criteria for testing the spirits (cf. 1 Thess 5:19-21). This approach coheres with the elder's acknowledgment that his readers are fully able, by virtue of their anointing, to decide matters of truth (2:26-27). Testing the spirits also tallies with the church's responsibility, urged throughout 1 John, to examine its religious experience, characterized by the elder in stark alternatives:

Walking in the light (2:7; cf. 2:6, 10)	**Walking in the darkness** (1:6; 2:9, 11)
Keeping his word or command (2:3, 5-6; 3:24; 5:2)	**Disobeying his commands** (2:4)
Loving one's brother (2:10; 3:14; 4:7, 21) **or God** (5:2)	**Hating/not loving one's brother** (2:9, 11; 3:15; 4:8, 20)
Doing righteousness/ not sinning (3:7, 9)	**Commiting sin/ not doing righteousness** (3:4, 8, 10)

What are the tests for whether spirits are "from God" and of truth, or not from God and of error? The elder notes two criteria: one, christological (vv. 2-3a); the other, experiential but theologically construed (vv. 5-6).

4:2-3a. The first criterion pertains to the identity or character of Jesus: "every spirit that confesses that Jesus Christ has come in flesh is from God, and every spirit that does not confess Jesus is not from God."[130] Like so many sentences in 1 John, this is so highly compressed that it is difficult to determine where the elder places the emphasis and what "errant preaching" he contests. Like 2:18-25, 1 John 4:1-6 suggests that the Johannine church has split over a christological issue. Appearing in both passages are similar accusations, expressed in much the same vocabulary: "antichrist" (2:18, 22; 4:3); "gone out" (2:19; 4:1); "truth" and "lie," "falsity" and "error" (2:21-22; 4:1, 6); "confessing" and "not confessing" or "denying" (2:22-23; 4:2-3). As we have seen, the deceitful ideas attacked in 2:18-25 are just as obscure as those challenged in 4:2-3. The one pericope does not offer us the help we need in ascertaining the other's intention.

Absent from 2:18-25 but present in 4:2 is a two-word phrase, around which swirls considerable debate: "in flesh" (ἐν σαρκί *en sarki*). The only other occurrence of "flesh" in 1 John is at 2:16, in connection with "boiling desire" for things of this world that are not of God's domain. Here, however, the term has a different connotation: Jesus' having come "in flesh" is a positive, nonnegotiable confession for anyone who is "of God." But exactly what does the elder mean by this? He may be challenging a super-spiritualized christology by asserting that Jesus' humanity is as theologically integral to his personality as is his divinity.[131] Or the elder may be correcting a view that granted Jesus' humanity without according it salvific consequence.[132] Perhaps the elder refutes those who accepted Jesus as the fully human, fully divine Christ but undervalued the saving significance of his death.[133] The second and third possibilities are subtle variations of the first. Any of them makes sense of 4:2. None, however, is ironclad, for the elder has not left us enough

---

130. Appearing in later MSS, the alternative wording of 4:3a in the NRSV footnote ("every spirit that dissolves Jesus") was probably devised by scribes to refute a gnostic separation of the human Jesus from the divine Christ. See Bart D. Ehrman, "1 John 4.3 and the Orthodox Corruption of Scripture," *ZNW* 179 (1988) 221-43.

131. See, among others, Bultmann, *The Johannine Epistles*, 62; Kysar, *I, II, III John*, 92; Strecker, *The Johannine Letters*, 134-35.

132. See, e.g., Schnackenburg, *The Johannine Epistles* 200-201; Brown, *The Epistles of John*, 76, 505; R. Alan Culpepper, *1 John, 2 John, 3 John* (Knox Preaching Guides; Atlanta: John Knox, 1985) 80.

133. Martinus C. de Boer, "The Death of Jesus Christ and His Coming in the Flesh (1 John 4:2)," *NovT* 33 (1991) 326-46; Marianne Meye Thompson, *1–3 John*, IVP New Testament Commentary Series (Downers Grove, Ill.: InterVarsity, 1992) 115.

pieces to reconstruct the puzzle without gaps. The most we can safely say is that 1 John opposes some kind of underestimation of Jesus' incarnation—the fact that he really lived and died—that compromised his messiahship and was, therefore, "anti-christ." In the elder's judgment, taking Jesus *in the flesh* with insufficient seriousness fails a primary test of the Spirit of God.

4:3b-6. The other criterion of spiritual discernment is somewhat easier to interpret than the first. Those who are of the world (ἐκ τοῦ κόσμου *ek tou kosmou*)—that is, those whose orientation is fundamentally wrongheaded (2:17; 2 John 7), in thrall to the evil one (5:19; John 14:30), and antagonistic to God (2:15-16)—gain the world's hearing. By definition, the world is the realm of antichrist (cf. 2:18-19) and the home of false prophets. The world does not listen to those who are of God (see also John 8:47*b*; 10:25-26; 15:19), because the world does not know them (3:1) and, indeed, hates them (3:13; John 15:18-25). Naturally it follows that whoever knows God—that is, whoever is begotten of God (3:4-10)—listens to "us," who are of God (4:6*b;* see also John 8:47*a;* 10:27; 18:37*d*). "We" who are of God are the ones who have not gone out (cf. 4:1*b*). "We" have no audience among those whose origin and orientation are worldly (4:6*c*).

This argument is entirely circular, but the conclusions follow if the premises are granted. Neither is 1 John's point of view as idiosyncratic as it first appears. Contrasts between the spirit of truth and the spirit of deceit (4:6) may be found in Jewish literature of the period, such as Qumran's *Manual of Disciple* (3:13–4:26) and the *Testament of Judah* (20.1). Moreover, the elder's analysis resembles the use of Isa 29:10 by Paul (Rom 11:1-10) and of Isa 6:9-10 by Mark (Mark 4:12), by Luke (Acts 28:26-27), and by John (John 12:40) to interpret the rejection of the Christian proclamation. In a distinctive way, 1 John articulates a theological explanation for faith and disbelief, as those phenomena were understood by early Christians. We need not read the elder's remarks as a rationalization for the defeat of his *kerygma* or as tantamount to the false prophets' success. The elder is trying to explain why different audiences fall on either side of a confessional divide. With thanks for "the one who is in you [who] is greater than the one who is in the world," the elder assures the faithful remnant of its *victory* over the church's schismatics and the world into which they have gone (4:4; cf. 2:13-14; 3:20; 5:4-5; John 16:33). In spite of its dualism, the perspective of 1 John assumes, not that the forces of good and evil are locked into a stalemate, but that God's triumph is already assured.

REFLECTIONS

1. First John 4:1-6 injects important caveats into our considerations of the Spirit and the church. In the elder's opinion, "captivating preaching" and "being spiritual" are not necessarily good things, because false prophecy and spirits counter to Christ really exist (see also 1 Cor 12:3). Furthermore, 1 John shows little patience and even less support for an understanding of the church as a club, a special interest group, a religious recreational facility, or a YMCA.

The elder's view of what should happen when the church gathers is very different: "Test the spirits to see whether they come from God!" This rallying cry is not aimed at dissidents who have seceded from the community, but at those with whom the elder is friendly. In 1 John, the church is where one ought to find hard questioning and reasoned deliberation about crucial matters of Christian faith and practice. In this endeavor no distinction is made or hinted at between the prerogatives of clergy and laity. All within God's family are equal participants in an ongoing, evaluative enterprise; no one occupying an official or demographic niche claims special purchase on theological insight. The church that takes its bearings from 1 John resembles a household with a flawed but venerable heritage, where the children of God are pondering what it means to be faithful to "what we have heard, what we have seen . . . concerning the word of life" (1:1 NRSV).

2. What are the terms under which such examination takes place? At other points in 1 John, moral considerations stand out: walking in the light, keeping God's commandments, loving one another. In 4:1-6, however, the elder puts before us an irreducibly theological criterion: the confession that Jesus Christ has come in the flesh. Seemingly bland, this test of the Spirit of God is a hot blade that slices deep into the fattest heresies of the church, ancient and modern. Docetism, the notion that Jesus was not really human but only appeared to be, did not vanish in the second century. Docetism flourishes with remarkable resilience among those of our day who play down the gospel of the Christ who really lived and really died, in deference to promises of fulfillment through this world's material goods. If our human potential can be realized by orchestrated political action, better schools, or the sheer affirmation of ourselves— as modern Christian rhetoric implies in its more reckless, vainglorious moments—then what need has the church for a Messiah at all? Lacking a grasp of the confession that Jesus Christ has come in the flesh—without *being grasped* by that reality—even our best-intentioned endeavors in practical love ring hollow, because we miscast ourselves in the role of the saving God and confuse the nature of love. It is simply not enough for the church to resemble the Democratic Party at work or the Republican Party at prayer. The church knows what love looks like only because the authentic Christ, Jesus of Nazareth, gave his life in love for us and for the world (1 John 2:2; 3:16).

3. The elder's antithesis in 4:5-6 ("They are of the world; we are of God") supports H. Richard Niebuhr's assessment of 1 John as a product of that type of Christianity that pits "Christ against culture."[134] For Niebuhr, this form of witness, while powerful, is neither the most appropriate nor the most effective for the church in the modern world. A growing number of NT scholars have collected such comments in John and 1 John as evidence of the sectarian tendency of the Johannine circle.[135] If valid, such appraisals would hardly endear this literature to Christians along the twenty-first century's mainline, among those inclined to engage, if not to embrace, the world beyond the church. Indisputably, the elder's sense of church and mission, formulated under particular conditions of stress, tends to be more polarized and centripetal than the expansive positions adopted in Paul's letters or the Acts of the Apostles. Compared with other such NT witnesses, 1 John's ecclesiological vision seems constricted.

Nevertheless, passages like 1 John 4:5-6 undeniably give us something to gnaw on. Throughout history and across the globe, Christians have so often identified themselves with their ambient culture that the church has lost its voice, abdicated its prophetic responsibility, and ended up a shabby burlesque of Paul's admonition in Rom 12:2: mentally enervated and thoroughly conformed to this world. If 1 John's witness strikes us as offensive, it is not because the letter's outlook is sectarian at bottom. (For real sectarianism, we may go to the Dead Sea Scrolls, whose community withdrew to the desert to await society's upheaval by God.) First John's offensiveness probably has more to do with its radically countercultural witness to Christ, which lances many of us at our most vulnerable point: our accommodation to secularity's "narcissism of similarity"[136] and our capitulation to society's nervous, loveless, self-absorbed values.

The *kerygma* of 1 John comes into focus on God's self-sacrificial atonement for sin through Jesus Christ. That message the world needs desperately to hear but will frequently refuse. "When we speak from the Spirit of God," sighed Luther, "the majority

---

134. H. Richard Niebuhr, *Christ and Culture* (New York: Harper and Bros., 1951) 46-49.
135. Thus Ernst Käsemann: "John is the relic of a Christian conventicle existing on, or being pushed to, the Church's periphery." See E. Käsemann, *The Testament of Jesus: A Study of the Gospel of John in the Light of Chapter 17* (Philadelphia: Fortress, 1968) 39. An even more influential expression of this view is Wayne A. Meeks, "The Man from Heaven in Johannine Sectarianism" *JBL* 91 (1972) 44-72.
136. Robert N. Bellah et al., *Habits of the Heart: Individualism and Commitment in American Life* (Berkeley: University of California Press, 1985) 72. Note also David Rensberger, *Johannine Faith and Liberating Community* (Philadelphia: Westminster, 1988) 135-54.

snore."[137] At other times the world may gladly approve of the church's proclamation. When that happens, 1 John 4:1-6 poses the critical question of whether the gospel has been proclaimed, subject to God's truthful Spirit or, to the contrary, enthralled by some anemic counterfeit like this: "A God without wrath brought men without sin into a kingdom without judgment through the ministrations of a Christ without a cross."[138]

137. *Luther's Works* 10 (1967) 290 (on 1 John 4:5).
138. H. Richard Niebuhr, *The Kingdom of God in America* (New York: Harper and Bros., 1937) 193. See also C. Clifton Black, "Christian Ministry in Johannine Perspective," *Int* 44 (1990) 24-41.

1 John 4:7-12, By This God's Love Was Manifested Among Us

COMMENTARY

Here we journey into the most profound analysis of Christian love in the NT, surpassing even the better-known 1 Corinthians 13. Although the elder takes up several matters, one appears foremost: the priority of God's love for us, which makes possible our love for one another.

4:7. The topic is signaled from the start: "Beloved" (Ἀγαπητοί *Agapētoi*), a mode of address employed by the elder throughout the letter (2:7; 3:2, 21; 4:1, 11; also 3 John 1-2, 5, 11). In the present pericope, where "love" appears as a noun or a verb thirteen times in six verses, the greeting *Agapētoi* perhaps serves as a subtle reminder that *already* the letter's recipients are loved—by the elder, of course, but in the first instance by God. This means that the exhortation to love one another (see also 3:11, 23; 4:12, 19) is by no means a strategic move, calculated to dispose God toward loving us. To the contrary, God loved us before we offered any loving response. The elder clarifies this further: Love comes from God, which implies that our love is not self-generated, but manifests our parentage (γεγέννηται *gegennētai*, "has been born") and kinship (γινώσκει *ginōskei*, "knows") with God (see also 2:3, 29; 3:6-10; 5:1). God's love for us is the source of our power to love God and one another.

4:8. In characteristically Johannine style, the elder underscores this point by inverting it. With few exceptions (most memorably, 4:18) love in 1 John is not personified as an active agent (as in 1 Corinthians 13). Nor does love define God. The elder is careful to say that "love is *of* God" (v. 7), not that love *is* God. Here, as elsewhere (see v. 16), it is God who defines love, not the other way around. In 1 John, love is not "presupposed as a universal human possibility, from which a knowledge of the nature of God could be derived."[139] God's self-giving, definitive mercy is the express source and presupposition of human love. Again, one may compare 1 Corinthians 13, throughout which God is implied, though not mentioned (cf. 2 Cor 13:11.)

4:9-10. God's love among us is manifested in the Son, whose description as the "only [begotten]" or "one and only" (μονογενή *monogenē*) harks back to the prologue of John's Gospel (John 1:14, 18; also John 3:16). The term is also linked with the claim, just made in v. 7, that the one who loves is begotten (γεγέννηται *gegennētai*) of God. Jesus is God's one-of-a-kind Son, through whom authentic life is made possible for the children of God (1:1-2; 2:25; 3:14-15; 5:11-13). In v. 10 the subject is expanded, again by reversing its presentation (cf. v. 8). Love is not known in the first place by our having loved God; rather, love is known by God's having loved us (see also v. 19), revealed in the sending of the Son (see also John 3:16-17; 5:38; 6:29; Rom 5:8).[140] The theater of that initiative is the world—an important reminder that, although Jesus is not *of* this world, and for that reason can extricate us

139. Bultmann, *The Johannine Epistles*, 66; Augustine "Seventh Homily: I John 4:4-12," §§4-6.
140. Without mentioning Jesus by name, the extra- or post-canonical *Odes of Solomon* reflect the conceptuality of 1 John 4:10: "For I should not have known how to love the Lord, if he had not continuously loved me. For who is able to discern love, except the one who is loved?" (3.3-4).

from its dominion (John 8:23; 1 John 5:4), he unquestionably came *into* this world for the purpose of expunging human sin (see Commentary on 2:2; cf. Rom 5:10).

4:11-12. From this inquiry the elder draws two conclusions. The first returns to the salutation and counsel with which this passage began (v. 7; see also 3:11, 23; 4:19): Mutual love is the responsibility of Christians, who have been so loved by God (see also 2:6; 3:16; Matt 18:33). The second conclusion points the way to the ensuing consideration of love in vv. 13-21. While no one has ever beheld God (cf. Exod 33:20; Matt 5:8; John 1:18; 3:13; 6:46), the sure sign of God's continued dwelling (μένει *menei*) among us is our love for one another (see Commentary on 2:6). Again, God's love for us does not depend on our love. Rather, divine love matures (τετελειωμένα *teteleiōmena*) among Christians by their love for one another (see also 2:5; 3:17; 4:16-18). (See Reflections at 1 John 4:13-21.)

1 John 4:13-21, By This We Know That We Abide in God and God in Us

COMMENTARY

Between 4:7-12 and 4:13-21, a temporal shift is observable. The earlier pericope is peppered with verbs inflected in the past tense, referring to God's loving initiative revealed in the sending of the Son. Punctuated with a glimpse of the church's future (v. 17), 4:13-21 is conjugated predominantly in the present tense, portraying the permanence (μένω *menō*, vv. 13-16) of God's love within the church that loves.

4:13. This verse resumes the theme of pervasive testing (see also 2:3; 3:24; 4:1). How may we be assured that we abide in God and God in us? By this: "he has given us of his Spirit." This comment essentially restates 3:24*b*: The Spirit is given by God to enhance the church's understanding of itself and its relationship to God (see also John 14:26; 16:13-14; Rom 8:9-17; 1 Cor 2:6-16). In this verse we also note that the church has received from God "a share in his own Spirit" (Moffatt). The community gathered in God's love partakes of the Spirit and in that sense partakes of God (v. 6), but Christians are not thereby deified. The church is not God. No matter how intimate its relationship to its Father through the Son (v. 9), the congregation remains distinct from God, the perpetual recipient of God's gifts.

4:14-16a. These verses reconstitute other themes that have recurred throughout the epistle. That "we have seen and testify" recalls the elder's introductory announcement to his readers of the tangible word of eternal life (1:1-2). In v. 14 the entire church claims that vision and testimony. Although "no one has ever seen God" (v. 12*a*), the community testifies to what it has seen: the Father's sending of his Son as Savior (see also 2:2; John 3:17; 4:42; 12:47). In 3:24 the mutual indwelling of God and the believer depends on the believer's keeping God's commands; since faith in Jesus Christ is, along with love for one another, God's commandment (3:23), it naturally follows that God abides in whoever confesses Jesus as God's Son (v. 15; see also 2:22-24; 3:23-24; 5:5, 10). The command to believe and the command to love are complementary, each fleshing out the other's meaning. It makes sense, accordingly, that "the love God has for us" (or "among us") would "have been known and believed" by the church on the strength of its dwelling in God, to whose love, revealed by Jesus, the church has borne witness (v. 16*a*; 5:10). The elder's thoughts are tightly knotted, but possible to disentangle.

4:16b-19. Reference in v. 16*a* to "the love God has for us" sets the stage for the next series of comments, pertaining to the character of love (ἀγάπη *agapē*). The note struck in v. 8*b* is repeated: "God is love." Therefore, to abide in love is to abide in God (see also 2:10; 4:13) and to sustain the conditions under which God abides in us (v. 16*b*; also 3:15; 4:12*b*). The elder does not consider this a static process, as clarified in the next breath. The purpose or result of the church's perfection, or maturity (τετελείωται *teteleiōtai*), in love (2:5; 4:12) is boldness (NRSV) or confidence (NIV) in "the day of judgment" (v. 17; cf. 2:28; 3:21-22; 5:14). This is another vivid instance of 1 John's delving into the apocalyptic imagery of future hope in order to interpret the church's identity (see also 2:18; 3:2-3; cf. Ezek 22:14; Matt 11:22, 24; 2 Pet 2:9; 3:7).

It is hard to see how the concluding clause of v. 17 ("because as he is, so are we in this world") follows logically from a promise of confidence on judgment day. Although there is an ellipsis in his thought, the elder's hope may be for a consummation of divine love that enables Christians to be not only beneficiaries but also God's (or Christ's) exemplary agents of love in a loveless world (cf. 2:6; 3:2-3, 16). Verse 18 flows more intelligibly from v. 17. The prospect of standing before the bar of God's judgment holds no terror for those growing up in love, "for when the love of God is properly known, it calms the mind."[141] The flip side of this observation follows: Since fear implies the threat of punishment (v. 18c), the fearful one, by definition, has not been perfected in love (v. 18d). In other words, Christians do not mature in divine love under the lash, because that love, by its very nature, springs from God's merciful sending of Christ for the annulment of our sin (v. 10). God's persistent, encouraging presence—not fear of judgment to come—is experienced in the lives of those who entrust themselves to Christ and who activate that trust in love for one another. As though to nail down the point that love is not an inherently human aptitude, even less a stratagem to evade condemnation when it is "our day in court," the elder returns to the divine origin of our loving, enunciated in the plainest terms: "We love[142] because he first loved us" (v. 19; cf. vv. 9-11; John 15:16).

4:20-21. Throughout 1 John the author has proved conspicuously reluctant to allow any concept of "vertical love"—God's love for us or our love for God—to ride unbalanced without its "horizontal" counterpart—our love for one another (see 2:5-6; 3:10-11, 16-18; 4:7-8, 11-12). It is no surprise that this pericope, focused on love's origin in God, marches relentlessly toward the coordinate love for one's brother or sister. This basic principle of verification is intensified with an *a fortiori* argument: If one cannot love a visible sibling, how much greater is the impossibility of one's loving an invisible God (cf. Matt 25:38-40, 44-45)? These verses ring the changes on this idea by drawing liberally from stock Johannine nomenclature: love's incompatibility with hate (2:9-11; 3:13-15); Christian duplicity as lying (1:10; 2:4, 21-22; 5:10b); what we have and have not seen (cf. 1:1-3; 3:2, 6; 4:12, 14); and the commandment from God (cf. 2:3-8; 3:22-24; 5:2-3; 2 John 4-6). The elder concludes this section with a command that equalizes the vertical and horizontal axes of Christian life: "those who love God must love their brothers and sisters also" (4:21; cf. Mark 12:29-31).

---

141. Calvin, *The Gospel According to St John 11–21 and the First Epistle of John*, 296.

142. The main verb in 4:19 could be rendered as an exhortation (thus JBP, "we are to love"). An indicative statement of fact best fits the context here.

REFLECTIONS

The interpreter of 1 John 4:7-21 is faced with a challenge: How does one approach a subject so shopworn and trivialized as love? Surely not by tacking our private enthusiasms onto the text, but by following its lead. The elder's view of love is surprisingly fresh and altogether different from those popularized by Hollywood, Tin Pan Alley, or Madison Avenue.

1. The elder's mode of discourse merits attention and invites reflection on his letter's interpretation in our day. The rhetoric of 1 John 4:7-21 spirals repetitively and is metrically balanced. Such a style perfectly matches what the elder is saying. What more appropriate way to speak of a cohesive love encompassing God and Christians,

Christians and Christians, than in phrases and sentences themselves so tightly braided? While a modern interpreter might preach this text in many ways, a logician's deductive arguments—much less a prosecutor's browbeatings—would scarcely constitute the happiest weddings of media and message.

In describing divine love, the elder's style vividly echoes that of Jesus' farewell address to his disciples (see esp. John 13:31-35; 14:15–15:17; 17:20-26). What better means for maintaining the church's tradition (1 John 1:1-3; 2:7, 24; 3:11) and recalling Jesus' sacrificial love (1 John 1:5-10; 4:2-3, 7-12) than to replicate the style of Jesus, as Johannine Christians remembered him? Modern congregations, less attuned to John's portrayal of Jesus, need help in recognizing the Master's "voice" as rendered in the Fourth Gospel or other NT witnesses. Again, 1 John does not require that a present-day preacher ape the elder's distinctive technique. The point is that a congregation should be reminded of its loving Lord in whatever homiletical style is adopted.

The rhetoric of 1 John 4:7-21 is elevated. It does not drone in an academic cellar. It soars, like the words of Martin Luther King, Jr., over the top of the Lincoln Memorial. The language of this text is performative. Like a wedding vow, it does not just convey information but does something to its listeners. The elder's style does not come naturally to every preacher for every audience; it cannot be forced. Nevertheless, an interpretation of 1 John that is in tune with the text will strive not merely to explain but also to lift its hearers up to the sheer grandeur, the height and expanse, of God's love for them. The church that is no longer caught up in the majesty of the gospel proclaimed by this text is the community that most needs to hear it.[143]

2. It is not as though 1 John 4:7-21 were style without substance, all shimmer and ribbons but nothing inside. Like a jeweler scrutinizing a gem's facets in sunlight, the elder trains our eye upon many dimensions of love. For instance, his constant emphasis on God's initiative in love signals a critical, theocentric difference between *agapē* and romantic love, friendship, political concourse, and altruism—the valuable, but relatively small, coin of our realm. Contrary to our inclination toward the *quid pro quo*, God has decided in our favor apart from our ability to reciprocate, gracing us with love prior to and independent of any response we might offer, for no reason other than that love is the very nature of God that is knowable by human beings (1 John 4:16*b*, 19). For the elder, love is not one thing among many that God does; *everything* that God does is loving, for God as revealed in Christ is nothing other than love. Nor is God's love abstract. To Augustine's question, "What sort of face hath love?"[144] the elder's answer is that love looks like Jesus, who sacrificed himself for human sin (1 John 4:10). Moreover, God's love is creative. As surely as God breathed life into our earthy frames (Gen 2:7), God continues to create and to sustain in us a capacity for love that, as Karl Barth put it, "does not ask or seek or demand or awaken and set in motion our love as though it were already present in us, but which creates it as something completely new, making us free for love as an action which differs wholly and utterly from all that we have done hitherto."[145] Our love, generated by God's, is not static; it matures in acts of obedience (1 John 4:12, 17-18), purified by God (1 John 3:3). God's love does not cancel out divine judgment, before which we still must stand (1 John 4:17); but God is no more prevented by justice from loving us than we should be shackled by fear from loving God and one another (1 John 4:18).

In communicating this testimony, the preacher does not have to strain for something novel or flashy. The elder's view is so generally underrated in society at large

---

143. See Black, "'The Words That You Gave to Me I Have Given to Them,'" 220-39. On a related subject, see Richard Lischer, *The Preacher King: Martin Luther King, Jr., and the Word That Moved America* (New York: Oxford University Press, 1995).
144. Augustine "Seventh Homily: I John 4:4-12," §10.
145. Karl Barth, *Church Dogmatics*, vol. 4: *The Doctrine of Reconciliation*, part 2, ed. G. W. Bromiley and T. F. Torrance (Edinburgh: T & T Clark, 1958) 777. Barth's "The Basis of Love" (*Church Dogmatics*, vol. 4, 751-83) is an elegant meditation on 1 John 4:7-21 and other biblical texts.

that we need do little more than restate it to get people's attention. Hungry congregations are familiar with love made insipid in the bromides and pabulum peddled by best-selling televangelists and pop psychologists. Deep down, however, Christians remember that love is not what supports our interests and makes us feel good or better adjusted. Love is what God through Jesus Christ has given the church to know about God and to communicate to others.

3. Perhaps the most astonishing thing about 1 John 4:7-21 is that it exists at all. In spite of the hate that the author and his readers felt aimed at them, the elder never advocates hatred in return (1 John 2:9-11; 3:13-15; 4:20). In a thick forest of malevolence, the community's compass remained oriented to Jesus, remembered as one who loved and was loved. To be claimed by a text like this will transform one's life. Mamie Mobley, the mother of Emmett Till, was asked if she harbored bitterness toward two white men, or toward whites generally, for the brutal murder of her son in 1955. This is what she said:

> It certainly would be unnatural not to [hate them], yet I'd have to say I'm unnatural. . . . The Lord gave me shield, I don't know how to describe it myself. . . . I did not wish them dead. I did not wish them in jail. If I had to, I could take their four little children—they each had two—and I could raise those children as if they were my own and I could have loved them. . . . I believe the Lord meant what he said, and try to live according to the way I've been taught.[146]

The church's love is progressively shaped by Christ and distilled of all corrupting naïveté, bitterness, and cynicism. As this happens, we may come to realize that, finally, we do not interpret 1 John. It interprets us.

146. Quoted in Studs Terkel, *Race: How Blacks and Whites Think and Feel About the American Obsession* (New York: New Press, 1992) 21-22.

1 John 5:1-5, By This We Know That We Love God's Children

COMMENTARY

Once more the elder has composed a passage that seems to defy parsing into logical thought. Motifs entwine, spiral, then interlace with such circularity that a reader may experience verbal vertigo. On closer inspection, however, a structure for this dense segment does emerge: a circular chain of tightly linked comments that restate previous claims or reply to latent questions.

Everyone who believes that Jesus is the Christ is a child of God. (v. 1a)
This claim echoes the elder's avowed interest in Jesus (4:2, 9-10, 15) and his recognition of believers as God's children. (3:1-2; 4:4)

How should one respond to God and to a child of God?
Everyone who loves the parent loves the offspring. (v. 1b)
This claim reaffirms the love of God and of brother and sister in 4:21.
But how do we know that we love God's children? (v. 2a)
Whenever we love God and carry out God's orders. (v. 2b; see 4:21)
And how do we know that we do love God? (v. 3a)
By keeping the commandments. (v. 3b, restating v. 2b)
How difficult is that?
God's commandments are not burdensome. (v. 3c)

What is the result of keeping the commandments?
Whatever is begotten of God (cf. v. 1a) conquers the world. (v. 4a)
What form does this conquest of the world take? (v. 4b)
Our faith. (v. 4b; see also v. 1a)
Who conquers the world? (v. 5a)
None other than the one who believes that Jesus is God's Son. (v. 5b)

This conclusion approximates the claim in v. 1a, which introduced this entire pericope.

5:1. The opening verse requires extended consideration, because it announces so many of the interlacing topics throughout vv. 1-5: faith (see also vv. 4b, 5b), the identity of Jesus (see v. 5b), the believer as begotten of God (also v. 4a), and love as definitive of the believer's conduct (thus vv. 2-3a). The governing theme in v. 1, however, is the significance of faith or belief in Jesus as the Christ. The verb "to believe" (πιστεύω *pisteuō*), which has already appeared three times in 1 John (3:23; 4:1, 16), occurs in chapter 5 six times (vv. 1, 5, 10 [3x], 13).[147] Throughout these verses the subject matter of faith is christologically concentrated: the entrustment of oneself to Jesus as the Christ (v. 1) or the Son of God (v. 5). As in 2:22-23, these two titles balance each other and appear to be practically synonymous. Similarly, in 3:23 the commandment is enunciated in terms of belief in the name of God's Son, Jesus Christ (see also vv. 10, 13). Likewise, the elder's comments in 4:15-16: It is in the light of Jesus Christ, the Son of God, that we know and believe the love that God has for us. And the basis on which we may confirm that a spirit is "of God" is the same: the confession of Jesus Christ come in the flesh (4:1-2). In 1 John faith is thus stripped to its basics. The love of God, the commandment of God, and the Spirit of God all converge, like the spokes of a wheel, upon one hub: Jesus Christ, the incarnate Son of God. In this regard the First Epistle of John chimes with the position of the Fourth Gospel, according to which belief in Jesus both defines and validates belief in God (John 1:12; 3:15-16, 36; 5:24, 37-38; 6:29, 40, 69; 12:44; 14:1; 20:31).

While 1 John's use of "Christ" (Χριστός *Christos*) may presuppose its messianic connotations within Jewish apocalypticism (2:22; 5:1; see also John 7:41; Acts 2:36), "Christ" appears to have become for the elder another name for Jesus (1:3; 2:1; 3:23; 4:2; 5:5, 20; 2 John 3, 7, 9). Typically, the elder characterizes Jesus as the Son of God (3:8; 4:15; 5:5, 10-13, 20; 2 John 3, "the Son of the Father"), the Son (4:14; 5:12; also 2 John 9), or God's Son (1:3, 7; 3:23; 4:9-10; 5:9-11). First John's emphasis on Jesus as God's Son is probably no accident. It stands in alignment with the elder's inclination toward family metaphors in speaking of God ("the Father": 1:2-3; 2:1, 14-16, 22-24; 3:1; 4:14; 2 John 3-4, 9) and of the church ("little children": 2:1, 12, 28; 3:1-2, 7, 10, 18; 4:4; 5:2, 21; 2 John 1, 4, 13; 3 John 4). To be sure, the elder employs other images to describe Jesus' significance (e.g., "expiation" [2:2; 4:10] and "Paraclete" [2:1]). Nevertheless, precisely because it highlights the intimate association of Jesus with God, Jesus' identity as the Son of God is for 1 John the confession that is most vital and least susceptible of compromise. To deny Jesus as the Son is, in a real sense, to lose God as one's Father. Belief in Jesus provides access to God; to dwell in the one is to dwell in the other (2:23-24).

In 5:1 the primary metaphor for the benefit of faith in Jesus is the believer's being "begotten of God." This image appears throughout 1 John (2:29; 3:9; 4:7), but, like the terms for "faith," is concentrated in chap. 5 (vv. 1 [3x], 4, 18 [2x]). Unlike Paul, who describes Christians as adopted "children of God" (Rom 8:15, 23 NRSV), the elder restricts language of "sonship" to Jesus alone. Unlike the Nicene Creed, which speaks only of Jesus as "begotten," in 1 John the metaphor of God's procreation is applied to believers as well. The translation "begotten" (γεγέννηται *gegennētai*; see KJV, JBP, NAB) is better than "born" (RSV, NIV, NRSV) or the paraphrastic "child of God" (NEB, GNB, REB); at vv. 1 and 4 the elder's primary interest is in the believer's point of origin, not in the process of birth or the progeny's identification.[148] Life that is

---

147. The noun "faith" (πιστίς *pistis*) appears in 1 John only at 5:4; neither the noun nor the verb appears in 2 or 3 John. By comparison, *pistis* occurs only four times in Revelation (Rev 2:13, 19; 13:10; 14:12), not at all in the Gospel of John. The verb πιστεύω (*pisteuō*) appears nowhere in Revelation but at least ninety-eight times throughout the Fourth Gospel.

148. See Keck, "Derivation as Destiny," 274-88.

begotten of God originates in an extraordinary act of God. Radically different from the life of ordinary human generation (vv. 11, 13, 20; see also John 1:12-13), it is life whose hallmarks are righteousness, love, and faith (2:29; 4:7; 5:1). First John does not work out the cosmological or anthropological implications of this divine derivation. Instead, the elder uses this imagery to encourage believers (2:28; 3:21; 4:17; 5:14) and to remind them of the responsibilities that ensue from their origin.

5:2-3. Another idea is more explicitly developed in these verses: love for God and for the children of God. Love for fellow believers has already been identified as an indicator of our dwelling in God's love (3:10-18; 4:7-12; 5:1; see also 1 Pet 1:22-23). Correlatively, the elder has stressed God's prior love for us (3:16; 4:9-11, 16, 19). Adumbrated in 4:20-21 and 5:1, a variation on this theme is now elaborated in 5:2-3: the believer's love for God, manifested in obedience to God's commands and in love for God's other children. In the elder's view, love flows in a continuous circuit, originating from and returning to God as depicted in Fig. 1.

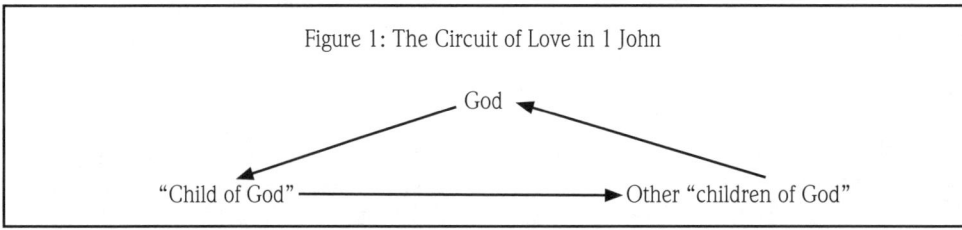

Figure 1: The Circuit of Love in 1 John

Love for God and for God's children is manifested in obedience to God's commandments (see also 2:3-4, 7-8; 3:22-24; 4:21; John 14:15, 23-24; 2 John 4-6). Obedience is the medium through which love is communicated. The elder's view of obedience is similar to Philo's: "God asks of you nothing burdensome or complicated or difficult, but only something quite simple and easy."[149]

5:4-5. The outcome of Christians' interconnected acts of faith, love, and obedience is "victory over the world" (author's trans.).

This claim by the elder draws together two lines of thought throughout 1 John: the world as a deluded realm in need of restoration (2:2, 15-17; 3:1, 13; 4:1, 3-5, 9, 14, 17, 19; also 2 John 7; Rev 11:15), and the Christian's present experience of triumph over evil forces that continue to assail (2:13-14; 4:4; John 16:33; Rev 2:7, 11, 17, 26; cf. Rom 8:37). In 1 John a life activated by faith and conducted in love *already* conquers a faithless, loveless world. This, in a sense, is the elder's commentary on his own aphorism in 2:8: "the darkness is passing away and the true light is already shining" (NRSV).

---

149. Philo *On the Special Laws* 1.55. 299; note also Deut 10:12-13; 30:11-14; Matt 11:29-30.

REFLECTIONS

1. Most sermons on 5:1-5 cannot linger in 1 John's mesmerizing rhetoric without losing the listeners. Still, we may applaud the elder's adoption of a mode of proclamation that fits his subject. The apparently seamless way in which his thoughts run together corresponds to his vision of life among God and the children of God, inseparably united in love. This passage also coordinates several important issues—Christian identity, faith, love, obedience, hope—with impressive concision and coherence. The elder implicitly invites us to consider and to enact these dimensions of Christian experience as an interconnected whole, not as detached points in our sermons or as fragments of our lives.

2. The elder's concentration on faith in Jesus as the Christ, the Son of God, may seem overly restrictive to some. Are there not more things in heaven and on earth that Christians should ponder than just what we think about Jesus? Of course there are—as, to judge from the whole of 1 John, the elder would surely agree. It is not a question of oversimplification, but of *focus*: At what point do our views of God, of humanity, of the church and of the world, of love and of ministry, of a hundred other matters come together? First John affirms that if we are Christians, all these things converge in Christ. If we know God, it is because God has known and claimed us through the life and death of Jesus. If we participate in life that is eternal, it is because we live it through Christ. We love, and we know what love is, because we have known him who laid down his life for us. The elder's testimony assumes that Christians do not approach God as generally religious people, praying to whom it may concern.

There is a scandalous particularity in the faith on which Christians stake their lives. In such a confession our centrifugal, frenzied existence may be calmed; in Christ we find what T. S. Eliot sought, "the still point of the turning world."[150] With such a core comes a stabilizing clarity that orders and relativizes our other beliefs. Spirits must be tested and assessed for their trustworthiness (1 John 4:1), but not every issue that comes before the church is of the same gravity as its confession of Jesus Christ (1 John 4:2). Christians may converse and at times disagree among themselves with equanimity, emancipated from anxious obsessions to "bleed and die" for every cause that comes their way. If Christ occupies the center at which faith comes into focus, then other things, however important, do not.

3. Gently and potently, 1 John 5:1-5 challenges a variety of baleful tendencies on our contemporary scene. Against the demeaning, dehumanizing forces that would grind away the souls of women and men throughout the modern world, the elder maintains that Christians enjoy an ennobling dignity that, apart from Christ, we could never know: that of "children of God," an unshakable and gifted status that is not ours to earn. Others in our day deny any respect for authority that could possibly be healthy, despite the fact that their lives are falling apart for lack of limits. By contrast, 1 John declares that love for and obedience to God are of one piece, that God's commandments are not oppressive, that in discipleship there is salutary discipline. In their careers and other pursuits, still others, sad to say, behave as though "for this life only we have hoped" (1 Cor 15:19 NRSV). Contrary to such tinsel aspirations, 1 John reminds us that this world does not have the last word, that our allegiance and our victory as Christians ultimately belong elsewhere.

4. God's love for us is, rightly, a recurrent theme of Christian preaching. Less often proclaimed is 1 John's reminder that as Christians we love God. In the elder's hands this subject remains refreshingly concrete. We love God by keeping the commandments (1 John 5:2-3*a*), which includes entrusting ourselves to Christ (1 John 3:23) and loving God's children (1 John 5:1). Abiding in God is not religious fire insurance, which we take out in nervous interest of our self-preservation. Just the opposite: Dwelling in God's love is the habitat for which human beings were originally created and, in Christ, are being re-created. With the Westminster Confession, the elder would have agreed that our chief end is to adore and enjoy God forever. With the Methodist baptismal covenant, he would have concurred that surrounding God's children with steadfast love is a primary means of expressing that adoration.

---

150. T. S. Eliot, from *Four Quartets:* "Burnt Norton," II (1935), in T. S. Eliot, *The Complete Poems and Plays, 1909–1950* (New York: Harcourt Brace, n.d.) 119.

1 John 5:6-12, The Testimony That God Has Borne to the Son

COMMENTARY

For Year B, the *Revised Common Lectionary* presents 1 John 5:1-6 and 5:9-13 as the epistle lessons for, respectively, the sixth and seventh Sundays of Easter. One may question this division of the material. It cuts out vv. 7-8, which, while undeniably obscure, could help us in the interpretation of their surrounding verses. Such help should not be refused; 1 John 5:6-12 is one of the letter's most tangled patches, presenting a challenge for any interpreter to find a footing.

To take our bearings, we may begin by noting the recurring topic throughout this pericope: "witness" or "testimony" (μαρτυρία *martyria*). This noun occurs nowhere else in the epistle, but six times in 5:9-11. The cognate verb, "to bear witness" (μαρτυρέω *martyreō*), appears in 5:6, 7, 9, 10 (as well as in 1:2; 4:14; 3 John 3, 6, 12). Clearly, 1 John's reflections on witness are concentrated in 5:6-12, but the idea's lack of development elsewhere means that we have sparse interpretive context to fall back on. If the elder and his readers assumed what is said about witness in the Fourth Gospel, this context is considerably filled out; witness is an important theme in John, especially testimony that is borne to Jesus by John the Baptist (John 1:7-8, 15, 19, 32-34), by the Beloved Disciple (John 19:25; 21:24), by God (John 5:31-40), by the Spirit of truth (John 15:26-27), and by Jesus himself (John 8:13-18).

5:6. Help provided by the Gospel could be critical for interpreting this verse, which emphasizes that Jesus Christ "came" (ἐλθών *elthōn*) in a particular way. Although we should not press a verbal conjugation for more information than it can offer, the verb *elthōn* is in the aorist (pointedly past) tense, which may suggest the finality of Jesus' once-for-all coming in history. According to the elder, the manner of Jesus' advent was "by water and blood . . . not with the water only but with the water and the blood" (v. 6*ab*). Most commentators agree that here we have a rhetorical device known as metonymy, the use of the name of one thing in place of another with which it is closely associated (as we might speak of "counting noses" when we are actually counting people). Opinions differ, however, on what v. 6 indicates with reference to "water" and "blood." Three possibilities have strong defenders: (1) Water represents Christian baptism, or the dispensing of living water by Christ (cf. John 4:1-2, 10-14; 7:38-39); blood represents the eucharist (John 6:53-56).[151] (2) Water alludes to Jesus' own baptism (John 1:29-34), blood symbolizes his crucifixion.[152] (3) Water and blood in v. 6 collectively recall the death of Jesus, from whose side blood and water issued after his death (John 19:34*b*).[153]

There is no way to be sure which of these alternatives was uppermost in the elder's mind. If choose we must, the last option seems more probable than the first.[154] Negatively, references to Christian ritual are rare in 1 John, although "anointing" in 2:26-27 may allude to baptism. Positively, "spirit," "water," "blood," "witness," and "truth" are all conjoined in both John 19:30, 34*b*-35 and 1 John 5:6, a coincidence that seems too great to be fortuitous. Perhaps some conjunction of the second and third alternatives underlies the elder's obscure comment in 1 John 5:6. Against a view that may have exaggerated Christ's spiritual endowment at his baptism ("with water only"; cf. John 1:31-33) to the denigration of his atoning death, the elder may be acknowledging Jesus' baptism while emphasizing his death ("with the water

---

151. Luther, "Lectures on the First Epistle of St. John," 314-15; Calvin, *The Gospel According to St John 11–21 and the First Epistle of John*, 302. M. C. de Boer, "Jesus the Baptizer: 1 John 5:5-8 and the Gospel of John," *JBL* 107 (1988) 87-106, and Strecker, *The Johannine Letters*, 182-86, offer modifications of this view.

152. Thus Bede *Commentary on 1 John* 216; Wesley, *Explanatory Notes Upon the New Testament*, (1755) (London: Epworth, 1950) 917; Brooke, *A Critical and Exegetical Commentary on the Johannine Epistles*, 133-36; Howard Marshall, *The Epistle of John*, NICNT (Grand Rapids: Eerdmans, 1978) 231-39; Smalley, *1, 2, 3 John*, 277-80.

153. Thus Augustine *Against Maximinum* 2.22; Thompson, *1-3 John*, 132-35.

154. Many commentators allow for more than one option. See Bultmann, *The Johannine Epistles*, 79-81; Schnackenburg, *The Johannine Epistles*, 232-338; Smith, *First, Second, and Third John*, 123-26.

and with the blood"; cf. John 19:34*b*).[155] Although intelligible, such a precise framing of the controversy says more than we can confidently confirm. Whatever imbalance the elder hopes to rectify, clearly he does so with stress on Jesus' blood, which almost surely refers to his death as atonement for sin (see 1:7; 2:2).

5:7-8. The elder assumes that the Spirit bears valid witness to Jesus (v. 6*b*; cf. 3:24; 4:6, 13; John 15:26). The problem, as 1 John has already conceded (4:1-6), is that an appeal to the Spirit can also be made by those whose perspectives on Jesus are distorted. Perhaps for this reason the elder makes a telling move. Without impugning the Spirit's testimony, he asserts the existence of not one but *three* witnesses (v. 7) whose testimony agrees: that of the Spirit, the water, and the blood (v. 8).[156] In a sense, this restates the elder's earlier insistence that the Spirit of God is known by the confession of Jesus Christ come in the flesh (4:2). Yet it is a restatement with some helpful elaboration. It enlarges the scope of the testimony and factors in the need for corroboration, even of the Spirit's truthful witness. (Here the elder alludes to, but characteristically does not cite, the biblical dictum for supporting witnesses: Deut 19:15; cf. Matt 18:16; John 8:17-18.) If my suggested interpretation of "water and the blood" (v. 6) is correct, the elder underscores a crucial aspect of Jesus' incarnation that under no circumstances may be soft-pedaled: his death. Just as the Spirit of God confesses Christ's having come in the flesh (4:2), so also we have life in the Son of God, who truly died—who came by way of water and of blood (5:6, 12).

5:9-12. Faith in the Son of God, thus understood, appears to be the criterion for verifying God's own testimony to the church. God has borne witness that eternal life was given by God through the Son (vv. 9*b*-10*a*, 11), much as victory over the world depends on faith that Jesus is the Son of God (v. 5). Having the Son, therefore, is equivalent to having life; not having the Son of God means not having life (v. 12; see also John 3:36; The NIV and the NRSV import into v. 10*a* "his [their] heart[s]," words not found in the Greek text. By thus implying "an inward witness of the Spirit," these translations may drag a red herring across the elder's trail of thought.[157]

Like v. 12*b*, vv. 9*a* and 10*b* could be considered hypothetical possibilities, which in Johannine thought attend the decision for or against faith. Given the elder's fighting words elsewhere in this letter, however, these verses could also be interpreted as polemical thrusts against mere human testimony or as challenges to the lack of trust in God's witness to Jesus that makes God[158] out to be a liar (cf. 2:18-25; 4:1-6; John 5:34, 37; 8:18).

---

155. This interpretation is favored by Brown, *The Epistles of John*, 574-78.

156. First appearing in a Latin recension of 1 John near the end of the fourth century, the famous "Johannine comma" (appearing in the KJV but reproduced as an italicized footnote in both the NIV and the NRSV) is absent from all of the ancient versions of the letter and from all but four Greek mss. Had the passage been original, there is no good reason for it to have been omitted. Commentators are virtually unanimous that it was added onto 1 John 5 in the light of later trinitarian debates. A full discussion of this gloss, its origins and textual history, may be found in Brown, *The Epistles of John*, 775-87.

157. As Howard Marshall observes, "The contrast [between v. 10*a* and 10*b*] is between accepting what God has said and rejecting it" (*The Epistles of John*, 241).

158. Some ancient texts and versions of 1 John 5:10*b* read, "The one who does not believe in the Son [of God]," which reflects a scribal attempt to draw this clause into closer parallelism with 5:10*a* ("Those who believe in the Son of God" [NRSV]).

REFLECTIONS

1. In some Christian traditions, "testimony" is regularly practiced within corporate worship. With this activity the author of 1 John would probably sympathize (1:2; 4:14). Yet for the elder the accent of bearing witness falls elsewhere. Testimony in 1 John, like love (4:19), is not something that we initiate: "If we receive human testimony, the testimony of God is greater" (5:9*a* NRSV). The primary witness is what *God* has borne to the Son; our testimony is a derivative acknowledgment of God's own accreditation of Jesus and its claim on our lives. Confession of Jesus Christ is for Christians an expression of their occupancy in God's indestructible life (2:23; 4:2, 15; 5:11-12), but by that testimony we do not validate Jesus. To believe that is to mistake hubris for piety. Before we open our mouths in response, God, through the Spirit (5:7), has already borne authenticating witness to "the man of God's own choosing."[159] The effectiveness of God's testimony—the fact that it *works* within us—is manifested by our faith, the trusting investment of our lives in Jesus as God's Son, who shows children of God the way to the Father (John 14:8-11; cf. Rom 8:16; Gal 4:6).

2. To none of us does God's testimony come unmediated. Not only do spirits need testing (4:1), but even the Spirit needs corroboration from concurring witnesses (5:8). Given 1 John's immediate concerns and location within formative Christianity, it would be unreasonable to expect that the letter could offer us a set of fully articulated principles by which the church may confirm God's witness. More important is the elder's recognition of the reality of God's Spirit, at work within the church, as well as the need for the Spirit's testimony to be coordinated with other resources for Christian judgment. In 1 John the essential criteria are adherence to the character of Jesus as he was remembered in Johannine tradition (1 John 1:1-3; 2:5*b*-6, 22-24; 3:23; 4:2-3; 5:5-6), obedience to God's nurturing commands (1 John 2:3, 7-8; 3:22-24; 4:21; 5:2-3), and practical love for one another (1 John 3:11, 18, 23; 4:7, 11-12). Churches of the Wesleyan tradition particularly will recognize in these emphases some of John Wesley's standards for Christian life and faith: tradition, which comes into focus on God's pardoning initiative for humanity in Jesus Christ; the Christian's vital assurance of identity as a child of God; responsive human love, prompted by God's own love for us.[160] In its consideration of norms and resources for testing the spirits, later Christian thought has evolved beyond the elder—but only because it could stand on the shoulders of witnesses like him.

3. First John insists that we perceive Jesus Christ as the one "who came by water and blood." This hint of Christ's death may sound strange to those who hear 5:9-13 preached as an Easter lection. Does not the resurrection of Jesus stand at the core of the Christian *kerygma?* Have we not, by the elder's own testimony, passed from death to life in God's Son (1 John 2:25; 3:14; 5:11-12)?

All of this is true. For 1 John, as for the rest of the NT, it is not, however, the whole truth. Unlike those modern churches whose pews overflow on Easter Sunday but are vacant on Good Friday, 1 John never loses sight of Christ's death in pondering "the word of life" (1 John 1:1 NRSV). The texture of the elder's theology would not allow it. To be sure, Jesus' death is in part an inevitable aspect of his coming "in flesh" (4:2); if he did not really die, then he was not truly human. But there is more to 1 John's christology than that. "In this is love, not that we loved God but that he loved us and sent his Son to be the atoning sacrifice for our sins" (4:10 NRSV; see also 1:7; 2:2). Expiation implies sacrifice, and sacrifice means death. But why death? "This is how we know what love is: Jesus Christ laid down his life for us" (3:16 NIV). God's raising of Jesus from death did not eradicate his crucifixion (to the contrary, see John 20:24-28; Rev 5:6-14). The resurrection was God's vindication of the crucified Jesus—this one and no other—as the Son of God.

This truth—so fundamental, so easily forgotten—literally surrounds many worshipers every Sunday morning. Viewing the magnificent stained glass in the Chapel at King's College, Cambridge, Sister Wendy Beckett commented on the perfect correspondence of that Christian medium and its message:

> The whole story of the passion can be such a dark story, can fill us with such grief and compassion. And of course so it should. But it was a story that always had light coming through: the resurrection was implicit in the passion right from the start. And to be

---

159. Martin Luther, "A Mighty Fortress Is Our God," *The United Methodist Hymnal: Book of United Methodist Worship* (Nashville: United Methodist Publishing House, 1989) 110.
160. Albert C. Outler, "The Wesleyan Quadrilateral—in John Wesley," in *The Wesleyan Theological Heritage: Essays of Albert C. Outler,* ed. Thomas C. Oden and Leicester R. Longden (Grand Rapids: Zondervan, 1991) 21-37.

looking at passion windows, where the light is always coming through, has a wonderful spiritual as well as an artistic meaning.[161]

[161]. Transcribed from "Pains of Glass," a television interview with the Reverend Dr. George Pattison, produced in the United Kingdom by BBC North (1995).

1 JOHN 5:13-21, REFRAIN: THAT YOU MAY KNOW THAT YOU HAVE ETERNAL LIFE

OVERVIEW

The symphony that is 1 John draws to a close with 5:13-21, a coda to the work commencing with a signal refrain: "I write to you . . . so that you may know" (v. 13; cf. 1:4; 2:1, 3, 7-8, 12-14, 21, 26; 3:2, 5, 14, 16, 19, 24b; 4:2, 6b, 13, 16). This epilogue contains two subunits: vv. 13-17, which are concerned with prayer, and vv. 18-21, concerned with the central dimensions of "what we know."

With an unexpected warning (v. 21), 1 John ends as abruptly as it began—and just as appropriately. Sounding the depths of divine love and human responsibility, an epistle like this cannot end. By its very nature, there can be for 1 John no full stop. There can only be, as it were, a colon, a directional indicator of how the rest of the church's life will continue, along the limitless horizon of God's love.

1 John 5:13-17, The Boldness in Our Asking

COMMENTARY

5:13. Just as 1 John opens (1:1-4) with comments redolent of John's prologue (John 1:1-18), so also the letter approaches its conclusion with a postscript of purpose similar to the colophon of the Fourth Gospel:

1 John 5:13	John 20:31
these things I write to you who believe in the name of the Son of God, that you may know that you have eternal life	these things are written so that you may believe that Jesus is the Christ, the Son of God, and that by believing you may have life in his name

Viewed within the letter's own framework, 1 John 5:13 consolidates some of the elder's main topics: "knowing" (εἰδῆτε *eidēte*) in the sense of relationship (2:3-4, 13-14; 3:1, 6, 16, 20; 4:6-8; 5:20); the Christian's experience of "eternal life" (1:2; 2:25; 3:15; 5:11, 20); "belief" or "faith" (3:23; 4:1, 16; 5:1, 4-5, 10); "the name [= the person; see 2:12;

3:23] of the Son of God" (3:8; 4:15; 5:5, 10, 12, 30). Even more clearly than John 20:31, the epilogue of 1 John conveys the author's intent to bolster his readers' faith and to leave them reassured of their standing with God.

5:14-15. Symptomatic of that certitude (see also 2:28; 4:17) is the community's engagement in prayer (vv. 14-17), a subject noted at 3:21-22 but developed here in more detail. It is unclear whether Christian confidence is directed toward Jesus (v. 13; cf. John 14:14) or toward God, to whom prayers in the Johannine tradition are typically offered (see John 11:22; 15:16; 16:23; 1 John 3:22). Either way, believers may adopt a frankness toward God, which assumes that requests made of God, in conformity with God's will (cf. John 4:34; 5:30), are heard (1 John 5:14; see also 3:21b-22; 4:17; cf. Eph 3:11-12; Phil 4:6; Jas 1:6). If read carelessly, the curiously worded v. 15 appears tautologous: "if he hears, then he hears." Actually, this point is less circular than subtle; if God *hears* whatever we ask, then we *receive* what we have asked for.

In prayer we have petitioned a hearing from God; what we receive is, by definition, God's reply to that petition and the confirmation that God has, indeed, heard us. This idea resembles Jesus' teaching on prayer in Matt 7:7-11 (= Luke 11:9-13; John 11:41-42; 1 John 3:22). In fact, 1 John 5:15 is even more subtle than my paraphrase suggests, for both the premise and the conclusion are formulated in terms of faith's knowledge: "And if *we know* that he hears . . . *we know* that we have." In trusting alignment with God's will, the church is sure that its prayers both *are* (not should be) heard and *are* (not will be) fulfilled. The thought approximates Jesus' stunning comment in Mark: "Whatever you ask for in prayer, *believe that you have received it,* and it will be yours" (Mark 11:24 NRSV, italics added; cf. Matt 21:22; John 14:13; 15:7, 16; 16:23).

5:16-17. We come now to remarks about sin mortal and not mortal, about those for whom one should and should not pray—comments, which have predictably stirred up a mare's-nest of interpretive debate. As in other patches of the letter, the author speaks so vaguely here that, while we can work out a rough idea of his meaning, precision remains unattainable.

Verse 16a focuses the elder's comments about prayer on a particular case: request made on behalf of a community member ("brother or sister") who commits a sin that is "not toward death" (μὴ πρὸς θάνατον *mē pros thanaton,* vv. 16ab-17). For such sinners, intercession may be made. Indeed, it must be made, since "all wrongdoing is sin" (v. 17). In response to that prayer, life is given, ultimately, though not explicitly in the Greek text, by God (v. 16a; cf. Jas 5:16). What is "a sin toward" (v. 16b) or "not toward death"? The preposition πρὸς (*pros*) usually carries a kinetic nuance of tendency toward something, which is concealed in translations of πρὸς θάνατον (*pros thanaton*) as "mortal sin" (RSV, NRSV) or "deadly sin" (Moffatt, JBP, NEB, REB). The suggestion of motion or heading is better preserved in the archaic KJV phrase, "unto death," and in the NIV and GNB formulations, "a sin that leads to death" (cf. John 11:4). Still the question stands: What is a deathward sin? The elder does not answer, which has spurred commentators to fill in the blank (see Reflections).

If we seek clues from elsewhere in 1 John, at least two possibilities emerge. (1) In 3:14-15 the refusal to love, or hatred for one's brother is equivalent to dwelling in death. This interpretation is favored among patristic and medieval commentators.[162] While it seems to fit the circumstances of this pericope, in v. 16bc the elder does not explicitly attribute the commission of "a sin unto death" *to a member of the community.* (2) If, by definition, a deathward sin is committed by one *outside* the community, beyond the purview of eternal life known by those "who believe in the name of the Son of God" (v. 13), then the sin heading toward death may be an outright denial of Jesus. Traceable at least as far back as Calvin, this interpretation is held by a majority of modern interpreters.[163] It presupposes the theology of the Fourth Evangelist, who describes sin as a refusal to believe Jesus' testimony (John 8:24; 15:22; 16:8-9). More immediately, in 1 John 2:18-25 the denial of Jesus is associated with secession from the church. Perhaps for these reasons John Wesley construed a sin *pros thanaton* in 5:16 as "total apostasy from both the power and form of godliness,"[164] even though such an interpretation outruns firm substantiation from 1 John itself.

162. Augustine *The Sermon on the Mount,* 1.22; Bede *Commentary on 1 John* 223-24.
163. A good argument in its favor is mounted by David M. Scholer, "Sins Within and Sins Without: An Interpretation of 1 John 5:16-17," in *Current Issues in Biblical and Patristic Interpretation: Studies in Honor of Merrill C. Tenney Presented by His Former Students,* ed. Gerald F. Hawthorne (Grand Rapids: Eerdmans, 1975) 230-46; cf. Calvin, *The Gospel According to St John 11–21 and the First Epistle of John,* 310-11.
164. Wesley, *Explanatory Notes Upon the New Testament,* 919.

REFLECTIONS

1. Jumping off from 1 John 5:16-17, Tertullian (c. 160–225) classified some sins as unpardonable: murder, idolatry, injustice, apostasy, blasphemy, adultery, and fornication.[165] Correlatively, in his interpretation of 1 John 1:6, Augustine drew attention to

165. Tertullian *On Modesty* 2, 19.

"light" sins, pervasive throughout humankind, whose forgiveness requires confession, charity, and humility.[166] Drawing from a broader biblical base that included not only 1 John but also the Torah's distinction between deliberate and inadvertent sins (Lev 4:1–6:7; Num 15:27-31), Thomas Aquinas (1224/25–74) differentiated sins that were mortal, or eternally damning, from those that were venial, or ordinary, and defined modes for their remission.[167] From the sixteenth century onward, Roman Catholic moral theology refined these distinctions: Mortal sin was considered a deliberate violation of a serious law of God, forgiveness of which normally entailed the sacrament of penance; venial sin was regarded as a violation of a minor law of God, forgiveness of which could be obtained in many different ways (prayer, sacraments, good works). Since Vatican II, Roman Catholic moral theologians have tended to view sin not primarily as an act against God's law but in terms of an individual's relationship to God: Mortal sin ruptures that relationship; venial sin weakens it. In the light of this newer understanding of sin, the theory and practice of the sacrament of penance are being reevaluated.[168]

Such developments go far beyond 1 John, which intends to describe the core and outer limits of the church's responsibility toward sinners. This more modest concern should be hurdle enough, however, for those in our day who find it hard to take seriously any understanding of sin. To the sobriety of the elder's counsel, much less the anguish of Paul's cry, "Wretched man that I am!" (Rom 7:24 NRSV), "I'm okay; you're okay!" is clearly an inadequate response.

2. Others see no escape for humanity from sin's quagmire apart from God's rescue. For them, the limitation on intercessory prayer in 1 John 5:16-17 may seem too harsh. Within the biblical context, however, the elder's views are neither unique nor strident. One thinks of Eli, who disallowed the possibility of mediation for sin committed against the Lord (1 Sam 2:25); of Jeremiah, who preached Yahweh's refusal to listen to idolatrous Judah (Jer 7:16; 11:14; 15:1); of Paul, who urged excommunication of a flagrant sinner from the Corinthian church (1 Cor 5:2, 5, 13); of Hebrews, which regarded atonement for post-baptismal apostasy impossible (Heb 6:4-8; 10:26-31); and of the Johannine Jesus, who intercedes with the Father for his disciples but not on behalf of the world, which refuses both Jesus and the Father who sent him (John 8:23-24; 17:9, 14). If our intuition about the "sin toward death" in 1 John 5:16 is correct, the elder is speaking of those who, by their denial of the Son and their schism from the community, have put themselves beyond the pale. The question would then be somewhat like that of "the unforgivable sin" (Matt 12:31-32 and par.), a view of God so utterly perverse that its holders place themselves under conditions in which reconciliation is impossible. Like the evangelists, the elder's point is that, while every sin is serious (1 John 5:17), not all sin is of the same magnitude. The church bears responsibility for a particular witness to God in the world and for discipline and prayer among its members. In the elder's opinion, prayer itself is a form of communal discipline. Still, the church is not God; its competence is limited. Only Almighty God, "who desires not the death of sinners, but rather that they may turn from their wickedness and live,"[169] can deal with sin so heinous that it could forever remove its perpetrator from the Giver of life.

3. Finally, however, 1 John 5:13-17 is a testimony of hope, from the pen of one convinced of the power of prayer. Prayer, for the elder, is not a form of abracadabra or self-interested manipulation. Prayer, rather, is a force that promotes restorative life,

---

166. Augustine "First Homily: I John 1:1–2:11," §6.
167. *St Thomas Aquinas: Summa Theologicae*, vol. 27: *Effects of Sin, Stain and Guilt (Ia2ae 86-89)*, ed. and trans. T. C. O'Brien (London: Blackfriars/Eyre & Spottiswoode, 1974) N.B. 110-24.
168. For a modern restatement of Roman Catholic doctrine on this matter, see *Catechism of the Catholic Church*, Libreria Editrice Vaticana (Liguori, Mo.: Liguori Publications, 1994) 454-56. I am grateful for Charles E. Curran's help in the formulation of this paragraph.
169. From the Litany of Penitence for Ash Wednesday, *The Book of Common Prayer and Administration of the Sacraments and Other Rites and Ceremonies of the Church* (n.p.: Seabury, 1979) 269.

bestowed on us by a mercifully responsive God (5:16). In intercession for their brothers and sisters, Christians actually participate in Christ's priestly ministry of atonement for the world (2:1-2; 5:16-17). More obviously, prayer molds the one who prays. It quells impertinent self-assertion, timidity, and apprehension, redirecting us toward alignment with God's will, confidence that God has heard us, and knowledge "that all we ask of him is ours" (5:15 REB). Whether framed as intercessions for others or petitions for ourselves, prayer in 1 John, as in the Bible generally, is enacted in the faith that a genuine conversation between God and humanity occurs, out of which God gives shape to the future. Thus not only is prayer performed in faith, but it is also an articulation of faith. "Therefore, to thee we hand over our existence—to thee, who has invited and commanded us to pray, to live for thy cause. Here we are. It is now up to thee to concern thyself with our human cause."[170] First John bears witness that God does hear and does uphold the cause of those who live in truth. As expressed by the condemned Sir Thomas More to his executioner, "[God] will not refuse one who is so blithe to go to him."[171]

170. Karl Barth, *Prayer*, ed. Don E. Saliers (Philadelphia: Westminster, 1985) 7.
171. Robert Bolt, *A Man for All Seasons* (New York: Vintage, 1962) 94.

1 John 5:18-21, What We Know

COMMENTARY

First John draws to a close with a capsule restatement of three of the epistle's primary topics: the believer's moral life (5:18), the believer's God-given identity (5:19), and the identity of Jesus, in whose truth the believer resides (5:20). Given the elder's penchant for wedding exhortation with declaration, we should not be surprised to find these affirmations immediately yoked to a final word of caution (5:21). As is also the author's wont, the rhetoric is finely wrought. The epilogue is a compressed series of assertions, each introduced by "We know" and structured in contrastive parallelism:

1 John 5:18
we are preserved by God;	we are untouched by the evil one.

1 John 5:19
we are of God;	the world is gripped by the evil one.

1 John 5:20-21
we are in the true God.	keep yourself from idols.

Like the epistle overall, this conclusion is obviously intended to bolster the community's confidence. To this end the elder returns to the metaphor of family: Christians are "little children" (v. 21), "begotten of God"[172] (v. 18) and "of God" (v. 19), whose perception of truth has been given to them by "the Son of God" (v. 20).

5:18. "Those who are born of God do not sin" restates the point of 3:6, 9, those verses so difficult to correlate with 1 John's acknowledgment of sin and its expiation within the church (1:9–2:2, 12). Instead of clarifying the elder's position, this verse heightens the problem. Immediately following his axiom that a community member may commit a sin for which Christians should offer intercessory prayer (vv. 16-17), the elder's comment here seems blatantly inconsistent. (This contradiction is softened by the NIV's interpretation, "does not continue to sin.") Although it may be possible to reconcile the elder's claims in terms with which he would agree (see the Commentary and Reflections on 3:4-10), that accommodation is not effected here or anywhere in the letter. The paradox persists: Undoubtedly, the Christian sins; undeniably, the one begotten of God does not sin. In

172. In 5:18, the translation of γεγέννηται (*gegennētai*) as "begotten" is preferable to "born" (NIV, NRSV), for the reasons given in the Commentary on 5:1-5.

1 John 5:18-21 Commentary

v. 18, however, the chief goal is not systematic rigor but encouragement in holiness; having acknowledged the community's sin and the means for its removal (vv. 16-17), the elder now emphasizes the Christian's divine parentage and protection from the power of the evil one, or Satan (see also 2:13-14, 29; John 17:15). The identity of that guardian is ambiguous. Those who are "born of" God may refer to the Christian believer (thus KJV; cf. 2:29; 3:9; 4:7; 5:1, 4; John 1:12-13; 3:3-8). Here the phrase probably refers to Christ, although the Greek text does not say "the Son of God," as some translations imply (Phillips, JBP, NEB, GNB, REB). While Jesus is not precisely described as "begotten of God" elsewhere in Johannine literature, he is characterized as God's only begotten Son in John 1:14, [18]; 3:16, 18.

5:19. This verse reaffirms the Christian's divine origin, in stark contrast with that of "the whole world" (ὁ κοσμός ὅλος *ho kosmos holos*). Considered within an apocalyptic framework, the world is gripped by the evil one, who cannot lay hold of the one begotten of God (v. 18; cf. 2:15-17; Gal 1:4).

5:20. Verses 18-19 specify the basis for the Christian's protection; this verse, the ground of Christian understanding. This verse's thought is so compressed that its components invite separation and labeling, in order to discern their interrelation:

a. And we know that the Son of God has come
b. and has given us understanding
c. so that we may know him who is true;
d. and we are in him who is true,
e. in his Son Jesus Christ.
f. He is the true God and eternal life.

This single verse coordinates at least four different kinds of claims. Segments a, e, and f are essentially *christological* affirmations: Jesus, the Son of God, is the true God and eternal life (see also 1:2; 5:11). The elder does not explain these affirmations of Jesus, whether in terms of pre-existence or some other concept. Rather, 1 John seems simply to presuppose the Fourth Gospel's radical reappraisal of who God is and of how God is revealed in the light of Jesus Christ (John 5:18-19, 30; 10:30; 14:6; 17:3; 20:28).[173] Because Jesus Christ is the Son of God, the true God and eternal life, it follows that those in Christ are also "in the truth" (d)—an *anthropological* comment about humanity in Christ. This statement presupposes a *soteriological* claim (b): Those who are in the truth enjoy Christ's gift of insight, the benefit of mental renewal. This soteriological assertion carries an *epistemological* implication (c): Since like recognizes like, those who are in the truth know Jesus as the one who is true and who is, indeed, the true God.

5:21. The letter's last words could not be more abrupt. Address to the author's "little children" is predictable (see 2:1, 12, 28; 3:7, 18; 4:4), but his reference to idols seems to come out of nowhere. Idolatry was a live option within religions of antiquity and a besetting temptation for early Christians (Acts 14:15; 1 Cor 10:14; 1 Thess 1:9; Rev 13:14-15), particularly those whose journey to Christ bypassed monotheistic Judaism (Ps 115:3-8; Isa 40:18-20; Jer 10:1-16). This problem, however, has been heretofore unmentioned in 1 John.[174] Perhaps the verse preceding offers an immediate, more direct context for understanding: We should "be on the watch against false gods" (NEB) if we abide in the One who is authentic reality, the true God (v. 20; cf. Ezek 14:4; 1QS 2:11-17; Col 3:5).[175]

---

173. For a well-balanced, elegantly nuanced account of Johannine christology in its complexity, see D. Moody Smith, *The Theology of the Gospel of John*, New Testament Theology (Cambridge: Cambridge University Press, 1995) esp. 75-135, 173-82.

174. A rebuttal is presented by Julian Hills, "'Little children, keep yourself from idols': 1 John 5:21 Reconsidered," *CBQ* 51 (1989) 285-310.

175. Thus Wesley's sermons, "Spiritual Worship" and "Spiritual Idolatry," in Outler, *The Works of John Wesley*, 3:88-114. Most commentators favor this interpretation, there is no consensus. See Brown, *The Epistles of John*, 627-29.

REFLECTIONS

The crucial issue before us in 1 John 5:18-21—the Christian's conjunction with Christ, who for the believer is "the true God and eternal life"—may be the hardest for the modern church to grasp, because our interpretive framework is so different from 1 John's.

We typically talk of membership in a church or participation in Christian belief and practice; the elder speaks of begetting from God and dwelling in Jesus Christ. Put differently, our reflex is to view things sociologically and anthropologically, whereas 1 John speaks ontologically and theologically. That difference is important, for in the elder's view God is not jockeying for a place among our everyday affairs, to add something useful to our βίος (*bios*; see 2:15-17). Through Jesus Christ, God is reconfiguring life itself into ζωή αἰώνιος (*zōē aiōnios* (5:20), life that dispels this world's illusions and conforms us with the indestructible reality that is God.

The elder's claims about life in Christ seem strange to us, preposterous really: We who are of God do not sin (5:18*a*, 19*a*); the evil dominating this world does not touch us (5:18*c*, 19*b*). First John is not an exercise in apologetics, which tries to prove such things. Even less is the message diluted, so that more might swallow it. The elder's interest is radically epistemological: to remind the church how it knows what it knows. In 1 John, such knowledge does not have its origin in more effective politics, extended therapy, better education, improved commentary, or anything else whose creation is of this world. To regard such provisional resources as definitive of eternal life is, as the elder knows (5:21) and as Paul Ramsey reminds us, to court idolatry: "absolutizing something finite, and in so doing seeking the interests of self."[176] Knowledge of eternal life issues only from trust in the one who *is* eternal life: the Son of God, Jesus Christ (5:20). Like a new program that reformats a computer's hard drive, *Christ reformats us*—the way we live and think, what we know, and how we know it. Testimony to Christ is offered, whether in the first century or the twenty-first, not with vaporings, lambastings, or longings for a dream come true. The tenor of 1 John is one of serenity under fire, confidence not in ourselves but in the One who gave us birth and will never desert us. Eternal life is where the church really is, because the life and truth that we know are nothing other than what the real and living God is.

---

176. Paul Ramsey, *Basic Christian Ethics* (Chicago: University of Chicago Press, 1950) 299. See Ramsey's acute analysis of "Idolatry: The Work of Self-Love," 295-306.

2 JOHN 1-13

THE SECOND LETTER

OVERVIEW

In the NT only the Third Epistle of John is briefer than the Second, whose Greek text contains 245 words. Either of the two smaller Johannine letters could have been accommodated on a single papyrus sheet of standard size (about 8" x 10". By modern standards, 2 and 3 John are more postcards than letters.

In length and presentation, 2 John exemplifies a common epistolary type in antiquity: the letter of petition, whose primary function was to request something of its addressee.[177] Ancient petitionary epistles adhered to a conventional format:

I. Opening
II. Body
   A. Background for the request
   B. The request itself
   C. How the addressee may benefit from complying
III. Closing

This format is modified in 2 John. Its salutation is more theologically developed. Its opening and closing adopt the language of family letters, another common epistolary type in antiquity. The request in 2 John has positive and negative elements, specifying the benefits of compliance and the liabilities of disregard.

I. Opening (vv. 1-3)
   Saluting the Elect Lady and Her Children
II. Body (vv. 4-11)
   A. Background: *Rejoicing in Truth* (v. 4)
   B. Requests: *Follow Love* (vv. 5-6); *Spurn Deception* (vv. 7-8)
   C. Benefits and Cautions: *Abide in the Teaching (vv. 9-11)*
III. Closing (vv. 12-13)
   Regrets, Hopes, and Greetings

(For further discussion of 2 John's authorship, religious setting, historical context, and major themes, see the Introduction to 1, 2, and 3 John.)

177. For more information, see John L. White, *Light from Ancient Letters*, FFNT (Philadelphia: Fortress, 1986) 194-96.

2 JOHN 1-3, SALUTING THE ELECT LADY AND HER CHILDREN

COMMENTARY

Verse 1. The sender of this note (and, apparently, of 3 John [1]) is "the elder" (ὁ πρεσβύτερος *ho presbyteros*). In texts of the NT era, this noun, inflected in the masculine gender, can refer either to a man of advanced years (Acts 11:30; 14:23; 15:2; 1 Tim 5:1-2) or to a "presbyter," a holder of administrative or juridical power, irrespective of age.[178]

Although the second of these alternatives is not impossible for the author of the Johannine letters,[179] it is unlikely. There is no evidence to suggest that 2 and 3 John were written by a member of a local presbytery; both letters imply an author who is not confined to a formal judicatory within a particular

178. See Ignatius *Eph.* 2.1; 4.1; *Magn.* 2; *Trall.* 2.2; 13.2; *Smyrn.* 8.1.

179. As argued by Karl Paul Donfried, "Ecclesiastical Authority in 2–3 John," in *L'Évangile de Jean: Sources, rédaction, théologie*, ed. M. de Jonge, BETL 44 (Leuven: Leuven University Press, 1977) 325-33.

congregation. Moreover, this elder's influence appears to be largely moral and closely associated with the tradition to which he testifies (2 John 5, 9-10). While he speaks as one with authority to advise (vv. 5, 8, 10-11; 3 John 6*b*, 9*a*, 11-12), even to threaten (3 John 10), there is no indication that he is an officeholder able to enforce his wishes or understanding of the tradition. Probably he was not in that position at this still early stage in Johannine Christianity. In the Fourth Gospel the only recognized teacher is the Paraclete, the Holy Spirit, who bears witness to Jesus (John 14:26; 16:13). First John acknowledges the bestowal of knowledge on the entire congregation, through its anointing by the Spirit (2:20, 27).

What of "the elect lady" (ἡ ἐκλεκτή κυρία *hē eklektē kyria*)? In the Greek texts of the NT, there is no differentiation between upper- and lower-case characters to denote a person's name; so it is not inconceivable that 2 John is addressed to "the chosen Kyria"[180] or even "the Lady Electa."[181] Still, the substance of 2 John, like that of 1 John, is clearly aimed, not at an individual, but at a Christian community apparently meeting in someone's home (see v. 10; cf. Rom 16:5; 1 Cor 16:19; Col 4:15; Phlm 2).[182] This leads most commentators to regard "the lady chosen"—by God or by Christ (John 15:16, 19; cf. Mark 13:20, 22, 27; 1 Pet 2:9; 5:13)—as a literary conceit for a local congregation (ἐκκλησία *ekklēsia*, a noun declined in the feminine gender), similar to the personification of Jerusalem as a woman in various biblical traditions (e.g., Isa 54:1-8; Bar 4:30–5:9; Gal 4:21-31).[183] From this inference it follows that the lady's "children" are members of that church.

Even as most of the primary concerns in Paul's epistles are announced in their salutations and statements of thanksgiving (see, e.g., 1 Cor 1:1-9), the initial comments of 2 John serve as an overture for this letter's themes. Of these the two most prominent are "love" (ἀγάπη *agapē*) and "truth" (ἀλήθεια *alētheia*), which in vv. 1-3 are presented as realities that bind the elder with this church. As in 1 John (3:23; 4:7, 11-12; see also John 13:34; 15:12, 17), the command to love one another is prominent in 2 John (vv. 5-6). Not surprisingly, the letter's salutation expresses love for "the lady and her children" (v. 1) and an assurance that love is the realm in which, along with truth, they all will exist (v. 3). Truth is the distinctive sphere within which the elder's (and others') love for this church is activated (v. 1; see also 3 John 1; John 17:17, 19), the medium through which they all will continue forever (2 John 2; see also John 14:17). More than a reference to the elder's honesty or sincerity, truth is that vital Christian force that empowers all who love (or "know," 2 John 1; see also 1 John 2:3, 13-14, 21; 4:6-7; John 8:32). Life "in the truth" is the elder's equivalent for Paul's understanding of "life in Christ" (e.g., Rom 8:2, 10-11; 9:1; 1 Cor 4:15; 2 Cor 1:21; 12:19; Gal 3:26-28). In 2 John 4 (also 3 John 3-4, 8) a different nuance of truth will be intimated by the elder's concern for enduring instruction, contrasted with the deception of unnamed impostors (2 John 7, 9-10; cf. 1 John 2:21-24).[184]

Verse 2. Closely related to truth's permanence is truth's "abiding" (μένουσαν *menousan*) among the elder and his addressees. Variations of this idea (the dwelling within the believer of God, Christ, God's word, or the Spirit) are found in John (John 5:38; 15:4) and extended in 1 John (2:14, 24, 27; 3:9, 24; 4:12, 15-16). The reciprocal notion, that the believer should dwell in truth (understood as truthful teaching), appears in 2 John 9. The continuance of divine reality with the church "forever" (εἰς τὸν αἰῶνα *eis ton aiōna*) is not developed further in 2 John, though this idea has echoes in the Fourth Gospel (John 4:14; 6:51, 58; 8:51-52; 10:28; 11:26; 14:16) and the First Epistle (1 John 2:17).

Verse 3. As in most NT and early patristic letters, the salutation of 2 John is more theologically elaborate than anything to

---

180. This is how Wesley interprets the wording (*Explanatory Notes Upon the New Testament*, 921).
181. In the Latin version of his *Outlines*, Clement of Alexandria (c. 150–215) suggests that 2 John was addressed to "a Babylonian woman named Electa who signifies the Catholic Church."
182. David C. Verner, *The Household of God: The Social World of the Pastoral Epistles*, SBLDS 71 (Chico, Calif.: Scholars Press, 1983) 27-81, explores the critical position of the household in Hellenistic and Roman society.
183. Brown theorizes that κυρία (*kyria*) may be intended to recognize this congregation's intimacy with "the Lord" (κύριος *kyrios*). That christological title does not occur in our best MSS of the Johannine epistles, though it is used with reference to Jesus more than fifty times in the Gospel of John. See Brown, *The Epistles of John*, 680.

184. While his argument probably outruns the evidence, with good reason R. Bergmeier, "Zum Verfasserproblem des II und III Johannesbriefes," *ZNW* 57 (1966) 93-100, perceives in 2 John a tendency toward doctrinal orthodoxy.

be found in the first century's business correspondence, which typically opens with the "banal Greeting" (Acts 23:26; cf. Acts 15:23; Jas 1:1). While its constituent ideas do not appear elsewhere in 2 John, the elder's assurance—not merely a wish—that "grace, mercy, and peace will be with us" (cf. 3 John 15) recalls benedictions in Revelation (Rev 1:4; 22:21), in Paul's letters (Rom 1:7; 1 Cor 1:3; 2 Cor 1:2; Gal 1:3; 6:16; Phil 1:2; 1 Thess 1:1; Phlm 3J), and in other NT epistles (Eph 1:2; Col 1:2; 2 Thess 1:2 Titus 1:4; 1 Pet 1:2; Jude 2). The elder's particular triad of spiritual gifts occurs elsewhere in the NT only in 1 Tim 1:2 and 2 Tim 1:2. Unlike Paul's letters (e.g., Rom 3:24; 5:15-21; 11:31), the term "grace" (χαρίς *charis*) occurs in the Fourth Gospel infrequently (John 1:14, 16-17); "mercy" (ἔλεος *eleos*) appears nowhere else in Johannine literature but in 2 John 3. "Peace" (εἰρήνη *eirēnē*), however, is an important Johannine term that characterizes eternal life: the life of God, presently and permanently shared by those who believe in Jesus (John 14:27; 16:33; 20:19, 21, 26).

One other aspect of 2 John's salutation is noteworthy: its emphasis on the church as family. Not only the elect lady but also her "children" are addressed (v. 1; see also 1 John 3:1-2; 5:2; 3 John 4); grace, mercy, and peace will be from "God the Father" and Jesus Christ, "the Father's Son" (v. 3; see also 1 John 1:2-3, 7; 2:1, 22-24; 4:14-15; 5:12). The same familial language recurs in 2 John beyond its salutation (vv. 4, 9, 13), cohering with the letter's emphasis on love (vv. 1, 3, 5-6) and its concern that "the home" not be poisoned (v. 10). As in 1 John, the family of believers in 2 John forms the backdrop for indications that some of the children are harshly at odds with one another (2 John 7, 10-11; cf. 1 John 2:18-25; 4:1-6). (See Reflections at 2 John 12-13.)

2 JOHN 4-11, REQUESTS, BENEFITS, AND CAUTIONS

2 John 4, Rejoicing in Truth

COMMENTARY

The confidence of the salutation is maintained by the elder's expression of rejoicing, another term with a Pauline ring (1 Cor 16:7; Phil 4:10; 1 Thess 5:16) that also recalls the character of Christian life as described in the Gospel of John (John 3:29; 14:28; 16:20, 22). "Walking in truth," the cause for that great joy, is an expression not found in John or 1 John, though it is repeated in 3 John 3-4.[185] On its face the idea appears similar to "walking in the light" (1 John 1:7; cf. John 11:9; 12:35), which in 1 John is equivalent to a life imitative of Jesus' love (1 John 2:6). The convergence of these ideas is reinforced by the elder's next comment; "walking in truth" coincides with the comprehensive command that he and the church received from God (v. 4). First John associates that command with faith in Jesus Christ (1 John 3:23) and love for God and one another (1 John 3:23; 4:21; 5:2-3). Intriguingly, the elder has found this way of life exhibited by "some"—by implication, not all—"of your children." Such reserve may suggest his caution of saying no more than he can verify. Alternatively, it may be this letter's first intimation that all is not well among communities within the Johannine circle. (See Reflections at 2 John 12-13.)

185. See also *T. Judah* 24:3.

2 John 5-8, Follow Love and Spurn Deception

COMMENTARY

Verses 5-6. Adopting a rhythm established in the First Epistle, the elder moves from a joyous statement of fact to an exhortation, framed as a request (v. 5). When finally articulated, that appeal seems unexceptional and thoroughly Johannine: that we "love one another" (see John 13:34-35; 15:12, 17; 1 John 3:11, 23; 4:7, 11-12). The construction of this sentence and the next is curiously clumsy, however. Before the encouragement to mutual love is expressed, the elder moves immediately to reassure his readers of its venerable antiquity, using language that practically duplicates his clarification in 1 John 2:7. Thus, while his petition substantiates the church's life in mutual love, the elder's emphasis rests on that prescription's confessional context—namely, the community's original experience of faith (see also 1 John 1:1; 2:13-14, 24; 3:11).

This accent persists in v. 6, which exemplifies the elder's tendency to link thoughts in a circular chain. From "truth and love" (v. 3), the connection between "truth" and "commandment" has been forged (v. 4), followed by the identification of the "commandment" with "love" (v. 5; see also 1 John 2:3-5a; 3:11-18). With the completion of one conceptual loop, another immediately opens and closes; "love" is defined as walking in God's commandments, and the command is that you "walk in it" (cf. John 14:15, 23-24). This translation (KJV, NRSV) captures the ambiguity of the Greek; it is unclear whether the church is commanded to walk in love (NIV, RSV), which inverts the ideas in v. 6a, or whether the church is commanded to walk in the commandment (Phillips, NAB), which is utterly tautologous! One aspect of vv. 4-6 becomes clearer when compared with 1 John. The latter usually defines "love" theologically and christologically, with reference to God's sending of the Son (1 John 4:10), who laid down his life for us (1 John 3:16). Second John describes love ecclesiologically, as the church's obedience to God's commands (v. 6), which is tantamount to "walking in truth" (v. 4). These approaches to love are not miles apart; 1 John also interprets love as the performance of God's orders (1 John 3:23; 5:3), and 2 John is definitely interested in Jesus Christ (vv. 7-9). It is a subtle difference in emphasis. In 2 John the language of love is used for the purpose of clarifying what it means to walk in truth, as God has commanded and as the church has heard "from the beginning."[186] (See Reflections at 2 John 12-13.)

Verses 7-8. Beginning in v. 7, the rupture of love and a threat to truth become evident. Here the fog enshrouding much of 2 John begins to lift, and the elder permits us to discern some of the real-life problems lending urgency to this letter. The terminology of v. 7 is instantly recognizable from 1 John:

2 John 7	1 John
Many deceivers (πολλοὶ πλάνοι *polloi planoi*)/the deceiver (ὁ πλάνος *ho planos*)	Those misleaders (τῶν πλανώντων *tōn planōntōn*, 2:26; cf. 1:8; 3:7; 4:6), [who are] many (2:18),
the antichrist,	the antichrist (2:22; also 2:18; 4:3),
went out	went out (2:19; also 4:1)
into the world,	into the world (4:1, 3; cf. 5:19),
those who do not confess	the one who does not confess (4:3; also 2:23; 4:2, 15)
Jesus Christ,	Jesus Christ (4:2; also 2:23; 4:3, 14)
coming (= has come)[187] in flesh.	having come in flesh (4:2).

186. Urban C. von Wahlde, "The Theological Foundation of the Presbyter's Argument in 2 Jn (2 Jn 4-6)," *ZNW* 76 (1985) 209-24, arrives at a similar conclusion along a different exegetical route.

187. Reviving a venerable interpretation in the history of 2 John's exegesis, some commentators think that this participle carries a future connotation: the expectation of Jesus' second coming in flesh. See Strecker, *The Johannine Letters*, 233-36; Charles H. Talbert, *Reading John: A Literary and Theological Commentary on the Fourth Gospel and the Johannine Epistles*, Reading the New Testament (New York: Crossroad, 1992) 10-11. Most interpreters, however, regard the position challenged by 2 John 7 as similar to that underlying 1 John 4:2: a depreciation of Jesus' humanity during his first advent. The present tense of the participle of 2 John 7 may be considered another example of the convergence of multiple temporal perspectives on Jesus in Johannine theology (see John 3:31; 6:14; 11:27). See Smith, *The Theology of the Gospel of John*, 101-3.

Second John 7 consolidates salient aspects of 1 John 2:15-25 and 4:1-6. A schism has erupted, turning on some unclarified issue involving the incarnation of Jesus Christ; the secessionists have defected into "the world," the realm of hostile delusion that rejects "the truth." (See the Commentary on those passages, as well as the Introduction, "The Adversaries Behind 1, 2, and 3 John.") Significantly present in the First Epistle, but absent from the Second, is a specification of the church from which the deceivers exited: "They went out *from us*" (1 John 2:19 NRSV, italics added). Although the elder may reserve judgment on how uniformly the church addressed by 2 John has cleaved to the truth (v. 4), it is not clear that 2 John's "elect lady" has experienced the schism that 1 John implies. The elder's comments in the Second Epistle suggest that he is trying to head off another breakdown before it happens (vv. 8, 10).

In this light, what course of action does the elder recommend? First, "Continue to stay on your guard, lest you lose [or wipe out] the things that we worked for, but rather that you may receive full compensation" (v. 8, author's trans.). The textual transmission of this verse is marred by pronoun problems, which account for its varied translations in different English versions. Along with the alternative proposed here and in the NRSV (thus also NEB, REB, NAB, GNB), v. 8 was copied by scribes as "that you do not lose what *you* have worked for, but that you may be rewarded fully" (NIV, RSV, Moffatt) and "that *we* lose not those things which we have wrought, but that *we* receive a full reward" (KJV). Though weakly attested in the manuscript tradition, the reading favored by the NRSV is the most difficult and, therefore, the most likely to have been reworded into one of the others.

Clear enough, the sense of this admonition in v. 8 may be filled out by John 6:29, where "the work of God" is "that you believe in him [Jesus] whom [God] has sent" (NRSV). In 2 John 8, the elder implies that he and others "who know the truth" (v. 1) have played a formative role in the development of these children's faith (similarly, see 1 John 1:1-4; cf. Gal 4:11). Still, mediators of the Johannine tradition do not constitute a magisterium, or teaching authority, to which the elect lady and her children are accountable. Rather, those in that church should keep on looking *to themselves* (an imperative in the ongoing present tense). This advice is consistent with that offered in 1 John 2:20-22, 26-27, which reminds another community that their anointing by the Holy One has bestowed on them all knowledge and resources necessary for them to "abide in him." That persistence may not be presumed upon, however, as though its fulfillment were a foregone conclusion. What was wrought by the elder within the church can be lost; that congregation's present reward may not be completely "paid out." This idea, which holds in tension the church's present election with its future reckoning by God, corresponds with 1 John 3:2 and is found throughout the NT (e.g., Matt 25:31-46; 1 Cor 3:14-15). (See Reflections at 2 John 12-13.)

2 John 9-11, Abide in the Teaching

COMMENTARY

Verse 9. The elder's second recommendation is almost an aphorism, barbed with tacit exhortation (cf. John 8:31). Once again, we hear echoes of 1 John. "Abiding" is, of course, the primary way in which the First Epistle expresses the enduring, reciprocal relationship that exists between the believer and God or Christ (1 John 2:24; 3:24; 4:15-16). "Having life" depends on "having the Son of God" (1 John 5:12), which is equivalent to believing in God (1 John 5:10). The one who confesses the Son also "has" God (1 John 2:23*a*).

To these ideas v. 9 adds some new ones. Appearing for the first and only time in the Johannine literature is the word ὁ προάγων (*ho proagōn*), "one who goes ahead" (RSV), "a progressive" (NAB) without proper restraint. Such a one is negatively contrasted with "the one who abides" (ὁ μένων *ho menōn*). Although the elder does not pinpoint the belief of those who are inappropriately advanced, the context suggests a refusal to confess Jesus' coming in flesh (v. 7).

Another fresh contribution to these considerations is 2 John's triple reference to "the teaching [διδαχή *didachē*] of Christ," in which the one who "has" or "holds on to" God or Jesus should abide (vv. 9-10). Although the elder may mean by this phrase "Christ's own teaching" (thus Phillips, JBP; cf. John 7:16-17; 18:19), "the teaching about Christ"—namely, his coming in flesh—probably captures the elder's primary intention. More so than modern interpreters, however, the elder would probably have equated, not distinguished, the church's proclamation about Jesus with Jesus' own (see 1 John 1:1-4). It is also debatable how heavily the elder would weight the term *didachē*—whether it is best translated here as "teaching" (NIV, NRSV, REB, GNB), roughly synonymous with "the instructional anointing" that dwells in believers (1 John 2:27), or as "doctrine" (KJV, Moffatt, RSV, NEB) with a recognized, corrective authority among some Johannine churches. The context of 2 John suggests that the elder intends, or at least hopes for, the latter (cf. Jude 3, "the faith that was once for all entrusted to the saints" [NRSV]).

Verses 10-11. The elder's final counsel is to refuse hospitality or even greeting to anyone who comes not bearing this teaching (διδαχή *didachē*). The Greek wording suggests that the possibility of such an "invasion" is more than hypothetical. If accepted, the elder's prescription would have had serious consequences at the time of 2 John's composition. Travel was much more hazardous then than it is now; travelers, including missionaries, were dependent on the kindness of friends and strangers (see Matt 25:35; Heb 13:2; 1 Pet 4:9; see also the Commentary on 3 John 5-8). Early Christians were directed to receive one another as they would receive Jesus or God, who sent Jesus (Matt 10:40; Mark 9:37). Accordingly, Paul, an itinerant apostle, commended the extension of hospitality to strangers and hinted that he would welcome such support for himself (Rom 12:13; 15:23-24). Hospitality is one of the attributes specified by the Pastoral Epistles for a "bishop," or overseer (1 Tim 3:2; Titus 1:8-9). Interestingly, the Pastorals couple that qualification with apt teaching or the ability to foster wholesome instruction. By urging the refusal of hospitality to such "progressives," the author of 2 John apparently hoped to prevent the spread of aberrant teaching and the contamination of Christian fellowship (κοινωνία *koinōnia*; cf. 1 Tim 5:22; 1 John 1:3, 6-7) with "wicked works" (τοῖς ἔργοις τοῖς πονηροῖς *tois ergois tois ponērois*; cf. 1 John 3:12). Similar concerns motivate directions by Paul (Rom 16:17) and writers in the Pauline tradition (Eph 5:11; 2 Thess 3:6, 14-15; Titus 3:10-11). The elder's recommendation for dealing with spurious teaching by itinerants is even more precisely paralleled in the letters of Ignatius of Antioch (d. c. 100)[188] and in the *Didache*,[189] an important manual of church discipline that may have been contemporaneous with 2 John. While the elder writes as though he expected his advice to be taken, there is no indication of his ability to enforce it. (See Reflections at 2 John 12-13.)

188. Ignatius *Eph.* 7.1; 8.1; 9.1; *Smyrn.* 4.1; 5.1; 7.2
189. *Did.* 11.1–12.5.

2 JOHN 12-13, REGRETS, HOPES, AND GREETINGS

COMMENTARY

The epistle closes conventionally, with Johannine embellishments. Typical in letters of this period are acknowledgments of the inadequacy of paper (actually, papyrus) and ink to convey an author's message and the superiority of a personal visit in which one can talk face to face (lit., "mouth to mouth"; see also Num 12:8; 3 John 13-14). Although customary, the elder's remarks are not necessarily *pro forma*. The hope attached to a real visit with this church—"that our joy may be fulfilled"—closes a ring opened by the elder's earlier expression of joy (v. 4). Verse 12 also recalls the conclusion of 1 John's prologue (1 John 1:4) as well as Jesus' express intention, in the Farewell Discourses, that his disciples' joy be fulfilled (John 15:11; 16:24; 17:13). The relay of greetings from "the children of your elect sister" (cf. 1 Pet 5:13) nicely complements the metaphor with which 2 John opened (v. 1), again emphasizing the family feeling that exists for the author with his "cousins" (vv. 1, 3-5) and contrasts with greetings that are not to be offered to those who go beyond "the teaching of Christ" (vv. 9-11).

REFLECTIONS

Second John is one of the usually neglected stepchildren in biblical interpretation. It occupies no place in the *Revised Common Lectionary*; one imagines a congregation going for years without ever hearing a lesson or a sermon on it. Among biblical scholars, 2 John is often regarded as slight and derivative. In fairness to pastors and professional exegetes, it must be said that the Second Epistle of John is scant and does reiterate themes more extensively considered in 1 John, itself hardly the church's most overworked scripture. (Reflections on the following topics in 2 John may be found in the ancillary treatment of 1 John: intramural love [see Reflections on 1 John 2:7-11], "the world" [1 John 2:15-17], Christian confidence [1 John 2:18-25], obedience and reassurance [1 John 3:19-24], the identity of Jesus Christ and Christian identity [1 John 4:1-6 and 5:1-5], and Christian love [1 John 4:7-21].)

More's the pity that the church so little exercises its intellectual muscles with 2 John. For the sheer challenge of serious theological conversation, few texts of its size will repay a congregation greater dividends. Curiously enough, the clue to its value in this respect may be found in many commentaries. While the First Epistle predictably and rightly elicits more painstaking examination than does the Second, no segment of 1 John has drawn more pained evaluation among interpreters than has 2 John, particularly its notorious prescription of Christian shunning (vv. 7-11). If ever a scriptural passage exposed the assumptions and commitments of its interpreters, surely 2 John 7-11 is such a text. Impressed by its exclusionist tendency, one commentator concludes that the fact that 2 John "found a way to acceptance by the wider church within its canon of Scripture remains one of those enigmatic ironies which must continue to stretch the imagination of both historian and theologian."[190] Simpler and sharper is the view of another scholar: "This passage . . . has, on any showing, an ugly look," and on closer inspection "it is even more drastic and unfortunate."[191] And this from another interpreter: "Perhaps the unique feature of this letter is best left unheeded. . . . There is a sufficiency of bigotry and intolerance about, so that we do not need the Second Epistle to encourage it."[192] Let the record show that these are the evaluations of some of this text's friendliest, most perceptive exegetes! If *they* find themselves stretched by this letter, then surely we fail the church of our day by not arranging at least an occasional interview between it and 2 John. If, after our exegesis of this letter, we determine its message so repugnant that we refuse to engage it, then we shall be practicing the very intolerance of which the elder stands accused.

Critical for our understanding of this text is its historical location. The impression that 2 John 7-11 counsels a provincial, seemingly unchristian response is based not only on modern sensibilities of civility and liberality, but also on the church's remembrance that Jesus preached kindness toward sinners (Matt 5:43-48; Luke 6:27-36) and

---
190. Lieu, *The Second and Third Epistles of John*, 165. In context, Lieu's assessment also includes 3 John.
191. Houlden, *A Commentary on the Johannine Epistles*, 146.
192. Smith, *First, Second, and Third John*, 146-47. Smith does not, however, allow this pejorative assessment to stand without qualification.

himself fraternized with society's despised (Matt 9:10-13 and par.). Yet we tend to forget that the early church, like other religious communities in antiquity, did practice exclusion under certain conditions. By putative order of Jesus, a house that proved unworthy of his missionaries was to be firmly rejected (Matt 10:11-15). Recalcitrant offenders within the church, whose sins tore the community apart, were to be excommunicated (Matt 18:15-17; 1 Cor 5:1-13; Titus 3:10-11). Sometimes the door should be opened; sometimes it should be shut (Matt 18:18; John 20:23; 2 Thess 3:14-15). Such decisions were not to be made capriciously or based on idiosyncratic taste; the nature of the offense, especially if committed by a fellow Christian, was to be carefully assessed and weighed against the maintenance of the church's integrity in Christ. Negatively, these principles were translated into an intolerance for self-styled apostles who, upon testing, were found to be practicing evil within the Christian community (see Rev 2:2). Underlying the welcome of someone as though he or she were Christ is the express assumption that the visitor is really a disciple, righteous as Jesus is righteous (Matt 10:40-42) and genuinely delegated by Christ (John 13:20).

We should read 2 John within this context. Admittedly, we are hampered by how little we know of the facts prompting the elder's comments. Moreover, we have only his view of things. Whether those against whom the elder inveighs would have recognized themselves in his description of them remains a good question to ponder. If, however, we give its author the benefit of the doubt, at least some matters in this letter are clear and still pertinent to the church in our day.

1. In 2 John we have what the elder reckons to be a pervasive emergency touching on the fundamental confession of the Johannine church: the coming of Jesus Christ in the flesh (v. 7), on which depends the Christian's relationship with God (v. 9). To acknowledge this at once limits and enhances the relevance of this text in another era. The crisis addressed by 2 John was apparently precipitated by habitual propagandists whose spurious claims about Christ were mangling one Johannine congregation after another. Although we are not able to verify the elder's reading of the situation, we can understand why "the elect lady," portrayed here as a protective mother, would be counseled to slam the door on such incursions. What pastor, charged to exercise supervision of the people committed to his or her care, would deliberately invite into the pulpit someone bent on undermining their faith?

A predicament of such magnitude, however, does not happen every day. Presupposed in the elder's comments are not those disagreements—some quibbling, others serious—that perennially arise among well-intentioned, faithful Christians. To the give-and-take of ordinary, though painful, conflict within a church still maturing, 2 John is not directed and may not be responsibly applied. It is true, as Raymond Brown observes, "that almost every dispute in church history has been judged by one of the parties as involving an essential question, and that almost every drastic action has been justified as done for the sake of the truth."[193] The fact that Christians remain susceptible to such self-delusion and smallness of heart reminds us of our continual need for repentance, discernment, and wisdom (see 1 John 4:1-6). It does not absolve the church of the responsibility of distinguishing those matters that strike at the root of Christian faith from the thousand other concerns, however deeply felt, that do not.

2. In the elder's estimate, the thing that has been put at risk is the identity of Jesus Christ, apart from whom the Christian cannot know the truth about God (see 2 John 1-3). Most Christians today would agree that this really is a matter of primary concern. As in 1 John 4:1-6, the theological controversy addressed by 2 John 7 turns in some way on the incarnation of Christ. Apparently the elder would have shared Luther's view of Jesus: "I begin with the swaddling clothes and accept the one who came, and

---

193. Brown, *The Epistles of John*, 693.

seek for the one that is in heaven; but I haven't got a ladder to climb up to heaven!"[194] That ladder, in the Johannine tradition, is none other than Jesus (John 1:51), the Word who became flesh and dwelt among us (John 1:14). Evidently this consideration has not gone cold for Christians living under modernity's pressures, as suggested by the fact that a quest for the Jesus of history has been renewed every forty or fifty years over the past two centuries. Whenever the acknowledgment of Christ's humanity is eclipsed by the confession of his exalted glory, the church risks substituting in place of Jesus someone or something else as the Messiah. One could argue, for example, that the loss of a meaningful confession of "Jesus, come in the flesh" among many Christians in the 1930s abetted the seduction of German Protestantism by Hitler's National Socialism. To this emergency, less remote for us than the one faced by the author of 2 John, Martin Niemöller and Karl Barth responded with another "exclusionary" testimony: the Barmen Declaration (1934), which asserted the loyalty of the German Confessing Church to the lordship of Jesus and not of the Nazi state.

> Jesus Christ, as he is testified to us in the Holy Scripture, is the one Word of God, whom we are to hear, whom we are to trust and obey in life and in death. . . . We repudiate the false teaching that the church can turn over the form of her message and ordinances at will or according to some dominant ideological and political convictions.[195]

3. The most problematic and least accessible aspect of the elder's advice may not be its defense under attack, but its defensiveness. This stance is partly attributable to a religious outlook, known to us also from Paul's letters, that feared contamination by demonic spirits (cf. 2 John 11 with 1 Cor 10:14-22). Such an assumption is aggravated by John's generally dualistic view, inclined to regard the world, even though under Christ's restorative conquest, as an evil and perilous place (John 15:18; 16:33; 17:14; 1 John 2:2; 3:13; 5:4-5). The fear that seems to animate 2 John 10-11 is that error, if given but a foothold, will drive out truth. That is a questionable assumption, assent to which is likely, in the long run, to retard truth's advance. Even if we do not accept it as our own, we can nonetheless understand the elder's alarm for an infant church, which did not enjoy the many religious and theological support systems that modern congregations take for granted—among others, a New Testament, the church's creeds and liturgy, judicatory guidelines, and professionally trained gatekeepers.

4. Finally, has the author of 2 John "incautiously expressed himself in terms which might seem to stigmatize any kind of 'advance' as disloyalty to the faith, and to condemn Christian theology to lasting sterility"?[196] Such an assessment overstates the case. The elder does *not* fault as faithless "any kind of advance." The risk of losing God is incurred, rather, by "anyone who is so 'progressive' that he does not remain rooted in the teaching of Christ" (v. 9).[197] An automobile must have *both* a driving gear to propel it *and* a steering wheel to keep it on the road. The chemist in research and development makes new discoveries that enlarge our understanding—but not by ignoring or pretending to reinvent the periodic table of elements. So, too, for the church. It is always a question of balancing theology (the exploratory reach of Christian self-criticism) with doctrine (the consensus grasp of the church's self-understanding).[198]

---

194. Martin Luther, *Weimarer Ausgabe: D. Martin Luthers Werke* 20 (1883–) 727.7-8, cited in Christof Windhorst, "Luther and the 'Enthusiasts': Theological Judgements in His Lecture on the First Epistle of John (1527)," *JRH* 9 (1977) 399-48 (here, 346).

195. For the complete text of the Barmen Declaration, see *Creeds of the Churches: A Reader in Christian Doctriune from the Bible to the Present*, ed. John H. Leith, 3rd ed. (Atlanta: John Knox, 1982) 517-22.

196. Dodd, *The Johannine Epistles*, 150. Dodd is among many commentators to be troubled by this possibility; his articulation of their uneasiness may be the clearest.

197. Translated by Brown, *The Epistles of John*, 645.

198. Thomas A. Langford, "Doctrinal Affirmation and Theological Exploration," in *Doctrine and Theology in The United Methodist Church*, ed. Thomas A. Langford (Nashville: Kingswood, 1991) 203-7.

Without theology, tradition, "the living faith of the dead," would calcify into traditionalism, "the dead faith of the living."[199] The elder emphasizes something else: Christians would be unable to move forward without a tradition to remind them of who they are, whose they are, and where they have been.

---

199. Jaroslav Pelikan, *The Vindication of Tradition* (New Haven, Conn.: Yale University Press, 1984) 65.

3 JOHN 1-15

THE THIRD LETTER

OVERVIEW

With only 219 words in its Greek text, the Third Epistle of John is the shortest document in the NT. Like the Second Epistle, 3 John corresponds closely, in conventional length and presentation, to an ancient private letter. Whereas 2 John appears to be a letter of petition, 3 John exemplifies another type of epistle in antiquity: the letter of introduction and recommendation. Such a communication was intended to acquaint the addressee with a creditable friend of the sender, even as letters of reference are used today in business or educational settings. Paul refers to this kind of letter in 2 Cor 3:1-3; recommendations of colleagues appear in his and other epistles in the NT (Rom 16:1-2; 1 Cor 16:3; Col 4:7-8; see also Acts 18:27).

Ancient letters of recommendation adhered to a standard format:

I. Opening
II. Body
   A. Identification of the one recommended
   B. The sender's recommendation
   C. Acknowledgment of the addressee's favor and the sender's promise to repay
III. Closing

Third John deviates slightly from this convention. Its opening and closing are heavily personalized and theologically elaborated. The body of 3 John has been modified in two ways: by withholding the identification and recommendation until near the end and by expanding, qualifying, and theologically formulating the recommendation's rationale, which has been moved to the first position:

I. Opening (vv. 1-4)
   A. *Saluting Gaius* (v. 1)
   B. *Praying for Health, Rejoicing in Truth* (vv. 2-4)
II. Body (vv. 5-12)
   A. *Supporting God's Missionaries* (vv. 5-8)
   B. *Condemning Diotrephes* (vv. 9-10)
   C. *Commending Demetrius* (vv. 11-12)
III. Closing (vv. 13-15)
   Regrets, Hopes, and Greetings

(For further discussion of 3 John's authorship, religious setting, historical context, and major themes, see the Introduction to 1, 2, and 3 John.)

3 JOHN 1-4, SALUTATION, PRAYER, REJOICING

3 John 1, Saluting Gaius

COMMENTARY

Third John opens like a Hellenistic personal letter, while differing in some obvious ways. First, its sender does not identify himself beyond the ascription, ὁ πρεσβύτερος (*ho presbyteros*), "the elder." This re-creates the interpretive problem in 2 John 1: whether the author (presumably the same as that of the First and Second Epistles) is a church official (a presbyter) or simply a figure of venerable age. Assumed throughout the letter (vv. 4, 9-10, 12b) is an authority that is evidently informal and unofficial, since the author's appeals rest on little more than theological and moral suasion. Particularly at 3 John's beginning and end, the elder speaks in the first-person singular (vv. 1-4, 9-10a, 13-14). In the epistle's central section he purportedly represents the point of view of others (see v. 7), who are referred to as "the brothers" (vv. 5, 10b), "the friends" (v. 15b), "the church" (v. 6), "such people" (v. 8), "all" (v. 12a), and at times simply "we" or "us" (vv. 9b, 10a, 12b).

We cannot establish the identity of the letter's recipient, since "Gaius" was a very common name in antiquity (see Acts 19:29; 20:4; Rom 16:23; 1 Cor 1:14). An associate of the elder, possibly one of his converts, Gaius appears to be affiliated with another Christian community within the Johannine circle, perhaps in the same or a neighboring locality. Matters of concern are addressed not only to Gaius (vv. 1-3, 5-7, 11, 12b-15), but also to "the children" (v. 4), "the church" (vv. 9, 10b), and "the friends" (v. 15c; see also John 15:13, 15). In this respect 3 John resembles Paul's letter to Philemon, which is further addressed "to the church in your house" (Phlm 2 NRSV). If they held prominent positions in households where Christians met, at a time before the construction of buildings for Christian religious activities, then Gaius and the elder would likely have exercised influence on and responsibility for the believers in their care.[200]

Third John's salutation is further distinguished from secular letters of the period by its overtly theological formulation. Gaius is "the beloved," whom the elder "loves in truth." Duplicating the elder's greeting of "the elect lady" in 2 John 1-2, this expression evokes the Johannine stress on love (ἀγάπη *agapē*) and truth (ἀλήθεια *alētheia*), which define the sphere of Christian existence (see John 17:17-19, 23-26; 21:15-16; 1 John 3:18-19; 4:7-21; 2 John 2-6). Brief though it is, 3 John will return to the topics of love (vv. 2, 5-6, 11) and truth (vv. 3-4, 8, 12). Just as "walking in the light" means the same as "walking as [Jesus] walked" in 1 John 1:7; 2:6, so also "truth" may be 3 John's oblique way of referring to life in Christ, who curiously goes unmentioned in this letter.

200. See Edwin Arthur Judge, *The Social Pattern of Christian Groups in the First Century: Some Prolegomena to the Study of New Testament Ideas of Social Obligation* (London: Tyndale, 1960).

3 John 2-4, Praying for Health, Rejoicing in Truth

COMMENTARY

Verse 2. In place of 2 John's benedictory hope for "grace, mercy, and peace" (2 John 3 NRSV) is 3 John's more conventional wish that its recipient is enjoying good health. That wish is couched as a prayer (cf. Acts 26:29; 27:29; Rom 9:3; 2 Cor 13:7, 9; Jas 5:16). The elder's prayer, or wish,[201] is that Gaius's soul may be proceeding as well and as soundly as Gaius is in all other respects. While "soul" (ψυχή *psychē*) can mean essentially the same thing as "life," neutrally understood (see 1 John 3:16), here the elder may be subtly differentiating the complementary physical and spiritual dimensions of Gaius's life (cf. Matt 10:28; John 12:27) in order to express the hope that each will be as whole and healthy as the other.

Verses 3-4. The elder adopts the familiar phraseology of 1 and 2 John in these verses. "To be overjoyed" that the "children are walking in the truth," or living out their Christian calling, repeats 2 John 4a almost verbatim. Both there and here great rejoicing accompanies an experience characteristic of eternal life (John 3:29; 15:11; 16:20-22, 24; 17:13; 1 John 1:4); "truthful walking" refers to the integrity of the believer's conduct (John 8:12; 11:9-10; 12:35; 21:18; 1 John 1:6-7, 2:6, 11). Also renewed in these verses is the elder's use of the family as a metaphor for the church: "some brothers" (see 1 John 2:9-11;

201. "I pray" acquires in some texts of this era a weaker, more secularized connotation. See Henrich Greeven, "εὔχομαι," *TDNT* 2 (1964) 775-808.

3:10-17; 4:20-21; 5:16) and "my children" (cf. 1 John 3:1-2, 10; 5:2; 2 John 1, 4, 13). "My children" appears to be the elder's affectionate expression for acquaintances who are younger than he.

While the reference to Gaius (and by implication the Christians in his home) as "my children" could imply that the elder founded that church (cf. 1 Cor 4:14; 2 Cor 6:13; 1 Thess 2:7, 11; Phlm 10), the author of 3 John never confirms, much less exploits, such a relationship. This is significant, when viewed in the context of the Roman institution of *patria potestas*—the legal system in which the father exercised full household dominion, with exclusive title to the family's property and ultimate power to discipline, to penalize, and to dispose of his wife and children. In the Johannine epistles the elder's approach stands in the sharpest possible contrast; no one exercises patriarchal dominion over an essentially egalitarian Johannine community (1 John 2:20, 26-27), whose only Father is God (1 John 1:2-3; 2:1, 13-16, 22-24; 3:1; 4:14; 2 John 3-4, 9; see also John 15:1-17).

Though absent from 2 John, the importance of "testimony" (μαρτύριον *martyrion*) is highlighted in 3 John 3 (see also vv. 6, 12; 1 John 1:2; 4:14; 5:6-7, 9-11). Obviously significant in Johannine vocabulary,[202] "testimony" acquires in this letter a distinctive nuance. In John (e.g., John 1:7-8, 15, 19, 32-34), 1 John 5:7-11, and Revelation (e.g., Rev 1:2, 9), witness typically has Christ as its object. In 3 John, testimony is ecclesiologically oriented; it is offered for a church (v. 3) or for individual Christians (vv. 6, 12) with regard to their truth or love. Witness that will be offered on behalf of Demetrius (v. 12) is mirrored here by the testimony of fellow Christians to Gaius's fidelity "to the truth" (v. 3). In these ways, 3 John exemplifies the ancient custom of public testimonials to a benefactor.[203] The elder's reference to associates who have repeatedly come bearing this kind of testimony touches on another of the letter's recurrent themes: the mobility of early Christians, characteristic of the Roman world in which they lived. There is, as Houlden notes, "an abundance of coming and going between the Johannine congregations."[204] In these verses we see one advantage of that mobility: the mutual encouragement of the elder and Gaius, prominent members of loosely affiliated congregations within a region (see also Acts 14:24-28; 2 John 12-13). (See Reflections at 3 John 13-15.)

---

202. The verb and its cognates occur 47 times in John, 18 times in Revelation.

203. Frederick W. Danker, *Benefactor: Epigraphic Study of a Graeco-Roman and New Testament Semantic Field* (St. Louis, Mo.: Clayton, 1982) esp. 442-47.

204. Houlden, *A Commentary on the Johannine Epistles*, 152. Inflected in the present tense, the two participles in 3 John 3, ἐρχομένων (*erchomenōn*, "coming") and μαρτυρούντων (*martyrountōn*, "testifying"), imply more than one visit.

3 JOHN 5-12, THE ELDER'S RECOMMENDATIONS

3 John 5-8, Supporting God's Missionaries

COMMENTARY

Verses 5-6. Taking up a topic that was briefly, and ominously, treated in 2 John 9-11, 3 John sketches a theological understanding of hospitality among Johannine congregations.[205] How should Christian missionaries and their hosts be regarded? Two principles inform the elder's remarks. First, whatever work is done for siblings in the faith is an expression of love by their benefactors, who are themselves beloved (see also John 13:34-35; 15:9-17; 1 John 3:11-24; 4:7-21). Second, there is no distinction between loving work done for a fellow Christian and the activity of faith: "whatever work you perform for the brothers, you do faithfully

---

205. John Koenig, *New Testament Hospitality: Partnership with Strangers in Promise and Mission*, OBT (Philadelphia: Fortress, 1985), provides a good general survey.

[πιστόν *piston*]" (author's trans.). The seeming contradiction between the views of the elder and those of Paul may be attributed to the different theological frameworks within which each understood "works." Johannine theology considers belief in Christ to be a "work" of God (John 6:29). In principle, Paul would not dispute this point, because he viewed faith as a response to God's prior act for human salvation through Jesus Christ (Rom 10:17; see also Rom 1:5; 1 Cor 12:9; Phil 1:6). Often, however, when Paul speaks of "works" he is distinguishing "works of the law"—human religious performance, by which no one may be justified to God—from grace: God's unmotivated goodness, which cannot be earned but can only be trusted (Rom 6:14; 11:5-6; Gal 2:16-21, 3:2-5). The distance between Paul and the Johannine elder may seem to be greater than it really is; in both Gal 5:6 and 3 John 5 love is the means by which faith is activated.

The beneficiaries of this faithful work in 3 John are itinerant Christians, "brothers—strangers as they are" (author's trans.). They may have been emissaries from other congregations, perhaps including the elder's own. Although they could claim no social status within their hosts' tightly knit households, in the elder's view they should be accepted as extended members of one Christian family (see also Matt 10:40-42; Acts 21:15-16; 28:7; Rom 12:13; Phlm 22; Heb 13:2; 1 Pet 4:8-10). Doing well by such strangers entails financial aid: "to send them on their way [προπέμψας *propempsas*]" connotes, not merely a polite farewell, but assistance in bearing their travel expenses (see also Acts 15:3; 20:38; 21:5; Rom 15:24; 1 Cor 16:6, 11*b;* 2 Cor 1:16; Titus 3:13-14).

Verse 7. On what basis do *strangers* receive such help? "They set out for the sake of the name" (author's trans.), presumably, the name of Jesus Christ (see Acts 4:17; 5:41; Rom 1:5; Phil 2:9-10; 1 Pet 4:14-16; 1 John 3:23; 5:13), though God was just mentioned in v. 6. Either way, this activity entitles these strangers to generous support, "in a manner worthy of God" (v. 6; cf. 1 Thess 2:12). That these missionaries received nothing from "the Gentiles" is probably not the ethnic slur that at first it may appear. (Given their names, Gaius [v. 9], and Demetrius [v. 12] would likely have been Gentiles.) Rather, these approved missionaries have refused any external assistance that might compromise the integrity of the gospel entrusted to them (cf. 1 Cor 9:1-27). Accordingly, their message is free from pollution by pagans or nonbelievers (cf. Matt 5:47; 6:7; 18:17; Gal 2:14). Such views, which for modern readers may seem standoffish, should be located within their historical context. As Abraham J. Malherbe observes, "When they spoke of 'outsiders,' early Christians revealed their minority group mind-set. They believed that they had been called to a higher quality of life than could be expected of their society, and they took measures to safeguard it through their communities."[206]

Verse 8. The conclusion naturally follows that it is *our* duty to undergird such people. Significantly, hospitality and financial aid are not offered in order that we may install ourselves in a position of leverage over those who, by our benefactions, have been made beholden to us. Such was the typical "patron-client" mentality of the ancient world.[207] To the contrary, the real benefit accrues to the hosts, "that we may become co-workers with the truth" (NRSV) or "that we may work together for the [cause of] truth" (NIV; cf. JBP; GNB). In addition, hospitality stimulates its recipients to bear witness, before another Christian assembly (ἐκκλησία *ekklēsia*), to the benefactors' love (v. 6). Wherever such hospitality is practiced, a binding of congregations occurs, a synergism of assistance. Appearing only here in the Johannine literature, συνεργός (*synergos*, "fellow-worker") is one of Paul's favorite epithets for his colleagues in faith (Rom 16:3, 9, 21; 1 Cor 3:9; 2 Cor 8:23; Phil 2:25; 4:3; 1 Thess 3:2; Phlm 1, 24). (See Reflections at 3 John 13-15.)

---

206. Abraham J. Malherbe, *Social Aspects of Early Christianity,* 2nd ed. (Philadelphia: Fortress, 1983) 69.

207. For a full discussion of the subject, see Richard P. Saller, *Imperial Patronage Under the Early Empire* (Cambridge: Cambridge University Press, 1982).

3 John 9-10, Condemning Diotrephes

COMMENTARY

In this section we encounter 3 John's burn and bite. The elder begins mysteriously: "I have written something to the church."[208] For those overhearing it centuries later, this comment clarifies nothing about what he wrote or the church that he addressed. The elder might be referring to what we know as 1 or 2 John; their content, however, does not obviously jibe with his comments here. The church alluded to in v. 9 may be the very one addressed by 3 John. But if Gaius were a member of that assembly, why would he need briefing on the matters recounted in vv. 9-10? Alternatively, let us imagine a network of Johannine churches: The elder may be updating Gaius, who lives in a community neighboring the elder's, on happenings in a third congregation, of which Diotrephes is a part. A reasonable hypothesis—and as sturdy as a house of cards. The exact circumstances, from here to the letter's end, are opaque.

Against Diotrephes, the elder registers five complaints. (1) Diotrephes is "the lover of preeminence" within a particular church. (2) Diotrephes does not "receive" or "accept" us, the elder and his sympathizers. (The NRSV translation, "[he] does not acknowledge our authority," depends not on the Greek wording but on a particular exegetical assessment of the overall situation.) (3) If the elder comes to Gaius's church, he aims to bring to mind what Diotrephes is doing—namely, "spreading evil nonsense about us" (NAB). This rendering captures the sense of the Greek—which indicates a misrepresentation of the elder by Diotrephes that is false, malicious, and slanderous—without importing a more vivid characterization than we can verify, whether "gossiping" (NIV) or "lay[ing] baseless and spiteful charges" (NEB). Thus, in contrast with Gaius's faithful works (v. 5), Diotrephes is accused by the elder of works and words that are evil (πονηρός *ponēros*; see also 1 John 2:13-14; 3:12; 5:18-19; 2 John 11).

(4) In addition, Diotrephes withholds hospitality from "the brothers," delegates of the elder (vv. 5-8). (5) Diotrephes hinders those willing to receive the elder's associates and throws these hospitable ones out of the church. How Diotrephes was capable of such draconian measures is undisclosed. Expulsion (ἐκβάλλει *ekballei*) of members from a Christian assembly is a power never claimed by the elder in 3 John or elsewhere. Not even Jesus excommunicates those whom the Father has given him (John 6:37; cf. John 9:34-35).

Presented from the elder's perspective, this dispute is just sharp enough, and vague enough, to tickle the commentators' imaginations. Who is this Diotrephes? What lies behind this controversy? There is no consensus on the answers, though several possibilities have been suggested. One explanation is theologically oriented, envisioning a doctrinal dispute. Along this line the usual interpretation assumes that the elder is a defender of Johannine orthodoxy and that Diotrephes is a heretic—though a provocative variant of this proposal reverses the roles for these characters![209] The weakness of such theories is that they explain too much; unlike 2 John 7-9, 3 John 9-10 contains no clear evidence of doctrinal contention between Diotrephes and the elder.

Other exegetes favor a sociopolitical explanation of vv. 9-10. The elder and Diotrephes are at odds over the reach of their respective jurisdictions and the failure of each to recognize the other's authority.[210] This sort of explanation risks reading into 3 John a later institutional hierarchy. In addition, these hypotheses explain too little; they do not account for the elder's characteristic theological motivations, not only in 1 and 2 John, but also in 3 John 3-8.

---

208. Some Greek texts delete the indefinite particle "something" (τι *ti*), which to some scribes may have sounded unbecoming of an author thought to be an apostle (thus NIV, REB, NAB). Other manuscripts read, "I would have written," perhaps trying to eliminate the suggestion that

209. Ernst Käsemann, "Ketzer und Zeuge: Zum johanneischen Verfasserproblem," *ZTK* 48 (1951) 292-311.
210. Thus Burnett Hillman Streeter, *The Primitive Church: Studies with Special Reference to the Origins of the Christian Ministry* (London: Macmillan, 1930) 83-89; Abraham J. Malherbe, "The Inhospitality of Diotrephes," in *God's Christ and His People: Studies in Honour of Nils Alstrup Dahl*, ed. Jacob Jervell and Wayne A. Meeks (Oslo: Universitetsforlaget, 1977) 222-32.

Perhaps we can compensate for the inadequacies of these theories with an explanation that consolidates them: Diotrephes may have refused hospitality to the elder and his associates out of the fear (unwarranted, in the elder's view) that his community's doctrinal standards might be contaminated.[211] The credibility of such a hypothesis is enhanced by the elder's concerns in 2 John 9-11, which yoke ecclesiological policy with theological integrity. If similar concerns underlie 3 John 9-10, then the irony is stunning: Diotrephes may have practiced a rigorous form of the elder's own doctrinal and communal discipline, preached in 2 John! (See Reflections at 3 John 13-15.)

211. See the careful examination in Lieu, *The Second and Third Epistles of John*, 148-65.

3 John 11-12, Commending Demetrius

COMMENTARY

The writer appeals to the beloved Gaius that he adopt the elder's appraisal of this affair and, accordingly, accept the testimony of one whom the elder supports. Verse 11 combines what appear to be maxims, the first of which is couched in terms not especially Johannine: "imitation" (only here in the Johannine literature); "evil" (τὸ κακόν *to kakon*, instead of the usual Johannine synonym, τὸ πονηρός [*to ponēros*]; 3 John 10; though cf. John 18:23, 30); "the good" (τὸ ἀγαθόν *to agathon*; only here and in John 1:46; 5:29; 7:12). Obviously Johannine in expression are "[being] of God" (see John 8:47; 1 John 3:10; 4:4-7), characteristic of those who are righteous, and "not having seen God" (see John 1:18; 1 John 3:6; 4:12*a*, 20), which is associated with sin. These aphorisms are honed by the context in which they are set: against Diotrephes, in favor of Demetrius. The elder's quiet reminder of the general resources of Johannine tradition contrasts with the aggressive, targeted action taken by Diotrephes against his adversaries.

In the face of the challenge mounted by Diotrephes, the elder's advocacy for a certain Demetrius emerges as 3 John's clearest motive. Although the elder does not exactly say it, by implication Demetrius is his envoy to the church with which Gaius is associated. (Demetrius may also have been the courier of this letter.) In the elder's opinion Demetrius bears the kind of Christian witness that deserves Gaius's hospitality (vv. 5-8), not Diotrephes' repudiation (vv. 9-10). Again it is interesting that the elder appears in no position to enforce Demetrius's reception. The elder most vigorously appeals to the tradition of authentic testimony (μαρτυρία *martyria*), so familiar to us from John, 1 John, and Revelation (see Commentary on 3 John 3). Accreditation of Demetrius comes from many sources: from the elder and his circle, "by all" (who know him), and "by the truth itself." The latter may refer to the coherence of Demetrius's witness with the Johannine understanding of truth as God's self-revelation in Christ (John 1:14, 17; 14:6; 17:17-19). The elder's own testimony is validated by its alignment with Johannine tradition: "Our testimony is true," even as it was said of Jesus' Beloved Disciple that "his testimony is true" (John 19:35 NRSV; 21:24; see also 1 John 1:1-4). (See Reflections at 3 John 13-15.)

3 JOHN 13-15, REGRETS, HOPES, AND GREETINGS

COMMENTARY

The conclusion of 3 John is similar to 2 John 12-13, though with enough variation in word selection and verb conjugation to suggest that these verses are the product, not of a copycat, but of one author closing two letters written at different times. Again the elder concedes the insufficiency of "ink and reed" ("pen and ink," we would say) to convey his thoughts, which he hopes to express "mouth-to-mouth" when he sees Gaius ("you" [sing.]). As noted in vv. 5-8, Christians expected to be received hospitably by other Christians. That customary hope acquires poignancy in this letter, which reveals the rupture of hospitality among Christians. Viewed in that light, the elder's express plans to visit Gaius may also imply a challenge to the inhospitable Diotrephes.

Verse 15 is a more complicated closing than that of the Second Epistle. In 3 John, the wish for peace (see also Eph 6:23; 1 Pet 5:14*b*; 2 John 3) is joined with greetings to Gaius from "the friends" of the elder, coupled with the elder's hope that his regards will be relayed individually, "name by name," to each of "the friends" with Gaius (cf. John 10:3; Jesus also departed from his disciples with "peace" for his "friends" [John 14:27; 15:14-15; 16:33; 20:19, 21, 26]). Obviously, the elder is paving the way for his own favorable reception, someday, by Gaius and others in that community. Among Johannine churches whose tradition stressed love for one another, it is equally manifest that hospitality cannot now be simply assumed. It must be deliberately cultivated.

REFLECTIONS

1. Like the Second Epistle, 3 John has attracted little attention among the church's teachers and preachers and has gotten a frosty reception among commentators who find it shallow. While the document does not exhibit the theological profundity of Romans or even 1 John, to denigrate or ignore 3 John hardly seems fair. The letter is not lacking a theological substructure, even if those premises are largely undeveloped. Viewed on its own terms, 3 John is concerned with some practical implications of the NT's Johannine testimony. In that sense it is a natural mate for 2 John, which offers a synopsis of some important issues in Johannine theology. Read in the light of the Christian canon, 2 and 3 John exemplify in tandem the dynamic that marks the structure of 1 John: God's begetting of those in Christ's fellowship, which impels them to "show forth in their lives what they profess by their faith."[212] By documenting moments in the continuing life of early churches molded in the Johannine tradition, all three letters are illuminating companions for the Fourth Gospel. They complement the NT's Johannine witness, even as the other catholic and deutero-Pauline epistles complement the testimony of Paul.

2. Another notable aspect of 3 John may be so obvious that at first it blinds us: its unfeigned human frailty. This letter addresses familiar tensions among ordinary Christians who quarreled mightily yet shared much. Reading 3 John is a bit like studying a cracked, sepia-tinted photograph in a family album. Although at first we do not recognize the faces of Gaius, Demetrius, Diotrephes, or the elder, and while their braided histories are long forgotten, slowly we perceive traces of ourselves in their affections and petulance, their grudges and gratitude.

In particular, 3 John holds a mirror to the church of our own day, inviting us to consider the sometimes divisive consequences of deep religious convictions. For its part, Johannine Christianity was permeated with a strong dualistic current. While its adherents did not withdraw from the world (John 17:6-19), they could not comfortably occupy the shadowlands between light and dark (1 John 1:5–2:10). Accordingly, they kept their doors tightly shut to perceived wickedness. This tendency may have been given unfortunate expression by Diotrephes (3 John 9-10), whose inhospitality to the elder and his envoys was formally justifiable on the elder's own terms (2 John 10-11). The elder does not identify Diotrephes as the antichrist (cf. 1 John 2:22*b*; 4:3*b*); yet he seems but a whisker away from ascribing to Diotrephes an evil that is not "of God" (3 John 11*b*), thereby practicing the same exclusion of which he accuses his adversary.

212. Collect for the Second Sunday of Easter, *The Book of Common Prayer,* 173.

Although a balanced assessment of this controversy is denied us by our ignorance of all its facts, perhaps we can sympathize with both the elder and Diotrephes. Since their time we, too, have found ourselves caught in the ambiguities of human experience, ensnarled by tensions within our own tradition, guilty of the very sins that we perceive so clearly in others within our Christian family. Like Johannine Christianity, most of our denominations have been wrenched and occasionally split by arduous questions of freedom and fidelity in Christian self-understanding. When ought the church that is loyal to the truth of Jesus Christ stand firm? When should it bend? Where should the lines of faith and practice be drawn sharply? Where should they be relaxed? For these questions, there can be no easy answers, because living as a Christian in this world remains inherently difficult for Christ's fallible followers.

Like Diotrephes and the elder, Christians of conviction in our generation will sometimes land in places diametrically opposed. Our reach for the truth of Jesus Christ exceeds the grasp of any of us. To recognize this is not to commend indifference; we must wrestle with major questions, for they often run to the root of our understanding of what it means to be Christian. With such questions we should strive to grapple in covenant with one another, for nothing so stains the integrity of our witness to God's reconciling peace as the disintegration of the church. And we should conduct our controversies with Christian humility, heeding Oliver Cromwell's entreaty to the General Assembly of the Kirk of Scotland: "I beseech you, in the bowels of Christ, think it possible you may be mistaken."[213]

3. Third John also raises thorny questions about the shape of authority within the church. The elder speaks, and Diotrephes acts, as though each were, or thinks he ought to be, in a position to decide some fundamental matters of community discipline. On its face the elder's position appears more creditable; it is hard to square Diotrephes' practice of excommunicating Christians with a church whose leaders were commissioned to tend and feed Christ's lambs (John 21:15-19). By what authority could a servant of Jesus expel any of those who came to him, those whom even Jesus would not cast out? The hunger for power of which Diotrephes is accused chimes with those tyrannical modes of ancient Roman governance that Jesus was remembered as criticizing: "the rulers of the Gentiles lord it over them, and their great ones are tyrants over them" (Matt 20:25 NRSV = Mark 10:42). In its most wrong-headed moments, even American ecclesiastical politics is tempted to engage in such malignant self-promotion, though it conforms not at all to a love like Christ's. Jesus, after all, knelt to wash his followers' feet (John 13:12-16; see also Matt 20:24-28 and par.; 1 Pet 5:2-3).

It would be simplistic, however, to judge as problem-free the elder's view of church order. Lacking a better articulated principle of authority than what we find in the Johannine letters, the elder can summon little for his position's support beyond insult of his adversary (3 John 9-10), in which vituperation Diotrephes also traded, and reassertion of the truth of the elder's own testimony (v. 12), which Diotrephes doubtless claimed as well. The confidence that all Christians enjoy knowledge that needs no human instruction (1 John 2:20, 27) harmonizes splendidly with an image of the church as branches of Christ, the one true vine (John 15:1-11). Such a defense, nevertheless, proved manifestly inadequate against "the action of a high-handed autocrat"[214] like Diotrephes. By his overt reliance on "what was from the beginning" and his self-presentation as a reliable guarantor of that tradition (1 John 1:1-4), the elder appears to have been reaching for some authoritative coordinates for reorienting the life of a church gone off-course. Somewhat later in patristic thought, such guidelines would gel into a doctrine of apostolicity, which gave clear expression to the church's hope for its own integrity across time. The Johannine epistles have not yet arrived at that point,

---

213. *The Writings and Speeches of Oliver Cromwell*, vol. 2: *The Commonwealth 1649–1653*, ed. Wilbur Cortez Abbott with Catherine D. Crane (Cambridge, Mass.: Harvard University Press, 1939) 303 (letter from Musselburgh, August 3, 1650).
214. Lieu, *The Theology of the Johannine Epistles*, 10.

as evidenced by the fact that the elder was unable to adjudicate some basic matters of doctrine and discipline in Johannine congregations. A principle of apostolicity probably could not have been grasped as normative within Johannine Christianity until after its consolidation with other Christian traditions into the church of the patristic era, to whose canon, creeds, and polity all Christians of the present day remain indebted for their variously inflected understandings of the church and its ministry.[215] Like the First and Second Epistles of John, 3 John thus testifies, inadvertently, to the need for a theologically responsible ordering of the church and its ministry, while it expressly demands of all preachers and teachers an accountability to the self-sacrificial love that God has bestowed.

4. Remarkably, in spite of all its introversion and avowed estrangement from the world, the Johannine church is summoned in this letter to welcome the stranger—the one who comes for the sake of the Name, who needs equipment for the next leg of the journey, who bears witness to the church's love and the truth in which the church walks (3 John 3, 6-7). No one knew better than did the elder that opening the door to the stranger carries risks, for the same road that brings to our door genuine need, worthy of support, also brings disturbance and even danger. But the elder also realized, and testifies to us, that the church that keeps its door locked cannot possibly be faithful to the truth or instrumental for love.

In the Third Epistle of John, hospitality is not talked about generally. It is fixed with a name: Demetrius. For us, too, the call for Christian hospitality is attached to specific names, special faces, particular pleas. In the face and voice of the Demetrius at our door, we recognize our own homelessness, our own hunger, our own ambivalent cries for help. And we remember, as clearly as we recall our last visit to the Lord's Table, those moments when the love of Christ beckoned us and welcomed us home:

> Love bade me welcome; yet my soul drew back,
>   Guilty of dust and sin.
> But quick-eyed Love, observing me grow slack
>   From my first entrance in,
> Drew nearer to me, sweetly questioning
>   If I'd lack'd anything.
> 'A guest,' I answer'd, 'worthy to be here:'
>   Love said, 'You shall be he.'
> 'I, the unkind, ungrateful? Ah, my dear,
>   I cannot look on Thee.'
> Love took my hand and smiling did reply,
>   'Who made the eyes but I?'
> 'Truth, Lord, but I have marr'd them: let my shame
>   Go where it doth deserve.'
> 'And know you not,' says Love, 'Who bore the blame?'
>   'My dear, then I will serve.'
> 'You must sit down,' says Love, 'and taste my meat.'
>   So I did sit and eat.[216]

Like the beloved Gaius, we do well to receive Demetrius at our doorstep, for the church knows, firsthand and repeatedly, what it means to have been a lonely stranger, embraced by God's sheer goodness and tender mercy. We are able to make a home for others because, through Christ, love first bade us welcome (1 John 4:19).

---

215. On the strengths and weaknesses of Johannine ecclesiology, see Eduard Schweizer, "The Concept of the Church in the Gospel and Epistles of St. John," in *New Testament Essays: Studies in Memory of Thomas Walter Manson*, ed. A. J. B. Higgins (Manchester: Manchester University Press, 1959) 230-45. The concept of apostolicity and its relevance for the widespread acceptance and eventual canonization of the four Gospels are considered in C. Clifton Black, *Mark: Images of an Apostolic Interpreter*, Studies on Personalities of the New Testament (Columbia: University of South Carolina Press, 1994) 251-59.

216. George Herbert (1593–1633), "Love," in *The Oxford Book of Prayer*, ed. George Appleton (Oxford: Oxford University Press, 1985) 206.

THE LETTER OF JUDE
INTRODUCTION, COMMENTARY, AND REFLECTIONS
BY
DUANE F. WATSON

THE LETTER OF
JUDE

INTRODUCTION

AUTHORSHIP, ORIGIN, AND DATE

Nothing definite can be said about the author, origin, or date of the Epistle of Jude.[1] The author calls himself Jude (Judas), brother of James. For the author to have identified himself through his brother James indicates that both Jude and James were well-known to the letter's addressees. The only brothers with the names Jude and James mentioned in the New Testament are the brothers of Jesus (Matt 13:55; Mark 6:3). Although several other men from the first century named Jude have been suggested as the author of this letter, the most likely reference is to the brother of James and Jesus, the leader of the church in Jerusalem (Acts 12:17; 15:13-21; 1 Cor 15:7; Gal 1:19; 2:9).[2] Jude did not believe that Jesus was the Messiah during Jesus' lifetime (Mark 3:21, 31; John 7:1-5). However, he came to faith after Jesus' resurrection and ascension (Acts 1:14), and probably became a missionary for the gospel (1 Cor 9:5).

The question is whether "Jude" is Jesus' brother's self-reference or a pseudonym used by someone within Jewish Christian circles, in which the memory of Jude and his brother James was prominent. On the one hand, the letter writer's familiarity with Jewish literature and traditions, as well as the Jewish Christian apocalyptic stance of the argumentation, supports Jude, Jesus' brother, as author. On the other hand, a pseudonymous author may have wished to use the name and authority of Jude to counter the false teachers in the postapostolic era. It is often argued that a pseudonymous author would have claimed to be the brother of Jesus rather than the brother of James, but claiming membership within the holy family offered considerable status to the writer. Eusebius mentions that many persons traced their ancestry to the holy family.[3]

Several prominent arguments in support of the author's pseudonymity can be readily countered. (1) The content of the letter requires a late date because it either reflects early Catholicism

---

1. For a discussion of the introductory issues of Jude, see R. J. Bauckham, *Jude, 2 Peter,* WBC 50 (Waco, Tex.: Word, 1983) 3-17, and *Jude and the Relatives of Jesus in the Early Church* (Edinburgh: T. & T. Clark, 1990) 134-78.
2. For a list of other identifications of Jude, see Bauckham, *Jude, 2 Peter,* 21-23.
3. Eusebius *Ecclesiastical History* 1.7.14. See J. H. Neyrey, *2 Peter, Jude,* AB 37C (New York: Doubleday, 1993) 45. For more on the holy family and Jude, see Bauckham, *Jude and the Relatives of Jesus in the Early Church,* 5-133.

or combats gnosticism of the post-apostolic era. However, these assumptions are unlikely (see "The Stance and Rhetorical Approach of the Letter," below). (2) The author excludes himself from the apostles, whom he presents as belonging to a previous generation (v. 17). However, he is only excluding himself from the apostles who founded the church(es) he addresses, and not from the apostolic era. (3) The brother of Jesus, a Galilean peasant whose native language would have been Aramaic, could not have produced this letter. The author appears to have had a scribal background, because he is able to write a letter, he uses literary Greek in which to write it, he possesses knowledge of Jewish tradition and writings and has access to those writings (e.g., *Testament of Moses, 1 Enoch*), and he is skilled in the use of rhetoric.[4] However, having an elementary education (which included some rhetorical training), hearing weekly exposition of the Old Testament in the synagogue, living in Galilee (an area dotted with Greek-speaking cities), and needing to increase proficiency in Greek to effectively preach to Greek audiences would have gone a long way toward explaining how Jesus' brother could come to possess competency in these skills. Thus there is really no strong reason to argue that the author could be anyone other than Jude, the brother of Jesus and James.

Decisions about the date of the writing of the letter depend on those for authorship and the nature of the false teachers involved. Dates offered range from the early apostolic age (50s CE) to the mid-second century CE. If the letter was written by the brother of Jesus, then a date in the mid-first century is warranted. If it is pseudonymous, a date in the latter part of the century of the post-apostolic era is logical. The letter's implication that the original converts of the church were still living (vv. 17-18), its use of a Jewish-Christian apocalyptic argumentative stance, and the use of the Epistle of Jude as an authoritative document by the author of 2 Peter (around 80–90 CE) indicate a date closer to the mid-first century. This places the letter's writing during the lifetime of Jude, Jesus' brother. A late first- or early second-century date loses still more appeal once it is recognized that the letter takes neither an early catholic nor an anti-gnostic stance of that period, nor does it necessarily look upon the apostolic era as being past (see "The Stance and Rhetorical Approach of the Letter," 476-77).

RECIPIENTS, OPPONENTS, AND HISTORICAL SITUATION

The letter is not a tract against heresy or a "catholic" letter addressed to all Christians, but a letter addressed to an unspecified church or group of churches. Jude did not found the church that he addresses, for it had learned the gospel from the apostles (v. 17). The church is probably Jewish Christian, for Jude quotes and alludes to Jewish documents and traditions without explanation, assuming the people's familiarity with them.

The geographical location of the church is unknown. The antinomian character of the false teachers' doctrine and their ability to influence the church indicate a predominantly Gentile context lacking the presence of strong Jewish moral teaching. Scholars have proposed Palestine, Syria, Egypt, or Asia Minor as the location of the recipient church(es). If the letter was written by Jesus' brother, then Palestine is the most likely candidate for the recipients' location, since Jude himself can be located there. If it is pseudonymous, then Asia Minor is a good candidate, for it boasted large Jewish populations within a Gentile environment, or Egypt, where the letter was popular with Clement of Alexandria and Origen. Syria is not likely because the letter was not accepted as canonical in churches there until the sixth century.[5]

The occasion of the letter is the infiltration of the church by a group whose doctrines and practices are at variance with the apostolic tradition the church had received (vv. 4, 17-19). The group is sectarian, having divided the church by rejecting its leadership (v. 8) and gathered a following of its own (vv. 19, 22-23). Their motivation is partially financial gain (vv. 11-12, 16). The description of them in v. 4, "certain intruders have stolen in among you" (NRSV), indicates that they may be itinerant prophets or teachers, who were common in early Christianity. Itinerant

---

4. See Neyrey, *2 Peter, Jude,* 29, 35.
5. Bauckham, *Jude, 2 Peter,* 16-17.

prophets and teachers could rely on the hospitality of their host church (1 Cor 9:4; *Did.* 13:1-3) and thus were in a position to misuse this privilege for financial gain (Rom 16:18; *Did.* 11:3-6, 12). The contorted doctrines of some of these itinerants, coupled with their desire for gain, often posed problems for the churches they visited (Matt 7:15; 2 Cor 10:1-11; 1 John 4:1; 2 John 10; *Did.* 11-12; Ign. *Eph.* 9:1).

The doctrine of these false teachers is antinomian—that is, they understand the gospel of freedom in Christ to relieve a Christian of ethical responsibilities, an understanding that "perverts grace" (v. 4). They deny the authority of the law of Moses (vv. 8-10) and of Christ himself (vv. 4, 8). This denial may be based on a claim of prophetic revelation (v. 8; cf. v. 19), a problem in early Christianity (Col 2:18), or it may be an overly realized eschatology that stressed that judgment was past rather than future for those in the Spirit. As a corollary of this rejection of authority, they are immoral, especially in sexual behavior (vv. 4, 6-8, 10, 16). They corrupt the church (vv. 22-24), even tainting the love feast, which is at the core of the fellowship (v. 12).

Such antinomianism is akin to that faced by Paul (Rom 3:8; 6:1, 15; 1 Cor 5:1-8; 6:12-20; 10:23; Gal 5:13), but there is no firm support for thinking that the false teachers were of the ilk encountered by Paul. Neither do the false teachers seem to be the gnostics of later times. Their reviling of angels who guard the law of Moses (vv. 8-10) is not part of a cosmic dualism in which angels are demigods of the material universe. Their indulgence in sin does not originate in the emphasis on spirit and knowledge to the disparagement of anything material (like the body). If gnosticism were involved, Jude would best have attacked the doctrine of the false teachers, not emphasized their immorality.[6]

Jude believes the situation may be spiritually fatal and, therefore, seeks immediate, drastic action. The presence of the false teachers, their teaching, and their behavior are precursors of the parousia, and they and their following will be destroyed with its coming (vv. 14-15, 17-18, 23). To save members of the church from destruction, Jude wants to convince them that the false teachers are the ungodly of prophecy (vv. 14-19) and that they are headed for destruction (vv. 5-16). The church is to cling to traditional doctrine (vv. 3, 5, 17, 20), bolster its spiritual life (vv. 20-21), and actively convince those persuaded by the false teachers to abandon them and their ways (vv. 22-23).

THE STANCE AND RHETORICAL APPROACH OF THE LETTER

Many interpreters have classified the Letter of Jude as an "early catholic" document. This designation refers to a reconstruction of early Christianity (needing serious rethinking) that postulates that beginning with the second generation of Christians there was a movement away from a hope in the imminent return of Christ and toward institutionalization of church offices and the understanding of faith as a body of doctrine rather than a personal commitment. This movement was fostered by the delay of the parousia and the encounter with heresy, which necessitated the creation of a central authority and clearly articulated doctrine.

Yet Jude should *not* be classified as early catholic. The parousia hope in the letter is strong. Jude tried to persuade the church to see that the false teachers of their day are those prophesied to appear in the last days. They are precursors of the parousia and designated recipients of its approaching judgment (vv. 4, 14-19). Their followers must be snatched quickly from the impending fire of judgment (v. 23). Jude does not address any church officers, but assumes that the church as a whole will respond as suggested. Jude also affirms that faith is not a set body of orthodox teachings but the gospel itself, which demands faith and which the church members received at the time of their conversion and instruction by the apostles (vv. 3, 17-18).[7]

As the use of Jewish sources, apocalyptic texts, and tradition (e.g., *1 Enoch, Testament of Moses*) indicates, Jude was working within the confines of Jewish Christianity, which had a

---

6. Bauckham, *Jude, 2 Peter,* 11-13.
7. Bauckham, *Jude, 2 Peter,* 8-9, 32-33; J. D. G. Dunn, *Unity and Diversity in the New Testament* (Philadelphia: Westminster, 1977) 341-66.

vibrant apocalyptic outlook,[8] and this outlook underlies his rhetorical approach.[9] The letter is predominantly deliberative rhetoric, which, by proofs and advice, tries to persuade an audience to embrace what is advantageous, necessary, and expedient and dissuade it from the opposite. The letter specifies that it aims to persuade the church "to contend for the faith" (v. 3)—that is, not to heed the false teachers' message and practice and thus come under like judgment at the encroaching parousia. In its effort to persuade the church, the letter also relies upon epideictic rhetoric, which both praises and blames. The aim of such rhetoric is to uplift what is honorable and to cast down what is dishonorable, especially with a view to increasing audience assent to honorable values. Verse 4 refers to the letter as a "condemnation" (τὸ κρίμα *to krima*). The false teachers are denounced as being (a) comparable to great sinners of the past and (b) the subject of prophecies of judgment. The denunciation of the false teachers is meant to strengthen the church in the faith received from the apostles and to preserve its members from impending judgment.

LITERARY GENRE, COMPOSITION, AND CONTENT

Jude is a genuine letter of the mixed variety. Its deliberative rhetorical style classifies it as a paraenetic letter meant to advise and dissuade.[10] The petition in vv. 3-4 classifies it as a letter of request or petition.[11] Jude's stated purpose is to persuade the church to "contend for the faith" (v. 3). The letter occupies a middle ground between documentary letters (e.g., personal, business) and literary letters written according to rhetorical conventions and meant for public consumption. Thus it contains both epistolary and rhetorical conventions, and its structure is best described by discussing both genres.[12]

The letter begins with a typical Jewish-Christian letter prescript, introducing the sender and the recipients, followed by a blessing (vv. 1-2). Verses 3-4 are the body opening of the letter, which establishes common ground between the sender and the recipients and informs the recipients of the main reason why the sender wrote the letter. In v. 3, the reason for writing is stated as a petition that the recipients "contend for the faith that was once for all entrusted to the saints." The background of, or reason for, the petition follows in v. 4: Ungodly false teachers have appeared in the church, as was foretold in prophecy. Verse 3 corresponds to the rhetorical convention of *exordium* and v. 4 to *narratio*. The *exordium* works to obtain the audience's goodwill and introduces the reason for an address. The *narratio* gives the facts to explain the need for that address and to outline the main point(s) the remainder of the address will develop.

Verses 5-16 are the body middle of the letter, which develops the material of the body opening. It begins with a typical disclosure formula, expressing the sender's desire that the recipients know something: "Now I desire to remind you . . . " (NRSV). The body middle corresponds to the rhetorical *probatio,* which presents proofs to verify the claims and propositions of the *narratio*. In Jude, the body middle proves that the false teachers in the church are ungodly and that they are the very ones foretold in prophecy. To make this assertion, the body middle uses proofs from example (vv. 5-10) and from prophecy (vv. 11-16) respectively.

Verses 17-23 are the body closing of the letter, which underscores the main reason for writing by reiterating and amplifying what has already been stated in the body of the letter. The body closing often urges that responsibility be taken for the matters discussed. Like the body middle, the closing begins with a disclosure formula: "But you, beloved, must remember . . . " (NRSV). It corresponds to the rhetorical device called *peroratio,* which reiterates the main points of the *probatio* and appeals to the emotion of the audience to persuade it to respond as desired. The

---

8. For a thorough study of Jude's use of Jewish traditions and source materials, see J. D. Charles, *Literary Strategy in the Epistle of Jude* (Scranton: University of Scranton Press, 1993); Bauckham, *Jude and the Relatives of Jesus in the Early Church*, 179-280.
9. For a rhetorical analysis of Jude, see D. F. Watson, *Invention, Arrangement, and Style: Rhetorical Criticism of Jude and 2 Peter,* SBLDS 104 (Atlanta: Scholars Press, 1988) 29-79.
10. Cf. Neyrey, *2 Peter, Jude,* 44.
11. Bauckham, *Jude, 2 Peter,* 28.
12. For a concise discussion of the ancient Greek letter genre, see John L. White, "Ancient Greek Letters," in *Greco-Roman Literature and the New Testament,* ed. David E. Aune, SBLSBS 21 (Atlanta: Scholars Press, 1988) 85-105.

repetition occurs in vv. 17-19, and the emotional appeal by exhortation is repeated in vv. 20-23. The letter ends in vv. 24-25 with a doxology for a postscript.

In proving that the false teachers are ungodly and that they are the ungodly of prophecy (v. 4), Jude uses Jewish types and prophecies sacred to the church as well as Christian instruction previously delivered to the church by apostolic missionaries (vv. 3, 5, 17-18). This material includes three OT narrative types (vv. 5-7), an OT prophecy (v. 11), a prophecy from *1 Enoch* (vv. 14-15), and a prophecy from the apostles (vv. 17-18). Each prophecy or narrative type is applied to the false teachers in order to identify them as ungodly and subject to judgment, those who were prophesied would appear in the end times (vv. 8-10, 12-13, 16, 19). The alternation of types and prophecy with interpretation is carefully constructed to underscore that the types and prophecies find counterparts and fulfillment in the false teachers. This alternation is accentuated by alternating verb tenses. The past tenses (vv. 5-6, 9), prophetic aorists (vv. 11, 14), and a future tense (v. 18) in the types and prophecies are juxtaposed with present tenses in the interpretations. Also, the interpretations are preceded with the Greek word "these" (οὗτοι *houtoi*) or "these are" (οὗτοι εἰσιν *houtoi eisin*), which clearly distinguishes them (vv. 8, 10, 12, 16, 19).

The entire letter is linked with the repetition of topics (sometimes called catchwords) in rhetorically strategic places. Take, for example, the topic of "keeping" (τηρέω *tēreō*, φυλάσσω *phylassō*). In the letter's prescript, the addresses are said to be kept for Jesus Christ (v. 1), and in the closing doxology God is the one said to be doing the keeping (v. 24). The saints are to keep themselves in God's favor (v. 21). In contrast, the angels and false teachers who have not been able to keep their place will be kept in deepest darkness (vv. 6, 13).

The letter is characterized by a rich vocabulary and many rhetorical figures of speech and thought. One particularly noteworthy feature is the appearance of triplets that amplify the message (vv. 1, 2, 5-7, 8, 11, 19, 20-21, 22-23, 25). For example, three types of ungodly persons are described, who find counterparts in the false teachers (vv. 5-7); and the application of these descriptions to the false teachers is a triplet (v. 8). In addition, words are carefully chosen for their associated imagery. Noteworthy are the images of the prophecy and the interpretation of vv. 11-13, which provide a strong negative characterization of the false teachers.

THE THEOLOGY OF JUDE

Jude is not concerned solely with doctrinal issues. Rather, the author is concerned with the moral implications of errant doctrine. This false teaching denies the parousia and judgment, thus removing moral constraints and, in effect, licensing immorality. In the light of this challenge, Jude's theological approach is to stress the need for adherence to the proclamation of the gospel as received from the apostles (vv. 3, 5, 17). This doctrine and the behavior it espouses are normative and can be used as the measure of new teaching that may be proposed in the church.[13]

Jude works with a vital eschatological expectation. He believes that the parousia and judgment will occur within the lifetime of the letter's recipients, and he points to the presence of the false teachers as an indication that they are, indeed, living in the end times (vv. 17-18). He affirms the reality of the divine judgment that will accompany the parousia. As surely as God acted in history to judge sinners, God will so judge sinners at the consummation of history (vv. 5-13). However, faithful Christians will be extended mercy and eternal life (vv. 2, 21, 24). The faithful themselves are to try to save sinners from the fire of judgment by pulling them away from the false teachers (v. 23).

Jude strongly affirms the lordship of Christ (vv. 4, 14, 17, 21, 25), a lordship based on his work of salvation, his current position of sitting at God's right hand, and his future role as Savior and Judge. Christians owe obedience to Christ as Lord for his work for their salvation, a salvation whose completion is based on a lifetime of obedience (v. 21). By contrast, immorality perverts the moral order of creation, which Christ enforces, and denies his lordship, leaving the

---

13. For discussion of the theology of Jude, see Bauckham, *Jude, 2 Peter*, 11-37; A. Chester and R. P. Martin, *The Theology of the Letters of James, Peter, and Jude*, New Testament Theology (Cambridge: Cambridge University Press, 1994) 65-86.

person who sins vulnerable to judgment (vv. 4, 8-16). In the light of eschatological expectation and the lordship of Christ, Jude provides ethical instruction for Christian living. Christians are to make a concerted effort to advance their individual and corporate spiritual lives (v. 3). The Christian life is sustained on two interdependent fronts. One is remaining in the love of God through one's own moral effort and obedience (v. 21), and the other is God's working for us to keep our salvation safe until it is complete (vv. 1, 24). Christians are to work for the spiritual good of all, to pray with the inspiration of the Holy Spirit, to obey God in order to remain in God's love, and to live in the expectation of the impending parousia (vv. 20-21). The faithful are to extend mercy to the errant, while remaining cognizant of the real danger of possibly being influenced by their doctrine and practice (vv. 22-23).

BIBLIOGRAPHY

Bauckham, Richard J. *Jude, 2 Peter.* WBC 50. Waco, Tex.: Word, 1983. The most comprehensive commentary in English that both summarizes previous scholarship and makes many new and helpful advances; places Jude within its Jewish, Christian, and Greco-Roman literary and theological contexts.

———. *Jude, 2 Peter.* WBT. Waco, Tex.: Word, 1990. A companion to the preceding commentary; discusses the theological themes of Jude.

———. *Jude and the Relatives of Jesus in the Early Church.* Edinburgh: T. & T. Clark, 1990. A thorough discussion of background issues, the holy family and its role in the early church, as well as Jude's exegesis, use of sources, and christology.

Charles, J. D. *Literary Strategy in the Epistle of Jude.* Scranton: University of Scranton Press, 1993. In-depth look at the literary strategy of the letter from its Palestinian Jewish apocalyptic context.

Chester, Andrew, and Ralph Martin. *The Theology of the Letters of James, Peter, and Jude.* New Testament Theology. Cambridge: Cambridge University Press, 1994. One of the finest discussions available on the theology of Jude within its context.

Neyrey, Jerome H. *2 Peter, Jude.* AB 37C. New York: Doubleday, 1993. An excellent commentary that breaks new ground by incorporating a social-science perspective; places the authors and audiences of these letters within their social world by using various social-science models or perspectives.

Watson, Duane F. *Invention, Arrangement, and Style: Rhetorical Criticism of Jude and 2 Peter.* SBLDS 104. Atlanta: Scholars Press, 1988. Demonstrates how the writer of Jude used Greco-Roman rhetorical conventions to persuade his audience to take a course of action deemed necessary to remain faithful in the face of the influence of false teachers.

OUTLINE OF JUDE

I. Jude 1-2, The Letter Prescript

II. Jude 3-4, A Petition to Contend for the Faith

III. Jude 5-16, Proof That the False Teachers Are Ungodly and Subject to Judgment
   A. Jude 5-10, Proof from Old Testament Examples
   B. Jude 11-13, Proof from Prophecy
   C. Jude 14-16, Proof from the Prophecy of *1 Enoch*

IV. Jude 17-23, An Apostolic Prophecy and Instruction on How to Respond to False Teachers

V. Jude 24-25, The Letter Closing as a Doxology

JUDE 1-2

THE LETTER PRESCRIPT

COMMENTARY

Jude begins with the three-part letter prescript typical of Jewish and early Christian letters: (1) identification of the sender and (2) the recipient(s), each often described theologically in relationship to God, to Christ, and to each other, and (3) a greeting (here a blessing) that originates in the Jewish wish for peace and prosperity for the recipients. Through the theological description and greeting the letter prescript functions rhetorically to establish by what authority the sender addresses the recipients and to obtain their goodwill so that the content of the letter may be heard (the letter would have been read aloud in a church setting) as well as to introduce topics to be discussed in the letter.

Verse 1. Jude identifies himself theologically as "a servant of Jesus Christ" and familially as the "brother of James" (see the section "Authorship, Origin, and Date" in the Introduction). Both identifications help to establish the writer's authority and honor. "Brother of James" identifies Jude as the brother of James, the leader of the church of Jerusalem, and indirectly as a brother of Jesus. "Servant" (δοῦλος *doulos*) is a title for any Christian, identifying him or her as one whom Christ has bought out of servanthood to sin and who now serves him (1 Cor 7:22-23; Eph 6:6; 1 Pet 2:16). As a self-designation, "servant" also denotes a Christian leader, especially when used in letter openings (Rom 1:1; Phil 1:1; Titus 1:1; Jas 1:1; 2 Pet 1:1). In this regard "servant" adapts the title "servants of God" used of great leaders of Israel (Exod 32:13; Deut 9:27; 34:5; Ps 89:3). The extended title "servant of Jesus Christ" implies that Jude exhibits the servant leadership that Christ exemplified.

The recipients are given a threefold theological identification: "those who are called, who are beloved in God the Father and kept safe for Jesus Christ." This identification is intended in part to obtain the goodwill of the recipients by showing in what high esteem they are held. It describes the church in terms applied to Israel, especially in Isaiah 40–55.[14]

That they have been "called" is a reminder of God's calling of Israel (Isa 41:8-9; 42:1, 6; 48:12, 15; 49:1, 7). The church has been called by God to be the new Israel.

"Beloved in God the Father" recalls God's love for Israel (Isa 43:4; 54:8). Israel became known as the "beloved" in the Septuagint (Ps 28:6; Isa 44:2 LXX), a love now the privilege of the church as the new Israel. The NIV's "beloved *by* God the Father" draws out the idea of God as the agent of love, an idea implicit in the participle "beloved." However, the NRSV's translation, "beloved *in* God the Father," is more accurate, although harder to understand. The Johannine literature speaks of Christians' relationship with God as being "in God," especially when they are obedient and abiding in love (John 17:21; 1 John 2:24; 3:24; 4:13, 15-16). "Beloved *in* God the Father" underscores the need to obey God in order to experience God's love. This idea is expressed by Jude in the command to "keep yourselves in the love of God" (v. 21 NRSV).

The phrase "kept safe for Jesus Christ" (dative of advantage, NRSV) is preferred over "kept by Jesus Christ" (dative of agent, NIV). In v. 24, a verse that, along with vv. 1-2, frames the letter, God keeps Christians safe from losing their salvation until it has been completed at the parousia of Christ. This idea was common in early Christianity (John 17:11-12, 15; 1 Thess 5:23; 1 Pet 1:5). God will keep the church safe from the deceptive teachings and practices of false teachers, which lead to destruction at the parousia.

---
14. As explained in Bauckham, *Jude, 2 Peter*, 25-26.

Verse 2. This threefold blessing also increases the recipients' goodwill. Mercy and peace were part of the Jewish blessing, and in the context of Jude their use connotes mercy in Christ and peace with God through Christ. This mercy will come to completion at the parousia (v. 21); in the meantime, mercy and grace should be extended in kind to those wavering in the faith (vv. 22-23). Peace is needed because the love feasts of the church are being disrupted by the false teachers (v. 12). They grumble (v. 16) and divide the church (v. 19). Love was an addition to the Jewish blessing of mercy and peace. Jude's blessing is that God (indicated by the divine passive) provide the recipients mercy, peace, and love in abundance.

The letter's opening also introduces topics that will be developed in the body of the letter and reiterated in its closing. One such topic is "keeping" (τηρέω *tēreō*; φυλάσσω *phylassō*). Whereas God keeps the recipients safe for Jesus Christ (vv. 1, 24), the recipients are to do their part to "keep" themselves in the love of God until the parousia (v. 21). This is in contrast to the angels, who did not "keep" their designated place in the universal order when they had sexual relations with women (Gen 6:1-4), and as a result are now "kept" in deepest darkness for judgment (v. 6)—a fate awaiting the false teachers as well (v. 13). As the topic is developed it provides the recipients with comfort in their status with God, instruction for how to resist the threat of the false teachers, and a warning of the consequences of not remaining steadfast.

REFLECTIONS

1. As a standard part of the opening, Jude identifies himself in such a way as to bring his authority to bear upon his letter. His authority and honor reside in his being the brother of James and of Jesus—and thus a member of the holy family—and in his servant leadership, which the Lord exemplified. As the letter was being read to the church, the authority of Jude would have transformed it into a powerful word of exhortation. As was the expectation of his era, Jude did not assume that the church members would automatically lend him their ears and heed his message; rather, his aim was to demonstrate his worthiness to address them.

When approaching the pulpit to preach, we cannot assume that we should be or will be heard simply because we preach the gospel. We are at a disadvantage because of the all too common television and movie stereotype of clergy as bald, middle-aged men who are out of touch and have no backbone. We also have to contend with the disheartening examples of televangelists who have publicly fallen from grace. Preaching is most effective when we bring authority or ethos to the pulpit that merits the attention and goodwill of our congregation. This authority may derive from association with a denominational body, from formal education, or from personal example of servant leadership and Christian virtues as witnessed and experienced by the congregation. This interdependence between the preacher's authority and the authority of the message is a reminder of how important one's own preparation and public walk are to the health of one's ministry.

2. In a time of challenge by false teachers who could lead his church to destructive judgment, Jude pastorally reminds the church of the basics of its spiritual status as the new Israel, the new people of God. He stresses how much of that spiritual status results from God's initiative, for it is God who called them, loves them, and keeps their salvation safe. Jude also prays that the blessings of mercy, peace, and love will be granted by God in abundance. Before he approaches the main problems, he gives the members of the church the broadest possible perspective or vision. He helps them to see their spiritual status and its blessings, to affirm who they are, and to muster their resources before discussing the threat posed by the false teachers. Jude provides us with a model for dealing positively with demoralizing situations in the church. Whether the church is faced with declining membership, infighting, or financial woes, we should affirm the spiritual blessings that are the bedrock of the faith and the mission to which that faith calls us.

3. Being called by God demands obedience in order to experience God's love and to enable God to keep our salvation sure until its completion after this life. Being called is not a matter of sitting back and letting God shower us with love and serve us by working for our salvation. Rather, being called mandates our being obedient servants of Jesus Christ. Such obedience keeps us from falling in our ethical walk (v. 24) and keeps us within the love of God (v. 21) so that God can and will provide us with the blessing of a sure salvation (v. 2).

JUDE 3-4

A Petition to Contend for the Faith

COMMENTARY

Jude 3-4 is the body opening of the letter in which the sender establishes common ground with the recipients and informs them of the main reason for writing. Here the common ground is the "salvation we share." The main reason for writing is related as a petition, something common to Greco-Roman letter openings: "contend for the faith that was once for all entrusted to the saints" (v. 3). The writer petitions the church to remain faithful despite the presence of ungodly false teachers, who were foretold in prophecy (v. 4).

From a rhetorical perspective, v. 3 is the *exordium* and v. 4 is the *narratio*. The *exordium* is an introduction that is designed to grab the attention and goodwill of the audience and to introduce the reasons for writing. The *narratio* follows the *exordium* and explains why the address is needed and outlines the main point(s) that the remainder of the letter will develop. Verse 4 presents the two main propositions to be developed: (1) The false teachers are ungodly and subject to judgment, and (2) they are the ungodly ones whose appearance and judgment in the last days have been foretold.

Verse 3. In his petition, the writer of Jude underscores the urgency of the situation presented by the false teachers. He mentions that he had intended to write (or perhaps had already begun to write) a letter about the salvation he shares with the church in the corporate body of Christ. Instead he has found it necessary to petition the church to contend for the faith, for the content of the gospel as preached and believed (Rom 10:8; Gal 1:23).

In the petition, "contending" (ἐπαγωνίζομαι *epagōnizomai*) and related metaphorical words in early Christian literature were borrowed from the jargon of Greek athletic events to compare the struggles of the moral life to an athletic contest (1 Cor 9:24-27; 1 Tim 6:12; 2 Tim 4:7). Paul uses this athletic metaphor to describe his apostolic mission as a contest against opponents (Rom 15:30; Col 1:29–2:1), as well as to describe the mission of his co-workers (Phil 4:3; Col 4:12-13) and of all Christians against opposition (Phil 1:27-30).[15] Like Paul, the writer of Jude uses the contending metaphor to describe (1) the struggle between the gospel and the teachings of false teachers and (2) the moral contest that the antinomianism of these teachers has made more difficult.

The faith was entrusted to the saints, the first generation of Christians converted at the preaching of the apostles (vv. 17-18). "Entrust" (παραδίδωμι *paradidōmi*) and the reciprocal term "receive" (παραλαμβάνω *paralambanō*), which is not found here, are technical terms for handing on tradition. That tradition includes the apostles' initial preaching of the gospel to a congregation as well as its initial instruction (1 Cor 11:2, 23; 15:1, 3; Gal 1:9; Phil 4:9; 1 Thess 2:13; 2 Thess 3:6). The faith was "once for all" entrusted to believers because its content cannot change. God's action in Christ is once for all (Rom 6:10; Heb 9:12, 26-28; 10:10; 1 Pet 3:18) and need not (and in fact cannot) be presented in any other fashion (like that of the false teachers). Tradition was highly respected in both the Greco-Roman world and Judaism. The traditions of the group provided guidance for living in the present and gave the group its identity. Jude's reference to contending for the apostolic preaching (which should be held sacrosanct) sends a strong signal that his

---

15. V. C. Pfitzner, *Paul and the Agon Motif*, NovTSup 16 (Leiden: E. J. Brill, 1967).

petition is in response to a serious threat to the church and its identity.

Verse 4. Here Jude gives the reason for his petition. Certain people have "stolen in" (NRSV) or "secretly slipped in" (NIV; παρεισδύ[ν]ω *pareisdy[n]ō*) to the church, which connotes that these people have something to hide. Their having come from outside the church suggests that they are itinerant prophets or teachers, who were common in the early church and who often caused confusion on doctrinal and ethical matters. Jude affirms the power and foreknowledge of God by identifying these infiltrators as the subject of ancient prophecy. The false teachers have not taken God by surprise, but "long ago were designated for this condemnation." Jude may refer to pre-Christian prophecy, which he uses in the forms of OT types (vv. 5-7), and to apostolic prophecy (vv. 17-18; cf. Acts 20:29-30; 1 Tim 4:1-3; 2 Tim 3:13), to the prophecy of *1 Enoch* 1:9 attributed "long ago" to Enoch (vv. 14-15), or to a Christian prophecy of unknown origin (v. 11).

The "condemnation" (τὸ κρίμα *to krima*) for which the false teachers have been designated is given in vv. 5-19. This section uses OT types or examples and prophecies to condemn the false teachers as being ungodly and as perverting the grace of God, denying Jesus Christ, and thus subject to judgment. Within this condemnation the topics of being ungodly and being subject to judgment are central. As used in Jewish-Christian literature, to be "ungodly" (ἀσεβεῖς *asebeis*) is to be irreverent toward God (manifested in immoral behavior and the rejection of the moral commandments), and to be subject to judgment (Rom 1:18).

The false teachers are ungodly and condemnable for two related reasons. First, they pervert the grace of God into "licentiousness" (NRSV) or "license for immorality" (NIV; ἀσέλγεια *aselgeia*)—that is, immoral sexual excess. Apparently they interpret the grace of God to mean that they are free from the bonds of sexual morality. This "perverts" God's grace; it moves it beyond accepted traditions (2 Macc 7:24; Gal 1:6).

Second, the false teachers deny "our only Master and Lord, Jesus Christ." "Master" (or "Sovereign," NIV) may refer to either God or Jesus, but the latter is more likely, since Jude has presented himself as a slave of Jesus in v. 1. Second Peter 2:1, which depends on this verse, understands Jude's referent to be to Jesus as a master. The term "master" (δεσπότης *despotēs*), a metaphor that would understand Jesus as a master who has bought Christians as his slaves (presumably through the shedding of his blood), was used to refer to the head of the Roman household, rulers like the Roman emperor, Greek deities, and God. By adding "only Master" to the title, Jude stresses the irony of the false teachers' denial of Jesus Christ. If Jesus Christ is the only Master and Lord, how can anyone claiming to be Christian deny his authority? In the Mediterranean culture of Jude's day, masters compelled honor from their slaves. A slave's disobedience brought shame to the slave and dishonor to the master. Since the false teachers were accepted as Christians in the church being addressed, they probably did not explicitly deny Jesus Christ with some doctrinal formulation, but did so implicitly through their libertine behavior, which dishonored both them and Jesus (cf. Titus 1:16). These circumstances are indicated in v. 8, where Jude accuses them of both defiling the flesh and rejecting authority.

REFLECTIONS

1. Jude's appeal to this church to contend for the faith is not a call to denigrate or abuse the false teachers or to form committees to discuss the problems they create. Such approaches cannot change the false teachers or prevent their teaching from taking further spiritual toll on the church. Rather, the church is to take the positive action of contending for the faith. Contending involves commitment to living according to what that faith proclaims, with the same dedication and drive that an athlete trains to win a sporting event. Contending involves building up the church in the faith (v. 20) and proclaiming the faith to those who are no longer contending for it in order to rescue them from judgment (vv. 22-23). Contending for the faith occurs in private and public prayer, in Bible study, in worship, and in outreach of any kind. Through these activities the truth and strength of the faith are established as faith transforms individuals, groups, and institutions.

2. Jude's approach to dealing with false teachers also reminds us that a community of faith needs to be fully informed and aware of its faith if it is to contend for it. Jude's primary reference to faith involves the apostolic preaching and the tradition based on that preaching that was taught to new converts in the early church. Today "the faith" includes the Bible and an enormous array of resources provided by church councils, the church fathers and mothers, theologians, scholars, and laity through the last two millennia. What portions of this material are held authoritative and to what degree and just how it helps to define "the faith" are understood differently by each Christian and by each Christian group. Christians should become familiar with what they and their affiliations affirm to be "the" faith. Such investigation will make living the Christian life an aware, informed, and purposeful walk. Such familiarity is a primary resource for living the Christian life and prevention for being led astray by attitudes and teachings promoted by a great variety of modern media outlets.

Jude's intolerance for what varies from the core of tradition cautions us in a relativistic and pluralistic age to be discriminating. Tolerance for variation from traditional doctrine and practice should not be extended without examining how these different teachings measure up to Scripture and to church tradition (as reinterpreted as much as possible without gender and cultural bias) and evaluating what impact they will have on the life and spiritual health of the faith community. The teaching ministry of the church does not have just an optional and ancillary role, but is especially vital to the witness and spiritual health of the church.

3. Jude also reminds us that the grace of God can be perverted when the moral precepts of the gospel are disregarded, especially those pertaining to sexual conduct. We can delude ourselves into thinking that sexual libertinism is compatible with salvation, when in reality it is a concession to the flesh and cultural attitudes and practices that are incompatible with a faith commitment. We may not be perverting the grace of God with any *teachings* that denigrate the value of moral behavior. However, our *behavior* may be perverting the grace of God, presuming that grace easily covers behaviors that we do not desire to submit to the scrutiny of the gospel because we do not want to forsake those behaviors and let Christ be Lord.

4. The opposite of confession is denial. Like the false teachers, we will probably not verbally mouth any denial of the lordship of Christ, but also like them, we may deny his lordship by our attitudes, words, and actions. The implication of denying Jesus Christ as Lord and Master is that we serve other lords and masters. Such denial places the person once more under servitude to sin, be it materialism, self-absorption, power, or a host of other common masters (Matt 6:24; Rom 6:12-23; Gal 4:3, 8-9; 2 Pet 2:19). At the time of judgment, a life lived in denial of Christ will receive his denial, because those who serve sin do not deserve the rewards of serving him (Matt 10:33; 2 Tim 2:12; cf. Mark 8:38).

JUDE 5-16

PROOF THAT THE FALSE TEACHERS ARE UNGODLY AND SUBJECT TO JUDGMENT

OVERVIEW

Jude 5-16 forms the body middle of the letter, which develops the topics and propositions of the body opening as well as introduces new material. It begins with a disclosure formula, "I desire to remind you." The body middle develops two interrelated propositions: The false teachers are ungodly and subject to judgment, and they are the same ungodly teachers whose presence and judgment in the last days were foretold in prophecy (v. 4). The first proposition is developed with proofs from example (vv. 5-10) and from prophecy (vv. 11-13), and the second is developed with a proof from prophecy (vv. 14-16). Jude reminds the church of previous instruction delivered "once for all" by the apostles—that is, they are not in need of being supplemented by the teachings of the false teachers (vv. 3, 5, 17).[16] He tries to persuade the church of the disadvantage, dishonor, and danger of following the false teachers, thus destroying their credibility. The body middle corresponds to the rhetorical *probatio,* which presents proofs to verify the facts and propositions of the *narratio.*

16. In v. 5, some MSS place "once for all" (ἅπαξ *hapax*) after "Lord" as if it pertained to the first example, the Israelites: "the Lord, who once for all saved a people" (NRSV). But the placement before "Lord" ("you are fully informed once for all"; cf. NIV) is more likely the original reading. It parallels v. 3, where faith was "once for all" (*hapax*) entrusted to the saints. See Carroll D. Osburn, "The Text of Jude 5," *Bib* 62 (1981) 107-15.

JUDE 5-10, PROOF FROM OLD TESTAMENT EXAMPLES

COMMENTARY

Jude 5-10 is a proof that the false teachers are ungodly and thus subject to judgment. It is composed of three OT examples or types of the ungodly, their sins, and their judgments (vv. 5-7), a threefold application to the false teachers (v. 8), and amplification of the proof by comparing the false teachers with the ungodly actions of the devil (vv. 9-10).

Verses 5-7. The three examples are the Israelites in the wilderness (v. 5), the fallen angels or watchers (v. 6), and Sodom and Gomorrah (v. 7). These three examples were often used together in Jewish and Christian writings as proof that ungodly behavior brings God's judgment (Sir 16:7-10; CD 2:17–3:12; 3 Macc 2:4-7; 2 Pet 2:4-10*a*). Early Christianity also often compared false teachers with the sinners of the OT (2 Tim 3:8-9; Rev 2:14, 20). The examples are given out of chronological order, illustrating Jude's love of climax. The punishment increasingly becomes more specific and more intense—from destruction in this life by natural death to being captured in chains until final judgment to being punished in eternal fire.

The first example of the ungodly who were judged is the Israelites in the wilderness, who, hearing the report of the spies on the power of the inhabitants of Canaan, refused to enter the land because they did not believe that God had the power to fulfill the promise to give them the land. Those persons twenty years old and over died in the wilderness, except Joshua and Caleb, who believed (Numbers 14; 26:64-65; Heb 3:7–4:11). The wilderness generation was also used as an example that disbelief expresses itself in disobedience (Deut 9:23-24; Ps 106:24-27; Heb 3:16-19). This example implicitly teaches that Christians, like the wilderness generation, can lose their salvation and become the object of judgment for their unbelief and disobedience. This is the counterpart to being "kept" by God until salvation is completed at the parousia (vv. 1, 24) by "keeping" in his love through obedience (v. 21). By not "keeping" in God's love through obedience, Christians work against God's effort to keep them for salvation and thereby expose themselves to judgment.

The second example of the ungodly who were judged are the evil angels of Gen 6:1-4. These angels became known as the "watchers" in Jewish tradition. They left their heavenly places of rule in order to have sexual union with human females, thus corrupting humanity with their teachings and precipitating the flood (cf. 1 Pet 3:19-20; 2 Pet 2:4). Jude depends on this tradition as developed in *1 Enoch* 6–19 (especially chap. 10), where the watchers are bound by the archangel Michael and are placed in darkness under the earth until the day of judgment, when they will be transferred to the fires of Gehenna. Jude's message is that the false teachers also corrupt the faithful with illicit sex and false teachings (vv. 8, 18); and like the evil angels, they will be so judged. Verse 6 is reiterated and amplified in v. 13, where the false teachers are explicitly compared to the evil angels (i.e., "wandering stars") and are said to share the same judgment of deepest darkness.

The third example is the premier example of sin and divine judgment in Jewish and Christian literature: Sodom and Gomorrah (Gen 19:1-29). For Jude's audience, these cities would still have served as an example of the judgment for sin, not only because they had become part of tradition, but also because they were thought to be observable. The hot springs and sulfur deposits of the region south of the Dead Sea were considered to be the smoldering ruins of those cities.[17]

At least three interrelated sins are involved in the example of Sodom and Gomorrah. One is the sin of inhospitality through attempted violence. In the ancient world, hospitality was a virtue with many social implications. The attempt of the men to rape Lot's two guests was an obvious and grave violation of hospitality. Rabbinic tradition also emphasized inhospitality in its interpretation of the text. Jesus partially interpreted the sin of Sodom and Gomorrah as the sin of refusing to accept those bearing God's Word, which involves neglect of hospitality as well (Matt 10:14-15; 11:23-24; Luke 10:12).

A second sin is that of homosexual practice and rape. The male inhabitants of the city were seeking to rape the two angels, who appeared as men, and even threatened Lot himself with the same (Gen 19:5, 9). Homosexual practice is forbidden in the holiness code of Leviticus (Lev 18:22; 20:13). Jewish pseudepigraphical writings emphasize this aspect of the behavior of the people of Sodom and Gomorrah. The author of 2 Peter, who depends on this passage of Jude, emphasizes the lawlessness of the inhabitants (2 Pet 2:8).

A third sin, and the one most in view here, is that of humanity's seeking sexual intercourse with angels—that is, members of another level of creation. Jude says that the inhabitants of Sodom and Gomorrah were "going after different flesh" ("pursued unnatural lust," NRSV; "perversion," NIV). This does not refer to other human flesh, male or female, for that would not be different in kind. Also, this sin is indicated by the contrast Jude makes with the previous example. In the previous example, angels lusted after humans, and here humans lust after angels. Both examples teach that violating the order for creation established by God leads to the judgment of eternal fire. This is a real concern for Jude, for in v. 23 he urges the church to "snatch from the fire" those who follow the false teachers and violate God's established moral order, subjecting themselves to the judgment of the parousia.

Verse 8. The three examples of the ungodly who were judged are summarized and applied to the false teachers in order to

---

17. See Josephus *The Jewish War* 4.483; Philo *Moses* 2.56.

prove that they "in the very same way" are ungodly and subject to judgment. There is a note of disbelief here that even with these examples of sinners and judgment the false teachers continue to act the same way! Like the watchers and the people of Sodom and Gomorrah, the false teachers defile the flesh (sexual impurity). Like the wilderness generation, the watchers, and the people of Sodom and Gomorrah, the false teachers reject divine authority (cf. vv. 4-5). Like the people of Sodom and Gomorrah, they slander the glorious ones (angels), probably those who gave, guard, and watch over the observance of the law of Moses and uphold the created order (Acts 7:38, 53; Heb 2:2).[18] Perhaps these angels are pictured as accusing the false teachers of antinomianism.

In making his application Jude calls the false teachers "dreamers" (ἐνυπνιάζομαι *enypniazomai*). This term refers to the prophetic experience of receiving revelatory dreams and is usually used of false prophets in the OT (Deut 13:1-2, 4, 6 LXX; Isa 56:10 LXX; Jer 23:25; 36:8 LXX). Apparently the false teachers grounded the authority for their antinomian behavior in personal revelations. However, Jude claims that their behavior clearly shows that their revelations are false (cf. v. 19).

18. See also *Jub.* 1:27-29; Josephus *Antiquities of the Jews* 15.136; *Herm. Sim.* 8:3:3.

Verses 9-10. Jude magnifies his application with a strong contrast. As told in the lost Jewish pseudepigraphical work the *Testament of Moses,* the devil disputed with the archangel Michael for the body of Moses. The devil accused Moses of murdering the Egyptian (Exod 2:11-12) and thus claimed that Moses was undeserving of an honorable burial by Michael. The archangel Michael did not dare act on his own authority to rebuke the devil for slandering Moses; rather, he invoked God's authority as the only one who could judge the devil for slander (v. 9). This Michael did by quoting Zech 3:2, "The Lord rebuke you!" which comes from God's rebuke of the devil's accusation of the high priest Joshua.

In contrast, by rejecting divine authority and slandering the good angelic guardians of the Mosaic law who accuse them of antinomianism (v. 8), the false teachers flagrantly act illegitimately as independent authorities. Such arrogant behavior is outrageous in the light of the reticence of the vastly more powerful archangel Michael to accuse the devil. Jude implies that the false teachers must answer to God's authority and to those, like the angels, who have been entrusted to uphold it. Defiling the flesh based on the authority of one's own personal revelation is akin to an irrational animal's acting upon instinct, which will result in its destruction.

REFLECTIONS

1. When presented with teachings and behaviors at odds with the standards of apostolic tradition, Jude does not hesitate to confront them, because they pose a threat to the spiritual lives of his church. However, he does not confront them primarily with his authority as a pastor. His authority might be challenged, as the false teachers no doubt had already done in gathering a following from within the church. Rather, Jude confronts the false teachers and their doctrine with the authority of the Old Testament, with traditions held authoritative by the church, and with apostolic preaching and tradition. These are the authorities that convinced the church members to make a faith commitment in the first place. These are the authorities that point to the judgment of God upon the ungodliness of the false teachers. Again we see the importance of grounding a faith community in biblical traditions, upon which faith commitment has been made, and upon the traditions that have established the church as a faith community. These are vital resources that help a church to maintain perspective in a world of competing allegiances, doctrines, and behaviors.

2. Although the three examples of ungodly persons in this section prove mainly that the ungodly are in the end judged, there is another implicit message in the example of

the wilderness generation. Membership in the people of God depends on obedience and keeping the faith. There is such a thing as being thrown out of the family of God, of being disinherited. "Once saved, always saved" is not the motto of Jude. Those "once saved, once for all instructed" can stop relying on the promises of God and God's power to fulfill them. The "once saved" can reject divine authority, can disbelieve, and can transgress the order of creation with sexual impurity and violence, guided by mere instinct. They can become subject to divine judgment, like the watchers and the inhabitants of Sodom and Gomorrah.

3. This passage, especially v. 7, has been an important element in the ongoing discussion of the Christian response to homosexuality. As the commentary points out, homosexual practice is at least one of the sins in view in Jude's use of the example of Sodom and Gomorrah. It is currently argued that sex between members of the same sex is not at variance with Christian teaching on morality. Proponents point to the model of homosexuality in the Greco-Roman era as oppressive—relationships between an older, powerful man who dominated a younger, powerless man. This type of relationship, it is claimed, is the target of biblical prohibitions against homosexuality, and not the mutual, loving relationships one might think of today. On the one hand it must be acknowledged that the sexual practice in view in Jude is on one level rape, which is always a sin. On the other hand, Jude uses the example of the behavior of Sodom and Gomorrah in general as worthy of judgment. The threat of the similar illicit sexual behavior of the false teachers is one reason why Jude rallies the churches to contend for the faith. As a scriptural text, Jude is part of the bedrock upon which Christian ethics have been based and should not be lightly dismissed from theological debates about homosexuality.

JUDE 11-13, PROOF FROM PROPHECY

COMMENTARY

The second proof that the false teachers are ungodly and subject to judgment is found in vv. 11-13. Like the first proof (vv. 5-10), three examples of ungodly persons are presented (here as a prophecy, v. 11), followed by application to the false teachers (vv. 12-13).

Verse 11. Whereas in the first proof the false teachers are compared with three groups of ungodly persons, here they are portrayed in terms of individual ungodly persons from the OT. This makes the accusation of ungodliness more specific. This verse is a prophecy in the form of a woe oracle, a form used by OT prophets to specify sins and to pronounce God's judgment upon them. That it is an actual prophecy and not simply a denunciation in the form of a woe oracle is indicated by the use of verbs in the past tense (aorist). The prophet used the past tense because he was so sure the prophecy would be fulfilled.

The origin of this prophecy is unknown, whether an early Christian prophet or Jude himself. On the one hand, Jude is proving that the condemnation of false teachers was "long ago designated" (v. 4), which indicates that the prophecy may have originated with an early Christian prophet from the past. On the other hand, this prophecy has no preface, and Jude usually prefaces prophecies that he quotes from others (vv. 14, 17). This points to the prophecy's having originated with Jude.

The prophecy presents three OT examples of ungodly persons who led others into sin: Cain, Balaam, and Korah. Cain is portrayed as a murderer in the OT (Gen 4:1-16), and in Jewish tradition he is the archetypal sinner, exemplifying the sins of envy, greed, and hatred. By his sins he taught others to sin.[19] "Walking in the way" is a metaphor for the ethical life. Depending on which traditions he is drawing upon, by acknowledging that

---

19. Josephus *Antiquities of the Jews* 1.52-66; Philo *On the Posterity and Exile of Cain* 38-39.

the false teachers "go the way of Cain" or have "taken the way of Cain," Jude may be claiming that they are ungodly, greedy, lustful (as in vv. 16, 18), and instructors of others in sin.

Although in the biblical account Balaam refuses Balak's temptation to curse Israel for money (Num 22:18; 24:13), Jewish tradition assumed that he was a greedy false prophet who did set out to curse Israel and later persuaded Balak to lead Israel into sexual sin and idolatry (Rev 2:14).[20] By describing the false teachers as hoping to profit from Balaam's error, Jude accuses them of being false prophets (cf. vv. 8, 19) who lead the church into sexual sin (vv. 4, 6-8, 10, 15-16, 18-19) for financial reward (cf. v. 16).

Korah led a rebellion against the authority of Moses. His punishment was to be swallowed by the earth, going down to Sheol alive (Num 16:1-35; 26:9-10). In tradition he is portrayed as a schismatic[21] and the primary example of an antinomian heretic who tried to modify the law of Moses.[22] By declaring that the false teachers will "perish in Korah's rebellion," the writer of Jude is probably accusing them of having rebelled against the authority of the Mosaic law (cf. v. 8, where they rebel against the angelic guardians of the law) and of Christ himself (v. 4), and of being schismatic (cf. v. 19) and subject to judgment. To be in chronological order, the example of Korah should precede that of Balaam, but Jude may have placed it last because it is such a striking example of punishment that follows judgment.

Verses 12-13. The application of the prophecy is composed of six metaphors that emphasize the sinful nature of the false teachers and undermine their claims to be leaders and teachers. First, they are blemishes or spots (σπιλάδες *spilades*) at the love feasts, or agape meals (cf. 2 Pet 2:13). They pollute the holiness of the fellowship meals because their participation amounts to feasting without reverence or fear or "eating with you without the slightest qualm," an outgrowth of their functioning on the level of animal instinct and solely focusing on satisfying their hunger (v. 10; 1 Cor 11:20-24, 33-34). "Blemish" may

also be translated metaphorically as "reef" with the understanding that the false teachers are as dangerous to the spiritual well-being of the church as reefs are dangerous to ships.

Second, they "shepherd themselves." The idea of "feeding" that is present in the NRSV and the NIV translations is inadequate, for it brings out only one aspect of shepherding. Shepherding was a commonly used metaphor for leadership in Judaism and Christianity. The writer of Jude, then, may be alluding to Ezek 34:2, which holds the leadership of Judah ("shepherds") accountable for enjoying the benefits of leadership, but not aiding the people (cf. Isa 56:11). While the false teachers claim leadership status, they do not tend to the church's welfare but their own gain (cf. v. 16).

The remaining four metaphors are drawn from the four regions of creation: sky, earth, sea, and the heavens. They are derived from *1 Enoch* 2:1–5:4, where nature, which follows the laws God has established for it, is contrasted with the wicked, who do not, and *1 Enoch* 80:2-8, in which nature transgresses those laws and misleads the wicked in the last days. These metaphors point out that the words and deeds of these teachers show them to be false. "Waterless clouds carried along by the winds" alludes to Prov 25:14: "Like clouds and wind without rain/ is one who boasts of a gift never given" (NRSV). The metaphor implies that the false teachers cannot deliver on their teachings or promises. "Autumn trees without fruit, twice dead, uprooted" relies on the common biblical metaphor of a tree and its fruit, often extended to describe the fate of those who do not bear spiritual fruit. Here the extended metaphor implies that the false teachers will not produce any benefit for the church. Like trees that do not produce good fruit, the wicked will be uprooted and destroyed (Prov 2:22), here by the second death ("twice dead"). The second death is the fate of those who do not have Christ as their advocate at the final judgment (Rev 2:11; 20:6, 14; 21:8).

The metaphor "wild waves of the sea, casting up the foam of their own shame" is an allusion to Isa 57:20:

---
20. Philo *Moses* 1.266-268. See also Philo *Moses* 1.295-299; Josephus *Antiquities of the Jews* 4.126-30.
21. *1 Clement* 51:1-4.
22. *Bib. Ant.* 16:1.

> But the wicked are like the tossing sea
>   that cannot keep still;
>   its waters toss up mire and mud. (NRSV)

Like the sea, which tosses up debris on the beach, the false teachers produce only what is shameful. "Wandering stars, for whom the deepest darkness has been reserved forever" alludes to *1 Enoch* 18:13-16; 21:1-6; 83–88 (esp. *1 Enoch* 88:1-3) and compares the false teachers with the watchers of Gen 4:1-6 (cf. v. 6), who are represented as wandering stars who disobeyed God and were cast from heaven down into the dark abyss. Confinement to "deepest/blackest darkness" (ὁ ζόφος τοῦ σκότους *ho zophos tou skotous*) is, along with consignment to fire, a form of eternal judgment in Jewish tradition (Tob 14:10; *1 Enoch* 63:6).

REFLECTIONS

1. The use of extra-biblical Jewish tradition in the prophecy of Jude 11 may be disturbing to some readers because the accounts of those mentioned from the OT have been elaborated in Jewish tradition without any corroboration from the OT. Such use of extra-biblical sources from tradition has various origins. For example, biblical narratives can be connected with extra-biblical sources and then interpreted in the light of shared words or themes. Sometimes the use of extra-biblical tradition is extensive. For example, in the book of Revelation, the idea of the antichrist arose from extra-biblical tradition spanning millennia. The image incorporates the legends of Leviathan the chaos monster from Mesopotamian myth and Jewish accounts of the deeds of Antiochus IV Epiphanes of the Maccabean era and the Roman Emperor Nero, both of whom were portrayed as the epitome of evil.

For the writer of Jude and other writers to have relied on extra-biblical traditions may seem to some readers today to detract from the truth of the Bible. Yet we need to remember that the elaboration of the received tradition by these Jewish writers was governed by the usefulness of this in understanding God's nature and will for a covenant people. The same governing principle was used for the gathering and preservation of the biblical tradition itself. We need to look beyond the elaborated tradition to determine the point that those appropriating it, like the writer of Jude, were trying to make about God. The canonization of the Epistle of Jude indicates that its contents are authoritative regardless of its sources.

2. The agape meal was a fellowship meal held by the first-century church, of which the eucharist was the final portion (Acts 2:46-47). It was patterned on the Passover meal, which Jesus celebrated with his disciples. There Jesus instituted the eucharist as a final element of the meal. As Paul found out, the agape meal was subject to abuse if the entire affair was used only to satisfy hunger or to display wealth and status (1 Cor 11:17-34). Jude reminds us that the purity of a church can be compromised by those who no longer place themselves under the lordship of Christ and have no concern about the spiritual lives of others with whom they commune.

3. This passage provides a synopsis of just what it means to fail as a leader in the church: a personal life characterized by envy, jealousy, and lust; the motivation for ministry rooted in the love of money and material gain; rebellion against scriptural and legitimate church authority; posing a threat to the spiritual well-being of the church by corrupt personal teaching and example; focusing on physical gratification rather than spiritual nourishment; picking up the paycheck without benefit to the church providing it; making great promises and never delivering on them; and producing no spiritual fruit within one's personal or church life. This type of destructive leadership is ultimately rooted, as it was for the false teachers of Jude, in resisting the lordship of Jesus Christ and making personal and natural inclinations the sole authority in one's life.

JUDE 14-16, PROOF FROM THE PROPHECY OF *1 ENOCH*

COMMENTARY

Verses 14-16 are proof that the false teachers are the ungodly prophets who were prophesied to appear and who will be subject to judgment in the last days. The proof is comprised of the prophecy of *1 Enoch* 1:9 (vv. 14-15) and the application of that prophecy to the false teachers (v. 16). Jude now provides a prophecy that the false teachers, with their rebellious words and licentious deeds, were designated for condemnation "long ago" (v. 4). *First Enoch* portrays Enoch, in the seventh generation since Adam (Gen 5:21-24), as prophesying the judgment of the false teachers for all their deeds and words against the Lord. The prophecy originally referred to God's coming with an army of angels ("holy ones") in apocalyptic judgment, but by inserting the term "Lord" (κύριος *kyrios*), Jude has made the prophecy refer to Christ's parousia, when he will return with his angels to execute judgment. The fourfold occurrence of the word "all" (or "everyone" [πᾶς *pas*]) in the quotation effectively emphasizes the complete scope of judgment: It is upon all the false teachers for their rebellious words and ungodly acts.

In v. 16 the application of the prophecy explicates both the rebellious words and the ungodly deeds of the false teachers, making it clear how easily they can be identified as the ungodly of prophecy. Their designation as "grumblers," "malcontents," and "faultfinders" recalls rebellion against divine authority. "Grumblers" characterizes the wilderness generation (Exod 16:1-12; 1 Cor 10:10), both for the incident at Kadesh, referred to in v. 5 (Num 14:2, 27, 29, 36), and Korah's rebellion, referred to in v. 11 (Num 16:11). These teachers "indulge their own lusts" and "follow their own evil desires," like the Sodomites (v. 11). The description that "their mouths speak bombastic words" ("boast," NIV) may be derived from *1 Enoch* 1:9 or 5:4, which pertains to the ungodly who speak against the commandments and authority of God. This would be Jude's attempt to tie prophecy and application together and define the nature of rebellious speech. "Flattering people to their own advantage" is probably a reference to teaching what others want to hear (i.e., freedom from moral constraint) in order to remain in their favor and retain their financial support.[23]

---

23. Bauckham, *Jude, 2 Peter*, 99-100.

REFLECTIONS

1. One question that frequently arises is, "Why does Jude quote a prophecy that was not in the Old Testament, especially one that did not originate with the writer to whom it is attributed?" By quoting a prophecy and understanding it as having been fulfilled in the false teachers, Jude understands that prophecy to have been inspired. It must be remembered that our current canon of Scripture did not exist in Jude's day. Both Jewish and early Christian communities valued literature that was held to be authoritative, but not all such works eventually were judged to be canonical. Also, Jude's modifications of the text of *1 Enoch* to make it apply to Jesus is akin to a common practice in Jude's time of making Old Testament texts originally referring to God's coming in the day of the Lord in judgment refer to the coming of Jesus at the parousia.

2. The judgment that Jude sets forth is against both word and deed. These ungodly words are not limited to insults spoken against Jesus directly, but include any speech that is not held subject to his lordship and authority. Grumbling against the direction

God may be providing (like the wilderness generation), speaking and teaching to please others rather than being faithful to the commandments of God, and following personal desires (often sexual) wherever they lead are actions that in essence say to God, "I am my own authority; I am my own god." Such spurning of Christ may be motivated by greed and power, as in the case of the false teachers here, or simply by ignorance of God's claims on our lives.

In many cases, spurning Christ's lordship boils down to fear of what he has in store for us if he is truly Lord of our lives. Any lessening of our control over our lives frightens us. We often find ourselves saying that we have to "get our lives under control," and not that "our lives are under too much control." The unknown adventure on which Christ will lead us according to the plan he has for our lives, in which we are not the guide, may take us outside the comfortable, the familiar, and the enjoyable. But under his lordship our lives will be under control, even if we cannot always see where his directions will lead us. We may leave the comfortable and the familiar, but we will experience what is purposeful and fulfilling, not only for ourselves as we exercise our gifts, but also for the working of the kingdom on earth.

JUDE 17-23

AN APOSTOLIC PROPHECY AND INSTRUCTION ON HOW TO RESPOND TO FALSE TEACHERS

COMMENTARY

Verses 17-23 comprise the letter's closing as indicated by the direct address and the disclosure formula beginning in v. 17: "But you, beloved, must remember." The closing reiterates and emphasizes what has been said and urges the recipients to attend to and take responsibility for the matters discussed. The letter closing corresponds to the rhetorical *peroratio,* the closing of an address, which both repeats the main points that have been made and appeals to the emotion of the recipients to help ensure that they will act as desired.

Verses 17-19. Jude's reiteration takes the form of a strong proof that the false teachers are ungodly. It is comprised of a "summary" prophecy from the preaching of the apostles to the church at its founding that in the last days ungodly people will appear (vv. 17-18) and the prophecy's threefold application to the false teachers (v. 19). At that time the most outstanding resource in argumentation was often kept until the closing of an address, and this prophecy of the church's apostles is perhaps the strongest of Jude's resources.

The summary of apostolic prophecies is similar to other summaries found throughout the NT concerning the appearance of false teachers and false prophets in the last days (Matt 7:15-20; 24:11 par. Mark 13:22; Acts 20:29-30; 1 Tim 4:1-3; 2 Tim 3:1; 4:3-4; 2 Pet 3:3). "In the last time there will be scoffers, indulging their own ungodly lusts" (v. 18). "Scoffers" (ἐμπαῖκται *empaiktai*) is a strong derogatory term denoting mockery of religion or of the righteous by attitude, word, or deed. It describes the false teachers' rejection of divine authority and dismissal of ethical constraints, which are manifested in indulgence in ungodly lusts or desires (vv. 4, 6-8, 10-11, 15-16).

In the threefold application of the prophecy, the statement "They are those causing divisions" recalls the example of Korah, who incited division among the Israelites (v. 11). "Worldly people" or those "who follow mere natural instincts" are described immediately as being "devoid of the Spirit." The false teachers have physical life without the gift of the Holy Spirit (cf. 1 Cor 2:14). The identification reiterates Jude's claim that the false teachers are "dreamers" and further refutes their claim that their visions derive from the Spirit (v. 8). This combination of being denied a claim to the Spirit and creating divisions implies that the factions the false teachers create are also devoid of the Spirit.

Verses 20-23. Jude has worked to persuade the church that the false teachers are ungodly and that they are the ungodly of prophecy (vv. 4-16), and he has reiterated his message (vv. 17-19). Here he turns to elaborate just what it means "to contend for the faith" (v. 3)—that is, how to work as a church against the ungodly influence of the false teachers. His strategy for contending for the faith is found in seven exhortations. The first four, common to early Christian instruction, exhort the faithful to do what they can for themselves (vv. 20-21). The remaining three, which allude to Zech 3:2-4, exhort the faithful to aid those who have fallen prey to the false teachers (vv. 22-23). In these exhortations, Jude clearly believes that he and the church are living in the last days, for the presence of the false teachers fulfills eschatological prophecy. This expectation adds urgency to the exhortations, for the time to act is short before the parousia judgment transpires.

In the four exhortations to the faithful to do what they can for themselves (vv. 20-21), Jude first advises them to "build yourselves up on your most holy faith." He pictures the faithful church as a temple where members are a holy priesthood offering spiritual sacrifices to God (Eph 2:20-22; 1 Pet 2:5). The "holy faith" includes moral instruction, and is in sharp contrast to the antinomian teaching of the false teachers, which produces an ungodly life-style. Members of this church build up one another on faith by looking out for their spiritual welfare, in contrast to the false teachers, who divide and tear down the church (v. 19).

Second, they should "pray in the Holy Spirit," which refers to prayer under the inspiration and control of the Holy Spirit, including charismatic prayer in which the Holy Spirit supplies the words.[24] This exhortation contrasts the church that is able to pray in the Spirit with the false teachers, who may claim to possess the Spirit but are, in fact, devoid of it (vv. 8, 19).

Third, he exhorts, "Keep yourselves in the love of God." This refers to God's love for us (NIV), and not to our love for God (v. 21). Our proper response is to obey God and remain in God's love (John 15:9-10; 1 John 4:16). Our moral effort works in conjunction with God, who keeps the Christian spiritually safe until the parousia (vv. 2, 24). This stands in contrast to the false teachers, who, like the watchers, are kept for deepest darkness (vv. 6, 13).

The fourth exhortation is for them to "look forward to the mercy of our Lord Jesus Christ that leads to eternal life." Here Jude provides the community with the basis for eschatological hope—the imminent parousia when Christ will bestow the mercy of eternal life upon the faithful (vv. 2, 21) and judgment upon the ungodly (vv. 14-15).

The remaining exhortations are to the faithful and to those who follow the false teachers (vv. 22-23).[25] First, they should "have mercy on some who are wavering" or who "doubt." The faithful are to offer those who have followed the false teachers the same mercy that they themselves expect to receive at the parousia (vv. 2, 21), with the hope of saving them from judgment (v. 23). Besides "waver" or "doubt," the verb διακρίνω (*diakrinō*) may also be translated "dispute"; thus translated, this exhortation would refer to those who defend their newly accepted doctrine when confronted by the faithful. That the faithful should "save others by snatching them out of the fire" (cf. Zech 3:2) implies that the false teachers and their followers are in danger of the punishment of eternal fire (v. 7), which will befall the ungodly at the imminent parousia (vv. 10, 12-13, 14-15).

Third, the exhortation to "have mercy on still others with fear, hating even the tunic defiled by their bodies" (NRSV; "clothing stained by corrupted flesh," NIV; cf. Zech 3:3-4) warns the faithful that, while associating with the false teachers and their followers, they must be fearful of being spiritually polluted by them (vv. 8, 12), especially by the tempting sins of the flesh, which these people indulge (vv. 6-8, 10, 16, 18). More broadly, they are to fear God, who judges—a fear that contrasts the false teachers' fearless attitude toward God (v. 12). The faithful must take as much care in dealing with false teachers as they would in avoiding contact with clothing soiled by human excrement. At baptism, early Christians put on new linen clothes to symbolize purity and were not expected ever again to don the soiled clothes of the flesh, which symbolize sin (Rev 3:4).

---

24. J. D. G. Dunn, *Jesus and the Spirit* (Philadelphia: Westminster, 1975) 246.

25. Verses 22-23 have numerous textual variants. The variants generally refer to either two or three parties, the three-party reading being preferred because of Jude's predilection for triple expression. This reading has been followed by both the NRSV and the NIV. For a clear, thorough discussion, see Bauckham, *Jude, 2 Peter*, 108-11; Sakae Kubo, "Jude 22-23: Two-division Form or Three?" in *New Testament Textual Criticism*, ed. E. J. Epp and G. D. Fee (Oxford: Clarendon, 1981) 239-53; S. C. Winter, "Jude 22-23: A Note on the Text and Translation," *HTR* 87 (1994) 215-22.

REFLECTIONS

1. A major strategy in the struggle against antinomian and immoral attitudes and behavior is not simply to denounce them, but to fortify personal and community holiness and promote spiritual growth. The plan is to keep within the love of God through obedience (v. 21) and not fail in the moral walk (v. 24). The desire to remain in the love of God and to obtain the full measure of salvation in eternal life through the mercy of Jesus Christ is a motivating factor in obedience to God's commandments.

2. Jude combines a strong condemnation of sin with a concern for the restoration of fallen Christians. He points out that mercy should pour forth from the community toward those Christians who have strayed. This mercy is rooted in the mercy that faithful Christians themselves enjoy from God (v. 2) and expect to receive in full at the parousia (v. 21). Having experienced the mercy of God, Christians should be willing to extend that mercy to others. The extension of mercy is motivated by concern for the eternal status of erring brothers and sisters.

3. Jude is concerned about the contagion of sin and remaining pure from it (vv. 12, 23-24). Being prepared for the judgment of Christ requires moral purity, being spotless and blameless (Eph 1:4; Phil 2:15). False teachers are impure because they follow the path set for them by their instincts (v. 10) and passions (vv. 16, 18). In helping those who follow the false teachers, the faithful must be careful not to be contaminated by sin themselves (vv. 23-24). We cannot underestimate the temptation posed by sin because it appeals to the strong forces of our natural drives and passions, which always seek expression.

4. We all try not to stick our noses in other people's business, but Jude reminds us by his admonitions in vv. 20-23 that looking out for the welfare of other Christians is our business. This may be the positive business of building one another up as a community in which each is looking out for the other as well as for self, but it may also include stepping in to help those who have veered from the path of faith in word or deed. The motivation for our commitment to the spiritual welfare of others is in part our concern for their eternal status and the purity of the community as a whole. The New Testament teaches us to lovingly confront brothers and sisters who have strayed (Luke 17:3; 2 Thess 3:14-15; 1 Tim 5:20; Jas 5:19-20), even instructing us on the procedure (Matt 18:15-17; Titus 3:10-11) while warning us to be careful not to fall into sin ourselves in the process (Gal 6:1).

5. Several questions arise here. If Jude is assuming from prophecy, both here and in vv. 14-16, that he and his community are living in the last days, did he falsely apply those prophecies? Was he wrong? In the company of the Christians of the early church, Jude was working with a vital expectation of the imminent, dramatic, and visible return of Christ. This expectation was based in part on sayings of Jesus that can be understood to infer that the parousia would occur within the lifetime of the apostolic generation (e.g., Mark 8:38–9:1; 14:62). Even though this expectation proved to be overly optimistic, our need to conduct our lives in the light of the judgment of the parousia remains vital. This is because Christian ethics are founded on the revealed nature, will, and promises of God, which are not affected by the timing of the parousia.

JUDE 24-25

THE LETTER CLOSING AS A DOXOLOGY

COMMENTARY

Rather than conclude his letter with the usual letter closing, personal greetings, or benedictions, typical of other NT letters, Jude uses a doxology. This is appropriate, considering that the letter would probably have been read to the people gathered for worship. The doxology reminds the church of God and Christ and of the Christian's future hope. It provides a perspective for the entire letter and motivation to respond as Jude has advised. It functions like the rhetorical *peroratio* of a speech in reiterating topics (keeping, ethical purity, and authority of God and Christ) and appealing to audience emotion.

Verse 24. This verse portrays the final goal that Jude has been steering the community toward: Do not fall into sin, but stand blameless in God's presence. "Keep you from falling" alludes to the metaphor of stumbling over rocks to speak of God's power to keep the faithful from falling into sin and death (Pss 56:13; 121:3). Jude assures the church members that God can protect them from falling prey to the ungodly ways of the false teachers and thus losing their salvation (v. 2; cf. v. 21), so that they will not end up like the false teachers in being kept for deepest darkness (v. 13; cf. v. 6). The phrase "to make you stand without blemish in the presence of his glory with rejoicing" recalls the church's ultimate state of being pure and spotless sacrifices presented to God (1 Cor 1:8; Eph 5:27; Col 1:22; 1 Thess 3:13), as well as the rejoicing of God's people when God's purposes are fulfilled (1 Pet 4:13; Rev 19:7).

Verse 25. This verse is ambiguous. It may mean either that God is the Savior through Jesus Christ our Lord or that through Jesus Christ our Lord, glory, majesty, power, and authority go to God our Savior (the usual usage in Christian doxologies); but perhaps both meanings are to be inferred. These are the attributes that Christ gives to God, but that the false teachers, by their actions, deny of God. These attributes were God's "before all time and now and forever" in spite of the false teachers' temporary challenge.

REFLECTIONS

The doxology attributes our salvation as a people of God completely to God. God is our Savior through Jesus Christ. Jesus Christ revealed the true nature of God as Savior to humanity as a being of glory, majesty, power, and authority (John 14:8-14). To stand rejoicing in the presence of God is the ultimate hope that God provides us (Matt 5:8; Rev 7:15; 22:3-4). It represents the consummation of our salvation, when we are free of sin and can stand before a holy God without fear of destruction. Assurance of this hope lies in the fact that God is the One able to keep us from falling into sin to stand sinless before the throne of grace.

THE BOOK OF REVELATION
INTRODUCTION, COMMENTARY, AND REFLECTIONS
BY
CHRISTOPHER C. ROWLAND

You say that I want somebody to Elucidate my Ideas. But you ought to know that What is Grand is necessarily obscure to Weak men. That which can be made Explicit to the Idiot is not worth my care. The wisest of the Ancients consider'd what is not too Explicit as the fittest for Instruction, because it rouzes the faculties to act.
—*William Blake, Letter to Dr. Trusler, 23 August 1799.*

THE BOOK OF REVELATION

INTRODUCTION

A. The Apocalypse of Jesus Christ
B. John, the Gospel of John, and the Revelation to John
C. The World of the Apocalypse
D. Contemporary Apocalyptic: 4 Ezra and Revelation
E. A History of the Interpretation of the Apocalypse
    1. The Early Christian Context: Apocalyptic Tradition in the New Testament
    2. The Patristic Period
    3. The Joachite School
    4. The Reformation
    5. William Blake and His Contemporaries
    6. The Eschatological Synthesis of Modern Fundamentalism
    7. Historical Criticism and Modern Exegesis
    8. The Apocalypse and Art
    9. An Apocalyptic Tone in Recent Theology and Philosophy
    10. Conclusion

THE APOCALYPSE OF JESUS CHRIST

Apocalypse, revelation, promises comprehensibility and freedom from opacity, with no need for an intermediary to interpret what is immediately available to disclosure. Yet in the Apocalypse of Jesus Christ "a host of perceptions suddenly come together to form a dazzling impression (to dazzle is ultimately to prevent sight, to prevent speech),"[1] provoking instead fear, awe, and even distaste, leading to avoidance and incomprehension rather than to understanding. John's book demands attention, but its arresting manner cannot mask the fact that it, too, is only

---

1. Roland Barthes, *A Lover's Discourse: Fragments* (Harmondsworth: Penguin, 1990) 18.

indirectly related to that awesome apocalyptic experience that took place on Patmos. We would not have John's vision unless he had been obedient to the command to write down what he had seen. It may momentarily seem to beckon us into the visionary's unconscious, but, whatever the sophistication of our psychoanalytic tools, that path into the mind of the prophet is barred to us. All that we have are traces of history and biography woven into the fabric of vision and transformed by it, no longer readily available as a means of explaining what now lies before us.

In its emphasis on revelation, apocalyptic can seem to offer easy solutions whereby divine intervention, by offering insight to unfathomable human problems, can cut the knot of those intractable problems. It can be an antidote to a radical pessimism whose exponents despair of ever being able to make sense of the contradictions of human existence except by means of the revelation of God. The kinds of answers offered by the apocalypses are by no means uniform, however. There are apocalypses (or at least parts of them) that use the concept of revelation to offer a definitive solution to human problems. For instance, in the book of *Jubilees,* an angelic revelation to Moses on Sinai, there is a retelling of biblical history following the sequence of what is found in Scripture. But there are also significant divergences, especially when halakhic questions emerge. The fact that the book is a revelation to Moses functions to vindicate one side in contentious moral matters in Second Temple Judaism and to anathematize opponents. In this situation the text's meaning is transparent and is promulgated as the final, authoritative pronouncement.

Not all apocalypses offer unambiguous and exclusive answers that seem to brook no dispute, however. They certainly offer revelation, much of which is, in effect, what was traditionally believed already. The horizon of hope is reaffirmed by revelation and the historical perspective of salvation supported. But sometimes the form of the revelation is such that it can produce as much mystification as enlightenment. There is frequently a need for angelic interpretation of enigmatic dreams and visions (e.g., Rev 7:14; 17:15). Even these angelic interpretations are not without problems. It proved necessary for revelations coined in one era to be the basis of "updating" and application in the different political circumstances of another. Thus the symbolism of the fourth beast of Daniel 7 was given new meaning in the Roman period when it ceased to refer to Greece and began to refer to Rome (a process that continued, as the history of the interpretation of Daniel 7 shows). Examples of this interpretive change may be found in both Revelation 13 and 4 Ezra 12. So some apocalypses do not provide answers through revelation and offer nothing more than the refusal of a complete answer as being beyond the human mind to grasp. Instead there is a plethora of imagery or enigmatic pronouncements that leaves the reader with either no possibility of ever knowing the mind of God or tantalizing glimpses into the enigmatic symbols of dreams and visions. In 4 Ezra, the seer wishes to know why Israel has been allowed to suffer and why God seems content to allow the bulk of humanity to perish. The role of revelation, akin to God's answer in the final chapters of the book of Job, is to stress the puny nature of human understanding in the face of the transcendence of God, to stress the ultimate victory of God's righteousness and to urge the need for those committed to the ways of God to continue in the narrow way that leads to salvation. No solution to the problem is posed by the human seer. The only enlightenment offered is the need to struggle, a theme paralleled in Revelation's demand for "the endurance of the saints" (14:12 NRSV).

The book of Revelation—paradoxically the most veiled text of all in the Bible—makes great demands on those who read or hear it in pursuit of the blessing it offers. Always there is the temptation to move too quickly to interpret or translate its imagery into a more accessible mode of discourse. But then it ceases to be apocalypse, whose distinctive blend of strange symbols and oscillating narrative confronts and engages the reader, and it becomes explanatory, more prosaic discourse, dependent on the enlightened interpreter to distill (and thereby reduce) the welter of images to the prosaic and accessible. That is what we find contained within Daniel, the other apocalyptic text in the Bible. There the perplexity of the apocalyptic seer is relieved by an enlightened, angelic, rather than human, interpreter, who explains the mysterious visions Daniel has seen. The images of statue, beasts, clouds, and thrones are reduced to historical prediction, less suggestive and more tied to specific events in the past. Daniel's images, however, and not historical prediction, are included in Revelation and become part of a new disclosure, here transformed as a catalyst of new visionary wisdom. But this time no key is offered to unlock their meaning.

There have been several ways of interpreting Revelation. First, the book has been treated as a relatively straightforward account of the end of the world. In such an interpretation it is usually linked with other prophetic and eschatological texts, like Daniel, Ezekiel, and 1 Thess 4:16ff. to produce a coherent eschatological chronology. Second, the visions are related to their ancient first-century context (the so-called preterist method of interpretation). Here questions are concerned with the meaning for the original author and readers and with the need to decode the complex symbolism and its relationship to (ancient) contemporary historical realities. Third, the images are regarded as an account of the struggles facing the journey of the soul to God. Fourth, the book has been used as an interpretative lens through which to view history. With this approach, one reads a text like Revelation as a gateway to a greater understanding of reality, both divine and human, spiritual and political, that not only includes, but also transcends the understanding offered by the human senses. "What must happen soon" refers to the apocalyptic disclosure, a way of illuminating the nature of politics and religion in every age. Some interpreters of Revelation relate the text to a single set of events, whether historical or eschatological, while other interpreters allow the possibility of a multiplicity of reference. There is also a distinction between those who regard prophecy as prediction and those who regard it as pronouncement. For the former, the apocalyptic imagery is a code that can be translated into another (usually historical) discourse and in which an alternative account can be offered of the various ciphers contained in the apocalyptic texts. We assume that we are in a less fortunate position than were the original readers. There may be some force in the suggestion that, like the modern political cartoon, related as it is to a very particular context, Revelation's imagery may have struck home in ways that are difficult, if not impossible, now that the original situation that provoked the images is no longer the case. But there is no evidence that the ancient readers found it any easier to understand than we do. The only difference is that they were probably less resistant to using, and being challenged by, this kind of literature than we are.

To decode Revelation, as if it were like Morse code—a language whose only function is to conceal and is a means to an end, namely, the communication of something that has to be kept secret—fails to take seriously the apocalyptic medium. John, as the recipient of a revelation from Jesus Christ, has bequeathed to us an apocalypse, a prophecy, not a narrative or an epistle, a text requiring of its readers different interpretative skills—imagination and emotion, for example. Like a metaphor, it startles, questions, even disorients before pointing to a fresh view of reality by its extraordinary imagery and impertinent verbal juxtapositions.[2] However difficult it may be for us, we must learn to exercise those faculties that are needed to engage such a medium.

Throughout the history of interpretation it has proved impossible to resist the temptation to decode, whether in the imaginative reconstruction of Revelation's past situation or in the distillation of its symbols into a historical program, past, present, or future. As soon as the interpreter does this, the images are left behind and the peculiar ethos of the apocalyptic narrative, the story, with all its abrupt transitions and allusive quality, is lost. To put it another way, the literal gives way to the allegorical as the other story, the "translation" of those images becomes the meaning of apocalypse rather than the interweaving of image and movement of the text itself, interacting with the reader's own social location and the mysterious action of the Spirit. Succumbing to the temptation to offer what the text *really* means, in another genre, can in fact mean intellectual and spiritual laziness, demonstrating a failure of nerve and a refusal to allow the imagination to be engaged by the letter of the text. It is impossible in interpreting to avoid some kind of decoding (Rev 17:9ff. pushes us in this direction); yet the force of Revelation depends on the ability of the reader to allow its images to inform by means of a subtle interplay of text, context, and imagination.

The words of Revelation do not offer a view of things in any kind of literal way. A word used frequently in the book is ὡς (*hōs*), "as" or "like," suggesting the world of metaphor, the

---

2. See D. Cooper, *Metaphor* (Oxford: Blackwell, 1986); J. M. Soskice, *Metaphor and Religious Language* (Oxford: Oxford University Press, 1985); P. Ricoeur, *The Rule of Metaphor* (London: Routledge, 1978); N. Wolterstorff, *Divine Discourse* (Cambridge: Cambridge University Press, 1994) 193-99.

juxtaposition of words and ideas that connote a mind groping for adequate expression, rather than precise, uncomplicated depiction. Apocalyptic imagery beckons us to suspend our pragmatism and to enter into its imaginative world. That means being prepared to see things from another, unusual, point of view and being open to the possibility that difference of perspective will enrich our view and lead to difference of insight. The Apocalypse, not itself biblical interpretation but Scripture commissioned by Christ, presents the symbols and myths of what was Scripture in a new visionary form, much as Blake was to do in his mythic writings.

The visions of Revelation do not provide the currency of our everyday exchange of ideas and patterns of existence. Yet in the ancient world (and today in non-Western cultures) visions and dreams are regarded as important. The world of dreams is akin to that less ordered imaginative part of us that becomes active only when our dominant intellectual equipment itself lies dormant. When it comes to the imagination, we are like people who, having had little exercise, find themselves severely taxed by strenuous physical effort. Our imaginations are out of condition; we lack the skills to exercise our imaginations. So we are in no fit state to read Revelation with real insight. Like those who fail to see the point of the mysterious in the material, we need to cultivate imaginations that can grasp profound truths:

"What," it will be Question'd, "When the Sun rises, do you not see a round disk of fire somewhat like a Guinea?" O no, [responds William Blake] no, I see an Innumerable company of the Heavenly host crying, 'Holy, Holy, Holy is the Lord God Almighty.' I question not my Corporeal or Vegetative Eye any more than I would Question a Window concerning a Sight. I look thro' it & not with it.[3]

Apocalyptic offers us no excuse for resorting to a life based solely on fantasy; however, an understanding of what apocalypse is can lead to a more informed and obedient life. As Revelation itself indicates, to live in this way may be controversial, costly to ourselves and to our public esteem, because to live such a life is to refuse to conform to the expectations of the world unless those demands are compatible with Christ's teaching. We cannot underestimate the extent of resistance required of us. And we must be wary of hermeneutical strategies that would prevent us from making full use of a resource that would enable us to understand what to resist.

For example, the whole scope of demythologizing is really linked with the decoding mentality that has a long history in Revelation's interpretation. Demythologization was intended to enable strange texts to keep their value by getting at their "spirit" or "essence"—a typical strategy of Christian hermeneutics down the centuries. The letter of the text seems to kill, and this seems to be particularly true in the case of Revelation. The spirit, the essential message of the myth, however, can live on. But the cost of such a reading is that the literal, the medium of the message, is lost and with it the message, too. Is it a coincidence that the demythologization project got off the ground in 1942, at the height of Nazi tyranny and the most diabolical perversion of the millennial hope in the Third Reich and the unspeakable horror of the Holocaust? Bultmann's seminal essay was published then, offering a modern explanation of the gospel.[4] In one respect, such a project marked a challenge to the way mythology had been appropriated for such demonic ends. What passed as rationality needed a critique that could interpret the horror and effects of evil, a perverted millennial dream destructive in its scope.[5] But demythologizing, which at its heart sought to explain the words and images of myth in other terms, also reduced its power by its individual focus. The church's suspicion of the Apocalypse did not help, epitomized by Bultmann's description of the book as "weakly christianized Judaism," an assessment, echoing Luther's negative opinion of 1522, that Revelation is "neither apostolic nor prophetic."

Dietrich Bonhoeffer, on the other hand, exhorted fellow church men and women to be "a community which hears the Apocalypse . . . to testify to its alien nature and to resist the false principle of inner-worldliness" and so to be at the service of "those who suffer violence and injustice." In his view "the Church takes to itself all the sufferers, [all] the forsaken of every party

---

3. William Blke, *A Vision of the Last Judgment*, in *Blake: Complete Writings*, ed. G. Kaynes (London: Oxford University Press, 1966) 617.
4. R. Bultmann, "The New Testament and Mythology," reprinted in *Kerygma and Myth*, ed. H. W. Bartsch (London: SPCK, 1964).
5. N. Cohn, *The Pursuit of the Millennium* (London: Paladin, 1984).

and status. 'Open your mouth for the dumb'(Proverbs 31:8)."[6] That witness and countercultural character of the church, so well exemplified by the dualistic contrasts of the Apocalypse, challenged church people to raise their voices in protest at the treatment of Jews. It is one thing to admit the importance of apocalyptic and Revelation for the understanding of the New Testament and to see it as the "mother of Christian theology";[7] it is rather different to allege that such ideas have a continuing resonance in contemporary life.

Contemporary interpreters of the book of Revelation are in a treble bind. First of all, they are confronted with an authoritative text that claims to reveal and turns out to be, at best, enigmatic and, at worst, off-putting. Second, a century and a half of historical exegesis has only served to underline the strangeness of the text and its distance from the sophisticated discourse of the First World. Third, Revelation has a reputation for fomenting an apocalyptic, irrational attitude of a catastrophic end for humanity or of fantasies about escaping from the problems and contradictions of life. In contrast to the situation of our ancestors, and many readers of this text in developing nations, Revelation has ceased to be a significant part of our linguistic currency. We are relieved that secularism and historicism have enabled us to tame the Apocalypse and subordinate its angularity to a liberal, apparently less threatening and more inclusive spirit by decoding its message and situating its significance in a previous, more credulous age. This text, which, despite its ambiguity and transgression of boundaries, is in large part about chaos, the loosening of the bands of historical order. It bears witness to aspects of our world that we fear. Ordering, and taming, the text enables us to avoid engaging our emotions and imaginations and, eventually, our wills and thereby evacuates the text of its power to change us.

If there is a text that required a reading "against the grain"[8] of what is accepted as normal in our current situation, it is Revelation. Read "against the grain," it may put us in touch with "utopian hopes and critical energies" as "a necessary corrective to the repetition of the ever-the-same in the guise of the new, the return of the seemingly repressed even amidst apparent enlightenment."[9] It can put us in touch with a subversive, apocalyptic memory "that seems so out of place against the more frequent hopes of bleak despair" that can characterize everyday life. The "unmasking of Babylon" and the truth about empire can enable us to see, perhaps to our discomfort and sadness, that "the cultural monuments celebrated by official, establishment history could not be understood outside the context of their origins, a context of oppression and exploitation." Apocalypse offers a fleeting glimpse of an alternative, the "involuntary memory of a redeemed humanity which contrasts with convention and false tradition."[10] It beckons us to rescue tradition from convention and to wrest it away from a conformity that is about to overpower it. Walter Benjamin's words, written at the end of his life, as he contemplated persecution and death, offer an eloquent description of the hermeneutics of the book of Revelation.

Revelation, and the apocalyptic tradition generally, has often been linked to the projects of agents of social change; yet it can be found buttressing the projects of those whose quest for utopia is firmly rooted in conventional values and the nostalgic yearning for a golden age of moral perfection based on hierarchy and subservience. In this nostalgic quest, apocalyptic symbolism serves to undergird a view of the world that supports the conviction of a comfortable elect that they will ultimately be saved. This outlook, with its alternative horizon beckoning toward a different future, enables a group to maintain clearly defined lines between the godly and the godless. On the other hand, apocalyptic symbolism can serve to enable the oppressed to find and maintain a critical distance from an unjust world, to claim the hope of a reign of justice. There is little new in this struggle over the language of apocalypse; apocalyptic symbolism has never been the sole preserve of the oppressed and the poor. Even in post-exilic Israel, in the very years when eschatological hope was being formed, there was a common stock of images that both sides in a struggle for power used to achieve pre-eminence for their own positions.[11] In our time,

---

6. Dietrich Bonhoeffer, *No Rusty Swords* (London: Collins, 1965) 324-25.
7. E. Käsemann, *New Testament Questions of Today* (London: SCM, 1969).
8. W. Benjamin, "Theses on the Philosophy of History," in *Illuminations*, ed. H. Arendt (London: Collins Fontana, 1978).
9. Benjamin, "Theses on the Philosophy of History," 255ff.
10. On the importance of the church as a place of alternative and healing memories see W. Benjamin, *Memory and Salvation* (London: Darton, Longman and Todd, 1995).
11. P. Hanson, *The Dawn of Apocalyptic* (Philadelphia: Fortress, 1974); cf. O. Plöger, *Theocracy and Eschatology* (Oxford: Blackwell, 1968).

the rhetoric of the "evil empire" is as likely to be found in the corridors of economic and political power as in the grassroots Bible study groups of developing nations.

In the last century, we have labored to reconstruct an original historical context with care and precision, thinking it would enable us to hear the message as it was heard originally. But we cannot achieve that aim, in spite of the sophistication of our endeavors and the extent of our knowledge. Few of us are either a frightened minority or a people saturated with the images and outlook of apocalypse (some may say, though, that those of us in the West or in the "North" are "Laodiceans" or "Ephesians," who are lukewarm or have lost our first love), desperately and unwittingly compromised in our allegiance to the beast and Babylon. We are resistant to a text that confronts our particular interests and the power structures in which we are so deeply implicated. So we either avoid it or simply cannot hear "what the Spirit says to the churches." We fulfill the pessimistic prophecy of Isaiah and become more deaf rather than more receptive. Our deafness is increased as we treat the text as marginal to most churches or simply ignore it.

It is a telling fact that few people may, in fact, hear this text in the normal course of Christian worship. *The Revised Common Lectionary* prescribes ten readings from Revelation over the three-year cycle. Of these ten readings, five are from Revelation 21–22, four from two passages (1:4-8; 7:9-17), and one from chapter 5. That what we read in the church is a matter of ecclesiastical politics is evident from the fact that for centuries the Church of England allowed only small parts of the book of Revelation to be read at morning and evening prayer.[12] In churches that assert in their formularies that the Scriptures contain everything necessary for salvation, this is a remarkable phenomenon. To paraphrase Bonhoeffer's words, we have ceased to be a community that hears the Apocalypse, for the simple reason that we do not allow ourselves the opportunity of hearing, let alone keeping, its words.

Any commentary can go only part of the way to enabling readers and hearers to become what Bonhoeffer describes as a community of the Apocalypse. What follows is divided into sections on "Commentary" and "Reflections." The Commentary sections will provide resources for reading the text, with attention given to vocabulary and textual and translation problems,[13] connections with other parts of the text, and, where appropriate, other biblical texts. It is intended to facilitate reading and to aid reflection on the book of Revelation. Commentary cannot replace reading, hearing, and keeping the words of this book, however. Neither is the particular experience of the commentator in the Reflections the last word on the meaning of this profound text. Indeed, often it is those who have been in Bonhoeffer's predicament or who more recently have had to be prophets against the injustice of empire nearer our own day who can find resonances in the images of the book.[14] A commentary is an ancillary tool; it should never stand in the way of the imaginative engagement provided by the text. Indeed, its very prosaic character may itself pose a problem: It cannot do justice to the character of apocalyptic discourse in the manner of picture or poem, for a pedestrian explanation, however suggestive and allusive, reduces and diminishes the power of symbolism and myth. Those images may be more allusive and less precise, but better able to stimulate those aesthetic faculties that enable us to read apocalyptic literature. In lieu of poem or vision, therefore, we must recognize the possible "scandal" caused by prosaic comments about our understanding and the tendency to mask rather than to unveil the meaning of the vision.

Hearing "what the Spirit says to the churches" is a complex interaction of text and interpreter at a particular time and place. It is the commentator's job to enable that interaction and not to pre-empt it by suggesting that *the* meaning of the text is readily available—if only one has the expertise to extract it. Commentators cannot avoid reflecting their own concerns and prejudices, whether academic or political, however. Commentary and reflection, therefore, are inevitably intertwined, and any commentator who has studied the text will be able to report on the way the constellation of text, reader, and social context has engendered meaning. Such

---

12. F. E. Brightman, *The English Rite* (London: Rivingtons, 1915) 1:51. In 1661, lessons from Revelation were to be read only on certain feasts. The situation changed later when Revelation (except chaps. 9; 13; and 17) was prescribed to be read in the month of December.
13. On the text of Revelation, see H. C. Hoskier, *Concerning the Text of the Apocalypse* (London: Quantch, 1929).
14. See A. Boesak, *Comfort and Protest* (Edinburgh: T. & T. Clark, 1987); P. Richard, *Apocalypse* (Maryknoll, N.Y.: Orbis, 1995).

particular readings of what I have discerned in Revelation have *largely* been explored in the Reflections sections.

A necessary check in our quest for understanding is to pay attention to the way the text has been interpreted in different theological and socioeconomic settings. Such a diachronic perspective ensures that the contemporary commentator's line is placed firmly in the broader context of the experience of a cloud of witnesses, whose insight is an essential context of any contemporary crystallization of meaning. Short of writing a commentary that included all strands of interpretation of this text in a vast compendium, there is the need to be selective, and so to constrict.

So determining the meaning of the text is always a contextual enterprise that cannot avoid an individual and social dimension. That will require of us discipline and self-critical awareness of what we bring to our reading. If we are going to seek to understand God's Word, we need honesty about ourselves, whether individually or socially. Like the biblical writers, we have a story to tell that we would do well not to avoid lest it reappear as a kind of unseen and, perhaps, unwelcome guest at our interpretative feast. We cannot put our experience to one side. Too often, unfortunately, the welter of concerns and opinions about matters religious, political, and psychological is unseen, but all too pervasive. We bring to our interpretation who we are, our personal and psychological history, and where we are, whether we approach the text from an inner-city community or a wealthy suburb, from a prosperous Western nation or from a poor shanty town of a developing nation.[15] It is helpful when we read any biblical book, but particularly one like Revelation, where the opportunity for variety of interpretation and application is much greater, to read with heightened awareness of ourselves and our own concerns. Feminist and liberationist perspectives in particular have pointed out how much we can miss in our reading. Recognizing what we most have to lose by taking the challenge of the text seriously or what it is we might need to learn to support or justify by reference to Scripture will help us to have ears to hear what the Spirit says in the text.

Although there are some peculiarities about the exegesis of Revelation, as with any biblical book, it is necessary to acknowledge the importance of the interaction of three dimensions in the hermeneutical process: text, context, and reader. The interaction constantly demands the highest level of awareness of self and of circumstance on the part of the interpreter. Space is created to reflect, so that the interpreter can explore the extent to which self-interest is projected onto the text or whether one is resistant to it. It is necessary for interpreters to distance themselves from the text in order not to make facile assumptions or to be controlled by unstated commitments to a particular tradition's reading of the text. Strategies of distancing can also call attention to the reasons for resistance to or too-ready acceptance of a text. We shall want to ask ourselves why we allow ourselves to be carried along by a text or a particular way of reading and what the resistance to a text says about us. Also, and most important, we must avoid treating texts as a problem that we as enlightened, modern interpreters can solve. Part of the process of reading is that critical self-awareness and attentiveness that may mean a reversal of roles in which interpreters in humility recognize that they need to become the ones who in some sense are being interpreted by the text.

In the Commentary, I attempt to avoid prematurely pushing the reader into any particular meaning for the text. A commentator on Revelation struggles to find ways to enable interaction with the text as we have it, thereby engaging the imagination, so that the book, with its peculiar network of imagery, may begin to pervade the reader's consciousness so that prejudice can be challenged. It is *this* text, *these* images that we need to read, not an explanation, however politically or theologically acceptable it may be. Revelation summons us into an apocalyptic world to be confronted by, infused with, and, perhaps, overpowered by (for good or ill) its images. Like John, we are called to "come up here, and I will show you what must take place"—not as interpreters or calculators of a precise eschatological program so much as co-participants in mental agony that wrenches us from our prejudice. The door of perception lies open, and we can experience apocalypse, just as John found himself reading or recalling, meditating upon,

---

15. See the general articles on reading the Bible from particular social locations in *The New Interpreter's Bible*, 12 vols. (Nashville: Abingdon, 1994) 1:150-87.

seeing again, writing, and being formed by the images of Ezekiel, Daniel, Isaiah, and the prophets. John sees the vision as Ezekiel would have seen it had the exilic prophet been inspired in John's circumstances. John repeats Ezekiel's experience in seeing the heavens opened (4:1; cf. Ezek 1:1) and seeing the awesome divine throne and the eating of the scroll (10:9; cf. Ezek 3:1ff.); like Daniel, John sees a divine figure who is the author of the revelations of what is to come (1:13ff.; cf. Dan 10:5-6).[16]

The way Revelation engages us and transforms us is as much a story of how apocalypse takes place with every reading, every "digesting" of this text, as an interpretation or commentary.[17] A new moment of unveiling occurs through the images and the configuration of visions that John has bequeathed to us, and not in spite of them. We may be curious about the meaning of symbols or perhaps distracted by the odd historical reference, but we need to remember that our fundamental task is to read, to hear, and to appropriate, in whatever way our faculties allow us, the contents of this book, having thereby our perspective transformed and our imagination engaged. What we have in Revelation is the opening of an interpretative space for readers or hearers to be provoked, to have their imaginations broadened, and to be challenged to think and behave differently. The words of the book resist neat encapsulation and the precision of definition. It is a classic example of art that *stimulates* rather than *prescribes*. Readers do not require explanation so much as the encouragement to explore its words and images, so that they may be able to see and behave differently. The point is put very succinctly by William Blake in response to a request for the elucidation of his images:

> You say that I want somebody to Elucidate my Ideas. But you ought to know that What is Grand is necessarily obscure to Weak men. That which can be made Explicit to the Idiot is not worth my care. The wisest of the Ancients consider'd what is not too Explicit as the fittest for Instruction, because it rouzes the faculties to act.[18]

From time to time in the Reflections, Blake's words and images are called upon. The most important reason for my doing so is that Blake was a visionary and thought of himself as a prophet. In this respect, he differs from most of us who are exegetes, who, whatever our desire to exercise a prophetic ministry, cannot pretend to have the kind of call that Blake had and that he shared with John, whose words were such a fundamental part of his life and writing.

Apocalypse is not a manual of eschatology, ethics, or theology, and yet it enables all of these. By refusing the predictable and by demanding that suspension of what counts for normality, we may perceive where the beast and Babylon are to be found. Whether as a result of reading and hearing the words of this prophecy we will see, understand, and repent of our allegiance to Babylon and to the beast—whose power over our minds and our social and economic structures is revealed to John in Revelation—and so choose to stand with the Lamb. What Revelation offers is the hope of a time when "the war of swords departed now" and "the dark Religions are departed & sweet Science reigns."[19]

JOHN, THE GOSPEL OF JOHN, AND THE REVELATION TO JOHN

External evidence concerning the apostle John and his relationship to Revelation comes relatively early in the Christian tradition. In commenting on Rev 20:4, Justin talks of John as one of the apostles of Christ who prophesied of the apocalypse that came to him.[20] Papias is reputed to have attested to the worth of Revelation,[21] though earlier Eusebius had a low opinion of Papias because of his millenarian views, as also did Melito of Sardis.[22] According to Tertullian, Marcion

---

16. D. Halperin, *Faces of the Chariot* (Tübingen: Mohr, 1988) 71.
17. See G. Loughlin, *Telling God's Story: Bible, Church and Narrative Theology* (Cambridge: Cambridge University Press, 1996).
18. William Blake, Letter to Dr. Tusler, 23 August 1799, in Keynes, *Blake*, 793.
19. William Blake, *The Four Zoas*, in Keynes, *Blake*, , 855.
20. Justin *Dialogue* 81:4.
21. See W. G. Kümmel, *Introduction to the New Testament* (London: SCM, 1975) 470.
22. A commentary on Revelation is listed among the works of Melito. See Eusebius *Ecclesiastical History* 4.26.2.

rejected Revelation as being a Jewish text,[23] and in the aftermath of the Montanist movement, Dionysius of Alexandria denied that Revelation was written by John the apostle.[24]

Traditionally the date of the book's writing has been set toward the end of the reign of Roman Emperor Domitian (the mid-90s), who took action against some members of the imperial household for their atheism; that may be a reference to Christianity, but equally could have been Judaism.[25] That may have been part of a much wider attempt to impose a tax on Jews and Jewish sympathizers (Christians would have fallen into that category). In that situation, there may have been a wave of sporadic persecution or harassment, but it is uncertain whether it was empire-wide in scope.

Evidence from Revelation itself suggests that an earlier date is equally likely. This derives from the most obvious reading of Rev 17:9-10. After Nero's death in 68 CE, there were four claimants to the throne in one year. So it may have been during the period of great upheaval in the empire while the power struggle was going on that John saw his vision. But the events of the 60s could easily have dominated the visionary horizon if he had his vision thirty years later (see the Commentary on 17:9).[26]

We know little other than what the book tells us about how John received this revelation. We will never know whether, like a poet, he exercised that mixture of imagination and attention to form that is characteristic of poetry, or whether he offers in the book the account of a true visionary experience. Many commentators suppose that Revelation is a conscious attempt to write an apocalypse, much as Paul would have written an epistle. Such an assessment is unsatisfactory, however. There are signs in the book of that dream-like quality in which the visionary not only sees but also is involved (e.g., 1:12, 17; 5:4; 7:13; 11:1; 17:3; cf. 1:10; 21:10). We should pay John the compliment of accepting his claim—unless we find strong reasons for denying it. There is in it a semblance of order, that, whatever the reservations of commentators, does yield a coherent pattern and deserves to be made sense of unless the juxtapositions seem totally contradictory. In some respects, Revelation differs markedly from a Jewish apocalypse like *1 Enoch*, which is a collection of heterogeneous material. The ordering in Revelation, however, need not exclude the possibility that it contains the visions that John saw, either on one single occasion or over a long period of time.

It has become something of a commonplace in New Testament scholarship to suppose that the Gospel of John represents the antithesis to the apocalyptic spirit of the Apocalypse. The Gospel of John at first sight seems a strange companion to Revelation, not least because its form and content are so markedly different. It has been so linked with Revelation because Christian tradition almost entirely asserts common authorship for the two works.[27]

The tradition that John the son of Zebedee ended his life in Ephesus offers an important connection with Revelation's setting in Asia Minor.[28] Obviously the narrative form of the Gospel places it at a significant distance from the Apocalypse. The Gospel contains few of the elements of an apocalypse, with the word ἀποκάλυψις (*apokalypsis*, "revelation") being used.

The Gospel of John is apparently the least apocalyptic document in the New Testament. It has frequently been regarded as an example of that type of Christianity that firmly rejected apocalyptic. By that is often meant that there is no imminent expectation of the end but rather the necessity of preparing for an unexpected and uncertain future for the church devoid of an apocalyptic horizon. Yet the main thrust of the message of the Gospel of John appears to have a remarkable affinity with apocalyptic. John Ashton rightly calls the Gospel of John "an apocalypse in reverse,"[29] for the heavenly mysteries are not to be sought in heaven but in Jesus, "the one who has seen the Father" (5:37) and makes the Father known. Admittedly, the mode of revelation stressed in the Gospel differs from that outlined in the apocalypses. The goal of apocalyptic

---

23. Tertullian *Against Marcion* IV.4.
24. Eusebius *Ecclesiastical History* vii.25.1ff.
25. Dio Cassius *Histories* 67-68.
26. See the discussion in Leonard L. Thompson, *The Book of Revelation: Apocalypse and Empire* (New York: Oxford University Press, 1990); and C. Rowland, *The Open Heaven: A Study of Apocalyptic in Judaism and Early Christianity* (London: SPCK, 1982) 403-13.
27. See M. Hengel, *The Johannine Question* (London: SCM, 1989).
28. Irenaeus *Against Heresies* iii.1.2. Cf. Eusebius *Ecclesiastical History* v.20.4.
29. J. Ashton, *Interpreting the Fourth Gospel* (Oxford: Oxford University Press, 1991) 381-406.

is the attainment of knowledge of the divine mysteries, in particular the mysteries of God. Much of what the Fourth Gospel says relates to this theme. Jesus proclaims himself as the revelation of the hidden God (1:18; 14:8). The vision of God, the heart of the call experiences of Isaiah and Ezekiel and the goal of the heavenly ascents of the apocalyptic seers, is in the Fourth Gospel related to the revelation of God in Jesus. All claims to have seen God in the past are repudiated; the Jews are told: "You have never heard his voice or seen his form" (John 5:37 NRSV; cf. Deut 4:12). Even when, as in Isaiah's case, Scripture teaches that a prophet glimpsed God enthroned in glory, this vision is interpreted in the Gospel of John as a vision of the pre-existent Christ (John 12:41). No one has seen God except the one who is from God; he has seen the Father (John 6:46). So the vision of God reserved in the book of Revelation for the fortunate seer (4:1) and for the inhabitants of the new Jerusalem, who will see God face to face (22:4), is found, according to the Fourth Evangelist, in the person of Jesus of Nazareth. Possibly in the Fourth Gospel an attempt is made to repudiate the claims of those apocalyptists who claimed to have gained divine knowledge by means of heavenly ascents to God's throne when Jesus says to Nicodemus: "No one has ever gone into heaven except the one who came from heaven—the Son of Man" (John 3:13 NIV). In the Gospel of John, the quest for the highest wisdom of all, the knowledge of God, comes not through the information disclosed in visions and revelations but through the Word become flesh, Jesus of Nazareth. Thus, even if there is a rejection of any claim to revelation except through Christ, there is presupposed a claim to revelation with many affinities to Revelation.

John's narrative seems, on the face of it, totally devoid of the apocalyptic symbolism of the cosmic struggle. There is nothing of Jesus' struggles with the powers of darkness, familiar to us from the synoptic exorcisms, or the eschatological discourse of Mark 13 and parallel texts; John's Gospel seems to be devoid of the prophetic message of institutional judgment and cosmic upheaval. It is striking how apparently matter-of-fact the account of the passion of Jesus appears to be in the Fourth Gospel. There are no portents like the rending of the veil or the darkness that attends Jesus' death.

Yet telling the merely human story is insufficient to give an adequate impression of its significance, perhaps hinted at in Jesus' words to Pilate in John 19:11. The confrontation between darkness and light, between truth and the lie, between God and Caesar is all bound together and acted out in the discussion with Pilate. These machinations of the political powers cannot be understood apart from the apocalyptic struggle—a moment of eschatological judgment is going on behind the scenes (e.g., John 3:19), which is not confined to individual members of humanity (as 12:31; 14:30; and 16:11 make clear). The advent of Christ effects a cosmic judgment in which the dominance of the rule of the present is both called into question and brought to an end.

In John 12:27ff. there is a rare appearance of apocalyptic discourse epitomized by the heavenly voice, for which the crowds, faced with the characteristic ambiguity of the heavenly revelation, offer differing interpretations. Jesus then asserts: *"Now* is the time for judgment on this world; now the prince of this world will be driven out" (John 12:31 NIV, italics added). There is a link with the cross (e.g., John 12:33; cf. 13:1; 17:1). But the emphatic "now" in John 12:31 suggests that the triumph is not solely focused on the cross. Indeed, according to John 3:19 the eschatological judgment has already been brought into effect by the coming of the Son into the world. The life of Jesus, therefore, is a struggle that reaches a decisive moment in John 12:31.

In Rev 12:7, the battle in heaven leads to Satan's ejection from heaven to earth with the consequent threat to its inhabitants and their corruption by the evil empire. It is then followed in Revelation 13 by the specific embodiment of the diabolical threat in the beasts of political power. In John 12, the moment of the judgment of the world comes shortly after the declaration of the ruler of the world's ejection and just before the reference to the devil's/Satan's entering Judas (John 13:2, 27; note the eschatological role of humans in 1 John 2:19-20; 3:12ff.) and the beginning of the political maneuverings that lead to Jesus' death. The apocalyptic struggle is acted out on the plane of human history and reaches its climax in the cross. We can go further and note that in Revelation 12 there is the juxtaposition of Satan's ejection and the snatching up of the messianic child to heaven, similar to the juxtaposition of Satan's ejection and the lifting up of the Son of Man in John 12.

As in Rev 11:5 and 12:7, there is a decisive moment at the end of John 12, suggesting that a moment of decision has come and passed. There is now division between those who follow Jesus and those who, like Judas, find themselves permeated by darkness, and follow the ruler of the world. Yet the diabolical initiative that leads to the crucifixion is in reality the moment of the lifting of the Son of Man to heaven. To put it in the language of the Apocalypse, it is the moment when the Lamb opens the heavenly book of judgment and takes a place in the throne of glory. In the "ordinary" world of narrative (with only the barest hints of the apocalyptic scenario acted out, as it were, behind the scenes), the crisis in John 12 reverberates throughout the universe. However much the Gospel seems to offer hope only to that small remnant of perceptive people (John 17:24), that wider vision of the decisive shift in the fundamental nature of things, symbolized by the fracture of the power of all that is opposed to God, is not lost completely. Those who identify with Jesus bear witness to that shift in power, which demands of them public and costly witness, much as is required of those who refuse to conform to the demands of the beast in Revelation. In this they are accompanied by the cosmic role of the Spirit, whose function is not merely ecclesial but social and cosmic also (John 16:9ff.).

According to Revelation 14:7, the hour of judgment will have come when God's just and true judgments are revealed (cf. 16:7; 18:10). That true judgment is stressed by the Johannine Jesus in John 8:16. The judgment is focused on the fact that "the light has come into the world, and people loved darkness rather than light because their deeds were evil" (John 3:19; cf. Rev 9:20; 16:9). Judgment comes through believing the Son (3:18) who is not sent as judge (3:17; 8:15; 12:47; cf. 8:50); the one who does not believe is judged already (3:18). Yet elsewhere it is for judgment that Christ came into the world (9:39) and exercises judgment as the Son of Man (5:27; cf. 12:10; Dan 7:13-14). Father and Son are linked together like the Lamb and the one seated on the throne in 7:17. In Revelation, the judgment belongs to God but is exercised, too, by the rider on the white horse (19:11). John 5:24 echoes the blessings of Revelation on those who hear and keep the words of the prophecy (Rev 1:3; 22:7, 14). Judgment is in the past tense for the one who "hears my word and believes him who sent me" (John 5:24 NRSV), just as in Revelation the martyr who participates in the millennium does not come to judgment and the second death that is linked with it (20:6; that judgment is described in John 5:28 in terms remarkably similar to Rev 20:13).

These similarities of theme cannot mask the difference of perspective that an apocalypse gives. Here the veil is removed, and the reader glimpses what goes on behind the scenes. This is only hinted at in the Gospel of John. Readers' attention is focused not on the "beyond" but on the Word become flesh: "Whoever has seen me has seen the Father" (John 14:9 NRSV). We shall never know whether the Gospel and the Apocalypse were written by the same author. Yet the ancient tradition that links the two has, on closer inspection, something to commend it and suggests that more than merely superficial similarity that may offer by connection and contrast fruitful interpretative avenues for the exegete.

THE WORLD OF THE APOCALYPSE

There are other works that offer revelations of divine secrets similar in form and content to the New Testament apocalypse; indeed, they derive their generic description "apocalypse" from Rev 1:1. It is not the way in which the writers of these works, which are formally so similar to Revelation, describe their writings, however. The use of the words "revelation" (ἀποκάλυψις *apokalypsis*) and "reveal" (ἀποκαλύπτω *apokaptō*) to describe a vision from God or a revealing of divine secrets is relatively rare in literature written around about the time of Revelation.[30]

---

30. The evidence is set out in M. Smith, "On the History of ἀποκαλύπτω/ἀποκάλυψις," in *Apocalypticism in the Mediterranean World and Near East*, ed. D. Hellholm, 2nd ed. (Tübingen: Mohr, 1989) 9ff. See also F. Mazzaferri, *The Genre of the Book of Revelation from a Source Critical Perspective* (Berlin: De Gruyter, 1989); M. Bockmuehl, *Revelation and Mystery* (Tübingen: Mohr, 1990); M. Freschkowski, *Offenbarung und Epiphanie* (Tübingen: Mohr, 1995–97); D. Aune, *Prophecy in Early Christianity and the Ancient Mediterranean World* (Grand Rapids: Eerdmans, 1983); J. C. VanderKam and W. Adler, *The Jewish Apocalyptic Heritage in Early Christianity* (Assen: Van Gorcum, 1996).

They include a work heavily interpolated by a Christian editor, the *Testaments of the Twelve Patriarchs*[31] and *Joseph and Aseneth,* a work written probably in Egypt around about the beginning of the Christian era (16:7; 22:9).

The words are more common in the New Testament. In the Gospels, *apokalypsis* is found at Luke 2:32 in Simeon's song in a context in which already the revelation of a mystery, which angels desire to look upon, had been celebrated (Luke 2:13; cf. 1 Pet 1:11-12). The salvation is described by Simeon as light and glory, suggesting a mystery revealed "for the Gentiles" (cf. Eph 1:17; Col 1:26). Elsewhere, *apokalypsis* appears in contexts dealing with the eschatological revelation of secrets (Matt 11:25 // Luke 10:21; Matt 11:27; 16:17; in the quotation of Isa 53:1 in John 12:38 [see also John 1:31; 2:11; 7:4; 9:3; 17:6; 21:1, where *phaneroō* is used]; and of the day of the Son of Man in Luke 17:30).

Apokalypsis is central to Paul's self-understanding (Gal 1:12). It is both something past and a future hope as well (1 Cor 1:7; cf. 2 Thess 1:7; 1 Pet 1:7; Rev 1:13; 4:13). Such revelations could be experienced both by him and by members of the church (1 Cor 14:26; 2 Cor 12:2ff.; Gal 2:2; Eph 1:17; Phil 3:15). The enigmatic passage in 2 Cor 12:2ff. is closest to what we find in Revelation. There Paul writes of an ascent to heaven and "visions and revelations" (ἀποκαλύψεις *apokalypseis*). The former (*optasia*) is used of angelic appearances in Luke 1:22 and of Paul's conversion experience in Acts 26:19. It is the word used for the translation of the Hebrew word מראה (*mar'eh*), the chief term for the visions in Daniel 10 (in Theodotion's Greek translation of the Old Testament, *apokalyptō* is introduced in passages where the earlier Greek versions used other words, e.g., Dan 2:19, 47; 10:1; 11:35). *Apokalyptō* is used of the present manifestation of God's wrath (Rom 1:17-18) and the divine mystery (1 Cor 2:10). Paul writes of the gospel as that which is made manifest (Rom 3:21), echoing the way he speaks of Christ's impact on him (Gal 1:16). The mystery of hidden things made manifest is found in Col 1:26 (*phaneroō*; cf. 3:4; Eph 3:3, 5) and in the doxology that concludes Romans (Rom 16:25). The terminology is used of eschatological unveiling as well. The coming of Antichrist has still to be revealed (2 Thess 2:3), as do the judgment of human works (1 Cor 3:13) and the demonstration of the identity of the children of God (Rom 8:18-19; a usage evident also in 1 Pet 1:5; 5:1).

"Apocalyptic" has passed into common parlance as a way of speaking of a doom-laden outlook on life or a pattern of thought replete with the symbols and imagery of Revelation, and it can often be found in discussions of contemporary economic, social, and political affairs.[32] There has been much confusion in the discussion of apocalyptic, in particular regarding its relationship to eschatology. Indeed, the two are often closely related and used virtually interchangeably.

A distinction is usually made in contemporary scholarly discussion between apocalyptic (or apocalypticism) and the apocalypse. Indeed, it is important to note that apocalyptic is used by modern interpreters as an interpretative device to explain certain features of Second Temple Jewish prophetic texts.[33] Apocalypse is used to describe a particular literary type found in the literature of ancient Judaism, characterized by claims to offer visions or other disclosures of divine mysteries concerning a variety of subjects. Usually in Jewish and early Christian texts, such information is given to a biblical hero like Enoch, Abraham, Isaiah, or Ezra, so pseudonymity is characteristic of these writings. The apocalypse is to be distinguished from apocalyptic, a cluster of mainly eschatological ideas having to do with the secrets of heaven and God's plan for the cosmos. Apocalyptic ideas may also be found in a variety of texts that are not revelatory in form or intent. In the New Testament, the book of Revelation is an obvious example of an apocalypse. But passages like Mark 13, where Jesus speaks of the future, and 1 Thess 4:16 have been regarded as examples of apocalyptic, with their descriptions of the irruption of the Redeemer into history and (in the case of Mark 13) the cosmic catastrophes that must precede the coming of the heavenly Son of Man (indeed, Mark 13 is often misleadingly called "the little apocalypse").

---

31. See Reuben 3:15; Judah 16:4; Joseph 6:6; Levi 1:2; 18:2; Benjamin 10:5.
32. See Rowland, *The Open Heaven*; J. J. Collins, *The Apocalyptic Imagination* (New York: Crossroad, 1985).
33. J. Barton, *The Oracles of God: Perceptions of Ancient Prophecy in Israel After the Exile* (London: Darton, Longman & Todd, 1986).

We may best understand the enormous variety of material in the apocalypses if we consider them not merely as eschatological tracts satisfying the curiosity of those who wanted to know what would happen in the future but as revelations of divine secrets whose unveiling will enable readers to view their present situation from a completely different perspective. So, in the case of Revelation, the letters to the churches offer an assessment of the churches' worth from a heavenly perspective: The vision of the divine throne room in Revelation 4 enables the churches to recognize the dominion of their God; in Revelation 5, the death and exaltation of Christ are shown to mark the inauguration of the new age; and in chapters 13 and 17 the true identities of the beast and Babylon are divulged.

The origins of the apocalyptic genre are much disputed. In their concerns with the mysteries of God and the fulfillment of the divine purposes, these works have a close affinity to the prophetic literature of the Old Testament. That only one apocalypse is included in the canon of the Old Testament, the book of Daniel, should not be taken as an indication that the compilers of the canon did not have much interest in the apocalyptic tradition, as there seems to have been a lively apocalyptic oral tradition in Judaism that had a long history. The discovery of fragments of the Enoch apocalypse at Qumran have pushed the date of this particular text back well before the second century BCE—back, in other words, into that obscure period when the prophetic voice began to die out in Israel. Apocalyptic continued to play a vital part within Jewish religion throughout the period of the Second Temple, and even in rabbinic circles it persisted as an esoteric tradition that manifested itself in written form in the much later *Hekaloth* tracts and later on in the Kabbalah.[34] There is a paucity of references to apocalyptic matters in early rabbinic literature,[35] and apocalypses like the books of Enoch are not quoted or thought of as authoritative.

During the period of the Second Temple and immediately after its destruction in 70 CE, there existed a mystical tradition among several prominent rabbis that was based on the startling description of the throne-chariot in the first chapter of Ezekiel and the account in Genesis 1. While there was considerable suspicion of this tradition among the rabbis, there is also evidence that many treasured apocalyptic ideas. It is likely that some of the rabbis who occupied themselves in the study of texts like Ezekiel 1 actually experienced ecstatic ascents to heaven to behold the divine throne-chariot, similar to that described by John in Revelation 4. The resort to apocalypticism by visionaries and writers took place in a variety of circumstances. While many of the apocalypses written during the Second Temple period in their present form are products of careful editing, it is possible that actual experiences may lie behind them, and this possibility should not be ruled out in the case of the New Testament apocalypse. The discovery of apocalypses in the Gnostic library at Nag Hammadi may indicate some relationship between apocalyptic and gnosticism, particularly in the light of their common concern with knowledge. As far as one can see, apocalyptic did not reach a stage where its revelation was of itself salvific, but at times it comes very close to being so.[36]

In the study of the antecedents of apocalyptic literature and its ideas, there have been significant differences of opinion about those origins. On the one hand are those who consider apocalyptic to be the successor to the prophetic texts of the Old Testament, and particularly to the future hope of the prophets.[37] The concern with human history and the vindication of Israel's hopes in Revelation all echo themes from the prophets, several of whom have contributed widely to Revelation's language, particularly Ezekiel, Daniel, and Zechariah. Some, on the other hand, see a subtle change taking place in the form of that hope in the apocalyptic literature as compared with most of the prophetic texts in the Bible. It is suggested that the future hope has been placed on another plane, the supernatural and otherworldly (e.g., Isaiah 65–66; cf. Revelation 21; 4 Ezra 7:50). But evidence for such a change from the earthly to the supramundane is not, in fact, widespread. More important is the subtle change of prophetic genre in the later

---

34. G. Scholem, *Major Trends in Jewish Mysticism* (New York: Schocken, 1955); D. Halperin, *The Faces of the Chariot* (Tübingen: Mohr, 1988).
35. In the Mishnah, *Hagigah* 2.1 is a solitary example.
36. I. Gruenwald, *Apocalyptic and Merkavah Mysticism* (Leiden: E. J. Brill, 1978); and *From Apocalyptic to Gnosticism: Studies in Apocalypticism, Merkavah Mysticism, and Gnosticism* (Frankfurt: Lang, 1988).
37. E.g., Hanson, *The Dawn of Apocalyptic*, though note the critical comments of R. Carroll, "Twilight of Prophecy or Dawn of Apocalyptic," *JSOT* 14 (1979) 3ff.

chapters of Ezekiel, with its visions of a new Jerusalem; the highly symbolic visions of Zechariah's early chapters and the cataclysmic upheavals of its last chapters; and the probably late eschatological chapters of Isaiah 24–27; 55–66. Also important is the emergence of the apocalyptic heavenly ascent, evident in texts like *1 Enoch* 14 (See Excursus: "The Fall in *1 Enoch*"). The glimpse into heaven, which is such a key part of John's vision from chapter 4 onward, has its antecedents in the call visions of Ezekiel (Ezekiel 1; 10) and Isaiah (Isaiah 6) as well as the parallel glimpses of the heavenly court of 1 Kings 22:1 and Job 1–2.

Antecedents of apocalyptic literature have been found in the wisdom tradition of the Old Testament as well, with its interest in understanding the cosmos and the ways of the world. Apocalyptic is concerned with knowledge, not only of the age to come but also of things in heaven (e.g., *1 Enoch* 72ff.) and the mysteries of human existence, akin to features of the wisdom literature. While it is the case that the concern with the destiny of Israel, so evident in parts of some apocalypses, is hardly to be found in works like Ecclesiastes and Sirach, both of which seem to discourage the kind of speculation found in the apocalypses (see Sir 3:21ff.), the activities of certain wise men in antiquity were not at all dissimilar from the concerns of the writers of the apocalypses. This includes interpretation of dreams, oracles, astrology, and divine mysteries concerning future events. There is some trace of the role of such figures in the Old Testament, for instance, in the Joseph stories in Genesis and in the book of Daniel. But the most obvious apocalyptic moment in the wisdom corpus is the opening and dramatic climax of the book of Job. The latter enables Job's entirely reasonable stance to be transcended and for Job to move from an understanding based on hearsay to one based on apocalyptic insight (Job 42:5).

A comparison of Revelation with Daniel reveals differences as well as similarities. In certain visions, Revelation is clearly indebted to Daniel (e.g., Daniel 10 in Rev 1:13ff.; Daniel 7 in Revelation 13; 17). Both books are eschatologically oriented. Unlike Revelation, however, Daniel is pseudonymous (probably written in the second century BCE at the height of the crisis in Jerusalem under the Seleucid king Antiochus IV, see 1 Maccabees). John's authority resides primarily in his prophetic call (1:9ff.) rather than in any claim to antiquity or apostolicity. The form of the visions differs also. Daniel's dream vision followed by interpretation is almost completely lacking in Revelation (chap. 17 is a solitary exception in which contemporary historical connections are most explicitly made).

A significant part of the book of Daniel has to do with the royal court in Babylon, and Daniel 2 offers an interpretation of Nebuchadnezzar's dream. Here are men who are comfortable, cosmopolitan Jews who have a good reputation in the land of their exile, though they are nostalgic for Zion (Dan 6:10) and there are limits on what they will compromise. As in Revelation, idolatry is a problem for the Jews (Daniel 3). The fiery furnace and the lions' den are the terrible consequences for those who refuse to conform to Babylonian worship. Yet Nebuchadnezzar (unlike Belshazzar) is depicted sympathetically; there is evidence of admiration on the part of the king for the young Jewish men (cf. the signs of that in Rev 11:13) and of his reluctance to see these significant courtiers die. And these men who resist the imperial system, and are thus prepared to face suffering, miraculously escape. This story contrasts with Revelation, where religious persecution is expected to include suffering and death (2:11; 6:9; 7:14; 11:7; 13:10; 12:11). In Revelation, there is the promise of vindication (11:7-8), but at the same time a clear recognition that there can be no escape from the great tribulation (7:14).

There is in Revelation a more distanced and antagonistic attitude toward empire. Although Revelation 18 briefly reflects on Babylon's fall from the perspective of the kings, the mighty, and the merchants, the position of the writer is that of vigorous rejection of the power and purposes of empire and satisfaction at the ultimate triumph of God's righteousness (14:11; 19:3). Whereas Daniel presents persons who are immersed in the life of the pagan court, Revelation countenances no such accommodation. The only acceptable stances are resistance and withdrawal (18:4). Accommodation may be a sign of apostasy (2:20ff.). Pagans react with awe (6:15), with fear (11:10), and with anger toward God (6:10; 9:20).

In the New Testament, Mark 13 and 1 Thess 4:16–5:11 have affinities with eschatological sections of Revelation, but particular attention should also be given to the many New Testament passages that refer to the importance of visions and revelations. Mark 1:10 records at the outset of Jesus' ministry a private vision, reminiscent of the apocalypses and the call visions of the prophets; the reference to the open heaven is a typical feature of visionary accounts (cf. Isa 49:1; Jer 1:5; Gal 1:12, 16). Matthew's Gospel gives an often missed but significant role to dreams and revelations (Matt 1:20; 2:12-13, 19; 27:19; 11:25-26; 16:17; 17:9). But it is Luke's account of the origins of the church that has most of the references to visions. Even allowing for Luke's special interest in the divine guidance of the church and its mission, the vision of the tongues of fire at Pentecost (Acts 2), the martyr Stephen's vision of the heavenly Son of Man (Acts 7:56-57), the twice-told decisive vision of the sheet descending from heaven, which preceded Peter's preaching to Cornelius (Acts 10:11), and the thrice-told account of Paul's conversion (Acts 9; 22; 26) all indicate the importance Luke attached to visions and revelations. The polemic of Paul against false teachers at Colossae (e.g., Col 2:18) indicates that they may have had an interest in visions of the activity of the angels in heaven and needed to be pointed to the centrality of Christ. Outside the New Testament, figures like Elchesai,[38] Cerinthus,[39] and the *Shepherd of Hermas*,[40] as well as the Montanist movement[41] may be mentioned.

Spatial categories form an important part of apocalyptic thought.[42] Such categories are presupposed by several New Testament writers; indeed, they form part of the argument of one or two documents. In Ephesians, for example, the author speaks of a heavenly dimension to the church's existence; by his use of the phrase "in the heavenly places," he links the church with the exalted Christ (Eph 2:6). An important part of the argument of the Letter to the Hebrews concerns the belief that the superiority of Christ's sacrifice is that his offering of himself enabled him to enter not the earthly shrine, but heaven itself, into the very presence of God (Heb 9:11, 24). This framework of contrast between the world below and the world above facilitates the writer's presentation of the saving work of Christ. Christ the heavenly pioneer has entered into the inner shrine, behind the veil (Heb 6:19-21). He has entered into not a sanctuary made with hands, a mere copy of the true one, but into heaven itself to appear in the divine presence on behalf of God's people.[43]

The book of Revelation fails to satisfy the desire for an unambiguous, final utterance on faith and morals. Revelation never allows the reader complete certainty. There is no simple division between the church and the world. There are no grounds for complacency—only watchfulness (3:3) and the constant endeavoring to keep one's robes clean (22:14). The practice of the church is confused and compromised. Despite the authoritative status it claims for itself, the book of Revelation hardly offers a definitive prescription of the religious life. There is in it an implied intense suspicion of the values of the surrounding culture and institutions, but nowhere does it set down precise rules of how one should exemplify the divine wisdom. We are not offered a detailed and immediately applicable code of laws but the revelation of divine mysteries that bemuse and perplex and seem to veil as much as they reveal. And unlike the interpretations of the visions in Daniel (see Dan 2:7), rarely is there an angelic interpreter on hand to tell readers what the imagery means.

To discern the true nature of a culture in thrall to war and virtue "calls for wisdom" (13:18 NRSV; see also 17:9). This means more than astute observation of the world. What is required is a recovery of imagination as a necessary complement to all-conquering reason. In *1 Enoch* 2–5, the wisdom deriving from observation of the world is juxtaposed with apocalyptic, revelatory, wisdom. Apocalyptic wisdom does not offer unambiguous and unequivocal answers. The appeal to revelation may seem to promise solutions to intractable human problems through divinely bestowed insight. Apocalypses produce as much mystification as enlightenment, however,

---

38. Hippolytus *Refutation of All Heresies* IX. 13.1ff.
39. Eusebius *Ecclesiastical History* III. 281-82.
40. E.g., *Shepherd of Hermas* Visions III.1.6ff.
41. Eusebius *Ecclesiastical History* V.16.6.
42. Thompson, *The Book of Revelation*; P. Minear, "The Cosmology of the Apocalypse," in William Klassen and Graydon Snyder, *Current Issues in New Testament Interpretation* (London: SCM, 1962) 23-27; Andrew T. Lincoln, *Paradise Now and Not Yet: Studies in the Role of the Heavenly Dimension in Paul's Thought* (Cambridge: Cambridge University Press, 1981) 198.
43. See further C. Rowland, "Apocalyptic, Mysticism, and the New Testament," in *Geschichte Tradition Reflexion: Festschrift für Martin Hengel*, ed. P. Schäfer (Tübingen: Mohr, 1996) 405ff.

revealing the extent of the problem of human perception and the complex strategies needed to compel an uncomprehending humanity to begin to see things differently. That is how apocalyptic visions function. We should not ask of apocalypses, What do they mean? Rather, we should ask, How do the images and designs work? How do they affect us and change our lives? The intellectual asceticism of 4 Ezra, the opacity of Revelation's symbolism, and the tantalizing parables of God's reign in the Gospels all indicate that until "sweet Science reigns" those whose minds are darkened will need a variety of ways to open their intellects to glimpse the mystery of apocalyptic wisdom.

CONTEMPORARY APOCALYPTIC: 4 EZRA AND REVELATION

Revelation's imagery and its hope in the messianic vindication and defeat of Rome parallels in many ways the roughly contemporary 4 Ezra (2 Esdras 3–14).[44] This work has for centuries been an important resource for understanding the milieu of the New Testament. It has a place in the Vulgate, and some Christian traditions have placed it among the books of the Old Testament. Its similarity of outlook in regard to human sinfulness with the Paul of Romans and Galatians sets it apart from other Jewish texts. Its messianic vision in chap. 13, dependent as it is on Daniel 7:1, has often been used as a resource for the discussion of the Son of Man in the canonical Gospels. The book of 4 Ezra is an apocalypse that emerged in the dark days of despair after the fall of the Second Temple in 70 CE. It offers "a fountain of wisdom" (4 Ezra 14:47) in its secret books.

In the dialogues between Ezra and the angel, which occupy the first part of the book, the contrast between human and divine wisdom and the inability of even the most righteous humans to understand the divine purposes are repeated themes (echoes here of Isaiah 40:21ff.). Ezra's words embody an enlightened, commonsense position with regard to the lot of humanity, the injustices of the world, and the perplexity at the fate of the chosen people in the wake of the destruction of the Temple. He is concerned for the majority of humanity whose unrighteousness seems to be about to consign them to perdition (4 Ezra 7:62ff.). The divine perspective is uncompromising, however, and only partially understandable. The dialogue between Ezra and the angel indicates the contrast between human and divine wisdom. At times it appears that Ezra's concerns are more merciful than the divine reply. Despair is dealt with by urging the righteous to concentrate on the glory that awaits those who are obedient to God (4 Ezra 8:52; 9:13). God's patience is not for the sake of humanity, but because of divine faithfulness to the eternal plan, which was laid down before creation (4 Ezra 7:74). Throughout the book, the ways of God, the Most High, are vindicated (parallels here with Paul's agony in Romans 9–11). God is the one who orders the times and the seasons, and God alone will bring about the new age (4 Ezra 6:5). Just as in the book of Job,[45] where the divine answer stresses the inadequacy of human wisdom, so here, too, the impossibility of understanding the divine purposes in the midst of the old order is stressed (4 Ezra 4:1ff., 21; 5:36). Ezra cannot presume to be a better judge than God or wiser than the Most High (4 Ezra 7:19). Humanity's problem is that despite being given a mind to understand, they have sinned. So torment awaits them (4 Ezra 7:72; cf. 4 Ezra 9:20), sentiments reminiscent of Paul's description of a benighted humanity in Romans 1. All speculation and argument are irrelevant compared to the eschatological concerns that should occupy the attention of the righteous (4 Ezra 9:13).

In 4 Ezra 6:11ff., Ezra is shown the signs of the end of the present order. These visions involve a dreadful period of disease and deprivation (4 Ezra 6:20ff.; see Excursus: "The Tribulations of the Messianic Age"). In 4 Ezra 7, there is a much longer and more explicit description of the future purposes of God. The hidden city and land will appear (presumably a reference to the fulfillment of the hidden purposes of God, vouchsafed to the seer and soon to be made manifest on earth). The Messiah also will be revealed, and those who are left on earth will reign with him for four hundred years. This will come to an end with the death of the Messiah

---

44. M. Stone, *Fourth Ezra*, Hermeneia (Minneapolis: Fortress, 1990).
45. M. Knibb, "Apocalyptic and Wisdom in 4 Ezra," *Journal for the Study of Judaism* 13 (1982) 56-74.

and all humanity, with the world returning to primeval silence for seven days. Only after that will the world, which is not awake, be roused; whatever is corruptible will perish (4 Ezra 7:32), and the resurrection will take place as a prelude to the judgment of all humanity, confronted by the furnace of hell and the paradise of delight.

What emerges in the work is a perceptive insight into the pervasiveness of evil, which makes difficult the attempts of men and women to fulfill the divine command. There is free will (4 Ezra 3:8; 8:50-51), but Adam's sin has had devastating effects on human life and understanding (4 Ezra 3:20; 4:30; 7:118). A blessed place is reserved for those who persevere to the end. The message is uncompromising. There is little of the arresting symbolism that permeates virtually the whole of the book of Revelation (though 4 Ezra 9ff. marks a change of mood). The effect of reading the early chapters of 4 Ezra is to disinfect the mind of any presumption of being able to fathom the wisdom of God and to warn against flights of metaphysical fancy. What the righteous need do is view all things in the light of the end rather than concentrate on the apparent injustices of the present time (4 Ezra 7:16). Eschatology offers the hope of final resolution. Those who, like Ezra, continue in obedience, a way of life that seems so pointless to the majority of humanity, receive reassurance that faithful endurance ultimately will pay off. If there can be any answer to human questioning in 4 Ezra, that is the only one on offer. The stark message is that the righteous need to view all things in the light of eschatological salvation and to persist in obedience to God rather than allow themselves to become depressed or allow their reason full rein to seek explanations to the apparent injustices of the present (4 Ezra 7:16).[46] The mystery that offers salvation is perseverance in the righteous way of life, whatever the apparent contrary indications (cf. Mark 13:13).

Revelation has several parallels with 4 Ezra and with Daniel. The beasts from the sea and land in Revelation 13 are dependent on the opening verses of Daniel 7 and, like 4 Ezra 11, focus on one beast only, which is an epitome of the awfulness and oppression of tyranny. Like the messiah in 4 Ezra 13, the Lamb can stand on Mount Zion (Rev 14:1); and at the dramatic parousia in Rev 19:11, the rider on the white horse is described in language reminiscent of Dan 10:6, with the same capacity as the messiah in 4 Ezra 13 to take effective action in judgment (here there is a sharp sword rather than a stream of fire, 19:15). Both 4 Ezra and Revelation agree in separating the political critique (the opening verses of Daniel 7, dealing with the beasts emerging from the sea) from the "messianic solution" focused on in Dan 7:13. So Revelation 13 focuses on the critique of empire, whereas Revelation 14 and 19 (though the latter is not formally dependent on Dan 7:13-14) present us with a contrasting scene in which the dominion of the Lamb under God is outlined. In 4 Ezra 11–12 the eagle vision is a critique of and prediction of the destruction of the last empire, while 4 Ezra 13 is a messianic vision. Both Revelation and 4 Ezra concentrate on the fourth beast of Daniel, a preoccupation that was to feature in a wide range of apocalyptic scenarios down the centuries.[47]

The vision in 4 Ezra 11–12 is a complicated account of an eagle with twelve wings and three heads that rises out of the sea. The complexity of this vision has often prompted the suggestion that it is an artificial construction reflecting recent Roman history. That assessment is entirely understandable, but needs to be set alongside the difficulties commentators have had in offering a historical explanation of the various details. The wings of the eagle spread over the whole earth. The eagle reigns over the earth with all things subjected to it. Out of the wings, eight rival small wings emerge. The first twelve wings rise and fall, and of these none rule as long as does the second (v. 16). Eventually the twelve large wings and two of the eight little wings disappear. Nothing remains except three heads, which are at rest, and six of the little wings. Two little wings separate from the six and remain under the head on the right side, while four little wings plan to rule. Two set up their kingdom and then disappear, leaving the two who plan to reign together. In v. 29 the head in the middle awakens and with the two remaining heads devours the little wings that are planning to reign. The head gains control over the world and oppresses

---

46. Note the similarities with Ludwig Wittgenstein's understanding of religion as outlined by Ray Monk, *Ludwig Wittgenstein: The Duty of Genius* (London: Vintage, 1990) 409-10.
47. D. Brady, *The Contribution of British Writings Between 1560–1830 to the Interpretation of Revelation 13:16-18* (Tübingen: Mohr, 1983).

its inhabitants. Eventually the head in the middle disappears, and the two remaining heads rule until the head on the right side devours that on the left.

Then the focus of interest changes. In v. 37 a lion is roused from the forest; it speaks to the eagle, the last of four beasts that were made to reign in the world and the sign that the end of time has come. This fourth beast conquers all that have gone before and holds sway in an oppressive manner. It is condemned in 4 Ezra 11:41-42: "You have judged the earth but not with truth, for you have oppressed the meek and injured the peaceable; you have hated those who tell the truth, and have loved liars; you have destroyed the homes of those who brought forth fruit, and have laid low the walls of those who did you no harm." Its destruction is "so that the whole earth may be freed from violence." The remaining head disappears, leaving two wings to set themselves up to reign, after which follows a period of tumult until they vanish; the body of the eagle is burned, and the whole earth is left terrified.

This vision, with its far-fetched multiplications of the wings of the eagle, demands an explanation. As we might expect from an apocalypse, the seer is offered an interpretation of this complicated vision by an angel. In 4 Ezra 12:11, we are told that the eagle from the sea is the fourth kingdom that appeared in Daniel's vision. This is more terrifying than all the kingdoms that came before it. This fourth kingdom will be ruled by a series of twelve kings, the second reigning the longest. After the second king's death there will be great conflicts. and the empire will be on the verge of collapse. Of the eight kings whose times will be short, two will perish; four will be kept for the time when the end approaches, but two will be kept until the end. According to 4 Ezra 12:22, the culmination of its dominion will come when three kings represented by the three heads raised up by the Most High in the last days will rule the earth more oppressively. They will sum up the wickedness of the regime. One of the kings dies in his bed; one will fall victim to the sword of another; and the last one will fall by the sword as well. The lion who appears is the Messiah, the offspring of David, kept for the end of days to execute judgment and bring about the liberation of the "remnant of my people" and to "make them joyful until the end comes."

Whereas in 4 Ezra the eagle is Daniel's fourth beast, in Revelation the beast that arises from the sea incorporates characteristics of the previous empires. The imagery of 4 Ezra 11–12 is more complicated than anything in Revelation, though something approaching that complexity is to be found in Revelation 17, where the seven heads of the beast upon which the woman is seated are both kings and hills (Rev 17:9). The Messiah in both texts is symbolized by a lion (Rev 5:5; 4 Ezra 12, probably dependent on Gen 49:9). Revelation lacks the pessimistic tone of 4 Ezra, though it, too, contemplates a world that is seduced by the power and brilliance of the Beast. The interpretation of the eagle vision suggests that the reign of the Messiah precedes the end and so is part of a two-stage eschatology. This twofold scheme of a messianic reign followed by a new age, possibly used for the first time in such an explicit form, is evidence in a Jewish apocalypse of the hope for a new age that is transcendent. It appears, however, alongside the conventional hope for a this-worldly reign of God (4 Ezra 7:28-29; cf. 4 Ezra 6:18ff.). In this it parallels Revelation, where the vision of the new heaven and new earth is preceded by the millennial messianic reign. This particular pattern represents a significant development of late first-century eschatology, when political despair may have contributed to the emergence of a transcendent eschatology alongside the hope for a messianic kingdom on earth.

For all their differences, a scheme of woes, messianic kingdom, resurrection, judgment, and new age is clearly discerned in both works. Revelation uses much more vivid imagery as compared with the prosaic prediction found in 4 Ezra (and the contemporary Syriac *Apocalypse of Baruch*). The role of the redeemer figure is much more obvious in Revelation. There is little sign in any of these works of the warrior role found in the *Psalms of Solomon* (and in 4 Ezra 13). Indeed, the Messiah's reign on earth in 4 Ezra 7:28-29 lasts only four hundred years, at the end of which he dies.

Eschatological concerns in 4 Ezra are to some extent eclipsed by another concern: the evil of humanity, the wrestling with the apparently merciless character of the divine purposes and human frailty in the face of God's inscrutable purposes. The issues raised are what we would have expected Jews to have struggled with after the traumatic experience of 70 CE. There was an inevitable reappraisal of attitudes with the need for more precise definitions of what was required of the people of God and an emphasis on the centrality of the law. The burning question in 4 Ezra is not so much, When will the end be? but, How can one make sense of the present and ensure participation in the kingdom of God? Apocalyptic insight is part of the way in which the impoverished character of existence and the injustices of the world are given a different perspective.

A HISTORY OF THE INTERPRETATION OF THE APOCALYPSE

The Early Christian Context: Apocalyptic Tradition in the New Testament. We cannot regard other New Testament texts as interpretations of Revelation, because most were contemporary with Revelation. Yet there are connections between them that should be noted.[48]

Eschatological passages in the Gospels (esp. Matthew 24–25; Mark 13; Luke 21) all have connections with passages from Revelation.[49] Luke's Gospel in particular, perhaps surprising given its reputation as the one least in touch with apocalyptic ideas, shows several points of contact. Thus whereas Mark's Gospel talks of the sea as the destination of the demons (Mark 5:13) in the struggle with Legion, Luke's version of the story uses the same Greek word as does Revelation (Luke 8:33; cf. Rev 19:20; 20:14).[50] Contacts between Luke's Gospel and Revelation deserve particular attention. Verbal connections between the two texts are quite striking (e.g., cf. Luke 16:19 with Rev 18:12 and 17:4; Luke 10:19 with Rev 9:3; Luke 4:5-7 with Rev 13:7-8; Luke 21:27 with Rev 14:14; and, most striking of all, Luke 12:8 with Rev 3:5). Several of these connections are apparent in Luke's version of the eschatological discourse (Luke 21). The features are distinctive and suggest that Luke has a broader horizon to the prophecy more in keeping with that found in Revelation. Thus in Luke 21:28 the reference to liberation suggests that more could have been said, but there has instead been concentration on the time of distress preceding it (Luke 21:23; cf. 1 Cor 7:26, 28). What Luke predicts are days of vengeance (picking up on Isa 61:2, but omitted from the quotation of these verses in Luke 4:19). The tribulation in Luke 21:25 reminds us of the chaos in Rev 6:8-9, as also does the reaction of humanity in Luke 21:26 (cf. Rev 6:15ff.) in the face of the time of wrath (cf. Luke 23:30). The allusive reference to the trampling of Jerusalem by Gentiles (Luke 21:24) recalls John's vision in Rev 11:1ff. Elsewhere in the story of Jesus, it is Luke who reports the absence of Satan from the life of Jesus (Luke 4:21; cf. Luke 22:3 with Rev 7:22 and 13:16; see also Rev 20:2ff., where Satan is bound and removed from the earth). It is the Gospel of Luke that portrays Jesus as offering an interpretation of the mission of the seventy and their triumph over the powers of darkness, which is linked with the vision of Satan's fall from heaven (cf. Luke 10:18 with Rev 12:7ff.). The critical moment of Jesus' death is marked by an eclipse (there is an explicit reference in Luke 23:45; cf. Rev 8:12; 16:10).[51]

Paul's doctrine of the parousia (see Excursus: "The Parousia in the New Testament"), the allusive eschatological description in Rom 8:18ff., with the tribulations of the messianic age, and, of course, the manifestation of God's wrath (Rom 1:17-18) and the gospel (Rom 3:21) all connect with the apocalyptic way Paul speaks of Christ's impact on him (Gal 1:16). Paul includes in the gospel message the revelation of God's justice and of God's wrath (Rom 1:16-17). It is a juxtaposition that is very much akin to the revelation of God's salvation and judgment (as is the case in Deuteronomy 28ff.) as interlocking manifestations of the divine purpose in Revelation.[52] As in Revelation, in Romans 1 the wrath mentioned is God's eschatological wrath against impiety and injustice, particularly evident in idolatry. In Rom 1:17ff. there is a repeated

---

48. See the surveys in A. Wainwright, *Mysterious Apocalypse* (Nashville: Abingdon, 1993); E. B. Allo, *L'Apocalypse de Saint Jean* (Paris: Lecoffre, 1921); W. Bousset, *Die Offenbarung Johannis* (Göttingen: 1906); R. H. Charles, *Studies in the Apocalypse* (Edinburgh: T. & T. Clark, 1910); G. Maier, *Die Offenbarung Johannis und die Kirche* (Tübingen: Mohr, 1981).
49. Survey in R. Bauckham, *The Climax of Prophecy* (Edinburgh: T. & T. Clark, 1993) chap. 3.
50. K. Wengst, *Pax Romana and the Peace of Jesus Christ* (London: SCM, 1988) 65-66.
51. On Luke and apocalyptic traditions, see S. Garrett, *The Demise of the Devil* (Minneapolis: Fortress, 1989) 128; M. E. Boismard, "Rapprochements litt'raires l'vangile de Luc et l'Apocalypse," in J. Schmid and A. Vögtle, *Synoptische Studien* (Munich: Mohr, 1953) 53-63.
52. See further G. Bornkamm, "The Revelation of God's Wrath," in *Early Christian Experience* (London: SCM, 1969) 47-70.

stress on revelation. The refusal to acknowledge God leads to a determined response from God. There is a threefold assertion that "God gave them up" (Rom 1:24, 26, 28 NRSV), a more direct assertion of divine judgment than the string of passives in Revelation suggesting the same thing (e.g., Rev 6:2, 4).

Humanity did not give God the glory (Rom 1:21). It is the proclamation of the eternal gospel in Rev 14:6 that humanity should fear God (cf. the quotation of Ps 35:2 in Rom 3:18) and give God the glory and worship God the Creator (cf. Rom 1:25). Idolatrous behavior leads to a perverted outlook on the world (Rom 1:21) and a failure to recognize the ways and acts of God (cf. Rev 9:20). Idolatry is the problem in Revelation, both generally in 9:20 and specifically in the context of worship of the Beast in 13:8, 12. "Uncleanness" (Rom 1:24; cf. Rom 6:19) is the mark of the dragon (Rev 16:9) and of Babylon (Rev 17:4; 18:2). The sexual immorality of Rom 1:25 parallels the warning to be ready and not to be found naked and "exposed to shame" in Rev 16:15. The concern with the natural and the unnatural in sexual activity in Rom 1:26 corresponds to that frame of mind seen so often in Revelation, where the clarity of boundaries is sharply defined and transgression of those boundaries that result in one's becoming "lukewarm" (Rev 3:14-16) is resisted. This state of mind is one of deceit, the heart of the activity of Satan and the beast (e.g., Rev 12:9; 13:14); in Revelation, it is focused on idolatrous practices (Rev 2:20).

The "lie" (Rom 1:25; cf. Rev 2:2; 21:8; 22:15) and false service (Rom 1:25) need to be replaced with the true service of those who are priests in the new world (Rev 7:15; cf. Rom 12:1). That threefold "giving up" by God covers three areas: the desires of the heart, shameful passions (Rom 1:26), and the undiscerning mind, which does that which is unbecoming; then follows a list of vices that result in disrupted and inharmonious living. We may compare Paul's focus on sexual misdemeanors in Romans 1 with the characterization of the offense of "fornication" throughout Revelation (e.g., Rev 2:20).

This also includes behavior that contributes to society's malfunctioning, all of which is a consequence of idolatry. In Romans, it is God who consigns the impious to particularly distorted patterns of behavior, just as in Revelation the source of the crisis for a disordered cosmos is in the divine book with seven seals, preserved in God's presence. The cataclysmic effects may not be immediately apparent in the list of consequences in Romans 1. What we are offered in Romans is a prose description of a world marked by deceit and human selfishness. Stripped of the apocalyptic symbolism, its message is much the same as that of Revelation 6 and 8–9, however. In Rev 6:4, the second horseman removes peace from the earth, so that people slay one another; here is the consequence of the strife, envy, and covetousness that Paul had spoken of in Rom 1:28.

While Paul's extant writings include no apocalypse, the opening chapters of 1 Corinthians reflect an apocalyptic perspective, access to which comes through revelation through the Spirit. The divine mystery precedes and is then backed up by Scripture (e.g., Rom 11:25-26). Paul describes himself and his companions as apocalyptic seers who are entrusted the privilege of administering the divine secrets (1 Cor 4:1). In 1 Cor 2:6-7, Paul talks of the content of the gospel itself as a mystery hidden from the rulers of the present age. The success of the saving act of God results from the inability of those who are dominated by the present age and its gods to see the significance of what they were doing in crucifying the Lord of glory (1 Cor 2:9). The cross, the sign of failure in human estimation, turns out to be the very heart of the divine mystery for the salvation of the world. It points to an apocalyptic mystery hidden before all ages and revealed only in the last days (cf. Luke 10:23-24; 1 Pet 1:11-12). The divine wisdom to which the true apostle has access is a mystery taught by the Spirit, and it can be understood only by those who have the Spirit (1 Cor 2:10). The divine wisdom is something revealed rather than something immediately clear and compelling to those whose minds are darkened and cannot understand its significance. It remains hidden until the veil is removed (2 Cor 3:14-15). The cross is a sign that transcends the plethora of apocalyptic imagery. Like every sign, it is ambiguous. To some it remains foolishness (1 Cor 1:18). Like the Lamb, which forms the centerpiece of the apocalypse, the cross stands at the fulcrum of history and is the determinant of a true understanding of reality. In continuity with the Jewish apocalyptic tradition, Paul thinks of another dimension of human existence, normally hidden from sight but revealed to those with eyes to see. His apocalypse of Jesus Christ is the basis for his practice, not the least that of admitting Gentiles into the messianic age without the law of Moses. His relegation of the Sinai covenant to a subordinate position to the new covenant in the Messiah contrasts with the firm subordination of the disclosures of the apocalyptic spirit to the Sinai theophany in the rabbinic traditions.

The contrasts in Hebrews between the sacrifice of Christ and the sacrifices of the levitical system have been taken as indications of Greek platonic influence. But the likelihood is that the apocalyptic tradition, with its contrasts between the heavenly world above and the earthly world below, may explain the distinctive soteriology of Hebrews.[53] The author seeks to understand the work of Christ as the important moment in the piercing of that barrier between heaven and earth that is so familiar to us from the apocalyptic literature. The climax of history has now occurred in Jesus, and he is the first to enter the heavenly sanctuary, which is at the same time the sign of the new age. Jesus, the pioneer, has gone into the innermost part of heaven and has sat down with God. He is behind the veil. Calvary becomes the moment when the unmediated access to God becomes a possibility. Paradoxically, the death outside the camp (Heb 13:12) becomes the place where heaven and earth coincide in that the sacrifice of Jesus opens up the way into the heavenly shrine. The cross has become a meeting point between heaven and earth. The place of reproach and rejection turns out to be the very gate of heaven.

In Hebrews (and in the Letter to the Ephesians also), apocalyptic categories are taken up and utilized in the expression of convictions about Christ's exaltation and its consequences. The cosmology of apocalyptic and the notion of revelation found in the apocalypses and the mystical literature was a convenient starting place for reflection on the understanding of revelation, which Christian writers believed had been inaugurated by the exaltation of Christ. The glory of the world above, which was to be manifested in the future, had now become a present possession for those who acknowledged that the Messiah had come and had already made available the heavenly gifts of the messianic age.

The Patristic Period.[54] There is a close link between the closing invocation in Rev 22:20 and the "maranatha" of *Didache* 10:6 (cf. 1 Cor 16:22):

> Let grace come, and let this world pass away. Hosanna to the Son of David. Whoever is holy, let them come; whoever is not, let them repent. *maranatha*. Amen.

The priority given to the prophetic in *Didache* 11–13 echoes what we find in Revelation (e.g., Rev 1:3; 2:20; 10:11; 11:2, 10; 16:6; 18:20, 24; 19:10; 22:2, 6-7, 9-10, 18-19), suggesting that distinguishing true from false prophecy is an issue in both writings.

In the struggle with gnosticism, insistence on the materiality of the doctrine of the resurrection and on this-worldly eschatology played their part in the writings of both Justin[55] and Irenaeus,[56] though Justin recognized that not all share his hope for a messianic reign on earth. Elsewhere in the earlier books of *Against Heresies,* however, Irenaeus regards Revelation as primarily about the first coming of Christ and the witness of the church. Thus the enmity between humanity and the devil is related to the advent of Christ viewed through the lens of Rev 20:2.[57] What is also evident in *Against Heresies* V is an integration of eschatology and creation. What began with creation, Adam, and the fall ends with the new creation, the new Adam, and the final temptation and overthrow of Satan. Irenaeus periodizes history into seven ages.[58] The parousia inaugurates the seventh millennium, when the sabbath rest comes (cf. Gen 2:2). The events of Genesis 1–3 are seen as archetypes of the last days. When Irenaues comes to discuss the Beast and its number in Rev 13:18,[59] he thinks that *Lateinos* or *Teitan* or *Evanthus* may be intended and so affirms an anti-imperial reference.

---

53. L. D. Hurst, *The Epistle to the Hebrews: Its Background of Thought* (Cambridge: Cambridge University Press, 1990) 199.
54. B. Daley, *The Hope of the Early Church* (Cambridge: Cambridge University Press, 1991); C. Helms, "The Apocalypse in the Early Church, Christ, Eschaton, and the Millennium" (D. Phil. diss., Oxford University, 1991).
55. Justin *Dialogue with Trypho* 80.
56. Irenaeus *Against Heresies* V.26.1–36.3.
57. Irenaeus *Against Heresies* III.23.7
58. Irenaeus *Against Heresies* V.28.3.
59. Irenaeus *Against Heresies* V.30.3.

Hippolytus, in his treatise on Antichrist, reads Revelation 12 as being of the church and the struggle to bring the gospel to a hostile world.[60] Revelation is seen as the completion of the journey of God's people, of which the exodus is a type, and there is a link between the Christ of Rev 1:13ff. and the prophets of old.[61] Rome and the kingdom of Antichrist merge;[62] and there is a Jewish dimension to the Antichrist figure, because he will come from the tribe of Daniel (see Daniel 14–15) and will rebuild the Temple. The two witnesses of Revelation 11 are identified with Enoch and Elijah. Hippolytus uses the cosmic week to show that only five and a half of the six periods have elapsed before the millennium (note the emphasis on the penultimate here, which we shall have reason to comment on in the context of the commentary), though he does not dwell on the delights of that age as Irenaeus had done.

Origen's reading of Revelation (he wrote no commentary on it) is decidedly anti-chiliastic—that is, he rejects the belief in a messianic reign on earth. His interpretation is christological. He sees Rev 19:13, for example, as an image of the victorious Logos (Word) marked by the signs of crucifixion. The prophecies of chaps. 12–22 are linked with the life of Christ and the church, and the millennium is seen as past.[63] The defeat and binding of Satan (Rev 20:3) has already occurred.[64] The heavenly Jerusalem is a spiritual reality, made possible by the resurrection; the new heaven and new earth began with Christ's resurrection.[65]

The earliest extant commentary on Revelation, used by Jerome, is by Victorinus of Pettau (c. beginning of the 4th cent.). His work is thoroughly contextual and relates the text to the circumstances of his day. The seven churches represent the universal church and are not intended for John's area alone. Although Victorinus was a chiliast, his method included a typological reading, which presented Revelation as a series of events recurring in sacred history. So the trumpet blasts of Revelation 8ff. relate not only to the period after the coming of Christ but also to both the Babylonian exile and the period of Antichrist, whose malevolence can be seen in the actions of Roman emperors as well as in the figure of the last days. His interpretive approach blends the christocentric and ecclesiological with the eschatological. He uses an exegesis that blends present relevance and eschatological prediction. Thus the two witnesses (Rev 11:3) represent the deaths of prophets, both those of the past and the ones to come under Antichrist,[66] and the sixth king is Nero, past and future persecutors of the saints.

The book of seven seals is the Old Testament, a legal document sealed until the death of its testator, Jesus Christ. The unsealing of the seals reveals that the Old Testament has been fulfilled in the person of Christ. In the Son of Man vision in Rev 1:13ff., the two-edged sword indicates that Christ uttered both the law and the gospel. Victorinus explains the images of Revelation 4:1–5 as symbols of the old and the new economies.[67] Just as Revelation 4 is seen as a résumé of salvation history, so also the seals fulfill the old and reveal the totality of the new. The repetition of the sequence of seven is the means whereby the Spirit provides the opportunity for fuller appreciation of the mystery of God. In Revelation 6 the white horse and its rider are the Holy Spirit and the gospel message: "after the Lord ascended to heaven . . . he sent the Holy Spirit, whose words the preachers sent forth as arrows reaching to the human heart . . . and the crown on the head is the promised Holy Spirit."[68] Whereas the white horse signifies the Christian revelation from Christ to eschaton, the other horses are primarily eschatological. In Revelation 11, Elijah is both the witness and the precursor of Antichrist. He is the angel of Rev 7:2[69] and the eagle of Rev 8:13. The woman in chap. 12 is both an Old and a New Covenant figure. The devil's attempt to devour the child is a reference to the temptation and passion of Christ. The flood of water from the dragon's mouth is the persecution of the church. The war in heaven in Rev 12:7 is the beginning of the eschaton, which then becomes the focus for the rest of the commentary.

---

60. Hippolytus *Antichrist* 61.
61. Hippolytus *Antichrist* 12.
62. Hippolytus *Antichrist* 25ff.
63. Origen *On Prayer* 27:13.
64. Origen *Commentary on John* 1.27.97.
65. Origen *Commentary on John* 10.35.22.
66. Victorinus *Commentary on the Book of Revelation* 102:16ff.
67. Victorinus *Commentary on the Book of Revelation* 46ff.
68. Victorinus *Commentary on the Book of Revelation* 66.
69. Victorinus *Commentary on the Book of Revelation* 82.

Antichrist is Nero redevivus.[70] Victorinus follows earlier commentators in seeing in the number 666 the Greek word *Teitan* or the Latin *Diclux*. The seven heads of the dragon refer to the seven emperors who reigned near the beginning of the Christian era, from Galba to Nerva.[71] Antichrist is associated with civil and religious corruption. Rome is Babylon, but the false prophet is associated with Judaism. He will cause an image of Antichrist to be set up in the Jerusalem Temple.[72] Antichrist sums up all evil in himself so that the condemnations of Babylon refer to one final embodiment of evil already partially glimpsed in earlier history. Victorinus stresses the concrete character of the new Jerusalem and the life enjoyed by the saints,[73] in a way similar to earlier evocations of the earthly eschatological delights in Papias and Irenaeus. Victorinus picks up on the element of inclusivism in the final vision and suggests that the gates are always left open because saving grace is always available.

Tyconius's (c. 400) reading of the book of Revelation, now no longer extant,[74] has been reconstructed from various sources. Its importance is great, because it had a profound influence on the mature Augustine and thence on later Christendom.[75] In his exegesis of Revelation, he uses the book to interpret contemporary reality. His work epitomizes those trends in exegesis that did not consign its message solely to the eschatological future. Tyconius encapsulates trends that had been in force at least since the time of Origen and of which there had been hints earlier in parts of Irenaeus' writings. The text becomes a tool to facilitate the discernment of the moral and spiritual rather than to search out the eschatological in the text. So the millennium becomes a medium for understanding the present rather than merely the eschatological future.

The mature Augustine continued in that tradition. He had originally believed that there would be a sabbath rest for the people of God that would last a thousand years, but, influenced by Tyconius, he accepted an approach to Scripture that enables Revelation to be a source of insight both eschatologically and for the contemporary church. Thus in his discussion of the millennium in *The City of God*[76] he argues that with the first coming of Christ and the establishment of the church the devil has been bound "in the innumerable multitude of the impious, in whose hearts there is a great depth of malignity against the church of God."[77] Eschatological elements, like Antichrist, Gog, and Magog, are stripped of their eschatological significance and relate to the experience of the church in this age.

Augustine's approach to empire is in certain key respects at one with the dualistic and suspicious attitude evident in earlier Christian apocalyptic interpretation. This contrasts with a different tone in the writing of Eusebius of Caesarea, a militant opponent of millenarian hope and an apologist for a Christian empire. For him the fulfillment of eschatological promise had come with the conversion of Constantine, which had enabled the divine peace to envelop the world.[78]

The Joachite School.[79] The Augustinian exegesis held sway for much of the next five hundred years. The later Middle Ages saw the emergence of the next influential reading by Joachim of Fiore (c. 1132–1202), which was to use Revelation as a way of understanding salvation history and thereby embolden people to see themselves as being part of the imminent apocalypse. In a highly complex interpretative method formulated by allowing one part of Scripture to offer the model for interpreting the whole (what he calls *concordia*), Joachim related closely the Old and the New Testaments. He divided the book of Revelation into eight parts: (1) 1:1–3:22, letters to seven churches; (2) 4:1–8:1, the opening of the seals; (3) 8:2–11:18, the trumpet blasts; (4) 11:19–14:20, the two beasts; (5) 15:1–16:7, the seven bowls; (6) 18:16–19:21, destruction of Babylon; (7) 20:1-10, the millennium; and (8) 20:11–22:21, the new Jerusalem. The parts

---

70. Victorinus *Commentary on the Book of Revelation* 120.
71. Victorinus *Commentary on the Book of Revelation* 110.
72. Victorinus *Commentary on the Book of Revelation* 128.
73. Victorinus *Commentary on the Book of Revelation* 152.
74. K. Steinhauser, *The Apocalypse Commentary of Tyconius* (Frankfurt: Lang, 1987).
75. See P. Fredriksen, "Tyconius and Augustine on the Apocalypse," in *The Apocalypse in the Middle Ages,* ed. R. Emmerson and B. McGinn (Ithaca, N.Y.: Cornell University Press, 1992) 20-37.
76. Augustine *The City of God* 20.
77. Augustine *The City of God* 6:3.
78. See Eusebius *Ecclesiastical History* X.9; *Oration* XVI.3-8.
79. Emmerson and McGinn, *The Apocalypse in the Middle Ages*; H. Lee, M. Reeves, and G. Silano, *Western Mediterranean Prophecy: The School of Joachim of Fiore and the Fourteenth Century Breviloquium* (Toronto: Pontifical Institute of Medieval Studies, 1989).

of the book correspond to the seven periods of the church, which are then followed by eternity. Each of the series of seven is then related to the seven ages (tempora) of the church. The seven seals relate to the seven ages of both Israel and the church. In the sequence of seven, the sixth assumes great importance as the penultimate period, anticipating the consummation of history. Thus the sixth letter is a prophecy of the sixth period, which is imminent in Joachim's day. In Israel's history and in the beginnings of the church, the Babylonian exile and the birth of Jesus, respectively, herald the renewal of the church in the sixth period of history. The preoccupation with the penultimate period, the sixth, is typical of exegesis in the Joachite tradition; it is the period of Antichrist and leads to the fulfillment of Joachim's final age of the Spirit.

So Joachim finds a parallel between the experience of Israel and that of the church, but he broke decisively from the Augustinian tradition in being willing to find significance in history. Joachim used a trinitarian reading of history in which a coming third age, that of the Spirit, would be characterized by an outburst of spiritual activity in the form of monastic renewal. That time, for him, was imminent. The opening of the sixth seal would be a time of persecution and exile, parallel to that of the Jews in Babylon, that would purify the church. The coming of the seventh era, the opening of the seventh seal, would herald the era of the Holy Spirit, and the seeds of that new age, sowed long before, would come to fruition. Revelation, therefore, offered the key to the reading of the Bible as a whole and to the interpretation of history.

Most daring of the commentators in this tradition is Peter Olivi (1248–98), who used Joachim extensively in his *Postilla in apocalypsim*.[80] Olivi's commentary on the book of Revelation was investigated and condemned in 1326. For him, the sixth period is the beginning of the time of renewal. Olivi places himself in the sixth period and identifies Francis of Assisi, whom he identifies with the angel of the sixth seal in Rev 7:2, as the inaugurator of that period.

What is remarkable about Olivi's exegesis are his predictions of the corruption of the church and the conflict over the issue of poverty in the Franciscan order, which dominated the early history of the order, which are to be seen as an eschatological tribulation. Olivi predicts that the pope and Franciscan leaders would reject the "true" Franciscan view of poverty. Like Joachim, he divided salvation history into three periods, corresponding to Father, Son, and Spirit. In the seven ages of the church, the sixth age is that of evangelical men, from Francis to the death of Antichrist; the final age will last from Antichrist until the end of the world. Olivi matched the seven heads of the dragon with seven persecutions of the church and the seven periods of the church to the seven ages of world history: Adam to Noah, Noah to Abraham, Abraham to Moses, Moses to David, David to Christ, Christ to Antichrist, Antichrist to the end of the world. He spoke of three advents of Christ: first in the flesh, then in the spirit of evangelical reform, and third in judgment. Just as Christ came in the sixth age to replace Judaism, so also in the sixth age of the church, it will be renewed, something initiated by the appearance of Francis of Assisi.

What is new in Olivi's interpretation is that he saw the forces of evil as being concentrated in a worldly church, a present, or at least imminent, reality, that is identified with the whore of Babylon. A mystic antichrist appears, possibly a false pope, though this is unclear from his writing. On the basis of the second half of Revelation 13, Olivi sees this mystic antichrist as one who excludes those who contradict ecclesiastical authority. During the time of Antichrist, the doctors of the church will take the side of Antichrist, and they will attack the life and spirit of Christ in the lives of those engaged in the renewal of the church. Like Augustine, Olivi declared that the millennium began with the church's reign, starting in the time of Constantine and lasting until the last judgment, which would take place at some point in the fourteenth century. In the light of views like this, it comes as no surprise that the later Middle Ages were a period of such intense upheaval fired by apocalyptic revivals.[81]

The Reformation.[82] Bullinger was the only magisterial Reformer to write a commentary on Revelation arising from lections and sermons, and the importance of that commentary to sixteenth-century theological study should not be underestimated. In the first edition of the

---

80. D. Burr, *Olivi's Peaceable Kingdom: A Reading of the Apocalypse Commentary* (Philadelphia: University of Pennsylvania Press, 1993).
81. See Cohn, *The Pursuit of the Millennium*.
82. K. Firth, *The Apocalyptic Tradition in Reformation Britain, 1530–1645* (Oxford: Oxford University Press, 1979); C. Hill, *The Antichrist in Seventeenth Century England*, rev. ed. (London: Verso, 1990); C. Hill, *The English Bible and the Seventeenth Century Revolution* (London: Penguin, 1993).

German Bible, however, which was richly illustrated (in the 1522 edition Babylon is depicted wearing a papal crown), Luther outlined his reasons for relegating the book to a subordinate place within the canon of the New Testament, in words that echo much earlier (and later) assessments in the Christian tradition:

> About this book of the Revelation of John, I leave everyone free to hold his own ideas, and would bind no man to my opinion and judgment: I say what I feel. I miss more than one thing in this book, and this makes me hold it to be neither apostolic or prophetic. First and foremost, the Apostles do not deal with visions, but prophecy in clear, plain words, as do Peter and Paul and Christ in the gospel. For it befits the apostolic office to speak of Christ and his deeds without figures and visions but there is no prophet in the Old Testament, to say nothing of the New, who deals so out and out with visions and figures. And so I think of it almost as I do of the Fourth Book of Esdras, and I can in nothing detect that it was provided by the Holy Spirit.
>
> Moreover, he seems to be going much too far when he commends his own book so highly—more than any other of the sacred books do, though they are much more important, and threaten that if any one takes away anything from it, God will deal likewise with him. Again, they are to be blessed who keep what is written therein; and yet no one knows what that is, to say nothing of keeping it. It is just the same as if we had it not, and there are many far better books for us to keep. Many of the fathers rejected, too, this book of old, though St. Jerome, to be sure, praises it highly and says that it is above all praise and that there are as many mysteries in it as words; though he cannot prove this at all, and his praise is at many points, too mild.
>
> Finally, let every one think of it as his own spirit gives him to think. My spirit cannot fit itself into this book. There is one sufficient reason for me not to think highly of it—Christ is not taught or known in it; but to teach Christ is the thing which an apostle above all else is bound to do, as He says in Acts 1:1 "Ye shall be my witnesses." Therefore I stick to the books which give me Christ clearly and purely.[83]

Revelation's theological shortcomings and the dangers it posed for the faithful meant that it was to be considered as little better than an apocryphal book. Luther subtly modified his view of Revelation in the later editions of his New Testament from 1530 onward, offering the advice: "The first and surest step toward finding its interpretation is to take from history the events and disasters that have come upon Christendom until now, and hold them up alongside these images and so compare them very carefully. If then the two perfectly coincided and squared with one another, we could build on that as a sure, or at least unobjectionable interpretation."[84] "In this book," wrote Luther in his Preface to Revelation of 1545, "we see that, through and above all plagues and beasts and bad angels, Christ is with his saints, and wins the victory at last."

Luther came to the view that the pope was Antichrist, a view held also by Calvin, who believed that "all the marks by which the Spirit of God has pointed out antichrist appear clearly in the Pope,"[85] a view worked out in detail by many Protestant commentators. This notion was repudiated by Roman Catholic expositors like Bellarmine, who argued that the advent of Enoch and Elijah (Revelation 11), the emergence of Antichrist from the tribe of Dan, and the universal proclamation of the gospel had to precede Antichrist, and so the Roman Catholic pontiff could not be that figure. [86]

A fascinating witness to the interpretation of Revelation in the early Calvinist tradition is provided by the Geneva Bible, which offers a historicizing interpretation typical of the day.[87] It enables us to see how Revelation was used as part of the ecclesiastical struggle of the time. Its Protestant leanings are everywhere apparent. On Rev 15:2, the promise is that the afflictions

---

83. Martin Luther, *Preface to the New Testament*, 12ff.
84. See R. Bauckham, *Tudor Apocalypse: Sixteenth Century Apocalypticism, Millenarianism, and the English Reformation* (Oxford: Sutton Courtenay, 1978) 41ff.
85. Firth, *The Apocalyptic Tradition in Reformation Britain*, 13.
86. Firth, *The Apocalyptic Tradition in Reformation Britain,*, 171.
87. Edinburgh 1579. See also Hill, *The English Bible and the Seventeenth Century Revolution*, 56-62. The notes were influenced by Bullinger's sermons and Bale's writing, see Firth, *The Apocalyptic Tradition in Reformation Britain*, 122-24. See also Bauckham, *Tudor Apocalypse*, 45-48.

of the world are all overcome by the saints of God. According to 14:1, Christ is ever-present with his church: "there can be no vicare; for where there is a vicare, there is no church." The mark on the forehead of the elect is "the mark of their election, their faith." The throne of Satan (2:13) is "all townes and countries whence God's words and good living is banished . . . and also the places where the word is not preched syncerly, nor manners right reformed." As may be expected, there is an identification of Rome with the antichrist (the papacy is the inheritor of the power of the Roman Empire, in the interpretation of the two beasts of Revelation 13). The beast from the sea has two horns, "which signifies the priesthode and the kingdoms, and therefore he giveth in his armes two keys, and hath two swordes caryed before him." The Roman Catholic character of Antichrist is supported by the interpretation of 666 as *lateinus* (an early patristic exegesis as well). The locusts of Rev 9:3 are "worldlie suttil Prelates, with Monkes, freres, cardinals, Patriarkes, Archbishops, Doctors, Bachelors and masters which forsake Christ to maintain false doctrine." There is explicit rejection of the Anabaptists (the Nicolaitans of Rev 2:6 are said to be "the heretics which helde that wives shulde be commune") and of their doctrine of the State in the comment on Rev 21:24: "here we see as in infinite other places that Kings and Princes (contrarie to what wicked opinion of the Anabaptists) are partakers of the heavenlie glorie, if they rule in the feare of the Lord."

The opening of the first seal in Rev 6:1 is the declaration of God's will, and the white horse signifies "innocence, victorie and felicitie which shilde come by the preaching of the gospel" (an echo of the exegesis of Victorinus). The plagues that come through the sequence of seals, trumpets, and bowls refer to the corruption of the church from within and the persecutions from without. The only remedy is to appear before God "by the meanes of Jesus Christ" (on 8:2). True ministry should resemble that of the two witnesses, who are types of "all the preachers that shulde buylde up God's church" (11:3).[88] The ministers "ought to receive the worde into their hearts and to have grace and deep judgment and diligently to studie it with zeale to utter it" (on 10:9). So zeal is required, for "nothing more displeaseth God than indifference and coldness in religion" (on 3:19).

The marginal note urges readers to recognize the contemporary relevance of the book: "this is not then as the other Prophecies which were commanded to be hid till the time appointed . . . because that these things shulde be quickly accomplished and did now begin" (on 22:10). Urgency and watchfulness are essential: "Seeing the Lord is at hand, we ought to be constant and rejoyce, but we must beware we esteme not the length or shortness of the Lord's coming by our own imagination." What is needed is to "read diligently: judge soberly, and call earnestly to God for the true understanding thereof" (the conclusion of The Argument, The Revelation of John the Divine). The interpretation of Revelation's imagery includes recognition of the historical background of the original work, evident also in the approach to passages like Dan 9:24ff. These passages have often been a subject of eschatological speculation, but in the Geneva Bible they are interpreted entirely in terms of Jewish history before Christ. So while Christopher Hill writes that "the main offence of the Geneva Bible lay in its notes,"[89] it cannot be said that they fomented eschatological enthusiasm, for "the time shall be long of Christ's second coming, and yet the children of God ought not to be discouraged" (on Dan 12:11). Rather, they are a testimony to a use of Revelation as a crucial tool for "the true kings and priests in Christ" whereby may be disclosed "the wicked deceit" in their midst (on 16:12) and acting in a way appropriate to their election and continued perseverance. Given that this historicizing and hortatory reading of Revelation rejects both Anabaptist and chiliastic enthusiasm, it is strange that Revelation should have a less favored position in the lectionary of the *Book of Common Prayer* than do apocryphal books (read in October and November).[90]

Joachite influence continued in differing forms. On the one hand, in his widely influential book *The Image of Both Churches,* John Bale combined the historical interpretation of the Joachite tradition with the Augustinian apocalyptic dualism of an eternal struggle between two

---

88. On the interpretation of these verses, see R. L. Petersen, *Preaching in the Last Days: The Theme of "Two Witnesses" in the Sixteenth and Seventeenth Centuries* (London: Oxford University Press, 1993) 199.
89. Hill, *The English Bible and the Seventeenth Century Revolution*, 64.
90. F. E. Brightman, *The English Rite* (London: Rivingtons, 1915) 1:51.

classes of people: those of Christ and those of Antichrist. Revelation, therefore, offers an important insight into the nature of this eternal struggle, which has gone on through the ages.[91] In the spirit of Joachim, Bale suggested that the sixth trumpet and seal introduced his own period: The sixth age is the age of reformation. Another interpreter who was influenced by the Joachite tradition, yet in an overtly revolutionary direction, was Thomas Muentzer (d. 1525). Despite his reputation as the epitome of apocalyptic radicalism, Muentzer's use of the book of Revelation itself is quite sparse. His political radicalism is rooted in the mystical tradition influenced by the writings of Tauler rather than in the Apocalypse,[92] which may have influenced early Anabaptism. Hans Hut, for example (who may have been part of Muentzer's army, which was routed at Frankenhausen in 1525 and who himself died in prison the following year), wrote of the situation at the time of the Peasants Revolt that "the final and most terrible times of the world are upon us."[93]

The evidence of an extensive use of Revelation is apparent, however, in the writings of Muentzer's contemporary Melchior Hoffman (d. c. 1534).[94] He saw Revelation as the key to the understanding of history, the meaning of the secrets of which had been revealed to him. There were three revelations of divine glory in the time of the apostles, the second at the time of Jan Hus, and the third at the time of the Reformation. Following each was a period of decline. He saw his own time as the coincidence of the last kingdom of Antichrist and the last outpouring of the Holy Spirit. He shared an Augustinian view of the millennium: There had been a Christian Jerusalem in which the elect, together with Christ, ruled the faithful for a thousand years. After Hus, God had given the church time to repent, but the papacy was antichrist and still prevailed. Hoffman, like Muentzer, identified his own mission with Elijah to come, one of the two witnesses of Revelation 11. Their defeat was a certain sign of the Second Coming, after which there would be a persecution of the true church, at the end of which a company of 144,000, inspired by the Spirit, would proclaim God's grace throughout the world (echoes here of Joachim's "spiritual men").

Although his own vision had no place for the exercise of violent retribution by the elect, Hoffman's views were an ingredient in the establishment of the millennialist commonwealth in the city of Münster. He appears to have given tacit support to the Münster commonwealth, as when he described one of the leaders, Jan Matthijs, as one of the divine witnesses of Revelation 11. His successor as prophet was Jan of Leyden, who believed himself to be the eschatological Davidide. A reign of terror in Münster in 1534 fueled by antinomianism ensued. The influx of people into the city was seen as the fulfillment of the gathering of 144,000 into the new Jerusalem in Revelation 14. The Melchiorite interpretation of Revelation is an unusual example of the use of Revelation in the practice of a millenarian politics that, like the revolutionary actions of Thomas Muentzer a decade earlier (and like the more recent example of the Branch Davidian compound at Waco, Texas), did not remain at the level of utopian idealism but resulted in violent attempts to establish an eschatological theocracy.[95]

The use of the sword by the elect was not accepted by all Anabaptists of this period, however. The catastrophic effects of Münster as well as the career of Thomas Muentzer led to reaction against notions of eschatological theocracy.[96] It was viewed as a diabolical exercise whose enthusiasm was to be repudiated by all Christian people. Menno Simons, for example, the key figure in the revival of the Anabaptist movement after the Münster debacle, attacked the Münster prophets as false. He talked of the kingdom of Christ as not being of this visible world. The church is the visible form of the kingdom. It is visible in this world to the extent that Christians are obedient to the teachings of Christ. Despite the sense of an expectation of imminent fulfillment, what one finds in the post-Münster Anabaptism is the sense of being in the penultimate period rather than in the eschatological commonwealth on earth.[97]

---

91. See Bauckham, *Tudor Apocalypse*, 54-90; Firth, *The Apocalyptic Tradition in Reformation Britain*, 32-68.
92. P. Matheson, *The Collected Works of Thomas Muentzer* (Edinburgh: T. & T. Clark, 1988).
93. Hans Hut, "On the Mystery of Baptism," in D. Liechty, *Early Anabaptist Spirituality* (London: SPCK, 1994) 64; and on anabaptism in England, I. B. Horst, *The Radical Brethren* (Nieuwkoop: de Graaf, 1972).
94. K. Deppermann, *Melchior Hoffmann* (Edinburgh: T. & T. Clark, 1987).
95. Cf. M. Walzer, *Exodus and Revolution* (New York: HarperCollins, 1985) 120-22.
96. On millenarian apocalypticism, see Cohn, *The Pursuit of the Millennium*.
97. W. Klaassen, *Living at the End of the Ages: Apocalyptic Expectation in the Radical Reformation* (Lanham, Md.: University Press of America, 1992).

Alongside the place of Revelation in radical religion in the sixteenth and early seventeenth centuries is a rich stream of interpretation in which the careful exposition of the book was carried out in a more measured and less heated atmosphere, encouraging a long tradition of apocalyptic speculation. Chief among such interpreters was Joseph Mede (1586–1638), whose work had enormous influence on subsequent generations (and whose interpretation of Revelation was taken up and used by more politically active groups during the Commonwealth period in England after the execution of Charles I).[98] By an interpretive method that viewed the book as a series of "synchronisms," or recapitulations in which several passages are said to relate to the same period of history, he calculated a period of 1,260 years from the rise of the papacy (dated to 365 CE) to its overthrow sometime in the seventeenth century. He considered his hermeneutical method to be based on a careful exegesis of the text: "The Apocalypse considered only according to the naked Letter . . . hath marks and signs sufficient by the Holy Spirit, whereby the Order, Synchonism and Sequele of all the Visions therein contained, may be found out . . . without supposall of any Interpretation whatsoever."[99]

In a diagram in the 1833 edition of *Clavis Apocalyptica,* the last in each of the three series of sevens is viewed together as a moment of climax. That synchronic approach to the visions has been typical of many commentators on Revelation down to the present day, and his work has been frequently quoted in subsequent centuries. Similar in approach (explicitly indebted to Mede's work) and dictated by a concern to manifest evidence of divine providence in history are Isaac Newton's commentaries on Revelation, written a century and a half later. These are detailed and exhaustive attempts to demonstrate the marvelous orderliness of the pattern of the history of church and world, condensed in the books of Daniel and Revelation and parallel to what may be observed in the physical world.[100]

A link between revelation and radical politics is particularly evident in English Civil War writing,[101] best exemplified in the brief radical career of Gerrard Winstanley, who, with others, laid claim to the common land of the basis of a belief that the earth was a common treasury. The rule of the beast is not merely eschatological but is seen in the political arrangements of the day. Professional ministry, royal power, the judiciary, and the buying and selling of the earth correspond to the four beasts in the book of Daniel. The struggle between the dragon and Christ is exemplified in the advocacy of communism over against the rival claims to private property. The new heaven and earth can be seen here and now. Royal power is the old heaven and earth that must pass away. The new Jerusalem is not "to be seen only hereafter." Winstanley asserts, "I know that the glory of the Lord shall be seen and known within creation, and the blessing shall spread within all nations." God is not far above the heavens; God is to be found in the lives and experiences of ordinary men and women. God's kingdom comes when God arises in the saints. The perfect society will come when there takes place "the rising up of Christ in sons and daughters, which is his second coming." Winstanley used apocalyptic imagery to speak of the present as a critical moment in the life of the nation. He was convinced that Christ would reign and judge the world in and through his saints.[102] This millenarian vision was to permeate English religion through the individualized reading of the apocalyptic narrative in Bunyan's *Pilgrim's Progress,* itself a product of a period when the revolutionary politics of the mid-seventeenth century were on the wane.[103]

William Blake and His Contemporaries. The German commentator Albrecht Bengel had an enormous influence on contemporary readers, not least John Wesley, who quotes from Bengel's *Gnomon* in his introduction to Revelation. Bengel speaks for many eighteenth-century

---

98. Firth, *The Apocalyptic Tradition in Reformation Britain, 1530–1645,* 240-46.
99. Quoted in Firth, *The Apocalyptic Tradition in Reformation Britain, 1530–1645,* 221.
100. C. Burdon, *The Apocalypse in England 1700–1834: Revelation Unravelling* (London: Macmillan, 1997).
101. See C. Hill, *The World Turned Upside Down* (London: Penguin, 1972); Hill, *The English Bible and the Seventeenth Century Revolution;* Firth, *The Apocalyptic Tradition,* 242.
102. On Winstanley and his relationship to radical interpretation of Scripture, see C. Rowland, *Radical Christianity: A Reading of Recovery* (Oxford: Polity, 1988). The millenarian tradition is evident in early American exegesis. See R. Bloch, *Visionary Republic, Millennial Themes in American Thought 1756–1800* (Cambridge: Cambridge University Press, 1985).
103. See C. Hill, *A Turbulent Seditious and Factious People: John Bunyan and His Church* (Oxford: Oxford University Press, 1989).

commentators in appreciating this quality in the prophetic literature in writing thus about Revelation:

> The whole structure of it breathes the art of God, comprising in the most finished compendium, things to come, many, various; near, intermediate, remote; the greatest, the least; terrible, comfortable; old, new; long, short; and these interwoven together, opposite, composite; relative to each other at a small, at a great distance; and therefore sometimes as it were disappearing, broken off, suspended, and afterwards unexpectedly and most seasonably appearing again. In all its parts it has an admirable variety, with the most exact harmony, beautifully illustrated by those digressions which seem to interrupt it. In this manner does it display the manifold wisdom of God shining in the economy of the church through so many ages.[104]

While the existential, individualistic appropriation of the book in early Methodism suggests a move from the world of politics to that of the human soul,[105] the approach to Revelation that saw in it an account of universal history in which contemporary events could be found had a new lease of life at the time of the French Revolution.[106] Throughout his life, Samuel Taylor Coleridge retained a fascination for Apocalypse, the visionary manifestation evident in the fragmentary "Kubla Khan."[107] In the context of the French Revolution, Coleridge, like his contemporary Joseph Priestley, saw the prophecy of Revelation being fulfilled, as is evident from his explicit use of Revelation in his "Religious Musing," published in 1796. As he became more conservative in his political views, however, he stressed the need for interpretation and set store by the emerging historical study of the text (e.g., in the work of Eichorn).

Arguably, the person who has understood most about Revelation without ever explicitly commenting on it was William Blake. He inhabited and was suffused with the world of the Bible in a way without parallel. Blake wrote no commentary on Revelation, but wrote his own prophecy, weaving images of Revelation into the fabric of his own visionary mythology. He read Revelation not as an end in itself but as a means to an end: the permeating of consciousness with the apocalyptic outlook. Blake recognized the prophets of the Old Testament as kindred spirits, and he wrote in their style and used their images, but for his own time and in his own way.

Blake's mythological writings challenge the God of the Bible, who had become a key figure in the creation of the ideology of the state.[108] Blake manifests the prophetic impulse that is in opposition to the kind of conformity to church and monarch typical of his day. Throughout the 1790s Blake's writing and designs returned to the themes of prophetic struggle and the need to be aware of the dangers of the prophetic spirit's degenerating into the apostasy of state religion.[109] For Blake, Revelation offered a supreme example of the prophetic impulse. And yet its authoritarianism, asceticism, and emphasis on divine transcendence are often implicitly criticized by him in the light of divine immanence and a spirit of forgiveness and mercy, which, according to Blake, characterized the religion of Jesus.

The Eschatological Synthesis of Modern Fundamentalism. The use of Revelation as a repository of prophecies concerning the future has been evidenced from the start and reached an influential climax in the work of Joseph Mede. In the last two hundred years, it has become very much a part of a growing trend toward eschatological interpretation. It was given an impetus from an unlikely source when an Anglican clergyman, John Nelson Darby, founder of the Plymouth Brethren, interpreted the book as unfulfilled prophecy. In his interpretation of the rapture, which is not in Revelation but is described in 1 Thess 4:17 (though Darby thought he could find

---

104. Albrecht Bengel, *Gnomon Novi Testamenti*, 1026 on Rev 1:1, quoted in John Wesley, *Explanatory Notes Upon the New Testament*, 2:313. See also the important attempt to make contemporary the message of Revelation in J. G. Herder, *Maran Atha*, English trans. (London, 1821), discussed by Burdon, *The Apocalypse in England*, 85-87.

105. See M. H. Abrams, *Natural Supernaturalism, Tradition and Revolution in Romantic Literature* (New York: Norton, 1973) 47; M. Butler, *Romantics Rebels and Reactionaries* (Oxford: Oxford University Press, 1981).

106. Burdon, *The Apocalypse in England 1700–1834*.

107. E. Shaffer, "Kubla Khan" and the Fall of Jerusalem (Cambridge: Cambridge University Press, 1975).

108. See D. V. Erdman, *Blake: Prophet Against Empire*, 3rd ed. (Princeton: Princeton University Press, 1977).

109. J. Mee, *Dangerous Enthusiasm* (Oxford: Oxford University Press, 1992) 211.

it alluded to in Rev 3:10), this event was to occur before the resurrection, thereby opening the way for a period of great tribulation.

This kind of reading is supported by the widely influential Scofield Reference Bible, first published in 1909. Here the letters in Revelation 2–3 have a prophetic as well as a local application, disclosing seven phases of the spiritual history of the church. Thus Thyatira is the papacy: "as Jezebel brought idolatry into Israel, so Romanism weds Christian doctrine to pagan ceremonies." There is a close link between Revelation and Daniel: Revelation 4–19 synchronize with Daniel's seventieth week (Dan 9:24), with the great tribulation of Rev 7:14 coming in the middle of the "week." This is brought to an end by the parousia and the battle of Armageddon. The day of the Lord is preceded by seven signs: the sending of Elijah; cosmic disturbances; the insensibility of the professing church; the apostasy of the church; the rapture of the true church (1 Thessalonians 4); the manifestation of the man of sin (2 Thessalonians); and the apocalyptic judgments of Revelation 11–18 ("the great tribulation"), which involve the people of God who have returned to Palestine. The beasts of Revelation 13 are the last civil and ecclesiastical heads respectively. The "ten horns" of Dan 7:24 and Rev 17:12 refer to the last form of Gentile power, "a confederated ten-kingdom empire covering the sphere of authority of ancient Rome." The return of Christ in glory, which will bring to an end Gentile dominion, is followed by the destruction of the beast, the millennium, the satanic revolt, the second resurrection and final judgment, and the coming of the day of God.

Although thoroughly influenced by the peculiar fears of the late twentieth century, most influential in this tradition has been Hal Lindsey's *Late, Great Planet Earth*.[110] For Lindsey, the seals predict war in the Middle East. The sixth seal concerns the beginning of nuclear war, and the trumpet heralds the terrible disasters of such a war. The 200 million cavalry are the army of China, which will do battle with the armies of the West at Armageddon. The beast from the sea is Antichrist, which will emerge from the European Union, whose member nations are symbolized by ten horns. The beast from the land is religious and seeks to unite all religions in a spurious faith. The decline in religious and moral life, castigated in the Laodicean letter, is addressed to the twentieth century's generations. It is a sign that the end is near. The book of Revelation encourages the elect to dream of a miraculous rescue by the rapture and is a license for escape from political struggle to change the present world order, doomed as it is to destruction. There is no role for humans in saving it. All that matters is to be found as part of the elect, who will enjoy the escape of the rapture. The panorama of destruction in Revelation offers no human solution but ensures flight from the world.[111]

The nature of Revelation's polyvalent imagery means that there is at the end of the day no refuting of readings like this. One can only appeal to consistency with the wider demand of the gospel and its application by generations of men and women in lives of service and involvement with the suffering and the marginalized to counter such world-denying and dehumanizing appropriations of Revelation and other biblical books.

Historical Criticism and Modern Exegesis. The rise of historical scholarship led to a different perspective on the book, which focused more on past meaning than on present use. Earlier critics, like Hugo Grotius (1583–1645) in his *Annotations on the New Testament,* had argued that the book's meaning was almost entirely related to the circumstances of John's own day (the so-called preterist method of interpretation). He considered that John's visions related to the fall of Jerusalem and the end of Rome and that the millennium had started with the accession of Constantine, though he did not exclude some eschatological fulfillment. Typical of the method that has dominated study not only of Revelation but of all biblical texts since is evident in the work of J. J. Wettstein (1693–1754). In his *Novum Testamentum,* he dated the work at the outbreak of the Jewish war against Rome (66–73 CE) and saw it in part as a prophecy about the collapse of Jerusalem and then of Rome, and a prediction about the fate of Domitian. The

---

110. Hal Lindsey, *The Late, Great Planet Earth* (London: Lakeland) 1971. According to *US News and World Report* (Dec. 13, 1997) 69, this book and its sequels had phenomenal sales: 40 million copies.

111. A. Mojtabai, *Blessed Assurance* (Boston: Houghton Mifflin) 1987; P. Boyer, *When Time Shall Be No More: Prophecy Belief in Modern American Culture* (Cambridge, Mass.: Harvard University Press, 1992); D. Thompson, *The End of Time: Faith and Fear in the Shadow of the Millennium* (London: Minerva, 1997).

form of his study is significant, and it exemplifies the subtle change that the rise of the historical method brought with it. Attention is paid entirely to the book in its ancient context. As well as detailed text-critical analysis, there are lengthy quotations from ancient sources, including rabbinic parallels that illuminate particular passages of Revelation. Ferdinand Christian Baur's (1792–1860) theory of texts as mirrors of church conflict (given a new impetus in recent years in the writing of Michael Goulder)[112] considered the Apocalypse as an example of a Jewish-Christian anti-Pauline text. Attacks on Balaam, Jezebel, and the Nicolaitans are thinly veiled attacks on Paul. Thus Rev 2:14, 20 contrasts with advice that Paul offers on the issue of food offered to idols in 1 Corinthians 8:1; 10:23ff. The early dating of Revelation by members of the Tübingen school of biblical exegesis led Friedrich Engels to regard Revelation as the prime witness to the character of primitive Christian religion.[113]

Perhaps the most distinctive contribution of historical study of the book has been the application of source-critical study to it. The recognition of inconsistencies led Grotius to think that the book was written at different times in John's life, a view that has had many variations. So, for example, Revelation 11, with its reference to Jerusalem under siege, may have been written in the 60s and later incorporated into a book written in the 90s. R. H. Charles, the doyen of source critics of apocalyptic texts, considered that the author was responsible for compiling much of the first twenty chapters, but a later redactor wrote most of chapters 20–22 and made additions to the rest of the book, bringing about severe dislocations to the original.

Questions about the authorship of the book are not confined to the modern period but go back to the early centuries of the church, when anti-Montanist polemic led writers like Dionysius of Alexandria to question its apostolic origin and to suggest that it may have come from the hand of the heretic Cerinthus because of its espousal of a messianic, this-worldly eschatology. Luther and Zwingli also questioned its apostolic origin. Doubts about a common author for it and the Johannine Gospel are now widespread, with the consensus being that it was written by an unknown John in Asia. In the light of source criticism, the view that the book contains non-Christian elements recurs from time to time.[114] Such a theory reflects the kind of source-critical ingenuity applied to other apocalyptic texts in which there is some evidence of Christian revision (e.g., the *Testaments of the Twelve Patriarchs,* the *Apocalypse of Abraham,* and the *Ascension of Isaiah*), but enough evidence remains of a Jewish work untouched by the Christian gospel (though what counts as Christian in this context is never really discussed).

A distinctive voice in modern interpretation of the book, particularly in British circles, has been Austin Farrer. His careful and ingenious treatment of Revelation's number symbolism as well as an eye for the visionary character of the book have given him a peculiar position in the interpretation of the book.[115]

The recognition of the importance of apocalyptic for the understanding of Christianity, particularly the New Testament, has meant that Christian theologians have had to wrestle with the visionary and the eschatological as central features of their interpretive agenda.[116] At one and the same time the strange world of the apocalypse, far removed from the demythologized world of the Enlightenment, has contributed a golden thread that runs through modern scholarship on early Christianity and, in part, on ancient Judaism also. The reasons for the rediscovery in the second half of the nineteenth century of eschatological beliefs as a significant aspect of earliest Christianity are complex. The books of Daniel and Revelation, and for some traditions 2 Esdras, were for centuries part of the Christian canon of scriptures. The exploration of Abyssinia led to the discovery of Jewish apocalyptic works like *1 Enoch,* which for centuries had been part of the Old Testament canon of the Ethiopic church. The *Apocalypse of Enoch,*[117] for example, now extant in full only in Ethiopic (though fragments have been found among the Dead Sea Scrolls),

---

112. M. Goulder, *A Tale of Two Missions* (London: SCM, 1994).
113. F. Engels, *Marx and Engels: Basic Writings on Politics and Philosophy,* ed. L. Feuer (London: Fontana, 1959).
114. J. M. Ford, *Revelation,* AB 38 (New York: Doubleday, 1975).
115. A. Farrer, *A Rebirth of Images: The Making of St. John's Apocalypse* (Westminster: Dacre, 1949); *The Revelation of St. John the Divine* (Oxford: Oxford University Press). Farrer's work is used in a judicious way by J. Sweet, *Revelation* (London: SCM, 1979).
116. E.g., J. C. Beker, *Paul the Apostle: The Triumph of God in Life and Thought* (Edinburgh: T. & T. Clark, 1980); E. Käsemann, *Commentary on Romans* (London: SCM, 1980).
117. On the apocalyptic character of the Qumran writings, see J. J. Collins, *Apocalypticism and the Dead Sea Scrolls* (London: Routledge, 1997).

contains ideas similar to Daniel and Revelation and the Gospels; it confirmed that the world of Jesus and the first Christians was very much that of the Jewish apocalypses.

Such ideas made perhaps their most dramatic impact on the study of the New Testament in the work of Albert Schweitzer. After reviewing the various attempts, over the previous hundred years, to go behind the pages of the New Testament to get at the historical Jesus,[118] he proposed that Jesus' mission could be understood only if one took seriously the eschatological convictions found in Jewish apocalypses. In Schweitzer's view, the early church had to deal with an initial and dramatic disappointed hope; the result is found in what Schweitzer calls Paul's Christ mysticism, the identification of the messianic age in the lives of believers and the church. Much of what has been written since Schweitzer's work has been an attempt to come to terms with the impact of the eschatological ideas brought to the fore in such a dramatic way by exegetical pioneers like him and Johannes Weiss. Yet despite its problematic character, eschatology paradoxically was the means whereby Jesus' apocalyptic message could continue to speak to every generation—precisely because its strangeness meant that it could never be transformed into the compromises of history.

A feature of modern discussion has been the extent to which Revelation corresponds to contemporary Jewish apocalypses. The flowering of scholarship on Second Temple Judaism after the Second World War (coinciding with the discovery of the Dead Sea Scrolls) has led to a renewed interest in and sophisticated analysis of apocalypses.[119] Revelation's apparent lack of pseudonymity, its tightness of structure, and its author's assertion that the book is prophecy have led some to question how well it fits into the genre of apocalypse, despite its title in 1:1 and the inclusion of some typical features of the apocalypses of Second Temple Judaism (e.g., symbolic visions and heavenly journeys).

Social sciences have made less of an impact on the study of Revelation than one might have expected, given that a significant part of the emerging study of the sociology of religion has been concerned with the rise and character of sectarianism and its ideology.[120] A sectarian origin for apocalyptic has been canvassed.[121] The influential theory of cognitive dissonance pioneered by L. Festinger, with its origins in the study of the millenarian movements in Melanesia, has been applied to early Christian eschatology.[122] The result is to suggest that the failure of the materialization of the millennial hope might prompt a community to engage in various forms of activism (e.g., proselytizing) to cope with their disappointment. Revelation, then, is viewed as a myth for an oppressed community that found itself confronted with the dissonance between its beliefs and the sociopolitical realities of a militant Roman Empire, by which the reader can overcome the contradiction between the present, with its threat of persecution and the hoped-for life of bliss. The link with millenarian movements has been explored historically by Norman Cohn, who has continued to explore the social psychology of a dualistic mind-set.[123] Perhaps the most relevant (though not specifically related either to Revelation or to the New Testament) work is Stuart Hall's study of the rise and character of the Rastafarian movement (which is itself indebted in various ways to passages from the book of Revelation).[124]

The social-psychological perspective is evident also in Adela Yarbro Collins's exploration of the extent to which reading can be a way of dealing with aggression. The process of engaging with the book can bring about catharsis and displacement of difficult emotion.[125] This follows in the footsteps of C. G. Jung, who juxtaposed the gospel and the Apocalypse as examples of different and unresolved aspects of human personality—the gospel a testimony to love, and the Apocalypse a cry of vengeance. The perfectionist teaching of the First Epistle of John has its dark

---

118. A. Schweitzer, *The Quest of the Historical Jesus* (London: A. & C. Black, 1931).
119. R. A. Kraft and G. Nickelsburg, *Early Judaism and Its Modern Interpreters* (Philadelphia: Fortress, 1986); J. M. Schmidt, *Die jüdische Apokalyptik* (Neukirchen: Neukirchener Verlag, 1969).
120. P. L. Esler, *The First Christians in Their Social Worlds* (London: Routledge, 1995).
121. Hanson, *The Dawn of Apocalyptic.*
122. See John Gager, *Kingdom and Community* (Englewood Cliffs, N.J.: Prentice Hall, 1975).
123. N. Cohn, *Europe's Inner Demons* (London: Paladin, 1976).
124. S. Hall, "Religious Ideologies and Social Movements in Jamaica," in R. Bobock and K. Thompson, *Religion and Ideology* (Manchester: Manchester University Press, 1985).
125. A. Y. Collins, *Crisis and Catharsis* (Philadelphia: Westminster, 1984); C. G. Jung, *Answer to Job* (London: Routledge, 1984); E. Drewermann, *Tiefenpsychologie und Exegesis Band II Vision, Weissagung, Apokalypse Geschichte Gleichnis* (Olten: Walter, 1985) 541-91.

side in Revelation, replete with its primal myths. The shadow side of the gospel of love is fear and vengeance, which are split off and removed from the character of God.

There is much evidence of the power and influence of the book of Revelation among the grassroots groups influenced by late twentieth-century liberation theology. Two commentaries written from that perspective reflect these concerns, though, strictly speaking, their interpretative approach differs little in most respects from the mainstream of historical exegesis. Allan Boesak, for example, favors what he calls "a contemporary historical understanding" of the book of Revelation.[126] By this he means that John's book cannot be understood outside his own political context, but as prophecy does not receive its "full and final fulfillment in one given historical moment only but will be fulfilled at different times and in different ways in the history of the world." That enables him to relate the images of beast and Babylon, for example, to the struggle against the apartheid regime in South Africa. Similarly, Pablo Richard[127] sees the bulk of Revelation until 19:10 to be about the present, the challenge to the community and its role in the world (through his examination of the structure of the book, chap. 14 becomes the center of the message) and its own struggles, only the final chapters being concerned with the eschatological judgment of the world.

In the liberationist perspective, the book of Revelation both offers hope and stimulates resistance. It is a way of looking at the world that refuses to accept that the dominant powers are the ultimate point of reference. Apocalyptic discourse, consisting of picture and symbol, asks the reader to participate in another way of speaking about God and the world that makes it more readily understood by all. It taps the well of human response in those whose experience of struggle, persecution, and death has taught them what it means to wash their robes and to make them white in the blood of the Lamb. Two other interpreters ought to be mentioned in this context: Jacques Ellul[128] and William Stringfellow.[129] Both are marginal to the mainstream of modern biblical exegesis, but each reflects the way in which the Bible, and particularly the book of Revelation, challenges ideology by unmasking the principalities and powers. Perhaps few have understood the meaning of an apocalyptic witness in Babylon better than these two.

The liberationist perspective is apparent in the marginal notes of *Biblia Sagrada,* published in Brazil.[130] The introduction declares that the work is explicitly geared to promote the relationship between text and life and thereby initiate a dialogue between the word of God and "our reality," albeit one qualified by the communal context of reading.[131] In the notes to the first verses of Revelation it is stated that "the Apocalypse is a book read and expounded in meetings of Christian communities." The final verses in 22:6ff. are seen as a dialogue between Christ and the churches, where the book should be read in a liturgical context in which it can be explained and meditated upon and its message applied (thereby asserting a degree of control over individualistic and idiosyncratic readings). Revelation urges that John's mission is that of all Christians: to be prophets, announcing the word of God and continuing the testimony of Jesus Christ. Main themes include warnings against syncretistic religion (particularly applicable in Brazil, where the Afro-Brazilian religions are prominent) and the domination of imperial religion. The sketch of the age in which Revelation was written, particularly the references to the decadence and the prevalence of autocratic regimes, echoes the recent experience of Latin American nations. John's aim, according to the marginal notes, is to recall Christians to their original option and involvement in liberating action, which has to be informed by an understanding of the oppressive situation in which the communities found themselves and the maintenance of a horizon of hope for a new society. John, in his visions, is said to analyze the nature of the victory over evil (on 12:1). Throughout the work are several resonances with the favorite terms within the 'theology of liberation: option for the poor, oppression, liberation, new society, and the "see,

---

126. A. Boesak, *Comfort and Protest* (Edinburgh: T. & T. Clark, 1987).
127. Richard, *Apocalypse.*
128. J. Ellul, *Apocalypse: The Book of Revelation* (New York: Seabury, 1977).
129. W. Stringfellow, *Conscience and Obedience* (Waco, Tex.: Word, 1977); *An Ethic for Christians and Other Aliens in a Strange Land* (Waco, Tex.: Word, 1973). Stringfellow's work is a precursor of Walter Wink's work on the principalities and powers. See W. Wink, *Engaging the Powers* (Philadelphia: Fortress, 1992).
130. *Bíblia Sagrada* (São Paulo: 1990).
131. C. Mesters, "The Use of the Bible in Christian Communities of the Common People," in *The Bible and Liberation,* ed. N. Gottwald (Maryknoll, N.Y.: Orbis, 1983) 119-33; C. Mesters, *Defenseless Flower* (London: CIIR, 1989).

judge, act" of popular pastoral practice. Salvation is said to consist, not in reform, but in radical transformation, "bringing to birth a new world of justice and fraternity."

Revelation offers the opportunity to discern "God's project in history," the title of a pamphlet about the life and history of the people of God down the ages, written by Carlos Mesters, and widely used by the basic ecclesial communities. The interpretation of chap. 13 in this edition as compared with the Spanish translation *La Nueva Biblia Latinoamerica* indicates the more overtly modern political reading of the Brazilian version. In the former the interpretative notes concentrate mainly on the original context of Revelation, whereas in the latter the beast is stated without qualification to be "absolute political power," which takes the place of God and enslaves humans, "totalitarianism, dictatorships and oppressive regimes." The crime of Babylon is to persecute those who reject absolute political power and who are not taken in by the ideological propaganda that ensnares those not vigilant enough to see through it. Although the (ancient) Roman context is not ignored, a general message is found in which the second beast represents manipulative power on the ideological and political levels. When Babylon's fate is lamented in chap. 19, the notes speak of the laments coming from wielders of political, economic, and commercial power. In addition to the eschatological dimension of the book there is the assertion that the coming of Jesus is something that is in process and is evident in the testimony of those who maintain the faith: "to manifest truth, reveal the love of the Father, and promote conversion. Whenever Jesus comes there is the destruction of an unjust world and the construction of a new one." The contextual character of the notes parallel, in their contemporary concern, the approach of those in the sixteenth-century Geneva Bible, whose marginal glosses occasionally suggest politically subversive readings.[132] The narrowly religious interpretations that are standard fare in most modern commentaries are replaced in the Latin American texts by an interpretative lens through which the world can be perceived afresh.

There are examples in abundance of the work's appealing to the oppressed, whether whether in our time or in the ancient world, and of its being the ideology of what Leonard Thompson calls a "cognitive minority." Nevertheless, it has appealed also to those well established in society, albeit through different reading strategies (Newton's interpretation contrasts sharply with the roughly contemporary Winstanley's in this respect). People can think in the manner of the Apocalypse without themselves being part of a minority or even discontented with their personal life circumstances. The neat correspondence between literature and life, in which an apocalyptic text reflects a persecuted or threatened minority, does not do justice to the wide dissemination of such ideas in the ancient or modern world. The appeal of Revelation to the oppressed in Latin America as they practice their liberation theology lends plausibility to the hypothesis that apocalyptic is peculiarly applicable to the situation of an oppressed minority. But when the images of the Apocalypse can contribute to the mind-set of a significant group within the mainstream of North American society, we should beware of supposing that we have a book that appeals only to persons on the fringes of society.

Liberal Christianity's distaste for Revelation's vindictiveness and lack of concern with love, viewed as prime among all Christian characteristics, has led to attempts to domesticate or tone down its barbarous tone.[133] Recent feminist scholarship has a different objection. Tina Pippin has examined the references to women in the book and found it impossible to regard them as anything other than negative; the transformation of the world is only partial, as gender relations remain untouched.[134] The disparagement of women's activism and encouragement of a passive, dependent attitude is so firmly rooted in the domain of patriarchy that women everywhere remain subject to male dominion.

The Apocalypse and Art.[135] The exegetical commentary on a biblical text like Revelation needs to be complemented by the artistic exposition of the text. Indeed, a commentary cannot

---

132. Hill, *The English Bible and the Seventeenth Century Revolution*.
133. See G. B. Caird, *A Commentary on the Revelation of Saint John the Divine* (London: A. & C. Black, 1984).
134. T. Pippin, *Death and Desire: The Rhetoric of Gender in the Apocalypse of John* (Louisville: Westminster/John Knox, 1992).
135. See Emmerson and McGinn, *The Apocalypse in the Middle Ages*; M. R. James, *The Apocalypse in Art* (London: Oxford University Press, 1931); F. van der Meer, *Apocalypse: Visions from the Book of Revelation in Western Art* (London: Thames and Hudson, 1978); R. M. Wright, *Art and Antichrist in Medieval Europe* (Manchester: 1996). See also the use of Kip Gresham's prints of scenes from Revelation in C. Rowland, *Revelation* (London: Epworth, 1993).

do justice to the character of apocalyptic discourse in the way that a picture or a poem can. An explanation, however suggestive and allusive, reduces and diminishes the hermeneutical power of symbol and myth. Thus art may be better able to stimulate our aesthetic faculties. A commentator on Revelation struggles to find ways to enable interaction with the text as we have it, so that the book, with its peculiar network of imagery, may begin to pervade the reader's consciousness. Whereas exegesis renders texts in ways that systematize and explain, art defies explanation. Art assists in the new moments of unveiling that can occur through the repristination of the apocalyptic images in artistic work. If what we have in Revelation is the opening of an interpretative space for readers or hearers to be provoked, to have their imaginations broadened and the incentive to think and behave differently, then that process requires new methods to ensure that the original impact of a metaphorical text is maintained in different circumstances. Readers of Revelation require a variety of explanatory mediums to explore its words and images, so that they may be able to see, and behave, differently.

Different artistic uses of Revelation may be found over the centuries, ranging from the iconography of ecclesiastical architecture to designs that accompany the text itself. Revelation also lent itself to the catena of illustrations evident in texts like the *Trier Apocalypse* and the long series of "Beatus" manuscripts, which go back to Beatus of Liebana. Apart from manuscripts, there are cycles from the Apocalypse in church murals, the Angers tapestry (late 14th cent.), and stained glass (e.g., the east window in York Minster, England, from the early 15th cent.). Artistic representation of the apocalypse continued in the Renaissance art form of the woodcut, the most famous being Albrecht Dürer's depictions (1497–98). The prominent place given to illuminations of the apocalypse in Luther's Bible of 1534 is an indication of the continuing role of artistic imagination in the exegesis of what continued to be a controversial text. In the eighteenth and nineteenth centuries the contrasting images of Revelation evident in J. M. W. Turner's (1775–1851) work *Death on a Pale Horse* (c. 1825) can be compared with William Blake's less abstract painting of the same title (c. 1800). In our more secular world, the dependence on the inspiration of Revelation is less direct and more subtle. Yet the evocation of cataclysm in art, often distasteful and even banal in the written word, affects a generation saturated with images, not least of human and cosmic disaster, and is a profound influence on the artistic work of a century that has witnessed humanity's worst evils.

The different exegetical approaches to Revelation are manifest in art. Revelation has had from the start of New Testament interpretation a pre-eminent place as the primary eschatological text of the Bible. Last judgment scenes are common in European ecclesiastical buildings. In addition to the eschatological, Van Eycks's *Mystical Lamb* (1432) indicates another way of appropriating the book, following a tradition of interpretation that goes back to Tyconius and Augustine. The division between heaven and earth is transcended in the eucharistic feast as the Lamb, in the midst of the throne, is found on an altar on earth. Contextual readings, in which visions are related to their ancient historical or contemporary contexts, and thus used as an interpretative lens through which to view contemporary history, are seen in severe medieval cycles of apocalypse illustrations and the later woodcuts (e.g., in the depiction of Babylon as papal Rome in the Luther Bible).

William Blake (1757–1827) offers a significant example of the artistic appropriation of the book of Revelation and the creative exploitation of its exegetical potential. He is a unique example of a visionary who was an accomplished artist and poet and whose visionary imagination was combined with creative productive techniques, very much in the tradition of the medieval combination of text and design, to give him a unique place among cultural critics.[136] Blake explicitly traced a continuity not only between his own mythology and the vision seen by John,[137] but also between his own vocation to prophesy and that of John of Patmos. While John's apocalyptic vision is a central component of many aspects of Blake's visionary world and informs Blake's understanding of his own political situation, Blake uses the Apocalypse as inspiration rather than a prescription of his own apocalyptic visions. He is not a conventional commentator

---

136. See *William Blake's Illuminated Books*, 6 vols., ed. David Bindman (London: Tate Gallery Publications/William Blake Trust) 1991-1995.
137. Blake, *The Four Zoas*, in *Blake*, 263-382.

on it, unlike the emerging German historical critics in his day. Blake's relationship with the text represents that of the visionary who stands in continuity not by visualizing again Revelation's images but by using Revelation as a means of true insight into vision, who sees more clearly by means of the ancient apocalyptic text. Unlike his medieval forebears, he does not illuminate the text of Revelation, for his work stands alongside Revelation, not as exegesis but as a further exemplification of the prophetic tradition.

For Blake, the visionary and imaginative is all important, and the Bible has an apocalyptic role in encouraging this. Allowing reason to triumph over imagination denies a wisdom "Permanent in the Imagination," through which one could be "open [to] the Eternal Worlds." This would "open the immortal Eyes/Of Man inwards into the Worlds of Thought, into Eternity/ Ever expanding in the Bosom of God, the Human Imagination."[138] A way in which he achieves this is to juxtapose text and design in his illuminated books. Readings of the text must be set in the context of the illuminations. He achieves hermeneutical creativity by this juxtaposition. Often text and illumination seem to have little contact. The indeterminate relationship between writing and illustration demands that readers engage with the text, and their own imagination contributes to making sense of the two. Language and portrait function in an apocalyptic way, a hermeneutical device that opens up the imagination. Blake demands of the reader imaginative participation to explore the tensions and problems that the text poses. Nature itself can function in this way, for "to the Eyes of the Man of Imagination, Nature [can be] Imagination itself."[139] Blake expects "to see a World in a Grain of Sand and a Heaven in a Wild Flower."[140] "The Old & New Testaments are the Great Code of Art"[141] are just the best examples of art that can, with proper use, open up the way to the eternal: The Bible is "more Entertaining & Instructive than any other book," because it is "addressed as to the Imagination, which is Spiritual Sensation, & but mediately to the Understanding or Reason."[142] For Blake, the exegetical task involved reading, hearing, and appropriating in order to break what he called the "mind forg'd manacles" that prevent imagination and human community from flourishing. Essays in apocalyptic exegesis of the Bible must involve a variety of ways, in which the artistic is paramount, of rousing the faculties to new moments of understanding.

An Apocalyptic Tone in Recent Theology and Philosophy.[143] There are alternative modern perspectives outside the Christian tradition. One is that of D. H. Lawrence.[144] Lawrence saw Revelation as representing the vengeful Christianity of self-glorification, contrasting with the tender religion of Jesus. At its heart is a vital pagan original that has been overlaid by subsequent editors who in each succeeding edition made the book more mean-spirited. And yet there is sufficient evidence of the link with the pagan religion of nature that it can be appropriated by those who will put aside the historical perspective of the final versions and relish the cyclical world of nature that lies dormant in the text.

Jacques Derrida[145] looks at the antimonies sketched by Kant between poetry and mysticism, on the one hand, and philosophy on the other hand (echoes of Blake). Just as the Enlightenment claimed to bring new awareness, so also do apocalypses. When viewed more closely, apocalypse turns out to be an unveiling that reveals only another enigma. Far from offering answers, "the apocalyptic tone" leads to indeterminancy. What apocalyptic unveiling achieves is the revelation of the metaphorical character of all languages, which thereby challenges the fantasy of "answers" by demonstrating in the starkest way possible the indeterminancy of all reality.

The influence of the apocalyptic dimension was not felt within biblical scholarship alone, for the eschatological emphasis found in the work of Weiss and Schweitzer was to spill over in dramatic form into the theology of the immediate post-war scene in Barth's commentary on the

---

138. William Blake, *Jerusalem*, plate 5, ll. 18-20, in Keynes, *Blake*, 623.
139. Blake, Letter to Dr. Trusler, in Keynes, *Blake*, 793.
140. William Blake, "Auguries of Innocence," ll. 1-2, in Keynes, *Blake*, 431.
141. William Blake, *The Laocoön*, in Keynes, *Blake*, 777.
142. Blake, Letter to Dr. Trusler, 794.
143. See the essays in M. Bull, *Apocalypse Theory* (Oxford: Blackwell, 1995).
144. D. H. Lawrence, *Apocalypse* (London: Penguin, 1960).
145. Jacques Derrida, "Of an Apocalyptic Tone Recently Adopted in Philosophy," *Semeia* 23 (1982) 63-97.

Epistle to the Romans.[146] Eschatology offered a stark alternative to the world of destruction and devastation of 1919 and the compromises that contributed to it. It was a situation that provoked acute pessimism about humanity's resources to build a better world. Barth asserted that knowledge of God could come only through God's own revelation, which humanity could only accept or reject. Like the apocalypses of old, which seemed to offer some explanation of human existence and God's purposes through a revelation, Barth stressed the subordination of the human intellect to the revelation of God. He repudiated human attempts to comprehend God (what is referred to as natural theology). Instead, he stressed the centrality of revelation as the only basis for understanding anything about God; that is an "unveiling" or apocalypse.[147]

Contemporary with Barth and equally committed to the eschatological inheritance of the Jewish tradition, but with a very different assessment of it, is Ernst Bloch. He rehabilitated the perspectives of Joachim of Fiore and Gerrard Winstanley and recognized the significance of utopian elements in a variety of cultures. He was committed to the rehabilitation of that millenarian, apocalyptic inheritance on the fringes of orthodox Christianity. His mammoth book, *The Principle of Hope*,[148] explores the ways in which that longing for a future age of perfection has colored the whole range of culture in both East and West. Bloch called attention to the power of the utopian inheritance and its contribution to Marxism as well as the Judeo-Christian tradition (though his views are tangential to the mainstream Marxist tradition and have been received with considerable skepticism by other Marxists). He promoted the eschatological traditions that mainstream Christianity has preferred to forget. It is as the philosopher of "utopia" that Bloch will be remembered. Bloch considers that utopia is not something far off in the future, but is at the heart of human experience; it is already at hand in an anticipatory and fragmentary way. These fragments are themselves an encouragement to human action in the present, even if the hoped-for utopia is not fully possible without changing the present order of things.

Despite its kaleidoscopic quality, Bloch's work often provides suggestive insights into the character of Christian doctrine and its mutation into an ideology.[149] He does not see the Bible as an elaboration of a social utopia, but it "does point most vehemently to exodus and kingdom.[150] Apocalypse is the breaking in of the "novum" (Rev 21:5 is a favorite text of Bloch's). The Apocalypse is the vehicle of an unparalleled phenomenon in the history of religion: "the apocalyptic transformation of the world into something as yet completely non-existent."[151] Not surprisingly, Bloch pays great attention to the chiliastic tradition: "Utopian unconditionality comes from the Bible."[152]

Bloch's own work, echoed in a more attenuated form in the later writing of Walter Benjamin[153] and even Theodor Adorno,[154] all of whom were close friends of Gershom Scholem, the great pioneer of the modern study of Jewish apocalypticism and mysticism,[155] reminds us of neglected aspects of the eschatological tradition and its political potential. In the light of Bloch's work it is not surprising that Christians and some Marxists influenced by this utopian tradition have been united in a common quest for change and a new social order based on peace and justice in this world. Modern political theology owes a great debt to Bloch's appropriation of the Christian chiliastic tradition. The German theologian Jürgen Moltmann is particularly indebted to him.[156] Political theology in Europe in the post-war period has echoes in turn in the influential political theology of Latin America: liberation theology, in which the language of utopianism has sometimes been used as a way of speaking of the relationship between the future kingdom and present movements for social change in church and state, particularly among the downtrodden

---

146. K. Barth, *The Epistle to the Romans* (London: A. & C. Black, 1933) 19. See further B. McCormack, *Karl Barth's Critically Realistic Dialectical Theology* (Oxford: Oxford University Press, 1995).
147. K. Barth, *Church Dogmatics* I/2 (Edinburgh: T. & T. Clark, 1961) 28ff.
148. E. Bloch, *The Principle of Hope*, trans. N. Plaice, S. Plaice, and P. Knight (Oxford: Basil Blackwell, 1986). For an introduction to Bloch's thought, see W. Hudson, *The Marxist Philosophy of Ernst Bloch* (London: Macmillan, 1982).
149. In Ernst Bloch, *Atheism in Christianity*, trans. J. T. Swann (New York: Herder and Herder, 1972).
150. Bloch, *The Principle of Hope*, 502.
151. Bloch, *The Principle of Hope*, 1274.
152. Bloch, *The Principle of Hope*, 509-15. On the links, see Rowland, *Radical Christianity*.
153. See Walter Benjamin, "Theses on the Philosophy of History," in *Illuminations* (London: Collins Fontana, 1970).
154. R. Wiggerhaus, *The Frankfurt School* (Oxford: Polity, 1994).
155. D. Biale, *Gershom Scholem: Kabbalah and Counter-History* (Cambridge, Mass.: Harvard University Press, 1982).
156. J. Moltmann, *Theology of Hope* (London: SCM, 1975).

at the base of Latin American society.[157] In their refusal to divide history and eschatology, the present from the future, liberation theologians have inherited the mantle of that alternative political eschatology championed by Bloch.

Conclusion. The shifting fortunes of the Apocalypse can be traced in the history of interpretation. That ambivalence manifest in the work of the earliest commentators, where an ecclesiological and eschatological hermeneutic are woven together without comment, has characterized the two poles of interpretation. Despite their theological and political differences, Augustine, Winstanley, and Melchior Hoffman all seem to agree that key images relate to contemporary realities. Those who interpret the book wholly eschatologically effectively diminish its contemporary significance, as do those who see the book as applying totally to the past. But the differences of the contemporizing approach suggest that the impact of the images has as much to do with the complex preferences and interests of the readers as it does with what the text demands. We can say that Augustine's interpretation of Revelation 20 as a reference to the rule of bishops in the church conveniently ignores the fact that the text itself places the rule firmly with the martyrs, only a few of whom could be expected to be bishops (particularly in the post-Constantinian age). Equally the realized eschatology that dominates the theocratic applications of Revelation, such as those of Melchior Hoffman, ignore the fact that although what is described may be coming soon there is still an unfulfilled dimension to its apocalyptic evocation.

The demand for understanding has gone hand in hand with attempts to find precise equivalence between history and every image in the book and has resulted in a long tradition of interpretation based on the decoding principle. An image has a particular meaning, and if the code is understood in its entirety the whole apocalypse can be rendered in another form when the code is cracked and the inner meaning laid bare. It is only the occasional reader who refuses to settle for simple meanings, who insists on leaving open the possibility of polyvalence. Instead we typically find meaning confined as the details of images and actions are fixed on some historical personage or event. That applies also to encapsulations of Revelation's theology, for the problem posed by this book is the difficulty imagination places on that desire for the ordered systematic presentation that lies at the heart of theology. A book that requires interpretation and seems to demand order in the face of the apparent chaos of its imagery in the end confounds such attempts, not least those that are furthest from its own prophetic impulse. Schüssler Fiorenza aptly summarizes the peculiar importance of the text and of the context in which it is read:

> Revelation will elicit a fitting . . . response . . . only in those socio-political situations that cry out for justice. When Christian groups are excluded from political power, Revelation's language of divine kingship and royal reward, as well as its ethical dualism, stands against unjust authority and champions the oppressed and disenfranchised. Whenever Christians join the power structures of their society and seek to stabilise them, the same rhetorical world of vision serves to sacralise dominant authorities and preach against their enemies.[158]

In situations where its imagery is allowed to work, however, it can disturb the convention maintained by the commonsensical. Like metaphors, whose function is to lay bare the realities of experience by the abrupt and jarring impact of their linguistic juxtapositions, apocalypse seeks to stop us in our tracks and get us to view things differently. For many, however, metaphors are "dead," themselves having become part of mere convention or habit without the effect they once had; they are salt that has lost its savor. Revelation requires the recovery of that ability to hear or read and to be stirred or shocked and scandalized into repentance and action rather than indifference or rejection: "Let any one who has an ear listen."[159]

---

157. See L. Boff, *Jesus Christ Liberator* (London: SPCK, 1980).
158. E. Schüssler Fiorenza, *Revelation: Vision of a Just World* (Edinburgh: T. & T. Clark, 1993) 139. On the language of Revelation, see D. Barr, "The Apocalypse of John as Oral Enactment," *Int.* 40 (1986) 243-56; G. B. Caird, *The Language and Imagery of the Bible* (London: Duckworth, 1980).
159. I am grateful to James Grenfell, Alan Kreider, and Rebekah Rowland for comments on earlier drafts of this commentary and for help with proofreading and the checking of references.

BIBLIOGRAPHY

Aune, D. E. *Revelation 1–5.* WBC. Nashville: Word, 1997. The most recent and comprehensive commentary in the historical critical tradition.

———. *Revelation 6–16.* WBC. Nashville: Word, 1997.

———. *Revelation 17–22.* WBC. Nashville: Word, 1997.

Bauckham, R. *The Theology of the Book of Revelation.* Cambridge: Cambridge University Press, 1993. An outline of the main theological themes of the book that manages to remain sensitive to the apocalyptic genre and its resistance to theological system.

Beale, G. K. *The Book of Revelation: A Commentary on the Greek Text.* Grand Rapids: Eerdmans, 1998. A comprehensive survey of the biblical antecedents of Revelation.

Bindman, D., ed. *William Blake's Illuminated Books.* 6 vols. London: Tate Gallery Publications/William Blake Trust, 1991–95. An indispensable aid to the understanding of apocalyptic prophecy.

Boring, M. Eugene. *Revelation.* Interpretation. Louisville: John Knox, 1989.

Burdon, C. *The Apocalypse in England 1700–1834: Revelation Unravelling.* London: Macmillan, 1997. An excellent introduction to apocalyptic aesthetics.

Cohn, N. *The Pursuit of the Millennium.* London: Paladin, 1957. An epochal account of medieval revolutionary millenarianism that, though dated in some respects, gives some indication of the enormous importance of Revelation in late medieval politics and religion.

Collins, J. J. *The Apocalyptic Imagination: An Introduction to the Jewish Matrix of Christianity.* New York: Crossroad, 1987. An indispensable guide to the varying characteristics of the apocalyptic genre in ancient Judaism.

Daley, B. *The Hope of the Early Church.* Cambridge: Cambridge University Press, 1991. The wider theological context of early Christian apocalypticism.

Emmerson, R., and B. McGinn. *The Apocalypse in the Middle Ages.* Ithaca, N.Y.: Cornell University Press, 1992. An authoritative account of the interpretation and effects of Revelation down to the late medieval period.

Hill, C. *The English Bible and the Seventeenth Century Revolution.* London: Penguin, 1993. Represents the climax of a life's work of study on radical groups in the early modern period and the enormous importance the book of Revelation had for them.

Rowland, C. *The Open Heaven: A Study of Apocalyptic in Judaism and Early Christianity.* London: SPCK, 1982. An attempt to explore the revelatory character of apocalyptic texts and the central place they have in Judaism and Christianity.

———. *Radical Christianity: A Reading of Recovery.* Oxford: Polity, 1988. An outline of the importance of apocalyptic religion for radical Christianity down to the twentieth century, including liberation theology.

Schüssler Fiorenza, E. *Revelation: Vision of a Just World.* Edinburgh: T. & T. Clark, 1993. A social-rhetorical analysis that shows how Revelation is a work of persuasion intended to enable people to embark on a new way of seeing the world.

Wainwright, A. *Mysterious Apocalypse.* Nashville: Abingdon, 1993. A concise history of the interpretation of the book of Revelation.

Wengst, K. *Pax Romana and the Peace of Jesus Christ.* London: SCM, 1988. An account of the countercultural gospel with an important place given to the book of Revelation.

OUTLINE OF REVELATION

I. Revelation 1:1-8, John Introduces His Book: The Apocalypse of Jesus Christ

II. Revelation 1:9-20, The Great Voice, the Vision of the Son of Man Who Commissions John to Write

III. Revelation 2:1–3:22, John Writes to the Angels
    A. 2:1-7, The Letter to the Angel at Ephesus
    B. 2:8-11, The Letter to the Angel at Smyrna
    C. 2:12-17, The Letter to the Angel at Pergamum
    D. 2:18-29, The Letter to the Angel at Thyatira
    E. 3:1-6, The Letter to the Angel at Sardis
    F. 3:7-13, The Letter to the Angel at Philadelphia
    G. 3:14-22, The Letter to the Angel at Laodicea

IV. Revelation 4:1-11, Vision of God's Throne in Heaven

V. Revelation 5:1-14, Vision of the Divine Scroll and the Lamb

VI. Revelation 6:1-17, John Sees the Seals Opened

VII. Revelation 7:1-17, Concerning Those Sealed and a Vision of the Great Multitude
    A. 7:1-8, The 144,000 of Israel Are Sealed
    B. 7:9-17, The Multitude from Every Nation

VIII. Revelation 8:1–9:21, The Seventh Seal and the Seven Angels with Seven Trumpets

IX. Revelation 10:1-11, The Vision of the Strong Angel and the Command to Prophesy

X. Revelation 11:1-19, The Two Witnesses

XI. Revelation 12:1-18, Signs in Heaven: The Woman and the Dragon

XII. Revelation 13:1-18, The Vision of Two Beasts

XIII. 14:1-20, The Lamb, the 144,000, the Eternal Gospel, and the Human Figure
    A. 14:1-5, The Song of the 144,000
    B. 14:6-13, The Message of the Three Angels
    C. 14:14-20, The Harvest of the Earth

XIV. Revelation 15:1-8, Another Sign in Heaven: The Sea of Glass and the Song of Those Who Conquered

XV. Revelation 16:1-21, Seven Angels and Seven Trumpets

XVI. Revelation 17:1-18, The Vision of Babylon

XVII. Revelation 18:1–19:10, The Fall of Babylon

XVIII. Revelation 19:11-21, Heaven Opens, and the Rider on the White Horse Appears

XIX. Revelation 20:1-15, Millennium and Judgment
  A. 20:1-6, Another Angel Descending from Heaven, the Binding of Satan, and the Millennium
  B. 20:7-10, The Release of Satan for the Last Battle
  C. 20:11-15, The Vision of the Great White Throne and Judgment

XX. Revelation 21:1–22:5, The New Heaven, the New Earth, and the New Jerusalem

XXI. Revelation 22:6-21, Concluding Sayings

REVELATION 1:1-8

JOHN INTRODUCES HIS BOOK: THE APOCALYPSE OF JESUS CHRIST

COMMENTARY

1:1-3. Revelation is a book without parallel in the New Testament. It is a revelation that comes from Jesus Christ. The authoritative quality of the book is announced, similar in some ways to the way Paul announces the authoritative character of his apostolic office at the beginning of Galatians (Gal 1:12, 16). In this respect, Revelation differs even from the biblical book with which, in other respects, it has most in common: Daniel, which opens with stories that set the scene rather than with the stark announcement of apocalypse. Revelation's closest parallels in vocabulary and style, however, are with the opening of Ezekiel's prophecy and the word of God written on tablets of stone at Sinai in Exodus and Deuteronomy, though Revelation is emphatically not a collection of law. A passage from Deuteronomy is alluded to in the words in Rev 22:18, which suggests that the words of this prophecy matter: It is *these* words that are to be heard and read, not a commentary or a paraphrase. Just as the Muslim hears and reveres the particular words of the Quran, so also it is the words of the Apocalypse that are the medium of the revelation of Jesus Christ, and it is these pre-eminently that are to be attended to and pondered.

The word "apocalypse" (ἀποκάλυψις *apokalypsis*) is used for the first and only time here to describe a written collection of revelations, though it is used to speak of divine revelations elsewhere in the NT (see Introduction). Elsewhere the book is described as prophecy; John's contemporary, the writer of the Epistle of Jude, writes of Enoch's "prophesying" (Jude 14) and then quotes a work that is conventionally categorized by modern scholars as an apocalypse, though the word is not used in the book itself (*1 Enoch* 1:9). As far as these writers are concerned, to be called to see and to write in this way is to utter prophecy.[160] The apocalypse is given by God and is something to be communicated to God's servants, who are elsewhere designated as prophets (19:10; 22:9).

An apocalypse is a peculiar form of writing. Whatever the experience that triggered these words, it is a collection of images that persuades not by appealing to "our logical faculties but to our imagination and emotions."[161] What we have in Revelation is a series of images relating to things that have been seen (1:12, 19), communicated by means of words. John *writes* (we may compare John with William Blake, who communicated a sense of vision both pictorially and verbally). While we have to read Revelation and recognize the importance of words, therefore, we need to appreciate that John communicates what he sees and what he hears (see Commentary on Revelation 7). In the imagery there is an attempt to evoke that visionary experience.[162] Unlike the letter to the Romans, which uses argument to persuade readers that the revelation to which it bears witness should be taken seriously, Revelation's word pictures seek to address and involve readers and relocate them in that divine economy. It is full of comparisons as the writer struggles to expand the boundaries of language to encapsulate what defies description. Paul's words summarize the problem for the visionary in the opening chapters of 1 Corinthians, where he renounces plausible words of wisdom (1 Cor 2:4) in favor of "God's wisdom, secret and hidden . . . revealed to us through the Spirit . . . [which] we speak of . . . in words

---
160. J. Barton, *Oracles of God: Perceptions of Ancient Prophecy in Israel After the Exile* (London: Darton, Longman, and Todd, 1986).
161. Schüssler Fiorenza, *Revelation*, 25.
162. See G. B. Caird, *The Language and Imagery of the Bible* (London: Duckworth, 1980).

not taught by human wisdom but taught by the Spirit" (1 Cor 2:7, 10, 13 NRSV). Apocalypse does not consist of "propositional, logical, [or] factual language" but persuades by means of "the evocative, persuasive power of its symbolic language compelling imaginative participation."[163]

The problem with a Bible commentary whose main concerns are authorship, date, purpose, and background is that it can fail to do justice to the peculiarities of a work that depends on imagination and the power of symbolic language. This caution is particularly appropriate for a work like Revelation. We may be tempted to "make sense" of it by offering an interpretation—what it *really* means. But to do that is to ignore the claim made in the words with which John introduces his book: ἐσήμανεν (*esēmanen*). The NRSV translates this expression as "he made it known," but a more literal translation, "he signified," makes clear the importance of the signification through which the apocalypse is communicated. In other words, the medium is the message. To understand Revelation is not to translate its message into another medium but to engage with those signs and juxtapose others to complement them. The verb σημαίνω (*sēmainō*; lit., "signifying") is the same word used by the narrator of the Fourth Gospel to comment on Jesus' use of a phrase like "lift up" (John 12:33), indicating that he would die by crucifixion (John 18:32; cf. John 21:19). How this revelation is signified is important, therefore. To read Revelation as if it were merely a code, reducible without remainder to another form of discourse, is to ignore the fact that it is this mode through which God has communicated to John and that has taxed, vexed, and provoked readers ever since.

So, to extract a message from Revelation and leave behind the images in favor of something more manageable and rational is to run the risk of evacuating the Apocalypse of its power by ignoring that which enables it to be the word of God. Commentators and readers of the book are beckoned to stay within the imagery and not too readily get diverted in their quest for a simple message lurking behind the words, which, it is supposed, history and reason can lay bare.

Revelation stands apart from the rest of the Bible. The bulk of it is presented as a vision that John received. An apostolic epistle or a gospel could legitimately be expected to have worked within received traditions; certainly Paul sought to respond to situations and problems and, in general, to have exercised a conscious effort to mold tradition, thought, and technique to meet an immediate need. Revelation is an altogether different work. It is possible that there are contacts with contemporary Jewish tradition or the hymns of praise of church or synagogue.[164] If we examine its relationship with the Old Testament,[165] we would find that there is hardly a verse in Revelation that does not have some kind of contact with the language and imagery of the Old Testament. But what kind of contact? Are we, for example, justified in thinking of it as an allusion,[166] in the way that an evangelist would cite Scripture to prove the fulfillment of prophecy in Christ (e.g., Matt 1:23) or that a gospel tradition is linked with Scripture (e.g., Gen 28:12 in John 1:51)? Did John sit down and write an apocalypse in much the same way Paul might have written an epistle, either himself or through an amanuensis? Or like an evangelist using sources, whether oral or written? If we take seriously John's claim to report a vision, then we would be wrong to consider the writing as a conscious recall of tradition with a particular intent. If we respect the writer's visionary claim, we will be wary of seeking allusions, as if they were deliberate attempts to echo biblical passages or to respond, in a pragmatic fashion, to particular circumstances, however much these might have affected the deepest levels of his consciousness. Rather, the immediate circumstances, as well as the language of the Bible, become a mode of discourse in which the original context and purpose ceases to be of primary concern (some of these issues are explored further in the Reflections on Revelation 17). The visionary language and its particular syntax are what demands the

---

163. Schüssler Fiorenza, *Revelation*, 31.

164. P. Prigent, *Apocalypse et Liturgie* (Paris: Delachaux, 1960).
165. On the major prophetic books and Revelation, see J. Fekkes, *Isaiah and the Prophetic Traditions in the Book of Revelation* (1988); J. M. Vogelsang, *The Interpretation of Ezekiel in the Book of Revelation* (1985); S. P. Moyise, *The Old Testament in the Book of Revelation* (Sheffield: Sheffield Academic, 1995).
166. See R. Hays, *Echoes of Scripture in the Letters of Paul* (New Haven, Conn.: Yale University Press, 1989).

reader's attention. In the visionary imagination, Ezekiel and Daniel echo in the minds of readers who know these texts well. This is an indication of the "visionary tradition" rather than a deliberate attempt to write a commentary on these texts. Such language is the appropriate—indeed, inevitable—mode of discourse for the visionary. Daniel's and Ezekiel's prophecies are quite simply the means whereby visions are expressed and, perhaps, even engendered.

Consider the opening vision, for example. Its relationship with Daniel is evident, as a comparison makes clear:

I looked up and saw a man clothed in linen, with a belt of gold from Uphaz around his waist. His body was like beryl, his face like lightning, his eyes like flaming torches, his arms and legs like the gleam of burnished bronze, and the sound of his words like the roar of a multitude. (Dan 10:5-6 NRSV)

I saw one like the Son of Man, clothed with a long robe and with a golden sash across his chest. His head and his hair were white as white wool, white as snow; his eyes were like a flame of fire, his feet were like burnished bronze, refined as in a furnace, and his voice was like the sound of many waters. (Rev 1:13-15 NRSV)

This is obviously not mere copying, though the parameters provided by the vision in Daniel are crucial for the Apocalypse's vision. It is as if the language is in some sense determinative for what John sees. Whether he believes he sees what Daniel saw or that the overwhelming vision of the risen Christ could only be written about in terms derived from the book of Daniel is unclear. Like contemporary believers who pray using the language and style of the version of Scripture familiar to them, this written description of the awesome apparition that confronted the seer on Patmos can only be written in the words of Scripture. To write in any other style might be to devalue what was there and reduce its significance.

The blessing promised by engagement with the book (1:3; cf. 14:13; 16:15; 19:9; 20:6; 22:7, 14) comes for both reader and listeners; interestingly, there is only one reference to the former, possibly indicating something about the situation in which a solitary reader might read, with the majority hearing the words of the book (cf. Mark 13:14). Reading and hearing are two very different activities: The reader's occupation allows the words on a page the possibility of cross-referencing, whereas the hearer engages the imagination more easily and makes connections that are perhaps less structured and predictable. Either way, the process leads to "keeping the words." This does not refer to mere preservation of what is contained in the book but, as is evident elsewhere, is the act of practicing them in a way that responds to the critical moment that is near (22:10).

1:4-8. In v. 4, John writes to the seven churches in Asia, which are then addressed individually in chaps. 2–3. Here the particularity of context seems important. We may wonder whether there were only seven churches in the area in John's day, for, as the letters of Paul (Colossians) and Ignatius (*Trallians* and *Magnesians*) indicate, it is likely that there were more. This raises the question of whether the number 7, like the number later in the book (seven seals, trumpets, and bowls; seven spirits, etc., contrasting with the threefold 666 in 13:18), represents the wholeness of the church, a point noted in the earliest extant commentary of Victorinus (see "The Patristic Period," in the Introduction).

Like the opening of Paul's letters (e.g., 1 Cor 1:1), there is a greeting from God, who is described as the one "who is and who was and who is to come" (cf. Rev 3:1; 4:8; 11:17; 16:5). The greeting is from the God of past, present, and future (whose name in Exodus [יהוה *yhwh*] is glossed as "I am who I am" [or "was" or "will be"]; see Exod 3:14; cf. Isa 41:4). The greeting is also from the seven spirits that are near God's throne (cf. 3:1; 4:5; 5:6) and from Jesus Christ, who is represented throughout the book (from chap. 5 onward) as a Lamb. It is a trinitarian juxtaposition reminiscent of 2 Cor 13:12 and Mark 1:10. Jesus Christ is further described in terms that are important for the rest of the book of Revelation. He is the firstborn from the dead (cf. Col 1:18) and ruler of the kings of the earth, a political dominion, a fact that will be stressed again at the parousia in 19:16. John's greeting is from himself as well as from Jesus Christ. This juxtaposition is in line with much else in these opening words, where the authority of

John is enhanced by the ease with which his words and the words of God or Christ (e.g., v. 8) mingle, affirming the divine origin of this particular word to God's servants (v. 1).

As the faithful witness (3:14; 19:11), Christ offers a model for subsequent acts of witness (e.g., 2:13; 11:3; cf. 22:20). John himself, on the isle of Patmos as a witness (v. 9), is engaged in recording the apocalypse itself (1:2; 22:18). The power of witness is evident (11:7; 12:11) and can be a costly affair (2:13; 6:9; 11:7-8; 17:6; 20:4), reflecting the will of God (cf. 15:3). Witness to the way of God is centered on lives of faithfulness and is encapsulated in the witness of the book of Revelation to the ways of God. There is a similar pattern in the Fourth Gospel, in which Jesus is said to have come in order to bear witness to truth (John 18:37), and the Paraclete and the disciples continue that witness (John 15:26-27). Likewise, the witness of John the Baptist assumes importance as a crucial means of adding to the testimony of Father and Son (John 1:7; 5:31ff.; 8:18).

Verse 5 is one of many examples of the departure from standard Greek grammar—not evident in English translations of the text, which inevitably tend to gloss over such grammatical infelicities and leave readers with a more fluent text and an impression of homogeneity. The idiosyncratic Greek syntax[167] underlines a message that does not, at least at first sight, conform to what is normal or common sense. John writes from Patmos, not one of the centers of influence or power. He is an outsider, an insignificant person, perhaps not even an apostle. Yet he is the one who glimpses the mystery of God's purposes. The Greek style, like the imagery, pulls readers up short, as we begin to recognize that God's ways are not our ways and that God's thoughts are not like our thoughts (see Job 40–41; Isa 40:12). Human wisdom, to paraphrase Paul, is stretched to its limit as "normal" language seeks to bear witness to the mystery of God.

A doxology starts in the second half of v. 5, reminiscent of similar interruptions in New Testament letters (e.g., Rom 11:33; 16:25; Jude 24). It continues to the end of v. 8. In v. 7 it takes the form of an assertion about a future coming and universal vindication, and then there is a first-person declaration, as if from the voice of God (v. 8).

One might note the emphasis on the love of God in these verses, not a particularly common theme in Revelation (cf. 2:4, 19; 3:9; 12:11). The praise is due to one who "loosed" (λύω *lyō*, preferring that reading to "washed us from our sins," which is found in some later MSS). The imagery is that of release, similar to the way in which the blood of the Passover lamb released the people of Israel from the curse on Egypt (see further on this in the Commentary on 5:5-6). With echoes of the vocation of the people in Exod 19:6 (cf. Exod 23:22; Isa 61:6), the constitution of "us as a kingdom, priests to our God" speaks of a present role, a theme that will be taken up in the hymn in 5:10.

We are immediately confronted with a contrast between the present state of "us" (an inclusive reference when the author joins with the addressees of v. 4) who have been made a kingdom and priests, and who still with patience have to endure tribulation (cf. v. 9). The climax of the book marks the fulfillment of the hope that they will reign with the Lamb (20:6; cf. 5:10). The abrupt introduction of the statement about the parousia in v. 7 points the reader to that future and sets it as the context in which the praise is uttered. Once again, as in v. 5, suffering is mentioned—presumably of Christ, though this is implied rather than stated. Here suffering is set in the context of the demonstration of the dignity of the one who is pierced. Verse 7 uses language from a variety of biblical sources, including Dan 7:13 and Zech 12:10, and resembles Gospel passages like Matt 24:30 and John 19:37. The praise and assertion are rounded off with a first-person pronouncement in a formula that recurs later in the book (11:17; 21:6; 22:13), together with a description of God as "almighty," taken up in the heavenly praise in the throne scene (4:8). (See Reflections at 1:9-20.)

---

167. Discussed by Dionysius of Alexandria in Eusebius *Ecclesiastical History* VII.25.24-27, and in R. H. Charles, *A Critical and Exegetical Commentary on the Revelation of St. John* (Edinburgh: T. & T. Clark, 1970) 1:cxvii-clix.

REVELATION 1:9-20

THE GREAT VOICE, THE VISION OF THE SON OF MAN WHO COMMISSIONS JOHN TO WRITE

COMMENTARY

1:9. The autobiographical explanation of the text is picked up after the divine pronouncement in v. 8 (cf. 22:8). We know nothing about John other than the fragmentary remarks in these verses: his prophetic vocation and the evidence of his deep immersion in the Scriptures and the Jewish visionary tradition. John's qualifications do not include companionship of the historical Jesus, membership in an apostolic circle, or any ecclesiastical status. John bids us dwell on different qualities than an authority based on knowing or listening to a person in the flesh, however important that may be in certain circumstances (cf. 2 Cor 5:16). He does not place himself in a position of superiority. So alongside the unique authority vouchsafed to one who has seen a vision, John describes himself as a "brother who share[s] with you in Jesus the persecution and the kingdom and the patient endurance," a situation that characterizes Christian witness (14:18; cf. Mark 13:13). In other words, he identifies himself with that group that has been released (v. 5) and now knows themselves part of the messianic reign, though the readers of the book must submit to the demands of the ensuing message. That bonding parallels a similar assertion by Paul in Philippians as he links his own and the Philippians' sufferings (Phil 4:14; cf. Phil 1:29). There is throughout the book a refusal to allow a hierarchy that detracts from the worship of Almighty God and God's service. Thus John, in his vision, when persuaded to fall down at the feet of an angel is told by the angel that he is a fellow servant (19:10). John's relationship with his hearers, then, is similar and involves a companionship in tribulation.

The word translated "persecution" (θλῖψις *thlipsis*) is used often in Revelation and has particular resonances within the eschatological tradition referring to the specific trials and tribulations that have to precede the coming of God's reign (e.g., Mark 13:19). Paul speaks of his suffering in such terms (2 Cor 1:4) and even suggests that his own life of suffering can vicariously relieve that of the church (Col 1:24). What that tribulation may have meant for John, we have no means of knowing. John tells us that he was on Patmos "because of the word of God and the testimony of Jesus." Whether that is the result of external circumstances (e.g., persecution) or the inner compulsion of the Spirit leading John to this island is not clear. It has been suggested that John was exiled by the proconsul of Asia Minor to an island within his jurisdiction.[168] The tribulation, however, is balanced by the participation in the reign of Christ, and the present is characterized by another important virtue: "patience," the cultivation of which, arguably, the book of Revelation as a whole seeks to encourage. Indeed, keeping the commandments of God in circumstances that are not conducive to that activity characterizes "the endurance of the saints" (14:12 NRSV).

The "testimony of Jesus" has been much debated, since it could mean the testimony about Jesus or the testimony that Jesus offered.[169] The hypothesis of John's exile

---

168. Caird, *A Commentary on the Revelation of Saint John the Divine*, 22.
169. See the essays by J. Sweet and G. Lampe in *Suffering and Martyrdom in the New Testament,* ed. W. Horbury and B. McNeil (Cambridge: 1981).

leads to a preference for the former, but the testimony Jesus offered might itself have been the reason for a separation or distancing from society. The phrase "testimony of *Jesus*" is found elsewhere (12:17; 14:12; 17:6; 19:10; 20:4), adding weight to the view that it may refer to the earthly life of Jesus (though Jesus is a present heavenly agent in 22:16).

1:10. The enigmatic "I was in the spirit" (cf. 4:2; 17:3) has been understood to indicate some kind of visionary state inspired by the Spirit.[170] The same phrase is used in 4:2 to speak of what seems to be John's heavenly ascent and in 17:3, where the Spirit is the means whereby John is taken, in his vision, to a desert place to see Babylon. The phrase is a marker that something different is occurring (an event of the spirit as opposed to flesh), and so what follows should be read in an appropriate way, "interpreting spiritual things to those who are spiritual" (1 Cor 2:13 NRSV). It signifies a change of gears and alerts us to what will be the case in so much that follows—e.g., that the metaphorical will dominate John's description of his vision.

Like the OT prophets, whose visions are recorded (e.g., Isa 6:1), John gives a general indication of time, "the Lord's day" (the adjective "belonging to the Lord" [κυριακός *kyriakos*] is found elsewhere in the NT only in 1 Cor 11:20, referring to the Lord's supper). It is probably a reference to Sunday rather than to the sabbath (cf. Matt 28:1; Acts 20:7; 1 Cor 16:2). It is a day when the Lord comes to John, anticipating the great day of God's wrath (see 6:17). Such an indication suggests that the actuality of or the memories of a setting of worship were the context for John's vision just as they had been for Isaiah in his Temple vision. We should recall that worship was widely seen as a communion with heaven, in which the earthly saints join with the heavenly people of God in lauding God. This is a matter of promise as well as a threat (see 1 Cor 16:21). The "Lord's day" belongs to God, who is Lord (1:8; 4:8; 11:4; 11:17) the one who will be seen as "King of kings and Lord of lords" (19:16 NRSV; cf. 11:8; 17:14). It is sacred time just as Patmos has, at least temporarily, become sacred space, hallowed by the vision. It was the day in particular when the risen Lord had appeared to disciples in the past (Luke 24:13ff.; John 20:1ff.).

1:11-16. In this setting, John hears a voice, which he compares to a trumpet (cf. Exod 19:16), blasts of which will herald the eschatological woes later in the book. The voice like a trumpet (cf. 4:1) speaks words and utters a command to write in a book (v. 11) to seven churches, already alluded to in v. 4 but now named. The voice is behind John, and John turns and sees as well as hears. But he turns in order to see, according to v. 12, a voice. Here is one of many awkward juxtapositions: How can John *see* a voice? Perhaps one should not ask such a prosaic question. But the text, with its surprising, even jarring, images has the effect of stopping us in our tracks by its idiosyncrasy. The voice seems to impinge so much on John's consciousness that it demands to be seen as well as heard. Indeed, eventually the voice will be seen, because what it says will be translated into writing and the words of the prophecy will be read as Scripture.

In the command to write lies a distinctive feature of Revelation. John functions as a scribe who will communicate with the angels of the churches, not by word of mouth but by "scripture" (19:9; Isa 30:8). John is commanded to write what he sees (v. 11). It is the written vision that assumes importance. That becomes a particularly important part of the message in 5:5, where John hears that the Lion of Judah has conquered but *sees* a Lamb standing as if it had been slaughtered.

What John sees is written about in differing ways; yet it is marked with the visionary qualifier "as if" (ὡς *hōs*), which is used scores of times in the book as John gropes to find the language to convey adequately the awesome and stirring images that have confronted him. The reader is confronted by the immediacy of the impact as words seek to convey what is seen, whether it be the glory of the Son of Man, the terrible color and appearance of the armed locusts, or the gaudy beauty of Babylon (17:4). That contrasts with a more prosaic, narrative style of reportage, albeit in summary form. Thus the actual end of Babylon is hinted at: It is burned with fire (e.g., 18:8), and the end of the armies that are

---

170. Cf. Ezek 3:12; 8:2, which seem to form the basis for the *Gospel of the Hebrews,* quoted in Origen *Commentary on John* ii.12.87: "My mother the Holy Spirit took me by one of the hairs of my head and brought me to the great mount Tabor."

ranged against the rider on the white horse in 19:21 are said to have been killed with the sword that proceeds from his mouth. Much of the book is not just an immediate report of what John has seen but includes what he hears from the various voices in heaven that contribute to a kaleidoscope of perspectives about what has happened (this is particularly true of chaps. 18–19). John's visions of God's throne and the beast rising from the sea are vivid and detailed. This contrasts with reportage that assumes a less vivid narrative style as what he has seen, which has made such an impact, is described in a more prosaic, concise manner (e.g., 13:5ff., 12-13).

The first things John sees are seven lampstands (v. 12), which he will be told are the seven churches (v. 20; cf. Exod 25:37; Num 8:1; Zech 4:2). A mysterious human figure ("one like the Son of Man"; cf. the similar figure in 14:14) confronts John, standing in the midst of the lampstands. The human figure is described with language drawn from several biblical passages, particularly Ezekiel 1 and Daniel 7; 10 (and there is a general similarity with the description of the beloved in Cant 5:10-16). In seeing something that looks like the mysterious divine figures in Ezekiel and Daniel, he is seeing again, in his own way and for his own time, the vision as Ezekiel or Daniel would have seen it (see Excursus: "God's Throne, the Heavenly Merkabah, and the Human Figure").

The details of the description of this figure are echoed in the letters to the seven churches: He "holds the seven stars in his right hand" (2:1 NRSV; cf. 3:1) and has a "sharp, double-edged sword" (2:12 NIV). He has "eyes like a flame of fire" and feet "like burnished bronze" (2:18 NRSV). The long robe, golden sash, hair, voice, and face are not mentioned in the letters. Three letters, however, refer to other qualities mentioned in chap. 1: "the first and the last, who was dead and came to life" (2:8) refers to 1:17, "the first and the last, and the living one. I was dead, and see, I am alive"; "the seven spirits of God" (3:1) refers to 1:4, "the seven spirits who are before his throne"; "the key of David" (3:7) refers to 1:18, "keys of Death and Hades"; "the faithful and true witness" (3:14) refers to 1:5, "the faithful witness." Those images picked up later in the letters preface different kinds of exhortations. The eyes and the feet stand at the beginning of a letter that criticizes tolerance of appearances (Jezebel thinks she is a prophet, 2:20) and affirms patience. The sharp sword prefaces a letter that is in part a recognition of Antipas's witness and the threat of judgment for the tolerance of the Nicolaitans (2:15). The first letter, to the angel of Ephesus, stresses the proximity of the one like the Son of Man to all the churches.

1:17-20. The dramatic appearance results in John's prostration (v. 17) and the typical command not to fear, reminiscent of Jesus' words of assurance to the disciples after the vision on the mount of transfiguration (Matt 17:6; cf. Dan 8:18; 10:15ff.). In v. 17, there is no command not to worship (unlike 19:10), suggesting that John's response of obeisance here is entirely appropriate. The word of comfort echoes v. 8, this time with "first" and "last" replacing "alpha" and "omega," together with a reference to the figure as one who "is alive," though he had been dead. As first and last, the human figure is linked with the divine statement in Isa 44:6 and 48:12. The power of life and death belongs to this figure (cf. Matt 16:19). The credentials of the divine envoy having been stated, the command to write is given.

Unusual for Revelation, an explanation is offered at the end of the chapter for one aspect of the vision (v. 20). This may be paralleled in 4:5, where the lamps are said to be the spirits of God, but it is found infrequently elsewhere. Even chap. 17, which includes heavy historical and geographical allusions, is not as explicit as this. This all contrasts with much apocalyptic literature (the book of Daniel is a good example in this respect), in which the details of a vision are offered a minute interpretation so that every atom of meaning can be extracted from the symbolism (e.g., Daniel 7 and the vision of the man from the sea in 4 Ezra 13). The mystery of the seven stars and seven lampstands has an immediate connection with what follows, where John writes to the angels of seven churches. In v. 20 the different and yet intimate relationship between Christ, the angels, and the churches is stressed. Christ stands in the midst of the lampstands (the churches) and holds the stars (the angels). The latter seem to stand closer to

Christ, whereas the lampstands, though overshadowed by his presence, stand somewhat apart. As we shall see in the ensuing message, it is going to be possible for the lampstand to be removed from its place as a result of judgment, though nothing is said about the removal of the angel of the church from Christ's right hand.

John is commanded to write down what he has seen (v. 19): "What is, and what is to take place after this" (cf. 1:1; 4:1; 22:7). "What must happen soon" may refer either to what is to take place in human history or, more probably, to what will take place in the narrative of the vision John is to receive and write down. Indeed, what actually follows is a revelation of the nature of the churches and in chaps. 4–5 a vision of heaven. The revelation, therefore, is not solely about the end of the age. John is about to have opened up to him reality, including the presence of the whole eschatological process in the midst of which the readers now stand, and in the light of which they have to make decisions about their present conduct.

REFLECTIONS

1. The opening and closing words of the book of Revelation indicate the special status of this book: It is revelation. To read its contents, and particularly to heed them, is to be blessed. Here for the first time is a Christian text that comes close to portraying itself as sacred scripture on a par with the writings of the old covenant. The book is grounded in the apocalyptic event: the revelation of God in Jesus Christ. And yet it is the one book of the New Testament that is most neglected or treated with suspicion.

New Testament writers want to signal something of world-shaking significance bursting over the horizon of human experience. That is the way in which Paul speaks of the cross in 1 Corinthians 1–3. It is folly to uncomprehending humanity, but those who have eyes to see can understand it as the means of God's ultimate saving purposes. Apocalypse demands a break from our present way of looking at things. It offers an alternative perspective—though not the authoritative, definitive statement for which we crave—that requires the recipient who understands to bear witness.

Despite its message "from beyond," as it were, there is a familiar greeting similar to those found in Paul's letters (1:4). John is not commissioned to write some abstract, ethereal collection of eschatological predictions. The language may seem strange and otherworldly, but it is rooted in the needs and obligations of specific communities.

The words of this text are important and encourage our preoccupation with detailed exegesis of them. But what this text, perhaps especially of all the biblical texts, encourages and requires is not preoccupation with the letter. Instead, it calls us to move through the letter to the spirit, not to become so bogged down in the minutiae of symbolic detail that we fail to experience these words as an organ for further imaginative insight into the ways of God and the world.

2. The figure standing in the midst of the lampstand is "like the Son of Man" (1:13 NRSV). Jesus frequently used the phrase "Son of Man" to refer to himself in all the Gospels. This is the weak human figure who must suffer many things (Mark 8:31) and has nowhere to lay his head (Luke 9:58), yet he is none other than the one whose coming manifests the injustice done to him (1:7; cf. Mark 13:26) as he comes in judgment (19:11ff.; cf. Matt 25:31ff.). This is no remote judge whom the nations will fear only in the future. John sees the risen Christ now standing in the midst of the lamps, which symbolize the Christian communities (1:20). This is a reminder that the *present* activity of the churches' angels and its individual members is of eternal significance. There is a distinctive pattern of behavior and witness that needs to be adhered to.

3. Three times within the opening nine verses of Revelation 1, John writes of witness. It is a word and an activity removed from the everyday experience of most of us, reserved for courts of law, but it was central to the understanding of Christian identity in the pre-Constantinian church. Persons in contemporary situations comparable to those of the first Christians, who were misunderstood, suspected, ostracized, and persecuted, yet carried on lives of faithfulness, can particularly resonate with John's words.

I recall a meeting in São Paulo, Brazil, during a period of military dictatorship in that country. Members of grassroots churches were studying these words from Revelation 1 with the help of biblical exegetes from a local university. There was an atmosphere of utter comprehension of, and accord with, John's situation, as trade union activists, catechists, and human rights workers shared their experiences of persecution and harassment as a result of their work with the poor and the marginalized. They found in John a kindred spirit as they sought to understand and build up their communities in the face of the contemporary beast of poverty and oppression. It was readily apparent as I listened to their eager attempts to relate Revelation to their situation that they had discovered a text that spoke to them. They had not been desensitized by an ordered and "respectable" life of accommodation and assimilation. But Revelation is not directed only to the persecuted. Several of the letters to the angels of the churches indicate that it is the comfortable who are being addressed, too. It is, however, more readily comprehended by those who, when they pray for God's reign to come on earth as in heaven, know that they live in Babylon and cannot be at ease with its habits and demands.

4. We may consider the claim in 1:7, that all peoples of the world will lament, to be outrageous when viewed from the perspective of isolated (and in some cases, for example at Smyrna) weak communities. After all, that claim sounds very far removed from these communities' everyday life. But these words remind such people of the significance of their position. The poor, the weak, the marginalized are the ones who, despite their lowliness, may be destined to share in the messianic governance. They follow in the steps of the crucified Messiah, whose death seemed to be another sad episode in the story of the world, yet who turned out to be the one whose way will ultimately be vindicated (1:7) when God will be recognized as Creator and Lord of the universe (1:8). Meanwhile, whenever Christians meet, they remind each other in their liturgy that the story of Jesus shakes the world. To worship is to have the opportunity to have one's eyes opened, to have a fresh, apocalyptic dimension to life.

5. At the start of John's vision Christ commissions him to be the divine envoy to the seven churches. It is the moment when John receives authority from Christ himself to act as the agent of that message of doom and encouragement. The prophet or witness is given a crucial role, something that will be explored further in later visions. The mind-blowing apocalyptic vision is laid upon weak human flesh to communicate to angels and to humans (cf. Eph 3:10). John's vision occurs not in some recognized holy place in the midst of a beautiful edifice or a lavish divine service but on an island, Patmos. The prophet Ezekiel long before had seen God in exile in Babylon, far removed from the ark in the holy place of Israel, the Temple in Jerusalem. The kingdom of God had appeared on the margins of Judaism's life with an eccentric prophet and his baptism in the Jordan. It was there that Jesus had seen the heavens open and the Spirit of God descending upon him in the wilderness (Mark 1:10). God identifies with Hebrew slaves, a humiliated people in exile in Babylon, a crucified Messiah. Patmos becomes a special place and moment. It is a moment "in the spirit" in which John could "stand outside" himself and his world to see things differently.

The spiritual illumination John speaks of here has resonances with the visionary call that is at the heart of the mystical experience throughout history. Such moments are not the preserve of a spiritual elite, however. The disciplines of using Ignatius of Loyola's *Spiritual Exercises* or of living in solidarity with the poor and the marginalized enable those who practice them to put themselves in a "Patmos situation" and, thereby, with imagination, to begin to see things differently. The coming One now stands in the midst of the world as a challenger and a comforter. If John's experience is anything to go by, the divine voice will be apprehended more clearly in places like Patmos, in moments like "the Lord's day." So liturgy, especially that of eucharist, is a moment of communion with the eternal purposes and the birth pangs of a new world and to those whose words and deeds make them marginal to the processes of the world.

6. John is commanded to write down what he has seen (1:19; cf. 4:1). The revelation is not solely, nor indeed primarily, about the future. Some of what he sees is past history (e.g., the death of Christ and his exaltation in chap. 5). From the perspective of those on earth, John's vision brings together the mind of God and human history. His vision portrays the relationship between the one who was, who is, and who is to come and what is now the case, between eternity and the finite, between the Holy One and the profanity of sinful and unjust institutions. The theme of the Apocalypse is that the two cannot co-exist. Human chronology is not that of the apocalyptic mind. The perspective of the Apocalypse cannot be tied down to a particular time scale. The reality of the significance of Christ's death at a particular point in human history is immediately present with God (see 13:8). The coming One now stands in the midst of the world. He demands that the mystery of that presence be heeded, particularly by those who acknowledge him as ruler of the kings of the earth (1:5).

REVELATION 2:1–3:22
JOHN WRITES TO THE ANGELS

OVERVIEW

John had been commissioned to write what he had seen (1:18). This task is expanded in chapters 2–3 when seven times over he is instructed to write to the angels of seven different churches. Writing is central to Revelation. John is commissioned as a scribe (cf. 1 John 1:4; 2 John 5; 12; 3 John 9, 13). Just as Paul writes to churches as an apostle of Christ, so also John is a witness of Christ (1:2), like the heavenly scribe Enoch of Jewish legend.[171] Revelation is a written text, a book, of ultimate importance (1:11; 22:18-19), whose contents can help to determine one's inclusion in another book: the book of life (13:8; 17:8).

There has been much discussion about the identity of the angel of each of the seven churches. Is a heavenly being referred to or an emissary or messenger who might be a church official? In the light of the use of ἄγγελος (*angelos*) throughout the rest of the book, the translation "heavenly being" is to be preferred. Nevertheless a sharp distinction should probably not be drawn between angels and humans. Other NT passages indicate that there was a close link between angels and humans. In Matt 18:10, for example, the "little ones" have angels who behold the face of God, and in Acts 12:15 the human Peter can be mistaken for his angel in circumstances when, in the estimation of the assembled company, the appearance of a flesh-and-blood person would seem to be out of the question. Even a reference like Matt 11:10, in which John the Baptist is hailed in the words of Mal 3:1 ("See, I am sending my messenger/angel" [NRSV]), may reflect a widespread belief that certain humans were incarnations of important angels. The early Christian writer Origen discusses this very possibility in his commentary on John 1:6. To support his argument that John the Baptist was the incarnation of an angel, he quotes a Jewish work, the *Prayer of Joseph,* which asserts that Jacob was the incarnation of an archangel named Israel.[172] Addressing an angel involves addressing the human or humans whose representative that angel is. The significance of the letters in Revelation is that communication with heaven is also communication with earth, as John is able to share this hidden knowledge. Indeed, the words of exhortation at the end of each letter presuppose a wider audience. The call vision itself has hinted as much, for the angels of the seven churches and the seven churches themselves are in the hand of the heavenly Son of Man. As we shall see in the letters to the angels, there is an oscillation between angel and church, suggesting the close relationship between the two (e.g., 2:10).

The letters to the seven churches raise in turn both historical and hermeneutical questions. Archaeological and literary study have found information that may assist readers in clarifying the contextual character of the address.[173]

Ephesus was an important Christian center and the base for Paul's work. A variety of groups inhabited the city, including Jews, disciples of John the Baptist (Acts 18:19ff.), and worshipers of Artemis. The crown in 2:10 may relate to the games at Smyrna. Pergamum was the center of the cult of the emperor. The stone of Pergamum is dark, in contrast to the white stones mentioned in 2:17. Lydia was in the province of Thyatira (Acts 16:14), a center of the dye goods

---

171. *1 Enoch* 12:1; *Jub.* 4:20; Pseudo-Jonathan Targum on Gen 5:24. See also J. W. Bowker, *The Targums and Rabbinic Literature* (Cambridge: Cambridge University Press) 1969.

172. See J. Z. Smith, "The Prayer of Joseph," in J. Neusner, ed., *Religions in Antiquity,* Supplement to *Numen* 1-2 (Leiden: E. J. Brill, 1968) 253-94.

173. The evidence is reviewed in C. J. Hemer, *The Letters to the Seven Churches in Their Local Setting* (Sheffield: Sheffield Academic, 1986).

industry. Inscriptions from Thyatira show that trade guilds were numerous. Membership in them involved participation in religious ceremonies. It has been suggested that the suddenness of the coming announced in 2:13 is an allusion to the attacks by Cyrus and Alexander the Great. Ignatius's letters to the Philadelphians and the Magnesians (beginning of the second century) indicate that the tension between church and synagogue was still an issue.[174] Laodicea was a prosperous city, and there are cutting allusions to its wealth in the letter. There are some links with the terminology of Colossians in Rev 3:14, language unique to Revelation. The angel's reference to a lukewarm attitude may have been derived from the Laodicean water supply, which came from hot springs. Laodicea's self-assertive prosperity (3:17) may reflect the city's refusal of imperial help to rebuild after the earthquake in 61 CE. The eye salve mentioned in 3:18 is said to reflect the medical school and famous Phrygian eye powder. This city also had a clothing industry.

The reference to Jezebel the prophetess (2:20) reminds us that Asia Minor became a center of Montanism[175] in the second half of the second century CE. This was a prophetic renewal movement in which, initially at least, female prophets played a major role. Montanism seems to have drawn inspiration from Revelation.[176] There does seem to be some concern in the Pastoral Letters, traditionally linked with Asia Minor, with the exercise of charisma (1 Tim 4:14; 2 Tim 1:6). A proto-Montanist movement might explain the sobriety of the Pastorals, their firm regulation of the conduct of women, and their support for regular ministry (1 Tim 1:3ff.; 2:8ff.; 5:1ff.).[177] Ignatius of Antioch wrote letters to communities in Asia Minor. A visionary,[178] he seems to have functioned in a mediating role between the prophetic tradition of Revelation and the traditional authority recommended in the Pastoral Epistles. While Revelation is a book whose slant would seem to be more "Montanist "than "Pastoral," its claim to unique authority means that it stands firmly against the claims of false prophets (Matt 7:15-16; 1 John 4:1ff.; *Didache* 11) and false apostles (2:2-3; 2 Cor 11:4ff.).

This information is of interest to the historian, and if our primary concern is to recover the original situation in which the letter was read and heard, finding such information is important. Nevertheless, these are hints that only in certain instances, particularly in the last letter, warrant any degree of certainty. The reconstruction of early Christianity and Judaism in Asia Minor is a tentative kind of exercise and cannot be the foundation of interpretation.[179] Barth's words in the preface to his commentary on Romans give us pause for thought: "Why should parallels drawn from the ancient world be of more value for our understanding of the epistle than the situation in which we ourselves actually are and to which we can therefore bear witness?" As in so much historical reconstruction, the hints and allusions are simply not sufficient to bear the weight of even the most tentative reconstruction. Exegetes who wrestle with the text as a resource for insight into the human condition may find themselves needing to resort from time to time to history, but must never be bound by that obligation. Biblical exegesis cannot depend on reconstruction, however valuable that might be for pursuing historical research into the history of Christian origins. There is no need to imagine ourselves in the situation of the first readers to enable the text to "speak" to us—unless, that is, we find that the text is so utterly opaque that we cannot discern any resonance at all with our own reading. That original context has been left behind in Revelation as we now have it, as the visionary imagination forges the elements of history into a new literary substance, just as William Blake took the events of his time and produced insightful comments.[180] The challenges and insights of Revelation are largely comprehensible and relevant in our time even without access to hypothetically reconstructed situations.

---

174. Ignatius *Letter to the Philadelphians* 6:1.
175. Montanism was a movement that sprang up in Asia Minor in the second century under the leadership of Montanus. Along with a strict asceticism, it proclaimed through ecstatic utterances the proximity of the end of this age, the imminent age of the Paraclete, and the establishment of the new Jerusalem.
176. Hemer, *The Letters to the Seven Churches in Their Local Setting*, 168-74.
177. Sweet, *Revelation*, 94.
178. Ignatius *Letter to the Trallians* 5.
179. For a judicious survey of material relating to this area, see J. Lieu, *Image and Reality* (Edinburgh: T. & T. Clark, 1947).
180. See William Blake, *Continental Prophecies;* and Erdman, *Blake*.

REVELATION 2:1-7, THE LETTER TO THE ANGEL AT EPHESUS

COMMENTARY

2:1. The reference to Ephesus relates the ethereal world of apocalypse to reality. Ephesus had an important place in the earliest Christian mission, being an important center for Paul (Acts 19:1ff.; 1 Cor 16:8), with letters addressed to it by him (depending on how we approach the variant reading in Eph 1:1; see also Acts 20:17ff.) and by the early second-century bishop of Antioch, Ignatius. Any precise understanding of the character of the Ephesian church cannot be discerned from this letter, nor do external sources offer much enlightenment.[181]

The message is addressed to the angel of a church that has "fallen" (v. 5; cf. the fate of Babylon in 18:2). The city's reputation is based on its past deeds, like that of the churches in Sardis (3:3) and Laodicea (3:17). The message comes from one who is depicted as being present with his church (cf. 1:19). Indeed, it is worth recalling that at the very beginning of John's vision the first thing he sees is not the human figure but seven golden lampstands (1:13), which are the churches. Christ is just as close to them as he is to John on Patmos. He walks in the midst of the seven lampstands, just as God had walked in the Garden of Eden when Adam and Eve had disobeyed God (Gen 3:8). The judge of all the world cannot be avoided; God is not an absent lord, but one who "knows your works, your toil and your patient endurance" (v. 2 NRSV).

2:2-3. The speaker stresses knowledge: "I know your works," a repeated phrase in the letters (see v. 19; 3:1, 8, 15). The angel of the church is first congratulated. The emphasis is on "deeds" (cf. 14:13; 20:13), often taken to indicate that Revelation propounds a religion of human endeavor and fails to connect that concern with the supportive action of grace. A goal is set before the readers, whose task is to be faithful amid toil, tribulation, and hardship. As the first verse of the chapter makes clear, however, the risen Christ stands in the midst of the church, both as judge and as comforter (more evident in the letters to weaker churches, like Smyrna and Philadelphia). Indeed, what is offered in the words of the book is itself "grace," enabling understanding and patient endurance to the end (1:3).

"Patient endurance" (ὑπομονή *hypomonē*, v. 2) is a characteristic of authentic Christian existence (cf. Luke 8:15; 21:19; Rom 5:3; 8:25; 15:5; 1 Thess 1:3), modeled by John himself (1:9). "Endurance" is persistence in faith (evident in the behavior of the ancestors in Hebrews 11 as they looked forward to a greater destiny) when all appears to be lost and there seems to be no good reason for carrying on to achieve one's eschatological goal (cf. 13:10; 14:12). The angel of the church is congratulated for not putting up with evil people and for exercising a test for true and false prophets. This issue emerges from time to time in the NT and elsewhere in early Christian literature (Matt 24:24; 2 Cor 11:13ff.; 1 John 4:1; *Didache* 11ff.). In Matt 7:15ff. rudimentary tests are set up to test true and false prophets ("by their fruits you will know them"). Prophecy is an activity that Paul includes as a gift of the Spirit (1 Cor 12:10). The perseverance of the church is such that it has not wearied. This is seen elsewhere as a characteristic of Christian ministry (e.g., John 4:38; Rom 16:6; 1 Cor 4:12; 16:16; 2 Cor 6:5; 11:23-24; 1 Thess 1:3; and note the offer of Jesus to the weary in Matt 11:28). Exactly what the church has had to put up with is not clear, though Paul gives some indication of what he had to endure in Ephesus in 1 Cor 15:32 (cf. Acts 20:31-32; 2 Cor 1:8). This affliction has taken place "because of my name," reminiscent of the ignominy predicted in Matt 10:22.

2:4-6. The opening compliment is then followed by a critical evaluation, which is found in a formulation repeated in vv. 14 and 20 and a parallel exhortation to "remember" in 3:3. What is described here is a fall (cf. 18:2; Gal

---

181. See J. T. Sanders, *Schismatics, Sectarians, Deviants: The First One Hundred Years of Jewish-Christian Relations* (London: SCM, 1993).

5:4). The major indictment is that the angel has lost its first love, an eschatological sign in Matt 24:12. There is little in Revelation of that insistent stress on the love of God reflected in the life of the disciples, so familiar from the Gospel of John (esp. John 13ff.; 1 John 4; cf. 1 Cor 13:1ff.) and 1 Pet 4:8. Power and its exercise (of which love is an aspect) are the constant concern of Revelation. Love is a necessary characteristic of discipleship (cf. 2:19) and reflects the love of God and Christ (1:5; 3:9). Love will not be self-centered (12:11; cf. Mark 8:34ff.; John 12:25). As elsewhere in the NT, the love of Christ as a distinctive experience and practice has as its corollary hatred by the world (John 15:18; cf. 15:25ff.).

Like the people addressed in Hebrews (Heb 6:1ff.) the angel of the church in Ephesus needs to be warned of the dangers of falling away. Here is the first of the insistent commands to repent (vv. 5, 16, 22; 3:3, 19), refusal of which (e.g., 9:20) is characteristic of a rebellious and uncomprehending humanity.

What is required is "the works you did at first" (v. 5). Christ's coming suggests a coming at the universal parousia (cf. 1:7; 19:11ff.). But the message to the angel suggests that the coming One comes without waiting for the end. The threat now extends to an unrepentant community and not just to an angel (it is the lampstand that is to be removed, symbol of the church in 1:20). Verses 5-6 mix positive assertion and a call to repentance with the hatred of the teaching of the Nicolaitans is an obscure reference that may be illuminated a little more by 2:13ff. Possible links with Acts 6:5 are of little help.[182]

182. Sweet, *Revelation*, 69.

2:7. This verse is a final summons, similar to those in Matt 13:9 and 11:15, using a repeated formula (vv. 11, 17, 29; 3:6, 13, 22; cf. 13:9). It is a portentous announcement that comes from the Spirit; the words of the Spirit and the words of Christ are thus closely linked, as in 22:17. There is then a promise to the one who "conquers" (νικάω *nikaō*), a favorite Johannine word (1 John 2:13-14; 4:4; 5:4-5), used fifteen times in Revelation (2:7, 11, 17, 26; 3:5, 12, 21; 5:5; 6:2; 11:7; 12:11; 13:7; 15:2; 17:14; 21:7). The idea of "conquest" is connected with achieving the eschatological goal (22:2). We shall see how the peculiar notion of conquest in Revelation is illuminated by 5:5: The lion of Judah turns out to be a Lamb, indicating that "conquest" differs from that of the beast (cf. 11:7; 13:7). That subversion of language becomes the model for the "conquests" of those who identify with the Lamb (e.g., 12:11).

Verse 7 provides the only reference to paradise in the book of Revelation (though 22:2 suggests an Edenic setting). "Paradise" (παράδεισος *paradeisos*), a word found occasionally in the NT (Luke 23:43; 2 Cor 12:4), is a Persian loan word meaning "enclosure" or "garden" (e.g., Cant 4:13; cf. John 19:41). The promise to eat of the tree of life (cf. Gen 2:9; 3:22ff.; Ezek 31:8) is one that is not explicitly described in the description of the privileges of the inhabitants of the new Jerusalem (22:2), where the ultimate joy is seeing God face to face (though note the reference to the feast in 19:17 in the context of judgment). (See Reflections at 3:14-22.)

REVELATION 2:8-11, THE LETTER TO THE ANGEL AT SMYRNA

COMMENTARY

The address to the angel of the church in Smyrna comes from one who is both eternal (cf. 1:17) and who has died and is alive (cf. 1:18). The letter is written to a church that is undergoing "affliction" (cf. 7:14). In their suffering, they are in the same situation as John himself (1:9). "Affliction" (θλῖψις *thlipsis*) is a word that is often used of the time of crisis and catastrophe that marks the climax of history (e.g., Matt 24:21), and it is in such terms that Paul might have construed his sufferings (2 Cor 1:4; 6:4; Phil 1:17; Col

1:24) and the suffering of his churches (Phil 4:14; 1 Thess 1:6; 3:3, 7). The contrast set up here, so typical of the function of apocalypse, which unveils reality as opposed to fantasy or illusion, is evident when the angel of the church, whose poverty Christ knows, is told that it is rich. It is subject to "blasphemy" (βλασφημία blasphēmia; cf. Mark 3:22) by the synagogue of Satan (v. 9; cf. 3:9; John 8:30ff.), which may be linked with that exercise of diabolical power that will be seen in the vision from chap. 12 onward. These are people who think they are Jews and are not. It is not necessary to suppose that ethnic Jews are referred to here. They may be Jewish Christians or Christians (like Paul's opponents in Galatia or Colossae) who claimed to be Jews or to practice Jewish law. Here the word "Jew" is seen as a positive term (in contrast to the Gospel of John), as in the Gospel of Matthew (with the exception of Matt 28:15). Blasphemy (NRSV, "slander") is characteristic of the beast (13:1, 5-6) and of Babylon, which is seated upon the beast (17:3).

Satan is introduced for the first time. In the vision proper, readers will learn that Satan has been thrown out of heaven and will be bound in prison (20:7; cf. 18:2), so his presence on earth is only to be expected (cf. 12:12; cf. 1 Pet 5:8). "Satan" (Σατανᾶς Satanas) and "devil" (Διάβολος Diabolos) are used interchangeably (cf. 12:9; 20:2). Like John, who is reassured by the touch and words of comfort of the risen Christ in 1:17, the angel receives words of reassurance in the midst of suffering (v. 10, "Do not fear"). The perspective of the letter now includes the church (note the change from singular to plural in v. 10). The devil is about to throw some of the church members into prison, where testing will take place. Babylon is a prison in 18:2 and is a particular site of testing for those who seek to resist the beast. This testing (cf. 2:2; 3:10; Matt 6:13) will be limited (only ten days) and, therefore, endurable (cf. Mark 13:12, 20; 1 Cor 10:13). Faithfulness to death (v. 10) reflects the life of the one addressing them (1:5). The promise of crowns (the property of the elders in 4:4-5; cf. 1:6; 20:4; 1 Cor 9:25), characterized by life, corresponds with the escape from the second death in 20:6, suggesting that some Smyrneans were dying for their witness (cf. 12:11; 20:4). Freedom from harm (v. 11) may offer a temporary respite for the witnesses in 11:5 and for the earth in 7:2, but what counts is one's ultimate destiny and integrity, whatever the cost. (See Reflections at 3:14-22.)

REVELATION 2:12-17, THE LETTER TO THE ANGEL AT PERGAMUM

COMMENTARY

2:12-13. The address to the angel in Pergamum picks up the reference to the sword that proceeds from the mouth of the Son of Man in 1:16. This is alluded to again in 19:15, 21 (cf. Isa 49:2), where the sword functions as a means of guiding the nations. There is an opening commendation as in the previous letters. The angel dwells where the throne of Satan is (cf. 13:2). Indeed, this is the place where Satan dwells (v. 13). Given that readers of Revelation will learn that Satan is down on earth, "seeking whom he may devour" (cf. 1 Pet 5:8), the presence of Satan in Pergamum is no surprise, though the angel of the church appears under particular threat because of emperor worship. In the ensuing vision the reader will learn which is the true throne before which one should worship (4:2ff. and, ultimately, in the new Jerusalem in chaps. 21–22). Despite the unpromising environment, the angel holds "fast to my name" and refuses to deny "my faith" (probably an objective genitive—"faith in me"). Denial (cf. 3:8) is an important theme, often used in forensic contexts elsewhere in the NT (e.g., Matt 10:33; 26:70; Acts 3:13; 2 Tim 2:12; 1 John 2:22-23; Jude 4). There has been a special time of difficulty because of the killing of Antipas, who is described in terms similar to Christ in 1:5 (cf. 14:12). Note here once more the basic errors in Greek syntax;

REVELATION 2:12-17 COMMENTARY

Antipas should be in the genitive, but instead is in the nominative.[183]

2:14-17. The contrast between the faithful witness and some members of the church is continued in v. 14: "You [presumably the angel] have [or tolerate] those who hold the teaching of Balaam" (similarly also in the next verse, possibly closely linking the Balaamites and the Nicolaitans; cf. 2:6).[184] The angel is held responsible for a group of people, and their repentance is needed in order to avoid the "war" on the offenders (v. 16). Heavenly and earthly responsibility are closely aligned.

It should come as no surprise to the reader that the message is negative (cf. the similar formulation in 2:4). First, there are those who hold the teaching of Balaam, whose offense was to put a stumbling block in the way of the people of Israel (a reference to Num 31:16; 25:1-2; cf. 2 Pet 2:15; Jude 11). Balaam is seen as having led Israel astray so that the people yoked themselves to Baal Peor (Num 25:1-2) and so engaged in idolatry. The contemporary "Balaams" are persuading people to eat food sacrificed to idols and to commit fornication (cf. 2:20). Eating food sacrificed to idols resembles the issue that was a problem for the Corinthian church, according to 1 Cor 8:1 (cf. Acts 15:18-19). In the light of the fact that Paul allowed the Corinthians in certain circumstances to eat meat offered to idols, the possibility arises that a Pauline Christian position is under attack here.

While Balaam became a type of a deceiver (Christ is seen as a reincarnation of Balaam in later Jewish texts),[185] throughout the bulk of the Balaam cycle of stories in Numbers 23–24 Balaam is presented as steadfastly refusing to curse Israel, despite the urgent demands of Balak. And Balaam is also presented as having insight into the divine wisdom, enabling him to predict Israel's future (most famously in the Balaam oracle about the star of Jacob in 24:17). This is the first of a number of places in Revelation where in the midst of the strong dualistic contrasts between good and evil the evil figures turn out, in fact, to be highly ambiguous (the obvious places are the descriptions of the Beast in Revelation 13, which has echoes of the description of the Lamb in chap. 5 and of Babylon and the bride of the Lamb in chaps. 17 and 21).

---

183. See G. Mussies, *The Morphology of Koine Greek as Used in the Apocalypse of St. John* (Leiden: E. J. Brill, 1971).

184. On Balaam, see G. Vermes, *Scripture and Tradition in Judaism* (Leiden: E. J. Brill, 1973) 127-77.

185. R. T. Herford, *Christianity in Talmud and Midrash* (New York: KTAV, 1975).

❖   ❖   ❖   ❖

EXCURSUS: "FORNICATION" AND IDOLATRY

In the LXX, particularly in Hosea 1–3, πορνεία (*porneia*) is used for the activities of Israel: "The land commits great whoredom by forsaking the LORD" (Hos 1:2 NRSV; see also Hos 2:2). In Wis 14:12, "the making of idols [is] the beginning of fornication [*porneia*]" (NRSV) and results in "false consciousness": "It was not enough for them to err about the knowledge of God,/ but though living in great strife due to ignorance,/ they call such great evils peace" (Wis 14:22 NRSV).

In the NT outside the book of Revelation, πόρναι (*pornai*) is used for "harlots" who precede the righteous into the kingdom (Matt 21:31; cf. Luke 15:30); for sexual immorality (1 Cor 5:9-10; 6:18; 1 Tim 1:10); for sexual intercourse with prostitutes (1 Cor 6:15-16); in a transferred sense for the sin of Israel in the wilderness (1 Cor 10:8), when they participated in sacrifices to Moabite gods and bowed to them (Num 25:1; cf. Exod 32:5-6); and it is used to describe Rahab (Heb 11:31; Jas 2:25). Elsewhere *porneia* is linked with characteristics like "greedy" (Eph 5:5) and "godless" (Heb 12:16).

Excursus: "Fornication" and Idolatry

The concept of fornication appears throughout Revelation. In the letters to the seven churches, the risen Christ challenges those who would be tempted to idolatry (2:14, 20). In this case, the eating of food sacrificed to idols is the issue. The denunciation of this practice contrasts somewhat with what Paul had to say in 1 Corinthians 8, though he is unequivocal in his repudiation of idolatry in 1 Corinthians 10. The prohibition against idolatry is a recognition of the close link between religious practice and beliefs and patterns of behavior. Rejection of idolatry in the OT is bound up with a countercultural attitude to holiness. The kings of the earth are castigated for committing fornication with Babylon (17:2; 18:3, 9). Revelation 21:8 and 22:15 use πόρνοι (*pornoi*) to describe a group of people who are excluded from the holy city.

It would appear that another body of teaching is being condemned in v. 15, unless "you also hold" is a further explanation of the foregoing teaching. Mention is made once more of Nicolaitans (cf. v. 6). As in the message to the Ephesian angel, Christ promises to come (cf. 22:12) if repentance is not forthcoming. The judgment implied in v. 12*b* is made explicit in v. 16. There is an interesting link between coming and repentance. Christ's *not* coming is dependent on repentance. This has an interesting connection to contemporary Jewish debates as to whether the coming of the Messiah was dependent on Israel's ability to repent fully.[186] Verse 16 represents an inversion of this idea:

Advent in judgment can be avoided by repentance—quite a contrast to the promise of, and yearning for, the coming of the Son of Man in 22:7, 17. Then comes a promise, not alluded to again in the book (though there is a reference to the messianic feast in 19:17): the offer of hidden manna and a white stone (a positive color in Revelation) with a new name on it (cf. 19:12; Isa 62:2; 65:15). In the light of the importance of "holding fast to the name" (v. 13) and of the name as a distinguishing mark of the rider on the white horse (19:12), we may have here a reference to the qualification of those who are in the possession of the "name," such as is the case for those who see God face to face (22:4). They contrast with the worshipers of the beast, who are distinguished by a mark and not by a name (14:1, 9). It is having that knowledge that enables them to sing a new song (14:3). (See Reflections at 3:14-22.)

---

186. See the contrasting positions set out in E. Urbach, *The Sages: Their Concepts and Beliefs* (Jerusalem: Magnes, 1975) 668.

REVELATION 2:18-29, THE LETTER TO THE ANGEL AT THYATIRA

COMMENTARY

2:18-19. The message to the angel of the church at Thyatira (cf. Acts 16:14) is the longest of the seven. It comes from the Son of God, a term used only here in Revelation (cf. 21:7), and picks up the reference to the eyes and feet of the Son of Man in the initial vision (1:14; cf. Dan 10:6). The angel is commended in terms similar to those of previous letters (esp. 2:2), but with the addition of "service" (διακονία *diakonia*; used only here in Revelation, though "servant"/"slave" [δοῦλος *doulos*] is widely used of those in the divine service [e.g., 11:18] as well as of all those who acknowledge God [e.g., 7:3]). Unlike the angel of Ephesus, this angel's situation has improved (v. 19).

2:20-23. The commendation is followed by criticism of toleration of Jezebel, who "calls herself a prophet and is teaching and beguiling my servants to practice fornication and to eat food sacrificed to idols" (v. 20). "Beguiling" is the activity of Satan (12:9) and the beast (13:14), which leads to the nations' being deceived and led away from the truth (18:23; cf. 20:3, 8).

Deception is the mark of the false prophet in Deuteronomy 13. Why the prophet should be called Jezebel can only be guessed, because there is nothing to suggest that the Jezebel who was the wife of Ahab had prophetic powers, unless that is hinted at in 2 Kgs 9:22. She is, however, an opponent of the true prophet Elijah, a zealous critic of idolatrous compromise with the religion of Baal, and she persecuted the prophets (1 Kgs 18:13; 19:2). Ahab's marriage to Jezebel (1 Kgs 16:31; 21:25) produced apostasy from the service of the true God, just as Balaam had led Israel astray.

The "fornication" referred to here is probably to be understood metaphorically (cf. 14:8; 17:2-4; 18:3; 19:2) as the compromises with a prevailing culture that result from idolatry and thereby compromise the distinctiveness of life and outlook that is a central feature of Revelation. We can discern what this might mean from 1 Corinthians 8, where social intercourse with non–church members might involve attendance at pagan worship (cf. 2:14). Separation rather than compromise is commended; the latter seems to be the message of "Jezebel" (1 Kgs 16:31). Jezebel is to be thrown onto the bed of her fornication; perhaps the extent of her compromise with society will be made manifest for all to see and her claim to piety and divine inspiration shown to be spurious. Those who commit adultery with her could be persons who follow her teaching or who have engaged in acts of compromise with her—that is, pagans who have been part of her circle. They are to be distinguished from "her children," who are her followers in the church (v. 23). They are threatened with death, like the children of the Egyptians (Exodus 11; cf. Ezek 33:27). Their fate is a warning to the churches (v. 23) that the risen Christ is not an absent lord but one who knows the very secrets of all and judges them accordingly (cf. Jer 11:20; Heb 4:12-13; see esp. Rom 8:27; 1 Cor 4:5, where it is the Lord's role to search the hidden things of the heart). Recompense will be according to works (20:12; Rom 2:6).

2:24-29. The "adultery" with Jezebel does not typify the whole of the church who have not known the deep things of Satan. In 1 Cor 2:10, there is reference to the Spirit, who "searches everything, even the depths of God" (NRSV; cf. Sir 24:5). Such a claim to insight and knowledge, which may characterize an intellectual elite, is of no value if it is not matched by appropriate behavior. Mystery and knowledge are useless and positively corrupting when divorced from appropriate practice. No other "demand" (lit., "burden" [βάρος baros]; cf. Acts 15:28) is made, save perseverance; this is needed "until I come" (2:25; cf. 3:11). Such a coming has about it a note of threat (as in 2:5, 16; cf. 16:15). It is to be set in the context of that cosmic "coming" on the clouds (1:7; 22:7, 12) and the judgment unleashed by the Lamb's coronation (6:1, 3, 5, 7, and esp. 17; 9:12; 11:14; 14:7). "Conquering" here means "holding fast to what you have" (v. 25) until "the end" (v. 26, used only here in this sense in Revelation, but note the similar sentiment in Matt 24:13). The promise is to share in the messianic role of "shepherding" the nations, which is the lot of the Messiah (v. 26; cf. 7:17; 12:5; 19:15; Ps 2:8-9, which is echoed), a rule that is fulfilled in the vision in 20:4 and 22:5. Similarly, the gift of the "morning star" (22:16; cf. Dan 12:3; Phil 2:15) is shared by the Son of God as agent of the Father (cf. John 5:19ff.) with the one who conquers (2:28). (See Reflections at 3:14-22.)

REVELATION 3:1-6, THE LETTER TO THE ANGEL AT SARDIS

COMMENTARY

3:1a. This letter to Sardis, another city with a church that received a letter from Ignatius on his way to martyrdom at the beginning of the second century CE, comes from the one who holds the seven spirits of God. This goes beyond 1:4, where the greeting comes from the seven spirits who are before the throne and alongside Christ. That Christ also holds the seven stars, which are the angels of the churches (1:20), is a reminder that the autonomy of the angels is circumscribed by the oversight of the Son of Man.

3:1b-2. Commendation is avoided, and a negative comment is immediately offered. The possession of a "name" here is not a strength but a weakness, since it is a "reputation" that is a deceit (cf. 3:17). It contrasts with the reality of Christ, who was dead and then alive (1:17). The angel is urged to strengthen what remains (a neuter plural) and is on the point of death. The verb "strengthen" (στηρίζω *stērizō*) is used elsewhere in the NT in eschatological contexts that concern the support needed to endure to the end (e.g., 2 Thess 3:3; cf. Rom 16:25; 1 Thess 3:13; 1 Pet 5:10). The command to the angel is to "watch" (γρηγορέω *grēgoreō*), a favorite word also used in eschatological contexts (16:15; cf. Matt 24:42; Mark 13:34ff.; 14:34ff.). The picture in v. 2 is of Christ as a prosecuting counsel opening the books (cf. 20:12; Luke 12:8). The deeds of the angel of the church are known in full detail in heaven.

3:3. The call to remember sets the present in the context of the past (cf. 2:5; cf. Luke 17:32, where the past is offered as a basis for present understanding of eschatological crisis). The consequences of not being alert are illustrated by the metaphor of the thief (cf. 16:15; Matt 24:42; 1 Thess 5:2). The threat of the coming (cf. 2:5, 16) seems to be an anticipation of the coming on the clouds (1:7; 22:7, 12) and the terrible judgment unleashed by the Lamb's vindication (6:1, 3, 5, 7).

3:4. A compliment is now paid to the angel. The church has a few "names" in Sardis who have not defiled their robes (cf. Jude 23). In the light of 14:4, these would be the ones identified with the Lamb. Those whose robes are pure have washed them in the blood of the Lamb (7:14), or as the result of their martyrdom are given white robes (6:9-10). The conquest leads to sharing in the privilege of wearing white robes (3:18; cf. 16:15), for the possession of white robes is a mark of proximity to the throne (4:4). "Walking with me in white" (cf. 2:1) is not alluded to elsewhere in Revelation, though in 14:4 the 144,000 follow the Lamb wherever it goes and in 19:13 the rider on the white horse, by implication, wears a white robe spattered with blood and leads an army of the saints (19:14). The "names" are deemed worthy, like God (4:11), the Lamb (5:12), and saints and prophets (16:6).

3:5-6. In v. 5, Christ is described as a heavenly scribe with the right to erase names from the book of life (cf. 1:19; 13:8; 17:8; 20:12, 15; 21:27). The criterion for being named in the book of life is one's works, specifically whether one had resisted being deceived by the beast (13:8; 17:8). Being included in the book of life means washing one's robes and making them white in the blood of the Lamb (see 7:14) and resisting the deluding power of the beast. There might be an allusion to the tradition in Matt 10:32 (cf. Luke 12:8; Rev 3:5). Christ here is depicted not as a judge but as an accuser (cf. Mark 8:38) or a defender (cf. Rom 8:34). In the Gospels, Christ is rarely portrayed as judge; according to John's Gospel, he comes not to judge the world (Matt 25:31ff. is a solitary example). He is also presented as a vindicator of the elect (Matt 24:30-31). (See Reflections at 3:14-22.)

REVELATION 3:7-13, THE LETTER TO THE ANGEL AT PHILADELPHIA

COMMENTARY

3:7. The epithets attached to the risen One are used of God in 6:10. With one exception, "true" (ἀληθινός *alēthinos*) is used in conjunction with other words, like "faithful" or "just" (e.g., 3:14; 15:3; 19:11; 21:5). "Holy" is used many times, particularly of "the saints" (e.g., 17:6), and occasionally of angels (14:10), the new Jerusalem (21:2, 10), and in the *trisagion* in 4:8 of God (cf. 6:10). It is used only here of Christ. Also unique is the reference to the "key of David" (closely following the words of Isa 22:22, where it is a promise to Eliakim son of Hilkiah to succeed Shebna the steward—a context not relevant for the interpretation of this passage and an indication of the way a piece of scripture could be transmuted in the visionary imagination to form a different message in a different context). This is one of three references to David (cf. 5:5; 22:16), indicating the continuing contribution of the Davidic messianic dimension, though, as we shall see, in 5:5 the nature of that messianism is thoroughly subverted.

3:8. The privilege granted the Holy One to open and close (reminiscent of the binding and loosing in Matt 16:19) leads into the very next verse, with its reference to the open door. The image of a closed door will form part of the challenge to the angel of Laodicea: Christ stands outside the door knocking and seeking entrance (v. 20). It is an open door that will introduce a new dimension of John's vision (4:1). That privilege afforded John to enter, to see, and to enjoy the glory of God is now accorded to the (outwardly) least promising of the angels. It is a promise from Christ to an angel who is weak (v. 8*b*). "Keeping my word" (vv. 8, 10) comes again in 22:7 in connection with the words of the apocalypse. The "word" (λόγος *logos*) is used in connection with the "testimony of Jesus" in 1:9 and 20:4 (cf. 12:11). "Keeping" is used in a positive sense of keeping the words of prophecy in the apocalypse (1:3; 22:7, 9), "my works" (2:26), the commandments of God (12:17; 14:12), and one's robes clean (16:15). Refusal to deny the name (cf. 2:13) echoes the positive statement in v. 5 and has its links with Mark 8:38 (cf. 2 Tim 2:12).

3:9. As in 2:9, the "synagogue" of Satan reappears (cf. 2:13), which suggests a division between ἐκκλησία (*ekklēsia*), John's word for the true religious community (chaps. 1–3; 22, as elsewhere in the NT) and συναγωγή (*synagōgē*), the word used twice in Revelation and elsewhere in the NT (with the exception of Jas 2:2) for the Jewish religious meeting. Whereas in 2:8 the synagogue of Satan was guilty of blasphemy, here they are lying and place themselves in the same category as the deceivers who appear later in the vision (cf. 2:2; 16:13) and are to be excluded from the new Jerusalem because of it (21:27; 22:15). A promise is made that members of "the synagogue of Satan" will be compelled to come to the angel and worship. There are here echoes of Isa 49:23 and 60:14 (cf. Ps 86:9). The use of "worship" (προσκυνέω *proskyneō*) is striking, because it is used in Revelation only for the true worship of God or for false worship of the beast and Satan. This kind of obeisance, which is due to God, will be enjoyed by the Philadelphian angel, suggesting once more the ultimate demonstration of the rectitude of those who are persecuted (cf. Wisdom 3–4).

This verse is a demonstration of the peculiar affection of God for the angel of the church (cf. Matt 18:10, where the angels of the little ones have the privilege of seeing God). The echo here of Isa 43:4, a particularly personal and warm address to Israel concerning the love of God for the chosen people, is striking in the context of a book in which the tenderness and graciousness of God is not always immediately evident.

3:10. The commendation is for keeping "my word of patient endurance," a key phrase in Revelation (1:9; 2:2-3, 19; 13:10; 14:12) that is found in eschatological contexts elsewhere (Luke 21:19; Rom 8:25; cf.

Matt 10:22; Mark 13:13). From Rev 13:10 and 14:12 we see that this characteristic is defined by resisting capitulation to the beast and thereby continuing the witness of Jesus. Faithful endurance means being kept from the hour (cf. 14:7, 15) of trial (cf. 2 Pet 2:9), which is to come on the whole world ("trial" [πειρασμός *peirasmos*] is found only here in Revelation, though it is possibly used elsewhere in the NT of eschatological trials; e.g., Luke 4:13; 11:4; 22:28, 40; 1 Cor 10:13). This may be an allusion to the temptation of the earth's inhabitants, who (according to chap. 13) seem to be led astray to follow the beast. Satan, having descended to the world (12:9), proceeds through the beast to lead humankind astray (13:8).

3:11. In this verse there is the ambiguous "I am coming soon," which in this context is an assurance rather than a threat (cf. 2:5, 16). Whether it refers to a coming before the parousia is unclear (cf. 22:7, 12). The angel is urged to hang on to ensure the bestowal of its crown (v. 11).

The promise to this weak angel is that the one who conquers will become a pillar in the temple of God (cf. Gal 2:9; 1 Tim 3:15). The use of temple imagery in connection with Christians is found in 1 Cor 3:16; 6:19 and corresponds with the priestly vocation of the new community (1:5; 7:15). The juxtaposition of temple and new Jerusalem in v. 12 contrasts with the description of the heavenly city, where there will be no temple (21:22; cf. 7:15), though the city's foundation has written on it the names of the twelve apostles (21:14). The one who conquers never has to leave the temple, and so is free from the threat posed by those outside in that shadowy, threatening land at its gate (21:27; 22:15).

3:12-13. The climax of the apocalypse is alluded to in v. 12: God's name will be on their foreheads (22:4). In addition to the name of God, there is the name of the city and Christ's new name (2:17; cf. 19:12). The act of writing, so important in the book, both as a sign of the definitive judgment of God (chaps. 5; 10) and as a mark of the authority of the book of Revelation itself and the message to the angels of the churches (1:3), is epitomized in the great privilege for the elect of having the names written on them (v. 12). (See Reflections at 3:14-22.)

REVELATION 3:14-22, THE LETTER TO THE ANGEL AT LAODICEA

COMMENTARY

3:14-16. This is the most negative letter of all. As elsewhere, knowledge of the angel's deeds (2:2, 19; 3:1, 8) anticipates a negative comment. There is no positive assessment to balance the negative, however, and the angel is described as neither cold nor hot, but lukewarm (v. 16). The state of being neither one thing nor another conflicts with Revelation's stark dualism. It is important to choose and not sit on the fence (cf. Luke 11:23). Christ's mouth (v. 16), from which the angel is to be spewed, is elsewhere a source of judgment (1:16; 2:16; 19:15, 21; cf. 9:17-18; 11:5). Although the message has nothing by way of commendation, it still manages to indicate the love of Christ for the angel (v. 19; cf. Prov 3:12; Heb 12:6) and the reality of the present Christ waiting to sup with them (v. 20). The message comes from the "Amen" (v. 14; cf. 2 Cor 1:20), "the faithful and true witness" (1:5). The epithet "origin of God's creation" is unique and is similar to Col 1:15: "the firstborn of all creation" (NRSV; Colossae and Laodicea were adjacent cities). It is the only place in Revelation that hints at pre-existence (divine foreknowledge is implied elsewhere; e.g., 13:8; 17:8) and links the text with the wisdom tradition of Proverbs (esp. Prov 8:22-23).

3:17-18. Like the angel at Sardis, which had a reputation for life but, in fact, was dead, the Laodicean angel brags of its wealth (cf. Ezek 28:1; Zech 11:5; 1 Cor 4:8). But it is wretched, poor, and naked. In Revelation, it is the rich (6:15) and those who have become wealthy (18:3, 15, 19) who are particularly under threat from the wrath of the Lamb, and true wealth is commended (2:9). The frank assessment of the extent of the angel's lack of self-knowledge is offered in v. 17. The angel's nakedness anticipates the fate of Babylon in 17:16, when it is stripped of wealth, a fate the reader is warned to avoid (16:15). The address to the angel (v. 18) repeats the importance of white robes to clothe nakedness (cf. 6:11; see also Commentary on 3:4).

The Son of Man explicitly offers words of counsel (v. 18). True wealth comes from the Son of Man, whose precious metal is refined (v. 18; cf. 1:15; Isa 55:1). The summons is like the summons of Wisdom to purchase from her (Sir 51:25; cf. Matt 11:28). "Purchase" (ἀγοράζω *agorazō*) is used elsewhere in Revelation of the purchase for God by the Lamb (5:9; cf. 1:5-6; 1 Pet 1:7). The ointment used to "anoint" (the same verb root [χρίω *chriō*] as in the phrase "Christ, the anointed one") the eyes parallels the anointing of the blind man in John 9:11, where sight and understanding are closely linked. The consequence of "sight" is insight into one's context and consequent separation from the prevailing wisdom and culture, as the man born blind discovered in persisting doggedly in his faithfulness (John 9:34-35).

3:19-22. The severe criticism is explained with a word derived from Prov 3:12 to indicate the need for the discipline of God, which may enable life rather than death (cf. 1 Cor 11:32; Heb 12:6). The Son of Man describes himself as standing outside the door, seeking entry just as Wisdom seeks to call people (Prov 1:20) and just as the beloved seeks entry (Cant 5:2). Those who open the door recognize his voice (cf. John 10:3), and they can share a meal with him (cf. John 14:23). The address in v. 20 appears to be to a wider group that extends beyond the church's angel. In contrast to the afflicted John, to whom a door opens in heaven (4:1), and the open door to God for the angel of the Philadelphian church (3:8), the door of the Laodicean angel is closed and needs to be opened to the one standing outside (cf. 1:13; 14:1). Throughout Revelation, John hears the voice, responds to it, and writes what he sees. That responsiveness is demanded in order to share a common meal with the Son of Man, an anticipation of that final messianic meal (19:9, 17; cf. 2:7) when Christ comes (cf. 3:11). In v. 21, participation in the royal reign (Luke 22:29-30; cf. Col 3:1) anticipates the vision of the Lamb's sharing the throne of God (7:17). As we shall see in chap. 5, the Lamb's "conquest" as a result of suffering equips it to share in God's throne.

REFLECTIONS

1. The very occasional references in the letters indicating local knowledge of the various cities remind us that the Word of God always occurs in the context of specific situations. The first readers of Revelation might have recognized the local allusions, and that would have heightened the impact of the message. The letters to the seven churches remind us that context is all-important in any theology or exegesis. The Word became flesh at a particular time and place, and it is by attention to particularity that one may hear what the Spirit says to the churches. In interpreting this text, we need to pay attention to context, to attend to the weakness and fallibility of Smyrna and Philadelphia and to the complacency and compromise of Laodicea and Pergamum. While there is no guarantee that people will hear what the Spirit says to the churches, the address is a present, not a past one, is contextual, and is linked to the particulars of existence.

2. Two churches receive unequivocally positive addresses, Smyrna and Philadelphia. They are fragile, like the crucified Christ, whose resurrection is offered as a source of hope (2:8; 3:7). Positive things are said about six of the churches (2:2, 10, 13, 19; 3:4, 10). Even the most negative letter of all, the one to the Laodiceans, which has no congratulatory note, indicates the love of Christ for the church (3:19) and the reality of the present Christ waiting outside the confines of their complacent existence to sup with them (3:20). A mixture of encouragement and criticism is a necessary prerequisite for pastoral practice. Affirmation is something we find difficult; it is much easier to find fault. The letters offer a pattern of affirmation and correction, challenge and comfort.

3. There may have been a struggle with rival Jewish congregations (2:9; 3:9), but it is possible that a Jewish-Christian community may be alluded to. In the letter to the Philadelphians, it appears that the people had been pressured to disown the name of Jesus (3:8), something that may have confronted some Jewish Christians who wished to continue to worship in the synagogues in the early years of the second century. We must not too quickly see these remarks as a judgment on Judaism. A historical approach to the New Testament reminds us that these texts were produced when Christianity was still loosely linked to Judaism and Christianity itself was a minority group. Anti-Jewish polemic takes on a far more sinister hue in later years when Christianity could enforce its will with the power of the empire.

4. What the letters offer is a catalog of church life: "loss of first love" (Ephesus), persecution (Smyrna), compromise (Pergamum), true and false prophecy (Thyatira), fragments of hope (Sardis), being lukewarm (Laodicea). Because these are often portraits of human failings, situations worthy of divine disapproval, these letters make uncomfortable reading. But there are surprises to be seen. Weakness and fallibility are opportunities for strength (2 Cor 12:9). The open door of revelation is granted to the weak. Insight, not least about the meaning of the Apocalypse, may sometimes be glimpsed by those we least expect to understand. Indeed, the book of Revelation may better be comprehended by non-academics than by those inside the academy, whose way of studying divinity can make them resistant. It is disconcerting for experts to discover the truth of Jesus' saying, "I thank you, Father, Lord of heaven and earth, because you have hidden these things from the wise and the intelligent and have revealed them to infants" (Matt 11:25 NRSV) and to realize that the understanding of the divine call may be better understood by the poor and outcast than by academics and ecclesiastics who think they know the depths of the text.[187]

5. The letters to the angels suggest that there are limits to how much the churches should compromise with contemporary culture. This is a major biblical theme, as is evident in the repeated rejection of idolatry throughout the Bible. In the wilderness, the people of Israel worshiped the golden calf (Exodus 32) and learned from their mistake what idolatry involved. Instead of the unseen God, who went before them, they wanted something dazzling and static, a tangible expression that accommodated itself to their desires. An idol is the work of human hands onto which is projected a quasi-divine, mystical status. The work of our hands achieves a mystical quality with superhuman characteristics that displace God. God stands over against humanity, pointing to other norms besides those to which nature and society give expression. Idols have to be unmasked and knocked down from their pedestals. Isaiah of the exile (Isaiah 40–55) does this by ridiculing idolatrous practices. The maintenance of idolatry is self-serving and exclusive of the interest of others, the quintessential expression of special interests. Revelation, like Old Testament prophecy, refuses to "baptize" the world as it is and accept the values of the surrounding culture. The readers of the letters are challenged about their unwillingness to dissociate from the regular habits of life of the ancient city and from easy and uncritical relations with the surrounding culture. Idolatrous compromise takes many forms. The Gospel of Luke hints at one way we might view the matter in Luke 16:15, where the "abomination" of idolatry is linked, not with

---

187. C. Rowland, "'Open Thy Mouth for the Dumb': A Task for the Exegete of Holy Scripture," *Biblical Interpretation* 1 (1993).

worship in a religious place, but with the idol Mammon (cf. Matt 6:24, "You cannot serve both God and Money" [NIV]).

Coming to terms with a culture involves recognizing conflicts of interest and being aware of the extent to which one's language and behavior are influenced by ideological power struggles. Revelation is a book about the exercise of power, and, disconcerting as it is to our modern sentiments, not primarily about the manifestation of divine love (ἀγάπη [agapē] occurs only twice [the verb four times]; ἐξουσία [exousia] is found twenty times; δύναμις [dynamis] twelve times). Divine power is manifested in the effects of the revelation, which is consequent upon the vindication of the Lamb who was a victim. It is that power of unmasking everything that runs like a thread throughout the vision.

6. In the opening chapters we find two sets of names: John and Antipas, who are faithful witnesses, and Jezebel and Balaam,[188] who are used as an attack on those who fall short of the standard required to "conquer." These names of biblical characters are used to both mask and illuminate the identity of the true offending parties. These names are given as we might give someone a nickname, which, whether affectionate or hurtful, point to some aspect of the person's character.[189] The name that betokens our identity under God, that reflects what it is to be true to our deepest selves, is utterly distinctive. It is not a matter of acting out, whether consciously or unconsciously, the character of others, past or present. This is what, according to Revelation, the Balaam and Jezebel who were contemporary with John were doing. Their being addressed in the names of others indicates that they repeat the identity of those characters from the past without fulfilling that distinctive vocation that is the fundamental property of each human being under God. The simple names "John" and "Antipas," without the mask of another persona, indicate a distinctive personality and vocation that enabled them to stand out from the sea of names merging into the undifferentiated, stereotypical "whole world" (which wandered, misguidedly, after the beast and Babylon) or the charismatic individuals whose identity was merely a repetition of the past. The people of Sardis stand out from the rest. But, as we shall read elsewhere in Revelation, standing out from the rest is an uncomfortable position to be in. Indeed, to "have a name of being alive" is not the same as being alive. Reputation in society and culture counts for little, as the angelic messengers learn: "Woe to you when people speak well of you" (Luke 6:26 NRSV).

7. The address of the letters to the angels rather than directly to the churches opens up a heavenly perspective, but not in a deterministic way, as if heaven were controlling human existence. Quite the reverse. The insight into the heavenly message offered by the apocalypse is a way for those on earth to see that what is said and done on earth determines the message from heaven to the angel. What is striking (as in the exaltation of the Lamb and the prayers of the saints) is that what happens on earth affects what happens in heaven. The angel of a church embodies those qualities (or lack of them) that make up the church as a whole. The angel, as it were, distills the character of the behavior and attitudes of the individual communities.

8. A theme that runs through the letters is the need for endurance. Habits of resistance are required in order to endure. Whenever we pray the Lord's prayer, we pray to be delivered from evil, words paralleled in the promise to the Philadelphian angel: "Because you have kept my word of patient endurance, I will keep you from the hour of trial that is coming on the whole world" (Rev 3:10 NRSV). Apocalypse offers a converted sense of history, so that one might see in every event not only the reality of death but also the Word of God; not only the demonic and the dehumanizing, but also the power of the resurrection; not only the portents of apocalyptic doom, but also hope for oneself and one's society.

---

188. See G. Vermes, *Scripture and Tradition* (Leiden: Brill, 1973).
189. See S. Kripke, *Naming and Necessity* (Oxford: Blackwell, 1980).

REVELATION 4:1-11

VISION OF GOD'S THRONE IN HEAVEN

COMMENTARY

In chap. 1, John had seen the way in which Christ was intimately concerned for the life of the churches. In chap. 4, John is allowed to see the reality of God's sovereignty. God is the creator of the universe (4:8, 11). Even if another lord appears to rule the world at present (chaps. 12–13), such a rule can be only temporary. The God who appeared at the exodus and made a covenant with Israel in thunder and lightning is at present only apparent to the eye of vision, but in due course will be apparent in all creation. Like Isaiah and Ezekiel before him, John describes the holy God, who seems far removed, yet is ever-present and active.

4:1-3. After giving John the letters to the angels, a door in heaven (v. 1) opens and a new visionary perspective is presented to John. The opening of heaven is also a prelude to a vision in Ezek 1:1 (cf. 19:11; Mark 1:10; John 1:51; Acts 7:56; 10:11). The continuity with the vision that opens Revelation is evident (1:10). John uses the same phrase, "in the Spirit" (v. 2), that he had used in 1:9, and the first voice speaks once more (1:10). The trumpet will be a significant feature of the later vision in the trumpet sequence (8:6ff). The trumpet is linked with the eschatological moment in 1 Thess 4:16 (cf. Matt 24:30-31) and is the first of several links with Exod 19:16ff. The voice summons John to "come up here," a summons similar to the dead witnesses in 11:12 (cf. 17:1; 21:9; Exod 19:24); and there is a repetition of the promise to show "what must take place after this" (v. 1; cf. 1:1, 19; Dan 2:29, 45).

John's experience of being "in the Spirit" (v. 2; cf. 1:10) leads him to the awareness of another space, in this case heaven (the Spirit will be the means of John's removal to a desert place in 17:3; cf. 21:10), the setting for the ensuing apocalyptic narrative. Heaven is the place where God's throne is set (4:2; cf. Ps 103:19) and the source of the crisis that unfolds (6:1; cf. 10:1; 20:1). Heaven's "cleansing" of Satan (12:7-8) is the prelude to earth's trial. The throne of God will play an important role in Revelation, though heaven plays virtually no part in John's vision of the new Jerusalem. We have already had reference to the throne with the promise to the Laodicean angel in 3:21. The throne is the dwelling of God, of the Spirit (1:4), and (after 5:7) of the Lamb (5:13; cf. 12:5). In v. 2, John sees a throne "in heaven" surrounded by other thrones and marked by the awesome appurtenances of the theophany (cf. Exod 19:16). The description of it owes much to OT theophanies, in which God is enthroned, mysterious, fiery, and glorious (Ezek 1:26; Isa 6:1-2; and see Excursus: "God's Throne, the Heavenly Merkabah, and the Human Figure"). The worship of God takes place around the throne (4:9; 7:11; 14:3). The One seated on the throne (4:2; cf. Ezek 1:26) will eventually "tabernacle" (σκηνόω *skēnoō*) with the multitude of the redeemed (7:15). Voices come from the throne (16:17; 19:5; 21:3). One voice will speak, finally (21:3), to affirm that the throne of God is with humanity on a new earth when the old heaven and old earth have passed away (21:1). Only at 21:5 is the voice of the one seated on the throne identified. The throne of God and the Lamb will be set in the midst of the new Jerusalem (22:3), the description of which marks the climax of the book. In 4:5, however, the throne pours forth lightning and thunder (cf. Exod 19:16), and before it is what appears to be a sea of glass. Later, the sea disappears (21:1), and instead of fire the throne pours forth a river of living water (22:1). Contrasting with the throne of God is the throne of Satan (2:13), the dragon (13:2), or the beast (16:10), two contrasting sites of dominion and obligation (cf. Rom 6:12ff.).

The indebtedness to the language of Ezekiel's vision in Ezekiel 1 and 10 (especially), to Isaiah 6, and to the great theophany at Sinai in Exodus 19 is everywhere apparent in Revelation 4. If we compare John's vision with Ezekiel's, we shall see that John starts where Ezekiel finishes. The fiery cloud that bursts on the prophet's life in Babylon leads to a description, often convoluted, of the divine chariot, with its wheels, fire, terrible faces of creatures, and crystal firmament, before culminating in the brief mention of the throne and the fiery human figure sitting upon it. John's vision does not ignore the terrible faces and the fire. There is little evidence here of the chariot (מרכבה *merkābâ*), its wheels, and its movement, which so captivated Ezekiel. John's gaze is fixed immediately on the climax of Ezekiel's vision: the throne and the One seated upon it. John does not linger over its description, nor does he describe details of his ascent "in the Spirit," in this respect differing from some contemporary visionary texts.[190] Whereas Ezekiel had dared to describe the vague outlines of a human form, John's vision notes that there is someone seated on the throne, and he compares that figure with jasper (cf. 21:11, 18-19; Ezek 28:13), carnelian (cf. 21:20), and emerald (cf. 21:19; Ezek 28:13). The bow around the throne also accompanies the angelic figure in 10:1 and echoes the description of Ezekiel's vision of God's glory: "Like the bow in a cloud on a rainy day, such was the appearance of the splendor all around" (Ezek 1:28 NRSV).

4:4-6a. The throne is encircled by twenty-four other thrones, occupied by elders clad in white (apparel linked with God's presence in 1:14; 2:17; 3:4-5; 6:11; 7:9; 20:11), with crowns on their heads (cf. Zech 6:11). These elders form the divine court (1 Kgs 22:19; Isa 6:1). They engage in worship (4:10; 5:5-8; 7:11; 11:16; 14:3; 19:4) without ceasing (4:8; 14:11). Occasionally, in the subsequent vision, one of the elders is given a role in communicating with John to enable him to understand what he sees (5:5; 7:13). The identity of the elders is unclear, though passages like Isa 24:23 and the twenty-four priestly families of 1 Chr 24:4ff. have often been cited as background.

The noise and fire that proceed from the throne (v. 5) appear elsewhere (8:5; 11:19; 16:18) and are reminiscent of the description of the Lord's descent on Mount Sinai to give the Torah (Exod 19:10ff.) and the fire that proceeds from the divine chariot (Ezek 1:13). The "flashes of lightning, and rumblings and peals of thunder" (v. 5) occur at significant points in the later vision: at the end of the seventh seal and immediately before the sequence of trumpet blasts (8:5); at the end of the sequence of seven trumpet blasts when God's temple in heaven is opened (11:19); and when a voice comes from the throne, asserting "It is done" at the end of the sequence of bowls (16:18).

Only once in the description of God's throne in heaven does John offer an interpretation of what he sees: The seven lamps before the throne are the seven spirits of God (v. 5; cf. Zech 4:2). We shall meet the seven spirits again in 5:6, where they are closely linked with the Lamb (cf. 1:4). That solitary interpretation is a warning not to read too much into the images without indicators in the text. It would be tempting—but questionable—to read, as many commentators have done, the rainbow as a sign of the covenant with Noah in Gen 9:13, an interpretation noted in the earliest extant commentary by Victorinus of Pettau. While John's use of colors and spatial contrasts has a degree of consistency, allowing us to speak of an "apocalyptic grammar," the exploration of the full extent of the intertextual references in this allusive text lies with the reader to exploit.

In front of the throne is a sea of glass (v. 6; cf. Ezek 1:22, 26). In 15:2, it is mingled with fire, and those who have "conquered" the beast are standing on its shore, singing a song, just as the people of Israel did after the destruction of Pharaoh and his host (15:3; cf. Exod 15:11). At this moment in John's vision, however, the sea of glass is not mingled with fire.

4:6b-8. John's gaze returns to the throne in v. 6, and (in a direct allusion to Ezek 1:5, 18) the terrible creatures that appear there are described. They are both in the midst of

---

190. E.g., *1 Enoch* 14:8ff.; *Ascension of Isaiah* 7ff. Cf. 2 Cor 12:2ff.

and around the throne (see Commentary on 5:6), full of eyes (eyes and insight or knowledge are occasionally linked; see 2:18; 5:6; cf. Zech 4:10). Like the elders, the creatures recur throughout the vision as part of the description of the throne (e.g., 5:6ff.; 7:11; 14:3; 15:7; 19:4), and as part of the worship of God (4:9; cf. 14:3). All four participate in summoning the procession that follows the opening of the seals in 6:1ff. The description of the creatures echoes Ezek 1:18 (cf. Ezek 10:12) but is much less convoluted. Whereas Ezekiel's creatures have four faces each, John sees four different creatures: a lion, an ox, a man, and an eagle (cf. the four beasts in Dan 7:4ff.). Another difference is that John's creatures have six wings (v. 8; derived from Isa 6:2 rather than Ezek 1:6) and are full of eyes all around (the eyes in Ezek 1:18 are attached to the wheels of the chariot). They engage in ceaseless praise, echoing the song of the seraphim of Isaiah's vision:

"Holy, holy, holy is the LORD of hosts;
  the whole earth is full of his glory."
(Isa 6:3 NRSV)

"Holy, holy, holy
  the Lord God the Almighty,
    who was and is and is to come."
(Rev 4:8 NRSV)

The praise in vv. 8-9 has become a praise of God's being. Isaiah's assertion that God's glory fills the earth is not denied; God is "Almighty" (παντοκράτωρ *pantokratōr*). God is past, present, and future (cf. 1:8; 11:17). The divine glory, hymned by the heavenly host, belongs peculiarly to the God *of heaven* (11:13; cf. 4:9; 7:2; 15:8). This is changed only when, as the divine judgment moves to its conclusion, the earth is permeated with the divine glory (18:1); in the new Jerusalem that glory will be found everywhere (21:11, 23; cf. 21:24, 26). This contrasts with the Gospel of John, where the divine glory is evident in the past on earth in the incarnation of the Logos: "We have seen his glory, the glory as of a father's only son, full of grace and truth" (John 1:14 NRSV)—though, of course, the divine glory does not pervade the whole world.

4:9-11. In the ritual of praise (v. 9) there is a close relationship between the praise of the creatures and the elders, actions that recur in the vision at 5:8, 14, and 19:4. The reference in the next chapter may possibly be connected with the action described in v. 9. The verbs in vv. 9-10 are consistently future (though there is important MSS evidence that has present tenses). Translations usually take these future-tense verbs as frequentative (e.g., the NRSV's "whenever the living creatures give glory"). If we take these future tenses literally (and there is a debate as to whether we should),[191] then they refer to acts of the attendants of the divine throne at some *future* point in the apocalyptic narrative. That is best understood as being 5:8, where that action is described with present-tense verbs. They form a response to the moment when the Lamb took the book and opened the seals. So this double action of praise and obeisance takes place *after* the exaltation of the Lamb in 5:6. If we give full weight to the future tenses, vv. 9-10 refer to a future fulfillment. John sees the elders here at a point *before* they perform their ritual of worship in response to the creatures' song, when the Lamb shares the divine throne (already seen by John, according to 4:8). The ritual in v. 9 takes place in his vision only once the Lamb has appeared. These future-tense verbs give weight to the view that what we have here, as Victorinus hinted long ago, is like a scene of the old covenant, devoid of any distinguishing marks of Christian interpretation, which could have been written by any Jewish apocalyptic visionary of John's day. But it will be transformed in the following chapter.

The act of casting crowns before God is one of the few uses of βάλλω (*ballō*, "throw") in Revelation that does not have connotations of the judgment of God (e.g., 8:5ff.). The crowns of the elders are shown to be subject to the authority of God, unlike the diadems on the heads of the beast, which are worn without any acknowledgment that such a sign of rule might derive from God (cf. Rom 13:1-2).

Hymns recur throughout Revelation (e.g., 5:12-13; 7:10, 12; 11:15, 17; 12:10-11; 15:3-4). They probably echo the worship in

---

191. See Thompson, *The Book of Revelation*; G. Mussies, *The Morphology of Koine Greek as Used in the Apocalypse of St. John* (Leiden: E. J. Brill, 1971).

synagogues and the early Christian communities and are reminiscent of doxological passages elsewhere in the NT (esp. Rom 16:27; Jude 24; cf. 1 Chr 29:11). But what passages like Isaiah 6 indicate to readers is that the uttering of the sanctus enabled humans to share in the language of the heavenly liturgy. Of the words of praise to God, "glory" (δόξα *doxa*) and "honor" (τιμή *timē*; along with "power") are often included (cf. 4:11; 5:13); "thanksgiving" is found only here and in 7:12. Glory is ascribed to God when the nations engage in an act of obeisance in the new Jerusalem (21:26). God is described as the One who "lives forever and ever" (v. 10; cf. 10:6; 15:7; Dan 4:34), parallel to v. 8: "who was and is and is to come" (cf. 1:4, 8; 11:17; 16:15) and similar to the description of Christ as the one who is now alive (though he was dead) in 1:18. That God is "worthy" (ἄξιος *axios*) is found only in 4:11, though the word forms part of the question asked as the search goes on for one worthy to open the seals (5:2, 4, 9; it is used of the Lamb in 5:12). Elsewhere it is used of those who are found worthy of attaining the bliss of the new age (3:4) and of the just judgment of God on the persecutors of the saints and the prophets (16:6).

One difference about this particular paean of praise (v. 11) is the inclusion of the praise of God as creator (parallel to Eph 3:9; Col 1:17):

What is the plan of the mystery hidden for ages in God who created all things. (Eph 3:9 NRSV)

In [or by] him all things in heaven and on earth were created, things visible and invisible. (Col 1:17 NRSV)

You are worthy, our Lord and God,
to receive glory and honor and power,
for you created all things,
and by your will they existed and were created.
(Rev 4:11 NRSV)

The only other place in Revelation where God is hailed as Creator is the moment when the great angel swears by the God who created heaven and earth (10:2) and declares that there will be no more delay (10:6). In Revelation, the created world, for all its rebellion (cf. 9:20), is *God's* creation.

Power is attributed to God (4:11). The Greek word δύναμις (*dynamis*) is used to describe the "power of God" (7:12; 12:10; 15:8; 19:1) and the Lamb (5:12; cf. 1:16). It is also used for the power given by the dragon to the beast (13:2) and the power bestowed in turn by the kings of the earth on the beast (17:13). In two other passages, it is used in an address to the angel at Philadelphia, where the lack of the angel's power prompts an offer of grace, an open door that no one will shut. "The power of her luxury" in 18:3 (NRSV) refers to the wealth accrued by the merchants of the earth. Babylon's luxury was a powerful means of creating wealth, therefore.

Closely related is the word "authority" (ἐξουσία *exousia*), also used in connection with "giving" (δίδωμι *didōmi*; 6:8; 9:3; 13:2, 4-5, 7; 17:13; cf. 9:10, 19). It refers to the rule (2:26), the right to participate in life in the holy city, the new Jerusalem (22:14), and the power the two witnesses have the right to exercise (11:6). Only occasionally is it used of God (16:9) or Christ (12:10). It is not always easy to make a clear distinction between the two (*exousia* and *dynamis* could probably be used interchangeably in passages like 2:26 and 20:6). Nevertheless, it often does have the sense of the specific exercise of power within the mystery of the divine providence. So the angels who have power over a quarter of the earth (6:8) exercise that authority within the providence of God (see also 14:18). In 17:13, where the two words are used together, there may be a contrast between undifferentiated and specific forms of the exercise of power, manifested in political and economic rule. That may be behind the use in 12:10, where the two words are juxtaposed, albeit in the very different rule of Christ.

In a vision largely devoid of sentiment, though not devoid of the ability to provoke emotion, the exercise of power and its specific authorization are examined. The exercise of love involves power in almost all circumstances. That is the case in the story of Jesus, whose self-giving love is also an exercise in power, albeit one that contrasts with the powers of this age.

REFLECTIONS

Worship plays a central role in Revelation.[192] The first of several hymnic passages is to be found in chapter 4. Three things can be said about these passages, which are interspersed throughout John's vision from chap. 4 to chap. 19.

1. There is the all-encompassing participation of the worshipers (4:10; cf. Mark 12:30). We can too readily dismiss the affective and confine worship to verbal or intellectual expression. Physical and sensory participation in worship (e.g., the smell of incense is hinted at in 8:3ff., and the strains of music in 14:2) are all important components of worship of God. There is no evidence of words of praise either in the account of the messianic reign or in the new creation in chaps. 20ff. That may suggest that in the new age, when men and women see God face to face and God tabernacles with them, they will serve God in a fashion that has no need of words (7:15; 22:3). Indeed, there will be no temple in the new Jerusalem (21:22), and so no need of mediation between humanity and God. However, as long as the old order exists, worship in words and action helps to maintain a true perspective on life focused on God and God's demands rather than on those of the beast or Babylon.

Later in the book the repeated concern to stress the justice of God's action reflects a concern with theodicy, which hints at some sensitivity to the horror of all that is happening in the eschatological process. The wrath of God is not arbitrary and capricious, even if the inscrutability of God's ways means that full understanding lies beyond human comprehension. The paeans of praise are related to God's actions in history and human response to do God's works.

2. We shall see as the vision progresses that singing hymns to God is incompatible with idolatry. An appropriate pattern of behavior is expected from worshipers. Those who worship God will not worship the beast (cf. 14:9). To have the character of God means above all being committed to a particular style of life. One cannot have true worship without doing the works of God (cf. 1 John 3:18).

When worship becomes an escape from life and from witness, it has lost touch with God. There is always a great temptation to allow worship and churchgoing to be ends in themselves. Of course, religious activity can be a haven from the rigors of everyday life, an evocation of a different kind of society, and a means of resistance to the dominant culture, as is evident in the hymns and songs of the African American slaves.[193] But when worship serves merely as an opiate, an anesthetic for the hurt of life rather than a divine discipline for an alternative way of life, it has moved into activity contrary to God's purposes.

3. In Revelation 4, with its obvious indebtedness to Ezekiel and Isaiah, the ancient scriptures provide the medium whereby John enters the door of perception to see, hear, and communicate the divine mysteries. The insight of apocalypse is not an avoidance of what is there, a diverting opiate to escape reality, but another way of perceiving that reality. "The 'visionary' is the man who has passed through sight into vision, never the man who has avoided seeing, who has not trained himself to see clearly, or who generalises among his stock of visual memories."[194] It is the product of insight into the nature of things, which recognizes the contradictions and sees "through" them to a more complete understanding. The eye of vision is not mere repetition of normal discourse or the words of the past. Revelation is not an exegesis, a conscious attempt by the sophisticated scholar to offer a precise interpretation of the biblical text. It is

---

192. On the importance of worship as a countercultural act, see A. Kreider, *Worship and Evangelism in Pre-Christendom* (Cambridge: Grove, 1995).
193. See L. Genovese, *Roll, Jordan, Roll* (New York: Vintage, 1975).
194. N. Frye, *Fearful Symmetry: A Study of William Blake* (Princeton, N.J.: Princeton University Press, 1947) 25.

an interpretation—but it comes through the use of Scripture as the medium of fresh apocalyptic insight. This is evident in every line of Revelation, where words and images of Scripture are subtly transformed, elements from earlier texts are dropped, and others are emphasized. Our use of Revelation may well be similar. We may find in our context that the Spirit now speaks to the churches in different ways, with new symbols, but always speaks of hope and in dialogue with the story of Jesus.

This is one reason why Revelation has been regarded as a dangerous book. Its own relationship with the biblical tradition indicates creativity and development rather than a rigid adherence to the meaning of the letter of ancient scriptures. Revelation licenses imagination and insight and the use of Scripture as the vehicle of new insight. It is a text that breathes the importance of the Spirit rather than the letter, and it stands at the fountainhead of that radical tradition in Christianity, where mere knowledge of Scripture or tradition is inadequate without the Spirit's enlightenment or from the gracious moment of insight into everyday life. Scripture, then, is a witness to the faith of the writer or visionary. The inner illumination that prompted the writing is at the heart of true discipleship.[195]

---

195. See Rowland, *Radical Christianity*, on the use of Scripture in the writings of Winstanley and Muentzer.

❖   ❖   ❖   ❖

EXCURSUS: GOD'S THRONE, THE HEAVENLY MERKABAH, AND THE HUMAN FIGURE

Interest in God's throne and the one seated upon it, as well as the cosmos and its origins, formed key aspects of Jewish mysticism. This interest almost certainly antedates the fall of Jerusalem in 70 CE and had a long history from the very earliest times after the return from exile in Babylon down to the hasidic movements nearer our own day.[196] Interest in Ezekiel 1 is attested mainly in apocalyptic writings that in part antedate the Christian era. The material from Qumran Caves 4 and 11 known as the *Songs of the Sabbath Sacrifice* has given considerable support to the view that the origin of the idea that the speculative, visionary interest in the heavenly temple, liturgy, and the existence of a complex angelology linked with attempts to pierce the veil surrounding the profound secrets of God's dwelling lies early in the Second Temple period.[197] According to the Mishnah, two biblical passages provide the foundation for this speculative interest: Genesis 1 and Ezekiel 1.[198] Jewish mysticism is divided into two main branches: one concerned with cosmogony and cosmology, based on Genesis 1 (מעשה בראשית *ma'ăśeh bĕrē'šît*), and the other based on Ezekiel 1 and the throne-chariot of God (מעשה מרכבה *ma'ăśeh merkābâ*). The latter is much more theologically oriented insofar as it deals specifically with God's nature and immediate environment in heaven. Reading Ezekiel 1 was severely restricted by ancient Jewish teachers because of its use by visionaries and the dangers to faith and life that such visionary activity posed.[199]

---

196. G. Scholem, *Major Trends in Jewish Mysticism* (New York: Schocken, 1955); I. Gruenwald, *Apocalyptic and Merkavah Mysticism* (Leiden: E. J. Brill, 1978); D. Halperin, *The Faces of the Chariot* (Tübingen: Mohr, 1988); Rowland, *The Open Heaven*, 1; P. Schäfer, *The Hidden and Manifest God* (New York: State University of New York Press, 1992).
197. On the expositions of the chapter in the apocalyptic tradition see C. Rowland, "The Visions of God in Apocalyptic Literature," *JSL* 10 (1979) 138ff.
198. *m. Hagigah* 2:1.
199. *m. Megillah* 4:10; *Tosefta Megillah* 4:3.11ff.; *b. Megillah* 24.6.

Excursus: God's Throne, the Heavenly Merkabah, and the Human Figure

The reconstruction of the content of the *merkabah* tradition in the late first century is not easy. The focus of the tradition was the throne-chariot of God and the glorious figure enthroned upon it. Meditation on passages like Ezekiel 1, set as it is in exile and in the aftermath of a previous destruction of the Temple, would have been particularly apposite as the rabbis sought to come to terms with the devastation of Jerusalem in 70 CE.

We know that Paul was influenced by apocalyptic ascent ideas (2 Cor 12:2ff.)[200] and that he emphasizes the importance of this visionary element as the basis of his practice (Gal 1:12, 16; cf. Acts 22:17). His apocalyptic outlook enabled him to act on his eschatological convictions, so that the apocalypse of Jesus Christ became the basis for his practice of admitting Gentiles into the messianic age without the Law of Moses. The threat posed by apocalyptic may be discerned elsewhere, particularly in its possibilities for christology.[201] There may have been a "seeing again" of that awesome vision of Ezekiel, or perhaps that vision becomes itself the object of analysis and speculation.[202]

Texts that resemble Revelation 4's vision of God and the throne and can be dated to the same period are now quoted.

1 ENOCH (AT LEAST 3RD CENTURY BCE AND PROBABLY MUCH OLDER)

And behold I saw the clouds: And they were calling me in a vision; and the fogs were calling me; and the course of the stars and the lightnings were rushing me and causing me to desire; and in the vision, the winds were causing me to fly and rushing me high up into heaven. And I kept coming (into heaven) until I approached a wall which was built of white marble and surrounded by tongues of fire; and it began to frighten me. And I came into the tongues of the fire and drew near to a great house which was built of white marble, and the inner wall(s) were like mosaics of white marble, the floor of crystal, the ceiling like the path of the stars and lightnings between which (stood) fiery cherubim and their heaven of water; and flaming fire surrounded the wall(s), and its gates were burning with fire. And I entered into the house, which was hot like fire and cold like ice, and there was nothing inside it; fear covered me and trembling seized me. And as I shook and trembled, I fell upon my face and saw a vision. And behold there was an opening before me (and) a second house which is greater than the former and everything was built with tongues of fire. And in every respect it excelled (the other)—in glory and great honor—to the extent that it is impossible for me to recount to you concerning its glory and greatness. As for its floor, it was of fire and above it was lightning and the path of the stars; and as for the ceiling, it was flaming fire. And I observed and saw inside it a lofty throne—its appearance was like crystal and its wheels like the shining sun; and (I heard?) the voice of the cherubim; and from beneath the throne were issuing streams of flaming fire. It was difficult to look at it. And the Great Glory was sitting upon it—as for his gown, which was shining more brightly than the sun, it was whiter than any snow. None of the angels was able to come in and see the face of the Excellent and the Glorious One; and no one of the flesh can see him—the flaming fire was round about him, and a great fire stood before him. No one could come near unto him from among those that surrounded the tens of millions (that stood) before him. He needed no council, but the most holy ones who are near to him neither go far away at night nor move away from him. Until then I was prostrate on my face covered and trembling. And the Lord called me with his own mouth and said to me, "Come

---

200. See M. Dean-Otting, *Heavenly Journeys: A Study of the Motif in Hellenistic Jewish Literature* (Frankfurt: 1984); M. Himmelfarb, *Ascent to Heaven in Jewish and Christian Apocalypses* (New York: Oxford University Press, 1993).

201. See A. F. Segal, *Two Powers in Heaven: Early Rabbinic Reports About Christianity and Gnosticism* (Leiden: Brill, 1977); J. Fossum, *The Name of God and the Angel of the Lord* (Tübingen: Mohr, 1985); Rowland, *The Open Heaven,* esp. 94ff.; L. W. Hurtado, *One God, One Lord: Early Christian Devotion and Ancient Jewish Monotheism* (London: SCM, 1988).

202. M. Lieb, *The Visionary Mode* (Ithaca, N.Y.: Cornell University Press, 1991); D. Halperin, *The Faces of the Chariot.*

near to me, Enoch, and to my holy Word." And he lifted me up and brought me near to the gate, but I (continued) to look down with my face.[203]

4Q405 20.ii.21-22 (PROBABLY 1ST CENTURY BCE)

The cherubim prostrate themselves before him and bless. As they rise, a whispered divine voice [is heard], and there is a roar of praise. When they drop their wings, there is a [whispered] divine voice. The cherubim bless the image of the throne-chariot above the firmament, [and] they praise [the majest]y of the luminous firmament beneath his seat of glory. When the wheels advance, angels of holiness come and go. From between his glorious wheels there is as it were a fiery vision of most holy spirits. About them, the appearance of rivulets of fire in the likeness of gleaming brass, and a work of . . . radiance in many-coloured glory, marvellous pigments, clearly mingled. The spirits of the living gods move perpetually with the glory of the marvellous chariots. The whispered voice of blessing accompanies the roar of their advance, and they praise the Holy One on their way of return. When they ascend, they ascend marvellously, and when they settle, they stand still. The sound of joyful praise is silenced and there is a whispered blessing of the gods in all the camps of God. And the sound of praise . . . from among all their divisions . . . and all their numbered ones praise, each in his turn.[204]

APOCALYPSE OF ABRAHAM (PROBABLY FROM THE END OF THE 1ST CENTURY CE AND CONTEMPORARY WITH REVELATION)

And as I was still reciting the song, the mouth of the fire which was on the firmament was rising up on high. And I heard a voice like the roaring of the sea, and it did not cease from the plenitude of the fire. And as the fire rose up, soaring to the highest point, I saw under the fire a throne of fire and the many-eyed ones round about, reciting the song, under the throne four fiery living creatures, singing. And the appearance of each of them was the same, each having four faces. And this (was) the aspect of their faces: of a lion, of a man, of an ox, and of an eagle. Each one had four heads on its body so that the four living creatures had sixteen faces. And each one had six wings: two on the shoulders, two halfway down, and two at the loins. With the wings which were on their shoulders they covered their faces, with the wings at their loins they clothed their feet, and they would stretch the two middle wings out and fly, erect. And when they finished singing, they would look at one another and threaten one another. And it came to pass when the angel who was with me saw that they were threatening each other, he left me and went running to them. And he turned the face of each living creature from the face which was opposite it so that they could not see each other's faces threatening each other. And he taught them the song of peace which the Eternal One has in himself. And while I was still standing and watching, I saw behind the living creatures a chariot with fiery wheels. Each wheel was full of eyes round about. And above the wheels was the throne which I had seen. And it was covered with fire and the fire encircled it round about, and an indescribable light surrounded the fiery crowd. And I heard the voice of their sanctification like the voice of a single man.[205]

---

203. *1 Enoch* 14:8-25, trans. E. Isaac, in *The Old Testament Pseudepigrapha*, vol.1, ed. J. H. Charlesworth (New York: Doubleday, 1983).
204. Translation from G. Vermes, *The Dead Sea Scrolls in English* (Harmondsworth: Penguin, 1961) 228. See C. Newsom, *The Songs of the Sabbath Sacrifice* (Atlanta: Scholars Press, 1985).
205. *Apocalypse of Abraham* 18:1-14, trans. R. Rubinkiewicz, in *The Old Testament Pseudepigrapha*, vol.1, ed. J. H. Charlesworth (New York: Doubleday, 1983).

Excursus: God's Throne, the Heavenly Merkabah, and the Human Figure

PARALLELS TO JOHN'S VISION OF THE HUMAN FIGURE

The opening of the book describes a christophany with few parallels in the NT (the transfiguration being a notable exception).[206] There are some similarities with various christophanies and angelophanies from both Jewish and Christian texts. The elements of Revelation 4 are inspired by several OT passages, one of which is the first chapter of Ezekiel, particularly the climax of his call-vision, in which the prophet catches a glimpse of the form of God on the throne of glory in the dazzling gleam of bronze. It is also similar to Dan 10:5-6, where we find a vision of a heavenly being, broadly based on Ezekiel 1. There are hints of a tradition of interpretation of Ezekiel 1, particularly in visionary contexts, in which the glorious figure on the throne acts in a quasi-angelic role.

> At that time I, Daniel, had been mourning for three weeks. I had eaten no rich food, no meat or wine had entered my mouth, and I had not anointed myself at all, for the full three weeks. On the twenty-fourth day of the first month, as I was standing on the bank of the great river (that is, the Tigris), I looked up and saw a man clothed in linen, with a belt of gold from Uphaz around his waist. His body was like beryl, his face like lightning, his eyes like flaming torches, his arms and legs like the gleam of burnished bronze, and the sound of his words like the roar of a multitude. I, Daniel, alone saw the vision; the people who were with me did not see the vision, though a great trembling fell upon them, and they fled and hid themselves. So I was left alone to see this great vision. My strength left me, and my complexion grew deathly pale, and I retained no strength. Then I heard the sound of his words; and when I heard the sound of his words, I fell into a trance, face to the ground.
> But then a hand touched me and roused me to my hands and knees. He said to me: "Daniel, greatly beloved, pay attention to the words that I am going to speak to you. Stand on your feet, for I have been sent to you. . . . Do not fear, Daniel, for from the first day that you set your mind to gain understanding and to humble yourself before your God, your words have been heard. (Dan 10:2-12 NRSV)

> And I stood up and saw him who had taken my right hand and set me on my feet. The appearance of his body was like sapphire, and the aspect of his face was like chrysolite, and the hair of his head like snow. And a kidaris (was) on his head, its look that of a rainbow, and the clothing of his garments (was) purple; and a golden staff (was) in his right hand. And he said to me, "Abraham." And I said, "Here is your servant!" And he said, "Let my appearance not frighten you, nor my speech trouble your soul. Come with me! . . . and I got up and looked at him who had taken my right hand and set me up on my feet; and his body was like sapphire, and his face like chrysolite, and the hair of his head like snow, and there was a linen band about his head and it was like a rainbow and the robes he was wearing were purple, and he had a golden staff in his right hand.[207]

> And a man came to her from heaven and stood by Aseneth's head. And he called her and said . . . "I am the chief of the house of the Lord and commander of the whole host of the Most High. Rise and stand on your feet, and I will tell you what I have to say."

> And Aseneth raised her head and saw, and behold, (there was) a man in every respect similar to Joseph, by the robe and the crown and the royal staff, except that his face was like lightning, and his eyes like sunshine, and the hairs of his head like a flame of fire of a burning torch, and hands and feet like iron shining forth from a fire, and sparks shot forth from his hands and feet. And Aseneth saw (it) and fell on her face at his feet on the ground. And Aseneth was filled with great fear, and all of her limbs trembled. And the

---

206. Thoroughly explored in L. Stuckenbruck, *Angel Veneration and Christology* (Tübingen: Mohr, 1995).
207. Rubinkiewicz, *Apocalypse of Abraham* 18:1-14.

Excursus: God's Throne, the Heavenly Merkabah, and the Human Figure

man said to her, "Courage, and do not be afraid, but rise and stand on your feet, and I will tell you what I have to say."[208]

With the book of Revelation we are in the midst of the world of apocalyptic mystery. Despite attempts over the years to play down the importance of this book, the indications suggest that its thought forms and outlook were more typical of early Christianity than is often allowed. The fact that there is no visionary material elsewhere in the NT accounts for some of the differences, but they are only superficial. Beneath the surface, we have here convictions about God, about Christ, and about the world that are not far removed from the so-called mainstream Christianity of the rest of the NT. The synoptic eschatological discourses are an obvious example of a similar outlook, but they are by no means alone. Revelation, with its indebtedness to a shadowy, perhaps embryonic mysticism of the Second Temple period, prompts us to look closer at other NT texts to see whether they, too, exhibit some of the telltale marks of mysticism. This unique early Christian example of the apocalyptic genre is profoundly indebted to Jewish apocalyptic ideas. In Revelation, the first chapter of Ezekiel, the *merkabah* chapter, has not only contributed to the visionary vocabulary of John, but also the initiatory visions (Rev 1:13ff.; 4:1ff.) are dominated by it. When taken alongside those other descriptions of the divinity that are now extant from the Second Temple period, we may suppose that we have in Revelation a glimpse of the tip of a mystical iceberg now largely lost from view. What is visible points to a distinctive use of prophecy parallel to, but in significant respects different from, other apocalyptic texts.

---

208. Vision of the angel in *Joseph and Asenth* 14:4-11, trans. C. Burchard, in *The Old Testament Pseudepigrapha*, vol. 2, ed. J. H. Charlesworth (New York: Doubleday, 1985).

REVELATION 5:1-14
VISION OF THE DIVINE SCROLL AND THE LAMB

COMMENTARY

One part of the heavenly scene described in chap. 4 now attracts John's attention. He sees a sealed scroll, which is a cause of consternation to him. Then he hears about the one who will open the seal, the lion from the tribe of Judah. But he sees something different. In the midst of the worship and movement in heaven, John sees a Lamb "bearing the marks of slaughter," who comes to God and takes the scroll, the opening of which heralds the manifestation of the crisis described in the subsequent chapters.

5:1-2. John's attention is focused on the right hand of the one seated on the throne, holding the churches in the right hand (1:16-17; cf. 10:5-6, where an angel raises his right hand to heaven and swears an oath). In contrast, the mark of the beast is found on the right hand of those who worship and thereby are effectively excluded from sitting at the right hand of the Holy One. John sees a scroll written "on the inside and on the back" (cf. Ezek 2:10 and also the eyes of the creatures in Rev 4:8; Dan 12:4, 9). The sealed scroll echoes Jer 32:9-10 and Isa 29:11. As we have already seen, books form an important part of Revelation. John's commission is to write a book (1:11; cf. 22:7, 10, 18-19), and he will be commanded to eat a book or scroll in 10:8. Key to the judgment are the books (20:12), particularly the book of life (21:27; cf. 3:5; 20:15, where βίβλος [*biblos*] is used). The opening of seals eventually results in a text that describes what John has seen and heard, the unsealed prophecy of the apocalypse itself (22:10; cf. 10:4). A mighty angel asks the question, "Who is worthy to open the scroll and break its seals?" (v. 2; cf. 10:1, where the mighty angel appears with the distinctive characteristics of the risen Christ of 1:13ff.; see also 18:21). The verb "loose" in v. 2 (λύω *luō*; NRSV, "open"; NIV, "break") is the same used of the "loosing from sin" in 1:5. In the light of what follows in the vision, we can surmise that the book contains the story of judgment, the opening of which initiates its performance.

5:3-5. No one is found anywhere in creation who is worthy (v. 4) to open the scroll or even to look into it.[209] Recall that Jesus' words reassured the disciples that their names are written in the heavens (Luke 10:20). John writes a heavenly book but does not read one; he sees actions in and from heaven that arise from the opening of this heavenly writing. John sees and writes (1:11; 22:8), and so the one who reads his book is counted as blessed (1:3), because the book witnesses to the mysteries of heaven.

Earlier in his vision, when John was confronted with the vision, he was overwhelmed with fear (1:17), and he was given commands that he could not but obey (4:1). He has so far been encountered by God, commissioned to "write," and observes the vision. Now he reacts. Immediately after the mighty angel has asserted that no one has been found worthy to open the scroll and look at its contents, John weeps (v. 4). Unlike the merchants and magnates who will weep because of its opening and the consequent judgment on Babylon (18:9ff.), John mourns the fact that the process of justice and judgment is being delayed (cf. 6:9). One of the elders commands him not to weep (cf. the word of assurance from the Son of Man in 1:17: "Do not be afraid"), for "the Lion of the tribe of Judah, the Root of David, has conquered" (v. 5; a lion appears among the creatures in 4:7; cf. 9:8, 17; 10:3; 13:2).

---

209. Looking into the secrets of heavenly books is one of the functions of apocalyptic, such as *1 Enoch* 81:1ff.; 93:2; 103:2.

The tribe of Judah is given a place of pre-eminence in the roll call in 7:5, and the Davidic origin of the Messiah (cf. 3:7; 22:16), well documented in the OT (e.g., Genesis 49; Isa 11:1; cf. Rom 1:3-4; 15:12; Heb 7:14; Rev 22:16) is asserted, only now to be juxtaposed with the Lamb (just as Davidic messianism is juxtaposed with the statement of Ps 110:1 in Mark 12:36, which seems to put that belief in question; cf. Mark 8:29ff.; 14:61-62). This standard messianic hope is represented in contemporary Jewish texts like *Pss Sol* 17:25-26, where military messianism, albeit clearly indebted to the language of Isaiah 11:1 as Revelation is, contributes to the expectation of the Messiah.

5:6-10. Despite the fact that the voice cries out that no one is able to break the seals and open the book, John *sees* who will do just that, a Lamb standing as if it had been slaughtered. Literally, the Lamb emerges "in the middle of the throne and of the four creatures and in the middle of the elders" to open the book. Whatever the precise meaning of the Greek, in comparison with 7:17, where the Lamb is said to be "at the center of the throne," here the Lamb's position is more ambiguous, being related in some way to creatures and elders as well as to the throne, and so not identified with either. In other words, the Lamb is in a liminal position, an intermediary. That position changes by the time John speaks of the Lamb and the throne in 7:17. The contrast between what John hears and what he sees is striking. It is the latter that offers him the insight into the nature of the liberation and its agent (see Fig. 2: "Hearing and Seeing in the Book of Revelation," pp. 1010-11).

Throughout the history of the interpretation of the book of Revelation, it has been assumed that the Lamb is a metaphor for Christ.[210] The lack of specific "Christian" elements (despite the expressions "as if it had been slaughtered" [5:6] and "the blood of the Lamb" [7:14; 12:11]) have occasionally raised doubts about such an identification. Connections have been made with the Lamb of God of John 1:29, plausibly interpreted there also as an apocalyptic symbol of the Messiah, though, as elsewhere, there is probably a closer link with Isa 53:7, as in Acts 8:32 and 1 Pet 1:19 (though in all these cases ἀμνός [*amnos*] is used, not ἀρνίον [*arnion*] as in Rev 5:6; cf. Jer 11:19). In the light of what follows, the apocalyptic background should remind us not to play down the element of power and messianic upheaval attached to the figure by concentrating on notions of suffering and powerlessness. Revelation is a text of messianism, and whatever its idiosyncrasies, it is in tune with much else in NT soteriology.[211]

The notion that the blood of the Lamb is a means of redemption is mentioned elsewhere (1:5; 7:14; 12:11; cf. 19:13). There has been much debate over the background to the imagery. The juxtaposition of buying/redeeming/loosing, blood, and a lamb suggests a Passover context, in which deliverance is effected for the children of Israel by the blood of a lamb, bringing deliverance from the angel of death and facilitating the process of liberation from Egypt (Exod 12:22-23, 31). As the hymn in v. 9 suggests, the death of the Lamb—who is no passive victim but one who was a "faithful witness" (1:5 NRSV)—has brought about release. The Lamb's death has "made them to be a kingdom and priests serving our God,/ and they will reign [assuming that the future rather than the present tense is the earlier reading] on earth" (v. 10). The similarity with 1:6 (cf. 20:6) is close:

To him who loves us and freed us from our sins by his blood, and made us to be a kingdom, priests serving his God and Father. (Rev 1:5-6 NRSV)

"You were slaughtered and by
  your blood you ransomed for God
 saints from every tribe and
language and people and nation;
you have made them to be a kingdom
  and priests serving our God,
 and they will reign on earth."
(Rev 5:9-10 NRSV)

Indeed, the whole earth is mine, but you shall be for me a priestly kingdom and a holy nation. (Exod 19:6)

---

210. Caird, *A Commentary on the Revelation of Saint John the Divine*, 75; J. M. Ford, *Revelation*, AB 38 (New York: Doubleday, 1975) 87-95.

211. C. Rowland, "The Meaning of the Resurrection," in *The Resurrection of Jesus Christ*, ed. P. Avis (London: Darton, Longman and Todd, 1993).

We are given no explanation, no story, that leads to this moment in the heart of heaven. It is a critical moment of deliverance. The identification of Christ with the Lamb, made throughout the book, suggests that an act of witness, at great cost, has turned the world upside down. The victim is shown to be in the right, and the demonstration of that witness shakes the fabric of the cosmos and its institutions to the core.

The figure of the one like the Son of Man (1:13ff.) now gives way to that of a Lamb, who has the decisive role (6:1ff.; 7:9; 12:11; 13:8; 14:1ff.; 22:4). John's description of the Lamb suggests death (hence the "as if"). The Lamb appears to have been slaughtered (σφάζω [*sphazō*, v. 6] is the word used by 1 John 3:12 for the primal killing of Abel by Cain; cf. Isa 53:7; Matt 23:35; Heb 11:37). This is the only time in Revelation that the Lamb stands as a suppliant (cf. 14:1, where the Lamb stands on Mount Zion with its armies, like the Messiah in 4 Ezra 13:6). Elsewhere it is the recipient of praise (5:8, 12-13), shares God's throne (7:9, 17), and is associated with death (5:6; 7:14; 12:11), with wrath and judgment (6:1; 17:14), with the messianic banquet (19:9), and with the life in the new age (21:9). The Lamb's slaughter (a fate shared by saints and prophets [6:9; 18:4]) is redemptive (5:9; cf. 1:5). It is a fate that is no random event but whose significance lies deep within the mists of time (13:8).

In describing the Lamb with the seven horns, John sets up a comparison with the dragon (12:3) and the beast that will arise from the sea (13:1). In other respects, too, the Lamb and the beast are comparable. In 13:3, the phrase "seemed to have received a death-blow" is used to describe one of the beast's seven heads.

In one respect, however, the Lamb is different. The eyes of the Lamb are not matched by those of the beast. Elsewhere in Revelation, we find reference to the eyes of the Son of Man (1:7; cf. 2:18) and to those of the rider on the white horse (19:12), but here the eyes are associated with the throne of God (4:6, 8); these are "the seven spirits of God sent out into all the earth" (v. 6; this picks up 1:4 and is inspired by the seven lamps of Zech 4:10). Note the link between the "spirits" of God and the Lamb here as well as the theme that runs throughout the NT of the immanence of God through the divine Spirit, which comes from the Messiah (cf. Isa 11:1; John 15:26; Acts 2:33).

One unusual parallel to this passage appears to be the fourth beast of Dan 7:7: "I saw in the visions by night a fourth beast, terrifying and dreadful and exceedingly strong. . . . It was different from all the beasts that preceded it, and it had ten horns" (NRSV). There the animal is a symbol of the mighty kings of the earth. In John's vision there is an unusual development of the apocalyptic tradition. Superficially, the scene is similar to that described in Dan 7:9 (cf. 1 Kgs 22:19). Whereas in Dan 7:13 a human figure comes to take divine authority, here it is an animal.

The contrast between Revelation and Daniel is striking. If we examine the Jewish apocalypses,[212] it is apparent that there are several types of visions. There is the report by the seer of what has been seen in heaven, usually after a mystical ascent (e.g., *1 Enoch* 14). Then there is the communication to the seer of divine secrets by an angel in which visions play no part (as in 4 Ezra). Finally there is the dream vision, in which the seer sees in a dream various objects (often animals) that afterward by means of an angelic interpretation are explained (Daniel 7; *1 Enoch* 89ff.). These objects have no independent existence in heaven except as part of the dream vision and are merely symbols of persons and events that take place on earth.

There is usually a fairly clear distinction in the apocalypses between visions in which a seer reports what he has seen in heaven and visions in which the contents of a dream are not direct glimpses of heavenly realities but need to be interpreted by earthly persons or events. For the first type of vision, there is an attempt to describe the environs of God using the terminology of Ezekiel and Isaiah. These visions are reports of what is actually believed to be occurring in the world above. Dream visions, with their extravagant symbols and interpretations, are not usually merged in the Jewish apocalypses with heavenly ascent visions, as they are in Revelation 4–5. The vision in Revelation 4 is a good example of the first type of vision. John glimpses the

---

212. J. J. Collins, *The Apocalyptic Imagination* (New York: Crossroad, 1984).

activities in heaven, normally hidden from human perception. If John had followed the conventions of apocalyptic, set out in chap. 4, he might have been expected to describe Christ, in language similar to that in 1:13ff., as a heavenly figure clad in divine glory. Instead, John introduced the language more typical of the symbolic vision. The use of animal imagery parallels the way *1 Enoch* 89–90 uses animals to represent humans. These images have symbolic significance, as representative of persons or nations (just as the beasts represent kings in Daniel 7). Humans are invariably animals and only become angelic in advance of the eschatological age (as in the case of Noah in *1 Enoch* 89:1). When viewed in the light of the *1 Enoch* material, the use of that animal symbolism suggests a stress on the humanity of the messianic agent. The juxtaposition of visionary types has few parallels. This awkwardness reflected also in the juxtaposition of "Lion" and "Lamb" in 5:4-5 may be taken to reflect the jarring nature of the eschatological reality to which John seeks to bear witness. The Lamb had affected the normal apocalyptic conventions, and hitherto accepted patterns of discourse are shattered, as well as the understanding and course of history. We may even speak of a mixing, perhaps even a subversion, of genres here, all the more apt when the message the text seeks to convey is of the cosmos-shattering effects of the triumph of Christ.

The Lamb takes the scroll (v. 8). No permission is given for him to do so; it is as if the qualifications have already been demonstrated and the action is a necessary consequence. That act prompts praise directed to the Lamb, similar to what had been described earlier as praise directed toward God (4:10); it should be noted, however, that the verb "worship" (προσκυνέω *proskyneō*) is not used here. It is worth noting also that *proskyneō* is used in Revelation either for worship of God alone (5:14 is ambiguous), for the worship of the beast (13:8), or to describe those occasions when humans show obeisance to others (3:9). The word is also used to describe the desire of John to worship the angel who accompanies him on his apocalyptic journey (19:10).

The elders now possess a harp and golden bowls of incense (cf. 14:2; 15:3). John offers an interpretation of them as the prayers of the saints, which will be referred to again, particularly with regard to their effect (8:3; cf. Ps 141:2). Praying is not referred to in Revelation apart from these passages, although one should not ignore that attitude of adoration and submission to God, which the divine presence prompts among those around the throne.

The elders sing a new song (v. 9). This anticipates the new song sung with harps before the throne, the creatures, and the elders by the 144,000 who have God's name written on their foreheads (14:1-2; cf. Ps 144:9). There is a connection in the words of both songs (v. 9; cf. 14:4). It is a new song, celebrating a new departure in salvation history with the Lamb's receipt of the scroll. The right to take it, which is hymned, recalls the declaration of the worthiness of God in 4:11. The right to take the scroll is based on the fact of the Lamb's slaughter, the consequence of which is the liberation of people from every tribe, tongue, and nation (v. 9; cf. 7:9; note the all-embracing inclusiveness suggested by the phrase "tribe, language, people, and nation" elsewhere in 10:11; 11:9; 13:7; 14:6; 17:15).

The Lamb's role is an active one (cf. Gal 1:4, where Christ is not a passive victim but the agent of deliverance). That role results in the formation of a kingdom and priests (cf. 1:6; Exod 19:16; Isa 61:6) who will reign on earth (20:6; 22:5). The formation of a kingdom and priests contrasts with the "priestly kingdom" of Exod 19:6, though Rev 1:6, where *priests* are in apposition to *kingdom,* may suggest that the sense of the Exodus passage is preserved. The democratization of holiness here is paralleled elsewhere in the NT and in Jewish sources (Rom 15:16, 27; 1 Pet 2:5, 9; 1QS 8).

5:11-14. In v. 11, John begins his description of what he hears with the expression "I saw," so typical of the style of apocalyptic narrative (e.g., Dan 7:2, 9). This time it is the heavenly hosts, countless angels who surround the throne, the creatures, and the elders, described in 4:10 (cf. Dan 7:10; Heb 12:22). The assertion of the Lamb's worthiness is here a statement *about* it, not *to* it, as in v. 9; thus it is similar to 4:10:

> "You are worthy, our Lord and God,
>   to receive glory and honor and power,
> for you created all things,
>   and by your will they existed
>   and were created." (Rev 4:11 NRSV)

> "Worthy is the Lamb that was slaughtered
> to receive power and wealth and
>   wisdom and might
> and honor and glory and blessing!"
> (Rev 5:12 NRSV)

Included in this list of what the Lamb is worthy to receive is wealth, which, when accumulated illicitly, is to be laid waste when Babylon's profligacy is judged (18:17). Babylon's luxury is the basis of the wealth of the merchants of the world (18:3, 15). But true wealth comes from purchasing from the Son of Man "gold refined by fire" (3:18 NRSV). The response to the Lamb's receiving the book, starting with the elders (v. 8), now moves to every creature in the universe, "on earth and under the earth and in the sea, and all that is in them" (v. 13), echoing and extending the phraseology of v. 3 (note that the sea ultimately will have no part in the new heaven and earth, 21:1).

The universal approbation of the Lamb seems strange at this juncture, when the force of wrath is about to burst upon a recalcitrant universe. It is as though there is a moment of recognition, short-lived yet full of insight. The Lamb is now added to the name of the one who sits upon the throne, an acknowledgment of the Lamb's status (cf. 11:14; Phil 2:10).

REFLECTIONS

1. Revelation 5 is the pivotal chapter in the book. The account of the opening of the seals, which in turn leads to the trumpet blasts and the pouring out of the bowls of wrath, starts here in the opening of the sealed scroll by the Lamb. Contrary to what might have been expected, a weak creature with no mark of triumph—only the marks of its own slaughter—is the agent of God's purposes. So, too, Paul declared: "We proclaim Christ crucified, a stumbling block to Jews and foolishness to Gentiles, but to those who are the called, both Jews and Greeks, Christ the power of God and the wisdom of God" (1 Cor 1:23-24 NRSV). This involves, to quote the words with which Nietzsche concludes *The Antichrist,* the "revaluation of all values."[213] The way of Christ cuts across all those "respectable" virtues. Those who would be disciples have to learn what it means to take up a cross and follow him.

2. The execution of Jesus was of little concern to the writers of his era. He was a troublemaker who received the just reward for his actions and cried out to heaven for vindication (Gen 4:10; cf. Acts 2:24). That event in Palestine, however, affected the way God relates to the world; it was, in Paul's words, "not done in a corner" (Acts 26:26 NRSV). God's relationship to creation could never be the same again. The Lamb, then, becomes the means of bridging the gap between heaven and earth. The one who was dead is now alive and shares God's throne. The experience of human life and death is taken into God. A human being shares the intimacy of God's throne (cf. John 1:18 where the Logos is in the bosom of the father).

3. In Revelation 5, the transformation of heaven rather than that of humanity is the issue, though the consequences of that transformation are for the cosmos as a whole. That is done not by the conquering of heaven through violence. The secret of the heart of God (cf. 13:8; 1 Pet 1:20) and the qualification for proximity to God are rooted in the death of the Lamb. The character of God is revealed in that God did not spare God's own Son but gave him up for us all (see Rom 8:32). This is the identity of the

---

213. Friedrich Nietzsche, *Twilight of the Idols and the Antichrist* (London: Penguin, 1990).

true ruler of the kings of the earth, whose sovereignty does not come by force of arms or by the exploitation of the inhabitants of the world and its resources, but by costly witness (cf. Phil 2:5ff.).

4. The striking character of the image of the Lamb should not lead us to suppose that complete passivity is encouraged. The juxtaposition of the Lion of Judah and the Lamb challenges our assumptions about the character of the Messiah. But the image of the Lamb—benign, defenseless, and passive—by no means exhausts what John wants to tell us about Jesus. (William Blake complements his poem "The Lamb" in Songs of Innocence with "The Tyger" in *Songs of Experience.*) The description of the Lamb must be complemented by passages like 1:13ff. and 19:11ff. The Lamb does not go to its death with a fatalistic acceptance of its lot. Nor is its death all that is important. The human one is, after all, the "faithful witness" (1:5). As we shall see in the discussion of the two witnesses in chap. 11, activity in pursuance of the witness to God leads to death in the midst of Babylon. It is testimony before the nations of that other way, the way of truth, in which messiahship consists. The writer of 1 Timothy gives expression to it when he speaks of Jesus as having made a "good confession" in his testimony before Pontius Pilate (see 1 Tim 6:13).

5. If it is the slain Lamb that merits the worship of the heavenly host, then we have to ask about the character of the lifestyle that is acceptable to God. It is not that of the mighty of the world, who attract fame and attention, those who are worldly wise, those who run the system best of all. It is those who are victims of the system of the beast and Babylon, just as the Lamb was, who are promised the blessings of the age to come (7:15). Revelation 5 compels us to consider a different understanding of the meaning of success and the exercise of power. This is so difficult to hold on to when we are pressured to conform to a culture of self-aggrandizement, epitomized by Babylon. Self-offering and weakness, recognized and accepted, are powerful and acceptable to God; but this is not about passivity (as is suggested by the more defiant stance of the Lamb in 14:1ff.).

6. John is not merely passive, a mere spectator, but an obedient servant to the divine will to act as scribe. Here he weeps. Such moments of participation may not seem important. But the expression of grief (cf. John 11:35) is a radical challenge to the status quo.[214] Weeping is "radical criticism."[215]

7. The vision of the slaughtered Lamb's place with God reminds us that the gospel offers an alternative story—in which the side of the victims is taken. In society's dominant version of the story, victims are perceived as troublemakers, subversives. The sentiment reported in John 11:50 ("It is better for you to have one man die for the people than to have the whole nation destroyed" [NRSV]) is the sentiment of the leaders of state security forces down the centuries. The gospel, in contrast, takes the perspective of the victim, the innocent victim. The Christian gospel exposes the distortions and delusions we tell about ourselves, the violence we use to maintain the status quo, and our ways of disguising from ourselves the oppression of the victim.

One of the most compelling explorations of the impact of the gospel on human culture is the work of René Girard.[216] According to Girard, human cultures originate in the basic human tendency to imitate (mimesis). This provokes conflicts of desire, which are resolved by the murder or scapegoating of an arbitrary victim. Events like

---

214. Itumeleng Mosala, *Biblical Hermeneutics and Black Theology in South Africa* (Exeter: Paternoster, 1989) 151.
215. W. Brueggemann, *The Prophetic Imagination* (Philadelphia: Fortress, 1978) 61.
216. For this section, I am indebted to the work of Steve Finamore ("God, Order, and Chaos" (D. Phil. diss. Oxford University, 1997), who has discussed R. Girard, *Violence and the Sacred* (Baltimore: Johns Hopkins University Press, 1977); *The Scapegoat* (Baltimore: Johns Hopkins University Press, 1989); and *Things Hidden Since the Foundation of the World* (London: Athlone, 1987). Girard's work has been used to interpret the apocalyptic and eschatological traditions of the Bible in J. Alison, *Living in the End Times: The Last Things Re-imagined* (London: SPCK, 1997).

this are remembered and retold, and the initial problems that led to the murder are wrongly attributed to the victim. Myths grow up to narrate the murder from the perspective of the killers, and, along with such myths, sacrificial rites provide an outlet for the actual violence generated by mimetic desire. In the Gospels, however, we have a story of a victim and a killing, but this story is told from the perspective of the scapegoated person, asserting his innocence. This has the effect of unmasking cultures based on violence. Humanity is challenged to follow Jesus in renouncing violence, lest we destroy ourselves.

These observations are relevant for the interpretation of Revelation, which is a text about the unmasking of human culture. At its start it reveals the vindication of the Lamb who was slain. The story of Jesus' death is a revelation of the false consciousness of the scapegoat mechanism and the violence that it institutionalizes. The gospel unmasks the fact that violence lies at the base of all human culture and does so by proclaiming the innocence of the victim. It offers an alternative pattern for human mimesis. The consequence of this (crucial for our understanding of Revelation) is the cross. Jesus identifies with the victims in his society, and as a result he sets in motion a process of victimization of himself. There is a violent reaction as the political elite plot to rid themselves of a troublemaker. As John's unfolding visions demonstrate, this leads to violence as the gospel shows up human culture for what it is. To bear witness to this alternative way is to risk the violence of the old system. The story of Christ's life and death subverts the "lie" of a culture based on violence, as do the lives of those who follow this pattern. That provokes a violent crisis as the lie is revealed, accelerating the process of cultural disintegration. With the gospel there can be no resolution other than acceptance of its alternative way. Culture based on violence is inherently unstable. Religion, myth, and ritual can only paper over the cracks in society. The gospel reveals God's wrath in that the human culture based on violence is shown for what it really is. Sooner or later the power of the gospel's alternative story becomes evident:

> We can see why the Passion is found between the preaching of the Kingdom and the Apocalypse.... It is a phenomenon that has no importance in the eyes of the world—incapable, at least in principle, of setting up or reinstating a cultural order, but very effective, in spite of those who know better, in carrying out subversion. In the long run, it is quite capable of undermining and overturning the whole cultural history and supplying the secret motive force of all subsequent history.[217]

---

217. Girard, *Things Hidden Since the Foundation of the World*, 209.

REVELATION 6:1-17

JOHN SEES THE SEALS OPENED

COMMENTARY

The outburst of praise at the Lamb's coming to open the book provokes, surprisingly, an outburst of a very different kind: the four riders of the apocalypse, heralding the gospel with conquest, war, famine, and death. The coming of the Lamb, the Lion of the tribe of Judah, heralds "the wrath of the Lamb." The gospel is news of the reality of death and destruction, which will be punctuated in chapter 7 by a vision of those who are sealed and those who will come through the great tribulation with integrity intact, even if they are not promised escape from the violence of an unjust world.

There is a close link between the sequences of trumpets and bowls, each of which resemble Exodus themes and echo the catastrophes that accompanied God's liberation of the people.[218] Despite the parallelism, there is a sense of progression as the bowls suggest a degree of finality (e.g. 15:1). It is only a *sense* of progression, however. There is no neat sequence. What we find in chaps. 6–16 is what Bengel described as "the admirable variety . . . with the most exact harmony, beautifully illustrated by those digressions which seem to interrupt it" (e.g., the sealing of the servants of God in chap. 7 and the witness of the two prophets in chap. 11). The reader may have a sense of frustrated anticipation in the way the penultimate event, the sixth, is halted before the seventh takes place (this is true of the first two sequences in 6:12 and 8:1; 9:13 and 11:15, though not the third sequence in 16:12ff.). That sense of being at the penultimate moment, on the brink of a special event in human history has been a consistent mark of interpretations of Revelation. Readers' attention will be drawn to their own time as special. John finds himself situated between the sixth and seventh trumpets when he is called to prophesy (10:1–11:13),

and the community is faced with the blasphemy that issues from the mouth of the false prophet (16:13ff.).

The angel of the sixth seal and the awesome destruction that causes the inhabitants of the world to cringe in terror only pave the way for delay in the apocalyptic narrative. There will be a promise in 10:6 that there will be no more delay when the seventh trumpet blasts; but that only marks a significant moment of assertion of the divine reign and the drastic and immediate consequences for earth as Satan inspires the institutions of beast and Babylon.

6:1-8. The opening of the first four seals by the Lamb follows a pattern. Each one in turn prompts a summons from one of the creatures around the throne and is a prelude to action, as is the case with all the sequences of sevens (with the exception of 8:1; 11:19; 15:5). The first creature speaks with a voice that sounds like thunder that proceeds from the throne (4:5; 14:2), similar to the (unwritten) speech of the seven thunders John is initially instructed to seal up (10:3-4).

The first four seals are related to one another and may well be inspired by Zech 1:8; 6:1-3. In Revelation, the four horses are colored white, red, black, and pale green, whereas in Zech 1:8 the horses are red, sorrel, and white, and in Zech 6:1-2 they are red, black, white, and dappled gray. In Zechariah, the horses patrol the earth (Zech 1:10) and are the four spirits of heaven (Zech 6:5; cf. 5:8).

6:1-2. The white horse comes first. Its rider is similar to the rider in 19:11 and may for that reason be separated from the rest. Doubt has been expressed as to whether this could be an image of Christ (as in 19:11), because Christ has been identified as the Lamb who opens the seals. Such a demand for consistency ignores the fluidity of the apocalyptic mind. Christ appears as a Lamb, as a fiery

---

218. Richard, *Apocalypse*, 84-86.

	Figure 1: The Sequence of Seven Seals, Trumpets, and Bowls	
S1 (6:1-2) first horseman conquers	T1 (8:7) hail and fire mixed with blood; third of earth burnt up	B1 (16:2) evil sores appear on those with mark of beast
S2 (6:3) second horseman removes peace from the earth, so humans would slay one another	T2 (8:8-9) third of sea creatures die after burning mountain thrown into sea and latter is turned to blood	B2 (16:3) sea becomes blood and every living thing in it dies
S3 (6:5-6) third horseman: famine and inflated prices	T3 (8:10-11) water made bitter after star fell from heaven; people died from drinking water	B3 (16:4) river and springs become blood
S4 (6:7-8) fourth horseman: quarter of earth killed by sword, famine, death, and wild beasts	T4 (8:12) third of sun does not shine nor do moon and stars	B4 (16:8-9) humans scorched by sun
	8:13: **THREEFOLD WOE**	
S5 (6:9) martyrs plead for vindication	T5 (9:1-6) air polluted by smoke from abyss after star falls from heaven. Locusts created from smoke harm humans not sealed. Humanity tormented by insects with scorpion stings	B5 (16:10) darkness over the kingdom of the beast
	9:12: **FIRST WOE PAST**	
S6 (6:12-17) earthquake; sun darkened; stars fall from heaven; heaven rolls up; kings and mighty hide themselves from God's presence	T6 (9:13ff.) third of humanity killed after release of the angels bound at the Euphrates	B6 (16:12) Euphrates dried up to prepare a way for the kings of the East. Spirits from dragon, beast, and false prophet work miracles to assemble kings at Armageddon
	10:1–11:13	
	11:14: **SECOND WOE PAST**	
S7 (8:1) silence in heaven followed by prayers of saints in the incense offering	T6 (11:15-19) celestial worship proclaiming the fact that God reigns. Sanctuary in heaven opened	B7 (16:17) earthquake that splits great city into three; every island vanishes

heavenly being, as well as through his angels (10:1; 14:14); in 1:1 and 22:16 explicit mention is made of Christ's angel. So there seems to be no insuperable objection, other than our desire for precision, to interpreting the first rider as the Christ who "conquers" (a use of νικάω [nikaō] here akin to other intransitive usage in which the emphasis seems to be on the overcoming of the forces of darkness through resistance and martyrdom [e.g., 12:11; 15:2]. The rider has a crown like those of the elders (4:4), the woman (12:1), and, most important, like that of the Christ-like angel in 14:14. The use of the word "bow" here is unique in Revelation. The Greek word for "bow" (τόξον *toxon*) used here is the same word used in Ezek 1:27-28 for the rainbow that is used in the prophet's attempt to describe the divine glory.

The other images associated with the first rider are more common in Revelation. The color white is associated with God or Christ (1:14; 19:11, 14; 20:11) and the followers of the Lamb (3:4-5; 4:4; 6:11; 7:9, 13-14; 19:14). Because the verb "come" (ἔρχομαι *erchomai*) is not used exclusively of Christ, or even of the process of judgment, identification of the rider with Christ at first sight seems improbable, not least because the Lamb is said to open the seals in v. 1. Nevertheless, such logic may be out of place in an apocalypse, particularly when Christ could send his angel as emissary of his purposes (22:16). In the earliest extant commentary on Revelation, Victorinus of Pettau wrote: "After the Lord ascended to heaven and opened all things, he sent the Holy Spirit, whose words the preachers sent forth as arrows reaching the human heart, that they might overcome unbelief."[219] Thus the rider on the white horse symbolizes the gospel, a proclamation of salvation that inevitably includes judgment on unrepentant persons and institutions (cf. Rom 1:17ff.; 1 Cor 1:18; 2 Cor 4:3). In artistic representations of this chapter, the four riders are often presented as a group, all of whom symbolize the death and destruction connected in popular imagination with an apocalyptic cataclysm. The gospel is an ambivalent phenomenon, however, and it effects a moment of crisis in which indignity, death, and disorder are seen for what they actually are.

The first horseman goes forth to "conquer." Nothing explicitly is said about death and destruction. As we have seen, "conquer" is used throughout the letters to the seven churches. Here, as there, the verb is used intransitively (cf. 11:7, where the beast is said to conquer and kill God's two witnesses; 13:7, where the beast is permitted to conquer the saints). This activity is closely related to that of the Lamb, who "conquers" and is able to open the scroll. To "conquer," therefore, is to be like the Lamb, to do the Lamb's works and to be faithful like the Lamb. The reward will be to share the state that Jesus has (3:21). In 12:11, we will read of the conquest of Satan by Christians, but the character of the "conquest" there reflects the terms set out in 5:5, 9. The principal use of *nikaō* in connection with Christ and his followers is defined in 5:9 and 12:11. It is connected with the faithful witness, which may be "unto death," and it indicates a new way of life, overcoming and resisting conventional patterns of existence. In other words, there is a deconstructing of the usual meaning of the idea of conquest based on military victory.

The language of conquering appears frequently in Johannine literature. Christ's conquest of the world (John 16:33) is closely linked with the casting out of Satan (John 12:32), a process that comes to completion with Jesus' declaration that "it is finished [τετέλεσται *tetelestai*]" on the cross (John 19:30). The diabolical initiative that leads to the crucifixion is in reality the moment of the lifting of the Son of Man to heaven. The cross, therefore, is the moment when the Lamb "as if it had been slaughtered" opens the heavenly book of judgment and takes a place on the throne of glory. "Conquering" comes through the victim, barely evident to those whose eyes are closed. In the ordinary world of the Johannine narrative, only the barest hints of the apocalyptic scenario are acted out, as it were, behind the scenes. Parallel to this, the word *nikaō* is used frequently in 1 John (2:13; 4:4; 5:4-5) in the context of triumphing over the way of evil by means of following a path that demands love of the "brethren." These observations suggest that the gospel is a demonstration of the values vindicated in the coming of the Lamb to God, a new understanding of what it means to conquer.

6:3-4. If little is said about the white horse other than its activity of "conquering," the second horse has a more sinister role. Its color matches that of the dragon that persecutes the woman in 12:3. Whereas the first rider was given a bow, the second rider is given a sword (μάχαιρα *machaira* rather than ῥομφαία *romphaia*; 13:10, 14; cf. 1:16; 2:12, 16; 6:8; 19:15, 21; all occurrences except 6:8 are associated with Christ) and permission to remove peace from the earth. "Peace"

---

219. Victorinus *Commentary on the Book of Revelation.*

(εἰρήνη *eirēnē*) is not a word found frequently in Revelation (only here and in the salutation in 1:4). Perhaps, in the light of the disruption of order in the Apocalypse, "peace"[220] is a word too easily misunderstood, since it is not that which comes from God, but a state of apparent stability under the dominion of the beast, in which the merchants are able to buy and sell, men and women end up as slaves, and people grow rich by their fornication with Babylon. The opening of the seals breaks the bonds that have kept human society in its previous patterns of so-called peace, releasing forces that hitherto have been kept in check (cf. 7:1; 9:1, 14).

6:5-6. The opening of the third seal heralds the rider on the black horse, a color only used to describe the conditions when the sixth seal is opened and the sun turns black (v. 12). The rider holds ζυγός (*zygos*), translated here as "pair of scales," but elsewhere in the NT it is used metaphorically as the yoke or burden laid upon a person (e.g., "slavery" in Gal 5:1; 1 Tim 6:1; the religious requirements in Acts 15:10; the "yoke" of Christ in Matt 11:29-30). The scales used for weighing wheat may be what is referred to in v. 6, but it is equally possible that it is a metaphor for the subjugation to forces of death-dealing hunger (perhaps a consequence of Babylon's insatiable desire for luxury in 18:11ff.?).

There is an additional comment on the third rider. A voice comes from the circle of the creatures who have each summoned a rider, "A quart of wheat for a day's pay, and three quarts of barley for a day's pay, but do not damage the olive oil and the wine!" (NRSV). This partial catastrophe contrasts with the awesome death and famine brought by the last plagues (18:8). We cannot know whether this reflects particular events in John's day, but the times must have been many when gross shortages led to inflation of the cost of basic necessities. Thus the memory of a time of famine and inflation may have been transformed into a symbol of the consequence of the Lamb's opening of the seals. Later in the text, wheat, olive oil, and wine will be listed among the food stuffs traded by the merchants who had profited from the wealth of Babylon (18:13). That the rider on the black horse is told not to harm the wine is ironic, for it is wine that many will continue to drink and end up intoxicated with Babylon (17:2), thereby discovering the wine of the wrath of God (14:8, 10; 16:19; 19:15).

6:7-8. The fourth creature summons a different rider, whose horse's color is rendered "sickly pale" by the REB, appropriately enough, given the fact that the rider's name is Death (probably appearing again in 20:13-14; cf. Hos 13:14; 1 Cor 15:55). Elsewhere this color is used to describe scorched grass (8:7; cf. 9:4). According to 1:18, however, death has been overcome and the fear of death should offer no peril for those who are faithful (2:10); they will participate in the new Jerusalem, where death will be no more (21:4). Hades, repository of the dead (20:13-14), over which Christ has power (1:18), accompanies the rider and will be thrown into the lake of fire (20:14).

The granting of power (v. 8) to be an agent of death, destruction, and trial is a feature found throughout the judgment section of Revelation (cf. 9:3; 13:2ff.). Such license has to be set in the context of the authority that belongs to God (16:9) and to Christ (12:10). A quarter of the earth is to suffer death and famine, taking up a combination familiar from prophetic sources (cf. Jer 14:12; 15:2; 21:7; Ezek 5:12ff.; 14:21; 33:27). Famine plagued the civilizations of antiquity,[221] and it is described as such in Rev 18:8. Famine and death are elements of the eschatological tribulation in Mark 13:8 as well (cf. Matt 24:7; Luke 21:11), and they form part of the list of things that Paul declares cannot triumph over the overwhelming love of God (Rom 8:35). Death, particularly the second death (20:14), is the ultimate threat. Physical death, say as the result of faithfulness unto death (cf. 12:11), is not what really matters (cf. Matt 10:28). Indeed, death comes as a relief for those who seek refuge from divine wrath (9:6; cf. Gen 4:13ff.).

The beasts of the earth and their threat are alluded to in v. 8 (cf. 19:18-19; Ezek 29:5). But the threat of "the beast" that comes from "the Abyss" is more to be feared. A breakdown of those bonds that prevent murder and strife and ensure a proper food supply prompts

---

220. See Wengst, *Pax Romana and the Peace of Jesus Christ.*

221. See P. Garnsey, *Famine and Food Supply in the Greco-Roman World: Responses to Risk and Crisis* (Cambridge: Cambridge University Press, 1988); P. Garnsey and S. Whittaker, ed., *Trade and Famine in Classical Antiquity* (Cambridge: Cambridge University Press, 1983).

the invasion of beasts of the earth into areas from which they are normally excluded. The beginning of the dissolution of the threads of society and civilization runs throughout this part of the vision. Proper order will be re-established in the new Jerusalem, for there no one will hunger or thirst anymore (cf. 7:15), and death will be destroyed (20:14; cf. 21:4). Proper boundaries will be set there, so that "unwelcome animals" will be excluded (22:15; cf. 21:27). The wrath of the Lamb will unravel those threads that have hitherto maintained civilization. The current order is under judgment and must be replaced by one with different values (cf. Mark 10:41ff.; Phil 3:20).

6:9-11. The opening of the fifth seal ends the sequence in which the creatures summon the riders. A different scene now confronts John. He sees under the altar the souls of those "slaughtered for the word of God and for the testimony they had given" (v. 9; cf. 1:2; 12:11; 20:4). The altar, presumably in heaven, appears elsewhere only at 8:3, where the saints once again feature: An angel stands on the altar with incense that accompanies the prayers of the saints. The cry to God in v. 10 (here called δεσπότης [*despotēs*; NRSV, "sovereign Lord"] for the only time in Revelation; cf. Luke 2:29; Acts 4:24; 2 Pet 2:1; Jude 4), who is holy and true (cf. 3:7), echoes the themes of Zech 1:12 and Ps 79:5, where the prophet remonstrates with God about the delay in showing mercy upon Zion (cf. Luke 18:7; Acts 4:24ff.). It is a cry for vindication and judgment (cf. Gen 4:10; Deut 32:43; Matt 23:35), and what follows is a description and an assertion of God's just judgment (16:5; 18:8, 20; 19:2, 11; 20:12). The loud cry in 19:2 indicates that with the destruction of Babylon the blood of God's servants has been avenged, though, as v. 9 indicates (cf. 11:10), it is the dwellers on earth who collude with the promotion and promulgation of that culture.

John sees "souls." In Revelation, the "soul" (ψυχή *psychē*) is the essence of a person (much as is implied in Matt 10:28). The enigmatic 8:9 suggests a distinction between creatures that have souls (the NRSV translates *psychē* as "living creatures") and those that do not. The word is used alongside "bodies" in 18:13 (cf. Matt 10:28), hinting that enslavement is not just a physical but also a mental or spiritual phenomenon that destroys any sense of autonomy. Verse 9, together with 20:4, might suggest that John sees disembodied souls whose cry for vengeance because of their desire to avoid continued nakedness (on the shame of nakedness, see the Commentary on 3:18; cf. 16:15; 17:16). Their pleas are met with the gift of white robes (cf. 7:9, 13-14; 22:14; see also the discussion of "garments" [ἱμάτια *himatia*] in the Commentary on 3:4-5, 18). In 2 Corinthians 5, Paul contemplates mortality and appears to wrestle with the possibility of nakedness, desiring to be clothed with a heavenly "tent" without any gap between the present and the hereafter (what he calls "being further clothed"). But he seems to accept the fact that it will be necessary to be undressed, even naked, before one can be dressed.

The souls under the altar are told to rest (see also 14:13; cf. Matt 11:28, with which Rev 14:13 has several affinities). Rest is an eschatological promise in Heb 4:10-11 (cf. Sir 24:7). There is a full complement of those who are to be killed (cf. 2:13; Heb 11:40) among their "fellow servants" and "brothers and sisters" (cf. 1:9; 12:10; 19:10; 22:9), a line of those who must engage in lives of witness and obedience, which will mean that they will have to wash their robes in the blood of the Lamb. The idea that there is a particular number or quota that has to be filled is evident, albeit in terms of a nation's misdeeds, in Matt 23:32, where "this generation" has fulfilled the full measure of the fathers in their rejection of the prophets (cf. Matt 23:35). In Rom 11:25, Paul claims that there are a number of Gentiles who have to come in before all Israel will be saved. A limit is set on the time of persecution and destruction (cf. 2:10); it is not a never-ending sequence without significance or terminus.

6:12-17. Cataclysmic events accompany the opening of the sixth seal (v. 12): earthquake (cf. Jer 10:22 LXX; Ezek 38:19; Joel 2:10), the darkening of the sun (Isa 50:3) and the moon (Ezek 32:7), stars falling from the sky (cf. Isa 13:10), and the heaven's being rolled up (cf. 16:20; 20:11; Isa 34:4; Heb 1:12). The reference to the earthquake appears in almost identical language in 11:13 and 16:18, though the unique character of the earthquake in 16:18 is stressed (thunders and earthquake are found together also in 8:5; 11:19). What is described here has its counterpart in 8:12 (cf. 9:2). The turning of the moon to blood (arising from Joel 3:4) is part of the Pentecost prophecy in Acts 2:20 (an important reminder of the apocalyptic character of that event in Luke's narrative). Within the context of Revelation, these cataclysmic events are telling reminders of the risk that those who are "stars" (the angels of the churches) in the hands of the Son of Man might also find themselves falling from their exalted positions. John uses an analogy of a fig tree that is shaken by the wind and loses its fruit to illustrate the falling of the stars, an apt analogy for overripe fruit (cf. 2:4-5; the fig tree is used as an analogy of the eschaton, though with a different purpose, in Mark 13:28-29; cf. Mark 11:13). The shaking of mountains and islands is referred to in a more climactic way in 16:20 (cf. Heb 12:26).

As well as the parallels in prophetic texts of judgment, there are apocalyptic elements in the discourses that precede the narratives of Jesus' death (Matthew 24–25; Mark 13; Luke 21)—not entirely inappropriate to mention in this context, given that the Lamb's death is the basis for the opening of the seals (5:5-6). Matthew describes an earthquake (Matt 27:54; 28:2; cf. 24:7). Both Matthew and Luke report a darkening of the sun (Matt 27:45; Luke 23:45; cf. Rev 8:12). The Gospels also include references to the moon (Matt 24:29; Luke 21:25; cf. Acts 2:20) and the stars (Matt 24:29; Mark 13:25). The "apocalyptic" character of the death of Jesus may be hinted at in Luke 23:30, where there is a reaction on the part of the crowd similar to that in Rev 6:16, and each quoting Hos 10:8.[222]

In the midst of the cosmic upheaval we find the first reactions from the earth's populace. There is a particular, though not exclusive, concentration on the mighty—kings, magnates, generals, rich (see Isa 24:21)—though the slave is included as well (cf. 13:16; 19:18). There can be no respite for anyone. There is no release from judgment for any, rich and poor alike, who capitulate to the beast (13:16), who fail to practice the way of the King of kings (19:16). The kings of the earth commit fornication with Babylon (17:2; 18:3) and are destined to bewail their folly (18:9) and pay for it (see 19:18, where the generals and the mighty are mentioned). Here the terror of the divine glory revealed in wrath prompts a reaction like that spoken of by the prophets Isaiah (Isa 2:10) and Hosea (Hos 10:8). The people's reaction is to hide in the face of apocalypse (the unveiling); the revelation of the day of wrath is too much to bear ("who can stand?"), and yet that is precisely what those who "conquer" will do (7:9; 11:4; 14:1; 15:2; cf. Jude 24). Mountains and their caves will prove utterly inadequate hiding places (16:20). The desire to hide is like that of the man and the woman in Eden when they realized their nakedness (Gen 3:8). The plea to the mountains and rocks to "fall upon us" will have a ghastly fulfillment in the destruction wrought by the falling stars (8:10; 9:1) and the falling dragon (12:7; cf. Luke 10:18). The cataclysm is described as a consequence of the wrath not only of God but also of the Lamb (cf. 14:10).[223] God's reign means the manifestation of wrath (11:18; cf. Rom 1:17ff.). It will be likened to a draft of wine (14:10; 16:19; 19:15), which those who bear the mark of the beast will taste. Only here and in 16:14 is there an explicit connection with the rich tradition of the Day of the Lord in the reference to "the great day" (v. 17; cf. Joel 2:1, 11; Amos 5:18; Nah 1:6; Zeph 1:14; Mark 13:32; Rom 2:5; 2 Thess 2:2).

---

222. See Ched Myers, *Binding the Strong Man: A Political Reading of Mark's Story of Jesus* (Maryknoll, N.Y.: Orbis, 1988), who brings out well the apocalyptic dimension of Mark's narrative.

223. On the theological implications, see A. T. Hanson, *The Wrath of the Lamb* (London: SPCK, 1957) 159-80; and G. B. Caird, *The Revelation* (London: A. & C. Black, 1966) 91.

REFLECTIONS

1. The uplifting hymn of praise in 5:9ff., which many readers may find themselves owning, cannot disguise the more difficult questions and emotions that may be unleashed on reading the words that follow in chapter 6. Revelation does not dwell on the issue of how a loving God, hymned so lovingly, can be the source of so much death and destruction. Its refusal to abstract God from the dark side of our world is a reminder not to protect God from the seamier sides of ourselves and the world in which we live. Revelation leaves us with the problems of theodicy, but not before demanding that we seek to recognize God in unexpected places:

> I form light and create darkness,
>   I make weal and create woe;
>   I the LORD do all these things.
> (Isa 45:7 NRSV)

What appears in chap. 6 and the following chapters contrasts starkly with the optimism generated by the paeans in the previous vision. Nevertheless, as the scroll of Ezekiel reminds us (which John is instructed to eat in Rev 10:10), "written on it were words of lamentation and mourning and woe" (Ezek 2:10 NRSV). Understanding their theological significance is another matter. Theologians long to be able to tie up loose ends. But texts like Revelation deny them the privilege, offering little sign of dealing with the questions they seek to have answered. Revelation only infrequently provides the satisfaction of interpretive certainty, involving as it does an appeal to the imagination rather than to logic. Unlike the philosophical essay, which demands its readers' intellectual submission by the force of argument, Revelation's word pictures seek to address and involve readers and relocate them in the divine economy. They deny us those "plausible words of wisdom" (1 Cor 2:4 NRSV) in favor of "God's wisdom, secret and hidden . . . revealed to us through the Spirit . . . in words not taught by human wisdom but taught by the Spirit" (1 Cor 2:7, 10, 13 NRSV).

Revelation offers no reasoned theodicy, unless the hymns asserting God's righteous judgment be understood as such. A danger with interpreting Revelation is to be too prescriptive and, therefore, too restrictive. Its surprises and abrupt transitions are part and parcel of the prophetic tradition, as Bengel noted long ago. If we cannot pin down apocalyptic symbolism, whose meaning will be conditioned by readings in very different contexts, we may nevertheless be able to offer some pointers for finding meaning in this turbulent and shocking sequence of images in the middle chapters, contrasting so markedly with the sublime evocation of heavenly worship in the previous chapters.

2. Interpreters of Revelation through the centuries have been struck by the repetition of references to the penultimate. Readers stand in the midst of the eschatological drama. It is partly complete, and we are offered a preview of the ending. In the midst of the trials and tribulations, we await their climax. All we can do is watch, wait, witness, and not be led astray (cf. Mark 13:13, 33). That sense of anticipation, of living in the penultimate time, characterizes New Testament eschatology. Paul criticizes the Corinthians for living as if the kingdom of God had already arrived (1 Cor 4:8), and he teaches the Romans that the present is a time of waiting, struggle, and anticipation (Rom 8:18). New Testament theology is characterized by this sense of being "in between" with the prospect not of release but of disorientation, of destruction and chaos before the new age can come. The weak Smyrnean Christians already know that tribulation, whereas the Laodiceans carry on, falsely confident. For all that the good news is about a present reality, the present remains, stubbornly, a time of exile from which deliverance is still awaited.

3. Apocalypse provokes crisis, and injustice is laid bare. The terror of that critical moment evokes prophetic passages where judgment comes on a people disobedient to the covenant. The apocalyptic imagery of Revelation could be seen as a consequence of the fracture of the cosmic covenant, whose repair was the function of the Messiah.[224]

---

224. See R. Murray, *The Cosmic Covenant* (London: Sheed and Ward, 1992).

Revelation demonstrates the world *dis*order, particularly through the activity of the Beast in which injustice and human self-centeredness have distorted the way society and the whole created order function. The world is out of joint, demonstrated in the destruction of the Messiah by the representatives of the present scheme of things. The Messiah's coming shows up the distorted and fractured nature of the world, humans, beasts, and the whole of creation for what it really is (cf. Isa 11:4).

There is in Revelation no bland indulgence of the status quo or easy inclusiveness, but a vision of covenant faithfulness that involves mutual responsibilities (John 14:15; cf. Deut 30:15ff.; 1 John 3). The God of the covenant will allow the cry of the weak and the oppressed to go unheard (Exod 3:7). Revelation 4 is linked to Sinai via Exod 19:15, and the sound of the trumpet in the latter is, of course, important in Rev 8:6ff. At the end of each series of plagues, the reference to theophany (and covenant) is reiterated (8:5; 11:19; 16:18ff.), and the plagues may relate to the covenant curses in Deut 28:15ff. and the prophecies of the day of the Lord, which turns out to be a day of disaster for people who have neglected the covenant demands (Amos 5:18ff.). Despite all this, humanity persists in carrying on in the same old way, ignoring the justice of God—indeed, cursing the very God who can offer life and true peace and harmony (9:20; 16:9, 11). And the disorder and disease continue.

4. Even allowing for the fact that the book offers prophetic insight into the misguided attitudes and practices of a deluded humanity, Revelation, understandably, has the reputation of being one of the most violent books in the New Testament. It is important to remember that in reading Revelation we are asked to share in the celebration of God's justice—to read it is to be open to feelings of passion, hatred, longing, and vindication as well as sorrow. But we are not asked to engage in barbarism or violence ourselves, nor is there ever any hint that we should. Revelation's portrayal of violence may (and has) encouraged imitation of the violent scenes, but that is a misunderstanding of Revelation and needs to be corrected by the positive traits it encourages: patient endurance, faithfulness, and steadfast witness. Revelation may draw us into the process of recognizing those feelings that are too big and too powerful to manage; but it persuades us to recognize the darker side of things—what we have become and the peril of staying as we are—while at the same time feeding our aspirations that things may be different. The process of reading or hearing is itself a means whereby the darker feelings may be brought to the surface, so that the effect of the book can be cathartic.[225]

Even the most revolutionary of texts, seeking to challenge the conventional and articulate the alternative, are written in fallible human language and are shot through with the values of the prevailing culture and prejudice. One of the features of apocalyptic is that it represents an alternative to conventional wisdom. Yet it is that which is most conventional—language—that often has to serve as the vehicle of what is subversive. Such texts, therefore, are inevitably related to the assumptions and ideas of their social formations, so often based on violence and oppression. We cannot expect a text to be devoid of the values of the prevailing culture, even if it struggles to bring to birth something different. The most we can hope for is (to quote Walter Benjamin) that "involuntary memory of a redeemed humanity," which contrasts with "convention and false tradition." Revelation is no exception. Its language, however unconventional, its themes, and its imagery still work within the dominant culture and inherit from it the values contaminated by it, alongside a glimpse of something different. There is no easy way out of this dilemma. Human language is pervaded with a culture that is opposed to sentiments that are, at best, ambiguous and, at worst, shot through with the strains of conflict and violence of the old order. Even this sublime vision will be no

---

225. A. Y. Collins, *Crisis and Catharsis* (Philadelphia: Westminster, 1984); E. Drewermann, *Tiefenpsychologie und Exegesis Band II Wunder. Vision, Weissagung, Apokalypse, Geschichte, Gleichnis* (Olten: Walter 1985) 541-91.

exception insofar as it is, of necessity, expressed in the words of human discourse. It, too, cannot quite shake off the culture of rejection and exclusion and violence.

Revelation, if we allow it to do so, may touch the reality of our anger and passion, too. The symbols are evocative means of bringing to the surface the horror of personal and corporate feelings of destructive power and the way to their transcendence. Unless we can recognize the passions and desires that have led to so much conflict, victimization, and destruction, then we shall continue to use the deceit that has covered up human conflict. Revelation is a text, a product of visionary imagination, that claims a privileged access to divine realities.

The church has long recognized the importance of our owning the whole spectrum of our feelings within the context of the liturgy. Hence, we read psalms that embrace the celebration of God's tenderness and deliverance as well as the fierce outbursts of pain and the demand for vengeance. We are unwilling to include words like those that conclude Psalm 137, because they express sentiments we would not always own. I do not want to identify with the righteous who "will rejoice when they see the vengeance done;/ they will bathe their feet in the blood of the wicked" (Ps 58:10 NRSV). These words, however, *in certain circumstances* might be true to our feelings. In avoiding those feelings, we may only end up in denial of the attitudes we would prefer not to acknowledge. But to deny them and drive them underground is to risk their bursting out in a far more virulent form. To own our feelings and to talk about them is the start of healing; to deny them is the insidious process of heaping up a bonfire of resentment whose destructive capability knows no bounds. Revelation reminds us that the darker side cannot be hidden from God, because God is in it as well. The message of Revelation 6, with its tale of destruction and death, is not apart from God.

REVELATION 7:1-17

CONCERNING THOSE SEALED AND A VISION OF THE GREAT MULTITUDE

OVERVIEW

This chapter picks up the sealing theme of chaps. 5–6, but uses it in a different way. There the opening of the seals means the beginning of the judgment of God, the wrath of the Lamb, but here there is hope for those who are sealed with God's name and have washed their robes in the blood of the Lamb. In the midst of death and destruction, some people have with integrity refused to conform and are willing to pay a price for it. There is a contrast here similar to that found in chaps. 13–14, where it is between bearing the mark of the beast (13:17; 14:9) and having the name of God written on the forehead (14:1). Washing their robes and making them white in the blood of the Lamb is no specifically "religious" matter. It is a matter of not conforming to the negative aspects of the prevailing culture.

REVELATION 7:1-8, THE 144,000 OF ISRAEL ARE SEALED

COMMENTARY

7:1. At this point in the vision five seals have been opened, and there is an interruption in the inexorable process, resumed at 8:1. John sees a vision not of death and destruction but of assembly and praise. An angel stands at each of the four corners of the earth (cf. Ezek 7:2; 37:9; Zech 6:5), preventing the wind from blowing and so harming the earth (see v. 3; cf. 6:6; 9:4). The loosening of restraint on the angels and on Satan has brought chaos to the natural order (cf. 9:14-15; 20:7).

7:2. Another angel ascends from the dawn (cf. 16:12; Isa 41:25). The use of "ascend" (ἀναβαίνω *anabainō*) often signifies a significant moment in Revelation: note John's and the witnesses' ascent (4:1; 11:12); the emergence of the beast (11:7; 13:11; cf. 17:8); the enduring evidence of judgment (9:2; 14:11; 19:3); and the ascent to the presence of God of the prayers of the saints (8:4). This angel holds a seal of the living God (cf. 4:9; 15:7; of Christ in 1:18) and cries with a loud voice (a phrase invariably used for heavenly commands [10:3; 14:15; 18:2; 19:17] or for the elect [6:10; 7:10]) to prevent the four angels from releasing the winds to harm the earth (note once again the notion of permission; see Commentary on 6:4).

7:3. The reason for the delay in releasing the destructive powers of the four winds is to allow time to mark "the servants of our God with a seal on their foreheads." This theme is reminiscent of Ezek 9:4-5, where a mark is placed on the heads of those who "sigh and groan" over all the abominations of the city while a man in white linen kills those who do not have the mark. Persons who have the mark are spared the torment of the locusts in Rev 9:4. Sealing as a metaphor of divine favor is found elsewhere in the NT, occasionally as a sign of eschatological deliverance (as in Eph 1:13; 4:30; cf. 2 Cor 1:22), and a sign of an esoteric book relevant for another generation (10:4; cf. Dan 12:4). John's writing is not to be sealed (22:10), however.

We have in this verse another reference to the "servants of God" (lit., "slaves"). John uses the word δοῦλος (*doulos*) to describe himself and others who are obedient to God (1:1; 2:20; 19:2, 5; 22:3), just as Paul does (Rom 1:1; Phil 1:1; cf. Titus 1:1). John's use of the term in Revelation is often linked with the prophetic ministry (10:7; 11:18; cf. 1:1; 22:6). In this usage, John and the other prophetic servants of God follow in the footsteps of Moses (Rev 15:3). In the context of the opening of the seals and the unleashing of the contents of the book, those who are the "slaves of God" are marked as such. Whereas in Ezekiel such a mark will preserve people from harm, we shall see in the ensuing chapters that not all of the "servants" of God can expect to be preserved from physical harm.

7:4-8. John hears the numbers of those sealed (v. 4) and begins to offer a list from "every tribe of the people of Israel" (v. 4)— one hundred and forty-four thousand in all (cf. 14:1-2). The NRSV translation uses "people" (v. 4), though the Greek reads "sons" (υἱοὶ *hyioi*). Though the issue of whether Revelation's vision of the future appears to be includisve of gender and race, there are contrary indications elsewhere in the book (e.g., 14:4). The 144,000 is composed of people from every tribe of Israel. The Jewish identity of this group is indicated by the fact that there is another multitude in v. 9 that comes from every nation, suggesting that those mentioned in v. 5 are Jews. The precise number suggests that it is a remnant of the children of Israel that has been sealed (Isa 10:20; Rom 9:27; cf. Rom 11:25-26).

If we compare the list in v. 5 with the names of the sons of Jacob/Israel in Gen 35:22; 49 (Reuben, Simeon, Levi, Judah, Zebulun, Issachar, Dan, Gad, Asher, Naphtali, Joseph, Benjamin), we note that Dan is absent from and Manasseh is included in the number in Revelation (but Ephraim, the other son of Joseph, is excluded; see the allocation of land in Joshua 13) and that the list starts with Judah rather than with the firstborn, Reuben, an indication of the priority given to Judah as the tribe of the Messiah (5:5; cf. Isaiah 11).

Numbering is important (cf. 5:11; 7:9; 9:16; 13:17-18; 15:2; 20:8), as is measuring (11:1-2; 21:15ff.). The numbers here, based on the number twelve, are linked explicitly with the twelve tribes. Elsewhere, the number seven (seals, trumpets, bowls, and letters) contrasts with a number like six (used in 13:18), which is one short of perfection. Numbering and measuring are a sign of possession, a sort of census of the full complement of God (cf. 6:11). It is an activity that indicates ownership rather than being a measure of the success of human endeavors. (See Reflections at 7:9-17.)

REVELATION 7:9-17, THE MULTITUDE FROM EVERY NATION

COMMENTARY

7:9-12. In addition to the 144,000 from the children of Israel who are sealed, there is another group, "a great multitude." This group John *sees* (v. 9) as opposed to *hearing* the report of the number of those who have been sealed (see Fig. 2, "Hearing and Seeing in the Book of Revelation").

No mention is made of this group's being sealed, and so they do not seem to be given the protection offered as the result of being marked with the angelic seal. The precision of the numbering of the children of Israel contrasts with the countless host "from every nation, from all tribes and peoples and languages," which John sees (v. 9; cf. 5:9; Gen 15:5). This multitude contrasts with the waters, interpreted as "peoples and multitudes and nations and languages" (NRSV), on which Babylon is seated in 17:15. John often uses a similar string of words to denote

Figure 2: Hearing and Seeing in the Book of Revelation

great voice commissioning John (1:10ff.)
vision of the Human Figure (1:13ff.)
    address to the seven angels (2-3)
    first voice speaks again (4:1)
the throne in heaven (4:1)
    praise of elders and creatures (4:8ff.)
the scroll (5:1f)
    the strong angel asks about scroll (5:2)
    elder's command not to weep (5:5)
the Lamb (5:6)
    new song (5:9)
    voice of many angels (5:11)
    whole creation (5:13)
John sees seals 1, 3, 4, 5, and 6 opened (6:1f., 2, 5, 9, 12)
    four living creatures summon (6:1, 3, 5, 7)
    voice from midst of creatures (6:6)
    reaction of terrified humanity (6:16)
four angels at the corners of the earth (7:1)
the angel ascending from the dawn (7:2)
    command not to damage the earth (7:3)
    number of sealed (7:4)
the great multitude (7:9)
    songs of multitude (7:10, 12)
    questions and answer about the multitude (7:13)
    song of multitude (7:15f.)
the seven angels with seven trumpets (8:2)
sight of the eagle (8:13)
    the threefold woe (8:13)
star falling from heaven (9:1)
    voice from horns of altar (9:13)
    number of cavalry (9:16)
the horses (9:17)
the strong angel (10:1)
    voice from heaven (10:4)
    oath of the angel (10:6)
    command to John to take scroll (10:8ff.)
John, the measuring rod and the vision of the two witnesses (11:1ff.)
    command to measure (11:1)
    transfer of sovereignty (11:15)
    praise by elders (11:16)
ark of covenant in heaven (11:19)
signs of woman and dragon (12:1ff.)
    loud voice proclaims transfer of sovereignty (12:10f.)
sight of dragon (12:13)

hearing = italic type
seeing = roman type

two beasts (13:2, 11)
    cry of inhabitants of world (13:4)
Lamb standing (14:1)
    voice from heaven (14:2)
angel with eternal gospel (14:6)
    eternal gospel (14:7)
    prediction of Babylon's fall (14:8)
    wrath on those who worship the beast (14:9)
    voice from heaven (14:13)
human figure on white cloud (14:14)
    command to commence reaping (14:15)
another angel (14:17)
    another command to reap (14:18)
another sign in heaven (15:1)
sea of glass (15:2)
    Moses' song (15:3)
temple opened (15:5)
    great voice from temple (16:1)
    angel of waters (16:5)
    altar speaks (16:7)
unclean spirits out of mouth of dragon (16:13)
the vision of Babylon (17:3, 6, 8, 12, 15, 16, 18)
    summons by one of angels of bowls (17:1)
    explanation by angel (17:7ff.)
another angel (18:1)
    mighty voice of angel (18:2)
    another voice from heaven (18:4)
    kings of earth lament (18:9)
    merchants of earth lament (18:14, 16)
    seafarers of earth lament (18:18)
    mighty angel casts stone (18:21ff.)
    voice of multitude (19:1, 6)
    responses from elders and throne (19:4f)
    angelic command to write and not worship (19:9f.)
heaven opened (19:11)
angel standing in the sun (19:17)
    summons to supper of God (19:17)
beasts and kings of earth assemble (19:19)
another angel descending from heaven (20:1)
thrones in millennium (20:4)
great white throne (20:12)
vision of new heaven and new earth & new Jerusalem (21:1)
    voice from throne (21:3ff)
    summons by one of angels of bowls (21:9)
John sees no temple (21:22)
    angel confirms importance of prophecy (22:6)
    Jesus speaks (22:16)

hearing = italic type
seeing = roman type

variety and universality (see 1:9; 5:9; 10:11; 13:7; 14:6; 17:15) and to add to the rhetorical effect. Theirs is a situation of subjection and oppression. This crowd is distinguished by its identification with the Lamb, and its status is dignified and defiant.

This crowd stands, as the Lamb had done, before the throne (cf. 5:6). Now the Lamb, in company with those around the throne, forms the environs for this gathering. In contrast with the very close link between the Lamb and the throne in v. 17 ("the Lamb at the center of the throne"), in vv. 9-10 the throne and the Lamb are described as two adjacent parts of the heavenly presence (cf. 22:1, 3).

The great multitude is clothed in white (cf. 3:4; 4:4; 6:11; Mark 16:5). They hold palm branches in their hands, as if celebrating the Feast of Tabernacles (Lev 23:40ff.; 2 Macc 10:7), and like the oppressed and insignificant crowd who welcomed Jesus the humble king (Matt 21:5) into Jerusalem (Matt 21:15; John 12:13). In antiquity, the palm branch was also a symbol of victory. The crowd in v. 10 (cf. 5:12) sings "with a great voice" of God's salvation (cf. 12:10; 19:1). The ascription of saving power to God (v. 10) is another link with Jesus' triumphal entry into Jerusalem. A great crowd of people was present in Jerusalem for the feast, and they met Jesus with shouts of "Hosanna!/ Blessed is the one who comes in the name of the Lord—/ the King of Israel!" (John 12:13 NRSV). The Pharisees complained that the whole world had "gone after him" (John 12:19 NRSV), an ironic foreshadowing of the vision of the host that assembles in praise of God's salvation and of the Lamb in Revelation 7.

In the Gospels, the widespread references to the crowds indicate that they are the special object of Jesus' ministry (e.g., Matt 9:36; 15:32; cf. Matt 4:25). Of particular relevance to this passage in Revelation is when the festival crowd sang similar songs at the triumphal entry (Matt 21:8). Unlike the crowd who later turned against Jesus, this festal gathering in Revelation 7 will not turn away from the Lamb.

The cry of salvation (v. 10) may echo the "Hosanna" of Ps 118:21, 25. There is a response to this shout of praise from the heavenly host (v. 11), the angels around the throne, and the elders and creatures (cf. 5:11). Interestingly, they worship God alone; there is no mention here of the Lamb. The ascriptions of praise are almost identical with 5:12 (cf. 4:11), there addressed to the Lamb, with the exception that thanksgiving rather than wealth is included in the praise (v. 12).

7:13-17. John is then met by one of the elders (v. 13; cf. 4:4; 5:5), who asks him a question about the vision (we must remember that John has only *seen* the great multitude and *heard* the number of those who are sealed). It may be tempting to suppose that the question is put by the elder only for John to confess ignorance and then be enlightened by his heavenly interlocutor, of whom such knowledge might be expected (2:2, 9, 13; 3:1; 19:12). As one of that great multitude and himself a martyr, John may know as much about them and their experience as does the heavenly elder. Hence, it is appropriate that John be asked who they are and from where they have come. Indeed, at two points later in the vision, John will be reminded that he is in no way inferior to the angelic companion whom he feels compelled to worship (19:10; 22:8), hinted at here in John's address to the elder as κύριος (*kyrios*; lit., "lord"; here it is "sir"), a word used elsewhere either for God (e.g., 1:8; 4:8) or for Christ (11:8).

The meaning of "the great ordeal" (v. 14) is unclear. The phrase τῆς θλίψεως τῆς μεγάλης (*tēs thlipseōsa tēs megalēs*) is found only here (see Commentary on 2:9) and echoes similar themes in the Gospels (e.g., Matt 24:21; cf. Dan 12:1). A passage like Rev 3:10 points to the whole gamut of upheaval described in the book. Such an ordeal would have a peculiar dimension for those who identify with the Lamb and who experience social ostracism or even persecution. What John is offered here is a proleptic glimpse of those who have made it through the time of trial, particularly as a result of resisting the pressure to conform to the beast and the allure of Babylon.

Although John uses the verb "whiten" (λευκαίνω *leukainō*) only here (v. 14; NIV and NRSV, "made them white"), whiteness in Revelation is associated with God and with Jesus, and it is associated with the clothes of the redeemed (3:4-5; 4:4; 6:11; 7:9, 13-14; 19:14). The washing of the robes in blood to make them white is a startling example of an oxymoron, a juxtaposition of contradictory ideas (another example is the lion who turns out to be a Lamb in 5:5-6). The meaning of the phrase "washed their robes and made them white in the blood of the Lamb" can best be gleaned from related passages in Revelation, though it may be inspired by passages like Gen 49:11 (the blessing of Judah by Jacob); Exod 19:14; and Isa 63:1. In Rev 22:14 and in the related references in 3:4-5, we are not told what is required to keep the robes white. Here, however, the multitude have washed their robes in the blood of the Lamb (cf. 1:5; 5:9; 12:11; 19:13; 1 John 1:7). In 12:10, the conquering of the "accuser" by "our brethren" comes about by the Lamb's blood and by the testimony of the faithful, which itself resembles the testimony of Christ, the faithful and true witness (1:5; 3:14; cf. 2:13). Engaging in the faithful testimony of Jesus, therefore, and being prepared, like him, to forsake life is the basis of "conquering" (cf. Mark 8:34-35). That includes resisting Babylon, which has gotten drunk on the blood of the witnesses to Jesus (17:6; cf. 18:24). In 16:15, the warning to readers, "See, I am coming like a thief! Blessed is the one who stays awake and is clothed, not going about naked and exposed to shame" (NRSV), comes immediately after John sees demonic spirits, linked with the beast, performing signs to lead the kings of the earth astray. So washing one's robes in the blood of the Lamb not only identifies one with his way but also means abstaining from the ways of the beast. It means that one will be prepared to face discrimination, and even death (12:11), for the sake of the Word of God and the witness to Jesus (6:9; cf. 12:11).

It is their active perseverance (v. 14; cf. 14:12) that enables the righteous to stand before God's throne (cf. 22:4), where they serve God day and night in the temple (v. 15; cf. 22:3). "Service" (λατρεύω *latreyō*) is a verb used of cultic service (see Acts 7:7, 42; Heb 8:6; 9:9, 14; 10:2; 13:10; it seems to be used in a transferred sense of general divine service in Luke 1:74; Rom 1:19). That divine service is one that, as the witnesses in 11:1ff. demonstrate, takes place outside the safe heaven of temple or cult in the place trampled by the nations. Thereby is fulfilled the command to "prophesy again about many peoples and nations and languages and kings" (10:11 NRSV).

The divine service that is described at the climax of the vision in 22:3 is priestly. The righteous will see God face to face (the divine "face" and its blessing are a theme of the priestly blessing in Num 6:24-25). The name of God will be written on their foreheads (cf. Exod 28:16), and they will enter the divine presence (cf. Leviticus 16; Num 12:8). God is described as hovering over them (cf. 21:3, where God tabernacles with the people), as the Spirit hovers over Jesus at his baptism (Mark 1:10; cf. Gen 1:2). "Tabernacling" (a verb used in 12:12; 13:6; 21:3) is also used for the dwelling of the incarnate Logos with humanity in John 1:14 (cf. Wis 24:8, 10, 21).

Freedom from hunger and thirst (v. 16; cf. 21:14) and the heat of the sun (cf. Isa 49:10) contrasts with the want implied in the death and destruction that was unleashed at the opening of the seals (e.g., 6:6) and that will intensify in the awesome visions that follow. In particular, being burned by the fierce heat of the sun is explicitly mentioned in 16:8-9. The reason why they are protected is that the Lamb "at the center" (ἀνὰ μέσον *ana meson*; used only here in Revelation; cf. 5:6) "shepherds" them (cf. Ezek 34:23). This guidance contrasts with the more aggressive shepherding in 12:5 and 19:15 (cf. 2:27). In a reversal of roles, a Lamb will be a shepherd for the people (cf. 5:5). The eschatological prophecy of Isa 25:8 is here fulfilled (quoted again in 21:4).

REFLECTIONS

1. The very striking image of washing robes in blood to make them white raises a question about the participation in God's saving work of the members of the great multitude. The image is an active rather than a passive one, "washing" rather than "being washed." As we shall see in chap. 11, the task of faithful witness, epitomized by Jesus, can be the vocation of others too. Revelation suggests that the saving work is to be shared and continued by men and women, just as the writer of Colossians

describes the apostolic task as "completing what is lacking in Christ's afflictions" (Col 1:24 NRSV). The sharing in the divine economy, being God's co-worker as Paul puts it in 1 Cor 3:9, has been typical of apocalyptic and mystical beliefs within Christianity through the centuries.[226] It is exemplified by the long tradition of martyrdom in the early church, in which Christians participated and continued the efficacious witness of the Lamb against and on behalf of the world.

As other passages of Revelation indicate (6:9; 11:1ff.; 14:12), there is no guarantee of either the spiritual or the physical well-being of God's servants. They are always under pressure to conform (chaps. 2–3; 13). When they resist, they will find themselves at the receiving end of the anger and retribution of those who seek to maintain the world as it is and who will see their deaths as a reason for rejoicing. That which pricks the conscience of these people has been removed (11:10; cf. John 16:2). That harsh juxtaposition of ideas, making robes white in blood, evinces an awesome purity that comes through costly and deliberate devotion to a better way. The vision here (like passages in Paul's letters; e.g., 2 Cor 4:10; Col 1:24) expresses the conviction that Jesus continues to suffer among those who, like him, are victims of the injustices of our world.

2. The graciousness of God to those who follow the Lamb is brought out in Rev 7:16. This passage injects a theme of tenderness and comfort, seemingly lacking elsewhere in Revelation. We should take care not to miss the odd hints of God's sustaining and enabling promise to support an enduring witness to Christ in the midst of death and destruction. But, as we have seen, the book of Revelation is realistic in its concern with power and the exercise of power, both in the divine way and in opposition to it. And to love is to be engaged in an exercise of power that itself needs to be examined with the eye of vision and devoid of any cloud of sentiment.

The promise fulfilled in 7:16 hints that the blessed are particularly those who have suffered hunger and thirst in the present age: "They will hunger no more, and thirst no more" (Rev 7:16 NRSV). The promise is focused on the needy and the outcast, therefore (cf. Matt 25:35ff.). This focus comes as no surprise after the letters to the seven churches. It is the, outwardly, least prosperous and famous churches (Smyrna and Philadelphia) that are singled out for commendation and support by the risen Christ. The distinguished and, outwardly, spiritually complete churches are shown to be dead and lukewarm (Sardis and Laodicea): "Woe to you when all speak well of you, for that is what their ancestors did to the false prophets" (Luke 6:26 NRSV). For those who have conformed to society and reflect its values, there is a much greater temptation to be "lukewarm" and to offer support, however tacit, to the beast and to Babylon. The poor and the marginalized often have nothing to gain from such a course of action, though, as we shall see, Revelation is not sanguine about their ability to resist the pervasive seduction of ideology.

3. The inclusiveness of the vision is striking (something that needs to be borne in mind when this passage is the subject of a sermon on All Saints Day). The multitude includes Jews and all those who have washed their robes in the blood of the Lamb and thereby have identified with the way of the Lamb. The neat equation that is often made between this image and the sense of having one's sins washed away christianizes something that is not necessarily so in the apocalyptic text. Such an interpretive move brings the vision a little too quickly within the ambit of a precise theological formula. Witnessing against the beast, refusing to compromise, and espousing the way of the Lamb, inside or outside the church, mean inclusion in that great multitude. "All Saints" means that. The great multitude includes many who never "named the name" of Jesus but who lived lives that continued in the way of the Lamb: "Not everyone who says to me, 'Lord, Lord,' will enter the kingdom of heaven, but only the one who does the will of my Father in heaven" (Matt 7:21 NRSV).

---

226. See Cohn, *The Pursuit of the Millennium*; Rowland, *Radical Christianity*.

REVELATION 8:1–9:21

THE SEVENTH SEAL AND THE SEVEN ANGELS WITH SEVEN TRUMPETS

COMMENTARY

The sequence interrupted by the report of the sealing of the children of Israel and John's vision of the great multitude is now resumed with the opening of the seventh seal (presumably by the Lamb, though that is not mentioned here). This section, with its vivid and alarming description of the agents of destruction, epitomizes Revelation's links with OT prophets like Nahum and Zephaniah. There is another sequence of seven, this time of trumpet blasts. Once more it is interrupted in 9:13ff. (cf. 6:12), with the final trumpet blast occurring at 11:15. The trumpets herald the longest sequence of catastrophes to befall the earth. The section starts with a pause in the sequence, with silence in heaven, and finishes with John reporting that the catalogue of disasters did not lead humanity to repent (9:20).

8:1. The opening of the seventh seal brings silence in heaven (cf. Hab 2:20; Zeph 1:7; Zech 2:13; Acts 15:12)—a marked contrast to the tumult of praise John has encountered in his vision. It is an opportunity to pause and, in the words of Ps 46:10, "Be still, and know that I am God!" (NRSV). Silence is a characteristic of heaven, and it is from the mysterious silence of God that the ultimate mystery comes (Rom 16:25).[227] Silence is a characteristic of the eschatological age in 4 Ezra 7:30-31: "And the world shall be turned back to primeval silence for seven days, as it was at the first beginnings; so that no one shall be left. And after seven days the world, which is not yet awake, shall be roused, and that which is corruptible shall perish."[228] Here, however, the silence serves to heighten anticipation.

8:2. John now sees seven angels (cf. Tob 12:15), standing before the throne of God (15:6; 16:1; 17:1; 21:9; cf. 1:4, 20; 4:5; 7:11), being given seven trumpets; note the passive once more, indicating the way in which things are allowed to happen within the divine providence (see, e.g., 6:1, 8; 7:2; 9:3; 11:1; 13:7, 14-15). The trumpet blast is a signal of alarm (see Joel 2:1) in the face of God's awesome presence (see Exod 19:16). John's commission and his ascent to heaven (1:10; 4:1) have been attended with a voice like that of a trumpet. The trumpet blast now has eschatological, doom-laden significance (cf. Matt 24:31; 1 Thess 4:16).

8:3-5. Before the trumpets are blown, another angel (cf. 10:1; 18:1) stands at the altar (cf. 14:18), holding a golden censer with incense (v. 3; cf. 18:3; Exod 30:1ff.; Luke 1:10-11). This angel offers to God the prayers of the saints (cf. 5:8). The smoke of the incense mingles with the prayers and ascends into the divine presence (Ps 141:2; cf. Tob 12:12). Just as John sees that the cries of the souls are heeded, so also he can see that the prayers of the saints ascend to the presence of God. The prayers of the saints are efficacious (v. 4). The angel takes the censer, fills it with fire from the altar (cf. Lev 16:12; Ezek 10:2), and casts it to earth, provoking a heavenly commotion such as had attended the vision of God's throne in 4:5. In 8:5 there is also an earthquake. Whether the ascent of the prayers to God causes this commotion is not clear, but there is a juxtaposition of the prayers ascending and the contents of the

---
227. Cf. Ignatius *To the Ephesians* 19.
228. 4 Ezra 7:30-31, trans. B. Metzger, in Charlesworth, *The Old Testament Pseudepigrapha*.

censer bringing upon earth what John had hitherto only seen in heaven (chap. 4).

8:6-7. The expression of downward movement (βάλλω *ballō*, "throw"; cf. πίπτω *piptō*, "fall"; 8:10; 9:1) suggests divine action toward the earth (cf. 12:8; 6:13). The trumpets themselves inaugurate a series of downward movements, linking heaven and earth in a chaotic and destructive way: hail mixed with blood; a mountain of fire; a star from heaven given the key of the abyss (8:7–9:1). Similarly, the seven last plagues involve angels pouring out bowls filled with God's wrath (16:1ff.). The verb καταβαίνω (*katabainō*, "come down") parallels this (10:1ff.; 18:1). It is only in 21:2, when the descent of the new Jerusalem resolves the division between heaven and earth, that the descent from heaven to earth will bring something other than judgment. Until that moment, the sharp dichotomy between the heaven and earth means that what proceeds from heaven is experienced on earth as judgment. Otherwise, only John's message, which comes from heaven, offers hope, but only for those who repent.

The first trumpet (v. 7) brings hail mingled with blood, which is cast upon the earth (cf. 16:21; Exod 9:23ff.; Ezek 38:22; Sir 39:29). The juxtaposition of hail and thunder, lightning, and earthquake in a theophany is found at 11:19, after the exposition of the ark in the heavenly temple. The consequence is disastrous for the ecology of the world (v. 7; cf. 7:3; 9:4), contrasting with the serenity of the rural idyll of the garden in the new Jerusalem, with the leaves of the tree for the healing of the nations (22:3); but that lies beyond the fiery judgment (cf. 17:16; 18:8; 1 Cor 3:13). Now one-third of the earth is destroyed, echoing Ezek 5:2, 12 and Zech 13:9.

8:8-9. With the blast of the second trumpet, the great, fiery mountain is cast into the sea, prefiguring the fall of Babylon (18:21), with whose rebellion Jerusalem itself is identified (11:8). The sea turns to blood, with terrible consequences for life in the sea and for mariners (cf. 18:19). It is possible that, if John was writing after the eruption of Vesuvius in 79 CE, this event (or rumors about something similar) might have insinuated itself into his imagination as he wrote this vision.

8:10-11. The third trumpet blast leads to a third fiery "bolt" from heaven, this time a star burning like a torch (Isa 14:12; cf. Rev 4:5), with dire consequences for rivers and springs (cf. 16:4). Once again we may compare the end of the vision, when thirst will be quenched from the spring of living water by the One who created the waters (14:7) and the river that flows through the heart of paradise (22:1-2). John names the star "Wormwood" (v. 11; cf. Amos 5:6-7; 6:12, where justice is turned to wormwood; see also Jer 9:15). Many die as a result of the waters' being made bitter (cf. Jer 23:15), anticipating the bitterness John experiences when he devours the scroll of judgment, with its "unpalatable" message for the nations (10:9-10).

8:12-13. The fourth trumpet blast leads to a third of the sun being "struck" (πλήσσω *plēssō*, the same cognate verb that is used of the plagues in chap. 15; cf. 9:18). The partial cataclysm here contrasts with what is described in the last plagues in chap. 16. Throughout the series of trumpet blasts, their effects befall a third of creation (vv. 7ff.; cf. 9:15, 18). Likewise, in v. 12 one-third of the sun, the moon, and the stars are afflicted, bringing darkness upon the earth (cf. 6:12; 9:2; 16:10; Exod 10:21; Amos 8:9, where these phenomena are linked with "that day," the day of the Lord). In v. 13 (and at 14:6), there is a solemn proclamation of woe, here by an eagle (cf. 4:7), on the earth's inhabitants, who are about to experience the consequences of the last three trumpet blasts (9:1, 3; 11:15):

"Woe, woe, woe to the inhabitants of the earth, at the blasts of the other trumpets that the three angels are about to blow!" (8:13 NRSV)

"Fear God and give him glory, for the hour of his judgment has come; and worship him who made heaven and earth, the sea and the springs of water." (14:7 NRSV)

The inhabitants of the earth seem to be oblivious to the significance of what is going on. They will gloat over the death of the witnesses (11:10), worship the beast (13:8; cf. 13:14), and become drunk with the wine of Babylon's fornication (17:2, 8). The angel of

Philadelphia has been warned of this time of trial that is to come (3:10).

9:1-11. The angel with the fifth trumpet (v. 1) heralds another star's falling from heaven to earth (cf. 8:10; Matt 24:29). A key is given to this star, probably referring to an angel, if 1:20 and Jude 6, 13 are anything to go by; this identification may be supported by Rev 20:1 (cf. Isa 14:12; Luke 10:18; *1 Enoch* 80:6-7). The key opens the bottomless pit (the abyss), the abode of the beast (11:7; cf. 17:8). The word "abyss" (ἄβυσσος *abyssos*) occurs only in Revelation, with the exception of Romans 10:17 and Luke 8:31, where Luke uses "abyss" in place of "sea" (cf. Mark 5:13), indicating an apocalyptic dimension to Luke's version of the story of the Gerasene demoniac.[229] The angel of the abyss is identified in v. 11 as Abaddon, the Destroyer.

When the angel opens the shaft of the "bottomless pit," smoke ascends. Unlike the smoke of the incense, which mingled with the prayers of the saints (8:4), this smoke resembles smoke from a furnace, which darkens the sun and pollutes the air (cf. Gen 19:28; Exod 19:18). The acrid nature of the smoke produces locusts on the earth (cf. Exod 10:12), which are given power "like scorpions." Unlike ordinary locusts, these have been told not to harm green things (cf. 7:3); instead, they are to torment for a period of five months those who "do not have the seal of God on their foreheads" (vv. 4-5; cf. 7:3; 9:10). Marking people as a prophylactic against destruction is the role of the man clothed in linen in Ezek 9:4ff., as he goes through the city marking those who sigh over the abominations—though being marked in this way is hardly a consolation in the midst of death and destruction. There can be no escape from the widespread effects of this.

Humanity is to be tormented, but not killed. According to v. 6, people will long for death, just as Job longed to be released from his torment (Job 3:21) and just as Cain, condemned to be a fugitive, was not allowed the release of death (Gen 4:13ff.; cf. Rev 6:15ff.; Luke 23:30). The torture typifies the judgment meted out on the earth (14:10; cf. 18:7, 10, 15) and that is carried out also by the two witnesses (11:10).

The description of the locusts becomes more terrible in vv. 7-8 (cf. Joel 2:4). They are like armored horses ready for battle. This sets the scene for the battles to come, which will be between the forces of evil and Christ and his followers (πόλεμος [*polemos*, "war"/"battle"] is used only here without an explicit eschatological sense; cf. 11:7; 12:7, 17; 13:7; 16:14; 19:19; 20:8). The description of the locusts is a terrible parody of the divine: What appears to be a golden crown is on the heads of these creatures (golden crowns belong to the elders in 4:4, 10, and to the human figure in 14:14). The horrific creatures have human faces, as did the third creature around the divine throne (4:7). The comparison of their hair with that of women (cf. 1:14; Luke 7:38, 44; John 12:3; 1 Pet 3:3) may relate to its length (cf. 1 Cor 11:14-15) and possibly to the frenzy of certain manic rituals.[230] The comparison of their teeth with the teeth of a lion recalls Joel 1:6, and the sound of their wings is loosely related to Joel 2:5. In John's visionary imagination, various OT passages seem to be linked and may have contributed to the terrifying description captured in John's words. The king over the locusts is an angel called Abaddon, "the destroyer" (from the Hebrew אבד [*'ābad*], meaning "destroy"; Abaddon is another name for Sheol, the realm of the dead; see Job 26:6; Prov 15:11). John's intention is to leave his readers in no doubt of the malevolent function of this angel, and so he includes the Greek term for "destroyer," Apollyon (cf. the phrase "were destroyed by the destroyer" [ἀπώλοντο ὑπὸ τοῦ ὀλοθρευτοῦ *apōlonto hypo tou olothreutou*] in 1 Cor 10:10, which is dependent on the story in Num 21:6; cf. also Heb 11:28).

9:12. John comments that the first woe has passed and that two more are to come. This comes at a point, roughly speaking, halfway through the sequences of seals, trumpets, and bowls. Four seals and five trumpet blasts have brought acts of destruction (seals 1, 5, and, possibly, 7 have not). Of the trumpet blasts, eight have brought about destruction on earth, as did the seven bowls, which are the last plagues. The second woe comes after the sixth trumpet blast and follows the vision

---

229. These elements are explored in Myers, *Binding the Strong Man*.

230. On the identification of the locusts with female heretics, see E. Schüssler Fiorenza, *In Memory of Her* (New York: Crossroad, 1983) 227; Wainwright, *Mysterious Apocalypse*, 42.

of the two witnesses. Although only one more woe is actually described in the book (11:14), with the promise that the third one is to come quickly, in 8:13 there is a threefold woe on the inhabitants of the earth, in 18:10, 16, 19 there is a threefold double woe on the great city, and, before that, in 12:12, a woe is pronounced on sea and land because of Satan's ejection from heaven.

The "messianic woes" are a consistent feature of the eschatological expectation of texts contemporary with Revelation (e.g., the Syriac *Apocalypse of Baruch* 25–26; see Excursus: "The Tribulation of the Messianic Age"); they are probably presupposed in Matt 24:19 and Mark 13:17. The eschatological character of the woes in Revelation casts fresh light on such passages elsewhere in the New Testament, especially in the Gospels. Thus the woes on the rich in Luke 6:24ff. and on the scribes and Pharisees in Matthew 23 should also be seen in this light (particularly the latter, coming as they do immediately before the eschatological discourse in Matthew 24–25). The woes of Jesus fall upon the cities (Matt 11:21) and upon the betrayer (Mark 14:21); perhaps also the woe Paul proclaims on himself if he does not preach the gospel (1 Cor 9:16) reminds readers that such woes have an eschatological significance.

9:13-15. At the blast of the sixth trumpet, a voice is heard from the altar (v. 13; cf. 6:9; 8:3), which sounds as if it comes from the horns of the altar (cf. Exod 30:1ff.). The angel is commanded to loose the angels that are bound at the Euphrates (cf. 16:12; 20:2). Once again chaos returns upon the earth (cf. Ps 104:9). They have been destined for this moment (v. 15); it is as if they were animals eager to be unleashed (cf. 20:3, 7). The sense of predestination evident here is curiously not often explicit in Revelation (cf. 12:6; 13:8; 17:8, which refers to the eternal destiny of the Lamb; see also 21:2). Still, they are allowed to kill only one-third of humanity.

9:16-19. John hears the enormous number of the horsemen: two hundred million (v. 16). This number is large, but finite (cf. 5:11; 7:4; 20:8). As in the previous vision, John describes the horses' armor. Their breastplates (cf. v. 9), which are multi-colored, in the colors of fire, sapphire (cf. 21:20), and sulphur (cf. 14:10; 19:20; 20:10; 21:8). They have heads like lions (cf. 4:7; 9:8; 13:2), and fire, smoke, and sulphur come out of their mouths. Their power resides in their mouths (cf. 1:16; 11:5; 12:15; 16:13; 19:15) and in their tails (cf. 9:10; 12:4). The tails are like serpents, and they have heads, with which they do harm (cf. 7:2; 9:10); this description indirectly links this vision with the serpent that gives power to a beast with seven heads (12:3, 9; 13:4). Although there are few verbal parallels, there is a general similarity between these creatures and Job's leviathan (Job 41:10ff.), which has similar teeth, breastplate, smoke, and fire.

9:20-21. This horrific picture of destruction, called "these plagues" (v. 20; cf. 15:8), is interrupted by a comment from John that will appear later in 16:9 (cf. 11:21). Instead of being led to repentance by these calamities, humankind continues in its old ways. The need for repentance is the insistent theme of the letters to the angels (2:5, 16, 21, 22; 3:3, 19), with the letters to the angels in Smyrna and Philadelphia being the only exceptions. The fragment of humankind that has survived the plagues does not repent of the "works of their hands" or their idolatry (cf. Isa 2:8; 17:8), the futility of which is expounded in words from Pss 115:4 and 135:15ff. This idol worship is nothing other than the worship of demons (v. 20; cf. Deut 32:17 LXX; Ps 95:5 LXX; 1 Cor 10:20). John might have gone on to complete Ps 135:18: "Those who make them/ and all who trust them/ shall become like them" (NRSV), but that is set forth in John's own vision in the surrounding context. The inability of human beings to act on the initial recognition that they have been confronted with the wrath of God and the Lamb (6:15ff.) suggests minds dulled to the awareness of God and the divine justice (cf. Rom 1:21 [NRSV]: "For though they knew God, they did not honor him as God or give thanks to him, but they became futile in their thinking, and their senseless minds were darkened").

The precious metals of which the idols were made are found elsewhere; gold is often used, for example, for crowns (14:14) and to describe Babylon (17:4; cf. 18:16; Isa 2:20; Dan 5:4), and silver and gold are among the cargo of the lamenting merchants (18:12). In addition, the misdeeds of this fragment of humanity are mentioned elsewhere (idolatry and murder: 21:8; 22:15; Genesis 4; Exod 20:15; sorcery: 18:23; 21:8; 22:15; Mic 5:12; Mal 3:5; and fornication: 2:14, 21; 14:8; 17:1-2, 5, 15-16; 18:3, 9; 19:2; [note the linking of sorcery and fornication in 2 Kgs 9:22; Isa 47:9; Nah 3:4]; theft is mentioned only here in Revelation). The plagues seem to be designed to bring people to repentance, similar to Wis 12:10: "you carried out your sentence by stages to give them room for repentance" (cf. Wis 12:20). But that has not occurred.

Revelation pauses in the midst of the final sequence of plagues to comment on the inability of humanity to understand and repent (16:9, 11, 21; cf. Mark 4:11-12). Humanity longs for release, but does not find it. It is as if humanity is brought face to face with the full horror of the world it has created and is not allowed to escape the consequences of its actions. That leads to darkness, disfigurement, and the unbalancing of the natural world. The death and destruction that have taken place up to this point constitute the first woe. The absence of any mention of the third woe may be an indication that the final consummation is still awaited. The readers stand in the midst of the eschatological drama. It is partly complete, and we are (as it were) offered a preview of the ending. In the midst of the trials and tribulations, we await the climax. All we can do is watch, wait, witness, and not be led astray (cf. Mark 13:9, 33ff.).

Despite all the terrible indications of disintegration, however, people's injustice toward one another still persists. It is as if death and destruction had become an anesthetic, preventing the recognition of the remedy for disorder. It is a seemingly unending forgetfulness, which prevents a change of mind ("metanoia") that can enable the world, and God, to be seen aright and the religion of the beast to be replaced by the way of the Lamb. At the top of the list of injustices people continue in is idolatry, accompanied by evil deeds that exhibit disorder. We shall be shown the ultimate demonstration of murder, idolatry, and robbery in Babylon's cruel regime (chaps. 17–18). Amid the growing chaos, life goes on as before with no sense on humanity's part that anything is amiss with the way in which they are conducting themselves:

They were eating and drinking, and marrying and being given in marriage, until the day Noah entered the ark, and the flood came and destroyed all of them. Likewise, just as it was in the days of Lot: they were eating and drinking, buying and selling, planting and building, but on the day that Lot left Sodom, it rained fire and sulphur from heaven and destroyed all of them—it will be like that on the day the Son of Man is revealed. On that day, anyone on the housetop who has belongings in the house must not come down to take them away; and likewise anyone in the field must not turn back. Remember Lot's wife. Those who try to make their life secure will lose it, but those who lose their life will keep it. (Luke 17:27-33 NRSV)

REFLECTIONS

1. The opening of the seventh seal causes silence in heaven. The seemingly inevitable process is interrupted, and the pause enables reflection on what is happening, even in heaven. Silence and reflection are appropriate in the midst of the tumult of life. Silence is an appropriate response in the light of this coming of God in wrath. Ludwig Wittgenstein finished a very different book with the words, "What we cannot speak about we must pass over in silence."[231] That is an appropriate warning for any commentator on the book of Revelation. The desire to explain and justify prompts many words, but perhaps silence, awe, fear, and dread are more appropriate responses to moments of apocalyptic insight. If reading Revelation leads to disorientation and bewilderment, then we shall begin to comprehend the moment of apocalypse, such as when

---

231. Ludwig Wittgenstein, *Tractatus Logico-Philosophicus,* trans. D. F. Pears and B. F. McGuiness (London: Routledge, 1974).

the women fled from the tomb in fear when they were confronted by the ultimate apocalyptic moment and words failed them (Mark 16:8).

2. In the sequence of seals and trumpets there emerge scenes even more nightmarish than our worst dreams. John's "nightmare" is the reality of judgment. The fantastic and horrifying description of the torments that await those who are not sealed (9:4) brings to our awareness our deepest, usually unacknowledged, fears, represented by poisonous insects and the disruption of the natural world so that it becomes a threat rather than an accepted, and acceptable, part of our existence, as the bonds of normality are loosened (7:1; 9:14). It is the reverse of that process described in Genesis 1, where (to use the words of Ps 104:9) God has set them their bounds, which they should not pass or turn again to cover the earth. As has been suggested, cosmological disorder is linked with neglect of God's way. To put it in the words of Gen 6:11, "Now the earth was corrupt in God's sight, and the earth was filled with violence" (NRSV). Violence marked the Lamb who was brought to God's throne and prompted the opening of the seals.

The worst fears surface in the gruesome catalogue that issues forth from the trumpet blasts. Locusts are a plague to humanity, and the sting of the scorpion is proverbially threatening. Yet the creatures are girded with weapons of war (9:9), and the threat of the angelic host who had been bound at the Euphrates (9:14) described in military terms. John's vision is of the awfulness and destructive potential of war. Creatures that are already frightening in themselves take on an even more fearsome aspect in John's vision. The full destructive power of nature is set loose as it is transformed into something far more threatening than the occasional plague of locusts or the poisonous sting. In nature and in society, the destructive power consequent to rebellion against God the Creator and the rejection of the coming Messiah leads to the dissolution of order.

Revelation 18–19 evoke a doomsday vision, a glimpse of what ecological disaster might mean. There has been much discussion about threats to the environment. But those of us in the affluent West like our way of life and are unwilling to do much more than make a half-hearted attempt to curb the profligate consumption and destruction of the world that our life-styles entail. Readers are asked whether they wish to side with Babylon, "which destroys the earth" (11:18; 19:2), or with God, whose order provides healing for the nations (22:2).

3. Revelation's grim picture of ecological catastrophe might seem to underline the belief of some that Christianity is not merely world-denying but also uncaring about the cosmos, destined, as it appears to be, for destruction. There are hints in passages like 11:18 and 19:2, however, that the destruction of the earth is not the result of a divine caprice but a consequence of the behavior of humanity. Revelation is about the return to chaos, symbolized by the relaxation of those arrangements that gave the world its order, an order, which the book as a whole demonstrates, is in reality disorder, because it is based on the luxury of Babylon (18:3) and the trade in human souls (18:13).

When New Testament writers, like the author of 1 John, speak of "the form of this world passing away," they are not referring to the imminent winding up of the world and the irruption of a new world from above. Rather, it is the desire and, where at all possible, the implementation of another way of being and behaving that demands an alteration in the nature of things so that they reflect the divine righteousness.

The world is the arena of God's saving purposes, past, present, and future; but the form of the world in its entirety had been demonstrated as being disordered in the light of the Messiah and the rejection of him. The cross points to human folly as well as pointing forward to another type of wisdom. It shows the order of the world and its institutions to be shot through with the disorder that had to be put right before the new age could come in all its fullness. Revelation 20, in the language of apocalyptic, links the dawn of the messianic era with the binding of Satan. The writer of 1 John addresses his readers with, "We are God's children now; what we will be has not yet been revealed. What we do know is this: when he is revealed, we will be like him, for we will see him as he is" (1 John 3:2 NRSV). So in saying that early Christianity was world-denying, we should be clear that it was not because Christians believed that the end of the world was imminent through some cosmic disintegration. Rather, its arrangements would be changed. Meanwhile, in the midst of disorder, it is important not to be conformed to the world as it is.

❖   ❖   ❖   ❖

EXCURSUS: THE TRIBULATIONS OF THE MESSIANIC AGE[232]

The occurrence of terrible calamities on earth before the coming of the messianic kingdom was a widely held belief and is well illustrated in the Old Testament deutero-canonical/apocryphal book 2 Esdras:

"And if the place where you are standing is greatly shaken while the voice is speaking, do not be terrified; because the word concerns the end, and the foundations of the earth will understand that the speech concerns them. They will tremble and be shaken, for they know that their end must be changed."

When I heard this, I got to my feet and listened; a voice was speaking, and its sound was like the sound of mighty waters. It said, "The days are coming when I draw near to visit the inhabitants of the earth, and when I require from the doers of iniquity the penalty of their iniquity, and when the humiliation of Zion is complete. When the seal is placed upon the age that is about to pass away, then I will show these signs: the books shall be opened before the face of the firmament, and all shall see my judgment together. Children a year old shall speak with their voices, and pregnant women shall give birth to premature children at three and four months, and these shall live and leap about. Sown places shall suddenly appear unsown, and full storehouses shall suddenly be found to be empty; the trumpet shall sound aloud, and when all hear it, they shall suddenly be terrified. At that time friends shall make war on friends like enemies, the earth and those who inhabit it shall be terrified, and the springs of the fountains shall stand still so that for three hours they shall not flow." (2 Esdr 6:14-24 NRSV)

"Now concerning the signs: Behold, the days are coming when those who dwell on earth shall be seized with great terror, and the way of truth shall be hidden, and the land shall be barren of faith, and unrighteousness shall be increased beyond what you yourself see, and beyond what you heard of formerly. And the land which you now see ruling shall be waste and untrodden, and men shall see it desolate. But if the Most High grants that you live, you shall see it thrown into confusion after the third period;

and the sun shall suddenly shine forth at night,
and the moon during the day.
Blood shall drip from wood,
and the stone shall utter its voice;
the peoples shall be troubled,
and the stars shall fall.

---

232. Further parallels in H. L. Strack and P. Billerbeck, *Kommentar zum NT aus Talmud und Midrasch* (Munich: Beck, 1924) 4:977ff.

Excursus: The Tribulations of the Messianic Age

And one shall reign whom those who dwell on earth do not expect, and the birds shall fly away together; and the sea of Sodom shall cast up fish; and one whom the many do not know shall make his voice heard by night, and all shall hear his voice. There shall be chaos also in many places, and fire shall often break out, and the wild beasts shall roam beyond their haunts, and menstruous women shall bring forth monsters. And salt waters shall be found in the sweet, and all friends shall conquer one another; then shall reason hide itself, and wisdom shall withdraw into its chamber, and it shall be sought by many but shall not be found, and unrighteousness and unrestraint shall increase on earth. And one country shall ask its neighbor, 'Has righteousness, or anyone who does right, passed through you?' And it will answer, 'No.' And at that time men shall hope but not obtain; they shall labor but their ways shall not prosper."[233]

In a similar vein, the Syriac *Apocalypse of Baruch* 25–27 treats the notion of calamities befalling earth before the coming of the kingdom of the Messiah, though with the added similarity of the clear periodization of the messianic woes, as in Revelation, and earlier *Jubilees* evokes the grim circumstances of the end of the age:

When horror seizes the inhabitants of earth, and they fall into many tribulations and further, they fall into great torments. And it will happen that they will say in their thoughts because of their great tribulations, "The Mighty One does not anymore remember the earth"; It will happen when they lose hope, that the time will awake. . . .

That time will be divided into twelve parts, and each part has been preserved for that for which it was appointed. In the first part: the beginning of commotions. In the second part: the slaughtering of the great. In the third part: the fall of many into death. In the fourth part: the drawing of the sword. In the fifth part: famine and the withholding of rain. In the sixth part: earthquakes and terrors. In the eighth part: a multitude of ghosts and the appearances of demons. In the ninth part: the fall of fire. In the tenth part: rape and much violence. In the eleventh part: injustice and unchastity. In the *twelfth* part: disorder and a mixture of all that has been before. These parts of that time will be preserved and will be mixed, one with another, and they will minister to each other.[234]

And in those days if a man will live a jubilee and a half, they will say about him, "He prolonged his life, but the majority of his days were suffering and affliction. And there was no peace, because plague (came) upon plague, and wound upon wound, and affliction upon affliction, and evil report upon evil report, and sickness upon sickness, and every evil judgment of this sort one with another: sickness, and downfall, and sleet, and hail, and frost, and fever, and chills, and stupor, and famine, and death, and sword, and captivity, and all plagues, and suffering." And all of this will come in the evil generation which sins in the land. Pollution and fornication and contamination and abomination are their deeds.[235]

---

233. 4 Ezra 5:1-13.
234. 2 (Syriac Apocalypse of) Baruch 25:1–27:14, trans. A. F. J. Klijn, in Charlesworth, vol. 1 of *The Old Testament Pseudepigrapha*.
235. *Jub.* 23:12-14, trans. O. S. Wintermute, in *The Old Testament Pseudepigrapha*, vol. 2, ed. J. H. Charlesworth (New York: Doubleday, 1985).

REVELATION 10:1-11

THE VISION OF THE STRONG ANGEL AND THE COMMAND TO PROPHESY

COMMENTARY

In the middle of the seemingly inexorable process of judgment, once more interrupting a sequence of seven at the penultimate, there are two complementary visions: one an account of a call to John to prophesy (chap. 10), and the other an account of the witness of two figures who prophesy for a time before being killed by the beast from the abyss (chap. 11). The deaths of these prophets, who are vindicated after their corpses have lain in the street, provokes enormous rejoicing among the world's inhabitants. Their vindication, parallel to that of the Lamb, provokes cataclysm and marks the assertion of the transfer of sovereignty to God and the Messiah.

10:1-2. The descents from heaven to earth continue. A mighty angel, "wrapped in a cloud, with a rainbow over his head," straddles sea and land (cf. 10:5; see also 7:2, 12, 18; 14:7). The physical destruction described in the preceding chapter is replaced by a different kind of devastation, that of the prophetic word. The "mighty angel" echoes the stronger one who is greater than John the Baptist (Mark 1:7) and who plunders the strong man's kingdom (Mark 3:27)

The angel descends from heaven (cf. 18:1; 20:1) clothed with cloud (cf. 12:1), something that accompanies Christ (1:7; cf. 11:12; 14:14-15; Mark 13:26; 1 Thess 4:17). The rainbow, which had been around the throne in 4:3, now surrounds this angel's head; his face, "like the sun," resembles that of Christ in 1:16 (cf. 12:1; Matt 17:2). His feet are like pillars of fire (cf. 1:15), and in his hand he holds an open scroll. There is some similarity between this chapter and 5:2, in which a mighty angel appears. In 5:1, as well, the one seated on the throne has a "scroll" (the Greek there is βιβλίον [*biblion*], as compared with βιβλαρίδιον [*biblaridion*] in 10:2, though the papyrus 𝔓47 and the *Textus Receptus* use *biblion*, making the link more explicit). Here, however, in contrast to chap. 5, the scroll is open, as the reader would expect, in the light of the Lamb's having opened the seals earlier in the vision. There are some connections between Revelation 4–5 and 10 with Ezekiel (here with Ezek 2:10; 3:3) as well.

10:3-4. The angel's "great shout" (v. 3; cf. 7:2; 14:15; 18:2; 19:17; Jer 25:30; Matt 27:50; Mark 5:7) is like a lion's roar (cf. 13:2; Amos 3:8). It prompts a response from the seven thunders (cf. the sevenfold voice of the Lord in Ps 29:3ff.; note also John 12:29, where the divine voice is mistaken for thunder). Elsewhere in Revelation, thunder accompanies the appearance of God (e.g., 4:5; cf. Exod 19:16) and the accomplishment of the judgment of God (11:19; 16:18). John is about to write down what the seven thunders have spoken in obedience to the command to "write what you have seen" (1:19 NRSV), but a voice from heaven (cf. 11:12; 12:10; 14:2; 18:4) commands him to "seal up" what they have said and not write it down (cf. 22:10; Dan 8:26; 12:4, 9). Like the contents of the sealed scroll in chap. 5, what the seven thunders said must remain a mystery and, thus, is to form no part of this book of prophecy, which is very much a public rather than an esoteric text (22:10). The word "mystery" is rare in Revelation, usually linked with explanations (1:20; 17:7; cf. 17:5; Rom 11:25; 1 Cor 15:51). The mystery of God is what is contained in John's prophecy (cf. 17:17). This apocalyptic mystery is not for some religious elite; rather, it is a public matter (14:6), as was the case for Paul (1 Cor 2:6-7; Eph 3:9-10; Col 1:26), who proclaimed the ultimate apocalyptic mystery in the word of the cross. What the content of the utterance of the seven thunders might have been can only be guessed.

10:5-7. To describe an oath by the God of earth and heaven, John uses words from Dan 12:7, adding a reference to God as Creator, based on Exod 20:11 (cf. Ps 146:6; Acts 4:24). The content of the oath is that "there will be no more delay." The word used for "delay" (χρόνος *chronos*, "time") is used also at 2:21; 6:11; and 20:3 having the sense of a duration of time (rather than καιρός *kairos*, a "particular, critical moment"; cf. Mark 1:15). The mystery of God will be fulfilled when the seventh trumpet is blown (10:7), marking 11:15 as a signal moment in the narrative.

The angel reveals that the mystery is moving to its climax. God had proclaimed that this would happen by means of his servants, the prophets (v. 7; cf. Jer 7:25; Dan 9:6; Amos 3:7; Zech 1:6), about whom the next vision speaks (11:10, 18) and among whom John sees himself (22:9). Whether John refers only to prophets contemporary to him or whether he includes those like Ezekiel, Daniel, and Amos, whose words are so often the vehicles of John's own prophecy in the book, is unclear. Nevertheless, as we have seen, John makes no attempt to refer to their works directly as authoritative texts, even if they do function as the language for his prophecy. John speaks of the proclamation of these words of judgment as "evangelizing" (εὐηγγέλισεν *euēngelisen*; NRSV and NIV, "announced"), a word that is used also in 14:6 of the eternal gospel proclaimed by the angel.

10:8-11. John is now commanded by the voice from heaven, which had spoken to him before (v. 4), to take the scroll from the angel. John asks that the book be given to him, and the angel commands him to take the scroll. In being made to take it, he is not merely a passive, perhaps even reluctant, recipient of the scroll's contents (prophets often find that they can do no other, Jer 20:8; Amos 3:8; cf. 1 Cor 9:16). In the spirit of Ezekiel, John takes the scroll and, having been told to do so, devours it (cf. Ezek 2:8; 3:1ff.):

But you, mortal, hear what I say to you; do not be rebellious like that rebellious house; open your mouth and eat what I give you. I looked, and a hand was stretched out to me, and a written scroll was in it. He spread it before me; it had writing on the front and on the back, and written on it were words of lamentation and mourning and woe.

He said to me, O mortal, eat what is offered to you; eat this scroll, and go, speak to the house of Israel. So I opened my mouth, and he gave me the scroll to eat. He said to me, Mortal, eat this scroll that I give you and fill your stomach with it. Then I ate it; and in my mouth it was as sweet as honey. (Ezek 2:8–3:3 NRSV)

"Go, take the scroll that is open in the hand of the angel who is standing on the sea and on the land." So I went to the angel and told him to give me the little scroll; and he said to me, "Take it, and eat; it will be bitter to your stomach, but sweet as honey in your mouth." So I took the little scroll from the hand of the angel and ate it; it was sweet as honey in my mouth, but when I had eaten it, my stomach was made bitter. Then they said to me, "You must prophesy again about many peoples and nations and languages and kings." (Rev 10:8-11 NRSV)

Having eaten the scroll, John is commissioned to prophesy to the nations *again* (v. 11), perhaps a reminder of the prophetic character of what has been contained earlier in the book. John finds the scroll to have a bitter as well as a sweet taste (v. 9), a reflection of the words of his prophecy and their awesome effects (cf. 8:11; Ezekiel's words, too, are words of lamentation and woe). Indeed, John and his prophetic companions find themselves experiencing the times of tribulation in persecution by the beast (11:7; 16:6; 18:24), the terrible effect of which is focused in this exquisitely piercing moment of commissioning. The temporary sweetness of the scroll's message cannot disguise the necessity of a word of judgment, which has to proceed from the prophet's mouth (v. 11; cf. 1:16; 2:16; 11:5; 19:15) and which thereby places the prophet at odds with other people, as Jeremiah understood well (Jer 15:10ff.).

There is another allusion to the experience of prophetic inspiration by means of the consumption, in this case, of drink, in a passage roughly contemporary with Revelation, 4 Ezra 14:38:

"Ezra, open your mouth and drink what I give you. I opened my mouth and was handed a cup full of what seemed like water, except that its colour was the colour of fire. I took it and drank and, as soon as I did so, understanding welled up in my mind."[236]

236. Metzger, 4 Ezra 14:38.

John's commission comes from "them" (v. 11, perhaps the voice from heaven and the strong angel). He is told that he must prophesy again about "many peoples and nations and languages and kings" (cf. Jer 25:30; Gal 1:15). John's prophecy is not mere words. It is the mystery of the One who is past, present, and future (v. 7; cf. 4:8), the promulgation of whose secrets, in the words of this book, are not just about overthrow and construction but effect judgment on a civilization constructed on unjust, and therefore shaky, foundations (cf. 17:3). (See Reflections at 11:1-19.)

REVELATION 11:1-19
THE TWO WITNESSES

COMMENTARY

11:1-2. The scene changes with the commissioning in 10:11, and the language moves from Jeremiah's influence back to Ezekiel's (esp. Ezek 40:3; cf. Zech 2:1). John is given a measuring rod, something that will be used once more when an angel measures the new Jerusalem (21:15; cf. 2:27; 12:5). John is once again no mere spectator of the vision but himself measures the temple of God, the altar, and the worshipers. The temple is probably to be distinguished from that in v. 19, God's temple in heaven. Attempts to relate the incident to specific events in the Second Temple period, particularly during the siege of Jerusalem by the Romans in 66–70 CE, have failed to carry conviction, though one cannot rule out the way in which a comparatively insignificant incident might have been taken up and altered in the visionary imagination.[237] John is given strict instructions not to measure the outer part of the temple. This is because it has been given over to the nations, who will trample upon the holy city for forty-two months (cf. Dan 8:14, where the trampling goes on for 2,300 days; see also Luke 21:24). The time span suggests a finite period (v. 3). The reason for measuring and not measuring is unstated. In Ezek 43:10-11, the temple measurement appears to be a blueprint for a restored Jerusalem.[238] The reference to the nations in v. 2 suggests that only what is measured belongs to God, at least for the moment. John's vision is of a space for God, restricted in scope, the outer margins of which do not belong, at least in the short term, to God and are not, therefore, to be measured. No such restriction will apply in Rev 21:15.

11:3-7. The witnesses prophesy (v. 3; cf. 1:5; 2:13; 3:14; 17:6) and thus offer exemplars of what John has been commanded to do (10:11). They prophesy for the duration of the nations' occupation. They are clothed in sackcloth (cf. 6:12; Isa 20:2; 22:12; 37:1), unlike the white robes of the multitude (7:14) and the angel (10:1). The further description of the witnesses as "olive trees" and "lampstands" is inspired by language from Zech 4:3, 11ff., where these terms are used to describe the priestly and royal messiahs. Lampstands are used in 1:12-13, 20 and 2:1 to symbolize the seven churches, suggesting that there is a role of prophecy and witness for the churches, too. These two witnesses are given authority to prophesy as they stand before the Lord of the earth (v. 4). They are protected from harm, but only for the time it takes to complete their testimony (v. 5). Fire from their mouths destroys their enemies (vv. 5-6; cf. 19:15; 2 Sam 22:9; 2 Kgs 1:10; Isa 11:4; Jer 5:14; 2 Thess 2:8). They have the same power that Elijah (v. 6; cf. 1 Kgs 17:1) and Moses had (v. 6; cf. Exod 7:17ff.; and the similarities with the Egyptian plagues in 8:8).

The activity of the two witnesses is variously described as testimony and prophecy (11:6-7; cf. 11:3). This is brought to an end when they are killed by the beast who comes up from the abyss (cf. 9:11; 13:2; see also Dan 7:3, where the beast emerges from the sea), the first reference to that terrible specter, which will dominate the second half of John's vision. The beast's oppressive actions (cf. Dan 7:21), culminating in the witnesses' death, brings to an end their prophetic activity. Conquest by the beast cannot overcome that true "conquest," inspired by the Lamb, however, which ends in martyrdom (12:11; cf. 5:5). The beast's power cannot last long. Michael and his angels will triumph over the host of Satan, the source of the beast's power (12:7; cf. 13:4).

11:8-10. The bodies of the dead witnesses will suffer the ultimate indignity of being left

---
237. Examples of this may be found in Erdman, *Blake*.
238. See J. Maier, *The Temple Scroll* (Sheffield: Sheffield Academic Press, 1982).

on the open street of the great city (v. 8)—a very public place (cf. Matt 6:5; Luke 10:10; 13:26), a place where life is unpredictable and the site of little protection for the injured and vulnerable (Mark 6:56; Luke 14:21). The place where they had testified is "prophetically called" Sodom and Egypt. It is a place of rebellion and persecution, and is linked with the place where "their Lord was crucified" (v. 8, the only reference to the means of Christ's death in the book). In the light of vv. 1-2, one might link v. 8's "great city" with Jerusalem, but this is visionary material, so precise identity is inevitably vague. Jerusalem becomes one among several places that have rejected God's envoys (Matt 23:37-38). A link is made between persecution anywhere and any act of witness for the Lamb or against the beast, the latter rooted in that crucial act of witness and faithfulness in Jerusalem (1:5).

Some of those "peoples and tribes and languages and nations" to whom John was commanded to prophesy now rejoice (cf. John 16:1-2, 20) when they see the corpses lying unburied. "Inhabitants of the earth" is a negative phrase (e.g., 1:7; 2:13; 3:10; 6:10; 8:13; 11:10; 12:9, 12; 13:8, 12, 14; 17:2, 8) suggesting a social as well as a geographical dimension, involvement with and conformity to the world's values. The exchange of gifts suggests celebration that life carries on as normal (cf. Luke 17:27-28), freed from the torment of the witnesses (cf. 9:5).

11:11-12. The resuscitation of the two witnesses, however, comes from God's life-giving Spirit (the phrase "breath of life from God" is used only here; cf. 4:5; 5:6). That action is followed by a summons from a great voice from heaven (v. 12; cf. 10:4; 12:10; 14:13; 19:1), which tells them, "Come up here!" This is the same command that was made of John by the voice "like a trumpet" (4:1; cf. Eph 4:8). The ascent of the witnesses to heaven in a cloud echoes the ascension of their Lord and is a moment when their enemies will see their vindication (and so echoes the parousia, when, according to 1:7b, "every eye will see him,/ even those who pierced him;/ and on his account all the tribes of the earth will wail" [NRSV]; cf. Matt 24:30-31).

11:13. A great earthquake follows their ascent (cf. 6:12; 8:5; 16:18), similar to the one that attended the resurrection of Jesus in Matt 28:2. The reaction to the earthquake here, however, is one of fear as people see the witnesses standing upright (cf. 18:10, 15). No mention is made of repentance here, so we should not assume that the people's giving "glory to the God of heaven" is a positive response to the prophetic witness.[239] We shall see that humanity instead blasphemes God (16:9, 11, 21; cf. 9:21). What we have here is a temporary recognition of God's greatness, such as we find at 6:15ff. (once more following an earthquake). The people have acknowledged that they are experiencing the wrath of God, but have not converted to the ways of God. Indeed, in the paean of praise in v. 18, the heavenly choir asserts that the nations rage.

11:14. At this juncture, the second woe has passed. So between the first and second woes (9:13–11:13) John's vision has concentrated almost entirely on his own involvement in the prophetic mission and a description of the costly witness of the two "lampstands." As we have seen earlier (9:13), the precise moment of the third woe, which "is coming soon," is not mentioned explicitly in the book. The second woe is a significant moment in the apocalypse, which seems to be hinted at in the following verse, when the series of trumpet blasts reaches its climax.

11:15. The seventh trumpet's blast is accompanied by great shouts in heaven. If the modern translations have it right, one can understand why: "The kingdom of the world has become the kingdom of our Lord/ and of his Messiah,/ and he will reign forever and ever" (v. 15). At this point in the vision, the heavenly voices assert the transfer of kingship to God.

We should be careful not to place much weight on that translation, however.[240] The verb γίνομαι (*ginomai*) is widely used in Revelation and is usually translated "is" or "was." Why, then, should we translate it here as "become"? There are two other places (12:10; 16:4) where "become" is the more obvious rendering as well. Of these two, 12:10 is the more important. There the presence of the word ἄρτι (*arti*, "now") makes

---

239. Cf. R. Bauckham, "The Conversion of the Nations," in *The Climax of Prophecy* (Edinburgh: T. & T. Clark, 1992) 238-338.
240. See further G. Mussies, *The Morphology of Koine Greek as Used in the Apocalypse of St. John* (Leiden: E. J. Brill, 1971); and Thompson, *The Book of Revelation*.

the translation "has become" the most natural way of taking the verb in that verse. The verb is used earlier in 11:15 in the sentence "there were loud voices in heaven." So we do well to explore whether a simple past may be the same meaning when it is used in the second half of the verse.

There is another reason to question whether we should translate *ginomai* as "has become." John was quite capable of using the perfect of *ginomai* (he does so in 16:17; 21:6) and of including an adverb (as in 12:10) to make his meaning clear. (The Greek perfect tense expresses completed action with ongoing results.) So we might consider translating the verse as "the kingdom of the world *was* [i.e., belonged to] our Lord's and his Christ's, and he will reign forever." This rendering should be considered, not least because it is theologically appropriate: The kingdom of this world has never belonged to anyone other than God (cf. Ps 10:16). What has happened, however, is that there has been a temporary usurpation of possession, authority, and administration—which is ending. In translating the Greek as an ordinary past tense, the heavenly voice is asserting what always has been the case (cf. 19:6). Perhaps the very assertion itself marks a claim of possession from those who trespassed on, and ignored, the divine dominion (cf. Zech 14:9). It is a divine illocutionary act in which the words bring about the reality on earth that John has already seen to be the case in heaven.

11:16-19. What is said in the second hymn in vv. 17-18 is that God has taken power and reigned. We have a similar translation problem in this verse with the word ἐβασίλευσας (*ebasileusas*). This follows a perfect tense and is widely taken as an inceptive aorist "you have . . . begun to reign" (so NRSV). This translation is based on the context. It is possible to render the Greek as a present: "you have taken power, and are king"; but the aorist in this verse, however, could be seen as a consequence of the taking of power *with the result that* God reigned. The words of such psalms as 47:8[46:9]; 96:10; and 99:1 add weight to the translation "the Lord has become king."

In vv. 15 and 17, readers hear an assertion of the divine reign (see also 12:7). It is as if hitherto that had been in doubt and the vision had allowed John to see that this doubt had been dispelled. What accompanies the assertion of divine sovereignty, however, is reaction and rebellion. This is a theme of Psalm 2, used several times in Revelation, which gives an account of a rebellion against the new king. A change of rulers results in a period of instability and disorder as the nations conspire against the Lord's anointed one. Their plot to shake off the yoke of God's dominion and the control of God's anointed one is thwarted by the divine proclamation reasserting the inheritance of the nations for the Messiah. Similar motifs are found elsewhere in Scripture (e.g., Ps 46:6; Isa 17:12ff.). Such a pattern (of change of rulers followed by chaos) is found also in Revelation, though here with a sense that it is part of the deliberate loosening of cultural and ecological constraints. The exaltation of the Lamb had led to a change of sovereignty in both the divine (cf. 12:7) and the human realms; the dominion of the beast and Babylon and the culture they represented was doomed. God's or Christ's rule would take time to establish (cf. 1 Cor 15:25). Transfer of sovereignty brings with it instability and chaos. The plagues of the middle chapters, then, may be understood as the process whereby the king's power and authority were established. It was only then that the benefits of the new reign could be felt, when all that stood in the way of the new rule had been put aside.

The assertion of divine sovereignty prompts further worship (v. 16), which we have not heard since 7:12 and will not hear again until 15:3 and then 19:4 and the rejoicing over Babylon's destruction. The hymn of praise recalls themes from earlier hymns (e.g., 1:8; 4:8; cf. 16:7, 14), though its beginning is unique. Thanks are offered to God, who was and is ("is to come" is omitted in most ancient versions; its omission in this hymn concentrates attention on the significance of the present rather than on what is still to come).

The nations' angry response (v. 18) is in the face of the imminent climax of God's wrath (15:1) and evokes Ps 2:5, a psalm that will be in the background on several occasions in the following chapters (e.g., 12:5; 14:1; 16:14; 17:18; 19:15, 19). The exercise of divine wrath will bring a reward for God's servants (cf. 19:2). "Reward" (μισθός *misthos*) is not a frequently used word in Revelation; the only other reference is in 22:12 (cf. Matt 5:12; 6:1-2; 10:41).

Assuming that the conjunction "and" is to be included after the word "saints" (v. 18), we have here a list of those who will be rewarded, which includes the saints and those who fear God. One wonders whether that extends to the people who "were terrified and gave glory to the God of heaven" after the witnesses' ascension or to those outside the ambit of the communities who fear God by not worshiping the beast (cf. Ps 115:13). Does it include those who respond to the proclamation of the eternal gospel (14:7; cf. 15:4; 19:5) and do not blaspheme the name of God (16:9)? Readers of Revelation are often left with this kind of tantalizing question. The temptation to tie up the loose ends of this allusive text by exegetical ingenuity are enormous. But the text remains, obstinately and uncompromisingly, resistant to our attempts to impose harmony and tidiness upon it.

There is judgment on those who destroy the earth (v. 18), expanded later in 19:2 by the reference to Babylon as having "corrupted the earth with her fornication" (NRSV). The destruction of the earth echoes the assessment of antediluvian humanity: "now the earth was corrupt [lit., "was destroyed" (διαφθείρω *diaphtheirō*)] in God's sight . . . and was filled with violence." Perhaps John's visionary imagination was fueled, as well, by knowledge of the Enochic myth of the angelic corruption of the world.

The emphasis on the just reward of God is followed by a first vision of the temple of God in heaven (cf. 15:5) and the ark of the covenant (referred to only here in Revelation; cf. 1 Kgs 8:6), accompanied by the marks of the theophany at Sinai (Exod 19:16; cf. the hail in Exod 9:24), which accompanied the giving of the Sinaitic covenant. It is a sign of the norms of judgment rooted in the covenant, the keeping of which led to blessing and the neglect of which to a curse (Deuteronomy 28–30).

❖   ❖   ❖   ❖

EXCURSUS: THE FALL IN *1 ENOCH*

The Apocalypse of Enoch has fascinated biblical scholars because of its similarities with parts of the New Testament. The myth of the fallen angels, the sons of heaven, appears in *1 Enoch* 6ff., which is an extended version of the allusive reference in Gen 6:4.[241] These fallen angels have sexual intercourse with women, and "they teach [humans] charms and spells and showed to them the cutting of roots and trees" and how to make swords, daggers, shields, and breastplates. The human women become pregnant and give birth to giants, who become a drain on human resources. Eventually, the giants turn against humanity and the created universe. In the face of the destruction, humans cry out, and their voices reach heaven. The angels Michael and Gabriel look down from heaven and see the blood that is being shed on the earth and bring the plight of humankind before the Most High (*1 Enoch* 6:1–9:5). God's response is to warn that the whole earth will be destroyed by a deluge before the earth, which the Watchers have ruined (*1 Enoch* 10:7), can be restored.

Enoch then appears on the boundary between angels and humans. He has access to divine secrets, which enable him to have an authentic perspective on the world and God's purposes for it (*1 Enoch* 12:1). He is the scribe of righteousness and mediates between God and the Watchers, who seek Enoch's assistance in pleading for God's forgiveness. In *1 Enoch,* there is a stress on misappropriated wisdom and the cosmic

---

241. On the importance of this myth in Second Temple Judaism, see M. Barker, *The Older Testament* (London: SPCK, 1987).

as well as the individual effects of it. The writer comments ominously: "And the world was changed. And there was great impiety and much fornication and they went astray and all their ways became corrupt." It is Enoch, a figure, like John, on the margins of society, who has wisdom and can intercede with God and reflect the message of divine judgment on a fallen world.

REFLECTIONS

Despite the universal and indiscriminate effects of the judgment as the seals are opened the vision does not ignore the reactions of particular groups. The opening of the fifth seal focuses on the martyrs (6:9). The cry for vindication and vengeance is an understandable one.[242] This honest expression of desire lies deep within those who have been victimized. God's response to their cries is to give comfort and an exhortation to patience. The witness (and death) of others has to take place first. This may seem at first sight rather a strange response. Yet, it is a reminder of the important task of witnessing. That cannot be bypassed; it must go ahead. Humanity has to be given the opportunity to listen and see things differently, even if at the same time there is despair of humanity's responding to the prophets in any way except by killing them. Indeed, in the midst of the crisis provoked by the proclamation of an eternal gospel, the prophets need to interpret the *dis*ease and disorder of the world. In the face of the continued deferral of the climax of the promise at the end of the first two sequences of sevens (8:1, 15), when the expected fulfillment does not quite materialize, humanity needs to take full advantage of the opportunity offered.

1. In Revelation 10–11, as in 1:19, there is a direct call to participate as a prophet rather than merely be a passive spectator. John's commission comes in a context of much urgency. Like the Lamb in chap. 5, the prophet takes the scroll and shares in the same kind of activity. Prophecy is no longer merely an uttering of oracles but involves the whole of life. The message is internalized (10:9) and forms part of the very being of the prophet. The prophetic role encompasses every aspect of life (and death), something experienced by all true prophets of God. Prophets could expect a life of witness, suffering, and death. Chapter 11 is an important reminder that the vast eschatological drama unfolding before John's visionary gaze leaves neither him nor his audience as passive spectators, uninvolved or unaffected. In the midst of superhuman forces, humans have a prophetic role—indeed, this is the role of the church as a whole. This prophetic vocation takes on a new dimension of urgency when one recognizes that, in reality, the holy community itself is riddled with compromise with Babylon, as the letters to the angels of the churches indicate.[243]

2. Resistance, dissent, and non-conformity are recurring themes of this commentary. They trip from the lips or drip from the pen and easily mask the enormous psychological and social cost that resistance engenders. The story of non-conformity, from the anguished agony of Jeremiah to contemporary prisoners of conscience, frequently involves enormous personal expense. A spirituality of resistance involves vigilance as well, lest, imperceptibly, non-conformity slip into an attitude of making a virtue out of difference. When resistance becomes a hardened habit of life, it can cause one's

---

242. See J. Kerrigan, *Revenge Tragedy: Aeschylus to Armageddon* (London: Oxford University Press, 1996).
243. There are important comments relating to this theme in A. Y. Collins, "The Political Perspective of the Revelation to John," *Cosmology and Eschatology in Jewish and Christian Apocalypticism* (Leiden: E. J. Brill, 1996) 198ff.

humanity to shrivel. To guard against this one needs the constant mutual support and correction that a network of solidarity can bring and critical reflection on one's position in the light of the consistent refusal of texts like Revelation to offer any consolation of certainty and self-righteousness. Indeed, Revelation and texts like 4 Ezra and the Gospel of Matthew hardly satisfy the lust for certainty and the self-satisfaction of an elect group, nor do they offer security to the readers. Arguably, they are among the least assuring texts of the first century CE.

3. A common temptation of religious people who claim to be prophets is to speak at a level of generality that ignores the specificity of context and situation. Christian speakers are too often quick with a general comment, manifesting a vagueness that floats over a situation at a sufficiently uncontroversial and unthreatening level. This ignores one of the major elements of prophecy, the necessity of commenting on specific matters, brilliantly summarized by Blake:

> Prophets, in the modern sense of the word, have never existed. Jonah was no prophet in the modern sense, for his prophecy of Nineveh failed. Every honest man is a Prophet; he utters his opinion both of private & public matters. Thus: If you go on So, the result is So. He never says, such a thing shall happen let you do what you will. A Prophet is a seer, not an Arbitrary Dictator.[244]

Blake frequently criticized abstractions or grand theories and attended to "minute particulars." It is a healthy sign that contemporary Christians are concerned with the debt of developing nations, threats to the environment, and the arms trade. But we need to guard against being so general in our concerns that we fail to engage specific concerns and, more important, miss the "angel at our door."[245]

---

244. William Blake, Annotations to "An Apology for the Bible in a Series of Letters Addressed to Thomas Paine by R. Watson, D.D., F.R.S.," in Keynes, *Blake*, 392.
245. William Blake, "Holy Thursday," in Keynes, *Blake*.

REVELATION 12:1-18

SIGNS IN HEAVEN: THE WOMAN AND THE DRAGON

COMMENTARY

Although the themes of persecution and vindication pick up where they left off in the vision of the two witnesses, the beginning of chap. 12 is one of the most abrupt transitions in Revelation. Two visions occur in this chapter: a woman pursued by a dragon and the heavenly war between the hosts of the angel Michael and Satan. This leads to the latter's ejection from heaven, paving the way for an immediate threat to the world's inhabitants.

12:1-2. John speaks of the appearance of a great sign in heaven, a pregnant woman "clothed with the sun" (cf. the angel in 10:1), with "the moon under her feet" (cf. 6:12; 8:12; 21:23) and a golden crown (cf. 14:14) with twelve stars on her head (cf. 1:16). She is crying out in labor pains (cf. Isa 66:7). She may be contrasted with Babylon in 17:4, who is clothed in purple and adorned with gold and precious stones. She is in "agony" or "torment" (βασανίζω *basanizō*), the word used to describe the experience of the inhabitants of the world as the judgment comes (9:5; 14:10-11; 18:7, 10, 15; cf. Luke 21:23). Thus she is not immune from that experience. Elsewhere in the NT, childbirth is used as a metaphor for the birth of the reign of God (Matt 24:8; Mark 13:8; 1 Thess 5:3). Paul uses the metaphor of childbirth to describe creation as it awaits its future glory: "We know that the whole creation has been groaning in labor pains until now; and not only the creation, but we ourselves, who have the first fruits of the Spirit, groan inwardly while we wait for adoption, the redemption of our bodies" (Rom 8:22 NRSV).

12:3-6. Another sign in heaven appears alongside the first (v. 3), a great dragon, whose identity is explained in v. 9 and whose effects on earth are envisioned in 13:1ff. (cf. 20:2). The dragon's appearance is "fiery" (cf. 6:4), and its seven heads, ten horns, and seven diadems resemble the beast in 13:1 (cf. 5:6; 19:12; Dan 7:7). Its tail (cf. 9:10) sweeps one-third of the stars of heaven to earth (cf. 6:13; 8:12; Dan 8:10). The dragon stands in the woman's presence, echoing language used of the Lamb and the great multitude that stand in God's presence. But the dragon is a lurking, threatening presence (v. 4; cf. Gen 4:7), because it intends to devour the woman's child as soon as it is born. She gives birth to a male child, "who is to rule the nations with a rod of iron" (v. 5; cf. 2:27; 7:17; 19:15; Ps 2:9).[246] The child is "snatched away and taken to God" (the verb ἁρπάζω [*harpazō*] is used elsewhere of being "snatched up" to heaven; see 2 Cor 12:2, 4; 1 Thess 4:17; cf. Acts 8:39; Wis 4:11).

The woman flees into the desert ("wilderness," NRSV), the place where John will later be taken to see Babylon (17:3). Just as in chap. 17, where the desert gives John a different perspective, so here, too, the desert should not be seen as a harsh and forbidding place. It is the place that God has prepared for the woman, where she will be nourished (v. 6). As the Gospels indicate, the desert is the place where the voice cries out and the Messiah emerges, on the very margins of life (Matt 3:3ff.).[247] It is unclear who will take care of the woman (if it is angels, then this is a parallel to the care Jesus received during his trial in the desert, according to Mark 1:13). The period of her nurture is 1,260 days, roughly the same amount of time the nations will "trample over the holy city" in 11:2 (1,260

---

246. This myth is found in a similar form in the gnostic *Apocalypse of Adam* from the Nag Hammadi texts. See J. M. Robinson, *The Nag Hammadi Library* (Leiden: E. J. Brill, 1977) 260-61.
247. On the role of the desert in early monasticism, see P. Brown, *The Body and Society* (London: Faber, 1991).

days are roughly equivalent to 42 months). The situation of the woman contrasts with that of the dragon, which will have no place in heaven (12:8, 14). The woman's flight is reminiscent of that of the parents of Jesus when they fled to Egypt with the infant Jesus (Matt 2:13), to a place "prepared" by God in the prophetic scriptures (Matt 2:15). Another parallel of this woman is Hagar, who found relief in the wilderness after being ill treated by Sarah (Gen 16:7) and rejected by Abraham (Gen 21:14). Even in a situation of exclusion, there is succor for Hagar (Gen 16:7; 21:19).

12:7. Juxtaposed with this vision is the mention, but not description, of a war in heaven.[248] Elsewhere in Revelation, war consists of the beast's persecuting God's people (11:7; 12:17; 13:7) and the final battle (16:14; 19:19; 20:8). This war, though waged in heaven, will have enormous significance for humankind. Michael leads the fight against the dragon (cf. 19:11ff.). This is the only reference to the archangel Michael in Revelation (elsewhere in the NT only at Jude 9, also in the context of a struggle with Satan). Michael is the angelic protector of the people of God (Dan 12:1), their advocate in heaven (cf. Rom 8:34, where that role is assumed by the ascended Christ; see also 1 John 2:1).

12:8-9. These verses suggest an assault from the devil, in line with the active pursuit of the interests of the beast in Revelation, but the dragon and "his angels" are defeated. It is worth noting that, while the immediate environs of God's presence may be one of perfection, no place this side of the new Jerusalem is immune from the struggle with the forces of darkness (cf. Eph 6:10). The dragon is cast out, and accompanies the stars, the fiery mountain and the hail that fell to earth (8:7).

The throwing down of Satan is a theme hinted at elsewhere in the New Testament (see Luke 10:18), but is particularly important in John 12:31. There the struggle is focused on the inner turmoil of Jesus, and the earthly presence of Satan is acted out in the person of Judas (John 13:2, 27). The apocalyptic moment comes abruptly and is described without any of the usual elements of cosmic upheaval. In John 12:27-36, Jesus appears to be in a state of inner conflict and asserts: "Now is the judgment of this world; now the ruler of this world will be driven out" (John 12:31 NRSV). There is a link with the cross (e.g., 12:33; cf. 13:1; 17:1), but the emphatic νῦν (*nyn*, "now") in John 12:31 suggests that the triumph is not solely focused on the cross. Indeed, according to John 3:19, the eschatological judgment has already been brought into being by the coming of the Son into the world.

The identity of the dragon is made quite clear, and the link with Gen 3:1, 14 is made explicit. The role of deceiver has been alluded to briefly in the description of Jezebel, the false prophet, in 2:20. There a church was threatened with deceit (cf. Matt 24:4-5, 11, 24); here it is the whole world (cf. 13:14; 18:23; 19:20; 20:3, 8, 10). Being led astray, particularly in a time of crisis (see Matt 24:5, 11, 24; 1 John 2:26), is an ever-present threat. False prophecy was always a problem within the Bible (Deuteronomy 13; 18; and Jeremiah 23 are obvious examples). As we shall see in Revelation 13, that deceit is found in the fascination with, and worship of, the beast. At the end of v. 9, John repeats the reference to Satan's being cast out but adds that his destination is earth.

12:10. A voice is heard in heaven (cf. 10:4; 11:12; 14:2; 18:4; 19:1). The emphatic "now" (cf. 14:13; John 12:31) stresses the significance of the moment that "has come" (see the Commentary on 11:15). As compared with 4:11 and earlier hymns to God and the Lamb, this hymn (and the related passage in 11:15) includes a reference to the kingdom and salvation (cf. 7:10) The kingdom is now seen to belong to God and the rule to God's Messiah (cf. Dan 7:14; Matt 28:18). The kingdom is closely related to Satan's ejection from heaven. Satan is called "an accuser of our comrades" who accuses them "day and night before our God," contrasting with the day-and-night praise of the elders (4:8; cf. 7:15; 14:11). This verse reflects an ancient understanding of Satan as a heavenly prosecutor in passages like Job 1:9ff. and Zech 3:1, another reminder that heaven, without its catharsis, is not without threat or conflict (cf. 15:2ff.). In the Gospels, Satan has a testing role, but the Pauline Epistles offer a picture of Satan as lord of a realm "outside" that of Christ (1 Cor 5:5; 2 Cor 4:4; 1 Tim 1:20)

---

248. See Bauckham, *The Climax of Prophecy*, 210-37.

and as a constant threat to Paul (2 Cor 2:11; 12:7; 1 Thess 2:18). For Paul, Satan can at times *appear* to be on the side of good (2 Cor 11:14).

12:11. The obstacle to access to God is removed, and salvation may be enjoyed by those who have "conquered" by the blood of the Lamb (cf. 7:9, 14; 14:3). In God's presence, the Son of Man acknowledges the name of the One who "conquers" (3:5). The comrades "conquered" Satan in three ways: through the blood of the Lamb, with the word of their testimony, and by virtue of the fact that "they did not cling to life even in the face of death" (cf. Matt 10:28; 16:25-26). The ejection of Satan from heaven and the lack of heavenly prosecution are here juxtaposed with the saints' earthly activities. What appears to be threatening is shown to be an empty sham (though that does not deny the physical and spiritual hardship to be endured). "Conquering" and the end of accusation parallel each other. The Lamb's blood (5:9; 12:11; cf. 1:5; 19:13) is linked with the "conquering" of "our brethren" (NRSV, "comrades"). The word of their testimony (cf. 1:5; 2:13; 3:14) is in continuity with that of the Lamb, provoking the same kind of response as that to the Lamb (11:7). Babylon will get drunk on the blood of the witnesses to Jesus (17:6; cf. 18:24). Solidarity with the way of the Lamb, the faithful witness, means suffering discrimination and possibly death, especially when following that way involves avoiding worship of the beast for the sake of the word of God and the witness to Jesus (6:9; cf. 12:11). Those who lose their lives are those who bear witness to the Lamb (11:5) and refuse to bow down to the beast (13:15). Such action, carried on with dogged perseverance (cf. 14:12), enables them, eventually, to stand before God's throne (cf. 22:4).

12:12. This verse returns to the theme of rejoicing, specifically directed to heaven and its inhabitants (cf. 18:20). The word used for "dwell" (σκηνόω *skēnoō*, "to tent," the word used of the incarnation in John 1:14) is different from the one used for "the inhabitants" of the earth (κατοικέω *katoikeō*), who are uniformly presented as being under the sway of the beast and rejoicing over the slaughter of the witnesses (11:10). But the carnival atmosphere of 11:10 was premature. It is heaven that can rejoice in a festal spirit (cf. 18:20; Isa 49:13), whereas a woe is pronounced on the earth and the sea (cf. 8:13; 9:12; 11:13). This is because the devil (cf. 2:10; 20:10; "Satan" [Σατανᾶς *Satanas*] and "devil" [διάβολος *diabolos*] are clearly interchangeable, as 12:9 and 20:2 indicate) has descended to it. But Satan's time is short. The little time Satan has left corresponds to that careful quantification of time allotted to the witness (11:2), to the nurture given to the woman (vv. 7, 14), and to the short span of the reign of one of the kings in 17:10 (cf. 2:10; Dan 12:7; Mark 13:20). It may be a vicious time for those who resist the devil, but it is not of indefinite duration.

In a passage that is directly analogous to this one and found only in Luke's Gospel, at the end of the temptations of Jesus (Luke 4:13), the devil departs from Jesus "until an opportune time." That leaves the time of Jesus' ministry as a period when evil is overcome (Luke 10:18-19; 11:18). It is brought to an end with the diabolical plot to murder Jesus (Luke 22:3; cf. Luke 22:31). Here in v. 12, as in Luke, Satan has his moment. And it is a time of wrath, a theme of the visions to come, but then it will be God's wrath (14:8, 10, 19; 15:1, 7; 16:1, 19) or "the wine of the wrath" of Babylon's fornication (14:8; 18:3; cf. 6:16-17; 11:18) that earth's inhabitants will need to avoid. Satan's power is ultimately ineffective and futile.

12:13-14. In the last mention of the woman who had given birth (v. 6), she had fled into the desert to be nourished. She reappears in these verses to be pursued by the dragon. Thus the defeat of Satan is sandwiched between the two parts of the narration of the vision of the woman clothed with the sun. Satan is defeated and cannot conquer the woman and her offspring, however vigorous the persecution. Earlier the dragon had stood in the presence of the woman as she prepared to give birth (v. 4). Now, ejected from heaven, it pursues the woman, who is now identified as the one who bore the male child. But she is given "the two wings of the great eagle" (cf. Isa 40:31, which echoes a favorite theme of Revelation, patient endurance). She escapes to her place in the desert, where she is nourished (cf. 6:16; 20:11).

12:15-18. The dragon, now referred to as "the serpent" (ὁ ὄφις *ho ophis*), poured "water like a river" from his mouth to persecute the woman, "to sweep her away with the flood" (v. 15; cf. 9:17-18; 11:5; 16:13). She is protected from the flood (cf. Isa 43:2), however, when the earth comes to help her and swallows the water (v. 16). The earth rises up, as it were, to aid the woman, against those who destroy the earth (11:18).

The devil's anger with the woman leads him to make war on the rest of her "seed" (σπέρμα *sperma*, v. 17; NIV, "offspring"; NRSV, "children"), an indication that the woman symbolizes the people of God. The "seed" of the woman (v. 17; cf. Gen 14:12; Gal 3:16-17) are "those who keep the commandments of God and hold the testimony of Jesus" (cf. 14:12). Just as earlier the recognition of the judgment of God and the assertion of God's reign had provoked the anger of the nations (11:18), so also now the defeat and ejection of Satan have provoked his wrath. It will mean war on the saints who are linked with the One who will rule the nations with an iron rod (v. 5; cf. 2:27). The war in heaven between Satan's host and the host of Michael in v. 7 now has its earthly counterpart,[249] as that multitude who have "washed their robes and made them white in the blood of the Lamb" (7:14 NRSV) must engage in the struggle with Satan's earthly representative, the beast, the evil empire. John's vision ends abruptly with the sight of Satan standing on the seashore on the brink of the abyss, that place from which the beast will rise to try the faithfulness of the saints (cf. 11:7).

249. Caird, *The Revelation*, 154.

REFLECTIONS

The two signs in heaven offer clues for reflection on Revelation 12: The woman is persecuted and bears a child, and the dragon is thrown out of heaven.

1. John's vision of the woman contrasts with the vision of Babylon in chap. 17. There a woman is supported by the beast; here the woman is nurtured by God—not in luxury, but in the wilderness, where she is taken on eagle wings:

> [God] gives power to the faint,
>   and strengthens the powerless.
> Even youths will faint and be weary,
>   and the young will fall exhausted;
> but those who wait for the LORD
>   shall renew their strength,
>   they shall mount up with wings like eagles,
> they shall run and not be weary,
>   they shall walk and not faint. (Isa 40:29-31 NRSV)

Babylon is supported by the beast and is subject to the vagaries of the beast's vicious behavior (17:16). The woman here is pursued by the dragon and is dependent on God. This kind of portrayal sits uneasily with an outlook on life that prefers action, responsibility, autonomy, and involvement. The picture offered of Jesus in the closing chapters of the Gospels is that of a victim, mostly passive though never fatalistic and powerless. To wait and to watch is a vocation that our age finds difficult, and yet it may be all that is politically possible as it was in John's day, confronted as he was with the apparently all-embracing power of the Roman imperium. "The one who endures to the end shall be saved" (Mark 13:12). Victorinus of Pettau linked the woman with the ancient church of the ancestors in the faith, the prophets, the saints, and the apostles; it comes as no surprise, though, that from the sixth century onward Christian tradition has connected the vision of the woman in this chapter with Mary, mother of the Messiah.[250]

It is in this dramatic chapter that the conflict between good and evil and the enormity of the threat to the vulnerable are most vividly portrayed. It is not always easy to comprehend how such potent images can relate to the ordinariness of our lives. Nor is it easy to give ourselves the permission to connect them with what appears to be the triviality of our everyday existence.

Threat and insecurity lie at the heart of the dramatic signs in Revelation 12. The vision of the woman clothed with the sun is one of glory. Yet at the same time she is vulnerable. She is pregnant and about to give birth, not a situation in which one can think of defending oneself. She shares the pain of the torment of creation. She gives birth, her offspring is preserved and nurtured, and the woman is cared for. Like Hagar (Gen 16:7), the woman in Revelation 12 finds relief in the wilderness. Even in that situation of exclusion and apparent God-forsakenness, there is succor for her

Revelation 12 suggests two ways in which the threat is overcome: (1) recognition of vulnerability and trust in God and (2) lack of defensiveness, obedience to God, and holding true to the witness of Jesus. Revelation's advice to its readers is not a defensiveness based on weapons of war or protection of oneself, but an admonition to continue the way of the testimony of Jesus. There is no guarantee that there will be no threat or freedom from threat or harm. Nevertheless, the reality of the threat is nothing compared to the nakedness that is exposed at the judgment of Christ and the impoverishment of one's own integrity by the (apparently sensible) strategy of self-protection through wealth, property, and accommodation with the beast.

Divine protection is the basis for real security and self-worth. There is no human nurture that can ultimately be relied upon or any defensive strategy that will ultimately protect. To be secure in oneself is to be secure in God and to accept oneself as worthy and glorious in the sight of God; to accept that we are loved even if we may not always be able to feel it. That is no easy task, but it is the root of a sense of worth that does not have to rely on the ephemeral nature of false gods, which, as Revelation reminds us, ultimately involve us in the worship of the beast. What is required is an unmasking, something that is grasped in a different way in the words of Thomas Cranmer: "to whom all hearts are open, all desires known and from whom no secrets are hid."[251] They remind us that the one with whom we have to deal searches the very depths of our being (Rev 2:23), and there is no point in hiding the reality behind the masks we have constructed to protect ourselves.

2. Talk about Satan is avoided by some liberally minded people. It seems to reflect the beliefs of simple-minded believers or the fantasies of infancy, which mature adults should have grown out of. The demonic world, particularly when it dwells on destruction, is one we may find distasteful—even pathological. We may find ourselves reacting negatively to images of hostility and polarization or, rightly, reluctant to "demonize" others. The symbolism of evil in the Bible is a problem,[252] and yet it is a potent resource to help us to comprehend the forces that upset and subvert our managed lives.

Satan symbolizes that which stands between humans and the divine presence, and the personification of him as a dragon or a serpent is a sign of the reality of evil. As Revelation indicates, the manifestation of Satan's power is complex. It is institutional and social as well as personal. Thus the beast is a concrete embodiment of evil power. Evil does not take the form of a single king but an imperial institution or structure; it is a way of operating, and its agents of propaganda take many shapes (13:1ff.). Likewise, Babylon is not an individual but a city with its whole network of relationships and institutions contributing to a pattern of life, involvement in which John calls "fornication."

---

250. P. Prigent, *Apocalypse 12. Histoire de l'exégèse* (Geneva: Labor et Fides, 1988).
251. The Collect for Purity, Service of Holy Communion, Anglican *Book of Common Prayer*.
252. P. Ricoeur, *The Symbolism of Evil* (New York: Beason, 1969).

Revelation beckons us to broaden our horizons to understand the scope of evil by not confining it to what we can manage (e.g., the person who is before us or who may seem a threat to us), just as it refuses to allow us to confine the horizon of hope and salvation to the individual person's destiny.

Revelation's unmasking of the extent of deception and the flattery of evil is entirely consistent with the practice of Jesus, who not only rooted out evil in the individual person but sought to do so in society as well. By his death, the veil of the Temple, which maintained the mystique of an institution and kept a ruling elite in power, was ripped in two. The agent of God's kingdom could not fulfill his role without dealing with the influence it had on both individuals and society. So he went up to Jerusalem and met the resistance of its operators. The system opposed him and apparently crushed him, but in so doing it was itself denuded and overcome (Mark 15:38).[253]

3. In Revelation what is opposed often is a slight perversion of something that is of God: a city (chap. 17; cf. chap. 21), a beast/Lamb bearing the marks of slaughter (chap. 5; cf. chap. 13), a prophetic spirit (2:20; cf. 11:5; 19:10), sexual impurity/purity (chaps. 2; 17; cf. chaps. 14; 21). So often evil is a distortion of what is good. The world is not to be rejected; its goodness is not to be despised, though its exploitation is. It is the way in which wealth is made that is the problem, and the disfiguration of humanity that takes place in that process are evil.

4. The bringing to birth of the messianic age and its different values is a threat to those who would maintain the status quo of the powers of this age. The symbolism of evil has a very "down-to-earth" dimension in Revelation (e.g., 12:12). The heavenly struggle is closely linked with the earthly struggle of those who seek to maintain their testimony of faith in Jesus (12:10). The letter to the Ephesians coincides with Revelation 12 in stressing the extraordinary character of the struggle Christians are engaged in (Eph 6:10). It is not just about wrestling with the temptation of individual peccadilloes or personal relations but with the effects of larger, superhuman forces. Only an apocalyptic language can give us some means of expressing the enormity of what confronts us. That is the privileged insight of those who seek an alternative way as they continue the cosmic struggle begun by Jesus (Eph 2:6; 3:5; cf. Matt 16:17).[254]

5. While Revelation differentiates sharply between good and evil, it refuses to allow the reader that complete certainty and satisfaction of knowing who is in the group of the elect and who is outside it. It does not countenance a simple division between the church and the world. The letters to the seven churches indicate that uncleanness and fornication are rife in the churches. The pollution (3:4) and nakedness that are later threats (14:4; 16:15; 17:16) can already be found in the churches. There are no grounds for complacency. There is need for vigilance (3:3) and the endeavor to keep one's robes clean (22:14). There is little suggestion that the present practice of the church is anything but confused and compromised. The only mark of true religion is based on a prophetic witness that refuses to accept the mark of the beast. This—not membership in the Christian church or being a pillar of society—is the criterion for inclusion in the book of life.

---

253. See Myers, *Binding the Strong Man*.
254. The historical background and meaning of NT passages concerning the principalities and powers is explored by Walter Wink, *Naming the Powers* (Maryknoll, N.Y.: Orbis, 1984); *Unmasking the Powers* (Maryknoll, N.Y.: Orbis, 1986); and *Engaging the Powers*.

REVELATION 13:1-18

THE VISION OF TWO BEASTS

COMMENTARY

Chapter 12 ended with the dragon standing on the seashore, angrily seeking to make war on the woman's offspring. Two more beasts appear in chap. 13. From the sea emerges a beast that exercises the authority of the dragon. It is aided by a beast that rises out of the earth. The immediacy of the threat to the earth and its inhabitants, which is the consequence of Satan's ejection from heaven, is set out in this vision. John sees the world's inhabitants falling in line and worshiping the beast. Those who refuse to worship the beast have to live (and die) with the consequences.

13:1-3. A beast had already emerged from the abyss to persecute the two witnesses (11:7). This new beast, which appears from the sea, will be the seat upon which the woman called Babylon will sit (17:3). The sea, which will disappear in the new creation (21:1), is a sign of chaos (cf. Gen 1:7; Ps 104:9; Dan 7:3). Like Satan, the beast has ten horns and seven heads and diadems on its horns (cf. 12:3). On its heads are names of blasphemy (NIV, "a blasphemous name"; NRSV, "blasphemous names"; cf. 17:3). These names contrast with the names of God and the Lamb, which are written on the foreheads of the inhabitants of the new Jerusalem (22:4; cf. 14:1). In appearance, the beast is like a leopard, with feet like a bear and the mouth of a lion. Three of Daniel's beasts are here merged into one (cf. Dan 7:4-6). The dragon of chap. 12 gives the beast its power (v. 2), its authority, and its throne, the very throne that the angel of Pergamum had been warned about earlier (2:13; cf. 16:10). One of the heads resembles the Lamb in that it is described as having "received a death-blow" (exactly the words used in 5:5), but the "mortal wound" (lit., "the plague of its death") had been healed and so can afflict the whole world at the climax of God's wrath in 19:21.

13:4. In the face of the dragon's power, the whole world follows after it in amazement (v. 4; cf. 17:8) and worships it—activity that should be reserved for God. Not even the Lamb is to be worshiped, and later John will be given strict instructions to worship God alone (22:9; cf. 19:10). The one exception to this is that the angel of Philadelphia is promised that the members of the synagogue of Satan will come and worship at the angel's feet (3:9).

Verse 4 repeats the fact of the transfer of the dragon's authority to the beast and the deception involved in worshiping the beast. The amazed question, "Who is like the beast?" (reminiscent of similar sentiments expressed about God in Exod 15:11), is followed by "Who can make war against him?" In other words, their amazement is a combination of a sense of awe at the beast's military power and a sense of despair: There is no alternative to capitulation.[255]

13:5-6. Permission is now given to the beast to "exercise authority" for forty-two months (cf. 11:2; 12:6).[256] The dragon has transferred its power and authority to the beast. This permission is now set in the context of another scheme of things, a higher power (δίδωμι *didōmi*, the passive "was given," often indicates the way in which things are allowed to happen within the divine providence; see 6:1, 8; 7:2; 9:3; 11:1; 13:7, 14-16; cf. Ezek 20:26; Acts 7:42; Rom 1:24).

The beast's arrogant speech echoes that of the horn of the fourth beast in Dan 7:8, 11, 20. It blasphemes not only the name of God (cf. Lev 24:15-16), but also God's dwelling, which may refer to the heavenly temple (cf. 21:2) or be used, in a transferred sense, to indicate the holy people (7:15; cf. 21:3). This

---
255. Wengst, *Pax Romana and the Peace of Jesus Christ*.
256. Wink, *Engaging the Powers*.

is suggested by the second explanatory gloss, "those who dwell in heaven" (cf. 12:12). While the present age of injustice lasts, heaven is the location of the divine glory (cf. 4:1); it, too, had been pervaded by the power of Satan (cf. Job 1) when he had accused "our comrades" (12:10). According to v. 7a, the beast is not just engaged in words of blasphemy but in hostile actions against the saints (as is the horn in Dan 7:21). The war on the saints recalls the war of Michael and Satan in heaven (12:7), won by the angels of light, particularly the war of the beast against the witnesses and its conquest of them (11:7). However, many MSS lack this sentence.

13:7-8. The apparent universality of worship offered to the beast is qualified, however, by the reference to the Lamb's book of life. Until the books are opened (20:12; cf. Dan 12:1) and judgment takes place, the names contained in it are unknown. Thus the threat remains for all on earth, believer and unbeliever alike, that one's name might be removed. *The* criterion for inclusion in the book of life is to resist worshiping the beast.

The "Lamb that was slaughtered before the foundation of the world" (see NRSV note) refers to a pre-existent truth that reflects the world of apocalyptic mysteries and truths, where things are known from eternity even if they are only now revealed eschatologically (cf. Rom 16:20; Eph 3:9; Col 1:26).[257] Although there is nothing in Revelation that takes us back further than the decisive event of the life and death of the Lamb (and so little apart from 3:14 that suggests a doctrine of pre-existence), a statement like v. 8 reminds us that the mystery of the saving events has been with God from eternity (cf. 1 Pet 1:20). The message NT writers believed they were sharing was the ultimate divine mystery, opaque and only glimpsed in a fragmentary way until now. Its disclosure is surprising: The ultimate apocalyptic sign is an executed victim (1 Cor 2:6ff.). The divine mystery is a Lamb who is slain, a victim of injustice, yet a faithful and true witness.

13:9-10. The vision is then interrupted by two aphorisms (similar to Jer 15:2; 43:11), written in awkward Greek, that suggest the necessity of accepting the constraints placed on discipleship by one's circumstances. These aphorisms are prefaced with a summons to attentiveness, which ran as a refrain throughout the letters to the angels (e.g., 2:7; cf. Matt 11:15; 13:9, 43), and concludes with a call for the patience and faithfulness of the saints (cf. 14:12). The first aphorism speaks of the acceptance of any captivity that may befall one (cf. 2:10). The second promises death by the sword for those who resist with the sword (cf. 13:14). Such death has already been experienced by some (according to 2:13) and is an imminent threat to those who refuse to worship the beast (13:15). Revelation is full of calls to resistance mingled with "patient endurance," particularly in the context of not being taken in by the allures of the beast. Nevertheless, what these two verses demand, in the midst of a description of the threat posed by the beast, is the need to accept the ill treatment meted out without rebellion (cf. Matt 26:52; 1 Cor 7:17ff.; 1 Pet 2:20ff.).

13:11-14. John returns to the description of his vision (v. 11) and sees another beast, this time arising from the land. It has "two horns like a lamb," but it speaks like a dragon (cf. 16:13, the only other place where mention is made of what comes out of the dragon's mouth). Verse 12 suggests that this beast acts as an agent of the first beast and exercises its authority as a kind of grand vizier (cf. 13:14). The function of this new beast is to make "the earth and its inhabitants worship the first beast." The created world is under thrall to the beast (cf. 11:18; 13:3; 17:5; 19:2). The beast is identified as possessing a mortal wound that has healed (v. 12; cf. v. 3). It "performs great signs" (ποιεῖ σημεῖα μεγάλα *poiei sēmeia megala*, the term also used for the "portents" of 12:1; 15:1; cf. 16:14), as did the false prophets predicted by Jesus (Matt 24:4-5, 11, 24; cf. 2 Thess 2:9). Indeed, later this beast will be associated with "the false prophet" (16:13; 19:20; 20:10; cf. Matt 7:15; Acts 13:6, where false prophecy and magic are linked; 1 John 4:1). The signs recall those of Elijah in 1 Kgs 18:38 (cf. Luke 9:54; Rev 11:6). Like Satan, the second beast is a deceiver (see Commentary on 12:9; cf. 20:3). Signs deceive in order to persuade the earth's inhabitants to make an "image"

---

257. This is discussed in the Babylonian Talmud, *b. Pesaḥim* 54a. See also the survey in R. Hamerton-Kelly, *Pre-Existence, Wisdom, and the Son of Man* (Cambridge: Cambridge University Press, 1973).

for the beast "that had been wounded by the sword," which will be an object of worship, something that is to be resisted, according to 14:9, 11; 15:2; 16:2; 19:20; and 20:4. In v. 14, we learn that the mortal wound is a wound of the sword that the beast survived.

The references to the image of the beast and the more specific description of the beast's wound have led commentators over the centuries to suppose these are specific historical allusions. The worship of the image of the beast (v. 14) has been plausibly linked with the promotion of the imperial cult, which was particularly widespread in the area of the churches whose angels are addressed by John.[258] Emperor worship had become part of the fabric of life, and John's vision in effect demands of readers that they unravel that fabric and weave a new fabric of living in which the persistent, even casual, participation in state religion and the social conventions that surround it form no part. The beast whose mortal wound was healed may reflect Nero, who was assassinated in 68 CE,[259] but was widely rumored to have escaped death and fled to the east, from whence he was on the point of coming back as emperor. This legend is included in Suetonius's *Life of Nero*: "In fact twenty years later (c. 90 CE) when I was a young man, a person of obscure origin appeared, who gave out that he was Nero, and the name was still in such favor with the Parthians that they supported him vigorously and surrendered him with great reluctance."[260]

13:15-17. The nature of charlatan is brought out in this verse; a specific series of miraculous occurrences in Asia Minor connected with the statue of the beast is hinted at here, but there is little hard evidence.[261] The instruction that proceeds from the mouth of the image is to be rejected, because it affects the eternal destiny of the readers of the book (v. 8; cf. 17:8). The spurious oracle that comes from the image threatens death to those who do not worship the image of the beast (cf. Dan 3:5-6). This threat is all-encompassing and covers all strata of society (cf. 6:15; 19:5, 18; 20:12). The inclusion of the small as well as the great is a reminder that, whatever the peculiar insight they may have (cf. Matt 11:25ff.), all persons are subject to the blandishments and ideological distortions of power and can be misled by it.

This act of worship is not a private matter, for those who worship the beast will receive a mark (χάραγμα *charagma*) on their right hand or on their forehead (cf. 14:9, 11; 16:2; 19:20; 20:4), contrasting with those who stand with the Lamb, who are marked with the name of the Lamb and of God (14:1; cf. 22:4). There are public, social, and economic consequences for those who resist; they are excluded from regular social intercourse. Without the name of the beast or the number of its name, it becomes impossible to buy or sell. Those "bought" with the blood of the Lamb (5:9; cf. 14:3) can do nothing other than resist, however. The present disruption of their pattern of life is a temporary hardship compared with the wider disruption of buying and selling, which will take place when Babylon is destroyed, provoking the merchants to lament (18:11).

13:18. Reference to the number of the beast's name prompts this word of exhortation (cf. v. 10). But now "anyone with understanding" or "insight" is required to calculate the number of the beast; people will also be asked to use wisdom to understand the mystery of Babylon and the beast in 17:9. The mysterious number 666 has attracted much attention.[262] Jews in antiquity were fond of working out the numerical value of letters, a technique called *gematria*. The numerical value of the name Nero Caesar in Hebrew is 666. This interpretation has a long pedigree in the history of the interpretation of Revelation as is confirmed by the variant reading 616 (a reading known along with 666 to the late second-century writer Irenaeus). One can understand the change, since the Greek form "Neron Caesar" (Νέρων Καῖσαρ *Nerōn Kaisar*) written in Hebrew characters (נרון קסר *Nerōn Kasar*) is equivalent to 666, whereas the Latin form "Nero Caesar" is equivalent to 616. Another suggestion, dependent on a similar numerical computation found in the *Sibylline Oracles*,[263] is that

---

258. S. R. F. Price, *Rituals and Power: The Roman Imperial Cult in Asia Minor* (Cambridge: Cambridge University Press, 1984).
259. R. Bauckham, "Nero and the Beast," in *The Climax of Prophecy* (Edinburgh: 1992) 384-452.
260. Suetonius *Life of Nero* 57.
261. W. Ramsay, *The Letters to the Seven Churches of Asia* (London: Hodder and Stoughton, 1904) 97ff.
262. The matter is dealt with in exhaustive detail in Bauckham, "Nero and the Beast."
263. *Sib. Or.* i.324ff.

666 represents a contrast with the numerical value of "Jesus" ((Ἰησοῦς *Iēsous*) in Greek, which is 888, a contrast that fits in well with the parody of Christ in the image of the beast in this chapter.

We need to exercise caution here and not assume that John summons readers to engage in this kind of complex calculation. Would Greek speakers have been able to latch on to the fact that the calculation is to be based on the numerical value of Hebrew, not Greek, letters? Maybe John's understanding of what constitutes wisdom may be different from ours. It is the wisdom of God (cf. 5:12; 7:12), not human wisdom, that determines true understanding (cf. 1 Cor 1:18ff.). Precise numbers clearly are important for John (see 5:11; 7:4; 9:16; cf. 20:8).

One issue that should give us pause for thought is the translation of the expression. The NRSV renders it as "it is the number of a person." The REB has "the number represents a man's name." But the RSV's "it is a human number" moves away from associating the number with a particular person. This latter translation seems more likely in the light of 21:17, the only other relevant use of the word ἄνθρωπος (*anthrōpos*) in Revelation, where most translations agree that the word means "human measurement." Could it be, then, that the translation "the number of a man" might be leading us into unnecessary speculations? Within the context of Revelation itself, the number 7 (used of angels, churches, seals, trumpets, and bowls) implies completeness, particularly evident in the sense of completion attending the description of the last sequence of sevens (15:1, 8; cf. 10:7). The number 6 three times over (666) falls one short of the number of perfection, 7. This falling short is evident also in the interruption after the sixth seal and the sixth trumpet in 6:12ff. and 9:13ff. The beast seems to be near perfection; it is, after all, a caricature of the Lamb who was slain (13:3). But what it lacks actually renders it diabolical and utterly opposed to God in supposing that it has ultimate power and wisdom (13:4). The numerical value of "Jesus" in Greek is 888, and in 17:11 it is an eighth king, the beast that was and is not, who is a kind of antichrist and who, together with the other kings, will make war on the Lamb. If there is a number game at work here, it is more likely this. But the simpler solution is to see the number 666 as a threefold falling short of perfection, that which is almost messianic but not quite so. It has most of the hallmarks of truth, and so it can easily deceive. For this reason, it must, at all costs, be resisted.[264]

---

264. See Karl Barth's comments on revolution in the context of the discussion of Romans 13 in his *The Epistle to the Romans* (London: A. & C. Black, 1933) 482-83.

REFLECTIONS

1. In Revelation 13 we are given a graphic portrait of the nature and operation of an ideology that cloaks its real goals and identity from those it has taken in. The beast is the incarnation of the powers of evil and attracts universal admiration for its military power and for acts that appear to be beneficial. The people feel pressure to conform (13:14). Those who refuse to do so face social ostracism (13:16). Because the beast has some of the characteristics of the Lamb (13:3, 14), we can understand how easy it is for people to be deceived and how watchful one has to be to avoid being taken in by what seems plausible and thereby colluding with everything that is opposed to the divine justice. We should not underestimate the impact of a prevailing set of ideas on us. When something different and challenging comes along, we consider it wrongheaded or misguided. That is exactly the effect of what is called ideology.[265] It makes you think that widely held ideas are "obvious," "commonsense," and "normal," when in fact they often cover up the powerful vested interests of a small group that has power and wants to retain it. In John's vision, the task of the beast that arises out of the land is to persuade ordinary people that what they see in the first beast is normal and

---

265. See the discussion in T. Eagleton, *Ideology: An Introduction* (London: Verso, 1991).

admirable, so that any deviation or counterculture is regarded as strange and anti-social and, therefore, to be repudiated. John's vision helps to unmask these processes and is a pointed reminder of the ease with which the powers of evil can seduce us. Despite the widespread assumption that it was evil men like Hitler, Stalin, and Pol Pot and their supporters who were responsible for crimes against humanity, they would not have been able to commit atrocities without the tacit support of ordinary people (including many Christians), who kept their noses clean, maintained a low profile, and avoided at all costs being seen as "political."

2. There has been a tendency to limit the applicability of Revelation 13 (if it is used at all; it was explicitly excluded from readings prescribed for the Daily Offices of Morning and Evening Prayer in the old Anglican *Book of Common Prayer*), either to an eschatological manifestation of evil or to specific cases of tyrannical regimes. Romans 13 (along with Titus 3 and 1 Pet 2:13) is then left as the mainstream New Testament teaching on the state, with its apparent exhortation to be subject to the ruling authorities. Such a limitation of the applicability of Revelation 13 limits the breadth of the New Testament witness. What Revelation 13 brings out most clearly is the, perhaps inevitable, demonic character of the state. The state or society in general is not a neutral enterprise, devoid of conflict of interest or human self-aggrandizement. Political theorists from Hobbes to Marx have shown how the state is a means of controlling or masking deep-seated conflicts of interest, and it is important that structures of society be subjected to searching criticism. As human agents, we are prone to use power (or to acquiesce by our lack of resolve) to promote institutions that will serve individual or sectional interests. That can lead to blasphemy when we do not acknowledge the interest of God. The faithful use of political power involves a substantial practical implementation of ways of behaving and the creation of institutions that will give attention to the goals of God's justice, while recognizing that, because we live in an imperfect age, we shall fall short of our ideals

Romans 13 makes a similar point, although indirectly. The blanket injunction to be subject to the ruling powers is qualified by the assertion that the powers are there as God's agents, working "for your good" (Rom 13:4 NRSV). Whatever the source of Paul's teaching on the state, the understanding of the "good" in this context must be informed by the wider Pauline context, in which the divine goodness is mentioned several times (particularly in Rom 12:12). It is true that Paul does not tell us to submit to the powers *only* if they promote our good. Rather, Paul exhorts the Romans to accept the reality of the constraints of life in "Babylon." Romans 13 needs to be balanced by the more realistic portrayal in Revelation 13, which indicates that states serve the interests of some—particularly those who consent to its sanctioned beliefs and practices—and not of all. But Revelation, like Romans 13 (though without the positive assertion of the powers' role in Rom 13), implies submission rather than revolution.[266] The repeated emphasis that "authority was given" indicates that what takes place is not to be resisted by revolution, except through non-conformity.

3. In one key respect, John's situation differs from that of most contemporary Western readers of Revelation. Christianity was the religion of a tiny minority, not in any way favored by or linked with the state. It was to be another two hundred years before the Christian religion was incorporated into the life of the state. The emergence of Christendom has resulted in situations very different from the ones contemplated by John, even if from time to time in history there are close analogies to those of the first Christians, such as the situation in Germany in the 1930s. Most Christians find themselves either having to come to some kind of accommodation with the state or gladly being part of a closer alliance between throne and altar in the promotion of national

---

266. See further J. H. Yoder, *The Politics of Jesus* (Grand Rapids: Eerdmans, 1972); W. Stringfellow, *Conscience and Obedience* (Waco, Tex.: Word, 1977).

welfare. Individual temperament, upbringing, and experience all condition the formation of our attitudes toward the state. The visions of Revelation present us with serious questions about an uncritical involvement with the state, particularly when it involves, tacitly or implicitly, too close a support for the values and practices of society. Too often churches have colluded with forces that oppose the gospel of Jesus Christ and have provided a veneer of religious respectability for attitudes and regimes that should be rejected by those who bear witness to Jesus Christ.

In the time of the apartheid regime in South Africa, the *Kairos Document* emerged as a Christian, biblical, and theological comment on the political crisis in that nation. It stands in the tradition of the book of Revelation, with its concern to unmask the reality of the situation, and offers a call to the church to engage in a prophetic ministry. Its major difference from Revelation, however, is that it includes a critique of the churches' collusion with the state. It is critical of a state theology that is based on a misreading of Romans 13. The composers of the *Kairos Document* reject the idea that Paul presents an absolute doctrine about the state, and they argue that the text must be interpreted in its own context, in which Christians thought that they were exonerated from obeying the state because Christ alone was their king. Paul's insistence is on the necessity of some kind of governmental authority. When a state does not obey the law of God and becomes a servant of Satan, however, it is passages like Revelation 13 to which one should turn to illuminate the situation. The use made of a divine sanction for the apartheid system in the constitution of South Africa can be seen as idolatrous: "The god of the South African state is not merely an idol or false god, it is the devil disguised as Almighty God—the Antichrist."[267]

Christian churches are criticized for advocating reconciliation as "an absolute principle that must be applied in all cases of conflict or dissension" when reconciliation is impossible without the removal of injustice. Neutrality is nothing but a means whereby the status quo of oppression can continue. The church should expose false peace and reject mere reform of a situation that is inherently evil: "God does not bring his justice through reforms introduced by the Pharaohs of this world."[268]

The document calls for "a prophetic theology," which involves "what Jesus would call reading the signs of the times." This means being aware of the interests of those maintaining the present system and the exploitation of those most vulnerable in it who labor to keep the privileged minority affluent. The churches should offer a message of hope to oppressed peoples, recognizing that suffering will be a necessary prelude to resurrection.

> The church of Jesus Christ is not called to be a bastion of caution and moderation. The church should challenge, inspire and motivate people. It has a message of the cross that inspires us to make sacrifices for justice and liberation. It has a message of hope that challenges us to wake up to act with hope and confidence. The church must preach this message not only in words and sermons and statements but also through its actions, programmes, campaigns and divine services.[269]

267. *The Kairos Document: Challenge to the Church* (Waco, Tex.: Word, 1977) 8-10.
268. *The Kairos Document,* 8-10.
269. *The Kairos Document,* 8-10.

REVELATION 14:1-20

THE LAMB, THE 144,000, THE ETERNAL GOSPEL, AND THE HUMAN FIGURE

OVERVIEW

In stark contrast to the previous vision, in which those who worshiped the beast had been marked with its sign, here the Lamb and its followers, with God's name on their foreheads, stand on Mount Zion. Angelic voices proclaim an eternal gospel and assert the destruction of Babylon. A final vision of judgment is seen by John in the form of a terrible harvest. This is followed in chapter 15 by a vision of a sea of glass mingled with fire, with those who have "conquered" standing beside it singing a song of deliverance.

REVELATION 14:1-5, THE SONG OF THE 144,000

COMMENTARY

14:1-3. The phrase "And I saw" (NIV and NRSV, "Then I looked") signals another vision, as so often in Revelation (e.g., 4:1; 13:11). "Seeing" is at the heart of John's message ("write what you see," 1:19). John sees the Lamb once more (cf. 5:6), but this time the Lamb is standing on Mount Zion. The picture of Zion as a site of salvation is familiar enough from the Old Testament (e.g., Isaiah 2; Micah 4), though Jerusalem is elsewhere in Revelation depicted as a place of rebellion (11:8). Mount Zion is here the site of God's presence, as the new Jerusalem will be in 21:4 (cf. Ps 46:5: "God is in the midst of the city"). Although the Lamb has been mentioned throughout the vision (e.g., 7:9-10; 12:11; 13:8), this is the first time that it has formed part of one of John's visions since 6:1, when it opened the first seal. The Lamb is here attended by 144,000 righteous persons (cf. 7:4). These persons are distinguished by the name of the Lamb and the name of the Father of the Lamb on their foreheads (cf. 7:3). This is an unusual christological conjunction: God as the Lamb's Father is found only here. Elsewhere, God is referred to as the heavenly Father of the Son of Man (e.g., 1:6; 2:27; 3:21-22). The description of God as the Lamb's Father is not surprising, however, given that the Lamb shares the throne of God. In 21:3, the inhabitants of the new Jerusalem are "sons" of God (cf. 2 Sam 7:14). There is an obvious contrast with the previous vision, where those who worship the beast are marked (13:16). But a *name* is written on the foreheads of the 144,000—not just a mark. What is written is important, even sacred, not only because it is the means of signifying that which is of God, but also because it is the name of God (cf. 22:4).

John hears a voice from heaven (v. 2; cf. 10:4), whose sound is like many waters (cf. 1:15; 19:6) and like thunder, but at the same time like harpists playing on their harps (cf. 5:8; 15:2). The 144,000 sing a new song (v. 3), as did the elders and creatures around the throne to mark the Lamb's taking the scroll (5:8; cf. Ps 144:9). Now the multitude "sing a new song" in the presence of the throne and its attendants (cf. 4:6-7). The song is a mystery to all but those who have been redeemed from the earth (5:9) as a first fruits (14:4; cf. Rom 8:23; 16:5; 1 Cor 15:23; 2 Thess 2:13; Jas 1:18). Only the 144,000 can learn this song (v. 3).

14:4-5. In these verses, John describes the multitude. They have not "defiled themselves with women" and are virgins. They follow the Lamb "wherever he goes" (cf. John 10:4). No lie can be found in their mouths, thus "they are blameless" (cf. Isa 53:9; 1 Pet 2:22). In 3:4, those who have not "soiled their clothes" are worthy to walk with the Lamb. Virginity and non-defilement are linked here, implying abstinence from sexual activity. The picture of the elect as virgins is also found in 2 Cor 11:2 (cf. Matt 25:1ff.).[270] Sexual activity can cause uncleanness (Lev 15:18), which requires ritual cleansing to avoid defiling the tabernacle (Lev 15:31) and the holy mountain (Exod 19:15).

How should we read these verses? Does John here bear witness to a misogynist, male-only world,[271] in which women are either a problem unless they are chaste and passive like the bride of the Lamb and the woman in heaven, or even completely absent from the eschatological vision? We should read this description of those who accompany the Lamb on Mount Zion in the same way in which we read so many of the other images in the vision—that is, metaphorically rather than literally. So it is unlikely that these are actual virgins. The idiom of sexual relations is used to evoke a sense of distinctiveness and purity. The followers of the Lamb are seen as an army of people who are in a state of ritual purity, appropriate for those who fight a holy war (Deut 23:9ff.; 1 Sam 21:5; 2 Sam 11:9ff.; 1QM 7:3ff.).[272] It is parallel to the use of the imagery of fornication as a metaphor for idolatry (e.g., 2:14, 21). That does not reduce the difficulty of the fact that the metaphor of defilement with women is being used to describe the singularity and lack of compromise that abstinence from sexual intercourse involves, reflecting the profound distaste throughout this book with whatever is ambiguous, mixed, or a compromise (cf. 3:15).

John describes the assembled host as a "first fruits" (v. 4). In other words, this is not the sum total of the elect but a foretaste of that great harvest of the elect, which is still to be revealed. Harvest imagery will dominate the second part of this vision (vv. 15-20). By contrast with what comes forth from the mouth of the beast in the previous vision (e.g., 13:5; cf. 3:9; 16:13), what proceeds from the mouths of these people contains nothing untruthful. That characterizes life in the New Jerusalem (21:27; cf. 22:15). Being without blame, here linked with their ransom (NRSV, "redeemed"; NIV, "purchased"; cf. 1 Pet 1:18-19), is expected of those who are found worthy to stand in the divine presence (Eph 1:4; Col 1:22; Jude 24).

The military imagery implicit in these verses suggests a comparison with the *War Scroll* from the Dead Sea Scrolls (1QM).[273] In one of the most fascinating texts found in the vicinity of the Dead Sea, we are offered in detail the inventory of preparations necessary for the fight between the sons of light and the sons of darkness. This is a conventional battle in that weapons of war are used. But like Revelation, it is apparent that this battle is not between humans alone but between angelic forces who fight alongside humans (cf. Josh 5:13-14).

But in the war that takes place in heaven in Rev 12:7, the elect do not fight. That does not mean, however, that their endurance and witness contribute nothing to the eschatological process. As in Eph 6:10, we are offered a picture of a battle conducted without weapons and rooted in the triumph of the Lamb (14:1), who (like the Messiah in the contemporary apocalypse 4 Ezra 13:10, 27) stands as a conqueror without indulging in any military action. The warfare of the elect is conducted with other weapons: endurance, witness, prophecy, obedience to God, and remaining loyal to Jesus (14:12). (See Reflections at 14:14-20.)

---

270. The historical context is surveyed in R. Lane Fox, *Pagans and Christians* (London: Penguin, 1987) 351ff. See also P. Brown, *The Body and Society* (London: Faber and Faber, 1991) 38, 351-74.
271. See T. Pippin, *Death and Desire: The Rhetoric of Gender in the Apocalypse of John* (Louisville: Westminster/John Knox, 1992).
272. See R. Bauckham, "The Book of Revelation as a Christian War Scroll," in *The Climax of Prophecy* (Edinburgh: T. & T. Clark, 1993).
273. Bauckham, *The Climax of Prophecy,* 210-37.

REVELATION 14:6-13, THE MESSAGE OF THE THREE ANGELS

COMMENTARY

14:6-7. John sees an angel flying in mid-heaven, proclaiming an eternal "gospel" (εὐαγγέλιον *euangelion*; cf. Matt 24:14; Mark 13:10). It is similar to the eagle in 8:13, which proclaims threefold woe. The angel's message is quite simple: "Fear God and give him glory, for the hour of his judgment has come." Such fear of God is hinted at elsewhere, explicitly on the part of the earth's inhabitants (11:11; cf. 11:18; 15:4; 19:5; 1 Pet 2:17). Glory is given to the God of heaven in 11:13 (cf. 16:9) and by the great multitude in 19:7. Giving God glory is the regular habit of the host that surrounds God's throne (4:9), and it contrasts with the devotion paid to the beast by the world's inhabitants. In Josh 7:19, giving glory to God is closely linked to confession of sin (cf. John 9:24), and that may be the case in the angelic pronouncement, too. The angel utters a demand to worship the Creator rather than the creature (cf. Acts 17:24; 1 Thess 1:9-10) in the light of the imminence of the hour of judgment (cf. 3:3; 18:10). The message of this gospel is not far removed from the summary in Mark 1:15: "The time is fulfilled, and the kingdom of God has come near; repent, and believe in the good news" (NRSV). In Revelation, the command is to fear God; in Mark, the command is to repent. In both passages, the presence of a time of crisis is stressed, and in both that crisis is set in the context of a struggle with the powers of the cosmos as the coming of the gospel provokes the possibility of rejection and judgment (cf. Matt 10:7, 15).[274]

14:8. The first angel is followed by another who proclaims the fall of Babylon (cf. Isa 21:9), the first reference to Babylon in the vision (cf. 16:19; 17:5; 18:2-3). Babylon's offense was having caused all the nations to "drink of the wine of the wrath of her fornication" (cf. Jer 51:7). This awkward phrase can be interpreted as Babylon's having intoxicated the people and caused wrath as the result of the forgetfulness of the true vocation to worship God and keep God's commandments (cf. 16:19; 17:2; 18:3; 19:15).

14:9-10. After the first two angels have proclaimed the need to fear God and the imminence of Babylon's fall, a third angel appears, pronouncing the torment of those who worship the beast. In 13:15, the social cost of *non-conformity* was stressed. Now the cost of *conformity* is set forth: "They will also drink the wine of God's wrath." Intoxication with Babylon can lead only to God's wrath, expressed in the image of anger as a strong wine drunk undiluted (cf. Isa 51:17; Jer 25:15), in the form of torment (cf. 9:5; 20:10) with fire (Matt 5:22; 25:41; Mark 9:43, 48; 1 Cor 3:13-14; 2 Thess 1:7; 2 Pet 3:7). The presence of the Lamb and the angels is not a blessing (cf. 7:11; 11:4) but judgment (cf. 3:5), consistent with the great day of the wrath of the Lamb, when all the inhabitants of the world will desire to hide themselves (6:16-17). Here the Lamb is not kept away from wrath; as is implied in its role in the opening of the seals, it is a witness to the judgment that takes place upon those who have been compromised by their involvement with the beast and Babylon (v. 10).

14:11-12. Those who surround the throne do not cease day and night praising God (cf. 4:8; 7:15), and in the same way the torment of those who worship the beast and its image and those marked with the beast's name carries on day and night (cf. 20:10). Theirs now is that constant threat of accusation that had hitherto been the fate of "our comrades" (12:10). Verse 11 repeats the words of v. 9, which set out the qualifications for those who receive the awful judgment: "those who worship the beast and its image and for anyone who receives the mark of its name." The dire warning concludes with a message to the saints: Endurance consists in keeping the commandments of God and holding fast to the faith of Jesus (v. 12). The

---

274. See Myers, *Binding the Strong Man*.

expression πίστιν Ἰησοῦ (*pistin Iēsou*, "faith of Jesus") is probably a subjective genitive and so refers to Jesus' faithfulness, which is exemplified in a particular way of life (and death). (If *pistin Iēsou* were an objective genitive, the phrase would mean "faith in Jesus." Interpreters face the same choice in Rom 3:22, 26.) This fidelity means resisting the devil, whose authority is given to the beast (cf. 12:10, 17; 13:15ff.). Endurance, which John himself practices (1:9) and which is a key characteristic required of the angels of the seven churches (2:2-3, 19; 3:10), is particularly necessary in the face of the demands of the beast (13:10). It enables "conquest" (cf. Mark 13:13; Luke 8:15; 21:19; Rom 8:24-25; 12:12; 2 Cor 1:6; 1 Thess 1:3). Perseverance is required to resist the blandishments of the beast and the peer pressure that persuades humans to conform.

14:13. Another voice from heaven commands John to write, just as he had been commanded in 1:19; 10:4 and will be again in 19:9. As in 12:10-11 (cf. 11:15) the heavenly voice effects a new situation for the dead who "die in the Lord," a phrase found only here in Revelation and reminiscent of the ethical injunctions of the Pauline tradition (e.g., Rom 14:14; 16:2ff.; 1 Cor 11:11; 16:19; 2 Cor 2:12; Eph 1:15; 4:1; 6:1; Phil 2:24, 29; 3:1; 4:1-2; Col 4:17; 1 Thess 3:8). There is an affirmative echo (cf. 1:7) from the Spirit (cf. 22:17; cf. 4:5), who addresses the churches (2:7, 11, 17, 29; 3:6, 13, 22). The rest from toil echoes 6:9, where the agony of waiting and nakedness is resolved by the granting of white robes. The deeds of the dead are not forgotten, however, for "their deeds follow them" (cf. Sir 44:1ff., esp. v. 9). The deeds of all persons have been written down, to be opened up to public gaze when the books are opened (20:12). The angels of the churches are shown that their deeds are all known as well (2:5). For example, the angel at Sardis is told that its deeds are not perfect in the sight of God (3:2). The prerequisite for humanity is to repent of their evil deeds (9:20; 16:11). (See Reflections at 14:14-20.)

REVELATION 14:14-20, THE HARVEST OF THE EARTH

COMMENTARY

14:14-16. John now sees a white cloud (cf. 1:7; 10:1) and on it one like a son of man (NRSV, "like the Son of Man"), resembling the vision in 1:13ff. (cf. Matt 24:30). Like the elders (4:4), the first rider (6:2, though the crown is not golden), and the locusts (9:7, though their crowns are *like* gold), this Son of Man figure has a golden crown. He also holds a sharp sickle in his hand (cf. 1:16, where the Son of Man has seven stars). An angel comes out from the temple (which in 11:19 is the repository of God's just laws) and bids the one seated on the cloud to reap, "for the hour to reap has come." In words reminiscent of Joel's "Put in the sickle,/ for the harvest is ripe" (Joel 3:13 NRSV; cf. Mark 4:29), he is commanded to begin "the harvest of the earth" (cf. Jer 51:33). Note that this is the harvest of the *earth*, and not just of its inhabitants (cf. 16:1ff.).

14:17-20. Another angel emerges from the temple in heaven with a sharp sickle. A third angel, "who has authority over fire," emerges from the altar and cries to the preceding angel (vv. 17-18) to use the sickle to "gather the clusters of the vine of the earth." The fruit that is gathered is cast into a wine press (cf. Isa 63:2; Lam 1:15). In the light of 19:15, this seems to be an image of judgment rather than of redemption (cf. 14:3). The wine press is said to be outside the city (v. 20), a place separated from the places of holiness, just as outside the new Jerusalem are the dogs, sorcerers, and immoral persons (22:15). But it is also the place, outside the camp, where followers of Jesus are summoned to go (Heb 13:13). Here the blood of judgment flows. Elsewhere in Revelation, there is no reference to the shedding of the blood of those being judged; instead the blood that is shed is that of the Lamb (1:5;

5:9; 19:13) and martyrs (6:10; 7:14; 12:11; 17:6; 18:24; 19:2). Hence this passage has been interpreted as describing the martyrdom of the saints, which, to the eye of faith, is the judgment meted out on Babylon.[275] If so, then the gory character of this passage might be related to the "judgment to begin with the household of God" (1 Pet 4:17 NRSV)—the slaughter of the martyrs, whose witness is, in some sense, vicarious. In the light of the rest of the vision and the reference to first fruits earlier in the chapter, we may see here an anticipation of judgment, described in other terms later in the book (e.g., 19:11ff.), from which the servants of God cannot escape. They, too, find that their time of trial comes when they must resist and that they, too, will be martyred.

275. See Caird, *A Commentary on the Revelation of Saint John the Divine*, 194.

REFLECTIONS

1. Chapter 14 offers a contrast to the chapter that precedes it. Those who conform to the ways of the beast may achieve a temporary respite and prosperity, but ultimately that cannot continue. John's vision offers hope to those who stand firm. The stress on integrity and truthfulness contrasts with the duplicity and deceit made manifest in chapter 13, where what is false leads astray and is met by the self-serving response of the world's inhabitants. Those who have compromised have demonstrated to them the error of their ways as the truth is revealed. In rather brutal fashion, the vision brings home the ultimate character of apparently harmless actions. Compromise with the old order is nothing less than being marked by the beast (14:9). For John, all action, however small, is ultimately significant and of infinite value in the divine economy.

The New Testament writers see in the mundane situations of life in the present the challenge, the threat, and the opportunity of the hidden life of God. They seek to offer readers a mixture of the mundane and the heavenly to convey the deeper character of reality. We see this perhaps most clearly in Matt 25:31-46 in the subtle relationship between the eschatological judge and his hidden presence in the least of his "brethren" in the midst of the present age: The consequences for final judgment, indeed, are now being gestated in the womb of history. This is true of the Bible as a whole.

All of life is an issue for the religious person, from eating to buying, from words and deeds, as well as what is narrowly regarded as worship. No area of existence is neutral and unaffected by religious significance. Christianity inherited from Judaism this perspective and has preserved an indissoluble link between the public and the private, the spiritual and political, which has become a central feature of catholic Christianity. To use contemporary religious terminology, "spirituality" is not a matter of private cultic devotion unconnected with the demands of ordinary life.

2. The clear contrast between the Lamb and the beast foreshadows Ignatius of Loyola's meditation on *Two Standards* in the *Spiritual Exercises* (incidentally, the Ignatian *Exercises* offer an excellent example of how to use texts that are, in Blake's words "not too explicit" to "rouze the faculties to act"):

"This is the history. Here it will be that Christ calls and wants all beneath his standard, and Lucifer, on the other hand, wants all under his." . . .

"This is a mental representation of the place. It will be here to see a great plain, comprising the whole region about Jerusalem, where the sovereign Commander-in-Chief of all the good is Christ our lord; and another plain about the region of Babylon where the chief of the enemy is Lucifer." . . .

". . . consider the address which Lucifer makes, how he goads demons to lay snares for humanity and bind them with chains. First they are to tempt them to covet riches (as

Satan is accustomed to do in most cases) that they may the more easily attain the empty honours of this world and then come to overweening pride." . . .

"Consider the address which Christ our Lord makes to all his servants and friends whom he sends on this enterprise, recommending them to seek to help all, first by attracting them to the highest spiritual poverty, and should it please the Divine Majesty . . . even to actual poverty. Secondly, they should lead them to a desire for insults and contempt, for from these springs humility."[276]

3. It is often difficult, when one is committed to a set of principles or to a particular community, to maintain one's stand when fear and public disgrace tempt one to retreat. This chapter of Revelation indicates that, while the price is worth paying, all those who are committed to causes continually need to assess their commitments, their motives, the cost to others and to themselves. On the one hand, caution may lead to never taking sides, and, consequently, never taking a stand about anything. On the other hand, certainty of the rectitude of one's cause may lead to intransigence and a mindless devotion to that cause. In this chapter the company of the redeemed is standing, not on their own, but with the Lamb. The criterion of the "good cause" must be the person, the activity, and the story of the Lamb. As Paul would put it, it must be conformity with the pattern of Christ's life that counts.

4. The imagery in the closing verses of Revelation 14 seems barbaric, unedifying, and theologically immature. This is one of the sections of the book that continues to be a scandal for modern readers. As with the material in chapters 6, 8, and 9, we cannot gloss over it, nor does an attempt to water down its shocking effect really do justice to the text. The Commentary suggests that the text stresses with the utmost seriousness the choices we make and the consequences of those choices. Given that Revelation is an allusive, suggestive text rather than a prescriptive one, its function is to move readers and hearers to think anew, to allow their perspective to be changed and to portray the consequences of failing to respond rather than to describe in minute detail the future of the world.

This does not diminish the sense of alienation that a modern reader has when confronted by these verses. Valiant attempts have been made to "christianize" the text, and yet the vision resists neat accommodation to our theological sensibilities. Most of us, as a result, read or use Revelation little. We have simply abandoned it to fringe religious groups and lost a resource that can help us to see what makes for our peace. Bonhoeffer reminded his contemporaries that the church is the church of Apocalypse, and it must not cut itself off from this important theological resource.[277] We may discern that what the Spirit says to the churches demands of Christians imagination, not slavish dependence on the minutiae of exegesis of this or that apocalyptic image, but openness to the process of disorientation to our understanding, which a metaphorical text sets in motion, just as the prophetic Scriptures themselves did for John.

---

276. Translation from *The Spiritual Exercises of St. Ignatius*, L. J. Puhl, S.J. (Chicago: Loyola University Press, 1950) paragraphs 137-48.
277. D. Bonhoeffer, *No Rusty Swords* (London: Collins, 1965).

REVELATION 15:1-8

ANOTHER SIGN IN HEAVEN: THE SEA OF GLASS AND THE SONG OF THOSE WHO CONQUERED

COMMENTARY

15:1. Another "portent" is seen by John (cf. 12:1, 3). This is said to be "great and amazing." Like the dragon in 12:3, it is threatening: "seven angels with seven plagues, which are the last" (cf. 21:9, where these angels are explicitly linked with the seven bowls). This indicates that what will be described in chap. 16 has the air of finality, which is confirmed by the end of 15:1, "with them the wrath of God is ended."

15:2-4. The scene changes to the sea of glass, which has already appeared in 4:6, but here it is mixed with fire (there is a similarity with the hail mixed with fire in 8:7, which is also found in the description of God's throne in *1 Enoch* 14). The sea seems to be of little threat in chap. 4, but its absence in 21:1 and its fiery aspect in chap. 15 suggest otherwise (cf. 8:8; 9:17-18; 11:5; 14:10; 16:8; 18:8; 19:20).

John sees those who have conquered the beast (v. 2; cf. 12:11), its image, and the number of its name (cf. 13:18). Like the Lamb (5:6; 14:1), the great multitude of 7:9, and the 144,000 of 14:1, these people are standing (cf. Rom 14:4), this time beside the sea. They hold "harps of God" (cf. 5:8) and "sing the song of Moses" and "the song of the Lamb." This same song was sung by the Israelites after they passed through the Red Sea and the army of Pharaoh was destroyed (Exod 15:1-18). By analogy, then, those who have conquered will be on the other side of the sea of glass—in other words, on God's side of the throne (4:6: "in front of the throne there is something like a sea of glass, like crystal" [NRSV]). Like the great host in 7:9, therefore, they stand in the divine presence beyond the threat of ultimate alienation from God, though still on the very margins of that threatening situation (beside the sea of glass).

The hymn (vv. 3-4) reflects the central verses of the song in Exodus 15, where God's character is lauded. As in the Exodus passage, there are echoes of the psalms (esp. Pss 111:2; 145:17). God's wonderful and mighty deeds are lauded in words without exact parallel in earlier hymns, though the just and true acts (here only "ways" [ὁδοί *hodoi*]) of God are themes that recur in 16:5, 7 and 19:2 (cf. 19:11). God is "Almighty" (cf. 1:8; 4:8; 11:17; 16:7, 14; 19:6, 15; 21:22) and, here alone, "King" (Christ is king in 1:5; 19:16). God is "King of the nations" (NRSV; NIV, "King of the ages") that threaten the holy place (11:2); elsewhere that sovereignty is shared with the one who conquers (2:26) as well as the Messiah (12:5). The song asks, "Who will not fear/ and glorify your name?" (v. 4; cf. Ps 86:8-9; Jer 10:7), reflecting the content of the eternal gospel in 14:7. The answer to that question will be a depressing negative in 16:9, 21, though in 11:13 a (temporary?) attitude of fear and a willingness to give God the glory were found. God's holiness is stressed in 16:5. The coming of the nations to worship before God will be fulfilled in the new Jerusalem (21:24; cf. Isa 2:2).

15:5-6. God's righteous deeds have been made manifest not only in the acts of judgment but also in the opening of the temple in heaven (11:19). Now the "temple of the tent of witness" is opened (v. 5), rather than the ark of the covenant, and from it proceed seven angels holding the seven last plagues. Here is the justice of divine judgment that is outlined in Revelation. The covenant forms the basis of judgment and vindication. The angels are clothed in "clean, shining linen" (v. 6; cf. 19:8, 14), possibly inspired by the man dressed in linen who exercises judgment on Jerusalem in Ezek 9:3-4 (though their appearance reflects also that of the Son of Man in Rev 1:13; cf. Dan 10:5-6).

15:7-8. One of the creatures then gives the angels the seven bowls that are full of the anger of God (cf. 6:1ff.). The golden bowls in 5:8 were full of incense, representing the prayers of the saints (cf. 8:3-4). But now these golden bowls are full of the wrath of God (cf. 16:1; 17:1; 21:9). The prayers for vindication of the souls under the altar who had asked, "How long?" are about to be answered (cf. 6:10). The temple is filled with smoke "from the glory of God" (cf. Exod 40:34), and no one can enter until the last plagues are completed (cf. Exod 40:35; 1 Kgs 8:10-11). Smoke is more usually linked with the fire of judgment than with God's glory (9:2-3; 14:11; 18:9, 18; 19:3), though in Isa 6:4 God's glory is linked with the smoke that fills the Temple. In Rev 8:4, smoke mingled with the prayers of the saints arises to the presence of God. What follows is final judgment.

REFLECTIONS

The significance of human behavior is expressed clearly in Revelation 15. When the people of Israel reached the other side of the Red Sea, they sang a song of deliverance (Exodus 15). This song is echoed in Revelation 15. "Those who had been victorious over the beast" (15:2 NIV) is a metaphor for non-conformity and the refusal to accept the beast's dominion and way of life. This action becomes equivalent to the redemptive crossing of that threatening sea to God's side

A neutral, apparently secular, action can be an event of supreme importance in the eyes of God, on a par with other fundamental redemptive moments like the exodus. The redemptive moment means siding with the Lamb by standing firm in one's convictions and one's commitment to the way of hope, symbolized by the Lamb who bears the marks of slaughter. The liberative character of participation in the outlook and practice of a movement that promises freedom from the bondage of culture and society is on every page of Revelation (cf. 1:6), but it differs from the revolutionary zeal of the mass movements mentioned by Josephus, whose leaders sought to replicate the events of the exodus.[278]

---

278. See Josephus *Antiquities of the Jews* XX.97ff.; 167ff. See also R. Gray, *Prophetic Figures in Late Second Temple Jewish Palestine* (Oxford: Oxford University Press, 1993); and M. Walzer, *Exodus and Revelation* (New York: HarperCollins, 1985).

REVELATION 16:1-21

SEVEN ANGELS AND SEVEN TRUMPETS

COMMENTARY

Chapter 16 contains the description of the seven last plagues, completing the sequence of sevens that starts with the letters to the angels of the seven churches in chaps. 2–3 and becomes more specifically focused on judgment in the series of seals and trumpets in chaps. 6; 8–9; and 11. In the series of seals and trumpets, the penultimate marks a moment of interruption and delay. It is less obvious in chap. 16, but still present in 16:15 before the process is completed with the judgment of Babylon in chaps. 17–19.

16:1. The temple is the site from which a loud voice proceeds (cf. 1:10; 11:12; 12:10; 14:13; 16:17; 21:3; Isa 66:6). This voice tells the seven angels: "Go and pour out on the earth the seven bowls of the wrath of God." Here "wrath" translates θυμός (*thymos*, "fury") instead of the usual ὀργή (*orgē*). The former word is used elsewhere in a context relating to God only at Rom 2:8, and there only implicitly. Elsewhere in the New Testament it is used of human anger (e.g., Luke 4:28; Acts 19:28; 2 Cor 12:20; Gal 5:20; Eph 4:31; Col 3:8; Heb 11:27, several of which are lists of vices). In Revelation, *thymos* is usually used to refer to the anger of Satan (12:12) and for Babylon's fornication (14:8; 18:3). In two places it is used with the word *orgē* (16:19; 19:15) and in a further four places of God's anger (14:19; 15:1, 7; 16:1). Elsewhere, *orgē* is used exclusively for the wrath of God and of the Lamb (cf. 11:18). There does not seem to be any significant difference between these words, though we may note the use of *orgē* in contexts of eschatological judgment in Matt 3:7; Luke 21:23; John 3:36; Rom 1:18; 5:9; Eph 5:6; Col 3:6; and 1 Thess 1:10; 2:16; 5:9.

16:2. The first angel pours out its bowl on the earth, and humankind is afflicted with sores (cf. Exod 9:10-11; Luke 16:20-21). Because of these sores, humanity will blaspheme God and be unrepentant (16:11). This plague specifically affects those marked with the mark of the beast and who worship its image (13:15-16; cf. 7:3; Ezek 9:4).

16:3-4. The second angel pours out its bowl on the sea (cf. 8:8-9; Exod 7:17ff.), which becomes like the blood of a corpse. Whereas in the aftermath of the eighth trumpet blast a third of the creatures in the sea were destroyed, here every living thing in the sea dies. The third bowl is poured out on the rivers and the "springs of water" (cf. 8:10; Exod 7:17-18). In 8:11, the waters were made bitter. Here they become blood. This prompts the angel of the waters to shout out in praise of God (note that in chaps. 2–3 an angel is linked with the created world).

16:5. Just as in 11:17, God is hailed as just, as both past and present (cf. 1:4). Here God is referred to as the "Holy One" (as in 15:4) and judge (cf. 6:10; 18:8, 20; 19:11; Ps 119:137). The increased amount of hymnic material in this part of the vision is noteworthy. The heavenly choir's comments on the eschatological process seem to intensify in direct proportion to the intensification of the woes that afflict the world. Although there is no explicit suggestion that theodicy is the motive for this, the effects of this passage on the reader raise this possibility, particularly as the justice of God is a theme of these chapters.

16:6-7. This hymn from the angel of the waters (v. 6) is based on the *lex talionis* (Exod 21:24): Humanity has shed the blood of the martyrs, so the water that they have to drink is turned into blood. Thus the "shedding" of blood occurs in a chapter where "shedding" the contents of the bowls is a central theme. At the end of v. 6, "It is what they deserve!"

(NRSV) freely renders ἄξιοί εἰσιν (*axioi eisin*, "they are worthy"). The phrase probably is an indication that humankind is getting its just deserts—that is, "they deserve" to drink blood, and thus fall foul of the prohibition in Lev 17:10. Or it may be a kind of parenthesis in which the angel pronounces the worthiness of the saints and the prophets: Since their blood has been shed, they deserve retribution in kind (cf. 4:11; 5:9, 12). In 9:13, John heard a voice from the four horns of the altar. Here the altar itself speaks, asserting God's true judgment (cf. 15:3-4; 19:2).

16:8-9. The fourth angel pours out a bowl on the sun, and the sun is given permission to scorch humanity with fire (cf. 7:16; 8:12; Matt 13:6). The consequence is that humankind blasphemes the name of God (cf. 13:6; 16:11, 21). The phrase "blasphemed the name of God" (NIV and NRSV, "cursed"), found also in Rom 2:24 (cf. John 10:33; Acts 6:11; 19:37; 1 Tim 6:1; Jas 2:7), echoes Isa 52:5. Such blasphemy is particularly linked with the last days in 2 Tim 3:2 and 2 Pet 2:2. The ultimate authority over the plagues rests with God, who permitted them. Unlike 11:11, where great fear spread among earth's inhabitants, here there is no sign of repentance (cf. 9:20) or of giving God glory (cf. 11:13; 14:7), rare indeed in the book (4:9; 19:7).

In contrast, God as giver is a theme that runs throughout. In the letters to the angels, God gives time for repentance (2:21) and promises the varied gifts that belong to life in the future (e.g., 2:7; 11:18). The use of the passive ἐδόθη (*edothē*, "was given") is widely used to express divine permission (6:4; 7:2; 9:3; 13:5; 20:4), and in 17:17 (cf. 11:3) God is specifically mentioned as the one who inspires the process of judgment. In the new Jerusalem, God gives liberally from the water of life (21:6), echoing the promise of the gifts in the letters.

16:10-11. The destination of the wrath of the fifth bowl is the throne of the beast (cf. 2:13; 13:2), and its kingdom is plunged into darkness (cf. 8:12; 9:2; Exod 10:22; Matt 24:29; 27:45; Acts 2:20). Strangely, the themes of light and dark are less prominent in Revelation than we would expect in a text in which dualistic contrasts are fundamental to its worldview (cf. John 1:5; 8:12; 12:35). The darkening of minds, which Paul refers to in Rom 1:21 and 11:10 (cf. Eph 4:18), however, is reflected in humanity's hostile attitude and failure to recognize the true significance of the cataclysm taking place. Revelation echoes the sentiments of the Fourth Gospel: "People loved darkness rather than light" (John 3:19 NRSV). These people gnaw their tongues and persistently refuse to repent; instead they blaspheme God because of their pain.

16:12-14. The pouring out of the sixth bowl prompts the longest description of the consequence of the plagues. The Euphrates dries up (cf. 9:14), making way for the "kings from the east" (cf. Isa 11:15), who are among those gathering for the last battle (cf. 19:19; 20:8), referred to in anticipation in v. 16. Apart from the submission involved in the donation to Zion in 21:24, the kings of the earth are invariably led astray (6:15; 17:2; 18:3; 19:19) and only too late recognize their folly (18:9). John's vision then turns to the dragon, the beast, and the false prophet, from whose mouths proceed unclean spirits, resembling frogs (cf. Exod 8:3; on the mouth as the source of evil, see Rev 12:15; 13:5-6). These froglike beings are "unclean spirits" (πνεύματα ἀκάθαρτα *pneumata akatharta*, v. 13; NIV, "evil spirits"; NRSV, "foul spirits"), and they characterize Babylon (cf. 17:4; 18:2; this expression is used for demons in Mark 1:23; 3:11; 5:13; 7:25; 9:25; cf. Luke 11:24). The "great day of God Almighty" (v. 14; cf. 6:17) echoes the ideas connected with the day of the Lord in the OT (e.g., Amos 5:18; cf. Rom 2:5; 2 Thess 2:2). The link between the day of the Lord and the sudden disruption caused by the thief in vv. 14-15 is found in 1 Thess 5:2.

16:15. In this verse the sequence of bowls is interrupted with a saying, probably from Christ, if this verse is a parallel to 1:3. As elsewhere in the vision, the interruption comes before the final event of the sequence of seven (after the sixth seal, the servants of God are sealed [7:2-8], and after the sixth trumpet blast come the prophetic commissioning and the vision of the two witnesses [10:1–11:14]). The warning immediately follows the reference to unclean spirits and the need to be ever watchful of their activities. Vigilance (cf. 3:2-3) is a necessary quality for survival in the last days (cf. Matt 24:42-43; 25:13; 26:38; 1 Thess

5:6; 1 Pet 5:8). A beatitude (cf. Matt 5:2) is pronounced on the one who remains alert (cf. 1:3; 14:13; 19:9; 20:6; 22:7). "Keeping" one's robes (NRSV, "is clothed") means avoiding the fate of Babylon (17:16) and the threat that confronts the Laodicean angel (3:17-18). In 22:14, washing one's robes (cf. 7:14-15) is the key to the tree of life.

16:16. The kings assemble at Armageddon (הר מגדו *har Mĕgiddō*, "the Mount of Megiddo"), which is explicitly referred to only here in Revelation.[279] John reminds his readers that the name is a Hebrew word (cf. 9:11). Megiddo was the site of the death of Jehu (2 Kgs 9:27) and more particularly of the defeat of the righteous and reforming king Josiah (2 Kgs 23:29). It had by the end of the period of the Hebrew Bible achieved a place in the events of "that day" (Zech 12:11).

16:17-19. The seventh bowl is now poured out on the air (cf. 9:2), which provokes the loud cry, "It is done!" from the Temple and the throne. If the NIV and the NRSV translations are correct in including both the temple and the throne as the origin of the cry, this is the only place where the two are juxtaposed (in 16:1, the temple alone is the origin of the voice; in 4:5, the voice comes from the throne). A parallel proclamation is to be found in 21:6, where the one seated on the throne speaks. The juxtaposition in v. 18 is like 11:19 (cf. 6:12; 8:5; 11:13), though John adds that the earthquake was without parallel (cf. Dan 12:1).

In Revelation earthquakes accompany significant moments: the opening of the sixth seal, which prompted a response of fear on the part of humanity (6:12); at the ascent of the prayers of the saints to God (8:5); in the aftermath of the witness of the "lampstands," which prompted fear in the inhabitants of the city (11:13-14); and following the seventh trumpet blast and the second woe, when God's reign is seen to be effective (11:19). As has been noted, in Matthew also earthquakes attended both the crucifixion and the resurrection (Matt 27:54; 28:2). The "great city" is destroyed (v. 19) as in 11:13, as well as the cities of the nations, which in this age have been led astray (14:8; 18:21; 20:8). In the age to come, however, under the rule of Christ in the new Jerusalem (12:5; 19:15), the nations are destined to be healed (21:24-25; 22:2).

All of this prefigures the fall of Babylon, called "the great city" in 18:10, 16, 18-19, 21. Its part in the outworking of God's wrath is remembered; like the prayers of the saints, Babylon will not be forgotten in the presence of God (cf. 8:4). Babylon is to be given the cup of God's wrath, a recompense (18:6) for the cup she has made others drink (14:10; 17:4).

16:20-21. As in 6:14, mountains and islands flee (cf. 20:11). Hail of enormous size (NRSV and NIV, "about a hundred pounds"; ὡς ταλαντιαία *hōs talantiaia*, "like talents") descends from heaven (v. 21; cf. 8:7; 11:19, where no reference is made to heaven as the source of the hail). Once again people (does the Greek ἄνθρωποι [*anthrōpoi*, "men"] include women?) blaspheme God because this plague is so great (NIV, "terrible"; NRSV "fearful"; cf. 15:1; Num 11:33), just as they had because of the sores (16:11).

---

279. See J. Day, "The Origin of Armageddon," in S. Porter, P. Joyce, and D. Orton, *Crossing the Boundaries* (Leiden: Brill, 1994) 315-28; and *God's Conflict with the Dragon and the Sea* (Cambridge: Cambridge University Press, 1985).

REFLECTIONS

In the light of passages like Isaiah 21, Jeremiah 8, or Nahum 2, the doom-laden words of Revelation 16 are a prophet's attempt to describe the tumult of forces in language of myth. Their images bring readers' attention to the chaos around them as a moment of opportunity to pursue a different course. We may imagine that the upheavals in the aftermath of the death of Nero, when the Roman Empire was on the verge of crumbling, may have been either a backdrop or a vivid memory for the prophet's imagination. The fragility of a seemingly invincible empire and the superhuman forces that, once let loose, could wreak havoc on the apparently impregnable foundations of a civilization defied adequate description in the language of conventional historiography and needed the distinctive language of prophecy or apocalyptic.

"All that the poet can do today is warn," wrote a modern poetic commentator on the chaos and destruction of war, drawing on the inspiration of imagination to enable some understanding of these awesome forces and the appropriate response to them. John sees behind the machinations of human beings a more profound disease in culture and society, which will mean doom if there is no change of attitude and practice. When cataclysmic forces are unleashed, people cower in fear and incomprehension and anger. It would have been a perplexing time for the tiny Christian groups who found themselves scapegoats in a crumbling social order. What was required of them was patient endurance and even the shedding of blood as they strove to resist the power of the beast.

Revelation may be seen as an imaginative commentary on the world, a prophetic critique of human delusion and the terrible consequences of social upheaval. It summons us to read the signs of the times with the visionary imagination and insight of prophecy and, at the same time, to recognize that the prophetic words are addressed to people with minds and habits so formed by culture and human interests that they cannot understand and repent. They need to be jolted from the slumber of incomprehension caused by the idolatrous habits of oppression, violence, and hedonism.

REVELATION 17:1-18
THE VISION OF BABYLON

COMMENTARY

The description of the awesome period of woe comes to an end, and one of the angels offers to show John the judgment of Babylon. John sees Babylon seated on a scarlet beast. The vision includes detailed interpretation of various parts of the vision, quite out of keeping with other parts of Revelation. This vision is then followed by a sequence of heavenly acclamations juxtaposed with earthly laments over Babylon's fate.

17:1-2. John is approached by one of the angels who had held one of the bowls containing the seven last plagues. John is summoned to witness the judgment of the great whore, Babylon (cf. 4:1; 21:9, there to view a very different kind of city). Babylon's destruction is a particular focus of the account of judgment that has preceded (cf. 15:1). Readers of the vision will already be aware of the threat of "immorality" (πορνεία *porneia*, 2:21; 9:21; 14:8), and now will see its embodiment in the great "whore" (πόρνη *pornē*) who is "seated on many waters" (cf. Jer 51:13, where Babylon is said to "live by mighty waters" [NRSV]), a phrase that evokes, and contrasts with, the vision of the Son of Man in 1:15 (cf. 14:2; 19:6). Babylon, with whom the kings of the earth have committed fornication (v. 2) resembles Tyre (Isa 23:17; cf. Nah 3:4), and her "golden cup" (17:4) has made all the earth drunk (v. 2; cf. Jer 51:7; cf. 18:3). Babylon, too, is drunk—with "the blood of the saints and the blood of the witnesses to Jesus" (v. 6).

17:3-4. John is taken away to the desert (cf. 12:6) by the Spirit (cf. 1:10; 4:1; 21:10; Ezek 8:3). It is in the desert, or wilderness, that John comes face to face with Babylon (cf. 12:6), just as Jesus had come face to face with Satan (Matt 4:1). The wilderness, then, could be a place of insight and renewal (Hos 2:14) and the place from which movements of renewal arose (Matt 3:1; cf. Acts 21:38).[280]

John sees a woman seated on a scarlet beast (v. 3; cf. 18:12, 16) that is "full of blasphemous names" (v. 4; cf. 13:1; 18:12, 16; Dan 7:25). It has seven heads and ten horns, like the beast that arose from the sea. Unlike the saints, who are clothed in white (3:5; 4:4; 7:9, 13; cf. 19:13), the woman is bedecked in purple and scarlet robes (v. 4; see 18:12 for the list of the different-colored cloths traded by the merchants and from which Babylon would have profited). She is adorned with gold, precious stones, and pearls, and holds a golden cup "full of abominations and impurities" in her hand (cf. 1:17).

We have here the first of a number of ideas and images derived from Ezekiel's dramatic condemnation of Tyre. In Ezek 28:13, Tyre is said to have "every precious stone [as] your covering . . . and worked in gold were your settings" (NRSV). Ezekiel depicts Tyre as being a proud city that has amassed great wealth through trade with other nations (Ezek 28:5). But that prosperity will ultimately end in devastation (Ezek 27:27-36). Babylon both resembles and contrasts with the "bride of the Lamb," the new Jerusalem in John's final vision. The cup she holds is full of abominations (v. 5; cf. 21:27; Matt 24:15; Luke 16:15, where the abomination has become associated with Mammon). The reference to "the impurities of her fornications" (v. 4) coincides with the concern throughout the vision to see things in clearly dichotomous ways: clean/unclean; heaven/earth; virginity/fornication; bride/whore. "Fornication" (*porneia*) refers to the transgression of

---

280. See Josephus *The Jewish War* VI.281-283, 301-315; *Antiquities of the Jews* XX.97-99; 167-172; 185-188; M. Goodman, *The Ruling Class of Judaea: The Origins of the Jewish Revolt Against Rome, A.D. 66–70* (Cambridge: Cambridge University Press, 1987) 51ff.; R. Gray, *Prophetic Figures in Late Second Temple Jewish Palestine* (Oxford: Oxford University Press, 1993).

clear, publicly recognized boundaries of what constitutes appropriate relations (for example, incest is strictly prohibited by levitical law; see Lev 18:6ff.). The "impurities" are not just the uncleanness caused by sexual intercourse (Leviticus 15), however, but defilement that is the result of "fornication" (cf. Deut 22:22).

17:5-6. The woman resembles the saints in having a name (v. 5), rather than merely a mark (cf. 13:16; 14:1), written on her forehead: "Babylon the great, mother of whores and of earth's abominations" (v. 5). This name is a "mystery" (μυστήριον *mystērion*; a word used only here and at 1:20; 10:7; cf. its use to speak of the mystery of salvation in Rom 11:25; Eph 3:6-11; Col 1:26; and of the eschatological process in 2 Thess 2:7). And this eschatological mystery needs explaining. Like the scandal of the cross, if left a mystery, it can be a stumbling block to those who do not recognize Babylon for what it really is.

"Babylon" is the woman's name (14:8; 16:9), linking her with the prediction of an imminent fall. What is said about her in this and the following chapters owes much to biblical oracles about Babylon's destruction (e.g., Jeremiah 51). Babylon was an alien culture and the place of exile, hence the reference in 1 Pet 5:13, a work for which the experience of exile is a significant theme (e.g., 1 Pet 2:11).[281] Babylon the great, the epitome of the earth's "abominations" (some of which will be described in chap. 18), commits "fornication" and is the source of other similar acts. Babylon is "drunk with the blood of the saints and the blood of the witnesses to Jesus" (1:5; 2:13; 11:3, 18; 18:20, 24), and she offends the prohibition of Lev 17:10: "If anyone of the house of Israel or of the aliens who reside among them eats any blood, I will set my face against that person who eats blood" (NRSV; cf. Rev 16:6). Babylon's drunken stupor is infectious, and it contaminates those with whom she commits her "fornications." So the inhabitants of the earth have become drunk from the wine of Babylon's "fornication" (v. 2). But Babylon is about to drink the cup of the wine of God's wrath (16:19; cf. 14:8).

John is "greatly amazed" by the wondrous spectacle (v. 6), language he had earlier used to describe the wonder of the earth at the might of the beast (13:3). This reaction, which will be replicated at v. 8, may itself be the prelude to captivation, however (cf. 13:4). This inclusion of the reference to John's reaction parallels other moments in the book of Revelation, for example, the weeping in 5:4 and the repeated attempts to worship angels in 19:10 and 22:8.

17:7-8. At this point an angel questions John about his amazement and proceeds to tell him about the mystery of Babylon and the beast who carries her. This passage is a unique one in Revelation in which the angelic messenger offers the meaning of a vision. Seldom used in Revelation, such interpretation is a typical feature of other works in the apocalyptic tradition. The second half of the book of Daniel, for instance, offers several examples of this kind of angelic explanation of events; Daniel 7 is an obvious example where Daniel's vision of the thrones, judgment, and the coming of the Human One is interpreted in terms of human history.

The beast that came up from the sea (v. 8) "was, and is not, and is about to ascend from the bottomless pit" (an allusion to the first reference to the beast in 11:7), the place from which the destruction of the fifth trumpet had started and into which Satan will be cast (20:3). The phraseology used for the beast in v. 8 is reminiscent of that used for God in 16:5, where God is referred to as the "Holy One, who are and were" (NRSV). As in 13:8, those whose names are not written in the book of life will be amazed when they see this beast, though, as in 13:8, they will not worship it. Such wonder is a spiritually dangerous attitude to take, and it makes the interruption by the angel in v. 7 all the more comprehensible. Seeing the beast that "once was, now is not, and yet will come" can easily lead people astray (cf. 13:14). To be in receipt of a heavenly vision is a threatening business.[282] The parody of the divine character in the description of the beast (the one who was and is to come) parallels similar descriptions, particularly the beast with the mortal wound that had been healed in 13:3.

---

281. See J. H. Elliott, *A Home for the Homeless* (London: SCM, 1982).

282. See G. Scholem, *Major Trends in Jewish Mysticism* (New York: Schocken, 1955).

John is fortunate to have revealed to him the true identity of the beast upon which Babylon sits and through that disclosure be saved from a profound mistake.

17:9-14. The angel continues to explain the vision by saying, "All this calls for a mind that has wisdom" (v. 9), a repeat of the formula John used in 13:18, another passage where there is a probable historical allusion. While the angel's purpose seems to be to decode the vision for John, one cannot ignore the fact that he has nearly been carried away by the wonder of what he has seen. True wisdom may consist, therefore, in making a correct identification of Babylon and the beast so that John and others like him are not deceived, as will be many of the inhabitants of earth.

In the explanation that follows (v. 9), various parts of the vision are explained. The seven heads stand for both seven mountains (elsewhere mountains are to be shaken and removed; see 6:14-15; 8:8; 16:20; cf. Mark 11:23) and seven kings (cf. 6:15; 18:3). It is the kings who will receive the focus of attention in vv. 10-14. Five of these kings have fallen already, one is still living, and the final king has not yet come. When this final king comes, he will reign for only a short time. The beast is said to be an eighth king (v. 11) who "belongs to the seven," and it will "go to destruction." The ten horns are ten kings who are still to come, and their authority will last for "one hour" (cf. 18:10, 19). These kings share a common purpose of bestowing their power and authority on the beast. They will make war with the Lamb (actually it is the rider on the white Horse in 19:16 who engages in the struggle; cf. 2:16; 11:7; 12:7; 13:4; 20:8). But the Lamb will conquer them (19:21; cf. Isa 11:4), for he is called "Lord of lords and King of kings" (cf. 19:16; 1 Cor 8:6). The Lamb is accompanied by the faithful "elect" (ἐκλεκτός *eklektos*, v. 14; NIV and NRSV, "chosen"; used only here in Revelation, though it is used several times in the synoptic eschatological discourse, e.g., Mark 13:20, 22, 27).

17:15-18. The angel now explains to John that the "many waters" upon which the woman is seated are "peoples and multitudes and nations and languages" (v. 15; cf. 5:9; 7:9; 11:9; 13:7). The ten kings of v. 12 unite with the beast to make the woman "desolate and naked." The focus now is on the pact between the kings and the beast to utterly destroy Babylon (v. 16; cf. 18:16, 19). They will "devour her flesh and burn her up with fire" (cf. 19:18; burning was the fate of a priest's daughter who had resorted to prostitution in Lev 21:9). So the beast will turn against what it supports, an example of a kingdom divided against itself being laid waste (Matt 12:25).

The purposes of God are at work in this self-destruction of Babylon and the beast (v. 17), stressing the omnipotence of God. Verse 17 is a striking sentence. God is seldom explicitly named as the author of such events (see 1:6; 7:17; 18:5, 8, 20; 19:6; 21:3, 22; 22:5, 18-19; of these instances, only 7:17, the references in chap. 18, and 22:18-19 compare with 17:17, which echoes the "permitting" affliction in passages like 1 Kgs 22:22 and Job 1:12). Such statements contrast with the passive verbs that are usually employed to convey the fulfillment of the divine purposes.

The common purpose of the ten horns in v. 13 to give their power and authority to the beast has become, in the interpretation in vv. 16-17, a common purpose to give their kingdoms to the beast as well. That conspiracy will last until the words of God are fulfilled (cf. 10:7, when the seventh angel's trumpet announces the fulfilling of the mystery of God), when the rider on the white horse emerges to complete the judgment (19:11), and when the marriage supper of the Lamb takes place (19:9).

The final word of interpretation in v. 18 concerns Babylon, the great city, which rules over the kings of the earth. Elsewhere Babylon's relationship with the kings is less explicitly monarchic; Babylon exercises power through her "fornication" (e.g., 17:2; cf. 16:20).

Along with chap. 13, Revelation 17 has rightly been seen as a fairly explicit point of contact with the history of John's own day. Assuming that Rome has inspired John's vision of Babylon in 17:9-18, the reference to the seven heads may be references to Roman emperors. It is not clear whether John intends readers to associate specific emperors with the seven kings, and if so, where to start the list of emperors. The computations are bound to be affected by assumptions we may have about the date of John's writing. If one favors a Domitianic date for the writing of Revelation, as early church tradition suggests (see the section "John, the Gospel of John, and the Revelation to John" in the Introduction), then one needs to find a way of interpreting 17:9-18 to include Emperor Domitian. The *Sibylline Oracles*,[283] a Jewish text contemporary with the book of Revelation, starts the list with Julius Caesar, even though he did not, strictly speaking, take the title of emperor. If, however, one starts with Augustus, one needs to decide whether to include the three emperors (Galba, Otho, and Vitellius) who reigned for only a short time in the upheaval that shook the empire after the death of Nero in 68–69 CE. If these emperors are excluded, then we are left with a date in Vespasian's reign. The simplest solution is to start with Augustus and, like Suetonius, the chronicler of the early Roman emperors, include the three emperors who briefly succeeded Nero (Galba, Otho, and Vitellius), meaning that the five who have fallen are the emperors before and including Nero.[284] The one who is to come would then be Galba, and the one who is to succeed Galba and is one of the five is probably Nero[285] (on the widespread belief that Nero would return, see the Commentary on 13:11-14). But for reasons that will be set out, care needs to be taken to avoid any kind of mathematical precision in correlating visionary imagination with historical events.

Figure 3: Roman Emperors 49 BCE–138 CE

Julius Caesar	49–44 BCE
Augustus (Octavian)	31 BCE–14 CE
Tiberius	14–37 CE
Gaius (Caligula)	37–41
Claudius	41–54
Nero	54–68
Galba	68–69
Otho	69
Vitellius	69
Vespasian	69–79
Titus	79–81
Domitian	81–96
Nerva	96–98
Trajan	98–117
Hadrian	117–138

As the report on the vision progresses, there is a change of interest in v. 11 away from the heads of the beast to the beast itself. The eighth head, which is one of the seven, is in fact the beast "that was and is not and is to come" (v. 8). There is a similar oscillation between the beast and its heads in 13:1-3, 12, where the beast as a whole is characterized by the head that has been mortally wounded, yet healed. The eighth king is the one who goes back to perdition, the last embodiment of the works of darkness. That this eighth king is one of the seven may reflect the widespread belief that Nero would rise again from death.

All this points to a date after the fifth king and before the last one, who is one of the seven, returns. That would seem to exclude the emperor Domitian, during whose reign the earliest commentators suggested that the book of Revelation was written.[286] Indeed, the evidence for persecution of Christians in Asia Minor at the time of Domitian is nonexistent apart from Revelation.[287] At the end

---

283. See *Sib. Or.* v. 12.
284. See also *Sib. Or.*, vv. 13ff.
285. See Bauckham, "Nero and the Beast," 384-452.
286. E.g., Irenaeus *Against Heresies* v.30:3.
287. See Thompson, *The Book of Revelation*, chap. 6.

of Domitian's reign there appears to have been harassment of Jews and those identified with Judaism (among whom Jewish Christians, like John, would have been numbered) as the scope of the *fiscus Iudaicus* (a tax imposed on all Jews after the destruction of the Temple in 70)[288] was extended. Dio Cassius tells us that certain prominent members of the imperial court had been charged with "atheism" in the dying years of Domitian's reign,[289] which may refer to sympathizing with the Jews rather than with Christians. Domitian claimed for himself the title *dominus ac deus noster* ("Our Lord and God"; cf. Rev 19:16), a move that no doubt presented a particular problem for Jews and Christians, who would have viewed the state cult and its idolatry as utterly blasphemous; that crisis passed with the accession of a new emperor, however (Nerva). Even if the vision reflects the turbulent events at the end of Nero's life instead of those of Domitian's time, it is entirely possible that persons and events of that era of upheaval imposed themselves on the visionary much later than the time in which they took place.

We are left with a situation in which the external evidence is strong for a date during Domitian's reign, but the internal evidence of this chapter points in the general direction of a date three decades earlier. Either way, the message is unaffected, though the hermeneutical implications are significant (see Commentary on 1:19). Readers are directed, rather as they are when they are confronted by Mark 13:14, to see in the beast and Babylon an ancient referent. This consideration suggests a reading of the book that is not exclusively concerned with eschatology but attends to prophecy as an act of insight into present circumstances rather than a prediction of the future. John's vision relates to social and political realities that confront his readers, even if such references are now transformed in the visionary's imagination. We need to remember that the vision John sees is of Babylon, not of Rome.[290] Thus it assumes a wider significance than the narrow focus on Rome in the vision could achieve. The image of Babylon resonates with passages that point back to the OT experiences of displacement, exile, the threat of idolatry, and the longing for Zion.

Too narrow a focus on vv. 8-14 can beguile us into a process of decoding. To leave interpretation at the level of identification of heads and horns, however, would be to end up engaged merely in a hermeneutic of decoding.

The allure of Babylon as well as its identity remain as pressing for modern as for ancient readers. Like John, readers today may be amazed at her description, stunningly evoked in the lament of her fall in the following chapters. As the vision in chap. 17 makes clear, she is no hapless victim who sadly ends up desolate at the hands of supposed supporters (vv. 16-17). Babylon, too, will be drunk with the blood of the saints (v. 6), because the horns of the beast on which she sits will make war against the Lamb (v. 14). Babylon is not merely a symbol of all that is dissolute, who ultimately will end up in her own dissolution. Rather, she colludes with "war" on the saints, which causes intoxication and lack of proper judgment. John's vision of the two witnesses in chap. 11 enabled readers to see where the threat to the prophetic witness of the church comes from: "the beast that comes up from the bottomless pit" (11:7 NRSV). That beast reappears in 17:8, and its horns are the kings who persecute the righteous and profit from the riches of Babylon (18:9-10). Not only is Babylon to be laid waste (v. 16), but also the beast, the supporter of Babylon, is destined for destruction (v. 11). The abomination of luxury, persecution, and military might also goes to desolation.

---

288. Rowland, *The Open Heaven*, 407-13.
289. Domitian *Histories* 16.14.1.
290. See P. Minear, *I Saw a New Earth: An Introduction to the Visions of the Apocalypse* (Washington: Corpus, 1968).

REFLECTIONS

1. Mention was made in the commentary of the way in which isolated historical events can be taken up and become part of a prophet's visionary insight. For the writer of Revelation, recollections of past events, whether from the late 60s, at the time of the

Jewish revolt and the chaos after the death of Nero, or from the time of Domitian, have infused the visionary's imagination and become part of the apparatus of the symbolic world and graphic scenery that confront us. The original historical significance of these events is transcended and ceases to determine their import within the framework of the prophecy.[291]

The discussion of such possible historical allusions raises an important hermeneutical question: Does it matter whether or not we can now pick up the precise allusions? That is a matter of interest only if we think that the sole way to make sense of an ancient text is to locate it precisely in its ancient context. That strategy may be necessary if a text remains utterly opaque. Revelation's opacity has little to do with our inability to understand the weft of allusion, however. The point at issue in Revelation 13, for example, is quite clear: Do not worship the beast or the dragon that stands behind the beast. We do not need to know the details of the Roman imperial cult or even economic life in Asia Minor in the last half of the first century (about which, unfortunately, we know all too little) in order to understand Revelation. History can satisfy our curiosity and occasionally enrich our exegesis. But it is not essential for it. What we have in Revelation 17 are traces of a first-century setting that have been taken up in the language of visionary imagery so that the contingent is rendered in a form that transcends the original circumstances to become prophetic pronouncement. Modern readers do not need the ancient allusion in order to make sense of the text.[292]

We assume that ancient readers would have been better equipped to make sense of apocalyptic texts than we are. This presupposes that there was a deliberate attempt on the part of the writer to couch the message in such a way as to facilitate the understanding of those "in the know" and to avoid having the message be understood by others if it fell into the wrong hands. We cannot be sure, however, whether this is what happened. The visionary used elements of the prophetic discourse of Ezekiel and Daniel, which would have been familiar to ancient readers. It may also be that those first readers were as much at a loss as we are, though in all likelihood they were more familiar with the ancient scriptures. Those persons involved in the life of their communities and for whom the imperial cult caused no offense might have reacted with the same mixture of incredulity and disdain that has always characterized the reaction to sharply worded prophetic messages. The problem now and then is not the opacity of the images but the inability of minds soaked in a dominant culture to be shaken from complacency by metaphorical texts.

2. At the time when John was writing, the Roman Empire had inspired his imagery, but the naming of the woman as Babylon gives a wider application to the image.[293] Bablyon is a symbol of military power and oppression. Above all, for those who witness to the ways of the Lamb, it is a place of exile and alienation (see Psalm 137; 1 Pet 5:13). Yet it is a place where the person with a visionary eye can see the glory of God, as Ezekiel did (Ezekiel 1), in whose footsteps John follows. John writes and readers read in the mist of the dominion of the beast and Babylon's luxurious consumption. However strong the desire of the saints to come out from the midst of Babylon (see 18:4), the book of Revelation is addressed to people who breathe Babylon's ethos, whether they like it or not, and need a vision of how to live under its imperial rule yet without becoming a part of it (parallel in some respects to the conduct of the Jews in the stories in the early part of the book of Daniel). There is no escape from exile this side of the millennium, except, that is, in the difference of perspective that comes with a vision of a common life based on different values.

---

291. Indeed, Caird comments: "We cannot expect to decipher the book unless we know what happened to account for John's visionary experience." See Caird, *The Revelation*, 6. See also Bauckham, *The Climax of Prophecy*, 450-52.
292. See P. Ricoeur, *Time and Narrative*, trans. K. McLaughlin and D. Pellauer (Chicago: University of Chicago Press, 1984) 157.
293. See Minear, *I Saw a New Earth*.

3. The kings of the earth commit fornication with Babylon, and the mighty of the earth are intoxicated by Babylon's power. As elsewhere in the Bible, sexual language is used here to capture certain aspects of the need for exclusivity in divine service and distinctiveness in ethical response. Throughout Revelation, John encourages resistance to compromise and the blurring of boundaries, except in the circumstances determined by God. So consummation comes only when the marriage of God and the bride takes place in the new age. A degree of exclusivity rather than promiscuity characterizes relationships between humans and between the divine and humans. Boundaries are set in place, transgression of which is proscribed. It is only in the new Jerusalem that the boundary between heaven and earth is swept away and the nature of God is shared by all its inhabitants; yet, even there the sense of exclusion and divine superiority remains.

Discrimination in intimacy, particularly when that involves one's vocation and integrity as a person created in God's image, matters; to be marked with the mark of the beast is, in fact, a denial of one's true self. To commit "fornication" or be "intoxicated" risks compromising both our ability to discern truth and justice and our sense of integrity. The book of Revelation is a challenge to see ourselves as we are seen by God and to see others without the corrupting lens of self-interested exploitation.

4. Harlotry involves selling one's body. The situation in which men and women are driven to that means that it is an epitome of ways of life in the distorted world of the beast and Babylon. Submission to the beast, enjoying Babylon, may seemingly save the lives of the kings of the earth and its inhabitants; but it will mean forfeiting their souls (Mark 8:36; Luke 12:5). The kings of the earth, through their involvement in trade with Babylon, accumulate great wealth. Even ordinary people enjoy some benefit, provided they become part of the system. They get drunk with the wine of Babylon's fornication, desensitized by the ideology and diversions of its culture. People become stupefied by the effects of Babylon's activities and by participating in that which makes Babylon "great." People are in no state of mind to see clearly the cost of involvement with Babylon, not least in human lives (18:13). Reading Revelation may enable some people to see the truth of what they are doing.[294]

5. Chapter 17 epitomizes the negative portrayal of women in Revelation.[295] To the modern reader, these negative images include: Jezebel, who personifies prophecy that is opposed to God; the new Jerusalem, which is portrayed as an adjunct of the bridegroom whose life is governed by pleasing "him"; the exaltation of celibacy; and the use of sexual imagery focusing on the woman as the harlot. The book seems to project images of women as either whores or brides, active Jezebels or passive wives and mothers. Women are viewed in terms of a patriarchal culture and its attendant economy. They can survive only by being harlots or wives and risk destitution if single or widowed.

The way women are pictured in Revelation is complicated, however. Revelation 12:1-2, with the woman clothed with the sun, has been a key text in the development of doctrine and iconography about Mary, whose ambiguous role within theology has been widely discussed.[296] There is nothing sexist about the reference to Jezebel. Like Balaam, Jezebel has come to embody the false prophet:[297] She "calls herself a prophet and is teaching and beguiling my servants to practice fornication and to eat food sacrificed to idols" (Rev 2:20 NRSV). Moreover, we need to bear in mind that the ultimate inspiration for the immoral behavior lies with the beast supporting the woman. While

---

294. Cf. W. Stringfellow, *An Ethic for Christians and Other Aliens in a Strange Land* (Dallas: Word, 1979).
295. Tina Pippin, *Death and Desire: The Rhetoric of Gender in the Apocalypse of John* (Louisville: Westminster/John Knox, 1992).
296. See P. Prigent, *Apocalypse 12: Histoire de l'exégèse* (Geneva: Labor et Fides, 1988); Y. Gabara and M. C. Bingemer, *Mary Mother of God, Mother of the Poor* (Tunbridge Wells: Burns and Oates, 1989); M. Warner, *Alone of All Her Sex: The Myth and Cult of the Virgin Mary* (London: Picador, 1985).
297. See G. Vermes, *Scripture and Tradition* (Leiden: Brill, 1973).

it would not be correct to describe Babylon as a victim of the beast and its allies, Babylon is consistently not the active partner in the "fornication" but the object of the attentions of the kings of the earth. They have played their part in making Babylon what it is. Without the support of the beast, Babylon will perish. So the apocalyptic imagery suggests the complexity of oppression. Babylon is culpable, but ultimately at the mercy of the beast.

Although in some instances women are idealized in the book of Revelation, the overall portrayal hardly evinces a sympathetic attitude to women. Yet, paradoxically, as a prophetic book, Revelation has offered space for women as well as men to enable their spirituality to flourish and for them to emerge as individuals in their own right, created in God's image, in the midst of a society steeped in patriarchy. Prophets and mystics have found in Revelation the inspiration to explore the inner life and to exercise a ministry denied by much else in Scripture and tradition (with the possible exception of the Song of Songs).[298] Teresa of Avila, Catherine of Siena, and Hildegard of Bingen, like the male radicals who turned to Revelation, found in this allusive text the freedom to resist received religion and practice. This canonical text opened a door for an experience of God that enabled them to transcend the boundaries imposed by what was conventionally possible.[299]

There was in John's day (and often still is) only a severely constrained range of possibilities for resisting the hegemony of the dominant culture. Yet even from within the constraints of patriarchy, however, insight emerges. For example, patient endurance might be required instead of grand gestures. Or better, Revelation helps us to see that "holding the testimony of Jesus" in patient endurance is the only grand gesture we need. Faith (14:12), readiness, and witness (11:2ff.), emotional involvement and perseverance have all been characteristic, for good or for ill, of women's lot in our male-dominated world. Such characteristics have been resistance and subversion, enabling a modicum of integrity in cultures that have been dominated by men.[300] Watching and waiting are the daily experience of women at times of crisis, in labor (of different kinds) or death, but also in the ordinariness of life: "There were also women looking on from a distance" (Mark 15:40 NRSV); "[Anna] never left the temple but worshiped there with fasting and prayer night and day" (Luke 2:37 NRSV). Patient endurance, so often characterized by women, seemingly futile and ineffectual, is a form of witness characteristic of the divine, powerful in its apparent weakness, and is part of the reconceptualization of what constitutes cosmos, order, in Revelation. The exploitation of small opportunities for change is not to be despised.

Revelation challenges the dominion and patterns of patriarchy in its key hermeneutical concept of the slaughtered Lamb.[301] In the new Jerusalem, God is not "father" but "God" (21:7; a subtle change of 2 Sam 7:14: "I will be a father to him, and he shall be a son to me" [NRSV]). Divine dominion is marked by a Lamb who shares the throne. One thing the reader should be used to by now about Revelation: To offer neat explanations and rationalizations of a text like this is to risk misreading it. As with so much else, its metaphorical form is not about tidy systems of satisfying exegetical solutions.

The medium can, understandably, detract from its message, so that the unpalatable character of its imagery becomes an obstacle. There is no easy answer, notwithstanding the attempts to understand and apologize for the language and imagery of Revelation. John's horizon in certain important respects differs from ours. Perhaps a way to a solution is offered by William Blake's prophetic mythology, in which the imagery of Revelation is taken up and expanded, different from but in continuity with the book of

---

298. On female visionaries, see S. Elm, *Virgins of God: The Making of Asceticism in Late Antiquity* (New York: Clarendon, 1996) 32; G. Jantzen, *Power, Gender, and Christian Mysticism* (Cambridge: Cambridge University Press, 1995).
299. I am grateful to Sara Maitland and Ros Hunt for helping me reflect on some of the contemporary hermeneutical issues posed by the book of Revelation.
300. See James Scott, *Domination and the Arts of Resistance: Hidden Transcripts* (New Haven: Yale University Press, 1990).
301. Blake, *The Four Zoas*, in Keynes, *Blake*.

Revelation itself.[302] Blake embarked on a new form of mythopoesis. He was not a commentator or an exegete; thus he is not closely tied to the text. He engaged with, and his work embodies, the "spirit of apocalypse." He was capable of leaving the detail of Revelation behind in exploring an apocalyptic vision for his own day. It can be said that he developed "voices of apocalyptic thunders."[303] For his own day, in a medium different from, but intimately linked with, Revelation, he was not tied to the ancient images and their context, historical or textual. Instead he sought to reimagine and recast them. As we engage with both Blake's and Revelation's ambivalent attitude toward women, we need to explore other apocalyptic media to find a discourse that will permeate contemporary minds dulled to the shock and insight of metaphorical language and at the same time not run the risk of putting a stumbling block in the way of those it seeks to persuade.

302. T. Pippin, *Death and Desire: The Rhetoric of Gender in the Apocalypse of John* (Louisville: Westminster/John Knox, 1992) 107.
303. See Stephen Moore, "The Heavenly Vision as a Posing Exhibition," *JSNT* 60 (1995) 27-55.

REVELATION 18:1–19:10

THE FALL OF BABYLON

COMMENTARY

The vision reported in 18:1–19:10 begins with a series of statements from representatives of heaven. By the end of the passage, however, the tone and the speakers have changed. The angel predicts that kings (18:9), merchants (18:11-17), and shipmasters and sailors (18:17-18) will weep over Babylon's demise. Chapter 18 ends with a mighty angel demonstrating the violence of Babylon's overthrow, followed by rejoicing in heaven (19:1-10). As well as an oscillation between voices, some rejoicing, some lamenting, Babylon's fall, the text moves between verse and prose.

18:1-2. John sees another angel descending from heaven (cf. 10:1; 20:1) with authority and with such splendor that the whole earth is illuminated (cf. 15:8; 21:23; 22:5; Isa 6:4). The angel cries out with a mighty voice, "Fallen, fallen is Babylon the great!" (cf. 18:2, 10, 21). There is a twofold assertion of Babylon's fall (cf. 14:8, where the proclamation of Babylon's fall has already been anticipated, and the threefold woe in 8:13 and Isa 21:9) and a statement about its present pitiable state (cf. 17:16): "It has become a dwelling place of demons." In the light of what has already been said in 16:14, Babylon had probably been an abode of demons and full of unclean things as a result of "fornication" (17:4) long before its fall. Its site as a place of impurity is affirmed by virtue of the fact that it has become a haunt of "every unclean and detestable bird" and "every foul and hateful animal" (cf. 17:16; 22:15; see the list in Deuteronomy 14), though there is some textual uncertainty here.

18:3. Once more we hear that the nations and the kings of the earth have "drunk of the wine of the wrath of her fornication" (cf. 14:8, as will the one marked with the beast in 14:19). The awkward Greek genitive construction ("the wine of the wrath of her fornication") seems to be a compressed way of speaking about collusion, thereby earning the wrath of God. In 16:19, God gave Babylon the "wine-cup of the fury of his wrath," and it is this wrath that Babylon now shares with the nations (cf. 17:2). The kings in particular have committed fornication with Babylon. The merchants have become rich as a result of Babylon's luxury (v. 3, already hinted at in the description of Babylon in 17:4 and to be expanded further in 18:11-19). True wealth is not what Babylon has offered (18:15); true wealth comes only from Christ (3:17-18).

18:4-5. John hears another voice out of heaven (cf. 10:4; 14:13), summoning God's people out of Babylon (implying that they had lived in the midst of it until that point) so as not to share in Babylon's sins (cf. Jer 51:45). God's people will share in the life of the new Jerusalem (21:3), so they must separate themselves (cf. 2 Cor 6:17, drawing on Lev 26:16) to avoid Babylon's "plagues" (cf. Ezek 9:4-5). As in Sodom and Gomorrah (Genesis 18–19), the righteous must evacuate Babylon, for its sins are "heaped high as heaven" (Jer 51:9). But coming out of Babylon is less about escaping the judgment that will fall upon the city than it is about avoiding the risk of contamination from Babylon's "plagues" (the word πληγή [$pl\bar{e}g\bar{e}$] is invariably used of the eschatological plagues; e.g., 9:18; 15:1; 16:9). Babylon's "plagues" will be the destruction and nakedness referred to in 17:16. Like the "abomination of desolation" that Jesus commands the disciples to flee (see Mark 13:14-15), Babylon's desolation is a reason to flee. God now remembers Babylon's misdeeds (cf. 16:19).

18:6-8. In v. 6, the summons to God's people turns into a plea to God to repay Babylon (cf. 16:6) and to double that recompense (cf. Isa 40:2; Jer 16:18), a double draft of the wine of wrath (14:8). The theme of recompense continues in v. 7 with the plea for Babylon's judgment to be in direct proportion to the glory and luxury Babylon had enjoyed. Instead of luxury, Babylon should now be in "torment and grief" (cf. 9:5; 14:11), a continuation of what the two witnesses had earlier carried out before the inhabitants of the great city (11:10). The grief Babylon is about to endure will not be part of the life in the other city, the new Jerusalem (21:4). The arrogance of Babylon's supposition that she will be free from grief because of her royal status is condemned (v. 7; cf. Isa 47:8; note the description of Zion as a woman in mourning in 4 Ezra 10:41). This arrogance echoes that of the king of Babylon who presumed to be a god in Isa 14:13-14. Babylon's particular plagues are mentioned in v. 8 (cf. 17:16): "pestilence and mourning and famine—and she will be burned with fire" (cf. 6:8), contrasting with the luxury and consumption that have characterized Babylon and will be set out in the merchants' lament in v. 11. This reversal is a manifestation of the almighty God's judgment upon her (v. 8; note that God is called "mighty" [ἰσχυρός *ischyros*], an adjective used of Babylon in v. 10).

18:9-10. The kings of the earth weep and wail at Babylon's demise (v. 9; cf. 1:7 and the similar juxtaposition of verbs in Jas 4:9; 5:1, the latter in a context of the condemnation of the rich). The kings have accommodated Babylon, who has been the means of their own enrichment. They now lament from afar on account of fear (cf. 11:11), just as the sailors wept over the fall of Tyre in Ezek 27:30ff.[304] The double woe of v. 10, "Alas, alas," will recur in vv. 16 and 19 (cf. 8:13). Babylon's judgment comes quickly, "in one hour" (v. 10; cf. 17:12).

18:11-19. Just as the kings of the earth had wept, so now do the merchants weep and lament, "since no one buys their cargo anymore" (v. 11). Babylon had been the hub of trade, and the merchants had depended on her. Those who refused to worship the beast had been excluded from buying and selling (13:17). These merchants had colluded with Babylon (they committed "fornication"), thus avoiding ostracism and enjoying the opulence of the wealth they amassed (v. 15).

---

304. See Nelson Kraybill, *Imperial Cult and Commerce in John's Apocalypse* (Sheffield: Sheffield Academic, 1996); R. Bauckham, "The Economic Critique of Rome," in *The Climax of Prophecy* (Edinburgh: T. & T. Clark, 1993) 338-83; P. Garnsey, K. Hopkins, and C. Whittaker, *Trade in the Ancient Economy* (Berkeley: University of California Press, 1983).

The list of the items of trade in vv. 12-13 echoes places in Revelation where these goods are linked with God and the Messiah. Gold, silver, and precious stones have bedecked Babylon (17:4; cf. 18:16), and precious stones will form the foundations of the new Jerusalem (21:19). Gold is mentioned throughout the book in connection with those who are opposed to God (9:7; 17:4; 18:12, 16), and it is often used to describe the apparel of the Son of Man (1:12), the crowns of the elders (4:4), the angel's crown (14:14), the golden measure (21:15), and the street of the new Jerusalem (21:21). Silver is mentioned only here in Revelation. Pearls adorn Babylon as well (17:4), and the twelve gates of the heavenly city will each be made of a single pearl (21:21). Fine linen is the clothing of the great city (18:16) and of the bride of the Lamb (19:8) and its armies (19:14), while purple and scarlet belong to Babylon alone (17:4). The different woods (ξύλον *xylon*) contrast with the wood of the tree (*xylon*) of life (22:2, 14, 19; *xylon* is used for the cross in Acts 5:30; Gal 3:13; 1 Pet 2:24). The feet of the Son of Man were compared to "burnished bronze" in 1:15, and it is with an iron rod that Christ will rule the nations (2:27; 12:5; 19:15). Incense is the vehicle of the prayers of the saints to God (8:3-4; cf. 5:8); frankincense (18:13) is contained in the golden censer with which the angel offers the saints' prayers at the altar before the throne (8:3, 5). Oil and wine had been spared in the first part of the judgment, when the seven seals were broken (chap. 6; cf. 9:7). But now they, too, have become unsalable merchandise. The culmination of the list is the brief, but poignant, reference to "human lives" (v. 13; cf. Ezek 27:13). The Greek merely has "bodies" (σώματα *sōmata*). Thus slaves were just bodies, mere commodities to add to the long list. But John cannot allow that to pass without glossing the word: They are human lives.[305]

The reference to human beings at the end of v. 13 prompts a short refrain on Babylon's loss: "The fruit for which your soul longed/ has gone from you" (v. 14). The word ἐπιθυμία (*epithymia*, "desire," "lust") echoes Exod 20:17 and the fruit in the garden in Gen 3:6. Babylon's soul is taken up with

---

305. See Wengst, *Pax Romana and the Peace of Jesus Christ*, 118ff.

"dainties" and "splendor." "Desire" is related to affluence and property in 1 John 2:16; it is the way of Cain, who hated and killed and who, according to Josephus, degenerated into amassing material property.[306]

Like the kings (v. 10), the merchants (v. 15), who had become rich, stand afar and weep. Again, there is a cry of woe because Babylon has been stripped of the purple, scarlet, gold and precious stones mentioned in v. 12. Wealth is laid waste (cf. 17:16; Ezek 26:19). Then the seafarers (v. 17; cf. Ezek 27:27ff.) from afar view the smoke that comes from the fire of Babylon's burning. Their cry, "What city was like the great city?" is meant to elicit pity and great sadness at Babylon's destruction (cf. Ezek 27:32). They throw dust on their heads as they cry out in sorrow for the loss of the place from which all who had ships had grown rich.

18:20-24. Such sentiments are interrupted, however, by a different kind of cry, one of rejoicing (v. 20), echoing the joy of heaven at Satan's ejection in 12:12 (cf. Jer 51:48). Apostles as well as saints and prophets are commanded to rejoice ("apostles" [ἀπόστολοι *apostoloi*] is used only here and at 2:2; 21:14 in Revelation), because God has judged in favor of them over Babylon (v. 20), who has been drunk "with the blood of the saints and the blood of the witnesses to Jesus" (17:6 NRSV). This alternative theme is taken up in the following verses. A mighty angel casts a millstone into the sea: "With such violence the great city of Babylon will be thrown down" (v. 21; cf. 5:2; 10:1; Jer 51:63). The once great city "will be found no more" (v. 21; cf. Ezek 26:21).

The tone of sadness resumes in v. 21, this time in the words of the mighty angel, who announces the end of Babylon's music, contrasting with the heavenly music that is often mentioned (e.g., the trumpets of apocalypse and the songs of deliverance accompanied by harps; 5:8; 14:2; 15:2). Babylon as a place of art, music, craft, and trade is no more. Lamps will no longer shine in the city's windows (cf. Jer 25:10), and the voices of "bridegroom and bride" will no longer be heard (cf. Matt 24:38). The merchants had been "the magnates of the earth" (v. 23; cf. 6:15), but now their goods go unsold. Readers will be in for a rude shock if they think that there is a neutral character to all the activity of trade, commerce, and socializing. Such commercial and cultural activities are described as "sorcery" (v. 23), an activity that will be excluded from the new Jerusalem (21:8; 22:15) and of which humanity has refused to repent (9:21). (God's witness against sorcery is closely linked with the oppression of the hired laborer, the widow, the orphan, and the stranger when the refining fire of judgment comes [Mal 3:5].) The lament for Babylon's culture and sophistication and wealth cannot pass without the reminder that in Babylon the blood of the prophets and of the saints had been shed (v. 24; cf. 6:10; 16:6; 17:6; 18:24; Matt 23:35ff.), as well as all those "who have been slaughtered on earth" (v. 24; cf. Jer 51:49). Babylon is not only a place of prosperity for kings and merchants, but also a place of viciousness toward human beings.

The contrast in the perspective of the different voices in chap. 18 is obvious. The kings and merchants lament Babylon's fall as a past event (vv. 9, 11, 14, 17), whereas some of the heavenly voices (not all, as v. 2 indicates) speak of the fall as imminent, rather than past: God has passed judgment against Babylon (v. 20), but the desolation is still to come (vv. 21-24; cf. v. 7). That is in line with the vision in chap. 17, which concerns a future desolation (17:16). Surrounded by all these voices, readers must choose between them. Each voice echoes deeply held sentiments, some more so than others. In this antiphonal dialectic, the prejudices and preferences of the readers and hearers are themselves subjected to scrutiny.

19:1-2. The focus shifts from Babylon and its fate to a voice like "a great multitude in heaven" (cf. 9:9; 19:6; Dan 10:6), declaring the attributes of God. This declaration is prefaced by "Hallelujah" (ἀλληλούια *hallēlouia*; cf. Ps 104:35), which will recur three more times at the beginning of proclamations in this part of the vision. Salvation is mentioned here as in 7:10 and 12:10 (in the latter used in the paean of praise after the ejection of Satan from heaven). As in 16:7, God's judgments are hailed as just and true. The condemnation of Babylon is on the grounds of having

---

306. See Josephus's telling of the story of Cain and Abel in *Antiquities of the Jews* 1:52-66. Cf. Augustine's use of the story in *The City of God* 1:52-66.

corrupted the earth through "fornication" (cf. 11:18). The kings of the earth, who have "lived in luxury with her" (18:9 NRSV), have thereby committed fornication with Babylon. The blood of God's servants is now avenged, fulfilling the plea of the souls of those who had been slaughtered (6:10; cf. Deut 32:43; 2 Kgs 9:7).

19:3-4. A response follows, introduced by the words "a second time" (δεύτερον *deuteron*; NRSV, "once more"; NIV, "and again"). The identity of those who utter the words is unclear: Is it the angelic host or God's servants? If the latter, it would help us to understand the vengeful, even gloating, tone of the pronouncement (cf. 8:4; 9:2-3; 14:11). Now John sees the twenty-four elders and the creatures fall down in worship with their own simple "Amen. Hallelujah" (cf. 4:10; 5:14; 7:11; 11:16).

19:5-8. A voice comes from the throne in v. 5 (for the first time in Revelation; cf. 16:17; 21:3). This voice commands God's servants and all those who fear God, "small and great," to "praise our God" (cf. 11:18; 13:16; 19:18; 20:12; Ps 115:13). This command is parallel in some respects to the summons contained in the eternal gospel in 14:7.

Again a voice that resembles "a great multitude" and the sound of "many waters" speaks (1:15; 14:2; cf. 19:1), asserting God's sovereignty. The words echo the cry of the psalms: "The LORD is King" (cf. Pss 93:1; 97:1; 99:1). God the Almighty reigns (parallel to 11:17; cf. 12:10). The joy in which hearers are asked to participate contrasts with the sorrow and lament of the kings and the merchants.

Verbs are used in v. 7 that have few parallels in Revelation. The word χαίρω (*chairō*) is elsewhere used only of the festive "rejoicing" of the inhabitants of the earth after the death of the two witnesses (11:10). Gladness is now that of the servants of God, who are vindicated (cf. Matt 5:12; see also Ps 118:24, alluded to in Rev 7:10; 22:14). Unlike 16:9, where the inhabitants of the earth refuse to repent, now God is given the glory (v. 7; cf. 11:12; 14:7). The reason for this joy is eschatological: "The marriage of the Lamb has come." Now licit, rather than illicit, sexual congress in marriage replaces fornication. The "bride" who has been prepared is none other than the new Jerusalem, in which the Lamb will dwell (21:2-3, 9). The bride is given a garment, "fine linen, bright and pure" (v. 8; cf. 18:12, 16; Isa 61:10). Note that in v. 8 a rare significance is given to an image: The fine linen is "the righteous deeds of the saints" (cf. 3:5; 5:8). The Lamb, the Son of Man, has communion with the churches; consummation is about communion of an explicit, demonstrable kind, rather than covert and illicit, requiring an apocalypse to reveal it (cf. Luke 12:2). The letters to the angels in chaps. 2–3 reveal as much. This consummation is the *demonstration* that the dwelling of God is with humanity (21:3), with the throne of God and the Lamb in the midst of it (22:3).

19:9-10. The sequence of voices leads to a command once more for John to write (cf. 1:11, 19; 10:4; 14:13). The identity of the speaker is not revealed, but is simply "the angel." The angel tells him to write these words: "Blessed are those who are invited to the marriage supper of the Lamb" (cf. Luke 2:7; 3:20; 14:15-16). Such beatitudes are common in the book (e.g., 1:3; 14:13; 16:15; 20:6; 22:7, 14). After having told John what to write, the angel states that "these are true words of God" (v. 9; cf. 21:5; 22:6). To these words, John has borne witness (1:2). In the next part of his vision, John will see one who is called "The Word of God" (19:13).

For whatever reason, John falls down at the angel's feet to worship the angel,[307] just as the elders and the living creatures had done before God. The angel sternly rebukes him and explains that the one who talks with John is "a fellow servant" of all those who hold the testimony of Jesus.

The reference to the voice from the throne might have suggested to John that the angel speaking to him was a divine figure, like the Son of Man. The angel refuses to accept such an exalted status. That is exactly what we should expect when John, though a human being,[308] has been granted the privilege of writing to angels about the secrets of God. But the angel refuses to accept such an exalted status. Angels are not superior to humans (cf. Heb 2:5ff.). Indeed, humans have a role in proclaiming the gospel to the angelic world

---

307. See L. Stuckenbruck, *Angel Veneration and Christology* (Tübingen: Mohr, 1995).
308. See P. Schäfer, *Rivilität zwischen Engeln und Menschen* (Berlin: de Gruyter, 1975).

(Eph 3:10). God alone is to be worshiped (cf. 11:16; 14:7; but note the exceptions in 3:9; 13:4ff.).

There has been much dispute as to whether the phrase "the testimony of Jesus" (μαρτυρία Ἰησοῦ *martyria Iēsou*) should be translated as a subjective genitive (Jesus' testimony) or an objective genitive (testimony about Jesus; cf. 12:17). In the concluding sentence ("the testimony of Jesus is the spirit of prophecy"), the former mode of translation is to be preferred. The witness that Jesus himself offered becomes the paradigm of all prophecy and is the foundation of the lives of God's servants thereafter, who may expect to share in his fate (cf. 7:14; 12:11). In fact, the difference in meaning is not great, except that the specific character of the life of the Lamb moves into greater prominence.

REFLECTIONS

1. This vision (particularly 18:13) gives a reader a glimpse of how the wealth of Babylon has been gained at the expense of millions. Luxury items here gravitate to the center to supply an insatiable need. Those on the periphery become merely the means of supplying the needs of others. John's vision is an evocation of the consequences of a narcissistic social order, in which everything revolves around the needs of a demanding upper class that makes itself the center of the universe and preserves that position by force, ideology, and demands for conformity. The beauty, sophistication, and splendor of its culture, arts, social life, and technology may be great, but it is in a condition of death. The prophet exposes that reign of death while pointing to ways whereby new life can be found.

This vision invites us to consider carefully the history of our wealth and to assess the extent to which the trade that forms a part of the business of our international order (18:13) is neutral in its inspiration and effects: "Trade as much as conquest violates the integrity of communities which become dominated by the influence of the stronger trading partner."[309] Babylon and the kings and the mighty have committed fornication; great lengths have been taken in order to achieve wealth, status, and power. And that has come about through trade, which is very starkly seen as fornication. International trade can be a form of cultural promiscuity by which one power exploits and drains the resources of many others. In extravagance and luxury lies hidden a cost in human lives and societies.

There is no view in Revelation of economic and political activity as autonomous enterprises devoid of any theological meaning. Trade and commerce are shown to be shot through with human interest (as in Rev 13:6). Many Christians feel out of their depths when they seek to explore contemporary politics and economics in the light of the gospel. But Christians are obligated to learn about and to understand through the lens of the story of Christ the nature of what confronts them. That story casts its shadow over every human transaction. No activity can be regarded as morally neutral and beyond critique and the need for redemption of the Lamb who was slain. That is one of the reasons why Revelation is such a difficult book to read. Its panorama is too big for most of us to grasp. However hard we try, we cannot tame its message and the scope of its concern. It compels us to recognize the vastness of God's concerns and the scope of God's justice. We would prefer a spirituality that concentrated on the individual. But the book of Revelation refuses to allow us to narrow our vision or to be anesthetized in our moral sense. We would prefer to believe that the dark side did not exist. It does, and we must face up to it, individually, socially, and economically, if we are truly to reflect the scope of God's concern. Our assumptions about how the world does and should work may need to be scrutinized in the light of another way of

---

309. O. O'Donovan, "The Political Thought of the Book of Revelation," *Tyndale Bulletin* 37 (1986) 85.

viewing things.[310] The striking imagery demands that we see the prosaic and ordinary as, in reality, extraordinarily threatening to God's way. Harmless words and actions are shown as being of ultimate significance. Revelation's symbolism refuses to allow us to remain indifferent.

2. The command in 18:4, "Come out of her, my people,/ so that you do not take part in her sins" (NRSV), is an indirect reminder that people have to live and work in Babylon for the time being. Jeremiah told the unsettled Jews of his day to "build houses . . . plant gardens and . . . seek the welfare of the city" of their exile (Jer 29:5-7 NRSV). There has to be some degree of acceptance of Babylon, but not conformity with it. There is no escape from the place of exile. There is no safe haven where the elect can remain unspotted by the world, particularly so in a world in which communications and the influence of dominant ideologies are all-pervasive. Until the time comes to leave, Chrisitans need to claim a distinctive identity and to develop habits of resistance that will enable witness and prophecy to take place.

3. One feature of chapters 18–19 is the welter of voices that confront the reader. They oscillate between cries of triumph at Babylon's fall and searing laments at the end of that sophisticated culture. Revelation is full of competing voices, symbolic systems, and worldviews. We are called to identify with John's visionary voice and any claim to vision (such as that of Jezebel, Balaam, or the false prophet) is to be rejected. Voices, even within John's own church, which commended the eating of meat sacrificed to idols and compromise of social mores, have their echoes in the merchants and the mighty who lament Babylon's fall. The unclean thing that has pervaded the life of Babylon still lurks at the gates of the city.[311]

The perspective of the beneficiaries of Babylon's wealth is included as well. Sadness is expressed at the passing of the splendor of Babylon, though none of the heavenly voices is raised in support of Babylon. The uncomfortable fact is that the perspective of those who have profited from Babylon's greatness includes all of us who have become prosperous. To the degree that we are honest, we may identify with the laments of the kings, the merchants, and sailors and bemoan the ease with which the seemingly eternal and beautiful can be destroyed, a waste of all that talent, time, and industry that has gone into making the fabric of society. The way in which John's lament looks at the event from the perspective of the merchants reminds those of us who are privileged that there is another side to our world in which impoverishment is the price to be paid for our ease and wealth. If we identify with the sorrow of the merchants at the end of civilization, we shall, as Allan Boesak has put it, share "the viewpoint which is so typically the one of those who do not know what it is like to stand at the bottom of the list."[312]

---

310. See U. Duchrow, *Alternatives to Global Capitalism* (The Hague: International Books, 1995); T. Gorringe, *Capital and the Kingdom* (London: SPCK, 1994).
311. See Schüssler Fiorenza, *Revelation* 132ff.; T. M. S. Long, "Narrator Audiences and Messages: A South African Reader Response Study of Narrative Relationships in the Book of Revelation" (Ph.D. diss. University of Natal, 1996).
312. Alan Boesak, *Comfort and Protest* (Edinburgh: T. & T. Clark, 1987) 121-22.

REVELATION 19:11-21

HEAVEN OPENS, AND THE RIDER ON THE WHITE HORSE APPEARS

COMMENTARY

In this passage, John describes a warriorlike rider on a white horse who goes forth to pass judgment upon human beings. This is the second judgment passage (there has been a vision of the eschatological harvest in 14:14), and there will be a universal judgment before the great white throne, described in 20:11ff. There is an eschatological battle, as in 20:7ff. The particular focus of judgment is the beast and the false prophet, the former having once supported Babylon (17:7).

19:11-16. The long concentration on Babylon comes to an end, and the vision takes another important turn. This is marked by the words, "I saw heaven opened" (v. 11; parallel to the door that opened in heaven in 4:1; cf. Ezek 1:1; Mark 1:10; Acts 10:11). John sees a white horse with a rider seated upon it, repeating words from 6:2, where the first of the four horsemen came forth to conquer. This rider is called "Faithful and True" (cf. 1:5). Christ is the faithful and true witness in 3:14 (cf. 2:13), but the term "witness" is lacking from this rider's description. Rather, he will be engaged in carrying out judgment in righteousness (cf. Pss 72:2; 96:13; Isa 11:4). The time for testimony is over; the case has been made, and the sentencing will begin.

Links with the figure of Christ earlier in the vision are confirmed by the description of the rider (v. 12), which harks back to the description of the Son of Man (1:14): "His eyes are like a flame of fire, and on his head are many diadems" (cf. 12:3; 13:1). He has a name "inscribed" that no one knows but himself (echoing 2:17), a name that contrasts with the widely used name of the beast (13:17). This rider's name is "The Word of God" (v. 13; cf. John 1:1; Wis 18:15 [NRSV]: "Your all-powerful word leaped from heaven, from the royal throne,/ into the midst of the land that was doomed,/ a stern warrior/ carrying the sharp sword of your authentic command,/ and stood and filled all things with death"). And on his robe and his thigh are inscribed the words, "King of kings and Lord of lords" (v. 16; cf. 1:5; 17:14; Deut 10:17; 1 Cor 8:6). The word κύριος (*kyrios*) is usually used to describe God, but here it describes the divine warrior. He is wearing a garment that has been dipped in blood (v. 13), a hint that he is the Lamb who stood as if it had been slaughtered (5:6; cf. Isa 63:1ff.), bearing the marks of his own blood. He leads the heavenly armies, who are riding white horses and are clad in white linen (cf. 18:12; 19:8), like the white garments of the elders and the righteous one (4:4; 6:11; 7:9; cf. 3:4). From this rider's mouth comes "a sharp sword with which to strike down the nations" (in 1:16 it is a two-edged sword; cf. 2:12; Isa 11:4; 49:2).

According to v. 15, he will rule (lit., "shepherd" [ποίμαινω *poimainō*]; see NRSV textual note) the nations "with a rod of iron." The role of the shepherd in Revelation has two aspects. On the one hand, as here, the shepherd is a stern ruler (2:27; 12:5); on the other hand the shepherd is a more gentle image, providing pasture for the sheep (7:17). Here the rider will smite the nations as a shepherd, a curious reversal of Zech 13:7 (quoted in Matt 26:31), where the shepherd himself will be struck down. The links to earlier items in the vision continue in v. 15*b* when the rider is described as treading "the wine press of the fury of the wrath of God the Almighty" (cf. Isa 63:2). So the identity of the one treading the wine press in 14:19 is now revealed.

19:17-18. An angel appears, standing "in the sun" (the subject of a dramatic painting by J. M. W. Turner [c. 1825]; see the insert in the Introduction, cf. 7:2). The angel summons the birds that "fly in midheaven" (cf. 8:13; 14:6) to a feast. Unlike the marriage feast of the Lamb (v. 9), this feast will be a "great supper of God," an occasion for the birds to gorge themselves on the flesh of the kings, the captains, and the mighty who (according to 6:15) had pleaded to be hidden from the great day of the wrath of God and the Lamb. It is an awesome destruction like that of Gog and Magog in Ezek 39:17. The inclusion of "small and great" (cf. 13:16) shows that Revelation contemplates no respite for anyone who has been taken in by the ideology of the beast and Babylon.

19:19-21. The summons for the birds to gather is matched in v. 19 by the gathering of the beast and the kings of the earth with their armies to make war on the rider on the white horse, who "in righteousness judges and makes war" (v. 11 NRSV). That gathering was alluded to in 16:14, in which evil spirits come from the mouths of the dragon, the beast, and the false prophet. This war continues the one that had been started with the assault on the two witnesses in 11:7. This time, however, the initial as well as the final victory will belong to the rider on the white horse and his army (v. 20), and the beast and the false prophet will be captured (πιάζω *piazō*; the word used of the attempts to arrest Jesus in John's Gospel, e.g., John 7:30).

In v. 20, the reader is reminded of the identity of the false prophet: He is the one "who had performed in its [the beast's] presence the signs by which he deceived those who had received the mark of the beast and those who worshiped its image" (cf. 13:13; 16:14). The mark of the beast here seems to be the possession of those who have been deceived, rather than something that is inflicted on them (cf. 14:9). But these people were no hapless victims who had been forced to submit; rather, they had willingly colluded with the culture of Babylon and the dominion of the beast. So those who worship the image of the beast "receive" (λαμβάνω *lambanō*) rather than "are given" the mark, as in 13:16. Those who worship the beast are active in their acceptance of this deceit. Ultimately, the beast and the false prophet are thrown alive into the lake of fire, a feature that anticipates the final vision (20:10, 14-15; 21:8; cf. 9:17-18; 14:10; and Num 16:33, where Korah and his household go down to Sheol alive). The people who have worshiped the beast and received its mark are killed by the sword that proceeds from the mouth of the rider on the horse.

The destruction of enemies links back to Isa 11:4 and parallels other passages indebted to it:

With righteousness he shall judge the poor,
    and decide with equity for the
        meek of the earth;
he shall strike the earth with the
        rod of his mouth,
    and with the breath of his lips
        he shall kill the wicked. (Isa 11:4 NRSV)

When he saw the onrush of the approaching multitude, he neither lifted his hand nor held a spear or any weapon of war; but I saw only how he sent forth from his mouth as it were a stream of fire, and from his lips a flaming breath, and from his tongue he shot forth a storm of sparks. All these were mingled together, the stream of fire and the flaming breath and the great storm, and fell on the onrushing multitude which was prepared to fight, and burned them all up, so that suddenly nothing was seen of the innumerable multitude but only the dust of ashes and the smell of smoke. (4 Ezra 13:9-11)[313]

And then the lawless one will be revealed, whom the Lord Jesus will destroy with the breath of his mouth, annihilating him by the manifestation of his coming. (2 Thess 2:8 NRSV)

"These are the words of him who has the sharp, two-edged sword. . . . I will come to you soon and make war against them with the sword of my mouth." (Rev 2:12, 16 NRSV)

From his mouth comes a sharp sword with which to strike down the nations. . . . And the rest were killed by the sword of the rider on the horse, the sword that came from his mouth. (Rev 19:15, 21 NRSV

---

313. Metzger, 4 Ezra 13:9-11.

All of these passages suggest that judgment in the context of an eschatological battle comes by means of the power of the Word of God rather than through force of arms. The effect is devastating, because it functions as a divine illocutionary act. The Word of God brings it into effect the moment it is uttered:

The word of God is living and active, sharper than any two-edged sword, piercing until it divides soul from spirit, joints from marrow; it is able to judge the thoughts and intentions of the heart. And before him no creature is hidden, but all are naked and laid bare to the eyes of the one to whom we must render an account. (Heb 4:12-13 NRSV)

REFLECTIONS

1. The vision described in Revelation 19 concerns the judgment on institutions that had been responsible for a disordered world and that had attracted to themselves absolute power and demanded conformity. It is a reminder to followers of Jesus that God cannot allow the injustices of human history to continue forever. We may prefer a God who will treat those who have accepted the ways and benefits of the beast in the same way as those who have refused to conform are treated. But a view of God that is merely supportive of our prejudices and desires is idolatrous. The challenging picture of Christ as judge is iconoclastic and disturbing.

Revelation represents one pole in the Christian gospel: the justice of God. Balancing justice and love lies in the depths of both Jewish and Christian wrestling with the character of God. No theodicy can answer the problem merely by showing revulsion at the consequences of justice. Love's ability to cover a multitude of sins in a vision of eternal inclusion is in danger of baptizing the status quo of this world's injustice, as the kings, magnates, and captains ride into the kingdom on the tide of the love of God. That sentimentality is ruthlessly challenged by the apocalyptic vision.

Nevertheless, the pattern of justice and judgment is gruesome in its execution (Rev 19:21*b*). Readings of Revelation must not dilute what seems to us the force of this "scandal," failing to grapple with its scandalous imagery. But apocalypse is untamed and perhaps untamable. Perhaps that is why the book of Revelation was canonized—so that the norms and orderliness of religion might channel its desire and prophetic energy into more constructive operations. But the vision remains chaotic and wild, hoping for the order of the new Jerusalem, but denouncing injustice and proclaiming dissolution.

2. Revelation offers a vision of another path for humanity than of the road of violence and evil. But it is a vision, not a prescription. It is more a warning of what to avoid than a manual of what to do. It shocks and disconcerts us so that we might begin to assess reality afresh. It is the means of beginning on a new path, rather than a precise guide for following that path. What proceeds from the mouth of the Messiah is seen to be devastating (cf. Isa 11:4; 2 Thess 2:8). "The two-edged sword" of the Word of God (19:13) is threatening, but it is also a metaphorical image. An effective word, but still only a word and not a violent action.

Perhaps our difficulty with Revelation's harsh words should prompt us to reflect on our easy use of words: Do we disguise from ourselves the wounding and destructive, as well as the creative, power of words? Words can torment hearers as much as does the eschatological judgment itself (as Rev 11:6 reminds us). Jesus' words, recalled by the Spirit, assist in the conviction of the reality of sin, righteousness, and judgment (John 16:8ff.). His words are the cornerstone of the indictment against a world that prefers darkness to light. John's vision is couched in words of frightening and forbidding tones, reflecting the ultimate seriousness of the choices and the extent of human imperviousness to the problems of this world.

3. The *future* dimension of Revelation 19:11-20 should not lead us to neglect the *present* effectiveness of the divine word. In Hos 6:5, God's prophetic word has the same devastating effect as does the manifestation of the eschatological rider: "I have hewn them by the prophets,/ I have killed them by the words of my mouth,/ and my judgment goes forth as the light" (NRSV). John's words, too, are prophecy (Rev 22:18), and their effect is like Jeremiah's: "to pluck up and to pull down,/ to destroy and to overthrow,/ to build and to plant" (Jer 1:10 NRSV; cf. Rev 10:11). That task is not reserved for just a prophetic elite.[314] As Blake said, "The voice of honest indignation is the voice of God."[315]

4. However awesome Revelation's images are, we should not allow ourselves to get too involved in speculating about what the future will be like. The description of judgment is economical in the extreme. Only what is necessary to make the point about the message of justice and judgment and the significance of present words and deeds is included. To this extent, Revelation differs little from the Gospel of John in placing all the emphasis on present decisions, attitudes, and conduct (John 5:24-25). In Rev 19:17-21 there is little attempt to satisfy the reader's curiosity about how it will all work out. The list of those upon whom the birds will gorge themselves in 19:18 is consistent with the perspective of the book: While the "small" can be expected to be led astray as they desperately seek for their own survival (13:16), it is the kings, the captains, and the mighty who are prominently mentioned as receiving judgment (cf. 6:15). Those who benefit most from Babylon are least likely to notice the effects of the culture Babylon creates.

314. See R. Bauckham, *The Theology of the Book of Revelation* (Cambridge: Cambridge University Press, 1993) 80ff.
315. William Blake, plates 12-13, in Keynes, *Blake*, 153.

EXCURSUS: THE PAROUSIA IN THE NEW TESTAMENT[316]

There is ample evidence of the belief in the Second Coming of Christ, most apparent in Rev 1:7; 19:11ff.; and 22:20 (the word παρουσία [*parousia*] is not used in Revelation, though it is a technical term elsewhere in the NT; e.g., Matt 24:3; 1 Cor 15:23; 1 Thess 5:23; 2 Thess 2:1; 2 Pet 1:16; 1 John 2:28; cf. Jas 5:7). In eschatological Jewish texts contemporary to Revelation, reference may be made occasionally to a messianic agent,[317] though even these texts are less concerned with the identity of the Messiah than with the conviction of some future reign of God on earth.

In Rev 19:11-21, there are explicit links with the vision of the Son of Man in Rev 1:14, which inaugurates John's vision. Revelation 19:11-21 forms part of a much longer symbolic account of the culmination of the manifestation of the divine wrath within human history, stemming from the exaltation of the Lamb and its claiming the right to open the sealed scroll.

After the diversion in Rev 17:1–19:10, which considers the character of Babylon and speaks of its destruction and the reaction in heaven to it, John's vision resumes with the heaven opened and the appearance of a rider on a white horse, which leads

316. See the survey in C. Rowland, *Christian Origins* (London: SPCK, 1985) 285ff.; G. B. Caird, *New Testament Theology* (Oxford: Oxford University Press, 1994) 250-56; A. L. Moore, *The Parousia in the New Testament* (Leiden: E. J. Brill, 1966); R. Bauckham, *Aufstieg und Niedergang der römischen Welt* (Berlin: de Gruyter, 1972) 2:28.3.
317. E.g., *Pss. Sol.* 17:24-25; *1 Enoch* 46:5-6; 90:37; 4 Ezra 7:29; 12:32; Syr. Baruch 29:3; 39:7; 72:2; *Sib. Or.* iii. 652ff.; *T. Levi* 2:11; 4QFlor; 1QS 9:11).

Excursus: The Parousia in the New Testament

to a holy war. Like the descendant of David, described in Isaiah 11, it is with the sword proceeding from his mouth that this rider will rule the nations. He comes as "King of kings and Lord of lords" (Rev 19:16 NRSV); his victory, therefore, in the struggle that is to take place has already been assured (exactly what we would expect in the light of Rev 11:17). There gather together the beast, the false prophet, and the kings of the earth to make war against the rider on the white horse (19:19). The beast and the false prophet are thrown into the lake of fire, and their allies are slain with the sword that proceeds from the mouth of the rider on the white horse.

This triumph immediately precedes the establishment of the messianic kingdom on earth (Rev 20:4). But this is not the end of the struggle against the forces opposed to the divine righteousness, because the messianic reign is temporary and depends on the binding of Satan in the abyss (Rev 20:2). Satan's release, however, leads to another terrible conflict. But whereas the rider on the white horse had conquered the beast and the kings of the earth, in the next battle, Satan, released from prison, gathers the armies of Gog and Magog to wage war against the camp of the saints and against the holy city—only to be destroyed by fire from heaven. The devil will join the beast and the false prophet in the lake of fire for eternal torment. This is then followed by the last assize, which paves the way for the new heaven and new earth and the establishment of God's dwelling with humankind.

The closest parallel in the New Testament to Rev 19:11–21 is the short eschatological account in 1 Corinthians 15. In a discussion focusing on the belief in the resurrection and the character of the resurrection body, Paul alludes to the future consummation in two passages. In the first passage (1 Cor 15:20-34), Paul outlines the order in which the resurrection from the dead will take place: Christ, "the first fruits" (which has already taken place), then those who belong to Christ at his coming (cf. 1 Thess 4:16). Then comes the end, when Christ hands over the kingship to God, "after he has destroyed every ruler and every authority and power" (1 Cor 15:24 NRSV). Paul then interpolates the comment that Christ must exercise the sovereignty until he has put all his enemies under his feet (an allusion to Ps 110:1); the last enemy to be destroyed is death itself. It is only when all things are subjected to the Messiah that the Son will himself be subject to the Father and God will be all in all (1 Cor 15:28).

Later in the chapter, in a discussion of the character of the resurrection body (1 Cor 15:35-58), Paul stresses that flesh and blood cannot inherit the kingdom of God and tells his readers of the mystery of the resurrection of the elect: Not all will die, but all will be "changed, in a moment, in the twinkling of an eye, at the last trumpet" (1 Cor 15:52 NRSV; cf. Matt 24:31; 1 Thess 4:17). When the heavenly trumpet sounds, the righteous dead will be raised, incorruptible. It is when what was corruptible has put on immortality in the form of the resurrection body that death will be swallowed up in victory. It is not clear whether this passage contradicts the earlier hint of a period of a messianic kingdom on earth at some point during the lordship of the Messiah, during which he puts under subjection the enemies of God. But it is possible to read 1 Cor 15:25-28 as indicating that Paul's eschatology follows the general outline of that found in Revelation 19–21 and presupposes a messianic reign on earth.

Also related to Revelation 19 is the account of the parousia in 2 Thessalonians 2. This eschatological passage is to be found in a context dealing with a particular pastoral problem. As such, like 1 Corinthians 15, it offers only a fragment of an eschatological scheme, sufficient to deal with the particular issue confronting the writer: the threat of disturbance to the community because of an outburst of eschatological enthusiasm, prompted by the belief that the day of the Lord had already arrived (1 Thess 2:2). In order to counteract such enthusiasm, Paul reminds his readers that a rebellion must first take place, and the "lawless one," who opposes God and sits in the Temple of God, "declaring himself to be God" (1 Thess 2:4 NRSV), must be revealed. This sign of the coming of Christ has not yet occurred, because it is being restrained until the proper time (1 Thess 2:6). It is unclear as to what the restraint Paul asks his readers to remember might be. Is it Paul himself? Is it the evangelization of the Gentiles? Is it the Roman Empire? Is it some divine/angelic restraint, such as that found in Rev 7:1? Meanwhile the mystery of lawlessness is already at work. In other words, the present is, in some sense, an eschatological time. The coming of the lawless one will be accompanied by signs and wonders that will deceive those who are on the way to destruction, just as the activity of the beast and the false prophet deceive the nations of the earth in Rev 13:7, 12-18. Finally, the Lord Jesus will slay the man of lawlessness with the breath of his mouth (2 Thess 2:8). So there is some similarity between this passage and Revelation, where the exaltation of the Lamb provokes the initiation of the whole eschatological drama, which moves forward according to its own apocalyptic logic. Until the restraint is removed, there can be no manifestation of the Antichrist figure (cf. the reason for delay given in Mark 13:10).

As it does for Rev 19:15, Isa 11:4 has contributed to this passage from 2 Thessalonians, particularly in the description of the destruction of the lawless one. A similar description turns up in *Ps. Sol.* 17:24 as well: "With a rod of iron he shall break in pieces all their substance; he shall destroy the godless nations with the word of his mouth. At his rebuke shall the nations flee before him." Likewise, in the vision of the man from the sea in 4 Ezra 13, we find a similar description of the destruction of his enemies (4 Ezra 13:8ff.). In the interpretation of the vision, we are told that, after a period of unrest when nation will rise up against nation (4 Ezra 13:30ff.), the one whom the Most High has been keeping for many generations will appear to reprove the assembled nations for their ungodliness (4 Ezra 13:37-38) and destroy them by the law. After this, the tribes of Israel will gather at Mount Zion, where they will live in peace. In all of these passages from 4 Ezra it is made quite clear that those forces opposed to God will be destroyed. Thus the appearance of the Messiah will be more than just a prelude to a better order, made quite explicit in passages like 4 Ezra 13 and Revelation 19, for he will act as the agent of destruction of the evil that stands opposed to the righteousness of God.

When viewed in the light of Rev 19:11-21, the eschatological discourses in the synoptic Gospels (Matthew 24–25; Mark 13; Luke 21) show some remarkable omissions. There are the messianic woes that are so characteristic of eschatological writings of this period of Judaism. While there may well be some kind of connection between the sort of focus on evil that is cryptically outlined in Mark 13:14 and the hubris of the man of lawlessness mentioned in 2 Thessalonians 2, nothing is said about the effects on the forces of evil of the coming of the Son of Man. Indeed, the description of the coming of the Son of Man in all three synoptic Gospels is linked primarily with the vindication of the elect, thus focusing on the final aspect of the messianic drama in the vision of the man from the sea in 4 Ezra 13:12. The certainty of vindication is there, but the lot of the elect when they have been gathered from the four corners of the earth is not touched on at all in Mark.

The element of judgment at the parousia of the Son of Man is not entirely absent from the synoptic discourses. The climax of the Matthean version is the account of the final assize, with the Son of Man sitting on God's throne, separating the sheep from the goats (Matt 25:31-46). Here, too, the focus of attention is on the present response of the elect. It is those who recognize the heavenly Son of Man in the brethren who are hungry, thirsty, strangers, naked, weak, and imprisoned in the present age who will inherit the kingdom prepared by God from the foundation of the world. There is a possible link here with the much disputed *1 Enoch* 3–71, where the Son of Man sits on the throne of the lord of the spirits and exercises judgment (*1 Enoch* 69:2).

The primary concern of the Markan discourse on the parousia is not satisfaction of curiosity about the details of the times and seasons so much as dire warnings of the threat of being led astray, of failing at the last, and of the need to be ready and watchful to avoid the worst of the coming disasters. In the bleak moments of the last days there is little attempt to dwell on the delights awaiting disciples in the messianic kingdom (though an eschatological promise is made a little later in Luke's Gospel in the context of the supper discourse; Luke 22:29-30). The reader's thoughts are made to dwell on responsibilities in the short and medium term as the essential prerequisite of achieving eschatological bliss. These sentiments are very much at the fore in 4 Ezra, where the emphasis is on the need to follow the precepts of the Most High in order to achieve eternal life.

In comparison with the more extended accounts of the coming of the new age to be found in other material, both Christian and Jewish, the synoptic discourses concentrate on the period of strife and tribulation leading up to the coming of the Son of Man, itself an expectation only hinted at in the *Similitudes of Enoch*. In the Gospels what happens after the coming of the Son of Man is not mentioned, though in the Lukan version there is the expectation that the arrival of the Son of Man will be the beginning of the process of liberation, for which the tribulations and destruction had been the prelude (Luke 21:26ff.). The implication is that the kingdom does not arrive with the coming of the Son of Man; that is only part of the eschatological drama, whose climax is still to come—exactly what we find in Revelation. The arrival of the rider on the white horse in Revelation is the prelude to the struggle that must precede the establishment of the messianic kingdom, an event still to come, when there will be a reversal of Jerusalem's fortunes (Luke 21:24).

In the Pauline letters, the word παρουσία (*parousia*) is used in the context of Christ's coming (e.g., 1 Thess 3:13; 2 Thess 2:8; cf. his revealing at 1 Cor 1:7), and also that of the apostle (2 Cor 10:10; Phil 1:26; 2:12) or his agent (1 Cor 16:17; 2 Cor 7:6-7). The present experience of the Christ who is to come can be discerned also in aspects of Paul's understanding of apostleship.[318] There is a close relationship between the parousia of Christ and the apostolic parousia, so that through the presence of the apostle, whether in person, through a co-worker, or through letter, the presence of Christ was confronting his congregations (Rom 15:14ff.; 1 Cor 4:14ff.; 1 Cor 5:3ff.; Phil 2:12). Paul's presence brings eschatological power, despite his human weakness and humility (2 Cor 10:10; cf. 1 Cor 4:9-10). According to 1 Corinthians 4–5, Paul is a father in Christ Jesus to the Corinthians (4:15); Paul's person is to be imitated (4:16) as he is the embodiment of Christ (11:1). Paul's coming will be with power (1 Cor 4:19). His emissary Timothy will remind the church of the way of Christ (1 Cor 4:17), and even Paul's absence will not diminish the force of the apostolic will (1 Cor 5:3). When he comes, it is either with discipline (1 Cor 4:21; cf. 1 Cor 2:27; 3:19) or with gentleness (cf. the gentler tone of the letter to the Philadelphian angel in Rev 3:7-13). And he promises the Roman church that when he finally reaches Rome his coming will bring blessing to them (Rom 15:29). Like the risen Christ, who stands in the midst of his churches as judge and sustainer (Rev 1:13), the apostle of Christ comes as a threat and a promise—a threat to those who have lost their first love or exclude the Messiah and his apostle; a promise of blessing for those who conquer.

The Fourth Gospel's account of the coming of Jesus has been seen as a development of the early parousia hope that moves away from the public cosmic scenes we find in the other Gospels. Jesus will come to his disciples (John 14:21, 23). The dwellings that Jesus goes to prepare for the disciples can be enjoyed by the one who loves Jesus and is devoted to his words (John 14:2; cf. John 14:23). Likewise, the manifestation of the divine glory is reserved not for the world, but for the disciple (John 14:19). Whereas all flesh will see the salvation of our God in Isa 52:7-10 and those who pierced the victorious Son of Man will look upon him in glory (Rev 1:9; cf. Mark 14:62), the world cannot see the returning Jesus. Indeed, the goal of the new age in Revelation, where

---

318. See R. Funk, "The Apostolic Parousia: Form and Significance," in W. R. Farmer, C. F. D. Moule, and R. Niebuhr, *Christian History and Interpretation* (Cambridge: Cambridge University Press, 1967) 249ff.

those who bear the name of God on their foreheads (Rev 22:3-4) and will see God face to face, is part of the bliss reserved for the disciples in heaven to be with God and to see God's glory (Rev 17:24). Just as Jesus comes again to the disciples, so too does the Paraclete (NRSV, "Advocate"). The world cannot receive Christ, and it is the Paraclete that enables the disciples to maintain their connection with the basic revelation of God, the Logos who makes the Father known (Rev 14:17ff.; 15:26). The Paraclete thus points back to Jesus, the Word made flesh, and is in some sense a successor to Jesus, a compensation by his presence for the absence of Jesus, who has returned to the Father.

An issue that always arises when the parousia is discussed is the problem caused for Christians by the non-fulfillment of the expectation of Christ's return. Explicit evidence that the delay of the parousia was a problem within early Christianity is not as vast as is often suggested; 2 Peter 3 is, in fact, a rather exceptional piece of evidence. Other passages that are often mentioned, for instance, in Matthew (the parables at the end of Matthew 24) and Acts 1:7 need to be seen as indirect rather than direct evidence of the supposed problem.

Within the eschatological tradition there was an attempt to come to terms with the delay of the coming of God's reign.[319] The apocalypses are an important resource for dealing with the non-appearance of God's reign on earth, since they reflect interest in the world above, where God's reign is acknowledged by the heavenly host and where the apocalyptic seer can have access to the repository of those purposes of God for the future world. Thus the visionary can either glimpse in the heavenly books about the mysteries of eschatology or be offered a "preview" of what will happen in the future of human history. The privilege of having the heavenly mysteries revealed could be extended to a wider group. The *Hodayoth* from the Dead Sea Scrolls (1QH) and the *Odes of Solomon* offer the elect group a present participation in the lot of heaven and a foretaste of the coming glory.

---

319. See R. Bauckham, "The Delay of the Parousia," *Tyndale Bulletin* 31 (1980) 3-36.

REVELATION 20:1-15

MILLENNIUM AND JUDGMENT

OVERVIEW

After the vision of the rider on the white horse in 19:11-21 comes one of the most controversial passages in this controversial book: the description of the thousand-year messianic reign on earth. During this period, Satan will be bound. The millennial kingdom, over which the martyrs preside, ends with the release of Satan, a final war with Gog and Magog, and another version of the judgment, parallel to 19:17-21, this time before the great white throne.

REVELATION 20:1-6, ANOTHER ANGEL DESCENDING FROM HEAVEN, THE BINDING OF SATAN, AND THE MILLENNIUM

COMMENTARY

20:1-3. John sees an angel descending from heaven (cf. 9:1; 10:1; 18:1; 21:2), holding the key to the abyss, which had been given to the star that fell from heaven in 9:1 (cf. 1:18). With the key, the angel is holding a great chain (cf. Mark 5:3; Acts 12:6-7; Eph 6:20). The angel seizes the dragon ("the ancient serpent, who is the Devil and Satan"; cf. 12:9), binds him for a thousand years, and throws him into the abyss (whence the beast had emerged, according to 11:7). The angel then locks and seals the pit (cf. 1:18; 3:7; 7:3; 10:4; 22:10), so that the nations will no longer be deceived (v. 3), as they had been previously, into worshiping the beast to whom had been given the dragon's authority (13:14). This act reverses the bondage by which Satan, through the beast and Babylon, had held the inhabitants of the earth in thrall (cf. Luke 13:16: "whom Satan bound").

After a thousand years, Satan must be released for a short time (cf. 2:21; 6:11; 10:6). The loosing of Satan contrasts with the loosing of the new community from their shackles, allowing them to become a kingdom of priests (1:6). Throughout Revelation, there is a balance of positive effect and negative consequences: the ejection of Satan from heaven in chap. 12 results in a threat to earth, and the loosing by the vindication of the Lamb leads to the opening of the seals of apocalypse in chaps. 5–6. Here Satan's being loosed brings deceit and war, the significance of which can be apprehended only by those who have been loosed from sin and so perceive the nature of deceit in the cosmos.

The word "thousand" ($\chi i \lambda \iota \alpha$ *chilia*) occurs only here in the book (cf. 7:4ff.; 14:1; the only other relevant NT passage in which the word is used is 2 Pet 3:8). In that text, in response to those who scoff at the delay of Christ's coming, the author alludes to Ps 90:4 ("with the Lord one day is like a thousand years, and a thousand years are like one day") as part of an argument to prove that the human and divine time-scales are very different, and that when the Lord does come it will be suddenly, "like a thief" (see 3:3; 16:15).

20:4-6. John sees thrones (v. 4), just as he had seen them earlier (4:4; cf. Dan 7:9). In

4:4 and 11:16, twenty-four elders, seated on thrones, surround the one who is seated on the throne and spend their time in worship of the one seated on the throne. Here people sit, and judgment is given to them. There has been a promise to the one who "conquers" to sit with Christ on his throne (3:20), now fulfilled in v. 4. That echoes the promise to the Twelve to sit with the Son of Man judging the twelve tribes of Israel (Matt 19:28; cf. Luke 22:28, where it is granted to "you who have stood by me in my trials").

John also sees the souls of those "beheaded." Earlier he had seen the souls of those slain for their testimony (12:17). This appears to be another group, who "refused to worship the Beast or his statue and did not have the brand-mark on their foreheads and hands" (JB). Most translations, however, refer to only one group (e.g., REB, "who for the sake of their witness to Jesus, had been beheaded, those who had not worshipped the beast"). Whether there is a different group alongside those who have been martyred is not clear; John's Greek is awkward. It could be that the group exercising judgment includes not only the martyrs but also those who did not worship the beast. The obvious parallel to the syntax of this passage is 1:7. As in 19:20, the whole litany of the nature of compromise with the beast is narrated (cf. 14:9, 11; 16:2), so that what is demanded to conform with the will of God, on the one hand, and to reject the beast, on the other hand, is made absolutely clear. If another group is referred to, then their distinctive characteristic is that they did not worship the beast. Whether or not they did so "for the sake of God's word and their witness to Jesus" is of secondary importance. We may have a vision, therefore, of those who resisted the beast and those who suffered for it, both inside and outside the church, sitting with the one who had himself been the faithful witness (1:5). They had held out against the compromises required of them in the old scheme of things (the extent of the nature of compromise with the beast and the resistance required is narrated in 14:9, 11; 16:2).

The righteous dead have come to life (like their Lord in 1:18; 2:8) to reign with Christ. The word "Christ" (Χριστός *Christos*) is seldom used in Revelation (1:1, 2, 5; 11:15; 12:10; 20:4, 6). Only on four occasions does the word appear in the vision proper, where it is probably best translated as "Messiah." In addition to reigning with Christ, the vivified also act as priests (v. 6; cf. 1:6; 5:10). The reign of Christ and the elect is still a future event in 5:10 and 11:15 (cf. 20:6; 22:5). Here, the past tense is used. "King" is used in 1:5; 15:3; 17:14; 19:16 of God or Christ as king, and "kingdom" is used of the kingdom of people that has been constituted by Christ's saving act (1:5; 5:10), in which John is also a participant (1:9). Like the verb "reign," "kingdom" is related to moments when God's sovereignty is demonstrated (11:10; 12:10). Thus the transfer of sovereignty over the kingdom of this world to God is given tangible expression in the thousand-year reign on earth of Christ and those who share in his kingdom.

Other parts of the NT offer little help in interpreting the character of this messianic kingdom. The meanings of the terms "kingdom" and "reign of God" in the Gospels are much contested. In Mark 1:15 and 14:25, the usage appears to be a clear future reference, while Luke 11:20 and 17:21 have elements of realization. Neat encapsulations of the meaning of the phrase come up against the stubborn fact that the Gospels consistently portray Jesus as telling parables, which by their allusive nature and accessibility might help hearers respond to God's reign rather than offer some definitive interpretation of it. What does emerge in the Gospels is a tension between present reality and future realization, which is evident elsewhere in the NT (e.g., future: 1 Cor 6:9-10; Gal 5:21; 2 Thess 1:5; present: Eph 5:5; Col 1:13; 1 Thess 2:12). Of most immediate relevance is the eschatological narrative in 1 Cor 15:24-25, which has been linked with the millennium in Revelation 20. The issue is whether in this sequence in 1 Corinthians there is a period during which Christ reigns and puts his enemies under subjection, much as the devil is bound in Revelation 20, or whether, as 1 Cor 15:52 suggests, the parousia is immediately followed by the resurrection with no intervening period.[320] It is possible to reconcile the two parts of 1 Corinthians 15, so that what 1 Cor 15:51 describes is exactly the same as

---

320. See C. Hill, *Regnum Coelorum: Patterns of Future Hope in Early Christianity* (Oxford: Oxford University Press, 1992).

Rev 20:4: "they came to life," which John identifies as the first resurrection (v. 5). But such attempts at harmonizing hardly do justice to the fluidity of the eschatological imagery of the NT.

A blessing is pronounced on those who share the first resurrection (v. 6; cf. 1:3; 14:13; 16:15; 19:9; 22:7, 14). The first resurrection, that of the martyrs (v. 6), is to be complemented with another resurrection in 20:12 (cf. v. 5, where John states that the rest of the dead will not be raised until the end of the millennium). Those who participate in the first resurrection are free from the threat of the second death, the lake of fire (21:8; cf. 20:14). It is this second death that will not harm the one who conquers in Smyrna, an angel that knows tribulation and poverty (2:11). Whether John's visionary zeal has led to the inclusion of various traditions of judgment and future fulfillment has been a matter of debate, particularly in the heyday of source criticism. The repetition of accounts of judgment scenes in 14:14ff.; 19:11ff.; and 20:11ff. and eschatological resolution in 20:1ff. and 21:1ff. may be seen as warnings to those who are "neither hot nor cold" and as encouragement to the faithful witnesses, "who lived not their lives even unto death." In any case, the first resurrection (v. 5) is a reward reserved for the faithful. The second is necessary to bring the dead to judgment. (See Reflections at 20:11-15.)

EXCURSUS: THE MILLENNIUM[321]

Views about the millennium have varied throughout the history of the Christian church. There are *premillenarian* ideas, held by exegetes who think that the parousia will take place before the messianic reign on earth (often linked with a cataclysmic eschatology that envisages a divine irruption into history), and *post-millennial* ideas, held by those who think that Christ's reappearance will take place at the end of the millennium (often linked with gradualist, evolutionary views of history, inexorably moving toward an eschatological goal). In addition, there are *amillennialists,* who reject the idea of the messianic reign on earth, either because they believe that this event has already happened in the cross and resurrection or in the emergence of the Christian church (Augustine's interpretation in *The City of God* is a good example of amillennialism).

In the earliest period of Christianity, resorting to the language and genre of apocalypse enabled NT writers to understand the significance of events and persons in the light of God's eternal purposes. It buttressed the belief of the first Christians, in their diverse social settings, that they were privileged to be the ones "on whom the ends of the ages have come" (1 Cor 10:11 NRSV). The nature of that eschatological background has been the subject of fierce debate, however. While few scholars would dispute the preoccupation with the ultimate purposes of God in the NT, there is a significant difference of opinion between those who argue that the first Christians, in contrast to their Jewish contemporaries, expected the winding up of history and ultimately the appearance of a spiritual kingdom and those who consider the expectation to be on the historical plane. Gershom Scholem neatly summarizes these differing views when he contrasts the spiritual messianism of Christianity with the political, this-worldly, messianism of Judaism:

> A totally different concept of redemption determines the attitude to messianism in Judaism and Christianity. . . . Judaism, in all its forms and manifestations, has always

---

321. Cohn, *The Pursuit of the Millennium*; Rowland, *Radical Christianity*.

Excursus: The Millennium

maintained a concept of redemption as an event which takes place publicly, on the stage of history and within the community. It is an occurrence which takes place in the visible world and which cannot be conceived apart from such a visible appearance. In contrast, Christianity conceives of redemption as an event in the spiritual and unseen realm, in the private world of each individual, and which effects an inner transformation which need not correspond to anything outside. Events which for the one which stood unconditionally at the end of history as its most distant aim, are for the other the true centre of the historical process, even if that process was henceforth peculiarly decked out as *Heilsgeschichte*.[322]

This contrast exists also in the messianic and eschatological doctrines of Christianity; indeed, they are endemic to Christianity. Even if Christianity has come to be identified with a spiritual messianism, there are important strands in the history of Christianity that bear witness to a political messianism akin to that which is characteristic of Judaism. Both forms of messianism are endemic to Christianity. There are significant strands within the New Testament that exhibit the "chiliastic mentality" (from χίλια [*chilia*], Greek for 1,000, hence "millennium") in which the present becomes an opportunity for transforming the imperfect into the perfect; history and eschatology become inextricably intertwined, and the elect stand on the brink of the millennium itself. We can see this in the story of Jesus of Nazareth as he proclaims the present as being decisive in God's purposes and himself as the messianic agent for change. Jesus' eschatological expectation was of an otherworldly kingdom of God, brought into being by God alone, where humankind were merely passive spectators of a vast divine drama with the cosmos as its stage. Similarly, Paul saw himself as the human agent in the eschatological act of God, whereby the Gentiles are offered the gospel and the last things are completed.

Some texts that are roughly contemporary with Revelation evince the material eschatology that pervades Jewish literature. The Syriac *Apocalypse of Baruch* includes this passage:

> And it will happen that when all that which should come to pass in these parts has been accomplished, the Anointed One will begin to be revealed. And Behemoth will reveal itself from its place, and Leviathan will come from the sea, the two great monsters which I created on the fifth day of creation and which I shall have kept until that time. And they will be nourishment for all who are left. The earth will also yield fruits ten thousandfold. And on one vine will be a thousand branches, and one branch will produce a thousand clusters, and one cluster will produce a thousand grapes, and one grape will produce a cor of wine. And those who are hungry will enjoy themselves and they will, moreover, see marvels every day. For winds will go out in front of me every morning to bring the fragrance of aromatic fruits and clouds at the end of the day to distill the dew of health. And it will happen at that time that the treasury of manna will come down again from on high, and they will eat of it in those years because these are they who will have arrived at the consummation of time.[323]

Millenarian beliefs are found in various other texts from Asia Minor. Cerinthus, for instance, is linked with such beliefs.[324] In the third century, in fact, Revelation was attributed to Cerinthus because of its millenarian ideas.[325] Papias of Hierapolis, in the early part of the second century, included in his now lost work a saying attributed to

---

322. E.g., *Pss. Sol.* 17:24-25; *1 Enoch* 46:5-6; 90:37; 4 Ezra 7:29; 12:32; Syr. Baruch 29:3; 39:7; 72:2; *Sib. Or.* iii. 652ff.; *T. Levi* 2:11; 4QFlor; 1QS 9:11).
323. Klijn, 2 Bar 29:3-8. See also 4 Ezra 7:26ff., a contemporary of the Syriac Baruch that contains similar ideas.
324. As well as an adoptionist christology. See Irenaeus *Against Heresies* I.26; Eusebius *Ecclesiastical History* III.27.
325. Eusebius *Ecclesiastical History* VII.25.1-3.

Excursus: The Millennium

Jesus in which the fruitfulness of the earth would be dramatically increased in the new age:

> "The days will come in which vines shall grow, each with ten thousand shoots, each shoot with ten thousand branches, each branch ten thousand twigs, each twig ten thousand clusters, each cluster ten thousand grapes; and each grape when pressed shall yield twenty-five measures of wine. And when any of the saints shall take hold of one of the clusters, another cluster shall call out, 'I am a better cluster; take me, and bless the Lord through me.' Likewise a grain of wheat shall yield ten thousand ears, each ear ten thousand grains, each grain ten pounds of pure white flour. And fruits, seeds, and grass shall yield in like proportion. And all the animals, enjoying these fruits of the earth shall live in peace and harmony, obedient to man in entire submission."

The authority for these sayings is Papias, who belonged to an earlier generation, who heard John speak and was a companion of Polycarp.[326]

Montanist expectation was for a new Jerusalem that would descend in Phrygia.[327] Justin looked forward to an earthly reign of the saints, where they would reign with Christ in peace and prosperity in a rebuilt and enlarged Jerusalem. This is but a prelude to judgment, however, though Justin recognizes that "not all Christians are of this persuasion."[328] Irenaeus, in his refutation of gnostic heresy, stressed the material character of salvation and supported Papias's view about the millennium.[329] Irenaeus made reference to biblical passages that speak of peace, prosperity, and material restoration, which he refuses to spiritualize. As in Revelation 20–21, at the end of the thousand years will come judgment:

> For it is only right that [the righteous] should receive the reward of their endurance in that created order in which they suffered hardship or affliction and were in all manner of ways tested by suffering; that they should be brought to life in that created order in which they were put to death for the love of God; and to reign where they had endured bondage. For God is "rich in all things" and all things are his. Therefore this created order must be restored to its first condition and be made subject to the righteous without hindrance.[330]

Tertullian also defended this belief:

> For we also hold that a kingdom has been promised to us on earth, but before (*we attain*) heaven. . . . This will last for a thousand years, in a city of God's making. Jerusalem sent down from heaven which the Apostle designates as "our mother from above" and in proclaiming that "our *politeuma*," that is, citizenship, "is in heaven," he surely ascribes it to a heavenly city. Ezekiel knew that city, and the Apostle John saw it, and the Word of the New Prophecy which dwells in our faith witnesses to it so that it even foretold the appearance of the likeness of that city to serve as a sign before its manifestation before men's eyes. . . . We say that this is the city designed by God for the reception of the saints at the *[first]* resurrection, and for their cherishing with abundance of all goods, spiritual goods to be sure, in compensation for the goods we have despised or lost in this age. For indeed it is right and worthy of God that his servants should also rejoice in the place where they suffered affliction in his name. This is the purpose of that kingdom; which will last a thousand years, during which period the saints will rise sooner or later, according to their degrees of merit, and then when the resurrection of the saints is completed,

---
326. Iraenaeus *Against Heresies* V. 33.3-4, in Bettenson, *The Early Christian Fathers*, 137.
327. *Epiphanius Pan.* XLIX; cf. Eusebius *Ecclesiastical History* V.18.2.
328. Justin *Dialogue* 113, 139.
329. Justin *Dialogue* 81.
330. Irenaeus *Against Heresies* V.32.1, in Bettenson, *The Early Christian Fathers*, 136.

Excursus: The Millennium

the destruction of the world and the conflagration of judgement will be effected; we shall be "changed in a moment" into the angelic substance, by the "putting on of incorruption," and we shall be transferred to the celestial kingdom.[331]

Elsewhere he is more sympathetic to a less materialistic hope.[332]

Hippolytus's commentary on Daniel is one of the oldest extant Bible commentaries. In it he affirms the view that the reign of Antichrist and the end of the world will be six thousand years after creation (a view echoed in the work of later commentators, like the early Augustine). That time would be five hundred years after Christ's birth,[333] after which will come a sabbath (cf. Heb 4:9-10), "the future kingdom of the saints when they will reign with Christ after his coming from heaven, as John narrates in the Apocalypse."[334] Origen rejects this tradition,[335] though he is elsewhere content to relate the imagery to actual history, as reflected also in the work of his pupil Dionysius.[336] Victorinus, whose commentary is the earliest extant commentary on the book of Revelation, approaches Revelation 20 literally as a hope for the just to rise from death and reign with Christ over all people. In his *Divine Institutes*, for Lactantius the victory of Christ ushers in an age of peace.[337] After a judgment of believers, the saints will be gathered into the holy city, and the just will rule with Christ.

Ambrose transformed the millennial tradition into an allegory about the interim state between death and general resurrection.[338] The influential Donatist commentator Tyconius was convinced that the apocalyptic scenario was imminent, evident in part in the persecution endured by his own church and soon to afflict the whole world. He interpreted the millennium as referring to the time of the church "from the passion of the Lord until his second coming."[339] In the present age, the saints are already enthroned with the triumphant Christ. Tyconius's work had enormous influence on Augustine, who distinguishes sharply between history and eschatology. The eschaton means the end of history. In *The City of God*, Augustine lists the following as elements of the consummation: the return of Elijah, the conversion of the Jewish people, the coming of Antichrist, the coming of Christ as judge, the resurrection of the dead, the separation of the good from the wicked, and the burning and renewal of the material world.[340] Earlier in his life, he understood the millennium as the future rest of the saints on earth.[341] In *The City of God*, he recognizes that some form of millenarian belief can be held,[342] but he developed an ecclesiological interpretation of Revelation 20 in which the kingdom stands for all the years of the Christian era and the thrones of judgment of Rev 20:4 are positions of authority in the church. Thus he follows Tyconius's lead.

Augustine's role in developing not only a Christian understanding of the state but also an attitude toward eschatology is enormous. Drawing upon his distinctive interpretation of the messianic kingdom in Revelation 20 as a description of the era of the church, Augustine argues that the church now on earth is both the kingdom of Christ and the kingdom of heaven:

---

331. Tertullian *Against Marcion* III.24, in Bettenson, *The Early Christian Fathers*, 226-27.
332. Tertullian *On the Resurrection* 26.
333. Hippolytus *Commentary on Daniel* IV.23-24.
334. Hippolytus *Commentary on Daniel* IV.23.
335. Origen *De Principiis*. II.11.2; *Commentary on Matthew* XVII. 35.
336. Dionysius vii. 24-25.
337. Victorinus *Commentary on the Book of Revelation*.
338. Ambrose Homily on Psalm 1:1.54.
339. See Friedriksen, "Tyuconius and Augustine," 24-29.
340. Augustine *The City of God* XX.30
341. Augustine *Ctr Adim* II.2.
342. Augustine *The City of God* XX.7.

Excursus: The Millennium

> Now some people assume . . . that the first resurrection will be a bodily resurrection . . . taking it as appropriate that there should be a kind of sabbath for the saints for all that time, a holy rest, that is, after the labours of the six thousand years since human creation. . . . This notion would be in some degree tolerable if it were believed that in that sabbath some delights of a spiritual character were to be available for the saints. . . . I also entertained this notion at one time. But in fact those people assert that those who have risen will spend their time in the most unrestrained material feasts, in which there will be so much to eat and drink that not only will those supplies keep within no bounds of moderation but will exceed the limits of incredibility. . . . the devil is bound throughout the whole period (of the millennium) embraced by the Apocalypse, that is from the first coming of Christ to the end of the world. . . . the Omnipotent did not debar Satan altogether from putting the saints to the test; but he threw out the devil from the inner man, the seat of belief in God. . . .
>
> . . . now the binding of the devil was not only effected at the time when the church began to spread beyond the land of Judea into other nations . . . it is happening now . . . for even now people are being converted to the faith from the unbelief in which the devil held them in power. . . .
>
> . . . the thrones are to be interpreted as the seats of authorities by whom the church is now governed, and those sitting on them the authorities themselves . . . the beast represents the godless city, and the people of the unbelievers contrasted with the people of the faith and the City of God . . . those who do not worship the beast or his image (are) those who follow the instruction of the apostle by not taking the yoke with unbelievers.[343]

In *The City of God,* a major contribution to political theology, Augustine seeks to combat the view that the sack of Rome was the result of the pagan divinities' anger at the people's abandonment of traditional Roman religious practices in favor of Christianity. He questions simplistic attempts to read off from the complexities of history evidence of the hand of God in the affairs of men and women. He does this by espousing a sharp division between the earthly city and the city of God. The city of God for him is a transcendent, heavenly reality. The earthly city is always characterized by corruption and violence and can never be identified in its entirety with the city of God. The best that can be hoped for in the earthly city is a modicum of peace and justice to ensure some kind of stability and harmony.[344]

In contrast, Joachim of Fiore[345] saw history as a process that pushes forward to a goal within history. He divided history into three periods (from the Trinity), the third being the age of the Spirit when the purposes of God will be fulfilled and humanity would manifest moral perfection under the guidance of the Spirit. Even among the radical followers of the Joachite tradition, the millennium was given an Augustinian interpretation, however. That is, the millennium was seen as having begun with the coming of Christ and was not a future event. Even an ardent interpreter of the book of Revelation like Melchior Hoffman, whose interpretation of the book had a significant influence on its use in the Münster commonwealth, understands the millennium as the early period of church history, ushered in by Paul's preaching the gospel to the Gentiles when the Spirit of Christ was still active.[346]

The case of Thomas Muentzer is instructive. Muentzer seems to exemplify the millenarian spirit, and yet he was not influenced in his revolutionary apocalypticism either by Revelation in general or by Revelation 20 in particular. Muentzer and six thousand poorly equipped peasants occupied a hill overlooking Frankenhausen in Saxony during the Peasant's Revolt of 1525. They carried a banner proclaiming "The Word of God

---

343. Augustine *The City of God* XX.7-8.
344. E.g., Augustine *The City of God* XV.4-5.
345. Survey of Joachism in M. Reeves, *Joachim and the Prophetic Future* (London: SPCK, 1976); and Emmerson and McGinn, eds., *The Apocalypse in the Middle Ages,* esp. 72ff.
346. For a survey of more recent opinions with regard to the millennium see Wainwright, *Mysterious Apocalypse,* part 1.

Excursus: The Millennium

endureth forever." Muentzer encouraged his supporters with biblical stories like that of Gideon, in which a small army aided by the power of God defeated a larger enemy. At the decisive moment of Muentzer's last battle, a rainbow appeared in the sky, and he and his followers took it as a sign that the God of the New Covenant would give them victory. That Muentzer and the peasants believed that they were engaged in a holy war is suggested by their singing "Veni Creator" as they prepared for battle. Any eschatological hopes were rudely shattered once the first cannon round had been fired, however, and the peasants were easily routed. Muentzer escaped but was later captured and was finally beheaded after having recanted of his theological "errors."[347]

In the Geneva Bible there is a rejection of a materialist millennium. The marginal note on Rev 5:10 ("You have made them to be a kingdom and priests" [NRSV]) adds "not corporally." There is a contrast between the kingdom of Christ and that of the pope: "as the kingdom of Christ is from heaven and bringeth men thither: so the Pope's kingdome is of the earth and leadeth to perdition and . . . is established by ambition, covetousnes, beastlines, craft, treason and tyranie" (note on Rev 13:11). The mention of the new heaven and the new earth is a reference to the time when "the faithful shall enter into heven with their head Christ." The millennium starts "from Christ's nativitie unto the time of Pope Sylvester the seconde; so long the pure doctrine shulde after as sorte remaine." At the end of the thousand years, "Satan had greater power than he had before." "Reigning with Christ" means "while they [i.e., the elect] have remained in this life." The first resurrection refers to receiving "Jesus Christ in true faith, and to rise from sinne in newness of life." The rest of the dead refers to those "which are spiritually dead, for in whom satan liveth he is dead to God." The binding of Satan is the proclamation of the gospel, and the loosing of Satan at the end of the millennium results in an era when "the true preaching of God's worde is corrupt."

Surprisingly, the millennium of Revelation 20 does not appear to have been an inspiration for many of the radical groups that have sought to establish an eschatological theocracy on earth. Instead, the realized eschatology, the view that the decisive moment in the divine economy is not just imminent but actually here and that humans are agents in bringing it about, has been predominant. Such a mingling of the future age of absolute perfection with mundane history is what Karl Mannheim termed "the chiliastic mentality."[348] He speaks of this conviction as one in which the present moment is of critical significance within the whole gamut of salvation history, in which action is necessary. It is no ordinary moment but one pregnant with opportunities to fulfill the destiny of humankind. The absolute perfection of the millennium ceases to be a matter of speculation and becomes a pressing necessity for active implementation. The reason for such urgency is that the *kairos*, or propitious moment, has arrived. As a result, the chiliastic mentality has no sense for the process of becoming; it is sensitive only to the abrupt moment, the present pregnant with meaning.

347. Rowland, *Radical Christianity*, 89ff.
348. Mannheim, *Ideology and Utopia*, 190-96.

REVELATION 20:7-10, THE RELEASE OF SATAN FOR THE LAST BATTLE

COMMENTARY

Satan is released (rather than escapes) from his prison (cf. 2:10; 18:2) at the end of the thousand-year reign of Christ and begins again to deceive the nations (13:14), called Gog and Magog. These are the hordes that descend on Israel, according to Ezekiel's prophecy, for easy plunder, only to fall in the open field (Ezek 39:4; cf. Ezek 38:22). The battle described in vv. 8-9 parallels the battle in 19:19, which was led by the beast, agent of the devil. This time, the devil himself leads the charge (prompting earlier commentators to suppose that different sources have been stitched together in this part of Revelation).[349] Satan gathers an innumerable host (cf. Josh 11:4; 1 Sam 13:5) and encircles the encampment of the saints (cf. Heb 13:11, 13) and the "beloved city" (cf. Ps 48:4). Military imagery was used earlier in connection with the conquest of the saints who stand with the Lamb on Mount Zion. There the followers of the Lamb were described as an army, and they were in a state of ritual purity appropriate for those who would fight a holy war (see Deut 23:9ff.; 1 Sam 21:5; 2 Sam 11:9ff.; and 1QM 7:3ff.). The reference to the beloved city (perhaps using language from 2 Kgs 6:14; Sir 24:11; and the mythology of Psalm 46; Isaiah 38–39) might appropriately describe the dwelling of those who have God with them (cf. 12:12; 13:6). No actual battle takes place in the vision (as at 19:20), because fire descends from heaven and consumes the enemy forces (v. 9; cf. 2 Kgs 1:10; Isa 11:4; Commentary on 19:21). The devil now shares the same fate of the beast and the false prophet by being thrown into the lake of fire (cf. 19:20), where they will endure eternal torment (cf. 14:10). (See Reflections at 20:11-15.)

[349]. R. H. Charles, *Revelation*, 2 vols., ICC (Edinburgh: T. & T. Clark, 1920) 2:144.

REVELATION 20:11-15, THE VISION OF THE GREAT WHITE THRONE AND JUDGMENT

COMMENTARY

The demise of the devil, the beast, and the false prophet paves the way for judgment by the one seated on the great white throne (vv. 11-12; cf. 4:2; 1 Kgs 10:18; Dan 7:9). Heaven and earth have fled from that presence (cf. 6:14; 21:1; 2 Pet 3:12). Just as no room was found for the devil in heaven (12:6), so also now the whole creation is removed.[350] The judgment of the dead takes place (v. 12). They stand, as the Lamb had done (5:5), as suppliants. Books are opened (another reminder of the importance of books as written records; 1:11; 5:1; 10:2; 22:7, 10, 18-19), reminiscent of the judgment scene in Dan 7:9-10; 12:1. Among these books is the book of life (v. 12; cf. 13:8; 17:8; 21:27). The assurance is given that no one whose name is in the book of life will be sentenced to eternity in the lake of fire (3:5). Inclusion in that book is not determined beforehand; it is possible, therefore, to have one's name blotted out of it (cf. 3:5). The book functions as a way of enabling readers to see what has to be avoided in order to "conquer" and to ensure that one's name remains listed in it.

Judgment is "according to their works," a phrase repeated twice in vv. 12-13 and throughout the letters to the angels in chaps. 2–3. One's deeds will not be forgotten (14:13; cf. 22:12). Although the criteria of judgment

[350]. Contrasting with the eschatological imagery in the Jewish text *1 Enoch* 91:12ff., where only heaven is removed and the old earth remains.

are not laid out, the emphasis throughout Revelation on holding fast to one's faith in Jesus (e.g., 14:12) and to the testimony of Jesus (e.g., 19:10), in contrast to the beguiling and seductive demands of the beast and Babylon, suggests difference, non-conformity with culture—exemplified in the conduct that led to the death of the Lamb.

REFLECTIONS

We can describe in detail what happens in Revelation, but the far more difficult task of determining what sense we should make of it remains. The imagery of the text, with its symbols and metaphors, suggests a new vision and a new practice, one that removes prejudice and blindness to God's purposes. It demands that we allow ourselves to be interrogated by those images and disturbed by a different way of looking at things, like the visually impaired person who puts on glasses and finally sees things clearly, or the adventurer who finds the mist disappearing from the mountaintops to reveal a vista different from any that may have been imagined. If we allow ourselves to be challenged by this text instead of rushing to explain everything in Revelation and to organize the images into a precise eschatological scenario, we may begin to discern that the vision of the millennium might disturb our complacency.

1. While one can understand a reluctance to take sides in contemporary political struggles, the New Testament itself is not neutral. It does take sides. The writers look not only to the future, but also to the present, which becomes a moment of opportunity for transforming the imperfect into the perfect; history and eschatology become inextricably intertwined. In the words and life of Jesus, the present is proclaimed as decisive in God's purposes, and he is the messianic agent for change. Paul took upon himself the role of the human agent, whereby the eschatological purpose of God, to bring the gospel to Gentiles, was completed.

If a veil lies over the timing of any future age of perfection, we may be tempted to avoid taking any decisive action. Such reserve is an understandable part of resistance to the notion that a perfect understanding of reality is available. A reading of both the Old and the New Testaments excludes the extremes of both revolutionary activism and political quietism.

In the apocalyptic tradition the seer is enabled to see the vague outline of the whole course of history. Until the historical process has come to fruition, we are obliged to remain faithful to the ways of God and to seek to take upon ourselves the yoke of the kingdom, both individually and corporately. This will require, as Revelation makes clear, a cost for those who hold out for a better way. And it will be necessary to resist, and wrestle with, the principalities and powers—whether of state, church, group, or nation—that would dominate and impoverish humans.

2. Theologically, the millennium deserves much greater prominence than it has had. At the center of Christian faith, after all, is the confession that Jesus has risen from the dead. Resurrection transforms death into new life in a renewed world. It is not an escape into a world beyond, therefore. In the Christian creeds we confess belief not in the immortality of the soul but in resurrection from the dead. The hope for the Messiah's reign on earth is consistent with that resurrection hope and is an attempt to encapsulate it in the images of apocalypticism. It is an evocation of a time when the deceiving of people by the ideology of contemporary society and the distortion of minds and lives by the beast of Mammon no longer takes place (cf. 12:9; 13:14), and it bids us to alter our present practice accordingly

Jesus promised the disciples the power to do exactly what the angel with the key to the abyss could do in Revelation 20 (Matt 16:17; 18:18; John 20:23). Although it is easy to let Satan loose and to cause chaos by looking at things from a human rather than a divine perspective (Matt 16:23), those who follow the way of the Messiah have the power to build foundations of a community against which the gates of hell can never prevail. It is that divine perspective that characterizes the millennium that now, amid all the perplexities and confusion of existence under the domain of the beast and the temptation to collude with Babylon, the Spirit of Christ summons the church to claim and live: "Let anyone who has an ear listen to what the Spirit is saying to the churches" (Rev 2:7 NRSV).

3. A perennial issue for Christians is how they deal with that strong exclusivist strand within their tradition, largely (though not entirely) due to the eschatological inheritance. The apocalyptic tradition based on Revelation has the reputation for being the most stringent of all. It does contain, however, a surprisingly inclusive aspect.

According to Revelation 13, dire consequences result from worshiping the beast and the dragon that stands behind the beast. No activity, not even buying or selling, can be regarded as morally neutral. In all situations of life, therefore, there is present a challenge, a threat, an opportunity of the hidden life of God. What is distinctive about Revelation is that those who resist the beast and Babylon are not church members alone. Indeed, those who compromise may well include many in the churches.

Similarly, in Matt 25:31ff. service to the hungry, the thirsty, the naked, and the imprisoned is the criterion for a place among the sheep or the goats, not membership in the church. The texts of Matthew and Revelation do not allow readers to be complacent in the face of judgment. In Matt 25:31ff., there is a subtle relationship between the eschatological judge and his hidden presence in the least of his "brethren" in the midst of the present age. Final judgment, indeed, is now being gestated in the womb of history.

Judgment texts like Matthew 25 and Revelation do not offer precise descriptions of what is to come, but challenge neat assumptions about priorities, inclusiveness, and values. They are most disturbing for any ecclesiology. As the letters to the seven churches indicate, who is "in" and who is "out" are not at all clear. Those who are most confident (the Laodiceans) turn out to be the least included. Confessing the name and being part of an ecclesial community is not what counts; it is whether one has worshiped the beast and drunk deep of the wine of the fornication of Babylon. Membership within a specific religious group is less important than non-conformity to the mores of the beast and Babylon. Confessing Christ does not guarantee either insight or salvation. There remains the possibility that resistance to the beast and Babylon can be discerned by all those who instinctively do what is required of them by God (cf. Rom 2:13-14).

REVELATION 21:1–22:5

THE NEW HEAVEN, THE NEW EARTH, AND THE NEW JERUSALEM

COMMENTARY

Revelation contains a repeated pattern of judgment and eschatological resolution. The advent of the rider on the white horse and the messianic reign (19:11–20:6) are completed with the last assize (20:11-15) and a vision of a new heaven and new earth. The focus is now on earth, not heaven, for it is to earth that the heavenly city descends. God's presence, until now hidden behind the vault of heaven, now tabernacles with those who dwell in the new Jerusalem. The throne of God is in the midst of the city, and the healing, sustenance, and relief, only glimpsed in 7:16, are described once more. The dimensions of the new Jerusalem are set out, and the glory, until now illicitly gained or used, now contributes to this new age. Still there remain discordant notes as the boundaries are set—even though the gates of the city are left wide open, some people will remain outside.

21:1. Picking up on a theme twice repeated in the final chapters of Isaiah (Isa 65:17; 66:22), John sees a new heaven and earth replacing the ones that have vanished. The theme of newness of Second Isaiah (e.g., Isa 42:9), hinted at in promises to the angels of the seven churches (Rev 2:17; 3:12) and in the song that greets the Lamb (Rev 5:9; 14:3), is now fulfilled. What is past, the "first," the provisional rather than the fundamental (cf. Rev 1:17; 22:13), is no more. There is a brief, unexplained mention that there will be no more sea. The sea in heaven (4:6) became a threatening place, to be endured or "conquered" (15:2), and the earthly sea had been the object of judgment (5:13; 7:1-2; 8:8-9; 12:12; 16:3; 18:21). It was a place to be exploited by the mariners (18:17), and above all the sea was the place out of which the beast had arisen to threaten the eternal destiny of humanity (13:1; cf. 12:12; Mark 5:13). That threat is now removed.

21:2. John sees the holy city descending out of heaven, referred to in 11:2 in the context of the vision of the witnesses (though it is not described there as new). This vision comes after chapters that have focused on the "great city" (e.g., 18:10). Babylon and Jerusalem are thereby implicitly juxtaposed and contrasted, reminiscent of the contrast between Jerusalem above and below in Gal 4:26 (cf. Heb 12:22).[351] That which descends from heaven is a blessing rather than a curse on humanity (cf. 12:12; 16:21), and this city is a place to enter rather than depart from (18:4); it is from God (cf. 3:12). The image of the city's being prepared in heaven reflects the apocalyptic view that heaven is, in some sense, a repository of what is to come, which can be revealed to the eye of vision before it descends in the last days (cf. 9:15; 12:6). Jerusalem is likened to a bride. The bride's voice had been silenced in Babylon (18:23), and the wedding feast seemed destined not to begin (19:7). The true bridegroom will appear, however, and will be summoned to come to the bride (22:17; cf. Matt 25:6).

21:3. There is a voice from the throne (cf. 16:17; 19:5), a "great voice" from heaven (NIV and NRSV, "loud voice"; cf. 11:12; 12:10; 16:1, 17; 19:1). God's dwelling ("tabernacle" [σκηνή *skēnē*], the word used of the incarnation in John 1:14) will be (taking the cue from the tense of the next verb σκηνόω [*skēnoō*; "dwell"]) with "mortals" (assuming that ἄνθρωποι [*anthrōpoi*, "men"] here is probably to be understood inclusively, fulfilling the promise of 7:15). God's

---

351. A. T. Lincoln, *Paradise Now and Not Yet* (Cambridge: Cambridge University Press, 1981).

tabernacle is found in heaven in 15:5, where it is the source of the seven last plagues. It is the object of the beast's blasphemy in 13:6, where it is interpreted as "those who dwell in heaven" (NRSV). God's dwelling with people characterizes the life of the holy nation in Lev 26:12 and Joel 2:27, and it is the new Jerusalem of Ezekiel's vision (Ezek 48:35; cf. Ezek 37:27; Zech 2:11). In the New Testament God's dwelling (tabernacle) is the life of a holy, and so separate, people (2 Cor 6:16).

Three times in this verse God is said to be "with them." The use of the preposition "with" (μετά *meta*) in the sense of accompaniment and belonging is found only in the promise in 3:4, 20-21, in the eschatological vision in 14:1, and in the description of the eschatological reign. This usage contrasts with its use in a hostile context (making war with or committing fornication with) earlier in the vision. In the new Jerusalem, mortals are now God's "peoples" (the Greek is plural here, contrasting with the singular in 18:4; cf. Jer 31:1; many MSS, however, leave the singular, as the NRSV footnote indicates). Verse 3 resonates with the theme of 5:9 and 7:9, where those who have been redeemed come from "every tribe and language and people and nation." God has not been totally absent from the world. Indeed, the burden of the letters to the angels has been the revelation of the intimate relationship between the one like the Son of Man and the churches (1:20), and the cataclysm following the opening of the seals is in some sense a revelation of the mystery of the divine presence, though in wrath, in the world.

21:4. The promise of 7:17 is once again stated (cf. Isa 25:8), and the end of death is repeated (cf. 20:10). There will be no more mourning, crying, or pain (cf. Isa 35:10; 51:11; 65:19), contrasting with what had been (18:7-8; cf. 11:15; 16:10-11). "The first" is replaced by "the new," expressed in words from the one seated on the throne, who now speaks and asserts responsibility: "I am making all things new" (see Isa 43:18-19).

21:5-6. This leads to another command from the one seated on the throne (v. 5), presumably to John, to write (cf. 1:11, 19; 14:13; 19:9), asserting that the words are faithful and true (see also 19:9; 22:6). This probably refers not just to the promise to make all things new but also, in the light of 19:9, to God's promise to dwell with people. Addressing John personally (v. 6), the one on the throne announces, "It is done!" (like the assertion from heaven at the culmination of the seven plagues in 16:17). God is both Alpha and Omega (v. 6; cf. 1:8), the beginning and the end (cf. 3:14; 22:13; the Greek equivalent of A and Z). In the declaration that God will "give water as a gift from the spring of the water of life," the promise of 7:16 is again alluded to; the spring of water (v. 6) will be described in 22:1 (cf. Zech 14:8; John 7:37). Water will no longer pose a threat (cf. 12:15; 15:2), for the waters have returned to the control of the one who created them (14:7). The nations, who are the waters on whom Babylon sat (7:1), are now peoples who can partake of the water of life freely (21:6).

21:7. The one who "conquers" (changed to plural by the NRSV) will inherit "these things." They are the ones who have overcome the beast and its image by means of the blood of the Lamb (15:2; 21:11). In being inheritors, human beings now have a familial relationship with God (cf. Matt 5:5; 19:29; 25:34). The promise to the dynasty of David in 2 Sam 7:14 is here extended to all people, as it is in the eschatological passage in *Jub.* 1:24; it is central to the eschatology of other parts of the New Testament as well (e.g., Rom 8:15; Gal 4:6). One difference between Revelation 21 and 2 Samuel 7 should be noted: though human beings inherit from God, God is not spoken of as Father in Revelation 21 (though that could be explained by the influence of Lev 26:12; cf. Zech 8:8 in 21:3).

21:8. The promise is immediately followed by a darker statement, paralleling the contrasts in eschatological passages elsewhere in the NT (e.g., 1 Cor 6:10; Gal 5:21). Interestingly, despite the comprehensive judgment in the previous chapter, there still exist those who are outside the gates and who are destined for the lake of fire (19:20; 20:6). But such a comment manifests a pedantic literalism that does not do full justice to the poetic license of apocalypse. In other words, v. 8 simply elaborates and reinforces what has already occurred: The condemned will have no place in the new Jerusalem. In the list of those intended for the "second death" (cf. parallel lists in Ezek 44:9; Rom 1:29; 1 Cor 6:10; Titus 1:16), the first two (the cowardly and the faithless) have no direct parallel in Revelation, though in the light of the repeated emphasis on being faithful even to death (2:10), we can see the need for courage to resist the allure of the beast, like the "faithful witness" (1:6; cf. 2:10). Babylon is said to be full of abominations (17:4), and so avoidance of fornication (cf. 22:15) may be suggested in the reference to "the polluted" and the "idolaters" who eat food sacrificed to idols (cf. 2:14; 9:20; 17:2). "Sorcery" was mentioned in 9:21 and 18:23 (and see the Commentary on 9:20).[352] No lie was found in those who stood with the Lamb on Mount Zion (14:5), and no liars enter the new Zion (cf. 2:2; 21:27; 22:15; see also 13:13; 2 Thess 2:9-10).

21:9-11. The link with the previous catastrophes is maintained in v. 9, where an angel who had held one of the seven bowls (15:1) comes to show John the bride of the Lamb (cf. 19:7). John's removal parallels his removal to see another city, Babylon, in 17:3. He is carried away (as in 4:1) "in the spirit." Like Ezekiel, who in visions was brought to a very high mountain to behold a city (Ezek 40:1), John is taken to a high mountain (cf. Matt 4:8; 17:1). There John again sees the holy city descending from heaven (v. 2), but this time he is "shown" the holy city (this is different from Ezekiel's city, which the prophet sees perched on the mountain rather than descending from heaven). Additionally, John speaks of the city as possessing the glory of God, as does Ezekiel's city, once the glory of God had entered the Temple (Ezek 43:4; cf. Isa 60:1). The "bride" (v. 9) who belongs to the Lamb contrasts with Jezebel (2:20) and with Babylon seated on the beast (17:3), but resembles the woman clothed with the sun (12:1). The radiance of the bride/holy city is like that of a precious gemstone, like that of God's throne in 4:3 (see also 21:18), and it is comparable to Babylon's adornment (17:4; 18:12, 16).

21:12-14. In these verses John describes the city in terms that evoke the conclusion of Ezekiel's vision of Jerusalem (Ezek 48:30ff.). Boundaries and separation are fundamental, as 21:8, 27 and 22:6 make clear (cf. Ezek 40:3). Thus a "great, high wall" with twelve gates surrounds the city. The three gates at each compass point resemble those described in Ezek 48:31; here, too, they are linked to the twelve tribes of Israel (explicitly named in Ezekiel). There are angelic gatekeepers (cf. Isa 62:6).[353] The tribes of Israel are mentioned earlier in the vision of the eschatological host, which was divided into two parts, Israel (7:4-8) and the multitude from "every nation, from all tribes and peoples and languages" (7:9-17 NRSV). A related juxtaposition follows in v. 14 between the tribes of Israel and the twelve apostles. Just as the names of the twelve tribes of Israel are inscribed on the gates of the wall, so also the names of the "twelve apostles of the Lamb" are inscribed on the wall's twelve foundations (cf. 2:2; 18:20). The idea of the apostles as foundation stones is found also in Eph 2:20, where the household of God is built on the foundation of the apostles and the prophets (cf. 18:20, where the two are linked), with Christ as the cornerstone. This is the only reference to apostles of the Lamb in Revelation. Elsewhere mention is made of false apostles (2:2; cf. 2 Cor 11:13), and the prophets and apostles in 18:20 are like the line of witnesses referred to in Luke 11:49 (cf. Matt 23:34). It would appear that in Revelation the prophet assumes more importance than does the apostle.

21:15. The angel (cf. v. 9) who shows the city to John is holding a golden measuring rod to measure the city, an operation that contrasts with that described in Rev 11:1 and Ezek 40:3. The measuring in the latter passage was done to offer an inventory of the city that is to come, to "declare all that you see to the house of Israel" (Ezek 40:4 NRSV). In Rev 11:1 John is given a measuring rod and is told to measure only a part of what he sees: the temple, the altar, and "those who worship there." There is no such restriction here, nor is a census taken of those who worship (this contrasts with the contemporary 4 Ezra, which makes explicit comment on the small number of those who will be saved; see 4 Ezra 7:70).

---

352. See P. L. Esler, *The First Christians in Their Social Worlds* (London: Routledge, 1994) 131-46.

353. Angelic gatekeepers are a feature of later gnostic and Jewish texts. See, e.g., *Ascension of Isaiah* 10:25, where heavenly gatekeepers demand a password before allowing anyone to pass through the gates.

21:16-17. The city is "foursquare" (cf. Ezek 48:16), being equal in height, width, and length (v. 16); in other words, it has the shape of a cube.[354] The interior of the inner sanctuary of Solomon's Temple was also a cube (1 Kgs 6:20; cf. the size of the altar in Ezek 43:16). So the city's shape is like an extended form of the innermost part of the sanctuary. The vocabulary of v. 16 is reminiscent of Eph 3:18 (three of the terms are found), where a complex of images is made up of the biological and the architectural, suggesting (not least in the light of Eph 2:20) that the city's dimensions are "the measure of the full stature of Christ" (Eph 4:13 NRSV). The angel measures the wall, and it is 144 cubits (cf. the figure used of the host in 7:4 and 14:1, and possibly paralleling the idea of a spiritual building in Ephesians). The angel is said to be using human measurement (cf. Deut 3:11; see also Commentary on 13:18).

21:18-20. The radiance of the city was likened to jasper in v. 11, and now John describes the walls of the city as being made of jasper (v. 18). The city itself is built of pure gold, "clear as glass." The word "pure" (καθαρός *katharos*) has been previously linked with special clothing identified with God (15:6; 19:8-14; 21:21; cf. Matt 5:8; Jas 1:27). Earlier the sea in heaven had been described as being like glass (4:6; 15:2), and the streets of the city will be described in similar terms in 21:21.[355] Precious stones were mentioned in a general way in v. 11, but here the foundations of the city are described in more detail and the stones composing it are listed (v. 19): jasper (cf. 4:3), sapphire (cf. 9:17), agate, emerald (cf. 4:3), onyx, carnelian (cf. 4:3), chrysolite, beryl, topaz, chrysoprase, jacinth, and amethyst. The jewels here are reminiscent of the descriptions of the high priest's breastplate and the Edenic splendor of the king of Tyre. The high priest's breastplate is adorned with gemstones set in four rows of stones.

A row of carnelian, chrysolite, and emerald shall be the first row; and the second row a turquoise, a sapphire and a moonstone; and the third row a jacinth, an agate, and an amethyst; and the fourth row a beryl, an onyx, and a jasper; they shall be set in gold filigree. (Exod 28:17-20 NRSV)

The king of Tyre is described in Ezekiel as:

full of wisdom and perfect in beauty.
You were in Eden, the garden of God;
    every precious stone was your covering,
carnelian, chrysolite, and moonstone,
    beryl, onyx, and jasper,
sapphire, turquoise, and emerald;
    and worked in gold were your settings
    and your engravings. (Ezek 28:12-13 NRSV)

21:21. Each of the twelve gates is made of a single pearl (cf. 17:4; 18:12, 16). The street of the city is pure gold (cf. Babylon's golden aspect in 17:4; 18:16), transparent as glass (cf. 2 Cor 4:4; Heb 1:3; 2 Pet 1:19).

21:22-23. John reports that he saw no temple in the new city (v. 22). It is possible that there will be no need for a temple, because the city is a sanctuary unto itself. But John's explanation is that the Almighty God and the Lamb are the city's temple (v. 22). If a temple marks a discrete place of divine presence in the midst of a world, here the divine is immediately present and all-pervasive; there is no need for a preserve that guarantees and identifies holiness. There is no need for light in the new Jerusalem, either, because of the radiance of divine glory (cf. v. 11; 22:5; Isa 60:19). The city's brilliance contrasts with the darkness of Babylon (16:10; 18:23), and it parallels the situation where the sun and the moon accompany the woman (chap. 12). The description of God's glory is like the radiance of Ezekiel's vision (Ezek 1:28; cf. 15:8; 18:1; 21:11).

21:24-27. The nations are guided by this glorious light (v. 24; cf. Isa 60:3, 5; Zech 8:20), contrasting with the delusion described earlier (14:8; 18:3), which led to the nations' wrathful response to God (11:18). The promise that the nations will be ruled by the messianic rod has appeared often in Revelation (e.g., 12:5; 19:15). The kings of the earth, until now thoroughly under the spell of the beast (e.g., 17:2; 18:3), reappear (v. 24); but now the kings will bring their "glory" (δόξα *doxa*, the same word used of God) into the city. In Isa 60:11, the kings will lead their nations in a procession to bring their wealth

---

354. See M. Rissi, *The Future of the World* (London: SCM, 1972).
355. It is interesting to compare the description of the city in Revelation with what Josephus has to say about the stunning sight of the high priest's vestments. See Josephus *The Jewish War* 5.233.

into Zion, whose gates are never closed (cf. Zech 14:7; John 13:30). Nothing profane will enter this city (v. 27; cf. Isa 35:8; 52:1), nor will anyone whose name is not written in the book of life. So no one who has committed fornication with Babylon (17:2), which was full of abominations (17:4), or anyone who lies (cf. 14:5) and has been ensnared in, or colluded with, the deceit of the beast and false prophet (19:20) will be allowed to enter the city.

22:1. Just as an angel pointed out the city in v. 10, so also in 22:1 John reports that the angel showed him the very heart of the city (elsewhere John is promised that he will be shown these things; e.g., 4:1; 17:1). John sees the river of the water of life, promised in 21:6. This river, in its limpid and life-giving quality, contrasts with the rivers that were poisoned in the eschatological catastrophes (8:10; 16:4, 12). It evokes paradise, a garden (cf. Gen 2:10).

The description of the water as being "bright as crystal" prompts a comparison with the sea in Rev 4:6 (cf. 21:11). The difference between the throne here and the one described in Dan 7:9 bears noting (cf. *1 Enoch* 14:18-19). In Daniel, the seer sees a throne of "fiery flames" with "a stream of fire" issuing from it. There is no stream of fire in Revelation 4, though the throne produces lightning and thunder, and seven flaming torches are in front of it (Rev 4:5). The fiery stream from Daniel (hinted at, perhaps, in Rev 4:5; 15:2) has been replaced by the stream of living water that proceeds from the throne and runs down the street of the new Jerusalem. Life-giving water is a feature of the new Jerusalem in Ezekiel's vision also, where water flows from the entrance of the Temple, fructifying the land (Ezek 47:1ff.; cf. Ps 46:4; Zech 14:8).

22:2-5. Verse 2 is awkward, as the variant in the NRSV attests. On either side of the river grows the "tree of life." That the tree produces twelve different kinds of fruit each month is characteristic of the trees irrigated by the water that runs from the temple in Ezek 47:12. The leaves of the tree are meant for the healing of the nations. The emphasis on the healing of the nations contrasts with the earlier statements that the nations would be ruled with an iron rod (e.g., 12:5). Nothing accursed enters in (v. 3; cf. Matt 25:41), which is in line with the harsher statement of vv. 11 and 15 (cf. 21:8, 27).

Here the throne of God and of the Lamb (cf. 7:17) is in the city. Earlier the throne in heaven was the locus of God's dwelling (4:1-2), and continues to be so when God's dwelling place is with humanity. But there is still a throne and so a limit to the extent to which God and humanity are identified. Heaven is now on earth, and God's servants will perform their service to God (cf. 7:15) without a temple. They will see God's face, the ultimate privilege denied to all until now—not even Moses was allowed to see God's face (Exod 33:20; cf. Num 12:6). For John the evangelist no one has seen God at any time, and it is only the Logos incarnate who has made God known (1:18; cf. 14:9). In Matt 5:6, it is the pure in heart who will see God. Here it is all of God's servants, those who have not worshiped the beast or committed fornication with Babylon and have God's name written on their foreheads (cf. 14:1). Once again John states that the glory of the place is such that there will be no night (cf. 21:25). God will shine upon them (cf. Isa 60:19), and they will reign forever (cf. Dan 7:18, 27). So, as in the millennium, God's servants share God's reign (cf. 3:21); they are a kingdom as well as priests who serve (1:5; cf. 7:15).

From the very beginning of the vision (2:17; 3:12) the righteous have been promised knowledge of the name of God. Understanding what one's name is, and should be, is crucial. Possession of the right name enables confession before God (Rev 3:5) and entry into the book of life. Fearing God's name means not blaspheming God, as the beast had done (13:6). To ensure that one's name stays in the book of life, one must not worship the beast (14:9). Possession of the divine name distinguishes those who follow the beast, who have a mark and not a name. Only Babylon had a name on her forehead: "Babylon the great, mother of whores and of earth's abominations" (17:5 NRSV).

Names link the present and the future, whether it be in terms of judgment (13:8) or the foundations of the new Jerusalem (21:12, 14). So the name is the person (e.g., 3:4: "you have still a few persons [lit., "names"] in Sardis who have not soiled their clothes" [NRSV]; cf. 3:12). "Holding the name" (2:13) is equivalent to maintaining the faith. The sin of the nations is having followed the beast and then blasphemed the name of God (16:9). But knowledge of God's name is not a talisman, some kind of protective charm. Possession of the name of God depends on appropriate behavior: not worshiping the beast or being intoxicated with Babylon.

❖   ❖   ❖   ❖

EXCURSUS: BIBLICAL SUSPICION OF THE TEMPLE[356]

In antiquity, every religion—the Jewish religion included—had its sacred space, a temple, the "house of God." It is remarkable, therefore, that in the new Jerusalem John "saw no temple in the city, for its temple is the Lord God the Almighty and the Lamb" (Rev 21:22 NRSV). Despite the importance of the Temple in Jerusalem in both pre-exilic and post-exilic times, there is a marked ambivalence toward temple religion in the Bible. The absence of a temple in the New Jerusalem reflects the triumph of a persistent critical attitude toward temple worship.

Although Genesis reports that the patriarchs had worshiped at a variety of holy places, after the exodus provision for liturgy centered on the portable tabernacle. Later, just as there was ambivalence toward the monarchy, important though it was, so also the role of the temple and (more often) other places of worship was viewed with a mixture of approbation, unease, and downright condemnation. Despite the divine sanction for the building of the Temple in Jerusalem and its conformity to the divine plan (1 Chr 28:12, 19) the description of its construction suggests that from its very inception the Temple's structures were infused with the spirit of Canaan. Temple worship involved compromise with local cults, the world of the senses, and the values of the Canaanite society. Solomon's departure from the worship of God (recorded in 1 Kings 11) continued in the deeds of his descendants, whose exploits, outlined in the books of Kings, become a litany of catastrophic decline from the singleminded devotion to the God of Israel's ancestors. God, though acknowledged to be beyond human comprehension in Solomon's prayer (1 Kgs 8:27), came to be too closely identified with a place, a temple made with human hands (cf. 1 Kings 8; Isa 66:1-2), a dynasty, a city, and oppression and injustice. God's approval of the building did not extend to the form, content, and actions in it, as the conditions laid out in the response to Solomon's prayer make clear (1 Kgs 9:3). The Temple, influenced by the culture of Canaan, rapidly became more a shrine to Baal than to Yahweh.

Subsequently, particularly in the reigns of Hezekiah and Josiah, some people began to recognize the extent of this departure from God's purposes. They became increasingly more aware of the extent of the discrepancy between the practice of the Temple and the demands of God. They kept alive the Sinaiitic vision of a people, formed in the desert, who had shed the false consciousness of Egypt and its fleshpots and had not yet been corrupted by Canaanite ways. Theirs was a vision of a God who demanded concern for the orphan, the widow, and the stranger and whose presence was particularly connected with the portable tabernacle, rather than the permanent and glorious edifice of the Temple. The exodus vision had almost disappeared in the Jerusalem of the monarchical period. It makes only a rare appearance in the psalmody of Solomon's Temple and in the oracles of Jerusalem's prophets. Even the celebration of the

---

356. A survey of biblical and patristic discussion is offered by Bede, *De Templo*, trans. S. Connolly, in *Translated Texts for Historians* (Liverpool: Liverpool University Press, 1995).

Excursus: Biblical Suspicion of the Temple

Passover had fallen into desuetude by Josiah's day (2 Kgs 23:22). In place of the story of the exodus and the giving of the Law, the myths of the Davidic dynasty and the invincibility of Zion and its Temple so dominated the culture that the austere story of the formation of a people with a religion of tabernacle and social justice was almost forgotten. Prophets like Isaiah called a people to seek justice, to rescue the oppressed, to defend the orphan, and to plead for the widow rather than "the multitude of your sacrifices" (Isa 1:11 NRSV). The prophetic critique reaches its climax in Ezekiel and Jeremiah, who regarded Solomon's Temple as a place of idolatry (Ezek 8:5), nowhere more stingingly rebuked than in the latter's temple sermon (Jer 7:4, 8-9).

For the temple culture, convinced that "God is in the midst of the city;/ it shall not be moved" (Ps 46:5 NRSV), it must have been a terrible shock when the Temple was destroyed after the invasion of Nebuchadnezzar. After the exile there seems to have been a struggle between those like Haggai and Zechariah, who wanted to see the Temple rebuilt as a symbol of Israel's life, and those who held out against such a move with a grander vision, more universal in scope. Haggai prophesied that the impoverishment of Israel was the result of the neglect of old-fashioned temple religion. If only the Temple were rebuilt (and scarce resources thereby diverted to the restoration of cultic activity), then all would be well in the land (Hag 1:4). It is likely that the oracles that make up the final chapters of Isaiah bear witness to the growing disillusionment of a prophetic group who found themselves outmaneuvered by the protagonists of temple reconstruction and consequently were marginalized in Israelite society. As Jews sought to survive in the hostile world of ancient Near Eastern power power struggles, figures like Ezra and Nehemiah consolidated the life of Jerusalem, centered in priesthood, temple, and law. The Temple continued to play a central role in the lives of Jews both inside and outside Judea in the years preceding the Christian era. The regular flow of income to the Temple from all parts of the empire enriched this institution and those who ran it. The Temple was the focus of religion and was a powerful economic factor in Judean life as well as an influential ideological symbol. The profaning of the temple by Antiochus IV and the prohibition of circumcision (1 Maccabees 1) precipitated the Maccabean revolt (168–165 BCE); the subsequent restoration of the Temple was (and still is) celebrated at Hanukkah (also called the Feast of Dedication in John 10:22). But the pre-eminence of the Temple did not silence the continued questioning of the temple cult in inter-testamental literature.[357]

The priests who held power in Jerusalem preserved the Temple as a holy space at the heart of Jewish life in the holy city in order to maintain the pattern of worship they believed God had prescribed for that place. Anything that might defile the holy place was excluded from the Temple. Because the preservation of this holy place was given the highest priority, in Jesus' day, the maintenance of the temple cult necessitated some kind of cooperation with the Roman authorities (cf. John 11:49). The maintenance of a holy space was not confined to the Temple, however. The Qumran sect, situated in the desert, created a holy environment where the holy angels were said to have assembled and shared their life. The Pharisees had a view of holiness that could be expressed in the midst of human communities, both near to and far from the Temple. The detailed regulations of the Mishnah (the earliest code of Jewish practice apart from the Bible, completed in the second century CE) bear witness to the seriousness of the endeavor of their rabbinic successors to preserve a holy space in all aspects of existence. That vision enabled Judaism to survive the destruction of its holy place in 70 CE and allowed Pharisaism to become the driving force of what was to emerge in the second century as rabbinic Judaism.

The Pharisees, like other Jews, may have been devastated by the destruction of the Temple in 70 CE. But the emerging practice of synagogue worship, which could be held anywhere and thus was not necessarily attached to particular places deemed to

---

357. E.g., *1 Enoch* 89:73; *Assumption of Moses* 4:5; *2 Enoch* 45:3.

be holy, was a factor in enabling the Pharisees to survive the events of 70. Buildings did not, in the last resort, matter in the life of the people of God, but obedience to the divine law in all circumstances was essential. Judaism has survived without a temple for the last two thousand years, maintaining a religion that does not depend on temple or even holy places, thereby paralleling the words of the third-century Christian writer Minucius Felix, "We have no temples; we have no altars"—a contrast with what Christianity has become.[358]

The synoptic Gospels report that Jesus, in the last days of his life, prophesied the destruction of the Temple (Mark 13:1-2 par.). In Mark's passion narrative (Mark 11 onward) a dominant theme is the Temple, which Jesus enters and "cleanses." The story of the cursing of the fig tree, which, frames the cleansing (Mark 11:12-14, 20-22), is a comment on the bankruptcy of the institution. The Temple's fate will be that of the cursed tree. In addition, before leaving the Temple for the last time, Jesus points to the impoverished widow who gives all the money she has to live on to the Temple, while the rest contribute out of their abundance (Mark 12:41). The incident is described without comment; but, in the light of Mark 12:40, where the scribes are condemned for devouring widows' houses, the fact that an institution allows an impoverished widow to give all that she has sits uneasily with the Torah's command to care for the widow (Deut 24:17; Jer 7:6; Jer 7:11 is quoted in Mark 11:17).

For Mark, the death of Jesus is the moment when the heart of the old economic, political, and religious institutions are destroyed, symbolized by the tearing of the veil that hides the holy of holies—truly the end of the world for those who set great store by it. Just as the heavens are rent apart at Jesus' baptism, so also is the veil of the Temple rent in two at Jesus' death (Mark 1:10; 15:38). Heaven and earth are then linked. But at the moment of Jesus' death, the tearing of the veil, symbolizing the mystique of the Temple's power, suggests something more destructive: the end of the Temple itself (cf. 1 Sam 15:27). The Temple is replaced by a way of life based on service and an alternative "holy" space focused on the commemoration of Christ: in place of the temple liturgy, Jesus offers his body—that is, his messianic practice in life and death.[359] The destruction of the Temple meant an end to an institution and an ideology that had dominated life, politically, religiously, and economically. So the stones of the Temple, which had so impressed the disciples, were destined to be monuments to an obsolescent form of religious life (Mark 13:1-2). In the days of Israel's exile, the departure of the divine glory from the Temple was a sign of imminent destruction (Ezekiel 1; 10). But unlike the prophecy of Ezekiel, the New Testament offers no promise that any building will ever again be set apart as a particular place in which the divine presence dwells—except, that is, the temple of Jesus' body (see John 2:19-22).

According to Acts, the first Christians continued to worship in the Temple (Acts 2:46) and made it the place of proclamation (Acts 3:1-22; 5:46). But not all did so, apparently, for Stephen's criticism of the Temple provoked a hostile response, leading to his death. In the speech attributed to him in Acts, he dwells on the rebelliousness of the majority of his ancestors. In his review of Israel's history, he points to Solomon, who built a house for God, a departure from the divine intention:

"Yet the Most High does not dwell in houses made with human hands;as the prophet says,
    'Heaven is my throne,
     and the earth is my footstool.
What kind of house will you build
    for me, says the Lord,

---

358. Minucius Felix *Octavius* 32.
359. See Myers, *Binding the Strong Man*, 364.

>   or what is the place of my rest?
>   Did not my hand make all these things?'"
> (Acts 7:48-50 NRSV, quoting Isa 66:1)

Bede, the great early medieval English writer, regarded Stephen as a spiritual pioneer who explained to his hearers that "the Lord does not place a high value on dressed stone, but rather desires the splendour of heavenly souls." What Jesus told the Samaritan woman expresses the outlook of the New Testament as a whole: "The hour is coming when you will worship the Father neither on this mountain nor in Jerusalem. . . . The true worshipers will worship the Father in spirit and truth, for the Father seeks such as these to worship him" (John 4:21, 23 NRSV).

Throughout the New Testament, sacred buildings, however glorious, seem to be of little concern to its writers. What is important is the reign of God, the witness to the ways of God's justice, and the hope of heaven on earth, anticipated in the common life of small groups of men, women, and children who began to explore a different way of being God's people. For them the priority was the temple of the Holy Spirit, men and women of flesh and blood (1 Cor 10:19). Immanuel, God with us (Matt 1:23), is not housed in a building, but is met in the persons of the hungry, the thirsty, the naked, and the imprisoned (Matt 25:31; cf. Matt 1:23), for the weak and the marginal are the ones with whom Jesus identified. In the Pauline Epistles we have glimpses of communities that struggled to maintain a style of life at odds with contemporary culture. As the locus of Christ's presence in the world, the church (found in various places) shares the holiness of God (1 Cor 1:2; 3:17; 6:19; cf. Rom 12:1; 15:16) as it seeks to live as a community under God, distinguished by the quality of its life and its practical service (Rom 15:16, 25, 31; 2 Cor 8:4, 19; 9:1, 12; Phlm 13). Heaven and earth meet no longer in tabernacle or Temple but outside the camp, a place of shame and reproach, where the blasphemers and Sabbath breakers are stoned (Exod 33:7; Lev 24:16; Num 15:35; Heb 13:13).[360] Those who share the way of Jesus can expect to go with him outside the camp, in the secular world. God's love and solidarity are among human beings in ways that the elaborate performance of cultic ritual never can be.

The sentiments of early Christian writers make disturbing reading, as Karl Barth appreciated in lectures of 1920:

> The church of the Bible is, significantly, the Tabernacle, the portable tent. The moment it becomes a Temple, it becomes essentially only an object of attack. One gathers that for the apostles the whole of the Old Testament is summarized in Stephen's apology. Undeniably the center of interest of both Testaments is not in the building of the church but in its destruction, which is always threatening and even beginning. In the heavenly Jerusalem of Revelation nothing is more finally significant than the church's complete absence: And I saw no Temple therein.[361]

When Christianity became the religion of the Roman Empire, things began to change, especially after the Constantinian settlement. From about 260 CE (but especially after 313), church buildings began to grow in size and become public structures. This growth reflected the increase in the size of congregations and (after 313) of imperial favor. (In the fourth century, church membership grew, according to one estimate, from 10 percent of the populace to about 50 percent). For the design of their new worship buildings, Christians chose the basilica (associated with the emperor and with law courts) rather than the temple (associated with paganism). Not only did their ornate decor reflect imperial iconography, but also their space was divided into areas

---

360. M. Isaacs, *Sacred Space: An Approach to the Theology of the Epistle to the Hebrews* (Sheffield: Sheffield Academic, 1992).
361. K. Barth, "Biblical Questions: Insights and Vistas," in *The Word of God and the Word of Man* (London: 1935) 72. See also K. Barth, *Church Dogmatics III.3* (Edinburgh: T. & T. Clark, 1961) 475-76.

for clergy and laity. Because of the large congregations, the worship became large-scale rather than relational and communitarian, and the importance of human relationship in divine service withered as ceremony flourished.[362] So there began to emerge a pattern of Christian activity that sits uneasily with the biblical vision of the common life. In the New Testament, the image of Christ as a temple, the divine presence in unexpected places and persons, and the priority given to human relationships in ministry should lead us to widen our quest for the gates of heaven.

362. See Kreider, *Worship and Evangelism in Pre-Christendom*, 7.

REFLECTIONS

1. Revelation 21 marks the climax of the whole book. In it we find the culmination of the process that began in chapters 2–3 with the promises made to the angels and chapter 5, where the Lamb receives the sealed scroll. The vision of God's "tabernacling" with humanity marks the climax in the eschatological drama. In Revelation 4, the seer is granted a glimpse into the environs of God. There God is hidden behind a closed door, in heaven. The contrast between heaven and earth disappears in the new creation. Now the tabernacle of God is with men and women, and they shall be God's people (21:3). God's dwelling is not to be found above the cherubim in heaven. The throne is set right in the midst of the new Jerusalem, where the living waters stream from the throne of God (22:1) and God's servants are marked with the divine name and will see God face to face (22:4). God is no longer far off but immediate and manifest—very much part of that world of perfection and as evident in it as God was in paradise (Gen 3:8). But (as Paul reminds us in 2 Cor 5:17) that new creation is not merely something to look forward to. In Christ there is already the possibility, in the power of God's Spirit, to bring about that new creation in individual lives, though with the clear recognition of the struggle of the birth pangs the whole of creation must undergo before paradise can be revealed (Rom 8:18ff.).

2. In the new Jerusalem the apostles, the vacillating faint-hearts of the Gospels, turn out to be founding members and contribute to the building of the new Jerusalem (21:14). This is a task not confined to apostles only, as those who conquer (15:2) will have the right to become pillars in the temple, just as Peter was a pillar (3:12; cf. Gal 2:9; 1 Tim 3:15). There has been much debate over the extent to which human endeavor can contribute to the new Jerusalem. Can human initiative help in any way with bringing about the coming of the reign of God, or should one just leave it in God's hands? In Revelation 21, the fact that the names of the apostles are written on the foundations of the wall and that the kings of the earth bring their glory into the city suggest that humans do contribute to its distinctive character. The city may be from heaven, but humans can be the means of channeling God's grace into it. So we have here some support for the notion of "building the kingdom." It is not all left to some eschatological miracle. Human agents infused with the Spirit of the new creation may contribute to that future reign of God here and now in the midst of the debris of the old world.

3. There will be no temple in the new Jerusalem because the glory of God and of the Lamb will pervade the whole city. The establishment of holiness in the midst of the world and in the lives of people is echoed elsewhere in the New Testament (e.g., 1 Cor. 3:16; 6:19; cf. 2 Cor 6:16). A renewed temple is often included in eschatological passages in contemporary Jewish writings, so its explicit omission here deserves to be noted. There was ambivalence, even hostility, toward the Temple in early Christianity (Acts 6:7; cf. Mark 14:58; John 4:25). Like the Pharisees, from whom Christianity derived so much, the first Christians had a view of holiness rooted in practical living in the midst of the variety of human community (Rom 12:1-2; 1 Pet 2:9).

The ambivalence toward buildings—and especially the Temple—in the Bible raises a question about the enormous investment in its buildings by the Christian church through the centuries (see Excursus: "Biblical Suspicion of the Temple"). Revelation uses evocative language about structure and space. But at its heart is the face-to-face relationship between God and humanity (22:4-5). The building is superfluous in the new Jerusalem. And yet special places seem to have become indispensable to Christians, often taking precedence over the promotion and sustenance of human relationships. Our need to create holy spaces often betrays our failure to understand that the holy space is the body of a crucified man (Mark 15:38) and a group of people who identify with him (Matt 18:20; 1 Corinthians 12).

4. With certain qualifications John's is not an exclusive vision. The light of God's glory is a light for the nations, and the glory of the old age is to be brought in. Only those who ignored God by raising the material to the level of a god and placed their own self-interest (cf. 12:11) above God's justice are barred from entering the city (21:27). Likewise, those whose names are not written in the book of life, who have compromised and collaborated with the old order (13:8), are excluded as well. At the head of the list of those who will be excluded from the new Jerusalem are cowards (21:8), who have refused to stand up and be counted when protest against injustice was needed.

5. John's vision is of a communal society, a reminder that biblical practice and hope center around humanity's relationship with God and with one another. Christianity has in its history focused so often on hope for the individual that it sometimes has lost sight of the central place community plays in past, present, and future expressions of human destiny. As we grow ever more fearful about life in our cities, and as people seek escape in some suburban or rural idyll, it is important to be reminded that the fulfillment of God's purposes is centered on a city, a community that reflects God's paradise.

6. The climax of the description of the new Jerusalem in 22:4 has the inhabitants sharing God's character (cf. Phil 3:20; 1 John 3:2) and seeing God face to face (cf. Matt 5:8). Moses was unable to see God, for no one can see God and live (Exod 33:20). That beatific vision, according to John 14:9 (cf. 1:18), was focused in Christ. It is now offered to all, because God will be all in all (1 Cor 15:28; cf. 2 Pet 1:4). All will share in the reign of God on earth (22:5), fulfilling all the promises that have been made (1:6; 5:10; cf. Matt 19:28). The beatific vision marks the climax of life in the new Jerusalem. Yet it is not merely something to be looked forward to in this life and experienced only after death. Jesus reminded his disciples that the one who sits on the throne of glory is present in the midst of the injustice of the old order (Matt 25:31ff.). In Revelation there is the faintest echo of this idea, though in slightly different tones. God is with those who wash their robes and make them white, the non-conformists who resolutely refuse to bow down to the beast.

7. As we watch a loved one die from a painful or lingering illness, we may be reminded of those passages from Revelation 21 that are frequently read at funerals in order to comfort the bereaved. But to reduce the meaning of Revelation to such a message of comfort feels like an escape and a betrayal of the prophecy of the Apocalypse that is not there to console but to challenge and warn. The vision confronts us not so much with relief that everything will turn out well in the end but with the reality that things, here and now, are profoundly *un*well and that repentance and change of life are required. Disease is present in a society where there is so much plenty, but there is inadequate provision for the sick and dying. The promise of a new heaven and a new earth is a vision of judgment on Babylon and its culture of death, where money and privilege can buy success, health, and care, and the dignity and well-being of people, young and old, are subordinated to the demands of economic accounting and ability to pay.

REVELATION 22:6-21

CONCLUDING SAYINGS

COMMENTARY

The vision proper stops abruptly at 22:5, with a sense of climax in the beatific vision and the sharing of God's character through the possession of God's name. It is not too much of an exaggeration to say that Paul's words "God may be all in all" (1 Cor 15:28 NRSV; cf. Eph 1:23) are an apt comment on these words. But the revelation goes on, albeit by means of a string of injunctions that take us back to the opening of the book. The beginning and the ending of the book of Revelation (1:1, 8; 22:6-20) are a mixture of isolated sayings, the speakers of which are not always evident. For example, who is speaking in vv. 10, 12? There is a sense of repetition in that these words are faithful and true (v. 6; cf. 19:9-11; 21:5). God is said to be God of the spirits of the prophets (cf. 1:4; 4:5; 5:6, where the seven spirits of God are referred to). A similar expression for God is used in the Jewish apocalypse *1 Enoch* 37–71, where God is called "Lord of the spirits" (cf. Num 27:16; Heb 12:9).

22:6. There are differences between the first and last chapters of the book of Revelation. In chap. 1, the revelation given is to Jesus, which he then communicates through an angel to John. In 22:6, it is God who sends an angel to show God's servants what will occur. This angel may be the "one like the Son of Man" of 1:13, who shows John the way to heaven (4:1) and what must take place on earth. It is possible, though, that this angel is one of the seven angels with the seven bowls full of the plagues (17:1; 21:9-10; 22:1). So the phrase "his angel" may refer either to one of the angels of the plagues or to the Son of Man. But that needs to be discussed in relation to 22:16, where Jesus speaks of having sent his angel with the testimony.

22:7. The blessing of 1:3, in which the angel blesses both those who read aloud the prophecy and those who hear and keep its words, is balanced by the blessing in this verse. The angel announces, "See, I am coming soon!" The difficulty in determining the precise time to which "soon" refers is compounded by the repetition of the promise "I am coming soon" in vv. 12 and 20 and the statement "the time is near" in v. 10 (cf. 2:16). That coming is eschatological in all cases, and the crisis is imminent, incorporating the event narrated in 19:11-21 as well as the Son of Man standing at the door of a church with the threat of judgment in the present (3:20). The sense of necessity (v. 6, "what must soon take place") is felt in the Gospels also, where it occurs in a similar eschatological context (Matt 24:6).

22:8-9. John identifies himself as the one to whom these mysteries have been revealed (v. 8). His reaction to having heard and seen these things is to fall down and worship at the feet of the angel who has revealed them to him. John had reacted in the same manner in 1:17, when he fell at the feet of the one like the Son of Man, and in 19:10, where the angel showed him the marriage supper of the Lamb. In 22:9, as in 19:10, the angel tells John that he must not worship the angel and uses the same expression to explain why: "I am a fellow servant with you and your comrades." In 19:10, John's "comrades" were those who "hold the testimony of Jesus" (NRSV); here they are the prophets and "those who keep the words of this book." The angel demands that John worship God alone.

22:10-11. The angel commands John not to seal the words of prophecy in the book (unlike the prophecy of Daniel; cf. Dan 12:9). These words are for the present, and so, because the book stands open, they are relevant not only to readers in John's day, but also for readers of all eras. The Apocalypse is not a collection of prophecies, like those of Nostradamus, for it relates as directly to the seven churches of Asia Minor as it does to the church today (cf. 1:3). It remains an open book (cf. 10:4). The series of sayings in 22:11 (reminiscent of 13:10) suggests a rather fatalistic attitude, contrasting with the much more vital, open-ended attitude throughout the book, which encourages change of heart rather than resignation to one's fate. But the deterministic tone may well be read as part of the book's challenge for us: to decide whether we belong among the unjust or the filthy (v. 11; cf. Dan 12:10; Ezek 3:27). Of all the biblical books, Revelation is the one most intended to lead the reader to change. A watchword of Revelation is "repent."

22:12-13. The identity of the speaker in these verses is unclear. In the light of phrases similar to v. 13 ("I am the Alpha and the Omega"; 1:8, 17; 3:11; cf. 21:6), we must assume that it is Christ. The speaker is one who comes with a reward, which he will "repay" according to people's deeds (cf. 20:12; Isa 40:10). The word rendered "reward" (μισθός *misthos*) is not widely used in Revelation (cf. Matt 5:12; 10:41-42).

22:14-15. There is another blessing (v. 14; in plural form, as in 14:13; 19:9), this time on those who "wash their robes" in the blood of the Lamb (see 7:14). In the light of 12:11 ("they have conquered him by the blood of the Lamb/ and by the word of their testimony" [NRSV]), their having washed their robes means that they have kept their witness despite the threat of the beast (cf. 3:4, where the church at Sardis had few people "who have not soiled their clothes" [NRSV]). Washing their robes will give human beings the right to the tree of life (v. 2; cf. 2:7) and allow entry into the city.

At the very climax of the vision, when resolution seems to be complete, when judgment is past and heaven has come down to earth, there is a stubborn refusal to abandon the language of contrast, dualism, and separation. Ambiguity remains. Even if there is no longer a boundary between God and human beings, even if the city gates remain open, some barriers to entry still remain. Those who are prohibited from entering the city have associated themselves with the beast; they are abominators (cf. 17:4), fornicators (17:2; 18:3), idolaters (cf. 13:16). They have refused to repent and give glory to God. And they have been shown to be liars (21:8; cf. 2:2), like the beast and the false prophet (13:13-14). They are called "dogs" (κύνες *kynes*, a term designating outsiders in Matt 7:6; 15:26; Paul uses it as a term of disparagement for his opponents in Phil 3:2).

The open-endedness of judgment is evident in the letters to the angels of the seven churches (2:1–3:22), communities that often were found to be on the wrong side of the boundary between good and evil.[363] So readers of Revelation are faced with the challenge from beginning to end, even after they have put the book down. Divine guarantee of ultimate salvation is not an unambiguous part of the Apocalypse.

22:16. The speaker now identifies himself as Jesus, and says that he was the one who sent his angel to bear witness to these things (possibly a reference to Christ as Son of Man; cf. 10:1; 14:14; see also Commentary on 1:1). What is included in the book is a continuation of the testimony by the one who had been the faithful witness (1:5), and it is the witness of Jesus that is the heart of prophecy (19:10). Prophecy, witness, and the life of Christ are bound together in Revelation, and its readers find that such commitments and activities have a price (11:3ff.; 12:11). Here testimony is said to have been for the churches themselves rather than, as in the introductions to the letters, being directed to the angel of each church. Davidic descent is once more asserted (something that has made its appearance from time to time throughout the book; e.g., 3:7; 5:5; 12:5). Here, however, it is linked with Balaam's prophecy (see Num 28:17; Luke 1:68, 78; Rev 2:14, 28).

22:17. The Spirit and the bride now speak in response to Jesus (cf. 2:7; 21:2, 9). The voice of the bride, the new Jerusalem, is heard only here, and its brief inclusion replaces the stilled voice of the bride in Babylon (18:23). They plead with Jesus to come (cf. v. 20), echoing the command of the creatures to the four riders of the apocalypse (6:2). Whether that coming is with clouds (1:9) or as a thief (16:15), it will be soon (vv. 7, 12; see also 2:16). They make this plea twice, the second time saying, "Let everyone who hears say, 'Come!'" That response is appropriate for all who hear the words of the prophecy (cf. v. 18; 1:3), which is what the Spirit says to the churches (2:7). Hearing

---

363. See Thompson, *The Book of Revelation*.

must be accompanied by heeding the command of 14:9 and not worshiping the beast. Those who do not hear will find that the One who comes is not a redeemer but a judge (cf. 3:10). The promise of 21:6 ("To the thirsty I will give water as a gift from the spring of the water of life" [NRSV]; cf. 7:16) is then made into an offer: "Let anyone who wishes take the water of life as a gift" (cf. John 7:37).

22:18-19. These verses, apparently spoken by John, solemnly emphasize the authority of the prophecy of this book and, like those of the book of life (13:8), are of utmost significance. In the warning that no one should add to or take away from the book, John repeats words from the Torah:

So now, Israel, give heed to the statutes and ordinances that I am teaching you to observe, so that you may live to enter and occupy the land that the LORD, the God of your ancestors, is giving you. You must neither add anything to what I command you nor take away anything from it, but keep the commandments of the LORD your God with which I am charging you. (Deut 4:1-2 NRSV)

This is a warning for the present, with the threat of plagues (cf. Deut 29:19) or loss of participation in the tree of life and the holy city for the offender. So ill treatment of the book brings a curse. It is, indeed, a holy book. Unlike Deuteronomy, the book of Revelation is not law but prophecy. Its words have a different function. It is not laws to be carried out but visions to be seen, heard, and responded to, so that the nature of reality can be viewed differently, certain acts avoided, and others followed.

Although John describes what he has written as prophecy (v. 19), it is also an apocalypse (1:1). But unlike other apocalypses, it was presented to John, an ordinary man, and not to a great figure of the past. Prophecy in Revelation is linked with the testimony of Jesus.[364] It is a means of witnessing, therefore, characterized by the vision of chap. 11. Hearing and reading must be matched by keeping (1:3)—but not preserving the message in some conservationist sense. Keeping the word means observing "my works" (2:26), "my word" (3:8, 10), "the commandments of God" (12:17; 14:12), washing one's robes (22:14), and keeping "the word of their testimony" (12:11).

22:20. The penultimate word is from the One who bears witness (cf. 1:15; 3:14), who asserts that he comes quickly (22:7, 12; cf. 1:7). The response, "Amen. Come, Lord Jesus!" echoes the response found in early liturgies, like the *Didache* and the enigmatic "Maranatha" of 1 Cor 16:22: "Let anyone be accursed who has no love for the Lord. Maranatha!" (see NRSV note).

22:21. John ends with a prayer that the grace of the Lord Jesus be "with all" (the NRSV does not represent the inclusiveness of the Greek [μετὰ πάντων *meta pantōn*] with its "with all the saints"; cf. 1 Cor 16:24). This benediction has many similarities with the conclusions of the Pauline letters (e.g., 2 Cor 13:13; 2 Thess 3:18). It is a final prayer of universal blessing at the end of a text in which threat and division have predominated. It is a final prayer of openness at the end of a text in which threat and division have predominated. At its end there is the promise of water given freely, a tentative refusal of closure or the offer of life.

---

364. On prophecy, see Aune, *Prophecy in Early Christianity and the Ancient Mediterranean World.* On the prophetic character of Revelation, see F. D. Mazzaferri, *The Genre of the Book of Revelation from a Source-Critical Perspective* (Berlin: de Gruyter, 1989).

REFLECTIONS

1. We are left in no doubt about the importance John attached to his book. It is ironic that the book in the New Testament with the most exalted claim to authority is the one that is least read and most widely despised. Even if we cannot understand its message in its entirety and are uncomfortable with the import of what we can understand, we must not ignore it. It stands not only at the end of the New Testament, but at the end of the Christian Bible. Thus it may offer us a key to understanding the whole story, because it points to the fulfillment of God's purposes, of which all else gives only a partial and fragmentary example. Its message is about God and about human history.

Its scope is panoramic, and its focus on Jesus as the key to understanding the fulfillment of God's justice is central. Revelation may enable us to look back over the biblical story and make sense of the whole as well as pointedly reminding us of the demands made on us by a God who regards every action as significant. We may begin to glimpse what the Spirit says to the churches and learn to respond accordingly: "Blessed are those who wash their robes, so that they will have the right to the tree of life and may enter the city by the gates" (22:14 NRSV; cf. 7:14).

2. Revelation is intended to be heard and read. Keeping the words is not about defensiveness or preservation, nor is it simply a matter of intellectual understanding confined to academy or church. Keeping the words means practicing their message in life. It is a matter of being so utterly informed and pervaded by the words that one can perceive that "the wisdom of this world is foolishness with God." John had to devour the book, and there is a sense in which the reader and the hearer must do that with Revelation—digest it so that one also can "prophesy about many peoples and nations and languages and kings." Thus the effect of reading the text is to condition an outlook on life whereby image and metaphor jar us awake and transform our actions as well as our attitudes. The temptation is to ask what this book is about and to seek references in history—past, present, or future. But first and foremost, Revelation is meant to be heard and to be read, so that the reader/listener is changed; that change means repentance and rebirth (cf. Matt 19:28).

3. The claim to prophetic insight is fraught with problems. Prophecy may enlighten, but there are occasions when such claims can be diabolically destructive. Throughout the Bible, prophecy is a central component of life, and yet it is also problematic. The very nature of prophecy means that it is not subject to control by any set of regulations. What happens when there are contrasting presentations of the word of God? John's apocalyptic prophecy obviously did not stand alone (and possibly not unchallenged) in the churches of his day. This issue confronts us in Revelation itself when John condemns "Jezebel" and the pseudo-prophetic witness of the beast and its agent (Revelation 13; cf. 19:20). In the Old Testament, the issue attracted attention as well (Jer 23:9ff.; Deuteronomy 13; 18).[365] According to Revelation, a prophet who claimed to speak for God but who also compromised with the existing order (Rev 2:20) is to be repudiated. Similarly, in Deuteronomy 13, the prophetic exhortation to worship other gods and be like the other nations is the mark of a false prophet.

Similarly, the voice from heaven is a frequent component of John's vision. Its presence raises the question of authenticity: How does one distinguish among voices? John offers no explanation, and yet the question remains a pressing one for any New Testament theology. At the start of Mark's story of Jesus (Mark 1:10) and in the conversion of Paul (Acts 9:4), voices from heaven are heard—unauthenticated and uncompromising. Why are these voices heeded? How do they relate to the voice of God in the pages of the Hebrew Bible? The answer in the Gospel of John is uncompromising (John 5:37). All claims to having heard the voice of God (including Sinai) are to be understood in the light of the One whom God has sent, who alone has heard and seen (John 6:46) and can speak the words of God. That voice, the voice of Christ, the voice that speaks with John on Patmos, is the medium and the standard for hearing and understanding what God says. All that is claimed as having been spoken through God must be examined and judged in the light of Christ's voice. Christ's words may slay the wicked (cf. Isa 11:4), but never give humans divine sanction to engage in violence.

---

365. On the importance of this theme in the Gospels, see N. T. Wright, *Jesus and the Victory of God* (London: SPCK, 1996).

ABBREVIATIONS

BCE	before the Common Era
ca.	circa
CE	Common Era
cent.	century
cf.	compare
chap(s).	chapter(s)
d.	died
Dtr	Deuteronomistic historian
esp.	especially
fem.	feminine
HB	Hebrew Bible
l(l).	line(s)
lit.	literally
LXX	Septuagint
masc.	masculine
MS(S)	manuscript(s)
MT	Masoretic Text
n(n).	note(s)
neut.	neuter
NT	New Testament
OG	Old Greek
OL	Old Latin
OT	Old Testament
par(r).	parallel(s)
pl(s).	plate(s)
SP	Samaritan Pentateuch
v(v).	verse(s)
Vg	Vulgate
\\	between Scripture references indicates parallelism

Names of Pseudepigraphical and Early Patristic Books

Apoc. Abr.	*Apocalypse of Abraham*
2–3 Apoc. Bar.	Syriac, Greek *Apocalypse of Baruch*
Apoc. Mos.	*Apocalypse of Moses*

Ascen. Isa.	*Ascension of Isaiah*
As. Mos.	*Assumption of Moses*
Barn.	*Barnabas*
Bib. Ant.	Pseudo-Philo, *Biblical Antiquities*
1–2 Clem.	*1–2 Clement*
Did.	*Didache*
1–2–3 Enoch	Ethiopic, Slavonic, Hebrew *Enoch*
Ep. Arist.	*Epistle of Aristeas*
Gos. Pet.	*Gospel of Peter*
Herm. Sim.	Hermas, *Similitude(s)*
Ign. Eph.	Ignatius, *Letter to the Ephesians*
Ign. Magn.	Ignatius, *Letter to the Magnesians*
Ign. Phld.	Ignatius, *Letter to the Philadelphians*
Ign. Pol.	Ignatius, *Letter to Polycarp*
Ign. Rom.	Ignatius, *Letter to the Romans*
Ign. Smyrn.	Ignatius, *Letter to the Smyrnaeans*
Ign. Trall.	Ignatius, *Letter to the Trallians*
Jub.	*Jubilees*
POxy	B. P. Grenfell and A. S. Hunt (eds.), *Oxyrhynchus Papyri*
Pss. Sol.	*Psalms of Solomon*
Sib. Or.	*Sibylline Oracles*
T. Benj.	*Testament of Benjamin*
T. Dan	*Testament of Dan*
T. Iss.	*Testament of Issachar*
T. Job	*Testament of Job*
T. Jud.	*Testament of Judah*
T. Levi	*Testament of Levi*
T. Naph.	*Testament of Naphtali*
T. Reub.	*Testament of Reuben*
T. Sim.	*Testament of Simeon*

Names of Dead Sea Scrolls and Related Texts

CD	Cairo (Genizah text of the) Damascus Document
DSS	Dead Sea Scrolls
8HevXII gr	Greek scroll of the Minor Prophets from Nahal Hever
Q	Qumran
1Q, 2Q, etc.	numbered caves of Qumran, yielding written material; followed by abbreviation of biblical or apocryphal book
1Q28b	Rule of the Blessings (Appendix b to 1QS)
1QH	Thanksgiving Hymns (Qumran Cave 1)
1QM	War Scroll (Qumran Cave 1)
1QpHab	Pesher on Habakkuk (Qumran Cave 1)
1QpPs	Pesher on Psalms (Qumran Cave 1)
1QS	Rule of the Community (Qumran Cave 1)
1QSa	Rule of the Congregation (Appendix a to 1QS)
1QSb	Rule of the Blessings (Appendix b to 1QS)
4Q175	Testimonia text (Qumran Cave 4)
4Q246	Apocryphon of Daniel (Qumran Cave 4)
4Q298	Words of the Sage to the Sons of Dawn (Qumran Cave 4)
4Q385b	fragmentary remains of Pseudo-Jeremiah that implies that Jeremiah went into Babylonian exile. Also known as ApocJer^C or 4Q385 16. (Qumran Cave 4)

4Q389a	several scroll fragments now thought to contain portions of three pseudepigraphical works including Pseudo-Jeremiah. Also known as 4QApocJer^e. (Qumran Cave 4)
4Q390	contains a schematized history of Israel's sin and divine punishment. Also known as psMos^e. (Qumran Cave 4)
4Q394–399	Halakhic Letter (Qumran Cave 4)
4Q416	Instruction^b (Qumran Cave 4)
4Q521	Messianic Apocalypse (Qumran Cave 4)
4Q550	Proto-Esther$^{a\text{-}f}$ (Qumran Cave 4)
4QFlor	Florilegium (or Eschatological Midrashim) (Qumran Cave 4)
4QMMT	Halakhic Letter (Qumran Cave 4)
4QpaleoDeutr	copy of Deuteronomy in paleo-Hebrew script (Qumran Cave 4)
4QpaleoExod	copy of Exodus in paleo-Hebrew script (Qumran Cave 4)
4QpNah	Pesher on Nahum (Qumran Cave 4)
4QpPs	Psalm Pesher A (Qumran Cave 4)
4QPrNab	Prayer of Nabonidus (Qumran Cave 4)
4QPs37	Psalm Scroll (Qumran Cave 4)
4QpsDan	Pseudo-Daniel (Qumran Cave 4)
4QSam	First copy of Samuel (Qumran Cave 4)
4QTestim	Testimonia text (Qumran Cave 4)
4QTob	Copy of Tobit (Qumran Cave 4)
11QMelch	Melchizedek text (Qumran Cave 11)
11QPs^a	Psalms Scroll (Qumran Cave 11)
11QT	Temple Scroll (Qumran Cave 11)
11QtgJob	Targum of Job (Qumran Cave 11)

Targumic Material

Tg. Esth. I, II	First or Second Targum of Esther
Tg. Neb.	Targum of the Prophets
Tg. Neof.	Targum Neofiti

Orders and Tractates in Mishnaic and Related Literature

To distinguish the same-named tractates in the Mishnah, Tosefta, Babylonian Talmud, and Jerusalem Talmud, *m., t., b.,* or *y.* precedes the title of the tractate.

'Abot	'Abot
'Arak.	'Arakin
B. Bat.	Baba Batra
B. Meṣ.	Baba Meṣi'a
B. Qam.	Baba Qamma
Ber.	Berakot
Dem.	Demai
Giṭ.	Giṭṭin
Ḥag.	Ḥagigah
Hor.	Horayot
Ḥul.	Ḥullin
Ket.	Ketubbot
Ma'aś.	Ma'aśerot
Meg.	Megilla
Menaḥ.	Menaḥot

Mid.	Middot
Moʻed Qaṭ.	Moʻed Qaṭan
Nazir	Nazir
Ned.	Nedarim
p. Šeqal.	pesachim Šeqalim
Pesaḥ.	Pesaḥim
Qidd.	Qudduŝin
Šabb.	Šabbat
Sanh.	Sanhedrin
Soṭah	Soṭah
Sukk.	Sukkah
Taʻan.	Taʻanit
Tamid	Tamid
Yad.	Yadayim
Yoma	Yoma (=Kippurim)

Other Rabbinic Works

ʼAbot R. Nat.	ʼAbot de Rabbi Nathan
Pesiq. R.	Pesiqta Rabbati
Rab.	Rabbah (following abbreviation of biblical book—e.g., Gen. Rab. = Genesis Rabbah)
Sipra	Sipra

Greek Manuscripts and Ancient Versions

Papyrus Manuscripts

$\mathfrak{P}^1$	third-century Greek papyrus manuscript of the Gospels
$\mathfrak{P}^{29}$	third- or fourth-century Greek papyrus manuscript
$\mathfrak{P}^{33}$	sixth-century Greek papyrus manuscript of Acts
$\mathfrak{P}^{37}$	third- or fourth-century Greek papyrus manuscript of the Gospels
$\mathfrak{P}^{38}$	fourth-century Greek papyrus manuscript of Acts
$\mathfrak{P}^{45}$	third-century Greek papyrus manuscript of the Gospels
$\mathfrak{P}^{46}$	third-century Greek papyrus manuscript of the letters
$\mathfrak{P}^{47}$	third-century Greek papyrus manuscript of Revelation
$\mathfrak{P}^{48}$	third-century Greek papyrus manuscript of Acts
$\mathfrak{P}^{52}$	second-century Greek papyrus manuscript of John 18:31-33, 37-38
$\mathfrak{P}^{58}$	sixth-century Greek papyrus manuscript of Acts
$\mathfrak{P}^{64}$	third-century Greek papyrus fragment of Matthew
$\mathfrak{P}^{66}$	second- or third-century Greek papyrus manuscript of John (incomplete)
$\mathfrak{P}^{67}$	third-century Greek papyrus fragment of Matthew
$\mathfrak{P}^{69}$	third-century Greek papyrus manuscript of the Gospel of Luke
$\mathfrak{P}^{75}$	third-century Greek papyrus manuscript of the Gospels

Lettered Uncials

א	Codex Sinaiticus, fourth-century manuscript of LXX, NT, Epistle of Barnabas, and Shepherd of Hermas
A	Codex Alexandrinus, fifth-century manuscript of LXX, NT, 1 and 2 Clement, and Psalms of Solomon
B	Codex Vaticanus, fourth-century manuscript of LXX and parts of the NT

Abbreviations

C	Codex Ephraemi, fifth-century manuscript of parts of LXX and NT
D	Codex Bezae, fifth-century bilingual (Greek and Latin) manuscript of the Gospels and Acts
G	ninth-century manuscript of the Gospels
K	ninth-century manuscript of the Gospels
L	eighth-century manuscript of the Gospels
W	Washington Codex, fifth-century manuscript of the Gospels
X	Codex Monacensis, ninth- or tenth-century manuscript of the Gospels
Z	sixth-century manuscript of Matthew
Θ	Koridethi Codex, ninth-century manuscript of the Gospels
Ψ	Athous Laurae Codex, eighth- or ninth-century manuscript of the Gospels (incomplete), Acts, the Catholic and Pauline Epistles, and Hebrews

Numbered Uncials

058	fourth-century fragment of Matthew 18
074	sixth-century fragment of Matthew
078	sixth-century fragment of Matthew, Luke, and John
0170	fifth- or sixth-century manuscript of Matthew
0181	fourth- or fifth-century partial manuscript of Luke 9:59–10:14

Numbered Minuscules

33	tenth-century manuscript of the Gospels
75	eleventh-century manuscript of the Gospels
565	ninth-century manuscript of the Gospels
700	eleventh-century manuscript of the Gospels
892	ninth-century manuscript of the Gospels

Names of Nag Hammadi Tractates

Ap. John	Apocryphon of John (also called the Secret Book of John)
Apoc. Adam	Apocalypse of Adam (also called the Revelation of Adam)
Ep. Pet.	Letter of Peter to Philip
Exeg. Soul	Exegesis on the Soul
Gos. Phil.	Gospel of Philip
Gos. Truth	Gospel of Truth

Ancient Versions

bo	the Bohairic (Memphitic) Coptic version
bo^{mss}	some manuscripts in the Bohairic tradition
d	the Latin text of Codex Bezae
e	Codex Palatinus, fifth-century Latin manuscript of the Gospels
ff^{2}	Old Latin manuscript, fifth-century translation of the Gospels
Ir^{lat}	the Latin translation of Irenaeus
latt	the whole Latin tradition (including the Vulgate)
mae	Middle Egyptian
sa	the Sahidic (Thebaic) Coptic version
sy	the Syriac version
sy^s	the Sinaitic Syriac version

Other Abbreviations
700*	the original reading of manuscript 700
ℵ*	the original reading of Codex Sinaiticus
ℵ¹	the first corrector of Codex Sinaiticus
ℵ²	the second corrector of Codex Sinaiticus
𝔐	the Majority text (the mass of later manuscripts)
C^2	the corrected text of Codex Ephraemi
D*	the original reading of Codex Bezae
D^2	the second corrector (c. fifth century) of Codex Bezae
f^1	Family 1: minuscule manuscripts belonging to the Lake Group (1, 118, 131, 209, 1582)
f^{13}	Family 13: minuscule manuscripts belonging to the Ferrar Group (13, 69, 124, 174, 230, 346, 543, 788, 826, 828, 983, 1689, 1709)
pc	a few other manuscripts

Commonly Used Periodicals, Reference Works, and Serials

AAR	American Academy of Religion
AASOR	Annual of the American Schools of Oriental Research
AB	Anchor Bible
ABD	*Anchor Bible Dictionary*
ABR	*Australian Biblical Review*
ABRL	Anchor Bible Reference Library
ACNT	Augsburg Commentaries on the New Testament
AcOr	*Acta Orientalia*
AfO	*Archiv für Orientforschung*
AfOB	Archiv für Orientforschung: Beiheft
AGJU	Arbeiten zur Geschichte des antiken Judentums und des Urchristentums
AJP	*American Journal of Philology*
AJSL	*American Journal of Semitic Languages and Literature*
AJT	*American Journal of Theology*
AnBib	Analecta Biblica
ANEP	J. B. Pritchard (ed.), *The Ancient Near East in Pictures Relating to the Old Testament*
ANET	J. B. Pritchard (ed.), *Ancient Near Eastern Texts Relating to the Old Testament*
ANF	*Ante-Nicene Fathers*
ANRW	*Aufstieg und Niedergang der römischen Welt*
ANTC	Abingdon New Testament Commentaries
ANTJ	Arbeiten zum Neuen Testament und Judentum
APOT	R. H. Charles (ed.), *The Apocrypha and Pseudepigrapha of the Old Testament*
ASNU	Acta Seminarii Neotestamentici Upsaliensis
ATANT	Abhandlungen zur Theologie des Alten und Neuen Testaments
ATD	Das Alte Testament Deutsch
ATDan	Acta Theologica Danica
Aug	*Augustinianum*
AusBR	*Australian Biblical Review*
BA	Biblical Archaeologist

BAGD	W. Bauer, W. F. Arndt, F. W. Gingrich, and F. W. Danker, *Greek-English Lexicon of the New Testament and Other Early Christian Literature*, 2nd ed. (Bauer-Arndt-Gingrich-Danker)
BAR	*Biblical Archaeology Review*
BASOR	*Bulletin of the American Schools of Oriental Research*
BBB	Bonner biblische Beiträge
BBET	Beiträge zur biblischen Exegese und Theologie
BBR	*Bulletin for Biblical Research*
BDAG	W. Bauer, W. F. Arndt, F. W. Gingrich, and F. W. Danker, *Greek-English Lexicon of the New Testament and Other Early Christian Literature*, 3rd ed. (Bauer-Danker-Arndt-Gingrich)
BDB	F. Brown, S. R. Driver, and C. A. Briggs, *A Hebrew and English Lexicon of the Old Testament*
BDF	F. Blass, A. Debrunner, and R. W. Funk, *A Greek Grammar of the New Testament and Other Early Christian Literature*
BEATAJ	Beiträge zur Erforschung des Alten Testaments und des antiken Judentum
BETL	Bibliotheca Ephemeridum Theologicarum Lovaniensium
BEvT	Beiträge zur evangelischen Theologie
BHS	*Biblia Hebraica Stuttgartensia*
BHT	Beiträge zur historischen Theologie
Bib	*Biblica*
BibInt	*Biblical Interpretation*
BibOr	Biblica et Orientalia
BJRL	*Bulletin of the John Rylands University Library of Manchester*
BJS	Brown Judaic Studies
BK	*Bibel und Kirche*
BKAT	Biblischer Kommentar, Altes Testament
BLS	Bible and Literature Series
BN	*Biblische Notizen*
BNTC	Black's New Testament Commentaries
BR	*Biblical Research*
BSac	Bibliotheca Sacra
BSOAS	*Bulletin of the School of Oriental and African Studies*
BT	The Bible Translator
BTB	Biblical Theology Bulletin
BVC	Bible et vie chrétienne
BWA(N)T	Beiträge zur Wissenschaft vom Alten (und Neuen) Testament
BZ	Biblische Zeitschrift
BZAW	Beihefte zur Zeitschrift für die alttestamentliche Wissenschaft
BZNW	Beihefte zur Zeitschrift für die neutestamentliche Wissenschaft
CAD	*The Assyrian Dictionary of the Oriental Institute of the University of Chicago*
CB	*Cultura Bíblica*
CBC	Cambridge Bible Commentary
CBOTS	Coniectanea Biblica: Old Testament Series
CBQ	*Catholic Biblical Quarterly*
CBQMS	Catholic Biblical Quarterly Monograph Series
ConBNT	Coniectanea Neotestamentica or Coniectanea Biblica: New Testament Series
ConBOT	Coniectanea Biblica: Old Testament Series
CP	*Classical Philology*
CRAI	Comptes rendus de l'Académie des inscriptions et belles-lettres

CRINT	Compendia Rerum Iudaicarum ad Novum Testamentum
CTM	*Concordia Theological Monthly*
DJD	Discoveries in the Judaean Desert
EB	Echter Bibel
EI	*Encyclopaedia of Islam*
EKKNT	Evangelisch-katholischer Kommentar zum Neuen Testament
Enc	*Encounter*
EncJud	C. Roth and G. Wigoder (eds.), *Encyclopedia Judaica*
EPRO	Etudes préliminaires aux religions orientales dans l'empire romain
ErIsr	*Eretz-Israel*
EstBib	*Estudios bíblicos*
ETL	*Ephemerides Theologicae Lovanienses*
ETS	Erfurter theologische Studien
EvQ	*Evangelical Quarterly*
EvT	*Evangelische Theologie*
ExAud	*Ex Auditu*
ExpTim	*Expository Times*
FAT	Forschungen zum Alten Testament
FB	Forschung zur Bibel
FBBS	Facet Books, Biblical Series
FFNT	Foundations and Facets: New Testament
FOTL	Forms of the Old Testament Literature
FRLANT	Forschungen zur Religion und Literatur des Alten und Neuen Testaments
FTS	Frankfurter Theologische Studien
GBS.OTS	Guides to Biblical Scholarship. Old Testament Series
GCS	Die griechischen christlichen Schriftsteller der ersten [drei] Jahrhunderte
GKC	Emil Kautzsch (ed.), *Gesenius' Hebrew Grammar*, trans. A. E. Cowley, 2nd ed.
GNS	*Good News Studies*
GTA	Göttinger theologischer Arbeiten
HALAT	*Hebräisches und aramäisches Lexikon zum Alten Testament*
HAR	*Hebrew Annual Review*
HAT	Handbuch zum Alten Testament
HBC	*Harper's Bible Commentary*
HBT	*Horizons in Biblical Theology*
HDB	*Hastings' Dictionary of the Bible*
HDR	Harvard Dissertations in Religion
HeyJ	Heythrop Journal
HNT	Handbuch zum Neuen Testament
HNTC	Harper's New Testament Commentaries
HR	*History of Religions*
HSM	Harvard Semitic Monographs
HSS	Harvard Semitic Studies
HTKNT	Herders Theologischer Kommentar zum Neuen Testament
HTR	*Harvard Theological Review*
HTS	Harvard Theological Studies
HUCA	*Hebrew Union College Annual*
IB	*Interpreter's Bible*
IBC	Interpretation: A Bible Commentary for Teaching and Preaching
IBS	*Irish Biblical Studies*
ICC	International Critical Commentary

IDB	*The Interpreter's Dictionary of the Bible*
IDBSup	supplementary volume to *The Interpreter's Dictionary of the Bible*
IEJ	*Israel Exploration Journal*
Int	*Interpretation*
IRT	Issues in Religion and Theology
ITC	International Theological Commentary
JAAR	*Journal of the American Academy of Religion*
JAL	Jewish Apocryphal Literature Series
JANESCU	*Journal of the Ancient Near Eastern Society of Columbia University*
JAOS	*Journal of the American Oriental Society*
JBL	*Journal of Biblical Literature*
JETS	*Journal of the Evangelical Theological Society*
JJS	*Journal of Jewish Studies*
JNES	*Journal of Near Eastern Studies*
JNSL	*Journal of Northwest Semitic Languages*
JPS	Jewish Publication Society
JQR	*Jewish Quarterly Review*
JR	*Journal of Religion*
JRH	*Journal of Religious History*
JSJ	*Journal for the Study of Judaism in the Persian, Hellenistic, and Roman Periods*
JSNT	*Journal for the Study of the New Testament*
JSNTSup	Journal for the Study of the New Testament Supplement Series
JSOT	*Journal for the Study of the Old Testament*
JSOTSup	Journal for the Study of the Old Testament Supplement Series
JSP	*Journal for the Study of the Pseudepigrapha*
JSS	*Journal of Semitic Studies*
JTC	*Journal for Theology and the Church*
JTS	*Journal of Theological Studies*
KAT	Kommentar zum Alten Testament
KB	L. Koehler and W. Baumgartner, *Lexicon in Veteris Testamenti libros*
KEK	Kritisch-exegetischer Kommentar über das Neue Testament (Meyer-Kommentar)
KPG	Knox Preaching Guides
LCL	Loeb Classical Library
LTQ	Lexington Theological Quarterly
MNTC	*Moffatt New Testament Commentary*
NCBC	New Century Bible Commentary
NHS	*Nag Hammadi Studies*
NIB	*The New Interpreter's Bible*
NIBC	*The New Interpreter's Bible Commentary*
NICNT	New International Commentary on the New Testament
NICOT	New International Commentary on the Old Testament
NIGTC	The New International Greek Testament Commentary
NJBC	*The New Jerome Biblical Commentary*
NovT	*Novum Testamentum*
NovTSup	Supplements to Novum Testamentum
NPNF	*Nicene and Post-Nicene Fathers*
NTC	New Testament in Context
NTG	New Testament Guides
NTS	*New Testament Studies*
NTT	*Norsk Teologisk Tidsskrift*

OBC	*The Oxford Bible Commentary*
OBO	Orbis Biblicus et Orientalis
OBT	Overtures to Biblical Theology
OIP	Oriental Institute Publications
Or	*Orientalia* (NS)
OTG	Old Testament Guides
OTL	Old Testament Library
OTM	Old Testament Message
OTP	*Old Testament Pseudepigrapha*
OTS	*Oudtestamentische Studiën*
PAAJR	*Proceedings of the American Academy of Jewish Research*
PEFQS	Palestine Exploration Fund Quarterly Statement
PEQ	*Palestine Exploration Quarterly*
PGM	K. Preisendanz (ed.), *Papyri Graecae Magicae*
PTMS	Pittsburgh Theological Monograph Series
QD	Quaestiones Disputatae
RANE	Records of the Ancient Near East
RB	*Revue biblique*
ResQ	*Restoration Quarterly*
RevExp	*Review and Expositor*
RevQ	*Revue de Qumran*
RSRel	*Recherches de science religieuse*
RTL	*Revue théologique de Louvain*
SAA	State Archives of Assyria
SB	H. L. Strack and P. Billerbeck, *Kommentar zum Neuen Testament aus Talmud und Midrasch,* 6 vols. 1922–61
SBAB	Stuttgarter biblische Aufsatzbände
SBB	Stuttgarter biblische Beiträge
SBL	Society of Biblical Literature
SBLDS	SBL Dissertation Series
SBLMS	SBL Monograph Series
SBLRBS	SBL Resources for Biblical Study
SBLSCS	SBL Septuagint and Cognate Studies
SBLSP	SBL Seminar Papers
SBLSS	SBL *Semeia* Studies
SBLSymS	SBL Symposium Series
SBLWAW	SBL Writings from the Ancient World
SBM	Stuttgarter biblische Monographien
SBS	Stuttgarter Bibelstudien
SBT	Studies in Biblical Theology
SEÅ	*Svensk exegetisk årsbok*
SJLA	Studies in Judaism in Late Antiquity
SJOT	*Scandinavian Journal of the Old Testament*
SJT	*Scottish Journal of Theology*
SKK	Stuttgarter kleiner Kommentar
SNTSMS	Society for New Testament Studies Monograph Series
SOTSMS	Society for Old Testament Studies Monograph Series
SP	Sacra Pagina
SR	*Studies in Religion/Sciences religieuses*
SSN	Studia Semitica Neerlandica
ST	*Studia Theologica*
SUNT	Studien zur Umwelt des Neuen Testaments
SVT	Supplements to Vetus Testamentum

SVTP	Studia in Veteris Testamenti Pseudepigraphica
SWBA	Social World of Biblical Antiquity
TB	Theologische Bücherei: Neudrucke und Berichte aus dem 20. Jahrhundert
TD	*Theology Digest*
TDNT	*Theological Dictionary of the New Testament*
TDOT	*Theological Dictionary of the Old Testament*
TextS	Texts and Studies
THKNT	Theologischer Handkommentar zum Neuen Testament
TLZ	*Theologische Literaturzeitung*
TOTC	Tyndale Old Testament Commentaries
TQ	*Theologische Quartalschrift*
TSK	*Theologische Studien und Kritiken*
TSSI	*Textbook of Syrian Semitic Inscriptions*
TToday	*Theology Today*
TynBul	*Tyndale Bulletin*
TZ	*Theologische Zeitschrift*
UBS	United Bible Societies
UBSGNT	*United Bible Societies Greek New Testament*
UF	*Ugarit-Forschungen*
USQR	*Union Seminary Quarterly Review*
UUÅ	Uppsala Universitetsårsskrift
VC	*Vigiliae Christianae*
VT	*Vetus Testamentum*
VTSup	Supplements to Vetus Testamentum
WA	M. Luther, *Kritische Gesamtausgabe* (= "Weimar" edition)
WBC	Word Biblical Commentary
WBT	Word Biblical Themes
WMANT	Wissenschaftliche Monographien zum Alten und Neuen Testament
WTJ	*Westminster Theological Journal*
WUNT	Wissenschaftliche Untersuchungen zum Neuen Testament
ZAH	*Zeitschrift für Althebräistik*
ZAW	*Zeitschrift für die alttestamentliche Wissenschaft*
ZNW	*Zeitschrift für die neutestamentliche Wissenschaft und die Kunde der älteren Kirche*
ZTK	*Zeitschrift für Theologie und Kirche*